Handbook of
Marriage and the Family

Handbook of
Marriage and the Family

Edited by
Marvin B. Sussman
and
Suzanne K. Steinmetz

University of Delaware
Newark, Delaware

Plenum Press • New York and London

Library of Congress Cataloging in Publication Data

Handbook of marriage and the family.

Includes bibliographical references and index.
1. Family—Handbooks, manuals, etc. 2. Life cycle, Human—Handbooks, manuals,
etc. 3. Marriage—Handbooks, manuals, etc. I. Sussman, Marvin B. II. Steinmetz,
Suzanne K.
HQ518.B154   1986   306.8   86-25135
ISBN 0-306-41967-X

© 1987 Plenum Press, New York
A Division of Plenum Publishing Corporation
233 Spring Street, New York, N.Y. 10013

Printed in the United States of America

To Reuben Hill

Contributors

Vern L. Bengtson
Department of Sociology
University of Southern California
Los Angeles, California

Pauline Boss
Department of Family Social Science
University of Minnesota
St. Paul, Minnesota

Carol A. Darling
Department of Home and Family Life
Florida State University
Tallahassee, Florida

Robert T. Francoeur
Department of Biological and Allied Health Sciences
Fairleigh Dickinson University
Madison, New Jersey

Frank F. Furstenberg, Jr.
Department of Sociology
University of Pennsylvania
Philadelphia, Pennsylvania

Patricia A. Gongla
Department of Psychiatry and the Biobehavioral Sciences
University of California
Los Angeles, California

Tamara K. Hareven
Clark University
Worcester, Massachusetts, and
Center for Population Studies
Harvard University
Cambridge, Massachusetts

Susan Losh-Hesselbart
Department of Sociology
Florida State University
Tallahassee, Florida

Reuben Hill
Late of the Minnesota Family Study Center
University of Minnesota
Minneapolis, Minnesota

Sharon K. Houseknecht
Department of Sociology
Ohio State University
Columbus, Ohio

Florence W. Kaslow
Florida Couples and Family Institute
Northwood Medical Center, Suite 404
2617 N. Flagler Drive
West Palm Beach, Florida

David M. Klein
Department of Sociology
University of Notre Dame
Notre Dame, Indiana

Lauren Langman
Department of Sociology
Loyola University
Chicago, Illinois

Robert E. Larzelere
Rosemead School of Psychology
Biola University
La Mirada, California

Gary R. Lee
Departments of Sociology and Rural Sociology
Washington State University
Pullman, Washington

Lora Liss
7207 Snowden Drive
San Antonio, Texas

Eleanor D. Macklin
Department of Child, Family, and Community Studies
Syracuse University
Syracuse, New York

Teresa Donati Marciano
Department of Sociology
Fairleigh Dickinson University
Teaneck, New Jersey

Paul Mattessich
Office of Research and Statistics
Amherst H. Wilder Foundation
919 LaFond Avenue
St. Paul, Minnesota

Brent C. Miller
Department of Family and Human Development
Utah State University
Logan, Utah

Phyllis Moen
Department of Human Development and Family
    Studies, and Sociology
Cornell University
Ithaca, New York

Marie Withers Osmond
Department of Sociology
Florida State University
Tallahassee, Florida

Gary W. Peterson
Department of Child and Family Studies
University of Tennessee
Knoxville, Tennessee

Chaya S. Piotrkowski
Department of Psychology
St. John's University
Jamaica, New York

Karen A. Polonko
Department of Sociology
Old Dominion University
Norfolk, Virginia

Rhona Rapoport
Institute of Family and Environmental Research
1–2 Castle Lane
London, England

Robert N. Rapoport
Institute of Family and Environmental Research
1–2 Castle Lane
London, England

Helen J. Raschke
West Texas Legal Services
Wichita Falls, Texas

Boyd C. Rollins
Department of Sociology
Brigham Young University
Provo, Utah

John Scanzoni
Department of Sociology
University of North Carolina
Greensboro, North Carolina

Alvin L. Schorr
School of Applied Social Sciences
Case Western Reserve University
Cleveland, Ohio

Barbara H. Settles
Department of Individual and Family Studies
University of Delaware
Newark, Delaware

Arthur B. Shostak
Department of Psychology and Sociology
Drexel University
Philadelphia, Pennsylvania

Graham B. Spanier
Vice President and Provost
Oregon State University
Corvallis, Oregon

Suzanne K. Steinmetz
Department of Individual and Family Studies
University of Delaware
Newark, Delaware

Marvin B. Sussman
Department of Individual and Family Studies
University of Delaware
Newark, Delaware

Maximiliane E. Szinovacz
Department of Individual and Family Studies
University of Delaware
Newark, Delaware

Jay D. Teachman
Department of Sociology
Old Dominion University
Norfolk, Virginia

Darwin L. Thomas
Department of Sociology and the Family and
    Demographic Research Institute
Brigham Young University
Provo, Utah

Edward H. Thompson, Jr.
Department of Sociology
Holy Cross College
Worcester, Massachusetts

Judith Treas
Department of Sociology
University of Southern California
Los Angeles, California

Jean Edmondson Wilcox
Department of Family and Human Development
Utah State University
Logan, Utah

Doris Wilkinson
Department of Sociology
University of Kentucky
Lexington, Kentucky

Foreword

The lucid, straightforward Preface of this *Handbook* by the two editors and the comprehensive perspectives offered in the Introduction by one of them leave little for a Foreword to add. It is therefore limited to two relevant but not intrinsically related points vis-à-vis research on marriage and the family in the interval since the first *Handbook* (Christensen, 1964) appeared, namely: the impact on this research of the politicization of the New Right[1] and of the Feminist Enlightenment beginning in the mid-sixties, about the time of the first *Handbook*.

In the late 1930s Willard Waller noted: "Fifty years or more ago about 1890, most people had the greatest respect for the institution called the family and wished to learn nothing whatever about it. . . . Everything that concerned the life of men and women and their children was shrouded from the light. Today much of that has been changed. Gone is the concealment of the way in which life begins, gone the irrational sanctity of the home. The aura of sentiment which once protected the family from discussion clings to it no more. . . . We want to learn as much about it as we can and to understand it as thoroughly as possible, for there is a rising recognition in America that vast numbers of its families are sick—from internal frustrations and from external buffeting. We are engaged in the process of reconstructing our family institutions through criticism and discussion" (1938, pp. 3–4).

In the postwar period, the constraints on research on marriage and the family did seem to be relaxing. Thus, about thirty years after Waller's first celebration of the growing freedom and four years after the first *Handbook,* Reuben Hill, in a talk at the twenty-fifth birthday of the American Association of Marriage Counselors, summarized the then-current status of marriage and family research and noted that, after many years of being hazard, it was now safe. Textbooks no longer had to deal primarily with ancient or exotic families because "to analyze the contemporary family dispassionately would offend the prevailing moral sentiments. It was thought a violation of the sanctity of the home and made researchers open to censorship from agents of the social order" (1968, p. 21). As recently as the 1930s, researchers had lost their jobs for disturbing the innocence of the young by studying courtship on campus. But now family research was free; free at last. It was no longer necessary to hide the fact that many families were sick; that there were such things as violence in the family; that not all families rode on sleighs to grandmother's house for Thanksgiving dinner. But again, such freedom was still precarious. Even studying ancient or exotic families was becoming less and less safe.

There is a long history of opposition to the uses to which research on marriage and family can be intrinsic to the ambience in which academic research must be carried on. Such opposition may rise and fall, take on varying issues to attack, and wax and wane in its impact. In the period since Christensen's *Handbook of Marriage and the Family* (1964) appeared, two aspects of the ongoing opposition deserve attention. One is that the opponents of the standard research and teaching tradition in academia are now more sophisticated, more educated; the other is that they are now politicized.

Until recently, the opposing sides were widely disparate in sophistication. Education, knowledge, science, and research were on the side of those whom John Scanzoni called the Progressives. Conviction and commitment were on the side of those whom he called the Conservatives. In recent years, the Conservatives have been going to college; they have become exposed to research of all kinds and have

---

[1] I am using the overall term *New Right* even though it is not a homogeneous entity but rather a congeries of groups that may disagree on specific issues though they agree on others. It includes, among other groups: Falwell's Moral Majority (more than half of whom do not even share his religious fundamentalism, 30% being Catholic, and a substantial number Jewish or Mormon); Evangelicals; Christian Voice; several fundamentalist Baptist Fellowships; and even an Orthodox Presbyterian group (D'Souza, *Washington Post,* 1984).

learned a vocabulary with which to state their case. They have become more knowledgeable research-wise, better armed to meet their opposite numbers with self-confidence. They are no longer the "Bible Belt booboisie" that H. L. Mencken had had so much fun with. They are now in a position to draw up a Family Protection bill that targets exactly the results of academic research that goes into textbooks. The researchers have armed them. They have become like the Jesuit who is trained to know his opponents' arguments as well as they do and to be prepared to state them even better.

The other great difference between present and past Conservatives is that today they are highly politicized. Political activism, once forbidden as a sin, has now become a duty; it is non-activism that has become a sin. As recently as 1965, a year after the first *Handbook,* one of their leaders, the Rev. Jerry Falwell, still believed that the Bible forbade political activism. Preachers were called soul-winners, not politicians. Preparing for the imminent end of the world was more pressing than gaining more political power. But in the 1960s and 1970s there was a radical change of heart among the New Right. They felt that the power structure in our society, including universities and the intelligentsia, was controlled by the Progressives. In part, the kind of research reported in the Sussman and Steinmetz *Handbook,* for example, chapters on nontraditional family forms, voluntary childlessness, single-parent families, and divorce, supplied them with their grievances.

In time, they learned the game of politics and played it to the hilt. It was no longer possible for the good Christian to stay out of politics. Of the several issues that concerned them, the most relevant here are those having to do with the family. Thus, in the 96th Congress, Senator Paul Laxalt introduced a Family Protection Act (S. 1808) aimed at restoring "the historical [read traditional] family." Among its 35 major provisions was one that would prohibit federal support for "any program that teaches children values that contradict demonstrated community beliefs or textbooks that denigrate, diminish or deny the historically understood role differences between the sexes" (X 13550). That bill was not passed but similar ones could be expected to be introduced in the future.[2]

In the 1980 NCFR program, Reuben Hill assessed some of the expectable consequences for family research of the new political climate. He saw a "pulling back" to "safer ground" and asked what did this "winding down" portend for family research in the eighties. "There will be an expedient retreat and regress, in the face of economic restrictions. . . . Leaving large-scale national studies to the better financed research bureaucracies, individual scholars will turn to exploratory descriptions of families in transition using small, local samples" (Hill, 1981, pp. 256–257).

Reuben Hill was not one to be pessimistic. He was reassuring. "We can make a virtue out of poverty, if that is what we face in the 1980's" (p. 256). Much of the small-scale, intimate, exploratory research "generates more discoveries per hour expended than large scale quantitative verification or experimentally designed studies in laboratories" (p. 256).

This insight ties in with the second point mentioned at the beginning of this Foreword: the rise of the Feminist Enlightenment in the mid-to-late 1960s *pari passu* with renascent feminism. A considerable amount of the research in renascent feminism was directed toward this kind of research and it did "generate more discoveries per hour expended" than large-scale studies in which human beings are transformed into "variables" and in which we learn a great deal more about "variables" than about marriage or families.

Jacqueline Wiseman (1980) reminded family researchers of a major missed cue: "Family theorists and researchers did *not* predict the onset of what we now term "the sexual revolution," a tidal wave of change in the mores of intimate behavior. Neither the women's liberation movement nor the gay liberation movement appears to have been reflected in our crystal ball. Rather, these phenomena had to be studied after they came into existence" (p. 263).

According to Scanzoni, "There was little or nothing in the 1960's body of research and theory. . . that would have stimulated analysts to move in this direction. Instead, the move was stimulated by happenings in the 'real world'—in particular the revival of feminism" (1983, pp. 237–238). He sees this inability of family theory to anticipate these changes as "indicative of the apparent irrelevance of that theory" (p. 238). And he challenges family scholarship to get with it (p. 238). A brief glance at the way some of the family textbooks were dealing with the women's movement and feminism may help to explain why they did not anticipate their renascence. Family sociologists did not approve of them. The treatment of the

[2]In 1984, a group of parents appealed to the Department of Education under an amendment to a 1978 education act, authored by Orrin Hatch, that called for parental consent before children could take part in federally funded activities including, among other such activities, research surveys. Under that amendment anything that was designed "to reveal information about . . . sexual behavior and attitudes . . . or to elicit critical appraisals of family members" was forbidden. Letters by parents to schools disapproved of participation in "role reversal" and "open-ended discussion."

women's movement or feminism in the 1920s and 1930s was either simply a straightforward historical sketch as a ''won'' case, as in Groves' 1934 or Baber's 1939 texts, or ignored as in Waller's 1938 text. In the 1940s textbooks, such as Burgess and Lock (1943) and Bossard (1948), the effects of war and depression on the status of women began to be included.

The 1964 *Handbook* appeared too early to catch the ''tidal wave of change,'' as Wiseman called it, that was already beginning to sweep over the country. Panos D. Bardis paid his respects to the emancipation of women and specified it as one of the seven main changes in the American family. He was not implying that complete sexual equality had been achieved (1964, p. 457);[3] this was still a male-centered world and many women preferred it that way.

In broad strokes, then, the trajectory had been one in which the textbooks in the first years after 1920 reported the end of the women's movement now that its major goal of achieving the suffrage had been reached and gave it mainly historical attention and a hopeful prognosis. Textbooks of the 1930s and 1940s were beginning to tip in a negative direction vis-à-vis feminism as its implications began to come clear, a trend which became more marked in the babyboom 1950s. The toting-up of pros and cons in the early 1960s tended to emphasize the cons for both women themselves and for society as a whole. It was a period when it was not at all clear what new role configurations were called for by all the new challenges of the times. The term *chaotic* was sometimes used in textbooks to describe the situation; chaotic, but also déjà-vu. Even the so-called sexual revolution had been in the textbooks a long time.

But just as the New Right was different from the prepoliticized Right of the past, so was the feminism emerging in the 1960s different in one major respect from that of the past. Women in the 1960s and 1970s were learning how to participate in the creation of knowledge. They were learning the skills of research, such as how to formulate the relevant questions and how to go about getting the data to answer them. Until then the creation of human knowledge had been an exclusively male prerogative. Now women could share in this powerful privilege.

This *Handbook* directly confronts the politicalization of the New Right and the Feminists Enlightenment in its authorship, subject matter, and in the arrangement of its chapters. First, a complete section is devoted to the diversity in life styles that are presented as viable alternatives to the traditional family and not as deviant or aberrant cases. This would not have been possible, regardless of the editor's persuasion, had there not existed extensive, empirically based research on these topics. Second, in Christensen's *Handbook* only three of the 26 chapters were authored by women. In the Sussman and Steinmetz *Handbook*, one of the editors and 23 of the 42 authors and/or coauthors are women. Equity is a standard-bearer for scholars who view and write their observations of marriage and family systems and behavior. Such internalization of the value of equity in the deep psyches of family scholars is a harbinger of tranformations of the layer body politic in the process of becoming. A critical mass of creative and sensitive professionals now exists, whose perceptions of reality are not limited by tunnel vision; and who are advocates of gender options, quality families, and quality family life.

JESSIE BERNARD

References

Baber, R. E. *Marriage and the family.* New York: McGraw-Hill, 1939.

Bardis, P. Family forms and variations historically considered. In H. T. Christensen (Ed.), *Handbook of marriage and the family.* Chicago: Rand McNally, 1964.

Burgess, E. W., & Lock, H. J. *The family from institution to comparionate.* New York: American Book, 1943.

Christensen, H. T. *Handbook of marriage and the family.* Chicago: Rand McNally, 1964.

Groves, E. R. *The American family.* Chicago: J.B. Lippincott, 1934.

Hill, R. Status of research about marriage and the family. In J. A. Peterson (Ed.), *Counseling: Perspective and prospect.* New York: Association Press, 1968.

Hill, R. Whither family research in the 1980's: Continuities, emergents, constraints, and new horizons. *Journal of Marriage and the Family,* 1981, *43,* 255–257.

Scanzoni, J. *Shaping tomorrow's family.* Beverly Hills: Sage, 1983.

Waller, W. *The family, a dynamic interpretation.* New York: Dryden Press, 1938.

Wiseman, J. The family and its researchers in the eighties: Retrenching, renewing, and revitalizing. *Journal of Marriage and the Family,* 1981, *43,* 263–266.

[3]The other six were: individual choice of mate based on romantic love; decline in parental authority; reduced family size; emphasis on child welfare; decline in the economic, educational, religious, recreational, and protective functions of the family; and prevalence of various forms of disorganization.

Preface

The *Handbook of Marriage and the Family* represents the combined talents of scholars from such fields as demography, history, psychology, social work, social psychology, and sociology who have been chosen because of their expertness as researchers and theoreticians of marriage processes and family systems. When attempting to define an area for inclusion in a publication, the perspectives of authors, editors, and publishers become considerations.

The handbook has been in development over nine years, beginning in 1977. Dr. Steinmetz joined the project in 1980 and contributed substantially in enlarging the concept and scope of the project. Chapter subjects were determined, authors were sought, and the authors' interests and skills with the subject matter were fine-tuned. The publisher gave us a free hand to proceed, with appropriate feedback regarding intellectual and contractual matters during the years of preparation.

The basic concept of the volume is for each chapter to contain a succinct synthesis of the best work done in the topical area. Authors have been encouraged to take advantage of their authorship by introducing new and stimulating ideas that students and scholars of family systems can critique and research. A handbook has a future. It is a sourcebook, referred to constantly, for the factual, theoretical, and empirical data that substantiate the analyses and postures of the author in a given methodological, substantive, or theoretical area. The *Handbook* is a compendium of ideas and authoritative sources, and it is a historical document. As history, it omits works completed after the chapters are written. This is not a serious limitation but a condition inherent in a large-scale publication. The power of a handbook is established by the robustness of its ideas, which stimulate the creative juices to develop new perspectives and patterns of viewing and studying families and their sociocultural milieus.

The Handbook of Marriage and the Family is the first comprehensive compendium to present ''state of the art'' chapters on a wide range of topics since Christensen's classic handbook (1964). This handbook is both similar to and different from Christensen's seminal work. Topics that are absent from the Christensen handbook, such as family power or family violence, now require an entire chapter to provide adequate coverage of factual data, complex theories, and matching methodologies. Christensen devoted four chapters to theory: institutional, structural-functional, interactional-situational, and developmental. We have chosen to combine these conceptual frameworks into one chapter, and we have devoted one chapter to the exposition of newly evolving/nontraditional theories. This approach was taken not to undermine the presentation and discussion of family theories but because of the availability of excellent edited volumes devoted to theory (Aldous, 1978; Rogers, 1973; Nye & Berardo, 1981; Burr, Hill, Nye, & Reiss, 1979a,b).

A similar decision based on the plethora of excellent research and methodology books resulted in a single chapter's being devoted to methodology rather than five chapters' examining separate dimensions of methodology.

Chapters devoted to new topics reflect the great difference of scholars' views of families in the 1980s from those in the 1960s, with recognition given to the diversity of family lifestyles. Five chapters that represent the growth and development of theory and research center on evolving family structures: experimental family forms, singlehood, voluntary childlessness, the single-parent family, remarriage, and reconstituted families. In the 1960s, these topics were usually discussed within the social context of abnormal or abberant behavior.

Five chapters on power, violence, divorce, work, and sex roles represent a recognition of the interface between societal (structural) external forces and family (interpersonal) interactions as found in research and theoretical studies. Marital power, family violence, and divorce are not new phenomena, but in the past two decades, family scholars have addressed these areas as legitimate and important ones in order to understand the full range of family dynamics. Because a majority of contemporary American families have dual earners, the impact of the labor force and sex-role renegotiation for families has become a major concern. Therefore, the need for a comprehensive review of research in these areas became evident.

However, a handbook, regardless of its level of comprehensiveness, cannot be all things to all people. This handbook was prepared for use by scholars interested in a state-of-the-art review of a wide range of marriage and family topics. In the future, we can expect that an awareness of new social problems will foster research in areas only briefly touched on here.

Any project such as this handbook is shaped by the philosophy of the editors and the contributors. Perhaps our philosophy is best exemplified by the organization of this handbook.

The first section, ''Family Perspectives and Analyses,'' provides a foundation of knowledge for students. The seven chapters supply the tools and perspectives for understanding marriage and family structures and processes. The inclusion of a chapter on families in the future is consistent with a section that also contains historical and comparative perspectives.

In the second section, ''Diversity in Family Life,'' diversity is used in its broadest sense to represent not only the nontraditional forms of marriage and families but also ethnicity, social stratification, work, and religion, which cut across all family forms.

Perhaps our inclusion of the chapter on divorce in the section on ''Life Cycle Processes'' best represents our concept that divorce is no longer viewed as pathological; rather, it is a normal part of the life cycle process, along with socialization, human sexuality, the development of gender roles, fertility, and family relationships in the later years.

Our final section, ''Family Dynamics and Transformation,'' focuses on power, stress, and violence, dynamics that have a critical impact on marriage and family life, as well as on institutions that can inhibit or foster change, that is, the law, social policy, family life, education, and marital and family therapy.

As we initially noted, many changes have occurred in the scope and intensity of marriage and family research, theory, and application during the decades since a handbook was first published (Christensen, 1964). We hope that our handbook will encourage continued growth and exploration in the field.

MARVIN B. SUSSMAN
SUZANNE K. STEINMETZ

References

Aldous, J. *Family careers*. New York: Wiley, 1978.

Burr, W., Hill, R., Nye, F. I., & Reiss, I. *Contemporary theories about the family* (Vol. 1). New York: Free Press, 1979. (a)

Burr, W., Hill, R., Nye, F. I., & Reiss, I. *Contemporary theories about the family* (Vol. 2). New York: Free Press, 1979. (b)

Christensen, H. T. *Handbook of marriage and the family*. Chicago: Rand McNally, 1964.

Nye, F. I., & Berardo, F. *Emerging conceptual frameworks in family analyses*. New York: Macmillan, 1981.

Rogers, R. H. *Family interaction and transition*. Englewood Cliffs, N.J.: Prentice-Hall, 1973.

Contents

Chapter 6 • Methodology 125

Robert E. Larzelere and David M. Klein

Chapter 7 • A Perspective on Tomorrow's Families 157

Barbara H. Settles

Chapter 11 • Families and Religions

Teresa Donati Marciano

Chapter 12 • Nontraditional Family Forms

Eleanor D. Macklin

Chapter 18 • Parent–Child Socialization 471

Gary W. Peterson and Boyd C. Rollins

Chapter 19 • Human Sexuality 509

Robert T. Francoeur

Chapter 20 • Development of Gender Roles 535

Susan Losh-Hesselbart

Chapter 21 • Marriage, Family, and Fertility 565

Brent C. Miller

Chapter 28 • Families and Social Policy 795

Phyllis Moen and Alvin L. Schorr

Chapter 29 • Family Life Education 815

Carol A. Darling

INTRODUCTION

From the Catbird Seat

OBSERVATIONS ON MARRIAGE AND THE FAMILY

Marvin B. Sussman

In the September 4, 1985, issue of *The Chronicle of Higher Education* there appeared an article on "Major Trends in Research: 22 Leading Scholars Report on Their Fields." Sociologist Sheldon Stryker resonated on the traditional macro/micro perspectives that have split the sociological enterprise into two camps, and the new emergent direction of linking macro processes with individual behavior. One presumes that a further extension of this direction would be the nexus between the networks of primary groups, such as families with large-scale systems, institutions, and organizations. Implied in Stryker's analysis of new directions is the search for meaning. How do individuals, family units, and their networks impact, influence, handle, neutralize, and adapt with larger social structures and the reciprocal impact of macro upon micro systems?

Another portentous happening according to Stryker is the increase in scholarly writing and research using a life-course perspective. Life stage, timing, transition, trajectory, change, and movement, and the use of now available longitudinal data are some of the components of this research paradigm that is seeking an understanding of the similarities and differences in behavior.

This brief report in the prestigious *Chronicle* should be of comfort to the family scholar. Even if it is not recognized by the body politic of sociology that these new directions have long been advocated and researched by students of the family, and that the concepts, processes, and methods endemic to macro/micro linkages and life-course analysis have been successfully employed, we should feel the power of this recognition. The marriage and family field has existed far too long in a strokeless economy. We stand now to be recognized, rewarded, and empowered.

Suggesting other new directions for research and scholarly work on marriages and the family is my primary task. The rationale for these trends and future directions is based on a set of assumptions, observations, and meanings given to marriage as a process and to the family as a primary group.

From primordial times families have been rooted in the legal and moral orders of their societies. The definition and concept of family as an interaction system of primary relationships, with reproductive and nurturing functions, exist in tandem with legal definitions of family. The legal family is established by the act of marriage. The parties in matrimony sign a contract that establishes their rights, responsibilities, and obligations and that defines the positions of wife/husband, parent/child, grandparents, in-laws, other immediate relatives, extended kin, and affines (Sussman, 1975a,b; Weitzman, 1981).

Within all cultures and in all times law is an all inclusive controlling system that sets the outer limits of permissible behavior to be engaged in by families and its members. It is primarily a latent system. It is difficult to realize the tremendous constraining power of law until one has a "legal problem," such as obtaining a divorce, going through probate on the death of a family member, damaging another person's car after one's insurance has expired, witnessing a crime, being sued for slander, or other anticipated and unexpected events (Sussman, 1983a).

The laws governing marriage and the family relationships are complex and conclusive in establishing the rights, responsibilities, and obligations of marital partners who are forming a bond by the act of marriage. The state has taken the position that it is an interested third party in what otherwise could be described as a private transaction between two persons who are formulating a contract in order to create a family (Jeter & Sussman, 1985).

The issuance of a marriage license and the taking of a blood test are but the tips of the legal iceberg in which the depths of the legal issues are only examined when the marriage turns sour and the partners seek either an annulment, separation, or divorce (Kitson & Sussman, 1977). A relatively small number of couples who marry in the United States every year realizes the full implications of their solemn commitment to each other in which their main source of information is the mass media. Even legal scholars are unaware of the profundity of regulations, obligations, responsibilities, and privileges the law establishes for both parties entering matrimony.

Marriage and family laws have generally been highly discriminatory of women who enter into marriage. The women are treated generally in the same class as children, paupers, the mentally incompetent, and the mentally retarded. Until recently, the law has viewed women to be no better than indentured servants unable to take care of their own resources or having the ability to make sound judgments. The removal of existing prejudicial laws to women and other minorities will take aeons. Spurred on by the gender revolution and other events that indicate we are in a radically changed society are the forces that are facilitating this rapid recodification of law to provide equal justice for women and other oppressed and underclassed persons (Weitzman, 1981).

The family conveys to its members status and position in the society and provides for the orderly transmission of resources over generational time. Our inheritance system provides for such transfers from testators to heirs and legatees (Sussman, Cates, & Smith, 1970). Inheritance is imbedded in legal and sociological doctrines of "natural law," testamentary freedom, distributive justice, "best interests" of family members and the state, the symbolic expression of closeness and intimacy, and the persistence of family lines over generational time.

In a study of 1,234 respondents from 651 randomly selected family units in Cuyahoga County, Ohio, in 1967, persons who comprised the population were heirs or legatees or were about to inherit property, equity, and other resources under the condition of intestacy. It was found that testamentary freedom was exercised within the tradition of the natural law (Sussman *et al.*, 1970). Testators felt a moral obligation to convey status and resources to family members, kith and kin, following encrusted cultural patterns—the paramount filial obligation being to care for one's own. Such behaviors in face of a disinheritance rate of less than 2% in this study had the tacit approval of the state. The state's interest is that individuals do not become wards or dependents of the state, thus increasing the welfare burden for taxpayers. Testamentary freedom (i.e., the right to convey title to persons of one's choice) was exercised within the family and kin network. Charitable contributions were made only after adequate economic provisions were made for family and kin. Testators gave fair shares to their surviving kin based on previous gifts conveyed to children and relatives and services provided by family members to them during the final stages of life. Such "distributive justice" was exercised in cases of intestacy, where no will existed. Those who stood to inherit under the Ohio statute of intestacy and succession elected not to take their fair share but allocated irrevocable rights to their portion to the family caretaker, usually the surviving spouse or child who provided the testator with nurturance and care in the final months or years of life (Sussman *et al.*, 1970).

Two critical family-legal issues emerged from this study. The first is that the inheritance of economic resources is of lesser importance than the bonding of generational ties through the gifting of family heirlooms, goods, and other remembrances. The lesser importance given to economic transfers by heirs and legatees was partially due to the *inter vivos* generational transfers, those which are made during the lifetime of the testator. Also recipients of transfers averaged 55 years of age and were established in their life-styles. Monies and properties transferred were reinvested, thus providing for the chain of generational transfers in a future time. No radical shift in work or family trajectories occurred.

The high significance attributed by inheritors to receiving family heirlooms, goods, and other remembrances is their expression of a lifetime relationship with the deceased. Such conveyances, often of insignificant monetary value, are a symbolic representation of the spiritual, nurturing, and caring relationships internalized in the deep consciousness of these family members and their ancestors.

Such bondings need to be examined in the context of current economic theories that postulate cost/benefit analysis as the most probable explanation. This is a view I held prior to undertaking the research just reported. I believed that the economic transfer was the principal test of generational continuity. One could measure the true meaning and significance of generational relationship by the amount of equities bequeathed and received. This is not the case. The power of these symbolic representations with past generations reinforces the primacy of generationally linked family connections and continuities in a modern urban society.

It is hypothesized that *inter vivos* transfers, those gifts of monies, properties, goods, heirlooms, and services that pass from the living older generations to the younger, far exceed in value and relational importance the conveying of equities at probate. The extent, type, and quantity of such generational transfers, expressive of the informal economy in modern complex societies, have not been studied. Such transfers, which are part of the interlocking family-support system, are the lifelines of generational continuity. Serial reciprocity is invoked. Within family transfers from the older to the younger generation conditions expectations of support when independent living of the elderly is problematic. The working of this critical family informal economic system begs for conceptualization and study.

The law and the legal system have clearly defined the family and have established the rules of marriage and the rights and responsibilities of family members. The law establishes the legitimate status of the family, such as the rights of those to inherit, to receive welfare, and to obtain social security survivor benefits. The law favors the nuclear family, consisting of a husband and wife living in a separate household with their offspring apart from either spouse's set of parents. There is no compelling reason or legal doctrine to establish this as the ideal form. Rather, it is the preferred one because the courts view the traditional nuclear unit to be best suited to express the interests of the state and to promulgate the doctrine of ''the best interests of the child.'' Furthermore, social scientists have speculated that the small-sized nuclear family is best suited to meet the requirements and demands of an industrial society. The cultural wave that worshiped the interchangeable part had to wrench individuals from cottage industries and the family hearth in order to fit them into the developing factory system. Geographic mobility was required because industries were located in areas where it was best for the development and the production of goods at least cost. Hence, the large-scale move of peoples from the farms, villages, and towns to the larger cities where industrialization in its early period experienced near cataclysmic development (Litwak, 1960a,b).

The need for workers to be free to move was real and probably cost efficient for the emergent factory system. The work system began to consume more and more families with the increasing dependency on the new industrial order.

Studies on the history of the family suggest, however, that the nuclear family always existed in preindustrial societies (Bane, 1976; Sussman, 1959). Living side by side with nuclear families were extended, single-parent, three- and four-generational, and blended families. The incidence of divorce compared to today's rate was less, but the incidence of family breakup due to death (largely the consequence of excessive childbearing), Indian wars, and disease produced an inordinate number of single-parent and blended families—those that were created by remarriage. Three- and four-generational households, particularly in rural areas, were in existence. Also found in reasonable numbers were extended families in which individual units had separate households but were tied together in economic, social, ritual, and political undertakings.

A careful mapping of family units of yesteryear and today finds that all forms in existence currently were present in the beginning settlements of society in the United States. The difference is the numbers found in each of the categories of the nuclear-intact household, the single-parent family, the blended family, the extended family, the three-generational family, the dual job, and other structures. In the preindustrial period, there were fewer nuclear units, single-parent, dual-job, and childless couples. Other major differences are in the society's allocation of power and authority to the adult male head of the household regardless of the family form, the birthrate of women of fertility-bearing age, and the family size. Families in early American society were large, childbearing was excessive with attendant high morbidity for women, and men had life and death control over their spouses and children (Hess & Sussman, 1984; Hareven, 1982; Sussman, 1978).

The demographers' population pyramid in the 1980s has been reshaped to resemble a nuclear missile with the smoothing out of cohorts to almost similar in size, becoming almost equal from age day 1 to age 50, and narrowing slightly after age 50 to form the cone of the missile. This configuration is a consequence of a severely lowered fertility rate that resulted in zero population growth after the baby boom of World War II, the increased standards of health of the American people that enabled more and more older adults to survive the trauma of retirement from jobs and to live until their eighties and nineties, and the increased availability of human services to sustain long-term care within families or in institutions (Glick & Norton, 1977; Shanas & Sussman, 1981; Riley, 1979; Uhlenberg, 1979).

The counting of numbers and the making of future projections about the size, shape, and form of the population, which is the basic intent of demographic analysis, are critical for determining policies and legislative programs for different segments and cohorts of the population. Demographic analysis is essential for reasonable planning of the use of current and potential resources. For example, with regard to the current growth of the population aged 65 and over demographers report that, by the year 2010, at least one out of five persons will be over the age of 65, with the largest increase seen among those 75 and older. The magnitude of this development, assuming that catastrophic conditions will not prevail and that the society will not develop a policy of genocide, indicates the need to develop the necessary institutional and other support systems to provide adequate care and protection of this growing population of vulnerable elderly. These demographics, along with pressure from those lobbying for the aged (such as the Grey

Panthers or the American Association of Retired Persons) have prompted legislative changes that extend the work life of the individual to age 70. The replacement rate through reproduction may provide an insufficient number of individuals in the working ages to produce enough goods and services to be able to pay the tremendous costs of support for retired and disabled populations (Sussman & Pfeifer, 1985).

In their analysis of the types, incidence, and prevalence of family structures over time, demographers provide new ways to perceive and think about families. Steinmetz (1974) presents convincing evidence of the sexual bias in the collection of demographic data by the Census Bureau since the beginnings of census taking. In the census of 1800, women who were housewives or who lived in their parents' homes were considered to have "no occupation." The census in 1940 included part-time employed women and those working in family businesses as participants in the labor force. Designating women as heads of households or co-heads did not occur until 1980, even though an increasing number of women (three million in 1971) had a larger earned income than their husbands (Steinmetz, 1974).

The changing demographic profile and the late recognition of women as economic contributors to families, with the subsequent availability of new statistical data, offer the family scholar exciting research possibilities. With the newly collected census data, it is now possible to undertake a more accurate mapping of family types, structures, and households. To date such analyses of varied family forms and household composition used multiple-data sources, and the conclusions were derived primarily from speculative inferences (Ramey, 1978; Sussman, 1971). Studies of women's social and occupational mobility compared to men's, the determination of the accurate socioeconomic status of the family unit, and the examination of family and work trajectories and their consequences for marital health and family well-being are critical and feasible investigations.

The nonpyramid shape of the demographic profile in the 1980s indicates that there is a continuous formation of new family forms and living arrangements. The prospects for the twenty-first century are for family systems in forms conducive to the consequences of the zero population growth rate of the World War II baby boom cohort. Low-fertility parents who might be in search of scarce relatives to assist them, when they are in need, will find few caretakers available in the years 2010 to 2020 when they reach late adulthood. New "like-family" units will be required in increasing numbers (Streib & Hilker, 1980; Sussman, 1984). The expected growth of institutional care facilities will be less than the need because of decreased support from federal and state legislatures and the administrative branches of Government. The increasing acceptance of the notion that smaller, homelike environments for those in need of care is superior to institutional arrangements, especially for the elderly, will support the quest for caretaking families where individuals may not be related by blood or marriage. Family researchers have the rare opportunity to observe the genesis of these emergent forms, their growth and development, as an alternative living arrangement, functioning in complementarity with legal families and institutional forms of care.

Family historians have been successful in using demographic analysis over time to demonstrate changes as well as the persistence and stability of family forms and patterns. Intensive probing of documents and the use of record-linkage techniques to gather data systematically have substantiated the findings that, in historical times, multiple family forms were in existence (Hareven, 1974, 1977, 1978; Bane, 1976; Chudacoff, 1975; Goode, 1963, 1964; Greven, 1970; Modell & Hareven, 1973). In the early history of the United States extended families engaged in help, exchange, support, and connecting. These same patterns can be found in today's urban environments. The number of family members living in a single household has decreased since the seventeenth century. Today, however, most individuals have family members living nearby (Shanas, 1979a,b, 1980; Sussman, 1983b). The result is an optional support system that has essentially the same functions found among seventeenth- and eighteenth-century families. Working-class families in the earlier period struggled to maintain themselves as self-sustaining economic units. Many families resorted to taking in boarders and roomers in order to replace their own members who formerly contributed to the family but had left to set up their own households. These boarders and roomers, who were largely immigrants or migrants, contributed to the family economy, and many became "like" family and were treated as family members (Model & Hareven, 1978).

Industrialization caused a separation of work from the living place as family members were now employed in factories, and service industries became increasingly dependent economically on the growing industrial system. As in the past, large numbers of families continued as production units, with some of their members working in the factories, creating thereby a multieconomic system. As a unit, families contributed to the production of goods and services while, at the same time, they used the wages of those persons working in factories to augment their living standards.

Family historians have provided evidence that this working-class family made great use of an "informal" economy whereby the members produced and exchanged goods and services for each other. They maintained a solidarity and a strong support system influencing decisions regarding the education and jobs of other family members and they developed skills and strategies that affected the individual's participation in the outside world.

The contrary image of an isolated nuclear family, child centered, autonomous, independent, and reserved, stemmed more from portrayals of middle- and upper-class families who were creating and controlling the patterns of industrial development. These families had the resources to afford a very private position. Concomitant with their marriage to the new industrial order and the promises of the new ideology, they were able to promulgate values befitting their high positions in the emerging social class system in the United States and other industrial societies. These middle- and upper-class families became the governing elites, and their life-styles were to be copied and emulated if one was to achieve status and power in society.

Careful research has led to the rejection of the grand theory of linear change in family behavior. Industrialism did not trigger the creation of a nuclear-family form. There was no evolutionary process involved, because nuclear units, along with extended and single parent and other types, existed coterminously in the preindustrial period.

Early historical analyses attempted to reconstruct the history of mankind, using evolution as the major concept whereby one form of family evolved out of another (Parsons & Bales, 1955; Weber, 1947; Zimmerman & Cervantes, 1960). This evolutionary focus is the essence of current theories of change and modernization; however, the contrary conclusion is derived from the work of family historians. Families have adapted and changed selectively in different life sectors, such as work and education, while still maintaining patterns of family life. This procedure occurs in highly sophisticated urbanized environments as it did in preindustrial societies.

Family historians have established what a number of sociologists have emphasized; namely, that there is a reciprocal influence between family systems and societies, organizations, and institutions. Families are not passive entities to be acted on and controlled. Families do take the initiative in effecting changes in the value systems, policies, and practices of organizations and institutions; they are active agents in dealing with outside systems and assist members to meet the normative demands of the more powerful bureaucratized systems.

Another view is that families have little influence over the powerful industrial order and can be detrimental to effective operations of a modern society. Industrial organizations and today's multinational corporations are perceived as requiring individuals to rid themselves of family obligations, especially those that would constrain their mobility and impose the family will over their individual will (Kahl, 1968; Parsons & Bales, 1955; Smith & Inkeles, 1966). In acceding to family control, members would be restrained in their efforts in the industrial system and would eventually partake in the system's largesse which is endemic to the successful production of goods and services. The further assumption is that the family would be a small unit. In the process of adapting and becoming absorbed by large-scale organizations, the family would change its habits, values, tastes, and aspirations. It would begin to measure its success as a modern family by the goods, wealth, and education it acquired.

Such theories are embedded in the concept of modernity and are of limited value to family social scientists, because they assume that family members are subordinate to the more powerful industrial organizations and institutions. Hence it is more comfortable to talk about the modernization of individuals rather than of families, because families are viewed to be insignificant units that always seem to have problems and that are shorn of their historic basic functions.

Soon after World War II, family sociologists began to question the dominance of functional theory which stipulated that the family was a small and fragile unit and limited in its contacts with kin; and therefore, most family units in industrial society were isolated, easily torn by conflict, and limited in their social supports. The major prerequisite for survival of the nuclear unit was its ability to adapt and accommodate the normative demands and power of larger social organizations. In one of the first studies of divorce and its consequences for women, Goode (1956) suggested that where there were social supports women and their offspring adjusted far better when such help was available from friends, family, and kin. No specific effort was made to measure the quality or quantity of such support, but it was strongly indicated that such assistance made a difference. In a study done as a doctoral dissertation and published in 1951, I indicated that in the urban culture of New Haven, Connecticut, there were strong intergenerational connections and that the leave taking of children from the family of orientation did in no way destroy the continuities existing between parents, children, and grandchildren. I noted that for parents in their mid 40s and 50s services and transfers of equities were occurring from parents to children. A variety of exchanges occurred between parents and their adult children, including the provision of services on a regular basis, especially when families lived close to one another, and the great use of holidays and other ceremonial events to maintain family continuity over generational time. In addition, there were exchanges of services and monies in times of crisis and need. All these events suggested that families were linked at least in generational units through the exchange of help, the conveyance of equities, and regular communication.

Litwak (1960a,b) using data available from the Detroit Area Survey, demonstrated the extent of such linkages and found connections that extended along bilateral kin lines. He proposed different descriptions of family networks and suggested that there existed in urban society a modified extended family that differed from the extended family of traditional times, in which individuals who did not live in the same household were linked together in terms of services, help patterns, and in some instances economic enterprises.

In the early 1960s, two review articles were published on intergenerational continuity and urban kin networks (Sussman & Burchinal, 1962) that suggested a plethora of research confirming the existence of a family unit and kin network, within a social and economic context, that had great power and that provided extensive support to member units. The image one receives from this evaluation is that the family is a viable and basic unit of society and is not as weak or dependent on large-scale bureaucracies as had been proposed by the functionalists in sociology and the students of modernity. In the remaining years of the 1960s, investigations continued at a very rapid rate to establish the validity of the existence of a pervasive and "hidden" support system for urban families. Of those I read, I catalogued about 500 studies done over a period of two decades and, undoubtedly, there were countless others.

In 1965, I became concerned about the excessive amount of research establishing the existence of an urban kin network, not only in this society but also in other modern countries like Japan, Greece, Australia, Austria, Yugoslavia, Great Britain, France, Denmark, The Netherlands, and Spain, that I felt obliged to suggest that the next level of investigation should be engaged (Sussman, 1965). This level would look at the meaning and significance of such connections embedded in patterns of service, mutual exchange, feelings of filial piety, and economic well-being. My concern was that the debate on the isolation and fragmentation of the nuclear family and the existence of a viable and optional urban family network would become polemical. Establishing the existence of a functioning kin network is not tantamount to being "good." An objectively described pattern of close connecting through the exchange of services, patterns of visitation, and communication may not bide well for the individuals involved. One classic but stereotypic example is the mother-in-law who visits almost daily and talks on the telephone with her daughter-in-law and who, by any objective measure, is maintaining a high level of intergenerational continuity. She functions as a communicator among all kin—those living close by and those far away. Her negative approach to life and her highly critical position regarding her daughter-in-law result in less than positive consequences for the young family that wishes to recognize the honored status of her as a parent but desires to be free from her repetitious criticism.

As investigators substituted establishing the viability of the urban family kin network and began to probe the impacts of involvement in such networks, a new paradigm emerged. These networks could have either positive or negative consequences for the individuals involved.

Active family networks did not mean the preservation of the traditional and ideal order of historic time—peace, harmony, and solidarity. Lesser credence was given from the point of view to the functionalist perspective that extended families created obstacles to the process of modernization and had a disquieting effect on achieving the goals of an industrial order.

The new paradigm embraced the meaning, significance, and timing of situations and events. When divorce occurs, for example, members of the family network are most effective when they provide warmth, intimacy, and various services to children, such as visits, meals, and general communication without reservation or question. It is ill advised for parents and other immediate family members to force discussion of the causes of the divorce or separation. Divorcing individuals report that family members are so emotionally involved that the divorcing pair cannot handle the interaction. They prefer to accept relief from their burden in any form other than advice or analysis of causes and conditions that led to the separation and eventual divorce (Kitson & Sussman, 1982; Kitson, Sussman, & Holmes, 1982).

In situations in which family or kin members are asked or respond willingly to provide care for an elderly relative, the overwhelming preference is for these family members to provide services rather than monies. The preference is to use extensively third-party payers and the resources of the individual who is in need of care. Only as the last resort does the family want to utilize its own resources and fervently seeks funds not tied to the family's budget (Sussman, 1979).

The effort to deepen the description of the family kin network and its importance to its members within the matrix of human and organizational relationships required attention to conceptual methodological problems and issues. Mapping and quantifying case data do capture the frequency of contacts, the visitation patterns, the economic and equity exchanges, and the overview of extended family connecting and continuity of relationships. These descriptions are of limited value because they gloss over the specific functionalities and consequences of a viable family network and do not indicate the conditions and situations in which a network activity can be detrimental or of benefit to the individuals involved.

One way to reduce gross analyses and descriptions of kin networks and their activities into micro-phenomena was to devise the concept-of-life sector. In order to capture the structure, dynamics, and interaction of family networks in a major cross-national study involving nine countries, it was necessary to consider a single sector of family activity (Sussman, 1974). These sectors included work, leisure, religion, welfare, social service, social control, health, and economy. The sector is composed of a myriad of institutions, organizations, and actors to which family members relate on a daily basis or turn to when there are specific issues and problems in need of solution. Each of these sectors can be subdivided, and the focus of the research activity is to delineate comprehensively the organizational connections of a family unit, the role of the extended family network, the patterns of family–organization interaction, and the complementarity of family and organization roles and functions.

Another technique for establishing the specificity of activities performed by extended family members is to discover their role expertise in different life sectors. In preparation for the cross-national family study just mentioned, a pilot investigation was conducted of family structure, interaction, and cohesiveness in a small city in Puerto Rico. Twenty family networks were mapped and described in great detail. It became apparent that specific family members developed skills based on lifelong experiences from their jobs, religious and political activities, and social relationships. For example, if Jose got in trouble in school, Aunt Rosetta was called since she was a school teacher and knew the principal and the other teachers at Jose's school. She was best suited to find out what the problem was and act as Jose's benefactor and advocate. When Luis needed a driver's license in order to obtain a good paying job after he graduated from high school, grandfather Marin knew how to take shortcuts around the bureaucracy and help Luis obtain the license without having to take the driver's course, which was mandatory. Luis could never get on the list to take the course while he was in high school and did not have the money to pay for private instruction. He had extensive driving experience as do most adolescent Puerto Ricans.

A social security card in Puerto Rico is essentially a work permit. When any member of the Rodriguez extended network needed a social security card, Uncle Pedro, who had long since retired and was a minor figure in local politics in the Bayomen district, could make the necessary arrangements so that the security card was obtained with a minimum of hassle. These are illustrations of how one can use family specialists who act in behalf of family members to describe how families connect, influence, and deal with large scale bureaucracies.

One premise of accepted sociological theory is that work is essential for survival, and that, in complex societies characterized by occupational differentiation, the work system dominates the family. It be-hooves families and their members to be adaptable and highly mobile, to go where the job is located. Those persons in jobs in which upward mobility in the corporate, service, and government systems is possible often face a consequence of geographic movement. The family members gather their belongings and pull up their community roots to establish in another location. Lynd (1929) called this phenomenon the "long arm of the job." The family moves where the breadwinner, usually designated as the male, can find work.

Questioning the verity of this sacrosanct premise is close to committing academic heresy. A truth is being questioned. A reasonable posture is that bureaucratic work systems in complex societies do have some control over families and their members particularly in times of job scarcity. One example would be the closing of the steel mills in the eastern United States as a consequence of their failure to compete successfully with foreign steel imports. A booming economy, on the other hand, creates a demand for workers who are in scarce supply, and it is at this time that families exert considerable influence over the work system, forcing the latter to accommodate to the needs and aspirations of families and their members. A supply and demand principle is operating in the family work bureaucracy nexus. A posture that the work system completely dominates the family's life-style, quality of life, directions, values, and behaviors is unfounded (Sussman & Cogswell, 1971).

A more tenable proposition is that families and their members are in patterns of reciprocal influence with work bureaucracies. This influence is uneven in its consequences and effects. The greater demand for the individual's services in the work bureaucracy, in tandem with positioning in the organizational hierarchy, results in greater consideration given by both the individual and the organization worker regarding family needs, aspirations, and values. Family versus job often becomes an issue.

In June, 1985, John Fabian won his third shuttle assignment which would put him on a crew for a space shuttle with a cargo ultimately destined to reach the planet Jupiter (O'Toole, 1985). This was to be his third mission. Two months after receiving this choice assignment, he resigned from the Astronaut Corps because it was putting too much pressure on his family life. He did not mind the 16-hour work days or the continuous Ph.D.-like training over a work career of 24 years. Fabian, who is age 44, felt that his family was getting short changed. ''Astronauts get a chance to fly in space,'' reported Fabian. ''The families don't get that pay off. All they see are the missed dinners and the trips out of town to Cape Canaveral or to some contractor's factory in California. I came home one night and my wife told me, 'I'm ready to move out of Houston this year, and I hope you are ready to move with me.' I got the message,'' Fabian said.

In a program in which there has been only one resignation a year for the last twenty years, there have occurred eight resignations in the last sixteen months. The causes for quitting the space program are multiple. There is weariness and burnout, feelings of having reached a goal and of now being on a plateau with lessening challenge, and, of course, family concerns. The point of this illustration is to indicate that we have underestimated the power of family values, family members' feelings, and the increasing expressed concerns of the noncareer marital partner, all of which have serious consequences for the work system. The early retirement of the astronauts resulted in the loss of millions of dollars expended for their training and education to accomplish the impossible and to do it successfully.

The questioning of the established proposition of families and their members being subordinate to the more dominant large-scale organizations, such as the work system, needs to continue with the anticipation that the theory will be reconceptualized after some grounded research. Collection of anecdotal and clinical cases such as John Fabian's resignation from NASA is a beginning. Studies are needed to examine systematically the geographical mobility of workers who are ''required'' to move as a consequence of plant closings or for upward mobility in their careers. Such investigations will provide empirical data on the myth of work system control over the lives of families and their members. These studies will establish the conditions, events, and situations in which the families may be influential over the work system and when and where the work system has a greater influence over families and the decisions they have to make.

The greatest task of families in the remaining decades of this century is linking and meeting the normative demands of large-scale organizations and institutions while keeping intact their essential primary group structure, value system, and patterns of interaction. There are several reasons for this posture. The majority of modern nations, including the United States, have reached their absorptive capacities to continue expending large sums of money, through the process of society-wide transfers, to provide formal and institutional care of dependent individuals. The growing numbers of retired persons who are removed from gainful employment and, therefore, unable to contribute to the gross national product, and disabled children kept alive largely by high-technology medicine will be increasingly a care and financial burden. Professional caretaking and support systems have reached the outer limits of their capacities to provide needed care and treatment. The inability of professional caretakers to meet the growing demand for services from the increasing number of children and adults in need is partly due to the unevenness in the geographical distribution of services and professionals. Consequently, there is little political appetite to increase such budgets for funding more health and service organizations that will follow the traditional distribution pattern of favoring the professional over the client or the patient.

In United States society, there is a marked pendulum swing to almost deification of the family. This honorific position had its most recent resurgence during the Carter administration and continued with great force and intensity during the Reagan administration. The family has been rediscovered as a primary unit of society and increasingly persons of all persuasions and ideologies are for the family although their behaviors may be quite contradictory. Efforts are currently underway to return to the family its lost rights and prerogatives. This is being expressed by both liberals and conservatives. There are current drives to make parents responsible for their children, not only in providing their economic support but in being responsible for parenting and accountable for their children's torts. Human service organizations, faced with diminishing resources and operating on Spartan budgets, are being forced to rely more heavily on families and kin networks for the care of chronically ill, disabled, and deviant individuals. To date, a complementarity of roles of such organizations and families has not emerged. Rather, the pattern has been to ''dump'' on the families those cases that are costly with the admonition that the organization has done all it could to help the individual and now ''it is up to the family.''

Families who care for their aged relatives are increasing in incidence. Although feelings of filial responsibility remain strong, the potential for families being burdened by such care, in effect, experiencing burnout, can result in an increased incidence of elder abuse, which will be a growing problem in the decades to come (Steinmetz, 1981, 1982). Despite the wide geographic distribution of family members of different generations and the prospects of burden, 80% of the respondents in one study indicated a willingness to care for an elderly relative under certain conditions (Sussman, 1979). These conditions limit physical and mental capacities. Although the respondents were willing if called upon to care for the older adult in their own homes, they preferred to look after the older person living in a separate but nearby residence. Motivations for providing such care were several: including expectations that the older person would contribute significantly to the life of the family by his or her presence and in the provision of services in a system of mutual exchange. The presence and availability of quality health care, not only for the older persons but also for all family members, were other important motivations to offer a creative environment for the older adult. Receiving a stipend of $200 a month from a support agency, monies which could be used by family members as they saw fit, was a high-priority request.

State and federal authorities and legislatures have responded to the new emphasis on the preeminence of the family by introducing strengthened filial responsibility laws, by developing strong child-support laws with mechanisms for enforcing payment, and by providing tax incentives for families to care for its disabled members. This combination of private- and public-sector action to restore the family to its former independent state of control by giving the family more and more responsiblity for the care of its deviant and disabled members is placing increasing demands on an already burdened family system.

Family researchers and advocates should undertake diligent investigations and actions that will socialize family members to be competent in examining available options for services provided by organizations and institutions. It is a matter of historic record that there is a plethora of services available to individuals and families. For a long time, service agencies have been in competition with one another to provide care for those individuals whose predicted outcomes were favorable. This process is known as creaming the pool of patients or clients in order to have a superb service record, which is helpful in obtaining funds for operations (Haug & Sussman, 1969; Scott, 1969).

American society and other complex societies are blessed with bountiful, humanly created organizations and institutions that exist for the purpose of providing services and the economic well-being of families. The task is to discover where these helping agencies exist, what is provided, what is the array of available options, and to select one that can be pursued with some prospect of success. The family's status in the society as well as the physical and mental capabilities of its members have to be considered in implementing a selected option.

For the researcher, the task is to establish how families discover and utilize these organizations and institutions for their benefit and to use appropriate techniques and strategies to transform the agency, organization, or institution so that they will be receptive to the needs and requirements of family and kin members.

Underestimation of the family as a dynamic force in change and in actions to protect its members is found in sectors other than work. In this age of awakening, there has been an increase in the incidence of religious cults that have directed their attention toward adolescents and young adults as potential recruits. Many cults have been extremely successful in converting adherents to their new religion (Kaslow & Sussman, 1982). Families have been in the forefront in efforts to divest their children from these cults and have used all types of techniques and strategies to effect their release (Hershell & Hershell, 1982; Schwartz & Kaslow, 1982). They have organized into collectivities and have hired legal counsel to pursue this quest.

Organized religion has been neutral with regard to the growth of religious cults and has attempted to modify their own programs to make them more attractive to the youth of the 1970s and 1980s. Government officials have responded to the admonitions and cries for help from families primarily by using their investigative procedures to determine whether the leadership of the different cults, especially those who are successful, may be in violation of income tax laws. Our intention is not to analyze the phenomenon of cults in this short introduction because we have information that many families approve of their children undergoing such a religious and spiritual transformation. Rather, this discussion indicates the dynamism of families who have had to dip deeply into their own resources and consciousness, to become highly innovative and imaginative in developing postures and programs of action, and to take matters into their own hands because institutional support is lacking.

The microelectronic revolution currently in process will provide the family with another tool in its armamentarium for effecting needed change in the practices and policies of large-scale systems so that the family can maintain itself with integrity and life satisfaction. In 1980, I predicted that by 1985 computers would be available for under $400, would have a more powerful memory, and would work faster than most advanced computers that existed in the world at that time (Sussman, 1980). The multiple advantages and disadvantages of families' using computers and the impact of the computer on the family are critical issues. Families will experience increments to a large body of instant information, growing daily, and will be able to examine multiple options in every life sector. The result will be a better base to evaluate the available options and processes required to pursue a choice to a successful conclusion. The dissemination and utilization of large bodies of information, condensed and simplified, will enable families to evaluate more readily the services they receive from human service professionals, merchants, and other providers; the value of purchased products; and the probable success of important choices, as, for example the selection of a college for a child, the taking of another job, or the purchase of property. They will become less dependent on specialists and experts who heretofore through control of information have exercised tremendous influence in family decision making.

It is predicted that families will continue to organize into viable social groups and movements around central issues and concerns. Families will strengthen their knowledge base and interpersonal competencies through the use of home computers, with resultant pressure for greater accountability on the part of government, business, and voluntary organizations. We will enter into a period of social accounting. There will be social auditing of corporate and human service systems with efforts to determine the consequences of social and economic activities of these systems.

One can anticipate that families through their representatives will become more involved in policy formation, program implementation and dissemination, and the use of information that affects their relationships with large-scale organizations within their communities, states, and nations.

Families have always been able to organize around a situation or condition that affects the members directly. The examples of the cults previously given as well as the chronic illnesses and disabilities that affect children have resulted in very strong and powerful organizations that are able to obtain policy changes and introduce legislation helpful to dependent family members and to the family as a unit.

One can anticipate that in the coming decades families will move into the politics of local governance. The policies of decentralized services, local autonomy in matters relevant to families and community well-being, greater reliance on individuals and families in local communities to get the job done with minimal federal support will catalyze increasing involvement of families in local politics and governance. Participation in local governance is best exemplified in membership on such boards as school, planning, sanitation, zoning, environmental, architectural, fire, police, finance, welfare, social service, and perhaps an additional 15 others, and in being elected to office such as on the city council. These units of government shape and control life in the respective communities. In the past, we have underestimated the power of these boards, the legal bases for their actions, and the legislative mandates that provide the bases for control over the lives of all residents.

This transformation from voluntary organization and participation in self-interest groups to political action and local governance has not been completed. Daily newspapers report repeatedly how Mr. X, Mrs. Y, or Ms. Z were automatically elected to the school board because there were no other candidates to run for that position. This practice will change in the coming decades, because family members will learn that active participation in the governing of their local neighborhoods and communities is the best protection of their integrity and utilization of available family and community resources.

In the 1970s, the environmental-impact statement emerged, the purpose of which was to determine the consequences of the introduction of a policy and the concomitant legislation for curing ills or meeting the needs of the community, state, or region. A few years later, the family-impact statement was introduced (Sawhill, 1977), the intent of which was to measure consequences for other family members and for the family as a functioning unit. Part of the impact process is to monitor and evaluate both proposed and current policies and their implementing legislation. There is much discussion in federal and other governmental circles about legislation that will restore to parents more responsibility for the misbehavior and torts of their children. In 1985, the legislature of the State of Wisconsin passed a law making grandparents responsible for the economic maintenance of a grandchild if no support was available from the parent(s). The target population in Wisconsin was the teenage unwed mother. The rationale was to involve parents more extensively in the supervision of sexually active children and, if they failed, to penalize them with child support.

This effort to restore the nineteenth-century image of an ideal family, in which parents are given power, control, and responsibility, is contrary to current policies of protecting the rights of family members especially those who are dependent. Children can sue their parents for abuse. Would a policy of giving parents sole and complete control over other family members increase the incidence of child and elder abuse?

Another component of family-impact assessment is ascertaining the consequences of current policies and programs that focus on remedial, therapeutic, and service activities for individuals on family continuity and well-being. There will be a shift from individual to group emphasis in policy formation and implementation. In the coming decades, families, through their organized strength, will create "family power," that is, they will demand and obtain family-impact statements on a regular basis similar to environmental-impact statements.

The concept of superordinate goals will become more viable and utilized by families and bureaucratic service agencies in the coming decades (Sherif & Sherif, 1964; Sussman & Weil, 1960). Families and service professionals will discover that they need each other and will have to develop a complementarity of their roles and functions, which will emerge as cost containment and concern over institutional control become more manifest. The experiences with deinstitutionalization of the mentally ill and more increasingly of the physically ill have not been an overwhelming success. Families and communities have not been prepared economically or psychologically to receive back family members who were once institutionalized. A new paradigm will emerge as professionals and family members work together around a common goal in which both need each other and neither can succeed in obtaining this goal without the help of the other. Professionals will experience an increase in self-esteem, being able to use their expertise without the need to exercise absolute control over others. Family members will develop the skills to utilize experts in areas in which they do not have the competence and skill required to aid their ill or disabled member, thereby feeling more comfortable in the supportive roles they perform.

The continued presence and persistence of pluralistic family forms will result in changes of federal regulations regarding a family's qualification for service programs. Such changes will be buttressed by court decisions that have and will continue to accept broader definitions of the family than current traditional and legal ones. Along with the relaxation of such regulations, new forms of the family will emerge in the coming decades that are currently highly "experimental." I refer to the everyday, focal, "natural" family whose members are not related by blood or marriage but function as if they were (Ramey, 1978; Sussman, 1975a,b). These are found in different neighborhoods and communities in which members provide the services, caring, love, intimacy, and interaction that all human beings require in order to experience a quality existence. In time, these forms will become institutionalized and legalized, bringing together individuals from different generational cohorts as well as persons of the same peer group.

The family will continue to be the primary unit of all social structures worldwide. Regardless of its size, shape, or membership, the family will carry on those primary functions that enable children to be reared and nurtured and to carry on the values and traditions of their culture. The task of the family scholar is to continue to map families over time and to provide the kinds of information for families to control their own futures and for governmental elites to use such information in the best interest of families.

References

Bane, M. *American families in the twentieth century*. New York: Basic Books, 1976.

Chronicle of Higher Education. Major trends in research: 22 leading scholars report on their fields. 1985, September 4: 12.

Chudacoff, H. *The evolution of American urban society*. Englewood Cliffs, N.J.: Prentice-Hall, 1975.

Glick, P. C. A demographer looks at American families. *Journal of Marriage and the Family*, 1975, 15–26.

Glick, P. C., & Norton, A. J. Marrying, divorcing, and living together in the U.S. today. *Population Bulletin*, 1977, *32*, 5.

Goode, W. *After divorce*. Glencoe, Ill.: The Free Press, 1956.

Goode, W. *World revolution and family patterns*. Glencoe, Ill.: The Free Press, 1963.

Goode, W. *The family*. Englewood Cliffs, N.J.: Prentice-Hall, 1964.

Greven, P. *Four generations: Population, land, and family in colonial Andover, Massachusetts*. Ithaca, N.Y.: Cornell University Press, 1970.

Hareven, T. The family as process: The historical study of the family cycle. *Journal of Social History*, 1974, 7, 322–329.

Hareven, T. Family time and historical time. *Daedalus*, 1977, *106*, 57–70.

Hareven, T. *Transitions: The family and the life course in historical perspective*. New York: Academic Press, 1978.

Hareven, T. *Family time and industrial time*. Cambridge, England: Cambridge University Press, 1982.

Haug, M., & Sussman, M. B. Professional autonomy and the revolt of the client. *Social Problems*, 1969, *17*, 153–161.

Hershell, M., & Hershell, B. Our involvement with a cult. In F. Kaslow & M. B. Sussman (Eds.), *Cults and the family*. New York: Haworth Press, 1982.

Hess, B., & Sussman, M. B. (Eds.). *Women and the family*. New York: Haworth Press, 1984.

Jeter, K., & Sussman, M. B. Each couple should develop a marriage contract suitable to themselves. In H. Feldman & M. Feldman (Eds.), *Current controversies in marriage and family*. San Francisco: Sage Publications, 1985.

Kahl, J. A. *The measure of modernism*. Austin: University of Texas Press, 1968.

Kaslow, F., & Sussman, M. B. *Cults and the family*. New York: Haworth Press, 1982.

Kitson, G., & Sussman, M. B. The impact of divorce on adults. *Conciliation Courts Review*. Los Angeles: Association of Family Conciliation Courts, 1977, *15*, 20–24.

Kitson, G. C., & Sussman, M. B. Marital complaints, demographic characteristics, and symptoms of mental distress in divorce. *Journal of Marriage and the Family*, 1982, *44*, 73–86.

Kitson, G. C., Sussman, M. B., & Holmes, W. M. Withdrawing divorce petitions: A predictive test of the exchange model of divorce. *Journal of Divorce*, 1982, *7*, 51–66.

Litwak, E. Occupational mobility and extended family cohesion. *American Sociological Review*, 1960a, *25*, 9–21.

Litwak, E. Geographic mobility and extended family cohesion. *American Sociological Review,* 1960b, *25,* 385–394.

Litwak, E. Extended kin relations in an industrial demographic society. In E. Shanas & G. Streib (Eds.), *Social structure and the family: Generational relations.* Englewood Cliffs, N.J.: Prentice-Hall, 1965.

Lynd, R. S., & Lynd, H. M. *Middletown.* New York: Harcourt Brace, 1929.

Modell, J., & Hareven, T. K. Urbanization and the malleable household: An examination of boarding and lodging in American families. *Journal of Marriage and the Family,* 1973, *35,* 467–479.

Modell, J., & Hareven, T. K. Transitions: Patterns of timing. In T. K. Hareven (Ed.), *Transitions: The family and the life course in historical perspective.* New York: Academic Press, 1978.

O'Toole, T. Astronauts are bailing out. *The Washington Post National Weekly Edition,* 1985, Vol. 3, No. 2, p. 32.

Parsons, T., & Bales, R. *Family, socialization and interaction process.* Glencoe, Ill.: Free Press, 1955.

Ramey, J. Experimental family forms. *Marriage and Family Review,* 1978, *1,* 1–9.

Riley, M. (Ed.). *Aging from birth to death: Interdisciplinary perspectives.* Boulder, Col.: Westview Press, 1979.

Sawhill, I. V. Economic perspectives on the family. In A. S. Ross, J. Kagan, & T. K. Hareven (Eds.), *The family.* New York: W. W. Norton, 1977.

Schwartz, L. L., & Kaslow, F. W. The cult phenomenon: Historical, sociological, and familial factors contributing to the development and appeal. In F. Kaslow & M. B. Sussman (Eds.), *Cults and the family.* New York: Haworth Press, 1982.

Scott, R. A. *The making of blind men.* New York: Russell Sage Foundation. 1969.

Shanas, E. Social myth as hypothesis: The case of the family relations of old people. *Gerontologist,* 1979a, *19,* 3–9.

Shanas, E. The family as a social support system in old age. *Gerontologist,* 1979b, *19,* 169–174.

Shanas, E. Older people and their families: The new pioneers. *Journal of Marriage and the Family,* 1980, 9–15.

Shanas, E., & Sussman, M. B. The family in later life: Social structure and social policy. In R. W. Fogel, E. Hatfield, S. B. Kiesler, & E. Shanas (Eds.), *Aging: Stability and change in the family.* New York: Academic Press, 1981.

Sherif, M., & Sherif, C. *Reference groups: Exploration into conformity and deviation of adolescents.* New York: Harper & Row, 1964.

Smith, D. H., & Inkeles, A. The OM scale: A comparative socio-psychological measure of individual modernity. *Sociometry,* 1966, *29,* 4.

Steinmetz, S. The sexual context of social research. *The American Sociologist,* 1974, *9,* 111–116.

Steinmetz, S. Elder abuse. *Aging,* 1981 (Jan.–Feb.), pp. 6–10.

Steinmetz, S. Dependency, stress and violence between middle-aged caregivers and their elderly parents. In J. I. Kosberg (Ed.), *Abuse and maltreatment of the elderly.* Littleton, Mass.: John-Wright PSG, Inc., 1982.

Streib, G., & Hilker, M. The cooperative family: An alternative life style for the elderly. *Alternative Lifestyles,* 1980, *3,* 167–184.

Sussman, M. B. The isolated nuclear family: Fact or fiction. *Social Problems,* 1959, *6,* 333–347.

Sussman, M. B. Relationships of adult children with their parents in the United States. In E. Shanas & G. Streib (Eds.), *Family, intergenerational relationships and social structure.* Englewood Cliffs, N.J.: Prentice-Hall, 1965.

Sussman, M. B. Family systems in the 1970's: Analysis, policies, and programs. *Annals of the American Academy of Political and Social Science,* 1971, *396,* 40–56.

Sussman, M. B. *Cross national family research: Report on conceptual development and pilot testing.* Cleveland, Ohio: Institute on Family and Bureaucratic Society, Case Western Reserve University, 1974.

Sussman, M. B. *Marriage contracts: Social and legal consequences.* Plenary address, 1975 International Workshop on Changing Sex Roles in Family and Society, Dubrovnik, Yugoslavia, 1975a.

Sussman, M. B. The four f's of variant family forms and marriage styles. *The Family Coordinator,* 1975b, *24,* 563–576.

Sussman, M. B. The family today: Is it an endangered species? *Children Today,* 1978, *48,* 32–37.

Sussman, M. B. *Social and economic supports and family environments for the elderly.* Washington, D.C.: Administration on Aging, Grant #90-A-316, Winston-Salem, N.C. Study, 142 pp., 1979.

Sussman, M. B. Future trends in society and social services. National Conference on Social Welfare: *Future Trends.* New York: Columbia University Press, 1980.

Sussman, M. B. Law and legal systems: The family connection. *Journal of Marriage and the Family,* 1983a, *45,* 9–21.

Sussman, M. B. Family relations, supports and the aged. In A. M. Hoffman (Ed.), *The daily needs and interests of older people,* Baltimore: Thomas, 1983b.

Sussman, M. B. The family life of old people. In R. H. Binstock & E. Shanas (Eds.), *Handbook of aging and the social sciences,* 2nd ed. New York: Van Nostrand Reinhold, 1984.

Sussman, M. B., & Burchinal, L. Kin family network: Unheralded structure in current conceptualizations of family functioning. *Marriage and Family Living,* 1962, *24,* 231–240.

Sussman, M. B., & Cogswell, B. E. Family influence on job movement. *Human Relations,* 1971, *24,* 477–487.

Sussman, M. B., & Pfeifer, S. *Children and youth connecting with older adults.* Newark, Del.: Department of Individual and Family Studies, University of Delaware, 1985.

Sussman, M. B., & Weil, W. B. An experimental study of the effects of group interaction upon the behavior of diabetic children. *International Journal of Social Psychiatry,* 1960, *6,* 120–135.

Sussman, M. B., Cates, J., & Smith D. T. *The family and inheritance.* New York: Russell Sage Foundation, 1970.

Uhlenberg, P. Demographic change and problems of the aged. In M. Riley (Ed.), *Aging from birth to death: Interdisciplinary perspectives.* Boulder, Col.: Westview Press, 1979.

Weber, M. *The theory of social and economic organization.* New York: Oxford University Press, 1947.

Weitzman, L. J. *The marriage contract.* New York: Free Press, 1981.

Zimmerman, C. C., & Cervantes, L. F. *Successful American families.* New York: Pageant Press, 1960.

PART I

Family Perspectives and Analyses

Theoretical perspectives are employed in marriage and family research for the purpose of providing explanations of what is being observed. Because scholars have different perceptions of reality and assumptions on how families, groups, institutions, and societies are organized and function, there is a plethora of views, which share some elements and diverge on others. These varied perspectives influence the topics chosen for research as well as the methods used in conducting the research. The theoretical constructs presented in this section of the *Handbook* provide multiple explanations of the phenomena reported in other chapters covering substantive marriage and family issues and problems.

The first chapter, by Jay D. Teachman, Karen A. Polonko, and John Scanzoni, contains an approach to family demography that encompasses structure, a set of statuses with associated roles and processes and discrete, observable events that alter previous structures. Using a life cycle modality, these authors analyze age at marriage; fertility; household size and composition; marital disruption and remarriage; female labor-force participation; and the impact that timing and sequence of events has on family formation and development.

In the second chapter, Tamara Hareven utilizes the historical method to gather evidence that families in colonial and nineteenth-century America were diversified in their structures; that nuclear families coexisted with multiple generation and extended households; and that boarders and lodgers had prominent roles in the lives of these families. Using census reports, occupational files, letters, diaries, and birth, marriage, and death registers, Hareven reconstructs the family patterns of the past and provides evidence that the nuclear family did not evolve from the extended one as a consequence of industrialization and urbanization.

Because the family is a universal institution found in all societies, examining families in other cultures allows one to differentiate the means by which families meet their needs. In Chapter 3, Gary R. Lee suggests that the comparative analysis of any behavior influenced by social systems will elicit and document the properties of the systems. Lee limits his analysis to research on family structure, family systems, marital power, and socialization in both industrialized and nonindustrialized societies.

There are two theory chapters. The first, Chapter 4, coauthored by Darwin L. Thomas and Jean Edmondson Wilcox, details the development of family theory through a growing interest in conceptual frameworks, interrelated propositions, and general theoretical models. These authors analyze the evolution of family theory through several phases: nineteenth-century attempts to explain family disorganization, which were influenced by Darwin, Compte, and Spencer and rooted in positivism and structuralism; the social psychologists James, Cooley, Thomas, and Znaniecki in the first half of the twentieth century who provided alternatives to positivism; and critical theory perspectives in more recent times professed by Popper, Kuhn, and Habermas.

In Chapter 5, Marie Withers Osmond focuses on alternatives to the traditional theories used in explaining marital and family behavior. Radical-critical theories have enjoyed a rich history in Europe and have been used recently and sparingly in the study of family in America. Osmond's contribution is a detailed understanding of the history and the application of critical theories. She develops a typology of social theories juxtaposing subjective versus objective analysis and radical change versus processes regulation. She illustrates applications of these theories to marital and family issues and problems.

Although theoretical perspectives influence our interpretation of marriage and family interactions and structures, the methodological perspective—what we study and how we study it—directly influences the body of knowledge available for interpretation. In Chapter 6, Robert E. Laszelere and David M. Klein note that the optimal methodology depends on the nature of the topic, specific research questions, existing research on the topic, and the available resources. There is a need to fit the theory (the significant question) with methods, techniques, and procedures. The authors have identified four characteristics of the family: it is a small group; its existence is lengthy; it is private and value-laden; and it is influenced by its social and physical environment. The conceptualization of research issues and problems, the research design, data collection, and analysis are described with recognition of these four basic characteristics of the family system.

Chapter 7, the final chapter in this section, is authored by Barbara H. Settles. Her discussion focuses on the family as an ideological abstraction; the presence and persistance of a romantic image in our culture; the family as a unit of analysis and treatment; the use of the family as a refuge and as the caretaker of its disabled and dependent members; the family as a process that evolves new pat-

terns, objectives, and procedures over time; and the family as a social and economic network. Specific commentary is on disinstitutionalization versus institutional
alternatives as they impact on medical care, educational
interventions, child care, care of the elderly, and care of
deviates and criminals.

CHAPTER 1

Demography of the Family

Jay D. Teachman, Karen A. Polonko, and John Scanzoni

Introduction

Family demography, a field increasingly investigated by sociologists, demographers, historians, economists, and family specialists, now contains a growing body of literature dealing with a range of topics that can be treated as elements of family demography. This chapter provides an overview of the field, with specific attention to significant research topics central to an understanding of the demographic analysis of families.

Before focusing on specific substantive areas within the field, it is useful to describe family demography, that is, what is unique about a demographic perspective on families and what implications this uniqueness has for data and methods. According to Bogue (1969):

Demography is the statistical and mathematical study of the size, composition, and spatial distribution of human population (structure), and of changes over time in these aspects through the operation of the five processes of fertility, mortality, marriage, migration, and social mobility. Although it maintains a continuous descriptive and comparative analysis of trends in each of these processes and in their net result, its long-run goal is to develop a body of theory to explain the events that it charts and compares. (pp. 1–2)

Several elements of this definition need to be emphasized. First, there is a notion of both structure and process. Second, structure is the result of changes induced by process, although variations in structure can also impact on process. Third, demography seeks both to describe and to explain structure and process, under the notion that *structure* refers to a set of statuses with associated roles that are important to the functioning of society. *Process* refers to the occurrence of discrete, or relatively discrete, observable events that serve to alter previous structure.

Family demography concerns itself with the structure of families and households (i.e., their size, composition, and distribution) and the family-related events (i.e., processes), such as marriage and divorce, that alter this structure through their number, timing, and sequencing. On the simplest level, changes in family and household structure can be "explained" by the processes that serve as transitions between the statuses or positions of which structure is composed. For instance, the increase in female-headed families as a status can be "explained" by increases in factors like divorce and illegitimacy (Ross & Sawhill, 1975). In large part, early demographic research on the family focused on these types of analyses. More recently, though, greater emphasis has been placed on providing explanations for the processes themselves, and thus on constructing a deeper explanation for shifts in structure. To account for variations in the number, the timing, and the sequencing of family-related events, a variety of social, economic, and demographic influences must be considered. Family demographers must therefore supplement their traditional demographic tools with those from other disciplines, recognizing that families and households, and therefore family-related events, are embedded in a milieu of larger social institutions.

The Family Life Cycle

As early as Rowntree's 1906 analysis of poverty over the life cycle, the family life cycle has been associated with family demography (Sweet, 1977). The family life cycle has generally been constructed as a varying number of predetermined stages—based on marriage, childbearing, child rearing, and dissolution through the death of a spouse—that characterize the development of family units (Aldous, 1978; Baltes & Brim, 1980; Cuisenier, 1977; Davids, 1980; Duvall, 1963; Glick, 1947, 1955, 1957; Glick, Heer, & Beresford, 1963; Glick & Parke, 1969; Hill & Rodgers, 1964; Loomis & Hamilton, 1936; Rodgers, 1964, 1973; Rodgers & Whitney, 1981). This framework has provided a scheme into which families can be sorted and has also been used as an independent variable predicting some other element of the social world (Glick, 1947; Lansing & Kish, 1957; Sandefur & Scott, 1981; Speare, 1970; Speare, Goldstein, & Frey, 1974; Waite, 1980; White, 1982). When combined with the concept of birth cohort or marriage cohort (Ryder, 1965), the family life cycle has also served as a convenient mechanism for studying changes in family structure and process (see especially Spanier & Glick, 1980a; Uhlenberg, 1974, 1978). More recent research in this area has expanded to include information on the interrelationships

Jay D. Teachman and Karen A. Polonko • Department of Sociology, Old Dominion University, Norfolk, VA 23508. John Scanzoni • Department of Sociology, University of North Carolina, Greensboro, NC 27514.

between the family life cycle and a variety of related life-cycle processes, such as schooling and employment (Elder, 1974, 1977, 1978, 1981; Furstenberg, 1979; Hogan, 1978b, 1980).

However, although the concept of a family life cycle has been useful in the past, family demography is now a more inclusive field of study, going beyond the delineation of developmental stages. Given the changes in family structure and process, the concept of a family life cycle has become overly rigid, having too great an emphasis on normatively constructed sequences of events, while ignoring variations in the timing of events and nonnormative sequencing (Nock, 1979, 1981; Spanier & Glick, 1980a; Spanier, Sauer, & Larzelere, 1979). To elucidate how families are organized and adapt to social and environmental conditions, family demography has expanded the concept of a life cycle into a more general concept of a life course that focuses on the number, timing, and sequencing of important family-related transitions without assuming predetermined stages. Thus, the life-course concept subsumes the family life cycle, while allowing events like premarital births and divorces to be examined. By focusing on transitions, as opposed to stages, the life-course approach is also better able to include explanations as well as description and categorization (Elder, 1978). In sum, although the family life cycle made, and still may make, sense in the biological realm, from which demographers originally borrowed it, it becomes less useful as an explanatory tool for contemporary analyses of the family. What is needed now, and in the future, are valid conceptions of the complexities of ongoing development and change in the family across the course of adult development.

Data

Data from the decennial census and the vital statistics registration system have provided the basis for most demographic research on the family. An important supplement to these data is the Current Population Survey, especially the periodic birth and marital histories that have been gathered. These data sources constitute a reasonably representative sample of the U.S. population and contain a large number of cases. In combination, they provide information on levels, trends, and differentials with respect to marriage, divorce, remarriage, and fertility, as well as family or household structure.

These data suffer from several limitations, however. First, the detail of information pertaining to social, economic, and other characteristics of individuals experiencing family-related events is limited. Second, most of the information on such characteristics refers to the time of enumeration, therefore opening up the issue of causality, as various transitions themselves affect the social and economic characteristics of individuals. Third, the continuity of data collected over time with respect to topical coverage, definitions used, and so on is often low, a circumstance leading to considerable difficulties in constructing a picture of long-term trends and plaguing researchers who attempt to perform historical analyses (see Hareven, 1978).

A full understanding of family structure and process, including explanations for the processes themselves, requires what Tuma, Hannon, and Groenevald (1979) have called event–history data, or data that contain the dates at which events occur in time. Along with information on social, economic, and other characteristics, such data can provide a very detailed description and explanation of family composition and change. The appropriate data may be gathered in longitudinal studies or by asking a series of retrospective questions in a cross section. Retrospective surveys, however, may suffer from problems of recall as well as misreporting. Panel studies are also useful but pose analysis problems not found when the dates of events are recorded (again, see Tuma *et al.*, 1979). A summary of the data available, including longitudinal and panel surveys, and of census and vital-statistics data has been provided by Glenn and Frisbie (1977). The authors also pay attention to the deficiencies of census and vital statistics for trend analysis.

Methods

Because family demographers deal with discrete, observable variables, their methods are mainly quantitative, making use of the descriptive and inferential statistics commonly found in the social science literature (see Glick, 1964). Some demographic analyses of family-related events have also relied heavily on mathematical models to illuminate underlying regularities and associations in family structure and process (Coale, 1971; Hernes, 1972; Krishnamoorthy, 1979).

Family demographers also rely on specific concepts and methodological tools to study population structure and process. A central concept is that of a rate, or the number of events during an interval relative to some population exposed to the risk of that event (i.e., divorces per 1,000 married couples). The body of literature surrounding the concept of a rate also includes procedures for separating changes due to rates from changes due to shifts in composition (Althauser & Wigler, 1972; Kitagawa, 1955, 1964). For example, such procedures can determine whether the increase in the number of divorces can be attributed to the growing number of marriages involving individuals in the most divorce-prone ages or to an increase in the rate of divorce irrespective of age (Michael, 1978).

Rates are also the main component underlying life table analysis. Although originally developed to study mortality, life tables are useful in studying the number and timing of family-related events (Elandt-Johnson & Johnson, 1980; Gehan, 1969; Gross & Clark, 1975). Thus, life tables focus on the incidence of events as they occur in a population of individuals exposed to the risk of experiencing the event. This emphasis is distinct from an emphasis on prevalence, which considers the number or percentage of individuals characterized by having experienced the event in question at some point in time. For instance, the prevalence of divorced persons in a population can be distinguished from the incidence of new divorces taking place. Recent advances have also enabled the multivariate analysis of life tables in a regressionlike fashion (Kalbfleisch & Prentice, 1980; Tuma, Hannon & Groeneveld, 1979).

Six major substantive areas are covered in this chapter: age at marriage, female labor-force participation, fertility, divorce, remarriage, and household size and composition. Emphasis is placed on an update of trends, differentials, and explanations that have occurred since 1960, and attention is also limited to the United States. The discussion of each substantive area begins with a general overview of trends in the recent past. Attention is then focused on differentials and explanations that have been covered in the literature. The review of previous work is selective, stressing what we perceive to be the most important findings from the most representative studies. At the end of the chapter, we summarize the significant trends and present a suggestive framework within which they may be interpreted.

Age at Marriage

From the turn of the century through the baby boom, age at marriage in the United States declined; a particularly steep decline occurred during the 1940s and 1950s. Since the mid-1960s, however, the trend has reversed. As shown in Table 1, between 1960 and 1979, the median age at first marriage rose from 22.8 to 23.4 for men, and from 20.3 to 21.6 for women, with the bulk of the increase occurring primarily after 1975. Also, the age difference between males and females at first marriage has declined from about 4 years at the beginning of this century to 2.5 years in 1960 and 1.8 years in 1979, because of the more rapid increase in recent years in the age of females at first marriage compared to that of males.

Period marriage rates, also shown in Table 1, are seemingly inconsistent with the rise in median age at first marriage, as they indicate that the number of marriages per 1,000 total population was higher in 1979 than in 1960. However, the number of marriages per 1,000 unmarried women aged 15 and over declined between 1960 and 1979, as shifts in the U.S. age structure were responsible for the increase in marriages per total population. Because of the baby boom, an increasing proportion of the population has moved into the most common marriage ages, shifting the crude marriage rate upward. But among those eligible to marry, the marriage rate has declined.

Another view of this phenomenon is shown in Table 2. Between 1960 and 1979, the percentage of never-married women aged 20–24 rose from 29% to 49%. Similarly, the percentage of never-married women aged 25–29 more than doubled, increasing from 9.5% to 19.6%. The delay in marriage, therefore, is particularly sharp for women reaching their 20s during the 1970s, primarily involving women born after 1945 (i.e., products of the baby boom). The percentages of those never married of women age 20–29 are now consistent with pre-1940 levels, and as Masnick and Bane (1980) pointed out, "the rate of increase in the proportion single for specific age groups [has been] greater than ever before experienced by any successive cohorts born in the twentieth century." (p. 27). The decrease in the percentage of those never married between 1960 and 1970 for women over age 30 and the lower rate of increase between 1970 and 1979 for this age group mainly involve women who reached marriageable ages during the baby-boom years, when marriage and birth rates were high.

Another element of changing marriage statistics is shown in Table 1. The percentage of marriages that are first marriages has declined over the 1970s from 75.8% to 64.3% for men, and from 76.2% to 65.9% for women. In part, this shift is due to the increasing delay in first marriages, as well as a consistent rise in divorce rates, which has increased the proportion of once-married persons in

Table 1. Median Age at First Marriage, Marriage Rates, and Percentage of Marriages That Are First Marriages: 1960–1979[a]

Year	Median age at first marriage		Marriage rate		Percentage first marriages	
	Male	Female	Crude[b]	General[c]	Male	Female
1979	23.4	21.6	10.7	63.6	64.3	65.9
1975	22.7	20.8	10.1	66.9	68.7	70.1
1970	22.5	20.6	10.6	76.5	75.8	76.2
1965	22.5	20.4	9.3	75.0	—	—
1960	22.8	20.3	8.5	73.5	—	—

[a]Source: Various issues of Monthly Vital Statistics Reports, National Center for Health Statistics.
[b]Rate per 1,000 total population.
[c]Rate per 1,000 unmarried women aged 15 and over.

Table 2. Percentage of Women Never Married by Age: 1960–1979[a]

Age	Percentage by year		
	1979	1970	1960
20–24	49.4	35.8	28.9
25–29	19.6	10.5	9.5
30–34	9.5	6.2	6.9
35–39	6.6	5.4	6.1

[a]Source: U.S. Bureau of the Census, 1980. "Marital Status and Living Arrangements: March 1979." Current Population Reports, Series P-20, No. 349, Table B.

the pool of eligibles. Further, divorce has been occurring at younger ages, increasing the probability of remarriage.

An adequate model of historical shifts in marriage age has not appeared in the literature. About all that can be generalized from the efforts of formal modeling is that marriage is heavily age-stratified (Coale, 1971; Trussell, 1976b) and that marriage markets are inherently unstable. One element in the instability of marriage markets has been termed a *marriage squeeze,* a term referring to the imbalance in the number of eligible persons of each sex (Akers, 1967; Muhsam, 1974) that may occur, for instance, when war losses reduce the number of marriageable men relative to the number of eligible women. More common are marriage squeezes caused by shifts in fertility. The escalating number of births in the United States during the late 1940s and through the 1950s has meant that females born during these years have faced a relative shortage of slightly older men, perhaps as much as 10%. Such an imbalance may be corrected in several ways: (1) women may marry later or remain permanently single; (2) they may shift the preferred age range of potential spouses to include younger men; or (3) they may marry men who previously would not have been selected in the marriage market (Sweet, 1977). It would also be expected that marriage rates for men would increase to meet the age-induced shift in demand. However, shifts in age differences between spouses have not coincided with the recent marriage squeeze (Presser, 1975). Further, age at first marriage for men has risen along with that for women, a trend opposite to what would be expected if only the marriage squeeze was in operation (Sweet, 1977).

Some researchers have argued that increases in economic uncertainty have slowed the rate at which individuals enter marriage, as, alternatively, the good economic times following World War II increased marriages at young ages (Easterlin, 1980). Modell (1980; see also Modell, Furstenberg, & Strong, 1978) has argued that economic opportunity during the baby-boom years allowed individuals to achieve early-marriage ideals and that poor economic times during the Great Depression kept individuals from achieving these goals. As discussed by Sweet (1977), other potential explanations for the recent rise in age at first marriage include the greater availability of contraception and abortion, rising levels of educational attainment, the increasing labor-force participation of women, and changing ideology consistent with the women's movement—in short, changes over time in the status of women. Since the mid-1960s to the late 1960s, through the 1970s, research suggests that there has been a gradual, but pervasive, shift toward more egalitarian sex-role preferences (see the review by Scanzoni & Fox, 1980). At the same time, women's level of educational attainment has been increasing, and their employment options have been expanding. In a mutually reinforcing manner, these changes have served to provide more women with increasingly attractive alternatives (e.g., prestige and income), which compete with the traditional rewards

of marriage and childbearing, resulting not only in delayed marriage but also in smaller families (Masnick & Bane, 1980; Scanzoni, 1972, 1975).

Although each of these factors has changed along with age at marriage, no study has provided a solid estimate of their effects. The evidence that does exist on the effects of these factors on marital timing is largely based on cross-sectional studies at one point in time. What is needed, then, are studies that adequately measure all of the variables in question and that assess their relative effects on changes in age at marriage, through either a series of cross sections or longitudinal data.

Differentials in Age at Marriage

A number of early studies focused on factors associated with marital timing, but many used small, nonrepresentative samples. Research using census data is limited in the range of variables available for examination, and seldom do these variables tap the circumstances or the characteristics of individuals at the time when they make the decision to marry. Thus, the differentials considered here are those examined in larger, more representative survey efforts, many of which are quite recent. A comprehensive review of some of the earlier studies is provided by Otto (1979).

Family Background Factors. Of all background variables, parental socioeconomic status has received the most attention. Although variation in measurement has obscured conclusions, earlier research suggests a positive relationship with marital timing (see the review and explanations in Otto, 1975, 1979). More recent multivariate studies, however, have failed to find strong direct effects. This is particularly true for males (Hogan, 1978a), although Waite and Spitze (1981) found that the socioeconomic status of parents does have a direct effect in reducing the chances of marriage for young teenage women, a finding suggesting that parents use their resources in a more direct fashion to prevent their daughters from marrying too early. Overall, the findings of research suggest that the effects of parental socioeconomic status on marital timing are primarily indirect, through such variables as high educational aspirations and achievement (Bayer, 1969; Marini, 1978) and later marriage plans (Bayer, 1969; Moore & Hofferth, 1980). Recent studies investigating other characteristics of the parental household have not systematically pursued several background variables on which previous research has been quite consistent, such as perceived dissatisfaction with the adolescent role (i.e., perceived disagreement with and estrangement from parents or otherwise poor home adjustment), which may serve to increase the costs associated with the adolescent role and to hasten marriage.

In summary, it appears that early background variables do not play an important direct role in creating differentials in age at marriage. Rather, the findings suggest influences that are primarily indirect, particularly as they impact on norms, values, preferences, and life-course plans and experiences that are formed in young adulthood, before marriage.

High-School Experience. Three groups of variables relating to plans and experiences during the high-school years have a more substantial impact on marital timing than earlier family background factors. First, research suggests that high grades or academic success, parental encouragement, and educational expectations and goals delay marriage, operating primarily through educational attainment (Bayer, 1969; Marini, 1978). Also, Voss (1975) has found that occupational aspirations have a positive effect on marital timing, controlling for educational attainment, but only for females. Overall, it appears that expectations and events that lead to the development of achievement (vs. familistic) orientations, combined with academic success, delay marriage, especially for females. Conversely, as Otto (1979) stated, it appears that "the early-married [have] reached a 'dead end' academically" (p. 109).

Second, perhaps the most important high-school experience predicting subsequent marital timing is dating (Bayer, 1968) or early heterosexual involvement and sexual experimentation (Bartz & Nye, 1970). Marini (1978) has documented the key direct and indirect impact of dating frequency on early marriage for both genders, but especially for females, beyond any other indicator of social activity or rebellion in high school. The effects of early heterosexual involvement may reflect, in part, increased opportunities for meeting a spouse (Becker, 1973, 1974) or experience of a premarital pregnancy. However, it is more likely that this association centers on traditional sex-role preferences or familistic orientations, as females who value marriage and children are "more likely to move faster and further into dating and into intimate, physical relationships" (Bartz & Nye, 1970, p. 266). Consistent with this finding and with Bartz and Nye's concept (1970) of anticipated satisfactions from marriage, research (Bayer, 1969; Moore & Hofferth, 1980) has also found that ideal or expected age at marriage affects marital timing.

Education. A consistent finding in the literature is that education delays marriage, although most individuals marry shortly after completing their education (Bayer, 1968, 1969; Call & Otto, 1977; Davis & Bumpass, 1976; Freiden, 1974; Hogan, 1978a; Keeley, 1977; MacDonald & Rindfuss, 1981; Preston & Richards, 1975; Voss, 1975). Recent research has begun to explore possible reciprocal effects by estimating structural equation models allowing for a simultaneous relationship between age at marriage and education. It is generally found that, for women, education delays marriage; in turn, early marriage has a negative, but much smaller, impact on educational attainment (Marini, 1978; Marini & Hodsdon,

1981; Moore & Hofferth, 1980). For men, education also acts to delay marriage, but less so than for women, and marital timing has no significant impact on educational attainment (Marini, 1978).

Alexander and Reilly (1981) have criticized these efforts for a number of methodological and substantive reasons and have suggested dynamic models as an alternative to structural equation models. Using such models, they concluded that previous studies are biased in overestimating the effect of marital timing on education. However, their substantive conclusion is not different from previous research: Early marriage reduces further educational attainment for females, but not for males.

Overall, the stronger relationships for women than for men point to the differential salience of socioeconomic achievements. In contrast to men, most women are socialized to view marriage and childbearing as primary goals and means of status attainment, thus allowing marriage to interfere with their educational attainments (Marini, 1978). However, among women, higher education does serve to increase the attractiveness of alternatives to the wife role and to increase the costs of marriage, in part because of the more egalitarian preferences or tastes of more educated women (Scanzoni, 1975) and the more rewarding occupational and income potential that this education affords them.

Labor Force Participation and Income. Research findings show that the proportion of never-married women in their early 20s is higher in urban areas where the industrial structure provides more opportunities for female employment and in areas where female earnings are higher (Preston & Richards, 1975; Freiden, 1974; White, 1981). Research on individual-level data (Keeley, 1977) also finds that higher income women delay marriage longer.

Findings on women's premarital employment are more complex. For example, Waite and Spitze (1981) found that premarital employment acts to hasten marriage, and they reasoned that employment may increase contact with potential spouses and make women more attractive in the marriage market. However, Cherlin (1981) found that prior employment had little effect on marriage two years later, and Scanzoni (1979a) found that working full time prior to marriage had a strong effect on delaying marriage. In contrast, though, both Cherlin (1981) and Waite and Spitze (1981) found that women who planned to be in the labor force at age 35 were more likely to delay marriage. Thus, it appears that commitment to the labor force (e.g., full-time employment and plans for employment) and actual career success (e.g., higher income) are key variables that serve to increase the costs of assuming the wife role. In contrast, more traditional women, who are not committed to the labor force, may use their paid employment as a resource to marry earlier.

With respect to males, the results are generally opposite to those for females, as higher earnings are associated with earlier marriage for men who have entered a career (Keeley, 1977; MacDonald & Rindfuss, 1981). The study by MacDonald and Rindfuss (1981) also found that current male income relative to parental income had no effect on marital timing. This finding is contrary to Easterlin's relative income hypothesis (1980) which predicts that men who experience greater financial success than their parental household when they were growing up will marry earlier. Current employment and a first full-time job are related to earlier marriage for men (Mac-Donald & Rindfuss, 1981), although men with higher status jobs are slightly more likely to delay marriage (Hogan, 1978a). Service in the military has also been found to delay marriage (Hogan, 1978a; MacDonald & Rindfuss, 1981).

These differential effects for males and females are most likely due to the difficulty that women have in combining attractive nonfamilial roles with marriage (Waite & Spitze, 1981; Marini, 1978; Scanzoni & Scanzoni, 1981). As women typically must make their occupational achievements secondary to their husband's career and to their responsibilities for housekeeping and childcare, the women who are most committed to their careers and who are the most successful have the most to gain from delaying marriage. Conversely, as men typically assume the primary provider role, marriage does not hold the same costs in terms of expected career sacrifices, and higher socioeconomic resources increase the male's attractiveness as a future wage earner.

Premarital Fertility. Early heterosexual involvement and sexual experimentation are related to early marriage. As Scanzoni and Fox (1980) noted, among teenage females, premarital sex is associated with more traditional sex-role preferences, which would reduce the perceived costs of a premarital pregnancy. Thus, it is not surprising that many early marriages are accompanied by a premarital pregnancy, and this proportion has been growing over time (Glick & Norton, 1977).

The aggregate impact of premarital conceptions on marital timing depends not only on the frequency of conception but on the availability of and willingness to obtain an abortion and the propensity to legitimize the pregnancy. Some evidence suggests that the advent of legal abortion may be one factor in the rising age at marriage as premarital pregnancies are increasingly terminated (Bauman, Koch, Udry, & Freedman, 1975).

Over time, a lower proportion of premarital pregnancies have been legitimized (O'Connell & Moore, 1980; Teachman & Polonko, 1982; Zelnick & Kantner, 1980). Although the impact of a premarital birth on marital timing varies by age at birth (Teachman & Polonko, 1984; Waite & Spitze, 1981), Ryder and Westoff (1971) reported that women with a premarital birth marry, on average, later than women without a premarital birth. This finding indicates that women who do not choose abortion or to legitimize the pregnancy operate differently in the marriage market.

Race and Ethnicity. Census data show that foreign-born individuals and native-born individuals of foreign parentage marry later than native whites or blacks, whereas native blacks marry later than native whites (Carter & Glick, 1976). Controlling for other variables, blacks still marry later than whites (Marini, 1978; Moore & Hofferth, 1980; Preston & Richards, 1975; Waite & Spitze, 1981). However, it may be inappropriate to assume that the same variables influence marital timing for each race. For instance, census data and data from the Current Population Surveys show that highly educated white women (with five or more years of college) are much less likely to have married than highly educated black women. High educational attainments thus appear to be more incompatible with marriage for white women than for black women, perhaps because of the greater responsiveness of blacks to individual rights for women (Scanzoni & Scanzoni, 1981).

Related conclusions may be drawn from a study by White (1981) that found that, for nonblack women, higher median female earnings and greater employment opportunities for women delayed marriage. Black women, however, were actually more likely to marry when median female earnings were higher. The black–white differential in marital timing is also likely to be affected by variations in premarital fertility, abortion, and legitimization. Unmarried black women are more likely than white women to become pregnant but are less likely to seek an abortion (although, overall, black women are more likely than white women to obtain an abortion) and are less likely to marry in order to legitimize a pregnancy (O'Connell & Moore, 1980; Teachman & Polonko, 1982; Zelnick & Kantner, 1980).

Other Factors. For both men and women, age at marriage is consistently higher in larger cities and in the Northeast (especially compared to the South). These differentials cannot be explained by compositional differences on a number of variables, such as race and education (Carter & Glick, 1976; Hogan, 1978a; Preston & Richards, 1975; Waite & Spitze, 1981). Similarly, shifts in age at marriage by birth cohorts of individuals remain after controlling for numerous control variables (Hogan, 1978a; Moore & Hofferth, 1980). It remains for future research to identify the factors responsible for geographic and birth cohort variations in marital timing.

Waite and Spitze (1981) have found that the effects of many variables on marital timing vary by the age of the woman, with most serving to enhance or decrease the probability of marriage at young and old ages. To some extent, this age grading may help to explain the failure of earlier research to find significant effects for some variables, as they operate differentially across age groups. Previous research has implicitly assumed the effects of any independent variables being researched to be linear across all ages. Waite and Spitze's results indicate that a nonsignificant effect in prior research could occur by forcing this assumption on the data. In other words, a variable that increases or decreases the probability of marriage within a specific age group may not appear to be as significant if it is assumed to have an equal impact on marriage at all ages.

Consequences

Marriage is a life-course transition with long-term consequences. Marrying at a young age, especially for women, can define the nature, content, and structure of future roles, often truncating the development of preferences for and participation in alternative roles (e.g., education, postmarital employment, and earnings) in which tastes competing with familial activities are generated and reinforced (Presser, 1971; Rossi, 1965; Scanzoni, 1979a).

Age at marriage also has implications for fertility. For instance, Gibson (1976) attributed about one fifth of the decline in U.S. period fertility rates between 1971 and 1975 to increased age at marriage. On the individual level, an early marriage is associated with higher completed parity and rapid birth spacing (Bumpass, 1969; Bumpass, Rindfuss, & Janosik, 1978; Marini & Hodsdon, 1981; Tsui, 1982; Westoff & Ryder, 1977a; Wilkie, 1981). In part, this association may reflect the greater amount of reproductive time available to couples who marry earlier, as well as their less efficient contraceptive use. It may also be that couples with higher fertility ideals may marry younger (Modell, 1980) or, more important, that younger married couples are less likely to participate in activities competing with childbearing.

Studies have also linked early marriage to higher levels of marital instability, for both males and females and blacks and whites (Bumpass & Sweet, 1972; Moore & Waite, 1980; Teachman, 1983). Weed (1974) found that age at marriage is a factor in explaining differentials in divorce rates by state. Marriage timing also has an impact on family and household structure (Masnick & Bane, 1980; Cherlin, 1981). With an older age at marriage, fewer children are being born. Delayed marriage, in conjunction with an increased propensity to leave the parental household, has also contributed to the rise in the number of individuals living alone.

Female Labor-Force Participation

In 1950, about 34% of women aged 16 and over were in the labor force, making up about 29% of all workers. By 1980, the percentage of women working or looking for work rose to nearly 52%, constituting 43% of the labor force. In contrast, over the same period, male labor-force participation dropped from 84% to 77%, and the male percentage of all workers declined from 71% to 57%. This trend is detailed in Table 3, showing increased female labor-force-participation rates for all marital statuses. The labor force participation rate of widowed and

Table 3. Percentage of Women in the Labor Force by Marital Status: 1960–1979[a]

Year	Percentage[b] by marital status		
	Single	Married	Widowed or divorced
1979	62.7	50.0	40.0
1975	56.8	45.0	37.7
1970	53.0	41.4	36.2
1965	40.5	35.7	35.7
1960	44.1	31.7	37.1

[a]Source: Various issues of Special Labor Force Reports, U.S. Bureau of Labor Statistics.
[b]Age 16 and over.

divorced women is weighted downward by the large number of widows receiving social security (see Table 5). Since 1960, single women have increased their employment by 18.6% and married women by 18.3%. Thus, the rapid increase in female labor-force-participation rates cannot be explained by the increase in the proportion of single women in the population.

A shift in the age structure is also an insufficient explanation for the increase, as there has been an increase in labor force participation for each age group between 1960 and 1980 (see Table 4). However, the increase has been strongest at the younger ages, when women have traditionally married, have started childbearing and child rearing, and have dropped out of the labor force. Over the 20-year period, employment increased between 27% and 29% for women aged 20–34 and 21.4% for women aged

Table 4. Percentage of Women in the Labor Force by Age, 1960–1980, and Percentage of Women Fully Employed by Age, 1960–1977[a]

Year	Percentage in labor force				
	20–24	25–34	35–44	45–54	55–64
1980	73.0	63.3	62.9	58.6	40.6
1970	57.7	43.2	49.9	53.7	42.6
1960	45.7	34.1	41.5	48.6	36.2

Year	Percentage fully employed[b]				
	20–24	25–34	34–44	45–54	55–59
1977	27.7	32.1	32.3	32.8	31.1
1970	25.6	22.7	26.9	32.9	31.6
1960	22.4	16.5	22.9	27.1	24.0

[a]Sources: Waite (1981); Masnick and Bane (1980).
[b]Employed 35 hours or more per week for 50 or more weeks per year.

35–44. Conversely, at the older ages, when children are older or have left home, labor force participation increased much less, including a drop of 2% between 1970 and 1980 for women aged 55–64.

The differential rate of growth in labor force participation by age has changed the employment status of each age group vis-à-vis other age groups. The cross section of labor force participation rates for 1960 and 1970, for instance, indicate what Masnick and Bane (1980) call an M-shaped pattern, with a dip in labor force participation at ages 25–34 because of responsibility of child rearing, and with employment higher at younger and older ages. However, the rates for 1980 show a considerable departure from the past. A dip below the rates observed for women aged 20–24 still occurs, but women aged 25–34 are actually more likely to be working than older women.

Regarding age patterns of female employment over the past century (see Lloyd, Andrews, & Gilroy, 1979; Oppenheimer, 1970, 1973; Smith, 1980; Sweet, 1973b; Waite, 1981), women born before the turn of the century generally had their highest rates of labor force participation at the youngest ages, leaving the labor force after marriage and not returning unless forced to support themselves or their family. Women born after the turn of the century (until recent cohorts) have generally been characterized by the M-shaped pattern of labor force participation, with each successive cohort experiencing higher peaks on both sides of the M. However, although their employment histories are truncated, women born after World War II appear to be generating a new profile of employment across their life course. Women in these more recent birth cohorts have increased their employment at all ages, with a gradual flattening of the M-shaped pattern, leading to the possibility that the shape of the curve as well as the levels of labor force participation for women will approach those for men in the next decade (Masnick & Bane, 1980).

Falling fertility may help explain why more recent cohorts of women have been more likely to enter and stay in the labor force. However, labor-force-participation rates for married women with children, especially preschool children, have gone up faster than for other women (see Table 5). In 1950, only about 12% of married women with children under 6 were in the labor force, a figure that increased to over 43% by 1979. The increase was also much greater for married women compared to divorced women, although women without a spouse are still much more likely to be working.

Even though married women with young children have increased their labor-force participation the most, they are the least likely to be working full time, followed by married women with older children. This finding underscores the point made by Masnick and Bane (1980) that participation in the labor force does not necessarily imply full-time or continuous employment and that high participation rates "can mask wide fluctuations in work schedules to accommodate childcare" (p. 65). As of 1978, about two thirds of all women workers were em-

Table 5. Percentage of Women in the Labor Force by Marital Status and Age of Children: 1960–1979[a]

Subject	Percentage in labor force		
	1979	1975	1960
Married husband present	49.4	44.1	34.7
No children under age 18	46.7	43.9	38.3
Women aged 16–34	81.9	77.2	62.4
Women aged 35+	38.3	35.5	34.3
Children aged 6–17 only	59.1	52.3	42.7
Children under age 6	43.2	36.6	23.3
Divorced	74.0	72.1	—
No children under age 18	69.9	69.9	—
Children aged 6–17 only	83.4	80.1	—
Children under age 6	68.9	65.6	—

[a]Sources: U.S. Bureau of the Census, 1980. Statistical Abstract of the United States: 1980. Table 672; Glick and Norton (1977).

ployed full time (a percentage that has changed little over time), and 44% of women workers were employed full time for a full year (Masnick & Bane, 1980; Waite, 1981). Thus, only about one third of all women were fully employed (i.e., employed 35 hours or more per week for 50 or more weeks per year; Masnick & Bane, 1980). As shown in Table 4, the percentage fully employed rose gradually, for all age groups, between 1960 and 1970, although continued increases appear only for younger women, especially those aged 25–34. Thus, trends for women born after 1945 may be foreshadowing a fundamental departure from past trends in attachment to the labor force, although even among younger women, two thirds are still not fully employed. Furthermore, among women with children under age 3, for example, only a small minority, about 10%, are fully employed (Masnick & Bane, 1980), and women cite "taking care of home responsibilities" as the most common reason for being employed only part of the year (Barrett, 1979). Such findings are consistent with Masnick and Bane's conclusions (1980; p.71) that, although fewer women are completely dropping out of the labor force in response to family contingencies, it appears that they are continuing to adjust their paid employment to the dictates of marriage and child rearing.

Research, using a variety of approaches, has reached opposite conclusions on the degree to which female employment is sequential (involving movement in and out of the labor force) or bipolar (involving women who remain either employed or not employed; Ewer, Crimmins, & Oliver, 1979; Heckman & Willis, 1977; Masnick & Bane, 1980; Scanzoni, 1979b). For example, Heckman and Willis argued that there is consistency over time in the percentage continuously employed versus the percentage continuously not employed. Based on a question on whether the wife did any work for money in a particular year, they found that 27% had worked five out of five years, 35% had not been employed in any of the five years, and 38% had moved in and out of the labor force. However, using the same data for a 10-year period and defining work as earning more than $100 in a year, Masnick and Bane stressed the continuing sequential nature of female employment in response to family demands, as only 20% of wives were in the labor force all 10 years, 18% never were, and 62% moved in and out. The youngest wives were the most likely to have ever been employed, but the least likely to have worked all 10 years. Also, if earnings greater than 20% of the family income or greater than 33% of the family income, respectively, are used as a crude proxy for being employed, then the same data suggest that between 2% and 7% of the wives were fully employed for all 10 years (Masnick & Bane, 1980; Table 3.4). Thus, the minimal definition of paid employment most commonly used (i.e., having worked for pay in a particular year) allows for substantial shifts from full to part-time employment as family needs dictate.

Conclusions regarding consistency in the labor market activity of women are therefore dependent on the time frame and the methods used. Also, to more fully understand the nature and implications of consistency or continuity in light of the increasing age at marriage, the postponement of having children, and the greater percentage remaining permanently childless, there is a need to examine employment patterns in relation to the presence or absence of children *per se*. Cramer's results (1980), for example, suggest that, in the short run, there is evidence for the bipolar, "mover–stayer" model of employment, but that "the effect of employment before birth on subsequent employment clearly diminishes over time as intervening events and contingencies become more common and more important" (p. 181).

The intent here is not to minimize changes in female employment that have been occurring, as a "revolution" in labor force participation among women has clearly taken place. However, although such changes are important, it is not yet clear whether parallel changes in the nature and continuity of market activities are as entrenched.

Female Labor: Demand and Supply

Oppenheimer (1970, 1973, 1976) has provided an attractive framework that helps to explain the large influx of married women into the labor force over this century. Starting with the point that occupations are typed by sex, she showed that females have traditionally monopolized several occupations that have expanded tremendously over this century (e.g., teachers, nurses, and secretaries). At first, this demand could be met by the supply of young single women preferred by employers and supported by prevailing norms. Over time, however, the supply of young single women declined, leaving the demand unmet. To meet the demand, older women first moved into the labor force, followed by younger married women with children. Therefore, at least part of the reason for the increase in female employment, particularly for married women, has been a structural transformation involving economic and demographic components: an economic component in the increasing demand for female labor and a demographic component in the changing relative supply of female labor by age and marital status.

Economic Necessity

In addition to structural changes, ther have been economic pressures to work because of recessions, unemployment among males, and inflation (Bowen & Finegan, 1969; Smith, 1979; Waite, 1981). The majority of female workers still are unmarried or are married to men with low incomes and thus work out of economic necessity (Barrett, 1979; Waite, 1981). Even though women earn only about 60% of what men earn for the same full-time full-year employment (Lloyd & Neimi, 1980), their contribution to the family income can be significant. Currently, husband–wife families with the wife employed have incomes roughly $6,000 greater than families in which the wife remains at home, and on average, working wives contribute about one fourth of total family income (Waite, 1981). The percentage that wives contribute in two- earner families ranges from 11% for part-time or part-year workers to 38% for full-time, full-year workers, and, interestingly, the percentage of contribution has not changed much over time (Masnick & Bane, 1980).

Oppenheimer (1979) noted that the economic position of men aged 20–34 vis-à-vis men aged 45–54 has declined since World War II, a period when consumption standards and aspirations rose. To meet consumption demands and to offset the relative economic deprivation of young males, more married women in their childbearing years have moved into the labor force. Once in the labor force, particularly given the rising educational levels of women and their own increasing taste for employment outside the home, they are not as likely to leave permanently.

Occupations and Income

Occupational segregation has not decreased over this century and may even have increased, especially in heavily female occupations like nursing and secretarial work. Half of all women in the labor force work in jobs where men constitute 20% or less of their co-workers (Waite, 1981). Since 1960, there has been a slight reversal, but even a this trend is far from a random assignment of new employees to jobs (Blau & Hendricks, 1979).

Segregation may be attributable to at least three factors: (1) the lower educational attainment of women (although this is changing); (2) discrimination on the part of employers; and (3) preferences on the part of women. Brown, Moon, and Zoloth (1980) found that the occupational attainments of women highly committed to the labor force are less than those of males, controlling for the effects of age, experience, and education (see also Barrett, 1979; Bergmann, 1971). However, data show that many women even among the more highly educated desire traditionally female jobs (Barrett, 1979). Undoubtedly, all three factors interact, so that even highly educated women may misperceive their chances for occupational success, limited partially by discrimination practices, and therefore aspire to a career dominated by females.

One consequence of this occupational segregation is that women earn less than men, as female occupations are traditionally low-paying (Barrett, 1979; Bergmann, 1971). However, women are paid less than men even within the same occupations, and this difference increases with age and is changed little by education (Waite, 1981). Furthermore, there is no indication of a decrease in the male–female earnings gap over time (Waite, 1981).

Differences in Female Labor-Force Participation

Research on the correlates of female labor-force participation has mainly focused on married, husband-present women. As this literature is extensive, only a few of the major studies and findings are reviewed here. Married women are more likely to be in the labor force if they are black, if they are highly educated, if their potential wage rate is high, if the local labor market provides greater opportunity for employment, if they have a history of prior employment, and if their husbands have lower incomes (Bowen & Finegan, 1969; Cain, 1966; Cramer, 1980; Heckman & Willis, 1977; Mincer, 1963; Mott, 1972; Smith-Lovin & Tickamyer, 1978; Waite, 1980; Waite & Stolzenberg, 1976). In addition, fewer and older children are associated with increased female employment (Cain, 1966; Sweet, 1973b; Waite, 1980), as are longer first-birth intervals and the use of birth control (Groat, Workman, & Neal, 1976). Employment plans and attitudes of both husbands and wives also affect the labor market activity of women, although they are largely dependent on the women's past employment behavior (Cramer, 1980; Ferber, 1982; Spitze & Waite, 1981).

The effects of these variables have also been found to vary according to factors like the race and the education of women (Leibowitz, 1974; Sweet, 1973b). Moreover, the labor force participation of married women has been found to respond differentially according to the presence or absence of children, their age and spacing, and expected future fertility (Clifford & Tobin, 1977; Groat, Workman, & Neal, 1976; Mott, 1972; National Center for Health Statistics, 1980b; Oppenheimer, 1979; Shapiro & Mott, 1979; Waite, 1980).

Consequences

One of most cited consequences of female employment is that it reduces fertility. Considerable effort has been expended in trying to determine the nature of the relationship between female employment and fertility, and much of the recent research focuses on a reciprocal relationship between these two variables. Waite and Stolzen-

berg (1976) found a strong effect of employment plans on reducing fertility expectations but only a weak effect of fertility expectations on reducing plans for employment. On the other hand, Smith-Lovin and Tickamyer (1978) found that actual fertility (number of live births) has a much greater effect on years in the labor market. Such divergent findings could be due to the use of plans versus behavior or to the use of different control variables. However, Cramer (1980), noting that both studies used structural equation models to estimate the reciprocal relationship, estimated a series of dynamic models and concluded that, "in the short run, fertility has a strong effect on employment, but, in the longer run, the effect of employment on fertility may be stronger" (p. 165). It may also be that increased female employment reduces the likelihood of marriage or at least delays entry into marriage, and delayed marriage is related to lower fertility (Bumpass, 1969; Rindfuss & Bumpass, 1978).

Once she is in a marriage, the employment of the wife does not change the household division of labor (Vanek, 1980), as men do not appreciably increase the amount of household labor they perform when their wives have paid employment outside the home, although most of these wives do not state a preference for extra household help from their husbands. Rather, working wives have reduced their total weekly labor input, mainly by cutting down on the amount of housework they perform (Stafford, 1980). Results from a recent study of faculty women similarly indicate that, even among dual-career couples, the traditional division of labor exists (Yogev, 1981). Regarding other areas in marriage, the results of employment on power are not clear, although it appears that employed wives may have greater power in certain areas of decision making (see Moore & Hofferth, 1979). Last, the evidence suggests that a wife's employment *per se* does not have a direct effect on marital satisfaction (Glenn & Weaver, 1978; Locksley, 1980).

Female employment may influence household structure by affecting rates of marital dissolution and remarriage. A growing body of literature indicates that working wives are more likely to dissolve their marriages than housewives (Cherlin, 1977, 1979; Moore & Waite, 1981; Mott & Moore, 1979; Ross & Sawhill, 1975). In addition, divorced and widowed women who work are probably less likely to remarry (Wolf & MacDonald, 1979). The net result is that increasing labor-force participation on the part of women is tied to the increasing proportion of female-headed households.

Fertility

Perhaps more than any other topic covered in this chapter, fertility has received the most research attention. Fertility is covered extensively in the decennial census, the Current Population Surveys and vital statistics (Cho, Grabill, & Bogue, 1979; Rindfuss & Sweet, 1977). In addition, much work has been done on documenting trends and differentials in childbearing (Grabill, Kiser, &

Whelpton, 1958; Ryder & Westoff, 1971; Westoff, Potter, Sagi, & Mishler, 1961; Westoff & Ryder, 1977a; Whelpton, Campbell, & Patterson, 1966); identifying and modeling the complex biosocial process by which childbearing varies across time and individuals (Bongaarts, 1978; Davis & Blake, 1956; Potter, 1963; Ryder, 1980, 1981; Sheps & Menken, 1973); examining socioeconomic differentials in fertility, offering theoretical orientations (see Andorka, 1978; Hawthorne, 1970; Bagozzi & Van Loo, 1978); and measuring fertility, recognizing that different views of the same phenomenon can suggest different explanations (Hendershot & Placek, 1981; Rindfuss & Sweet, 1977; Ryder, 1975).

Given the richness of detail concerning fertility, only very broad trends on general fertility trends in number and timing, illegitimacy, planning status, and contraception are covered here.

Trends in Number

Between 1917 and 1935, the nation's total fertility rate, a period measure, dropped from 3,333 to 2,145 per 1,000 women, or an average decline of over one child per woman. By 1957, the total fertility rate had risen to 3,682, or an average increase of over one and one-half children per woman. Since 1957, fertility levels have dropped precipitously, with the 1979 total fertility rate being 1,856, or about one half the 1957 level. The increase in fertility during the baby-boom years and its subsequent decline occurred among virtually every major subgroup of the U.S. population, although with variation in the magnitude of rise and decline (Rindfuss & Sweet, 1977).

The upward shift in completed fertility for cohorts of women producing the baby boom was largely due to fewer women remaining childless or having only one birth compared to women passing through their childbearing years during the Great Depression (Cutright & Shorter, 1979; Ryder, 1969). Thus, the baby boom was not the result of more women having very large families. In addition, Ryder (1969, 1980, 1981) has shown that period fertility rates for the baby-boom years were inflated because of the rapid tempo in childbearing. Thus, the baby boom represented a convergence around the two-to-three-child family, with early marriage and closely spaced births.

Explanations for the baby boom are still subject to debate and focus on a variety of factors, including the promarriage and pro-natalist norms of the period (Blake & Das Gupta, 1975; Bouvier, 1980; Gibson, 1976) and the privileged economic position of young adults in the 1950s compared to that of their parents (Easterlin, 1973, 1980). It may be that, after a decade of depression and four years of war, as well as a postwar economic boom, Americans were especially anxious to enjoy the perceived security of a strong family life (Cherlin, 1981; Modell, 1980). Other explanations include shifts in the timing of births in reaction to anticipated female wages and labor force participation (Butz & Ward, 1977, 1978) and to

high levels of unwanted births, with later fertility declines due to reductions in unwanted births via improved contraceptive technology (Westoff & Ryder, 1977a). Masnick and McFalls (1978) showed, however, that the fertility decline since the baby boom is due less to changes in contraceptive technology *per se* than to changes in the rigor of contraceptive use once sexual activity is begun. This is an important point, because modern contraceptive innovations cannot explain the low fertility of the Depression years.

Table 6 shows the decline in fertility between 1967 and 1979, accompanied by changes in expected lifetime fertility for wives aged 18–34. As fertility has dropped, so has expected fertility. Although fertility expectations are not always a sure indicator of future childbearing (Hendershot & Placek, 1981), the magnitude of the declines indicates a substantial downward revision in preferences, both within and across cohorts of women. Indeed, 1979 levels of expected lifetime fertility imply replacement levels of childbearing.

In addition, part of the fertility decline since the 1960s reflects increases in the proportion of women at each age who are childless (Bloom & Pebley, 1982). Between 1967 and 1976, the percentage of all wives aged 14–39 intending to remain childless increased from 3.1% to 5.4%. The increase was more pronounced for white women and highly educated women (i.e., 4.5% of white wives aged 14–39 with one or more years of college intended to remain childless in 1971 vs. 8.7% in 1976; the corresponding figures for white women with less than a high-school education were 3.1% and 3.4%). As of 1980, about 6% of wives aged 18–34 expected to remain childless, and about 11% of all women in this age group expected to do so. Bloom (1981), at the high end of the spectrum, projected that about 30% of younger cohorts of all white women may remain childless. There have also been substantial increases in the percentage expecting to

Table 6. Total Fertility Rates and Expected Lifetime Births per 1,000 Married Women Aged 18–24, 25–29, and 30–34: 1967–1979[a]

Year	Total fertility rate[b]	Lifetime births expected by age[c]		
		18–24	25–29	30–34
1979	1,865	2,164	2,193	2,282
1975	1,799	2,173	2,260	2,610
1971	2,275	2,375	2,619	2,989
1967	2,558	2,852	3,037	3,288

[a]Source: Various issues of Monthly Vital Statistics Reports, National Center for Health Statistics, and various issues of Series P-20, Current Population Reports.
[b]Births per 1,000 women aged 15–49 over their lifetime under current fertility levels.
[c]Per 1,000 married women.

have one child. In 1967, about 5% of wives aged 18–34 expected to have only one child, as opposed to about 12% in 1979. Numerous other researchers have also noted a trend toward increased childlessness and the one-child family over that experienced by baby-boom mothers (Blake, 1981; Cutright & Polonko, 1977; DeJong & Sell, 1977; Freshnock & Cutright, 1978; Hastings & Robinson, 1974; Houseknecht, 1978; Polonko & Scanzoni, 1981; Poston & Gotard, 1977; Veevers, 1979).

The total fertility rate of 1856 per 1,000 women for 1979 is a 3% increase over that recorded for 1975. Although this percentage reflects a slight increase in the number of births and in age-specific fertility, most of the rise can be attributed to births delayed from previous years. Whereas age-specific fertility rates have inched upward in recent years for first, second, and third births, the parity-specific birth probabilities have not changed and have even decreased in some cases. In other words, because of population increase and delayed childbearing, there has been an increase in the number of women eligible for first, second, and third births. Combined with even constant parity-specific birth probabilities, this increase has led to increased fertility rates, both overall and specific by age. The amount of increase involved does not portend a shift in completed fertility. Rather, it indicates a small bulge in period fertility because of changes in the timing of childbearing. It appears likely that fertility in the future will generally remain low, with variations being the result of shifts in timing.

Trends in Timing

As the above discussion implies, it is difficult to abstract trends in number from changes in timing, especially for cohorts of women still in their childbearing years. As shown in Table 7, for women first married in 1950–1954, over 60% had a first birth within two years of marriage. The corresponding percentage for women first married in 1955–1959, the peak years of the baby boom, was over 68%. Starting in 1960–1964, the percentage dropped, so that, for the 1970–1974 marriage cohort, less than half the women experienced a first birth within two years of marriage. These figures illustrate the quickening and subsequent slowdown in the pace of childbirth linked to the rise and decline of the baby boom.

Table 7 also shows a countervailing trend with respect to first childbirth. The sequencing of marriage and childbirth has changed in intensity, with more marriages involving a premarital birth or pregnancy. Between 1950–1954 and 1970–1974, the percentage of marriages involving a premarital birth increased from 6.5% to 9.5%, and the percentage of marriages involving a legitimized birth increased from 14.5% to 22.1%. By 1965, nearly one third of all first marriages involved either a premarital birth or a pregnancy legitimized by marriage. Because premarital conceptions are included in the percentage of women experiencing childbirth within two years of marriage, they obscure an even greater trend in delayed child-

Table 7. Premarital Fertility and Spacing of First Births after Marriage by Marriage Cohort: 1950–1954 to 1970–1974[a]

| Year of first marriage | Percentage involving a | | | Months after marriage to first birth | |
	Premarital birth[b]	Premarital pregnancy[c]	Premarital conception[d]	12	24
1970–1974	9.5	22.1	31.6	32.9	48.4
1965–1969	8.3	22.9	31.2	39.6	57.2
1960–1964	8.2	21.6	29.8	43.8	67.3
1955–1959	7.6	18.7	26.3	42.0	68.2
1950–1954	6.5	14.5	21.0	35.0	60.6

[a]Source: U.S. Bureau of the Census, 1978. "Trends in Childspacing, June 1975." Current Population Reports, Series P-20, No. 315, Table 26.
[b]Born before marriage.
[c]Born within seven months after marriage.
[d]Premarital births plus premarital pregnancies. Does not include spontaneous fetal loss or induced abortion.

birth among women with postmarital conceptions. The figures for premarital conceptions and delayed births also indicate a growing tendency for childbirth to be disassociated from marriage, that is, with respect to increasing fertility before marriage (premarital births and pregnancies), as well as the considerable postponement of childbearing after marriage for the remaining women.

Significant differentials exist with respect to premarital fertility and child spacing. Most important, perhaps, blacks are much more likely to experience premarital fertility and a rapid first birth than are whites (U.S. Bureau of the Census, 1976a). Rapid first childbirth is also more likely to occur among women who marry early, have less education, are Catholic, and do not participate in the labor force (Davidson, 1970; Hastings, 1971; Hastings & Robinson, 1975; Namboodiri, 1964; National Center for Health Statistics, 1981; Tsui, 1982; Whelpton, 1964; Wilkie, 1981).

For subsequent births, however, the above differentials in birth spacing are considerably diminished. The spacing of second and subsequent births has not changed as significantly over time as that of first births (National Center for Health Statistics, 1981; Tsui, 1982). Rather, a major determinant of subsequent birth timing is the spacing of the first birth (Bumpass, et al., 1978; Marini & Hodsdon, 1981; Millman & Hendershot, 1980; Presser, 1971; Tsui, 1982).

Another way to look at the timing of fertility is to consider the percentage of women who have remained childless to particular ages. Table 8 shows that the percentage childless at various ages has been increasing since at least 1965. In 1965, about 20% of all women aged 25–29 were childless. By 1979, this figure had increased to almost 38%. Indeed, by the late 1970s, almost one

Table 8. Percentage of All Women and Ever-Married Women Who Were Childless at Selected Ages: 1960–1979[a]

	Percentage of all women			Percentage of ever-married women		
Year	25–29	30–34	35–39	25–29	30–34	35–39
1979	37.8	18.7	11.7	26.2	13.1	7.1
1975	31.1	15.2	9.6	21.1	8.8	5.3
1970	24.4	11.8	9.4	15.8	8.3	7.3
1965	19.7	11.7	11.4	11.7	7.2	8.7
1960	20.0	14.2	12.0	12.6	10.4	11.1

[a]Source: Various issues of Series P-20, Current Population Reports.

Table 9. Percentage of Marital Births by Planning Status: 1961–1965 to 1975–1976[a]

	Percentage by planning status[b]		
Period	Planned	Mistimed	Unwanted
1975–1976[c]	69	23	9
1970–1973	63	25	12
1966–1970	57	29	14
1961–1965	45	31	24

[a]Source: Anderson (1981).
[b]Among currently married women aged 15–44.

third of all first births were occurring to women aged 25 or older. This delay in childbearing is also evident in the proportions childless at ages 30–34 and 35–39. The figures for ever-married women follow the same general pattern as for all women, showing that the trend toward delaying childbearing cannot be fully explained by the concurrent rise in age at first marriage.

Bloom (1981) showed that the mean age at first birth for women turning age 14 and over increased from 22.1 in the early 1950s to 22.9 in the late 1960s. For white women, the change was from 22.4 years to 23.4 years. Among black women, however, there was actually a decrease, from 20.7 to 20.3 years. Bloom also found that, although the overall mean age at first birth had been going up in recent years, there had been a drop in the age at which appreciable numbers of women had first births. This finding is consistent with the data contained in Table 7, which show increases in premarital conceptions. It is also consistent with the increasing tendency toward bifurcation in the childbearing experience of women: fertility increasingly either occurs at a young age or is delayed. Also, as discussed earlier, the analyses by Bloom and others indicate increases in the proportion who will remain childless permanently, representing another example of the apparently increasing tendency to disassociate childbearing from marriage. Thus, women are more likely to be entering the parent role either early, late, or never. The birfurcation of childbearing experiences reflects not only more varied alternatives to family life but also a greater consistency between gender-role preferences and fertility behavior: egalitarian women delay or forgo childbearing, and women with a familistic orientation become young parents.

Contraception and Birth Planning

Congruent with the decline in fertility from levels observed during the baby-boom years, there have been significant changes in the wantedness status of births (Anderson, 1981; Weller & Hobbs, 1978; Westoff, 1981; Westoff & Jones, 1977), as shown in Table 9. For the period 1961–1965, only about 45% of marital births were wanted and planned with respect to timing, whereas 31% were mistimed and 24% were unwanted. By 1975–1976, only 9% of marital births were unwanted, and 69% were planned and timed correctly. The shift away from unwanted and mistimed births was registered across race, education, religion, and income groups, although by 1975–1976, differentials still persisted, with blacks and low-income families subject to higher levels of unwanted births.

Table 10 shows that these changes in the wantedness status of births were accompanied by changes in contraceptive use patterns among married women. Although the percentage of nonusers did not change significantly between 1965 and 1976, the distribution of methods among users shifted considerably, with increases in the proportion of women relying on sterilization, the IUD, or the pill (although the pill and IUD usage appear to have

Table 10. Percentage of Married Women Using Contraception by Method and Abortion Rate: 1965–1979[a]

	Percentage by year			
Method	1979	1976	1973	1965
Contraception[b]	—	67.7	69.6	63.9
Sterilization	—	18.6	16.4	7.8
Pill	—	22.5	25.1	15.3
IUD	—	6.3	6.7	0.7
Other methods	—	20.3	21.4	40.1
Nonusers[c]	—	20.9	22.9	21.7
Abortion rate[d]	30.2	24.5	16.6	-

[a]Sources: National Center for Health Statistics, 1981. "Contraceptive Utilization: United States 1976." Series 23, No. 7, Table A; Henshaw, Forrest, Sullivan, and Tietze (1982).
[b]Among currently married women aged 15–44.
[c]Excludes those noncontraceptively sterile, pregnant, postpartum, or seeking pregnancy.
[d]Abortions per 1,000 women aged 15–44.

dropped slightly between 1973 and 1976). By far the most dramatic increase was in sterilization, from nearly 8% to over 18%. The net effect of these changes was a substantial increase in overall contraceptive efficiency, which may partially explain the decline in unwanted births over this period. Still, very low fertility was achieved by women living their childbearing years during the Depression through the use of methods currently believed to be "unattractive and inefficient" (Dawson, Meny, & Ridley, 1980). Blake and Das Gupta (1975) also showed that over 70% of the decline in marital fertility between 1961 and 1970 was due to downward shifts in family-size expectations, and that only about 22% was due to less unwanted fertility. Thus, the process of recent fertility reduction is more complex than a simple reduction in unwanted births.

The trends in legal abortion between 1973, the year of the U.S. Supreme Court decision, and 1979 are also presented in Table 10. In 1973, there were 16.6 abortions per 1,000 women aged 15–44, rising to 24.5 in 1976 and 30.2 in 1979. Increases in abortion have been slowed because of problems with geographic location, cutbacks in medicaid funding, increased use of parental notification and consent, and restrictions placed on abortions by clinics that perform them (Forrest, Tietze, & Sullivan, 1978; Henshaw, Forrest, Sullivan, & Tietze, 1982). It is probable that increases in abortion helped to lower unwanted fertility among married women, although women seeking abortion disproportionately represent unmarried women.

Illegitimacy

As overall fertility dropped during the years following the baby boom, rates of illegitimacy continued their historical upward trend (Cutright, 1972a). In 1940, there were 7.1 illegitimate births per 1,000 unmarried women aged 15–44, and by 1979, the figure had increased to 27.8. Although a decrease in the rate of illegitimacy occurred between 1970 and 1974, the upward trend resumed in 1975. For a historical view on illegitimacy, see Cutright (1971a, 1972a, b) and Smith an Hendus (1975). Illegitimacy rates for nonwhites are much higher than for whites, but the general trend for nonwhites since 1960 has been downward, whereas that for whites has been upward (see Table 11). However, the percentage of all live births outside of marriage has increased for both races. Only about 2% of all white births were illegitimate in 1960, rising to over 9% in 1979. For nonwhites, the jump was from about 22% to 49%. Part of this increase, among whites, can be explained by rising illegitimacy rates, but the major determinant for both races has been the substantial decline in legitimate fertility.

Illegitimacy has been increasingly concentrated among teenage women and thus has been more likely to involve first, premarital births (O'Connell, 1980). Focusing on premarital births among young women under age 24, O'Connell and Moore (1980) reported findings confirm-

Table 11. Trends in Illegitimacy: 1960–1979[a]

	Rate[b]			Percentage of all live births	
Year	Total	White	Nonwhite	White	Nonwhite
1979	27.8	15.1	80.9	9.4	48.8
1975	24.8	12.6	80.4	7.3	44.2
1970	26.4	13.9	89.9	5.7	34.9
1965	23.5	11.6	97.6	4.0	26.3
1960	21.6	9.2	98.3	2.3	21.6

[a]Source: Various issues of Monthly Vital Statistics Reports, National Center for Health Statistics.
[b]Rate per 1,000 unmarried women aged 15–44.

ing those listed for illegitimacy in general, documenting a strong differential between blacks and whites. They also found that, since 1970, premarital fertility had changed little for women aged 20–24, whereas premarital fertility for women under age 20 had risen substantially.

Attention has also been devoted to premarital sexual activity and contraceptive use (Kantner & Zelnik, 1972; Zelnik & Kantner, 1974, 1977, 1978a, 1978b, 1980; Zelnik, Kim, & Kantner, 1979). These studies show that, during the 1970s, rates of premarital sexual intercourse rose for both black and white women, although the values for blacks stabilized around 1976, and the differential between blacks and whites declined. Still, on average, black women initiate intercourse about one year earlier than white women (aged 15.5 vs. age 16.4). In 1979, among women aged 15–19, 47% of the whites and 66% of the blacks had engaged in premarital intercourse.

With respect to contraceptive use, the Zelnik–Kantner studies show that the 1970s witnessed more sexually active young women having ever used a contraceptive method prior to a pregnancy and declines in never users. Yet the level of premarital pregnancy among women aged 15–19 increased from 9% to 16%, as increased levels of premarital sexual activity more than offset the increased use of contraception. Pregnancy levels also rose among ever users of contraception as there was a shift away from the most efficient methods. This increase in premarital pregnancies was translated into more premarital births, despite an increased propensity to abort, because a decline occurred in the likelihood of marriage before the birth.

Static versus Dynamic Perspectives

Although there are several competing perspectives with respect to fertility (see Bagozzi & Van Loo, 1978), an emerging distinction has been made between a static versus a dynamic approach. To the static approach (Becker, 1960, 1981; Becker & Lewis, 1979; Mincer, 1963; Willis, 1974), fertility represents an economic choice, made at the time of marriage, between fertility and competing goods and services, depending on income, prices, and opportunity costs. The assumption of a static family-size decision made at marriage has received much criticism, and a dynamic perspective has been formed as an alternative (Namboodiri, 1972, 1981). Several studies have shown the variability of fertility expectations and desires of individuals over time, especially downward revisions during the 1960s and 1970s (Butz & Ward, 1978; Coombs, 1979; Freedman, Freedman, & Thornton, 1980; Westoff & Ryder, 1977b). Attitudes toward and actual timing of births have also changed (Pebley, 1981; Tsui, 1982). Morgan (1981) illustrated the considerable indecision characterizing fertility decisions after minimal acceptable family size has been reached. Rindfuss and Bumpass (1978) argued that fertility interacts with the age of the woman, as norms exist about the appropriate ages for parity-specific births.

A dynamic perspective views fertility as an ongoing, decision-making process. Not only do the social and economic conditions of women and couples change over time, and in directions that cannot always be anticipated, but they are also affected by the birth of a child. These changing conditions make it unlikely that fertility decisions made at marriage, if they are made at this time, will not be questioned or modified in the future.

Consequences

Basically, two sets of consequences of fertility can be identified: those for parents and those for children (Clausen & Clausen, 1973; Pohlman, 1968, 1969). Consequences for parents involve the number of children, as well as their timing and spacing. Children are expensive in terms of time and monetary costs (Espenshade, 1977) and in terms of cost due to the wife's leaving the labor force or reducing her hours of paid employment (Cramer, 1979; Smith & Ward, 1980). Aside from constraints on consumption patterns, the presence of children, particularly preschool children, also affects the marital relationship by shifting it toward a more traditional or segregated division of labor in terms of more traditional sex-role ideology; a decrease in the wife's labor force participation; an increase in the number of household chores she performs and a decrease in the husband's participation; and an increase in the husband's power (Hoffman & Manis, 1978; LaRossa & LaRossa, 1981; Lloyd, 1975; Polonko & Scanzoni, 1981; Rossi, 1968). Other effects of the presence and/or number of children on the marital relationship include decreased spouse companionship and marital satisfaction (Figley, 1973; Glenn & Weaver, 1978; Houseknecht, 1979; Miller, 1976; Polonko, Scanzoni, & Teachman, 1982; Rollins & Galligan, 1978) and decreased parental satisfaction (Marini, 1980; Nye, Carlson, & Farrett, 1970). Although marital satisfaction declines with the advent of children, research suggests that the vast majority of mothers view "being a parent" as a source of high satisfaction (Hoffman & Manis, 1978).

Timing or spacing of children has also been related to consequences for parents, especially with respect to the first birth. Early fertility and premarital fertility have been associated with reduced education for women (Bacon, 1974; Pohlman, 1968; Presser, 1971; Waite & Moore, 1978); rapid subsequent childbearing and higher levels of fertility (Bumpass et al., 1978; Marini & Hodsdon, 1981; Millman & Hendershot, 1980); economic deprivation and reduced asset accumulation relative to those who delay childbearing (Baldwin, 1976; Coombs & Freedman, 1970; Coombs, Freedman, Freedman, & Pratt, 1970; Freedman & Coombs, 1966a, b; Hofferth & Moore, 1979; Smith & Ward, 1980; Trussell, 1976a); and subsequent marital dissolution (Bumpass & Sweet, 1972; Teachman, 1983).

Concerning the consequences of fertility for children, Menken (1972) documented that children of young mothers are more likely to be premature, to have low birth weight, and to have higher rates of mortality. Berkov and Sklar (1976) showed that illegitimate children are more subject to infant mortality, are more likely to grow up in a broken home, and are more likely to require public assistance than legitimate children. Card (1981) found that children of teenage parents are likely to show relative decrements in academic achievement, are more likely to live in single-parent or stepparent homes, and are more likely to repeat the early-marriage, early-parent, high-fertility tendencies of their parent or parents.

Marital Disruption

The long-term trend in marital disruption in the United States has been upward, whether measured by the number of divorces, by period divorce rates, or by marriage-cohort-specific divorce rates (Preston & McDonald, 1979). With the exception of a brief "divorce boom" following World War II, the upward trend in divorce was gradual until the mid-1960s, when a very steep increase in the divorce rate was observed. The 1950s were a period of relative stability with respect to marital dissolution, with lower than expected divorce rates based on the long-term upward trend, serving to heighten the magnitude of increase observed over the 1960s and 1970s.

Table 12 presents various period indicators of the trend in divorce between 1960 and 1979, showing that divorces went up from approximately 400,000 in 1960 to well over 1 million in 1979, with a corresponding increase in the crude divorce rate, divorces per 1,000 total population, from 2.2 to 5.4. Relating the number of divorces to the exposed population, estimated by the number of married women aged 15 and over, the divorce rate increased from 9.2 to 22.8 per 1,000. Similarly, the number of divorced persons per 1,000 married persons increased from 35 in 1960 to 92 in 1979.

As marital disruption occurs most often in the early years of marriage, period measures are dependent on the distribution of current marriages by duration. Therefore, the steep rise in divorce rates since 1965 could be ex-

Table 12. Number of Divorces, Divorce Rates, and Divorced Persons per 1,000 Married Persons: 1960–1979[a]

Year	Number	Divorce rate		Divorced persons per 1,000 married persons[d]
		Crude[b]	General[c]	
1979	1,181,000	5.4	22.8	92
1975	1,036,000	4.9	20.3	69
1970	708,000	3.5	14.9	47
1965	479,000	2.5	10.6	—
1960	393,000	2.2	9.2	35

[a]Sources: National Center for Health Statistics, 1981. "Advance Report of Final Divorce Statistics, 1979. Monthly Vital Statistics Reports, Vol. 30, No. 2 (Supplement), Table 2; U.S. Bureau of the Census, 1980. "Marital Status and Living Arrangements: March 1979." Current Population Reports, Series P-20, No. 349, Table C.
[b]Rate per 1,000 total population.
[c]Rate per 1,000 married women aged 15 and over.
[d]Married persons with spouse present.

Table 13. Percentage Divorced by Anniversary of Marriage and Percentage of Marriage Cohort Projected to Experience Divorce: 1960–1973[a]

Year of marriage	Percentage divorced by year after marriage			Percentage projected to end in divorce[b]
	3	5	10	
1973	—[c]	—	—	49.2
1972	9.4	—	—	48.7
1971	9.0	—	—	48.0
1970	8.6	16.4	—	47.8
1969	8.2	15.6	—	47.1
1968	7.7	14.6	—	45.9
1967	7.6	14.1	—	45.3
1966	7.3	13.4	—	44.3
1965	6.8	12.5	24.8	43.7
1964	6.6	11.9	23.5	42.2
1963	6.5	11.4	22.1	41.0
1962	6.3	11.0	21.1	40.0
1961	6.1	10.6	20.0	39.1
1960	6.3	10.5	19.3	38.8

[a]Sources: National Center for Health Statistics, 1979. "Divorces by Marriage Cohort." Series 21, No. 34, Table 4; National Center for Health Statistics, 1980. "National Estimates of Marriage Dissolution and Survivorship: United States." Series 3, No. 19, Table A.
[b]Assuming national duration-specific divorce rates for 1976–1977.
[c]No estimate available.

plained, in part, by the influx of baby-boom cohorts into marriage, tipping the distribution of marriages toward those with short durations. Components analyses by Michael (1978) and Horiuchi (1979), however, indicate that this has not been the case. Also, certain compositional changes have occurred, such as an upward shift in the educational distribution and a rise in age at marriage, which should operate to lower divorce rates, as more highly educated individuals and those who marry older are less likely to experience marital dissolution (Norton & Glick, 1976; Sweet, 1977).

On the other hand, changes have occurred that could explain increased divorce rates. Although no estimate of their effects is available, a number of factors have been discussed in the literature, including the negative impact of the war in Vietnam on family life (Glick & Norton, 1977; Preston & Richards, 1975); the impact of the welfare system (Norton & Glick, 1976); and an increase in the proportion of marriages involving premarital births. However, lower fertility overall has been cited as a contributor to increased divorce rates, as smaller families are associated with greater labor-force participation among wives and, hence, financial independence (Norton & Glick, 1976). As sex roles have become more egalitarian and labor force participation rates have risen, women have increased their bargaining power in marriage, including the ultimate threat to dissolve the relationship (Scanzoni, 1979a, p. 30).

Another way to measure the trend in marital disruption, one in which a control for marital duration can be made, is to compare the incidence of divorce in successive marriage cohorts (Carlson, 1979; National Center for Health Statistics, 1979, 1980a; Preston & McDonald, 1979; Schoen & Nelson, 1974; Schoen, Greenblatt, & Mielke, 1975). Table 13 presents the percentage of marriage cohorts, married between 1960 and 1973, divorcing within

3, 5, and 10 years of marriage and gives estimates of the percentage expected to divorce given the marriage-duration-specific divorce rates observed for 1976–1977. At each marriage duration, later cohorts show a greater percentage divorced. The percentage expected to divorce eventually has also increased from 38.8% of the 1960 marriage cohort to nearly 50% of the 1973 marriage cohort.

The data presented in Tables 12 and 13 refer to divorce alone, as separations are not counted in the national reporting system. However, separations plus divorces constitute a better indicator of marital disruption than does divorce alone (Bumpass & Sweet, 1972; Norton & Glick, 1976; Sweet, 1977), and most analyses based on survey data include separation as a form of marital disruption. Blacks, for instance, are more likely to terminate a marriage through separation than divorce and to take longer to divorce once separated, compared to other groups. Failure to recognize this point and subsequent reliance on divorce statistics alone can lead to incorrect conclusions about differential levels of marital disruption. Upward shifts in marital disruption may also be underestimated by divorces alone, as separations may occur more rapidly than divorces. Liberalized divorce laws, however, may increase divorce rates by shortening the period between separation and divorce and by encouraging divorces among separated couples who might not have otherwise divorced (Schoen et al., 1975).

Differentials in Marital Disruption

Significant differentials in marital disruption are considered below.

Stability of Parental Marriage. The notion that there is a modest intergenerational transmission of marital instability has received some support in the literature (Bumpass & Sweet, 1972; Moore & Waite, 1981; Mott & Moore, 1979; Mueller & Pope, 1977; Pope & Mueller, 1976). As Sweet noted, though, much of this association can be explained by the social characteristics of the spouses at marriage. In other words, individuals coming from broken homes are more likely to have characteristics associated with a high risk of marital dissolution, such as premarital fertility and lower education. It also appears that the relationship is stronger for whites than for blacks.

Education. Individuals with less than a high-school education experience the highest level of marital dissolution, whereas the lowest level occurs at four years of college for women and at five years of college for men (U.S. Bureau of the Census, 1976b, 1977). Both men and women with six or more years of college experience increased rates, although the increase is greatest and the pattern most clear for women, because highly educated women are more likely to have a career and are less financially dependent on their husbands (Houseknecht & Spanier, 1980). Over time, however, differentials in marital instability according to education level have been declining (Glick & Norton, 1977; Norton & Glick, 1976).

In multivariate models, the effects of education for either blacks or whites, or for men or women, are generally attenuated or nonsignificant (Becker, Landes, & Michael, 1977; Bumpass & Sweet, 1972; Cherlin, 1977; Cutright, 1971b; Hannon, Tuma, & Groeneveld, 1977; McCarthy, 1978; Mott & Moore, 1979). Only individuals with less than a high-school education appear to run an increased risk of marital disruption. The lack of a strong net effect for education is probably due to its relationship with age at marriage and other factors like income or work experience.

Premarital Fertility. Premarital fertility, either a premarital birth or a premarital pregnancy, has been associated with an increased risk of marital disruption (Furstenberg, 1976a,b; McCarthy & Menken, 1979), with premarital births representing a greater risk to marital stability (U.S. Bureau of the Census, 1976c; Bumpass & Sweet, 1972). An early marriage combined with a premarital birth represents a set of characteristics related to very high levels of marital instability (Teachman, 1983).

Age at Marriage. The risk of marital disruption declines sharply from marriage during the teen years to marriage in the early 20s and thereafter tends to level off. This general pattern appears to be true for both males and females and blacks and whites. Carter and Glick (1976),

however, noted, that the risk of marital disruption for women marrying after age 30 is greater than the risk for women marrying in their early to mid-20s. This difference reflects the greater likelihood that women who marry at an older age will have some postgraduate education and therefore a career (Glick & Norton, 1977). Results from multivariate analyses indicate that the extent to which early marriage increases martial disruption is much greater for white women than for blacks or for men (Becker *et al.,* 1977; Teachman, 1983).

Religion. Evidence suggests that Catholics, controlling for other factors, are slightly less likely to divorce or separate than are Protestants (Teachman, 1983), although the difference is small in comparison to differences observed for other variables. In addition, religiosity, measured as the frequency of church attendance or communion, has been related to marital disruption. If one controls for religious affiliation and other variables, more religious individuals are less likely to divorce or separate (Ross & Sawhill, 1975; Teachman, 1983).

Race and Ethnicity. Recent data show that blacks experience the highest rate of marital dissolution, followed by whites, and then other racial/ethnic groups (National Center for Health Statistics, 1978). Over time, differences between racial and ethnic groups have tended to converge (Norton & Glick, 1976). In multivariate analyses, the black–white difference in marital instability is reduced slightly but remains considerable (Houseknecht & Spanier, 1980; Moore & Waite, 1981; Sweet & Bumpass, 1974; Ross & Sawhill, 1975). A full accounting of racial and ethnic differences is complex, however, as the same factors do not always affect marital dissolution for each racial or ethnic group, and common factors are often of varying importance (McCarthy & Menken, 1979; Moore & Waite, 1981; Mott & Moore, 1979; Pope & Mueller, 1976; Teachman, 1983). A discussion of black patterns of marital dissolution can be found in Bernard (1966), Cutright (1971b), Farley and Hermalin (1971), and Udry (1966, 1967). Hispanic patterns are discussed by Eberstein and Frisbie (1976), Frisbie, Bean, and Eberstein (1978), and Uhlenberg (1971, 1972).

Heterogamy. Heterogamous marriages are more likely to experience marital dissolution than homogamous marriages (Becker, 1977; Bumpass & Sweet, 1972; Cherlin, 1977; Norton & Glick, 1976; Teachman, 1983). Differences with the largest effects include interfaith marriages where one spouse is Catholic; marriages involving considerable age differences between spouses, especially if the wife is older; and interracial marriages. Heterogamy raises the likelihood of marital disruption more among whites than among blacks (Teachman, 1983). The reason is not clear, but it may be that problems associated with heterogamy are less salient in a population where rates of marital disruption are high because of low education and unstable financial conditions. Huber and Spitze (1980), looking at the probability of having ever thought about divorce, also found that heterogamy has little effect on wives but is much more likely to spur husbands to consider divorce.

Income and Employment. Greater income of the husband has been related to greater marital stability (Becker *et al.*, 1977; Bernard, 1966; Cutright, 1971b; Mott & Moore, 1979), although differences have declined over time (Norton & Glick, 1976), and a few studies have reported no significant effect (Moore & Waite, 1980; Ross & Sawhill, 1975). A more important factor appears to be the husband's history of unemployment or earnings trajectory. Husbands with a history of unemployment or earnings that are below those for men with comparable market resources are the most likely to experience marital dissolution (Cherlin, 1979; Ross & Sawhill, 1975). For women, higher earnings are consistently related to greater marital instability, as their greater economic resources make them less financially dependent on their husbands (Cherlin, 1977, 1978; Moore & Waite, 1980; Mott & Moore, 1979; Ross & Sawhill, 1975). Similarly, wives who have had consistent labor-force participation and who work full time are more likely to divorce or separate (Mott & Moore, 1979).

Overall, the evidence suggests that economic factors are most important when a family's financial condition varies across time. Even at low income levels, marital disruption is not higher than expected if consistent financial and employment conditions have been maintained (Cherlin, 1979; Ross & Sawhill, 1975). The failure to measure economic changes within the family in an adequate fashion may explain why income measures have traditionally explained less variance in marital stability than have factors such as age at marriage and premarital fertility (Mott & Moore, 1979).

Public Assistance Programs. Studies using census data to study the effects of level of public assistance benefits on marital dissolution have had contradictory results, with some studies finding a positive association (Honig, 1973; Moles, 1976; Ross & Sawhill, 1975) and others finding no relationship (Cutright & Scanzoni, 1973). Relating average welfare payments per recipient to having ever been divorced among men and women aged 25–44 living in the 123 largest urban areas, Bane (1975) found no association. However, higher welfare payments were related to a lower probability that divorced or widowed men and women had remarried.

Bane's results suggest that the cross-sectional separation ratios or proportions of women who head families may be biased because public assistance payments may influence such measures not by inducing separation or divorce, but by slowing the process of remarriage. Though several studies have used longitudinal data to focus on the probability of separation or divorce over some period of time, consistent findings have not appeared, as several studies have reached different conclu-

sions about the existence of an association, even using the same data (Cherlin, 1979; Cutright & Madras, 1976; Mott & Moore, 1979; Ross & Sawhill, 1975).

Moles (1979) argued that the evidence is not sufficient to support a realtionship between public assistance programs and marital disruption, especially a strong relationship. However, he also noted that no study has been conducted using a set of data specifically designed to test the hypothesis of a direct relationship. In addition, no study has adequately addressed the potential reciprocal relationship between public assistance programs and marital disruption.

Children. The presence of children has often been argued to be a barrier to separation or divorce, but conclusive results have not been presented in the literature. Issues of causality and spuriousness are also difficult to sort through, as marital fertility, at least, is an event that occurs within and is affected by marriage (Sweet, 1977; Thornton, 1977). It is also not clear whether the question should address the simple presence or absence of children or, in addition, the number and ages of children.

Bumpass and Sweet (1972) found no substantial impact of a postmarital birth on the subsequent probability of separation or divorce. A similar finding for the simple presence of a child under age 18 was reported by Ross and Sawhill (1975). Cherlin (1977), though, indicated that the presence of a preschool child deters marital disruption, but that the presence of an older child does not. Becker *et al.*, (1977) obtained estimates suggesting that both younger children and fewer children act to inhibit marital dissolution, whereas greater numbers of children may act to increase marital instability. However, subsequent analyses that also controlled for the ages of children (but not the number of children in all cases) have tended to find no effect (Hannon *et al.*, 1977; Moore & Waite, 1981; Mott & Moore, 1979).

Life-Course Events. The influence of previous life-course events on marital disruption is visible from the importance of differences observed by age at marriage and premarital fertility. For instance, women who marry young or who have a premarital birth are subject to an increased risk of marital disruption. Preston and McDonald (1979) also found that divorce within a marriage cohort is greater than expected following periods of armed-service mobilization, an event that typically alters the life course of males. Hogan (1978b, 1980) reported that men who have nonnormative sequencing of major life-course events (schooling, then job, then marriage as a normative sequence) are more likely to experience marital dissolution, as societal institutions are not geared to nonnormative sequencing patterns, and a variety of role conflicts may therefore occur among those who deviate from the norm. Similar arguments can be constructed to apply to individuals who follow normative sequencing but who time events or space them in a nonnormative fashion.

Other Factors. A variety of factors have also been found to influence marital disruption. For instance, whites who experience multiple marriages are more likely to divorce than couples in their first marriages (Becker, *et al.*, 1977; Bumpass & Sweet, 1972; Cherlin, 1977; McCarthy, 1978; U.S. Bureau of the Census, 1976b, 1977), but the converse is true for blacks (McCarthy, 1978). Moreover, the factors associated with the disruption of first marriages do not appear to be the same as those associated with the disruption of subsequent marriages (McCarthy, 1978). Cherlin (1978) noted that second and subsequent marriages may involve problems of child rearing and kinship interaction that produce stress not found in first marriages. Overall, blacks are less likely to remarry than are whites, however, a fact maybe indicating a greater selectivity in spouses.

Rates of marital dissolution also vary according to urban-rural, farm-nonfarm, and regional residence (Carter & Glick, 1976; Houseknecht & Spanier, 1980; Mott & Moore, 1979; Moore & Waite, 1981; National Center for Health Statistics, 1978; Ross & Sawhill, 1975; Weed, 1974). In general, urban residence, a nonfarm background, and residence in a western state are all related to higher rates of marital instability. Commonly, the differentials by geographic location are not large but remain significant.

Consequences

As discussed elsewhere in this chapter, marital instability has played a significant role in changing the structure of U.S. households over time (Masnick & Bane, 1980) in conjunction with other processes, like the availability and choice of housing alternatives and remarriage. Although the data are not available, marital disruption and changes in household structure may be reshaping the socialization experiences of American youth. The average number of children involved per divorce has decreased from 1.36 in 1966 to 1.0 in 1980, because of declining fertility. However, because there are more divorces, the absolute number of children experiencing marital disruption has continued to climb. Bumpass and Rindfuss (1979), using data from the 1973 National Survey of Family Growth, indicated that one third of all children spend a portion of their lives in a single-parent home, with an average duration of four and one-half years. For blacks, the numbers involved are even greater.

Marital disruption is also closely related to the economic status of women, as Hoffman (1977) showed that separated and divorced women suffer a considerable drop in income from married levels. A similar drop in income is not observed for men. This drop in income and the relative disadvantage experienced by women in the labor force may help to explain the usually high rates of remarriage and the higher labor-force-participation rates of separated and divorced women.

Many studies have also noted the lower fertility of ever-divorced compared to continuously married women.

Thornton (1978) showed that this deficit in fertility for ever-divorced women is not found at the time of separation and therefore results from lower fertility after separation and during the period between divorce and remarriage. Cohen and Sweet (1974) also attributed the fertility deficit of ever-divorced women to time lost in the married state. Levin and O'Hara (1978) expanded on these results by showing that the fertility of remarried women depends on the prior fertility history of the second husband, with higher fertility occurring if the woman marries a man with no children of his own. Rindfuss and Bumpass (1977) also showed that fertility between marriages varies according to the social and economic characteristics of the women; that is, women who are less educated, are of lower parity, are younger, and are black are more likely to have children between marriages.

Remarriage

The long-term, upward trend in marital disruption for the United States has nearly been matched by remarriage, reflecting an overall preference for marriage as opposed to single life (Glick & Norton, 1977). The rate of remarriage, though, stopped increasing in the early 1970s and declined slightly through 1978 before shifting upward again in 1979. As shown in Table 14, the rate of remarriage (remarriages per 1,000 widowed and divorced women aged 14 and over) varied from 56.1 in 1965 to 75.6 in 1979. Glick and Norton (1977) estimated that, in the recent past, about 80% of people ever divorced remarried, although this figure may now be closer to 75% and varies according to sociodemographic characteristics (see also Sweet, 1973a; Thornton, 1975). Besides eventually remarrying, most individuals have also done so rapidly. The median duration between divorce and remarriage has been estimated to be 2.3 years for those divorcing before 1970 and 3.0 years for those divorcing after 1970 (National Center for Health Statistics, 1980a).

Table 14. Median Age at Remarriage, Difference between Median Age at First Marriage and Remarriage, and Remarriage Rates: 1965–1979[a]

Year	Median age at remarriage		Difference[b]		Rate[c]
	Male	Female	Male	Female	
1979	35.3	31.9	11.9	10.3	75.6
1975	35.5	32.0	12.8	11.2	74.0
1970	37.5	33.3	15.0	12.7	64.2
1965	39.6	35.5	17.1	15.1	56.1

[a]Source: Various issues of Monthly Vital Statistics Reports, National Center for Health Statistics.
[b]Calculated as difference between median age at first marriage and median age at remarriage.
[c]Remarriages per 1,000 widowed and divorced women aged 14 and over.

Table 15. Cumulative Probabilities of Remarriage by Years since Divorce: Women Divorcing before and after 1970[a]

	Year of divorce	
Years since divorce	Before 1970	After 1970
1	.24	.18
2	.46	.33
3	.60	.50
4	.70	.58

[a]Source: National Center for Health Statistics, 1980. "Remarriage of Women 15–44 Years of Age Whose First Marriage Ended in Divorce: United States, 1976." Advance Data, No. 58.

Other indicators of change in remarriage are also presented in Table 14. The median age at remarriage declined considerably between 1965 and 1979, to 35.3 years for males and 31.9 years for females. Over time, the difference between median age at remarriage and median age at first marriage has also declined, from 17.1 to 11.9 years for males and from 15.1 to 10.3 years for females. Each of these declines, influenced by delayed age at first marriage for both men and women, as well as changes in age at divorce and remarriage, indicates an increasing concentration of marital life-course events.

Remarriage tends to occur most often at short durations (measured from either separation or divorce), so that the distribution of separated or divorced individuals by duration influences period remarriage rates like those presented in Table 14. The information presented in Table 15 examines remarriage probabilities using two broadly defined divorce cohorts, thus largely negating the influence of duration of marital disruption. These remarriage probabilities indicate a downward shift in the proportion remarrying by each duration since divorce for women divorcing after 1970 (but before 1976). By four years after divorce, 70% of those women divorcing before 1970 had remarried, compared to 58% of those women divorcing after 1970. This finding suggests a downturn in remarriage during the 1970s, even though it may indicate a change in timing as opposed to a decline in the probability of eventually remarrying.

Differentials in Remarriage

Unlike marital disruption, remarriage has received relatively little attention in the literature, despite the growing numbers of those eligible to remarry. Therefore, differentials with respect to remarriage are not as well documented, especially when examined in a multivariate framework. In part, this lack of research stems from less adequate data (Sweet, 1977). Census data, for instance, provide no information on when after separation or divorce remarriage occurs or on characteristics of individuals at the time of marital disruption and remarriage.

Basically, the same limitations apply to data gathered in the vital statistics registration system. Most of the information on remarriage differentials thus comes from surveys.

Males tend to remarry more than women (Glick & Norton, 1977; Sweet, 1973a), although the remarriage probabilities of women are strongly affected by the presence or absence of children (Spanier & Glick, 1980b). Becker et al. (1977) found that women without children are actually more likely to remarry than men, suggesting that the customary awarding of child custody to wives plays a role in affecting their remarriage probabilities. Research by Koo and Suchindran (1980) also indicates that the effects of the presence of children on remarriage are dependent on the woman's age at divorce, with childless women being more likely to remarry if they divorce before age 25 and less likely to remarry if they divorce after age 35. The presence or absence of children appears to have little effect on the remarriage chances of women who divorce between ages 25 and 34. Remarriage among women is also affected by their age at marital disruption and widowhood, with younger women and women who divorce being more likely to remarry (Becker et al., 1977; Spanier & Glick, 1980b; Sweet, 1973a).

Hispanics are the most likely to remarry and to remarry quickly, followed by whites and then blacks (National Center for Health Statistics, 1980c). Blacks, especially, are more likely to remain separated, lowering their remarriage probability and increasing the length of time between marriages. Even controlling for the greater reliance on separation versus divorce for marital disruption, blacks are less likely to remarry and take longer to do so (Hannon, Tuma, Groeneveld, 1977; McCarthy & Menken, 1979; Spanier & Glick, 1980b). Furthermore, Hannon and his colleagues (1977) noted significant differences in the impact of income maintenance on the probabilities of remarriage. Specifically, income transfers significantly delay remarriage among Hispanics, act to hasten remarriage among blacks, and have no significant pattern among whites.

Men with higher incomes are more likely to remarry than men with less income (Becker et al., 1977; Sweet, 1973a), although Wolf and MacDonald (1979), considering several indicators of male income, including current earnings, earnings stability, income relative to other men, and permanent income, found that only permanent income has a significant net positive effect on the probability of remarriage. Most of the discussion has centered on the income of males, although some concern about the effects of income transfers focuses on women (Hannon et al., 1977).

Census data indicate that men with higher education, income, and occupation are more likely to remarry after divorce, whereas the converse is true for women (Carter & Glick, 1976). Among women, those with an early age at first marriage, an early first birth, and not an illegitimate birth have a great likelihood of remarriage (McCarthy & Menken, 1979; Spanier & Glick, 1980b). Many of these factors have not been considered in a multivariate framework, though, and it would be difficult to do so without large sample sizes, because many are highly correlated (e.g., an early first birth and an early age at first marriage).

Consequences

As a demographic event, remarriage plays an important role in altering households and families. It acts to combine households—often separate families—into a single unit. As mentioned in the section on marital disruption, remarriage plays an important role in determining the size and the growth of the separated and divorced population. Remarriage also acts to change the economic situation and the living conditions of husbands, wives, and children. Depending on its timing and earlier life-course transitions, it can affect fertility and child spacing. Cherlin (1978, 1981) and Furstenberg (1979) have noted that remarriage implies consequences for patterns of kinship terminology, child rearing responsibilities, and the structure of interaction across split families. As noted earlier, these factors may be related to the higher rate of marital disruption among second and subsequent marriages than among first marriages.

Household Size and Composition

Over time, the United States has experienced considerable variation in household and family structure. To some extent, changes in household and family structure can be predicted by changes in the age–sex–marital-status structure, which, in turn, is a product of change in fertility and mortality. Much of the long-term decline in household size is due to the fertility and mortality declines occurring since the early nineteenth century. On the other hand, discretionary shifts in living arrangements, such as those associated with divorce or remarriage, have also had an impact, especially after World War II.

Kobrin (1973, 1976a,b) has outlined the historical decline in size of households. Fertility decline has reduced household size by decreasing the proportion of large units, and falling mortality has meant that more husband–wife couples survive past their childbearing years, increasing the proportion of small units. Fertility and mortality declines have also acted together to increase the proportion of small units by lowering the age at which couples bear their last child and by lengthening the "empty-nest" stage in the life course. Over time, separated and divorced women have been less likely to return to their parents' home and have been more likely to set up separate households. Smaller units have also increased because of the upward trend in marital disruption and have increased in periods during which there is greater delay in marriage. Since about 1950, another trend has emerged, the rise of primary individuals (most of whom live alone), leading to an increase in the proportion of single-member households.

Table 16. Average Number of Persons per Household and per Family, by Age: 1960–1979[a]

Year	Households			Families		
	All ages	Age < 18	Age ≥ 18	All ages	Age < 18	Age ≥ 18
1979	2.78	0.81	1.97	3.31	1.08	2.23
1975	2.94	0.93	2.01	3.42	1.18	2.23
1970	3.14	1.09	2.05	3.58	1.34	2.25
1965	3.29	1.21	2.09	3.70	1.44	2.26
1960	3.33	1.21	2.12	3.67	1.41	2.26

[a]Source: U.S. Bureau of the Census, 1979. "Households and Families by Type: March 1979 (Advance Report)." Current Population Reports, Series P-20, No. 345, Table 2.

Table 16 illustrates the fall in household size between 1960 and 1979. Both the number of children and the number of adults per household have declined since 1960. The decline in the number of children per household is particularly dramatic, falling from an average of 1.2 to an average of 0.8. This is the result of two processes: the continuing decline in fertility since the baby boom and the increasing proportion of nonfamily households. The decline in the number of adults per household largely reflects the increasing propensity for living alone among those who are single, separated, divorced, or widowed.

Table 16 also shows the change in family size between 1960 and 1979. Unlike household size, which has continuously declined, family size has increased slightly and then decreased. The trend in the mean number of adults per family, though, has been consistently downward, so that the fluctuation in average family size has been mainly due to shifts in fertility (Treas, 1981). The decline in the mean number of adults per family has been gradual since the early 1950s, as the major shift of adult members out of family units occurred rather abruptly after World War II. Declines in the mean number of children per family since 1965 have been substantial because of lower fertility. Overall, the reduction in the number of adults per family has acted to attenuate the increases in family size brought about by the baby boom and has exacerbated decreases associated with the lowered fertility of the 1960s and 1970s.

Treas (1981) also found that changes in mean family size have varied according to family type, age of family head, and race. Husband–wife families are larger than female-headed families, which, in turn, are larger than male-headed families. Since about 1950, however, female-headed families have been converging with the average husband–wife family size, while diverging from the average male-headed family size. This shift has occurred as declines in adult members in female-headed families have been largely offset by increases in children. Families characterized by the age of the head have also varied differentially, with younger-headed families being more affected by trends in fertility and older-headed families being more affected by the consistent decline in adult members. Black families have begun to converge with mean white family size because of their greater fertility decline in recent years. This decline was preceded by a period of divergence during the baby boom, though, as blacks increased their fertility more than whites. Racial differences in family size have not been strongly affected by the decline in adult members.

As mentioned above, household size has been affected by changes in household type (see Table 17). In 1970, over 81% of households were family households, and about 70% were husband–wife households. By 1979, less than three fourths of households were family households, and only about 62% were husband–wife households, as single-parent families and nonfamily households gained an increased share of the total number of households. Over the decade, family households increased by about 12%, husband–wife families by about 7%, and all other categories by at least 30%. Of the growth in new households over the decade, about 43% were family households, but only 21% were husband–wife families. In other words, nearly 80% of the increase in households between 1970 and 1979 were due to nontraditional family and nonfamily units. Almost 20% of the increment in households was attributable to newly formed female-headed families. The largest proportion of the increase in new households, however, stemmed from the creation of nonfamily households, most of which involved persons living alone.

Female-headed families were the fastest growing family type during the 1970s, as they were in the 1960s, growing at a rate over seven times as fast as husband–

wife families and one and one-half times as fast as male-headed families. Increasingly, female headship also involves younger women and children (Ross & Sawhill, 1975). Female-headed families containing children have been growing half again as fast as all families headed by women. Furthermore, nonwhite female-headed families have grown more rapidly than white families headed by women (Bianchi, 1980, 1981).

Since 1960, the economic position of families headed by women has declined, relative to husband–wife families, for both blacks and whites (Bianchi, 1980). Table 18 illustrates the economically disadvantaged status associated with female headship in a comparison with all other families. Female-headed families are more likely to exist in poverty, irrespective of age of head, presence or absence of children, and employment status. In 1979, families headed by females were over five times as likely to be under the poverty line as all other families. In 1959, this ratio was just under three times, reflecting the more rapid exodus from poverty by families not headed by women. Table 18 also indicates that female headship accompanied by children is a particularly disadvantaged status.

Controlling for population growth alone, the major contributor to the increase in female-headed families with children was increased marital separation and divorce involving children (Ross & Sawhill, 1975), followed by illegitimacy (see also Masnick & Bane, 1980). More specifically, increased marital dissolution has increased the proportion of female-headed families, a process not matched by remarriage or other factors. Although widows make up a large (but declining) proportion of female-headed families, widowhood has declined over time as an important growth mechanism. Similarly, changes in the propensity for spouse-absent women to create new house-

Table 17. Change in Households by Type: 1970–1979[a]

Household type	Percentage by year 1979	Percentage by year 1970	Percentage change[b]	Percentage of total increase[c]
Family households	74.4	81.2	11.7	43.3
Married couple	61.6	70.5	6.6	21.1
Male head, spouse absent	2.1	1.9	31.6	2.8
Female head, spouse absent	10.6	8.7	49.5	19.5
Nonfamily households	25.6	18.8	66.0	56.7
Male householder	10.4	6.4	98.5	28.7
Female householder	15.2	12.4	49.3	27.9
Persons living alone	22.2	17.1	36.9	45.6

[a]Source: U.S. Bureau of the Census, 1979. "Households and Families by Type: March 1979 (Advance Report)." Current Population Reports, Series P-20, No. 345, Tables 1, 3.
[b]Percentage change in household type between 1970 and 1979.
[c]Percentage of total increase in households between 1970 and 1979 according to household type.

Table 18. Percentage of Families under the Poverty Line by Household Type: 1959–1979[a]

Household type	Percentage by year 1979	Percentage by year 1969	Percentage by year 1959
Headed by female	30.2	32.6	42.6
Aged 25–44	35.9	43.3	57.9
Aged 65 and over	13.5	23.5	31.5
No children	9.3	13.9	20.1
With children	43.3	50.1	65.7
Employed	14.8	18.9	27.9
All other families	5.5	6.9	15.8
Aged 25–44	4.9	4.9	13.0
Aged 65 and over	8.3	16.6	29.7
No children	4.6	7.6	15.4
With children	8.9	8.9	22.8
Employed	3.4	4.3	11.8

[a]Source: U.S. Bureau of the Census, 1981. "Characteristics of the Population below the Poverty Level: 1979." Series P-60, No. 130, Table 5.

holds has not been an important factor in the growth of female-headed families. Although the above conclusions on female-headed families hold for both blacks and whites, illegitimacy is a significant difference between the races, as illegitimacy is a more important source of female headship among blacks.

Primary Individuals

Even more dramatic than the growth in female headship of families has been the growth in nonfamily households (again, see Table 17). Persons living alone accounted for over 85% of nonfamily households in 1979 and were responsible for some 45% of the growth in households over the decade. Females are more likely to head a nonfamily household than are males, but male-headed nonfamily households have been the most rapidly growing category of households in recent years.

Nonfamily households are created by several processes. Although a detailed components analysis of the relative effects of each of these processes has not been conducted, it is known that headship rates among those eligible to form nonfamily households have increased over time, and therefore, the growth in these units cannot be explained by changes in age–sex–marital-status structure alone (Kobrin, 1976a; Masnick & Bane, 1980).

Studies of the socioeconomic determinants of living alone suggest shifts in either income or tastes as reasonable explanations for the growth in single living (Beresford & Rivin, 1966; Carlinger, 1975; Chevan & Korson, 1972; Troll, 1971). In an analysis of the proportions of persons living alone among never-married males and females aged 25–34 and widows aged 65 and over, using 1970 state-level data, Michael, Fuchs, and Scott (1980) found income to be an important predictor. Using results from their cross-sectional model, they also found that changes in the propensity to live alone between 1950 and 1976 could be largely explained by changes in income. A similar analysis by Pampel (1982), using individual-level data from the 1960 and 1970 U.S. Censuses and the 1976 Current Population Survey, supports the notion that income shifts have allowed or prompted more persons to live alone, controlling for other factors like age, education, labor force participation, and race. Pampel's study, however, which was not restricted by age and used a time series of cross sections, found a significant upward shift in single living between 1960 and 1976 that could not be explained by income shifts or shifts in any of the other variables considered, possibly reflecting an increased taste for living alone.

A third study, by Kobrin (1981), used 1970 U.S. Census data to determine factors associated with living with nonfamily members (including living alone) as opposed to living in a family. Consistent with the research described above, greater income was related to a greater propensity to live away from family members, even when controls for other variables were introduced. Additional findings from this study include (1) never-married persons were more likely to live with kin than ever-married persons; (2) males were more likely to live with unrelated household members or by themselves than were females; (3) males and females "aged" differently with respect to living arrangements, as males moved away from kin more abruptly; (4) the availability of kin reduced the propensity to live alone or with unrelated individuals; and (5) the effects of marital status and income on the propensity to live away from kin did not vary by age.

Living Arrangements of Children

The 1970s decade was a period of change in children's living arrangements, as shown in Table 19. The percentage of children living with two parents dropped by nearly 8 percentage points, from 85.2% to 77.4%. For black children, the figures are even more striking, with less than half living with two parents (Glick & Norton, 1977). An increasing percentage of children were therefore living with one parent, usually the mother. In 1979, around 17% of children lived with their mother only.

The changing living arrangements of children is a result of the changing living arrangements of adults. Marital disruption, remarriage, and illegitimacy are all factors involved in this process. Since 1960, marital disruption, operating at a rate greater than that of remarriage, has been the most important contributor to shifting children out of two-parent families (Ross & Sawhill, 1975). Among blacks, though, illegitimacy has also played an important role.

Cohabitation

Although they still represent a small percentage of all households (see Table 20), cohabiting couples are an increasingly common occurrence (Cherlin, 1981; Clayton & Voss, 1977; Glick & Spanier, 1980; Macklin, 1978). In 1979, unmarried heterosexual couples made up 1.7% of all households, a doubling of the 1970 percentage. The percentage of such couples with children has declined

Table 19. Living Arrangements of Children (Age < 18): 1970–1979[a]

	Percentage by year	
Living with	1979	1970
Two parents	77.4	85.2
One parent	18.5	11.9
Mother only	16.9	10.8
Father only	1.6	1.1
Other relatives	3.4	2.2
Nonrelatives	0.7	0.7

[a]Source: U.S. Bureau of the Census, 1980. "Marital Status and Living Arrangements: March 1979." Current Population Reports, Series P-20, No. 349, Table H.

**Table 20.   Adults Living as Unmarried Couples:
1970–1979**[a]

	Year	
Subject	1979	1970
Percentage of all households	1.7	0.8
Percentage unmarried couples with children present	26.7	37.5
Percentage unmarried couples with male householder	63.5	50.9
Percentage unmarried couples with female householder	36.5	49.1

[a]Source: U.S. Bureau of the Census, 1980. "Marital Status and Living Arrangements: March 1979." Current Population Reports, Series P-20, No. 349, Table E.

over time, from about 38% in 1970 to under 27% in 1979, because of the large increase in young never-married couples in the cohabiting population. These figures, because they represent proportions at two points in time, considerably underestimate the proportion of individuals who ever experience cohabitation. In a national study of men aged 20–30 in 1975, for instance, Clayton and Voss (1977) found that 18% had lived with a woman to whom they were not married. A review of the literature by Macklin (1978) also indicates that 25% of college students have experienced cohabitation, and that a much larger percentage would do so given the chance.

Knowledge about cohabitation before 1970 is virtually nonexistent, but Glick and Spanier's (1980) data for the 1970s suggest that it involves at least two distinct groups of couples. The first group consists of better educated, younger, and never-married couples who apparently try cohabitation as a temporary alternative to marriage or as a transitional stage before marriage. A second group is made up of less well-educated, older couples in which at least one of the partners has been previously married.

Consequences

The changes in household size and composition considered here—as well as others not given specific attention, such as the timing of the move of younger adults out of the parental household (see Carter & Glick, 1976; Duncan & Morgan, 1976; Hill & Hill, 1976; Kobrin & Goldscheider, 1978; Sweet, 1972)—imply a variety of different consequences. Most obvious is that if present trends continue, individuals will continue to experience increasingly different household and family environments during their life times. This experience will serve to further distinguish various birth cohorts of individuals, as each has tended to experience these changes in household and family-living arrangements differently, and it will therefore act to exacerbate existing forms of age segregation (Masnick & Bane, 1980). These different family environments may also serve to alter the role of families

in providing satisfying personal relationships and thus may enhance the importance of nonfamily relationships (Cherlin, 1981). It is probable that completely new lifestyles will continue to emerge as alternatives to the traditional husband–wife family.

Changes in household size and composition also mean changes in the demand for housing and other goods and services. Over the past few decades, the number of households has grown much more rapidly than the total population, spurring the demand for housing. Shifts in household type and declines in household size have also altered the type of housing that is in demand. In addition, greater pressure may be put on government to supply various services, such as child care, medical care, welfare, and other forms of support traditionally supplied by families.

There is emerging evidence that household structure is closely related to income and housing inequality (Bianchi, 1981; Kuznets, 1976, 1978). Research has also indicated a link between the living arrangements of individuals and their mental and physical health status, as well as levels of mortality (Hughes & Gove, 1981; Kobrin & Hendershot, 1977; Pearlin & Johnson, 1977). Increasingly, differences in household size and composition are being related to cross-national differences in culture, development, and modernization processes (Burch, 1980; Kuznets, 1976, 1978; Young, 1975).

Summary

The past several decades have witnessed a substantial change in the demography of the family. Following an all-time low, the 1970s saw a tremendous increase in age at marriage and the percentage never married, primarily involving cohorts born after 1945. These increases have placed the percentage never married among younger women consistent with pre-1940 levels and have occurred at rates greater than ever before experienced in this century (Masnick & Bane, 1980). Similarly impressive increases have occurred in the labor force participation of women of all marital statuses and ages, but particularly among women during their prime childbearing years. These changes have been characterized as a "revolution" in female labor-market activity and point to women's growing commitment to paid employment. Although changes of a similar magnitude have not yet occurred in the nature of women's labor-force participation (e.g., in work continuity, in the proportion employed full time, full year; and in the percentage contributed to total family income), trends for younger women, again born after 1945, represent a break from prior patterns in their higher participation rates during their childbearing years and their more rapid move into full-time, full-year employment. Although employment histories are truncated, these and other findings for young women suggest that a "revolution" in the nature of labor market activity may be under way.

Not surprisingly, given the strong interconnections between employment and fertility, significant declines in actual and expected fertility have also taken place, with impressive increases in the proportion of women expecting to have one child or to remain childless permanently. There have also been notable increases in the postponement of childbearing, in the use of more effective methods of birth control, and in the percentage of births planned. Congruent with the greater bipolar tendency for women to remain either in or out of the labor force, at least in the short run, there is also tentative evidence of an increasing bipolar tendency among women either to engage in lengthier postponement and have fewer children, or to have premarital births or pregnancies. The latter trend has grown to the point where nearly one third of all first marriages between 1970 and 1974 involved a premarital conception. Overall, the events of marriage and childbearing are becoming increasingly disassociated (Modell *et al.*, 1978).

Although the changes in the above areas have been considerable, the upsurge in divorce as well as in remarriage has been even more widespread during this period. Also, in contrast to other areas, such as age at marriage, increases in divorce over the past several decades have been greater than long-term historical trends would predict (Cherlin, 1981). Projected estimates for the marriage cohorts of the early 1970s to the mid-1970s indicate that close to 50% of marriages will end in divorce, with most individuals also remarrying. Moreover, changes in the timing of divorce and remarriage imply an increasing concentration of marital life-course events.

Finally, to a large extent, changes in all the above areas are reflected in changes in household composition. As Masnick and Bane (1980) stated, "the once typical household—two parents and children, with a husband breadwinner and a wife-homemaker—has faded in prominence" (p. 95). The increase in nonfamily households—including for instance, the growing number of cohabitors, unrelated individuals living together, and never-married and divorced persons living alone—has been significant. Likewise, increases in divorce as well as in illegitimacy have resulted in substantital increases in female-headed households and in the proportion of children not living in the traditional husband–wife structure. Overall, the evidence is not only for growth in nontraditional family and nonfamilial living arrangements, but also for a more fluid set of arrangements, with a greater likelihood of experiencing several different household environments over one's lifetime (Cherlin, 1981).

An additional example of this fluidity may be the evolution of "dual households." Persons in such households maintain separate living quarters but spend several days and nights per week at a "friend's" residence. This type of arrangement may be as socially significant as cohabitation but would be classified as living alone. As a consequence, increases in living alone since the 1950s may involve not only a quantitative shift but also a qualitative shift in the lifestyle arrangements of singles and, hence, in the social meaning of "singleness." The development of "dual-household" arrangements could be an additional reason for the trend in delayed marriage reported in this chapter.

Numerous factors have been cited in attempts to explain historical shifts in the areas reviewed in this chapter. On one level are the more straightforward demographic factors that "explain" change, at least partially, as the result of shifts in population structure (e.g., the marriage squeeze in relationship to marital timing) and that remain specific to certain areas. On another, deeper level are factors that appear as more general explanations across areas, two of which are changes in the economic structure and changes in women's roles. The former, for example, stresses the importance of changing economic conditions as a causal agent in determining marital timing, female labor-participation, fertility, divorce, and remarriage (Becker, 1981; Cherlin, 1981; Easterlin, 1978, 1980). The latter emphasizes the importance of shifts in sex-role ideology and behavioral changes on the part of women, reflecting a general decline in familism and a growth of individualism and alternative opportunities outside the family (Cherlin, 1981; Modell, 1980; Scanzoni, 1979b; Sweet, 1977; White, 1979). Because we lack research to provide solid estimates of the impact of these factors on historical changes in the six areas covered, attention was focused on the research and theory on predictors/differentials to provide some preliminary insight. What was reviewed under changes in women's roles can be drawn on in an illustrative fashion to provide just one example of how family sociology and family demography can work in concert.

Beginning with the findings reviewed in this chapter on marital timing, women who delay marriage are, on average, more likely to come from a high socioeconomic-status family background where there is a greater emphasis on developing egalitarian preferences and achievement orientations (Scanzoni, 1975). These, in turn, facilitate higher educational and occupational aspirations and, bolstered by actual successful academic performance, are likely to increase the costs inherent in early heterosexual involvement and experimentation, which might interfere with highly valued goals concerning future attainments. Subsequent achievements in line with these preferences (i.e., higher education, career commitment, and economic success) then serve to further delay both marriage and children, as the attractiveness of alternatives to marriage increases, as do the costs of trying to combine a career and a family.

These same types of factors are related not only to marital timing but also to the likelihood of adolescent childbearing. As Chilman's intensive review of the literature (1980) indicates, lower socioeconomic status, poor academic performance, low educational goals, and traditional sex-role preferences are related to one or more of the following: increased likelihood of adolescent coitus, failure to use birth control, and unwillingness to abort. In turn, premarital fertility and early marriage tend to truncate further the female's educational attainment and participation in nonfamilial roles.

The changes that have occurred in labor force participation and fertility suggest that, once married, sex-role-egalitarian women are more likely to minimize incursions into nonfamilial roles. They evidence greater commitment to employment and, to facilitate it, use more effective birth control, plan and postpone childbearing, and have fewer children. Thus, trends in fertility, labor force participation, and labor market continuity point to an intensification of the "deferral syndrome" characterizing sex-role-egalitarian preferences and behaviors consistent with the attainment of individualistic goals. However, the preliminary evidence concerning the increasing tendency for women to stay in or out of the labor force, and to have children very early or to engage in postponement, also suggests that links between traditional preferences and behaviors consistent with familistic goals (e.g., early childbearing and nonparticipation in the labor force) are becoming more distinct for a subset of women.

At the same time, data on the family can further inform us about the nature and implications of the specific changes that have occurred. For example, although there have been substantial increases in female employment, the majority (two thirds) of women, even younger women, are not fully employed. In addition, the evidence suggests a bipolar model of labor market continuity in the short run, as well as a core of women showing strong commitment even in the long run. However, the data also indicate that the majority of women still move in and out of the labor force over their life course. It appears that the concept of marital structures (Scanzoni, 1972, 1980) provides one vehicle for understanding these different and seemingly ambiguous findings on the nature of changes in women's commitment to the labor force.[1] Previously,

[1]For the reader who is not familiar with this typology, a brief description is provided here. Scanzoni (1972) stated that the vast majority of marriages in the United States are characterized by one of the two variations of the traditional marital structures: the head–complement and the senior–junior structures. The key distinguishing feature of the head–complement structure is that the wife is not in the labor force and the husband is, therefore, the sole wage earner. The wife has the right to be supported financially and her chief tasks include child care and household duties. Given this unique access to economic resources, the husband has much more power than the wife in marital decision-making. When the wife is in the labor force, her position of complement changes to that of junior partner. Although she is in the labor force, the junior partner is also characterized by intended or actual intermittent labor-force participation. She views her occupation as secondary in importance to her husband's, as he continues to be defined as the primary chief provider. Thus, although the junior partner shares more marital power than the complement because of the economic resources she is bringing into the marriage, the junior partner still has less power than her husband because he maintains the primary provider role. It should be stressed that many wives move back and forth between the positions of complement and junior partner. Finally, there is a third structure (i.e., equal-equal partners), which represents a fairly radical departure from the way in which traditional marriages are structured. The key distinguishing features of the equal partnership are equal career commitment of both spouses; equal power shared by the husband and wife in decision making; and role inter-

when first married, the woman assumed the position of junior partner (i.e., in the labor force), but her job was viewed as secondary to that of her husband, and her primary responsibility was home and children. When children arrived, the woman moved to the position of complement (i.e., out of the labor force and responsible for home and children), with a concomitant loss in marital power and increase in traditionalism (Hoffman & Manis, 1978). Subsequent shifts between these statuses then varied according to family demands.

Currently, it appears that women are increasingly unwilling to accommodate these demands in such an extreme fashion. Instead, they are attempting to minimize the amount of time spent out of the labor force and thus to maintain the status of junior partner by shifting between various part- and full-time employment schedules. If such is the case, women would not only be accruing benefits in the labor market but also might be minimizing many of the changes in marriage typically associated with the interrelated events of dropping out of the labor force and having a child, such as decreased power and lower marital satisfaction (Polonko & Scanzoni, 1981). However, even maintaining the status of junior partner cannot be expected to result in large-scale, fundamental changes in the nature of female labor-force activity (e.g., in the proportions working full time, full year over the life course and in contribution to total family income) or even in marriage (e.g., equally shared household division of labor). Such changes cannot be expected because junior partners still make their careers secondary to the needs and responsibilities of children and the husband's career.

Expecting that greater changes have occurred is not, at this time, supported by extant data on the family. First, although women are postponing having children and are having fewer children, with increases in the percentage voluntarily remaining childless, the majority of wives still have at least two children. Second, the traditional division of labor still prevails in most marriages today, even among high-status, dual-career couples (Poloma, 1972; Rapoport & Rapoport, 1977; Yogev, 1981). Women continue to assume responsibilities for child care and housework because of little recourse to large-scale, quality day-care centers and/or equal husband participation in housework and child care. Thus, it is reasonable that increasing preferences for a commitment to labor market activity among women take the form of minimizing costly prolonged stays out of the labor force. The result is high labor-force participation rates, but primarily part time for women in the peak years of family demands, and shifts in work "attachment" as subsequent events demand or permit.

changeability with respect to the occupational/economic and domestic roles. This structure also differs from the others in that parenthood is no longer automatically assumed; rather, the ramifications for the wife's career are taken into account, and if the decision is made to have children, both parents assume equal responsibility for their care.

Overall, it would seem that the more substantial changes resulting in commitment to full-time, full-year careers throughout the life course can flourish only among truly equal partners. This is a slowly emerging alternative to traditional marital structures, and only a small minority of couples are thought to be characterized by it (Scanzoni, 1972, 1980). Moreover, it is interesting to note that there are both theoretical (Movius, 1976; Scanzoni & Scanzoni, 1981) and empirical (Bram, 1978; Polonko & Scanzoni, 1981) reasons for suspecting strong interconnections between the equal-partner marital structure and the decision to remain childless. Given the crucial role that children play in reinforcing the traditional division of labor, and given the apparently higher attainments and career commitment of voluntarily childless wives (Bram, 1978; Silka & Kiesler, 1977; Veevers, 1979), the decision to forgo children can, in this sense, be seen as one logical extension of the "deferral syndrome" among egalitarian women.

With respect to other areas, the concept of shifts in marital structures seems similarly useful in offering some insight into the nature of the changes that have taken place. For example, Scanzoni (1979a) argued that recent increases in divorce can be understood within the context of the rapid increase in junior-partner marriages, as this marital type is more apt to experience separation or divorce than the complement type of marriage. Of wives experiencing lower levels of economic and expressive rewards from their husbands, it is the junior partner who has alternative occupational rewards, thus "her potential threat of dissolving the marriage often becomes a reality" (Scanzoni, 1979a, p. 30).

However, the findings for women can also be viewed as further evidence of the incompatibility of marriage with significant achievement and career success for women. An equal partnership, for women desiring one, is difficult to find, as it implies that the careers of both spouses will be given equal weight and that housework and child care will be equally shared. Further, once married, these women are likely to be tougher bargainers on issues relating to their own interests, to have higher economic resources to back up their demands, and to reject pleas for "inherent male authority"; the result is a high potential for marital dissolution (Scanzoni, 1979a). Finally, even though the overall propensity toward remarriage is high, reflecting continued commitment to the rewards of marriage for most men and women, it is the women with the highest socioeconomic achievements who are not only the most likely to divorce but also the most likely not to remarry.

Thus, the shifts in the areas reviewed in this chapter, although impressive, certainly do not indicate a large-scale rejection of marriage and childbearing; rather they suggest changes in the direction of making family life more compatible with women's individualistic achievements. Consequently, although people's (gender-role) preferences are indeed shifting, the outcomes are not unrecognizable compared to those of the past.

Concepts regarding women's roles and family structures suggest ways in which the articulation between family demography and family sociology can and should be occurring not only with respect to women's roles, but also with respect to changing economic conditions and so on. Consequently, the task of family sociology and family demography, working in concert, will be to identify the array of newly developing predictors that will enable us to understand and accurately predict variations, as well as trends, in life-course patterns. Ideally, the emphasis will be on understanding changes over time in family structure and process.

The future of family demography is likely to follow several paths, one of which is the effort to theoretically blend the micro- and macrolevels of analysis. Blalock and Wilken (1979) accomplished this blend by using reemerging notions of goal-seeking processes to question the assumption that there is a break between the two levels. For example, they asserted that, as individuals pursue interests or preferences, these pursuits, if widespread, may subsequently influence societal trends in matters such as marriage, divorce, and living arrangements. In turn, those trends may influence the preferences—and thus the behaviors—of increasing numbers of individuals. Hence, argued Blalock and Wilken, the researcher's goal should be to formulate, and then to investigate, the conceptual and empirical links between micro- and macrolevel phenomena, rather than merely observing one-way effects.

Collins (1981) carried this type of reasoning one step further by arguing for an "effort" to "reconstitute macro-sociology upon radically empirical micro-foundations" (p. 82). He asserted that

the dynamics as well as the statics of the larger world ultimately depend upon its only living elements, people in micro-situations. Structural aggregates of micro-situations in time and space [i.e., family demographic issues] *are on another level of analysis and play a part in social causation only as they bear upon people's situational motivations. It is within micro-situations that we find both the glue and the transforming energies of these (aggregate) structures.* (p. 105)

Pondering these sorts of theoretical arguments rekindles interest in Max Weber's notions regarding the formation of interest groups and their subsequent impact on social organization (see Bendix, 1962). Both Collins and Blalock and Wilken have revived Weber, contending that, as individuals with similar preferences cluster together, they tend to form interest groups that seek to alter macrotype matters. In his analysis of demographic changes in family and household in England between 1500 and 1800, Stone (1977) explicitly acknowledged his debt to Weber and then proceeded to show how micropreferences shaped the formation of interest groups, which, in turn, influenced family demographic patterns. Matthews (1977) used this same theoretical posture—the impact of interest-group influences on demographic patterns—to help account for the emergence of the nineteenth-century American family. Not that one can ignore traditional demographic "explanations." Instead, one incorporates those traditional explanations into a more comprehensive framework in which macrophenomena are analyzed in terms of interest-group influences as well.

For example, there is a body of literature from both Europe and the United States suggesting that macrolevel struggles between what might be called *conventionals* and *progressives* may have some impact on demographic matters such as divorce, remarriage, living arrangements, and fertility control (Connecticut, 1981; Granberg & Denney, 1982; Lory, 1980; Scanzoni, 1983). In the United States, the conventionals include the so-called New Right, a collection of diverse interest groups united for the purpose of, among other things, marshaling unaligned citizens to support their efforts to control policy and legislation regarding the sorts of microbehaviors that, according to Collins, ultimately influence demographic patterns (e.g., marriage, divorce, abortion, sex education along with contraceptive delivery systems, and single parenthood). Hence, future research into certain demographic topics will need to take these sorts of interest-group perspectives into account.

ACKNOWLEDGMENTS

We wish to thank Phillips Cutright, Fred Pampel, and Geoffrey Leigh for their many helpful comments on this chapter.

References

Akers, D. On measuring the marriage squeeze. *Demography,* 1967, *4,* 907–924.

Aldous, J. *Family careers.* New York: Wiley, 1978.

Alexander, K., & Reilly, T. Estimating the effects of marriage timing on educational attainment: Some procedural issues and substantive clarifications. *American Journal of Sociology,* 1981, *87,* 143–156.

Althauser, R., & Wigler, M. Standardization and component analysis. *Sociological Methods and Research,* 1972, *1,* 97–135.

Anderson, J. Planning status of marital births, 1975–76. *Family Planning Perspectives,* 1981, *13,* 62–70.

Andorka, R. *Determinants of fertility in advanced societies.* New York: Free Press, 1978.

Bacon, L. Early motherhood, accelerated role transition, and social pathologies. *Social Forces,* 1974, *52,* 333–341.

Bagozzi, R., & Van Loo, M. Fertility as consumption: Theories from behavioral sciences. *Journal of Consumer Research,* 1978, *4,* 199–220.

Baldwin, W. Adolescent pregnancy and childbearing— Growing concerns for Americans. *Population Bulletin,* 31(2). Washington, D.C.: Population Reference Bureau, 1976.

Baltes, P., & Brim, O. *Life span development and behavior* (Vol. 3). New York: Academic Press, 1980.

Bane, M. *Economic influences on divorce and remarriage.* Cambridge: Center for the Study of Public Policy, Harvard University, 1975.

Barrett, N. Women in the job market: Occupations, earnings, and career opportunities. In R. Smith (Ed.), *The subtle revolution: Women at work.* Washington, D.C.: Urban Institute, 1979.

Bartz, K. and Nye, F. Early marriage: A propositional formulation. *Journal of Marriage and the Family,* 1970, *32,* 258–268.

Bauman, K., Koch, G., Udry, J., & Freedman, J. The relationship between legal abortion and marriage. *Social Biology,* 1975, *22,* 117–124.

Bayer, A. Early dating and early marriage. *Journal of Marriage and the Family,* 1968, *30,* 628–632.

Bayer, A. Life plans and marriage age: An application of path analysis. *Journal of Marriage and the Family,* 1969, 31, 551–558.

Becker, G. An economic analysis of fertility. In National Bureau of Economic Research (Ed.), *Demographic and economic change in developed countries.* Princeton: Princeton University Press, 1960.

Becker, G. A theory of marriage: Part I. *Journal of Political Economy,* 1973, *81,* 813–846.

Becker, G. A theory of marriage: Part II. *Journal of Political Economy,* 1974, *82,* 511–526.

Becker, G. *A treatise on the family.* Cambridge: Harvard University Press, 1981.

Becker, G., & Lewis, H. Interaction between quantity and quality of children. In T. Schultz (Ed.), *Economics of the family.* Chicago: University of Chicago Press, 1979.

Becker, G., Landes, E., & Michael, R. An economic analysis of marital instability. *Journal of Political Economy,* 1977, *85,* 1141–1187.

Bendix, R. *Max Weber: An intellectual portrait.* New York: Anchor Press, 1962.

Beresford, J., & Rivin, A. Privacy, poverty and old age. *Demography,* 1966, *3,* 247–258.

Bergman, B. The effects on white incomes of discrimination in employment. *Journal of Political Economy,* 1971, *79,* 294–313.

Berkov, B., & Sklar, J. Does illegitimacy make a difference? A study of the life chances of illegitimate children in California. *Population and Development Review,* 1976, *2,* 201–217.

Bernard, J. Marital stability and patterns of status. *Journal of Marriage and the Family,* 1966, *28,* 421–439.

Bianchi, S. Racial differences in per capita income, 1960–1976: The importance of household size, headship, and labor force participation. *Demography,* 1980, *17,* 129–143.

Bianchi, S. *Household composition and racial inequality.* New Brunswick, N.J.: Rutgers University Press, 1981.

Blake, J. The only child in America: Prejudice versus performance. *Population and Development Review,* 1981, *7,* 43–54.

Blake, J., & Das Gupta, P. Reproductive motivation versus contraceptive technology: Is recent American experience an exception? *Population and Development Review,* 1975, *1,* 229–247.

Blalock, H., & Wilken, P. *Intergroup processes: A micro-macro perspective.* New York: Free Press, 1979.

Blau, F., & Hendricks, W. Occupational segregation by sex: Trends and prospects. *The Journal of Human Resources,* 1979, *24,* 197–210.

Bloom, D. *What's happening to the age at first birth in the United States? A study of recent white and nonwhite cohorts.* Paper presented at the Annual Meeting of the Population Association of America, Washington, D.C., 1981.

Bloom, D., & Prebley, A. Voluntary childlessness: A review of the evidence and implications. *Population Research and Policy Review,* 1982, *3,* 203–224.

Bogue, D. *Principles of demography.* New York: Wiley, 1969.

Bongaarts, J. A framework for analyzing the proximate determinants of fertility. *Population and Development Review,* 1978, *1,* 1978, *1,* 105–132.

Bouvier, L. America's baby boom generation: The fateful bulge. *Population Bulletin* 35(1). Washington, D.C.: Population Reference Bureau, 1980.

Bowen, W., & Finegan, T. *The economics of labor force participation.* Princeton: Princeton University Press, 1969.

Bram, S. Through the looking glass: Voluntary childlessness as a mirror of contemporary changes in the meaning of parenthood. In W. Miller & L. Newman (Eds.), *The first child and family formation.* Chapel Hill, N.C.: Population Center, 1978.

Brown, R., Moon, M., & Zoloth, B. Occupational attainment and segregation by sex. *Industrial and Labor Relations Review*, 1980, *33*, 506–517.

Bumpass, L. Age at marriage as a variable in socio-economic differentials in fertility. *Demography*, 1969, *6*, 45–54.

Bumpass, L., & Rindfuss, R. Children's experience of marital disruption. *American Journal of Sociology*, 1979, *85*, 49–65.

Bumpass, L., & J. Sweet. Differentials in marital instability: 1970. *American Sociological Review*, 1972, *37*, 754–766.

Bumpass, L., Rindfuss, R., & Janosik, R. Age and marital status at first birth and the pace of subsequent fertility. *Demography*, 1978, *15*, 75–86.

Burch, T. The index of overall headship: A simple measure of household complexity standardized for age and sex. *Demography*, 1980, *17*, 25–37.

Butz, W., & Ward, M. *The emergence of countercyclical U.S. fertility*. Santa Monica, Calif.: Rand Corporation, 1977.

Butz, W., & Ward, M. *Completed fertility and its timing: An economic analysis of U.S. experience since World War II*. Santa Monica, Calif.: Rand Corporation, 1978.

Cain, G. *Married women in the labor force*. Chicago: University of Chicago Press, 1966.

Call, V., & Otto, L. Age at marriage as a mobility contingency: Estimates for the Nye-Berado model. *Journal of Marriage and the Family*, 1977, *39*, 67–78.

Card, J. Long-term consequences for children of teenage parents. *Demography*, 1981, *18*, 137–156.

Carlinger, G. Determinants of household headship. *Journal of Marriage and the Family*, 1975, *37*, 28–38.

Carlson, E. Divorce rate fluctuation as a cohort phenomenon. *Population Studies*, 1979, *33*, 523–536.

Carter, H., & Glick, P. *Marriage and divorce: A social and economic study*. Cambridge: Harvard University Press, 1976.

Cherlin, A. The effect of children on marital instability. *Demography*, 1977, *14*, 165–172.

Cherlin, A. Remarriage as an incomplete institution. *American Journal of Sociology*, 1978, *83*, 634–650.

Cherlin, A. Work life and marital dissolution. In G. Levinger & O. Moles (Eds.), *Divorce and separation*. New York: Basic Books, 1979.

Cherlin, A. *Marriage, divorce, remarriage*. Cambridge: Harvard University Press, 1981.

Chevan, A., & Korson, J. The widowed who live alone: An examination of social and demographic factors. *Social Forces*, 1972, *51*, 45–53.

Chilman, C. Social and psychological research concerning adolescent child-bearing: 1970–1980. *Journal of Marriage and the Family*, 1980, *42*, 793–805.

Cho, L., Grabill, W., & Bogue, D. *Differential current fertility in the United States*. Chicago: Community and Family Study Center, 1970.

Clausen, J., & Clausen, S. The effects of family size on parents and children. In J. Fawcett (Ed.), *Psychological perspectives on population*. New York: Basic Books, 1973.

Clayton, R., & Voss, H. Shacking up: Cohabitation in the 1970s. *Journal of Marriage and the Family*, 1977, *39*, 273–284.

Clifford, W., & Tobin, P. Labor force participation of working mothers and family formation: Some further evidence. *Demography*, 1977, *14*, 273–284.

Coale, A. Age patterns of marriage. *Population Studies*, 1971, *25*, 193–214.

Cohen, S., & Sweet, J. The impact of marital disruption and remarriage on fertility. *Journal of Marriage and the Family*, 1974, *36*, 87–96

Collins, R. Micro-translation as a theory-building strategy. In K. Knorr-Cetina & A. Cicourel (Eds.), *Advances in social theory and methodology: Toward an integration of micro and macro sociologies*. Boston: Routledge & Kegan Paul, 1981.

Connecticut Mutual Life Insurance Co. *The Connecticut Mutual Life report on American values in the '80s: The impact of belief*. Hartford, 1981.

Coombs, L. Reproductive goals and achieved fertility: A fifteen-year perspective. *Demography*, 1979, *16*, 523–534.

Coombs, L., & Freedman, R. Premarital pregnancy, childspacing, and later economic achievement. *Population Studies*, 1970, *24*, 389–412.

Coombs, L., Freedman, R., Freedman, J., & Pratt, W. Premarital pregnancy and status before and after marriage. *American Journal of Sociology*, 1970, *75*, 800–820.

Cramer, J. Employment trends of young mothers and the opportunity cost of babies in the United States. *Demography*, 1979, *16*, 177–197.

Cramer, J. Fertility and female employment: Problems of causal direction. *American Sociological Review*, 1980, *45*, 397–432.

Cuisenier, J. *The family life cycle in European societies*. The Hague: Mouton, 1977.

Cutright, P. Illegitimacy: Myths, causes, and cures. *Family Planning Perspectives*, 1971, *3*, 26–48.(a)

Cutright, P. Income and family events: Marital stability. *Journal of Marriage and the Family*, 1971, *33*, 291–306.(b)

Cutright, P. Illegitimacy in the United States: 1920–1968. In C. Westoff & R. Parke (Eds.), *Social and demographic aspects of population growth*. Washington, D.C.: U.S. Government Printing Office, 1972. (a)

Cutright, P. The teenage sexual revolution and the myth of an abstinent past. *Family Planning Perspectives*, 1972, *4*, 24–31. (b)

Cutright, P., & Madras, P. AFDC and the marital and family status of ever married women aged 15–44: United States, 1950–70. *Sociology and Social Research*, 1976, *60*, 314–327.

Cutright, P., & Polonko, K. Areal structure and rates of childlessness among American wives in 1970. *Social Biology*, 1977, *24*, 52–61.

Cutright, P., & Scanzoni, J. Income supplements and the American family. In Joint Economic Committee (Ed.), *The family, poverty, and welfare programs: Factors influencing family instability*. Washington, D.C.: U.S. Government Printing Office, 1973.

Cutright, P., & Shorter, F. The effects of health on the completed fertility of nonwhite and white U.S. women born between 1867 and 1935. *Journal of Social History*, 1979, *13*, 191–217.

Davids, L. Family change in Canada, 1971–1976. *Journal of Marriage and the Family*, 1980, *42*, 177–183.

Davidson, M. Social and economic variations in child spacing. *Social Biology*, 1970, *17*, 107–113.

Davis, K., & Blake, J. Social structure and fertility: An analytic framework. *Economic Development and Cultural Change*, 1956, *4*, 211–235.

Davis, N., & Bumpass, L. The continuation of education after marriage among women in the United States. *Demography*, 1976, *13*, 161–174.

Dawson, D., Meny, D., & Ridley, J. Fertility control in the United States before the contraceptive revolution. *Family Planning Perspectives*, 1980, *12*, 76–86.

DeJong, G. & Sell, R. Changes in childlessness in the United States: A demographic path analysis. *Population Studies*, 1977, *31*, 129–141.

Duncan, G., & Morgan, J. Young children and "other" family members. In G. Duncan & J. Morgan (Eds.), *Five thousand American families: Patterns of economic progress*. Ann Arbor: Institute for Social Research, University of Michigan, 1976.

Duvall, E. *Family development*. New York: Lippincott, 1963.

Easterlin, R. Relative economic status and the American fertility swing. In E. B. Sheldon (Ed.), *Family economic behavior: Problems and prospects*. Philadelphia: Lippincott, 1973.

Easterlin, R. What will 1984 be like? Socioeconomic implications of recent twists in age structure. *Demography*, 1978, *15*, 397–432.

Easterlin, R. *Birth and fortune: The impact of numbers on personal welfare*. New York: Basic Books, 1980.

Eberstein, I., & Frisbie, W. Differences in marital instability among

Mexican American, blacks, and anglos: 1960 and 1970. *Social Problems, 1976, 23, 609–621.*

Elandt-Johnson, R., & Johnson, N. *Survival models and data analysis.* New York: Wiley, 1980.

Elder, G. Age differentiation in the life course. In A. Inkeles, J. Coleman, & N. Smelser (Eds.), *Annual review of sociology* (Vol. 1). Palo Alto, Calif.: Annual Reviews, 1974.

Elder, G. Family history and the life course. *Journal of Family History, 1977, 2, 279–304.*

Elder, G. Family history and the life course. In T. Hareven (Ed.), *Transitions: The family and the life course in historical perspective.* New York: Academic Press, 1978.

Elder, G. History and the family: The discovery of complexity. *Journal of Marriage and the Family, 1981, 43, 489–519.*

Espenshade, T. The value and cost of children. *Population Bulletin,* 32(1). Washington, D.C.: Population Reference Bureau, 1977.

Ewer, P., Crimmins, E., & Oliver, R. An analysis of the relationship between husband's income, family size and wife's employment in the early stages of marriage. *Journal of Marriage and the Family, 1979, 41, 727–738.*

Farley, R., & Hermalin, A. Family stability: A comparison of trends between blacks and whites. *American Sociological Review, 1971, 36, 1–17.*

Ferber, M. Labor-market participation of young married women: Causes and effects. *Journal of Marriage and the Family, 1982, 44, 457–468.*

Figley, C. Child density and the marital relationship. *Journal of Marriage and the Family, 1973, 35, 272–282.*

Forrest, J., Tietze, C., & Sullivan, E. Abortion in the U.S., 1976–1977. *Family Planning Perspectives, 1978, 10, 271–279.*

Freedman, R., & Coombs, L. Childspacing and family economic positions. *American Sociological Review, 1966, 31, 631–648.* (a)

Freedman, R., & Coombs, L. Economic considerations in family growth decisions. *Population Studies, 1966, 20, 197–222.* (b)

Freedman, R., Freedman, D., & Thornton, A. Changes in fertility expectations and preferences between 1962 and 1977: Their relation to final parity. *Demography, 1980, 17, 365–378.*

Freiden, A. The United Stated marriage market. *Journal of Political Economy, 1974, 82, 534–553.*

Freshnock, L., & Cutright, P. Structural determinants of childlessness: A nonrecursive analysis of 1970 U.S. rates. *Social Biology, 1978, 25, 169–178.*

Frisbie, W., Bean, F., & Eberstein, I. *Recent changes in marital instability among Mexican Americans: Convergence with black and anglo trends?* Austin: University of Texas, Texas Population Research Center, 1978.

Furstenberg, F. Premarital pregnancy and marital instability. *Journal of Social Issues, 1976, 32, 67–86.* (a)

Furstenberg, F. *Unplanned parenthood: The social consequences of teen-age childbearing.* New York: Free Press, 1976. (b)

Furstenberg, F. Recycling the family: Perspectives for a neglected family form. *Marriage and Family Review, 1979, 2, 11–22.*

Gehan, E. Estimating survivor functions from the life table. *Journal of Chronic Diseases, 1969, 21, 629–644.*

Gibson, C. The U.S. fertility decline, 1961–1975: The contribution of changes in marital status and marital fertility. *Family Planning Perspectives, 1976, 8, 249–252.*

Glenn, N. & Frisbie, W. Trend studies with sample survey and census data. In A. Inkeles, J. Coleman, & N. Smelser (Eds.), *Annual review of sociology* (Vol. 3). Palo Alto, Calif.: Annual Reviews, 1977.

Glenn, N., & Weaver, C. A multivariate, multisurvey study of marital happiness. *Journal of Marriage and the Family, 1978, 40, 269–282.*

Glick, P. The family cycle. *American Sociological Review, 1947, 12, 164–174.*

Glick, P. The life cycle of the family. *Marriage and Family Living, 1955, 18, 3–9.*

Glick, P. *American families.* New York: Wiley, 1957.

Glick, P., & Norton, A. Marrying, divorcing, and living together in the U.S. today. *Population Bulletin,* 32(5). Washington, D.C.: Population Reference Bureau, 1977.

Glick, P., & Parke, R. New approaches in studying the life cycle of the family. *Demography, 1969, 2, 187–202.*

Glick, P., & Spanier, G. Married and unmarried cohabitation in the United States. *Journal of Marriage and the Family, 1980, 42, 19–30.*

Glick, P., Heer, D., & Beresford, J. Family formation and family composition. In M. Sussman (Ed.), *Sourcebook in marriage and the family.* Boston: Houghton-Mifflin, 1963.

Grabill, W., Kiser, C., & Whelpton, P. *The fertility of American women.* New York: Wiley, 1958.

Granberg, D., & Denney, D. The coathanger and the rose: Comparison of pro-choice and pro-life activists in the contemporary United States. *Transaction/Society, 1982.*

Groat, H., Workman, R., & Neal, A. Labor force participation and family formation: A study of working mothers. *Demography, 1965, 13, 115–125.*

Gross, A., & Clark, V. *Survival distributions: Reliability applications in the biomedical sciences.* New York: Wiley, 1975.

Hannon, M., Tuma, N., & Groeneveld, L. Income and martial events: Evidence from an income maintenance experiment. *American Journal of Sociology, 1977, 82, 1186–1211.*

Hareven, T. *Transitions: The family and the life course in historical perspective.* New York: Academic Press, 1978.

Hastings, D. Child-spacing differentials for white and non-white couples according to educational level of attainment for the 1/1000 samples of the United States population in 1960. *Population Studies, 1971, 25, 105–116.*

Hastings, D., & Robinson, J. Incidence of childlessness for United States women: Cohorts born 1891–1945. *Social Biology, 1974, 21, 178–184.*

Hastings, D., & Robinson, W. Open and closed birth intervals for once-married spouse-present white women. *Demography, 1975, 12, 455–466.*

Hawthorne, G. *The sociology of fertility.* New York: Macmillan, 1970.

Heckman, J., & Willis, R. A beta-logistic model for the analysis of sequential labor force participation by married women. *Journal of Political Economy, 1977, 85, 27–58.*

Hendershot, G., & Placek, P. *Predicting fertility.* Lexington, Mass.: Lexington Books, 1981.

Henshaw, S., Forrest, J., Sullivan, E., & Tietze, C. Abortion services in the United States, 1979 and 1980. *Family Planning Perspectives, 1982, 19, 5–15.*

Hernes, G. The process of entry into first marriage. *American Sociological Review, 1972, 37, 173–182.*

Hill, D., & Hill, M. Older children and splitting off. In G. Duncan & J. Morgan (Eds.), *Five thousand American families: Patterns of economic progress.* Ann Arbor: Institute for Social Research, University of Michigan, 1976.

Hill, R., & Rodgers, R. The developmental approach. In H. Christensen (Ed.), *Handbook of marriage and the family.* Chicago: Rand McNally, 1964.

Hofferth, S., & Moore, K. Early childbearing and later economic well-being. *American Sociological Review, 1979, 44, 789–815.*

Hoffman, L., & Manis, J. Influences of children on marital interaction and parental satisfactions and dissatisfactions. In R. Lerner & G. Spanier (Eds.), *Child influences on marital and family interaction: A life-span perspective.* New York: Academic Press, 1978.

Hoffman, S. Marital instability and the economic status of women. *Demography, 1977, 14, 67–76.*

Hogan, D. The effects of demographic factors, family background, and job achievement on age at marriage. *Demography, 1978, 15, 155–175.* (a)

Hogan, D. The variable order of events in the life course. *American Sociological Review*, 1978, 43, 573–586. (b)

Hogan, D. The transition to adulthood as a career contingency. *American Sociological Review*, 1980, *45*, 261–276.

Honig, M. The impact of welfare payment levels on family stability. In Joint Economic Committee (Ed.), *The family, poverty, and welfare programs: Factors influencing family instability*. Washington, D.C.: Government Printing Office, 1973.

Horiuchi, S. Decomposition of the rise in divorce rates: A note on Michael's results. *Demography*, 1979, *16*, 549–551.

Houseknecht, S. Voluntary childlessness: A social psychological model. *Alternative Lifestyles*, 1978, *1*, 379–402.

Houseknecht, S. Childlessness and marital adjustment. *Journal of Marriage and the Family*, 1979, *41*, 259–265.

Houseknecht, S., & Spanier, G. Marital disruption and higher education among women in the United States. *Sociological Quarterly*, 1980, *21*, 375–389.

Huber, J., & Spitze, G. Considering divorce: An expansion of Becker's theory of marital instability. *American Journal of Sociology*, 1980, *86*, 75–89.

Hughes, M., & Gove, W. Living alone, social integration, and mental health. *American Journal of Sociology*, 1981, *87*, 48–74.

Kalbfleisch, J., & Prentice, R. *The statistical analysis of failure time data*. New York: Wiley, 1980.

Kantner, J., & Zelnik, M. Sexual experience of young unmarried women in the United States. *Family Planning Perspectives*, 1972, *4*, 9–18.

Keeley, M. The economics of family formation. *Economic Inquiry*, 1977, *15*, 238–250.

Kitagawa, E. Components of a difference between two rates. *Journal of the American Statistical Association*, 1955, *50*, 1168–1194.

Kitagawa, E. Standardized comparisons in demographic research. *Demography*, 1964, *1*, 296–315.

Kobrin, F. Household headship and its changes in the United States, 1940–1960, 1970. *Journal of the American Statistical Association*, 1973, *68*, 793–800.

Kobrin, F. The fall of household size and the rise of the primary individual in the United States. *Demography*, 1976, *13*, 127–139. (a)

Kobrin, F. The primary individual and the family: Changes in living arrangements in the United States since 1940. *Journal of Marriage and the Family*, 1976, *38*, 233–239. (b)

Kobrin, F. Family extension and the elderly: Economic, demographic and family cycle factors. *Journal of Gerontology*, 1981, *36*, 307–377.

Kobrin, F., & Goldscheider, C. *The ethnic factor in family structure and mobility*. Cambridge, Mass.: Ballinger, 1978.

Kobrin, F., & Hendershot, G. Do family ties reduce mortality: Evidence from the United States, 1966–1968. *Journal of Marriage and the Family*, 1977, *39*, 373–380.

Koo, H., & Suchindran, C. Effects of children on women's remarriage prospects. *Journal of Family Issues*, 1980, *1*, 497–515.

Krishnamoorthy, S. Family formation and the life cycle. *Demography*, 1979, *16*, 121–129.

Kuznets, S. Demographic aspects of the size distribution of income: An exploratory essay. *Economic Development and Cultural Change*, 1976, *25*, 1–94.

Kuznets, S. Size and age structure of family households: Exploratory comparisons. *Population and Development Review*, 1978, *4*, 187–223.

Lansing, J., & Kish, L. Family life cycle as an independent variable. *American Sociological Review*, 1957, *22*, 512–519.

LaRossa, R., & LaRossa, M. *Transition to parenthood: How infants change families*. Beverly Hills: Sage Publications, 1981.

Leibowitz, A. Education and the allocation of women's time. In F. Juster (Ed.), *Education, income and human behavior*. New York: McGraw-Hill, 1974.

Levin, M., & O'Hara, C. The impact of marital history of current hus-

bands on the fertility of remarried white women in the U.S. *Journal of Marriage and the Family*, 1978, *40*, 95–102.

Lloyd, C. The division of labor between the sexes: A review. In C. Lloyd (Ed.), *Sex, discrimination, and the division of labor*. New York: Columbia University Press, 1975.

Lloyd, C., & Niemi, B. *The economics of sex differentials*. New York: Columbia University Press, 1980.

Locksley, A. On the effects of wives' employment on marital adjustment and companionship. *Journal of Marriage and the Family*, 1980, *42*, 337–346.

Loomis, C., & Hamilton, C. Family life cycle analysis. *Social Forces*, 1936, *15*, 225–231.

Lory, B. Changes in European family policies. In J. Aldous & W. Dunon (Eds.), *The politics and programs of family policy*. Notre Dame, Ind.: University of Notre Dame Press, 1980.

MacDonald, M., & Rindfuss, R. Earnings, relative income, and family formation. *Demography*, 1981, *18*, 123–136.

Macklin, E. Nonmarital heterosexual cohabitation: A review of the recent literature. *Marriage and Family Review*, 1978, *1*, 1–12.

Marini, M. The transition to adulthood: Sex differences in educational attainment and age at marriage. *American Sociological Review*, 1978, *43*, 483–507.

Marini, M. Effects of the number and spacing of children on marital and parental satisfaction. *Demography*, 1980, *17*, 225–242.

Marini, M., & Hodsdon, P. Effects of the timing of marriage and the first birth on the spacing of subsequent births. *Demography*, 1981, *18*, 529–548.

Masnick, G., & Bane, M. *The nation's families: 1960–1990*. Boston: Auburn House, 1980.

Masnick, G., & McFalls, J. *Those perplexing U.S. fertility swings: A new perspective on a 20th century puzzle*. Population Reference Bureau Occasional Report, Washington, D.C., 1978.

Matthews, D. *Religion in the old south*. Chicago: University of Chicago Press, 1977.

McCarthy, J. A comparison of the probability of the dissolution of first and second marriage. *Demography*, 1978, *15*, 345–360.

McCarthy, J., & Menken, J. Marriage, remarriage, marital disruption, and age at first birth. *Family Planning Perspectives*, 1979, *11*, 21–30.

Menken, J. Teenage childbearing: Its medical aspects and implications for the United States population. In C. Westoff & R. Parke (Eds.), *Demographic and social aspects of population growth* (Vol. 1). Washington, D.C.: U.S. Government Printing Office, 1972.

Michael, R. The rise in divorce rates, 1960–1974: Age-specific components. *Demography*, 1978, *15*, 177–182.

Michael, R., Fuchs, V., & Scott, S. Changes in the propensity to live alone: 1950–1976. *Demography*, 1980, *17*, 39–53.

Miller, B. A multivariate developmental model of marital satisfaction. *Journal of Marriage and the Family*, 1976, *38*, 643–657.

Millman, S. & Hendershot, G. Early fertility and lifetime fertility. *Family Planning Perspectives*, 1980, *12*, 139–149.

Mincer, J. Market prices, opportunity costs, and income effects. In C. Christ, (Ed.), *Measurement in economics: Studies in mathematical economics and econometrics in memory of Yehuda Grunfeld*. Stanford: Stanford University Press, 1963.

Modell, J. Normative aspects of American marriage timing since World War II. *Journal of Family History*, 1980, *5*, 210–234.

Modell, J., Furstenberg, F., & Strong, D. The timing of marriage in the transition to adulthood: Continuity and change, 1860–1975. In J. Demos & S. Boocock (Eds.), *Turning points: Historical and sociological essays on the family*. Chicago: University of Chicago Press, 1978.

Moles, O. Marital dissolution and public assistance programs: Variations among American states. *Journal of Social Issues*, 1976, *32*, 87–101.

Moles, O. Public welfare payments and marital dissolutions: A review of recent studies. In G. Levinger & O. Moles (Eds.), *Divorce and separation*. New York: Basic Books, 1979.

Moore, K., & Hofferth, S. Effects of women's employment on marriage: Formation, stability and roles. *Marriage and Family Review*, 1979, *2* (1), 27–36.

Moore, K., & Hofferth, S. Factors affecting early family formation: A path model. *Population and Environment*, 1980, *3*, 73–96.

Moore, K., & Waite, L. Marital dissolution, early motherhood, and early marriage. *Social Forces*, 1981, *60*, 20–40.

Morgan, S. Intentions and uncertainty at later stages of childbearing: The United States 1965 and 1970. *Demography*, 1981, *18*, 267–285.

Mott, F. Fertility, life cycle stage, and female labor force participation in Rhode Island: A retrospective overview. *Demography*, 1972, *9*, 173–185.

Mott, F., & Moore, S. The causes of marital disruption among young American women: An interdisciplinary perspective. *Journal of Marriage and the Family*, 1979, *41*, 355–365.

Movius, M. Voluntary childlessness—The ultimate liberation. *The Family Coordinator*, 1976, *25*, 57–63.

Mueller, C., & Pope, H. Marital instability: A study of its transmission between generations. *Journal of Marriage and the Family*, 1977, *39*, 83–93.

Muhsam, H. The marriage squeeze. *Demography*, 1974, *11*, 291–299.

Namboodiri, N. The wife's work experience and child spacing. *Milbank Memorial Fund Quarterly*, 1964, *42*, 65–77.

Namboodiri, N. Some observations on the economic framework for fertility analysis. *Population Studies*, 1972, *26*, 185–206.

Namboodiri, N. On factors affecting fertility at different stages in the reproductive history: An exercise in cohort fertility. *Social Forces*, 1981, *59*, 1114–1129.

National Center for Health Statistics. *Divorce and divorce rates: United States*. Series 21, No. 29, 1978.

National Center for Health Statistics. *Divorce by marriage cohort*. Series 21, No. 34, 1979.

National Center for Health Statistics. *National estimates of marriage dissolution and survivorship: United States*. Series 3, No. 19, 1980. (a)

National Center for Health Statistics. *Patterns of employment before and after childbirth*. Series 23, No. 4, 1980. (b)

National Center for Health Statistics. *Remarriages of women 15–44 years of age whose first marriage ended in divorce: United States, 1976*. Advance Data, No. 58, 1980. (c)

National Center for Health Statistics. *Socioeconomic differentials and trends in the timing of births*. Series 23, No. 6, 1981.

Nock, S. The family life cycle: Empirical or conceptual tool. *Journal of Marriage and the Family*, 1979, *41*, 15–26.

Nock, S. Family life cycle transitions: Longitudinal effects on family members. *Journal of Marriage and the Family*, 1981, *43*, 703–714.

Norton, A., & Glick, P. Marital instability: Past, present, and future. *Journal of Social Issues*, 1976, *34*, 5–20.

Nye, F., Carlson, J., & Farrett, G. Family size, interaction, affect, and stress. *Journal of Marriage and the Family*, 1970, *32*, 216–226.

O'Connell, M. Comparative estimates of teenage illegitimacy in the United States, 1940–1944 to 1970–1974. *Demography*, 1980, *17*, 13–23.

O'Connell, M., & Moore, M. The legitimacy status of first births to U.S. women aged 15–24, 1939–1978. *Family Planning Perspectives*, 1980, *12*, 16–25.

Oppenheimer, V. *The female labor force in the United States: Demographic and economic factors governing its growth and changing composition*. Population Monograph Series, No. 5. Berkeley: University of California, 1970.

Oppenheimer, V. Demographic influences on female employment and the status of women. *American Journal of Sociology*, 1973, *78*, 946–961.

Oppenheimer, V. The Easterlin Hypothesis: Another aspect of the echo to consider. *Population and Development Review*, 1976, *2*, 433–437.

Oppenheimer, V. Structural sources of economic pressure for wives to work: An analytical framework. *Journal of Family History*, 1979, *4*, 177–197.

Otto, L. Class and status in family research. *Journal of Marriage and the Family*, 1975, *38*, 315–332.

Otto, L. Antecedents and consequences of marital timing. In W. Burr, R. Hill, F. Nye, & I. Reiss (Eds.), *Contemporary theories about the family* (Vol. 1). New York: Free Press, 1979.

Pampel, F. *Changes in the propensity to live alone: Evidence from consecutive cross-sectional surveys, 1960–1976. Demography*, 1982, *20*, 433–448.

Pearlin, L., & Johnson, J. Marital status, life strains, and depression. *American Sociological Review*, 1977, *42*, 704–715.

Pebley, A. Changing attitudes toward the timing of first births. *Family Planning Perspectives*, 1981, *13*, 171–175.

Pohlman, E. The timing of first births: A review of effects. *Eugenics Quarterly*, 1968, *15*, 252–263.

Pohlman, E. *The psychology of birth planning*. Cambridge, Mass.: Schenkman, 1969.

Poloma, M. Role conflict and the married professional woman. In C. Safilios-Rothschild (Ed.), *Toward a sociology of women*. Lexington, Mass.: Xerox College Publishers, 1972.

Polonko, K., & Scanzoni, J. *Patterns compared for the voluntary childless, undecided childless, postponing childless, and others*. Final Report to the National Institute for Child Health and Human Development, Contract No. 1-HD-92805, 1981.

Polonko, K., Scanzoni, J., & Teachman, J. Assessing the implications of childlessness for marital satisfaction. *Journal of Family Issues*, 1982, *3*, 545–573.

Pope, H., & Mueller, C. The intergenerational transmission of marital instability: Comparisons by race and sex. *Journal of Social Issues*, 1976, *32*, 49–66.

Poston, D., & Gotard, E. Trends in childlessness in the United States: 1910–1975. *Social Biology*, 1977, *24*, 212–224.

Potter, R. Birth intervals: Structure and change. *Population Studies*, 1963, *18*, 155–166.

Presser, H. The timing of the first birth, female roles, and black fertility. *Milbank Memorial Fund Quarterly*, 1971, *49*, 329–361.

Presser, J. Age differences between spouses: Trends, patterns, and social implications. *American Behavioral Scientist*, 1975, *19*, 190–205.

Preston, S., & McDonald, J. The incidence of divorce within cohorts of American marriages contracted since the Civil War. *Demography*, 1979, *16*, 1–25.

Preston, S., & Richards, A. The influence of women's work opportunities on marriage rates. *Demography*, 1975, *12*, 209–222.

Rapoport, R., & Rapoport, R. *Dual career families re-examined*. New York: Harper & Row, 1977.

Rindfuss, R., & Bumpass, L. Fertility during marital disruption. *Journal of Marriage and the Family*, 1977, *39*, 517–528.

Rindfuss, R., & Bumpass, L. Age and the sociology of fertility: How old is too old? In K. Taeuber, L. Bumpass, & J. Sweet (Eds.), *Social demography*. New York: Academic Press, 1978.

Rindfuss, R., & Sweet, J. *Postwar fertility trends and differentials in the United States*. New York: Academic Press, 1977.

Rodgers, R. Toward a theory of family development. *Journal of Marriage and the Family*, 1964, *26*, 262–270.

Rodgers, R. *Family interaction and transaction: The developmental approach*. Englewood Cliffs, N.J.: Prentice-Hall, 1973.

Rodgers, R., & Whitney, G. The family life cycle in twentieth century Canada. *Journal of Marriage and the Family*, 1981, *43*, 727–740.

Rollins, B., & Galligan, R. The developing child and marital satisfaction of parents. In R. Lerner & G. Spanier (Eds.), *Child influences on marital and family interaction: A life-span perspective*. New York: Academic Press, 1978.

Ross, H., & Sawhill, L. *Time of transition: The growth of families headed by women.* Washington, D.C.: Urban Institute, 1975.

Rossi, A. Women in science: Why so few? *Science,* 1965, *148,* 1196–1202.

Rossi, A. Transition to parenthood. *Journal of Marriage and the Family,* 1968, *30,* 26–39.

Rowntree, B. *Poverty: A study of town life.* London: Macmillan, 1906.

Ryder, N. The cohort as a concept in the study of social change. *American Sociological Review,* 1965, *30,* 843–861.

Ryder, N. The emergence of a modern fertility pattern: United States, 1917–1966. In S. Behrman, L. Corsa, & R. Freedman (Eds.), *Fertility and family planning: A world view.* Ann Arbor: University of Michigan Press, 1969.

Ryder, N. Fertility measurement through cross-sectional surveys. *Social Forces,* 1975, *54,* 7–35.

Ryder, N. Components of temporal variations in American fertility. In R. Hiorns (Ed.), *Demographic patterns in developed societies.* London: Taylor & Francis, 1980.

Ryder, N. A time series of instrumental fertility variables. *Demography,* 1981, *18,* 487–509.

Ryder, N., & Westoff, C. *Reproduction in the United States, 1965.* Princeton: Princeton University Press, 1971.

Sandefur, G., & Scott, W. A dynamic analysis of migration: An assessment of the effects of age, family and career variables. *Demography,* 1981, *18,* 355–368.

Scanzoni, J. *Sexual bargaining: Power politics in the American marriage.* Englewood Cliffs, N.J.: Prentice-Hall, 1972.

Scanzoni, J. *Sex roles, lifestyles, and childbearing: Changing patterns in marriage and the family.* New York: Free Press, 1975.

Scanzoni, J. A historical perspective on husband-wife bargaining power and marital dissolution. In G. Levinger & O. Moles (Eds.), *Divorce and separation.* New York: Basic Books, 1979. (a)

Scanzoni, J. Work and fertility control sequences among younger married women. *Journal of Marriage and the Family,* 1979, *41,* 739–755. (b)

Scanzoni, J. Contemporary marriage types: A research note. *Journal of Family Issues,* 1980, *1,* 125–140.

Scanzoni, J. *Is family possible: Theory and policy for the 21st century.* Beverly Hills, Calif.: Sage, 1983.

Scanzoni, J., & Fox, G. Sex roles, family, and society: The seventies and beyond. *Journal of Marriage and the Family,* 1980, *42,* 743–756.

Scanzoni, L., & Scanzoni, J. *Men, women, and change.* New York: McGraw-Hill, 1981.

Schoen, R. & Nelson, V. Marriage, divorce, and mortality: A life table analysis. *Demography,* 1974, *11,* 267–290.

Schoen, R., Greenblatt, H., & Mielke, R. California's experience with nonadversary divorce. *Demography,* 1975, *12,* 223–243.

Shapiro, D., & Mott, F. Labor supply behavior of prospective and new mothers. *Demography,* 1979, *16,* 199–208.

Sheps, M., & Menken, J. *Mathematical models of conception and birth.* Chicago: University of Chicago Press, 1973.

Silka, L., & Kiesler, S. Couples who choose to remain childless. *Family Planning Perspectives,* 1977, *9,* 16–25.

Smith, D., & Hendus, M. Premarital pregnancy in America, 1640–1971: An overview and interpretation. *Journal of Interdisciplinary History,* 1975, *5,* 537–570.

Smith, J. *Female labor supply.* Princeton: Princeton University Press, 1980.

Smith, J., & Ward, M. Asset accumulation and family size. *Demography,* 1980, *17,* 243–260.

Smith, R. *The subtle revolution: Women at work.* Washington, D.C.: Urban Institute, 1979.

Smith-Lovin, L., & Tickamyer, A. Nonrecursive models of labor force participation, fertility behavior, and sex role attitudes. *American Sociological Review, 1978, 43,* 541–557.

Spanier, G., & Glick, P. The life cycle of American families: An expanded analysis. *Journal of Family History,* 1980, *5,* 97–111. (a)

Spanier, G., & Glick, P. Paths to remarriage. *Journal of Divorce,* 1980, *3,* 283–298. (b)

Spanier, G., Sauer, W., & Larzelere, R. An empirical evaluation of the family life cycle. *Journal of Marriage and the Family,* 1979, *41,* 27–38.

Speare, A. Home ownership, life cycle stage, and residential mobility. *Demography,* 1970, *1,* 449–458.

Speare, A., Goldstein, S., & Frey, W. *Residential mobility, migration and metropolitan change.* Cambridge, Mass.: Ballinger, 1974.

Spitze, G., & Waite, L. Wives' employment: The role of husbands' perceived attitudes. *Journal of Marriage and the Family,* 1981, *43,* 117–124.

Stafford, F. Women's use of time converging with men's. *Monthly Labor Review,* 1980, *103,* 57–59.

Stone, L. *The family, sex, and marriage: England 1500–1800.* New York: Harper & Row, 1977.

Sweet, J. The living arrangements of separated, widowed, and divorced mothers. *Demography,* 1972, *9,* 143–157.

Sweet, J. *Differentials in remarriage probabilities.* Madison: Center for Demography and Ecology, University of Wisconsin, 1973. (a)

Sweet, J. *Women in the labor force.* New York: Academic Press, 1973. (b)

Sweet, J. Demography and the family. In A. Inkeles, J. Coleman, & N. Smelser (Eds.), *Annual review of sociology* (Vol. 3). Palo Alto, Calif.: Annual Reviews, 1977.

Teachman, J. Early marriage, premarital fertility, and marital dissolution: Results for blacks and white. *Journal of Family Issues.* 1983, *4,* 105–126.

Teachman, J., & Polonko, K. *An exploratory analysis of factors associated with the legitimation of premarital pregnancies.* Population Studies and Training Center, Brown University and Department of Sociology, University of Iowa, 1982.

Teachman, J., & Polonko, K. Out of sequence: The timing of marriage following a premarital birth. *Social Forces,* 1984, *63,* 245–260.

Thornton, A. *Marital instability and fertility.* Ph.D. thesis, University of Michigan, Ann Arbor, 1975.

Thornton, A. Children and marital instability. *Journal of Marriage and the Family,* 1977, *39,* 531–541.

Thornton, A. Marital dissolution, remarriage, and childbearing. *Demography,* 1978, *15,* 361–380.

Treas, J. Postwar trends in family size. *Demography,* 1981, *18,* 321–334.

Troll, L. The family and labor life: A decade review. *Journal of Marriage and the Family,* 1971, *33,* 263–290.

Trussell, T. Economic consequences of teenage childbearing. *Family Planning Perspective,* 1976, *8,* 184–190. (a)

Trussell, T. A refined estimator of measures of location of the age at first marriage. *Demography,* 1976, *13,* 225–234. (b)

Tsui, A. The family formation process among U.S. marriage cohorts. *Demography,* 1982, *19,* 1–27.

Tuma, N., Hannon, M., & Groeneveld, L. Dynamic analysis of event histories. *American Journal of Sociology,* 1979, *81,* 820–851.

Udry, J. Marital instability by race, sex, education, and occupation using 1960 census data. *American Journal of Sociology,* 1966, *72,* 203–209.

Udry, J. Marital instability by race and income based on 1960 census data. *American Journal of Sociology,* 1967, *72,* 673–674.

Uhlenberg, P. Demographic correlates of group achievement: Contrasting patterns of Mexican-Americans and Japanese-Americans. *Demography,* 1971, *9,* 119–128.

Uhlenberg, P. Marital instability among Mexican-Americans: Following the patterns of blacks? *Social Problems,* 1972, *20,* 49–56.

Uhlenberg, P. Cohort variations in family life cycle experiences of U.S. females. *Journal of Marriage and the Family*, 1974, *36*, 281–292.

Uhlenberg, P. Changing configurations in the life course. In T. Hareven (Ed.), *Transitions: The family and life course in historical perspective*. New York: Academic Press, 1978.

U.S. Bureau of the Census. *Fertility history and prospects of American women: June 1975*. Current Population Reports, Series P-20, No. 288, 1976. (a)

U.S. Bureau of the Census. *Number, timing, and duration of marriages and divorces in the United States: June 1975*. Current Population Reports, Series P-20, No. 297, 1976. (b)

U.S. Bureau of the Census. *Premarital fertility*. Current Population Reports, Series P-23, No. 63, 1976. (c)

U.S. Bureau of the Census. *Marriage, divorce, widowhood, and remarriage by family characteristics: June 1975*. Current Population Reports, Series P-20. No. 312, 1977.

U.S. Bureau of the Census. *Trends in Childspacing, June, 1975*. Current Population Reports, Series P-20, No. 315, 1978.

U.S. Bureau of the Census. *Marital status and living arrangements: March 1979*. Current Population Reports, Series P-20, No. 349, 1980. Table B.

Vanek, J. Household work, wage work, and sexual equality. In S. Berk (Ed.), *Women and household labor*. Beverly Hills, Calif.: Sage, 1980.

Veevers, J. Voluntary childlessness: A review of issues and evidence. *Marriage and Family Review*, 1979, *2*, 1–26.

Voss, P. *Social determinants of age at first marriage in the United States*. Ph.D. thesis, University of Michigan, Ann Arbor, 1975.

Waite, L. Working wives and the family life cycle. *American Journal of Sociology*, 1980, *86*, 272–294.

Waite, L. Women at work. *Population Bulletin*, 36(2). Washington, D.C.: Population Reference Bureau, 1981.

Waite, L., & Moore, K. The impact of an early first birth on young women's educational attainment. *Social Forces*, 1978, *56*, 845–865.

Waite, L., & Spitze, G. Young women's transition to marriage. *Demography*, 1981, *18*, 681–694.

Waite, L., & Stolzenberg, R. Intended childbearing and labor force participation of young women: Insights from nonrecursive models. *American Sociological Review*, 1976, *41*, 235–252.

Weed, J. Age at marriage as a factor in state divorce rate differentials. *Demography*, 1974, *11*, 361–375.

Weller, R. & Hobbs, F. Unwanted and mistimed births in the United States: 1968–1973. *Family Planning Perspectives*, 1978, *10*, 168–172.

Westoff, C. The decline in unwanted fertility, 1971–1976. *Family Planning Perspectives*, 1981, *13*, 70–72.

Westoff, C., & Jones, E. Contraception and sterilization in the United States, 1965–1975. *Family Planning Perspectives*, 1977, *9*, 153–157.

Westoff, C., & Ryder, N. *The contraceptive revolution*. Princeton, N.J.: Princeton University Press, 1977. (a)

Westoff, C., & Ryder, N. The predictive validity of reproductive intentions. *Demography*, 1977, *14*, 431–453. (b)

Westoff, C., Potter, R., Sagi, R., & Mishler, E. *Family growth in metropolitan America*. Princeton: Princeton University Press, 1961.

Whelpton, P. Trends and differentials in the spacing of births. *Demography*, 1964, *1*, 83–93.

Whelpton, P., Campbell, A., & Patterson, J. *Fertility and family planning in the United States*. Princeton: Princeton University Press, 1966.

White, L. The correlates of urban illegitimacy in the United States, 1960–1970. *Journal of Marriage and the Family*, 1979, *41*, 715–726.

White, L. A note on racial differences in the effect of female economic opportunity on marriage rates. *Demography*, 1981, *18*, 349–354.

White, R. Family size composition differentials between central city-suburb and metropolitan-nonmetropolitan migration streams. *Demography*, 1982, *19*, 29–36.

Wilkie, J. The trend toward delayed parenthood. *Journal of Marriage and the Family*, 1981, *43*, 583–591.

Willis, R. A new approach to the economic theory of fertility behavior. In T. Schultz (Eds.), *Economics of the family*. Chicago: University of Chicago Press, 1974.

Wolf, W., & MacDonald, M. The earnings of men and remarriage. *Demography*, 1979, *16*, 389–399.

Yogev, S. Do professional women have egalitarian marital relationships? *Journal of Marriage and the Family*, 1981, *43*, 865–872.

Young, C. Factors associated with the timing and duration of the leaving home stage of the family life cycle. *Population Studies*, 1975, *29*, 61–73.

Zelnik, M., & Kantner, J. The revolution of teenage first pregnancies. *Family Planning Perspectives*, 1974, *6*, 74–80.

Zelnik, M., & Kantner, J. Sexual and contraceptive experience of young unmarried women in the U.S., 1976 and 1971. *Family Planning Perspectives*, 1977, *9*, 55–71.

Zelnik, M., & Kantner, J. Contraceptive patterns and premarital pregnancy among women aged 15–19 in 1976. *Family Planning Perspectives*, 1978, *10*, 135–142. (a)

Zelnik, M., & Kantner, J. First pregnancies to women aged 15–19: 1976 and 1971. *Family Planning Perspectives*, 1978, *10*, 11–20. (b)

Zelnik, M., & Kantner, J. Sexual activity, contraceptive use and pregnancy among metropolitan area teenages: 1971–1979. *Family Planning Perspectives*, 1980, *12*, 230–237.

Zelnik, M., Kim Y., & Kantner, J. Probabilities of intercourse and conception among U.S. teenage women, 1971 and 1976. *Family Planning Perspectives*, 1979, *11*, 177–183.

CHAPTER 2

Historical Analysis of the Family

Tamara K. Hareven

Introduction

The family is one of the most complex social institutions. It is affected by biological processes, psychological dynamics, cultural values, market conditions, demographic changes, the institutions of industrial capitalism, churches, government welfare-planning agencies, and long-term historical change. Nor is the family itself a static, homogeneous unit; rather, it is a complex organization of different age and sex configurations. Families contain husbands and wives, parents and children, brothers and sisters, grandparents and grandchildren, and various other kin bound to one another by blood ties as well as by a variety of social, emotional, and moral bonds.

The roles and status of each family member in relationship to other members, and in relation to the collective family unit at large, are defined differently in different cultural and historical contexts. The meaning of family and the expectations from it also differ among its members. Individual and family life transitions are timed and synchronized differently. The family is a process, involving varying relationships and configurations of family members that change over the life course.

Until recently, however, in much sociological and historical writing, the simple, uniform model of the American nuclear family has been not only upheld as the ideal pattern but imposed on the interpretation of family life in the past, an approach thus idealizing and oversimplifying patterns of historical change. One of the most fruitful recent directions in the study of the family has been a departure from the quest for uniformity in family behavior, the abandonment of blanket concepts such as "universal" functions of the family and "the" American family, and the acceptance of complexity. The historical study of the family, although itself still in its early youth, has contributed to these developments.

This chapter provides a brief sketch of the emergence of the field of family history and its interdisciplinary origins; it then proceeds with a discussion of several major areas of endeavor in historical research on the family: the

organization of the family and the household; the functions of kin, family development and the life course, and the family's relation to social change.

A relatively new field, the history of the family provides a time perspective on contemporary issues as well as an understanding of behavior in the past. The questions asked by family historians have much in common with those of psychologists, anthropologists, sociologists, and economists. (Elder, 1978a; Hareven, 1971, 1974, 1976; Stone, 1981; Tilly & Cohen, 1982). The uniqueness of historical research on the family lies not only in its providing a perspective on change over time, but also in its examining family behavior within specific social and cultural contexts. Historians have thus contributed not just to examinations of diachronic changes, but to investigations of synchronic patterns within discrete time periods as well. The cumulative impact of studies in the history of the family has been to revise a simplistic view of social change and family behavior over time. These revisions have also generated a host of new questions, which have yet to be answered (Elder, 1981; Hareven, 1977b).

The most important impetus for the history of the family came from the "new social history" in the 1960s. Historical studies of the family share with the "new social history" an interest in reconstructing the life patterns of ordinary people rather than simply the elites or celebrated individuals; a commitment to linking individual and group behavior to larger social processes and to social structures; and a view of people in the past as actors confronting historical forces, rather than as passive victims. Much of this research has represented an effort to reconstruct patterns of people's behavior and perceptions from their own experience and point of view.

By delving into census records; birth, marriage, and death registers; occupational files; and family letters and diaries, historians have reconstructed the family patterns of large numbers of ordinary people in the past. The history of the family has thus served to reintroduce human intimacy into historical research and to generate a realistic view of the complexities in the relationship between the family and other institutions confronting historical change. Beyond the specific topic of the family, an understanding of how individuals and families have responded

Tamara K. Hareven • Clark University, Worcester, MA and Center for Population Studies, Harvard University, Cambridge, MA 02138.

to historical change and how they, in turn, have affected such change has considerably broadened our understanding of the process of change itself.

As the field developed, historians expanded their inquiry from the classification of households and family structures to a broad range of subjects, encompassing marriage and sexual behavior, childrearing, and relations between kin and between generations. In trying to understand the role of the family and its internal dynamics, historical research has gradually moved from a concentration on the family as an isolated unit to an exploration of its interaction with other social processes and institutions, notably the role of the family in the processes of industrialization and urbanization (Anderson, 1971; Hareven, 1975a, 1977a, 1978b, 1982; Smelser, 1959).

Over the past half decade, research in the history of the family has moved from a narrow view of the family as a household unit at one point in time to a view of it as a process over the entire lives of its members; from a study of discrete domestic family or (household) structure to a study of the nuclear family's interaction with the wider kinship group; and from a study of the family as a separate domestic unit to an examination of its interaction with the worlds of work, education, correctional and welfare institutions, and such processes as migration. Efforts to explore internal decision-making processes within the family have also led to an investigation of the strategies and choices that individual family members and family groups make (Elder, 1978a, 1981; Modell, 1978). Finally, the life course approach, which has greatly influenced historical research on the family in recent years, has added an important time dimension to the history of the family by focusing on age and cohort comparisons in ways that link individual and family time to historical development (Elder, 1978a,b; Hareven, 1978a; Vinovskis, 1977).

Origins of the Field

Historical studies of the family have come into vogue only since the publication of Philippe Ariès's *Centuries of Childhood* (1962), but not exclusively as a result of that book's impact. Prior to its appearance, historians' references to the family were generally limited to institutional treatments, with occasional allusions to changes in manners and mores. Childhood and youth, insofar as they were discussed, were treated in a monolithic, idealized fashion, as if they had remained constant throughout history. Little attention was given to the possibility that the meaning of various stages of the life cycle has changed over time, and that the treatment, perception, and experience of the stages of life have differed in various societies and social groups.

This narrow treatment was symptomatic of historians' general tendency to focus exclusively on public events and the lives of elites rather than on private experience (except where biography was concerned) and common people. Even those historians who recognized the importance of the family were daunted by the scarcity and the fragmentary nature of documentary materials and the need to assimilate concepts and methods from the social sciences. Yet, as more recent work has demonstrated, the obstacles derived less from a shortfall in methodology or material than from the failure to ask certain questions.

Before the 1960s, the research effort closest to the history of the family was focused on child rearing and national character, while neglecting the actual experience of childhood or the status of children (Erikson, 1950; Mead & Wolfenstein, 1955; Potter, 1954, 1966; Wishy, 1968). The weakness in the historical national-character studies was their attempt to portray the "typical" family as a representative of the social order, without analysis of the family as an institution reflecting class differences, population movements, and economic change. In treating the family as representative of the social order, they failed to focus on the dynamics shaping family life and organization. The result was a study of cultural attitudes rather than of social conditions and interaction. Another limitation was the fact that "national character" represents only the dominant culture, leaving out the varieties of family experience among other groups in a society. Historical studies of childhood and the family that were influenced by this approach focused primarily on attitudes, rather than on social structure and experience, and used proscriptive materials as their major sources (Wishy, 1968; Welter, 1966).

Ariès's book opened up a new direction for historians by focusing attention both on the concept of childhood and on the changing experience of children in French society. His conclusion that childhood as a distinct experience and stage of life had been discovered only in the early modern period and that its discovery was closely linked to the emergence of the "modern family" has provided a model for subsequent historical studies of the origins of the "modern" family, most notably those by Shorter (1976) and Stone (1977). In linking child development to family structure, social class, and economic and demographic changes, Ariès provided a model for studies of the life cycle in relation to the changing conditions of the family in society. Even though Ariès's methods, approach, and basic conclusions have drawn criticism, his seminal work has been used as the major reference point for the study of the major historical transition to the "modern" family by historians who focus on cultural rather than socioeconomic and demographic factors.

The field of family history has sprung from social history and historical demography. However, it owes its major development to the theoretical and methodological influences of the social sciences, namely, psychology, sociology, demography, and anthropology. As the field developed, new findings in the history of the family have led to the revision of generalizations about family behavior, individual development, and social change in these disciplines as well.

The French demographers, particularly those of the *Annales* school, provided historians with techniques of family reconstitution that were essential for reconstructing patterns of migration, fertility, mortality, and nuptiality. They used individual and family data rather than aggregate data alone. The family reconstitution technique has enabled historians to reconstruct the family patterns of vast numbers of anonymous people in the past; to trace them over several generations; and to relate their demographic behavior and family organization to other behaviors. Family reconstitution made possible the linking of demographic patterns of fertility, nuptiality, mortality, and migration with family and household structure in preindustrial populations (Goubert, 1970; Henry, 1968; Vann, 1969; Wrigley, 1959, 1972). While the French demographers focused primarily on demographic patterns, the Cambridge Group for the History of Population and Social Structure in England and, subsequently, historians of colonial American society reconstructed household and inheritance patterns as well (Demos, 1970; Greven, 1970; Lockridge, 1966).

Family reconstitution in other Western European countries as well and in the United States and Canada facilitated a major reinterpretation of population and family behavior in the preindustrial period. The initial conclusions that emerged from this research were that geographic mobility in preindustrial society was more pervasive than had been generally assumed, that the predominant forms of family (household) structure in preindustrial society was nuclear rather than extended, and that some forms of birth control had come into practice by the eighteenth century (Laslett & Wall, 1972; Wrigley, 1966b, 1977).

Using the family reconstitution technique, Philip Greven (1970) analyzed the demographic patterns of the population of Andover, Massachusetts, from 1650 to 1800 and reconstructed the patterns of family organization over four generations. Greven's study linked demographic data to landholding patterns in the family and concluded that the family unit thus emerged as a crucial focus of all economic transactions and as the basis of stability in an agrarian society. John Demos (1970), in contrast, used demography as the backbone for a psychosocial reconstruction of family experience in Plymouth colony. Demos related the demographic data—marriage age, birth rates, longevity, and occupation—to "themes of individual development" in various stages of the life cycle and, in turn, linked these to basic concepts of Puritan culture.

Despite some efforts on the part of "psychohistorians" to study childhood and the family, Demos's work remains the key contribution to the history of the family that uses psychological theories to document individual and family development within a specific historical context. The application of psychological theory to such purposes has been limited almost entirely to Erik Erikson's developmental model (1950), which is a composite of psychoanalytic theory, anthropological concepts of culture and personality, and a historical perspective. Demos (1970) chose Erikson's model because of the "need to discover the dynamic interconnections between experience at an earlier stage and a later stage, to appreciate that a child is always *developing* according to influences that proceed from within as well as from the wider environment" (p. 130). This development would hold equally true for all stages of human growth. With sufficient data, the historian should be able to understand the experience itself, not only the social and cultural attitudes toward a developmental stage.

Unfortunately, Demos's psychological reconstruction of the lives of ordinary people, which places individual development in a social and demographic context, has not yet been followed by similar psychohistorical studies of the family. Most of the subsequent historical studies of childhood have been reductionist in approach, establishing links between childhood conditions and specific historical circumstances, without adequate recognition of the complexity of family patterns (deMause, 1974). As will be detailed below, the life course approach and the sociology of age stratification have since replaced the mechanistic use of stages with an emphasis on process and transitions. The study of the later years of life, on the other hand, has progressed in a direction that combines both behavioral and attitudinal patterns. But its emphasis has been cultural, social, and economic, rather than psychological (Achenbaun, 1978; Chudacoff and Hareven, 1979; Fischer, 1977; Hareven, 1976). As will be suggested below, the life course approach has integrated the study of stages (individual and family collective) into a more comprehensive framework, but one that, at the moment, is primarily structural.

Sociology has had a far-reaching influence on historical research on the family, particularly on the analysis of family and household structure and kinship, in the study of the relation between the family and work, changing family functions, and the relationship between the family and social change, most notably the impact of urbanization and industrialization. The basic theoretical framework underlying recent work in the history of the family, including the analyses of household structure and kinship patterns, and the fundamental concepts of family development, the family cycle, and the life course approach are derived from sociology.

Talcott Parsons's structural-functional model of the family served as the dominant framework in the first stage of the emergence of family history. Even though historians and sociologists have now revised Parsons's generalizations about the impact of industrialization on the family, the Parsonian model still dominates historical research to some extent (Parsons, 1951; Parsons & Bales, 1955; Smelser, 1959). Although following a basic structure-function approach, historians have been successful, nevertheless, in revising general key characteristics of the Parsonian approach. Recent historical research has thus questioned the Parsonian assumptions that there is a harmonious "fit" between the family and the larger social system; that it is the family's major task to serve that system; and that the family is a static unit, rather than a conglomerate of interacting personalities. In this respect, the most promising direction in the development of the field has come from the life course approach, which has not provided an alternative to structural-functional perspective but has nevertheless provided a dynamic model for the study of family development internally and over historical time (Elder, 1978b).

Family and Household Structure

Before systematic historical study of the family began, other social sciences had generated their own myths and grand theories about continuities and changes in family behavior in the past. These prevailing assumptions claimed that "modern" family and population behaviors (earlier age at marriage, family limitation, and population mobility) were innovations introduced with industrialization, and that the predominant household form in preindustrial society had been the extended family, in many cases involving the coresidence of three generations. Industrialization was thus considered a major watershed between the preindustrial and the postindustrial modes of family organization and demographic behavior. Most important, the prevailing assumption was that industrialization destroyed a three-generation *coresident* family structure and led to the emergence of the isolated nuclear family—a type functionally more compatible with the demands of the "modern" industrial system than the "traditional" extended family. Also associated with these generalizations by social scientists were popular myths that, in the preindustrial period, family life (along with community life) was more harmonious, and that industrialization had eroded a traditional three-generational family pattern.

Work on the history of the family in the 1960s demolished some of these myths and led to the revision of a simplistic linear view of historical change. Laslett and his group (Laslett & Wall, 1972) firmly established the predominance of a nuclear household structure in preindustrial western Europe and its persistence over at least the past three centuries. (The definition of *nuclear family*, following Laslett's is a family unit consisting of parents and their children, or of a childless couple, or of one parent and his or her children. In this definition, it is necessary, however, to distinguish between "family" and "household.") The most important distinguishing characteristic of a nuclear family is the absence of extended kin. A nuclear *family* is not, however, identical with a nuclear *household*, as the domestic group may have included nonrelatives as well (Laslett & Wall, 1972). These findings, combined with those for colonial American communities, have shown the prevalence of the three-generation household in preindustrial society— what William Goode (1963) called "The Great Family of Western Nostalgia to be a myth with little basis in historical fact" (see Demos, 1970; Greven, 1970). These studies of preindustrial communities in the United States and western Europe, followed by studies of household structure in nineteenth-century American communities, have laid to rest the assumption that the dominant preindustrial family structure was extended and three-generational; they have established, instead, the continuity of a nuclear household structure since the Industrial Revolution. In most early American communities, the typical form of household structure was nuclear. Members of the nuclear family were, however, engaged in close ties with extended kin; and as Greven found in Andover, Massachusetts, aging parents did not reside in the same household with their adult son but lived in his vicinity, on the same land, in what would be labeled a *modified extended family structure* (Demos, 1970; Greven, 1970; Smith, 1979).

In American urban communities in the nineteenth century, the dominant household structure, once again, was nuclear. Only about 9%–12% of these households were extended, and only about 1%–3% contained solitary residents. The remaining households were nuclear (Hareven, 1977; Sennett, 1970). The most important conclusion emerging from this first stage of historical research was that industrialization did not break down a great extended family and lead to the emergence of an isolated nuclear family. In fact, as some studies have shown, industrialization and urbanization may have led to an increase in household extension (Anderson, 1971; Hareven, 1982).

Historians who have emphasized the persistence of the nuclear family structure have drawn their major evidence from the household rather than from the family. In emphasizing this continuity, they have unwittingly implied that the unit that persisted over time was the nuclear *family* rather than the *household*. In most of these studies, the major unit of analysis, however, was the *household*, not the family. In reality, it was the household that was nuclear (Hareven, 1974). The household generally contained a nuclear family within it but often also included nonrelatives. Nor was the nuclear residential family unit itself isolated; rather, it was extended through kinship ties outside the household (Anderson, 1971; Greven, 1970; Hareven, 1978b, 1982; Yans-McLaughlin, 1977). The mistaking of "household" for "family" arose in part because the measurable entity in most studies of the family, particularly for the nineteenth century, was the residential unit. Historians' use of the census manuscript schedules as their major data source tended to reinforce this concentration on the domestic unit, as if it were the entire family unit. It was only in the next stage in the development of the field that more serious attention was given to the pervasive kinship ties outside the individual household. Another limitation in the studies emphasizing the continuity in a nuclear household structure was their being limited to one point in time, rather than viewing the household as a process that changes over the family's cycle and in relation to the organization of production and inheritance (Berkner, 1972; Goody, 1973; Hammel, 1972).

Unlike anthropologists and economists, who have

made important progress in this direction, historians have not yet developed a theory of the household that differentiates its functions from those of the family unit and the wider kin group. Thoughtful attention to this question would suggest several characteristics that distinguish the household as somewhat separate from the nuclear family unit within it and from the wider kin group outside its confines. Some of these are worth noting here for methodological as well as theoretical reasons.

The household was the basic organizational unit of the family in Western society. Households formed the cells that together made up the fiber of neighborhoods and entire communities. In American cities in the late nineteenth century, only about 3% of the population lived alone. Almost all men and women expected to live out their lives in familial or surrogate familial settings. The household was also the basic unit of economic activity in preindustrial society, as well as the locus of vocational training and welfare. With industrialization and the concomitant transfer of these activities to industrial enterprises and to vocational and welfare institutions, the household ceased to be the major locus of production and welfare, but it continued to fulfill a central economic role: household production, although limited in scale, persisted in rural areas and even in urban areas, where food processing was still done at home. Through the family's control of housing space, its members were engaged in economic exchange relations with nonrelatives, servants, apprentices, and boarders and lodgers—and at times, with extended kin as well. In many respects, the household continued to function as an economic unit, beyond consumption, even after it had been stripped of its major function as the primary site of production. As a flexible unit, the household expanded and contracted in accordance with the family's needs and over the life course. The very changes in the organization of the household over the life course of its members suggest its responsiveness to the family's development, to economic need or opportunities, and to changing historical conditions.

Inherent in the dynamic processes of the household, however, was a contradiction in its functions: The household served as a source of order, stability, and continuity, while at the same time encouraging population movement. It was in the households that new families were formed and children were reared. It was the household to which young people returned in times of need; and it was the place where migrants and older people without families found a familial setting. The household was also a source of continuity in the lives of older people. At the same time, the household also dislodged family members from its midst—thus generating instability in the population. Households launched children into the world when they reached adulthood, sent out members that they were unable to support, or dissolved if their heads or crucial members were stricken by illness or death or became too old to maintain their independence (Hareven, 1982).

Households engaged in indirect exchanges of members across neighborhoods and wide geographic regions. As some members went out into the world, in moved newcomers. Those whose lives were disrupted by migration or death were absorbed into other families. Young people could move to new communities, confident that they could coreside with relatives or strangers. Similarly, working mothers placed young children in the homes of relatives or strangers, and dependent older people moved into other people's households. Such exchanges between relatives, neighbors, or complete strangers were laced through the entire society (Anderson, 1971; Hareven, 1982; Katz, 1975).

The emphasis on the continuity in a nuclear household structure over time should not mislead us to assume that the households of the preindustrial period or of the nineteenth century were identical with the nuclear households of our time, which generally consist of husband, wife, and children. The "nuclear" household in earlier times was far more complex in its structure, often including nonrelatives along with the nuclear family. The presence of young people as servants and apprentices or of older people as dependent members of the household was part of the multiplicity of functions that the domestic family performed in the preindustrial period. Their presence added a significant dimension to the membership of the household that is rarely experienced in contemporary families (Laslett, 1965). Because the household held numerous functions as a workshop and a vocational training and welfare institution, its boundaries expanded to include nonrelatives who were engaged in various degrees of economic and social relationships with the members of the nuclear family. In the preindustrial period, these nonrelatives were usually apprentices or servants; at times, they were dependent individuals who were placed with families by town authorities. For young people, leaving home and living with another family was a common pattern of transition to adult roles. In the nineteenth century, following the decline of apprenticeship, and particularly of the practice of live-in apprentices, nonrelatives residing in the household were predominantly servants, boarders, and lodgers (Demos, 1970; Modell & Hareven, 1973).

The "discovery" of boarding and lodging in nineteenth-century American and western European families represents an important historiographic benchmark in the study of the family: It suggests that the distinguishing historical variant in the organization of the household was not its extension through the presence of other kin, but its augmentation by nonrelatives who joined in the household at certain points in the head of the household's life. In nineteenth-century American communities, only 12%–15% of urban households contained relatives other than the nuclear family, compared to 20%–30% of all households that included boarders and lodgers. Clearly, the majority of urban households were much more likely to include nonrelatives than extended kin. Boarders and lodgers were as common in the household as servants and apprentices had been in preindustrial families. Boarding and lodging were articulated to the life cycle and were therefore part of the regular process of individual and family development, but they were also part of a migration process (Modell & Hareven, 1973).

For young men and women in the transitional stage between departure from their parents' households and marriage, boarding offered housing that they could afford in a family setting. It provided some surrogate family arrangements without the accompanying obligations and parental controls. For migrants and immigrants, boarding represented a creative use of the household as a means of access to jobs and social supports, through the connections of the head of the household with whom one was boarding. It was no coincidence, therefore, that migrant boarders clustered in the households of members of the same ethnic group, often former fellow townspeople (Modell & Hareven, 1973). For head of households, taking in boarders augmented the family income and provided surrogate children after their own sons and daughters had left home. Boarding thus fulfilled the function of the "social equalization of the family" (Taeuber, 1969). In working-class families in Massachusetts during the late nineteenth century, the contribution of boarders and lodgers to family income was most significant as a substitute (or, depending on family need, as a supplement) for the work of women or children, especially after the children had left home. Taking in boarders thus enabled wives to stay out of the labor force and old people to retain the headship of their household after their children had left home (Hareven, 1982; Modell & Hareven, 1973). Although the economic and social role of boarders and lodgers in the family awaits further exploration, it is clear that, in nineteenth-century American society, the presence of nonrelatives in the household was much more widespread and significant than that of the presence of extended kin. However, ongoing and future research will have to distinguish between those aspects of family behavior where strangers were more central and those that were more commonly dependent on kin.

The realization that households expanded and contracted over their members' lives and in response to external circumstances, as evidenced in the practice of boarding and lodging, has helped historians to recognize the importance of a developmental view of the family and the household over their cycle. With several exceptions for the colonial period, the majority of studies in the earlier stage of the field were limited in their concentration on family and household structure at one point in time or, at best, at several points in time, thus conveying the impression that household and family structure were constant over the entire life of their members. This static view of family organization was a result of historians' excessive reliance on snapshots of family organization as recorded in the census, rather than on an examination of changes in the membership configuration and structure of the family and the household over its life. As will be discussed below, this limitation has been overcome gradually, first by applying the family cycle construct, and subsequently by following the life course approach, which offers a more comprehensive way of examining family development in a historical context.

Kinship

Historians' transcendence of the boundaries of the household as a research unit and their examination of kinship patterns outside the household have been slow and spotty. Historians had not initially asked meaningful questions about kinship, perhaps because of an excessive concern with the nuclearity of the household, and because of a reliance on the household record in the census as the major unit of analysis. The difficulty of determining and reconstructing familial relationships outside the household further discourages investigations of kinship ties. Historians' confusion of "household" with "family" and the evidence of only a small proportion of extended kin present in the household tended to reinforce historians' assumption that nineteenth-century American urban families were isolated from extended kin. Thus, historical reinforcement was provided for Parsons's assertion of the "isolated nuclear family" as the dominant form of family organization in Western society.

The most marked oversight of extended kinship ties was in Richard Sennett's analysis of family patterns in a late-nineteenth-century Chicago suburb (1970). Sennett based his conclusion that the nuclear family was isolated—and therefore ill adapted to urban life—on a small proportion of the households with kin present. It was ironical that historians of nineteenth-century family structure tended to accept this Parsonian view, when sociologists—especially Marvin Sussman and Lee Burchinal (1962) and Eugene Litwak (1960)— pointed to the pervasiveness of extended kinship ties and assistance in contemporary American society, thus challenging the thesis of an "isolated nuclear family." Extended kinship ties were even more widespread in the nineteenth and the early twentieth centuries; before the emergence of the welfare state, kin formed the very base of social security and assistance in times of crisis.

Under the influence of some of these sociological studies of contemporary society, and particularly Anderson's study of kinship in nineteenth-century Lancashire (1971), historians began to document the continuity of kinship ties in the process of migration and the important role of kin as sources of resilience and assistance in settlement in the new environments. Historians have thus recognized that the prevailing historical pattern in England and the United States was one of nuclear households embedded in extended kinship ties outside the household. The overall tendency and the inferred preference of the population were to include nonrelatives in the household rather than kin, at the same time engaging in mutual assistance with kin outside the household. Whenever individuals had kin available nearby, they turned to them for assistance rather than to strangers (Anderson, 1971; Hareven, 1978b, 1982). Thus, nuclear units must be viewed as parts of a larger network of households linked through extended kinship ties. Especially in a regime of economic insecurity with hardly any other available institutional supports, the very autonomy of the nuclear family depended on reciprocity with extended kin.

Kin fulfilled a central role in mediating between the nuclear family and other institutions. They were central in organizing migration, in facilitating settlement, in finding employment, and in cushioning the shock of adaptation to new conditions. The movement of individuals or family clusters to urban areas followed a pattern of chain migration; it was directed, organized, and supported by kin.

A study of working-class life in Manchester, New Hampshire, documents the carryover of kinship ties from rural to industrial settings. Kinship networks effectively interacted with the modern, industrial system in the late nineteenth and early twentieth centuries (Hareven, 1978b, 1982). Kin fulfilled a major role in labor recruitment, the organization and support of migration to the industrial community, and the placement of workers in the factory. Relatives acted as major brokers between the workers and the industrial corporations. Kinship networks also facilitated the movement of job seekers from one industrial town to another. Within the textile factory, kin also offered their relatives basic protection on the job, initiated the young and the new immigrants into the work process, and manipulated the machinery and work procedures in order to effect slowdowns during periods of speedup and pressure (Hareven, 1975b, 1978b, 1982).

This analysis of the internal work relations inside a major industrial corporation shows the extent to which the relationship between the workers' families and the corporation was reciprocal. Both the corporation and the workers recognized and utilized kin as key agents in their relationship. The family trained its members for industrial work as well as cushioned them from potential shocks and disruptions in the workplace. In this process, the family developed its own defenses and brought its cultural traditions to bear on work processes and relations between workers, and between workers and management.

While kin initiated young workers or newly arrived immigrants into industrial work procedures and technology and into work disciplines and social relations among workers, they also socialized newly arrived immigrant workers to collective working-class behavior. The active role performed by family and kin group in these circumstances suggests that the family type most "fit" to interact with the factory system was not the isolated nuclear one, as has frequently been argued, but a family with extended kinship that called on the resources of a network. At the same time, in cushioning the adaptation of young workers and of newly arrived immigrants, without excessively restricting their mobility, kin were instrumental in serving the industrial employer as well as in advancing the interest of their own members and trying to protect them (Hareven, 1982).

These important roles that kin fulfilled in their interaction with the workplace in a modern corporation exemplifies both the continuity in the functions of kin as mediators and their taking on new functions in response to the requirements of the industrial system.

Among immigrant populations, the vital functions of kin were not restricted to the local community. The salient role of kin extended beyond the immediate community to encompass long-distance functions as well. To be sure, kinship ties were most effective in interaction with local institutions and in meeting immediate crises. Yet, kinship networks typically stretched over several communities and were most useful when conditions failed in the local community. The strength of locally based kin groups lay in stability; the strength of extended networks lay in their fluidity and their continuous reorganization. Under certain historical or life course conditions, intercommunity kinship networks were more instrumental, and under other conditions, long-distance ties were more critical (Hareven, 1978b, 1982).

In Manchester, New Hampshire, as in mid-nineteenth-century Lancashire and twentieth-century East London, kinship networks were embedded in the industrial town (Anderson, 1971; Bott, 1957; Young & Willmott, 1957). By contrast, the social space of French-Canadian kin extended from Quebec to Manchester and spread over other New England industrial towns. Long-distance kinship networks, besides serving as important backup systems, also enabled workers to experiment with different kinds of roles, to send their sons to scout out better jobs, or to marry off their daughters. During periods of failure in the factory, kin continued to prove effective migration agents. Under these conditions, the route of migration was reversed. Earlier, workers had brought their kin into the factory; now, other kin enabled them to find temporary or more permanent work in other towns or to migrate back to Canada. The existence of fluid kinship networks throughout New England ensured that the needs of unemployed workers for temporary jobs and housing would continue to be met (Hareven, 1982).

Kinship networks were salient in both one's immediate neighborhood and one's workplace, as well as in the persistence of long-distance kinship ties that were laced through larger communities. Long-distance kin performed significant functions for migrant populations and were particularly helpful to temporary migrants, at least at the initial stages of their migration. Geographic distance did not disrupt basic modes of kin cooperation; rather, it led to the diversification of priorities and modes of kin interaction. Under certain conditions, migration strengthened kinship ties and imposed new functions on them. Kin affiliations in the new setting not only facilitated migration and settlement there but also served as a reminder and reinforcer of obligations and ties to the premigration communities.

Appalachian mountain migrants to Ohio industrial communities in the post–World War II period followed similar patterns. In their study of migration from Appalachia to Ohio, Schwarzweller and his colleagues (Schwarzweller, Brown, & Mangalam, 1971) concluded that the kinship structure

provides a highly persuasive line of communication between kinsfolk in the home and in the urban communities. It channels information about available job opportunities and living standards directly, and therefore, it tends to orient migrants to those areas where kin groups are already established.

In this context, their definition of a "migration system" is particularly pertinent to this study:

Two subsystems (the community of origin and community of settlement) together form the interactional system in which we wish to consider the adjustment of a given group of migrants, individually and collectively. We have then, one migration system to consider, namely, the Beech Creek-Ohio migration. (pp. 94–95)

Kinship is a process; kinship ties may be latent for a time and may be revived when circumstances change. The functions of kin are best examined by looking from the nuclear family outward—not only as it relates to extended kin, but also in its relationship to larger social institutions.

Patterns of family integration with the workplace and the active role of kin as labor brokers between individual workers and corporations were more intensive in the textile industry. Were they as important in industries that employed males predominantly or totally? At present, we lack the studies of kin involvement in other industries that would permit precise comparison. Existing studies about steel towns, such as Pittsburgh, where the labor force was male predominantly, suggest different patterns in the family's relationship to the workplace (Byington, 1910; Kleinberg, 1977). Here, families did not work as units, but male relatives often tended to work together and to assist one another in ways similar to those common in the textile industry. Even in male-dominated industries, kin were active both in the workplace and in family life, but the forms of assistance tended to be sexually segregated. Whereas male kin influenced the workplace, female kin assisted each other in handling personal and family crises and in securing employment wherever it was available for women in the community. A fuller understanding of the family's interaction with the industrial process depends, however, on future systematic comparisons of the role of kin in different types of industry—a question that is also relevant to the developing countries today.

Underlying family relations, both in the nuclear family and in the wider kin group during the nineteenth century and the first two decades of this century, was a corporate view of family relations, which required an almost total commitment of individual preferences to collective family needs. Work careers of individual members were integrated in a collective family economy. Family and household structure, as well as the time of life transitions, was to some extent determined by collective family needs (Chudacoff & Hareven, 1978, 1979; Hareven 1978a; Modell, Furstenberg, & Hershberg, 1976; Modell &

Hareven, 1978). This commitment to collective goals was also a major determinant of the participation of children, teenagers, and married women in the labor force. The view of the family as a collective economic unit and the expectation that family members would forgo or modify their own career choices in the service of their families were carryovers from rural society that served as a major form of adaptation in working-class life.

Although historians are now recognizing that the overall pattern of historical change over the past century has been one of an increasing shift from a commitment to family collectivity to individual goals and aspirations, the central question is: What was the basis of interdependence between family members? What made possible the strong commitment of individuals to the family and to mutual assistance between kin that led individuals to sacrifice personal preferences?

Anderson (1971) saw reciprocity and economic exchange as the key explanation for interdependence between kin in nineteenth-century Preston, Lancashire. Defining relations among kin as "instrumental," he saw a calculative motive underlying reciprocity. Although calculativeness may have been the most central motive in the lower strata of working-class communities, consisting of a high proportion of immigrants, they in themselves do not fully explain the sacrifices that relatives made for each other when no direct benefits could be anticipated. Short-term, daily, routine exchanges may have offered visible returns, but long-range investments were more demanding and less certain in their future returns.

Although benefits in short-term exchanges were more clearly tangible, it would be difficult to conceive of long-range exchanges as resting exclusively on calculativeness. For example, when young men and women sacrificed their opportunity for marriage or gave up opportunities for careers because of the need to support their parents, they hardly did so out of expectations of immediate or even long-range rewards. The young women who postponed their marriage or never married did so because they were socialized to have a sense of responsibility for their parents or siblings; but affection and loyalty were also important parts of their attitude. When they acted as surrogate parents to their siblings rather than sending them to orphanages, they did so because they placed a higher value on the preservation of family autonomy, self-respect, and good standing in the neighborhood and ethnic community than on personal happiness. Loyalty and a commitment to "family culture" dictated such priorities in the lives of individuals, even if they were trapped into sacrifices that they resented. Within the economic constraints and insecurities that the majority of the population experienced in the nineteenth century, personal preferences clearly had to give way to collective family strategies. In addition to exchange, there were thus other reasons that prompted individuals to sacrifice their own preferences to collective family needs. Future work on the history of the family will have to address these questions of reciprocity and mutuality between kin and to identify the historical transition from a kin-oriented to an egocentric approach.

Family Development

The Family Cycle

The early work on the history of the family, which was based on a profile of the household limited to one point in time, obscured the constant movement of family members in and out of different forms of household organization over their lives. In vigorously criticizing the "snapshot" approach to the hsitorical study of the family, Berkner (1972) drew historians' attention to the importance of the changes that households and families undergo over their cycle, particularly in relation to the transmission of property and inheritance. The application of the family cycle approach to nineteenth-century patterns of household structure revealed that the household and family structure was fluid and variable over the family's life from marriage to dissolution, and that individuals went through several forms of household organization over their lives. The very label of *nuclear* or *extended* household type was meaningless, therefore, unless one accounted for various changes in household organization over the life of its members. In reality, households were like a revolving state into which individual members entered and from which they exited, under their own momentum or under the impact of external conditions (Hareven, 1974).

Historians initially found in the family cycle a flexible framework for the developmental analysis of changes in household and family structure. Its major value was in leading historians to shift the analysis of family behavior in the past from one point in time to a developmental sequence, even in the use cross-sectional data. The family cycle, as formulated by Duvall (1957) and Hill (1964, 1970), measures role and structural changes in the family unit as it moves from stage to stage over the life of its members, from its formation with marriage, to its dissolution with the death of its head. Essentially, as Elder (1978b) has pointed out, the family cycle is organized around stages of parenthood.

The family cycle construct has enabled historians to identify the variability of patterns that appeared constant at one point in time over the lives of the household's head and of different family members. Changes in the structure of the household and in the age configurations of its members were affected to a large extent by the movement of family members through their prescribed roles over the course of their lives. The life transitions of young family members—particularly their leaving home, getting married, and setting up independent households—all affected the structure of the family of orientation as well as the family of procreation (Glasco, 1977; Hareven, 1974). Individuals living in nuclear households at one point in

their lives were likely to live in extended or augmented households at other points. The age configurations and memberships of individuals living in nineteenth-century households thus varied over the family cycle in accordance with patterns of migration, the availability of housing, and changing economic needs (Chudacoff & Hareven, 1978; Modell & Hareven, 1973).

Studying the family cycle also offers an effective way of examining the family as a collective unit, engaged in various activities and decisions, which changed in relation to the roles and the social characteristics of its members and in response to external conditions. In the area of economic behavior, for instance, the extent to which inheritance practices, the availability of housing, or migration patterns caused variation in family and household configurations may be best understood by studying family behavior along its cycle, rather than at one point in time.

The family cycle has proved especially valuable for studying those conditions under which the family unit was economically vulnerable. In his study of poverty in England at the turn of the century, Rowntree (1901) identified two stages at which the family was most likely to slip into poverty: first, when the children were too young to work, and second, when the grown children had left home and the parents were too old to work. This approach, leading from Frederick LePlay through Rowntree into American sociological and economic studies of the family, has also influenced historical analysis. Modell (1978), for example, followed the family cycle in analyzing changing patterns of labor force participation and expenditure of U.S. workers in the late nineteenth century. This approach enabled him to identify both the family's economic strategies and the rhythms of insecurity over the family's cycle.

Systematic efforts to apply the family cycle to historical data, however, have revealed some limitations inherent in this approach. Elder (1978b) saw one of its major failings in its measurement of stages. He suggests that although we may be able to identify the children's stage in the life cycle in terms of age-pattern roles, we may not know the parents' stage. Therefore, timing is a critical variable in the family-cycle model in relation to both the children and their parents. The family cycle, from this perspective, is unable to do justice to its primary target, the temporal features of stages of parenthood.

Within a historical context, additional limitations of the family cycle concept become apparent. The *a priori* stages in the family cycle, as defined by sociologists studying contemporary populations, cannot be consistently applied to the diverse patterns of the late nineteenth century. Glick's model (1947, 1955, 1977; Glick & Parke, 1965), followed by demographers and more recently by historians, measures mean patterns of change in states of the family cycle from the late nineteenth century on, but it does not examine variance from the norm or differentials by sex, ethnicity, or occupation within specific time periods. Largely because of higher levels of mortality, nineteenth-century families were less likely to experience an orderly progression than are contemporary families, except when the latter are disrupted by divorce. As Uhlenberg (1974, 1978) has shown, voluntary and involuntary demographic factors affected age configurations within the family, causing considerable differences between nineteenth-century families and modal twentieth-century patterns. From his examining of the family cycle patterns of white American women from 1870 to 1930, he concluded that the sequence of marriage, family formation, child rearing and launching, and survival until age 50 with the first marriage still intact unless broken by divorce, although always modal, was by no means prevalent for most of the population before the twentieth century.

Before the late-nineteenth-century decline in mortality and fertility, discontinuities between different stages of the family cycle were less clearly demarcated. Children were spread along a broader age range within the family; frequently, the youngest child was starting school when the oldest was preparing for marriage. Parenthood, by contrast, often encompassed the entire adult life span. The combination of a later age at marriage and earlier mortality meant that the "empty nest" was a rare phenomenon. Fathers surviving the child-rearing years rarely lived beyond the marriage of their second child. Because the boundary between family of orientation and the family of procreation was less clearly demarcated than it is today, and because transitions from one stage of the family cycle to the next were less rigidly timed, nineteenth-century families did not go through clearly marked stages. For example, leaving home did not so uniformly precede marriage, and the launching of children did not necessarily leave the nest empty. Frequently, a married child would return to his parents' home, or the parents would take in boarders or lodgers. (Recent developments in the 1970s have begun to revive some of the "historical" patterns, thus blurring the contrast between past and present. Among these, most notably, are late marriages and late commencement of childbearing among professionals, the return of young adults to the parental home, or their delayed leaving.)

For all these reasons, the application of *a priori* stages, borrowed from contemporary sociology, to past conditions did not always fit the historical reality. It was important, therefore, to identify the transitional points at which individuals and families moved through different family configurations and roles over their lives. Rather than merely calculating median differences between stages, historians began to measure the pace at which a cohort completed its transition from one stage to the next (Modell *et al.*, 1976).

Although the family cycle continues to be a valuable construct, developmental analysis of the family in the past has been amplified through the use of the life course approach in several directions: first, by utilizing a framework that captures with greater sensitivity the erratic and complex trajectories of families and careers in nineteenth-century population groups (Elder, 1978b; Hareven, 1978a; Vinovskis, 1977); second, where stages do exist, by analyzing transitions from stage to stage and the accompanying roles within each stage; and third, by focusing on the synchronization of individual transitions with changes in the family as a collective unit. The life course offers an approach that can address the complexities of family development in the past more effectively.

The Life Course

The life course has provided a theoretical orientation for our understanding of the link between family time, individual time, and historical time. Originating from the sociology of aging, from the concept of cohorts as defined by demographers, and from the life history traditions in sociology and social psychology, the life course is historical by its very nature (Baltes, 1979; Elder, 1978b; Neugarten & Hagestadt, 1976; Riley, 1978; Riley, Johnson, & Foner, 1972). Its influence on family history has been most powerful in three areas: the synchronization of individual life transitions and collective family changes, the interaction of both individual and collective family transitions with historical conditions, and the impact of earlier life transitions on later ones. "Timing" takes into account the historical context defining the social circumstances and cultural conditions that affect the scheduling of life events, on both an individual and a familial level (Hareven, 1978c).

Following a life course approach, historians have begun to pursue the question of how people plan and organize their roles over their lives and how they time their life transitions on both the nonfamilial and the familial levels in areas such as entering and leaving school, joining or quitting the labor force, migration, leaving or returning home, marriage, and setting up an independent household, or how, in the later years of life, individuals and couples move out of active parental roles into the "empty nest" or retire from work careers. Historians have discovered that much of what would be considered "individual" timing today was closely articulated to collective family timing in the past.

In a society and time period when most educational, economic, and welfare functions were concentrated within the family, decisions on the timing of transitions were family-based and were regulated according to family needs; but in the nineteenth and twentieth centuries, decisions on timing have been closely articulated to external economic and institutional factors. Institutional and legislative changes, such as compulsory school attendance, child labor laws, and mandatory retirement, affect the transitions of different age groups into and out of the labor force. At the same time, however, the ways in which people respond to these opportunities or constraints is also shaped by their cultural traditions.

As people move over their life course, they group and regroup themselves in various family units. Their individual roles and their functions vis-à-vis the family in these different clusters also vary significantly over their lives. Most individuals are involved simultaneously in several family configurations, fulfilling different roles in each. A married person, for example, is part of both a family of origin and a family of procreation, occupying a different position and fulfilling a different role in each; in addition, such an individual also figures in his or her spouse's family of orientation and in the spouse's kin network. Because of the integration of individuals in earlier periods with the collective goals of the family, historically life transitions such as leaving home, which appeared to be individual moves, were in reality integrated with the family collectivity.

Similarly, marriage, which today would be considered the act of an individual or a couple, impinges on at least three families: the man's family of origin, his wife's family of origin, and the couple's newly founded family. In situations where remarriage follows a spouse's death or divorce, the new spouse's family enters the orbit of relationships, and the former spouse's family does not necessarily disappear. Thus, the multiplicity of familial relationships in which individuals are engaged changes over the life course, and along with them, an individual's transitions into various roles are also timed differently. Age, although an important variable defining life transitions, is not the primary one. Changes in family status and in accompanying roles may be as important, if not more so.

The Timing of Life Transitions

Central to an understanding of any life-course pattern is the impact of historical processes on the timing of individual or family transitions. Such timing is influenced by the interaction of demographic, social, and economic factors, as well as by familial preferences shaped by the family members' cultural background. Thus, for example, in the nineteenth century, the timing of marriage was not strictly related to age; rather, it was related to a complex interaction between social and economic factors, cultural preferences, and institutional constraints.

The changes in the timing of life transitions and in the synchronization of individual timetables with the collective timetable of the family since the late nineteenth century have been related to demographic and institutional changes as well as to cultural factors guiding internal family choices. On the one hand, as Uhlenberg (1978) suggested, over the past century, demographic developments have tended to effect greater uniformity in the life course of American families and have made it considerably more likely that the family unit will survive intact over the lifetime of its members. The decline in mortality, especially in the earlier years, has enabled an increasing proportion of the population to enter prescribed family roles and, except in cases of divorce, to live out their lives in family units (Uhlenberg, 1974). The decline in mortality has meant that the chances of children's surviving into adulthood and growing up with their siblings and

both parents alive have increased considerably. Similarly, the chances of women's surviving to marry, raise children jointly with a husband, and survive with the husband through the launching stage (Uhlenberg, 1974) increased steadily from the late nineteenth to early twentieth centuries. For women, these changes, combined with earlier marriages and earlier completion of maternal roles, have meant a more extended period of life without children in their middle years. At the same time, women's tendency to live longer than men has resulted in a protracted period of widowhood in later life. Men, on the other hand, because of lower life expectancy and a greater tendency to remarry in old age, normally remain married until death (Glick, 1977; Glick & Parke, 1965).

The most marked discontinuity in the life course that has emerged since the nineteenth century has occurred in the middle and later years of life, namely, the emergence of the empty nest in a couple's middle age. The combination of earlier marriage and fewer children, with childbearing occurring in the early stages of the family cycle and children leaving home at an earlier point in their parents' lives, has resulted in a greater prevalence of the empty nest as a characteristic of middle and old age (Glick, 1977).

In the nineteenth century, later marriage, higher fertility, and shorter life expectancy rendered different family configurations from those characterizing contemporary society. For large families, the parental stage with children remaining in the household extended over a longer period of time, sometimes over the parents' entire life. Because children were spread in families along a broad age spectrum, younger children could observe their older siblings and near relatives moving through adolescence and into adulthood. Older siblings, in turn, trained for adult roles by acting as surrogate parents for younger siblings (Hareven, 1977a). Most important, the nest was rarely empty because, under conditions of economic insecurity, usually one adult child remained at home throught the parents' lives (Chudacoff & Hareven, 1979; Hareven, 1982).

Demographic factors account only in part for the occurrence or the nonoccurrence of the empty nest. Children did not remain in their aging parents' household only because they were too young to move out. Even when sons and daughters were in their late teens and early 20s, and therefore old enough to leave home, at least one child remained at home to care for the aging parents if no other assistance was available. Familial obligations, dictated by the insecurity of the times and by cultural norms of familial assistance, took precedence over strict age norms (Chudacoff & Hareven, 1979; Hareven, 1982). Even though the nest is now being refilled through the return of young adult children to the parental home, the flow of assistance reverses the historical pattern: Children now return home because of their need for parental support, whereas earlier in the century, at least one child was expected to remain at home in order to provide support for the aging parents.

The important historical change in the timing of life

transitions since the beginning of this century has been the emergence of a greater uniformity in the pace at which a cohort accomplishes a given transition. This is particularly evident in the transitions to adulthood (leaving home, marriage, and the establishment of a separate household). As Modell *et al.* (1976) have shown, over the past century transitions have become more clearly marked, more rapidly timed, and more compressed. In contrast to our times, in the late nineteenth century transitions from the parental home to marriage, to household headship, were more gradual and less rigid in their timing. The time range necessary for a cohort to accomplish such transitions was wider, and the sequence in which transitions followed one another was flexible. In the twentieth century, transitions to adulthood have become more uniform for the age cohort undergoing them, more orderly in sequence, and more rigidly defined. The consciousness of embarking on a new stage of life and the implications of movement from one stage to the next have become more firmly established.

The historical changes over the past century, particularly the increasing rapidity in the timing of transitions and the introduction of publicly regulated and institutionalized transitions, have converged to isolate and segregate age groups in the larger society and, at the same time, have generated new pressures on timing within the family as well as outside its confines. The timing of life transitions has become more regulated according to specific age norms rather than in relation to the family's collective needs. The major historical change over the past century has been from a timing that is more closely articulated to collective family needs and to a more individualized timing.

This pattern is even more visible in the timing of later life transitions in the late nineteenth century, when the empty nest, widowhood, and being relieved of household headship followed no ordered sequence, were not closely synchronized, and extended over a relatively long period of time. For most men who survived to old age, labor force participation and family roles generally resembled those of their earlier adult years. Only at very advanced ages did a substantial number experience definite changes in their household status. These men, however, represented only a small proportion of their age group. On the other hand, because widowhood was such a common experience, older women went through more marked transitions than did older men, although the continuing presence of adult children and others in the household meant that widowhood did not necessarily represent a dramatic transition to the empty nest (Chudacoff & Hareven, 1979; Hareven, 1982; Smith, 1979). The timing of earlier life transitions was interlocked with the timing of later ones through the common bond of interdependence within the family. Aging parents' need for support from their children affected the latter's transitions into independent adulthood.

The crucial turning point in the trend has not been determined yet, although there is considerable evidence to suggest that it may have occurred around the turn of the century. Chudacoff (1980) found a marked change in the timing of life transitions to adulthood among women in Providence, Rhode Island, between 1865 and 1900, which confirms the general trend outlined by Uhlenberg and the comparison of two points in time found by Modell *et al.* The age at which native-born Providence women left home, married, and had their first child became more compressed by 1900. At the same time, the span of childbearing in the lives of these women was contracting, and parenthood thus occupied a more limited segment of these women's lives. Significantly, this pattern was more typical of the lives of native-born women, whereas immigrant women experienced less clearly marked transitions, with childbearing extending over a considerably longer period of their lives. To what extent these changes in timing in the lives of native-born women are an expression of greater age-consciousness and conformity to age norms is an important issue that deserves further exploration.

Both class and ethnicity had an important effect on timing. So far, it has been difficult, however, to disentangle ethnicity from class when examining the factors that had the greatest effect on life course decisions. In Essex County, Massachusetts, for example, in the late nineteenth century, native-born women married earlier and completed their childbearing earlier than foreign-born women. Whereas native-born women were already beginning to segregate motherhood to their earlier years of marriage, Irish women both delayed the commencement of childbearing and spread it over a longer period of their lives. Because it is impossible to know from the census whether the *foreign-born* women were married in their country of origin or in the U.S., it would be difficult to determine the exact life-course stage from which their attitudes originated. The delay may have facilitated the establishment of an independent household among the Irish upon marriage, but it was also a result of the greater propensity of the daughters of Irish immigrant parents to stay longer in the labor force than the daughters of native-born parents (Hareven & Vinovskis, 1975; Modell & Hareven, 1978). The same pattern held true in Manchester, New Hampshire, where young French-Canadian immigrant women entered the labor force earlier and married later than native-born women (Hareven, 1982).

The timing of marriage in the lower class in the Essex County communities analyzed seems to have been considerably less contingent on the establishment of residential independence either before or after marriage. When controlling for class, the ethnic culture in which families developed affected the way they managed their children's transitions. Immigrant children left school earlier than native-born children, entered the work force earlier, left home later, and married later, because of their family's dependence on their contribution, and because of the longer time period they needed to amass resources in order to establish an independent household (Modell & Hareven, 1978).

In assessing the relative impact of class and ethnicity on timing, it is also necessary to differentiate immediate decisions on timing from long-range ones. Sending a child to work, leaving home, or taking in a boarder are immediate decisions with limited consequences (although they may turn into permanent moves), whereas the decisions affecting the timing of marriage and the number and spacing of children are more lasting and consequential ones. Such decisions require careful planning that might be influenced by cultural background as well as by one's social status and economic constraints. In the urban population in the late nineteenth century, where economic insecurity was pervasive, economic needs often took priority over normatively established time schedules. But the ways in which different groups in the population went about meeting these economic constraints may have been dictated by their cultural backgrounds, emanating from ethnic traditions. Ethnicity may have affected timing in several ways: indirectly, through its impact on earlier behavior that affects subsequent timing (fertility), and directly, in guiding immediate choices pertaining to schooling, women's labor-force participation, or leaving home. Modell's analysis (1978) of family expenditure patterns in American cities in the late nineteenth century suggests that, as Irish families adopted American tastes and standards of living, they gradually adjusted their timing and family labor strategies accordingly. As immigrants, and especially their children, adopted ''American'' patterns, timing became more homogenized (Hareven, 1977b; Uhlenberg, 1974, 1978).

The broad changes in the timing of family transitions sketched out here do not take into account detailed cohort comparisons. As historical research in this area becomes more refined, it will be possible to discern differences in the timing of life transitions within cohorts as well as between cohorts. Ryder (1965) has suggested that social change occurs when there is a distinct discontinuity between the experiences of one cohort and those of its predecessors. Important historical discontinuities, however, may also occur within a cohort, as a result of earlier life experiences that members of a cohort may have encountered. For example, the cohort that reached adulthood during the Great Depression experienced major discontinuities in family and work life that were not only part of an overall process of social change, but that may, in turn, have catalyzed further social change. Such an approach views a cohort as an age group moving through history whose social experience is influenced not only by contemporary conditions but also by experiences of earlier life events, which, in turn, were affected by specific historical circumstances. Variations in people's earlier life histories and in exposure to historical events by class, ethnic background, and community type would generate important differences within the same cohort.

As Elder's *Children of the Great Depression* (1974) has shown, experiences in childhood and early adulthood encountered during the Great Depression had a major impact on adjustment in later life. Within the same cohort of unemployed adults caught in the Great Depression, coping with economic stress differed not only in accordance with differences in personality, family background, and the availability of other resources, but also in terms of earlier transitions experienced—how long the individual had been working and whether his or her career had been continuous and stable or had been disrupted before the onset of the Depression.

The continuous cumulative and spiral impact of earlier life transitions as affected by historical conditions on subsequent ones is important both in individual lives and in the collective experience of the family as a unit. Thus, history has an impact on people's lives both directly, at any moment of their interaction with historical forces, and indirectly, through the cumulative impact of earlier historical circumstance on their lives.

To date, historians have not had many opportunities to examine the cumulative impact of earlier life transitions on subsequent ones. In the absence of longitudinal data, historians have not yet investigated sufficiently the ways in which earlier life transitions are linked to later ones, as Elder (1974) has been able to demonstrate from his study of the Berkeley and Oakland cohorts who experienced the Great Depression in their childhood.

The significance of this approach in historical research cannot be sufficiently emphasized. The major difficulty in following it is the absence of longitudinal data that would enable historians to construct these patterns over time. But as some of ongoing research has suggested, a life course perspective enables one to infer longitudinal patterns even from cross-sectional data limited to one or several points in time (Hareven, 1978c).

Family Strategies

Most of the prevailing historical and sociological literature has concentrated on the impact of institutions on the family, but the most important development in historical research has been to redirect attention to the family members themselves. The emphasis has shifted to the ways in which families take charge of their lives and allocate their resources in the struggle to survive and to secure their own and their children's future.

Once we view the family as an active agent rather than a passive victim of social change, the crucial questions focus on the internal dynamics of families' strategies: How did families plan their lives, particularly under conditions of adversity and rapid social change? What kinds of strategies did they follow in their adaptation to changing conditions over their life course and over historical time? How did family members juggle multiple roles and obligations as children, parents, workers, and members of a kinship network? How were decisions made within the family, who made the decisions, and how were individual careers synchronized with collective family ones? The most important implication of this perspective is an emphasis on the family as a dynamic process and as a constantly changing interaction of personalities within it, rather than as an organization and institution. This approach is strongly linked to a life course perspective because it assumes change and redefinition of familial strategies over the life course and in relation to external historical conditions (Elder, 1981).

Historical research on the family has begun to address these issues, particularly in relation to the family's interaction with the industrial system, family labor-force strategies, and internal family economic strategies such as the allocation of resources. Economists may have exaggerated the degree to which families plot strategies rationally and calculate the respective economic value of the members' services to one another. Without assuming conscious calculation as the overwhelming mode of action, historians have nevertheless identified purposeful planning and weighing of options as the base of families' interaction with the economy. In the context of recent historical studies, ''strategies'' do not always entail clear plans and are not always consciously defined. The use of the term *strategies* presupposes, nevertheless, that individuals and families make choices and exercised priorities when responding to external pressures or internal needs.

The internal dynamics of such a collective decision-making process in a historical context need to be explored more precisely. Family collectivity did not necessarily imply mutual deliberation or ''democratic'' participation in the process. It is possible that such decisions were imposed by the male head of the family on its members, although there is sufficient evidence that consultation and bargaining took place between husbands and wives and between parents and children. The historical pattern of change has been one of transition, from authoritarian parental (expecially paternal) control over the life transitions of young-adult children to greater independence, and from husband-dominated decisions to a companionate relationship between husbands and wives (Degler, 1980; Hareven, 1982; D. B. Smith, 1980; D. S. Smith, 1973). The most important contribution of recent research has been to emphasize the role of the actors' cultural heritage as well as economic considerations in shaping the kinds of choices that family members make within given economic limits.

Family strategies cover various aspects of family life, ranging from inheritance to the decision to migrate and the organization of migration, and from decisions on the membership of one's household to family limitation and child-rearing. Some such choices involve trade-offs made in order to achieve solvency, to buy a house, to facilitate occupational advancement for one's children, to save for the future, and to provide for old age. The underlying assumption is that the family makes decisions as a collective, corporate unit, rather than as the sum of individual members. For that very reason, family strategies determine the timing of life transitions, particularly leaving home, marrying, and forming a household. Examples of consciously articulated strategies are the use of kin not only to organize migration to new industrial communities, but also to provide backup in the community of origin; the selection of relatives or godparents to act as custodians of children in times of crisis; residence in proximity to one's kin; and prudential planning for the future, such as education, savings, and insurance (Hareven, 1982).

The areas of family decision-making that have received the closest attention from historians are the labor force participation of women and of children and family (household) income and expenditure patterns. The gainful employment of children and married women outside the home posed a critical dilemma for working-class families. Economic constraints and aspirations for mobility required the contributions from women's and children's labor. The participation of women and children in a collective family effort was sanctioned by the cultural values that immigrant workers brought with them from rural society. But gainful employment of mothers outside the home was not always consistent with premigration views of wives' work and was in conflict with middle-class norms. In this area, family strategies had to accommodate economic constraints and cultural traditions, as well as the values of the dominant culture. The conflict between family needs and the values of the native middle class, which censored the employment of married women and of mothers in particular, necessitated major adjustments by immigrant and working-class families.

Throughout the nineteenth and early twentieth centuries, women's labor-force participation followed a life cycle pattern. Working-class women commenced work in their teens and dropped out after marriage, or after the birth of their first child. Unlike in the 1950s and 1960s, they rarely returned into the labor force after the completion of child rearing. Those mothers who worked did so intermittently throughout their childbearing years. For the most part, wives, especially mothers, were kept out of the labor force, except in textile communities, with their female-intensive and family-intensive employment patterns.

The recurring pattern in the late nineteenth and the early twentieth centuries reflects a response to economic conditions that was shaped by the dictates of one's own culture. In this pattern, families relied first on the labor of their children to supplement their head's income or to substitute for a missing, unemployed, or sick father. If one infers strategies from these labor-force-participation patterns, a ranking of the priorities that people followed would become apparent: The widespread preference was to send one's children to work, take in boarders, or both, rather than to send one's wife to work. But families on the margin of subsistence followed all three routes: They sent women and children into the labor force and took boarders into the household. The economic contribution from children's work, especially that of older children, was the steadiest crucial supplement or substitute for the head's earnings (Goldin, 1981; Hareven, 1978c, 1982; Mason, Vinovskis, & Hareven, 1978). Children's labor was considered even more crucial in the later years of life, as the head's earning power was declining, or in the case of widows, where child labor was the only source of support, as widows rarely reentered the labor force. The stage in the life course in which the family found itself was one of the most crucial determinants of the labor force participation of children. The older the head of household, the greater was the family's reliance on the work of children (Haines, 1981).

Child labor in itself was not a uniform practice. As Goldin (1981) found, in Philadelphia in the late nineteenth century, family strategies caused differentials within child labor patterns. Whether a child worked depended on family income, sex, age, the labor force participation of other siblings, and the presence or absence of a parent. Whether older siblings worked or not determined whether a younger child would seek employment. Daughters were less likely to work if they had older brothers working—a clear expression of cultural preferences. Such preferences were evident in the fact that native-born families were less likely than ethnic families to send their children or wives to work.

The differences in employment patterns of white and black women and children in Philadelphia confirms the impact of cultural considerations as well as economic constraints. The fact that both married and widowed black women were more likely than white women to be gainfully employed could be interpreted as an expression of the poverty of black families. But the lower tendency of black children than of white children to be employed may reflect a trade-off within black families—a strategy of keeping children in school longer as well as a greater acceptance of married women's work among blacks. Or does it reflect the absence of employment opportunities for black children, which increased the family's dependence on the work of wives (Goldin, 1981)?

To the extent to which it is possible to reconstruct these patterns for the nineteenth century, it appears that, although children's work was viewed as a basic source of income, wives' work outside the home was viewed as a supplement to the family's budget. Despite the reluctance to send wives to work, women's labor force participation was much more widespread than one would be led to believe from a ''snapshot'' gleaned from the census. Women tended to move in and out of the labor force, in accordance with childbearing, familial needs, and the availability of employment (Hareven, 1982). The propensity of married women to work in such industries as textiles and food processing reflects both the greater availability of opportunities for women in such female-intensive occupations and a cultural preference for sending wives and daughters to jobs related to what had been traditional home industries (Yans-McLaughlin, 1977). When alternatives were available, wives and daughters tended to work, especially in industries where several other members of their family were employed, which provided continuity between the family and the workplace, as well as supervision and protection of young people, especially females, by their older relatives. But

even when married women pursued regular and continuous careers, they considered their work supplementary to the family economy rather than primary (Hareven, 1982; Scott & Tilly, 1975).

Most of the recent examinations of family strategies have drawn on cross-sectional data that prohibit the analysis of changing family strategies over the life course, except through cohort comparison of families at different points in their life (using age or family status as a proxy). Nor has it been possible to reconstruct perceptions and priorities from census and family budget schedules, except by inference from behavior. Historians have been unable, therefore, to reconstruct the decision-making process within the family as articulated by the actors themselves. The very focus on the *family* as a decision maker tends to obscure the dynamics within the family: Who made the major decisions? How did various family members respond to the collective decisions imposed on them?

Interviews used to supplement quantitative behavioral data have suggested areas of tension surrounding the trade-offs and sacrifices that individuals were expected to make for the collective good of their families. Strain and conflict revolved around such issues of family timing as when to leave home, when to marry, how to allocate responsibilities for parental support among different siblings, and how to divide resources (Hareven, 1982). Most individuals and families living under conditions of economic insecurity found themselves in a double bind: On the one hand, the family's collective requirements imposed enormous pressures and burdens on individuals, and on the other hand, the individual was dependent on family collectivity for assistance in time of need (Anderson, 1971). Thus, a rebellion against familial requirements, however onerous, would deprive the individual of access to the only source of support under conditions of insecurity.

History of the Family and the Understanding of Social Change

Recent work on the history of the family has had a profound impact on our understanding of the family's response to changing social and economic conditions; it has also contributed to an understanding of the broader question of how people react to social change and what change means in their lives. Because the family has served as mediator between individuals and the social forces and institutions affecting them, it has both facilitated the adaptation of individuals to social change and initiated change itself.

The area in which this dual role of the family has been most explicitly documented is in its relationship to industrialization. Until recently, standard sociological theory has argued that the family broke down under the impact of industrialization. Adherents of the Chicago School of Sociology maintained that, throughout the history of industrial development, migration from rural to urban centers uprooted people from their traditional kinship networks, and that the pressures of industrial work and urban life caused a disintegration of the family unit (Linton, 1959; Thomas & Znaniecki, 1918–1920; Wirth, 1938).

Even sociologists who questioned the theory of social breakdown agreed with Parsons and Bales (1955) that the family became increasingly nuclearized to fit the requirements of the new industrial system and that the nuclear family was the unit most compatible with that system. These analysts have argued that, because the occupational system is based on achievement rather than on detachment from the obligations and controls of extended kinship networks, individuals are more mobile and therefore more adaptable to the labor demands of industrial society. Goode (1963), a major exponent of this view, saw the conjugal family as an entity that serves industry while placing workers at the mercy of the factory:

The lower-class family pattern is indeed most "integrated" with the industrial system, but mainly in the sense that the individual is forced to enter its labor market with far less family support— his family does not prevent industry from using him for its goals. He may move where the system needs him, hopefully where his best opportunity lies, but he must also fit the demands of the system, since no extended kin network will interest itself greatly in his fate. (pp. 12–13)

During the 1970s, several historical studies have convincingly refuted the claim that industrialization destroyed a three-generational family structure and have challenged the assumption that families and kin groups break down under the impact of migration to urban industrial centers and under the pressures of industrial work. There is considerable evidence that industrial life actually strengthened family ties and may have increased cohesion: Housing shortages in industrial areas necessitated at least temporary coresidence with extended kin. Hence, one witnesses a higher degree of household extension in industrial communities than in preindustrial ones (Anderson, 1971). Rather than "forcing" sons and daughters to leave sooner, the availability of employment in industrial areas enabled young adults to work in the community, live at home, and contribute to the support of their family.

Industrial work itself did not break up the family unit. As Smelser (1959) has shown in his study of the early stages of the Industrial Revolution in Britain, textile factories recruited entire family groups as work units. Fathers contracted for their children, collected their wages, and often disciplined them in the factory. Entire families relied on the factory as their employer; the factories, in turn, depended on the recruitment of family groups to maintain a continuous labor supply. Smelser argued, however, that, by the early 1830s, the development of new machinery had introduced specialization, which meant that families no longer worked together in the factory.

In a later study, Anderson (1971) has shown, however, that, in Lancashire, recruitment of workers in family groups continued in the textile industry. Most important,

Anderson stressed the survival of kinship ties and the continuing importance of kin in migration and adaptation to industrial conditions, even when relatives were not working in the same place. The family survived as a work unit in different forms throughout the nineteenth century. In the United States, particularly in the textile industry, the family continued to function as a work unit, and kin continued to fulfill a vital role even under more complex industrial conditions in the late nineteenth and early twentieth centuries (Hareven, 1982).

As suggested above, in New England industrial communities, the family served as a crucial intermediary in the recruitment of workers from rural areas and in organizing the migration of workers to factory towns, both during the initial period of industrialization in the late eighteenth and early nineteenth centuries and later on. Kinship ties with the workers' communities of origin were reinforced by the back-and-forth migration of individuals and the transfer of resources.

This continuity was evident as the factory system emerged as a major force in New England in the early nineteenth century. It was observable in both styles of recruitment of rural laborers for the emerging textile mills—the "family system" and the "mill girl" system. Even in the planned large-scale textile towns founded and developed during the first half of the nineteenth century, where the typical employee was a single woman, factory work represented a transitional one- or two-year phase in her life between domestic work in her parents' farm home and marriage. In many instances, the savings that women accumulated from their factory labor were sent back to their families on the farm. Families that sent one or more members to work in nearby textile mills often maintained subsistence farming as a backup if the factory failed (Ware, 1931). The interdependence of countryside and factory was strengthened by back-and-forth migration. Thus, factory workers and their relatives in rural communities were linked into a common social system through their family ties.

Family employment emerged once again as the dominant pattern in the mid-nineteenth century, when new Irish, French-Canadian, Portuguese, and eastern European migrants were recruited to replace the mill girls as a cheaper labor force. Even long-distance overseas migration did not entirely sever the immigrants' links with their native bases. Relatives on both sides of the Atlantic maintained ties and transmitted assistance. Kinship ties from rural areas were carried over into industrial settings, and kin assumed new functions in mediating between workers and the modern organizations, as well as in maintaining the earlier function of support in critical life situations.

Two conclusions that considerably revise the prevailing interpretations emerge from these historical studies: first, that industrial capitalism in itself did not cause a breakdown of the family, and second, that the family type most "fit" to interact with the modern factory was not the isolated nuclear type, but a nuclear family embedded in an extended kinship network: As the experience of textile workers in Manchester, New Hampshire, shows, the role of the family and the kin group went beyond assistance to its members to an interaction with the industrial employer on several levels: influencing the placement and transfer of workers to desirable jobs, socializing novices, and, at times, manipulating work schedules and procedures. Rather than simply carrying over premigration traditions, the family actually addressed the factory system on its own terms (Hareven, 1982).

In summary, this means that the family was a broker between its members and the institutions of industrial capitalism and a facilitator of their adaptation. Of course, this does not mean that the family was in full control of its destiny; nor does it mean that workers and their relatives succeeded in changing the structure of industrial capitalism. It means, rather, that families were facilitating change as well as responding to it. In doing so, families and individuals charted their own strategies and drew on their own culture and traditions.

As recent work has begun to suggest, the crucial historical question is not merely whether the family was an active or passive agent. Rather than an either-or question, this is a complex issue about the nature of historical circumstances. Under what conditions was the family in control of its destiny, and under what circumstances did this control diminish? How did the family reorder its priorities to respond to new conditions, and how did this reordering affect internal family relations?

To answer these questions in the context of industrial capitalism, one needs to consider not only how industrial work affected family organization and work roles, but also how the family affected conditions in the factory. Thus, an understanding of the family's relation to the factory requires examining the family's internal economic strategies and labor force configurations, as well as its interaction with larger economic processes and institutions outside its confines. Hareven's study (1982) of the factory workers shows that the internal structure of the family, its economic conditions, and the changes it experienced during the life course of its members affected its response to industrial time and historical time. Externally, the family's ability to retain some control over employment and work processes depended on business cycles; on changes in management and in the organization of work in the factory; and on the social, economic, and cultural forces in the larger society. For example, because of its central role in the recruitment of workers, it becomes clear from the Manchester, New Hampshire, study that the family was more in control of its destiny during periods of labor shortage, and that it began to loose control under conditions of labor surplus. Thus, supply and demand was an important factor in the family's ability to control its enviroment. The family's active role did not cease, however, once its influence diminished or collapsed in the workplace, as the textile industry began to decline. The family devised new responses to cope with the insecurities resulting from unemployment, strikes, and the final collapse of the industry.

Future work addressing these questions will have to expand the inquiry into the family's interaction with the industrial process, by further identifying and defining the circumstances under which the family was able to influence its environment or the conditions under which it had to succumb to external pressures.

Now that historians have rejected grand theories of linear change in family behavior, a new set of questions emerges: If, as the new consensus now maintains, industrialization did not cause the first major decline in fertility, did not generate simple nuclear households, and did not effect a drastic reorganization of family structure, did industrialization cause any significant changes in family behavior at all? If, for centuries for western European families, the prevailing form of household organization has been nuclear, then the historical search for the origins of the nuclear family must press further into the past; and if some of the important characteristics of ''modern'' family behavior preceded the Industrial Revolution, what did cause the change in family structure and behavior over the past three centuries?

Although they have rejected the assumption that industrialization generated a new type of family structure, historians have agreed that industrialization has had an impact on changes in family functions, in family values, and in the timing of family transitions. Many of these changes were not necessarily linked directly to industrialization but emerged as consequences of the restructuring of the economy and of increased urbanization following industrialization. Historians accept that the most crucial change wrought by industrialization was the transfer of functions from the family to other social institutions. In Parsonian terms, what occurred here was a process of differentiation in which one social group, becoming antiquated because of changing historical conditions, is split into two or more groups or roles functioning more efficiently in the new historical context. (Smelser, 1959). As has been often pointed out, the preindustrial family served as a workshop, a church, a reformatory, a school, and an asylum (Demos, 1970). Over the past century and a half, these functions have become, in large part, the responsibility of other institutions. The household has been transformed from a place of production to a place of consumption and the nurturing of children. The family has withdrawn from the world of work, extolling privacy and intimacy as its major sources of strength, and the workplace has generally become nonfamilial and bureaucratic.

The home is viewed increasingly as a retreat from the outside world. The family has turned inward, assuming domesticity, intimacy, and privacy as its major characteristics as well as ideals. The privacy of the home and its separation from the workplace have been guarded jealously as an essential feature of family life (Cott, 1977; Degler, 1980; Welter, 1966). The commitment to the domesticity of the family is itself the outcome of a long historical process, which commenced in the early modern period in western Europe, a process characterized by Philippe Ariès (1962) as follows:

The modern family . . . cuts itself off from the world and opposes to society the isolated groups of parents and children. All the energy of the group is expended in helping the children to rise in the world, individually and without any collective ambition, the children rather than the family. (p. 404)

Aries (1962), by contrast, states that the premodern family was identified by the large amount of sociability it maintained. The family and the household, therefore, were the bulwark of the community. Under the impact of economic growth and industrialization, the family became a specialized unit, its tasks limited primarily to consumption, procreation, and child rearing. The question is still open, however, as to what impact the loss of many of its former functions, combined with shrinking household membership, has had on the internal dynamics and the quality of family relationships. According to Ariès, the contracting of family functions and the resulting privatization of family life marked the emergence of the modern family—nuclear, intensive, inward-turning, and child-centered—at the expense of sociability and greater integration with the community. Ariès concluded that these developments weakened the family's adaptability and deprived children of the opportunity to grow up in a flexible environment with a variety of role models to follow. To date, however, historians have done little to document and to explore closely the effect of these changes on internal relations within the family.

As change in the family is slower than in other social institutions, and because, as has been shown, the family does not simply respond to change but also generates it, it has been difficult for historians to develop a typology of change over time in the family. Historians attempting to date the emergence of "the modern family" in the West place it somewhere between 1680 and 1850. Ariès (1962) and Stone (1977) have singled out the late seventeenth and early eighteenth centuries, whereas Shorter (1976) has dated its emergence as being in the late eighteenth and early nineteenth centuries. Stone has identified the emergence of the "closed domestic nuclear family" as being between 1640 and 1800. American historians generally date its emergence to the late eighteenth and early nineteenth centuries (Degler, 1980).

Stone, Ariès, and Shorter have focused on the rise of affective individualism as the major criterion of the modern family. They have generally agreed that the "modern" family is privatized, nuclear, domestic, and child-centered, and that the sentimental bond between husband and wife and parents and children is the crucial base of family relations. They have all pointed to the weakening influence of extended kin, friends, and neighbors on family ties, and to an isolation of the family from interaction with the community as the consequence of privacy and child-centeredness. Marriages are based on "emotional

bonding" between husband and wife and are a result of personal and sexual attraction rather than alliances between sets of parents or lineages. Stone, and to some extent Degler, see the weakening of bonds with kin as an inevitable consequence of this type of family.

Although historians have generally agreed on these characteristics of modern family life, there is some disagreement and, at times, some lack of clarity about which class first initiated these changes. The scholars discussed above follow basically a "trickle-down" theory. Ariès, Stone, and, more implicitly, Degler have viewed the bourgeoisie and the gentry as the vanguard, whereas Shorter has assigned a crucial role to peasants and workers. For American society, Degler has placed the origins of the "modern" family in the middle class, although he has generalized from the experience of the middle class to the entire society. The most important aspect still absent from the historical studies of long-term changes in the family over time are more systematic distinctions between social classes and a more detailed understanding of the historical process by which modes of family behavior were adopted by other classes, if indeed that was the case, and conversely what class differences have survived (Ariès, 1962; Degler, 1980; Stone, 1977; Shorter, 1976). These studies of broad change over time also hold in common their acceptance of ideological and cultural factors as the major explanations of change in family behavior rather than social and economic ones. Shorter is the only one among them to cite "market capitalism" as the major cause for the emergence of family sentiment, but as his critics have pointed out, he has not provided an explicit connection between these economic forces and the transformation of family relations (Tilly & Cohen, 1982).

Stone (1981) offered a "multicausal" explanation, rather than one single factor but has tended to favor the predominance of cultural and ideological explanations over social and economic ones, as has Degler (1980). This is precisely where the most fundamental disagreements about social change and the family are likely to emerge among historians. Not only is there a disagreement among historians over the relative importance of ideological or socioeconomic causes in long-term changes in the family, there is also a greater need to know how the changes took place and what the nature of the interaction among these different factors was. The "grand" explanations of change are vulnerable, particularly in some of these studies' claim for linear change over time. This is precisely the area where the critique that social historians have made against modernization theory applies as well.

The broad pattern of historical change that was based primarily on the experience of the upper and middle classes has tended to obscure the persistence of earlier forms of behavior among other classes. Among working-class and ethnic families, some preindustrial family characteristics have persisted, although in modified form. As discussed above, although industrialization caused a separation of the workplace from the home, the working-class family continued to function as a production unit in certain aspects of its economy. Even if all members did not work in the same place, the family experienced a continuity between work outside the home and household production, especially in women's work. The family continued to be a major economic decision-making unit, organizing the careers of its members and plotting collective strategies, and, in certain instances, affecting the workplace (Scott & Tilly, 1975; Hareven, 1982).

Nor should one take for granted that the characteristics of the "modern" family that were typical of the middle class also held true for other classes. In the United States, for example, there has not been sufficient research over time to identify specific differences between middle-class, working-class, black, and immigrant families. There is, however, sufficient evidence to suggest that privatism, child-centeredness, affective individualism, and isolation from kin, which emerged as characteristic traits of urban middle-class families (the carriers of the "modern" family type), were not necessarily typical of the other groups. Over the nineteenth century and into the twentieth century, historians have been able to identify major differences between native-born, urban, middle-class families, on the one hand, and immigrant, working-class, and black families on the other hand. We still lack adequate systematic studies for comparisons within and among these groups. Historians such as Degler (1980) may have paid too much attention to similarities in household structure, at the expense of other differences: There were differences in fertility patterns, in the presence of boarders and lodgers in the household, in women's labor-force participation, and in the timing of life transitions. Differences in fertility not only affected the size of the household and the age configurations within it, but they also reflected the wife's ability to exercise control over decisions of family limitation; the presence or absence of boarders and lodgers is an important indicator of variations in a family's economic needs, in the style of meeting them, and in the degree of a family's commitment to privacy; and differences in the timing of life transitions, particularly in the age of young people's entry into the work life, leaving home, and marriage, indicate important variations in adherence to a collective family economy.

Nor should one overemphasize the similarities in women's and children's labor-force participation across classes and racial and ethnic groups. As suggested above, immigrant, working-class, and black families were more dependent on the labor of their children. Even though married women in general tended not to be employed, all existing studies show a higher propensity toward labor force participation on the part of immigrant and working-class and especially black women than on the part of their middle-class counterparts. All these differences converge around what I would argue is the most central dividing line between the native middle-class family, on the one hand, and black, immigrant, and working-class families,

on the other hand, namely, a commitment to a collective family economy. Although the central ideal and practice of middle-class family life was the separation of the spheres between the world of the home and the world of work, working-class and immigrant family life revolved around economic responsibilities in which the work of each member was considered an integral part of the family's economy, and in which instrumental relations may have taken precedence over sentiment.

Unquestionably, the overall pattern of historical change has moved in the direction of an adoption by other classes and ethnic groups of the middle-class, companionate, private, child-centered family patterns. As Modell (1978) showed, even the consumption patterns and the tastes of immigrant families began to conform to those of native-born families. But the adoption of native-born, middle-class family styles by other classes and ethnic groups was by no means linear and uniform (Hareven & Modell, 1980). How the process of adaptation took place, and at what pace, is still a major subject for future research. But it is clear from several studies that the adoption of "modal" patterns of behavior by different ethnic groups and various classes was selective and unevenly paced.

The realization that historical changes in the family have not taken place uniformly throughout society has led historians to react against a simplistic, linear interpretation of change and to focus instead on research that is carried out on a synchronic level, examining family interaction with societal processes and institutions within specific community contexts. Although such work has already contributed to a revision of earlier generalizations, historians still have to face the challenge of welding ongoing research into a more systematic pattern ranging over a longer historical period.

At the moment, the contribution of historical knowledge to the overall understanding of social change and the famiy lies in three major points: first, that in the process of change, families are *active* agents in their contacts with social, economic, and cultural forces; second, that changes in family behavior do not conform perfectly to the traditional periodization of Western history; and third, that changes in family behavior (as well as in many other aspects of society) do not follow any simple linear trend, as postulated in modernization theory. Historians of the family have identified a checkered pattern of change that belies any continuous linear pattern encompassing the entire society and moving inevitably to a more "modern" level.

References

Achenbaum, A. W. *Old age in the new land.* Baltimore: Johns Hopkins University Press, 1978.

Anderson, M. *Family structure in nineteenth-century Lancashire.* Cambridge: Cambridge University Press, 1971.

Ariès, P. *Centuries of childhood*, trans. by R. Baldick. New York: Knopf, 1962.

Baltes, P. B. Life span development psychology: Some observations in history and theory. In P. B. Baltes & O. G. Brim, Jr. (Eds.), *Life span development and behavior* (vol. 2) New York: Academic Press, 1979.

Berkner, L. K. The stem family and the developmental cycle of the peasant household: An eighteenth century Austrian example. *American Historical Review,* 1972, *77* (April), 398–418.

Bott, E. *Family and social network: Roles, norms, and external relationships in ordinary urban familes.* London: Tavistock, 1957.

Byington, M. F. *Homestead: The households of a mill town* (Vol. 5). *The Pittsburgh survey.* New York: Russell Sage Foundation, Charities Publication Committee, 1910.

Chudacoff, H. P. The life course of women: Age and age consciousness, 1865–1915. *Journal of Family History,* 1980, *5,* 274–292.

Chudacoff, H., & Hareven, T. K. Family transitions and household structure in the later years of life. In T. K. Hareven (Ed.), *Transitions: The family life and the life course in historical perspective.* New York: Academic Press, 1978.

Chudacoff, H., & Hareven, T. K. From the empty nest to family dissolution. *Journal of Family History,* 1979, *4* (Spring), 59–63.

Cott, N. F. *The bonds of womanhood: Woman's sphere in New England, 1780–1835.* New Haven, Conn.: Yale University Press, 1977.

Degler, C. N. *At odds: Women and the family in America from the Revolution to the present.* New York: Oxford University Press, 1980.

deMause, L. (Ed.). *The history of childhood.* New York: The Psychotherapy Press, 1974.

Demos, J. *A little commonwealth: Family life in Plymouth Colony.* New York: Oxford University Press, 1970.

Duvall, E. M. *Family development.* Philadelphia: Lippincott, 1957.

Elder, G. H., Jr. *Children of the Great Depression: Social change in life experience.* Chicago: University of Chicago Press, 1974.

Elder, G. H., Jr. Approaches to social change and the family. In J. Demos & S. Boocock (Eds.), *Turning points: Historical and sociological essays on the family.* Chicago: University of Chicago Press, 1978. (a)

Elder, G. H., Jr. Family history and the life course. In T. K. Hareven (Ed.), *Transitions: The family and the life course in historical perspective.* New York: Academic Press, 1978, pp. 17–64. (b)

Elder, G. H., Jr. History and the family: The discovery of complexity. *Journal of Marriage and the Family,* 1981, *43* (3), 489–519.

Erikson, E. *Childhood and society.* New York: Norton, 1950.

Fischer, D. H. *Growing old in America.* New York: Oxford University Press, 1977.

Glasco, L. A. The life cycles and household structure of American ethnic groups: Irish, Germans and native-born whites in Buffalo, New York, 1885. In T. Hareven (Ed.), *Family and kin in American urban communities, 1700–1930.* New York: Franklin Watts, New Viewpoints, 1977.

Glick, P. The family cycle. *American Sociological Review,* 1947, *12* (April), 164–174.

Glick, P. The life cycle of the family. *Marriage and Family Living,* 1955, *17* (February), 3–9.

Glick, P. Updating the life cycle of the family. *Journal of Marriage and the Family,* 1977, *39* (February), 5–13.

Glick, P. C., & Norton, A. J. Marrying, divorcing and living together in the U.S. today. *Population Bulletin,* 1977, *32* (October), 1–39.

Glick, P. C., & Parke, R., Jr. New approaches in studying the life cycle of the family. *Demography,* 1965, *2,* 187–212.

Goldin, C. Family strategies and the family economy in the late nineteenth-century: The role of secondary workers. In T. Hershberg (Ed.), *Philadelphia.* New York: Oxford University Press, 1981.

Goode, W. *World revolution and family patterns.* New York: Macmillan, Free Press, 1963.

Goody, J. Strategies in heirship. *Comparative Studies in Society and History,* 1973, *15,* 3–20.

Goubert, P. Historical demography and the reinterpretation of early modern French history: A research review. *Journal of Interdisciplinary History,* 1970, *1,* 37–48.

Greven, P. *Four generations: Population, land, and family in colonial Andover, Massachusetts.* Ithaca, N.Y.: Cornell University Press, 1970.

Haines, M. Poverty, economic stress, and the family in a late-nineteenth-century American city: Whites in Philadelphia, 1982. In T. Hershberg (Ed.), *Philadelphia.* New York: Oxford University Press.

Hammel, E. A. The Zadruga as process. In P. Laslett & R. Wall (Eds.), *Household and family in past time.* London: Cambridge University Press, 1972, pp. 335–373.

Hareven, T. K. The history of the family as an interdisciplinary field. *Journal of Interdisciplinary History,* 1971, *2* (Autumn), 399–414.

Hareven, T. K. The family as process: The historical study of the family cycle. *Journal of Social History,* 1974, *7* (Spring), 322–329.

Hareven, T. K. Family time and industrial time: Family and work in a planned corporation town, 1900–1924. *Journal of Urban History,* 1975, *1* (May), 365–389. (a)

Hareven, T. K. The laborers of Manchester, New Hampshire, 1900–1940: The role of family and ethnicity in adjustment to industrial life. *Labor History,* 1975, *16* (Spring), 249–265. (b)

Hareven, T. K. Modernization and family history: Perspectives on social change. *Signs,* 1976, *2* (Autumn), 190–206.

Hareven, T. K. (Ed.). *Family and kin in American urban communities, 1700–1930.* New York: Franklin Watts, New Viewpoints, 1977. (a)

Hareven, T. K. Family time and historical time. *Daedalus,* 1977, *106* (Spring), 57–70. (b)

Hareven, T. K. Cycles, course, and cohorts: Reflections on the theoretical and methodological approaches to the historical study of family development. *Journal of Social History,* 1978, *12* (September), 97–109. (a)

Hareven, T. K. The dynamics of kin in an industrial community. In J. Demos & S. Boocock (Eds.), *Turning points: Historical and sociological essays on the family.* Chicago: *American Journal of Sociology,* Supplement, *84,* S151–182, 1978. (b)

Hareven, T. K. (Ed.). *Transitions: The family and the life course in historical perspective.* New York: Academic Press, 1978. (c)

Hareven, T. K. *Family time and industrial time.* New York: Cambridge University Press, 1982.

Hareven, T. K., & Modell, J. Family patterns. In S. Thernstrom (Ed.). *Harvard encyclopedia of American ethnic groups.* Cambridge: Harvard University Press, Belknap Press, 1980.

Hareven, T. K., & Vinovskis, M. A. Marital fertility, ethnicity and occupation in urban families: An analysis of South Boston and the South End in 1880. *Journal of Social History,* 1975, *18* (Spring), 69–93.

Henry, L. Historical demography. *Daedalus,* 1968, *97,* 385–396.

Hill, R. Methodological issues in family development research. *Family Process,* 1964, *3* (March), 186–206.

Hill, R. *Family development in three generations.* Cambridge, Mass.: Schenkman, 1970.

Katz, M. B. *The people of Hamilton, Canada West: Family and class in a mid-nineteenth-century city.* Cambridge: Harvard University Press, 1975.

Kleinberg, S. J. The systematic study of urban women. In M. Cantor & B. Laurie (Eds.), *Class, sex, and the woman worker.* Westport, Conn.: Greenwood Press, 1977.

Laslett, P. *The world we have lost.* London: Methuen, 1965.

Laslett, P., & Wall, R. (Eds.). *Household and family in past time.* Cambridge: Cambridge University Press, 1972.

Linton, R. The natural history of the family. In R. N. Anshen (Ed.), *The family: Its function and destiny* (rev. ed.). New York: Harper & Row, 1959.

Litwak, E. Geographical mobility and extended family cohesion. *American Sociological Review,* 1960, *25* (June), 385–394.

Lockridge, K. The population of Dedham, Massachusetts 1636–1736. *Economy History Review*, 1966, *XIX* (second series), 318–344.

Mason, K. O., Vinovskis, M. A., & Hareven, T. Women's work and the life course in Essex County, Massachusetts, 1880. In T. K. Hareven (Ed.), *Transitions: The family and the life course in historical perspective*. New York: Academic Press, 1978.

Mead, M. & Wolfenstein, M. (Eds.). *Childhood in contemporary culture*. Chicago: University of Chicago Press, 1955.

Modell, J. Patterns of consumption, acculturation, and family income strategy in late-nineteenth-century America. In T. K. Hareven & M. A. Vinovskis (Eds.), *Family and population in nineteenth-century America*. Princeton, N.J.: Princeton University Press, 1978.

Modell, J., & Hareven, T. K. Urbanization and the malleable household: An examination of boarding and lodging in American families. *Journal of Marriage and the Family*, 1973, *35* (August), 467–479.

Modell, J., & Hareven, T. K. Transitions: Patterns of timing. In T. K. Hareven (Ed.), *Transitions: The family and the life course in historical perspective*. New York: Academic Press, 1978.

Modell, J., Furstenberg, F., & Hershberg, T. Social change and transition to adulthood in historical perspective. *Journal of Family History*, 1976, *1* (Autumn), 7–32.

Neugarten, B., & Hagstad, G. O. Age and the life course. In R. H. Binstock & E. Shanas (Eds.), *Handbook of aging and the social sciences*. New York: Van Nostrand Reinholt, 1976.

Parson, T. *The social system*. Glencoe, Ill.: Free Press, 1951.

Parsons, T., & Bales, R. *Family, socialization, and interaction process*. Glencoe, Ill.: Free Press, 1955.

Potter, D. *People of plenty*. Chicago: University of Chicago Press, 1954.

Riley, M. W. Aging, social change, and the power of ideas. *Daedalus: Denerations*, 1978, *107*(1), 39–52.

Riley, M. W., Johnson, M. E., & Foner, A. (Eds.). *Aging and society: A sociology of age stratification*. New Port: Russell Sage Foundation, 1978.

Rowntree, E. S. *Poverty: A study of town life*. London: Longmans, Green, 1901.

Ryder, N. B. The cohort as a concept in the study of social change. *American Sociological Review*, 1965, *30*, 843–861.

Schwarzweller, H. K., Brown, J. S., & Mangalam, J. J. *Mountain families in transition: A case study of Appalachian migration*. University Park: Pennsylvania State University Press, 1971.

Scott, J., & Tilly, L. Women's work and family in nineteenth-century Europe. *Comparative Studies in Society and History*, 1975, *17* (January), 36–64.

Sennett, R. *Families against the city: Middle-class homes of industrial Chicago, 1872–1890*. Cambridge: Harvard University Press, 1970.

Shorter, E. *The making of the modern family*. London: Rollins, 1976.

Smelser, N. J. *Social change and the Industrial Revolution*. Chicago: University of Chicago Press, 1959.

Smith, D. B. *Inside the great house: Planter family life in eighteenth-century Chesapeake society*. Ithaca, N.Y.: Cornell University Press, 1980.

Smith, D. S. Parental power and marriage patterns: An analysis of historical trends in Hingham, Massachusetts. *Journal of Marriage and the Family*, 1973, *35* (August), 419–428.

Smith, D. S. Life course, norms, and the family system of older Americans in 1900. *Journal of Family History*, 1979, *4*, 285–298.

Stone, L. *The family, sex, and marriage in England 1500–1800*. New York: Harper & Row, 1977.

Stone, L. Family history in the 1980s. *Journal of Interdisciplinary History*, 1981, *12*, 51–87.

Sussman, M. B., & Burchinal, L. Kin family network: Unheralded structure in current conceptualizations of family functioning. *Marriage and Family Living*, 1962, *24* (August), 231–240.

Taeuber, I. B. Change and transition in family structures. In *The family in transition*. Washington, D.C.: Fogarty International Center Proceedings, 1969.

Thomas, W., & Znaniecki, F. *The Polish peasant in Europe and America* (3 vols.). Chicago: University of Chicago Press, 1918–1920.

Tilly, L. A., & Cohen, M. Does the family have a history: A review of theory and practice in family history. *Social Science History*, 1982, *6*(2), 131.

Uhlenberg, P. Cohort variations in family life cycle experiences of U.S. females. *Journal of Marriage and the Family*, 1974, *36* (May), 284–292.

Uhlenberg, P. Changing configurations of the life course. In T. K. Hareven (Ed.), *Transitions: The family and the life course in historical perspective*. New York: Academic Press, 1978.

Vann, R. T. History and demography. *History and Theory*, 1969, *9*, 64–78.

Vinovskis, M. A. From household size to the life course: Some observations on recent trends in family history. *American Behavioral Scientist*, 1977, *21* (November), 263–287.

Ware, C. F. *The early New England cotton manufacture*. Boston: Houghton Mifflin, 1931.

Welter, B. The cult of true womanhood: 1820–1860. *American Quarterly* 1966, *18* (October), 151–174.

Wirth, L. Urbanism is a way of life. *American Journal of Sociology*, 1938, *64*, 1–24.

Wishy, B. *The child and the republic: The dawn of modern American child nurture*. Philadelphia: University of Pennsylvania Press, 1968.

Wrigley, E. A. *Population and history*. New York: McGraw-Hill, 1959.

Wrigley, E. A. Family limitation in pre-industrial England. *Economic History Review*, 1966, *19* (April), 82–109. (a)

Wrigley, E. A. Family reconstitution. In Laslett, (Eds.), *An introduction to English historical demography*. 1966. (b)

Wrigley, E. A. The process of modernization and the Industrial Revolution in England. *Journal of Interdisciplinary History*, 1972, *3*, 225–229.

Wrigley, E. A. Reflections on the history of the family. *Daedalus*, 1977, *106*, 71–85.

Yans-McLaughlin, V. *Family and community: Italian immigrants in Buffalo, 1880–1930*. Ithaca, N.Y.: Cornell University Press, 1977.

Young, M. D., & Willmott, P. *Family and kinship in East London*. London: Routledge & Kegan Paul, 1957.

CHAPTER 3

Comparative Perspectives

Gary R. Lee

Introduction

Comparative social research has long played a critical role in the scientific study of the family, partly because most scholars recognize that the family is a universal social institution—that is, that all cultures at all times have had some form of family system—although there is a great deal of disagreement about which precise aspects or components of family structure are universal (Hendrix, 1975b; Lee, 1975; Murdock, 1949; Reiss, 1965; Weigert & Thomas, 1971). Murdock (1949) provided the most explicit and detailed hypothesis about the constant factors in human family systems. He asserted that family systems everywhere consist of or include the nuclear family (husband-father, wife-mother, and dependent children) as the basic unit, and that a minimum of four societal functions is performed by this group: the regulation of sexual relationships, reproduction, primary socialization, and economic cooperation between husband and wife. Reiss (1965), Weigert and Thomas (1971), and Hendrix (1975b), however, have all provided evidence of societies in which either the nuclear family is not the basic family unit, or one or more of the four functions stipulated by Murdock are accomplished by some social structure other than the nuclear family.

Reiss (1965) offered an alternative that is much less detailed, but that is more defensible on empirical grounds as a statement of the constant factors of human family systems (see Lee, 1975). He argued that only two characteristics may be common to family systems in all societies: (1) structurally, families are small groups based on kinship; and (2) they perform the function of nurturant socialization of the newborn. All other characteristics of human family systems, according to Reiss, vary across social systems. It is the variation in these properties that is the subject matter of comparative family sociology, and that concerns us here.

The purpose of this chapter is to apply the logic and the method of comparative sociology to the subject of family structure and interaction. Before launching into substantive issues, we should briefly discuss the nature, poten-

tials, and limitations of the method of comparative sociology. Then, we will deal with three kinds of issues that have been addressed by comparative family sociology: family structure, conjugal power relations, and socialization. This is not at all an exhaustive list of the subjects examined by comparative family researchers, nor are these issues necessarily representative of those that might be discussed. However, each topic illustrates in its own way how comparative research has contributed to the resolution of a substantive or theoretical issue that could not be approached as well in any other fashion. Comparative family sociology is not a subarea or special topic within the general field of family sociology. It is instead a unique method, by means of which we may attack any substantive issue in the discipline. This method offers advantages in the construction of explanatory theory that are simply unavailable without it. The objectives of this chapter are therefore twofold: to demonstrate the utility of comparative research in the task of explaining human behavior, and to illustrate this utility by showing how comparative study has contributed to knowledge about variation in family structure, marital power, and socialization.

The Method of Comparative Sociology

The term *comparative sociology* is, if literally interpreted, at least partially redundant. Sociology is inherently and necessarily comparative. The business of describing and explaining human behavior and experience, which is the mandate of all behavioral science, cannot be conducted without comparison. Any statement purporting to convey knowledge about the behavior of human beings must be, explicitly or implicitly, a comparative statement. Even an apparently simple descriptive statement such as ''The human is a featherless biped'' is an implicit comparison: it implies that members of the category ''human'' have been compared with members of some residual category (''not-human''), with the resulting observation that members of the former category were found to be featherless bipeds, whereas at least some members of the latter category were not. (If all members of both categories were found to be featherless bipeds, the statement in question would convey no information.) Empirical knowledge in sociology consists of com-

Gary R. Lee • Departments of Sociology and Rural Sociology, Washington State University, Pullman, WA 99164.

parative statements. Any correlational statement involves a comparison. When we report that income is positively correlated with education, we mean that we have compared people who have had a lot of education with people who have had less education, and we have found that the more educated typically earn more money.

What, then, is the unique domain of comparative sociology? If all sociology is comparative, how can the adjective *comparative* distinguish one type or subarea of sociology? The resolution of this dilemma involves a consensual rather than a literal interpretation of the term. By *comparative sociology,* we mean any sociological endeavor in which two or more *social systems* are compared (Lee, 1982; Marsh, 1967). That is, at least some of the units of analysis in comparative sociological research must be social systems. If all observations employed in a study are drawn from one social system, the study is not comparative according to this definition.

Although this definition is quite simple (in theory if not in practice), it is easily misinterpreted. The most common distortion is the widespread assumption that sociology done elsewhere (e.g., research by an American sociologist done in France) is *ipso facto* comparative. It isn't comparative because the research involves only one social system. This is not comparative research in the same sense that a case study of one individual is not a survey. No analyses can be conducted on a sample of one, and even a sample of thousands of individuals is a sample of one on the comparative level if it is drawn exclusively from one society or social system.

We do need to point out, however, that data obtained from one society may subsequently be employed for comparative purposes if the properties of the data are "comparable" with those of data obtained from other societies. The method known as *comparative ethnology* (Goodenough, 1956; Marsh, 1967) or *cross-cultural research* (Lee, 1982, p. 9) consists of secondary comparisons of data collected by ethnographers from single societies. The ethnographic research in itself is not comparative, but the subsequent use of ethnographic data in cross-cultural research clearly is. Furthermore, Straus (1968) and others have pointed out that other kinds of data (survey, experimental, and so on) collected in single societies may also be employed in subsequent comparisons with data from other societies, provided that the rules of comparability are observed.[1] Thus, studies conducted in single societies are not in themselves comparative, but may be employed for comparative purposes under certain cir-

cumstances. We shall do some of this in the pages which follow.

If comparative sociology is defined as the systematic comparison of two or more social systems, it is necessary to define social systems, in order that they may be distinguished from one another and from phenomena that are not social systems (or societies; these terms may be employed interchangeably for current purposes). This definition has proved to be one of the most difficult problems in comparative sociology, in terms of both abstract definitions and the application of these definitions to concrete cases. There is no single "correct" definition. However, one of the most general and representative attempts was offered by Marsh (1967), who defined a society as "a plurality of interacting individuals" that possesses at least four properties: (1) a definite territory; (2) recruitment of new members primarily by means of sexual reproduction; (3) a comprehensive culture; and (4) at least partial political independence (p. 12).[2] These criteria are obviously difficult to apply in specific instances. For example, much of the debate surrounding the universality of the nuclear family as defined by Murdock (1949) revolves around the issue of whether observed counterinstances of his definition, such as the Nayar of south India or the Israeli kibbutz, are independent social systems or subunits of other, more inclusive systems (see Reiss, 1965, 1980, p. 23).

Comparing units of different levels of complexity (for example, societies with communities or cultures with subcultures) can cause empirical and theoretical problems too extensive to investigate here (but see Stolte-Heiskanen, 1972, and Zelditch, 1971, pp. 280–281). The possible consequences of comparing units of differing complexity include confusion between the properties of social systems and subunits of systems, nonindependence of cases in both a statistical and a logical sense, and difficulties in uniquely assigning observations to cases (systems). No simple definition of social systems, at either the conceptual or the operational level, will clearly and simply resolve all of these possible problems. The point here, however, is that comparative sociology is the comparison of multiple social systems, which are known and distinguished from one another according to criteria similar to those expounded by Marsh (1967). The lines between social systems—and between systems and subsystems—are not always clear, and there is no real consensus among comparative researchers on the appropriateness of any one set of defining criteria. Nonetheless, comparisons may be successfully made as long as the possible criteria are, insofar as possible, clearly stipulated

[1]It is not possible in this context to satisfactorily discuss and analyze rules of comparability. The issues involved in the determination of comparability include measurement, the sampling of social systems and of units within systems, and the nature of theoretical statements. For thorough and excellent discussions of factors that affect the comparability of data from multiple social systems, see Straus (1969), Przeworski and Teune (1970), and Zelditch (1971), among others. Some of these issues are discussed, in introductory fashion, in Lee (1982, pp. 17–47).

[2]According to these criteria, comparisons between communities or subcultures (such as ethnic groups) within single societies do not constitute comparative sociology as we have defined it. This is, however, more a matter of semantics than of theoretical or methodological principles. The logic and method of comparative research may certainly be applied to such comparisons, as long as the units to be compared are of the same level of complexity or abstraction (Zelditch, 1971).

and systematically applied in each instance of comparative inquiry.

Comparative sociology analyzes variation in the properties of social systems. It therefore requires for its conduct that observations be made on at least two social systems, so that these observations may be compared. However, the systems themselves are not the objects of these comparisons; the focus of interest is instead the *properties* of the systems. There is some descriptive value in the observation that Trobriand Islanders practice polygynous marriage whereas the English do not. On the other hand, there is no *explanatory* value in such an observation. The primary objective of comparative research is explanation: How and why do the properties of social systems affect human behavior? Knowing which societies practice polygyny is not explanation, although it is an important first step in the explanatory process. The next step involves the identification of systematic properties that distinguish societies practicing polygyny from societies that do not practice polygyny: that is, a search for the system-level correlates of polygynous marriage customs. This search, to be effective, must be guided by a good theory. This theory must inform all phases of the research process: the selection of social systems for comparison, the selection and measurement of critical variables, and the mode of data analysis (see Lee 1982, pp. 17–47).

The point of this discussion has been phrased most succinctly by Przeworski and Teune (1970), who argued that "the goal of comparative research is to substitute the names of variables for the names of social systems" (p. 8). Their message is that it is not enough to know that two or more identifiable social systems differ on some criterion (dependent) variable. We wish to know *why* such a difference occurs. The pursuit of this issue involves the identification of other differences between the systems, which are empirically coincident with the difference in question and logically or theoretically connected to that difference. To determine why systems differ on one property, we must determine whether they differ on other properties, and how these differences are causally or logically interrelated. The focus, then, is on the properties that vary across systems, not on the systems themselves.

A comparison I have previously employed (Lee, 1982, p. 14) may help to illustrate this point. Consider the following generalizations derived from Rodman (1967, 1972):

1. The relationship between a husband's socioeconomic status and his marital power is positive in the United States and France but is negative in Greece and Yugoslavia.
2. The relationship between a husband's socioeconomic status and his marital power is positive where cultural norms are relatively egalitarian but is negative where the norms are more patriarchal.

The first of these statements is an empirical generalization, reporting an apparent fact about differences between

social systems. The second statement is a theoretical (explanatory) generalization, which may explain the fact contained in the first statement. Statement 1 typifies the data base from which the comparative sociologist works; it is a "thing to be explained." Statement 2 exemplifies the kind of product that may result from comparative sociology: a statement that one property of social systems affects other properties of those systems—or the behavior of individuals within those systems—in ways that may be logically apprehended and thus understood.

Many methodological difficulties beset comparative research and hinder the development and testing of social theory. This is not, however, the place for an examination of comparative methods. The methodological principles governing sampling, measurement, and data analysis are the same in comparative social inquiry as in any other form of research, but for a great variety of reasons, these principles are more difficult to implement and ideal solutions are more difficult to realize. Nonetheless, comparative research is the only means by which the properties of social systems—and the effects of these properties on human behavior—can be examined and analyzed.

We will now proceed with an attempt to synthesize some of the existing knowledge regarding family structure and interaction that has been generated by comparative social research. We begin with an examination of family structure. This term, as employed here, is intended to refer to the composition of the residential family group in terms of structural positions. The question at issue involves the kinds of persons, in kinship terms, who typically comprise the family unit.

Family Structure

Industrialization and the Conjugal Family

A major focus of comparative family research since its inception has been cross-systemic and chronological variation in family structure. The fact that the modern American family system is different from the systems prevalent at other times and places is common knowledge—perhaps too common, as popular stereotypes tend to exaggerate and overgeneralize the actual differences. Comparative research has been productively employed to document these changes and differences and, more important, to attempt to explain them. Questions about differences between cultures in family organization are distinctively comparative questions and therefore cannot be addressed without comparative data.

The family system of the contemporary United States constitutes a very clear empirical example of a nuclear family system. A nuclear family consists of three and only three social positions: husband-father, wife-mother, and offspring-sibling (a fancy word for children). There may be more than one incumbent of any of these three positions, but a family is defined as nuclear for our purposes as long as it contains no positions other than these three (Lee, 1982; Murdock, 1949). Thus, a family that includes one husband, two wives, and seven children is nuclear; the two wives make the *marriage* polygynous, but the *family* remains nuclear. A family containing a husband, a wife, one child, and a mother-in-law is not nuclear, however, as the latter position is not one of the three nuclear positions. Family structure is thus not the same thing as family size, although, on the average, nuclear families are usually smaller than others.

Although more complex families do, of course, appear in the United States, particularly among the poor and among ethnic minorities (Adams, 1970; Allen, 1979; Lee, 1980; Stack, 1974), our family system is clearly nuclear in both statistical and normative terms. Winch (1977, pp. 19–20) estimated that only about 2% of all families in the United States are nonnuclear, and that no more than 4% of all persons who reside in families are nonnuclear kin (see also Kobrin, 1976).

Any family that contains more than the three nuclear positions is termed *extended*. There is an almost infinite number of possible kinds of extended families. For purposes of categorization, however, three types delineated by Murdock (1949) subsume most of the empirically extant family systems. In order of increasing complexity, these are the stem family, the lineal family, and the fully extended family. The stem family occurs when one child, and only one child, remains a member of his or her parents' family after marriage, bringing his or her spouse to this home and raising children as members of this family. The stem family has been fairly common in many rural areas of Europe (see Arensberg & Kimball, 1940; Berkner, 1972). The lineal family occurs when all the children of one sex remain in their parents' home after marriage. The Indian joint family (Gore, 1965) is a variation of the lineal family theme; here, it is typical for brothers to break up and form their own families following the death of their father. If they remained together, the result would be a fully extended family system, which consists of two or more related nuclear families in each of at least two adjacent generations. Thus, if two brothers remained together, and if their sons each married and brought their wives to live in their fathers' household, we would have a (patrilineal) fully extended family. Such a family system was the cultural ideal of traditional China (Lang, 1946; Levy, 1949), although it is likely that relatively few families were actually able to attain such complexity, for reasons that we will discuss below.

A central theme in both comparative and historical research and theory on family structure is that increasing societal complexity or differentiation is associated with decreasing family structural complexity. In other words, according to this position, modern industrial societies such as the United States are typified by nuclear family systems, whereas extended family systems characterize at least some nonindustrial societies. Although Laslett (1976) and many others have correctly warned against overly simplistic comparisons of "before" and "after" the Industrial Revolution, this logic also implies change in family structure coinciding, at least loosely, with the advent of industry.

The idea that economic or technological complexity and family structural complexity are inversely related is by no means new. Social scientists in the nineteenth century used the presumed transition from extended to nuclear family systems as an indicator of modernization, a tradition that was continued into the twentieth century by scholars such as Ogburn (1922), Parsons (1943), Wirth (1938), and Zimmerman (1947). There are many systematic attempts to explain this trend (see, for example, Mogey, 1964; Winch, 1979; Zelditch, 1964), but the most explicitly stated and thoroughly documented analysis of family structural change is undoubtedly Goode's *World Revolution and Family Patterns* (1963). As Goode's logic is, in general terms, quite representative of the sociological tradition in this area of inquiry, we will examine his theory in some detail (see also Lee, 1982, pp. 107–140).

Goode's analysis shows that, as industrialization proceeds, family systems throughout the world are moving toward a "conjugal" family model. By this term, Goode meant a family structure that is nuclear, and that also possesses certain other distinctive characteristics. These include a bilateral mode of reckoning kinship and the consequent absence of unilineal kin groups, relatively free or autonomous mate-selection practices, the absence of the bride price or dowry, and a fairly egalitarian family authority structure in terms of both husband–wife and parent–child relations (Goode, 1963, pp. 7–10; 1964, pp. 51–52). Although different systems may be converging on the conjugal family model from different directions, the system it is supplanting is usually a more extended, more structurally complex family. Goode provided evidence of the trend toward the conjugal family from virtually all areas of the world. Although Goode recognized that there are many causes of this trend and that it is ultimately impossible to separate cause from effect, his central premise is that the movement toward the conjugal family may be attributed in large part to the forces of industrialization, although he stipulated that causal priority cannot be unequivocally assigned to either variable. His logic may be summarized by four related points (see also Lee, 1982, pp. 114–119).

First, an industrial economy requires geographic mobility. People must move with some frequency to obtain jobs, promotions or advancements, and even the training required for their occupations. Thus, their dependents must also be mobile. Extended families, of course, tend to be large and thus cumbersome to move. But in addition, a family containing several employable adults must reconcile the income needs of the family with the occupational skills and needs of each employable member. The geographic mobility necessary for the occupational placement or advancement of one member may be antithetical to the same needs of other members. This conflict is currently a great source of difficulty even for the increasing number of two-career families in the United States, but the nuclear family structure, containing no more than two workers, is much more compatible with the geographic mobility frequently required by an industrial economic and occupational system than an extended family structure would be.

Second, industry also produces and requires social mobility. As industry expands, it creates a demand for more professional, managerial, and administrative workers, thus creating opportunities for upward mobility. Thus, parents and their grown children often have markedly different socioeconomic characteristics, pursue quite different occupations, and have correspondingly different lifestyles, attitudes, values, and interests. Such differences may make extended family living less attractive, if not less possible. These generational or cohort differences increase the value of generational independence, at least in living arrangements, compared to situations where children inherit occupations or other sources of livelihood directly from their parents, as is often the case in agricultural societies.

Third, the high rate of social mobility is related to another feature of the industrial occupational system: positions in such systems are "achieved" rather than "ascribed"; that is, positions in the occupational system tend to be allocated to individuals according to training, experience, and other objective qualifications that they possess rather than according to family or kin group membership. The resources possessed by a family are far from irrelevant in determining the ultimate occupational placement of children, but in the normal case, although these resources assist and contribute to such placement, they do not ensure it. The ascription of occupation by birth is a virtual impossibility in industrial systems in light of the specialized knowledge, skills, and motivations required for the successful performance of many occupations. Because individuals must make their own way in the occupational world beyond a certain point, the instrumental importance of the family with regard to social placement is relatively low. Individuals are, in fact, rewarded for breaking loose from their families of orientation at some point, in order to participate with greater freedom in the mobility so frequently necessary for occupational success. Parents may instill in their children values conducive to higher education and may finance that education, but they cannot provide it. Nor do most people rely on inherited wealth for their livelihood. This situation contrasts greatly with that in sedentary agricultural societies, where a son's only hope of occupation in adulthood may be the inheritance of his father's farm or some fraction of it. This circumstance, as well as the absence of other opportunities, means that the son's self-interest is best served by remaining a member of his parents' family until he succeeds to the family headship. In brief, occupational systems based on achievement encourage children to break away from their parents in early adulthood, whereas those based on ascription encourage the younger generation to bond itself to the elder, which controls resources and dispenses them according to kinship.

Fourth, industrialization inevitably brings with it a concomitant increase in specialization and functional differentiation of the social structure. The most important aspect of this differentiation, which underlies the previous three points, is that work and family are separated. That is, the family unit is not the unit of economic production in a fully industrial system, as it usually is in an agricultural economy, where families work the land and subsist on the direct product of their collective labor. The separation of work and family means that, as individuals attain adulthood, most must find a source of livelihood independent of their parents and the resources that their parents control. In conjunction with this change, specialized institutions for the provision of education, protection, decision making, health care, and religion emerge and develop. In nonindustrial societies, these functions are often fulfilled by the family, but this is not possible in complex systems. As functional differentiation proceeds, it becomes increasingly possible for individuals to survive without being family members, as more and more of their needs are satisfied by nonfamily agencies. This situation facilitates the minimization of bonds between the generations, reduces the dependence of young adults on their elders, and thus promotes a conjugal rather than an extended family system.

For these reasons, then, societies with industrial economies should evince conjugal family systems, whereas nonindustrial societies may be typified by extended family systems. However, several kinds of data have been marshaled against this theory. These data are of three related, but somewhat distinct, types: (1) evidence that kinship relations are strong, viable, and important in many industrial societies, including the United States; (2) historical evidence to the effect that, in currently industrial or industrializing societies, no change in family structure has occurred in conjunction with industrialization; and (3) evidence that conjugal, or at least nuclear, family systems occur in many nonindustrial societies. Each of these objections to the theory is worthy of a fairly detailed examination.

Kinship in Industrial Societies

Much of family sociology in the 1950s and 1960s was concerned with the issue of the "isolated nuclear family." This phrase was coined by Parsons (1943), but the general idea, as noted above, was not original with him. Its implication is that the American nuclear family is isolated spatially, economically, and interactionally from nonnuclear kin. Parsons's logical and empirical basis for this assertion was similar to—and was, in fact, an intellectual precursor of—Goode's position; Parsons located the causes of nuclear family isolation primarily in the realms of industrialization and urbanization (see also Wirth, 1938).

For the next several decades, research concentrated heavily on the question of whether the American nuclear family was "really" isolated from kin (see Adams, 1968, 1970; Gibson, 1972; and Sussman, 1965 for reviews of these studies). Although some disagreement still exists (Gibson, 1972), most scholars answered the question in the negative: strong, viable ties between kin, including substantial mutual aid as well as social interaction, were quite consistently found even in the most industrialized and urbanized segments of the American population. Many observers thus concluded that, contrary to Goode's theory, industry does not result in the destruction of kinship ties.

Unfortunately, the debate over the isolated nuclear family was conducted in large part in a noncomparative context. Goode (1963)—and Parsons as well (see especially Parsons, 1965)—argued that industrialization coincided with changes in family and kinship structure, including an attenuation of kinship ties, but not that kinship ceases to exist or to be functionally significant in industrial societies. There are no absolute criteria of isolation from kin or of the strength of kin ties against which data from any single family system may be compared to determine whether the nuclear family is "really" isolated from kin (Lee, 1980; Lee & Cassidy, 1981). As the theory in question posits a relationship between type of family and type of economy, its merits cannot be empirically evaluated by data from industrial societies alone. Instead, we need evidence bearing on the hypothesis that conjugal family systems are more likely to coincide with industrial than with nonindustrial economic systems. Such evidence is necessarily comparative in nature.

Goode (1963) made it perfectly clear that the attenuation of kin ties in the conjugal family is a relative attenuation:

The most important characteristic of the ideal typical construction of the conjugal family is the relative exclusion of a wide range of affinal and blood relatives from its everyday affairs: There is no great extension of the kin network. (p. 8; emphases added)

This situation is contrasted with that in societies with extended family systems and multifunctional kin groups: "Neolocality and the relative freedom from control by an extended kin network prevent the maintenance or formation of a powerful lineage system" (p. 9).

The conjugal family system, then, implies not the absence of ties between related nuclear families, but only that these ties are less strong and less significant than is the case in societies with consanguineous (extended) family systems and organized kin groups or lineages. Thus, evidence to the effect that kinship relations exist, or that they perform certain functions in industrial societies with conjugal family systems, does not bear directly on the issue.

Historical Trends in Family Structure

Evidence regarding change over time in family systems and structures is much more germane to this issue than synchronic data proving the existence of kin ties in industrial societies. However, its relevance also needs to be thoroughly and carefully assessed.

Goode's theory (1963) does imply that family systems change in the conjugal direction over time, as urbanization and industrialization proceed. If the emergence of the conjugal family is a direct consequence of these processes, then the family systems of the United States and of other currently industrialized societies should now conform more closely to the conjugal model than they did before, or earlier in the progress of, industrialization. Recent methodological developments in sociohistorical research have resulted in data that bear on this question. In addition, relevant observations have been made in a number of societies that are currently industrializing.

There are quite a few studies that show that, under certain conditions at least, the industrialization process affects family structure more or less as the theory says it should. Roy (1974) and Ramu (1972, 1974) have both shown that industrialization, particularly insofar as it entails spatial mobility in pursuit of employment, decreases the frequency of extended family households in India, and Conklin (1977) found that Indian urbanites were more likely than rural dwellers to hold attitudes favorable to the conjugal, as opposed to the joint, family.[3] Wong (1975) documented a clear connection between stages of industrialization and a progression from "broken extended" to stem to small nuclear family structure for Hong Kong. Petersen (1969) demonstrated that Egyptian married couples have stronger kin networks than do Americans, although because of problems of comparability, she warned against overenthusiatic conclusions. Shanas (1973) reported substantially higher rates of the coresidence of aging parents and their adult children for the more agricultural, less industrialized societies of Poland and Yugoslavia than for Britain, Denmark, or the United States. Many other studies have come to similar conclusions. However, many studies have also discovered patterns that appear to contradict the theory.

A great deal of historical information on the United States, England, France, and other societies indicates that extended family households were quite uncommon—and perhaps even less common than they are today—before the Industrial Revolution (Anderson, 1973; Demos, 1970; Furstenberg, 1966; B. Laslett, 1975, 1977; P. Laslett, 1969, 1971, 1973, 1977; Laslett & Wall, 1972; Netting, 1979; Parish & Schwartz, 1972; Ramos, 1978; E. Smith, 1978). Anderson (1973), in fact, found a higher frequency of extended family households in an English city during the most intense period of industrialization

---

[3]The astute reader will note that these studies are not comparative according to the definition given earlier in this chapter and may wonder why they are mentioned in connection with an issue that can be addressed only in a comparative context. The reason is that these studies bear directly on hypotheses derivable from Goode's theory. If geographic mobility and urbanization, both of which are correlates of industrialization, are related to family structure in ways consistent with this theory, the theory becomes more credible. Furthermore, historical studies may be used for comparative purposes (that is, assessing the effects of systemic properties on one another and on human behavior) if the properties of the social system under investigation vary sufficiently over the time period considered by the study (see Lee, 1982).

than in either a comparable rural sample or a broader sample of England for the previous two centuries. These findings correspond with those of several studies of contemporarily industrializing societies, which have often reported greater frequencies of extended families in urban-industrial areas than in rural regions (Burch, 1967; Chu, 1974; Conklin, 1974, 1976; Khatri, 1975; Paydarfar, 1975; Stinner, 1977, 1979).

Such findings would appear to contradict directly the theory that we are evaluating. If industrialization causes the nuclear family, how can the extended family be more prevalent during the industrialization process than before it? If urbanization is also part of the causal process, why do we often find higher proportions of extended families in the cities than in the countryside, particularly in developing nations? Do such empirical findings warrant the rejection of the theory?

Although the last question is undeniably debatable, the most defensible position at this point is that these data do not disprove the theory, although they do suggest or require several modifications in it. This is the case for a variety of reasons, which have to do with the nature of the data as well as with the nature of the theory.

Statistical data on the prevalence of extended families in preindustrial times and cultures must be employed with great caution in the evaluation of this theory. One qualification of the use of such data revolves around a necessary distinction between the cultural and structural dimensions of social systems. By *culture,* in this case, I mean collectively shared, ideational representations of social structure. This is similar to Parsons' usage of the term when he referred to "the basic cultural orientations as systems of ideas or beliefs, systems of expressive symbols, and systems of value-orientation" (Parsons, Shils, Allport, Kluckhohn, Murray, Sears, Sheldon, Stouffer, & Tolman, 1951, p. 21).[4] The concept of culture directs attention to norms (behavioral expectations) and values (desired goals or outcomes) that are held more-or-less uniformly or collectively by the members of the society. It is perfectly possible for a society to be characterized by an extended family system on the cultural level, yet to evince very low statistical frequencies of extended families. In fact, many scholars contend that the majority of families in any society are and always have been nuclear, regardless of the cultural elements favoring extended families.

For example, Levy (1965) and others have shown that, under the medical and nutritional conditions that prevail

in most nonindustrial societies, it is most unlikely that a high proportion of families will be extended at any given time, regardless of cultural norms. Life expectancies under such conditions are almost invariably quite low; the life spans of grandparents and grandchildren rarely overlap. Under these conditions, few families can be generationally extended (that is, to contain three or more generations) because usually only two generations are alive simultaneously. Thus, the culture may stipulate that families should be extended or that the multigenerational household is the preferred or ideal form of family living, but this ideal may be attainable by only a few families or under rare circumstances, and then only for short periods of time. Ring (1979), for example, found that only about 5% of all households in a ninth-century Italian village contained extended families. However, by using reasonable assumptions about life expectancies, infant mortality, age at marriage, and other demographic factors, he determined that only about 5.5% of all households could possibly have contained extended families. Ring therefore concluded that some form of the extended family was indeed normative in this village in spite of its infrequent occurrence.

Levy's major point (1965) is that cross-systemic variation in actual family structure is likely to be much less than cross-systemic variation in ideal or normative family structure. This is true primarily because societies in which some form of extended family is culturally prescribed or favored tend to have relatively low life expectancies. Thus, Levy argued that most families in all societies are nuclear, by default if not by design. Burch (1967) found support for this position in a cross-societal analysis of census data, although he still observed some fairly substantial differences in certain measures of family structure. The United States, for example, had an average of 0.19 nonnuclear kin per household, whereas the average for India was over six times as high (1.2).

Because of the demographic factors specified by Levy and others, it is undoubtedly the case that changes in cultural systems with respect to family structure are much more marked than changes in actual family structures as given by census data. The existence of an extended family *system* does not imply that a statistical majority of all families are in fact extended, particularly at any one point in time.

If most families are indeed nuclear regardless of the nature of the family system, does it matter whether the system is nuclear or extended? The answer here is definitely in the affirmative. Cultural norms regarding family structure exert strong influences on authority patterns, inheritance rights, family roles and role relationships, the potential for industrialization, rural-to-urban migration, and many other aspects of social structure (see, for example, Goode, 1963; Habakkuk, 1955; Lee, 1982; Levy, 1955; Winch, 1977). Recent cross-cultural research has shown positive relationships between family structural complexity, measured on the systemic level, and such diverse variables as the status of the elderly (Lee & Kezis,

[4]This definition is similar to the anthropological rendition of cultures as systems of shared meanings (see, for example, Geertz, 1973, p. 5) but differs from other anthropological definitions, such as Kluckhohn's conception of culture as "the total way of life of a people" (1949, p. 17). The latter definition is congenial to the objectives of ethnography, which involves comprehensive descriptions of cultures, but it has little explanatory utility because its inclusiveness allows any behavior pattern to be attributed to culture, making all "cultural explanations" tautological.

1979) and parental control over mate selection (Lee & Stone, 1980). Thus, the fact that historicodemographic research does not invariably show clear changes in the statistical frequency of extended families coinciding with indicators of industrialization does not mean that no change has occurred. Demographic factors may, in many instances, prevent cultural changes from being unambiguously reflected by statistical realities, but the cultural change is real and significant in itself.

There are other reasons that cultural and statistical representations of family structure may correspond rather poorly. Berkner's analysis of family structure in rural Austria during the eighteenth century (1972) shows quite conclusively that the patrilineal stem family was normative; however, only about one quarter of all families in the 1763 census contained any nonnuclear kin.[5] But Berkner pointed out that families in a stem-family system are actually extended (in terms of household composition) for only a very small portion of the family life cycle: the period between the marriage of the inheriting son and the death of the parents. The length of this period is obviously decreased by late marriage and low life expectancies, both of which were characteristic of rural Austrian society at this time. Also, of course, virtually all noninheriting children in stem-family systems form nuclear families when they marry, as only one son and his spouse (in the patrilineal case) remain with the parents. But, unless the death of the parents precedes the inheriting son's marriage, almost all families will pass through a period of extended family living, however brief, during the course of the family life cycle. Stem- and nuclear-family systems may therefore be virtually indistinguishable by census data, but the differences between them are nonetheless real.

It is also important to note here that the theory relating industrialization and the conjugal family, as proposed by Goode (1963) and others, does not imply that families will be extended, on either the cultural or the individual family level, whenever industrialization is not present. Many scholars (Berkner, 1972, 1973, 1977; Berkner & Shaffer, 1978; Goubert, 1977; Kertzer, 1977; Mitterauer & Seider, 1979; Parish & Schwartz, 1972), have shown that extended families have predominated at various times and in various places in European history, but only under certain conditions. The conditions facilitating extended family systems are perhaps less numerous—and less frequent in occurrence—than those facilitating the

nuclear family. They will be discussed more intensively below; however, they have been summarized by Berkner and Shaffer (1978) as consisting of an agricultural economy with relatively large family landholdings, together with some restrictions (*de facto* or *de jure*) on families' rights to subdivide their lands at points of inheritance. Goode's point (1963) is that conjugal family systems tend to appear in conjunction with industrial economies; if this is true, it does not mean that extended families should prevail whenever the economy is other than industrial.

In fact, a more thorough analysis of Goode's logic shows that he did not identify industrialization as the *immediate* cause of the conjugal family system. As we noted above, he stipulated four consequences of industrialization that are, in their turn, causes of the conjugal family. These are (1) high rates of geographic mobility; (2) high rates of social mobility; (3) a relatively minimal role of the family in occupational placement; and (4) a high degree of functional differentiation in the social structure. The effect of industrialization on family structure is thus indirect, and the four factors act as intervening variables that impact family structure more directly.[6] Industrialization, however, is not the only cause of these intervening variables. It is thus quite possible for the proximate causes of the conjugal family system to occur without industrialization.

For example, high rates of geographic mobility can—and often do—occur in nonindustrial societies. Hunting-and-gathering peoples are almost necessarily nomadic. The early American colonists were migratory by definition: Had they not migrated from Europe they would not have been colonists. And the westward expansion that typified the United States for the better part of two centuries was antithetical to extended families, even though it was not a consequence of industrialization. It is not surprising that the United States has never been characterized by extended families. The reasons, furthermore, are consistent with Goode's theory rather than contrary to it.

A similar logic may account for the fact that a number of researchers (Anderson, 1973; Burch, 1967; Stinner, 1977, 1979) have found higher proportions of extended families in the urban-industrial areas of industrializing societies than in the rural regions. For none of these cases (Venezuela, nineteenth-century England, and the Philippines, respectively) do we have information to the effect that the conditions facilitating extended family households prevailed in the rural areas. Burch (1967) suggested that urban houses may be larger in Venezuela, and that it may be easier for related nuclear families to build separate dwellings in rural areas. It is also likely that the higher proportions of extended families in the cities of indus-

---

[5]Berkner (1975, 1977) also showed that measuring family structural complexity by computing the percentage of all households containing nonnuclear kin is not necessarily the best or most accurate method, and that it may understate the importance of extended familism. He pointed out, for example, that, in a sample of French peasant families in 1820, only one third of all households contained nonnuclear kin, but these households contained nearly 55% of all married couples and widowed persons (Berkner, 1977, p. 162).

[6]See Winch (1979) for an example of a similar, but more explicitly stated, logical system that employs a somewhat different and more extensive set of intervening variables.

trializing societies are attributable to the rapidity of rural-to-urban migration, a shortage of housing in the cities, and the typically low industrial wages that make sharing a home and sharing other tasks, such as child care, economically advantageous (Lee, 1982). But the urban extended family may well be a temporary adaptation to such exigencies.

Handwerker (1973) found, among the Bassa of Monrovia, that there was no clear trend toward a nuclear family structure among recent urban migrants. However, those with higher incomes were much more likely to form nuclear families, whereas extended families prevailed among the economically marginal migrants. Handwerker thus hypothesized that, as urban economic conditions improve, nuclear families become the norm in the city. As we noted earlier, extended family living offers the opportunity to share resources for minorities and other economically disadvantaged groups even in the contemporary United States (see Adams, 1970; Lee, 1980; Stack, 1974). This advantage may be of even greater importance in times of rapid industrialization and urban migration. We also know that, at least in the United States, rural-to-urban migrants have a tendency to move toward kin (Hendrix, 1975a). But the extended families resulting from this process tend to be transitory and are, in all likelihood, replaced by nuclear families as industrialization progresses and prosperity increases. As Gordon (1973) concluded, "Family life during the beginnings of industrialization may, then, represent a distinctive transitional stage, rather than a full-blown picture of later patterns" (p. 59).

To summarize, a considerable amount of historical evidence shows that, in many parts of the world, no great reduction in the proportion of extended family households occurred in conjunction with industrialization. These findings have often been employed as counterevidence to the theory that industrialization is causally related to the conjugal family system. But the theory is not necessarily disproved by such data, for at least four reasons: (1) Life expectancies are quite low in most societies with extended family systems, limiting the frequency with which such families can occur empirically even though they may be culturally normative. (2) In many types of extended family systems, such as the stem family, the family is actually extended for only a small fraction of its life cycle; therefore, only a small proportion of all families are extended at any single point in time. (3) The baselines chosen for comparison with industrial systems (rural areas and/or preindustrial times) may be inappropriate for testing this theory, if they are not characterized by the conditions that facilitate extended families. And (4) the proximate causes of nuclear (if not conjugal) family systems, as specified by the unabridged theory, may occur under conditions other than industrialization.

The latter two points may be clarified by a more detailed discussion of a third objection to Goode's theory (1963). This objection is based on evidence to the effect

that nuclear family systems—on the cultural as well as the statistical level—occur frequently in many types of nonindustrial societies.

Family Systems in Nonindustrial Societies

Goode's (1963) theory has frequently been interpreted as stating that an inverse relationship exists between family structural complexity and "societal complexity" (Blumberg & Winch, 1972; Lee, 1982; Marsh, 1967), That is, as societies become progressively more complex, families become structurally simplified: Extended family systems give way to nuclear family systems. Such an interpretation has frequently found empirical support. Osmond (1969), for example, found that the "general" family (including fully extended systems along with any type involving frequent polygyny) occurs most frequently in societies with only rudimentary agricultural technologies and simple stratification systems, whereas the "limited" family type (nuclear, stem, or lineal) is more common in societies with more complex agricultural and stratification systems.

Osmond's categorization scheme, however, is not precisely comparable to Goode's. It also confounds family structure with marital structure (see Lee, 1982). Furthermore, Osmond's and Goode's findings both appear to contradict the results of an earlier study by Nimkoff and Middleton (1960), who demonstrated the existence of a clear *positive* relationship between societal complexity and familial complexity.

Nimkoff and Middleton (1960) employed the World Ethnographic Sample, a precursor of the Ethnographic Atlas (Murdock, 1967), which contained ethnographic data on over five hundred nonindustrial cultures. Their primary measure of societal complexity was type of economy, which ranged in this sample from hunting and gathering at the "low" end to intensive or sedentary agriculture combined with animal husbandry at the "high" pole of the continuum. They classified family systems as "independent" (nuclear) or "extended" (stem, lineal, or fully extended). Their findings showed that extended families were more common among agricultural societies, and that nuclear systems were more prevalent among hunters and gatherers.

It should be apparent by now that these findings do not contradict Goode's conclusion (1963) at all; rather, they complement it (see also Lee, 1982, pp. 119–124). Both studies show that extended family systems are most likely to occur in sedentary agricultural societies and are less likely in other types of economies; the studies simply arrive at this conclusion from different directions. Nimkoff and Middleton (1960) showed that nuclear family systems are more common in societies where agriculture has not been highly developed, whereas Goode (1963) showed that the conjugal family type (which includes the nuclear structure) is more prevalent among economic systems that have progressed beyond the agricultural stage in the direction of industry. As we noted above, the range of conditions under which extended family systems are likely to occur is limited, and an important limitation in this regard is an economy based on some form of agriculture. What we really need to explain is why extended family systems tend to coincide with agricultural economies.

Nimkoff and Middleton (1960) offered a sound basis for this explanation in their examination of the differences between hunting-and-gathering and agricultural societies. They made three key points:

First, hunting-and-gathering technologies typically do not produce food supplies of sufficient size and stability to permit large concentrations of people to subsist in any one place for a significant period of time. Agriculture not only allows such large concentrations but, within certain limits, requires them for maximum efficiency. Nonmechanized agriculture or horticulture is labor-intensive; that is, per capita production increases with an increase in the size of the labor force, again within limits (Boserup, 1970; Lee, 1982). Thus, small nuclear families are better adapted to exploitative technologies, whereas extended families can provide the larger and more differentiated work groups appropriate for agriculture.

Second, the basis of agricultural wealth is property. Land is owned or possessed by a group, usually a family. It is to the advantage of the junior generation to stay on the family lands, to ultimately inherit that land, and to earn their living from it as adults. Thus, children, or at least some of the children, need to retain membership in their parents' families after adulthood and marriage. This residential compounding of adult generations is what makes families extended. No such processes operate in hunting-and-gathering economies, however, as "wealth" comes from individual labor and initiative rather than from property. In most cases, children are wise to separate themselves from their parents once they reach adulthood, as their continued presence would not increase the group's ability to exploit resources and would, in fact, accelerate the use of these resources. Parents have little or no real (immovable) property to pass on to their children, so residential separation of the generations maximizes the efficient exploitation of the land.

Third, geographic mobility is a virtue and a necessity for most hunters and gatherers, but an impossibility for most agriculturalists. Farmers are tied to specific plots of land, but hunters must move in pursuit of game and gatherers must migrate when they use up the available vegetation in any single area. As in the case of industry, high rates of geographic mobility promote nuclear family systems, which are more mobile; because they are also smaller, they do not use up resources as rapidly. The parallel to the industrial case was clearly recognized by Nimkoff and Middleton (1960):

The modern industrial society, with its small independent family, is then like the simpler hunting and gathering society and, in part, apparently for some of the same reasons, namely, limited need for family labor and physical mobility. The hunter is mobile because he pursues the game; the industrial worker, the job. (p. 225)

The relationship between societal "complexity" and family structural complexity should thus be curvilinear, with the frequency of extended family systems reaching its peak among sedentary agricultural societies. This hypothesis was supported by Blumberg and Winch (1972), who employed data from the Ethnographic Atlas supplemented by information on industrial societies collected by Adelman and Morris (1967). Further examination and analysis of these data (Winch, 1977, 1979) show clearly that it is not societal "complexity" *per se*, but the specific subsistence base of the society, that influences family structure. It is intensive agriculture on permanent fields that is most strongly related to the prevalence of extended family systems; nuclear systems are more typical in both preagricultural and postagricultural economies. Clearly, the nuclear family structure is not a modern invention, and its causes or antecedents do not always involve industry. However, we are likely to find nuclear family systems where individuals must be mobile for economic reasons, where there is a premium on individual achievement and ability, where the individual rather than the family is the unit of labor, and where the primary source of wealth for most people is labor rather than real property. Nuclear *families* also occur with great frequency under almost all other conditions, but nuclear family *systems* are relatively unlikely to characterize societies with agricultural economies, sufficiently large family landholdings, and a rudimentary agricultural technology. Thus, the nuclear family system typifies both the simplest and the most complex technological systems. Extended family systems prevail at the cultural level where agriculture provides the means of subsistence, but even here, the statistical frequency of extended families is generally low if life expectancies are low and if family landholdings are small or unproductive.

Throughout this section, we have used Goode's theory (1963) linking the conjugal family with industrialization as a linchpin for discussion. However, we have concentrated on only one aspect of the conjugal family as Goode defined it: its nuclear structure. As noted earlier, the conjugal system is composed of nuclear families with several additional characteristics that, except for the relative minimization of kin ties, involve intrafamily relations: husband-wife and parent-child. In relating family structure to societal complexity, the term *nuclear* has been consistently employed because the theory does not imply that conjugal family systems exist in hunting-and-gathering societies. Nonetheless, there is substantial variation across social systems in the nature of marital and parent–child relations. We shall investigate certain aspects of this variation in the next two sections.

Marital Power

Goode (1963) and many others have contended that one characteristic that distinguishes the conjugal family system from other types is the relative egalitarianism of marital relations in the conjugal family. According to this logic, the process of modernization brings with it a movement away from the traditional, patriarchal norms that typify extended family systems and toward shared or joint decision-making patterns and greater overall equality between spouses. In Brickman's terms (1974), this process represents a shift from "fully structured" relationships, in which the norms completely specify authority patterns, to "partially structured" relationships, in which the power to make decisions is the subject of bargaining and negotiation between husband and wife (see also Scanzoni, 1979).

Marital power is one of the most difficult concepts to define and measure in the field of family sociology (Cromwell & Olson, 1975). For our purposes, we may employ McDonald's definition of power (1980) as "the ability of an individual in a social relationship to carry out his or her will, even in the face of resistance by others" (p. 842). Power is frequently measured, at the level of individual marriages, by asking which spouse usually makes decisions in a number of salient areas; this strategy was pioneered by Blood and Wolfe (1960). This method has a number of obvious shortcomings, not the least of which is that it fails to generate information on who decides who makes which decisions. That is, decisions in many areas may be left to wives because husbands have little or no interest in making these decisions or in their outcomes; the reverse situation, of course, is also possible, although probably less frequent. In spite of its inadequacies, however, the substantial majority of the available data on marital power, in both cross-national and intrasocietal research, has been obtained by measures such as this one.

The most prominent current theory of marital power, known as *resource theory,* emanated most directly from the work of Blood and Wolfe (1960; see also Wolfe, 1959) in the United States. These authors, employing data from a sample of married women in the Detroit vicinity, began their study of marital power by testing hypotheses derived from "normative theory." This theory takes as its premise the assumption that contemporary American culture is changing from patriarchal to egalitarian with respect to marital relations. That is, traditional norms of male dominance are, under the pressures of urbanization and industrialization, giving way to norms favoring equality between spouses in family decision-making. There is, incidentally, little doubt that this process has occurred on the cultural level during the twentieth century (see, among others, Brown, 1978; Scanzoni, 1979). Blood and Wolfe thus hypothesized that husband dominance should be most frequent among the most "traditional" categories of the population: farm families, immigrants, Catholics, the elderly, and the less educated. These hypotheses, however, were not supported (Blood & Wolfe, 1960, pp. 24–29).

Blood and Wolfe (1960) went on to develop alternative hypotheses derived from what they initially termed "pragmatic theory," based on the premise that "the power to make decisions stems primarily from the re-sources which the individual can provide to meet the needs of his marriage partner and to upgrade his decision-making skills" (p. 44). In other words, the decision-making power of each spouse should vary directly with the resources provided by that spouse. A resource is something that gives an actor the ability to reward (or punish) another actor (Emerson, 1976; Scanzoni, 1979). Resources thus include tangible socioeconomic factors such as the education, the occupational status, and the income of each spouse, which may be used to the material advantage of the married couple, as well as less tangible skills and competencies developed by community participation, organizational memberships, and so on. The greater the number of resources possessed by a spouse, and the greater the value of those resources to the other spouse, the greater the power of the first spouse should be. Hypotheses derived from this theory were generally supported by Blood and Wolfe's data (1960) and by many subsequent studies in the United States (for one example, see Centers, Raven, & Rodriguez, 1971).

In the years since the original publication of this theory, most research has concentrated on the effects of socioeconomic and material resources on conjugal power. The results of this research, particularly that done in the United States and other Western societies, have usually supported resource theory, although relationships between resources and conjugal power have often been found to be fairly modest (for reviews of these studies, see Burr, 1973; Cromwell & Olson, 1975; Lee, 1982; Rodman, 1972; Scanzoni, 1979). The general conclusion has been that the power to make decisions in families is subject to bargaining and negotiation between spouses, that the resources possessed by each spouse provide "leverage" in the exchange relationship, and that each spouse's level of resources positively affects that spouse's power.[7]

However, several tests of resource theory in non-Western societies have discovered interesting reversals of the predictions of resource theory involving the effects of husbands' resources. Studies in Greece (Safilios-Rothschild, 1976) and Yugoslavia (Buric & Zecevic, 1967) specifically found that the relationships between socioeconomic resources and marital authority for husbands were negative; that is, high-status husbands had lower conjugal power scores than low-status husbands. Similar findings were subsequently reported for Japan by Blood (1967) and for Turkey by Fox (1973).

Blood's results (1967) caused him to conclude that the "resource theory of marital power must be limited in its application to modern, emancipated social conditions" (pp. 168–169). Rodman (1967, 1972), however, went

[7]In this form, resource theory is a specific application of the more general exchange theory to the issue of marital power. Exchange theory, as explicated by authors such as Ekeh (1974) and Emerson (1976), is much more complex and powerful than the simplified version of resource theory presented here. For a more thorough treatment of resource theory and its relationship to exchange theory, see Scanzoni (1979).

further in his attempt to reconcile these findings with the theory of resources. He distinguished sharply between marital power on the behavioral level (as measured, however imperfectly, by decision-making indices) and cultural norms and values regarding relationships between the sexes in general and spouses in particular. Blood and Wolfe (1960), as we noted above, found no support for hypotheses about marital power drawn from "normative theory." Rodman (1967, 1972), however, argued that cultural norms do influence marital power, but in indirect fashion under many circumstances. Rodman's contribution is known as the *theory of resources in cultural context*.

Rodman (1972) conceptualized four categories of cultural or normative systems, including patriarchy, modified patriarchy, transitional egalitarianism, and egalitarianism. Under the fully patriarchal and fully egalitarian conditions, Rodman argued, the norms are so strong and clear that there is little variation between marriages in power structure; the strong norms suppress this variation, thereby also suppressing any effects of structural variables, such as resources, on actual power. In consequence, resource theory (or any other theory of power implicating structural variables) is not applicable.

In transitional egalitarian societies such as the United States, Rodman contended, the norms are becoming egalitarian but are not sufficiently unequivocal to ensure that all marriages will, in fact, be egalitarian. This situation of normative ambiguity leaves other factors, such as resources, free to operate. Conjugal power is a matter of negotiation because there is no "spontaneous consensus" (Fox, 1974; Scanzoni, 1979) that the husband's interests should predominate. When power is negotiable, resources become relevant in the manner described by resource theory, and they correlate positively with power in marriage.

In modified patriarchal societies, however, the predictions of resource theory do not hold; with regard to the husband's resources, they are, in fact, reversed. These are the societies that are undergoing, for whatever reason, a change in the normative system away from strong traditional patriarchy. We know that, in virtually all instances of social change, new knowledge and ideas diffuse differentially through social structures, generally affecting the more privileged strata first. Thus, in modified patriarchal societies, the standard socioeconomic measures of resources (income, occupational status, and particularly education) actually measure the exposure of individuals to "modern" egalitarian norms. In Rodman's words (1972):

Greece and Yugoslavia would typify this kind of modified patriarchy, in which patriarchal norms are retained in the lower classes while "modern," equalitarian norms are adopted from the top down. . . . The lower-income man does not therefore suffer any loss of authority, and it is only the upper-income man, adopting more equalitarian marital patterns, who modifies the patriarchal tradition. (p. 64)

For modified patriarchal societies, then, the "theory of resources in cultural context" implies a positive correlation between resources and power for wives, but a negative correlation for husbands. Fox's data (1973) from Turkey give perhaps the clearest illustration of this process: The husband's power was found to decrease as the resources of both husbands and wives increased.

Some relatively recent research on cultures that might be defined as "modified patriarchal" has lent modest support to the theory of resources in cultural context (see, for example, Kim & Kim, 1977, for Korea, and Conklin, 1979, for India). Buehler, Weigert, and Thomas (1974) found that predictions based on resource theory were supported a bit more strongly for the more "modern"—and presumably more egalitarian—cultures in their five-society analysis; this finding supports Rodman's position, but rather weakly. Szinovacz (1978) observed weak positive relationships between family status and the husband's power for an Austrian sample, a finding that is consistent with resource theory if Austrian culture is defined as transitional egalitarian rather than modified patriarchal, which is probably more accurate.

There have also been studies that fail to support Rodman's theory. Burr, Ahern, and Knowles (1977) tested Rodman's predictions on a sample of American college students, measuring norms about marital power on the individual level rather than by cross-cultural comparison, and found no support. However, Rodman's hypotheses were not formulated on the individual level; there is no particular reason to expect that intracultural variation in individual beliefs should have the same effects as cross-cultural variation in normative systems. Kumagai (1979a,b; Kumagai & O'Donoghue, 1978) has reported that resources and conjugal power are not related in any systematic fashion in a Japanese sample, in slight contradiction to Blood (1967), who found a negative relationship for men. Kumagai argued that traditional sex-role distinctions in Japanese culture may give wives most of the authority in family decision-making; thus, traditional norms and increased resources for wives would both have the same effect if the theory of resources in cultural context were operative in Japan, so no differences in conjugal power according to level of resources would be expected.

Overall, then, empirical tests of the theory of resources in cultural context in transitional egalitarian and modified patriarchal cultures have been moderately supportive. There are indications, however, that the theory in its current form may be less applicable to traditional patriarchal and, possibly, fully egalitarian cultures. Rodman (1972) argued that, in cultural contexts in which the norms regarding the distribution of marital authority between spouses are very clear, these norms suppress variation in power across individual marriages and thus prevent structural factors such as resources from affecting power. In other words, in cultures with strong patriarchal normative systems, marital power structures are almost uniformly patriarchal, and in those with fully egalitarian cultures, marriages are egalitarian, regardless of spouses' resources. Resources and power are therefore uncorrelated under these two cultural conditions.

On the other hand, anthropologists studying patriarchal

cultures have for years employed a line of reasoning very similar to resource theory to explain many instances of the exercise of power by wives (see, for example, Bossen, 1975; Friedl, 1967; Riegelhaupt, 1967; Rogers, 1975). It is clear from studies such as these that women often exercise considerable power even in strongly patriarchal cultures, and that this exercise of power may be attributable to the possession or provision of economic resources by women (see Lee, 1982, pp. 224–231, for a summary). Boserup (1970) showed that the introduction of modern agricultural technology decreases women's role in economic production, and that this decreased productivity may eventuate in a loss of status and power for women. Employing data from the Ethnographic Atlas (Murdock, 1967), Murdock and Provost (1973) demonstrated that increments in technological complexity across cultures coincide with the shifting of many productive endeavors from the female to the male domain; thus, women are least involved in economic production in the most complex societies.[8] It may be that modernization influences cultural systems in the direction of greater status for women and sex-role equality, but on the behavioral level, it results in decreased power for women because it removes them, at least temporarily, from critical productive roles in the economic system. If women do lose power through this process, it is because their production of and control over resources decline. And if this line of reasoning is correct, then resources must influence conjugal power even in patriarchal cultures.

Among nonindustrial societies, we know that women contribute the most to subsistence, by their labor, in economic systems based on gathering or on rudimentary agriculture (Lee, 1979, p. 708; see also Aronoff & Crano, 1975; Winch, 1979). Data obtained from the Standard Cross-Cultural Sample (Murdock & White, 1969), together with original codes of marital power for these societies from the Human Relations Area Files, show a moderate positive relationship between wives' power in marriage and proportionate female contributions to subsistence (see Table 1). The 113 cultures in this sample are all nonindustrial and, with few exceptions, indisputably patriarchal at the normative level. Nonetheless, behavioral power structures do vary across these cultures, and this variation is related to variation in the relative contributions of resources by men and women, as resource theory would predict. Rodman's argument (1972) that resource theory does not apply to patriarchal cultures is not supported by these data. We should note, however, that the data in Table 1 pertain to variation *between* cultures, whereas Rodman's generalizations are directed toward variation *within* cultures. But in combination with the anthropological evidence cited above, we have considerable empirical documentation for the effectiveness

[8]The Ethnographic Atlas, of course, does not contain data on modern industrial societies. The most complex societies in this sample, in technological terms, are those with economies based on intensive agriculture, often with irrigation, and with complex (differentiated) craft specialization.

Table 1. Wives' Power in Marriage by Proportionate Female Contribution to Subsistence across Patriarchal Cultures (in Percentages)[a]

	Proportionate female contribution to subsistence		
Wives' power	<30%	30%–39%	≥40%
Low	50.0	30.4	24.1
Medium	33.3	43.5	44.4
High	16.7	26.1	31.5
Total	100.0	100.0	100.0
N	(36)	(23)	(54)
		Gamma = +.315	

[a]Source: Standard Cross-Cultural Sample (Murdock & White, 1969) and Human Relations Area Files. Estimates of wives' power were coded from the HRAF by five judges working independently; each culture was coded twice. The correlation (Pearsons's r) between the two coders' ratings for these 113 societies was +.854. Reprinted from Lee and Petersen, 1983, p. 31.

of resource theory in the explanation of marital power both across and within patriarchal cultural systems.

Several more extensive cross-cultural studies, however, have found little or no relationship between proportionate female contribution to subsistence and more general measures of the status of women. In a pilot study of 12 cultures, Sanday (1973) found women's status to be highest in the intermediate range of female subsistence contribution, and lower at either extreme. However, neither Whyte (1978) nor Blumberg (1978), both of whom employed larger samples, found any relationship whatsoever between these variables. Results such as these caused Osmond, in a major review article (1980), to conclude that ''we find no evidence that women's work in the subsistence economy increases their social status'' (p. 1003). After investigating relationships between many measures of the status of women and proportionate female contribution to subsistence, Whyte (1978) concluded that ''there now seem to be no grounds for assuming that the relative subsistence contribution of women has any general status implications'' (p. 169).

Blumberg (1978), however, did find that women's status (which she operationalized as ''life options'') is strongly related to women's ''economic control.'' The latter variable indexes women's control over the means of production, the extent to which women allocate surplus, and the rights of women to inherit and accumulate wealth (for a concise summary, see Osmond, 1980, pp. 1002–1003). Thus, women's role in economic production may indeed have a great deal to do with their status in society, although this relationship may be poorly reflected by simple measures such as their proportionate contribution to subsistence. It is also quite possible, in light of data such as those reported in Table 1, that the direct contribution of women to subsistence-producing activities may have more to do with their power in marriage than with their overall status in society. A high level of proportionate female contribution to subsistence for a given society may indicate that women are members of the laboring class, whereas men direct and supervise; however, within individual marriages, the more food a wife produces (proportional to her husband), the more her husband is dependent on her for his own subsistence and that of their family. Although they are undoubtedly connected, both conceptually and empirically, wives' power in marriage and the societal status of women are in many ways distinct phenomena and should be treated as separate variables in research and theory.[9]

The evidence discussed above suggests that, at the behavioral level, there is variation in marital power both across and within societies that are clearly patriarchal on the cultural (normative) level, and that this variation may be related to wives' resources. Thus, Rodman's assertion (1972) that resource theory is not applicable to patriarchal cultures may have been premature, although more and better evidence is certainly needed.

There is also some evidence, contrary to Rodman, to the effect that resource theory may have some utility in fully egalitarian cultures, although it is not clear that any society is yet characterized by such a normative system. Denmark, however, may come as close as any society. Kandel and Lesser (1972) found, for a sample of Danish women, that both relative education and wife's employment were positively related to conjugal power; however, neither income nor occupational status affected power in the manner predicted by resource theory. This support is quite equivocal, but it does not diverge widely from that provided by many studies conducted in the United States.

Furthermore, Scanzoni (1979) argued persuasively and correctly that egalitarian norms will not automatically result in uniformly egalitarian marriages. Instead, he contended that marital power becomes a matter of negotiation, bargaining, and conflict—that is, it becomes problematic—to the extent that norms do *not* clearly stipulate a hierarchial authority structure:

In short, it is utopian sentiment to assume, as some persons evidently do, that movement toward equalitarian role structures somehow signals the "end of power" as a viable theoretical and research interest. Quite the contrary—as power becomes more problematic, it shall become more significant and require more rigorous investigation. (pp. 305–306)

Therefore, we might expect that, when and if an egalitarian culture appears, resource theory will be no less effective in predicting and explaining marital power than it is in contemporary "transitional egalitarian" cultures.

[9]This decision to treat marital power and social status of women as separate phenomena is consistent with Whyte's finding (1978) that, across nonindustrial cultures, various indicators of the status of women are only slightly intercorrelated, if at all. Although Whyte employed no measure precisely comparable to our concept of marital power, his data and logic clearly suggest that wives' power may not be strongly related to other dimensions of the status of women. If this is true, then these variables may also have different correlates.

On the basis of the evidence currently available, one might conclude that resource theory is, without modification, moderately useful in explaining variation in conjugal power under all normative (cultural) conditions except what Rodman called "modified patriarchy." Even here, the predictions of resource theory (that resources and power are positively related) are generally supported for women. But there may be negative relationships between resources and conjugal power for men in modified patriarchal cultures because the diffusion of egalitarian ideals from "modern" societies is likely to affect men with greater resources (income, occupational status, and education) first.

Several points need to be made to conclude this section: First, neither resource theory nor the theory of resources in cultural context provides a sufficient explanation of the distribution of conjugal power. Even the studies that support these theories most strongly show that the substantial majority of the variation in power remains unexplained. Other theories, or extensions of these theories, are obviously necessary. One possibly fruitful strategy would be to expand the range of resources considered in empirical tests of resource theory beyond the range of socioeconomic factors, provided that measurement difficulties can be resolved and minimized. Safilios-Rothschild (1976), for example, showed that Waller's "principle of least interest" (Waller & Hill, 1951) may be applied to the analysis of conjugal power. For a Greek sample, Safilios-Rothschild found that the spouse rated lower on romantic (love) involvement tended to have the most decision-making power. Emotional independence can thus be defined and employed as a resource. We should not evaluate the utility of resource theory solely on the basis of studies that measure only tangible, economic resources.

Second, the effects of modernization and cultural change on the bases and distribution of marital power have probably been seriously overrated in recent research and theory. It is true, as we have noted, that norms have changed in many cultures from strongly patriarchal to relatively egalitarian. But the accumulated evidence does not allow us to conclude that wives actually have more power in egalitarian than in patriarchal cultures. In fact, if resources do affect power in patriarchal cultures, then women may well have less power in egalitarian cultures because, in many ways, they may control fewer resources as their role in economic production changes (Boserup, 1970). Furthermore, it does not appear to be the case that there is "spontaneous consensus" (Scanzoni, 1979) regarding the distribution of power between spouses in traditional patriarchal cultures: actual power structures may vary across societies regardless of the normative system, and power is thus the object of negotiation, bargaining, and exchange even when the norms prescribe male dominance. Modernization, then, may produce a change from patriarchal to egalitarian norms without necessarily causing a comparable change in the distribution of power at the behavioral level (see Conklin, 1979, for examples drawn from India).

Finally, in a related vein, cultural change may affect

the way in which power is distributed between spouses without changing the overall balance of power. For example, Kumagai (1979a) showed that, although Japanese and American wives have very comparable average total power scores, they arrive at these scores quite differently. In Japan, decision-making spheres are clearly divided into husband- and wife-dominated arenas, and each spouse makes autonomous decisions within his or her arenas. In the United States, however, most kinds of decisions are made jointly, without the degree of segregation evident in Japan (see also Szinovacz, 1978, for Austria). Modernization may therefore cause some trend toward "syncratic" rather than "autonomic" decision-making structures, and thus influence the way in which decisions are made, without causing dramatic changes in the overall balance of marital power.

This treatment of comparative research on marital power has been very superficial; we have avoided important issues of measurement, conceptualization, and theory that are necessary for a full understanding of the phenomenon. The point here, though, is that comparative research has facilitated the development of explanatory theory in this area far beyond what would have been possible had all research been conducted in one social system. Variation in cultural normative systems appears to be important in the explanation of conjugal power, but in subtle rather than obvious ways: the nature of the normative system influences relationships between other variables. Without comparative research, such variation cannot be taken into account, and explanations are necessarily incomplete.

Socialization

Comparative social research has, over the years, made substantial contributions to the development of explanatory theory with regard to the socialization of children. This research has been addressed to many specific topics in the area of socialization, but some of the most important contributions have occurred in the explanation of parental values. Much of the comparative research and theory hinge on the work of Melvin Kohn (1959, 1963, 1976, 1977; Kohn & Schooler, 1969). Although Kohn's empirical work was conducted in the United States, his ideas have spawned many attempts at replication in other societies (Coburn & Edwards, 1976; Pearlin, 1971) and have also been integrated with a number of anthropological and comparative theories of socialization values, leading to theoretical formulations of considerable generality (see Lee, 1982).

Kohn's specific focus has been the documentation and explanation of a relationship between social class and parental values in socialization. He and others have found that, in the United States and elsewhere, white-collar and blue-collar parents differ in their emphasis on the value of self-reliance relative to conformity in their children. In Kohn's words (1977),

The higher a person's social class position, the greater is the likelihood that he will value self-direction, both for his children

and for himself, and that his orientational system will be predicated on the belief that self-direction is both possible and efficacious. The lower a person's social class position, the greater the likelihood that he will value conformity to external authority and that he will believe in following the dictates of authority as the wisest, perhaps the only feasible, course of action. (p. xxvi)

Research in the United States has generally found modest positive relationships between socioeconomic status and the valuation of self-reliance, as well as modest negative relationships between socioeconomic status and the valuation of conformity (for reviews, see Gecas, 1979; Kohn, 1977). The important aspect of this correlation for current purposes, however, is not its existence or its magnitude but its explanation.

Kohn argued, and to a considerable extent demonstrated, that the source of the relationship between social class and parental values resides in the differential occupational experiences of the members of the middle and working classes.[10] These differences may be classified along three dimensions: closeness of supervision, routinization, and substantive complexity of work (Kohn, 1977, p. xxxv). Blue-collar workers are more closely supervised on the job, perform more standardized and repetitive tasks, and work with physical objects rather than with people or ideas. These factors, separately and in combination, serve to instill in blue-collar workers the value of comformity to the directions of authority figures, as they are rewarded for such conformity in their work. White-collar workers, on the other hand, are less closely supervised and thus more autonomous, must deal with varied rather than repetitive phenomena, and work with people and ideas more than with things. Creativity and self-reliance are virtues in such situations, and workers are rewarded largely for independence of action, initiative, and autonomy. Thus, the members of the two occupational classes find, through their occupational experiences, their own pathways to success. The criteria of good performance are different in the different kinds of jobs, leading blue-collar and white-collar workers to value differently the traits of conformity and self-reliance. These differing occupational values are generalized to other arenas, including the socialization of children, so that blue-collar workers are likely to prize conformity and obedience, whereas white-collar workers reward their children for self-reliance and autonomy.

The comparative implications of this theory emanate largely from the generalizability of the occupational conditions that we have discussed. These conditions, particu-

---

[10]The differential education of members of the middle and working class also appears to play a substantial role in the explanation of the relationship in question (see Wright & Wright, 1976; Kohn, 1977, pp. xlii–xliii). We are interested here, however, in the generalizability of explanatory variables across societies and behavioral domains, and most of the relevant research has taken the relationship of occupational characteristics to parental values as its point of departure. We will thus concentrate on the implications of occupational differences.

larly those involving closeness of supervision and routinization of work, pertain to many domains of behavior other than the occupational lives of American workers. But even within the realm of economic behavior, there are striking parallels between Kohn's work and earlier anthropological attempts to explain cross-cultural variation in socialization values and practices.

Barry, Child, and Bacon (1959) found, in an analysis of ethnographic data from 104 primarily nonliterate societies, that parents in societies with economic systems based on pastoralism and agriculture tend to emphasize "compliance" in child socialization, whereas parents in hunting and/or fishing economies are more likely to value "assertive" behaviors. The compliant-assertive dimension is very similar to Kohn's distinction between conformity and self-reliance. Barry *et al.* suggested that the association they found between socialization values and type of economy may be explained by variation between subsistence types in the extent to which food can be stored and accumulated: compliance is valued in high-accumulation technologies (pastoral and agricultural), and assertiveness is valued in low-accumulation technologies (hunting and fishing). This distinction would seem, at least superficially, to have little to do with Kohn's distinction between white- and blue-collar occupational conditions, but in fact they have much in common:

Pressure toward obedience and responsibility should tend to make children into the obedient and responsible adults who can best insure the continuing welfare of a society with a high-accumulation technology, whose food supply must be protected and developed gradually throughout the year. Pressure toward self-reliance and achievement should shape children into the venturesome, independent adults who can take initiative in wresting food daily from nature, and thus insure survival in societies with a low-accumulation economy. (Barry *et al.*, 1959, p. 62–63)

This logic suggests that adult workers in different types of economies are productive for different reasons and are thus rewarded for different kinds of behavior. In hunting and fishing economies individual skill and initiative are at a premium; the successful hunter must be creative, resourceful, and independent. But in agricultural and pastoral societies, success comes from long-term planning, organization, and group cooperation. The work tends to be routine and repetitive, and the members of the work groups must cooperate with one another and conform to the directions of supervisors; these constraints are comparable to those faced by industrial blue-collar workers. It is reasonable, then, to expect self-reliance or assertiveness to be a valued characteristic among hunters and fishers, and conformity to be a desirable trait among farmers and herders. Thus, the association observed by Barry *et al.* (1959) may be explicable by reference to Kohn's theory (1977).

The generalizability of this theory beyond the realm of economics was suggested by Nancy Olsen (1974) in a study of Taiwanese parents, in which mothers in nuclear families were compared with mothers living in extended families containing the husband's mother. Olsen argued that mothers who live in the same household with their mothers-in-law are subject to supervision in the performance of domestic and maternal tasks in much the same way that blue-collar workers are subject to supervision on the job. If this analogy is useful, then mothers in three-generation families should place a higher value on conformity than those in nuclear family households, whereas the latter should place a higher value on self-reliance. This is, in fact, what she found. There are several possible explanations for these differences, of course. Olsen found that the difference between mothers from nuclear and extended families in the value of self-reliance was attributable primarily to family size rather than family structure. It is also possible that mothers in extended families have less need to instill the value of autonomy in their children because of the availability of alternative adult caretakers in such families (Olsen, 1973; Whiting, Chasdi, Antonovsky, & Ayres, 1966). Nonetheless, Olsen's work shows that a hypothesis drawn from Kohn's theory regarding the effects of occupational conditions on socialization values also yields accurate predictions when applied to family structural conditions.

There is also evidence that political conditions influence socialization in ways consistent with this theory. Research in both anthropology and sociology has consistently found that people in societies with complex or autocratic political structures are more likely to value conformity and obedience (Barry, Josephson, Lauer, & Marshall, 1976; Bronfenbrenner, 1970; Schooler, 1976; Stephens, 1963); self-reliance is a more highly valued trait in societies with less autocratic political systems. These findings again suggest that adults who find that conformity is functional in their own roles are likely to value conformity in their children (see Lee, 1982, pp. 258–259). Political self-direction, like occupational and familial self-direction, appears to affect parents' values for their children in a manner predictable from Kohn's theory.

A study by Ellis, Lee, and Peterson (1978) attempted to test one hypothesis drawn from this theory on ethnographic data from a sample of 122 cultures. This hypothesis concerned the supervision of parents in the performance of adult roles in a variety of structural settings. The dependent variable was emphasis on conformity versus self-reliance in socialization values. The closeness of supervision of adults was measured with respect to economic, familial, political, and religious behaviors. In each case, an emphasis on conformity in socialization was expected to vary directly with closeness of supervision.

Supervision in economic activities was indexed by ordering primary subsistence bases from fishing and hunting (low supervision) to intensive agriculture (high supervision), under the assumption that agriculture requires the most cooperative, coordinated group effort for success in production, whereas fishing and hunting are highly individualistic activities. Familial supervision was measured in three ways: family structural complexity, ranging from nuclear through fully extended family types; complexity of kinship groupings, ranging from bilateral kinship with no corporate kin groups to patrilineal systems with highly developed kinship-based organizations; and the extent to which mate-selection practices were controlled by cultural rules stipulating community endogamy or exogamy. Each of these variables serves as an inverse indicator of the extent to which individuals are autonomous in their familial behavior. Political supervision was measured by the complexity of the political system in terms of a number of distinct jurisdictional levels, under the assumption that a "highly differentiated political system exercises more control and supervision than a less differentiated or nonexistent structure" (Ellis, Lee, & Petersen, 1978, p. 394). Finally, religious supervision was indexed by the extent and severity of religious behavioral taboos, and by the existence of ancestor worship.

An emphasis on conformity in socialization was found, in both bivariate and multivariate analyses, to be positively related to economic supervision, the complexity of the kinship system, cultural control over mate choice, political complexity, the extent of religious taboos, and ancestor worship. These results clearly support the hypothesis and, indirectly, the theory from which it was derived. In societies where adults are closely supervised in the performance of economic, familial, political, and religious role behaviors, socialization values emphasize conformity; in societies where individual adults are more autonomous, there is a greater emphasis on the value of self-reliance for children.

The one variable that did not behave as expected was family structural complexity, which was simply uncorrelated with socialization values. This finding is surprising in light of Olsen's clear support (1974) for a similar hypotheses on a Taiwanese sample, discussed above. Closer inspection of the Ellis *et al.* data, however, suggests that family structural complexity in itself is not a direct indicator of supervision of the mother, who is generally the primary agent of socialization. Olsen's observations (1974) consisted of comparisons between nuclear families and patrilocal extended families, in which the mother shared a household with her mother-in-law; not all extended families contain this combination of household members. A more detailed analysis of family structural complexity (Ellis *et al.*, 1978, p. 400) showed that it is uncorrelated with socialization values in nonpatrilocal societies, but that, in societies with patrilocal residence customs, there are clear differences between nuclear and extended family systems. The emphasis on conformity is lowest in nuclear family systems, as expected and as Olsen found. It is highest, however, in *small* extended families (stem or lineal families) rather than in fully extended families, perhaps because fully extended families contain more members of each generation, so that there is a dispersion of authority. In smaller three-generation families, it is more possible for mothers-in-law to exercise direct and immediate control over their daughters-in-

law. Thus, familial supervision of the mother may indeed be greatest in small patrilocally extended families. If this is the case, then these results also support Kohn's theory.

The indicated conclusion from these comparative studies is that parental values in socialization are attributable to certain properties of adult role behaviors as specified in a more abstract and general version of Kohn's theory (1977). This theory was originally developed to explain class-related differences in socialization values in an industrial society; comparative research has shown that its utility is much greater. When economic tasks are highly routinized, and when adults are subject to a high degree of supervision in the performance of virtually any social role, parents tend to value conformity, obedience, or compliance in their children. But when adult role behaviors demand autonomy or creativity, self-reliance is a more desired socialization outcome.

Of course, many other systemic factors influence parental values in socialization. Swanson (1967, 1969) related socialization practices to features of both political and kinship systems. He argued that matrilineal descent systems coincide with "communal" polities, in which emphasis is placed on common interests, cooperation, and socioemotional skills. Patrilineal descent, on the other hand, occurs in conjunction with "factional" political systems, in which special interests, competition, and instrumental skills are highly valued.[11] Matrilineal descent symbolizes maternal values and is thus associated with participatory socialization and leniency in child rearing, whereas patrilineal descent, symbolizing masculine values, is related to more restrictive and coercive socialization patterns (see also Farber, 1975).

The data presented by Ellis *et al.* (1978) are consistent with Swanson's logic to a certain extent because they show that conformity is more likely to be valued in patrilineal than in matrilineal societies. However, if Swanson was correct, bilateral societies should be intermediate between matrilineal and patrilineal, as bilaterality represents a balance of or compromise between maternal and paternal symbolism. But Ellis *et al.* found bilateral kinship to be associated with less emphasis on conformity than either type of unilineal descent; they argued (1978, p. 393) that this relationship is attributable to lower degrees of parental supervision by kin in bilateral systems. Further analyses (Petersen, Lee, & Ellis, 1982) have shown that the same ordering of kinship systems obtains with respect to the use of physical punishment as a disciplinary technique: it is most likely to be employed in patrilineal societies and is least likely in bilateral systems. Farber (1975) also showed that socialization practices vary among cognatic (bilateral) societies according to rules of postmarital residence.

A number of studies have suggested that, as indus-

---

[11]See Paige (1974) and Swanson (1974) for an interesting and enlightening debate over the causal ordering of political and kinship variables. The issue is summarized by Farber (1975) and by Lee (1982, pp. 162–66).

trialization, urbanization, and other aspects of modernization proceed, socialization values tend in the direction of self-reliance and away from conformity. Smith and Schooler (1978) demonstrated that, for mothers in Japan, environmental complexity (urbanization, education, and high occupational status) is directly related to individualistic values and inversely related to "traditional" values such as obedience and neatness. Pearlin (1971) found Italian parents to be more similar to American blue-collar than white-collar parents on socialization values overall, although class differences in values followed the same lines as in the United States. Studies of the correlates of adolescent conformity in six cultures (Thomas, Gecas, Weigert, & Rooney, 1974; Weigert & Thomas, 1979) show that conformity is inversely related to urbanization and industrialization on the cross-societal level.

However, the broader range of comparative research on socialization values reviewed here suggests that it is not "modernization" *per se,* nor even industrialization, that is the direct cause of this change. We know that parental socialization values in the least complex technological systems, such as hunting and fishing, are more likely to emphasize self-reliance than are the values of parents in rather highly developed agricultural technologies. The relationship between societal complexity and parental values is not linear. These data indicate instead that there are certain similarities in the conditions of life between the most and the least technologically complex societies, which affect the social behavior of adults and thus the valued traits that they attempt to inculcate in their children in the direction of self-reliance. Societies with pastoral and/or agricultural technologies, in the intermediate ranges of complexity, are characterized by emphases on conformity and obedience in the socialization of children. Insofar as modernization entails a change in the mode of production from agricultural to industrial, decrease in the prevalence and power of extended families and unilineal kin groups, a loosening of the control of religion over individual behavior, and decreasingly autocratic political regimes, we may expect that socialization values will accordingly change in the direction of self-reliance. But because these changes occur differentially across social systems, there are differences between industrial societies in socialization values that correspond to political, religious, and familial system differences.

Furthermore, the differences within societies, to which the work of Kohn and others was originally addressed, persist. It is, in fact, reasonable to hypothesize that intrasystemic variation in socialization values is greater in more modern, differentiated systems than in the nonindustrial societies of the past or present. The concept of differentiation implies, virtually by definition, that there are greater differences between the conditions of life faced by adults in the more differentiated societies, and that these differences, in turn, are likely to produce greater differences in socialization values between various categories of their populations. Kohn's theory—and the others to which it is related—is of great value because it allows explanations of variation between societies as well as within societies. The explanatory concepts are of sufficient generality and abstractness so that they can be applied to familial, political, and religious as well as economic institutions, and to systemic as well as intrasystemic properties.

In concluding this section, it is important to point out that parental values do not precisely and directly determine the outcomes of socialization. That is, parents who value conformity do not automatically get conforming children; there is, in fact, some evidence that the opposite may be true (see, for example, Devereux, 1972; Lee 1982, pp. 265–272). There is instead a much more complex causal process, in which the social environment affects parental values, which affect parental behaviors,[12] which, in turn, partially determine the behaviors of the children (Kohn, 1977). We have, in this context, examined only a part of the link between the social environment and parental values, which is itself only a small part of the causal chain. Much more work has been done, by both comparative and noncomparative methods, and much more remains to be done. But even from this brief example, the value of comparative research is apparent. The theory with which we began this section is now known to be much more general—and therefore much more powerful—than it was earlier perceived to be because it has been tested and expanded in a comparative context.

Conclusions

Within the confines of this chapter we have been able to cover only three topics addressed by comparative family research. The first, variation in family structure across cultures, was for many years one of the very few family-related issues examined by comparative means, for the simple reason that it is an inherently comparative question and cannot be approached in any other way. This issue is certainly important, and it deserves a great deal of additional research, as the answers that we now have are partial, and because these answers themselves raise more questions.

But perhaps the most significant development in comparative family sociology in the past generation or so is the general realization of the fact that, although there are a few inherently comparative questions, there are no inherently noncomparative questions. Any issue that may be studied in one social system may be profitably studied in two or more. We now examine, by comparative means,

---

[12]For example, we now know from cross-cultural research (Petersen *et al.,* 1982) that parents in societies where conformity is highly valued employ physical punishment as a disciplinary technique much more often than do parents in societies where self-reliance is valued. This finding is consistent with, but to some degree independent of, the effect of kinship structure on coercive socialization, which was mentioned above.

family behaviors ranging from mate selection to marital relations to socialization to the role of the aged in the family. Chapters (and books and classes) on comparative family sociology can no longer be single-issue treatises. Virtually every issue addressed by family sociology is now addressed by comparative family sociology: those examined here are only small samples from a large and growing discipline.

Although there are many reasons for the increasing scope of comparative family research, a major cause is an increased realization among family scholars of the benefits of intersystemic comparisons for theory construction. We have long known that a hypothesis that has been supported in two societies is more "general" than a hypothesis supported in only one, and that it is therefore more valuable. But this simplistic interpretation of the concept of generality obscures the real benefits of comparison. Although it is nice to know whether a theory that "works" (yields accurate predictions) in the United States also works in Belgium or India or Sweden, this is not the real point of comparison. The point lies in the potential variation in systemic *properties or conditions* between the particular social systems in the analysis. Systemic properties may vary if and only if two or more social systems are compared, and only by such comparisons may we observe the effects of these properties on human behavior and incorporate these effects into our explanations. Thus, when we find that the resource theory of marital power yields incorrect predictions for Greece or Yugoslavia, we are able to develop a theory that explains the conditions under which resource theory is applicable and those under which it is inapplicable (Rodman, 1972). By generalizing and testing a theory of socialization values developed in and for the United States (Kohn, 1977), we find that differences between white- and blue-collar workers in industrial societies are similar to differences between hunters and horticulturalists, and that they may be explained by reference to the same principles (Ellis *et al.*, 1978).

Thus, any aspect of human behavior that is affected by the properties of social systems, or that might be so affected, is a worthy object of comparative study. The effects of social, cultural, political, ecological, and other systemic factors on behavior can be apprehended and explained only by comparing multiple social systems that differ on these factors. The real objects of explanation are not the systems themselves, but their properties. They affect family behavior in many diverse ways; we are now slowly beginning the process of documenting and understanding these effects.

References

Adams, B. N. *Kinship in an urban setting*. Chicago: Markham, 1968.

Adams, B. N. Isolation, function, and beyond: American kinship in the 1960s. *Journal of Marriage and the Family*, 1970, *32*, 575–597.

Adelman, I., & Morris, C. T. *Society, politics, and economic development*. Baltimore: Johns Hopkins University Press, 1967.

Allen, W. R. Class, culture, and family organization: A review, assessment, and extension. *Journal of Comparative Family Studies*, 1979, *10*, 301–313.

Anderson, M. Family, household, and the industrial revolution. In M. Gordon (Ed.), *The American family in social-historical perspective*. New York: St. Martin's Press, 1973.

Arensberg, C. M., & Kimball, S. T. *Family and community in Ireland*. Cambridge: Harvard University Press, 1940.

Aronoff, J., & Crano, W. D. A re-examination of the cross-cultural principles of task segregation and sex role differentiation in the family. *American Sociological Review*, 1975, *40*, 12–20.

Barry, H., III, Child, I. L., & Bacon, M. K. Relation of child training to subsistence economy. *American Anthropologist*, 1959, *61*, 51–63.

Barry, H., III, Josephson, L., Lauer, E., & Marshall, C. Traits inculcated in childhood: Cross-cultural codes. *Ethnology*, 1976, *15*, 83–114.

Berkner, L. K. The stem family and the developmental cycle of the peasant household: An eighteenth-century Austrian example. *American Historical Review*, 1972, *77*, 398–418.

Berkner, L. K. Recent research on the history of the family in Western Europe. *Journal of Marriage and the Family*, 1973, *35*, 395–405.

Berkner, L. K. The use and misuse of census data for the historical analysis of family structure. *Journal of Interdisciplinary History*, 1975, *5*, 721–738.

Berkner, L. K. Household arithmetic: A note. *Journal of Family History*, 1977, *2*, 159–163.

Berkner, L. K., & Shaffer, J. W. The joint family in the Nivernais. *Journal of Family History*, 1978, *3*, 150–162.

Blood, R. O., Jr. *Love match and arranged marriage: A Tokyo-Detroit comparison*. New York: Free Press, 1967.

Blood, R. O., Jr., & Wolfe, D. M. *Husbands and wives: The dynamics of married living*. New York: Free Press, 1960.

Blumberg, R. L. *Stratification: Socioeconomic and sexual inequality*. Dubuque, Iowa: William C. Brown, 1978.

Blumberg, R. L., & Winch, R. F. Societal complexity and familial complexity: Evidence for the curvilinear hypothesis. *American Journal of Sociology*, 1972, *77*, 898–920.

Boserup, E. *Women's role in economic development*. London: George Allen & Unwin, 1970.

Bossen, L. Women in modernizing societies. *American Ethnologist*, 1975, *3*, 587–601.

Brickman, P. *Social conflict*. Lexington, Mass.: D. C. Heath, 1974.

Bronfenbrenner, U. *Two worlds of childhood: U.S. and U.S.S.R.* New York: Russell Sage Foundation, 1970.

Brown, B. W. Wife employment and the emergence of egalitarian marital role prescriptions. *Journal of Comparative Family Studies*, 1978, *9*, 5–17.

Buehler, M. H., Weigert, A. J., & Thomas, D. L. Correlates of conjugal power: A five culture analysis of adolescent perceptions. *Journal of Comparative Family Studies*, 1974, *5*, 5–16.

Burch, T. K. The size and structure of families: A comparative analysis of census data. *American Sociological Review*, 1967, *32*, 347–363.

Buric, O., & Zecevic, A. Family authority, marital satisfaction, and the social network in Yugoslavia. *Journal of Marriage and the Family*, 1967, *29*, 325–336.

Burr, W. R. *Theory construction and the sociology of the family*. New York: Wiley-Interscience, 1973.

Burr, W. R., Ahern, L., & Knowles, E. M. An empirical test of Rodman's theory of resources in cultural context. *Journal of Marriage and the Family*, 1977, *39*, 505–514.

Centers, R., Raven, B., & Rodrigues, A. Conjugal power structure: A re-examination. *American Sociological Review*, 1971, *36*, 264–278.

Chu, S. S. Some aspects of extended kinship in a Chinese community. *Journal of Marriage and the Family*, 1974, *36*, 628–633.

Coburn, D., & Edwards, V. L. Job control and child-rearing values. *Canadian Review of Sociology and Anthropology*, 1976, *13*, 337–344.

Conklin, G. H. The extended family as an independent factor in social change: A case from India. *Journal of Marriage and the Family*, 1974, *36*, 798–804.

Conklin, G. H. The household in urban India. *Journal of Marriage and the Family*, 1976, *38*, 771–779.

Conklin, G. H. Family modernization values and factory employment: An example from South India. *Journal of Comparative Family Studies*, 1977, *8*, 315–326.

Conklin, G. H. Cultural determinants of power for women within the family: A neglected aspect of family research. *Journal of Comparative Family Studies*, 1979, *10*, 35–53.

Cromwell, R. E., & Olson, D. H. (Eds.). *Power in families*. New York: Halsted Press, 1975.

Demos, J. *A little commonwealth*. New York: Oxford, 1970.

Devereux, E. C., Jr. Authority and moral development among German and American children: A cross-national pilot experiment. *Journal of Comparative Family Studies*, 1972, *3*, 99–124.

Ekeh, P. P. *Social exchange theory*. Cambridge: Harvard University Press, 1974.

Ellis, G. J., Lee, G. R., & Petersen, L. R. Supervision and conformity: A cross-cultural analysis of parental socialization values. *American Journal of Sociology*, 1978, *84*, 386–403.

Emerson, R. M. Social exchange theory. In A. Inkeles, J. Coleman, & N. Smelser (Eds.), *Annual review of sociology*. Palo Alto, Calif.: Annual Reviews, 1976.

Farber, B. Bilateral kinship: Centripetal and centrifugal types of organization. *Journal of Marriage and the Family*, 1975, *37*, 871–888.

Fox, A. *Beyond contract: Work, power, and trust relations*. London: Faber & Faber, 1974.

Fox, G. L. Another look at the comparative resources model: Assessing the balance of power in Turkish marriages. *Journal of Marriage and the Family*, 1973, *35*, 718–730.

Friedl, E. The position of women: Appearance and reality. *Anthropological Quarterly*, 1967, *40*, 97–108.

Furstenberg, F. F., Jr. Industrialization and the American family: A look backward. *American Sociological Review*, 1966, *31*, 326–337.

Gecas, V. The influence of social class on socialization. In W. R. Burr, R. Hill, F. I. Nye, & I. L. Reiss (Eds.), *Contemporary theories about the family (Vol. 1): Research-based theories*. New York: Free Press, 1979.

Geertz, C. *The interpretation of cultures*. New York: Basic Books, 1973.

Gibson, G. Kin family network: Overheralded structure in past conceptualizations of family functioning. *Journal of Marriage and the Family*, 1972, *34*, 13–23.

Goode, W. J. *World revolution and family patterns*. New York: Free Press, 1963.

Goode, W. J. *The family*. Englewood Cliffs, N.J: Prentice-Hall, 1964.

Goodenough, W. H. Residence rules. *Southwestern Journal of Anthropology*, 1956, *12*, 22–37.

Gordon, M. (Ed.). *The American family in social-historical perspective*. New York: St. Martin's Press, 1973.

Gore, M. S. The traditional Indian family. In M. F. Nimkoff (Ed.), *Comparative family systems*. Boston: Houghton Mifflin, 1965.

Goubert, P. Family and province: A contribution to the knowledge of family structures in early modern France. *Journal of Family History*, 1977, *2*, 179–195.

Habakkuk, H. J. Family structure and economic change in nineteenth-century Europe. *Journal of Economic History*, 1955, *15*, 1–12.

Handwerker, W. P. Technology and household configuration in urban Africa: The Bassa of Monrovia. *American Sociological Review*, 1973, *38*, 182–197.

Hendrix, L. Kinship and economic-rational migration: A comparison of micro- and macro-level analyses. *Sociological Quarterly*, 1975, *16*, 534–543. (a)

Hendrix, L. Nuclear family universals: Fact and faith in the acceptance of an idea. *Journal of Comparative Family Studies*, 1975, *6*, 125–138. (b)

Kandel, D. B., & Lesser, G. S. Marital decision-making in American and Danish urban families: A research note. *Journal of Marriage and the Family*, 1972, *34*, 134–138.

Kertzer, D. J. European peasant household structure: Some implications from a nineteenth-century Italian community. *Journal of Family History*, 1977, *2*, 333–349.

Khatri, A. A. The adaptive extended family in India today. *Journal of Marriage and the Family*, 1975, *37*, 633–642.

Kim, O. L., & Kim, K. A causal interpretation of the effect of mother's education and employment status on parental decision-making role patterns in the Korean family. *Journal of Comparative Family Studies*, 1977, *8*, 117–131.

Kluckhohn, C. *Mirror for man*. New York: McGraw-Hill, 1949.

Kobrin, F. E. The primary individual and the family: Changes in living arrangements in the United States since 1940. *Journal of Marriage and the Family*, 1976, *38*, 233–239.

Kohn, M. L. Social class and parental values. *American Journal of Sociology*, 1959, *64*, 337–351.

Kohn, M. L. Social class and parent-child relationships: An interpretation. *American Journal of Sociology*, 1963, *68*, 471–480.

Kohn, M. L. Social class and parental values: Another confirmation of the relationship. *American Sociological Review*, 1976, *41*, 538–545.

Kohn, M. L. *Class and conformity: A study in values* (2nd ed.). Chicago: University of Chicago Press, 1977.

Kohn, M. L., & Schooler, C. Class, occupation, and orientation. *American Sociological Review*, 1969, *34*, 659–678.

Kumagai, F. Family egalitarianism in cultural contexts: High-variation Japanese egalitarianism vs. low-variation American egalitarianism. *Journal of Comparative Family Studies*, 1979, *10*, 315–329. (a)

Kumagai, F. Social class, power, and husband-wife violence in Japan. *Journal of Comparative Family Studies*, 1979, *10*, 91–105. (b)

Kumagai, F., & O'Donoghue, G. Conjugal power and conjugal violence in Japan and the U.S.A. *Journal of Comparative Family Studies*, 1978, *9*, 211–221.

Lang, O. *Chinese family and society*. New Haven: Yale University Press, 1946.

Laslett, B. Household structure on an American frontier: Los Angeles, California in 1850. *American Journal of Sociology*, 1975, *81*, 109–128.

Laslett, B. Social change and the family: Los Angeles, California, 1850–1870. *American Sociological Review*, 1977, *42*, 268–291.

Laslett, P. Size and structure of the household in England over three centuries: Mean household size in England since the 16th century. *Population Studies*, 1969, *23*, 199–223.

Laslett, P. *The world we have lost* (2nd ed.). London: University Paperbacks, 1971.

Laslett, P. The comparative history of household and family. In M. Gordon (Ed.), *The American family in social-historical perspective*. New York: St. Martin's Press, 1973.

Laslett, P. Societal development and aging. In R. H. Binstock & E. Shanas (Eds.), *Handbook of aging and the social sciences*. New York: Van Nostrand Reinhold, 1976.

Laslett, P. Characteristics of the Western family considered over time. *Journal of Family History*, 1977, *2*, 89–115.

Laslett, P., & Wall, R. (Eds.). *Household and family in past time*. Cambridge: Cambridge University Press, 1972.

Lee, G. R. The problem of universals in comparative research: An attempt at clarification. *Journal of Comparative Family Studies*, 1975, *6*, 89–100.

Lee, G. R. Marital structure and economic systems. *Journal of Marriage and the Family*, 1979, *41*, 701–713.

Lee, G. R. Kinship in the seventies: A decade review of research and theory. *Journal of Marriage and the Family*, 1980, *42*, 923–934.

Lee, G. R. *Family structure and interaction: A comparative analysis* (2nd ed.) Minneapolis: University of Minnesota Press, 1982.

Lee, G. R., & Cassidy, M. L. Kinship systems and extended family ties. In R. T. Coward & W. M. Smith (Eds.), *The family in rural society.* Boulder, Colo.: Westview Press, 1981.

Lee, G. R., & Kezis, M. Family structure and the status of the elderly: A preliminary empirical study. *Journal of Comparative Family Studies,* 1979, *10,* 429–443.

Lee, G. R., & Petersen, L. R. Conjugal power and spousal resources in patriarchal cultures. *Journal of Comparative Family Studies,* 1983, *14,* 23–38.

Lee, G. R., & Stone, L. H. Mate-selection systems and criteria: Variation according to family structure. *Journal of Marriage and the Family,* 1980, *42,* 319–326.

Levy, M. J., Jr. *The family revolution in modern China.* New York: Atheneum, 1949.

Levy, M. J., Jr. Contrasting factors in the modernization of China and Japan. In S. S. Kuznets, W. E. Moore, & J. J. Spengler (Eds.), *Economic growth: Brazil, India, Japan.* Durham, N.C.: Duke University Press, 1955.

Levy, M. J., Jr. Aspects of the analysis of family structure. In A. J. Coale et al. (Eds.), *Aspects of the analysis of family structure.* Princeton: Princeton University Press, 1965.

Marsh, R. M. *Comparative sociology.* New York: Harcourt, Brace & World, 1967.

McDonald, G. W. Family power: The assessment of a decade of theory and research, 1970–1979. *Journal of Marriage and the Family,* 1980, *42,* 841–854.

Mitterauer, M., & Seider, R. The developmental process of domestic groups: Problems of reconstruction and possibilities of interpretation. *Journal of Family History,* 1979, *4,* 257–284.

Mogey, J. M. Family and community in urban-industrial societies. In H. T. Christensen (Ed.), *Handbook of marriage and the family.* Chicago: Rand McNally, 1964.

Murdock, G. P. *Social structure.* New York: Free Press, 1949.

Murdock, G. P. Ethnographic atlas: A summary. *Ethnology,* 1967, *6,* 109–236.

Murdock, G. P., and Provost, C. Factors in the division of labor by sex: A cross-cultural analysis. *Ethnology,* 1973, *12,* 203–225.

Murdock, G. P., & White, D. R. Standard cross-cultural sample. *Ethnology,* 1969, *8,* 329–369.

Netting, R. M. Household dynamics in a nineteenth century Swiss village. *Journal of Family History,* 1979, *4,* 39–58.

Nimkoff, M. F., and Middleton, R. Type of family and type of economy. *American Journal of Sociology,* 1960, *66,* 215–225.

Ogburn, W. F. *Social change.* New York: Viking Press, 1922.

Olsen, N. J. Family structure and independence training in a Taiwanese village. *Journal of Marriage and the Family,* 1973, *35,* 512–519.

Olsen, N. J. Family structure and socialization patterns in Taiwan. *American Journal of Sociology,* 1974, *79,* 1395–1417.

Osmond, M. W. A cross-cultural analysis of family organization. *Journal of Marriage and the Family,* 1969, *31,* 302–310.

Osmond, M. W. Cross-societal family research: A macrosociological overview of the seventies. *Journal of Marriage and the Family,* 1980, *42,* 995–1016.

Paige, J. M. Kinship and polity in stateless societies. American Journal of Sociology, 1974, *80,* 301–320.

Parish, W. L., Jr., & Schwartz, M. Household complexity in nineteenth century France. *American Sociological Review,* 1972, *37,* 154–173.

Parsons, R. The kinship system of the contemporary United States. *American Anthropologist,* 1943, *45,* 22–38.

Parsons, R. The normal American family. In S. Farber, P. Mustacchi, & R. H. Wilson (Eds.), *Man and civilization: The family's search for survival.* New York: McGraw-Hill, 1965.

Parsons, T., Shils, E. A., Allport, G. W., Kluckhohn, C., Murray, H. A., Sears, R. R., Sheldon, R. C., Stouffer, S. A., & Tolman, E. Some fundamental categories of the theory of action: A general statement. In T. Parsons & E. A. Shils (Eds.), *Toward a general theory of action.* New York: Harper & Row, 1951.

Paydarfar, A. A. The modernization process and household size: A provincial comparison for Iran. *Journal of Marriage and the Family,* 1975, *37,* 446–452.

Pearlin, L. I. *Class context and family relations: A cross-national study.* Boston: Little, Brown, 1971.

Petersen, K. K. Kin network research: A plea for comparability. *Journal of Marriage and the Family,* 1969, *31,* 271–280.

Petersen, L. R., Lee, G. R., & Ellis, G. J. Social structure, socialization values, and disciplinary techniques: A cross-cultural analysis. *Journal of Marriage and the Family,* 1982, *44,* 131–142.

Przeworski, A., & Teune, H. *The logic of comparative social inquiry.* New York: Wiley-Interscience, 1970.

Ramos, D. City and country: The family in Minas Gerais, 1804–1838. *Journal of Family History,* 1978, *3,* 361–375.

Ramu, G. N. Geographic mobility, kinship and the family in South India. *Journal of Marriage and the Family,* 1972, *34,* 147–152.

Ramu, G. N. Urban kinship ties in South India: A case study. *Journal of Marriage and the Family,* 1974, *36,* 619–627.

Reiss, I. L. The universality of the family: A conceptual analysis. *Journal of Marriage and the Family,* 1965, *27,* 443–453.

Reiss, I. L. *Family systems in America* (3rd ed.). New York: Holt, Rinehart & Winston, 1980.

Riegelhaupt, J. Saloio women: An analysis of formal and informal political and economic roles of Portuguese peasant women. *Anthropological Quarterly,* 1967, *40,* 109–126.

Ring, R. R. Early medieval peasant households in central Italy. *Journal of Family History,* 1979, *4,* 2–25.

Rodman, H. Marital power in France, Greece, Yugoslavia, and the United States: A cross-national discussion. *Journal of Marriage and the Family,* 1967, *29,* 320–325.

Rodman, H. Marital power and the theory of resources in cultural context. *Journal of Comparative Family Studies,* 1972, *3,* 50–69.

Rogers, S. C. Female forms of power and the myth of male dominance: A model of female/male interaction in peasant society. *American Ethnologist,* 1975, *2,* 727–756.

Roy, P. K. Industrialization and ''fitness'' of nuclear family: A case study in India. *Journal of Comparative Family Studies,* 1974, *5,* 74–86.

Safilios-Rothschild, C. A comparison of power structure and marital satisfaction in urban Greek and French families. *Journal of Marriage and the Family,* 1967, *29,* 345–352.

Safilios-Rothschild, C. A macro- and micro-examination of family power and love: An exchange model. *Journal of Marriage and the Family,* 1976, *38,* 355–362.

Sanday, P. R. Toward a theory of the status of women. *American Anthropologist,* 1973, *75,* 1682–1700.

Scanzoni, J. Social processes and power in families. In W. R. Burr, R. Hill, F. I. Nye, & I. L. Reiss (Eds.), *Contemporary theories about the family (Vol. 1): Research-based theories.* New York: Free Press, 1979.

Schooler, C. Serfdom's legacy: An ethnic continuum. *American Journal of Sociology,* 1976, *81,* 1265–1286.

Shanas, E. Family-kin networks and aging in cross-cultural perspective. *Journal of Marriage and the Family,* 1973, *35,* 505–511.

Smith, E. C. Family structure and complexity. *Journal of Comparative Family Studies,* 1978, *9,* 299–310.

Smith, K. C., & Schooler, C. Women as mothers in Japan: The effects of social structure and culture on values and behavior. *Journal of Marriage and the Family,* 1978, *40,* 613–620.

Stack, C. B. *All our kin: Strategies for survival in a black community.* New York: Harper & Row, 1974.

Stephens, W. N. *The family in cross-cultural perspective.* New York: Holt, Rinehart & Winston, 1963.

Stinner, W. F. Urbanization and household structure in the Philippines. *Journal of Marriage and the Family,* 1977, *39,* 377–385.

Stinner, W. F. Modernization and family extension in the Philippines: A social demographic analysis. *Journal of Marriage and the Family,* 1979, *41,* 161–168.

Stolte-Heiskanen, V. Contextual analysis and theory construction in cross-cultural family research. *Journal of Comparative Family Studies,* 1972, *3,* 33–49.

Straus, M. A. Society as a variable in comparative study of the family by replication and secondary analysis. *Journal of Marriage and the Family,* 1968, *30,* 565–570.

Straus, M. A. Phenomenal identity and conceptual equivalance of measurement in cross-national comparative research. *Journal of Marriage and the Family,* 1969, *31,* 233–239.

Sussman, M. B. Relationships of adult children with their parents in the United States. In E. Shanas & G. F. Streib (Eds.), *Social structure and the family: Generational relations.* Englewood Cliffs, N.J.: Prentice-Hall, 1965.

Swanson, G. E. *Religion and regime.* Ann Arbor: University of Michigan Press, 1967.

Swanson, G. E. *Rules of descent: Studies in the sociology of parentage.* Ann Arbor: Anthropological Paper No. 39, Museum of Anthropology, University of Michigan, 1969.

Swanson, G. E. Descent and polity: The meaning of Paige's findings. *American Journal of Sociology,* 1974, *80,* 321–328.

Szinovacz, M. E. Another look at normative resource theory: Contributions from Austrian data—A research note. *Journal of Marriage and the Family,* 1978, *40,* 413–421.

Thomas, D. L., Gecas, V., Weigert, A. J., & Rooney, E. *Family socialization and the adolescent.* Lexington, Mass.: D. C. Heath, 1974.

Waller, W., & Hill, R. *The family: A dynamic interpretation* (rev. ed.). New York: Dryden Press, 1951.

Weigert, A. J., & Thomas, D. L. Family as a conditional universal. *Journal of Marriage and the Family,* 1971, *33,* 188–194.

Weigert, A. J., & Thomas, D. L. Family socialization and adolescent conformity and religiosity: An extension to Germany and Spain. *Journal of Comparative Family Studies,* 1979, *10,* 371–383.

Whiting, J. W. M., Chasdi, E. H., Antonovsky, H. F., & Ayres, B. C. The learning of values. In E. Vogt & E. Albert (Eds.), *People of Rimrock: A study of values in five cultures.* Cambridge: Harvard University Press, 1966.

Whyte, M. K. *The status of women in preindustrial societies.* Princeton: Princeton University Press, 1978.

Winch, R. F. *Familial organization: A quest for determinants.* New York: Free Press, 1977.

Winch, R. F. Toward a model of familial organization. In W. R. Burr, R. Hill, F. I. Nye, & I. L. Reiss (Eds.), *Contemporary theories about the family (Vol. 1): Research-based theories.* New York: Free Press, 1979.

Wirth, L. Urbanism as a way of life. *American Journal of Sociology,* 1938, *44,* 3–24.

Wolfe, D. M. Power and authority in the family. In D. Cartwright (Ed.), *Studies in social power.* Ann Arbor: University of Michigan Institute for Social Research, 1959.

Wong, F. Industrialization and family structure in Hong Kong. *Journal of Marriage and the Family,* 1975, *37,* 985–1000.

Wright, J., & Wright, S. Social class and parental values for children: A partial replication and extension of the Kohn thesis. *American Sociological Review,* 1976, *41,* 527–537.

Zelditch, M., Jr. Cross-cultural analyses of family structure. In H. J. Christensen (Ed.), *Handbook of marriage and the family.* Chicago: Rand McNally, 1964.

Zelditch, M., Jr. Intelligible comparisons. In I. Vallier (Ed.), *Comparative methods in sociology: Essays on trends and applications.* Berkeley: University of California Press, 1971.

Zimmerman, C. *Family and civilization.* New York: Harper & Brothers, 1947.

CHAPTER 4

The Rise of Family Theory
A HISTORICAL AND CRITICAL ANALYSIS

Darwin L. Thomas and Jean Edmondson Wilcox

Introduction

In 1957, Hill, Katz, and Simpson published a prospectus for an inventory of marriage and family research from 1900 to 1956. A goal of this inventory was "the theoretical organization, where possible, of research findings into a set of interrelated hypotheses and propositions" (p. 89). This article also continued Hill's earlier work (1951a,b, 1955) of organizing previous research projects by "major conceptual apparatus" (1957, p. 89). Two years later, William J. Goode (1959) published an article on family theory with the subtitle "Horizons in Family Theory." The content and format of these two articles were dramatically predictive of what was to happen during the 1960s and 1970s in family theory.

The two articles called attention to what would become the central concerns of family theory, namely, conceptual frameworks and propositions. Goode talked of propositions and in his own way ordered some propositions, although in a discursive fashion, so that logical conclusions could be derived from them. Our own condensed reformulation of some of Goode's illustrative propositions highlights some of the theoretical assertions contained in his discursive presentation. *If* upper strata families

1. spend greater resources on training the young and
2. exercise greater social control over adults, *then*
3. upper strata families will exercise greater control over the social interaction of young adults so as to control with whom they will fall in love, consequently ensuring the desired social placement of offspring.

Goode made no pretension that his review of family theory was comprehensive, but he suggested that what he had done could be a useful illustration of what family theory should be like. For Hill *et al.* and Goode, theory is clearly not armchair thinking nor grand theoretical for-

mulation, but interrelated sets of empirically grounded propositions. To what extent has family theory followed the general theoretical model of propositions found in these presentations? Consideration of Volume 1 of *Contemporary Theories About the Family* (Burr, Hill, Nye, & Reiss, 1979a) shows that, in the 22 substantive areas covered in the book, 19 contain detailed interrelated sets of propositions generally induced from research findings. In those 19 chapters, there are a total of 719 propositions, or an average of 1.3 propositions per page. That is a remarkable change, from a few illustrative propositions coming from Goode in 1959 to 719 in one volume in a short 20 years.

Various assessments have already been formulated that recount in detail the organizational developments and the accomplishments that have taken place in family theory since the 1950s (Aldous, 1970; Burr, 1973; Burr, Hill, Nye, & Reiss, 1979a,b; Christensen, 1964; Goode, 1959; Goode, Hopkins, & McClure, 1971; Hill, 1966; Hill & Hansen, 1960; Nye & Berardo, 1966). In addition to these, there have now been two decade reviews published in the *Journal of Marriage and the Family* (Broderick, 1971; Holman & Burr, 1980). All of these have mirrored the introspective aspect of those working in family theory. They have charted their course and recounted their travels (Aldous, 1970). What has not been done is to assess theory in the family field as it relates to the social sciences in general. Our purpose, then, is to render salient some developments in the social sciences as a backdrop against which to analyze the theoretical developments in the family field, drawing from philosophy of science and hermeneutics.[1] Our focus is on sociology because of its close relationship to theory in the family field. Highlighting the developments in family theory along with some

[1]Originally the term *hermeneutics* was used to identify a problem encountered by translators of ancient texts. The problem was not just to make a word-for-word translation but to translate the text according to the intent of the original author. Thus, interpretation of original meaning as experienced by the original author was sought by the translator. Here, knowledge of cultures, times, places, and purposes were used. In the social sciences, the term is used to identify this central concern about interpretation of meaning. Just as in the literary work, a word

Darwin L. Thomas • Department of Sociology and the Family and Demographic Research Institute, Brigham Young University, Provo, UT 84602. **Jean Edmondson Wilcox** • Department of Family and Human Development, Utah State University, Logan, UT 84322.

developments in the social sciences permits us to under-score some of the distinguishing characteristics of family theory emerging from its positivist heritage. The basic thesis is that, in form and content, family theory is an instance of mainstream sociological theory,[2] which was in large measure shaped by a positivist heritage in West-ern thought. This positivist heritage is reflected in the particular type of theory that emerged in the family field after 1950.

Emergence of the Received View of Family Theory

This analysis of family theory is limited to the period of the 1800s to the present and emphasizes the post-1950 era

---

gets its meaning from the sentence, the paragraph, and the discourse context within which it is embedded, so, too, in the social world, meaning is understood or apprehended from the social context before individual bits of behavior are defined or understood. For humans, self-understanding and interpretation are possible precisely because of the reflexive nature of lan-guage, and to "decipher this self-interpretation is the task of hermeneutics (Habermas, 1971, p. 169).

[2]The intellectual position underlying our discussion is most sim-ilar to positions developed and articulated by Bernstein (1976), Suppe (1977), and Alexander (1982). Our use of the term re-ceived view follows Suppe's analysis of mainstream develop-ments of theory in philosophy of science. It is our effort to identify the most widely accepted view of theory underlying the family field. We characterize the major theoretical develop-ments in the family field as an application of the view of theory contained in mainstream sociology, but we realize that there are many types of theoretical endeavors that we do not discuss that fall outside this type of family theory. Our purpose is to discuss the major trend-setting emphasis. Likewise, we use the term positivism at various places in the chapter to identify the basic underlying philosophical position of the received view. Gid-dens (1974, pp. 3–4) identified those suppositions of the "positivistic attitude": (1) The methodological procedures of natural sciences may be directly adapted to sociology. (2) The outcome or the goal is to formulate laws or lawlike generaliza-tions. (3) The knowledge produced will be instrumental in form. The findings do not carry any logically given implications for practical policy or the pursuit of values. We use the term positivism in this basic philosophical sense and not as a descrip-tive term for family theorists who might use variables, proposi-tions, and generalizations in their work. We recognize that many researcher-theorists take the typical American pragmatic position in using theory, namely, "If it works, use it." The decision by any theorist to develop theory of the received-view type, which in our analysis is seen as being founded on basic positivistic assumptions, should not be interpreted to mean that the user necessarily believes in the underlying positivistic view of the nature of social reality. Our use of positivism is similar to Suppe's description of the tenets of positivism. Our charac-terization of family theory as an instance of mainstream so-ciological thinking is similar to and has been influenced by Bernstein's work (1976) in defining characteristics of main-stream social and political theory. Our conceptualization of the received view of theory and its connection to positivism has affinities to Alexander's discussion (1982) of what he called the "positivist persuasion" in sociological theory. See these above sources for additional background analysis of philosophical is-sues underlying the received view of theory.

as the time when the received view of theory was accepted and promulgated (Christensen, 1964, pp. 5–6). Three foci underlie our treatise: (1) an orientation toward social problems; (2) European influences on American thought; and (3) a philosophical rift between positivist and human-istic orientations.

Developments during the 1800s

One of the most important aspects of family study in the 1800s was the emergence of a deep fundamental belief in the need to solve or ameliorate social problems. The family was inextricably linked to many of these social problems. The outcry in the 1800s by persons wishing to preserve and protect families from a variety of social problems focused the attention of professionals (clergy, lawyers, social reformers, and charity workers) on both social problems and the family. Pressing problems were seen as rising divorce rates, effects of slavery, women's suffrage movement, and effects of industrialization on the family—all giving rise to the need for parent education (Bridgman, 1930; Gordon, 1978, p. 288; Howard, 1981, p. 16). Social reformers of the day held a view of the family that was quite different from that held by some professionals, who would later be known as sociologists. Social reformers viewed the family as fundamental to the health of society (Howard, 1981, p. 16). The family was a fragile institution in need of protection from prevailing social conditions. Divorce was one of the greatest threats to the family's survival. The ideal family was seen as "a patriarchal rural family, tied to tradition, the primary ve-hicle of socialization" (Howard, 1981, p. 19). By 1890, in the wake of rapid social change, industrialization and urbanization were viewed as causes of family disor-ganization (Howard, 1981, p. 39), and a reactionary movement began against the evils of industrialization and urbanization. This reactionary movement favored a re-turn to the patriarchal, rural family as a way of combating these social problems.

The "sociologists" held different perceptions of the family, influenced by social Darwinism. These early American sociologists, including William Sumner, Lester Ward, and Franklin Giddings, developed their basic theoretical position, which Hinkle (1980) called "evolutionary naturalism" (p. 68), growing out of the European works of Charles Darwin and Herbert Spencer[3] and later Auguste Comte. From Comte, American so-ciology was given a name and a positivist heritage (Mar-tindale, 1960, pp. 73–75). As part of this positivist

---

[3]There appears to be some disagreement about which so-ciologists were most instrumental in disseminating the works of Charles Darwin and Herbert Spencer. For example, Martindale (1960, pp. 69–72) credited Ward with adapting Spencerian notions to America, whereas Becker and Barnes (1961, pp. 955–963) credited Charles Sumner and his student Albert Kel-ler with this accomplishment. Howard (1981, pp. 12–16) viewed Ward, Giddings, and Sumner as having great influence in popularizing the evolutionary perspectives of Spencer in America.

heritage, general laws of the social order were hypothesized to exist, and efforts were initiated to discover them through systematic societal comparisons (Martindale, 1960, p. 174).

The intellectual underpinnings of American sociology were similar to those of Europe (Becker & Barnes, 1961, p. 953). In fact, some argued that "theorizing in American sociology represents the application of European philosophical ideas to the changing problems of a materialistic, pragmatic, and utilitarian society in which idealism has given way to empiricism and utilitarianism" (Kinloch, 1977, p. 280).

This utilitarian, pragmatic theme can be seen throughout the history of American sociology and therefore characterizes much of the work in family theory against the larger philosophical background of evolutionary naturalism.

Ward integrated evolutionary ideas with the social changes occurring in American society. He viewed the women's rights movement as an attempt to reestablish equality in the family (Howard, 1981, p. 14). Sumner viewed evolution as an automatic, unchangeable process. From this view, the changes occurring in American society were seen as functional and necessary (Becker & Barnes, 1961, pp. 955–959). Giddings believed that individual rights had been unduly stressed and that through education Americans would come to accept their social responsibility (Howard, 1981, p. 14). Even though their conclusions varied, each of these American sociologists shared "a common faith in the adaptability of the family as an institution to new social conditions" (Howard, 1981, p. 16) as part of societal evolution.

From the preceding, it is apparent that the social problems perspective of the family led to assumptions about families that differed from those of an evolutionary perspective, and that these divergent perspectives were influential in determining how families should be studied and when and if intervention was necessary, and in molding theories about the family. For the social reformer, the family represented a fragile institution battered by a variety of social problems. For the sociologist, the family represented an adapting institution that had evolved over centuries, and the social problems were signals that family roles needed to change. These two perspectives of the family led to divergent methodologies as well as differing theoretical approaches to the study of the family.

The social reformers (some of whom would later be called social workers[4]) sought to study families from an individual case approach, so that the situational specifics could be considered. Many social reformers were outspoken against the objective, scientific view of the family characteristically used by sociologists:

[4]Howard's book (1981) traces the relationship between social work and sociology from the 1880s to 1940. In fact, this vacillating cooperation and contempt between social work and sociology set the tone for many of the research and methodology issues that surfaced in family sociology. Howard appears to be quite convinced of the mutual impacts of these two disciplines on each other, particularly regarding family issues.

For the social worker, becoming scientific was seen in terms of modeling their profession upon the profession of medicine, especially on its clinical methodology of diagnosis, the prescription of treatment on the basis of diagnosis, and the careful observation and recording of the results of treatment. The sociologists viewed the development of a scientific sociology in terms of pure empirical research into social phenomena, free from the biases of moral scruples of meaning. Becoming scientific led to divergent professional goals for the two disciplines. Sociologists came to view the goal of their profession as social knowledge, while social workers saw their goal as social therapy. (Howard, 1981, p. 41)

The sociologists followed Comte's lead in developing their methodologies. As Martindale (1960) noted,

Positivism, the view that the methods which had proved their worth in the physical sciences were appropriate to the study of social phenomena, was inseparably built into Comte's sociology. . . . Sociological knowledge is not in principle different from other forms of scientific knowledge: it is merely more complex and less general. (p. 73)

American sociologists adhering to the positivistic view achieved legitimacy for their approach by creating academic departments of sociology (Chicago in 1892 and Columbia in 1894), by writing textbooks (by Albion Small, Giddings, Ward, and Thorstein Veblen), and by publishing professional journals (*The American Journal of Sociology*, 1895).

1900–1950

In the early twentieth century, social reformers, social workers, and sociologists continued to raise the public awareness of pressing social problems (Komarovsky & Waller, 1945, p. 443). Journals of the times discussed these problems. For example, the *Annals of the American Academy of Political and Social Science* devoted entire volumes to the topics of child labor (Vol. 25, 1905; Vol. 27, 1906); women's work and organizations (Vol. 28, 1906); the living wage of women workers (Vol. 37, 1911), and uniform child labor laws (vol. 38, 1911). Similar themes appeared in the *American Journal of Sociology* and in sociological books of this same era (Komarovsky & Waller, 1945, p. 444). Sociologists generally described these as inevitable aspects of social change and did not necessarily believe that urbanization and industrialization would harm the family or other social institutions.

The concerns about social problems were also manifest in the new field of social psychology growing out of the works of William James, Charles Cooley, W. I. Thomas, and Florian Znaniecki (Martindale, 1960, pp. 339–353). It was Cooley who took James's original ideas about the self and applied them to society, characterizing primary groups as the chief socializers. Peer groups, neighborhood gangs, and the family were some of the important primary groups (Howard, 1981, p. 49–50; Martindale, 1960, p. 345). In this view, reform of the family would not necessarily resolve social problems, as other socialization agents were also evolved. The impact of these other influences on the family could be better understood by spotlighting the internal workings of the family. As Howard (1981) noted, Thomas's and Zaniecki's work focused

upon the need to study the internal and subjective processes of social disorganization [which] anticipated the growing preoccupation of family sociologists in the 1920's and 1930's with the internal relationships of family interaction, rather than the external relationships of the family with larger institutions of society. (pp. 53–54)

Burgess promoted this microscopic, social psychological perspective in the study of the family. He defined the family as a "unity of interacting personalities" (1926). This perspective "came to dominate the output of family sociology in the United States until at least 1955" (Mogey, 1981, p. xi). The study of the family was further legitimized by the creation of a family section at the American Sociological Society meetings of 1924. During this same year, Ernest W. Groves began teaching university courses on marriage and family life (Mogey, 1981, p. xi).

European influences on the American family field were particularly evident in the first half of the twentieth century. During the 1920s and 1930s, various European works were translated into English and influenced the American family field. Among these were the works of Piaget (1926a,b, 1929, 1932) and Freud (1938). These works influenced research and theory in child development and parenting and were incorporated into the growing family-life education movement of this era. The writings of various European sociologists were also translated into English and influenced the research and theory efforts of American family scholars. Stryker (1972) portrayed the European-American exchange of ideas as follows:

The intellectual heritage of contemporary American sociology is heavily European, as is evidenced by the almost ritualistic tracing of starting points in virtually any work to (variously) Weber, Marx, Durkheim, Pareto, Michels, Tocqueville, or Simmel. Historically, the flow of the intellectual ideas has been from Europe to America. (p. 18)

The migration of several European scholars to America before World War II influenced social sciences through their many publications. Among these were Kurt Lewin, Fritz Heider, Wolfgang Köhler, Max Wertheimer, George Katona, Paul Lazarsfeld, and Egon and Else Brunswik (Cartwright, 1979). The European-American influences were not all unidirectional, however. When many of these social scientists returned to Europe, they took with them a more Americanized version of social science in general and of social psychology in particular. The mix of European philosophical ideas with the Americanized social psychology generated considerable controversy about the nature of scientific theory from some quarters, such as the Frankfurt school and its critical theory approach, to be discussed later.

World War I, the Great Depression, and World War II had dramatic influences not only on American families but also on family research and theory. In the wake of these worldwide stressor events, family researchers and theorists were faced with a myriad of social problems to study. Adaptation of families to crisis was studied by Angell (1936), Cavan and Ranck (1938), and Morgan (1939). A devastating worldwide depression sandwiched between two cruel world wars created a heap of rubble out of the evolutionary naturalism of the social sciences. How could societies be evolving and produce these worldwide disasters? Was the family as an institution evolving into a more adaptable form, or was it fragile and hence in danger of extinction? What type of family was best able to handle crisis? Zimmerman, influenced by Frederic LePlay's empirical research on French families in the 1840s, carried out a similar study in the United States with Frampton (1935). Although their findings did not totally corroborate LePlay's, they did conclude that an interdependent, rural family system adapted better to the Depression than did a more urbanized family system. Family researchers and theorists began to develop a view of the family as a beleaguered institution.

This change of family researchers and theorists to a position similar to that of the earlier social reformers is obvious in their philosophy about the resiliency of the family. Instead of reiterating the social-Darwinian view of the family as adapting to various social conditions (problems), many family researchers of this period espoused a "fragile family" view. What is now apparent is that the dominant notion of the declining and decaying family was developed and maintained by social scientists on the basis of very inadequate theoretical or empirical evidence (See Caplow, Bahr, Chadwick, Hill, & Williamson, 1982, for a more detailed discussion of the emergence and maintenance of this myth). The felt need to strengthen the crumbling family is apparent in the nature of research questions of the 1930s and 1940s, and in the growing involvement of the federal government in amelioratory family programs.

The involvement of the federal government, encouraged by social scientists, can be seen in the functioning of the typical American family. For example, when Robert and Helen Lynd first studied the families of "Middletown" in the 1920s, there was virtually no input from the federal government into household income. By 1977, however, "$4,000 per household was spent by the Federal Government in Middletown every year" (Caplow *et al.*, 1982, p. 26). These Middletown researchers found a myriad of federal agencies providing scores of social programs directed at strengthening the very "fragile" family.

Along with a concern about social problems, this period saw an increased emphasis on the scientific study of social phenomena. Actual research procedures were stressed more than a match between the physical science model and the social sciences. A look at the type of theory envisioned by the leaders in family theory points out that those family theorists trained as sociologists brought with them a view of theory from mainstream sociology. The one sociologist as responsible as any for having developed a general consensus about theory and research in mainstream sociology is Robert Merton (for a more detailed analysis of Merton's work, see Alexander, 1982, pp. 1–15, 127–136; Bernstein, 1976, pp. 7–18). Merton's writings did more than perhaps anyone else's to identify the necessary and salutary interplay between theory and research and to argue against theory as the development of grand theoretical schemes designed to explain how societies operate. This mainstream sociological view of theory argued for identification of variables, generation of propositional formulations, and creation of interrelated sets of propositions. Many family researchers and theorists espoused a type of theory very similar to the mainstream sociological view. Rossi (1956, p. 22) noted three emphases among family researchers and theorists of this era: (1) an increased emphasis on theories of the middle range; (2) the prevalence of mathematics in the language of theory; and (3) a considerable interest in stock taking. He typified this stock taking as "building inventories of theory, speculations, and empirical findings in a particular area" (p. 26). All three of these emphases have remained in the family field from 1950 to the present.

Family Theory since 1950

The years since 1950 have been the most active for theoretical developments in the study of the family (Howard, 1975, p. 183). During these three and a half decades, the field has been characterized by stock-taking articles focusing on conceptual frameworks and systematic effort at theory construction. These efforts, when seen in light of previously referred to developments in social science in general and sociology in particular, have created a particular view of theory similar to that existing in sociology here referred to as the received view.

As Howard (1975) noted, one of the results of the stock-taking articles by family researchers and theorists was to develop "a tradition of introspection and reassessment" (p. 183). The stock-taking articles of Hill (1951a,b, 1955), Hill, Katz, and Simpson (1957), Foote (1957), Goode (1959), Hill and Hansen (1960), Sussman (1968), Christensen (1964), and Broderick (1971), along with the theory construction work in the 1970s (Burr, 1973; Burr et al., 1979a,b; Goode, Hopkins, & McClure, 1971), emphasized the importance of conceptual frameworks, empirical findings, generalizations, variables, propositions, and finally a view of theory as interrelated sets of propositions.

Conceptual Frameworks. The 1950s saw the emergence of a focus on family theory characterized by identifying and clarifying what conceptual orientations had been used by students of the family. The conceptual framework emphasis grew out of the study of the family as a multidisciplinary phenomenon. In the two articles by

Hill published in 1951, he placed his work in this multidisciplinary perspective and indentified the most commonly used conceptual frameworks as the (1) institutional; (2) structure function; (3) interactional-role analysis; 4) situational; 5) learning-developmental; and 6) household economics. The first four are essentially the work of sociologists, with some minimal input by anthropologists, social psychologists, and psychologists. The learning-theory–developmental approach is largely the product of psychologists studying children, and the household economic approach comes from home economics.

Because part of Hill's purpose in the reviews was to assess what had been done in the study of marriage and the family and hopefully to move the field along, he identified "obstacles to progress" (1951a, p. 16). One of the four major problems holding back progress was "the vested interests and perceptions of competing ways of viewing the family." He lamented the chaos resulting from the multidisciplinary approach to family study:

> With so many approaches to the study of the family, it is no wonder our findings do not add up. We have been delayed in our development of a body of theory because of disciplinary separation and are just beginning to develop a generation of research workers who can bridge the distances between the disciplines. (1951a, p. 17)

Some four years later, Hill (1955) repeated his list of obstacles to progress and added a fifth one that he called "prima donnism." He then combined it with the "confusion of competing conceptual approaches" and discussed the two:

> Two obstacles to progress in family research have been linked together; prima donnism and the discipleship which develops around prima donnas. Our system of graduate study, of individual bylines in publication, and promotion based on individual publication has rewarded the solitary worker, giving him recognition and public attention. European sociology is even more plagued by this pattern of rewarding the individual who builds up his own system and differentiates himself sharply from his colleagues.
>
> A good explanation for our failure to develop any significant theory in the family field has been the Tower of Babel we have built conceptually during the transition in family research. Several competing approaches for studying the family have grown up within sociology, social anthropology, psychology, and home economics. These approaches provide relatively incompatible conceptual systems for viewing the family, each with its own peculiar focus, definitions of the family, and key concepts. Generalizations made by one approach cannot easily be added to generalizations made by other competing systems. (p. 274)

Two aspects of Hill's arguments developed in these early pieces are important for the general thesis of this chapter. Confusion among the multitude of findings published on the family can be reduced by codifying the research findings and (1) identifying the underlying conceptual frameworks used by the various researchers, and (2) generating a multidisciplinary conceptual framework that focuses directly on the family. With respect to the latter point, Hill identified the emerging family-development conceptual framework as having real potential. At the close of his 1955 critique of marriage and family research, he identified where the framework's key concepts had come from and held out the hope for an eventual payoff:

> Family development as a multi-disciplinary framework has borrowed the concept of stages of the family life cycle from the rural sociologists, the concept of development needs and tasks from the child psychologists and human-development specialists, and has taken from the family sociologist and social theorist the concepts of age and sex roles, plurality patterns, functional prerequisites, and the family as an arena of interacting personalities. All these concepts have been fused fruitfully to produce a frame of reference for studying the internal growth and development of families from formation to dissolution. . . .
> As this approach to family study is rendered researchable by more rigorous definition of concepts and by methods of data collection which can provide analyzable data, the dynamics of family development may be tested over a family's life span with living families. The outcome of that research may some day produce a companion volume on the growth and development of families comparable to Dr. Benjamin Spock's pocketbook Baby and Child Care, written by one of our successors who will have grown up in a new age of family research. (p. 276)

In 1957, Hill *et al.* published their progress report on the codification project. They discussed the seven conceptual frameworks that Hill had earlier delineated and argued that the time was "ripe for codification" (p. 89) of research findings and conceptual approaches. This inventorying project under the direction of Hill was then located at the Institute for Research in Social Sciences at the University of North Carolina and had five major objectives. The first four dealt with summarizing research findings and identifying conceptual frameworks. The fifth was "the theoretical organization . . . of research findings into interrelated hypotheses and propositions" (p. 89). By 1960, Hill, with the inventory project, had moved to the University of Minnesota, where he and Hansen published their most influential piece on identifying conceptual frameworks.

With the publication of the Hill and Hansen's article (1960), theoretical work in the family field could be characterized as repeatedly emphasizing the need to systematically codify research findings. This emphasis on codification was explicitly based on Merton's earlier work on codification in sociology (Hill *et al.*, 1957, p. 89, footnote 1). Second, it identified the generation of propositions as a necessary and worthwhile goal if theory was to be developed. It defined a proposition as an "empirically validated generalization" (Hill & Hansen, 1960, p. 299, footnote 1). This emphasis on the empirical side of theorizing reflects the influence of Merton, who argued for the combinations of theory and research by underscoring the empirical dimension (Alexander, 1982, p. 13). Third, this emphasis on codification has explicitly called for the use of conceptual frameworks as a means of developing "Middle range theories about marriage and the family" (Hill & Hansen, 1960, p. 300). In this latter case, the influence of Merton is not referenced by the authors, but it is self-evident.

The Hill and Hansen article is important for raising issues related to conceptual frameworks in two ways. First, it changed the number of major conceptual frameworks used in the study of the family from the seven previously given to five. The learning-maturational (earlier called *learning-developmental*) and the household-economic approaches were dropped. Hill and Hansen indicated that the household-economic approach was not generating enough research to qualify as a major conceptual framework, and that the learning-maturational approach, although generating an abundance of research, was carried out by psychologists who focused on individuals and not families. This emerging and declining nature of frameworks continues to characterize family theory in the 1980s (see Figure 1).

The second importance of the Hill and Hansen publication is that it raised a question about how propositions as they had defined them were related to conceptual frameworks. Because their propositions were research propositions or empirical generalizations, they were not seen "ideally" as part of the frameworks. But presumably, by creating bridging concepts and integrating findings, propositions of a more general nature could be created that would further theoretical work. In short, codification would lead to "theoretical propositions derived from the findings" and "conceptual frameworks, then, [were] the key to fruitful codification" (Hill & Hansen, 1960, p. 299). This issue of the relationship of conceptual frameworks to propositions and how they both relate to theory continues to be discussed in family literature in the 1980s (Rodman, 1980; Klein, 1980).

During the 1960s, important publications gave further examples of conceptual frameworks, identified central concepts in each, discussed the underlying assumptions characteristic of each framework, and reviewed research findings relevant to the framework (Christensen, 1964; Nye & Berardo, 1966). The first handbook to be published in the marriage and family area (Christensen, 1964) gave major treatises on the interactional, structure-function, institutional, and developmental approaches but combined the situational with the interactional (see Klein, 1980, for discussion of this decision). Nye and Berardo (1966) did likewise and included a number of other conceptual frameworks. They argued that the psychoanalytic approach could be seen as a major framework.

In his review of 1960s research and theory on the family, Broderick (1971) saw only the symbolic interactional and the developmental as frameworks that still remained as major approaches to the study of the family. The structure-functional and institutional were clearly declining, whereas systems and perhaps exchange were emerging as major theoretical approaches.

In family theory, then, the emphasis on conceptual frameworks was clearly established during the 1950s, largely through the work of Hill and his colleagues. The

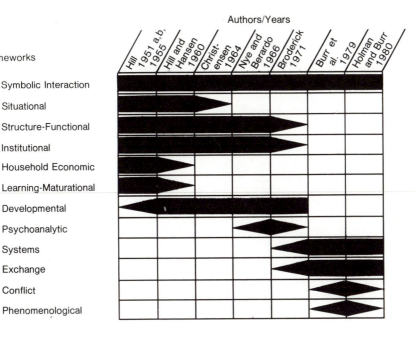

Figure 1. Major conceptual frameworks presented in family research and theory publications from 1950 to 1980. We have included those frameworks that the authors say or imply are the major or dominant conceptual orientations existing in the family field of study. Many of the authors discuss other frameworks, which are seen as minimal or peripheral approaches, such as the anthropological, social psychological, or Western Christian (Nye & Berardo, 1966), balance, or game (Broderick, 1971). We are indebted to David Klein for some information used in this figure from work that he did as archivist for the Theory and Research Methods Workshop at the National Council on Family Relations.

1960s saw a refinement of and an addition to the various frameworks as more researchers and theorists published their work. Our reading of the literature leads us to observe that, over these two decades, there was a clear shift away from a concern about the confusion arising out of the multidisciplinary study of the family first identified by Hill in the early 1950s. The major publications in the 1960s, which discussed the confusion did not necessarily lay this confusion at the doors of the various disciplines. The failure to do so may be partly understood by noting that the two frameworks first dropped (see Figure 1) were those most closely tied to psychology and home economics. The remaining frameworks are those with greatest affinity to sociology. Thus, competitiveness between the disciplines tends to be deemphasized. We also see a more careful and discerning questioning of what family theory should look like. And we see a general agreement in the literature (Christensen (1964; Goode, 1959; Hill & Han-

sen, 1960; Nye & Berardo, 1966) about the central place of propositions in family theory.

Propositions were initially seen as empirical generalizations rising out of research. Although the above literature, with its emphasis on conceptual frameworks, had not identified procedures for creating sets of interrelated propositions, it had clearly created an intellectual climate conducive to that task.

In 1966, Hill specifically addressed the problem of creating "partial theories out of discrete propositions" (p. 11) and suggested how that could be done. In that important formulation, Hill integrated the work of Zetterberg with the conceptual framework emphasis and turned family theory in the direction that it would travel in through the 1970s. He clearly saw Zetterberg's approach to the construction of theoretical sociology as holding the key for the family field. He urged family theorists and researchers to "go beyond journalistic-type descriptive writing . . . to the level of explanation and verification; that is, to the formulation of propositions'' (1966, p. 15). He still advocated more codification, but building propositions and linking them into sets of propositions (of lower and higher orders) would produce theory. Emphasis on propositions could transform conceptual framework description into theories. He then pointed to work currently under way that attempted to build theory of this type. In his view, such development would show "that family theory in 1965 is not limited to naming and classifying of family behaviors. We are indeed developing more and more encompassing propositions which when linked together, permit deduction of higher-order partial theories'' (p. 17). It remained, then, for the work of the 1970s to make explicit the procedures recommended for constructing theories and actually to create theory by interrelating propositions.

Theory Construction

With the intellectual climate of the 1950s and 1960s having been prepared by Hill, Goode, and Christensen, who all emphasized propositions, and with Hill (1966) in addition pointing to the significance of Zetterberg's treatise on theory construction, the groundwork was laid for rapid accomplishments in theory construction during the 1970s. These rather remarkable accomplishments were achieved by following and extending leads published by sociologists of the theory-construction variety and organizing coordinated theory-construction projects involving large numbers of leading family researchers and theorists.

In the 1960s, several sociologists addressed the need for methodologies of theory construction (Blalock, 1969; Dubin, 1969; Homans, 1964; Stinchcombe, 1968; Zetterberg, 1965). These sociological works had a noticeable influence on the theory construction movement in the family field. As noted above, Hill first used Zetterberg's strategies. Ivan Nye and his students applied the Zetterbergian techniques of theory construction advocated by creating chains of propositions in three substantive areas of the family. Bartz and Nye (1970) developed propositions attempting to explain and understand early marriage. Nye, White, and Frideres (1973) created propositional formulations in family stability, and Nye, Carlson and Garrett (1970) did the same for family size. These theoretical efforts represent the first attempt by family sociologists to systematically create interrelated sets of propositions in different areas. Some observers have referred to this as axiomatic theory building (Burr *et al.*, 1979, p. 8), which underscores the interrelatedness of propositions with higher and lower levels. Some more general propositions are created out of lower level propositions, usually more closely tied to empirical research. Some type of inductive logic is used to create the more general propositions, which presumably give the theory greater explanatory power.

Burr's publication in 1973 further focused attention on the theory construction effort. He took as his central task that identified by Blalock (1969):

The careful reworking of verbal theories is undoubtedly one of the most challenging tasks confronting us. The major portion of this enterprise will undoubtedly consist of clarifying concepts; eliminating or consolidating variables, translating existing verbal theories into common languages, searching the literature for propositions, and looking for implicit assumptions connecting the major propositions in important theoretical works. (p. 27)

Burr's book-length work (1973) was a progress report on his project of "theoretical reformulation.'' The project was begun in 1968 with the stated purposes being

(1) to identify theoretical propositions that seem to be useful in understanding processes in the social institution of the family, (2) to analyze the nature of these propositions to determine what is asserted and the circumstances under which it is asserted to occur, (3) if there is no defensible way to improve the original theoretical formulations, an attempt is made to integrate them with other theoretical ideas when this is possible, (4) to improve the propositions if possible by such techniques as clarifying concepts or relationships, relabeling variables when they are the same as other variables but have different labels, identifying clearly those assertions that are made in the formulation and those that are not, and identifying the logical relationship of the propositions with other propositions, (5) to examine the relevant empirical data to determine the amount of proof that exists either for or against various aspects of the theoretical ideas, (6) to identify how the theoretical ideas can be used in applied professions such as teaching, counseling, and community action, and (7) to develop computer simulations with some of the theoretical models. (p. vii)

The first four purposes call attention to the central role of propositions in theory construction and to how the theory can be improved. The fifth goal is to test the theory by examining empirical data, and the sixth points toward practical application.

Burr's treatise begins with an attempt to spell out his view of theory, which is essentially that espoused by the above-mentioned authors of theory construction works in sociology, with some recourse to philosophers of science such as Ernest Nagel, Richard Braithwaite, and Abraham Kaplan. In theory construction in sociology, the influence of Zetterberg's work is very apparent. His work, when compared to that of the other theory construction sociologists, is most often referenced by Burr. There is a difference of emphasis between the two, with Zetterberg's formulations emphasizing the inductive process, whereas Burr's emphasize deductive processes in theory building.

Burr (1973) repeated the assertion of Zetterberg (1965) and Homans (1964) that the "goal of theorizing is to acquire laws about nature that can be used to explain and predict more specific phenomena'' (p. 1). Next follows a discussion of the various components of theory: concepts, variables, and "propositions as statements of relationship among variables.'' Although these are necessary components of theory, they are not sufficient to constitute a theory because the propositions may not form a logically interrelated set of propositions capable of explaining family phenomena. Burr (1973) identified the additional necessary component:

It would be possible to have a large conceptual framework (list of concepts or taxonomy), to have a large number of proposi-

tions, but if this additional component of deductive theory is not present there is no theory. There is no explanation and the concepts and propositions are scientifically useless without this additional component, which is thus an extremely valuable part of deductive theories. Unfortunately, it is also the part that social scientists tend to have the most difficulty understanding and using. This component is the particular type of logical relationship between propositions that provides explanation or understanding, referred to as deduction—the process of using certain propositions and other identifiable conditions as a basis for explaining why other propositions or conditions exist. (p. 19)

When the above components of theory are present, Burr (1973) argued, "there is enough explanation that theory genuinely exists" (p. 22). He then noted that Homans (1964) had made a similar argument. Development of this type of theory will produce scientific knowledge because, as Burr (1973) wrote, "the end of science is not prediction but understanding through the use of theory" (p. 23).

The remainder of the 1970s was largely a continuation of the theory construction emphasis, following the general pattern initated by Nye's and Burr's trend-setting work. The most notable accomplishment is the two-volume *Contemporary Theories about the Family* (1979a,b), edited by Burr, Hill, Nye, and Reiss.

This impressive two-volume publication grew out of years of organizing and work among some of the recognized leaders in research and theory in the family field. By using organizations such as the National Council on Family Relations and the family section of the American Sociological Association, the editors were able to enlist the efforts of 45 researchers and theorists from over 25 universities to build theory in 22 "theoretical domains" (Burr *et al.*, 1979a, p. 13). The initial idea for the project occurred in the summer of 1972 and ended in 1979 with the 1,020-page publication.

The overall plan of the project was broken into two phases; the second phase consisted of two parts. In Phase 1, the 45 theorist authors constructed their theory according to guidelines provided by the editors. Some of the points emphasized in the seven guildelines were (1) that areas would be included only where it could be demonstrated that enough previous research and theory existed to justify inclusion. The intent was to build on previous empirical and theoretical work and not to engage in "speculative thinking." The authors would (2) make explicit statements of propositions and evaluate the level of proof for them; (3) create a diagrammatic presentation depicting the basic causal formulations represented by their theory; (4) organize each chapter around theoretical ideas (i.e., propositions) rather than around "previous studies" or "historically oriented" organizational strategies; (5) not use various "conceptual frameworks . . . to illuminate their area of study"; as the testability of the theory against empirical findings "should be paramount throughout the work." The last guideline to be followed was (7) that the propositions should be "indented and set off from the other text" (Burr *et al.*, 1979a, pp. 12–13). The results of Phase 1 were published in Volume 1.

In Part 1 of Phase 2, a selected group of scholars each wrote a chapter that would integrate theoretical ideas generated by the authors in the 22 areas in Volume 1 with a particular theoretical orientation: exchange theory, symbolic interaction, systems theory, conflict theory, and phenomenological theory. Part 2 was to have followed Merton's codification procedures. The formulations from Phase 1 were to have been used to "induce more general formulations than had been achieved" by the various authors. In addition to making the project more manageable, the editors believed that the two-phase strategy would (1) integrate the context-bound theories into the more widely used theories and (2) systematically integrate the 22 substance-bound theoretical formulations with each other in the more general theory created in Part 2 of Phase 2. The completion of this theoretical project would correct the problem of isolation of the family field from "mainstream theoretical developments in the basic disciplines that inform the family field" (Burr *et al.*, 1979a, p. 12).

The project completed all of the proposed work except the second part of Phase 2. The chapters were written that attempted to integrate the findings from the first phase into the general theoretical orientations. The degree to which the various authors succeeded is debatable. In the introduction to Volume 2, the editors noted the difference between the degree to which the authors integrated the theories from Phase 1 into their chapters. In the epilogue to Volume 2, the editors explained the difference in the degree of integration of middle-range theories from Volume 1, into more general theory as being due to the length of time that the theoretical orientations had been used. Symbolic interaction and exchange were the oldest and very likely "guided the thinking of many of the theorists and researchers who were developing middle range theories in Volume I" (Burr *et al.*, 1979b, p. 207). Systems, conflict, and phenomenology were newer and therefore were less useful in integrating the middle-range theories from Volume 1.

Volume 2 makes one thing clear: The relationship between conceptual framework and theory is still ambiguous. If theory is taken to be an interrelated set of propositions, then constructing more general theory by integrating middle-range theories through the use of different theoretical perspectives did not necessarily produce theory in the form of interrelated sets of propositions. The authors of the systems, conflict, and phenomenology chapters made it explicit that they were writing about conceptual frameworks and/or theoretical orientations rather than theory. To talk of theory would have been premature (Broderick & Smith, 1979, p. 126; Sprey, 1979, p. 130). The authors of the symbolic interaction chapter wrote about the need to identify and clarify a "conceptual framework that is within this theory" (Burr *et al.*, 1979b, p. 42). Their use of the word *theory* seems to refer to the general theoretical perspective rather than to specific propositional formulations. Our judgment is that the chapters appearing in Volume 2 have much in common with earlier work referred to as conceptual frameworks. These chapters may be called *theoretical perspectives,* but the terms appear to be used synonymously.

The absence of the family development framework from Burr *et al.* (1979b) is enigmatic. Up to the publication of the two-volume work, virtually all review pieces had identified it as a major conceptual framework, but it does not appear in Burr *et al.* (see Figure 1). In our judgment, its absence should not be taken to mean that the framework is no longer an important approach used in family analysis. Rather, we suspect that its absence is more a historical accident resulting from the fact that Hill, a long proponent of the family development framework, was not able to complete Part 2 of Phase 2. We suspect that, had he been able to induce more general theory (see the discussion below), it would have contained much from the family development framework. Chapter 17 in this book on family development is evidence of its continued relevance to the study of the family.

If the terms *conceptual frameworks, theories,* and *theoretical perspectives* are still used with different meanings, our impression is that the term *middle-range theories* is used rather consistently throughout the project. In that sense, the theory-building project was very successful in generating theories of the middle range defined as interrelated sets of propositions in 22 areas of family study. This outcome corroborates what others have noted, namely, that one of the reasons that Merton's admonition to create middle-range theories was so popular was that it opened the theory construction door to virtually all research-oriented social scientists who wanted to pass through: "Whatever theory 'really' was, the important theorizing was no longer the monopoly of philosophically oriented theorists" (Burr *et al.,* 1979a, p. 6). Zetterberg, Homans, and others increased the flow of traffic through the door opened by Merton.

If the project was singularly successful in creating middle-range theory, it was just as singularly unsuccessful in creating general theoretical formulations. Not only was there difficulty in the integration work of Part 1 of Phase 2, discussed above, but Part 2 of Phase 2 never materialized. The strategy in Part 2 was to follow Merton's procedures of codification of the middle-range theories from Volume 1 into more general theories by means of inductive processes. Hill was the theorist commissioned to carry out this part of the project. He reported some initial success, but overall, the project was a dismal failure. In a statement that is remarkable for its candor in the social sciences, which generally do not publish results of projects that fail (nonfindings), Hill refreshingly identified some perceptions about what didn't work:

The inductively oriented scholar encountered serious trouble, however, in his attempts to deal with the hundreds of partial theories, chain propositions, and empirical generalizations across some twenty domains. This was the central task of conceptual and theoretical integration across domains using inductive procedures. Hill failed first of all because of the lack of semantic equivalence across domains and the lack of iso-

morphism of the phenomena treated in the several chapters. Moreover, in the theory domains where the authors had concluded their theory building by summary theoretical models, the complexity of these models defied mergers. The usual rules for simplifying by subsumption, which enabled the scholars within domains to pare down the number of propositions in a given model, proved almost useless in attempting model mergers.

Finally, Hill reported serious problems of equivalence of propositions and theories at the macro level of changes and continuity in family forms and functions in Western civilization, at the meso level of family transactions with social networks and community agencies and at the micro level of family problem-solving patterns, all of which are represented in the twenty-two domains of Volume I. It appeared that no readily available vocabulary of concepts and partial theories was forthcoming to encompass these disparate levels of analysis.

Hill concluded that a summary chapter aimed at achieving a less substance-bound general theory by the method of induction across the theory domains in Volume I was not viable at this time, given the state of the art of inductive theory building and the time available. (Burr *et al.,* 1979b, pp. xiii–xiv)

This is an informative comment and causes one to reflect on the field of family study and on theory construction in particular, especially given that, some 30 years earlier, Hill (1951b) had noted the chaos in the field and observed that "our findings do not add up . . . because of disciplinary separatism" (p. 17). This realization led him to his two-decade-long work on conceptual frameworks and finally into the inventorying and theory-building efforts. Did the nonadditivity of the middle-range theories result from research and theory generated in the competing disciplines that Hill had observed 30 years earlier? Although the theoretical and research chaos of the 1940s and the 1950s may have resulted from the competition of scholars from various disciplines, we think that cannot be the cause of the observed chaos in general theory at the end of the 1970s.

In looking carefully at those 45 authors working in the theory construction project, we are impressed much more by their similarity in training and orientations than by their differences. Of the 45 authors in Volumes 1 and 2 (including the editors), 34 were trained as sociologists and/or members of sociology departments, 4 were in psychology departments, 5 were in child and family departments, and 2 were in other settings. When one looks at the two chapters authored chiefly by the 4 psychologists, which would have been the most unusual according to disciplinary difference, it is obvious that their theoretical formulations were not the chief source of Hill's problems in integration. The theory construction effort is clearly the work of sociologically oriented family theoreticians, and it mirrors that in most of the chapters. The source of the failure to achieve more general knowledge must be sought elsewhere.

As the family field analyzes the failure to achieve more general knowledge, we suspect that one source that ought to be carefully considered is the general process of theory construction used during the 1970s. Here, we think that the debate that has been going on in general sociological theory can be informative. For example, Alexander (1982) looked at some of the theory construction work of Zetterberg, Homans, Stinchcombe, and others and argued that this positivist heritage unduly emphasizes the "observational and verificational dimensions: and inevitably leads to the atomization of scientific knowledge." He wrote that the "positivist thrust of contemporary sociology impoverishes not only the realm of empirical inquiry but also what remains of the theoretical tradition itself" (pp. 9, 15). Alexander saw the results of the theory-building efforts, along with other developments in sociology, as resulting in a pressing "need for a general theoretical logic in Sociology" (p. 33). We see the experience of those researchers and theorists working in the family arena during the 1970s as corroborating Alexander's observations.

Because family theory in its general outline is seen in this treatise as a specific instance of mainstream sociological theoretical thinking, it has brought with it the accompanying positivist view of the nature of its subject matter. Family theory reflects the union of empiricism and rationalism[5] that had occurred centuries earlier in the physical sciences and had fundamentally influenced the social sciences. This natural-law approach to the study of the social order and of the family emphasizes the necessity of clearly identifying the key variables that characterize family reality, both theoretically and operationally. It emphasizes the necessity of carrying out sufficient empirical research so that the underlying regularities in the nature of that social order can be discovered, the essential varying components can be abstracted, and the reduced number of variables can be logically ordered into higher order propositions, from which a number of specific and testable hypotheses can then be derived. Family theory conceptualizes social order as a knowable reality and portrays the rational side of theory building as consisting of the use of both inductive and deductive reasoning.

The combination of empiricism and rationalism in a natural-law framework applied to the study of the family as part of the social order creates its own particular view of knowledge. Knowledge and explanation are very closely related. Family phenomena will be explained, and hence, knowledge will be generated when the observable family phenomena in question can be deduced from a more general law. The most explicit statement of this

particular view of theory in the family field was given by Burr (1973) in the chapter "The Nature of Deductive Theory." With the family field operating from this basic view of theory, knowingly or unknowingly it has also operated according to underlying positivist views of the nature of family phenomena. From this received view of theory, "Scientific progress (is) dependent upon: (a) a calculus composed of a set of axioms deductively generating theorems, (b) a set of bridge principles linking the calculus to observable phenomena, and (c) a set of deductively generated empirical claims that can be tested against empirical reality" (Alexander, 1982, p. 131).

This received view of family theory is similar to mainstream sociological thought in that it highlights the break between theory and fact. Facts are seen as existing independently of the theoretical formulations. The yardstick against which any theory is to be measured is the array of empirical facts. This general strategy elevates the empirical evidence in any epistemological discussion of knowledge. The empirical side tends to be treated as "unproblematic" and "questions of a theoretical or general nature can correctly be dealt with only in relation to such empirical observation." In family theory in particular and in mainstream sociology in general there has been "a continual . . . effort . . . to reduce every theoretical whole to the sum of its more empirical, more specific parts" (Alexander 1982, p. 7). The emphasis in family theory on empirical findings and on building higher order propositions from them flows logically from the positivist persuasion. When the major publications in the field and activities such as those of the theory construction workshop of the National Council on Family Relations are analyzed for the period from 1950 to 1980, it is obvious that many of the leaders in the family field saw much of merit in the received view of family theory.

We think, however, that the family field has begun to assess more carefully some of the implications of the received view of theory for the field. We suspect critiques of the received view of theory to be important parts of the theoretical works of the 1980s. The first attempt at such critiques was offered by Thomas, Kleber, and Galligan (1980) in the theory workshop of the National Council on Family Relations. This critique was followed, a year later, by Osmond's examples (1981) of alternative approaches to positivist family theory. In the 1982 theory workshop, Harris and Berlin (1982) asked some very fundamental and insightful questions about what family theory of the received view says about families. They observed that family theories, as they had been created during the 1970s, were not necessarily "benign. They produce paradox with no escape" (p. 17).

Aldous (1980), reacting to the first effort at critique by Thomas et al. (1980), observed that the critique seemed "to mark the end of an era, an era in which it was thought that there was a simple 'how to' scheme for creating theory and that any number could play" (p. 1). We doubt that such critiques will end an era, but we do think that the field is ready to reassess some of the positivist heritage

---

[5]For a typical discussion of the union of rationalism and empiricism in Western thought, see Martindale (1960, pp. 425–427, and 1962, pp. 424–458, especially his Chapter 17, "The Humanistic and Scientific Policies of Western Intellectuality") Martindale observed that, for science to emerge, the social order had to be willing to elevate empirical proof to be equal to or perhaps even more important than rational proof (pp. 447–448). Merton (1957) made a similar point, observing that, in America, these two forces combined in the early historical setting: "Puritanism and the scientific temper are in most salient agreement, for the combination of *rationalism and empiricism* which is so pronounced in the puritan ethic forms the essence of the spirit of modern science" (p. 579).

underlying its views of theory. Part of the impetus for this reassessment, we suspect, may well come from the clinically oriented family researchers and theorists who have not been in the forefront of the theory-building movement.

The Clinical Emphasis. Although individuals had been performing marital and family therapy for decades, the period 1946–1963 has been called the professionalization era for marital and family therapy (Broderick & Schrader, 1981, p. 13). During this period, standards for clinicians and centers were established, training centers were developed, and landmark publications appeared. Broderick and Schrader (1981) characterized the 1960s and 1970s as the time of the amalgamation of four movements that laid the groundwork for the present marriage and family therapy emphasis in the family field: the marriage counseling movement, psychoanalysis, the family therapy movement, and sex therapy. As is evident from the diversity of these four founding movements, marriage and family clinicians represent a broad range of approaches to the theoretical study of the family. Academic disciplines and training of marriage and family clinicians include medicine, law, education, the ministry, and the social sciences. Conceptual frameworks and techniques run the gamut from behaviorism to systems theory and include techniques as varied as structural family therapy, contextual family therapy, and marital contracts.

As a group, marriage and family clinicians have not been heavily involved in the theory-building efforts of family researchers and theorists described previously.[6] For example, *The Handbook of Family Therapy* (Gurman & Kniskern, 1981b) organizes conceptual frameworks into four different approaches: psychoanalytic and object relations, intergenerational, systems theory, and behavioral. In the almost 600 pages of text describing these approaches, there are no central discussions of formal propositions, linear versus curvilinear relationships, or how respective variables might vary (i.e., are they dichotomous, continuous, or interval variables?). If variables and propositions are at the heart of the family theory-building efforts, then marriage and family clinical theory is of a very different order. The emphases by clinicians is on the background of the approach, definitions of functional and dysfunctional marriages and families seen

within the framework, assessment, goal setting, treatment applicability, structure of the therapeutic process, role of the therapist, techniques of therapy, curative factors, effectiveness of the approach, and training issues (Gurman & Kniskern, 1981a, pp. xv–xvii).

Although it is certainly possible for clinicians to build propositional theory, they have done little theorizing of this type. Some marriage and family clinicians find more practical use out of typologies rather than theoretical models constructed out of variables and propositions. Olson, Russell, and Sprenkle (1980, p. 983), marriage and family clinicians, argued that efforts to create typologies of families is more useful in therapeutic work with families than is a concern about variables, while Rollins and Thomas (1979, pp. 343–348), family researcher-theorists, argued for an emphasis on variables and not typologies. Their argument is that better scientific research and theorizing will result when variables rather than typologies are used because the relative effects of a variable "singly and in conjunction with other variables" can be assessed (p. 348). The relative merits of typologies and variables is currently unresolved in the discussion between clinicians and those with a theory construction emphasis in family theory. Reiss, Olson, and Kantor (1983) marriage and family clinicians, argued for typologies in the 1983 theory and method workshop at the annual National Council on Family Relations (NCFR) meetings, whereas theory construction proponents urged that the clinicians ought to move past typologies, which are seen as preliminary to better theoretical work with variables and propositions. Whatever the outcome of this and future discussions, it is clear that the received view of family theory is being used by a minority of marriage and family clinicians.

One attempt has been made by family theorists and researchers to apply the received view of theory to the practical setting (Burr, Mead, & Rollins, 1973). Examples are given for using generalizations from empirical research in both education and counseling settings. Even though this article was published more than a decade ago, it has not generated many published attempts at application by clinicians.

This difference of opinion about the use of empirical research and theory is currently being discussed in the clinical literature. Many marriage and family clinicians see empirical research as a necessary means of evaluating process and outcome in marriage and family therapy (Pinsof, 1981; Gurman & Kniskern, 1981b). However, a growing number of marriage and family clinicians, calling themselves the *new epistemologists* (Gurman & Kniskern, 1983), challenge even the use of traditional theory and research methods (Colapinto, 1979; Sheehan, Storm, & Sprenkle, 1982).

The current differences between the family theorists and the clinical theorists have much in common with differences between social workers and sociologists in the late 1800s, discussed earlier. The different approaches to becoming scientific discussed by Howard (1981) reflect

---

[6]The clear exception that tends to prove this generalization is seen in the career of Carlfred Broderick. He has been prominent over the years in the National Council on Family Relations and active specifically in the theory construction workshop, as well as contributing to the family theory literature during the 1960s and 1970s. However, most of his work has been in the area of stock-taking articles, such as his 1970 review article and his chapter with J. Smith on systems theory in Volume 2 of *Contemporary Theories about the Family* (1979). Our own judgment is that, in his work as a clinician, the literature on theory construction in the family here called the *received view* does not readily inform his therapeutic strategies or his work in family theory.

different views of research and practical application. His observation that "sociologists came to view the goal of their profession as social knowledge, while social workers saw their goal as social therapy" (p. 41) could, with only slight modification, be used to describe differences between the received view of family theory and theory as it is discussed in clinical literature.

We suspect that part of the difference is related to the nature of explanation. In the received view of theory, explanation is achieved when the specific instance of human behavior can be deduced from the more general law. We suspect that this type of explanation is not very informative to many clinicians, who live with the pressures of trying to help solve the family's practical problems. The emphasis of contemporary marriage and family therapists, just as that of therapists in the late 1800s, is continuing the scientist–humanist split that has characterized much social science thought for the last century.

Some Accomplishments of Family Theory

The application of mainstream sociological theoretical thinking to family theory has generated some notable accomplishments. Up to the emphasis on theory beginning in the 1950s, the family field had been burdened from its inception with an atheoretical social-problems approach that tended to produce vast bodies of rambling, opinion-laden literature, which, as Hill observed, did not add up. The concern with conceptual frameworks (Hill & Hansen, 1960; Klein, 1980; Nye & Berardo, 1966) and the more systematic theory-building efforts (Burr, 1973; Burr et al., 1979a; Goode et al., 1971; Reiss, 1967) forced the field to clarify its theoretical formulations. These stock-taking and theory-building efforts have forced the theorists in the various areas to be much more specific about what they assert theoretically. Heiss (1980) extolled this more systematically developed view of theory in the field:

> We have come a long way in our requirements (of what theory should be). No conceptual schemes or theoretical approaches need apply. They want propositions which state relationships between variables, and they want these variables to be fairly abstract. Limited hypotheses will not do. And they will not settle for a rationale or explanation for each proposition, and the propositions must be connected. The explanations should be higher level propositions. The lower level propositions can be connected in a variety of ways, but they must be connected. They do not believe that discreet lower level propositions, all derived from different explanatory propositions, deserve the label of theory. (p. 201)

Another result of this particular approach to theory is that it calls attention to issues of causality. The view of the family from a natural-law perspective sees social realities operating in a time-dependent, linear fashion in the sense that all events are conceptualized as having a cause or causes. The theories that have been developed are not simplistic sets of bivariate relationships but often consist of multivariate formulations. One purpose of the multi-variate formulations is to identify contingent variables that may aid in understanding basic relationships. The theorist constructing the multivariate formulation is forced to clarify and make more explicit the underlying causal relationships that are being posited.

A consequence of this emphasis on propositions and variables in attempts at causal explanation is that it calls attention to the necessity of specifying the nature of underlying relationships between variables. Thus, the family theoretician is concerned with determining the direction of the relationship (positive or negative), the degree of linearity (straight-line or curved) and the direction of effects (causal, covariational, or nonrecursive). To appreciate the centrality of this concern is to understand why some of the writings stemming from this tradition emphasize the relationships as much as or more than the constructs (Burr, 1973; Burr et al., 1979a,b). The result of this concern about relationships is that energies and efforts in family theory are devoted to a clarification of the nature of one basic relationship (for example, see Holman, 1981).

The final accomplishment that we note here of this received view of family theory is a faith in the eventual payoff of many research and theory efforts of many social scientists. Building increment on increment of one research project after another in any area of the family field is seen as necessary foundation work that will eventually succeed in creating theory capable of explaining the phenomena under investigation. Better theory will increase the power of explanation, predictions, and control. These will all result in a payoff in the practical realm of helping families to solve problems (Hill, 1966; Burr, 1973; Burr et al., 1979a,b). The authors' hope is very similar to the one enunciated by Merton early in his formulations about what good theory would do for sociology. Merton believed that sociology had such a poor record of explanation as a science, compared to the physical sciences, chiefly because of its immaturity. Before major breakthroughs could occur, hundreds and hundreds of hours of carefully conducted research would have to be done. Only after the painstaking research had been completed could major theoretical formulations be expected. In 1949, Merton wrote, "Perhaps sociology is not yet ready for its Einstein because it has not yet found its Kepler" (p. 7). He wrote 20 years later: "Perhaps sociology is not yet ready for its Einstein because it has not yet found its Kepler—to say nothing of its Newton, Laplace, Gibbs, Maxwell or Planck" (1968, p. 47). Over the two decades, Merton increased the number of middle-range theorists and researchers needed to build the foundation, but he never stopped believing that, if enough work was done, a foundation would be built for major breakthroughs.

This same faith in the eventual payoff has been an important theme in most of the central works in family theory (Aldous, 1970; Burr, 1973; Burr et al., 1979a,b; Christensen, 1964; Goode, 1959; Hill & Hansen, 1960). It was also repeated by Holman and Burr (1980) in their review of the 1970s. For them, however, the payoff will come not only from more empirical research but from applying the theory construction tools to already-published research. One of the consequences of this incremental view of the nature of family theory and research is that the best work may well be done by groups of family researchers and theorists. Hill (1966) espoused this view, and Holman and Burr (1980) reiterated it. Faith in the eventual payoff, in terms of both better theory and better practice, helps one to understand the remarkable accomplishment of the 4 editors and the 45 authors who produced the two-volume *Contemporary Theories about the Family*—a most visible and influential product of such joint efforts.

Alternates to the Positivist View

From 1950 on, family theory espoused a traditional sociological mainstream view of the nature of theory. This traditional view is enunciated clearly in the first handbook (Christensen, 1964). Christensen discussed what should be the attitude of science and then observed that family theory was moving in that direction. Once family theory was improved, it would become better science in Christensen's view. He wrote, "the attitude of science is that of value-free truth-seeking: the method is that of the objective analysis of empirical data and the aim is that of predictive theory" (p. 11). He argued that the scientist must become free of bias or vested interest in the research process so that she or he can create a "value-free science" (Christensen, 1964, p. 27). The positivist suppositions behind this argument are self-evident.

This same objectivist's view underlay much family theory and research during the 1970s. At the same time that the received view of theory was being built on positivist suppositions, other branches of the social sciences were continuing to develop critiques of the received view of theory. Two streams of thought that seriously questioned the positivist view of theory came from philosophy of science and the hermeneutic emphasis.

Philosophy of Science

Although the general union of rationalism and empiricism as philosophical orientations is seen as underlying the early development of the physical sciences, it is generally conceded that the last half of the 1800s and the first two decades of the 1900s were the periods in which theory in the physical sciences came to be defined specifically as an axiomatic, interrelated set of propositions. Positivism as such was seen as being a mainstream intellectual approach during the last half of the 1800s and specifically influenced much of the social science tradition through Comptean formulations. As a chief explanatory mode of thought (Suppe, 1977), positivism, with its mechanistic view of the nature of the world, was developed to its greatest heights in the German intellectual circles culminating in the Vienna circle, where a number of mathematicians systematized and formalized the basic

view of scientific theory. Thus, by 1920, it was commonplace "to construe scientific theories as axiomatic calculi which are given a partial observational interpretation by means of correspondence rules" (Suppe, 1977, p. 2). Suppe further noted that this classical view of the nature of theory became so accepted in science that "it is little exaggeration to say that virtually every significant result obtained in philosophy of science between the 1920's and 1950 either employed or tacitly assumed" this basic view of the nature of theory (Suppe, 1977, pp. 2–4). (See Brown, 1977, or Suppe, 1977, for more detailed descriptions of the rise of this traditional view of theory.)

Although positivist thinking was an important part of conventional wisdom in philosophy, social sciences, and the physical sciences during the early 1900s, the seeds of its destruction were being sown on the frontiers of physics. The period from 1890 to 1910 saw the development of James Maxwell's electromagnetic theory, Albert Einstein's early work on relativity, and Max Planck's atomic theories. It was out of the clash between these ideas and classical mechanics that physicists realized that their ability to build models of reality was limited by the concepts through which they viewed phenomena and the assumptions that they used in constructing their models. The physicists were gradually forced to reject the radical break between theory and fact, as well as the possibility of objective empirical observation. In short, some of the presuppositions of positivism were being seriously questioned in the philosophy of science.[7]

The 1950s is generally seen as beginning the "demise of positivism" (Suppe, 1977) in philosophy-of-science circles. A number of people's works, when taken together, offered such a fundamental critique of this view of theory that, by the end of the 1960s, it was generally agreed that the philosophers of science had been forced by the weight of the argument to drastically reformulate their view of the nature of theory and the scientific enterprise.

One of the more dominant forces suggesting a fundamental reformulation of the basic view of theory came from the work of Karl Popper (Brown, 1979; Suppe, 1977). Whereas traditional positivist theoretical formulations assume an incremental growth of science through the process of adding more and more instances of confirmation to the underlying theory, Popper gave much greater emphasis to falsification than to confirmation. For Popper, inductive logic could never lead to the verification of theories, but theoretical formulations could be falsified. In Popper's formulation, the most adequate theory is the one that would generate the possible greatest number of falsifiable statements or deductions, and that would, in fact, have the least amount of evidence that could be taken as falsification of the theoretical formulations.

[7]There is a considerable body of literature on the the "new philosophy of science," which emerged during the 1960s and 1970s. The general thrust of this literature is to document how developments in physics had forced a new and radically different view of the nature of scientific theories. For some of these sources see Brown (1977) or Suppe (1977).

Although controversy surrounds some of Popper's formulations (Brown, 1979; Suppe, 1977; Alexander, 1982), the first important point for our analysis is the nature of the knowledge generated by scientific theories according to Popper. Here his ideas diverge markedly from the traditional positivist view. Whereas in positivism, generalizations in the form of scientific laws are taken to be true, for Popper (1963) "all scientific knowledge is hypothetical or conjectural" (p. 965) because theories can never be proved. As induction can never prove the truth of a universal statement, any theory must be evaluated according to whether it is the most adequate theoretical formulation at present. In Popper's view of the nature of science, current theoretical formulations may be falsified in the future, revised drastically, or overturned completely, and the theory that used to be false could, in fact, later be shown to be true. If scientific theories have this chameleon character, it makes little sense to attach truth claims to them. Many examples can be given of the changing status of theories. For instance, in the 1920s, the theory of continental drift was considered false, whereas by the 1970s continental drift had become an integral part of the present theory of plate tectonics and is now held as the most adequate theoretical formulation (Brown, 1979, p. 153).

The *second* important emphasis in Popper's model is the relationship of observation and facts to theory. In the traditional positivist theoretical formulations, there exists a radical break between fact and theory. The assumption is that the best test of a theoretical formulation is the untainted observation of a central phenomenon. As Alexander (1982) noted, this particular emphasis can be accepted only if one elevates empirical proof by seeing observation as unproblematic. This point logically leads to the necessity for the observers to free themselves of biases in order to make the untainted observation. This is the basic argument that Christensen (1964) brought into the family theory literature, where he emphasized the role of value-free science. In Popper's model (1963), this type of observation is not even possible. He wrote, "There is no such thing as 'pure' observation, that is to say, an observation without a theoretical component. All observation . . . is interpretation of facts in light of some theory" (pp. 962–963). Indeed, Popper's emphasis on the role of falsification in a theory requires that the community of scientists agree among themselves that a particular theoretical formulation is the most adequate. Once this assumption has been made and people are expecting particular outcomes to follow, it is possible for unusual findings to emerge that, in fact, contradict the expectations. In Popper's model, scientific knowledge begins when an observation creates a problem by "disappointing some of our expectations."

The other major emphasis growing out of the 1950s and 1960s that called for a radical reformulation of positivist theory is represented in the work of Kuhn (1962, 1972). His major publication appeared in 1962 and was the culmination of 15 years of work. His formulations exerted a tremendous influence on the philosophy of science during the 1960s and into the 1970s. As in Popper's formulation, Kuhn's emphasis on paradigms and his concern with anomalies that are generated from these generally accepted theoretical paradigms call attention to the tentative nature of knowledge. Kuhn's formulation also calls for a different conceptualization of progress in science. In short, Kuhn rejected the incremental notion of progress in science. In the Kuhnian formulation, major progress comes when any one scientific paradigm has existed long enough to produce a series of anomalies, that is, findings that cannot be explained by means of that particular theoretical formulation. When enough of these anomalies have accumulated over time, a crisis exists until a scientist or scientists generate a different paradigm and its accompanying different worldview. If this new theoretical formulation is more successful in explaining the observed phenomena, then it is gradually accepted by the scientific community as the dominant paradigm.

Taken together, the above and other critiques generated a fundamental skepticism about the adequacy of the traditional view of theory. In short, these formulations argued convincingly for an acknowledgment of theory-laden observations, the hypothetical and tentative nature of scientific knowledge, and the nature of the social organization inherent in a scientific community at any one point in time that leads to the acceptance or the rejection of basic scientific knowledge. In commenting on the transforming nature of this critique of the received view of theory, Suppe (1977) noted that

by the end of the decade [1960's] these [critiques] have been so successful that most philosophers of science had repudiated [the traditional view of theory in science]. . . . The consequences of this rejection were far reaching and catastrophic. Reinforced by sustained attacks on positivistic treatment of reduction, explanation, induction, and confirmation, the result was widespread confusion and disagreement. (p. 618)

In 1969, a conference of many of the leading philosophers of science was held to survey the damage and to assess the directions in which philosophy of science should go. Although the 1970s brought some clarity, it is too early to clearly discern how philosophy of science will finally reorganize itself. What is not disputable, however, is the conclusion reached by Suppe (1977) that "Positivistic philosophy of science has gone into a near total eclipse" (p. 618). Those emphases that have called for a more tentative view of the nature of scientific knowledge and for different ways of looking at explanation, induction, and confirmation have had a tremendous impact. Whatever direction philosophy of science takes, it will obviously come up with a different view of the nature of scientific theory. The new theory will undoubtedly see as much more central the role of the scientist in constructing theory and its accompanying worldview. The constructed theory will be seen as much more responsible for any conclusions reached than the traditional objectivist view, which attributes any conclusions to the nature of the real world: "Causes certainly are connected with effects; but this is because our theories connect them, not because the world is held together by cosmic glue" (Hanson, 1977, as cited in Suppe, 1977, p. 159).

Thus, somewhat paradoxically, at a time when philosophy of science was turning away from an objectivist view of theory, family theory was moving in a different direction. Philosophy of science was moving to overhaul its basic view of the nature of theory while family theory was building its theoretical foundation on the positivist rubble being discarded by the philosophy of science.

During the 1960s and 1970s, there was little in the family literature that attempted to articulate what the movements in philosophy of science meant to the theory development movement in the family field. Likewise, there was little attempt during those same decades to analyze the received view of family theory in light of another tradition in the social science literature that called attention to the socially constructed nature of scientific knowledge, namely, the hermeneutic tradition.

Hermeneutics

The term *hermeneutics* is selected here to stand for a particular emphasis that has generated considerable discussion in the social sciences. *Hermeneutics* has been selected because it is generally used to describe intellectual traditions concerned with meaning or the science of interpretation. The interpretive emphasis that we wish to call attention to under the general hermeneutic label is present in both phenomenology and critical theory.

Phenomenology had made its appearance in the family literature by the end of the 1970s. Volume 2 of *Contemporary Theories about the Family* contains a chapter by McLain and Weigert entitled "Toward a Phenomenological Sociology of Family: A Programatic Essay" (1979). In this chapter are some assumptions about the nature of the social order as well as the nature of theorizing that are fundamentally different from those in the other chapters in Volume 2, which generally reflect the received view of theory. This difference is not commented on by the editors of the handbook. Coming out of the phenomenological approach of Martin Heidegger, Edmund Husserl, and Alfred Schultz, the McLain and Weigert chapter brackets the question of correspondence between the knowledge as experienced by the knower and the question of the existence of the real world taken to be independent of the observer. Their purpose is to study the process or the processes that the knowing subject uses in constructing his or her view of the everyday world. The focus then becomes one of intentional action on the part of the knowing person and how this intentional action is related to the individual's constructed reality. It is clear that the authors see the phenomenological formulations as lying outside the traditional scientific mode of investigation, which espouses an epistemology based on the degree of correspondence between the knowledge obtained and the characteristics of the real world taken to exist

independent of the observer (see specifically the discussion of "blood's lament," McLain & Weigert, 1979, p. 197).

What puts the McLain and Weigert chapter outside the traditional view of positivist sociology of the family is their concern with phenomenology as an interpretive discipline. One way to understand this interpretive dimension is to briefly consider the critique of the received view of theory from a critical theory perspective.

The critical theory movement is generally seen as beginning with the Frankfort school, a group of German intellectuals who fled Germany during World War II. Many returned and continued their critical evaluation of Western society in an effort to formulate an approach that would allow them to address fundamental issues of their times.

Theodor Adorno, Max Horkheimer, and Jürgen Habermas were some of the more important representatives of a social theory that would be critical in its basic analysis. Of primary concern was an attempt to make an extrasocietal critique of social processes, that is, to develop an analysis of the social process that would not be bound by the particular society within which it was generated. In their development of this concern, these theorists outlined a basic and fundamental critique of positivism as a way of knowing. Habermas (1970, 1971), as a current proponent of critical theory, has set himself the task of developing nothing less than a systematic approach to social analysis that will (1) be critical in nature; (2) be objective and therefore scientific, and not just another ideological formulation; and (3) be emancipative.

A central characteristic of Habermas's critical theory is the insistence on two types of knowledge. Building upon the works of Immanuel Kant, Georg Hegel, Karl Marx, and Wilhelm Dilthey, he further elaborated the basic distinction between physical and cultural sciences. The methods of investigation and the resulting knowledge are quite different in each.

In the physical sciences, the positivist methodologies produce technical knowledge. Positivism, when applied to the study of the human condition, distorts the nature of human knowledge. The contemporary industrialized world, with its emphasis on production and technology, fits very well into the traditional scientific mode of analysis. Feelings of alienation arise in those caught in technocratic organization, which sees humans as objects to be manipulated. Science of society in the positivist vein compounds the error because it fails to see humans as reflexive beings who, because of the reflexive nature of language (Habermas, 1971, p. 169), create their own social reality.

The critical theorists' critique of positivism, applied to the social structure, can be characterized in the following manner. Positivist social scientists make fundamental errors much like those of the early religionists, who out of their own needs created their gods and then worshiped them. When applied to the social world, positivism takes humankind's social constructions (norms, rules, customs, institutions, and relations among them) and treats them as "things" in the real world without seeing them as constructed realities. Like the religionists and their gods, positivist social scientists profess to be trying to discover underlying laws, and all the while fail to realize that whatever laws they discover are of their own making.

For critical theorists, the thing that makes the difference in hermeneutic interpretation is a consideration of this reflexive dimension of human behavior. In this sense, Habermas's formulations are similar to the phenomenological emphasis growing out of Alfred Schutz. Schutz (McLain & Weigert, 1979) espoused the notion that self-understanding is vital. Habermas sees his formulations as going beyond the phenomenology of Husserl and Schutz. His formulations are presented as scientific and, in that sense, are assumed to be a valid critique of that social order. Not only is the critical theorist expected to expose the distortions of false consciousness generated by a given social order, but the critical theorist is also expected to identify what ought to exist.

If critical theory is to be taken seriously as a scientific critique, it must be able to demonstrate that it, unlike other ideologies, is generalizable whereas they are non-generalizable or particularistic (Sensat, 1979, p. 32). McCarthy (1978) asked,

to what standard does [critical theory] appeal in unmasking ideological world views and forms of life? To what perception or theory of reality does it appeal in characterizing other perceptions and theories as distorted . . . ? In short, to what "emphatic concepts of truth," normative and theoretical, can Habermas appeal to justify his critical enterprise? (p. 108)

Although the detailed answers to these very central questions are yet to be developed by critical theorists, it is clear from the writings of Habermas that one answer will ultimately lie in an analysis of language as well as an emphasis on the inherent nature of the human being, who has the unique capacity to utilize language in her or his communicative and social world (see McCarthy, 1978).

The Habermasian formulations emphasize language, communication, and the norms underlying language. In language, Habermas (1970) sees an inherent push toward communicative competence. From the nature of language, Habermas (1971) concluded that knowledge of autonomy and responsibility is fundamental. The

human interest in autonomy and responsibility is not mere fancy, for it can be apprehended a priori. What raises us out of nature is the only thing whose nature we can know—language. Through its structure autonomy and responsibility are positive for us. Our first sentence expresses unequivocally the intention of universal and unconstrained consensus. Taken together, autonomy and responsibility constitute the only idea that we possess apriori in the sense of the philosophical tradition. (p. 314)

As Sensat (1979) observed,

according to Habermas, the partisanship of critical theory is a partisanship in favor of the norms of rational speech, so that the question of the legitimacy of the emancipatory interest reduces itself to that of the legitimacy of the norms of rational speech. But the legitimacy of those norms, Habermas claims, cannot be [reasonably] disputed because to dispute it would require an act of communication, and every act of communication implicitly endorses these norms. For first, every act of communication endorses the values of truth and correctness: whenever we assume a theoretical attitude, whenever we engage in a discourse—indeed whenever we engage in communication at all, we thereby at least implicitly make certain pre-suppositions: namely, that true propositions are preferable to false propositions and that correct (i.e., justifiable) norms are preferable to incorrect ones. (p. 34)

Thus, the beginning point for Habermas in establishing an universally applicable critique of the social order is the nature of language. The assumption is that there is an inherent push in the nature of language toward correct statements or truth in a generalizable sense.

From the foregoing, it can be seen that critical theory has an affinity with social psychology. As Habermas wrote,

A sociology that accepts meaning as a basic concept cannot abstract the social system from structures of personality; it is also social psychology. The system of institution must be grasped in terms of the imposed repression of needs and of the scope for possible individualization. Just as personality structures must be grasped in determination of the institutional framework and the role qualifications. (cited in McCarthy, 1978, pp. 334–335)

The concepts of communicative competence and interactive competence make Habermas's position a full-fledged social-psychological formulation.

Interactive competence for Habermas is similar to communicative competence. It retains the central emphasis on the reflexive dimension but refers to a much broader setting than merely speech. He sees interactive competence as the ability "to take part in increasingly complex interactions" (McCarthy, 1978, p. 344). This ability is seen as the central dimension of Habermas's formulation about identity formation and rests on the basic assumption that, inherent in each person, is a push for competence. This characteristic is a species characteristic. Thus, it is a universal competence.

Interactive competence is seen as developing in stages that are "hierarchically ordered in a developmental logic" (McCarthy, 1978, p. 345). Here, Habermas has developed formulations akin to those of symbolic interaction, specifically those of George H. Mead, as well as utilizing Noam Chomsky's views of the nature of generative grammar and Piagetian developmental stages. In the latter area, Habermas relies on Lawrence Kohlberg's formulation of the developmental stages inherent in moral development as a basis for understanding interactive competence. By giving the human being inherent predispositions toward language, as well as more broadly defined social interactional competencies, it is clear that Habermas has moved epistemologically to a position close to Piagetian formulations, which ultimately require a biological base to carry his ethics.

In summary, the critique of positivism from the critical theory perspective insists on a knowledge duality by arguing that, unlike in the physical sciences, understanding, not causal explanation, is the goal of the human sciences. Only by focusing on the knower can one begin to understand intentional behavior and human choice, which are fundamental to an understanding of the human condition. In addition, whereas knowledge gained in the physical sciences tends toward neutrality in the realm of what ought to be, understanding in critical theory carries with it a commitment of emancipation from oppressive social orders. Theory and practice are not separate, but inseparably joined (Habermas, 1971, pp. 311–317).

The Postpositivist Future

Assuming that the general outline of this treatise has some validity—namely, that (1) family theory brought with it a mainstream sociological view of theory based on positivist presuppositions, and that (2) since 1950, this received view of theory has been described as needing reformulation by philosophy of science and hermeneutic analysis, what directions will family theory take in the future? Given its history and its current state, we think we can see some basic issues that will receive attention in the coming years.

Epistemological questions centering on the nature of knowledge will emerge with more frequency in the family literature. We anticipate that the tentative and hypothetical view of knowledge coming from the philosophy of science will increasingly become a more central part of the Western world's view of science. As Bronowski (1973) noted, one of the accomplishments of physics in the twentieth century has been to prove that it is impossible to give an exact description of the physical world. He concluded:

There is no absolute knowledge . . . all information is imperfect. We have to treat it with humility. That is the human condition and that is what quantum physics says. . . .

The world is not a fixed, solid array of objects, out there, for it cannot be fully separated from our perception of it. It shifts under our gaze, it interacts with us and knowledge that it yields has to be interpreted by us. There is no way of exchanging information that does not demand an act of judgment. (pp. 353–364)

If physics has arrived at that basic conclusion, then critical theory's insistence on different types of knowledge may invite careful analysis. If physical science, as Bernstein (1976) noted, is moving to a conceptualization of knowledge that is very similar to a subjective view of the nature of knowledge encountered in the cultural sciences (e.g., in Dilthey, Habermas, and Marx), then perhaps the postulated knowledge duality may need rethinking and reformulation. If the physical world as well as the social world has to be interpreted by humankind, the knower, then what is the fundamental difference between physical and social sciences?

We expect that knowledge that is created by any scientific theory will be increasingly seen as constructed knowledge rather than as discovered knowledge in the positivist sense. This view of knowledge in relationship

to theories will force a much less radical separation between fact and theory. Alexander (1982) recently argued that this view should be part of a "postpositivist persuasion" in contemporary social thought. In this view, all facts or "scientific data are theoretically informed" (p. 30). If they are theoretically informed, and if theory is always partly constructed out of the sociocultural milieu within which it is embedded, constructing theory is always the "social activity of science" (Bhaskar, 1975, p. 48). Even Bhaskar and followers such as Outhwaite, who argue for a realist's view of knowledge and insist on the fundamental assumption that the natural order is partly responsible for knowledge gained by a probing scientist independent of the particular observer's worldview, say that a solution can be achieved to the knowledge question only by accepting the "theory-laden nature of all description" (Outhwaite, 1983, p. 323). Once the constructed dimension of scientific knowledge is accepted, questions of truth claims become very important: Will family theory attempt to continue to ground its truth claims on the traditional positivist correspondence nature of truth? To what extent will truth claims emanating from family theory be based on a consensus of the scientific community rather than on a correspondence between the "real" world object and the knower's conception of that object?

One consequence of adopting an epistemological position based on a consensus criteria of truth is to become more subjectivistic and relativistic in one's view of knowledge. For example, some have objected to the inherent subjectivism and relativism of Kuhn's formulations (Alexander, 1982). Traditionally, scientific knowledge relying on correspondence criteria of truth has been able to evaluate truth claims by assessing the degree of fit (Thomas & Weigert, 1973) between a theoretical assertion and evidence from the empirical world. However, as Alexander (1982) noted, such evaluations can be done only by assuming that the empirical evidence is unproblematic (i.e., that it is an accurate description of real-world processes). The empirically unproblematic thesis can no longer be justifiably defended. Thus, the relativity of knowledge based on the position of the observer underscored in both philosophy of science and hermeneutic discourse emphasizes the consensus basis of scientific knowledge. How adequately will the consensus criteria of knowledge serve family theorists, researchers, and practitioners who believe that they have an emancipatory responsibility when it comes to the study of the family? This is an especially important question, which focuses on the relationship between theory and practice. The social problems history of much of family theory and research highlights the importance of the very central question about what the relationship should be between theory and practice.

As indicated, the received view of family theory was developed essentially as a neutral position with respect to social action issues or the implementation of value-laden social-change strategies. A theory assumed to be value-neutral that discovered the nature of social laws, which were themselves constructed by value-laden social actions, would of necessity be a value-laden theory in defense of the status quo. Thus, some observers such as Baumrind (1980) argue that "not only is it impossible for scientists to be objective in the positivist sense, but they should not be so. That is, empirical work directed at describing what *is* should do so within a framework of clarifying and justifying what *ought* to be" (p. 647). In what way will the family theorist, advocating that a given family structure *ought* to be, be similar to or different from any other rhetorician speaking for a given value position (athlete, criminal, lawyer, politician, religionist, and so on)? This issue bears directly on both the research and theory and the family action sections in the National Council on Family Relations. The theory and the action sections of the national organization may find increasing needs for collaborative efforts.

The last issue that we think will emerge in family theory in the coming decades differs from the foregoing in that it is at base an ontological issue, whereas the above are, for the most part, epistemological concerns. Whereas epistemological questions focus on *how* one knows what is known, ontological questions focus on the fundamental nature of those things taken to exist: "Ontology asks, 'What is there?' [and] social ontology asks the same question but with specific reference to the social world . . . what are the 'solid facts' . . . ?" (Lewis & Smith, 1980, p. 8).

A traditional ontological distinction important for our discussion is that between nominalism and realism. Nominalism locates social reality in "properties of individuals and their interrelations" (Lewis & Smith, 1980, p. 8). Much of American social thought has been characterized by the nominalist view of social reality in the individual and has seen social structure as reducible to the individual and to interactions between people. Voluntarist nominalism further locates social reality in the intentionality of the human social actor (Hinkle, 1980). Wolfe (1959) argued that voluntarist nominalism has characterized most American social thought and that this voluntarist nominalism tends to mesh well with the dominant individualistic and pragmatic social milieu. The dominance of nominalist thought in the social realm is analogous to its dominance in philosophy in general. Lewis and Smith (1980) asserted that "the history of modern philosophy . . . is the history of competing nominalist systems: skepticism, subjective idealism, materialism, empiricism, positivism, analytic philosophy, rationalism, existentialism, and numerous others" (pp. 12–13).

Social realism rejects the nominalists' view of social reality and asserts that there are "characteristics of collective units not fully definable and explicable in terms of properties of the individuals comprising them" (Lewis & Smith, 1980, p. 8). The realists argue that their ontological position is more compatible with science (Outhwaite, 1983). As Lewis and Smith (1980) noted, nominalism makes "science awkward if not impossible" (p. 23). As the purpose of science is to ask questions of the

natural order, it would be impossible to conceive of a natural order if particulars (individuals, in the case of social reality) were all that is real. Science demands the existence of universals in the sense of general classes and scientific laws. For that reason, "science, as it must, has remained realistic" (Lewis & Smith, 1980, p. 13).

Although there is an emerging body of literature[8] attempting to develop realism in the social sciences, it is too early to see in detail the characteristics of a fully developed, contemporary social realism. However, some aspects are already apparent. Outhwaite (1983) argued for incorporating elements of the social construction of reality into a realist's perspective. Not only has Bhaskar (1975, 1979) argued that the realists' position is useful for the social sciences, but he has actually insisted that a science of society must be based on an ontological view of the individual that highlights the *agency* of and the *reasons* for behavior; thus, intentionality is fundamental to social realism. Furthermore, Bhaskar (1979) argued for a very different analysis of explanation. The positivist conception of deduction from higher order laws built on the notion of the constant conjunction of events that reduces such "laws to empirical regularities" (p. 27) must be rejected. Instead, Bhaskar's ontology argues for a conception of causality where "reason can and must be causes for any theoretical or practical activity to be possible" (p. 205). Lewis and Smith (1980) argued for the strong presence of social realism in the symbolic interaction tradition growing out of G. H. Mead's work. As such attempts continue to identify and develop the ontology and epistemology inherent in social realism, we expect that discussion to influence the nature and type of theory about the family likely to emerge in the coming decades.

For example, we see the general area of parent–child relations in the study of the family as being ripe for the inclusion of the concepts of agency and reason in theoretical developments. Traditionally, parent–child relations have been studied from a social mold perspective (Rollins & Thomas, 1979); however, social realism as well as common sense argues for an active, change-producing child in the family rather than a passive lump of clay molded by parental behavior. If at a very young age the child experiences itself as a central agent in the construction of its social world (Rollins & Thomas, 1979, p. 350), then family theorists ought to attempt to formulate theories that reflect that central reality.

We await the coming discussion about the nature of family theory with considerable interest. We fully expect family theorists to struggle with questions about the nature of our knowledge about the family as a social order. The decline of certainty has rendered important the base on which knowledge claims are founded. The ever-

---

[8]See Bhaskar (1975, 1979) for some of the philosophical literature on which he based his argument for the relevance of social realism as having the possibility of solving some of the problems left unresolved by traditional positivism and the hermeneutic critiques.

present concern for solving family problems, we believe, will confront those knowledge claims in any strategy designed to change human conditions. And finally, questions about what aspects of the family are taken to be real will become more salient. Perhaps, family theorists of the coming decades will develop a body of literature devoted to laying bare what the solid social facts of family life really are. In one sense, the ontological questions, we believe, are really propaedeutic to epistemological endeavors.

ACKNOWLEDGMENTS

From the beginning of this work to its completion, numerous people have made important contributions. Appreciation is expressed to Richard Galligan for extensive suggestions on earlier drafts of this chapter. We thank a number of other colleagues who at various times offered valuable criticisms, ideas, and moral support: Joan Aldous, Carfred Broderick, Wes Burr, Dave Connelly, Vik Gecas, Don Herrin, Reuben Hill, Tom Holman, Margie Holmes, Dave Klein, Bill Marshall, Boyd Rollins, Jim Smith, and Andy Weigert. James E. Faulconer, professor of philosophy, made important suggestions about the philosophical content of the chapter. Although many have helped, the authors take full responsibility for the form and content of this chapter.

References

Aldous, J. Strategies for developing family theory. *Journal of Marriage and the Family,* 1970, *32,* (May), 250–257.

Aldous, J. *A brighter view: Discussion of "through the glass darkly."* Paper presented at the NCFR Theory Construction and Research Methodology Workshop, October 1980, Portland, Oregon.

Alexander, J. C. *Theoretical logic in sociology* (Vol. 1). Berkeley: University of California Press, 1982.

Angell, R. *The Family Encounters the Depression.* New York: Scribner, 1936.

Bartz, K. W., & Nye, F. I. Early marriage: A propositional formulation. *Journal of Marriage and the Family,* 1970, *32,* 258–268.

Baumrind, D. New directions in socialization research. *American Psychologist,* 1980, *35,* 639–652.

Becker, H., & Barnes, H. *Social thought: From lore to science* (Vol. 3), *Sociological trends throughout the world to the start of the twentieth century's seventh decade* (3rd ed.). New York: Dover, 1961.

Bernstein, R. J. *The restructuring of social and political theory.* New York: Harcourt Brace Jovanovich, 1976.

Bhaskar, R. *A realist theory of science.* Leeds: Leeds Books, 1975.

Bhaskar, R. *The possibility of naturalism.* Brighton, Sussex: Harvester Press, 1979.

Blalock, H. *Theory construction.* Englewood Cliffs, N.J.: Prentice-Hall, 1969.

Bridgman, R. P. Ten years' progress in parent education. *Annals of the American Academy of Political and Social Science,* 1930, *151,* 32–45.

Broderick, C. B. Beyond the five conceptual frameworks: A decade of development in family theory.'' *Journal of Marriage and the Family,* 1971, *33,* 139–159.

Broderick, C. B., & Schrader, S. S. The history of professional marriage and family therapy. In A. S. Gurman & D. P. Kniskern (Eds.), *Handbook of family therapy.* New York: Brunner/Mazel, 1981.

Broderick, C. B., & Smith, J. The general systems approach to the family. In W. R. Burr, R. Hill, F. I. Nye, & I. L. Reiss (Eds.), *Contemporary theories about the family* (Vol. 2). New York: Wiley, 1979.

Bronowski, J. Knowledge and certainty. In J. Bronowski (Ed.), *The Ascent of Man.* Boston: Little, Brown, 1973.

Brown, H. I. *Perception, theory and commitment: The new philosophy of science.* Chicago: University of Chicago Press, 1977.

Burgess, E. W. The family as a unity of interacting personalities. *Family,* 1926, *7,* 3–9.

Burr, W. R. *Theory construction and the sociology of the family.* New York: Wiley, 1973.

Burr, W. R., Mead, D. E., & Rollins, B. C. A model for the application of research findings by the educator and counselor: Research to theory to practice. *The Family Coordinator,* 1973, *22,* 285–290.

Burr, W., Hill, R., Nye, F. I., & Reiss, I. *Contemporary theories about the family* (Vol. 1). New York: Free Press, 1979. (a)

Burr, W., Hill, R., Nye, F. I., & Reiss, I. *Contemporary theories about the family* (Vol. 2). New York: Free Press, 1979. (b)

Caplow, T., Bahr, H. H., Chadwick, B. A., Hill, R., & Williamson, M. H. *Middleton families: Fifty years of change and continuity.* Minneapolis: University of Minnesota Press, 1982.

Cartwright, D. Contemporary social psychology in historical perspective. *Social Psychology Quarterly,* 1979, *42*(1), 82–93.

Cavan, R., & Ranck, K. *The family and the Depression.* Chicago: University of Chicago Press, 1938.

Christensen, H. T. Development of the family field of study. In H. Christensen (Ed.), *Handbook of marriage and the family.* Chicago: Rand McNally, 1964.

Colapinto, T. The relative value of empirical evidence. *Family Process,* 1979, *18,* 427–441.

Dubin, R. *Theory building: A practical guide to the construction and testing of theoretical models.* New York: Free Press, 1969.

Foote, N. N. The appraisal of family research. *Marriage and Family Living,* 1957, *19,* 92–99.

Freud, S. *The basic writings of Sigmund Freud,* trans. and ed. by A. A. Brill. New York: Modern Library, 1938.

Giddens, A. *Positivism and sociology.* London: Heinemann, 1974.

Goode, W. J. Horizons in family theory. In R. K. Merton, L. Broom, & L. S. Cottrell (Eds.), *Sociology today* (Vol. 1). New York: Basic Books, 1959.

Goode, W., Hopkins, E. H., & McClure, H. M. *Social systems and family patterns: A propositional inventory.* Indianapolis: Bobbs-Merrill, 1971.

Gordon, M. *American family: Past present and future.* New York: Random House, 1978.

Gurman, A. S., & Kniskern, D. P. Family therapy, outcome research: Knowns and unknowns. In A. S. Gurman & D. P. Kniskern (Eds.), *Handbook of family therapy.* New York: Brunner/Mazel, 1981. (a)

Gurman, A. S., & Kniskern, D. P. *Handbook of family therapy.* New York: Brunner/Mazel, 1981. (b)

Gurman, A. S., & Kniskern, D. P. Family therapy research and the "new epistemology." *Journal of Marital and Family Therapy,* 1983, *9*(3), 227–234.

Habermas, J. Towards a theory of communicative competence. *Inquiry,* 1970, *13,* 360–375.

Habermas, J. *Knowledge and human interests.* New York: Beacon Press, 1971.

Harris, L. M., & Berlin, D. *Meta theoretical considerations for family theory: An apology to families.* Paper presented at NCFR Theory Construction and Research Methodology Workshop, October 1982, Washington, D.C.

Heiss, J. Family theory—Twenty years later. *Contemporary Sociology,* 1980, *9* (March), 201–203.

Hill, R. Interdisciplinary workshop on marriage and family research. *Marriage and Family Living*, 1951, *13*(1), 13–28. (a)

Hill, R. Review of current research on marriage and the family. *American Sociological Review*, 1951, *16*(5), 694–701. (b)

Hill, R. A critique of contemporary marriage and family research. *Social Forces*, 1955, *33*, 268–277.

Hill, R. Contemporary developments in family theory. *Journal of Marriage and the Family*, 1966, *28*(1), 10–25.

Hill, R., & Hansen, D. The identification of conceptual frameworks utilized in family study. *Marriage and Family Living*, 1960, *22*, 299–311.

Hill, R., Katz, A., & Simpson, R. An inventory of research in marriage and family behavior: A statement of objectives and progress. *Marriage and Family Living*, 1957, *19*, 89–92.

Hinkle, R. C. *Founding theory of American sociology 1881–1915.* Boston: Routledge & Kegan Paul, 1980.

Holman, T. B. The influence of community involvement in marital quality. *Journal of Marriage and the Family*, 1981, *43*(1), 143–149.

Holman, T. B., & Burr, W. R. Beyond the beyond: The growth of family theories in the 1970's. *Journal of Marriage and the Family*, 1980, *42*(4), 729–741.

Homans, G. Bringing men back in. *American Sociological Review*, 1964, *29*(6), 809–818.

Howard, R. L. *A social history of American family sociology, 1865–1970.* Unpublished doctoral dissertation, University of Missouri, 1975.

Howard, R. L. *A social history of American family sociology, 1865–1940*, ed. by J. Mogey. Westport, Conn.: Greenwood, Press, 1981.

Kinlock, G. *Sociological theory: Its development and major paradigms.* New York: McGraw-Hill, 1977.

Klein, D. Commentary on the linkages between conceptual frameworks and theory development on sociology. *The Social Quarterly*, 1980, *21*(Summer), 443–453.

Komarovsky, M., & Waller, W. Studies of the family. *American Journal of Sociology*, 1945, *50*(6), 443–451.

Kuhn, T. S. *The structure of scientific revolutions.* Chicago: University of Chicago Press, 1962.

Kuhn T. S. *The structure of scientific revolutions* (2nd ed.). Chicago: University of Chicago Press, 1972.

Lewis, J. D., & Smith, R. L. *American sociology and pragmatism: Mead, Chicago sociology, and symbolic interaction.* Chicago: University of Chicago Press, 1980.

Martindale, D. *The nature and types of sociological theory.* Boston: Houghton Mifflin, 1960.

McCarthy, T. *The critical theory of Jurgen Habermas.* Cambridge: M.I.T. Press, 1978.

McLain, R., & Weigert, A. Toward a phenomenological sociology of family: A programatic essay. In W. Burr, R. Hill, F. I. Nye, & I. Reiss (Eds.), *Contemporary theories about the family* (Vol. 2). New York: Free Press, 1979.

Merton, R. *Social theory and social structure.* Glencoe, Ill.: Free Press, 1949.

Merton, R. *Social theory and social structure* (rev. and enlarged ed.). Glencoe, Ill.: Free Press, 1957.

Merton, R. *Social theory and social structure* (enlarged ed.). New York: Free Press, 1968.

Mogey, J. Preface. In R. Howard (Ed.), *A social history of American family sociology, 1865–1940.* Westport, Conn.: Greenwood Press, 1981.

Morgan, W. L. *The family meets the Depression: A study of a group of highly selected families.* Minneapolis: University of Minnesota Press, 1939.

Nye, F. I., & Berardo, F. *Emerging conceptual frameworks in family analysis.* New York: Macmillan, 1966.

Nye, F. I., White, L., & Frideres, J. A preliminary theory of marital stability: Two models. *International Journal of Sociology of the Family*, 1973, *3*(1), 102–122.

Nye, F. I., Carlson, J., & Garrett, G. Family size, interaction, affect and stress. *Journal of Marriage and the Family*, 1970, *32*, 216–226.

Olson, D. H., Russell, C. S., & Sprenkle, D. H. Marital and family therapy: A decade review. *Journal of Marriage and the Family*, 1980, *42*(4), 793–993.

Osmond, M. W. *Rethinking family sociology from a radical-critical perspective: Applications and implications.* Paper presented at NCFR Theory Construction and Research Methodology Workshop, October 1981, Milwaukee, Wisconsin.

Outhwaite, W. Toward a realist perspective. In G. Morgan (Ed.), *Beyond method: Strategies for social research.* Beverly Hills: Sage Publications, 1983.

Piaget, J. *Judgment and reasoning in the child,* ed. and trans. by M. Warden. New York: Harcourt, Brace, and World, 1926. (a)

Piaget, J. *The language and thought of the child,* ed. and trans. by M. Gabain. London: Routledge & Kegan Paul, 1926. (b)

Piaget, J. *The child's conception of the world,* ed. and trans. by J. and A. Tomlinson. New York: Harcourt, Brace, and World, 1929.

Piaget J. *The moral judgment of the child,* ed. and trans. by M. Gabain. New York: Harcourt, Brace, and World, 1932.

Pinsof, W. M. Family therapy process research. In A. S. Gurman & D. P. Kniskern (Eds.), *Handbook of family therapy.* New York: Brunner/Mazel, 1981.

Popper, K. Science: Problems, aims, responsibilities. *Proceedings of the American Societies for Experimental Biology*, 1963, Part 1, No. 4, (July–August), 961–972.

Reiss, I. *Social context of premarital sexual permissiveness.* New York: Holt, Rinehart, & Winston, 1967.

Reiss, P., Olson, D., & Kantor, D. *Planning research on family classification: A discussion of questions posed by current theory and method.* Paper presented at NCFR Theory Construction and Research Methodology Workshop, St. Paul, Minnesota, 1983.

Rodman, H. Are conceptual frameworks necessary for theory building? The case of family sociology. *The Sociological Quarterly*, 1980, *1*(21), 429–441.

Rollins, B. C., & Thomas, D. L. Parental support, power, and control techniques in the socialization of children. In W. R. Burr, R. Hill, F. I. Nye, & I. L. Reiss (Eds.), *Contemporary theories about the family* (Vol. 1). New York: Wiley, 1979.

Rossi, P. Methods of social research, 1945–1955. In H. Zetterberg (Ed.), *Sociology in the United States of American: A trend report.* Paris: UNESCO, 1956.

Sensat, J. *Habermas and Marxism: An appraisal.* Beverly Hills, Calif.: Sage Publications, 1979.

Sheehan, R., Storm, C. L., & Sprenkle, D. H. *Therapy based on a cybernetic epistemology: Problems and solutions for the researcher.* Panel presented at the Annual Meeting of the American Association for Marriage and Family Therapy, October 1982, Dallas, Texas.

Sprey, J. Conflict theory and the study of marriage and the family. In W. Burr, R. Hill, F. I. Nye, & I. Reiss (Eds.), *Contemporary theories about the family* (Vol. 2). New York: Free Press, 1979.

Stinchcombe, A. L. *Constructing social theory.* New York: Harcourt, Brace, and World, 1968.

Stryker, S. Interaction theory: A review and some suggestions for comparative family research. *Journal of Comparative Family Study*, 1972, *3*(1), 17–32.

Suppe, F. *Structure of scientific theories,* (2nd ed.). Urbana: University of Illinois Press, 1977.

Sussman, M. B. Current states and perspectives of research on the family. *Social Science Information*, 1968, *7*(3), 35–52.

Thomas, D. L., & Weigert, A. Sociological theory and the family: The problem of fit between form and content. *Social Science Information,* 1973, *12*(April), 139–155.

Thomas, D. L., Kleber, J. E., & Galligan, R. *Through the glass darkly: Family theory, the new philosophy of science and hermeneutics.* Paper presented at NCFR Theory Construction and Research Methodology Workshop, October 21, 1980, Portland, Oregon.

Wolfe,, K. H. The sociology of knowledge and sociological theory. In L. Gross (Ed.), *Symposium on Sociological Theory.* Evanston, Ill.: Row, Peterson, 1959.

Zetterberg, H. L. *On theory and verification in sociology* (3rd ed.). Totowa, N.J.: Bedminister Press, 1965.

Zimmerman, C., & Frampton, M. *Family and society: A study of the sociology of reconstruction.* New York: Van Nostrand, 1935.

CHAPTER 5

Radical-Critical Theories

Marie Withers Osmond

Sociology (and here we refer specifically to family sociology) "is a science whose progress is marked less by a perfection of consensus than by a refinement of debate. What gets better is the precision with which we vex each other." Geertz (1973, p. 29)

Introduction

The goal of this chapter is to explicate a perspective termed *radical-critical theory* that questions the most fundamental assumptions of traditional family sociology. Basically, radical critics claim that family sociology, one of the oldest areas in the discipline, reflects its subject matter (rather than explaining it) and, as a consequence, constructs a deeply conservative sociological approach that limits its contribution to sociology and serves to justify the status quo in society.[1]

Radical-critical theory is virtually unexplored in American family sociology. Its origins are primarily European, and its proponents are largely from academic areas outside the sheltered boundaries of family sociology. The author embarked into this foreign territory as a result of nagging dissatisfactions with contemporary family theory and research methodology: concerns about our preoccupation with theory constructed on the basis of mountains of data that had not, themselves, been validated; concerns about our theoretical schisms and endless debates; and concerns about our narrow focus on the interior of families in the American middle class.

The chapter is an account of a journey into a "new" and quite irreverent theoretical viewpoint that questions traditional assumptions and goes beyond sheer critique to pose alternative ways of uncovering the realities of marriage and the family. There is no intent to offer radical-critical theory as a replacement for other models. However, there is sufficient evidence that radical-critical theory offers a unique perspective that will generate consider-

able theory and research as well as debate. Thus, the purpose of the chapter is to offer the student a compelling alternative to what has been a relatively restricted range of theoretical applications to the study of marriage and the family.

The chapter is organized in three sections. The first section is designed to provide a background in radical-critical theory. Unlike our familiar theoretical frameworks, the radical-critical model has received no description of founders and history, no elaboration of concepts and assumptions, in the family literature. Thus, a basic introduction is necessary to familiarize the reader with theorists, assumptions, and concepts that reappear when the chapter turns directly to the goal of theoretical application to the area of family sociology. In this introductory section, the emergence of radical-critical sociology is traced through three major sources: the European developments of both critical theory and radical structuralism and the American construction of radical sociology.

The second section attempts to locate the radical-critical perspective within the mainstream of sociological theories currently applied in family sociology. A fourfold typology of social theories is offered that distinguishes them on the basis of two major dimensions: the subjective versus the objective dimension and the radical change versus the regulation dimension. Major social theories (from symbolic interactionism to general systems theory, exchange, role, and so on) are located within this general model, and some of the basic differences in assumptions that divide these theories are discussed. Emphasis is given to how critical theory and radical structuralism view each other and the positions from which they criticize traditional sociological approaches. The section concludes with a critical overview of the development of American family sociology.

The third section illustrates applications of radical-critical theory. Radical critics contend that we must go beyond the claim that a certain theory is useful for understanding marriage and the family. The persuasiveness of the claim is in its demonstration. Two topics in family sociology are delineated as examples of the application of a radical-critical approach: family history, as related to the assumption of a "public-private" dichotomy, and the

---

[1]It is recognized that there are individual exceptions to the general picture of family sociology depicted here. The purpose is to critique the broad field of family sociology and not to extol or blame those individual members who are attempting to develop the area today.

Marie Withers Osmond • Department of Sociology, Florida State University, Tallahassee, FL 32306.

politics of sexuality. For each of these subjects, the traditional approach in family sociology is outlined and the radical-critical alternative is documented with examples from the literature.

The chapter concludes with an overview of the basic critique of family sociology and suggested guidelines for the development of a radical-critical approach. The critique and guidelines are then placed in the broader perspective of the central concepts, assumptions, and methodological positions of radical-critical theory. The emphasis is on a combination of critical theory and radical structuralism for the most heuristic development of a radical alternative for family sociology.

Emergence of Radical-Critical Sociology

It should be emphasized at the outset that the definition of *social theory* in this chapter is a broad one. The issue of what constitutes a theory in sociology continues to be debated (cf. Martindale, 1981, Chapter 3). McNall's sixfold classification of social theory (1979, pp. 1–12) is useful in delineating a number of approaches in sociology: (1) theory as science—formal, logical deductive theory; (2) theory as method—ethnomethodology is a primary example; (3) theory as a technique of illumination—the use of minitheories or concepts to gain insight; (4) theory as a belief system or ideology or model of interpretation—humanist and minority sociology offer examples; (5) theory as critique—the use of theory to demystify the social world, to explain the sources of human constraints, and to point out the possibilities of liberation; and (6) theory as praxis—the wedding of thought and action. What is termed *radical-critical sociology* in this chapter endorses each of these positions with the explicit exception of the first approach: theory as science. Radical critics are united, as is discussed at length in subsequent sections, in their "antiscientism" with regard to both social theory and research. At a basic level, contemporary radical critics call for sociological theory to be a body of explanation that "makes sense" of the social world (following Mills, 1959, and Gouldner, 1971).

Radical-critical sociology includes a number of perspectives whose integrative characteristics are the radical critique of society and of "establishment" sociology. One difficulty in explicating the approach is the diversity of theories that are currently labeled radical or critical. A commonly shared intellectual tradition of social criticism, of course, lies in Marxism. However, as Mayhew (1980) pointed out, the varieties of Marxist sociology number possibly in the thousands. Also, radical sociology should not be taken only as a euphemism for Marxist sociology. As Flacks and Turkel (1978, p. 194) asserted, radical sociology can be as critical of certain varieties of Marxism as it is of "bourgeois" or "academic" sociology. A primary distinction among these various approaches appears to be that between "critical" and "radical" theory. Both theories attempt to develop a sociology of radical change but do so from somewhat divergent viewpoints. The critical, more "humanist," approach emphasizes the subjective aspects of Marxism with a primary analytic focus on social ideology or belief systems. The radical, more "structuralist," camp advocates objective approaches and concentrates primarily on political-economic systems.[2] The intellectual histories of critical theory and of radical structuralism are traced in the following subsections, mainly by identification of the intellectual leaders in each school, along with their most visible contributions to the theoretical approach.

Critical Theory

The term *critical theory* has a relatively specific connotation and refers to the variety of Marxism originating in the 1920s when Georg Lukács and Antonio Gramsci revived interest in the subjectivist interpretations of Marx's early work. The young Marx, influenced by Hegelian idealist philosophy, sought to develop an emancipatory theory that emphasized how individuals, through self-consciousness, could create and change their society. Marx's central premise had to do with the "alienation" of the individual. In essence, he saw capitalist society as dominating human experience and as objectifying the individual's essential nature (Marx, 1844).

Lukács. Seeking to formulate a critical theory that provided an alternative to the orthodox Marxism of his time, Lukács emphasized the early humanistic, more subjective side of Marxism (for a discussion of both Lukács and Gramsci, see Burrell & Morgan, 1979; Martindale, 1981). His aim was to develop a theory of radical change that underscored the role of the proletariat, particularly its class consciousness, in the revolution against capitalist society. Thus, Lukács stressed consciousness and ideology (Marx's superstructural factors) as being basic to understanding capitalist society. In the development of theory, Lukács stressed the concept of "totality": the

[2]The distinction between subjective and objective Marxism can be traced to the publication in French in 1966 and in Britain in 1969 of Althusser's *For Marx*. Althusser saw an "epistemological break" in Marx's work. The young Marx, influenced by Hegelian idealism, stressed the domination of human consciousness by the ideological superstructures. In his later work, Marx moved from the idealist perspective to a more realist interpretation of the nature of society. Particularly in his work with Engels, Marx focused on the materialist (economic) base of society. Burrell and Morgan (1979) labeled these two camps "radical humanism" and "radical structuralism." Burroway (1978), following Althusser, termed the positions "expressive" and "structured." Mullins's distinction of "radicals" and "criticals" (1973) is quite similar to the classification in this chapter. It should be noted that, although Gouldner (1980) emphasized two orientations within Marxist sociology (which he called "scientific Marxism" and "Marxism as critique"), he insisted that these orientations reflect not different periods in Marx's life but contradictory tendencies that were always present in Marx's theory.

tenet that no partial aspect of social life and no isolated phenomenon can be comprehended unless it is related to the historical whole, the social system conceived as a global entity.

Another central concept in Lukács critique is what he called "reification." The term *reification* refers to the fact that, although individuals' everyday activities create their social world, these activities and their products are seen as independent, objectified "things" (Burrell & Morgan, 1979, p. 287). Reified ideas about the nature of social reality are constructs created in response to present social orders. When a given social structure restricts or limits possible alternatives, the structure appears to be independent of human activities. In response, people may regard the existing social arrangement as a "necessary" or even a "universal" requirement. Lukács pointed, for illustration, to social theories that claim that social relations are due to biological or ecological forces or to inherent laws of the economy. A classic example of reification in contemporary family sociology would be the idea of a "natural" differentiation of marital roles into "instrumental" and "expressive." Regardless of their content, reified ideas emphasize the permanence of the present; they direct social practice to the maintenance of the status quo; and they limit or downplay alternative assumptions of social reality. In sum, Lukács saw the political, constraining aspects of reification as the major form of alienation to be overcome in the transformation of capitalist society.

Gramsci. Gramsci was likewise convinced that ideology is the key both to social change and to social order. According to Gramsci, domination in capitalism rested, in large part, within the people's consciousness through "ideological hegemony." He maintained that the ruling class always seeks to legitimate its power through the creation (and perpetuation) of a brief system that emphasizes the need for order, authority, and discipline. Gramsci argued that it is first in the family and then in the schools and workplaces that capitalism develops and increases the invisible power of the ruling class by infiltrating the consciousness of the individual. Gramsci believed also in ideological resistance that could lead to a workers' revolution. More than other critical theorists, Gramsci emphasized "praxis," the union of theory and practice. His social theory was intended not only to explain social domination but also to serve as a political methodology to guide the working class to revolution (Hoare & Nowell-Smith, 1971). Thus, praxis is equated not with "practical" or "pragmatic" but with emancipatory social action. Praxis, as an operating condition in a society, is the opposite of alienation (Wardell & Benson, 1979, p. 239). Contemporary critics, although less revolutionary than Gramsci, still call for praxis in sociology; that is, they argue that sociologists must aim their research at the alleviation of social problems; must become closer to (be a part of) the people they study; and must make their results available and informative to the people they concern (cf.

Fasola-Bologna, 1970; Gouldner, 1973; Szymanski, 1970).

Frankfurt School. Members of the German "Frankfurt school" of critical theory were influenced by the work of Marx, Lukács, and Gramsci. The Institute for Social Research was established in Frankfurt in 1923 and has housed such social scientists as Theodor Adorno, Erich Fromm, Max Horkheimer, Leo Lowenthal, Herbert Marcuse, and Jürgen Habermas (for a history of the school, see Jay, 1973). The original effort of the Frankfurt school can be seen as an attempt to account for the failure of the western European proletariat to become revolutionary. Traditional Marxism (the late, or mature, Marx and particularly the works of Marx and Engels) appeared to rely too heavily on the concept of "mode of production" (the economic base of society). What was needed was an explanation of how ideological, cultural, and psychological factors (the superstructure) deflected the workers' class consciousness from the idea of revolution. A union of Marxism and Freudianism seemed to offer insight into the problems of individual submissiveness, repression, and conformity (i.e., an insight into how societal constraints are internalized). Marx's historical materialism would offer a critical theory of society and psychoanalysis, a critical theory of the individual.

Most reviewers agree that there is no "one" critical theory but rather the critical theories of the individual members of the Frankfurt school (cf. Tar, 1977, p. 204). For this chapter, the more pertinent theorists are Horkheimer (the original director at the school) and Marcuse and Habermas, two of the school's leading contemporary theorists.

According to Horkheimer, the task of critical theory is to penetrate the world of things to show the underlying relations between persons. The appearance of capitalist social interaction, for example, is that of equal exchange between things. The goal of critical theory is to demystify this surface form of equality. Horkheimer (1972) claimed that "the social function of philosophy lies in the criticism of what is prevalent" (p. 13). Postivism, by accepting the role of science as the careful recording of facts and limiting generalizations to surface phenomena, neglects the question of historical development and, further, becomes instrumental to the prevailing power system. Horkheimer sought to explain the rise of fascism (and other forms of authoritarian politics) through a comprehension of the process of "social reproduction" that underlies the institutions of everyday life and their relations to economic production. He maintained that the relationship between the traditional family and the maintenance of capitalist society is mutually determining. The patterns of authority characteristic of the economic sphere are "reproduced" in the family in the person of the father: "In consequence of the seeming naturalness of paternal power and its twofold foundation in the father's economic position and his physical strength with its legal backing, growing up in the restricted family is a first-rate schooling in the authority behavior specific to this society'' (Horkheimer, 1972, p. 107). Moreover, the familial role of the woman strengthens the authority of the status quo. Not only is she economically dependent on her husband's position and earnings, she is also circumscribed by the fact that her husband conforms to the economic situation and often, ambitiously, strives to better his position. In essence, the concept of ''reproduction'' is used to explain the continuity of social relations over time, especially those relations that have to do with domination or power.

Marcuse was more recognized for his attack on the ''one-dimensional'' nature of modern technological society, and his special contribution to critical theory lies in the attempt to incorporate the ideas of Sigmund Freud and Max Weber within an Hegelian-Marxist perspective (Burrell & Morgan, 1979, p. 292). In *Eros and Civilization* (1955), Marcuse linked the human personality and society through the Freudian concepts of the ''pleasure principle'' and the ''reality principle.'' Marcuse's position was that the ''reality principle'' is historically specific to eras of scarcity. He argued that, as scarcity is no longer characteristic of technically advanced societies, the need to repress instinctual drives is no longer strong. However, it continues, and Marcuse termed this ''surplus repression.'' According to Marcuse, this surplus repression, which supports the system of production, lies at the core of the individuals' psychological domination by modern society. In *One-Dimensional Man* (1964), Marcuse moved toward a more Weberian perspective in his argument that technology produces a ''one-dimensional'' society in which there is a flattening out of the human character and an erosion of the capacity for fundamental opposition. The industrial system appears to have a logic of its own. Consciousness is molded and controlled through the media. The ''welfare'' and ''warfare'' states are instruments for maintaining the level of consumption necessary for sustaining a ''happy'' work force. The logic of purposive rationality pervades both consciousness and material organization. For Marcuse, critical theory must examine historical alternatives to this technological rationality to discover possibilities for human liberation.

In the 1970s, the writing of Habermas attracted increasing attention to critical theory. Habermas's work can be understood as a reaction against the shortcomings of both interpretive sociology and sociological positivism. He sees the empirical, strict sciences as serving the interests of technological control. Further, the interpretive, hermeneutic sciences aim at understanding meaning without influencing it. The critical sciences, however, aim both to understand the world and to change it (see Schroyer, 1971, 1973, for an extended analysis of Habermas's critical theory of science). Currently, Habermas (1971) is most known for his development of a communication theory of society. According to Habermas, recent developments in structural linguistics demonstrate that today the ''problem of language'' has replaced the traditional ''problem of consciousness.'' The current goal of critical theory is to understand the role that *language* plays as an alienating force in all aspects of social life. Toward this goal, Habermas has developed a theory of ''communicative competence.'' The heart of this theory concerns the extension of economic rationality to spheres of symbolic interaction, with the resulting suppression of communicative prerequisites for self-reflective consciousness. Self-reflection is seen as necessary for emancipation from the ''seemingly'' natural forces that are, in fact, legitimations of existing control systems. Habermas has distinguished between the ''ideal speech situation,'' in which consensus develops without the operation of power (i.e., free debate), and one characterized by ''communicative distortion,'' in which a supposed consensus is arrived at within the context of unequal power relations. In short, Habermas sees communicative distortion as the very basis of human alienation.[3] Habermas's more recent work (1976) deals with the variety of crises that might affect modern society. He argued that a permanent economic crisis is no longer likely because of the pervasive intervention of the State. Thus, Habermas sees the key problem within advanced capitalism to be the ''legitimation crisis,'' that is, the capacity of the State to perpetuate the sense that its actions of authority are valid.

It appears that the most basic notion underlying the perspective of critical theory is that of the emergence of a totalitarian order in which domination is exercised through the manipulation of consciousness, rather than force, and which results in a world of one-dimensional robots. Critical theorists see the members of society as constrained by ''false consciousness,'' which inhibits true human fulfillment. The emphasis on human consciousness characterizes the perspective as a subjectivist approach to social theory. Its intellectual foundations derive from the German idealist tradition, particularly as expressed in the works of Immanuel Kant, Georg Wilhelm Hegel, and the young Karl Marx. Critical theory is generally identified with the Frankfurt school. However, members of the Frankfurt Institute were greatly influenced by Lukács and Gramsci, and the most contemporary representative of a critical viewpoint, Habermas, has departed from his institute affiliation.

Radical Structuralism

''Radical structuralism,'' sometimes termed *Marxist structuralism* or *neo-Marxism,* is identified with Marx's later work, particularly *Capital.* Here, Marx moved away from philosophical interpretations to analyses of the political economy of capitalism. His emphasis changed to a focus on ''crises, contradictions, and structures'' rather than the concepts of ''alienation, consciousness, and critique'' stressed in his earlier work. Basically, Marx's

---

[3]For a trenchant analysis of Habermas's reconstruction of Freudian psychoanalysis as a theory of distorted communication, see McCarthy (1978, pp. 193–213).

model of society consists of two structures. The "substructure" consists of the economic base of the society. The "superstructure" refers to noneconomic structures within the society, such as the State, mass culture, epistemology, and ideology. Radical structuralism concentrates on the substructure of society and sees the superstructure as being basically determined by the nature of economic production. Critical theory, as discussed above, places primary emphasis on the ideological characteristics of the superstructure. One of the goals of radical structuralism is to provide a critique of the societal status quo. Equally important is the aim toward radical social change. Analysis concerns the interrelationship of structures within society. These interrelationships are viewed as containing contradictions that generate political and economic crises that eventually lead to the breakdown of the mode of production and its related social formations. It is important to note that the idea of contradiction is central to the radical explanation of social change.[4] In contrast to the perspective of critical theory, the radicals place less emphasis on the role of the individual. Common to both camps, however, is the vision of human liberation from the forms of domination seen as basic characteristics of capitalist industrial society (see Burrell & Morgan, 1979, Chapter 10, for a discussion of "radical structuralism").

Althusser. The position of radical structuralism is perhaps best illustrated in the work of Althusser, a French Marxist scholar. Althusser's perspective can be interpreted as a reaction against the Hegelian Marxism of the Frankfurt school and an effort to develop an alternative in the tradition of a materialist Marxism. For Althusser (1969), individuals do not make history; history is made by the specific interrelationship of structures at a given historic time. The concept of "totality" is viewed as a structured totality (as opposed to the Hegelian totality of a single dominating principle or spirit). Althusser's structural totality consists of four "practices": economic, political, ideological, and scientific. Although the economic is seen as the most determinative practice (i.e., it defines the contributions of the different parts of society and thus the relations among them), at any given historic time each of the practices has relative independence despite the possible domination of one practice over others.

In essence, Althusser rejected economic determinism for a multicausal theory of history. For example, from such a structuralist perspective, the family would be viewed as performing a number of necessary functions for the capitalist economy: reproducing labor power; preparing youth for the alienating experience of work; socializing children; maintaining women as a reserve labor force; consuming; and so on. However, the family not only changes with the changing requirements of the capitalist

economy but also has a structure of its own and, therefore, a relative independence in carrying out its activities (see Burroway, 1978, for a lucid discussion of Althusser's notion of structural and expressive totalities). For Althusser, social change depends on the type and extent of contradictions in the structural totality. Some contradictions can be antagonistic, and their interrelationships will produce sweeping social change; other contradictions can be absorbed by the system. Thus, revolution will depend on particular conjunctions of contradictions and structures in domination. Also, change is uneven: it is the combination of the disparate histories of the separate practices. Because these practices move with their own relative independence, revolutionary situations (conjunctures) can be unpredictable. Thus, the focus on "times of crisis." The role of individuals as political activists receives little emphasis in Althusser's work. In sum, Althusser argued for a historical analysis of the interrelationship of social structures (and their relative dominance) as related to specific historical events.[5]

Godelier. The French structuralist Maurice Godelier identified himself, perhaps more than Althusser did, with contemporary sociological structuralism (McQuarie, 1978). Godelier focused on the contradiction between the everyday, taken-for-granted, "visible" functioning of social relations and the "hidden" nature of the social structures that govern and explain these relationships. He emphasized that Marx's most important contribution to the social sciences was in the study of social structures and their "hidden" and multiple evolutions. Godelier argued that social reality presents itself as a multiplicity of layers (structures). The role of social science is to peel back the surface layers of taken-for-granted (ideological) representations of everyday life and penetrate to the "hidden" forms of social relations. For example, the wage exchange, which on the surface appears to be a "fair exchange" of equivalents, is shown to conceal an asymmetrical exchange: the exploitation of surplus value.

In one incisive article, Godelier (1970) explicated the controversial idea of "contradiction" in Marx's *Capital*. Godelier asserted that there are contradictions internal to the system and others that exist between systems. For example, the contradiction between capital and labor is an internal contradiction of a structure. The contradiction is antagonistic: the function of one class is to exploit the other. This contradiction reveals itself (becomes manifest) in the class struggle. Godelier interpreted the notion of contradictions between structures as explaining the objective *limits* on the possibilities of their reproduction. Beyond these limits, a change in structure becomes necessary. Instead of starting with individuals and their social norms of prescribed behavior to explain the role and

---

[4] For a very negative critique of critical theory in general and Habermas's work in particular, see Van Den Berg (1980).

[5] See Althusser (1969) and Althusser and Balibar (1970). For further discussion of Althusser's approach see Burroway (1978), Collinicos (1976), and Glucksmann (1974). My interpretation owes much to Burrell and Morgan (1979).

the hierarchical relation of the structures of a society, Go-delier posited that it is necessary to explain the role and the relation of structures in all their aspects, known or unknown by individual members, and to look to the struc-tures for the basis of norms and values.

It should be emphasized that radical structuralism re-flects a revolutionary view of social change that is in marked contrast to a number of critical theorists' vision of nonviolent change through the alteration of con-sciousness. Structures are viewed as being changed pri-marily through economic and political crises that generate such a degree of conflict that the status quo is necessarily dislocated and replaced by radically different systems. It should likewise be understood that there is a wide range of debate within the structural Marxist perspective and, in particular, that different theorists stress the role of differ-ent social forces in their explanation of social change (Bottomore, 1975).

American Radical Sociology. In concluding the histor-ical review of the background of critical and radical theo-ries, it is pertinent to note how very recently these per-spectives entered American sociology. The "radical movement" in American sociology, which began in the 1960s, acknowledged C. Wright Mills (who was more influenced by Thorsten Veblen than by Marx) as found-er.[6] Mills rejected both the abstract theorizing of Talcott Parsons and the bureaucratic ethos of the survey research institute. He called for the study of large-scale so-ciological problems that would interrelate the individual, social structure, and history. During the 1960s, so-ciology's neglect of the issues of power, protest, and ideology laid the groundwork for the radical critiques of social theories that appeared to be biased toward system maintenance. Gouldner's presidential address at the an-nual meeting of the Society for the Study of Social Prob-lems ("The Myth of a Value-Free Sociology," 1962) and his best-known book, *The Coming Crisis of Western So-ciology* (1971), set the tone and the targets for American radical sociology.

Overall, the radical attack included analyses of the ideological foundations of theoretical frameworks (es-pecially functionalism); a criticism of survey research methodology (Mills's "cheerful robots" of computer analysis); charges of ahistoricism, ethnocentrism, natu-ralism, and universalism; and an exposure of university sociologists' conservative liberalism and dependence on financial support from governmental agencies whose goal was to maintain the status quo (cf. Flacks & Turkel, 1978, and the special issue of *Sociological Inquiry,* Winter 1970).

In short, the origins of the American radical movement were, first, a rebellion against the values of establishment sociology and its blindness to power relations; second,

the participation of academics (graduate students and fac-ulty) in contemporary social movements (such as antiwar, black-power, and women's liberation); and currently, the American rediscovery of intellectual Marxism in the forms of both critical theory and radical structuralism (cf. Birnbaum, 1971; Brown, 1970; Colfax & Roach, 1971; Connerton, 1976; Lehmann & Young, 1978; Stein & Vidich, 1963; Wells, 1978).

Theoretical Schisms

Sociology has long been preoccupied with debates over different combinations of theoretical and methodological assumptions about the nature of social life and how best it might be studied. Also, it has become somewhat of a tradition among social theorists to attempt to organize their arguments into some type of model (a typology or a cross-classificatory scheme) to delineate the major schisms among existing theories (cf. Martindale, 1981, p. 622).[7] It appears heuristic to attempt to locate the radi-cal-critical perspectives within the mainstream of so-ciological theories currently applied to family sociology. Figure 1, therefore, represents an analytic "map," or classificatory device, that locates social theories accord-ing to their shared and divergent underlying assumptions. The classification in Figure 1 is a modified version of Burrell and Morgan's typology (1979) of sociological paradigms for organizational analysis.

The most basic schism in views of social reality con-cerns the very nature of the phenomenon to be studied: the objective-subjective split on the horizontal axis of Figure 1. Is the reality under investigation external to the indi-vidual, objective, a given that imposes itself on indi-viduals from without? Or is the reality a product of individual consciousness, subjective, a creation of indi-vidual cognition? This debate has taken various labels, all having to do with the assumptions that follow from each position: holism-elementarism; realism-nominalism; sci-entism-humanism; nomothetic-hermeneutic; objective-subjective. As shown in Figure 1, the basic split between the critical (humanist) and the structuralist perspectives centers on this issue.[8]

From the basic position of subjectivist or objectivist, other assumptions follow. Here, these assumptions are stated as polar extreme positions, and in Figure 1, the various theories can be located on a continuum of the polarity. It should be emphasized that the arrows in Fig-ure 1 do represent continua, and that no workable theory would be found at the extremes. These extremes are dis-cussed only in an attempt to locate actual theories in a relational context.

---

[6]For a thorough discussion of Mills as the leading voice of radi-cal opposition to the sociological establishment, see Binns (1977, Chapter 6).

[7]Eckberg and Hill (1979) reviewed 12 such organizational schemes. See also Ritzer's reply (1981) as one of the 12 re-viewed by Eckberg and Hill.

[8]Other family theorists who have concentrated on critical theory view this split as being between "positivistic" and "in-terpretive" theory (Paolucci & Bubolz, 1980).

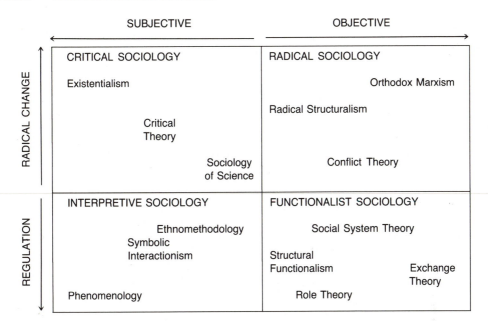

Figure 1. Theoretical schisms in assumptions about the nature of social science and the nature of society. This is a modification of a model developed by Burrell and Morgan (1979).

The extreme *subjectivist* view of social reality also subscribes to nominalism, voluntarism, ideographic understanding, and antipositivist method. The nominalist assumption is that the individual is the primary reality in human social life; that organizations, from small groups to society, are something created by individuals; and that society is the extension of individuals. The assumption of voluntarism views the individual as autonomous, free-willed, purposive, and goal-directed. From the ideographic position, one can understand the social world only by gaining firsthand knowledge of the subject studied; by analysis of subjective accounts obtained by "getting inside" situations and allowing the subject to unfold its characteristics during the research process; and by *Verstehen*. The antipositivist viewpoint, similarly, views social behavior as essentially relativistic and as being understood from the point of view of the individuals directly involved in the subject of study; rejects the standpoint of an "objective observer" as the means of understanding human behavior; questions the ideals of scientific objectivity and value neutrality in social research; and strongly objects to the search for "laws" or underlying "universals" in social life.

An extreme *objectivist* view of social reality, on the other hand, posits realism, determinism, nomothetic understanding, and positivist method. The realist assumption is that the social world exists independently of individuals; that it has an objective reality; that the individual is created by society; and that society is an entity *sui generis*—greater than and different from the sum of its parts. From a deterministic perspective, individuals and social behavior are determined by the situation or environment; human experience is a product of the environment; and humans are conditioned by their external circumstances. From a nomothetic viewpoint, the scientific endeavor is to focus on the analysis (taking the ground rules of the natural sciences) of relationships and regularities among the various elements that comprise the social world; at its most extreme, it is to search for universal laws that explain and govern the observed reality. The positivist approach to research seeks to apply methods derived from the natural sciences to the study of the social world; assumes that the growth of knowledge is a cumulative process in which new ideas are added and false hypotheses are eliminated; and endorses "scientific objectivity," the rigid separation of the observer and the facts observed.

In attempting to locate radical-critical perspectives relative to traditional sociological theories, the second major schism concerns the approach to social change: the regulation versus radical change split on the vertical axis of Figure 1 (Burrell & Morgan, 1979, pp. 16–19; Martindale, 1981, p. 622, terms this the "right and left wing" of social theory). This schism represents a much more extreme polarity than the traditional order–conflict debate. As presented in Figure 1, when compared with radical-critical approaches, the majority of mainstream sociological theories are relatively more concerned with social regulation. The extreme positions of this debate can be outlined as follows:

The sociology of *regulation* is concerned with the status quo, social order, consensus, social integration, cohesion and solidarity, and actuality. The theoretical goal is to provide explanations of social order and organization. The basic questions are directed at why society is maintained; why it holds together; and what social forces prevent the Hobbesian version of "war of all against all." In its need to understand the status quo, it directs attention to what remains unchanged. The characteristic view of the functional interdependence of parts assumes a basic compatibility among the various elements of social structure. Functional interdependence also implies homogeneity, equilibrium, and essentially convergent social forces. The work of Émile Durkheim is most illustrative of a sociology of regulation.

At the opposite extreme, the basic concern is to understand and explain *radical social change*. The emphasis is on radical change, structural conflict, modes of domination, contradiction, emancipation, and potentiality. The emphasis is on control of (rather than adaptation to) the environment. The characteristic view of contradiction assumes a basic incompatibility among various elements of the social structure. Contradiction also implies heterogeneity, dialectic, and essentially antagonistic and divergent social forces. There is an explicit concern with human emancipation from social structures that limit human potentials for development. At its most extreme, the sociology of radical change appears visionary and utopian in positing alternatives to the status quo. The writings of Marx offer the clearest example of a theory of radical change.

Figure 1 shows the major cleavage between the radical-critical perspectives and traditional sociological theories as being one between radical change and regulation. The major schism *within* the radical-critical positions is along the subjective versus objective dimension. Critical theory, as discussed earlier, derives from the German idealist tradition and attempts to develop a sociology of radical change from a *subjectivist* perspective. Whereas the critical theorists focus on human consciousness as the basis for their critique of society, the radical structuralists emphasize structural relationships from a realist, *objectivist* theoretical position. Although there is considerable debate both within and between critical and radical structuralist schools, the disagreements do not appear to include differences in "micro-macro" perspectives nor divisions on the merits of positivism.

The Micro-Macro Issue

In microsociology, the individual is the unit of analysis and the goal is to "interpret" (explain) "human behavior" (e.g., attitudes, values, motives, and experiences). Macrosociology, on the other hand, takes the social system as the unit of analysis and asks how the emergence, or stability, or change of this system explains social phenomena. The system under analysis may range from small groups to families to communities and on up to society itself. Macrosociology does *not* ask how the behavior of individuals explains social phenomena (see

Mayhew, 1980, 1981). In essence, my claim is that both critical theory and radical structuralism attempt to explain individuals and institutions in terms of their interrelationships within society as a *whole*. Both camps emphatically underscore the importance of understanding the historical *totality:* the objective and subjective worlds that characterize a given epoch. The critical theorists tend to emphasize the subjective world, and the radical structuralists, the objective world. In sum, at their most basic level, both critical theory and radical structuralism tend to be macrosociology.[9]

The Positivist Issue

It is implausible to make a general statement that radical-critical sociologists are not positivists.[10] One purpose of this chapter is to provide applications of a radical-critical approach to family sociology. From these applications, it is apparent that some radical critics are more positivist in their approach than are others. Inasmuch as they proceed deductively from certain ideas and tenets and arrive at certain conclusions that they attempt to relate to the concrete world, they are positivists.

It is emphasized, however, that radical-critical sociologists are *not* empiricists. On this issue, the stance of radical critics ranges from cautious to negative. Empiricism draws conclusions about the concrete world on the basis of induction. It treats the world of appearances as the real world. A primary goal of radical-critical sociology is to try to penetrate appearances and to try to demonstrate that what appears to be common sense, to be natural and necessary, really rests on the existence of conditions that are socially produced. Burroway (1978), in reference to Marxist sociologists, asserted:

> They try to advance a theory *of social structure; they try to show how networks of social relations into which we enter as individuals are produced by an underlying structure. This underlying structure then becomes the object of analysis: its dynamics, its contradictions, and its effects on the experience of particular individuals.* (p. 51; emphases in the original)

Thus, radical-critical sociologists are dismayed by the traditional emphasis on survey research, which they see as "methodological individualism" (cf. Birnbaum,

---

[9]See Bottomore (1975) for support and Shalin (1978b) for opposition to this position. Individual theorists, of course, vary in their applications of micro- and macroperspectives.

[10]It is not the intention of this chapter to enter a philosophy-of-science debate about the nature of positivism or its alternatives. For discussions on these issues see, for example, Martindale (1981), Paolucci and Bubolz (1980), Thomas, Kleber, and Galligan (1980), and Walls (1979). It is notable, however, that among radical critics there is a wide divergence in the stance toward positivism. For example, Marcuse's statement in *Reason and Revolution* (1941) represents an extreme negative reaction to all forms of positivism. On the other hand, there are contemporary radical critics whose works tend toward the opposite extreme (cf. the "reification scale" of Harvey, Harvey, Warner, & Smith, 1980).

1971; Colfax & Roach, 1971; Gerhardt, 1980; O'Neill, 1974; Stein & Vidich, 1963). They are equally critical of the logical positivism of theory construction: the goal of arranging existing generalizations (often derived from survey research) into axiomatic systems to derive a set of laws matching those of the natural sciences (e.g., Zetterberg, 1966). They claim that such "scientific sociology" purports to analyze the existing society but only mystifies it. The rhetoric of "measurement" and "variables" is predicated on the assumption that human society can be analyzed in terms of objective facts and laws. This assumption ignores the historical nature of society, that is, that this particular social system is qualitatively different than those that preceded it and has, itself, only a limited historical existence. Moreover, this assumption appears blind to the fact that any study of society is located within society and so, necessarily, both affects and is affected by that society. To the extent that sociologists avoid these problems, they actually justify existing social relations and structures by making them appear "natural" and "eternal": These sociologists deny the possibility of alternative forms of relations and structures (Birnbaum, 1971, pp. 126–129; Offe, 1977, pp. 4–5).[11]

Critical Views of Other Sociological Theories

In relation to the subjective-objective and the regulation–radical-change dimensions, critical theory and radical structuralism can be understood as complementary to several other social theories and as diametrically opposed to others (see Figure 1). Without attempting exhaustive treatment, those divergences and conjunctions are examined briefly. The section concludes with a radical-critical overview of the development of American family theory.

Divergences

Perhaps the strongest invective that radical critics apply to divergent theories is that they are "ideological." In the Marxist sense of the term, ideologies are defined, first, as legitimizing an existing social condition with justifications derived from the status quo, and, second, as repressing the possibility of historical alternatives, denying the historical limitedness of any given social condition (Offe, 1977, pp. 12–14). Ideologies simultaneously provide an interpretation of the present and offer, through this interpretation, the future as the extrapolation of an existing trend. Ideologies present social structure ahistorically, as natural, inevitable, unchangeable, or universal features of human existence. Such a perspective serves to legitimize and reinforce the given system regardless of that system's deficiencies.

In general, from a radical-critical perspective, theories that focus on social regulation tend to be ideological. If

such theories also take an objectivist view of social reality, they are even more suspect. Thus, radical critics direct severe criticism at functionalist, role, and exchange theories. Basically, they view these theories as mirror images of the social order that serve to support its reproduction rather than to understand or explain it.

Parsonian functionalism has borne the brunt of such frequent criticism that sociologists have been tempted to say that the debate over functionalism is dead (cf. Burrell & Morgan, 1979; Silverman, 1970). However, radical critics continue to point out how the tenets of functionalism reflect the basic ideology of contemporary capitalist society.

Role theory is viewed as one of the more ideological aspects of functionalism. Basically, functionalism views the social order of society as maintained ("determined") by interlocking sets of shared norms and assumes consensus on these rules of action among the members of society. Further, different institutions in the society are related by the way in which they contribute to society as a whole, that is, by their "functions." Radical critics view what functionalists term "norms" not as the reflection of a basic consensus but as ideology (in Mills's term, "master symbols of legitimation," 1959). Moreover, functionalism insists that social institutions, and society itself, be conceptualized as a system of "roles." Roles are defined by norms that delineate the rights and duties of role occupants (and actually prescribe how the individual is recruited into the role originally). Functionalist theory assumes that these role expectations are "affectively neutral." Gerhardt (1980) argued that role theory ignores the power dimension of roles. It implies that impersonal "normative forces" are at work whereas, in fact, normative rules function according to the interests of power groups, and role obligations may be created at the discretion of the more powerful and may be used in their interest. Role theory focuses on the formal question of whether a behavior conforms with expectations, but it does not examine the contents of norms to which the individual is supposed to conform: "No matter how cruel or humiliating a role task, it is argued, the sociologist only looks at whether the individual conforms or deviates from norms" (Gerhardt, 1980, p. 559).

From a radical-critical perspective, exchange theory is another branch of functionalism. Mullins (1973, p. 13) argued that, if one accepts the basic assumptions of functionalism, one will also accept those of exchange theory. Exchange theory is viewed as the very essence of the "human capital model." It is a utilitarian model in which people are rational, calculating actors exchanging resources to maximize satisfactions. It fails to question why some have more "resources" than others. It assumes that life is a free market of individual competitors. Thus, it is entirely compatible with the embedded American ideology of exchange equality and meritocracy. Mayhew (1980, p. 352) remarked that it is the close fit between this individualistic social theory and American ideology that makes it so imminently acceptable and obviously true:

---

[11]For concrete outlines of a "radical methodology," see, for example, Barton (1971), Fasola-Bologna (1970), and Szymanski (1970).

"telling people what they already believe is a very effective way to gain a wide audience" (p. 352). Miley (1981) claimed that the reality (as opposed to the ideology) is actually one of "false reciprocity," which does not restrain absolute self-interest but is used to legitimize exploitation by creating the illusion that a just exchange process exists in society. The reduction of all social relations to exchange relations is justified by presenting exchange psychology as a description of a "universal" human nature. The radical critics emphasize that exchange, profit-maximizing perspectives are not features of human nature but a normative aspect of modern capitalism.

Convergences

Radical structuralists see some compatibility—but admit to *no* overlap—with orthodox Marxism, conflict theory, and general systems theory. Orthodox Marxism, labeled "Russian Social Theory" by Burrell and Morgan (1979), is modeled strictly on Engels's reformulation of Marx. It is explicitly based on historical materialism and is more extremely objectivist ("scientific sociology") than radical structuralism. In its formulations, it has some parallels with systems theory, but it differs, very basically, in its orientation toward radical social change (for developments in contemporary Russian social theory, see Heydebrand, 1981; Plekhanov, 1974; Shalin, 1978a; Wineberg, 1974).

With regard to conflict theory, a major difference is the radical critics' emphasis on contradiction rather than conflict. Wardell and Benson (1979, p. 239) underscored that traditional conflict theory (as typified by Coser, 1967, and by Dahrendorf, 1959) suggests that conflict arises because of unequal shares in power, wealth, and so on, accompanied by the imposition of the dominant group's values on the subordinate group. In contrast, from a dialectical viewpoint, power conflicts stem from basic contradictions residing in the limitations of social structures.

On the complementarity of general systems theory, there are diverse opinions. This is not surprising as all sociologists are interested in systems and the sociological systems approach remains very loosely organized (Koestler & Smythies, 1971). On the one hand, Wardell and Benson (1979, p. 235) are quite negative about any alignment. They asserted that general systems theory emphasizes the "givenness" of society, fails to grasp the process through which a social formation is produced, and deals instead with the orderly relations within a produced formation. It does not deal adequately with a society's contradictions nor with potential transformation. Ball (1979), on the other hand, offered an intriguing example of an integration between the "dialectical method" and general systems theory: a new conceptualization of "dialectical equilibrium."[12]

Turning to critical theory, one can find several alliances among the subjectivist models. Perhaps the closest link is that with the sociology of science (see Figure 1). The view that science is a "socially constructed reality" as opposed to an "absolute truth" that is "discovered" by bright researchers was held by both Marx and Karl Mannheim in the early developments of the "sociology of knowledge" (for an overview, see Curtis & Petras, 1970). Sociologists of science seek out the relationship between the production of scientific knowledge and the sociopolitical context in which scientific ideas are pursued (Eigen, 1980).[13]

Schroyer (1971), for example, argued that the "scientistic image of science is the fundamental false consciousness of our epoch. . . . If the technocratic ideology is to loosen its hold on our consciousness, a critical theory must lay bare the theoretical reifications of this scientistic image of science" (p. 253). Connerton (1976) claimed that the current increasing attention to critical theory is based on the growing awareness in the Western world that it is necessary to distinguish between the liberating effects of science and the *use* of scientific empiricism, together with the language of pseudoscience, to underwrite particular distributions of social power.

Existentialism, especially the existential theory of Jean-Paul Sartre, shares the critical sociological (radical humanist) perspective (Burrell & Morgan, 1979). They have a common concern with the domination of consciousness by various aspects of the ideological superstructure of modern society. The existential perspective differs from phenomenology in its vigorous humanism and in its political commitment to the desirability of change in the existing social order (cf. Manning, 1978). As shown in Figure 1, the phenomenological focus on understanding the world "as it is" cannot be viewed as complementary to critical theory.

Of all the interpretive sociologies, ethnomethodology has been most frequently linked to critical theory. Young (1974) and Lehmann and Young (1978) have called ethnomethodology the new "conflict methodology" for radical sociology. In the sense that ethnomethodology attempts to discover the grounds of human social existence, it has the potential not only for understanding particular social worlds but also for changing them altogether (Lehmann & Young, 1978, p. 215). McNall and Johnson (1975) took an opposite position. They characterized ethnomethodologists, along with symbolic interactionists and phenomenologists, as "the new conservatives." All three of these models are charged with being ahistorical, astructural, and apolitical. Ethnomethodology, in particular, neglects the significance of values, power, status, and even the economic base that influences social action. It implies that individuals are "free" to develop their own reality and does not try to understand the reality that can be used as a basis to facilitate social change (McNall & Johnson, 1975, p. 54). Chua (1977), viewing eth-

---

[12]A penetrating discussion of general systems theory by leaders in Western Social theory (e.g., Bruner, Frankl, Koestler, and Piaget) can be found in Smythies and Koestler (1971).

[13]See Mullins's pioneering work (1973) on mapping networks of social theorists in America.

nomethodology from a Marxist perspective, claimed that ethnomethodological analysis can be useful (to radical sociology) only in the study of the "reproduction" of ideology, that is, in the task of demystification and deobjectification. In essence, ethnomethodology could be of value if it attempted to understand the operations that reproduce ideology: the social practices that produce socially constructed reality as objectively, naturally, observable phenomena (Chua, 1977, p. 30).[14] However, to complement radical sociology, ethnomethodologists would have to discard their value-neutral stance and criticize this social construction and the content of this reality; that is, they cannot just describe reality but must explore the critical implications of the description.

American Family Theory

American family sociology originated in the first school of sociology, at the University of Chicago, Here, Albion Small, Lester Ward, W. I. Thomas, and Ernest Burgess were colleagues at various times and presented relatively consistent views on marriage and the family. It is most striking that, although these scholars took a liberal-reformist stance on most social issues, they were extremely conservative in regard to marriage and the family. Small, for example, considered the family the primary institutional means of achieving social stability (Timasheff, 1957, p. 65). Ward emphasized that the function of marriage is to preserve social order by preventing males from mutual destruction (Schwendinger & Schwendinger, 1971). Thomas (1907) explained gender roles in terms of biological analogies in which the female's "metabolism" is like that of plants, thus stable and enduring, whereas the male's metabolism is more fitted for motion, feats of strength, and bursts of energy. These complementary characteristics enabled men and women to constitute the functionally necessary units of marriage and family.

Ernest Burgess is considered the true father of American family sociology. Although Small, Ward, and Thomas all wrote about the family at various times, Burgess was the first to make family sociology his major focus. Moreover, Burgess (with Herbert Blumer, Ruth Cavan, and Everett Hughes) was part of the initial core of Chicago colleagues who emphasized what was to become symbolic interactionism. They were the "Chicago School" and called themselves "social psychologists" (see Mullins, 1973, Chapter 4). The dual influences of the social problems' orientation of the early Chicago sociologists and the symbolic interactionism perspective are shown in Burgess's early publication of his research on families with delinquent children (1926). It was here that he defined the family as "a unity of interacting person-

alities existing chiefly for the development and mutual gratification of its members . . . held together by internal cohesion rather than external pressures" (p. 3). Burgess (with Cottrell) emphasized the importance of complementary "role patterns" in *Predicting Success or Failure in Marriage* (1939). Burgess claimed that the family had moved *From Institution to Companionship* (1945). Burgess (with Wallin) conducted a pioneering longitudinal survey-research project that was reported in *Engagement and Marriage* (1953). Burgess was one of the original organizers of The National Council on Family Relations in 1938.

Many of the basic assumptions of family theory, assumptions that radical critics see as continuing to permeate the field today, originated in the work of Burgess and his colleagues. These assumptions, summarized from Burgess's books, are as follows:

1. The family is the bastion of social order. It is integrated by complementary role patterns, especially the complementary roles of husband and wife. These role divisions in the family are natural and universal. Women's place is in the home performing the important tasks of childhood socialization and husband nurturance. Men's place is in the competitive world of work and their family function is to be the "breadwinner."

2. Family functions have diminished in importance. Specifically, the family has lost its economic function. Its social-psychological function has become of central importance. The family has changed from institution to companionship. It can be defined as a network of interpersonal relationships.

3. The family sphere is qualitatively different from the public sphere. The public and private spheres are separate social realms. The family is a psychological relief station from the public world.

4. Marriage precedes the family. Marital solidarity is the heart of family sociology. The major foci for study are the prediction of marital success, adjustment, and happiness.

5. Family sociology is different from the general sociology of society because the family world is distinct from the public world. To study the family, one must focus on the interacting individuals *within* it. These individuals can be studied through questionnaire surveys of their attitudes, values, and belief systems. Because families function homogeneously, usually one member's account of a family process can be used to represent the perceptions of other family members.

6. Methodologically, family sociology should stress quantitative research and scientific objectivity.

A radical-critical view of the foregoing legacy of family sociology would see it as a reflection of the ideology of the particular historical period and of specific academic networks. In brief, several objections are raised. First, the approach emphasizes social regulation at the expense of the individual. Second, no account is taken of racial, class, sexual, ethnic, and religious differences (the scope is limited to the modern, American, middle-class family as viewed by male academics). Third, the approach is

---

[14]Maynard and Wilson (1980), in an argument similar to Chua's (1977), claimed that ethnomethodology is most useful in understanding reifications of social structure; they illustrated their claims with conversational analyses.

unduly optimistic: The system may have problems but not contradictions. Fourth, there is little attempt to address the admittedly difficult question of the interrelationship between the family and society. The question is negated by the focus on marriage and on the individual as the unit of analysis. One of the most crucial, and ideological, assumptions here is that of a strict duality between public and private worlds.

The founders of family sociology (along with their liberal-reformist colleagues) viewed the "public" world quite critically. Specifically, the world of work was seen as harshly competitive, calculating, brutal, mechanistic, and artificial in its rationality. In sharp contrast, the "private" world of the family was assumed to be (like nature) inherently egalitarian. This assumption was based on a belief in the internal freedom of the family and its determination by the emotional (social-psychological) needs of its members. In addition, it contained a parallel belief in the distinct and separate worlds of men and women: Men are identified with the struggle for existence, and women, with emotional life. With the assumption of a public-private duality, "the family" becomes an abstraction, divorced form the real-life societal variation, and the family world is defined as subjective. By viewing this "split" as natural and/or inevitable in advanced industrial society, family sociologists thus ruled out as not being the business of family theory any challenge or exploration of a basic analysis of the interrelationship between the family and society, for example, the degree of public-private overlap among various social strata and the functionality of a public-private ideology for capitalist society.

The advent of the "golden age" of Parsonian functionalism in the 1940s did little to change the assumptions of family sociology. In fact, functionalism's reflection of the ideology of the times made it appear to be obviously "true" to family sociologists. Parsons's microfunctionalism—his view of the family as a small group and his Freudian interpretation of personality—was especially amenable to family sociologists. Functionalism emphasized the concept of role differentiation: Parsons's industrial model for the study of the family with the father as "chairman of the board" (instrumental leader) and the mother as "personnel manager" (expressive leader). Parsons viewed the central function of the family as "tension management and pattern maintenance," that is, minimizing the potentially disruptive effects of frustration generated by the social system.

With the mounting criticisms of functionalist theory in the 1960s, many family sociologists settled back comfortably to their original concentration on symbolic interactionism (cf. the review by Klein, Schvaneveldt, & Miller, 1977). Of course, there have been variations. General systems theory, as a more process-oriented neofunctionalism, has appealed to counseling-oriented family sociologists. Exchange theory, even more ideological than functionalism (as discussed earlier), was popularized in the 1970s. Also, Reuben Hill's developmental theory,

which is quite complementary to symbolic interactionism, has continued to have its advocates.[15]

The mode of expressing theory changed in the 1970s from the explication of conceptual frameworks to axiomatic theory construction, that is, from verbal frameworks of concepts to diagrammatic models of variables, and from applications of theory to the construction of "minitheories" on the basis of empirical "evidence." The goal for family sociology, however, remained consistent: to build cumulative theory in the scientific sense of theory generalizable across time and place.

From a radical-critical perspective, the underlying paradigms of family theory preclude the most crucial questions about the nature of the family and its relationship to society. Preoccupation with social regulation and the insistence on a subjectivist focus cause family theory to celebrate the very structure it describes and blinds it to basic alternatives. In effect, little theoretical development can occur if one begins by knowing the answers and then searches for the questions that fit them (Mayhew, 1981). The radical critic would also question the advisability of building a "general" family theory. First, generalizations from individualistic survey-research data are apt to be superficial. Second, observed regularities and thus major theoretical propositions are firmly intermeshed in historical conditions. Finally, family theory cannot "accumulate" (in the manner of, say, biochemical theory) because such theory does not transcend its historical boundaries (see Gergen, 1973, for further discussions of the issue of social theory as history).

Substantive Applications

The strength of a theoretical position is demonstrated in its application to substantive questions. For purposes of illustration, this section delineates two areas in which a radical-critical approach shows promise of having a catalytic impact on family sociology. The examples were selected because they either challenge established formulations in the field, or provoke new questions and methods of study, or both.[16] The increasing number of family-related studies that are based on a radical-critical perspective provides a visible indicator that the critics have gone beyond polemic and are engaged in the devel-

[15]It should be underscored that this is an overall perspective on the field as a whole. Theoretical perspectives of individual family sociologists vary enormously.

[16]As of this writing (1985), there is no systematic statement of how radical critics approach the substantive areas of family sociology. The works discussed in this section appear to illustrate one or more of the basic tenets of critical theory and/or radical structuralism. The authors, however, may or may not consider themselves radical critics. This lack of identification is reflected in the less-than-perfect consensus among them. The goal in this initial presentation is to organize selected writings into themes without creating the appearance of a false unity among various writers.

opment of new substantive knowledge of marriages and families.[17]

The topics of family history and human sexuality have been the basis for a number of current works that illustrate a radical-critical perspective. In the following two subsections, these topics are viewed, in radical-critical terminology, as (1) historical totality versus public-private dichotomy and (2) the politics of sexuality. For each topic, the conventional approach in family sociology is outlined, and the radical-critical alternative is documented with selected publications.

Historical Totality versus Public-Private Dichotomy

This section illustrates the application of the radical-critical premise of historical totality to the explication of one of the most pervasive assumptions in family sociology. The traditional assumption is that families are natural (biological) units that can be understood in relative isolation from other social institutions. More specifically, it is assumed that *private family life* (as a haven or retreat) is dualistically opposed to the ruthless and alienating world of *public life*. Radical critics claim that the basic assumption of a public-private dichotomy has limited family research and theory from the time of its inception.

A major premise of the radical-critical perspective is that social systems must be viewed in their historic totality, that is, that social explanation must be historical and historically specific. As noted earlier, the methodological implications of the analysis of totality requires an effort to show that what appears to be "natural" or "universal" or "commonsense" actually rests on socially produced conditions. The radical critic asserts that the view of the family as an isolated retreat from society is ideology, that is, that it precludes questions of how the family mirrors and supports other institutions (such as economy and polity) and, in turn, is supported by them. This ideology serves a number of functions; for example, it obscures the economic function of the family and, thus, a realistic view of the operations of capitalism; it places ultimate responsibility on the family for the "personal" needs of individuals and, thus, relieves the obligations of and the questioning of other institutions; and it serves as a basic justification of a "natural" split between male and female worlds. The assumption of a public-private dichotomy can be attacked from either a critical perspective (which emphasizes ideology and consciousness) or a radical-structural one (which stresses the overlap of structures) or both. As is noted in the following review, both approaches appear in the current literature.

Rapp, Ross, and Bridenthal (1979) reviewed a number of works, structural-historical in emphasis, that demon-

strate that the family should be conceived of not simply as a biological entity but as one shaped by social forces. Ariès (1962) detailed the social rather than the biological nature of childhood. Davis (1977) showed the wide historical variation in what have been defined (by the church) as blood relations. Stone (1977) described the legal, governmental changes that define and redefine family relationships. Shorter (1975), offered persuasive evidence that modern "private" families are social products and are closely intertwined with the public sphere, much as extended family relations were interpenetrated by preindustrial village society in Europe. Both MacFarlane (1978) and Poster (1978) have shown the uneven historical changes in family structure and have questioned the utility of assuming that the contemporary modal American family type is the ultimate in "progress."

The most ambitious attempts to demonstrate the complex historical interplay between society and family are those of Donzelot (1977), Lasch (1977), and Zaretsky (1976). These three works, summarized below, cover a broad sweep of family change through time.

Donzelot. Donzelot's *The Policing of Families* (1977) focuses on the changing nature of sociopolitical *control* over families in France at both the structural and the ideological levels. He mapped out the emergence and expansion of the modern "hybrid" family over the last two centuries—the merging of the public and the private spheres. Donzelot posited the family "not as a point of departure, as a manifest reality, but as a moving resultant," a form understood only from studying its relation with the sociopolitical world.

In both a broad and a deep coverage of changes in ideology, class relations, and family life, Donzelot's historical treatment of the control of children is original and thought-provoking. He showed in great detail that the relationship between state and family is reflected in the history of foundling hospitals, the French juvenile court system, the structure of housing developments, and so on. He carried this analysis forward to the dilemmas of the modern family, which is charged with the socialization of "successful citizens," yet lacks the autonomy to do so: "Parents no longer have the right, as they had in the Dark Ages, to turn their children into failures . . . the Parents School is standing by, and there is guidance counseling, and mass-circulation magazines to consult with such advice as 'protect him,' 'expose him,' 'don't give up,' 'don't interfere' " (p. 225). Donzelot attributed much of the modern policing of the family to the ideology of psychoanalysis and the adoption of more general psychologistic approaches by the expanding "helping professions." A pervasive psychologism protects the state by locating problems in the individual "mind" and the blame for problems in individual families (p. 233).

Lasch. Lasch's *Haven in a Heartless World* (1977), similar to Donzelot's work, asserts that the family is not a private retreat but is "besieged" by the interventionism

---

[17]A number of sociologists have attacked radical-critical approaches as being only negative and polemical (cf. Wrong, 1974).

of "social services" in health, education, and welfare. Lasch claimed that the family did not simply evolve but was deliberately transformed by social engineers with social scientists as participants in the process. His specific target is the psychiatric-medical model of the 1940s, which assumed that the helping professions could cure the entire society. One of Lasch's major themes is that capitalist-industrial society has proletarianized parenthood by making parents unable to provide for their children's needs without professional help. This is analogous to the proletarianization of the labor force, which made workers more dependent on the managerial and professional classes. The system maintains legitimacy by placing the cause of any friction not in real conflicts of interest, but in the psychology of individuals. In essence, Lasch underscored that the modern nuclear family is *not* isolated, and that the world intrudes at every point—from the expropriation of children to the organization of family leisure as an industry. Family changes result from and serve a capitalist-industrial system that no longer requires autonomous, self-controlled, rational individuals; rather, it requires unbridled consumption and "other-directed" behavior.

Zaretsky. Zaretsky's *Capitalism, the Family, and Personal Life* (1976), from a more ideological-subjectivist perspective, argues that perceptions of the family and the economy as separate realms are specific to (and functional for) capitalist society and that these two realms must be understood as one integrated system (as we must also learn to integrate the "personal" and the "political"). Zaretsky traced the history of the development of the ideology of a public-private dichotomy from the rise and decline of the bourgeois family to the increasing proletarianization of the family.[18] Before industrialization, it was the political realm that seemed to be apart from "natural" family and subsistence activities. With the advance of capitalism, occupation came to be glorified as a "calling," and high moral and spiritual value was placed on work and private property. Thus, the split appears to be one between work and the family. Zaretsky analyzed the separation of work and "life" as this separation carries over to the dichotomy of male versus female worlds. For the average middle-class male, occupation is idealized and housework is trivialized to the extent that these *appear* to be two separate and nonoverlapping realms.

In conclusion, the assumption of a public-private dichotomy constitutes the foundation of a "social psychology," as opposed to a genuine sociology, of the family; that is, it focuses on relationships *within* the family to the neglect of asking how family relations and family structures are influenced and how they, in turn, influence relations and structures *outside* the family. Radical critics, regardless of their substantive focus, consistently question the "privatization" of marriage and the family in family sociology.

---

[18]See also Rosaldo (1980) for a brief but penetrating history of this development.

The Politics of Sexuality

Perhaps no other area in sociology is surrounded by a greater aura of "privatization" than human sexuality. Traditionally, sociologists have approached the area very cautiously. First, the sociology of human sexuality has been limited in scope and almost totally relegated to the area of family sociology. The equating of sex and family further privatizes the study of sexuality; it also creates a dualism between "marital" sex (normative) and "premarital" or "extramarital" sex (deviant).[19] Moreover, sex research in family sociology has been for the last several decades marked by a singular preoccupation with quantitative analyses of survey-questionnaire data on "premarital sexual permissiveness" (see the decade reviews by Cannon & Long, 1971, of the 1960s, and by Clayton & Bokemeier, 1980, of the 1970s).[20] Thus, much of the extant information on human sexuality is concerned with what the field defines as deviant behavior, whereas the treatment of adult sexuality in marriage is virtually nonexistent (cf. articles in the *Journal of Marriage and the Family* and in texts of family sociology). The only apparent rationale for this imbalance is that marital sex is considered dull, or stated more in accordance with family texts, sex declines in salience after marriage (cf. the critique by Miller & Fowlkes, 1980).

To the radical critic, the gap between the everyday world as experienced and the sociological world as theorized is nowhere so apparent as in the area of sexuality (Morgan, 1975, p. 171). Critics claim that the field is dominated by male sociologists and that, despite efforts toward "scientific objectivity," male norms (which Laws, 1979, p. 229, called a "phallocentric worldview" on the subject) intrude on both data collection and interpretation. For example, a myopia pervades the sexual permissiveness research on the effects of power relations as they define and restrict female sexuality. In capsule, radical critics claim that contemporary research on human sexuality is atheoretical (primarily descriptive and isolated from other social systems); ahistorical (with the assumption that existing relations in American society are "normal"); and reductionistic (sexuality is reduced to physical behavior and highly abstracted from social and interactional settings). Examples of radical-critical approaches to the sociology of sexuality are summarized under three subheadings: (1) sexuality as identity (the socialization approach); (2) sexuality as ideology (the comparative and historical approach); and (3) sexuality as power (the political-economic approach).

Sexuality as Identity. The socialization of sexuality

---

[19]Sociologists have questioned the terms *premarital* and *extramarital* as being based on the assumption that everyone marries. Some years ago, Sprey (1969) theorized, realistically, that sexuality in our society is becoming an autonomous institution separate from marriage and the family.

[20]Laws (1979, pp. 184–186) offered a critical overview of Reiss's work on standards of premarital sexual behavior. More recently, Reiss (1981) also critiqued the field.

was of interest to early critical theorists (notably Theodor Reich and Herbert Marcuse) and continues to be important in the writings of radical critics. One of the most remarkable works from this perspective was published by the "Red Collective" (1978) in England. The authors tenaciously challenged the assumption of public-private divisions in modern life and attempted to show that "personal" relationships are both social and political. More specifically, they argued that personal problems should be viewed as socially determined rather than in terms of individual "failings." This type of recognition allows for the possibility of changing existing relations and constructing new social realities. The central theme of the Red Collective is that families are "untheorized practice," that is, that family members live the effects of social relations as they have been structured and interrelated over time as distinguished from consciously constructing these relations themselves. The goal is to develop a conscious practice of constructing relationships as opposed to pursuing the dynamics of emotional needs created within the traditional family. On the unconscious level, needs formed in family contexts can be satisfied only by re-creating emotional relationships like those in one's family; that is, family relations are then reproduced, and "personal" couple relationships are created not by bonds formed between adults but by emotional needs created in childhood. Furthermore, because of the contradiction between sex and affection in the family, the adult carries over from childhood an uneasy relation between sex as love and sex as dissociated from an emotional relationship.

Whereas the family structures the child's emotional patterns, the educational system structures the child's mind. In school, children first learn to split thought (intellectuality) from feeling (experience). Sexuality, however, receives little mention either at school or in the home. As a consequence, sexuality is formed "undercover" and comes to be seen as the antithesis of thought: it is thus closed to conscious attempts to change traditional sexual relations.

This capsule summary fails to do justice to the intricacy of the Red Collective's attempts (1978) to explicate the dissociations within the family among economic, sexual, and political relations; to penetrate problems in power relations caused by the ideology of emotional individualism; and to offer their own case histories to illustrate the "idea of consciously constructing the way sexual and political relations can combine in an emotional-sexual relationship" (p. 73).

Thus, a radical-critical perspective poses basic sociological questions about the social construction of human sexuality as opposed to the orthodox family sociological tradition of quantifying sexual behavior and/or attributing psychological "motivations" to it. An example is Person's elaboration (1980) of the process by which the power of parents over children gives rise to the conceptualization of sexuality in terms of submissive-dominant connotations. Person also noted that many cultures place an extreme emphasis on the sexuality of males, with

the consequence that male sexuality often becomes driven and competitive. Thus, it is ironic that sociologists frequently take male sexuality as the norm or characterize it as "liberated." Chodorow (1978), in analyzing the reproduction of mothering, similarly emphasized that, as long as women remain the nurturers of children, sons will continue to grow up looking only to women for compassion and will resent traits of strength in women as attempts to "control."

Sexuality as Ideology. Radical critics argue that the analysis of human sexuality would benefit from comparative cross-cultural and historical treatment. A number of efforts in this direction are illustrated below.

Critical attempts to trace the changing ideologies surrounding sexuality and sexual relationships have used data from the comparative analysis of religion. As Ruether (1974) asserted, "religion traditionally has been highly political in its reality and highly sexual in its imagery" (p. 10). Carmody (1979) traced variations in sexual imagery from early hunting-and-gathering societies through the development of the major world religions. In early, "archaic" societies, the sacred permeated much of nature, and important events such as birth, puberty, and death were laden with exceptional significance. Because women experienced many of these times differently from men, ceremonial rites became sexually differentiated. In hunting-and-gathering societies (which embrace the longest time period in human history), however, high gods were regularly seen as androgynous (that is, as being at once both male and female). The relatively positive status of women in these societies was reflected in the sacredness of female fertility and the carryover to the worship of the Earth Mother. As Ruether (1974) underscored, religion is highly associated with political power. With the historical development of intensive agriculture, large settlements, and social stratification, the ascendancy of patriarchy was reflected in the basic ideology of early religions. Beginning with Hinduism in its earliest forms, and pervading each of the following religions, there was an increasing separation of the sacred from the sexual. Carmody's historical analysis emphasizes the lengthy heritage of an ideological dualism regarding female sexuality: the female as both profane (hated, the "Devil's Gateway") and sacred (adored, the "Virgin Mother").

Turning to more recent history, Barker-Benfield (1978) offered provocative analyses of nineteenth-century views of marital and family sexuality. A male masturbation phobia and general concern with the "wastage" of semen reflect the ambiguity and ambivalence about sexuality during this period. These phenomena are linked to the growth of capitalism in American and "the two overriding preoccupations of nineteenth-century Western man, sex and money, which were rapidly becoming the only measures of his identity" (1978, p. 379). Barker-Benfield (1978) also documented a penetrating critique of the growth of gynecological surgery during this period; for example, "The gynecologists' underlying aims cannot be separated from the society in which they moved—these aims were retaliation against and control of women, and the assumption of as much of their reproductive power as possible" (p. 387).

Other writers have focused on the historical and political-economic influences on women's reproductive rights (cf. Janeway, 1980; Petchesky, 1980). Gordon (1977) laid the groundwork of a critical theory of reproductive freedom as she documented, throughout history, the recurring moral and/or legal prohibitions on birth control. This history is permeated with examples of the ways that nineteenth- and twentieth-century American women's birth control possibilities were directly affected by their social class (e.g., the diaphragm was virtually inaccessible to working-class and poor women). As Petchesky (1980, p. 763) emphasizes, the critical issue is not and has never been women's "right to choose" but the social and material conditions under which such choices are made. Women must make reproductive choices under conditions that they are powerless to change; for example, in cultures where illegitimacy is stigmatized or female infants are devalued, women have the "right" to choose abortion or infanticide. Until women have a *choice* about whether or not to accept total responsibility for child rearing, however, there cannot be reproductive "freedom."

Sexuality as Power. There is a sizable and growing radical-critical literature on the political dimension of sexuality as a significant aspect of the power relations between men and women. A number of writers have contended that the very basis of women's subordination in society lies in male control over female sexuality (cf. Barry, 1979; Brownmiller, 1975; Daly, 1978; Hosken, 1979). Rich (1980), elaborating on Gough's (1975) list of eight characteristics of male power, began with the following two traits:

The power of men: (1) to deny women sexuality (by means of clitoridectomy and infibulation; chastity belts; punishment, including death, for female adultery; . . . denial of the clitoris; strictures against masturbation; denial of maternal and postmenopausal sexuality; unnecessary hysterectomy; . . .) (2) or to force male sexuality upon them (by means of rape, including marital rape, and wife beating; father-daughter, brother-sister incest; the socialization of women to feel that male sexual "drive" amounts to a right; . . . prostitution, the harem, . . . doctrines of frigidity and vaginal orgasm; pornographic depictions of women responding pleasurably to sexual violence and humiliation). (p. 638)

Radical critics emphasize that male sexual violence toward and harassment of women have no association with male sexual "drive" or sexual "interest" but are directly linked with male hostility and attempts to dominate and control. The growing incidence of rape and the manner of its perpetuation (with beatings and artificial penetration) is evidence that rape is not a sexual act (cf. Johnson, 1980). The traditional use of rape on female war victims provides another illustration. Diamond (1980) argued that the common belief that pornography is about

sex is similar to the notion that rape is about sex. In essence, Diamond claimed that the raw biological material of sex is shaped by society and especially by its relations of domination. The basic dynamic of pornography is hostility (in varying degrees from "soft" to "hard" pornography), and power is what pornography celebrates. Millett (1969) similarly claimed that our greater "sexual permissiveness" has given greater latitude to expressions of male domination in sex. In the last decade, the greatest change in the subject matter of pornography, according to Morgan (1978), is the marked concentration on the "pleasures" to women of anal intercourse.

Finally, the argument that pornography is "harmless" tends to overlook the evidence, for example, that in a national survey, a large proportion of high-school males reported that pornography (movies, books, and magazines) "provides information about sex" and agreed that women are sexually aroused by abuse (Berger, Gagnon, & Simon, 1970). Other surveys of high-school youth report frequent physical coercion by males to obtain sex with an accompanying "blaming of the victim" via dress, attitude, behavior, and so on (see Bachman, Johnston, & O'Malley, 1981).

In capsule, radical critics raise questions that have been overlooked in mainstream family sociology with regard to how sex is *used* in power relations. These questions include the interaction of sexuality and economics. Prostitution and pornography are, of course, billion-dollar industries (*Dollars and Sense*, 1978). Other writers have analyzed the less publicized subjects of the sexualization and the sexual abuse of women on the job; the increasing use of "kidporn" to reach the lucrative teenage market; and women as the consumer victims of every conceivable sex-related product from cosmetics to menstrual aids, treatments, pads, tampons, a range of contraceptives, douches, sprays, creams, and lotions for "personal hygiene" (cf. Ehrenreich & English, 1978; MacKinnon, 1979; Schulman, 1980).

Radical critics view the reluctance of society to pay serious attention to sexual violence against women as the product of the mystification and privatization of sex (as biological, individual, and personal). This mystification buttresses male control and preserves the power of economic interests. Radical critics call for peeling back the surface layers and revealing the full extent of sexual violence and domination of women. Barry (1979), for example, asserted that, until sexual relations are conceptualized as power relations in contemporary American society, "those who are the most obvious victims will also not be able to name or define their experience" (p. 100). Zaretsky (1976) similarly underscored the twentieth-century assertion of sexuality as an abstraction. It has not included a critique of the social relations of sexuality: male supremacy and authoritarianism. Zaretsky (1976, p. 123) asserted that movements to enable women to gain control over their bodies, like the birth control movement, have not questioned or criticized male domination. Zaretsky concluded that sexuality may have been "liberated''—to become a commodity, an ideology, and a form of leisure—but men and women have not.

Summary

In recent years, a number of social scientists have begun to study various aspects of the family from a radical-critical perspective. The critique that has evolved has been wide-ranging, but it has developed, and has been reported, largely outside the traditional boundaries of family sociology. This chapter has attempted to open up radical-critical theory to family sociologists and to demonstrate that behind the rather scathing critique of mainstream family sociology also lies a unique and heuristic approach to the understanding of marriage and the family.

The chapter first examined the origins of critical theory and radical structuralism. These approaches were then viewed within a fourfold classification of social theories. The purpose of this introduction was to underscore both the complementarity of radical structuralism and critical theory and the opposition of these perspectives to many assumptions of traditional social theories. In spelling out in some detail the assumptions of these theories, the concern was to emphasize their individuality. My argument is that there is no shortcut to the application of any theory. It is a real necessity to ground the perspective in the philosophical and sociological assumptions from which it derives. In a parallel sense, there is no way to incorporate (merge or integrate) one theory with theories based on diametrically opposed assumptions. Such a fusion would not do justice to the respective foundations and problematics from which the approaches derive, and further, it would demand a dilution of their tenets and, as a predictable consequence, a misunderstanding of their very nature. This should be construed not as a limitation of social theories but as an opportunity to select among several distinct theoretical positions. Thus, one of the major conclusions prompted by this journey through various contemporary social theories is that family sociologists face a number of viable alternatives to the subject.

The chapter traced the development of American family sociology to its founders and delineated a traditional perspective that continues to dominate much of the field. The final section attempted to illustrate radical-critical approaches to two broad areas in family sociology. Throughout, it was a conscious decision not to include in the chapter critiques of the radical-critical approach. Merely by locating oneself in the position of a rival perspective, attacking the critics would be a relatively easy task. However, as the intent of the chapter is to present a new approach to family sociology, it appeared more suitable to allow proponents of the radical-critical perspective the opportunity to state their case before they were required to debate it.

As yet, there is no integrated radical-critical approach to the multifaceted domain of family sociology. However, it is apparent that radical critics are united on certain fundamental criticisms of conventional family sociology

and, to some extent, on suggestions for alternative approaches. The articulation of these critiques and suggestions provides the flavor of the radical-critical argument and offers directions for the initial development of a radical-critical family sociology. Outlined below are six critiques of conventional family sociology. By implication, the critiques suggest a parallel set of six guidelines for radical-critical family sociology.

Critiques of Conventional Family Sociology

1. Family sociology is locked into a social-psychological approach. It is basically unaware of the crucial importance of macrosocietal factors external to the family.

2. Family theorists, consciously or unconsciously, reinforce the subordinate role of women.

3. Family sociology is ahistorical and noncomparative.

4. It is static and conservative. It emphasizes social regulation and exaggerates consensus and homogeneity.

5. It is basically empiricist. It treats the world of appearances as the only "real" world. It takes the individual as the unit of analysis.

6. Its recurrent attempts to construct theory on the basis of reviewing and summarizing research publications are sterile.

Guidelines for a Radical-Critical Family Sociology

1. Radical-critical sociology would start with the basic assumption that families are social products (social structures or social organizations) and proceed to study the mutual interpenetration with other social structures. It would deprivatize marriage and the family. Analysis would shift from exploring relationships within families to asking how these relations are influenced by structures outside families. It would politicize the study of marriage and family. Particular attention would be given to how the political economy, in its historic setting, affects family organizations and processes. In capsule, it would expand a radical *sociology* of families as a complement to the conventional social psychology of families.

2. It would take considerations of gender seriously (cf. Morgan, 1981, for specific suggestions for sociological research). Analysts would recognize that, in the majority of contemporary societies, the subordination of women derives from economic factors that promote the division of labor by sex. Considerations of gender would be emphasized from the point of view of scholarship and, further, in the light of ethical and political ramifications.

3. Radical-critical sociology would add a historical dimension to any proposition about marriage and the family. It would compare and contrast family differences by race, social class, ethnicity, religion, gender composition, and so on, rather than limiting its scope to "the" modern American middle-class family. It would expand its international consciousness and place high priority on cross-national research.

4. It would be dynamic and conceive of all social structures, including the family, as processes that contain the interplay of contradictory forces, which can result in disorganization and radical change. It would redefine "the" family to include the variety of existing family structures.

5. It would seek to peel back the surface layers of appearances in order to unmask the reifications of the everyday world and to recognize and understand the factors that make people define social reality in certain ways. It would avoid methodological individualism and analyze networks of interaction as the smallest unit of analysis.

6. It would attempt to develop theories that are of practical and political relevance. Rather than offering empirically based theoretical descriptions of the family status quo, such theories would elaborate a counterdefinition of social reality. Radical-critical sociology would explicate the problems and contradictions in the way in which the present system functions, underscore oppressive institutional arrangements, and detail alternative structures that promise to maximize human potential. Moreover, radical-critical theory would be committed to the development of practical strategies to join theory with practice.

The Radical-Critical Perspective

The above critique and guidelines, however, are only elements—directed here toward the realm of family sociology—of the broader perspective of radical-critical theory. Their significance for the development and refinement of an alternative approach in family sociology can be understood only within the context of the basic tenets and concepts (i.e., the intellectual tradition) of critical theory and radical structuralism.

The concepts of totality and dialectic are unifying themes of radical-critical theory. In the area of family sociology, they have the following implications:

Totality. The radical-critical approach calls for as complete an understanding as possible of total social formations.[21] To understand any aspect of social life, radical critics emphasize, it is crucial to include some consideration of history, biography, institutional processes, and cultural value and belief systems. Families can be understood only in terms of their place within a total context, in terms of the wider social processes within which they live and which they reflect. The concept of totality carries with it specific methodological implications. Not only is historical analysis essential, but it must be followed by an examination of the subject in its contemporary manifestations. Contemporary analysis should not be narrowly focused only within the family but should include an integrated analysis of family phenomena at various levels of

analysis and within the context of the various institutions in which family members participate. This method sharply contrasts with the bulk of conventional family research, which attempts to abstract and isolate social processes from their wider social context, for example, confining inquiry only to individuals or to specific types of families, which leads to the partialling out of those individuals or families from the wider social, economic, and political world. The approach explicitly rejects the assumption of a public-private dichotomy that has been reified in family sociology.

Dialectic. To the radical critic, all social relations imply their opposites. The concept of the dialectic helps to explain how social structures tend to be reproduced and also how they can change because of internal contradictions.

The dialectical viewpoint is quite different from the conventional role analysis in family sociology. In family theory, the idea of "role complementarity," for example, is frequently invoked to explain family transactions. Complementarity implies "separate but equal" (or at least equitable) rewards for normative behavior. In essence, there is no visible exploitation. The dialectical approach, however, reveals that underneath the visible transactions lie the actual relationships between asymmetrical power positions, that is, husbands over wives and parents over children. The contradiction between the expectation of equally rewarding role relationships and the actuality of power differentials creates many of the problems and crises characteristic of contemporary family life. Further, it is within the family (and associated relations, such as courtship, divorce, and remarriage) that many contradictions within society are revealed. Families can be viewed as the screen on which some of the most deep-seated schisms within the larger society and culture are made visible. Not all radical critics address these contradictions in the same way. Critical theorists are more likely to analyze contradictions in ideology or belief systems, such as the contradiction between the idealized conception of the partner in courtship and the reality of marital responsibilities. Radical structuralists, on the other hand, focus on the contradictions within and between structures, such as that between women's work in the home and in the labor market. Both of these approaches are quite distinct from conventional family sociology, where the greatest attention is given to exploring marital relationships within the home—often posing a dualism between husband and wife. The radical critic asks how family members are placed in contradictory situations by the impingement of ideologies and structures outside the immediate marital relationship.

Radical critics also analyze the way in which social relations are reproduced. Again, there are differences in perspective. Critical theorists emphasize ideological hegemony, such as how the ideology of patriarchy is reproduced by socialization in the family, by dogma in the world's religions, and by law in the state or, as another

[21]Critics sometimes dismiss the radical-critical approach on the ground that it is impossible to understand each problem in terms of its "totality." In my viewpoint, such a dismissal is an extreme stance taken in response to an extreme interpretation of the radical critics' position.

example, the reification of a "natural" division of marital roles into husband as "instrumental" and wife as "expressive." Radical structuralists are more likely to concentrate on how structural arrangements are reproduced, for example, the reproduction of mothering if women continue to bear the major responsibility for child rearing, or the mutual reinforcement of women's subordination in the family and the economy.

A basic assumption, integral to the dialectical perspective, is that of ubiquitous social change. The extreme form of radical social change is characterized by continuous and intense contradictions that result in crises and dislocation of the totality itself. In many ways, family organizations reflect the totality as it moves from crisis to crisis (and adjusts or fails to adjust). Contemporary family-related changes and crises are numerous: high rates of divorce and remarriage with reconstituted families; increasing teenage pregnancy; family violence; and growing reliance on the helping professions for marital and family-related issues. These are of particular significance to radical critics not necessarily—as conventional family sociology would view them—as "problems," but as indicators that can yield insights into the nature of the totality itself and the interrelationship of family processes with specific subsystems.

Methodology. The methodological position of radical critics is also a distinguishing characteristic. Radical critics reject the abstract empiricism and the abstract theoretical models of family sociology. They criticize family sociologists' multifactor approach to research that seeks to describe or to discover various factors related to specific family phenomena. Although this method may specify certain ingredients, it is weak on the interpretation of their relative significance. In general, radical critics point out that the tendency in much of the research on marriage and the family has been for methodologies to overshadow substantive and theoretical issues. Researchers tend to communicate only in terms of abstract variables. Currently, the abstraction process has reached an extreme, with many family research articles describing families in SPSS computer language.

Abstract empiricism, according to the radical critic, is mirrored by the deductive efforts of family sociologists interested in constructing theories of family behavior. Faith in the scientific procedure and in empirical data results in a family sociology that is ahistorical, noncomparative, and oriented largely to technical problems relating to theory construction and to measurement. The goal of understanding families is forgotten, and the flowcharts of theoretical models expand in length and complexity. The models are so abstract and generalized as to be of little use in the analysis of any particular types of family behavior. Radical critics reject much of this model building as purely an intellectual exercise that abstracts and thus removes human beings from the family and the larger social setting.

From a radical-critical position, the stress would be on developing methods that are true to the nature of the phenomenon that is being studied. The radical-critical aim is not to discard traditional methods but to use an appropriate *combination* of methods and to develop the full potential of each. This is a key issue for the further development of the radical-critical approach (cf. Barton, 1971, and Eichler, 1981, for specific suggestions on how to do critical research). Two current research practices in family sociology are viewed as particularly problematic: methodological individualism and static research designs. If survey methods, for example, were designed to provide data not only on individuals but also on their family and community contexts, the data could be linked with macrosociological information (on organizations, classes, ethnic groups, and societies) in an effort to understand the reciprocal influences between behavior in families and behavior in the larger contexts. Further, radical critics point out that the survey method would produce more heuristic data if the sampling frame included specific types of families rather than just the general public, for example, elites, the disadvantaged, and exceptional cases.

Similarly, there would be a greater potential for understanding family dynamics if, for example, experimental procedures were incorporated into simulation studies of family crises, conflicts, and change. The typical approach of interviewing family members in times of relative stability and daily routine gives little hint of their unarticulated needs, frustrations, or potentials. Asking family members who have never experienced different forms of family organization or personal relationships how they feel about conflict resolution, decision making, socialization values, and so on tends to produce answers with a status quo bias. When subjects are confronted by alternatives, even in a simulation, the answers and the actions may be quite different.

Perhaps most distinctive is the radical critics' commitment to social action, to human emancipation, to practice. The call for social action and change is quite different from the individualistic humanism reflected in family texts and family-therapy-oriented books and articles. The radical critics' purpose is to transform "private troubles" into "public issues." The goal is to explain social problems (not just to measure them) in a way that provides evidence that relates to social action. This goal calls for a consideration of the question of not only how to do better research but also how research relates to the social, economic, and political world of which it becomes a part. Radical critics also underscore the artificiality of the assumptions of objectivity and value neutrality. They argue that relative objectivity resides in the presentation of reproducible findings rather than in adherence to the "scientific method," where truth need only be applied rather than established. The underlying view of the radical critics is that theories and preconceptions always limit and shape social research. However, as long as researchers do not share the same limiting beliefs (a critique aimed at mainstream sociology), there is a chance that a certain degree of "truth" will emerge from exchanges among them.

The ideas associated with the core concepts of totality and dialectic, together with the methodological positions on research, theory, and social action, constitute a basic foundation from which a radical-critical sociology of family life can be shaped. At the present, such an approach is largely embryonic, and its various explications are scattered in a diverse body of literature, often outside mainstream family periodicals and books. This chapter has attempted to develop an initial statement about the nature of the radical-critical approach.[22] Current applications of radical-critical theory to family-related topics not only constitute frameworks for continuing research but are very likely to have an impact even on those family sociologists who are unlikely to identify themselves as radicals.

In conclusion, a combination of critical theory and radical structuralism appears to offer a new frontier for family sociologists: critical theory because it sensitizes us to the process of everyday theory construction, to the ideologies that mold human consciousness, and to the fact that all theories are political; and radical structuralism because it alerts us to the powerful influence of social structures, to the contradictions inherent in their interrelationship, and to the necessity for historical-comparative perspectives. At the outset, a radical-critical approach requires that its proponents believe in the possibility of radical social change.

"One can't believe impossible things," said Alice. "I daresay you haven't had much practice," replied the Queen. "When I was your age I always did it for half-an-hour a day. Why sometimes I've believed as many as six impossible things before breakfast." (Carroll, 1920, pp. 176–177)

Viewing marriages and families from a radical-critical perspective will provide a good exercise for family sociologists. Most possible things were thought to be impossible at some time.

References

Althusser, L. *For Marx.* Harmondsworth, England: Penguin, 1969.

Althusser, L., & Balibar, E. *Reading Capital.* London: New Left Books, 1970.

Ariès, P. *Centuries of childhood* (R. Baldick trans.). New York: Vintage, 1962.

---

[22]A major difficulty with a review essay lies in the attempt to bring organization to a wide-ranging topic without creating the appearance of false unity or consensus among proponents of various approaches. I have made rather free use of the term *radical-critical theory,* which is a shorthand expression for a combination of critical theory and radical structuralism. I understand quite well that these two systems of thought are complex and varied, and that there are conflicts and differences within each group as well as between them. The radical-critical synthesis is my own proposal, and its explication represents my understanding of what would constitute a radical-critical approach to family sociology.

Bachman, J. G., Johnston, L. D., & O'Malley, P. M. *Monitoring the future: Questionnaire responses from the nation's high school seniors.* Ann Arbor, Mich.: Institute for Social Research, 1981.

Ball, R. A. The dialectical method: Its application to social theory. *Social Forces,* 1979, *57* (March), 785–798.

Barker-Benfield, G. J. The spermatic economy: A nineteenth-century view of sexuality. In M. G. Gordon (Ed.), *The American Family in Social-Historical Perspective.* New York: St. Martin's Press, 1978.

Barry, K. *Female sexual slavery.* Englewood Cliffs, N.J.: Prentice-Hall, 1979.

Barton, A. H. Empirical methods and radical sociology: A liberal critique. In J. D. Colfax & J. L. Roach (Eds.), *Radical sociology.* New York: Basic Books, 1971.

Berger, A. S., Gagnon, J. H., & Simon, W. Pornography: High school and college years. *Technical Reports of the Commission on Obscenity and Pornography.* Washington, D.C.: Government Printing Office, 1970.

Binns, D. *Beyond the sociology of conflict.* London: Macmillan, 1977.

Birnbaum, N. *Toward a critical sociology.* New York: Oxford University Press, 1971.

Bottomore, T. Competing paradigms in macrosociology. *Annual Review of Sociology,* 1975, *1,* 191–202.

Brown, C. A history and analysis of radical activism in sociology. *Sociological Inquiry,* 1970, *40* (Winter), 27–34.

Brownmiller, S. *Against our will: Men, women and rape.* New York: Simon & Schuster, 1975.

Burgess, E. The family as a unity of interacting personalities. *The Family,* 1926, *7*(March), 3–9.

Burgess, E. *The family from institution to companionship.* New York: American Book, 1945.

Burgess, E. & Cottrell, L. *Predicting success or failure in marriage.* New York: Prentice-Hall, 1939.

Burgess, E., & Wallin, P. *Engagement and marriage.* Philadelphia: Lippincott, 1953.

Burrell, G., & Morgan, G. *Sociological paradigms and organizational analysis.* London: Heinemann, 1979.

Burroway, M. Contemporary currents in marxist theory. *The American Sociologist,* 1978, *13,* 50–64.

Cannon, K. L., & Long, R. Premarital sex behavior in the sixties. *Journal of Marriage and the Family,* 1971, *33,* 36–49.

Carmody, C. Influence of the world's religions on the status of women. In E. C. Snyder (Ed.), *The study of women.* New York: Harper & Row, 1979.

Carroll, L. *Alice's adventures in wonderland and through the looking-glass.* New York: Illustrated Editions, J. J. Little & Ives, 1920.

Chodorow, N. *The reproduction of mothering: Psychoanalysis and the sociology of gender.* Berkeley: University of California Press, 1978.

Chua, B. H. Delineating a Marxist interest in ethnomethodology. *The American Sociologist,* 1977, *12* (Feb.), 24–32.

Clayton, R. R., & Bokemeier, J. L. Premarital sex in the seventies. *Journal of Marriage and the Family,* 1980, *42,* 759–776.

Colfax, J. D., & Roach, J. L. *Radical sociology.* New York: Basic Books, 1971.

Collinicos, A. *Althusser's Marxism.* London: Pluto Press, 1976.

Connerton, P. *Critical sociology.* Harmondsworth, England: Penguin, 1976.

Coser, L. A. *Continuities in the study of social conflict.* Glencoe, Ill.: Free Press, 1967.

Curtis, J. E., & Petras, J. W. *The sociology of knowledge: A reader.* New York: Praeger, 1970.

Dahrendorf, R. *Class and class conflict in industrial society.* London: Routledge & Kegan Paul, 1959.

Daly, M. *Gyn-ecology: The metaethics of radical feminism.* Boston: Beacon Press, 1976.

Davis, N. Z. Ghosts, kin and progeny: Some features of family life in early modern France. *Daedalus,* 1977, *106* (Spring), 87–114.

Diamond, I. Pornography and repression: A reconsideration. *Signs,* 1980, *5* (Summer), 686–701.

Dollars and Sense. Pornography: Obscure profits at the expense of women. Boston; September 1978.

Donzelot, J. *The policing of families.* New York: Pantheon Books, 1977.

Eckberg, D. L., & Hill, L. The paradigm concept and sociology: A critical review. *American Sociological Review,* 1979, *44,* 925–937.

Ehrenreich, B., & English, D. *For her own good: 150 Years of the experts' advice to women.* Garden City, N.Y.: Doubleday, 1978.

Eichler, M. Monolithic model of the family. *The Canadian Journal of Sociology,* 1981, *6,* 367–388.

Eigen, J. P. On the importance of the sociology of science to the goals of general education. *The American Sociologist,* 1980, *15* (Nov.), 214–

Fasola-Bologna, A. The sociological profession and revolution. *Sociological Inquiry,* 1970, *40,* 35–43.

Flacks, R., & Turkel, G. Radical sociology: The emergence of neo-Marxian perspectives in U.S. sociology. *Annual Review of Sociology,* 1978, *4,* 193–238.

Geertz, C. *The interpretation of cultures.* New York: Basic Books, 1973.

Gergen, K. J. Social psychology as history. *Journal of Personality & Social Psychology,* 1973, *26* (3), 309–320.

Gerhardt, U. Toward a critical analysis of role. *Social Problems,* 1980, *27,* 556–569.

Glucksmann, M. *Structuralist analysis in contemporary social thought.* London: Routledge & Kegan Paul, 1974.

Godelier, M. System, structure and contradiction in *Das Capital.* In Michael Lane (Ed.), *Introduction to structuralism.* New York: Basic Books, 1970.

Gordon, L. *Woman's body, woman's right: A social history of birth control in America.* New York: Penguin, 1977.

Gouldner, A. W. *The coming crisis of Western sociology.* New York: Basic Books, 1971.

Gouldner, A. W. *For sociology.* New York: Basic Books, 1973.

Gouldner, A. W. *The two Marxisms: Contradictions and anomalies in the development of theory.* New York: Seabury Press, 1980.

Habermas, J. *Towards a rational society.* London: Heinemann, 1971.

Habermas, J. *Legitimation crisis.* London: Heinemann, 1976.

Harvey, D., Harvey, E., Warner, L., & Smith, L. The problem of reification. In S. G. McNall & G. Howe (Eds.), *Current perspectives in social theory.* Greenwich, Conn.: JAI Press, 1980.

Heydebrand, W. V. Marxist structuralism. In P. Blau & R. Merton (Eds.), *Continuities in structural inquiry.* Beverly Hills, Calif.: Sage, 1981.

Hoare, Q. & Nowell-Smith, G. *Selections from the prison notebooks of Antonio Gramsci.* London: Lawrence & Wishart, 1971.

Horkheimer, M. *Critical theory: Selected essays,* trans. by Matthew J. O'Connell *et al.* New York: Herder & Herder, 1972.

Hosken, F. P. *The Hosken Report: Genital and sexual multilation of females.* Lexington, Mass.: Women's International Network News, 1979.

Janeway, E. Who is Sylvia? On the loss of sexual paradigms. *Signs,* 1980, *5,* 573–589.

Jay, M. *The dialectical imagination.* London: Heineman, 1973.

Johnson, A. G. On the prevalence of rape in the United States. *Signs,* 1980, *6,* 136–146.

Klein, D., Schvaneveldt, J., & Miller, B. The attitudes and activities of contemporary family theorists. *Journal of Comparative Family Studies,* 1977, *8* (Spring), 5–27.

Koestler, A., & Smythies, J. R. *Beyond reductionism.* Boston: Beacon Press, 1971.

Lasch, C. *Haven in a heartless world: The family besieged.* New York: Basic Books, 1977.

Laws, J. L. *The second X: Sex role and social role.* New York: Elsevier, 1979.

Lehmann, T., & Young, T. R. From conflict theory to conflict methodology: An emerging paradigm for sociology. In A. Wells (Ed.), *Contemporary sociological theories.* Santa Monica, Calif.: Goodyear Publishing, 1978.

MacFarlane, A. The origins of English individualism: Some surprises. *Theory and Society,* 1978, *6* (Sept.), 255–277.

MacKinnon, C. A. *Sexual harrassment of working women: A case of sex discrimination.* New Haven: Yale University Press, 1979.

Manning, P. K. Existential sociology. In A. Wells (Ed.), *Contemporary sociological theories.* Santa Monica, Calif.: Goodyear Publishing Company, 1978.

Marcuse, H. *Reason and revolution: Hegel and the rise of social theory.* New York: Oxford, 1941.

Marcuse, H. *Eros and civilization: A philosophical inquiry into Freud.* Boston: Beacon Press, 1955.

Marcuse, H. *One-dimensional man: Studies in the ideology of advanced industrial society.* Boston: Beacon Press, 1964.

Martindale, D. *The nature and types of sociological theory.* Boston: Houghton Mifflin, 1981.

Marx, K. *Early writings,* trans. by R. Livingston & G. Benton. Harmondsworth, England: Penguin, 1844.

Mayhew, B. H. Structuralism versus individualism, Part 1: Shadowboxing in the dark. *Social Forces,* 1980, *59,* 335–375.

Mayhew, B. H. Structuralism versus individualism, Part II: Ideological and other obfuscations. *Social Forces,* 1981, *59,* 627–648.

Maynard, D. W., & Wilson, T. R. On the reification of social structure. In S. G. McNall & G. Howe (Eds.), *Current perspectives in social theory.* Greenwich, Conn.: JAI Press, 1980.

McCarthy, T. *The critical theory of Jurgen Habermas.* Cambridge: M.I.T. Press, 1978.

McNall, S. G. *Theoretical perspectives in sociology.* New York: St. Martin's Press, 1979.

McNall, S. G., & Johnson, J. C. M. The new conservatives: Ethnomethodologists, phenomenologists, and symbolic interactionalists. *Insurgent Sociologist,* 1975, *5,* 49–65.

McQuarie, D. *Marx: Sociology/social change/capitalism.* London: Quartet Books, 1978.

Miley, J. D. *False reciprocity and the theory of exchange.* Paper presented at the annual meetings of the Southern Sociological Society, Louisville, Kentucky, 1981.

Miller, P. Y., & Fowlkes, M. R. Social and behavioral constructions of female sexuality. *Signs,* 1980, *5,* 783–800.

Millett, K. *Sexual politics.* New York: Doubleday, 1969.

Mills, C. W. *The sociological imagination.* New York: Oxford University Press, 1959.

Morgan, D. H. J. *Social theories and the family.* London: Routledge & Kegan Paul, 1975.

Morgan, R. Theory and practice: Pornography and rape. In R. Morgan (ed.), *Going too far: The personal chronicle of a feminist.* New York: Vintage, 1978.

Mullins, N. C. *Theories and theory groups in contemporary American sociology.* New York: Harper & Row, 1973.

Offe, C. *Industry and inequality.* New York: St. Martin's press, 1977.

O'Neill, J. *Making sense together: An introduction to wild sociology.* New York: Harper & Row, 1974.

Paolucci, B., & Bubolz, M. *Toward a critical theory of the family.* Paper given at Research and Theory Workshop, National Council of Family Relations Annual Meeting, Portland, Oregon, 1980.

Person, E. S. Sexuality as the mainstay of identity: Psychoanalytic perspectives. *Signs,* 1980, *5,* 605–630.

Petchesky, R. P. Reproductive freedom: Beyond "a woman's right to choose." *Signs,* 1980, *5,* 661–685.

Plekhanov, G. *Selected philosophical works* (Vol. 1). Moscow: Progress, 1974.

Poster, M. *Critical theory of the family.* New York: Seabury Press, 1978.

Rapp, R., Ross, E., & Bridenthal, R. Examining family history. *Feminist Studies,* 1979, *5,* 174–200.

Red Collective. *The politics of sexuality in capitalism.* London: Publications Distribution Cooperative, 1978.

Reiss, I. Some observations on ideology and sexuality in America. *Journal of Marriage and the Family,* 1981, *43* (May), 271–284.

Rich, A. Compulsory heterosexuality and lesbian existence. *Signs,* 1980, *5,* 631–660.

Ritzer, G. Paradigm analysis in sociology: Clarifying the issues. *American Sociological Review,* 1981, *46,* 245–248.

Rosaldo, M. Z. The use and abuse of anthropology: Reflections on feminism and cross-cultural understanding. *Signs,* 1980, *5,* 389–417.

Ruether, R. R. *Religion and sexism: Images of women in the Jewish and Christian traditions.* New York: Simon & Schuster, 1974.

Schroyer, T. A reconceptualization of critical theory. In J. D. Colfax & J. L. Roach (Eds.), *Radical sociology.* New York: Basic Books, 1971.

Schroyer, T. *The critique of domination: The origins and development of critical theory.* Boston: Beacon Press, 1973.

Schulman, A. K. Sex and power: Sexual bases of radical feminism. *Signs,* 1980, *5,* 590–604.

Schwendinger, J., & Schwendinger, H. Sociology's founding fathers: Sexist to a man. *Journal of Marriage and the Family,* 1971, *33,* 783–799.

Shalin, D. N. The development of Soviet sociology, 1956–1976. *Annual Review of Sociology,* 1978, *4,* 171–191. (a)

Shalin, D. N. The genesis of social interactionism and differentiation of macro- and microsociological paradigms. *Humboldt Journal of Social Relations,* 1978, *6,* 3–38. (b)

Shorter, E. *The making of the modern family.* New York: Basic Books, 1975.

Silverman, D. *The theory of organizations.* London: Heinemann, 1970.

Smythies, J. R., & Koestler, A. *Beyond reductionism: The Alpbach symposium 1968.* Boston: Beacon Press, 1971.

Sociological Inquiry. Radical perspectives in sociology. *Special Issue,* 1970, *40* (Winter), 3–185.

Sprey, J. On the institutionalization of sexuality. *Journal of Marriage and the Family,* 1969, *31* (August), 432–440.

Stein, M., & Vidich, A. *Sociology on trial.* Englewood Cliffs, N.J.: Prentice-Hall, 1963.

Stone, L. *The family, sex and marriage in England 1500–1800.* New York: Harper & Row, 1977.

Szymanski, A. Toward a radical sociology. *Sociological Inquiry,* 1970, *40,* 3–25.

Tar, Z. *The Frankfurt school: The critical theories of Max Horkheimer and Theodor W. Adorno.* New York: Wiley, 1977.

Thomas, D. L., Kleber, J. E., & Galligan, R. *Through the glass darkly: Family theory, the new philosophy of science, and hermeneutics.* Paper presented at Research and Theory Workshop, National Council of Family Relations Annual Meeting, Portland, Oregon, 1980.

Thomas, W. I. *Sex and society.* Boston: Richard G. Badger—The Gorham Press, 1907.

Timasheff, N. S. *Sociological theory.* New York: Random House, 1957.

Van Den Berg, A. "Critical theory: Is there still hope?" *American Journal of Sociology,* 1980, *86* (November), 449–478.

Walls, D. S. Dialectical social science. In S. G. McNall (Ed.), *Theoretical perspectives in sociology.* New York: St. Martin's Press, 1979.

Wardell, M. L., & Benson, K. "A dialectical view: Foundation for an alternative sociological method." In S. G. McNall (Ed.), *Theoretical perspectives in sociology.* New York: St. Martin's Press, 1979.

Wells, A. *Contemporary sociological theories.* Santa Monica, Calif.: Goodyear Publishing, 1978.

Wineberg, A. E. *The development of sociology in the Soviet Union.* London: Routledge & Kegan, 1974.

Wrong, D. H. On thinking about the future. *The American Sociologist,* 1974, *9,* 26–30.

Young, T. R. The politics of sociology: Gouldner, Goffman, and Garfinkel. In S. Denisoff, O. Callahan, & M. Levine (Eds.), *Theories and paradigms in contemporary sociology.* Itasca, Ill.: F. E. Peacock, 1974.

Zaretsky, E. *Capitalism, the family, and personal life.* New York: Harper & Row, 1976.

Zetterberg, H. L. *On theory and verification in sociology.* Totowa, N.J.: Bedminster, 1966.

CHAPTER 6

Methodology

Robert E. Larzelere and David M. Klein

What we know about families is largely determined by *how* we know what we know. An earlier era without cumulative knowledge, scientific tools, or cross-cultural information believed the world to be flat and families in other cultures to be like families in their own. Since then, our picture of the universe has changed much more than our understanding of families. Astronomy has achieved qualitative jumps in its methods, whereas family research has depended primarily on improved forms of the same verbal data used for conclusions so long ago. Supporters of current research on families could argue that the differences in methodological progress are due to the differing topics of study. Critics might see the slow progress as evidence of a general methodological shortcoming in family studies. In either case, it is important to take a fresh look at family research methodology occasionally in order to critique and improve it.

This chapter provides a selective overview of the state of family research methodology, emphasizing issues particularly relevant to the family as an object of study. General characteristics of families are used to identify the issues of most importance for family researchers. Alternative strategies for dealing with those issues are then discussed and contrasted with each other.

A one-chapter overview of the methodology of family research has to be somewhat limited in its goals. It cannot cover all relevant methods both in breadth and in depth. Duplicating material in general methods texts would be pointless. So we have opted to emphasize selected methodological issues of particular relevance to family researchers (see Brown & Kidwell, 1982).

In addition to what cannot be accomplished, a methodological overview can have some unique benefits. It can directly compare and contrast methodologies that are ordinarily isolated from each other. By juxtaposing methodologies, characteristics that initially appear to be different in kind turn out to be merely differences in degree. Issues that are emphasized in one methodology become salient for alternative strategies as well. These benefits will help researchers to borrow methodologies associated with one research topic and apply them to another topic. In addition, innovative methodologies could be constructed from pieces of existing methodologies.

One assumption should be clarified before continuing: The optimal methodology for a particular study depends on several factors, including the nature of the topic, the specific research question, what is already known in the literature, and the resources available to the researcher. There is no single best methodology. Multivariate statistics are sometimes assumed to be invariably superior to simpler statistics. In contrast, we would argue for the KISS (Keep It Short and Simple!) principle. Then the reader can better understand the statistical support for conclusions. Multivariate statistics are certainly called for at times, but only when the user can specify what is gained by them. Fit the method to the research situation—that is the watchword.

Family research methodology has generally been borrowed from the major social-scientific disciplines with little selectivity or modification. Such nonselective borrowing is inappropriate at times, partly because family studies are not central to any of their host disciplines. For example, the family is more micro than most other sociological topics and more macro than most other psychological topics.

Macrosociology focuses on subcultural and cross-cultural influences on a particular topic of interest (e.g., marital power). It tends to ignore how these cultural influences are mediated at the level of the individual (e.g., by what process patriarchal vs. egalitarian norms affect how married partners coordinate their individual interests). It also ignores individual differences within a subculture (e.g., why working-class couples differ among themselves in marital power). Individual differences within the family are of minimal importance; the relationship of external variables to family charactersitics is of primary importance.

In contrast, microsociology and psychology emphasize the influences of situations and/or individuals. Thus,

Robert E. Larzelere • Rosemead School of Psychology, Biola University, La Mirada, CA 90639. David M. Klein • Department of Sociology, University of Notre Dame, Notre Dame, IN 46556. NIMH Grant No. 5 T32 MH15161-04 provided support for part of the work on this chapter.

macrosociology's blind spot becomes microsociology's focal point, and vice versa. Consistent with this conclusion, psychological research on marital power has often ignored how social norms and personal resources affect power. Similar points could be made concerning other host disciplines.

Although these specific problems caused by nonselective methodological borrowing have been recognized and are being corrected to some extent, no alternative to nonselective methodological borrowing has been proposed. One contribution of this chapter is to move us toward an alternative by highlighting the methodological implications of several general characteristics of the family. A similar strategy has been used by Baltes, Nesselroade, and their colleagues for advancing methodology in life-span developmental psychology (e.g., Baltes, 1973). They first identified the characteristics of life-span developmental psychology relevant to methodology (e.g., intra-individual change), then identified the important methodological issues implied by these characteristics (e.g., age-related variability in the validity of measures), and subsequently explored strategies to handle such issues effectively (e.g., comparative factor analysis; Baltes & Nesselroade, 1970).

This chapter uses a similar strategy. It identifies four distinctive characteristics of the family and then discusses the methodological issues implied by each one along with research strategies relevant to those issues. The following four characteristics of the family are considered: (1) It is generally a small group, (2) has a lengthy existence, (3) is relatively private and value-laden, and (4) is influenced by its societal context. For each family characteristic, the following broad aspects of research methodology are considered in turn: (1) conceptualization, (2) research design, (3) data collection, and (4) data analysis. After discussing the methodological implications of the four family characteristics, a few other methodological topics that are applicable to all four characteristics will be discussed.

The Nature of the Family as a Small Group

The family is a *group* of two or more individuals. This definition distinguishes it from most psychological research, in which some aspect of the *individual* is the primary interest. Of course, an adequate understanding of the family also requires an understanding of the individuals within the family. But one central aspect of the family concerns the organization and functioning of the family group. Further, family functioning is not simply the summed total of the functioning of the individual members. Each member of a three-person family group may be intelligent and may have the ability to cope with complex problems. But communication patterns and the power structure of the group might interfere with their ability to organize their joint activities in a way that enables the family unit to function effectively in coping with problems (Straus, 1968).

Implications for Conceptualization

Because the family is a group, one recurring issue for the conceptualization of family research is the most appropriate unit of analysis. Hodgson and Lewis (1979) identified four units of analysis used in family research: individuals, dyads, nuclear families, and extended families. Levinger (1977) used similar units of analysis to produce a matrix for generating research questions about close relationships. Table 1 presents a modified version of his matrix as applied to family research. Our discussion of corresponding research possibilities borrows heavily from Levinger.

The first row of Table 1 represents how variables at the individual level influence variables at each of four levels of analysis. Examples of Cell 1,1 are the effects of husbands' self-esteem on their problem-solving skills or on their wives' problem-solving skills. Cell 1,2 is illustrated by the influence of husbands' self-esteem on marital cohesion, and Cell 1,3, by the effect of their self-esteem on the problem-solving efficiency of the nuclear family unit. The association of husbands' self-esteem with the frequency of social gatherings of the extended family illustrates Cell 1,4.

Other rows represent other units of analysis for the independent variable. Whereas dependent variables in research about the family generally involve characteristics of family members as individuals or as a group, additional types of variables may be useful as independent variables. Situational and societal characteristics represent the kinds of variables external to the family that may be of interest as independent variables. For some research purposes, Table 1 might be expanded to allow for the effects of families, family subsystems, and individual members on situational or societal characteristics. The section on "Implications for Data Collection" will consider how the conceptual unit of analysis relates to the unit of analysis for data collection.

Table 1. A Matrix for Generating Research Questions about the Family[a]

Unit of analysis: Antecedent variable	Unit of analysis: Consequent variable			
	1. Individual	2. Dyad	3. Nuclear family	4. Extended family
1. Individual	1,1	1,2	1,3	1,4
2. Dyad	2,1	2,2	2,3	2,4
3. Nuclear family	3,1	3,2	3,3	3,4
4. Extended family	4,1	4,2	4,3	4,4
5. Situation	5,1	5,2	5,3	5,4
6. Society	6,1	6,2	6,3	6,4

[a]Source: Adapted from Levinger (1977).

Implications for Research Design

Research design has a wide variety of meanings. The implications for research designs in this chapter focus on research strategies and on methods for controlling for extraneous variables.

One of the most basic aspects of a research strategy is how an investigator chooses to slice up the complexity of families: What will the research focus be? What will be ignored? What will be controlled for? What will not be?

The choice of units of analysis for research variables tends to create emphases and blind spots in the overall research strategy. For example, a microsociological or psychological approach generally uses an individual unit of analysis and ignores variables external to the family.

Such a practice was characteristic of family process research on marital power (for example, Jacob, 1975), which compared dominance patterns in families with a psychologically disturbed adolescent with dominance patterns in control families. The individual was the unit of analysis (e.g., talking time for each member). The major research issue was intrafamilial: the relationship between parental or marital dominance and the psychological adjustment of the adolescent.

A macrosociological approach, on the other hand, generally uses the marital dyad or the nuclear family as its conceptual unit of analysis. Blood and Wolfe's classic study of marital power (1960), for example, obtained data only from wives. The implicit assumption was that the wife could speak for the entire family as a unit because distinctions between the perspectives of different family members were unimportant. But on the positive side, this approach highlighted cultural and subcultural effects on family power, leading to Rodman's theory (1972) of resources in a cultural context.

Thus, effects within the family are emphasized in microsociological research strategies and are minimized in macrosociological studies. Cultural and subcultural effects are minimized in microsociology and emphasized in macrosociology. In each case, the blind spot of the one strategy is the strength of the other. Micro and macro approaches should, therefore, be quite complementary. If sufficient resources are available, a single study could combine both strategies.

Implications for Data Collection

The fact that the family is a small group has two implications for data collection to be discussed here. The unit of analysis will be the first issue, followed by the consistency of data from different family members.

Unit of Analysis. As is obvious from the examples above, the conceptual unit of analysis often does not match the unit of analysis used in data collection. In family process research, the individual is the conceptual unit of analysis, but the entire family is observed in the research session. In sociological research on the family (e.g., Blood & Wolfe, 1960), the family or marital group is the conceptual unit of analysis, but usually, only one family member is used for data collection. This pattern is typical: If *intra*family differences are of interest, at least two sources of data within each family are required; but if *inter*family differences are of primary interest, then a single source of data per family may be warranted. A single data source assumes intrafamily consistency of data, a topic to be discussed shortly.

The conceptual unit of analysis is reflected more directly in the nature of the questions asked. Questions are completely *individualistic* when no family member is included in the question as target person, explicitly or implicitly. For example, questions about personality or personal income are individualistic in this sense.

Alternatively, questions may measure group properties in one of four ways. The first is a *simple combination* of individual characteristics, such as family income. The second is a *unilaterally target-specific* question. One such item on Spanier's Dyadic Adjustment Scale (1976a) is "Do you confide in your mate?" Alternatively, a question could be *bilaterally target-specific* (or "multilaterally"), as in "Do you and your mate confide in each other?" Finally, an item could be *emergent* in the sense that the indicator would not be directly reducible to individual characteristics. For example, "Indicate the extent of your agreement or disagreement about handling family finances."

The same categories would also apply to behavioral observations. Suppose a family of two parents and two children was observed. The total talking time of one family member is an individualistic measure. The sum of the total talking time of both parents is a simple combination. A unilaterally target-specific measure is illustrated by the portion of talking time that is directed by the husband toward the wife. The time that the spouses spend talking to each other could be considered a bilaterally target-specific measure. The number of interruptions is an emergent measure.

Consistency of Data among Family Members. Some frequently used units of analysis and question formats assume intermember consistency of data, an assumption that is often questionable. For example, correlations between husband and wife scores on marital adjustment have ranged from .04 to .88, with typical interspouse correlations between .40 and .60 for the most widely used scales (Spanier, 1973).

One implication of the previous discussion is that consistency between family members should vary with the type of question. Emergent measures should yield higher consistency than other types of measures. As illustrated above, marital adjustment scales also include unilaterally target-specific items. Differences between spouses on those items represent differences in perspective as well as error variance. An initial attempt to verify empirically such systematic differences in interspouse consistency failed to support these implications (Van Buren & Larzelere, 1984).

Implications for Data Analysis

When only one score represents each group in the sample, the data about a group, such as the family, are statistically analyzed just as are data about individuals. It often is useful, however, to include similar measures on two or more members (e.g., fathers and mothers) as independent variables. A study of family influences on student political behavior (Braungart & Braungart, 1975), for example, included separate measures of mothers' and fathers' religious preferences, political affiliations, and 1972 presidential votes. Data analysis problems arise in such cases if the independent variables correlate too closely with each other, a situation called the *multicollinearity problem*. In the Braungarts' study, the mothers' responses correlated with the fathers' responses from $r = .60$ to $r = .91$. This can be a serious problem for many types of analyses, including analysis of variance and multiple regression (Kidwell & Brown, 1982; Schumm, Southerly, & Figley, 1980).

There are four basic options for handling multicollinearity problems. One is to combine the set of highly interrelated variables into a summary variable, yielding one score on each variable per family (e.g., parents' religious preferences). By conceptually combining factor analysis with path analysis, structural equation models (Jöreskog & Sörbom, 1979) provide a technically sophisticated way to combine highly correlated variables. In either case, summary scores may be less desirable when the research questions require separate estimates of the influence of each family member on a dependent variable (e.g., do fathers or mothers have greater influence on childrens' political actions?).

A second option is to ignore the multicollinearity problem. This option is more feasible if the multicollinearity is less extreme.

A third option is to drop all but one of the highly interrelated variables from the analysis. A useful version is to do separate analyses for each family member (e.g., one analysis for mothers' data and one for fathers' data).

A fourth option would be to use a biased estimator instead of the usual unbiased estimators in ordinary-least-squares (OLS) regression. The usual criterion that an OLS estimator be unbiased is relaxed in order to achieve greater reliability in the estimator. The best known biased-estimation procedure is ridge regression (Draper & Van Nostrand, 1979; Fennessey & D'Amico, 1980; Kidwell & Brown, 1982). Kidwell and Brown (1982) described how to detect multicollinearity in a data set and how to use ridge regression to reduce this problem.

Most methodological implications of the family as a small group have centered on the unit of analysis. The choice of a particular unit of analysis has implications for how investigators conceptualize the family, what re-

search strategies they favor, whom they collect data from, and how they analyze those data (Thompson & Walker, 1982; Thomson & Williams, 1982; Walters, Pittman, & Norrell, 1984). Our second characteristic of the family, its time-ordered nature, also has numerous implications for family research methodology.

The Time-Ordered Nature of the Family

The family is distinct from most other social groups in the duration of family members' close association with each other. Despite an increasing rate of divorce, the family remains the most stable group of close personal relationships for most people.

Several studies have found that members of ongoing groups interact differently from the members of newly formed groups (e.g., Gottman, 1979, pp. 50–53; Hall & Williams, 1966). This finding suggests the need for methodologies to describe and explain the development of distinctive types of interaction that emerge over time in families.

Implications for Conceptualization

An important conceptual issue in each piece of family research is whether or not change in important variables needs to be taken into account. If so, then the issue shifts to the pace of change: slow versus rapid. Some features of family life change rather rapidly over time, others more slowly, and others only trivially. Variables such as the number of children and the socioeconomic level change slowly, if at all. In contrast, the amount of interpersonal interaction fluctuates from day to day and from hour to hour. Further, some variables could be modified dramatically by changing from a static perspective to a dynamic perspective, which incorporates change over time. A recent innovative approach for studying marital satisfaction focuses on daily fluctuations in satisfaction (Jacobson, Follette, & McDonald, 1982) in contrast to the static view of marital satisfaction in previous research. Daily fluctuations highlight the correlates of daily changes in marital satisfaction, whereas the traditional approach emphasizes the correlates of differences among couples. How we conceptualize change over time in our variables has direct implications for measurement strategies and indirect implications for the type of findings obtained.

The estimated time for causal effects to occur becomes an important conceptual issue in studies concerned with the *explanation* of family phenomena. Some antecedent variables have their major influence immediately, whereas others require a longer period of time for their maximal influence to occur. Research strategies should be carefully chosen to fit the most likely causal lag. Focusing on daily fluctuations in marital satisfaction has allowed researchers to determine the influence of the daily frequency of positive and negative interactions on marital satisfaction (Jacobson *et al.*, 1982). Prior marital satisfaction studies had identified independent variables with more long-term effects, a result of the more static research approach.

Antecedent and consequent variables are often measured simultaneously, even though only previous levels of antecedent variables (e.g., of socioeconomic status) could explain current consequent variables (e.g., parenting values). An unstated assumption in such research is that current measures of the antecedent variables accurately represent previous levels of those variables. Sometimes, this assumption is warranted; at other times, it reflects a failure to consider how variables change over time.

When time-ordered change is relevant to conceptualizing variables, it will also be relevent to the next topic: research-design options for handling time-ordered change.

Implications for Research Design

As most families stay together a long time, time-ordered research designs should be used frequently to investigate them. Such is far from the case. Almost all family research continues to use static cross-sectional designs (Klein, Jorgenson, & Miller, 1978). Apparently, the greater practicality of a cross-sectional design outweighs the perceived advantages of designs that directly investigate change over time. As practicality carries so much weight in these years of declining research support, we will consider some practical modifications of time-ordered designs.

Two major kinds of time-ordered designs have emerged in relative isolation from each other: family process designs and longitudinal designs. Although they have each been contrasted with static or cross-sectional designs, they have rarely been compared with each other. To emphasize such comparisons here, we are introducing new labels to distinguish these two designs from designs that ignore time-ordered data.

Although a cross-sectional design yields time-related conclusions, it has only one data collection point and is therefore called here a *brief-occasion design*. Brief-occasion designs also include static research strategies that ignore the time dimension in their conclusions. A family process design includes multiple data-collection points during one lengthy session with brief time gaps between data collection points. This is referred to here as an *extended-occasion design*. A typical longitudinal study has two or more data-collection points separated by longer time gaps, usually months or years. This is called here a *multi-occasion design*. Each of these designs could be used with any data-collection method, although observational data have been traditionally associated with the extended-occasion design and survey data with the multi-occasion design.

Brief-Occasion Designs. Brief-occasion designs handle the time dimension with the convenient assumption that the time-ordered influence of an antecedent variable on a subsequent consequent variable is reflected in the persisting levels of both variables. Thus, it is thought that time can be ignored with minimal loss in research quality.

When time-related conclusions are made from brief-occasion designs, the implicit assumption is that the older families would have had results like the younger families when they were younger. Cross-sectional research has found older couples to be more satisfied than middle-aged couples. But to conclude an improvement in marital satisfaction from such data requires the assumption that the older couples were like the middle-aged couples in satisfaction when they were that age. In addition, it assumes that the effect of research mortality is inconsequential, that is, that families that have not survived intact into older ages are as satisfied as families that have lasted longer. This is an unreasonable assumption, as less satisfied couples have a higher research mortality because of divorce.

Although most brief-occasion designs do not have such explicit developmental implications, they often make conclusions about the effects of antecedent variables on consequent variables. Generally, the measured value on the antecedent variable (e.g., marital power) is assumed to have preceded the measured value on the consequent variable (e.g., marital happiness), even though both variables were measured at the same time. Thus, in most brief-occasion designs, change over time is directly relevant to central conclusions even if time is ignored in the strategy for data collection.

Extended-Occasion Designs. Extended-occasion designs follow rapidly changing variables intensively over a period of one to several hours, usually with a focus on interpersonal processes. Although family process research has been done for several decades (Doan, 1978; Jacob, 1975), new technological and methodological developments have dramatically increased its utility (Filsinger & Lewis, 1981). Previous extended-occasion studies were motivated by a desire to get valid measures of family interaction, but they generally did not exploit time in investigating the relationships among variables. Comparisons of interaction patterns were usually made between well-adjusted and deviant families in such studies. Recently, an increasing focus of extended-occasion studies has been the sequential influences of interpersonal actions on subsequent actions of the persons involved. For example, Lytton (1979) used home observations to investigate how several parental disciplinary techniques influenced the immediately subsequent probability of children's compliance with parental requests.

More Practical Extended-Occasion Designs. The major practical problems of extended-occasion designs are the overwhelming amount of data and the usual necessity to use trained coders and, sometimes, taping equipment for data collection. The data-overload difficulty can be reduced with computerized data-collection devices, or it can be circumvented by limiting the amount of information. The coding difficulty can be reduced somewhat by computerized data-collection devices or by using one or more family members as data collectors.

Portable computerized data-recording systems have recently become available that enable researchers to manage observational data in extended-occasion designs in a fraction of the time previously necessary (Holm, 1981; Stephenson & Roberts, 1977). Alternatively, data can be limited to a particular type of incident that is especially relevant theoretically. The target incident might have occurred recently, or it might be elicited with a structured situation. Harris (1980) and Peterson (1979) have both developed intriguing procedures for selecting a recent relevant marital-interaction sequence and having the participants describe the sequence of actions and feelings in detail. Such infrequent incidents are often more relevant theoretically than are typical everyday interactions in a family. Another approach is to focus on one specific recurring incident. For example, Patterson (1976) had parents of aggressive boys carefully record the occurrence or nonoccurrence of the boys' aggressive behavior daily for an extended period of time.

For some purposes, a structured situation can elicit appropriate data even when the target events usually occur infrequently. Good examples in family research include the "strange situation" (Ainsworth, Blehar, Waters, & Wall, 1978), SIMFAM (Straus & Tallman, 1971), and the Inventory of Marital Conflicts (Olson & Ryder, 1970). These structured situations were explicitly developed to represent naturally occurring events (Olson & Ryder, 1970); are similar to related events in natural settings (Ainsworth *et al.*, 1978); and get the participants so involved that they seem to ignore the fact that they are being observed for research (Straus & Tallman, 1971). A structured situation enables a researcher to use an extended-occasion design even though the relevant interactions occur infrequently in everyday life. Advanced coding schemes using new data-collection devices often improve on the original coding procedures of these older structured situations (Vincent, 1979), but the situations themselves are very useful if they fit the research topic well.

Otherwise, the use of targeted, naturally occurring situations require data reported from research participants. Such a solution to the data-overload problem forces the investigator to have family members assume a larger role in data collection. This can be an advantage when the subjective perspectives of the participants about the data are crucial to the investigation (Harris, 1980; Peterson, 1979), or when parents' active involvement helps to meet the therapeutic objectives (Patterson, 1976). If an appropriate structured situation cannot be designed, subjects' reports seem to be essential to modify an extended-occasion design, as the *a priori* selection of a target event implies that a participant will be required to recall such an event or to notice and report on such an event when it occurs. If the investigator is present, waiting for the target event to occur, there is little reason not to have fairly complete data collection, especially with the new data-collection systems.

A choice between an extended-occasion design and a modified version, then, should be made not only on the basis of practicality and the available resources but also on the basis of the appropriateness of survey versus observational data for important variables, the naturally occurring frequency of the target events, and the feasibility of designing a structured situation to elicit the target events. Relevant target events would have to occur frequently or be elicited fairly easily to warrant a complete extended-occasion design rather than a modified version using subjects' reports.

Quasi-Experimental Extended-Occasion Designs. Most previous extended-occasion designs have used only passive observation of the variables of interest. As will be seen under "Implications for Data Analysis," complex statistical problems often undermine the researcher's ability to make clear-cut causal interpretations, even with time-ordered designs. Thus, if the research goals include explanations as well as descriptions, it would be worth considering quasi-experimental or experimental modifications of the usual extended-occasion design. There are many situations in which it is feasible to randomly assign some families to different treatments (Campbell, 1969; Cook & Campbell, 1979, pp. 371–384). One example is with families who have no preference concerning alternatives (e.g., therapeutic strategies) and who are willing to be randomly assigned to one of them. Then, family interaction can be examined in the two therapeutic conditions to contrast the therapeutic effects more clearly than is possible without such an experimental manipulation.

Alternatively, an interrupted time-series design (Cook & Campbell, 1979, Chapter 5) may be combined effectively with an extended-occasion data-collection strategy. Among family research designs, extended-occasion designs are most likely to have the 30–50 data-collection points necessary for a time-series analysis.

Multi-Occasion Designs. A multi-occasion design, the other type of time-ordered design, is appropriate when investigating causal influences over a longer period of time. Several sophisticated versions have been developed for research in the social sciences, including simple longitudinal designs and more complex sequential designs (Baltes, 1968; Fienberg & Mason, 1978; Glenn, 1977; Nesselroade & Baltes, 1979; Schaie, 1973). An illustrative study using a longitudinal design might collect data on marital quality throughout the duration of each couple's marriage. A sequential version replicates a longitudinal design like this for two or more cohorts, where a cohort is a group of couples marrying in the same year.

Simple longitudinal designs bring with them a set of problems not faced by cross-sectional designs: statistical regression toward the mean, sample dropout, autocorrelations (i.e., correlations between two measures of the same variable at two different times), and cohort effects

(Baltes & Nesselroade, 1979; Heise, 1977). Longitudinal research can appear "to be a design panacea" but may turn out to be "a Pandora's box for the interpreter" (Baltes & Nesselroade, 1979, p. 31; Palmore, 1978; Riley, 1973).

Nevertheless, multi-occasion designs need to be used more frequently in family research. The time-ordered nature of families and the advantages of time-ordered data for causal interpretations both imply that such designs are often optimal. Recent critiques make it clear, though, that methodological problems must be fully considered and minimized before such designs are implemented.

Compromises between ideal multi-occasion designs and brief-occasion designs also need to be considered more frequently by researchers. Such compromises approximate ideal designs in certain respects but are more practical to implement than full-fledged multi-occasion designs. Greater practicality is achieved by sacrificing some of the quality of the more ideal designs.

More Practical Multi-Occasion Designs. Three modifications of multi-occasion designs will be considered here: a segmented longitudinal panel, a follow-up study, and a retrospective design.

The *segmented longitudinal panel* was introduced by Hill (1964). It uses two or more data-collection points that bracket a crucial transition in the family, such as the transition to parenthood. This strategy yields a short-term rather than a long-term description and/or explanation of development in families. Feldman (1971) used such a design to examine the effects of the arrival of children on marital quality. He interviewed parents during the second trimester of pregnancy and two times after childbirth. He also interviewed childless couples three times, separated by the same time intervals. This procedure enabled him to track the course of marital quality around the time of childbearing and to compare the trajectory with that of similar couples not experiencing childbirth during the study. By adding studies of the effects of other critical transition points on marital quality, researchers could build a developmental picture of the course of marital quality throughout a typical marriage (Harvey, 1983; Klein *et al.*, 1978). In short, a segmented longitudinal panel is more manageable than a longitudinal design because it focuses on one important transition point.

A second alternative to a full-fledged multi-occasion design is to do a *follow-up* of a previous brief-occasion study. Two research teams (Call & Otto, 1982; Clarridge, Sheehy, & Hauser, 1977) have given successful accounts of locating research participants from previous studies. Such procedures demonstrate the feasibility of designing a longitudinal follow-up to a previous study when the identifications of the original participants are available.

A *retrospective design* is a third strategy for obtaining time-ordered data in a more practical way. It can cover as long a time period as a longitudinal design, but it uses retrospective reports to accomplish this.

For example, Huston and his colleagues (Huston, Sur-ra, Fitzgerald, & Cate, 1981; Surra & Huston, in press) used this type of design to investigate the developmental course of premarital relationships leading to marriage. They asked newlyweds to recall important events in their relationship and when each one occurred. The respondents then recalled the likelihood of marriage when they first met and at the time of each event. Finally, the partner and the interviewer charted the trajectory of the perceived probability of marrying throughout the history of the relationship. These developmental trajectories fit one of three general patterns: accelerated, prolonged, or intermediate courtship, according to how quickly and smoothly they progressed toward marriage. Some of the more surprising results included the following: Couples increased in conflict and negativity as well as love as they progressed from casual to serious dating. Men fell in love faster and disclosed more about themselves early in the relationship than did women. (The differences in self-disclosure had reversed by the time they married.) Those in an accelerated courtship felt *less* love in the early stages of the relationship than did those in the slower developmental trajectories.

Such a retrospective design has both advantages and disadvantages relative to other strategies. As these pros and cons apply more directly to data collection than to research design, they will be discussed in the next section.

It must be reemphasized that these modified versions of time-ordered designs are not wholly adequate substitutes. Rather, they are alternatives to brief-occasion designs that should be carefully considered when resources are inadequate for a complete extended-occasion or multi-occasion design. Furthermore, the findings from modified time-ordered designs should improve subsequent planning of the more ideal time-ordered designs in a programmatic sequence of studies. Thus, the net effect of modified time-ordered designs should be to improve, not to replace, subsequent extended-occasion and multi-occasion studies.

Implications for Data Collection

The time-ordered nature of the family also has implications for issues relevant to data collection. As previously noted, brief-occasion designs simply assume that current measures of family variables adequately represent previous levels of certain variables. Aside from this issue, considerations about data collection in brief-occasion designs are similar for time-ordered variables as for any other variables. Several distinctive issues arise for extended- and multi-occasion designs, however.

Extended-Occasion Designs. Most older studies that used extended-occasion designs yielded only one score per variable. In contrast, recent extended-occasion designs have yielded multiple scores over time for each variable, using either continuous measurement, discontinuous samples, or interval samples (Sackett, 1978). If one is interested in interruptions, for example, every interruption is recorded if continuous measurement is being used. With discontinuous or interval samples, the occurrence or nonoccurrence of interruptions in each time interval (e.g., 30 seconds) is recorded. Discontinuous sampling would be based on selected periods of interaction, whereas interval sampling would include the entire interaction session. Only continuous measurement would yield an exact count of the number of interruptions, as frequency is ignored in the other two methods.

Sackett (1978) discussed the advantages and disadvantages of these alternative approaches (see also Bakeman, 1978; Lamb, 1979). In general, continuous measurement is harder to do but yields more adequate data, especially for analyses of sequential influences of one event on another.

Multi-Occasion Designs. Three issues relevant to multi-occasion designs or their modifications are discussed in this section: problems with longitudinal data, the pros and cons of retrospective data, and the optimization of the time gap between data collection points.

There are three major problems with longitudinal data: sample attrition, testing effects, and the consistency of the meaning of measures across time. Sample attrition, called "research mortality" in Campbell and Stanley's influential book (1966), is a more severe difficulty in multi-occasion research than in other types of studies. Attrition can be due to residential change, noncooperation, illness, or death. In family research, it can also be due to divorce or marital problems. If it is essential to include multiple family members in the entire study, the attrition of any member causes that family to be dropped, a procedure making the attrition rate higher for families than for individuals.

Testing effects can also modify the nature of the data in multi-occasion studies. That is, people who have previously been research participants often yield data systematically different from those who are participating for the first time. Such differences may be due to familiarity with the research process, boredom with it, or sensitization to the research variables.

The meaning of the measures of a variable often changes from one occasion to another. Cultural-historical changes, maturation, and changes in wording all reduce such measurement consistency across time. Cultural-historical changes include societal changes that modify how respondents understand an item. The feminist movement, for example, has modified perceptions about items related to women's roles. Maturation indicates any personal changes that affect how an item is understood. A change in meaning due to maturation could explain the following puzzling inconsistency from the same national survey: 92% of parents of 3-year-olds reported spanking their child in the past year (Straus, 1983), whereas only 71% of all parents reported ever spanking their child (Straus, Gelles, & Steinmetz, 1980). It could be that the meaning

of *spanking* to a parent changes as children grow up. A third source of a change in meaning is modification in wording. The wording of many items is changed in subsequent waves of longitudinal data collection, usually to improve the clarity (Glenn & Frisbie, 1977). In such cases, time-ordered differences can be explained by changes in meaning as well as by actual differences across time.

One modification of a multi-occasion design discussed previously is a retrospective design. Its major distinction is that it relies on retrospective data rather than on data collected in multiple waves. This approach can have both advantages and disadvantages. The advantages include an efficient use of resources, measurement consistency, flexibility to focus on theoretically relevant events, less sample attrition, and better generalizability to the later parts of the time period examined (Featherman, 1980). Efficiency in the use of resources is the most obvious advantage; one interview is easier to complete than are multiple interviews.

Measurement consistency over time is better for retrospective data than for longitudinal data. By asking about previous points in time during one interview, a retrospective design keeps meanings consistent. Compared to longitudinal data, retrospective data allow the investigator more flexibility to focus on theoretically relevant events for two major reasons. First, the same theoretical focus is applied across all time periods of interest, and second, there is a greater flexibility to focus on important events regardless of whether they fit into the same time schedule for all subjects. To some extent, longitudinal data are limited to the theoretical issues conceived by the originator of the study. Subsequent advances in theoretical understanding can be used only to the extent that relevant variables were measured in the first waves of data collection. Thus, the early waves of longitudinal data are like secondary data for an investigator who becomes involved during the later stages of the study. In addition, longitudinal studies are ordinarily limited to fixed time periods between waves of data collection, whereas the events of interest may not be timed similarly for different people. In the study of courtship patterns (Huston *et al.*, 1981; Surra & Huston, in press), for example, the retrospective measures allowed greater flexibility to focus on significant events in the development of the premarital relationship regardless of the timing of those events.

Compared to longitudinal studies, retrospective studies have fewer problems with sample attrition, but more problems with sample bias. Sample attrition is minimized, but the sample excludes those who begin the developmental sequence but do not complete it (e.g., those whose courtship ends before marriage). Thus, in a time-ordered sequence of events, longitudinal studies generalize better to early periods, and retrospective studies generalize better to later periods.

The major disadvantages of retrospective data are falsified accounts and faulty recall (Spanier, 1976b). Falsified accounts are usually motivated by a tendency to distort self-descriptions in a socially desirable direction. The crucial issue is whether retrospective reports are more subject to conscious distortion than concurrent reports (Featherman, 1980). As most survey data are also confounded with a social desirability response bias (Edwards, 1957), it is not clear that concurrent data are any less subject to falsification. Huston *et al.* (1981) found that couples were just as consistent with each other in describing their past relationship as they were in describing their current relationship.

Faulty recall is another matter. Regardless of motivational factors, certain kinds of information are not available for recall. It is difficult to reconstruct a characteristic that changes gradually (e.g., mental ability) as it was at a previous time. Further, requested information must have been salient at the time it was available. Failure at this point seems the best explanation for the surprising finding that over half of a teenage sample incorrectly reported the handedness of their left-handed parents (Porac & Coren, 1979). When initial information has been incomplete, people tend to use their general knowledge and beliefs to fill in the holes to produce a convincingly complete memory (Myers, 1980). Thus, faulty recall yields apparently complete data that are biased toward normative expectations. Faulty recall is minimal when the initial event was prominent and its memory continues to be salient.

The relative severity of the problems of falsified accounts and faulty memory differ for different research questions. These differences, in turn, affect the optimal amount of detail requested in retrospective items. If falsified accounts are more problematic (e.g., in research on first sexual intercourse), then retrospective items should call for specific, objective details (e.g., "When did you first experience sexual intercourse?"). If faulty memory is more problematic (e.g., an adult's perceptions of relationships with parents during childhood), then items calling for less detail and more inference may be preferable (e.g., a Likert-scaled item on parental warmth).

In sum, there are both advantages and disadvantages to retrospective data. Whether concurrent or retrospective data are more appropriate is not an either-or matter but a matter of degree. In fact, most survey items are either retrospective (e.g., educational level) or a current summary of retrospective information (e.g., marital satisfaction). The usual methods of determining reliability and validity that are used for concurrent measures can also be applied to retrospective measures (Featherman, 1980).

A final consideration in multi-occasion data is determining the best time gap between data collection points. It should be set to maximize the chance of detecting causal influence. Gaps between occasions are often too long. For example, Lefkowitz, Eron, Walder, and Huesmann (1977) collected data relevant to parental characteristics, television watching, and children's aggression in their third and "thirteenth" grade. This 10-year gap is too long for many important causal influences to be detected. Empirical evidence concerning the time period

of maximal causal influence would aid in planning subsequent extended-occasion designs (Bakeman, 1978) and multi-occasion designs (Rogosa, 1979).

Implications for Data Analysis

Some statistical analyses are designed to take advantage of time-ordered data, whereas others are thought to circumvent the need for time-ordered data. This section reviews some of these alternatives. The central issue concerns what conclusions are appropriate when two variables, such as parental punitiveness and child aggressiveness, are associated with each other.

Analyses of Brief-Occasion Designs. Some social scientists (e.g., Schuessler, 1978) have argued that new multivariate analyses enable causal conclusions to be just as strong with brief-occasion data as with time-ordered data. The major statistical procedures claimed to accomplish this feat are path analysis and structural equation models.

When a simple correlation coefficient shows an association between two variables (e.g., punitiveness and aggressiveness), that association could be due to one or more causal influences. Punitiveness could influence aggressiveness, aggressiveness could influence punitiveness, or some third variable (e.g., parental approval of aggression) could influence both variables of interest. *Path analysis* can only rule out the third option and then only for other variables specified in the path analysis model. It is useful, therefore, for determining whether an association is due to another *measured* variable, but it is not a panacea for determining causal influences. Clear evidence for causal influence from one variable (A) to another (B) can be derived from path analysis only if two conditions hold. First, there must be some rationale external to path analysis for ruling out B's influencing A. Time-ordered designs are better suited to providing this rationale than are brief-occasion designs. Second, all variables that could simultaneously influence both A and B must be included in the path analysis. This is called the *specification problem*, and it is crucial for making interpretations from panel analysis (Hannan & Tuma, 1979), structural equation models (Bielby, Hauser, & Featherman, 1977), and time series (Cook & Campbell, 1979; McCleary & Hay, 1980), as well as path analysis. As Cook and Campbell pointed out, leaving relevant independent variables out of the causal model can lead to incorrect estimates of both the magnitude and the sign of causal paths. That is, conclusions about the strength of the effect of parental punitiveness on child aggressiveness and whether it increases or decreases aggressiveness could both be wrong.

Conceptually, *structural equation models* (Jöreskog & Sörbom, 1979) combine a path analysis model with a factor analysis model of the dependent variables and a factor analysis model of the independent variables. Thus, the above arguments against using path analysis as a cure-all for causal ambiguity apply to structural equation models as well. If, however, specific alternative causal interpretations are built into such models, then evidence can often be provided for or against the specified alternatives. Thus, path analysis and structural equation models can best be used together with strong inference (discussed later; see also Cook & Campbell, 1979, Chapter 7; Platt, 1964).

Analyses of Extended-Occasion Designs. Most family studies using extended-occasion designs before 1975 were analyzed primarily in terms of group differences (Jacob, 1975). The time-ordered nature of the data was not used directly in such analyses.

Recently, *sequential probability analyses* have been developed for extended-occasion designs (Bakeman, 1978; Gottman, 1979; Gottman & Bakeman, 1979). This procedure uses the conditional probability of a target event, given that a second specified event has occurred previously. Evidence supporting the causal influence of the specified event on the target event is found if the conditional probability of the target event is significantly different from its unconditional probability.

Lytton and Zwirner (1975) used a sequential probability analysis to study how several kinds of parental control attempts were related to the immediately subsequent compliance or noncompliance of a 2-year-old child. They found that physical control and negative action increased the probability of noncompliance more than it increased the probability of compliance. In contrast, positive and neutral parental actions increased the likelihood of compliance more than of noncompliance.

Time series analysis has been developed in econometrics for handling time-ordered data. Family research data are often not suitable for time series analysis, as a minimum of about 50 data-collection times are recommended (Cook & Campbell, 1979; Glenn & Frisbie, 1977). Some recent extended-occasion research, however, has approached that number of data points (e.g., Gottman, 1979). Further, the logic of time series analysis may be useful even when the number of data points falls far short of the recommended 50 (Cook & Campbell, 1979). Good introductions to time series analysis for social scientists are presented by Cook and Campbell (1979) and by McCleary and Hay (1980).

Analyses of Multi-Occasion Designs. Many analyses of multi-occasion data do not take advantage of the time-ordered nature of the data. Instead, there is some tendency for longitudinal research to evolve into a series of repeated cross-sectional analyses (Featherman, 1980). This section summarizes three methods that do use multi-occasion data: cross-lagged panel analysis, path analysis, and structural equation models.

When first introduced, *cross-lagged panel analysis* seemed to be an ideal method for discriminating between the causal influence of variable *A* on variable *B* versus the influence of *B* on *A* (Campbell & Stanley, 1966). Recent criticisms (Bielby & Hauser, 1977; Rogosa, 1979, 1980), however, have raised serious questions about it. Misleading conclusions can be made about the relative strengths of the two causal directions because of the differential stability of the variables over time, because of differences in variances of the two variables, or because of changes in the causal influences over time (Cook & Campbell, 1979; Rogosa, 1979, 1980). The first two problems could be corrected by using standardized variances and partial (Hannan & Tuma, 1979) or semipartial correlations (Nunnally, 1967, pp. 154–155). It is not clear that alternative analytic procedures do any better in handling the problem of instability of the causal model (Cook & Campbell, 1979; Rogosa, 1979, 1980). At any rate, cross-lagged correlational analysis provides, at best, a low power test that does not guarantee valid causal interpretation by itself (Bielby & Hauser, 1977; Cook & Campbell, 1979; Rogosa, 1980). Users should consult Cook and Campbell (1979) and Kenny (1979) for the analysis of continuous variables or Duncan (1979) for the analysis of dichotomous variables.

Multiple-regression analyses can be used to analyze time-ordered data. This is the type of analysis with which cross-lagged correlational analysis was compared by Rogosa (1979). *Path analysis* is a form of regression analysis that has been discussed under brief-occasion designs. If some of the variables are measured on two or more occasions, then some of the alternative causal possibilities can be ruled out. However, any regression analysis that uses ordinary least squares has difficulty handling autocorrelation of a variable with itself over time. Some statisticians have suggested generalized least squares or pseudo-generalized least squares as an alternative for handling autocorrelations in regression analyses (Hibbs, 1974; Ostrom, 1978).

Structural equation models, in contrast, can build the autocorrelations into the model directly (Jöreskog, 1979). Thus, such models may have more potential for analyzing time-ordered data. However, this approach requires a large sample size, is often misused (Bielby *et al.*, 1977), and can be difficult to interpret.

Other analytic strategies are at least potentially useful for some purposes but have not been widely used or evaluated to this point. Gain score analyses (Cook & Campbell, 1979, pp. 182–185) use difference scores in traditional analysis of variance or analysis of covariance. A selection cohort design regresses pretest scores on age (or some other time marker), using the regressed scores to predict posttest scores. Life-table techniques (Potter, 1966) have proved particularly useful for correcting for sample attrition in fertility studies, and have recently been adapted to the study of other transitions (Espenshade & Braum, 1982; Teachman, 1982). Finally, cohort tables (Glenn, 1977) may be analyzed by bivariate or multivariate contingency-table analysis (Bishop, Fienberg, & Holland, 1975).

The time-ordered nature of the family thus has direct implications for all aspects of the research process: conceptualization, research design, data collection, and statistical analysis. There remain many questions concerning how best to analyze time-ordered data, but investigators should seriously consider the implications of the time-ordered nature of their variables for each research phase. Methodologists need to develop statistical procedures for analyzing time-ordered data less ambiguously.

Let us turn now to the methodological implications of two closely interrelated characteristics of the family: the private and value-laden nature of the family.

The Private and Value-Laden Nature of the Family

Because of cultural norms concerning family privacy, and because of the intimacy and interdependence of family members over a long period of time, families develop private, idiosyncratic norms and meanings about their own activities. The private and idiosyncratic nature of the family has important implications for the external (ecological) validity of data: To what extent do the reports and actions of family members elicited by outsiders correspond with characteristics of the family in private?

Closely related to the private nature of the family is the value-laden nature of the family. Research on families elicits more than its share of strong opinions, probably because the family is such a central part of most people's lives. Researchers are no exception. Nonconscious value positions have led white male social scientists to make conclusions about families that have been criticized by blacks (e.g., Allen, 1978) and by feminists (e.g., Millman & Kanter, 1975).

Implications for Conceptualization

Information from families is often interpreted by the researcher differently from how it would be interpreted by the participating families themselves. Sometimes, such differences are random; in other cases, they are systematically biased. Differences in interpretations arise from the idiosyncratic norms and meanings in private family life. Another source is the reluctance of families to share their own private experiences completely and accurately. One way to deal with such issues is to collect and use data on the participants' own interpretations of their family life.

Systematic differences in interpretations may arise because of a social desirability response bias or because of value differences between investigators and participants. Issues concerning the social desirability response bias are considered in a later section. It is sufficient for now to note that families may distort reports of their private experiences to appear more typical to the investigators.

Value differences between researchers and participants are more specifically related to research conceptualization. The history of family studies illustrates some of the ways in which values have inadvertently influenced the conceptualization and interpretation of research. Until the last decade, for example, black families were generally ignored by family researchers or were viewed in terms of deviancy from the implicit standards of the white majority (Peters, 1978). Thus, Moynihan (1965) concluded that "at the heart of the deterioration of the fabric of Negro society is the deterioration of the Negro family" (p. 5). Allen (1978) pointed out two alternatives to this culturally deviant perspective on black family life: the culturally equivalent perspective and the culturally variant perspective. The culturally equivalent perspective minimizes differences between black families and white families. The culturally variant perspective recognizes subcultural differences but does not evaluate the minority patterns by the majority pattern; rather, it views the characteristics of both groups as outgrowths of their respective sociocultural contexts.

Allen noted further that the conclusions of investigators have been influenced by their values as well as by the objective data. Allen's analysis applies to any minority group outside the mainstream of family researchers, whether a minority of race, sex, creed, or lifestyle. Various studies have challenged outsiders' viewpoints concerning the families of such minority groups as blacks (Allen, 1978; Peters, 1978); Mormons (Wilkinson & Tanner, 1980), the working class (Rubin, 1976); the remarried (Albrecht, 1979); and women (Millman & Kanter, 1975).

Values about the family are more directly involved in some areas than in others. For example, evaluation research is particularly influenced by value positions. Outcome measures are so intertwined with evaluations of what is good in family life that it is impossible to construct value-free outcome measures.

Sensitivity about these issues has usually been increased by family specialists who are also members of the minority group that is being studied. Input from such professionals is advisable during the conceptualization of the research. Other recommendations are to facilitate feedback from research participants about the investigators' interpretations (Foote & Cottrell, 1955; Peters & Massey, 1979) and to aim for heterogeneity of values in a research team (Baumrind, 1971).

Implications for Research Design

Careful consideration of conceptual issues will help researchers deal adequately with private aspects of the family and with value differences in the design of their studies. For example, investigators should routinely evaluate whether various socioeconomic and ethnic groups should be included in their study. From 1959 to 1968, only 7% of articles in the *Journal of Marriage and the Family* focused on lower-class samples, and another 25% explicitly reported on socioeconomic differences (Stolte Heiskanen, 1971).

Handling problems with reactivity and the social desirability response bias is an important issue at every phase of the research process. At the research strategy level, several things can be done to minimize such problems. Obtaining data separately from two or more family members can provide a partial check on motivated distortions. Young children seem particularly resistant to social desirability response biases, although research is needed to demonstrate how the validity of children's reports varies with age. Using interviewers of the same ethnic group as the subjects decreases the social desirability response bias. Bielby *et al.* (1977) found that black but not white responses tended to be distorted in a socially desirable direction. The most reasonable explanation is that expectations of ethnic prejudice influence members of minority groups to modify data that could otherwise be used to reinforce prejudicial stereotypes.

Implications for Data Collection

Modifications of data collection procedures are the most frequent way of dealing with problems of reactivity and the social desirability response bias. After discussing how to deal with reactivity and social desirability, subsequent sections consider the extreme response bias and methods for collecting data on sensitive topics.

Reactivity and Social Desirability. Reactivity is the extent to which people's actions are influenced by knowing that they are participating in a research study. The *social desirability response bias* is the most common systematic bias due to reactivity. Although the social desirability response bias is usually considered only for self-report measures, it is hard to believe that subjects are not similarly motivated when they know that their behavior is being observed for research purposes. It may be easier to distort a self-report indicator than to distort an observational one, but that does not make reactivity trivial, even after subjects adapt to being observed.

Several strategies can be used to reduce reactivity in observational data. Several research tasks (e.g., Straus & Tallman, 1971; Strodtbeck, 1951) are so engrossing that participants often "forget" that they are being observed. High levels of role-playing involvement do seem to counter socially desirable distortion (Geller, 1978). Further, role playing can be used to examine people's abilities (e.g., in interpersonal communication) even when it is not representative of how they actually use those abilities. This approach circumvents the reactivity problem by requesting research participants to perform to their maximum ability.

The research setting can also be selected to decrease reactivity. Gottman (1979) has shown that marital interaction is more negative at home than in a research laboratory, suggesting that reactivity is less in a familiar setting than in an unfamiliar one. When public settings are suitable for a research topic, they may be used to reduce reactivity. For example, Brown (1979) observed the disciplinary practices of parents in a shopping mall.

Young children are relatively unaffected by social desirability concerns, as any parent can testify. This trait can be used to reduce reactivity, especially for research on parent–toddler relationships. It may be useful for reducing reactivity on other topics. For example, an investigator could study spousal interaction by focusing on how they interact about their child in a situation with the child present.

Some investigators have used special recording devices to obtain data without having observers present (Christensen, 1979; Johnson, Christensen, & Bellamy, 1976). Christensen, for example, placed recording instruments in high-interaction areas in the home, such as the eating area. By means of timers, interaction was randomly sampled during the times when the family was expected to be there.

Nonverbal behavior is more difficult to modify in a socially desirable direction than is verbal behavior (Vincent, Friedman, Nugent, & Messerly, 1979). Measures of nonverbal behavior, then, are less subject to reactivity than are measures of verbal behavior. In her study of the effects of father absence on young adolescent daughters, for example, Hetherington (1972) included measures of the daughters' proximity to males to evaluate their attitudes toward men.

Social desirability is also a common confounding variable in family research. Self-report measures of marital power are more associated with the perceived appropriateness of male authority (as measured by self-report) than with observational power measures (Olson, 1969; Turk & Bell, 1972). There are several methods for reducing the social desirability response bias in survey measures.

Measurement scales can be developed to reduce the effects of social desirability (Larzelere & Huston, 1980). Items can be selected not only according to their correlations with the total score on an initial item pool, but also according to how closely the correlation with a social desirability scale approaches zero. Jackson's Differential Reliability Index (1971) combines these two criteria for item selection. An alternative approach is to use forced-choice items in which the respondents must choose between two or more distinct items that are equated on social desirability (Klein, 1978). A potential problem with forced choice is that respondents are reluctant to select between two equally undesirable items; thus, the response rate for those items is decreased.

The forced-choice strategy assumes that items can be reliably judged for social desirability and that social desirability differs little for the different individuals or groups that are going to be compared in the data analysis. The other methods depend on a valid measure of social desirability. The Marlowe–Crowne Social Desirability Scale (Crowne & Marlowe, 1964) has well-established validity and is not heavily laden with references to psychologically abnormal behavior (Robinson & Shaver, 1973) as is the Edwards (1957) scale. However, the Marlowe–Crowne scale has not proved to be highly related to family variables (Hawkins, 1966; Larzelere & Huston, 1980). It may be that the Marlowe–Crowne scale is not as suitable for controlling for social desirability in family research as is the Edmonds (1967) scale, which was specifically constructed for such a purpose. However, some questions have been raised recently about the construct validity of Edmonds's scale (Schumm, Bollman, & Jurich, 1982).

Two matters seem to be confounded in all social desirability scales: the extent to which respondents distort their responses in a socially desirable direction and the extent to which respondents actually do behave in a socially desirable manner. Social desirability distortion obviously should be reduced as much as possible. The usefulness of controlling for the social desirability of the actual characteristics of families depends on the research purpose. About one half of respondents make a socially desirable response on a typical item on a social desirability scale, a result that seems rather high for an unbelievably extreme response. Edmonds's items (1967), for example, have from 32% to 64% answering in a socially desirable direction. Items that elicited fewer than 32% socially desirable responses might have indicated socially desirable distortion more than the items in Edmonds's final scale, but the former were eliminated in the item selection process (Edmonds, 1967), partly because of the lower biserial correlations possible for skewed dichotomous items (see Nunnally, 1967, p. 133). As the resulting scale controls for actual social desirability as well as for social desirability distortion, it is not surprising that partialing out scores on Edmonds's scale eliminates correlations between indices of conventionality and marital adjustment (Edmonds, Withers, & Dibatista, 1972). But it remains to be shown whether conventional correlates of marital quality are spurious or not. (For an early debate on this point, see Ellis, 1948; Terman & Wallin, 1949).

Extreme Response Bias. The strong evaluative nature of central aspects of the family implies that the extreme response bias will be especially problematic for some family variables. The extreme response bias occurs because some people give extreme responses (e.g., "very strongly agree") much more readily than do other people. The tendency to give extreme responses is negatively correlated with age and intelligence (Achenbach, 1978, p. 183). When the mean score of items is near the neutral point (on a Likert-type item), the extreme response bias is uncorrelated with scores on the scale. When, however, most of the range of respondents' scores is on one side of the midpoint, the extreme response bias can be a serious confounding factor. Such is the case for measures of positively valued dimensions of intimate relationships, such as trust, love, and marital satisfaction (Larzelere & Huston, 1980; Rubin, 1970; Spanier, 1976a). The usual method of controlling for this has been to construct scales such that the mean score is near the neutral point. However, following this recommendation conflicts with the careful conceptualization of such variables (e.g., what kind of measure of love would put the average couple at the neutral midpoint?). Thus, it would be better to use a relatively content-free measure of the extreme response

bias, such as Arthur's scale (1966), which correlated .30 ($p < .01$) with the Dyadic Trust Scale (Larzelere, Poelstra, Olson, & Waitschies, 1984).

Sensitive Topics. In research on sensitive topics, reluctance to disclose information, reactivity, and social desirability distortion are accentuated further whether because of the undesirable nature of the phenomenon examined (e.g., physical abuse) or because of the private nature of the phenomenon (e.g., details about sexual technique). Several procedures have been suggested for data collection on sensitive topics (Gelles, 1978). The funneling technique begins with socially desirable aspects of the topic and gradually decreases the social desirability of the potential answers (Straus, 1979). Another strategy is to phrase the question so that the respondent must deny socially undesirable behavior (Kinsey, Wardell, & Martin, 1948), for example, asking *when* the respondent first experienced it instead of whether she or he ever did.

Sampling is also more problematic for research on sensitive topics. Probability sampling is rarely used in studies of divorce, spouse abuse, or child abuse (for an exception, see Straus *et al.*, 1980). Potential subjects for sensitive family topics are usually identified through private or public records or through social networks (Gelles, 1978). Such methods use resources efficiently to obtain a useful sample, but generalizations are often limited. Generalizations to a limited target population (e.g., child abuse cases that come to the attention of social agencies) can be confidently made if the investigator has a probabilistic sample of that population. Conclusions about differences between such special populations and other types of families are limited unless a probabilistic sample is used of all types of families that are included in the conclusions. When a probabilistic sample is not feasible, however, demographic comparisons of the research sample (and, ideally, nonrespondents) with census data or another relevant comparison group would be helpful.

Research on sensitive topics is not as problematic as it appears to be on the surface. DeLamater (1974; DeLamater & MacCorquodale, 1975) has examined several potential sources of bias in research on premarital sexuality and concluded that:

> The difficulty of obtaining valid data from respondents about sensitive topics may have been consistently overestimated. . . . Reports of sexual and other "threatening" behaviors may be relatively uninfluenced by methodological variations. (DeLamater & MacCorquodale, 1975, p. 234)

Implications for Data Analysis

Statistical analysis can be used to control for the social-desirability response bias if it has not been dealt with adequately in data collection. A measure of social desirability must be included in the data set to control statistically for this response set. Given that prerequisite, any regression-based statistical procedure could be used. For example, Edmonds *et al.* (1972) used partial correlations to control for the effect of marital conventionalization. Such a statistical control eliminated the correlation between religious activity and marital adjustment.

A second approach is to limit the analyzed data to those participants with relatively low social desirability scores. This approach reduces the sample size but requires less stringent statistical assumptions. Schumm, Bollman, and Jurich (1982) found that religiosity remained a substantial predictor of marital adjustment among those who scored low on conventionalization. Until the reasons for this discrepancy are better understood, it would be best to use both strategies as statistical controls for social desirability.

The central methodological questions concerning the private and value-laden nature of the family have been how to handle value differences and how to cope with the social desirability (or reactivity) response bias. These issues take different forms during different phases of a research project and can be handled in distinct ways at each of those phases.

The Family as Part of a Larger Social System

To this point, we have considered the family almost as an isolated aspect of society. Except for our discussion of value differences, we could be accused of giving the impression that the societal context of the family is irrelevant to understanding families. Of course, that is far from the case. This section, then, considers the methodological implications of the fact that the family is intimately embeded in a larger societal context.

The relationship of the family to the larger social system was a common concern of scholars during the nineteenth century. Microscopic studies using social psychological perspectives that focus on intrafamily processes have come to dominate the intellectual scene in more recent decades (Christensen, 1964, pp. 6–10; Hill, 1980; Howard, 1981). Nonetheless, the family's relationship to social structure remains important, and it reflects a general orientation that argues that family life cannot be adequately understood unless families are situated in their social environments.

This section covers two types of methods used to investigate the family in its social context. The more commonly used type is *comparative analysis.* Cross-cultural research compares families across geographical, political, or ethnic boundaries. Historical research compares families across relatively broad sweeps of time. Comparative analysis within a society can also take either of these two forms but in a more limited way, yielding data on subcultural differences or generational differences. Cross-cultural research and historical research are usually treated separately (e.g., Lee, 1977), although some previous writers have, like us, emphasized their similarities (e.g., Keniston, 1971; Sirjamaki, 1964). Lee (1984) has recently discussed some of the problems and erroneous

assumptions concerning cross-cultural research which have inhibited its use in family studies.

A second type of research, *transactional analysis,*[1] refers to the study of the family's relationships with its social network, which involves the study of role relationships linking family members simultaneously to their positions in the family and to their positions in other social systems (e.g., the interactions of people at home and at work). This approach assumes that family roles are mutually interdependent with roles performed outside the family unit by the same persons. Whereas comparative analysis contrasts families in different cultural settings, transactional analysis investigates hypotheses about how other societal groups more directly influence the family.

Because of the distinctions between comparative analysis and transactional analysis, this section is organized slightly differently from the previous sections. It first considers the four types of methodological implications for comparative analysis and subsequently considers those implications for transactional analysis.

Comparative Analysis

Implications for Conceptualization. In comparative research, one must be prepared to conceptualize important variables that vary meaningfully either among sociocultural units or across historical time. In cross-cultural research, it is important to go beyond merely naming nations to specifying what is thought to distinguish them (Lee, 1977, p. 16). A variety of general variables have been proposed for this purpose. Among the more popular are "modernization" (Cogswell & Sussman, 1972), "complexity" (Winch, 1979), and "heterogeneity" (Cogswell & Sussman, 1979). According to Osmond (1980, p. 1010), most studies based on these ideas assume a model of economic determinism, and she encourages the employment of other approaches also.

Similar points apply to historical family research. We need to go beyond merely naming historical epochs to specifying the important ways in which different historical periods have varied from each other and from the current era. Modernization and economic determinism are at least as applicable to historical research as they are to cross-cultural research. Especially given the tendency to view family life as evolving in one direction, from traditional to modern forms (cf. Goode, 1963), it is crucial to demonstrate that family life has such a unilinear progression. In our judgment, this is the most important lesson of the recent research by family historians.

In both cross-cultural (Elder, 1976, p. 210; Lee, 1977, pp. 47–50) and historical research (Boocock, 1978), there are differences of opinion about whether a particular

---

[1]This use of the term *transactional analysis* is derived from Rodgers (1973, Chapter 7) and is unrelated to Berne's (1961) use of the same term to refer to a neo-Freudian dynamic view of personality.

culture can best be studied on its own terms or by explicit comparison with others. At one extreme of cross-cultural researchers are those who hold that cultures constitute distinctive wholes. Adopting this position, one would study the family by embedding it in the unique and total cultural context of which it is a part. At the other extreme are those who hold that a key mission of social science is to search for and discover cross-cultural universals. Adopting this position, one would study the family in various cultures, expecting to find functionally equivalent practices or homologues. Neither approach is inherently superior, but one's position on the issue is likely to affect the design of a particular study. As an illustration, there is still some controversy over whether or not the division of labor by gender is cross-culturally universal, with adult males always being the instrumental leader and adult females always being the expressive leader (Aronoff & Crano, 1975). The controversy may in large part be due to differences between studies in their samples of cultures or in their measures of the division of labor. Even if a case could be made for some universal principle of gender-role differentiation, the reasons for it may be unique to each culture studied.

A similar debate in the historical study of the family centers on whether to adopt a conventional historical approach or a conventional sociological approach. The former emphasizes descriptive detail and is idiographic, focusing on the unique sequence of events that happened during a particular period of time. The latter emphasizes the reduction of detail to general variables for explanatory purposes and is therefore nomothetic (Boocock, 1978, p. S367). A study of family life in colonial New England, for example, would be idiographic unless it compared that setting with family life in a different period of history in an effort to use general principles to explain why they were similar or different.

Another issue that is similar in cross-cultural and historical research is the difficulty of drawing boundaries between cultures or epochs. Perhaps the problem is clearest in historical research, as historical periods are inherently subject to precarious definitions. The contrast between families in the twentieth century and in the nineteenth century, for example, assumes that the calendar itself provides a meaningful boundary between periods. We can speak of periods, such as the Great Depression, but it is not so easy to specify when they began or ended. The important point is that, although periods of history may develop conventional meanings, the researcher is obligated to defend the scheme adopted for a particular study.

A related issue is whether historical change can best be conceptualized in terms of specific events or in terms of processes. A major discovery of contemporary family historians has been that key features of the ''modern'' family emerged before the Industrial Revolution experienced in Western societies around the middle of the last century (cf. Degler, 1980, Chapter 1), although the veracity of this idea is still subject to vigorous debate (cf. Gordon, 1978, pp. 12, 201). The focus on industrialization as a pivotal concept highlights the methodological issue of events versus process. The term *industrialization* refers to a process rather than to a specific event, although that process can be decomposed into a series of events that might involve, for example, the adoption of an assembly line in a factory.

The vagueness of boundaries between cultures is sometimes called *Galton's problem* in cross-cultural research. When two or more cultures are found to be similar on a variable or in a relationship between variables, the researcher cannot always be sure that the evidence has come from truly independent cultures. Instead, the similarity may have resulted from interaction between the cultures, resulting in a diffusion of practices from one to the other. Several solutions have been proposed to deal with this problem (Elder, 1976, pp. 27–218; Lee, 1977, pp. 44–46). One is to classify nations into culturally distinct subsets and to limit one's comparisons to nations in different subsets. Methods of stratifying samples by geography, calculating ''diffusion arcs'' (Naroll, 1961), or using the standard cross-cultural sample (Murdock & White, 1969) have also been proposed. Most of these solutions can be anticipated and applied when samples are being selected. They may also be introduced as statistical controls during the data analysis phase.

Comparative analyses of different groups of families can also be applied within a particular culture. Generational comparisons could be made between the families of different generations (e.g., Hill, Foote, Aldous, Carlson, & MacDonald, 1970). In this sense, historical research need not be limited to data collected in previous time periods (Boocock, 1978, p. S366). Interviews with grandparents and other mature persons can sometimes be obtained to provide oral histories of past events and situations.

Subcultural analyses contrast families of distinct groups within a society, such as socioeconomic groups or ethnic groups. Contextual analysis is a type of subcultural analysis that we discuss later as a research design that bridges the gap between macrosociology and microsociology. The next section first considers more general implications of comparative analyses for research strategies.

Implications for Research Design. One research strategy that has rarely been used in family research is the cross-cultural replication of a true experiment (Elder, 1976). Important beginnings in this direction have been made (Straus, 1970; Tallman, 1980), but cross-cultural family research continues to be dominated by survey, demographic, and ethnographic studies. Osmond (1980) has provided an overview of cross-cultural research published in three English-language journals during the 1970s. Among the findings from her content analysis are that English-speaking and Western European countries are overrepresented, that most studies are descriptive rather than explanatory, that the majority are based either on nonprobability samples or secondary analysis, and that the majority of studies present data on the families of only one country. We agree with Osmond that remedies for these deficiencies ought to have a high priority. Most experienced researchers are aware of such problems. It seems to us, therefore, that obtaining the necessary resources to meet these problems is bound up in the practical and political context of doing research and is not so much a matter of inadequate methodological standards in the research community.

Contextual analysis is a research strategy that investigates the relationship between macro, societal-level variables and micro, family-level variables. Classic examples of contextual effects include the discovery that attitudes among enlisted men toward the army's promotion system varies inversely with the proportion of enlisted men in a military unit who are highly ranked (Stouffer, Lumsdaine, Lumsdaine, Williams, Smith, Janis, Star, & Cottrell, 1949, pp. 250–254), and that consensus on politics in union shops is positively related to the degree of the union members' interest in politics (Lipset, Trow, & Coleman, 1956, pp. 163–171). "Proportion highly ranked" and "consensus" in these examples are contextual variables because they are not attributes of individuals but of the group itself.

Contextual analysis is a comparative strategy in the sense that the effects of contexts can be ascertained only if contexts are permitted to vary in the design of the research. Much cross-cultural family research might be classified as contextual in that cultural variables serve as contextual parameters. It is also true that contexts can be arrayed along a historical dimension. *Capitalism,* for example, refers to a type of economic system that has changed historically and that may affect family life.

Family researchers have often generated findings that may be interpreted as contextual effects. Whenever features of the family group, such as its size or the consensus among its members, are treated as independent variables affecting the behaviors of the members, a form of contextual analysis has been employed. Sometimes, the context is not a property of the family but some aspect of the larger community. Examples include the findings that marriage rates for men and women vary in opposite directions with the sex ratio of the communities in which they live (Groves & Ogburn, 1928, pp. 193–205), that the proportionate size of a minority group affects its intermarriage rate (Reiss, 1971, p. 327), and that the status of women in a state (e.g., legal rights) inversely affects the probability that wives will be victims of spouse abuse (Ÿllo, 1980). The ecological perspective in human development research (cf. Bronfenbrenner, 1979; Garbarino, 1977) can also be understood as explicitly incorporating contextual effects in its explanatory models.

Despite the examples of contextual arguments in family studies, it seems to us that this approach has been used infrequently, perhaps because of the tendency for family researchers to view the family as a closed system of relationships unaffected by variables operating at a more macrosocietal level.

There are two specific methodological issues in contextual analysis that we will treat here. One is the selection of appropriate contexts. We have already suggested that some aspect of the composition or organization of the family itself may be selected, or that, alternatively, some larger and often territorial unit may be selected. Straus (1980) has argued, for example, that data aggregated at the state level offer considerable potential for family research. The choice of contextual units is problematic because effects may be observed at one level and not at another. For example, the size of a family may be important to what goes on in families, but the average size of a family in a particular region may be more or even less important for the same purpose. Systematic comparisons across different aggregation schemes should help us to better identify the crucial contextual effects on family behavior.

The second issue involves whether or not the effects of contextual variables are entirely mediated by variables at a more microlevel and, further, how to determine this. The issue remains unresolved in sociology generally (Erbring & Young, 1979; Farkas, 1974; Firebaugh, 1979; Hauser, 1974). Some hold that contextual variables are only indirect measures of individual variables unless it can be demonstrated that they explain variance beyond that accounted for by variables measured at the individual level. Even if the effects of contextual variables are entirely mediated in this way, a contextual analysis can still be helpful in suggesting interventions at a macrolevel, such as decisions about social policy. Suppose, for example, that the communities with the most available programs of marital enrichment have higher average marital quality. Suppose further that the differences between communities are mediated entirely by the effects of marital enrichment programs. The higher marital quality in certain communities is entirely due to improvements in those couples completing marital enrichment. The likelihood of a particular couple's being helped (microlevel) would seem to depend on the availability of services in the community (macrolevel). To improve the service, and thus the chances of any particular couple's being helped, the policy should be to get as many therapists as possible working in a community.

Implications for Data Collection. One fundamental issue in cross-cultural family research is whether to obtain original data through field study or to rely on the secondary analysis of existing data sets (Hill, 1962). For the researcher engaged in primary data collection, important considerations include administrative control over the research process. Attention to the details of forming collaborative teams and of staffing, training, coordinating, and monitoring the quality of work by the team members is central to the success of this kind of research. Helpful suggestions are provided by Hill (1962), Sussman and

Cogswell (1972), and Elder (1976, pp. 224–225). Perhaps the most distinctive position was taken by Sussman and Cogswell (1972), who argued for a "parity model" designed to overcome the colonialism and dehumanization that can develop when a foreign scholar collects data in a host country. They attributed the shortcomings of past cross-cultural studies "more to inadequacy in interpersonal competence among potential collaborators than the unavailability of a sophisticated scientific technology" (p. 211).

Another issue that has received considerable attention is the sampling of cultural units. Usually, the researcher wants to maximize the range of variation in the sample (Elder, 1976, p. 211), although it is sometimes argued that the study of a single society has merit (Osmond, 1980, p. 997). Sampling depends on the researcher's ability to establish criteria for deciding that the units are similar or dissimilar and then on assignment of the units to categories in line with the criteria (Elder, 1976, pp. 214–215). A variety of stratified random-sampling procedures have been discussed by Elder (1976, pp. 218–221) and Lee (1977, pp. 22–30).

Once the cultural units have been selected, the researcher engaged in an original field study must still face the problem of securing an adequate sample of cooperating families. Hill (1962, p. 435) noted that refusal rates tend to be higher outside than inside the United States, although this circumstance may have changed in recent years. He offered several ideas for maximizing response rates, including careful attention to sponsorship and interviewer training (Hill, 1962, pp. 434–438). The protection of human subjects in cross-cultural family research is complicated by the fact that cultures vary in their norms about privacy as well as about the risks and benefits of participating in research. Sussman and Cogswell (1972, pp. 220–221) proposed that, to deal with this problem, the researcher should imvolve the participating families very early in the design of the project.

Secondary analysis has always been typical of historical research. Its attractiveness for cross-cultural research has been greatly enhanced by the existence of the Human Relations Area Files and the Ethnographic Atlas developed by Murdock and his colleagues over the last several decades (cf. Lee, 1977, pp. 23, 45). An endemic problem in the sampling of cultures for the secondary analysis of family data is that less than half of those cultures that have ever existed have written records. An even smaller proportion have recorded information of interest to the family researcher. Furthermore, among those cultures with relevant data available, the quality of the data varies considerably. In light of these considerations, it is usually very difficult to support claims about the representativeness of one's sample or to make confident generalizations from research findings.

The further back in time one goes, the more severe is the problem of the limited availability of relevant data from a given culture. Great strides have been made in recent years to unearth new sources, such as parish records, but the fact remains that family historians must continuously operate in a situation of information scarcity (Boocock, 1978, pp. S367, S373). As a result, sampling issues take on special importance. There is, for example, a bias created by the fact that better educated persons are most likely to produce and maintain records of their family lives (Boocock, 1978, S374–376).

Another implication of limited data is that historical research on the family tends to concentrate on demographic characteristics reflected in the events of birth, marriage, divorce, and death, or on such structural features as household size. The further back in history one moves, the more difficult it is to reconstruct the social and emotional fabric of family interaction, the very stuff that occupies so central a role in research on contemporary families. One exception to the demographic focus in historical family research is the analysis of popular culture by means of documents from the mass media (cf. Lantz, Schultz, & O'Hara, 1977). Even here, however, reliability and validity are often questionable. Accounts in the mass media may often be caricatures or may oversample dramatic aspects of family life and ignore its more mundane and common features.

Without question, the most frequently addressed measurement issue in the area of cross-cultural family research is *conceptual equivalence* (cf. Straus, 1969). This issue is just as relevant to historical family research. Formally equivalent items may be administered to members of different cultures, but there is no guarantee that they mean the same thing in these cultures. Hence, effort is normally directed toward obtaining functional equivalence in original field studies, even if this means that the instruments administered in the different settings are themselves quite different.

Many suggestions have been offered to promote conceptual or functional equivalence. Collaborating with experts in the host country helps to ensure that the biases of foreign scholars will be checked (Hill, 1962, pp. 443–445; Sussman & Cogswell, 1972, p. 218). Starting out with careful pilot testing and becoming enmeshed in the fieldwork helps investigators to get a feel for the meaningfulness of behavior patterns (Sussman & Cogswell, 1972, p. 217). Utilizing "confrontation interviews" encourages family members to discuss matters of importance to them and to clarify meanings for the interviewer (Hill, 1962, p. 442–443). Using multiple methods of data collection helps to assess convergent validity (Sussman & Cogswell, 1972, p. 218).

Utilizing open-ended questions enables responses to be coded with sensitivity to the categories used by the respondents (Elder, 1976, p. 222). Being multilingual (Sussman & Cogswell, 1972, p. 218) and using back translations or multiple independent translations (Elder, 1976, pp. 222–223; Lee, 1977, pp. 35–36) sensitize the researcher to problems of nonequivalent meaning. Additional methods for assessing and maximizing conceptual equivalence across cultures are discussed by Lee (1977, pp. 37–40). It should be noted that most of the listed suggestions have wide applicability. In general, whenever the researcher suspects that his or her own cultural background is different from that of the family members participating in a study, problems of interpretation may arise, and corrective measures are appropriate. When secondary data are employed, the original data may need to be regrouped or recoded.

Because the reliability and validity of secondary data often cannot be assessed easily, researchers are advised to reconstruct the process by which the data were originally obtained wherever possible (Boocock, 1978, p. S367). Estimating the extent to which historical data were based originally on samples of elite respondents, for example, may help the analyst guard against generalizing beyond certain social strata. Boocock (1978, pp. S369–372) has also provided a useful typology, cross-classifying the nature of the data (verbal vs. nonverbal) with the purposes for which they were generated. Strategic combinations are encouraged so that the inherent strengths and weaknesses of the various types may be counterbalanced. Verbal sources, for example, depend on the literacy of the people studied and therefore introduce biases that can be partially determined by also including nonverbal sources.

Implications for Data Analysis. A number of technical issues arise in the course of analyzing cross-cultural data. Elder (1976, p. 220) proposed the use of ordinal designations of variables within cultures to standardize scores and to facilitate comparisons across cultures. It may be more important to know, for example, that a particular Yugoslavian family scores high on a measure of problem-solving compared with other Yugoslavian families than that it scores low compared with American families. Other issues, such as resolving contradictory findings (Elder, 1976, p. 224) and handling overidentified models (Lee, 1977, pp. 42–44), have also received attention.

A common issue in cross-cultural research has recently become more salient in historical research on the family: the debate over qualitative versus quantitative approaches (Boocock, 1978, pp. S379–380). Historiography before World War II was mostly qualitative and descriptive, and only in recent decades have the more systematic quantitative techniques of historical demography come into vogue. As with any research on the family, qualitative and quantitative techniques are best viewed as complementary rather than as rivals.

Perhaps the most discussed historical analysis technique in recent years is *family reconstitution* (Boocock, 1978, pp. S388–390; Wrigley, 1966). The basic idea behind this technique is that it draws on multiple data sources to build up a file of information about specific families. Instead of having to make inferences about aggregates of families, the reconstitution technique helps to ensure that each family will be measured on each variable of interest. Boocock (1978, p. S389) provided useful warnings about the added costs of time and diligence required to perform family reconstitution. For example,

the names of persons may not be uniformly identified across types of records. Also, as most records are maintained for geographic or political units, the mobility of persons in and out of an area often leads to incomplete data on the families of these mobile persons. Another limitation is the 72-year anonymity rule currently in force (Boruch & Cecil, 1979), which means that U.S. Census and vital data more recent than 1910 cannot now be used for the purpose of family reconstitution.

To date, family reconstitution has been restricted to studies on a modest scale with farily small and immobile samples. An interesting anecdote in the history of science is that a family sociologist (Christensen, 1958) independently developed a version of the reconstitution method that he called "record linkage." Most historians appear to be unaware of Christensen's efforts.

Transactional Analysis

Whereas comparative analyses contrast groups that differ on important independent variables, transactional analysis addresses links between macro- and microlevel variables directly. Comparative research might compare families from industrial societies with those from agrarian societies. Transactional research investigates the effects of industrialization by examining the relationship between family variables and variables in the work setting of the family members. A transactional analyst would argue that, however important external, large-scale conditions might be, they can have an effect on family life only if they are transmitted through those interpersonal contacts that sum up to the relationships that family members have with outsiders.

Implications for Conceptualization. As with other approaches to the study of the relationship between the family and the larger social system, a key issue in the conceptualization of transactional research is whether to focus on description or to focus on explanation. Because transactional analysis is less well developed than the other approaches, we see the advantage of devoting considerable effort to descriptive studies in the near future.

If the researcher does adopt an explanatory objective, a decision must be made about whether to view roles and behaviors in one setting as causally influencing roles and behaviors in another setting, or whether, instead, to view causality as bidirectional. The habit of treating the properties of family organization and activity as dependent variables is as likely to infect this type of research as it has cross-cultural and historical research on the family. Transactional designs may have a built-in safeguard against blinding assumptions about causality, however. This type of research deals with concrete patterns of interaction in two or more settings. At this microlevel it is reasonably apparent that intrafamilial patterns of behavior impact family members' interactions with outsiders as well as being influenced by relationships with those outsiders.

The fundamental research-design issue in the transactional approach is the selection of settings. We suggest that there are at least eight primary settings that the family researcher may wish to investigate in conjunction with the family setting: the occupational setting, the social network (or affiliative) setting, the extended kin setting, the economic consumption setting, the religious or spiritual setting, the human services setting (governments and their agencies and so on), the educational setting, and the media consumption setting (TV, magazines, and so on). In each of these settings, family members interact directly or vicariously with other persons who are playing the role of representatives of the myriad groups, organizations, firms, or institutions that exist outside the boundaries of the nuclear family unit. Most of these representatives also have family roles to play. The investigator may wish to envision role chains as follows: One person's family roles are linked to the family roles of other members in the family. That same person has extrafamilial roles that link him or her to "outsiders" through their extrafamilial roles. The outsider, in turn, has family roles linking him or her to other members of his or her own family. Each role player has multiple sets of roles, one set for each social group in which the person participates.

For a useful application of the transactional approach, the reader is encouraged to consult Reiss (1981, Chapters 7–8). After discussing conceptual and theoretical issues, he presents and analyzes data on two linkages: between families and a psychiatric hospital and between families and their kinship networks.

Implications for Research Design. Ordinarily, the family researcher wants to select one extrafamilial setting and to explore the transactions that occur between it and the family setting. So, for example, the relationship between job satisfaction (or other aspects of the job environment) and family satisfaction might be explored. One difficulty here is that the boundaries around settings can be rather arbitrary or diffuse. The job setting, for example, is a place where friendships (social networks) are often formed and sustained. Similarly, contacts with the media might serve educational, religious, economic consumption, or other functions. We expect that family researchers will be making greater efforts in the future to distinguish settings, and that they will want to sample from multiple settings in order to compare the relative importance of each. With regard to a topic like socialization, for example, it would be valuable to know how involved each member of a family is with each extrafamilial setting and to determine the relative influence of these contacts on child-rearing practices.

As transactional family research is a microanalytic strategy for assessing the relationship between family variables and extrafamilial variables, it involves the collection of data about intrafamilial interaction *and* about interaction that occurs between family members and nonmembers of the family. This raises a question about units of analysis. Should a family member be considered the unit (individual level), or should the whole family be considered the unit (group level)? The individual level permits an emphasis on intrafamilial differences in patterns of relating to the environment, especially when the family members are unevenly involved in the web of relevant transactions. In some cases, the family itself may be an appropriate unit, especially where the whole family conducts its transactions as a group. Examples might include camping trips, the family business enterprise, or family therapy.

Selecting a unit of analysis is also required for the extrafamilial setting(s) included in a study. Contacts with the school, for example, may be aggregated to the level of the educational system itself, or distinctions between various school personnel may need to be taken into account.

Although transactional analysis places one's attention directly on the interchanges between family members and nonmembers of the family, one would ordinarily hypothesize that the nature of these linkages are systematically related to some aspect of intrafamily dynamics. Of course, the extrafamilial setting has some internal dynamics of its own. To illustrate, the decision of a school board to cut back educational services may affect the quality of teacher–student interaction, which, in turn, may affect the interaction between the student and the student's parents. The flow of effects may run in the other direction as well. Family life can affect the decisions of school boards. The basic point is that transactional analysis is not concerned only with the transactions between groups but can encompass data about intrasetting phenomena. As a consequence, family transaction researchers may wish to design their studies to investigate a two-step model (as in the school-board example above) or they may wish to concentrate on any number of the links in the role chains that tie other groups to families.

Implications for Data Collection. Access to data sources is a problem in all research, but it takes on special importance in transactional family research. For each setting that is included, the access problem is compounded. In studies of work and the family, for example, one may be able to observe interaction in the home but not at the place of employment, or vice versa. The transactional researcher ordinarily wants to collect information about the same people as they move between settings. Although cross-cultural researchers also deal with multiple settings, they usually have the advantage of studying different people in each setting.

In transactional designs, available resources must be distributed across settings rather than being focused on only one. This spreading of resources may force transactional researchers to scale down the depth and the detail of the information they set out to collect, and it places an extra burden on researchers to employ measures with proven reliability and validity. One way to improve the quality of such studies and to ensure a balanced treatment of settings is to form collaborative research teams. For example, a family sociologist might team up with a political scientist to conduct a transactional study of the family and government.

Because many transactions occur in public places, unobtrusive methods of observation may be particularly suitable for this type of research (cf. Rosenblatt, 1974; Rosenblatt, Titus, & Nevaldine, 1979; Webb, Campbell, Schwartz, & Sechrest, 1966). If the researcher decides instead to rely on traditional survey techniques, a great deal of information can be obtained from home-based interviews or from questionnaires. The task simply becomes one of designing questions about transactive behavior to supplement those ordinarily asked about intrafamily phenomena.

The problem of conceptual equivalence, so central in cross-cultural research, also arises in transactional research. Some variables, such as the amount of time spent in various settings, may be relatively unambiguous. It remains to be determined, however, that formally equivalent items are also conceptually equivalent across settings. It seems likely, for example, that measures of the quality of relationships in each of several settings would require some nonparallel items because quality can mean different things in different settings. One rather obvious illustration is the concept of physical affection. In many families, the demonstration of affection through forms of physical contact is highly valued and is considered a symbol of the quality of relationships. Hugging one's coworkers at the office is likely to have quite different meaning and significance.

Implications for Data Analysis. Multioccasion designs or other forms of longitudinal data collection and analysis seem especially crucial in transactional studies. Delayed effects of interactions in one setting on interactions in another should be common, especially if family members consciously strive to insulate each other from changes in the environment. The recreational travel behavior of families, for example, may depend on changes in international relations in the Middle East, mediated by changes and anticipated changes in prices at the gas pump. We must be concerned here with how long international affairs persist before the consumption behaviors of families are affected. The simultaneous decision of a large number of consuming families to forgo certain expenditures may also affect—quite indirectly, of course— the pattern of international relations.

One approach to the analysis of transactional data has already received considerable attention in the literature. It involves the study of social networks, pioneered by Bott (1971). Others have explored this approach for the study of developing relationships (Ridley & Avery, 1979) and the coping behaviors of families under stress (McCubbin, Joy, Cauble, Comeau, Patterson, & Needle, 1980, pp. 862–864). The basic idea is that the researcher determines the extent to which family members are connected to persons outside the nuclear family and the extent to which the latter are connected to each other. We expect

greater use to be made of the sociometric techniques of social network analysis as transactional studies accumulate.

General Methodological Issues

To this point, we have discussed the methodological implications of four characteristics of the family: it is a small group, has a lengthy existence, is relatively private and value-laden, and is influenced by its societal context. The remainder of this chapter focuses on methodological issues that are particularly important in family research, even though they are not specifically related to one of our four family characteristics. In most cases, they apply too generally to all research to be considered an implication of just one family characteristic.

Conceptualization: Interaction between Theory and Research

The relationship of theory to research is crucial to the conceptualization of research, encompassing all four of our family characteristics. Theory has three major purposes relative to research. First, theory has a summarizing function. It brings systematic order to an otherwise disconnected set of research findings. Second, theory provides clarification of important concepts, which are interdefined in terms of one another. Most family-theory development in the past decade has focused on these two objectives, culminating in *Contemporary Theories about the Family* (Burr, Hill, Nye, & Reiss, 1979a,b). But this type of work has less successfully implemented the third function of theory: to generate new research directions. Even deductive theory building in the family field has yielded few new testable hypotheses. Rather, the focus has been on making deductions from general sociological theories relevant to *previous* findings in family research (Burr *et al.*, 1979b).

In contrast, other research traditions in family research are nearly atheoretical. This is characteristic of observational research on marital interaction, for example. The measures of interaction typically bear little relationship to any theory beyond the position that an understanding of interaction is crucial to the understanding of families. This atheoretical stance partially explains why measures of marital power rarely correlate with one another (Turk & Bell, 1972) and why Jacob (1975) found few consistencies across studies of marital interaction. The overload of data in an observational study is conducive to a fishing expedition that may produce findings that are little more than Type I errors. For example, in one of the most methodologically sophisticated observational studies of its time, Mishler and Waxler (1968) had nearly as few significant findings as could be expected by chance.

What is sorely needed is a type of interplay between theory and research that will yield new research directions. Some new directions could come from the summarizing and conceptually clarifying functions of theories. Research hypotheses could be based on plausible implications of theoretical propositions.

It would also be profitable to design hypotheses to provide potential disconfirmations of theoretical propositions. This approach is particularly lacking in family research. Few theoretical propositions about families are disconfirmed or modified because of a set of research findings (one partial exception is Winch's [1958] complementary needs theory of mate selection). Many inductive theoretical propositions about families have obvious exceptions (Burr *et al.*, 1979a).

Where several exceptions to an accepted theoretical proposition exist, investigators should be trying to understand what accounts for the discrepant findings rather than simply adopting the majority of results as the best summary statement. Such strategies would yield improved modifications of a relevant theoretical proposition, indicating more precisely when it applies and when it does not. An increased research focus on plausible *disconfirmations* corresponds closely to Popper's (1935/1959) view that science progresses most efficiently by attempted disconfirmations that are well conceived (see also the discussion of strong inference in the next section on research design).

In sum, family research needs to be more relevant to family theory. Both new evidence for and new evidence against a theoretical proposition are relevant. But research that has little possibility of yielding important evidence either pro or con has little justification, at least with respect to family theories.

Research Design Issues

This section considers several important research strategies that can be applied across a wide range of family research. First, two types of intensive research strategies are considered: qualitative methodology and small sample designs. Then, several approaches to experimental research are discussed, including true experimental designs, experimental analogues, quasi-experimental designs, and strong inference.

Research energies are distributed differently in intensive research strategies than they are in more typical quantitative designs, such as multiple regression or analysis of variance. In an intensive approach, the investigator strives for a more complete picture of a small sample. With multiple regression, the researcher focuses on selected information about a larger sample.

Intensive Research Strategies. One form of intensive research uses *qualitative methods* (LaRossa & Wolfe, 1985; Rubin, 1981). Rubin (1976), for example, summarized open-ended interviews with working-class couples about their marriages. This strategy is particularly useful as an exploratory investigation or as a corrective to the sterility of quantitative research. The comprehensive descriptions of people's lives yielded by such research give a better feel for their own perspectives and experiences.

In short, qualitative research describes living people, not just a few cold facts about them.

It must be remembered, however, that qualitative research faces the same problems of external and internal validity as does quantitative research. Thus, it is not a panacea for overcoming the limitations of quantitative methods (Cook & Campbell, 1979, pp. 92–93). Rather, qualitative and quantitative methods are best used together so that their respective strengths complement each other.

The second type of intensive study focuses on a *small sample* over an extended period of time, often using intrasubject comparisons. It is most useful when the dependent variable can be expressed in terms of frequent, specific events that can be counted during successive intervals. For example, Patterson, Reid, Jones, and Conger (1975) used such a design to evaluate the success of several intervention strategies for decreasing the frequency of aggressive acts by certain children referred to their clinic. Robinson and Foster (1979) provided an introduction to this type of design, whereas Kratochwill (1978) and Hersen and Barlow (1976) have covered the technical issues in greater depth. Harvey (1983) discussed the application of this design to the study of close relationships, and Kazdin (1978) related it to clinical research.

Approaches to Experimental Research. For practical or ethical reasons, it is usually difficult to use true experimental research designs with families. The major alternative, passive-observational (correlational) research, makes it difficult to untangle various possibilities of causal influences. In order to obtain the strongest evidence concerning causal influences, the researcher should use the best available approximation to a truly experimental design.

A *true experimental design,* with random assignment to treatment groups and experimental manipulation of the independent variable, is generally the best method for ruling out alternative interpretations relevant to internal validity and "statistical conclusion validity" (Cook & Campbell, 1979). Unfortunately, a true experimental design is rarely used in family research, partly because of practical and ethical considerations. Such considerations, though important, should not shortcut family investigators' search for innovative possibilities for true experimentation. Campbell (1969; Cook & Campbell, 1979, pp. 370–384) has identified many possibilities for such experiments. As one possibility, it would be ethical to randomly assign people to different treatment options when they have no preferences among the options. We might take research on corporal punishment and children's aggression as an example. Passive-observational research has been unable to provide consistent evidence concerning the causal direction between these two positively associated variables. To overcome this problem, new parents who are undecided about using corporal punishment could be randomly assigned to spanking or nonspanking groups. Although this strategy would still have to be planned carefully to protect the rights of the parents and their children, such a strategy would have more internal validity than previous research on this topic. The findings might generalize only to parents undecided about spanking, but those would be the parents most open to influence by expert opinion.

Another possibility for true experiments exists when a fair rationale for random assignment is applicable. For example, when a new intervention program for parents can be delivered to only some of the first-time parents, random assignment seems a fair way to distribute the opportunities available. Random assignment is also fair when two or more types of intervention appear to be equally desirable.

Experimental analogues are often possible when true experiments are not. An experimental analogue is a true experiment in an artificial situation designed to represent the topic under investigation. A series of studies used experimental analogues to investigate the effects of punishment on children (e.g., LaVoie, 1974; Parke, 1974). Typically, these studies focused on the effect of some mild punishment, such as a noxious noise or a verbal reprimand, on subsequent play with an attractive toy that the child was told not to handle. The influence of confounding variables can be ruled out with such a strategy, but applicability to real life may be questionable (Hoffman, 1975).

A third strategy is a *quasi-experimental design* (Cook & Campbell, 1979). This strategy maximizes evidence relevant to causality when randomization is not feasible. Cook and Campbell (1979) identified two major types of quasi-experiments. *Nonequivalent group designs* include control groups that have not been formed by random assignment. Research on the effects of divorce could be improved with this type of design. For example, an investigator could begin with a sample of intact families contemplating separation or divorce. Subsequently, those who chose to separate or divorce could be compared on selected characteristics with those who remained intact. Although the two groups would still not be completely comparable, pretest measures could be used to evaluate whether changes in the families (e.g., the adjustment of the children) are related to the decision to separate or to stay together. Cook and Campbell (1979) also recommended the use of multiple dependent variables, some hypothesized to be affected and others to be unaffected by the independent variable (e.g., divorcing vs. not divorcing). Such discriminant validity of effects can rule out some alternative explanations of the data.

In *interrupted-time-series designs,* changes following an intervention can be compared with random fluctuations in the dependent variable over time (i.e., within a base line). Such a design could resolve an uncertainty noted by Price-Bonham and Balswick (1980): One cannot conclude whether low income increases the likelihood of divorce or whether divorce decreases income. To untangle this causal ambiguity, a study could use the annual income of people over about a 10-year period that spanned a time of divorce. Better, the study could compare this time series with that of a control group that did not experience divorce. Whether a study is quasi-experimental or passive-observational, the investigator must carefully consider plausible alternative interpretations and design the research to rule out as many as possible. Cook and Campbell (1979) have identified four classes of plausible alternative interpretations. Each class threatens one type of validity, either external validity, internal validity, statistical conclusion validity, or construct validity. Specific forms of such alternative interpretations need to be systematically considered and ruled out one by one in quasi-experimental designs. Such a process was called "strong inference" by Platt (1964).

Platt (1964) examined a wide range of scientific disciplines and concluded that those that progress most rapidly are those that systematically use *strong inference.* The key elements of strong inference are the systematic consideration of plausible alternative interpretations of data, the design of research so that the outcomes predicted by different interpretations are mutually exclusive, and systematic repetitions of this process to refine the possible interpretations. These elements fit Popper's (1935/1959; Cook & Campbell, 1979, pp. 20–25) view of the philosophy of science, that science progresses via falsifications, not from confirmations, of plausible interpretations.

There are three current tendencies in the field of family studies that undermine the use of strong inference in research (Larzelere & Skeen, 1984). The first is the tendency to see research as the servant of theory rather than as a tool for improving theories. Thus, there is a focus on confirmations of theoretical propositions and a corresponding dismissal of conflicting findings (e.g., in many chapters of Burr *et al.,* 1979a). It is difficult to find an instance in which empirical findings have modified a previously accepted theoretical proposition. Family scholars have devoted a great deal of attention to cataloging the existing conceptual frameworks and theories in the field. This work could now serve as a base on which to conduct theoretically relevant research according to the principle of strong inference.

Second, strong opinions about many family issues result in corresponding conclusions' gaining wide acceptance despite insufficient empirical support. Fifteen years ago, for example, it was assumed that family violence was limited to a very small portion of families, which were psychologically pathological. Only when investigators began tentatively adopting an alternative view, at least for research purposes, did the high rates of spouse abuse and child abuse become apparent (Straus *et al.,* 1980). The principle applies regardless of how well intentioned the current *Zeitgeist* may be. Premature conclusions about family-related topics, whether motivated by concerns about sexism, racism, the goodness of the nuclear family, or whatever, tend to undermine the soundness of the very conclusions that we would most prefer to make. For example, in the contemporary climate, it is often seen as socially and professionally inappropriate to do research to find out under what conditions corporal punishment may be *positively* related to desirable child characteristics (e.g., Feshbach, 1976; Humphreys, 1976; Welsh, 1976). Precisely because such alternatives have not been systematically pursued and ruled out, the empirical base for an *anti*spanking recommendation is weak.

Third, there is growing opinion that sophisticated multivariate statistics can resolve questions about alternative causal inferences. Thus, Schuessler (1978) stated, "Sociologists have undermined the dogma that correlation does not prove causation by fitting structural equation models to batches of nonexperimental data" (p. xv). Generally, such complex statistical techniques can compare only the causal alternatives specified in the model. They are only a tool for strong inference, not a replacement for careful consideration of plausible alternative interpretations.

In sum, several research strategies should be used more frequently by family social scientists. For certain topics, intensive studies, either qualitative or small-sample designs, would provide profitable breakthroughs in the area. In other cases, better approximations to true experimentation should be used. Options include true experiments, experimental analogues, and quasi-experiments. In most family research, strong inference should be used more systematically.

Data Collection Issues

Four additional issues concerning data collection remain to be discussed. The relative strengths of survey versus observational data are considered first, followed by considerations of ratings and behavioral self-reports and molecular versus molar units of data.

Survey versus Observational Measures. Most research reported in the major family journals uses survey measures (Harvey, 1983; Hodgson & Lewis, 1979; Klein, 1984), but the methodology of the behavioral observation of families has developed rapidly during recent years (Filsinger & Lewis, 1981). One issue that raises itself immediately concerns the consistency of survey versus observational measures of the same variables. Wicker (1969) reviewed studies that included both attitudinal and behavioral indicators (usually associated with surveys and observations, respectively) and found a median correlation of +.14 between the two types of measures of the same construct. Furthermore, the attitude–behavioral-consistency problem is probably even more severe for characteristics of ongoing relationships in families. Liska (1974) concluded that social support factors influence behavior relatively more than do relevant attitudes when the situation involves high group cohesiveness, high frequency of interaction, long duration of group membership, and strong group identification. All of these would be characteristic of family relationships.

Accordingly, there are many examples of inconsistency between attitude surveys and behavioral observations

in research on family relationships. Survey and observational measures of marital power have been found to be uncorrelated with each other (Olson & Rabunsky, 1972; Turk & Bell, 1972). Rubin (1970, 1973) predicted three behavioral correlates of his Love Scale, but all three correlations failed to reach the .05 level of significance. Marital adjustment scales provide a rare instance of consistency. They are significantly associated with marital stability and, negatively, with an expressed desire for marital counseling (Gottman, 1979).

All of these correlations can be explained by Ajzen and Fishbein's analysis (1977) of the consistency between attitudes and behaviors. They pointed out that attitude measures are usually *target*-specific with no reference to particular *actions* toward that target, nor to particular *contexts* or *times* for such actions. In contrast, an observed behavior incorporates a specific action toward the specific target at a specific time in a specific context. These authors argued from an extensive literature review that attitudes and behaviors are consistent when they correspond in generality versus specificity on all four dimensions. In the studies of marital power and love, the survey and observational measures did not correspond in specificity of action, context, or time. Marital adjustment scales and decisions to divorce or seek counseling, on the other hand, both reflect general evaluations of a marriage across a variety of actions, contexts, and times. Decisions to divorce or to seek therapy are behavioral indications of a general evaluation, like voting, which correlates well with related attitude measures (Ajzen & Fishbein, 1977).

The inconsistency of attitudinal survey versus behavioral observation measures has led some to recommend the use of both types of measures in a multimethod research strategy (e.g., Clayton & Bokemeier, 1980; Harvey, 1983; Walters & Walters, 1980). Validation checks can best be done in a research study if both types of measures are used (Straus, 1964). Convergent validity would be demonstrated to the extent that the two types of measures of the same concept are correlated (Campbell & Fiske, 1959).

A thorough understanding of the strengths and weaknesses of the two methods is necessary to maximize the usefulness of multiple-method strategies (Fiske, 1975). Olson's discussion (1977) of insiders' versus outsiders' perspectives is very helpful in this regard. Survey data, he pointed out, are generally more suitable than observational data for measuring people's *subjective* reality, including measures of knowledge, attitudes, perceptions, expectations, self-concept, personality, evaluations of self and others, and meanings given to various actions (Harvey, 1983; Olson, 1977; Parke, 1978). Behavioral observation is usually more appropriate for measuring *objective* reality about people, including overt actions, interaction processes, and nonverbal communication (Olson, 1977).

Attribution theory (Kelley, 1977) is also useful for highlighting strengths of survey versus observational research. A research participant is more likely than an observer to attribute his or her behavior (especially when evaluated negatively) to influences of the research situation rather than to stable characteristics of the person (see also Levinger, 1977). Further, research participants' self-reports are based on observing themselves and their relationships in different situations over a long period of time. In contrast, researchers observe behavior in a limited situation for a brief period of time, but they observe a wide range of people and relationships in that type of situation (see Figure 1).

In research on marital interaction, for example, a husband and wife may become upset with each other in a discussion of a vignette about whether a wife should have bought an additional new pair of shoes (Olson & Ryder, 1970). The couple may feel that such a heated argument is atypical of them and that it occurred in the experimental setting because the woman had to cut short her shopping time to go to the research session, which had been scheduled by her husband (a situational attribution). The experimenter, in contrast, may record their interaction as very conflictual because they score higher on a conflict scale than do other couples interacting about that vignette (a

relational attribution). Neither judgment is necessarily more correct than the other. The couple are more aware of their previous interactions; the researcher is more aware of how other couples interact about that vignette. Survey measures then emphasize the attributions of the participants and take the history of the relationship into account. Observational measures emphasize the attributions of the observer and take into account systematic comparisons of couples in the same situation. Thus, differences between survey and observational measures are related to differences in perspectives between the participant and the investigator.

Investigators sometimes assume that observational measures are exempt from problems of reliability and validity. Such is far from the case. Verbal responses on well-developed scales are usually more reliable than most observational measures. Several researchers have begun to give thorough consideration to the reliability of behavioral measures (Gottman, 1979; Hartmann, 1977; Johnson & Bolstad, 1973). For both observational and survey measures, there is usually a trade-off between reliability and content validity. For example, Fiske (1978) achieved high reliability on observational measures of interaction by eliminating verbal content and meaning from consideration (Craik, 1979; see also Waxler & Mishler, 1966). On survey scales, high reliability can be achieved by focusing on a narrow concept. At the extreme, the highest reliability can be achieved when a scale consists of the same item repeated a large number of times.

Observational measures are regarded as more valid even if they are less reliable than survey scales. Typically, the validity of observational measures is taken as self-evident and is therefore not examined as thoroughly. Observational measures would be enhanced by subjecting them to the same validation procedures commonly used in developing survey scales.

Ratings and Behavioral Self-Reports. Although verbally reported data have been used to measure the subjective characteristics of the person reporting and observational data have generally focused more on the objective behaviors of a target person in a specific situation, other possibilities exist. One alternative is the use of ratings, that is, reports of one person about another. Another possibility is a behavioral self-report, where research participants record their own specific actions.

Little seems to be known about the relative reliability and validity of the ratings of one family member by another. Levinger and Senn (1967) concluded that ratings of a spouse's behavior or feelings reveal more about the perceptions of the relationship than do descriptions of one's own behavior or feelings. Ratings could be based on a larger sample of naturally occurring situations than is typical in structured observations (Achenbach, 1978). On the negative side, memory distortion, biases, the halo effect, and unreliability are potential problems.

Ratings can also be used to summarize extensive data from open-ended interviews so that the information can

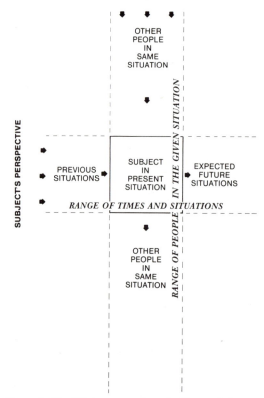

Figure 1. The differing perspectives of subjects and observers. (Adapted from Levinger, 1977.)

be managed quantitatively. Block and Haan (1971) did this with data from a previous longitudinal study. As they were interested primarily in the developmental associations of variables across three time periods, they used different raters for different time periods for any particular subject. Further, they used a minimum of three judges to rate the characteristics of a subject in one given time period and required a standard of reasonable consensus among the raters before completing the rating process. They argued convincingly that such use of multiple raters substantially enhances the replicability of research based on ratings (see also Epstein, 1979). Thorough training of the raters also improved the reliability of the data.

The behavioral self-report (Olson, 1977) is another innovation that combines some aspects of both observational and survey methods. For example, Straus (1979) asked respondents how many times they had used particular behaviors (e.g., ''stomped out of the room or house'') to resolve conflicts with a particular other person in the past year. Such behavioral reports reduce the subjectiveness of self-report measures but enable the researcher to get at information that could not be obtained with observational methods (e.g., the frequency of verbal and physical aggression in the family).

Molar versus Molecular Variables. One general issue in data collection concerns whether to use molar or molecular variables. Molar variables are global, multifaceted dimensions; molecular ones are narrower in focus. The historical emphasis on molar variables, such as marital adjustment and power, carried some limitations with it. The multidimensional nature of marital power, for example, may account for the finding that most measures of marital power are uncorrelated with each other.

A promising alternative is to focus on more specific components of such molar variables. For example, several studies have found that the negative and the positive dimensions of marital quality are somewhat independent of each other (McNamara & Bahr, 1980) and relate distinctly to other variables (Gilford & Bengtson, 1979; Jacobson, Waldron, & Moore, 1980).

Although a good case can be made that power and marital adjustment are too molar to produce consistent associations with other variables, it is more difficult to determine how molecular a variable should be (Patterson & Moore, 1979). The more molar a variable is, the more practical it is to use and the better it captures subjective meanings (Craik, 1979). A more molecular variable is usually more reliable and may highlight important distinctions that are confounded in molar variables. In survey research, molecular variables may reduce confounding response sets, such as the social desirability response bias, more than do molar variables.

For observational measures, molecular units require fewer inferences while coding, but are less directly related to important theoretical constructs. One suggested rule of thumb is to select the variable specificity that will permit the level of distinctions that research participants

make about themselves and each other (Lamb, 1979). This guideline sometimes yields an impractically large amount of data and, at other times, misses useful distinctions, such as gaze patterns during interactions, that are not consciously made by many people (Kendon, 1967). Molar variables can always be formed by combining molecular variables, but the reverse is not possible (Suomi, 1979).

Conclusions

Many other methodological issues are also relevant to family research but were left out of this chapter because of space limitations. Important topics not considered include family measurement scales (Cromwell, Olson, & Fournier, 1976; Straus & Brown, 1978); scale development (Nunnally, 1978; Straus, 1964); survey techniques (Gorden, 1975; Sudman & Bradburn, 1982); research on family therapy (Gurman & Kniskern, 1981; O'Leary & Turkewitz, 1978); sampling (Kitson, Sussman, Williams, Zeehandelaar, Schickmanter, & Steinberger, 1982); and research ethics (American Psychological Association, 1973). Other topics have potential importance for family research, although they are not in the current mainstream of family research methodology (e.g., exploratory data analysis: Leinhardt & Wasserman, 1978; Tukey, 1977). References such as these should be consulted for information on these methodological issues. Our purpose has been to provide not exhaustive coverage but a selected overview of methodological issues that, in our judgment, are most critical for the improvement of family research.

Critical assessments of research methods in a scientific field typically identify deficits, strengths, and weaknesses in current practice and propose modifications to the research community. This has basically been our emphasis in this chapter. In closing, let us turn from the world of the methodological ideal to the practical side of doing research.

Family researchers appear to be pragmatic in orientation, just like other social scientists and most people in general. We respond to funding opportunities, adopt popular research tools, cut corners, and publish in a style that will win recognition from peers. Given much pragmatism, when a methodological deficit persists over a period of years in a field, it is instructive to ask how the incentive system may be responsible for this condition. For example, the scarcity of time-ordered longitudinal research designs in the family field has been recognized and deplored for a long time. It seems unrealistic to expect this situation to change if the balance of costs and rewards for doing stronger research methodologically does not also change.

It should be obvious that family research is being done and has always been conducted in a context of scarce resources and competition for them. Furthermore, shifts in the political and economic climate of a society influence the degree to which methodological ideals can be achieved in practice. Therefore, the challenge to family researchers is twofold. On the one hand, we need to press for a competitive advantage by convincing sponsors and the public that we make important contributions to knowledge and to society. On the other hand, we need to be clever enough to develop methodological techniques and strategies that are both scientifically sound and cost-effective. Emphasizing one of these criteria at the expense of the other is doomed to failure. The tension between them is perhaps the single most important practical issue with which family researchers will have to cope.

ACKNOWLEDGMENTS

This chapter has benefited from helpful reviews of previous drafts by Lynne Harrington Brown, Steven W. Cornelius, Erik E. Filsinger, Ted L. Huston, Marie F. Peters, Walter R. Schumm, Graham B. Spanier, the 1979–1980 Family Violence Research Seminar at the University of New Hampshire (B. Carson, J. Dingman, D. Finkelhor, L. M. Harris, J. C. Harvey, S. Herrick, and K. Ÿllo), and especially Murray A. Straus.

References

Achenbach, T. M. *Research in developmental psychology.* New York: Free Press, 1978.

Ainsworth, M. D. S., Blehar, M. C., Waters, E., & Wall, S. *Patterns of attachment: A psychological study of the strange situation.* Hillsdale, N.J.: Erlbaum, 1978.

Ajzen, I., & Fishbein, M. Attitude-behavior relations: A theoretical analysis and review of empirical research. *Psychological Bulletin,* 1977, *84,* 888–918.

Albrecht, S. L. Correlates of marital happiness among the remarried. *Journal of Marriage and the Family,* 1979, *41,* 857–867.

Allen, W. R. The search for applicable theories of black family life. *Journal of Marriage and the Family,* 1978, *40,* 117–129.

American Psychological Association. *Ethical principles in the conduct of research with human participants.* Washington, D.C.: American Psychological Association, 1973.

Aronoff, J., & Crano, W. D. A re-examination of the cross-cultural principles of task segregation and sex role differentiation in the family. *American Sociological Review,* 1975, *40,* 12–19.

Arthur, A. Z. Response bias in the semantic differential. *British Journal of Social and Clinical Psychology,* 1966, *5,* 103–107.

Bakeman, R. Untangling streams of behavior: Sequential analyses of observational data. In G. Sackett (Ed.), *Observing behavior (Vol. 2): Data collection and analysis methods.* Baltimore: University Park Press, 1978.

Baltes, P. B. Longitudinal and cross-sectional sequences in the study of age and generation effects. *Human Development,* 1968, *11,* 145–171.

Baltes, P. B. Prototypical paradigms and questions in life-span research on development and aging. *Gerontologist,* 1973, *13,* 458–467.

Baltes, P. B., & Nesselroade, J. R. Multivariate longitudinal and cross-sectional sequences for analyzing ontogenetic and generational change: A methodological note. *Developmental Psychology,* 1970, *2,* 163–168.

Baltes, P. B., & Nesselroade, J. R. History and rationale of longitudinal research. In J. R. Nesselroade & P. B. Baltes (Eds.), *Longitudinal research in the study of behavior and development.* New York: Academic Press, 1979.

Baumrind, D. Current patterns of parental authority. *Developmental Psychology Monograph,* 1971, *4* (1, Pt. 2), 1–103.

Berne, E. *Transactional analysis in psychotherapy.* New York: Grove Press, 1961.

Bielby, W. T., & Hauser, R. M. Structural equation models. *Annual Review of Sociology,* 1977, *3,* 137–161.

Bielby, W. T., Hauser, R. M., & Featherman, D. L. Response errors of black and nonblack males in models of the intergenerational transmission of socioeconomic status. *American Journal of Sociology,* 1977, *82,* 1242–1288.

Bishop, Y. M. M., Fienberg, S. E., & Holland, P. W. *Discrete multivariate analysis.* Cambridge: M.I.T. Press, 1975.

Block, J., & Haan, N. *Lives through time.* Berkeley, Calif.: Bancroft Books, 1971.

Blood, R. O., & Wolfe, D. M. *Husbands and wives.* Glencoe, Ill.: Free Press, 1960.

Boocock, S. S. Historical and sociological research on the family and the life cycle: Methodological alternatives. In J. Demos & S. S. Boocock (Eds.), *Turning points: Historical and sociological essays on the family.* Chicago: University of Chicago Press, 1978.

Boruch, R. F., & Cecil, J. S. On solutions to some privacy problems engendered by federal regulation and social custom. In M. L. Wax & J. Cassell (Eds.), *Federal regulations: Ethical issues and social research.* Boulder, Colo.: Westview, 1979.

Bott, E. *Family and social network* (2nd ed.). New York: Free Press, 1971.

Braungart, R. G., & Braungart, M. M. Family, school, and personal political factors in student politics: A case study of the 1972 presidential election. *Journal of Marriage and the Family,* 1975, *37,* 823–839.

Bronfenbrenner, U. *The ecology of human development.* Cambridge: Harvard University Press, 1979.

Brown, B. W. Parents' discipline of children in public places. *Family Coordinator,* 1979, *28,* 67–71.

Brown, L. H., & Kidwell, J. S. (Eds.). Methodology: The other side of caring [Special issue]. *Journal of Marriage and the Family,* 1982, *44*(4).

Burr, W. R., Hill, R., Nye, F. I., & Reiss, I. L. *Contemporary theories about the family* (Vol. 1). New York: Free Press, 1979. (a)

Burr, W. R., Hill, R., Nye, F. I., & Reiss, I. L. *Contemporary theories about the family* (Vol. 2). New York: Free Press, 1979. (b)

Call, V. R. A., & Otto, L. B. *Tracking respondents: A multi-method approach.* Lexington, Mass.: Lexington Books, 1982.

Campbell, D. T. Reforms as experiments. *American Psychologist,* 1969, *24,* 409–429.

Campbell, D. T., & Fiske, D. W. Convergent and discriminant validation by the multitrait-multimethod matrix. *Psychological Bulletin,* 1959, *56,* 81–105.

Campbell, D. T., & Stanley, J. C. *Experimental and quasi-experimental designs for research.* Chicago: Rand McNally, 1966.

Christensen, A. Naturalistic observation of families: A system for random audio recordings in the home. *Behavior Therapy,* 1979, *10,* 418–422.

Christensen, H. T. The method of record linkage applied to family data. *Marriage and Family Living,* 1958, *20,* 38–43.

Christensen, H. T. Development of the family field of study. In H. T. Christensen (Ed.), *Handbook of marriage and the family.* Chicago: Rand McNally, 1964.

Clarridge, B. R., Sheehy, L. L., & Hauser, T. S. Tracing members of a panel: A 17-year follow-up. In K. F. Schuessler (Ed.), *Sociological methodology 1978.* San Francisco: Jossey-Bass, 1977.

Clayton, R. R., & Bokemeier, J. L. Premarital sex in the seventies. *Journal of Marriage and the Family,* 1980, *42,* 759–775.

Cogswell, B. E., & Sussman, M. B. Advances in comparative family research. In M. B. Sussman & B. E. Cogswell (Eds.), *Cross-national family research.* Leiden, Netherlands: E. J. Brill, 1972.

Cogswell, B. E., & Sussman, M. B. Family and fertility: The effects of heterogeneous experience. In W. R. Burr, R. Hill, F. I. Nye, & I. L. Reiss (Eds.), *Contemporary theories about the family* (Vol. 1). New York: Free Press, 1979.

Cook, T. D., & Campbell, D. T. *Quasi-experimentation: Design and analysis issues for field settings.* Chicago: Rand McNally, 1979.

Craik, K. H. The smile or friendliness? The speaking turn or talkativeness? (Review of *Strategies for personality research*, by D. W. Fiske). *Contemporary Psychology,* 1979, *24,* 374–375.

Cromwell, R. E., Olson, D., & Fournier, D. Diagnosis and evaluation in marital and family counseling. In D. H. L. Olson (Ed.), *Treating relationships.* Lake Mills, Iowa: Graphic Publishing, 1976.

Crowne, D. P., & Marlowe, D. *The approval motive.* New York: Wiley, 1964.

Degler, C. N. *At odds: Women and the family in America from the Revolution to the present.* Oxford: Oxford University Press, 1980.

DeLamater, J. Methodological issues in the study of premarital sexuality. *Sociological Methods and Research,* 1974, *3,* 30–61.

DeLamater, J. D., & MacCorquodale, P. The effects of interview schedule variations on reported sexual behavior. *Sociological Methods and Research,* 1975, *4,* 215–236.

Doan, J. A. Family interaction and communication deviance in disturbed and normal families: A review of research. *Family Process,* 1978, *17,* 357–376.

Draper, N. R., & Van Nostrand, R. C. Ridge regression and James-Stein estimation: Review and comments. *Technometrics,* 1979, *21,* 451–466.

Duncan, O. D. Testing key hypotheses in panel analysis. In K. F. Schuessler (Ed.), *Sociological methodology 1980.* San Francisco: Jossey-Bass, 1979.

Edmonds, V. H. Marital conventionalization: Definition and measurement. *Journal of Marriage and the Family,* 1967, *29,* 681–688.

Edmonds, V. H., Withers, G., & Dibatista, B. Adjustment, conservatism, and marital conventionalization. *Journal of Marriage and the Family,* 1972, *34,* 96–103.

Edwards, A. L. *The social desirability variable in personality assessment and research.* New York: Dryden Press, 1957.

Elder, J. W. Comparative cross-national methodology. In A. Inkeles (Ed.), *Annual Review of Sociology* (Vol. 2). Palo Alto, Calif.: Annual Reviews, 1976.

Ellis, A. The value of marriage prediction tests. *American Sociological Review,* 1948, *13,* 710–718.

Epstein, S. The stability of behavior: I. On predicting most of the people much of the time. *Journal of Personality and Social Psychology,* 1979, *37,* 1097–1126.

Erbring, L., & Young, A. A. Individuals and social structure: Contextual effects as endogenous feedback. *Sociological Methods and Research,* 1979, *7,* 396–430.

Espenshade, T. J., & Braun, R. E. Life course analysis and multistate demography: An application to marriage, divorce, and remarriage. *Journal of Marriage and the Family,* 1982, *44,* 1025–1036.

Farkas, G. Specification, residuals and contextual effects. *Sociological Methods and Research,* 1974, *2,* 333–363.

Featherman, D. L. Retrospective longitudinal research: Methodological considerations. *Journal of Economics and Business,* 1980, *32,* 152–169.

Feldman, H. The effects of children on the family. In A. Michel (Ed.), *Family issues of employed women in Europe and America.* Leiden, Netherlands: E. J. Brill, 1971.

Fennessey, J., & D'Amico, R. Collinearity, ridge regression, and investigator judgment. *Sociological Methods and Research,* 1980, *8,* 309–340.

Feshbach, N. D. Corporal punishment. *American Psychological Association Monitor,* February 1976, p. 3.

Fienberg, S. E., & Mason, W. M. Identification and estimation of age-period-cohort models in the analysis of discrete archival data. In K. F. Schuessler (Ed.), *Sociological methodology 1979.* San Francisco: Jossey-Bass, 1978.

Filsinger, E. E., & Lewis, R. A. (Eds.). *Marital observation and behavioral assessment: Recent developments and techniques.* Beverly Hills, Calif.: Sage Publications, 1981.

Firebaugh, G. Assessing group effects: A comparison of two methods. *Sociological Methods and Research,* 1979, *7,* 384–395.

Fiske, D. W. A source of data is not a measuring instrument. *Journal of Abnormal Psychology,* 1975, *84,* 20–23.

Fiske, D. W. *Strategies for personality research: The observation versus interpretation of behavior.* San Francisco: Jossey-Bass, 1978.

Foote, N. N., & Cottrell, L. S., Jr. *Identity and interpersonal competence: A new direction in family research.* Chicago: University of Chicago Press, 1955.

Garbarino, J. The human ecology of child maltreatment: A conceptual model for research. *Journal of Marriage and the Family,* 1977, *39,* 721–735.

Geller, D. M. Involvement in role-playing simulations: A demonstration with studies on obedience. *Journal of Personality and Social Psychology,* 1978, *36,* 219–235.

Gelles, R. J. Methods for studying sensitive family topics. *American Journal of Orthopsychiatry,* 1978, *48,* 408–428.

Gilford, R., & Bengtson, V. Measuring marital satisfaction in three generations: Positive and negative dimensions. *Journal of Marriage and the Family,* 1979, *41,* 387–398.

Glenn, N. D. *Cohort analysis.* Beverly Hills, Calif.: Sage, 1977.

Glenn, N. D., & Frisbie, W. P. Trend studies with survey sample and census data. *Annual Review of Sociology,* 1977, *3,* 79–104.

Goode, W. J. *World revolution and family patterns.* New York: Free Press, 1963.

Gorden, R. L. *Interviewing: Strategy, techniques, and tactics* (rev. ed.). Homewood, Ill.: Dorsey, 1975.

Gordon, M. *The American family: Past, present, and future.* New York: Random House, 1978.

Gottman, J. M. *Marital interaction: Experimental investigations.* New York: Academic Press, 1979.

Gottman, J. M., & Bakeman, R. The sequential analysis of observational data. In M. E. Lamb, S. J. Suomi, & G. R. Stephenson (Eds.), *Social interaction analysis: Methodological issues.* Madison: University of Wisconsin Press, 1979.

Groves, E. R., & Ogburn, W. F. *American marriage and family relationships.* New York: Holt, 1928.

Gurman, A. S., & Kniskern, D. P. Family therapy outcome research: Knowns and unknowns. In A. S. Gurman & D. P. Kniskern (Eds.), *Handbook of family therapy.* New York: Brunner/Mazel, 1981.

Hall, J., & Williams, M. S. A comparison of decision-making performances in established and ad hoc groups. *Journal of Personality and Social Psychology,* 1966, *3,* 214–222.

Hannan, M. T., & Tuma, N. B. Methods for temporal analysis. In A. Inkeles, J. Coleman, & R. H. Turner (Eds.), *Annual Review of Sociology* (Vol. 5). Palo Alto, Calif.: Annual Reviews, 1979.

Harris, L. M. Analysis of a paradoxical logic: A case study. *Family Process,* 1980, *19,* 19–33.

Hartmann, D. P. Considerations in the choice of inter observer reliability estimates. *Journal of Applied Behavior Analysis,* 1977, *10,* 103–116.

Harvey, J. H. Research methods. In E. Berscheid, A. Christensen, J. Harvey, T. Huston, H. Kelley, G. Levinger, E. McClintock, A. Peplau, & D. Peterson (Eds.), *The psychology of close relationships.* New York: W. H. Freeman, 1983.

Hauser, R. M. Contextual analysis revisited. *Sociological Methods and Research,* 1974, *2,* 365–375.

Hawkins, J. L. The Locke Marital Adjustment Test and social desirability. *Journal of Marriage and the Family*, 1966, *28*, 193–195.

Heise, D. R. Prologue. In D. R. Heise (Ed.), *Sociological methodology 1977*. San Francisco: Jossey-Bass, 1977.

Hersen, M., & Barlow, D. H. *Single case experimental designs: Strategies for studying behavior change*. New York: Pergamon Press, 1976.

Hetherington, E. M. Effects of father absence on personality development in adolescent daughters. *Developmental Psychology*, 1972, *7*, 313–326.

Hibbs, D. A., Jr. Problems of statistical estimation and causal inference in time-series regression models. In H. L. Costner (Ed.), *Sociological methodology 1973–1974*. San Francisco: Jossey-Bass, 1974.

Hill, R. Cross-national family research: Attempts and prospects. *International Social Science Journal*, 1962, *14*, 425–451.

Hill, R. Methodological issues in family development research. *Family Process*, 1964, *3*, 186–205.

Hill, R. Status of research on families. In J. A. Calhoun, E. H. Grotberg, & W. R. Rackley (Eds.), *The status of children, youth and families, 1979*. Washington, D.C.: U.S. Department of Health and Human Services, 1980.

Hill, R., Foote, N., Aldous, J., Carlson, R., & MacDonald, R. *Family development in three generations*. Cambridge, Mass.: Schenkman, 1970.

Hodgson, J. A., & Lewis, R. A. Pilgrim's Progress III: A trend analysis of family theory and methodology. *Family Process*, 1979, *18*, 163–173.

Hoffman, M. L. Moral internalization, parental power, and the nature of parent-child interaction. *Developmental Psychology*, 1975, *11*, 228–239.

Holm, R. Mechanized data collection. In E. E. Filsinger & R. A. Lewis (Eds.), *Observing marriage: New behavioral approaches*. Beverly Hills, Calif.: Sage Publications, 1981.

Howard, R. L. *A social history of American family sociology, 1895–1940*. Westport, Conn.: Greenwood Press, 1981.

Humphreys, L. G. Corporal punishment. *American Psychological Association Monitor*, April 1976, pp. 2, 12.

Huston, T. L., Surra, C. A., Fitzgerald, N. M., & Cate, R. M. From courtship to marriage: Mate selection as an interpersonal process. In S. Duck & R. Gilmour (Eds.), *Personal relationships* (Vol. 2): *Developing personal relationships*. London: Academic Press, 1981.

Jackson, D. N. The dynamics of structured personality tests: 1971. *Psychological Review*, 1971, *78*, 229–248.

Jacob, T. Family interaction in disturbed and normal families: A methodological and substantive review. *Psychological Bulletin*, 1975, *82*, 33–65.

Jacobson, N. S., Follette, W. C., & McDonald, D. W. Reactivity to positive and negative behavior in distressed and nondistressed married couples. *Journal of Consulting and Clinical Psychology*, 1982, *50*, 706–714.

Jacobson, N. S., Waldron, H., & Moore, D. Toward a behavioral profile of marital distress. *Journal of Consulting and Clinical Psychology*, 1980, *48*, 696–703.

Johnson, S. M., & Bolstad, O. D. Methodological issues in naturalistic observation: Some problems and solutions for field research. In L. A. Hamerlynck, L. C. Handy, & E. J. Mash (Eds.), *Behavior change: Methodology, concepts, and practice*. Champaign, Ill.: Research Press, 1973.

Johnson, S. M., Christensen, A., & Bellamy, G. T. Evaluation of family intervention through unobtrusive audio recordings: Experiences in "bugging" children. *Journal of Applied Behavior Analysis*, 1976, *9*, 213–219.

Jöreskog, K. G. Statistical estimation of structural models in longitudinal-developmental investigations. In J. R. Nesselroade & P. B. Baltes (Eds.), *Longitudinal research in the study of behavior and development*. New York: Academic Press, 1979.

Jöreskog, K. G., & Sörbom, D. *Advances in factor analysis and structural equation models*. Cambridge, Mass.: Abt Associates, 1979.

Kazdin, A. E. Evaluating the generality of findings in analog therapy research. *Journal of Consulting and Clincial Psychology*, 1978, *46*, 673–686.

Kelley, H. H. An application of attribution theory to research methodology for close relationships. In G. Levinger & H. L. Raush (Eds.), *Close relationships*. Amherst: University of Massachusetts Press, 1977.

Kendon, A. Some functions of gaze direction in social interaction. *Acta Psychologia*, 1967, *26*, 1–47.

Keniston, K. Psychological development and historical change. *Journal of Interdisciplinary History*, 1971, *2*, 329–345.

Kenny, D. A. *Correlation and causality*. New York: Wiley, 1979.

Kidwell, J. S., & Brown, L. H. Ridge regression as a technique for analyzing models with multicollinearity. *Journal of Marriage and the Family*, 1982, *44*, 287–299.

Kinsey, A., Wardell, B., & Martin, C. *Sexual behavior in the human male*. Philadelphia: W. B. Saunders, 1948.

Kitson, G. C., Sussman, M. B., Williams, G. K., Zeehandelaar, R. B., Shickmanter, B. K., & Steinberger, J. L. Sampling issues in family research. *Journal of Marriage and the Family*, 1982, *44*, 965–981.

Klein, D. M. Developmental context, coorientation, and conflict management in marriage (Doctoral dissertation, University of Minnesota, 1978). *Dissertation Abstracts International*, 1979, *39*, 5750A. (University Microfilms No. 7906338).

Klein, D. M. *The problem of multiple perception in family research*. Paper presented at the Theory Development and Research Methodology Workshop at the annual meeting of the National Council on Family Relations, San Francisco, October 1984.

Klein, D. M., Jorgensen, S. R., & Miller, B. C. Research methods and developmental reciprocity in families. In R. M. Lerner & G. B. Spanier (Eds.), *Child influences on marital and family interaction: A life-span perspective*. New York: Academic Press, 1978.

Kratochwill, T. R. (Ed.). *Single subject research: Strategies for evaluating change*. New York: Academic Press, 1978.

Lamb, M. E. Issues in the study of social interaction: An introduction. In M. E. Lamb, S. J. Suomi, & G. R. Stephenson (Eds.), *Social interaction analysis: Methodological issues*. Madison: University of Wisconsin Press, 1979.

Lantz, H., Schultz, M., & O'Hara, M. The changing American family from the preindustrial to the industrial period: A final report. *American Sociological Review*, 1977, *42*, 406–421.

LaRossa, R., & Wolf, J. H. On qualitative family research. *Journal of Marriage and the Family*, 1985, *47*, 531–541.

Larzelere, R. E., & Huston, T. L. The Dyadic Trust Scale: Toward understanding interpersonal trust in close relationships. *Journal of Marriage and the Family*, 1980, *42*, 595–604.

Larzelere, R. E., & Skeen, J. H. The method of multiple hypotheses: A neglected research strategy in family studies. *Journal of Family Issues*, 1984, *5*, 474–492.

Larzelere, R. E., Poelstra, P., Olson, T., & Waitschies, D. [Dyadic trust anf two measures of the extreme response bias]. Unpublished raw data, 1984.

LaVoie, J. C. Type of punishment as a determinant of resistance to deviation. *Developmental Psychology*, 1974, *10*, 181–189.

Lee, G. R. *Family structure and interaction: A comparative analysis*. Philadelphia: J. B. Lippincott, 1977.

Lee, G. R. The utility of cross-cultural data: Potentials and limitations for family sociology. *Journal of Family Issues*, 1984, *5*, 519–541.

Lefkowitz, M. M., Eron, L. D., Walder, L. O., & Huesmann, L. R. *Growing up to be violent*. New York: Pergamon Press, 1977.

Leinhardt, S., & Wasserman, S. S. Exploratory data analysis: An introduction to selected methods. In K. F. Schuessler (Ed.), *Sociological methodology 1979*. San Francisco: Jossey-Bass, 1978.

153

Levinger, G. Re-viewing the close relationship. In G. Levinger & H. L. Raush (Eds.), *Close relationships*. Amherst: University of Massachusetts Press, 1977.

Levinger, G., & Senn, D. J. Disclosure of feelings in marriage. *Merrill-Palmer Quarterly*, 1967, *13*, 237–249.

Lipset, S. M., Trow, M., & Coleman, J. S. *Union democracy*. Glencoe, Ill.: Free Press, 1956.

Liska, A. E. Emergent issues in the attitude-behavior consistency controversy. *American Sociological Review*, 1974, *39*, 261–272.

Lytton, H. Disciplinary encounters between young boys and their mothers and fathers: Is there a contingency system? *Developmental Psychology*, 1979, *15*, 256–268.

Lytton, H., & Zwirner, W. Compliance and its controlling stimuli observed in a natural setting. *Developmental Psychology*, 1975, *11*, 769–779.

McCleary, R., & Hay, R. A., Jr. *Applied time series analysis for the social sciences*. Beverly Hills, Calif.: Sage, 1980.

McCubbin, H. I., Joy, C. B., Cauble, A. E., Comeau, J. K., Patterson, J. M., & Needle, R. H. Family stress and coping: A decade review. *Journal of Marriage and the Family*, 1980, *42*, 855–871.

McNamara, M. L. L., & Bahr, H. M. The dimensionality of marital role satisfaction. *Journal of Marriage and the Family*, 1980, *42*, 45–55.

Millman, M., & Kanter, R. M. (Eds.). *Another voice: Feminist perspectives on social life and social science*. New York: Octagon, 1975.

Mishler, E. G., & Waxler, N. E. *Interaction in families*. New York: Wiley, 1968.

Moynihan, D. P. *The Negro family: The case for national action*. Washington, D.C.: U.S. Department of Labor, 1965.

Murdock, G. P., & White, D. R. Standard cross-cultural sample. *Ethnology*, 1969, *8*, 329–369.

Myers, D. G. *The inflated self*. New York: Seabury Press, 1980.

Naroll, R. S. Two solutions to Galton's problem. *Philosophy of Science*, 1961, *28*, 15–39.

Nesselroade, J. R., & Baltes, P. B. (Eds.). *Longitudinal research in the study of behavior and development*. New York: Academic Press, 1979.

Nunnally, J. C. *Psychometric theory*. New York: McGraw-Hill, 1967.

Nunnally, J. C. *Psychometric theory* (2nd ed.). New York: McGraw-Hill, 1978.

O'Leary, K. D., & Turkewitz, H. Methodological errors in marital and child treatment research. *Journal of Consulting and Clinical Psychology*, 1978, *46*, 747–758.

Olson, D. H. The measurement of family power by self-report and behavioral methods. *Journal of Marriage and the Family*, 1969, *31*, 545–550.

Olson, D. H. Insiders' and outsiders' views of relationships: Research studies. In G. Levinger & H. L. Raush (Eds.), *Close relationships*. Amherst: University of Massachusetts Press, 1977.

Olson, D. H., & Rabunsky, C. Validity of four measures of family power. *Journal of Marriage and the Family*, 1972, *34*, 224–234.

Olson, D. H., & Ryder, R. G. Inventory of Marital Conflicts (IMC): An experimental interaction procedure. *Journal of Marriage and the Family*, 1970, *32*, 443–448.

Osmond, M. W. Cross-societal family research: A macrosociological overview of the seventies. *Journal of Marriage and the Family*, 1980, *42*, 995–1016.

Ostrom, C. W., Jr. *Time series analysis: Regression techniques*. Beverly Hills, Calif.: Sage, 1978.

Palmore, E. When can age, period, and cohort be separated? *Social Forces*, 1978, *57*, 282–295.

Parke, R. D. Rules, roles and resistance to deviation: Recent advances in punishment, discipline, and self-control. In A. D. Pick (Ed.), *Minnesota Symposia on Child Psychology* (Vol. 8). Minneapolis: University of Minnesota Press, 1974.

Parke, R. D. Parent-infant interaction: Process, paradigms, and problems. In G. P. Sackett (Ed.), *Observing behavior* (Vol. 1): *Theory and applications in mental retardation*. Baltimore: University Park Press, 1978.

Patterson, G. R. The aggressive child: Victim and architect of a coercive system. In L. S. Hamerlynck, L. C. Handy, & E. J. Mash (Eds.), *Behavioral modification and families: I. Theory and research*. New York: Brunner/Mazel, 1976.

Patterson, G. R., & Moore, D. Interactive patterns as units of behavior. In M. E. Lamb, S. J. Suomi, & G. R. Stephenson (Eds.), *Social interaction analysis: Methodological issues*. Madison: University of Wisconsin Press, 1979.

Patterson, G. R., Reid, J. B., Jones, R. R., & Conger, R. E. *A social learning approach to family intervention* (Vol. 1): *Families with aggressive children*. Eugene, OR: Castalia, 1975.

Peters, M. Notes from the guest editor. *Journal of Marriage and the Family*, 1978, *40*, 655–658.

Peters, M. F., & Massey, G. *Socialization and childrearing in black families: An innovative approach*. Paper presented at the annual meeting of the National Council on Family Relations, Boston, August 1979.

Peterson, D. R. Assessing interpersonal relationships by means of interaction records. *Behavioral Assessment*, 1979, *1*, 221–236.

Platt, J. R. Strong inference. *Science*, 1964, *146*, 347–352.

Popper, K. R. *The logic of scientific discovery*. New York: Basic Books, 1959. (Originally *Die Logik der Forschung*, 1935).

Porac, C., & Coren, S. A test of the validity of offsprings' report of parental handedness. *Perceptual and Motor Skills*, 1979, *49*, 227–231.

Potter, R. G. Application of life table techniques to measurement of contraceptive effectiveness. *Demography*, 1966, *3*, 297–304.

Price-Bonham, S., & Balswick, J. O. The noninstitutions: Divorce, desertion, and remarriage. *Journal of Marriage and the Family*, 1980, *42*, 959–972.

Reiss, D. *The family's construction of reality*. Cambridge: Harvard University Press, 1981.

Reiss, I. L. *The family system in America*. New York: Holt, Rinehart & Winston, 1971.

Ridley, C. A., & Avery, A. W. Social network influence on the dyadic relationship. In R. L. Burgess & T. L. Huston (Eds.), *Social exchange in developing relationships*. New York: Academic Press, 1979.

Riley, M. W. Aging and cohort succession: Interpretations and misinterpretations. *Public Opinion Quarterly*, 1973, *37*, 35–49.

Robinson, J. B., & Shaver, P. R. *Measures of social psychological attitudes* (rev. ed.). Ann Arbor: Institute for Social Research, University of Michigan, 1973.

Robinson, P. W., & Foster, D. F. *Experimental psychology: A small-N approach*. New York: Harper & Row, 1979.

Rodgers, R. H. *Family interaction and transaction: The developmental approach*. Englewood Cliffs, N.J.: Prentice-Hall, 1973.

Rodman, H. Marital power and the theory of resources in cultural context. *Journal of Comparative Family Studies*, 1972, *3*, 50–67.

Rogosa, D. Causal models in longitudinal research: Rationale, formulation, and interpretation. In J. R. Nesselroade & P. B. Baltes (Eds.), *Longitudinal research in the study of behavior and development*. New York: Academic Press, 1979.

Rogosa, D. A critique of cross-lagged correlation. *Psychological Bulletin*, 1980, *88*, 245–258.

Rosenblatt, P. C. Behavior in public places: Comparison of couples accompanied and unaccompanied by children. *Journal of Marriage and the Family*, 1974, *36*, 750–755.

Rosenblatt, P. C., Titus, S. L., & Nevaldine, A. Marital system differences and summer-long vacations: Togetherness-apartness and tension. *American Journal of Family Therapy*, 1979, *7*, 77–85.

Rubin, L. B. *Worlds of pain: Life in the working-class family*. New York: Basic Books, 1976.

Rubin, L. B. Sociological research: The subjective dimension. *Symbolic Interaction,* 1981, *4,* 97–112.

Rubin, Z. Measurement of romantic love. *Journal of Personality and Social Psychology,* 1970, *16,* 265–273.

Rubin, Z. *Liking and loving.* New York: Holt, Rinehart & Winston, 1973.

Sackett, G. P. Measurement in observational research. In G. P. Sackett (Ed.), *Observing behavior* (Vol. 2): *Data collection and analysis methods.* Baltimore: University Park Press, 1978.

Schaie, K. W. Methodological problems in descriptive developmental research on adulthood and aging. In J. R. Nesselroade & H. W. Reese (Eds.), *Life-span developmental psychology: Methodological issues.* New York: Academic Press, 1973.

Schuessler, K. F. (Ed.). *Sociological methodology 1979.* San Francisco: Jossey-Bass, 1978.

Schumm, W. R., Southerly, W. T., & Figley, C. R. Stumbling block or stepping stone: Path analysis in family studies. *Journal of Marriage and the Family,* 1980, *42,* 251–262.

Schumm, W. R., Bollman, S. R., & Jurich, A. P. The "marital conventionalization" argument: Implications for the study of religiosity and marital satisfaction. *Journal of Psychology and Theology,* 1982, *10,* 236–241.

Sirjamaki, J. The institutional approach. In H. T. Christensen (Ed.), *Handbook of marriage and the family.* Chicago: Rand McNally, 1964.

Spanier, G. B. Whose marital adjustment? A research note. *Sociological Inquiry,* 1973, *43,* 95–96.

Spanier, G. B. Measuring dyadic adjustment: New scales for assessing the quality of marriage and similar dyads. *Journal of Marriage and the Family,* 1976, *38,* 15–28. (a)

Spanier, G. B. Use of recall data in survey research on human sexual behavior. *Social Biology,* 1976, *23,* 244–253. (b)

Stephenson, G. R., & Roberts, T. W. The SSR System 7: A general encoding system with computerized transcription. *Behavior Research Methods & Instrumentation,* 1977, *9,* 434–441.

Stolte Heiskanen, V. The myth of the middle-class family in American family sociology. *American Sociologist,* 1971, *6,* 14–18.

Stouffer, S. A., Lumsdaine, A. A., Lumsdaine, M. H., Williams, R. M., Jr., Smith, M. B., Janis, I. L., Star, S. A., & Cottrell, L. S., Jr. *The American soldier* (2 vols.). Princeton, N.J.: Princeton University Press, 1949.

Straus, M. A. Measuring families. In H. T. Christensen (Ed.), *Handbook of marriage and the family.* Chicago: Rand McNally, 1964.

Straus, M. A. Communication, creativity, and problem solving ability of middle- and working-class families in three societies. *American Journal of Sociology,* 1968, *73,* 417–430.

Straus, M. A. Phenomenal identity and conceptual equivalence of measurement in cross-national comparative research. *Journal of Marriage and the Family,* 1969, *31,* 233–239.

Straus, M. A. Methodology of a laboratory experimental study of families in three societies. In R. Hill & R. Konig (Eds.), *Families in East and West.* Paris: Mouton, 1970.

Straus, M. A. Measuring intrafamily conflict and violence: The Conflict Tactics (CT) Scales. *Journal of Marriage and the Family,* 1979, *41,* 75–88.

Straus, M. A. *The state and regional data archives: A national resource for family research.* Roundtable presentation at the annual meeting of the National Council on Family Relations, Portland, Oregon, October 1980.

Straus, M. A. Ordinary violence, child abuse, and wife-beating. In D. Finkelhor, R. J. Gelles, G. T. Hotaling, & M. A. Straus (Eds.), *The dark side of families: Current family violence research.* Beverly Hills, CA: Sage, 1983.

Straus, M. A., & Brown, B. W. *Family measurement techniques: Ab-*

stracts of published instruments, 1935–1974. Minneapolis: University of Minnesota Press, 1978.

Straus, M. A., & Tallman, I. SIMFAM: A technique for observational measurement and experimental study of families. In J. Aldous, T. Condon, R. Hill, M. A. Straus, & I. Tallman (Eds.), *Family problem solving.* Hinsdale, Ill.: Dryden Press, 1971.

Straus, M. A., Gelles, R. J., & Steinmetz, S. K. *Behind closed doors: Violence in the American family.* New York: Doubleday, 1980.

Strodtbeck, F. L. Husband-wife interaction over revealed differences. *American Sociological Review,* 1951, *16,* 468–473.

Sudman, S., & Bradburn, N. M. *Asking questions.* San Francisco: Jossey-Bass, 1982.

Suomi, S. J. Levels of analysis for interactive data collected on monkeys living in complex social groups. In M. E. Lamb, S. J. Suomi, & G. R. Stephenson (Eds.), *Social interaction analysis: Methodological issues.* Madison: University of Wisconsin Press, 1979.

Surra, C. A., & Huston, T. L. Male selection as a social transition. In S. Duck & D. Perlman (Eds.), *Heterosexual relations, marriage, and divorce.* Beverly Hills, Calif.: Sage, in press.

Sussman, M. B., & Cogswell, B. E. Interpersonal competence: An issue in cross-national family research. In M. B. Sussman & B. E. Cogswell (Eds.), *Cross-national family research.* Leiden: E. J. Brill, 1972.

Tallman, I. Social structure, family socialization, and children's achievement goals: A comparative analysis. In J. Trost (Ed.), *The family in change.* Västerås, Sweden: International Library, 1980.

Teachman, J. D. Methodological issues in the analysis of family formation and dissolution. *Journal of Marriage and the Family,* 1982, *44,* 1037–1053.

Terman, L. M., & Wallin, P. The validity of marriage prediction and marital adjustment tests. *American Sociological Review,* 1949, *14,* 497–505.

Thompson, L., & Walker, A. J. The dyad as the unit of analysis: Conceptual and methodological issues. *Journal of Marriage and the Family,* 1982, *44,* 889–900.

Thomson, E., & Williams, R. Beyond wives' family sociology: A method for analyzing couple data. *Journal of Marriage and the Family,* 1982, *44,* 999–1008.

Tukey, J. W. *Exploratory data analysis.* Reading, Mass.: Addison-Wesley, 1977.

Turk, J. L., & Bell, N. W. Measuring power in families. *Journal of Marriage and the Family,* 1972, *34,* 215–222.

Van Buren, J. H., & Larzelere, R. E. [A search for systematic differences in inter-spouse consistency of marital adjustment scores by type of item]. Unpublished raw data, 1984.

Vincent, J. P. *Observations of couple interaction: Convergent and discriminant validity.* Paper presented at the meetings of the American Psychological Association, New York, September 1979.

Vincent, J. P., Friedman, L. S., Nugent, J., & Messerly, L. Demand characteristics in observations of marital interaction. *Journal of Consulting and Clinical Psychology,* 1979, *47,* 557–566.

Walters, J., & Walters, L. H. Parent-child relationships: A review, 1970–1979. *Journal of Marriage and the Family,* 1980, *42,* 807–822.

Walters, L. H., Pittman, J. F., Jr., & Norrell, J. E. Development of a quantitative measure of a family from self-reports of family members. *Journal of Family Issues,* 1984, *5,* 497–514.

Waxler, N. E., & Mishler, E. G. Scoring and reliability problems in interaction process analysis: A methodological note. *Sociometry,* 1966, *29,* 28–40.

Webb, E. J., Campbell, D. T., Schwartz, R. D., & Sechrest, L. *Unobtrusive measures: Nonreactive research in the social sciences.* Chicago: Rand McNally, 1966.

Welsh, R. S. Tongue-in-cheek? *American Psychological Association Monitor,* July 1976, pp. 12–13.

Wicker, A. W. Attitudes versus actions: The relationship of verbal and overt behavioral responses to attitude objects. *Journal of Social Issues,* 1969, *25,* 41–78.

Wilkinson, M. L., & Tanner, W. C., III. The influence of family size, interaction, and religiosity on family affection in a Mormon sample. *Journal of Marriage and the Family,* 1980, *42,* 297–304.

Winch, R. *Mate-selection: A study of complementary needs.* New York: Harper, 1958.

Winch, R. F. Toward a model of familial organization. In W. R. Burr, R. Hill, F. I. Nye, & I. L. Reiss (Eds.), *Contemporary theories about the family* (Vol. 1). New York: Free Press, 1979.

Wrigley, E. A. Family reconstitution. In E. A. Wrigley (Ed.), *An introduction to English historical demography.* New York: Basic, 1966.

Ÿllo, K. *The status of women and wife-beating in the U.S.* Paper presented at the annual meeting of the National Council on Family Relations, Portland, Oregon, October 1980.

CHAPTER 7

A Perspective on Tomorrow's Families

Barbara H. Settles

Introduction

The purpose of this chapter is to examine ideas about families in the future, from the viewpoint both of what is likely and of what may be possible. Usually considerable energy is expended in defining the family as a term in theoretical discussions of the family. However, in this essay, six approaches to the family as a concept are summarized: the family as used in ideological abstraction, as a romantic image, as a unit of treatment, as a last resort, as a process, and as a network. Although these topics do not exhaust the question of definition, they are suggestive of the range of ideas available. The difficulties of assessing the potential for change are discussed. The future itself, as an environmental setting for families, is examined to the limits of our imagination, invention, and innovation.

Family substitutes, alternatives, and varieties in terms of trends and opportunities are described. Deinstitutionalization versus institutional alternatives are examined as these trends are found in medical care, educational intervention, child care, care of the elderly, and care of deviates and criminals. The family is often peripheral to the policy decisions made in these areas, although family-centered programs and parent involvement are desired. The legal and value systems that underlie our current concerns with the rights and responsibilities of family members are characterized by the theme of blood versus emotional ties. Attention is given to current thinking about the future of ethnic and regional differences in family style and function.

Three substantive areas of family life in the future are considered. The first is the area of lifestyle and life course transitions. The potential for change, as current technology and demographic facts are played out over time, is anticipated. The second area, for prevalence and durability of family types and individual lifestyles is examined, primarily from the American perspective. Third, family dynamics, in the areas of intimacy, involvement, and conflict, are discussed for potential change in relationships.

Barbara H. Settles • Department of Individual and Family Studies, University of Delaware, Newark, DE 19716.

Instead of reviewing all the literature on the future of the family, the task was defined as extracting from a variety of sources some of the more relevant ideas and issues that will be shaping the future for families.

Family Definitions

An analysis of how families are currently defined and viewed is needed in order to access the potential for change in both the perception and the actuality of family life. Six approaches to the family are explored: (1) ideological abstraction, (2) romantic image, (3) unit of treatment, (4) last resort, (5) process, and (6) networks.

The Family as an Ideological Abstraction

The family has been defined by scholars of many persuasions: law, religion, social science, medicine, and therapy. These definitions are used to label, diagnose, treat, harass, reward, and separate spheres of influence. Definitions that fit theories of political and religious order are developed for different purposes, for example, to discover the death of the family (Cooper, 1970) or to posit a profamily political position or to oppose divorce on theological grounds. The "family" as a concept is useful in strategic political planning because it has no common empirical referent. If you refer to the government, most listeners picture the same real government in their society, but with the idea of family, most people picture either their own real family or the advertising world's stereotype of a family. Consequently, the content of the conclusions about a course of action and its impact on "the family" can vary greatly and yet be supported by the same arguments.

If one sees the past as a stable framework for family members, a classical view is developed of the family. This view or myth posits a standard for comparing today's families and for suggesting either a return to virtue or the total demise of the family in the future. Even popular magazines are now reexamining the myths about family (Gottschalt, 1977; *U.S. News and World Report*, 1980). Lantz, Schultz, and O'Hara (1977) called attention to this view as a refrain about "families not being what they once were'' and noted examples from mid-nineteenth-century magazines.

The use of familial terminology in the structure of the church and in actual doctrine about familial regulation in religious organizations indicates the functionality of sacred definitions of family order. Although the specific content of the prescriptions and mandates varies from one religious persuasion to another, the essential element that the family is sacred, not secular, and thus the business of religion, has continued into the present.

The grouping of issues, which have been identified as profamily by conservative religious groups in America, is particularly interesting because of the basic conflicts among modernization, technological innovations, and family policy. Antiabortion, anti-secular-sex-education, anti-family-planning, anti–Equal Rights Amendment, and anti-genetic-research movements have been brought together under the rubric of being positive for the family as an institution. The uniting of the Fundamentalist Protestants, the Catholics, and the Orthodox Jews in America around these concerns has been a spectacular strategic success. Whether the coalition can hold together in the near future is more questionable. The unifying theme is the rejection of newer family forms and the availability of choice about family matters (Schulz, 1981), The fear of choice and change is often extremely high when innovations are introduced in any culture. However, the benefits that often occur to early adopters of innovation can undermine the penalties that traditionalists seek to impose.

Some prohibition-style regulation and enforcement are still likely in the immediate future as the profamily organizations influence legislative processes and bureaucratic policy enforcement. It would not be surprising to find abortion becoming a very scarce and expensive resource because of policy shifts (Ebaugh, Fuchs, & Haney, 1980; Isaacson, 1981) and to find sex education remaining an undeveloped component of the school curriculum in the next decade (Brown, 1981). However, it is much less likely that the total package of conservative family policies will, in fact, take hold in ordinary practice in family life.

Other social forces make impractical the rigid and traditional sex roles and marital interaction (Bernard, 1972; Giele, 1979). The real likelihood of single parenthood and survivorship in old age makes it risky for women to be untrained and to remain outside the labor market. People cannot easily afford to invest for extended periods of time in social forms that are not compatible with the demands of daily life. For example, it is clear that Catholic couples in this society have adopted contraceptive practices not supported by religious doctrine and have worked out rationalizations to handle their conflicting beliefs and actions. On other issues, the society may have a short era of public policy on the family that is counter to public practice and that requires the service of an underworld to maintain current practice. Certainly, we have precedents in this century for prohibition strategies, and we know some of the costs and benefits.

The Family as a Romantic Image

In contrast to the politicizing of a religious definition of the family, the romanticizing of the family found in the media and the peer group makes an impact not by forcing issues, but by structuring thought so that only certain choices are apparently good. Feminist scholars have studied intensely the way in which images of the family—and of men and women—in the media define our sense of self-worth (Elshtain, 1982). In the media, the woman who fails the ''Ring around the Collar'' or ''Snoopy Sniffer'' tests of good housekeeping is led to believe that her family is in grave peril. The man whose charcoal or mower won't start loses his manly leadership role in the family. These images and ideals of family competence do evoke laughter and ridicule, but they sell products and direct behavior.

The picture of the composition, the age, and the sex of family members has evolved in recent times. It is no longer so common to find the definitely older husband, the younger wife with the adolescent son, the elementary-school-aged daughter, and the baby as the ideal family. But other images linger on. Public opinion polls suggest that families have changed in how they view children's sex roles, but they still expect mothers to do the housework and fathers to be the breadwinners (Yankelovich, Skelly, & White, Inc., 1976–1977). For example, the husband's attitudes toward household work have changed from cohort to cohort (Wheeler & Avery, 1981), although housework is still not equitably shared in dual employment homes (Giele, 1979; Walker & Woods, 1976). Cherlin and Walters (1981) saw steadily increasing support for nontraditional sex roles over the 1970s. Identifying one's own family in the midst of these images leads to some evaluation of the quality of life and the success to be attributed to the family. If your experience comes close to these images and ideals, then the family situation is declared to be successful.

Revision in images can cause a previously positively evaluated situation to be rejected or vice versa. When behavior changes, the image or the family has to change also. In the twentieth century, this dictum has often meant that the specific family had to go: separating, divorcing, and remarrying (Bane, 1976). The process has been fixing the situation by changing who the players were rather than changing what the people themselves did. Some observers do find second marriages to have less similar marital partners than first marriages (Dean & Gurak, 1978), but in many cases, the new arrangement may simply repeat the problems of the old. The continuing future of a romantic view of a family is likely to continue to be emphasized by advertising and individuals because it simplifies the complexity of life for the moment.

The Family as a Unit of Treatment

The growth of therapeutic intervention and family support systems demonstrates the possibility of the alteration of the internal family. Although the data are not complete on the efficacy of family therapy, the emotional and economic response has been positive. Families are willing to pay for intervention, and professionals are flocking to train as therapists (*Newsweek*, 1978).

The movement away from ordinary educational and media approaches to family intervention and toward peer counseling and family therapy is pronounced in professional circles. Peer counseling has the virtue of apparent economy because the peers volunteer their time. Supervision by professional family-life personnel may be quite minimal, and the support groups that have developed around every stress of family or public life are run on the commitment of the people involved. Marriage enrichment has developed as an approach to giving a similar experience to those who have no presenting problem (Mace & Mace, 1975).

Family therapy is far more expensive than peer counseling and seems to have a ''severe'' problem orientation. Families come into therapy after exhausting the resources of other areas of support, or by direct referral from these support systems. Commonly, a member of the family has been acting out in some labeled deviance that serves as the initial problem, for example, alcoholism, anorexia nervosa, juvenile delinquency, suicide attempts, drug abuse, school failure, job loss, mental or physical illness, or child or spouse abuse (Malcolm, 1978). (See also Kaslow, Chapter 30, in this book.) The various approaches to therapeutic intervention are based on differing views of how families maintain interaction and structure within society and how the presenting problem is related to this family process. In the future, it may be possible to evaluate these approaches for relative quality, and families may be better advised about how to select supportive therapeutic intervention. In some cases, as the presenting problem itself is better understood, the family's role in the treatment or the alleviation of the problem may be reduced.

Family problems may be redefined as technological change alters how families relate to these problems. Corrective surgery reduced the need for the family of a child with a cleft palate to deal with stigma. As asthma and allergies have become better understood and the symptoms have become treatable, the family has been relieved of assuming the major responsibility for the allergic member's attacks. Schizophrenia, which has been seen as a family anomaly or biological fault, although not as well understood, is being reexamined for the scope and substance of the family's contribution (Falloon, Boyd, McGill, Razoni, Mosi, & Gilderman, 1982; Sheehan, 1982). The family may become less a unit of treatment in many situations when symptomatology becomes better understood. However, helping the family to adjust to the medical therapies will continue to be necessary even if the problems are redefined.

The Family as a Last Resort

The family has often been viewed as the resource of last resort, as Robert Frost's poem (1946) suggested, ''Home is the place where, when you have to go there, They have to take you in.'' The literature has long suggested that families, to the extent that they can manage the stress and continue as family units, provide for continuity in the care and treatment of the member with special needs (Hill & Hansen, 1964). The literature on singleness also notes that a person with few family ties may become lost in the institutional settings that replace the family support; hence, he or she may remain institutionalized long after the need has passed because no advocate asks questions. Stein (1981) suggested that the crucial issue may not be marriage versus singlehood, but the strength of the support network.

The availability of family members and the concern of extended kin are crucial to the life course of elderly people. Shanas and Sussman (1981) found that old people without immediate kin are more likely than their contemporaries to be institutionalized. They further suggested that the twenty-first century will be characterized by the elderly ''in search of a relative'' to look after them or to take appropriate action on their behalf.

When a major institution such as the economy fails to function positively for individuals, they turn to family even in younger adult life. One of the rationales for keeping the large family home that was achieved when children were young is now to shelter adults and grandchildren in times of crisis.

Current conservative political groups suggest that the family might be the first resort for the solution of problems if other agencies and government do not intervene. The civil defense and disaster research has suggested that families use their family ties as emergency resources before turning to emergency programs (Drabek & Boggs, 1968).

The Family as a Process

Intimacy and continuity are basic needs that have been served by family units. When successful, the basic marital dyad has the capacity for enlarging the individual's experience in trust that supports both intimacy and a sense of continuity. In rapidly changing societies, shared meaning is a precious commodity. The game is far more often that of guessing if one understands another's gestures, words, and linguistic structure. The easy informality of the salesperson's use of list names or of the party introductions that identify people by name and job gives the appearance of closeness without the substance.

No one will claim that all or even a majority of families provide the meaningful relationships so widely discussed as a goal in the 1960s and 1970s. Families are strategic hunting grounds for such potential relationships. In contrast to work, school, and leisure settings, where temporary relationships and direct exchange are built into the institutions, families provide an opportunity for stability and indirect exchange as normative options. The fragility of the marital bond documented by divorce and separation seems not to be so closely paralleled in the parental role

(Ryder, 1974). Although there has been some weakening of the parent's exclusive control, elasticity and continuity seem more typical of parents' and children's relationships. Adults today complain not of the empty nest, but of the returning "adult" child with his or her children in tow. Now that adoption has lost much of its stigma to the adoptee and the adopting parents, birth parents are seeking to contact the child, or the young adult seeks to open his or her records to find those parents (Cole, 1976). Often, foster parents care for children for longer than standards of practice recommend because the birth parents continue to make some efforts to continue duties.

The Family in Networks

The individually mobile nuclear family may attenuate extended kin ties during periods of stress in the movement between social positions. However, even these groups often reconstitute an interaction at life passage moments such as weddings, funerals, and hospitalizations. In addition to the kin of Western nostalgia, families today create their own relatives as needed. These friends who are called on to fill in for missing or nonfunctioning kin add substance to the potentiality for continuity, intimacy, and shared meaning as they are recruited for their commitments rather than by accident birth. The open family, as Constantine (1977) proposed it, may be quite purposeful in seeking such additional interactions.

Divorce and remarriage are adding great complexity to the potential for kin and family support systems (Kent, 1980). The child who is grandchild to a dozen other adults may surely find one or two suitable "soul affiliates." The price paid in loss of continuity may be regained in the intimacy and speciality of such relationships. The boundaries of these reconstituted families are more permeable, and a definition of new roles must be achieved (Walker & Messinger, 1979). The family chronicler who can keep the story straight and tell the great-grandchildren how the blended family all came about will have an important function.

In addition to the rearrangements of marriages and nuclear family units, improved health and life expectancy have added to the complexity of arranging each family vis-à-vis kin and friendship support systems. The family of four and five generations may become more frequent in spite of trends toward later marriage and childbearing (Glick, 1977; Reed, 1982). When elders are "deserted" by their children, the real situation is not that of young adults neglecting their parents but of already old "children" of 60 or 70 being unable to care for a 90-year-old parent and themselves as well (Steinmetz, 1981). There seems to be no reason not to expect this expansion of the population of the frail elderly to continue (Uhlenberg, 1980). The opportunity to recycle earlier friendship relationships is found because of these demographic trends. The widow may find her high-school sweetheart. The divorced may remarry. Friends may live together, pooling their pensions. Although new friendships and mar-

riages are made possible by the extension of both life and good health, the actual prevalence depends on many other opportunity factors.

In the future, although family support may well increase, families are not likely to be designed around the concept of dependency. Financial and emotional dependency was fundamental to many of the restrictive norms on family dissolution and was sanctioned and supported the authority patterns within families. Continued dependency does not appear to be as essential as was previously thought, and it may be contrary to the demands of loving relationships (Saflios-Rothchild, 1977). The wave of married women with young children returning to the labor force has challenged the assumption of dependency by wives and has worried those desiring to continue patriarchal authority. Certainly, the many divorced women who support their children with little or no help from the father are not impressed by the dependency arrangements within nuclear families that ensure continued support (Schorr & Moen, 1979; see also Chapter 28 of this book).

Children may also be "liberated" both from dependency and from parental sponsorship for access to status and position. Currently, only a few children—those who have trust funds or social security benefits, those who are in foster care, and those who have their own jobs—are free of total reliance on family functioning for lifestyle. Child-rearing payments or family allowances are considered frequently in discussing family policy, but to date, they have met with little organized support (Kamerman & Kahn, 1978).

Implications of Definitions for the Future of the Family

These six ways of defining the family project different outcomes in futurist speculations:

1. *Ideological Abstraction.* These definitions appear to have considerable power for use by social movements. Currently, the traditional definitions are being used as rationales by the profamily coalitions in America and by religious groups throughout the world to promote more restrictive public policy on the family. A more clearly articulated statement of egalitarian family organization might have a similar utility for the women's movement.

2. *Romantic Image.* Romanticizing families continues to have great impact, especially in the public media. Although this view is generally rejected in family and women's studies literature and teaching, the fact that it must be countered as an approach suggests a tenacity in the concept. Today, there is an attempt to incorporate working wives and homemaking husbands into advertising. No doubt, the romantic image can be stretched to accommodate change without indicating the complexities underlying the change.

3. *Unit of Treatment.* This approach to refining an understanding of the family is the "cornerstone" of the conceptualization of family. The professions related to family therapy and family support services are still grow-

ing. The one caution is that some "family" problems may later be understood more fundamentally as medical, individual, or social problems.

4. *Last Resort.* Both the conservative political groups and the more liberal professional social-welfare service groups agree that this residual role is critical in understanding individuals and their resources. There is controversy over how to exploit the potentiality of the family to serve as last resort, but there is not much pressure, even from the political left, to replace the family in this function.

5. *Process.* Attention to definitions based on process have become important both for research and for therapeutic practice. Since Burgess and Locke (1945) presented the rationale of a contemporary "modern" family based on companionship, the interest has shifted to analyzing how such a family may operate.

6. *Networks.* Both kin and friends as both interactive and integral parts of the family constellation are receiving scholarly attention and public policy notice. The complexity and the individualization of these networks appear to be increasing, but dependency as an organizing principal is declining.

These six approaches to the definition of the family illustrate a vast literature that refines, defines, argues, posits, and develops what the family may or may not be. If cross-cultural comparisons are included, there is a geometric progression of the amount of consideration of the idea of family. The fluid quality of the word *family* makes it especially useful for political propagandizing and as a residual variable in societal studies. In the future, it is not likely that the job of specifying what is meant by *family* will progress rapidly. Consensus would be costly for politicians and improbable for scholars.

Assessing the Potential for Change in the Family

The future of the family and of families on the world scene, and more particularly in American society, hinges on several interrelationships. A worldview of families suggests that social and technological change continues to intrude on family lifestyles and that the tensions caused by these changes are played out at the microlevel of individual families. From a pessimistic worldview, the family emerges as a survival mechanism for the few who are not consumed by war, pestilence, famine, and poverty. This shrinking-resource paradigm puts a premium on those family forms that emphasize flexibility and problem solving. Small, tightly knit units appear to have survival qualities, especially if they have excellent brokerage skills for finding support both in the traditional extended kin and in the larger social milieu.

A more positive view of the future sees invention, social management, and the balancing of interests providing new options and supporting some traditional arrangements. This more synergetic view allows for more variability and individuality of lifestyle arrangements (Sussman, 1979). If there is an increasingly responsive world,

where products can be made to order by computer and fitted to individual requirements, and where resources are allocated without waste and confusion, the resources available to humanity may expand as needed (Toffler, 1980). Current-day families' investments in a worldview may be predictive of their approaches to making choices and accepting strategies. Families today have as windows to the future (1) the media; (2) the government; (3) religious organizations; (4) political and social organizations; and (5) informal social networks. The twentieth-century fantasy of the future has invested heavily in technological innovation, rapid duplication and dissemination of information, symmetry of solutions, and reduction of human energy by replacement with other energy sources. The classic futurist description places a forever-young population on a moving sidewalk dressed in sequined long underwear with a communicator-light-ray gadget in the hand. Pickett (1977) suggested that these artists' conceptions may indeed be sharper and closer to the truth than some of the more academic models. He sees this utopian thinking as rediscovering personal alternatives that have always existed.

In addition to this limited vision, an animal husbandry approach to the application of technology to human families has been anticipated by some futurists. Therefore, if one can grow a child in an outside medium without a person's carrying the fetus (Francoeur & Francoeur, 1974), the picture presented has been of a "chick incubator" factory away from home rather than a "fish tank" in one's own living room. In the popular press, the weird and the threatening are more interesting to emphasize (Andrews, 1981). Technology itself is rather value-free, but its applications are built on the society's expectations and fantasy. Today, *in vitro* fertilization has been welcomed by the public and by the couples who are involved.

Another example of perceptual narrowness is the way in which some of the ideological commitment to conservation of the earth has developed. It is interesting how surprised many conservationists were by the eruptions of Mount Saint Helens. A few of them really seemed to want it put back "right" as it was before. The changing of the lake, the burning of forests, and the flooding were not viewed as natural change to be welcomed, like many changes in the last 4,500 years (Decker & Decker, 1981), but as a human tragedy. There has been alienation from the human as one of the animals sharing the world, which suggests that things might be better if we were not around to ruin the trails and the wildflowers.

The immediacy of counterrevolutions and conservative trends in both Third World nations and the nations of the great powers suggests that we should be cautious in assuming that all that is possible is probable. Family and religious systems have shown great tenacity in hanging onto practices that seem on the surface nonfunctional or even dysfunctional.

This contradiction was illustrated in the recent Iranian revolution, where the veil was first used as a symbol of the overthrow of the old authoritarian regimen and then as the symbol of the reestablishment of traditional values in the new authoritarian government. Many politically active women were caught in the middle of the change and did not accept the latter stabilization of their role as easily as the former symbolism. Lindsey (1980) maintains that the decline in the status of women worldwide is a consequence of the way the development of the third world has proceeded.

Even when a society professes an ideological commitment to changing the relationship between the family and the community (for example, the kibbutz life in Israel), the stability of these forms is precarious. Beit-Hallahmi (1981) discussed the changes from the classical kibbutz of 1920–1950 and emphasized the ties between economic improvement and the resurgence of the nuclear family. He saw women as the familistic underground undercutting the traditions and the ideology of the kibbutz.

Hertz (1982) suggested that the driving force toward a return to familism was the desire for a privacy and intimacy not possible in a more complex communal society, as well as the development, over time, of the extended family as a political pressure group within the kibbutz. In examining the arguments about the resurgence of the more separate gender-based roles for men and women in the kibbutz and the assumption that household work is primarily women's work, Hertz questioned those who use a biological explanation and saw a need for a closer examination of economic contingencies and the political processes that define and interpret communal needs.

Most societies today have some involvement in an individualistic, future-oriented political economy, and the strength of the religious influence on family systems is challenged.

Contemporary societies bridge the values of religion and technology that have not been integrated into the society by developing norms of evasion. These norms put a premium on discretion and privacy, both of which can be plausibly obtained in the urban, technologically complex social society. Family members can isolate parts of their lives and shelter ''meaningful others'' from the impact of their new behavior. The family can live by traditional ideas to the extent that barriers are enforced within the changing society. In the ''soap operas'' of contemporary life, the ultimate terror is the discovery of secret worlds in a loved one's life.

In many of the developing nations, an intricate web of evasions has been organized to minimize the direct conflict between new technology, wealth, and work lives and the sacred family-religious forms of social interaction. For example, different dress and behavior are tolerated in different locations. This symbolic use of clothing establishes which values are in force. An upper-class Arab family may be undistinguishable from other jet-setters in London, but as they return to Saudi Arabia, the wife will assume traditional veiling and clothing and slip quietly into the background and privacy of the family compound (Fertile-Bishop & Gilliam, 1981).

It is generally assumed that the trend toward secularization and nuclearization will continue in the Third World, although not all the variety of lifestyles will necessarily be adopted. So far, most of the spread of social change has gone out from the Western industralized nations into the Third World. As the barriers among nation-states do soften, the opportunity for families to move about and to have cosmopolitan experience could readily be enhanced. American families that have had the opportunity to experience family life outside the country often report new priorities and practices when they return. Perhaps there will be some ''feedback'' to the technologically developed nations.

In utopian literature, a common approach to the future of the family simplifies modern living to a more rural, gemeinschaft-type unit. The idea is to overcome tensions by simplifying lives. There have been numerous attempts in recent years to implement communal and cooperate groups (Berger, 1981). This strategy runs counter to the social complexity needed to maintain norms of evasion. Why large numbers of people would want to forgo the current extra variations in lifestyle for the security of a simpler social system is not clear.

The basis for comparison of current trends in family change is not secure because our historical baseline is often based on wishful thinking. Hareven (1980) reviewed historical perspectives on the family for the White House Conference in 1980 and noted a number of myths not supported by historical research on American families:

1. Great extended families did not exist in preindustrial America.

2. Outsiders, not kin, augmented the household as boarders and lodgers. Chain migration kept many family ties active during industrialization. Even though the workplace changed to the industrial setting, work was still a family's effort.

3. The family as a retreat and the glorification of motherhood as a career were a relative late phenomenon, developing primarily in the middle class in the nineteenth century.

4. The birth rate decline was quite evident by the beginning of the twentieth century.

5. Greater stability and uniformity in family-life-cycle transitions have been achieved in this century.

Historical accuracy can help us to avoid trying to explain trends that never were and can keep us from seeing present and future situations as stranger than they are. The family systems of the twentieth century seem less threatening and awkward when they are related to a historical perspective that does not romanticize the past. Edwards and Kluck (1980) pointed out in an article on patriarchy that frequently, when negative data on a concept are found, definitions are created to incorporate the new data without challenging the concept. Elder (1981) noted that recent historical research has opened up more complex views of past family patterns.

Classic family scholars have had an important impact

on our current understanding of future prospectives. Og-burn and Nimkoff (1955) codified the perception that technological innovation was linked inexorably to changes in family structure and practice. Burgess and Locke (1945) defined the outcome of these changes as a shearing away of family functions, so that the family became a companionship unit. Carl Zimmerman (1971) viewed this lighter, tighter, more fragile family form as indicating alarming social change, indicative of dec-adence in the society. In his Burgess Award address, he reaffirmed this point of view and commented that he found himself usually to be right about outcomes, if sometimes wrong about the timing and sequence of events. Etzioni (1977) continued this theme in his more recent popular and scholarly publications. He has found the current family system to be unstable and inadequate in its socialization functions for both children and adults over the life cycle and divorce to indicate the disintegra-tion of the family. Although conservative in his in-terpretation of the features of family life, Winch (1952) was more optimistic about the meaning of the statistics. For example, he found high remarriage rates to be a positive outcome.

The White House Conference on Children and Youth (Forum 14, 1970) used as its theme diversity in family structure, and a number of papers and presentations indi-cated a positive view of changes in family.

Glick's Burgess Award address (1975) pulled together a statistical picture of the family, which scholars found satisfying without creating a longing for so-called better, previous times. The diversity that Glick presented was not as alarming as earlier writings by other scholars. Per-haps this diversity has simply become less shocking to the profession. Sudia (1976) reviewed historical trends in family behavior at the bicentennial and emphasized the consistency of diversity as a feature of American society.

The nuclear family system received the theoretical seal of approval through Parsons and Bales's presentation (1955) of theory linking a psychoanalytic individual de-velopment to a universalistic nuclear family. Using cross-cultural data and small groups research studies, they made a case for traditional sex roles, characterizd as in-strumental and expressive, being the general, appropri-ate, and institutionalized situation worldwide and through history. The isolation and emphasis on the tightly orga-nized nuclear unit were subjected to criticism early on. For example, in 1959, Sussman reviewed the question by examining data from his research that did not support the concept of an isolated family structure in an urban setting. Litwak (1960) found similar evidence in other data on other contemporary families. Further work on genera-tional interaction (Adams, 1968; Shanas & Sussman, 1981) also produced a picture of a nuclear family with important ties to other kin. The feminist critiques that emerged in the 1970s have made the Parsonian "mod-ern" formulation of the contemporary family appear old-fashioned and reactionary (Eichler, 1980).

The developmental approach to the family, as pro-posed and expanded by Duvall (1957, 1977) and Hill (1978), accommodated to the perception of diversity in family life. When Rogers (1973) amplified and docu-mented developmental theory, he related his work to the major work on family studies. He used it to tie together family scholarship into a meaningful whole. Although criticized for describing the intact "normative" family's life cycle as the model, the basic dynamic of change bringing challenge to family interaction and requiring ad-justment seems to have stretched to include alternative family forms as adjustments to these changes (Aldous, 1978). Hill (1978) based on this development approach an optimistic view of the family's future as a process of renewal in each family.

Family relationships have remained central to most people in both contemporary modern and traditional so-cieties, as both a component of personal life and a poten-tial force for organizing and disorganizing everyday exis-tence (Sussman, 1981). Whether one is included in a nuclear family or only at the edge of a kinship network, she or he is continuously negotiating how much of family life will encompass her or his total life space.

In traditional societies, the person may have only a few options for separating from the family setting, and most of life may be defined in family terms (Lindsay, 1980). Exceptions found in these traditional settings include sub-stituting intense religious participation for family, as well as individuals' migrating away from the family of origin. In the modernizing social situation, more possibilities for separating family relationships from the whole of life's existence are available, and the individual more fre-quently makes conscious decisions about which family relationships to nurture and develop and which to let lapse or survive. The pressure from other family members to be an active family member varies in intensity, but it is part of the dynamic process of an individual's definition of his or her family life.

The scripts for family life vary from one society to another and within subcultures, but they are well known and demand response from each person. Laswell and Laswell (1982) summarized the scripting process and noted that families continue to respond to larger societal ideals. For example, a family scholar may find his or her own family run by the same scripts as the "others" iden-tified in the family studies research. These scripts have a life of their own, little altered by academic understand-ing. The scholar attends a family reunion, a wedding, a graduation, or a funeral and repeats the lines from a Broadway play or a television miniseries, faintly amused at the irony, but unable or unwilling to find any fresher words. In the intimacy of the marriage bond, this classi-cism in the scenario seems even more intense.

The variety of current family lifestyles is seen in both historical and present cultural themes. Current issues that affect prediction for the future are (1) the impact of further technological change; (2) the visions that we have devel-oped of the future; (3) the incomplete integration of new technologies and concepts into current societies; (4) the incomplete and unsophisticated understanding of the past as an influence on today's and tomorrow's family choices; and (5) the ability and opportunity of individuals to separate their destiny from that of their families.

The Future as the Setting for Families

Imagination and Images

The future is a dry and uninteresting place because of our failure in imagination (Ornaurer, Wiberg, Sicinski, & Galtung, 1976). We see it as only more of what we have now or the loss of everything we hold dear. The story lines shown on television or in movies are borrowed either from Greek myth or from medieval legend. These images may be as good as any, for they have durability. Space fiction and games such as "Traveler" and the other fantasy role-playing games integrate the images taken from the real and the fictional past and give them new life. King Arthur's legendary sword in the stone becomes a laser. The dragon becomes hundreds of specialized characters. Thus, we tend to expect new technology to support old ideology.

In fact, the ideological and theoretical changes of the twentieth century have been as interesting as the accompanying technological innovations. The technological inventions are the material evidence of changed thinking and innovations. The thinking is far more revolutionary because the view of the reality and the possibilities is altered so completely. Physics has given us arguments about the universe that shake our sense of time, physical space, and knowledge. Biology has begun to specify the mechanics of the life process at a much more fundamental level, which leaves us wondering what is the "nature" we have so often used as an explanation for our ideology. Cybernetics has overloaded our sense of what must be included in our systematic examination of knowledge. Even architecture has been an expression not just of technological possibilities but also of the ideology in fashion at the moment. Images of future cities and environments emphasize the manufactured interior not the vista. For example, Buckminster Fuller's geodesic dome is an expression not just of the technological possibilities, but also of the controlled environment as an ideal. These and other ideas of physics, biology, and cybernetics have affected our view of reality and our religious and explanatory frameworks. Boulding (1978) discussed a few of these worldviews and how they affect the other questions we ask of the future. For example, we predict a future that we believe has the capability of changing the future itself.

Progress and Change

The idea of progress itself has its own history and is linked to a view of time as linear, flowing, and cumulative (Nisbet, 1980). Currently, we must deal with time as a variable that is shapable and a growing sense that progress is not inevitable.

Change in any society includes a process of innovation, adoption, and conservative challenge. When the transitions are rapid, these processes overlap, and predicting the future is especially difficult. Incorporating the new reality of technological change into the philosophical foundations of thought is often much slower than adopting the technology itself. Daniel Bell's development (1973) of the thesis of a postindustrial society attempts to show how thoughts and reality have been linked and finds many gaps in explanation and overlaps in modalities. For example Bell (1973) wrote that three different power systems (property, political position, and skill) operate concurrently in America today:

Base of power	Mode of access	Social unit
Property	Inheritance	Family
Political position	Entrepreneurial ability	Group/party
Skill	Education	Individual

Bell suggested that the movement is away from the family as the dominant power and the direct access system. The family's continued influence on the child's opportunities for the other access routes, however, remains important.

Individual families who are on the front edge of social change are often adaptable and flexible. In contrast to this flexibility, the family as part of philosophy and religion is usually seen as conservative and traditional (Elshtain, 1981). Rights, duties, and mobility opportunities are especially important in predicting family change. Equity as the ideal of the twentieth century has made great progress in infiltrating ideology and practice. For example, the opinions expressed in public opinion polls suggest that such issues as equal pay, equal opportunity, personal credit, and freedom to choose childbearing are established American values for men and women and in all racial groups (Harris, 1981; Yankelovich, 1981).

Pluralism versus Single Ideologies

In reviewing recent research on nontraditional family forms, Macklin (1980) saw continued pluralism and emphasis on individual choices as the trend (see also Chapter 12 of this volume). Some feel that these trends are reaching a plateau and even predict some return to earlier social structures and traditional discriminations. Among the fastest growing religious groups in the Third World are those with more traditional doctrines on family structure and class/race status, for example, Islam, the Church of Jesus Christ of the Latter Day Saints (Kephart, 1976), and the Roman Catholic Church (Reed, 1982). Secular humanism and science are under attack by conservative religious groups in both the Western and the Eastern worlds. For example, recent polls reflect the American opinion that both biblical and evolutionary theories should be covered in public school classes on science. Legislation efforts to ensure this practice have not been effective, but scholars are concerned about the impact on academic decision-making (see "Creationism," 1982).

The political problems associated with the attempt to ratify the Equal Rights Amendment for women is another illustration of the power of these conservative views. Heer and Grossbard-Schectman (1981) speculated that some of the current interest in cohabitation may have resulted from the demographics of a "marriage squeeze" on women. They believe that there will be a return to the traditional values accorded the wife–mother role as the ratio of women to men of marriageable age becomes more favorable to women.

In speculating on the future of lifestyle diversity, David Schulz (1981) suggested that traditionalists such as Jerry Falwell are not a voice of the lunatic fringe of American society, but a clear articulation of widely held American values. Although Schulz does not believe that these views will endure for the majority, he predicted less celebration of diverse family forms in the near future.

Other scholars and political figures believe that the momentum for change is so strong that the organized groups working for equity in family policy will continue the fight (Aldous & Dumon, 1980). It may be impossible for those who have experienced freedom and equity to return to traditional forms and practices. The conflicts among ideologies, religious institutions, and current technological reality affect distant and adverse groups because of the easy communication and travel within countries and throughout the world. Although citizens of nations experiencing new development express optimism over the technological promise they see in the more developed countries, many express "development fatigue" and see few advantages to come in the future (Ornaurer *et al.*, 1976).

Invention and Innovation

Although an article on the future of the family cannot anticipate the nature of continued invention and innovation in the technical world, it is likely that new technologies may invalidate old adjustments and may require further change in individual and family lifestyles. There is little to suggest that we may assume family stability. For example, Toffler's extremely popular book *The Third Wave* (1980) has emphasized how computer wizardry, video display, telephone interface, and automation could create opportunities for flexibility in the workplace and the return to the home of many tasks currently carried on outside. This technology is already being promoted and marketed and is decreasing in cost ("Window on the World," 1981). Bernard (1972) noted that this opportunity is not as well received by women as by the men who propose it. For example, the opportunity to work in one's home may appeal to men who are not expected to balance the demands and conflicts of both homemaking and career but may be viewed by women as a narrowing of the choice between work inside or outside the home.

Another promising area of continued innovation is biological research and health care applications (M. Pines, 1976). The potential for bringing even more areas of life into the realm of choice and decision making is close at hand. Intervention in the early development of the fetus, the prevention of anomalies, and the understanding of brain function all appear to be within this generation's grasp. The family is faced with major changes in responsibility for participation in these opportunities. Providing informed consent for dependents such as elders and children is a tremendous burden for family members when consequences are as yet unknown, for example (see Crutchfield, 1981a; Rodman, 1981; Zimmerman, 1981). These three authors each look at different aspects of the evolving status of parents and children in relationship to consent and required information. In the brief time since the publication of these works, public policy has addressed the question of more parental involvement in another issue: contraceptive prescriptions to minors. However, this attempt to tighten regulations in federally funded programs was not supported by the courts in 1983 (Rossoff, 1982a,b).

The relationship of the family to the outcomes and the responsibilities generated by the new medical technologies has not been refined. Basic questions about the beginning or cessation of life have not yet been thoroughly addressed by philosophy or religion as current technical innovations have allowed this border to be stretched.

Beyond the question of giving informed and adequate consent for procedures related to these technological intervention in life and death, there is the whole range of implications that flow from these decisions. For example, the handicapped child or elder who might not have lived without intervention is assumed to be the family's responsibility, until the family breaks down. However, the quality of life that the society expects to be provided to those for whom a medical miracle has been performed seems to be rising along with the trends toward intervention. The question for each family and the society is: Who is saved for what kind of life?

When death is not clear, deciding when to mourn becomes a real problem for the family. Is it when the relative ceases to function as a family member? Is it when hope is thought to vanish? Is it at each medical crisis? Is it when the individual or the family no longer has room in their lives for the problem? People who have been thought to be dead and have been revived have expressed a new perspective and a different relationship to their families following the event.

In the Western religious tradition, medical decisions made by families and practitioners have followed the general guideline that "reasonable means" should be used to preserve life and functioning. This concept of *reasonable means* has been a particularly difficult idea to adapt to the changing technological scene for dealing with the family's and society's responsibility for the person at risk for death. One year's clearly dramatic intervention is next year's standard practice. The expectation of new scientific breakthroughs suggest that families hold onto hope for a possible discovery and a new miracle. Simple necessities such as good food, shelter, and a healthy emotional climate have not been available for all persons in society, but kidney machines and open-heart surgery are potentially available to some patients. In addition, families can not know all the consequences of their decisions and therefore endure ''guilt trips'' when their decisions are evaluated later in terms of newly discovered knowledge.

For example, those of us over 40 remember when playing with the foot X-ray machine was our entertainment or reward while our mothers shopped for clothes, and dentists used X-rays regularly in each examination. Now we know enough to worry about the accumulated radiation. Such little things, which accumulate over a lifetime of new discoveries and recommendations, need to be integrated into the family's experience. Families must find some way to accommodate this ordinary chaos within their reality. Hopefully, some insightful philosophical breakthrough will make it easier in the future to incorporate such changes into family life.

The two areas briefly discussed here (information processing and biological understanding) are relatively well-known technical areas. No doubt, there are hundreds of other researches now being analyzed or proposed that may have equal or greater impact on families.

Planning and Strategies

In addition to the generation of new understanding, the dissemination and application of currently available knowledge are not certain. One of the greatest coordinated efforts in world history was accomplished recently when smallpox was eliminated worldwide (Henderson, 1976). This model of a program that has a narrow goal with worldwide cooperation has not been used widely yet, but numerous problems affecting the everyday quality of life for families could lend themselves to such a strategy. For most of the world, family life still revolves around simply providing fuel, water, food, clothing, shelter, and clean air. In 1980, to review these issues, the *Scientific American* commissioned a series of articles on these topics that suggest strategic interventions to deal with these worldwide concerns.

Another example is the current public attention being given to questions about energy: its limits, distribution, equity, and effective utilization. So far, this concern has resulted not in any unified strategy, but in increasing polarization and differentiation of interest groups, increasing conflict, and an increasing exertion of power to control the availability and cost of energy. The quality of life of the individual family is related directly to how these kinds of problems are attacked by the larger social order.

Human energy in production is not being replaced by other sources at the same rate as earlier in the century. In addition to identifying new sources of energy, reclamation and distribution, and the reduction of the energy requirements of technology have some promise. For example, transistor chips use energy much more efficiently than the vacuum tube. Ginzberg (1981) maintained that

the long-term trend is still toward improving human capital and the growth of service industries over industrial sectors.

It has been fashionable in the twentieth century to attempt long-term social and economic planning, and some magnificent failures have dotted the epoch in both the capitalist and the socialist countries. For example, in the United States, our government farm programming has been successful in developing great productive capacity which is based on high capital, information, and maintenance investments. Marketing problems and inadequate return on investment have been cushioned by governmental support programs. Now, the whole program of price supports and controlled markets appears shaky (Schrimshaw & Taylor, 1980). In contrast, long-term agricultural planning in the USSR has had a mixed outcome, with many shortfalls in product and distribution to consumers.

Another example of mixed results in programming has been the development of the social security system in the United States. Demographic and economic anomalies, as well as changing standards for the scope and adequacy of programming for the elderly, have opened the debate about whether this program can survive in its present form. Young people and those nearing retirement have lost confidence in the program's ability to deliver the product. Rainwater (1978) maintained that many lost opportunities for developing a life cycle approach to security stemmed from turning the concept into a joke and from not recognizing that the economic structure as it now operates does not need all of the people who, according to our cultural standard, should work.

A future that has uncertainty as its organizing feature gives the individual family little sense of control or of managing their own destiny, because taking prudent action as a family member requires some insight into the future's character. Although our elders are the survivors of the modern era, we have seldom really sought to know what mental gymnastics and social adjustments they used to retain internal order in an uncertain world (Shanas, 1980). Because these specific adjustments are not easily applicable to the next generation, young people have assumed that there is no *Hitchhiker's Guide to the Galaxy* (Adams, 1979) handbook to the new era.

Family Substitutes, Alternatives, and Varieties

The literature on the family in the 1970s focused on opening up the definitions of familial ties and studying the varieties of personal lifestyles that had familial qualities. Textbooks devoted chapters to alternate lifestyles, single parents, living-together arrangements, communal groups, and group marriages. (Much more of the population were studied as normal family life.) It was more important to view the arrangements as alternatives rather than as problems (Sussman, 1980b). Not only did the family scholar take a new look at emergent family forms, but the law and the folkways also responded. The advice columnists and etiquette books discussed the role of divorced parents at their child's wedding ceremony and counseled mothers on how to arrange sleeping accommodations for the cohabitants of their adult children when they visited. The law has begun to recognize financial obligations between members of shared households that parallel those of family law (Myricks, 1980). These developments have been counterbalanced by conservative political groups, who have seen this view of the family as dangerous and subversive. This controversy still appears to have a lot of energy and will exert considerable influence in defining the lifestyles that will be included as familistic and those that will be treated as deviant.

As reports on the alternatives begin to evaluate the outcomes and patterns of group marriage (Constantine, 1973) and communal life (Berger, 1981), the likelihood of major shifts in personal living arrangements seems quite modest. The toleration of these small minorities, when openly recognized, is less certain now than when these ideas were seen as signals for social change. Three categories of substitutes, varieties, and alternatives are examined as illustrating this range: (1) deinstitutionalization versus institutionalization; (2) blood versus emotional ties; and (3) regional and ethnic subcultural variations versus national cultural uniformity.

Deinstitutionalization versus Institutional Substitutes

The rise of the institutional household for living arrangements and as a substitute for the family seems to have reached its crest, except in the area of criminal justice. Orphanages and long-term-care hospitals for the disabled, the deficient, and the mentally and physically ill have been reexamined, and community- and family-based alternatives have been advocated. The institutional household in the twentieth century grew in complexity and specialization and now seems to be retreating to smaller, less complex, and less specialized facilities. Even within traditional settings, the least restrictive alternatives have been sought, and patients have been reclassified to take advantage of this new approach. This trend toward downscaling institutions and turning to in-home care significantly affects family lifestyles and choices. Several general problems have been identified: (1) role overload and the stereotyping of the homemaker as caregiver; (2) an extension of the dependency phase of the family life cycle; (3) failure to serve some individuals whose families reject the responsibility for special needs care; (4) conflict between family and institutional expectations; and (5) increased alternative costs to family members. The usual benefits include (1) improved individualized care of the individual in the family setting; (2) some economies in costs to larger social institutions; and (3) greater family control of and responsibility for quality of life.

In order to explore more specifically the costs and benefits of this trend for families, the following institutional alternatives are examined: medical, educational, child-care, elder-care, and criminal justice.

Medical Alternatives

Quality care in institutional settings is often evaluated by comparison to home- and family-care alternatives. One of the major forces in promoting deinstitutionalization has been the availability of drugs that control "acting-out" and aggressive behavior and medical regimens adapted to the less trained paraprofessional's or layperson's skills (Bassick & Gerson, 1978). Throwaway syringes, premeasured medicine, paper goods, disposal thermometer tips, and prepared dietetic foods are all part of the supporting technology for smaller care facilities and home-care alternatives. As home computers and assessment devices become more common and more cost-effective, further decentralization of substitute care may be possible.

Partial institutional solutions and respite care may be more common in the future and will allow kin and "future" kin to care for their relatives with special problems intensively, but not exclusively. Hospices for the terminally ill and birthing clinics for normal births are both contemporary examples of the trend toward partial institutions that encourage familial involvement. The barrier between hospitals and families appears to be weakening and is being replaced by a flexible interchange and the incorporating of family members into the health-care team. This trend seems to have good reason to continue and expand as technology, cost-benefit analyses, and social values run in the same direction (Sussman, 1980a). The assumption that the wife/mother is the appropriate family member to be on that medical team has not been examined in light of today's employment situation and egalitarian values. Alternative costs for home care have not always included an estimate of the lost earnings of the wife or other family members. In addition, actual expenditures beyond third-party payments or by the "patient" family member have often been omitted.

Educational Alternatives

In the area of education, the relationship between families and the educational institutions in the United States has not been clearly articulated. Many families have rejected the philosophy of education proposed by the public school system. The result is a proliferation of alternative private schools that propose to respond to parental values. In addition to literacy and cultural unification, educational institutions have been designated by law to press for integration of racial, ethnic, and socioeconomic groups; equal treatment of the sexes; and affirmation action for all. These mandates have not been thoroughly incorporated into public education and certainly have been unevenly recognized by families as normative. Scanzoni and Scanzoni (1976) noted that the continuing controversies among scholars contribute to the uncertainty.

To some extent, the need to use schools to accomplish these goals stemmed from the interaction between families and the housing market. Families made decisions about housing on the basis of assumed permanency in the school districts and patterns of education that supported race, class, and ethnic segregation, whether or not that was the family's immediate goal. The changes in schooling were a direct challenge to these decisions and values. Social-psychological researchers suggest that attitudes are changed by participation in group life and the experiencing of interaction with peers, role models, and persons of various religious and cultural backgrounds. It will not be surprising that some children of this generation may arrive at conclusions different from those of their parents. However, the ability of parents to prevent their children from participating in integrated schools has narrowed the number who may change (Weale, 1978). The continued proliferation of learning environments and individualized home instruction is feasible technologically and may be used to avoid confronting this social conflict between families and schools.

Although enchantment with the primary and secondary schools has decreased, participation by adults in various educational enterprises is still expanding. Longer life spans and good health, changing job requirements, and the expansion of education to adult learners in a variety of degree and nondegree programs support the future commitment to expanding adult education. More specifically, family life education itself has become popular. The current expansion of parent education and marriage enrichment education will continue, providing possibilities for a rapprochement with schooling and family life in the future (Brown, 1981).

Child-Care Alternatives

Child-care institutions have reexamined adoptability, foster-care styles, and group treatment thoroughly in recent times. Through the development of adoption exchange networks and changes in policy about appropriate families, many children thought nonadoptable have been successfully placed in substitute homes (Cole, 1976). *Accountability* is the word currently in vogue in foster care, and to some extent, it is becoming a reality, with closer supervision and periodic citizen and legal review (Fanshel, 1976; Pike, 1976; Settles, Van Name, & Culley, 1976). Permanency planning programs mean that children should be moved more quickly back into their own homes, with appropriate supports, or into adoption or permanent foster care. Foster care in the future may be more specialized and fine-tuned. Foster parents can be better trained to handle children with very special needs—physical, emotional, or social. Primary prevention and services in one's own home are being emphasized. The movement away from institutionalization and toward diversification of services is well established (Kadushin, 1976). Wiltse (1979) sees the attention to children's rights and developing contracts and written agree-

ments as major changes in the 1970s in child welfare services. These refinements in the foster-care and adoption systems may improve the way children are involved in alternatives to their families of origin. Aspiring to excellence in such services is an appropriate goal.

Day care and after-school care are currently in limbo. The need and utility of education for the preschool child are well established in the research work (Hoffreth, 1979). Group care, although it has been shown to be without negative outcome in the past few decades, has not taken the public fancy (Dail, 1982). Nursery schools are usually not counted as day care, although they may serve the purpose (Hoffreth, 1979). Beyond the fact that group care has been limited in availability, it has been without any glamour. It has been seen as allowing the welfare mother to get back to work rather than as a route to "prep" school for the middle class upwardly mobile family. In addition, a taint of presumed socialist or communist values is still attached to the concept.

Child care has been resistant to technological and marketing solutions, and little cost-effectiveness is generated by scaling up. No shortcuts to child care have appeared (Giele, 1979). Even though several franchising operations have attempted to create "McDonald's" standardization and availability of day care, these are still relatively modest efforts. Whether this problem can be addressed by a creative inventor or advertising specialist in the next few years is an open question.

After-school care appears to be less difficult to solve because of the length of the school day. Extracurricular activities involve less costly outside supports. Space is available in schools, on playgrounds, and at "Y's" and churches. Exemplary programs are being reported (Mayesky, 1979). Both parents' having jobs is now expected and even approved by most community members so that movement toward after-school care may be consistent with the community's values. Bringing together some of the extracurricular and enrichment activities of elementary-school children to common locations would conserve energy both in transportation and in the parents' own resources. Marketing and conceptual packages appear to be the major requirement for the expansion of child-care service in the future. The demand for child care, however, depends on both the fertility and the labor force participation of young women in the future (Hoffreth, 1979).

Elder-Care Alternatives

For the elderly, institutional substitutes for home environments have also been under reevaluation. Retirement communities and real estate/care-combination offerings are becoming more complex, offering the well-to-do elderly flexible options that change as the person's health needs change.

The enrichment of lifestyle alternatives for the affluent elderly has been recognized by a private industry as an opportunity to relieve the elderly of their resources. Alternatives for the middle class and the poor still tend to be single choices, for example, to enter or not to enter a nursing home or a state institution, or to sell out and live in an apartment. Dressel and Hess (1981) suggested that there is a wide variety of independent lifestyles that can serve elderly people in avoiding institutionalization, but they recognized the limited evidence of their success.

Increasing the range of choice for those less advantaged groups requires imagination, flexibility, and a more careful assessment of the needs and resources of both the elderly and their families. In discussing the family life of old people, Sussman (1976) suggested a number of innovations that could increase the possibilities of avoiding institutionalization. These "halfway-to-institutionalization" programs are not suitable for everyone but may expand choices for families of more limited means, if they can be made available at reasonable costs.

However, whether the current legislative push to support home care of the "frail" elderly will succeed or not depends not only on the financial incentives but on the availability of relatives who can care for the elderly (Steinmetz, 1981, 1983). As earlier noted, with secure health care, the "frail" elderly are often in their 80s or 90s, and their children are "spring chickens" of 60 or 70. It may be necessary to widen the search for grandchildren, siblings, and good friends to serve kinship functions.

Shanas and Sussman (1981) suggest that the elderly of the twenty-first century may need to search for a relative to care for them or to take appropriate action on their behalf.

Criminal Justice and Deviant-Behavior-Care Alternatives

The current technology for dealing with those deviants whose problems involve violence, conflict with the law, and repeated convictions is inadequate. With an increasingly heavy reliance on institutionalization and unevenly administered work rehabilitation and counseling programs, the offender has few opportunities to make a new life or to relate to his or her family in any meaningful way. The punishment is primarily to deprive these persons of family, friends, and support and to bring them into contact with criminals who have greater deviant skills. Although some alternatives have been tried, including probation and victim compensation, the deinstitutionalization of criminals is usually more a consequence of prison overcrowding or inadequate prosecution than a positive program of achieving the least restrictive settings.

Considerable political action has been mounting to increase the available prison space and to seek longer prison terms. This movement suggests a rejection of community- and family-centered approaches and a return to institutional solutions. Families of adjudicated criminals are not included in any meaningful way, in most programs for rehabilitation, although they are expected to absorb the person on release, and release itself may be predicated on the family's accepting the responsibility.

Summary of Care Alternatives. Institutionalization as a substitute for family support and care has continued to be seen as essential in criminal control, but it has fallen out of favor for the handicapped, the mentally ill, the elderly, and children. With the present medical and household technology, it has been assumed that these latter groups can be handled at home by women. Policymakers have assumed that women can be encouraged to care for persons with special needs in the family setting. However, the resources and support for this solution have not been forthcoming. Also, the competition with the marketplace for women's time will need to be altered by financial and emotional incentives.

Blood versus Emotional Ties: Variations in Family Structure

Defining one's family as those who function for one in familistic ways puts the emphasis on emotional and social support and networks. Residual in the American view of the family is a sense that the kinship charting itself has important meaning. When Alex Haley's romantic story of *Roots* (1976) took hold of America's imagination, part of the interest aroused was in finding out about individuals who had not functioned directly in one's close family. These latent ties were thought to give meaning to today's experiences. In another example of interest in kinship history, the Church of Jesus Christ of the Latter Day Saints has assembled an immense library that has as its primary purpose searching for ties so that members may bring these ancestors into the church's system (Kephart, 1976).

Although psychological theory and research have tended to emphasize the parent figure as most important, the current movement is toward identifying kin even when these kin have expressed the wish to be unknown. Adoption agencies are torn between their belief that ethically they owe clients of the past the confidentiality that they were promised and the reality of grown adoptees demanding to meet, to know, and to have records about their parents and other "lost kin" (Simpson, Timm, & McCubbin, 1981). Foster parents now commonly seek to adopt and to continue their ties with foster children in spite of being originally oriented toward acknowledging foster parenthood as a temporary tie. The termination of parental rights to free children for adoption is still a difficult process demanding great skill of agency workers and lawyers, as public attitudes about permanently breaking the blood ties are so negative. In divorce and remarriage, the child's relationship to the expanded family is not clearly defined. A long-lost father or mother who was denied custody or visitation or failed to fight for these rights may turn up with expectations of resurrecting the relationship. Children of divorce become couriers for sending messages among all the new families and households created out of the divorce. Divorce may also create extremely small units with few supports. These single-parent units may experience great alienation from other relatives.

Separated, divorced, never-married, and widowed single-parent homes may deal with relationships in a multitude of ways (Verazo & Hermon, 1980). They may become imbedded in their families of orientation and bring grandparents into the household. Remarriage, cohabitation, and friendship patterns add to the complexity of the alternatives. Fictive kin, neighbors, and colleagues have become more important to many families as the need for support networks has become identified. Research on resources for the nuclear family has drawn attention to how these patterns can be encouraged and developed.

Confusion over the functioning and meaning of emotional and kinship ties apparently will continue in the next few years with tests in the courts and confrontations among vested interests.

Regional and Ethnic Subcultural Variations versus National Cultural Uniformity

Ethnic and regional pride has reasserted itself both in America and in the world at large (Mendel & Habenstein, 1976). Fragmentation into smaller and more specific heritage groups has been encouraged both by scholarship and by public policy. Nationally, demands for representation are being solidified, and rationales and doctrines are being developed. Scholarship has encouraged a historic reexamination of earlier images and perceptions. In addition, the discovery of "unremembered" events, people, and data has enlarged the view of the past family as a part of one's subcultural and ethnic experience, and individual families have been encouraged to develop rituals and a greater expression of their relationship to older generations. Families are where the ethnic content is transmitted and used.

Among the indicators of these more positive attitudes toward separatism by cultural heritage has been the development of folk festivals, gourmet food magazines featuring ethnic foods, associations and organizations for ethnic groups, genealogical services, language instruction in so-called minor languages, and bilingualism in the schools (Naisbitt, 1982). Some searches for a connection to past immigration have led to young people's changing their names back to the more clearly identified form of the name, even when they propose to be in television or movies or to publish books (e.g., Wallace and Wallinsky). American Indian, Hispanic, and black organizations have particularly demonstrated the power of identity to shape public policy toward families. The point is that "ethnicity is the result of a process which continues to unfold" (Yancey, Eriksen, & Juliani, 1976).

In retrospect, the major changes that these sectors of the population have made in their access to the American society and the tempering of public discrimination has been one of the most dramatic changes ever made in a few

decades in any large country. These official changes have made a great deal of difference to many families in their interaction, their aspirations, and their actual quality of life. Although this shift is not conclusive and leaves many problems untouched, the negative stereotypes have been undermined, and the entry of these groups into the professions and trades provide opportunity for a further power base to be developed.

The maintenance of the identity of separate cultural heritages and the free access to a larger society present an extremely difficult problem of social balance. In many countries today, major conflicts are being fought in the streets over perceived inequities (e.g., in Southeast Asia, Ireland, Iran, South Africa, South and Central America, and the Middle East); less dramatic but as strongly felt differences appear in other countries (e.g., Canada, Belgium, India, and Pakistan). There are many possibilities for conflict in this country. A Mexican border-crosser in the Southwest, a Haitian landing in Florida, or a Cuban or Vietnamese arrived in the Northeast is definitely not in a secure situation in which to preserve her or his cultural background. Very likely, tensions will continue for families as to their identity vis-à-vis their subculture and social mobility. For example, the life course trajectory of black women varies more than that of white women (Spanier & Glick, 1980), including a greater range in the timing of life events such as marriage, children, employment, divorce, and remarriage. Staples (1976) noted a fairly large number of upwardly mobile blacks who also want to preserve some of their cultural traditions, usually associated with the lower class. If the opportunity for social mobility becomes more limited in the future, the ethnic support system may be more valuable. If economic recovery is successful and mobility opens up again, families may have less time and energy for investment in these subcultures as they learn the ways of their new occupations. Yancey *et al.* (1976) suggested that ethnicity, as it now operates, is embedded in the larger social structures and occupational patterns and merges with regionality.

Regional differences in family lifestyles reflect migration patterns and the ethnic groups represented in the population. In addition, family decisions about economic and recreational opportunities shape daily life and interest. Shaping life around an industry (e.g., chemical, automobile, mining, or high technology); an enterprise (e.g., farming, ranching, or fishing); or a service (e.g., government, fast foods, or education) gives a common meaning and destiny to the families in a community. Finding an outlet in the regional scene for family and individual tastes varies in potential. For example, sailing, hiking, hunting, music, theater, dance, organized sports, and hobbies are not evenly distributed across society, yet participation in such activities may well replace the support of kin strength of a subcultural experience.

The pull against ethnic and regional differentiation is found in the national and multinational efforts to develop a common set of expectations and tastes. Both governments and corporations seek some standardization. When one stops at the ''Burger King'' in Madrid, Spain, or in Newark, Delaware, the experience with young children is much the same for families. Brand names, quality standards, and media blitzes are organized to bring some symmetry to the vision and opportunities that families have in their lives. Continued interest in the variety and complexity of ethnic and regional subcultures is likely, but the movement toward national and international shared perspectives and artifacts is strong.

Transitions in Lifestyle over the Life Course

Family continuity has provided opportunities for vicarious satisfaction from one generation to the next. Using family relationships for a source of life's meaning and a handle on immortality has been a common experience over the centuries. With longer average life spans and lower overall fertility, some new opportunities and limitations are occurring. Smaller family size results in a more costly investment in each person. Unexpected early death is a threatening possibility, especially if small family size has been permanently guaranteed by sterilization. A ''black sheep'' or other nonresponsive family member is more costly when the group is small and each person is more crucial to its existence. Outliving one's friends and colleagues, as well as family members, is a real possibility for many people. The family may be reconstituted, or one may live with family memories and artifacts providing continuity. The responsibility for achievement and failure when one lives through others is a critical question. Will the child continue to have the implied responsibility to ''do his or her parent proud?'' Zimmerman (1971) maintained that this coloration of the family by the actions of one is an essential aspect of the family as an institution. Goffman (1963) examined stigma in a similar way. If this responsibility endures, at what level can the child be said to have sufficiently performed this task? Do the parents continue to have the responsibility to rescue their adult ''child'' from failures that may be blamed on parental interaction in childhood? It may be quite common for the child to return home several times after ''launching.'' The filial responsibility to support the family's elders has been diluted with social security, pension plans, and the decline of family businesses, but the future of these programs is questionable. However, the so-called Family Protection Act that has been proposed for legislation suggests creating incentives for intergenerational support. Inheritance becomes less important as a downward link between generations when elders live long past the point in children's careers where an inheritance could be helpful. Sussman (1982) maintained in his Burgess Award address that transfers during the lifetime of the elders are increasing.

Although new legislation has increased the amount of an estate that is exempted from federal taxation, many families argue more about how to pay the taxes than about who will benefit from the estate. Although the nuclear family size has been decreasing, the number of living generations is increasing. The overlap provides the possibility of long and intricate interaction and includes the opportunity to skip generations in seeking and giving support.

Continuity in family life provides the context for current events. One of the tragedies of divorce is the need to forget the good with the bad. The minor miracles and irritations of everyday life lose some of their interest when one lives alone, without the chatter of companions. When older people talk to any stranger and on any topic, it is often because they do not have anyone with whom they can have a real conversation. Peer solidarity may supply some of the interchangeable parts, especially on general events and nostalgic items, but seldom does the cohort generation have access to specific family events.

Family continuity provides recurring opportunities for people to do out-of-character and cross-generational activities that provide the materials for further elaboration. Taking the children or the grandparents to the fair or on a picnic reinforces the texture of the relationship. Second chances for families and individuals are more likely in future.

Prevalence and Durability of Various Family Types and Individual Lifestyles

In addition to recognizing the qualitative trends in family variations and alternatives, demographic findings suggest the future prevalence and durability of these arrangements and their relative influence on our culture.

Statistically, the current young-adult population appears to be postponing both marriage and children (Jones, 1980). This large element of our population has had a major impact on all our social institutions as they have grown up. The postponement of or potential permanent shift from the formation of nuclear families has concerned business and governmental planners. One of the major alternatives to marriage, cohabitation, has been increasing both in prevalence and in social acceptability (Macklin, 1978; also see Chapter 12 in this book). Although most cohabitation arrangements have a life history moving toward marriage or dissolution, the greater acceptance of these arrangements provides an alternative to marriage for many people at different life stages (Macklin, 1978). These postponements of marriage may finally result in fewer marriages, a substantially lower number of children for the cohort, and longer periods of child-free adult life (Glick, 1979). Glick (1979) believes that there will be a dampening effect, with smaller demographic changes in the next two decades than in the past two decades. Demographers who made inaccurate predictions during the Great Depression that were overturned by the baby boom after World War II are reluctant to predict a lower completed family size (''Changing American Family,'' 1977; Westoff, 1979).

Beale (1982) identified a number of areas in which forecasts for the 1970s failed to account for the trends that took place in population. Birth rates were 17% below the lowest projection and 23% below the most widely accepted projections. The simple fact is that, in the final analysis, cumulative decisions were made by the individuals making their own predictions about the future.

Also, there is the new interest in having children at an older age. A practice that was primarily confined to professional women and the poorest of the poor only a decade ago, having babies in middle age has become fashionable and even preferable for many (Golden, 1982). Although a reduction in overall fertility may be an artifact of age distribution and the economy, some demographers believe that there is a strong likelihood that a catch-up pattern of childbearing will *not* occur (Westoff, 1979). Child spacing is apparently being confined to shorter spans of time (Glick, 1977). Perhaps the fear of two children in diapers has vanished with the disposable diaper; more realistically, the need to limit the impact of childbearing on work patterns has become crucial.

The high rates of divorce and remarriage appear to be stabilizing (Glick, 1979). The actual length of marriages may not be changing very rapidly. Longer life expectancies make it possible for people to survive several marriages, each of which is as long as many lifetime marriages were in colonial days. In addition, those committed to long-term marriages have the potentiality for records in length and durability of relationships (Bane, 1976). Certainly, in comparison to other personal relationships, families are among the more stable sources of long-term relationship. Adults can expect longer periods of child-free older married life (Glick, 1979). Widowhood continues to be more common for women than is widower status for men. Most men and women will live alone several times during their adult lives. As Glick (1980) noted, the ideal of marriage is still highly regarded, but satisfaction often requires the second attempt. Women should expect to spend a major portion of their lives in a postmarriage period (Lopata, 1973). Guttentag and Secord (1983) detailed many implications of the larger ratio of women to men in some cohorts today. Children are more likely to have a single parent as they grow up. Single parenthood is becoming a normal phenomenon that is not as frequently being treated as deviant, but that is still being associated with poverty (Glick, 1979). Teenage mothers and children continue to be a major component of this sector of families. (See also Chapter 21 in this book.)

Rural living has had an infusion of interest, and for the first time, many rural areas are experiencing the immigration of younger families (Coward, 1980; Hauser, 1981). Some decayed inner cities have bottomed out and are being redeveloped as family-centered, somewhat elite communities (Steinlab & Hughes, 1980). Both extremes of the urban and rural situation look more promising. Family-environment suburban areas developed after World War II are now declining, and new housing starts and renovation projects are not expected soon. Pressure on families to accommodate to smaller homes and apartments or to double up with other family units is a long-term trend.

Family Dynamics: Intimacy, Involvement, and Conflict

Most people have their longest and most intimate contacts with others in the family setting. The length of family and marital contact may be longer than previously because of increased longevity and frequency of marriage. Even after divorce and remarriage occur, these original contracts are probably the most permanent of any that people have (Furstenberg, 1979). Instead of viewing affection and sexuality as by-products of a marital union that were simply outcomes of other processes making the marriage viable, these items have become for many the primary rationale for marriage. Quality of life in intimate personal relationships has become the standard for measuring marital success and continued commitment, at least in Western industrialized societies (Campbell, Converse, & Rodgers, 1976).

Although these matters have assumed primary consideration, families have not found them easy to discuss. There has been a strong reaction against formal education in sexuality and family relationships in the schools and churches, and there has not been a concurrent growth of informal education between parent and child (Brown, 1981). The demand to inform parents of children's seeking birth control materials seems not to be based on closer family communication, but on the need to control the agencies' service to minors (Rossoff, 1982a). The potentiality of sexual overtones or action between parents and children and other family members apparently is still so anxiety-producing that communication on these matters is inhibited.

The expression of affection between generations appears to have become more prevalent. Fathers find it easier to express warmth and support to children of both sexes, both as infants and as young adults. The consequences of expressing more feelings between generations may be seen in the next few years as young adults decide how to interact with their older parents and how they want to relate to their own children. Some of the consequences are likely to differ from the classical psychoanalytic model of development or the Parsonian expressive-instrumental view of parental roles, because of the other normative changes that have occurred. The "new fatherhood," as James Levine (1982) characterized these changes, has important benefits for the parent as well as for the child.

Expressiveness has also been attached to the process of having children. The enrichment of both fathers' and mothers' roles in the birth of their babies and the subsequent child care has been a strong trend in the past two decades. Birth and parent education classes have grown rapidly and have affected the style and content of the medical regimen (Block, Norr, Meyering, Norr, & Charles, 1981). The success of these programs suggests that families perceived the need for such support at the transition to parental status and were open to the forum in which it was given. This kind of education for family life will continue to be important.

Involvement in close family interaction provides an opportunity not only for the expression of affection, but also for playing out negative emotions and actions.

In addition, to the positive aspects of increased expressiveness within the family the opportunity for sexual assault, incest, and mental and physical violence occur in this same private setting (Steinmetz, 1981; see also Chapter 26 of this book).

Grand conflicts require family ties to mature in complexity, scope, and impact. Families can cling to incidents over time and organize current life around them. Lesser groups give up too soon, and only ''world'' powers have more weapons to throw into disputes. Case studies from family therapy (Minuchin, 1974; Walsh, 1982) and stage plays illustrate the intrigue and power of family conflicts across generations and eras. Shakespeare told the stories on a grand scale, and modern authors find smaller, but equally intense, tragedies. Even when stressed to the breaking point, families have the enduring ability to fight.

For example, divorce is an interesting institution in the process of family conflict. Although the legal aspects of the conflict are resolved and the family unwinds as a unit, the argument may continue unabated. Children and former relatives can carry messages, and certainly, murder and mayhem are still possible. Conflict, stress, and violence have been major foci for research in the last decade, and a more complete understanding of these processes may be forthcoming. The relationships among the family processes, individual adjustment, and the ecological milieu in producing and continuing conflicts are being delineated.

Perceptions of conflicts in the outside world influence the internal dynamics of family life. For the young people, who never knew a world without the potential for nuclear war and total devastation, it is hard to imagine how many of their elders do not see a flaming holocaust as a possible future. Living closer to the present in imagination is a protection against the unthinkable. Burying oneself in everyday existence has often been the way of families fighting for elementary survival. Unless much greater security is delivered to families in the near future, there is unlikely to be great innovation in family lifestyle or commitment to future change. In cross-cultural surveys, people express short-range pessimism and long-range optimism over the issue of world war and armament (Ornaurer et al., 1976), and people see the nation-state as the actor, not the individual or the family. Currently, the popular press (Kelly, 1982; Lifton & Falk, 1983; Schell, 1982) is focusing on these visions. Political and social action groups are actively seeking to draw attention to these critical decisions and to involve families in socialization.

It is not clear that outside factors are going to change enough to radically alter the amount, the type, or the intensity of family conflicts in the near future, although intervention to resolve conflicts may improve. However, the growth of self-help groups, group therapy, family counseling, and family service programs suggests that intervention and change may alleviate some of the long-term effects.

Models for Describing the Futures of Families

Predictive models for describing the futures of families are still in the process of development. The codification, explication, and integration of theories applied to families were a major scholarly enterprise of the 1970s. Interest in theory and related methodological concerns was expressed in the organization of a theory workshop at the National Council on Family Relations. Family research has been reviewed and explained in terms of selected theoretical perspectives (Burr, Hill, Nye, & Reiss, 1979). The number and complexity of relationships to outside variables and among family members is overwhelming, when it comes to selecting what warrants a judgment for the future. Five major theoretical schemes are examined in detail in the Burr, Hill, Nye, and Reiss volume (1979): choice exchange and the family (Nye); symbolic interaction and the family (Burr, Seigh, Day, & Constantine); a general systems approach to the family (Broderick & Smith); conflict theory and the study of marriage and the family (Sprey); and the phenomenological sociology of the family (McLain & Weigart).

Each of these approaches has some mechanisms for understanding change and stability in families and presents some specific comments about the future. For example, Sprey noted in his conclusion that the deep structure—which contains the potential for *orderly* change—is limited. To discover what is and what is not possible must be a major part of the conflict approach. Also, McLain and Weigart suggested that the family is likely to remain a universal form of human organization and experience because it balances objective and subjective experience for the individual.

At the same time as family scholars have pursued the integrative and application tasks related to family theories that are not political, scholars in black and women's studies have been interested in theories that analyze the family for enhancing a potential for change. For example, housework has received more scholarly attention in this last decade because of its theoretical importance to the relationships of the family, the political economy, and change (Malos, 1980; Millet, 1970; Oakley, 1974; Strasser, 1982).

The 1970s were a productive time for theoretical development in family therapy. Theories that specify the processes by which an individual family may be assisted in making changes and predictions (Kantor & Lehr, 1975) note the importance of the family's future-orienting behavior in the way family strategies operate. However, theoretical statements and therapy are, of course, centered on the individual family as a point in time and do not attempt to link it to the trends of society.

My own current thinking about models of family change tends toward an eclectic borrowing from several of these views. Especial debts are owned to Sussman and Shanas for the linkage concept and to Nye for exchange and choice; however, neither those nor others need be blamed for my estimate of the future prospects of the family (based on Settles, 1976).

Briefly, to review my perspective, four figures are used to summarize the main components in this simple approach: (1) areas of choice for the individual are affected by constraints in the society that may be modified by social processes; (2) mechanisms that link the family to other institutions may inhibit or promote change; (3) these

mechanisms of interface affect change by social processes; and (4) families (and individuals) may take action to change their relationship to other institutions, but the costs vary.

Areas of Choice and Social Processes

The life space of an individual varies from culture to culture, within societies, and over a lifetime. In Figure 1, seven of these constraints are identified with the social processes that tend to be relevant to them adjacent to the constraint. For example, roles tend to be less clearly specified and more flexible when there is rapid social change in general and when individuals participate in numerous separate groups. More freedom is not necessarily more pleasant for individuals; they may experience feelings of insecurity and may be overwhelmed by complexity. However, constraint, after flexibility has been experienced, often leads to boredom and a felt loss in indi-

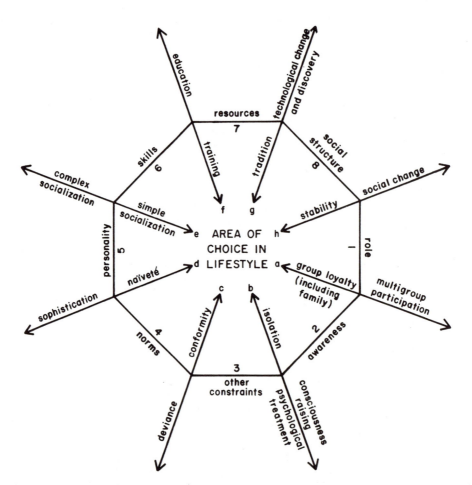

Figure 1. Areas of choice in lifestyle and processes which restrict or enlarge choice. Cross bars indicate movable or variable states. Spokes suggest processes for affecting the states, the direction of greater choice moving outward on the spokes.

Table 1. Mechanisms Which Link Specific Families to Social Institutions and Potentiality for Change

Mechanism	Family	Society
Brokerage	1. An individual or individuals may develop skills in finding and relating to appropriate institutional supports, e.g., parent education.	1. Institutions may train and appoint brokers to relate to families or individuals, e.g., social workers, public health nurses, lawyers, doctors, peer counselors.
	2. Family representatives may form interest groups to deal with institutions, e.g., PTA, Parents without Partners, Parents Anonymous.	2. Institutions may attempt to bring families or individuals together as populations to be handled as groups, e.g., community organizations.
		3. Institutions may develop information, propaganda, advertising, and other outreach to the brokers in each family, e.g., television, direct mail.
Participation	1. Individuals from the family may become involved in other institutions, e.g., go to school or out to work.	1. Institutions may become involved with family, e.g., family therapy, parent support groups.
Isolation and/or privacy	1. Families may withdraw from institutions that threaten their equilibrium in subcultural groups such as Amish, communes, at-home alternative education.	1. Barriers for participation or brokerage from families may be made to exclude some types of families and/or individuals, e.g., referral required by a doctor, records confidentiality, eligibility requirements.
	2. Families may evade institutional norms by use of closed doors, etc., e.g., child abuse, wife beating.	2. Institutions may not collect or analyze information to access the needs of targeted families and present unattractive programs, e.g., some public schools, churches, government agencies.
Incentives and disincentives	1. Families may evaluate the impact of the changes for themselves, e.g., decisions on savings and investment, choice of home.	1. Institutions may change their mandates, e.g., access to the handicapped, disintegration, equity hiring policies.
	2. Familial behavior may change, requiring institutional response, e.g., proportion of women in work force.	2. Families may change the institutions costs–benefits equilibrium by behavior demanding evaluation, e.g., legal suit, grievance, publicity.

viduality and freedom. With modernization, the overall trend in these processes has been toward greater choice, and an occasional countertrend has occurred toward more rigid definitions for individuals and families.

Linking Families to Other Institutions and Potentiality for Change

Four of the mechanisms that link families to other institutions are examined (see Table 1). Each of these mechanisms may be encouraged or discouraged by both the family and the institution.

Brokerage. The terms *broker* and *brokerage* are used in the context of this discussion to indicate the special role that both families and other institutions may create to deal specifically with interaction between social institutions. In a complex society, knowledge of the potential resources and ideas that an individual could use is difficult to obtain. Information overload is one strain. The indexing and accesses are complex and are often phrased in technical language. (There is a long-standing ''No one cares as much as you.'') In a myriad of problem areas these homilies are true. The family may, however, serve this role of broker for the individual. For example, the health care of a dependent child is almost wholly at the mercy of the values and the sophistication of the family members. A diversity of health care is available even for the poorest family, if a family member can make a meaningful contact with the healthy delivery system. Apparently, the most useful contact is ordinarily with another institution that can make referral. In the office, job hotlines and guidance counselors have been used. Families have, for example, tapped the skills of teenagers in relating to educational institutions when the mother wants to return to school to update her job skills. Although in a traditional, rather stable society brokers may be designated and identified by ascription, in a society where complexity and change are the mode, knowledge, skill, and assertiveness may be more important determinants of the brokers.

Participation. A participant can be a good broker but may or may not have the large picture of resources and the range of possibilities. Being involved with a family in a participatory manner is a risky enterprise for an institution. In most cases, the institution is not able to take long-term total responsibility for the family or its individuals. At best, such participation is a therapeutic interval or an intensive educational experience that has some built-in closure. At worst, the institutional interaction breaks down the familial boundaries without achieving some new organizational level. The participation of a family member can provide information, resources, skills, awareness, and so on, which allow more choice, or it may reinforce more rigid definitions. Consciousness raising has been one of the important participation experiences that has led to change in families.

Isolation and/or Privacy. Many of the changes in the occupational world that have been influenced by sex roles result in a breaking down of private communication networks within institutions and between families. When mandated change requires intrusion into the ''sacred'' privacy of the home, for example, laws protecting children and elderly, then resistance occur. Institutions can also enforce isolation. The exclusively men's luncheon club is an example that women come across in the occupational scene. In dealing with families, institutions frequently maintain their boundaries by elaborate application forms and the demand for referrals and recommendations. It is quite clear that the mechanism of

isolation may be used to reduce contact between certain families and certain institutions. This reduction can be initiated by either the family or the institution or both.

Incentives/Disincentives. The society does change the costs and benefits to families for different actions. There are limitations on the manipulations of these mechanisms for possible change. Questions of equity in terms of the family may be quite differently answered when individuals are considered. Enforcement of the new pattern of incentives or disincentives may not be simply achieved; achieving consensus in the community may be difficult. Those sanctions that have quick, sure consequences are likely to be the most effective. It is difficult to keep up interest in preschool day-care reform when your children are growing up and need after-school care or alternatives to the Little League. Affirmative action suits wear down a family's energy and interest. Many legal schedules simply overwhelm families and prevent their use. Another example from foster care and adoption procedures is that children simply grow up before any solution is developed. By the time some questions of equity for the child and the family may be decided legally, they are simply not relevant to that family. The family, as an institution, may gain some overall change out of the use of test cases, but usually, the isolated family unit rarely benefits directly from participation in any enforcement procedures that they initiate through the legal system. Some incentives are being discussed today to encourage families to assume more care of members throughout their lifetime.

Effect of the Mechanisms on Potential for Change. In Figure 2, the hypothesized effect of the mode of interface on the social processes leading to change is noted. Again,

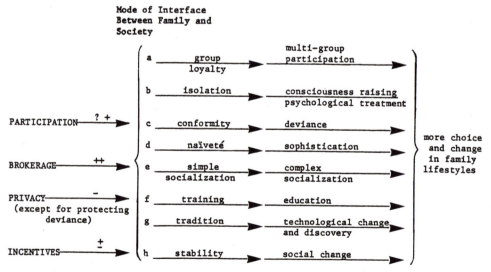

Figure 2. Effect of mechanism of interface on social processes that support change in family lifestyle: + = toward change; − = toward stability.

the general picture is toward more choice and change for families overall. Even privacy may have a protective function in those deviant behaviors related to long-term change.

The Family's Impact on Change in Other Institutions. Although families are usually analyzed from the direction of how outside institutions impact on them, there is more attention to the choices available to families in impacting on institutions. Table 2 details how a family might analyze the costs and benefits of different types of action in effecting change. For example, families and individuals may use a formal grievance procedure in affirmative action, handicapped access, age discrimination,

Table 2. A Comparison of the Utility of Formal and Informal Action Effecting Change for a Family in Dealing with an Outside Institution

Situations	Formal action	Informal action
1. The stakes are high:	High	Low
—survival: professional, personal dignity, familial unity		
—many people have the problem	High	Low
2. The person and family are strong:		
—mentally	High	Low
—physically	High	Low
3. Group support is available to the family:		
—social	High	Low
—monetary	High	Low
—agency	High	Low
4. The institution is strongly resisting change.	High	Low
5. The emotional state of the individual and the family members is:		
—unrelenting anger	High	Low
—depressed	Low	High
—mixed	Low	High
6. The issue, although relevant, is not crucial.	Low	High
7. The individual (and the family) has an idiosyncratic grievance.	Low	High
8. The person and the family are unable to handle long strain:		
—physical	Low	High
—emotional	Low	High
9. The family knows influential people who have resources to apply.	Low	High
10. The institution desires to comply with the mandated change.	Low	High

and complaints or may choose to use an informal inquiry to attempt to get a resolution of the problem. A family may be able to develop a strategy to make the institution more responsive to its needs. Although conservative countertrends have received a great deal of attention in recent years, it is unlikely that these forces will, in the long term, stem the overall increase of the choices and options of families.

More specifically, the following ideas appear to have vigor for the future of families. Making estimates and predictions is always a dangerous occupation for families or writers, but our lives are based on making predictions.

Return to Restricted Options.

1. Conservative trends in defining and regulating the family have sufficient energy to be important in both the industrial and the developing nations.

2. Individual families will bridge the two trends with a variety of evasions and compartmental thinking.

3. Relating secular and sacred views of the family will continue to frustrate philosophers and theologians dealing with new realities about choice and decision making.

Continuity in Trends for Families.

1. Images of historical and cross-cultural descriptions of family life will continue to be revised as scholarship becomes more intense and refined.

2. The classic tie of technological change and family change will be redefined to include more individual solutions because of more flexible, diffuse technologies.

3. The trend toward employment outside the home for men, women, and older children will continue even in Third World nations, although some tasks can be done in the home "workshop."

4. Women will continue to bear most of the costs of technological and family change in the near future.

5. Redefinition of family roles toward equity will continue in spite of the trend to maintain traditional roles.

6. Providing continuity for individual life transitions will continue to be an important function of life in the family.

7. Family life will continue to be the major opportunity to have intense relationships of long-term endurance expressing both affection and conflict.

8. Adult dyadic relationships resulting in marriage will continue to be long-term, but they are also likely not to be lifelong or monagamous.

9. The primary tie between parents and children will continue to be the most enduring of familial relationships, including both the adopted and the foster child.

10. Single-parent families will continue to be a common experience for children, at least for a portion of their childhood.

11. Complexity in family arrangements will continue to increase with former spouse; and longer lifetimes, rearrangements contributing the range of potential interactive people.

12. Continuity and functionality of kinship ties will be further refined, accounting for divorce, remarriage, and more surviving generations.

13. Small family size in the nuclear family appears likely in the next few years as the result of decisions already made by the present childbearing cohort, including the teenagers.

14. Families will continue to be the most convenient and cost-effective living arrangement across the life span, but not the exclusive choice for all.

Trends in Family Substitutes and Alternatives.

1. Family substitutes are more likely to be small-scale informal "families" than major formal institutions such as schools, hospitals, and day-care centers.

2. The current trend of building large-scale prisons will result in large capital investments; these prisons will soon be as vacant as the elementary schools and the tuberculosis hospitals, but there will not be a major shift in the direction of family-centered care for deviant behavior.

3. The family will continue to be the institution that handles the leftover problems of society and that provides the advocate for the person with special needs; brokerage skills will be even more important.

4. Cohabitation, communal arrangements, and other group-oriented alternatives to traditional marriage and family will continue to serve the needs of selected groups.

5. Single lifestyles will be a major part of most people's lives.

Anticipated Changes in Family Life.

1. The present concern with ethnicity and regional differences in family lifestyles will be less pervasive when economic mobility opportunities reopen and the barriers to migration are relaxed.

2. Families will have more opportunity to choose therapeutic and support strategies with a more precise knowledge of their efficiency and results.

3. A major redrafting of family law and practice will be needed to incorporate the family's increasingly sophisticated responsibilities toward one another and over the life cycle.

4. Coordinated social action for narrowly defined humanitarian goals will become more common among nation-states, bringing improved quality of life to families.

5. Families will be organized not around the concept of dependency but around interdependency.

6. Living arrangements may be more closely related to current family needs, with investment in housing as homeplace less critical to family definition.

Families of the future will no doubt be more inventive and interesting than this discussion has suggested. If we can catch up to these decisions in our research as they happen, we will indeed be fortunate.

ACKNOWLEDGMENTS

I wish to thank David Schulz, Suzanne Steinmetz, and Marvin Sussman for their many helpful suggestions on this chapter, as well as the graduate students in family studies at the University of Delaware, whose reactions helped to clarify the presentation.

References

Adams, B. N. *Kinship in an urban setting.* Chicago: Markam, 1968.

Adams, D. *The hitchhiker's guide to galaxy.* New York: Pocket Books, 1979.

Aldous, J. *Family careers.* New York: Wiley, 1978.

Aldous, J., & Dumon, W. *The politics and programs of family policy.* Notre Dame: University of Notre Dame and Leuvan University Press, 1980.

The American family bent, but not broken. *U.S. News and World Report,* June 16, 1980.

Andrews, L. B. Embryo technology. *Parents Magazine,* May 1981, 63–69.

Bane, M. J. *Here to stay: American families in the twentieth century.* New York: Basic Books, 1976.

Bassick, E. L., & Gerson, S. Deinstitutionalization and mental health services. *Scientific American,* 1978, *238*(2), 46, 53.

Beale, C. L. The six population surprises of the 1970's. *Intercom,* 1982, *10*(5), 6.

Beit-Hallahmi, B. The kibbutz family: Revival or survival. *Journal of Family Issues,* 1981, *2*(3), 259–274.

Bell, D. *The coming of the post-industrial society.* New York: Basic Books, 1973.

Berger, B. *The survival of a counter culture.* Berkeley: University of California Press, 1981.

Bergesen, A. Political witch hunts: The sacred and the secular in cross national perspective. *American Sociological Review,* 1977, *42*(2), 220–223.

Bernard, J. *The future of marriage.* New York: World Publishing, 1972.

Block, C. R., Norr, K. L., Meyering, S., Norr, J. l., & Charles, A. G. Husband gatekeeping at birth. *Family Relations,* 1981, *30*(2), 197–204.

Boulding, K. E. *Ecodynamics.* Beverly Hills, Calif.: Sage Publications, 1978.

Brown, L. (Ed.). *Sex education in the eighties: The challenge of healthy sexual revolution.* New York: Plenum Press, 1981.

Burgess, E. W., & Locke, H. J. *The family: From institution to companionship.* New York: American Book, 1945.

Burr, W. R., Hill, R., Nye, E. I., & Reiss, I. L. *Contemporary theories about the family,* (Vols. 1, 2). New York: Free Press, 1979.

Campbell, A., Converse, P. E., & Rodgers, W. L. *The quality of American life.* New York: Russell Sage Foundation, 1976.

The Changing American Family. *Editorial Research Reports,* June 3, 1977, 430.

Cherlin, A., & Walters, P. B. Trends in United States men's and women's sex role attitude 1972–78. *American Sociological Review,* 1981, *46*(4), 453–460.

Cole, E. *Trends in family formation and dissolution: The case of adoptions, Implications for Policy.* Groves Conference, Kansas City, Missouri, March 1976.

Constantine, L. L. Open family: A life style for kids and other people. *The Family Coordinator,* 1977, 113–131.

Cooper, D. *The death of the family.* New York: Vintage Books, 1970.

Constantine, L. L. Group marriage: A study of contemporary mutilated marriage. New York: Macmillan, 1973.

Coward, R. T. Rural families changing but retaining distinctiveness. *Rural Development Perspectives,* USDA RDP 3, October 1980, 4–8.

Creationism. *Academe,* 1982, *68*(2), 10.

Crutchfield, C. F. Medical treatment for minor children: The roles of parents, the state, the child and the Supreme Court of the United States. *Family Relations,* 1981, 30(2), 165–178. (a)

Crutchfield, C. F. Medical treatment for minor children: Replies to Zimmerman and Rodman. *Family Relations,* 1981, 30(2), 185–186. (b)

Dail, P. Who will mind the child—A dilemma for many employed parents. *Journal of Home Economics*, 1982, *74*(1), 22–23.

Dean, G., & Gurak, D. T. Marital homogamy, the second time around. *Journal of Marriage and the Family*, 1978, 40(3) 559–569.

Decker, R., & Decker, B. The eruptions of Mount St. Helens. *Scientific American*, 1981, *244*(3), 68–91.

Drabek, T. E., & Boggs, K. S. Families in disaster: Reactions and relatives. *Journal of Marriage and the Family*, 1968, *30*, 443–51.

Dressel, P., & Hess, B. B. *Alternatives for the elderly*. Groves Conference, May 1981, Mount Pocono, Pennsylvania.

Duvall, E. M. *Family development*. Philadelphia: J. B. Lippincott, 1957.

Duvall, E. M. *Marriage and family development*. Philadelphia: J. B. Lippincott, 1977.

Ebaugh, H. R. F., & Haney, A. C. Shifts in abortion attitudes: 1972–1978. *Journal of Marriage and the Family*, 1980, *42*(3), 491–499.

Edwards, J. N., & Kluck, P. Patriarchy—The last universal. *Journal of Social Issues*. 1980, *3*, 317–337.

Eichler, M. *The double standard, A feminist critique of feminist social science*. New York: St. Martin's Press, 1980.

Elder, G. H., Jr. History and the family: The discovery of complexity. *Journal of Marriage and the Family*, 1981, *143*(3), 489–515.

Elshtain, J. B. *The family in political thought*. Amherst: University of Massachusetts Press, 1982.

Etzioni, A. The family: Is it obsolete? *Journal of Social Issues*, 1977, 47–51.

Falloon, I. R. H., Boyd, J. L., McGill, C. W., Razoni, J., Mosi, H. B., & Gilderman, A. M. Family management in the prevention of the exacerbations of schizophrenia: A controlled study. *The New England Journal of Medicine*, 1982, *306*(24), 1437–1440.

Fanshel, D. Computerized information systems and foster care. *Children Today*, 1976, *5*(6), 14–18, 44.

Fertile-Bishop, S., & Gilliam, M. In view of the veil: Psychology of clothing in Saudi Arabia. *Journal of Home Economics*, 1981, *73*(4), 24–26.

Francoeur, A. H., & Francoeur, R. (Eds.). *The future of sexual relations*. Englewood Cliffs, N.J.: Prentice-Hall, 1974.

Frost, R. *The poems of Robert Frost*. New York: Random House, Modern Library, 1946.

Furstenberg, F. F. Recycling the family: Perspectives for a neglected family form. *Marriage and Family Review*, 1979, *2–3*, 1–21.

Giele, J. Z. Changing sex roles and family structure. *Social Policy*, 1979, *9*(4), 32–44.

Ginzberg, E. The professionalization of the U.S. labor force. *Scientific American*, 1981, *240*(3), 48–53.

Glick, P. C. A demographer looks at American families. *Journal of Marriage and the Family*, 1975, *37*, 15–26.

Glick, P. C. Updating the life cycle of the family. *Journal of Marriage and the Family*, 1977, *39*(1), 5–13.

Glick, P. C. The future of the American family. *Current Population Reports: Special Studies*, Series D-23, No. 78, January 1979.

Glick, P. C. Remarriage: Some recent changes and variations. *Journal of Family Issues*, 1980, *1*(4), 455–478.

Goffman, E. *Stigma: Notes on the management of spoiled identity*. Englewood Cliffs, N.J.: Prentice-Hall, 1963.

Golden, F. Here come the micro kids. *Time*, May 3, 1982, 50–51.

Gottschalk, E. C., Jr. Exploring the myths about the American family. *Family Circle*, December 13, 1977.

Guttentag, M., & Second, P. F. *Too many women?* Beverly Hills, Calif.: Sage Publications, 1983.

Haley, A. *Roots*. Garden City, N.Y.: Doubleday, 1976.

Hareven, T. *American families in transition: Historical perspectives on change*. Research Forum on Family Issues, White House Conference on Families, Washington, D.C., April 1980.

Harris, L., & Associates, Inc. The General Mills, American Family Report, 1980–81, *Families at Work, Strength and Strains*. Minneapolis, Minn.: General Mills, 1981.

Hassinger, E. W. *The rural component of America*. Danville, Ill.: Interstate Printers and Publishers, 1981.

Hauser, P. The Census of 1980. *Scientific American*, 1981, *245*(5), 53–61.

Heer, D. M., & Grossbard-Schectman, A. The impact of the women's liberation movement in the U.S., 1960–1975. *Journal of Marriage and the Family*, 1981, *43*(1), 49–63.

Henderson, D. The eradication of smallpox. *Scientific American*, 1976, *235*(4), 25–33.

Hertz, R. Family in the kibbutz: A review of authority relations and women's status. *Marriage and Family Review*, 1982, *5*(2), 29–50.

Hill, R. *Deos the family have a future?* Presented at Cooperative Extension Workshop, November 7, 1978.

Hill, R., & Hansen, D. A. Families under stress. In H. Christensen (Ed.), *Handbook on marriage and the family*. Chicago: Rand McNally, 1964.

Hoffreth, S. L. Day care in the next decade. *Journal of Marriage and the Family*, 1979, *41*(3), 649–658.

Isaacson, W. The battle over abortion. *Time*, April 6, 1981. 20–24.

Jones, L. Y. *Great expectations*. New York: Coward, McCann and Geoghegan, 1980.

Kadushin, A. Child welfare service past and present. *Children Today*, 1976, *5*(3), 16–23.

Kamerman, S. B., & Kahn, A. J. (Ed.). *Family policy, government, and families in fourteen countries*. New York: Columbia University Press, 1978.

Kantor, D., & Lehr, W. *Inside the family*. San Francisco: Jossey-Bass, 1975.

Kaslow, F. W. History of family therapy: A kaleidoscopic overview. *Marriage and Family Review*, 1980, *3*, 77–111.

Kelly, J. Thinking the unthinkable, rising fears about nuclear war. *Time*, March 29, 1982, 10–14.

Kent, O. Remarriage: A family systems perspective. *Social casework*, 1980, 146–154.

Kephart, W. M. *Extraordinary groups: The sociology of unconventional life styles*. New York: St. Martin's press, 1976.

Laswell, M., & Laswell, T. *Marriage and family*. Lexington, Mass.: D. C. Heath, 1982.

Levine, J. *The new fatherhood*. Groves Conference, Ocean City, Maryland, June 1982.

Lifton, R. J., & Falk, R. *Indefensible weapons*. New York: Basic Books, 1983.

Lindsay, B. (Ed.). *Comparative perspectives of Third World women*. New York: Praeger, 1980.

Litwak, E. Geographic mobility and extended family cohesion. *American Sociological Review*, 1960, *25*, 385–394.

Lopata, H. Z. *Widowhood in an American city*. Cambridge, Mass.: Schenkman, 1973.

Mace, D. Marriage and family enrichment: A new field. *The Family Coordinator*, 1975, *24*, 171–173.

Macklin, E. D. Nonmarital heterosexual cohabitation. *Marriage and Family Review*, 1978, *1*(2), 1–12.

Macklin, E. D. Nontraditional family forms: A decade of research. *Journal of Marriage and the Family*, 1980, 905–922.

Malcolm, J. A reporter at large: Family therapy, the one way mirror. *The New Yorker*, May 15, 1978, 39.

Malos, E. *The politics of housework*. London: Allison & Busby, 1980.

Mayesky, M. E. Extended day programs in a public elementary school. *Children Today*. 1979, *8*(3), 6–10.

Mendel, C. H., & Habenstein, R. W. *Ethnic families in America*. New York: Elsevier, 1976.

Millet, K. *Sexual politics.* Garden City, N.Y.: Doubleday, 1970.

Minuchin, S. *Families and family therapy.* Cambridge: Harvard University Press, 1974.

Myricks, N. Palimony: The impact Marvin vs. Marvin. *Family Relations,* 1980, *29*(2), 210–215.

Naisbett, J. *Megatrends.* New York: Warner Books, 1982.

Nisbit, R. *History of the idea of progress.* New York: Basic Books, 1980.

Oakley, A. *The sociology of housework.* New York: Pantheon Books, 1974.

Ogburn, W. F., & Nimkoff, M. F. *Technology and the changing family.* Boston: Houghton Mifflin, 1955.

Ornaurer, H., Wiberg, H., Sicinski, A., & Galtung, J. (Eds.). *Images of the world in the year 2000: A comparative ten nation study.* Atlantic Highlands, N.J.: Humanities Press, 1976.

Parsons, T., & Bales, R. F. *Family, socialization and interaction Process.* Glencoe, Ill.: Free Press, 1955.

Pickett, R. S. Tomorrow's family. *Intellect,* April 1977, 330–332.

Pike, V. Permanent planning for foster children. *Children Today,* 1976, *3*(6), 14–18, 44.

Pines, M. Genetic profile will put our health in our own hands. *Smithsonian,* 1976, *4,* 86–90.

Rainwater, L. Notes on U.S. family policy. *Social Policy,* March–April 1978, 28–30.

Reed, J. D. The new baby boom. *Time,* February 22, 1982, 52–58.

Rodman, H. Understanding the United States Supreme Court's position on parental consent requirements: In defense of Danforth and Bellotte, A response to Butchfield. *Family Relations,* 1981, *30*(2), 182–184.

Rogers, R. H. *Family interaction and transition.* Englewood Cliffs, N.J.: Prentice-Hall, 1973.

Rossoff, J. L. New data shed light on parent notice impact. *Washington Memo.* New York: Alan Guttmoucher Institute, April 9, 1982. (a)

Rossoff, J. L. *Washington memo.* New York: Alan Guttmoucher Institute, March 19, 1982. (b)

Ryder, N. B. The family in developed countries. *Scientific American,* 1974, *231*(3), 122–132.

Saflios-Rothschild, C. *Love, sex, and sex roles.* Englewood Cliffs, N.J.: 1977.

Saving the family: Special report, families on the couch. *Newsweek.* May 15, 1978, 63–90.

Scanzoni, J., & Scanzoni, J. *Men, women and change.* New York: McGraw-Hill, 1976.

Schell, J. *The fate of the earth.* New York: Avon Books, 1982.

Schorr, A., & Moen, P. The single parent and public policy. *Social Policy,* March–April 1979, 15–20.

Schrimshaw, N. S., & Taylor, L. Food. *Scientific American,* 1980, *243*(3), 78–88.

Schulz, D. A. *Speculation on the future of the family: Before bearing.* Groves Conference, Mt. Pocono, Pennsylvania, May 1981.

Settles, B. H. *The interface of family and society in sex role changes.* Theory and Methodology Workshop, National Council on Family Relations, 1976, unpublished.

Settles, B. H., Van Name, J. B., & Culley, J. D. Estimating costs in foster family care. *Children Today,* 1976, *5*(6), 19–21, 40–41.

Shanas, E. "The New Pioneers". *Journal of Marriage and the Family,* 1980.

Shanas, E., & Sussman, M. B. *Aging: Stability and change in the family.* New York: Academic Press, 1981.

Sheehan, S. *Is there no place on earth for me?* New York: Houghton Mifflin, 1982.

Simpson, M., Timm, H., & McCubbin, H. L. Adoptees in search of their past: Policy induced strain on adoptive families and birth parents. *Family Relations,* 1981, *30*(3), 427–434.

Spanier, G. B., & Glick, P. C. The life cycle of American families. *Journal of Family History,* 1980, *15*(1), 97–111.

Staples, R. *Introduction to black sociology.* New York: McGraw-Hill, 1976.

Stein, P. J. *Singlehood.* Presented at Groves Conference on Marriage and the Family, Mt. Pocono, Pennsylvania, May 1981.

Steinlab, G., & Hughes, J. W. The changing demography of the central city. *Scientific American,* 1980, *243*(2), 4–53.

Steinmetz, S. K. *Elder care and the middle aged family.* Presentation at American Home Economics Association, June 1981, Atlantic City. NJ. Elder abuse *Aging,* 1981, 315–316.

Steinmetz, S. K. Dependency stress and violence between middle aged caregivers and their elderly parents. In J. Kosberg (Ed.), *Abuse and maltreatment of the elderly: Causes and intervention.* Boston: John Wright/PGS, 1983.

Strasser, S. *Never done.* New York: Pantheon Books, 1982.

Sudia, C. E. Historical trends in American family behavior. In E. Gerotberg (Ed.), *200 years of children.* DHEW, #OHD 77-30103, 1976.

Sussman, M. B. The family life of old people. In E. Shanas & R. Binstock (eds.), Handbook of aging and the social sciences. New York: Van Nostrand Reinhold, 1976.

Sussman, M. B. Actions and services for the new family. In D. Reiss & H. Hoffman (Eds.), *The American Family.* 1979.

Sussman, M. B. Future trends in society and social services. *National Conference on Social Welfare.* Columbus and New York: Columbia University Press, 1980. (a)

Sussman, M. B. *Positive family functioning.* National Research Forum, White House Conference on Families, Washington, D.C., April 11, 1980. (b)

Toffler, A. *The third wave.* New York: William Morrow, 1980.

Uhlenberg, P. Death and the family. *Journal of Family History,* 1980, *15*(3), 313–320.

Verazo, M., & Hermon, C. B. Single parent families: Myth and reality. *Journal of Home Economics,* 1980, *72*(3), 31–33.

Walker, K. E., & Woods, M. E. *Time use: A measure of household production of family goods and services.* Washington, D.C., American Home Economics Association, 1976.

Walker, K. N., & Messinger, L. Remarriage after divorce: dissolution and reconstruction of family boundaries. *Family Process,* 1979, *18,* 185–191.

Weale, A. *Equality and social policy.* London: Routledge & Kegan, 1978.

Westoff, C. F. Marriage and fertility in the developed countries. *Scientific American,* 1979, *239*(6), 32–33.

Wheeler, C., & Avery, R. D. Division of household labor in the family. *Home Economics Research Journal,* 1981, *10*(1), 10–20.

Wiltse, K. R. Foster care in the 1970's: A decade of change. *Children Today,* 1979, *8*(3), 10–15.

Winch, R. F. *The modern family.* New York: Henry Holt, 1952.

Winch, R. F. *The modern family* (3rd ed.). New York: Holt Rinehart & Winston, 1971.

Window on the world: The home information revolution. *Business Week,* June 29, 1981, 74–83.

Yancey, W. L., Eriksen, E. R., & Juliani, R. N. Emergent ethnity: A review and reformation. *American Sociological Review,* 1976, *41*(3), 391–401.

Yankelovich, D. New rules in American life: Searching for self-fulfillment in a world turned upside down. *Psychology Today,* April 1981, 35–91.

Yankelovich, Skelly, & White, Inc. *Raising children in a changing society.* The General Mills Report, 1976–1977.

Zimmerman, C. C. *The future of the family in America.* Burgess Award Address, National Council on Family Relations, Estes Park, Colorado, July 1971.

Zimmerman, S. L. More than a matter of parent's versus children's rights: Response to Crutchfield. *Family Relations,* 1981, *30*(2), 179–181.

PART II

Diversity in Family Life

The chapters in this section, "Diversity in Family Life," have several interrelated foci. "Ethnicity," "Social Stratification," and "Families and Religions" examine the influence of ethnic background, membership in a particular social class, or religious affiliation on the family's structure, lifeways, processes, values, and ideologies. The writers of the "Families and Work" chapter demonstrate the transformation of the nuclear family as a consequence of the increasing number of women employed in jobs for pay outside the home. The structure of such families has not changed; what has occurred is a dramatic shift in roles, relationships, power, values, beliefs, ideologies, and—in some instances—behavior. Authors of the chapters "Nontraditional Family Forms," "Singlehood," "Voluntary Childlessness," "Single-Parent Families," and "Remarriage and Reconstituted Families" examine the variation in household and family composition, which is increasing in incidence in countries worldwide but at very high rates in westernized postindustrial societies.

The authors use historical frameworks to catalog theoretical and research developments over time. The results are state-of-the-art reviews, where antecedents explain the current condition of families—its dynamics and forms—and the potentials for new research and theory in the future.

Ethnicity, as Wilkinson notes, functions to transmit the native tongue, which is the instrument that preserves the fundamental beliefs and folkways of the group. Ethnicity is a powerful tool in maintaining bondings and supports in an alien culture. Four ethnic groups have been intensively examined: Hispanics, Afro-Americans, Asian-Americans, and American Indians. Unique to this chapter is the attempt to counter the more frequent view of ethnic groups—one in which the minority group is viewed from the perspective of, and is compared to, the dominant culture. Ethnic groups are miniature societies with their own cultures and as such entities have an existence all their own, the cross-sectional comparison is ethnocentric.

Lauren Langman, in "Social Stratification," describes how the hierarchies of classes or status groups reflect variation in the available resources, values, and lifestyles. This posture follows a tradition in which class preorders one's lifeways. Theories of stratification and profiles of specific status groups are presented to provide better understanding of the impact of status on family life. This posture is in the tradition that class determines one's lifeways and life chances. Class movement is a limited process, and change in the distribution of a society's resources can come only with overwhelming political and social action.

In a society in which achieved status has taken precedence over ascribed status for the vast majority of members excluding elites, work becomes a critical resource. No longer does the myth of a separate world of joy and family hold credence. Piotrkowski, Rapoport, and Rapoport, using a mesolevel analysis, examine the relationship of work to the internal dynamics of family life. The effects of occupational status, women's employment in the work force, and perceptions and feelings regarding dual work careers on marital and family relationships are the major topics in this chapter.

Although the family has always been closely linked to religion, as the family transmits religious values and supports institutional ties, this connection has often been neglected in explaining family or individual behavior. Religious beliefs and practices or the lack of them are interwoven into the cultural fabric that individuals carry with them into groups and relationships. Similarly, gender and social class become variables to be included in one's research design. In recent decades, religious issues have become major constitutional decisions (e.g., prayer in schools, abortion, and Amish schooling). The Carter and Reagan presidencies have moved religion from the personal domain and the family setting into the public arena, making it a public policy issue. The result is ideological conflict and polarization of the public regarding religious worthiness and moral values. Marciano, in her examination of religious diversity, discusses these developments with a focus on religious options for a highly differentiated public, where choice is still possible to fit one's needs. Topics include the electronic church, cults, women and the church, and the new meanings given to religiosity by family members.

Defining *traditional* is required before defining what is a nontraditional or a nonnormative family unit. Macklin examines the lifestyles of heterosexual never-married singles, heterosexual cohabitants, homosexual relationships, extramarital intimacies, and swinging. Voluntary childlessness, coparenting, the remarried, and the single-parent family are emerging either as consciously chosen family forms or as a consequence of societal conditions. With more women in the work force, dual careers are becoming normative. Commuter marriages, however, are a consequence of limited job opportunity, nepotism rules, and a desire by both partners to take advantage of career opportunities. Thus, couples have to work in different locations and have to communicate when possible. Macklin concludes her chapter with a discussion of communes and intentional communities—forms with lifestyles bound to catalyze an examination of current traditional family types and to serve as experiments for transforming and modifying traditional families.

The next four chapters provide an in-depth analysis of major family forms that in an earlier era might have been considered nontraditional but that today describe a growing number of families.

Arthur Shostak, in his chapter on singlehood, views singlehood as a state of being with its satisfactions and fulfillments. Singlehood is a lifestyle. The singlehooder is not to be pitied as a lonely bachelor or old maid. Five major aspects of the lives of the never-married are examined. "Ambivalents," "wistfuls," "resolveds," and "regretfuls" comprise a typology that is based on how singles feel about their status. Shostak concludes with an analysis of their coping mechanisms and social policy options.

Although some couples face childlessness with remorse, today a growing number are consciously choosing to remain childless. Houseknecht's chapter on voluntary childlessness covers five topics: trends and incidence; motives; correlates; the decision-making process; and so-

ciety's view of childlessness. Current methodological and theoretical issues are examined in relation to their potential impact on future research.

Gongla and Thompson, in the chapter on single-parent families, critique the most commonly used approach to single-parent families. This is the conceptual model that single parenthood is beset with problems and is a pathological state. The authors note serious theoretical and methodological inadequacies, such as regarding all single-parent families as similar; focusing on a single individual rather than on the family unit; and failing to consider other environmental factors. Thus, the usefulness of these studies is limited. An eight-cell typology of single- and two-parent families is developed that describes psychological and interactional processes with the family. The investment of one or both parents in the relationship, whether the parents live in one or two households, is proposed by the authors as a viable characteristic for classifying a family, structurally, as having one or two parents.

In the final chapter of this section, Spanier and Furstenberg examine remarriage and reconstituted families cross-culturally and historically, presenting a demographic profile of remarriage; parenting, stepparenting, and generational ties; and the transition to remarriage. The authors present the conditions and characteristics common to marriage and remarriage and those unique to remarriage, and they discuss the impact of these on the family.

CHAPTER 8

Ethnicity

Doris Wilkinson

Introduction

Despite the universal and inevitable social, political, and technological changes that affect family structure and functioning, families in some form survive. Yet they differ significantly on a number of important variables: cultural histories, ethnic identities, bonds of kinship, patterns of residence, forms of lineage, integenerational relationships, socioeconomic characteristics, and an array of institutionalized attitudes and beliefs. Because of variations in their social biographies and the centrality of these nurturing units in all societies, each system should be examined with sensitivity and caution (Allen, 1978a,b; McLanahan, Wedemeyer, & Adelberg, 1981; Palisi, 1966; Staples, 1971a,b; Staples & Mirandé, 1980).

It has been aptly expressed that families are the primary agents for perpetuating social class, lifestyle, value, nationality and racial distinctions, and concomitant cultural histories. With respect to ethnic traditions, they function to transmit "the native tongue"—a language system—and hence the fundamental beliefs and folkways of an ethnic heritage. In highly heterogeneous societies like ours, where race has been established as paramount in status ascription, families respond differently to the legacies and the social interpretations of race in their unique modes of coping with the consequences of those definitions (Thompson & Van Houten, 1970, p. 43). Differential responses reflect the immense heterogeneity in all facets of life among ethnic populations.

This chapter has several objectives. The primary one is to review and discuss selected works that provide a general picture of the diversity in family constellations among four prominent ethnic groups. Another aim is to present selected quantitative data and research results on significant demographic processes that impinge on family systems. To date, most of the information on minority[1] families

lies has tended to mirror biases intrinsic in the nation's dominant culture. To counteract these biases an attempt has been made to incorporate the array of conceptual frameworks, vocabularies, theoretical arguments, and models offered by contemporary minority scholars. Many who are members of the ancestral groups presented have focused not only on social science assumptions about the family but also on family strengths from their perspectives (Lewis, 1981; Montiel, 1973).

The family characteristics of four racially distinct ethnic populations will be examined: Afro-American,[2] Asian,[3] American Indian,[4] and those of Hispanic ances-

---

[1]Minority families differ from those in the majority population on the basis of race, ancestry, and other characteristics. They are part of a socially, politically, and economically subordinated population. Differential treatment is a significant consequence of minority status. The dominant minority groups (or populations) in the United States are blacks or Afro-Americans, Chicanos or Mexican-Americans, Puerto Ricans, Japanese, Chinese, and Filipinos.

[2]In the 1980 U.S. Census of population, *black* was used to designate persons who identified themselves as black or Negro as well as others who indicated their ancestry or national origin as Jamaican, black Puerto Rican, West Indian, Haitian, or Nigerian (see the 1980 Census of Population: Supplementary Reports. *Age, Sex, Race, and Spanish Origin of the Population by Regions, Divisions, and States: 1980.* PC80S1-1. U.S. Government Printing Office, Washington, D.C., 1981). In this discussion, *Afro-American* will be used interchangeably with *black*. This classification refers to any American of African descent.

[3]In many population reports, Asians and Pacific Islanders are often combined. The category *Asian* includes persons who indicate their race as Asian Indian, Chinese, Filipino, Hawaiian, Guamanian, Korean, Japanese, Samoan, or Vietnamese (1980 Census report, p. 7.) Only three Asian groups are examined in this presentation: Chinese, Japanese, and Filipinos.

[4]Frequently, American Indians are referred to as *native Americans.* In recent years, they have requested to be identified as American Indians. They are combined with Eskimos and Aleuts in the 1980 Census. Also included as American Indians are persons who classified themselves as members of an Indian tribe but who did not specify their race or ethnicity as American Indian.

Doris Wilkinson • Department of Sociology, University of Kentucky, Lexington, KY 40506.

try or Spanish origin.[5] The criteria used in selecting and designating these as minorities were ancestry and social history; placement in the stratification hierarchy in the country of settlement; race; nationality and cultural heritage as these differ from those of the dominant sector. Restricted access to sources of economic and political power constitutes the essence of the minority classification. This discussion thus relies on a systematically derived and realistic conceptualization of the term *minority* as having as basic components *ancestry* and *locus in the stratification system.*

The labels used indicate self-identification by the respondents who participate in population surveys. It is of interest to note here that the ethnic designations emerge both from formal criteria, such as national heritage or country of birth, and from self-classification, although they may not denote clear-cut scientific definitions of biological stock. Defining ethnic populations in terms of descent, ethnicity, or ancestry means that the reference is to the origin, the lineage, the nationality group, or the country in which the person or the person's ancestors or parents were born. With respect to this definition, in a 1979 special census report on ethnicity and language, "persons reported their ancestry group regardless of the number of generations removed from their country of birth. Responses to the ancestry question reflected ethnic group(s) with which persons identified but did not necessarily indicate the degree of attachment or association the person had with the particular ethnic group(s)" (U.S. Bureau of the Census, 1982a, p. 19).

The rationale for concentrating on the families of the four populations selected is based on several historically salient and socially relevant facts: (1) they are separated from the dominant group by racial heritage and access to the sources of economic and political power; (2) they constitute the largest ancestral minorities in the United States, and their numbers are growing individually and collectively; (3) the histories of American Indians and Afro-Americans predate those of many of the other ethnic immigrants; (4) although quantitative studies are few, their cultures, lifestyles, and forms of social organization have been described extensively in the social and behavioral science literature; (5) as groups, they represent politically active and potent voting blocks; (6) a large proportion of their families have an association with federal, state, and local governments, particularly in the area of public assistance; and (7) some of these racial and ethnic

minorities have had a major impact on changes in American society and culture (Wilkinson, 1969).

Delineating boundaries for racial and ethnic minority populations is not an easy task. Designations vary depending on research objectives and the responses of the groups surveyed. As a result, the lack of consistency in definitions often means that data about ethnic minorities, in particular, are not comparable. For example, in the 1980 U.S. Census, the mother's heritage was used to classify persons who could not provide a single response to the race item on the questionnaire. In contrast, earlier Census procedures relied on the respondent's father's race. This procedural modification has altered the comparability of 1970 and 1980 data.

Data comparability is also affected by inconsistencies in self-classification. Disparities in such reporting specifically modify the counts and the comparability of the "white" and "other" categories (U.S. Bureau of the Census, 1981b). In 1980, persons of Spanish ancestry reported their racial status differently than in the 1970 census. A much larger proportion specified their race as "other." Further, most of those who marked this category and wrote in a Spanish affiliation such as Mexican, Venezuelan, or Latino were reclassified as "white" a decade later (U.S. Bureau of the Census, 1981a, p. 3). These fluctuations in self-racial designation thus resulted in a much larger proportion of the Spanish origin population being classified as "other" in 1980 than in the previous decade.

In the 1970 census, 93% of the population of Spanish heritage was classified as "white," whereas in 1980, only 56% reported "white" as their race. It is important to mention such shifts in identification as they are pertinent to our understanding of the beliefs, the changing consciousness, and the collective self-perceptions of the families of ethnic minorities. Not only does the practice of fluctuating ethnic/racial classifications indicate modifications in census methodology, it also symbolizes transitions in the social structure and reveals the political significance assigned to ethnic status and race in American society. What is sociologically relevant is that changes in ethnic identity are correlated with the historical epoch as well as with age, age at arrival in the country for immigrants, educational status, place of residence (Rogler & Cooney, 1980), and family identities and interactional patterns.

Definitions

Some of the basic concepts to be used in this discussion require clarification. In sociology, the concept of *minority* represents a generic, all-inclusive label used to refer to persons who are not simply a numerical minority but who also constitute a socially, politically, and economically subordinated population. The term has referred to specific racial and ethnic groups that share a common race, national heritage, and language and who are not in the dominant sector.

---

[5]Persons designated as Hispanic or of Spanish origin are those who report themselves as Chicanos, Mexican-Americans, Mexicans, Mexicanos, Puerto Ricans, Cubans, Central or South Americans, or others of Spanish ancestry. Self-identification or perceived ethnic identity and national heritage constitute the basis for classifying participants in the U.S. Census as persons of Spanish descent. Such persons may be of any race (see 1980 Census of Population: Supplementary Reports. *Age, Sex, Race, and Spanish Origin of the Population by Regions, Divisions, and States: 1980.* PC80S1-1. U.S. Government Printing Office, Washington, D.C. 1981.)

Despite multiple interpretations of the concept, in this discussion of ethnic diversity in family life, *minority* will be used in the conventional sociological sense. Most of the criteria for the designation are applicable to the aforementioned racial and ethnic populations. Each has a common ancestry and is smaller in size than the dominant group. Each has fewer opportunities, less political power, a lower economic status, and hence lower family income than the majority population. Further, all of the minority sectors have experienced social discrimination, exclusion, and political subordination in some form. These varied experiences have resulted in specific behavioral modes of adaptation ranging from mass revolts and passive resistance to acquiescence. Predictably, family life has been affected by the experiences of and the responses to minority status.

By *racial* is meant an anatomical designation based on biological criteria. More precisely, a *race* is a category of persons who are related by a common heredity or ancestry and who are perceived and responded to in terms of external features or traits. Although the members of a racial subdivision are characterized by a relatively distinct combination of physical attributes, those in an ethnic *group* share not only a national heritage but also a distinct set of customs, a language system, beliefs and values, indigenous family traditions, rituals, and ceremonials. Ethnicity thus includes a common cultural history and familial and other institutions. Basically, an ethnic population is a "group"[6] of people who are of the same nationality or ancestry and who enact a shared culture and lifestyles. Individuals and hence families may, however, be in the same racial category but in different ethnic groups.

Rationale for Study Period

For this summary of specific research emphases, the period under discussion is 1960–1980. One rationale for this time frame is that it permits closer inspection of the recent past and of potential future trends. In addition, more analytic work was carried out during this era, and new perspectives on minority families were introduced. Earlier studies were primarily descriptive, and a considerable number concentrated on negative aspects of ethnic family structure and behavior. Between the 1940s and the early 1960s, an overwhelming body of sociological and psychological research centered on the alleged pathological features of Afro-American, Puerto Rican, Mexican-American, and American Indian families.

[6]Although *population* has a specific demographic and statistical meaning, it will be used here synonymously with *group*. In this sense, *population* will refer not only to the total number of individuals occupying a given area but also to a group of persons or individuals having qualities or characteristics in common, such as ancestry, cultural backgrounds, and racial and ethnic identities. Although the standard definitions of *population* differ from the sociological conception of *group, population* does provide a useful general translation of the latter concept.

Some analysts, for example, stressing the culturally variant nature of minority families, suggested that they represented essentially deviant forms. Many described them as permeated with disorganization. In contrast, more recently, a number of studies of Puerto Rican and Mexican-American families have highlighted difficulties such as the emotional problems of children and the economic pressures on family members with a view toward evaluating these in the context of displacement, patterns of mobility, and the increasing exposure and expectations associated with adjusting to a new environment. From the mid-1970s to the present, growing numbers of scholars began to emphasize internal bonds and cohesion as well as the need to understand the nature and causes of family problems (Canino, Earley, & Rogler, 1980; Hill, 1972; Jiménez-Vásquez, 1980; Lacy, 1975; Martin & Martin, 1978; Maunez, 1973; Mirandé, 1979; Montiel, 1970; Nievera, 1980; Nobles, 1974; Padillo & Ruiz, 1973; Peters, 1974; Sue & Wagner, 1973; Wilkinson, 1978a, 1980a).

It is important to point out here that this literature review does not involve making extensive contrasts in differential family functioning nor unwarranted comparisons among racial and ethnic minority families that have vastly distinct and cumulative social histories. Rather, the aim is to present variations *within* given populations and to accent similarities in salient demographic and family institutional properties where these exist.

Demographic Patterns

Population Distributions

During the 1960s and 1970s, growth was evident in racial and ethnic minority populations in the United States. The largest sector continues to be the Afro-Americans; Hispanics rank second. Although persons of Spanish descent now number between 12 million and 15 million and constitute the second largest minority in this country (Alvirez, 1981, p. 11), the classification denotes an extremely dissimilar ethnic category. Its heterogeneity is demonstrated by the inclusion of the following Hispanics: Latinos, Mexican-Americans or Chicanos, Puerto Ricans, Dominicans, Cubans, and other persons from Central and South America and of Spanish heritage. The diversity represented is anchored in biological heritage, as well as in unique cultural histories and experiences that interlace the institutional character of the family (Mann & Salvo, 1985).

Table 1 provides a summary of recent estimates for the racial and ethnic minorities being discussed. The size of each of the groups is quite variable. A number of ecological processes and demographic trends, such as fertility and the numbers immigrating, along with the reporting of multiple ancestry (U.S. Bureau of the Census, 1982), have contributed to the population differentials between and within the categories for the years shown. For example, "persons of Spanish origin reported their race differ-

Table 1. U.S. Population By Race and Ethnicity for Selected Racial and Ethnic Groups, 1970 and 1980[a]

Racial/ethnic category	1970	1980	Percentage change
American Indian	792,730	1,361,869	+71.8
African American black	22,580,289	26,488,218	+17.3
Chinese	435,062	806,027	+85.3
Filipinos	343,060	774,640	+125.8
Japanese	591,290	700,747	+18.5
Mexican-American	7,000,000[b]	9,000,000	+28.6
Puerto Rican	1,000,000	2,100,000	+1.1

[a]Source: U.S. Bureau of the Census. Race of the Population by States: 1980. *Supplementary Reports* PC80-S1-3 (July, 1981): Table 1.
[b]The 1970 figures for Mexican-Americans and Puerto Ricans are rough estimates and are derived from U.S. Census reports of the population. The 1980 total Spanish-origin population was about 15 million. Differences between 1980 and 1970 U.S. Census counts by Spanish origin affect the comparability of data.

ently in the 1980 census than in the 1970 census," and this discrepancy in identification has altered the counts and the comparability of the available population data on Hispanics (U.S. Bureau of the Census, 1980e, 1981a,b, p. 3). Further, as previously indicated, the 1980 Census relied on the mother's ancestry to classify persons who did not give a single response on the racial status item. A decade earlier, the procedure involved using the race of an individual's father for respondents participating in the Census.

Hispanics. Hispanics, or persons of Spanish origin, constitute a highly diverse population (U.S. Bureau of the Census, 1980e, 1981a; U.S. Department of Labor, 1971; Ventura, 1982). This ancestral and cultural diversity pervades family lifestyles. As the data in Table 1 show, at the beginning of the 1970s, there were about 7 million persons of Mexican heritage in this country. An estimated 1 million were of Puerto Rican descent. Of the total estimate of 15 million Hispanics in 1980, three fifths were of Mexican ancestry. The others were distributed approximately as follows: 15% were Puerto Rican; 7% were Cuban; 7% were of Central or South American origin; and 11% were classified by the Census Bureau as "other" Spanish (Gurak, 1981, p. 6; Nieves & Martinez, 1980; U.S. Bureau of the Census, 1980c,f).

Afro-Americans. Afro-Americans, or blacks, are the largest racial minority in the United States with a history in the country dating back to the 16th century. One notable characteristic of this group is that it is young: approximately 37% of its members are under age 18. As the data in Table 1 show, Afro-Americans totaled about 26 million in 1980, representing a 17% increase over the 1970

figure. In contrast to most of the other racial and ethnic minority populations, the 1980 figure constituted only a slight increase (U.S. Bureau of the Census, 1981b). Current estimates put the population at around 30 million.

Asian-Americans. Like Hispanics, Asian-Americans are an exceptionally dissimilar ethnic minority (Endo, 1980; Endo, Sue, & Wagner, 1980; Fujii, 1980b; Lyman, 1970, 1971, 1974; Pian, 1974). There is no complete consensus on who is an Asian. With respect to the classifications used in population surveys and in the U.S. Census, the groups most often included in this category are Burmese, Cambodians, Chinese, Filipinos, Japanese, Koreans, Malaysians, Guamanians, Pakistanis, Indonesians, Vietnamese, and Samoans. In the U.S. Census, some of these have been designated as "others," meaning unclassified ethnic or racial populations. Yet, classifying these diverse ethnics as Asians obscures the extent of variation in their national heritage, language, beliefs, customs, and family organization (Johnson, 1977; Kalish, 1973; Liu, 1966; Liu & Yu, 1975; Muramatsu, 1960; Sue & Kirk, 1973).

In 1970, Asians comprised about 1% of the U.S. population (U.S. Bureau of the Census, 1973). With the dramatic entry of Indochinese refugees in 1975, the counts rapidly increased (Cordova, 1980, p. 139). Of those admitted since the spring of 1975, an estimated 89% were Vietnamese. The remaining percentages were divided among Laotians, Hmongs (mountain-dwelling peoples from China, Laos, Vietnam, and Thailand), and Cambodians (Aylesworth, Ossorio, & Osaki, 1980, p. 64). Contrary to newspaper accounts, the Vietnamese and the other Asians were quite different with respect to skills, occupational status, educational attainment, and family lifestyles and values.

Asian-Americans have always been a culturally diversified population, the dominant subdivisions in the United States being the Chinese, the Filipinos, and the Japanese (Endo, Sue, & Wagner, 1980; Pian, 1974). The Japanese are the largest group, presently approaching 1 million. With sustained immigration and a reduction in mortality for the nation as a whole, their numbers continue to rise. Chinese and Filipinos rank second and third, respectively. Existing data reveal that these sectors also increased in the 1970s. Although most of the growth in these two ethnic populations has been the result of immigration, in contrast it is estimated that about two-thirds of the Japanese increment can be attributed to births (Kaplan & Van Valey, 1980, p. 216). It is of interest that, at the beginning of this decade, Koreans constituted the fourth largest and fastest growing Asian group (U.S. Bureau of the Census, 1981b, p. 7).

American Indians. The American Indian population is increasing, but the patterns of growth are difficult to measure precisely because of shifts in racial identification and delays in the dissemination of current statistics. The growth shown in Tables 1 and 2 is due both to a rise in the

Table 2. American Indian Population in the United States: 1900 to 1980[a]

Year[b]	Estimated population	Change from preceding year (percentage increase or decrease)
1980	1,361,869[c]	+71.8
1970	792,730	+51.4
1960	523,591	+46.5
1950	357,499	+3.5
1940	345,252	+0.6
1930	343,352	+40.5
1920	244,437	−11.7
1910	276,927	+16.8
1900	237,196	—

[a]Source: U.S. Department of Commerce, Bureau of the Census, General Population Characteristics, PC(1)-B1, and Race of the Population by States: 1980, *Supplementary Reports of the 1980 Census.*
[b]The year is the census year; *change* refers to change from the preceding census.
[c]This figure has been projected to 1.5 million.

birth rate and to changes in classification procedures. A number of other factors have also contributed to growth in the American Indian population: increased life expectancy at birth, improved census procedures, the value placed on children, residential mobility, and tribal folkways and mores.

Around 1500, about 840 million Indians were residing in the United States. Over four centuries later, the numbers claiming Indian and Alaskan native ancestry had not been altered appreciably. Recent data reveal, however, that the Indian population is growing at a rate that is four times the national average (Kaplan & Van Valey, 1980, p. 214). Several demographic processes have influenced this growth rate: (1) a sustained rise in the birth rate; (2) a reduction in infant mortality; and (3) increasing numbers of persons identifying themselves as having Indian ancestry. Further, the growth reflects modifications in the methods for classifying persons of Indian heritage and improved data-gathering procedures. Table 2 presents the estimated population counts and percentage changes for American Indians from 1900 to 1980.

Regional Variations

Residential patterns vary; these patterns are associated with differing community values and mores and hence with variations in the institutional nature of the family. Whereas Puerto Rican families are disproportionately clustered in New York (Gurak & Rogler, 1980), those of Mexican-Americans constitute only a small portion of the Hispanic population in New York City. Their families and communities are located primarily in the southwestern part of the country.

Like Puerto Ricans, the majority of Afro-Americans reside in metropolitan areas. At the end of the 1970s, an estimated 56% were central-city residents, and only 20% lived in the suburbs of metropolitan areas. At the beginning of the 1980s, "twelve states had a Black population of 1 million or more," with New York ranking first, followed by California and Texas (U.S. Bureau of the Census, 1981b, p. 1). Most, however, continued to live in the southern part of the country. In seven southern states and in the District of Columbia, they comprised 20% or more of the total population. Among the southern cities of at least 50,000 with black majority populations were Atlanta, Birmingham, New Orleans, Richmond, and Wilmington. This spatial clustering in a specific region of the country "reflects a change in the long-term pattern of a large net outmigration of Blacks from the South" (U.S. Bureau of the Census, 1981b, p. 1). Further, the current ecological distribution of black families is based on economic and social variables (Edwards, 1970).

Moreover, among American Indians, place of residence and residential mobility are intricately interwoven with family behavior (Ablon, 1964; DeGeyndt, 1973). For the American Indian, life on the reservation merges with the family life cycle. The Bureau of Indian Affairs estimated that more than 75% of Indians were living on or near reservations in 1977. Excluding Alaska, the areas designated as reservations at the time totaled about 267. Slightly over 51% of these were tribally owned lands (Passel, 1976). Some were individually owned allotted lands, the majority of this type being dual-allotted tribal lands. The relationship of Indian customs, beliefs, rituals, and daily life to the land has been vividly captured in the historical and contemporary literature (Blanchard, 1975; DeLoria, 1970; Hostbjor, 1965; Passel, 1976; Red Horse, 1981).

In recent years, several land-related issues have emerged. For example, in New Mexico, Navaho Indian ranchers, Pueblo leaders, and social workers informed a U.S. Civil Rights Commission panel that traditional customs were being disrupted by energy development. Because family and tribal beliefs incorporate the sacredness of ancestral burial sites, abuse of such areas is perceived as desecration of valued observances. In Connecticut, several Indian tribes requested laws to protect the burial grounds of their ancestors. As recently as 1982, Kumeyaay Indians filed a suit in Los Angeles for permission to exhume the remains of ancestors so that they could rebury them on the reservation. The year before, a group of Navahos and an allied group of Hopis requested that a federal judge stop a proposed ski resort in Arizona. Manifesting the deeply entrenched values of their culture, they felt that construction would desecrate the sacred mountain range and anger their gods. Such events illustrate the traditional links between Indian customs, family practices, and tribal lands. Many tribes today are involved in land disputes.

Although American Indians live in all parts of the

country, nearly half of the population is concentrated in the West. Slightly over 25% reside in the South, and this region of the country is experiencing an increase in its Indian population. Such changes in community of residence eventually become cultural transitions because regions have not only differing geographies, but also modes of production, social customs, folkways, religious beliefs, and dietary practices. Thus, the place where families reside forms a cultural settlement.

In the 1970s, nearly half of American Indian families lived on or near reservations located in Arizona, Alaska, California, Minnesota, New Mexico, North Carolina, Oklahoma, South Carolina, South Dakota, Washington, and Wisconsin. Ten years later, California had the largest population, with Oklahoma, Arizona, New Mexico, and North Carolina ranking second, third, fourth, and fifth. As a proportion of the total population, the American Indian sector was highest in two states: New Mexico and South Dakota.

In addition to regional variability, there are numerous tribal affiliations with distinct languages and customs. In 1970, the largest tribes were the Apache, Cherokee, Chippewa, Choctaw and Houma, Creek, Alabama and Coushatta, Iroquois, Lumbee, Navajo, Pueblo, and Sioux tribes. The Navaho ranked first in size and the Cherokee ranked second. Other well-known tribes included the Cahuilla, Cheyenne, Comanche, Delaware, Menominee, Mandan-Hidatsa, Mohawk, and Osage (Kaplan & Van Valey, 1980, p. 214). Recognizing and understanding the nature of distinct tribal identities are essential, because these identities are associated with diversity in language, family forms, traditions, life cycle rituals and ceremonials, patterns of lineage, and kinship relationships (Association of American Indian Affairs, 1974; J. Brown, 1970; Deloria, 1978; Farris, 1976; Harmsworth, 1965; Medicine, 1969, 1975; Virgil, 1980; Wissler, 1966).

The social consequences of urban versus rural residence must also be considered in analyses of Indian family organization. Often, there is continuous movement between reservations and urban communities for some individuals and families. Further, growing numbers are leaving rural areas and reservations for city life. Many also return to the reservation. In 1960, about one third resided in urban centers. Yet, 10 years later, nearly half lived in such communities. Thus, the American Indian population, like other earlier rural and traditional people, is increasingly becoming an urbanized one. Lifestyles originating from prior tribal affiliations and customs interacting with urban migration have an effect on the character of the family. Future studies of these relationships must take into account the fact that the existing data are general and do not lend themselves to detailed descriptions of the specific ways of life of any one tribe. It is, however, important to understand that tribal identities vary and that these are integrated with family organization.

Unlike the regional patterns for Afro-Americans and

Puerto Ricans, most Asian-American families are concentrated in California. In 1970, an estimated 40% of Filipinos, 39% of Chinese, and 36% of Japanese lived in that state alone. A decade later, large numbers of Pacific Islanders and Asian families resided in California, Hawaii, New York, Illinois, Texas, New Jersey, and Washington (U.S. Bureau of the Census, 1983). Although recent immigrants have not been settling exclusively in the western part of the country, that section continues to have a larger proportion of Asians than any other region. Although California ranked first for each group except Hawaiians and Asian Indians, other states varied in distributions of the different populations. At the beginning of the 1980s, New York was second, with the highest concentrations of Chinese and Koreans. Also, Hawaii had the largest proportion of Filipinos and Japanese, and Texas had the largest number of Vietnamese. Asians and Pacific Islanders comprised 60% of the total Hawaiian population (U.S. Bureau of the Census, 1981b, p. 2). What may be ecologically pertinent, because of the impact of regional location on family behavioral codes, is that Asians and Pacific Islanders are becoming more dispersed (U.S. Bureau of the Census, 1973, 1983).

Data in Table 3 show the 1970 and 1980 populations and the percentage change for Chinese, Filipinos, and Japanese by regions. The Chinese live in larger numbers outside the western part of the country in contrast to the other Asian ethnics. At the beginning of the 1970s, slightly over 25% lived in the Northwest, and nearly 20% lived in New York State (Kaplan & Van Valey, 1980, p. 216). Although the country of origin and its accompanying norms and values contribute to family diversity

Table 3. Population of Chinese, Filipinos, and Japanese for 1970 and 1980 by Regions[a]

Ethnic group and region	1970 population	1980 population	Percentage change
Chinese			
Northeast	115,777	217,730	+ 88.1
North Central	39,343	72,905	+ 85.3
South	34,284	90,616	+ 164.3
West	245,658	424,776	+ 72.9
Filipinos			
Northeast	31,424	75,104	+ 139.0
North Central	27,824	79,945	+ 187.3
South	31,979	82,596	+ 158.3
West	251,833	536,995	+ 113.2
Japanese			
Northeast	38,978	46,930	+ 20.4
North Central	42,354	44,426	+ 4.9
South	30,917	44,636	+ 44.4
West	479,041	564,755	+ 17.9

[a]Source: U.S. Department of Commerce, Bureau of the Census. Race of the Population by States: 1980, *Supplementary Reports*, PC80-S1-3, July 1981.

among Asians, regional location and patterns of residential mobility have an impact on family income status and behavior. Place of residence can affect family member occupational opportunities and thus the economic security of the household.

In contrast to Asian-American families, Puerto Ricans are disproportionately clustered in New York (Gurak & Rogler, 1980; Mann & Salvo, 1985). Mexican-Americans, on the other hand, form only a small portion of the Hispanic population in New York City (Samora & Lamanna, 1967; Thurston, 1974). Their families are located primarily in the southwestern part of the country. It has been observed that this phenomenon of residential selection "creates numerous distinct Hispanic communities" (Gurak & Rogler, 1980, p. 2) and consequently distinct family milieus (Alvarez, 1973; Baca Zinn, 1980, 1982; Samora & Lamanna, 1967). For example, large numbers of Hispanics are "concentrated in ethnically specific pockets or enclaves" (Zavaleta, 1981, p. 1; Samora & Lamanna, 1967). These residential boundaries, interacting with unique histories, predictably contribute to community and family diversity. This relevant social fact explains the variability in intergenerational relationships, family customs, and marital patterns, particularly rates of "outgroup" marriage. With respect to the latter, it has been found that where ethnic groups such as Puerto Ricans are closely grouped, rates of ethnic intermarriage decrease (Collado, 1980, p. 5).

Moreover, a number of sociological investigations have focused on a subculture that evolves in ethnically specific areas (Penalosa, 1967). What we have discovered about children of Hispanic ancestry is that those who grow up in Hispanic communities maintain close ties with their cultural heritage. Growing up, they play with other children whose backgrounds are similar to theirs. Unlike American Indians and Asians, they share not only values and beliefs that are rooted in indigenous family traditions, but also a language. Basically, their regional distributions are as follows: (1) Mexican-American children and their parents reside primarily in southwestern states and selected parts of the Midwest; (2) Puerto Rican families are concentrated in three Middle Atlantic states: New York, New Jersey, and Pennsylvania; and (3) large numbers of Cuban and Central and South American families are found in Florida, New York, and Texas (Zavaleta, 1981, pp. 1–2).

Size and Composition

Ethnic diversity in family structure is revealed in variations in size and composition. For example, compared to all families in the United States, those of Afro-American and Hispanic descent tend to be large. In 1979, nearly 33% of Hispanic families consisted of five or more persons, as compared with 18% of all families in the United States (U.S. Bureau of the Census, 1980f, p. 50). Although the proportions of Hispanic and non-Hispanic ever-married women who had at least five children de-

creased between 1970 and 1978, Hispanic women continued to have large families. Yet like other ethnics, Hispanic families vary in size and composition.

By the end of the 1970s, 3 of every 10 families of Hispanic origin and 1 of every 4 Afro-American families had five or more members. About 41% of Afro-American families had female householders,[7] "as compared with 15 percent for families of all races combined" (U.S. Bureau of the Census, 1980f). The average size of Afro-American households in the mid-1970s was 3.3 persons. If this reduction in household size indicates a pattern, it would coincide with national trends: declining fertility and increases in the numbers of young people living alone (U.S. Bureau of the Census, 1978, p. 100).

According to the data available from the U.S. Department of the Interior (1977), American Indian families are reported as large, primarily because of more accurate statistical reporting, greater interest in Indian history and family life, a measurable reduction in infant mortality, and a sustained high birth rate. In the mid-1970s, the "rate of 30.5 live births for each 1,000 Indians and Alaska Natives was 2.1 times as high as the U.S. 'All races' rate of 14.8" (U.S. Department of the Interior, 1977, p. 2).

Birth and fertility rates vary among Hispanics, and Hispanic mothers tend to be younger than most non-Hispanic mothers, with the exception of Afro-Americans. In 1979, the Hispanic birth rate was 25.5 births per 1,000 population. The fertility rate was 100.5 births per 1,000 women 15–44 years old. The fertility rate for Mexican-American women (119.3) was greater than the rate for Puerto Rican women (80.7) (Ventura, 1982, p. 2). No special meaning, however, can be attributed to these differences other than the uniqueness of family values (Fernandez-Marina, Maldonado, & Trent, 1958; Steward & Steward, 1973).

Age Distributions

In contrast to Asian-Americans, the child population for American Indians, Afro-Americans, and Hispanics is relatively large (U.S. Bureau of the Census, 1980f, p. 2). Of persons of Hispanic parentage, 32% were under age 14 in 1980, whereas nearly 29% of Afro-Americans were

---

[7]*Householder* and *head of family* are used interchangeably, although the former term replaced the latter in the 1980 U.S. Census. This shift in labeling is the consequence of social changes and has resulted in the Bureau of the Census "reconsidering its longtime practice of always classifying the husband as the head when he and his wife are living together. . . . In the 1980 census, the householder is the first adult household member listed on the census questionnaire" (see U.S. Bureau of the Census, 1980b, p. 149).

All persons who occupy a house, an apartment, or a single room occupy a *household*. Thus, a household includes persons living alone, related family members, and unrelated persons, if any, such as lodgers (U.S. Bureau of the Census, 1980b, p. 150).

Table 4. Percentage Distribution of Characteristics of Nonfarm Black and Hispanic Husband–Wife Families by Number of Own Children under 18, 1981[a]

Own children under 18, all families	Nonfarm	
	Afro-American families	Hispanic families
No own children under 18	41.5	30.5
With own children under 18	58.5	69.5
1 child	22.3	22.6
2 children	19.3	22.7
3 children	9.2	13.1
4 children	4.3	5.9
5 children	1.8	3.3
6 or more children	1.7	1.8

[a]Source: U.S. Department of Commerce, Bureau of the Census, *Household and Family Characteristics: March 1979. Current Population Reports,* Series P-20, No, 352, July 1980, Table 1.

under 14, 25% of Asian and Pacific Islanders and an estimated 33% of American Indians were under this age (U.S. Bureau of the Census, 1980f, Table 1). Differences in age distributions and in family size contribute to family structural diversity on the mainland and in Alaska, Hawaii, and Puerto Rico. Because of the absence of comparative data for all ethnic groups, Table 4 presents data only on the similarities in the distributions of children under 18 for Afro-American and Hispanic families in nonfarm areas. The data indicate that nearly 70% of Hispanic husband–wife families have children younger than 18 years of age; 24% of these and 17% percent of Afro-American nonfarm families have three or more children under this age.

One-Parent Structures

Unlike the modal family forms among Asians and American Indians, those of Puerto Ricans and Afro-Americans are characterized by a high proportion of one-parent households. These are typically headed by females. Yet, for the nation as a whole, there was a dramatic growth in single-parent households in the 1970s. Whereas two-parent families decreased by 4%, those with one-parent increased by 79%: "In 1970, about 11 percent of all families with children living at home were maintained by one-parent, but by 1979, this proportion had increased to 19 percent" (U.S. Bureau of the Census, July, 1980b, p. 3). At present, the majority of these single-parent families are maintained by mothers, despite a rise in the number supported by fathers. One distinguishing feature of single-parent families is a large number of children.

It has been observed that for Afro-Americans, "as income increases, the proportion of female-headed families

decreases and conversely, male-headed family structures increase" (Blackwell, 1975, p. 41). This premise appears to apply to other minorities when family structure is associated with socioeconomic status. Current estimates reveal that "one in three Puerto Rican families is headed by a woman" (Nieves & Martinez, 1980, p. 94). These households tend to be poor and disproportionately concentrated below the poverty level. There are some predictions that such family forms, which have a historical basis, will continue to increase among Puerto Ricans and other ethnic populations (Cooney, Rogler, & Schroeder, 1980).

At present, the rate of increase in single-parent households among Puerto Ricans appears to be increasing. In 1970, whereas about 13% of Mexican families were maintained by women, 24% of Puerto Rican families had a female householder with no husband present. By the end of the 1970s, the Puerto Rican rate had escalated to 40%, whereas the rate for Mexican-Americans had increased only slightly (Gurak, 1981, p. 7). This structural dissimilarity emanated from variations in male and female responses to displacement and exposure to Anglo lifestyles, as well as from differences in their cultural origins. Thus, at the end of the 1970s, Mexican-American families had fewer one-parent households and fewer children than Puerto Rican families. Along with fertility differentials, ethnicity, and familial values, socioeconomic factors have also contributed to the variability among Hispanics in single-parent units.

The available data on the single-parent form are consistent in presenting a direct correlation between the sex of the householder and family economic status. Recently, it was suggested that Afro-American women who work and maintain their families might serve as models for "all women of the proletarianized class" (Dobbins & Mulligan, 1980, p. 209). But the position of the female head of a household operates against this possibility, for, as noted, one of the striking changes in the poverty population in the last two decades has been the rise in the number of *poor* families with a female householder. This occurrence has been referred to as the *feminization of poverty.* Further, the poverty rate for persons in Afro-American families supported by a woman remains much higher than the rate for persons in comparable white families. These minority women are not members of a proletarian class. Even if they were, their social history and sustained ascriptive status are unparalleled.

Family History and Culture

Because the family ancestral and cultural histories of Asian-Americans are highly diverse and their life experiences in the United States have been quite varied (Liu, 1966; Lyman, 1974; Sue & Kirk, 1973) only African-Americans, Mexicans, and Puerto Ricans are discussed in this section (P/AAMHRC Research Review, 1983). Each family institution for these groups has also had a distinct historical biography (Berry, 1958). In addition, each has encountered, in unique ways, external events such as value and behavioral transformations resulting from immigration and movement to and from central cities. Unlike all other ancestral groups, American Indian or native American families and those of African heritage have occupied an unprecedented status in the social structure (Billingsley & Green, 1974; Blassingame, 1972; Frazier 1968; Gutman, 1976; Haley, 1976; Hare, 1976; Lammermeier, 1973; Pinkney, 1975; Wilkinson, 1969, 1974b, 1978b, 1980b).

For Americans of African ancestry, the system of slavery, with its concordant attitudes, "may have militated against black family stability" (Pinkney, 1975, p. 98). The family's mode of adaptation to this form of social organization gave rise to prototypical and enduring kinship systems, which, in turn, may have contributed to the emergence of distinct cultural traditions (Gutman, 1976; Mack, 1971; Staples, 1971a). What we do know is that, in its evolution, the African-American family persisted because of its affectional ties, the maintenance and strength of bonding, and multigenerational networks (Martin & Martin, 1978; Nobles, 1978; Wilkinson, 1978a, 1979).

The unique nature of the contemporary Afro-American family as a system interrelated with other institutions in the larger social milieu has required articulation for some time. In the analysis of any family constellation, a number of theoretical perspectives is possible. Unfortunately, in the majority of instances where families of African ancestry have been studied, these families have been evaluated primarily using the frame of reference of social problems.

In this chapter, minority families are not considered from a social problems perspective. Rather, the Afro-American family is described within the context of the social ecology and culture of both black and white America, the family's historical character in a plantation system, the prevailing disparities in opportunities for members' upward mobility, and the differing sources of achievement. These social facts, in turn, have contributed to class and cultural variations in family organization and functioning. Despite economic and value distinctions, the family remains an essential part of the fabric of black communities.

Further, within each community, there are a variety of strata, each with class-specific lifestyle behaviors. Socioeconomic factors impinge on the modes of family interaction, child-rearing practices, and customs, as well as member life chances. The ability of contemporary Afro-American families to meet their basic needs is directly linked to their placement in the stratification hierarchy.

Under slavery, class distinctions were obliterated; and as a sanctioned form of social organization, enslavement constituted a massive disintegration of the former cultural life of Africans. One of the most disastrous results of slavery for the African family was that the slave husband was not the head of the household. This point is relevant here because the powerlessness of the male to support and protect his family for two and a half centuries has had a deleterious, pervasive, and enduring impact on family relationships (Blackwell, 1985; Cade, 1970; Wilkinson & Taylor, 1977).

American Indians

Before the seventeenth century, most of the inhabitants of this country were American Indians (U.S. Bureau of the Census, 1982, p. 2). Sharing a similar history of subordination with Americans of African heritage, American Indians were forced to adapt to pervasive disruptions in tribal society and later to what has been described as government indecisiveness on policies of assimilation versus pluralism (Berry, 1958). American Indians' family lives have been intertwined with government policies and with social changes and acculturation. Unlike the families of the other ancestral groups in the United States, American Indian parents and their children have had a long-term association with the federal government. This relationship has been defined by a territorial arrangement that influences tribal and family life extensively. For example, the United States has held in trust millions of acres of land for Indian tribes. The administrative responsibility for this territory, which continues to serve as the land base for most Indian families, rests with the Bureau of Indian Affairs.

Although their families have not been subjected to enslavement as have those of Americans of African descent, as a group Indians have experienced conquest, dislocation, cultural disintegration, spatial segregation, and consequently predictable ethnic identity and family problems (Brown, 1970). Recent case studies have shown that their personal estrangement and continued isolation are correlated with family problems and high rates of alcoholism, suicide, runaways, and crime on the reservations (Westermeyer, 1977). In order for individuals or families to be eligible for social services, they must be members of tribes recognized by the federal government. For some services, it is necessary to claim one-fourth or more Indian heritage (U.S. Department of the Interior, 1977, 1980).

According to some social scientists, the unparalleled historical conditions of Afro-Americans and American Indians are associated in the present with unique types of family patterns, particularly composition, lifestyles, husband–wife and parent–child interaction, the form and content of socialization, and modes of family adaptation. Because of intense emotional and economic needs, nuclear families in isolation from relatives and even from older members have not been found frequently in the past. Although variable, kinship bonding and obligations to relatives remain essential in famlial interaction. Even today, relations with kin involve much more than long-distance "help patterns." They include residential propinquity, obligatory mutual aid, active participation in life cycle events, and central figures around whom family ceremonies revolve. These patterns are similar in some respects to the role sets found in many Hispanic families (Baca Zinn, 1975). Relatives live near each other and become involved in the daily lives of the members of the kinship unit. Women play fundamental roles in these extended systems (Red Horse, Lewis, Feit, & Decker, 1978; Rubel, 1966; Spindler, 1962; Williams, 1980; Witt, 1974). In many American Indian tribes, the descent of children and the ownership of property are traced through the mother's line. The observation has been made that "as matrilineal people, American Indian women are carriers of tribal credentials" (Keshena, 1980, p. 250). It is important to point out here also that the centrality of women is a major aspect of the family configurations of all the ethnic groups described.

Puerto Ricans

Frequent social mobility and residential dispersion have affected relations among Puerto Rican parents and their children. Traditional norms of obedience and respect for adults, rules pertaining to endogamy, and those governing male–female behavior have been modified. Many coping behaviors have emerged. One indicator of "adjustment to life on the mainland has been the increase of marriage of Puerto Ricans with non-Puerto Ricans" (Fitzpatrick, 1971, p. 94), although their rate of intermarriage is lower than that for more recent immigrant groups (Gurak & Rogler, 1980, p. 5).

Most Puerto Rican families live in inner cities and in "ethnically specific enclaves" (Zavaleta, 1981, p. 1) and thus have an opportunity to interact with other Puerto Ricans. Life in central cities, however, has its own peculiar problems: unemployment, frequent residential mobility, high crime and drug abuse rates, and marital dissolution. Puerto Rican females, for example, appear to have higher divorce rates than other Hispanic women (Alvirez, 1981, p. 12). Further, in urban centers, Puerto Ricans appear to remain single in greater proportions than most of the other Hispanics. This may simply be a consequence of the age distribution, which includes large numbers of young among the population. It is essential to understand these demographic and ecological patterns and trends among Puerto Ricans and other ethnic minorities that affect family organization.

Moreover, Puerto Rican women on the island have been exposed to social situations in which their roles reflect mainland values. They are accustomed to working, to occupying positions of prestige, and consequently to being out of the home. On the island, historically, they have been represented in the political and literary spheres: "Throughout Puerto Rico, one will find female mayors; and in the legislature, there are senators and assembly women" (Correa, 1980, p. 5). Women have thus played active integrated roles as wives, mothers, and workers. Like Mexican-American women, they have also been socialized to a set of cultural norms anchored in a belief in male authority, but this sex-typed ethic is not the negative feature that it has been claimed to be in much of the family literature.

The explicit codes of conduct for the sex-specific behaviors of Hispanic males and females are integral parts of their cultural ideology and their learned system of status differentiation. Historically, male dominance has been a prominent aspect of Hispanic social organization; and in Puerto Rican and Mexican-American families, expressive and conventional duties for mothers and wives prevail (Gonzales, 1980; Sánchez, 1973). But, as previously indicated, this fact discloses the premium placed not only on effective family organization but on a rational division of labor. The prevailing distorted notions about extreme paternal rigidity and a negative *machismo* ethic do not reveal the affectional roles of husbands and fathers (Goodman & Beman, 1971; Ruben, 1966).

Mexican-Americans

Many of the external influences on Puerto Rican families also affect those of Mexican heritage. It has been asserted that the fundamental beliefs of Mexican culture do not coincide with those of Anglo society (Fernandez, Maldonado, & Trent, 1958; Hamilton, 1973; Mirandé, 1977). Although there are predictable generational and class differences within Mexican-American communities and among families, understandably those reared in a Mexican environment do not share an assumed ideal middle-class Anglo-American norm, such as deferred gratification (Burma, 1963, p. 22), for example. In Mexican culture, there is a greater emphasis on the present and on meeting the needs of the collective: la familia (Mirandé, 1979; Rubel, 1966).

Furthermore, there are several distinguishing aspects of Mexican-American expectations and family interaction that should be discussed. Although these are similar to the behavioral precepts of other Hispanics, they vary by virtue of differences in history and culture, family customs, immigrant status, regional location, and occupational and economic positions. Like other families of Spanish descent in the United States, those of Mexican ancestry tend to ascribe significance to solidifying beliefs such as (1) the integral nature of the family in daily living; (2) the functional dominance of males, complemented by a positive and traditional role for women; (3) the reinforcement of sex-role distinctions through child-rearing practices; (4) strong kinship bonds; (5) the "centrality of children"; (6) the repression of feminine attributes in males; and (7) a precedent for the male as head of the household (Penalosa, 1968; Mirandé, 1979, 1980; Mirandé & Enriquez, 1979). As previously indicated, these differ in scope and intensity from the beliefs of other Hispanics because of separate histories, behavioral prescriptions, and the configuration of familistic values to which the members are socialized.

Family interaction is of paramount importance among Mexican-Americans (Kenkel, 1985). The intimate involvement of personalities is a prominent feature, and children are at the center of family life. However, a number of dramatic social events and conditions, such as migration, unemployment, illegal-alien status, and discrimination, have resulted in modifications in some of these fundamental traits. Increasingly, families are becoming similar to Anglo-American middle class structures (Penalosa, 1968, p. 407, 409). This trend perhaps indicates a class metamorphosis from a lower socioeconomic status to an ethnic group similar to European immigrants of a few generations ago, such as the Italian-Americans (Penalosa, 1967).

Exposure to a changing political environment has had a direct effect on women's roles in the family system. There has been, for example, a lessening of the woman's customary adherence to the values and conventions of her family of origin. New levels of aspiration for independence and professional status, as well as less dependence on male authority, also characterize contemporary role shifts for women. Despite modifications in the traditional habits and behaviors that have shaped Mexican-American culture and have affected husband–wife interaction, particularly role expectations for women, the family remains the strongest source of emotional strength and support (Díaz-Guerrero, 1955; Mirandé & Enriquez, 1979). Although the family constitutes the nucleus of Hipanic life, it is undergoing transformation (Kenkel, 1985).

As indicated earlier, there is considerable heterogeneity within the Hispanic population, resulting in significant differences in family styles and customs. For example, Puerto Rican women in their childbearing years, like Mexican American women, tend to have large numbers of children: "First and second generation Mexican women have a greater tendency to continue having children after the age of 35" (Gurak, 1981, p. 9). In addition to fertility differentials, there are basic marital and residential distinctions. These result not only from established practices but also from variations in immigrant status, employment opportunities, and encounters with discrimination. There are also considerable differences in these experiences from those of the other racial and ethnic groups. For example, "direct discrimination does not hit the Mexican American as severely" as it does the Afro-American (Bullock, 1978, p. 159).

For Mexican-Americans and Puerto Ricans, migration and adjustment to a new status and cultural environment—specifically American middle-class folkways—are among the processes contributing to change in family organization. Some of the internal transitions are reflected in the family life of Asians and American Indians, such as (1) an increase in the participation of mothers in occupational activities outside the home; (2) a rise in nontraditional male and female role expectations, which are modifying conventional family observances; (3) decreasing authoritarian structure with respect to the father role and a greater emphasis on egalitarianism (Cromwell & Cromwell, 1978); (4) the acquisition of knowledge of the English language on the part of children, with accompanying redefinitions of the father–offspring relationship in particular; and (5) status attainment increasingly based on individual achievement rather than on family productivity (Jiménez-Vásquez, 1980). The content and form of these changes vary considerably with the cultural histo-

ries and experiences of Hispanic families (Baca Zinn, 1980; Durrett, O'Bryant, & Pennebaker, 1975; Fitzpatrick, 1971; Mirandé, 1980; Montalvo, 1974; Murillo-Rohde, 1976; Perez, 1979; Project on the Status and Education of Women, 1975).

Kinship Relationships

Despite the sharp demarcation in sex-role behaviors, male and female relatives provide basic integenerational links in ethnic families. Arrangements based on cohesiveness and kinship bonding were illuminated in the social science literature at the end of the 1950s, when prevailing theories of isolated nuclear structures were questioned (Sussman, 1959). Decades later, social scientists unveiled help patterns that continue to filter throughout American Indian, Afro-American, Asian, Mexican-American, and Puerto Rican family life cycles.

Hispanics

Although the basic unit for Mexican-Americans tends to be nuclear with strong emotional ties (Thornburg & Grinder, 1975, p. 352), as Chicano culture is exposed to constant and rapid environmental changes and modernization, extended kin associations become more and more important (Mirandé, 1979).

Generally, in Hispanic families, close relationships with maternal and paternal grandparents are fundamental. Of special importance are the emotional ties with the mother's relatives. Maternal aunts often serve as brokers, providing a link between parents and other adults in the family. Actually, the aunt functions as a "second mother" or a mother substitute. She is the one who responds to the problems of all family members, which range from requests for financial assistance to consultations (Jiménez-Vásquez, 1980, pp. 224–255). She thus enacts a set of roles that are quite similar to those found in Afro-American families, especially among the lower and working classes.

Kinship forms vary among the different ethnic populations. For example, la familia among Hispanics is quite distinct in structure and composition from the extended bonds found among Asians and Afro-Americans. In the Spanish language, la familia is a broad concept that may include single households, combinations, and/or all extended relatives. Thus, its form and function depend on the emotional and financial capabilities of the central families. Although the most frequent household type among Chicanos is nuclear-centered, the norm is geographic propinquity and strong kinship ties among family units, especially in times of need (Sena-Rivera, 1979).

Like those for others of Spanish ancestry, extended kin units function as connecting links to basic institutions such as the church and the school in Puerto Rican communities. Although families are becoming spatially nuclear, emotional closeness and mutual aid networks among relatives have been preserved. Puerto Rican parents and their adult offspring tend to reside close to each other. This practice is manifested in their regional distribution in central cities. As noted earlier, minicommunities of families live in the same block of a neighborhood. A similar ecological pattern of neighborhood concentration is found among the Japanese, the Chinese, the Filipinos, and other Asian-Americans. Apparently, the legacy of the extended system with strong emotional ties clustered in nearby residential areas remains as an important aspect of Hispanic, Asian, American Indian, and Afro-American family bonding (Billingsley, 1970; Conner, 1974; Johnson, 1977; Martin & Martin, 1978; McAdoo, 1978a; Palisi, 1966; Wilkinson, 1979).

Afro-Americans

Although kinship relations are salient, the majority of Afro-American families reflect a nuclear model. Extended relatives often reside in the immediate household. One trend that is transforming composition and family form has been the decline in the proportion of families with a husband and wife present. In the mid-1970s, those with a husband and wife accounted for slightly over 60% of all American families of African heritage. In contrast, three decades earlier, that figure was estimated at 77% (U.S. Bureau of the Census, 1978, p. 100). A significant consequence of this change in structure has been a substantial rise in the proportion of Afro-American households maintained by a woman (U.S. Bureau of the Census, 1980b, p. 3). Such families often encounter emotional and financial difficulties. Yet frequently these are offset by social support and financial assistance provided by relatives.

Kinship systems among Afro-Americans tend to be interdependent and multigenerational. In many respects, they resemble those of other ethnic minority families (McAdoo, 1978b). They are characterized by intimate involvement and a set of unwritten obligations to consanguineal and conjugal relatives regardless of age. Among the most important properties are affectional bonds connecting several generations; a central family member who occupies a leadership position, establishes behavioral codes, and participates in the socialization of the children; an expectation of responsibility for the children on the part of the fathers; an intense communal orientation toward family members; the interdependency of relatives on each other for emotional, social, and material support; an absorption mechanism for taking in those unable to care for themselves; and a mutual aid system (Martin & Martin, 1978; Wilkinson, 1979, p. 397). Despite class distinctions and social changes that influence family solidarity as well as upward mobility, relations with kin are fundamental in the Afro-American family system (Billingsley, 1970; McAdoo, 1978a,b).

Asian-Americans

Variations in cultural backgrounds, class differences, and recency of immigration contribute to diversity in the kinship forms among Asian-American families (Lyman, 1971). However, the retaining of functional liaisons with relatives through established customs and a chain-migration pattern are typical (Boyd, 1971, 1974; Pian, 1980). Such occurrences mirror and amplify the unique placement of families in the economic and social structure of the United States.

Furthermore, all of the different Asian populations have entrenched norms and role expectations pertaining to caring for the aged, who are usually older relatives. Most often, an elderly parent lives in the same household as the adult children (Fujii, 1980a; Kalish & Moriwaki, 1973; Osako, 1980, p. 227). Responsibilities to aged parents and to close relatives are fundamental to the family institution among Japanese, Chinese, and Filipinos, although changes are taking place in the modes of assisting kin, the degree of internalization of contemporary American family values, and economic and cultural backgrounds and lifestyles (Cheung, Cho, Lum, Tang, & Yau, 1980; Conner, 1974, 1977; Ishizuka, 1978; Johnson, 1977; Kalish & Yuen, 1971; Kim & Mejia, 1976; Li, 1975; Liu, 1966; Liu & Yu, 1975; Lyman, 1974; Montero, 1980; Muramatsu, 1960; Osako, 1976; Yanagisako, 1975).

American Indians

Although American Indians, like Asians, are a people experiencing continuous transitions, there are qualities of strength within their families; and affinal and consanguinal bonds are sustained through profoundly embedded customs (Lewis, 1981). Despite tribal as well as urban versus rural residential distinctions, kinship ties are of supreme importance. In fact, "extended family networks remain as a constant regardless of family life style patterns" (Red Horse, Lewis, Feit, & Decker, 1978, p. 71). These networks include several households of significant relatives which tend to assume a "village-type" character. Transactions within and among them occur within a community context (Red Horse et al., 1978, p. 68). Variations in household composition and in intergenerational relationships are indicators of unique tribal histories, customs, and values; life on particular reservations and in urban communities; the changing roles of women (Gilfillan, 1901; Granzberg, 1973; Harmsworth, 1965; Jimson, 1977; Medicine, 1969); techniques of adaptation to urban dislocation; past "deculturation" (Ablon, 1964; Boggs, 1953; Hallowell, 1963; Westermeyer, 1977; Williams, 1980; Unger, 1977); and individual and family problems and needs (Ackerman, 1971; Kuttner & Lorinez, 1967; Streit & Nicolich, 1977; Tyler & Thompson, 1965). Yet, the community–family configuration is a mark of an integrated social organization that serves to offset the ravages of perpetual displacement (Attenave, 1977).

Marital Patterns

Urbanization, industrialization, "deculturation," war, evolving roles, and social changes have affected marriage and divorce trends. Because of their relevance to diversity in family interaction and the attention given them in the past four decades, two events are of particular concern here: (1) trends in the marital status of women and (2) the phenomenon of interethnic and interracial exogamy. Residential mobility (specifically movement to urban centers), new contacts in the workplace, and changing mate selection and marital practices have resulted in an increase in interracial and interethnic marriages and a dramatic rise in the divorce rate.

Asian-Americans

In the traditional Asian family, marriage and unity were the foundation of social organization. Divorce and intermarriage were simply not characteristic. For example, "the ancient Chinese family was patriarchal, family centered, male dominated" (Mirandé, 1979, p. 97), and stable. These traits remain, and marriage continues to be essential to family solidarity and cultural transmission (Fillmore & Cheong, 1980; Osako, 1980).

Recent studies have shown that Asian-American families share strong kinship associations, fewer children than the national average, declining authoritarianism, a high proportion of marriages outside one's specific ethnic group (Kitano & Kikumura, 1980), and a smaller percentage of divorced women than in other ethnic populations. Moreover, in contrast to U.S. families as a whole, those of Chinese, Japanese, and Filipino heritage tend to be more stable, to have lower divorce rates, and to have fewer families with female heads.

Nearly "half of Asian American women are primarily housewives" (Hirata, 1980, p. 173), a position that differs from the marital status of significant proportions of Puerto Rican, Mexican-American, and Afro-American women. In 1970, over 60% of women from the three dominant Asian ethnic populations were married. Among Japanese women alone, age 16 and older, two thirds were married. This proportion contrasts sharply with the marital status of Puerto Rican and Afro-American women today, a large number of whom resided in households with no husband present (U.S. Bureau of the Census, 1980b,c).

The frequent occurrence of interracial marriage among Asians is worth noting because of its relevance to the family environment. As early as the 1930s, researchers discovered that the Japanese in Hawaii had high rates of "outgroup" marriage (Adams, 1937). Since then, studies of exogamous unions have dealt specifically with the numbers of women marrying outside their ethnic group. Although a larger proportion of Japanese women who practice exogamy marry white males than either Chinese or Filipino women, a significantly higher percentage of Filipino women who practice exogamy marry males of Spanish descent (U.S. Bureau of the Census, 1973). There are several sociological explanations for this phenomenon. Place of residence and occupation are important explanatory variables. Further, many Asian-American women who marry outside their ethnic group live in

urban centers. They tend to have high-status jobs and to emphasize upward mobility for themselves and their families (Cheng & Yamamura, 1957; Kikumura & Kitano, 1973). The desire to enhance status and the tendency toward assimilation are prominent.

The assumption of marital mobility for Asian women who practice exogamy has been scrutinized. In fact, one study of Asian intermarriage in Los Angeles County for 1960–1961 found that, on the average, Japanese, Chinese, and Filipino women married men with lower occupational statuses than they themselves held (Mittlebach & Moore, 1968). Despite the limited data in this important area of marital relations, correlations have been found between socioeconomic status and intermarriage. It has been suggested that, if Asian women do marry downward, there may still be a compensatory element in marrying a member of the majority group (Hirata, 1980, p. 330). What is known from most of the available literature is that social class factors, interacting with a multiplicity of personality needs, play a prominent role in exogamous unions (DeVos, 1973).

Moreover, the increasing numbers of Chinese, Japanese, and Filipino interethnic marriages portend new social changes. Macrosocietal developments and their consequences not only impact on family interaction and traditional institutions but may eventually alter the conventional system of ethnic classification (Kikumura & Kitano, 1973, p. 34). Further, the social-psychological and familial consequences of those marriages that experience difficulties include some of the same ones encountered by the other ethnic minorities: planning where to live, selecting a school for the children, deciding how to rear the children to have a positive identity, and being concerned about peer-group pressures and community attitudes toward the family. Asians, however, experience fewer of these problems than other racial minority families (Endo, Sue, & Wagner, 1980).

Afro-Americans

Although marriage provides the foundation for the Afro-American family, single households and divorce have become common. An important indicator of changes in traditional family structure is the proportion of families that include both a husband and a wife (U.S. Bureau of the Census, 1978, p. 100). In the 20-year period between 1940 and 1960, the marital status distribution for the Afro-American population showed a larger proportion of men and women who were married than had been true in earlier years. It has been asserted that, "in this century, the percent of married was at its peak for Blacks" during that 20-year period (Glick, 1981; U.S. Bureau of the Census, 1978, p. 101).

The trends in marital status patterns for blacks have been basically similar to those for the white population. In the mid-1970s, 81% of Afro-American males who were 35 to 44 years old were married. For females in this same age range, only 73% were married (U.S. Bureau of the

Census, 1978, p. 110), and an estimated 11% were divorced.

In most of the census years since 1890, larger proportions of men than of women in their middle years have consistently been reported as married (U.S. Bureau of the Census, 1978, p. 101). The factors that account for the disparities in marital status between the sexes include age at first marriage, rate of remarriage, variations in the age structure, and differential rates of intermarriage, as well as the possibility of misreporting and census errors in calculations. What is important here is that, like other racial and ethnic minority families, those of African ancestry are experiencing considerable reorganization and structural change. The rise in the divorce rate, the escalating economic insecurity of husbands and fathers, the growing number of single households headed by females, and an increase in interracial marriages since the 1960s have all eroded the traditional Afro-American family institution.

As a consequence of the historical position of Americans of African descent in the stratification system, the subject of interracial marriage has elicited a multiplicity of behavioral science interpretations and emotional responses. Because racial status and associated symbolic meanings are entrenched in the dominant political structure and ideological system, these variables assume distinct connotations in the context of black-white dating, mating, and marriage. Although social controls both within the family and outside it have operated against such liaisons, racial exogamy has become a frequent occurrence. On the other hand, endogamy does prevail as the norm for the selection of marital partners in the majority of racial and ethnic minority families.

With the advent of social changes in the 1960s, interracial marriages, primarily between Afro-American males and white females rose. Of the estimated 65,000 interracial married couples in 1970, over 63% involved a black husband and white wife. By 1977, the number of such couples constituted an estimated 95,000, a 131.7% change in that seven-year period! However, there have been few studies of the life styles, child-rearing practices, and marital behaviors in these families. It has been suggested that the "small amount of scientific investigation of racial intermarriage in this country is testimony to what could be termed a degree of myopia in contemporary American sociology" (Barnett, 1975, p. 23).

Several social consequences for family organization and interaction emanate from interracial unions. These involve collective status incongruence and ambiguities in the content of socialization, particularly with respect to the self-concept development of the children. Recently, the serious ramifications of these issues have been revealed in divorce cases where some fathers have requested custody of children on the grounds that their offspring are genetically black and that, therefore, *their* offspring would be denied an Afro-American identity and heritage. The potential psychological pressures on children have been observed as critical. Among the most

frequent tensions for interracial families as a whole are having difficulty deciding where to live in relative comfort; not being able to maintain close affectional ties with kin; being constantly exposed to public responses to the emotional symbolism of the black-male–white-female union (Golden, 1975, p. 9); occupational adjustment difficulties; and awareness by children of the subordinated position and inferiorized status of the father throughout history (Beigel, 1975; Wilkinson, 1975a, 1980b; Wilkinson & Taylor, 1977).

American Indians

Interracial marriage is also increasing among American Indians. It is estimated that more than one third of all Indians marry outside their ethnic group (Scheirbeck, 1980). These alliances are the result of a number of social conditions: residence in metropolitan areas, new occupational opportunities, frequency of contact with other ethnic groups, higher educational status, and the desire for and perceptions of the possibility of assimilation. Although tribal marital customs remain, the practice of interethnic marriage has affected Indian cultural identity, traditional tribal values, and the institutional context of the family (Boggs, 1953; Boyer, 1964; Williams, 1980).

Hispanics

Converging with the marital patterns among Asian-Americans, there has been considerable exogamy among Hispanic ethnics (Bean & Bradshaw, 1970; Fitzpatrick & Gurak, 1979). Although Puerto Ricans have relatively low rates of exogamy, Hispanics from Central America and Cuba tend to have high rates of interethnic marriage. Duration of time in the country of residence, the degree of racial similarity and perceptions of assimilation, regional location, social class variables such as education and occupation, and frequency of contact contribute to variations in intermarriage rates (Murguia & Frisbie, 1977; Wilkinson, 1975a). Within each occupational stratum, exogamy tends to increase with distance from immigrant status for Asians and Hispanics. In addition, within each generation, marriage outside one's ancestral group "increases steadily with the socioeconomic status of the groom" (Mittlebach & Moore, 1968). Interestingly, "the second generation exogamy rates for the non-Puerto Rican Hispanics are high even when compared to European ethnic groups, while those of Puerto Ricans are relatively low" (Gurak, 1981, p. 8). More recent data suggest that the intermarriage rates for Mexican-Americans may be on the decline (Murguia & Frisbie, 1977). Women of Hispanic origin have higher rates of intermarriage than the males, especially in the second and third generations. Interestingly, marriages between Puerto Ricans and other Hispanics are relatively frequent (Gurak, 1981, p. 8). The variable forms of exogamy are indicative of differences in values, social class position, frequency of contact, the extent of assimilation, and the degree of internalization of the dominant sector's social distance attitudes.

Over a decade ago, the majority of Puerto Rican and Mexican American women were married (U.S. Bureau of the Census, 1980e). However, as noted earlier, there has been a substantial increase in female-headed families among Puerto Ricans. For example, in the 1960 and 1970 U.S. Census data, an increase in such households with own children under 18 was found in the states of New York, New Jersey, and Pennsylvania (Cooney, Rogler, & Schroeder, 1980). Despite the structural transitions, family and kinship ties are highly valued.

Socioeconomic Characteristics

Family Income

It is axiomatic that diversity among minority families is manifested in lifestyle characteristics based on income and the educational and employment status of the head of the household. Most of the available data on income, however, are confounded for Hispanics and Asians by the combining of ethnic populations. Yet, it can be safely stated that, with the exception of Asians and Pacific Islanders, the economic position of racial and ethnic minority families is low.

Hispanic and Afro-American families are underrepresented at the higher income and educational levels. The proportion of Hispanic families with incomes less than $5,000 is about twice the proportion for families not of Hispanic heritage. For Afro-Americans, the proportion is about three times that for white American families (NCHS, 1979, p. 4). Thus, the stratification pyramids are quite distinct for the different populations and consequently for the families within them.

A number of values, behavioral customs, and life cycle events in ethnic families are directly correlated with disparities in social and economic status. Understandably, the ability of families to meet the fundamental needs of their members is intricately interwoven with their placement on the economic ladder (Billingsley, 1968, p. 145).

Among Afro-Americans, upper-class persons are more likely than working- and lower-class persons to have grown up in nuclear families with norms of obedience to adults and with strong fathers (Billingsley, 1968). These values are characteristic of upper- and upper-middle-class families, regardless of race or ethnicity. Although the poor occupy an economically powerless location in the stratification system, it has not yet been empirically substantiated that their families share a "culture of poverty."

In addition to exceedingly high poverty rates, a rise in the proportion of poor families, and low family median income, fewer Afro-American children in the 1970s were living with both parents than in 1960. In fact, data showing the relationship between income and structure clearly demonstrated that the lower the socioeconomic status, the less was the likelihood that children would grow up in two-parent families. Although detailed information is not available on the economic position of American Indian families, it is known that a large proportion of them also live under conditions of poverty (Kitagawa, 1965; U.S. Department of Interior, 1977).

Educational Attainment

Asian-Americans. Significant relationships have been found among ethnicity, lifestyles, and socioeconomic status. Yet, it is difficult to translate the dimensions of the latter variable for some groups, such as Asian-Americans (Bonacich, 1980; Suzuki, 1980), because of the greater dissimilarity in occupational statuses, economic levels, and educational achievements within the Asian population (Cordova, 1980) than in the other ethnic populations. For example, although Chinese and Japanese rank above whites in educational attainment, Filipinos rank lower than all three groups on this variable. This distributional pattern parallels the income component of social class.

Like all other ancestral groups, Asian-American families differ with respect to family income, occupational mobility, and educational attainment. Although the median number of years of schooling completed for Chinese, Filipinos, and Japanese is basically the same, their incomes vary considerably. Moreover, in comparison with the total U.S. female population, the three ethnic populations have larger proportions of women with college degrees (Jaco & Wilbur, 1975; Osako, 1980; U.S. Bureau of the Census, 1973) than the other racial and ethnic minorities. In fact, there are regional variations for the population as a whole in educational attainment. Among all regions, the West had the highest educational level at the end of the 1970s.

When compared with other families in Los Angeles, New York, and San Francisco—cities where Asians are concentrated—the proportion of their families in poverty receiving public assistance is much lower (Cabezas, 1978); and those with advanced educational levels is higher. These facts explain differences as well as similarities in family rules and customs and the content of intrafamilial interaction.

Many impoverished Asian families have members with less than a high-school education. On the other hand, a sizable proportion of impoverished families have members who have completed high school and who are found in the laborer and service occupations (Baxa, 1973; Cordova, 1980, p. 142). These data not only reinforce the empirically demonstrated relationships among education, income, and occupation, they suggest intergenerational occupational continuity. It is, however, important to comprehend the significance of regional variations in this relationship, for these are directly associated with family functioning, especially with husband–wife relationships and patterns of child rearing.

Hispanics and Afro-Americans. At the end of the 1970s, 42% (41.9) of married Hispanic females aged 35–54 and 39% (39.9) of married males in this age range had completed high school. These data are confounded by the fact, previously mentioned, that the Hispanic population is a diverse one with respect to country of origin, family customs, educational attainment, recency of arrival in the United States, and place of residence within the country.

Residents of metropolitan communities are more likely to be high-school graduates than those living in non-metropolitan areas. For example, in 1979, 72% of Afro-American males aged 25–44 who were living in metropolitan areas of 1 million or more were high-school graduates. In sharp contrast, only 57% of those residing in nonmetropolitan areas, both nonfarm and farm, had completed high school. Similarly, of the population of Afro-American females in the same age category residing in metropolitan regions the majority were high-school graduates. In contrast, fewer in this age group in nonmetropolitan communities had completed high school.

American Indians. Although information on the educational achievements of many other ethnic minorities and their family members is sparse, it is known that American Indians have exceedingly low attainment levels. Although changes have been observed in the educational position of urban Indians, nearly half of those residing in rural communities have not gone beyond elementary school (Scheirbeck, 1980, p. 64). Less than one fourth have graduated from high school. It is in this population that traditional tribal customs and place of residence play highly significant roles in the socialization of children and in the establishment of family values (Keshena, 1980; pp. 231–250; Scheirbeck, 1980). Despite low achievement levels, education is important among American Indians. Those who leave the reservation for training tend to return with the skills to assist in building a modern tribal economy.

Occupational Status

Asian-Americans. The position of women in the professions and as members of families varies with ethnicity and with customary definitions of the woman's roles. For example, in comparison to other ethnic minorities, Filipino and Chinese women have a "higher percentage employed in the professions" (Osako, 1980, p. 163). For both males and females, the "majority of Filipino immigrants settling in the East are younger highly educated professionals (e.g., medical doctors, registered nurses, accountants, engineers, etc.)" (Cordova, 1980, p. 142). These achievements elevate the socioeconomic status of the family and enrich its values (Kim & Mejia, 1976; Loo, 1980).

Puerto Ricans. With respect to the employment status of Puerto Ricans, over one-third live at or below the poverty level. The majority of single-parent families live in poverty. In two-parent households, women are less likely to work outside the home, and fewer of them are in the

labor force. Generally, unemployment rates are high; and the median family income is slightly more than one half the nation's average (Nieves & Martinez, 1980, p. 93). Overall, median family income tends to be lower for Puerto Rican than for other Hispanic families. The men tend to have longer periods of unemployment than other Hispanic males (Alvirez, 1981, p. 13). Even in families with the husband present, Puerto Rican males often encounter difficulty securing jobs (Mizio, 1974, p. 81). In contrast to Mexican-American males, they also have longer periods of being without work. What accounts for these disparities in socioeconomic levels and the concomitant experiences? There are several explanations for the low socioeconomic attainment of Puerto Rican males: stresses of migration, concentration in lower paying jobs, difficulties related to life in central cities, the preponderance of families with unskilled female heads, language and structural barriers.

American Indians. Rural and urban American Indian families also have organizational and interactional characteristics that are associated with social and economic factors as well as with distinct tribal histories. They have large families (Scheirbeck, 1980, p. 64), and their occupational and income status are low. Husbands and fathers tend to be unskilled or lack the training for jobs in urban communities, and they hold low-paying jobs. If families reside in rural communities, the women who work outside the home are likely to be found in semiskilled service occupations. Where families live in urban centers, the women can be found holding white-collar positions. Low educational achievement, combined with a large proportion of men and women relegated to service and semiskilled jobs results in the Indians' having one of the lowest median incomes of any sector in the U.S. population. Recently, they have expressed dismay about the recession and federal budget cuts. Tribal and family living are being affected by widespread unemployment among Indians across the country.

Themes in the Literature: Changing Historical Perspectives

Although the civil rights revolution ushered in a widespread concern about the varied depictions of ethnic family life, thorough analyses of Hispanic and American Indian families, in particular, are relatively recent. In the 1950s, writings about ethnic minorities were primarily anecdotal presentations, limited case studies, subjective essays, and time- and space-restricted ethnographies by social workers and others (Díaz-Guerrero, 1955; Dohen, 1959). With the advent of the politically conscious 1960s, studies were designed to explore a wide range of topics pertaining to majority–minority relations and ethnic families and communities. Some of the results, based on an array of data collection techniques, expanded foci on realistic issues such as employment needs and mental health problems (J. Brown, 1970; Cabezas, 1977; Correa, 1980;

Diàz-Guerrero, 1955; Fong & Cabezas, 1980; Ikeda & Yamamura, 1965; Jaco & Wilber, 1975; Nagel, 1975; Nava, 1973).

Hispanics

Descriptions of Hispanic families in the previous decade provided insights into demographic, social, and cultural distinctions within this multiethnic population (Gurak & Rogler, 1980). In fact, ethnically specific frames of reference for examining Chicano parents and their children were not crystallized until the 1970s (Mirandé 1977; Sena-Rivera, 1979). One of the insightful contributions about those of Mexican heritage appeared in the late 1960s in which a perspective for analyzing their cultures and traditions was offered (Penalosa, 1968). It was based on the premise that earlier studies tended to display positive tones about Mexican-American families, but that those centering on families *in the country of origin* carried negative tones. Other Chicano social and behavioral scientists criticized the myths, the pathological models, and the pejorative depictions of Chicano family organization. "Insider" views were based on the assumption that a general model of life among Mexicans was necessary to fully understand husband–wife and parent–child interaction and to reduce cultural biases on the part of researchers.

In the 1970s, a growing portion of the data collected on Hispanics began to be produced by Hispanic scholars. Emphasis was placed on the history of Mexicans in America (Cabeza de Baca, 1972; Carrillo-Beron, 1974; Grebeler, Moore, & Guzman, 1970; Rendón, 1971); their general family characteristics (Alvirez & Bean, 1976; Mirandé, 1979; Murillo, 1971; Padilla & Ruiz, 1973; Temple-Trujillo, 1974); and the evolution of their adaptations to American culture (Alvarez, 1973). Simultaneously, many young writers initiated systematic inquiries into the subjective and conflicting images of Chicano people and their culture, as well as into the myths in the literature about Mexican-American men, women, and family environments (Mirandé, 1977; Montiel, 1970; Riccatille, 1974; Rincón, 1974; Nieto, 1974; Suárez, 1973). It was observed that, as no hard data existed on Mexican-Americans, myths and generalizations abounded (Mirandé, 1977, p. 747). These portrayed Mexican-American men and women and their families and customs in negative ways (Montiel, 1978; Shepro, 1980, p. 120) and thus perpetuated under the "banner of science," stereotypical images and distorted interpretations (Montiel, 1973).

The economic development of Chicano communities (Alvirez & Bean, 1976) and earnings differentials for male workers (Poston, Alvirez, & Tienda, 1976) were the subject of research in the mid- to late 1970s, along with the tensions associated with marital decision-making power and methods of family conflict resolution (Cromwell, Corrales, & Torsiello, 1973). One study of particular interest, using a sample of 274 spouses (88 Anglos, 88 Afro-Americans, and 98 Chicanos), found that ethnicity did not constitute a sufficient explanation for variance in perceptions by spouses of decision making. The emphasis was on who makes the determination about purchasing a car or contacting a doctor, whether or not the wife will work, how much the family will spend on food per week, and what will be the interaction among the children and with whom they will play (Cromwell & Cromwell, 1978, p. 754). In one hypothesis, it was assumed that "the relative degree of patriarchy perceived by husbands and wives will be greatest for Chicanos, intermediary for Anglos, and least for Blacks" (Cromwell & Cromwell, 1978, p. 752). The informative result was that, for the three ethnic groups, egalitarianism in conjugal decision-making was the norm as defined by the wives and their husbands. Whereas Chicano couples tended to agree on who dominated, Afro-American husbands and wives disagreed on the outcomes (Cromwell & Cromwell, 1978, p. 755).

It should be noted here that the components of decision making typically examined are not problems fundamental for husbands and wives in ethnic minority families. Rather, their collective concerns revolve around meeting basic economic needs, providing quality life experiences for children, maintaining employment, developing coping strategies in response to mobility, and controlling perpetual external pressures.

As indicated in the previous discussion, ethnic endogamy has been another important topic studied in the social science literature. A considerable portion of the data on Hispanic intermarriage indicates that there are generational differences in the practice of marrying outside one's ancestral group. Younger Mexican-Americans are more antitraditionalist and thus tend to practice exogamy more frequently than older generations (Mittlebach & Moore, 1968). Among Mexican-Americans, as well as other minority groups, there is also an association between the socioeconomic status of the man and the rate of interethnic marriage. In the Mittlebach and Moore study (1968) of marriage licenses in Los Angeles county in the 1960s, 40% of the marriages involving Mexican-Americans were exogamous. Interestingly, women were found to practice exogamy more frequently than men. Perceptions of opportunities for assimilation and expectations for upward social mobility are among the explanations for this occurrence.

Coinciding with the feminist movement, Puerto Rican and Chicano women and their families began to be studied in the social and behavioral science literature in more positive or appreciative tones (Delgado, 1971; García, 1980; Longeaux y Vásquez, 1972; Lopez, 1973; Montiel, 1973; Suárez, 1973; Viera, 1980). A few of the findings revealed that, despite exposure to the women's movements, Mexican-American women's feelings about their traditional roles and family responsibilities were only slightly altered (Gonzales, 1980; Nieto, 1974). Basically, the deeply rooted sex-role behaviors, sexual mores, and the familistic conventions associated with being wives and mothers, as well as feelings of estrangement from the Anglo women's movement (Hamilton, 1973; Mirandé, 1979; Nieto, 1974, 1980; Vidal, 1971)—sentiments shared with Asian, Afro-American, and American Indian women—have remained intact. Explanations for this adherence to ingrained role definitions are based on the "centrality of children" and internalized husband–wife and mother-father role relationships that oppose the goals of the women's movement. In fact, extreme feminists have been viewed by many in ethnic minority groups as antifamily.

Between 1960 and 1970, two divergent foci monopolized the sparse writings on Puerto Rican families and their communities in the United States and on the isalnd (de Rodriguez, 1973). As indicated earlier, these were the "culture of poverty" thesis (Lewis, 1965; Sexton, 1965) and migration trends. Because migration transformed family structure and functioning in a myriad of ways, patterns of social mobility and subsequent changes in Puerto Rican culture were studied (Fitzpatrick, 1971; Taeuber, 1966). Of special concern has been the impact of migration to the mainland on parent–child interaction, effective parental role functioning, and consequently the significance of the helping professions in meeting the needs of family members (Mizio, 1974). In the 1970s, critiques of earlier behavioral science and historical portrayals of families of Hispanic origin escalated (Mirandé, 1977; Montiel, 1970; Riccatille, 1974; Vásquez, 1970; Vidal, 1971; Ybarra, 1977).

Some of the literature of the 1970s provided a new perspective on prevailing disputes over "momism" versus "machismo," (Sánchez, 1973), as well as on the nature of Puerto Rican community social habits that affect family member interaction and adjustment. Investigations in the late 1960s and early 1970s by Hispanic and non-Hispanic scholars explored Puerto Rican families' experiences with child rearing and emphasized socialization and the emotional development of children (Maunez, 1973; Moran, 1973; Muñoz, 1973; Santiago, 1973). Home–school conflicts were found to be frequently encountered in Puerto Rican families (Canino & Canino, 1980; Montalvo, 1974).

American Indians

Before the 1960s, there were ethnographic portraits and social work reports on Indian family life and the experiences of children in tribes such as the Chippewa (Hilger, 1951) and the Arapaho (Hilger, 1952). The writings tended to be descriptive personal accounts of daily activities, tribal rituals, and ceremonials. There were no analyses of the needs of different tribal families.

In later years, there were case studies on the hazards of boarding schools (Beiser, 1974; Brightman, 1971), the mental health risks of such schools (Krush & Bjork, 1965), the dilemmas associated with adoption practices (Byler, Deloria, & Gurwitt, 1974; Davis, 1961; Farris, 1976; Lacy, 1975), and the emotional difficulties encoun-

tered in attempts to adapt to dislocation (Fitzpatrick, 1971). There were calls for assistance in finding solutions. Yet, many of these problems remain and warrant not merely descriptive accounting but practical resolutions. Increasingly, Indians are becoming more vocal about their family and community needs.

Many of the difficulties that American Indians continue to confront, which affect their life chances and family functioning, were disclosed in the 1970s. Juxtaposed with poverty and its correlates—substandard housing, high infant mortality rates, tuberculosis, and other health problems—persistent bureaucratic neglect of children was divulged. Among the prevailing *issues* are those that center on the quality of education for Indian children, the disadvantages of boarding schools (Dlugokinski & Kramer, 1974), and the psychological stresses related to adoption (Byler *et al.*, 1974). Simply keeping children in school is a continual family and community problem for many tribes on the reservations, as well as for those families living in urban areas. Although the majority of Indian children of school age are enrolled in school, the dropout rate for those in both public and private high schools tends to be high.

With the advent of the 1970s, descriptions of the physical and mental health of Indian children as well as their educational achievements were offered along with accounts of American Indian history (Bird, 1972; D. Brown, 1970; Deloria, 1970; McLuhan, 1974), the status of Indian women (Brown, J., 1970; Spindler, 1962; Williams, 1980; Witt, 1974), and the totality of family experiences, which differ by tribal affiliations. As a result of the ideological and value orientations underlying the women's movement, more recently specific attention has been devoted to the educational needs of Indian girls (Scheirbeck, 1980).

In the mid-1970s, the various images and multiple intersecting roles of Indian women as mothers, wives, and workers began to constitute a subject of interest (Green, 1975). It was recognized that, although modern Anglo roles are not compatible with Indian tribal customs, many fundamental needs of Indian women had been neglected in the literature *and* in their own societies. In 1976, a Conference on the Educational and Occupational Needs of American Indian Women, sponsored by the National Institute of Education, explored a number of Indian women's problems and their unfulfilled expectations (Blanchard, 1980; Keshena, 1980; Williams, 1980). Today, there is a North American Indian Women's Association, which has as its mission the improvement of the home, of family life, and of the community (Blanchard, 1980).

Asian-Americans

Understandably, Asian families differ not only from those of American Indians but also among themselves. Asian children do not have a history of boarding schools and high dropout rates or severe emotional traumas resulting from continual displacement (Aylesworth, 1980). Further, their families have manifested a high degree of stability, less internal modification, and fewer conflicts revolving around women's roles. These differences are understandable, as the cultures and social experiences of Chinese, Japanese, and Filipinos are substantially distinct from those of the American Indians. In fact, as pointed out earlier, in contrast to the marriages of Puerto Rican and Afro-American women, the marriages of Chinese, Japanese, and Filipinos display a greater degree of permanence, and there is a high level of family solidarity. The majority of Asian women are housewives with husband present (Hirata, 1980, p. 173), although not all of them are married to Asian-American men.

Aside from the studies in the 1960s of internal family dynamics and, more specifically, of child-rearing practices of Asian parents (Guthrie & Jacobs, 1966; Kitano, 1961, 1964; Kurokawa, 1968; Scoffield & Sun, 1960), a frequent focus of social science research has been on changing marital customs, particularly on mate selection among women. As early as the 1950s, interracial marriages began to dominate inquiry into Asian marital patterns. Following the Korean War, interest centered specifically on the cultural changes that affected Filipino–American marriages (Hunt & Coller, 1956) and the adjustment problems of Japanese war brides (Kim, 1972, 1980; Kimura, 1957; Schnepp and Yui, 1955; Strauss, 1954). Soon attention was directed not only to interethnic marital trends among Japanese, Chinese, and Filipinos in the aftermath of the war (Barnett, 1963; Burma, 1963), but also to the psychological motives and the relational problems underlying these marriages (Biegel, 1975; Gordon, 1964; Strauss, 1954; Teicher, 1968).

Twenty years after World War II and during the height of the Vietnam era, the sociological subjects of interest were war brides, identity conflicts of children, and the general adjustment difficulties faced by Chinese and Japanese women married to white servicemen (DeVos, 1973). Deviance and social problems were often the key analytic concepts. The relevance of ethnic boundaries for Japanese who practiced exogamy became a topic of consideration (Kikumura & Kitano, 1973; Kim & Mejia, 1976; Tinker, 1973). Specifically emphasized were the tensions in transethnic families as evidenced by the clinical casework examinations of Japanese wives of Americans (Kim, 1972).

Patterns of acculturation in Chinese-Caucasian dating (Weiss, 1970) were also explored. Interracial marriages were viewed within the context of assimilation and social class factors. It was found that the higher the socioeconomic status, and the more frequent the contact with persons of another ethnic or racial group, the greater the likelihood of "outgroup" dating and marriage. This substantiated proposition provided one explanation for the intermarriage trends among the members of other ethnic minorities. There were also studies of the economic status and employment patterns in Asian families in which special attention was given to the marital and pa-

rental roles of women and to the mental health consequences of urbanization and migration (Berk & Hirata, 1972; Ikeda, Ball, & Yamamura, 1962; Homma-True, 1980; Sue & McKinney, 1975; Sue & Sue, 1971; Sue & Wagner, 1973).

Afro-Americans

Historical and social science inquiries were simultaneously designed in the 1970s to focus on the significance of the family institution in the Afro-American population. One highly perceptive analysis of kinship functioning enriched current thinking about the structural, emotional, and economic continuity among many generations (Martin & Martin, 1978). Black social scientists investigating social class and value differences among Afro-American families were the first to capture their strength and resiliency rather than the presumed deviant and negative features (Blackwell, 1975; Hill, 1972; Staples, 1971a,b; Willie, 1977). They provided extensive descriptions of the supportive and instrumental functions of kinship linkages. Among the most salient were the provision of mutual aid and emotional support to the nuclear household.

Research findings indicate that, like Mexican-American families, those of African heritage were and still are familistic, with paternal and maternal relatives perpetuating vital ties in multigenerational and in nuclear units. The bilateral kinship bonds actually represent economic arrangements penetrated by intense emotional loyalty. These bonds complement the nuclear structures that evolved after World War II with the migration of Afro-Americans to northern industrial communities. During that era, individualism emerged as an orientation dominating family values.

As a result of critiques of the matriarchy thesis (Staples, 1977), new concepts and interpretations were introduced in research on Afro-American families. Many social scientists observed that, although there have been innumerable macrostructural barriers to manhood in families of African ancestry, the female-headed household is not an obstacle; rather, it is the consequence of "the marginal economic position of the black male" (Staples, 1977, p. 136). In recent years, the matriarchical concept has been reexamined and is now considered neither a "reality" nor a deviant form when it is simply a matrifocal or matricentric arrangement. Sociologists have recognized that the instrumental roles of wives who work continue to be essential in helping to maintain middle-class status for large numbers of households (Hill, 1972). In most Afro-American two-parent families, men, not women, are the householders or heads (Blackwell, 1975). Thus, in husband–wife units, "dominance is shared between the mother and the father *or* is vested in the father" (Pinkney, 1975, p. 107). In fact, family stability is correlated with maternal employment, with dual-career patterns, with kinship associations, (McAdoo, 1978), and with the male as head of the household.

As the 1970s came to an end, the findings from research on Afro-Americans tended to accentuate familial continuity and stability, the survival of kinship linkages, social class variations in husband–wife and parent–child interaction and in family size and composition, the survival strategies of women (Cazenave, 1980; Kane & Wilkinson, 1974; Nobles, 1978) heterogeneity in lifestyles, the affectional bonds with aged parents, patterns of friendship among the elderly (Jackson, 1972), and the socialization and the value orientations of youth (Wilkinson, 1975b). Themes from earlier investigations were summarized in an insightful critique of three prevalent conceptual models of Afro-American families: structural-functional, interactional-situational, and developmental or life cycle. Three competing perspectives dominant in the research literature were also presented: the cultural equivalent, the cultural deviant, and the cultural variant (Allen, 1978b). Since World War II, the cultural deviant scheme has generated numerous deficit-oriented studies (Wilkinson, 1978b; 1980a). Yet, the appropriate model for analyses of American families of African ancestry is perhaps the cultural variant one. Concomitantly, the developmental frame of reference is viewed as the most useful *conceptually* (Allen, 1978a).

Moreover, it has been suggested that a unitary theoretical paradigm should not be used to generate research for the study of black family organization. Considerable diversity exists and emanates from significant differences in demographic origins, social class backgrounds, economic status, residential location, and patterns of mobility (Blackwell, 1975). This diversity and the varying conceptual perspectives for examining it negate the likelihood of constructing a single empirically testable and useful model for probing the differing types of Afro-American family organization (Allen, 1978a, p. 126). This principle is applicable to attempts to develop monolithic schemes for examining the structure and functions of other racial and ethnic minority families as well.

Research Priorities

Although each ethnic and racial minority family complex presented has been described primarily within its own demographic and cultural structure, three important similarities have been found to be characteristic: kinship bonding, multigenerational links, and the "centrality of children" (Cazenave, 1980). Of special interest has been the maintenance of generational continuity in a decade of nucleated and single-parent households. Although cohesiveness for American families in general, via kinship associations, was made prominent at the end of the 1950s (Sussman, 1959) and in the early 1960s (Litwak, 1960a,b), thorough analyses of the functioning of extended support systems among racial and ethnic minorities did not occur until the mid-1960s (Bernard, 1966; Billingsley, 1980; Boyd, 1974; Hays & Mindel, 1973; Heiss, 1975; Hill, 1977; Martin & Martin, 1978; Martineau, 1977; McAdoo, 1978a,b). There is a need for research on the network of relations in minority families and on those psychological forces that sustain them in an era of continuous social change and economic stress.

Status of Women

Awareness of the changing roles of ethnic minority women, another important area for future analysis, is a recent subject that is less a consequence of the women's movement than of the civil rights revolution (Cade, 1970; Hamamsy, 1957; Lott, 1980; Nieto, 1974, 1980; Wilkinson, 1970). Most policy-directed emphases in government and special funding programs pertain to women in the dominant population. One specific direction for social science inquiry might be the major status transitions experienced by minority women and the accompanying changes in their role expectations and achievement aspirations as wives, mothers, and workers. Among the questions for which we might seek answers are: (1) What are the consequences of modifications in women's roles for family stability among racial and ethnic minorities? (2) What are the fundamental concerns of these women as mothers and wives and as blue- and white-collar workers? (3) What can local, state, and federal governments, as well as the private sector, do to meet the needs of minority women who are single parents and those who are in dual-career marriages? (4) What processes occur in ethnic family integration and functioning when *emergent* role definitions are internalized and enacted? (5) How can opportunities for the advancement of minority women in the managerial, technical, and professional work force be enhanced so that these women will be able to meet their families' economic, health, and educational needs?

The employment problems and accompanying stresses confronting women in ethnic minority families require adequate documentation in the behavioral and social science literature (Green, 1975; Medicine, 1975; Metcalf, 1976; Spindler, 1962; Williams, 1980; Witt, 1974). It has been observed that, "while the women's movement has sought to liberate all women, it has focused more on the needs of middle-class Anglo women" (Mirandé & Enriquez, 1979, p. 1) than on the unique experiences of minority women. What this statement reveals is the necessity for useful data on the demographic, occupational, and marital trends among those who are politically powerless and for practical and realistic studies of the impact of changes in their roles on the family. Hispanic social and behavioral scientists, recognizing this need, have called for research in the following areas: the cultural and ecological factors correlated with the acquisition of new roles, with family tensions, and especially with the emotional difficulties experienced by children and youth (Canino and Canino, 1980; Canino et al., 1980; Moran, 1973; Santiago, 1973; Zambrana, 1980); the occupational positions of Puerto Rican women (Correa, 1980); and the consequences of these. Further inquiry is needed into intrafamilial dynamics among ethnic populations and particularly into the changing status of women as this affects family functioning (Baca Zinn, 1975, 1980; Delgado, 1971; García, 1980; Longeaux y Vásquez, 1972; Lopez, 1973; Mirandé & Enriquez, 1979; Suárez, 1973; Viera, 1980; Ybarra, 1977).

Health

One of the most important topics requiring attention is the physical and mental health status of racial and ethnic minority family members (Ikeda, Ball, & Yamamura, 1965; Livingston, 1982; Sue, 1977; Wilkinson, 1974a, 1980a). The family's economic position and its accompanying stresses are related to the likelihood of disease and emotional disorders. Judging from the results of existing case data and research, chronic unemployment and lack of marketable skills, poverty, marital instability and its impact on the emotional well-being of children, unplanned teenage pregnancies, alcoholism, and drug abuse, continue to plague minority families (Ackerman, 1971; Blanchard & Warren, 1975; Blackwell et al., 1978; Davis, 1974; Harper, 1976; Hostbjor, 1961; Spivey, 1977; Swanson, Bratrude, & Brown, 1971; U.S. Bureau of the Census, 1980d).

For Hispanics, particularly Puerto Ricans, many health problems, such as emotional disorders, are associated with the strains that accompany structural displacement and feelings of isolation on the mainland, resulting from linguistic and other forms of discrimination, redefinitions of their social identities, and lack of employment skills. Inconsistencies in beliefs and norms are experienced when recent immigrants are exposed to abrupt cultural transformations (Zavaleta, 1981). Puerto Rican families, like those of other minority groups, undergo adjustment difficulties following continuous residential dislocation, migration, high rates of unemployment, and reclassification in the class/race system (Rogler & Cooney, 1980; Unger, 1977).

Ramirez (1980) examined the mental health status of urban Mexican-Americans within the context of extended kin ties. The conclusions suggest that the incorporation of all Hispanic family members into the economic life of the society will result in improvements in their health and overall life chances. In fact, clinicians' recognition of the health relevance of disparities in economic position and in family sociodemographic backgrounds will ensure more successful clinical work with minority family members (Bithorn, 1980; Gurak & Rogler, 1980; Nieves & Martinez, 1980; Tyler & Thompson, 1965).

If one considers mental disorders specifically, in contrast to Afro-American and Asian-American adolescents, Puerto Rican and other Hispanic youth have double the rate of psychiatric hospitalization (Canino and Canino, 1980, p. 7). However, it is difficult to sift out whether such differences constitute true incidence, variations in utilization behavior, or merely discrepancies in diagnostic evaluations (Wilkinson, 1980a). It has been observed that, for some groups, extended kin interaction functions to offset mental disorders (Padilla, Carlos, & Keefe, 1976; Hawkes & Taylor, 1975). Maternal and paternal aunts and grandparents play meaningful nurturing roles in this connection in all ethnic minority families.

At present, the effectiveness of community health centers is of special concern. One central issue revolves around the question: "How can we devise more responsive services for minority groups" (Sue, 1977, p. 623)? Future studies of family health status and health behaviors for Hispanic and Asian populations as well as the other racial and ethnic minorities, must be ethnically specific. With respect to the Spanish-speaking population, for example, the generic label *Hispanic* may have to be reconceptualized because it does not denote racial, cultural, ancestral, or ethnic homogeneity. In fact, persons designated as Hispanic are of mixed parentage or combinations of Spanish, Mexican, African, Portuguese, and Indian descent (Jiménez-Vásquez, 1980). Labeling them in fixed classifications, particularly where diverse cultural histories exist, and subjecting them to categorical treatment in health care and other essential areas, intervenes in family-member self-conceptions and aspirations. By evaluating individuals in terms of racial ascription, it has been observed that the "society plays havoc with Puerto Rican" (Mizio, 1974, p. 79) and other minority families.

Research on the problems faced by Hispanics, Afro-Americans, new immigrants, the elderly, and the handicapped (Kim, 1973), as well as the mental health stresses on Asian-Americans that became prominent in the 1970s, should be continued (Sue & McKinney, 1975; Sue & Sue, 1971; Sue & Wagner, 1973). The prevailing insensitivity to the emotional, social, and educational needs of Asian women in their roles as wives, mothers, and workers has been documented (Kim, 1980; Cheung, Cho, Lum, Tang, & Yau, 1980). The questions that could be addressed include: How do we reduce barriers to the access and use of community services? What kinds of training and language programs could be designed to teach social workers and other clinical personnel how to relate to the multilingual and mutlicultural character of American society?

Among the priorities for minority parents and kin are the following: obtaining stable employment, elevating family economic position, strengthening resources, securing adequate health care and other necessary services, locating affordable housing, finding constructive ways to rear children in impoverished communities, controlling husband–wife and parent–child conflict, establishing educational priorities for offspring, and maintaining responsibilities for elderly parents (Cheung et al., 1980; Montero, 1980). Understanding the traditions of families in the same racial category but in different social strata will permit the discernment of adaptative and lifestyle distinctions among them and an interpretation of the uniqueness of their needs. Actually, *needs* should constitute the focus of attention rather than family *forms*.

Summary

This chapter has incorporated, for the most part, writings reflecting indigenous, though varied, and relatively positive orientations to four minority family configurations. Although the contributions are sparse and are different in emphases, techniques of analysis, and conceptual models, many of the social science biases about minority husband–wife relationships and parent–child interaction can be offset by the perspectives offered (Montiel, 1973; Wilkinson, 1978b, 1979). Blending the frames of reference used by scholars writing in the 1950s and 1960s with those of a new generation of scientists will enable us to make better predictions about minority family life.

Specifically, kinship network paradigms (Litwak, 1960a,b; Litwak & Szelenyi, 1969; Sussman, 1959, 1970) should be incorporated in studies of ethnic minority families. Given the economic constraints and the depletion of resources, it is important to comprehend how mutual aid among relatives can be sustained. Where to house elderly parents and grandparents will become an increasing problem. Two decades ago, it was recognized that, because the aged population is growing, "studies of housing for older people cannot ignore the aid variable" (Sussman & Burchinal, 1962, p. 329).

The research topics formulated and even the interpretations of the results in the future should be culturally specific. Assumptions regarding ethnic family organization must not emanate from models of pathology or deviance or structural determinism. Rather, theories ought to be based on the fact that, despite disparities in form and in functioning, families remain the primary types of social arrangements for American Indians, Afro-Americans, Mexican-Americans, Asian-Americans, and Puerto Ricans. Differences among them are merely the consequence of unique demographic and ancestral backgrounds, cultural histories, ecological processes, and economic origins and statuses. These have been considered here to enable us to understand the diverse contextual and institutional nature of minority families.

References

Ablon, J. Relocated American Indians in the San Francisco Bay Area: Social interaction and Indian identity. *Human Organization*, 1964, *23*, 296–304.

Ackerman, L. A. Marital instability and juvenile delinquency among the Nez Perces. *American Anthropologist*, 1971, *73*, 595–603.

Adams, R. *Interracial marriage in Hawaii*. New York: Macmillan, 1937.

Allen, W. R. Black family research in the United States: A review, assessment, and extension. *Journal of Comparative Family Studies*, 1978, *9*, 167–190. (a)

Allen, W. R. The search for applicable theories of black family life. *Journal of Marriage and the Family*, 1978, *40*, 117, 129. (b)

Alvarez, R. The psycho-historical and socio-economic development of the Chicano community in the United States. *Social Science Quarterly*, 1973, *53*, 920–942.

Alvirez, D. Socioeconomic patterns and diversity among Hispanics. *Research Bulletin*, 1981, *4*, 11–14.

Alvirez, D., & Bean, F. The Mexican American family. In C. H. Mindel & R. W. Habenstein (Eds.), *Ethnic families in America*. New York: Elsevier, 1976.

Association of American Indian Affairs. The destruction of Indian families. In *Indian Family Defense*. New York: Author, 1974.

Attenave, C. L. The wasted strengths of Indian families. In S. Unger (Ed.) *The destruction of American Indian families*. New York: Association on American Indians, 1977.

Aylesworth, L. S., Ossorio, P. G., & Osaki, L. T. Stress and mental health among Vietnamese in the United States. In R. Endo, S. Sue, & N. Wagner (Eds.), *Asian Americans: Social and psychological perspectives*, Vol. 2. Palo Alto, Calif.: Science and Behavior Books, 1980.

Baca Zinn, M. Political familism: Toward sex role equality in Chicano families. *Aztlan: Chicano Journal of the Social Sciences and the Arts*, 1975, *6*(Winter), 13–26.

Baca Zinn, M. Employment and education of Mexican-American women: The interplay of modernity and ethnicity in eight families. *Harvard Educational Review*, 1980, *50*(February), 47–62.

Baca Zinn, M. (Ed.). Social science research on Chicanos: A symposium. *The Social Science Journal*, 1982, *19*(April).

Barnett, L. D. Interracial marriage in California. *Marriage and Family Living* 1963, *25*, 424–427.

Barnett, L. D. Interracial marriage in California." In D. Wilkinson (Ed.), *Black male/white female: Perspectives on interracial marriage and courtship*. Morristown, N.J.: General Learning Press, 1975.

Baxa, A. *Report on Filipino immigration and social challenges in Maui County*. Project of County of Maui, March 5, 1973.

Bean, F., & Bradshaw, B. Intermarriage between persons of Spanish and non-Spanish surname: Changes from the mid-nineteenth to the mid-twentieth century. *Social Science Quarterly*, 1970, *51*(September), 389–395.

Beigel, H. G. Problems and motives in interracial relationships." In D. Wilkinson (Ed.), *Black male/white female: Perspectives on interracial marriage and courtship*. Morristown, N.J.: General Learning Press, 1975.

Beiser, M. A hazard to mental health: Indian boarding schools." *American Journal of Psychiatry*, 1974, *131*, 305–306.

Berk, B., & Hirata, L. C. Mental illness among the Chinese: Myth or reality." *Journal of Social Issues*, 1972, *29*, 149–166.

Bernard, J. *Marriage and family among Negroes*. Englewood Cliffs, N.J.: Prentice-Hall, 1966.

Berry, B. *Race and ethnic relations: The interaction of ethnic and racial groups*. Boston: Houghton Mifflin, 1958.

Billingsley, A. *Black families in white America*. Englewood Cliffs, N.J.: Prentice-Hall, 1968.

Billingsley, A. Black families and white social science. *Journal of Social Issues*, 1970, *26*, 127–142.

Billingsley, A., & Greene, M. C. Family life among the free black population in the 18th century. *Journal of Social and Behavioral Sciences*, 1974, *20*, 1–17.

Bird, G. B. *The Cheyenne Indians: Their history and ways of life*, Vol. 2. Lincoln: University of Nebraska Press, 1972.

Bithorn, M. A. Hispanic women move forward—Out of a marginal status. In *Conference on the Educational and Occupational Needs of Hispanic Women*. Washington, D.C.: U.S. Department of Education, National Institure of Education, 1980.

Blackwell, J. E. The black family in American society." In J. Blackwell, *The black community: Diversity and unity*. New York: Dood, Mead, 1985.

Blackwell, J., Sharpley, R., & Hart, P. S. *Health needs on urban blacks*. Cambridge, Mass.: Solomon Fuller Institute, 1978.

Blanchard, E. L. Organizing American Indian women. In *Conference on the educational and occupational needs of American Indian women.* Washington, D.C.: Department of Education, National Institute of Education, 1980.

Blanchard, J. D., and Warren, R. L. Role stress of dormitory aides at an off-reservation boarding school. *Human Organization,* 1975, *34,* 41–49.

Blassingame, J. W. *The slave community.* New York: Oxford University Press, 1972.

Boggs, S. T. Cultural change and the personality of Ojibwa children. *American Anthropologist,* 1953, *60,* 47–58.

Bonacich, E. Small business and Japanese American ethnic solidarity. In R. Endo, S. Sue, & N. Wagner (Eds.), *Asian-Americans: Social and psychological perspectives,* Vol. 2. Palo Alto, Calif.: Science and Behavior Books, 1980.

Boyd, M. Oriental immigration. *International Migration Review,* 1971, *5,* 48–61.

Boyd, M. The changing nature of Central and Southeast Asian immigration to the United States: 1961–1972. *International Migration Review,* 1974, *8,* 489–519.

Boyer, R. M. The matrifocal family among the Mescaleroi: Additional data. *American Anthropologist,* 1964, *66*(June), 593–602.

Brightman, L. Mental genocide: Some notes on federal schools for Indians. In *Inequality of Education.* Cambridge, Massachusetts: The Center for Law and Education, Harvard University, 1971.

Brown, D. *Bury my heart at Wounded Knee: An Indian history of the American West.* New York: Holt, Rinehart & Winston, 1970.

Brown, J. Economic organization and the position of women among the Iroquois. *Ethnohistory,* 1970, *17,* 151–167.

Bullock, P. (Ed.). *Minorities in the labor market: American Indians, Asian Americans, blacks, and chicanos.* Los Angeles: Industrial Relations Institute, UCLA, 1978.

Burma, J. Interethnic marriage in Los Angeles, 1948–1959. *Social Forces,* 1963, *42,* 156–165.

Byler, W., Deloria, S., & Gurwitt, A. American Indians and welfare: The problem of child adoption. *Current,* 1974, 30–37.

Cabeza de Baca, F. The pioneer women. In L. Valdez & S. Steiner (Eds.), *Aztlan, an anthology of Mexican American literature.* New York: Random House, 1972.

Cabezas, A. Evidence for the low mobility of Asian Americans in the labor market. In P. Bullock (Ed.), *Minorities in the labor market.* Los Angeles: Institute of Industrial Relations, University of California, 1977.

Cade, T. (Ed.). *The black woman: An anthology.* New York: New American Library, 1970.

Canino, I. A. The Puerto Rican child: A minority risk. *Research Bulletin* (Hispanic Research Center), 1980, *3*(January), 6–7.

Canino, I. A., & Canino, G. Impact of stress on the Puerto Rican family: Treatment considerations. *American Journal of Orthopsychiatry,* 1980, *50,* 535–541.

Canino, I. A., Earley, B. F., & Rogler, L. H. *The Puerto Rican child in New York City: Stress and mental health.* Bronx, New York: Hispanic Research Center, 1980.

Carrillo-Beron, C. *Traditional family ideology in relation to locus of control: A comparison of Chicano and Anglo Women.* San Francisco: R. and E. Research Associates, 1974.

Cazenave, N. A. Alternate intimacy, marriage, and family life styles among low-income black Americans. *Alternate Lifestyles,* 1980, *3*(November), 425–444.

Cheng, C. K. & Yamamura, D. S. Interracial marriage and divorce in Hawaii. *Social Forces,* 1957, *36,* 377–384.

Cheung, L., Cho, E. R., Lum, D., Tang, T. Y., Yau, H. B. The Chinese elderly and family structures: Implications for health care. *Public Health Reports,* 1980, *95*(September–October), 491–495.

Collado, E. Hispanic intermarriage in New York City. *Research Bulletin,* 1980, *3*(January), 5–6.

Conner, J. Acculturation and family continuities in three generations of Japanese Americans. *Journal of Marriage and Family,* 1974, *36,* 159–165.

Conner, J. *Tradition and change in three generations of Japanese Americans.* Chicago: Nelson-Hall, 1977.

Cooney, R. S., Rogler, L. H., & Schroeder, E. Puerto Rican fertility: An examination of social characteristics, assimilation, and minority status variables. *Research Bulletin* (Hispanic Research Center), 1980, *3,* 3–4.

Cordova, D. Educational alternatives for Asian-Pacific women. In *Conference on the Educational and Occupational Needs of Asian-Pacific-American Women.* Washington, D.C.: U.S. Department of Education, National Institute of Education, 1980.

Correa, G. Puerto Rican women in education and potential impact on occupational patterns.'' In *Conference on the Educational and Occupational Needs of Hispanic Women.* Washington, D.C.: U.S. Department of Education, National Institute of Education, 1980.

Cromwell, R., Corrales, R., & Torsiella, P. Normative patterns of marital decision-making power and influence in Mexico and the U.S.A.: A partial test of resource and ideology theory. *Journal of Comparative Family Studies,* 1973, *4,* 177–196.

Cromwell, V., & Cromwell, R. Perceived dominance in decision-making and conflict resolution among Anglo, Black, and Chicano couples. *Journal of Marriage and the Family,* 1978, *40,* 749–759.

Davis, F. Alcoholism among American blacks.'' *Addiction,* 1974, *3,* 8–16.

Davis, M. Adoptive placement of American Indian children with non-Indian families: Part II, One agency's approach to the Indian adoption project. *Child Welfare,* 1961, *40,* 12–15.

DeGeyndt, W. Health behavior and health needs in urban Indians in Minneapolis.'' *Health Service Reports,* 1973, *88*(April), 360–366.

Delgado, S. Chicana: The forgotten woman. *Regeneración,* 1971, *2,* 2–4.

Deloria, V. *Custer died for your sins: An Indian manifesto.* New York: Avon Books, 1970.

Deloria, V. Kinship with the world. *Journal of Current Social Issues,* 1978, *15*(Fall), 19–21.

de Rodriguez, L. V. Social work practice in Puerto Rico. *Social Work,* 1973, *18*(March), 32–40.

DeVos, G. *Personality patterns and problems of adjustment in American-Japanese intercultural marriages.* Taiwan, 1973.

Díaz-Guerrero, R. Neurosis and the Mexican family structure. *American Journal of Psychiatry,* 1955, *112,* 411–417.

Dlugokinski, E., & Kramer, L. A system of neglect: Indian boarding schools. *American Journal of Psychiatry,* 1974, *131,* 670–673.

Dobbins, M. P., & Mulligan, J. Black Matriarchy: Transforming a myth of racism into a class model. *Journal of Comparative Family Studies,* 1980, *11*(Spring), 195–217.

Dohen, D. Religious practice and marital patterns in Puerto Rico. *American Catholic Sociological Review,* 1959, *20*(Fall), 203–218.

Durrett, M., O'Bryant, S., & Pennebaker, J. Child-rearing reports of white, black, and Mexican-American families. *Developmental Psychology,* 1975, *11,* 871.

Edwards, O. L. Patterns of residential segregation within a metropolitan ghetto. *Demography,* 1970, *7* (2,May), 185–192.

Endo, R. Social science and historical materials on the Asian American experience. In R. Endo, S. Sue, & N. Wagner (Eds.), *Asian-Americans: Social and psychological perspectives,* Vol. 2. Palo Alto, Calif.: Science and Behavior Books, 1980.

Endo, R., Sue, S., & Wagner, N. (Eds.). *Asian Americans: Social and psychological perspectives,* Vol. 2. Palo Alto, Calif.: Science and Behavior Books, 1980.

Farris, C. Indian children: The struggle for survival. *Social Work*, 1976, *21*, 386–389.

Fernández-Marina, R., Maldonado Sierra, E., & Trent, R. Three basic themes in Mexican and Puerto Rican family values. *The Journal of Social Psychology*, 1958, *48*, 167–181.

Fillmore, L. W., & Cheong, J. The early socialization of Asian-American female children. In *Conference on the Educational and Occupational Needs of Asian-Pacific-American Women*. Washington, D.C.: U.S. Department of Education, National Institute of Education, 1980.

Fitzpatrick, J. *Puerto Rican Americans: The meaning of migration to the mainland*. Englewood Cliffs, N.J.: Prentice-Hall, 1971.

Fitzpatrick, J. P., & Gurak, D. T. *Hispanic intermarriage in New York City*. Bronx, New York: Hispanic Research Center, 1979.

Fong, P., & Cabezas, A. Economic and employment status of Asian-Pacific women. In *Conference on the Educational and Occupational Needs of Asian-Pacific-American Women*. Washington, D.C.: U.S. Department of Education, National Institute of Education, 1980.

Frazier, E. F. *The free Negro family*. New York: Arno Press, 1968.

Fujii, S. Elderly Asian Americans and use of public services. In R. Endo, S. Sue, & N. Wagner (Eds.), *Asian-Americans: Social and psychological perspectives*, Vol. 2. Palo Alto, Calif.: Science and Behavior Books, 1980. (a)

Fujii, S. Elderly Pacific Island and Asian-American women: A framework for understanding. In *Conference on the Educational and Occupational Needs of Asian-Pacific-American Women*. Washington, D.C.: U.S. Department of Education, National Institute of Education, 1980. (b)

García, F. The cult of virginity. In *Conference on the Educational and Occupational Needs of Hispanic Women*. Washington, D.C.: U.S. Department of Education, National Institute of Education, 1980.

Gilfillan, J. The Ojibwe in Minnesota. *Collections of the Minnesota Historical Society*, Vol. 9. St. Paul: Minnesota Historical Society, 1901.

Glick, P. C. A demographic picture of black families. In H. McAdoo (Ed.), *Black families*. Berkeley, Calif.: Sage Publications, 1981.

Golden, J. Patterns of Negro-White intermarriage. In D. Wilkinson (Ed.), *Black male/white female*. Morristown, N. J. General Learning Press, 1975.

Gonzales, S. La Chicana: An overview. In *Conference on the Educational and Occupational Needs of Hispanic Women*. Washington, D.C.: U.S. Department of Education, National Institute of Education, 1980.

Goodman, M. E., & Beman, A. Child's-eye-views of life in an urban barrio. In N. Wagner & M. Haug (Eds.), *Chicanos: Social and psychological perspectives*. St. Louis: C. V. Mosby, 1971.

Gordon, M. *Assimilation in American life*. New York: Oxford University Press, 1964.

Granzberg, G. The psychological integration of culture: A cross-cultural study of Hopi type initiation rites.'' *Journal of Social Psychology*, 1973, *90*, 3–7.

Grebler, L., Moore, J. W., & Guzman, R. *The Mexican American people: The nation's second largest minority*. New York: Free Press, 1970.

Green, R. The Pocahontas perplex: The image of Indian women in American culture. *The Massachusetts Review*, 1975, *16*, 698–714.

Gurak, D. T. Family structural diversity of Hispanic ethnic groups. *Research Bulletin*, 1981, *4*, 6–10.

Gurak, D., & Rogler, L. Hispanic diversity in New York City. *Research Bulletin*, 1980, *3*, 1–5.

Guthrie, G., & Jacobs, P. *Child rearing and personality in the Philippines*. University Park: Pennsylvania State University Press, 1966.

Gutman, H. *The black family in slavery and freedom, 1750–1925*. New York: Pantheon, 1976.

Haley, A. *Roots: The saga of an American family*. New York: Doubleday, 1976.

Hallowell, A. I. American Indians, white and black: The phenomenon of transculturation. *Current Anthropology*, 1963, *4*, 519–531.

Hamamsy, L. S. The role of women in a changing Navajo society. *American Anthropologist*, 1957, *59*, 101–111.

Hamilton, M. The women of la raza. In D. Moreno (Ed.), *La mujer—En pié de lucha*. Mexico-San Francisco: Espina del Norte, 1973.

Hare, N. What black intellectuals misunderstood about the black family.'' *Black World*, 1976, *20*, 4–14.

Harmsworth, H. Family structure on the Fort Hill Indian reservation. *Family Life Coordinator*, 1965, *14*, 7–9.

Harper, F. D. (Ed.). *Alcohol abuse in black America*. Alexandria, Va.: Douglass Publishers, 1976.

Hawkes, G. R., & Taylor, M. Power structure in Mexican and Mexican-American farm labor families. *Journal of Marriage and the Family*, 1975, *37*(November), 807–811.

Hayes, W. C., & Mindel, C. H. Extended kinship relations in black and white families. *Journal of Marriage and the Family*, 1973, *35*, 51–56.

Heiss, J. *The case of the black family: A sociological inquiry*. New York: Columbia University Press, 1975.

Hilger, I. M. Chippewa child life and its cultural background. *U.S. Bureau of American Ethnology Bulletin*, 1951, 146.

Hilger, I. M. Arapahoe child life and its cultural background. *U.S. Bureau of American Ethnology Bulletin*, 1952, *148*, 1–269.

Hill, R. *The strengths of black families*. New York: Emerson-Hall, 1972.

Hill, R. *Informal adoption among black families*. Washington, D.C.: National Urban League, 1977.

Hirata, L. C. Social mobility of Asian women in America: A critical review. In *Conference on the Educational and Occupational Needs of Asian-Pacific-American Women*. Washington, D.C.: Department of Education, National Institute of Education, 1980.

Homma-True, B. Mental health issues among Asian-American women. In *Conference on the Educational and Occupational Needs of Asian-Pacific-American Women*. Washington, D.C.: Department of Education, National Institute of Education, 1980.

Hostbjor, S. Social services to the Indian unmarried mother. *Child Welfare*, 1961 (May), 7–9.

Hunt, L., & Coller, R. Intermarriage and cultural change: A study of Philippine-American marriage.'' *Social Forces*, 1957, *35*, 223–230.

Ikeda, K., Ball, H., & Yamamura, D. Ethnocultural factors in schizophrenia: The Japanese in Hawaii. *American Journal of Sociology*, 1962, *68*, 242–248.

Indians seek to rebury remains of ancestors. *New York Times* (March 14, 1982), p. A22.

Ishizuka, K. *The elder Japanese*. San Diego: Campanile Press, 1978.

Jackson, J. Comparative life styles and family and friend relationships among older black women. *The Family Coordinator*, 1972, *21*, 477–486.

Jaco, D., & Wilber, G. Asian Americans in the labor market. *Monthly Labor Review*, 1975, *98*, 33–38.

Jiménez-Vázquez, R. Some issues confronting Hispanic American women. In *Conference on the Educational and Occupational Needs of Hispanic Women*. Washington, D.C.: U.S. Department of Education, National Institute of Education, 1980.

Jimson, L. B. Parent and child relationships in law, and in Navajo custom. In Steven Unger (Ed.), *The destruction of American Indian families*. New York: Association of American Indian Affairs, 1977.

Johnson, C. L. Interdependence, reciprocity and indebtedness: An analysis of Japanese American kinship relations. *Journal of Marriage and the Family*, 1977, *39*(May), 351–363.

Kalish, R., & Moriwaki, S. The world of the elderly Asian American. *Journal of Social Issues*, 1973, *29*, 187–209.

Kalish, R., & Yuen, S. Americans of East Asian ancestry: Aging and the aged. *The Gerontologist*, 1971, *11*, 36–47.

Kane, P., & Wilkinson, D. Survival strategies: Black women in *Ollie Miss* and *Cotton Comes to Harlem*.'' *Critique: Studies in Modern Fiction*, 1974, *16*, 101–109.

Kaplan, C., & Van Valey, T. *Census '80: Continuing the factfinder tradition.* Washington, D.C.: U.S. Bureau of the Census, 1980.

Kenkel, W. *The family in perspective* (5th ed.). Houston, Texas: Cap & Gown Press, 1985.

Keshena, R. Relevancy of tribal interests and tribal diversity in determining the educational needs of American Indians. In *Conference on the Educational and Occupational Needs of American Indian women.* Washington, D. C.: U.S. Department of Education, National Institute of Education, 1980.

Kikumura, A., & Kitano, H. Interracial marriage: A picture of the Japanese Americans. *Journal of Social Issues,* 1973, *29,* 67–81.

Kim, B.-L. C. Casework with Japanese and Korean wives of Americans. *Social Work,* 1972, *53,* 273–279.

Kim, B.-L. C. Asian Americans: No model minority. *Mental Health Digest,* 1973, *5*(September), 42–46.

Kim, B.-L. C. Asian wives of U.S. servicemen: Women in triple jeopardy. In *Conference on the Educational and Occupational Needs of Asian-Pacific-American Women.* Washington, D.C.: U.S. Department of Education, National Institute of Education, 1980.

Kim, H., & Mejia, C. *The Filipinos in America: 1898–1974.* New York: Oceana Publications, 1976.

Kimura, Y. War brides in Hawaii and their in-laws. *American Journal of Sociology,* 1957, *63,* 70–76.

Kitano, H. Differential child rearing attitudes between the first and second generation Japanese in the United States. *Journal of Social Psychology,* 1961, *53,* 13–19.

Kitano, H. Inter- and intra-generational differences in maternal attitudes towards child rearing. *Journal of Social Psychology,* 1964, *63,* 215–220.

Kitagawa, D. The American Indian. In A. Rose & C. Rose (Eds.), *Minority problems: A textbook if readings in intergroup relations.* New York: Harper & Row, 1965.

Kitano, H., & Kikumura, A. The Japanese American family. In R. Endo, S. Sue, & N. Wagner (Eds.), *Asian-Americans: Social and psychological perspectives* (2 vols.). Palo Alto, Calif.: Science and Behavior Books, 1980.

Krush, T., & Bjork, J. Mental health factors in an Indian boarding school. *Mental Hygiene,* 1965, *49,* 94–103.

Kurokawa, M. Lineal orientation in child rearing among Japanese. *Journal of Marriage and the Family,* 1968, *30,* 129–136.

Kuttner, R., & Lorinez, A. Alcoholism and addiction in urbanized Sioux Indians.'' *Mental Hygiene,* 1967, *51,* 530–542.

Lacy, S. Navajo foster homes. *Child Welfare,* 1975, *4,* 127–128.

Lammermeier, P. Urban black family of the nineteenth century: A study of black family structure in the Ohio Valley, 1850–1880. *Journal of Marriage and the Family,* 1973, *35,* 440–456.

Lewis, O. *La vida: A Puerto Rican family in the culture of poverty, San Juan and New York.* New York: Random House, 1965.

Lewis, R. Patterns of strengths of American Indian families. In Proceedings of the Conference on Research Issues, *The American Indian Family: Strengths and Stresses.* Isleta, N.M.: American Indian Social Research and Development, 1981.

Li, P. S. S. *Occupational mobility and kinship assistance: A study of Chinese immigrants in Chicago.* Unpublished dissertation, Northwestern University, 1975.

Litwak, E. Geographic mobility and extended family cohesion. *American Sociological Review,* 1960 *25*(June), 385–394. (a)

Litwak, E. Occupational mobility and extended family cohesion. *American Sociological Review,* 1960, *25*(February), 9–21. (b)

Litwak, E., & Szelenyi, I. Primary group structures and their functions: Kin, neighbors, and friends.'' *American Sociological Review,* 1969, *34*(August), 465–481.

Liu, W. T. Family interactions among local and refugee Chinese families in Hong Kong. *Journal of Marriage and the Family,* 1966, *28*(August), 314–323.

Liu, W., & Yu, E. S. Asian-American youth. In R. J. Havighurst (Ed.), *Youth: The seventy-fourth yearbook of the National Society for the Study of Education,* Part 1. Chicago: NSSE, 1975.

Livingston, I. L. ''Awareness of hypertension among black college students: An exploratory study with counseling implications.'' *Journal of Non-White Concerns in Personnel and Guidance,* 1982, *10*(3, April), 102–111.

Longeaux y Vásquez, E. The women of La Raza. In L. Valdez & S. Steiner (Eds.), *Aztlán, an anthology of Mexican American literature.* New York: Random House, 1972.

Loo, F. V. Asian women in professional health schools with emphasis on nursing. In *Conference on the Educational and Occupational Needs of Asian-Pacific-American Women.* Washington, D.C.: U.S. Department of Education, National Institute of Education, 1980.

Lopez, J. Chicana women's statement. In D. Moreno (Ed.), *La mujer— En pie de lucha.* Mexico-San Francisco: Espina del Norte, 1973.

Lott, J. T. Migration of a mentality: The Filipino community. In R. Endo, R. Sue, & N. Wagner (Eds.), *Asian-Americans: Social and psychological perspectives,* Vol. 2. Palo Alto, Calif.: Science and Behavior Books, 1980.

Lyman, S. *The Asian in the West.* Reno: Western Studies Center, Desert Research Institute, University of Nevada, 1970.

Lyman, S. Marriage and the family among Chinese immigrants to America, 1850–1960. *Phylon,* 1971, *29,* 321–330.

Lyman, S. *Chinese Americans.* New York: Random House, 1974.

Mack, D. Where the black matriarchy theorists went wrong. *Psychology Today,* 1971, *4*(24), 86–87.

Mann, E. S., & Salvo, J. J. Characteristics of new Hispanic immigrants to New York City: A comparison of Puerto Rican and non-Puerto Rican Hispanics. *Research Bulletin* (Hispanic Research Center), 1985, *8,* 1–8.

Martin, E., & Martin, J. *The black extended family.* Chicago: University of Chicago Press, 1978.

Martineau, W. Informal social ties among urban black Americans. *Journal of Black Studies,* 1977, *8,* 83–104.

Maunez, J. The Puerto Rican community: Its impact on the emotional development of children and youth. In R. E. Móran (Ed.), *Ecological and cultural factors related to emotional disturbances in Puerto Rican children and youth.* Río Piedrás: College of Education, University of Puerto Rico, 1973.

McAdoo, H. Factors related to stability in upwardly mobile Black families. *Journal of Marriage and the Family,* 1978, *40,* 761–776. (a)

McAdoo, H. Minority families. In J. Stevens & M. Matthews (Eds.), *Mother/child, father/child relationships.* Washington, D.C.: National Association of Young Children, 1978. (b)

McLanahan, S. S., Wedemeyer, N. V., & Adelberg, T. Network structure, social support, and psychological well-being in the single-parent family. *Journal of Marriage and the Family 43* (August):601–612.

McLuhan, T. C. *Touch the earth: A self-portrait of Indian existence.* New York: Outerbridge & Dienstfrey, 1974.

Medicine, B. The changing Dakota family and the stresses therein. In *Pine Ridge Research Bulletin,* 9. Washington, D.C.: U.S. Government Printing Office, 1969.

Medicine, B. The role of women in native American societies. *The Native Historians,* 1975, *8,* 50–54.

Metcalf, A. From schoolgirl to mother: The effects of education on Navajo women.'' *Social Problems,* 1976, *23*(June), 535–544.

Miller, D. Alternative paradigms available for research on American Indian families: Implications for research and training. In Proceedings of the Conference on Research Issues, *The American Indian Family: Strengths and Stresses.* Isleta, N.M.: American Indian Social Research and Development Associates, 1981.

Mirandé, A. The Chicano family: A reanalysis of conflicting views. *Journal of Marriage and the Family,* 1977, *39,* 747–756.

Mirandé, A. Machismo: A reinterpretation of male dominance in the

Chicano family. *The Family Coordinator,* 1979, *28*(October), 473–479.

Mirandé, A. The Chicano family. *Journal of Marriage and the Family,* 1980, *42*(November), 892–896.

Mirandé, A., & Enriquez, E. *La Chicana: The Mexican American woman.* Chicago: University of Chicago Press, 1979.

Mittlebach, F., & Moore, J. Ethnic endogamy—The case of Mexican Americans. *American Journal of Sociology,* 1968, *74,* 50–62.

Mizio, E. Impact of external systems on the Puerto Rican child. *Social Casework,* 1974, *55,* 76–83.

Molotsky, I. Census indicates a sharp decline in whites in city. *New York Times* (April 6, 1981), pp. A1, B4.

Montalvo, B. Home-school conflict and the Puerto Rican child. *Social Casework,* 1974, *55,* 100–110.

Montero, D. The elderly Japanese Americans: Aging among the first generation immigrants. *Genetic Psychology Monographs,* 1980, *101,* 99–118.

Montiel, M. The social science myth of the Mexican-American family. *El Grito: A Journal of Contemporary Mexican American Thought,* 1970, *3*(Summer), 56–63.

Montiel, M. The Chicano family: A review of research. *Social Work,* 1973, *18*(March), 22–31.

Montiel, M. (Ed.). *Hispanic families: Critical Issues for Policy and Programs in Human Services.* Washington, D.C.: COSSMHO, 1978.

Moran, R. (Ed.). *Ecological and cultural factors related to Emotional disturbances in Puerto Rican children and youth.* Rio Piedras: College of Education, University of Puerto Rico, 1973.

Muñoz, R. Family structure and the development of the child. In R. Moran (Ed.), *Ecological and cultural factors related to emotional disturbances in Puerto Rican children and youth.* Rio Pedras: College of Education, University of Puerto Rico, 1973.

Muramatsu, M. Family planning practice among the Japanese. *Eugenics Quarterly,* 1960, *7*(March), 23–30.

Murguia, E., & Frisbie, W. P. Trends in Mexican-American intermarriage: Recent findings in perspective. *Social Science Quarterly,* 1977, *58*(December), 374–389.

Murillo-Rohde, I. Family life among mainland Puerto Ricans in New York City slums. *Perspectives on Psychiatric Care,* 1976, *14,* 174–179.

Murillo, N. The Mexican-American family. In N. Wagner & M. Haug (Eds.), *Chicanos: Social and psychological perspectives.* St. Louis: C. V. Mosby, 1971.

Nagel, G. American Indian life: Unemployment, ill health, and skid rows. *Current,* 1975, No. 169, 34–43.

National Center for Health Statistics. *Health United States—1979.* DHEW Pub. No. (PHS) 80-1232. Office of Health Research, Statistics, and Technology. Washington, D.C.: U.S. Government Printing Office, 1979.

Nava, Y. The Chicana and employment: Needs analysis and recommendations for legislation. *Regeneración,* 1973, *2,* 7–8.

Nieto, C. Chicanas and the women's rights movement, a perspective. *Civil Rights Digest,* 1974, *6,* 36–43.

Nieto-Gómez, A. La feminista. *Encuentro Femenil,* 1974, *1,* 34–47.

Nievera, F. C. Some effects of childrearing practices on the value systems of Asian-American women. In *Conference on the Educational and Occupational Needs of Asian-Pacific-American Women.* Washington, D.C.: U.S. Department of Education, National Institute of Education, 1980.

Nieves, J., & Martinez, M. Puerto Rican women in higher education in the United States. In *Conference on the Educational and Occupational Needs of Hispanic Women.* Washington, D.C.: U.S. Department of Education, National Institute of Education, 1980.

Nobles, W. African root and American fruit: The black family. *Journal of Social and Behavioral Sciences,* 1974, *20,* 52–64.

Nobles, W. Toward an empirical and theoretical framework for defining black families. *Journal of Marriage and the Family,* 1978, *40,* 679–688.

Osako, M. Intergenerational relations as an aspect of assimilation: The case of Japanese Americans. *Sociological Inquiry,* 1976, *46.*

Osako, M. The effects of Asian-American kinship systems on women's educational and occupational attainment. In *Conference on the Educational and Occupational Needs of Asian-Pacific-American Women.* Washington, D.C.: U.S. Department of Education, National Institute of Education, 1980.

Pacific/Asian American Mental Health Research Center Research Review (P/AAMHRC), 1983, *2*(January), 1–11.

Padilla, A., & Ruiz, R. *Latino mental health: A review of literature.* Washington, D.C.: National Institute of Mental Health, 1973.

Palisi, B. J. Ethnic generation and family structure. *Journal of Marriage and the Family,* 1966, *28*(February), 49–50.

Penalosa, F. The changing Mexican-American in Southern California. *Sociology and Social Research,* 1967, *51*(July), 405–417.

Penalosa, F. Mexican family roles. *Journal of Marriage and the Family,* 1968, *30,* 680–689.

Perez, J. *A profile of the Puerto Rican community in the United States.* New York: National Puerto Rican Forum, 1979.

Peters, M. The black family—perpetuating the myths: An analysis of family sociology textbook treatment of black families. *The Family Coordinator,* 1974, *23,* 349–357.

Pian, C. Immigration of Asian women and the status of recent Asian women immigrants. In *Conference on the Educational and Occupational Needs of Asian-Pacific-American Women.* Washington, D.C.: U.S. Department of Education, National Institute of Education, 1980.

Pinkney, A. "The family." In A. Pinkney, *Black Americans.* Englewood Cliffs, N.J.: Prentice-Hall, 1975.

Poston, D., Alvirez, D., & Tienda, M. Earnings differentials between Anglo and Mexican American male workers in 1960 and 1970: Changes in the "cost" of being Mexican American. *Social Science Quarterly,* 1976, *57,* 618–631.

Project on the Status and Education of Women. *Spanish speaking women and higher education: A review of their current status:* Washington, D.C.: Association of American Colleges, 1975.

Ramirez, O. Extended family phenomena and mental health among urban Mexican Americans. *Dissertation Abstracts,* 1980, *41*(August), 698.

Red Horse, J. American Indian families: Research perspectives. In *Proceedings of the Conference on Research Issues, The American Indian family: Strengths and stresses.* Isleta, N.M.: American Indian Social Research and Development Association, 1981.

Red Horse, J. G., Lewis, R., Feit, M., & Decker, J. Family behavior of urban American Indians. *Social Casework,* 1978, *59*(February), 67–72.

Rendón, A. *Chicano manifesto: The history and aspirations of the second largest minority in America.* New York: Collier Books, 1971.

Riccatille, R. The sexual stereotypes of the Chicana in literature. *Encuentro Femenil,* 1974, *1,* 48–56.

Rincón, B. La Chicana, her role in the past and her search for a new role in the future. *Regeneración,* 1974, *2,* 36–39.

Rogler, L. H., & Cooney, R. S. Intergenerational change in ethnic identity in the Puerto Rican family. *Research Bulletin,* 1980, *3*(January), 1–3.

Rubel, A. L. *Across the tracks: Mexican-Americans in a Texas city.* Austin: University of Texas Press. 1966.

Samora, J., & Lamanna, R. *Mexican-Americans in a Midwest metropolis: A study of East Chicago.* Los Angeles: Division of Research, Graduate School of Business Administration, University of California at Los Angeles, Advance Report No. 8, 1967.

Sánchez, E. Machismo vs. momism in Puerto Rico. In R. Moran (Ed.), *Ecological and cultural factors related to emotional disturbances in*

Puerto Rican children and youth. Rio Piedras: College of Education, University of Puerto Rico, 1973.

Santiago, G. The impact of some factors to the Puerto Rican community on children's development. In R. Moran (Ed.), *Ecological and cultural factors related to emotional disturbances in Puerto Rican children and youth.* Rio Piedras: College of Education, University of Puerto Rico, 1973.

Scheirbeck, H. Current educational status of American Indian girls. In *Conference on the Educational and Occupational Needs of American Indian Women.* Washington, D.C.: U.S. Department of Education, National Institute of Education, 1980.

Schnepp, G., & Yui, A. Cultural and marital adjustment of Japanese war brides. *American Journal of Sociology,* 1955, *61,* 48–50.

Scoffield, R., & Sun, C. A comparative study of the differential effect upon personality of Chinese and American child training practices. *Journal of Social Psychology,* 1960, *52,* 221–224.

Sena-Rivera, J. Extended kinship in the United States: Competing models and the case of La Familia Chicana.'' *Journal of Marriage and the Family,* 1979, *41*(February), 121–129.

Sexton, P. *East Harlem.* New York: Harper & Row, 1965.

Shepro, T. Impediments to Hispanic women organizing. In *Conference on the Educational and Occupational Needs of Hispanic Women.* Washington, D.C.: U.S. Department of Education, National Institute of Education, 1980.

Spindler, L. Menominee women and culture change. *American Anthropological Association Memoir 91.* Menasha, Wisconsin: American Anthropological Association, 1962.

Spivey, G. H. The health of American Indian children in multiproblem families. *Social Science and Medicine,* 1977, *11,* 357–359.

Staples, R. *The black family: Essays and studies.* Belmont, Calif.: Wadsworth, 1971. (a)

Staples, R. Towards a sociology of the black family: A theoretical and methodological assessment. *Journal of Marriage and the Family,* 1971, *33,* 119–138. (b)

Staples, R. The myth of the black matriarchy. In D. Wilkinson & R. Taylor (Eds.), *The black male in America.* Chicago: Nelson Hall, 1977.

Staples, R., & Mirandé, A. Racial and cultural variations among American families: A decennial review of the literature on minority families. *Journal of Marriage and the Family,* 1980, *42,* 887–903.

Steward, M., & Steward, D. The observations of Anglo, Mexican, and Chinese-American mothers teaching their young sons. *Child Development,* 1973, *44,* 329–337.

Strauss, A. Strain and harmony in American-Japanese war-bride marriages. *Marriage and Family Living,* 1954, *16,* 99–106.

Streit, F., & Nicolich, M. J. Myths versus data on American Indian drug abuse. *Journal of Drug Education,* 1977, *7,* 117–122.

Suárez, C. Sexual stereotypes-psychological and cultural survival. In *Education for Survival.* Washington, D.C.: National Education Association, 1973.

Sue, S. Community mental health services to minority groups: Some optimism, some pessimism. *American Psychologist,* 1977, *32,* 616–624.

Sue, S., & Kirk, B. Differential characteristics of Japanese and Chinese American college students. *Journal of Counseling Psychology,* 1973, *20,* 142–148.

Sue, S., & McKinney, H. Asian Americans in the community mental health care system. *American Journal of Orthopsychiatry,* 1975, *45,* 111–118.

Sue, S., & Sue, D. Chinese-American personality and mental health.'' *Amerasia Journal,* 1971, *1,* 36–49.

Sue, S., & Wagner, N. (Eds.). *Asian Americans: Psychological perspectives.* Palo Alto, Calif.: Science and Behavior Books, 1973.

Sussman, M. The isolated nuclear family: Fact or fiction. *Social Problems,* 1959, *6,* 333–340.

Sussman, M. The urban kin network in the formulation of family theory. In R. Hill & R. Konig (Eds.), *Families in East and West.* Paris: Mouton, 1970.

Sussman, M., & Burchinal, L. Kin family network: Unheralded structure in current conceptualizations of family functioning. *Journal of Marriage and the Family,* 1962 (August), 231–240.

Suzuki, B. Education and the socialization of Asian Americans: A revisionist analysis of the ''model minority'' thesis. In R. Endo, S. Sue, & N. Wagner (Eds.), *Asian-Americans: Social and psychological perspectives,* Vol. 2. Palo Alto, Calif.: Science and Behavior Books, 1980.

Swanson, D., Bratrude, A., & Brown, E. Alcohol abuse in a population of Indian children. *Diseases of the Nervous System,* 1971, *32,* 835–842.

Taeuber, I. Migration and transformation: Spanish surname populations and Puerto Ricans.'' *Population Index,* 1966, *32,* 3–34.

Teicher, J. Identity problems in children of Negro-white marriages. *Journal of Nervous and Mental Disease,* 1968, *146.*

Temple-Trujillo, R. Conceptions of the Chicana family. *Smith College Studies in Social Work,* 1974, *45,* 1–20.

Thompson, J. D., & Van Houten, D. R. *The behavioral sciences: An interpretation.* Reading, Mass.: Addison-Wesley, 1970.

Thornburg, H., & Grinder, R. Children of Aztlán: The Mexican-American experience. In R. Havighurst (Ed.), *Youth: The seventy-fourth yearbook of the National Society for the Study of Education.* Chicago: NSSE, 1975.

Tinker, J. Intermarriage and ethnic boundaries: The Japanese American case.'' *Journal of Social Issues,* 1973, *30,* 49–66.

Tyler, I. M., & Thompson, S. Cultural factors in case work treatment of a Navajo mental patient. *Social Casework,* 1965, *46,* 215–220.

Unger, S. (Ed.). *The destruction of American Indian families.* New York: Association on American Indian Affairs, 1977.

U.S. Bureau of the Census. Subject Reports: *Japanese, Chinese and Filipinos in the U.S.,* PC(2)-1G, Washington, D.C.: U.S. Government Printing Office, 1973.

U.S. Bureau of the Census. Current Population Reports, Special Studies, Series P-23, No. 80. *The Social and Economic Status of the Black Population in the United States: An Historical View, 1790–1978.* Washington, D.C.: U.S. Government Printing Office, 1978.

U.S. Bureau of the Census. Current Population Reports, Series P-20, No. 356. *Educational Attainment in the United States: March 1979 and 1978.* Washington, D.C.: U.S. Government Printing Office, 1980. (a)

U.S. Bureau of the Census. Current Population Reports, Series P-20, No. 352. *Household and Family Characteristics: March 1979.* Washington, D.C.: U.S. Government Printing Office, 1980. (b)

U.S. Bureau of the Census. Current Population Reports, P-20, No. 349. *Marital Status and Living Arrangements: March 1979.* Washington, D.C.: U.S. Government Printing Office, 1980. (c)

U.S. Bureau of the Census. Current Population Reports, Series P-60, No. 125. *Money Income and Poverty Status of Families and Persons in the United States: 1979* (Advance Report). Washington, D.C.: U.S. Government Printing Office, 1980. (d)

U.S. Bureau of the Census. Current Population Reports, Series P-20, No. 354. *Persons of Spanish Origin in the United States: March 1979.* Washington, D.C.: U.S. Government Printing Office, 1980. (e)

U.S. Bureau of the Census. Current Population Reports, Series P-20, No. 350. *Population Profile of the United States: 1979.* Washington, D.C.: U.S. Government Printing Office, 1980. (f)

U.S. Bureau of the Census. Census of Population: 1980 Supplemental Reports. PC80S1-1, *Age, Sex, Race, and Spanish Origin of the Population by Regions, Divisions, and States: 1980.* Washington, D.C.: U.S. Government Printing Office, May 1981. (a)

U.S. Bureau of the Census. *Race of the Population by States: 1980.* Supplemental Reports, PC80-S1-3. U.S. Government Printing Office, Washington, D.C., 1981. (b)

U.S. Bureau of the Census. Current Population Reports, Series P-23, No. 116. Ancestry and Language in the United States. November, 1979, U.S. Government Printing Office, Washington, D.C., 1982.

U.S. Bureau of the Census. Census of Population, 1980. *General Social and Economic Characteristics: U.S. Summary.* PC80(1)-C1. Washington, D.C.: U.S. Government Printing Office, 1983.

U.S. Department of Interior. *Facts on American Indians and Alaskan Natives.* Washington, D.C.: Bureau of Indian Affairs, 1977.

U.S. Department of Interior. *The Indian people.* Washington, D.C.: Bureau of Indian Affairs, 1980.

U.S. Department of Labor. The New York Puerto Rican: Patterns of work experiences, poverty profiles. *Regional Reports No. 4.* New York: Author, 1971.

Vásquez, E. The Mexican American woman. In R. Morgan (Ed.), *Sisterhood is powerful.* New York: Vintage Press, 1970.

Ventura, S. J. Births of Hispanic parentage, 1979. *Monthly Vital Statistics Report,* 1982, *31*(May 13), 1–11.

Vidal, M. Women: New Voice of La Raza. In *Chicanas Speak Out.* New York: Pathfinder Press, 1971.

Viera, S. The need for an anthropological and cognitive approach to the education of Hispanic women. In *Conference on the Educational and Occupational Needs of Hispanic Women.* Washington, D.C.: U.S. Department of Education, National Institute of Education, 1980.

Virgil, J. *From Indians to Chicanos: A sociocultural history.* St. Louis: C. V. Mosby, 1980.

Weiss, M. Selective acculturation and the dating process: The patterning of Chinese-Caucasian interracial dating. *Journal of Marriage and the Family,* 1970, *32*, 273–278.

Westermeyer, J. The ravage of Indian families in crisis. In S. Unger (Ed.), *The destruction of American Indian families.* New York: Association of American Indian Affairs, 1977.

Wilkinson, D. (Ed.). *Black revolt: Strategies of protest.* Berkeley, Calif.: McCuthan, 1969.

Wilkinson, D. Tactics of protest as media: The case of the black revolution. *Sociological Focus,* 1970, *3*, 13–21.

Wilkinson, D. For whose benefit? Politics and sickle cell. *The Black Scholar,* 1974, *5*(May), 26–31. (a)

Wilkinson, D. Racial socialization through children's toys: A socio-historical examination. *Journal of Black Studies,* 1974, *5*, 96–109. (b)

Wilkinson, D. *Black male/white female: The sociology of interracial dating and marriage.* Morristown, N.J.: General Learning Press, 1975. (a)

Wilkinson, D. Black youth. In R. Havighurst (Ed.), *Youth: The seventy-fourth yearbook of the National Society for the Study of Education.* Chicago: NSSE, 1975. (b)

Wilkinson, D. The black family: Past and present—A review essay. *Journal of Marriage and the Family,* 1978, *40*, 829–835. (a)

Wilkinson, D. Toward a positive frame of reference for analysis of black families: A selected bibliography. *Journal of Marriage and the Family,* 1978, *40*, 707–708. (b)

Wilkinson, D. Review of *The Black Extended Family. Contemporary Sociology,* 1979, *8*, 296–297.

Wilkinson, D. Minority women: Social-cultural issues. In A. M. Brodsky & R. Hare-Mustin (Eds.), *Women and psychotherapy.* New York: Guilford Press, 1980. (a)

Wilkinson, D. Play objects as tools of propaganda: Characterizations of the African American male. *The Journal of Black Psychology,* 1980, *7*, 1–16. (b)

Wilkinson, D., & Taylor, R. (Eds.). *The black male in America: Perspectives on his status in contemporary society.* Chicago: Nelson Hall, 1977.

Williams, A. Transition from the reservation to an urban setting and the changing roles of American Indian women. In *Conference on the Educational and Occupational Needs of American Indian Women.* Washington, D.C.: U.S. Department of Education, National Institute of Education, 1980.

Willie, C. The black family and social class. In D. Wilkinson & R. Taylor (Eds.), *The black male in America.* Chicago: Nelson-Hall, 1977.

Wissler, C. *Indians of the United States.* New York: Anchor Books, 1966.

Witt, S. Native women today, sexism and the Indian woman. *Civil Rights Digest,* 1974, *6*, 29–35.

Yanagisako, J. The process of change in Japanese-American kinship. *Journal of Anthropological Research,* 1975, *31*, 196–224.

Ybarra, L. *Conjugal role relationships in the Chicano family.* Unpublished doctoral dissertation, University of California, 1977.

Zambrana, R. Research issues: Family, health, and employment patterns of Hispanic women. *Research Bulletin,* 1980, *3*, 10–12.

Zavaleta, N. Variations in Hispanic health status. *Research Bulletin,* Hispanic Research Center, 1981, *4*, 1–6.

CHAPTER 9

Social Stratification

Lauren Langman

Introduction

Complex societies are stratified—divided into a hierarchy of classes or status groups that show systematic variations in available resources, values and lifestyles. The basis of stratification differs, of course, in various societies. Our present concern is with advanced industrial society, particularly the United States—though certain similar patterns are found in many other societies (Lenski, 1966). It is much easier to observe stratification than to conceptualize the reasons that it occurs and its consequences.

To observe people at work, one might stand at a larger construction site for a few hours. Some men, and even women now, drive up in trucks filled with building materials and manufactured products. Laborers unload cement, bricks, steel, and lumber; others use these materials to erect the structure. As the people work, some give orders, and some take them. Some people work with ideas and plans, others manage people, and some work with their hands. An architect may appear with blue prints to check a detail, then mutter something to a supervisor. A limousine may pull up; some bankers, lawyers, or the project's owners may want to see how things are going. Just behind them may arrive some building inspectors from the city or a utility crew to connect gas, phone, or electrical service. Some pedestrians pass by and comment on what is happening. At lunch hour, hordes of office workers become sidewalk superintendents.

In traveling through any large city and/or its various suburbs, one may pass through neighborhoods of stately old mansions or elegant modern structures as well as crowded and deteriorating slums or ghettos. Between these extremes can be found the large, comfortable houses with two-car garages, the modern "restorations" in once proud and now upgraded neighborhoods, and the modest bungalows that are scrupulously maintained—"neat and tidy" in the words of the owners. However, about one third of all households rent rather than own, and the apartments may range from elegant rooftop penthouses with gardens to small multifamily dwellings to public housing. It is evident that these communities and their dwellings reflect economic differences and/or, in many cases, one's location in the life course, for example, the "singles" community, the young couples neighborhood, or a haven of retirement.

If we spend enough time looking at *what* people do, *how* they do it, *where* they do it, what they *wear*, what they *say* to each other, and *how* they say it, certain recurrent patterns become visible. These patterns of daily life—*how* one lives and works and *where* one lives and works—constitute the raw materials for an understanding of social class. If we could follow the workers home and systematically observe their family life and their relationships to each other, watch them shop and pray and play, listen to their hopes and dreams, and tune in to their joys and fears, we could then show how family life differs in each class.

This chapter will attempt to illustrate the profound ways in which the social status differences of families influence sexual behavior, the dynamics of marriage, kinship and friendship patterns, the development of the individual personality, and the way in which people construct, negotiate, and communicate social life. The attempts of social scientists to explain stratification remain a lively, still unsettled, debate. Further, as time goes on, not only do the society and its class structure change, but various explanations gain ascendency and then decline into obscurity.

As our goal is the illumination of class differences, it will be necessary to examine the theories of stratification that organize our perceptions, direct our empirical research, and explain our findings.

Theories of Stratification

Social theories are neither right nor wrong; they are ever-changing conceptual frameworks meant to explain empirical realities. Our theoretical and methodological sophistication has vastly increased since Warner (1949) studied Yankee City, yet his observations remain valid regardless of how we explain them, even if the alternative explanations look at different aspects of class and family life.

Lauren Langman • Department of Sociology, Loyola University, Chicago, IL 60626.

The Marxist Perspective

In the Marxist perspective, the inequality of economic resources between labor and capital, proletariat and bourgeois classes, is the major determinant of social organization and collective values. The means of production determine the social relations of production and the ideologies of production. The bourgeois class owns capital resources in the forms of wealth and/or the means of production, namely, factories, transportation systems, financial organizations, and the means of marketing products. The exploited proletariat has nothing more than labor to exchange for wages. Profit is the difference between the "true" value of work and the wages paid. The capitalist retains this profit based on labor and uses it for further investment or personal indulgence.

The Marxist theory of stratification maintains that the dominant economic class tries to increase its profits and to maintain its economic, social, and ideological domination. Control of economic resources enables control of the State, the political process, the schools, the churches, the mass media, and even family life. The dominant class tries to preserve its privileges and to ensure not only that the masses will consider inequality legitimate, but that this inegalitarian social structure will be perpetuated in each generation. As the dominant class *increases* its wealth and political control, the quality of life for the workers deteriorates to little more than a subsistence level.

The Marxist perspective has made us aware of the inequalities of resources between classes and between the sexes within a class. The consequences of differential resource allocation remain a crucial aspect of family life. However, we take strong exception to two central tenets of Marxist theory (Marx's economic and political theories are outside our purview). First, its designations of the class structure as concerned primarily with capitalists and workers is too simple. For purposes of placing the family in the current class system, the Marxist typology of classes is less useful. Second, there are a number of resources *other than* economic that affect family life. Prestige and/or authority, occupational skills, interpersonal skills, cognitive abilities and strategies, physical attributes, and even sexual attractiveness can be considered resources often related to but not reducible to economic resources. These resources vary in each group and/or by sex; what may be a resource in one group may not be so in another.

Critical Theories of Social Class and Family

The central themes of classical Marxist theory are domination, exploitation, and alienation. Critical theory emerged when these classical Marxist explanations for the rise of fascism became inadequate. A unique group of scholars that came to be known as the *Frankfurt school* attempted to understand the consequences of capitalism and its unique value system, stressing reason and individuality over human subjectivity and consciousness.

They further argued that Freud's understanding of character and its familial basis added a needed dimension of depth psychology to the Marxist perspective. For Reich (1970), the bourgeois family, especially lower-middle-class merchants and farmers, repressed sexuality as a means of instilling a compliant authoritarian character structure with fascist leanings, suited to the demands of a capitalist economy. Horkheimer (1972) placed less emphasis on sexual repression and focused on the development of the superego. The internalization of the parent and of parental values not only was based on the parent as an individual personality, but the parental behavior and values as reflecting class-determined social roles. The superego thus engendered was an internalization of repressive bourgeois authority relationships that maintained the capitalist system by thwarting the emancipatory potential of humankind. Critical theory established the importance of considering the interpersonal and emotional aspects of the family life of different classes under capitalism.

Capitalism engendered a separation of household and economy. This bifurcation, by enhancing subjectivity and individualism (narcissism), led to the end of a public life and culture and a destructive emotional dependency between marital partners (Sennett, 1976). Family life and unpaid household work were subordinated to the spheres of commodity production by the working class and to commodity exchange by the bourgeoisie. The family structures and socialization practices served to reproduce these classes, as well as the class relationships and ideologies that maintained capitalism. The modern family was a privatized, serialized realm that oppressed women and dehumanized all its members (Brittan, 1977; Zaretsky, 1976) and separated them from public life (Sennett, 1976). The personality socialized by this family, although "adapted" to perform his or her economic roles, suffered guilt, anxiety, depression, and loneliness. Depending on sex, social class, and historical period, personality types produced by capitalism have included frigid hysterics, inhibited obsessive compulsives, and sadomasochistic authoritarians. Some now argue that late consumer capitalism fosters the self-absorbed user of other people, the narcissistic personality (Lasch, 1978; Langman & Kaplan, 1978). Although there has been an increase in the various strains of radical or conflict theory critique, the critical theorists and the feminists have most directly addressed issues of social class and family life.

The Weberian Perspective

Weber (1968) felt that Marx's approach was too limited. To be sure, classes differed in their economic resources, but there were also group differences in political power and social status that were not simply reducible to variations in wealth. For Weber, class as an economic category referred to a group's "life chances," the extent to which monetary resources enabled the consumption of food, housing, health care, education, leisure, and so on.

Power, the ability to influence the actions of others, was not simply a function of wealth. Many of the very rich had little political interest or power, whereas people of modest means, such as Mahatma Ghandi, Fidel Castro, or Martin Luther King, Jr., could influence, if not change, an entire society. For Weber, there was no honor in the marketplace. "Honorific status," what we generally call social status, was a measure of prestige, an evaluation of social honor, not wealth. Criminals often garnered enormous wealth but were rarely honored. Many who served the poor, led the religious, contributed to art and letters, or otherwise made important contributions to society had little wealth but were highly esteemed. Status was based on "style of life" and patterns of social relationships that led to relatively homogeneous status groups.

In his view, a social grouping based on inequalities of status, a *judgment* of social honor, was analytically different from a class as a dimension of economic ranking. Status groupings differed in style of life, cultural tastes, and interests. These nonmaterial aspects of social differentiation were more subtle than income and/or material possessions. Weber could be interpreted as a conflict theorist; groups compete as much over the honor of their status as over their wealth (Collins, 1975). Finally, Weber noted that groups differed by power, which he analyzed in terms of political parties. In Europe, in Weber's time, parties may have better reflected economic or occupational differences. Dahrendorf (1959) took this suggestion to reconsider the Marxist approach. He claimed that groups differ in *authority*. Private property in the Marxist sense was a historically determined particular form of authority; class differences were based on authority relationships. In modern society, the control of knowledge, information and communication by people of authority (politicians, scientists, and professionals) may be more important than control of capital. Collins (1975) therefore conceptualized status differentials as patterns of *deference:* some give orders and take none, some take orders and give many, and some only take orders. From this perspective, families differ in resources, such as goods or talent, that enable authority. Such differences further affect the family's lifestyle—especially relationships to kin, husband–wife relationships, relationships to children, and cultural pursuits.

Functionalism

Although Emile Durkheim, the father of functionalism, was primarily concerned with society as a whole and with how particular social arrangements and rituals maintained a social structure. His work influenced social class and family research in several ways. First, in his analysis of suicide, he saw that the higher social classes were less "constrained" and protected from suicide by solidarity networks. Second, as will be discussed subsequently, he influenced Lloyd Warner, a pioneer of American family research. Finally, the functional theory of stratification depends on accepting Durkheim's view.

The cultural and subcultural approaches to social status that emphasize differential norms, behaviors, and constructions of meaning were rooted in Durkheim's functionalism. Collins (1975) tried to look at differing "class cultures," how class specific norms, values, and meanings are articulated in behavior and ritual (see below). Most of the research on social class and family relations is concerned with behavioral and psychosocial processes.

The scientific study of the family and class relations was the indirect consequence of Durkheim's functionalism. Durkheim argued that we must look at "social facts," not myths, folklore, or other "evidence" of prehistoric social life. For Durkheim, society was, *sui generis,* reality. Social institutions such as law, religion, and education all served to maintain cohesiveness and solidarity in industrial society. Various shared symbols, collective rituals, and representations served to provide beliefs and practices that maintained social solidarity.

The functional theory of stratification maintains that the differences in allocation of scarce rewards, such as income, power, or prestige, is based on the "functional importance" of each job and the amount of talent and/or training required. The high incomes of executives and doctors reflect the importance of maintaining and increasing a society's economic and physical health. If the Marxist perspective is based on a hierarchy of wealth, the functionalists see a hierarchy of talent.

Measuring Social Class

Given the variations in the ways of conceptualizing social class, it has, of course, been difficult to operationalize its meaning and to differentiate it from concepts like *status* and *prestige.* Do classes vary in relation to a specific variable, or are they discreet social groupings?

Weber and Durkheim were grand theorists, and they were not very precise in measuring social class. In the nineteenth century, when Marx and Weber wrote, perhaps the class system was more evident. Class differences were closely linked to occupation. A banker, an industrialist, a shopkeeper, a landowner, and a factory worker were clearly of different classes. But the growth of industrial corporate capitalism, the separation of ownership and management, the decline in proprietorship to about 10% of the population, and the growth of the service sector in public and private bureaucracies have complicated the relationship of occupation to class. The relationship of capital to class has also changed. Capital is no longer held and controlled by a few individuals; it is held by institutions, profit-sharing plans, insurance plans, pension funds, and ESOPs (employee stock-owning plans), which have widened the range of "owners" of capital.

The concept of class involves several levels of analysis. For Marx and Weber, class was a *structural* category for understanding societal patterns or class relationships, for example, bourgeois control of the State, petit bourgeois political conservatism, union legitimacy, or the religious orientations of workers. Some authors define *class* as a "cultural pattern" (Schneider, 1968; Farber, 1971). Class differences are seen as subcultural variations (Cavan, 1964; Collins, 1975). The cultural approach places primacy on class-specific normative values, role relationships, and interaction patterns. Although based on objective dimensions of ranking, class is not reducible to these measures. Rather, it is an embodiment of deep cultural principles, implicit assumptions, modes of perception, and evaluations that regulate the person's behavior and his or her evaluations of others. These principles are the "rules" by which people negotiate relationships and construct reality. As a conceptual component of a cultural framework, class is an organization of meanings through which people view themselves and the world. They try to make sense of everyday experience and to relate these experiences to each other and to a temporal perspective.

For most family researchers, class is used as an interactional pattern; it represents the social boundaries within which certain interpersonal relationships and negotiations take place. As every introductory Sociology teacher tells his or her students, class is who you have dinner with. Thus, class is used as a perspective to explain differential patterns of interaction, such as husband–wife power allocation, marital stability, and socialization practices. Social class at a *cultural* or subcultural level of values or a *structural* pattern of hierarchical organization at the macrosocial level and as an *interactional* category at the microsocial level represents *different* levels of analysis. In many studies what the author *means* by class or status differs from the way the concept was measured and the various theoretical meanings. Thus, a study may use the term *class* when the author really means "community status," uses perhaps a measure of occupational prestige to arbitrarily designate families as "middle or working class"—and the class categories so created have nothing to do with theoretical perspectives of the sociological tradition. Most family researchers are less concerned with the macrosocial level and/or debates on functional versus conflict theory. They opt for a "neutral" or "objective" measure. But the attempts to use an "objective" measure raise many questions and problems for research and for understanding its results. Failure to adequately consider class may obscure real differences or create "artificial" findings that are artifacts of measurement rather than subgroup differences.

Studies of social class and the family have generally fallen into three categories; the case study, the community study, and the survey. In the case study, the investigator generally lives with or close to her or his subjects. This approach gives the richest data, vignettes of everyday life are explored in depth. But such studies cannot indicate the ranges of variation within a social class, nor can they generate data that can be compared with the data of other studies. Finally, such studies cannot offer generalizations.

The community study is like the case study, but it involves a larger, usually homogeneous, sample. Most of the data come from participant observation, and the larger sample gives a broader perspective—though comparisons between communities of the same or different classes are difficult to make. The focus of investigators often differs, and many community studies are not done by family sociologists and therefore only touch on these issues.

Surveys tend to be broader, and the data are more likely to be based on interviews or questionnaires. When semistructured interviews are used, the qualitative data tend to offer rich portrayals of family life, which, however, lack the depth of the case study or the precision of the stratified random survey. Surveys based on a large number of respondents with a structured interview or questionnaire give the largest range of variation as well as the most easily quantified and comparable data. But in addition to the problems inherent in *all* survey research, family and social class studies face problems of social class influences on motivation, social desirability and response sets that might artificially *inflate* class differences. Conversely, there may be no *objective* class differences in response frequencies, which nevertheless have profound differences in *subjective* meaning. The *frequency* of physical punishment shows little class difference (Erlanger, 1974), but there are important contextual differences between punishment based on control and punishment based on intent (Kohn, 1969). The survey with objective measures of social class has been widely used in family research.

There have been a number of attempts to develop a measure of social class or status. Warner and Lunt (1941, 1963) used "reputational" status as the measure of social class. In Yankee City, people were asked what they thought of the "Smith" family or of the "Browns," and so on. Warner and Lunt also asked people how they ranked the different families. There was a considerable degree of agreement on where different families ranked—although how families were ranked differed. The rich saw the poor as animals, whereas the poor divided the classes into "decent folks" (themselves) and into "snobs pushing up," "way up but not society," and "them what gots" (the rest of society). The research of Warner was criticized for lacking an *objective* measure of class. Reputational status was not clearly applicable in a large city of which it is impossible for a person to know the status reputations of other families. Urban life is impersonal and anonymous. People often do not know their neighbors. Further, the high-status elites of small towns would hardly fit into the national or international elite. Warner then developed an Index of Status Characteristics based on occupation, education, source of income (fee, profit, wage, salary, etc.), and area of residence (Warner, Meeker, & Eels, 1949).

The most important early attempt to develop an objective measure of social status was Hollingshead's measure of socioeconomic status (SES) based on a weighted score of seven levels of occupational skills and seven levels of education.[1] For many years, this measure was widely used, but its flaws became evident.

In a series of opinion surveys of occupational prestige by NORC (National Opinion Research Center), Duncan developed a measure of occupational prestige, the socioeconomic index (SEI), which has become more widely used in family research than the SES (Otto, 1975). The attempts to ''objectively'' measure social status have as many problems as merits. Almost every reviewer who has addressed the relationships of social class to the family or some aspect of it has raised a number of methodological questions (Cavan, 1964; Haug & Sussman, 1971; Hess, 1970; Kerckhoff, 1972; Otto, 1975; Steinmetz, 1974b).

In the family literature, *social class, social status, socioeconomic status* (SES), *socioeconomic index* (SEI), *occupational level,* and *occupational prestige* are often used interchangeably to indicate differential rankings. Americans have different concepts of class, such as money, job, education, or life style (Coleman & Rainwater, 1978). Whether or not these concepts are interchangeable is not usually considered. Different measurements of class show little correlation; the number of classes designated shows little consistency; the SES has only a .74 correlation with the SEI, and only 55% of the variance is explained (Haug & Sussman, 1971). Some concepts of class put upper-level managers, professionals, and skilled technical workers with postgraduate degrees in the same ''middle-class'' category as sales representatives, who can range from highly educated computer salespeople and stockbrokers to used-car salespeople, office workers, and bank tellers. Other studies place higher level managers and professionals in the ''upper class'' and consider lower-level white-collar workers and skilled blue-collar workers in the same ''middle-class'' category. This categorization ignores manual and nonmanual distinctions.

The Hollingshead index of SES considers certain white-collar jobs more prestigious than blue-collar jobs, but this designation is highly arbitrary and ignores variations of education within an occupational rank (Haug & Sussman, 1971). On the other hand, Steinmetz (1974a), using Holland's concept (1959) of ''occupational worlds,'' found that when people worked with their hands, ''motoric'' skills versus ''supportive'' interpersonal skills had better predictive power for parental use of physical punishment than did class or education. She gave an example of a man with an M.S. in engineering. He might be a university teacher, an executive managing a company or a division, a designer of new products, or a worker on equipment.

Large-scale surveys show that many blue-collar jobs are seen as more prestigious than some white-collar jobs. Educational differences may affect cultural tastes and interpersonal patterns that have *more* influence on family

life than occupation. Level of education (grade school, high school, college, postgraduate) does not indicate its quality, for example, a rural high school versus an elite ''prep'' academy, or a community college versus an elite university. Further, the choice of curriculum (e.g., liberal arts vs. engineering) can affect family life. Finally, there are historical differences in the relationship of education to class: Some ''differences'' in white-collar–blue-collar values and lifestyles may have been found 40 years ago, but as educational differences have narrowed, there seems to have been a greater convergence in areas such as marital communication and social behavior. A composite measure like the SES often masks or obscures significant relationships that may be due to a single factor (such as education or occupational status) or even another factor correlated with the measure but not directly measured (such as class of origin, degree of mobility, age of first child, family size, intelligence, media or cultural exposure, or neighborhood; cf. Kriesberg, 1979).

The Duncan measure of occupational prestige (SEI) was not designed to differentiate social classes or to be used for family research. Duncan is a demographer concerned with the social mobility of aggregates (Blau & Duncan, 1967). Haug and Sussman (1971) listed some of the problems of the SEI when it is used in family research. There are very small gradients of prestige between levels. At the upper levels, all tend to require high levels of education, usually postgraduate, but there are wide income differentials between a physician and a university professor. The public awareness of higher skill jobs is unequal and idiosyncratic. Professors are rated higher than sociologists, and physicians are rated higher than psychiatrists. The SEI pays too much attention to deviant cases, masks educational and income differences, and creates some ''strange'' combinations where M.D.'s, Ph.D.'s, and J.D.'s are in the same ''middle class'' as assembly-line supervisors or clerks.

Perhaps the greatest single problem has been the failure to empirically differentiate class as an economic position from prestige or social status as a social evaluation. According to the survey research measuring the prestige of different occupations, there is a relative stability over time of these evaluations, and there is even consistency across various cultures (Inkeles & Rossi, 1956). The top levels of prestige are political or intellectual-professional elites of authority, such as judges, cabinet members, governors, physicians, scientists, and professors. At the upper levels of prestige, only members of boards of large corporations and bankers are present and they are given *less* prestige than the political or intellectual elites. Sennett and Cobb (1972) suggested that people who perform the interpretive-nurturance work of the society are given more honor than the owners or controllers of wealth. Although most of these occupations are highly remunerated they do not constitute an economic elite or ruling class (Domhoff, 1967, 1971). Although there are some individuals from the upper economic strata, like the Kennedys, Roosevelts, Rockefellers, or Harrimans, who seek

---

[1]Occupational levels were (1) high executives, proprietors of large business, some professional; (2) managers, lesser professional; (3) administrators, functionaires; (4) clerical, sales; (5) skilled manual; (6) machine operators; and (7) unskilled.

public office, most of the males in this class gravitate toward business, usually a family enterprise.

What is the *internal differentiation* within a class? Coleman and Rainwater (1978) differentiated upper middle, lower middle, and working classes into elite, core, and marginal subgroups. Gans (1967) divided the upper middle class into conservative-managerial and liberal-professional factions. The former were the businesspeople or corporate executives, the latter more likely to be doctors, lawyers, or other professionals. But these differences also reflected religion: The managers were more likely to be Protestant; the professionals, Jewish. Further, both groups in this study were relatively young; some may have become owners of businesses and, as entrepreneurs, may have differed from bureaucrats at the same status level (Miller & Swanson, 1958).

The lower-middle-class small proprietors, functionaries, and lower-echelon clerical workers of Levittown could be divided into *expansive* and *restrictive* subgroups (Gans, 1967). The former were largely upwardly mobile from blue-collar urban Catholic backgrounds. They were more impulsive, expressive, and indulgent. The restrictives were more likely to be nonmobile and from rural Protestant backgrounds. They were more likely to value restraint, moderation, and respectibility (see p. 228). This is the group that has historically mobilized behind crusades for conservative morality (e.g., temperance or chastity).

The importance of intraclass differences has not been systematically studied in family research, where they are lumped together. Further, in terms of family dynamics, there can be a number of permutations in many combinations of husband and wife: a managerial husband, an intellectual wife, a traditional housewife, a professional wife, a professional husband. If we further consider househusbands, student spouses, and homosexual "marriages," the possibilities are enormous.

Much the same problem of intraclass variation exists in the lower class, beginning with variations of ethnic rank. Many studies consider lower-class ethnic variation less salient than class, but Gordon (1964) argued that the lower the class, the greater the variations due to ethnicity. Further, the lower class can be divided into several subgroups: the stable working poor (perhaps the largest single group); the unstable poor who go in and out of welfare; the permanent welfare class; skidders and hobos; criminals, drug addicts, and some prostitutes; and so on (cf. Hannerz, 1969). Many sociologists question whether the lower class is even part of the stratification system. Lenski (1966) saw them as a modern class of expendables. Although many argue that the number of poor is relatively lower today, those who are poor are ever less likely to find jobs. Most labor-intensive menial jobs have been automated, exported to countries with lower labor costs, or channeled to illegal immigrants.

Another problem is that different social-class groups are used in these various social-class schemata. For example, Warner's framework did *not* include a "working class." Skilled blue-collar workers were put in the lower middle class, and semiskilled workers were upper lower class. Studies (using Warner's schema and/or theory) that have used white-collar–blue-collar or manual–nonmanual may thus be making comparisons *within* the lower middle class. If blue-collar workers *include* semiskilled workers, then there is even more confusion, given the internal differentiations of blue-collar status (Le Masters, 1975).

The occupational roles of manual and nonmanual workers are quite different, the former deal with manufacturing, producing, or servicing concrete objects, the latter with people and/or procedures. Thus, the occupational skills and the social roles of white-collar and pink-collar workers are quite different from those of blue-collar workers. It is, of course, true that there are wide variations of skill and income within each stratum. As will be shown below, the cultural and social variations between these groups are far greater than within them. Thus, we will consider them separate strata with different historical origins, values, and current lifestyles.

Broom and Selznick (1981) suggested that, although the working and lower middle classes differ in cultural orientations and mobility patterns, they may be viewed as being at about an equal or parallel social rank. Educationally, they are similar, many having post-high-school education in trade or business schools. White-collar workers may often have more prestige than blue-collar workers, but the NORC prestige ratings of electricians and printers are *higher* than those of bookkeepers, insurance agents, or store managers. Further, some higher skilled blue-collar trades may pay much more: skilled construction workers often make $15/hour ($600/40-hour week) whereas a sales representative might make $250/week. In the following discussions, the lower middle class will be discussed before the blue-collar workers, although this order does not represent a clear status differential.

Another problem in the study of class is the Marxist claim of the *proletarianization* of the work force, that 90% exchange labor for wages and own little or no capital. Work at all levels is often boring and dehumanizing (Braverman, 1974). At the same time, there is a mass *embourgeoisement*, a diffusion of common "middle-class" tastes and patterns of consumption, though the "evidence" is more often a tacit assumption by Marxists to explain working-class political conservatism than actual evidence of value similarity (see Goldthorpe, 1969). Some class distinctions are blurred, and there is often much similarity between classes, which is often based on religion, ethnicity, rural-urban background, and so on.

The Marxists have made us aware of the influence of historical change on the class structure and of how class relations are reproduced over time. Classes change in size, composition, and occupation over time and/or affected by historical changes. The independent artisans of one era became organized workers of another and are now becoming less-skilled service workers. Many jobs that were once primarily male are now largely female (e.g., real-estate agents and insurance adjusters; see

"Gender Bias" below). Often the feminization of an occupation means that the tasks are more routine and less-skilled; thus, the status of the job declines. Many lower-echelon jobs have been upgraded and require a college education, not for particular skills but for status inflation (Collins, 1979). Thus, the class structure and individual classes are not fixed structures. Classes have a dynamic aspect, with changing internal composition and changing lifestyles, values, and interpersonal relationships. The relationships of classes to each other change over time. Finally, classes experience social, economic, or political events in different ways. Such issues are rarely addressed in the empirical measures of class.

Gender Bias

A significant problem is the male bias of independent measures of class and the empirical measures of family structure, dynamics, socialization and mobility (Haug & Sussman, 1971). Steinmetz (1974b) indicated the extent to which family status is based on *male* resources, a wife's status being seen as the same as her husband's and/or, if unmarried, of her father—even though *large* numbers of women have incomes, education, or occupational status *higher* than that of their husband or father. Just as Eve was religiously portrayed as derived from Adam's rib, women are still seen as appendages of the male—and rudimentary ones at that. Bernard (1981) suggested that women fall into a separate—and not equal—stratification system of celebrities, intellectuals, housewives, white, pink, or blue collar workers, welfare recipients, and outcasts. The problem of the status of women raises questions of historical change and cohort effects. The role of women in society has changed. Similarly, the general levels of education have increased.

Status Inconsistency

Many people simply do not fit: they are either highly status inconsistent or *déclassé*. Thus, a singer in a night club has a low-ranked status, but some Las Vegas singers command huge salaries and translate income into property. Conversely, the performers of high-brow culture often have very low incomes: ballet, for example, often requires more years of training than are spent in performance, at very low wages except for superstars. Finally, the place of the intelligentsia, artists, novelists, and critics is really not clear. Professors rank high in prestige, often have "high-brow" cultural tastes and low income relative to their level of education, and may live in lower-middle- or working-class neighborhoods.

Measuring Social Class: An Unresolved Problem

We have now seen that the measurement of social class incorporates a number of problems, beginning with the attempt to operationalize macrosocial concepts into measures by which individuals and their families can be grouped, ranked, analyzed, and compared to other groups. We have seen that rankings along single dimensions, such as income, education, or occupational prestige, do not clearly differentiate groups, address questions of internal variations within a particular status level, or consider the role of historical changes or of gender or status inconsistency. Further, the cultural tradition of the United States, which stresses equality, obscures group differences in rank.

Despite all the problems of conceptualizing and measuring social class or status, variations in values, lifestyles, and social relationships are associated with a group's relative social and economic rank. At this time, it does not seem that there is a social class measurement without serious shortcomings. The more one considers the question and examines prior efforts, the more elusive seems the task. Although this author cannot suggest a better measure, perhaps the problem comes from how the question is asked. It would seem that classes are less defined by "objective" measures than by social-psychological attributes based on, but not reducible to, these measures. Haug and Sussman (1971) suggested that we use a social-psychological approach to the designation of status. Therefore, we should more carefully look at such factors as resources and amount of authority (Collins, 1975; Dahrendorf, 1959), occupational role requirements (Kohn, 1969, 1971), and occupational worlds (Holland, 1959). Those who command others, those who seek to maximize profit, those who utilize or create specialized knowledge, those who master complex mechanical skills, and those who master and/or control little have different resources, values, and modes of relationships. These differential qualities of occupational roles affect relationships between adult family members and between parents and children. Those who control responsibility and knowledge and/or procedures tend to value egalitarian social relations and a person or child's inner life and its development. They tend to be future-oriented. Those who are more controlled tend to stress hierarchical relations and the control of behavior. Although a clear-cut, objective class measure of rank is wanting, we suggest that the class system be considered a hierarchy of "status cultures" (see discussion below). Status cultures differ in economic resources, as Marx would remind us, but there are many other resources, such as authority, education, intelligence, entrepreneurial skill, and motivation. Such resources influence normative and interpersonal processes. Although our discussion may use the terms *class* and *status* interchangeably, such usage is frequent in the literature and is not meant to wed us to particular theoretical usage.

Social Class and Family Life in Historical Perspective

In the 1970s, there was a growth of historical research examining the every-day qualities of family structure, marriage, the status of women, sex, child rearing, and the life course. However, in many of the studies of Demos, Degler, Bane, Hareven, or Laslett, for example, there is little, if any, explicit reference to social class. We will try however, to show some of the class differences of family life that have been reported. One of the important consequences of this research has been the questioning of some of our images of family life, past and present. There are questions, for example, about the prevalence of the multi-generational extended family under one roof (Bane, 1976; Demos, 1970; Laslett, 1965). In earlier (preindustrial) times, later marriage and a shorter life span made this pattern rare. Further, young people not only made their own marital choices long before industrialization (a pattern frequent in the English lower classes since the thirteenth century) but established their own households.

A variety of family structures are associated with different levels of colonization, urbanization, and industrialization. Greven's study (1970) of seventeenth-century Andover, a farming community in New England, indicated a modified extended-family network centering on the father and his control of land allocation. Farber (1971) found that the early New England pattern emphasized patrilinear descent, whereas midwestern kinship was more bilateral. These patterns continue to show social class differences. Anderson's analysis (1971) of Preston, an English (Lancashire) cotton town in the mid-nineteenth century, found that early industrialization led *not* to "isolated nuclear families," but to an *increase* of multigenerational households among the working class. Laslett (1965) claimed that these were rare, and Berkner (1973) has challenged him. Tilly (1979) reported a similar pattern in Roubaix, a French textile town. It would seem that the social and economic forces influencing the early-nineteenth-century proletarian family led to an *increased* salience of working-class kinship ties, which has endured until this day (cf. Young & Willmott, 1957). The allocation of jobs was often based on kinship ties to current workers, just as union memberships today favor relatives. Family structures seem to have been and still remain organized in ways that *maximize* the available resources, whether land, capital, or wages.

Historical changes in the economy—namely, capitalism—brought a change to the class system that affected the family and changes its interaction patterns and emotional relationships. Among the bourgeoisie, there occurred an "emotional revolution," a withdrawal from wider social networks to the private realm of the family, with new attitudes and forms of intimacy (Ariès, 1962). The bourgeois household became an emotional realm separate from the world of work that was quite unlike the households of the aristocracy or the peasantry (Hunt, 1970; Poster, 1978). The family household took on new patterns, from a loosely defined structure to a cohesive unit. These changes in the family affected its internal dynamics and emotional climate.

Social Status and the Changing Role of Women

According to Shorter (1975), capitalist industrialization, which enabled women to work outside the home, led to female emancipation and sexual liberation. Women became individualistic and free of social or parental constraints, at least as indicated by lower-class illegitimacy. Tilly, Scott, and Cohen (1976) took sharp issue with Shorter's interpretations of the rise in illegitimacy in the eighteenth century and the role of lower-class women: They argued that none of the evidence found supported Shorter's argument in any way. These authors concluded that capitalism did *not* offer women freedom but a *loss* of power, economic deprivation, and the "freedom" to be economically and/or sexually exploited. Women worked for the wages needed to supplement family resources—*not* for independence from constraints. In traditional families, women were neither dependent nor powerless. In the "new" capitalist system, women went to the cities and performed "traditional" female work—domestic service, garment making, and textiles manufacture—with less power than before. The rise in illegitimacy was less an individualistic pursuit of sexual pleasure than "the traditional wish to marry," intensified by the loneliness of city life and meager wages; most illegitimacies were preceded by promises of marriage. The loss of traditional community constraints increased a woman's vulnerability and exploitation rather than her freedom. These conditions often led to prostitution out of desperation rather than sexual desire. With the rise of prosperity, illegitimacy began to wane.

Although there was a rise and fall in illegitimacy, the extent of infanticide and/or infant abandonment decreased. Further, the number of pregnant brides declined. Thus, the changing economic system, the growth of industrialization, and the market economy increased the options of work or motherhood for women.

Degler (1980) showed the same emotional pattern of bourgeois marriage, affective individualism, was emerging in the early nineteenth century in America. By 1830, four basic characteristics of the family emerged: (1) Marriage was based on affection and respect; (2) the woman was primarily concerned with child rearing and domestic service, the doctrine of "separate spheres"; (3) there was more concern with and investment in child rearing (childhood was now seen as a separate stage); and (4) families were smaller in size. Degler has been criticized by some feminists, who argue that he legitimized the traditional female role ("the cult of true womanhood") even though he was sympathetic to the isolation of the woman's family life and her need to incorporate work and career. He argued that his title, *At Odds,* deals with the very conflict between female equality and the family's traditional dependence on female subordination. In the colonial period, women's status was hierarchical: A woman's status was based on that of her husband or father, despite the shortage of women and the importance of women's work. After the American Revolution, the era of Jacksonian democracy, particularly the more egalitarian values, opened up new opportunities for men. In the early nineteenth century, the more affluent classes married later. Single women of the middle and lower classes also showed a great deal of autonomy and independence. They traveled about quite freely, unlike European women of the same class (cf. Toqueville, 1840). (Among U.S. southern upper-class women, chaperonage continued until the late nineteenth century.) Ironically, women's status deteriorated with their relegation to "the proper sphere" of the house if they were middle class or to semiskilled work in the mill if they were lower class (Lerner, 1979). By 1830, mill work lost status because of greater mechanization and immigration. The prosperity of the nineteenth century gave the middle-class "lady," now a symbol of her husband's conspicuous consumption, a leisure that enabled her to acquire cultural sophistication and social refinement. Whatever their cultivation, the lady and the mill girl were excluded from the centers of genuine power.

The notion of "separate spheres" for men and women had many consequences for the middle classes. It increased the emotional dependence of women, and it also increased the importance of the affectional ties of marriage. It also intensified intimate sororal ties between women. Finally, it enhanced the power of middle-class women (Lantz, Keyes, & Scholtz, 1975). These factors led to the formation of various middle-class women's groups whose social concerns were perceived as extensions of the woman's role and her familial domestic concerns. Temperance, abolition, moral (sexual) reform, education, church service, and aid to poor families were seen as profamily activities.

Women found greater opportunities for education and/or work in fields such as domestic service and the textile mills (for working class women) and writing, teaching, social work, and nursing (for middle-class women). Women then began to organize over issues less directly of concern to the family: suffrage, the working conditions of women, and the treatment of the mentally ill and others who were incarcerated. Some middle-class women went into labor organizations (e.g., the Consumers League and the Women's Trade Union League) or political activities like suffrage and the League of Women Voters. Other middle-class women joined leisure and social groups such as the DAR and Junior Leagues. One half of all contemporary women's organizations had been begun by the end of the nineteenth century (O'Neill, 1969).

For segments of the more affluent, the enhancement of the women's power in the home not only increased individualism and involvement outside the family but ultimately challenged the very family structure that engendered this pattern. A sense of domestic oppression and/or common college experiences strengthened emotional ties between middle-class women. This pattern, together with women's intensified individualism and emerging alternatives outside the family, led to conflict between the traditional role of domesticity and aspirations for genuine autonomy in the late nineteenth century. Professional (educated) women of that time were less likely to marry. The same forces that led some middle-class women to pursue domestic causes, such as moral propriety, led others to rebel and advocate free love, contraception, and defiance of "traditional" concerns. There was a rise in divorce in the late nineteenth century.

In the course of time, and with the growth of industrial affluence, many working- and lower-class women adapted some of the middle-class values of domesticity and moral crusade. In the course of westward migration and/or farming, these women often assumed male responsibilities (e.g., handling guns, money, and land), which increased their self-esteem and power. But class became a divisive issue for women. Middle-class women sought the vote and job opportunities; work was seen as self-fulfilling. Working-class women began to experience more opportunities. But for the working-class women work was (1) in addition to household and child rearing and (2) dull, boring, and dehumanizing. These class differences in women's concerns are still with us. Many of the issues of women's role, family life, and sexuality that seem so new can be traced to changes in the family that were evident in the early nineteenth century.

What led to the Victorian ideology among the late-nineteenth-century bourgeoisie? Marxists argue that capital formation required sexual repression via the conservation of sperm (Cominus, 1963; Marcus, 1964; Marcuse, 1955). But the economic problem of the Victorian era was *consumption*, not investment. Advertising emerged to stimulate family consumption (Ewen, 1977). Collins (1975) and Smith (1978) tried to explain nineteenth-century Victorianism as a means of maintaining and enhancing the status of the middle-class women. Marriage was (is) an exchange relation. For the middle-class woman, without economic resources, control over sexuality and fertility enhanced her exchange value. She could provide sexual gratification and children in return for her husband's economic support, social status, and "autonomy" within her "proper sphere" of domesticity. The increasing autonomy of these women, their supposed "moral" superiority, and their involvement in "moral purity" movements (temperance and anti-prostitution, which were attempts to limit competition) enhanced the market for sexuality *within* marriage and increased their autonomy and equality in their "separate domestic sphere" and the general status of married women. Victorian morality was a luxury for middle-class women. Working-class and/or black women were suitable for male sexual exploitation. For a working-class woman, looks and/or sexual favors were more likely to enhance chances for upward mobility than the very remote chance of education (Elder, 1969; Lerner, 1979).

The Role of Children. Demos (1970) noted that, in seventeenth century, colonial society childhood was barely recognized as it is known and understood today. The major concern was breaking the child's will and selfishness through Puritan religion and an occasional whipping. By 6 or 7, the child was expected to act as a little adult in family relations and at work or church. But the open frontier and "unlimited" economic opportunity undermined parental authority and community constraint. Toqueville (1840) noted the independence and egalitarianism between man and wife and parent and child: the more egalitarian relation of parent and child was seen as leading to greater independence by Toqueville. How independent, unruly, undisciplined, and disrespectful to adults American children were! A modern egalitarian family and a more indulgent childhood thus emerged by the time of the American Revolution and continued to become more prevalent (see also Degler, 1980; Greven, 1970).

By the middle of the 1800s, doctors had replaced midwives in the delivery of middle-class children, a pattern later adopted by working- and lower-class mothers. Mother of the middle and upper classes became concerned with the child-rearing advice of "experts." They were more likely to breast feed their infants and assume the primary role in child rearing. There was a decline in the use of money and power to control the child by middle-class and upper-class fathers. The use of physical punishment declined in the early nineteenth century, especially among the middle class. There was less concern about subduing the child's will and more concern with psychological techniques, love, shame, deprivation, isolation, and so on (Degler, 1980; Greven, 1970; Wells, 1975). By the end of the Civil War, this middle-class pattern had diffused to the working class, and most working-class children were kept in school until the eighth grade. Finally, it might be noted, that, part and parcel of the greater emotional investment in child rearing and concern about the child's emotional state, in the late nineteenth century some American writers were advising parents to be cognizant of the child's natural sexuality—before Freud even turned to psychiatry.

The Role of Young Adults. By the end of the nineteenth century, the concentration of teenagers in the city—often immigrants—coincided with the growth of high schools. *Adolescence,* the term used by G. Stanley Hall in 1904, was now defined as a social problem. Many young men became delinquents. In the early twentieth century, sociology, the new science of society, began to study gangs (Thrasher, 1927) and maladjusted girls (Thomas, 1923). We now see that the growth of adolescent youth cultures is necessary for the socialization of identity in a society in which there is a separation of household and economy (Eisenstadt, 1956). This was the case among the urban middle and working classes.

Industrialization and urbanization in the nineteenth century were also associated with patterns of boarding. Younger individuals or couples with limited resources rented a room and often took meals in the homes of older people, where, because of their place in the life cycle, "extra rooms" were available. Modell and Hareven (1973) reported this pattern for the urban middle class, especially among younger unmarried workers. Anderson (1971) argued that, for the working classes with limited

resources, it was advantageous to share or reduce costs by multigenerational coresidence and/or boarding. Modell and Hareven suggested that, by the end of the nineteenth century, boarding had lost its "middle-class" respectability and was "overshadowed" by lower-class boarding—which elicited moralistic responses.

Black Families and Immigrant Families

Most of this discussion has concerned native-born white middle-class and working-class families. There were other groups as well. Perhaps one of the most important directions of the new historical research has been to cast doubt on the "accepted" thesis that slavery, like a concentration camp, destroyed the black family and infantilized the personality (Elkins, 1959). Rather, research by Gutman (1976) and by Fogel and Engerman (1974) suggests that, among the plantation slaves, there were stable two-parent marriages, strong attachments, kinship patterns, absence of polygamy, avoidance of cousin marriage, and so on. Premarital sex and pregnancy were common, often by white exploitation, but patterns of stable marriage were frequent. After emancipation, former slaves entered Union camps as families, and most sought marriage licenses. After emancipation, there was a higher percentage of black women working than whites (employed in the lowest echelon of domestic service, to be sure).[2] It seems that the migration to the urban North was more deleterious to family stability than slavery and sharecropping. In this setting, extended kinship patterns became important means of adaptation (see Stack, 1974; and p. 232).

Immigrant families that were mostly working class were more likely to be nuclear than extended. Continuing certain European patterns, they were more likely to marry later and to have more children than natives. However, males with higher incomes married earlier. The women ran the house and controlled the expenses (cf. Thomas & Znaniecki, 1927/1958). Irish, Italian, and Polish women were more likely to work than natives.

We have seen how feudalism, early capitalism, and industrialization not only changed the class system and the family but established certain patterns of class-specific family differences. As the economic system changed, so did familial and individual means of maximizing resources. In some cases, the nuclear family was best suited for enhancing resources. In others, modified extension kinship patterns were more profitable. For the working class, kinship ties were advantageous. But resources changed—not only economic resources but so-

---

[2]See Lerner (1979) for the history of black women's involvement in self-improvement through education, social service, and so on. But these black women's clubs had to await a certain critical mass of educated middle-class women. Because of both the white patterns of discrimination and black traditions of the family, black women were more likely to achieve higher education and job mobility than black men.

cial and psychological resources—and they varied by historical time and class. For example, female sexuality could be a resource by either allocation or limitation (Victorianism). Similarly, as societal wealth increased, especially for the bourgeoisie, economic resources were less scarce and psychological rewards gained value. The marital relation, as well as child rearing, became somewhat less an economic relation or investment. Psychological gratifications became resources to be negotiated for economic resources, social status, and other psychological gratification. The increased leisure time and education available to middle-class women, as a resource, enabled cultural elevation and social activism. The price was paid in subordination and relegation to "the proper sphere" of "true womanhood." But as societal resources increased, along with women's resources of time, education, and wages, the price became too high. Female radicalism emerged. But many of the "radical" achievements of the nineteenth-century middle-class women (e.g., voting, improved work conditions, and birth control) are now used by all classes.

The Functionalist View of the Twentieth-Century Family

Lloyd Warner was one of the first to empirically examine the connection between family life and social status. The classical community studies of the 1930s and 1940s by Warner, Hollingshead, Dollard, Gardner, Davis, and the Lynds viewed social class as patterns of social interaction and ritual among people at particular locations in the community's perceived status hierarchy. Families fell into about five or six classes, though *status groupings* might be a more accurate term. The class system and its distributions in Warner's study of a Yankee city (Newburyport, Massachusetts) are summarized in Table 1.

The upper class, the "old families" with inherited wealth, owned and/or controlled most of the economic and political life of the community. These families were highly endogamous, participating in select clubs, attending high-status churches (Episcopal and Presbyterian), and living in "exclusive" neighborhoods in the best part of town. Just below them were the newly rich, often wealthier, who attempted to join the same clubs and cliques. Although the degree of their acceptance varied, their children nevertheless entered the upper class. The children of these families went to the same (e.g., the "better") schools and/or dominated the social, cultural, and academic life of communitywide schools. The upper middle class, the professionals, independent businesspeople, and some managers were successful but not wealthy. They were less likely to socialize with the upper class(es). They had their own clubs, churches, and social activities. The lower middle classes, white-collar workers, small businesspeople, and tradespeople were hardworking "respectable" people. They stuck to their families and church groups. The upper-lower-class working people were factory workers or tradespeople, poor but

Table 1. The Class System of Yankee City[a]

1. Upper-upper, 1.4% of the total population. This group was the old-family elite, based on sufficient wealth to maintain a large house in the best neighborhood, but the wealth had to have been in the family for more than one generation. This generational continuity permitted proper training in basic values and established people as belonging to a lineage.
2. Lower-upper, 1.6%. This group was, on the average, slightly richer than the upper-uppers, but their money was newer, their manners were thus not quite so polished, and their sense of lineage and security were less pronounced.
3. Upper-middle, 10.2%. Business and professional men and their families who were moderately successful but less affluent than the lower-uppers. Some education and polish were necessary for membership, but lineage was unimportant.
4. Lower-middle, 28.1%. The petty businessmen, the schoolteachers, the foremen in industry. This group tended to have morals that were close to those of Puritan Fundamentalism; they were churchgoers, lodge joiners, and flag wavers.
5. Upper-lower, 32.6%. The solid, respectable laboring people, who kept their houses clean and stayed out of trouble.
6. Lower-lower, 25.2%. The "lulus" or disrespectable and often slovenly people who dug for clams and waited for public relief.

[a]From Warner and Lunt, 1941, p. 88.

honest. Finally, the lower classes consisted of the "animals, on the other side of the tracks," whose morals were nonexistent and whose family patterns were unstable. The women were loose, the men drunkards. They would never amount to a hill of beans.

The analysis of Yankee City followed the functional approach that Warner had used in his study of the Australian "aborigines." The organization of that society was based on the interdependencies of the various clans, each of which claimed a particular ancestral progenitor as its totem. Each clan was responsible for protecting the integrity of its own totem for the sake of society as a whole. Once a year, the clans gathered together for religious rituals that strengthened the solidarity of the group and established new marriages.

Warner saw the U.S. classes as a hierarchy of totemic clans, each performing its rituals and serving its purpose in maintaining the solidarity of the community. The classes were, however, endogamous, unlike the clans, which were exogamous. Annual ceremonies like Memorial Day, July Fourth, and the town's three hundredth birthday party were seen as solidarity rituals uniting the classes in a common pursuit. The churches and social organizations of each class had their own floats and/or ritual performances. Further, there were rituals linking the living to the dead ancestors of the community and the nation. Homage to Lincoln was seen as a collective representation.

The Yankee City studies inspired similar research in other cities, such as social class and adolescence in a midwestern town, Elmtown (Hollingshead, 1949); social class and mental illness in New Haven (Hollingshead & Redlich, 1958); and social class and racial caste in a southern town (Davis & Dollard, 1940; Davis, Gardner, & Gardner, 1941). This research considered the ramifications of class from the functional viewpoint. Social classes maintained themselves by limiting friendship patterns to those within the same class. Higher status youth were looked up to by peers and were differentially treated by social authorities. They were college-bound. Lower status youth were looked down on; they were rated "dirty," were harshly treated for infractions, and went to work. The higher classes were less likely to be mentally ill, but when so afflicted, they were more likely to be judged neurotic or manic-depressive, syndromes with a good prognosis for psychotherapy (especially by *private* practitioners). The lower classes were more likely judged schizophrenic, less suitable for psychotherapy. In the Deep South, the blacks were not even part of the class system; they were more like an "untouchable" caste. They were found in deplorable shacks, had poor schools, and had jobs limited to sharecropping or menial labor. This inequality raised questions about its functions. Some thought it was the legacy of a preindustrial economy. Although scholars such as Davis, Warner, and Havighurst were never radicals, they were among the earliest to document the inequality of education.

The final stage in the development of the functional theory of the family and its relationship to social class was the Parsonian framework. In 1937, Parsons's *Structure of Social Action* established the basis for the subsequent functionalist approach. In the 1940s, Parsons began to apply functionalism to the study of age, sex, and generations. Parsons (1953) presented a unified conceptual scheme of the interrelationships between biological, psychological, sociological, and cultural systems. The primary unit of analysis was social action expressed as the interaction of social actors in role relationships that were motivated by the actor's socialized need dispositions and patterned according to particular value orientations. Industrial society required values of rationality, universal standards, achievement, specific relationships, and a self-orientation that legitimized economic activity and integrated the new social order. The functionalist theory of stratification saw the class system as a means for the differential allocation of scarce rewards (status and income) according to the functional importance of the occupational role to the society and its requirements of talent and arduous training. Accordingly, the isolated conjugal nuclear family, separated from the economy, was a small group that valued emotion, diffuse total relationships, and a commitment to the family unit. At the same time, the family socialized the talents, motives, values, and skills required in the outside world.

An Examination of Social Status and Family Life

We have now considered some of the theory, history, and early research on the relation of stratification to family life. We will now indicate some of the qualities of family life typical of each status level. For the current approach, status as indication of lifestyle is more relevant than class as an economic grouping. But we must remember that status levels are based on unequal distributions of resources, although many resources are not economic *per se*. The resources of each status level affect its "culture," which we see as a dynamic enactment of norms and values expressed in people's relationships to each other. These resource-dependent processes can be considered "status cultures."

This view of "status cultures" comes close to the way in which Gans (1962) described subcultures:

Subcultures are responses that people make to the opportunities and the deprivations that they encounter. More specifically, each subculture is an organized set of related responses that has developed out of people's efforts to cope with the opportunities, incentives, and rewards, as well as the deprivations, prohibitions, and pressures which the natural environment and society—that complex of coexisting and competing subcultures— offer to them. The responses which make up a subculture are compounded out of what people have retained of parental, that is, traditional response, the skills and attitudes they have learned as children, and the innovations they have developed for themselves in their own encounters with opportunity and deprivation.

These responses cannot develop in a vacuum. Over the long range, they can be seen as functions of the resources which a society has available, and of the opportunities which it can offer. In each of the subcultures life is thus geared to the availability of specific qualitative types and quantities of income, education, and occupational opportunities. (p. 249)

It is difficult to highlight the distinctive features of each "status culture." Unequal attention has been paid to each group, and there have been differing methods of investigation or sources of information, different research concerns, locations, periods, and so on. Nor have the data necessarily been collected and organized according to the historical-dynamic perspective of this review. There are few survey data that include the upper classes. In fact, some of our knowledge of the upper classes is based on writers like Cleveland Amory (1960), Stephen Birmingham (1968), and the biographers of upper-class people. The studies consulted here are generally those done since 1960.[3] The early research in the Warner and Hol-

---

[3]The general portraits of each group were based on the following works. For the upper class, see Amory (1960), Birmingham (1968), Baltzell (1958, 1964, 1980), Daniels (1975), Lundberg (1968), and Domhoff (1971). Gans (1962, 1967), Schneider (1968), Seeley (1956), Farber (1971), and Dobriner (1963) contributed to the knowledge of the middle class. The informa-

lingshead perspective mentioned was reviewed by Cavan (1964). In our highlights of each status culture, we will try to mention some of the historical roots of each status culture; its resources; its distinctive values; its the norms of marital and family life; its social, cultural, and religious patterns; and its modes of self-presentation. Following common usage, the term *class* is more often meant as a dimension of status.

Upper-Class Families

Upper-class families were born into wealth gained by earlier generations. Some Yankee families trace their descendents to the *Mayflower*. The northeastern traders, whalers, and merchants of the eighteenth century were usually shrewd, hard-working Puritans who managed to parlay their fortunes and establish dynasties. In the middle colonies, Quaker businesspeople did the same (Baltzell, 1980). In the southern states, Anglican plantation owners raised tobacco and cotton to establish neofeudal estates and to gain the wealth that enabled a rural-gentry lifestyle modeled after that of the English aristocracy. In the nineteenth century, an upstart faction of merchants, railroad barons, and industrialists, often Methodists and Baptists, began to emerge. New urban centers of commerce, finance, and manufacturing emerged in the Midwest, Cleveland, Detroit, and Chicago. By the early twentieth century, a number of indigenous Catholics and immigrant Jews had become successful entrepreneurs and had founded families that now, three generations later, are also upper class. In most cases, the grandchildren of the founder(s) of the dynasty are fully integrated into the upper class. There are several variations within this class by region, religion, or ancestry. In the Far West, in San Francisco, Los Angeles, and Seattle, fortunes were also made in oil, agriculture, and entertainment, and a new economic elite emerged.

The primary resource of upper-class families is inherited wealth, which carries with it power, especially power to command others and/or to influence events. Not only do their resources affect their family life, but extended family networks and well-placed "connections" with political elites can also be considered resources.

Quite naturally, the values of this group are justifica-

tions to maintain and preserve privilege. The paramount values of the upper class are social domination and perpetuation of lineage and wealth (Adams, 1980). They need to justify their inherited status in a supposedly egalitarian society. Therefore, they perform the vital economic services of managing and controlling large businesses.[4] Given their self-identification as an aristocracy, they also provide leadership in cultural and philanthropic activity. Successful businesspeople are usually successful fund raisers for charities as well. Participation in charitable activity offers a paternalistic rationalization for their social dominance and an easy access to the ceremonial leadership of the community (Collins, 1975). The philanthropy of course, increases the public visibility and social power of their class. "Charitable" contributions are tax deductible; some deductions are often greater than actual costs. These activities often provide "useful" roles and careers for upper-class women (Daniels, 1975). The women clearly see their role in philanthropic activity as being a means of maintaining the dominance of their class by limiting the encroachment and the involvement of the public sector, which they feel lead to communism (Ostrander, 1979). The women of this class further maintain the style of "gracious living" in fashion benefits and charitable banquets.

Aware that their privileged status came through inheritance, the upper class pay homage and respect to lineage, revere the past, and maintain extensive collections of heirlooms and genealogies. Much of the "gossip" of this class concerns relatives of earlier generations. Oral histories of the family's economic and political deeds are passed to each generation. Each generation must increase the family fortune for future generations. Therefore, this class values achievement and competence, but to a lesser extent than the anxious strivers of the middle class whose status is less assured. Further, the hustling and the wheeling and dealing of aggressive entrepreneurship are considered vulgar. Having great wealth leads to a most ingenuous indifference to pecuniary concerns. In fact,

---

[4]This also increases the capital for future generations. Sometimes members of this class serve in high elective or appointive offices. A few even choose careers in the public sector, as governors, lawyers, judges, or members of the Commerce and State departments. In such pivotal positions in the government, they are able to defend their class interests (Useem, 1979). There are many variations in occupational choice among this class. They are not all high-placed executives. Some become professionals. Doctors constitute about 8% of the listings in social registers. Others may start new businesses, especially those catering to cultured tastes. Nelson Rockefeller became a dealer in art reproduction, and his brother David started Rock Resorts, a chain of vacation retreats for the very affluent where the daily rates are $275 per person—meals included (1980). Such rates aid the maintenance of privacy. "Celebrity" women of this class sometimes establish businesses (Bernard, 1981). Gloria Vanderbilt entered the high fashion and cosmetic business. Others, like Jacqueline Kennedy Onassis, may work in journalism or literary fields.

---

tion on blue-collar families was drawn from Howe (1970), Komarovsky (1962), Ryan (1973), Sexton and Sexton (1972), Rainwater (1959), Rubin (1976), Howell (1972), Shostak (1969), Shostak and Gomberg (1964), Fried (1973), Aronowitz (1974), Sennett and Cobb (1972), Berger (1960), and Le Masters (1975). The perspectives on the lower class were based on Stack (1974), Billingsley (1968), Hannerz (1969), Liebow (1967), Ladner (1971), Valentine (1968), Suttles (1968), Schneider and Smith (1973), Rainwater (1970), Scanzoni (1971), and Martin and Martin (1978). For general overviews, see Collins (1975), Lenski (1966), Adams (1980), Rapp (1978), and Farber (1971).

discussions of personal finance breach the codes of etiquette.

For the upper class, marriage is more than a legal-emotional commitment. It is also a means of concentrating capital and maintaining the ingroup solidarity of the "symbolic estate" (Gordon & Noll, 1975). Though marital choice is "free," there is a high degree of surveillance and scrutiny by the extended kinship groupings (Goode, 1963). Marriage between cousins is often encouraged. Social networks, including elite schools and social activities, generally limit contact with people of other classes. There are a variety of means to limit marrying "down," as this class does not always reproduce itself. When this does occur, the prospective entrant must be carefully screened and approved, as the heirs will continue the family life. An "upstart" bride or groom is often reminded of her or his ambiguous position in the family—and at the same time is expected to raise the offspring as a full member of the family.

The marital unit shows a high degree of sexual segregation and traditional sex-role ideology. Independent economic resources, however, limit gross power differentials. Most of the women pursue "traditional" female concerns, such as domestic management and the charitable or cultural activities mentioned (Daniels, 1975), but the interesting irony is that such "careers" often put these women in strategic positions of community power (Ostrander, 1979).

The family structure usually consists of nearby nuclear households that maintain extensive kinship ties, especially as the control of the inherited wealth often requires concerted decisions and actions (Lundberg, 1968). There are frequent reconstitutions of the clan, usually at summer homes or winter resorts (Baltzell, 1964). The adult males may be present only on weekends because of work responsibilities. The family network often has a central authority, a matriarch, a patriarch, or an eldest sibling whose authority is based on age, wealth, and ability to integrate the kinship grouping and influence its financial decisions. There are extensive patterns of deference to this figure. Upper-class kinship tends to follow the New England or "Yankee" pattern (Farber, 1971; Goodenough, 1956). Relatives by marriage and consanguines (by blood) are *both* considered relatives. The midwestern pattern, more typical of lower classes, emphasizes kinship along blood lines (Farber, 1971; Schneider, 1968). Among higher-status groups, parental inlaws are addressed as "Father" and "Mother," and collaterals (cousins) are treated as relatives. In lower classes, such inlaws are treated as friends but not kin and are called by their first names. Cousins are treated with cordiality but not as relatives.

The social life of elite families further expresses a lifestyle of "gracious living." Support of cultural activity also reflects the gracious and expensive living characteristics of the elite classes. They also stress elegant but subdued taste in clothes, houses, home decor, entertainment, and *haute cuisine*. They are likely to have formal dinner parties indicating the "latest" trends in cuisine. They are joiners of "exclusive" clubs, which are often by invitation only and require sponsorship by a number of gatekeepers. Many of these clubs are sexually segregated. Family recreation is at the elite country clubs. As patrons of the arts and exemplars of cultural sophistication, such families frequent classical music performances, museums, and galleries, especially those supported by the family. The children often receive specialized art instruction. This class is likely to read "great" literature or poetry and to attend theater, opera, and ballet. Families participate in expensive recreation, such as skiing, yachting, tennis, curling, and horsemanship. Their religion tends to be the higher-status denominations of Protestantism or the more liberal branches of Judaism or Catholicism. Weber (1968) indicated that the religion of such elites is worldly and ritualistic. Yinger (1970) claimed that elite religions, based on bourgeois Puritanism, have an intellectual concept of faith, liberal social ethics, and a reaffirmation of individuality and self-reliance.

The upper-class demeanor and modes of self-presentation come from being born into a lifestyle of command and self-designation as an elite. Even as children, these people have a number of maids, servants, and drivers who pay them deference. Because this is an aristocracy, there is a strong emphasis on ritual forms of association, refined manners, and displays of awe (Collins, 1975). Wealth makes possible the elaborate show of elite lifestyle in clothes or possessions that are some of the "props" of self-presentation (Goffman, 1959). Being in command and expecting obedience give rise to an air of confidence based on self-importance, cool composure, and an unconscious arrogance (Collins, 1975). These people project an attitude of deliberateness and finality. Being in command of organizational networks also promotes a sociability expressed in highly formalized codes of etiquette. Toward those of lower classes, there are polite displays of a condescending air of superiority that maintains social distance.

Lower-Upper-Class Families

The history of America can be seen as a "circulation of elites," to use Pareto's term, whatever may be the inequality of opportunity in capitalism, there are opportunities for those with certain skills and values to take advantage of new products, services, or business opportunities. Thus, we can view the history of our class structure as a history of status competition, one central element of which is the attempt by the newly rich, the lower-upper class, to gain the status of the established elites—who in turn defend their ranks from encroachment (Collins, 1975). In most cases the *arrivistes* do not gain full acceptance by the elites, but their children, if socialized by the "right" schools and organizations, will very likely gain entry. Thus, although there have always been groups of the *nouveau riche*, it is a status culture without a history; it is transitional status that is assimilated into the old elites and reconstituted from below, or loses its wealth and descends back to the class of origin.

We have previously noted the extent to which the rise of capitalism and its ever-changing patterns of finance, technology, and/or marketing have enabled various groups to gain economic fortunes and establish family dynasties. As the economic system and its technologies have changed, certain groups have successfully created or utilized new opportunities. In the 1960s and 1970s, fortunes have been made in real estate, electronics, and so on. The former multimillionaire president of one computer company was in his late 20s. Thus, "status competition" is typical of America (Collins, 1975). In fact, the number of groups "competing" has increased.

The primary resources of the lower upper class are, of course, the various economic skills—professional, managerial, or entrepreneurial—that allowed the rapid increase in wealth and thus their achievement of this status. For many professionals (especially doctors and lawyers) with a combination of highly remunerated services and surplus capital for investment, it is not uncommon to eventually earn more money and to amass greater wealth through investments than from professional fees. Although most upper-echelon corporate executives come from middle- and upper-income backgrounds, a small but significant number of corporate elites come from less advantaged status groups. Some estimate that over 25% of top executives came from "poorer" families (most of the top corporations recruit their upper management from their financial and production divisions; engineers, typically from blue-collar backgrounds, often climb the corporate ladder from production to upper management). Upper-level executives are not only highly remunerated but often have a number of perquisites—cars, planes, club memberships, stock options, and so on—that supplement their salaries.

Perhaps the largest number of persons attain lower-upper status through entrepreneurship. Such entrepreneurs have a wide range of class and/or ethnic backgrounds. The only thing that entrepreneurs have in common is their ability to innovate, organize, and take risks. In recent years, entrepreneurs have made fortunes in real estate, fashion, shipping, electronics, computers, oil, marketing, fast foods, and so on. Finally, a relatively small number of the newly affluent come from the entertainment field, including a few virtuosos of song, dance, instruments, or conducting, writers of best-sellers, or stars and celebrities of various other media. At the time of this writing, the president of the United States is a former "B" movie actor of humble origin, best known for his costarring with a chimpanzee named Bonzo.

Significant numbers of people from minority groups, such as blacks and Hispanics, are now also gaining economic success. Some might even consider women a separate group, and there is now a small but growing number of businesswomen who have become successful on the basis of their own talents, such as Mary Kay (cosmetics),

Helen Gurley Brown (publishing), and Mary Wells (advertising). The resources of the newly rich, from so many backgrounds, are the skills and talents that produced their economic success and the material resources that have resulted.

Although the values of lower-upper-status families reflect the diverse origins of their members, one of the most typical values is "conspicuous consumption," the display of newly gained wealth in expensive homes, furniture, art objects, cars, fashions, club memberships, and so on. One function of such display is the attempt to secure entry into or at least acceptance by the older established upper class. Another function is to command deference and awe from lower classes. However, having gained wealth without the early socialization experiences of the upper class, these people do not have the same tastes and social manners. Thus, they often seem garish and ostentatious compared to the established upper classes, who prefer more subdued tastes and who shun publicity. Newly gained wealth does, however, buy the services of architects, decorators, and designers to provide the "latest" trends and fashions; the established elites prefer more traditional designs.

In many cases, the newly rich are likely to be politically conservative, for a number of reasons. Though not a concern of this chapter, part and parcel of "status competition" is "status anxiety" (Lipset, 1970). Conservative politics can serve to gain entry into the elite class and to justify the individualistic ideology associated with aggressive entrepreneurship. Insofar as their success is attributed to individual effort rather than to opportunity, the self-esteem of these people is enhanced.

The marital patterns of the lower-upper class are highly influenced by their prior status. Because they have now moved upward in the social hierarchy, friends and relatives of the prior status are now less valued. Full acceptance by the elites is problematic. Therefore, the marital unit becomes especially important for support and intimacy. Despite many exceptions, for the most part such families are likely to have a traditional division of labor. The wives of successful men usually attempt to secure newly gained status and frequently join the social, cultural, philanthropic, and civic organizations controlled by the established elites. They are likely to work especially hard in hopes of securing social acceptance and personal invitations from the older families. Further, as the husbands are usually very hard-working men, it is up to the wives to regulate social activities, to purchase goods and services, and otherwise to control domestic life. Thus, the marital unit is extremely important as a source of psychological and emotional support in the new-found status, and as the means of securing acceptance in the newly attained rank and/or by the old aristocracy. In most cases, the ties to extended kin are less salient. Warner (1959) noted that, in some cases, the newly rich have transferred parental remains to "high-status" cemeteries.

The social life of the newly affluent attempts to emulate the "gracious-living" styles associated with old wealth.

Such families are joiners of those "elite" social philanthropic and cultural organizations that are open for membership. The wives of the *nouveaux riches* attempt to "secure" the newly gained family status. Thus, being on the women's auxillary of an orchestra, an opera company, museum, or theater group may serve both cultural and social functions.

The cultural orientations of the newly rich again show a great variety in tastes, reflecting the influence of the cultural tastes of their origins and those of the upper class with whom they now interact. Those with college backgrounds typically enjoy the upper-middle-brow tastes of adventure or romantic novels on best-seller lists, show tunes, "known" artists, some nineteenth-century symphonic music, and "hit" plays. There are a few academics (successful text writers, for example) and some producers, directors, artists, and performers of various "culture" industries who are very successful financially and also appreciate the more esoteric tastes of introspective writing (Proust and Nin), poetry, avant-garde art, "modern" music, chamber music, and more sophisticated theater, ranging from the Greek tragedies and comedies to twentieth-century writers such as Beckett or Anouilh.

The religions and the religious orientations of the newly rich show wide patterns of diversity, reflecting the variety of backgrounds from which the members are drawn. Those with Jewish and Greek Orthodox backgrounds, having cultural traditions of entrepreneurship, are likely to be overrepresented. Given the patterns of immigration of the 1960s and 1970s, a small number of Asian professionals and entrepreneurs have been very economically successful. Indian, Pakistani, Korean, Vietnamese, and Chinese immigrants may be of Christian, Islamic, Sikh, Hindu, or Buddist backgrounds. As Weber (1968) observed, the religions of merchants tend to pragmatic, "this-worldly," and ascetic.

In many cases, especially among Protestants, upward mobility may be associated with denominational change, those from lower-status denominations such as Baptists or Methodists joining the more prestigious Presbyterian or Episcopal congregations, which are likely to be found in the more affluent urban enclaves and/or exclusive suburbs. This is not to suggest that upward mobility is regularly associated with denominational change. It sometimes happens that those of conservative (fundamentalist) origins may attribute their success to their faith and may become prosyletizers and/or supporters of a conservative faith.

The most typical route to lower-upper status has been "aggressive entrepreneurship." Interpersonal qualities, rituals, and modes of demeanor are closely associated to occupation rather than background. Such manners and styles are quite different from those of inherited wealth (Collins, 1975). They are less subdued and lack the ritualized social graces and cultural refinements that come from a lifetime of elite socialization. Further, the newly rich are often loud and crudely assertive and expect deference based on their newly gained fortunes and the expression of the wealth in consumption. Given their brash manners and patterns of ostentation, interaction with the elites usually occurs in more public or impersonal settings, rather than in the more intimate settings of the home.

Upper-Middle-Class Families

The antecedents of the upper middle class were the "free" professionals of the clergy, the law and medicine, and some merchants or artisans. With the growth of urbanization, more merchants and entrepreneurs joined their ranks. After the growth of industrialization in the late nineteenth century, groups such as scientists, engineers, and other highly trained technical workers became part of this class (Noble, 1977). Finally, the growth of corporations led to a vastly expanded managerial class. Therefore, this stratum now consists of the free professionals in law, accounting, or medicine, and higher-level businesspeople, primarily middle management or successful entrepreneurs. This stratum also includes service professionals, that is, teachers, especially at university levels; mental health workers; and administrators in social service or governmental organizations.

The resources of this group include the occupational skills that result from college education and, often, postgraduate studies. The type and amount of education and subsequent careers are the basis for the differentiation of this stratum. The free professionals and salaried intellectuals in universities, research centers and government usually have postgraduate education in a specialized field. They can "disinterestedly" apply their expertise either to solve or to understand medical, legal or social problems; to formulate policy, to make scientific discoveries; or to train subsequent generations. The people in the managerial or business sector have resources that include knowledge of procedures and capacities to persuade, organize, or lead others to implement organizational goals. If successful, they can even rise to positions of formulating goals and policies. Some members of either group may also have entrepreneurial skills and may establish or take over businesses. The occupations of this class, careers of sequential progression (Wilensky, 1961), lead to greater income, status, and authority. Cognitive and interpersonal skills enable this class to get a great deal of authority and to make above-average incomes.

The upper-middle stratum values place primary emphasis on rationality and individualism, expressed in achieving occupational success. Economic and work values that express individualism and personal achievement are central avenues to success and respectability (Adams, 1980). Values of self-control, discipline, rational control of impulses, and fulfillment in work emerged with the very rise of capitalism. As Schneider and Smith (1973) noted, the average suburban commuter hardly seems the villain of the bourgeois Protestant ethic, yet embodies these values.

The upper-middle-class family establishes its own

household, and the integrity of this unit is the primary emotional obligation of its members. This stratum is likely to be geographically mobile in pursuit of career goals (Adams, 1978; Osborn & Williams, 1976). There is, however, extensive visiting, communication, and aid even between parents and grown children who are mobile. For the middle classes, aid is likely to be parental financial help (Lee, 1979).

The ideal marital pattern is an egalitarian allocation of decision making based on rational expertise, a high degree of intimate communication, and primary commitment to each other. We see the greatest saliency of the marriage and the maximal dependency of the partners on each other to provide intimacy, emotional gratifications, and happiness. The conjugal unit stresses the unity of the relationship. The wife's social activities are often integral parts of the husband's career. "Social" activities with bosses, clients, or professional colleagues often become central aspects of marital life. There is a strong future orientation and long-term planning. Budget allocations and plans, as well as employee benefits, include certain amounts for future security, such as mortgages, insurance, savings, or investments. Discretionary income is more frequently spent on goods that enhance family status rather than on personal enhancement. It would be a breach of norms for a parent to fail in his or her breadwinner role and to place personal indulgence above family needs. There is an emphasis on personal ability and competence based on career performance. Individual achievement becomes a most crucial aspect of the person's role and his or her self-esteem. Self-realization and creativity in the career are more important than income (Kohn, 1969). Thus, self-control, internal discipline, and planning are crucial to accruing social rewards and to maintaining one's self-conception. These qualities are important for both work and home. Rational behavior also serves as a role model for the child and a socialization technique (see pp. 239–243). The child is highly important to the parents, and although he or she is highly indulged, there are also strong pressures to achieve (see pp. 243–244). But achievement is viewed as his or her self-realization (Gans, 1967). Families of higher status and education are egalitarian in sex-role norms and encourage female education (Holter, 1970).

For more and more wives in this sector, the wife's career is as important to her as her husband's is to him. In the last decade or so, as variety of economic and cultural factors have led to greater female occupational pursuit. Women at this level, usually highly educated, are now likely to pursue a "career" that provides rewards both intrinsically and extrinsically. Whereas women in other classes may work out of economic necessity in the "dual-career family," *both* parties have professional or managerial status in the upper-middle class. Competence in a career as a "central self-concept" for both husband and wife is becoming more frequent (Bernard, 1981; Rapaport & Rapaport, 1971). Some of the patterns of traditional sex-role differentiation have become blurred, men performing more household and child-care tasks

(though this may be rare) and moving when the wife gets a promotion, for example.

Occupation and family roles are part of an intertwined career. One's occupation makes possible home life, certain leisure and cultural pursuits, children's expenses, their education, and long-term financial security. For the upper-middle-status family, the intertwining of work, career, and stratum values affects marital relationships. Thus, the time of marriage, usually later than in lower classes, and family planning are highly stressed (cf. Cogswell & Sussman, 1979).

The family interaction patterns are learned as part of earlier sex-role socialization. Cross-sex *non*erotic friendships after puberty are frequent. A variety of school, leisure, and cultural activities show little sexual segregation (student council and newspapers). This socialization prepares the person for mutual activities (sharing, cooperation, and empathy) in a variety of cross-sex relationships. As a worker, he or she may be in collegial relations with the opposite sex.

In general, the degree of happiness and the quality of the marital relationship are strongly tied to the resources of education and income that determine status (Lewis & Spanier, 1979). The upper-middle group reports the most satisfaction (Orden & Bradburn, 1968). (Upper-class families were not included.) Such families also report greater satisfaction from the sexual aspect of their marriage (Rainwater, 1965). But we should note that in some marriages of this stratum, the husband may work so hard and long that there is little interaction and hence no satisfaction. For example, Cuber and Haroff (1965) reported five types of marriages among such families: Conflict-habituated marriage are maintained on the basis of hostility; devitalized marriages are those in which initial intimacy has been lost but duties, responsibilities, and psychological inertia have maintained the union; passive-congenial marriages seem never to have had an initial vitality; vital marriages are those in which there are shared interests and the partners focus on the marital relationship; and total marriages make openness, sharing, mutual interests, and healthy, nondestructive tension-resolution central interests. Cuber and Haroff (1965) suggested that only about 16% achieve this ideal.

The upper-middle families are joiners and are often active in professional, business, community, religious, political, and leisure organizations. Activities within such organizations and/or with other couples are an important part of the family's social life. Because many of this status are mobile, geographically and socially, this group is likely to have a wide number of friends, but sustained relations and activities are more infrequent than in other groups. Visiting and social activities are usually with other couples of the same status that link either the male or the female to the other couple. Not only are activities likely to be sex-linked, but a certain degree of cross-sex flirtation is expected.

Social and cultural orientations differ between the managerial and the professional sectors (Glenn & Alston, 1968). The professionals are more liberal and humanistic in social political orientation (Gans, 1967). But as Gans (1967) noted, Jews are more likely to be overrepresented in this sector, and such "marginal" groups usually have liberal values. The cultural orientations also differ. The professionals are more likely to appreciate the "high-brow" culture supported by the upper class. The managers are more likely to enjoy the "middle-brow" culture of monthly book clubs, best-sellers, Broadway musicals, and pop or soft rock. Jazz appeals to both groups. The leisure patterns of this status are likely to involve participation rather than observation (Carlson, 1979). Leisure is quite often filled with joint family activity that may require a degree of expense. These are the families that have the resources and the inclination for foreign travel, winter skiing, or outdoor backwoods activities (Carlson, 1979). The greater the family's resources, the greater the ability to purchase leisure goods and the greater the options for leisure activity (Carlson, 1979). Families of this status are joiners, and church-going is no exception. The higher the status, the more likely people are to go to church and to participate in church activities, but less orthodox, doctrinal, and parochial are their beliefs (Glock & Stark, 1965). Upper middle class Protestants are most likely members of "higher-status" denominations such as Episcopal, Presbyterian, Unitarian, or Quaker (cf. Yinger, 1970).

The modes of demeanor reflect the resources and authority of the members of this class. The upper-middle-status groups have specialized knowledge and skills, moderately high incomes, and a high degree of authority. This is especially true of self-employed professionals like doctors and lawyers. They are usually highly adept in conversation, especially when expressing opinions on political, economic, cultural, and psychological matters. The highly educated frequently take a flat emotional tone to lend credence to their pontifications (Collins, 1975, p. 122). Women of this class, even when not employed, must be able to demonstrate the appropriate graces of trivialized conversational ritual (cf. Collins, 1975). They are usually quite active in community affairs, organizationally conscious, and cosmopolitan in outlook. Formalized sociability is frequent among this class, though much of their dinner and cocktail party discussion tends to be both impersonal and self-aggrandizing. Their resources allow self-assuredness and confidence—but with less of the complacent gentility and self-important arrogance of the upper class. They do, however, borrow some expensive tastes, ritual forms, and subtle manners from the elite (Collins, 1975, p. 70).

Lower-Middle-Class Families

The lower-middle class of small proprietors, bureaucratic functionaries, lower-echelon white-collar workers, salespersons, and clerks also emerged with the growth of capitalism. There were (are) at least two origins of this class. There are the more rural Protestant businesspeople and artisans descended from the early settlers. They are

the more restrictive in the analysis by Gans (1967). Upwardly mobile Catholics, more typically expansive, whose families were immigrants, are likely to find political jobs as bureaucrats or public servants (police officers and fire fighters). The Irish, for example, were able to translate citizenship and command of English into urban political power and to wrest local control from old Yankees. Such power meant public jobs and business favors. The different origins of each segment of the lower middle class explain in part how these constrictive and expansive sectors emerged and still remain (Gans, 1967).

The major distinguishing values of the members of this status are respectability and achievement. Although they do not achieve much prestige in their lower-echelon white-collar jobs or small businesses, they attempt to gain respect on the basis of their moral qualities, such as hard work and honesty. Respectability as a value in the more constrictive segments of this stratum is further expressed in highly traditional sexual attitudes, traditional patriotism, and puritanical religion. This sector is especially concerned with differentiating themselves from the more hedonistic classes below it. The lower-middle stratum believes in the values of independence and achievement. With limited levels of education or career options, they are unable to attain the American dream of mobility. They nevertheless encourage their children to fulfill their own frustrated hopes. Although their levels of education and income are similar to those of blue-collar workers, their children are more likely to achieve mobility through education (Broom & Selznick, 1981). However, much of the "mobility" of first-generation college graduates, especially of less prestigious colleges or state universities, may be more a function of status enhancement and upgrading of job entry requirements (Collins, 1979).

The lower-middle-class family structure is similar to the upper-middle-class structure in that the (not so) isolated conjugal nuclear family is the primary orientation of the adult members. Within the family, there tends to be a traditional pattern of authority and sex-role division of labor. The wife defers to the husband's authority yet maintains control over personal and familial household realms. There is little segregation by sex. Joint family activities are frequent; for example, children are taken to museums to "further" their education. The family tends to be "child-oriented." Some parents may read Dr. Spock or child-care experts and are highly concerned about the child's development. However, they emphasize *control* over the child's aggression (fighting or stealing) or sexual impulses that violate norms of respectability. Such restrictive norms may threaten the child's upward mobility (Blau, 1981). This pattern toward children is rooted in the Puritan tradition (Farber, 1972). There are extensive patterns of leisure, social, and religious activities within *kinship* networks that may or may not live close together. Sussman's now-classical study (1959) of Cleveland's lower-middle-class families reported extensive visiting and helping patterns, such as child care, advice, and financial aid. Holiday gatherings among kinship networks were frequent. Sussman (1966) explained kinship reciprocity in terms of exchange theory; that is, the reciprocal exchanges of gifts, services, advice, and so on were rewarding to the parties involved.

The lower-middle stratum is highly sociable—for some, primarily within kinship groups. Among bureaucratic functionaries and the small businesspersons, there is much sociability outside the family networks. Like the higher-status groups, many segments of this class are joiners. But this stratum is usually localistic; therefore, we see less of the urban cosmopolitan forms of ritualized impersonality and informal personalistic exchange. There is a good deal of coffee-klatching and many bridge clubs among wives (Gans, 1967). Concerned with their children's future character development and career mobility, such women and, occasionally, their husbands are often involved with PTA, Little Leagues, Scouting, and church activities. Such groups may often include upper-middle-status parents.

The males of this group often join luncheon clubs and business groups that may cross status lines. Organizations such as the Elks, Rotary, Kiwanis and the Chamber of Commerce go beyond simple class lines and unite to promote business interests, community service, and charitable work. Within such groups, lower-middle-status men often work especially hard to implement programs and to gain respect from the higher-status members. Occasionally, they secure business contacts and/or an invitation to dinner or cocktails (Collins, 1975). Despite status *differences,* the small businessmen are culturally and politically close to the high-status executives and businessmen (Glenn & Alston, 1968). This stratum is the target of much mass culture, such as television, popular magazines, and "middle-brow" culture. They are not particularly interested in "high-brow" literature or cosmopolitan concerns, and they disdain the erotic and nihilistic themes of youth culture. Some of the religious sectors enjoy inspirational books. Among the functionaries and the business class, sedentary rule-bound games like bridge are popular (Collins, 1975). These are usually joint husband-wife activities with other couples who may be business friends, neighbors, or kin. The sectors of this stratum with more limited resources usually have more limited recreational pursuits (Carlson, 1979). The Protestant religious of this group generally tend toward more fundamentalist puritanical denominations, such as the Baptists (cf. Demerath, 1965; Yinger, 1970). Many consider themselves evangelical. They tend to be ascetic, pietistic, moralistic, community-oriented, respectable, and hard-working (Collins, 1975, p. 69). Such an orientation legitimizes their occupational roles and their somewhat restrictive child-rearing practices. This orientation was evident among the artisan class in early Salem (Farber, 1972).

The demeanor of the lower-middle class, especially functionaries and small businesspeople, is a moralistic, self-disciplined respectability. They show a rigid orientation to organizational rules or business practices. They adhere to procedures and knowledge of rules and forms that enable them to have a certain degree of power over subordinates and/or clients (Collins, 1975). Collins (1975) claimed that their level of education, the nature of their jobs, and their modest incomes allow for little cosmopolitanism or for subtle manners or refined tastes; rather, they display a crude asceticism and tasteless respectability. There is often a ritualized informal familiarity that was typical of and advantageous to early bourgeois entrepreneurs. Conversational skills and sociability are important, but without the refinement or cosmopolitan sophistication of higher strata; there is a distinctive style of loudness, gregariousness, and physical and verbal intimacy (Collins, 1975, p. 208).

Working-Class Families

The blue-collar or working class (construction workers, factory operatives, repair and maintenance workers) generally came from rural backgrounds. At the time of the American Revolution, only 5% of the population was urban. The small preindustrial working class consisted of construction workers, shipbuilders, blacksmiths, and so on. The growth of industrialization, first in textiles and then in mining and steel, required large numbers of minimally skilled workers. As technology progressed more and more, skilled labor was needed to use more complex machines and to construct urban houses, offices, and factories. Three patterns of rural colonial life seem to have endured, given a certain structural similarity in occupational roles: (1) role segregation of husband and wife; (2) an emphasis on obedience of children and sharp limits within which much freedom is allowed; and (3) the husband as a patriarchal authority (Adams, 1980). The cultural and social values of blue-collar manual workers remains similar to those of small farmers (Glenn & Alston, 1968).

The primary resources are, of course, skills of service or production. A number of the working-class jobs are well remunerated, but for most, there just never seems to be enough money (Howell, 1972; Rubin, 1976). The possibilities of career mobility are limited, and they define the American dream of success in terms of owning homes, cars, and possessions—especially related to leisure (e.g., campers, vacation homes, and small boats). Job skills sometimes become resources exchanged for "favors"—a system of reciprocal interpersonal obligations of auto repair or help in building a bathroom in exchange for another skill or the use of a camper. The men of this class often have a number of mechanical skills that must be considered resources. This is the do-it-yourself market.

The values of the working class are a function of their resources, their position in the occupational hierarchy, and their historical origins (Gans, 1962). These jobs rarely have genuine power to initiate and innovate. The largely rural past of this class, often several generations ago, similarly allowed little control over natural caprice.

Nor could they produce enough crops to allow a sizable cash income. The conditions of their life, past and present, make central the values of security and obedience. Thus, their values tend to be authoritarian (Lipset, 1960). Authoritarianism does seem to capture some of the values of conformity, obedience, patriarchal family attitudes, masculine toughness, anti-intellectualism, conservatism (except on economic issues), racism, and disdain of homosexuality. But in some ways, the members of this class do not fit certain stereotypes. Le Masters (1975) reported that they generally distrust political leaders and were quite critical of the Vietnam war. The values of younger, more educated members of the working class are not much different from those of middle-class youth (Yankelovich, 1974). Orderliness of relationships and material things are necessary. Working-class people show deference to bosses on the job and demand it at home; women and children are subordinate (cf. McKinley, 1964). Conformity is frequent on the job, where the peer group is a source of social control over activities (Homans, 1950). Further, insofar as their jobs are physical, they value a degree of toughness. They tend to stress traditional sex-role ideology and socialize along same-sex lines (this is changing). Finally, given the conditions of a hard and unpredictable life and their available resources, there is little incentive for repression—they are hedonistic. They take advantage of what pleasure comes their way. There is little use in long-term planning. Their hedonism is, however, situational rather than a central aspect of their lifestyle (Le Masters, 1975).

Blue-collar marriage shows traditional sex-role patterns, especially among older couples and families with less educated husbands (Komarovsky, 1962). The husband is the breadwinner; the wife, whose preferred place is in the home, does most of the housework and the child care. The father may act as the ultimate authority and disciplinarian. There are less joint husband–wife activities than in the middle strata, but this is a matter of degree in comparison to the middle-class ideal of companionship. The adult relationships are more important than the parent–child relation. There is, however, more joint marital activity today, especially before and after child-rearing duties and when the wife works (Fried, 1973). In the "tavern culture," Friday night is "ladies night" (Le Masters, 1975). The men take their wives (or dates) to dinner and then to the bar for a few drinks. Shared activities do enhance marital satisfaction in blue-collar families (Fried, 1973). There is less gratification from the restrictive sexually segregated patterns. Further, when working-class families interact as *couples,* marital solidarity is enhanced (Komarovsky, 1962).

Fathers stress traditional male virtues to their sons of toughness, ability to defend oneself, and avoidance of being taken advantage of by a woman, but they actually do little to either exemplify or socialize these values (Le Masters, 1975). Daughters generally do well in school, but they receive less encouragement to pursue education. Children tend to be less important and/or involved in parental activities compared to the middle class. The family tends to be more "adult-centered" (Gans, 1967). Children have more "unsponsored freedom" in Farber's terms (1964) but, at the same time, are more behaviorally restricted at early ages (Kohn, 1969).

Marriage among blue-collar individuals is often a way of leaving the parent's home. But marriage for blue-collar women often includes a romanticized fantasy of love and attaining the American dream, which their own home lives did not realize—nor often does their marriage (Rubin, 1976). General social changes are creating strains and changes in blue collar marriages. Almost half of working-class wives now work at lower-echelon clerical or service jobs, which increase their relative resources, their independence, and their exposure to the outside world. Today, most have completed high school and are exposed to the mass media. The women have more "middle-class" outlooks (Fried, 1973; Le Masters, 1975). Women's magazines provide more exposure to middle-class ideals of marital communication and intimacy. Working-class wives are often frustrated by their husband's limited degree of intimacy and sharing. Thus, they experience an emotional "relative deprivation" (cf. Komarovsky, 1962; Rubin, 1976). This is a frequent factor in divorce. Komarovsky (1962) found blue-collar wives even more frustrated when the husband did not do very well as a provider.

For blue-collar wives, especially those not employed, the typical form of social extension is along either kinship or "old friend" networks, which provide empathy, intimacy, and social support (Komarovsky, 1962). These networks often become disrupted when such families move to the suburbs (Berger, 1960). With greater role segmentation and less husband–wife communication, when the wife's support networks are ruptured, she becomes more dependent on the husband to deal with the psychological consequences of the lost or disrupted relations previously provided by the kinship group.

Blue-collar jobs and lifestyles tend to limit acquaintance with middle-class life, especially the nonmaterial aspects of tastes, social patterns, and cultural values. Thus, there is a lack of diffusion of cultural change and diversity; more egalitarian, communicative relationships; shared leisure-time activities; and mobility (Komarovsky, 1962). As this class achieves greater education and exposure to the media, often combined with suburban residence, these forces are changing the interaction pattern to the more communicative, companionate, "symmetrical" pattern of the middle class.

We previously noted that English industrialization fostered an extensive pattern of kinship solidarity, focused on "Mum" (Young & Willmott, 1957; Hoggart, 1967). This pattern is also typical in some American blue-collar groups, where socializing with family members is frequent (Cohen & Hodges, 1963). Families are likely to exchange a number of services (Sussman & Burchinal, 1962). Family ties are very important, given rural origins, large families, and socioeconomic continuity (Fried,

1973; Gans, 1962; Le Masters, 1975). In families that are more sexually segregated, the extended kinship networks influence the husband–wife relation and reinforce the separate activities of each sex (Bott, 1957; Lee, 1979). The working class are usually not joiners. Most of their social life centers on kinship networks, neighbors, and old friends, usually from high school youth cultures. Blue-collar families are less likely to move to areas of job opportunities (Adams, 1978). Movements are likely to be no further than what will maintain frequent kinship or friendship ties (Lee, 1979). In many cases, especially in ethnic communities, friendships with neighbors are important (Fried, 1973; Gans, 1967). Because visiting and dining in each other's homes is less frequent than in the middle classes, earlier research failed to show the importance of neighborhood ties.[5] The members of this class are not often involved in organized community activities. However, relationships with neighbors and social ties to nearby families are very important (Gans, 1962). There were serious psychological disturbances when the West End community of blue-collar Italians was moved to make way for "progress" (Fried, 1973). The tavern culture depends on long-term residential propinquity (Le Masters, 1975).

Male social activities include drinking; motor sports like bowling, pool, or baseball; and craft projects (Collins, 1975). Hunting and fishing are also enjoyed. Men who do physical work enjoy violent spectator sports of contact like boxing or wrestling (Collins, 1975). In general, the less affluent are more likely to enjoy craft, spectator, commercial, and home-centered activities (Carlson, 1979).

Working-class culture is a mass culture of simple drama or melodic music. Abstract discussions of political or intellectual topics are rare. The people are not avid readers. When they read, the men prefer dramatic adventure magazines or mechanical and craft publications, and the women prefer home-oriented publications. They both are likely to watch television a great deal. However, they see it as quite phony and unrealistic (Gans, 1962). For many, it is the only source of news.

Working-class religion is rarely moralistic or ascetic; it tends to be worldly and cathartic. The people like to celebrate periodic events with boisterous festivity. Religion often has a tone of magic, luck bringing, and future predicting that uses religious ceremony for worldly ends or emotional release. It is in some ways similar to rural or peasant religion (Collins, 1975; Weber, 1968). Many of the descendants of immigrants from central and southern Europe are Catholic. Protestant denominations include Methodists, Baptists, and Lutherans. Bellah (1975) maintained that, Puritan asceticism was the religion for the entrepreneurs, Methodism, with its cyclic pattern of restraint and order, followed by emotional release in church, appealed to the working classes in factories.

The working classes are little involved in occupational, social, or community organizations. They rarely show the patterns of cosmopolitanism, ritualized sociability, and impersonal ritual of the upper classes. Even those with high incomes do not develop the more cosmopolitan worldviews (Glenn & Alston, 1968). They tend to express distrust and cynicism toward superiors and wariness toward strangers, and to see the world from an aggressive personal point of view. They display physical strength and project an air of marked toughness. They disdain the "weakness" of women and the "sissy" paperwork or the "smooth talk bullshit" of the upper classes (Le Masters, 1975). The socialization of young boys encourages "motoric" expressions rather than cognitive or verbal skills (Miller & Swanson, 1960). Although such males are more likely to display and value courage and barroom brawls, they do not go around seeking combat; actual fighting is rare and is usually broken up quickly (Le Masters, 1975). They tend to show great loyalty to friends. They are worldly in orientation and take what pleasures they may. However, there is also a dual sex standard. The males tend to be hedonistic and to express interest in sex (Le Masters, 1975). Much barroom talk (fantasy?) concerns sexuality. The more traditional women are somewhat sexually repressed, although enjoying romanticized fantasy (Rubin, 1976). The younger women of today are less traditional and more sexually open. The general emotional tone of blue-collar self-presentation is relatively uninhibited, whether in discourse or in celebration (Collins, 1975, p. 72). This side is rarely seen by bosses, researchers, or those outside the friendship and kinship networks.[6]

Lower-Class Families

Before the growth of capitalism, the majority of people were poor peasants; farmers barely produced subsistence crops and a small surplus to support the aristocracy. In modern times, most of today's lower classes are only a generation or two removed from a sparce rural existence. The urban poor are largely minority groups, especially black, Hispanic, and some Appalachian stock. Depending on the figures used, 13%–20% of the society are poor. The growth of technology and its complex skills, together with the economic problems of the 1970s and 1980s, seems to make it more difficult to make the transition from poverty into the mainstream of society (Auletta, 1982).

Lower-class families have the fewest resources for adapting to the larger society. They have the most limited educations and job skills. In the United States, govern-

---

[5]This was true in lower-class communities as well. However, Suttles (1968), Hannerz (1969), and Liebow (1967) demonstrated the importance of neighborhood ties.

[6]We note that those who use extensive participant observation see blue-collar families as more expressive and hedonistic than those who read survey data or do short interviews.

ment programs to provide education, job skills, and welfare support are among the most poorly funded and administered of those in any industrial society (Grønbjerg, Street, & Suttles, 1977). Lower-class positions, which usually involve unskilled or semiskilled jobs, tend to be unstable and intermittent, to have no clear line of promotion, and so on. Lower-class jobs do not generally reward individual effort; any benefits or increased wages come from overtime, collective gains, and so on. Many lower-class males engage in a variety of economic endeavors termed *hustling,* some of which are clearly illegal (drug dealing, theft, pimping, and gambling); ''semilegal'' (ambulance chasing and auto sales); or perfectly legal (catch-as-catch-can part-time labor or junk collecting).

The limited and precarious resources of the poor make survival one of their most salient values (Adams, 1980). A consistent theme in delinquency and criminology research is the extent to which scarce resources, marginal status, and blocked channels of opportunity encourage criminal or delinquent behavior (Block, 1977; Cohen, 1955; Cloward & Ohlin, 1961). There are few stable commitments to organizations that might encourage honesty, suppress violence, or limit extreme self-indulgence; the outlook is essentially amoral and individualistic (Collins, 1975). Miller (1958) identified several ''focal concerns'': toughness, daring, adroitness in repartée, excitement, and rejection of authority. Gans (1962) termed these ''thrill seeking,'' the only means by which gratifications can be found in a world of few resources and little expectation of a better future through participation in the larger society. With little expectation of a better future, hedonistic self-expression is more likely than long-term goal-oriented achievement (Kluckhohn & Strodtbeck, 1961; Spiegel, 1971). The conditions of life encourage momentary pleasures, whether sexual, aggressive, or retreatist drug addiction (cf. Cloward & Ohlin, 1966). When economic resources are limited, gratifications are few, and the future is uncertain, hedonistic consumption is likely. The lower class are therefore likely to purchase items for self-aggrandizement and personal displays that bring momentary esteem from peers. Expressive clothes or jewelry is likely to impress others and to bring immediate gratification (Hannerz, 1969; see also Rainwater, 1966).

Lower-status family life, adapting to scarce resources, is based on cultural assumptions and behavioral norms that are *different* from those of the middle class (Ladner, 1971; Rodman, 1963; Schneider & Smith, 1973; Staples, 1971). The family pattern is highly ''organized,'' but in different ways from the higher strata to maximize the meager resources available. Extended kinship groups linked along female lines facilitate current adaptations to scarcity and enhance survival. There is a sharp degree of sex-role segregation or ''matrifocality,'' so that relationships among female kin are more salient and permanent than the husband–wife relation (Stack, 1974). In the case of poor American black families, this family pattern

is more an adaptation to current conditions than an intergenerationally transmitted ''culture of poverty.'' Gutman's work (1976) shows that this pattern was not frequent among slave families. Among the poorer families of London, there was a matrifocal family structure centered on ''Mum'' (Bott, 1957; Young & Willmott, 1957). However, the father was usually present and participated in child rearing and family decision-making (see also Hoggart, 1957). The essential features of this family pattern occur in many other poor cultures. It has been reported in Trinidad and among several caucasian groups, Latins, Appalachians, and so on. Limited status and resources seem to be the determining factors, not race or ethnicity (Billingsley, 1968; Schneider, 1968; Schneider & Smith, 1973; Stack, 1974). Safa (1971) and Rainwater (1965) reported that ''matrifocal'' families are typical when males are intermittent providers who may leave the family or find another woman. When socioeconomic forces deprive a man of stable and adequate resources, he loses authority in the community as well as in the family.

Poor families in America today are generally large and headed by minority-group women who tend to be unemployed or underemployed and are likely to depend in whole or in part on state entitlements (Chilman, 1975; Ross & Sawhill, 1975). Matrifocality is, by default, an adaptation to poverty rather than a desired option. Most such mothers would prefer a stably employed husband present. There are families of stable working poor (with a traditionally monogamous father). Most males that work, however, find their income to be irregular (Schultz, 1969).

Among the lower lower classes, there is a coherent organized family system with patterns of kinship solidarity along female lines that differs from the middle-class conjugal family (Schneider & Smith, 1973; Stack, 1974). In considering the lower-class family, we must look at the distinction between *household* and *family.* Households are units of production, reproduction, and consumption; families are normative relations of husband, wife, and children and the broader kinship ties that define reciprocal obligations (cf. Goody, 1972). Kinship ties extend *across* family and household boundaries. Women share a variety of domestic and economic resources with each other: child care, household help and redistribution of income. The household is *not* a centrally budgeted unit of rational accounting (Schneider & Smith, 1973). There are extensive (but often fragile) networks of help, redistribution, cooperation, and solidarity. A number of ''relatives'' may be created by association rather than by blood or marriage; these are ''play kin'' (Stack, 1974) or ''fictive kin'' (Liebow, 1967). Black males often refer to each other as ''blood'' or ''brother.'' However, these ''kinship'' relations, like those in any culture, create certain obligations of aid and reciprocity that are often difficult to fulfill. The degree of this kinship solidarity is also a function of geographical mobility. Recent entrants to a community are less likely to have these networks, but conversely, migration to an area may often be due to the existence of these extended networks (Schneider & Smith, 1973).

Lower-class marriage is based on a variety of peer pressures more than on individual ''attraction'' or romantic ideals. For the woman, being married (or having been married) leads to a certain degree of respectability and acceptance into a kinship grouping that often endures after divorce or separation (see Stack, 1974). For males, however, integration into the peer group may encourage sexuality but serve to delay marriage (Lee, 1979).

In the lower class, the marital relationship is not the basis for family structure. Nor is the conjugal relation of family life the primary basis of interpersonal gratifications, peer-group evaluation, or social activity. Conjugal solidarity does not assume the same degree of importance or perform the same purpose of intimacy, trust, and sharing that it does in the middle class. The conditions of limited resources are more likely to lead to distrust and fear of exploitation. The household has less saliency for family and/or social life than in other classes. The dwelling, most often a substandard rental unit, tends to be smaller and more crowded, affording less privacy. Social and leisure activities are usually outside the home; ''home life'' is less an arena of family interaction. The females have extensive kinship networks that cut across residential units (Stack, 1974). Male solidarity networks, less often along kinship lines, are also frequent (Liebow, 1967). Given the sex-role segregation of activities, marital disruption or broken homes are less disruptive to the family and more easily accommodated by extended kinship networks (Schneider & Smith, 1973; Stack, 1974).

Relations between men and women are quite different in lower-status families. Sexuality, for example, cannot be judged by middle-class norms, which are based on different resources and historical traditions. Such norms can represent self-righteous hypocrisy, and lower-class sexuality may be more honest, open, and free of hangups (Ladner, 1971; Rodman, 1963).[7] Schultz (1969) described several types of ''husbands.'' The *pimp* exploits women financially whether their income is legitimate (work or welfare) or actual prostitution. *Supportive companions* regularly spend a weekend with the women and offer some financial support in exchange for sexual favors; they avoid permanent family commitments. *Supportive fathers* contribute to biological children even if married to someone else. There are *free men* who pursue many women: the *indiscreet*, whose wives know of ''other women,'' and the *discreet*, whose extramarital affairs are covert. In lower-class adultery (by the male), the wife is more likely to be angered by the diversion of time and money from the family than by the act *per se*. The conditions of poverty in a modern society contribute to unstable, ungratifying marital relationships. Money is a major source of conflict (Liebow, 1967). Poverty leads to distrust between family members and little communication or sharing (Chilman, 1975). Divorce, separation, and desertion are more frequent.

The mother–child relation is more important than the father–child relation (Liebow, 1967; Safa, 1971). Child rearing is perceived as a ''female'' activity (Safa, 1971; Stack, 1974; Rainwater, 1965). This is not to imply a lack of warmth or commitment by the father but rather a reflection of sex-role norms. In fact, fathers are often warm and emotionally and financially indulgent, but this behavior tends to be intermittent (Liebow, 1967; Schultz, 1969). Liebow (1967) found that his fathers were not together with their children very often, nor were they very involved in the children's socialization. Contacts were brief, infrequent, and irregular. The men were *more* affectionate to their children when they did not live with them. Biological fathers often maintain relationships with their children even when they have never been married to the mother or after divorce (Schultz, 1969). Mother–daughter and sister–sister relations are closer than relations with males, who tend to be more independent of family ties (Schneider & Smith, 1973).

Most friendship groupings and activity patterns are among the same sex; men and women have few common interests. Even though sexual relations may begin early and occur at greater frequency than in upper classes (perhaps no longer true), adolescent sexual activity is separate from peer-group activity. However, male peer-group evaluations of men's heterosexual activity, especially the personal qualities that are its antecedents (wit, charm, popularity, cleverness, and expressive style of self-presentation) are of extreme importance.

The members of the lowest stratum are least likely to participate in formal organizations. They do not see how remote goals and events will affect their lives; rather, goal attainment is more likely through networks of personal relationships (Cohen & Hodges, 1963). Similarly, they are the least likely to vote and are the most cynical (or perhaps realistic) about the extent to which the electoral process or political action can affect their lives. Those who feel alienated and powerless to change social conditions may be *right* in their assessment. The lower classes are most likely to value motoric skills and physical abilities and to value contact sports, especially those that involve aggression. For some, athletics offer the rare pos-

---

[7]But Rainwater (1964) found that lower-class women are *less* likely to enjoy sexuality. Lower-class women often feel sexually exploited (Schneider & Smith, 1973). We should note, however, that class-specific sexual norms have undergone a rapid change since the 1960s. Sexual behavior is so complex a topic as to warrant a complete chapter (see Chapter 19). A number of recent surveys conducted by *Cosmopolitan, Redbook,* and *Playboy* magazines have suggested a great deal of liberalization of sexual attitudes and behavior among younger college-educated professionals. Many of the class-based differences in premarital sexuality, masturbation, extramarital sexuality, and sexual practices that were reported in early studies are no longer found (see pp. 234–235).

sibility of escape from poverty through professional sports, such as baseball, basketball, or boxing. In general, however, the lower classes are more likely to be "spectators" than "doers" (Hodges, 1964).

The lower-status religions may come the closest to being the "opiate of the people." For Weber (1968), lower-status religion consists of sporadic waves of chiliastic beliefs and fantasies of imminent world destruction. Pentacostal sects provide emotional catharsis as a compensation for economic deprivation; a haven for the lonely; emotional gratifications for the psychologically deprived; and "esteemed" religious status for those without any economic status (Yinger, 1970). Attendance is least frequent (Glock & Stark, 1968). Most studies of lower-class communities, as compared to middle- and upper-class communities, do not find religion a central theme of family life (Demerath, 1965). There are, however, some fundamentalist sects and store-front churches that attract many of the dispossessed and alienated. Within lower-status subcultures, there are what Gans (1967), following W. B. Miller (1958), termed "routine seekers" who tend to have stable jobs, to organize their lives, to live by ethical religious norms, and to be regular churchgoers. Hannerz (1969) called such ghetto families "mainstreamers" and described them as similar to the stable working class.

The modes of demeanor of lower-status cultures indicate the most limited organizational ties and the fewest resources. The social life of the lower stratum rarely occurs in the more private, structured locations of the higher groups but in more public places with little privacy or regard for the taboos of politeness typical of higher strata (Collins, 1975). There are few social constraints on self-indulgent hedonism (sex, drugs, and alcohol). The resulting patterns of self-presentation are highly individualistic, stylized forms of expressive hedonism. This individualism is expressed in personal display rather than in self-realization in a career. The upper classes, which often have that "lean and hungry look," present subdued dignity; the lower classes, at least the "swinger elements," tend to be more expressive in style of dress and exaggerated physical gesture (Hannerz, 1969). The higher classes, especially the constrictive sector of the pietistic lower-middle class, finds the lower-class patterns of sensuality, language, undignified musical tastes, and so on vulgar if not immoral. The highly stylized language is freely laced with obscenities (Labov, 1972). One of the most important aspects of the lower status (demeanor) is a personalized ritual of manipulative charm "soul" in black cultures. "Jiving" and "shucking" modes of verbal discourse are particularly salient in this group. Bantering, joking, verbal contests of insult, "playing the dozens," and frequent use of slang and obscenity are typical of the black lower class (Hannerz, 1969; Labov, 1972; Liebow, 1967). The ritual of conversation and propriety of grammar, vocabulary, and accent reflect the limited resources and social power of the "status culture."

Status, Sex, and Marriage

The patterns of courtship, sex, and married life again reflect a person's status. One's status influences whom one is likely to meet, date, and mate, and the nature of one's sexuality and married life. For the sake of brevity, Simon and Gagnon (1969) indicated the patterns of marriage, class, and sexuality. Although their table (Table 2) was meant to be somewhat humorous, it nevertheless summarizes a great deal of information. Their use of *brow* comes close to the meaning of *status* in this review.

It is very difficult to specify relationships of status differences to sexuality for two reasons. First, there has been a great change in sexual norms since 1960. Findings such as those of Kinsey are no longer valid. In the 1940s and 1950s, it seemed that lower-status groups were more sexually active before marriage, especially males. But this "fact" obscured the relation of premarital sexuality to age of marriage, and the middle classes married later. Premarital sex was also associated with marital infidelity. In the early 1960s, sociologists argued that the "sexual revolution" that began after World War I had arrived but was of attitudes rather than behavior. Sexual researchers such as Bell, Reiss, Kanter, Hite, and Hunt found that, since 1960, there had been a gradual increase in the rates of premarital sexuality and decreased differences between the working class and the middle class (see also Yankelovich, 1974, who reported few class differences in sexual values). Further, the male–female gaps have narrowed. Thus, by the 1980s, more than half of the youth population had experienced premarital intercourse by the age of 19. (In one *Playboy* survey, over 70% of the sample had experienced sexual relations by age 19. Over 25% by 16, and the females a few percentage point *more* active than males.) Once again, we must conclude that changing values and lifestyles mandate a more dynamic perspective for understanding status differences. Today, over 95% of married couples report premarital sexual activity.

The data collected by researchers, especially the surveys of large samples of *Redbook, Cosmopolitan* and *Playboy* readers, were not collected or analyzed in ways useful for considering subgroup variations. Specifically, the respondents were *self-selected* from the readership of sexually liberal publications. Such readers tend to be young adults (20–30 years of age) with a higher education. As has been argued, at any given level of income or education, there are normative variations of each "status culture." Among the lower class are both libertines and religious fundamentalists. Among the lower-middle class are the "restrictive" and "expansive" sectors, whose "objective" rankings are similar to those of the working classes.

It has been remarked that sociologists were more concerned about counting virgins than about exploring the meaning of sexuality. The findings of surveys that correlate sexual values or behaviors with income or education do not clearly address our interest in the values, meanings, and lifestyles of a particular "status culture." Given the various limitations in approach and method, a few brief but tentative comments are in order.

The lowest-status group, especially those without the constraints of close-knit families, restrictive religions, or organizational ties, tend to be hedonistic. This is especially true among the "thrill-seeking" elements. There are few rewards for premarital chastity and many inducements for sexuality. The illegitimacy rates among poor girls showed a rapid increase in the 1970s (see Furstenberg, 1976). Sexual relations are often one of the few sources of pleasure for those without access to the material rewards and/or the occupational gratifications of higher-status groups. Erotic modes of self-presentation in dress, body language, and verbal styles may be rewarded in some subcultures. However, sexuality can also be the basis of a great deal of jealousy, distrust, and exploitation, as was described above.

We previously noted that the working-class "status culture" is hedonistic and generally tolerant of premarital sexuality for both sexes (Le Masters, 1975). Among the younger generations, there has been a greater convergence with certain middle-class norms of communication, intimacy, sharing, and, it would seem, sexuality. If publications like *Playboy* and *Penthouse* cater to the upper-middle classes, *Hustler* is more oriented to working-class males. Though any leap from readership to sexuality is speculative, *Hustler* tends to focus on scatological, sadistic, and domination themes. On the other hand, much of the family research has also reported a good deal of puritanism, male chauvinism, traditional moral codes, and sexual frustration (cf. Rubin, 1976). Little research speaks to this discrepancy. It would seem that such "differences," if they exist, may be a function of generation, religion, or ethnicity. (Recent immigrants of the working class often come from less industrial and more traditional societies.)

It is among the "restrictive" sectors of the lower-middle class, especially among members of more conservative Protestant denominations, that the traditional values of premarital chastity are most salient. Such groups constitute much of the membership of various anti-ERA and prolife organizations. (The leadership, however, is more likely to be from high classes.) But there are far too few empirical data on the sexual values and behaviors of either the "restrictive" or the "expansive" segments of this "status culture." The extent to which "respectability" and upward-mobility affect sexuality is unclear. Youth encouraged to attend college often find themselves in a more liberal, permissive milieu with values that differ from those of their families and communities.

The upper-middle classes, especially youth attending college, have been the vanguard of changing sexual norms. Indeed, premarital sexual intimacy, if it does not hinder educational or occupational attainment, may itself reflect certain norms of psychological intimacy, open communication, and self-realization. Whatever may be the variations in politics and lifestyles between the managerial and the professional segments, the attitudes toward premarital sexuality are similar. The same *Playboy* issue with the survey on marital sexuality also featured a female stockbroker—subsequently fired. It is among certain segments of the upper-middle class that sexual gratification, experimentation with various techniques, use of devices, and enhancement through drugs have become salient goals. Of the 100,000 or so respondents to the *Playboy* survey, about 95% practice oral sex, 50% practice anal sex, 50% use drugs, about 33% have had group sex, 40% report oral-anal contact, and 70% use devices. (The women were generally a bit more liberal than the men. We should also mention that extramarital affairs are frequent; close to half of the 30- to 39-year-olds and two-thirds of the 40- to 49-year-olds so reported; male–female differences were slight. We must again note the bias in sample selection.)

For males there was a relation of income to infidelity: 70% of those with 1982 incomes of over $60,000 reported affairs. Educated women pursuing careers were more likely to have extramarital affairs than housewives. If, as some argue, the upper-middle class in strategic positions of communication and opinion shaping is the most salient segment of society in establishing its norms, values, and lifestyles, the sexual revolution is over. All that remains are some futile rear-guard actions.

Among the lower-upper class, sexual values are likely to be formed by the experiences of the prior status. As was just noted, the higher the income, the more likely is male infidelity. Some have suggested that men with strong needs for power and achievement may also have the needs (and financial means) for frequent sexual conquest. For the very upper classes, who zealously guard their privacy, we have perhaps the very least amount of concrete knowledge. There have recently been a number of public divorce trials and "palimony" suits that suggest that whatever the "differences between the very rich and the rest of us," their sexual behavior is not very different—only more private.

These brief comments indicate that the relation of social status to sexual values and behaviors is especially long on theory (speculation) and short on data. We need not only more research into the meaning of sexuality but more specific research on variations according to "status culture." One universal consequence of sexuality is children, the rearing of which is our next concern.

Socialization and Social Status

The family is the initial setting and context for early childhood socialization, one of its primary functions. Other agencies, such as schools, church, peers, and the mass media, all of which show class differences, further socialize the growing child. The first years of the child's life are especially critical in establishing the motivations

Table 2. How Fashionable Is Your Sex Life?[a]

	Highbrow	Upper middlebrow	Lower middlebrow	Lowbrow
1. How girl meets boy:	He was an usher at her best friend's wedding	1. At college, in the psychology lab	1. In the office, by the water cooler	1. On the block
2. The proposal:	In his room during the Harvard–Princeton game	2. In the back seat of a Volkswagen	2. After three drinks in an apartment he borrowed	2. In her home one night when Mom and Dad were at the movies
3. The wedding:	In her living room, by a federal judge	3. College chapel (nondenominational)	3. City Hall	3. Neighborhood church
4. The honeymoon:	Mediterranean	4. Bahamas	4. Any Hilton hotel	4. Disneyland
5. Marriage manual:	*Kama Sutra*	5. *Sexual Efficiency in Marriage*, volumes I and II	5. Van de Velde	5. None
6. Sex novels she reads:	Jane Austen	6. *Lady Chatterley's Lover*	6. *Myra Breckinridge* and any novel by Harold Robbins	6. *Valley of the Dolls*
7. Sleeping arrangements:	Double bed	7. King-size bed or twin beds with one headboard	7. Twin beds with matching night tables	7. Double bed
8. Sleeping attire:	He: nothing. She: nothing	8. He: red turtleneck nightshirt. She: gown with matching peignoir	8. He: pajamas. She: pajamas	8. He: underwear. She: nightgown
9. Background music:	Ravi Shankar or the Beatles	9. Wagner	9. Sound track of *Dr. Zhivago*	9. Jackie Gleason and the Silver Strings
10. Turn-ons:	Pot	10. Champagne and oysters	10. Manhattans and whisky sours	10. Beer
11. The schedule:	Spontaneously, on an average of 2.5 weekly (that means 2 times one week and 3 times another)	11. Twice a week and when the kids go to the Sunday matinee	11. Twice a week and when the kids go to Sunday school	11. Twice on Saturday night

12. Number of children:	1 each by a previous marriage, or as many as God provides	2.4	3	As many as God provides
13. Anniversary celebrations:	A weekend in Dublin	He gives her a new dishwasher. She gives him a power lawn mower	Corsage and dinner out	Whitman Sampler and dinner at Howard Johnson's
14. Quarrels:	"I don't care what your analyst says"	"I don't care if he is your brother"	"What do you think I'm made of?"	"Drop dead!"
15. If the marriage needs help:	He consults her analyst. She consults his	They go (a) to a marriage counselor; (b) to the minister	He: to his successful brother. She: to her best friend	He: to the bartender. She: to her mother
16. The affair:	"But I assumed you knew"	"It was basically a problem in communication"	"It was bigger than both of us"	"Some things no woman should have to put up with"
17. Sex education:	"Ask Doctor Grauber, dear, when you see him tomorrow"	"Well, you see, Daddy has something called a . . . etc. And Daddy and Mommy love each other very much"	"Well, you see, Daddy puts the seed in Mommy's tummy, etc., etc."	"We got you at the hospital"
18. Vacations:	Europe in May. She takes the children to the Cape. He commutes	Europe in July. Family camping in Yosemite	He hunts or fishes. She visits Mother with the children	They visit Brother Charlie in Des Moines
19. Financial arrangements:	Separate trust funds	Joint checking account	She budgets	He gets weekly allowance
20. Who raises the children:	English nanny, boarding school, and Dr. Grauber	Mommy and Daddy, Cub Scouts, and Dr. Freud	Mom and Dad, the Little League, and Dr. Spock	Mom, the gang, Ann Landers, and good luck

ᵃFrom Simon and Gagnon, 1968, pp. 58–59.

and cognitive abilities that enable later educational and occupational success and/or mobility.

Every society attempts to foster the motives, values, self-conceptions, and skills (cognitive, behavioral, and social) necessary to perform the required adult roles and activities (Inkles, 1968). Parents are the major providers of early nurturance, stimulation, rewards, and frustrations. Status differences that affect parental attitudes, behavior, and role relationships therefore have a profound influence.

The socialization process reflects the norms of the appropriate techniques of child rearing, what the child means to the parents, and parental expectations for his or her current and future behavior. The norms, values, and techniques of child rearing differ by status, as well as undergo long-term historical changes. Current practices, then, represent an interaction of early traditions and current realities. Further, there are short-term events that affect particular cohorts. A father's loss of job in a depression, rapid promotion in a boom, or going off to war can affect family patterns and the child's experiences, which, in turn, affect his personality (Elder, 1974).

The authority of the parent as a worker affects his or her qualities as a role model. Socialization can be considered an exchange relationship in which parental resources, psychological or physical, are exchanged for the child's behavioral control and/or psychological development. Parents attempt to secure certain types of relationships with the child, to foster certain types of behavior, and to ensure particular outcomes in the future.

Social Status, Occupational Role, and Socialization

Kohn's analysis (1969) of occupational roles argues that different positions in the occupational hierarchy vary in authority and control. There are also variations in type of job skills: motoric, cognitive or interpersonal (Holland, 1959). As a result of such differences in daily work life, people see the world differently and have varied conceptions of social reality, different hopes and fears, and different ideologies of childhood (Kohn, 1969, p. 7). Middle-class occupational roles require self-direction, initiative, creativity, and responsibility. There is little control by superiors. White-collar jobs involve the manipulation of symbols, ideas, and/or interpersonal relations and involve complexity, thought, and judgment. Working-class roles require conformity, standardization, and obedience to external authority. Working class jobs have less authority. They deal more often with concrete objects and require fewer interpersonal skills. These occupational role demands are translated into socialization values. The self-direction of the middle-class job is generalized to the parental role. Middle-class parents are more psychologically aware and concerned with their child's intent and controls. Parents are more tolerant of the expression of their child's impulses and thus encourage the child's

creativity, curiosity, and achievement. Higher-status parents tend to be more "proactive," more concerned with the child's acquisition of internalized principles of self-control, on which she or he may base *future* behavior and/or judge the implications of potential actions. The middle-class orientation, more aware of the child's inner life and stressing its intrinsic potential, has been termed *developmental*. The working- and lower-class pattern, emphasizing compliance with parental authority and suppression of impulse, is a more "traditional" orientation rooted in preindustrial Puritanism. The child is expected to conform to external rules and to be obedient to authority. The parents are more concerned with the child's overt behavior. They stress neatness, cleanliness, and so on as the means of success.

At the upper echelons, people value a job in terms of *intrinsic* qualities, such as how much freedom it offers, how interesting it is, and how many opportunities it affords for expressing talents or helping people (Kohn, 1969). Therefore, there is more concern with the *child's* intrinsic qualities: his or her psychological needs and their expression, his or her curiosity about the world and intellectual growth. Conversely, at lower-status levels, there is more concern with the job's *extrinsic* qualities: work conditions, pay, security, and hours. Accordingly, there is more concern with the *child's* extrinsic qualities: his or her behavior, especially limiting disruptive expression. These parents stress orderliness.

The middle-class roles, especially in the upper echelons, require abstract knowledge and the manipulation of symbols. Middle-class parents have more subjective involvement in their jobs and are more likely to discuss job activities at home (Piotrkowski, 1979). Intellectual discussion is more frequent in the home. These parents are more concerned with the abstract qualities of the child. As part of their own upbringing and/or college experience, as well as their daily experience, middle-class parents are more aware of the nonmaterial aspects of cultural tastes, theories of child psychology, and "expert" advice (Blau, 1981). They are more likely to use cultural resources such as museums, libraries, and camps. They are better able to help children with homework. Thus, their occupational roles and educational level encourage the child's intellectual and cultural development. For some upper-class families, the mother is, in fact, an active participant in the cultural activities of the community (Daniels, 1975). Parents of less education read fewer books or magazines and watch more television. There is less intellectual stimulation for the child.

The middle-class occupational roles, and those of the upper class as well, are more concerned with a future perspective and with long-range planning. As parents, these people are more aware of the long-range consequences of child rearing. Informed about theories of child development, they not only are aware of the effects of their behavior on the child's personality but have greater feelings of control over their children and confidence in their methods of child rearing (Walters & Stinnett, 1971).

Lower-class parents are more concerned with immediate consequences and try to control disruptions. They are less aware of the effects of their socialization practices. They have less confidence in their ability to control children and are less likely to feel that they can influence the long-term future of their children (Walters & Stinnett, 1971). It has been argued that the relevant factor of status differences in socialization is not occupational role but level of education (Wright & Wright, 1976).

Socialization Techniques

Socialization research, initially inspired by Freudian theory, attempted to relate class position to child-rearing practices concerned with "training" biologically based motives. Research focused on *overt* measures of impulse control and management of biological needs. Attempts to "objectively" measure "oral fixations," "anal traits," or Oedipal feelings were of little avail (Orlansky, 1949; Sewell, 1952). The "variables" suggested by Freud were based on *individual's subjective* meanings expressed in transference or symptoms, not *overt* aspects of a group's typical parent–child relationships. Although precise measurement was elusive and evidence of significant consequences fleeting, there were historical changes in socialization practices (Wolfenstein, 1953). There was more indulgent breast feeding on demand, relaxed toilet training, and greater toleration of sexuality, which reversed reported class differences (Bronfenbrenner, 1958). Early research suggested that the lower classes relied primarily on physical punishment, whereas the middle classes used psychological punishments (e.g., love withdrawal, guilt induction, reason, and verbal explanation). Recent research suggests that there are *few*, if any, class differences in the use of physical punishment *per se* (Erlanger, 1974). Kohn (1969) showed that the *context* of physical punishment was more important than its frequency. Middle-class parents, concerned with the child's *self-control,* punish failures of *self-restraint;* working-class parents punish *overt* acts of disobedience (cf. Gecas & Nye, 1974).

Given the parental views and expectations of childhood, which are dependent on status, what socialization techniques are most typical of each status? Socialization practices themselves depend on a group's resources, values, current realities, and historical tradition. Lower-class socialization tends to be concerned with the consequences of immediate behavioral disruption. The households tend to be smaller and populated by more *persons.* High-density households stress the suppression of disruption (Whiting, 1975). Discipline tends to be more arbitrary, inconsistent, coercive and stresses *submission* to adult fiat. Socialization places more emphasis on the child's submission to adult power than on his or her internalization of adult norms and rational self-control.

Power-assertive techniques include the parental capacity to do harm or violence, control over resources, and the ability to deprive their child of privileges. Power-assert-

ive techniques are used more frequently in the working and lower classes than the psychological techniques of discipline used by the middle classes (Gecas, 1979; Hoffman, 1970; Kerckhoff, 1972). Power assertion, especially physical punishment, is usually associated with "expressive" behavior, such as anger and rage (Kerckhoff, 1972). The child is expected to obey authority and to conform to the rules—but these rules and the quality of the respect demanded for authority tend to be arbitrary, particularistic, and egocentric. Obedience comes from fear of superior parental power based on the parent's hierarchical position and her or his physical capacity to do harm. Positional appeals foster compliance because the parent demands it—and has power-assertive techniques at his or her disposal. Middle-class parents more often use *personal* appeals; compliance happens because the person requests it and usually gives a reason for the request. Middle-class parents are less likely to assert hierarchical domination, power and coercion through commands, deprivations, or force. The parent–child relation is more democratic and egalitarian. The lower classes are more autocratic and restrictive (Elder & Bowerman, 1963; Waters & Crandall, 1964). The lower-class father, denied status and prestige at work, gains "respect" from his children via their obedience to his commands (Cohen & Hodges, 1963). McKinley (1964) suggested that the frustrations of low-status work leads fathers to stern, aggressive, or restrictive behavior toward their children.

Psychological techniques, used more frequently in the middle class, stress the *relation* to the parent. Love withdrawal may be used to induce guilt or shame. Verbal explanations, praise, and reasoning are inductive techniques; the children learn general principles for behavior rather than simply inhibiting a particular action (Hoffman, 1970). They are more likely to learn role taking and/or empathy, the effects of their behavior on the feelings of another person.

The major polarity of socialization techniques is thus the use of power assertion versus the use of psychological or love techniques. Love techniques may be either positive ("induction," through praise, reasoning, and negotiation) or negative (love withdrawal, isolation, or shame; Steinmetz, 1979). Maternal power assertion usually results in "aggressive dependent boys who are low in conscience, and aggressive but nondependent girls low in conscience" (Steinmetz, 1979). Negative love techniques produce similar patterns but with moderate conscience development. Finally, positive techniques produce dependent children with a strong conscience. It would seem that power assertion is used more frequently in lower- and working-class families, negative love in lower-middle-class families, and induction in the upper-middle class.

Why do parents of differing status groups use particular techniques? "Parents use the techniques they can best afford" (Collins, 1975, p. 267). The techniques used, consistent with the resources and the values of each "status culture," are attempts by the parents to produce certain desirable outcomes in their offspring. We do not claim that parents are any more certain of cause-and-effect relations than scientific researchers. Rather, we suggest that, of the variety of techniques potentially available, the ones most likely to produce results more-or-less consistent with the group's values are likely to become intentionally practiced and hence most frequent (cf. Le Vine, 1973). Socialization techniques can be considered negotiation strategies to gain the child's current compliance and to secure enduring patterns of behavior and, at least in the higher classes, to foster psychological development.

Power-assertive techniques are cheap: They are readily available to groups with few other resources of control (Collins, 1975). Thus, they are more likely found in lower-status groups. Further, working-class and lower-class occupations involve "motoric" skills. Physical punishment is more often used in groups that use such skills (Steinmetz, 1974a). This may also be true at other strata where the occupation roles attempt to gain advantage through compliance by others. Certain salespeople or lawyers who try to use "persuasive" powers may, as parents, use force as a last resort (Steinmetz, 1974a). Power-assertive practices may gain momentary control of behavior. These lead not to internalized constraints but to fear of punishment. In fact, they more often lead to limited impulse control, especially the expression of aggressive behavior. Such techniques facilitate authoritarianism, inhibit cognitive development, impair self-esteem, and limit achievement. Power-assertive techniques that breed resentment are less frequently used when family solidarity is important. Further, these techniques limit the possibility of educational and occupation success.

Parents may also attempt to control rewards as a means of social control. Material rewards may gain momentary compliance or even short-term results, but these alone are less likely to produce an internalization of parental desires. Some parents reward good grades with money. Parents may also reward children with praise, attention, or play, which, in turn, depend on available parental time and their interest in sociability with their children. Praise is usually more effective than punishment in shaping behavior. The use of praise is more common in modern middle-class families. Children who often play with their parents tend to be more sociable and expressive.

Shaming or ridicule produces self-control, especially over public demeanor and emotional expressiveness to outsiders. Shame produces external conformity to group expectations. But shame depends on extensive surveillance by an audience of peers or adults. Its continued effect into adulthood depends on the prevalence and importance of family links throughout one's career (Collins, 1975, pp. 267–268). It is most often found in high-density agrarian societies and, to an extent, among the upper-class family units that maintain a high degree of surveillance and solidarity. For such a family, public dishonor or scandal is worse than losing its wealth. The middle-class-

es sometimes use shaming techniques in conjunction with guilt induction.

Control by love deprivation and guilt induction depends on parental resources of time, attention, and limited dilution of affection (see also p. 241). It is therefore most likely to be found in middle-class homes with few children. Harsh socialization would threaten the child's future achievement potentials and the friendly parent–child relationships that such parents anticipate. Love deprivation leads to internalized constraints of guilt that enable autonomous self-control in the future.

The use of reasoning, discussion, and explanation also fosters internalized controls (Hoffman, 1970). Such internalized controls stand as principles to live up to rather than restraints on impulse expression. These inductive techniques foster internalized strategies without necessarily arousing anxieties. The necessary verbal skills and parental empathy are typically found in the more educated sectors of the upper-middle class. This is probably especially true among those who deal in interpersonal relationships of a supportive or communicative nature. Explanation and discussion facilitate an acquisition of general principles of behavior rather than the inhibition of a particular action. They also help to foster role taking or empathy on the part of the child, who learns the consequences of behavior in others. Thus, pulling the dog's tail or a sister's hair is not just wrong; it violates an abstract principle, the Golden Rule, and causes pain to the other party.

Parent–Child Relationships

Certain socialization techniques, such as deprivation of love, presuppose a strong affective bond between parent and child. The quality of the parent–child relation varies by social status. The "adult"-centered versus "child"-centered orientation varies by class (Gans, 1967). The middle class is more child-centered. In the working and lower classes, joint parent–child activities are less frequent. The sexual segregation of adult activities results in a similar pattern of segregated parent–child activities. The father might take a son hunting while the wife visits friends or relatives with the daughter.

The relation between middle-class parents and their children is more egalitarian and reciprocal. We noted earlier the greater degree of exchange between parties. The working and lower classes are more hierarchically patterned. There is greater emphasis on positional authority between parent and child.

The middle-class father is more likely to be supportive of his child of either sex. His role as an authority imposing punishment or restraint is secondary (Kohn, 1969). Support includes discussing events, aid with school work, and praise for accomplishment. The working-class father is more likely to see child rearing as a mother's responsibility and to leave discipline to her (Kohn, 1969). Lower-class fathers play an even more minor role in socialization—and the mothers prefer it that way (Rainwater, 1965).

In general, the higher the parental status, the greater the degree of parental warmth and expression of affection, especially by the father. This is not to suggest that lower-class fathers are cold; they are often highly indulgent, but the frequency of interaction is often sporadic. Further, the differences in family and household previously indicated suggest that the lower-class child receives a good deal of warmth from other members of the family, including aunts, grandparents, and even "fictive kin." However, in general, fathers of higher social classes are usually warmer and play a more supportive role.

Children who are raised in an atmosphere of warmth and who have with autonomy-granting parents show leadership, achievement, and creativity (Walters & Stinnett, 1971). Parental warmth promotes internalized controls and higher levels of moral development (Hoffman, 1970). When parents seek interpersonal gratification from socializing with their children, they tend to show more warmth and affection. This is the case in middle-class families. In upper-class families, the child is also expected to become part of a kinship network that maintains a high degree of family solidarity. Parental warmth facilitates this attachment to the family network. Further, the attachment of the family network is a prerequisite for the extended surveillance that makes possible the use of shame as a means of social control.

Parental warmth is said to enable the use of love deprivation as a means of guilt induction in the middle class. The child fears abandonment, internalizes the parental values, and develops capacities of self-surveillance, inhibitions from transgressions, and guilt for engaging in prohibited activities. Collins (1975) suggested that the process is better explained by understanding the child's cognitive development. His argument is too complex to be easily summarized. The main thrust is that the child develops the capacity for intentionality (self as agent of action) before attaining object constancy (retaining a memory of an object not present). By maintaining the child's anxiety over the cognitive world, the mother fosters a permanently internalized worldview based on her interpretations of reality. The middle-class child depends less on the direct manipulation of objects than the child in the working or lower classes. By the time the child attains preoperational structures of thought, including object constancy, she or he will have internalized the parental worldviews as enduring cognitive structures. If parents have the resources to exploit the special vulnerability of this early age, they can establish a strong, internally controlled personality (Collins, 1975, p. 270). These resources include love and empathy.

Cognitive Development and Social Class

Most of the research on socialization has been concerned with parental values, socialization practices, and particular motives. There has recently been a renewed interest in Piaget's theories of child development and concern with cognitive development and intelligence. Research has examined the relationships of social status to intellectual growth, levels of attainment, patterns of cognition, and language. The literature suggests that the cognitive milieu, the child-rearing practices, and the verbal patterns of more highly educated middle- and higher-class parents foster greater cognitive development, verbal skills, and capacities for abstraction in the child.

The middle-class family places greater stress on *verbal* skills. There is a higher level of abstraction and more concern with general principles. Middle-class jobs and marital and social relationships stress explanation, verbal negotiation, and reasoning. This pattern is extended to relationships with children. In this milieu, more time is spent in family interaction. Smaller families, more typical of higher-status groups, mean that each member has more one-to-one interaction and verbal interchange. Middle-class parents tend to be more supportive. Further, such parents encourage curiosity and reward verbal behavior. These factors, individually and in together, foster higher levels of cognitive development. Zigler and Child (1973) argued that social class differences represent populations at *different* levels of cognitive development that perceive and experience the world differently. The more educated groups are more likely to use "formal operations" in their daily lives and negotiations.

Kohlberg (1969) and his students have found that differences in sex-role identity, self-conceptions, and morality are related to rates of cognitive development, and that the levels attained are closely related to social status. Kohlberg's concept of morality—or, more specifically, moral principles—can be thought of in terms of three broad levels of interiorization: (1) "premoral" expedience (what you can get away with); (2) "conventional" conformity (the law-and-order morality of conformity to group standards to gain approval); and (3) "postconventional" principles (internalized universal principles of justice that prevent self-condemnation). The lower classes are more likely to have a morality based on expediency. The fear of external punishment is the only constraint on seeking immediate rewards. The working and lower-middle classes are more likely to value conformity to the law as a means of gaining social approval. The college-educated upper-middle class, which use higher levels of abstraction, is more likely to value universal principles of democratic law and/or avoidance of self-condemnation. Moral development, as one aspect of cognitive development in general, is accelerated and increased by varied role-taking experiences as a form of cognitive stimulation. Such experiences, as we have seen, are more likely in a middle-class environment with socialization practices that emphasize verbal interaction, foster empathy and role taking. Cognitive development is another crucial link between the social status of the family and personality development.

One of the most important status differentials in socialization is in language and verbal communication. Research by Bernstein (1960, 1971, 1973), Cook-Gumperz (1973), and others (e.g., Hess & Shipman, 1965) has suggested that patterns of linguistic usage show significant status differences that shape worldviews and modes of cognition. Bernstein has distinguished two linguistic patterns, which he has called "restricted" and "elaborated" codes. The working class is more likely to use the former; the middle class, the latter. Restricted codes tend to be more concrete, more emotive, and more specific to a particular situation. These codes tend to be subjective and "egocentric." They require the addressed party to exert more conceptual effort to understand the message. Not infrequently, the statement may end with "d'y'know what I mean," indicating that the communication may be egocentric and not easily comprehended. Elaborated codes are more abstract and complex. There is a larger vocabulary, more adjectives, adverbs, and subordinated clauses. Meanings are clearly expressed and are clear to the listener. Such codes better express relationships between events.

To clarify Bernstein's approach, let us use the following example. Two mothers take a young child to the food store. There is a display of cans stacked in a six-foot pyramid. The child removes one from the bottom. The middle-class mother might say, "Mommy's little darling shouldn't do that. A good boy (girl) should know better. Now the poor stock person will have to stack all those cans up again." The lower-class mother would say, "Don't do that again or I'll let you have it." In the former case, the middle-class mother uses an "elaborated" code. We see greater complexity describing the event. The particular act or event is a deviation from the abstract categories of "Mommy's little darling" and a good boy or girl.[8] The mother expresses a moral imperative of "should *know* better." Finally, the mother indicates the consequences of the child's action as inconveniencing another person (the stock person), which encourages role taking and empathy. In the restricted code, the concrete *act* leads to a vague egocentric power-assertive command and threat: What "it" is is not made explicit. "It" is some veiled threat of retaliation that the child must decipher. The child is more likely to be given a spank. Again, the middle class are more concerned about *intent* and interpersonal consequences; the working class, about behavior.

Bernstein (1971) tried to link language and the social order. First, more-educated high-status families use a more complex language to enunciate meanings. There is a greater effort to express the nuances of the message and to express the speaker's intent in ways more easily comprehensible to the listener. The middle classes have more "organic" solidarity. Their social roles, relationships, and experiences are more differentiated and require more elaborated codes to make meanings explicit. Middle-

class roles show more flexibility and openness. They are what Bernstein called "person-oriented" roles. Lower-class families have more "mechanical" solidarity and cohesive social networks. Restricted codes stress solidarity based on shared but implicit (egocentric) meanings. Lower-class roles tend to be more closed and "position-oriented" (Cook-Gumperz, 1973). Person-oriented families stress the *psychological* qualities of the members; they tend to be more democratic. Position-oriented families stress the *power* of the members and tend to be more authoritarian.

The evidence linking social class, family, and language is significant. But Bernstein's theoretical linking of language with solidarity patterns and role flexibility are more tenuous (see Gecas, 1979, for a more comprehensive critique). The cognitive aspects of class-based socialization differences are highly suggestive and warrant more careful scrutiny. Indeed, there is a good deal of compatibility with some of the other approaches indicated. Kohn's stress (1969) on middle-class concerns about the child's intent and Hoffman's work (1970) on internalization through induction are consistent with Bernstein's work on language.

Socialization, Personality, and Social Status

The socialization values, techniques, and cognitive milieus of each status group encourage or discourage certain individual potentials and/or restraints. Middle-class parents stress autonomous achievement to prepare the child for a higher echelon career; working-class parents stress conformist compliance to attain secure jobs. There are several dimensions of individual personality—such as aggression, sexuality and sex role, moral development, self-conceptions, and achievement—that show differences according to status group membership.

Middle-class parents are more tolerant of a child's impulses, especially aggression and sexuality (Langman, 1969; Le Vine, 1970). Given the child's greater levels of norm internalization, parental empathy, and concern with intent, parental toleration of aggression is constrained by the child's own empathy and his or her internalized limits on doing harm to others and/or breaking expensive toys. For the working class, the patterns of child rearing suppress the expression of aggression from within or without. One consequence is greater authoritarianism (Lipset, 1960). Impulses are more often handled by denial, projection, and acting out (Miller & Swanson, 1960). Thus, greater aggression is expressed toward and projected onto outgroups; this, in short, is one factor in the greater prejudice of the working class (Adorno *et al.*, 1950; Langman, 1969). Lower-class children, especially boys, are more frequently punished through power-assertive techniques for the expression of aggression within the household. Suppression in the house leads to expression outside it. Further, when parents express aggression, they may act as role models. If power-assertive techniques and aggressive displays are expressions of parental anger, the

---

[8]The implicit threat of love withdrawal should be noticed.

child learns that aggression is the "appropriate" response to anger and frustration. The lower-class values of male qualities, such as aggression and toughness, further contribute to aggressive behavior and the prevalence of violence in lower-status subcultures (Miller, 1958). Finally, the context of structural inequality facilitates the expression of aggressive behavior, often in an antisocial form.

There are class differences in sex-role socialization. In all classes, boys are encouraged to show greater independence, aggression, rational control, and so on. Girls are socialized toward dependency, submissiveness, and affectivity. The stories that parents read to children, the toys that they buy, and the games that they play further reinforce these different expectations. But the *degree* of these differences is greater at the lower-status levels, where each sex is more integrated into sexually segregated networks of kinship extension (Kohn, 1969). Within this milieu, more traditional patterns of sex role are encouraged. Higher-status groups are more likely to tolerate less sex-role differentiation. There is more encouragement of female achievement in school and career.

An important line of sex-role research has been concerned with the role of father absence for lower-class boys. This was said to lead to impaired sex-role identity, hypermasculinity, hedonism, criminal behavior, gang membership, lower achievement motivation, and limited levels of aspiration. More recent research has questioned some of the "measures" of the effects of father absence (e.g., deferred gratification, impaired sex-role identity, poor grades, and low motivation). It would seem that, when divorce rates among the upper-middle class began to rise, and the father began to be "absent" most of the time in many "intact" nuclear families, father absence was no longer defined as a social problem.

Sexual values, such as emphasis on modesty, toleration of masturbation, and explanations of sexuality, vary. Working-class parents offer little or no sex education (Rubin, 1976). Nor do lower-class parents (Furstenberg, 1976; Rainwater, 1964). The lower-middle class—at least, the more *constrictive* sectors—try to actively suppress sexuality and knowledge of it. The more educated upper-middle class are more tolerant of "natural" impulses. They are more likely to stress the importance of privacy for "natural" functions than to punish their expression. Although they may induce guilt over such things as achievement, today they are more likely to accept sexuality, sexual curiosity, and masturbation as a normal part of a child's development.

The parental use of reasoning, verbal explanation, praise, guilt induction, and so on in combination with parental warmth and empathy has been shown to be related to the child's moral development (conscience) (Hoffman, 1970). This socialization pattern is more typical of more highly educated middle-class parents. There is greater identification with parents and a higher degree of internalization of parental norms, resistance to temptation, and guilt upon transgression. As has been noted, the

more frequent role-taking experiences and the stimulating cognitive milieu foster higher levels of cognitive development in general and moral principles in particular. A persistent theme in child development literature, psychotherapy, and even popular literature is middle-class guilt (Slater, 1970).

Kerckhoff (1972, p. 57) argued that middle-class practices provide more information and greater motivation for developing a clear self-image. Self-esteem has *not*, however, shown a strong relation to class (Coopersmith, 1967; Gecas, 1979). Coopersmith did, however, show that self-esteem is associated with clear-cut rules, achievement pressures, and low levels of coercion, which seem to be associated with social class. Parental support and inductive techniques also show a relation to self-esteem and social competence (Rollins & Thomas, 1979). There does seem to be some evidence that higher social status is associated with a greater feeling of efficacy compared to fatalism, as well as with an internal versus an external locus of control. Whether or not this is a dimension of personality versus realistic appraisals of the different allocations of political and economic power is uncertain.

Perhaps the most important aspect of the individual is his or her educational and occupational achievement. From what we have already said, in relation to social status and career, this is a function of the norms of each "status culture" and individual motivation and ability. A number of factors contribute to mobility, beginning with the expectations of each "status culture." The upper classes stress achievement to maintain their social domination and patterns of luxurious consumption. The upper-middle class values self-realization, whereas the lower-middle class sees achievement as leading to a respectable career. Parents of every class value achievement, but its translation into concrete expectations and techniques varies. (There are independent effects of the opportunity structure based on the larger economy that we will not consider here; see Elder, 1974.)

The socialization techniques of higher-status parents, such as warmth and induction, encourage achievement through the "deferred-gratification pattern" maintained by guilt. Parental concerns with intent, inner development, and self-direction encourage autonomous achievement. Democratic socialization gives the person a sense of mastery over events. Finally, the verbal patterns and symbolic environments of the higher-status cultures facilitate cognitive development and achievement.

Certain child-rearing practices have been shown to be associated with parental status, on the one hand, and the child's subsequent achievement, on the other. In a pioneering study, McClelland (1961) translated Weber's theory of the Protestant Ethic into psychological terms. The "need for achievement" was a result of early encouragement of independence, mastery, and achievement. Middle-class parents have higher expectations for their children and stress early achievement to a greater degree (Rosen, 1956, 1959; Strodbeck, 1958; Veroff, 1960).

Winterbottom (1958) found parental practices that stress early and independence training to be related to the child's need for achievement. Langman (1969) found that middle-class parents expected their children to perform certain tasks (e.g., to carry money and to dress themselves) at age 6½, working-class parents at age 7½, and lower-class parents at age 9. Farber (1964) suggested that middle-class parents reward *responsible* independence; it is "sponsored." Similarly, Scanzoni (1971) reported that lower-status parents feel more passivity than do higher-class parents.

The early stratification and family literature noted that the children of higher-status groups were more likely to pursue higher education and, in turn, to obtain higher-status jobs (Cavan, 1964). In the past two decades, sophisticated methods of analyzing large amounts of data have shown that the social status and/or the educational level of the father is a powerful predictor of social mobility. In one of the most ambitious of such projects, Sewell and Shah (1967) traced 20% of the high-school students in Wisconsin. The higher-status youth did better in school and obtained more education. A high-status youth had nine times the chance of receiving a postgraduate degree of a low-status youth (Sewell, 1971). Sewell claimed that several other intervening variables, such as academic abilities, school performance, and parental attitudes, also contributed to mobility. Teachers and peers also played a role.

In a complex model of intergenerational mobility, Blau and Duncan (1967) traced the course of male mobility. The education of the father influenced the son's level of educational attainment. The son's level of education influenced the status of his first full-time, entry-level job. This, in turn, determined the subsequent degree of mobility. This model was replicated (Hauser & Featherman, 1977).

In a telling critique of the literature, Jencks (1972) and his colleagues have argued that education is *not* the basis of upward mobility but its manifestation. Rather, the socialization practices and cognitive environment of the person's family background influence one's career. Further, a certain degree of luck and on-the-job competence affects mobility. One of Jencks's coworkers has since argued that education is a means of social reproduction; it ensures that each social stratum will *maintain* its relative position in the social hierarchy (Bowles & Gintiss, 1976). Educational experience socializes the values necessary for each social class. High school socializes the conformity and obedience required in working-class jobs. College provides the autonomy and self-direction required in middle-class jobs. Finally, education reinforces the myth that anyone who works hard will succeed. The lower classes can look with awe to the educated managers and justify their servitude as legitimate.

Early socialization is thus one of the means by which each "status culture" begins the shaping of subsequent generations. Many will remain in the same status, some will become upwardly mobile, and some will "skid" downward. Socialization, values, and practices are rooted in the history of the status culture and are modified by current realities, such as the daily life of the parents and social, economic, or political events. Although the young person is most influenced by his or her early family experiences, subsequent personality development occurs throughout the life cycle as a result of peers, schools, church, and so on. Yet, even the "extrafamilial" influences on the life cycle are influenced by the "status culture" into which the person is born.

Summary and Conclusions

Despite the various limitations of and differences in theoretical conceptualizations and methodological approaches, we have seen that social status is perhaps the most important influence on family life. Although conceptions and measures of status leave much to be desired, we have seen how status differences are associated with varying marital norms and dynamics, relations with family members or friends, leisure, cultural and religious orientations, modes of self-presentation, and the socialization of the next generation. If early explorations have been fruitful, the next generation of research strategies should be even more illuminating. Therefore, we begin our conclusions by claiming that any statement about family life that does not consider the role of social status is limited. Much family research either ignores status variation or relegates it to a formality. But any study that has used social status should also be scrutinized. How was status conceived of? How was it measured?

Marx made us aware of the role of inequality, conflict between the classes and/or the sexes, the importance of historical factors and the deleterious aspects of domination and exploitation. But his approach placed too much emphasis on relation to capital (profit, fee, rent, or wage) as the determining factor of social class. Perhaps, for those at the very top and bottom of income distribution, economic class may be relevant, but for most groups in the middle, status seems more salient. Yet Marx's insights into the role of work and the economy as a powerful influence remain cogent. In current society, it seems that the *nature* of work activity, especially its social-psychological aspects, is more influential in shaping worldviews, family relations, and socialization patterns (cf. Kohn, 1971, 1976). Further, we argue that there are many resources besides economic ones. Authority varies by status. It may be based on control of resources or lineage, capacity to organize or innovate, knowledge of abstract principles, or knowledge of forms or mechanical skills. Knowledge and/or the interpersonal skills of management, leadership, or selling ability are resources. Similarly, family and/or kinship relations may be a resource. Employable family members can be resources, especially during difficult times.

Further, the Marxist typology of class is too simplistic to differentiate the normative, interactional, and symbolic variations in family processes that constitute the very essence of status differences. We are not at a point where we can give a comprehensive index or list of resources, but we hope to encourage more a systematic understanding of how families of different status have access to and the use of certain resources.

The functional theories of stratification and/or family life, especially the Parsonian integrations, were at one time the dominant perspective in American sociology. That conception of the family not only was biased toward the middle class but was not even a realistic portrait of that class. The nature of family life in general and the woman's role have undergone enormous changes since 1960. Therefore, recent explorations into the family's history and life cycle have made us more cognizant of the dynamic aspects of social life as a set of interactive process within a larger social-historical process. Many family researchers now regard status differences as processes rather than structures (Moen, Kain, & Elder, 1981). Elder (1981) has been especially critical of structural conceptions of social status. His work examining the influence of historic change on family career and individual development requires a dynamic social-psychological understanding linking class to occupational roles, family dynamics, and socialization processes that vary over time in response to changes in the economy as a whole. Structural approaches tend to be static and ahistorical, and to ignore the intersection of historical change and the ecological context of the life cycle of the family and the individual. Historical change in family life has been primarily in the emotional and behavioral realms, not in the structure *per se*. We have seen that the two-generation nuclear-family *structure* has changed less than the social-psychological processes (cf. Bane, 1976). To be sure, in earlier times, families were larger—but death was more certain. The predictability of the life cycle was less certain. Living to adulthood with both parents still alive was less frequent.

Current directions in family research require a process view of status differences. This process view of social status was required by certain issues in family research. Haug and Sussman (1971) argued that status was a *judgment*. Therefore, the determination of status was a social-psychological process. Further, the very essence of status is manifested in the enactment of norms, the negotiation of relationships, the construction of reality, and the presentation of the self (cf. Berger & Kellner, 1964). A social-psychological approach to status is therefore mandatory (cf. Block, 1971). Kohn (1969, 1971) has similarly maintained that the basis of status differences in socialization values comes from what men—and now women—*do* in their jobs. Do they control, initiate, and have responsibility? Do they have a command of knowledge or work procedures by which they influence others, or do they perform physical labor in which the tasks assigned are controlled from without? Lower-status men, who have the least control and self-direction in their work, felt more alienated and powerless (Kohn, 1976). Current work realities influence the person's worldview,

sense of personal competence, marital relations, and parental roles.

A current perspective on status variations must then emphasize the different resources and competition of groups; must focus on process, especially at the social-psychological level; and must attend to historical change. Weber's concept of "status culture" most captures these criteria. For Weber (1968), a status group was bound by personal ties, a common sense of social honor, and shared values. These, in turn, generated a "status culture" of shared lifestyles and cultural tastes. Further, Weber argued that status groups *compete* for scarce social, economic, or cultural resources. Therefore, the group's "status culture" serves an important function in the competition for resources: It provides solidarity to the group and, in the case of elite status groups, extracts deference from subordinate groups.

With Weber's insights, we have further considered the social-psychological aspects of daily behavior, in order to make sense of the data and to provide a coherent framework for group variations in status based on control of resources. These resources, especially authority, generate normative processes expressed in social interaction and self-presentation. The values of each status group are based on historical tradition, the group's available and potential resources, and current social realities. These resources and values then influence the interpersonal processes by which status groups communicate, enact, and negotiate relationships, self-conceptions, a concept of reality, and parent–child transactions.

Further, a status group has social, cultural, leisure, and religious orientations that articulate its lifestyle. The totality of these processes are considered "status cultures." Status cultures are not enduring structures of social organization but cognitive and behavioral processes enacted in day-to-day social life. Status cultures may show a great deal of continuity over time. They may also change as available resources and/or values change in response to long-term and short-term social change. A status culture is thus an interaction between its historical origins and current events. Further, status cultures can influence social change. Privileged groups try to retain their advantage; others may seek material improvement, cultural domination, greater social honor, or political power (Lipset has long indicated the role of status politics in America). Finally, for our understanding of family life, the important qualities of each status culture are not so much its rankings compared to others, but how it expresses its available resources.

Our discussion of status cultures attempted to indicate the historical background from which each status group emerged and now influences its current reality. The aggressive entrepreneurship of one generation led to the genteel arrogance of subsequent generations of the upper class. The harsh Puritanism of the early artisans endures in some segments of the lower-middle class. The growth of the familial extension of the working class *because of* industrialization has long endured. Similarly, some of the qualities of its rural heritage, especially the patriarchal sex roles, endure. But now education, female employment, and media exposure are influencing and seemingly changing certain traditional patterns of blue-collar life. At the same time, our examination of family history indicated that many of the "modern" questions of family life, the role of women, the emotional relation between partners, and the "modern" conception of childhood emerged in the nineteenth century. However, many of these patterns were typical only of the relatively small urban middle class. Not until 100 years later did these questions become salient political issues.

We then proceeded to indicate the resources of each stratum, especially the source and nature of its authority. The values of each stratum represent attempts to maximize or legitimize the group's resources, especially its authority, status, and wealth. Further, its values express its differences from the other strata. Finally, each group's values are goals for its members to attain honor and prestige. The interpersonal processes of marital and family life are best understood as attempts to maximize the rewards of each person as spouse, family member, and parent in ways consistent with the norms of the group. Similarly, the social and cultural orientations of each stratum differ, as do the modes of self-presentation and interpersonal demeanor. We saw how status affects socialization, values, practices, and outcome.

The measures of social status (SES, SEI, and so on) suffer a variety of methodological problems. They often try to rank strata along some dimension such as income, education, or occupational prestige. Do individuals with similar scale scores, levels of education, or job prestige ratings form interacting entities that share and articulate a culture? Do strata vary along a continuum of some objective index of income, education, or job prestige, or do classes represent discrete categories? Classes designated by scales often include "strange combinations." There is little agreement on what constitutes a status group and how it is objectively measured and differentiated from other groups. The differentiation between strata is not easily measured or always clear. At what point does a bureaucratic worker go from lower to upper-middle status or does a cardiologist enter the lower-upper class? What are the ranges of variations found within a class? How many classes are there? Typologies of class range from two classes to nine. Are classes "objective" categories or subjective entities?

In this review, we have offered some tentative answers to these questions while remaining aware of the objections and the alternatives. The central concern has not been to propose either a theory of status differences or a way of measuring these differences. Rather, the concern has been to point out the effect of status differences on family life. But given the current limitations on theory and methods, any conclusions are not only tenuous but likely to change over time. Those interested in the theoretical and methodological issues raised, (class vs. status, scale score vs. lifestyle) will find the pursuit of such subjects exciting. Those who deal with broad sectors of the society will find the understanding of status differences essential.

References

Adams, B. W. Kinship in an urban setting. Chicago: Markham, 1978.

Adams, B. W. The family: A sociological interpretation. Boston: Houghton Mifflin, 1980.

Adorno, T., et al. The authoritarian personality. New York: Harper, 1950.

Amory, C. Who killed society? New York: Harper, 1960.

Anderson, M. Family structure in nineteenth century Lancashire. Cambridge: Cambridge University Press, 1971.

Ariès, P. Centuries of childhood. New York: Random House, Vintage Books (1965 ed.), 1962.

Aronowitz, S. False promises. New York: McGraw-Hill, 1974.

Auletta, K. The underclass. New York: Random House, 1982.

Baltzell, E. D. Philadelphia gentlemen: The making of a national upper class. Glencoe, Ill.: Free Press, 1958.

Baltzell, E. D. The Protestant establishment. New York: Random House, 1964.

Baltzell, E. D. Puritan Boston and Quaker Philadelphia. New York: Free Press, 1980.

Bane, M. J. Here to stay: American families in the twentieth century. New York: Basic Books, 1976.

Bellah, R. The broken covenant. New York: Seabury Press, 1975.

Berger, B. Working class suburb. Berkeley: University of California Press, 1960.

Berger, P., & Kellner, H. Marriage and the construction of reality. Diogenes, 1964, 46, 1–25.

Berkner, L. Recent research on the history of the family in Western Europe. Journal of Marriage and the Family, 1973, 35, 395–405.

Bernard, J. The female world. New York: The Free Press, 1981.

Bernstein, B. Language and social class. British Journal of Sociology, 1960, 11, 271–76.

Bernstein, B. Class, codes and control. Vol. 1: Theoretical studies toward a sociology of language. London: Routledge & Kegan Paul, 1971.

Bernstein, B. Class, codes, and control. Vol. 2: Applied studies toward a sociology of language. London: Routledge & Kegan Paul, 1973.

Billingsley, A. Black families in white America. Englewood Cliffs, N.J.: Prentice-Hall, 1968.

Birmingham, S. The right people: A portrait of the American social establishment. Boston: Little, Brown, 1968.

Blau, P., & Dunca, O. D. The American occupational structure. New York: Wiley, 1967.

Blau, Z. Black children-white children: Competence, socialization and social structure. New York: Free Press, 1981.

Block, J. Lives through time. Berkeley, Calif.: Bancroft, 1971.

Block, R. Violent crime: Environment, interaction and death. Lexington, Mass.: Lexington Books, 1977.

Bott, E. Family and social network. London: Tavistock, 1957.

Bowles, H., & Gintiss, G. Schooling in capitalist America. New York: Basic Books, 1976.

Braverman, H. Labor and monopoly capital: The degradation of work in the twentieth century. New York: Monthly Review Press, 1974.

Brittan, A. The privatized world. London: Routledge & Kegan Paul, 1977.

Bronfenbrenner, U. Socialization and social class through time and space. In E. E. Maccoby et al. (Eds.), Reading in social psychology. New York: Holt, 1958.

Broom, L. A., & Selznick, P., with Darroch, D. Sociology. (7th ed.). New York: Harper & Row, 1981.

Carlson, J. The family and recreation: Toward a theoretical development. In W. Burr *et al.* (Eds.), *Contemporary theories about the family,* Vol. 1. New York: Free Press, 1979.

Cavan, R. Subcultural variations and mobility. In H. Christianson (Ed.), *Handbook of marriage and the family.* Chicago: Rand McNally, 1964.

Chilman, C. A. Families in poverty in the early 1970's: Rates, associated factors, some implications. *Journal of Marriage and the Family,* 1975, *37,* 57–58.

Cloward, R., & Ohlin, L. *Delinquent and opportunity.* Glencoe, Ill.: Free Press, 1966.

Cogswell, B., & Sussman, M. B. Family and fertility. In W. Burr *et al.* (Eds.), *Contemporary theories about the family,* Vol. 1. New York: Free Press, 1979.

Cohen, A. K. *Delinquent boys: The culture of the gang.* Glencoe, Ill.: Free Press, 1955.

Cohen, A. K., & Hodges, H. Characteristics of the lower-blue collar class. *Social Problems,* 1963, *10,* 303–334.

Coleman, R. P., & Rainwater, L. *Social standing in America: New dimentions of class.* New York: Basic Books, 1978.

Collins, R. *Conflict sociology.* New York: Academic Press, 1975.

Collins, R. *The credential society.* New York: Academic Press, 1979.

Cominus, P. T. Late victorian sexual responsibility and the social system. *International Review of Social History,* 1963, *8,* 18–48.

Cook-Gomperz, J. *Social control and socialization.* London: Routledge & Kegan Paul, 1973.

Coopersmith, S. *Antecedents of self esteem.* San Francisco: Freeman, 1967.

Cuber, J. F., & Harroff, P. B. *The significant Americans: A study of sexual behavior among the affluent.* New York: Appleton-Century, 1965.

Dahrendorf, R. *Class and class conflict in industrial society.* Stanford, Calif.: Stanford University Press, 1959.

Daniels, A. *Room at the top.* Unpublished draft, 1975.

Davis, A., & Dollard, J. *Children of bondage.* Washington: American Council on Education, 1940.

Davis, A., Gardner, B., & Gardner, M. *Deep South.* Chicago: University of Chicago Press, 1941.

Degler, C. *At odds.* New York: Oxford University Press, 1980.

Demerath, N. *Social class in American Protestantism.* Chicago: Rand, McNally, 1965.

Demos, J. *A little commonwealth.* New York: Oxford University Press, 1970.

Dobriner, W. *Class in suburbia.* Englewood Cliffs, N.J.: Prentice-Hall, 1963.

Domhoff, W. *Who rules America?* Englewood Cliffs, N.J.: Prentice-Hall, 1967.

Domhoff, W. *The higher circles.* New York: Random House, 1971.

Elder, G. Appearance and education in marriage mobility. *American Sociological Review,* 1969, *34,* 519–533.

Elder, G. *Children of the Great Depression.* Chicago: University of Chicago Press, 1974.

Elder, G. History and the family: The discovery of complexity. *Journal of Marriage and the Family,* 1981, (August), 489–519.

Elder, G., & Bowerman, C. Family structure and childrearing patterns: The effect of family size and sex composition. *American Sociological Review,* 1963, *28,* 891–905.

Elkins, S. *Slavery: A problem in American institutional and intellectual life.* Chicago: University of Chicago Press, 1959.

Erlanger, H. Social class and corporal punishment in child rearing: A reassessment. *American Sociological Review,* 1974, *39,* 68–85.

Ewen, S. *Captains of consciousness.* New York: McGraw-Hill, 1977.

Farber, B. *Family: Organization and interaction.* San Francisco: Chandler, 1964.

Farber, B. *Kinship and class: A midwestern study.* New York: Basic Books, 1971.

Farber, B. *Guardians of virtue: Salem families in 1800.* New York: Basic Books, 1972.

Fogel, R., & Engerman, S. *Time on the cross.* Boston: Little, Brown, 1974.

Freid, M. *The world of the urban working class.* Cambridge: Harvard University Press, 1973.

Furstenberg, F. *Unplanned parenthood.* New York: Free Press, 1976.

Gans, H. *The urban villagers.* New York: Free Press, 1962.

Gans, H. *The Levitowners.* New York: Pantheon, 1967.

Gecas, V. The influence of social class on socialization. In Burr *et al.* (Eds.), *Contemporary theories about the family.* New York: Free Press, 1979.

Gecas, V., & Nye, F. I. Sex and class differences in parent-child interaction: A test of Kohn's hypothesis. *Journal of Marriage and the Family,* 1974, *35,* 742–749.

Glenn, N., & Alston, J. P. Cultural distances among occupational categories. *American Sociological Review,* 1968, *33,* 365–382.

Glock, C., & Star, R. *Religion and society in tension.* Chicago: Rand, McNally, 1965.

Glock, C. Y., & Stark, R., *Patterns of religious commitment.* Berkeley: University of California Press, 1968.

Goffman, E. *The presentation of self in everyday life.* New York: Doubleday, 1959.

Goldthorpe, J. The affluent worker and the thesis of embourgeoisment. *Sociology,* 1969, *1*(January), 11–31.

Goode, W. *World revolution and family patterns.* New York: Free Press, 1963.

Goodenough, W. H. Componential analysis and the study of meaning. *Language,* 1956, *32,* 195–216.

Goody, J. The evolution of the family. In P. Laslett & R. Wall (Eds.), *Household and family in past time.* Cambridge: Cambridge University Press, 1972.

Gordon, M. *Assimilation in American life.* New York: Oxford University Press, 1964.

Gordon, M., & Noll, C. E. Social class and interaction with kin and friends. *Journal of Comparative Family Studies,* 1975, *6,* 239–248.

Greven, P. *Four generations: Population, land and family in colonial Andover, Massachusetts.* Ithaca, N.Y.: Cornell University Press, 1970.

Grønbjerg, K., Street, D., & Suttles, G. *Poverty and social change.* Chicago: University of Chicago Press, 1977.

Gutman, H. *The black family in slavery and freedom.* New York: Pantheon, 1976.

Hannerz, U. *Soulside.* New York: Columbia University Press, 1969.

Haug, M., & Sussman, M. B. The indiscriminate use of social class measurement. *Social Forces,* 1971, *49*(4), 549–562.

Hauser, R., & Featherman, D. *The process of stratification.* New York: Academic Press, 1977.

Hess, R. Social class and ethnic influence on socialization. In P. Mussen (Ed.), *Carmichaels manual of child psychology,* Vol. 2. New York: Wiley, 1970.

Hess, R., & Shipman, V. Early experience and the socialization of cognitive modes in children. *Child Development,* 1965, *36,* 869–886.

Hodges, H. *Social stratification.* Cambridge, Mass.: Schenkman, 1964.

Hoffman, M. Moral development. In P. Mussen (Ed.), *Carmichaels handbook of child psychology,* Vol. 2. New York: Wiley, 1970.

Hoggart, R. *The uses of literacy.* London: Chatto & Windus, 1957.

Holland, J., A theory of vocational choice. *Journal of Counseling Psychology,* 1959, *6*(1), 35–45.

Hollingshead, A. *Elmtown's youth.* New York: Wiley, 1949.

Hollingshead, A., & Redlich, F. *Social class and mental illness.* New York: Wiley, 1958.

Holter, H. *Sex roles and social structure.* Oslo, Norway: Universitetsforleget, 1970.

Homans, G. *The human group.* New York: Harcourt Brace, 1950.

Horkheimer, M. Authority and the family. In *Critical Theory.* New York: Herder and Herder, 1972. (originally published, 1936.)

Howe, L. K. (Ed.). *The white majority: Between poverty and affluence.* New York: Random House, 1970.

Howell, J. *Hard living on Clay Street.* New York: Doubleday, 1972.

Hunt, D. *Parents and children in history.* New York: Basic Books, 1970.

Inkeles, A. Society, social structure and child socialization. In J. Clausen (Ed.), *Socialization and society.* Boston: Little, Brown, 1968.

Inkeles, A., Rossi, P. National comparisons of occupational prestige. *American Journal of Sociology,* 1956, *61*(January), 529–539.

Jencks, C., *et al. Inequality.* New York: Basic Books, 1972.

Kerckhoff, A. *Socialization and social class.* Englewood Cliffs, N.J.: Prentice-Hall, 1972.

Kohlberg, L. Stage and sequence: The cognitive developmental approach to socialization. In D. Goslin (Ed.), *Handbook of socialization theory and research.* Chicago: Rand, McNally, 1969.

Kohn, M. *Class and conformity.* Homewood, Ill.: Dorsey Press, 1969.

Kohn, M. Bureaucratic man. *American Sociological Review,* 1971, *36*(June), 461–474.

Kohn, M. Occupational structure and alienation. *American Journal of Sociology,* 1976, *82,* 111–130.

Komarovsky, M. *Blue collar marriage.* New York: Random House, 1962.

Kriesberg, L. *Social inequality.* Englewood Cliffs, N.J.: Prentice-Hall, 1979.

Labov, W. Rule for ritual insults. In D. Sudnow (Ed.), *Studies in social interaction.* New York: Free Press, 1972.

Ladner, J. *Tomorrow's tomorrow: The black woman.* New York: Doubleday, 1971.

Langman, L. *The effects of subsistence economy on motives, values and socialization practices.* Unpublished Ph.D. dissertation, 1969, University of Chicago.

Langman, L., & Kaplan, L. The crisis of self and state in late capitalism. *International Journal of Law and Psychiatry,* 1978, *1,* 343–374.

Lantz, H., Keyes, J., & Schultz, M. The American family in the preindustrial period: From baseline in history to Change. *American Sociological Review,* 1975, *40*(February), 29–30.

Lasch, C. *The culture of narcissism.* New York: Norton, 1978.

Laslett, P. *The world we have lost.* New York: Scribners, 1965.

Lee, G. Effects of social networks on the family. In W. Burr *et al.* (Eds.), *Contemporary theories about the family,* Vol. 1. New York: Free Press, 1979.

Le Masters, E. E. *Blue collar aristocrats.* Madison: University of Wisconsin Press, 1975.

Lenski, G. *Power and privilege: The theory of social stratification.* New York: McGraw-Hill, 1966.

Lerner, G. The majority finds its past. New York: Oxford University Press, 1979.

Le Vine, R. Cross-cultural study in child psychology. In P. Mussen (Ed.), *Carmichaels handbook of child psychology,* Vol. 2. New York: Wiley, 1970.

Le Vine, R. *Culture, behavior and personality.* Chicago: Aldine, 1973.

Lewis, R., & Spainer, G. B. Theorizing about the quality and stability of marriage. In W. Burr *et al.* (Eds.), *Contemporary theories about the family,* Vol. 1. New York: Free Press, 1979.

Liebow, E. *Tally's corner.* Boston: Little, Brown, 1967.

Lipset, M. *Political Man.* New York: Doubleday, 1960.

Lipset, M. *The politics of unreason.* New York: Harper & Row, 1970.

Lundberg, F. *The rich and the super-rich.* Secaucus, N.J.: Lyle Stuart, 1968.

Marcus, S. *The other Victorians.* New York: Basic Books, 1964.

Marcuse, H. *Eros and civilization.* Boston: Beacon Press, 1955.

Martin, E., & Martin, J. M. *The black extended family.* Chicago: University of Chicago Press, 1978.

McClelland, D. *The achieving society.* New York: Van Nostrand, 1961.

McKinley, D. *Social class and family life.* New York: Collier Books, 1964.

Miller, D., & Swanson, G. *The changing American parent.* New York: Wiley, 1958.

Miller, D., & Swanson, G. *Inner conflict and defense.* New York: Holt, 1960.

Miller, W. B. Lower class culture as a generating milieu of gang delinquency. *Journal of Social Issues,* 1958, *14,* 5–14.

Modell, J., & Hareven, T. Urbanization and the malleable household: An examination of boarding and lodging in American families, *Journal of Marriage and the Family,* 1973, *35,* 467–479.

Moen, P., Kain, E., & Elder, G. *Economic conditions and family life.* Unpublished manuscript, 1981.

Noble, D. *America by design.* New York: Alfred Knopf, 1977.

O'Neill, W. *Everyone was brave.* Chicago: Quadrangle Books, 1969.

Orden, S., & Bradburn, N. Dimensions of marital happiness. *American Journal of Sociology,* 1968, *73,* 615–631.

Orlansky, H. Infant care and personality. *Psychological Bulletin,* 1949, *46,* 1–48.

Osborn, R., & Williams, J. I. Determining patterns of exchange and expanded family relationships. *International Journal of Sociology of the Family,* 1976, *6,* 205–218.

Ostrander, S. Class consciousness as conduct and meaning: The case of upper class women. *Insurgent Sociologist,* 1979, *9*(Fall), 38–50.

Otto, L. Class and status in family research. *Journal of Marriage and the Family,* 1975, *37,* 315–332.

Parsons, T. *The structure of social action.* New York: McGraw-Hill, 1937.

Parsons, T. *Toward a general theory of action.* Cambridge: Harvard University Press, 1953.

Piotrkowski, C. *Work and the family system: A naturalistic study of working class and lower middle class families.* New York: Free Press, 1979.

Poster, M. *The critical theory of the family.* New York: Seabury Press, 1978.

Rainwater, L. *Workingman's wife.* New York: Oceana Publications, 1959.

Rainwater, L. Marital sexuality in four cultures of poverty. *Journal of Marriage and the Family,* 1964, *26,* 457–466.

Rainwater, L. *Family design: Mental sexuality, family size and contraception.* Chicago: Aldine, 1965.

Rainwater, L. Crucible of identity. *Daedulus,* 1966, *59*(Winter), 172–216.

Rainwater, L. *Behind ghetto walls.* Chicago: Aldine, 1970.

Rapoport, R., & Rapoport, R. *Dual career families.* New York: Penguin Books, 1971.

Rapp, R. Family and class in contemporary America. *Science and Society,* 1978, *42,* 278–300.

Reich, W. *The mass psychology of fascism.* New York: Farrar, Straus & Giroux, 1970. (Originally published, 1933.)

Rodman, H. The lower class value stretch. *Social Forces,* 1963, *42,* 205–215.

Rodman, H. *Lower class families: The culture of poverty in Negro Trinidad.* New York: Oxford University Press, 1971.

Rollins, B., & Thomas, D. Parental support, power and control techniques in the socialization of Chicago. In W. Burr *et al.* (Eds.), *Contemporary theories of the family,* Vol. 1. New York: Free Press, 1979.

Rosen, B. The achievement syndrome: A psychocultural dimension of social stratification. *American Sociological Review*, 1956, *21*, 203–211.

Rosen, B. Race ethnicity and the achievement syndrome. *American Sociological Review*, 1959, *26*, 574–585.

Ross, H., & Sawhill, I. *Time of transition: The growth of families.* Washington, D.C.: The Urban Institute, 1975.

Rubin, L. *Worlds of pain.* New York: Basic Books, 1976.

Ryan, J. *White ethnics: Their life in working class America.* Englewood Cliffs, N.J.: Prentice-Hall, 1973.

Safa, H. I. The matrifocal family in the black ghetto: Sign of pathology or pattern of survival. In C. Crawford (Ed.), *Health and the family: A medical-sociological analysis.* New York: Macmillan, 1971.

Scanzoni, J. *The black family in modern society.* Boston: Allyn & Bacon, 1971.

Schneider, D. *American kinship.* Englewood Cliffs, N.J.: Prentice-Hall, 1968.

Schneider, D., & Smith, R. *Class differences in sex roles in American kinship and family structure.* Englewood Cliffs, N.J.: Prentice-Hall, 1973.

Schultz, D. *Coming up black.* Englewood Cliffs, N.J.: Prentice-Hall, 1969.

Seeley, J., *et al. Crestwood Heights.* New York: Basic Books, 1956.

Sennett, R. *The fall of public man.* New York: Vintage Books, 1976.

Sennett, R., & Cobb, J. *The hidden injuries of social class.* New York: Knopf, 1972.

Sewell, W. Infant training and the personality of the child. *American Journal of Sociology,* 1952, *58*(2), 150–159.

Sewell, W. Inequality of opportunity for higher education. *American Sociological Review,* 1971, *36,* 793–809.

Sewell, W., & Shah, V. P. Socioeconomic status, intelligence, and the attainment of higher education. *Sociology of Education,* 1967, *40,* 1–23.

Sexton, P., & Sexton, B. *Blue collars and hard hats.* New York: Vintage Books, 1972.

Shorter, E. *The making of the modern family.* New York: Basic Books, 1975.

Shostak, A. *Blue collar life.* New York: Random House, 1969.

Shostak, A., & Gomberg, W. (Eds.). *Blue collar world: Studies of the American worker.* Englewood Cliffs, N.J.: Prentice-Hall, 1964.

Simon, W., & Gagnon, J. How fashionable is your sex life. *McCall,* 1969, *94*(October), 58–59.

Slater, P. *The pursuit of loneliness.* Boston: Beacon Press, 1970.

Smith, D. The dating of the American sexual revolution. In M. Gordon (Ed.), *The American family in social historical perspective* (2d ed.). New York: St. Martins Press, 1978.

Stack, C. *All our kin.* New York: Harper & Row, 1974.

Staples, R. *The black family.* Belmont, Calif.: Wadsworth Press, 1971.

Steinmetz, S. Occupational environment in relation to physical punishment and dogmatism. In S. Steinmetz & M. Straus (Eds.), *Violence and the Family.* New York: Dodd Mead: 1974. (a)

Steinmetz, S. The sexual context of social research. *American Sociologist,* 1974, *9,* 111–116. (b)

Steinmetz, S. Disciplinary techniques and their relationships to aggressiveness, dependency and conscience. In W. Burr *et al.* (Eds.), *Contemporary theories about the family,* Vol. 1. New York: Free Press, 1979.

Strodbeck, F. Family interaction, values and achievement. In D. McClelland *et al.* (Eds.), *Talent and Society.* New York: Van Nostrand, 1958.

Sussman, M. B. The isolated nuclear family: Fact or fiction? *Social Problems,* 1959, *6,* 333–340.

Sussman, M. B. *Theoretical basis for an urban network system.* Cleveland: Case Western Reserve University (mimeo).

Sussman, M. B., & Burchinal, L. Kin family network: Unheralded structure in current conceptualization of family functioning. *Marriage and Family Living,* 1962, *24,* 231–240.

Suttles, G. *The social order of the slum.* Chicago: University of Chicago, 1968.

Thomas, W. I. *The unadjusted girl.* Montclair, N.J.: Patterson Smith, 1923.

Thomas, W. I., & Znaniecki, F. *The Polish peasant in Europe and America.* New York: Dover, 1958.

Thrasher, F. *The gang.* Chicago: University of Chicago Press, 1927.

Tilly, L. The family wage economy of a French textile city: Roubaix, 1872–1906. *Journal of Family History,* 1979, *4,* 381–393.

Tilly, L., Scott, J., & Cohen, M. Women's work and European fertility patterns. *Journal of Interdisciplinary History,* 1976, *6,* 447–476.

Tocqueville, A. de *Democracy in America.* New York: Langley, 1840.

Useem, M. Which business leaders help govern? *Insurgent Sociologist,* 1979, *9*(Fall), 107–120.

Valentine, C. *Culture and poverty.* Chicago: University of Chicago Press, 1968.

Veroff, J. A perception to assess motivation in a nation-wide interview study. *Psychological Monographs,* 1960, *74,* 12.

Walters, J., & Stinnett, N. Parent child relationships: A decade review of research. In C. Broderick (Ed.), *A decade review of research and action.* Minneapolis: National, 1971.

Warner, L. *Social class in America.* Chicago: Science Research Associates, 1949.

Warner, L., *The living and the dead.* New Haven: Yale University Press, 1959.

Warner, L., & Lunt, P. *The social life of a modern community.* New Haven, Conn.: Yale University Press, 1941.

Warner, L., & Lunt, P. *Yankee City.* New Haven, Conn.: Yale University Press, 1963.

Warner, L., Meeker, M., & Eells, K. *Social class in America.* Chicago: Science Research Associates, 1949.

Waters, E., & Crandall, V. Social class and observed maternal behavior from 1940–1960. *Child Development,* 1964, *35,* 1021–1032.

Weber, M. *Economy and society.* New York: Bedminster Press, 1968.

Wells, R. Family history and demographic transition. *Journal of Social History,* 1975, *12,* 1–20.

Whiting, B. *Children of six cultures.* Cambridge: Harvard University Press, 1975.

Wilensky, H. Orderly careers and social participation. *American Sociological Review,* 1961, *26,* 521–539.

Winterbottom, M. The relation of need for achievement to learning experiences in independence and mastery. In J. Atkinson (Ed.), *Motive in fantasy action and society.* Princeton, N.J.: Van Nostrand, 1958.

Wolfenstein, M. Trends in infant care. *American Journal of Orthopsychiatry,* 1953, *23,* 120–130.

Wright, J. D., & Wright, S. R. Social class and parental values for children: A partial replication and extension of Kohn's thesis. *American Sociological Review,* 1976, *41*(3), 527–537.

Yankelovich, D. *The new morality.* New York: McGraw-Hill, 1974.

Yinger, M. *The scientific study of religion.* New York: Macmillan, 1970.

Young, M., & Willmott, P. *Family and kinship in East London.* New York: Free Press, 1957.

Zaretsky, E. *Capitalism: The family and personal life.* New York: Harper & Row, 1976.

Zigler, E., & Child, I. *Socialization and personality development.* Reading, Mass.: Addison-Wesley, 1973.

CHAPTER 10

Families and Work

Chaya S. Piotrkowski, Robert N. Rapoport, and Rhona Rapoport

Introduction

The broad links between the family as an institution and the economic and social structure have traditionally constituted important areas of inquiry within the social sciences. Still, as Kanter (1977) noted, the connection between working and loving in the everyday life of families has been obscured by what she called the "myth of separate worlds." In this view, work and family represent two distinct worlds that operate according to their own laws. In Victorian imagery, the family was a woman's place—a haven of comfort and peace (Degler, 1980; Lasch, 1977). In contrast, the realm of work seemed naturally to be a man's world—harsh and competitive.

Theory in the social and behavioral sciences reflected these cultural beliefs. Max Weber saw the separation of kin obligations from enterprise as a crucial element in the development of capitalism. Talcott Parsons viewed the conventional family, with its gender-linked division of labor, as ideally adapted to the needs of modern industrial society and as separate from but complementary to it. These ideas were also embodied in the specialization within disciplines. Family sociology, for example, was distinct from the sociology of work and occupations. In psychology, the study of human development in the context of the family was clearly separated from occupational and industrial psychology (Kanter, 1977; Piotrkowski, 1979; Rapoport & Rapoport, 1965).

The study of the social-psychological connections between families and the work of their members has emerged as a recognized field of inquiry only since the 1960s. The revival of interest in Marxist theory, the new feminist scholarship, and the emergence within psychology of theory and research on adult development through the life span helped to establish the intellectual climate in which the study of work and family links became feasible (Kanter, 1977). But perhaps the most important single influence has been the increased participation of married

women in the labor force—particularly mothers. This important development, along with the increased scrutiny of traditional sex roles in the family and in the workplace, has highlighted the importance of work and family transactions. Whereas the men interviewed by Aberle and Naegele (1952) saw little connection between their work and family lives, 30 years later most of Crouter's respondents (1982) perceived some significant connections between the two realms.

Scholars in a variety of disciplines and specialty areas—including demography, history, social policy analysis, and economics, as well as sociology and psychology—are contributing to our knowledge of the connections between work and family life. Macroanalytic research includes demographic studies of family variables and women's labor-force participation, social policy studies of day care, and social-historical research on broad work and family relations. This chapter focuses on "mesolevel" studies (R. Hill, 1981) of the relationship of work life to *the internal dynamics of the family*. Considered are household organization, the socioemotional quality of relationships (i.e. solidarity, adjustment, and satisfaction), power and decision making, and socialization processes. Although this area of work–family studies has experienced rapid development in the last decade, it still constitutes a "social science frontier" (Kanter, 1977). We treat the macroanalytic studies of work–family relations as the context for understanding the specific transactions between families and the work life of their members. The extensive, related literatures on maternal employment (e.g., Bronfenbrenner & Crouter, 1982; Etaugh, 1974; Hoffman, 1974a,b, 1979, 1980, 1984a,b; Maccoby, 1958), on social policy (e.g., Kamerman, 1980b; Kamerman & Kahn, 1978, 1981), and on family factors and women's labor-force participation (e.g., Rallings & Nye, 1979) are used when they are relevant to an understanding of the internal dynamics of the family.

In the first part of the chapter, the conceptual bases for research in this area of work–family studies are described, along with the historical and social context in which this research has occurred. Second, we focus on theory and on empirical research. The research is drawn primarily from the United States and Great Britain. The

Chaya S. Piotrkowski • Department of Psychology, St. John's University, Jamaica, NY 11439. **Robert N. Rapoport and Rhona Rapoport** • Institute of Family and Environmental Research, 1–2 Castle Lane, London, SW1E 6DR, England.

extent to which the findings from these countries can be generalized to those with different social and economic systems remains an open question.[1] Three major lines of research within sociology and psychology are integrated: studies of the effects on families of men's occupations; studies of the consequences for families of women's employment; and studies describing the strains and the satisfactions in dual-career families. Given the rapidly proliferating studies in these areas, an exhaustive review of all research is not possible.[2] Instead, the chapter has four related aims: (1) to provide an overview of the major theoretical positions and of some research bearing on them; (2) to evaluate the findings and to draw some general conclusions from them; (3) to point out particularly important conceptual, empirical, or methodological problems, with suggestions for how they can be approached; and (4) to identify neglected research areas that deserve further attention. The themes of gender relations—so crucial in shaping both family relations and research on them—and the family life cycle are woven throughout the discussion. A concluding section covers directions for further theory development and research.

Setting the Context

Theoretical Context

We use the term *family* to designate persons sharing a residence and household who are related by biological ties, marriage, social custom, or adoption. This conceptualization allows the inclusion of diverse family structures, including single-parent families, childless couples, and other newly emerging family forms. Our conception of *work* is similarly broad. It refers generally to instrumental human activity, whose aim, at minimum, is the provision of goods and services for supporting human life. Variations in the demands and rewards of occupations, as well as the structure of work settings, have been assumed to be important for family relations.

Although most research in the field of work–family studies has focused on paid work, it is important to recognize that work can be unpaid and outside the formal economy. The ''informal economy'' includes unreported work for pay, exchanges of goods and services on a non-

cash basis, and the household production of goods and services (see, for example, Burns, 1975; Ferman & Berndt, 1981; Gersuny, 1978; R. Pahl, 1980). Such work activities are not included in public accounts of wages. They produce undeclared income, are sometimes illegal, and are difficult to conceptualize and measure. In this view, unpaid housework—which has become a recent focus of feminist sociologists—is work (e.g., Ferree, 1976; Gavron, 1966; Glazer-Malbin, 1976; Lopata, 1971; Oakley, 1974a,b).[3] Although this chapter necessarily concentrates on *paid employment* in the formal economy, the possible importance of the informal economy as a future area of study within the work–family field should not be overlooked.

Given the multiple and complex links between work and family spheres, no one unifying theoretical framework exists within the field. Nonetheless, the many theoretical orientations that have been used do share some important assumptions. One assumption is that the individual constitutes the basic autonomous unit, so that attitudes, coping behavior, individual strain, and so on are sometimes included as moderator and mediating variables. A second assumption is that families are relatively ''open'' social systems that engage in complex transactions with their environments, including the institutions and structures of work (see Bell & Vogel, 1960). A third assumption is that families and individuals are dynamic; that is, they change and develop over time. Consequently, work–family relations can be expected to change over the life cycle. This latter assumption reflects theoretical developments within family sociology and developmental psychology (e.g., Aldous, 1978; Bronfenbrenner, 1979; Duvall, 1977; Goulet & Baltes, 1970; R. Hill, 1974; Neugarten, 1968).

A final assumption, which is less often reflected in actual research, is that relationships between families and work settings are reciprocal: Each setting influences the other. The majority of studies attempt to demonstrate the effects of work settings on families. Less-well-documented empirically is the extent to which family life influences work. Such influence is asserted widely but is rarely examined (Kanter, 1977; Portner, 1978). (For exceptions, see Hareven, 1975a,b; Crosby, 1982; Crouter, 1984.)

Kanter (1977, 1978) identified at least three conditions under which families may serve as strong ''independent variables'' that affect work life: where strong, ethnic traditions exist; among upper-class families; and in family-based businesses. Reciprocal influences also are especially evident for women. For example, women's work plans may influence their age of marriage (Cherlin,

---

[1]The research of the Vienna Center's working party on work and family life in Eastern and Western European countries since 1950 will make a major contribution to this effort. However, the results were not available at the time of this writing.

[2]Specialized reviews relevant to the work–family field include those by J. Pleck (1983), L. S. Walker and Walston (1985), Rapoport and Rapoport (1980b), Gecas (1979), Rallings and Nye (1979), Portner (1978), Aldous, Osmond, and Hicks (1979), Kanter (1977), Bahr (1974), Nye (1974), Bronfenbrenner and Crouter (1982), Mortimer and London (1983), Hoffman (1974a,b, 1979, 1980, 1984a,b), Piotrkowski and Repetti (1984), and Voydanoff (1983a.b). The rapid proliferation of such reviews reflects the rapid increase in the number of studies in the field.

[3]Modern ideologies of the family have designated housework as a ''labor of love,'' thereby obscuring its work components (Piotrkowski, 1979). The ''new'' home economics (e.g., Robinson, 1980; Berk & Berk, 1979; K. Walker & M. Woods, 1976), as well as recent feminist scholarship, has begun to correct this bias.

1980). At the same time, the impact of family roles and life-cycle stage is evident in the limitations that marriage and motherhood have placed on women's labor-force participation and their occupational advancement (e.g., Broschart 1978; Duncan & Perrucci, 1976; Ewer, Crimmins & Oliver, 1979; Faver, 1981; Mortimer, Hall, & Hill, 1978; Poloma, Pendelton, & Garland, 1981; Nieva & Gutek, 1981).

In some European countries, social policy legislation mandates workplace policies that take family needs into account. In the United States and Britain, where such policies are negligible, individual families can exert relatively little influence on workplace policies and structure, even though they may influence the occupational decisions of individuals. In general, individuals are reporting that work affects or interferes with their family life more than the reverse.[4] Thus, the assumption of reciprocal influences needs to be considered within specific historical and social contexts.

Historical Context[5]

Although social historians disagree about the generality of the phenomena (see E. Pleck, 1976), there is some consensus that family life in the United States and England was less clearly separated from productive activity prior to industrialization than after it. In the preindustrial society of the United States and England, the family household was the primary economic unit. In the peasant and laboring classes, the production of food, clothing, and goods for market was often a family affair. Surplus family members sometimes worked for a wage, but these wages were then incorporated into the family economy. Among artisans, economic activity also was not clearly differentiated from family life. For many artisans, workplace and family residence were one, and all family members participated in economically useful activity.

With the coming of industrialization, relations between productive life and the family changed considerably. In the earliest cotton-spinning mills, family members were sometimes employed together and were even remunerated as a single unit. Paternal discipline at home was transferred to the factory. The boardinghouses of the Lowell mill girls in New England were also modeled on the family. These family-based methods were eventually replaced with more impersonal modes of organizing the labor force. With their centralized labor force, factories

began to replace the household and the small workshop as the center of production.

As industrialization proceeded, it had several important consequences for work–family relations. It resulted in a spatial separation between the location of much productive activity and the family residence. As Scott and Tilly (1975) noted, "The first industrial revolution in England broke the locational unity of home and workshop by transferring first spinning and then weaving into factories" (pp. 163–164). However, as Hareven's studies (1975a,b) of immigrant families in New England at the turn of the century demonstrate, kin networks may have been used to place workers in factories and to provide them with security there.

The introduction of so-called protective legislation restricting employment hours for women and children restricted women's employment opportunities and resulted in married women's staying at home to care for their children. Wives were no longer full economic partners. They were dependents in the home. Wilensky (1961) estimated that, with industrialization, the working day and year of male laborers in England and France increased. Long working hours away from family members hindered men from taking an active part in domestic life, reinforcing the division of labor within the family household.

There were class differences in women's patterns of work in the nineteenth century. In the middle class, productive work outside the home came to be reserved entirely for men. Women were responsible for the household, though the affluent relied on servants. The ideal of the housewife who could remain home because her husband was a good provider eventually extended to the working class. By the early twentieth century in both England and the United States, only about one tenth of white married women were employed (Chafe, 1976; Scott & Tilly, 1975), although nonwhite women in the United States were employed at higher rates (Beckett, 1976; Chafe, 1976; Degler, 1980). The majority of employed women were single and left the labor force on marriage.

In the early twentieth century, many services and products formerly produced at home were transferred outside it. The domestic science movement in the United States hoped to fill the "domestic void" by creating new tasks for women, who became responsible for the health of family members. The household germ was discovered, and it became the enemy (Cowan, 1976; Ehrenreich & English, 1975). The nineteenth-century "cult of domesticity" reinforced the ideal of married women being located in a now-shrunken household, asserting that women's natural place was in the home, caring for the physical and moral development of children and nurturing husbands after their daily travails in the world outside. Thus, the modern role of housewife was created (Oakley, 1974b). Home, as the antithesis of work, came to be viewed in popular sentiment as a "haven in a heartless world," to borrow a term from Lasch (1977). As employment opportunities in clerical and other sectors

---

[4]In a study of employees working in a setting that had participatory management, Crouter (1982, 1984) found that spillover from family to work was reported less frequently than spillover from work to family. In their analysis of a national probability sample of men and women, J. Pleck, Staines, and Lang (1978) found that reports of jobs interfering with family life were relatively rare.

[5]Our discussion draws on the work of Degler (1980), G. Lerner (1979), Cott (1977), Scott and Tilly (1975), Demos (1970), Laslett (1965), Thompson (1966), and Smelser (1959).

opened up for single women, domestic servants became scarce, and the positions of white middle-class and working-class housewives grew closer. The so-called traditional nuclear family of England and the United States, composed of a husband breadwinner and a housewife restricted to domestic activities in the home, is partly a product of the way industrialization took shape.

Recent Social Trends

Social and economic changes since World War II have altered, once again, the nature of work–family relations. Four such changes and their implications for work–family relations are presented: changing patterns of women's employment, changes in family structure, changes in sex-role attitudes, and shifts in the structure of the work force.

Women's Employment. From 1900 to 1940, the major change that occurred in patterns of women's employment was in the *type* of paid work that women performed. The proportion of women employed in factories and as domestics and agricultural laborers decreased, and the proportion of those employed in clerical and similar jobs increased dramatically, a change reflecting the growth in new economic sectors (Chafe, 1976; Hesse, 1979). In the aftermath of World War II, the labor-force-participation rates of women rose steadily. In the 1940s, approximately one quarter of women were employed. By the early 1950s, this proportion had more than doubled.

Associated with the increased proportion of employed women were changes in the *pattern* of labor force participation (Degler, 1980; Oppenheimer, 1973). Whereas single women's employment rates remained approximately constant, the percentage of employed married women—particularly those with young children—rose dramatically. Over 60% of married women with school-aged children were employed in the United States in 1981. Among mothers with preschoolers, the percentage was approximately 47% (Moore, Spain, & Bianchi, 1984). Similar percentages are reported in Britain (Moss, 1980).

Rather than returning to work only after their children are grown or in school, many women are remaining in the labor force with the birth of their children. The rapid monetary inflation of the 1970s makes women's wage work necessary for many families. In both the United States and Britain, over half of two-parent families with dependent children are now "dual-earner" families (Moss, 1980; Waldman, Grossman, Hayghe, & Johnson, 1979).[6] Keniston (1977) noted that "this is the first time in our history that the *typical* school-age child has a mother who works outside the home" (p. 4).

Aldous (1981a) warned us against overemphasizing

[6]We use *dual-earner* rather than *dual-worker* to denote those families in which husbands and wives are gainfully employed. As commonly used, the term *dual-worker* implies that unpaid household work and other work activities are not "work" (Aldous, 1981a; Piotrkowski & Repetti, 1984).

the newness of the dual-earner phenomenon. She noted that early U.S. Census data may have underestimated the financial contributions made by working-class and non-white women, as well as by women on farms, because they tended to do their work at home. The economic contributions of working-class women have also been overlooked because of the emphasis on dual-career families in the scholarly literature. Moreover, even though a majority of families are now dual-earners, only about one half of wives are employed full time (Hayghe, 1982). Women have always worked. What is a modern phenomena is the emergence of a *predominant* family form in which both husbands and wives work outside the home.

Changing Family Structure. A second important trend with implications for work–family relations is the dramatic rise in divorce rates. Since 1960, the divorce rate has increased 400% in Britain (Dominian, 1982). Norton and Glick (1979) predicted that 4 of every 10 marriages of women born between 1945 and 1949 in the United States will end in divorce. Many factors may affect the divorce rate, including the liberalization of divorce laws, earlier marriage, the growth of secularism, the growing ideology of personal self-fulfillment, the strains of poverty, and the opportunity that women now have for economic independence. Whatever the causes, an important implication of such increases in the divorce rate is the rise in single-parent families, usually headed by women (Ross & Sawhill, 1975). In the United States, the proportion of such households remained fairly constant, at about 10% of all families. By 1977, such families had increased to over 13% (Johnson, 1978). Previously, the death of a husband accounted for most single-parent families. More recently, divorce and separation have provided the main stimuli, and the age groups are younger.

Single-parent families are at a disadvantage because they are generally poorer than two-parent families. Lone parents are more likely to be employed than their married counterparts, except among black families (Beckett, 1976; Ferri, 1976), but they are concentrated in low-paying jobs. They also may be disadvantaged because there are fewer backup resources for child care in such families. Child-care services, needed both by employed single parents and dual parents, cannot readily take up the slack. In their reports on child-care facilities in relation to the specific issue of women's employment, Kamerman and Kahn (1978, 1981) concluded that the pattern of provision that is emerging for child care and family benefits is only loosely linked to the actual growth in demand, as reflected in the rates of maternal employment (also, see Hofferth, 1979). Child-care services are a variable amalgam, not commensurate with the actual needs and wants of today's families. Where and how national policy investments have been made and will be made in the future depend on factors such as public concern, advocacy efforts, and national priorities.

Sex-Role Attitudes. With the growth in women's employment and the changes in family structure have come somewhat modified attitudes toward traditional sex roles. Women's employment outside the home has become more acceptable, and child rearing is increasingly viewed as the responsibility of both parents (e.g., Harris & Associates, 1981; Mason, Czajka, & Arber, 1976). The relative importance of work and family life also appears to be converging for both men and women. Men are reporting greater psychological involvement with their families than with their jobs (see Campbell, Converse, & Rodgers, 1976; Fogarty, Rapoport, & Rapoport, 1971; Glenn & Weaver, 1981; J. Pleck, 1983), and most women are reporting noneconomic commitments to employment (Iglehart, 1979).

Despite these changes, the cult of feminine domesticity and other traditional sex-role attitudes remain (see Komarovsky, 1973). Employment of mothers with preschool children is still not readily accepted (Harris & Associates, 1981; Mason et al., 1976; Szinovacz, 1984), an attitude indicating that the equation of maternal employment with maternal deprivation persists. Changes in men's family roles lag behind changes in women's employment roles (J. Pleck, 1977). Women, whether or not they are employed, still perform the major proportion of domestic work (Hartmann, 1981; J. Pleck, 1977, 1983; Vanek, 1974; Walker, 1973), even in dual-career families (Bryson, Bryson, Licht, & Licht, 1976; Epstein, 1971; Portner, 1978; Rapoport & Rapoport, 1971; Yogev, 1981). Reviewing U.S. national survey data, J. Pleck (1983) concluded that only a minority of the population report believing that men should increase their level of housework and child care. Although the general value that men attribute to family may now be higher, on a daily *behavioral* basis men may value their jobs more (Veroff & Feld, 1970). In other words, men's daily behaviors do not reflect their reported attitudes. In the absence of adequate outside supports, the persistence of traditional arrangements in the family place married women with children at a disadvantage in the workplace, a circumstance constituting a *de facto* form of indirect discrimination.

Changes in the Workplace. A final important trend relevant to work–family relations involves changes that have occurred in the workplace. Prominent among them are the sectoral shifts that have occurred in both the United States and Britain. Proportional employment in manufacturing and industry has declined, with a concurrent increase in service and clerical work, reflecting increases in public sector employment (Elias, 1980; Job, 1978; Sekscenski, 1981). These changes in the *types* of work that people perform may have significant implications for families.

Finally, the increase in shiftwork is also important in shaping the nature of the relations between work and families. Whereas 12% of British manual workers in manufacturing were shiftworkers in 1954, it is estimated that this proportion had risen to 30% by 1978 (Moss, 1980). In the United States, an estimated one in six full-time employees worked a night, evening shift, or other nontypical shift in 1978, and this figure is most likely to

nontypical shift in 1978, and this figure is most likely an underestimate (Finn, 1981). A disproportionate number of shiftworkers are drawn from the 25–44 age group, when the presence of young children at home may make shiftwork a special problem.

Conclusion

The social and economic changes described above have shaped inquiry in the work–family field, to a considerable extent defining the questions that have been asked. The influx of married women into the labor force spurred psychological research on the effects of maternal employment, sociological research on the impact of such employment on marriages, and analytic case studies of dual-career couples. The close link between inquiry and social and economic conditions also introduced cultural biases into our investigations, limiting theory development and systematic research. For example, much initial research on women's employment focused on its possible detrimental effects on family relations, including little else about women's paid work than the fact of their employment. The effects on parent–child relations of fathers' employment—considered normative—were rarely addressed, except as fathers' occupational status influenced the attainment of their sons. The continuing designation of housework as nonwork means that there have been few studies on the transactions between domestic work in the household and family relationships (Piotrkowski, 1979).

As social and economic conditions continue to change, such biases are being corrected. The emphasis on the deleterious effects of women's employment is giving way to a more sympathetic attitude toward the potential costs and benefits of being a dual-earner family. Research has become increasingly sophisticated and less tied to traditional sex-role attitudes (Piotrkowski & Repetti, 1984).

Structural Links between Work and Family Systems

In this section, empirical research on structurally based connections between work and family spheres is examined. As used here, *structure* refers to the relatively stable organization and sequence of roles and activities within work and family systems. Thus, the structure of work time, occupational rewards, and the nature of work tasks are considered. Consistent with the orientation outlined in the introduction, the discussion is limited to those studies relevant to the dynamics of family life, that is, the division of household labor, marital power, the quality of marital and parent–child relationships, and socialization processes. The studies considered fall within a fairly limited methodological range. Generally, they are either cross-sectional correlational studies, qualitative studies based on a small number of cases, or descriptive surveys. Each of these methodologies has its advantages and limitations. A major strength of research in the work–family field is this methodological diversity. Our strategy is to present the major questions that have concerned researchers in this area, along with some empirical findings. These presentations are followed by summary and discussion sections in which the findings are evaluated and recommendations are made for further research.

Work Time and Family Relations

The separation of work setting from family residence and kin from coworker that characterizes industrialization means that time spent in paid work is time not spent performing family functions nor being with family members. Work-related separations involve the regular absence of sustained face-to-face contact between family members (Piotrkowski & Gornick, 1986). Time is also a basic resource used to accomplish family tasks and to maintain family solidarity (Kantor & Lehr, 1975). Two aspects of work time have been viewed as relevant to family relations: (1) the amount of time spent at work and (2) the weekly and daily timing of those hours (Aldous, 1969a; Kanter, 1977; Piotrkowski, 1979; Staines & J. Pleck, 1983). Although men and women report similar levels of work–family conflicts, men are more likely to report conflict because of excessive work hours, whereas women are more likely to mention scheduling difficulties (J. Pleck, 1983; J. Pleck, Staines, & Lang, 1980).

It has been widely assumed that time spent at work interferes with the performance of family roles because of conflicts between work and family roles and because of quantitative role overload and role strain, that is, the experience of difficulty in enacting one's roles. Many employed people complain of insufficient time for family activities and of difficulties in balancing work and family roles. Because of their heavy family responsibilities, employed women are especially subject to the experience of role strain (Herman & Gyllstrom, 1977; Keith & Schafer, 1980; National Commission on Working Women, 1979; Pleck *et al.*, 1980; Rapoport & Rapoport, 1971, 1977). Several studies have found that the number of hours worked is associated with work–family conflict and with difficulties in managing personal and family activities (Bohen & Viveros-Long, 1981; Keith & Schafer, 1980; Pleck *et al.*, 1980).

Social policy analysts, home economists, and sociologists have been concerned about conflicts between employment and "family work." If women are employed, who will care for the children and perform other household functions? Family sociologists have emphasized the effects of employment time on marital solidarity. Conflicts between paid work and family roles or sheer role overload can result in inadequate role performance. The "role discrepancies" (Burr, 1973) resulting from differences between role performance and role expectations are seen as potentially detrimental to marriage. Psychologists have attended to the question of whether the time that mothers spend at work interferes with the development of adequate mother–child relationships, in particular the development of secure attachments between mothers and their children. Early attachment theory postulated that any departure from full-time mothering was a type of maternal deprivation, with devastating effects on the social and cognitive development of the children (e.g., Bowlby, 1951; Spitz, 1964).

There have been no systematic investigations of the hypothesized links between time spent at work, role conflict and overload, role strain, family role performance, and other family outcomes. Instead, most research has focused on the first and last of these variables, that is, time spent at work and family outcomes. The general research paradigm used to consider the association between these two variables is to compare dual-earner and traditional male-breadwinner families on household work variables, on marital solidarity, and on the quality of mother–child relationships.

Conflicts between Paid Work and Family Work. Traditionally, women have had the primary responsibility for household maintenance and child care. Women's employment therefore leads to the possibilities of role overload and conflicts between performing paid work and family work. The question of how to provide for child care is one of the most pressing problems faced by employed parents, as there are not enough places in child-care centers (Hofferth, 1979; Kamerman, 1980a,b; Kamerman & Kahn, 1978, 1981; Moore & Sawhill, 1976). How are such problems managed? In general, child care seems to involve an "informal system" that depends on families themselves, on relatives, and on neighbors (Wattenberg, 1980). For children under the age of 3, care is still most likely to be provided by relatives and neighbors. Finding child care after school remains a serious problem (Bane, Lein, O'Donnell, Stueve, & Wells, 1979; Bone, 1977; Land & R. Parker, 1978; Waite, 1981). The Working Family Project (1978) reported that many lower-middle-income parents in their sample staggered their work schedules to alternate child-care responsibilities (also see Hood & Golden, 1979; Presser & Cain, 1983). Thus, conflicts between obligations to working and caring for children are being managed by innovative family strategies and by a reliance on social networks.[7]

Similarly, families are faced with the potential for conflict between time spent at work and time spent performing other basic household functions. In their sample of employed black mothers, Katz and Piotrkowski (1983) found that the more hours mothers were employed, the more difficulty they reported finding time to do household chores. The few families that utilize hired help are concentrated among upper-middle-class families (Angrist, Lave, & Mickelsen, 1976; Safilios-Rothschild, 1970a; K. E. Walker & Woods, 1976). Most household work is still performed by women, employed or not (Fox & Nickols, 1983; J. Pleck, 1983; Meissner, Humphreys,

---

[7]It should be noted that the parents who still have the major responsibility for child care, irrespective of employment status, are the mothers.

Meis, & Scheu, 1975; K. E. Walker & Woods, 1976). One strategy that employed women have used to deal with conflicting role obligations is to reduce the time they spend doing housework, particularly routine cleaning and maintenance (Robinson, 1980), and to increase their efficiency (Elman & Gilbert, 1984).

Another coping strategy for dealing with role overload and conflicts between time spent at work and time spent performing basic household tasks is to redistribute household chores. Several studies relying on global self-report indicate that the older children of employed mothers do more household work than the children of nonemployed mothers (e.g., Douvan, 1963; Propper, 1972; Roy, 1963). However, studies that have used time-diary methods found insubstantial increases and even some decreases in children's housework contribution (Cogle & Tasker, 1982; K. E. Walker 1973; K. E. Walker & Woods, 1976).

The relative distribution of household work between employed husbands and wives has received special empirical attention because of its implications for changes in sex roles (J. Pleck, 1983). In their early study of wives in Detroit, Blood and Wolfe (1960) developed the concept of "comparative availability" to account for the levels of household work performed by husbands and wives. According to their formulation, household tasks are divided according to traditional gender roles when time and the skills to perform housework are equally available to both partners. Under conditions of strain, as when wives are employed, tasks are reallocated to the more available partner. This resource model of the distribution of household work is based on an assumption that rational, essentially economic, considerations readily override sex-role attitudes and prior socialization.

Blood and Wolfe's findings were consistent with their model: Husbands of employed women did a greater share of housework than the husbands of nonemployed wives. J. Pleck (1977, 1979, 1983) has critically reviewed the research on husbands' participation in housework. He warned that data such as those gathered by Blood and Wolfe are misleading because they consider proportional effort. Because employed wives decrease the time they spend doing housework, the proportion of other family members' time may increase, even though their absolute contribution remains constant. Some data indicate that there has been a slight increase in husbands' household work time when their wives become employed (Nickols & Metzen, 1982; J. Pleck, 1983), particularly in the area of child care (J. Pleck & Rustad, 1980). Hood (1983) has described the subtle negotiations over housework that occur on becoming a dual-earner family. Still, decreases in husbands' paid work time are not associated with equivalent increases in household work time, and women still perform more housework than men, even with equivalent hours in paid work (J. Pleck, 1983).

Hours spent in employment are not a sufficient explanation of why husbands do a small share of housework. Consequently, researchers have also considered other work-related variables that might explain the differential between husbands and wives. Eriksen, Yancey, and Eriksen (1979), for example, found that the more husbands earn, the less housework they perform. Other findings indicate that husbands do more housework as their wives' income approaches theirs (Model, 1981; Scanzoni, 1978). Men's greater financial contribution to the family may give them the power to avoid doing housework (Aldous, Osmond, & Hicks, 1979; Hartmann, 1981). Pleck is optimistic that men's increasing involvement in the family offers the basis for change. Meanwhile, women are adjusting to the conflicts inherent in having two major work roles by reducing the time they spend in housework and, probably, by reducing the time they spend in paid employment (J. Pleck & Rustad, 1980).

Time at Work and Marital Solidarity. Empirical research has also demonstrated no simple relationship between the amount of time spent at work and marital solidarity. Interview and qualitative studies of the wives of husbands who travel extensively or are away for extended periods disclose that the extreme hours that these husbands spend away from home can result in marital strain and lonliness among wives (see, for example, Hollowell, 1968; Hunter & Nice, 1978; Renshaw, 1976). However, in a study of husbands' working hours, Clark, Nye, and Gecas (1978) found that wives' marital satisfaction and perceptions of their husbands' role competence were not significantly associated with husbands' work hours. It may be that the *direct* effect on marriage of the hours husbands spend at work is apparent only when absences are "extraordinary"—as in the military, the merchant marine and long-distance truck driving—and when long working hours are combined with high job involvement and low family commitment.

The numerous studies comparing the marriages of dual-earner and traditional male-breadwinner families on indices of marital solidarity also show no straightforward associations between wives' employment and marriage. Recent comparisons of the marital adjustment of employed and nonemployed wives have revealed few significant differences between them when employment status alone is considered (e.g., Locksley, 1980; Orden & Bradburn, 1969; Staines, J. Pleck, Shepard, & O'Connor, 1978; Safilios-Rothschild, 1970a; Simpson & England, 1981).[8] An exception appears among lower-class women: Whereas the slight differences favoring housewives' marital adjustment in the middle class appear to have disappeared over time, lower-class employed women still report less satisfaction (see Feldman & Feldman, 1974; Nye, 1974; Staines *et al.*, 1978). Despite the fairly consistent evidence for this social class difference, the data

[8]Although Burke and Weir (1976) reported slight differences favoring employed wives, the comparison groups differed on significant background variables.

must be interpreted cautiously. We cannot be certain what lower marital satisfaction represents. Employed lower-class women may be less psychologically or financially dependent on marriage and therefore may be less defensive in reporting dissatisfaction than their nonemployed counterparts.

Few studies of wives' employment have directly measured the number of hours that wives are employed. Treating the fact of employment as the independent variable confounds employment hours with other job factors such as income. Another methodological strategy is to treat employment hours as a continuous variable, distinct from other job variables, and to control for employment status. This strategy was used in a study of employed married women. Controlling for wives' income and job satisfaction, Piotrkowski and Crits-Christoph (1981) found no association between hours spent at work and wives' reported marital satisfaction in either the high-status or the low-status occupational groups. Negative findings, of course, must be interpreted cautiously, but these results are consistent with those reported by Clark et al. (1978) for husbands' employment time. Because their sample of low-status women was highly educated, these results are not comparable to those of other studies of lower-class women that found decrements in wives' marital adjustment as a function of employment status.

An indirect approach to determining whether wives' employment is associated with marital solidarity has been to examine *husbands'* well-being in dual-earner and male-breadwinner families. If wives' employment interferes with their traditional caretaking functions, we might expect husbands to suffer some deleterious health or psychological consequences. Some studies indicate that husbands of nonemployed wives fare better (e.g., Axelson, 1963; Burke & Weir, 1976; Kessler & McRae, 1982; Scanzoni, 1970), while others do not (e.g., Booth, 1977, 1979; Glenn & Weaver, 1978; Locksley, 1980; Orden & Bradburn, 1969; Simpson & England, 1981; Staines et al., 1978). These latter studies show either no effects for husbands or positive effects. The study by Kessler and McRae (1982) is especially important because of the representative nature of their sample and the multiple control variables. They found husbands of employed wives to be more depressed and to have lower self-esteem than sole breadwinner husbands. Neither distress about their provider role nor increased child care responsibilities explained these findings. In fact, the least distressed husbands were those who helped most with child care. Since marital satisfaction was not assessed, it remains unclear if increased distress is related to reduced marital solidarity. Further research is required to examine this connection, as well as to understand the sources of husbands' distress.

"Commuter marriages," in which spouses maintain separate residences and are apart for several days each week, represent an extreme case—albeit a highly self-select one—of separation. These arrangements have arisen because of the relative insensitivity of career and workplace to personal needs (Gerstel & Gross, 1984). Unlike extensive separations because of husbands' jobs, these commuting arrangements occur because of the career needs of *both* spouses. They are chosen as a temporary expedient for career development (Gross, 1980). The arrangement works best when there are no children at home, when career commitments are high and are accepted by both spouses, when careers and marriage are well established, and when work schedules are flexible (Gerstel, 1977; Gerstel & Gross, 1984; Gross, 1980; Kirschner & Walum, 1978). Young marriages appear most vulnerable in these circumstances (Gerstel, 1977; Gross, 1980). Despite young couples' fears of growing apart, separate residences do not increase sexual infidelity (Gerstel, 1979), and couples evolve strategies for maintaining intimacy (Kirschner & Walum, 1978). Even in the face of extreme separations, these marriages appear to be viable, although not without costs.

Time at Work and Parent–Child Relations. Young people mention work time (bad schedules and excessive hours) and insufficient contact as what they like least about their fathers' and mothers' jobs (Piotrkowski & Stark, 1984). Similarly, men and women mention excessive hours and scheduling conflicts as the major sources of work–family incompatibility (J. Pleck et al., 1980). Yet research relevant to the consequences of time spent at work on parent–child relations has focused almost exclusively on mothers. Fathers' work-related absences from home have been viewed as normative, whereas the mother–child bond—based on constant face-to-face contact—has been located at the heart of healthy child development. Consequently, mothers' absences because of employment have been viewed as critical for children and therefore worthy of investigation. Again, maternal employment has been treated as a dichotomous variable, although part-time employment occasionally has been considered.

Research on maternal employment has followed the patterns of women's labor force participation, with research on early childhood emerging only recently. Because excellent reviews on the effects of maternal employment exist (see Introduction), only a summary will be provided here. Consistent with the orientation of this chapter, the emphasis is on parent–child relations, rather than on child outcomes.

Existing research evidence does not support the dire predictions from clinical and developmental theories regarding the direct adverse impact of employment-related separations on mother–child relationships. In the case of preschoolers, for whom the concerns are greatest, two lines of research are relevant. First is research on the effects of daycare. Blehar's (1974) early study notwithstanding, recent reviews of the literature on the effects of daycare indicate that, overall, there are no reliable differences between daycare and home-reared children on the quality of the mother–child relationship or the security of the children's attachments to their mothers (e.g., Belsky & Steinberg, 1978; Clarke-Stewart, 1982; Kagan, Kearsley & Zelazo, 1978; Rutter, 1982). It should be noted, of course, that most dual-earner families do not utilize daycare centers (see above) and that the studies of daycare have been conducted primarily in high-quality centers.

Second, studies of maternal employment and infant attachment demonstrate no reliable differences in the security of babies' attachment to employed and non-employed mothers (see Hock, 1980; Hoffman, 1984a; Owen, Easterbrooks, Chase-Lansdale, & Goldberg, 1984).[9] Although employed mothers spend less time with their preschoolers than nonemployed mothers do, the two groups may not differ in the amount of meaningful, direct interaction (Hoffman, 1984a). When differences in the quality of attachment or interaction have been found, they appear to be related to methodological problems (e.g. S. Cohen, 1978); to unstable or poor quality substitute care (Vaughn, Gove, & Egeland, 1980); or to maternal role satisfaction (Hock, 1980; Stuckey, McGhee, & Bell, 1982), especially in the case of nonemployed mothers (J. Lerner & Galambos, 1985). More satisfied women seem to be more adequate mothers, regardless of their employment status (Lamb, 1982).

Still, the picture is not entirely sanguine, as recent studies have found that young boys in middle-class, dual-earner families may be viewed by both parents less positively than daughters (Bronfenbrenner, Alvarez, & Henderson, 1984) and may receive less positive attention from them (Stuckey *et al.*, 1982; Zaslow, Pedersen, Suwalsky, & Rabinovich, 1983). Perhaps in these families boys are viewed as more independent or more troublesome than girls and are therefore given short-shrift when parents feel strained. In these cases, the absence itself may be less important than the ways reunions are handled (Piotrkowski & Gornick, 1986). Still, these remarks are speculative. This apparent gender difference cannot be accounted for by existing data and requires further research (see Hoffman, 1980).

These studies also indicate the importance of considering maternal employment in the context of a family system that includes fathers. In fact, Owen *et al.* (1984) found that changes in maternal employment affected father–child attachment rather than mother–child attachment. Similarly, Pedersen, Cain, Zaslow, and Anderson (1982) found that fathers in dual-earner families played less with their infants than fathers in male breadwinner families. Employed mothers showed the most intense interaction with their infants at homecoming. The authors suggested that mothers in these dual-earner families were

compensating for their employment and, as a result, were literally "crowding out" their husbands.

Employment also diminishes the amount of time that employed mothers spend with their school-aged children (Hauenstein, 1979). But again, maternal role satisfaction and job-related morale seem more important for the quality of parent–child relations than simple absence because of employment (Harrell & Ridley, 1975; Hoffman, 1963; Piotrkowski & Katz, 1983; Yarrow, Scott, DeLeeuw, & Heinig, 1962). Children of employed and nonemployed mothers report no significant differences in feelings of closeness to their mothers (e.g., Douvan & Adelson, 1966; Peterson, 1961; Propper, 1972). (A major strength of Propper's study was that the employed comparison group was composed only of children whose mothers had been fully employed for at least seven years since the child's birth, thereby maximizing the possibility of obtaining differences between groups.) Treating employment hours as a continuous variable and looking only at employed mothers, Piotrkowski and Katz (1983) also found no significant relationship between the number of hours mothers were employed and the extent to which their daughters reported them to be supportive and available. Although some studies have found more frequent or serious disagreements between children and parents in dual-earner than in traditional families, such conflict is not accompanied by lessened closeness (Propper, 1972). Evidence from research on adolescents suggests that disagreement can result from parental encouragement of autonomy (Douvan & Adelson, 1966), and parents in dual-earner families are more likely than those in male breadwinner families to encourage independence in their children (Hoffman, 1979).

The father–child relationship may be more vulnerable to maternal employment. In the past, school-aged sons in lower-class and working-class dual-earner families have been found to express greater disapproval of or to admire their fathers less than sons in traditional families (e.g., Douvan, 1963; McCord, McCord, & Thurber, 1963; Propper, 1972). These sons may view their mothers' employment as indicators of their fathers' failure (Hoffman, 1979) or as threats to their parents' marriages (King, McIntyre, & Axelson, 1968). However, it is not the hours that mothers are absent that are implicated in these findings. Rather, it is the *meaning* children attach to maternal employment. In nonwhite families, for example, mothers' employment may be viewed as a positive contribution to the family (Woods, 1972).

If the hours mothers spend at work have little direct effect on the quality of mother–child relations, it is unlikely that fathers' ordinary absences are critical. However, an important difference between mothers and fathers is that the latter are more likely to work long hours and on weekends (Staines & J. Pleck, 1983). They are also more likely to be employed in occupations (like trucking) that involve extraordinary absences.

Some research, although very limited, suggests that

---

[9]Although Thompson, Lamb, and Estes (1982) found that a mother's return to work changed the nature of a baby's attachment, the change was not necessarily to greater insecurity. Some babies became more attached. Owen *et al.* (1984) did not find such instability, however.

such extensive separations of fathers and their children may have costs. Cohen (1977) found that young managerial and professional fathers who travelled frequently or worked long hours did not play significant roles as companions or disciplinarians for their children. At the less extreme end of the separation continuum, in an exploratory analysis, Piotrkowski and Stark (1984) found that the greater the number of hours working-class fathers worked regularly, the more symptoms of depression their daughters reported and the poorer they performed at school. Several British studies have found decreased cognitive performance in children whose fathers frequently are away from home (see Shinn, 1978). In a study of the 8- and 9-year-old children of Norwegian maritime officers, who regularly were away at least nine months each year or more, Lynn and Sawrey (1959) found, as expected, that the father-absent boys showed greater immaturity, increased hypermasculinity, and poorer peer adjustment than the control boys. The sailors' daughters showed greater dependency on their mothers than the girls in the control group. Children with fathers in the military also may exhibit difficulties (McCubbin, Dahl & Hunter, 1976; Hunter, 1982). We do not know, of course, if negative effects are due to paternal absence *per se* or to some unmeasured changes in the relationship between mothers and children that are related to the fathers' absences.

The Timing of Work Hours. Many service occupations, such as health care and law enforcement, require employees to work nonstandard shifts, and shiftwork is most common among married men with children (Finn, 1981). Presser and Cain (1983) found that at least one spouse worked a nonstandard shift in one out of every three couples sampled with children under the age of fourteen. Despite its prevalence, the extent to which the nonstandard timing of work hours may facilitate or hinder performance of family roles has received little attention. We do know that working a nonstandard shift increases reports of job–nonjob and work–family conflict (House, 1980; J. Pleck *et al.*, 1980; Young & Willmott, 1973). The few studies examining the familial correlates of husbands' shiftwork indicate that it may affect the marital and the father–child relationship.

Afternoon–evening shiftworkers are not home during weekday evenings, and night shiftworkers may need to prepare for work during the evening. These schedules can infringe upon couples' precious evening time, so that opportunities for developing consensus and managing tensions and intimacy become limited (Piotrkowski & Gornick, 1986). Consistent with these notions, Mott, Mann, McLoughlin, and Warwick (1965) found that husbands in blue-collar jobs who worked a nonday shift reported greater difficulties in coordinating family roles and managing tensions and lower marital happiness than husbands on the day shift. The night shift and rotating shifts posed special difficulties for marriage. Couples with husbands on these shifts reported greater difficulties in achieving mutual understanding and in their sexual relations than couples with husbands on afternoon–evening shifts. Since the split-shift arrangement is most common among young couples with children and among lower socioeconomic groups (Presser & Cain, 1983; Staines & J. Pleck, 1983), shiftwork may affect couples that already are most vulnerable to disruption. Of course, shiftwork as a refuge for the unhappily married should not be overlooked (Mott *et al.*, 1965).

Shiftwork also may affect parent–child relations and children. But once again, the evidence is sparse. Male shiftworkers report feeling especially inadequate as parents (Mott *et al.*, 1965). Crouter (1982) found that familial difficulties resulting from work timing was a special problem for mothers of girls and fathers of boys. She speculated that, in these cases, working hours interfered with parent–child companionship. Landy, Rosenberg, and Sutton-Smith (1969) looked at child outcomes directly. Their findings, though limited in scope, suggest that the cognitive development of the daughters they studied was adversely affected by having fathers who worked night shifts before the girls were 10 years old.

But the effects of shiftwork are not necessarily negative. Hood and Golden (1979) described a case in which a father on a nonstandard shift became involved in caring for his preschoolers, thereby developing a close, warm relationship with them. Whereas an afternoon–evening shift may facilitate involvement with a preschooler, it can drastically curtail contact with a school-aged child, who returns from school just as the father leaves. Mott *et al.* (1965) found that afternoon–evening shift fathers believed they had more difficulty being companions to their children, teaching them skills, maintaining close relationships with them, and controlling and disciplining them than if they worked during the day. These findings underscore the importance of considering family life-cycle stage, as well as the age and sex of children, in studies of shiftwork.

Job control is a variable that may moderate some of the negative effects of nonstandard shifts (Piotrkowski, 1979). Staines and Pleck (1983) found that schedule control substantially increased the time fathers on nonstandard shifts spent in child care. More broadly, flexibility in work schedules has been heralded as an important innovation in making workplaces more responsive to the needs of families (Bohen & Viveros-Long, 1981). Flexible work schedules, usually involving some discretion in starting and ending times, were developed in West Germany in the late 1960s and are widely available in some European countries (Winnett & Neale, 1980a). In the United States, federal legislation mandating such experiments in federal agencies was passed in 1978 (Bohen & Viveros-Long, 1981). It has been estimated that approximately 141,000 federal employees were on some sort of flexible schedule in 1977 (Silverstein & Srb, 1979). In nongovernmental firms with more than 50 employees, between 2.5 and 3.5 million employees were on flexible schedules (Nollen, 1979).

Using time diaries, Winnett and Neale (1980a,b) found

that parents on flexible schedules increased their afternoon and evening time with their families. This increase was interpreted as having positive consequences for families because evening time was viewed as being of higher "quality," as the respondents found evenings more enjoyable than mornings. In their study of flexible working hours within government agencies, Bohen and Viveros-Long (1981) found that the modest flexibility available benefited two groups: fathers whose wives were not employed and wives in childless dual-earner couples. For both groups, the work schedule was a more important determinant of ease or difficulty in managing family activities than the total number of hours worked (cf. Holmstrom, 1972).

Summary and Discussion. Several tentative conclusions can be drawn from the available research evidence regarding the extent to which time spent in employment interferes with family roles. Employment is related to difficulties in finding adequate child care and in fulfilling other household tasks. Child-care problems are managed by relying on social networks and complex arrangements such as two parents working "split shifts." Rather than any appreciable redistribution of household tasks, employed women simply spend less time doing housework. Despite the relationship between the number of hours worked and the reports of strain, there is little evidence that wives' employment necessarily reduces marital solidarity, although some husbands may be distressed by spouses' employment. Husband's work time also is not necessarily problematic. Two exceptions may be lower-class marriages, as viewed by the women in them, and families in which husbands are away from home for extended periods of time.

Maternal employment *per se* appears to have few direct effects on the mother–child relationship. Given loving, consistent substitute care and mothers who are sensitive to their children's needs, it appears that families with employed mothers can provide "good enough" environments for their children's healthy development. More important than the number of hours mothers work—at least within reason—is the mothers' satisfaction with their roles.

Viewing the family as a system of interrelationships is important so that indirect effects on father–child relations of maternal employment can be assessed. Also, the gender of the child may affect how parents manage role strain in dual-earner families—with sons appearing to be somewhat vulnerable. There are two notable research gaps: the available evidence points to the importance of the timing of working hours for marriage and for parents and children, making it an important research priority. A second glaring omission is the lack of research on fathers' employment hours and father–child relations.

Rallings and Nye (1979) suggested that the general lack of reliable differences between dual-earner and male-breadwinner families in family relationship variables is due to the fact that few married women actually work full time. Piotrkowski and Repetti (1984) questioned this interpretation, arguing instead that a substantial proportion of wives in dual-earner families now work full time and that many studies have used samples of such wives.

Other possible explanations for the lack of positive findings are more plausible. Possibly, the proposition that work time influences family relations has not been adequately tested, as work time has rarely been measured directly. For women, the use of employment status (employed/not employed) as an indicator of work time presumes that extreme and moderate departures from being a full-time wife and mother are equivalent and confounds work time with other differences between employed and nonemployed groups. At best, employment status provides only a gross measure of time spent at work and confounds work hours with income (Burr, 1973). As reviewers have repeatedly noted, comparing dual-earner with male-breadwinner families to determine the effects of employment variables is a questionable research strategy (Piotrkowski & Katz, 1982b; Piotrkowski & Repetti, 1984; Sussman, 1961). Although some studies have controlled for background characteristics, dual-earner and male-breadwinner families are not essentially equivalent. Moreover, processes within the two groups may differ even though the net effects on family outcome variables are similar.

The implicit assumption that time not spent at work is time spent enacting family roles also is overly simple. It is important to distinguish between simple presence at home and the adequacy of family role performance there. As a number of observers have noted, employment hours *per se* may not limit the amount of mutually satisfying interaction among family members (Etaugh, 1974; Hoffman, 1974a). Individual and familial values may determine whether or not nonwork time is spent enacting family roles and whether or not work-related absences are a problem (Kantor & Lehr, 1975). The amount of necessary contact among family members probably varies with a family's stage in the life cycle and the developmental stage of the children. Mothers who spend no time in paid employment may become overinvolved with their adolescent children, for example (Hoffman, 1974a, 1979; Maccoby, 1958). It also is possible that there has been an overemphasis on time at work as a factor in the adequacy of role performance. Recent studies indicate that job satisfaction, degree of autonomy at work, and extent of job demands are as important as the sheer number of hours worked in predicting time shortages in trying to perform family roles (Katz & Piotrkowski, 1983; Voydanoff & Kelly, 1983).

Finally, the studies of dual-career families have provided particularly rich descriptions of the multiple coping strategies used by dual-earner families—and particularly the women in them—to protect families from the potential negative effects of role conflict and role overload. Some women try to work harder and more efficiently (e.g., Elman & Gilbert, 1984). Women also create role hierarchies and give children priority over clean homes and careers (Bryson *et al.*, 1976; Gilbert, Holahan, & Manning, 1981; Harrison & Minor, 1978; Herman & Gyllstrom, 1977; Poloma, 1972; Poloma *et al.*, 1981; Rapoport & Rapoport, 1971). Some mothers compensate for time spent in paid work by engaging in specially planned activities with the children (Rapoport & Rapoport, 1971; Yarrow *et al.*, 1962). Family and work roles also are given priority over leisure and work activities (Herman & Gyllstrom, 1977; Rapoport & Rapoport, 1971). Parents may evolve strategies to facilitate children's adaptations to daily work-related separations and to parents' working hours (Piotrkowski & Gornick, 1986). Children themselves may develop active coping mechanisms (see Piotrkowski, 1979). These, too, need to be studied. The strategies that wives use to minimize difficulties created by their husbands' work-related absences include acceptance of the situation, viewing it as temporary or under control, becoming more independent, and developing a strong social network for support (Boss, McCubbin, & Lester, 1979; G. Cohen, 1977; Dennis, Henriques, & Slaughter, 1956; Hollowell, 1968; Maynard, Maynard, McCubbin, & Shao, 1980; J. Pahl & R. Pahl, 1971; Renshaw, 1976). Devoting nonwork time to family activities may be a strategy used by men (Clark *et al.*, 1978). The role of social support may be especially relevant. Mortimer (1980) found that husbands' perceptions of their wives' supportiveness mediated the link between husbands' work–family strain and their marital adjustment. Houseknecht and Macke (1981) also found that supportive husbands eased professional women's difficulties in managing their multiple roles.

Some developments in the measurement of family role strain (e.g., Bohen & Viveros-Long, 1981; Parry & Warr, 1980) and coping strategies used by dual-earner families (e.g., Skinner, 1982) make feasible the study of the complex relationships among the amount of hours worked, the timing of those hours (e.g., days/nondays), family role strain, and the quality of relationships between family members.

Occupational Resources and Marriage

In return for time and skill sold in the labor market, family members receive certain "rewards" or "resources" that may enter into transactions within the family. Family sociologists have concentrated on two types of such work-related resources: income and the symbolic reward of the prestige associated with occupations (Kanter, 1977). These have been viewed as especially important for marital *power* and for marital *solidarity* (i.e., satisfaction and adjustment).

Resources and Marital Power. In their classic monograph, Blood and Wolfe (1960) proposed a type of social exchange theory to connect the occupational resources of both spouses to the marital power structure. Arguing that normative authority has become relatively unimportant as

the basis for power in American marriages, they proposed a "comparative resource" theory instead. Defining a resource as "anything that one partner may make available to the other, helping the latter satisfy his needs or his goals," they proposed that power will accrue to a spouse according to the resources that he or she contributes to the marriage. The partner who contributes resources controls them, so that power is gained in the relationship. The partner who contributes the greater number of resources will have the greater power.

Blood and Wolfe tested their theory on a sample of married women, using a measure of decision making to indicate marital power. Their data supported the hypothesis that a husband's power is positively related to his occupational resources (see Aldous *et al.*, 1979; Centers, Raven, & Rodrigues, 1971). Elder's (1974) study of children growing up during the Great Depression provides further evidence of a link between husbands' occupational resources and their power, at least over decision making. These children perceived their mothers' power in decision making to increase as their fathers' income dropped, regardless of class.

Blood and Wolfe also predicted that wives' employment would increase their marital power because employment provides them with economic and other, less tangible, resources to bring to the marriage. Blood and Wolfe originally interpreted their data as supporting their hypothesis. However, critiquing their reliance on a summary measure of decision making, Blood (1963) reexamined their data and concluded that wives' employment increased their power over economic decisions ("external decisions") but not over daily household matters ("internal decisions").[10] In his review of the subsequent research literature on wives' employment and marital power, Bahr (1974) found further support for this distinction. He speculated that the effect of wives' employment is less powerful in the middle class than in the working class, where employed wives' comparative resources are greater (see Heer, 1963a).

Husbands' Occupational Resources and Marital Solidarity. It has been a truism of sociology that marital satisfaction and happiness are positively associated with the husband's socioeconomic status, and that divorce and other signs of marital instability are negatively associated with it (e.g. Aldous *et al.*, 1979; Glick & Norton, 1971; Renne, 1970). Scanzoni (1970) presented the most comprehensive model linking the occupational attainment of *husbands* to marital adjustment. The strength of his theoretical achievement lies in his translation of socioeconomic structural factors into processes and out-

[10]It is unlikely that Blood and Wolfe's comparative resource theory could adequately account for the distribution of marital power, because societal supports for male authority and limitations on female power also affect power within the family (Rodman, 1972; Gillespie, 1971; Scanzoni, 1978; Safilios-Rothschild & Dijkers, 1978).

comes within the family. Using exchange theory, he hypothesized that the greater the occupational rewards a husband provides his wife, the more she feels her "rights" are being met and the more positively she performs her instrumental and expressive duties. As each spouse feels his or her expressive and instrumental rights being met, each is more satisfied with his or her situation, a satisfaction that, in turn, motivates the husband to perform his occupational duties. This model is based on the structural-functionalist assumption that the key to family solidarity is the husband's articulation with the opportunity structure. The model also assumes that wives value the symbolic meaning of their husbands' occupational resources and that they vicariously experience their husbands' successes or failures.

A close look at the data that Scanzoni presented in support of this model indicates that neither the husbands' income nor their occupational prestige was closely related to marital satisfaction. The husbands' income was associated with the men's and the women's hostility toward their spouses, but not with marital satisfaction. Although the husbands' occupational prestige showed a stronger association with marital satisfaction, the differences between the lowest and the highest prestige levels were quite small, and the wives' satisfaction dropped or leveled off in the highest socioeconomic group.

In attempting to account for the curvilinear relationship between husbands' occupational attainments and marital satisfaction, Aldous et al. (1979) proposed a "success constraint theory." The underlying processes are hypothesized to differ within low and high socioeconomic groups. Highly successful men use their power to escape family responsibilities (i.e., basic caretaker tasks). Their lowered family participation leads to increased role segregation and role requirements for wives, as well as a lowered value consensus that reduces marital satisfaction.

Success constraint theory also attempts to account for lowered marital satisfaction at the low end of the socioeconomic hierarchy. Here, an inverse exchange process is proposed. The "blue-collar" man's inability to adequately provide for his family leads his wife to withhold affection and to limit her performance of household duties. The husband becomes discouraged from participating in the family, and marital satisfaction declines (see Aldous, 1969b; Liebow, 1967).[11] This model, like Scanzoni's, posits the centrality of husbands' occupational success as the basis for men's power and involvement in the family.

Empirical findings have raised questions about the link between husbands' occupational resources and marital solidarity. Several methodologically sophisticated longitudinal studies have found that family assets, rather than husbands' income, significantly predict marital stability

(Galligan & Bahr, 1978; F. Mott & S. Moore, 1979; Ross & Sawhill, 1975). The possible mechanisms that underlie the hypothesized relationship between husbands' occupational resources and marital solidarity have also received some empirical scrutiny. Brinkerhoff and White (1978), who studied an economically disadvantaged white population, found no association between family income—determined primarily by the husbands' income—and the wives' participation in household tasks. Jorgensen (1979) found that husbands' occupational rewards engendered wives' satisfaction with those rewards but not necessarily with love or empathic "services." He noted that objective occupational rewards may have declined in their significance for marriage. These findings are inconsistent with the model presented by Aldous et al. However, the finding that husbands' income is negatively associated with their participation in housework is consistent with their model (Ericksen et al., 1979). Subsequent research by Scanzoni (1975) suggests that it is the degree of satisfaction with occupational rewards, such as income, that is the crucial variable in the exchange process.

The complex nature of the link between husbands' occupational resources and marriage becomes clear from Mortimer's work (1980). Studying a sample of young, high-status professional and managerial men, she found that their socioeconomic status was positively related to their marital satisfaction directly and indirectly, through its positive effect on their wives' supportiveness of their occupational roles. At the same time, socioeconomic status *reduced* their marital satisfaction by increasing family strain, thereby reducing the wives' supportiveness. In this study, socioeconomic status was measured by income, education, and occupational prestige.

Wives' Occupational Attainment and Marital Solidarity. Whereas husbands' occupational attainment has been viewed as a basic contributor to marital solidarity, it has been proposed that wives' occupational attainment threatens it. Parsons (1949) first elaborated this view by proposing that marital solidarity depended on complementary but discrete spousal roles. Husbands served as the family's "instrumental leaders" and were the link to the community and to status there. Wives were responsible for maintaining family cohesion and were the family's expressive leaders. Labor market competition between husbands and wives could introduce tensions into the family, undermining the functional complementarity of spousal roles. If wives did work outside the home, marital solidarity could be protected only if they earned less than their husbands and had occupations of lower status.[12]

The proposition that wives' labor-force participation by itself undermines marital solidarity has not been supported by those studies comparing marital satisfaction in dual-earner and male-breadwinner families (see above).

---

[11]Aldous et al. also suggested that the blue-collar man's extra efforts to provide by working long hours can lead, ironically, to lessened family participation.

[12]See Oppenheimer (1977) and Richardson (1979) for more complete discussions and critiques of this formulation and its subsequent development.

Several investigators have tested the status competition hypothesis more directly by examining employed wives' occupational status relative to that of their husbands. Although these researchers have used different measures of occupational status, the results do not support the Parsonian status-competition hypothesis (Philliber & Hiller, 1983; Richardson, 1979; Simpson & England, 1981).

Safilios-Rothschild (1976) suggested that the dominant status determinant of a culture determines whether wives' occupational status or income threatens marriage. In the United States, spouses' relative earnings may be more important in the marital relationship than their occupational statuses (Oppenheimer, 1977; Philliber & Hiller, 1983). The husbands whom Garland (1972) interviewed, for example, were not threatened by their wives' occupational accomplishments as long as their wives placed family above career and did not earn more than their husbands. Simpson and England (1981) found some negative effects on husbands' marital satisfaction as a function of their wives' income. Piotrkowski and Crits-Christoph (1981) found a negative relationship between wives' earnings and their satisfaction with family relations in the low-status occupational group only. Their marital satisfaction, however, was not affected.

These studies did not examine the relative earnings of husbands and wives directly. But Kessler and McRae (1982) found no effects on husbands' self-esteem of wives' earnings relative to their husbands' earnings. Cherlin (1979) measured wives' actual or expected wages (estimated) relative to their husbands'. He found that the greater a wife's real or possible wage relative to her husband's, the greater the probability of marital dissolution. This effect was small but significant. Because Cherlin measured wives' *potential* income, as well as actual wages, these findings lend more support to the proposition that wives' earnings increase their independence relative to marriage and their husbands, than to the "threat" hypothesis (also see Haavio-Mannila, 1971).

Summary and Discussion. Some tentative conclusions can be drawn from the current research on occupational resources and marriage: While husbands' occupational resources appear to be associated with greater power over decisions in the family, wives' employment is related to their power in limited areas such as financial matters. Husbands' occupational attainments are not directly related to marital solidarity and wives' occupational status attainment does not threaten marriage. It remains to be seen if their financial success has some negative consequences for marriage. Perhaps the firmest conclusion is that spouses' occupational resources appear to be relevant to marriage, but in what ways remains uncertain.

Several conceptual and methodological issues need to be addressed in further research on occupational resources and marriage. Occupational "attainment" and "resources" are multidimensional constructs, and evidence is accumulating that their components may have

differing effects on marriage (cf. Otto, 1975). Education, for example, has independent effects on marriage that need to be separated from the effects of occupational prestige and income (e.g., Locksley, 1982). Mortimer's research (1980) also indicates the importance of directly measuring hypothesized intervening variables and indirect pathways of influence. Consequently, variables such as husbands' self-esteem, power, and family participation could be measured as intervening between occupational resources or attainment and marital outcomes. Mortimer's work has also alerted us to the possibility that a given resource may have both positive and negative effects. Advances in causal modeling make such complex analyses possible.

Difficulties in measuring marital power present a significant stumbling block in the study of occupational resources and marital power. A number of authors have noted that the study of family power is fraught with conceptual and methodological difficulties (e.g., Cromwell & Olson, 1975; Heer, 1963b; McDonald, 1980; Safilios-Rothschild, 1970b). Methodological studies also indicate a lack of convergence of different measures of marital power and of husbands' and wives' reports (e.g., Turk & Bell, 1972). The use of multiple measures and methods would constitute an important methodological advance.

Power is a slippery concept. It might be more useful to focus on a more limited construct, such as decision making, commonly treated as an indicator of family power. An alternative approach is to focus not on outcomes but on the processes that lead to outcomes (Hood, 1983; Scanzoni, 1978; Scanzoni & Polonko, 1980). For example, Chafetz (1981) proposed that resources—including those from employment—influence the *strategies* used in conflict resolution. Although an empirical test did not support the general model, the methods developed for assessing spousal conflict strategies might prove useful in further research (Bell, Chafetz, & Horn, 1982). A more ambitious approach was described by Hill and Scanzoni (1982), who analyzed the sequential processes involved in decision making, the contextual variables that may influence it (e.g., income disparity between husbands and wives), and objective and subjective outcomes. The method they developed shows promise in helping us to understand how occupational resources may influence the processes of negotiation and conflict resolution.

A clear test of the proposition that wives' financial attainment threatens marital solidarity is especially important. Occupational prestige and education need to be held constant in such an analysis. It is likely that sex-role attitudes moderate this relationship (Oppenheimer, 1977; Safilios-Rothschild & Dijkers, 1978). Husbands' attitudes toward their wives' employment *per se* may be less important than the fit between the spouses' attitudes and the congruence between the husbands' attitudes and the wives' actual situation (Eiswirth-Neems & Handal, 1978; Nye, 1974; Staines *et al.*, 1978).

Hiller and Philliber (1982) developed a theory that considers the joint effects on marriage of wives' occupational achievements and spouses' sex-role attitudes. They proposed that, when either or both spouses have a traditionally masculine or feminine gender identity, marital strain is created when wives have higher achievement than their husbands, because of the incongruity between role expectations and perceptions of performance. Such strain can lead to either divorce or job change, depending on whether the wives have a stronger commitment to their careers or to their marriages. Marriages between people with androgynous gender identities are not expected to experience such strains. Their formulation is particularly interesting because it considers the sex-role identities of wives as well as husbands, and because it allows for several alternative outcomes.

Early theories of the effects of wives' attainments on marriage reflected prevailing sex-role ideologies in their emphasis on negative outcomes (Piotrkowski & Repetti, 1984). More recently, formulations have been proposed that emphasize the possible *benefits* to a marriage of the wife's occupational attainments (Oppenheimer, 1977; Simpson & England, 1981). Further development and tests of such theories would be particularly welcome.

Finally, this body of research also reflects a glaring omission: There is very little research on the effects of parents' occupational attainment on the quality of parent–child relationships. As early as 1958, Maccoby noted that wives' earnings may cause children in low-income families to devalue their fathers. This hypothesis was also suggested by Hoffman as late as 1979, for subsequent studies found that sons in low-income families admired their fathers less when their mothers were employed. Maccoby cautioned against drawing causal conclusions from such data. Nonetheless, she suggested a complex set of interactions among mothers' attitudes toward their husbands, the husbands' self-esteem, and father–child interaction as a function of the wives' employment. Thus, a promising research direction would be to include additional family subsystems in the study of family effects of occupational resources.

Individuals at the Interface

Conceptualizations of the links between work time, occupational resources, and family adjustment have emphasized familial roles and processes as the major intervening variables. For some, the psychological effects of work on *individuals* is the major pathway whereby work life can influence family life (Kanter, 1977). The wage earner, who is a member of both occupational and family systems, regularly crosses the boundaries between them. As Piotrkowski (1979) noted, if we assume that roles are compartmentalized or that human behavior is, at most, a response to the demand characteristics of specific settings, questions about the individual psychological processes that may connect both social systems do not arise. These points of view—now somewhat outmoded in sociology and psychology—are consistent with the "myth of separate worlds" that has been called into question by

research in the work–family field. Once we acknowledge that individuals do not necessarily compartmentalize life roles, the question of what psychological processes mediate the relations between work and family systems must still be answered. We have already mentioned role strain as one such mediating variable. Here, other psychological variables are examined: job satisfaction and strain, as well as occupationally derived values. These variables have not yet received much empirical attention in work and family studies. We focus on them because they represent especially promising research avenues.

Job Satisfaction and Strain

Occupations vary in their demands and the conditions under which tasks are performed. Consequently, they vary in their physical and psychological consequences for jobholders. Organizational and industrial psychologists have focused on job satisfaction as a work-related consequence for psychological well-being. Our purpose is not to enter into the debate on the proper conceptualization and measurement of job satisfaction but to utilize a general definition that can be useful to those doing research on work and family life. *Job satisfaction* refers generally to the feelings of pleasure with intrinsic and extrinsic aspects of a job.[13] *Job dissatisfaction* refers to feelings of displeasure with job facets. As used here, *job strain* refers to the harmful psychological and physical consequences (e.g., psychosomatic complaints) of repeated exposure to job stressors that tax the adaptive capacities of workers. Job characteristics that increase dissatisfaction and strain include piece-rate work, routinization, machine pacing, time pressure, and lack of control (e.g., Frankenhaeuser & Gardell, 1976; Friedman, Rosenman, & Carroll, 1958; Gardell & Gustavsen, 1980; Karasek, 1979; Karasek, Baker, Marxer, Ahlbom, & Theorell, 1981; Kasl, 1978). Job satisfaction tends to increase as one moves up the occupational hierarchy (Quinn, Staines, & McCullough, 1974).

Implicit in the work–family literature are two contrasting perspectives on the relationship between job satisfaction and satisfying family relations. Usually applied to men, the dominant perspective assumes that there is an inverse relationship between job satisfaction and satisfying family relationships. In this view, an intrinsically interesting and therefore satisfying job becomes "salient" for the individual, giving rise to a competition between work and family for his "emotional involvement." Job satisfaction thus leads to lessened family participation and, implicitly, to less satisfactory family relationships (Rapoport & Rapoport, 1965; Aldous, 1969a). This perspective identifies the families of managers, executives, and professionals as potentially experi-

[13]*Intrinsic aspects* of the job usually refer to the job content itself. *Extrinsic factors* refer to the general conditions of work, including pay, security, quality of supervision, and safety conditions.

encing the greatest amount of work–family conflict and disruption from the work role.

Two mechanisms have been proposed to link *lack* of job satisfaction to increased family participation: A worker in an unsatisfying job will not invest his energies there and will have "leftover" energy for family participation. Alternately, the compensation hypothesis states that nonwork activities provide the worker with satisfactions not derived at work (see Aldous, 1969a; Dubin, 1956; Hammond, 1954; Young & Willmott, 1973). A related set of hypotheses is that satisfying work leads to lowered family participation, whereas unsatisfying work leads to a "natural" segmentation of work and family realms (e.g., Blood & Wolfe, 1960). Parker (1967) proposed that such segmentation occurs in jobs that are neither satisfying nor unsatisfying (i.e., "neutral" jobs).

A second perspective predicts that job satisfaction is *positively* associated with satisfying family relations. Kemper and Reichler (1976) hypothesized that the satisfied worker brings home little "residual discontent" to interfere with family participation and also demands less of his or her spouse. Consequently, marital solidarity is enhanced. Piotrkowski similarly outlined a "spillover" model (Piotrkowski, 1979; Piotrkowski & Katz, 1983). In this view, the degree of job satisfaction or strain affects a worker's interpersonal availability to family members, that is, the extent to which he or she makes positive initiations and responses to others. Interpersonal availability is positively associated with satisfaction in family relations. In her qualitative study of 13 families, Piotrkowski (1979) identified one positive and two negative spillover patterns: An interesting job that provides autonomy leads to satisfying work experiences and to increased interpersonal availability. A boring, routine job leads to lack of satisfaction and to passivity and withdrawal at home. A stressful job leads to feelings of dissatisfaction and to symptoms of strain, with consequent irritability and displacement of tension at home (cf. McKinley, 1964). In the latter two cases, interpersonal availability decreases. Thus, job satisfaction and morale—particularly daily job-related moods—intervene between the characteristics of a job and relationships within the family. This perspective, in contrast to the first one, identifies the families of service workers, blue-collar workers, and others in low status occupations as facing special difficulties because of the unsatisfying and stressful nature of their work.

For men, the empirical evidence regarding the relationship between job satisfaction and family satisfaction is mixed. There is no evidence to support the hypothesis linking lack of job satisfaction to compensatory participation in nonwork realms and to increased satisfaction there (Kabanoff, 1980; Near, Rice, & Hunt, 1980).[14] However, qualitative studies of the families of male managers

and executives offer some support for the hypothesis that intrinsically interesting and satisfying jobs are associated with family difficulties. These studies paint a similar picture: The executives and managers studied experienced a great deal of job satisfaction, they reported strong work–family conflict, they did not spend enough time with their wives and children, and they often had poor relationships with them (e.g., J. M. Pahl & Pahl, 1971; Young & Willmott, 1973). In their sample, Young and Willmott found that the executives, compared to the manual laborers, reported more work-related intrusions into their home lives. The downturn in marital satisfaction at the upper levels of the occupational hierarchy has already been noted (see above.)

At the same time, studies that have correlated measures of men's job and family satisfaction demonstrate consistently positive—if modest—associations (Rice, Near, & Hunt, 1980). Several studies have reported positive associations between husbands' job satisfaction and their marital satisfaction (e.g., Haavio-Mannila, 1971; Kemper & Reichler, 1976; Ridley, 1973; Scanzoni, 1970). Job dissatisfaction or tension has been related to father–son and marital tensions (Bradburn & Caplovitz, 1965; McKinley, 1964). Studies of "burnout" among police officers indicate that job stress is associated with tension, irritation, and withdrawal at home (Jackson & Maslach, 1982). Crouter (1982) found some empirical support for the patterns of spillover described by Piotrkowski. Respondents reported negative spillover from work that took the form of depletion, tension and frustration, preoccupation with work matters at home, bad moods at home, and psychosomatic complaints. Crouter did not relate such spillover to job characteristics or satisfaction. More recently, Piortrkowski and Stark (1984) found that stressful job conditions were related to father–son tension and to the quality of the marital relationship.

Women's job satisfaction has been linked most consistently with the mother–child relationship; greater job satisfaction is associated with more positive relationships. Harrell and Ridley (1975), for example, reported a significant positive association between mothers' work satisfaction and their reports of satisfaction with the quality of mother–child interaction. The few studies that include data from both children and mothers found positive associations between mothers' enjoyment of their work and children's reports of their mothers' affection and supportiveness (Hoffman, 1963; Piotrkowski & Katz, 1983). Piotrkowski and Stark (1984) found that stressful job conditions were associated with sons reporting less support from their mothers. Though Peterson (1961) found that mothers' work enjoyment was negatively associated with daughters' reports of maternal interest in some groups, the extent of interest may be independent of the affective quality of that interest. Work-enjoying mothers were also seen as exerting less control. Mothers who enjoy their jobs may allow their children greater independence in their own activities (see Douvan, 1963).

Studies of women's job satisfaction and marital soli-

[14]A study by Spreitzer, Snyder, and Larson (1979) that claims to have found some evidence for compensatory relationships among life roles is severely flawed, so that few clear conclusions can be drawn from it.

darity have resulted in no clear pattern of findings. Several studies confound job satisfaction with commitment to the work role, so that conclusions cannot be drawn from them (e.g., Locksley, 1980; Safilios-Rothschild, 1970a). Other studies suggest complex interaction effects. Ridley (1973) reported that female teachers' job satisfaction was positively associated with their marital adjustment only when the work was salient for them. Ridley interpreted these results as support for the theory that only when roles are dominant can they influence secondary roles. Other findings further complicate this picture. In a Finnish sample, Haavio-Mannila (1971) found job satisfaction to be significantly associated with employed married women's reported satisfaction with family life in general but not with their satisfaction with spousal relations. Using very different measures of satisfaction, Piotrkowski and Crits-Christoph (1981) reported similar results in a sample of employed women in the United States. They suggested that the marital relationship may be more sensitive to husbands' than to wives' job satisfaction (see also Bailyn, 1970; Kemper & Reichler, 1976; Ridley, 1973).

Occupational Conditions, Values, and Socialization

Job satisfaction and strain represent relatively obvious mediators of the relationship between work and family. Occupational conditions may also affect workers' personality and values and, consequently, their behavior within the family. Early theorists proposed that occupations and work settings may influence adult personality (e.g., Hughes, 1958; Merton, 1952). Subsequent research on adult socialization has demonstrated the relevance of occupational factors to personality development in employed men and women (Kohn & Schooler, 1973, 1978; J. Miller, Schooler, Kohn, & Miller, 1979; Mortimer & Lorence, 1979).

Early researchers also observed the relationships between fathers' occupations and the values the fathers held for their children (Aberle & Naegele, 1952). Research on the potential impact of occupational conditions on values and family behavior derives primarily from studies of social class differences in child-rearing values and practices (Gecas, 1979). The "occupational linkage hypothesis" (Lueptow, McClendon, & McKeon, 1979) specifies linear, causal connections between nonvertical aspects of fathers' occupations, their personalities, socialization values and practices, and child outcomes. Although this model has usually been applied to men, it may be especially appropriate for employed mothers, who are primary socialization agents (Morgan, Alwin, & Griffin, 1979; Piotrkowski & Katz, 1982a).

An early theoretical and empirical contribution to research on occupation and child-rearing values and practices was the classic study by Miller and Swanson (1958). In investigating child rearing, they hypothesized that the key determinant of differences in parental values and practices was "integration setting," that is, the type of setting in which work was carried out. They distinguished

two such settings: entrepreneurial settings, in which risk taking and creation or enterprise are values, and bureaucratic settings, in which security and accommodation are valued. Proposing that parents train their children for the world that they themselves know and that they believe their children will occupy, these authors hypothesized that entrepreneurial parents value self-control, individuation, and active, independent behavior. They socialize their children accordingly. Bureaucratic parents train their children to be spontaneous and accommodative and to seek external direction. Their hypotheses, tested on a sample of Detroit mothers, were only partially supported.

The most systematic research program on occupational socialization and child-rearing values derives from the model developed by Kohn (1969, 1977, 1979). Kohn attempted to account for social class differences in child rearing. He proposed that differences in occupational circumstances associated with social class position result in substantially different learning experiences and "world-views." These are expressed in the child-rearing values and practices of parents through processes of generalization. *Values* are defined as conceptions of what is desirable (Kohn, 1969, 1980). Like Miller and Swanson, Kohn proposed that parents value in their children traits that they perceive as being adaptive in their own occupational world. He focused on self-direction as a key occupational variable, that is, the substantive complexity of the work, the closeness of supervision that one receives, and the degree of task routinization (Kohn, 1981). Working-class parents, whose work requires little self-direction, come to value their children's conformity to external authority. In contrast, the work of middle-class parents is self-directed, and they come to value independence in their children. Kohn viewed such "structural imperatives" of the job as being more psychologically important than the income and prestige that the job provides (Kohn, 1980; Kohn & Schooler, 1973).

Kohn and his colleagues have demonstrated that the extent of fathers' self-direction at work predicts their child-rearing values, independent of background variables such as education (see Coburn & Edwards, 1976; Kohn, 1977). Kohn's research is exemplary because it is theoretically based and systematic and includes attempts at cross-cultural replication (see Kohn, 1977). Some data have also been gathered regarding the relationship between occupation and parental socialization practices. Following Kohn's suggestion, Gecas and Nye (1974) found that white-collar and blue-collar parents reported punishing their children for different reasons: White-collar parents stressed their children's motives; blue-collar parents tended to stress the consequences of their children's behavior.

Also following Kohn's lead, Steinmetz (1974) considered the relationship of the task requirements of fathers' "occupational environments" to college students' reports of their fathers' use of physical punishment. She found that fathers in "persuasive" occupations (e.g., business executives and salesmen), who identify with power and use physical skills and control in interpersonal relationships, were more likely to use physical punishment or its threat than fathers in "supportive" (e.g., teachers) or "conforming" (e.g., clerks) occupations. These latter environments require the use of verbal skills rather than strength. McKinley (1964) also reported that fathers' job autonomy was inversely associated with severity of socialization practices and hostility directed toward sons, although no statistical tests are reported. These findings are consistent with Kohn's notion that the actual conditions under which people work and the requirements of their jobs are related to socialization practices.

If parental occupation affects socialization values and practices, the process should result in measurable child outcomes (see Bronfenbrenner, 1979). The evidence linking occupational conditions and child outcomes is inconsistent. Arguing for the importance of controlling for extrinsic occupational factors such as prestige and income, Lueptow *et al.* (1979) found no relationship between the substantive complexity of fathers' jobs and sons' academic outcomes and work orientations. These authors concluded that the linkage hypothesis was not empirically viable. However, they did acknowledge that their dependent variables (e.g., achievement) may have been inappropriate. Morgan *et al.* (1979) did argue, in fact, that achievement in school may be valued by conformist and independence-valuing parents alike. They found employed mothers' valuation of conformity or self-direction to be unrelated to adolescents' grade-point averages but significantly related to extracurricular activities and type of curriculum in white, but not black, children.

Suggesting that the search for general associations between occupations, values, and child outcomes is not an adequate test of the linkage hypothesis, Piotrkowski and Katz (1982a) tested relatively precise hypotheses in a sample of low-status nonwhite women and their children. They correlated specific features of the mothers' jobs with objectively measured school outcomes (attendance, skill acquisition, and productivity). Consistent with their hypotheses, they found that the mothers with more opportunities to use their skills at work had children with higher mathematics achievement, and that the mothers' job autonomy was negatively related to their children's attendance. Job demands showed a more complex relationship to school outcomes. Statistically controlling for the mothers' education and for family income did not alter the results.

In a series of studies on the relationship of fathers' occupational subcultures to child outcomes, Mortimer found associations between fathers' occupations and sons' work values and later occupational attainments (Mortimer, 1975, 1976; Mortimer & Kumka, 1982). These relationships were moderated by the socialization context, that is, the closeness of the father–son relationship. Professional fathers were hypothesized to value intrinsic occupational rewards (e.g., service and autonomy), whereas businessmen valued extrinsic rewards (e.g., income). Mortimer found that sons' closeness to

their professional fathers was associated with the sons' having intrinsic work values, whereas closeness to business fathers was related to the sons' valuation of extrinsic rewards. The fathers' education, occupational prestige, and income were statistically controlled. Mortimer and Kumka concluded that it is important to consider familial conditions, such as closeness, that facilitate or hinder the transmission of parental values.

Summary and Discussion

The available evidence, although sparse, points to the importance of individual psychological dynamics as one type of intervening link between occupational conditions and family relationships. Several trends in the data can be noted: Men's job satisfaction appears to be positively associated with satisfying relations between spouses and, perhaps, between fathers and their (male) children. The families of managers and executives appear to be exceptions. Women's job satisfaction has a consistently positive relationship to the adequacy of the mother–child relationship, but their job satisfaction may not be relevant to marriage. Although the data are incomplete, the proposition that occupational conditions influence socialization practices within the family is viable and worth systematic attention. Further research on fathers' job satisfaction and their relations with their children is especially needed, as are studies on the connections between mothers' occupational conditions and their socialization attitudes and practices.

In general, the reliability of the trends noted above need to be determined. Some findings that are especially puzzling warrant special attention. For example, if husbands' job satisfaction is generally positively related to marital solidarity, why do the families of job-satisfied managers and executives appear to suffer? Aldous *et al.* (1979) proposed a curvilinear relationship between job satisfaction and satisfactory family relations. They hypothesized that both low and high levels of job satisfaction lead to lowered family participation and lessened marital solidarity. However, the link between job satisfaction and family participation remains unspecified.

Alternately, it may be that job *satisfaction* and job *involvement* are confounded in studies of managers and executives. Job involvement is a construct developed by organizational psychologists to account for the observation that some individuals tend to become especially absorbed in their work roles. Such involvement appears to be a function of both present occupational circumstances and prior socialization (see Gannon & Hendrickson, 1973; Hall & Mansfield, 1971; Kanungo, 1982; Lodahl, 1964; Lodahl & Kejner, 1965; Rabinowitz & Hall, 1977; Saal, 1978).

Although moderately correlated, job satisfaction and involvement are conceptually distinct (Gannon & Hendrickson, 1973; Gechman & Wiener, 1975; Rabinowitz & Hall, 1977) and they may have opposite effects on family relationships. Whereas job satisfaction may facilitate family involvement, job involvement may interfere with it. The highly job-involved individual devotes personal time and attention to work (Gechman & Wiener, 1975) at the cost of family participation. Job involvement and job satisfaction are especially confounded in managerial occupations because job-involved people may be drawn to and selected for such "absorptive" occupations (Kanter, 1977; Lodahl & Kejner, 1965). Evidence for a negative relationship between job involvement and the adequacy of family relationships comes from studies of "workaholics" (Machlowitz, 1980). Burke, Weir, and Duwars (1979) also found that Type A behavior in prison wardens was associated with poor marital adjustment in their wives. Their measure of Type A behavior was highly correlated with a measure of job involvement (Burke & Weir, 1980). The greatest difficulties may arise for families in which individuals are both highly job-involved and job-dissatisfied.

The negative relationship between job involvement and family satisfaction may further be moderated by the sex-role traditionality of wives. In such cases, the husband's job involvement is viewed as consistent with his primary role as breadwinner, so that there is little discrepancy between role expectations and role performance. Support for such a moderator effect comes from several interview studies. Bailyn (1970) found that marital satisfaction did not suffer when career-oriented men were married to relatively traditional women. Marital satisfaction was especially low in couples in which both partners were highly career-oriented. Handy (1978) and Pahl and Pahl (1971) found that marriages between highly job-involved men and traditional wives did not suffer because such wives did not expect companionate marriages. They supported their husbands in their jobs and did not burden them with problems. Another successful adaptation may be the "two-person career" in which the wife actively contributes to her husband's career and may derive vicarious fulfillment from it (see Helfrich & Tootle, 1972; Hochschild, 1969; Papanek, 1973; Taylor & Hartley, 1975). Nonetheless, wives may pay a high personal price for their supportiveness (Macke, Bohrnstedt, & Bernstein, 1979; Seidenberg, 1975).

A second puzzle to be addressed is the apparent lack of a direct relationship between wives' job satisfaction and marital solidarity. There is some evidence that women's satisfaction with their current situation is more relevant to the marital relationship than job satisfaction *per se*. Several studies have demonstrated that the congruence between a woman's preferred role status and her actual situation predicts her marital satisfaction (e.g., Orden & Bradburn, 1969; Safilios-Rothschild, 1970a).[15] Others have found that the fit between mothers' desired and actu-

al work status is associated with adequacy of mothering and child outcomes (Farel, 1980; Hall & Gordon, 1973; Lerner & Galambos, 1985; Stuckey *et al.*, 1982; Yarrow *et al.*, 1962). These studies suggest that it is the family of the full-time houseworker who prefers to be employed that suffers.

Associations between job satisfaction and satisfaction in family relationships do not indicate the direction of causality. Klenke-Hamel (1982) proposed a model that includes family factors as determinants of job satisfaction among dual-career couples. Empirical evidence also indicates that job satisfaction may be affected by family life, especially in the case of women. Andrisani and Shapiro (1978) found that women's job satisfaction was correlated with their perceptions of their husbands' attitudes toward their own employment. The more favorable the attitude, the greater the wives' job satisfaction. Married women also reported less job satisfaction than unmarried women. This latter finding is contradicted by Crosby's research (1982). She found that job satisfaction in both men and women varied with family status. Parents were most satisfied and single people were least satisfied, even when other characteristics were controlled for. She speculated that family roles help to enhance satisfying experiences at work and to dampen negative experiences. The more family roles one has, the stronger the effects. Although she did not examine job satisfaction *per se*, Crouter (1984) found that parents reported more negative spillover from family to work than nonparents, and that mothers reported more negative spillover than fathers, when children were young. Similarly, Cooke and Rousseau (1984) found that number of family roles (parent, spouse) is associated with increased work/nonwork conflict. Such research findings make it reasonable to assume that there are reciprocal influences between job and family life that require elucidation.

Research on occupation and socialization would benefit from the further development of precise hypotheses, as well as the direct measurement of working conditions and socialization practices. Two further directions are especially promising. First is the exploration of how the sex of the parent interacts with the sex of the child to affect socialization practices and outcomes. Are mothers' and fathers' jobs equally salient for the socialization of their male and female children? Second is the exploration of the possibility that occupational conditions socialize spouses into particular styles of marital interaction. Crouter (1984) reported that some respondents learned styles of communication in their participative management teams that had both positive and negative effects on their marriages. Anecdotal and case-study evidence in studies of police also suggests that styles of behavior learned at work may influence behavior in the marital dyad (Piotrkowski, 1979; Reiser, 1974). Gold and Slater's attempt (1958) to use Miller and Swanson's model (1958) to predict marital orientations had only limited success, as did the attempt by Kemper and Reichler (1976) to link power relations at the husbands' workplace

---

[15]Locksley (1980) found no association between such congruence and marital adjustment. However, her indicator of employment involvement was seriously confounded with motives for employment.

to conjugal power. Possibly, extending Kohn's work to the marital relationship would be more fruitful.

Measurement and statistical advances make it possible to test some of the more complex propositions advanced above. For example, measures exist to test both Aldous *et al.*'s curvilinear hypothesis (1979) and the proposed effects of job satisfaction and job involvement, as moderated by wives' traditionality (For such measures, see Kanungo, 1982; Lodahl & Kejner, 1965; Spence & Helmreich, 1978.) Including measures of parent–child relations also would constitute an important advance. The proposition that the marital relationship is differently sensitive to husbands' and to wives' job satisfaction could be readily tested in dual-earner families. Multivariate analyses would allow the inclusion of the fit between the wives' actual and desired employment status as an additional predictor variable.

Two methodological strategies can help to eliminate the possibility that personality factors or individual response biases inflate associations between reports of job and family satisfaction. The first strategy is to use reports by several family members. If one is studying husbands' job satisfaction, then reports by wives and children should be included. A second strategy is to use measures of job and family satisfaction that are as different in format as possible. Advances in measurement also make it possible to consider coping strategies as moderators of the relationship between occupational stressors and family outcomes (e.g., Maynard *et al.*, 1980). Finally, longitudinal studies and causal modeling procedures can help to untangle complex reciprocal influences, as well as the effects of self-selection factors. This latter issue is especially important in studies of occupational conditions and socialization practices. Studies that illustrate the possibilities of such analyses already exist (e.g., Kohn & Schooler, 1978; Mortimer & Kumka, 1982; Orpen, 1978).

Critical Events

The discussion of structural interactions has focused on the interplay of regular, fairly stable arrangements within and between work and family systems. Rapoport and Rapoport (1980a) distinguished "event impacts" from more stable "structural impacts" of one system on the other. *Event impacts* refer to the effects on one system of identifiable, critical occurrences in the other. Critical events taking place in either work or family system may alter established patterns that link one system with the other. Divorce, for example, may lead women to seek employment or, if already employed, to devise new work–family arrangements (cf. Hetherington, Cox, & Cox, 1979). Job relocation is a potentially stressful event with implications for family functioning. The ways in which employing organizations handle such events can mitigate or exacerbate the difficulties (e.g., Ammons, Nelson, & Wodarski, 1982; Brett, 1980; Hunter, 1982; Kilpatrick, 1982; Renshaw, 1976). Retirement is another

occupational event with implications for marriage. For some, it may pose special difficulties; for others, it is a boon (Szinovacz, 1980).

Some critical events, such as the birth of a child or retirement, are normative. Others, such as unwanted job loss, are not (Pearlin & Lieberman, 1979). We examine job loss as a significant workplace event because high rates of unemployment have made it a major concern in many industrialized countries. It also illustrates the complexity of familial responses to critical events in the workplace.

The effects on families of chronic unemployment are difficult to separate from the effects of poverty in general. Therefore, the discussion focuses on the critical event of job loss and its psychosocial impact on families. However, the event itself is variable. It may occur suddenly, without warning, or it may be anticipated for several months. It may involve a whole community—as in a plant closing—or isolated individuals. For some individuals, job loss is a recurrent experience. For others, it occurs after many years of stable employment. The economic context of job loss is also an important variable. Losing a job during times of high unemployment has different implications from losing a job during periods of economic well-being (Liem & Rayman, 1982). Unfortunately, little is known about the consequences of these various job-loss experiences. The discussion also focuses on men's job loss because the bulk of research has concerned white men. Still, it is important to note that joblessness affects women; it befalls the young, the unskilled, and the nonwhite disproportionately (Moen, 1979; Pearlin & Lieberman, 1979).

The Consequences of Job Loss

Recent research on job loss has followed two paths. First are the macroanalytic studies that attempt to link unemployment with communitywide indices of suicide, mental health admissions, child abuse, and so forth (e.g., Brenner, 1973; Catalano, Dooley, & Jackson, 1981; Steinberg, Catalano, & Dooley, 1981). A second line of research considers the physical and psychological consequences of job loss for individuals (e.g., Bakke, 1940b; Cobb & Kasl, 1977; Pearlin & Lieberman, 1979). These latter studies indicate that job loss can have deleterious consequences for people, affecting their physical and psychological well-being. Job loss may result in withdrawal and in difficulties organizing meaningful ways to spend time. It can mean the loss of a valued provider role and of status in the family (Komarovsky, 1940). It may have a stigma attached to it, along with the lingering suspicion that one is not "really trying" or that one is not good enough to hold a job (Bakke, 1940b). Several studies have identified stages that individuals go through following job loss. As the search for employment proves futile, boredom, declining self-respect, self-doubt, and malaise set in (Hill, 1978; Jahoda, 1979; Powell & Driscoll, 1973). Given the psychological importance of paid work to most people (Morse & Weiss, 1955), it is not surprising that lowered self-esteem is often mentioned as an individual's response to job loss.

Recent studies have just begun to document the familial costs of unemployment. Moen (1979, 1980, 1982) has detailed the economic hardships faced by families experiencing unemployment. The extent of the hardship varies with factors such as family structure and family life-cycle stage. Single-parent families, those headed by women, and nonwhite families are especially vulnerable. Researchers have also begun to identify difficulties for family members not directly experiencing the loss of a job. Liem and Rayman (1982) reported that wives in their samples showed signs of stress reactions several months after their husbands' job loss. They hypothesized that the women were responding to changes in family relationships. Their respondents also commented on signs of strain in their children. Margolis and Farran (1981) found that the children of workers who lost their jobs were at risk of developing health problems. They also hypothesized that family strain mediated the association between parental unemployment and children's health.

Job loss has been linked to strained family relationships directly. At the individual level, fathers' unemployment has been associated with increases in violence toward their children by both mothers and fathers (Belsky, 1980; Gelles, 1980; Gelles & Hargreaves, 1981). In a longitudinal study, Steinberg et al. (1981) found that declines in the work force were associated with subsequent increases in reported child abuse. Longitudinal studies on separation and divorce indicate that the employment instability of husbands, independent of the absolute level of family income, increases the probability of separation and divorce (Cherlin, 1979; Ross & Sawhill, 1975).

Loss of economic support for basic household maintenance can tax the adaptive capacities of families. Among the working poor, who have few assets, the reduction of an accustomed financial base may be critical. Marital tension and conflict over inadequate resources to support family expenditures are a problem common to working-class families (Komarovsky, 1962; Liker & Elder, 1983; Rubin, 1976). Without assets or wealth, unstable employment may precipitate repeated crises that deplete a family's adaptive capacities (Howell, 1973). In Brinkerhoff and White's study (1978) of working-class families with both low income and unstable employment, the wives' marital satisfaction was related to their satisfaction with their families' standard of living (also see Moen, 1982). Ironically, job loss occurs most often among the working poor. Families with wealth not only suffer job loss less frequently but also have greater financial resources to cushion its negative economic impact.

As researchers are increasingly aware that job loss may have significant consequences for families, as well as individuals, family variables are being included in studies of unemployment (Liem & Rayman, 1982). Still, the richest descriptions of the familial consequences of job loss come from the qualitative studies conducted during the Great Depression (e.g., Angell, 1936; Bakke, 1940a; Cavan & Ranck, 1938; Jahoda, Lazarsfield & Zeisel, 1971; Komarovsky, 1940). These studies were concerned with the job loss of husband-fathers. They identified two major psychosocial consequences for families: family disorganization and changes in the family role structure. These studies also identified major variables intervening between job loss and family consequences: the psychological effects of job loss on individuals within the family and the reduction of financial and other occupationally related resources (see Cavan, 1959).

Several studies noted the negative consequences for family relationships when irritability, occasioned by unemployment, spilled into interactions between husbands and wives (Liker & Elder, 1983). Conflict escalated when husbands attempted to assert their failing authority (e.g., Cavan & Ranck, 1938; Komarovsky, 1940). Komarovsky noted that the fathers in her study were more likely to vent their irritability on their children than on their spouses. Belsky (1980) suggested that the economic frustrations and feelings of powerlessness experienced by unemployed parents may underlie the connection between unemployment and child abuse. Even when job loss is not associated with such extreme reactions, parent–child relations may suffer. In his study of children of the Depression, Elder (1974) reported that sons whose families were severely deprived economically viewed their fathers as less desirable companions than sons in control families.

Economic deprivation occasioned by job loss may also affect power relations in families. In her study of Depression families, Komarovsky (1940) concluded that fathers' loss of authority with children was confined to older children, with whom the unemployed father could no longer use money as a source of reward or punishment. In the marital relationship, loss of authority accompanied economic deprivation only when the husbands' authority was based on fear and when the spouses' orientations to each other were instrumental (Bakke, 1940a; Komarovsky, 1940). Elder (1974) found that mothers gained power in decision making as deprivation increased, irrespective of social class.

A uniform finding of the Depression studies was that not all families suffered the same amount of disorganization following job loss. There were significant differences in the ways in which individuals and families responded to unemployment. Similar differences have been noted in more recent studies. In England, Hartley (1980) found that some unemployed managers recovered their equanimity even without formal reemployment, through the development of new interests and activities. Cavan and Ranck (1938) concluded that individual reactions to deprivation were consistent with personality traits observed before the job loss (see also Catalano & Dooley, 1979).

An important contribution of the Depression studies was the identification of the moderators that affected the severity of a family's response to unemployment. The level of family integration and the degree of adaptability before the job loss were crucial determinants of its impact, so that some families were able to adapt successfully after a period of disorganization (Angell, 1936; Cavan & Ranck, 1938). In some cases, the extreme disorganization of one family member served to unify the family (Cavan & Ranck, 1938). When a wife's primary attitude toward her husband was one of love, his personality deterioration did not necessarily result in a loss of his authority (Komarovsky, 1940). Similarly, when the relationship between a father and his children was good before job loss and the father took a special interest in his children's lives, Komarovsky found that relations between fathers and children could improve. Such improvements have also been reported in more recent studies (Thomas, McCabe, & Berry, 1980). In Elder's study (1974), the increased responsibility assumed by adolescent children actually had positive consequences for their later development.

Summary and Discussion

It remains unclear to what extent the findings of studies from the Great Depression in the 1930s can be generalized to the present social context, when wives' employment has become normative and income transfers help cushion the financial impact of unemployment. Still, taken together, the studies that consider familial consequences of job loss point to three general conclusions: (1) Job loss is a significant, critical event for families that may lead to family disorganization; (2) families vary in their response to job loss—whereas some families become disorganized, others manage to cope successfully after an initial period of readjustment; and (3) family members other than the person experiencing the loss may suffer psychological and health consequences. The third conclusion underscores the importance of conceptualizing the family as a system. Further systematic research on family responses to different types of job loss experienced by men *and* women is clearly necessary. Unemployment is a social problem that is not likely to disappear in the next decade.

Future research on the familial consequences of job loss would benefit from two conceptual developments. First, Moen's research (1979, 1980) has demonstrated the importance of the family life-cycle stage in moderating the economic hardships occasioned by unemployment. Family life-cycle stage may also be important for understanding psychosocial outcomes. Second, recent developments in family stress theory (Burr, 1973; Hill, 1949, 1965; McCubbin, 1979; McCubbin & Patterson, 1982; McCubbin, Joy, Cauble, Comeau, Patterson, & Needle, 1980) can be fruitfully applied to research on unemployment. Voydanoff (1983a,b) has taken this approach. She has described how strategies that families use to cope with unemployment may themselves become stressors, contributing to a "pileup" of hardships. Wives' em-

ployment, for example, may lead to role reorganization in the family that itself may be stressful. McCubbin and Patterson's formulation (1982) is especially relevant. They provide a dynamic theory that considers family responses to crisis over time and the processes underlying adaptation to crisis. Especially important is their distinction between a family's responses to the stressor event (e.g., job loss) and the family's responses to the ensuing crisis (e.g., family role disorganization). These authors recognize that family coping strategies are not static but develop continuously as a response to stressors.

A family resource especially important for understanding the impact of job loss is social support. McCubbin has identified the procurement of social support as a coping strategy that can facilitate a satisfactory adaptation to stress (McCubbin, 1979; McCubbin *et al.*, 1980). Liem and Liem (1979) identified three "moments" when supportive relations are especially important: the anticipation or threat of job loss, the initial experience of stress, and the coping process itself. Family relationships thus may serve as "victims" of job loss and, simultaneously, as moderators of the relationship between job loss and individual and familial outcomes. The recent development of measures of family adaptability and cohesion can facilitate research into these family moderators of unemployment effects (Olson & McCubbin, 1982; Olson, Sprenkel, & Russell, 1979, 1983).

Concluding Remarks

Many of the topics discussed in this chapter were not under general discussion 20 years ago, when the first *Handbook of Marriage and the Family* was published (Christensen, 1964). But the "myth of separate worlds" is no longer tenable. The recognition of significant work–family relationships has become normative. In part, women's participation in the formal economy, as well as the increased scrutiny of men's traditional roles, has forced us to acknowledge the transactions between life in the family and life in the workplace. For males and females alike, adulthood has come to mean being economically active, as well as being mates and parents.

For clarity of presentation, men's and women's work roles, as well as aspects of family dynamics, were discussed in separate sections. This organizational framework may have obscured an important truth, namely, that families are complex social systems. The classic early studies of dual-career couples recognized the complex nature of family systems in their descriptions of the interaction and development of husbands' and wives' work and family roles (Bailyn, 1970; Epstein, 1971; Holmstrom, 1972; Rapoport & Rapoport, 1969, 1971, 1977). These studies were limited by their focus on what may be a "minor variant" of dual-earner families (Hunt & Hunt, 1982; Benenson, 1984). Quantitative studies also increasingly look at the interaction of husband and wife job factors as they can affect families (e.g., Pleck &

Staines, 1982). Unfortunately, studies of children and studies of marriages have been the province of separate disciplines. Recent research in developmental psychology, however, reminds us that many dual-earner families must be conceptualized as at least a three-person system.

The importance of gender as an organizing category was evident throughout the chapter. Sex-role attitudes have biased the ways in which men and women's work roles have been treated, as well as the questions that have been asked (Feldberg & Glenn, 1979; Piotrkowski, 1984). Wives' employment and husbands' unemployment have been viewed as problems for families. An important development since the 1970s is the emergence of a more balanced approach and a sympathetic stance toward women's employment and the strains inherent in combining several primary life roles (Piotrkowski & Repetti, 1984). Gender has also been important in understanding empirical results. Women's jobs seem to have different "effects" from men's jobs with respect to variables such as marital power and marital satisfaction. Differences in sex-role obligations also mean that women may be bearing a disproportionate share of the burden in trying to accommodate work and family roles (Gutek, Nakamura & Nieva, 1981). It is also clear that gender cannot be overlooked as a critical moderator variable in understanding how parents' employment roles may affect parent–child relationships (see Hoffman, 1984a,b). As long as family and work roles continue to differ for men and women and male and female children have different socialization experiences, gender-dependent patterns of work–family relationships will continue.

Theoretical Directions

The field is entering a stage of development in which the need for dynamic process-oriented theories that address the complex transactions between work and family systems is evident. It is important that such theories not be time-bound and tied to existing gender arrangement (Aldous, 1981b; Rapoport & Rapoport, 1978). Movements toward greater equality between the sexes—at home and in the workplace—can be expected to change the nature of work–family relations, introducing strain where it did not exist before, as well as facilitating new, more gratifying arrangements.

Two theoretical frameworks offer special promise for their utility in studying work–family relationships. The *developmental framework* in family sociology offers a particularly useful approach to conceptualizing the family over its "life cycle" or "career" (Aldous, 1978; Duvall, 1977; Hill & Rodgers, 1964; Rodgers, 1964).[16] This

---

[16]With Aldous (1978), we prefer the term *career* because, as she pointed out, *life cycle* implies that the family returns to where it started. However, given the widespread usage of the term *life cycle*, the two terms are used here interchangeably.

framework attempts to specify the normative transitions in a family's history and the tasks associated with them. Although the family developmental framework has been criticized on theoretical and empirical grounds (e.g., Nock, 1979; Spanier, Sauer, & Larzelere, 1979), it has heuristic value in initial attempts to develop a dynamic formulation of work–family relationships.

The family career can be viewed as a moderator variable that influences family outcomes. Throughout the chapter, we tried to include discussions of moderator effects. For example, working a night shift has implications for the parent–child relationship when a child is a preschooler different from those when he or she is of school age. Two examples of this use of the developmental framework are seen in the work of Hareven (1975a, 1978a,b) and Moen (1979, 1980).

A more comprehensive approach is to focus on the dynamic interaction of family life-cycle stage with the career stages (broadly conceived) of employed family members. Rapoport and Rapoport (1965) were among the first to explicitly examine the interaction of occupational and family careers on patterns of work–family adaptation. They focused on relatively simultaneous significant role transitions in work and family spheres that presented a complex of "tasks" for families and individuals. In their classic study of dual-career families, Rapoport and Rapoport (1971, 1977) used the concept of "multiple-role cycling" to indicate the possibilities of integrating work and family roles through the life cycle of dual-career couples. Oppenheimer (1974, 1979) has also explicitly considered the interaction of "occupational and family life cycles." She examined the relationship between men's earning curve over their occupational careers and the economic needs of families as they vary through the life course. Blue-collar men and low-income white-collar men are caught in what Wilensky (1963) termed a "life-cycle squeeze," in which earnings are not adequate to meet the economic needs created by children (Oppenheimer, 1974).

Voydanoff (1980a) proposed a systematic typology that attempts to conceptualize patterns of work–family integration over time. The intersection of stages in work and family careers make up what she termed the "work–family life cycle." She considers work–family role staging (sequential or simultaneous), as well as role allocation (traditional or symmetrical), between husbands and wives as techniques for reducing the "asynchronies" of work–family overload and interference, as well as the role strain that can result from the interaction of these multiple careers (also see Bailyn, 1978). Combining the possible types of role staging and role allocation, Voydanoff was able to derive a typology of "work–family life cycles." This typology is useful because it leads to a number of predictions of the costs and benefits associated with the various patterns. For example, the continuous involvement of husbands and wives in work and family roles is associated with high role overload and interference, especially during the new-parent–early-career stage, when the demands of work and family systems are intense.

This typology shares the limitation of the developmental framework in its emphasis on stereotypical conceptions of family careers (Aldous, 1978). It could be expanded, for example, to include single-parent families. The emphasis on familial techniques that deal with work–family asynchronies is vital because it emphasizes the active role that families take in developing varying patterns of work–family integration over the life course. But as Tilly (1979) noted, family strategies may have different effects on individuals, depending on their family roles. Consequently, both individual and family outcomes need to be considered in the test of this typology.

The developmental framework can also be helpful in understanding the effects of unscheduled, sometimes unwanted, or even traumatic events on established work–family relationships. Oppenheimer's research (1974) would suggest, for example, that job loss is especially detrimental to family well-being during the school-age stage and the midcareer stage of the work–family life cycle. Placing such critical events in a developmental context may allow us to specify their impact with increasing precision.

A second theoretical framework that offers the prospect of being especially useful in the study of work–family relationships is *family stress theory*. Its utility in the study of the familial consequences of critical events has been discussed. Its application, however, is not limited to critical work-related stressors, such as job loss or relocation, that may confront families with potential crises. Stress theory can also be applied to chronic stressors that arise from the structural features of the workplace. Voydanoff (1980b) defined family stressors as problems that families must solve or adapt to in order to maintain (adequate) family functioning. For example, shiftwork, highly demanding tasks, and excessive work hours are *chronic* stressors that families confront. Piotrkowski, Stark, and Burbank (1983) identified three processes whereby chronic stressors can affect family relationships: (1) By affecting a worker adversely, job conditions may impair the performance of family roles; (2) some job conditions may affect family functioning directly, as when job instability limits a family's ability to make long-range plans; and (3) some job conditions may directly affect other family members adversely, as when the spouses of shiftworkers experience "night fear" (Mott *et al.*, 1965). In such cases, family role performance also may be impaired. The capacity of such chronic stressors to induce family disorganization varies with the family life cycle and with family circumstances.

Finally, the dilemmas created by families' attempts to manage work and family roles simultaneously, as well as the accommodations that families make to manage such dilemmas, may become stressors. Such dilemmas have been amply documented in the literature on dual-career families (e.g., Hall & Hall, 1980; Rapoport & Rapoport,

1971; Skinner, 1980). Role overload is a dilemma that commonly faces these families. Typologies such as those developed by Bailyn (1970), Handy (1978), and Hall and Hall (1980) are useful in helping to identify such stressors in various types of dual-earner families.

Methodological Directions

Research in the work–family field has made important progress in moving away from simple comparisons of dual-earner and traditional male-breadwinner families. Instead, researchers are using multivariate techniques to understand the processes that might underlie given outcomes *within* dual-earner groups. The increasing emphasis on within-group analyses reflects the realization that a finding of no group differences or measurable group differences is only the beginning of understanding. It also reflects the decreased concern with the potential harm of women's employment and a less biased approach to research questions (Piotrkowski & Repetti, 1984). Studies of dual-career families, which continue to rely heavily on qualitative analyses and small samples, have turned to focused questions that can be studied with greater precision (Rapoport & Rapoport, 1980b). The investment of effort in longitudinal data collection and "natural experiments" (Bronfenbrenner, 1979) also represents an important methodological improvement. Two further necessary steps are the assessment of multivariable models, with intervening links specified, and the inclusion of an array of outcome variables that simultaneously attend to individuals, family subsystems, and the family as a whole. This latter strategy would allow us to understand the complex costs and benefits associated with various work–family combinations.

It also is vital that researchers in the family field attend carefully to measurement validity (Miller, Rollins, & Thomas, 1982). There are several ways in which validity can be improved. When possible, existing measures with known psychometric properties should be used. For example, organizational psychologists have developed a variety of measures to assess workplaces. A most significant development is the introduction of measures designed specifically to assess work and family relations. In addition to the coping inventory developed by Skinner and her colleagues (Skinner, 1982), measures are being developed to assess relevant features of dual-career families (Pendleton, Poloma, & Garland, 1980) and work–family conflicts and spillover (Fournier, 1981; Fournier & Engelbrecht, 1982). The use of multiple measures and multiple methods of data collection is also important. Obtaining data from more than one family member is not overly difficult. The integration of observational techniques, though costly and time-consuming, would constitute an important forward step. Finally, greater attention needs to be paid to the meaning of traditional outcomes. It is possible, for example, that expressions of marital dissatisfaction and even divorce are not entirely negative outcomes (Laws, 1971).

Directions for Further Research

The research directions outlined by Kanter in 1977 and by the Rapoports in 1982 still are pertinent. In a field so dynamic, it is imprudent to suggest research priorities in any detailed, specific way. We can, however, review general substantive research areas that would benefit from further development:

1. *Structural effects* of the workplace on families need further study. Instead of focusing on the fact of employment or vertical aspects of occupations, the multiple aspects of work should be examined. Workplace policies and practices should be viewed as potential facilitators or inhibitors of family functioning. In addition, the extent to which workplace structures shape family dynamics and individual development is a key research area. Research needs to look at not only the work of managers and professionals, but also the work of those in clerical, service, semiskilled, and unskilled jobs. Changes in microtechnologies and workplace structure (e.g., home-based work) offer the opportunity to study experiments in nature. Finally, nonformal work—such as housework—needs to be studied for its potential impact on family life.

2. Research into how workplace *events* affect families, both positively and negatively, are needed. The consequences, for example, of job loss and then geographic relocation to search for work require systematic investigation.

3. Systematic *descriptions* of various patterns of work–family accommodations through the life cycle are still needed. With some exceptions, such descriptions have focused on corporate and dual-career families. But in most dual-earner families, the members' jobs are not prestigious and rewarding. Although the dual-earner family type is now the norm for husband–wife families, the growing interest in such families should not obscure the existence of other family structures, such as the single-parent employee family. Research is sorely needed on how the work–family strains of such households differ from those of other family types (Gutek *et al.*, 1981). Finally, descriptive research needs to be conducted on minority families (Ybarra, 1982). Currently, most research on work–family relations is based on white middle-class samples.

4. Finally, how *families* affect the work performance and behavior of employees is a theoretically important topic (Crouter, 1984).

To deal adequately with these issues requires a multidimensional approach that attends to individual strains and satisfactions, family dynamics, social participation, economic productivity and work life satisfaction. The work and family field represents a direct challenge to the treatment of families as "closed" systems. But care must be taken that the work–family complex itself not be treated as closed. The interaction of work, family, and community systems, as well as the influence of informal and formal social systems on the pattern of work–family arrangements through the life cycle, offers important possibilities for conceptual development and research. The study of these complex connections and the extent to which they are beneficial or detrimental to families provides us with a challenge for the future.

ACKNOWLEDGMENTS

We wish to extend our thanks to Shirby Strang and Kathy Washenko for their assistance in the preparation of this chapter. We also wish to thank the editors of this volume and the anonymous reviewers for their helpful comments.

References

Aberle, D. E., & Naegele, K. D. Middle class father's occupational roles and attitudes toward children. *American Journal of Orthopsychiatry*, 1952, *22*, 366–378.

Aldous, J. Occupational characteristics and males' role performance in the family. *Journal of Marriage and the Family*, 1969, *31*, 707–712. (a)

Aldous, J. Wives' employment status and lower-class men as husband-fathers: Support for the Moynihan thesis. *Journal of Marriage and the Family*, 1969, *31*, 469–476. (b)

Aldous, J. *Family careers*. New York: Wiley, 1978.

Aldous, J. From dual-earner to dual-career families and back again. *Journal of Family Issues*, 1981, *2*, 115–125. (a)

Aldous, J. Second guessing the experts: Thoughts on family agendas for the eighties. *Journal of Marriage and the Family*, 1981, *43*, 267–270. (b)

Aldous, J., Osmond, M., & Hicks, M. Men's work and men's families. In W. Burr, R. Hill, F. I. Nye, & I. Reiss (Eds.), *Contemporary theories about the family*, Vol. 1. New York: Macmillan, 1979.

Ammons, P., Nelson, J., & Wodarski, J. Surviving corporate moves: Sources of stress and adaptation among corporate executive families. *Family Relations*, 1982, *31*, 207–212.

Andrisani, P. J., & Shapiro, M. B. Women's attitudes toward their jobs: Some longitudinal data on a national sample. *Personnel Psychology*, 1978, *31*, 15–34.

Angell, R. *The family encounters the depression*. New York: Scribner's, 1936.

Angrist, S. S., Lave, J. R., & Mickelsen, R. How working mothers manage: Socioeconomic differences in work, child care and household tasks. *Social Science Quarterly*, 1976, *56*, 631–637.

Axelson, L. J. The marital adjustment and marital role definitions of husbands of working and nonworking wives. *Marriage and Family Living*, 1963, *25*, 189–195.

Bahr, S. J. Effects on power and division of labor in the family. In L. W. Hoffman & F. I. Nye (Eds.), *Working mothers*. San Francisco: Jossey-Bass, 1974.

Bailyn, L. Career and family orientations of husbands and wives in relation to marital happiness. *Human Relations*, 1970, *23*, 97–113.

Bailyn, L. Accommodation of work to family. In R. Rapoport & R. N. Rapoport (Eds.), *Working couples*. New York: Harper & Row, 1978.

Bakke, E. W. *Citizens without work*. New Haven, Conn.: Yale University Press, 1940. (a)

Bakke, E. W. *The unemployed worker*. New Haven, Conn.: Yale University Press, 1940. (b)

Bane, M. J., Lein, L., O'Donnell, L., Stueve, C. A., & Wells, B. Child care arrangements of working parents. *Monthly Labor Review*, 1979, *102*(10), 50–56.

Beckett, J. O. Working wives: A racial comparison. *Social Work*, 1976, *21*, 463–471.

Bell, D. C., Chafetz, J. S., & Horn, L. H. Marital conflict resolution: A study of strategies and outcomes. *Journal of Family Issues*, 1982, *3*, 111–132.

Bell, N. W., & Vogel, E. F. Toward a framework for functional analysis of family behavior. In N. W. Bell & E. F. Vogel (Eds.), *A modern introduction to the family*. New York: Free Press, 1960.

Belsky, J. Child maltreatment: An ecological integration. *American Psychologist*, 1980, *35*, 320–335.

Belsky, J., & Steinberg, L. D. The effects of day care: A critical review. *Child Development*, 1978, *49*, 929–949.

Benenson, H. Womans' occupational and family achievement in the U.S. class system. A critique of the dual career family analysis. *British Journal of Sociology*, 1984, *35*(1), 19–41.

Berk, R., & Berk, S. F. *Labor and leisure at home*. Beverly Hills, Calif.: Sage, 1979.

Blehar, M. C. Anxious attachment and defensive reactions associated with day care. *Child Development*, 1974, *45*, 683–692.

Blood, R. O., Jr. The husband-wife relationship. In F. I. Nye & L. W. Hoffman (Eds.), *The employed mother in America*. Chicago: Rand McNally, 1963.

Blood, R. O., Jr., & Wolfe, D. M. *Husbands and wives*. New York: Free Press, 1960.

Bohen, H. H., & Viveros-Long, A. *Balancing jobs and family life*. Philadelphia: Temple University Press, 1981.

Bone, M. *Pre-school children and the need for day-care*. London: HMSO, 1977.

Booth, A. Wife's employment and husband's stress: A replication and refutation. *Journal of Marriage and the Family*, 1977, *39*, 645–650.

Booth, A. Does wives' employment cause stress for husbands? *Family Coordinator*, 1979, *28*, 445–449.

Boss, P. G., McCubbin, H. I., & Lester, G. The corporate executive wife's coping patterns in response to routine husband-father absence. *Family Process*, 1979, *18*, 79–86.

Bowlby, J. A. *Maternal care and mental health*. Geneva: World Health Organization, 1951.

Bradburn, N., & Caplovitz, D. *Reports on happiness*. Chicago: Aldine, 1965.

Brenner, M. H. *Mental illness and the economy*. Cambridge: Harvard University Press, 1973.

Brett, J. M. The effect of job transfer on employees and their families. In C. L. Cooper & R. Payne (Eds.), *Current concerns in occupational stress*. New York: Wiley, 1980.

Brinkerhoff, D. B., & White, L. K. Marital satisfaction in an economically marginal population. *Journal of Marriage and the Family*, 1978, *40*, 259–268.

Bronfenbrenner, U. *The ecology of human development*. Cambridge: Harvard University Press, 1979.

Bronfenbrenner, U., & Crouter, A. C. Work and family through time and space. In S. B. Kamerman & C. D. Hayes (Eds.), *Families that work: Children in a changing world*. Washington, D.C.: National Academy Press, 1982.

Bronfenbrenner, U., Alvarez, W. F., & Henderson, C. R. Working and watching: Maternal employment status and parents' perceptions of their three-year-old children. *Child Development*, 1984, *55*, 1362–1378.

Broschart, K. R. Family status and professional achievement: A study of women doctorates. *Journal of Marriage and the Family*, 1978, *40*, 71–78.

Bryson, R. B., Bryson, J. B., Licht, M., & Licht, B. The professional pair: Husband and wife psychologists. *American Psychologist*, 1976, *31*, 10–16.

Burke, R. J., & Weir, T. Relationship of wives' employment status to husband, wife and pair satisfaction and performance. *Journal of Marriage and the Family*, 1976, *38*, 279–287.

Burke, R. J., & Weir, T. The type A experience: Occupational and life demands, satisfaction and well-being. *Journal of Human Stress*, 1980 (December), 28–38.

Burke, R. J., Weir, T., and Duwars, R. E., Jr. Type A behavior of administrators and wives reports of marital satisfaction and well-being. *Journal of Applied Psychology*, 1979, *64*, 57–65.

Burns, S. *Home, Inc.* Garden City, N.Y.: Doubleday, 1975.

Burr, W. R. *Theory construction and the sociology of the family*. New York: Wiley, 1973.

Campbell, A., Converse, P., & Rodgers, W. *The quality of American life*. New York: Sage, 1976.

Catalano, R., & Dooley, D. Does economic change provoke or uncover behavioral disorder? A preliminary test. In L. Ferman & J. Gordus (Eds.), *Mental health and the economy*. Kalamazoo, Mich.: Upjohn Institute, 1979.

Catalano, R., Dooley, D., & Jackson, R. Economic predictors of admissions to mental health facilities in a non-metropolitan community. *Journal of Health and Social Behavior*, 1981, *22*, 284–298.

Cavan, R. S. Unemployment—crisis of the common man. *Marriage and Family Living*, 1959, *21*, 139–146.

Cavan, R. S., & Ranck, K. H. *The family and the depression*. Chicago: University of Chicago Press, 1938.

Centers, R., Raven, B. H., & Rodrigues, A. Conjugal power structure: A re-examination. *American Sociological Review*, 1971, *36*, 264–278.

Chafe, W. H. Looking backward in order to look forward: Women, work and social values in America. In J. M. Kreps (Ed.), *Women and the American economy*. Englewood Cliffs, N.J.: Prentice-Hall, 1976.

Chafetz, J. S. Conflict resolution in marriage: Toward a theory of spousal strategy and marital dissolution rates. *Journal of Family Issues*, 1981, *1*, 397–421.

Cherlin, A. Work life and marital dissolution. In G. Levinger & O. C. Moles (Eds.), *Divorce and separation*. New York: Basic Books, 1979.

Cherlin, A. Postponing marriage: The influence of young women's work expectations. *Journal of Marriage and the Family*, 1980, *42*, 355–366.

Christensen, H. T. (Ed.). *Handbook of marriage and the family*. Chicago: Rand McNally, 1964.

Clark, R. A., Nye, F. I., and Gecas, V. Work involvement and marital role performace. *Journal of Marriage and the Family*, 1978, *40*, 9–22.

Clarke-Stewart, A. *Daycare*. Cambridge: Harvard University Press, 1982.

Cobb, S., & Kasl, S. V. *Termination: The consequences of job loss*. DHEW (NIOSH) Publication No. 77-224, 1977.

Coburn, D., & Edwards, V. L. Job control and child rearing values. *Canadian Review of Sociology and Anthropology*, 1976, *13*, 337–344.

Cogle, F. L., & Tasker, G. E. Children and housework. *Family Relations*, 1982, *31*, 395–399.

Cohen, G. Absentee husbands in spiralist families: The myth of the symmetrical family. *Journal of Marriage and the Family*, 1977, *39*, 595–604.

Cohen, S. E. Maternal employment and mother-child interaction. *Merrill-Palmer Quarterly*, 1978, *24*(3), 189–198.

Cooke, R. A., & Rousseau, D. M. Stress and strain from family roles and work-role expectations. *Journal of Applied Psychology* 1984, *69*, 252–260.

Cott, N. F. *The bonds of womanhood*. New Haven, Conn.: Yale University Press, 1977.

Cowan, R. The "Industrial Revolution" in the home: Household technology and social change in the 20th century. *Technology and Culture*, 1976, *17*, 1–23.

Cromwell, R. E., & Olson, D. *Power in families*. New York: Wiley, 1975.

Crosby, F. J. *Relative deprivation and working women*. New York: Oxford University Press, 1982.

Crouter, A. C. *Participative work and personal life: A case study of their reciprocal effects.* Unpublished doctoral thesis, Cornell University, 1982.

Crouter, A. C. Spillover from family to work: The neglected side of the work-family interface. *Human Relations,* 1984, *37,* 425–442.

Degler, C. N. *At odds—Women and the family in America from the revolution to the present.* New York: Oxford University Press, 1980.

Demos, J. *A little commonwealth.* New York: Oxford University Press, 1970.

Dennis, N., Henriques, F., & Slaughter, C. *Coal is our life.* London: Eyre & Spottiswoode, 1956.

Dominian, J. Divorcing families. In R. N. Rapoport, M. Fogarty, & R. Rapoport (Eds.), *Families in Britain.* London: Routledge & Kegan Paul, 1982.

Douvan, E. Employment and the adolescent. In F. I. Nye & L. W. Hoffman (Eds.), *The employed mother in America.* Chicago: Rand McNally, 1963.

Douvan, E., & Adelson, J. *The adolescent experience.* New York: Wiley, 1966.

Dubin, R. Industrial workers' worlds. *Social Problems,* 1956, *3,* 131–142.

Duncan, R. P., & Perrucci, C. C. Dual occupational families and migration. *American Sociological Review,* 1976, *41,* 252–261.

Duvall, E. M. *Marriage and family development* (5th ed.). Philadelphia: J. B. Lippincott, 1977.

Ehrenreich, B., & English, D. The manufacture of housework. *Socialist Revolution,* 1975, *5*(4), 5–40.

Eiswirth-Neems, N., & Handal, P. Spouse's attitudes toward maternal occupational status and effects on family climate. *Journal of Community Psychology,* 1978, *6,* 168–172.

Elder, G. H., Jr. *Children of the Great Depression.* Chicago: University of Chicago Press, 1974.

Elias, P. Employment prospects and equal opportunity. In P. Moss & N. Fonda (Eds.), *Work and the family.* London: Temple Smith, 1980.

Elman, M. R., & Gilbert, L. A. Coping strategies for role conflict in married professional women with children. *Family Relations,* 1984, *33,* 317–327.

Epstein, C. F. Law partners and marital partners: Strains and solutions in the dual career family enterprise. *Human Relations,* 1971, *24,* 549–563.

Ericksen, J., Yancey, W. L., & Ericksen, E. P. The division of family roles. *Journal of Marriage and the Family.* 1979, *41,* 301–314.

Etaugh, C. Effects of maternal employment on children. *Merrill-Palmer Quarterly,* 1974, *20*(2), 71–98.

Ewer, P. A., Crimmins, E., & Oliver, R. An analysis of the relationship between husband's income, family size and wife's employment in the early stages of marriage. *Journal of Marriage and the Family,* 1979, *41,* 727–738.

Farel, A. M. Effects of preferred maternal roles, maternal employment, and sociodemographic status on school adjustment and competence. *Child Development,* 1980, *51,* 1179–1186.

Faver, C. A. Women, careers and family. *Journal of Family Issues,* 1981, *2,* 91–112.

Feldberg, R. L., & Glenn, E. N. Male and female: Job versus gender models in the sociology of work. *Social Problems,* 1979, *26,* 524–538.

Feldman, H., & Feldman, M. The relationship between the family and occupational functioning in a sample of urban welfare women. *Cornell Journal of Social Research,* 1974, *9,* 35–52.

Ferman, L., & Berndt, L. E. The irregular economy. In S. Henry (Ed.), *Informal institutions.* New York: St. Martins Press, 1981.

Ferree, M. M. Working class jobs: Paid work and housework as sources of satisfaction. *Social Problems,* 1976, *23,* 431–441.

Ferri, E. *Growing up in a one-parent family.* London: National Children's Bureau, 1976.

Finn, P. The effects of shiftwork on the lives of employees. *Monthly Labor Review,* 1981, *104*(10), 31–35.

Fogarty, M., Rapoport, R., & Rapoport, R. *Sex, career and family.* Beverly Hills, Calif.: Sage, 1971.

Fournier, D. G. *Profiles.* Oklahoma State University, 1981.

Fournier, D. G., & Engelbrecht, J. D. *Assessing conflict between family life and employment: Conceptual issues in instrument development.* Unpublished manuscript, Oklahoma State University, 1982.

Fox, K. D., & Nickols, S. Y. The time crunch. *Journal of Family Issues,* 1983, *4,* 61–82.

Frankenhaeuser, M., & Gardell, B. Underload and overload in working life: Outline of a multidisciplinary approach. *Journal of Human Stress,* 1976, *2,* 35–46.

Friedman, M., Rosenman, R. H., & Carroll, V. Changes in the serum cholesterol and blood clotting time in men subjected to cyclic variations of occupational stress. *Circulation,* 1958, *17,* 852–861.

Galligan, R. J., & Bahr, S. J. Economic well-being and marital stability: Implications for income maintenance programs. *Journal of Marriage and the Family,* 1978, *40,* 283–290.

Gannon, M. J., & Hendrickson, D. H. Career orientation and job satisfaction among working wives. *Journal of Applied Psychology,* 1973, *57,* 339–340.

Gardell, B., & Gustavson, B. Work environment research and social change: Current developments in Scandinavia. *Journal of Occupational Behavior,* 1980, *1,* 3–17.

Garland, T. N. The better half? The male in the dual profession family. In C. Safilios-Rothschild (Ed.), *Toward a sociology of women.* Lexington, Mass.: Xerox Publishing, 1972.

Gavron, H. *The captive wife.* London: Routledge & Kegan Paul. 1966.

Gecas, V. The influence of social class on socialization. In W. Burr, R. Hill, F. I. Nye, & I. Reiss (Eds.), *Contemporary theories about the family,* Vol. 1. New York: Macmillan, 1979.

Gecas, V., & Nye, F. I. Sex and class differences in parent-child interaction: A test of Kohn's hypothesis. *Journal of Marriage and the Family,* 1974, *36,* 742–749.

Gechman, A. S., & Wiener, Y. Job involvement and satisfaction as related to mental health and personal time devoted to work. *Journal of Applied Psychology,* 1975, *60,* 521–523.

Gelles, R. J. Violence in the family: A review of research in the seventies. *Journal of Marriage and the Family,* 1980, *42,* 873–885.

Gelles, R. J., & Hargreaves, E. F. Maternal employment and violence toward children. *Journal of Family Issues,* 1981, *2,* 509–530.

Gerstel, N. R. The feasibility of commuter marriage. In P. Stein, J. Richman & N. Hannon (Eds.), *The family: Functions, conflicts and symbols.* Reading, Mass.: Addison-Wesley, 1977.

Gerstel, N. R. Marital alternatives and the regulation of sex. *Alternative Lifestyles,* 1979, *2,* 145–176.

Gerstel, N. R. & Gross, H. *Commuter marriage.* New York: Guilford Press, 1984.

Gersuny, J. I. *After industrial society.* London: Macmillan, 1978.

Gilbert, L. A., Holahan, C. K., & Manning, L. Coping with conflict between professional and maternal roles. *Family Relations,* 1981, *30,* 419–426.

Gillespie, D. Who has the power? The marital struggle. *Journal of Marriage and the Family,* 1971, *33,* 445–458.

Glazer-Malbin, N. Housework. *Signs,* 1976, *1,* 905–922.

Glenn, N. D., & Weaver, C. N. A multivarate, multisurvey study of marital happiness. *Journal of Marriage and the Family,* 1978, *40,* 269–282.

Glenn, N. D., & Weaver, C. N. The contribution of marital happiness to global happiness. *Journal of Marriage and the Family,* 1981, *43,* 161–168.

Glick, P. C., & Norton, A. Frequency, duration, and probability of marriage and divorce. *Journal of Marriage and the Family,* 1971, *33,* 307–317.

Gold, M., & Slater, C. Office, factory, store and family: A study of integration setting. *American Sociological Review,* 1958, *23,* 64–74.

Goulet, L. R., & Baltes, P. B. (Eds.). *Life span developmental psychology.* New York: Academic Press, 1970.

Gross, H. E. Dual-career couples who live apart: Two types. *Journal of Marriage and the Family,* 1980, *42,* 567–576.

Gutek, B. A., Nakamura, C. Y., & Nieva, V. F. The interdependence work and family roles. *Journal of Occupational Behavior.* 1981, *2,* 1–16.

Haavio-Mannila, E. Satisfaction with family, work, leisure, and life among men and women. *Human Relations,* 1971, *24,* 585–601.

Hall, D. T., & Gordon, F. E. Career choices of married women: Effects on conflict, role behavior and satisfaction. *Journal of Applied Psychology,* 1973, *58,* 42–48.

Hall, D. T., & Hall, F. S. Stress and the two-career couple. In C. L. Cooper & R. Payne (Eds.), *Current concerns in occupational stress.* New York: Wiley, 1980.

Hall, D. T., & Mansfield, R. Organizational and individual response to external stress. *Aministrative Science Quarterly,* 1971, *16,* 533–547.

Hammond, S. B. Class and family. In O. A. Oeser & S. B. Hammond (Eds.), *Social structure and personality in a city,* Vol 1. New York: Macmillan, 1954.

Handy, C. Going aginst the grain: Working couples and greedy occupations. In R. Rapoport & R. N. Rapoport (Eds.), *Working couples.* New York: Harper & Row, 1978.

Hareven, T. K. Family time and industrial time: Family and work in a planned corporation town, 1900–24. *Journal of Urban History,* 1975, *1,* 365–389. (a)

Hareven, T. K. The laborers of Manchester, New Hampshire, 1912–22: The role of family and ethnicity in the adjustment to industrial life. *Labor History,* 1975, *16,* 249–265. (b)

Hareven, T. K. Family time and historical time. In A. S. Rossi, J. Kagan, & T. K. Hareven (Eds.), *The family.* New York: W. W. Norton, 1978. (a)

Hareven, T. K. The historical study of the life course. In T. K. Hareven (Ed.), *Transitions.* New York: Academic Press, 1978. (b)

Harrell, J., & Ridley, C. Substitute child care, maternal employment and the quality of mother-child interaction. *Journal of Marriage and the Family,* 1975, *37,* 556–564.

Harris, L., & Associates, Inc. *Families at work: Strengths and strains.* Minneapolis: General Mills, 1981.

Harrison, A. D., & Minor, J. H. Interrole conflict, coping strategies, and satisfaction among black working wives. *Journal of Marriage and the Family,* 1978, *40,* 799–805.

Hartley, J. The impact of unemployment on the self-esteem of managers. *Journal of Occupational Psychology,* 1980, *53,* 147–155.

Hartmann, H. I. The family as the locus of gender, class, and political struggle: The example of housework. *Signs,* 1981, *6,* 366–394.

Hauenstein, L. Married women: Work and family. *Families Today,* 1979, Vol. 1, DHEW Pub No. (ADM) 79–815.

Hayghe, H. H. Dual-earner families: Their economic and demographic characteristics. In J. Aldous (Ed.), *Two paychecks: Life in dual-earner families.* Beverly Hills, Calif.: Sage, 1982.

Heer, D. M. Dominance and the working wife. In F. I. Nye & L. W. Hoffman (Eds.), *The employed mother in America.* Chicago: Rand McNally, 1963. (a)

Heer, D. M. The measurement and bases of family power: An overview. *Journal of Marriage and Family Living,* 1963, *25,* 133–139. (b)

Helfrich, M., & Tootle, B. The executive wives: A factor in promotion. *Business Horizons,* 1972, *15,* 89–95.

Herman, J. B., & Gyllstrom, K. K. Working men and women: Inter- and intra-role conflict. *Psychology of Women Quarterly,* 1977, *1,* 319–333.

Hesse, S. J. Women working: Historical trends. In K. W. Feinstein (Ed.), *Working women and families.* Beverly Hills, Calif.: Sage, 1979.

Hetherington, E. M., Cox, M., & Cox, R. The aftermath of divorce. In J. H. Stevens, Jr., & M. Matthews (Eds.), *Mother-child, father-child relations.* Washington, D.C.: NAEYC, 1979.

Hill, J. *The psychological impact of unemployment.* London: News Society, 1978.

Hill, R. *Families under stress.* New York: Harper & Row, 1949.

Hill, R. Generic features of families under stress. In J. J. Parad (Ed.), *Crisis intervention: Selected readings.* New York: Family Service Association of America, 1965.

Hill, R. Modern systems theory and the family: A confrontation. In M. B. Sussman (Ed.), *Sourcebook in marriage and the family.* Boston: Houghton Mifflin, 1974.

Hill, R. Whither family research in the 1980's: Continuities, emergents, constraints, and new horizons. *Journal of Marriage and the Family,* 1981, *43,* 255–258.

Hill, R., & Rodgers, R. H. The developmental approach. In H. T. Christensen (Ed.), *Handbook of marriage and the family.* Chicago: Rand McNally, 1964.

Hill, W., & Scanzoni, J. An approach for assessing marital decision-making processes. *Journal of Marriage and the Family,* 1982, *44,* 927–941.

Hiller, D. V., & Philliber, W. W. Predicting marital and career success among dual-worker couples. *Journal of Marriage and the Family,* 1982, *44,* 53–62.

Hochschild, A. The role of the ambassador's wife. *Journal of Marriage and the Family,* 1969, *31,* 73–87.

Hock, E. Working and nonworking mothers and their infants: A comparative study of maternal caregiving characteristics and infant social behavior. *Merrill-Palmer Quarterly,* 1980, *26,* 79–101.

Hofferth, S. L. Day care in the next decade: 1980–1990. *Journal of Marriage and the Family,* 1979, *41,* 649–658.

Hoffman, L. W. Mother's enjoyment of work and effects on the child. In F. I. Nye & L. W. Hoffman (Eds.), *The employed mother in America.* Chicago: Rand McNally, 1963.

Hoffman, L. W. Effects of maternal employment on the child: A review of the research. *Development Psychology,* 1974, *10,* 204–228. (a)

Hoffman, L. W. Effects on child. In L. W. Hoffman & F. I. Nye (Eds.), *Working mothers.* San Francisco: Jossey-Bass, 1974. (b)

Hoffman, L. W. Maternal employment: 1979. *American Psychologist,* 1979, *34,* 859–865.

Hoffman, L. W. The effects of maternal employment on the academic attitudes and performance of school-aged children. *School Psychology Review,* 1980, *9,* 319–335.

Hoffman, L. W. Maternal employment and the young child. In M. Perlmutter (Ed.), *Parent–child interaction and parent–child relations in child development, The Minnesota Symposia on child development.* Hillsdale, N.J.: Lawrence Erlbaum. 1984. (a)

Hoffman, L. W. Work, family, and the socialization of the child. In R. D. Parke (Ed.), *The review of child development research,* Vol. 7. Chicago: University of Chicago Press, 1984. (b)

Hollowell, P. G. *The lorry driver.* London: Routledge & Kegan Paul, 1968.

Holmstrom, L. *The two-career family.* Cambridge, Mass.: Schenkman, 1972.

Hood, J. C. *Becoming a two-job family.* New York: Praeger, 1983.

Hood, J. C., & Golden, S. Beating time/making time: The impact of work scheduling on men's family roles. *The Family Coordinator*, 1979, *28*, 575–582.

House, J. S. *Occupational stress and the mental and physical health of factory workers*. Ann Arbor, Mich.: Survey Research Center, Institute for Social Research, 1980.

Houseknecht, S. K., & Macke, A. S. Combining marriage and career: The marital adjustment of professional women. *Journal of Marriage and the Family*, 1981, *43*, 651–661.

Howell, J. T. *Hard living on Clay Street*. Garden City, N.Y.: Doubleday, 1973.

Hughes, E. C. *Men and their work*. Glencoe, Ill.: Free Press, 1958.

Hunt, J. G., & Hunt, L. L. Dual-career families: Vanguard of the future or residue of the past. In J. Aldous (Ed.), *Two paychecks: Life in dual-earner families*. Beverly Hills, Calif.: Sage, 1982.

Hunter, E. J. *Families under the flag*. New York: Praeger, 1982.

Hunter, E. J. & Nice, D. S. (Eds.) *Military families*. New York: Praeger, 1978.

Iglehart, A. P. *Married women and work*. Lexington, Mass.: Lexington Books, 1979.

Jackson, S. E., & Maslach, C. After-effects of job-related stress: Families as victims. *Journal of Occupational Behavior*, 1982, *3*, 63–77.

Jahoda, M. The impact of unemployment in the 1930's and 1970's. *Bulletin of the British Psychological Society*, 1979, *32*, 309–314.

Jahoda, M., Lazarsfield, P., & Zeisel, H. *Marienthal, the sociography of an unemployed community*. Chicago: Aldine, Atherton, 1971.

Job, B. C. More public services spur growth in government employment. *Monthly Labor Review*, 1978, *101*(9), 3–7.

Johnson, B. Women who head families, 1970–77: Their numbers rose, income lagged. *Monthly Labor Review*, 1978, *101*(2), 32–37.

Jorgensen, S. Socioeconomic rewards and perceived marital quality: A reexamination. *Journal of Marriage and the Family*, 1979, *41*, 825–835.

Kabanoff, B. Work and nonwork: A review of models, methods, and findings. *Psychological Bulletin*, 1980, *88*, 60–77.

Kagan, J., Kearsley, R. B., & Zelazo, P. R. *Infancy: Its place in human development*. Cambridge: Harvard University Press, 1978.

Kamerman, S. B. Child care and family benefits: Policies in six industrialized countries. *Monthly Labor Review*, 1980, *103*(11), 23–28. (a)

Kamerman, S. B. *Parenting in an unresponsive society: Managing work and family life*. New York: Macmillan, 1980. (b)

Kamerman, S. B., & Kahn, A. J. (Eds.). *Family policy: Government and families in fourteen countries*. New York: Columbia University Press, 1978.

Kamerman, S. B., & Kahn, A. J. *Child care, family benefits and working parents*. New York: Columbia University Press, 1981.

Kanter, R. M. *Work and family in the United States: A critical review and agenda for research and policy*. New York: Russell Sage, 1977.

Kanter, R. M. Families, family processes and economic life: Toward systematic analysis of social historical research. In J. Demos & S. S. Boocock (Eds.), *Turning points*. Chicago: University of Chicago Press, 1978.

Kantor, D., & Lehr, W. *Inside the family*. San Francisco: Jossey-Bass, 1975.

Kanungo, R. N. *Work alienation: An integrative approach*. New York: Praeger, 1982.

Karasek, R. J. Job demands, job decision latitude and mental strain: Implications for job redesign. *Administrative Science Quarterly*, 1979, *24*, 285–301.

Karasek, R., Baker, D., Marxer, F., Ahlbom, A., & Theorell, T. Job decision latitude, job demands and cardiovascular disease: A prospective study of Swedish men. *American Journal of Public Health*, 1981, *71*, 694–705.

Kasl, S. V. Epidemiological contributions to the study of work stress. In C. L. Cooper & R. Payne (Eds.), *Stress at work*. New York: Wiley, 1978.

Katz, M. H., & Piotrkowski, C. S. Correlates of family role strain among employed black women. *Family Relations*, 1983, *32*, 331–339.

Keith, P. M., & Schafer, R. B. Role strain and depression in two-job families. *Family Relations*, 1980, *29*, 483–488.

Kemper, T. D., & Reichler, M. L. Work integration, marital satisfaction, and conjugal power. *Human Relations*, 1976, *29*, 929–944.

Keniston, K. *All our children: The American family under pressure*. New York: Harcourt Brace Jovanovich, 1977.

Kessler, R. C., & McRae, J. A., Jr. The effects of wives' employment on the mental health of married men and women. *American Sociological Review*, 1982, *47*, 216–227.

Kilpatrick, A. C. Job changes in dual-career families: Danger or opportunity? *Family Relations*, 1982, *31*, 363–378.

King, K., McIntyre, J., & Axelson, L. J. Adolescents' views of maternal employment as a threat to the marital relationship. *Journal of Marriage and the Family*, 1968, *30*, 633–637.

Kirschner, B. F., & Walum, L. R. Two-location families. *Alternative Lifestyles*, 1978, *1*, 513–525.

Klenke-Hamel, K. Causal determinants of job satisfaction in dual career couples. In H. J. Bernardin (Ed.), *Women in the work force*. New York: Praeger, 1982.

Kohn, M. L. *Class and conformity*. Homewood, Ill.: Dorsey Press, 1969.

Kohn, M. L. *Class and conformity: A study in values* (2nd ed.). Chicago: University of Chicago Press, 1977.

Kohn, M. L. The effects of social class on parental values and practices. In D. Reiss & H. Hoffman (Eds.), *The American family: Dying or developing?* New York: Plenum Press, 1979.

Kohn, M. L. Job complexity and adult personality. In J. M. Smelser & E. H. Erikson (Eds.), *Themes of work and love in adulthood*. Cambridge: Harvard University Press, 1980.

Kohn, M. L. Personality, occupation and social stratification: A frame of reference. In D. J. Treiman & R. V. Robinson (Eds.), *Research in social stratification and mobility*, Vol. 1. Greenwich, Conn.: JAI Press, 1981.

Kohn, M. L., & Schooler, C. Occupational experience and psychological functioning: An assessment of reciprocal effects. *American Sociological Review*, 1973, *38*, 97–118.

Kohn, M. L., & Schooler, C. The reciprocal effects of the substantive complexity of work and intellectual flexibility: A longitudinal assessment. *American Journal of Sociology*, 1978, *84*, 24–52.

Komarovsky, M. *The unemployed man and his family*. New York: Dryden, 1940.

Komarovsky, M. *Blue collar marriage*. New York: Random House, 1962.

Komarovsky, M. Cultural contradictions and sex roles: The masculine case. *American Journal of Sociology*, 1973, *78*, 873–884.

Lamb, M. E. Maternal employment and child development: A review. In M. E. Lamb (Ed.), *Nontraditional families: Parenting and child development*. Hillsdale, N.J.: Erlbaum, 1982.

Land, H., & Parker, R. United Kingdom. In S. B. Kamerman & A. J. Kahn (Eds.), *Family policy: Government and families in fourteen countries*. New York: Columbia University Press, 1978.

Landy, F., Rosenberg, B. G., & Sutton-Smith, B. The effects of limited father absence on cognitive development. *Child Development*, 1969, *40*, 941–944.

Lasch, C. *Haven in a heartless world: The family besieged*. New York: Basic Books, 1977.

Laslett, P. *The world we have lost*. New York: Scribner's, 1965.

Laws, J. L. A feminist review of the marital adjustment literature: The

Rape of the Locke. *Journal of Marriage and the Family*, 1971, *33*, 483–516.

Lerner, G. The lady and the mill girl: Changes in the status of women in the age of Jackson, 1800–1840. In N. F. Cott & E. H. Pleck (Eds.), *A heritage of her own*. New York: Simon & Schuster, 1979.

Lerner, J. V., & Galambos, N. L. Maternal role satisfaction, mother-child interaction, and child temperament: A process model. *Developmental Psychology*, 1985, *21*, 1157–1164.

Liebow, E. *Tally's Corner: A study of Negro streetcorner men*. Boston: Little, Brown, 1967.

Liem, G. R., & Liem, J. H. Social support and stress: Some general issues and their application to the problem of unemployment. In L. Ferman & J. Gordus (Eds.), *Mental health and the economy*. Kalamazoo, Mich.: Upjohn Institute, 1979.

Liem, R., & Rayman, P. Health and social costs of employment. *American Psychologist*, 1982, *37*, 1116–1123.

Liker, J. K., & Elder, G. H., Jr. Economic hardship and marital relations in the 1930's. *American Sociological Review*, 1983, *48*, 343–359.

Locksley, A. On the effects of wives' employment on marital adjustment and companionship. *Journal of Marriage and the Family*, 1980, *42*, 337–346.

Locksley, A. Social class and marital attitudes and behavior. *Journal of Marriage and the Family*, 1982, *44*, 427–440.

Lodahl, T. M. Patterns of job attitudes in two assembly technologies. *Administrative Science Quarterly*, 1964, *39*, 482–519.

Lodahl, T. M., & Kejner, M. The definition and measurement of job involvement. *Journal of Applied Psychology*, 1965, *49*, 24–33.

Lopata, H. Z. *Occupation: Housewife*. New York: Oxford University Press, 1971.

Lueptow, L. B., McClendon, M. J., & McKeon, J. W. Father's occupation and son's personality: Findings and questions for the emerging linkage hypothesis. *Sociological Quarterly*, 1979, *20*, 463–475.

Lynn, D. B., & Sawrey, W. L. The effects of father absence on Norwegian boys and girls. *Journal of Abnormal and Social Psychology*, 1959, *59*, 258–262.

Maccoby, E. Effects upon children of their mothers' outside employment. In *Work in the lives of married women*. Proceedings of the National Manpower Council. New York: Columbia University Press, 1958.

Machlowitz, M. *Workaholics, living with them, working with them*. Reading, Mass.: Addison-Wesley, 1980.

Macke, A. S., Bohrnstedt, G. W., & Bernstein, I. N. Housewives' self-esteem and their husbands' success: The myth of vicarious involvement. *Journal of Marriage and the Family*, 1979, *41*, 51–58.

Margolis, L. H., & Farran, D. Unemployment: The health consequences in children. *North Carolina Medical Journal*, 1981, *42*, 849–850.

Mason, K. O., Czajka, J., & Arber, S. Change in U.S. women's sex-role attitudes, 1964–75. *American Sociological Review*, 1976, *41*, 573–596.

Maynard, P., Maynard, N., McCubbin, H. I., & Shao, D. Family life and the police profession: Coping patterns wives employ in managing job stress and family environment. *Family Relations*, 1980, *29*, 495–501.

McCord, J., McCord, W., & Thurber, E. Effects of maternal employment on lower-class boys. *Journal of Abnormal and Social Psychology*, 1963, *67*, 177–182.

McCubbin, H. I. Integrating coping behavior in family stress theory. *Journal of Marriage and the Family*, 1979, *41*, 237–244.

McCubbin, H. I., & Patterson, J. M. Family adaptation to crises. In H. I. McCubbin, A. E. Cauble, & J. M. Patterson (Eds.), *Family stress, coping, and social support*. Springfield, Ill.: Charles C Thomas, 1982.

McCubbin, H. I., Joy, C. B., Cauble, A. E., Comeau, J. K., Patterson, J. M., & Needle, R. H. Family stress and coping: A decade review. *Journal of Marriage and the Family*, 1980, *42*, 855–871.

McCubbin, H. I., Dahl, B. B., & Hunter, E. J. Research on the military

family: A review. In H. I. McCubbin, B. B. Dahl, & E. J. Hunter (Eds.), *Families in the military system*. Beverly Hills: Sage, 1976.

McDonald, G. W. Family power: The assessment of a decade of theory and research, 1970–1979. *Journal of Marriage and the Family*, 1980, *42*, 841–854.

McKinley, D. G. *Social class and family life*. New York: Free Press, 1964.

Meissner, M., Humphreys, E., Meis, C., & Scheu, J. No exit for wives: Sexual division of labor and the cumulation of household demands. *Canadian Review of Sociology and Anthropology*, 1975, *12*, 424–439.

Merton, R. K. Bureaucratic structure and personality. In R. K. Merton, A. P. Gray, B. Hockey, & H. C. Selvin (Eds.), *Reader in bureaucracy*. Glencoe, Ill.: Free Press, 1952.

Miller, B. C., Rollins, B. C., & Thomas, D. L. On methods of studying marriages and families. *Journal of Marriage and the Family*, 1982, *44*, 851–872.

Miller, D. R., & Swanson, G. E. *The changing American parent*. New York: Wiley, 1958.

Miller, J., Schooler, C., Kohn, M. L., & Miller, K. A. Women and work: The psychological effects of occupational conditions. *American Journal of Sociology*, 1979, *85*, 66–94.

Model, S. Housework by husbands. *Journal of Family Issues*, 1981, *2*, 225–237.

Moen, P. Family impact of the 1975 recession: Duration of unemployment. *Journal of Marriage and the Family*, 1979, *41*, 561–572.

Moen, P. Developing family indicators: Financial hardship, a case in point. *Journal of Family Issues*, 1980, *1*, 5–30.

Moen, P. Preventing financial hardship: Coping strategies of families of the unemployed. In H. I. McCubbin, A. E. Cauble, & J. M. Patterson (Eds.), *Family, stress, coping, and social support*. Springfield, Ill.: Charles C. Thomas, 1982.

Moore, K., Spain, D., & Bianchi, S. Working wives and mothers. *Marriage and Family Review*, 1984, *7*, (3/4), 77–98.

Moore, K. A., & Sawhill, I. V. Implications of women's employment for home and family life. In J. M. Kreps (Ed.), *Women and the American economy*. Englewood Cliffs, N.J.: Prentice-Hall, 1976.

Morgan, W. R., Alwin, D. F., & Griffin, L. J. Social origins, parental values, and the transmission of inequality. *American Journal of Sociology*, 1979, *85*, 156–166.

Morse, N. C., & Weiss, R. The function and meaning of work and the job. *American Sociological Review*, 1955, *20*, 191–198.

Mortimer, J. T. Occupational value socialization in business and professional families. *Sociology of Work and Occupations*, 1975, *2*, 29–53.

Mortimer, J. T. Social class, work and family: Some implications of the father's occupation for familial relationships and son's career decisions. *Journal of Marriage and the Family*, 1976, *38*, 241–256.

Mortimer, J. T. Occupation-family linkages as perceived by men in the early stages of professional and managerial careers. *Research in the interweave of social roles: Women and men*, Vol. 1. Greenwich, Conn.: JAI Press, 1980.

Mortimer, J. T., & Kumka, D. A further examination of the "occupational linkage hypothesis." *Sociological Quarterly*, 1982, *23*, 3–16.

Mortimer, J. T., & London, J. The varying linkages of work and family. In P. Voydanoff (Ed.), *Work and family: Changing roles of men and women*. Palo Alto, Calif.: Mayfield, 1983.

Mortimer, J. T., & Lorence, J. Occupational experience and the self-concept: A longitudinal study. *Social Psychology Quarterly*, 1979, *42*, 307–323.

Mortimer, J. T., Hall, R., & Hill, R. Husbands' occupational attributes as constraints on wives' employment. *Sociology of Work and Occupations*, 1978, *7*, 285–313.

Moss, P. Parents at work. In P. Moss & N. Fonda (Eds.), *Work and the family*. London: Temple Smith, 1980.

Mott, F. L., & Moore, S. F. The causes of marital disruption among young American women: An interdisciplinary perspective. *Journal of Marriage and the Family,* 1979, *41,* 355–365.

Mott, P. E., Mann, F. C., McLoughlin, Q., & Warwick, D. P. *Shift work: The social, psychological, and physical consequences.* Ann Arbor: University of Michigan Press, 1965.

National Commission on Working Women. *National survey of working women: Perceptions, problems, and prospects.* National Manpower Institute, Washington, D.C., 1979.

Near, J. P., Rice, R. W., & Hunt, R. G. The relationship between work and nonwork domains: A review of empirical research. *Academy of Management Review,* 1980, *5,* 415–429.

Neugarten, B. L. (Ed.). *Middle age and aging: A reader in social psychology.* Chicago: University of Chicago Press, 1968.

Nickols, S. Y., & Metzen, E. J. Impact of wives' employment upon husbands' housework. *Journal of Family Issues,* 1982, *3,* 199–216.

Nieva, V. F., & Gutek, G. A. *Women and work: A psychological perspective.* New York: Praeger, 1981.

Nock, S. L. The family life cycle: Empirical or conceptual tool? *Journal of Marriage and the Family,* 1979, *41,* 15–26.

Nollen, S. *New patterns of work.* Scarsdale, N.Y.: Work in America Institute, 1979.

Norton, A. J., & Glick, P. C. Marital instability in America: Past, present and future. In G. Levinger & O. C. Moles (Eds.), *Divorce and separation.* New York: Basic Books, 1979.

Nye, F. I. Husband-wife relationship. In L. W. Hoffman & F. I. Nye (Eds.), *Working mothers.* San Francisco: Jossey-Bass, 1974.

Oakley, A. *The sociology of housework.* New York: Pantheon, 1974. (a)

Oakley, A. *Women's work.* New York: Pantheon, 1974. (b)

Olson, D. H., & McCubbin, H. I. Circumplex model of marital and family systems: V. Application to family stress and crisis intervention. In H. I. McCubbin, A. E. Cauble, & J. M. Patterson (Eds.), *Family stress, coping, and social support.* Springfield, Ill.: Charles C Thomas, 1982.

Olson, D. H., Sprenkle, D. H., & Russell, C. S. Circumplex model of marital and family systems: I. Cohesion and adaptability dimensions, family types, and clinical applications. *Family Process,* 1979, *18,* 3–28.

Olson, D. H., Russell, C. S., & Sprenkle, D. H. Circumplex model of marital and family systems: VI. Theoretical update. *Family Process,* 1983, *22,* 69–83.

Oppenheimer, V. K. Demographic influence on female employment and the status of women. In J. Huber (Ed.), *Changing women in a changing society.* Chicago: University of Chicago Press, 1973.

Oppenheimer, V. K. The life-cycle squeeze: The interaction of men's occupational and family life cycles. *Demography,* 1974, *11,* 227–245.

Oppenheimer, V. K. The sociology of women's economic role in the family. *American Sociological Review,* 1977, *42,* 387–405.

Oppenheimer, V. K. Structural sources of economic pressure for wives to work: An analytic framework. *Journal of Family History,* 1979, *4,* 177–197.

Orden, S. R., & Bradburn, N. M. Working wives and marriage happiness. *American Journal of Sociology,* 1969, *74,* 391–407.

Orpen, C. Work and nonwork satisfaction: A causal-correlational analysis. *Journal of Applied Psychology,* 1978, *63,* 530–532.

Otto, L. B. Class and status in family research. *Journal of Marriage and the Family,* 1975, *37,* 315–332.

Owen, M. T., Easterbrooks, M. A., Chase-Lansdale, L., & Goldberg, W. A. The relation between maternal employment status and the stability of attachments to mother and to father. *Child Development,* 1984, *55,* 1894–1901.

Pahl, R. E. Employment, work and the domestic division of labour. *International Journal of Urban and Regional Research,* 1980, *4*(1), 1–19.

Pahl, J. M., & Pahl, R. E. *Managers and their wives.* London: Penguin, 1971.

Papanek, H. Men, women and work: Reflections on the two person-career. *American Journal of Sociology,* 1973, *78,* 852–872.

Parker, S. R. Industry and the family. In S. R. Parker, R. K. Brown, J. Child, & M. A. Smith (Eds.), *The sociology of industry.* London: Allen & Unwin, 1967.

Parsons, T. The social structure of the family. In R. N. Anshen (Ed.), *The family: Its function and destiny.* New York: Harper, 1949.

Parry, G., & Warr, P. The measurement of mothers' work attitudes. *Journal of Occupational Psychology,* 1980, *53,* 245–252.

Pearlin, L. I., & Lieberman, M. A. Social sources of emotional distress. *Research in community and mental health,* Vol. 1. Greenwich, Conn.: JAI Press, 1979.

Pedersen, F. A., Cain, R. L., Jr., Zaslow, M. J., & Anderson, B. J. Variation in infant experience associated with alternative family roles. In L. Laosa & I. Sigel (Eds.), *Families as learning environments for children.* New York: Plenum Press, 1982.

Pendleton, B. F., Poloma, M. M., & Garland, T. N. Scales for investigation of the dual-career family. *Journal of Marriage and the Family,* 1980, *42,* 269–276.

Peterson, E. T. The impact of maternal employment on the mother-daughter relationship. *Marriage and Family Living,* 1961, *23,* 355–361.

Philliber, W. W., & Hiller, D. V. Relative occupational attainments of spouses and later changes in marriage and wife's work experience. *Journal of Marriage and the Family,* 1983, *45,* 161–170.

Piotrkowski, C. S. *Work and the family system.* New York: Macmillan, 1979.

Piotrkowski, C. S. Impact of women's work on family health. In B. G. F. Cohen (Ed.), *The human aspect of office automation.* Amsterdam, Netherlands: Elsevier, 1984.

Piotrkowski, C. S., & Crits-Christoph, P. Women's jobs and family adjustment. *Journal of Family Issues,* 1981, *2,* 126–147.

Piotrkowski, C. S., & Gornick, L. The impact of work-related separations on children and families. In J. Bloom-Feshbach & S. Bloom-Feshbach (Eds.). *The psychology of separation.* San Francisco: Jossey-Bass, 1986.

Piotrkowski, C. S., & Katz, M. H. Indirect socialization of children: The effects of mothers' jobs on academic behaviors. *Child Development,* 1982, *53,* 1520–1529. (a)

Piotrkowski, C. S., & Katz, M. H. Women's work and personal relations in the family. In P. W. Berman & E. R. Ramey (Eds.) *Women: A developmental perspective.* NIH Publications, No 82-2298, 1982. (b)

Piotrkowski, C. S., & Katz, M. H. Work experience and family relations among working-class and lower middle-class families. In H. Z. Lopata & J. H. Pleck (Eds.), *Research in the interweave of social roles,* Vol. 3: *Families and jobs.* Greenwich, Conn.: JAI Press, 1983.

Piotrkowski, C. S., & Repetti, R. L. Dual-earner families. *Marriage and Family Review,* 1984, *7,* (3/4) 99–124.

Piotrkowski, C. S., & Stark, E. *Job stress and children's mental health: An ecological study.* Final report to the W. T. Grant Foundation, 1984.

Piotrkowski, C. S., Stark, E., & Burbank, M. Young women at work: Implications for individual and family functioning. *Occupational Health Nursing,* 1983, *31,* (11) 24–29.

Pleck, E. Two worlds in one: Work and family. *Journal of Social History,* 1976, *10,* 178–195.

Pleck, J. H. The work-family role system. *Social Problems,* 1977, *24,* 417–427.

Pleck, J. H. Men's family work: Three perspectives and some new data. *The Family Coordinator,* 1979, *28,* 481–488.

Pleck, J. H. Husbands' paid work and family roles: Current research issues. In H. Z. Lopata & J. H. Pleck (Eds.), *Research in the inter-*

weave of social roles, Vol. 3. *Families and jobs.* Greenwich, Conn.: JAI Press, 1983.

Pleck, J. H., & Rustad, M. *Husbands' and wives' time in family work and paid work in the 1975–76 study of time use.* Wellesley, Mass.: Wellesley College Center for Research on Women, 1980.

Pleck, J. H., & Staines, G. L. Work schedules and work-family conflict in two-earner couples. In J. Aldous (Ed.), *Two paychecks: Life in dual-earner families.* Beverly Hills, Calif.: Sage, 1982.

Pleck, J. H., Staines, G. L., & Lang, L. *Work and family life: First reports on work-family interference and workers' formal child care arrangements, from the 1977 quality of employment survey.* Wellesley, Mass.: Wellesley College Center for Research on Women, 1978.

Pleck, J. H., Staines, G. L., & Lang, L. Conflicts between work and family life. *Monthly Labor Review*, 1980, *103*(3), 29–32.

Poloma, M. M. Role conflict and the married professional woman. In C. Safilios-Rothschild (Ed.), *Toward a sociology of women.* Lexington, Mass.: Xerox Publishing, 1972.

Poloma, M. M., Pendleton, B. F., & Garland, T. N. Reconsidering the dual-career marriage. *Journal of Family Issues*, 1981, *2*, 205–224.

Portner, J. *Impacts of work on the family.* Minnesota Council on Family Relations, 1978.

Powell, D., & Driscoll, P. Middle-class professionals face unemployment. *Society*, 1973, *10*, 18–25.

Presser, H. B., & Cain, V. S. Shift work among dual-earner couples with children. *Science*, 1983, *219*, 876–879.

Propper, A. M. The relationship of maternal employment to adolescent roles, activities, and parental relationships. *Journal of Marriage and the Family*, 1972, *34*, 417–421.

Quinn, R. P., Staines, G. L., & McCullough, M. R. *Job satisfaction: Is there a trend?* U.S. Department of Labor, Manpower Research Monograph No. 3. Washington: U.S. Government Printing Office, 1974.

Rabinowitz, S., & Hall, D. T. Organizational research on job involvement. *Psychological Bulletin*, 1977, *84*, 265–288.

Rallings, E. M., & Nye, F. I. Wife-mother employment, family and society. In W. R. Burr, R. Hill, F. I. Nye, & I. Reiss (Eds.), *Contemporary theories about the family*, Vol. 1. New York: Macmillan, 1979.

Rapoport, R., & Rapoport, R. N. Work and family in contemporary society. *American Sociological Review*, 1965, *30*, 381–394.

Rapoport, R., & Rapoport, R. N. The dual-career family: A variant pattern and social change. *Human Relations*, 1969, *22*, 3–30.

Rapoport, R., & Rapoport, R. N. *Dual-career families.* Baltimore: Penguin, 1971.

Rapoport, R., & Rapoport, R. N. *Dual-career families re-examined.* New York: Harper Colophon, 1977.

Rapoport, R., & Rapoport, R. N. (Eds.). *Working couples.* New York: Harper & Row, 1978.

Rapoport, R., & Rapoport, R. N. The impact of work on the family. In P. Moss & N. Fonda (Eds.), *Work and the family.* London: Temple Smith, 1980. (a)

Rapoport, R., & Rapoport, R. N. Three generations of dual-career family research. In F. Pepitone-Rockwell (Ed.), *Dual-career couples.* Beverly Hills, Calif.: Sage, 1980. (b)

Rapoport, R., & Rapoport, R. N. The next generation in dual-earner family research. In J. M. Aldous (Ed.), *Two paychecks: Life in dual-earner families.* Beverly Hills, Calif.: Sage, 1982.

Reiser, M. Some organizational stresses on policemen. *Journal of Police Science and Administration*, 1974, *2*, 156–159.

Renne, K. S. Correlates of dissatisfaction in marriage. *Journal of Marriage and the Family*, 1970, 32, 54–67.

Renshaw, J. R. An exploration of the dynamics of the overlapping worlds of work and family life. *Family Process*, 1976, *15*, 143–165.

Rice, R. W., Near, J. P., & Hunt, R. G. The job-satisfaction/life-satisfaction relationship: A review of empirical research. *Basic and Applied Social Psychology*, 1980, *1*, 37–64.

Richardson, J. G. Wife occupational superiority and marital troubles: An examination of the hypothesis. *Journal of Marriage and the Family*, 1979, *41*, 63–72.

Ridley, C. A. Exploring the impact of work satisfaction and involvement on marital interaction when both partners are employed. *Journal of Marriage and the Family*, 1973, *35*, 229–237.

Robinson, J. P. Housework technology and household work. In S. F. Berk (Ed.), *Women and household labor.* Beverly Hills, Calif.: Sage, 1980.

Rodgers, R. H. Toward a theory of family development. *Journal of Marriage and the Family*, 1964, *26*, 262–270.

Rodman, H. Marital power and the theory of resource in cultural context. *Journal of Comparative Family Studies*, 1972, *3*, 50–69.

Ross, H. L., & Sawhill, I. V. *Time of transition: The growth of families headed by women.* Washington, D.C.: Urban Institute, 1975.

Roy, P. Adolescent roles: Rural-urban differentials. In F. I. Nye & L. W. Hoffman (Eds.), *The employed mother in America.* Chicago: Rand McNally, 1963.

Rubin, L. B. *Worlds of pain.* New York: Basic Books, 1976.

Rutter, M. Social-emotional consequenses of day care for pre-school children. In E. Zigler & E. Gordon (Eds.), *Day care: Scientific and social policy issues.* Boston: Auburn, 1982.

Saal, E. F. Job involvement: A multi-variate approach. *Journal of Applied Psychology*, 1978, *63*, 53–61.

Safilios-Rothschild, C. The influence of the wife's degree of work commitment upon some aspects of family organization and dynamics. *Journal of Marriage and the Family*, 1970, *32*, 681–691. (a)

Safilios-Rothschild, C. The study of family power structure: A review, 1960–1969. *Journal of Marriage and the Family*, 1970, *32*, 539–552. (b)

Safilios-Rothschild, C. Dual linkages between the occupational and family systems: A macrosociological analysis. *Signs*, 1976, *1*, 51–60.

Safilios-Rothschild, C., & Dijkers, M. Handling unconventional asymmetries. In R. Rapoport & R. N. Rapoport (Eds.), *Working couples.* New York: Harper & Row, 1978.

Scanzoni, J. H. *Opportunity and the family.* New York: Free Press, 1970.

Scanzoni, J. H. Sex roles, economic factors and marital solidarity in black and white marriages. *Journal of Marriage and the Family*, 1975, *37*, 130–144.

Scanzoni, J. H. *Sex roles, women's work, and marital conflict.* Lexington, Mass.: D. C. Heath, 1978.

Scanzoni, J., & Polonko, K. A conceptual approach to explicit marital negotiation. *Journal of Marriage and the Family*, 1980, *42*, 31–44.

Scott, J. W., & Tilly, L. A. Women's work and the family in nineteenth-century Europe. In C. E. Rosenberg (Ed.), *The family in history.* Philadelphia: University of Pennsylvania Press, 1975.

Seidenberg, R. *Corporate wives—Corporate casualties?* New York: Doubleday, 1975.

Sekscenski, E. S. The health services industry, a decade of expansion. *Monthly Labor Review*, 1981, *104*(5), 9–16.

Shinn, M. Father absence and children's cognitive development. *Psychological Bulletin*, 1978, *85*, 295–324.

Silverstein, P., & Srb, J. H. Flexitime: Where, when, and how? *Key Issues: Background reports on current topics and trends in labor-management*, No. 24. Ithaca, N.Y.: Cornell University, 1979.

Simpson, I. H., & England, P. Conjugal work roles and marital solidarity. *Journal of Family Issues*, 1981, *2*, 180–204.

Skinner, D. A. Dual-career family stress and coping: A literature review. *Family Relations*, 1980, *29*, 473–481.

Skinner, D. A. The stressors and coping patterns of dual-career families. In H. I. McCubbin, A. E. Cauble, & J. M. Patterson (Eds.), *Family stress, coping, and social support.* Springfield, Ill.: Charles C Thomas, 1982.

Smelser, N. *Social change in the industrial revolution: An application of theory to the Lancashire cotton industry 1770–1840.* London: Routledge, 1959.

Spanier, G. B., Sauer, W., & Larzelere, R. An empirical evaluation of the family life cycle. *Journal of Marriage and the Family,* 1979, *41,* 27–38.

Spence, J. T., & Helmreich, R. L. *Masculinity and Femininity: Their Psychological dimensions, correlates, and antecedents.* Austin: University of Texas Press, 1978.

Spitz, R. A. Hospitalism. In R. L. Coser (Ed.), *The family: Its structure and functions.* New York: St. Martin's Press, 1964.

Spreitzer, E., Snyder, E. E., & Larson, D. L. Multiple roles and psychological well-being. *Sociological Focus,* 1979, *12*(2), 141–148.

Staines, G. L., & Pleck, J. H. *The impact of work schedules on the family.* Ann Arbor: Survey Research Center, 1983.

Staines, G. L., Pleck, J. H., Shepard, L. J., & O'Connor, P. O. Wives' employment status and marital adjustment. *Psychology of Women Quarterly,* 1978, *3,* 90–120.

Steinberg, L. D., Catalano, R., & Dooley, D. Economic antecedents of child abuse. *Child Development,* 1981, *52,* 975–985.

Steinmetz, S. K. Occupational environment in relation to physical punishment and dogmatism. In S. K. Steinmetz & M. Strauss (Eds.), *Violence in the family.* New York: Harper & Row, 1974.

Stuckey, M. F., McGhee, P. E., & Bell, N. J. Parent-child interaction: The influence of maternal employment. *Developmental Psychology,* 1982, *18,* 635–644.

Sussman, M. R. Needed research of the employed mother. *Marriage and Family Living,* 1961, *23,* 368–373.

Szinovacz, M. E. Female retirement: Effects on spousal roles and marital adjustment. *Journal of Family Issues,* 1980, *1,* 423–440.

Szinovacz, M. E. Changing family roles and interaction. *Marriage and Family Review,* 1984, (3/4), 163–201.

Taylor, M. G., & Hartley, S. F. The two-person career: A classic example. *Sociology of Work and Occupations,* 1975, *2,* 354–372.

Thomas, L. E., McCabe, E., & Berry, J. E. Unemployment and family stress: A reassessment. *Family Relations,* 1980, *29,* 517–524.

Thompson, E. P. *The making of the English working class.* New York: Vintage, 1966.

Thompson, R. A., Lamb, M. E., & Estes, D. Stability of infant-mother attachment and its relationship to changing life circumstances in an unselected middle-class sample. *Child Development,* 1982, *53,* 144–148.

Tilly, L. A. Individual lives and family strategies in the French proletariat. *Journal of Family History,* 1979, *4,* 137–152.

Turk, J. L., & Bell, N. W. Measuring power in families. *Journal of Marriage and the Family,* 1972, *34,* 215–222.

Vanek, J. Time spent in housework. *Scientific American,* 1974, *231,* 116–120.

Vaughn, B. E., Gove, F. L., & Egeland, B. The relationship between out-of-home care and the quality of infant-mother attachment in an economically disadvantaged population. *Child Development,* 1980, *51,* 1203–1214.

Veroff, J., & Feld, S. *Marriage and work in America: A study of motives and roles.* New York: Van Nostrand Reinhold, 1970.

Voydanoff, P. *Work-family life cycles.* Paper presented at the annual workshop on Theory Construction and Research Methodology, National Council on Family Relations, October 1980. (a)

Voydanoff, P. Work roles as stressors in corporate families. *Family Relations,* 1980, *29,* 489–494. (b)

Voydanoff, P. Unemployment and family stress. In H. Z. Lopata & J. H. Pleck (Eds.), *Research in the interweave of social roles,* Vol. 3: *Families and jobs.* Greenwich, Conn.. JAI Press, 1983. (a)

Voydanoff, P. Unemployment: Family strategies for adaptation. In C. R. Figley & H. I. McCubbin (Eds.), *Stress and the family,* Vol. 2: *Coping with catastrophe.* New York: Bruner/Mazel, 1983. (b)

Voydanoff, P., & Kelly, R. F. Determinants of work-related family problems among employed parents. *Journal of Marriage and the Family,* 1984, *46,* 881–892.

Waite, L. J. U.S. women at work. *Population Bulletin,* 1981, 36(2), 1–44.

Waldman, E., Grossman, A. S., Hayghe, H., & Johnson, B. L. Working mothers in the 1970's: A look at the statistics. *Monthly Labor Review,* 1979, *102*(10), 39–49.

Walker, K. E. Household work time: Its implication for family decisions. *Journal of Home Economics,* 1973, *65,* 7–11.

Walker, K. E., & Woods, M. E. *Time use: A measure of household production of family goods and services.* Washington, D.C.: American Home Economics Association, 1976.

Walker, L. S., & Wallston, B. S. Social adaptation: A review of dual earner family literature. In L. L'Abate (Ed.), *Handbook of family psychology and therapy.* 2. Homewood, Ill.: Dorsey, 1985.

Wattenberg, E. Family day care: Out of the shadows and into the spotlight. *Marriage and Family Review,* 1980, *3,* 35–62.

Wilensky, H. L. The uneven distribution of leisure: The impact of economic growth on "free time". *Social Problems,* 1961 (Summer), 32–54.

Wilensky, H. L. The moonlighter: A product of relative deprivation. *Industrial Relations,* 1963, *3,* 105–124.

Winett, R. A., & Neale, M. S. Modifying settings as a strategy for permanent, preventive behavior change: Flexible work schedules and the quality of family life. In P. Karoly & J. J. Steffan (Eds.), *Improving the long-term effects of psychotherapy.* New York: Gardner Press, 1980. (a)

Winett, R. A., & Neale, M. S. Results of experimental study on flexitime and family life. *Monthly Labor Review,* 1980, *103*(11), 29–38. (b)

Woods, M. B. The unsupervised child of the working mother. *Developmental Psychology,* 1972, *6,* 14–25.

Working Family Project. Parenting. In R. Rapoport & R. N. Rapoport (Eds.), *Working couples.* New York: Harper & Row, 1978.

Yarrow, M. R., Scott, P., DeLeeuw, L., & Heinig, C. Child-rearing in families of working and non-working mothers. *Sociometry,* 1962, *25,* 122–140.

Ybarra, L. When wives work: The impact on the Chicano family. *Journal of Marriage and the Family,* 1982, *44,* 169–178.

Yogev, S. Do professional women have egalitarian marital relationships? *Journal of Marriage and the Family,* 1981, *43,* 865–871.

Young, M., & Willmott, P. *The symmetrical family.* New York: Pantheon, 1973.

Zaslow, M., Pedersen, F. A., Suwalsky, J., & Rabinovich, B. *Maternal employment and parent-infant interaction.* Paper presented at the Biennial Meeting of the Society for Research in Child Development, Detroit, 1983.

CHAPTER 11

Families and Religions

Teresa Donati Marciano

Introduction

The family until now has been the social institution most closely linked to religion. Yet, the extent and direction of these ties in the modern United States have been only sporadically examined. Explanations for what religion does in family and society are found in each of the three major theoretical orientations in sociology—structural-functionalism, conflict theory, and interactionism—as well as in newer world-system theory.[1] The study of religion in the past 30 years, however, has been marked by a shift from structural to personal levels of meaning, from Parsonian to interactionist frameworks. Luckmann's "invisible religion" (1967), which locates the functions of religion in personal meanings, and Bellah's "civil religion" (1967), the cultural backdrop of religious symbols providing new legitimation for American unity, are major instances of the new sociological approach. These have, however, been challenged for their sufficiency. Lemert (1975), for example, questioned their assumptions, in which he saw a failure to elaborate person–structure relationships. Lemert saw the need to hold onto person-and-meaning, "but now in a necessary dialectical relationship to *social structure* which . . . retains its capacity to convey religious meanings." (p. 104, italics in original). Another view locates civil religion as an activist dimension of religions (e.g., the Unification Church) that appeal to community-oriented youth (Robbins, Anthony, Doucas, & Curtis, 1976).

Most of the sociological data that we have on religion, though, are individual in nature. That is, the workings of religion in family groups (which are part of the social structure) are less understood than patterns of individual religious attendance, affiliation, or change. Ongoing research by D'Antonio (among others) may correct this imbalance in the near future. In his summary of previous research on family–religion connections (1980), he saw both old and new family–religion relationships "in eclipse," with an apparently newly developing relationship "which links the values of love and personal autonomy to the larger community" (p. 90). An older view of personal autonomy in the pursuit of self-interest seems to be giving way to a new religious consciousness:

there have been declines in belief, in ritual practice, in knowledge, and, most clearly, in the social consequences of traditional belief and knowledge. But these dimensions, designed to measure American religion of the 1940s and 50s, don't seem as relevant to the kind of religious consciousness that is emerging in recent research. (p. 98)

Autonomy is now exercised in the pursuit of love, interpersonally and at the community level. Interestingly, D'Antonio viewed the new consciousness, in part, as the *result* of a new heterogeneity of family forms (e.g., singles, experimenters in alternatives, childless couples, and working women). In this new consciousness, the young emphasize the value of religion according to how well it teaches love. D'Antonio's research is now focused on links between family, love, and religion; he is examining how the young perceive these links, and how they feel the links should be manifested.

That very focus, however, does come back to the question of autonomy, with its freedom to choose, criticize, or reject religious values. Thus, although the interplay of individual with structure is examined in this chapter, the importance of individual choice cannot be underestimated precisely because of the structural possibilities for such choices. A relatively open structure permitting high levels of individual freedom in religion and cultural-religious pluralism characterizes our society. Even if there is no single unifying "civil religion" as Fenn (1972) contended in emphasizing the pluralistic nature of religion, this openness would create a greater number of options for the individual.

It is the pluralistic nature of American life that is manifested in major religious trends today. The trends often

---

[1]For the various theoretical orientations in their application to family and religion, see Davis (1948, pp. 509–548) for the functionalist approach; Marx and Engels (1964) for the bases of the conflict approach; Berger and Luckmann (1963) for an important interactionist approach; and Wuthnow (1980) for world-system theory on religion. Useful texts include those by Winter (1977), Robertson (1970), and Scharf (1970).

Teresa Donati Marciano • Department of Sociology, Fairleigh Dickinson University, Teaneck, NJ 07666.

appear contradictory in their directions, as one would expect of our multiinterest-subcultural American society. Those trends are treated here as structural influences on individuals, having different strengths in different populations. The effect of these trends on families also varies, but to an extent not yet well explored by research, and often necessarily inferred from individual action.

The trends in American life today that have attracted interest include widespread pronouncements that we are a "secular" or "secularized" society; a concomitant proclamation of a "religious revival," with the growth of fundamentalist groups both in Christianity and Judaism; the rise of an "electric church" in large-scale television and radio ministries; reduced church attendance in the older, more "established" churches and denominations; diminishing numbers of celibate religious, such as priests and nuns, yet high Protestant seminary enrollments, which exceed the reduced congregational needs for such ministers; highly visible sects and cults,[2] many of which are Eastern in origin (e.g., Hare Krishna and the Unification Church, whose adherents are known as "Moonies"); feminist movements within and against the patriarchal churches, asserting rights to full participation and ordination; new or renewed religiously oriented lifestyles in and out of churches, including Catholic charismatic renewal, communes, and fellowships such as the havurot among Jews; the growth of religious themes in the popular arts, especially music; and the publishing industry's expansion of the number of religious titles offered, with growing sales of such literature.

All of these trends can be viewed both as responsive to and creative of needs: responsive in that they result from individual wishes or group decisions, and creative in that they then become choices open to others whose needs might have been, until that time, inchoate. Of these trends, this chapter focuses special attention on three: the evangelical "media" ministries, or "electric churches"; the cults; and the feminists in the churches. In each case, the family represents a special counterpoint to individual religious expression.

Synthesized Religion

All of the trends that have been listed affect all age groups and races and have had (at least initially) a more individual than familial impact. The family does remain the primary source of religious belief, however much and in whatever form it is taught to children. At the same time, there is today a newly powerful "synthesized" religion that can alter much or all of the previously assumed continuity of family religious teachings.[3]

[2]The term *cult* is used generically in this chapter. Treatments of the analytic distinctions among *sect, cult, church,* and *denomination* are found in many standard texts, for example, Johnstone (1975), Salisbury (1964), Robertson (1970), and Yinger (1970).

[3]Two works based on the questioning of these transmission assumptions are Robert Ellwood's *Alternative Altars* (1979), and Theodore Roszak's *Where the Wasteland Ends* (1973).

The term *Synthesized religion* means the result of personal synthesis, the bringing together of elements from personal biography as they fit with structural choices, to find religious beliefs that are internally satisfactory. These may agree or disagree, to varying extents, with the teachings of the institutional churches. Synthesis operates for individuals who are born into and remain members of a given church or denomination; individuals moving into new religious affiliations, including new affiliations that make far higher demands on them; and those whose beliefs do not lead to religious group membership. It is the many-directional potential of synthesis, its ongoing interactive quality with the social structure, that accounts for the variety of trends in American religious life. In the search for fulfillment, the compound of elements from personal biography finds a variety of expressions in and out of older religious forms.

Synthesis may lead to an increase in religious orthodoxy (and thus, it is not simply "privatized" religion); it may lead as well to a heterodox blending of religious and nonreligious beliefs and practices. An example of greater orthodoxy as the result of personal search is found in the striking new vitality of Orthodox Jewish congregations, as reported, for example, by Kaiser (1980). He found that growth to have been spurred by individual choices rather than by affiliations of families with these congregations. Once the choices are made, affiliation occurs; then, those centers of orthodoxy also become the settings for mate selection and the creation of families established out of strong common religious beliefs. Snook (1973) saw the new forms of orthodoxy and variety in Judaism, Protestantism, and Catholicism as varieties of modern unconventional belief. Arising out of the hunger for deep personal experiences, he wrote: "In some cases the people involved seem to feel that new kinds of religious relationships are necessary, and so the result is a new kind of religious group. For others . . . the effort goes into giving life to older religious forms" (p. 16).

Synthesis and Syncretism

Religious synthesis in the sociology of religion is typically described as *syncretism.* That term denotes a reconciliation of opposing philosophical or religious principles and has been used mainly to describe new types of religious *groups* among poor or Third World populations. Thus, the term is more likely to appear in descriptions of religion among American slaves (e.g., Raboteau, 1978) or among colonized peoples (e.g., Messenger, 1968) than in general texts and essays on religion and social life. One text that does examine the term to distinguish it from *pluralism,* is Robertson's (1970):

In the strictest terms all religious doctrines are syncretic. . . . The real sociological interest in the phenomenon of syncretism arises when we can examine precisely the processes *of syncretization and when the relationships between the component aspects of the overall syncretic products are problematic for the individuals and groups within the society in question.* (p. 103; emphasis in original)

Even here, though, the discussion of syncretism uses Javanese and other Third World examples.

Syncretic movements have tended to blend tribal and Christian (or Muslim) worship; sacred figures include gods, spirits, and saints; and sacred rituals may combine prayer with magical formulations and dancing. Two or more cultures are thereby coalesced in a significant group accommodation to oppression, cultural diffusion, and external pressures to adopt a colonial belief system. Syncretism may also be the outcome of the introduction of a nondominant religion into a larger culture, altering both in the process. Early Christianity was one example. Today, American Buddhism is a case of highly adaptive religious belief, to a point where it may constitute a syncretic movement as it evolves further in this culture (see, e.g., Cox, 1977; Prebish, 1978; Vecsey, 1979).

There is also evidence that the American culture constitutes a syncretic backdrop against which individual syntheses occur. For the purposes of this chapter, then, the term *syncretism* will be used to refer to collective expressions of blended beliefs, from whatever sources, whereas *synthesis* will refer to sets of personal beliefs shaped out of individual choices.

The Movement toward Synthesis

Durkheim (1965) saw in the late nineteenth and early twentieth centuries "contemporary aspirations towards a religion which would consist entirely in internal and subjective states, and which would be constructed freely by each of us" (p. 62). This religion would be a synthesis of those beliefs learned in the family with those acquired through structural and interpersonal influences in the life course. It represents by definition a departure from the collective tribal religions that Durkheim had studied. Such religious change paralleled the differences he saw between preliterate and the industrial societies. The "mechanical solidarity" of preliterate tribal groups is promoted by sameness, high degrees of conformity, and low degrees of individual difference. By contrast the "organic" bonding of urban, industrialized societies was made possible by the division of labor and the consequent socioeconomic interdependence; in such contexts, there was much room for high degrees of individualism (Durkheim, 1960). There is room as well for the "individual cult," which is explained by the general increase in individualism:

the existence of individual cults . . . are only the individualized forms of collective forces. . . . We are now able to appreciate the value of the radical individualism which would make religion something purely individual: it misunderstands the fundamental conditions of the religious life. (Durkheim, 1965, pp. 472–473)

Those fundamental conditions are the interactive process between individual and society. If faith raises the individual above mere self, it must be transcendent by communicating with others. Durkheim (1965) saw the drive to proselytize as characteristic of all religions because of this need to transcend self through communica-

tion. Yet, he saw religion as an embodiment of the community's ideals, so that, ultimately, society worships itself. If we are a "narcissistic" culture, as Lasch (1979) has described, individual religion can be the worship of the narcissistic object: the self.

So, today, transcendence may take on forms that are not recognized as specifically "religious." EST may be experienced as transcendence, just as congregational worship or participation in certain sports may be. A highly individualistic culture with a variety of options available to each person also makes possible a synthesis of the *sacred* and the *profane*, elements that traditional religions strove to keep sharply separate (Durkheim, 1965; p. 62). The sacred-profane synthesis is bred of the influences on religious belief of science, technology, and social science (particularly psychology) in a complex society. Bellah (1976), for example, described a Mormon meeting that he attended in rural New Mexico:

in a number of respects—the use of music with sexual and aggressive overtones, the coffeehouse atmosphere, the movies . . . —what was being included was not merely the religiously neutral but the consciously profane. . . . Durkheim, among others, has pointed out the ambivalence of the sacred and how the sacrilegious can be easily, much more easily than the religiously neutral, transformed into its opposite. (p. 212)

Richard Fenn (1978), in another view, saw secularization as an outcome of the struggle over what is "sacred" as opposed to "secular." And by derivation, these works provide an insight into such apparently contradictory tendencies as the pronouncements both of "secularization" and of "religious revival." Secularization is the blending of the sacred and the profane at the cultural level, a cultural syncretism of modern life. As a general phenomenon, it denotes a blurring of the lines between the realm of the holy and that of the everyday.

Personal syntheses of the sacred and the profane are facilitated by the large number of normative and subcultural systems available for individuals to choose in a diverse ("organic") society (see Berger, 1969; Berger & Luckmann, 1963). In an "organic" society, the performance of specific contractual obligations, such as work, leaves us free to express our individuality once the contract is fulfilled. Religion in its formal exercise is separated from economic and political functions (see Berger, 1969; Chapter 6). It becomes the vehicle, in the individual realm, of personal fulfillment and integration. Because the voluntaristic scope of interaction between person and structure is widened in such a society, religion is affected along with other structural forms. There is no longer the collective religion of the "mechanical" society, which asserts the moral superiority of society over individuals.

Where individual options were more limited, those limitations applied to religion (just as voluntarism now does). The eternal tension between individual and collectivity can be suppressed or restrained where physical and tribal survival are prime imperatives, in the face of visible threat. Once the perception of threat diminishes, the salience of survival tends to be lost to the group. Although survival needs may remain salient to subgroups within the larger collectivity, that group's capacity to maintain religious homogeneity and orthodoxy must wane. This lesson has been learned, often with much anguish, in several American religious and other social groups. One example is found among American Jews, who now experience a very high intermarriage rate (Sklare, 1971). As external definitions of a religious collectivity diminish in number and specificity, and as acceptance of the collectivity by the larger society increases (as in the case of Jews, Catholics, and Mormons), the external reinforcements of "orthodox" religious self-identification decline. The family as the building block of the collectivity has a diminished capacity to be a "haven" where religious definitions are formed around "outsider–insider" feelings about the larger society. As the barriers fall, geographic mobility detaches individuals from family control and the family from community control. Other normative systems in the pluralistic society, meanwhile, constitute competing avenues of self-identification, promoting a tendency toward personal synthesis in beliefs. The synthesis may take one further from childhood religion or more deeply into its practice, or into another religious system.

Berger (1969) noted the outcome of pluralism as one where "religion can no longer be imposed but must be marketed" (p. 145). As in any market situation, the consumer can pick and choose even apparently unlikely combinations of what is available; these, in turn, can be used to build something quite different from their originally intended uses.[4]

This synthesizing process underlies Lofland's counsels on the use of his study, with Stark, of the Unification Church (Lofland & Stark, 1965) to derive "conversion models." Predisposing and situational factors were set forth in that work to account for the attraction of the cult for the young. In his more recent statement, Lofland (1977) rejected that "passive" actor approach embodied in the interactionist perspective (derived from Blumer): "I have lately encouraged students of conversion to turn the process on its head and *to scrutinize how people go about converting themselves*" (p. 817; emphasis added).[5]

Family, Synthesis, and Selectivity

Synthesized religious choice immediately calls into question any automatic assumptions about the influence of religion on other actions, including family formation, fertility, and the socialization of children. Although religion–fertility correlates are common in the literature,

along with various attempts to test the link between Protestantism and economic success posed by Weber (1958), we do not have the qualitative materials necessary to know how religious behavior is actually taught and modeled in families today.[6] For now, given the proposal of synthesis as the process of coming to religious belief (or unbelief), one assumes the following: One or both spouses, having chosen a set of religious beliefs suitable to their personal needs, transmit them to their children. Children enter the same religious market and are subject to the various competing normative systems offered by religious and secular culture. As they grow older, children synthesize their own beliefs, which may involve changes in religious affiliation by intensity, or by denomination, or it may involve disaffiliation.

In the case of affiliation, it may involve continued formal ties to childhood religion, observed and practiced with greater orthodoxy as noted previously; or it may result in observance and practice that is highly selective.

Selectivity according to preferences evolving out of personal biography, and the resultant synthesis, is evidenced in all the major churches of the United States. The Roman Catholic Church is the single largest Christian group in America, numbering approximately 132 million. Selectivity is apparent in various Catholic doctrinal and observance aspects. The use of birth control is a major area where church teachings are rejected in practice. The Princeton Office of Population Research reported in 1977 that its 1975 data showed 76% of Catholics using birth control; that rate hardly differed from reported rates of usage among non-Catholics. Of Catholics, just under 6% used the church-accepted rhythm method, 26% reported sterilization (a sevenfold increase in one decade), and 34.2% used the pill. So many public statements condemning the use of "artificial" birth control methods have been made, including the one by the Pope on his 1979 visit to the United States, that some powerful deterrent must be operating on Catholic compliance with this teaching. Economics would seem to be the major deterrent, although, again, such values as time, self-actualization, and early completion of childbearing have not been measured to any significant extent or may be confounded by the economic variable.

There is also a lack of qualitative data on the rising number of divorced Catholics. Divorce creates sacramental separation from the church, a fact that has been reported as extremely anguishing and difficult; yet the salience of religion in the option to get divorced or to stay

[4]Wuthnow (1977) offered still another elaboration of the religious marketplace.
[5]The "passive convert" model of conversion was called into question before Lofland's statement (e.g., Straus, 1970); others have reaffirmed the "activist" model of conversion (e.g., Bromley & Shupe, 1979).

[6]Even the more "institutional church" era of the 1950s saw Catholic preschool training of the children in the home falling short of expectations (Thomas, 1951). Furthermore, the extent and nature of childhood religious socialization was related to a "felt need" for religion later, as shown in a 1948 study by Allport, Gillespie, and Young. Lenski's study (1963) of Detroit indicates that the family shapes a framework of general orientation to the world, even where religious practice diminishes in adulthood.

married, and how it actually operates in the decision-making process, is not known.

Attendance at weekly mass, a requirement for Catholics, is dropping throughout the country, though individual areas of high attendance do persist.

Catholic use of abortion is another instance of action severely condemned by church teachings. Although Leon and Steinhoff (1975) did find lower Catholic use of abortion, in those choosing abortion no differences were found between Catholics and non-Catholics in the timing of abortion in the pregnancy.

None of these points, however, by themselves indicate the disaffection already present when the selective behaviors occurred, or the felt religiousness of the individual despite any of the behaviors.

Selectivity has long been noted for the 6.7 million American Jews. Sklare (1971) noted that the choice of *mitzvot* (obligations/blessings) observed by Conservative and Reform Jews (who still outnumber Orthodox and Hassidic Jews) tends to be observance that accommodates the secular society. Thus, the Sabbath is less observed than *kashruth* (kosher laws); and *kashruth* is less practiced than the Passover seder.

America's 93.3 million Protestants manifest selective behavior most obviously in the traditionally proscribed behaviors such as drinking, gambling, dancing, and smoking. It is far more a matter of personal choice than the church's power to enforce the proscriptions.

One may therefore claim to be a member of a church—and, in fact, remain affiliated—yet maintain a highly selective observance of the teachings. This practice is not condoned by religious leaders, but it certainly occurs with wide understanding among coreligionists. We do not know how a framework is synthesized that accommodates apparently contradictory sets of beliefs, nor do we know the directions in which felt dissonance tends to be resolved. There may simply occur a compartmentalization of "religious" and "other" areas of life; or contradictions may be acknowledged and accepted as unavoidable; or a person may simply decide that, in certain areas, religion has no authority to teach or compel.

Synthesis, Family Transmission, and Religious Change

Not only may a person synthesize beliefs out of childhood religion, but that synthesis may also lead to the choice of another religion. The extent to which individual conversions occur can be found in the records of various churches. But we do not know the effect of individual conversion on the convert's family, except in occasional biographical accounts or some cases of children's conversion to sects or cults; nor do we know the likelihood of a person's converting a spouse, parents, siblings, or friends. Religious switching is, though, historically prevalent in the United States (Newport, 1979; Roof & Hadaway, 1977; Yinger, 1967). Recent data on switching are provided by Roof and Hadaway (1979). Using com-

posite findings for 7,500 people in Gallup, Roper, and NORC surveys, they found that 40% of Protestants belonged to denominations different from the ones in which they had been raised. Interdenominational switching has probably been the most prevalent type of switching until now, but they show that church membership today changes less for status reasons (upwardly mobile people changing to higher status denominations) than for theological reasons. The fulfillment of personal needs was sought in literal interpretations of scripture and in evangelical theology, swelling the ranks of Pentecostal and evangelical churches.[7] To estimate family impact, we must consider what these churches represent, together with other findings on switching during this current "revival."

The growth of Pentecostal groups and churches, together with that of evangelical churches (of which the Southern Baptists are the largest)[8] have important implications not only for family religious authority, but for evangelical church authority itself over time. Pentecostal and evangelical religion are at heart profoundly individual. Pentecostal groups, though somewhat famous for "speaking in tongues" (glossolalia), only manifest that as evidence in their eyes of the working of the Holy Spirit. The Spirit in the person and a holy life are true hallmarks of Pentecostal belief and practice. The implicit diffusion of personal revelation, as the Spirit works, reduces or obliterates a sense of absolute teaching authority in family or church.

This is true also of the evangelical churches. A church is "evangelical" if it emphasizes scriptural teachings and authority rather than the institutional authority of the church. Such churches teach the need for a personal ac-

---

[7]By comparison, Stark and Glock (1968), using a 1963 sample of 3,000 Protestant and Catholic church members in northern California, and a 1964 NORC sample of 1,976 respondents drawn nationwide, found that 46% of Protestants had been members of a denomination different from their current membership. In their sample, Southern Baptists had shown a decline of 34% whereas Episcopalians had increased by 40%. They said, "people who change their church tend to move from more conservative bodies to theologically more liberal ones" (p. 187). They went on to say that their figures "are likely to *underestimate* the extent to which shifts from conservative to more liberal bodies characterize denominational changing in our society" (p. 189; italics in original). Although acknowledging the limitations of their sample size, they pointed to two trends important for today: Baptists showed great attractiveness to those previously unchurched; and the increased affiliation with liberal churches had not swelled their numbers, most likely because of the dropping out of those born into them. Thus, liberal churches were attractive, but not necessarily retentive. For a critique of Stark and Glock, see Roof and Hadaway (1979).

[8]Jacquet (1980) showed that the fastest growing and largest of the Pentecostals is Assemblies of God (founded in 1914). Their membership in 1940 was 198,834; in 1978, it was 932,365. The Southern Baptist Convention shows a growth from nearly 5 million in 1940 to a 1978 figure of 13,191,394.

knowledgment of one's own sins and "accepting Christ" for reconciliation with God if one is to be saved.

In these churches, the special link to the holy is through the personal component of conscience and the inner workings of the heart. As children grow up, they must at some point consciously (sometimes publicly) make their own decision to "accept Christ." A baptismal ceremony may follow that decision, according to the practice of the church.

A question therefore arises of religious orientation among the young that remains to be explored. In the family, literal interpretations of Scripture (especially the New Testament) involve submission to parental authority, the man's "headship" of the family, the obedience of children, and the indissolubility of Christian marriage by divorce. Yet, where children are taught and are witnessing at home a religion in which their teenage or adult decision to accept the religion must be made individually, the child's orientation to the family and the world may be different from cases where one's religion is a "given." In the mainline churches one *is* Catholic or Jewish or Presbyterian or Episcopalian; these churches do not require the same kind of conscious decision to be saved that is part of the evangelical process. That emphasis on individual salvation outside institutional forms—salvation by faith, where good works are not enough to be saved, in a religious "market" society—may promote an individual religion or crystallize the quest for it. It would certainly tend to reinforce individualistic strains within the evangelical movement. Larsen (1978) reported that these strains have led large numbers of families to seek therapy and suggested therapeutic techniques to ameliorate the intertwining of religion and dysfunction in evangelical families.

There is another psychosocial question for family groups in the idea of the gift of salvation. In the Christian tradition from Augustine through Calvin to the present day, the doctrine of predestination has haunted the churches. Salvation is a free gift of God and comes from divine choice rather than free will. One cannot "will" to be saved, but one can accept the offer of salvation, trusting that one is, indeed, among the saved. "Backsliding" (relapse into a type of life defined as sinful) is believed by many evangelists to signify that one really was not saved in the first place. Given the potential diversity of character and inclination within any given family, what are the consequences for family affection, interaction, and solidarity when some members show signs of being saved whereas others do not? The introduction of Western literacy to tribal areas could upset the balance between old and young, transferring the power of literacy and technology to youth while devaluing the verbal lore acquired with age; in the same way, the idea of predestined individual salvation may transfer the locus of bonding, authority, and the formation of a self-image to religious rather than familial sources. Evangelists argue the need to remain committed to witnessing for one's family, but where sal-

vation may appear to have been given only to some family members (rather than all), a distancing or sense of separation may mark that family, with unknown effects.

The increasingly popular evangelical churches are not monolithic but manifest variations in aspects of doctrine and internal struggles over such issues as scriptural "inerrancy." Two cases occurred among Southern Baptist and the Lutheran Church–Missouri Synod in the 1970s.[9] In both churches, strong doctrinal debate and schism (among the Lutherans) were outgrowths of these struggles. In each case, each side had strong views on what a faithful teaching of scripture entailed and, therefore, on who was rendering fit ministry. One appreciates the seriousness of these divisions by understanding that rendering unfit ministry, or following such a minister's teachings, imperils the very promise of salvation.

The evangelical religious market, therefore, grows by dissent and regrouping. (This happened also in the Episcopal Church in the 1970s, in which a breakaway diocese was formed in dissent over the ordination of women and homosexuals).

When such congregational variation and dissent occur, which families go where? We do not know that families move as much as we have a sense of individual movement in such cases. The reform tradition that bred the Pentecostal and evangelical groups is the same tradition that became ongoing anti-institutional elements in those churches. A dialectical process is built into these congregations; this process reflects and parallels the submission–free-will paradox for families as they raise children in these traditions.

Families have not been unaware of the antifamily potential of the religious marketplace. The "deprogramming" of children who enter cults is the most visible aspect of the family in contention with its individual members; yet, the extent of divisiveness in evangelical choices is not really known. In terms of what is known, Shupe, Spielmann, and Steigall (1977) found an interesting by-product of anticult activities for families who have used "deprogrammers": the family is unified as never before by the external threat (the cult) to its integrity as a group. The rediscovery of the devil, whether in cults or in the traditional guise of Satan posed by the evangelicals, has as yet unstudied consequences for family cohesion.

Still, the family as a group is problematic to some extent at least, where salvation is a matter of personal acceptance. A family's internal normative system always

---

[9]*Inerrancy* is also a watchword of the Jesus People Movement. A study by Balswick (1974) distinguished the Jesus People's views from traditional orthodox views and Christian existentialist views of the Bible: "Jesus people use the Bible more in the manner of the Christian fundamentalist, who accepts the Bible as the Word of God without being too concerned about working towards any 'systematic theology,' and who rather subjectively interprets Scripture as he understands how it relates to his life at the moment" (p. 363).

poses a possible threat to the norms of the church.[10] In the same way, every set of religious teachings poses, ultimately, an authority different from, and alternative to, that of the parents. It is so in all cases and may become salient under conditions of individual "acceptance" of salvation.

Furthermore, although the churches teach that the fellowship with other believers as a public witness to faith is a necessary part of one's religious life, this is not a call to families so much as it is to individuals. The church's or group's role in personal transcendence is promoted far more by Judaism, Catholicism, and the "liberal" Protestant churches; yet, these are the very groups where formal membership declines have been most severe.[11]

Whereas fundamentalist Christianity's and Orthodox and Hassidic Judaism's numbers are growing, the young have dropped away from "mainline" or "liberal" churches (e.g., Catholic, Episcopal, United Church of Christ, United Methodists, and United Presbyterians). The declines will have interesting implications for family formation and the transmission of "liberal" religious values. Postconfirmation declines in attendance are noted by the largest denominations, as well as in Conservative and Reform Judaism. Although there are some indications of "returning" after children are born, today's higher ages at first marriage and longer postponements before the birth of the first child reduce the sense of continuity that would "automatically" affiliate young families with the religion of their childhood (see, e.g., Johnson, 1976).

Who drops away, then, and who comes in? Kleugel (1980) attempted to account both for higher nonaffiliation and for higher conservative church growth, using merged national survey data for the years 1973–1977. He found the Protestant/Catholic/Jewish cleavage—and the geographic region—still influential in switching. But he showed a trend toward nonaffiliation that affected all denominations and regions uniformly. The switching, he found, was not, as Stark and Glock (1968) contended, a conservative-to-liberal movement. If anything, there was a moderate gain in conservative involvement. Most

important, Kleugel showed that there is increased choice of no affiliation by those raised in a religion, but a constant tendency of those raised with no affiliation to adopt one.

Although the family as a basis for reactive behavior would appear to be indicated by these data, longitudinal studies will be necessary to determine if there is, indeed, an ongoing pendulum effect in affiliation, based on family conditions. There is the assumption that affiliation with the conservative churches provides answers to questions of meaning ("Why am I born?" "Why do I live?" "Why must I die?") not provided by religionless homes or "liberal" churches. Bibby (1978) attacked this assumption about the attractions of fundamentalism. Rather, he provided evidence of three factors in higher conservative church growth: higher birth rates and stronger religious socialization; switching into conservative religion; and the maintenance of high participation levels in the conservative churches. Of course, switching in may well be a result of a "better answer" to the question of meaning, the assumption that Bibby attacked. The familial components found directly in his data—fertility and socialization—leave a need to clarify the link between fundamentalism and family size, and why (and how) family size should operate so much more powerfully than among Catholics or Presbyterians.

The high-fertility–high-participation links to conservative churches found by Bibby are illustrated in the Mormon family process. Family nights, the family home evening (one night per week, generally Monday), are a specific and well-publicized (within the church) part of Mormon religious practice. Wilkinson and Tanner (1980) cited the strong encouragement of large families among Mormons, coupled with family group activities, as supportive of high affectional ties among family members. These authors' data contradict earlier findings of inverse relationships between family size and affection, intelligence, and children's emotional adjustment. Given the Mormon setting of this study, however, this may be not a general contradiction, but one that specifies the range, or delimits the applicability of, the previously found inverse relationship. Religion may have been an unexamined intervening variable in earlier studies, particularly as religion operated to enhance or reduce self-image and satisfaction in a large-family setting. For the Mormon study, the researchers found the embedding of families (especially mothers) in same-value networks supporting the eternal value of the family and the importance of motherhood; this value may have enhanced parental status and strengthened affectional ties.

The study of Mormon families does point out the extent to which adults can be reinforced in their beliefs after they have made role commitments in family formation. Some of the structure (family nights, supported by normative values) for socializing children to religious-familial values is also shown. Mormons can thus provide a good area of study for processes of continuity in the transmission of

---

[10]We are not really sure of the penetration or integration of religion's teachings for families. For example, how deeply did the Christian ethic penetrate European families before the Reformation? Scholarship such as Trexler's (1973) on the children that were abandoned in relatively large numbers in Renaissance Florence and the findings that girls were abandoned more than boys create wonder. If the building of cathedrals is an indication of religious fervor, whose fervor is it, and where, structurally, is it located? Even Glock's classic exposition (1965) of the dimensions of religiosity—ideological, intellectual, ritualistic, consequential, and experiential—is *individually* applicable. This individual level is well discussed by Winter (1977, pp. 8–9).

[11]Total church membership has, however, grown; 7% in the United States, a pace equal to that of the general population growth. Ongoing membership and large-scale growth, then, would not be a simple reflection of population size.

religious beliefs and practices, but such study raises questions about the transmission in family settings expressing different religious and structural forms.

Continuity and Discontinuity

Although Mormons are one of the growing churches in America, all cases of growth conceal degrees of *discontinuity:* (1) To what extent is growth greater than had been suspected because it conceals members who dropped away? And (2) what are the family foundations for radical discontinuity, as where the young embrace such culturally "extreme" religious forms as the cults?

It is far more difficult to find out who is gone from than who is present in the churches. In either case, additionally, church attendance may not be a proper measure of a synthesized religious orientation. Finally, one may be formally affiliated with a church yet have ceased to regard that church as a major point in one's life.

The effect on family members where some choose to ignore the family religion, or to switch away from it, is relatively unexplored both when the switch is to a "respectable" religion and when it is to a cult. How do Protestant parents, for example, feel about children who convert to Catholicism or Judaism? How do the children feel about their parents? What are the conditions under which intrafamilial switching is a relatively low-stress situation? Older data provide some answers to these questions, though their current validity is not really known. Vidich and Bensman (1968), for example, provided data for the 1950s on family membership in a small town's churches:

Kinship, marriage and family tradition all play a part in explaining the mixed class compositions of the congregations [in Springdale]. Children, with few exceptions, adopt the church of their parents. However, affiliation by kinship does not assure family continuity in a given church. In the Protestant churches, unless the husband is without a church, the wife upon marriage affiliates with the church of her spouse and any children who are products of this mating do likewise. Siblings and first cousins who all trace their descent to a common maternal grandfather can belong to different churches. . . . Beyond the nuclear family, kinship groups are not identified with a particular church.

Characteristically, church membership is determined by the husband's church preferences and these preferences are determined by family tradition. (p. 230)

It would be interesting to test this pattern in small towns today, with similar and different socioeconomic profiles, as well as in higher density areas.

Older data also exist on the higher anxiety levels and intolerance of disagreement among believers, compared to nonbelievers (Rokeach, 1970). Data on interfaith marriages reflect these findings, in that conflict rises as dissimilarity of religion increases; parental objections as one source of conflict were included in the measures on interfaith marriages.

The effect of parental opposition to an interfaith marriage presumes a possible solution in compartmentalizing

the relationship with children into nonreligious areas. But it is not known whether disaffection actually results in such cases, or what other effects exist on intrafamily bonding, as with siblings or grandparents.

This question becomes even more obvious when children adopt another religion before marriage, where that religion is an "umbrella" set of beliefs covering all aspects of daily life (as in the cults), and where the legitimacy of the new religion is not recognized by the rest of the family. In such cases, the family is faced with radical discontinuity; and because many cults reduce contact with the members' biological families, there is radical discontinuity of physical contact as well as religious belief.

The literature on the cults does provide some insights into what happens to families when their members join, though such information must often be gleaned from a variety of sources and opens more questions than it answers. The extent of *actual* continuity or discontinuity is the first question raised by cult membership.

Cults and Continuity

Cults in the United States have been regarded as quasi religions, or "extreme" religions. They certainly represent a break between parents and children in the transmission of external forms and settings of religious practice. This transmission process, however, has been mostly neglected in the research, so that the extent of (dis)continuity is difficult to generalize. Weiting (1975) reported out of his search for such studies: "I have not located any studies where a range of religious variables was investigated and where an intrafamilial design was employed." (p. 137)

Examining the studies of intergenerational continuity and discontinuity, he showed a growing recognition of the idea that "intergenerational differences may not be so much a matter of kind as of degree. . . . This suggests that attitudes to intergenerational relationships should be sensitive to both patterns of difference and commonality" (p. 139). His empirical data support the mixed-pattern approach. The research looked at mother, father, and oldest adolescent in high school in 66 families ($n = 198$), who separately answered and returned self-administered questionnaires in 1970–1971. He found a similarity between adolescents and their parents in their levels of belief in external control (defined as a bipolar continuum, where external orientation signified belief in a deity who is "omnipotent, ordering, external and controlling in human affairs," p. 140); the other pole, internal orientation, placed control within the self). Similar belief levels were also found for individualistic religion. This term also denoted a bipolar continuum where "An individualistic orientation refers to the tendency to value highly individualistic qualities of belief and private forms of religious expression" (p. 140). The other end of that continuum is "communalistic," valuing denominational doctrines and institutional, communal forms of religious expression.

The major differences that emerged were in the religious activity dimensions, which included the number of times per month attending church; the proportion of friends and relatives in the socioreligious community; parish involvement—the proportion of one's five closest friends in the same parish; and the relative importance of church compared to other activities. Parents scored higher in institutional orientation, based on those measures. Thus, belief continuity was strong (even to the extent that "in the adolescent-father comparison on external control the adolescents actually scored higher," p. 44).

A major discontinuity was in the "importance of religion." Weiting pointed out that this is considered a belief dimension in research; yet it may be one where adolescents associate the question with religious institution, and this would fit with the lower level of adolescent institutional orientation.

Examining some of the work on religious expression among the young, Weiting cited the Jesus People, transcendental meditation (TM), Maharishi Mahesh Yogi (TM's "founder"), and Meher Baba. In all these cases, he saw religious beliefs as strong but their institutional forms as different from Christianity. Youth roles, which are neither leadership nor financial support roles in the church, lead to a different institutional experience. (In effect, we experience a situation according to our roles in it; as roles differ, experience and relationship to the institution differ.)

By contrast, financial support roles for the young are integrated into such religions as the Unification Church and Hare Krishna. Bromley and Shupe (1980) showed how public solicitation rituals are raised to sacramental significance in these groups. To raise funds effectively, the groups have constructed "role definitions that legitimate and motivate such activity" (p. 231).

Support for role theory is also found in the older studies of the Meher Baba movement that were done by Robbins (1969) and Robbins and Anthony (1972). Weiting (1975) wrote: "the role of the "young person" simultaneously leads to divergent institutional practices but within some enduring and global set of values and belief complexes that remain from early experience" (p. 146).

Of course, as stated, role theory does not explain who remains in and who tries another institutional form in any generation of youth. But the use of role theory has proved valuable to other researchers. It was used, for example, by Bromley and Shupe (1979) to explain religious value discontinuity. They did a 4½-month study of the Unification Church (UC), using in-depth focused interviews (open-ended) on 42 respondents: 41% (n = 15) were from white-collar or professional families, and 32% (n = 12) were from blue-collar or manual-labor backgrounds. The research examined the rapid conversion to the UC, which has been called "brainwashing," and also the variety of predisposing motives uncovered in the sample. The re-

searchers found that interaction with the cult group *preceded* commitment; as attraction to the group increased, interest in the group broadened. *Psychological* commitment developed later, after affiliation, rather than before it. Whatever the predisposing motives, then, once they resulted in interaction, the psychological process could be set in motion. This finding of action's preceding belief as a key to cult involvement helps to explain the successful use by the cults of high-intensity welcoming sessions and marathon-activity weekends.

The research does not typically account for why cults are attractive in the first place (if, indeed, *attraction* is the correct word for that part of the conversion process). Robbins *et al.* (1976) asked the same question in examining the attractiveness of the UC, compared to that of the Eastern cults, which emphasize meditation and personal transformation. The UC's attractiveness is believed by Robbins *et al.* to be based, as noted earlier (see "Introduction"), in its communal dimension. Rather than concentrating on meditation and personal change as avenues toward harmonizing external relationships, the unification principles specifically address interpersonal and communal harmony and unity. The social ideology of the UC therefore appeals to those who feel in their lives the effects of the isolated nuclear family and reduced neighborhood/communal viability. Yet, in embracing the civil dimension of the UC (theistic patriotism, specifically countering political communism as a satanic phenomenon), the UC's activism in the secular sphere increases the tensions between itself and the larger society. The authoritarian and totalistic nature of the UC is an outcome of its sense of being at war with evil (communism). Ironically, the UC becomes in form as totalistic as the system it opposes. A major difference, however, lies in the freedom to leave the UC, and there is ample evidence that, among the cults, dropping away or drifting away, occasional participation, and limited involvement lead to far more fluid states of cult membership than is generally assumed (see, e.g., Judah, 1974; Robbins & Anthony, 1972, 1980; Wuthnow, 1978).

The cults in America are far from being a single entity or type of organization. Stark and Bainbridge (1979) distinguished among audience cults, where formal organization is lacking and ideas are received as part of a lecture or media audience; client cults, analogous to the client–therapist relationship, where those offering services are organized but where clients are mostly unorganized; and cult movements, which are true religions, though they show a range of organization from looser to greater organizational structure, and among which the less organized are numerically more prevalent. Correlates of relative interest and participation in such a variety of groups (though not using the Stark and Bainbridge typology) are examined in Wuthnow's study (1978) of the Bay Area (San Francisco) data on religious experimentation. It will be from a closer synthesis of grounded theoretical works such as these that we will better understand how families may, even unwittingly, set the stage for their children's attraction to cults.

Cults and Families

Many cults in America today are, from the data available, more feared than is warranted by their numerical strength. The data also show that, where their appeals are effective, they are to white middle- and upper-middle-class youth more than to lower-class or black youth. (However, lower-class or black youth are not excluded from the successful appeals. All classes and races are found in the cults, though the proportion of the white middle class seems highest, from the available data.)

Several cults prominent in the past decade have faded from their once-salient positions in the media and on campuses, whereas others have persisted either as increasingly ''acceptable'' additions to the religious scene (e.g., TM) or are perceived as ''continuing threats'' to the young. Those that have faded from immediate prominence (sometimes by the desire to do so, as with the Alamo Foundation) include the Divine Light Mission (followers of the Maharaj Ji) and the Children of God (COGs). The latter are estimated by Cohen (1975; p. 8) to have had perhaps 3,000 members at their 1972 peak. They have emigrated in large numbers to Europe and Latin America, apparently spurred by the same feelings of ''danger'' in their leader, David Berg, that led James Jones to take his followers to Guyana. But later research does show growth in this group. Davis and Richardson (1976) cited the figure of about 4,500 members for mid-1976, not counting about 800 young children of the members. The basic unit of the COGs is the colony, and the authors cited more than 600 colonies in existence, in over 70 countries (1976; p. 321). The value of this research lies in the information derived from the authors' direct experience with the COGs outside the United States and from the extensive, detailed history of the movement that they provide. Still another group whose current status and numbers are unclear is the ''Jesus People,'' an umbrella term for many groups arising out of Christian ministries to the hippies in the 1960s.

Most visible today are Hare Krishna and the Unification Church, though many other cults do continue to exist in the United States. The visually dramatic Hare Krishna were estimated by Cohen (1975; p. 80) to have 1,500 members in the United States and an additional 1,500 worldwide. Far higher estimates were offered by Conway and Siegelman (1979), perhaps, in part, because of their general alarm over the cults and their consequent ignoring of any fluidity in membership in that movement; Snow, Zurther, & Ekland-Olson (1980) obtained an estimate of 4,000 members from Krishna sources. The UC has a far higher estimated membership, though, again, the estimates vary. Cohen (1975; p. 45) put their numbers as between 300,000 and 3 million, and Conway and Siegelman (1979; p. 35) estimated 60,000–80,000 members.

Among Hare Krishna, the Jesus People, and also apparently the UC, major pools of recruitment have been drug-using, alienated youth. The extent to which this is true for the UC is problematic because they do recruit heavily on campuses, where hard drug use has diminished; studies of ''deprogrammed Moonies'' do not, moreover, consistently deal with previous drug use. Loneliness and alienation, more than drug use, appear to precede conversion. All the literature reports at least some level of ''alienation'' for converts to cults. If, however, some valid measure of alienation could be agreed on, there would still be the question of whether that alienation is specific to persons sensing themselves unintegrated into the larger society generally, and whether it includes or is specific to family relations.

Much of the literature on the cults dwells on their youth appeal and the ''deprivation'' hypothesis (Glock, 1964; Peterson & Mauss, 1973; Robbins & Anthony, 1972); it shows that cults become places for alternative status attainment and social gratification. Also widely reported in the literature are cult practices, activity levels, and demands on members; relations with families, however, are far less focused and far more incidental to many reports. Now, however, the studies, the journalistic reports, the autobiographical descriptions of life in cults, and the ''warning'' literature are beginning to deal with family problems and reactions to cults (e.g., Robbins & Anthony, 1980). The ''warning'' literature is particularly addressed to parents and therefore deals most strongly with the consequences (all bad) to families whose children join cults. That literature often provides ''clues,'' guides to preventing children from becoming attached to cult groups. Conway and Siegelman's *Snapping* (1979) is one of the most alarmist and polemical of this type, along with the more recent addition of Rudin and Rudin (1980) to the literature attacking the cults. The family anguish that these authors have seen and reported among cultists' families cannot be denied; the alarmist literature is to be faulted mainly for its tendency to see only evil and dire consequences in cult membership.

Prince's description (1974) of cult appeals to youth treats the family more structurally. He called youth concern with the mystical, ''neotranscendentalism''; it is characterized by a rejection of Western economic and acquisitive values. His respondents were mostly under age 30 and usually from affluent homes. He wrote:

Neotranscendentalism . . . can be regarded as a self-imposed rite of passage. . . . The essential task is a psychological metamorphosis—a kind of cocoon work—shocking parental authority and making ready to accept spouse and family. Brainwashing is a major feature of the task: the freeing of the initiate from his childish attitudes, beliefs, fears. (p. 265)

For Prince, the concern with the mystical bridges the gap between childhood and adulthood. Other writers, however, have pointed out the control over marriage by cults and the inability to come out and resume normal adulthood (e.g., Singer, 1979). A concern with the mystical, then, must be distinguished from commitment to cult life; the cult may be an extreme form of mystical concern, but it is only one such avenue available in the American religious marketplace.

The picture of cults that emerges from the literature, in terms of cult–family relationships, shows high degrees of commonality. A major pattern is the 24-hour-a-day commitment, which reduces the likelihood of frequent family contact. Cult teachings and practices in regard to recruits' families vary a bit, although as a recruit becomes more deeply involved in a totalistic cult, where the recruit's family remains unreconciled to the conversion, family contact may be eliminated completely, with the cult's encouragement. Cohen's journalistic account (1975) of the various groups is one of the few that consistently makes at least some mention of cult member–family relations for each of the groups he studied. He used a descriptive approach, letting readers draw their own conclusions from the material he presented. Some striking facts nonetheless appear in his presentation, as well as new points for speculation. As an example of the latter, his description of the COGs leads one to conclude, at least tentatively, that the strength of parental opposition to any given group is a direct function of the group's pressure against the members' families. The antifamily nature of the COGs was described by Cohen (1975):

Berg was not content merely to get young people off drugs, and into church and straight society in general. He wanted "one hundred percent discipleship." That meant cutting all ties with home, family, church and established society, living communally and spending all one's time in spreading Berg's version of Christianity to other young people.

Given so radical an antifamily attitude, the family reactions to the cult should not be unexpected. Family anticult activities are mentioned in Conway and Siegelman (1979), as well as in Rudin and Rudin (1980). The latter listed the names and addresses of nine anticult groups ("countercult organizations," as they called them). Four of the nine were in California, two in Massachusetts, and one each in New Hampshire, Minnesota, and North Carolina.

A more scholarly study of the anticult movement (ACM) was offered by Shupe and Bromley (1979), specifically as it had been shaped around the Unification Church. They saw two sources of the ACM: family and organized religion, with the major countercult activity being "deprogramming." Where organized religion focuses on the theology of the Unification Church (UC), the reaction to the loss of young members is specifically religion against religion; isolation of cult members from families is attacked as a violation of religious precepts. (Enroth, 1979, is an example of the specific religious objections to the way in which the UC uses Christian scripture to explain and justify its message.) Families object to their children's full-time commitment to cults, which involves "wholesale abandonment of former careers, obligations, and associations, often including the

biological family" (Shupe & Bromley, 1979; p. 328). The time demands of the UC reduce the opportunity for and the frequency of family contacts; parents thus perceive a breach of reciprocity in family love and commitment.

Parental values and lifestyles are implicitly or explicitly condemned by cult lives and values. Without conventional recourse against such a breach, parents formed the first major ACM, known as FREECOG (Free Our Children from the Children of God) in 1972. By 1974, it had expanded into the largest ACM, the Citizens Freedom Foundation, whose goals are to locate and rescue children in cults, and to discredit the cults. An important point made by Bromley and Shupe is a condition that has been called *pluralistic ignorance:* parents often feel that they are "alone" in the loss of a child to a cult until they discover (often accidentally) the existence of the ACM.

Not all cults demand this exclusivity and severance, nor do cults such as the UC and Hare Krishna object to the involvement and support of friendly parents. The ACM is directed heavily against them partly because, although they do accept the friendliness of parents, there is no compromise in the totality of commitment to the cult. And although the ACM is heavily directed against the "cult movement" (in the Stark and Bainbridge typology), groups such as Meher Baba are far more loosely organized, with members working at their jobs in the world, in a sense of service to others (Anthony & Robbins, 1974).

Where parental friendliness is not maintained, or is prohibited, the cult is after a while presented as the member's "true family," the new life source and life focus, the new source of gratification, the giver and receiver of love. Newcomers find a sense of belonging, a sense of "making sense" out of life for the first time, in the new group. It must be remembered, though, that not only in cults, but also in mainline religions (e.g., Episcopal, Catholic, and Jewish), converts report their conversions as a process of "coming home." From a process viewpoint, the differences are not in conversion itself, but in the continuing intensity demanded of the follower after the initial commitment, on a daily or weekly basis. For "mainline" converts, family ties may have to be consciously rejected, at least insofar as the family holds strongly to negative feelings about the convert's new religion. Yet none of the more established churches in America advocate hatred for and wariness of one's biological family. Even active opposition tends to be interpreted by them as "testing" and an opportunity for "witnessing" their faith, rather than as the work of evil. Cults may fall into a theological trap by their very totalism in calling family opposition "satanic," and by fostering a countermovement fueled by their own virulence.

It has also been very apparent that the loudest protests against cults come from parents and "deprogrammed" members, but that no follow-up has been done on parents who have immediately distanced themselves from children in cults, or who have held onto their hostility without attempting some kind of resolution. The number of cult members far exceeds the number of attempts to deprogram them, but more important, unknown numbers of members receive continued angry rejection by hostile parents.

Also, parents' reactions to their children's conversion to a cult has not been uniformly negative, and cults have been willing to accept some parents as friendly outsiders. Although the UC is a major target of deprogramming at parental behest, for example, there was reported in 1976 (Brozan, 1976) an international parents' group approving of the UC and their children's membership in it. Ironically, the more "open" structure of the UC in this regard (though the openness is, of course, relative to that of other cults) is one of the reasons that parents can get hold of their children for deprogramming. Edwards (1979) reported his parents' maintaining cordial relations with him after he joined the UC, and they used their continued contact to get him to a meeting alone, whereupon he was "kidnapped" and deprogrammed. He wrote:

I had broken off completely from "Old Life," as the Family called it. I phoned my parents every two weeks to reassure them that I cared, since Family members were told not to alienate their biological parents but to prepare them for conversion. (pp. 160–161)

Edwards had lied to his parents, denying that he belonged to UC when they asked him. The amount of lying about one's religious status is generally unknown, and certainly, cults such as the UC work through groups where the church's name is not mentioned.

By contrast to the UC, where reports reflect continued parental contact even after membership is formalized, Cohen (1975) found that most of the COGs he talked with had broken with their parents and families long before conversion. Most of them, including the high number of ex-Catholics and Jews he found, reported that religion was unimportant at home. He also discovered a substantial minority from fundamentalist churches who had found their previous religious lives to be not strict enough (pp. 18–19). The fundamentalists were the leadership pool within the COG, evidently because their family socialization had already provided the groundwork for the extreme commitment demanded in that group. And for all the antifamily teaching of the COGs, Cohen reported that "COGs have been accused of having members put heavy pressure on their parents to continue contributions" (p. 15). One can speculate that previous alienation might make members susceptible to using parents from whom they had been alienated, and on whom they could now make specific, aggression-expressing demands. Again, however, the extent of this pressure, or its success, was unstudied.

Harrison (1979) did a journalistic study of one case of a UC conversion. This was of a young woman who entered the cult during her freshman year at college and then dropped out of school. (School dropouts after conversion are frequently reported.) Preceding the conversion, the young woman had experimented with macrobiotics and Zen Buddhism. Her UC conversion at age 18—and her marriage in the cult at age 22 (though engagements in the UC are supposed to occur only at age 24 for women)—marked four years in which there had been two attempts to deprogram her. The first deprogramming had resulted in her signing a notarized statement requesting her parents to remove her from the UC should she ever return to it. At the time of the writing of the Harrison article, the young woman was firmly within the fold. But the descriptions do provide some insight into family relations, as Harrison was able to interview the young woman after having interviewed her family. The young woman claimed that she had never been understood by her parents, though the parents and their pastor evidently did not agree. There were other children in the family, who shared their parents' displeasure at their sister's conversion, though it was not made very clear. Besides opening the question of assumed levels of mutual understanding in families, the article also shows the need to explore how different children in the same family experience "different" family life. Birth order and conversion certainly have not been researched in connection with the cults.

Sex ratios, however, have been mentioned in several studies: The more lowly the status of women, the lower their proportions in the cult. Cohen (1975) reported many more men than women among the COGs and the Jesus People, though Davis and Richardson (1976) saw the COGs as "less sexist in practice than some other [Jesus] groups" (p. 338). One defense of their claim is in the "shepherd couple" (a married couple) who together head a colony. Yet, the general literature on sex roles in marriage seems to indicate high power imbalances under general societal conditions, let alone those of a fundamentalist religious colony.

The sexism of the Jesus People (and the need to temper it in order to attract more women) has also been reported by Harder (1972) and by Harder, Richardson, and Simmons (1976). For the UC, Galanter, Rabkin, Rabkin, and Deutsch (1979), who had access to UC records, reported that 62% of the national membership was male. By contrast, "excursis religion" described by Ellwood (1979) as "a spiritual movement away from ordinary social and psychic structures alike" (p. 21), showed both female leadership and the perception of female aspects of divine order.

Another area of family–cult relationship research is the extent to which friendly overtures to families may alleviate the sense of break or discontinuity in intergenerational religious beliefs. Hare Krishna is an example of a cult that many parents have attempted to get their children out of (Sage, 1976), yet Cohen (1975) wrote of this group:

While many parents are horrified when their children join the sect, at least a small percentage are deeply relieved. Parents of the Hare Krishna people do not see their children often, but one of the first rules of the sect is reconciliation with parents. (p. 92)

Other family reaction, though, was reported by Singer (1979). She wrote of her four years of counseling and discussion groups with about 100 former cult members. Given Singer's support of deprogramming and the consequent underrepresentation of those who drift away from or voluntarily leave cult life, it must be understood that her data are particularly applicable to those who have been for the most part "forced out" of cults. One point she emphasized is the need for ex-cult members to obtain help in adjusting to life after leaving the cult. From her research on current and former cult members and their families (using interviews on nearly 300 ex-cult members), she wrote:

many participants joined these religious cults during periods of depression and confusion, when they had a sense that life was meaningless. The cults had promised—and many had provided—a solution to the distress of the developmental crises that are frequent at this age. (p. 72)

This precult mental state was also found by Galanter *et al.* (1979) who found for their 237 respondents (on self-administered questionnaires) "a fair amount of psychological difficulty before joining the church" (p. 166). More than a third (39%) retrospectively saw serious emotional problems, and almost one-third (30%) had had professional help. Serious drug problems had existed for 23% and the use of drugs at all was higher than for a comparable national sample (e.g., 45% of the respondents had used hallucinogens, whereas 14% of a national sample had done so.)

In Singer's study, the average age of the respondents was 23; they were typically from middle- or upper-middle-class families; and they had had two or more years of college. This similarity to other findings raises the problem of the extent to which parental education (as reflected in family class standing) functions to resist children's vulnerability to cults. Education as it is obtained in typical school systems neither inherently transmits, nor enables the educated to transmit, a set of trusted internal resources for finding (or against which to measure) meanings. Neither is there an automatic spillover from education into the possession of a framework of values. Here is what appears to be the most critical disjuncture between education, values, and family transmission of meanings. The whole idea of alienation, loss of control over one's life, and loss of meaning speaks of important gaps in the socialization of children that simply never may be noticed until parents are confronted with the cults. Of course, the problem is to determine not only *how* to control one's life, but from what value standpoint a person will do so. Cults evidently do all of this, as the more established churches cannot or will not.

Ironically, once a child is kidnapped from a cult and "deprogrammed," previous difficulties with family and friends may find a way to resolution through the new status and recognition derived from the former member's having been deprogrammed. Robbins and Anthony (1980) noted (perhaps with unintentional bitterness at the betrayals involved) that the deprogrammed cult member acknowledges cult membership to have been "coercive persuasion" (brainwashing). The ex-members can thereby

facilitate reintegration with relatives and former friends, who may now attribute past conflicts with the ex-convert to ego-alien mind controlling forces. . . . Recriminating against alleged cultic brainwashing and an associated quasi-career as a de-programmer may provide the ex-convert with a new sense of identity and a new sense of meaning and purpose.

In the absence of a clear value framework, and in the context of pluralism's competing normative systems, the youth who join totalistic cults apparently do so in a state of mental exhaustion over choices and decisions. Singer reported that her respondents had immersed themselves in their cults, relieved of the need to make decisions, finding the meaning they sought. After a time, though, disillusionment once more set in. Questions of meaning began to arise again. Although a number of Singer's discussion group members had left the cults on their own after this point, 75% had been brought out by family legal action in the California courts (conservatorship), a process still under debate for its constitutionality. Deprogrammers had also been engaged by many parents as a follow-up to legal custody. (Objections to deprogramming and conservatorships as violations of First Amendment freedoms, imperiling the general free exercise of religion, can be found, e.g., in Judah, 1978).

Singer's ex-cultists were generally grateful for help in getting out, as they reported a sense of powerlessness to come out of their own volition. Yet, the research here and elsewhere is only beginning to show what deep and continuing satisfactions are derived from remaining in the cults. Moreover, families entering at the point of disillusionment to get their children out of cults do not necessarily resolve the problems that the children seem to have solved by joining in the first place. An example of these problems is provided by Singer (1979):

Many of our informants had been struggling with issues of sexuality, dating, and marriage before they joined the cults, and most cults reduce such struggles by restricting sexual contacts and pairings, ostensibly to keep the members targeted on doing "the work of the master." (p. 76)

Extreme sexual reactions often set in after leaving the cult: sexual "binges" or sexual avoidance. (A very small number had been in orgiastic cults that had required participation in sexual activities.)

Singer was one of the few to deal with family formations in cults, or families entering cults (though the issue is touched tangentially in most of the literature cited in this section). Singer (1979) wrote:

Fear may be most acute for former cult members who have left a spouse or children behind in cults that recruited couples and families. Any effort to make contact risks breaking the links completely. Often painful legal actions ensue over child custody or conservatorship between ex- and continuing adherents. (p. 79)

This would be a special problem for such groups as the Jesus Movement commune studied by Harder *et al.* (1976) over a four-year period. A movement from communal living arrangements for married couples, to neo-local forms, was found. This was partly spurred by the weakening of male authority in the communal situation, as several men shared decision making. It also produced identity confusion for children, centering on whom the children had to answer to, and who the adults were whom they could depend on. How children react if a parent leaves such a movement family and what the significance is of the sex of the leaving parent (together with which parent is more likely to leave, as a pattern) are unknown.

Compared to the family socialization of youth who join cults, the cult's socializing processes appear to be far more long-lasting and effective. Cults show a capacity to imbue their members with long-term beliefs and a belief in damnation if they defect from the cult; these beliefs continue after the member leaves. Singer (1979) reported residual cult beliefs among many of the former members she had spoken to. She did not indicate, however, whether those leaving voluntarily showed as much residual belief as those who had been taken from the cults forcibly or through legal processes. She also found that former cult membership could continue to direct the judgments of family and friends. The cultic, hypercritical attitudes made reentry into noncult life much more difficult: "When parents, friends, or therapists try to convince them to be less rigid in their attitudes, they tend to see such as evidence of casual moral relativities" (p. 80).

Where these ex-cultists were torn between cultic moral beliefs and gratitude for their freedom, Harrison (1979), Cohen (1975), and Sage (1976) all reported on children who managed to escape from the deprogrammers, and who were thenceforth disillusioned with and distrusting of their parents' intentions and true feelings.

Although the cults present a sense of family unity to members, when deprogramming succeeds it often displaces cult family feelings back onto the biological family. Sage (1976; p. 46) reported that, in deprogramming, there is assertion of parental love, a call to view critically and cynically the cult's practices, and an emphasis on the primacy of the biological family's caring. Aside from the fact that any type of religious practice may be held up to ridicule, including the practices of Catholicism and Judaism or the belief in Jesus, there is also the real possibility that the cults simply reflect a point of displacement of problems between parents and children. Sage (1976, p. 49) cited Zaretsky on this last possibility. Agreements with this last position are found in Robbins and Anthony (1980), Anthony and Robbins (1974), and Eister (1972).

The search for "other ways," outside one's nuclear family and leading to cult membership, is apparent in the literature. The cults' recruiters intersect with the lives of recruits at critical times. The search that ends in the cult is preceded by experimentation and, often, transient lives. Harrison (1979) reported this, as did Galanter *et al.* (1979):

> Most (67%) reported themselves at least moderately committed to their family's religion before the age of 15. At some point thereafter, one-third (34%) became at least moderately committed to one of the Eastern religious sects, such as the Divine Light Mission, Zen, and Muktananda, and a smaller proportion (19%) to fundamentalist Christian sects. However, fully 90% reported a history of at least some prior commitment to these sects. (p. 166)

Robbins and Anthony (1969; 1972) reported the same pattern among the followers of Meher Baba. Dropping out of school and into drug-dependent subcultures had occurred among these youth in the late 1960s, before coming to the Meher Spiritual Center in South Carolina, where the study was conducted in 1970. Both studies, like others, pointed to a particular process after the age of 15 and into the college years. As mentioned earlier, postconfirmation reductions in personal religious involvement occur both in Christianity and in Judaism. Correlated with this reduction is an apparent normative void, a removal of prior values that, held with whatever intensity, could have had some physical expression in the confirmation ceremonies of the various faiths.

Even though Galanter *et al.* did their study with the cooperation of the Unification Church, there was no significant difference in the patterns found, compared to what was found among Singer's ex-cult members. All reported periods of disillusionment in the cult. Additionally, Galanter *et al.* showed higher and continued neurotic disorders among cult members, particularly where these had already been high at the onset of conversion. Intensity of theistic belief was found to reduce the UC distress scores, but on the whole, the sample showed greater distress than a matched-age comparison group. Galanter *et al.* did not see the UC conversion process as "brainwashing," which is one of the strongest accusations made by anticult parents' groups and ex-member activists (such as Edwards, 1979). By contrast, Conway and Siegelman (1979) and Rudin and Rudin (1980) were most emphatic in describing cult conversions as trickery, in describing psychological damage during and after cult membership, and in advocating action to control the cults. Conway and Siegelman also included among the "dangerous" groups those that advocate deeper levels of TM, EST, and other "mass marketed group therapies and self-help techniques."

The Family and Susceptibility to Cults

A family is "susceptible" to cults if it or one of its members becomes a cultist. The family is therefore a counterpoint to the effectiveness of recruitment by cults.

Two sets of findings emerge on the recruitment patterns of cults: The older, composite pattern, derived from the literature cited, shows individually focused recruitment; recent findings (Snow *et al.*, 1980) examine group effects on recruitment.

The older pattern is as follows: Somewhere between ages 15 and 20, young people who have experienced certain questions, misgivings, and difficulties in their lives and in problems of meaning become vulnerable to cult recruitment. Typically, at the time they are recruited, they are separated from their families (living away at school, emotionally disaffected, and/or in a physically transient existence); strong emotional ties to the family have been weakened; and the recruit may not be locked into a strong friendship network. The quest for meaning, love, friendship, and community intersects with the cult's recruitment processes. Once the recruit is in the cult, the emphasis on switching off critical attitudes toward the cult (as would be the case with any conversion) and gaining acceptance by conformity to cult practices further separates the new member from previous ties. Heavy indoctrination into cult beliefs, including the belief that a defector will be damned and that families are agents of Satan (which justifies threats to the defectors' families), reduces the likelihood that a person will voluntarily leave the cult. Except for the previously fundamentalist minority, cult members evidently encounter strong normative direction and control for the first time in their lives. These may contribute, in turn, to the sense of powerlessness if they cannot leave the cult on their own. A normative and affectional void therefore appears to exist in the person's life at the time of conversion; this void is promoted and reinforced by the dwindling of salient religious values, which, however weak or strong they were in the family, are no longer supported by the presence of family members. (Note that this description can also apply to conversion to certain types of fundamentalism in Christianity or even to Hassidic Judaism).

The newer findings link social networks to recruitment into social movements. Snow et al. (1980) attempted to answer questions on the influence process raised by Useem (1975) and by Zald and McCarthy (1979) about the recruitment of social movement members. Snow et al. examined (1) 10 studies containing quantitative data on the function of social networks in their relationship to differential recruitment (why some join and others do not), with a combined n of 1,200; (2) Snow's data on recruitment to Nichiren Shoshu of America (NSA), a Buddhist movement seeking individual change as the basis of world change, with 330 cases of published recruitment testimony plus 15 informally obtained testimonies ($n = 345$), and 25 informal interviews with Hare Krishna members; and (3) a questionnaire ($n = 300$ used, of 550 administered) given to students at a Texas university in Spring 1979. The authors acknowledged predisposing individual social-psychological factors in the recruitment, but they added the contact dimension, the conditions of contact with the recruiting agents:

It is a basic sociological tenet that social phenomena are not distributed randomly, but are structured according to aggregate or group membership, role incumbency, and the like. It thus seems reasonable to assume that movement recruitment, rather than being random or merely the function of social-psychological predispositions, will also be structured by certain sociospatial factors. (p. 789)

The authors then questioned whether public places, where one is recruited by strangers, are more successful than recruitment by friends, kin, and acquaintances already in a movement. They saw in the movement literature strong evidence that social networks are the richest recruiting source. But the 10 studies providing data on network recruitment showed a very mixed picture of "movements": they include March of Dimes, Sokkagakkai, Pentecostal, Catholic Pentecostal, Evangelistic Protestantism, Anti-Abortion, and Hare Krishna. A comparison of Nichiren Shoshu (NS) recruitment (and NS is not a totalistic group) with Hare Krishna (which is totalistic for those who embrace it fully) showed 82% of NS recruits obtained through social networks, but only 4% of Hare Krishna obtained that way. The public-places recruiting-techniques of NS were, in fact, far less productive (17%) than those of Hare Krishna (96%) in obtaining recruits.

One of the authors' conclusions on participation is stated as a function of countervailing influences: How much opposition to a movement exists in one's social networks *outside* a movement? Where they saw "minimal countervailing risk or sanctions" (p. 793) in successful recruitments, they were speaking exactly to the conditions of recruitment reported in the older patterns. Just as strong links to promovement friends may draw one in, weak links to (potentially) antimovement networks (e.g., the family) may be a structural impetus *by default* to cult recruiters. Snow et al. admitted that social bonds to movement members are not sufficient conditions for participation; neither are the weakened links of the older model. Snow et al. offered a balanced conclusion:

we argue that initial and sustained participation is largely contingent on the countervailing influence of alternative networks and intensive interaction with movement members. Whereas the first factor determines whether one is structurally available for participation, the second factor gives rise to the rationale for participation. (p. 795)

They set forth the propositions that, whereas exclusive participation movements (e.g., Hare Krishna and the UC) primarily attract recruits from public places, nonexclusive movements benefit from social network contacts.

These findings are complementary to the older model of recruitment derived from the literature on the cults. A significant implication drawn by Snow et al. is the relationship between rapidity of growth and network linkage: The very totality of some cults precludes their growth through extramovement networks. In all cases, values are also an issue involved in recruitment (which point brings us back, full circle, to the question of family and the instilling of values).

Although the specific function of religious values in tying families together has been only fragmentarily studied, those values appear to operate against the cults most strongly under particular conditions.

The first is when the values taught provide a clear set of guidelines against which to set questions. The clearer the religious beliefs, the clearer the objections that can be framed. Rather than a vague uneasiness or sense of insufficiency in "religion," there is a clear focus for questions of meaning, the sense of rebellion, and the place/values against which to rebel.

Second, where family religious values are clearly taught and reinforced (whatever such values are called, and whether or not church affiliation is involved), the family can transmit some kind of theodicy (an explanation of why evil and suffering exist in the world) that is accepted or rejected by the young, but for which the young person must establish clear thought concerning why it is (not) acceptable. Interestingly, clues to this susceptible time in the literature point out the need for continuing reinforcement (by implication) precisely at the time when parents typically are "letting go," and permitting ever-higher levels of mobility and autonomy among children. One clue is found in a somewhat unlikely place but shows the process of age-linked reinforcement; it is an older study of the religion–fertility–education linkages done by Westoff and Potvin (1966). They found that the transmission of religious values in the family was affected by the type of education the children received (though sending children to nonsectarian schools may also indicate lower intensity of certain parental religious values). Women in Catholic colleges had maintained higher fertility norms than Catholic women who had gone to nonsectarian colleges. The most significant change the authors found in fertility preferences was among Catholic women in nonsectarian colleges who had gone to Catholic high schools. Again, the choice of a nonsectarian college may also have meant lower religious salience, though the women had come out of the Catholic high schools with generally high fertility norms. These educational correlates with fertility points up the malleability of teenage norms, particularly religious norms and implies that "young adulthood" is so vulnerable to such changes that one might call it "older childhood." The importance of Westoff and Ptovin's study is precisely its examination of normative change in different settings, and if families are concerned about cult influences, they will have to be concerned about the person–environment interaction that will occur when their children leave home. The greater the value conflicts, the greater the disaffection with the family, the more likely it is that a search for intimacy and meaning will be found in groups offering sure normative values and (inter)personal harmony.

A difficulty and a paradox in families' conveying clear religious values against which children can rebel are that certain rational processes in families tend to be discouraged by the affectional setting. As family affections are diffuse, it is likely that certain kinds of intellectual or rational probings will be seen as personal betrayals, or as a diminution of affection on the prober's part. The extent to which families, in transmitting their own values, are capable of valuing critical thought about those values is problematic. For if children are taught critical distance, that process would apply also to all parental ideas, so that

critical detachment could be perceived as a lack of love or trust or respect for parental authority. And where parents may not wish to be authoritarian, another paradox arises in the freedom granted to children: Withdrawing strict parameters of behavior in the early teens, combined with reduced strength of religious socialization after the 12- to 14-year-old's transition to religious adulthood (confirmation, bat and bar mitzvah), may result in a sense of emptiness whose origins are not recognized as religious. Research would have to separate the variables of religious teaching, personal autonomy, and general behavioral norms, over time, to determine the actual effect of reduced religious salience on children's susceptibility to cults.

Again, from the literature, unfocused discontent and an incapacity to deal with autonomy (or fatigue in exercising it) seem most likely to create vulnerability to totalistic cult recruitment when the person is isolated. Nor is the recruitment of families the same as the recruitment of friendship or peer groups. The relative power of spouses to influence each other to join a cult is unexplored; and children will go where their parents take them. So although families are an area of research as they are targets of recruitment, the vast majority of accounts of totalistic cult conversion tell of being approached when the single person is alone. Also, the frequently voiced advantage that recruits find in the cults is "new friends." The unasked question has been: If the convert is so eager to find friends, how did the isolation occur in the first place? Eister's structural theory of cults (1972) proposes that they are the results of cultural crises, in which communicational and orientational institutions (families?) undergo dislocation. The structure for discourse on values and meanings has broken down, with a resultant confusion especially among the young, but reflecting confusion in the larger society. The discourse, to the extent that it now exists, has no center; cults can flourish in such a context.

There is a subculture that proposes strong, coherent sets of answers, which oppose the cults' practices, religiosity, and recruitment, and which raise questions of person–family conflicts as a result of cult conversion (see, e.g., Enroth, 1979). These are the evangelicals, who have already been discussed to some extent; their national prominence increased in 1980 through the actions of Jerry Falwell and his Moral Majority, which helped promote the successful Reagan presidential candidacy. The impact of the evangelicals has been strengthened through the transmission of their messages in the broadcast media, in what has been called the "electric church."

Evangelizing in the Media

In 1978, there were an estimated 1,200 religious radio stations in the United States, increasing at the rate of one per week, and beginning to use communications satellites to broadcast to other parts of the world. Twenty-five television stations existed, increasing at the rate of one per month (Montgomery, 1978).[12] TV broadcasting also occurs on nonreligious channels and stations, so that these figures underestimate total religious broadcast time. The media religious broadcasts, moreover, were and are overwhelmingly fundamentalist or evangelistic in nature.

Mainline churches have been worried by this development. Much religious broadcasting (about half) is listener-supported, and such figures as Martin Marty have expressed concern about this financial drain and the loss of religious community. All segments of the religious world, however, concede the success of media ministries. The numerical success is certainly impressive. By 1980, "television evangelists like Oral Roberts, Pat Robertson and Jerry Falwell reached an estimated 128 million viewers" (Kaufman, 1980, p. 1). Where cult converts sought and found meaning in Hare Krishna or the UC, older people, as well as the young, find evangelical messages the answer to their quest. Specific advice on living the Christian life daily, in families, is reported by mainline church ministers to be the single most important subject of religious teachings, as expressed by their congregants. The personalization of religion, the message of "how to be a Christian," is seen even by those ministers as a powerful attraction of the evangelicals. In addition to highlighting once again the idea of a "normative void" in the application of values, a description of typical sermons shows how the norms are brought home to individuals: "The sermon typically deals with problems that bother most men and women today, invariably discussing practical ways to overcome difficulties." The quotation is from Armstrong (1979, p. 112), describing the "Hour of Power" sermons by Robert Schuller to 4 million viewers each Sunday. But although there are strong indications of a desire to translate religious values into family relationships, the patterned outcomes are unstudied.

The personalism of the message is also paradoxical in terms of evangelical messages for families. Kaufman (1980) wrote:

this turning inward would seem to conflict with the efforts of preachers to mobilize evangelicals into a strong political force [e.g., to oppose abortion and homosexual rights bills]. Indeed, although Moral Majority [Falwell's political action group, whose message through his teachings reaches 25 million television viewers each Sunday on his "Old Time Gospel Hour"] has registered impressive numbers of voters, the group concedes that it often fights a losing battle against apathy and evangelism's strong individualistic strain. (p. 13; emphasis added)

---

[12]Sloan and Bagamery (1980) gave the following figures: of 4,600 AM stations, 500 were religious; of 5,200 FM stations, 280 were religious. One half of the religious stations were commercial, and the others were nonprofit educational. Specialization in religious programming is also described by them; they cited the 5 religious stations in Fort Lauderdale's area, aimed at 5 different types of religious market. Cable TV outlets also expand the reach of religious programs. National Religious Broadcasting (NRB) reports 35 TV stations in its group, not including cable.

It remains to be seen whether the physical isolation of cult recruits is matched to any extent by evangelical conversions. From the variety of testimonies made available, there is considerably less isolation of those who are "born again," and this evidence raises the question of how social location affects the choice of messages leading to radical life-change. Where the cults insist on conformity and group action, the evangelical message concentrates on the *person's* redeemed life. On the continuum of options in the religious market structure, then, where a search for personal values is occurring, individuals whose location makes them resistant to the highly structured, total-demand cult may join the fundamentalist movement; at bottom, it remains always a personal choice, and as such, it may be highly resistant to the fundamentalist groups' leveling influences.

Personalism is enhanced by the media nature of the evangelical appeal. The ability to take or leave the message (by turning the radio or the TV on or off) is realized by such media ministers as Ben Armstrong, who wrote (1979):

we see a reversal of the long-established roles between the person in the pulpit and the person in the pew. In the electric church, power does not rest with the radio or television speaker . . . but with the individual who has the power to turn the dial. (p. 9)

Armstrong is highly aware of the advantages and pitfalls of media ministry, advocating that ministry as a step toward church involvement. His description of the "electric church" is at once a history, a defense, and a set of goals for religion in the broadcast media. Again, the impact on families is derived from his statements and other data on audiences as they report their feelings and actions in letters and telephone calls. It is difficult to know if, as a general rule, families listen *together* to various programs. There are indications that radio is addressed to the specific needs of different family members in its programming, together with general-appeal programs. The monitoring of one 24-hour religious radio station, part of the Family Radio Network originating in Oakland, California, shows a number of general-audience programs (sermons on scripture; call-in question programs on the Bible; radio dramas of "born again" individuals—"Unshackled!" and "Stories of Great Christians"; the reading of new books to the listeners, day by day until each book is finished; and religious music) and programs addressed to individuals in their specific family roles (children's programs; Christian psychologists discussing child rearing and marital problems; singles programs—all of which support family-oriented interaction in conformity with evangelical thinking (Marciano, 1980).

The impact of the media in these tasks is clarified by a comparison: Whereas 42% of Americans attend a church service each week, 47% listen to at least one religious program on radio or television (Armstrong, 1979, p. 7). Media popularity has raised the whole question of ministry in that form: The National Council of Churches denounces it as neither real nor good (Sloan & Bagamery, 1980).

Of the centrifugal potential in the media, the individualistic appeal that may drive individuals more into themselves than into religious community, Armstrong (1979) has used several arguments: First, he sees the media as a return to the practices of the early church, in which a few people at a time gathered together to worship; he defines the electric church as complementary to traditional public church worship, citing letters to media ministers declaring that going to church has taken the place of listening to and viewing religious programs; and he says:

we fear the absence of koinonia, *the gathering together in community of believers, will suffer. Central to our understanding of the church is this element of fellowship one with another. That must never be eclipsed by the electric church, but the electric church has been and is being used to draw people into that kind of local church worship.* (p. 9; emphasis in original)

Religious broadcasting in a suburbanized and rural world is often a substitute for the urban neighborhood or village church that is more convenient to visit or is open daily for services, counseling, or private worship. Distance (especially in an energy-conscious age) and scattered congregations make broadcasting a useful service for many. Just as political and social expression have found their way to radio and television, so has religion. The major advantage of religious broadcasting is that it can go just about anywhere (including on family outings), at just about any time (including all night long). Those who protest the media ministry's popularity do so out of a preference for physical proximity and active collectivity among coreligionists. But group life does exist, religiously oriented and otherwise. Religious broadcasting reflects one part of the widened range of individual religious options; although voluntary associations of all types exist, broadcasting obviously meets needs that other kinds of voluntary religious forms do not.

Religious broadcasting has existed since the 1920s, and its continuing, growing popularity points to its missionary vigor. In fact, it is the missionary aspect of the media ministry that may be the key to its success, given its often stern message. Wilson (1969) argued, for example, that American churches are vigorous because they have secularized, have gone with the people. In Europe, the empty churches reflect a people moving while the churches stand still. In America, religious forms continue while the content of the message changes, so that religion has continued to be a strong force in American life. Wilson did see consequences, however, saying that all American religions have become denominations, whereas religions in Europe have become sects; the latter are marked by the intensity of commitment. And Luckmann (1967) made the same points about the secularization of church messages . Perhaps it is not enough for the message to change; the forms may have to change as well, including into the media. It may also be that if the form is more suitable to a cultural lifestyle, the message may vary considerably more.

By way of illustration of the missionary and form aspects of evangelical messages, from the end of World War II to the early 1960s mainline churches began to absorb liberal secular concerns into their messages; during that time, they held and increased their congregations. They had succeeded in growing because, however unwittingly, they had done what missionaries have been accustomed to doing: going where the unsaved were, learning the native language, preaching in its idiom, and relating the gospels to local problems. It was, of course, absurd to convey a message in a language that its hearers did not understand. Now, the idiom has changed; whereas the formerly successful liberal churches are wondering what happened, the media ministry has found the idiom of personalistic religion, going where the people are (in their homes, or highly mobile) via broadcasting. Because the media are capable of so personalistic a choice and reception, we may have a case where, to paraphrase Marshall McLuhan, the media and the idiom are one. In fact, McLuhan's views of broadcasting and the ministry have been cited by Armstrong (1979, pp. 11–12, 81–82) as keys to understanding the appeal of the religious broadcast media. Robertson (1970, pp. 237–243) classified McLuhan's views of the media as immanentist (one of the directions that secularization has taken). He sees evidence of this in McLuhan's contention (1964) that television and film (tactile, visual, and nonlinear in message) make possible a participation by people in the Body of Christ for the first time.

Thus, the media go with people; religious success occurs when the religion follows the people in terms of their needs; the evangelists have epitomized this process, and the results have been their huge audiences. That the mainline churches can also successfully follow this path today was shown by Armstrong (1979, p. 152), who cited a Presbyterian church that had been losing attendance until it took to the airwaves. Televising its services on alternate Sundays, it averaged 45,000 viewers and raised in-church attendance to over 3,000.

The capacity of the media to strengthen existing churches and the consequences of that process for families pose another set of questions. Armstrong (1979, p. 154) looked at the hidden costs of the media for the congregation from which a broadcast originates. The orientation of such a congregation, if its broadcasts are to be successful, must be one that places the needs of the unchurched over the needs of the churched. To present the broadcasts, there must also be perfected presentation (sermon, singing, and congregational response); high congregational participation in the broadcast process is therefore required. Some congregations resist this participation, and others share a high conviction with their pastor of the importance of the media ministry. But in perfecting their performance roles, family groupings in the congregation may experience division, although this is another area that has not been studied. The time and performance demands of media use also raise the problem of time allocated to daily pastoral work, including family-oriented and family-counseling activities by the pastor, a pitfall for any public figure, but a double danger for those whose message is supposed to exemplify humility and pastoral work.

Another family aspect of media and families is that because media can be experienced privately, perhaps as a "trial step" toward more religious involvement, one need not enter into a discourse about nor a defense of what one is hearing. The amount of privatism within a given family, the phenomenon of unshared reception, is unknown.

The fundamentalist media ministry, in its success, can also indicate that the content of the message *may* be less important than its immediacy, as long as it has religious content confidently presented as making sense in its own right. The immediacy of friendships, caring, and normative structure for the young that is offered by the cults is, after all, one of the recruiters' great reported attractions.

Immediacy also shapes to the medium: a single message can be driven home very effectively. Themes from the scriptures are clear-cut to the evangelist and are presented in straightforward language. The clearly developed plot, with its problems and conflicts elaborated and then clearly resolved, is the essence of American broadcasting generally, and of successful religious broadcasting by the evangelists. The Bible is a ready-made set of plots; daily-life conflicts can be framed in reference to them (e.g., temptation, infidelity, and trust in God), and an answer can be provided by biblical resolutions (rewards to the just and punishment of the unrighteous).

The immediacy and the instant availability of religious media messages reflect the qualities of other sectors of American life. Media ministries provide round-the-clock counseling and receiving centers for prayer requests, by mail and phone. The Family Radio Network, for example, broadcasts programs from the Moody Bible Institute (Chicago) and the Garden Mission, followed by 24-hour numbers that people can call who wish to begin living a Christian life, and who want to talk to someone about it. The Christian Broadcasting Network's (CBN) "700 Club" has more than 7,000 prayer counselors, nationwide, on duty 24 hours a day. McLuhan's "global village" created by the media is thus realized in access to the ministry that might otherwise be unavailable in a mobile, individualistic nation.

It is easy to be cynical in equating a 24-hour, fast-service, instant-gratification society with religious broadcasting. That attitude, however, would be to make the same mistake that Wilson (1966) saw in the European churches: they were content to preserve form and content; meanwhile, American churches preserved form and altered content, and the media ministry has changed both, in response to the culture in which it does its missionary work to the unsaved. It is ironic that convenience, availability, and "fit" with the culture should be the bases of condemnation by the "new traditionalists," the mainline churches that oppose and resist involvement with the media on the evangelical scale. Yet the use of radio and television by mainline churches on a large scale (e.g.,

"The Lutheran Hour" on radio and Bishop Sheen on television) has been a part of religious broadcasting history. In citing the effects of such broadcasts as Bishop Sheen's, Armstrong (1979) mentioned that the programs were often subjects of discussion at work the next day. In fact, anyone who has worked in an office or in a workplace where conversation with one's co-workers is part of the workday knows that television programs of all types become subjects of conversation. Again, however, research does not tell us much, particularly in terms of religious content media. It remains to be found how much the peer group at work or among friends becomes a center for religious discourse, compared with the family as such a center. (What outcomes would have resulted among cult recruits had friendship groups tried to argue them out of conversion?) The existence of an evangelical subculture (churchgoers, listeners, those who purchase the books and send financial support to media ministers, and those whose voluntary activities center on evangelical work) is known by those in and out of the subculture (Kaufman, 1980). It is the internal family processes of that subculture, as affected by the media, that would set up a model for how options are taken and continued in religious life toward or away from evangelical (or cultic) action.

There is also not much understanding of how religious broadcast audiences actually grow. Some report their parents' leaving on religious programs so the children will hear them; others happen on a radio or television program (in a car, flipping channels at home, or in a hospital bed, or in a motel while on vacation) at a point where the message being offered has an immediate relevance to their problems. These incidents are reported in individual accounts or letters but are not understood as a general pattern.

Finally, there is the question of whether and how *family* churchgoing may originate out of the media. Armstrong (1979, pp. 115–116) reported that local ministers beginning to use radio and TV find higher degrees of recognition and warmer receptions in their towns when they begin to canvas for new congregants. Once this contact is made, though, who influences whom to respond to the invitation to go to church, and how does churchgoing model role formation in the family?

Just as going to church is more likely after seeing the congregation or the pastor on television, or after hearing the sermon on radio, radio audiences for religious messages increased rather than decreased with the advent of TV. Radio has an audience today that is eight times larger than that of television (Armstrong, 1979, p. 122), a testament to its "fit" with American mobility and differentiation. Radio can specialize as television cannot, partly because so many more frequencies are available to radio, and particular markets can be specially targeted. Armstrong (1979) wrote:

If you live in Philadelphia, for example, you have a choice of twenty-four radio stations, and you can find religious programs

on at least eight of them. Across the country one out of every dozen stations devotes its schedule to religious programs full time. (p. 123)

Another evidence of popularity is the capacity of religious programming to rescue a station from financial difficulties, a fact noted both by Armstrong and by Sloan and Bagamery (1980). Stations have gone from secular and popular musical formats to religious broadcasting to find their audiences multiplying at astounding rates.

Radio ministries also provide an accessibility in time and place that television cannot. Among the places where first (and continued) listening has been reported are in the car, in a prison, lying in a hospital bed, out camping, and while working at home or in a workplace (using the radio to reduce the boredom of repetitive tasks). Impressionistically, listeners seem to report two directions of influence on family and friends: as the listener finds a sense of meaning and new happiness in listening, friends and family want to share in its source, and they begin listening too; or a strong negative reaction sets in, so that the listener reports a sense of being alone among the unsaved. Media ministers (especially on radio) give warnings about alienating people by giving testimony at every opportunity. There are also reports of suspicion of the "born again" individual, a wariness, and a sense that the convert has been fooled or has stopped being "sensible." Although a parallel process occurs for the new cult member, the major difference is that the "born again" individual remains in interaction networks with friends and family and is not shielded from external criticism as is the case in cult group life. Effects on family role satisfactions and performance are unknown.

There are writers (e.g., Wills, 1978) who see evangelistic growth as a fad, characterized by greater awareness rather than greater spirituality. But public awareness of certain values cannot be underestimated, especially in the light of research deficits in so many areas of religion. The degree to which evangelicals are promoting what will come to be taken-for-granted, everyday assumptions (paradigms for daily constructions of thought and reality) will be the degree of their power and effect.

Given the audience figures, the amount of money spent in spreading the Christian evangelical message on the air (see Armstrong, 1979, for a discussion of costs), the enormous volume of mail generated by the programs, and the reported increases in churchgoing as a reflection of "born again" status, the electric church is probably the most underestimated religious force in America today.

Evangelism and Women

While the fundamentalists in their congregations and broadcasts reassert traditional roles for women and men, a countertrend exists in the feminist movement vis-à-vis the churches and patriarchal religious doctrine in general. Women have not been immune to the religious revival; they are a strong part of the evangelists' followings. But

the religious market offers other options, arising from the resurgence of the women's rights movement. Termed generically the Women's Movement, it has not been monolithic, just as the cults and the evangelistic revival have not been single, unified phenomena. They are all "movements" in that they share common goals, and the separate groups within each movement tend to reflect similar global orientations to what they perceive as needed change. Movements may also organize to resist certain social changes, attempting to substitute new or older goals for current changes that they see occurring. (The case of Iran and the fall of the shah was one such countermovement, substituting the traditional orientations of Shiite Islam for the westernizing influences and political system of the shah). In America, the anti-ERA women led by Phyllis Schlafly have linked up with women who advocate what they see as traditional, biblically validated sex-role differences.[13] Other women, who have a different perspective on sex roles as shaped by religious meanings, have gone in several directions: out of the churches completely, holding a personal synthesis of beliefs; or into the churches to struggle for a reorientation of the patriarchal structures and teachings; or into some combination of selective church participation where feminist goals seem to be met; or into the formation of "women's religions," small, mostly unstudied groups of women who claim the continuing divine nature of Aphrodite, Artemis, Gaia, Isis, Magna Mater, and women's animism/naturalism in the worship of trees (their spirits).

As with the other phenomena examined, family consequences tend to be derived from the individual or collective actions of women in relation to others, and women's collective actions toward the churches.

Feminists and the Churches

The basic dilemma faced by all women in major religious structures is the misogyny of practice and transmitted doctrine, compared to the equality of love and compassion for all people in the original prophetic messages. The global orientation of religious feminists is the calling forth of that equality in the original messages, as a step toward changing current practices that discriminate against women. Therefore, feminists press above all for reinterpretations of theology that will lead to equally shared access to opportunities for action, leadership, sacramental participation, and church policy formation. Feminism can and has, in these aims, divided churches and families along sex lines and doctrinal lines, just as youth in the cults have divided families along generational lines. Little is known, however, about the direct action of religious feminism on the feminists' own fami-

---

[13]The women's movement and the fundamentalist women have been linked in antipornography campaigns. The fundamentalists' campaign against erotic material accords with the thinking of feminists who see pornography as glorifying violence toward and exploiting women.

lies, or on the family transmission of feminist religious values. Presumably, feminism is most divisive in families and churches where the old forms most favor male power and status. For the churches, there is ample evidence that this is so; church resistance and the resultant high levels of conflict occur where a church has refused to accede to a single major feminist demand, as, for example, with Roman Catholics and Mormons in Christianity, and in Orthodox Judaism. Although religious feminists may be male as well as female, the woman's feminism in a family context where parents, spouse, or children do not agree with her makes her an "enemy within." It would be most enlightening to have research on the degree to which religious feminists feel or grow conscious of a distance between themselves and their families over the issue; specific links between feminist orientations and the decision not to marry; and the withdrawal of family members from support of feminist members.

Churches apparently become an arena for feminist struggle after the women's attitudes have been influenced by values equated with feminist consciousness. Logically, injustice is perceived in a structure according to some point of comparison, so that alternative claims of right and wrong can be measured. McClain (1979) showed that feminists and nonfeminists differ in their orientation to life values, with feminists scoring very high on autonomy scales. This valuation of autonomy, set against the religious message of submission to the (external) will of God, illustrates the continuing interaction of person and structure in the formation of a feminist religious synthesis. There is a willingness among many religious feminists to submit to the discipline of their churches (as that discipline presumably expresses the will of God), but under the condition that they have some voice in the shaping of the discipline. To do so, they must first have a voice in the interpretation of the scriptures and the traditions that shape the discipline. It is to justify their remaining within the churches, then, that feminists lay claim to rights of leadership and full participation in all aspects of religious life, rather than simply following the rules laid down for them. The feminist synthesis is, in essence, the acceptance of the word of God, but a rejection of its sex-biased interpretation and implementation in daily life.

The primary appeal of feminists in the Christian churches is to the specific actions and attitudes of Jesus as recorded in the gospels; feminists oppose the presumed scriptural justifications of a secondary role for women in the words and works of those who went out after Jesus' death to preach the gospel message. Where the feminists deal with biblical injunctions against full female participation (in New Testament books such as Acts and St. Paul's Epistles), they call into question culturebound translations of scriptures and point out that, in their original languages, these books showed women occupying leadership roles in early Christianity.

Jewish feminists tend to emphasize the sexually nonexclusive appeal of the Law (Torah) and the sociohistorical forces creating patriarchal rather than androgynous religious leadership and practices. They emphasize the value placed on all human life that runs so powerfully through scripture and commentaries. Of particular concern to the Jewish feminists are the laws of ritual purity, which, by their restrictions on women generally, and on menstruating women particularly, are held to imply inferiority and uncleanness. (Christian feminists also struggle with this tradition as it came into Christianity through the Church Fathers.) Another major question is the binding of *mitzvot*[14] on women as well as on men, as full participation is contingent on fully shared obligation. The exemption of women from religious requirements that bind men has been set forth as freeing women to pursue their (primary) marital and child-rearing obligations. Steinsaltz (1976) listed some of the exemptions, though this is far from a complete list:

These include many of the familiar rituals of Jewish life: wearing the tzitzit *(fringed four-cornered garmet), laying* tefilin *(phylacteries), reciting the* Shema Yisrael *prayer, blowing the* shofar, *constructing the* sukkah, *and pilgrimage. Women are not permitted to join a* minyan *(quorum of ten) for prayer, nor are they assigned active functions in the community. As for their social status, they are not eligible for administrative and judicial positions. And, most significant of all, they are exempt from the important* mitzvah *of studying Torah, a fact that inevitably precludes them from playing a part in Jewish cultural and spiritual life.* (p. 137; emphasis in original)

These exemptions, which amount in some parts of Judaism to imposed restrictions, are not conceded by many Jewish feminists, who study the Torah, use phylacteries, pray at the hours when men are obliged to pray, and lead or join in sex-mixed prayer groups.

Both Christian and Jewish feminism have brought about the rewriting of prayers and liturgical services, the sponsorship of feminist religious publications (books, journals such as *Lilith,* and newspapers such as *Womanspirit*), and participation in feminist prayer and action groups that include both women and men. Both groups of feminists are involved in the reformulation of theology to eliminate male biases in its traditional formulation. Traditions and commentaries are also subjected to scholarly scrutiny to reveal the human biases and sexism imposed as divine law.

All of these activities occur in a range of ways: There are feminists who remain in traditional structural roles (e.g., nuns) working within the churches for ordination and full rights of participation; others stand outside totally, or in selective participation.

Those who struggle from within the structures face enormous conflict with families and peers who are not committed to feminist religious goals. Sister Theresa Kane's challenge to Pope John Paul II on his visit to the United States in 1979, wherein she called on him to ordain women to the priesthood, evoked as much criticism as approbation. Certainly, women do not automatically

---

[14]The 613 precepts binding all males in Judaism.

embrace feminist religious goals, just as men do not automatically reject them. Mary Daly (1975), a leader in feminist theological reconstruction, reported: "Often in the late sixties I encountered hostility in women, not toward the patriarchs whose misogynism I was exposing, but toward me for exposing them" (p. 14).

There are also women who feel that something very important is said by religion about sex-role differences, as expressed in the separation of sexes in rabbinical/ministerial functions (see, e.g., Wisse, 1979). At the same time, Priests for Equality is an example of a men's group (with women members) pressing for women's access to ordination, just as many women oppose that access (see also Daly, 1973, 1978; Williams, 1977).

The actions of Mormon feminists have begun to focus attention on the implications of feminist debate for family roles. (The literature still shows far more church-versus-person action, with family conflict implicit in that action.)

Mormon feminists (or anyone who violates certain precepts of the church) face the extreme sanction of excommunication and are torn by contradictions between the church and the feminist orientations that they concurrently feel. As non-Mormon women point to Jesus and to St. Paul (who is cited by the evangelicals as having told women to keep silent in the churches, but who is cited by the feminists for having said that in Christ there is neither male nor female), Mormon feminists point additionally to the words of Brigham Young, who encouraged women in roles other than the exclusively familial (Warenski, 1978, p. 198).

Special difficulty for Mormon feminists lies in the Mormon incorporation of family into the plan of salvation. These Mormon doctrines on marriage and family are unique in the Christian tradition and provide the closest thing to an "ideal type" for the category of woman-as-guerrilla in a traditionally religious family structure. Mormons marry for time and eternity, and that marriage continues through the present life into the afterlife. Salvation is contingent on marriage and is necessary for the achievement of the highest bliss after death. Thus, heaven is experienced in the family unit through eternity. Besides heavily penalizing single people through this doctrine (see Warenski, 1978, pp. 225–251), the Mormon family structure embodies eternal headship by the father not only as part of Christian tradition, but also because he is part (as all adult Mormon males are expected to be) of the Mormon priesthood.[15]

When a Mormon is excommunicated, she or he is cut off not only from full church participation but also from the family-based afterlife. The excommunication of Sonia Johnson from the Mormon church for her pro-ERA activities has been notable in highlighting the religious/familial/feminist conflicts that deserve more study in all faith contexts. Feminists have taken up Johnson's cause, publicizing her excommunication as an example of sexism and injustice in religious structures. One article also points up a dialectical process in the Mormon structure paralleling that within evangelical Christianity; describing the personal religious crisis faced by Johnson as a result of her first encounter with feminist literature, Wohl (1980) wrote:

She was finally reconciled to her faith, she says, "when I realized that I had confused the church leaders with God. . . ." After deciding that she still held to the Mormon religious faith, Johnson set out to oppose the church's political position on the ERA, relying on the Mormon doctrine of "free agency"—that is, the right of each individual to act according to her or his conscience. (p. 40)

The dialectical process in all churches, then, resides in the equality of human conscience pitted against the sex-based inequality of religious rights. It is also indicative of the individual-versus-group conflicts always implicit in the freedom–conformity balance that each person must strike.

The conflicts of women and their more religiously traditional peers and families were recorded long before the Equal Rights Amendment. Novels and essays from the past 200 years are being reprinted and are receiving renewed attention for their similarity to current feminist problems with family and social structure generally.[16] In the "second wave" of the women's movement that dates from the 1960s, Betty Friedan (1963, whose work crystallized the beginning of the second women's movement in this country) cited cases similar to Sonia Johnson's, though with less drastic and nonpublic results at the time (pp. 339–340). In those cases, women were persuaded by the weight of their religious traditions to discontinue their own careers or other interests outside the home. The women remained uneasy and dissatisfied with the choices forced on them by their beliefs and their socialization, and out of such conflicts came the beginning of the popular base (whose extent is unknown) of religious feminism.

Of all the feminist issues, however, religious feminism has received a relatively small amount of attention compared to that paid the advocacy of equal jobs, income, and educational opportunities for women. Yet, religious feminists may succeed more rapidly in dismantling patriarchal structures because they are attempting to dismantle partriarchal worldviews as they influence action generally in society.

---

[15]The exclusion of black men from Mormon priesthood was in force until the 1970s, after which the head of the Mormon church, by revelation, declared an end to racial restrictions on male priesthood.

[16]Some of the novels being reprinted include two first published in 1899: Charlotte Perkins Gilman's *The Yellow Wallpaper* and Kate Chopin's *The Awakening*. Authors receiving more attention include Virginia Woolf (whose nonfiction *A Room of One's Own* is popular, as are her novels), Dorothy Richardson, Dorothy Canfield Fisher, Sarah Orne Jewett, Willa Cather, Jean Rhys, and Edith Wharton. Nonfiction works include Elizabeth Cady Stanton's *The Woman's Bible* and Matilda Josly Gage's *Woman, Church and State*.

In attempting this reconstruction, however, religious feminists, with few exceptions (such as Mary Daly, who calls herself "postchristian"), have not chosen the ultimate weapon available against the religious institutions in society. Where the church is not legally established (i.e., state-supported, as in England), the church is a voluntary association in that it cannot compel financial or spiritual support. Except by a socialization of its believers, the church cannot force attendance, belief, conformity, or defense against attackers. Any such association, furthermore, tends to be strengthened by its capacity to take a deliberate stance against attack, buttressing itself by calling attention to the need for solidarity in the presence of an external enemy. In such a condition, the ultimate weapon against religious institutions is indifference. If the call went out to ignore the churches, to cease all participation, to be indifferent (in action at least) to spiritual and financial appeals of the patriarchal institutions, there would be two immediate consequences: First, with public arguments against the churches discontinued, opponents would no longer provide a public opportunity for the restatement of patriarchal views, or for a summons for public support against a feminist threat; second, church attendance (by contrast with cult membership) is more heavily female than male in the mainline churches, so the absence of women, at least in their former numbers, would be a statement against which no sermon could prevail. In that second case, the targets of the sermons simply would not be there to hear them. The family consequences of such action would be problematic: Sermons preached to men that condemn women could exacerbate intrafamilial conflict, and the religious norms of family stability and mutual devotion would be undercut. Alternatively, because such preaching would place the men in conflict, they might opt for conflict resolution through their own withdrawal from the churches.

As it now stands, the religious feminists implicitly legitimate the idea of church, and thereby its patriarchal phase, by attempting to change it rather than finding an alternative to it. *De facto* indifference to religion by feminists has been mentioned in passing in women's literature but has not been explored in terms of how the churches came to be irrelevant to women's concerns as a *process* in the evolution of the feminist consciousness.[17]

On the positive side, where religious feminists do not choose the route of indifference, they may experience continued frustration but may also act more forcefully on

the social construction of womanhood than would be possible elsewhere in the women's movement. The reason is that they are challenging the very categories of thought by which we construct and legitimate the world (see Berger & Luckmann, 1963), particularly the bases on which differences are drawn between "men" and "women." Those who remain within are working in several areas for change: as scholars and theologians; as activists in public demonstrations and conferences; and in the remaking of liturgies. All of these are aimed at redirecting the concept of the transcendent into one that incorporates the idea of the female as fully as it has, until now, incorporated the male. The areas of reconstruction and activism are interlocked, for theology supports action, and the insufficiency of these efforts for some leads to the search for alternative women's religions, as noted earlier.

Religious feminists work for women as women, for women as a class, and for the idea of women more than for any particular women's status in the family and religion. New status simply reflects new concepts of "woman." Thus, in 1980, Espiscopal women clergy and laity formed the Mother Thunder Mission in New York City. They still had to struggle with the fact that their nonsexist services are held on Saturday nights rather than on Sundays (Dullea, 1980).

To change the consciousness of womanhood, religious feminists have focused their theological and traditional research on views of women's sexuality and implicit impurity. Those are the foundations on which women have been held to be disqualified for clerical office and full religious participation as well as, through scriptural justification, for coequality with the husband in the family.

Sexuality and purity are the focus of so much religious thought[18] precisely because they have been implicit and explicit bases for constructing the day-to-day structures of ongoing religious institutions.[19] A most ironic commentary on this state of affairs has been written by Gloria Steinem to point up the absurdity of using physiology as a basis for theology. In "If Men Could Menstruate" (1978), Steinem wrote:

---

[17]Judith Antares (1978) described a prevalent feminist view of religion and the religious feminists' answer: "The strongest critics of spirituality see it as escapist, as focusing on inner subjective reality as opposed to external objective conditions—thus taking away from the 'real' political work that needs to be done. . . . Spirituality is seen simply as 'an opiate of the people'—i.e., as a way of diverting people's attention from their oppression in the here and now. While this can be said of patriarchal religion, it is not necessarily the essence of spirituality itself" (p. 11).

[18]A clue to changed categories of thought regarding women, reflecting changed attitudes and action, is found in Komarovsky (1972): "It is this ideal of intellectual companionship with women, we suggest, that may explain the relative adjustment of the men in this sphere. As long as the expectation of male superiority persisted, anything near equality on the part of the woman carried the threatening message to the men: 'I am not the intellectually *superior* male I am expected to be.' But when the ideal of intellectual companionship between equals replaces the expectation of male superiority, the pressure upon the man eases and changes. . . . Once the expectation of clear superiority is relinquished, varieties of relationships may be accommodated" (pp. 876–877; italics in original).

[19]The issues of sexuality and purity are the clearest links between family and religion, though how these links function and where else the bonds are are unresearched for modern-day America.

Military men, right-wing politicians, and religious fundamentalists would cite menstruation ("men-struation") as proof that only men could serve in the Army ("you have to give blood to take blood"), occupy political office ("can women be aggressive without that steadfast cycle governed by the planet Mars?"), be priests and ministers ("how could a woman give her blood for our sins?"), or rabbis ("without the monthly loss of impurities, women remain unclean"). (p. 110)

Women's Purity: The Family Connection

The scriptural work of Jewish feminists (e.g., Bird, 1974; Hauptman, 1974)[20] and Christian feminists such as Reuther (1974) and Daly (1975) detail the creation of inequality by religious outlook, based on women's "impurity" and stemming from the Fall.

The essence of "impurity" resides in those aspects of the female body's workings that are different from those of men. Hearts, lungs, livers, and legs are not of concern in the Scriptures except as they belong to animals, in which case they may or may not be ritually pure for consumption. Rather, the concern with the female's body's is in her having breasts, a womb, and menstrual cycles. Men's bodies are of concern insofar as circumcision is a sign of the covenant between God and Abraham. Beyond that, most of the injunctions on Jewish men (and many on Christian men) toward women are contingent on the woman's menstrual and marital status. In Christianity, menstruation does not debar sexual intercourse as it does for observant Jews, but the heritage of "uncleanness" remains, evolved from the Jewish blood taboo and other sources.[21] Catholic women do report, however, that where they use the rhythm method of birth control and do not want more children right away or at all, they experience emotional relief at the onset of menstruation as well as confidence that sex during this time is safe against conception.

Menstruation and childbearing, with their attendant "debilities" and shame, are the sign of God's displeasure with Eve in her fall from grace. Because woman was made from man (Eve from Adam's rib, rather than the mythical first woman Lilith, who was made from earth and therefore refused to serve Adam because she was made the same way as he), and because she was deceived into disobedience and seduced Adam into sin ("Eve was framed," say feminist posters), she was made subject to her husband by God.

What tends to be ignored is that Adam was also roundly cursed by God for eating the forbidden fruit. He would

have to struggle and sweat to get his food from the ground, and the earth would yield brambles and thistles and weeds rather than the abundance of Eden. Thus, if one is to accept the Fall at all, coequality of sinfulness would be a major step toward coequality of everyday existence between women and men.

There is nothing in Scripture explaining why Eve rather than Adam was approached by the serpent. It is the exposition of this "why" that sets in motion legitimations of patriarchy. If Eve were adjudged simply friendlier, more receptive to strangers, more eager for knowledge, less repelled by wildlife, or more open to new ideas, she would be a human being possessing qualities that are valued in the twentieth century. But by emphasizing the foolishness of Eve, her weakness, her gullibility, and her inherent flaw of character, the interpretation is completely slanted toward female unthoughtfulness and her need to be protected against herself. So it is with children, and adults consider themselves superior to children. If the woman is a child, and the man must protect her, the conditions of inequality are ready-made.

How, though, out of Eve's "foolishness," do her daughters become "impure"? For what is impure is to be feared, as it contaminates not only oneself in the present but also imperils salvation. Where there is fear of a peril, there also tends to be hatred of the cause of that fear. Thus, the continuing ambivalence of the love–hate relationships between men and women.

A functional explanation can be offered for the "impure" pronunciations on women's bodies. (As it is a value, countervalue explanations are of equal weight.) There is nothing inherently harmful to men in women when they menstruate, nor after parturition. But if Moses learned in Egypt about the oestral cycle and then had to lead a small band a long way, maximizing their reproductive capacities despite arduous travel and many enemies, knowledge of women's fertility cycle would have helped to maximize their reproductive potential. This actually is done (in the absence of contraception) by confining intercourse to the most fertile part of the menstrual cycle: approximately two weeks after the onset of menstruation. The laws of ritual purity demand seven "clean days" (i.e., free of any showing of blood) before the spouses can resume sexual intercourse. To compel this matching of sex and fertility, sanctions had to be powerful—and internalized. One hardly encourages reproduction, after all, by having guards poking about in a married couple's tent. Religious sanctioning would be most likely to evoke obedience in so religion-oriented a situation.

Reinforcement of the idea of menstrual and other types of female (and male) impurities was provided by contact with other cultures; Bird (1974, pp. 68–69) cited the Israelite knowledge of and reaction to cultic practices in Canaan (see also Shulman, 1974). The question of how any sex-based taboo arises in the first place continues to fascinate psychologists and other scholars, but the syncretic nature of "impurity" is somewhat evident in Judaism, and even more so in Christianity. In the latter case,

[20]John H. Otwell (1977) has also examined Old Testament texts to point out the high status of women in ancient Israel.

[21]It must also be understood that Judaism, since about 600 C.E. (Common Era), has existed in a Christian world. It cannot have failed to have been shaped at least somewhat by the dualistic Christian framework in which it found itself, or to protect its followers from the dualism of their Christian age peers. The implicit dualism already in Judaism, in the emphasis on female impurity, has been extended by Christian contact.

described in excellent detail by Reuther (1974), the syncretism vis-à-vis women involved the absorption of a dualistic view of creation (from the Greeks, among others). Such a view equates man with spirit and godliness, and woman with flesh and sin. Durkheim (1965) defined the profane as anything that contaminates the sacred, and by this definition, if men are sacred (godly), and women are not, women contaminate men. Thus female "impurity." Redemption for women is possible only if they deny their female (reproductive) nature, in virginity.

How does this attitude affect the view of women in the family? First, to become a wife is to lose virginity, which is the "best" status for women. It is also the best status for a man, though his virginity is owned by God, whereas a woman's is owned by her father, and then her husband. They are at least as dishonored as she by the loss of her virginity outside marriage.

Marriage is a sacrament in Christian belief; in Judaism, it is one of the 613 precepts, a blessing, and a step toward transcending self to live a godly life. How then does loss of virginity equate with inferiority for women? Because it presumes the beginning of the childbearing period, which is the punishment of Eve.

From this perspective, this view of virginity/sexuality must be seen as anachronistic. Who, today, is concerned with such matters? The continuing religious concern about premarital purity and extramarital restraint so well documented by Kinsey and his associates (1953), and later by Masters and Johnson (1970), shows a direct correlation between active religious status and sexual dysfunction, guilt, and conflict. (See Burlage, 1974, for a treatment of these findings in light of church doctrine.) In the area of sexuality, religion directly and indirectly transmits values whose origins and implications may have been forgotten. If the rules of etiquette, bound by class, take so long to change, the rules of sexual behavior, bound by the mores, certainly take far longer to change. The mores, the core of religious teachings on sexuality, are by their nature more resistant to adaptation, more powerful in their sanctions, more deeply internalized, and slower to be influenced by new knowledge and technology. William Ogburn's term "cultural lag" expresses precisely this. When it comes to sexual attitudes (and the resultant sex-role attitudes), the survival and persistence of old ideas tend to last very long indeed. And when these ideas continue to receive reinforcement from a subculture that is growing (the religious orthodoxies) and are promoted by public action (as in the political arm of the evangelical ministries), old ideas can maintain their force even where the "punishment" for "sinful sex" (out-of-wedlock pregnancy) can be avoided by the contraceptive technology available. In fact, the continuation of older attitudes is illustrated by the seemingly paradoxical finding that the best predictor of premarital pregnancy is the belief that premarital sex is wrong (Furstenberg, 1971). One million teenage pregnancies in 1979 exemplify, in part, the persistence of the older attitudes among the young. If, then, religion can instill guilt yet not inhibit completely a guilt-provoking act, there are important implications for women's religious equality: Women can occupy formal leadership positions in congregations, but congregations may well persist in their negative views of women, and in their doubt about the legitimacy of the woman's ministry.

Even sex in its sacramental aspect in marriage does not completely eradicate the view that sex is a "lower" choice than abstinence for women particularly, and for men as an ideal. Sherrard (1977) described how physical-sacramental confusion of sexuality continues to infuse Christian thought:

in spite of the fact that marriage is recognized as a sacrament by the Church, the attitude of Christian thought toward the sexual relationship and its spiritual potentialities has been singularly limited and negative. From the start Christian authors have been ill at ease with the whole subject. . . . Although precluded by their basic doctrine from subscribing to an out-and-out dualism in this matter . . . their practical attitude differs little from that of dualists of a Manichaean type. Sexuality is tainted. It is impure. (p. 307)

How much change has occurred? In April 1980, Hans Kung publicized a letter to the Pope that included the following: "How many more priests do we have to lose before we recognize the legitimacy of marriage?"

Men have made the theology; historically, their socialization has also been less sexually inhibiting. As a result, even the sight of a woman has been more likely to arouse men, and even more so where men have been prolongedly continent, as with the woman-denouncing Desert Fathers. Arousal and sexual desire represent a carnality that detracts from spirituality; women, therefore, cause sin and impurity and, thus, must be inherently sinful and impure.

All women are part of this impure caste, and female spiritual leadership is an endeavor that is therefore a contradiction. The inherently sinful cannot lead a congregation into godliness. Thus comes about the problem of women in the ministry, women performing sacramental functions, and women coequal with men, so that sex might cease to be the most salient point of recognition in the religious community.

Even where women have achieved ministerial/rabbinical ordination, the caste nature of women has been reported to continue to affect leadership perceptions and resultant performance (see Morton, 1974; Neville, 1974; Briggs, 1980). In his famous study *Streetcorner Society* (1966) Whyte showed that a leader embodies the norms, is more of what others want to be. In religious leadership, it is still normative to be male. Women cannot and do not embody this most basic leadership or value norm. Their socialization reinforces this, even where they have aspired to the ministry from early in their lives (Neville, 1974).

Thus, the apparent breakthroughs made by women in the ministry—as Reform rabbis in Judaism, as priests in the Episcopal church, and as ministers in Methodist, Lutheran, UCC, and other churches—would seem to leave just a few areas for women to overcome in order to achieve coequal leadership. Unfortunately, women in the ministry are marked by tokenism and all the problems that token status brings. Finding a congregation at all in a contracting market, being a pastor or a head rabbi rather than an assistant, at rates that approach males in the ministry—all would be true marks of a breakthrough. These have not happened (Morton, 1974), and token status does not indicate real progress. Kanter's research (1976) shows clearly the debilitating effects of tokenism on social change in the area of sex roles. Women in the ministry are tokens that are highly visible, in the same way that blackness or whiteness is visible in a race-conscious setting. Polarization occurs in the differences between the majority of male ministers and the token minority of female ministers. The stereotyped expectations about the minority prevail through the distorted perceptions of the majorities. Kanter (1976) saw all of this in the workplace, and it is no different where the workplace is a religious structure.

The token women in the ministry are also in churches or denominations that have lost congregants. Sex-exclusive ministry prevails among those churches that are growing (Mormons and evangelicals) and also among Roman Catholics, who are losing numbers.[22] What is the commonality that makes them so resistant to the inclusion of women, or to a revision of sex-role teachings that would relax the salience of *woman* in the term *woman minister*? All feel an exclusive, unerring heritage of truth that those "outside" cannot or will not recognize. The very pressure by women for admission reinforces the sense that this pressure stems from a willful refusal to submit to the will and word of God. Where the male-based stranglehold on "truth" was broken by feminists in churches that now ordain women, the breaking may have been caused by those churches' very weaknesses as institutional settings for a spiritual quest. Did the churches that now ordain women give in because their smaller

numbers (and consequent loss of status) make the ministry less important? Generally, the higher the stakes in a status, the more power it wields and the greater are the limitations on access. In the case of the growing churches, power derives from numerical growth. In the case of the Catholics, power resides in control over a worldwide apparatus, a bureaucracy staffed and controlled by men. And this male-oriented view of power and priesthood has extended so far as to allow married male Anglican priests, disaffected by the "liberal" tendencies in the Anglican Communion (e.g., female ordination), to become Roman Catholic priests (DeWitt, 1980).

It is also known historically that, as women enter a given job area, it declines in status. The feminization of a job is another way of saying that it matters less, is paid less, and has less power attached to it. Secretarial status declined when women began to fill those jobs in this century, replacing the more important males who had previously done secretarial work. Many studies show that, even where an occupation is predominantly female (elementary-school teaching, nursing, and library work), the supervisory positions are predominantly male (principals, hospital administrators, and head librarians) (see, e.g., Oppenheimer, 1968, 1973). Will ministerial status decline as women enter the ministry, in churches that have less to lose by granting this status to them? Lehman (1980) pointed to an affirmative answer to this question. He showed that churches struggling with budgets or membership declines are more likely to call women to their pulpits.

If status decline is in fact occurring, one must wonder how it will affect the capacity of women as ministers to model new ideas and attitudes toward women in their congregations and communities. The research questions, and needs, are phenomenal in this area.

Women in the ministry, as linked to the family, provide a new point of view from which counseling and preaching can be done. Whatever the consequences for status in the female ministry, the ministerial role still provides a way to make major incursions into old attitudes about female "purity," sinfulness, foolishness, and childlikeness. The symbol of woman-as-minister may be able finally to carry a religious force into sanctions on sexism. Women ministers would become structural models for individual syntheses, as has already happened to a small degree, changing ideas more forcefully than economic action has done so far. The link to the family from such a change would be as strong as the whole linkage between current sex disadvantage and religious belief. And perhaps, as a "heresy," it will be stronger than its parent doctrine ever was.

Conclusion

What becomes clear from these trends in churches today, specifically in the United States but to a large degree in other industrialized countries as well, is (1) how much the churches are voluntary associations; (2) how little direct influence they have in maintaining a hegemony in

---

[22]Jacquet (1980; pp. 258–259) showed the following figures for Protestant seminary enrollment: In 1974 there were 36,830 seminarians in 191 schools; in 1979, there were 48,433 in 193 schools. Women's enrollment in those seminaries had increased 203.9% since 1972. In 1972, 10.2% (3,358) of the students were women; in 1979, 21.1% were women (10,208). The increase for men between 1972 and 1979 was 28.8%. Some of the men's growth in numbers reflects the growth and vitality of the conservative churches (e.g., the Southern Baptist Convention).

For Catholics in 1969, Jacquet (1980, p. 261) showed combined seminary figures (religious orders and diocesan seminaries) of 33,990 (men) candidates for priesthood. In 1978 (the latest available data), there were 20,030 men preparing for ordination. The number of seminaries was decreasing as well: There were 26 fewer seminaries of all types in 1978 than in the previous year.

In all cases, the number of seminarians exceeds the number actually ordained, and this fact is a particular caution in examining Catholic seminary figures.

the structure of values; and (3) how vital they are as arenas for preservation, challenge, and change. The Judeo-Christian tradition of believers as supplicants has, in secular democracy, turned mainstream churches themselves into supplicants for believers. The churches compete with each other and with new groups and sects (''cults'') for centrality and salience. Religion, like other sources of meaning, must negotiate its authority with those who will recognize it. Yet, religion remains a powerful center in the quest for meaning, and in expressions of new forms of transcendence. Religious beliefs that express people's needs survive. Those that hold fast against change either become ''scenery'' in the background of nominal adherents' lives or are ignored completely.

Ironically, even where the church is a bastion for the people against an oppressor—as in modern Poland, where the church is an intermediate group helping to buffer people from the state—the church has gone where the people are. The state there, the major competitor for the people's sense of meaning historically, lacks a legitimacy that the church has still maintained. That legitimacy, however, must place the church constantly in danger of further repressions; yet, church negotiations with the state for its survival are bound to be viewed by the people with suspicions of betrayal. Thus, the church's legitimacy is defined perhaps as much by what it opposes as by what it teaches doctrinally. In the past, other countries (e.g., France and Italy) have been no less Catholic than Poland is today. The changes came when the church could not be separated from the state, when the failing legitimacy of one was defended by the failing legitimacy of the other. To defy one was to defy both; and for greater freedom, that defiance resulted in a revolution in France and the overthrow of centralizing fascism in Italy. In Poland, however, as in similar cases, the latent function of the political repression of the churches is to make their doctrines a matter of honor, liberty, and the assertion of individual rights against the state.

Perhaps the Irish Catholic tradition is a precursor of a future Polish experience. For the Irish Catholics, the church stood as its claim in national history against England—which was conveniently Protestant—in terms of the Irish cause. Yet, even in modern Ireland, the church's authority has eroded under conditions of modern laws and demands for greater rights. So even if Poland does finally have a democracy that the world would recognize as truly free, affection for the church does not guarantee doctrinal adherence or high numbers of public worshipers, or the maintenance of family religious practices. There are recent reports of high numbers of abortions in Poland because of the severity of its financial crisis (*New York Times*, May 23, 1983). This apparent anomaly speaks most clearly to the historical precedent: that the churches are valued for the liberties that they give and, modernly, are ignored for the liberties that they attempt to restrain or remove. In the absence of rights or with them, then, the church—even in Poland—is a voluntary association.

If Poland becomes even less free and falls into despair as political controls tighten—as Lawrence Wechsler's reports out of Poland have indicated might happen—then the church may not be able to maintain its posture as the basis of hope and freedom and will have to defend itself to the people as well as to the state. But secular states have never provided sufficient meanings in technology or science or industry to eliminate religion. Therefore, where a national church weakens, as it may in Poland, other meaning systems will arise—whether in Catholic splinters or variations, or in other religious streams.

Although the question of Catholic strength in Poland continues its course in history, the weakening of the churches and of all forms of absolute authority has long since proceeded in the West. The structures of social activity (work, family, politics, religion, education, and substructures such as the professions, science, and the arts) each contain embedded systems of values and meaning. These may to some degree overlap with and support the others, or each may be partly or wholly antagonistic to the others. These systems of value and meaning, however incomplete from an observer's standpoint, still compete with each other at least for physical presence (whether it be in the form, for example, of worship, work, or parental activities). Work–family conflicts are examples of such competition. The conflicts are often difficult to resolve and are provisional in resolution at any given point, because each offers benefits, satisfactions, fulfillments, and identity locations, as well as exacting costs. The weighing of costs and benefits, at whatever level of consciousness, is an ongoing process. Life changes reflect shifts in the equation. Radical reevaluations of one's life are now patterned and have acceptability and currency, as in the case of ''mid-life crisis.'' Old cost–benefit balances become unlivable.

Life crises may be patterned also by the adolescent's search for identity, when he or she is overwhelmed by the appearance of freedom of choices in schooling, occupation, sex, and family life. As these choices individually occur, and as biography intersects with other cultural factors, syntheses of meaning are formed that may include leaving religion, entering religion, embracing a religion more fervently, or adopting religious practices ''marginal'' to the culture, as in the cults.

The choices multiply uncertainly; family is itself one among many choices. In the absence of a single authority, where, in fact, authority is negotiated rather than imposed, youth will have fewer experiences (by definition) to serve as criteria for decisions. And those who would offer new choices—like the ''new religions''—will look to the young for support. Youth are always targets in attempts to create a new order. To recruit the young is to recruit the future. But the relatively small numbers in U.S. cults and the large number of competing appeals to youth indicate how varying is the ability of any church (or of the state) to compete successfully in open structures for the attention of individuals, let alone of family groups. Yet, this is not a one-way force. In social life, as in Newton's physics, forces produce counterforces, and families are not passive recipients of the play of history on their internal structures. Parental determination to maintain the integrity of the family structure is still promoted through the religious bond. Part of the evangelical appeal is a family structure where the lines of authority are clear, and where a transcendent order justifies the internal order and authority of the family. The growth of fundamentalist/evangelical churches surely reflects this appeal. Yet, even there, the personal and media ministries may not successfully embrace whole families, and the young are still free to depart from parental ways. Even there, authority must be negotiated so that, in a geographically mobile society, the young choose to stay close. This process is not openly admitted. It is seen, rather, in content analyses of sermons, counseling, and inspirational literature and in interpretations of the Bible.

Meanwhile, for the society as a whole, in a secular and democratic order, the loci of belief and meaning multiply, and these points of belief vary in the depth and breadth of the answers that they purport to offer. Their value and relative weight at any given time are determined by the intersection of life history with larger forces around the individual, and they may be synthesized into a set of beliefs serving personal needs. What they give is measured against what they demand.

In these cost–benefit equations of belief and action structures—as in work and the family and just as in religion—constraints of money and felt obligation may bind people to patterns that are not fully comfortable or satisfactory. Demographic and cultural changes, however, indicate how these equations may be resolved in the future. Some of these changes are an unusually large (historically) number of unmarried people (never-married, divorced, separated, and widowed); an outnumbering of males by females that is projected to last until the late 1980s; a family structure that seems beset by internal and external pressures, including questions of roles, rights, and control; a loss of the intrinsic "sacredness" of the family that mirrored the family–religion bond; media that are ever-present and increasingly powerful in presenting alternative lifestyle and consumption patterns; and the placement of an ever higher value on autonomy and personal freedom. The web of structural and subjective constraints thus may not have diminished, but it certainly shows qualitative change over time. The "market" for meaning has widened, in the variety of meaning systems available (from the "cult of good health" to the ascetic life in monasteries), and in the number of individuals who seek meaning systems.

The secularization of society—the substitution of this-worldly for other-worldly values—has been, in one sense, a great spiritual leveler: Because no single place such as the church can claim singular and sole legitimate authority over the spiritual realm, other spheres are at least potentially arenas for spirituality. Interestingly, Calvin's doctrines provide an explanation: Life in the world and work in particular were the battlegrounds of religious life. Belief in God was the background against which the spirit struggled in the world to realize Christian perfection. But then, all parts of life become, potentially at least, arenas of meaning. This heritage has remained while the power of the churches has declined. Without some institutional hegemony of the churches over the transcendent, other spheres of meaning can increase in strength. Internal competition among forms of belief can likewise multiply.

Looking at lifestyles, which have increased in variety, it becomes apparent that not only the churches, but families, too, have become voluntary associations. Non-marital lifestyles and reduced power of extended kin and ascription loosen bonds both physically and psychologically. Nor is work a "different matter": It is an individual rather than a collective enterprise. The job or career is an individual rather than a family-based activity. Educational systems, meanwhile, compete for students, a consequence of fertility decline. Even the military is voluntary, adapting to its soldiers in unprecedented ways. An industry of self-actualizing therapies has arisen, and leisure pursuits have become shapers of self-image. Thus, it becomes clear that churches and families and work and education and the military and leisure time take on voluntary-participatory characteristics. Any authority external to the self challenges the authority that has come to be felt in the self. That authority is exercised by the "shopping around" that is done, for the set or combination of sets of meanings that provide the most satisfactory individual synthesis of meaning systems. Most important among these factors is that, after age 18, the family is a legally voluntary system, as legal majority sets the individual's rights and duties in the context of the state, beyond the umbrella of family (Marciano, 1981). The family's power to mediate religious beliefs is reduced insofar as it cannot compel the physical presence of its children; its power is reduced by the autonomous capacities existing in laws permitting "divorce by consent," and by expanding labor-market roles for women. The "religious market," the competing beliefs among systems of meaning, becomes a set of selections and choices.

Both for family influence and the actual relationship between formal affiliation and practice, then, lists of church membership mean relatively little. *Process* is absent from most membership data available, and especially the process occurring after age 14 (confirmation, Bar or Bat Mitzvah); after that time, family and religious beliefs seem to move into a different phase of children's activity and parental belief. In "shopping around," successive areas of activity may be the primary focus of meaning, as family roles undergo their own evolution over time. After the formal rites of passage, work, family, and extra-familial processes may be sequentially salient for parents and/or children. As a given system of meaning is found wanting, as work or study or family ceases to be "enough" to fulfill spiritual longings, other sources of meaning may be sought. An adequate description of this fluid, ongoing stream of affiliation/disaffiliation, of surge and decline in commitment, of interior growth or external observance, would require far more intense qualitative study than is now available. The kind of information we now have—mostly quantitative, mostly individual—simply does not locate families in religious systems, or religion in family systems.

Finally, however, religion does not cease to offer and claim a most powerful and complete set of transcendent meanings. By its presence in the world that it wants to win, religion also becomes a target and an arena of change. The role of women in religion is the leading current indicator of this religious process. Women work within and outside the churches to make them available resources of meanings compatible with sexual equality. The *New York Times* (April 10, 1983) reported what is being heard from many sources: The number of women in the ministry is rising rapidly, and their proportions in seminaries are rising as well.

Women in the ministry are only the latest way in which religion has accommodated social change. Although traditional views, updated to include scientific and social-scientific terminology, pervade the evangelical and orthodox forms of religion, the very number of churches and denominations makes it possible to find an accommodating area of religion to reflect new personal demands. Although the ranks of the evangelicals grow, so do the ranks of those who have challenged the fundamentalist view of ministry.

How challenges arise from and reflect on the families of those who make new ministries is only beginning to be studied. Husband–wife ministries are increasing in percentages (though in absolute numbers, they are still small); the degree to which the ministry is a life model for congregants and the effect of minister parents on the parenting practices of congregants will be new areas of qualitative study. Feminism as an alternative set of meanings has already shown itself to be a powerful force. For women in religious life, that feminism may synthesize with religion to produce a powerful new synergy—or it may simply continue to be yet another variation on the landscape of the multiple meaning systems available in the society. The last eventuality seems more likely, given the persistence and the independent evolutions of the variations that have already shown themselves.

What we will probably find is more, rather than fewer, sets of meaning systems in the value landscape. More synthesis seems likely, rather than straitened choices. Although a growing number will probably choose a return to older orthodoxies (which still show an adaptation to modernity), the success of those family processes in holding their young will be an object of great interest to scholars of family and religion.

References

Allport, G. W., Gillespie, J. M., & Young, J. The religion of the post-war college student. *Journal of Psychology*, 1948, *25*, 3–33.

Antares, J. Feminist spirituality: The politics of the psyche. *Chrysalis*, 1978, *No. 6*, 11–13.

Anthony, D., & Robbins, T. R. The Meher Baba movement: Its effects on postadolescent youthful alienation. In I. Zaretsky & M. Leone (Eds.), *Religious movements in contemporary America*. Princeton, N.J.: Princeton University Press, 1974.

Armstrong, B. *The electric church*. New York: Thomas Nelson, 1979.

Balswick, J. The Jesus people movement: A sociological analysis. In P. H. McNamara (Ed.), *Religion American style*. New York: Harper & Row, 1974.

Bellah, R. N. Civil religion in America. *Daedalus*, 1967, *96*, 1–21.

Bellah, R. N. *Beyond belief: Essays on religion in a post-traditional world*. New York: Harper & Row, 1976.

Berger, P. L. *The Sacred Canopy*. New York: Doubleday Anchor, 1969.

Berger, P. L., & Luckmann, T. Sociology of religion and sociology of knowledge. *Sociology and Social Research*, 1963, *47*, 417–428.

Bibby, R. W. Why conservative churches *really* are growing: Kelley revisited. *Journal for the Scientific Study of Religion*, 1978, *17*, 129–137.

Bird, P. Images of women in the old testament. In R. R. Reuther (Ed.), *Religion and sexism*. New York: Simon & Schuster, 1974.

Briggs, K. A. Her long road to consecration as a bishop. *New York Times*, Sept. 8, 1980, C16.

Bromley, D. G., & Shupe, A. D., Jr. Just a few years seem like a lifetime: A role theory approach to participation in religious movements. In L. Kriesberg (Ed.), *Research in social movements, conflict and change*, Vol. 2 Greenwich, Conn.: JAI Press, 1979.

Bromley, D. G., & Shupe, A. D., Jr. Financing the new religions. *Journal for the Scientific Study of Religion*, 1980, *19*, 227–239.

Brozan, N. The Moon church: From parents who approve. *The New York Times*, Sept. 16, 1976, 44.

Burlage, D. D. Judaeo-Christian influences on female sexuality. In A. L. Hageman (Ed.), in collaboration with the Women's Caucus of Harvard Divinity School, *Sexist religion and women in the church: No more silence!* New York: Association Press, 1974.

Cohen, D. *The new believers*. New York: Ballantine Books, 1975.

Conway, F., & Siegelman, J. *Snapping*. New York: Delata, 1979.

Cox, H. *Turning east*. New York: Touchstone, 1977.

Daly, M. *Beyond God the Father*. Boston: Beacon Press, 1973.

Daly, M. *The church and the second sex*. New York: Harper, 1975.

Daly, M. *Gyn-ecology*. Boston: Beacon Press, 1978.

D'Antonio, W. V. The family and religion: Exploring a changing relationship. *Journal for the Scientific Study of Religion*, 1980, *19*, 89–104.

Davis, K. *Human society*. New York: Macmillan, 1957.

Davis, R., & Richardson, J. The organization and functioning of the Children of God. *Sociological Analysis*, 1976, *37*, 321–340.

DeWitt, H. K. Married Anglican priests may join Catholic church, the Vatican says. *New York Times*, Aug. 21, 1980, A21.

Dullea, G. Nonsexist mission engenders a new worship service. *New York Times*, Sept. 12, 1980, A14.

Durkheim, E. *The division of labor in society*. Glencoe, Ill.: Free Press, 1960.

Durkheim, E. *The elementary forms of the religious life*. New York: Free Press, 1965.

Edwards, C. *Crazy for God*. Englewood Cliffs, N.J.: Prentice-Hall, 1979.

Eister, A. W. An outline of a structural theory of cults. *Journal for the Scientific Study of Religion*, 1972, *ll*, 319–333.

Ellwood, R. S., Jr. *Alternative altars*. Chicago: University of Chicago Press, 1979.

Enroth, R. *The lure of the cults*. Chappaqua, N.Y.: Herald Books, 1979.

Fenn, R. Toward a new sociology of religion. *Journal for the Scientific Study of Religion*, 1972, *11*, 16–32.

Fenn, R. *Toward a theory of secularization* (monograph). Society for the Scientific Study of Religion, 1978.

Friedan, B. *The feminine mystique.* New York: Dell, 1963.

Furstenberg, F. Birth control experience among pregnant adolescents: The process of planned parenthood. *Social Problems,* 1971, *19,* 192–203.

Galanter, M., Rabkin, R., Rabkin, J., & Deutsch, A. The "Moonies": A psychological study of conversion and membership in a contemporary religious sect. *American Journal of Psychiatry,* 1979, *1363,* 165–170.

Glock, C. Y. The role of deprivation in the origin and evolution of religious groups. In R. Lee & M. Marty (Eds.), *Religion and social conflict.* New York: Oxford University Press, 1964.

Glock, C. Y. On the study of religious commitment. In C. Y. Glock & R. Stark (Eds.), *Religion and society in tension.* Chicago: Rand McNally, 1965.

Harder, M. Jesus People. *Psychology Today,* 1972, *6,* 37–43.

Harder, M. W., Richardson, J. T., & Simmonds, R. Life style: Courtship, marriage and family in a changing Jesus movement organization. *International Review of Modern Sociology,* 1976, *6,* 155–172.

Harrison, B. G. The struggle for Wendy Helander. *McCall's,* 1979, Oct., 87–94.

Hauptman, J. Images of women in the Talmud. In R. R. Reuther (Ed.), *Religion and Sexism.* New York: Simon & Schuster, 1974.

Jacquet, C. H. (Ed.). *Yearbook of American and Canadian Churches 1980.* Nashville: Abingdon, 1980.

Johnson, G. E. The impact of family formation patterns on Jewish community involvement. *Analysis,* 1976, *60,* 1–5.

Johnstone, R. L. *Religion and society in interaction.* Englewood Cliffs, N.J.: Prentice-Hall, 1975.

Judah, H. S. *Hare Krishna and the counterculture.* New York: Wiley, 1974.

Kaiser, R. B. New vitality growing in orthodox Jewish congregations. *The New York Times,* July 6, 1980.

Kanter, R. M. Some effects of proportions on group life: Skewed sex ratios and responses to token women. *American Journal of Sociology,* 1976, *82,* 965–990.

Kaufman, J. Old-time religion. *Wall Street Journal,* July 11, 1980.

Kleugel, J. R. Denominational mobility: Current patterns and recent trends. *Journal for the Scientific Study of Religion,* 1980, *19,* 26–39.

Komarovsky, M. Cultural contradictions and sex roles: The masculine case. *American Journal of Sociology,* 1972, *78,* 873–884.

Larsen, J. A. Dysfunction in the evangelical family: Treatment considerations. *The Family Coordinator,* 1978, *27,* 261–267.

Lasch, C. *The culture of narcissism.* New York: Norton, 1979.

Lehman, E. C., Jr. *Organizational resistance to women in ministry.* Paper presented to the Association for the Sociology of Religion, New York, August 1980.

Lemert, C. C. Social structure and the absent center: An alternative to new sociologies of religion. *Sociological Analysis,* 1975, *36,* 95–107.

Lenski, G. *The religious factor.* New York: Doubleday Anchor, 1963.

Leon, J., & Steinhoff, P. G. Catholics' use of abortion. *Sociological Analysis,* 1975, *36,* 125–136.

Lofland, J. "Becoming a world saver" revisited. *American Behavioral Scientist,* 1977, *20,* 805–818.

Lofland, J., & Stark, R. Becoming a world-saver: a theory of conversion to a deviant perspective. *American Sociological Review,* 1965, *30,* 862–874.

Luckmann, T. *Invisible religion.* New York: Macmillan, 1967.

Marciano, T. D. *Traditional family-role support by a religious radio station.* Unpublished paper, 1980.

Marciano, T. D. Families and cults. *Marriage and Family Review,* 1981, *3–4,* 101–118.

Marx, K., & Engels, F. *On religion.* New York: Schocken, 1964.

Masters, W. H., & Johnson, V. E. *Human sexual inadequacy.* Boston: Little, Brown, 1970.

McClain, E. W. Religious orientation the key to psychodynamic differences between femininists and nonfeminists. *Journal for the Scientific Study of Religion,* 1979, *18,* 40–50.

McLuhan, M. *Understanding media.* New York: Macmillan, 1964.

Messenger, J. C., Jr. Religious acculturation among the Anang Ibibio. In W. R. Bascom & M. J. Herskovits (Eds.), *Continuity and change in African cultures.* Chicago: University of Chicago Press, 1968.

Montgomery, J. The electric church. *Wall Street Journal,* May 19, 1978.

Morton, N. Preaching the Word. In A. Hageman (Ed.), *Sexist religion and women in the church.* New York: Association Press, 1974.

Neville, G. K. Religious socialization of women within U.S. subcultures. In A. L. Hageman (Ed.), *Sexist religion and women in the church.* New York: Association Press, 1974.

Newport, F. The religious switcher in the United States. *American Sociological Review,* 1979, *44,* 528–552.

Oppenheimer, V. K. The sex-labeling of jobs. *Industrial Relations,* 1968, *7,* 219–234.

Oppenheimer, V. K. Demographic influence on female employment and the status of women. *American Journal of Sociology,* 1973, *78,* 946–961.

Otwell, H. H. *And Sarah laughed: The status of women in the Old Testament.* Philadelphia: Westminster Press, 1977.

Peterson, D. W., & Mauss, A. L. The cross and the commune: An interpretation of the Jesus People. In C. Y. Glock (Ed.), *Religion in sociological perspective.* Belmont, Calif.: Wadsworth, 1973.

Prebish, C. Reflections on the transmission of Buddhism to America. In J. Needleman & G. Baker (Eds.), *Understanding the new religions.* New York: Seabury Press, 1978.

Prince, R. H. Cocoon work: An interpretation of the concern of contemporary youth with the mystical. In I. I. Zaretsky & M. P. Leone (Eds.), *Religious movements in contemporary America.* Princeton, N.J.: Princeton University Press, 1974.

Raboteau, A. J. *Slave religion.* New York: Oxford University Press, 1978.

Reuther, R. R. Misogynism and virginal feminism in the Fathers of the church. In R. R. Reuther (Ed.), *Religion and sexism.* New York: Simon & Schuster, 1974.

Robbins, T. Eastern mysticism and the resocialization of drug users: The Meher Baba cult. *Journal for the Scientific Study of Religion,* 1969, *8,* 308–317.

Robbins, T., & Anthony, D. Getting straight with Meher Baba: A study of mysticism, drug rehabilitation, and postadolescent youth conflict. *Journal for the Scientific Study of Religion,* 1972, *11,* 122–140.

Robbins, T., & Anthony, D. The limits of "coercive persuasion" as an explanation for conversion to authoritarian sects. *Political Psychology,* 1980, *2,*(2), 22–37.

Robbins, T., Anthony, D., Doucas, M., & Curtis, T. The last civil religion: Reverend Moon and the Unification Church. *Sociological Analysis,* 1976, *37,* 111–125.

Robertson, R. *The sociological interpretation of religion.* New York: Schocken, 1970.

Rokeach, M. Paradoxes of religious belief. In J. K. Hadden (Ed.), *Religion in radical transition.* New Brunswick, N.J.: Transaction Books, 1970.

Roof, W. C., & Hadaway, C. K. Shifts in religious preferences—The mid-seventies. *Journal for the Scientific Study of Religion,* 1977, *16,* 409–412.

Roof, W. C., & Hadaway, C. K. Denominational switching in the seventies: Going beyond Stark and Glock. *Journal for the Scientific Study of Religion,* 1979, *18,* 363–377.

Roszak, T. *Where the wasteland ends.* New York: Anchor Books, 1973.

Rudin, J., & Rudin, R. *Prison or paradise? The new religious cults.* Philadelphia: Fortress Press, 1980.

Sage, W. The war on the cults. *Human Behavior*, 1976, *5*, 40–49.

Salisbury, W. S. *Religion in American culture*. Homewood, Ill.: Dorsey Press, 1964.

Scharf, B. *The sociological study of religion*. New York: Harper, 1970.

Sherrard, P. The sexual relationship in Christian thought. In J. Needleman, A. K. Berman, & Janes Gold (Eds.), *Religion for a new generation* (2nd ed.). New York: Macmillan, 1977.

Shulman, G. B. View from the back of the synagogue. In A. L. Hageman (Ed.), *Sexist religion and women in the church*. New York: Association Press, 1974.

Shupe, A. D., & Bromley, D. G. The Moonies and the anti-cultists: Movement and countermovement in conflict. *Sociological Analysis*, 1979, *40*, 325–334.

Shupe, A. D., Spielmann, R., & Stigall, S. Deprogramming: The new exorcism. *American Behavioral Scientists*, 1977, *20*, 941–956.

Singer, M. T. Coming out of the cults. *Psychology Today*, 1979, *12*, 72–82.

Sklare, M. *America's Jews*. New York: Random House, 1971.

Sloan, A., & Bagamery, A. The electronic pulpit. *Forbes*, July 7, 1980, 116–124.

Snook, J. B. *Going further: Life-and-death religion in America*. Englewood Cliffs, N.J.: Prentice-Hall, 1973.

Snow, D. A., Zurcher, L. A., & Ekland-Olson, S. Social networks and social movements: A microstructural approach to differential recruitment. *American Sociological Review*, 1980, *45*, 787–801.

Stark, R., & Bainbridge, W. S. Of churches, sects, and cults: Preliminary concepts for a theory of religious movements. *Journal for the Scientific Study of Religion*, 1979, *18*, 117–133.

Stark, R., & Glock, C. Y. *American piety*. Berkeley: University of California Press, 1968.

Steinem, G. If men could menstruate. *Ms.*, 1978, *8*, 110.

Steinsaltz, A. *The Essential Talmud*, trans. by C. Galai. London: Weidenfeld & Nicolson, 1976.

Straus, R. A. Religious conversion as a personal and collective accomplishment. *Sociological Analysis*, 1970, *40*, 158–165.

Thomas, J. L. Religious training in the Catholic family. *American Journal of Sociology*, 1951, *62*, 178–183.

Trexler, R. C. The foundlings of Florence, 1395–1455. *History of Childhood Quarterly*, 1973, *1*, 259–284.

Useem, M. *Protest movements in America*. Indianapolis: Bobbs-Merrill, 1975.

Vecsey, G. Buddhism In America. *The New York Times Magazine*, June 3, 1979, 28–30, 93–99.

Vidich, A. J., & Bensman, J. *Small town in mass society* (rev. ed.). Princeton, N.J.: Princeton University Press, 1968.

Warenski, M. *Patriarchs and politics: The plight of the Mormon woman*. New York: McGraw-Hill, 1978.

Weber, M. *The Protestant ethic and the spirit of capitalism*. New York: Scribner's, 1958.

Westoff, C. F., & Potvin, R. H. Higher education, religion, and women's family-size orientations. *American Sociological Review*, 1966, *31*, 489–496.

Weiting, S. G. An examination of intergenerational patterns of religious belief and practice. *Sociological Analysis*, 1975, *36*, 137–149.

Whyte, W. F. *Streetcorner society* (2nd ed.) Chicago: University of Chicago Press, 1966.

Wilkinson, M. L., & Tanner, W. C., III. The influence of family size, interaction, and religiosity on family affection in a Mormon sample. *Journal of Marriage and the Family*, 1980, *42*, 297–304.

Williams, R. M. Women against women: The clash over equal rights. *Saturday Review*, 1977, *4*, 7–9.

Wills, G. What religious revival? *Psychology Today*, 1978, *11*, 74–81.

Wilson, B. R. *Religion in secular society*. Baltimore: Penguin, 1969.

Winter, J. A. *Continuities in the sociology of religion*. New York: Harper & Row, 1977.

Wisse, R. Women as Conservative rabbis? *Commentary*, 1979, *68*, 59–64.

Wohl, L. C. A feminist Latter-Day Saint: Why Sonia Johnson won't give up on the ERA—or the Mormon church. *Ms.*, 1980, *8*, 39–42.

Wuthnow, R. A. A religious marketplace. *Journal of Current Social Issues*, 1977, *14*, 38–42.

Wuthnow, R. A. *Experimentation in American Religion*. Berkeley: University of California Press, 1978.

Wuthnow, R. A. Religion in the world-system. In A. J. Bergesen, (Ed.), *Studies of the modern world system*. New York: Academic Press, 1980.

Yinger, J. M. Pluralism, religion, and secularism. *Journal for the Scientific Study of Religion*, 1967, *6*, 17–28.

Yinger, J. M. *The scientific study of religion*. New York: Macmillan, 1970.

Zald, M. N., & McCarthy, J. D. (Eds.), *The dynamics of social movements*. Cambridge, Mass.: Winthrop, 1979.

CHAPTER 12

Nontraditional Family Forms

Eleanor D. Macklin

Introduction

Any review of the literature on variant, nontraditional, or alternative family forms must begin with a discussion of the meaning of these terms. *Variant* suggests variation on the norm, but what is the norm? The ideal to which most aspire or the manner in which most persons actually live? To define *nontraditional*, one must first determine what is traditional, recognizing that traditions change. What period of time shall be held as the tradition for the present? Even the word *alternative* creates problems; some authors reserve the word for those instances when the lifestyle is chosen freely as a result of ideology and personal preference, using *alternate* when the lifestyle develops out of necessity or personal circumstance (e.g., Cazenave, 1980).

For the purposes of this review, the traditional family pattern is characterized as a "legal, lifelong, sexually exclusive marriage between one man and one woman, with children, where the male is primary provider and ultimate authority" (Macklin, 1980, p. 905). This has been the pattern most clearly supported by legal practice and the Judeo-Christian heritage; hence, variant family forms will be seen as those that deviate from this structure (see Table 1). This chapter is limited to research focusing on these nontraditional patterns.

It must be recognized that what is considered traditional here has not always been either the real or the idealized norm, even within Western society; such factors as economics, demographics, and religion have strongly influenced the marriage and family patterns of any given time (Laslett & Wall, 1972; Murstein, 1974; Shorter, 1975; Pickett, 1978a,b). One must also realize that, although categorized here as polar opposites, variations on the traditional family form a broad continuum from traditional to nontraditional, with any given lifestyle varying in its position on that continumm as a function of such factors as the values of the persons involved, their reason for living the particular lifestyle, and their commitment to that lifestyle.

To what extent is the traditional family, as defined above, the norm in American society? The question is not easily answered. Attitude surveys suggest that the great majority still wish eventually to marry, to stay married, to have children, and to be sexually exclusive and heterosexual (White & Wells, 1973; Bower & Christopherson, 1977; Strong, 1978; Glenn & Weaver, 1979; Weis & Slosnerick, 1981). Census data indicate that most persons marry, remain married, and have children (see Glick, 1979b). Even though more wives are working, they still tend to earn less than men (U.S. Department of Labor, 1980), and household tasks still tend to be determined by gender (Scanzoni & Fox, 1980). Although at any given point in time the majority of adults are not living in traditional nuclear households (see Table 2), over the course of a lifetime most will do so. On the other hand, increasing numbers are living together unmarried and in single-person or one-parent households, electing to remain childfree, striving for dual careers, remarrying, and forming stepfamilies. There is a growing acceptance of egalitarianism, particularly of shared parenting and decision-making, and a greater tolerance of persons who choose to live in nontraditional ways (Yankelovich, 1981).

The dramatic changes of recent years have led some alarmists to proclaim the demise of the institution of the family (e.g., Cooper, 1970; Gordon, 1972). It seems more reasonable to conclude that the family is continuing its age-old process of gradual evolution, maintaining many of its traditional functions and structures while adapting to changing economic circumstances and social ideologies. This normal process of change merely accelerated during the late 1960s and the early 1970s, as a consequence of the resurgence of the women's movement, improvements in contraceptive technology, and a general climate of concern about human rights and personal growth made possible by a period of relative affluence. Experimentation with ways to maximize human potential and to develop more meaningful relationships, particularly by the educated white middle class, led to widespread interest in alternatives of various kinds. There

Eleanor D. Macklin • Department of Child, Family, and Community Studies, Syracuse University, Syracuse, NY 13210.

Table 1. Variant Family Forms in Contemporary United States

The "traditional" family	The "nontraditional" alternative
Legally married	Never-married singlehood; non-married cohabitation
With children	Voluntary childlessness
Two-parent	Single-parent (never-married; once-married); joint custody and the binuclear family; the stepfamily
Permanent	Renewable contract; divorce and remarriage
Male as primary provider and ultimate authority	Androgynous marriage (e.g., O'Neill's open marriage; dual-career marriage; commuter marriage)
Sexually exclusive	Extramarital relationships (e.g., sexually open marriage; swinging; Ramey's "intimate friendship"; coprimary relationships)
Heterosexual	Same-sex intimate relationships
Two-adult household	Multiadult households (e.g., multilateral marriage; communal living; home sharing; the "affiliated family")

Table 2. Composition of U.S. Households, 1960–1980 (in Percentages)[a]

Type of household	1960	1970	1979	1980
Family households				
Married couple, no children under 18	30.3	30.3	29.9	
Married couple, children under 18	44.1	40.3	31.7[b]	60.9
One parent, children under 18	4.4	5.0	7.3	
Other (e.g., extended)	6.4	5.6	5.4	13.0
Total	85.3	81.2	74.4	73.8
Nonfamily households[c]				
Persons living alone	13.1	17.1	22.2	22.6
Other	1.6	1.7	3.4	3.6
Total	14.7	18.8	25.6	26.2

[a]Percentages for 1960–1979 are derived from the U.S. Bureau of Census, 1979 (Table A) and 1980a (Table A); for 1980, from U.S. Bureau of the Census, 1980b (Table 3).
[b]Slightly over half of all children under 18 living in two-parent families in March 1979 had mothers who were in the labor force, as compared to 38% of such children in 1970 (U.S. Department of Labor, 1979).
[c]Maintained by a person or persons who do not share their quarters with any relatives.

was a flurry of research and publication as students of marriage and the family set out to describe and analyze the changing patterns, and exploration of the increasing pluralism was a major focus of family studies during the 1970s (see Macklin, 1980; Macklin & Rubin, 1983).

The trend toward pluralism was noted in the Report of Forum 14 of the 1970 White House Conference on Children, "Changing Families in a Changing Society" (Sussman et al., 1971), which argued for the recognition of "variant family forms," long existent but now more visible and more common. The theme was reechoed in the title of the 1972 meeting of Groves Conference on Marriage and the Family, "Societal Planning for Family Pluralism," and again in the program for the 1981 meetings. Two issues of The Family Coordinator (Sussman, 1972, 1975) were devoted to the topic. Innumerable newsletters and new journals appeared (e.g., Alternative Lifestyles, Communities Magazine, Journal of Divorce, and Journal of Homosexuality). A multitude of edited collections were published (Otto, 1970; Gordon, 1972; Libby & Whitehurst, 1973, 1977; Smith & Smith, 1974; Delora & DeLora, 1975; Murstein, 1978a; Butler & McGinley, 1978; Gross & Sussman, 1982; Macklin & Rubin, 1983). Numerous books championed or chronicled "the new way" (Bernard, 1972; Rogers, 1972; Mazur, 1973; Rimmer, 1973; Casler, 1974; Thamm, 1975; Seal, 1975; Stinnett & Birdsong, 1978; Butler, 1979). A host of support groups emerged, for example, the National Organization for Non-Parents (now the National Alliance for Optional Parenthood), the National Organization for Women, Family Synergy, Future Families of the World, and Parents without Partners.

Research on variant family forms has not been easy. Operational definitions of the various lifestyles had to be agreed on; subjects were often difficult to locate and, hence, samples were usually small and not representative; relevant questions had to be discerned; and appropriate instruments had to be designed. Most of the initial research was exploratory, based on interviews with a few subjects painstakingly located or on data ferreted out of larger studies done for other purposes. Increasing efforts are being made to use systematically selected samples, and a few short-term longitudinal studies have recently been reported (e.g., Eiduson, 1979b; Newcomb & Bentler, 1980a; Risman, Hill, Rubin, & Peplau, 1981; Watson, 1981; Lewin, 1982; Bram, 1985). Researchers have tended to focus on white, relatively youthful, middle-class samples, although growing attention is being given to variant family forms among the elderly (Dressel, 1980; Dressel & Hess, 1983) and in the black community (Cazenave, 1980; Peters & McAdoo, 1983), and to cross-national comparisons (Buunk, 1980a, 1983). Although there are many ways in which alternative lifestyle research could be improved, much important work has been done, and much can be learned from a pooling of the many studies carefully reported by a wide variety of researchers. This chapter summarizes the major research on variant family forms published since 1970 and examines the issues raised by the reported findings.

Never-Married Singlehood

"Never-married singles" form the largest group of unmarried persons in this country. In 1980, about 34% of American men and more than 40% of American women aged 18 and over were never-married, separated, divorced, or widowed, and 24% of the men and 17% of the women were in the never-married group (U.S. Bureau of the Census, 1981). How many of these unmarrieds will experience a lifetime of singlehood is unclear. Although few college students indicate a desire never to marry (Macklin, 1976; Bower & Christopherson, 1977; Strong, 1978), young adults are increasingly postponing their entrance into marriage (U.S. Bureau of the Census, 1981, Tables A and B). The median age for first marriage for women was 20.8 in 1970 and 22.1 in 1980; for men, 23.2 in 1970 and 24.6 in 1980. Of women aged 20–24, 36% were still single in 1970, and 50% in 1980; of those aged 25–29, 10.5% were single in 1970 and 21% in 1980.

Because the longer one postpones marriage, the more likely it is that one will remain unmarried, it is predicted that 8–9% of adults now in their 20s will experience a lifetime of singlehood as opposed to 4–5% of those now 50 years old (Glick, 1979b). This growth in never-married singlehood has been explained by (1) the expanding range of lifestyle and employment options for women; (2) the increased number of women in higher education; (3) the ease with which singles can enjoy an active social and sexual life, and the growing acceptance of nonmarital cohabitation; and (4) the fact that there are more women than men of marriageable age, resulting in what Glick calls "the marriage squeeze" (Glick, 1979b). Males, Catholics, blacks, persons with more education, and persons living in urban areas have higher rates of nonmarriage, with education being the single most significant predictor (see Stein, 1983).

With the increased divorce rate (from 2.5 per 1,000 persons in 1965 to 5.2 in 1980), the growth in single-person households (from 13% of all households in 1960 to 23% in 1980) and the trend toward postponement of marriage, research on singlehood has become increasingly important (e.g., see Libby, 1977; Stein, 1978, 1983). Because of the tremendous heterogeneity among singles, resulting from such factors as reason for singlehood, age, social class, and living arrangement, it is relatively useless to refer to singles as a global category. In reviewing research on singles, it is important to distinguish between the never-married and the once-married, the widowed and the divorced, and persons who live alone and those living in a stable cohabiting or communal relationship or with their family of origin. To aid in analysis, Stein (1976, 1978, 1983) has suggested a typology of singles, based on whether the singlehood is voluntary or involuntary, stable or temporary. It is important to note that one's position within this typology may well shift over one's life course, and that the boundary between voluntary and involuntary is often very unclear.

Research has explored the lifestyles, coping strategies, mental health, and backgrounds of the never-married, with particular focus on the urban professional and the college graduate (e.g., Starr & Carns, 1972; Adams, 1976; Darling, 1976; Stein, 1976; Cockrum & White, 1985) and the single elderly (Gubrium, 1975; Scott, 1979). For instance, Starr and Carns (1972) interviewed 70 single college graduates living in Chicago and found that many of their concerns related to finding meaningful work, satisfying living arrangements, and congenial friends. Darling (1976) compared the life histories of 20 never-married men over the age of 35 with those of 20 men first married after the age of 35 and found that marriage tended to occur in conjunction with a major career transition when one needed the support of significant others.

Increasingly large proportions of black adults are single, partially because of the unbalanced sex ratio and the relative lack of eligible black males (see Peters & McAdoo, 1983), and it is predicted that, if current trends continue, a majority of black adults will be unmarried in the year 2000 (Stein, 1983). In a study of 500 black, urban, college-educated singles between the ages of 25 and 45, Staples (1981) found that because of their relative isolation, middle-class black singles have difficulty establishing a satisfactory social life.

Studies of the never-married elderly (approximately 5% of those 65 and older) indicate that marrieds and lifelong singles report similar levels of life satisfaction (Gubrium, 1975; Scott, 1979; Ward, 1979). Gubrium (1975), who interviewed 22 singles in Detroit and found them more independent and socially isolated than other elders but reporting relatively little loneliness, argued that lifelong singlehood, with its well-developed strategies for dealing with aloneness, becomes particularly functional in old age. Scott (1970), comparing 30 rural never-marrieds with a sample of married and widowed elderly, found them to report similar degrees of general life satisfaction, but more loneliness than the married and less than the widowed. It is suggested that, in the balancing of life's costs and benefits, elder never-marrieds find lack of intimacy to have been offset by factors such as opportunity for personal achievement and independence. When comparing elderly marrieds and never-marrieds, it should be remembered that persons still married at age 65 are the selected survivors of their marriage cohort, and that respondents, irrespective of lifestyle, may need to view their life choice as having been a wise one.

The relationship between health and marital status has been a topic of some controversy (e.g., Knupfer, Clark, & Room, 1966; Radloff, 1975; Warheit, Holzer, Bell, & Arey, 1976; Anderson & Braito, 1981). Research suggests that long-term singlehood has traditionally been a more positive state for women than for men, and that women who remain single are superior to single men in terms of education, occupation, and mental health (Bernard, 1972; Gove, 1972; Gilder, 1974; Glenn, Ross, & Tully, 1974). Spreitzer and Riley (1974), in an analysis of interview data from a probability sample of applicants for social-security disability benefits (median age, 55), found that males with higher levels of intelligence and occupational achievement were least likely to be single, the reverse being true for women (see also Havens, 1973), and that persons who had experienced poor family life situations during their childhood were two to three times more likely to remain single, particularly in the case of men. Using stepwise regression models, Cockrum and White (1985) found different variables predictive of life satisfaction in middle-aged never-married men and women: emotional loneliness and availability of attachment relationships were predictive for women, and self-esteem and availability of social integration for men.

Historically, studies have shown that, as a group, marrieds live longer and use healthcare facilities less often (Stein, 1983). However, current research indicates that the picture changes when one controls for institutionalization and differentiates among divorced, widowed, and never-married. The total singles population is less healthy than the total married population, but this may be largely because the former includes more persons with serious congenital or childhood health problems, more elderly, more incarcerated, and more divorced and widowed persons.

In a comprehensive review of data from two national health surveys, Verbrugge (1979) suggested that non-institutionalized never-marrieds tend to be healthier than marrieds, take less time off for health reasons, and make less use of physicians and healthcare services. Divorced and separated singles tend to have poorer physical and mental health than do never-marrieds (Verbrugge, 1979; Cargan & Melko, 1982), with degree of economic hardship, social isolation, and parental responsibility serving as major determinants of the health of the single individual (Pearlin & Johnson, 1977). It seems reasonable that the extent to which singlehood is a voluntary choice will also impact directly on the life satisfaction and the mental state of the individual.

With the growing population of singles and the increasing likelihood that a given individual may be single several times in his or her adult life (i.e., before marriage, after divorce, and after remarriage and widowhood), it is important that attention be given to understanding and preparing persons for this lifestyle. The question of whether there are, in fact, important differences between marrieds and never-marrieds, and whether these are due to the experience of being married or to characteristics possessed independent of marriage, is yet to be adequately resolved (see Anderson & Braito, 1981). Research is also needed on singlehood as a conscious life choice in contemporary society, controlling for class, ethnicity, age, and marital history; on the experience of being single at different points in the life cycle; and on which societal adaptations are most likely to facilitate the experience of singlehood as a fulfilling lifestyle.

Nonmarital Heterosexual Cohabitation

There has been a recent and dramatic increase in the number of U.S. couples living together unmarried, the major shift coming in the early 1970s (see Macklin, 1983). Reported households consisting of two unrelated persons of the opposite sex increased gradually from 1960 to 1970 and tripled from 1970 to 1980 (523,000 to 1,560,000). The trend shows no sign of leveling off, with a 14 percent increase from 1980 to 1981 (Spanier, 1983). Although persons living together as unmarried couples are still a small proportion of all "couple households" (3.6% in 1980), they include a wide age range; the majority are under 35 and the men are somewhat older than the women. In 1981, 38% of the women and 25% of the men were under 25; 36% of the women and 41% of the men were aged 25–34; 20% of the women and 28% of the men were aged 35–64; and 6% of both sexes were 65 years and older (U.S. Bureau of the Census, 1981, p. 5, Table G).

Unmarried cohabiting couples can be roughly divided into three major categories (extrapolated from U.S. Bureau of the Census, 1981, pp. 45–46, Table 7): those composed of two never-married persons (37%), those composed of one never-married and one currently or previously married person (31%), and those composed of two persons currently or previously married to others (32%). Three quarters of the households consist of two adults only, and one-quarter include one or more children under age 15; it is not known how many others include children who visit periodically.

Nonmarital cohabitation in the United States serves primarily as a part of the courtship process and not as an alternative to marriage. The great majority of young persons plan to marry at some point in their lives (e.g., Macklin, 1976; Bower & Christopherson, 1977; Risman et al., 1981), and most cohabiting relationships either terminate or move into legal marriage within a year or two (e.g., Macklin, 1976; Clayton & Voss, 1977).

A somewhat different situation exists in some of the European countries, where nonmarital cohabitation is more common and more generally accepted. In Holland, in 1977, 7% of all cohabiting couples were unmarried; 50% of single persons aged 18–25 and 20% of those aged 30–65 were cohabiting nonmaritally (Straver, 1981). In Sweden, it is estimated that 19–20% of all marriagelike relationships consist of living together unmarried, and that more than 99% of those marrying today cohabit before marriage, most for two or more years (see Trost, 1979, 1981, for an extensive review of European cohabitation rates). Trost maintained that cohabitation without legal marriage has become so common in Sweden that, unlike in the United States, it is a social institution rather than a deviant phenomenon and a variant of marriage rather than of courtship. Almost all of the Swedish unmarried cohabiting couples view themselves as essentially married (Lewin, 1982). Because of tradition, at least 50% do eventually marry, but usually after they have cohabited for a long time, and often the children of the couple are included in the wedding party. As Trost wrote, marriage in Sweden is becoming more of a *rite de confirmation* than a *rite de passage.*

The question, of course, is whether cohabitation in the United States will follow the pattern now apparent in Scandinavia. The trend is certainly in that direction, and it seems increasingly likely that couples will live together before marrying. Jacques and Chason (1979), reporting on a random sample of students from two southern universities in 1974–1975, found that 65% of the married couples had cohabited at least once before marriage. Newcomb and Bentler (1980b) found in a sample of 159 marriage-license applicants in Los Angeles that 35% had cohabited for three or more months with their current partner, and almost 47% had lived together for some period. In a sample of 87 Canadian couples whose wedding announcements had appeared in the local press, 43% had cohabited for three or more months and 64% for some shorter period (Watson, 1983). However, the normative pressures to marry (see Kotkin, 1985)—and in particular, to marry before childbearing—are so great in the United States that it seems likely that, for the majority, cohabitation will remain part of the "decision-to-marry" process rather than an alternative form of marriage, at least in the foreseeable future. In this culture, commitment tends to be indicated by legal marriage and, hence, marriage is still a very important end-step in the courtship process.

Research on nonmarital cohabitation in the United States has focused on the following topics:

1. *Prevalence rates:* Lack of a generally accepted operational definition of cohabitation and the difficulty of obtaining adequate samples have interfered with obtaining accurate prevalence rates. It has been estimated that about 25% of the undergraduate population has had at least one cohabitation experience (e.g., Arafat & Yorburg, 1973; Henze & Hudson, 1974; Peterman, Ridley, & Anderson, 1974; Macklin, 1976; Bower & Christopherson, 1977). Clayton and Voss (1977) reported that 18% of a national sample of 20–30-year-old men had cohabited nonmaritally for six months or more. In a review of data collected from a 1976 national area-probability sample of 2,500 adults living with a member of the opposite sex, Yllo (1978) found that 1.9% of the sample were unmarried, a figure comparable to the estimated 1.8% based on census data at the time (Glick & Spanier, 1980). It must be remembered that, because cohabitation is usually a transition phenomenon, "currently cohabiting" rates are much smaller than "ever-cohabited" rates.

2. *Attitudes toward nonmarital cohabitation:* Research has repeatedly documented the increasing acceptance of cohabitation, particularly by younger persons (e.g., Arafat & Yorburg, 1973; Henze & Hudson, 1974; Macklin,

1976; Bower & Christopherson, 1977). Over 50% of persons surveyed in a 1978 public-opinion poll indicated that they did not consider it morally wrong for couples to live together unmarried (Yankelovich, 1981).

3. *Nature of the cohabiting relationship:* It is clear that there is no such thing as "the" cohabitation relationship. The degree of emotional involvement in and commitment to the relationship, as well as the length of the relationship, are important differentiating variables. To facilitate discussion, researchers have noted at least five types of cohabiting relationships: temporary casual convenience; affectionate "going steady"; trial marriage; temporary alternative to marriage; and permanent alternative to marriage (e.g., Storm, 1973; Petty, 1975). The ages of the couple and their previous marital history should perhaps also be considered in any typology of cohabitation. What percentage of the 1.5 million cohabiting couples identified by the 1980 U.S. Census fell into each of the suggested categories is not known, and it is possible that, over time, any given cohabiting couple would fit into several categories, depending on where they are in their commitment process when they are surveyed.

4. *Characteristics of cohabitors:* Cohabitors tend to perceive themselves as more androgynous, to hold more liberal attitudes, and to have lower rates of religious affiliation than noncohabitors, but they are not more likely to come from unhappy or divorced homes, to perform less well academically, or to have lower personal-adjustment scores (e.g., Arafat & Yorburg, 1973; Henze & Hudson, 1974; Peterman, *et al.*, 1974; Catlin, Croake, & Keller, 1976; Macklin, 1976; Newcomb & Bentler, 1980b; Risman *et al.*, 1981).

As a group, cohabitors tend to be somewhat younger than marrieds (Yllo, 1978; Glick & Spanier, 1980), and in the case of divorced persons, the incidence of cohabitation is negatively related to the age of the children involved (Hanna & Knaub, 1981). Blacks tend to have higher rates of nonmarital cohabitation than whites, but blacks represent a very small proportion of the total number of cohabitors (Clayton & Voss, 1977; Glick & Spanier, 1980). Research has shown no consistent relationship between socioeconomic status, educational background, and likelihood of nonmarital cohabitation (see Macklin, 1983). As cohabitation becomes more widespread within the general population, the differences between persons who have and have not cohabited premaritally appear to become increasingly insignificant (Newcomb & Bentler, 1980b; Hanna & Knaub, 1981).

5. *Comparison of cohabiting, dating, engaged, and married couples:* Researchers have investigated such variables as reported satisfaction, commitment, decision-making, division of labor, sexual satisfaction, and communication. When compared to dating couples (with control for length of relationship), cohabitors expressed more satisfaction, more intimacy, and less behavioral egalitarianism; thus they looked much like married couples (Risman *et al.*, 1981). Whether the cohabitation was

a cause or an effect of these differences is not clear. With the exception of degree of commitment, few differences have been found between married and cohabiting couples (e.g., Johnson, 1973; Budd, 1976; Segrest & Weeks, 1976; Lewis, Spanier, Atkinson, & LeHecka, 1977; Stafford, Backman, & diBona, 1977; Polansky, McDonald, & Martin, 1978; Yllo, 1978). Because of the wide variation in types of cohabitation, it is important that comparison research match couples for their point on the courtship continuum.

6. *Comparison of married couples who have and have not cohabited before marriage:* The initial studies, which focussed primarily on married student couples who had and had not cohabited prior to marriage, found few significant differences between the groups with regard to degree of marital satisfaction, conflict, egalitarianism, or emotional closeness (Budd, 1976; Olday, 1977; Jacques and Chason, 1979; Risman *et al.*, 1981).

More recent studies, on broader populations, have reported somewhat different results. Watson (1983) found non-premarital cohabitors to have somewhat higher mean Dyadic Adjustment scores during the first year of marriage than cohabitors, perhaps because of the honeymoon effect for the former. Clatworthy and Scheid (1977) reported that couples who cohabited premaritally more frequently disagreed, were less dependent on their spouses and their marriages, and were more likely to have sought marriage counseling. DeMaris and Leslie (1984), in a study of 309 recently married couples whose names were obtained from Florida marriage records (72 percent of whom had cohabited before marriage), found that first-marriage wives who had cohabited reported significantly lower quality of communication and that both spouses reported lower marital satisfaction, with the modest differences not accounted for by differential commitment to the relationship or duration of the relationship. Premarital cohabitation was not found to be related to current marital satisfaction in the case of remarried persons (DeMaris, 1984).

Without longitudinal data, it is impossible to determine whether the above differences in the marital relationship were due to the premarital cohabitation or to preexisting personality and value characteristics of the individuals. It is possible that persons who cohabit before marriage expect more out of marriage or are persons who adapt less readily to the role expectations of traditional marriage, and that the apparent differences would have existed irrespective of the premarital cohabitation.

The one study to find premarital cohabitation positively correlated with marital quality compared 80 remarried families, half of whom had lived together before marriage (Hanna & Knaub, 1981). Remarried couples who had cohabited premaritally reported significantly greater happiness, closeness, concern for the partner's welfare, positive communication, family adjustment, and environmental support. However, they also tended to have somewhat younger children, a circumstance that could account for much of the difference.

Newcomb and Bentler (1980a), reporting on a four-year follow-up of couples first interviewed soon after marriage, half of whom had cohabited premaritally, indicated no significant difference in marital adjustment or divorce rate, although divorce was curvilinearly related to length of premarital cohabitation. Premarital cohabitants in more successful marriages tended to be older, previously divorced, more educated, and more traditional on some measures. Premarital cohabitants who later divorced tended to have higher marital-adjustment scores than noncohabitants who divorced, although it is unclear whether this result was due to a tendency to give up on a relationship more easily, more capacity for autonomy on the part of women who cohabit, or greater skill in dealing with dissolution.

Rank (1981) found greater differences between couples who stayed married and couples who divorced than between couples who had and had not lived together before marriage. Couples who were still married two to five years after the wedding tended to be couples who reported that the partners had had similar expectations of married life, had made a special effort to minimize the transition, and had treated the marriage as a natural continuation of the premarital relationship. Persons who divorced tended to report having married for inappropriate reasons (e.g., parental pressure, fear of losing the partner, or an assumption that marriage would improve the relationship) and unrealistic expectations of how the partner would behave after marriage. Because the data are from retrospective interviews and often from one person, they are merely suggestive.

It is clear that premarital cohabitation does not help persons to select more appropriate partners and does little to improve the quality of the marital relationship. Jacques and Chason (1979) concluded that "premarital cohabitation may not provide the type of learning experiences that significantly alter—in either a positive or negative direction—an individual's preparation for marriage" (p. 8). Ridley and colleagues (1978) agreed and suggested that

The degree to which cohabiting experiences prepare individuals for marriage depends in particular on the needs, goals, motivations, and competence of the persons involved. . . . Future research is sorely needed. . . . to identify the person and relationship characteristics that play an important role in determining the long-range effects of living together before marriage. (pp. 134, 136)

It would appear that, as with marriage, simply living with someone does not ensure a quality relationship. Nor does cohabitation, when compared to dating without cohabitation, result in a greater rate of termination before marriage (Risman *et al.*, 1981), as might be expected were it to play a significant and effective screening role. There has been little effort to help couples use their premarital cohabitation as a time for conscientious assessment and relationship enhancement and, hence, there is no way of knowing if such an effort would make a significant difference in the later marital relationship.

It is obvious that nonmarital cohabitation, which became highly visible less than 15 years ago, is rapidly becoming part of the normative culture. It is not clear what effect this increasing rate of premarital cohabitation will have on U.S. society. There is no evidence that it will lead to reduced marriage rates as it has in the Scandinavian countries. There has been an increase in median age at first marriage, but probably more because of the changing roles of women than because of changing courtship patterns; cohabitation is relatively temporary, and persons who marry with and without first living together report similar lengths of time between first date and marriage (Newcomb & Bentler, 1980a,b; Hanna & Knaub, 1981; Rank, 1981). There is no clear impact on birth rate. Persons who cohabit tend to desire fewer children (Bower & Christopherson, 1977) and to have fewer children during the first four years of marriage (Newcomb & Bentler, 1980a), but whether this pattern will continue as cohabitation becomes more widespread is not known. As noted above, there is no reason to think that premarital cohabitation will affect marital quality or divorce rates.

The effect of cohabitation on other societal institutions—religious, legal, financial, educational, and human service—has been more profound, often requiring important changes in policy and procedure. Perhaps the most widely publicized has been the legal controversy arising from the precedent set by the California Supreme Court in the *Marvin* v. *Marvin* (1976) case, in which it held that ''the fact that a man and woman live together without marriage, and engage in a sexual relationship, does not in itself invalidate agreements between them relating to their earnings, property, or expenses'' and granted Michelle Marvin the right to sue Lee Marvin for a property settlement when they separated after a seven-year cohabitation. The extent to which this case will affect judgments by other courts is not clear (see review of ''palimony'' decisions in Myricks, 1980, 1983). Some have speculated that, in time, all discrimination based on marital status will be held unconstitutional (Lavori, 1976; Straver, 1981).

Research on nonmarital cohabitation has been prolific since the 1970s, and although the samples have often been small and nonrandom, the findings have been sufficiently consistent to allow important conclusions. Although the original research focused on college populations and on cohabitation before first marriage and without children present, there have been substantial efforts in the past few years to include research on a wider range of cohabitants. There is a need for more longitudinal research that would place cohabitation in a life course perspective, for greater understanding of cohabitation among once-married and older persons, and for a testing of the assumption that increased efforts to help persons learn from the cohabitation experience would lead to greater marital quality. As nonmarital cohabitation *per se* does not appear to be a sufficient explanatory variable, more attention must be given to such factors as the meaning that the participants attach to the relationship (at the very least, where it falls on the courtship continuum); the age, educational level, marital history, values, and interpersonal competencies of the participants; and relationship variables, such as the length of time together, commitment balance, self-disclosure, and conflict management (e.g., see Cole & Goettsch, 1981; Hennon, 1981).

Voluntary Childlessness

Conservative estimates are that about 5% of all ever-married U.S. women are voluntarily childless (Veevers, 1979). Given the present tendency to postpone marriage and childbearing (Wilkie, 1981), as well as the increase in educational and career options for women, it has been predicted that voluntary childlessness will reach a rate of at least 10% (Veevers, 1979). How far above this percentage it will go is not clear. Some data suggest a leveling off of the trend toward childlessness (Houseknecht, 1982a), and the percentage of persons expecting or preferring to remain childless is still small (11% of women aged 18–34 in 1980 and 16% of those with four or more years of college, U.S. Bureau of the Census, 1982, Table 11).

Houseknecht (1982b) concluded that, although the degree of female education, labor-force participation, and career commitment play a key role in determining the incidence of voluntary childlessness, societal norms regarding childlessness are a significant factor, and in this country, these norms continue to be strongly traditional. Although the 1970s saw a slight increase in the percentage of persons who viewed nonparenthood as ideal (1% of the men and less than 1% of the women in 1970, and 3.5% of the men and 2.5% of the women in 1977; Blake, 1979), there is still a high degree of pronatalism among Americans. Researchers have uniformly reported that voluntarily childless couples experience some degree of disapproval from others (e.g., Magarick, 1975; Marcks, 1976; Cooper, Cumber, & Hartner, 1978; Ory, 1978; Callan, 1985). Undergraduates, when asked to characterize voluntarily childless wives, rated them as less loving, less happy, and less well adjusted than persons with children (Jamison, Franzini, & Kaplan, 1979; Calhoun & Selby, 1980).

There has been much recent research on voluntary childlessness—that is, the deliberate decision of husbands and wives to forego either procreation or adoption—and the achievement of a lifetime commitment to that decision (see Veevers, 1979, 1980, 1983, and Houseknecht, 1979a, 1982a, and Chapter 14 in this book, for extensive reviews of related research). The areas explored include (1) the characteristics of persons who elect childlessness and the differences between them and those who elect parenting; (2) the process involved in deciding to remain childless and the reasons for that decision; and (3) the consequences of childlessness, both for the individual and for the couple.

Much of the early research looked at childlessness as a global category and lumped together those unable to parent with those who preferred not to, and those postponing parenthood with those who intended never to parent. More recent research has sought to find samples of persons who have purposefully remained childless and who plan to continue to do so, although this research has usually necessitated small self-selected samples, often located through organizations such as the National Organization for Non-Parents (Barnett & MacDonald, 1976; Lichtman, 1976; Marcks, 1976; Marciano, 1978) or sterilization clinics (Gustavus & Henley, 1971; Magarick, 1975; Kaltreider & Margolis, 1977). There has been little use of carefully matched control groups and little effort to ensure that the parenting sample has been successful in controlling the number and spacing of their children, an important factor when relating presence of children to satisfaction.

Characteristics of Persons Who Decide Not to Have Children

When compared to parents, persons who choose childlessness are more likely to come from urban areas (Rhee, 1973); to have delayed their first marriage (Ritchey & Stokes, 1974); to have been previously married (Rhee, 1973); to be college-educated or to hold advanced degrees (e.g., Gustavus & Henley, 1971; Mommsen, 1973; Magarick, 1975; Nason & Poloma, 1976); to report "no religion" (virtually all studies); to have both husband and wife employed in relatively high-income positions (e.g., Rhee, 1973; Ritchey & Stokes, 1974; Ramu, 1985); to be disproportionately firstborn (e.g., Barnett & MacDonald, 1976; Thoen, 1977; Ory, 1978), lastborn (Pupo, 1980), or only children (e.g., Baum & Cope, 1980); to report that the advent of children negatively affected their parents' lives (Lichtman, 1976; Toomey, 1977); to be in good mental health (e.g., Malmquist & Kaij, 1971; Teicholz, 1977; Magarick & Brown, 1981); to be more androgynous (Teicholz, 1977); and to be less conventional (Magarick, 1975; Bram, 1985). It is not always clear to what extent these variables are cause or effect.

The Decision to Remain Childfree

Research has explored when the decision was made, who made it, and the reasons persons choose to remain childfree. Almost all data have been retrospective and, hence, may suffer from distortion. In about one third of the cases (the so-called early articulators, Houseknecht, 1979b), the decision was made independent of spouse and prior to marriage. The majority, however, have been classified as "postponers," who make the decision gradually through a series of postponements after marriage (Veevers, 1973; Houseknecht, 1979b). Of the latter, about half of the couples reached agreement easily and half experienced conflict and the need for negotiation, with the more powerful or least ambivalent partner winning (Cooper et al., 1978; Marciano, 1978).

Veevers (1979) suggested that there are two major groups of the voluntarily childless: the "repudiators," who are primarily motivated by the disadvantages of parenthood and are highly committed to being childfree, and the "aficionados," who like children but have developed a lifestyle to which children would be an impediment. Research by Cooper et al. (1978), in which "more personal freedom" and "greater time and intimacy with spouse" were major reasons for remaining childfree, suggests that the "aficionados" are the more common.

Consequences of Voluntary Childlessness

Researchers have looked at the relationship between childlessness and life satisfaction in old age, mental health, occupational success, and quality of the marital relationship. Because so much of the research has lumped together voluntarily and involuntarily childfree couples and has made no effort to control for the degree of volition among the parenting group, or to match for such variables as level of education, one must view comparison research with some caution.

Because of the concern that, with age, persons may come to regret their earlier decision to be childfree, researchers have compared the physical isolation and the social adjustment of older parents and nonparents (e.g., Singh & Williams, 1981; Beckman & Houser, 1982; Keith, 1983). The findings suggest few social, economic, or psychological differences between the two groups and indicate that most nonparents find alternative sources of satisfaction (Kivett & Learner, 1980; Bell & Eisenberg, 1985; Rempel, 1985), although the degree of satisfaction will differ as a function of social class and physical health (Bachrach, 1980). It can be concluded that the presence or absence of children does not appear to appreciably alter the life satisfaction of older adults.

As might be expected, childfree persons tend to be more successful professionally, and childfree academics of both sexes tend to publish more in a given period of time (Hargens, McCann, & Reskin, 1978). However, this positive correlation with career success appears to hold true only for those jobs that allow an extra investment of time, energy, and money in one's performance (e.g., self-employment and the professions).

The effect on marital interaction was investigated by Houseknecht (1979a) in a carefully controlled study that matched mothers and voluntary nonmothers on education, religion, and work participation. The childless women scored significantly higher on overall marital adjustment and, in particular, on spousal cohesion, but the differences were small. These findings were supported by data from a stratified random sample of white women married after age 21, which indicated that voluntarily childless, undecided, and postponing wives had higher mean levels of marital satisfaction than did mothers, and that factors associated with marital satisfaction for the voluntarily childless and the undecided differed from those for postponers and mothers (Polonko, Scanzoni, & Teachman, 1982). In order to test whether the higher marital satisfaction was due to absence of children, Hoffman and Levant (1985) studied 25–35-year-old voluntarily childfree and child-anticipated couples and found no significant differences between the groups on marital adjustment scores.

In one of the few studies to control for intentionality of parenthood, Feldman (1981) noted similar levels of marital satisfaction for voluntarily childless couples and intentional parents with a 6-month-old child. However, childless couples did report significantly more positive marital interaction and more frequent spousal conversation than did parents, and the frequency decreased for the parents after the birth of the child. Feldman suggested that the degree to which one is living a lifestyle of choice is most predictive of level of satisfaction. Follow-up data are required to determine whether these intentional parents will experience a decline in level of marital satisfaction with an increase in length of parenting and number of children.

Many questions remain: To what extent is the degree of reported marital satisfaction for parents and childfree couples related to the presence or absence of children, to intentionality of lifestyle, to the level of marital interaction, to the opportunity for sex-role equality, and to differential rates of dropout through divorce? To what extent is there an easing of the strong coercive pronatalism common in the United States, thus allowing couples real freedom to choose the lifestyle that may be best for them? Patterson and DeFrain (1981), in a review of family textbooks, noted that over half presented childlessness as a legitimate choice, but is this finding indicative of changes in the broader society? What would be the probable effect on society (e.g., productivity, use of time and resources, degree of individualism, quality of child care, and concern for others) if there was a dramatic increase in voluntary childlessness? To answer these questions will require carefully selected comparison groups, sample sizes appropriate for multivariate analyses, and increasingly precise operational definitions that take into account both social and biological parenthood as well as the degree of commitment to childlessness.

The Binuclear Family, Coparenting, and Joint Custody

Traditionally, divorce has been seen as synonymous with family dissolution, child custody has been granted to the mother, and the noncustodial father has played a minimal role in the rearing of his children. However, with the movement toward sex-role equality, increased participation by fathers in parenting, and a growing awareness of the loss experienced by the noncustodial parent (Keshet & Rosenthal, 1978; Greif, 1979, 1986; Fischer & Cardea, 1981, 1982) and by postdivorce children with little or no father contact (Hetherington, 1979; Wallerstein & Kelly, 1980), there has been a search for ways that would allow both adults to continue active parenting roles (e.g., Gal-

per, 1978; Abarbanel, 1979; Ahrons, 1980a,b; Folberg, 1984; Melli, 1986).

Ahrons (1979; Ahrons & Perlmutter, 1982) coined the term "binuclear family" to refer to the postdivorce family in which the child is a member of a family system composed of two nuclear households, maternal and paternal, with varying degrees of cooperation between and time spent in each. A related concept is the principle of coparenting, in which ex-spouses acknowledge the right of the other to share in the privileges and responsibilities of parenting (Galper, 1978). Coparenting may or may not be coupled with joint custody, in which the courts assign the divorcing parents equal legal rights and responsibilities to the minor child irrespective of the particular residential arrangement (Milne, 1979). Although there has been growing interest in these options, and numerous states have enacted legislation allowing for joint custody, as yet there have been few published studies on their effects or on the variables predictive of their success (see Abarbanel, 1979; Ahrons, 1979, 1980b; Greif, 1979; Steinman, 1981; Clingempeel and Reppucci, 1982; Lowery and Settle, 1985).

Ahrons (1979), in a study of 41 divorced parents awarded joint custody, noted three characteristic co-parental relationship patterns: "good friends," "neither friend nor foe," and "bitter enemies," with about one-fifth of the joint custody parents in the latter category (see Ahrons and Perlmutter, 1982). Interpersonal conflict and support were crucial variables determining both the type of parental interaction and the functionality of the joint custody arrangement. The lower the level of conflict and the higher the level of support, the more cooperative the co-parenting relationship and the higher the amount of non-residential parental involvement.

After a review of the research, Lowery and Settle (1985) conclude that two aspects of the custody arrangement which appear to affect the child's adjustment to divorce are the sex of the custodial parent and the nature of the custody. Children are better adjusted when in the custody of the parent of the same sex (Santrock and Warshak, 1979), and joint custody appears to have more advantages and fewer disadvantages than sole custody if the parents are able to interact constructively (Leupnitz, 1982). In examining court records for a two year period, Ilfeld, Ilfeld, and Alexander (1982) found the relitigation rate for joint custody cases to be half that for sole custody cases (16% vs. 32%).

The effect of joint custody on children was explored by Steinman (1981) in a study of 24 joint custody families characterized by strong parental commitment to co-parenting, mutual support, and relatively equal residential time with each parent. In spite of this relatively ideal situation and the fact that the parents reported satisfaction with the arrangement, the children had mixed reactions. While they valued the equal access to each parent, evidenced good emotional adjustment, and appeared to master the logistical problems of commuting, they still objected to the divorce and wished that the family could live together. About one-third felt burdened by the need to relate to two homes, with latency-aged children appearing to adapt more easily. Consistent with other research findings (e.g., Wallerstein and Kelly, 1980), the divorce was still a source of sadness for most of the children, even though for 70% of them half a lifetime had elapsed since the separation. However, until there is research comparing children in joint custody with children in sole custody, and children in dual residence with those in single residence, controlling for quality of the coparental relationship, there can be no assumption that children in sole custody/single residence would have fared any better or even as well.

It is important to note that while there has been increasing interest in joint custody and co-parenting, evidence suggests that these family forms may be a reality for only a small fraction of divorced families. Using data from a 1981 nationally representative sample of children aged 11–16 in single parent and stepparent families, Furstenberg and Nord (1985) point out that almost half of the children had not seen their nonresidential parent in the past year and that residential parents had disproportionately assumed responsibility for child care. They conclude that in the majority of cases, marital disruption results in a serious disruption of the parenting relationship for the nonresidential biological parent.

At the moment, one must conclude that divorce is painful irrespective of the circumstances. Its effects are mitigated by a positive coparental relationship and the possibility of equal access to each parent; however, it is clear that the legal decree of joint custody does not necessarily ensure parental cooperation. The growing research interest in the ex-spousal relationship and the factors affecting the nature of that relationship (e.g., Walker & Messinger, 1979; Ahrons, 1981; Clingempeel, 1981; Kitson, 1982; Clingempeel & Brand, 1985) is particularly significant, given the importance of the continued coparental relationship. (See Emery, 1982, for a proposed multilevel-multivariable family life-cycle approach to the study of the postdivorce parent–child relationship.)

The Stepfamily

The stepfamily, in which one or both of the married adults have children from a previous union with primary residence in the household, is not a new phenomenon. It has, however, traditionally followed the widowhood of one or both of the spouses. With the increase in divorce, and the fact that the great majority who divorce remarry and that many of these remarriages involve an adult with one or more children from a previous marriage, the stepfamily is becoming an increasingly common and complex family form (see Espinoza & Newman, 1979; Pasley & Ihinger-Tallman, 1984). In 1978, 10% of all children under 18 were reported living with a natural parent and a stepparent (Glick, 1979a). Many others living in a single-parent household have a stepparent married to their noncustodial parent.

As with most family forms, one should be cautious in describing "the" stepfamily. There are important subtypes that have many, as yet not well understood, differences among them. There are, for example, stepfamilies based on widowhood and those based on divorce; families with young children and those with older children and adolescents; families with or without an outside parent; stepmother and stepfather families; and one- and two-stepparent families. Each has unique structural and, hence, socioemotional characteristics.

The most common structure is a mother, her children, and a stepfather. Consequently, research has focused on the stepfather family (e.g., LaRoche, 1973; Bohannon, 1975; Buhr, 1975; Wilson, Zurcher, McAdams, & Curtis, 1975; Perkins & Kahan, 1979; Pink & Wampler, 1985). Early research suggested that stepfathers tend to establish better relationships with their stepchildren than do stepmothers, who have better relations with younger than with older stepchildren (Bowerman & Irish, 1962; Bohannon, 1970; Duberman, 1973, 1975). When compared to fathers in intact families, stepfathers tend to report a more negative image of themselves as fathers and to play a more passive role in child rearing (Bohannon, 1975; Pink & Wampler, 1985).

A major topic of both clinical and research interest has been the psychological health of the stepfamily and its members. Research to date suggests few significant long-range differences between children who grow up in stepfamilies and those who live in intact families (Wilson *et al.,* 1975; Bohannon & Yahraes, 1979; Ganong & Coleman, 1984). In an intensive study of 88 stepfamilies, Duberman (1975), using self-ratings and observation of degree of family integration as indicators of family adjustment, found that only 21% of the families showed poor integration and that the quality of the family relationship was highly related to the quality of the spousal relationship.

One of the few studies to compare stepfather families and first-marriage families found a wide range of family functioning and no difference in marital quality, with stepfamily members rating their families as less cohesive and less adaptive and the father–adolescent relationships as less positive (Pink and Wampler, 1985). The extent to which these differences are functional, given the family structure, is not clear. Clingempeel and Brand (1985) found no difference in marital quality between simple stepfather and stepmother families, but evidence of lower marital quality in complex stepfather families, perhaps due to increased role ambiguity, more permeable external boundaries, and competing commitments.

Whether living in a stepfamily is better or worse than some alternative pattern, clinical evidence and interview data suggest that it *is* different, having its own particular set of stressors. The problems commonly experienced by stepfamilies include a complex kin network with issues of divided loyalties, jealousy, guilt, and unclear boundaries; role ambiguity of stepparents and stepkin; unrealistic expectations; conflict over finances and child rearing; instant parenting with little time for the development of the spousal unit; and the fact that many new stepparents are unprepared for the stresses that they will experience or how to deal with them (Bowerman & Irish, 1962; Fast & Cain, 1966; Maddox, 1975; Messinger, 1976; Roosevelt & Lofas, 1976; Noble & Noble, 1977; Visher & Visher, 1979; Walker & Messinger, 1979; Keshet, 1980; Kompara, 1980; Fishman & Hamel, 1981). Much of the current literature emphasizes that the traditional nuclear family is not an adequate model for the stepfamily, and there is some question about whether the criteria traditionally used to assess family well-being are appropriate for assessing the well-being of stepfamilies.

Research on stepfamilies is difficult, both conceptually and methodologically, and therefore the findings have often been conflicting and confusing. Few studies have used a control group, and there has been considerable debate about the appropriate characteristics of such a group. Some have suggested that the most relevant comparison group would be divorced-not remarried single-parent families or first-marriage families with a high degree of marital dissatisfaction, since these are the most realistic alternatives for the majority of stepfamilies (Chilman, 1983). Since most standardized instruments have been developed for use with traditional nuclear families, there has been some concern about the use of these instruments with stepfamilies. The diversity of stepfamilies makes it difficult to adequately control for the wide range of crucial differentiating variables or to achieve sufficiently homogeneous samples. Most samples have been convenience samples of white middle class populations.

There is a need for more demographic data from national probability samples; more systematically selected samples, including minority and low-income families; controls for such variables as custody arrangements, age when child became a stepchild, length of time in stepfamily, and degree of structural complexity; multi-method analyses of the structural and interactional differences between nuclear families and stepfamilies (see Perkins and Kahan, 1979); longitudinal studies designed to identify the processes involved in establishing a stepfamily, the developmental changes over time, and the factors predictive of successful stepfamily functioning; and an assessment of the kind of community services most effective in facilitating stepfamily functioning.

The Single-Parent Family

The single-parent family, in which the children reside with one parent who has primary responsibility for their day to day care, has become a significant family form in the United States and a subject of extensive research (see Hanson & Sporakowski, 1986; Schlesinger, 1986). Because of increasing divorce rates and the growing incidence of unmarried motherhood, 1 out of every 5 families with children under 18 in 1984 was a one-parent family, as compared with 1 out of every 10 in 1970 (Norton and

Glick, 1986). In 1983, one-fifth (22.5%) of all children under 18 were living with one parent only; 20.5% of them with mothers and 2% with fathers (U.S. Bureau of the Census, 1984, p. 46). Norton and Glick (1986) have estimated that nearly 60% of all children born in 1986 will spend a large part of a year or longer in a single-parent home before age 18 (12% because of premarital birth, 40% because of divorce, 5% because of long-term separation, and 2% because of death of a parent), and that 37% of women in their late 20's in 1984 will at some point in their lives maintain a one-parent household involving children under 18.

Single-parent families are disproportionately represented among black families. In 1983, 51% of all black children under 18 were living with a single-parent mother, as compared with 15% of all white children of the same age (U.S. Bureau of the Census, 1984, p. 46). Whereas in 1970, 31% of all black families were female-headed with one or more own children and no spouse present, this had risen to 48% in 1983 (U.S. Bureau of the Census, 1984, p. 46). It is clear that the increase in single-parent households has been one of the most dramatic demographic changes in the past fifteen years.

As always, it is important to recognize the great variation that exists among single-parent families, both structurally and economically. One must distinguish between single-father and single-mother families; among single-parent families resulting from adoption, unmarried motherhood, widowhood, or divorce; by class, race, and age of the parent; and probably most important, by the degree of involvement of the outside parent. Because considerable parenting is often provided by the noncustodial parent, the single-parent family might more appropriately be labeled the *single-parent household*. Given this reality, Mendes (1979) suggested a typology of single-parent families based on the degree of responsibility carried by the residential parent for the care of the children. It is also important that a distinction be made between the census term "female-headed (or male-headed) family household" and the single-parent household, as the former includes households without children or where the children are not the sons and daughters of the head of the house (see Thompson & Gongla, 1983).

Because single parents are more likely to be women, most of the research has focused on the "father-absent" household (e.g., Kopf, 1970; Herzog & Sudia, 1971; Ross & Sawhill, 1975; Bould, 1977; Chapman, 1977; Hetherington, Cox, & Cox, 1979; Wattenberg & Reinhardt, 1979; Staples, 1980). However, with an increasing number of fathers acquiring custody of their children (single-parent fathers do not represent an increasing *proportion* of the single-parent population), the single-parent father has become a growing topic of inquiry (e.g., George & Wilding, 1972; Gasser & Taylor, 1976; Mendes, 1976; Orthner, Brown, & Ferguson, 1976; Bartz & Witcher, 1978; Rosenthal & Keshet, 1978; Schlesinger, 1978; Greif, 1985a & b; Risman, 1986).

Researchers have explored: (1) *the economic problems*

faced by the single-parent household and, in particular, the low-income single parent (e.g., Weiss, 1984; Gladow & Ray, 1986; Norton & Glick, 1986; Pett & Vaughan-Cole, 1986); (2) *the social-emotional problems faced by the single parent* and how transition to that role affects the lifestyle of that parent (e.g., Gasser & Taylor, 1976; Rosenthal & Keshet, 1978; Greenberg, 1979; Weiss, 1979; Staples, 1980; McLanahan, 1983; Burden, 1986; Gladow & Ray, 1986; Sanik & Mauldin, 1986); (3) *the characteristics of persons reared in single-parent homes,* in particular, the sex-role identity, self-esteem and mental health of the offspring (e.g., Muir, 1977; Singer, 1978; Langer, McCarthy, Gersten, Simcha-Fagen, & Eisenberg, 1979; Wallerstein & Kelly, 1980; Blechman, 1982; Krein, 1986; Mueller & Cooper, 1986), with a special interest in boys growing up in father-absent homes (Kopf, 1970; Herzog & Sudia, 1971; Lowenstein & Koopman, 1978); (3) *the structural and interactional characteristics of the single-parent family* (Cline, 1977; Savage, Adair, & Friedman, 1978; Weiss, 1979; Glenwick & Mowrey, 1986); and (4) *external support systems and programs designed to facilitate single-parent functioning* (Clayton, 1971; Weiss, 1973; Heger, 1977; Muro, Hudgins, Shoudt, Kaiser, & Sillin, 1977; Parks, 1977; Geffen, 1978; Schorr & Moen, 1979; McLanahan, Wedemeyer, & Adelberg, 1981; Turner & Smith, 1983). An important adjunct to the single-parent literature is the recent interest in the experience of the noncustodial parent (e.g., Keshet & Rosenthal, 1978; Greif, 1979, 1986; Fischer & Cardea, 1981; 1982).

The most common problems experienced by single parents—and particularly by single-parent mothers—are economic (e.g., Jauch, 1977; Bianchi & Farley, 1979; Bradbury, Danziger, Smolensky, & Smolensky, 1979; Espenshade, 1979). Data from 1968 and 1974 surveys of a nationally representative sample of one-parent families conducted by the University of Michigan Panel Study of Income Dynamics indicated that over one-half (2/3 of those who retained their single status) lived below the poverty level (Smith, 1980). In a study of the 5-year effect of marital dissolution on the income and consumption of single-parent women, using 1968–1979 data from the same research, Weiss (1984) concludes that "loss of the income of the former household head (who on the average had provided 80% of the household income) results in a precipitous drop in household income" (p. 126). For all income groups, this reduction persists as long as the household is headed by a female single parent. It is indicative that a review of admission data from mental health facilities found the single most depressed group of mental health service clients to be young, single-parent mothers with young children and low incomes (Guttentag, 1977).

Although it is true that single parents tend to report a number of problems, such as conflicting home and job responsibilities, role overload, the stress of having to make parenting decisions alone, finding enough time for their children and their own personal life, a need for ade-

quate child-care facilities, and social isolation (e.g., Orthner *et al.,* 1976; Schlesinger, 1978; Weiss, 1979; Turner & Smith, 1983; Burden, 1986; Sanik & Mauldin, 1986), one cannot assume that the single-parent family is a dysfunctional unit (Thompson & Gongla, 1983). Research suggests that the majority of single parents, both male and female, function effectively (e.g., Gasser & Taylor, 1976; Wilkinson & O'Connor, 1977; Bartz & Witcher, 1978; Rosenthal & Keshet, 1978; Orthner & Lewis, 1979; Schorr & Moen, 1979), particularly when one controls for the socioeconomic status of the custodial parent (Blechman, 1982).

Although single-parent fathers tend to have more education, income, opportunity to date, and environmental supports than do single-parent mothers, the problems and satisfactions of being a single parent appear to be similar for men and women (Greenberg, 1979; DeFrain & Eirick, 1981). Single fathers as a group tend to perceive themselves as competent and comfortable in their role as single parent, and to report satisfying relationships with their children, particularly in the case of men who elected custody (e.g., Gasser & Taylor, 1976; Santrock & Warshak, 1979; Rosenthal & Keshet, 1981; Risman, 1986), perhaps because single-parent males often played significant parenting roles prior to the divorce. Limited research indicates no significant difference in the self-esteem of children living with single-parent mothers and single-parent fathers, although there is a positive relationship between self-esteem and frequency of contact with the noncustodial parent (Lowenstein & Koopman, 1978). The data suggest an important interaction among child behavior, parental coping, and social resources, mediated by the gender and the economic status of the custodial parent (Ambert, 1982).

Research to date suggests that growing up in a single-parent household has a negative impact on the later educational, occupational, and economic attainment of the individual (e.g., Hetherington, Camara, and Feathermore, 1983). It is not clear, however, to what extent this is due to the lower socio-economic status of many of these families or to the reduced parental resources (e.g., less time to parent). Two recent studies are indicative. Using data from the Center for Human Resource Research, Krein (1986) found that, for men aged 28–38 in 1980, having lived as a child in a single-parent family had a negative impact on later educational attainment and in turn on earnings. Men who had spent even a short period of time in a single-parent home tended to complete fewer years of school than those from intact homes, even when one controlled for family income, race, mother working, and parents' education. Impact varied with length of time and age in the single-parent home, with the most adverse effects associated with having a single parent during the preschool years. Data from a 1982 survey of 19–34 year olds in a metropolitan county in the midwest showed that, when compared with persons from intact homes, persons who had been reared by single parents tended to have lower educational, occupational, and economic attainment and were more likely to be separated or divorced and to have had children at a young age. However, these differences were reduced when one controlled for economic conditions of the family of origin.

Although it is acknowledged that single-parent families, both adults and children, tend as a group to evidence more emotional problems than do members of stable nuclear families (e.g., Wallerstein & Kelly, 1980), there is some question about whether these problems result from external stressors, such as lack of community support and the aftermath of marital distress and separation, or from the structure of the single family *per se* (Schorr & Moen, 1979; Staples, 1980; Thompson & Gongla, 1983). Socioeconomic status, and the factors associated with it, probably play only a minor role. In a study of 256 custodial parents, most of them drawn randomly from public divorce records, SES accounted for only 15% of the variance in self-report social adjustment and general well-being (Pett & Vaughan-Cole, 1986).

Observers have noted the tendency for the single-parent family to have more open boundaries between the parent–child subsystems, with greater equity, more frequent interaction, and heightened cohesion (Weiss, 1979). The extent to which these qualities verge on enmeshment varies greatly from family to family and depends on numerous factors, such as culture, the ages and number of children (Cline, 1977), and the personality and parenting skills of the parent (Glenwick & Mowrey, 1986). It seems likely that there is more variation in intrafamily dynamics within one- and two-parent families than between them (Savage *et al.*, 1978; Thompson & Gongla, 1983).

In recognition of the special needs of single parents, efforts have been made to provide peer support networks (Parks, 1977) and training in parenting skills (Heger, 1977; Muro *et al.*, 1977; Geffen, 1978), with varying degrees of success. Repeated emphasis has been placed on the need for society to acknowledge the high proportion of single-parent families and to accommodate to their needs with more institutional supports, flexible work hours, and easily available child-care facilities (Schlesinger, 1978; Schorr & Moen, 1979; Thompson & Gongla, 1983; Turner & Smith, 1983). Society has tended to minimize the needs of the single-parent family, seeing it as a transitional stage and, hence, as temporary. This view no longer seems appropriate, given the increasing numbers of such families and the growing evidence that, for many, it is not a temporary lifestyle (Smith, 1980; Staples, 1980).

Although the research to date has generally consisted of interviews with small nonprobability samples and only recently has there been data from large samples with appropriate controls, findings have done much to remove the myths regarding the single-parent family and to outline the major issues in the life of the single parent. There is now a need for more studies designed to (1) identify the major factors affecting the functioning of single-parent families; (2) compare single-parent families, controlling for ethnic, economic, and structural characteristics; (3) examine the interaction effects of race, class, and family structure on the mental health of the family members; (4) explore the intrafamily dynamics of the single-parent family and how these impact on the later relationships of both parent and child; (5) identify techniques for parent education that will affect parenting behavior as well as attitudes; and (6) document the extent to which the single-parent family is negatively affected by present institutional constraints and identify those societal changes that would be both beneficial and realistic.

Open Marriage and the Open Family

Open marriage is a term that was coined in the early 1970s to refer to a marital relationship based on spousal equality and a commitment to both personal and relationship growth (O'Neill & O'Neill, 1972). The concept developed as a reaction to traditional marriage, which was seen as having rigid roles, unequal statuses, and possessive exclusivity, and in recognition of the growing importance of autonomy and mutuality in contemporary relationships. As the term was used by the O'Neills (1972), an open marriage was characterized by functioning in the "here-and-now" with realistic expectations, respect for personal privacy, role flexibility, open and honest communication, open companionship, equality of power and responsibility. pursuit of identity, and mutal trust. Basic to open marriage was a belief in synergy, or the assumption that, by acting together, two or more organisms can achieve an effect that neither is capable of alone, hence the emphasis on allowing space for individual growth and on sharing the process of that growth with one's partner (Rogers, 1972).

Although *Open Marriage* (O'Neill & O'Neill, 1972) became a national best-seller, there has been only one published study of open marriage. Using a 40-item scale, with 5 items for each of the eight open marriage (OM) components, Wachowiak and Bragg (1980) assessed the degree of self-reported openness in the marriages of 26 college-educated couples. Marital openness was found to be positively related to having fewer children, to less frequent church attendance, to younger age, and, for wives, to higher scores on the Locke–Wallace Marital Adjustment Scale. It is indicative that, in general, the couples appeared to be relatively traditional, although there is no way of knowing if they were less traditional than similar couples a decade before. It has been suggested that, given the level of ego development theoretically required for successful open marriage, it would be unrealistic to expect to find large numbers of persons actually practicing this lifestyle (Rejals & Foster, 1976).

Although there has been little work on open marriage *per se*, the growing attention to sex roles has led to much interest in its modified version, the "androgynous" or "egalitarian" marriage (Osofsky & Osofsky, 1972), in which decision making and division of labor is accomplished without regard to gender. However, as with open

marriage, studies suggest that, although androgynous relationships may be becoming more popular, few couples
are truly androgynous in their interaction. A review of
sex-role research suggests that behaviors are shifting
more slowly than attitudes (see Scanzoni & Fox, 1980).
Although there is an increasing preference for sex-role
equality (particularly among women and the college-educated), household task-performance continues to be sex-
typed, with women carrying the primary responsibility
for child rearing, housework, and the day-to-day functioning of the family (Yogev, 1981). Why this disparity
exists between attitude and behavior is not clear. It is
likely that individuals differ widely with regard to sex-
role attitudes and that the more egalitarian partner adapts
to traditional expectations in order to minimize conflict
and because of the residual power of socialization.

In a report of a study of 31 couples who had successfully implemented a role-sharing relationship, Haas (1980)
emphasized the problems faced by role-sharing couples
and concluded that such a lifestyle demands ''the whole-
hearted and enthusiastic willingness of both spouses to
participate'' (p. 296). The necessary commitment to do
so came more from the discovery that such a lifestyle
provided practical benefits than from an ideological belief
in androgyny. The benefits included the wife's having a
chance to work outside the home for personal fulfillment
without the typical overload dilemmas faced by most
working wives; the husband's being relieved of the provider role and its accompanying stresses; reduced economic and domestic dependence; increased financial security; and greater couple togetherness. Problems were
experienced with regard to the division of household
chores (e.g., discrepancy in standards, reluctance to delegate responsibility, lack of skills and efficiency, and a
disinclination to try nontraditional tasks) and accommodation to the outside world of work (e.g., the conflicting demands of the spouses' jobs and conflicts between
job and family responsibilities). (See the section on dual-
career families for further discussion.)

The concept of the *open family* (McGinnis & Finnegan,
1976; Constantine, 1977a, 1983) extends the principles of
open marriage to the entire family system, applying them
to parent–child as well as spousal interaction. Advocates
of the open family emphasize flexible role prescriptions,
clear communication with extensive negotiation and decision by consensus, open expression of emotion, and mutual respect across age as well as gender. This family style
has received no explicit research attention, although the
family therapy and family enrichment literature speaks of
similar goals (e.g., L'Abate, 1974; Guerney, 1977;
Olson, Sprenkle, & Russell, 1979; Sawin, 1979).

Dual-Career Families and Commuter Marriages

Dual-Career Families

One of the striking changes in the American family has
been the increase in the employment of married women.
Over one-half (53.3%) of all woman aged 16 and over

were in the labor force in 1984, compared to 41.4% in
1970 (U.S. Bureau of the Census, 1984). In 1979, 50.9%
of all husband–wife families reported both husband and
wife as earners, compared to 45.7% in 1970 (U.S. Department of Labor, 1979). Slightly over half (50.2%) of
all mothers in two-parent families with children under age
18 were employed in 1978, compared to 39.9% in 1970
(Waldman, Grossman, Hayghe, & Johnson, 1979). Concomitantly, there has been an increase in dual-career families, in which ''both heads of household pursue careers
and at the same time maintain a family life together''
(Rapoport & Rapoport, 1969, p. 18). It is impossible to
determine what proportion of dual-worker families are, in
fact, dual-career families.

Research on the dual-career family developed out of a
growing interest in the changing roles of women and a
concern about those factors that constrain women from
participating in careers commensurate with their abilities
(see Hopkins & White, 1978; Rapoport & Rapoport,
1978; Skinner, 1980). As part of a late-1960s study of
highly educated British women, the Rapoports (1969)
identified a subgroup of career-oriented women married
to career men and first introduced the concept of the *dual-
career family*. Much of the initial research was descriptive, consisting of interviews or questionnaire data from
relatively small samples, with the primary focus on the
stresses and coping strategies characteristic of this family
pattern (e.g., Rapoport & Rapoport, 1969, 1971; Poloma, 1970, 1972; Garland, 1972; Holmstrom, 1972).

Increasingly, studies have explored specific aspects of
the dual-career experience, looking in particular at (1) the
degree of marital satisfaction, with findings suggesting
that rates of satisfaction are related to the degree of ''fit''
between the husband's and the wife's attitudes and aspirations (e.g., Bailyn, 1970; Hornung & McCullough, 1981;
Houseknecht & Macke, 1981; Hiller & Philliber, 1982)
and that those with more traditional sex-role attitudes tend
to experience more stress (Keith & Schafer, 1980); (2)
early socialization experiences, indicating that many
dual-career wives experienced early acclimation to high
levels of stress, little reinforcement for conventional marriage, and a close relationship with parents who supported
their career aspirations (Bebbington, 1973; Allen & Kalish, 1984); (3) the *personality characteristics of dual-
career and traditional couples,* indicating some differences in degrees of desired and expressed affection and
control, but it is not clear whether these differences are
cause or effect (Burke & Weir, 1976); (4) the *effect of
having husband and wife in the same career,* indicating
that wives in the same field as their husband tend to produce more than those not married to fellow professionals,
but that they are less productive and less professionally
satisfied than their husbands (Epstein, 1971; Martin, Berry, & Jacobsen, 1975; Bryson, Bryson, Licht, & Licht,
1976; Heckman, Bryson, & Bryson, 1977; Bryson,
Bryson, & Johnson, 1978); (5) *consequences of status
differences between husbands and wives,* indicating that
degree of stress is related to the extent to which status

difference is congruent with the gender role identities and expectations of the persons involved (Hunt & Hunt, 1977; Hornung & McCullough, 1981; Hiller & Philliber, 1982; Philliber & Hiller, 1983; Atkinson & Boles, 1984); (6) *effect of dual careers on family task-sharing,* indicating that two-career couples tend to do more sharing of traditionally female tasks than do one-career or career/earner couples (Atkinson & Boles, 1984; Bird, Bird, & Scruggs, 1984); (7) the *impact of the work world on the dual-career family,* indicating the negative impact of traditional business, which operates on the assumption that career takes precedence over family and that there is a full-time support system at home (Rosen, Jerdee, & Prestwich, 1975; Bailyn, 1978); (8) the *effect of geographic mobility,* indicating that mobility has a negative impact on the wife's career and that her needs tend not to be the determining factor in the decision to move (Duncan & Perrucci, 1976; Ferber & Huber, 1979); and (8) the *effect of particular structural variations,* such as job sharing (e.g., Arkin & Dobrofsky, 1978) and commuting couples (Gerstel, 1977; Farris, 1978; Kirschner & Walum, 1978; Gross, 1980; Gerstel & Gross, 1983, 1984). Although couples who share less than two full-time equivalent positions favor a continuation of the arrangement, devote more time, and are more productive than the average full-time employee, employers tend to view the policy with some reservation.

Atkinson and Boles (1984) coined the term WASP (wives as senior partners) to refer to marriages in which the wife's career is considered by the couple to be more important than the husband's. Data from the 1982 Census (U.S. Bureau of the Census, 1983) indicate that wives earn more than husbands in 12% of all U.S. couples and 15.5% of all dual-career couples, suggesting that WASPs are relatively rare. An exploratory study of 31 such marriages (Atkinson and Boles, 1984) revealed that a major issue was the need to minimize the cost of being perceived as deviant, using such devices as concealing or deemphasizing the lifestyle and compensating by doing special things for one another. Even in these marriages, the wives assumed primary responsibility for traditional female household chores, although husbands contributed more time to such tasks than in other marital patterns.

Skinner (1980) classified the stresses confronting dual-career families into those that arise primarily from (1) stress internal to the family (i.e., role overload, identity issues resulting from the discontinuity between gender-role socialization and current lifestyle, role-cycling issues resulting from the need to mesh individual career and family career cycles, and presence of children) and (2) stress external to the family (i.e., normative dilemmas resulting from the expectations of others, occupational inflexibility and demands for geographic mobility and full-time primary commitment to the job, and social-network dilemmas resulting from lack of free time for socializing and kin relationships). Women experience more of these problems than do men; women make more frequent sacrifices and compromises in their career ambi-

tions (e.g., Epstein, 1971; Holmstrom, 1972; Poloma, 1972; Heckman *et al.,* 1977; Bryson *et al.,* 1978; Ferber & Huber, 1979). Characteristic coping strategies include "stress optimization," that is, the recognition that stress is both inevitable and outweighed by the advantages of the lifestyle; prioritizing, compartmentalizing, and compromising; and seeking outside support through hired help and associating with other career couples (e.g., Holmstrom, 1972; Poloma, 1972; Bebbington, 1973; Rapoport & Rapoport, 1976).

In a study of factors differentiating high and low quality dual-career marriages, Thomas and colleagues (1984) found the following to be characteristic of high quality marriages: adequate family income with husbands earning more than their wives, couple consensus that husband's career was to be preeminent, husbands supported their wives' careers, older children, satisfying social life, husband empathic to wife's stress, good sexual relationship, discussion of work-related problems, role complementarity and role sharing, and shared activities and companionship.

Given the changing norms and economic realities, it is likely that the great majority of families will have both spouses simultaneously employed at some point in the family cycle. With increased education and pressure for equality on the part of women, the proportion of men and women seeking careers will become more similar. Because of these increasing numbers and the degree of normative change implicit in the dual-career lifestyle, it can be predicted that the dual-career family will be the variant family form that promotes the most profound societal change. The extent to which this change will involve changes in the occupational structure as well as in family structure is not clear. With more college-educated women wishing both a high-status career and a full family life (Regan & Roland, 1985), the scene is set for serious future role conflicts which are not likely to be easily resolved.

There is a great need for further research on the consequences of the dual-career family, using carefully operationalized variables and appropriate control groups over time. A step in this direction has been taken by Pendleton, Poloma, and Garland (1980), who developed a series of scales to facilitate the quantitative study of dual-career wives and their attitudes regarding the relative importance of career and family. It is important to control for stage in the family cycle (Keith & Schafer, 1980) and to recognize the limitations of studying only currently married couples (Hornung & McCullough, 1981).

Commuter Marriages

There is a growing research interest in the "commuter," "two-location," or "long-distance" marriage, in which dual-career spouses voluntarily live in separate residences for at least three or four days a week because of geographically separated jobs (Gerstel, 1977; Farris, 1978; Kirschner & Walum, 1978; Gross, 1980; Gerstel &

Gross, 1983, 1984). Such an arrangement usually results from the two spouses' each wishing to pursue a career simultaneously and usually evolves as an accommodation to a wife's career. The commuter marriage is to be differentiated from the marriages of those couples who live apart because the husband's job requires that he travel while the wife maintains the family home (e.g., Merchant Marines, migrant workers, and construction workers). Preliminary research comparing dual-career commuter marriages and more traditional "husband-away" marriages suggests that each form has its own characteristic set of costs and benefits, and that there is a major difference in the pattern of values, expectations, and resources typically associated with each (Gerstel & Gross, 1983).

Research findings on the commuter marriage have emphasized the difficulties associated with this lifestyle, which most couples view as a temporary alternative. Interview data suggest that such a system works best when there are high career motivations, the husband's acceptance of the wife's career needs, a high income, geographic propinquity, a long-established marriage, and minimal child-rearing responsibilities. The length of separation and the degree of the regularity of visits appear to play a major role in determining the effect of the commuting experience; couples who see each other every weekend function most effectively. Dissatisfaction tends to increase with length of time apart and irregularity of visits.

The expressed advantages of commuting include the opportunity to pursue occupational opportunities, the freedom to concentrate more fully on work, the excitement of reuniting, and the redistribution or equalization of chores. The obvious disadvantages are lack of involvement in day-to-day "home-sharing" activities and a consequent reduction in feelings of interconnectedness, the often unrealistic expectations placed on time together, the continual adjustments demanded by repeated transition, and the frequent strain on relations with kin and friends. Most commuter marriages are not prompted by financial gain, as the added income typically does not equal the costs of the commuting arrangement, nor by a desire to end the marriage, given the apparent willingness to invest so much time, money, and effort in continuing the relationship (Gerstel & Gross, 1983). The findings to date indicate no increase in extramarital relationships during time apart, and most couples continue to behave extramaritally as they did when living together (Gerstel, 1979).

Gross (1980) distinguished between two types of two-career commuter marriages: (1) the "adjusting" or younger couple, who are beset by simultaneously establishing two careers with little history as a spousal unit, and (2) the "established" or older couple, who possess a backlog of experience to cushion the impact of the separation and who see the separation as the wife's rightful chance to have her turn at a career. However, even older couples suggest that "they are coping with the lifestyle

rather than enjoying it" (Gross, 1980, p. 574). Because it can be anticipated that an increasing number of couples will be faced with this lifestyle option, it is important that researchers work to further document the factors related to minimal stress and to identify techniques for enhancing the family functioning.

Extramarital Sex

General

Although traditionally prohibited in the majority of human societies (Murdock, 1949; Ford & Beach, 1951), the sexual interaction of a married individual with someone other than his or her spouse has been widely practiced and researched in the United States (Macklin, 1980). Although it is broadly referred to as *extramarital sex* (EMS), a distinction must be made between the clandestine affair and the comarital or sexually open marital relationship (SOM) in which the extramarital activity is conducted with the knowledge and consent of the spouse. Some researchers have even expanded the concept of EMS to include "affairs of the heart", contrasting EMS which is emotional (in love) but not sexual (intercourse), sexual but not emotional, and both emotional and sexual (Thompson, 1984).

The study of EMS has consisted primarily of surveys given to relatively large nonrandom samples in order to measure attitudes toward and establish rates of EMS. Multivariate analysis of the resulting data has been used to investigate the relationship between EMS and a host of possibly predictive variables. Specifically, research efforts have focused on:

1. *Rates of extramarital coitus:* In the 1940s and early 1950s, Kinsey and associates (1948, 1953) estimated that 50% of American men and 26% of American women had had at least one experience of extramarital intercourse. Since then, data from nonprobability studies of large numbers of people have suggested that, in middle-class educated samples, the rate of reported EMS has increased, especially for younger women; that the first incident is occurring at an earlier age; and that the rates for men and women are becoming more similar (Athanasiou, Shaver, & Tavris, 1970; Hunt, 1974; Bell, Turner, & Rosen, 1975; Levin, 1975; Maykovich, 1976; Thompson, 1984). It is now predicted that EMS rates for the cohort of women aged 30 years and younger in 1975 will eventually reach about 50% (Bell *et al.*, 1975; Levin, 1975; Atwater, 1979; Weis, 1983). Few women limit the experience to one occasion (Bell *et al.*, 1975), but most have three or fewer partners and the majority report an emotional involvement with those partners (Atwater, 1979; Spanier & Margolis, 1979).

2. *Attitudes toward EMS and variables predictive of "permissive" attitudes:* As is true of other types of sexual behavior, attitudes toward EMS tend to be more conservative than behavior. The results from a variety of studies consistently indicate that the great majority (70%–80%)

of Americans, college students as well as older adults, continue to disapprove of EMS (Singh, Walton, & Williams, 1976; Bukstel, Roeder, Kilmann, Laughlin, & Sotile, 1978; Strong, 1978; Glenn & Weaver, 1979; Ericksen, 1980; Rao & Rao, 1980; Reiss, Anderson, & Sponaugle, 1980; Weis & Slosnerick, 1981; Weis, 1983). In an analysis of responses from a 1974 National Opinion Research Center (NORC) sample of persons aged 18 and above, Singh *et al.* (1976) found that those who approved of EMS were likely to be young, male, black, and unmarried, the single best predictor being degree of liberality in general and, in particular, degree of liberality regarding premarital sexual behavior. Based on a sample of college students, Weis and Slosnerick (1981) suggested that an even more powerful predictor, accounting for 16% of the variance, may be the degree to which one associates sex with love and marriage, a variable that is highly related to premarital permissiveness. They noted that, although not approving EMS, college students do accept *nonsexual* extramarital relationships (NERs) with people of the opposite sex if these are not seen as likely to lead to sexual encounters. By focusing solely on extramarital coitus, researchers may have overlooked the significant liberalization that is taking place with regard to extramarital heterosexual friendship.

Using NORC data and a path analysis approach based on eight variables (age, gender, religiosity, attitude toward gender equality, political liberality, education, premarital sexual permissiveness, and marital happiness), Reiss *et al.* (1980) were able to explain 17% of the variance (25% among the college-educated sample) in attitude toward EMS, the last three variables being sources of direct influence. It was suggested that the addition of the following six variables would further increase the predictive capacity of the model: the degree of marital sexual satisfaction and experimentation, the degree to which one holds power in the marital relationship, the extent to which one focuses one's satisfaction of intimacy needs solely on one's mate, the extent to which one takes a pleasure-oriented approach to sexuality, and the degree of freedom and opportunity to be in contact with potential nonmarital partners.

Weis and Jurich (1985) also sought to find a winning combination of variables most predictive of attitudes toward EMS, using NORC data from five national surveys between 1973 and 1980 and the variables of gender, age, race, education, religiosity, marital status, marital happiness, political liberality, premarital sexual permissiveness, and size of present community. When premarital sexual permissiveness was used in the stepwise regression analysis, it was consistently the first and most predictive variable; when not used, religiosity was the best predictor. However, surprisingly, size of community was usually the second most predictive variable, more powerful than marital happiness, liberality, gender, age, or race.

Building on variables suggested by Reiss and colleagues (1980), and the assumption that background vari-

ables do not explain as much of the variance in sexual permissiveness as does the present marital situation, Saunders and Edwards (1984) developed a predictive model using only dyadic variables: marital satisfaction, marital sexual satisfaction, diffuse intimacy conception (degree to which one shares one's private feelings with persons other than spouse), perception of power (or ability to influence one's partner), autonomy of heterosexual interaction (perceived lack of social constraints to interact heterosexually), comparision level of alternatives (extent to which one finds their marriage best of available alternatives), number of life stations (work, home, and leisure), and priority of family roles (primacy given to spousal, parental, and family roles). Using a sample of 140 women and 70 males in occupations allowing varying degrees of heterosexual interaction, the model explained 34% of the variance in female attitudes and 16% of the variance in male attitudes, with diffuse intimacy conception proving to be the strongest predictor. They conclude that focusing on additional aspects of the dyadic relationship will prove the most fruitful direction in developing more effective models of EMS permissiveness, both attitudes and behavior.

The most successful model to date has been that suggested by Buunk (1980b). Using data from a Dutch sample, he found that the following variables explained 60% of the variance in the respondents' expressed *intent* to engage in EMS: need for intimacy, marital need deprivation, facilitative social context, approval by spouse, and sex-role egalitarianism. Persons who anticipate that they may experience EMS are, according to this model, likely to be individuals who have a high need for intimacy that is not being satisfied by their marriage, who perceive EMS as consistent with their value system and as acceptable to their peers and spouse, and whose social setting provides an opportunity for such interaction.

3. Factors predictive of EMS experience: Efforts to identify those variables correlated with actual involvement in EMS suggest findings very similar to the above. Research consistently shows that demographic variables such as religion, socioeconomic status, and education contribute only marginally. The following variables play a significant role but are only partially predictive: attitudes, such as acceptance of sexual liberality, liberal lifestyles, and sex-role egalitarianism (Bell *et al.*, 1975; Buunk, 1980b); characteristics of the marital relationship, such as perceived marital quality and length of marriage (Bell *et al.*, 1975; Edwards & Booth, 1976; Spanier & Margolis, 1979); and personality characteristics, such as high need for intimacy and low level of emotional dependency on spouse (Buunk, 1980b). Several authors have emphasized the importance of "perceived opportunity for involvement" (e.g., Johnson, 1970a,b; Maykovich, 1976; Atwater, 1979) and the anticipated cost–benefit ratio (Walster, Traupmann, & Walster, 1978).

Based on a review of the literature, it seems likely that actual involvement in EMS is dependent on the interaction of at least the following variables: (1) *perceived opportunity*, in particular, the availability of a potential partner and sufficient privacy; (2) *readiness to take advantage of the opportunity*, as indicated by the level of marital satisfaction and the pattern of personality needs and values, in particular, the need for intimacy, the degree of dependence on the spouse, and liberality of values; (3) *expectation of satisfaction*, as determined by role models, past experiences, and the degree of attraction to the potential partner; and (4) *expectation of negative consequences*, based on the perceived likelihood of being found out, or of being accepted by spouse and friends if found out, and the degree of significance attached to any possible consequences of being found out.

Using in-depth interviews with 40 middle-class EMS women, Atwater (1978, 1979) explored the dynamics of the "transition to unconventionality" and the process of resocialization involved in the initiation of EMS. Rather than drifting into EMS, most of her sample spent time in conscious deliberation before actual involvement. She argued that the first EMS experience is a symbolic marker-event in a woman's sexual career, akin to the first premarital sexual experience, and she urged that researchers view EMS in the context of individual social development. Based on her exploratory interviews, she hypothesized that participants typically follow one of two scripts: (1) the more traditional one, where EMS is motivated primarily by a bad marriage and falling in love and is accompanied by much guilt, which occurred less frequently in her sample, and (2) the more "humanistic, expressive" script, in which EMS results from curiosity and the desire for self-discovery and personal growth, which Atwater sees as the more common model for the future. Her work underlines the need for longitudinal studies that examine experience with alternative lifestyles from the perspective of a total life cycle.

A major concern of researchers and clinicians has been the relationship between EMS and marital satisfaction, and whether EMS is either an indicator or a precursor of a failing marriage. The evidence to date comes solely from retrospective self-report data. Although EMS is significantly related to low levels of marital happiness, and marital dissatisfaction is an important predisposing factor, large numbers of EMS participants report happy marriages and a sexually satisfying relationship with their spouse (Hunt, 1969, 1974; Johnson, 1970a,b; Bell *et al.*, 1975; Levin, 1975; Edwards & Booth, 1976; Atwater, 1979; Buunk, 1980b). Glass and Wright (1977) concluded, after an analysis of the survey data reported by Athanasiou and colleagues (1970), that, although EMS is generally associated with lower marital satisfaction, the relationship between the two variables varies with the length of the marriage and the gender of the respondent.

Without longitudinal data regarding the quality of the marital relationship prior to EMS, it is difficult to determine the effect of EMS on marriage. In interviews with a sample of divorced and separated persons, about one-third (38% of the men and 37% of the women) reported having engaged in EMS before their separation, but most viewed the EMS as indicative of, rather than a cause of, marital problems (Spanier & Margolis, 1979). The respondents were likely to perceive their partner as having been more often involved in EMS than they, and their partner's behavior as having had a more negative impact on the relationship than their own (49% reported their partner's EMS to have been detrimental, whereas only 6% reported their own to have been). Although there was no apparent relationship between participation in EMS and the quality of the postmarital adjustment, those who strongly disapproved of their spouse's EMS indicated lower levels of postmarital self-esteem and satisfaction with life. This finding suggests that it is not the EMS *per se* but one's reaction to it that is most indicative of its impact.

Swinging

Swinging is a form of comarital sex in which the couple engages in sex with other couples as a form of social recreation (Gilmartin, 1977). It is estimated that about 2% of the U.S. adult population in the early 1970s had engaged in swinging at least once, with about three-quarters dropping out within one year (Athanasiou *et al.*, 1970; Hunt, 1974; Levin, 1975; Murstein, 1978b). There was considerable research interest in the phenomenon of swinging in the early 1970s, and most of the data come from that period (e.g., Denfield & Gordon, 1970; Smith & Smith, 1970; Bartell, 1970, 1971; Palson & Palson, 1972; Varni, 1972, 1973; Henshel, 1973; Cole & Spanier, 1974; Gilmartin, 1974, 1977, 1978; Walshok, 1974; Symonds, 1976). Only four studies have been published since 1978 (Dixon, 1984; Duckworth & Levitt, 1985; Jenks, 1985; and Murstein, Case, & Gunn, 1985). Whether the lack of recent information is reflective of lack of current research interest or a fading of a fad is not clear.

The term *swinging* covers a wide variation in actual behavior, ranging from the "hard-core" swingers, who entertain no emotional involvement, to those who seek long-term intimate relationships with other couples (Varni, 1972). Most couples who continue the extramarital involvement gradually expand their activities from participating as a couple together in the same room, or at the same party, to more individual sexual involvements and more stable relationships (Smith & Smith, 1970). Husbands usually introduce their wives to swinging, and those wives who come to accept it as a lifestyle tend to have family backgrounds and values similar to those of their husbands (Bartell, 1970, 1971; Varni, 1972; Henshel, 1973; Jenks, 1985; Murstein *et al.*, 1985).

Descriptions of persons who swing vary with the particular study. Although some describe the typical swinger as white, middle-class, college-educated, politically liberal, and in professional or white-collar positions (Denfield & Gordon, 1970; Gilmartin, 1974, 1977), Bartell (1970, 1971) found his midwestern sample to be politically conservative and non-college-educated. In a comparison of swinging and nonswinging couples, Gilmartin (1974, 1977, 1978) found swingers to report less rewarding relationships with their parents, to interact less with kin and neighbors, to be more detached from religious or political activities, to have dated earlier, to have married younger, and to have experienced more divorce. They reported more frequent sexual interaction with their spouses and more marital happiness than did couples engaging in conventional EMS. These findings have been generally confirmed by the more recent research by Jenks (1985) and Murstein and colleagues (1985), who found that swingers are more liberal on matters related to their sexual lifestyle but more conservative on other issues.

There has been little research on the effect of swinging on the individual or on the couple relationship. Interviews with currently active participants emphasized the positive effects and the increased openness and sharing (Denfield and Gordon, 1970; Smith and Smith, 1970; Bartell, 1971). Data from dropouts are contradictory. A survey of 467 counselors indicated that clients who were ex-swingers often reported having experienced problems with jealousy, guilt, competing emotional attachments, and fear of discovery by family and neighbors (Denfield, 1974). A survey of 30 ex-swingers obtained through swinger-referrals and advertisements in magazines found that ex-swinger husbands were very similar to swinger husbands, while ex-swinger wives were more conventional than swinger wives, and that it was the wives who were primarily responsible for the dropout (Murstein *et al.*, 1985).

All of the research to date suggests that while swingers possess an unusually high interest in sex with relatively weak ties to parents, religion, and societal conventions, they are reasonably well-functioning individuals who have concluded that their sexual needs cannot be adequately satisfied in their marriage. The likelihood of continuing to swing appears to depend on the couple's value orientation and the extent to which the lifestyle is the result of a mutual decision (Gilmartin, 1977).

Sexually Open Marriage

The sexually open marriage (SOM) is one in which the spouses have mutually agreed to allow their partner to have openly acknowledged, independent sexual relations with secondary or satellite partners who maintain separate residences. Unlike in swinging, dating is done separately, and the emphasis is on the emotional as well as the sexual aspects of the outside relationship. SOM as a lifestyle usually develops out of a philosophical commitment to open companionship, spousal equality, and nonpossessiveness, and it is seen as a way to provide freedom for individual growth and experience within the security of an ongoing, committed relationship (Lobell & Lobell, 1972; Mazur, 1973; Francoeur & Francoeur, 1974).

In general, research on the sexually open marriage has been limited to interviews and questionnaires given to small samples of persons who either are or have been in such relationships (Ziskin & Ziskin, 1973; Knapp, 1976; Knapp & Whitehurst, 1977; Buunk, 1980b; Watson, 1981). Based on interviews of 34 persons in SOM relationships and their scores on the Myers–Briggs Type Indicator, Knapp (Knapp & Whitehurst, 1977) concluded that SOM participants tend to be individualistic, independent, future-oriented, risk-taking, stimulated by complexity, nonconforming, creative, and guided by their own personal ethical system. When the California Psychological Inventory was given to 71 persons who had experienced SOM, they scored high on independence, flexibility, and self-acceptance (Watson, 1981).

Although persons in SOM relationships tend to speak favorably about the lifestyle and to see it as having many personal and relationship benefits, they also report numerous complications, including jealousy, guilt, difficulty in apportioning time and attention, pressure from the extramarital partner, need for continuous negotiation and accommodation, loneliness, and the difficulty of integrating their lifestyle with their broader social network (Knapp & Whitehurst, 1977; Buunk, 1980b; Watson, 1981). In order to cope with the actual or potential pressures, couples frequently establish mutually agreed-upon ground rules (Buunk, 1980c; Watson, 1981), the most common being complete honesty, primacy of the marital and family relationship, and limits set on the intensity of the outside relationship.

The available evidence suggests that SOM works as a lifestyle only when (1) the primary relationship is characterized by high degrees of mutual affection, respect, understanding, and consensus regarding lifestyle; (2) the individuals involved possess the personality traits and interpersonal skills necessary to deal effectively with complex and potentially stressful relationships; and (3) the outside partner(s) has no desire to compete with the spouse for primacy in the relationship.

Evidence regarding the effect of SOM on the marital relationship is limited. Data from a two-year study of 38 individuals in on-going SOM, 13 separated/divorced persons who had been involved in SOM, and 20 persons who had been an outside partner to a SOM relationship suggested that SOM is not necessarily indicative of marital dysfunction, and that SOM is a lifestyle which couples find difficult to continue over time (Watson, 1981). Interviews with the secondary partners indicated that they had anticipated that the relationship would be temporary, supportive, and present-oriented, and those who continued in the relationship were persons who perceived it as equitable. SOM participants whose marriage ended in divorce were likely to report that their SOM had been motivated by a desire to leave an unfulfilling marriage and that they did not wish a subsequent open relationship. Two years after the initial interview, all persons in the ongoing SOM group were still married and, with one exception, had turned to a monogamous relationship, although they perceived that there might be other periods in their relationship when they would again choose nonexclusivity.

Watson (1981) concluded that "open marriage may best be conceived as a stage, perhaps recurring, in the developmental process of a couple's relationship, rather than as an on-going lifestyle" (p. 18).

The above study provides some exploratory data on how sexually open parents handle the disclosure of their lifestyle to their children (Watson & Watson, 1982). Although 75% of the 71 adults in the study wanted their children ideally to be aware of their lifestyle and values, they differed as to the appropriate age for disclosure and only 21% had chosen to inform their children of their extramarital relationship(s). There was no correlation between disclosure and age of parent or child, and the tendency toward discretion was evident even in families with adult children. The authors conclude that because their behavior was nontraditional, the parents experienced cognitive dissonance between their values and their behavior, an explanation supported by the fact that after a two-year follow-up all but one of the couples in the open marriages had returned to a monogamous lifestyle (Watson, 1981).

Ramey (1975, 1976) reported on a variation of SOM that he called "intimate friendship" (IF: friendship that allows intimacy on many levels, including sexual). He was able to identify 380 persons in primary relationships who had practiced IF for an average of 15 years, noting that a number of these had evolved into what he called "intimate friendship networks." Given that the great majority of his sample reported satisfaction with their primary relationship and with their lifestyle, one must conclude that it is a viable relationship choice for some persons.

Only one study to date provides a comparison of marital quality in sexually open and sexually exclusive marriages (Rubin, 1982). The sample consisted of respondents from two groups matched for stage in family life cycle, education, occupation, income, and marital status: 130 persons from sexually open marriages (82 still together, 48 now separated) and 130 persons from sexually exclusive marriages (82 together, 48 separated). There was no significant difference in the scores of persons in sexually open and exclusive marriages on the Dyadic Adjustment Scale, although persons no longer living with their spouse scored significantly lower irrespective of whether or not they had been open or exclusive sexually.

Coprimary Relationships

Coprimary relationships refer to those in which an individual is committed to maintaining a sexual and emotional relationship with two or more other persons who may or may not know about or be involved with one another and who do not reside together. The only research specifically devoted to this lifestyle is that by Scott (1980a), who reported on the custom of "man-sharing" in the black community. In this case, a man who is legally married to one woman takes on a second "consensual wife"; each of his "wives" live in separate and distinct

households, composing two separate families. Scott referred to these as "polygynous families," in that the male has two or more simultaneous mates, with economic, biological, and social bonds and subjectively perceived reciprocal rights and obligations. (The extent to which these relationships are truly polygynous has been a topic of considerable academic controversy; see Allen and Agbasegbe 1980; McAdoo, 1980; Scott, 1980b.)

Man-sharing is described as resulting from the unbalanced sex ratio among blacks, and from the lack of available black males eligible for marriage (Jackson, 1971). In most cases, women drift into the role of consensual wife via the path of early dating, unwanted pregnancy, single parenthood, and economic impoverishment. With limited marital prospects and few life chances, they are willing to settle for a relationship with a man who is already married in exchange for the limited economic and emotional security that he may provide. Man-sharing is a good example of an alternate lifestyle that results not from a philosophical orientation or a desire for personal growth and experience, but out of a series of forced choices heavily conditioned by the limitations of one's life circumstances. There is a need for research to determine the extent to which coprimary relationships exist and persist among persons who are not economically thrust into this lifestyle.

In conclusion, it appears that, for the great majority of Americans, exclusivity will continue as a value. Although there may be a gradual increase in nonexclusive behavior, most of it will probably continue to follow the secretive, nonconsensual pattern. Given the complexity of SOM and the conflicts involved in maintaining several simultaneous emotional involvements, consensual love-oriented EMS will probably represent no more than 10% of all extramarital relationships in this country (Reiss *et al.*, 1980). It is important that future research differentiate among types of EMS experience, specifying the extent to which the outside relationship is deficit-motivated, the degree of open approval from the spouse, and the extent of emotional investment in the outside relationship (see Reiss *et al.*, 1980, for one proposed typology). Research should go beyond a report of frequency to examine the dynamics and context of the relationships under study; and efforts must be made to develop longitudinal research, including dropouts as well as those currently practicing a given lifestyle.

Same-Sex Relationships

The early research on homosexuality consisted primarily of work with clinical samples of male homosexuals and focused on issues of etiology and treatment (Morin, 1977). More recently, attention has been given to community-based samples and to the coping strategies and living patterns of gay men and lesbian women. This change in research focus is, in many ways, a reflection of a broader social change, symbolized by such events as the formation of the Gay Liberation Front in 1969 and the removal in 1973 by the American Psychiatric Association of homosexuality from its listing of psychiatric disorders (Spector, 1977). The current focus on homosexuality as a lifestyle rather than an illness can be traced to the pioneer efforts of Kinsey and associates (1948, 1953), Ford and Beach (1951), and Hooker (1957), who first presented the public with evidence that homosexual behavior is widespread, not only in our culture but throughout human history, and that homosexuality is not a sign of psychological impairment.

Since the late 1960s and early 1970s, research has further challenged the image of the homosexual as deviant and disturbed. Three landmark studies have used data gathered during that period. In 1973, Saghir and Robins published a study based on in-depth psychiatric interviews with 165 nonpatient male and female homosexuals and 84 single heterosexuals, which concluded that the majority of homosexuals present little or no psychopathology and are very similar psychologically to heterosexuals. In 1978, the Institute for Sex Research (Bell & Weinberg, 1978) reported on a study of 979 homosexual males and females in the San Francisco area and a heterosexual comparison group, emphasizing the wide diversity among homosexuals and the high degree of similarity between homosexuals and heterosexuals. The great majority of homosexuals were in stable couple relationships or leading satisfying personal lives, with lesbians more likely than gay men to be in close-coupled relationships. After comparing homosexual and heterosexual samples composed primarily of persons with above-average education involved in committed relationships, Masters and Johnson (1979) reported no difference in physiology of sexual response and equal success in the treatment of sexual dysfunction. It is increasingly clear that, because of the great diversity among both heterosexuals and homosexuals, one can say very little about an individual based solely on knowledge of his or her sexual orientation.

Of particular interest is the growing research on the homosexual relationship as a variant family form (see Peplau, 1982). Much of the work has been on the lesbian and her relationships (e.g., Martin & Lyon, 1972; Jensen, 1974; Rosen, 1974; Bryant, 1975; Blumstein & Schwartz, 1976, 1977; Oberstone & Sukoneck, 1976; Moses, 1978; Peplau, Cochran, Rook, & Padesky, 1978; Ponse, 1978; Tanner, 1978; Lewis, 1979; Wolf, 1979; Caldwell & Peplau, 1980; Pagelow, 1980; Raphael & Robinson, 1980; Peplau & Amaro, 1982). Research suggests that, for the majority of lesbians, sexual interaction takes place within the context of a relatively stable, sexually exclusive, living-together relationship, and that the first sexual-romantic involvement grows out of an established friendship between the women (Vetere, 1982). Most lesbians describe their relationship as extremely close, personally satisfying, and egalitarian, with degree of satisfaction related to degree of equality within the relationship (Bell & Weinberg, 1978; Tanner, 1978; Jay & Young, 1979; Peplau & Amaro, 1982; Peplau,

Padesky, & Hamilton, 1982). When one compares lesbian and heterosexual couples on standardized measures, there is little significant difference in dyadic adjustment (Cardell, Finn, & Marecek, 1981), although women in lesbian relationships are more likely to report that lovemaking leads to orgasm and to indicate less satisfaction with unequal power (see Peplau & Amaro, 1982, for review of related research). The great majority have had sexual relationships with men, and about a quarter have been heterosexually married (Peplau & Amaro, 1982).

Sex-typed role playing is rare in contemporary lesbian relationships (Tuller, 1978; Jay & Young, 1979; Cardell et al., 1981; Pelau & Amaro, 1982), although data from earlier decades indicated a tendency for lesbians to play out traditional sex roles in a "butch/femme" pattern (e.g., Jensen, 1974, based on data gathered for a 1968 thesis). Almost 100% prefer equal power in relationships, and about two-thirds report that this is the case in their own relationship, with equality dependent on such factors as equal resources and equal involvement in the relationship (Peplau et al., 1978, 1982; Caldwell & Peplau, 1980; Peplau & Amaro, 1982).

Research on gay male relationships indicates that few gay couples pattern their relationship according to traditional sex roles, with degree of equality primarily related to the age differential between the partners (Tuller, 1978; Harry, 1982, 1983, 1984). Contrary to popular stereotype, the majority of gay men are interested in long-term relationships, and the more committed one is to the gay community (i.e., the more one has gay friends and is committed to a gay identity), the more likely one is to have been involved in an emotionally intimate, sexually exclusive marriagelike relationship (Harry & Lovely, 1979). However, gay relationships are less likely than heterosexual or lesbian relationships to be sexually exclusive, and there is less agreement among gays regarding the importance of exclusivity (Tuller, 1978; Peplau & Amaro, 1982; Harry, 1983). The extent to which this attitude is a function of male genetic predisposition or of socialization may never be determined. Research suggests that, at any given time, 40%–50% of gay men are currently involved in a couple relationship, with the probability of being coupled related curvilinearly to age. The latter may be an artifact of the fact that samples are selected from gay bars and gay organizations, which older and/or coupled gay men may be less likely to frequent (Harry, 1983).

When one looks at the degree of behavioral and attitudinal commitment in relatively long-term living-together gay and lesbian couple relationships using the Dyadic Formation Inventory, one finds few significant differences between male and female couples (Lewis, Kozac, Milardo, & Grosnick, 1981). However, there is a suggestion that lesbians may exhibit higher levels than gay men of dyadic interaction (e.g., doing things together and confiding in one another), perhaps because they have been socialized as women to place a higher value on togetherness or perhaps as a defense against the lack of external social supports for the relationship (Lewis *et al.*, 1981). Issues of attachment versus autonomy appear to be highly salient for lesbian couples, as lesbian women as a group typically place a high value on both autonomy and intimacy (Peplau *et al.*, 1978).

Two additional studies of gay and lesbian couples deserve special mention. Blumstein and Schwartz (1983), in their large scale non-random study of American couples, report survey and interview data from married heterosexual, cohabiting heterosexual, gay, and lesbian couples. It is interesting to note that 16% of the gay men and 26% of the lesbian women had been previously married, and 14% of the lesbians had children from that marriage. Based on their interviews, the authors conclude that "couplehood, either as a reality or an aspiration, is as strong among gay people as it is among heterosexuals" (p. 45). However, the lack of institutional support for their relationship, and the fact that the gay social world is organized around singlehood and promoting one's sexual marketability, puts gay relationships in more jeopardy than is true for heterosexual couples. A major issue for gay couples is the subtle underlying theme of male competitiveness, and the constant need to negotiate power and protect against domination and dependency, with neither wishing to take on roles which seem gender inappropriate. Female partners seek both an intense emotional home life and a strong commitment to career, and struggle with the inevitable tensions which this implies.

Faced with the fact that traditional family developmental theory is based on the heterosexual experience of marriage and children, McWhirter and Mattison (1984) offer an alternative theory for the development of same-sex relationships. After studying 156 male couples, they proposed the following 6 stages: blending (first year), nesting (years 2 and 3), maintaining (years 4 and 5), building (years 6–10), releasing (years 11–20), and renewing (after 20 years).

Further research is needed on the interaction between sexual orientation and relationship characteristics. It remains to be seen whether, as homosexuals feel free to openly engage in relationships with persons of the same sex and heterosexual couples move toward greater equality and away from traditional sex roles, the same set of variables will determine the quality and duration of these relationships (see Spanier and Lewis, 1980).

Increasing attention has been given to bisexuality as a lifestyle, and to the effect of bisexuality on the heterosexual marriage (Brownfaun, 1985; Coleman, 1985 a and b; Dixon, D., 1985; Dixon, J. K., 1985; Matteson, 1985; Wolf, 1985). Data to date suggest that heterosexual marriage may prove more satisfactory for bisexual men than women, and that some heterosexual marriages can adapt to bisexuality if the couple makes an effort to accept, understand, and communicate.

Although most research has focused on the couple or "spousal" unit, there is growing interest in homosexual parents, both fathers and mothers (Bryant, 1975; Voeller & Walters, 1978; Hitchens, 1979–1980; Miller, 1979;

1979; Bozett, 1980, 1981; Pagelow, 1980). Bozett (1980, 1981) and Miller (1978,1979) have explored the efforts of gay fathers to integrate their two identities, noting that such integration is possible and that men who attempt it often experience more acceptance than anticipated. Although it has traditionally been difficult for gay parents to gain custody of their children, more parents are doing so and, except for the fear that they may lose their children because of their lifestyle, the problems of single gay parents appear to be little different from those of any single parent (Bryant, 1975; Miller, 1978).

Although there has been little systematic research on the effect of growing up as the child of a homosexual parent, evidence to date suggests that the young children in these families demonstrate sex-appropriate play behavior and clothing, and that the erotic fantasies and overt sexual behavior of the older children is heterosexually oriented (see Green, 1978; Nungesser, 1980; Hoeffer, 1981; Kirkpatrick, Smith, & Roy, 1981). It should be noted that using sex-appropriate play behavior as an indicator of heterosexuality is probably ill advised, for it may say more about sex-role identity than about potential preference regarding gender of partner, and these two concepts must be clearly differentiated.

Unfortunately, the research to date on same-sex relationships has had to rely on self-selected volunteer samples, largely obtained through homosexual bars and organizations, and on responses from only one person in the relationship. In the case of women, samples have been almost entirely young, white, educated, and middle-class (the research by Raphael & Robinson, 1980, on the older lesbian is an exception). It remains impossible to obtain representative samples and, hence, conclusions about the homosexual population must be drawn from those findings that are consistent across research studies. One of the most consistent findings is that homosexuality is not a unitary phenomenon, and that persons who may be self- or researcher-designated homosexuals vary greatly with regard to their degree of same-sex orientation (both behaviorally and cognitively), the extent of their ideological commitment and openness of lifestyle, and the nature of their intimate relationships. There is a need for specificity in the selection of samples, for samples inclusive of more diverse age groups and cultural backgrounds, and for researchers to control for degree of involvement in ongoing relationships in the selection of comparison groups ("married" and "single" are no longer adequate indicators; see Bell & Weinberg, 1978, for a possible typology).

Multiadult Households

Multilateral Marriage

The first published research on multilateral or group marriage in the United States was done by Constantine and Constantine (1973), who studied over 100 such relationships in the early 1970s. They used the term "multilateral marriage'' to refer to a relationship in which ''three or more people each considered themselves to have a primary relationship with at least two other individuals in the group'' (pp. 159–160). Usually, the members lived together communally and shared goods, services, money, and the raising of children, as well as sexual access to one another (Salsberg, 1973).

The average family unit consisted of two couples and their respective children or a single adult and a couple with their children (see Constantine, 1978, for a discussion of the differences between triads and groups of four or more). The majority of persons entered such relationships with their spouses and, in most cases, the pair bonds of the original marriage continued to be primary. The participants tended to be young and college-educated, with liberal attitudes and normal childhoods, and to have high needs for change, autonomy, heterosexuality, and intraception. The majority reported that their prior marriage had been happy, and that a desire for companionship, sexual variety, love, and personal growth was the primary motive for joining a group marriage.

As a lifestyle, group marriage is rare in this society and is disapproved of by the vast majority (e.g., White & Wells, 1973; Strong, 1978). Most such relationships do not last more than a year; communication and personality conflicts are the primary problems. The Constantines (1973) reported that, of their groups, 44% lasted for a year or more, 17% for three years or more, and 7% for more than five years. They suggested that the bonds between the same-sex members of the group appeared to be particularly salient in determining group success and concluded that only a small minority of families would be based on multilateral marriage, for it represents the most difficult and extreme departure from prevailing models.

Communes and Intentional Communities

The decade between 1965 and 1975 was a period of dramatic communal development in this country. More communes were begun during this period than in all previous American history (see Zablocki, 1980, for a historical overview). In 1975, Conover estimated that there were about 50,000 communes with roughly 755,000 residents. This sudden growth can be seen as a reflection of the general radical and countercultural activity characteristic of American society during these years, and it was contributed to by demographic factors resulting in large numbers of unemployed and unwed youth. The communes that developed during this period tended to differ in significant ways from earlier communes. They were smaller, were more likely to be urban (see Zablocki, 1977, for a review of urban communes), were less authoritarian, placed more emphasis on individualism and personal freedom, had more unrestricted admission and less long-term member commitment, and subsisted more on the wages earned by members at outside jobs (Zablocki, 1980).

Persons joined contemporary communes for many rea-

sons: to live with others who shared a common spiritual or ideological belief system, to change society by providing an alternative economic or political model, to retreat from the perceived injustices and meaninglessness of the larger society, and to develop a sense of a caring community. Berger, Hackett, and Millar (1972) distinguished between urban and rural, creedal and noncreedal communes (see Zablocki, 1980, for an alternate typology). Although communes and their memberships vary greatly from one another, their members tend to be young, white, middle children from intact middle-class homes who are experiencing personal or societal alienation.

Based on a longitudinal study of 120 rural and urban communes between 1965 and 1978, Zablocki (1980) reported that communes in this country are typically unstable; one half disintegrate within the first two years, and almost half of those remaining disappear after four years. The major reported problems are relational issues (especially power and authority issues) and ideological issues. Zablocki concluded: ''Communal systems, in their search for consensus, tend to generate intense networks of interpersonal interaction, which, in the absence of periodic charismatic renewal, tend to be associated with communal instability'' (p. 354). Those most likely to survive are religious communes, with strict admission requirements, strong commitment mechanisms, controls on sexuality, and links with other communes. Mowery (1978), after a review of 58 past and present communes, noted that those that survived for more than three years tended to be well financed and to have a high degree of social organization. These findings were substantiated by Cornfield (1983), who found in a study of 32 secular urban communes that duration and satisfaction were significantly related to relatively conventional variables such as economic prudence, regular housework, sufficient private time, and parental responsibilities. (See Kanter, 1972, 1973a, for a further discussion of communes.)

Researchers have studied the impact of communal living on the nuclear family units that join or develop within this lifestyle. One apparent effect is the opening of external family-boundaries and the shifting of the locus of social control. Based on his sample of 120 communes, Zablocki (1980) reported high rates of marital dissolution, except in religious communes, which tend to support and strengthen the marriage relationship. Of the couples in religious communes, 76% were intact after a year of study, as compared to only 27% of those in secular communes. Kanter and her associates (Kanter, 1973b; Kanter, Jaffe, & Weisberg, 1975; Jaffe & Kanter, 1976) indicated that couples and parents in communal households tend to report a loss of control over their territory and their partner. Couples experience pressure toward individuation and eqalitarianism and, with added adult caretakers, parents find themselves less able to make and enforce rules (Weisberg, 1975b, 1977; Blanton, 1980).

Communes vary greatly from one another and some are more satisfactory for families than others. Using data from a large three-year panel study of 65 urban communes in the mid-70's, Ferrar (1982) found that parents of young children are more likely to remain in those communes which are set up to accommodate to the special needs of parents than in those where family life is only incidental to the purpose of the commune.

Because of the tremendous diversity among American communes (e.g., in size, structure, ideology, and socialization practices), the fact that many children do not spend all of their child-rearing years in the communal setting, and the difficulty of obtaining adequate measures, it is hard to generalize about the impact of communal living on the child. However, some patterns can be detected (see Eiduson, 1979a): intense mother–infant relationships coupled with multiple-caretaker experience; early independence from adults, with peers becoming potent socializing agents; and emphasis placed on group decision-making skills. The result is that children evidence a pluralistic outlook and the capacity to relate to many different people; a sensitivity to the needs of their peers and the ability to relate in prosocial modes; independent decision-making and the ability to verbalize their needs; and a resistance to routines and scheduling. The extent to which self-reliance is a defense against dependency needs, and whether the ability to relate to many is developed at the expense of true intimacy, is not clear.

In a review of seven studies involving more than 150 communal and group marriage families, Constantine and Constantine (1976) reported that most children appear to develop a trusting relationship with adults, to maintain a strong identification with their natural parents, and to be generally self-reliant, cooperative, friendly, and self-confident. These authors concluded that, "with few exceptions, children have fared uncommonly well in these families; fear of major emotional damage can be laid to rest'' (Constantine, 1977b, p. 260).

A longitudinal study of the effect of child rearing in four different family forms (single-mother families, cohabiting unmarried couples, communal settings, and two-parent married nuclear families), beginning with the third trimester of pregnancy, is being conducted by the Family Life Styles Project at UCLA (Eiduson, 1979, 1980, 1981). Results at the end of three years (Weisner & Martin, 1979) and six years (Weisner, 1981, personal communication) indicated no significant group-mean differences in outcome scores on tests of motor and mental development. One must be cautious, however, about concluding that lifestyle has no impact on child development, for there may be important long-term differences in such areas as emotional expressiveness and value orientation that are not easily tapped by standardized measures. Moreover, the degree of within-group variation in home environment, socialization practices, and outcome scores suggests that family structure is only one of a host of interacting factors, and probably not the most influential one. As of 1981, there had been considerable lifestyle shifting by families over the course of the study period, with about 40% having changed lifestyles. One may need to pay more attention to degree of parental commitment to

a given lifestyle and to the nature of the household over time than to the family form at time of childbirth. It seems likely that such factors as the nature of the parent–child interaction, the emotional maturity of the parent, and the value orientation modeled by that parent are more significant in a child's development than the structural characteristics of the home environment, and that family structure bears only a minimal relationship to these more crucial variables.

Voluntary group living is predicted to become an increasingly viable option for older adults in our society (Dressel & Hess, 1983). Uneven sex ratios and the fact that elderly persons are more frequently living independently of kin has created a situation that invites solutions for ensuring companionship and care as health and income decline. Polygyny is a logical answer but is unlikely to receive much support (Kassel, 1970; Rosenberg, 1970; Windemiller, 1976). More likely options are "share-a-home" arrangements, in which persons pool resources, share responsibilities, and perhaps hire a manager (Streib, 1978; Streib & Hilker, 1980); the rental of space to younger unrelated persons in return for services and income (Usher & McConnell, 1980); and the "affiliated family," in which older nonkin are integrated into a younger family unit (Claven & Vatter, 1972). These and other arrangements should increase in popularity as younger cohorts who bring with them a greater awareness of and tolerance for alternatives reach old age, and as the elderly increase in numbers.

Some mention should also be made of the nonresidential "expanded family" forms that are quietly and unobtrusively being explored by numbers of families. In 1970, Stoller described his concept of the "intimate family network" (not to be confused with Ramey's "intimate friendship network''), in which three or four families meet together on a regular basis for the reciprocal sharing of services and friendship. A step in this direction is the "family cluster" workshops and groups developed by Sawin (1979). Allied concepts are the *new extended family,* a term used to refer to the integration of relatives from previous marriages and remarriages (Furstenberg, 1979), or the "fictive kin" networks common to low-income and minority cultures. There is still little research on the incidence or viability of these alternatives.

Where to from Here

The demographic evidence is fairly clear. In 1980, the Joint Center for Urban Studies of MIT and Harvard University (Masnick & Bane, 1980) published a detailed analysis of current and projected trends for U.S. families from 1960 to 1990. They predicted a continued decline in the size of the average household, in the proportion of households headed by a married couple, and in the proportion of households without children, as well as a continued increase in the divorce rate, in the number of working mothers (and the number of women working in full-time, continuous work), in the number of persons who live alone, and in the proportion of children living with one parent. They concluded:

These changes show the population to be more evenly spread across several household types in 1990. Because no one arrangement will be "typical," there will be demands for a wide range of different kinds of housing, consumer goods, and public and private services. As they move through life from youth to old age, people will have more diverse experiences. Men and women will spend fewer years in conventional nuclear families and more years living apart from close relatives. They will move from one type of household to another more frequently than in the past, and will undoubtedly develop greater flexibility in adapting to new ways of life. . . . People will have more complicated histories and probably more complicated sets of relationships from one stage of life to another. . . . We project by 1990 a very diverse world of households, families, and individual life histories. (pp. 4,5,9)

The value changes are not as well documented but seem equally evident. Different writers attach different labels to the perceived patterns. Francoeur (1983) wrote of the gradual shift from an absolutist, past-oriented, authoritarian, patriarchal, monogamous morality, which he hypothesized was necessary for social stability in the days before reproductive technology, to a more creative, pluralistic, future-focused, process-oriented perspective. He argued that the latter is more functional in a society where there is less need to control sexual behavior in order to protect the well-being of families and their members.

Buunk (1983) argued that the observed structural changes in family forms are indicative of broad historical changes in basic family value patterns. He wrote of a three-stage evolution: (1) the "functional, patriarchal, community-dependent" family characteristic of preindustrial Europe, with marriage founded on rational and economic grounds and little affection between family members; (2) the "affectionate, private, male-dominated" nuclear family, which developed with industrialization, where the family was a social-emotional enclave and the permanent exclusive affectionate bond between spouses the cornerstone of the family; and (3) the "individualized, open, equal" value pattern that is evolving today, where independence, close emotional ties with persons outside the family, individual interests, and personal desire are given high priority.

Yankelovich (1981), using data from public opinion surveys, demonstrated the dramatic shifts in attitudes that are accompanying the changes in family forms. For example, in the late 1970s, although about three-quarters of the respondents still felt that a woman should put her husband and children ahead of her career and disapproved of married men having affairs, three out of four said it was morally acceptable to be single and have children, and only 10% wanted to return to the sex mores and gender-role norms of the past.

The challenge is for researchers and theorists to find a way to conceptualize this growing pluralism. Much has been done to identify and describe the evolving alternatives to the traditional family pattern, to develop typologies for delineating the subforms of each alternative, and to define the characteristics of the participants. There is a growing recognition that one must differentiate within any given family form between those who choose that living pattern out of ideological or personal preference and those who are thrust into it by the particular circumstances of their lives (e.g., between singlehood resulting from a limited number of potential partners versus singlehood chosen because one prefers to live alone). There is an increasing awareness that there is more variation within particular family forms than there is among them, and that labeling a person as living in a given structural form actually tells very little about the realities of that person's life. The label of *single parent,* for example, indicates little about one's economic status; the degree and nature of one's environmental support; the number, ages, and needs of one's children; and the recency and degree of stress involved in the transition to that lifestyle.

Much of the work to date has focused on the structural aspects of nontraditional family forms and on assessing the extent to which these are becoming institutionalized within the broader society. More remains to be learned from this approach. There is an obvious need for larger samples reflecting a broader spectrum of society, and for an exploration of the interactive relationships between families and the other social structures that impact on and are affected by changing families. For instance, if it is true, as Masnick and Bane (1980) predicted, that "a revolution in the impact of women's work is on the horizon," particular attention must be given to the phenomenon of the dual-worker–dual-career family and to the interface between work and family life.

Two other foci seem particularly important at this juncture. First, there must be an identification of those factors that affect the quality of family life regardless of family form, as well as an understanding of how best to ensure their existence in any given individual's living situation. Second, we need more understanding of the process by which individuals become involved in their particular living patterns, and of the factors affecting the successful transition from one pattern to another.

There has been some beginning movement toward the first. A special issue of *Alternative Lifestyles* on cohabitation research is indicative of the change. Whereas articles in the 1970s typically dealt with a description of cohabitation and its participants, four of the five articles in this issue focused on what could be learned from cohabiting couples about the dynamics of couple relationships and the factors leading to relationship success (Cole & Goettsch, 1981; Hanna & Knaube, 1981; Hennon, 1981; Rank, 1981).

Relatively little systematic attention has been devoted to the study of individual living patterns and how these evolve over time. Family sociologists have tended to look at family patterns as isolated structural forms (e.g., single-parent, dual-career, or sexually open marriage). In order to view life from the perspective of the participant, however, it is necessary to look at the particular *cluster* of forms that comprise an individual's living pattern at any given time, realizing that each combination is unique to that individual and is changing over time. For example, to understand an individual's lifestyle, it is only minimally helpful to know that she or he is, for instance, a never-married single. It is much more meaningful to be able to say, using the categories listed in Table 1, that she is a never-married single who voluntarily has no children, is cohabiting in what is intended to be a permanent alternative to marriage with a once-married single who has two adult children from a previous marriage, in an androgynous, dual-career, sexually exclusive heterosexual relationship, with no other adults in the house.

However, classification, although helpful in describing a phenomenon, does little to explain and, given the above reality, is soon very complex. To understand individual living patterns, or what may be referred to as individual lifestyles, will require a conscious joining of forces with the developmental and social psychologists. Given that there is no longer a standard life-course script that the majority follow, that the list of possible variables determining life scripts is too long to be very helpful, and that a person's lifestyle can change dramatically over the course of a lifetime, the emphasis must move to an analysis of process: the process of lifestyle choice and the process of transition from one lifestyle to another.

It makes sense to assume that, at any given time, one's lifestyle is the result of past opportunities and of decisions made with regard to those opportunities. Social exchange theory would suggest that whether or not one moves to, and stays in, a given lifestyle depends on the degree of perceived satisfaction with one's present lifestyle, the barriers to or perceived costs of leaving that lifestyle, the number of perceived alternatives or options to the present lifestyle, and the perceived costs and benefits of those possible alternatives (e.g., see Spanier & Lewis, 1980).

As the central issue in most contemporary relationships is the ambiguity of roles and the lack of commonly accepted scripts or patterns of interaction with significant others, another fruitful approach to understanding such relationships comes from symbolic interaction theory (see Burr, Leigh, Day, & Constantine, 1979). Symbolic interactionists see interpersonal interaction as a sequence of mutually interrelated behaviors on the part of two or more persons, each behavior arising out of and determined by the actor's *interpretation* of the preceding behavior and *anticipation* of succeeding behavior. As a result, one can assume that the better able each person in the family system is to interpret and anticipate accurately the behavior and expectations of significant others, the more successful that relationship will be (i.e., the easier it will be to make a transition into the relationship, the better the role performance, the less role strain, and the more satisfaction with the relationship). More specifically, it is hypothesized that the following variables will significantly affect the degree of relationship success experienced in a nontraditional role relationship (see Macklin, 1982, for further elaboration):

1. *Clarity of role expectation:* The greater the degree to which the participants are able to accurately articulate their expectations of themselves and of others, and to predict what others expect, the greater the degree of relationship success.

2. *Anticipatory socialization:* The more extensive the opportunity that participants have had to prepare for the role by reading, observing, or rehearsing the role, the greater the degree of role clarity and, hence, the greater the degree of relationship success.

3. *Congruence of role expectations:* The more congruent the role expectations—that is, the more role consensus among various members, congruence among multiple roles, and congruence between self-concept and the role—the greater the degree of relationship success.

4. *Degree of interpersonal competence:* The greater the ability to function effectively in long-term and fairly complex interpersonal relationships, the greater the degree of relationship success. Degree of interpersonal competence will be affected by such things as role-taking ability, role skills, tolerance of ambiguity and change, capacity for negotiation, and degree of differentiation of self.

5. *Extent of investment in the role:* The greater the importance attached by participants to success in the role, and to the success of the relationship, the greater the relationship success.

6. *Degree of system complexity:* The less complex the system, the greater the chance of relationship success. Complexity is determined by the number of subsystems, the number of actors within those subsystems, and the nature of the boundaries between the subsystems.

The above hypotheses deserve to be tested. Their validation would suggest that in order to facilitate effective functioning in contemporary relationships, persons must be educated regarding their possible lifestyle options and the behaviors and attitudes that these may necessitate. They may then enter relationships with more realistic expectations, may be better prepared for the fact that the scripts into which they have been socialized may no longer be appropriate for their present relationships, and may be assured of the communication skills necessary for the ongoing negotiation that will be required (see Macklin, 1981).

Conclusions

Since the late 1960s, research on nontraditional family forms has increased dramatically, reflecting a period of rapid social change in society as a whole. Although most persons still marry, have children, live in single-family households, prefer heterosexuality, and wish for permanence and sexual exclusivity, increasing numbers choose other lifestyles at some point in their lives, and even more acknowledge the right of others to do so.

Variants on the "traditional nuclear family" are not new, but many who have previously lived in alternative patterns have had to do so because of the social and economic realities of their lives. What is new is the increasing acceptance of nontraditional options by the majority culture, as well as the growing freedom to voluntarily decide how one will live. Slowly students of the family are identifying the prevalence of these lifestyles, the characteristics of the persons who engage in them, the relative costs and benefits associated with the various options, and the variables predictive of satisfaction. There is a need to continue these efforts and, in turn, to ensure that the findings will become general knowledge so that persons may begin early to make informed choices regarding the living and relationship patterns which will be most functional for them.

Research on alternative family patterns is no longer in its infancy. The necessary exploratory work, involving questionnaires and intensive interviews with small self-selected convenience samples of persons actively involved in a given pattern, has established the great range of variations within each lifestyle and has helped to suggest appropriate typologies, has identified the variables that must be controlled in future research, and has provided a basis for the development of meaningful hypotheses. Beginning efforts have been made to build predictive models (e.g., Reiss *et al.*, 1980) and to develop scales to measure relevant variables (e.g., Pendleton *et al.*, 1980). The findings to date indicate that each of the reviewed alternatives can be viable for some persons, but for how many and under what circumstances is only beginning to be understood.

There must now be concerted efforts to expand samples beyond easy-to-reach populations and to include persons who have ''dropped out'' of any given lifestyle; to build in the necessary control variables; to focus less on frequencies and more on the dynamics of the various lifestyles; to explore cross-cultural variations (see Bianchi & Farley, 1979; Cazenave, 1979, 1980; Buunk, 1983; Peters & McAdoo, 1983); to pursue longitudinal designs that permit a developmental perspective; and to continue to be sensitive to the implications of increasing pluralism for the larger society (e.g., Cogswell & Sussman, 1972; Weisberg, 1975a; Bernstein, 1977; Hauhart, 1977; Myricks & Rubin, 1977; Ramey, 1977; Roman, Charles, & Karasu, 1978; Myricks, 1983; Phillips, 1983).

A distinction must be made between voluntary and involuntary participation in any given living pattern and, in turn, we need a better understanding of the role of external social constraints on the choice of lifestyle and on the experiencing of that lifestyle. We must revise traditional family-developmental theory, which assumed that persons progress through identifiable stages of courtship, marriage, children, and retirement. It is now clear that adulthood is not as ordered as it may once have been, and that persons may cycle in and out of similar living patterns at different points in their life course. It may be more helpful to think in terms of life spirals (Etzkowitz & Stein, 1978) or alternative life paths or life scripts (e.g., see Libby, 1977; Weis, 1979; Scott, 1980a), both for family units and for individuals, and of lifestyle choice-points

that influence the available options at later points in time. Instead of continued focus on the structural characteristics of the various family forms, efforts should be made to identify factors affecting the quality of family life irrespective of family form, and to understand the process by which individuals make lifestyle decisions and transitions.

The alternative family forms that have been reviewed here are best seen as evolving modifications of the structure of the family, caught at a moment in time in the family's continual process of adaptation to changing societal conditions. Those alternatives that are being adopted by large numbers of persons (i.e., nonmarital cohabitation, dual-work and dual-career families, single-person and one-parent households, and stepfamilies) reflect broader social changes: the growing equality between men and women, improved contraceptive technology and the more general acceptance of nonmarital sexuality, and the increasing ability of the individual to survive independent of a kinship support system. Those alternatives that have not proved to be as functional, and hence are practiced by fewer persons, involve complex relationship systems (i.e., communal living, open marriage, and multilateral marriage), where the stresses involved tend, for most persons, to outweigh the benefits, at least at this stage of human development.

Viewed in this light, alternative family forms are merely part of the universal dialectic of change and evolve out of humankind's ongoing search for more effective ways of living while maintaining the necessary balance between growth and stability. Having been through a period of rapid change, we can now predict a period of relative retrenchment as society seeks to integrate what it has learned from the experimentation of the recent past. Students of the family will continue to watch the process with fascination.

References

Abarbanel, A. R. Shared parenting after separation and divorce: A study of joint custody. *American Journal of Orthopsychiatry*, 1979, *49*(April), 320–329.

Adams, M. *Single blessedness*. New York: Basic Books, 1976.

Ahrons, C. R. The binuclear family: Two households, one family. *Alternative Lifestyles*, 1979, *2*(4), 499–515.

Ahrons, C. R. Divorce: A crisis of family transition and change. *Family Relations*, 1980a, *29*(4), 533–540.

Ahrons, C. R. Joint custody arrangements in the post-divorce family. *Journal of Divorce*, 1980b, *3*(3); 189–205.

Ahrons, C. R. The continuing coparental relationship between divorced spouses. *American Journal of Orthopsychiatry*, 1981, *51*(3), 415–428.

Ahrons, C. R., & Perlmutter, M. S. The relationship between former spouses: A fundamental subsystem in the remarriage family. In J. C. Hansen & L. Messinger (Eds.), *Therapy with remarried families*. Rockville, Md.: Aspen Systems Corp., 1982.

Allen, S. M., & Kalish, R. A. Professional women and marriage. *Journal of Marriage and the Family*, 1984, *46*(2), 375–382.

Allen, W. R., & Agbasegbe, B. A. A comment on Scott's ''Black Polygamous Family Formation.'' *Alternative Lifestyles*, 1980, *3*(4), 375–381.

Ambert, A. Difference in children's behavior toward custodial mothers and custodial fathers. *Journal of Marriage and the Family*, 1982, *44*(1), 73–86.

Anderson, D., & Braito, R. The mental health of the never-married: Social protection, social reaction, and social selection models. *Alternative Lifestyles*, 1981, *4*(1), 108–124.

Arafat, I., & Yorburg, B. On living together without marriage. *Journal of Sex Research*, 1973, *9*, 97–106.

Arkin, W., & Dobrofsky, L. R. Shared labor and love: Job-sharing couples in academia. *Alternative Lifestyles*, 1978, *1*(4), 492–512.

Athanasiou, R., Shaver, P., & Tavris, C. Sex. *Psychology Today*, 1970, *4* (July), 39–52.

Atkinson, M. P., & Boles, J. WASP (wives as senior partners). *Journal of Marriage and the Family*, 1984, *46*(4), 861–870.

Atwater, L. *Women in extramarital relationships: A case study in sociosexuality.* New York: Irvington Press, 1978.

Atwater, L. Getting involved: Women's transition to first extramarital sex. *Alternative Lifestyles*, 1979, *2*(1), 38–68.

Bachrach, C. A. Childlessness and social isolation among the elderly. *Journal of Marriage and Family*, 1980, *42*(August), 627–636.

Bailyn, L. Career and family orientations of husbands and wives in relation to marital happiness. *Human Relations*, 1970, *23*(2), 97–113.

Bailyn, L. Accommodation of work to family. In R. Rapoport & R. N. Rapoport (Eds.), *Working Couples*. New York: Harper & Row, 1978.

Barnett, L. D., & MacDonald, R. H. A study of the membership of the National Organization for Non-Parents. *Sociology Biology*, 1976, *23*(Winter), 297–310.

Bartell, G. D. Group sex among the mid-Americans. *Journal of Sex Research*, 1970, *6*, 113–130.

Bartell, G. D. *Group sex: A scientist's eyewitness report on the American way of swinging.* New York: Wyden, 1971.

Bartz, K. W., & Witcher, W. C. When fathers get custody. *Children Today*, 1978, *7*(5), 2–6, 35.

Baum, F., & Cope, D. R. Some characteristics of intentionally childless wives in Britain. *Journal of Biosocial Science*, 1980, *12*(3), 287–299.

Bebbington, A. C. The function of stress in the establishment of the dual-career family. *Journal of Marriage and the Family*, 1973, *35*(3), 530–537.

Beckman, L. F., & Houser, B. B. Consequences of childlessness on the social-psychological well-being of older women. *Journal of Gerontology*, 1982, *37*, 243–250.

Bell, A. P., & Weinberg, M. S. *Homosexualities: A study of diversity among men and women.* New York: Simon & Schuster, 1978.

Bell, J. E., & Eisenberg, N. Life satisfaction in midlife childless and empty-nest men and women. *Lifestyles*, 1985, *7*(3), 146–155.

Bell, R. R., Turner, S., & Rosen, L. A multi-variate analysis of female extra-marital coitus. *Journal of Marriage and the Family*, 1975, *37*(2), 375–384.

Berger, B., Hackett, B., & Millar, R. M. The communal family. *The Family Coordinator*, 1972, *21*(4), 419–427.

Bernard, J. *The future of marriage.* New York: World Publications, 1972.

Bernstein, B. E. Legal problems of cohabitation. *The Family Coordinator*, 1977, *26*(4), 361–366.

Bianchi, S., & Farley, R. Racial differences in family living arrangements and economic well-being: An analysis of recent trends. *Journal of Marriage and the Family*, 1979, *41*(3), 537–551.

Bird, G. W., Bird, G. A., & Scruggs, M. Determinants of family task-sharing: A study of husbands and wives. *Journal of Marriage and the Family*, 1984, *46*(2), 345–355.

Blake, J. Is zero preferred? American attitudes toward childlessness in the 1970's. *Journal of Marriage and the Family*, 1979, *41*(2), 245–257.

Blanton, J. Communal child rearing: The Synanon experience. *Alternative Lifestyles*, 1980, *3*(1), 87–116.

Blechman, E. Are children with one parent at psychological risk? A methodological review. *Journal of Marriage and the Family*, 1982, *44*(1), 179–195.

Blumstein, P. W., & Schwartz, P. Bisexual women. In J. P. Wiseman (Ed.), *The social psychology of sex*. New York: Harper & Row, 1976.

Blumstein, P. W., & Schwartz, P. Bisexuality: Some social psychological issues. *Journal of Social Issues*, 1977, *33*(2), 30–46.

Blumstein, P. & Schwartz, P. *American Couples: Money, Work, Sex.* New York, N.Y.: William Morrow, 1983.

Bohannon, P. (Ed.) *Divorce and after.* Garden City, N.Y.: Anchor, 1970.

Bohannon, P. (Ed.). *Stepfathers and the mental health of their children: Final report to National Institute of Mental Health.* Washington, D.C.: Department of Health, Education, and Welfare, 1975.

Bohannon, P., & Yahraes, H. Stepfathers as parents. In E. Corfman (Ed.), *Families today: A research sample on families and children.* NIMH Science Monograph, Washington, D.C.: U.S. Government Printing Office, 1979.

Bould, S. Female headed families: Personal fate control and the provider role. *Journal of Marriage and the Family*, 1977, *39*(2), 339–351.

Bower, D. W., & Christopherson, V. A. University student cohabitation: A regional comparison of selected attitudes and behaviors. *Journal of Marriage and the Family*, 1977, *39*(3), 447–453.

Bowerman, C., & Irish, D. Some relationships of stepchildren to their parents. *Marriage and Family Living*, 1962, *24*(1), 113–121.

Bozett, F. W. Gay fathers: How and why they disclose their homosexuality to their children. *Family Relations*, 1980, *29*(2), 173–179.

Bozett, F. W. Gay fathers: Identity conflict-resolution through integrative sanctioning. *Alternative Lifestyles*, 1981, *4*(1), 90–107.

Bradbury, K., Danziger, S., Smolensky, E., & Smolensky, P. Public assistance, female headship, and economic well-being. *Journal of Marriage and the Family*, 1979, *41*(3), 519–535.

Bram, S. Childlessness revisited: A longitudinal study of voluntarily childless couples, delayed parents, and parents. *Lifestyles*, 1985, *8*(1), 46–66.

Brownfraun, J. J. A study of the married bisexual male: Paradox and resolution. *Journal of Homosexuality*, 1985, *11*(1/2), 173–188.

Bryant, B. S. *Lesbian mothers.* Unpublished master's thesis, California State University, Sacramento, 1975.

Bryson, R., Bryson, J. B., Licht, M., & Licht, B. The professional pair: Husband-wife psychologists. *American Psychologist*, 1976, *31*(1), 10–16.

Bryson, R., Bryson, J. B., & Johnson, M. F. Family size, satisfaction, and productivity in dual-career couples. In J. B. Bryson & R. Bryson (Eds.), *Dual-career couples.* New York: Human Sciences Press, 1978.

Budd, L. S. *Problems, disclosure, and commitment of cohabiting and married couples.* Unpublished doctoral dissertation, University of Minnesota, Minneapolis, 1976.

Buhr, K. S. *Stress, marital interaction, and personal competence in natural parent and stepfather families.* Unpublished doctoral dissertation, University of Michigan, 1975.

Bukstel, L. H., Roeder, G. D., Kilmann, P. R., Laughlin, J., & Sotile, W. M. Projected extramarital sexual involvement in unmarried college students. *Journal of Marriage and the Family*, 1978, *40*(2), 337–340.

Burden, D. S. Single parents and the work setting: The impact of multiple job and homelife responsibilities. *Family Relations*, 1986, *35*(1), 37–43.

Burke, R. J., & Weir, T. Some personality differences between members of one-career and two-career families. *Journal of Marriage and the Family*, 1976, *38*(3), 453–460.

Burr, W. R., Leigh, G. K., Day, R. D., & Constantine, J. Symbolic interaction and the family. In W. R. Burr, R. Hill, F. I. Nye, & I. L. Reiss (Eds.), *Contemporary theories about the family*, Vol. 2. New York: Free Press, 1979.

Butler, E. W. *Traditional marriage and emerging alternatives.* New York: Harper & Row, 1979.

Butler, E. W., & McGinley, R. L. (Eds.). *The other Americans: Living in emerging alternative lifestyles.* Buena Park, Calif.: Lifestyles Press, 1978. (Obtain from Western Periodicals Company, 13000 Raymer St., North Hollywood, Calif. 91605.)

Buunk, B. (Ed.). Alternative lifestyles in The Netherlands. (Special Issue) *Alternative Lifestyles,* 1980, *3*(3), 251–368. (a)

Buunk, B. Extramarital sex in the Netherlands. *Alternative Lifestyles,* 1980, *3*(1), 11–39. (b)

Buunk, B. Sexually-open marriages: Ground rules for countering potential threats to marriage. *Alternative Lifestyles,* 1980, *3*(3), 312–328. (c)

Buunk, B. Alternative lifestyles from an international perspective: A trans-Atlantic comparison. In E. D. Macklin & R. Rubin (Eds.), *Contemporary family forms and alternative lifestyles: Handbook on research and theory.* Beverly Hills, Calif.: Sage Publications, 1983.

Caldwell, M. A., & Peplau, L. A. *The balance of power in lesbian relationships.* Unpublished paper, 1980. (Write author at Department of Psychology, University of California, 405 Hilgard Avenue, Los Angeles, Calif. 90024.)

Calhoun, L. G., & Selby, J. W. Voluntary childlessness, unvoluntary childlessness, and having children: A study of social perceptions. *Family Relations,* 1980, *29*(2), 181–183.

Callan, V. J. Perceptions of parents, the voluntarily and involuntarily childless: A multidimensional scaling analysis. *Journal of Marriage and the Family,* 1985, *47*(4), 1045–1050.

Cardell, M., Finn, S., & Marecek, J. Sex-role identity, sex-role behavior, and satisfaction in heterosexual, lesbian, and gay male couples. *Psychology of Women Quarterly,* 1981, *5*(3), 488–494.

Cargan, L., & Melko, M. *Singles: Myths and realities.* Beverly Hills, Calif.: Sage Publications, 1982.

Casler, L. *Is marriage necessary?* New York: Human Sciences Press, 1974.

Catlin, N., Croake, J. W., & Keller, J. F. MMPI profiles of cohabiting college students. *Psychological Reports,* 1976, *38*(April), 407–410.

Cazenave, N. A. Social structure and personal choice: Effects on intimacy, marriage, and the family alternative lifestyle research. *Alternative Lifestyles,* 1979, *2*(3), 331–358.

Cazenave, N. A. (Ed.), Black alternative lifestyles. (Special Issue) *Alternative Lifestyles,* 1980, *3*(4), 371–504.

Chapman, M. Father absence, stepfathers and the cognitive performance of college students. *Child Development,* 1977, *48*(3), 1155–1158.

Chilman, C. S. Remarriage and stepfamilies: Research results and implications. In E. D. Macklin & R. Rubin (Eds.), *Contemporary families and alternative lifestyles: Handbook on research and theory.* Beverly Hills, Calif.: Sage Publications, 1983.

Clatworthy, N., & Scheid, L. A. *A comparison of married couples: Premarital cohabitants with non-premarital cohabitants.* Unpublished paper, Ohio State University, 1977.

Clavan, S., & Vatter, E. The affiliated family: A continued analysis. *The Family Coordinator,* 1972, *21*(4), 499–504.

Clayton, P. N. Meeting the needs of the single parent family. *The Family Coordinator,* 1971, *20*(4), 327–337.

Clayton, R. R., & Voss, H. L. Shacking up: Cohabitation in the 1970's. *Journal of Marriage and the Family,* 1977, *39*(2), 273–283.

Cline, B. J. *A construct validity study of disengagement-enmeshment: Some individual, family, and sociocultural correlates.* Unpublished doctoral dissertation, George Peabody College for Teachers, Nashville, 1977.

Clingempeel, G. W. Quasi-kin relationships and marital quality in stepfather families. *Journal of Personality and Social Psychology,* 1981, *41*, 890–901.

Clingempeel, W. G. & Brand, E. Quasi-kin relationships, structural complexity, and marital quality in stepfamilies: A replication, extension, and clinical implications. *Family Relations.* 1985, *34*(3), 401–409.

Clingempeel, W. G., & Reppucci, N. D. Joint custody after divorce:

Major issues and goals for research. *Psychological Bulletin,* 1982, *91*(1), 102–127.

Cockrum, J. & White, P. Influences on the life satisfaction of never-married men and women. *Family Relations,* 1985, *34*(4), 551–556.

Cogswell, B. E. & Sussman, M. B. Changing family and marriage forms: Complications for human service systems. *The Family Coordinator,* 1972, *21*(4), 505–516.

Cole, C. L., & Goettsch, S. L. Self-disclosure and relationship quality: A study among nonmarital cohabiting couples. *Alternative Lifestyles,* 1981, *4*(4), 428–466.

Cole, C. L., & Spanier, G. B. Comarital mate-sharing and family stability. *Journal of Sex Research,* 1974, *10*, 21–31.

Coleman, E. Bisexual women in marriages. *Journal of Homosexuality,* 1985, *11*(1/2), 87–99. (a)

Coleman, E. Integration of male bisexuality and marriage. *Journal of Homosexuality,* 1985, *11*(1/2), 189–207. (b)

Conover, P. W. An analysis of communes and intentional communities with particular attention to sexual and gender relations. *The Family Coordinator,* 1975, *24*(4), 453–464.

Constantine, L. L. Open family: A lifestyle for kids and other people. *The Family Coordinator,* 1977, *26*(2), 113–121. (a)

Constantine, L. L. Where are the kids? Children in alternative life styles. In R. W. Libby & R. N. Whitehurst (Eds.), *Marriage and alternatives: Exploring intimate relationships.* Glenview, Ill.: Scott, Foresman, 1977. (b)

Constantine, L. L. Multilateral relations revisited: Group marriage in extended perspective. In B. I. Murstein (Ed.), *Exploring intimate lifestyles.* New York: Springer Publishing, 1978.

Constantine, L. L. Dysfunction and failure in open family systems, I: Application of unified theory. *Journal of Marriage and the Family,* 1983, *45*(4), 725–738.

Constantine, L. L., & Constantine, J. M. Group and multilateral marriage: Definitional notes, glossary, and annotated bibliography. *Family Process,* 1971, *10*, 157–176.

Constantine, L. L., & Constantine, J. M. *Group marriage: A study of contemporary multilateral marriage.* New York: Macmillan, 1973.

Constantine, L. L., & Constantine, J. M. *Treasures of the island: Children in alternative families. Studies of marriage and family.* Monograph 90-038. Beverly Hills, Calif.: Sage Publications, 1976.

Cooper, D. G. *The death of the family.* New York: Pantheon Books, 1970.

Cooper, P. E., Cumber, B., & Hartner, R. Decision-making patterns and postdecision adjustment of childfree husbands and wives. *Alternative Lifestyles,* 1978, *1*(1), 71–94.

Cornfield, N. The success of urban communes. *Journal of Marriage and the Family,* 1983, *45*(1), 115–126.

Darling, J. *An interactionist interpretation of bachelorhood and late marriage: The process of entering into, remaining in, and leaving careers of singleness.* Unpublished doctoral dissertation, University of Connecticut, Storrs, 1976.

DeFrain, J., & Eirick, R. Coping as divorced single parents: A comparative study of fathers and mothers. *Family Relations,* 1981, *30*(2), 265–274.

DeLora, J. R., & DeLora, J. S. (Eds.). *Intimate life styles: Marriage and its alternatives* (2nd ed.). Pacific Palisades, Calif.: Goodyear Publishing, 1975.

DeMaris, A. A comparison of remarriages with first marriages on satisfaction in marriage and its relationship to prior cohabitation. *Family Relations,* 1984, *33*(3), 443–449.

DeMaris, A., & Leslie, G. R. Cohabitation with the future spouse: Its influence upon marital satisfaction and communication. *Journal of Marriage and the Family,* 1984, *46*(1), 77–84.

Denfield, D. Dropouts from swinging. *The Family Coordinator,* 1974, *23*(January), 45–49.

Denfield, D., & Gordon, M. The sociology of mate-swapping. *Journal of Sex Research*, 1970, *6*, 85–100.

Dixon, D. Perceived sexual satisfaction and marital happiness of bisexual and heterosexual swinging husbands. *Journal of Homosexuality*, 1985, *11*(1/2), 209–222.

Dixon, J. K. The commencement of bisexual activity in swinging married women over age thirty. *Journal of Sex Research*, 1984, *20*, 71–90.

Dixon, J. K. Sexuality and relationship changes in married females following the commencement of bisexual activity. *Journal of Homosexuality*, 1985, *11*(1/2), 115–133.

Dressel, P. L. (Ed.). Alternative lifestyles and the elderly. (Special Issue) *Alternative Lifestyles*, 1980, *3*(2), 131–248.

Dressel, P. L., & Hess, B. B. Alternatives for the elderly. In E. D. Macklin & R. Rubin (Eds.), *Contemporary family forms and alternative lifestyles: Handbook on research and theory*. Beverly Hills, Calif., Sage Publications, 1983.

Duberman, L. Stepkin relationships. *Journal of Marriage and the Family*, 1973, *35*(2), 283–292.

Duberman, L. *The reconstituted family: A study of remarried couples and their children*. Chicago: Nelson-Hall, 1975.

Duckworth, J. & Levitt, E. E. Personality analysis of a swingers' club. *Lifestyles*, 1985, *8*(1), 35–45.

Duncan, R. P., & Perrucci, C. C. Dual occupation families and migration. *American Sociological Review*, 1976, *41*(April), 252–262.

Edwards, J. N., & Booth, A. Sexual behavior in and out of marriage: An assessment of correlates. *Journal of Marriage and the Family*, 1976, *38*(1), 73–81.

Eiduson, B. T. The commune-reared child. In J. D. Call, J. D. Noshpitz, R. L. Cohen, & I. N. Berlin (Eds.), *Basic handbook of child psychiatry, Vol. 1: Development*. New York: Basic Books, 1979 (a)

Eiduson, B. T. Emergent families of the 1970's: Values, practices, and impact on children. In D. Reiss & H. Hoffman (Eds.), *The American family: Dying or developing*. New York: Plenum Press, 1979 (b)

Eiduson, B. T. Changing sex-roles of parents and children in alternative family styles: Implications for young children. In E. J. Anthony & C. Chiland (Eds.), *The child in his family, Vol. 6: Preventive child psychiatry in an age of transitions*. Yearbook of the International Association for Child Psychiatry and Allied Professions. New York: Wiley, 1980.

Eiduson, B. T. The child in the non-conventional family. In M. Lewis & L. A. Rosenblum (Eds.), *Genesis of behavior, Vol. 3: Uncommon Child*. New York: Plenum Press, 1981.

Emery, R. Interparental conflict and the children of discord and divorce. *Psychological Bulletin*, 1982, *92*(2), 310–330.

Epstein, C. D. Law partners and marital partners: Strains and solutions in the dual-career family enterprise. *Human Relations*, 1971, *24*, 549–563.

Ericksen, J. A. Race, sex, and alternate lifestyle choices. *Alternative Lifestyles*, 1980, *3*(4), 405–424.

Espenshade, T. The economic consequences of divorce. *Journal of Marriage and the Family*, 1979, *41*(3), 615–625.

Espinoza, R., & Newman, Y. *Step-parenting*. DHEW Publication No. (ADM) 78-579, Washington, D.C.: U.S. Government Printing Office, 1979.

Etzkowitz, H., & Stein, P. The life spiral: Human needs and adult roles. *Alternative Lifestyles*, 1978, *1*(4), 434–446.

Farris, A. Commuting. In R. Rapoport & R. N. Rapoport (Eds.), *Working couples*. New York: Harper & Row, 1978.

Fast, I., & Cain, A. C. The stepparent role: Potential for disturbance in family functioning. *American Journal of Orthopsychiatry*, 1966, *36*, 485–491.

Feldman, H. A comparison of intentional parents and intentionally childless couples. *Journal of Marriage and the Family*, 1981, *43*(3), 593–600.

Ferber, M., & Huber, J. Husbands, wives, and careers. *Journal of Marriage and the Family*, 1979, *41*(2), 315–327.

Ferrar, K. Experiences of parents in contemporary communal households. *Alternative Lifestyles*, 1982, *5*(1), 7–23.

Fischer, J. L., & Cardea, J. M. Mothers living apart from their children: A study in stress and coping. *Alternative Lifestyles*, 1981, *4*(2), 218–227.

Fischer, J. L. & Cardea, J. M. Mother-child relationships of mothers living apart from their children. *Alternative Lifestyles*, 1982, *5*(1), 42–53.

Fishman, B., & Hamel, B. From nuclear to stepfamily ideology: A stressful change. *Alternative Lifestyles*, 1981, *4*(2), 181–204.

Folberg, J. (Ed.) *Joint Custody and Shared Parenting*. Washington, D.C.: Bureau of National Affairs and Association of Family and Conciliation Courts, 1984.

Ford, C., & Beach, F. *Patterns of sexual behavior*. New York: Harper & Row, 1951.

Francoeur, R. T. Religious reactions to alternative lifestyles. In E. D. Macklin & R. Rubin (Eds.), *Contemporary families and alternative lifestyles: Handbook on research and theory*. Beverly Hills, Calif.: Sage Publications, 1983.

Francoeur, R. T., & Francoeur, A. *Hot and cool sex*. New York: Harcourt Brace Jovanovich, 1974.

Furstenberg, F. F. Recycling the family: Perspectives for a neglected family form. *Marriage and Family Review*, 1979, *2*(Fall), 12–22.

Furstenberg, F. F. and Nord, C. W. Parenting apart: Patterns of child rearing after marital disruption. *Journal of Marriage and the Family*, 1985, *47*(4), 893–904.

Galper, M. *Co-Parenting: A sourcebook for the separated or divorced family*. Philadelphia: Running Press, 1978.

Ganong, L. H. & Coleman, M. The effects of remarriage on children: A review of the empirical literature. *Family Relations*, 1984, *33*(3), 389–406.

Garland, T. N. The better half? The male in the dual profession family. In C. Safilios-Rothchild (Ed.), *Toward a sociology of women*. Lexington, Mass.: Xerox, 1972.

Gasser, R. D., & Taylor, C. M. Role adjustment of single parent fathers with dependent children. *The Family Coordinator*, 1976, *25*(4), 397–403.

Geffen, M. S. *The value of a course in parent effectiveness training for single parents*. Unpublished doctoral dissertation, California School of Professional Psychology, Fresno, 1978.

George, V., & Wilding, P. *Motherless families*. London: Routledge & Kegan Paul, 1972.

Gerstel, N. R. The feasibility of commuter marriage. In P. J. Stein, J. Richman, & N. Hannon (Eds.), *The family: Functions, conflicts and symbols*. Reading, Mass.: Addison-Wesley, 1977.

Gerstel, N. R. Marital alternatives and the regulation of sex: Commuter couples as a test case. *Alternative Lifestyles*, 1979, *2*(2), 145–176.

Gerstel, N. R., & Gross, H. Commuter marriage: Couples who live apart. In E. D. Macklin & R. Rubin (Eds.), *Contemporary family forms and alternative lifestyles: Handbook on research and theory*. Beverly Hills, Calif.: Sage Publications, 1983.

Gerstel, N. R. & Gross, H. *Commuter Marriage: A Study of Work and Family*. N.Y.: Guilford Press, 1984.

Gilder, G. *The naked nomads*. New York: Quadrangle, 1974.

Gilmartin, B. G. Sexual deviance and social networks: Study of social, family and marital interaction patterns among co-marital sex participants. In J. R. Smith & L. S. Smith (Eds.), *Beyond monogamy: Recent studies of sexual alternatives in marriage*. Baltimore: Johns Hopkins University Press, 1974.

Gilmartin, B. G. Swinging: Who gets involved and how? In R. W. Libby & R. N. Whitehurst (Eds.), *Marriage and alternatives: Exploring intimate relationships*. Glenview, Ill.: Scott, Foresman, 1977.

Gilmartin, B. G. *The Gilmartin report.* Secaucus, N.J.: Citadel Press, 1978.

Gladow, N. W. & Ray, M. P. The impact of informal support systems on the well-being of low income single parents. *Family Relations,* 1986, *35*(1), 113–123.

Glass, S. P., & Wright, T. L. The relationship of extramarital sex, length of marriage, and sex differences on marital satisfaction and romanticism: Athanasiou's data reanalyzed. *Journal of Marriage and the Family,* 1977, *39*(4), 691–703.

Glenn, N. D., & Weaver, C. N. Attitudes toward premarital, extramarital, and homosexual relations in the U.S. in the 1970's. *Journal of Sex Research,* 1979, *15,* 108–118.

Glenn, N. D., Ross, A. A., & Tully, J. C. Patterns of intergenerational mobility of females through marriage. *American Sociological Review,* 1974, *39*(October), 683–699.

Glenwick, D. S., & Mowrey, J. D. When parent becomes peer: Loss of intergenerational boundaries in single parent families. *Family Relations.* 1986, *35*(1), 57–62.

Glick, P. C. Children of divorced parents in demographic perspective. *Journal of Social Issues,* 1979, *35*(4), 170–182. (a)

Glick, P. C. Future American families. *The Washington COFO MEMO 2,* 1979, (Summer/Fall), 2–5. (b)

Glick, P. C., & Spanier, G. B. Married and unmarried cohabitation in the United States. *Journal of Marriage and the Family,* 1980, *42*(1), 19–30.

Gordon, M. (Ed.). *The nuclear family in crisis: The search for an alternative.* New York: Harper & Row, 1972.

Gove, W. R. The relationship between sex roles, marital roles, and mental illness. *Social Forces,* 1972, *51,* 34–44.

Green, R. Sexual identity of 37 children raised by homosexual or transsexual parents. *American Journal of Psychiatry,* 1978, *135,* 692–697.

Greenberg, J. B. Single-parenting and intimacy: A comparison of mothers and fathers. *Alternative Lifestyles,* 1979, *2*(3), 308–330.

Greif, J. B. Fathers, children and joint custody. *American Journal of Orthopsychiatry,* 1979, *49*(April), 311–319.

Greif, G. L. Children and housework in the single father family. *Family Relations,* 1985, *34*(3), 353–357. (a)

Greif, G. L. Single fathers rearing children. *Journal of Marriage and the Family,* 1985, *47*(1), 185–191. (b)

Greif, G. L. Mothers without custody and child support. *Family Relations* 1986, *35*(1), 87–93.

Gross, H. E. Dual-career couples who live apart: Two types. *Journal of Marriage and the Family,* 1980, *42*(3), 567–576.

Gross, H., & Sussman, M. (eds). *Alternatives to Traditional Family Living.* N.Y.: Haworth Press, 1982.

Gubrium, J. F. Being single in old age. *International Journal of Aging and Human Development,* 1975, *6,* 29–41.

Guerney, B. *Relationship enhancement.* San Francisco: Jossey-Bass, 1977.

Gustavus, S. O., & Henley, J. R. Correlates of voluntary childlessness in a select population. *Social Biology,* 1971, *18*(September), 277–284.

Guttentag, M. Women, men and mental health services. *Final Report,* NIMH Grant *MH-26523,* 1977.

Haas, L. Role-sharing couples: A study of egalitarian marriages. *Family Relations,* 1980, *29*(3), 289–296.

Hanna, S. L., & Knaub, P. K. Cohabitation before remarriage: Its relationship to family strengths. *Alternative Lifestyles,* 1981, *4*(4), 507–522.

Hanson, S. M. H. Healthy single parent families. *Family Relations,* 1986, *35*(1), 125–132.

Hanson, S. M. H. & Sporakowski, M. J. The single parent family. Special issue of *Family Relations,* 1986, *35*(1), 3–224.

Hargens, L. L., McCann, J. C., & Reskin, B. R. Productivity and re-

productivity: Fertility and professional achievement among research scientists. *Social Forces,* 1978, *57*(September), 154–163.

Harry, J. Decision-making and age differences among gay male couples. *Journal of Homosexuality,* 1982, *8*(2), 9–21.

Harry, J. Gay male and lesbian relationships. In E. D. Macklin & R. Rubin (Eds.), *Contemporary family forms and alternative lifestyles: Handbook on research and theory.* Beverly Hills, Calif.: Sage Publications, 1983.

Harry, J. *Gay Couples.* N.Y.: Praeger, 1984.

Harry, J., & Lovely, R. Gay marriages and communities of sexual orientation. *Alternative Lifestyles,* 1979, *2*(2), 177–200.

Hauhart, R. C. Children in communes: Some legal implications of a modern lifestyle. *The Family Coordinator,* 1977, *26*(4), 367–371.

Havens, E. M. Women, work, and wedlock: A note on female marital patterns in the United States. *American Journal of Sociology,* 1973, *78*(January), 975–981.

Heckman, N. A., Bryson, R., & Bryson, J. Problems of professional couples: A content analysis. *Journal of Marriage and the Family,* 1977, *39*(2), 323–330.

Heger, D. T. A supportive service to single mothers and their children. *Children Today,* 1977, *6*(5), 2–4, 36.

Hennon, C. B. Conflict management within cohabitation relationships. *Alternative Lifestyles,* 1981, *4*(4), 467–486.

Henshel, A. Swinging: A study of decision-making in marriage. *American Journal of Sociology,* 1973, *78*(January), 885–891.

Henze, L. F., & Hudson, J. W. Personal and family characteristics of cohabitating and non-cohabitating college students. *Journal of Marriage and the Family,* 1974, *36*(4), 722–726.

Herzog, E., & Sudia, C. E. *Boys in fatherless homes.* Washington, D.C.: U.S. Government Printing Office, 1971.

Hetherington, E. M. Divorce: A child's perspective. *American Psychologist,* 1979, *34,* 851–858.

Hetherington, E. M., Camara, K. A., & Feathermore, D. L. Achievement and intellectual functioning of children in one-parent households. In J. T. Spence (Ed.), *Achievement and Achievement Motives.* San Francisco: W. H. Freeman, 1983.

Heatherington, E. M., Cox, M., & Cox, R. The development of children in mother-headed families. In D. Reiss & H. Hoffman (Eds.), *The American family: Dying or developing.* New York: Plenum Press, 1979.

Hiller, D. V., & Philliber, W. W. Predicting marital and career success among dual-worker couples. *Journal of Marriage and the Family,* 1982, *44*(1), 53–62.

Hitchens, D. Social attitudes, legal standards, and personal trauma in child custody cases. *Journal of Homosexuality,* 1979–1980, *5*(1,2), 89–95.

Hoeffer, B. Children's acquisition of sex-role behavior in lesbian-mother families. *American Journal of Orthopsychiatry,* 1981, *51*(3), 536–544.

Hoffman, S. R. & Levant, R. F. A comparison of child-free and child-anticipated married couples. *Family Relations,* 1985, *34*(2), 197–203.

Holmstrom, L. L. *The two-career marriage.* Cambridge, Mass.: Schenkman, 1972.

Hooker, E. The adjustment of the male overt homosexual. *Journal of Projective Techniques,* 1957, *21,* 18–31.

Hopkins, J., & White, P. The dual-career couple: Constraints and supports. *The Family Coordinator,* 1978, *27*(3), 253–259.

Hornung, C. A., & McCullough, B. C. Status relationships in dual-employment marriages: Consequences for psychological well-being. *Journal of Marriage and the Family,* 1981, *43*(1), 125–141.

Houseknecht, S. K. Childlessness and marital adjustment. *Journal of Marriage and the Family,* 1979, *41*(2), 259–265. (a)

Houseknecht, S. K. Timing of the decision to remain voluntarily childless: evidence for continuous socialization. *Psychology of Women Quarterly*, 1979, *4*(1), 81–96. (b)

Houseknecht, S. K. Voluntary childlessness in the 1980's: A significant increase? *Marriage and Family Review*, 1982, *5*, 51–69. (a)

Houseknecht, S. K. Voluntary childlessness: Toward a theoretical integration. *Journal of Family Issues*, 1982, *3*(4), 459–471. (b)

Houseknecht, S. K., & Macke, A. S. Combining marriage and career: The marital adjustment of professional women. *Journal of Marriage and the Family*, 1981, *43*(3), 651–661.

Hunt, M. *The affair*. New York: World, 1969.

Hunt, M. *Sexual behavior in the 1970's*. Chicago: Dell, 1974.

Hunt, J. G., & Hunt, L. L. Dilemmas and contradictions of status: The case of the dual-career family. *Social Problems*, 1977, *24*(4), 407–416.

Ilfeld, J. W., Jr., Ilfeld, H. Z., & Alexander, T. R. Does joint custody work? A first look at outcome data of relitigation. *American Journal of Psychiatry*, 1982, *139*, 62–66.

Jackson, J. But where are all the men? *Black Scholar*, 1971, *3*, 30–41.

Jacques, J. M., & Chason, K. J. Cohabitation: Its impact on marital success. *The Family Coordinator*, 1979, *28*(1), 35–39.

Jaffe, D. T., & Kanter, R. M. Couple strain in communal households: A four-factor model of the separation process. *Journal of Social Issues*, 1976, *32*(1), 169–191.

Jamison, P. H., Franzini, L. R., & Kaplan, R. M. Some assumed characteristics of voluntarily childfree women and men. *Psychology of Women Quarterly*, 1979, *4*(2), 266–273.

Jauch, C. The one-parent family. *Journal of Clinical Child Psychology*, 1977, *6*(2), 30–32.

Jay, K., & Young, A. *The gay report*. New York: Summit Books, 1979.

Jenks, R. J. A comparative study of swingers and non-swingers: Attitudes and beliefs. *Lifestyles*, 1985, *8*(1), 5–20.

Jensen, M. S. Role differentiation in female homosexual quasi-marital unions. *Journal of Marriage and the Family*, 1974, *36*(2), 360–367.

Johnson, M. P. Commitment: A conceptual structure and empirical application. *Sociological Quarterly*, 1973, *14*, 395–406.

Johnson, R. E. Extramarital sexual intercourse: A methodological note. *Journal of Marriage and the Family*, 1970, *32*(2), 279–282. (a)

Johnson, R. E. Some correlates of extramarital coitus. *Journal of Marriage and the Family*, 1970, *32*(3), 449–456. (b)

Kaltreider, N. B., & Margolis, A. B. Childless by choice: A clinical study. *American Journal of Psychiatry*, 1977, *134*(February), 179–182.

Kanter, R. M. *Commitment and community: Communes and utopias in sociological perspective*. Cambridge: Harvard University Press, 1972.

Kanter, R. M. (Ed.). *Communes: Creating and managing the collective life style*. New York: Harper & Row, 1973. (a)

Kanter, R. M. The family and sex roles in American communes. In R. M. Kanter (Ed.), *Communes: Creating and managing the collective life*. New York: Harper & Row, 1973. (b)

Kanter, R. M., Jaffe, D. T., & Weisberg, D. K. Coupling, parenting, and the presence of others: Intimate relationships in communal households. *The Family Coordinator*, 1975, *24*(4), 433–452.

Kassel, V. Polygamy after sixty. In H. A. Otto (Ed.), *The family in search of a future*. New York: Appleton-Century-Crofts, 1970.

Keith, P. M. A comparison of resources of parents and childless men and women in very old age. *Family Relations*, 1983, *32*(3), 403–409.

Keith, P. M., & Schafer, R. B. Role strain and depression in two-job families. *Family Relations*, 1980, *29*(4), 483–488.

Keshet, H. F., & Rosenthal, K. M. Fathering after marital separation. *Social Work*, 1978, *23*(1), 11–18.

Keshet, J. K. From separation to stepfamily: A subsystem analysis. *Journal of Social Issues*, 1980, *1*(4), 517–532.

Kinsey, A. C., Pomeroy, W. B., & Martin, C. E. *Sexual behavior in the human male*. Philadelphia: W. B. Saunders, 1948.

Kinsey, A. C., Pomeroy, W. B., Martin, C. E., & Gebhard, P. A. *Sexual behavior in the human female*. Philadelphia: Saunders, 1953.

Kirkpatrick, M., Smith, C., & Roy, R. Lesbian mothers and their children: A comparative survey. *American Journal of Orthopsychiatry*, 1981, *51*(3), 545–551.

Kirschner, B. F., & Walum, L. R. Two-location families: Married singles. *Alternative Lifestyles*, 1978, *1*(4), 513–525.

Kitson, G. C. Attachment to the spouse in divorce: A scale and its application. *Journal of Marriage and the Family*, 1982, *44*(2), 379–393.

Kivett, V. R., & Learner, R. M. Perspectives on the childless rural elderly: A comparative analysis. *The Gerontologist*, 1980, *20*(December), 708–716.

Knapp, J. J. An exploratory study of seventeen open marriages. *Journal of Sex Research*, 1976, *12*, 206–219.

Knapp, J. J., & Whitehurst, R. N. Sexually open marriage and relationships: Issues and prospects. In R. W. Libby & R. N. Whitehurst (Eds.), *Marriage and alternatives: Exploring intimate relationships*. Glenview, Ill.: Scott, Foresman, 1977.

Knupfer, G., Clark, W., & Room, R. The mental health of the unmarried. *American Journal of Psychiatry*, 1966, *122*(February), 841–850.

Kompara, D. R. Difficulties in the socialization process of stepparenting. *Family Relations*, 1980, *29*(1), 69–73.

Kopf, K. E. Family variables and social adjustment of 8th grade father-absent boys. *The Family Coordinator*, 1970, *19*(2), 145–151.

Kotkin, M. To marry or live together? *Lifestyles*, 1985, *7*(3), 156–170.

Krein, S. F. Growing up in a single parent family. *Family Relations*, 1986, *35*(1), 161–168.

L'Abate, L. Family enrichment programs. *Journal of Family Counseling*, 1974, *2*, 32–44.

Langner, T. S., McCarthy, E. D., Gersten, J. C., Simcha-Fagen, O., & Eisenberg, J. G. Factors in children's behavior and mental health over time: The family research project. *Research in Community and Mental Health*, 1979, *1*, 127–181.

LaRoche, S. S. *The role of the stepfather in the family*. Unpublished doctoral dissertation, University of New Mexico, 1973.

Laslett, P., & Wall, R. (Eds.). *Household and family in past time*. New York: Cambridge University Press, 1972.

Lavori, N. *Living together, married or single: Your legal rights*. New York: Harper & Row, 1976.

Leupnitz, D. A. *Child Custody*. Lexington, Mass.: Lexington Books, 1982.

Levin, R. J. The Redbook report on premarital and extramarital sex: The end of the double standard? *Redbook*, 1975 (October), 38–44, 190–192.

Lewin, B. Unmarried cohabitation: A marriage form in a changing society. *Journal of Marriage and the Family*, 1982, *44*(3), 763–773.

Lewis, R. A., Spanier, G. B., Atkinson, V. L., & LeHecka, C. F. Commitment in married and unmarried cohabitation. *Social Focus*, 1977, *10*, 367–374.

Lewis, R. A., Kozac, E. B., Milardo, R. M., & Grosnick, W. A. Commitment in same-sex love relationships. *Alternative Lifestyles*, 1981, *4*(1), 22–42.

Lewis, S. G. *Sunday's women, A report on lesbian life today*. Boston: Beacon Press, 1979.

Libby, R. W. Creative singlehood as a sexual life-style: Beyond marriage as a rite of passage. In R. W. Libby & R. N. Whitehurst (Eds.), *Marriage and alternatives: Exploring intimate relationships*. Glenview, Ill.: Scott, Foresman, 1977.

Libby, R. W., & Whitehurst, R. N. (Eds.). *Renovating marriage: Toward new sexual life styles*. Danville, Calif.: Consensus Publishers, 1973.

Libby, R. W., & Whitehurst, R. N. (Eds.). *Marriage and alternatives: Exploring intimate relationships*. Glenview, Ill.: Scott, Foresman, 1977.

Lichtman, C. H. *Voluntary childlessness: A thematic analysis of the person and the process.* Unpublished doctoral dissertation, Columbia University Teacher's College, New York, 1976.

Lobell, J., & Lobell, M. *John and Mimi: A free marriage.* New York: St. Martin's Press, 1972.

Lowenstein, J. S., & Koopman, E. J. A comparison of the self-esteem between boys living with single-parent mothers and single-parent fathers. *Journal of Divorce,* 1978, 2(2), 195–208.

Lowery, C. R., & Settle, S. A. Effects of divorce on children: Differential impact of custody and visitation patterns. *Family Relations,* 1985, 34(4), 455–463.

Macklin, E. D. Unmarried heterosexual cohabitation on the university campus. In J. P. Wiseman (Ed.), *The social psychology of sex.* New York: Harper & Row, 1976.

Macklin, E. D. Non-traditional family forms: A decade of research. *Journal of Marriage and the Family,* 1980, 42(4), 905–922.

Macklin, E. D. Education for choice: Implications of alternatives in lifestyles for family life education. *Family Relations,* 1981, 30(4), 567–577.

Macklin, E. D. *Dramas without scripts: The challenge of contemporary relationships.* Unpublished paper given at Conference on Families and Close Relationships, Texas Tech University, 1982.

Macklin, E. D. Nonmarital heterosexual cohabitation: An overview. In E. D. Macklin & R. Rubin (Eds.), *Contemporary families and alternative lifestyles: Handbook on research and theory.* Beverly Hills, Calif.: Sage Publications, 1983.

Macklin, E. D., & Rubin, R. H. (Eds.). *Contemporary families and alternative lifestyles: Handbook on research and theory.* Beverly Hills, Calif.: Sage Publications, 1983.

Maddox, B. *The half-parent: Living with other people's children.* New York: M. Evans, 1975.

Magarick, R. H. *Social and emotional aspects of voluntary childlessness in vasectomized childless men.* Unpublished doctoral dissertation, University of Maryland, College Park, 1975.

Magarick, R. H., & Brown, R. A. Social and emotional aspects of voluntary childlessness in vasectomized childless men. *Journal of Biosocial Science,* 1981, 13, 157–167.

Malmquist, A., & Kaij, L. Motherhood and childlessness in monozygous twins. Part 2: The influence of motherhood on health. *British Journal of Psychiatry,* 1971, 118(February), 22–28.

Marciano, T. D. Male pressure in the decision to remain childfree. *Alternative Lifestyles,* 1978, 1(1), 95–112.

Marcks, B. R. *Voluntary childless couples: An exploratory study.* Unpublished master's thesis, Syracuse University, Syracuse, New York, 1976.

Martin, D., & Lyon, P. *Lesbian/woman.* San Francisco: Glide Publications, 1972.

Martin, T. W., Berry, K. J., & Jacobsen, R. B. The impact of dual-career marriage on female professional careers: An empirical test of a Parsonian hypothesis. *Journal of Marriage and the Family,* 1975, 37(4), 734–744.

Marvin v. Marvin. 18 Cal. 3d 660, 134 *Cal. Reptr.* 815, 557 P. 2d 106, 1976.

Masnick, G., & Bane, M. J. *The Nation's Families: 1960–1990.* Boston: Auburn House 1980.

Masters, W. H., & Johnson, V. E. *Homosexuality in perspective.* Boston: Little, Brown, 1979.

Matteson, D. R. Bisexual men in marriage: Is a positive homosexual identity stable marriage possible? *Journal of Homosexuality,* 1985, 11(1/2), 149–171.

Maykovich, M. K. Attitude vs. behavior in extramarital sexual relations. *Journal of Marriage and the Family,* 1976, 38(4), 693–699.

Mazur, R. *The new intimacy: Open-ended marriage and alternative lifestyles.* Boston: Beacon Press, 1973.

McAdoo, H. P. Commentary on Joseph Scott's "Polygamous Family Formation." *Alternative Lifestyles,* 1980, 3(4), 383–387.

McGinnis, T. C., & Finnegan, D. G. *Open family and marriage: A guide to personal growth.* Saint Louis: C. V. Mosby, 1976.

McLanahan, S. S. Family structure and stress: A longitudinal comparison of two-parent and female-headed families. *Journal of Marriage and the Family,* 1983, 45(2), 347–357.

McLanahan, S. S., Wedemeyer, N. V., & Adelberg. T. Network support, social support, and psychological well-being in the single-parent family. *Journal of Marriage and the Family,* 1981, 43(3), 601–612.

McWhirter, D. P. & Mattison, A. M. *The Male Couple: How Relationships Develop.* Englewood Cliffs, N.J.: Prentice-Hall, 1984.

Melli, M. S. The changing legal status of the single parent. *Family Relations.* 1986, 35(1), 31–35.

Mendes, H. A. Single fathers. *The Family Coordinator,* 1976, 25(4), 439–445.

Mendes, H. A. Single-parent fathers: A typology of lifestyles. *Social Work,* 1979, 24(3), 193–200.

Messinger, L. Remarriage between divorced people with children from previous marriages: A proposal for preparation for remarriage. *Journal of Marriage and Family Counseling,* 1976, 2(2), 193–200.

Miller, B. Adult sexual resocialization: Adjustments toward a stigmatized identity. *Alternative Lifestyles,* 1978, 1(2), 207–234.

Miller, B. Unpromised paternity: The lifestyles of gay fathers. In M. Levine (Ed.), *Gay men: The sociology of male homosexuality.* New York: Harper & Row, 1979.

Milne, A. L. (Ed.). *Joint custody: A handbook for judges, lawyers, and counselors.* Portland, Ore.: Association of Family Reconciliation Courts, 1979. (10015 Terwilliger Blvd. S.W., Portland, Ore. 97219.)

Mommsen, K. G. Differentials in fertility among black doctorates. *Social Biology,* 1973, 20(February), 20–29.

Morin, S. F. Heterosexual bias in psychological research on lesbian and male homosexuality. *American Psychologist,* 1977, 32(August), 629–637.

Moses, A. *Identity management in lesbian women.* New York: Praeger, 1978.

Mowery, J. Systemic requisites of communal groups. *Alternative Lifestyles,* 1978, 1(2), 235–261.

Mueller, D. P., & Cooper, P. W. Children of single-parent families: How they fare as young adults. *Family Relations,* 1986, 35(1), 169–176.

Muir, M. F. *Differential effects of father absence on sex-role identity as a function of sex, age at time of divorce, and step-parent availability.* Unpublished doctoral dissertation, University of Oklahoma, 1977.

Murdock, G. P. *Social structure.* New York: Macmillan, 1949.

Muro, J. J., Hudgins, A. L., Shoudt, J. T., Kaiser, H. E., & Sillin, P. C. HRD and parent training groups. *Elementary School Guidance and Counseling,* 1977, 12(1), 59–61.

Murstein, B. I. *Love, sex, and marriage through the ages.* New York: Springer, 1974.

Murstein, B. I. (Ed.). *Exploring intimate life styles.* New York: Springer, 1978. (a)

Murstein, B. I. Swinging, or comarital sex. In B. I. Murstein (Ed.), *Exploring intimate life styles.* New York: Springer, 1978. (b)

Murstein, B. I., Case, D., & Gunn, S. P. Personality correlates of ex-swingers. *Lifestyles,* 1985, 8(1), 21–34.

Myricks, N. "Palimony": The impact of *Marvin v. Marvin. The Family Coordinator,* 1980, 29(2), 210–215.

Myricks, N. The law and alternative lifestyles. In E. D. Macklin & R. Rubin (Eds.), *Contemporary families and alternative lifestyles: Handbook on research and theory.* Beverly Hills, Calif.: Sage Publications, 1983.

Myricks, N., & Rubin, R. H. Sex laws and alternative life styles. *The Family Coordinator,* 1977, 26(4), 357–360.

Nason, E. M., & Poloma, M. M. *Voluntarily childless couples: The emergence of a variant lifestyle.* Beverly Hills, Calif.: Sage Publications, 1976.

Newcomb, M. D., & Bentler, P. M. Assessment of personality and demographic aspects of cohabitation and marital success. *Journal of Personality Assessment,* 1980, *44*(1), 11–24. (a)

Newcomb, M. D., & Bentler, P. M. Cohabitation before marriage: A comparison of married couples who did and did not cohabit. *Alternative Lifestyles,* 1980, *3*(1), 65–85. (b)

Noble, J., & Noble, W. *How to live with other people's children.* New York: Hawthorne Books, 1977.

Norton, A., & Glick, P. C. What's happening to households? *American Demographics,* 1979, *1*, 19–23.

Norton, A. J. & Glick, P. C. One parent families: A social and economic profile. *Family Relations,* 1986, *35*(1), 9–17.

Nungesser, L. G. Theoretical bases for research on the acquisition of social sex-roles by children of lesbian mothers. *Journal of Homosexuality,* 1980, *5*(3), 177–187.

Oberstone, A. K., & Sukoneck, H. Psychological adjustment and lifestyle of single lesbians and single heterosexual women. *Psychology of Women Quarterly,* 1976, *1*(Winter), 172–188.

Olday, D. *Some consequences of heterosexual cohabitation for marriage.* Unpublished doctoral dissertation, Washington State University, 1977.

Olson, D. H., Sprenkle, D. H., & Russell, C. Circumplex model of marital and family systems: I. Cohesion and adaptability dimensions, family types, and clinical application. *Family Process,* 1979, *18,* 3–28.

O'Neill, N., & O'Neill, G. *Open marriage: A new life style for couples.* New York: M. Evans, 1972.

Orthner, D., & Lewis, K. Evidence of single-father competence in childrearing. *Family Law Quarterly,* 1979, *3*(1), 27–47.

Orthner, D., Brown, T., & Ferguson, D. Single-parent fatherhood: An emerging family lifestyle. *The Family Coordinator,* 1976, *25*(4), 429–437.

Ory, M. G. The decision to parent or not: Normative and structural components. *Journal of Marriage and the Family,* 1978, *40*(3), 531–539.

Osofsky, J. D., & Osofsky, H. J. Androgony as a life style. *The Family Coordinator,* 1972, *21*(4), 441–444.

Otto, H. A. (Ed.). *The family in search of a future: Alternative models for moderns.* New York: Appleton-Century-Crofts, 1970.

Pagelow, M. D. Heterosexual and lesbian single mothers: A comparison of problems, coping, and solutions. *Journal of Homosexuality,* 1980, *5*(3), 189–204.

Palson, C., & Palson, R. Swinging in wedlock. *Society,* 1972, *9*(February), 28–37.

Parks, A. Children and youth of divorce in Parents Without Partners. *Journal of Clinical Child Psychology,* 1977, *6*(2), 44–48.

Pasley, K. & Ihinger-Tallman, M. (Eds.) Remarriage and stepparenting. Special issue of *Family Relations,* 1984, *33*(3), 351–500.

Patterson, L. A., & DeFrain, J. Pronatalism in high school family studies texts. *Family Relations,* 1981 (April), 211–217.

Pearlin, L. I., & Johnson, J. S. Marital status, life strains, and depression. *American Society Review,* 1977, *42*(October), 704–715.

Pendleton, B. F., Poloma, M. M., & Garland, T. N. Scales for investigation of the dual-career family. *Journal of Marriage and the Family,* 1980, *42*(2), 269–276.

Peplau, L. A. Research on homosexual couples: An overview. *Journal of Homosexuality,* 1982, *8*(2), 3–8.

Peplau, L. A., & Amaro, H. Understanding lesbian relationships. In W. Paul & J. D. Weinrich (Eds.), *Homosexuality.* Beverly Hills, Calif.: Sage Publications, 1982.

Peplau, L. A., Cochran, S., Rook, K., & Padesky, C. Loving women: Attachment and autonomy in lesbian relationships. *Journal of Social Issues,* 1978, *34*(3), 7–27.

Peplau, L. A., Padesky, C., & Hamilton, M. Satisfaction in lesbian relationships. *Journal of Homosexuality,* 1982, *8*(2), 23–35.

Perkins, T. F., & Kahan, J. P. An empirical comparison of natural-father and stepfather family systems. *Family Process,* 1979, *18*(2), 175–183.

Peterman, D. J., Ridley, C. A., & Anderson, S. M. A comparison of cohabiting and non-cohabiting college students. *Journal of Marriage and the Family,* 1974, *36*(2), 344–354.

Peters, M. F., & McAdoo, H. P. The present and future of alternative lifestyles in ethnic American cultures. In E. D. Macklin & R. Rubin (Eds.), *Contemporary families and alternative lifestyles: Handbook on research and theory.* Beverly Hills, Calif.: Sage Publications, 1983.

Pett, M. A. & Vaughan-Cole, B. The impact of income issues and social status on post-divorce adjustment of custodial parents. *Family Relations,* 1986, *35*(1), 103–111.

Petty, J. A. *An investigation of factors which differentiate between types of cohabitation.* Unpublished master's thesis, Indiana University, Bloomington, 1975.

Philliber, W. W., & Hiller, D. V. Relative occupational attainments of spouses and later changes in marriage and wife's work experiences. *Journal of Marriage and the Family,* 1983, *45*(1), 161–170.

Phillips, R. A., Jr. Clinical issues in alternative lifestyles. In E. D. Macklin & R. Rubin (Eds.), *Contemporary families and alternative lifestyles: Handbook on research and theory.* Beverly Hills, Calif.: Sage Publications, 1983.

Pickett, R. S. Monogamy on trial: An analysis of historical antecedents to monogamy and its alternatives. Part I: The premodern era. *Alternative Lifestyles,* 1978, *1*(2), 153–189. (a)

Pickett, R. S. Monogamy on trial: An analysis of historical antecedents to monogamy and its alternatives. Part II: The modern era. *Alternative Lifestyles,* 1978, *1*(3), 281–302. (b)

Pink, J. E. T., & Wampler, K. S. Problem areas in stepfamilies: Cohesion, adaptability, and the stepfather-adolescent relationship. *Family Relations,* 1985, *34*(3), 327–335.

Polansky, L. W., McDonald, G., & Martin, J. A comparison of marriage and heterosexual cohabitation on three interpersonal variables: Affective support, mutual knowledge, and relationship satisfaction. *Western Sociological Review,* 1978, *9*(Summer), 49–59.

Poloma, M. M. *The married professional woman: An empirical examination of three myths.* Unpublished doctoral dissertation, Case Western Reserve University, 1970.

Poloma, M. M. Role conflict and the married professional woman. In C. Safilios-Rothchild (Ed.), *Toward a sociology of women.* Lexington, Mass.: Xerox, 1972.

Polonko, K. A., Scanzoni, J., & Teachman, J. D. Childlessness and marital satisfaction: A further assessment. *Journal of Family Issues,* 1982, *3*(4), 545–573.

Ponse, B. *Identities in the lesbian world, The social construction of self.* Westport, Conn.: Greenwood Press, 1978.

Pupo, A. M. A study of voluntary childless couples. Unpublished doctoral dissertation, U.S. International University, 1980.

Radloff, L. Sex differences in depression: The effects of occupation and marital status. *Sex Roles,* 1975, *1,* 249–265.

Ramey, J. W. Intimate groups and networks: Frequent consequence of sexually open marriage. *The Family Coordinator,* 1975, *24*(October), 515–530.

Ramey, J. W. *Intimate friendships.* Englewood Cliffs, N.J.: Prentice-Hall, 1976.

Ramey, J. W. Legal regulation of personal and family life styles. *The Family Coordinator,* 1977, *26*(4), 349–355.

Ramu, G. N. Voluntarily childless and parental couples: A comparison of their lifestyle characteristics. *Lifestyles,* 1985, *7*(3), 130–145.

Rank, M. R. The transition to marriage: A comparison of cohabiting and dating relationships ending in marriage or divorce. *Alternative Lifestyles,* 1981, *4*(4), 487–506.

Rao, V. V., & Rao, V. N. Alternatives in intimacy, marriage, and family lifestyles: Preferences of black college students. *Alternative Lifestyles*, 1980, *3*(4), 485–498.

Raphael, S. M., & Robinson, M. K. The older lesbian: Love relationships and friendship patterns. *Alternative Lifestyles*, 1980, *3*(2), 207–229.

Rapoport, R., & Rapoport, R. N. The dual-career family. *Human Relations*, 1969, *22*(February), 3–30.

Rapoport, R., & Rapoport, R. N. *Dual-career families*. Harmondsworth, England: Penguin, 1971.

Rapoport, R., & Rapoport, R. N. *Dual-career families reexamined*. New York: Harper & Row, 1976.

Rapoport, R., & Rapoport, R. N. (Eds.). *Working couples*. New York: Harper & Row, 1978.

Regan, M. C., & Roland, H. E. Rearranging family and career priorities: Professional women and men of the eighties. *Journal of Marriage and the Family*, 1985, *47*(4), 985–992.

Reiss, I. L., Anderson, R. E., & Sponaugle, G. C. A multivariate model of the determinants of extramarital sexual permissiveness. *Journal of Marriage and the Family*, 1980, *42*(2), 395–411.

Rejals, K., & Foster, D. Open marriage: A question of ego development and marriage counseling? *The Family Coordinator*, 1976, *25*(3), 297–302.

Rempel, J. Childless elderly. What are they missing? *Journal of Marriage and the Family*, 1985, *47*(2), 343–348.

Rhee, J. M. *Trends and variations in childlessness in the United States*. Unpublished doctoral dissertation, University of Georgia, Athens, 1973.

Ridley, C. A., Peterman, D. J., & Avery, A. W. Cohabitation: Does it make for a better marriage? *The Family Coordinator*, 1978, *27*(2), 129–136.

Rimmer, R. H. (Ed.). *Adventures in loving*. New York: New American Library, 1973.

Risman, B. J., Hill, C. T., Rubin, Z., & Peplau, L. A. Living together in college: Implications for courtship. *Journal of Marriage and the Family*, 1981, *43*(1), 77–83.

Risman, R. J. Can men "mother"? Life as a single father. *Family Relations*, 1986, *35*(1), 95–102.

Ritchey, P. N., & Stokes, C. S. Correlates of childlessness and expectations to remain childless. *Social Forces*, 1974, *52*(March), 349–356.

Rogers, C. *Becoming partners: Marriage and its alternatives*. New York: Delacorte Press, 1972.

Roman, M., Charles, E., & Karasu, T. B. The value system of psychotherapists and changing mores. *Psychotherapy: Theory, Research and Practice*, 1978, *15*(4), 409–415.

Roosevelt, R., & Lofas, J. *Living in step*. New York: Stein & Day, 1976.

Rosen, B., Jerdee, T. H., & Prestwich, T. L. Dual-career marital adjustment: Potential effects of discriminatory managerial attitudes. *Journal of Marriage and the Family*, 1975, *37*(3), 565–572.

Rosen, D. H. *Lesbianism: A study of female homosexuality*. Springfield, Ill.: Charles C. Thomas, 1974.

Rosenberg, G. S. Implications of new models of the family for the aging population. In H. A. Otto (Ed.), *The family in search of a future*. New York: Appleton-Century-Crofts, 1970.

Rosenthal, K. M., & Keshet, H. F. The impact of childcare responsibilities on part-time or single fathers: Changing patterns of work and intimacy. *Alternative Lifestyles*, 1978, *1*(4), 465–492.

Rosenthal, K. M. & Keshet, H. F. *Fathers Without Partners*, Towota, N.J.: Rowan and Littlefield, 1981.

Ross, H., & Sawhill, I. *Time of transition: The growth of families headed by women*. Washington, D.C.: Urban Institute, 1975.

Rubin, A. M. Sexually open versus sexually exclusive marriage: A comparison of dyadic adjustment. *Alternative Lifestyles*, 1982, *5*(2), 101–108.

Saghir, M., & Robins, E. *Male and female homosexuality: A comprehensive investigation*. Baltimore: Williams & Wilkins, 1973.

Salsberg, S. Is group marriage viable? *Journal of Sex Research*, 1973, *9*, 325–333.

Sanik, M. M., & Mauldin, T. Single versus two parent families: A comparison of mother's time. *Family Relations*, 1986, *35*(1), 53–56.

Santrock, J. W., & Warshak, R. A. Father custody and social development in boys and girls. *Journal of Social Issues*, 1979, *35*, 112–125.

Saunders, J. M., & Edwards, J. N. Extramarital sexuality: A predictive model of permissive attitudes. *Journal of Marriage and the Family*, 1984, *46*(4), 825–835.

Savage, J. E., Adair, A. V., & Friedman, P. Community-social variables related to black parent-absent families. *Journal of Marriage and the Family*, 1978, *40*(4), 779–785.

Sawin, M. M. *Family enrichment with family clusters*. Valley forge, Pa.: Judson Press, 1979.

Scanzoni, J., & Fox, G. L. Sex roles, family and society: The seventies and beyond. *Journal of Marriage and the Family*, 1980, *42*(4), 743–756.

Schlesinger, B. Single-parent fathers: A research review. *Children Today*, 1978, *7*(3), 12, 18–19, 37–39.

Schlesinger, B. Single parent families: A bookshelf: 1978–1985. *Family Relations*, 1986, *35*(1), 199–204.

Schorr, A. L., & Moen, P. The single-parent and public policy. *Social Policy*, 1979, *9*(5), 15–21.

Scott, J. P. Single rural elders: A comparison of dimensions of life satisfaction. *Alternative Lifestyles*, 1979, *2*(3), 359–378.

Scott, J. W. Black polygamous family formation: Case studies of legal wives and consensual ''wives.'' *Alternative Lifestyles*, 1980, *3*(1), 41–64. (a)

Scott, J. W. Reprise: Conceptualizing and researching American polygyny—and critics answered. *Alternative Lifestyles*, 1980, *3*(4), 395–404. (b)

Seal, H. *Alternative life styles*. Hamilton, New Zealand: Family Synergy, 1975.

Segrest, M. A., & Weeks, M. O. Comparison of the role expectations of married and cohabiting students. *International Journal of Sociology of the Family*, 1976, *6*(Autumn), 275–281.

Shorter, E. *The making of the modern family*. New York: Basic Books, 1975.

Singer, K. *A comparative study of self-concepts: Children from one-parent home environments, children from two-parent home environments*. Unpublished doctoral dissertation, Florida Atlantic University, 1978.

Singh, B. K., & Williams, J. S. Childlessness and family satisfaction. *Research on Aging*, 1981, *3*, 218–227.

Singh, B. K., Walton, B. L., & Williams, J. S. Extramarital sexual permissiveness: Conditions and contingencies. *Journal of Marriage and the Family*, 1976, *38*(4), 701–712.

Skinner, D. A. Dual-career family stress and coping: A literature review. *Family Relations*, 1980, *29*(4), 473–481.

Smith, J. R., & Smith, L. S. Co-marital sex and the sexual freedom movement. *Journal of Sex Research*, 1970, *6*, 131–142.

Smith, J. R., & Smith, L. S. (Eds.). *Beyond monogamy: Recent studies of sexual alternatives in marriage*. Baltimore: Johns Hopkins University Press, 1974.

Smith, M. J. The social consequences of single parenthood: A longitudinal perspective. *Family Relations*, 1980, *29*(1), 75–81.

Spanier, G. B. Married and unmarried cohabitation in the United States: 1980. *Journal of Marriage and the Family*, 1983, *45*(2), 277–288.

Spanier, G. B., & Lewis, R. A. Marital quality: A review of the seventies. *Journal of Marriage and the Family*, 1980, *42*(4), 825–839.

Spanier, G. B., & Margolis, R. L. *Marital separation and extramarital sexual behavior.* Unpublished paper presented to International Academy of Sex Research, Prague, Czechoslovakia, 1979.

Spector, M. Legitimizing homosexuality. *Society,* 1977, *14*(5), 52–56.

Spreitzer, R., & Riley, L. E. Factors associated with singlehood. *Journal of Marriage and the Family,* 1974, *36*(3), 533–542.

Stafford, R., Backman, E., & diBona, P. The division of labor among cohabiting and married couples. *Journal of Marriage and the Family,* 1977, *39*(1), 43–57.

Staples, R. Intimacy patterns among black, middle-class, single parents. *Alternative Lifestyles,* 1980, *3*(4), 445–462.

Staples, R. *The world of black singles.* Westport, Conn.: Greenwood, 1981.

Starr, J., & Carns, D. Singles in the city. *Society,* 1972, *9,* 43–48.

Stein, P. J. *Single.* Englewood Cliffs, N.J.: Prentice-Hall, 1976.

Stein, P. J. The lifestyles and life chances of the never-married. *Marriage and Family Review,* 1978, *1*(4), 1–11.

Stein, P. J. Singlehood. In E. D. Macklin & R. Rubin (Eds.), *Contemporary family forms and alternative lifestyles: Handbook on research and theory.* Beverly Hills, Calif.: Sage Publications, 1983.

Steinman, S. The experience of children in a joint custody arrangement: A report of a study. *American Journal of Orthopsychiatry,* 1981, *51*(3), 403–414.

Stinnett, N., & Birdsong, C. W. *The family and alternative life styles.* Chicago: Nelson-Hall, 1978.

Stoller, F. H. The intimate network of families as a new structure. In H. A. Otto (Ed.), *The family in search of a future.* New York: Appleton-Century-Crofts, 1970.

Storm, V. *Contemporary cohabitation and the dating-marital continuum.* Unpublished master's thesis, University of Georgia, Athens, 1973.

Straver, C. J. Unmarried couples: Different from marriages? *Alternative Lifestyles,* 1981, *4*(1), 43–74.

Streib, G. F. An alternative family form for older persons: Need and social context. *The Family Coordinator,* 1978, *27*(4), 413–420.

Streib, G. F., & Hilker, M. A. The cooperative "family": An alternative lifestyle for the elderly. *Alternative Lifestyles,* 1980, *3*(2), 167–184.

Strong, L. D. Alternative marital and family forms: Their relative attractiveness to college students and correlates of willingness to participate in non-traditional forms. *Journal of Marriage and the Family,* 1978, *40*(3), 493–503.

Sussman, M. B. (Ed.). *Non-traditional family forms in the 1970's.* Minneapolis: National Council on Family Relations, 1972.

Sussman, M. B. (Ed.). The second experience: Variant forms and lifestyles. (Special Issue) *The Family Coordinator,* 1975, *24*(4), 391–576.

Sussman, M. B., *et al. Changing families in a changing society.* Forum 14 in Report to the President: White House Conference on Children, 1970. Washington, D.C.: U.S. Government Printing Office, 1971.

Symonds, C. L. Swingers: Backgrounds and norms of participants. In J. P. Wiseman (Ed.), *The social psychology of sex.* New York: Harper & Row, 1976.

Tanner, D. M. *The lesbian couple.* Lexington, Mass.: Lexington Books, 1978.

Teicholz, J. G. *A preliminary search for psychological correlates of voluntary childlessness in married women.* Unpublished doctoral dissertation, Boston University School of Education, 1977.

Thamm, R. *Beyond marriage and the nuclear family.* San Francisco: Canfield Press, 1975.

Thoen, G. A. *Commitment among voluntary childless couples to a variant lifestyle.* Unpublished doctoral dissertation, University of Minnesota, Minneapolis, 1977.

Thomas, S., Albrecht, K., & White, P. Determinants of marital quality in dual-career couples. *Family Relations,* 1984, *33*(4), 513–521.

Thompson, A. P. Emotional and sexual components of extramarital relations. *Journal of Marriage and the Family,* 1984, *46*(1), 35–42.

Thompson, E. H., Jr., & Gongla, P. A. Single parent families: In the

mainstream of American society. In E. D. Macklin & R. Rubin (Eds.), *Contemporary family forms and alternative lifestyles: Handbook on research and theory.* Beverly Hills, Calif.: Sage Publications, 1983.

Toomey, B. G. *College women and voluntary childlessness: A comparative study of women indicating they want to have children and those indicating they do not want to have children.* Unpublished doctoral dissertation, Ohio State University, Columbus, 1977.

Trost, J. *Unmarried cohabitation.* Vasteras, Sweden: International Library, 1979.

Trost, J. Cohabitation in the Nordic countries: From deviant phenomenon to social institution. *Alternative Lifestyles,* 1981, *4*(4), 401–427.

Tuller, N. E. Couples: The hidden segment of the gay world. *Journal of Homosexuality,* 1978, *3*(4), 331–343.

Turner, P. H., & Smith, R. M. Single parents and day care. *Family Relations,* 1983, *32*(2), 215–225.

U.S. Bureau of the Census. Household and family characteristics: March 1978. *Current Population Reports,* Series P-20, No. 340. Washington, D.C.: U.S. Government Printing Office, 1979.

U.S. Bureau of the Census. Household and family characteristics: March 1979. *Current Population Reports,* Series P-20, No. 352. Washington, D.C.: U.S. Government Printing Office, 1980. (a)

U.S. Bureau of the Census. Households and families, by type: March 1980 (advanced report). *Current Population Reports,* Series P-20, No. 357. Washington, D.C.: U.S. Government Printing Office, 1980. (b)

U.S. Bureau of the Census. Marital status and living arrangements: March 1980. *Current Population Reports,* Series P-20, No. 365. Washington, D.C.: U.S. Government Printing Office, 1981.

U.S. Bureau of the Census. Fertility of American women: June 1980. *Current Population Reports,* Series P-20, No. 375. Washington, D.C.: U.S. Government Printing Office, 1982.

U.S. Bureau of the Census. Wives who earn more than their husbands. *Special Demographic Analyses,* CDS-80-9. Washington, D.C.: Government Printing Office, 1983.

U.S. Bureau of the Census. *Statistical Abstract of the U.S.: 1985 (105th Edition),* Washington, D.C.: U.S. Government Printing Office, 1984.

U.S. Department of Labor. Multi-earner families increase. *News,* U.S. Department of Labor 79-747 (Oct. 31, 1979), 1979.

U.S. Department of Labor. *Employment in perspective: Working women—1979 summary.* U.S. Department of Labor, Bureau of Labor Statistics, Report 587, February 1980.

Usher, C. E., & McConnell, S. R. House-sharing: A way to intimacy? *Alternative Lifestyles,* 1980, *3*(2), 149–166.

Varni, C. An exploratory study of spouse swapping. *Pacific Sociological Review,* 1972, *15,* 507–522.

Varni, C. Contexts of conversion: The case of swinging. In R. W. Libby & R. N. Whitehurst (Eds.), *Renovating Marriage: Toward new sexual life styles.* Danville, Calif.: Consensus, 1973.

Veevers, J. E. Voluntary childlessness: A neglected area of family study. *The Family Coordinator,* 1973, *22*(2), 199–205.

Veevers, J. E. Voluntary childlessness: A review of issues and evidence. *Marriage and Family Review,* 1979, *2*(2), 1–26.

Veevers, J. E. *Childless by choice.* Toronto: Butterworths, 1980.

Veevers, J. E. Voluntary childlessness: A critical assessment of the research. In E. D. Macklin & R. Rubin (Eds.), *Contemporary families and alternative lifestyles: Handbook on research and theory.* Beverly Hills, Calif.: Sage Publications, 1983.

Verbrugge, L. M. Marital status and health. *Journal of Marriage and the Family,* 1979, *41*(2), 267–285.

Vetere, V. A. The role of friendship in the development and maintenance of lesbian love relationships. *Journal of Homosexuality,* 1982, *8*(2), 51–65.

Visher, E. B., & Visher, J. S. *Stepfamilies: A guide to working with stepparents and stepchildren.* New York: Brunner/Mazel, 1979.

Voeller, B., & Walters, J. Gay fathers. *The Family Coordinator*, 1978, *27*(2), 149–157.

Wachowiak, D., & Bragg, H. Open marriage and marital adjustment. *Journal of Marriage and the Family*, 1980, *42*(1), 57–62.

Waldman, E., Grossman, A. S., Hayghe, H., & Johnson, B. L. Working mothers in the 1970's: A look at the statistics. In *Young workers and families: A special section*. Special Labor Force Report 233. U.S. Department of Labor: Bureau of Labor Statistics, 1979.

Walker, K., & Messinger, L. Remarriage after divorce: Dissolution and reconstruction of family boundaries. *Family Process*, 1979, *18*(2), 185–192.

Wallerstein, J., & Kelly, J. *Surviving the breakup: How children and parents cope with divorce*. New York: Basic Books, 1980.

Walshok, M. L. The emergence of middle-class deviant subcultures: The case of swingers. In J. R. Smith & L. G. Smith (Eds.), *Beyond monogamy*. Baltimore: Johns Hopkins University Press, 1974.

Walster, E., Traupmann, J., & Walster, G. W. Equity and extramarital sexuality. *Archives of Sexual Behavior*, 1978, *7*(March), 127–142.

Ward, R. A. The never-married in later life. *Journal of Gerontology*, 1979, *34*, 861–869.

Warheit, G. J., Holzer, C. E., III, Bell, R. A., & Arey, S. A. Sex, marital status, and mental health: A reappraisal. *Social Forces*, 1976, *55*(December), 459–470.

Watson, J., & Watson, M. A. Children of open marriages: Parental disclosure and perspectives. *Alternative Lifestyles*, 1982, *5*(1), 54–62.

Watson, M. A. Sexually-open marriage: Three perspectives. *Alternative Lifestyles*, 1981, *4*(1), 3–21.

Watson, R. E. L. Premarital cohabitation vs. traditional courtship: Their effects on subsequent marital adjustment. *Family Relations*, 1983, *32*, 139–147.

Wattenberg, E., & Reinhardt, H. Female-headed families: Trends and implications. *Social Work*, 1979, *24*, 460–467.

Weis, D. L. *Toward a theory of social scripting: The measurement of extramarital sexual scripts*. Unpublished doctoral dissertation, Purdue University, 1979.

Weis, D. L. "Open" marriage and multilateral relationships: The emergence of non-exclusive models of the marital relationship. In E. D. Macklin & R. Rubin (Eds.), *Contemporary families and alternative lifestyles: Handbook on research and theory*. Beverly Hills, Calif.: Sage Publications, 1983.

Weis, D. L. & Jurich, J. Size of community of residence as a predictor of attitudes toward extramarital sexual relations. *Journal of Marriage and the Family*, 1985, *47*(1), 173–178.

Weis, D. L., & Slosnerick, M. Attitudes toward sexual and nonsexual extramarital involvements among a sample of college students. *Journal of Marriage and the Family*, 1981, *43*, 349–358.

Weisberg, D. K. Alternative family structures and the law. *The Family Coordinator*, 1975, *24*(4), 549–559. (a)

Weisberg, D. K. *Children and communal life*. Unpublished doctoral dissertation, Brandeis University, 1975. (b)

Weisberg, D. K. The Cinderella children: Growing up in an urban commune. *Psychology Today*, 1977, *10*(11), 84–86, 103.

Weisner, T. S., & Martin, J. C. Learning environments for infants: Communes and conventionally married families in California. *Alternative Lifestyles*, 1979, *2*(2), 201–242.

Weiss, R. S. The contribution of an organization of single parents to the well-being of its members. *The Family Coordinator*, 1973, *22*(3), 321–327.

Weiss, R. S. *Going it alone: The family life and social situation of the single parent*. New York: Basic Books, 1979.

Weiss, R. S. The impact of marital dissolution on income and consumption in single-parent households. *Journal of Marriage and the Family*, 1984, *46*(1), 115–127.

White, M., & Wells, C. Student attitudes toward alternative marriage forms. In R. W. Libby & R. N. Whitehurst (Eds.), *Renovating marriage: Toward new sexual life styles*. Danville, Calif.: Consensus Publishers. 1973.

Wilkie, J. R. The trend toward delayed parenthood. *Journal of Marriage and the Family*, 1981, *43*(3), 583–591.

Wilkinson, C. B., & O'Connor, W. A. Growing up male in a black single-parent family. *Psychiatric Annuals*, 1977, *7*(7), 50–51, 55–59.

Wilson, K. L., Zurcher, L. S., McAdams, D. C., & Curtis, R. L. Stepfathers and stepchildren: An exploratory analysis from two national surveys. *Journal of Marriage and the Family*, 1975, *37*(3), 526–536.

Windemiller, D. *Sexuality, pairing and family forms*. Cambridge, Mass.: Winthrop, 1976.

Wolf, D. G. *The lesbian community*. Los Angeles: University of California Press, 1979.

Wolf, T. J. Marriages of bisexual men. *Journal of Homosexuality*, 1985, *11*(1/2), 135–148.

Yankelovich, D. New rules in American life: Searching for self-fulfillment in a world turned upside down. *Psychology Today*, 1981 (April), 35–91.

Yllo, K. A. Non-marital cohabitation: Beyond the college campus. *Alternative Lifestyles*, 1978, *1*(1), 37–54.

Yogev, S. Do professional women have egalitarian marital relationships? *Journal of Marriage and the Family*, 1981, *43*(4), 865–871.

Zablocki, B. *Alienation and investment in the urban commune*. New York: Center for Policy Research, 1977.

Zablocki, B. *Alienation and charisma: A study of contemporary American communes*. New York: Free Press, 1980.

Ziskin, J., & Ziskin, M. *The extra-marital sex contract*. Los Angeles: Nash Publishing, 1973.

CHAPTER 13

Singlehood

Arthur B. Shostak

Introduction

One of the fastest growing segments of the population, never-married Americans, is also one of the least well understood . . . or appreciated. Viewed historically as self-centered, irresponsible sowers of wild oats, they were thought to be redeemed only by marriage, and that as soon as possible. Those few who came to be regarded as permanent "bridesmaids," regardless of gender, were privately judged exceedingly unfortunate: life lived forever as a lonely bachelor or as an "old maid" spinster was regarded as a most pitiful outcome. To make matters even worse, many were secretly thought to be witless complicitors in their own hapless fate, being somehow personally responsible for this sorry turn of events.

More recently, thanks largely to the reassessment of gender roles demanded by the women's movement, the status of never-married adulthood has begun to be seen for the first time as complete and worthwhile in its own right. Custom-tailored routes to happiness other than "wedded bliss" are hailed for reducing pressure on the very institution of marriage itself, thereby providing breathing space for its possible reform. And at least one future-looking commentator speculated that "if the contemporary family continues to slip in general appeal, given its steady loss of distinctive functions, its opposite number, a deliberate and longterm singlehood, may become the accepted dominant social pattern" (Adams, 1976, p. 18).

Detractors, in turn, persist in characterizing marriage as the only reasonable, healthy, and natural route for all level-headed heterosexuals. They treat singlehood as a dependent variable, a temporary status meaningful only as a way station for marriageable young adults. They refuse to see it as a discrete entity in its own right, one capable of providing its advocates with more than a short-term, very haphazard, and fairly marginal existence. Accordingly, many American parents remain vexed when their offspring approach a thirtieth birthday without at least one marriage in the record (albeit the average age at

marriage has risen for both partners every year since 1958); (Feinsilber & Mead, 1980).

Despite a rapid rise in the absolute number of never-married Americans, a seeming gain in their public repute (marriage-prescribing parents not withstanding), and the likelihood that their ranks may expand substantially through the 1980s, far too little has been reliably known about unwed men and women. Until recently, for example, few texts on marriage and the family have discussed singles at any length or in any depth. A rare volume on the topic, first published in 1976, noted that in contrast to marriage, which has been subject to a spotlight of critical scrutiny, singleness has received almost no serious attention (Adams, 1976). A 1979 article observed that "we don't know who remains single or for how long, because social scientists never before thought it was important what happened to individual singles. They assumed that being single was a transition stage in life" (Ramey, 1979, p. 3).

Unanswered to date, accordingly, are persisting questions about five major aspects of the subjects of this essay: their *characteristics,* their *typology,* their *well-being,* their *coping mechanisms,* and the *social policy options* bearing on the contemporary world of never-married Americans. Just who are these men and women, and how do they define their state of well-being? What sort of coping tactics do they employ to change the environment on their own behalf? And, what reforms might the public adopt in order to enhance the status of singlehood?

To help illuminate the lives of the largest type of single American, or the nation's 31 million *never-married* individuals, this chapter draws on four particular resources: statistics from the 1980 U.S. Census; a typology of the four leading variations on the never-married life; a secondary analysis of national attitudinal data collected by pollsters from never-married Americans between 1972 and 1980; and the small body of social science literature that distinguishes never-married types from other varieties of single Americans (such as separated, divorced, and widowed individuals). Although the typology draws on Stein's pioneering analysis (1981a), its four key concepts are original to this chapter, as are the data from special computer reruns done by me on national at-

Arthur B. Shostak • Department of Psychology and Sociology, Drexel University, Philadelphia, PA 19104.

Table 1. Marital Status, Age 18 and Over, 1980[a]

	Single	Separated	Divorced	Widowed	Married
Males	16,970,000	1,513,000	3,471,000	1,945,000	48,816,000
Percentage	23	2	5	3	67
Females	13,644,000	2,409,000	5,355,000	10,499,000	48,771,000
Percentage	17	3	7	13	61

[a]U.S. Bureau of the Census, *Current Population Reports*, February 1980, Table E-1.

titudinal data to separate never-married answers from those of all others.

Never-Married Americans: Characteristics

The first of this chapter's five basic questions, "just who *are* the never-married singles?" can be answered with census data that suggest that never-married Americans are more often male than female (see Table 1). This sex ratio varies considerably across the age blocs, with males predominating in all but the oldest group (see Table 2). Evident in the numbers given in the tables is the cultural pressure on females to marry at least once, especially before the end of their safest childbearing years, a pressure that may explain why the proportion of women who never marry actually fell from almost 9% in 1900 to 7% in the 1970s (Rubin, 1981). All the more provocative, therefore, is the fact that, in 1979, as many as 50% of women between the ages of 20 and 24 were never-married, as compared to only about 30% twenty years before (the male figure went from 54% to 67%, a much smaller increase) (Stein, 1981a).

Never-Married Americans: A Typological Approach

Depending on whether the status of being unwed is voluntary or involuntary, a life lived as a single can vary greatly in quality of well-being. Similarly, depending on whether the status is considered stable or temporary, a single adult life may vary in self-assessment and commitment (see Table 3). Naturally, each of this chapter's four basic types—known hereafter as *ambivalents, wishfuls, resolveds,* and *regretfuls*—contains people who may shift among the types over time.

Ambivalents include especially younger males and females who are temporarily postponing marriage in favor of the pursuit of higher education, career building, self-development, or the like. As well, their ranks include singles who are living together, one of the fastest growing new forms of family life ("the most likely explanation of this increase is that young Americans are becoming increasingly attracted to this life style, and their parents are becoming less critical of this behavior as long as it does not result in childbearing and as long as those involved directly are economically independent," Glick & Spanier, 1981, p. 196).

Wishfuls are adults who hope to marry in the near future. Many are actively seeking mates, as they consciously prefer matrimony to singlehood and are earnestly working to get married. (Wolfe, 1982, noted of this type that "singles are a slippery bunch. No sooner do they get counted as singles than they rush off to City Hall and emerge as doubles" [p. 35].)

Resolved singles, in contrast, are confirmed in their

Table 2. Never-Married Singles, 1979[a]

Age	Males	Females	Total	% Difference
18–19	3,813,000	3,475,000	7,277,000	4.6% more men
20–24	6,545,000	5,003,000	11,548,000	13.4% more men
25–29	2,661,000	1,789,000	4,450,000	19.6% more men
30–34	1,180,000	777,000	1,957,000	20.6% more men
35–39	528,000	448,000	976,000	8.2% more men
40–44	460,000	299,000	759,000	21.2% more men
45–54	761,000	520,000	1,281,000	18.8% more men
55–64	510,000	504,000	1,014,000	.6% more men
65–74	358,000	504,000	862,000	17.0% more women
75 and over	154,000	324,000	478,000	35.6% more women
Totals	16,970,000	13,644,000	30,614,000	

[a]U.S. Bureau of the Census, *Current Population Reports*, Series P-20, No. 349, "Marital Status and Living Arrangements: March 1979," as reported in Stein (1981).

Table 3. Typology of Singlehood[a]

	Voluntary	Involuntary
Temporary	I. *Ambivalents* Those not seeking mates, but open to the idea of marriage.	II. *Wishfuls* Those actively seeking mates, unsuccessfully to date.
Stable	III. *Resolved* Those who consciously prefer singlehood; also, religionaries.	IV. *Regretful* Those who would rather marry but are resigned to singlehood.

[a]Typology from Stein (1981b). The descriptive labels are by this writer, and not by Stein.

choice of singlehood and do not intend ever to marry. A small percentage have lifestyles that preclude that possibility (as in the case of priests and nuns), and some are single parents who are raising their children alone and prefer it that way. The vast plurality, however, are an altogether different breed of singles—people who *choose* singlehood, out of conviction and with commitment—whose ranks may be swelling:

What remains the most resoundingly significant finding (in the 1980 Census data) is the growth rate of the hard-core single, the single qua single, the people who live by themselves, without children, friends, lovers, or family members. . . . This group has increased by 64 percent, a rate more than five times that of the total population's increase (in the last 10 years). (Wolfe, 1982, p. 34)

Nearly half (46%) of the males in this "hard-core" bloc were never-married, in contrast to only 23% of all such females. In fact, although the number of never-married females living alone increased from 1970 to 1980 by 89%, the male tally of seemingly confirmed bachelors rose by 118% ("there are more men than ever queuing up for that hard to-find studio apartment," Wolfe, 1982, p. 34).

The fourth and final category, *regretfuls*, includes people who have always wanted to eliminate their unwelcome single status in favor of marriage, but who have felt compelled instead to regard singlehood as a "life sentence." Because men tend to marry by dipping into an age pool of females younger than themselves, the regretful status is an especially high risk of women over 30, particularly highly educated, high-earning women:

The fact is, there is a real shortage of men. The fault lies not in our stars or ourselves but in a grim set of demographic data. We are in a state of single shock, a crisis of numbers. It is not that there are, literally, no men at the top, but there are precious few. (Doudna & McBride, 1981, p. 22)

Although 84% of single women surveyed in 1978 thought that a woman could enjoy life without ever marrying

(Norback, 1980, p. 47)—a much higher figure than ever true in the 1950s—only 44 percent thought that singlehood had more advantages than married life (as did only 30% of the men surveyed; Norback, 1980). Above all, regretfuls of both sexes have to contend with the fact that 94% of the population, excluding only themselves and resolved singles, marry at some point in their lives.

Three of these four types—ambivalents, wishfuls, and regretfuls—share at least one common characteristic of major significance: They are generally intent on graduating from a lonely form of singlehood to a romantic couple's status, "the avowed goal of almost everyone living without a special person in his or her life" (West, 1982, p. 24). Regardless of how they position themselves concerning the prospects of marriage, the vast majority of never-married adults work at securing and enjoying romance, as there are very few loners in their ranks. In at least this critical regard (the high value they place on achieving intimacy and sharing love with a special other), never-married and married Americans are as one.

Never-Married Americans: Well-Being

Questionnaire responses from 710 never-married adults (over 18 and employed) collected by the National Opinion Research Center (NORC) from 1972 through 1976 provide useful insights into the self-reported quality of life of singles. When asked, for example, how they found life in general, 55% said exciting; 41%, routine; and only 4% dull. Nearly three out of four felt that their friendships gave them a "very great deal" or "a great deal" of satisfaction; 68% responded in the same way about their health and physical condition; and 76% similarly lauded their own financial situation (NORC, 1979).

Where discontents are concerned, much can be learned by turning to another national survey, a thoroughgoing study of attitudes and well-being prepared in 1978 by the Harris polling organization for the U.S. Department of Housing and Urban Development (HUD, 1978). Nearly 1,200 never-married singles (and 4,700 married respondents) were interviewed for this "Survey on the Quality of Community Life," and its voluminous data offer unique insights into the contemporary scene.

Never-married Americans expressed concern over employment uncertainty (unemployment was termed a "serious problem" by 43%, as compared with only 29% of the married respondents). They worried about crime in the cities ("getting worse," or so reported 76% of their number and 83% of the married group). They worried about living alone, and about their vulnerability to criminal harm (36% reported keeping a gun in their place of residence, though far more, or 56%, of the married group did likewise). And they complained about various urban discontents (67% judged local traffic congestion a problem; 64%, lack of interesting things to do; 61%, lack of parks; 57%, air pollution; 55%, dirty streets and sidewalks; 52%, noise; and 49%, fires . . . in numbers seldom matched by the married group).

Consistent with their residence discontent, the singles expected to move more often than did their home-buying married counterparts (27%, versus 12%, thought they would move within two years). Ironically, the singles who expected to move identified a large city as their probable next place of residence (53%, versus 43% of the married respondents), despite the various discontents that seem inherent in their city living experience. When asked by Harris pollsters what was going "downhill" in the American city, the singles spotlighted housing (47%), shopping (32%), job opportunities (28%), and social activities (18%), a list quite different from that of more settled and less disaffected married types. These discontents seemed to be linked to economic need, along with the struggle that the singles make to expand and improve their social network.

If we look into the well-being of singles in still more detail, never-married women in their 20s rated themselves happier than did single men. Female discontent, however, grew after age 30 or so, a change seemingly linked to the approaching end of the years of relatively safe childbearing and fertility. The social life options of the over-30 single female also seemed to decline, as males of the same age commonly marry or begin to date younger women. Never-married middle-aged women may begin to doubt their own sex appeal, personal worth, and capacity to be any happier than a grim "spinsterhood" will permit when faced with the media image of married women: happy, sexy, and desirable. Sociologist Jonathan Freedman (1978) concluded from considerable survey data that "a single female over 35 to 40 has a hard time finding happiness in our society" (p. 81).

Never-married males, in turn, appear to experience their singlehood in a smoother, less change-marked fashion. For one thing, they can become fathers from puberty through old age. For another, as they reach middle age, they can date younger females with impunity (though a woman of the same age behaving in the same way may be censured as indecent). Above all, society seems to more easily accept older single males:

They are not seen as pathetic, lonely creatures; they are not dried-up spinsters (indeed, there is no comparable word for men). They are "confirmed bachelors" who are often envied by married men . . . our society incessantly bombards us with the notion older men are interesting and distinguished while older women are simply old. (Freedman, 1978, p. 80)

Being never-married, in short, may be somewhat easier for males than for females in our culture, though the new social and cultural climate being promoted by assertive, "liberated" females may soon secure more equity in positive well-being for singles of both genders.

Race also influences the well-being of never-married adults, and black Americans are apparently less satisfied with singlehood than whites (see Table 4). Discontent here seems to be connected with a disparity in personal attainment by gender that discourages males from seeking the consent of females to marriage (black males commonly have less schooling and lower earnings than do

Table 4. Never-Marrieds: Attitudes, by Race[a]

| | Rating of general happiness (percentages) | | |
	Very happy	Pretty happy	Not too happy
Whites	23	67	11
Nonwhites	12	63	25

| | Rating of life (percentages) | | |
	Exciting	Routine	Dull
Whites	57	40	3
Nonwhites	40	53	7

[a]From NORC (1972–1978).

black females, and, at least among the black middle class, "a troublesome singlehood is preferred to a compromise of standards for a mate," Staples, 1981, p. 41).

Where the variable of income is concerned, the NORC 1972–1978 survey makes clear a positive relationship: Regardless of race, sex, or age, the higher the income level, the greater the self-reported well-being (NORC, 1979). This finding, of course, may explain part of the appeal to singles of the "living-together" relationship, a form of family life that doubled in size between the 1970 Census and the 1980 Census, and that allows two unwed adults to share their dual incomes.

Never-Married and Married Americans: Comparative Well-Being

Given the diversity now apparent in the ranks of 31 million singles (by type of single—ambivalent, wishful, resolved, and regretful—along with further variation by sex, race, and income), any general comparison of never-married with their married counterparts must be regarded with considerable caution. As evident in Table 5, married people claim to be much happier than all four types of singles: "When asked how happy they have been over the past six months, the past ten years, and how happy they expect to be in the future, married people say they are happier on all measures than single people. On practically every question that has been asked in a great many different studies on love, sex, life, sense of recognition, personal growth, job, and so on—the same pattern of responses emerges." (Freedman, 1978, p. 49)

Although the relationship above has been accepted for years, several researchers are now beginning to question such long-established findings. Martin Hamburger, for one, urged a fresh approach:

In the old epidemiological studies, the single people were considered inadequate to begin with. Those were the days when everyone who was anyone gets married. If you didn't, it was because you were an emotional isolate, or you were in poor health. The single people were the leftovers, the ones who

Table 5. Single and Married Adults: Happiness Data[a]

	"Very happy" and "pretty happy" (percentages)
Singles	84
Widowed	72
Separated	75
Divorced	84
Never-married	87
Married	91

[a]From NORC (1972–1978).

couldn't *marry. Today we have an altogether different breed of singles—people who* choose *singlehood. . . . So it's time to question the gross statistics about the mental health of the single.* (Wolfe, 1982, p. 33)

Comparisons, in short, between *types* of never-marrieds and *types* of married Americans (matched for style of life, sex, race, age, income, and similarly revealing variables) continue to elude the careful and refined attention that the subject merits.

What few new data exist offer encouraging news for singles. A major study now suggests that when singles do suffer mental depression they recover just as rapidly as do married people, and that they experience no greater rate of relapse into depression than do those living in a state of married bliss: "It may be that it's better, if you're depressed, to be in no relationship than it is to be enmeshed in a bad one" (Keller, in Wolfe, 1982, p. 33).

Never-Married Americans: Coping Mechanisms

The third of this essay's five major questions asks: What sort of tactics and tools do singles employ on their own behalf?

To understanding coping mechanisms here is to keep in mind certain revealing characteristics of the 1972–1978 NORC and 1978 Harris samples: The never-married respondents were youthful, well educated, and generally satisfied with life and selected aspects of their own situation (friendships, financial condition, and personal health). On the other hand, however, many were cautious, or even caustic, about the motives of other people, and an air of hard-boiled defensiveness, an attitude of wary protectiveness, came through their survey responses about life in general. Overall, they appeared somewhat less ebullient and optimistic than their admirers might wish, though hardly as morose and hapless as suggested by their detractors.

Not surprisingly, these adults have evolved numerous and diverse coping mechanisms. They appear to rely on six major aids, three of a more traditional approach (per-

missive social attitudes, same-sex friendships, and marriage-deriding attitudes) and three of a more recent character (assertive social attitudes, dating aids, and prosinglehood options).

Permissive Social Attitudes

To rely again on the 1972–1978 NORC survey data, employed never-married Americans claimed to hold rather permissive views on many controversial social matters, views that not surprisingly backed a freewheeling, risk-taking style of life popularly associated with "sowing one's wild oats." Unlike the general public, for example, a majority of the singles (52%) thought that the use of marijuana should be legalized. Similarly, where homosexuality was concerned, 43% declined to judge it "always" or "almost always wrong," a liberal position similarly taken by as many as 30% in the case of adultery.

Additional light is shed here by a 1976–1977 Harris poll commissioned by *Playboy Magazine*, a survey that separated 684 never-married men into four blocs, according to their acceptance of new attitudes and behavioral options:

Traditionalists *are defenders of the past, men who are deeply committed to time-honored values. They rally round what is secure and familiar, persisting in old allegiances and finding little value in new alternatives.*

Conventionals *also prefer what is established and familiar; but, unlike Traditionalists, these men are more ready to consider new alternatives—after they have gained acceptance and approval by society in general.*

Contemporaries *prefer the new, but their inclination is tempered by a concern for continuity within the established order. Men in this category are usually fashionable but rarely* avantegarde.

Innovators *show a strong enthusiasm for what is new. Their preference is marked by a willingness to experiment with traditional forms. These men are not the inventors of new alternatives, but they are generally the first to try them out.* (Harris et al., 1979, p. 27)

Attitudes toward three selected social issues were used to help determine a respondent's designation, or his receptivity to change: (1) decriminalization of "victimless" crimes, such as smoking marijuana, using the services of a prostitute, or gambling with any but state agencies; (2) attitude toward sexual relations outside marriage; and (3) attitude toward changes in the status of women, such as the respondent's readiness to accept the appointment of a woman as his new boss or supervisor at work. To be designated a *traditionalist,* a respondent had to oppose all three items; a *conventionalist* had to oppose two items; a *contemporary* had to approve of any two of the three; and an *innovator* had to approve of all three items.

When the resulting designations of 684 never-married men were combined with those from a separate sample of 108 divorced, separated, or widowed men, and with answers from a third sample of 1,195 married men, the total

Table 6. Male Attitudinal Styles (Percentages)[a]

Type	All males	Never-married		Married		Postmarried	
		% of NM	% of type	% of M	% of type	% of PM	% of type
Traditionalist	23	13	20	29	76	17	4
Conventional	27	23	29	30	66	23	5
Contemporary	25	29	40	23	55	23	5
Innovator	25	35	48	18	44	27	8
N = 1,990		684		1,198		108	

[a]From Harris *et al.*, 1979.

sample of 1,990 male respondents divided fairly evenly. But when the men were reclassified according to their marital status, the permissive social attitudes of the never-married males clearly stood out (see Table 6). Almost twice as many of the never-married as of the married males were designated *innovators,* the most liberal of the four possibilities, and less than half as many singles as married men were labeled *conservative traditionalists.*

Single women have been similarly profiled in the sparse and uneven research data of direct relevance here. The 1980 Virginia Slims American Women's Opinion Poll, for example, shed helpful light on several attitudinal dimensions (Roper, 1980). To draw cautiously from the incomplete data in Table 7, never-married women stand out, as did their male counterparts in the NORC and Harris polls, in their comparative permissiveness, liberality, and acceptance of change.

Lacking the clarity of widely acclaimed success models or the support of society as a whole, singles appear to shape their lives by daring to take risks and forging into uncharted territory. Highly adaptive pioneers of cosmopolitan cultural lifestyles, singles decline to censor the controversial private acts of any "consenting adults," even though demonstrating considerable approval of controversial social developments (e.g., gains for women and the private use of "soft" drugs) of clear relevance to their own experimenting lifestyles.

Same Sex Friendships

Much of the popular literature on singles highlights the toll that can be taken by loneliness. Typical examples include these two excerpts from fairly bleak accounts:

There are many single women [at this downtown discotheque], and as the night wears on, their aloof, sophisticated demeanor is betrayed by their eyes, eyes that bespeak sadness, hunger and, in some cases, despair. Among the women over 30, the ravages of loneliness have left scars; their faces are hard and sour, with

Table 7. Female Survey Answers (Percentages)[a]

1980 Issues	All females	Never-married	Married	Postmarried (divorced/separated)[b]
1. Favor most of the efforts to strengthen and change women's status in society today.	(3,007)	(304)	(2,015)	(301)
	64	75	64	75
2. Prefer the *Ms.* form of address.	16	32	12	38
3. More advantages in being a woman than a man.	9	12	9	7
4. If you were free to work or stay home and care for a house and family, would you prefer to go to work?	46	73	41	63
5. Premarital sex is not necessarily immoral.	46	61	ND[c]	57
6. The new morality makes for more honest relationships.	45	48	ND	ND
7. The new morality makes for better marital choices.	42	48	ND	ND
8. The new morality ultimately makes for better marriages.	36	40	ND	ND
9. Approve of single, married parents.	45	55	ND	ND

[a]From Roper Polling Organization, *The 1980 Virginia Slims American Women's Poll*, 1980.
[b]Data from 340 widowed respondents were excluded from this table.
[c]ND = no data.

lines of worry etched indelibly in their brows; the corners of their mouths turned down permanently. (Carney, 1980, p. 14)

Loneliness is the most-often cited consequence of singleness and, as one man who moved back home put it, the stress of "silence.". . . It is not uncommon for singles who live alone to go from five in the evening till the next morning at work without face-to-face contact with anyone. (Barkas, 1980, p. 148)

Coping with this challenge often entails making several close friends of the same sex and developing a strong support network of such friends as a self-conscious antidote for the loneliness and silence that otherwise threaten.

A circle of girlfriends, a weekly group of card players, a "reserved" barstool with fellow "elbow benders" at a neighborhood "watering hole"—all these are the sort of same-sex alliances used by singles across the country to help secure a satisfactory social life. By associating with other never-married adults of the same sex, they can swap anecdotes about the dating game, trade "war stories" from the battle of the sexes, offer the precious gift of emotional "stroking" to one another, listen with a non-judgmental air to each other, counsel in a selfless and judicious way, and bolster morale with the sharing of common perceptions of the opposite sex, the ways of life and love, and the risks and gains of singlehood versus marriage.

Ties of friendship forged in this way can course deep, though some of the men may wonder at times—as in the movie classic *Marty*—if the bonhomie masks a poignant failure of nerve:

Hanging out with the boys used to be an end in itself; now, as an adult, it . . . often seems like an evasive maneuver—willed amnesia. It's an evasion of the responsibilities of adulthood: specifically, the problems of relating—emotionally and sexually—to women. (Rainer, 1980, p. 136)

Still other singles, however, are likely to have few such doubts, and trust instead to the warmth and security of same-sex fellowship for much that is vital in life. Indeed, of these well-connected singles, another writer has noted, this time quite approvingly, that "same-sex friends are not abandoned—or appointments cancelled—because a romantic prospect suddenly appears" (Barkas, 1980, p. 138). Same-sex friendships, in short, occupy a critical role in explaining the happiness, worldliness, and tenure of the single experience of many never-married adults—for better and for worse.

Marriage-Deriding Attitudes

Not surprisingly, some singles deride marriage to help justify their own unwed state of affairs. To hear them talk, there are few marriages that are not bad ones, and the single life is therefore preferable to an unfulfilling matrimonial union. (Ironically, many married people "idealize singleness. It is a fantasy that they need to cling to." Barkas, 1980, p. 15). Fanned by the counterculture propagation of antimarriage views in the turbulent 1960s and early 1970s, the jibes that some singles aim at marriage

help to keep them persuaded that they are well off—at least in comparison to their hapless married peers.

Quick to refer to high divorce statistics, horror tales of bitter battles over alimony or child support, spouse abuse, and occasional cases of spouse murder, those singles who want to castigate matrimony do not seem to lack material. Others take a less direct tack and deride marriage as an unromantic choice made largely under economic duress. Above all, detractors insist that they themselves cannot trust marriage, even if it seems to work for others, as marriage constricts their personal growth, change, and freedom (Shapiro, 1980). Stereotyped as a poor risk, marriage is maligned as an enemy of individualism and personal "space"—all the better to bolster the commitment of the unmarried critic to a sustainable and sustaining singlehood.

Assertive Attitudes

Typical of this relatively new coping option is the assertion that marriage is no longer necessary for its traditional lure, or the exclusive right of respectable parenthood. Instead, many singles note the end of legal sanctions against out-of-wedlock offspring, the relaxation of cultural attacks on bastardy, and the emergence of institutional supports, such as affordable nursery and preschool care for infants being raised by (unwed) parents.

Some singles, a well-publicized few, go so far as to advertise in the counterculture media for another single with whom to conceive a child out of wedlock. This especially defiant move understandably exasperates members of the Moral Majority and others who believe the marriage unit the *only* appropriate setting for parenthood. Singles, however, feel increasingly free to reassess such time-honored claims to exclusive privilege and weigh instead an option untenable as recently as two or three decades ago.

A second relatively new assertion focuses on the drawbacks of having any children whatsoever. Singles who feel a need to defend their nonparenting role may stockpile media items on the various drawbacks of parenting, for example:

A poll in 1978 of 50,000 parents allegedly established that as many as 70 percent would not have children were they to live their lives over again. (Vivano, 1980, p. 44)

A study in 1980 estimated that the costs to middle-class parents of rearing a baby to age 18 would reach $85,000. When the "lost earnings" of a mother who reduced her job hours to help raise the children were added in, the figure climbed to nearly $140,000 (where the mother had completed college). As well the costs rose about 30 percent from 1977 to 1980. Another study conducted in 1981 raised the $85,000 estimate to $134,000, based on an expectation of a constant 8 percent inflation rate over the lifetime of the 18-year-old. (Elson, 1980, p. 18)

Singles who take this stance raise the hackles of many pronatal Americans, though their nonparenthood argument can get a sympathetic hearing from the 82% of American women who told a pollster in 1980 that having children was not essential for a full and happy marriage (Roper, 1980). Opposition to becoming a parent, in short, gains increasing acceptability—although the position still goes against the cultural grain.

Lest the misimpression be created that the coping mechanism of assertive attitudes pivots on natalist issues alone, a very different topic like tenants' rights can be used to illustrate the remarkable range here of coping assertions seldom, if ever before, raised by never-married Americans.

Singles have faced landlord bans against renting to never-married applicants. However, some of these would-be tenants have begun to sense both their growing numbers and their potential collective power in the housing market:

Within this decade, according to a 1980 report of the MIT-Harvard Joint Center for Urban Studies, only 50 percent of households will be headed by married couples—compared to 80 percent in 1950. People will spend more years living alone or with roommates or partners. They will increasingly delay marriage, divorce more, remarry more slowly. (Pierce, 1980, p. 5)

Slowly and hesitantly, a militant tenants' movement has been struggling to emerge across the nation, spurred along by young adults from middle-class homes who refuse to accept the powerlessness and insecurity inherent in renting: "Their frustrations have triggered this new round of tenant activism—and account for much of its success" (Atlas & Dreier, 1980, p. A-27). Singles are conspicuous in the leadership of the various tenant groups, and they assert thereby a novel and a feisty claim to "tenants' rights"—a dramatic new frontier on which to struggle to clarify both their prerogatives *and* their responsibilities.

One final example of a controversial assertive attitude valuable in coping with life's vicissitudes is known as the *new celibacy* (Brown, 1980). Devotees make what they consider a good case for celibacy by choice rather than by default, and they insist that they *can* enjoy abstention from sex. (Critics, however, challenge them to ask: "Did it ever bother you that you felt bored and drained by sex? Did it ever occur to you that there might be something wrong with you, or with the relationship?" Levine, 1980, p. 35). Given well-publicized difficulties in efforts made by singles to achieve a satisfactory sex life, the coping technique of "taking a vacation" from sexual relations is likely to remain topical—and widely disputed—for years to come.

Dating Aids

Forcing oneself to search for new romantic friends tries the coping abilities of many singles to the fullest:

It takes energy and confidence to constantly put your best foot forward, maneuver through a social occasion or manage the silly and the scary parts of opening up to someone else. It can be tiring to have a love life that wobbles between feast and famine. (Lowe, 1977, p. 86)

Accordingly, the nation's singles have begun to draw on a wider range of dating aids than ever previously available, for example, computer dating services, specialized singles' clubs, singles' bars, singles' apartment complexes, and singles' magazines.

Barkas (1980), relying on in-depth interviews with 200 singles (previously married as well as never-marrieds), has arranged their coping options in the order of decreasing frequency shown in Table 8. Later in her 1980 volume, Barkas observed that the majority of disgruntled singles believed they lacked opportunities to meet eligible dating partners, whereas those who were far happier being single felt that such opportunities were absolutely there but were not always taken advantage of.

Each of the new dating aids has its own distinctive strengths and weaknesses, of course, along with an aura of strategic appropriateness, for example:

One of the perils of being a single woman, I used to complain, is that well-meaning married friends seem to think it's their duty to help you find a mate . . . those of us who have never been wed are reminded that we're not getting any younger. For years I resented and resisted their warnings and pleas—blind dates were for losers, I said, not for me. . . . Still, on the whole, I'd recommend blind dating. It's fun and exciting and reminds me of a lottery—you never know, you may be lucky. (Shocket, 1980, p. 10)

People are so afraid [in a singles bar] of being rejected that they become unnaturally guarded. You put yourself in a position where you give every man permission to approach, but then when men you consider unacceptable come, you quickly brush them off. Men who've been rebuffed a lot then try to be first to reject. The result is that everybody in this milieu develops a defensive stance. (Schwartz, 1981, p. 203)

Singles events and organizations are fine . . . but, I have found it's better to try to meet someone engaging in an activity you enjoy. Go to the public library and take a look at the Encyclopedia of Associations. Every group you can imagine is listed there, even a bowling association for truck drivers. Find which ones hold public meetings, and go. Who knows? You might meet a bowling truck driver you really like. (West, 1982, p. 29)

Table 8. Mechanisms for Meeting Dates[a]

Most frequent	Less frequent	Least frequent
Through a friend	Blind dates	Professional intro-
At parties	Singles' bars	duction
Through a hobby	Bars	services
or interest	Any kind of social	Video dating ser-
Through school or	or community	vices
work	function	Call girls or pros-
Talking to a	Joining a health	titutes
stranger	club	Singles' resorts
	Answering or plac-	Singles' clubs
	ing an ad	

[a]From Barkas (1980).

The Georgetown Connection is one of about a dozen of so-called videodating services around the country, all operating on the principle that viewing a videotape of a potential date is far less risky than a blind date or even a computer-matched date. . . . The clientele join to shortcut the often time-consuming social routes to romance and to meet people they wouldn't ordinarily come across in their daily lives. (Larson, 1980, p. 1)

Expensive, at fees of about $300 for men and perhaps $250 for women in 1980, video dating services are typical of singles-oriented options with "high-tech" allure, social class exclusivity, and a seeming ability to help "deliver the goods."

Comparatively staid singles, in turn, can choose from an ever-expanding list of highly specialized and sedate introduction clubs, as for booklovers, bird-watchers, politically concerned types, epicureans, opera fans, and chess enthusiasts:

Co-Founder, Singles Book Club: *We don't take everyone who wants to be a member. We want cultivated, single people, and we only advertise in publications like* Saturday Review, Psychology Today, Friends Journal, The Nation, The New Republic, *and the* New York Review of Books. . . . *People have a bad image of singles groups; they think of members as losers. But our members aren't like that. They want something better from life, and you can't go to a bar for that.* (Sachs, 1981, p. A-12)

Whereas some singles, in short, find locales like that of the exotic and unabashedly hedonistic "Club Med" made to order, others snub its likes in favor of a more low-keyed and cerebral type of meeting ground.

The diversity in these coping options is quite remarkable, as indicated by the contents of a typical issue of a typical singles' guidebook (the Westchester, New York, *Datebook,* November 1980): A reader is treated to a day-by-day calendar of hundreds of events and activities, including country club parties (singles only), cash admission; "perfume mixer" parties at private homes, both sexes invited ("learn about fragrances, win prizes, have fun"); rap sessions for singles (sponsored by churches, mental health groups, and so on); hikes and backpack trips (singles only); rap sessions for single men only; lecture on "investment alternatives for the 1980s," singles only; coed volleyball; dialogue, "making a will"; lecture, speaker from Women Against Pornography; single "grape intro," wine and cheese party; Scorpio party, 21 plus, singles only; singles Bible study; rap session, "The Independent Women" (never-married support group); talk, discussion, "Turning Points: Critical Moments and Making the Most of Them"; tennis and Greek Festival party; film/discussion, "Images of Acting," "Lies My Father Told Me;" racquetball party; and candlelight gourmet dinner party (Expensive Professional Singles International). Scattered throughout the guidebook's 40 crowded pages are catchy and revealing ads from singles-oriented restaurants ("a great place to relax and unwind"), dance halls ("average attendance is 200"), travel agencies ("spectacular vacations for singles"), and dating services ("a dignified method of screening and searching for the qualities you want in a person, *prior to any meeting*").

Dating aids—especially the many "discreet personal ads" printed in the Westchester *Datebook* and in innumerable other such sources—reflect the centrality of the human search for intimacy, ease, and support. Barkas (1980), after interviewing singles for two years across the country, was drawn to observe:

I have found that almost all singles, no matter how content they are living alone, fantasize about someday having a special partner. . . . It did not matter how long a man or woman had been single. . . . Of course friends or work may compensate if a lover is unavailable, but that simply does not replace an intimate romantic relationship. (p. 172)

Fortunately, the new range of relatively novel dating aids offers considerable support for singles seeking relationships.

Prosingle Options

The last of the six coping tactics examined in this chapter involves the emergence in recent years of coed dorms, singles' educational and counseling services, and other such aids in the life of singles.

Coed Dorms, with the sexes nominally segregated by floors, wings, or suites, were introduced amidst much controversy in the early 1970s. Parents feared that this relaxation of *in loco parentis* might undermine student morality and invite promiscuity. Related liberal changes in curfew hours, dormitory rules, and off-campus norms concerning "overnight unchaperoned mixed company" were rooted, however, in broader social changes that included

a change in the status of women which makes it difficult to justify different regulations for men and for women, youth's increasing demand that they no longer be treated as children, a questioning of the rigid sexual mores which have traditionally governed people's lives, a greater willingness to grant individuals the right to select their own life-style, and the increasing availability of contraception and abortion services. (Macklin, 1981, p. 213)

Most college campuses now provide the option of residing in a structure that also houses persons of the opposite sex.

Hailed as far friendlier residences than single-sex dorms, these coed residences *may* be having an intriguing impact on personal lives:

In what only seems to be a paradox, proximity has put a damper on carnal passion and even on what used to be called "romance." . . . Living together, instead of promoting sexuality and sexual relations, has demythologized and demystified sex. . . . "Platonic," that good old-fashioned word, has come to describe the new connections between young men and women. (Gittleson, 1980, p. 14)

In support of this analysis, a 1980 survey of 543 singles residing in coed dorms found that nearly 85% dated only outside their own dorm, and 80% reported that coed living had made it easier for them to form nonsexual relationships with the opposite sex: "Co-ed dorms seem to have provided one of the main arenas for the important recognition that men and women can know one another in ways that are intimate, complex and fulfilling without being—necessarily—erotic" (Gittleson, 1980, p. 158).

Singles educational and counseling services are called for, in turn, by a rapid increase in the uncertainties inherent in new personal freedom. Helpful here is Macklin's study (1981) of 44 never-married college students who had lived with a lover for at least four nights a week for three consecutive months. She found three dominant areas of stress in these generally positive relationships: emotional problems, sexual problems, and problems with space. Barkas (1980), in turn, found unhappy singles characterized by special problems in being able to tolerate intimacy. Many seemed to her to need outside help to decide which situation actually was theirs: "a practical problem of not having found a suitable potential mate or a deeper problem of personal intolerance of closeness and its other side, separation" (p. 161).

Fortunately, the institutional response here has come to include the provision for singles, and for others, of a "hot line" for the use of despondent callers, as well as proliferation of self-help paperbacks focused on life improvement insights. Better still, it also includes custom-tailored experiential learning options:

Around the country, hundreds of discussion groups and workshops for singles are mapping out the space between the old image and the new. One such workshop, called "The Challenge of Being Single," has enjoyed a six-year run at the University of Southern California and other campuses across the country. Psychologist Marie Edwards, who leads the program has put the ideas and suggestions of workshop participants into a successful book by the same name. (Lowe, 1977, p. 86)

Singles living off a college campus can turn to counseling efforts run by groups like the National Association of Christian Singles or the Task Force of Jewish Singles of the Federation of Jewish Philanthropies. At the local level, sponsorship often comes from self-help support groups hosted by a "Y," a church, a synagogue, or the like.

Some of the gestures here break new ground, as in the 1979 series of Joyce Brothers's telephone messages (changed daily) on "how to make the single life the good life," along with the provision of computer software for home computer guidance to a more satisfying singlehood. Whether novel or more conventional, however, these coping options offer much to singles learning how to establish and develop a fulfilling relationship—regardless of the seeker's preference for remaining single or soon joining the married crowd.

Summary

Coping mechanisms for never-married Americans range far beyond the six major types briefly discussed above, of course, and a far lengthier review would include such frontier items as (1) advances in medical technology that make childbirth after 30 safer than ever before, and that thereby extend the range of the conception decision years for nonparents; (2) advances in contraception and abortion technologies; (3) advances in the legal protections afforded couples living together outside marriage, as in the ability to make contracts and wills; (4) advances in the public and legal attention to issues raised by the 1976 California "palimony" case ("The very fact that the Marvin case has been as widely publicized as it has been, in and of itself, may be said to change the nature of unmarried relationships in the future"—Mitchelson, 1979, p. 220); (5) advances in the norms governing the adoption process, whereby single males and females have been able—although in very few cases—to adopt a child as a single parent; (6) advances in the availability of no longer illicit recreation options (never-married Americans, for example, outdo the general public, 70% to 61%, in their resort to legalized gambling; (Michener, 1980); and (7) advances in the know-how necessary to make a success of "the new American commune—the polymorphic, multigenerational, economically sensible middle-class commune of the 1980s, [a response to the fact that] many singles want to come home to somebody at night" (Konigsburg, 1980, p. 56).

Even this partial list illustrates the remarkable turbulence in the contemporary singles' scene, as a broad array of forces—the singles industry, the helping professions, the medical and legal change-makers, and, most especially, never-married adults themselves—work in combination to strengthen the quality of life characteristic of single Americans.

Social Policy Options

Improvements are earnestly needed, as the record still leaves much to be desired where single well-being is concerned: "Severe loneliness appears to be unusual among married men, somewhat more prevalent among married women, and quite prevalent among the unmarried of both sexes" (Weiss, 1981, p. 161).

Overall, being without a spouse is more likely to result in depression when one is also enmeshed in a context of unrelenting strains, especially strains of an economic nature. It is apparent that single people withstand these conditions of hardship less well than do married people. (Pearlin & Johnson, 1979, p. 176)

Given this situation, it is hardly surprising that only 2% of 3,000 women and 2% of 1,000 men, in a representative 1980 poll (Roper, 1980), identified the state of being never-married as their choice for an ideal life (about 52% of both sexes opted instead for a modern marriage of shared responsibilities; the remainder preferred a more traditional marriage).

If the six major coping options previously discussed come to reward their adherents as fully as possible, and if the repute of singlehood gains substantially, certain key public policies must be altered—although this may prove a difficult matter. Never-married Americans need reforms in their roles as learners, as citizens, as renters, as cohabitators, as parents, as purchasers of "singles-only" services, and especially, as the subjects of social-science research attention.

As *learners*, singles confront the challenge of caring for themselves, entering the world of work, holding their own in the dating game, and, in many other overlapping ways, standing on their own for the first time in their lives. Unfortunately, few get any directly relevant preparation in their high-school education for this challenge. To be sure, a small number of progressive high schools accept responsibility and offer an elective course in "living-alone" skills for both sexes that covers such topics as research insights into single lifestyles; what to look for in signing a lease; how to design and maintain a nutritious personal diet; the features of natural and synthetic clothing materials; preparing and keeping to a budget; protecting oneself; seeking and keeping quality friendships; ways of relating well to parents and siblings; and guides to emotional and sexual well-being. Unfortunately, the "back-to-basics" focus and budget-cutting pressures felt in public education threaten this type of reform. Singles deserve more substantial educational preparation for the years they will spend as unwed young adults than their high schools currently offer, and school-board decision-makers need help in reconsidering just what is and isn't a "basic" lesson in the education of their graduates (Shostak, 1981).

As *citizens*, singles confront every stressor known to the nation's 240 million Americans, of course, but in one particular, their situation appears to be unique: Many are especially vulnerable as neophytes in the world of work. In the role of new entrants into the labor force, never-married females and nonwhites have gained much in recent years from controversial antidiscrimination laws and the government's fair-employment-practices agencies. These laws and agencies, however, have recently come under fire by "deregulation" enthusiasts, and singles who suspect workplace victimization because of non-job-related issues (such as gender, age, race, or marital status) may continue to want effective governmental help in these delicate and career-critical matters.

As *renters*, as young adults not yet ready to buy a home of their own, singles confront the challenge of recognizing, clarifying, claiming, and extending their rights as tenants. Some have been using chapters in 50 cities of the embryonic National Tenants Union to promote a "tenants' bill of rights" that includes

1. *Protection against arbitrary evictions even with "just cause," including evictions for condominium and cooperative conversions;*
2. *Tax credits for tenants, as the current regulations discriminate against them; and*
3. *Recognition of tenants as a legitimate constituency with its own concerns.* (Atlas & Dreier, 1980, p. A-27)

Singles can join with married renters in a sound alliance to compel tenant reforms from city councils, state legislatures, and the U.S. Congress—and can learn much from such tenant activism of value elsewhere in life.

As *cohabitors*, singles confront three unusual policy stressors. For one, the antiabortion campaign threatens the continued availability of legal, confidential, safe, and economical abortion services. For another, contradictory rulings issued by various state courts since California's 1979 "palimony" case (*Marvin v. Marvin*) raise serious questions about the rights of "living-together" parties. And finally, certain never-married adults are nettled by censorship attacks aimed at commercial sources of erotic sexual stimulation (e.g., massage parlors, porno book shops, "XXX" movie houses, and male striptease dancers) and oppose any social-policy shifts aimed at impeding the right of access by overage "consenting" adults.

As *purchasers of "singles-only" services*, never-married Americans confront an absence of adequate consumer education and consumer protection measures. Typical are the problems encountered with computer dating services since their introduction in 1965. The early years were marred by the employment of high-powered, commission-hungry salespeople and by the related use of preposterous claims about potential matches. Media exposure and costly, lengthy, bothersome, and embarrassing legal suits were required to achieve the toning down of much of this "hype."

Singles as potential buyers, however, are still uninformed about two fundamental weaknesses: The matches can be only as good as the subscribers in the company's "talent bank" itself, and the computer matchup process can be only as good as the quantity and quality of attributes explored in the basic questionnaire. (An evaluation of the business in 1980 came away vastly unimpressed: "If the two problems of image and poor questionnaires are not solved, computer dating is likely to remain an insignificant force in the dating and mating of the public"—Rodgers, 1981, p. 8).

Consumer education services, including fair-minded TV, newspaper, and magazine coverage, are needed if never-married Americans are to minimize their marketplace gullibility to the $40-billion-a-year singles industry (Barkas, 1980):

> Singles may not yet look or act as childish as they're drawn, but they are as vulnerable as children, and the singles hustlers appreciate this. . . . they know their market, know that loneliness will prevail over dignity every time, and that even the most sensible people in the world will eventually crawl for company, if necessary. (Rosenblatt, 1979, p. 14)

Perhaps, but if the singles are to have a fighting chance here, social policies *could* be strengthened on behalf of consumer rights (e.g., new legal protections and enforcement staff) and against the rapacious designs of the singles hustlers.

Finally, in their role as *subjects of social-science research attention*, never-married Americans are owed much more field research than they have ever received. The list of significant questions still unanswered about singles is dismaying in the extreme; for example:

1. How do ambivalents, wishfuls, resolveds, and regretfuls *really* differ from and resemble one
   another?
2. How does the singles' life differ in various regions
   (e.g., the Sunbelt, the Frostbelt, and the "mellow"
   West)?
3. How do singles of various ethnic, religious, and
   racial backgrounds create different singlehood experiences for themselves?
4. How many singles seem to thrive on the experience
   or appear discontent? How are their numbers
   changing over time?
5. How does media coverage influence the singles experience, for example, in TV sitcom and "soap
   opera" stereotypes?
6. How might we apply some sort of cost–benefit
   analysis to the existence of the single way of life and
   assess its significance for the larger community?

Not surprisingly, our current understanding of never-
married Americans remains weakened by unsettled controversy and data-starved questions: Adams (1976) is
enthusiastic about the likelihood that "some single individuals (not necessarily all) will develop heightened skill
in adapting to the shifting trends and rapidly changing
exigencies of present-day society as well as being sensitive barometers to vital currents of the future" (p. 132).
Barkas (1980), however, represents the unattached singles whom she interviewed as unable to read situations
accurately, and as lacking in self-reliance. Schaffer
(1980) thinks "we might optimistically predict
that . . . it will no longer be assumed that marriage is a
necessary requirement for mental health for either women
or men" (p. 201). Bronfenbrenner, however, views an
increase in the numbers of unwed adults as a "danger
sign," a part of the unraveling of American society, for
"with people who live alone, a lot of the skills people
learn from living together don't get learned" (Reinhold,
1977, p. 4). Until research on singles becomes well established, the singles scene will remain far more contentious
and far less comprehensible than is good for never-married singles, or for any of us.

Summary

As recently as 1957, four out of five Americans stigmatized never-married individuals as neurotic, selfish, or
even immoral. By the mid-1970s, however, the detractors included only one in four citizens, a decline of 55
percentage points in only 20 years. Similarly, whereas in
1957 only one in five Americans thought the single life
just about as good (and bad) as married life, that figure
rose to over 60% by 1976 (Tarshis, 1981). And finally, an
18-year intergenerational study of 916 families in the Detroit area, plus data from several national studies, has led
two researchers to conclude that *both* young people and
their parents see the single life as a legitimate alternative
to marriage, and most do not disapprove of somebody
who chooses not to marry (Thorton & Freedman, 1982).

Further relaxation of prejudice in this matter hinges on
four types of progress: For one thing, social scientists
must continue to refine their grasp of the ratio, the dynamics, and the significance of key types among never-marrieds (ambivalents, wishfuls, resolveds, and regretfuls).
For another, proud singles must speak out and defend
themselves, as in this excerpt from a "letter to the editor"
penned by a never-married 30-year-old female. After
reading a sensationalized journalistic essay about lustful,
bar-hopping singles, she fired back her insistence that

*What so few [of the married crowd] realize is that many of us
simply are not the "swinging singles" created by the media, nor
are we society's lonely misfits, old maids, awkward bachelors,
gays or bookish bores. . . . thousands of us love our work, enjoy
our friends and our solitudes, and don't give a damn about
scoring or settling down because that's what's "normal."*
(Ciciola, 1979, p. 30)

Third, the quality of singlehood may especially turn on
how singles elect to relate to one another:

*Knowing what we've come to know, we surely are bound to
behave toward one another with a certain kindness, civility, and
tact, to ease one another's passage through this changeable and
occasionally brutal world with consideration and gentleness—
just plain common decency, not to put too fine a point on it.*
(Schickel, 1981, p. X)

Finally, progress here may require unprecedented efforts
by never-married Americans to win reforms in key public
policies and private market controversies.

As these four campaigns are successful, and as we
steadily gain more sociological research, stronger sin-
gles-initiated retorts, more common decency, and more
prosingle reforms, we will help assure a worthy maturity
in the unapologetic status of being never-married.

ACKNOWLEDGMENTS

An exceedingly helpful reading of the first draft of this
essay by a pioneering specialist, Peter J. Stein, went far in
guiding this version, as did also advice from a Drexel
University colleague, Professor Doreen Steg, and from
four of my undergraduate students (Michael Agovino,
Elizabeth Bond, Michelle Grossman, and Elizabeth
Schneider), all of whom have my sincere appreciation.
Mr. Michael Halperin of the Drexel University Library
staff competently conducted the computer-based analysis
of the NORC General Social Survey data and continues
even now to help me carry this line of research forward.

References

Adams, M. *Single blessedness: Observations on the single status in mar-
ried society.* New York: Basic Books, 1976.
Atlas, J., & Dreier, P. Tenants' new clout. *New York Times* (October 23,
1980), A-27.
Barkas, J. L. *Single in America.* New York: Atheneum, 1980.
Brown, G. *The new celibacy.* New York: McGraw-Hill, 1980.
Carey, A. The sad flight of single women. *Today* (November 30, 1980),
14.

Ciciola, G. The single's scene as seen by a single. *Today* (February 25, 1979), 30.

Date Book Publications, Inc. *Datebook*. Pleasantville, N.Y.: Date Book Publications, 1981.

Doudna, C., & McBride, F. Where are the men for the women at the top? In P. J. Stein (Ed.), *Single life: Unmarried adults in social context*. New York: St. Martin's Press, 1981.

Elson, M. Parents take note: Cost to raise a child: $85,000. *Chicago Tribune* (October 3, 1980), 1, 18.

Feinsilber, M., & Mead, W. B. *American averages: Amazing facts of everyday life*. New York: Doubleday, 1980.

Freedman, J. L. Love and marriage = happiness (still). *Public Opinion* (November–December 1978), 49–53.

Gittleson, N. Co-ed dorms. *McCall's* (September 1980), 14.

Glick, P. C., & Spainer, G. B. Cohabitation in the United States. In P. J. Stein (Ed.), *Single life: Unmarried adults in social context*. New York: St. Martin's Press, 1981.

Harris, L., *et al. The Playboy report on American men*. Chicago: Playboy Enterprises, 1979.

Konigsburg, D. If rent is killing you, and loneliness is a major problem, think about a commune. *Next* (November–December 1980), 56.

Larson, E. Look out, Redford: Our man is bursting onto singles scene. *Wall Street Journal* (July 29, 1980), 1.

Levine, J. Lust bust. *Village Voice* (July 30–August 5, 1980), 35.

Lowe, W. The single experience. *The Graduate* (1977), 86.

Macklin, E. D. Cohabiting college students. In P. J. Stein (Ed.), *Single life: Unmarried adults in social context*. New York: St. Martin's Press, 1981.

Michener, J. A. The quality of American life and the statistical abstract. In N. Cousins (Ed.), *Reflections of America: Commemorating the statistical abstract centennial*. Washington, D.C.: Government Printing Office, 1980.

Mitchelson, M. M. *Made in heaven, settled in court*. New York: Warner, Brooks, 1979.

National Opinion Research Center. *Codebook for the general social survey, 1972–1978*. Chicago: Author, 1979.

Norback, C. (Ed.). *The complete book of American surveys*. New York: New American Library, 1980.

Pearlin, L., & Johnson, J. S. Marital status, life-strains, and depression. In I. Hanson Frieze *et al.*, (Eds.), *New approaches to social problems*. San Francisco: Jossey-Bass, 1979.

Pierce, N. R. City census news isn't all bad: Fewer people, but more households. *Pittsburgh Post-Gazette* (September 8, 1980), 5.

Rainer, P. His. *Mademoiselle* (April 1980), 136.

Ramey, J. The advantages of being single. *Forum* (1979), unpaged.

Reinhold, R. Young people living alone: New trend in U.S. *Chicago Tribune* (April 3, 1977), 4.

Rodgers, N. N. *Computer dating*. Unpublished MBA term paper, Drexel University, Philadelphia, 1981.

Roper Polling Organization. *The 1980 Virginia Slims American Women's Poll*. Storrs, Conn.: Author, 1980.

Rosenblatt, R. The self as sybarite. *Harper's* (March 1979), 14.

Rubin, L. B. *Women of a certain age*. New York: Harper Colophon, 1981.

Sachs, S. Singles club books dates for readers. *Pittsburg Press* (January 16, 1981), A-12.

Schaffer, K. F. *Sex-role issues in mental health*. Reading, Mass.: Addison-Wesley, 1980.

Schickel, R. *Singled out: A civilized guide to sex and sensibility for the suddenly single man—or woman*. New York: Viking Press, 1981.

Schwartz, P., in Houck, C. Women in the social sciences. *Cosmopolitan* (January, 1981), 203.

Shapiro, J. How to be happy-alone-in the world's most romantic city. *Mademoiselle* (April 1980), 109.

Shocket, K. Why I'll never get used to blind dates. *Ladies' Home Journal* (February 7, 1980), 10.

Shostak, A. B. Abortion as fatherhood lost: Problems and reforms. *The Family Coordinator* (October 1979), 569–574.

Shostak, A. B. Tomorrow's family reforms: Marriage course, marriage test, incorporated families, and sex selection mandate. *Journal of Marital and Family Therapy*, 1981 (October) 521–526.

Staples, R. Black singles in America. In P. J. Stein (Ed.), *Single life: Unmarried adults in social context*. New York: St. Martin's Press, 1981.

Stein, P. J. (Ed.), *Single life: Unmarried adults in social context*. New York: St. Martin's Press, 1981. (a)

Stein, P. J. Understanding single adulthood. In P. J. Stein (Ed.), *Single life: Unmarried adults in social context*. New York: St. Martin's Press, 1981. (b)

Tarshis, B. *The "average American" book*. New York: Mentor, 1981.

Thorton, A. & Freedman, D. Changing attitudes on singlehood. *Family Planning Perspective*, 1982 (November–December), *14*(6), 297–303.

U.S. Bureau of the Census. *Current population reports*. Washington, D.C. U.S. Government Printing Office, February, 1980, Table E-1.

Viviano, F. The new lost generation. *Working Papers* (September–October 1980), 44.

Weiss, R. S. The study of loneliness. In P. J. Stein (Ed.), *Single life: Unmarried adults in social context*. New York: St. Martin's Press, 1981.

West, R. Looking for love in so many places. *New York* (December 28–January 4, 1982), 24.

Wolfe, L. The good news. *New York* (December 28–January 4, 1982), 35.

CHAPTER 14

Voluntary Childlessness

Sharon K. Houseknecht

Introduction

What do we know about voluntary childlessness? For a decade now, there has been an accelerating accumulation of research on this topic, especially since 1975. That the proliferation of data has been fairly recent is indicated by the fact that only 10 of the 47 studies that were located for the purposes of this chapter were completed before 1975. As might be expected in the early stages of investigation, most of the research that has been done is either exploratory or descriptive. Although it has been invaluable in the generation of insights, the time has come to move beyond these initial steps in the research process.

In this chapter, the existing work on voluntary childlessness is reviewed. If progress is to be made, it is necessary at some point to assemble the various pieces of information in one place and to integrate them. In the process of categorizing and critiquing all of the methodologies and results, a wealth of insight stands to be gained.

The specific plan of this chapter reflects, for the most part, what has been done in the area. The study of voluntary childlessness has typically focused on five questions: (1) What are the trends and incidence of this phenomenon? (2) What are the statements of motive for remaining childless? (3) What are the correlates of voluntary childlessness? (4) What is involved in the decision to remain childless (who makes the decision, when is it made, what is the degree of commitment, and so on)? (5) How does society feel about voluntary childlessness, and how do the voluntarily childless cope with their deviant status?

A second objective of this work is to clearly define, both conceptually and operationally, what is meant by voluntary childlessness. These issues are considered at the very beginning of this chapter.

The last section summarizes and discusses methodological and theoretical issues that need to be taken into account in future studies of voluntary childlessness. In addition, ideas for future projects are contained throughout the essay. In sum, it is hoped that, by assembling and critiquing all of the research that has been done in the past, this chapter will represent progress and lead to future yields.

Defining Childlessness

Voluntary or Involuntary Childlessness

To what does the term *childlessness* refer? Simply stated, it denotes the absence of children. It is generally recognized, however, that there are several different types of childlessness. Most basic, perhaps, is the distinction between childlessness that is voluntary and childlessness that is involuntary. This distinction is based on motivation and questions whether the people who prefer no children are the same as those who cannot have them even though they want them. The majority of childless couples with fecundity impairments (63.5% or about 848,000) would like to have a baby but have diminished ability to do so because of certain medical, physical, or behavioral conditions (National Center for Health Statistics, 1980). The inability to be self-determining in a sphere where most people have been socialized to think they are self-determining is a factor with potentially negative consequences for the individuals involved. Because it is not clear how and to what extent the voluntarily childless differ from the involuntarily childless, researchers would do well to consider these two groups as separate entities for the purpose of analysis.

Permanent or Temporary Childlessness

In addition to the issue of choice, there are several other points to consider when defining voluntary childlessness. First, *future intent* must be ascertained. Even though an individual may identify himself or herself as childless at a given time, this may be a temporary state. Some people simply delay childbearing until some future time and so should not be confused with those who are permanently childless. In fact, the available evidence suggests that there are significant differences between them (Bram, 1978; den Bandt, 1980; Hamilton, 1976; Hoffman & Levant, 1980; Houseknecht, 1977a, 1978b; Polonko, 1978; Poston, 1976; Scott, 1979; Silka & Kiesler, 1977).

A second point to consider when defining voluntary

Sharon K. Houseknecht • Department of Sociology, Ohio State University, Columbus, OH 43210.

childlessness is degree of commitment. An expression of future intent does not imply anything about the intensity of feeling that is associated with that intent. For example, individuals may report a desire to remain childless but may indicate a fairly low level of certainty. Nason and Poloma (1976), in fact, suggested a fourfold typology of commitment: (1) the irrevocably committed; (2) the strongly committed; (3) the reasonably committed; and (4) the committed with reservations. The extent to which the uncertains differ from the more strongly resolved is unclear at present (Kiesler, 1977; Moore & Moorman, 1977). The point is that, in order to identify permanent childlessness, it is necessary to ascertain not only future intentions but also the degree of commitment to those intentions.

To summarize, it is the combination of choice and permanence that serves to distinguish voluntary childlessness from childlessness that is due to impaired fecundity, delayed childbearing, or uncertainty. Although researchers, in general, recognize the distinctions, they frequently lump the various types of childlessness together. This kind of gross categorization is especially typical of aggregate-level surveys that have been conducted in the past. The reason, of course, is that motivational information has not generally been available, particularly as secondary data sources have commonly been used. Unfortunately, a number of microlevel studies have also failed to distinguish among the various types of childlessness.

Early Articulators or Postponers

In addition to specifying different kinds of *childlessness,* it is also possible to designate different kinds of *voluntary childlessness.* In one of the first exploratory studies of deliberately childless wives, Veevers (1973b) suggested that there are two different types of people involved. One type expresses the intention to remain childless relatively early in life, even before marriage. The other type arrives at a childless decision through a series of postponements after marriage. These two types have been referred to as *early articulators* and *postponers,* respectively (Houseknecht, 1974, 1977a, 1979b).

Typologies such as this one are an important kind of conceptual model, useful in guiding research. Although they are tentative and limited, they are the building blocks of empirical discoveries (Theodorson & Theodorson, 1979). In fact, two studies so far have empirically investigated the different types of voluntary childlessness mentioned here. One compared young *early articulators* with young females who desired children (Houseknecht, 1977a; 1978), and the other explored the similarities and differences between *early articulators* and *postponers* (Houseknecht, 1979b). With these two exceptions, however, researchers have tended to consider voluntary childlessness a single phenomenon.

Operational Definitions of Voluntary Childlessness

Commonly Applied Criteria. In the remainder of this section, we will take an in-depth look at the way in which voluntary childlessness has been operationally defined in studies that have been conducted thus far. With few exceptions, it was ascertained either directly or indirectly (1) that there were no biological children at present; (2) that none were expected in the future; and (3) that it was an *intention* or *choice* not to have children. It is interesting that four studies (Goodbody, 1977; Jones, 1978; Marciano, 1978; Raphael, 1975) out of the six (Mommsen & Lund, 1977; Townes *et al.,* 1977) that do not mention the second and third criteria obtained their *voluntarily* childless respondents through the National Alliance for Optional Parenthood (NAOP). There seems to have been an assumption that, if one is either a member of this organization or an interested person, the childless state is both permanent and voluntary. This is an assumption that needs to be seriously questioned. It is conceivable that some persons would seek support for their childless state even though they are involuntarily childless. Also, can it be assumed that people have made a firm decision before becoming members of NAOP? Some might join because they are seeking additional information to help them in making a choice.

Important but Infrequently Applied Criteria. The fact that most of the studies did ask about the presence of biological children, future expectations, and choice confirms that permanence and choice are generally recognized by researchers as the essential components in the definition of voluntary childlessness. Unfortunately, these three measures alone are insufficient for determining permanence and choice. Table 1 presents some important but infrequently applied criteria that could be used in a supplementary sense to enhance validity. (It should be noted that precise operational definitions are not always reported, and so, in some instances, it is difficult to know whether the problem is due to incomplete description, faulty definitions, or both.)

Ruling Out Biological and Genetic Reasons. First, knowing that an individual intends to remain childless or has made a choice or decision to do so is necessary but insufficient information for determining that the childless state is voluntary. For example, it may be a genetic problem that results in the choice to remain childless. Also, some persons who recognize that they are unable to have children because of biological limitations may misinterpret the meaning of the word *intend* and may report that they do not intend to have children because they know that they cannot. For these reasons, an operational definition of voluntary childlessness should include the respondents' perceptions of their fecundity status and potential genetic problems.

Ruling Out Children Who Are Not One's "Own." A second point to consider when operationally defining vol-

**Table 1. Operational Definitions of Voluntary Childlessness in 47 Studies:
Some Important but Infrequently Applied Measures**

Study	Absence of biological or genetic reasons	Spouse: no previous children	No plans to adopt	Attitude certainty	Length of marriage requirement (years)	Age requirement	Currently married[j]
Baum & Cope (1980)		X			1		X
Bellman (1974)							Mixed
Benson & Hoover (1978)			X		1		X
Bram (1974)[a]	X				1	Over 21	X
Burnside (1977)					5[i]		X
Centers & Blumberg (1954)							?
Chalfant (1979)[b]					5		X
Cumber (1977)[c]	X				1	23–40	X
den Bandt (1980)					3	Under 35	X
Denniston (1978)							?
Dietz (1979)	X						Mixed
Fisher (1979)							?
Gil (1978)							?
Goodbody (1977)							X
Gustavus & Henley (1971)							X
Hall (1979)					1	18–44	X
Hamilton (1977)	?	?	?	?	?	?	?
Hersch (1974)							X
Hoffman & Levant (1980)				X	2	25–35	X
Hotz (1975)							X
Houseknect (1974)[d]				X			All single
Houseknecht (1977b)[e]	X	X	X	X	5[i]	25–40	X
Jones (1978)							?
Kaltreider & Margolis (1977)							Mixed
Levine (1978)		X			5		X
Lichtman (1976)							X
Lindenmayer et al. (1977)							Mixed
Magarick & Brown (1981)							X
Marciano (1978)							X
Marcks (1976)							X
McLaughlin et al. (1974)							Single compared with married
Mommsen & Lund (1977)	?	?	?	?	?	?	?
Nason & Poloma (1976)							X
Ory (1976)[f]				X			X
Polonko (1978)	X						X
Popenoe (1936)							X
Popenoe (1943)							X
Poston (1977)	X						X
Raphael (1975)							Mixed
Rebecca (1977)[g]	X				1	Over 21	X
Scott (1979)							Mixed
Silka & Kiesler (1977)						Under 30	X
Teicholz (1978)	X					25–35	X
Thoen (1977)		X					X
Toomey (1977)				X			Mixed
Veevers (1972)[h]	X	X			5[i]		X

(continued)

Table 1. (*Continued*)

Study	Absence of biological or genetic reasons	Spouse: no previous children	No plans to adopt	Attitude certainty	Length of marriage requirement (years)	Age requirement	Currently married[j]
Welds (1977)	?	?	?	?	?	?	Mixed

[a]Also applies to the paper by Bram (1978).
[b]Also applies to the paper by Heller, Tsai, and Chalfant (1979).
[c]Also applies to the paper by Cooper, Cumber, and Hartner (1978).
[d]Also applies to the papers by Houseknecht (1977a, 1978b).
[e]Also applies to the papers by Houseknecht (1978a, 1979a,c).
[f]Also applies to the paper by Ory (1978).
[g]This study is a follow-up of Bram's study (1974).
[h]Also applies to the papers by Veevers (1973a,b; 1975a,b).
[i]The requirement here was five years of marriage *or* surgical sterilization of at least one spouse for contraceptive purposes.
[j]*Mixed* indicates that there was no distinction made in the sample between married and unmarried respondents.

untary childlessness has to do with establishing that there are no children at the present time and that none are intended for the future. Questions in this regard need to be expanded to include more than the individual's own biological offspring. One spouse may have children from a previous marriage who live with the couple at least part time, or there may be plans to adopt children in the future. In either case, the lifestyle cannot be considered childless because there are children involved. It does not matter that they are not one's own children.

Ascertaining Attitude Certainty. A third improvement that needs to be made in the operational definition of voluntary childlessness pertains to the degree of commitment. One step in this regard is to include an attitude certainty measure, something that very few studies have done (Table 1). The purpose, of course, is to exclude people who express uncertainty even though they have stated a perference for a childless lifestyle. It is inconsistent to measure attitude certainty and still to count as voluntarily childless those persons who say that they are "extremely likely to change their minds" (Toomey, 1977). If, in fact, permanence is an important component of the definition of voluntary childlessness, then the *uncertains* need to be considered separately from the *voluntarily childless*. Likert response categories can be used effectively to make this determination.

Duration of Marriage Requirement. In addition to attitude certainty, there are other measures that can be used to help determine degree of commitment. For example, the longer a person has been married without having children or wanting them the greater would seem to be the commitment to a childless lifestyle. Table 1 shows that although one fourth (12) of the studies being reviewed here had a duration of marriage requirement, only a tenth of them (5) stipulated as much as five years (in some cases, only if one of the spouses had not been sterilized for contraceptive purposes, which is, of course, an extreme behavioral measure of commitment). Failure to

specify a length of marriage requirement or requiring just one or two years does not allow adequate time for the decision to evolve and for commitment to develop, particularly as the major route to voluntary childlessness is *delayed* childbearing after marriage (Houseknecht, 1979b,c).

Age Requirement. Age is still another criterion that can be used to provide greater assurance of commitment to the childless decision. If a woman is older and believes that she will remain voluntarily childless, the chances are greater that she will because she is getting closer to her final reproductive years. Unfortunately, only 15% of the studies being reviewed here (Table 1) stipulated a minimum age requirement, and even then, it was only 18 in one study (Hall, 1979) and 21 in another (Bram, 1974). For Silka and Kiesler (1977), it was simply "under 30." The benefits to be gained by instituting very low age requirements are highly questionable. Whatever they may be, however, it is almost certain that greater assurance of commitment is not one of them.

Additional Methodological Considerations in Sample Selection

A final consideration, marital status, does not pertain directly to the definition of voluntary childlessness but will still be considered in this section because it is a frequently used criterion in sample selection. As seen in Table 1, many of the studies being reviewed do require that the respondents be currently married. The intent here is not to suggest that all but the currently married be excluded from participation in studies but to stress the need to control for marital status. Accepting only the currently married is one way of achieving this control, but an even better way would be to consider all the different categories *separately*. Unfortunately, a large number of studies simply mix the various marital statuses together. This procedure represents a serious methodological limitation because it cannot be assumed that there are no differences between single, married, separated, divorced, and widowed persons. Very different situations characterize people in each of these various categories, and for this reason, an effort should be made to hold them constant.

A similar but less common problem in studies of voluntary childlessness involves accepting for participation persons who are past childbearing age, the assumption being that this criterion represents a measure of commitment. Individuals who fall into this category should be considered separately from those who are still capable of reproducing, as there is typically a wide gap in age between the two groups, a difference that has many implications.

In summary, researchers who study voluntary childlessness need to say exactly what they mean when they use this term. If progress is to be made, conceptualization and operational definitions are important. In general, voluntary childlessness is conceptualized in terms of choice and permanence. These two concepts, however, are not always measured with the same degree of accuracy. Very often, in fact, operational definitions fail to specify *adequately* the measurable counterparts that are represented by these concepts. A number of infrequently applied criteria are described in this section that could be used in a supplementary sense to enhance validity in this regard.

Childlessness: Incidence and Trends

What is the incidence of voluntary childlessness in the United States today? Has there been a steady increase in the phenomenon over the past several years? What does the demographic evidence suggest for the future? These are widely discussed questions to which there are no clear-cut answers. Most of the aggregate-level surveys that have been conducted in the past have not differentiated between childlessness that is voluntary and that which is involuntary. Despite the absence of motivational information, however, numerous attempts have been made to infer the trends and incidence of deliberate childlessness. In these instances, conclusions are frequently drawn in terms of *voluntary* childlessness even though the stated focus is *childlessness* in general (Grindstaff, 1976; Mattessich, 1979; Poston & Gotard, 1977). This point is intended as an observation and not as a criticism. Researchers must do the best they can with the data that are available. To say that direct evidence is lacking is not to say that estimates are necessarily whimsical. A comprehensive understanding of the broader social context and the changes that are taking place within it can provide a solid foundation on which to draw such inferences.

Incidence

In examining rates of childlessness, it is important to determine whether they refer to *actual* or *expected* fertility behavior. These are the two major modes of reporting

that are used by the U.S. Bureau of the Census. Actual childlessness simply means that no children have been born by the survey date. It includes women who are intending to have children at some future time as well as those who are either voluntarily or involuntarily childless. Expected childlessness, in contrast, encompasses only those women who are childless at the time of the survey and who report zero as the number of lifetime births that they expect. Postponers, then, are excluded in the calculation of expected childless rates as they intend to become mothers eventually. Of course, in the older age categories, the difference between *actual* and *expected* childlessness becomes minimal as the postponers are slowly weeded out as they fulfill their childbearing expectations.

A significant point here is that, in order to evaluate the current so-called high rate of childlessness, it is necessary to ascertain whether it is the actual or expected rate that is being described. The figures in Table 2 demonstrate that it would be quite misleading if one rate were erroneously substituted for the other. (These data, like the others in this section on incidence, are presented in terms of white women rather than all races because, even though black/white differentials in childlessness have converged over the past three decades, a significant gap still exists in all age categories; Grindstaff, 1976; U.S. Bureau of the Census, 1980b). It is apparent that expected childlessness, unlike actual childlessness, does not vary much by age. The major reason, of course, is that it does not include postponers. Furthermore, the overall expected rate has not varied much with time (U.S. Bureau of the Census, 1978b). For almost two decades now, it has not changed by more than a few percentage points. The range for wives 18–39 years old has been from about 3% to 6% (Table 3).

Once again, it must be emphasized that the expected childless rate incorporates both voluntary and involuntary childlessness. However, recent data on reproductive impairments suggests that most childlessness is now voluntary. In 1976, it was estimated that only 1.5% of all currently married couples in the United States (with wife 15–44 years of age) were childless and noncontraceptively sterile (National Center for Health Statistics, 1980). Except in the case of sterility, where women know

Table 2. Actual and Expected Rates of Childlessness for White Married Women, 1978

Age categories	Expected childlessness[a] (wives)	Actual childlessness[b] (women ever married)
20–24	5.5	43.0
25–29	5.9	26.3
30–34	5.4	11.8

[a]U.S. Bureau of the Census (1979a, Table 4).
[b]U.S. Bureau of the Census (1979a, Table 7).

Table 3. Percentage of Wives 18–39 Years Old Who Expect to Remain Childless for Selected Years between 1960 and 1978[a]

Year	All races	White	Black
1978[b]	5.6	5.6	4.5
1977[c]	5.7	5.9	4.4
1976[d]	5.4	5.6	3.6
1975[e]	4.6	4.8	3.6
1974[e]	5.0	5.1	4.6
1973[e]	4.2	4.2	4.6
1972[e]	4.1	4.1	3.9
1971[d]	4.2	4.1	4.1
1967[d]	3.1	3.0	4.0
1960[d]	4.0	4.0	?

[a]1979 Census figures are for wives 18–34 years old and so are not reported here with the data for those 18–39 years old.
[b]U.S. Bureau of the Census (1979a, Table 4).
[c]U.S. Bureau of the Census (1978a, Table 3).
[d]U.S. Bureau of the Census (1978b, Table 3-3).
[e]U.S. Bureau of the Census (1976b, Table 2).

that it is *impossible* (not *difficult*) for them to conceive or carry a pregnancy to term, they probably would not report an expectation to remain childless, unless, of course, their preference is to remain childless (voluntarily).

Trends

It is fascinating and perhaps surprising to some that the *expected* childless rate has changed relatively little over time. Certainly, there is not the dramatic increase that many believe has accompanied the expansion in educational and occupational opportunities for women in recent years. The reason for this misconception, in large part, is that only census data through 1975 and only *actual* childless rates have been used by those endeavoring to substantiate such claims (DeJong & Sell, 1977; Mattessich,

1979; Poston & Gotard, 1977; U.S. Bureau of the Census, 1976a). An examination of the most recent census data suggests that, although viable, voluntarily childless marriages are not likely to become any more common in the 1980s.

Table 4 presents the percentage of ever-married white women who were *actually* childless by age for selected years between 1940 and 1979. It is clear that actual childless rates have varied considerably over time. From 1940 to 1960, there was a persistent *decline* for all age groups, which was probably due in large part to reductions in involuntary childlessness as a result of advances in nutrition and medicine (Glick, 1977). Looking just at the 20–24 age category, we see that there was a steady *increase* from 1960 until 1975. However, starting with 1976 and continuing each year through 1979 (except for one very minor exception), the rate consistently declined. The proportion of white women who were in the 20–24 age category and childless went from 45.1 in 1975 to 42.4 in 1979. More important than this 2.7 percentage-point decrease is the consistently declining pattern over the five-year period, which may indicate the beginning of a downward trend.

Thus far, this downward prediction is based only on the experience of the 20–24 age group. However, in the analysis of fertility, this category is the most important one because it is these women that have most of their reproductive life span ahead of them (U.S. Bureau of the Census, 1978b). A decrease in the actual childless rate has implications for voluntary childlessness because it suggests that the postponement of childbearing that became prevalent in the early 1970s (Gibson, 1976) may be subsiding. Postponement is directly related to the childless decision as the majority of voluntarily childless wives do not decide at a relatively early age in life, before marriage, to remain childless. Rather, they make their decision after they have developed a lifestyle that they do not want to give up (Bram, 1974; Houseknecht, 1979b,c; Marcks, 1976; McLaughlin, Rohrer, & Toomey 1974; Nason & Poloma, 1977; Veevers, 1973b). Therefore, a

Table 4. Percentage of Ever-Married White Women Who Were Actually Childless by Age for Selected Years between 1940 and 1979

Age categories	Year									
	1940[a]	1950[b]	1960[c]	1965[d]	1970[e]	1975[f]	1976[g]	1977[h]	1978[i]	1979[j]
20–24	36.9	34.0	25.0	28.7	37.7	45.1	44.2	44.4	43.0	42.4
25–29	27.2	20.1	12.3	11.8	16.1	21.7	22.4	25.5	26.3	27.4
30–34	20.6	15.8	9.7	7.0	8.1	9.0	10.8	11.6	11.8	13.4
35–39	17.1	17.5	10.2	8.1	7.0	5.3	6.4	6.9	7.0	7.1

[a]U.S. Bureau of the Census (1943, Table 1).   [f]U.S. Bureau of the Census (1976a, Table 6).
[b]U.S. Bureau of the Census (1955, Table 2).   [g]U.S. Bureau of the Census (1977b, Table 4).
[c]U.S. Bureau of the Census (1976a, Table 6).   [h]U.S. Bureau of the Census (1978a, Table 6).
[d]U.S. Bureau of the Census (1969, Table 1).   [i]U.S. Bureau of the Census (1979b, Table 4).
[e]U.S. Bureau of the Census (1976a, Table 6).   [j]U.S. Bureau of the Census (1980b, Table 4).

reduction in postponement would mean that fewer women would have sufficient time for the childless decision to evolve.

It was noted earlier that *actual* childlessness includes women who are intending to have children at some future time as well as those who are either voluntarily or involuntarily childless. That the continuing decrease in actual childlessness within the 20–24 age group is largely due to postponement is supported by the fact that the proportion of childless wives (as opposed to all wives) who considered themselves to be postponers declined between 1976 and 1978 (U.S. Bureau of the Census, 1977a, 1979a). This decrease can be linked to a trend in society at large. Many believe that young people specifically and the society generally have changed in recent years so that there is now a greater inclination to be traditional, conservative, and family-oriented. The anti-ERA, antiabortion, and traditional family movements are all part of the change. This assessment fits with the finding that more young women are having children earlier in life.

It might be argued that predicting voluntary childless rates on the basis of 20-to-24-year-old ever-married women is misleading. After all, growing numbers of women are postponing marriage beyond this age category, and it may be that, for them, childlessness is increasing at a phenomenal rate. To rule out this possibility, data for 20-to-24-year-old never-married white women are examined for the period 1976–1979 in Table 5. Interestingly, these women were characterized not by a phenomenal increase but by a small decline in *actual* childlessness. The most important question, of course, is whether increasing proportions of 20-to-24-year-old single women expect to remain childless after they are married. The figures presented in Table 5 suggest that this was *not* the case for the time period under consideration.

The 1976–1979 decline in the percentage childless for 20-to-24-year-old single and ever-married women is not observed when both marital categories are combined

Table 6. Percentage of White Wives Who Expected No Lifetime Births by Age, 1975–1979

Age categories	Year				
	1975[a]	1976[b]	1977[c]	1978[d]	1979[e]
20–24	4.7	4.3	5.7	5.5	5.7
25–29	4.9	6.7	6.6	5.9	5.5
30–34	5.5	5.8	6.1	5.4	6.4

[a]U.S. Bureau of the Census (1976b, Table H).
[b]U.S. Bureau of the Census (1977a, Table 12).
[c]U.S. Bureau of the Census (1978a, Table 3).
[d]U.S. Bureau of the Census (1979a, Table 4).
[e]U.S. Bureau of the Census (1980a, Table 5).

(Table 5). This seeming anomaly is due to the fact that single women were becoming a bigger part of the whole and they had higher rates of childlessness than ever-married women.

It is true that the data presented in Table 4 evidence a continuing *increase* in *actual* childlessness for the 25–29, 30–34, and 35–39 age groups. However, we can also see that the increase in childlessness that first began between 1960 and 1965 for the 20–24 age group only gradually spread to the older age categories at about five-year intervals. This means, of course, that it was the same people for the most part who were responsible for the initial change in each age group.

Even though the increase in *actual* childlessness continues for the older age categories, there has recently been a leveling off in the proportions of wives who *expect* to remain childless. In fact, Table 6 shows that this was the case for both the 20–24 and the 25–29 age categories between 1977 and 1979. Women 30–34 years old were the only exception. This latter finding does not negate the argument, however, as a *short-term* increase in the phenomenon in the older age categories was to be expected, given the importance of the postponement factor in the decision to remain voluntarily childless.

In conclusion, the *long-term* trend in the voluntary childless rate appears to be downward, or at least not upward. To suggest that there will not be a significant increase in childlessness in the United States is to take a rather controversial stance, as it disputes the commonly held notion that the phenomenon will continue to become more widespread (Bumpass, 1973; Grindstaff, 1976; De-Jong & Sell, 1977; Poston & Gotard, 1977; Westoff, 1978; Marciano, 1978; Veevers, 1979). However, based on the analysis of the most recent census data, it does seem unlikely that voluntary childlessness will soon reach Veevers's predicted rate of "at least 10 percent" (1979, p. 7).

"Wives" versus "Reporting Women"

In this section on trends and incidence, one final addendum is in order. Regardless of whether actual or expected

Table 5. Actual and Expected Childless Rates for 20- to 24-Year-Old White Women[a] for Selected Years and Marital Statuses

Year	Single women		All women	
	Actual	Expected	Actual	Expected
1979[b]	93.8	18.3	66.5	11.8
1978[c]	94.2	19.5	66.1	11.9
1977	95.7[b]	18.6[d]	66.6[b]	11.8[d]
1976	95.3[c]	19.2[e]	65.2[c]	10.5[e]

[a]The only exception in this regard are the actual rates for all women, and they apply to all races.
[b]U.S. Bureau of the Census (1980a, Tables 5, 6, 7).
[c]U.S. Bureau of the Census (1979a, Tables 4, 5, 6, 8).
[d]U.S. Bureau of the Census (1978a, Tables 3, 4).
[e]U.S. Bureau of the Census (1977a, Tables 4, 14).

childless rates are being studied, care must be taken not to confuse data bases. For example, rates for *wives* cannot be directly compared with rates for *reporting women*. The 1978 range for childless *expectations* in the different age groups of wives was 5%–6%, whereas for reporting women, it was 10%–12%. That this discrepancy exists is interesting in itself. In addition to wives, the category "reporting women" includes widowed, divorced, separated, and never-married persons. The fact that expected childless rates are higher for single women at *all* levels than for those who are married, widowed, divorced, or separated (U.S. Bureau of the Census, 1979a) suggests that the considerable difference in expected childlessness that exists between wives and reporting women can be attributed largely to single women. At least for some people, it may be that there is a tendency to forgo not only one, but two, of society's major role expectations. Two studies that lend support to this idea found that young women who desired no children, in contrast to those who did, were much more likely to reject the notion of marriage (Houseknecht, 1974, 1978b; Toomey, 1977).

Although discrepancies such as this one do need to be explained, the major point here is that they do exist. It is precisely for this reason that caution must be exercised when trends and incidence of childlessness are the subject of interest.

Statements of Motive for Voluntary Childlessness

Blake and Davis (1963) noted that population trends are the product of human behavior, and that human behavior involves motivation. Therefore, they feel that attitudes and motives are not simply relevant, but essential to population study. Twenty-nine studies that have looked at statements of motive for childlessness will be considered in this review.[1] Together, they contribute not only substantive points but methodological insights. All of them used the same source to elicit motivations, the voluntarily childless themselves.

In an effort to maintain consistency, one study will not be integrated with the others because the information was not obtained from childless individuals.[2] Popenoe (1936) presented a description of the motivations of voluntarily childless couples based on the perceptions of close friends and relatives. He asked these people what they thought was the real motive for the couple's childlessness. He felt that there was a need for such a study as individuals might rationalize their own feelings regarding negative fertility desires.

It is interesting to speculate in greater detail about who constitutes the most appropriate source for determining childless motivations, as the issue apparently remains unresolved. Individuals who wish to remain childless deviate from the dominant societal norm, which prescribes children. Therefore, according to Scott and Lyman (1970), it is necessary that such nonconformity be accounted for. These authors defined an *account* as "a statement made by a social actor to explain unanticipated or untoward behavior—whether that behavior is his own or that of others, and whether the proximate cause for the statement arises from the actor himself or from someone else" (p. 490). In their opinion, a range of alternative accounts is culturally appropriate to a variety of recurrent situations.

Based on Scott and Lyman's concept of accounts, therefore, it would seem that, regardless of who gives the reason, it is a rationalization that has been selected from an acceptable vocabulary of motives previously established by the historical epoch and the social structure in which one lives. According to this perspective, Popenoe's objection—that the reasons stated by the individuals themselves are not valid because they are probably rationalized—would not be improved upon by the use of the opinions of close others. In fact, Mills (1970) noted that what is a reason for one person is a rationalization for another.

Even though statements of motivation and causation are not necessarily related, it is still interesting and worthwhile to examine the rationales provided by persons who choose to remain permanently childless. These represent the language of situations and so can provide the basis for a deeper probe into the effects that different structural conditions have on vocabularies of motive (Mills, 1970). To this end, the results of a content analysis are presented in Table 7. Of the 47 studies reviewed, 29 were found to contain motivational data.

---

[1]There are eight studies concerned with rationales for voluntary childlessness in which *couples* were the unit of analysis: Gustavus and Henley (1971), Hersch (1974), Raphael (1975), Lichtman (1976), Marcks (1976), Nason and Poloma (1976), Ory (1976), and Burnside (1977). Nineteen studies concerned with childless rationales looked at *females* separately: Veevers (1973a, 1973b), Bram (1974), Houseknecht (1974, 1978b), Hotz (1975), McLaughlin *et al.* (1974), Cumber (1977), Goodbody (1977), Kaltreider and Margolis (1977), Lindenmayer *et al.* (1977), Rebecca (1977), Silka and Keisler (1977), Gil (1978), Levine (1978), Marciano (1978), Polonko (1978), Dietz (1979), Scott (1979), Baum and Cope (1980), and den Bandt (1980). Seven studies concerned with childless rationales looked at *males* separately: Bellman (1974), Bram (1974), Cumber (1977), Rebecca (1977), Silka and Keisler (1977), Marciano (1978), and Magarick and Brown (1981). The total number of studies concerned with rationales for voluntary childlessness is 28 (5 of those listed above included both males and females, although the data were presented separately for each sex).

[2]There is a second study that looked at rationales for voluntary childlessness that will also be omitted from this analysis. Centers and Blumberg (1954) posed questions in terms of the advantages of parenthood, and recent evidence suggests that the advantages associated with having children are different from the advantages associated with childlessness (Houseknecht, 1978b). Centers and Blumberg's study, therefore, would not be comparable with the 28 other studies, which investigated why people did *not* want to have children.

Table 7. Rationales for Voluntary Childlessness by Occurrence in Studies to Date and by Sex

Rationale	All studies concerned with childless rationales (Total = 29)[a]	Studies considering female rationales separately (Total = 19)[b]	Studies considering male rationales separately (Total = 7)[c]
Freedom from child-care responsibility/greater opportunity for self-fulfillment and spontaneous mobility	79% (23)	79% (15)	71% (5)
More satisfactory marital relationship	62% (18)	63% (12)	57% (4)
Female career considerations	55% (16)	74% (14)	29% (2)
Monetary advantages	55% (16)	42% (8)	57% (4)
Concern about population growth	38% (11)	32% (6)	14% (1)
General dislike of children	38% (11)	26% (5)	43% (3)
Early socialization experiences/doubts about ability to parent	31% (9)	37% (7)	0% (0)
Concern about physical aspects of childbirth and recovery	24% (7)	21% (4)	14% (1)
Concern for children, given world conditions	21% (6)	21% (4)	0% (0)

[a]The percentages are proportions of this total. Included are eight studies in which "couples" were the unit of analysis (see Footnote 1 for a list of these studies); in these instances, it is not possible to differentiate between male and female responses.
[b]The percentages are proportions of this total. (See Footnote 1 for a list of the studies that looked at female rationales separately.)
[c]The percentages are proportions of this total. (See Footnote 1 for a list of the studies that looked at male rationales separately.)

Before examining the findings, a word of caution is in order. The unit of analysis is *studies* and not *women, men,* or *couples.* The figures in the first column of the table represent the proportion of studies (total = 29) in which a particular rationale was mentioned. The second and third columns show the proportion of studies that looked at females separately (total = 19) and the proportion of the studies that looked at males separately (total = 7) that contained the various rationales. The data, then, provide some clues to what the most commonly stated motives are among studies. (It is not possible to determine what the most commonly stated motives are among individuals in all of these studies because there is a lack of consistency in reporting this kind of information, if it is reported at all.) It is important to note that the data do not suggest anything regarding importance. Regardless of whether studies or individuals are the unit of analysis, ranking statements of motive on this criterion would require knowing the importance of the ratings assigned by the respondents. Unfortunately, very few studies have dealt systematically with the issue of significance in connection with rationales for voluntary childlessness.

Specific Rationales for Voluntary Childlessness

Freedom from Child-Care Responsibility: Greater Opportunity for Self-Fulfillment and Spontaneous Mobility. What are the stated motives for the childfree lifestyle that appear most often across studies? As shown in Table 7, most of them fall into one of nine categories. The one with the highest frequency is freedom from child-care responsibility and greater opportunity for self-fulfillment and spontaneous mobility. This rationale was given in 79% of all the studies concerned with childless rationales.

It was also the most likely to occur in studies considering females (79%) and males (71%) separately. There was little difference in likelihood of mention between female and male samples. Veevers (1975a) remarked that it is the potential for new experience that is important to the voluntarily childless, not whether the opportunity is actually used.

More Satisfactory Marital Relationship. The rationale of a more satisfactory marital relationship was of the second highest frequency. It was reported in 62% of the 29 studies concerned with statements of motive. It was somewhat more likely to occur in studies considering females separately (63%) than in those considering males separately (57%). However, the difference is not great and it clearly was a common rationale among both males and females. Using marital interference as a rationale for remaining childless is particularly interesting because it contradicts a commonly held notion that children are necessary for a happy marriage (Houseknecht, 1978b). A review of the literature on childlessness and marital adjustment is presented later in the section on correlates of voluntary childlessness.

Female Career Considerations. Two rationales were tied for third highest frequency of occurrence. Both female career considerations and monetary advantages were mentioned in 55% of the studies concerned with motives for voluntary childlessness. The female samples, however, differed from the male samples in their tendency to offer these explanations. For example, 74% of the studies considering females separately reported female career considerations, in contrast to only 29% of the studies considering males separately. Nearly all of the males in these studies were married; thus, children were not widely perceived as having a negative impact on the wife's career. It may be that those men believed that children, in fact, would impact on the wife's career but did not view the effect itself as a reason for remaining childless. There is an expectation on the part of many husbands that the wife's primary commitment will be familial regardless of her employment status.

Monetary Advantages. The sex difference was reversed with regard to the rationale of monetary advantages. Although it was a fairly common one for both male and female samples, it was more likely to be mentioned in studies considering males separately (57%) than in studies considering females separately (42%). This difference may be related to the traditional view of males as providers; they may have been reacting to what they perceived as a reduction in their primary role obligation.

Concern about Population Growth. Two rationales were tied for fourth highest frequency of occurrence in studies concerned with statements of motivation. Both concern about population growth and general dislike of children were mentioned in 38% of the studies. Once again, there was a sex difference in the tendency for samples to offer these explanations. Female samples were much more likely than male samples to express a concern about population growth; still, only about one third of them did so (32% versus 14%). The sex difference is puzzling but might reflect a proclivity on the part of females to give socially acceptable explanations for their desire to remain childless. After all, motherhood has traditionally been a major role for women, whereas fatherhood has not been a major role for men. Because rejection of a major role would probably be associated with more severe sanctioning, there might be a greater effort by women to provide legitimization.

General Dislike of Children. Along these same lines, male samples revealed a greater tendency than female samples to say that their motive for childlessness was a general dislike of children. Close to half of the studies considering males separately contained this response (43%) in contrast to only a fourth of the studies considering females separately (26%). To reiterate the previous notion, it may be more culturally acceptable for men than for women to express a dislike of children. A major component of the female role has traditionally been to care, to give, and to nurture.

Early Socialization Experience/Doubts about Ability to Parent. The last rationales in Table 7 were mentioned in less than a third of the studies that have explored motivations for voluntary childlessness: early socialization experiences and doubts about ability to parent (31%); concern about physical aspects of childbirth and recovery (24%); and concern for children, given world conditions (21%). All three rationales were more characteristic of

female samples than of male samples. For example, 37% of the studies considering females separately mentioned early socialization experience and doubts about ability to parent. This explanation did not appear in any of the studies that considered males separately. Once again, this sex difference may be related to the fact that parenthood has traditionally represented the primary role for women but not for men. This being the case, females might be somewhat more scrutinizing in their analysis of what is involved.

Concern about Physical Aspects of Childbirth and Recovery. Concern about physical aspects of childbirth and recovery was mentioned by 21% of the female samples and 14% of the male samples. It seems reasonable that women would be more concerned than men about this particular aspect of parenthood because it affects them so directly. This rationale, however, was not a very typical one for either male or female samples.

Concern for Children, Given World Conditions. Finally, concern for children, given world conditions was reported in 21% of the studies considering females separately but was totally absent from those in which males were considered separately. Perhaps here, as was proposed for the greater tendency of female samples to express concern about population growth, there may have been an effort to provide socially acceptable explanations for the rejection of what is considered by society at large to be the primary role.

Methodological Considerations

The Need to Distinguish between Female and Male Data. In addition to identifying the most frequently occurring rationales for voluntary childlessness across studies, these findings suggest a number of differences between the male and the female samples. In general, the female samples were more likely to give collective responses, to present themselves as altruistic (concern for population; doubts about ability to parent; concern for children, given world conditions). The male samples, on the other hand, were less hesitant to offer individualistic rationales (general dislike of children; monetary advantages). Sex, then, seems to be one aspect of social structure that affects *vocabularies of motive* (Mills, 1970). Researchers, therefore, need to recognize the importance of distinguishing between male and female data, even if their sample is comprised of couples. Of the 29 motivational studies being reviewed, 7 did not make this distinction (see Footnote 1).

Status positions other than sex might also be investigated in future research to see how they affect childless rationales. Age, education, and race are examples, as they affect behavioral expectations. A study by Rebecca (1977), a follow-up of an earlier study by Bram (1974), found that there was more change than stability among stated motives for childlessness. This observation provides further support for the influence of structural conditions on vocabularies of motive.

Open or Closed Questions? This analysis of rationales for voluntary childlessness must be viewed as suggestive and not definitive as there were differences in sampling and methodology among the studies that make direct comparisons hazardous. For example, it is not always clear whether open or closed questions were used to obtain the information. In those cases where the format was closed, the list might not have been exhaustive and so may have excluded some of the rationales that appear in Table 7. In this connection, it is interesting to contemplate why 4 of the 19 female samples and 2 of the 7 male samples did not mention concern about personal freedom, the most commonly expressed motive among the studies reviewed (and among individuals within specific studies as well).

Reasons or Advantages? A second methodological consideration needs to be taken into account in interpreting the data in Table 7. Were the questions posed in terms of *reasons* for childlessness or *advantages* of childlessness? Although it is not always possible to discern this information from descriptions of techniques, it is apparent that each term was used in at least some of the 29 studies that looked at statements of motivation. Previous research indicates that differences may occur depending on which of these designations is used (Houseknecht, 1974); in fact, it suggests a way to increase specificity in the measurement of motivations for childlessness.

When asked the *reason* they decided not to have children, a number of the respondents in Houseknecht's study simply said, "Dislike children." Although dislike of children was cited as an *advantage* for not having them, it was mentioned much more frequently as a reason. It is conceivable that a number of the advantages for not having children that were reported by the respondents were subsumed under the vague reason "dislike children." It appears that by analyzing the decision to remain childless in terms of perceived advantages, it is possible to more precisely relate certain attitudes to that decision. The result, perhaps, may be a more accurate picture of the individual's motivation in this regard.

Given the sampling and methodological limitations that characterize this analysis of rationales for voluntary childlessness, it is important to stress once again that the major objective is to suggest directions for future research. Furthermore, because extensive data on statements of motive have not been obtained, it is proposed that the categories in Table 7 be used to classify free response data and not as a comprehensive domain of rationales.

Correlates of Voluntary Childlessness

The major objective of this section is to identify the correlates of voluntary childlessness. First, however, it is important to examine briefly the connection between determinants and consequences. As respondents themselves do not know the exact timing of their decision, it is difficult to precisely specify the order of some variables. We do know, though, that voluntarily childless individuals tend to be postponers rather than early articulators (Bram, 1974; Houseknecht, 1979b,c; Marcks, 1976; McLaughlin *et al.*, 1974; Nason & Poloma, 1976; Veevers, 1973b). In other words, they make their decision to remain childless after they have married and have developed a lifestyle that they do not want to give up. It appears, therefore, that some factors may be the consequences of having no children but the determinants for making a childless decision.

Once again, it must be emphasized that only those studies that deal specifically with *voluntary* childlessness will be considered in this section on correlates.

Birth Order

Investigations of the relationship between birth order and parental status have often shown that the voluntarily childless tend to be either firstborns or only children. In four separate studies (Hotz, 1975; Marcks, 1976; Nason & Poloma, 1976; Toomey, 1977), approximately half the female respondents were found to be firstborns. Veevers (1973b), too, reported that the incidence of firstborns in her all-female sample was "much larger than would ordinarily be expected." Two additional studies (Thoen, 1977; Burnside, 1977) did not distinguish between males and females but still found the incidence of firstborns to be extremely high (65% and 54%, respectively).

Although higher proportions of first-borns than only children constituted the childless samples, several studies found a higher incidence of only children than would ordinarily be expected (Baum & Cope, 1980; Bram, 1974; Nason & Poloma, 1976; Ory, 1976; Veevers, 1973a). One exception is Hotz (1975), who reported that there were no only children in her sample of 11 women.

It is important not to confuse data bases in this analysis and to conclude that firstborns are more likely than only children to be voluntarily childless. The foregoing results are based on the proportion of the childless who are either onlies or firstborns and not on the proportion of onlies and firstborns who are voluntarily childless. It may be that only children are more likely than firstborns to choose a childless lifestyle, but because they are fewer in number, they make up a smaller part of the childless total. Further research is needed in this area.

It can be inferred from the birth order findings that the voluntarily childless, like other early-borns, have a unique socialization experience as children. Marjoribanks (1978), for example, noted that earlier-borns have access to a more favorable intellectual environment. In fact, there is accumulating evidence that eldest and only children tend in adulthood to be high achievers (Lieberman, 1974; Polit, Nuttall, & Nuttall, 1980) and relatively autonomous (Feldman, 1978; Falbo, 1978).

Research showing that these same two variables are related to voluntary childlessness among women is presented later.

Family Background

If achievement and relative autonomy characterize voluntarily childless women in adulthood, the various family-background factors that have been associated with these variables should also characterize these women. A review of the literature has indicated that, for females, these experiences include moderate (not high) levels of family warmth, a relatively permissive rather than a coercive pattern of parental authority, independence training, and encouragement of achievement (Stein & Bailey, 1973). In fact, an association has been found between each of these family-background factors and voluntary childlessness.

The most extensive evidence pertains to the overall level of warmth in the family of orientation. (Findings regarding marital and family happiness are integrated here as they would seem to have an impact.) Three studies indicate that it was not high for the female respondents (Houseknecht, 1978a; McLaughlin et al., 1974; Veevers, 1973a). In two other surveys, childless women reported experiencing a significantly lower overall level of warmth than either parents (Bram, 1974) or intended parents (Bram, 1974; Toomey, 1977). The comparative findings are similar in two additional studies in which couples were the unit of analysis (Centers & Blumberg, 1954; Ory, 1976).

Only one study has looked at the remaining family-background factors that have been associated with female autonomy and achievement in adulthood (Houseknecht, 1978a). As expected, most of the childless women were reared with a noncoercive pattern of parental authority. They scored highest on principled discipline (democratic order). On the average, parental encouragement of assertive autonomy and of achievement was reasonably common. Kaltreider and Margolis (1977) also found that voluntarily childless women had an "early sense of identity as the achieving daughter rather than as the little mother in the family" (p. 182).

A limited number of researchers have investigated the notion that women who are deliberately childless have achievement-oriented mothers. It appears that they do not. Veevers (1973a), for example, noted that almost all of her voluntarily childless wives had mothers who had never participated in the labor force. Three comparative studies (Bram, 1974; Burnside, 1977; Toomey, 1977) found no differences between parent and nonparent women in terms of their mother's employment outside the home.

Whether the mothers of voluntarily childless women are satisfied with their traditional role is unclear. Veevers (1973a) reported that they are not and Toomey (1977) found that they are less satisfied than the mothers of those who intend to have children. Houseknecht (1974), however, found no difference between these two groups in this regard. Further research on maternal role models is needed before any definite conclusions can be drawn.

One final point in this section on background factors pertains to marital disruption in the families of orientation. Even though their parents' marriages are viewed by childless individuals as relatively unhappy (Ory, 1976; Toomey, 1977, Veevers, 1973a), there is evidence that they tend to remain intact (Marcks, 1976; Veevers, 1973a). Additional support for the not-higher-than-average incidence of parental divorce and separation is provided in comparison studies that have found no group differences in this regard for parent and nonparent women (Bram, 1974; Toomey, 1977), parent and nonparent men (Bram, 1974; Magarick & Brown, 1981), and parent and nonparent couples (Hersch, 1974; Ory, 1976; Silka & Kiesler, 1977). The single exception to these findings is a study by Burnside (1977) that revealed that parents were significantly more likely than nonparents to come from "stable natal homes."

Autonomy

In 1970, Pohlman wrote that a person who desires no children is probably rather strongly individualistic as the culture exerts severe pressures against childlessness. Although it will be seen in the next section that the childless are not without some reinforcement for their decision, it is understandable that, given this social context, they would need to be relatively autonomous.

A number of studies have investigated the possible association between autonomy and voluntary childlessness. With one exception (Levine, 1978), the results are consistent for females. Women intending to have no children were found to be more independent than those in other parent-status categories (Bram, 1974; Burnside, 1977; Houseknecht, 1977a, 1978b; Jones, 1978; Silka & Kiesler, 1977; Toomey, 1977) One researcher (Hersch, 1974) who used couples as the unit of analysis reported a similar difference between parents and nonparents. The findings for males, on the other hand, are limited and mixed. Magarick and Brown (1981) found that childless men scored higher on independence than fathers, but Silka and Kiesler (1977) observed no difference.

Achievement

Increased educational and employment opportunities have enabled more and more women to participate in the academic and occupational worlds both before and after marriage. This situation, combined with the postponement of childbearing that became prevalent in the 1970s (Gibson, 1976), has provided time for women to become aware of the advantages of reduced family size. Alternative sources of satisfaction outside the home compete with motherhood because every woman has only a limited supply of time and energy.

Career involvement has been found to play a significant role in the decision to remain voluntarily childless. This is not to say that most career-oriented women want to remain childless, as the tendency is to choose the lower limit of the acceptable fertility norm: to have two children rather than three or four (U.S. Bureau of the Census, 1979a). Nevertheless, it is understandable that the rejection of a major social role would be associated with commitment to another sphere of life.

The various measures of achievement (career involvement) considered here include education, employment, income, and sex-role attitudes.

Education. Research indicates that most voluntarily childless women have had at least some university experience; in fact, bachelor's and graduate degrees are common (Baum & Cope, 1980; Goodbody, 1977; Gustavus & Henley, 1971; Hall, 1979; Hotz, 1975; Marciano, 1978; Nason & Poloma, 1976; Scott, 1979; Thoen, 1977). That their level of education is higher than that of other women has been widely documented (Bram, 1974; Burnside, 1977; Houseknecht, 1978a; Magarick & Brown, 1981; McLaughlin *et al.*, 1974; Toomey, 1977).

Although four studies did not find educational differences between women who are voluntarily childless and those who are not, certain explanations could account for the discrepancies. For example, the respondents in one survey (den Bandt, 1980) were from another culture, The Netherlands. In another (Polonko, 1978), they had to have married after age 21; age at marriage, of course, is positively related to education. In the two remaining studies (Silka & Kiesler, 1977; Teicholz, 1978), the respondents were volunteers, so that sampling bias could have been involved. These comments are intended not to dismiss the contradictory findings as incorrect, but to suggest that there may be unexplored variables leading to the inconsistent outcomes.

In sum, the general consensus is that voluntarily childless women have unusually high levels of education. The comparative results for men, in contrast, show little agreement. In two studies, their educational level was found to be higher than that of other males (Bellman, 1974; Magarick & Brown, 1981); in two studies, it was found to be lower (Houseknecht, 1977b; Ory, 1976); and in four studies, there was no difference (Bram, 1974; Burnside, 1977; Hoffman & Levant, 1980; Silka & Kiesler, 1977). Nevertheless, these studies, as well as others that are descriptive in nature (Baum & Cope, 1980; Gustavus & Henley, 1971; Marciano, 1978; Thoen, 1977) have evidenced that voluntarily childless males, like females, tend to be college-educated.

Employment. Female employment is another variable that seems to be an important correlate of voluntary childlessness. Most comparative studies have found that women who choose never to have children are more likely than other women to participate in the labor force (Bram, 1974; Dietz, 1979; Magarick & Brown, 1981; Polonko,

1978; Scott, 1979). It is very interesting that the two exceptions in this regard (no difference was reported) are the same two studies that used volunteers and found no educational differences between women who were voluntarily childless and those who were not (Silka & Kiesler, 1977; Teicholz, 1978). Some indication of how high the labor-force-participation rates actually are is provided by several descriptive studies. In all of the samples, approximately 90% or more of the childless women were employed outside the home (Baum & Cope, 1980; Hall, 1979; Hotz, 1975; Marciano, 1978; Thoen, 1977; Veevers, 1975a).

Female educational attainment, in addition to being related to a propensity to be in the labor market, is also related to a specific position in the occupational hierarchy. Voluntarily childless women tend to be working in high-status jobs (Baum & Cope, 1980; Gustavus & Henley, 1971; Hall, 1979; Hotz, 1975; Teicholz, 1978). In fact, it is fairly well documented that, in comparison with other women, their occupational level is higher (Bram, 1974; Houseknecht, 1979a; McLaughlin *et al.*, 1974; Polonko, 1978; Silka & Kiesler, 1977; Scott, 1979). Only one study, and it was done in The Netherlands (den Bandt, 1980), did not find childless women comprising a more occupationally elite group. Recall that this same study did not find that they were more highly educated either.

Although less research has been done on males than on females, it appears that voluntarily childless husbands are also likely to be engaged in high-status occupations (Baum & Cope, 1980; Gustavus & Henley, 1971; Hoffman & Levant, 1980; Magarick & Brown, 1981; Silka & Keisler, 1977). The specific occupational choices of both sexes, however, seem to be fairly traditional (Bram, 1974; Thoen, 1977). This finding was also reported in two studies in which couples were the unit of analysis (Benson & Hoover, 1978; Marciano, 1978).

As indicated previously, research has shown that, for women in particular, a frequently stated motive for remaining childless is the opportunity for career involvement (Baum & Cope, 1980; Bram, 1974; den Bandt, 1980; Hotz, 1975; Houseknecht, 1978b; Marciano, 1978; McLaughlin *et al.*, 1974; Lindenmayer, Steinberg, Bjork, & Pardes, 1977; Polonko, 1978; Rebecca, 1977; Scott, 1979; Silka & Keisler, 1977; Veevers, 1975a). That childless women find their work rewarding is also indicated by the high level of work commitment that they express. Based on her exploratory study, Veevers (1975a) noted that approximately half of her childless wives were dedicated to their work and took a large part of their identity from it. Half of Bram's sample (1974) of childless women stated that work was "as important as marriage and family." Sixty-three percent of the childless women in still another study (Houseknecht, 1977b) felt that employment and marriage/family had equal importance in their lives and that was the way they preferred it. Eighty-two percent stated that their motivation for working was either personal or a combination of personal and financial. Although measures vary, several other studies have reached similar conclusions regarding work commitment (Nason & Poloma, 1976; Polonko, 1978; Rebecca, 1977; Thoen, 1977; Toomey, 1977).

Income. There is extensive evidence that the earnings of voluntarily childless women are far above average (Burnside, 1977; Dietz, 1979; Goodbody, 1977; Gustavus & Henley, 1971; Hotz, 1975; Houseknecht, 1979c; McLaughlin *et al.*, 1974; Polonko, 1978). Interestingly, there is some indication that the income situation for voluntarily childless females may not hold for voluntarily childless males. Dietz (1979), for example, using data from the 1965 National Fertility Survey, found that the husband's income is inversely related to voluntary childlessness; that is, the higher the husband's income, the more likely it is that a couple will intend a first birth. Burnside (1977) also reported that the parent husbands in her sample earned higher median incomes than voluntarily childless husbands.

When combined family income is considered, the results are less consistent than when males and females are examined separately. In three studies, family income was higher for voluntarily childless families (Hersch, 1974; Magarick & Brown, 1981; Ory, 1976); in two studies, it was lower for childless families (Burnside, 1977; Chalfant, 1979); and in two studies, no difference was found (Hoffman & Levant, 1980; Houseknecht, 1977b). With these anomalous results, it would appear that the family income of voluntarily childless families is not significantly different from that of parent families.

An interpretation of the combined-family-income results requires that two previously elaborated points be kept in mind. First, women who choose never to have children are more likely than other women to participate in the labor force, and second, they tend to earn higher-than-average incomes. The fact that voluntarily childless families seem to earn incomes that are more-or-less equivalent to those of parent families, even with these two apparent advantages, is further evidence that the childless male's contribution to family income is proportionately lower than average. Thus, although the voluntarily childless male tends to be employed in a high-status position (as indicated previously), his job does not seem to provide remuneration that is comparable to its status. On the other hand, the data indicate that the voluntarily childless working woman is contributing a larger proportion to the total family income than is the employed mother. Together, these findings suggest that the voluntarily childless may have a more egalitarian spousal relationship.

Sex-Role Attitudes. We have seen that voluntarily childless women are typically highly educated, are employed at relatively high occupational levels, and earn above-average incomes. Thus, they can be characterized as high achievers. Previous research has shown that a strong determinant of aspiration among women is sex-role ideology (Lipman-Blumen, 1972). Those with more egalitarian sex-role definitions are more likely to be achievement-oriented.

That voluntarily childless women tend to have a less traditional view of the female role than other women has been demonstrated in many studies (Bram, 1974; den Bandt, 1980; Fisher, 1979; Hamilton, 1977; Hoffman & Levant, 1980; Houseknecht, 1978b, 1979a; Polonka, 1978; Teicholz, 1978; Toomey, 1977; Welds, 1977). In only two instances in which women were considered separately were these findings not supported (Ory, 1976; Levine, 1978).

When *males* and *couples* are the units of analysis, the association between childbearing intentions and sex-role ideology is less clear-cut. Bram (1974) and Fisher (1979) reported that their voluntarily childless males had less stereotypical sex-role attitudes than other males, but Magarick and Brown (1981) and Hoffman and Levant (1980) found no difference. Focusing on *couples,* Burnside (1977) and Silka and Kiesler (1977) also reported no difference.

The measures of sex-role emancipation that were used in these various studies included domestic division of labor, decision making, attitude toward sex-role liberation, and androgyny/femininity/masculinity scale scores. Although sex-role attitudes and marital role attitudes are analytically distinct, they were combined for the purpose of this analysis.

Marital Adjustment and Divorce

Do voluntarily childless couples find other sources of fulfillment for the so-called gap in their marriages that many assume would exist without children? Apparently they do, as they commonly report that their marriages are happy and satisfying (Bram, 1974; Cooper, Cumber, & Hartner, 1978; Houseknecht, 1979a; Hotz, 1975; Lichtman, 1976; McLaughlin *et al.*, 1974; Rebecca, 1977; Teicholz, 1978; Veevers, 1975a). Description is not comparison, however, and a number of researchers have studied whether childless individuals have a higher or a lower level of marital adjustment and satisfaction than do people with children. Unfortunately, the term *childless* in several of these studies referred to more than just voluntary childlessness (Feldman, 1971; Renne, 1970, 1976; Ryder, 1973). People who were simply postponing childbearing, as well as the involuntarily childless, were also included.

Only two studies (Bram, 1974; Houseknecht, 1979a) have compared *voluntarily* childless persons and parents in terms of marital adjustment and satisfaction. Houseknecht (1979a) precision-matched voluntarily childless wives and mothers (all between 25 and 40 years of age) on education, religion, and participation in the labor force to eliminate the possibility that these variables might account for any observed differences. The findings revealed that women who were childless by choice scored significantly higher than mothers in overall marital adjustment as measured by Spanier's Dyadic Adjustment Scale (1976). This difference, however, was not uniform across the four subareas of adjustment (marital satisfaction, dyadic consensus, dyadic cohesion, and affectual expression). The component that possessed the greatest discriminatory power was cohesion. That the childless scored higher in this regard is not surprising, as they would seem to have more opportunity to do things together (the theme of most of the cohesion items).

In contrast to Houseknecht's study (1979b), Bram (1974) reported no difference in marital adjustment and satisfaction between current parents and childless persons. Her evaluation, however, was limited to a single global question: "How happy is your marriage compared to most couples you know?" There are problems with such a global question, including the possibility of bias resulting from socially acceptable responses.

Some limited but thought-provoking research suggests that the childless may not be better adjusted than others at all stages of the life cycle. For example, Silka and Keisler (1977) and Hoffman and Levant (1980) found no difference in marital adjustment and satisfaction between couples who intended to have children and the voluntarily childless. These findings suggest that it is the presence of children that is important, as those that were planned for had not yet arrived. However, it appears that the effects of pre- and postparenthood may be different. Former mothers (i.e., women with no children under 18 years of age) in Houseknecht and Macke's study (1981) scored higher on marital adjustment than childless women (voluntary was not distinguished) even when age and duration of marriage were controlled. The higher marital adjustment that these women perceived may have been, in part, a reaction to their newly found freedom to participate more extensively in companionship activities with their spouse. Miller (1976) found this variable to be one of the strongest predictors of adjustment, particularly for females. Women who have never had children would not experience this feeling of relief.

To suggest that the voluntarily childless may not have higher marital adjustment than others at *all* stages of the life cycle does not imply that their marriages are not happy and satisfying. We have seen that they are. Furthermore, the results of this review do not seem to indicate that the voluntarily childless are more divorce-prone than others (Hersch, 1974; Houseknecht, 1979a; Thoen, 1977). One study that did find a significant difference in favor of parents was characterized by a definitional problem (Ory, 1976), in that voluntary childlessness included people who had had children in previous marriages.

Religion

Demographic research has shown time and again that religion is a correlate of family size (Bogue, 1969; *Family Planning Perspectives*, 1977; Ryder, 1973). It appears

that childlessness is not an exception. A number of researchers have reported that the voluntarily childless commonly claim no current religious affiliation (Gustavus & Henley, 1971; Marcks, 1976; Thoen, 1977; Veevers, 1973b). In fact, there is extensive evidence that they differ significantly from others in this regard (Bram, 1974; Centers & Blumberg, 1954; Hersch, 1974; Houseknecht, 1979a; Magarick & Brown, 1981; Toomey, 1977). Apparently, however, this difference does not hold across the life cycle. Findings indicate that, in childhood, they tend to have identified with an organized religion (Bram, 1974; Houseknecht, 1979a; Thoen, 1977). The modal religious background that has been reported is Protestantism (Bram, 1974; Houseknecht, 1977b; Nason & Poloma, 1976; Silka & Keisler, 1977; Thoen, 1977; Toomey, 1977; Veevers, 1973b).

Considering the lower rate of religious affiliation that characterizes the voluntarily childless in adulthood, it might be expected that they would also have lower levels of religiosity and lower rates of church attendance than parents. In fact, this appears to be the case for women (Bram, 1974; Houseknecht, 1977b; Polonko, 1978; Toomey, 1977) but not for men (Bram, 1974) or couples (Burnside, 1977; Chalfant, 1979); Ory, 1976; Silka & Keisler, 1977).

Finding no difference for men may be related to the fact that church attendance and religious commitment are low for men in general (Hoge & Roozen, 1979). Furthermore, including them with women in *couple* analyses could account for that weakened relationship. Women, on the other hand, score typically higher than men in terms of church attendance and religious commitment (Hoge & Roozen, 1979). Those who choose to remain childless, though, have been found to be nontraditional in many spheres of life, and religion, it seems, is not an exception. The low level of religious involvement that characterizes voluntarily childless females is not surprising, given that most Western religions present childbearing as an obligation; in fact, some even define it as the primary purpose of marriage.

Other Assorted Demographic Characteristics

Information on the voluntarily childless is very sparse as far as several demographic variables are concerned. For example, little is known about age at marriage, race, and place of residence. It is true that a number of studies have found that an urban residence is most common (Dietz, 1979; Gustavus & Henley, 1971; Hotz, 1975; Marcks, 1976; Nason & Poloma, 1976; Veevers, 1973b) but some of these samples had been drawn from metropolitan areas. Although adequate data on these variables are not available for voluntary childlessness *per se*, they do exist for childlessness in general. For the latest statistics in this regard, see U.S. Bureau of the Census (1980a) and Veevers (1979).

The Decision to Remain Voluntarily Childless

Timing of the Childless Decision

It was previously noted that the majority of voluntarily childless individuals do not decide at a relatively early age in life, before marriage, to remain childless. Rather, they make their decision after they have developed a lifestyle that they do not want to give up (Bram, 1974; Houseknecht, 1979b; Marcks, 1976; McLaughlin *et al.*, 1974; Nason & Poloma, 1976). These two types have been referred to as *early articulators* and *postponers*, respectively.

Who Is Responsible for Initiating the Childless Decision?

In addition to the two general types of voluntary childlessness, four types of husband–wife decision-making have been identified: independent, mutual, husband-influential, and wife-influential (Cumber, 1977). The available data suggest that the most common type is the wife-influential. In other words, it is women who are generally the first to consider not having children (Bram, 1974; Burnside, 1977; Houseknecht, 1977b; Nason & Poloma, 1976; Ory, 1976; Silka & Keisler, 1977). Nason and Poloma (1976) contended that this is the case even when the decision is reached over time during the marriage. They wrote that the wife begins to give cues about not wanting children, which the husband picks up and supports. Only two researchers do not concur that the childless choice is predominantly female-initiated: one found no difference (Cumber, 1977), and one found a discrepancy in favor of males (Marciano, 1978).

Several studies lend support to the idea that males are less ego-involved in the issue of fertility than females and, therefore, are more susceptible to influence. Houseknecht (1974), for example, found that a disproportionate number of males, in contrast to females, (1) changed their family-size preferences between the screening questionnaire and the interview and (2) expressed doubts about the seriousness of the male interviewer when he asked about plans for parenthood. Many of them indicated that they had not yet thought seriously about the issue of childbearing because it was too far in the future. Their modal age was 20. Harrell, McCunney, and Kithcart (1976) also conducted a study with unmarried undergraduate male students and found that the number of children a male desired changed significantly when he anticipated that his spouse would prefer no children. In fact, having a spouse who desired no children ranked first in influencing the male to reduce his desired family size. Silka and Kiesler (1977) focused on voluntarily childless couples and found that nearly one half of the married men who did not intend to have children volunteered that they would change their minds if their wives decided to have children. None of the wives said they would do so. Finally, Lichtman (1976)

reported that the decision to remain childless was a more cogent and salient issue for the wife than for the husband. In sum, these various studies provide further support for the notion that it is the female who tends to be responsible for initiating the childless choice.

It is interesting that, although disagreement over the childless decision is relatively rare (Hotz, 1975; Houseknecht, 1977b), it seems to be most common when husbands try to convince their wives to remain childless (Cooper *et al.*, 1978; Marciano, 1978). This finding is not surprising, given that parenthood has traditionally been *the* major role for women but not for men. In fact, it can provide an explanation for Marciano's discrepant finding (1978) that the childless decision is predominantly male-initiated. Although her sample consisted of 40 couples, her analysis was based only on the 20 that were conflicted—those that tended to be husband-initiated.

Gaining the Spouse's Acceptance

Career development, which includes higher levels of education, enhances the likelihood that a woman will consider a childless lifestyle. It also promotes a higher level of communication between herself and her husband (Hollenbach, 1980), which enables her to convey her preferences to him. Exactly how a wife might persuade her spouse to forgo the parenting role, however, is unclear. Quite possibly, it is through the use of *legitimate* power, or authority. According to Raven, Centers, and Rodrigues (1975), this type of power is based on the acceptance of a particular role structure giving the other person the right to request compliance and giving one the duty to comply. To reiterate an earlier point, parenthood is generally recognized as a primary role for women but not for men, probably because the major responsibility for children is assumed by women, so that their lives are more affected. In fact, we have seen that research supports the idea that males are less ego-involved in the issue of fertility than females (Harrell *et al.*, 1976; Houseknecht, 1974; Lichtman, 1976; Silka & Kiesler, 1977). In this connection, decision making in general has been found to vary by specific area and to reflect the specific interests, involvement, and time constraints of the individuals involved (Douglas & Wind, 1978; Morelock, 1976). Thus, it is understandable that the wife's preference might carry more weight than the husband's in the final fertility decision.

To specify some of the dynamics of spousal acceptance is not to imply that consensus is always achieved. In fact, the findings that early articulators are much more committed to the childless decision and also much more likely to experience divorce (Houseknecht, 1979b) suggest that consensus with the spouse is harder to attain when the preference is stated by an early articulator than when the preference is stated by a postponer. It does seem that the efforts of one spouse to persuade the other to accept a childless lifestyle would be effective and less stressful if the preference evolved after marriage and out of the couple's relationship as opposed to an early, determined announcement before the relationship had been firmly established—before both persons had had an opportunity to experience the benefits of a childless lifestyle.

Commitment to the Childless Decision

It was noted earlier that an important point in defining voluntary childlessness is degree of commitment. Unfortunately, most studies have reported mixed levels in this regard. This situation, of course, is not surprising, given that attitude certainty is not a common criterion for sample selection (see Table 1).

Two variables that have been found to be related to commitment to the childless decision are sex and, as indicated earlier, the type of voluntary childlessness. Rebecca (1977) and Silka and Kiesler (1977) reported that the females in their studies were more committed than the males. This finding is in agreement with Cumber's discovery (1977) that couples in the wife-influential group were more committed than couples in the mutual group. Houseknecht's conclusion (1979b) that early articulators were more committed than postponers is based on the fact that voluntary sterilization of the wife and/or the husband characterized 74% of the early articulators in contrast to only 31% of the postponers.

High rates of sterilization for contraceptive purposes, in fact, have been found in a number of studies that have not distinguished between types of voluntary childlessness (Burnside, 1977; den Bandt, 1980; Hall, 1979; Hotz, 1975; Houseknecht, 1977b; Veevers, 1973b). The various percentages were 25%, 36%, 31%, 46%, 33%, and 31%, respectively. That some people are quite committed to the childless decision is also indicated by the finding that the voluntarily childless are more consistent and effective contraceptors than parents (Bram, 1974; Burnside, 1977; Silka & Keisler, 1977). Furthermore, there is evidence that they are willing to obtain an abortion if the wife does become pregnant (Hotz, 1975; Houseknecht, 1974, 1977b; Veevers, 1973b).

An analysis of the *decision* to remain voluntarily childless has been the focus of this section. The research to date, for the most part, has shed light on the *outcome* of decision making (i.e., the timing of the childless decision, who is responsible, and commitment to the decision). Although such information is valuable, this approach has provided little detail regarding the *processes* of decision making. The discussion on gaining the spouse's acceptance is a step in this direction, but additional research on the extent and the quality of interaction and communication between the spouses is needed for a comprehensive understanding of the decision to remain voluntarily childless.

Voluntary Childlessness: Deviance or Conformity

How Are the Voluntarily Childless Viewed by Society at Large?

Researchers have reported that people who do not desire children are perceived by society as deviant, not only in terms of this specific "transgression" but also in terms of their total personalities. In 1916, Hollingworth noted that "the desire for the development of interests and aptitudes other than the maternal is stigmatized as dangerous, melancholy, degrading, abnormal, indicative of decay" (p. 24). Twenty years later, Popenoe (1936) analyzed the perceptions of those close to voluntarily childless individuals and concluded that "the great bulk of the voluntarily childless marriages are motivated by individualism, competitive consumption economically, and an infantile, self-indulgent, frequently neurotic attitude toward life" (p. 472). This negative image did not change much over the next 30-year period. In 1965, Rainwater found the image of the deliberately childless woman to be completely negative, "either totally self-involved, neurotic or in poor health" (pp. 140–141).

There are some who believe that the voluntarily childless are no longer so discredited. Bram (1978), for example, noted that this phenomenon "is becoming increasingly acceptable in society which indicates changes in the meaning of parenthood" (p. 388). She believes that voluntary childlessness will soon be a legitimate option for married men and women. Fortunately, it is possible to assess whether such a change has occurred as several recent studies have been concerned with attitudes toward people choosing this family size.

In 1976, Ory found that "When differences were perceived, parents tended, in most cases, to characterize childless couples in terms of the undesirable meanings of nonparenthood, such as more selfish, less religious, less responsible, less happily married, less mature, less natural, less feminine or masculine and for females, more likely to have mental problems." (p. 150) Selfishness was the modal response. In 1978, Polit looked at family size effects and reported that "the voluntarily childless person was perceived as less socially desirable, less well adjusted, less nurturant, more autonomous, more succorant, and more socially distant than individuals of other fertility statuses" (p. 108). Jamison, Franzini, and Kaplan (1979) considered attitudes toward women and men separately. Their results show that the childfree woman was rated as more selfish, less happy, less well adjusted emotionally, less likely to get along with her parents, significantly less sensitive and loving, and less likely to be happy and satisfied at age 65 than mothers. Similarly, the childfree husband was seen as significantly less well adjusted emotionally, as less sensitive and loving, and as having a less fulfilling life than the otherwise identical father of two. In 1979, Blake published data on attitudes toward childlessness that had been obtained through a

1977 Gallup survey of voting-age adults in the United States. She concluded that "Despite the claims of the nonparenthood literature, the childless are not seen as enjoying the most satisfying lifestyle, nor are they seen as having the most satisfying marriages" (p. 249). In 1980, Calhoun and Selby found that "The husband with children was perceived as less disturbed than either the voluntarily or involuntarily childless husband" (p. 182).

That there is very limited support for encouraging people to consider options and to make a choice with regard to parenthood was further demonstrated on June 27, 1979, on QUBE TV in Columbus, Ohio, an experimental system in which the viewing audience can make instant responses to posed questions. A surprising 69% would not approve of classroom discussions that included even a mention of nonparenthood as a possible lifestyle choice.

It seems clear, after reviewing the stereotype findings, that the voluntarily childless are still not considered normal; rather, they are imputed to have a number of undesirable attributes. It is interesting that the stereotyping of couples with no children is more negative than the stereotyping of couples with more than four children (Ory, 1976). In fact, Hoffman and Manis (1978) found that 58% of both mothers and fathers would choose to have six children rather than none at all.

A limited amount of research has been done on the characteristics associated with an intolerance of voluntary childlessness. Polit (1978) identified four factors: Catholics were more likely than non-Catholics to negatively stereotype; respondents with large numbers of children were more likely to do so than those with few or no children; people with less formal education were more likely to do so than those who had attained higher educational levels (findings by Blake, 1979, concur on this point); and older respondents were more likely to do so than younger ones. In addition to these variables, Jamrozy (1972) and Blake (1979) noted that sex exerts a strong effect on attitudes toward childlessness. In both studies, men were significantly more likely than women to express negative feelings. There is a discrepancy, however, between these findings regarding sex and those reported by Griffith (1973). Her results indicated that, overall, women appeared to be *somewhat* less tolerant than men of childless families. In further contrast, Calhoun and Selby (1980) found no rating effect based on sex. Clearly, there is a need for additional research on social perceptions as they relate to family size before any definite conclusions can be drawn.

Awareness of Pressures and Sanctions

The choice to remain childless would seem to be rational, at least to the extent that an individual recognizes that a negative reaction by the larger society will accompany such a decision. A number of studies have specifically dealt with the awareness of pressures and sanctions that are levied for deviation from the dominant societal norm prescribing children. As shown in Table 8, the re-

Table 8. Sanction Awareness and Concern Associated with Voluntary Childlessness

Source	Extensive sanction awareness	Extensive sanction concern
Baum & Cope (1980)	Yes	
Benson & Hoover (1978)		No
Bram (1974)	Yes	
Burnside (1977)	No	No
Cooper, Cumber, & Hartner (1978)		Yes
Cumber (1977)	Yes	
den Bandt (1980)	Yes	No
Hall (1979)	Yes	No
Hoffman & Levant (1980)		Yes
Hotz (1975)	Yes	No
Houseknecht (1974, 1977a)	Yes	No
Houseknecht (1977b, 1978a)	Yes	No
Jones (1978)		Yes
Magarick & Brown (1981)	Yes	
Marcks (1976)	Yes	
McLaughlin (1975)	Yes	
Nason & Poloma (1976)	No	
Ory (1976)	Yes	
Veevers (1973b)	Yes	No

sults reveal extensive recognition (Baum & Cope, 1980; Bram, 1974; Cumber, 1977; den Bandt, 1980; Hall, 1979; Hotz, 1975; Houseknecht, 1974, 1977a, 1978a; Magarick & Brown, 1981; Marcks, 1976; McLaughlin, 1974; Ory, 1976; Veevers, 1973b). (This extensive recognition is found among individuals as well as among studies).

In only two research projects were the voluntarily childless not very aware of pressures to conform to the socially defined ideal number of children. Burnside (1977) reported that "few of the childless in her sample saw themselves as social deviants or felt that they were so labeled in the community" (p. 117). Similarly, Nason and Poloma (1976) noted that "regardless of the degree of commitment, the vast majority of the couples in the sample did not perceive the social pressure that Veevers argues is present" (p. 32). Although the discrepancy between these 2 studies and the other 13 is difficult to explain, it is conceivable that the wording of the questions could have played a role. For example, Burnside's respondents may have been reluctant to label themselves as "social deviants" or to admit that the community viewed them as such if, in fact, the question contained this term.

An alternative explanation can be suggested for Nason and Poloma's finding that relates to their observation that the "experience of social pressure" varied with degree of commitment. Those with the least and the most commitment perceived little or no pressure from family and friends, whereas those with a middle-range commitment perceived the most. Although these results are not consistent with those of Baum and Cope (1980) (the definitely decided English wives in their sample were subject to the greatest pressure), they do suggest the need for more extensive research on the role that commitment to the childless decision plays in the social control process.

In addition to commitment, several additional factors appear to be related to childless individuals' perceptions of social pressure and sanctions. The one that has been most frequently identified is sex. There is growing agreement that voluntarily childless women are subjected to a greater degree of pronatalist pressure than voluntarily childless men (Cooper et al., 1978; Marcks, 1976; Nason & Poloma, 1976; Ory, 1976). The results of three studies also concur that those married less than five years tend to feel more pressure than those married five years or more (Veevers, 1973b; Ory, 1976; Hall, 1979). Living in smaller towns and country areas, as opposed to large urban areas, has also been related (Baum & Cope, 1980). Finally, membership in the National Alliance for Optional Parenthood (NAOP) has been linked to the perception of unfavorable reactions (Ory, 1976; Burnside, 1977).

Concern about Pressures and Sanctions

Being aware that there are negative pressures and sanctions that accompany noncompliance to the dominant social norm prescribing children is not the same as being concerned. Although this important distinction is not always made, a number of studies have investigated the degree of discomfort resulting from pressure to conform (Table 8). The data strongly suggest that, even though the voluntarily childless are aware of direct and indirect pressures to become parents, they are rarely very upset by them (Bram, 1974; Benson & Hoover, 1978; Burnside, 1977; den Bandt, 1980; Hall, 1979; Hotz, 1975; Houseknecht, 1974, 1977a, 1978a; Veevers, 1973b).

Only 3 out of 12 studies found that childless individuals had problems dealing with the reactions of others (Cooper et al., 1978; Hoffman & Levant, 1980; Jones, 1978). It is interesting that in all three of these, the respondents were largely members of the National Alliance for Optional Parenthood. Earlier, an association was noted between NAOP membership and the awareness of unfavorable reactions to the childless state (Ory, 1976; Burnside, 1977). Apparently, these people are not only more aware but also more concerned. It is a well-known fact that NAOP serves as a support group for many. Perhaps there is a tendency for those who have an *unusually* low level of support in their immediate environment to seek membership in this organization. Some limited support for this notion was provided by Burnside (1977), who found that the NAOP members in her sample had significantly lower social-support scores than nonmembers.

In sum, there is extensive evidence that the voluntarily childless in the United States are negatively stereotyped, that they are aware of it, but that, in general, they are

relatively unconcerned. An important question, of course, is how they maintain an attitude of indifference in this social context. Part of the answer lies in the fact that stereotypes refer to one group's perception of another group—we/they. Therefore, to assume that stereotypes serve as a measure of social sanctions is to assume that people outside one's reference groups have the power to sanction.

Although stereotypes do help to enforce the norm that prescribes children, direct, personal pressures by important people in one's life (reference groups) are perhaps the most potent. It is for this reason that the effectiveness of social sanctions applied to nonparents by *people in general* is weakened. The lack of concern that the voluntarily childless espouse is understandable if they are being informally sanctioned by groups to which they have delegated little or no importance in deciding whether or not to have children. The important consideration should be which groups exercise the greatest influence with regard to an individual's childbearing decision (as defined by the individual) and whether those particular groups are levying sanctions or are supporting the person's decision to remain childless.

One group in which every individual has membership is society at large. As the norms of society prescribe children, the individual wishing to remain childless can be regarded as deviating from the dominant societal norm. At the same time, however, the person may be conforming to the fertility norms of another reference group. In other words, as norms, even extreme fertility norms, do not exist apart from groups within which they are formed over time or which adopt them, it seems logical to infer the voluntary membership of childless individuals in groups that support their attitudes. Such reference-other support would help to alleviate the affects of pressures and sanctions levied by dissenting groups or individuals.

Some support for these ideas is available. In two separate studies (Houseknecht, 1977a, 1978a), most of the female respondents had some reference-group approval for their childless state. The extent of the approval increased considerably when only those reference groups that they had considered in their childbearing decision were included. Although the research has not been very systematic, it appears to be the family (Bram, 1974; Burnside, 1977; Cooper et al., 1978; Hall, 1979; Houseknecht, 1977b; Marcks, 1976; Nason & Poloma, 1976) and the spouse (Cooper et al., 1978; Hall, 1979; Hotz, 1975; Houseknecht, 1977b; Veevers, 1975b) who provide the main sources of support. It does not seem to be provided by other voluntarily childless individuals. That the deliberately childless have relatively little interaction with their own (Goffman, 1963), that is, with other deliberately childless individuals, has been reported by a number of researchers (Bram, 1974; Benson & Hoover, 1978; Hotz, 1975; Nason & Poloma, 1976; Veevers, 1975b).

Thus far, this discussion has focused on who provides

support. Some evidence suggests that *acquaintances* are predominantly responsible for applying social pressures (Hotz, 1975; Houseknecht, 1977b; Nason & Poloma, 1976; Ory, 1976) The findings related to these two issues (support and social pressure) support the normative explanation of childlessness that was previously elaborated. They indicate that it is, in fact, significant others who provide reinforcement for the voluntarily childless and nonsignificant others who tend to exert pressure for conformity to the childbearing norm. It appears that, although voluntarily childless individuals can be viewed as deviating from the dominant societal norm, they are, at the same time, conforming to the fertility norm of another reference group, one whose acceptable family-size range encompasses zero.

A Normative versus a Structural Explanation of Voluntary Childlessness

Trying to decide whether childlessness is normatively based or structurally based is an issue that two studies have addressed (Ritchey & Stokes, 1974; Ory, 1978). In considering these two possible explanations of childlessness, Ritchey and Stokes pointed out that persistent differentials occur in a number of sociodemographic factors. They suggested, therefore, that social structural influences operate selectively to counter the prevailing norm and to produce deviance. Thus, the explanation for differential childlessness, in their view, is structural rather than normative. They base this notion on their finding that certain sociodemographic factors vary consistently with *actual* childlessness but not with *projected* childlessness. Expectancies were felt to reflect the normative position of couples on remaining childless.

Throughout Ritchey and Stokes's article, the implication is that they were discussing voluntary childlessness. Despite their focus, however, actual childlessness included both the intentionally and the unintentionally childless, as well as postponers, the latter probably representing by far the largest category. In contrast, projected childlessness included only those who expected to remain childless. Perhaps this is the reason that sociodemographic factors did not vary in the same manner with projected childlessness as they did with actual childlessness.

Beyond this methodological limitation that characterizes Ritchey and Stokes's research, there is also a theoretical issue. This same theoretical issue applies to a study by Ory (1978), who was also interested in testing the utility of the normative versus the structural explanation of childlessness. Can a distinction be made between the normative and the structural components in this regard? This author does not think so. Norms cannot be separated from the social structure because they are a part of it. The dominant societal norm defines an acceptable family size range of two to four children (*Family Planning Perspectives*, 1977). However, there are subgroups within the dominant society, each of which possesses its own normative fertility range. Although social structural

conditions (sociodemographic factors, as defined by Ritchey and Stokes) probably do influence normative fertility ranges, they do not exercise influence independent of the norms. In other words, they do not "counter the prevailing norm and produce deviance" (Ritchey & Stokes, 1974), p. 349). The existing norms are a reflection of the particular social structure, however small, and are manifested and enforced in the interaction of the individuals who comprise that structure.

Future Needs in the Study of Voluntary Childlessness

Some directions for future research have emerged from this effort to understand voluntary childlessness. They can be generally categorized as methodological and theoretical. Although these two spheres are separated for the purpose of this assessment, it is essential to recognize the links between them. Theory provides a foundation for the interpretation of empirical data and for the generation of researchable hypotheses. If we are to derive systematic explanations and predictions, the two ultimate goals of scientific research, we must recognize the need for research that is simultaneously theoretical and methodological (Blalock, 1979). Having acknowledged the interplay between theory and research, this section focuses on specific methodological and theoretical problems that relate to the study of voluntary childlessness (Table 9). Important methodological issues include sampling, research design, measurement, and analysis. Conceptual clarifications and theory development are major concerns in the theoretical realm.[3]

Methodological Problems

Sample. It is a fact that the voluntarily childless comprise a very small percentage of the total population. Therefore, probability samples, unless they are quite large, will not produce a sufficient number of respondents to permit a detailed analysis. For this reason, most of the research to date has utilized small, nonprobability, purposive samples. Although the difficulties associated with sample improvement are great, they are not insurmountable, and efforts must be made to overcome them. Representative samples are necessary if results are to be generalized. As shown in Table 10, only 13% of the studies thus far have been able to do this. Also, researchers need to obtain samples that are at least large enough to be statistically analyzed. A third of the studies to date (Table 10) have contained fewer than 30 voluntarily childless respondents; thus, the level of statistical sophistication was considerably limited.

In addition to the size and representativeness of the samples, a related sampling issue pertains to the selection

[3]Many of these categories were used by Lewis and Spanier (1980) in their review of marital quality.

Table 9. Voluntary Childlessness:
Specific Methodological and Theoretical Needs

Methodological	Theoretical
Sample	Conceptual clarifications
1. Adequate sample size	Theory development
2. Representative samples	
3. Unbiased sample selection	
Research Design	
1. Comparison groups	
2. Longitudinal designs	
3. Cross-cultural studies	
4. Hypothesis testing	
Measurement	
1. Details as to *what* measures are used	
2. Internal validity (matching in the absence of statistical controls)	
3. Improved operational definition of voluntary childlessness	
Analysis	
1. Multivariate analysis	
2. Unit of analysis: Individuals rather than couples	

of voluntarily childless respondents. The data in Table 10 indicate that a rather common source is the NAOP. In fact, nearly a fourth of the study samples to date were made up largely of NAOP members. Findings were presented earlier in this paper suggesting that these people may be different in some regards from others who choose not to have children. Detailed comparisons are needed, and until they have been made, researchers must be careful not to generalize from this select group to voluntarily childless persons in general. Also, caution must be urged in the use of "volunteers," as there was some indication earlier that they, too, may produce biased results.

Another aspect of the sample selection issue is the fact that the research to date on voluntary childlessness has tended to focus on females. For example, Table 10 shows that 81% of the samples included females; only 43% included males. That there is a lack of information on males is even more apparent when one considers that, in some of the studies involving males, the data were presented in terms of couples.

A final consideration, marital status, needs to be mentioned in this discussion of sampling needs. Many of the studies reviewed in this work do require that the respondents be currently married. The intent here is not to suggest that all but the currently married be excluded from participation in studies but to stress the need to control for marital status. Accepting only the currently married is one way of doing it, but an even better way

would be to consider all the different categories separately. Unfortunately, a large number of studies simply mix the various marital statuses together.

Research Design. Another area that is in need of improvement is design. The use of comparison groups is a start, and we see in Table 10 that a number of studies have used them. However, there has not been a lot of progress in this regard as the percentage of studies using comparison groups before and after 1978 is 60% and 65%, respectively. Most of the research that has used comparison groups has focused on actual or intended parents. Although these groups are very important, it would also be enlightening to make detailed comparisons between the voluntarily and the involuntarily childless; between different types of voluntary childlessness, (i.e., early articulators and postponers); between the voluntarily childless and future parents; and between the voluntarily childless and former parents. Some research has been done along these lines, but it is very limited.

In terms of the time dimension, longitudinal studies are desirable because they eliminate the problems associated with retrospective reporting and make possible a better understanding of the causal sequencing of the variables associated with the childless lifestyles. Unfortunately, because a very small proportion of persons remain voluntarily childless, it is extremely difficult to carry out long-term longitudinal studies. Still, it would be useful to do follow-ups of those persons who have been so identified. Rebecca's follow-up (1977) of Bram's study (1974) is the only example to date.

The gathering of comparable data from different cultures in order to see which generalizations or concepts have applicability only within certain cultures is also an important consideration in terms of design. Table 10 shows that only three studies on the topic of voluntary childlessness have been done outside the United States thus far; they were conducted in Canada, England, and the Netherlands.

Finally, it seems that much of the research on voluntary childlessness continues to be exploratory or descriptive. Although these types of design are useful, they are best applied in the early stages of research, as their greatest contribution is the generation of insights. It is appropriate to consider them as initial steps in the research process, the next step being the formulation of testable hypotheses. In short, the need for exploratory and descriptive studies has diminished. The time has come to use the existing information for the development of more sophisticated research designs.

Measurement. Perhaps the most common measurement problem characterizing the research on voluntary childlessness is the failure to report what measures are used, at least in any systematic way. This omission may be related to the previously mentioned observation that much of the research to date has been either exploratory or descriptive. At any rate, it is difficult to assess measure-

Table 10. Voluntary Childlessness: Selected Design Characteristics of 47 Studies

Study	Number of voluntarily childless respondents	Sex		Largely NAOP members	Use of comparison group(s)	Matched comparison group	Representative sample	Cross-cultural study
		Males	Females					
Baum & Cope (1980)	161		161					England
Bellman (1974)	70	70						
Benson & Hoover (1978)	40	20	20					
Bram (1974)[a]	60	30	30					
Burnside (1977)	26	13	13	X	X			
Centers & Blumberg (1954)	93	?	?		X		X	
Chalfant (1979)[a]	?	?	?		X		X	
Cumber (1977)[a]	44	22	22	X	X			
den Bandt (1980)	65		65		X			The Netherlands
Denniston (1978)	23	23						
Dietz (1979)	28		28		X			
Fisher (1979)	71	?	?		X		X	
Gil (1978)	8		8					
Goodbody (1977)	6		6	X				
Gustavus & Henley (1971)	144	72	72					
Hall (1979)	16		16					
Hamilton (1977)	?	?	?					
Hersch (1974)	64	32	32	X	X			
Hoffman & Levant (1980)	64	32	32	X	X			
Hotz (1975)	11		11	X				
Houseknecht (1974)[a]	27		27		X	X		

Study									Canada
Houseknecht (1977b)[a]	50		50	X	X	X		X	
Jones (1978)	36		36	X	X		X		
Kaltreider & Margolis (1977)	33		33	X	X			X	
Levine (1978)	25		25	X	X	X			
Lichtman (1976)	40	20	20	X		X			
Lindenmayer et al. (1977)	7		7						
Magarick & Brown (1981)	44	44	40	X	X	X	X		
Marciano (1978)	80	40	21			X			
Marcks (1976)	42	21	10			X			
McLaughlin et al. (1974)	10		10						
Mommsen & Lund (1977)	24	?	30	X		X			
Nason & Poloma (1976)	60	30	27						
Ory (1976)[a]	54	27	95	X		X		X	
Polonko (1978)	95		95	X	X				
Popenoe (1936)	1,164	582	582	X					
Popenoe (1943)	3,210	1,605	1,605	X		X		X	
Poston (1976)	119		119	X	X	X			
Raphael (1975)	21	?	?						
Rebecca (1977)[a]	22	11	11						
Scott (1979)	11		11			X			
Silka & Kiesler (1977)	42	21	21	X	X	X			
Teicholz (1978)	38		38	X			X		
Thoen (1977)	214	107	107						
Toomey (1977)[a]	63		63	X	X	X		X	
Veevers (1972)[a]	52		52	X					
Welds (1977)	72		72	X					

[a]Also applies to other paper(s); see same study in Table 1 and its associated footnote.

ment adequacy when details are not provided. Furthermore, the absence of such information makes it unlikely that replication research can be conducted.

It was noted earlier that many of the voluntarily childless samples have been small. Thus, the ability to control statistically during analysis is seriously limited. In the absence of sufficiently large samples, which would allow controls to be instituted after data collection, it is possible to control in advance by employing a matching technique. The purpose of matching in this case is to isolate the effect of the independent variable by eliminating alternative explanations. In other words, matching can enhance internal validity. It is clear from Table 10 that, to date, very few samples have been matched.

A final point regarding measurement is how voluntary childlessness has been operationally defined in the studies that have been conducted. With few exceptions, it has been ascertained either directly or indirectly (1) that there were no biological children at present; (2) that none were expected in the future; and (3) that it was an intention or choice not to have children. Unfortunately, these three measures alone are insufficient for determining permanence and choice. Earlier in this paper, some important but infrequently applied criteria were described that could be used in a supplementary sense to enhance validity. They include (1) ruling out biological/genetic reasons; (2) ruling out children that are not one's own; (3) ascertaining attitude certainty; (4) having a duration of marriage requirement; and (5) having an age requirement.

Analysis. It was earlier noted that a third of the studies to date have contained fewer than 30 voluntarily childless respondents. Such small sample sizes are not sufficient to permit a detailed multivariate analysis, especially when a large number of variables are being investigated, as is frequently the case in exploratory and descriptive research. It is therefore not possible to separate any related effects or to identify possible interactions. The failure to examine a number of variables simultaneously has not been limited to studies with very small sample sizes, however. If progress is to be made in understanding voluntary childlessness, it is of the utmost importance that researchers in this area of inquiry increase their efforts to use multivariate analysis.

A second point regarding analysis has to do with the unit of analysis. The findings throughout this work suggest a number of differences between male and female childless samples. Researchers, therefore, need to recognize the importance of distinguishing between male and female data, even if their sample is comprised of couples. Of the 29 motivational studies being reviewed, 7 did not make this distinction (see Footnote 1).

Theoretical Problems

Conceptual Clarifications. We have seen that there is a need to become more concerned about conceptual issues, about defining voluntary childlessness, for exam-

ple. Researchers need to say exactly what they mean when they use this term. In other words, clarity in conceptual as well as operational definitions is important. It is the combination of choice and permanence that serves to distinguish voluntary childlessness from childlessness that is due to impaired fecundity, delayed childbearing, or uncertainty. Although researchers, in general, recognize these distinctions, they frequently lump the various types of childlessness together.

Furthermore, in addition to specifying different kinds of childlessness, it is also possible to designate different kinds of voluntary childlessness. The two types described thus far have been referred to as *early articulators* and *postponers*. Such typologies, although tentative and limited, can be the building blocks of empirical discoveries.

Theory Development. Last, but not least, the need for theoretical development must be stressed. This need cannot be separated technically from the need for conceptual clarifications. Conceptual clarifications provide the foundation for the formulation of propositions and theories, particularly when the operational definitions adequately specify the measurable counterparts that are represented by these concepts.

In the future, too, investigators must recognize that, in order to contribute to the theoretical understanding of voluntary childlessness, they must incorporate and build on earlier findings. Other research that deals with the same variables must be taken into account. Only in this way can similarities be acknowledged and differences explained. The review contained in the foregoing pages demonstrates that integration can produce a wealth of insights. Such an approach is necessary for theoretical development. Without it, many of the gains that otherwise might be achieved will be sacrificed.

Acknowledgments

Thanks are due to Constance S. Tully for her extremely conscientious help in organizing the material for this essay.

References

Baum, F., & Cope, D. R. Some characteristics of intentionally childless wives in Britain. *Journal of Biosocial Science*, 1980, *12*, 287–299.

Bellman, P. *Vasectomy and childless men.* Unpublished manuscript, Reed College, 1974.

Benson, D. E., & Hoover, W. *The stigmatization of intentionally childless couples.* Unpublished manuscript, Kent State University, 1978.

Blake, J. Is zero preferred? American attitudes toward childlessness in the 1970's. *Journal of Marriage and the Family*, 1979, *41*, 245–257.

Blake, J., & Davis, K. Population and public opinion: The need for basic research. *American Behavioral Scientist*, 1963, *5*, 24–29.

Blalock, H. M., Jr. The presidential address: Measurement and conceptualization problems: The major obstacle to integrating theory and research. *American Sociological Review*, 1979, *44*, 881–894.

Bogue, D. J. Principles of demography. New York: Wiley, 1969.

Bram, S. *To have or have not: A social psychological study of voluntarily childless couples, parents-to-be, and parents.* Unpublished doctoral dissertation, University of Michigan, Ann Arbor, 1974.

Bram, S. Through the looking glass: Voluntary childlessness as a mirror of contemporary changes in the meaning of parenthood. In W. B. Miller & L. F. Newman (Eds.), *The first child and family formation.* Chapel Hill, N.C.: Carolina Population Center, 1978.

Bumpass, L. L. Is low fertility here to stay? *Family Planning Perspectives,* 1973, *5,* 67–69.

Burnside, B. *Gender roles and lifestyle: A sociocultural study of voluntary childlessness.* Unpublished doctoral dissertation, University of Washington, Seattle, 1977.

Calhoun, L., & Selby, J. W. Voluntary childlessness, involuntary childlessness, and having children: A study of social perceptions. *Family Relations,* 1980, *29,* 181–183.

Centers, R., & Blumberg, G. H. Social and psychological factors in human procreation: A survey approach. *The Journal of Social Psychology,* 1954, *40,* 245–257.

Chalfant, H. P. *Childlessness: A multivariate profile of a national sample.* Unpublished manuscript, Texas Tech University, 1979.

Cooper, P., Cumber, B., & Hartner, R. Decision making patterns and post decision adjustment of childfree husbands and wives. *Alternative Lifestyles,* 1978, *1,* 71–94.

Cumber, B. *To have or not to have: Married couple's decision to remain childfree.* Unpublished master's thesis, University of Connecticut, Storrs, 1977.

DeJong, G. F., & Sell, R. R. Changes in childlessness in the United States: A demographic path analysis. *Population Studies,* 1977, *31,* 129–141.

den Bandt, M.-L. Voluntary childlessness in The Netherlands. *Alternative Lifestyles,* 1980, *3,* 329–347.

Denniston, G. C. The effect of vasectomy on childless men. *The Journal of Reproductive Medicine,* 1978, *21,* 151–152.

Dietz, T. *Factors influencing childlessness among American women.* Unpublished doctoral dissertation, University of California, Davis, 1979.

Douglas, S. P., & Wind, Y. Examining family role and authority patterns: Two metholdological issues. *Journal of Marriage and the Family,* 1978, *40,* 35–47.

Falbo, T. Only children and interpersonal behavior: An experimental and survey study. *Journal of Applied Social Psychology,* 1978, *8,* 244–253.

Family Planning Perspectives. U.S. wives 18–24 expect 2.1 children, singles 1.9. 1977, *3,* 133–134.

Feldman, G. The only child as a separate entity: Differences between only females and other first born females. *Psychological Reports,* 1978, *42,* 107–110.

Feldman, H. The effects of children on the family. In A. Michel (Ed.), *Family issues of employed women in Europe and America.* Lieden, The Netherlands: E. F. Brill, 1971.

Fisher, P. J. Optional parenthood: Do young adults really have a choice? *Optional Parenthood Today,* 1979, *7,* 7.

Gibson, C. The U.S. fertility decline, 1961–1975: The contribution of changes in marital status and marital fertility. *Family Planning Perspectives,* 1976, *8,* 249–252.

Gil, E. *Expectations for parenting.* Unpublished manuscript, 1978. (Available from San Francisco Child Abuse Council, Inc., 4093 24th Street, San Francisco, Calif. 94114).

Glick, P. Updating the life cycle of the family. *Journal of Marriage and the Family,* 1977, *39,* 5–13.

Goffman, E. *Stigma.* Englewood Cliffs, N.J.: Prentice-Hall, 1963.

Goodbody, S. T. Psychosocial implications of voluntary childlessness. *Social Casework,* 1977, *58,* 426–434.

Griffith, J. Social pressure on family size intentions. *Family Planning Perspectives,* 1973, *5,* 237–242.

Grindstaff, C. F. Trends and incidence of childlessness by race: Indicators of black progress over three decades. *Sociological Focus,* 1976, *9,* 265–284.

Gustavus, S. O., & Henley, J. R., Jr. Correlates of voluntary childlessness in a select population. *Social Biology,* 1971, *18,* 277–284.

Hall, D. D. *Coping behaviors of voluntarily childless wives.* Unpublished master's thesis, Ohio State University, Columbus, 1979.

Hamilton, M. R. Application of a utility-cost decision model to a comparison of intentionally childless couples and parent couples (doctoral dissertation, University of Maryland, 1976). *Dissertation Abstracts International,* 1977, *38,* 2360-A. (University Microfilms No. 77-21, 353).

Harrell, J. E., McCunney, N., & Kithcart, B. *Exploring fertility behavior: Sex roles and the couple relationships from the male's perspective.* Paper presented at the annual meeting of the National Council on Family Relations, New York, October 1976.

Heller, P. I., Tsai, Y., and Chalfant, H. P. *Childlessness: Contrary findings from a national sample.* Paper presented at the annual meeting of the American Sociological Association, Boston, 1979.

Hersch, Lee. *Self-actualization as it relates to the decision to have children.* Unpublished manuscript, U.S. International University, 1974.

Hoffman, L., & Manis, J. Why couples choose parenthood. *Institute for Social Research Newsletter,* University of Michigan, Ann Arbor, 1978, pp. 3; 7.

Hoffman, S. R., & Levant, R. F. *A comparison of childfree and child-anticipated married couples in relation to marital and psychological variables.* Unpublished manuscript, Northeastern University, 1980.

Hoge, D. R., and Roozen, D. A. Research on factors influencing church commitment. In D. R. Hoge and D. A. Roozen (Eds.), *Understanding church growth and decline: 1950–1978.* New York: Pilgrim Press, 1979.

Hollenbach, P. E. *Center for Policy Studies Working Papers,* No. 53. Power in families, communication, and decision-making. New York: Population Council, January 1980.

Hollingsworth, L. S. Social devices for impelling women to bear children. *The American Journal of Sociology,* 1916, *22,* 19–29.

Hotz, J. N. *An investigation of the nature and defense of voluntary childlessness.* Unpublished manuscript, Douglass College, 1975.

Houseknecht, S. K. *Social psychological aspects of voluntary childlessness.* Unpublished master's thesis, Pennsylvania State University, University Park, 1974.

Houseknecht, S. K. Reference group support for voluntary childlessness: Evidence for conformity. *Journal of Marriage and the Family,* 1977, *39,* 285–292. (a)

Houseknecht, S. K. *Wives but not mothers: Factors influencing the decision to remain voluntarily childless.* Unpublished doctoral dissertation, Pennsylvania State University, University Park, 1977. (b)

Houseknecht, S. K. *Achieving females and the decision to remain childless: A missing link.* Paper presented at the annual meeting of the Groves Conference on Marriage and the Family, Washington, D.C., April 1978. (a)

Houseknecht, S. K. A social psychological model of voluntary childlessness. *Alternative Lifestyles,* 1978, *1,* 379–402. (b)

Houseknecht, S. K. Childlessness and marital adjustment. *Journal of Marriage and the Family,* 1979, *41,* 259–265. (a)

Houseknecht, S. K. Timing of the decision to remain voluntarily childless: Evidence for continuous socialization. *Psychology of Women Quarterly,* 1979, *4,* 81–96. (b)

Houseknecht, S. K. *Female employment and reduced family size: Some insight on the direction of the relationship.* Paper presented at the annual meeting of the American Sociological Association, Boston, August 1979. (c)

Houseknecht, S. K., & Macke, A. S. Combining marriage and career: The marital adjustment of professional women. *Journal of Marriage and the Family,* 1981, *43,* 651–661.

Jamison, P. H., Franzini, L. R., & Kaplan, R. M. Some assumed characteristics of voluntarily childfree women and men. *Psychology of Women Quarterly*, 1979, *4*, 266–273.

Jamrozy, L. H. *Attitudes towards voluntary childlessness*. Unpublished master's thesis, California State College, Los Angeles, 1972.

Jones, S. H. *Toward a psychological profile of voluntary childfree women*. Unpublished doctoral dissertation, California School of Professional Psychology, Los Angeles, 1978.

Kaltreider, N. B., & Margolis, A. G. Childless by choice: A clinical study. *American Journal of Psychiatry*, 1977, *134*, 179–182.

Kiesler, S. B. Choosing childlessness (letters from readers). *Family Planning Perspectives*, 1977, *9*, 246, 297.

Levine, J. O. *Voluntarily childfree women and mothers: A comparative study*. Unpublished doctoral dissertation, Michigan State University, 1978.

Lewis, R. A., & Spanier, G. B. Theorizing about the quality and stability of marriage. In W. R. Burr, R. Hill, R. I. Nye, & I. L. Reiss (Eds.), *Contemporary theories about the family* (Vol. 1). New York: The Free Press, 1979.

Lichtman, C. H. "Voluntary" childlessness: A thematic analysis of the person and the process (doctoral dissertation, Columbia University Teacher's College, 1976). *Dissertation Abstracts International*, 1976, *37*, 1484–1485.

Lieberman, J. The one-child family. *Dialogue*, 1974, *7*, 28.

Lindenmayer, J.-P., Steinberg, M. D., Bjork, D. A., & Pardes, H. Psychiatric aspects of voluntary sterilization in young, childless women. *Journal of Reproductive Medicine*, 1977, *19*, 87–91.

Lipman-Blumen, J. How ideology shapes women's lives. *Scientific American*, 1972, *226*, 34–42.

Magarick, R. H., & Brown, R. A. Social and emotional aspects of voluntary childlessness in vasectomized childless men. *Journal of BioSocial Science*, 1981, *13*, 157–167.

Marciano, T. D. Male pressure in the decision to remain childfree. *Alternative Lifestyles*, 1978, *1*, 95–112.

Marcks, B. R. *Voluntary childless couples: An exploratory study*. Unpublished master's thesis, Syracuse University, Syracuse, New York, 1976.

Marjoribanks, K. Birth order, age spacing between siblings, and cognitive performance. *Psychology Reports*, 1978, *42*, 115–123.

Mattessich, P. W. Childlessness and its correlates in historical perspective: A research note. *Journal of Family History*, 1979, *4*, 299–307.

McLaughlin, M., Rohrer, K., & Toomey, B. *Exploratory study of childless women choosing sterilization as the contraceptive method*. Unpublished manuscript, Ohio State University, Columbus, 1974.

Miller, B. C. A multivariate developmental model of marital satisfaction. *Journal of Marriage and the Family*, 1976, *38*, 643–657.

Mills, C. W. Situated actions and vocabularies of motive. In G. P. Stone & H. A. Farberman (Eds.), *Social psychology through symbolic interaction*. Waltham, Mass.: Xerox College Publishing, 1970.

Mommsen, K. B., & Lund, D. A. *Zero parity in the black population of the United States*. Paper presented at the annual meeting of the Population Association of America, St. Louis, Missouri, April 1977.

Moore, M. J., & Moorman, J. E. Choosing childlessness (letters from readers). *Family Planning Perspectives*, 1977, *9*, 246.

Morelock, J. C. *Sex differences in compliance*. Paper presented at the annual meeting of the Midwest Sociological Society, St. Louis, Missouri, April 1976.

Nason, E. M., & Poloma, M. M. *Voluntary childless couples: The emergence of a variant lifestyle*. Beverly Hills, Calif.: Sage Publications, 1976.

National Center for Health Statistics. *Advance Data*, No. 55. Reproductive impairments among currently-married couples: United States, 1976. Hyattsville, Md.: Scientific and Technical Information Branch, January 24, 1980.

Ory, M. *The decision to parent or not: Normative and structural components*. Unpublished doctoral dissertation, Purdue University, Lafayette, Indiana, 1976.

Ory, M. The decision to parent or not: Normative and structural components. *Journal of Marriage and the Family*, 1978, *40*, 531–539.

Pohlman, E. Childlessness: Intentional and unintentional. *The Journal of Nervous and Mental Disease*, 1970, *151*, 2–12.

Polit, D. Stereotypes relating to family size status. *Journal of Marriage and the Family*, *40*, 105–116.

Polit, D. F., Nuttall, R. L., & Nuttall, E. V. The only child grows up: A look at some characteristics of adult only children. *Family Relations*, 1980, *29*, 99–106.

Polonko, K. *A comparison of the patterns associated with voluntary childlessness and low birth intentions*. Paper presented at the annual meeting of the American Sociological Association, San Francisco, September 1978.

Popenoe, P. Motivation of childless marriages. *Journal of Heredity*, 1936, *27*, 467–472.

Popenoe, P. Childlessness: Voluntary or involuntary. *Journal of Heredity*, 1943, *34*, 83–84.

Poston, D. L. Characteristics of voluntarily and involuntarily childless wives. *Social Biology*, 1976, *23*, 198–209.

Poston, D. L., Jr., & Gotard, E. Trends in childlessness in the United States, 1910–1975. *Social Biology*, 1977, *24*, 212–224.

Rainwater, L. *Family design: Marital sexuality, family size, and family planning*. Chicago: Aldine, 1965.

Raphael, D. A. The childfree marriage: Its social and psychological implications. *Smith College Studies in Social Work*, 1975, *46*, 32–33.

Raven, B. J., Centers, R., & Rodrigues, A. The bases of conjugal power. In R. E. Cromwell & D. H. Olson (Eds.), *Power in families*. New York: Sage Publications, 1975.

Rebecca, M. *Stability and change in the lives of voluntarily childless couples*. Unpublished doctoral dissertation, University of Michigan, 1977.

Renne, K. S. Correlates of dissatisfaction in marriage. *Journal of Marriage and the Family*, 1970, *32*, 54–66.

Renne, K. S. Childlessness, health and marital satisfaction. *Social Biology*, 1976, *23*, 183–197.

Ritchey, P. N., & Stokes, S. Correlates of childlessness and expectations to remain childless: U.S. 1967. *Social Forces*, 1974, *52*, 349–356.

Ryder, N. B. Recent trends and group differences in fertility. Charles F. Westoff *et al.* (Eds.), *Toward the end of growth: Population in America*. Englewood Cliffs, N.J.: Prentice-Hall, 1973.

Ryder, R. G. Longitudinal data relating marriage satisfaction and having a child. *Journal of Marriage and the Family*, 1973, *35*, 604–606.

Scott, L. *Intentionally childless women: An exploration of psychosocial and psychosexual factors*. Unpublished manuscript, Fielding Institute, 1979.

Scott, M. B., & Lyman, S. M. Accounts. In G. P. Stone & H. A. Farberman (Eds.), *Social psychology through symbolic interaction*. Waltham, Mass.: Xerox College Publishing, 1970.

Silka, L., & Kiesler, S. Couples who choose to remain childless. *Family Planning Perspectives*, 1977, *9*, 16–25.

Spanier, G. Measuring dyadic adjustment: New scales for assessing the quality of marriage and other dyads. *Journal of Marriage and the Family*, 1976, *38*, 15–25.

Stein, A. H., & Bailey, M. M. The socialization of achievement orientation in females. *Psychological Bulletin*, 1973, *80*, 345–366.

Teicholz, J. G. *Psychological correlates of voluntary childlessness in married women*. Paper presented at the annual meeting of the Eastern Psychological Association, Washington, D.C., March–April 1978.

Theodorson, G. A., & Theodorson, A. G. *Modern dictionary of sociology*. Keystone Industrial Park, Scranton, Pa.: Harper & Row (Barnes & Noble Division), 1979.

Thoen, G. A. *Commitment among voluntary childfree couples to a variant lifestyle.* Unpublished doctoral dissertation, University of Minnesota, Minneapolis, 1977.

Toomey, B. G. *College women and voluntary childlessness: A comparative study of women indicating they want to have children and those indicating they do not want to have children.* Unpublished doctoral dissertation, Ohio State University, Columbus, 1977.

Townes, B. D., Beach, L. R., Campbell, F. L., & Martin, D. Birth planning values and decisions: The prediction of fertility. *Journal of Applied Social Psychology,* 1977, *7,* 73–88.

U.S. Bureau of the Census. *United States census of population: 1940.* Washington, D.C.: Government Printing Office, 1943.

U.S. Bureau of the Census. *United States census of population: 1950.* Washington, D.C.: Government Printing Office, 1955.

U.S. Bureau of the Census. *Current Population Reports,* Series P-20, No. 186. Marriage, fertility and childspacing: June 1965. Washington, D.C.: Government Printing Office, August 1969.

U.S. Bureau of the Census. *Current Population Reports,* Series P-20, No. 288. Fertility and prospects of American women: June 1975. Washington, D.C.: Government Printing Office, January 1976. (a)

U.S. Bureau of the Census. *Current Population Reports,* Series P-20 No. 301. Fertility of American women: June 1975. Washington, D.C.: Government Printing Office, November 1976. (b)

U.S. Bureau of the Census. *Current Population Reports,* Series P-20, No. 308. Fertility of American women: June 1976. Washington, D.C.: Government Printing Office, June 1977. (a)

U.S. Bureau of the Census. *Current Population Reports,* Series P-20, No. 307. Population profile of the United States: 1976. Washington, D.C.: Government Printing Office, April 1977. (b)

U.S. Bureau of the Census. *Current Population Reports,* Series P-20, No. 325. Fertility of American women: June 1977. Washington, D.C.: Government Printing Office, September 1978. (a)

U.S. Bureau of the Census. *Current Population Reports,* Series P-23, No. 70. Perspectives on American fertility. Washington, D.C.: Government Printing Office, July 1978. (b)

U.S. Bureau of the Census. *Current Population Reports,* Series P-20, No. 341. Fertility of American women: June 1978. Washington, D.C.: Government Printing Office, October 1979. (a)

U.S. Bureau of the Census. *Current Population Reports,* Series P-20, No. 336. Population profile of the United States. Washington, D.C.: Government Printing Office, April 1979. (b)

U.S. Bureau of the Census. *Current Population Reports,* Series P-20, No. 358. Fertility of American women: June 1979. Washington, D.C.: Government Printing Office, December 1980. (a)

U.S. Bureau of the Census. *Current Population Reports,* Series P-20, No. 350. Population profile of the United States: 1979. Washington, D.C.: Government Printing Office, May 1980. (b)

Veevers, J. E. The violation of fertility mores: Voluntary childlessness as deviant behavior and societal reaction. Toronto: Holt, Rinehart, and Winston, 1972.

Veevers, J. E. The child-free alternative: Rejection of the motherhood mystique. In M. Stephenson (Ed.), *Women in Canada.* Toronto: New Press, 1973. (a)

Veevers, J. E. Voluntarily childless wives: An exploratory study. *Sociology and Social Research,* 1973, *57,* 356–366. (b)

Veevers, J. E. The life style of voluntarily childless couples. In L. Larson (Ed.), *The Canadian family in comparative perspective.* Toronto: Prentice-Hall, 1975. (a)

Veevers, J. E. The moral careers of voluntarily childless wives: Notes on the defense of a variant world view. *Family Coordinator,* 1975, *24,* 473–487. (b)

Veevers, J. E. Voluntary childlessness: A review of issues and evidence. *Marriage and Family Review,* 1979, *2,* 1, 3–26.

Welds, K. *Voluntary childlessness in professional women.* Paper presented at the annual meeting of the American Psychological Association, San Francisco, August 1977.

Westoff, C. F. Some speculations on the future of marriage and fertility. *Family Planning Perspectives,* 1978, *10,* 79–83.

CHAPTER 15

Single-Parent Families

Patricia A. Gongla and Edward H. Thompson, Jr.

With the increase in the number of single-parent families in recent years, the attention paid to this family form has grown considerably—in both the academic and the public media. This increased concern with single-parent families has, however, often manifested itself as a concern about a growing "problem," a problem that may threaten the American family.

Many times, single-parent families are viewed as abnormal and broken. They are blamed for their inadequacies and problems in living, because the families are assumed to contain within themselves the causes of their own "pathology." Other times, children growing up in single-parent families are credited with causing many of the major social problems in America, such as the rise in adolescent pregnancies, educational failure, and delinquency.

Many of these negative claims, however, have been inadequately investigated. When "pathology" assumptions guide research, bias in both focus and design becomes apparent. In addition to the deviance assumption, much of the existing research shows additional problems. Some of the investigations assume that all single-parent families are alike. Other studies tend to focus on an individual family member rather than on the family unit. Still other studies fail to examine the interplay between the family and the environment. Almost all investigations assume that the "missing parent" is indeed absent.

To begin to understand single-parent families, we need to reconsider these biases; replace them with a view of single-parent families as an existing family form; and design research to allow positive and neutral, as well as negative, aspects to emerge.

The purpose of this chapter is to help with the reconceptualization of the single-parent family as a family form and then to examine these families in the context of their environment, particularly at the macrolevel of analysis. Specifically, this chapter (1) provides a demographic profile of the single-parent family and briefly examines the

problems in estimating the numbers of single-parent families; (2) reconsiders whether the single-parent family is indeed a family by comparing one-parent and two-parent families along three dimensions of family organization—structural, psychological, and interactional; (3) examines the single-parent family in relation to the macroenvironment of major social institutions, particularly economics and employment; (4) examines the microenvironment that single parent-families inhabit; and (5) examines the relations occurring within single-parent families.

Demographic Profile

During the 1970s, the single-parent family emerged as an increasingly significant family form. Before this period, single-parent families constituted a rather constant proportion of all American families, at least since the mid-nineteenth century. From that time until the 1970s, roughly 10% of American families were maintained by a single mother or a single father (Bane, 1976; Farley & Hermalin, 1971; Sennett, 1974; Seward, 1978).

This consistency ended, however, during the 1970s. By the 1980 U.S. Census, the proportion of single-parent families had doubled (U.S. Bureau of the Census, 1981a), so that they represented 21.4% of all families with dependent children at home.

Barring extraordinary changes, the *proportion* and *number* of single-parent families will become even greater. Outside the rapid increase in the number of cohabiting couples (Glick & Spanier, 1980; U.S. Bureau of the Census, 1981b, Table F), single-parent families are the fastest growing family lifestyle in America today, having grown at 21 times the rate of the traditional two-parent family during the 1970s (U.S. Bureau of the Census, 1981a). Over the course of the 1970s, the number of single-parent families increased by 107% to an unprecedented 6.7 million families, whereas the number of two-parent families actually decreased by 4%, to 24.8 million families. The net result has been a sharp increase in both the absolute and the relative number of families maintained by one parent. Moreover, these figures do not begin to estimate the number of people or the proportion of the population who, by 1980, had lived in a single-parent family at some time in their lives. Nor do these figures

Patricia A. Gongla • Department of Psychiatry and the Biobehavioral Sciences, University of California, Los Angeles, CA 90024. **Edward H. Thompson, Jr.** • Department of Sociology, Holy Cross College, Worcester, MA 01610.

include the number of households where an unmarried adult assumed responsibility for an unrelated child.

By 1980, the paths through which single-parent families had evolved suggested that single parenting has become a more intentional and less transitional lifestyle choice for many. Separation and divorce have replaced the death of a parent as the most common pathway. Many Americans may be choosing single parenthood over unhappy marriages or immediate remarriage. In addition, during the 1970s, an increasing number of never-married women chose to create single-parent families by carrying unplanned pregnancies to term and keeping their children. As a result of both the sharp increase in numbers and the emergence of single parenting as a lifestyle option, it is estimated that a quarter of the mothers and fathers who have minor children at home will be single parents at some time in the 1980s, and that half of the children born in the 1980s will spend part of their childhood living with either their mothers *or* their fathers (cf. Norton & Glick, 1979; Weiss, 1979). If current trends continue, it is conceivable that a majority of Americans will, at some point in their lives, experience living for a period in a single-parent family.

Thus, far from being an aberration, the single-parent family is becoming a very common type of family, already representing over one fifth of the families in the white community and nearly half of the families in the black community (Staples, 1980; U.S. Bureau of the Census, 1981a).[1] Any expected reduction in the total number of single-parent families created by the slowdown in divorce (Glick, 1979a,b) is likely to be replaced by the upsurge of families maintained by never-married mothers (U.S. Bureau of the Census, 1981b). Recent trends also suggest that proportionally fewer single-parent families will be maintained by the father, even though the absolute number of single-parent fathers will continue to rise (U.S. Bureau of the Census, 1980b, p. 3).[2] Single parents will be younger than in the past (Glick & Norton, 1977) and more likely to have responsibility for younger, yet fewer, children (U.S. Bureau of the Census, 1978); and single-parent families will very likely continue the trend of living alone as opposed to

moving in with relatives (Bianchi & Farley, 1979; U.S. Bureau of the Census, 1981a).

In devising these estimates of continued growth for single-parent families, it is important, when reviewing census figures, to be clear about the definition of a family in order not to overestimate or underestimate the numbers. As illustrated in Figure 1, a distinction must be made between *female-headed family households* (or male-headed family households) and *single-parent households*. The former category can include households where the children present are not the sons or daughters of the person who heads the household; for example, a grandmother raising a grandchild, or a parent who provides a residence for a two-parent subfamily of daughter, son-in-law, and grandchild. To ignore the distinction can result in an inflated estimate of the number of single-parent families. Mendes (1976b), Lewis (1978), and Katz (1979), for example, overestimated the number of single fathers by reporting the generic category male-headed families with children.

In this chapter, single-parent families are strictly defined as those *families*—and not family households—in which there is a single father *or* a single mother raising his or her own children (cf. Weiss, 1979). Although some single-parent families live with a relative or with a nonrelative and may not be readily visible (see Figure 1), the vast majority of these families do not share their home with others.

The Dimensions of Family Life

The need to reexamine and to understand the nature and functioning of single-parent families is prompted at least by their significant number and visibility. Initially, two critical and interrelated issues emerge: First, is the single parent family really a family? And second, how different are single-parent families from (the norm of) two-parent families? We will discuss each of these issues in turn.

Is the Single-Parent Family a Family?

The term *single-parent family* has become a generally accepted term for a particular kind of family structure, one in which only one parent lives with and has the major responsibility for the care of dependent children. The existence of the term, however, does not necessarily mean that single-parent families are viewed as desirable or even as real families. Indeed, the term conveys deviation from the ideal of the nuclear family, which consists of a wife and a husband and their children. From the well-known works of Anna Freud (Freud & Burlingham, 1944) and Talcott Parsons (1951; Parsons & Bales, 1955) onward, the two-parent nuclear unit (whether isolated or not) has been repeatedly identified as "the contemporary American family."

At the heart of this definition is the assumption that a husband–wife bond defines the nucleus of a new family (see, e.g., Duvall, 1971; Leslie, 1979). Such an assump-

---

[1]Glick (1979a) presented a convincing argument that the proportion of black single-parent families in the United States is probably overestimated by underestimating the number of black husbands actually living at home: "probably one-fourth to one-third of the difference between the proportion of black families and white families reported as maintained by a [single-parent mother] could be explained by the much larger undercount of black men than that of white men" (p. 4).

[2]There is some disagreement about the accuracy of the official figures. The question is whether the official statistics underestimate the number of single-parent fathers in the United States as well as in Great Britain. Pleck (cited in Rapoport, Rapoport, & Strelitz, 1980; p. 97) estimated that the 10% figure for the share of father-headed single-parent families in America is much closer to 16%. In England, the Finer Report (cited in Rapoport, Rapoport, & Strelitz, 1980) reported an estimate of 20%.

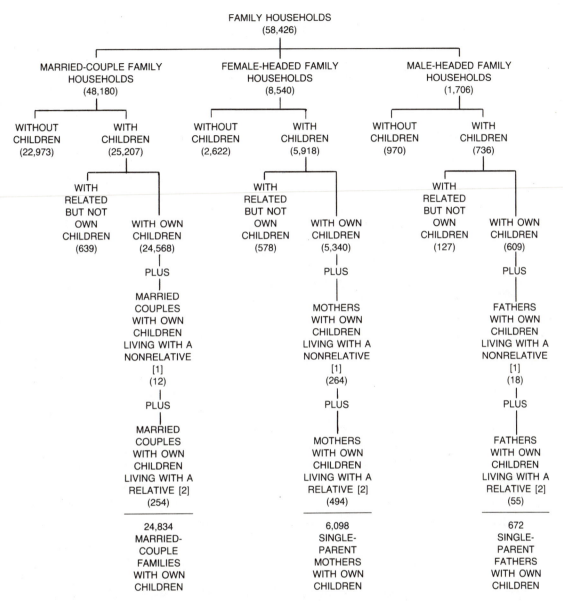

Figure 1. Distribution of family households by type and presence of children, and parent–child families by type, 1980 (numbers in thousands). (1) These families do not maintain their own household, rather they share a house or apartment with a nonrelative, who is head of the household. Formerly called secondary families, the Bureau of the Census now identifies them as "unrelated subfamilies," because they are imbedded within someone else's household. A very common example is a single parent mother and her child(ren) living with a friend in whose name the home is owned or rented. (2) "Related subfamilies" however, share a relative's house or apartment. A very common example is a single parent mother and her child(ren) living in her parents' home. (Source: U.S. Bureau of the Census, *Current Population Reports,* Series P-20, No. 366, *Household and Family Characteristics: March 1980,* Tables 1, 14, and 21. Washington, D.C.: U.S. Government Printing Office, 1981a.)

tion is, of course, not the only one possible. Margaret Mead (1949) suggested that both marriage and the father role are merely social conventions that are precariously integrated into the family system. Some theorists, therefore, point to the parent–child bond—and not to the hus-band–wife bond—as the nucleus of the family unit (e.g., Rossi, 1977; Slater, 1961). However, the institutionalized standard in American culture has been that the married couple is necessary for a "family," and difficulty occurs in seeing a family nucleus when the married couple does not exist. The literature, conforming to public opinion, has often proposed that, where there is no married couple, there is no family. If the marriage dissolves through divorce or one parent's death, the family is "broken" or "disorganized." If a marriage has never existed, the parent–child unit is "incomplete."

This emphasis on the husband–wife bond may be misplaced. As Sprey (1979) wrote, "Divorce (or any form of marital separation) ends a marriage but not a family" (p. 155). The family changes, but it can remain a family. Similarly, in the case of the never-married parent, family processes such as child socialization and boundary maintenance begin with the arrival of the child (Clapp & Raab, 1978; Plionis, 1975; Sprey, 1967).

It is our thesis that both marriage and marital disruption change families; these transitions do not necessarily create or end families. Yet researchers have traditionally emphasized the importance of the husband–wife bond, maintaining a normative perspective that seems theoretically inadequate. Sociologically considered, families can be defined more broadly, not only in terms of their structural characteristics, but also in terms of their psychological and interactive nature. Families clearly vary in structure (e.g., the number of spouses present and the degree of embeddedness in the kinship network), and they also vary in terms of the members' interactive and psychological presence. This interactive dimension of family organization refers to the ongoing process of communication and contact among the members, and it varies both across and within families by at least the expectations for boundary maintenance, the frequency of contact, and its predictability and quality (cf. Heiss, 1968; Turner, 1970). The psychological dimension, as we see it, includes the saliency of each member and the sense of attachment and identification among members (cf. Boss, 1974, 1980a; Laing, 1972).

If we include all three dimensions within our purview for defining families, then the fact that some families may be missing one parent does not automatically preclude them from being defined as families. Rather, whether the parent–child(ren) group sees itself as a family, has a common identity, includes defined patterns of exchange and reciprocity, forms rules for management of conflict, satisfies the members' affiliation and emotional support needs, and so on become the critical criteria for deciding whether a family exists. With these criteria, one-parent family systems do not need to be disqualified *a priori* from the realm of families. Families with one parent do indeed exist, whether headed by the mother or the father, and they are probably as diverse as two-parent families along the psychological and interactional dimensions.

Are Single-Parent Families Different from Two-Parent Families?

Most previous literature, using the structural framework of the number of parents present in the household to differentiate families, proceeded from an assumption that single-parent family households, because of their one-parent structure, had little affinity with the two-parent family. Grouped on the basis of an absent parent, single-parent families came to be viewed as a homogeneous group. This research tradition also introduced an additional assumption. In the view that single-parent families were a "unitary phenomenon" (Billingsley & Giovannoni, 1971), it was assumed that these families would produce different interaction patterns among members and consequently affect individual family members differently from the two-parent family system. Thus, one sees, for example, the large body of literature searching for the (usually detrimental) effects on children in "father-absent" as opposed to "father-present" families.

These assumptions not only have hindered the research on the single-parent family as a family system (Sprey, 1967) but also have limited exploration of the commonalities shared by one-parent and two-parent families (Gongla, 1982). Therefore, it is difficult not to invoke the usual plea that "more research needs to be done" that breaks away from these assumptions. This new research tradition would foster an awareness that the question of dissimilarities between one- and two-parent families requires a complex response.

To begin this reconceptualization, let us reconsider the traditional, structural classification of families. The structural distinction of one-parent families versus two-parent families has usually been made (by the public and by researchers alike) on the basis of an unfilled spouse role. However, the criteria for defining when the role is unfilled has been restricted to four conditions: the occurrence of separation, divorce, death, or the birth of a child to an unmarried woman. This distinction raises the question: Do these criteria thoroughly distinguish single-parent families from two-parent families?

Consider, for example, the two-parent family where the father is in the military and has lengthy absences from the family during tours of duty. During his absences, his role tasks are often performed by the remaining parent, perhaps in conjunction with the children. Such a family is often subject to boundary ambiguity, a stress situation where it is unclear whether the father is psychologically inside or outside the family, and therefore whether his role tasks should remain open (Boss, 1980a,b). During the long periods of father absence, is the family really a two-parent family? Similar boundary ambiguity occurs in families where one parent is imprisoned, hospitalized for long periods, traveling frequently on business, and so on. Nor does the parent need to be physically separated from the home for these issues to emerge. If an unhappy marriage exists, for example, various strategies of escape may be used. As Bernard (1964) noted years ago, strategies of "absorption in work, in travel, in entertaining, in clothes, in church work; or retreat through alcohol; or illicit alliances" (p. 723) are available. In all of these situations, when one of the parents is frequently absent so that interaction is minimal, when the role tasks for both parents are performed by one parent, when a parent is psychologically distanced from the family, does a two-parent family exist?

From another viewpoint, one might consider the single-parent family where, after a divorce, both parents maintain a strong commitment to the children. The children stay with the noncustodial parent every weekend; the parents maintain friendly relations with each other and frequently discuss the welfare of the children; both parents perform parenting tasks; and both (even if one parent predominates) have frequent interaction with the children. This pattern can occur whether joint custody has been awarded or not, as long as a coparenting relationship is maintained. In these circumstances, two interrelated households form one family system, which Ahrons (1979) identified as the binuclear family system. Should such a family really be classified as having only one parent?

It becomes clear from such examples that single-parent families and two-parent families are not discrete entities. Whether we really have a one-parent or a two-parent family depends on the particular viewpoint used and the dimensions of family life explored.

A Typology of Single-Parent Families and Two-Parent Families

For the sake of conceptualizing, one can focus on the major dimensions of family functioning that were outlined previously: the structural, the psychological, and the interactional. A typology of families can be created by considering the extent of involvement of one parent on each of these dimensions. For this typology, two conditions are made. First, although only the presence or absence of one parent's involvement in each dimension is referenced, the degree of involvement is actually on a continuum. Second, the viewpoint used is that of the parent who may or may not be absent from the family (see Figure 2).

In both the structural one-parent and two-parent families, it is thus possible to consider whether the parent in question is psychologically or interactionally involved with the family. Theoretically, there are family types to fit each one of the cells, but certain types are much more prevalent than others. An explanation or example for each one of the cells is presented.

Cell A represents the traditional "intact" family: two married parents, residing in the same household, continually interacting and psychologically involved with the family. Society has viewed this as the ideal family, using it as the norm by which to judge all families.

Cell B is a family where one of the parents has little or no interaction with the other members yet remains psychologically incorporated in the family. Such families may exist where a parent is hospitalized or imprisoned or has long business-related absences.

In *Cell C*, the involvement of one of the parents is on a *pro forma* basis. Interaction continues but the parent invests his or her psychic energy elsewhere, such as in work or in another person outside the family (e.g., an extramarital affair.)

An example of *Cell D* would be a family where one parent has a serious mental disturbance, such as severe depression, and withdraws from interaction and from affective investment in the family. A very different example exists in the case of a wealthy family where the spouses become estranged, but the marriage is maintained, perhaps for economic reasons. One of the spouses may divest herself or himself of the family, eliminating almost all interaction and psychological involvement. Economic resources allow separate households and a continuation of the same lifestyle without the necessity of much contact with the rest of the family.

As such examples indicate, the families that are socially labeled *two-parent* can have great variation in terms of the extent and type of involvement that the parents maintain with the family. Similar variation exists among the families labeled as *one-parent*, as the examples below indicate.

The most prominent example of *Cell E* is the family where the two parents are granted joint custody of their children after divorce. The levels of psychological in-

STRUCTURAL						
TWO PARENTS			**SINGLE PARENT**			
	INTERACTIONAL				INTERACTIONAL	
	Presence	Absence			Presence	Absence
PSYCHOLOGICAL				PSYCHOLOGICAL		
Presence	A	B		Presence	E	F
Absence	C	D		Absence	G	H

Figure 2. Typology of single-parent and two-parent families.

volvement and interaction of both parents with the children remains high. The parents themselves maintain significant contact as they share the responsibilities of raising their children. Observers of custody arrangements (Abarbanel, 1979; Ahrons, 1980; Galper, 1978; Greif, 1979; Newsome, 1977) estimate that this coparenting pattern may soon be the rule rather than the exception.

Cell F is a situation where one parent ceases continual interaction with the family yet remains psychologically attached to it. The parent still views the family members as significant others and modifies her or his behavior in line with her or his perception of their expectations. If we switch viewpoints for a moment, Cell F could include families where the death of a parent has occurred. The memories of the deceased parent are invoked by the remaining family members to guide current behavior, thoughts, and emotions. The "absent parent" is psychologically inside the family boundary, even though the parent is physically absent (Boss, 1980b; Lopata, 1979).

Examples of families in *Cell G* are more difficult to hypothesize than the other family types. However, it is possible to imagine a situation where a parent might, after divorce, eliminate most of his or her psychological attachments to the family yet, perhaps out of a sense of duty, maintain some interaction with the family, such as telephone calls on all special occasions and regular letter contact when sending support checks.

Cell H is the counterpart of Cell A. The families here are the single-parent families portrayed in the literature and recognized by society. Only one parent lives with and has sole responsibility for the children. The absent parent has almost no interaction with and little psychological investment in the family.

In summary, the typology shows that, in order to understand the nature and functioning of families, we need to consider how much investment *both* parents have in the family, whether it is structurally classified as one-parent or two-parent. As Boss (1974) pointed out, "Just because the father (or mother) is not visible we cannot automatically conclude that he (she) is absent" (p. 6).

This conclusion seems deceptively simple. However, the examples used in the typology have been presented from the perspective of one parent's physical, psychological, and interactive presence or absence. How the family members within the family system perceive and respond to that parent also needs to be considered. According to Boss (1974), "the perceptions of the members of the system create an important variable if not the most important variable of all" (p. 6). A second issue that needs to be considered is one mentioned earlier: Because parental roles differ from spousal roles, though they are closely intertwined, we need to untangle the extent to which the psychological and interactive investment in one is similar to or dissimilar from the other.

The Making of Single Parenthood

Given a conceptual model that indicates that some families labeled as single-parent actually have two parents'

strong involvement, whereas some two-parent families have only one parent involved, the question can still be asked: Is there any value in using only the structural dimension to define and classify single-parent families as being different from two-parent families? If so, under what conditions?

Recall that the structural dimension is the dimension by which society often defines and labels families. This fact has real consequences for families. A family defined as single-parent is treated differently from a two-parent family. A family that becomes labeled as *single-parent* inhabits a different social world from that of the family defined as "intact." Social institutions and social networks treat the two classes of family differently (Thompson & Gongla, 1983). Because of this different treatment, many single-parent families share common problems, issues, concerns and may thus adopt similar repertoires of coping. It is open to investigation how these external social forces affect the interior of family life and move families along the continua of the psychological and interactional involvement of both parents. Schorr and Moen (1979), for example, contended that, given the problems faced by single-parent families and the societal reaction that reinforces two-parent norms, single-parent families come to define themselves as different from two-parent families; members of single-parent families come to believe the false dichotomy between Cell A and Cell H families.

Therefore, whether to continue to consider a family single-parent or two-parent is not a simple matter, nor is it detached from normative meaning. The particular issue that we study may help to determine the definition. If we study the family in relation to the larger social environment, the structural definition may be sufficient. If we study the psychosocial interior of the family, then we need to consider as well the psychological and interactional dimensions.

The foregoing section suggests that single-parent families differ from two-parent families largely on the basis of their *family household:* One natural parent does not reside in the household. Single-parent families are structurally different from the modal (and normative) two-parent family household. However, this is not the only basis of comparison. How the behavior of the family members is organized constitutes a second point of comparison, and how the family as a system is perceived by the family members becomes a third point of comparison.

We have suggested that some single-parent and two-parent families may well be more similar than dissimilar when compared along their interactional and psychological dimensions. Families in Cells C and G of the typology, for example, similarly characterize a situation in which the present or absent parent minimally engages himself or herself in the family system, though occasionally being involved in some family activities. As one of Rubin's (1976) respondents commented:

My father was a very quiet man. He almost never talked, even when you asked him a question. He'd sit there like he didn't hear you. Sometimes, an hour later (it was like he'd come out of a

spell), he'd look at you and say, "Did you want something?"
Most of the time, he just didn't know you were there. (p. 36)

Or as one middle-class, two-parent child described his family:

My mother was always busy—too busy for us. At least that's the
way it felt when I was little. She was always out doing her thing—
worrying about the poor people or the black people or on one
damn committee to save the world or another. I used to be
jealous of those people because she didn't seem to spend nearly
as much time worrying about me or caring that I felt lonely or
scared. (Rubin, 1976, p. 26)

These two recollections of life in a two-parent family, one characterizing the parent's preoccupation and the other the parent's withdrawal, typify families within Cell C. From the point of view of the child, these two images would seem very comparable to what a single-parent child may remember if he or she grew up in what Mendes (1979) identified as the sole-executive family: "[This] single parent is the only parental figure actively involved in the lives of the children . . . the other parent voluntarily or involuntarily has no contact with the family and performs no parental functions" (p. 193).

Our thesis is that, on the one hand, the inside of a family system is an endless process of movement, sometimes from connectedness and attachment to separateness and withdrawal; and that, on the other hand, there are social forces and policies external to the family system that help to dissolve family connectedness along both its psychological and interactive bonds. We thus see patterned movement in some two-parent families from Cell A to Cell D and in many single-parent families from Cell E to Cell H. That patterned movement, or adaptation to both internal and external factors, may follow the path from both adults' participation within the family (Cell A or E), to one parent's psychological divestment of the family (Cell C or G), to his or her subsequent withdrawal from family activities and interaction (Cell D or H). Alternatively, the pattern of a family's adaptation could follow the process from connectedness (Cell A or E) through one parent's withdrawal from the family's everyday interaction, decision making, and child-rearing responsibilities (Cell B or F) to the parent's eventual psychological withdrawal and absence (Cell D or H).

Some family systems may "decompose" as a result of one parent's interactional absence or psychological absence. When the parental role is not actively taken by the person whom the children call mother or father, the family system is viewed as having an ambiguous boundary. How families go about resolving the ambiguity of who is in and who is out of the family system could potentially produce both detrimental and beneficial outcomes (cf. Boss, 1980a; Laing, 1972).

It would seem that decomposition within families along the *interactional continuum* follows from the family's adaptations to social forces that are external to the family system. For example, employment in our postindustrial society often demands a full-time commitment and thus pulls a parent away from the family. Such divestment of involvement with the family system, while investing oneself in an occupation, has been called the *invisible-American-father syndrome* (Biller & Meredith, 1972). This parent is so frequently absent from the family system (though maybe not from the home) that the family functions in many respects as if it were a single-parent family. The physically absent parent in a single-parent family is also frequently pulled away from the family system by societal forces, for example, the imposition of legal visitation restrictions (Greif, 1979; Stack, 1976). Here, the parent's investment in family interaction is proscribed. Thus, whether the parent (usually the father) is pulled from the family system while coping with societal prescriptions or has to abdicate the parental role to comply with proscriptions, the outcome is that the parent's interactional involvement in the family system is reduced. Interactional absence and subsequent family decomposition therefore seem to result from one member's adaptation to forces outside the family system.

Rather than being pulled from the family system, some parents may consciously withdraw their interactional involvement. The Academy Award–winning film *Kramer vs. Kramer* appeared to emphasize this type of withdrawal. However, we see such individual adaptations to dissatisfaction with parenting as unable to fully account for many families' decomposition. Often, parents want to engage themselves in their parental role, yet their interactional involvement is constrained.

Family decomposition along the *psychological continuum*, however, appears to be a by-product of one parent's separateness and the family system's subsequent accommodation to the loss. That "absent" parent may be interactively present on a *pro forma* basis but emotionally divested, as illustrated in Rubin (1976); or the parent may be both interactively and physically absent, as in the case of desertion. Psychological absence seems to be a "secondary absence." It need not always appear. Physical events such as death or divorce or long-term separation may not mean that the interactively absent parent is perceived by the other members of the family system as absent (cf. Boss, 1977). Family decomposition along the psychological continuum may best reflect how the family system secondarily adapts itself to changes in the members' investment and interactional presence.

In summary, the suggestion is that social forces and policies outside the family system encourage a family's patterned movement from connectedness toward separateness, whether the family system is two-parent or single-parent. Each parent is in a position in a social system that is defined in terms of a set of interconnected, though not necessarily consistent, expectations. In concert, other statuses outside the family system pull at a parent's interactional involvement with or commitment to his or her family. Although the general expectation is that the parent should parent, the specific expectations that each parent faces often cause role conflicts and demand some degree of separation of one's time and energy from the family. The family system is therefore vulnerable, and the single-parent family would seem to be especially vulnerable: The noncustodial parent in a single-parent family system is most often legally required to curtail the time spent within the (single-parent) family; thus, interactional absence and decomposition occur along the psychological continuum.

Which families decompose along what pathways and under what conditions is still an empirical problem. Whether single-parent and two-parent families follow similar pathways is also an empirical problem.

Macroenvironment: Major Social Institutions

Single-parent families, like all other families, live in a bureaucratic society. Major social institutions and service organizations—education, government, health care, housing, and so on—are governed by large-scale bureaucracies and impersonal business forces. The American family system, whether the two-parent or single-parent, must deal with these institutions to acquire the basic products and services that it needs.

In the early 1970s, Cogswell and Sussman (1972) noted that bureaucratized services

make certain assumptions about the family. They gear their services toward an ideal of what the family ought to be, namely, a nuclear traditional one. . . . Because agencies idealize the traditional family, their programs are aimed at restoring this form and, thus, are ill-equipped to provide relevant supportive services to variant family forms. (p. 513)

Furthermore, as Smith (1980) observed, single parenthood is often viewed as a temporary condition or as a transitional phase in the family life cycle; thus, government and business often gear their policies and programs only to the traditional, two-parent family.

Given the usually slow rate of change in large-scale service organizations, whether much change has occurred since Cogswell and Sussman's article is doubtful. For example, they noted that health-care services for children were organized for the convenience of the medical-care professionals and not around the availability of adults to accompany children to the health-care agency. A decade later, clients are still supposed to accommodate to the schedules of the health-care agency, regardless of whether a nonemployed mother is available to attend to the child's medical-care needs. Yet, the single parent (like other working parents) may lose income and even jeopardize a job by meeting the time demands of a health organization. Additionally, Horowitz and Perdue (1977) and Wilk (1979) noted that health professionals' institutionalized approach to single-parent families is to treat these families as if they were two-parent, or to view whatever clinical problems appear as being a result of the family's deviant, one-parent structure.

Although many schools have begun to hold parent–teacher conferences and other parental-participation activities during evening hours, school hours remain truncated, so that working parents must continue to seek, and often to pay for, child-care arrangements during their working hours. Trends in the public financing of education in some states threaten to further shorten school hours, cut after-school activities, and extend single parents' need for child care.

Market forces and economic policies have created problems with housing availability for one-parent families. The cost of owning a home has escalated tremendously, climbing beyond the reach of many single-parent families. Suitable apartment space has become more costly and less available in many areas. Some apartment owners may not accept children, and many apartments have been converted to condominiums too expensive for many single-parent families.

In some major religions communities, single parents may still have a difficult time. If divorced or never-married, they may still be viewed as having committed a moral wrong. If they turn to their church for consolation in times of stress, they may instead be saddled with blame, losing a former source of support. Pais and White (1979) noted this case when they listed commitment to a religion that maintains negative sanctions for divorce as a negative correlate of adjustment and family redefinition. Although there are signs of change, such as the divorced Catholics movement (Young, 1978), change is slow in the large-scale, bureaucratized churches.

Legislation and social policy have often not been supportive of the single-parent family. Major needs such as child-care services and long-term educational and vocational upgrading for single mothers (Brown, Feldberg, Fox, & Kohen, 1976) are not only unfilled but spark controversy and negative sentiments (Woolsey, 1977). With the emergence of a more conservative era, Ross and Sawhill's hope (1975) for neutrality in public policy with regard to family organization may be too liberal. The quest, as with the proposed U.S. Senate bill called the Family Protection Act (1979), appears to be toward federal governmental support of the traditional, two-parent family.

Nowhere is the impact of social institutions on single-parent families as prominent as in the combined areas of economics and employment. Because of the large differences in information about families headed by mothers versus those headed by fathers, we consider these two types of families separately in discussing economics and employment.

Single Mothers

Throughout the 1970s, the income of single-parent families headed by mothers remained less than one third of the income for husband–wife families. More important, the income difference appears to be getting larger. In 1976, for example, single-parent families maintained by the mother had a median income of $5,942, which was only about one third the median income for husband–wife families (Johnson, 1978). By the end of the 1970s, single mothers commanded half the income of single fathers, and half again the average income of the two-parent family (U.S. Bureau of the Census, 1980c, Tables 25 and D).[3]

Families headed by a lone mother are over three times more likely than those of single fathers, and six times more likely than two-parent families, to have an income below the poverty threshold (U.S. Bureau of the Census, 1980a, Table 19). Single-parent families maintained by the mother now represent the largest fraction of all the various types of families in poverty (Wattenberg & Reinhardt, 1979), and throughout the 1970s, they continued to account for a large proportion of the families who lived in poverty (Hoffman, 1977). The reality is that about one third of all white families maintained by a single mother (33.5%) and over one half of the black families headed by a single mother (58.8%) were in poverty in 1978 (U.S. Bureau of the Census, 1980a, Table 19).

Obviously, one implication of these income and poverty figures is that a substantial portion of separated, divorced, and never-married mothers must at some time depend on public assistance. The majority of single-parent mothers qualify for public assistance (Sibbison, 1974; Stein, 1970). Yet, Schorr and Moen estimated that a ''third of the women-headed, single parent families never receive welfare.'' Of the two thirds that do require assistance, the typical single-parent mother in a 10-year period is assisted for 2 years, leaves welfare, and eventually depends on it again to make ends meet for a few more years (Schorr & Moen, 1979, p. 16).

What these data suggest is that the gap between single- and two-parent family incomes cannot be readily explained by the small proportion of single mothers who might be identified as ''welfare-dependent.'' Rather, public assistance is more an emergency fund to make ends meet: ''The chief source of income for single parents is own earnings, particularly for mothers who obtain a divorce'' (Bane & Weiss, 1980, p. 14). Welfare dependency, when it does exist, seems to be more associated with the recipient's age, education, and health status than with the recipient's single-parent status *per se*.

A number of possible explanations have been advanced for the wide economic gap between one- and two-parent families. Some of these explanations do not hold up when empirically tested. For example, there is a belief about single-parent mothers' propensity to use welfare: Families in or near poverty become single-parent in order to take advantage of public assistance. The data, however, tend not to support the proposition that ''welfare breaks up marriage'' or that ''welfare triggers out-of-wedlock parenting'' (Bould, 1977; Bradbury, Danziger, Smolensky, & Smolensky, 1979; Chief, 1979; Dinerman,

1977; Ross & Sawhill, 1975). Neither can the economic inequity that separates single-parent and two-parent families be readily explained by the increasing size of the population living in families with the lowest income—families headed by a single-parent mother (Bianchi & Farley, 1979). Nor is the widening economic gap between single- and two-parent families simply explained by the slightly greater tendency of lower-income families to separate or to divorce (Espenshade, 1979).

Rather, one major explanation for the income differential between one- and two-parent families, which remains after empirical testing, lies in the effects of marital disruption. Most single-parent families evolve from marital disruption, and a sizable reduction in family income generally follows that disruption. To some extent, whether the custodial parent is male or female, a drop in family income following marital disruption is predictable and reflects the loss of the absent spouse's income and unpaid services. In recent years, the size of this reduction has become more severe.

This reduction in income largely explains the economic gap between single-parent and two-parent families, as well as the prevalence of single-parent mothers' poverty or near-poverty (Bane & Weiss, 1980; Bianchi & Farley, 1979; Espenshade, 1979; Hoffman, 1977; Mallan, 1975). Bradbury *et al.* (1979) analyzed the aggregate census data and found that women in 1975 could expect a 40% reduction in income were they to become the head of the household. Several analyses of the Michigan prospective study on 5,000 families (the Panel Study of Income Dynamics) similarly indicate that the economic costs for single-parent mothers following marital disruption have become severe, even with welfare funds. In 1973, divorced or separated mothers suffered nearly a 30% drop in family income (Hoffman, 1977). Bane and Weiss (1980) found that, by 1978, the average income of widows had fallen 31%, whereas divorced mothers experienced a 43% drop and separated mothers a 51% drop. One would guess that the never-married would be worse off, on the average, given the generally younger age, lower education, and higher percentage of minority families (Johnson, 1978).

These data strongly suggest that, for single-parent mothers, poor economic conditions are attached to the state of single parenthood itself. Becoming a single parent is detrimental to the mother's and her family's economic well-being.

The reasons for this decline in fortune seem to be tied to macrosocial forces rather than to psychosocial processes within the family. Simply stated, large-scale social institutions provide little support for mother–child families. Specifically, two major social factors seem to affect the family's economic status:

The first factor, the low status of women in the work force, is widely recognized. Women are relegated to lower paying jobs and may receive lower pay than men for similar work. Often, less opportunity exists for career advancement and upward mobility. In addition, the social ideology of ''appropriate'' sex roles has left many wom-

---

[3]The $16,000 family income noted for single-parent fathers is a ''Guestimate.'' The available official statistics do not break down the average incomes for males with no wife present, only for husband–wife families and females with no husband present. The figure is derived from the income for divorced males with related (though not necessarily their own) children in the family household.

en ill prepared, in terms of education, job skills, motivation, and work attitudes, to compete successfully for better paying jobs.

The second factor is the general organization of work within our society. Employer organizations view employees as workers, not as family members with family responsibilities. Family-related tasks, such as child care and household maintenance, usually cannot be performed by the worker during working hours. Flexible working hours have not become a widespread option. Nonetheless, as many of these family tasks cannot be accomplished during nonworking hours, the assumption underlying the work organization is that someone other than the worker will perform those family tasks. Traditionally, this has meant a two-parent family with the mother remaining out of the labor force to care for family needs. Although this pattern creates problems for the increasing number of two-parent families where both parents are employed, it is particularly burdensome to single-parent families, which are much less likely to have the resources to pay for appropriate services. In addition, single parents can rarely make trade-offs with the noncustodial parent about who will assume responsibility for the family tasks each time there is a conflict between family and employment responsibilities.

Other issues, such as a dearth of child-care options, a lack of flexible business and social-service provision, and generally low social prestige and power for women, contribute to the single mother's burdens (Brandwein, Brown, & Fox, 1974). Single mothers are at a particular disadvantage in seeking better paying and upwardly mobile jobs that require work beyond the standard eight-hour day, such as attendance at evening meetings, travel, weekend report-writing, or a general willingness to devote as much time as necessary to complete business. Such a schedule is impossible for many single parents, as they could not fulfill their child-care and household responsibilities. Economic status is further affected by low and irregular child-support payments and low levels of public assistance for the minority of single mothers who remain out of the labor force (Bane, 1976; Espenshade, 1979). It is important to note that all of these forces contributing to the low income-potential of single-parent mothers usually occur at a time in the family life cycle when the children are young and in need of care, and when family expenses are high (Dinerman, 1977).

The effects of lowered economic status on single-parent families are manifold. Families must often reduce consumption and move to a poorer neighborhood. Subsequent problems with reduced personal safety, higher delinquency rates, and poorer schools are likely (Bane & Weiss, 1980; Brandwein *et al.*, 1974). Low economic status is also likely to affect child development, although this factor is rarely examined in research on single-parent mothers (Herzog & Sudia, 1971). Low income, combined with the unstable or demeaning sources of income that many single mothers must rely on, may be related to a low sense of one's personal control of fate and one's ability to plan for the family's future (Bould, 1977).

In summary, the economic reality of single-parent mothers "going it alone" has not improved. Bianchi and Farley (1979) asked:

[Do] the recent shifts in living arrangements of adults and children suggest that our society has gradually moved away from a family system which maximized the economic well-being of women and children and toward one which appears to minimize their well-being but maximize that of men? (p. 544)

Alternatively, rather than gradually moving away from supporting one family system, could it be that our society has not moved toward supporting various family systems, and especially those headed by women?

Single Fathers

From the sparse evidence available, it seems that single-parent fathers are in much better financial condition than are single mothers (Johnson, 1978, p. 32). Probably because divorced fathers who receive custody of their children are in good financial circumstances to begin with (Duncan & Morgan, 1976), single fathers' level of economic well-being is comparatively less austere, and their reduction in family income is much less dramatic (Espenshade, 1979).

In one study, a concerted effort to locate lower-income single fathers met with failure (Orthner, Brown, & Ferguson, 1976). As Orthner and his colleagues indicated: "For a man to get custody of minor children, he has to demonstrate a degree of resource availability that will be respected by the courts, his peers, and perhaps his former spouse" (p. 432). Thus, although not facing the poor economic conditions that women face, men are still confronted by an inflexible work organization that is not concerned with the worker's family responsibilities. Sacrifices have to be made, and as Gersick (1979) found, raising the children is very often perceived as worth the occupational sacrifices. Such men felt that time flexibility at work would be most helpful in alleviating the conflict between their work and their child-care tasks.

Keshet and Rosenthal (1978) reported that a majority of fathers thought that their child-care duties did limit their job mobility: Their work lives were hampered in terms of working hours, earnings, and job transfer. Men may also face a lack of understanding from co-workers when they must place child-care needs above their work. Men are still identified in this society in terms of their work roles; child care is not supposed to be their primary domain. Similarly, fathers who are poor may face discrimination in trying to obtain welfare or AFDC funds, which are culturally identified as being for families of mothers and children.

In summary, although families maintained by single fathers seem to be in much better financial shape than those headed by single mothers, these fathers may similarly be hampered in their occupational roles by the parental tasks and household responsibilities of going it alone. Life inside these families and the effect of single parenting on fathers, nonetheless, remain virtually uncharted.

Microenvironment: The Community

Just as the family redefines and reorganizes itself when it becomes a single-parent family, so also does the community redefine its response to this family (Bohannon, 1970). Changes in the informal social networks of relatives and friends, in turn, affect the family's reorganization. Previous research, however, has not often examined the social relationships of the single-parent family, thus leaving questions about changes in the networks and the effects of changes on the family largely unanswered. With few exceptions, it is only the more recent research that has begun to recognize the importance of examining the interchange between the family and the microsocial environment. Most of this work has been restricted to discussing the social relationships of the parent rather than those of the children.

As indicated in the available studies, what needs to discussed is: How do the social networks of the family change when it becomes defined as a single-parent family? And what are the effects on the family when networks change, particularly the levels and types of social support?

Change in Social Relationships

The literature has suggested that single parents, in general, have a "roleless role" (Hiltz, 1978). The thesis holds that American culture has no clearly defined role for the separated, divorced, widowed, or unmarried parent, nor does it have clear norms for other individuals and groups to follow when interacting with the single parent (e.g., Adams, 1975; Udry, 1974). But what does this mean in terms of the changes in social relationships? If there is no role, are both the single parent and all former friends and relatives in a state of complete ambiguity over whether and how to maintain or change their relationships? Alternatively, are there any cultural norms that would reduce this ambiguity and help to determine the nature of relationships after a person becomes a single parent? To what degree does one's marital status or change in marital status affect one's relationships with friends and relatives?

To consider these questions, we need to distinguish between relationships with relatives and those with friends, as norms differ for the two groups.

Relationships with Relatives. A starting point for examining the changes in the single parent's relationships with relatives is a consideration of kinship norms. The perspective employed here is a structural one: We assume that, although kin statuses and roles are not rigidly determined, there is some degree of structure or patterning in the kinship system. In addition, the norm for marriage in American society is "free choice": The selection of the spouse is made by the individual rather than by his or her kin group. Free-choice marriage is usually correlated with kinship systems so that the choice of a mate has little

effect on the kin groups of either spouse, as few or no economic or political alliances are made between the kin groups of the husband and the wife (Zelditch, 1964). The marriage, instead of linking kin groups, links only the spouses themselves. From this brief overview, it could be hypothesized that (1) access to the spouse's relatives would be primarily indirect, gained through the spouse's interactive bonds, and, therefore, (2) norms of kinship that apply to one's own relatives (consanguine kin) do not fully extend to the relatives of a spouse (affinal kin).

Within the kinship structure, there are more specific norms governing behavior: the norms which revolve about the issue of autonomy for the adult child. Adult children are expected to live relatively independently of their parents, maintaining separate households and supporting themselves financially. What does all of this mean for the parent who divorces or who loses a spouse through death? Based on these kinship norms, one could further hypothesize that a single parent's (1) relationships with in-laws will tend to worsen as compared with relationships with blood kin; (2) relationships with blood relatives will tend to remain unchanged; and (3) relationships with blood kin will tend to remain unchanged or to improve if the single parent maintains a degree of autonomy similar to that maintained while the parent was married.

Although more research is needed, the initial evidence supports the hypotheses. First, after the loss of a spouse, single parents seem to maintain or increase their ties—both behaviorally and affectively—with their own blood relatives, and the children have patterns of contact similar to those of their parent (Anspach, 1976; Gongla, 1977; Hiltz, 1978; Spicer & Hampe, 1975; Stack, 1974).

In contrast, the parent's ties with in-laws tend to worsen, particularly after separation or divorce. In this case, the child may be able to maintain ties with those relatives, provided that the noncustodial parent maintains contact with the child and thus provides an access route to his or her own blood kin (Anspach, 1976; Gongla, 1977; O'Brien & Garland, 1977).

If the single parent's relationships with his or her consanguine kin worsen, issues about the single parent's autonomy may be a major factor in the decline. As Weiss (1979) indicated, relatives—particularly the single mother's parents—may criticize the single parent, not understanding or approving of the situation, as well as offer unsolicited advice. The worst case occurs when the single mother with her children moves into her parents' household. Here, she is likely to lose much autonomy and to decline in status as her parents reassert their authority. This situation leads to tension and strong dissatisfaction within the home environment (Colletta, 1979; Weiss, 1979). The children may have problems in determining where authority lies, as role boundaries become confused (Dell & Appelbaum, 1977). The children may offer less support to the single mother and may assume less responsibility than do children who live only with their mothers. Thus, to maintain good relationships with blood kin, it seems valuable for previously married single parents to keep some distance and independence from their relatives and to continue the autonomy that the parents had when they were married.

Although there is less research about the never-married, the literature does suggest that the never-married maintain ties with their blood kin. In particular, the large subgroup of young, especially adolescent, mothers seems to rely heavily on support from relatives, with the greatest support coming from the young mother's own parents. Besides receiving financial aid and help with child care, a large subgroup (perhaps a majority) of unmarried mothers live for some period with their relatives, usually their own mother (Bolton, 1980; Grow, 1979; Presser, 1978). Although the young mothers are not ''giving up'' the autonomy of an adulthood that they have not yet reached, there is a potential for role conflicts between the two generations; for example, the young mother may claim more autonomy in child care than her own parents wish (Bolton, 1980, p. 112).

These findings on single parents' relations to blood kin—whether the parent be previously married or never-married—seem to hold for both blacks and whites. There may be some difference, however, in the degree to which single parents and their children are incorporated into the kin groups. Black single parents may rely more heavily on aid from kin, and the kin are more ready to offer aid. Maintaining autonomy, particularly by keeping a separate household, may not be as important for black single parents, particularly if economic resources are low. Probably more than in the white community, the one-parent family has a secure position in the kin group, and the kin group gives stability to the family. The extended-family structure has more often remained viable among blacks (Martin & Martin, 1978; St. Pierre, 1980; Stack, 1974), although today there is some evidence that the viability of this extended-family system is being threatened, ironically by the rise in separate single-parent households (Cazenave, 1980).

In summary, the social situation for single parents is not completely ambiguous with regard to the single parent's relatives. The single parent is not left ''roleless.'' Although day-to-day interactions with relatives are far from fully determined by norms, the patterns of contact, support, and attachment do seem to be governed to some degree by the structures and norms of kinship. The single parent remains incorporated in his or her own blood-kin group. The single parent still has the kin status and role that she or he had before becoming a single parent. What may be lost, however, is the kin role in the spouse's kin group.

Relationships with Friends. Friendships are not governed by the same norms as kinship. For the most part, friendships are based on personal commitment. One must earn the status of friend, rather than being ascribed the status, as is true of kin relationships. One achieves the status of friend by reciprocating the support offered by the other. Friends are often in similar life circumstances,

which enable each one to understand the other's situation and thus to provide mutual support.

Because of these qualities, friendships are likely to be called into question when a person becomes a single parent. The person's life circumstances are changed significantly, so that a disparity can develop among friends; others may find it difficult to understand the new situation of the single parent or to identify with it. Ironically, at the same time, the single parent's needs for support and aid become greater. As Weiss (1979) wrote:

Single adults, more than the married, need ties outside their homes, for they are without that fellow adult within the household who can provide the married with assistance and companionship. But the single parent's need for ties outside the home is greater even than that of other single adults because the single parent, as head of a family, is more likely to need the help of others. All the forms of assistance—advice, relief, availability in emergencies—that a married parent could expect of a spouse, must be sought by a single parent from relationships outside the home. (p. 167)

In effect, as the need for support becomes greater, the single parent's resources for reciprocating become smaller.

Given these conditions, we might expect significant changes to occur in the friendship circles of new single parents. Although the research evidence is tentative, it supports this statement. For the divorced and the widowed, the network of married friends may be lost over time, and the single parent begins to feel marginal to this ''married'' community. For the divorced, in particular, a sense of being a ''fifth wheel'' may develop (Kitson, Lopata, Holmes, & Meyering, 1980). For those not previously married, difficulty develops in having one's single, non-time-constrained friends understand the problems, responsibilities, and lack of freedom associated with being a single parent; these friendships are likely to fade (Clapp & Raab, 1978; Weiss, 1975, 1979). Although single mothers and fathers are likely to maintain ties with a few close friends from ''before'' (Clapp & Raab, 1978; Rosenthal & Keshet, 1980), it is also likely that a degree of social isolation will ensue (Hetherington, Cox, & Cox, 1979; Kitson et al., 1980). This seems particularly true for men, who are less likely than women to have formed an affectively rich social-support system and who are thus more likely to experience loneliness (Greenberg, 1979; Schlesinger, 1978).

Whether the single parent is the father or the mother, a reduction in the friendship network is likely after a person becomes a single parent. A new circle of friends who understand the single parent's situation may eventually be formed, but this formation takes time. The new circle is often other single parents (Goode, 1956; Greenberg, 1979; Hunt, M., & Hunt, B., 1977; Staples, 1980; Weiss, 1979). This new circle may be smaller because the single parent has less ability to reciprocate and less time to invest. With regard to cross-sex friendships, single mothers appear to experience more difficulties, as they have less behavioral latitude than men because of social norms (Greenberg, 1979).

In summary, because of the nature of friend relationships, single parents are likely to undergo a period of significant change in the friendship network, losing former friends and thus, perhaps, lacking the social support that they need. Although new networks of friends are likely to form eventually, whether these networks provide adequate support has been inadequately investigated.

Effects of Support on the Single-Parent Family

Social support is often viewed as a positive mediating influence in family stress situations (McCubbin, Joy, Cauble, Comeau, Patterson, & Needle, 1980, p. 864). However, not many investigations have assessed how social support and participation in informal social networks affect the one-parent family.

Direct assistance from family and friends (e.g., help with child care, economic aid, and the performance of household repairs) can help the family accomplish the necessary tasks. But in addition, social support may play a much larger role in both family and individual functioning. Colletta (1979), for example, found that a lack of or a dissatisfaction with social support was associated with restrictive and punishment-oriented child-rearing practices by the single mother. Brassard (1979) also reported a link between the custodial parent's informal support systems and positive parenting styles. In terms of individual functioning, Brown, Feldberg, Fox, and Kohen (1976) mentioned the presence of more hopeful attitudes among those with limited support. Loge (1977) and McLanahan, Wedemeyer, and Adelberg (1981) noted that positive adjustment to the single parenting role was directly related to the parent's finding new social roles and an identity outside the family. Social supports, therefore, do appear to affect the parent's functioning.

A particularly valuable suggestion of the *need* for social support comes from epidemiology. Although the results are only tentative, research suggests that support from social networks is important in reducing the occurrence of illness and death (Berkman & Syme, 1979; Cassel, 1976; Cobb, 1976; Mueller, 1980; Turner, 1980). As unmarried adults seem to be subject to higher rates of physical and psychological morbidity and death than are married adults (Bachrach, 1975; Berkman, 1969; Bloom *et al.*, 1978; Gove, 1972; Parker & Kleiner, 1966; Renne, 1971; Verbrugge, 1979), it would seem that single parents are not receiving adequate support from their social networks. Lacking a spouse to give support, they are not "protected" from illness (Bloom, Asher, & White, 1978; Kessler, 1979; Pearlin & Johnson, 1977). Single parents generally do not turn to their children for support (Chiriboga, Como, Stein, & Roberts, 1979), so support must come from people outside the family. Thus, single parents seem to have greater unmet needs for informal social support.

Microenvironment: Single-Parent Family Relations

The widespread belief that single-parent families are necessarily harmful to those members going it alone is a sociological problem: Are single-parent families' relations and their effects detrimental to family members, and if so, how? We first examine the literature that assumes that single-parent family relations are detrimental or even "pathological" and then review the literature in which single-parent family life is more systematically analyzed and the psychological and interactional dimensions are considered.

The Research Tradition

Considerable research on single parenthood has been published in professional journals since the 1930s (e.g., Shaw & McKay, 1932). Much of the research purportedly dealing with single-parent families, however, does not study the family. Rather, it examines the individual family members who are residents of single-parent households; and typically, the investigator's focus is on the effects that this single parent condition has on individual family members, especially the children. That research is flawed methodologically and is based on various biases.

Although occasionally distinguishing among the specific types of single parenthood that arise from separation, divorce, death, or the birth of a child to an unmarried woman, the traditional research usually classifies all single-parent families in the same manner, as father-absent (single-parent) *households*. This research implies that all one-parent *families* are psychosocially identical. Grouping all single-parent families together, this homogeneity assumption resulted in a long tradition of studies that assumed that father-absent (single-parent) conditions would produce direct (and usually detrimental) effects on the individual family members, especially boys.

A typical study divided children into only two groups, pairing those from two-parent families with those from father-absent (single-parent) households; the study then typically attributed whatever differences existed between the children to the children's family life, that is, to the father's absence or presence. The effects commonly investigated fall into four categories: sex-role development (e.g., Badaines, 1976; Biller, 1968; D'Andrade, 1973; Greenstein, 1969; Hetherington, 1966, 1972, 1973; Santrock, 1970); general personality functions or emotional disturbances (e.g., Baker, 1967; Biller, 1971; Hoffman, 1971; Pederson, 1966; Trunnell, 1968); cognitive development (e.g., Atkinson & Ogston, 1974; Carlsmith, 1964; Consortium for the Study of School Needs of Children from One-Parent Families, 1980; Landy, Rosenberg, & Sutton-Smith, 1969; Rosenthal & Hansen, 1980; Santrock, 1972; Shinn, 1978); and various other pathological behavioral adaptations, such as delinquency or suicide (e.g., Dorpat, Jackson, & Ripley, 1965; Goldstein, 1972; Lester & Beck, 1976; Miller, 1958).

This body of literature assumes that father absence or presence by itself explains the observed difference among the children. The implied psychoanalytic perspective appears to force the assumption that father absence deprives the children of the role models and the childhood experiences necessary for "healthy" development, and it further tacitly suggests that the unmarried mother cannot manage the family environment. Assumptions such as these have resulted in a body of literature so biased that it is of limited use; it can be characterized as "impressionistic journalism" (Raschke & Raschke, 1979, p. 367). Sprey (1967) commented, "The traditional research design in which one parent families—often of different nature—are compared with intact ones is methodologically irrelevant and will easily lead to misleading generalizations" (p. 31).

Not only have studies following the traditional research design continued the homogeneity assumption by pitting father-absent against "intact" family systems, they have failed to consider the extent to which the (absent) father is absent. Such researchers have viewed the father as being completely absent from the family system when (as previously discussed) the spouse role is unfilled. Current research suggests, however, that fathers rarely vanish magically from the family system (Hetherington, Cox, & Cox, 1976; Rosenthal & Keshet, 1978), nor is their complete absence often preferred by family members (Goldsmith, 1979; Wallerstein & Kelly, 1980; Weiss, 1979). Nonresidential parents are expected to continue their parental role, and many do for a time, whether previously married to the child's mother or not (Abarbanel, 1979; Earls & Siegel, 1980). In addition, "father presence" in the two-parent household does not automatically ensure the father's interaction with his children or a warm, accepting relationship (Blanchard & Biller, 9971; Boss, 1974; Nye, 1957; Raschke & Raschke, 1979; Rubin 1976).

The main point, however, is that this research tradition has created a conceptual and methodological quagmire by assuming that the father-absent (single-parent) condition has a direct and usually detrimental effect on individual family members. Researchers have often failed to consider variables associated with the single-parent condition, even such obvious factors as sociodemographic differences. The Consortium for the Study of School Needs of Children from One-Parent Families (1980), for example, continued this crude *post hoc* explanatory design. Finding a high prevalence of troubled children living in single-parent households, it made three unwarranted assumptions: that single-parent family relations bred the pathology; that the troubled behavior emerged after the children and the fathers had lived apart; and that single-parent families, in fact, shared the same opportunities and life chances in their community as two-parent families.

An additional problem with this literature is that it often disregards single-parent families that function normally; many researchers focus on only those single-parent families found in a variety of "clinical" populations, such as juvenile courts and outpatient clinics (e.g., Kalter, 1977).

Findings from this large body of literature have not been unconditionally accepted by all scholars (see, e.g., the critical reviews by Biller, 1971; Blechman, 1982; Blechman & Manning, 1976; Herzog & Sudia, 1968, 1971, 1973; Hetherington & Duer, 1971; Kadushin, 1970; Lamb, 1976; Sprey, 1967). Herzog and Sudia (1968), for example, argued that some of the effects of father absence could be accounted for entirely by the economic poverty that many single-parent families cope with everyday. McCord, McCord, and Thurber (1962) pointed out that a mother lives in the father-absent household, and that her relationship with her child(ren) might account for some of the "father-absent" effects (cf. Biller & Bahm, 1971; Hetherington, 1972, 1973; Hoffman, 1971; Pederson, 1966). Reports of child pathology resulting from the father's absence from the household have rarely been confirmed in a study that controlled for a previously ignored concomitant variable. Moreover, when representative samples of single-parent and two-parent families have been studied, and when their differences in socioeconomic status have been controlled for, the hypothesized detrimental effects on the children attributable to the single-parent family structure have generally failed to appear. What is found is that there are fewer differences between children in single-parent families and two-parent families than within each family type (Blechman & Manning, 1976, p. 66; Herzog & Sudia, 1971).

New Research Direction

Some investigators, recognizing the weaknesses of the traditional parent-absent–parent-present research design, began studying families and how they interact, that is, whether the interaction within single-parent and two-parent families affects individual members differently. Although most of this research still focuses on the individual and thus does not directly assess families as families, it is nonetheless important.

First, it has begun a new research tradition in which single-parent family relations are more thoroughly analyzed. Second, it does not assume that single-parent families are a homogeneous group, even though they are structurally similar and may share a number of common problems. Third, these studies pay attention to the presence of the "absent" parent and his or her effect on the members of the single-parent household. Last, and most important, this new research substantiates the idea that family processes often supersede family structure. For example, research on how mothers interact with their children (Aldous, 1972; Biller, 1971; Hetherington, 1972, 1973; Longabaugh, 1973), on the inaccessibility of the "absent" parent both *before* separation (Blanchard & Biller, 1971; Kagel, White, & Coyne, 1978; Minuchin, 1974; Reuter & Biller, 1973) and *after* separation (Boss, 1977, 1980a; Earl & Lohmann, 1978; Kagel *et al.*, 1978;

Wallerstein & Kelly, 1980; Weiss, 1979), on the frequency and types of interaction between parents after marital disruption (Raschke & Raschke, 1979), and so on has changed our understanding of single-parent family relations. These findings strongly suggest that a number of single-parent families are more similar to two-parent families than they are to other single-parent families.

Effects on Children

Herzog and Sudia (1971) argued, "There has been repeated evidence that when factors within the home are studied, family climate has been a more potent variable than father absence, per se" (p. 85). Nonetheless, few family-interaction studies have yet been able to isolate which family-interaction patterns and what climate reliably differentiate troubled from nontroubled families (Jacobs, 1975, p. 56). Rather, the general finding is that living in a single-parent family does not necessarily harm children. That finding, however, appears to be both conditional and dependent on what Herzog and Sudia (1971, 1973) identified as the family's quality, harmony, or climate. Thus, although particular family patterns have not been isolated, the general family environment or climate has been proposed as crucial.

The weight of what little available evidence there is appears to support Herzog and Sudia's premise. Nye (1957) reported that adolescents living in family environments characterized as "unhappy" showed significantly poorer adjustment in areas of psychosomatic illness, delinquent behavior, and parent–child adjustment; no effect for family structure was noted. Kagel, White, and Coyne (1978) found that what differentiated disturbed adolescents from normals was the latters' perception of their family environment as expressive, warm, and cohesive; family structure showed no effect. Similarly, Raschke and Raschke (1979) found that public-school children's self-concept was lower in "unhappy" homes and when the children perceived the family environment as conflict-ridden; again, no significant differences across types of families was found. Berg and Kelly (1979), however, showed that not only did children's feelings of acceptance or rejection by their parents covary with self-esteem, but an interactive effect also showed the rejecting intact families as causing their children to suffer the lowest self-esteem.

In general, these studies suggest that family environment, independent of family structure, can limit or exacerbate children's social and psychosocial problems. Only the study by Berg and Kelly (1979) shows that family structure and family environment combine in a double-barreled effect, and these results challenge the assumption that single-parent families automatically jeopardize children's well-being.

One interesting explanation that helps to account for these findings has been suggested elsewhere (Blechman & Manning, 1976; Wolff, 1950). It could be that the decreased size of the single-parent family gives rise to more frequent and intense interaction, an increase in statements of affection, and a decrease in hostile statements. The reduced family size "changes not only communication rate but communication content" (Blechman & Manning, 1976, p. 78). Reduced family size further reduces the status inequities between parent and child (Weiss, 1979).

This hypothesis is consistent with the research findings that children who report that their home environment is filled with turmoil, conflict, and rejection *before* their parents' separation also experience less trauma after the separation. That is, the exit of the parent, in this case, reduces the tension in intrafamilial relationships, permits an increase in the frequency and intimacy of interaction among the single-parent family members, and thus enhances the child's self-esteem and self-concept. Family relations move toward a new equilibrium with the exit of the parent from the household (Boss, 1974; Burchinal, 1964; Lamb, 1977; Magreb, 1978).

That the evolution of a two-parent household to a single-parent household may enhance the *family system's* move toward a new equilibrium does not imply that the exiting parent necessarily disappears. On the contrary, physical absences need not be synonymous with psychological absences. For the child, two separate parent–child relationships often continue after marital separation, one with the "absent" father and one with the "present" mother. Do both these relationships become more intimate and introduce favorable changes in communication? Do physically absent fathers become more interactively and psychologically present in their relationship with their children? Whether or not children maintain the same frequency of interaction with their father, does the father remain psychologically salient in the child's phenomenological family?

The answer to each of these three questions seems to be an affirmative although conditional one. Children do frequently develop close relationships with both parents, if their noncustodial parent is accessible and the custodial parent "accepts" the other parent (Abarbanel, 1979; Cline & Westman, 1971; Earl & Lohmann, 1978; Rosenthal & Keshet, 1978; Wallerstein & Kelly, 1980; Weiss, 1979). The children continue to think of themselves as the children of two parents: "Although the mother's caretaking and psychological role became increasingly central in these families, the father's psychological significance *did not* correspondingly decline" (Wallerstein & Kelly, 1980, p. 307; italics in the original). In addition, as Weiss (1979) noted, "most single parents do what they can to foster their children's relationships with their non-custodial parents. They do so despite their own feelings, because they believe it important for the children" (p. 159).

As a result, these tentative findings do suggest that the quality of the father–child relationship after marital disruption improves, at least for a while (Earl & Lohmann, 1978; Grief, 1979; Hetherington, *et al.*, 1976). Over time, however, father–child relationships become more emotionally shallow if the frequency of encounters decreases as a result of the restrictions on visitation. However, it would be misguided to assume that the father decreases in saliency in the eyes of the child. Although many children would generally prefer more frequent contact with the father and often desire free, unrestricted access to this parent (Rosen, 1979; Wallerstein & Kelly, 1980), they think of themselves as having two parents. The father remains psychologically present if not also interactionally inside the child's (single-parent) family boundary.

Another area of research, that on "children of divorce," has examined the impact of marital disruption on children, looking closely at children's reactions and adjustments to the disruption of the family and the loss of everyday contact with a parent (e.g., Despert, 1953; Landis 1960; Hetherington, 1973; McDermott, 1970; Wallerstein & Kelly, 1980). The earlier investigations in this body of literature were particularly inclined to conceptually mix two analytically distinct issues: single-parent family relations and the effects of marital disruption. They were additionally likely not to distinguish whether the observed effects of the divorce or a parent's death were immediate, short-term, or long-term; and frequently, the samples of children coping with the postdivorce situation were drawn from clinical populations.

The literature on single-parent family relations presents the thesis that hostile or rejecting family relations result in negative effects whether the observed family structure is one-parent or two; the children-of-divorce literature similarly suggests that the quality, harmony, or climate of the marital disruption shapes the effects on the children (Sorosky, 1977; Weiss, 1975, 1979). If the milieu of the divorce situation has an air of hostility or includes hostile interaction between the spouses over their parenting roles, the children appear to be especially vulnerable to negative feelings (guilt and fear) and behaviors (irritability and aggressiveness). As Anthony (1974), Cline and Westman (1971), Landis (1960), and others have suggested, angry parents may well jeopardize their children's well-being.

Because the hostile feelings and interaction are probably most visible before the divorce, the predivorce rather than the postdivorce phase may well be the most stressful. Luepnitz (1979), for example, asked a small group of (normal) college students who were children of divorce to recall which aspect of divorce acted as the major stressor. She found that the household conflict before the divorce presented the major problems. Using a clinical sample of children and adolescents who asked for help in the midst of the divorce, Wallerstein and Kelly (1980, p. 304) similarly found that the predivorce phase had the greatest impact and produced the most stress.

What these limited data from the two bodies of literature suggest is twofold:

First, the quality of the child's family environment in a single-parent family may be less detrimental than the quality of his or her family environment preceding the marital disruption. This idea is consistent with Bohannon's (1970) and Wallerstein and Kelly's (1980) conceptualization of divorce as a several-stage process. It is also consistent with the interpretation that divorce is an adaptive strategy for the family in a postindustrial society (Bane, 1976; Parsons, 1970, p. 166). Whether the short-term or long-term costs, therefore, outweigh the gratification and benefits is an empirical question.

Second, the impacts on children caused by marital disruption and the impacts caused by single-parent family relations, when controlling for families' socioeconomic status, need to be analytically and methodologically distinguished. Studies have shown that the event producing the single-parent family structure is a stressful one, probably producing greater stress than events such as the birth of a sibling or moving to a new community. Yet, studies have not shown whether the stress actually results from the parents' separation as spouses, the antecedent conflict, or a parent's interactional and/or psychological absence before, during, or immediately after the marital separation. Neither have studies shown whether the impacts that persist past the initial stressor(s) are diminished or fueled by single-parent family relations. In other words, there is a need to consider the crucial differences between marriages and families and to shift the focus from the conduct of spouses to the relations within families (Sprey, 1979, pp. 155–157).

In summary, because of the history of methodologically flawed—then partly improved—studies that have successively reported contradictory findings, because of the analytical and methodological needs to untangle the effects of the precipitating stressor from single-parent family relations, and because of single-parent families' unequal access to societal resources, we cannot reject the null hypothesis: There is no known detrimental effect (on children) directly attributable to single-parent family *relations*. Single-parent families do not appear automatically or necessarily to result in a pathological environment for children. The crucial variable seems to be the manner in which the family members (including the absent parent) redefine their joint situation. In some families, that redefinition is likely to cause troubles for the child(ren). But it is still uncharted whether this redefinition is more detrimental than the unspoken redefinition that occurs in some two-parent families with a psychologically absent parent.

Children in single-parent families do, of course, face special circumstances and problems. To be sure, some children pay a penalty. They live in a single-parent household in a two-parent society. In a typical situation, their father lives elsewhere, and their mother must "deprive" them of her complete attention as she attends to her head-of-the-household responsibilities. Children do feel deprived (Schorr & Moen, 1979; Weiss, 1979). They also cope with fewer resources and more frequent residence changes than many of their (two-parent) peers (Bane & Weiss, 1980; Brandwein *et al.*, 1974; Ferri & Robinson, 1976), as well as with other people's misconceptions of life in a single-parent family. But these special problems emerge as a result of their membership in a family that society defines as abnormal and as one that will go away with "family reconstitution." The problems have not been known to be reflections of single-parent family relations; rather, they seem to reflect the economic, psychological, and social difficulties that result from the family's inability to command access to the same resources as two-parent families (Blechman & Manning, 1976; Brandwein *et al.*, 1974; Schorr & Moen, 1979). Thus, some children do pay a penalty, particularly when the family is headed by a female who has less access to financial, material, and social rewards, and when "the relative *social acceptability of the cause* of parental absence may result in a *real* change in a family's access to pleasant and aversive consequences" (Blechman & Manning, 1976, p. 69; italics added).

Effects on Parents

In comparison to the volume of literature on children in single-parent families, relatively little attention has been addressed to the single parent. This small body of literature presents the thesis that most single parents, particularly mothers, must shoulder more exclusively the responsibilities, pains, and joys of being both the head of the household and a single adult.

Single parents share problems with all parents. The needs of the children, role conflicts, and insufficient resources to meet aspirations—all of these affect single parents, who also cope with special troubles because of their situation as single parents. Weiss (1979) identified

the fundamental problem in the single parent's situation [as] the insufficiency of immediately available support. The married parent can rely on a partner. . . . The single parent must make do with much more limited help from children, kin, friends and professional helpers. (p. 265)

Their insufficiency of immediate supports means, effectively, that the single parent may suffer from what Weiss (1979) called an "overload."

First, single parents, who have the sole responsibility for the household, must meet alone whatever the children need emotionally, physically, and intellectually. This *responsibility overload* carries beyond children's needs, to include meeting the demands imposed by the physical environment (e.g., house repairs) as well as the demands of making decisions virtually alone, without someone with whom issues can be regularly discussed. As Glasser and Navarre (1965) argued, the effect is that the single parent's "responsibilities to home and children tend to never be completed" (p. 102). Such open-ended, largely unshared, and potentially burdensome responsibilities can result in a sense of role strain.

Not all single parents, however, confront role strain. This cognitive stress, generated when the single parent feels unable to comply with normative expectations, is often mitigated by the pattern of role distribution before marital disruption (Blechman & Manning, 1976) as well

as by the single parent's access to social supports. For example, single fathers may experience less role strain than single mothers, probably because of their greater access to scarce resources, more favorable community attitudes, and special treatment by the children's schools, neighbors, and work associates (Mendes, 1976a,b; Orthner *et al.*, 1976). One study (Rosenthal & Keshet, 1978), however, suggests that the strains experienced by fathers are similar to those identified by mothers. At first, fathers do feel overwhelmed with child care and household maintenance because of their inexperience. But motivated, first, by the fear of losing a relationship with their children and, second, by finding satisfaction in the parenting role, fathers adapt and sense their effectiveness. Whether or not fathers' strategies for adjusting are, in fact, effective remains an empirical question.

Second, single parents who assume the responsibility for housekeeping, child rearing, and employment become committed, thus, to two full-time jobs (Weiss, 1979, p. 272). This *task overload* largely results from what Blechman and Manning (1976) identified as "leader strain" (p. 72). This construct refers to the behavioral consequences of a situation where the single parent must carry out disparate tasks that overburden his or her available time and energy. All single parents must endure some leader strain. Thus, Glasser and Navarre (1965) suggested that we can also expect some behavioral resolution. Resolution could hypothetically evolve in three directions, yet it empirically appears to follow one path. Although single parents could overload their children with a variety of tasks to reduce their own role conflict or could curtail their involvement with the children as a secondary avenue to reducing the strain and conflict, they are more likely to simply neglect some tasks, particularly those associated with the traditional housewife role (M. Hunt & B. Hunt, 1977; Loge, 1977; Weiss, 1979). Thus, it appears that the options to overload the children or to cut back one's involvement with the children involve too many significant sacrifices for the parent and the child.

That two pathways to reduce the task overload are "unselected" does not mean that they are unused. Single-parent families are organizationally different from two-parent families; therefore, there is a blurring of the distinction between the statuses of adult and child in the single-parent family. In comparison to most two-parent families, this blurring leads both to having the children assume some responsibilities formerly assigned to the parent and to "depriving" the children of a large quantity of time. The blurring of the adult and child statuses also changes the quality of family interaction and encourages more negotiation. As Weiss (1979) suggested:

The absence of [a] parental echelon . . . permits the development of a new relationship between parent and children in which the children are defined as having responsibilities and rights in the household not very different from the parent's own. (p. 74)

Single parents thus do make demands on their children to assume greater responsibility within the household's division of labor, though they worry about overloading the children (Weiss, 1979). Single parents are also structurally constrained from as much involvement (i.e., time spent) with their children as two parents can afford, though they do worry about "depriving" the children of children's needs (Weiss, 1979).

Third, single parents cope with a sense of *emotional overload*. Weiss (1979) observed that

Emotional overload occurs because the parent's emotional resilience proves inadequate for the number and intensity of the children's demands. The absence of relief from constant availability to the children produces emotional depletion. (p. 275)

Simply stated, a child's love is demanding rather than supporting. Whereas adolescents are capable of serving as companions and sources of support (Weiss, 1979, p. 11), children, in general, become an obstacle to a single parent's intimacy needs.

In a study of single parenting and intimacy, Greenberg (1979) found:

The majority of the parents interviewed saw single parenting as directly constraining their sexual activities because of location constraints (having to go away from home), reduced amount of sexual activity, and reduced quality as a result of tiredness or intrusion by children. (p. 316)

For single parents, the very physical responsibility of caring for children acts as a major constraint: Intimacy and sharing cannot be left to chance but must be actively planned (Greenberg, 1979, p. 324). Adjustment to single-parenting demands thus may require considerable time (Hetherington *et al.*, 1979; Weiss, 1979) and may require finding new roles outside the family unit as a single adult, not as a single parent (Clayton, 1971; Loge, 1977; Rosenthal & Keshet, 1978).

Although these three problem areas are indigenous to the single-parent family system, they are not restricted to the single-parent family. Many two-parent families are likely to cope with similar problems, especially when one of the parents is physically or psychologically absent for long periods of time. It is our belief that many of these personal troubles are social issues, arising from various kinds of cultural norms and social policies. The responsibility and task overloads, for example, are exacerbated by the lack of child-care facilities, the presumption that dual parenting is harmful to the well-being of children, and the present adversary system in which separating spouses and lawyers barter parenting time with the children for money (Abarbanel, 1979; Grief, 1979; Kohen, Brown, & Feldberg, 1979). As Gordon (1980) suggested:

It is, after all, not just task and responsibility overload that lead to emotional overload. It is also the strain of living in a society which contains members who insist upon forcing all people into a mold, while ignoring the consequences of poverty, inequality. . . . single parents need, as other people do, a society that uses its resources to shape policies based on the recognition of the diversity of human experiences. (p. 287)

Discussion

The purpose of this chapter was to present a specific conceptual framework that would help social and behavioral scientists and clinicians to rethink their views on single-parent families. The framework presented is, we think, fairly parsimonious, even though it intentionally complicates the image of *the* single-parent family. Suggesting diversity among single-parent families, we do not claim to have uncovered and reviewed all the relevant issues, nor have we thoroughly analyzed each of those included. Rather than presenting such a review, we see this chapter as beginning to differentiate single-parent families from the stereotype of the single-parent family household. Much of that argument lies in the chapter.

Considering the number of studies on single-parent families that have been published, it is surprising that more systematic attention has not been given to middle-range theory-building. It is also surprising how few empirically grounded generalizations can be made in this area of family studies. In this chapter, however, some tentative directions have been suggested. Four in particular stand out.

First, a major task facing researchers interested in pursuing the distinction between single-parent households and single-parent families involves reassessing the extent to which the "absent" parent is absent. Despite marital status and household arrangements, we cannot assume that the noncustodial parent is interactively and/or psychologically absent. For example, from the perspective of the children, the family may evolve from occupying a single household to occupying two households. That is, a family boundary that includes two parents may continue to exist despite multiple households. Similarly, the custodial parent may view the other parent as still partially responsible for the children and therefore may include the other parent psychologically and/or interactively within the family boundary. Thus, the issue is how the family defines itself. Is the "absent" parent completely absent? Do the family members share a common, sense of the family boundary? Is the noncustodial parent more likely first to disengage interactively than to disengage psychologically? Are multiple-household (single-parent) families an emergent lifestyle? Is the multiple-household (single-parent) family only a probable stage in boundary definition?

Second, we need to examine the positive effects of single-parent family relations. Much has been written about the "broken," "unsuccessful" single-parent family, yet little attention has been given to how single-parent families successfully adapt. What are the benefits of becoming a single-parent family to the children, to the custodial parent, to the nonresidential parent, and to the family system?

Third, Simmel (Wolff, 1950), in his insightful treatment of intimacy, suggested that the mere number of affiliated individuals has a bearing on the qualitative aspects of relationships. Thus, what are the effects of various structural variables (e.g., family size and the age of the children) in determining the family's abilities to adapt? Do one-child single-parent families fare differently in their ability to successfully redefine the family boundary from single-parent families with more than one child? When more than one child is present, is there a coalescing among siblings? What effects would such a coalition have on redefining the family's authority structure and patterns of communication?

Last, more attention needs to be paid to the role that society has in aiding and thwarting single-parent families' ability to effectively reorganize and survive. We need more systematic attention to issues that go beyond the economics of single-parent family life. The normative expectation is that single-parent status is temporary. But this type of assumption is misleading, for it eliminates the need to examine whether other social institutions, like medicine, education, or religion, meet the needs of single-parent families.

References

Abarbanel, A. Shared parenting after separation and divorce: A study of joint custody. *American Journal of Orthopsychiatry*, 1979, *49*, 320–329.

Adams, B. *The family: A sociological interpretation* (2nd ed.). Chicago: Rand McNally, 1975.

Ahrons, C. "The binuclear family: Two households, one family. *Alternative Lifestyles*, 1979, *4*, 499–515.

Ahrons, C. Joint custody arrangements in the postdivorce family. *Journal of Divorce*, 1980, *3*, 189–205.

Aldous, J. Children's perceptions of adult role assignment: Father-absence, class, race, and sex influences. *Journal of Marriage and the Family*, 1972, *34*, 55–65.

Anspach, D. Kinship and divorce. *Journal of Marriage and the Family*, 1976, *38*, 323–330.

Anthony, E. Child at risk from divorce: A review. In E. Anthony & C. Koupernik (Eds.), *The child in his family, Children at psychiatric risk*, Vol. 3. New York: Wiley, 1974.

Atkinson, B., & Ogston, D. The effects of father absence on male children in the home and school. *Journal of School Psychology*, 1974, *12*, 213–221.

Bachrach, L. *Marital stress and mental disorder: An analytical review.* (DHEW Publication No. ADM 75-217). Washington, D.C.: U.S. Governmental Printing Office, 1975.

Badaines, J. Identification, imitation and sex role preference in father-present and father-absent black and Chicano boys. *Journal of Psychology*, 1976, *92*, 15–24.

Baker, L. Impact of father absence on personality factors of children. *American Journal of Orthopsychiatry*, 1967, *37*, 269–273.

Bane, M. Marital disruption and the lives of children. *Journal of Social Issues*, 1976, *2*(5), 11–117.

Bane, M., & Weiss, R. Alone together: The world of single-parent families. *American Demographics*, 1980, *2*(5), 11–15.

Berg, B., & Kelly, R. The measured self-esteem of children from broken, rejected and accepted families. *Journal of Divorce*, 1979, *2*, 363–369.

Berkman, L., & Syme, S. L. Social networks, host resistance, and mortality: A nine-year follow-up study of Alameda County residents. *American Journal of Epidemiology*, 1979, *109*, 186–204.

Berkman, P. Spouseless motherhood, psychological stress and physical morbidity. *Journal of Health and Social Behavior*, 1969, *10*, 323–334.

Bernard, J. The adjustment of married males. In T. Christensen (Ed.), *Handbook of marriage and the family*. Chicago: Rand McNally, 1964.

Bianchi, S., & Farley, R. Racial differences in family living arrangements and economic well-being: An analysis of recent trends. *Journal of Marriage and the Family*, 1979, *41*, 537–551.

Biller, H. A note on father absence and masculine development in lower-class negro and white boys. *Child Development*, 1968, *39*, 1003–1006.

Biller, H. The mother-child relationship and the father absent boy's personality development. *Merrill-Palmer Quarterly*, 1971, *17*, 227–241.

Biller, H., & Bahm, R. Father absence, perceived maternal behavior, and masculinity of self-control among junior high school boys. *Developmental Psychology*, 1971, *4*, 178–181.

Biller, H., & Meredith, D. The invisible American father. *Sexual Behavior*, 1972, *2*, 16–22.

Billingsley, A., & Giovannoni, J. Family, one parent. In R. Morris (Ed.), *Encyclopedia of social work*, Vol. 1. New York: National Association of Social Workers, 1971.

Blanchard, R., & Biller, H. Father availability and academic performance among third-grade boys. *Developmental Psychology*, 1971, *4*, 301–305.

Blechman, E. Are children with one parent at psychological risk? A methodological review. *Journal of Marriage and the Family*, 1982, *44*, 179–195.

Blechman, E., & Manning, M. A reward-cost analysis of the single-parent family. In E. Mash (Ed.), *Behavior modification and families*. New York: Brunner/Mazel, 1976.

Bloom, B., Asher, S., & White, S. Marital disruption as a stressor: A review and analysis. *Psychological Bulletin*, 1978, *83*, 867–894.

Bohannon, P. *Divorce and after*. Garden City, N.Y.: Doubleday, 1970.

Bolton, F. *The pregnant adolescent*. Beverly Hills, Calif.: Sage Publications, 1980.

Boss, P. *Psychological absence in the intact family: A systems approach to a study on fathering*. Paper presented at the Theory Construction Workshop, National Council on Family Relations, St. Louis, 1974.

Boss, P. A clarification of the concept of psychological father presence in families experiencing ambiguity at boundary. *Journal of Marriage and the Family* 1977, *39*, 141–151.

Boss, P. Normative family stress: Family boundary changes across the life-span. *Family Relations*, 1980, *29*, 445–450. (a)

Boss, P. The relationship of psychological father presence, wife's personal qualities and wife/family dysfunction in families of missing fathers. *Journal of Marriage and the Family*, 1980, *42*, 541–549. (b)

Bould, S. Female-headed families: personal fate control and the provider role. *Journal of Marriage and the Family*, 1977, *39*, 339–349.

Bradbury, K., Danziger, S., Smolensky, E., & Smolensky, P. Public assistance, female headship and economic well-being. *Journal of Marriage and the Family*, 1979, *41*, 519–535.

Brandwein, R., Brown, C., & Fox, E. Women and children last: The social situation of divorced mothers and their families. *Journal of Marriage and the Family*, 1974, *36*, 498–514.

Brassard, J. *The ecology of divorce: A case study analysis of personal social networks and mother-child interaction in a divorced and a married family*. Paper presented at the annual meeting of the National Council on Family Relations, Boston, 1979.

Brown, C., Feldberg, R., Fox, E., & Kohen, S. Divorce: Chance of a new lifetime. *Journal of Social Issues*, 1976, *32*, 119–137.

Burchinal, L. Characteristics of adolescents from unbroken, broken, and reconstituted families. *Journal of Marriage and the Family*, 1964, *26*, 44–51.

Carlsmith, L. Effect of early father absences on scholastic aptitude. *Harvard Education Review*, 1964, *34*, 3–21.

Cassel, J. The contribution of the social environment to host resistance. *American Journal of Epidemiology*, 1976, *104*, 107–123.

Cazenave, N. Alternative intimacy, marriage, and family lifestyles among low-income Black Americans. *Alternative Lifestyles*, 1980, *3*, 425–444.

Chief, E. Need determination in AFDC program. *Social Security Bulletin*, 1979, *42*(9), 11–21.

Chiriboga, D., Coho, A., Stein, J., & Roberts, J. Divorce, stress and social supports: A study in help-seeking behavior. *Journal of Divorce*, 1979, *3*, 121–135.

Clapp, D., & Raab, R. Follow-up of unmarried adolescent mothers. *Social Work*, 1978, *23*, 149–153.

Clayton, P. Meeting the needs of the single parent family. *Family Coordinator*, 1971, *20*, 327–336.

Cline, D., & Westman, J. The impact of divorce on the family. *Child Psychiatry and Human Development*, 1971, *2*, 78–83.

Cobb, S. Social support as a moderator of life stress. *Psychosomatic Medicine*, 1976, *38*, 301–314.

Cogswell, B., & Sussman, M. Changing family and marriage forms: Complications for human services systems. *Family Coordinator*, 1972, *21*, 505–516.

Colletta, N. Support systems after divorce: Incidence and impact. *Journal of Marriage and the Family*, 1979, *41*, 837–846.

Consortium for the Study of School Needs of Children from One-Parent Families. *The most significant minority: One-parent children in the schools.* First-year report of a longitudinal study cosponsored by the National Association of Elementary School Principals and the Institute for Development of Educational Activities, Arlington, Virginia, 1980.

D'Andrade, R. Father absence, identification, and identity. *Ethos*, 1973, *1*, 440–445.

Dell, P., & Appelbaum, A. Trigenerational enmeshment: Unresolved ties of single parents to family of origin. *American Journal of Orthopsychiatry*, 1977, *47*, 52–59.

Despert, J. *Children of divorce*. New York: Doubleday, 1953.

Dinerman, M. Catch 23: Women, work and welfare. *Social Work*, 1977, *22*, 472–477.

Dorpat, T., Jackson, J., & Ripley, H. Broken homes and attempted and completed suicide. *Archives of General Psychiatry*, 1965, *12*, 213–216.

Duncan, G., & Morgan, J. Introduction and overview. In *Five thousand American families—Patterns of economic progress*, Vol. 4. Ann Arbor, Mich.: Institute for Social Research, 1976.

Duvall, E. *Family Development* (4th ed.). Philadelphia: Lippincott, 1971.

Earl, L., & Lohmann, N. Absent fathers and black male children. *Social Work*, 1978, *28*, 413–415.

Earls, F., & Siegel, B. Precocious fathers. *American Journal of Orthopsychiatry*, 1980, *50*, 469–480.

Espenshade, T. The economic consequences of divorce. *Journal of Marriage and the Family*, 1979, *41*, 615–625.

Farley, R., & Hermalin, A. Family stability: A comparison of trends between blacks and whites. *American Sociological Review*, 1971, *36*, 1–17.

Ferri, E., & Robinson, H. *Coping alone*. London: NFER Publishing, 1976.

Freud, A., & Burlingham, D. *Infants without families*. New York: International University Press, 1944.

Galper, M. *Co-parenting*. Philadelphia: Running Press, 1978.

Gersick, K. Fathers by choice: Divorced men who receive custody of their children. In G. Levinger & O. Moles (Eds.), *Divorce and separation: Context, causes and consequences.* New York: Basic Books, 1979.

Glasser, P., & Navarre, E. Structural problems of the one-parent family. *Journal of Social Issues*, 1965, *21*, 98–109.

Glick, P. Future American families. *COFO Memo 2*, 1979 (Summer/Fall), 1–7. (a)

Glick, P. The future of the American family. *Current Population Reports*, Series P-23, 1979, *78*, 1–7. (b)

Glick, P., & Norton, A. Marrying, divorcing, and living together in the U.S. today. *Population Bulletin*, 1977, *32*, No. 5, Washington, D.C., Population Reference Bureau.

Glick, P., & Spanier, G. Married and unmarried cohabitation in the United States. *Journal of Marriage and the Family*, 1980, *42*, 19–30.

Goldsmith, J. *Relationships between former spouses: Descriptive findings.* Revision of a paper presented at the annual meeting of the National Council on Family Relations, Boston, 1979.

Goldstein, H. Internal controls in aggressive children for father present and father absent families. *Journal of Consulting and Clinical Psychology*, 1972, *39*, 512.

Gongla, P. *Social relationships after marital separation: A study of women with children.* Unpublished doctoral dissertation, Case Western Reserve University, 1977.

Gongla, P. Single parent families: A look at families of mothers and children. In H. Gross & M. B. Sussman (Eds.), Alternatives to Traditional Family Living, New York: Haworth Press, 1982, 5–27.

Goode, W. *Women in divorce.* New York: Free Press, 1956.

Gordon, J. Single parents' personal struggles and social issues. In P. Stein (Ed.), *Single life: Unmarried adults in social context.* New York: St. Martin's Press, 1980.

Gove, W. Sex, marital status and suicide. *Journal of Health and Social Behavior*, 1972, *13*, 204–213.

Greenberg, J. Single parenting and intimacy. *Alternative Lifestyles*, 1979, *2*, 308–330.

Greenstein, J. Fathering characteristics and sex-typing. *Journal of Personality and Social Psychology*, 1969, *3*, 271–277.

Greif, J. Fathers, children and joint custody. *American Journal of Orthopsychiatry*, 1979, *49*, 311–319.

Grow, L. Today's unmarried mothers: The choices have changed. *Child Welfare*, 1979, *58*, 363–371.

Heiss, J. *Family roles and interaction: An anthology.* Chicago: Rand McNally, 1968.

Herzog, E., & Suida, C. Fatherless homes: A review of research. *Children*, 1968, *15*, 177–182.

Herzog, R., & Sudia, C. *Boys in fatherless families.* Washington, D.C.: U.S. DHEW Office of Child Development, 1971.

Herzog, R., & Sudia, C. Children in fatherless families. In B. Caldwell & H. Ricciuti (Eds.), *Review of Child Development Research*, Vol. 3. Chicago: University of Chicago Press, 1973.

Hetherington, E. Effects of paternal absence on sex-typed behaviors in Negro and white pre-adolescent males. *Journal of Personality and Social Psychology*, 1966, *4*, 87–91.

Hetherington, E. Effects of father-absence on personality development in adolescent daughters. *Developmental Psychology*, 1972, *7*, 313–326.

Hetherington, E. Girls without fathers. *Psychology Today*, 1973, *47*, 49–52.

Hetherington, E., & Deur, J. The effect of father absence on child development. *Young Children*, 1971, *26*, 233–248.

Hetherington, E., Cox, M., & Cox, R. Divorced fathers. *Family Coordinator*, 1976, *25*, 417–428.

Hetherington, E., Cox, M., & Cox, R. The development of children in mother-headed families. In D. Reiss & H. A. Hoffman (Eds.), *The American family: Dying or developing.* New York: Plenum Press, 1979.

Hiltz, S. Widowhood: A roleless role. *Marriage and Family Review*, 1978, *1*, 1–10.

Hoffman, M. Father absence and conscience development. *Developmental Psychology*, 1971, *4*, 400–4U6.

Hoffman, S. Marital instability and the economic status of women. *Demography*, 1977, *14*, 67–76.

Horowitz, J., & Perdue, B. Single parent families. *Nursing Clinics of North America*, 1977, *12*, 503–511.

Hunt, J., & Hunt, L. Race, daughters and father loss: Does absence make the girl stronger? *Social Problems*, 1977, *25*, 90–102.

Hunt, M., & Hunt, B. *The divorce experience.* New York: McGraw-Hill, 1977.

Jacobs, T. Family interaction in disturbed and normal families: A methodological and substantive review. *Psychological Bulletin,* 1975, *82,* 33–65.

Johnson, B. Women who head families, 1970–1979: Their numbers rose, income lagged. *Monthly Labor Review,* 1978, *101,* 32–37.

Kadushin, A. Single-parent adoptions: An overview and some relevant research. *Social Services Review,* 1970, *44,* 263–274.

Kagel, S., White, R., & Coyne, J. Father-absent and father-present families of disturbed and nondisturbed adolescents. *American Journal of Orthopsychiatry,* 1978, *48,* 342–352.

Kalter, N. Children of divorce in an outpatient psychiatric population. *American Journal of Orthopsychiatry,* 1977, *47,* 40–51.

Katz, A. Lone fathers: perspectives and implications for family policy. *Family Coordinator,* 1979, *28,* 521–528.

Keshet, H., & Rosenthal, K. Single parent fathers: A new study. *Children Today,* 1978, *7,* 13–17.

Kessler, R. C. Stress, social status and psychological distress. *Journal of Health and Social Behavior,* 1979, *20,* 259–272.

Kitson, G., Lopata, H., Holmes, W., & Meyering, S. Divorcees and widows: Similarities and differences. *American Journal of Orthopsychiatry,* 1980, *50,* 291–301.

Kohen, J., Brown, C., & Feldberg, R. Divorced mothers: The costs and benefits of female family control. In George Levinger & Oliver Moles (Eds.), *Divorce and separation: Causes, contexts, and consequences.* New York: Basic Books, 1979.

Laing, R. D. *The politics of the family.* New York: Vintage, 1972.

Lamb, M. The role of the father: An overview. In M. Lamb (Ed.), *The role of the father in child development.* New York: Wiley, 1976.

Lamb, M. The effects of divorce on children's personality development. *Journal of Divorce,* 1977, *1,* 163–174.

Landis, J. The trauma of children when parents divorce. *Marriage and Family Living,* 1960, *22,* 7–13.

Landy, F., Rosenberg, B., & Sutton-Smith, B. The effect of limited absence of cognition development. *Child Development,* 1969, *40,* 941–944.

Leslie, G. *The family in social context (4th ed.).* New York: Oxford University Press, 1979.

Lester, D., & Beck, A. Early loss as a possible "sensitizer" to later loss in attempted suicides. *Psychological Reports,* 1976, *39,* 121–122.

Lewis, K. Single-parent fathers: Who they are and how they fare. *Child Welfare,* 1978, *57,* 643–651.

Loge, B. Role adjustment to single parenthood: A study of divorced and widowed men and women. *Dissertation Abstracts International,* 4647-A, 1977.

Longabaugh, R. Mother behavior as a variable moderating the effects of father absence. *Ethos,* 1973, *1,* 456–465.

Lopata, H. *Women as widows: Support systems.* New York: Elsevier, 1979.

Luepnitz, D. Which aspects of divorce affect children. *Family Coordinator,* 1979, *28,* 79–85.

Magreb, P. For the sake of the children: A review of the psychological effects of divorce. *Journal of Divorce,* 1978, *1,* 233–245.

Mallan, L. Young widows and their children: A comparative report. *Social Security Bulletin,* 1975, *38,* 3–21.

Martin, E., & Martin, J. *The black extended family.* Chicago: University of Chicago Press, 1978.

McCord, J., McCord, W., & Thurber, E. Some effects of paternal absence on male children. *Journal of Abnormal and Social Psychology,* 1962, *64,* 361–369.

McCubbin, H., Joy, C., Cauble, A., Comeau, J., Patterson, J., & Needle, R. Family stress and coping: A decade review. *Journal of Marriage and the Family,* 1980, *42,* 421–428.

McDermott, J. Divorce and its psychiatric sequelae in children. *Archives of General Psychiatry,* 1970, *23,* 421–428.

McLanahan, S., Wedemeyer, N., & Adelberg, T. Network structure, social support, and psychological well-being in the single-parent family. *Journal of Marriage and the Family,* 1981, *43,* 601–612.

Mead, M. *Male and female.* New York: Dell, 1949.

Mendes, H. Single fatherhood. *Social Work,* 1976, *21,* 308–312. (a)

Mendes, H. Single fathers. *Family Coordinator,* 1976, *25,* 439–444. (b)

Mendes, H. Single-parent families: A typology of lifestyles. *Social Work,* 1979, *24,* 293–300.

Miller, W. Lower class culture as a generating milieu of gang delinquency. *Journal of Social Issues,* 1958, *14,* 5–19.

Minuchin, S. *Families and family therapy.* Cambridge: Harvard University Press, 1974.

Mueller, D. Social networks: A promising direction for research on the relationship of social environment to psychiatric disorder. *Social Science and Medicine,* 1980, *14A,* 147–161.

Newsome, O. *Postdivorce interaction: An explanation using exchange theory.* Dissertation Abstracts International, 37:8001-A, 1977.

Norton, A., & Glick, P. What's happening to households? *American Demographics,* 1979, *1,* 19–23.

Nye, F. I. Child adjustment in broken and unhappy unbroken homes. *Marriage and Family Living,* 1957, *19,* 356–361.

O'Brien, D., & Garland, T. N. Bridging the gap between theory, research, practice, and policy-making: The case of interaction with kin after divorce. Paper presented at the annual meeting of the National Council on Family Relations, San Diego, 1977.

Orthner, D., Brown, T., & Ferguson, D. Single parent fatherhood: An emerging family life style. *Family Coordinator,* 1979, *25,* 429–437.

Pais, J., & White, P. Family redefinition: A review of the literature toward a model of divorce adjustment. *Journal of Divorce,* 1979, *2,* 271–281.

Parker, S., & Kleiner, R. Characteristics of Negro mothers in single-headed households. *Journal of Marriage and the Family,* 1966, *28,* 507–513.

Parsons, T. *The social system.* New York: Free Press, 1951.

Parson, T., *Social structure and personality.* New York: Free Press, 1970.

Parsons, T., & Bales, F. *Family, socialization and interaction processes.* Glencoe, Ill.: Free Press, 1955.

Pearlin, L., & Johnson, J. Marital status, life-strains and depression. *American Sociological Review,* 1977, *42,* 704–715.

Pedersen, F. Relationship between father absence and emotional disturbance in male military dependents. *Merrill-Palmer Quarterly,* 1966, *12,* 321–323.

Plionis, B. Adolescent pregnancy: Review of the literature. *Social Work,* 1975, *20,* 302–307.

Presser, H. *Sally's corner: Coping with unmarried motherhood.* Paper presented at the annual meeting of the American Sociological Association, San Francisco, 1978.

Rapoport, R., Rapoport, R., & Strelitz, Z. *Fathers, mothers, and society.* New York: Vintage, 1980.

Raschke, H., & Raschke, V. Family conflict and children's self concepts: A comparison of intact and single-parent families. *Journal of Marriage and the Family,* 1979, *41,* 367–374.

Renne, K. Health and marital experience in an urban population. *Journal of Marriage and the Family,* 1971, *33,* 338–350.

Reuter, M., & Biller, H. Perceived paternal nurturance—Availability and personality adjustment among college males. *Journal of Consulting and Clinical Psychology,* 1973, *40,* 339–342.

Rosen, R. Some crucial issues concerning children of divorce. *Journal of Divorce,* 1979, *3,* 19–25.

Rosenthal, D., & Hansen, J. Comparison of adolescents' perceptions and behaviors in single- and two-parent families. *Journal of Youth and Adolescence*, 1980, *9*, 407–417.

Rosenthal, K., & Keshet, H. Childcare responsibilities of part-time and single fathers. *Alternative Lifestyles*, 1978, *1*, 465–491.

Rosenthal, K., & Keshet, H. *Fathers without partners: A study of divorced fathers and their families*. Totowa, N.J.: Rowman and Littlefield, 1980.

Ross, H., & Sawhill, I. *Time of Transition: The growth of families headed by women*. Washington, D.C.: Urban Institute, 1975.

Rossi, A. A biosocial perspective on parenting. *Daedalus*, 1977, *106*, 1–32.

Rubin, L. *Worlds of pain: Life in the working-class family*. New York: Basic Books, 1976.

St. Pierre, M. *Black female single parent family: A preliminary sociological perspective*. Paper presented at the annual meeting of the American Sociological Association, New York, 1980.

Santrock, J. Paternal absence, sex typing, and identification. *Developmental Psychology*, 1970, *2*, 264–272.

Santrock, J. Relation by type and onset of father absence to cognitive development. *Child Development*, 1972, *43*, 455–469.

Santrock, J. Effects of father absence on sex-typed behaviors in male children: Reason for the absence and age of onset of the absence. *Journal of General Psychology*, 1977, *130*, 3–10.

Schlesingler, B. Single parent fathers: A research review. *Children Today*, 1978, *7*, 12–39.

Schorr, L., & Moen, P. The single parent and social policy. *Social Policy*, 1979, *9*, 15–21.

Sennett, R. *Families against the city*. New York: Vintage Books, 1974.

Seward, R. *The American family: A demographic history*. Beverly Hills, Calif.: Sage Publications, 1978.

Shaw, C., & McKay, H. Are broken homes a causative factor in juvenile delinquency? *Social Forces*, 1932, *19*, 514–525.

Shinn, M. Father absence and children's cognitive development. *Psychological Bulletin*, 1978, *85*, 295–324.

Sibbison, V. *Pennsylvania's female-headed households: Families in distress*. University Park, Pa.: Institute for the Study of Human Development, 1974.

Slater, P. Parental role differentiation. *American Journal of Sociology*, 1961, *67*, 296–311.

Smith, M. The social consequence of single parenthood: A longitudinal perspective. *Family Relations*, 1980, *29*, 75–81.

Sorosky, A. The psychological effects of divorce on children. *Adolescence*, 1977, *12*, 123–136.

Spicer, J., & Hampe, G. Kinship interaction after divorce. *Journal of Marriage and the Family*, 1975, *37*, 113–119.

Sprey, J. The study of single parenthood: Some methodological considerations. *Family Coordinator*, 1967, *16*, 29–34.

Sprey, J. Conflict theory and the study of marriage and the family. In W. Burr, R. Hill, F. I. Nye, & I. Reiss (Eds.), *Contemporary theories about the family*, Vol. 2. New York: Free Press, 1979.

Stack, C. *All our kin*. Chicago: Aldine, 1974.

Stack, C. Who owns the child? Divorce and custody decisions in middle-class families. *Social Problems*, 1976, *23*, 505–515.

Staples, R. Intimacy patterns among black, middle-class single parents. *Alternative Lifestyles*, 1980, *3*, 445–462.

Stein, R. The economic status of families headed by women. *Monthly Labor Review*, 1970, *93*, 3–10.

Thompson, E., & Gongla, P. Single parent families: In the mainstream of American society. In E. Macklin & R. Rubin (Eds.), *Contemporary families and alternative lifestyles: Handbook on research and theory*. Beverly Hills, Calif.: Sage Publications, 1983.

Trunnell, T. The absent father's children's emotional disturbances. *Archives of General Psychiatry*, 1968, *19*, 180–188.

Turner, R. *Family interaction*. New York: Wiley, 1970.

Turner, R. J. *Experienced social support as a contingency in emotional well-being*. Paper presented at the annual meeting of the American Sociological Association, New York, 1980.

Udry, J. R. *The social context of marriage* (3rd ed.). Philadelphia: Lippincott, 1974.

U.S. Bureau of the Census. *Marital status and living arrangements, March 1977*. Current Population Reports, Series P-20, No. 323. Washington, D.C.: U.S. Government Printing Office, 1978.

U.S. Bureau of the Census. *Characteristics of the population below the poverty level: 1978*. Current Population Reports, Series P-60, No. 124. Washington, D.C.: U.S. Government Printing Office, 1980. (a)

U.S. Bureau of the Census. *Marital status and living arrangements, March 1979*. Current Population Reports, Series P-20, No. 349. Washington, D.C.: U.S. Government Printing Office, 1980. (b)

U.S. Bureau of the Census. *Money income of families and persons in the United States*. Current Population Reports, Series P-60, No. 123. Washington, D.C.: U.S. Government Printing Office, 1980. (c)

U.S. Bureau of the Census. *Household and family characteristics: March, 1980*. Current Population Reports, Series P-20, No. 366. Washington, D.C.: U.S. Government Printing Office, 1981. (a)

U.S. Bureau of the Census. *Marital status and living arrangements: March, 1980*. Current Population Reports, Series P-20, No. 365. Washington, D.C.: U.S. Government Printing Office, 1981. (b)

U.S. Senate. Senate Bill 1808, The Family Protection Act, 1979.

Verbrugge, L. Marital status and health. *Journal of Marriage and the Family*, 1979, *41*, 267–285.

Wallerstein, J., & Kelly, J. *Surviving the breakup: How children and parents cope with divorce*. New York: Basic Books, 1980.

Wattenberg, E., & Reinhardt, H. Female-headed families: Trends and implications. *Social Work*, 1979, *24*, 460–467.

Weiss, R. S. *Marital separation*. New York: Basic Books, 1975.

Weiss, R. S. *Going it alone*. New York: Basic Books, 1979.

Wilk, J. Assessing single parent needs. *Journal of Psychiatric Nursing*, 1979, *17*(6), 21–22.

Wolff, K. *The sociology of Georg Simmel*. New York: Free Press, 1950.

Woolsey, S. Pied piper and the child care debate. *Daedalus*, 1977, *106*(2), 127–145.

Young, J. The divorced Catholic movement. *Journal of Divorce*, 1978, *2*, 83–97.

Zelditch, M. Cross-cultural analysis of family structure. In H. Christensen (Ed.), *Handbook of marriage and the family*. Chicago: Rand McNally, 1964.

CHAPTER 16

Remarriage and Reconstituted Families

Graham B. Spanier and Frank F. Furstenberg, Jr.

Cross-Cultural and Historical Perspectives

Remarriage is not a new social invention for repairing marital disruption. The earliest recorded histories document that remarriage was a recognized option for some, but not all, individuals whose marriages were disrupted by the death of the husband or wife. Some societies accorded the same status to remarriages as they did to first marriages, others a lesser or greater status. Many societies developed rules designating the particular person in the extended family network, such as a brother or sister of the deceased, who was obligated to support an individual whose spouse had died, and rules specifying that that support ought to take the form of marriage (Murstein, 1974).

For example, among the ancient Hebrews, divorce was rare but widowhood was common. When homes were broken by death there were definite provisions for the survivors (Queen & Habenstein, 1974). Some men had other wives or concubines or could obtain them. Remarriage was possible for both men and women, but a childless woman was sometimes expected to marry her deceased husband's brother. If she were to have a son, this child would be considered the descendant of her first husband, a custom known as *levirate*. A similar custom, know as *sororate*, was a cultural rule specifying that the preferred mate for a widower was the sister of his deceased wife (Leslie, 1967).

In the early Christian family, widows had considerable status, particularly if they pledged themselves to refrain from second marriages and to do religious and charitable work for the church (Murstein, 1974; Queen & Habenstein, 1974). Remarriage after the death of a spouse, although sometimes practiced, was considered evil by many Church Fathers, and it was condemned. Paul, however, believed that remarriage was a lesser evil for young widows. The norms for remarriage following divorce similarly discouraged second marriages. All of the first three Gospels forbid the remarriage of divorced men and women alike, although Paul took a somewhat equivocal position (Murstein, 1974; Queen & Habenstein, 1974). These examples illustrate the diversity of remarriage practices suggesting, at the same time, that remarriage was known to members of different societies throughout history.

Another example is the traditional Chinese family, where divorce was regarded as tragic. Three types of divorce were allowed: by mutual agreement; by order of authorities such as the family head, the clan head, or governmental authority; or by either husband or wife, although after feudal times divorce became almost exclusively a man's privilege (Leslie, 1967; Queen & Habenstein, 1974). Remarriage after divorce was unthinkable for women. Divorce was rare, however, and most marriages were terminated by the death of the husband or the wife. But whereas widows generally went to live with their sons following the death of the husband and rarely remarried, widowers had the option of remarriage, perhaps to a concubine.

In preindustrial England, there were few or no legal restrictions on remarriage. Many men and women were widowed at relatively young ages, and a liberal approach to remarriage most readily met many societal functions: constituting a complete household unit, providing for the care of surviving children, and providing for further childbearing (Griffith, 1980). Griffith (1980) also argued that remarriage was particularly important for widows in preindustrial England because poverty in old age was common, and remarriage helped to ensure security and care in ill health.

In modern times, remarriage has increasingly allowed individuals to seek the satisfactions of marriage after an earlier marriage has been disrupted by death or divorce. Unlike first marriage, which is expected in virtually all contemporary societies, the norms governing remarriage are ambiguous. Some societies, for example, have been reported to restrict the remarriage of widows (Dandekar, 1961; Fried, 1959), whereas others discourage the remarriage of divorcées (Goode, 1963). Remarriage seems to exist in all societies, but the rates of remarriage and the social rules governing this transition vary significantly (Chamie & Nsuly, 1981).

For example, the Baganda of central Africa and the

Graham B. Spanier • Vice President and Provost, Oregon State University, Corvallis, OR 97331. Frank F. Furstenberg, Jr. • Department of Sociology, University of Pennsylvania, Philadelphia, PA 19104.

peoples of Arabic Islam (Goode, 1963; Queen & Habenstein, 1974) illustrate the great diversity.

The Baganda are a primarily agricultural people living in the nation of Uganda. Polygyny, the marriage of a husband to more than one wife, is both the preferred and the dominant form of marriage for the Baganda (Queen & Habenstein, 1974). Following her husband's death, a first wife typically joins the family of the husband's brother living closest to the burial ground, her primary duty being to attend the grave of her husband. The other wives are claimed by relatives or become the property of the husband's heir. Permission for the first wife to remarry must be granted by her brother, who then refunds the bride price to her first husband's relatives. A widower typically takes a new wife from the clan of his former wife, but must pay the customary bride price. Little is known about remarriage after divorce, as divorce is rare. Marriages are defined as permanent and can be canceled only with the husband's consent and the return of the bride price (Queen & Habenstein, 1974).

Although there is much diversity in customs and laws in the Mideast, some meaningful generalizations can be made about remarriage in Arabic Islam (Goode, 1963). Arab tradition does not regard divorce very favorably, but the supremacy of the male in Arab culture traditionally allowed husbands to divorce their wives with essentially no external oversight. A wife, on the other hand, had no such rights in the Arab culture, although she could try to persuade a court to order the husband to divorce her. In Arab countries such as Egypt, contemporary wives have more freedom to initiate divorce actions. When divorce does occur, it appears that remarriage is common and accepted. A tradition peculiar to Arabic Islam is the remarriage of a husband and wife to each other after a divorce, sometimes without the divorce's being publicly known. Goode (1963) estimated that in Egypt in the 1950s, for example, 95% of divorced persons eventually remarried, and at least 10% remarried their former spouse. In some cases, the divorce action is "reversed"; in others, a new marriage contract is established. In fact, in traditional Arabic Islam, a first husband could not remarry his wife until she had married and cohabited with another man, who might divorce her (Goode, 1963).

In the United States, remarriage after divorce has become especially relevant. The proportion of marriages that ultimately end in divorce has increased from about 4% at the time of the Civil War to a projected 50% in the coming generation (Davis, 1972; Glick, 1980; National Center for Health Statistics, 1980b). By the mid 1970s marriages dissolved by divorce began to outnumber marriages dissolved by the death of one of the partners (Glick, 1980). Moreover, 90% of individuals remarrying in the United States today are doing so after a divorce; 10% of new unions follows widowhood (Glick, 1980). The phenomenon of remarriage, then, has been viewed increasingly in the shadow of divorce. It is often examined as a response to the failure of an earlier marriage.

Research History and Definitions

There are, of course, important differences between remarriage after death and remarriage after divorce. In the case of remarriage after death, the deceased spouse and parent is replaced; after divorce, the new spouse—and perhaps the surrogate parent—typically augments rather than supplants the former spouse and biological parent (Furstenberg, 1980). This structural difference is far from trivial because it raises numerous issues not provided for in our nuclear-based kinship system. We have no set of beliefs, no language, and no rules for families with "more than two parents." As has been previously pointed out, too little attention has been given to the conditions that have transformed our system of marriage from one that placed tremendous value on permanence into one that permits—at times, even promotes—conjugal succession (Furstenberg, 1980). As we shall demonstrate, family researchers have only recently begun to adequately describe the properties of this emergent family system.

All events studied by social scientists can be seen in the midst of a never-ending causal chain of interrelationships. The theorist or researcher has the task of deciding where in the chain to begin and end her or his consideration of the event in question. This is not a trivial issue in the study of remarriage; it can be viewed alternatively as part of the aftermath of a previous marriage or as a discrete event, a new chapter in one's life unrelated to past history. It can furthermore be considered in the former light for one participant in the remarriage and in the latter light for the other partner. It is tempting to argue, of course, that it must be viewed in all of these ways by the responsible scientist, but this view poses potentially complex questions, especially when the participants themselves have different definitions of the entrance into a second marriage. We are sensitive to how marriage is constructed as a social event in this chapter, for we believe that, in the lives of the individuals who are involved in a remarriage, the theme of remarriage as a transition from a previous marriage versus remarriage as a new beginning is a fundamental issue with important implications.

The presence or absence of children—in the household or outside the household—may be especially predictive of the influence of a previous marriage—and of the relationship with a previous spouse—on the remarriage. For this reason, our review gives considerable attention to the issues of parenthood, stepparenthood, and family networks.

Before the 1970s, very little research had been done on remarriage. Willard Waller's book *The Old Love and the New* (1930) was the first work on the subject by a social scientist. It was not until 1956, when Jessie Bernard published her book *Remarriage,* that the next major work appeared on this topic. Meanwhile, a small number of sociologists and demographers began to include remarriage as part of the growing interest in the demographic analysis of marriage and the family (e.g., Bowerman, 1953; Glick, 1949; Jacobson, 1959; Monahan, 1951, 1952, 1958, 1959). A few small-scale substantive studies were also conducted during the 1940s, the 1950s, and the 1960s (e.g., Smith, 1953; Burchinal, 1964; Landis, 1950; Locke & Klausner, 1948). One large-scale study was conducted by Bowerman and Irish (1962), but it included only limited data pertaining to remarriage and reconstituted families. One empirical study in early 1970s focused exclusively on remarriage and reconstituted families, examining in particular parent–child and step-parent–stepchild relations (Duberman, 1975).

It should also be noted that Goode's classic study (1956) of divorce included a brief but sophisticated discussion of remarriage. His study examined such topics as the chances of remarriage for women in varying social circumstances, the effect of children on remarriage, remarriage and adjustment to separation, and redivorce following remarriage.

As might be expected, however, great interest in remarriage did not develop in the scientific community until the divorce and remarriage rates began to accelerate in the 1960s and 1970s. Thus, the bulk of the existing literature on remarriage is less than a decade old.

It should not be surprising that much of the recent work on remarriage is conceptual as well as empirical, and that the definitions are of particular concern. Several writers (e.g., Price-Bonham & Balswick, 1980) have distinguished between "remarriage" and "reconstituted families." *Remarriage* typically refers to a marriage involving at least one individual who has been previously married. Some, however, might argue that a particular union might be defined as a remarriage for one spouse, but a first marriage for the other—and thus, remarriage could be considered a status applying to an individual *or a* couple, depending on one's view. A *reconstituted family* is defined as a remarriage that includes at least one child residing in the household of the remarried spouses (Bohannan, 1970; Duberman, 1975). This definition is too narrow, we believe. Biological, adopted, or stepchildren who may be living with a former spouse or with a new partner's former spouse are likely to be a significant part of an individual's extended family network, even though the child is not living in the household. Parental relations can be severed legally or structurally, but they can never be terminated sociologically. Thus, we prefer to consider remarriage and all of its variations, recognizing that families may be reconstituted in many different ways following divorce or the death of a spouse.

Remarriage should be viewed in the broadest sense, then, with terms such as *blended families, reconstituted families,* and *reconstructed families* considered synonymous. These concepts should reflect remarriages that may or may not involve children, who, in turn, may or may not live in the household with the remarried couple. It should also be remembered that what is a remarriage for one spouse may be a first marriage for the other spouse.

Moreover, as only 60% of divorces involve children under the age of 18, children consequently are involved in only a portion of remarriages (Spanier & Glick, 1981).

The purpose of this chapter is to expand existing perspectives on remarriage and reconstituted families. We do not attempt to present an exhaustive review of the literature nor to summarize all that is known about the topic. We begin our overview with a summary of the demography of remarriage in America. This section is followed by a summary of recent literature. Our attention is then turned to the transition to remarriage, discussions of remarriage and well being, children in reconstituted families, and remarriage and generational ties; we highlight findings in areas that we regard as especially promising ones for further research.

Demography of American Remarriage

Remarriage, if viewed as a variation from traditional lifelong marriage to one person, must certainly be characterized as the most prevalent "alternative lifestyle." In 1979, for example, 32% of American marriages involved a previously married woman and 33% of marriages involved a previously married man. These figures represented significant increases from the beginning of the decade (24% and 25% in 1970, respectively). As mentioned earlier, nearly 90% of the remarrying individuals had been previously divorced; slightly more than 10% had been previously widowed (National Center for Health Statistics, 1980a, 1981).

Demographic data on remarriage are available from several sources, including many national surveys conducted in recent years. Two sources in particular provide the majority of demographic information about the nature and extent of remarriage in the United States: vital statistics data from the National Center for Health Statistics and statistical survey data from the U.S. Bureau of the Census. Vital statistics analyses are based on actual reports of each marriage and divorce submitted by most counties and states through the vital statistics reporting program. Analyses of data from the Bureau of the Census use both the decennial census and data from special Current Population Surveys. The Current Population Survey is conducted monthly, and, from time to time, collects special information on household living arrangements, marital history, and fertility. This survey is based on a sample of at least 120,000 individuals living in at least 60,000 households in the United States.

U.S. Marriage in Relation to That in Other Societies

The incidence of remarriage today is the highest in the United States, where about 40% of marriages involve at least one spouse who has been married previously (National Center for Health Statistics, 1980a). Sweden, Denmark, England and Wales, Egypt, and the German Democratic Republic follow. Countries in which remarriage is low relative to first marriage include predominantly Roman Catholic countries, such as Peru, the Philippines, Portugal, the Dominican Republic, Ecuador, Italy, Chile, and Northern Ireland (Chamie & Nsuly, 1981), where divorce is still relatively rare.

Using combined information from vital registration data and census data, Chamie and Nsuly (1981) were able to estimate remarriage rates through 1976 for a substantial number of countries in the world. They pointed out that, except for a number of Catholic countries, the overwhelming majority of remarriages consisted of divorced persons. Among countries having a high proportion of remarriages, the percentage involving at least one divorced person was generally 80% or more. This rate can be contrasted with that of some Catholic countries, where the proportion of remarriages involving at least one divorced person was less than 30%.

In all but one country (Austria), the ratio of remarriages to all marriages is greater for males than for females. Remarriage rates for divorced males and females are higher than remarriage rates for widowed males and females in virtually all countries. In fact, across countries divorced men and women are about 7 and 18 times as likely to remarry as widowed men and women, respectively (Chamie & Nsuly, 1981).

U.S. Remarriage Rates

Remarriage rates are three times as high for men as for women. In 1978, the remarriage rate was 121.8 for men and 40.0 for women. The rate refers to the number of previously married individuals who marry in a given year per 1,000 divorced and widowed individuals eligible for remarriage. In other words, about 1 in 8 men eligible to remarry does so each year, compared to 1 in 25 women. When one distinguishes between the divorced and the widowed, however, the differentials are more revealing. Widowed men remarry at a rate five times greater than widowed women, but divorced men remarry at a rate only 60% greater than divorced women (National Center for Health Statistics, 1980a).

Several demographic considerations undoubtedly account for these differentials. First, mortality rates are higher for men than for women. There is a substantial excess of women over men who are widowed. Thus, at any given age, fewer men are available for marriage. Second, men tend to marry women who are younger than they, and this tendency increases with increasing age (Glick & Norton, 1979; Spanier & Glick, 1980a). Third, a divorced man is more likely to wed a woman who has never before been married than is a divorced woman to wed a never-married man (U.S. Bureau of the Census, 1978). These facts combine to result in a narrower field of eligible marriage partners for women than for men.

While the divorce rate was rising during the 1960s, so was the remarriage rate. However, during the 1970s, the remarriage rate slightly declined. This decline may be accounted for in part by a trend to postpone remarriage after divorce. One related trend supports this interpretation: A substantial proportion (approximately half) of unmarried individuals who are living together have been married previously (Glick & Spanier, 1980). Thus, cohabitation with a new partner after divorce may be extending the period between divorce and remarriage (Glick & Spanier, 1980).

Antecedents of Remarriage

The increasing propensity to divorce in the United States has forced social scientists to reconsider their notions about the permanence of individual marriages. As mentioned previously, the majority of marriages are now terminated by divorce, as opposed to the death of a spouse. This situation has existed since 1974, when the number of divorces in a given year exceeded the number of deaths of married persons for the first time (Glick, 1980). It has been true every year since and is likely to be true for several more years. Not until the turn of the century will the large postwar baby cohort reach the point in the life span when mortality rates begin a significant rise. Yet, this cohort is experiencing continued exposure to divorce. For example, it is projected that approximately half the marriages formed in the early 1970s will ultimately end in divorce (National Center for Health Statistics, 1980b). This projection will continue to apply to individuals marrying for the first time in the early 1980s, as divorce rates have remained comparable to the level used for projecting the survivability of first marriages for those married in the 1970s.

Divorce more often affects young marrieds, and widowhood more often affects older marrieds. Moreover, each divorce introduces two additional persons to the field of eligibles, whereas widowhood adds only one person to the field of eligibles. Consequently, remarriage is much more likely to involve divorced individuals than widowed individuals.

Timing of Remarriage

The median interval from marriage to divorce fluctuates around seven years; the modal length of time between a first marriage and divorce is two to four years (U.S. Bureau of the Census, 1976). The median length of time between divorce and remarriage is about three years, although there are indications that this period might increase as nonmarital cohabitation increases among previously married individuals (National Center for Health Statistics, 1980a; Spanier, 1983). Widowed men and women who do remarry tend to take longer to remarry than do divorced individuals, even when age is considered. Rates of remarriage after divorce are higher than rates of first marriage (National Center for Health Statistics, 1973); thus, a divorced person at any given age has a greater likelihood of marrying a second time than a never-married person ever has of marrying a first time. Thus, the idea that divorce involves a rejection of the institution of marriage is not well founded.

Factors Associated with Remarriage

There are several variations in the paths to remarriage. White women are more likely than black women to remarry, and they remarry more quickly (Glick, 1980; National Center for Health Statistics, 1973; Spanier & Glick, 1980b). The extent to which remarriage tends to be more likely to occur after divorce than after widowhood is considerably diminished for women whose first marriage terminated when they were young. The women who are most likely to remarry quickly after divorce are those whose first marriage was relatively brief, who were under 30 at the time of divorce, who were married at a relatively young age, and who had less than a college education (Glick, 1980; Spanier & Glick, 1980b).

Widowed women of both races remarry sooner if their husband died early in the marriage, if they were young when the husband died, and if they had married at a relatively young age. Education is not a powerful predictor of the propensity of widows to remarry, perhaps in part because most widows are middle-aged or older at the time of the death of their husbands (Glick, 1980; National Center for Health Statistics, 1973; Spanier & Glick, 1980b).

Children and Remarriage

An estimated 1.2 million children are involved in divorce each year (Spanier & Glick, 1981). Approximately 90% of these children live with the mother following the divorce. Fathers are unlikely to obtain sole custody of children regardless of the socioeconomic characteristics or the marital history of the wife. There is reason to believe that public attitudes concerning custody awards may be changing, but there is as yet no evidence to indicate that fathers are actually obtaining custody any more often than they did in the 1960s and 1970s.

Fathers are somewhat less likely to have custody of all their children if their former wives are still divorced rather than remarried (Spanier & Glick, 1981). Fathers increase their chances of having custody of very young children if the mother has remarried. Fathers appear to be more likely to obtain custody of their children if the children are all boys, and they are least likely to obtain custody if the children are all girls.

Spanier and Glick (1981) were able to estimate the extent of split custody in the United States by comparing data on household composition with data on child-custody arrangements. *Split custody* is defined as a situation where the father has the custody of one or more of the children *and* the mother has the custody of one or more of the children. In other words, brothers and sisters may find themselves living in different households. This arrangement contrasts with joint custody, where both parents are designated as the joint custodians of one or more children.

Although about 9% of all children under 18 live with their father following divorce, only 4% of children live with fathers who have custody of *all* the children from the previous marriage. Thus, roughly half of the fathers with the custody of any of their children have custody of only some of the children; half have custody of all the children. Split custody, then, involves about 5% of divorced mothers and fathers. But a man who receives the custody of any of his children is much more likely than a woman to be a part of a split-custody arrangement. Studies of child-care patterns following divorce suggest that split-custody arrangements may assign parents the children of the same sex, and that older children may be somewhat more likely to be in the father's care, whereas younger siblings are apt to remain with the mother (Furstenberg & Spanier, 1981; Spanier & Glick, 1981).

Although there has been some speculation that a greater proportion of fathers are obtaining custody of their children than they previously did, there are as yet no data to support this claim. The data presented above are consistent with the overall proportion of mother-versus-father custody determinations during the 1960s and 1970s. However, there is some evidence that, in the cases where the father challenges a custody determination, or where the father goes to court to seek custody, judges have been increasingly willing to grant custody to the father (Orthner & Lewis, 1979).

How do children affect the parents' chances of entry into remarriage? Spanier and Glick (1980b) found that, overall, children seem to be somewhat of a deterrent to remarriage. However, the effect of having children on the timing and the likelihood of remarriage is probably less than one would expect. Indeed, Koo and Suchindran (1980) found that the *age* of the parents at the time of divorce may be especially important in understanding the impact of children. Among women divorcing before age 25, having children decreased the likelihood of remarriage. Among women divorcing at 35 or older, however, having children increased the chances of remarriage. For women divorcing at ages 25–34, there was no effect. Nevertheless, more than one third of white divorced women and about one half of black divorced women with three or more children never remarry (Spanier & Glick, 1980b).

Age Differences in Remarriage

Men and women in remarriages tend to differ in age by a greater margin than do men and women in first marriages. In both first marriages and remarriages, the man is the same age or older than the woman in about 80% of marriages (Glick, 1980; National Center for Health Statistics; 1973; Spanier & Glick, 1980a). However, the magnitude of the difference is significantly greater in remarriages than in first marriages. Glick (1980) speculated that persons who are marrying for the first time, because of their relative youth, may be more sensitive about the difference between their age and that of their marriage partner than are older persons who are entering marriage for the second time. Another explanation might be that the marriage pool provides less selection at younger ages.

Parenting and Stepparenting

It is conservatively estimated that, in 1978, 6.5 million children under 18 were living with a biological parent and a stepparent, representing about 10% of all children under age 18. By 1990, it has been estimated that the number will grow to 7 million and the percentage to 11% (Glick, 1980). Among the families of remarried mothers, an estimated 70% of the children are living with their biological mother and a stepfather. The other 30% are living with both natural parents—in other words, these children have been born after their mother remarried (Glick & Norton, 1979).

Women who remarry after divorce have lower fertility than do women in first marriages, but higher fertility than women who divorce and do not remarry. Thus, a woman whose first marriage is interrupted by divorce can expect ultimately to have slightly lower fertility than other women in her first marriage cohort, even if she remarries (Glick, 1980).

Stability of Remarriages

Is the quality and stability of marriage "the second time around" greater than in the first marriage? The data suggest not. Divorce rates are actually greater among the remarried than among the first-married. Goode (1956) discovered this in his divorce study, and subsequent studies have confirmed this finding consistently. For example, whereas about 50% of all first marriages formed in the 1970s are projected to end in divorce, about 55% of remarriages can be expected to terminate this way. The difference is not substantial but nevertheless exists (National Center for Health Statistics, 1980b).

There are different explanations for this phenomenon. Andrew Cherlin (1978) explained the higher divorce rate of remarriages primarily by suggesting that remarriage poses special challenges. He theorized that remarriage is an incomplete institution with few clearly defined norms to help guide the new relationship. The presence of stepchildren, for example, may pose unusually difficult adjustments not normally found in first marriages. We (Furstenberg & Spanier, 1981) challenged Cherlin's reasoning, however, suggesting that an analysis of the difference ought to focus primarily on a unique attribute that all remarried people have in common: They have been married—and, typically, divorced—before. The previous experience of divorce suggests the possibility that they are more willing to terminate a marriage that fails than are many individuals in a first marriage. This greater willingness, however tempered, means that previously divorced persons are more likely to divorce a second time than are never-divorced persons, many of whom are unlikely to divorce no matter what the quality of their mar-

riage. Moreover, even if a previously divorced person is, in principle, opposed to divorce and is reluctant to divorce, he or she has nevertheless survived the experience once, and the knowledge that it can be survived may make him or her more likely to allow it to happen again.

Summary of Recent Literature

Little is known about remarriage even though numerous papers about it have been published in the past decade. Unfortunately, most of the articles on remarriage and reconstituted families represent very limited contributions, and the striking inconsistencies in what is known make it misleading to suggest that a meaningful integration could be accomplished (Furstenberg & Spanier, 1984).

Several authors have written limited reviews of the literature, and these reviews are instructive (e.g., Chilman, 1981; Walker, Brown, Crohn, Rodstein, Zeisel, & Sager, 1979; Walker, Rogers, & Messinger, 1977). Apart from such reviews, as well as demographic studies of remarriage, the literature falls into three general categories.

First, several empirical studies tend to examine very particular questions (e.g., Hutchens, 1979; Oshman & Manosevitz, 1976; Parish & Copeland, 1979; Perkins & Kahan, 1979; Touliatos & Lindholm, 1980). Much of this literature is of limited use because of the highly specialized nature of the samples; the small sample sizes, which preclude extensive data analysis; or inadequate research designs.

Second, there are essays, conceptual discussions, and summaries of clinical impressions that attempt to enlighten the reader, to suggest frameworks for the study of remarriage and reconstituted families, or to suggest important questions and approaches for studying and helping reconstituted families (e.g., Draughon, 1975; Johnson, 1980; Kleinman, Rosenberg, & Whiteside, 1979; Ricci, 1979; Walker & Messinger, 1979). These essays rarely rely on empirical data and give little evidence of how the authors reached the conclusions they have presented. When data are mentioned, they are primarily from clinical cases.

Third, clinical research, consisting primarily of case-study presentations, serve as the basis for much of the remarriage and reconstituted-family literature. Such studies suggest interpretations of the dynamics of stepfamilies, offer hints for working with stepfamilies, suggest new intervention programs, and present case-study material to support various conclusions about the phenomenon (e.g., Goldmeier, 1980; Messinger, 1976; Messinger, Walker, & Freeman, 1978; Mowatt, 1972; Nichols, 1980; Ransom, Schlesinger, & Derdeyn, 1979; Visher & Visher, 1978). These clinical studies do not offer much support for the findings presented, and the analysis is frequently descriptive rather than exploratory.

There are even a few articles that purport to identify and then dispel "myths" about topics such as stepfamilies (e.g., Jacobson, 1979; Schulman, 1972), but they offer little or no empirical evidence to demonstrate that the myths are incorrect or that their own alternative explanations are correct.

In summary, there has been an expansion in the literature on remarriage and reconstituted families. This literature encompasses review articles, conceptual pieces, clinical or case studies, and empirical studies. However, we believe that the limitations in this body of work have created as much uncertainty as clarification about the dynamics of family life following remarriage. It can only be concluded that much is yet to be learned. Our chapter, then, seeks more to help guide future investigations than to remedy the inadequacies in the literature.

The Transition to Remarriage

About 75% of the persons who divorce have the opportunity to try marriage again (U.S. Bureau of the Census, 1976). As Furstenberg (1982) pointed out, what little research exists on the reentrance into marriage has been preoccupied with the question of the success of second marriages; the studies ignore altogether what is involved in moving from one marriage to the next. Of course, all marriages, including remarriages, have elements in common. With remarriage, however, individuals must revise the definition of the first marriage, establish new commitments associated with the new relationship, develop working rules to bridge both marriages, and perhaps structure a new belief system. The process may be a minor adjustment for some and a radical adjustment for others.

There are several reasons to suspect that the process of remarriage is different from and probably more complicated than the initial entry into marriage (Furstenberg, 1982):

1. Although difficult to factor out, the first marriage undoubtedly has lingering effects on the second. The person's psychological experience of the first marriage may create a layer of expectations and habits that may or may not be imported into the second union. The first marriage may provide a kind of baseline against which the second relationship is judged. Couples take considerable pains to differentiate the marital styles of their first and second relationships, a circumstance suggesting an unavoidable tendency on the part of remarried couples to apply the experience of their first marriage to their second.

2. Apart from any lessons from the failure of the first marriage, second marriages bear the continuing imprint of the previous relationship. Remarried persons, particularly if they are parents, often cannot avoid continued interaction with the first spouse. In particular, when children are present, formerly married partners must continue to do business with one another, and their current and previous mates are unwittingly linked together in what has been described elsewhere as a "remarriage chain" (Bohannan, 1970; Furstenberg, 1981).

3. First and second marriages take place at divergent points in the individual's life span. Variations in personal maturity, life experience, and social status create a different set of constraints in the two marriages if they are contracted at disparate ages. Because of these life-span variations, people who remarry usually do so under circumstances dissimilar to those of their first marriage, so that they too perceive their first and second marriages as distinctively different events.

4. Finally, a remarried individual is a member of two different marriage cohorts and accordingly is exposed and then reexposed to the current cultural standards of how a marriage should operate. Individuals who marry at two very different historical moments—for example, those who were first married in 1970 and then married a second time in 1980—may be subject to very different expectations of how to behave in marriage. The process of remarriage may compel the marriage partners to rethink marriage according to contemporary standards.

Remarriage and Well-Being

Dozens of studies conducted over the last decade have confirmed Goode's earlier finding (1956) that divorce poses threats to the well-being of a substantial proportion of persons whose marriages are disrupted (Bloom, White, & Asher, 1979; Chiriboga, Roberts, & Stein, 1978; Hetherington, Cox, & Cox, 1976; Kitson, 1982; Kitson & Sussman, 1982; Rubin, 1979; Spanier & Casto, 1979; Thompson, 1981; Weiss, 1975). Despite the strong and consistent evidence of risk to such persons, little is known about the circumstances that may help to moderate such risk. As we have pointed out elsewhere (Spanier & Furstenberg, 1982), much of the growing body of research on divorce focuses on the immediate postdivorce transition; little information is available on long-term adjustment patterns. Because studies have relied almost exclusively on cross-sectional data, the well-documented range of problems encountered by those who divorce has not been examined in the context of changing personal and social circumstances after divorce. Many researchers and clinicians, as well as those who experience divorce, assume that remarriage following divorce may constitute a significant, if not *the* most significant, alteration in the social circumstances influencing enhanced well-being.

Drawing on data from a longitudinal study of divorce and remarriage among some 200 divorced persons in central Pennsylvania, Spanier and Furstenberg (1982) concluded that well-being following the dissolution of a marriage is not significantly altered by a transition to marriage or cohabitation.[1] Although considerable indi-

---

[1] The respondents were first studied in the spring of 1977 through in-depth, structured, face-to-face interviews focusing on the social, psychological, and economic adjustments of males and females who had experienced a marital separation within approximately 2 years preceding the interview, whether or not they had divorced. These individuals were then reinterviewed in the summer and fall of 1979, approximately 2½ years after

vidual variation in well-being during the postseparation period was found, remarriage alone was not related significantly to enhanced well-being. Most individuals reported greater well-being three to four years after their final separation, regardless of their marital status subsequently. Moreover, there appeared to be no significant differences between men and women or between individuals with children in the household and individuals without children in the household.

Undoubtedly, then, changes in well-being during the postseparation period must be attributed to as-yet-undiscovered influences that await further study. One must question what may have become a common wisdom that remarriage following divorce is, in general, a precursor to enhanced well-being. An important serendipitous finding of the Spanier and Furstenberg (1982) study, however, suggested that the likelihood of remarriage following divorce may be related to one's well-being during the postseparation period: The individuals with the greatest well-being were most likely to be remarried three to four years after their final separation.

Furthermore, among those who remarried, the quality of the remarriage was positively related to well-being. This discovery may have accounted for the absence of any overall differential in well-being between divorced and remarried persons. The study strongly indicated that remarried persons are heterogeneous, as is the remarriage experience.

When second marriages are successful and rewarding, individuals typically fare better, it appears, than they would have if they had remained divorced. The individual's marriage experience is viewed through the lens of his or her past biography of failure, and the current evaluation of well-being is enhanced. Just the opposite effect may occur when a remarriage experience is unrewarding. A sense of initial failure is reinforced, and in all likelihood, the individual's sense of well-being is reduced. Thus, the remarriage experience may have a conditional impact on personal adjustment. Although it cannot be said that remarriage generally enhances psychological well-being, it clearly does so in certain cases. This finding may account for the popular impression that remarriage improves a divorced person's psychological well-being. We suspect that for every person who benefits from a remarriage, there is another whose psychological status is adversely affected by an unsuccessful remarriage.

---

the initial interview. Complete interviews were obtained in 1979 with 181 of the 210 respondents interviewed in 1977. Thus the follow-up rate was 86%. The interview schedule at Time 2 repeated approximately half of the questions asked at Time 1 and, in addition, added approximately 200 new items, mostly related to remarriage, stepparenthood, kinship patterns, and long-term adjustments and changes in lifestyles. At Time 2, data were also obtained from the partners (married or cohabiting) of persons who were interviewed at Time 1. Unstructured, open-ended, tape-recorded interviews were also obtained with a subsample of remarried couples.

Children in Reconstituted Families

The recent rise in marital disruption means that a substantial proportion of America's children will spend part of their childhood either living with a single parent, living with one biological parent and a stepparent, or if shared custody after divorce becomes a more common arrangement, dividing their time between two households. A number of studies have appeared on the impact of divorce on the socialization process, examining the child's immediate adjustment to marital disruption as well as its long-run effect on the child's situation in later life (Levinger & Moles, 1979). The principal defect of most existing studies is their tendency to regard divorce as a static event, adopting what some critics of cross-sectional research have labeled a *states-and-rates approach*. The most creative longitudinal studies have shown that divorce has very different meanings to children over time, and that one cannot understand divorce without viewing it as a highly differentiated process that impacts on children differently depending on their age, their gender, their support within the family, and, not least of all, their parents' management of the divorce transition (Levitin, 1979; Hetherington, Cox, & Cox, 1978; Kitson & Sussman, 1982; Wallerstein & Kelly, 1980). Yet, even the studies that have adopted a longitudinal perspective on divorce have generally continued to treat divorce as a terminal event when, in fact, it is typically a transitional stage in a conjugal career that includes remarriage.

There is little doubt that marital separation and divorce can be stressful for a significant proportion of the children in the families involved (Hetherington, 1979; Hetherington et al., 1978; Wallerstein & Kelly, 1980). Wallerstein and Kelly (1980), for example, found that the initial period following the end of the marriage was especially difficult for the children in their longitudinal study. Five years after the divorce, approximately one third of the children were viewed as having made a good adjustment to the divorce; about one third displayed signs of some positive adjustment but also some negative adjustment; and the additional one third could be classified as suffering from more significant problems. Regardless of their status, all looked back at the transition as an unhappy one.

Because most parents report continuing commitments to their children, regardless of custody arrangements, it is reasonable to assume that the remarriage of a parent will, in some cases, complicate a child's life and present the child with additional adjustments, some of which may be stressful and psychologically and socially difficult (Langer & Michael, 1963; Duberman, 1975; Messinger, 1976; Visher & Visher, 1979; Wilson, Zucker, McAdams, & Curtis, 1975). There are very few data, however, to address this issue directly. Bowerman and Irish (1962) studied more than 2,000 high-school stepchildren in three states. Stepfamilies were found to be more likely to experience stress, negative feelings, and low self-esteem than first-marriage families. Burchinal (1964), however, found no differences between adolescents in first-marriage, broken, or remarriage families in his study of 1,500 Iowa high-school students. Not only are the data inconsistent, but as Bernard (1956) pointed out, it is ill advised simply to compare children in different statuses. Chilman (1981), for example, suggested that one needs to compare children in stepfamilies with children in first-marriage families in which there is a high degree of marital dissatisfaction.

Furstenberg, Spanier, and Rothschild (1980) examined patterns of parenting in the transition from divorce to remarriage in their Pennsylvania sample of divorced persons. They found conspicuous gender differences in the management of parenthood after divorce and remarriage. As women typically are awarded the custody of their children, the fathers are likely to become less and less involved in parenthood. Of course, there are notable exceptions. Some fathers become closer to their children following divorce. However, in the typical case, the traditional division of labor becomes even sharper, with women assuming most of the child-rearing responsibilities. Furthermore, remarriage seems to intensify this pattern because males frequently reduce their participation in their first family as they become involved in a new relationship, especially if their former spouse remains single. In general, Furstenberg *et al.* (1980) found that, when men or women defer marriage, they are more likely to share parental responsibilities more equally than when one or both remarry. It can be argued that the "his-and-her" perspective on divorce is not so much a product of gender differences as it is of the divergent situations of the parent who has custody and the parent who does not. Fathers who obtain custody adopt an outlook that is very similar to that of mothers who obtain custody, and when mothers relinquish custody, they have much more in common with the males who are living apart from their children.

Chilman (1981) attempted to summarize some of the central themes of problems and adjustments experienced by children, their parents, and their stepparents in reconstituted families:

1. *Discipline is a particularly thorny issue in many stepfamilies. The stepparent (usually a stepfather) often moves into the new marriage eager to play the role of an effective dad. He tends to strive for instant love and intimacy as well as firm control over the children's behavior. During courtship, preceding the marriage, he probably tried to be popular with the youngsters, as an easy-going "pal," but with marriage his perceptions of his role tend to change. Children are apt to strongly resent the stepfather's discipline, especially if the norms and methods are different from those practiced by the mother and biological father. . . .*

2. *Open communication between the marital pair and the children regarding many issues, including discipline, seems to be essential. Too frequently, the newlyweds are so focussed on their relationship that they overlook the needs and feelings of the children. These needs and feelings are apt to be acute and complex. This is particularly so when the reconstituted family consists of two sets of children: the biological children of each remarried parent—offspring of a former marriage. Rivalry between the two sets of young-*

sters, value conflicts, and psychological incompatibility are some of the common difficulties.

3. *Difficulties are apt to intensify if there are shifts or deficits in the physical environment. For example, a remarriage means that either the bride or groom (or both) moves to a new residence. When children are involved, this may mean changes in neighborhoods and schools, as well as housing. Especially if family finances are limited and the combined family has a large number of children, living conditions can become cramped. If a child is displaced as sole possessor of his or her room and play equipment. there can be a strong sense of invasion and loss of "turf."*

4. *A close, positive relationship within the marital dyad generally reduces conflicts between the stepsiblings and stepparent-stepchild relationships. When marital conflicts are unresolved, the children tend to act out the problems of the marriage.*

5. *It is recommended that reconstituted families use open discussions with all members and set superordinate goals for the family as a whole. Without such goals, the remarried family is apt to disintegrate into two separate families—returning to their earlier pre-marriage systems.*

6. *. . . Biological grandparents who resent the divorce and the remarriage may seek to form a coalition with their grandchildren against the new family. They may especially resent the remarriage of their biological child who has no youngsters and marries a spouse who already has children and does not want to have any more. Then, too, some grandparents discriminate between their biological grandchildren and their stepgrandchildren. Grandparents can make an important contribution of security and stability to their grandchildren especially during stressful periods of death, divorce, and remarriage. . . . Of course, many contemporary grandparents do not offer the stable model of the traditional family: they, too, may be involved in divorce and remarriage. Moreover, many are widowers or widows, especially the latter.*

7. *Grandparents and their grown children may be interacting in a continuing troubled relationship of unresolved dependencies, rivalries, ambivalences and so on. It should be recognized that reconstituted families may be especially haunted by ghosts of the past, not only of earlier marriages but of the various families of origin. Children can, therefore, become the battlegrounds for the earlier family wars of both their biological parents and their stepparents.*

It must be added that the evidence for many of these observations is largely anecdotal. It is prudent to regard Chilman's conclusions as hypotheses warranting further investigation. Preliminary evidence from a nationally representative survey of children between the ages of 11 and 16 conducted between 1976 and 1981 by Furstenberg and Zill indicates that most stepfamilies report high levels of parental satisfaction, low levels of intrafamily conflict, and relatively harmonious relations between stepparents

[2]The study collected data from a nationally representative sample of children between the ages of 7 and 11. Up to two children in the appropriate age category were selected from each eligible household. In order to contrast racial subgroups, blacks were oversampled and the final data were adjusted with sample weights to correct for this procedure. In all, 2,279 people from 1,747 households were interviewed at Time 1 in 1976. In addition to personal interviews with each child, information was collected from the parent or the parent-surrogate in the house-

and their children.[2] The national data suggest that clinically based studies may exaggerate—at least to some extent—the number of problems experienced by stepfamilies. Most stepfamilies appear to negotiate successfully the complications of a more complex and normatively ambiguous family situation.

Remarriage and Generational Ties

It is important to observe that divorce and remarriage have a profound effect on the structure of the extended-family system, in addition to the effects on the immediate nuclear family. In particular, divorce disrupts ties between grandparents and grandchildren, particularly when such marital dissolution separates parents from their children. Furstenberg and Spanier (1980) pointed out that physical and emotional distance between parent and child lessens the likelihood that relations will continue between the first and third generations. Except in the rare instance in which a noncustodial parent continues to preserve intimate bonds with his or her in-laws, grandparent–grandchild relations are almost entirely dependent on the custodial parent's mediating role.

The potentially unsettling effects of divorce and remarriage on intergenerational relations have not gone completely unnoticed. Several gerontologists have observed that increases in divorce may disturb the flow of assistance between young and middle-aged adults and their parents and may jeopardize the maintenance of ties between the senior generation and the grandchildren (Brody, 1978; Sussman, 1976). The two most widely cited studies, one by Rosenberg and Anspach (1973) and the other by Spicer and Hampe (1975), have examined the frequency of contact between divorced parents and their close relations (parents and siblings). They demonstrate rather convincingly that relations between blood relatives intensify somewhat following a divorce, whereas relations between in-laws are severely curtailed following the dissolution of the marriage.

Though the contact between the grandparents and the grandchildren has not been studied directly, the implica-

tion drawn from these two studies is that a similar pattern of attrition occurs between the child and his or her grandparents on the side of the noncustodial parent. If the child's mother, for example, ceases relations with her former parents-in-law, it is assumed that the child will suffer a similar loss of contact with his or her grandparents. However, this assumption has not been tested adequately. The children's father, for example, could take them to visit his parents from time to time. But even if intergenerational relations are, in fact, adversely affected by divorce, it does not necessarily follow, as previous researchers have generally concluded, that marital disruption shrinks the child's pool of available kin. As we pointed out earlier, divorce is generally a transitional rather than a terminal status. If and when remarriage occurs, the child is exposed to a new set of relations who may or may not become active figures in the child's life.

Little or no attention has been paid to the problems for the elderly of incorporating new relations after remarriage. In their comprehensive summary of the family situation of older people in contemporary society, Troll, Miller, and Atchley (1979) remarked:

Most writers refer only to the in-law adjustment problems of young married couples; few note the adjustment problems of middle-age parents and even older grandparents to the new families introduced into kin networks upon each new marriage in the family. (pp. 126–127)

After reviewing the existing literature on the impact of remarriage on kinship patterns, Troll and her associates concluded that so little is known about kinship relations among reconstituted families that one cannot even speculate about them.

Few studies, then, have examined the impact of remarriage on kinship bonds. In a small study of women still in their first marriages, divorced women, and remarried women, Anspach (1976) discovered that all three marital subgroups enjoyed about the same contact with their own parents. Divorced and remarried women had little contact with their former in-laws, though approximately a third of each group continued to maintain regular relations with their ex-spouse's family. Both women in first marriages and those in remarriages had nearly as much contact with their (current) spouse's family as with their own kin. In short, remarried persons were in an especially advantageous position in the kinship network, able to draw support from members of their own family, from their present in-laws, and to some degree from their former in-laws. As in the other studies discussed, the implications for grandparent–grandchild relations were unstated. But it would seem that, to the extent that children continue to see the family of their noncustodial parent, they might experience an enlargement of kin as a result of divorce and remarriage.

Of course, such a conclusion is not firmly grounded in empirical evidence, especially direct data on the extent and the quality of relations between children and their grandparents (biological and affinal). It may well be that

---

hold who had the greatest knowledge of the child. In more than 90% of the households, the respondent was the child's biological mother. Finally, a mailed questionnaire was sent to the schools attended by the children interviewed, soliciting data on their academic records and performance in the classroom. In 1981, the families were followed up in an examination of the effects of marital disruption on the development and well-being of the children. At Time 2, all children in families that had experienced a marital disruption by the time of the earlier survey were studied, as well as children whose parents had previously reported a high-conflict marriage, and a randomly selected subsample of children from stable marriages with low or medium conflict. An important difference between the two data collections was that the Time 2 interviews were conducted by telephone. Much of the information obtained at Time 1 was also obtained at Time 2. In addition, moreover, the data collected at Time 2 focused on issues pertaining to divorce, remarriage, custody, and related issues.

children have only a fixed amount of time to spend with their grandparents. If they spend more time with one set, they will have to reduce their interaction with another. Moreover, it is possible that even if children do continue to see their grandparents on the noncustodial parent's side, relations may be strained as a result of the divorce. Conversely, it is possible that affinal grandparents may not develop the same emotional commitment to the child as do biological grandparents.

Furstenberg and Spanier (1980), in their central Pennsylvania longitudinal study, found that, generally speaking, most noncustodial parents did continue to see their children on a fairly regular basis, and hence, the children had access to extended kin. Moreover, noncustodial parents, typically fathers, relied heavily on their parents for child-care assistance. These grandparents played a critical role in helping parents to manage unfamiliar or difficult child-care tasks when divorce occurred. (For more recent evidence, see also Cherlin and Furstenberg's 1986 national study of grandparents.) Accordingly, we might have anticipated that relations between the first and third generations on the noncustodial parent's side would decline after remarriage. But there was no indication in the study that grandparents were squeezed out of the picture when the crisis of divorce was over. As long as parent–child relations continued, which was usually the case, the grandparents' position was not jeopardized by a second marriage. In fact, it can be argued that extended kin, by their continued interest in the child, help to anchor the relationship between parent and child.

Remarriage appears to add relatives to, rather than subtracting them from, the extended-family network. Schneider (1980), among others, has suggested that an important feature of our kinship system is its discretionary quality. Individuals have the option but not the obligation to define people as relatives when they are not closely related by blood. Kinship is often achieved rather than ascribed. Remarriage illustrates this principle by creating an enlarged pool of potential kin. To a large extent, it is up to the various parties involved to determine the extent to which potential kin will be treated as actual relatives.

Conceptual Issues in the Study of Remarriage

A theorist would be obliged to ask whether there is anything conceptually important to ask about remarriage that could not be answered through a study of marriage more generally. As we have noted earlier, remarriage shares only certain elements with first marriage. Remarriage tends to involve more complex role relationships, extended-family networks, and ties to chil-

dren. These potential complexities are illustrated in Figures 1, 2, and 3. These three figures introduce the progression of complexity associated with marital extension, family reconstitution, and extended relations in reconstituted families. Ahrons (1980) referred to this restructured kinship organization as a binuclear family system.

The figures feature one small family network, highlighting the formal relationships between members. Figure 1 shows that John and Mary were previously married, as were Dick and Ellen. Both couples divorced, with Dick marrying Mary, and John marrying Sue. A relatively simple situation, involving two marriages that ended in divorce, results in an informal network of five adults who have some relationship to each other. Before the divorces and remarriages, each couple may have had no knowledge of the other. Not atypically, all five of these individuals may now have some contact with each of the other four, as well as children and other family members related to the other four adults. Several salient issues for these relationships can be noted. These issues demonstrate potential research questions for the field:

1. How does the transition from the first marriage to the second (or subsequent) marriage differ from couple to couple and from individual to individual?

2. How do remarried couples meet the challenge of family re-formation, particularly when children and others in the extended-family network are involved?

3. How do the lingering commitments to a former spouse influence the initiation and the subsequent course of the current marriage?

4. What styles of interaction develop between the new partners of former spouses or the former partners of one's current spouse?

5. What norms, if any, have developed regarding the socialization to remarriage?

6. How does the transition to remarriage differ from the transition to marriage?

7. In what ways do the dynamics differ in the socialization to remarriage when one partner is in a first marriage from when both partners are remarrying?

8. How important are age at divorce, age at remarriage, and the difference between the two?

9. Are there differences in the socialization to remarriage following divorce versus following widowhood?

10. What are the most challenging adjustments to divorce and remarriage, and what coping strategies do individuals use to help with the adjustments?

11. Are there intervention programs that can effectively meet the needs of persons experiencing adjustment problems in the transition to remarriage?

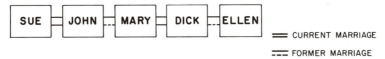

SUE — JOHN ⊟ MARY — DICK ⊟ ELLEN

═══ CURRENT MARRIAGE

╌╌╌ FORMER MARRIAGE

Figure 1. A diagram of marital extension.

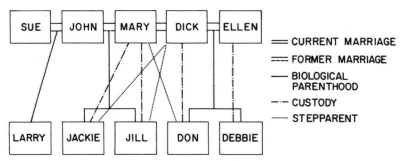

Figure 2. A diagram of family reconstitution.

Figure 2 shows the same five adults and adds their children to the picture. When the children are considered, two types of relationships can exist between parent and child: *biological parenthood* and *stepparenthood*. In addition, *custody* is a relevant consideration apart from the type of parenthood. Superimposed over each of these three roles is the possibility of *sociological parenthood*. Some adults and children develop relationships that ignore the formally stated roles. A girl who is in the custody of her biological mother, for example, might consider the new wife of her nonresidential biological father an especially significant other. A boy lives with his biological mother, who has been married three times. He is the biological child of his mother's first husband and the stepchild of his mother's third husband. The boy, however, considers his second father, with whom he has no current formal tie, his "real" father. This is a powerful sociological relationship not reflected in the formal presentation of the family network.

Figure 2 shows that two children were born to John and Mary in their first marriage (Jackie and Jill). Dick and Ellen also had two children in their first marriage (Don and Debbie). John, after remarrying, had an additional child (Larry) with Sue, who was marrying for the first time. Apart from these biological links, then, there are matters of custody and stepparenthood. Mary was awarded custody of Jackie and Jill, and thus, her new husband Dick has become a stepparent of two children. Dick was granted custody of one of his two biological children, Don. Therefore his new wife, Mary, is a stepparent as well. Dick and Mary thus have three children living with them, all by virtue of a custody award. This reconstituted family faces potential adjustments related to parenthood, custody and visitation, stepparenthood, stepsibling relationships, and, for Don, having a sister (Debbie) whom he grew up with but who is now living with her mother. A relatively simple family of two adults and three children can become a complex kinship configuration extending over several households.

Because John had given up custody of his children, and Sue married for the first time, they decided they wanted to have a child. Larry, their only child, also has a special relationship to John's other children, even though they do not live together. John's visitation rights often put Larry in the same household with Jackie and Jill, adding a visiting sibling for the residential children to deal with on occasion. Similarly, Debbie often visits the new home of her father, thus introducing a fourth child, who is partially affiliated with her stepsiblings by virtue of a common parentage, into the family world of Jackie and Jill.

Such complexity of interrelationships provides a sociologist or a social psychologist with many interesting questions to examine:

1. How do custody arrangements affect the relationships between spouses?

2. How are the responsibilities of parenthood modified when families are reconstituted?

3. How does the presence of children influence the relationships between former spouses, between current spouses, and between a current and former spouse?

4. How well are children able to adapt to the various roles that they may have to assume relating to other children in their reconstituted family network?

5. To what degree do children become intermediaries, and how are they affected by this role?

6. Does the age of a child make a difference in how he or she will adjust to the special demands of a reconstituted family?

7. How important is the particular constellation of children in reconstituted families according to age, gender, and the number children brought to the new household by each adult?

8. If the first marriage is terminated by the death of a parent, do the challenges of adjustment become easier for the child?

9. When there are children in the household with different biological parents, what special issues may exist?

10. How do changes in custody awards after a new household has been established influence the ability of the children and the parents to adjust?

11. Are innovative intervention programs that could successfully address some of these special challenges possible or advisable?

Figure 3 completes our illustration of the complexity of reconstituted families by adding the parents of the indi-

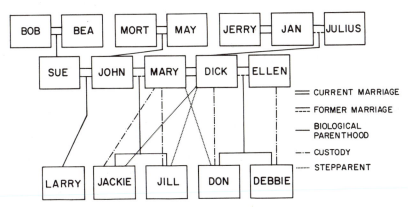

Figure 3. A diagram of extended relations in reconstituted families.

viduals first portrayed in Figure 1. The extended-family network often can be a powerful influence in decisions about marriage, divorce, and remarriage. Given the special status that most societies give to grandparenthood, there is interest in how divorce and remarriage influence the nature of such grandchild–grandparent relations. Moreover, it should be noted that there may have been one or more remarriages in the grandparent generation, thus adding another element of complexity to the family network.

In our illustration, we show only some of the grandparents, for simplicity. Sue's parents (Bob and Bea) and John's parents (Mort and May) fit the traditional picture in that they have each married once. Dick's parents (Jan and Julius) are divorced, however, and his mother has remarried Jerry, with whom she now lives. Recall that Dick has a relationship with four children, who, in turn, have three grandparents through Dick. The children all have somewhat different situations in relation to their grandparents. Given the split custody of Don and Debbie, they rarely see their grandparents on the same visit. Don sometimes sees his grandparents by himself, and at other times, Jackie and Jill come along. However, Jackie and Jill, because they are Dick's stepchildren, have a qualitatively different relationship with Dick's parents and stepparent. Furthermore, it should be noted that all of the children have two grandparent households through Dick.

Although John and Mary have little contact, their children (Jackie and Jill) still have a relationship to Mort and May, their paternal grandparents. Thus, situations where Jackie and Jill find themselves around Larry are not uncommon, even though John and Mary have virtually no contact anymore. For the children shown in Figure 3, then, the grandparent generation may introduce a new array of relationships that the parent generation sought to avoid. It is not uncommon in reconstituted family networks for children to have some relationship to as many as five or six sets of "grandparents." In reality, however, it would be difficult to maintain closeness with this many

relatives, and some selection on the part of the parents and the child undoubtedly operates. We make the point, nevertheless, that such family reconstitution can pose numerous additional questions for researchers:

1. What are the mechanisms by which children and their parents determine which grandparents they will become closer to, versus which ones they may choose to be more distant from?

2. To what degree does the termination of the parent's marriage influence the grandchild–grandparent relationship?

3. What terminology do children and their families adopt to handle the complexities of reconstituted extended-family networks?

4. To what degree do grandparents complicate issues of custody and visitation, beyond those presented by the parents?

5. To what degree are grandparent relationships maintained even when relationships with a parent have become infrequent or nonexistent?

6. Are grandparents themselves able to adapt to the divorce of their children to the extent that they are able to maintain commitments and attachments to their grandchildren?

7. How is the well-being of grandparents affected when they suffer the "loss" of a grandchild through divorce and remarriage?

8. What issues can develop concerning the transfer of equity, inheritance, and familial culture across generations?

Perspective for the Future

Certainly, no informed observer can question that the family, at least in the United States, is experiencing some profound alterations. As always, the magnitude of the perceived change depends in part on what is taken to be the baseline. Depending on whether we begin at the end of the nineteenth century (the first period for which we have a large amount of reliable quantitative data) or in the middle of the twentieth century (when we have a much richer variety of demographic and social information), somewhat different pictures emerge (Hareven, 1978; Demos & Boocock, 1978; Tufte & Myerhoff, 1979). Ironically, short-term family changes (those over the last few decades) are much more dramatic than the long-term changes (those over the last century) because in the period immediately following World War II, certain long-standing cyclical trends were temporarily upset. The age at marriage, which had been relatively stable, plummeted, giving the impression of a ''marriage rush.'' Fertility, which had been on the decline, increased dramatically, creating the well-known baby boom. Divorce rose precipitously at the end of the war but then declined nearly to prewar levels. In short, for reasons that are not yet well understood, in the middle of the twentieth century, Americans observed an unusually high commitment to domestic life. We might think of this period as an era of mass production of families (Cherlin, 1981; Masnick & Bane, 1980).

It is against this backdrop that we now view the period since the 1950s as a period of ''recession,'' or even ''depression,'' in family formation. The marriage age has risen close to historical highs for women, and fertility has declined to historical lows. Married women have moved out of the home, joining men in the workplace. It must be conceded that we are exaggerating these changes because our point of comparison is the baby-boom period. In reality, these changes are less discrepant with long-term trends in family formation. Nevertheless, the end of the baby boom signaled some profound changes that have no historical precedent. The one that we have considered in this chapter is the emerging pattern of conjugal succession—the increasingly common tendency for couples to divorce and remarry, and its associated implications for their children and extended-family networks.

Elsewhere, we have argued that this pattern of conjugal succession is probably related to a series of demographic developments that have taken place since the 1950s (Furstenberg, 1981, 1982; Furstenberg and Spanier, 1980, 1981). Briefly summarized, the argument is that, whereas marriage was once closely bound to departure from the parental home, the establishment of a new household, the onset of sexual activity, and parenthood, today marriage has become detached from these other transitions. Marriage no longer serves as the master event in the sequence of family formation; it is now merely one of a series of increasingly independent transitions that make up the process of creating a new family. Individuals can leave the parental household, set up their own residence, become sexually active, cohabit with a member of the opposite sex, and even have a child without getting married. All of these events are discrete acts that may or may not be linked to the decision to marry.

As marriage has become less central in the process of family formation, its meaning has changed accordingly. Matrimony is viewed today as more voluntary; that is, no longer do we take for granted that a person should marry, even though most individuals, in fact, do enter wedlock. Moreover, marriage is also regarded as involving a much more conditional commitment. A substantial proportion of the population accepts the inevitability—even the desirability—of divorce in the event of serious marital discord.

In the 1970s, researchers conducted a large number of studies on the causes of divorce and its consequences for family functioning (Hetherington *et al.*, 1978; Levinger & Moles, 1979; Levitin, 1979; Wallerstein & Kelly, 1980). For reasons that are not entirely clear, almost all of the current research on divorce regards marital dissolution as a terminal rather than a transitional status. Even studies that purport to look at the long-term effects of divorce ignore the well-known fact that most divorced persons remarry, parents and nonparents alike. Clearly, it is difficult to understand the consequences of divorce without examining the continuing conjugal career of the partners who terminated a marriage.

In this chapter, we have attempted to highlight some of what is known about remarriage and reconstituted families, and to suggest some conceptual and research issues that are likely to be important in the future study of these topics. It is common to conclude such presentations with calls for additional research. Unlike other areas of study within the family field, however, where masses of data already exist, we can safely say that few data exist that can help to guide our understanding of remarriage and reconstituted families. Thus, the present call for additional research must be considered more seriously than the usual request. Remarriage has become a reality for such a substantial proportion of Americans that it must capture as much attention from social scientists as many of the other social phenomena we routinely study.

References

Ahrons, C. R. Divorce: A crisis of family transition and change. *Family Relations*, 1980, *29*, 533–540.

Anspach, D. F. Kinship and divorce. *Journal of Marriage and the Family*, 1976, *38*(2), 323, 330.

Bernard, J. *Remarriage: A study of marriage*. New York: Dryden Press, 1956.

Bloom, B. L., White, S. W., & Asher, S. J. Marital disruption as a stressful life event. In G. Levinger & O. C. Moles (Eds.), *Divorce and separation: Contexts, causes, and consequences*. New York: Basic Books, 1979.

Bohannan, P. Divorce chains, households of remarriage, and multiple divorces. In P. Bohannan (Ed.), *Divorce and after*. New York: Doubleday, 1970.

Bowerman, C. E. Assortative mating by previous marital status, Seattle, 1939–1946. *American Sociological Review*, 1953, *18*, 171.

Bowerman, C. E., & Irish, D. P. Some relationships of stepchildren to their parents. *Marriage and Family Living*, 1962, 113–121.

Brody, E. The aging of the family. *The Annals of the American Academy of Political and Social Science*, 1978, *438*, 13–28.

Burchinal, L. G. Characteristics of adolescents from unbroken, broken, and reconstituted families. *Journal of Marriage and the Family*, 1964, *26*,(1), 44–51.

Chamie, J., & Nsuly, S. Sex differences in remarriage and spouse selection. *Demography*, 1981, *18*(3), 335–348.

Cherlin, A. Remarriage as an incomplete institution. *American Journal of Sociology*, 1978, *84*(3), 634–650.

Cherlin, A. J. *Marriage, divorce, and remarriage: Changing patterns in the postwar United States*. Cambridge: Harvard University Press, 1981.

Cherlin, A. J., & Furstenberg, F. F. *The new American grandparent: A place in the family, a life apart*. New York: Basic Books, 1986.

Chilman, C. S. *Remarriage and stepfamilies: An overview of research, observations, and some implications for further study and program development*. Paper presented at the annual meeting of the Groves Conference on Marriage and the Family, 1981.

Chiriboga, D. A., Roberts, J., & Stein, J. A. Psychological well being during marital separation. *Journal of Divorce*, 1978, *2*, 21–36.

Dandekar, K. *Widow remarriage in six rural communities in Western Africa*. International Population Union Conference, Paper No. 56, 1961.

Davis, K. The American family in relation to demographic change. In C. F. Westoff & R. Parke, Jr., (Eds.), Volume 1 of the technical reports of the Commission on Population Growth and the American Future, *Demographic and social aspects of population growth*, 1972.

Demos, J., & Boocock, S. S. (Eds.). *Turning points: Historical and sociological essays on the family*. Chicago: University of Chicago Press, 1978.

Draughon, M. Stepmother's model of identification in relation to mourning in the child. *Psychological Reports*, 1975, *36*, 183–189.

Duberman, L. *The reconstituted family: A study of remarried couples and their children*. Chicago: Nelson-Hall, 1975.

Fried, M. H. The family in China: The people's Republic. In R. N. Anshern (Ed.), *The family*. New York: Harper, 1959.

Furstenberg, F. F. Reflections on remarriage. *Journal of Family Issues*, 1980, *1*, 443–453.

Furstenberg, F. F. *Renegotiating parenthood after divorce and remarriage*. Paper presented at the biennial meeting of the Society for Research in Child Development, 1981.

Furstenberg, F. F. Conjugal succession: Reentering marriage after divorce. In P. B. Baltes & O. G. Brim (Eds.), *Life span development and behavior*, Vol. 4. New York: Academic Press, 1982.

Furstenberg, F. F., & Spanier G. B. *Marital dissolution and generational ties*. Paper presented at the annual meeting of the Gerontological Society, 1980.

Furstenberg, F. F., & Spanier, G. B. *The risk of dissolution in remarriage: An examination of Cherlin's hypothesis of incomplete institutionalization*. Paper presented at the annual meeting of the American Sociological Association, 1981.

Furstenberg, F. F., & Spanier, G. B. *Recycling the family: Remarriage after divorce*. Beverly Hills, California: Sage, 1984.

Furstenberg, F. F., Spanier, G. B., & Rothschild, N. *Patterns of parenting in the transition from divorce to remarriage*. Paper presented at the NICHD, NIMH, and NIA conference on Women, A Developmental Perspective, 1980.

Glick, P. C. First marriages and remarriages. *American Sociological Review*, 1949, *14*, 726–734.

Glick, P. C. Remarriage: Some recent changes and variations. *Journal of Family Issues*, 1980, *1*(4), 455–478.

Glick, P. C., & Norton, A. J. Marrying, divorcing, and living together in the U.S. today. *Population Bulletin, 32*(5). Washington, D.C.: Population Reference Bureau, 1979.

Glick, P. C., & Spanier, G. B. Married and unmarried cohabitation in the United States. *Journal of Marriage and the Family*, 1980, *42*, 19–30.

Goldmeier, J. Intervention in the continuum from divorce to family reconstitution. *Social Casework*, 1980, *61*(1), 39–47.

Goode, W. J. *Women in divorce*. New York: Free Press, 1956.

Goode, W. J. *World revolution and family patterns*. New York: Free Press, 1963.

Griffith, J. D. Economy, family and remarriage: Theory of remarriage and application to preindustrial England. *Journal of Family Issues*, 1980, *1*, 479–496.

Hareven, T. K. (Ed.). *Transitions: The family and the life course in historical perspective*. New York: Academic Press, 1978.

Hetherington, E. M. Divorce: A child's perspective. *American Psychologist*, 1979, *34*(10), 851–858.

Hetherington, E. M., Cox, M., & Cox, R. *The aftermath of divorce*. Paper presented at the annual meeting of the American Psychological Association, Washington, D.C., 1976.

Hetherington, E. M., Cox, M., & Cox, R. The aftermath of divorce. In J. H. Stevens & M. Matthews (Eds.), *Mother-child, father-child relations*. Washington, D.C.: National Association for the Education of Young Children (NAEYC), 1978.

Hutchens, R. M. Welfare, remarriage, and marital search. *The American Economic Review*, 1979, *69*(3), 369–379.

Jacobson, D. S. Stepfamilies: Myths and realities. *Social Work*, 1979, 202–207.

Jacobson, P. H. *American marriage and divorce*. New York: Rinehart, 1959.

Johnson, H. C. Working with stepfamilies: Principles of practice. *Social Work*, 1980, *25*(4), 304–308.

Kitson, G. C. Attachment to the spouse in divorce: A scale and its application. *Journal of Marriage and the Family*, 1982, *44*, 379–393.

Kitson, G. C., & Sussman, M. B. Marital complaints, demographic characteristics, and symptoms of mental distress in divorce. *Journal of Marriage and the Family*, 1982, *44*, 87–101.

Kleinman, J., Rosenberg, E., & Whiteside, M. Common developmental tasks in forming reconstituted families. *Journal of Marriage and Family Therapy*, 1979, *5*, 79–86.

Koo, H. P., & Suchindran, C. M. Effects of children on women's remarriage prospects. *Journal of Family Issues*, 1980, *1*(14) 497–516.

Landis, P. H. Sequential remarriage. *Journal of Home Economics*, 1950, *42*, 625–628.

Langer, T. S. & Michael, S. T. *Life stress and mental health*. New York: Free Press, 1963.

Leslie, G. R. *The family in social context*. New York: Oxford University Press, 1967.

Levinger, G., & Moles, O. C. *Divorce and separation: Contexts, causes, and consequences*. New York: Basic Books, 1979.

Levitin, T. E. Children of divorce. *Journal of Social Issues*, 1979 *35*, 1–25.

Locke, H. J., & Klausner, W. J. Marital adjustment of divorced persons in subsequent marriages. *Sociology and Social Research*, 1948, *33*, 97–101.

Masnick, G., & Bane, M. J. *The nation's families: 1960–1990*. Cambridge: Joint Center for Urban Studies of MIT and Harvard University, 1980.

Messinger, L. Remarriage between divorced people with children from previous marriages: A proposal for preparation for remarriage. *Journal of Marriage and Family Counseling*, 1976, *2*, 193–199.

Messinger, L., Walker, K. N., & Freeman, S. J. J. Preparation for remarriage following divorce: The use of group techniques. *American Journal of Orthopsychiatry*, 1978, *48*(2), 263–272.

Monahan, T. P. One hundred years of marriage in Massachusetts. *American Journal of Sociology*, 1951, *56*, 538–539.

Monahan, T. P. How stable are remarriages? *American Journal of Sociology*, 1952, *57*, 280–288.

Monahan, T. P. The changing nature and instability of remarriages. *Eugenics Quarterly*, 1958, *5*, 73–85.

Monahan, T. P. The duration of marriage to divorce: Second marriages and migratory types. *Marriage and Family Living*, 1959, *21*(2), 134–138.

Mowatt, M. H. Group psychotherapy for stepfathers and their wives.

Psychotherapy: Theory, Research, and Practice, 1972, *9*(4), 328–331.

Murstein, B. I. *Love, Sex, and marriage through the ages.* New York: Springer, 1974.

National Center for Health Statistics. *Remarriages: United States*, Series 21, No. 25. Department of Health, Education, and Welfare: Public Health Service; Health Resources Administration, Rockville, Md., 1973.

National Center for Health Statistics. *Monthly vital statistics reports: Advance report of final marriage statistics, 1978.* DHHS Publication No. (PHS) 80-1120, Vol. 29, No. 6, September 12, 1980. (a)

National Center for Health Statistics. *National estimates of marriage dissolution and survivorship: United States*, Series 3, No. 19. U.S. Department of Health and Human Services, Public Health Service, Office of Health Research, Statistics, and Technology, *National Center for Health Statistics*, Hyattsville, Md., 1980. (b)

National Center for Health Statistics. *Monthly vital statistics reports: Advance report of final marriage statistics, 1979.* DHHS Publication No. (PHS) 81-1120, Vol. 30, No. 4, July 31, 1981.

Nichols, W. C. Stepfamilies: A growing family therapy challenge. In L. Wolberg & M. Aronson (Eds.), *Group and family therapy.* New York: Brunner/Mazel, 1980.

Orthner, D. K., & Lewis, K. Evidence of single-father competence in childrearing. *Family Law Quarterly*, 1979, *13*(1), 27–47.

Oshman, H. F., & Manosevitz, M. Father absence: Effects of stepfathers upon psychosocial development on males. *Developmental Psychology*, 1976, *12*(5), 479–480.

Parish, T. S., & Copeland, T. F. Relationship between self-concepts and evaluations of parents and stepfathers. *Journal of Psychology*, 1979, *101*(1), 135–138.

Perkins, T. F., & Kahan, J. P. Empirical comparison of natural-father and step-father family system. *Family Process*, 1979, *18*(2), 175–183.

Price-Bonham, S., & Balswick, J. O. The noninstitutions: Divorce, desertion, and remarriage. *Journal of Marriage and the Family*, 1980, *42*(4), 959–972.

Queen, S. A., & Habenstein, S. A. *The family in various cultures* (4th ed.). Philadelphia: Lippincott, 1974.

Ransom, J. W., Schlesinger, S., & Derdeyn, A. P. A stepfamily in formation. *American Journal of Orthopsychiatry*, 1979, *49*(1), 36–43.

Rosenberg, G. S., & Anspach, D. F. *Working class kinships.* Lexington, Mass.: Lexington Books, 1973.

Rubin, L. B. *Women of a certain age.* New York: Harper & Row, 1979.

Schneider, D. M. *American kinship: A cultural account* (2nd ed.). Chicago: Phoenix Books, 1980.

Schulman, G. L. Myths that intrude on the adaptation of the stepfamily. *Social casework*, 1972, 131–139.

Smith, W. C. *The stepchild.* Chicago: University of Chicago Press, 1953.

Spanier, G. B. Married and unmarried cohabitation in the United States, 1980. *Journal of Marriage and the Family*, 1983, *45*(2), 277–288.

Spanier, G. B., & Casto, R. F. Adjustment to separation and divorce. A qualitative analysis. In G. Levinger & O. C. Moles (Eds.), *Divorce and separation: Contexts, causes, and consequences.* New York: Basic Books, 1979.

Spanier, G. B., & Furstenberg, F. F. Remarriage after divorce: A longitudinal analysis of well-being. *Journal of Marriage and the Family*, 1982, *43*, 709–720.

Spanier, G. B., & Glick, P. C. Mate selection differentials between whites and blacks in the United States. *Social Forces: An International Journal of Social Research*, 1980, *58*(3), 707–725. (a)

Spanier, G. B., & Glick, P. C. Paths to remarriage. *Journal of Divorce*, 1980, *3*(3), 283, 298. (b)

Spanier, G. B., & Glick, P. C. Marital instability in the United States: Some correlates and recent changes. *Family Relations*, 1981, *31*, 329–338.

Spicer, J. W., & Hampe, G. D. Kinship interaction after divorce. *Journal of Marriage and the Family*, 1975, *37*(1), 113–119.

Sussman, M. B. The family life of old people. In R. H. Binstock & E. Shanas (Eds.), *Handbook of aging and the social sciences.* New York: Van Nostrand Reinhold, 1976.

Thompson, L. *The aftermath of separation and divorce.* Unpublished doctoral dissertation, Pennsylvania State University, 1981.

Touliatos, J., & Lindholm, B. W. Teachers' perceptions of behavior problems in children from intact, single-parent, and stepparent families. *Psychology in the Schools*, 1980, *17*(2), 264–269.

Troll, L. E., Miller, S. J., & Atchley, R. C. *Families in later life.* Belmont, Calif.: Wadsworth, 1979.

Tufte, V., & Myerhoff, B. (Eds.), *Changing images of the family.* New Haven, Conn.: Yale University Press, 1979.

U.S. Bureau of the Census. *Number, timing and duration of marriages and divorces in the United States: June 1975.* Current Population Reports, Series P-20, No. 197. Washington, D.C.: U.S. Government Printing Office, 1976.

U.S. Bureau of the Census. *Perspectives on American husbands and wives.* Current Population Reports, Special Studies, Series P-23, No. 77. Washington, D.C.: U.S. Government Printing Office, 1978.

Visher, E. B., & Visher, J. S. Common problems of stepparents and their spouses. *American Journal of Orthopsychiatry*, 1978, *48*(2), 252–262.

Visher, E. B, & Visher, J. S. *Step-families: A guide to working with stepparents and stepchildren.* New York: Brunner/Mazel, 1979.

Walker, K. N., & Messinger, L. Remarriage after divorce: Dissolution and reconstruction of family boundaries. *Family Process*, 1979, *18*, 185–192.

Walker, K. N., Rogers, J., & Messinger, L. Remarriage after divorce: A review. *Social Casework*, 1977, *58*(5), 276–285.

Walker, L., Brown, H., Crohn, H., Rodstein, E., Zeisel, E., & Sager, C. J. An annotated bibliography of the remarried, the living together, and their children. *Family Process*, 1979, *18*, 193–212.

Waller, W. *The old love and the new.* Carbondale: Southern Illinois University Press, 1930.

Wallerstein, J. S., & Kelly, J. B. *Surviving the breakup.* New York: Basic Books, 1980.

Weiss, R. S. *Marital separation.* New York: Basic Books, 1975.

Wilson, K. L., Zucker, L., McAdams, D. C., & Curtis, R. L. Stepfathers and stepchildren: An exploratory analysis from two national surveys. *Journal of Marriage and the Family*, 1975, *37*, 526–536.

PART III

Life Cycle Processes

In this section, "Life Cycle Processes," focus is on the family and its expansion. Examined are the processes of family formation; parenthood; interaction and marital dissolution; and life patterns in middle and later adulthood. Included are chapters on fertility, human sexuality, and gender roles; events and situations that effect the life course transition of individuals; the behavior of members during various stages; and the family's course over the life cycle.

In the first chapter, "Life Cycle and Family Development," Mattessich and Hill introduce the family development perspective and provide a historical overview of family development. The authors pose several questions that form the basis of their essay: Does the family development perspective adequately describe family organizational change? Do family stages increase our understanding of life cycle changes? Is the concept of stages useful in describing change in the structure of families and their behavior as they move over the life cycle? Does this approach provide an adequate theory of how families develop over time? This chapter provides a foundation for understanding many of the life cycle processes discussed in depth in later chapters.

In "Parent–Child Socialization," Peterson and Rollins introduce symbolic interaction approaches to analyzing the parent–child dyadic relationship. The authors evaluate research on parental characteristics and child outcomes, as well as the impact of societal factors—such as social class, gender, culture, and ethnicity—on parent–child relationships. In order to gain an understanding of the impact that a theoretical perspective has on research methods, procedures, and techniques, the authors search, review, and integrate the literature on the parent–child dyad by using the symbolic interactional framework.

Francoeur, in his chapter "Human Sexuality," provides an overview of sexual development from conception to adolescence. Theories of social-sexual development are discussed, and a heterosexual/homosexual continuum is presented. Francoeur reviews research on religious variations and socioeconomic and ethnic differences between members of black, Jewish, Japanese, Mexican, and Islamic traditions for their impact on sexual development, values, and roles.

"Development of Gender Roles," by Susan Hesselbart, summarizes the research on the evolution of traditional gender roles; sex difference in personal traits; and the mechanics by which gender roles, societal positions, and reward are perpetuated. Housework, education, values, and labor force participation are examined as they are related to the development of gender roles. Hesselbart warns against the socialization "copout," which she defines as researchers' avoidance of the impact of adult socialization. For example, organizational patterns and social prejudice are ignored by researchers studying career patterns, and "fear of success" in women or "inexpressiveness" in men, purported to be the result of early childhood socialization, are emphasized. A discussion of the impact of gender roles throughout the life cycle and of the theories and models of gender-role development are included in this chapter.

An examination of fertility trends is provided by Miller in his chapter "Marriage, Family, and Fertility." Miller's analysis encompasses societies around the world, covering research on age of intercourse, celibacy, marital disruption, extended-family structures, and frequency of intercourse for its impact on fertility. Also examined are fertility controls, the value and cost of children, motivations for childbearing, and teenage pregnancy.

The chapter on divorce by Raschke focuses on the multiple circumstances, conditions, and situations that make marital separation and divorce a normative event at different stages of the family life cycle. Research on trends, characteristics of the divorced, and theories are reviewed in this chapter.

In "The Family in Later Years," Treas and Bengtson synthesize multiple macrosocial and microsocial perspectives on aging, the aged, and the families of old people. Demographic trends, labor-force-participation patterns, marital status, and intergenerational relationships are described. The authors note that dramatic changes occurring in society have altered traditional assumptions regarding aging, the family, and the social supports required to meet the needs of the elderly. They conclude with an examination of the burdens of family caregiving to the elderly and of public policy issues.

CHAPTER 17

Life Cycle and Family Development

Paul Mattessich and Reuben Hill

Introduction: The Family Development Perspective

The developmental perspective on the family has placed the nuclear family, as a group, with its regular patterns of expansion, transition, and contraction, in the forefront for research, theory, and practice. Family development, as a conceptual framework for orienting research, and as a set of theoretical propositions that invite empirical testing, has uniquely pioneered the effort to describe and explain the processes of change in families. Family time—the sequence of stages precipitated internally by the demands of family members (e.g., biological, psychological, and social needs) and externally by the larger society (e.g., social expectations and ecological constraints)—is the most significant focal point of the family development perspective. It is a focal point that distinguishes the developmental perspective from other approaches to the study of the family; and it is a focal point that produces an affinity between family development (research and theory concerning the life cycle of families) and life course analysis (research and theory concerning the life cycle of individuals). Since its germination in the 1930s and its accelerated evolution from the 1950s to the present, the family development perspective has attempted to explicate the phenomenon of development in families—not simply change, which may occur arrhythmically, but *development:* an underlying, regular process of differentiation and transformation over the family's history.

Has this perspective resulted in an intelligible and useful rendering of the phenomenon of family organizational change? Has the motion of family stages (the categorical system of operationally slicing the family career into segments that modally represent families whose incumbents display particular configurations of characteristics) increased our understanding of how families change from marriage to dissolution? Has the stage notion contributed significant, independent explanatory power, beyond much less complex notions, in research applica-

tions where the "family life cycle" is an antecedent to some dependent variable(s) of primary interest? Has the developmental perspective, either alone or in tandem with life course analysis, adequately established a theory of how families develop over time? These are among the challenging questions that this chapter addresses.

A Historical Overview of the Perspective

Let us turn first to a brief history of the family development perspective and to an exposition of major concepts that the perspective has borrowed, synthesized, and/or created. As Hill and Mattessich (1979) noted, scholars working on the family developmental perspective have intentionally and unashamedly assimilated concepts from other disciplines in order to tailor-make a relevant framework for analyzing the process of family change. Figure 1 contains the genealogy of the developmental perspective.[1] On the left-hand side of the tree appear rural so-

---

[1]Readers may wish to know the criteria for including and excluding works in Figure 1. The "rules of descent" that we used may also require elucidation to explain the meaning of the connecting lines among ancestors and descendents. The primary criterion for the inclusion of a work in Figure 1 was the degree to which the work was seminal for the developmental perspective. Hill's central participation in the early formulation of the family development perspective enabled him to make judgments about the seminal impact of the early works in the literatures listed as "Life Cycle Categories," "Social System Theories," "Human Development Theories," and "Life Events and Life Crisis Theories." We were helped in the identification of the early works from "Life Span and Life Course Theories" by reading the histories of life span development by Havighurst (in Baltes & Schaie, 1973) and Reinert (in Baltes & Brim, 1979). For the inclusion of later works, both authors have traced the impact of the writings listed by scanning acknowledgments and citations in admittedly less than systematic fashion. The "rules of descent" that determined the connecting lines included evidence of participation in the same academic lineages or as colleagues within literatures. For family development writers, we noted citations that evinced borrowing from other academic lineages. The life-span-development movement has been particularly active in making the links explicit across the literatures of which family development has been the beneficiary. For example, in Baltes and Brim (1979), the ties between life events

Paul Mattessich • Office of Research and Statistics, Amherst H. Wilder Foundation, 919 LaFond Avenue, St. Paul, MN 55104. **Reuben Hill** • Late of the Minnesota Family Study Center, University of Minnesota, Minneapolis, MN 55455.

ciologists, demographers, and economists. This set of scholars established family-life-cycle categories as demographic, independent variables that could conveniently and parsimoniously explain how family needs and demands interact with a finite set of family resources to produce, over the family life span, a sequence of characteristically stage-specific patterns of family behavior. The types of behavior that interested these early scholars fell primarily within a narrowly delimited range: economic activities, such as expenditure and consumption patterns, and labor force participation. Little attention was paid by them to family interaction within stages, to the process of interstage transition, or to continuities and discontinuities over the life cycle. In short, the ancestors of the family development perspective who appear on the upper-left side of the tree in Figure 1 constructed and exploited a powerful and useful explainer of variance in the behaviors that interested them. However, they did not concern themselves with the process of family development as a phenomenon deserving of investigation and explanation.

Hill and Rodgers (1964) credited Glick (1947, 1955, 1977) with reorienting the focus of family-life-cycle analysts. Glick, a demographer, concerned himself with the content of family living over the family life span. He teased out of historical, demographic data the implications of demographic phenomena at the societal level for the microorganizational and individual behaviors occurring within families and for the scheduling or timing of these behaviors. In the article, "Updating the Life Cycle of the Family," Glick (1977) stated, for example: "The life cycle of the family is a term that has been used in reference to the succession of critical stages through which the typical family passes . . . such as marriage, birth of children, children leaving home, the "post children" or "empty nest" period, and ultimate dissolution of the marriage through death of one of the spouses" (p. 5). He was squarely on target in his conceptualizing, which led him to transform aggregate data into parameters that differentiated phases of family development over historical time periods.

Toward the middle of the tree in Figure 1 appear the developmentally oriented scholars, who established theories of child development and personality formation. Rodgers (1977) noted that theoretical and empirical work

---

and life span by Hultsch and Plemens, between life course and life span by Elder, and between family development and life span by Hill and Mattessich are explicated in depth. Primarily as an exposition device, we began constructing Figure 1 from work that we had already done for a similar chart in Hill and Mattessich (1979). Because of the density of connections among literatures, we found it necessary to prune and cut to avoid shortchanging our exposition. More systematic attention should surely be given in future reviews to the validity of our judgments. We would welcome an early revision by those for whom the history of family development may become a major preoccupation.

in the area of human growth and development contributed at least two significant elements to the developmental study of the family. First, this work emphasized longitudinal analysis—that is, the study of the same individuals over time—to discover patterns of development. Longitudinal analysis enables the researcher to identify continuities and discontinuities in families over time and to test propositions about the causes and consequences of family change without taking the risks associated with testing propositions by means of cross-sectional data, which can only synthetically represent developmental change. A second contribution of the human development scholars, as noted by Rodgers, was the notion of *developmental tasks*. Families, as groups, were seen as having developmental tasks, the successful completion of which ensured optimal progression through the stages of the family career. Family developmental tasks were conceptualized as highly related to the individual developmental tasks of the family members.

An additional contribution of the human development scholars derives from the controversy among them over the nature of development. The existence of competing developmental theories led to greater awareness and specification of each theory's assumptions and metatheoretical foundation. The work of recent life-span developmentalists such as Looft (1973) and Lerner (1978) enabled Hill and Mattessich (1979) to specify many of the taken-for-granted assumptions of the family development model concerning the nature of family development, and thus to enhance the ability of contemporary scholars to test and refine that model.

The work of Duvall and Hill (1948), as the genealogy indicates, joined the life cycle and human development approaches. The Duvall–Hill cochairmanship of the Committee on the Dynamics of Family Interaction at the 1948 National Conference on Family Life established what Rodgers (1977) termed "the basis for a new level of sophistication in family cycle analysis." They drew on the symbolic interactionism of G. H. Mead, E. Burgess, and W. Waller for their view of the family as an arena of interacting personalities, and from Havighurst and Erikson for their views of human development as marked by mastery over the life span of progressively more complex developmental tasks. Duvall and Hill (1948) conceptualized the family as an organization and setting for facilitating the growth and development of its members. Subsequent collaborative work by these two scholars (at the University of Chicago) and their work along independent pathways (Duvall's writing of *Family Development*, 1957, 1962, 1967, 1971, 1977, a widely used text and reference, and Hill's seminars at the universities of North Carolina and of Minnesota) accelerated the developmental framework's chief concepts.

The culmination of a decade and a half of research and theory concerning family development was the chapter on the developmental framework by Hill and Rodgers in the first edition of the *Handbook of Marriage and the Family* (Christensen, 1964). This constituted a clearly defined,

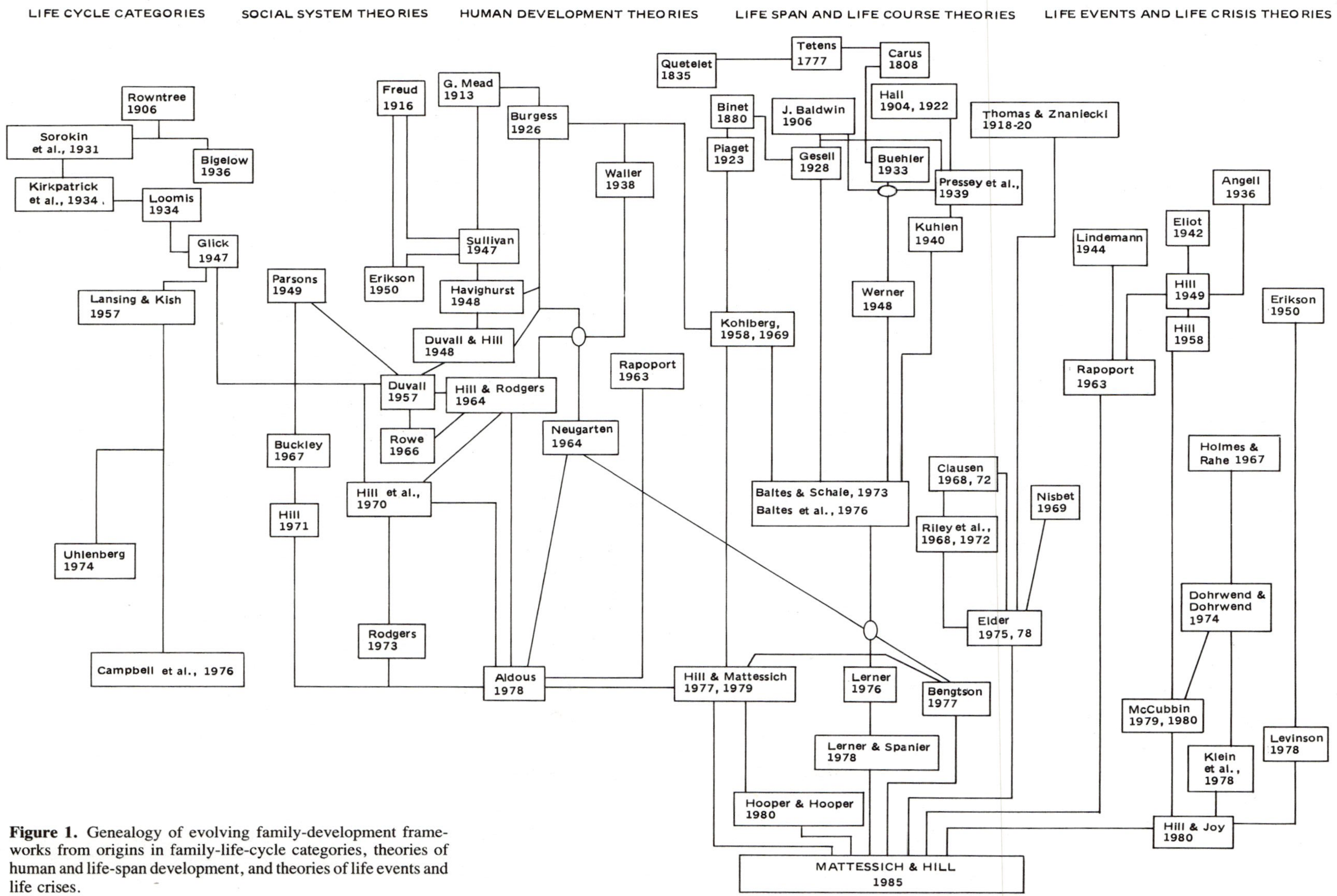

Figure 1. Genealogy of evolving family-development frameworks from origins in family-life-cycle categories, theories of human and life-span development, and theories of life events and life crises.

comprehensive examination of the framework, and it emphasized that the framework was an eclectic one, acquiring concepts from different approaches to the study of the family, in order to present a unified frame of reference for the study of the family in its own right. Contributions to the framework were drawn from symbolic interactionism (role, role taking, role playing, and role differentiation); structural functionalism (position, role, norm, boundary maintenance, and equilibrium); and the sociology of work and the professions (career, role sequences, and the family as a convergence of intercontingent careers of its members). Although not explicitly acknowledged by Hill and Rodgers, the systems theoretical approach also contributed to the developmental framework (semiclosed system, interdependence of parts, and goal attainment) and was explicitly integrated into family development theory by Hill (1971), who drew on Buckley's (1967) "modern systems theory."

Since 1964, Hill and his colleagues have continued to assess the isomorphism for the family development orientation of formulations from other literatures (noted in Figure 1) that have addressed the issues of development. The chief synthesizers for family development during this period have been Rodgers (1973, 1977), Aldous (1978), and Hill and Mattessich (1977, 1979). The literatures drawn upon have each challenged different sectors of the family development taxonomy, contributing, for descriptive purposes, new sensitizing concepts to its vocabulary and offering occasional general analytic propositions about the nature of family development.

The theories to the right of "Human Development" in Figure 1 were developed later by family scholars, although each of them can claim a remote ancestry. Life-span-development thinking originated in the remote prescience past in the writings of Tetens (1777) and Carus (1808). The Belgian statistician Quetelet (1835) gave quantitative form to life span phasing more than a century and a half ago, but legitimation for examining development over the life span in America waited until the mid-twentieth century, attracting the attention of family development scholars in the late 1970s (Hill & Mattessich, 1977, 1979). The scale of scholarly activity devoted to life span development in the 1970s, in conferences, publications, and training programs, approximated a social movement (Baltes & Schaie, 1973; Baltes, Reese, & Nesselroade, 1976; Golet & Baltes, 1970).

Life course analysis as an orientation was pioneered by the epoch-making work of Thomas and Znaniecki, *The Polish Peasant in Europe and America* (1918–1920); but it was almost 50 years before its formulations were used as theoretical guidelines in what has become known as the *sociology of age stratification and the life course* (Clausen, 1968; Elder, 1974; Riley & Foner, 1968; Riley, Johnson, & Foner, 1972). The effects of timing of major life events differently by birth cohorts and the de-formation of family and occupational careers as a consequence of economic depressions, military service, and wars impressed family scholars with the importance of studying the historical and social contexts of family development (Hill & Mattessich, 1977). A series of exchanges has occurred between Bengtson (1977), representing life course and age stratification, and these family development scholars, as well as between them and Hooper and Hooper (1979), representing life-span-development orientations. The Hoopers have questioned, among other things, the degree of isomorphism between individual development and family development. Bengtson has questioned the fruitfulness of the translation of findings about the normative scheduling of age group aggregates (assessed by intracohort and intercohort analyses) to the family level, with the goal of tracing longitudinally the typical course of family development. Some of these questions are addressed later in this chapter.

The final set of intellectual ancestors of contemporary family-development theory has in common an interest in life stress and crisis but differs on the implications that such stressor experiences may have in family development. The early work of Angell (1936) and Eliot (1942) saw crises as the product of external events, largely unpredicted and unanticipated, and not covered by culturally defined solutions: unemployment; catastrophes (such as floods, fires, and tornadoes); family dismemberment and accessions (such as untimely deaths and war separations and reunions); and so on. Hill (1949, 1958) integrated the generic aspects of family crises from this early literature into the familiar ABC-X theory of family crisis. Rapoport (1963) is credited with noting that all families encounter certain crises, which she termed "normal critical transitions," such as the crisis of getting married, of first parenthood, of deparentalization, of launching children, of retirement, and of family dissolution. Independently, other life-stress researchers (Holmes & Rahe, 1967; Dowhrenwend & Dowhrenwend, 1974) found both the types of life event stressors and the piling up of events in a short period of time to be highly predictive of mental disorder. McCubbin, Joy, Cauble, Comeau, Patterson, and Needle (1980) adapted the Life Event Scales prepared by these scholars for administration to families and created the Family Inventory of Life Events (FILE). The inventory differentiates among families in and out of crisis. Hill and Joy (1980) joined these several formulations from life stress events, family crisis theory, and normal crises of transition to operationalize a new criterion for demarcating stages of family development. They reconceptualized stages of development as equilibrium states punctuated by critical transitions. Critical transitions occur whenever multiple changes in the family's role complex are accompanied by a pileup of internal or external life-event stressors. This new view of the developmental dynamic is examined in more detail later.

In sum, the imagery of the genealogical tree represented by Figure 1 has identified the diverse ancestral origins of the concepts and assumptions that make up contemporary family development as a theoretical orientation. As in most such developments, the ancestors can not be held responsible for the transformations of their thinking by their beneficiaries. The exposition tells of intellectual imperialism and eclecticism in the appropriating of concepts from six diverse literatures and offers a partial explanation of the density, the richness, and the diffuse character of contemporary family-development theory.

Major Concepts of the Family Development Perspective

Major concepts of the developmental perspective (most of which are well explicated and illustrated by Aldous, 1978) fall into three categories: (1) Concepts about the family as a system, including concepts of goal orientation and direction, as well as allocation of resources and coordination of activities; (2) structural concepts; and (3) concepts of orderly sequence.

Before examining these concepts in detail, it is worthwhile to note the fundamental assumptions that provide a rationale for their acquisition and development. These five assumptions were advanced by Hill and Hanson (1960):

1. Human conduct is best seen as a function of the preceding as well as the current social milieu and individual conditions.
2. Human conduct cannot be adequately understood apart from human development.
3. The human is an actor as well as a reactor.
4. Individual and group development is best seen as dependent on stimulation by a social milieu as well as on inherent (developed) capacities.
5. The individual in a social setting is the basic autonomous unit.

Systemic Concepts

The family has four systemic features: its interdependence, its selective boundary maintenance, its ability to adapt to change, and its task performance.

A readily apparent systemic feature of the family is its *interdependence*. A member of a family does not live or act in isolation. That member's behaviors have consequences for all other members. Positions and roles in the family (defined below) are often complementary. They "interlock" so that a change in any part of the family affects the other parts. Aldous (1978) emphasized that interdependence extends beyond overt behavior to physical and emotional dependencies. Whether cooperating or competing, liking or loathing, family members find themselves enmeshed in a total system of interpersonal relationships.

Another systemic feature of the family is *selective boundary maintenance*. Families themselves and the larger society of which they are a part establish the nuclear family as a circumscribed entity and reinforce its differentiation from other groups in the society. Although family members engage in interaction with outsiders, as-

similate values and beliefs from the larger kin network, the community, and the society, and pursue nonfamily careers (interactions can contribute to the "pileup" of family crises at specific points in the family life cycle), family boundaries are only selectively permeable to outsiders. Families create and retain their own cultures and identities as fostered and/or manifested by physical boundaries (separate residences for nuclear families), kinship terminology, family rituals, and family "vocabularies" (i.e., modes of verbal expression, "inside jokes," and so on, which only family members can understand). As is true of any social group, a distinct family history gives family members a heritage that no outsider can share.

Families, as organizations, are resilient. They have the capacity to *adapt to changes* precipitated both internally by the members themselves and externally by the larger society; and this capacity constitutes another systemic feature. In light of the often, and sometimes abrupt, changing of family composition (e.g., husband and wife with no children to husband and wife with one child, two children, and so on, or families with teenaged young adults to postparental couples), and in light of the often changing needs and demands of family members (e.g., children's maturation and parents' midlife career changes), it is no wonder that adaptability to change is an organizational property of families. If it were not, the family career would be short, indeed, as members would find the nonadapting family atmosphere to be stultifying and dysphoric. The biological concept of *morphogenesis* has been used to describe how families reorganize their role structures as they attempt to attain their goals. Change in families is not merely the motion attendant on the maintenance of dynamic equilibrium. It frequently involves a major reordering of behaviors, including the creation of new behavior patterns and a discarding of the old.

Task performance is a fourth systemic feature of families on which the developmental perspective has focused attention. Families, as all social organizations, must accomplish certain necessary tasks in order to ensure their survival. The performance of these tasks is functional not only for family members but also for the larger society. At least five types of family tasks are salient throughout significant portions of the family career. These tasks are physical maintenance; socialization for roles inside and outside the family; the maintenance of family morale and of motivation to perform roles inside and outside the family; the maintenance of social control; and the acquisition of family members (by birth or adoption) to be launched from the family when mature.

Structural Concepts

Three structural concepts have served as elementary building blocks for the framework. They entered the framework from structural functionalism.

A *position* is a location within a group, in this case, within the family. Attached to every position are roles.

Roles are sets of norms that specify appropriate or required behaviors for the incumbents of positions. Family members generally have multiple roles, some of which are wholly internal to the family, and others that link the family to external networks and associations.

Norms are rules for behavior. They are expectations that guide the conduct of persons with particular roles.

Concepts of Orderly Sequence

The concepts of position and role have their dynamic counterparts. The *positional career* represents the changing role content of a family position. Such changes in content generally occur because of changes in age expectations for the position (which entail the adding or deletion of family-related roles).

A *role sequence* represents the changing normative content of a role. Roles may remain attached to a family position for a long time, but the behaviors associated with the role may change.

The product of the intercontingent positional careers of the incumbents of family positions is the *family career*. As became evident in the discussion of the family as a social system, no family member exists or acts in isolation. He or she affects—and is affected by—the behaviors of other family members. Shifts in the role content of any family member's position occur concomitantly with shifts in the role content of positions with reciprocally related roles.[2]

Facets of Family Dynamics

Rodgers (1973), recognizing that family behavior is a complex whole, suggested that attention to three facets of family behavior can provide developmental scholars with a holistic perspective on the process of family development. These facets are not new analytic concepts. Rather, they comprise a categorical device that ensures that all aspects of family behavior will be analyzed.

The family career has a *societal-institutional* facet. That is, the family is linked, throughout its career, with elements of the larger society of which it is a part. From the larger society, family members develop expectations concerning appropriate family behavior. Many of these expectations stimulate the accomplishment of individual and family developmental tasks. Families make use of the technologies of culture (e.g., language, forms of shelter, and media) in order to meet their needs and to reach their goals. Furthermore, many family roles are tied conjunctively (to use Rodgers's term) to roles in positions outside the family. For example, the provider roles of husband-father and/or wife-mother occur in conjunction with occupational roles played in work organizations.

Finally, an important element of the societal-institutional facet is the dual function of many family tasks. For example, physical maintenance accomplished by the family functions dually to satisfy the members' needs for food, clothing, and shelter to survive, and to satisfy society's needs for healthy, nourished societal members.

The family career has a *group-interactional* facet. Expectations concerning behavior arise within the family group itself. The socialization process involves not only the learning of values, norms, and behaviors, which are relatively fixed, but also the negotiation and making of roles that occur over time between and among family members. Plurality patterns within the family and the age and sex composition of the family members have an impact on the family as a group and on its individual members.

The family career has a third component, an *individual-psychological* facet. Family members have individual personalities, which are, in part, shaped by the family, but which, conversely, also affect family behavior. Variance in personalities across families accounts for differences in styles of performing family roles. The insightful characterization by Burgess (1926) and Waller (1938) of the family "as a unity of interacting personalities" draws attention to the fact that the family is, indeed, a group in its own right, but that its members maintain a certain measure of autonomy.

What Is Development for the Family as an Organization?

The concepts described in the preceding section have been essentially taxonomic. They provide heuristic tools for defining, identifying, measuring, and describing the continuous, complex phenomenon of family development. They offer the means of analyzing family processes generically and nomothetically—abstracting the commonalities across families in their everyday lives from the idiosyncratic behaviors that are classified only by ideographic examination. However, these concepts themselves do not define development. Just what is development for the family as an organization? What germinates or induces family change to provide the family with a developmental dynamic? What stimulates a process of orderly change?

Definition of Family Development

Let us turn to the working definition of development proposed by Hill and Mattessich (1979):

Family development refers to the process of progressive structural differentiation and transformation over the family's history, to the active acquisition and selective discarding of roles by incumbents of family positions as they seek to meet the changing functional requisites for survival and as they adapt to recurring life stresses as a family system. (p. 174)

This definition has at least three aspects that are crucial to an understanding of the phenomenon of family devel-

[2]Aldous (1978) has provided a fuller discussion of the concepts discussed in the sections on pp. 441–442.

opment. First, it establishes family development as an organizational, interactional phenomenon. Second, it emphasizes a relatedness or continuity of family behaviors across the family career. Third, it identifies two sources of developmental change: changing functional requisites and recurring life stresses.

The organizational quality of family development is evident with respect to structural differentiation (a property of the family as a system), which occurs over time as roles emerge and change to meet the needs of the family at each stage in its development. Three elements of the family organization appear and disappear during the course of the family career: persons (who enter through marriage and birth, for example, and who leave through launching, social placement, or death); roles (which become attached to family positions when certain family activities must be carried out); and patterns of roles or other interactive and transactive behavior (which is adjusted to meet the changing demands of family members and society, in accordance with the resources available to the family at any point in its career). The notion of family-life-cycle stages provides an index of the allocation of roles within the family and serves as one means of operationalizing developmental structural differentiation.

The relatedness of changes within the family across its life cycle implies that the family moves from stage to stage, restructuring its pattern of organization, yet with common threads tying all stages together. Hill and Mattessich (1979) suggested that each stage influences its successor by containing the embryonic elements that will eventually produce movement into the next stage and by setting limits (a product of family decisions and other actions) on the types of behavior in which the family can engage during the next stage. Aldous (1978) drew on the "game tree" formulation of Magrabi and Marshall (1965) to suggest that "limited linkage" is an appropriate way of conceptualizing the relatedness of family changes and family behaviors throughout the family career. Limited linkage implies that family behavior at one point in time does not wholly determine later behavior; but it does set limits on later behavior and predisposes the family toward familiar options for resolving problems.

The stimuli to developmental growth, or the pressures to move from one stage to the next in the family career, have been postulated to arise from two highly interdependent sources: family developmental tasks, which require that family members develop, or alter, or re-allocate important roles within the family, and recurrent life stresses (often produced either by the structural differentiation noted above or by the need to accomplish developmental tasks), which can force families into major reorganization.

Family developmental tasks are, for the family, analogous to individual developmental tasks, for the individual. The latter tasks arise as a product of the changing needs of individuals as they age and of the societal expectations regarding appropriate, age-related behaviors. (See Aldous, 1978; Duvall, 1957; Havighurst, 1953, 1956;

Havighurst, Prescott, & Kedl, 1942; Rodgers, 1965). Individual developmental tasks become salient for a family member because of his or her own maturation, aided and abetted by parents, siblings, and peers, who activate age norms for behavior. For example, a child must acquire the ability to cooperate with others in order to have playmates. In other cases, however, individual developmental tasks arise for a family member as the result of the reciprocal roles that he or she has vis-à-vis other family members. For example, the husband-father must develop nurturing competence as infants enter the family and mature. The infant's dependence and responsiveness set the contingencies for the activation and mastery of this developmental task (Goldberg, 1977).

Family developmental tasks include the five basic tasks mentioned earlier: physical maintenance; socialization; morale maintenance; social control; and acquisition of members and launching. Each of these is a function performed by the family for both individual family members and the larger society. The concrete activities associated with task performance differ according to the life cycle stage. As well, the salience of certain tasks waxes and wanes throughout the family career. That is, the extent to which the family needs to muster its resources to accomplish its tasks depends on the developmental demands of family members and on the assignments of the larger society.

A different focus on the developmental dynamic has been provided by Rapoport (1963), Hill and Joy (1980), and others, who noted that "pileups" of stresses or "crises of transition" usher in new stages of family development. Families can maintain a relatively stable pattern of organization for as long as no major role changes are provoked. However, the occurrence of several significant stressor events within a short period of time forces families into major reorganization. Virtually all families do experience the discontinuity that results from marked changes in the total role complex of the family. The term *normal crisis of transition* has been applied to the disordered periods in the family career that constitute disjunctures in the family's role complex before its reorganization into a new stage of development.

An effort to further explicate the qualities of the developmental process in families was undertaken by Hill and Mattessich (1979) in their juxtaposition of the family developmental model with four developmental psychology models with reference to several model issues:

1. *External versus internal locus of the developmental dynamic.* Does development occur because of changes within the family or because of changes external to it? In its present formulation, the developmental perspective posits the family as a semiclosed system, selectively open to societal demands and environmental changes requiring adaptations in family structure. Evident in the concept of the family developmental task is that the needs of maturing human beings interact with societal expectations or demands. Family development occurs because of this interaction effect of forces internal and external to the fami-

ly. Thus, the impetus for development may principally arise from internal stimuli; but such stimuli are clearly magnified by external influences.

2. *Continuous versus discontinuous family change.* Does growth throughout the family life cycle proceed steadily and continuously: Or does it occur spasmodically, with discontinuous transition periods punctuating developmental stages? It appears that family change, at disjunctures in the family's role complex, or at "critical transition points," is qualitative and discontinuous. Such discontinuity precipitates the major reorganization of roles that occurs in a new life-cycle stage. The modal type of family within each stage, demarcated by the discontinuities (i.e., major breaks in the family's role complex), can be distinguished from the modal type of family in each other stage. However, within each stage, some growth also tends to occur (not enough to tip the scales and provoke reorganization) that is essentially continuous and quantitative.

3. *Reductionism versus emergence.* Can all family developmental phenomena be reduced and analyzed in terms of events or entities of a lower level? Or is the developmental process one that, at least in part, must be analyzed in its own right? Although this issue is far from resolved, the predisposition among scholars is to treat family development as an emergent process. The family is a social system; and certain phenomena are much better understood and dealt with by examining the family as a whole, not just its component members.

4. *The nature of individual and family differences.* How does the family development model cope with differences among families? Is it committed to a rigid view of development that admits of no variations, regressions, or other differences among families that have progressed to the same stage? The model seems to lean toward an ipsative approach in which the focus is on intrafamily consistencies and changes over time. All the components of every family (recall the "unity of interacting personalities") do not necessarily grow and develop along rigidly defined, invariant tracks. Nonetheless, it is expected that movement from one developmental stage to the next will pull all family members along, engendering change in their individual positional careers as well as in the family career.

5. *The significance of chronological age.* Many developmental psychologists are unconcerned about chronological age, claiming that, in and of itself, it has little relevance to individual development. Others consider age intrinsic to the process of development, and they assume that age is correlated to invariant, sequential changes. Most methods for determining family-life-cycle stages use the age of the oldest child for the operational purpose of demarcating stages. In addition, the developmental process itself is stimulated by age-related, societal expectations (school age, retirement age, the "best age to have children," and so on); and a family is considered dysfunctional if it is recalcitrant in meeting age-related de-

mands. Thus, because of the central use of age markers, age norms, and age composition in formulating stages of development, and because of the importance of age with respect to developmental tasks, age appears to be intrinsic in the family development model.

6. *Universality versus relativity of development.* In what ways do the culture, the subculture, and the changing historical context influence the universality of development for families? Is there an identifiable course of development common to all families? Or do family uniquenesses render impossible the task of identifying a general developmental process? The basic premise of the family development perspective is that the ordering, sequence, and general shape of family development are essentially universal, although the timing of family events, the content of family roles, and societal expectations concerning the family do differ culturally and historically. Evidence of the cultural and historical universality of family developmental processes as stages of increasing and decreasing complexity comes from historians, anthropologists, and sociologists (e.g., see Berkner, 1972; Cuisenier, 1977; Desai, 1964; Goody, 1962; Hareven, 1974; Koyama, 1961). The contemporary demographics of the family life cycle in the United States and the implications of those demographics for the applicability of the family development model are discussed in the section on page 445.

Operationalizing the Family Career

The ultimate value of a dynamic framework lies in its utility for the analysis of real families. Such an analysis can occur at either of two levels: at the level of the individual family and at an aggregate level.

In the analysis of a specific family, the researcher or clinician is interested in determining the history of changes (type, sequence, effects, and so on) that the family has experienced. The analyst asks: How has this family, as a unit, developed patterns of organization and coped with the demands placed on it from the time of its inception to the present? The concepts of the developmental framework sensitize the analyst to many types of change that a family can experience, and they offer the means for a perspicuous and comprehensive portrait of a family's unique pattern of growth. Sequences of change for the family as a whole, as well as for its individual members, can be identified and described in detail. The time of family events, down to the very dates of their occurrence, can be plotted. Sequential, and even causal, relationships among individual, interactional, and transactional events can be inferred. In short, the life history of a specific family, with all of its idiosyncrasies, can be roughly portrayed through the use of concepts applicable to any family. Such a use of the developmental framework has significant benefits in clinical and educational settings.

At the aggregate level, for the purpose of making generalizations about developmental commonalities that all families share, family researchers have found useful the demarcation of stages of the family career. Such stages represent a modal pattern of development that families experience. The demarcation of stages enables researchers both to describe, in a summary or synthetic fashion, the changes that occur in families and to analyze the relationship between family change and other phenomena. In this latter application, the stages of the family career (or *family-life-cycle stages,* as they are also called) comprise an index that can be related to any other measures of the investigator's choosing. The use of stages is predicated on the assumption that modal families do experience very similar changes throughout their careers, even though each individual family will have its own idiosyncratic features.

How many life cycle stages are necessary for optimal representation of the family career? This question is not completely resolved. Stage formulations have ranged from as few as 2 categories to as many as 24 (see Rodgers, 1962). The number of categories necessary for representing the family career may vary, depending on the goals of a researcher. Two categories generally lack adequate descriptive power, whereas 24 categories can frequently be too unwieldly to handle analytically. A seven-stage model is often used (e.g., Aldous, 1978), and the intuitive appeal of this model in describing significant portions of the family career is very evident. The stages derive from three criteria offered by Duvall and Hill (1948): changes in family size (and hence, in family positions); changes in age composition; and changes in the occupational status of the breadwinner(s). The seven stages are

1. Newly established couples (childless)
2. Childbearing families (infants and preschool children)
3. Families with schoolchildren (one or more children of school age)
4. Families with secondary-school children (one or more children in adolescence)
5. Families with young adults (one or more children aged 18 or over)
6. Families in the middle years (children launched from parental household)
7. Aging families (parents in retirement)

Note that the use of summary categories to carve up the family career is a critical ingredient of any aggregate-level analysis, but that it is unnecessary (although possible) for the analysis of a specific family. The use of stages in aggregate-level studies is so critical because the social-scientific enterprise demands that social phenomena be captured by summary measures that can be meaningfully related to one another. Statistics such as an average can be used to describe a salient characteristic of a group of individuals, with no implication that these individuals identically resemble one another, or even that any one individual has exactly a mean rating on the characteristic. So also, life cycle stages can be used to describe groups of families without the implication that all families within the same stage are absolutely identical.

Thus, the life cycle stages provide an index of development. Using the stages enables the analyst to place in categories families that are experiencing similar events, facing similar crises, and attempting to accomplish similar developmental tasks. The index can be related quantitatively to any other measure(s) of the analyst's choosing. Use of the family-life-cycle stages for classifying families does not blind the analyst to the heterogeneity that exists among families in the same stage. Nonetheless, heterogeneity that can be portrayed ideographically in detailed family histories is simply viewed as dispersion around a modal family type for any given stage. Of course, some families may have characteristics that preclude the use of listed stages. Such families can be represented as groups for which the modal developmental pattern does not apply, but paths of development for these families may still be identifiable. For example, it is likely that all single-parent families experience a standard set of stresses and need to accomplish developmental tasks at relatively uniform points in their life cycles. They need to establish patterns of organization, and their members need to acquire and discard roles in order to adapt adequately. Therefore, Aldous (1978), for example, proposed that single-parent families have family careers that can be meaningfully described by a set of stages—stages that resemble, but are not identical to, the stages experienced by two-parent families. The next section also contains a discussion of this issue.

A Statistical Overview of Family Development

From U.S. Census and sample surveys, it is apparent that the vast majority of families are maintained by intact married couples (80.7% in 1979). A rising proportion since 1970, however, has been maintained by women with the husband absent (separated, divorced, or widowed), up from 10% in 1970 to 17.4% in 1979. Male-maintained families (with the wife absent) have remained negligible at 1%–2% of all families (Rawlings, 1980).

In this statistical overview, the new category for which the course of development over the life span demands attention is the female-maintained family. By ethnic background, the proportion of female-maintained families varied dramatically in 1979 (13.5% of white, 21.6% of Hispanic, and 45.6% of black families). We will therefore attempt to compare the paths of development not only of married couples and of female-maintained families, but also of white and black female-maintained families.

Female-maintained households encompass dwelling groups of varied age and marital-status compositions. Our focus on family development over the life span requires us to single out those involved in child rearing and to differentiate among widowed and divorced female heads. Of the 8.5 million families maintained by females, 63% have children under 18 present (colloquially termed *single-parent families*). These fractured homes are disproportionately due to divorce (42.2%) or separation (23.8%), but 17% are single (never-married) and 12.8% are widowed. Eighty-two percent of the women who head female-maintained families with children under age 18 are 45 years old or younger. By contrast, the female-maintained families with no children under 18 are generally surviving widows (56.3%) at the end of the family life span, whose children have left home.

Complicating the developmental trajectory over the life span in recent decades are unscheduled changes in marital status and in parental status as couples marry, become parents, divorce, and remarry, often bringing to the second marriage children from previous marriages, and then adding progeny after remarriage. We will therefore give attention to the paths followed by divorced and widowed single-parent families that remarry as well as to those that do not. Before turning to this intriguing task, let us say a word about the constraints and the contextual limitations to which female-maintained households are subject, drawing from U.S. sample surveys (Rawlings, 1980).

Female-maintained households face major economic constraints, particularly among divorced or separated families in which children are being reared. Whereas maternal employment, making possible two incomes, occurs in 49% of couple-headed child-rearing families, 60% of female households were in the labor force in 1979. The percentage would probably have been higher if it were not for a 158% increase (1970–1979) in unemployment among this single-parent group. Underpaid compared with men doing the same work, more vulnerable to unemployment and more frequently to unemployability, child-rearing female householders earned predominantly less than $10,000 (58%) in 1978. If we compare intact husband–wife households (median income $17,640 in 1978) with families maintained by women (median income $8,540 in 1978), the constraints are clear. A woman with no husband contributing directly to the family income can expect to have only about $1 for essential expenses to every $2 available to most families. The plight of the single-parent mother is even worse for mothers under 25 (median income $3,960 in 1978). Tragically, female householders with children under 6 have incomes ($4,500) well below those with older children, over 6 ($8,690), and a fraction of those reported by female heads with no children under 18 to support ($11,970). The income levels of young divorced women rearing preschool children, cited above, were well below the poverty line for 1978 of $6,662 for a family of four. Indeed, the poverty rate of children in families maintained by women was strikingly higher (51%) than for children in families overall (16%).

With such inhospitable conditions facing the divorced with children, the attractiveness of a second marriage would be understandable. The younger the woman, and the fewer the children she brings to a second marriage, the higher the probability of a remarriage. We will therefore examine the subsequent family careers of the divorced and widowed who don't remarry as well as of those who do. A comparison of these family careers against the schedule of phases characteristic of the modal careers of intact families will reveal how badly "off schedule" are the families that experience female-headedness, and whether they manage to get back "on schedule" later in the life span.

Table 1 is a revised, theoretically constructed schema formulated originally by Hill and Rodgers (1964) to depict the stages of family development and the accompanying changes in family structure and functioning, using the criteria for stage demarcation developed by Duvall and Hill (1948). The schema displays the average ages of husband and wife at marriage, the average interval between marriage and first birth, and the spacing of four children, two of each gender, to be married off later in the life span at the average age of marriage. The family's career ends with the death of one of the spouses at the actuarial average for women of 77 years and for men of 69.3 years. The advantage of this schema is that it provides in one heuristic the theoretical, modal career of the nuclear family, on which empirically constructed careers can be overlaid to ascertain phases that fit and that depart from the modal course.

Table 1 shows, in successive rows, the variability stage by stage over the life span of family size, number of interpersonal relations maintained within the family, years in stage, duration of marriage, complexity of positional structure and of derived positional tasks, and stage-specific major family goals. The model portrays increasing complexity in interpersonal relationships, because of expanding numbers, over the first 15 years of the marriage, with a 7-year period of stability in numbers in Stage 4. However, the coming of children into adolescence and young adulthood during Stage 4 adds to the complexity of this allegedly stable period. From this numerically stable stage, the launching of children into homes of their own precipitates a rapid decline in numbers, ending with the simple dyad of the postparental period. The postparental stage lasts an average of 14 years, concluded by the changes occasioned by retirement and allegedly dominated by the family goal of disengagement from organizations and occupational networks.

Later in this chapter, we will review and respond to the criticisms leveled against this model. The most frequent of these is that the model doesn't encompass the great variety of family careers in contemporary American society. A heuristic model can be expected, at its best, to point to empirically modal patterns. The empirical constructions that we now present offer evidence that even family careers very different from the modal career conform in some respects to the theoretical staging of family development in the Hill–Rodgers model depicted in Table 1.

Table 1. Stages of Family Development and Accompanying Changes in Family Structure and Functioning[a]

	Stage 1: Establishment	Stage 2: Childbearing preschool family	Stage 3: School age	Stage 4: Adolescence	Transition of launching young adults[b]	Stage 5: Postparental	Stage 6: Retirement years
Age composition	H 22–23 W 20–21	F 24–30 M 22–28 S_1 0–6 S_2 0–4 S_3 0–2	F 30–37 M 28–35 S_1 6–13 S_2 4–11 S_3 2–9 S_4 0–7	F 37–44 M 35–42 S_1 13–20 S_2 11–18 S_3 9–16 S_4 7–14	F 44–52 M 42–50 (S_1 20–28,f) (S_2 18–26,m) (S_3 16–24,f) (S_4 14–22,m)	H 52–65 W 50–64	H 66–69.3 W 64–77.1
Size	2	3–5	5–6	6	6–2	2	2–1
Interpersonal relations maintenance	1	3–10	10–15	15	15–1	1	1–0
Years in stage	1	6	7	7	8	14	3–13
Years married	1	7	14	21	29	43	43–46
Positions in family	Husband Wife	Husband-father Wife-mother Son-brother Daughter-sister	H-F W-M S-B D-S	H-F W-M S-B D-S	H-F-GF W-M-GM S-B-Uncle D-S-Aunt	H-GF W-GM	H-GF W-GM
Positional developmental tasks (age and relatedness positions)	Young adult DT	Parent DT Infant DT Child DT	Parent DT Infant DT Child DT Preadolescent DT	Parent DT Child DT Preadolescent DT Teenage DT	Grandparent DT Parent DT Teenage DT Young adult DT	Postparental adult DT Grandparent DT	Grandparent DT Aging DT
Major family goal	Adjusting to living as married pair	Reorganization of unit around needs of infants and preschool children	Reorganization of family to fit into expanding world of school-agers	Loosening of family ties to permit greater freedom and heavier responsibility to members	Reorganization of family into equalitarian unit and releasing of members	Reorganization of family around married pair; strategy of disengagement	Disengagement

[a] From Hill and Rodgers (1964), Figure 3, p. 118.
[b] Parentheses indicate the departure of the children during this stage.

Table 2. Timing of Stages of Family Development for Black and White Intact Families Based on Aggregate Performance of Birth Cohorts of Women, 1900–1949

	Stage 1: Childless	Stage 2: Childbearing and preschool	Stage 3: School age	Stage 4: Adolescents	Period of transition: Launching of young adults[a]	Stage 5: Postparental	Stage 6: Retirement years
		Black families (husband and wife present)					
	H 23.6–23.9 W 21.1–21.3	F 24.0–29.9 M 21.4–28.3 S_1 0–5.9 S_2 0–4.0 S_3 0–2.1	F 30–35.9 M 28.4–33.3 S_1 6–12.9 S_2 4.1–11.0 S_3 2.2–9.1 S_4 0–6.4	F 36–43.9 M 33.4–41.3 S_1 13–20.9 S_2 11.1–19.0 S_3 9.2–17.1 S_4 6.5–14.4	F 44–52.0 M 41.4–49.4 (S_1 21–29.0) (S_2 19.1–27.1) (S_3 17.2–25.2) (S_4 14.5–22.5)	H 52.0–64.9 W 49.4–62.4	H 65 at death W 62.4–72.1 at death
No. of interpersonal relations	1	1–10	10–15	15	15–1	1	1–0
Years in stage	0.4	6	7	8	8	13	0–10
		White families (husband and wife present)					
	H 23.6–25.7 W 21.1–23.2	F 25.7–31.6 M 23.3–29.2 S_1 0–5.9 S_2 0–3.9 S_3 0–1.9	F 31.7–38.6 M 29.3–36.2 S_1 6–12.9 S_2 4–10.9 S_3 2–8.9	F 38.7–46.6 M 36.3–44.2 S_1 13–20.9 S_2 11–18.9 S_3 9–16.9	F 46.7–52.2 M 44.3–49.8 (S_1 21–26.5) (S_2 19–24.5) (S_3 17–22.5)	H 52–65.0 W 49.8–62.6	H 65–69.3 at death W 62.6–77.1 at death
No. of interpersonal relations	1	1–10	10	10	10–1	1	1–0
Years in stage	2.2	6	7	8	5.5	12.8	4–14

[a]Parentheses indicate the departure of the children during this stage.

Table 2 compares white and black couple-headed families, from family formation to family dissolution, using census survey data for calculating the aggregate performance of families of women of the birth cohorts 1900–1949. (Many of the calculations for Tables 2–4 are adapted from Graham B. Spanier and Paul C. Glick, 1980, "The Life Cycle of American Families: An Expanded Analysis.") Although beginning marriage at comparable ages (23.6 for husbands and 21.1 for wives), the white cohorts experience a childfree period of companionship of 2.2 years before first parenthood, compared to 0.4 years for black couples (about half of whom begin marriage as parents). Among whites, in contrast to blacks, children are spaced more widely apart, and the family is completed with fewer children (2.9 children for whites vs. 3.7 children for blacks). In Table 2, whites rear three children spaced two years apart, with the last child born after six years of childbearing, whereas black families bring four children into the world in seven years. Both white and black couple-headed families conform closely (except for the brevity of the establishment stage for black families) with the theoretically constructed model with respect to the first stages of family development. Major differences between black and white couple-headed families appear for the length and timing of launching children into households of their own. Black families take 8 years to accomplish launching, compared to 5.5 years for white families. The close fit between the phases of family development of the theoretical model (Table 1) and the course of development of the two major ethnic categories of couple-headed families in Table 2 was anticipated. Table 1 faces a more rigorous test in confrontation with data on single-parent families whose life course may be expected to deviate from the modal, couple-headed families.

Table 3 arrays the timing of stages of family development for three different categories of single-parent families: (1) The divorced who don't remarry; (2) the divorced who remarry; and (3) the widowed who remarry. Family formation for both categories of divorced begins earlier than for widows or for marriages that persist. The divorced who don't remarry have a longer period of childbearing and produce more children than do the divorced who remarry: 1.2 at divorce for those who remarry versus 1.5 for those who don't remarry (see U.S. Bureau of the Census, 1977). Divorce, for both those who do and do not remarry, occurs in this model as the eldest child is entering school and while other siblings are infants or toddlers, for whom full-time child care would be needed if the now single parent returns to school or enters the labor force. We treat this pileup of stressor events in Table 3 not as a stage of the life cycle, but as a critical transition of disequilibrium experienced before achieving the reorganization required for entering a new stage of development. The critical transition of divorce to single parenthood is impoverishing in that there is a loss of one earner's income and the added costs of breaking up household arrangements. During this period, intact families in the

school-age stage are buying homes and other amenities—leaving single-parent families with the sense of falling behind schedule in their development. Midway in the school-age stage, the divorced who are destined to remarry do so, experiencing still another critical transition in regaining the married status and in adding the role of stepparent. They finish the school-age stage, therefore, as a reconstituted family.

Family development theorists have come to think of the age composition of families with children of school age as the most stable and livable of the child-rearing periods because the rates of growth of the children have slowed down to tolerable levels and because communication among the children and the parents is likely to approach levels of adequacy. It is therefore the more tragic that the timing of divorce, the return to the labor force, and remarriage, with the further complications of stepparenthood, should disturb this oasis of stability in the family's career. Further complicating the adjustment to the transition from the single-parent family to the reconstituted family is the return to childbearing and the consequent overlapping of stages of development, with family developmental tasks arising simultaneously in response to the needs of the infant-toddler and the preadolescents brought to the marriage. Furstenberg (1979) referred to this phenomenon as "recycling the family." The recycling involves more than reliving earlier stages of development, as the transition of launching children into jobs and marriage is prolonged over a 13-year period, compared to the 4 years required for the single-parent family that did not remarry. The divorced who don't remarry, although economically and socially more deprived, pursue a less complicated, if more lonely, family career over the remaining stages of the family life span.

The third, variant family career depicted in Table 3 is that of the family of widows who remarry. We selected from the vital statistics report on remarriage (Williams, 1973) and from the report of census surveys (U.S. Bureau of the Census, 1977) families of widows 14–39 years of age at widowhood, which encompass most families for which the death of a spouse was drastically off schedule (i.e., several years before the actuarially expected age at death). The remarriage of such widows provides a stepparent for children still at home and makes the later social placement of the children in jobs and marriage less of a problem economically. The age of the spouses at marriage is more mature for the widowed, and the widowed encounter single parenthood five years later than do the two divorced categories also shown in Table 3 (age 32.3 for widows and 27.0 for the divorced). The period of single parenthood is relatively short (4.2 years) before remarriage. The timing of the transition into a remarriage is early in the stage of families with adolescents. Thus, the available data imply differences in the timing of transitions to single parenthood and of remarriage between the widowed and the divorced who remarry. The latter experience adolescence as a reconstituted family but complicate matters by adding an infant during this period,

Table 3. Comparison of Stages of the Life Cycle for U.S. Divorced, Widowed, and Remarried Families Based on Birth Cohorts of Women, 1900–1949

Divorced who doesn't remarry

	Stage 1: Childless establishment	Stage 2: Childbearing and preschool	Period of transition: Divorce and return to labor force	Stage 3: Single parent, school age	Stage 4: Single parent with adolescents	Period of transition: Launching of young adults[a]	Stage 5: Postparental (living alone)	Stage 6: Retirement years (living alone)
	H 21	F 23–27	M 27–27.9	M 28–33	M 34–41	M 42–46	M 46–61.9	M 62–77.1 at death
	W 19	M 21–26.9	S₁ 6–6.9	S₁ 7–12.9	S₁ 13–20.9	(S₁ 21–24.9)		
		S₁ 0–5	S₂ 4–4.9	S₂ 5–10.9	S₂ 11–18.9	(S₂ 19–22.9)		
		S₂ 0–3	S₃ 2–2.9	S₃ 3–8.9	S₃ 9–16.9	(S₃ 17–20.9)		
		S₃ 0–1						
Years in stage	2	5	1	6	8	4	16	15.1
Interpersonal relations	1	1–10	10–6	6	6	6–0	0	0

Divorced who remarries

	Stage 1: Childless establishment	Stage 2: Childbearing and preschool	Period of transition: Divorce and return to labor force	Stage 3a: Single parent, school age I	Period of transition: Remarriage and stepparenthood	Stage 3b: Reconstituted family, school age II	Stage 4: Reconstituted family, adolescents	Period of transition: Launching young adults	Stage 5: Postparental	Stage 6: Retirement
	H 21	F 23–28	M 27–27.9	M 28–30.9	SF 34–34.9	SF 35–37.9	SF 38–45.9	SF 46–58.9	SF 59–64.9	SF 65–69.3 at death
	W 19	M 21–26.9	S₁ 6–6.9	S₁ 7–9.9	M 31–31.9	M 32–34.9	M 35–42.9	M 43–55.9	M 56–61.9	M 62–77.1 at death
		S₁ 0–5	S₂ 3–3.9	S₂ 4–6.9	S₁ 10–11.9	S₁ 11–12.9	S₁ 13–20.9	(S₁ 21–32)		
		S₂ 0–3			S₂ 7–8.9	S₂ 8–10.9	S₂ 11–18	(S₂ 19–30)		
							S₃ 0–7.9	(S₃ 8–20)		

	Stage 1: Childless establishment	Stage 2: Childbearing	Stage 3: School age	Stage 4: Single parent family with adolescents but remarrying mid-stage	Transition: Remarriage and stepparenthood	Transition: Launching of young adults	Stage 5: Postparental family	Stage 6: Retirement years		
				Widow who remarries						
Years in stage	2	6	1	3	1	3	8	13	6	4.3–15.1
Interpersonal relations	1	1–6	6–3	3	3–6	6	6–10	10–1	1	1
Ages	H 22.4 W 20.6	F 24.4–30.3 M 22.6–28.5 S$_1$ 0–5.9 S$_2$ 0–3.9 S$_3$ 0–1.9	F 30.4–34.1 at death M 28.6–34.5 (Widow at 32.3) S$_1$ 6–12.9 S$_2$ 4–10.9 S$_3$ 2–8.9	M 34.6–42.5 S$_1$ 13–20.9 S$_2$ 11–18.9 S$_3$ 9–16.9	SF 38.7–39.6 M 36.7–37.6 S$_1$ 14.1–15.0 S$_2$ 12.1–13.0 S$_3$ 10.1–11.0	SF 40–43.9 M 42.6–46.5 (S$_1$ 21–24.9) (S$_2$ 19–22.9) (S$_3$ 17–20.9)	SF 44–64.9 M 46.6–66.6	SF 65–69.3 at death M 66.7–77.1		
Years in stage	6	7	8	1	4	20	2			4.3–10.4
Interpersonal relations	1–10	10	10–6	6–10	10–1	1	1			1

ᵃParentheses indicate the departure of the children during this stage.

and as a consequence, the divorced who remarry prolong the period of launching children. The reconstituted widowed family launches its closer spaced children over a short period of four years and faces the longest postparental period of any of the family types we have charted.

In conclusion, a comparison of Tables 2 and 3 reveals great variability within stages created by the transitions of remarriage and launching, which change the subsequent scheduling of family stages in the postparental and retirement years. The divorced who don't remarry and the white intact family remain nearly on schedule compared to the theoretical model in Table 1. The divorced who remarry and add an infant deviate furthest from the model, although they come close to catching up in fertility with the intact family type of Table 1.

Before closing this discussion, one more specification seems useful, namely, the comparison of the family careers of black and white reconstituted families where remarriage occurrs following divorce. Table 4 presents these comparisons, adapting data from Spanier and Glick (1980). Black families experiencing divorce and remarriage marry at about the same age as white families, but about 50% are already parents at marriage. Thus, black parents get a head start on the demanding roles of parenthood, coping with the dependencies and economics of this stressful period. It is perhaps remarkable that the period before divorce is no shorter for black than for white families (roughly seven years), in light of the pileup of stressors in the first months of marriage. It is in the speed with which the black single parent remarries that the differences appear between black and white families (2.7 years for black vs. 5.2 years for white). The transition to remarriage and the incorporation of a stepparent occur when the children are in middle childhood for both categories. It is the sequelae of adding a third child, with all of the attendant diversion of attention from the older children still adjusting to a stepparent, that prolong the transition. Indeed, the combination of the rapid growth of adolescents, with their questioning of rules and privileges, and the rapid growth of infant and toddler may leave little opportunity for achievement of family equilibrium during roughly 25 years from the moment of remarriage (when the oldest child is 10–11 and the parents are in their early 30s) until the launching of the youngest child (when the postparental companionate has been reached). The launching of the youngest child occurs late enough in life so that both black and white couples face only about 13 years together before family dissolution.

To conclude this statistical overview, Figure 2 graphically summarizes the statistical data from Tables 1 through 4, offering a visual representation of the career paths followed by different family types. The career of the modal intact family (all races) is depicted, with the careers of six variant family types above and below: the intact black family; the single-parent black family; the single-parent family (all races); the reconstituted family; the childless marriage; and the childless–remarriage–late-childbearing family. The points at which the variant types "break" from the modal type are shown. In this single display, one can gain an understanding of the differences among family types with respect to the length of the family career; the chronology of life cycle events; and the length of time spent in specific phases of the family career.

Testing the Developmental Model

What is necessary to test the validity of the family development model? Is the model merely heuristic—fruitful for stimulating research, but incapable of proof or disproof? The Hill and Mattessich (1979) "confrontation with developmental psychology" constituted a test of a sort. Their metatheoretical examination of the developmental paradigm exposed the underlying assumptions and premises of the developmental perspective, making those assumptions and premises visible for debate and disconfirmation, as well as testable, rendering the perspective more rigorously theoretical than it had been. Such work constitutes necessary, but insufficient, testing of family development. Empirical testing is necessary, but what kind of empirical testing?

To respond to this question, the concept of development itself must be distinguished from the correlates of development. Or as Hill and Rodgers (1964) stated, the family life cycle as process must be distinguished from the family life cycle as a demographic, independent variable. The historical discussion in this chapter revealed that early use of the family life cycle in social research occurred in the service of explaining the economics of families: patterns of income and expenditure and the match or mismatch between the two (see, for example, Bigelow, 1936; Rowntree, 1906; Sorokin, Zimmerman, & Galpin, 1931). Economists and rural sociologists in those early days had little or no interest in the internal workings of the family. They employed crude and atheoretical classifications of the family life cycle because such classifications enabled them to better understand economic phenomena of primary research interest. Even now, some scholars continue to put the family life cycle to good use as an explainer of social or psychological phenomena (which transcend economics) of interest to them. (See, for example, the research described in the section on page 456.) All of this research focuses on potential correlates of development, not on the process of development itself.

The definition of the process of family development offered in this chapter entails a regular, ordered sequence of changes within the family as a system that occurs as an adaptation to the needs and demands of the family members and of society. Note that the proposed definition does not make reference to individual psyches or to the emotional states of family members. The psychological attributes of family members (e.g., happiness and adjustment) may be correlated with the phenomenon of family development (or they may not be), but their variance over the family life cycle is not postulated to be intrinsically

Table 4. Comparison of Stages of the Life Cycle for Black and White Reconstituted Families (Women of 12 Years of Education of Birth Cohorts, 1900–1949)

	Stage 1: Establishment	Stage 2: Childbearing and preschool	Period of transition: Divorce and return to labor force	Stage 3: Single parent, school age	Period of transition: Remarriage and stepparenthood	Stage 4: Reconstituted family, adolescents and school age	Period of transition: Launching young adults[a]	Stage 5: Postparental	Stage 6: Retirement years
Black reconstituted families									
	H 22.0–22.4 W 19.9–20.3	F 22.5–28.4 M 20.4–26.3 S_1 0–5.9 S_2 0–3.8	M 26.8–27.7 S_1 6.5–7.4 S_2 4.3–5.2	M 26.4–32.3 S_1 6.0–11.9 S_2 3.9–9.8	SF 30.5–31.4 M 29.6–30.5 S_1 9.7–10.6 S_2 7.5–8.4	SF 31.4–39.3 M 33.4–41.3 S_1 13–20.9 S_2 11–18.9 S_3 0–7.9	SF 39.4–52.3 M 41.4–54.3 (S_1 21–33.9) (S_2 19–31.9) (S_3 8–20.9)	SF 52.4–64.9 M 54.4–66.9	SF 65 at death M 67–72.1 at death
Years in stage	0.5	6	1	6	1	8	13	12.5	0–5.1
Interpersonal relations	1	1–6	6–3	3	3–6	6–10	10–1	1	1
White reconstituted families									
	H 22.0–24.8 W 19.7–22.5	F 24.9–30.8 M 22.6–28.5 S_1 0–5.9 S_2 0–2.9	(F 30.9–32.1) M 26.6–27.5 S_1 7.3–8.2 S_2 4.3–5.2	M 28.6–33.0 S_1 6.0–10.4 S_2 3.0–7.4	SF 34.0–34.9 M 31.8–32.7 S_1 10.5–11.4 S_2 7.5–8.4	SF 34.9–43.2 M 34.0–42.3 S_1 11.5–20.9 S_2 8.4–16.7 S_3 0–8.4	SF 43.2–55.7 M 42.3–54.8 (S_1 21–33.5) (S_2 16.8–29.3) (S_3 8.5–20.9)	SF 55.8–64.9 M 54.9–64.1	SF 65–69.3 at death M 64.1–77.1 at death
Years in stage	2.9	6	1	4.4	1	8.4	12.5	9.2	4.3–13.0
Interpersonal relations	1	1–6	6–3	6–3	3–6	6–10	10–1	1	1

[a]Parentheses indicate the departure of the children during this stage.

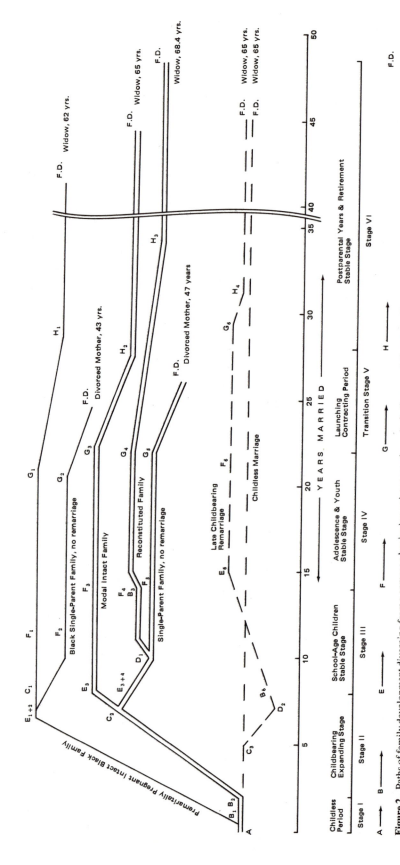

Figure 2. Paths of family development diverging from a common beginning point at marriage, including a modal intact family type and six divergent types based on aggregate performance of birth cohorts of women, 1900–1949 (for details documenting this display see Tables 1–4). Key: A = Marriage, B = First parenthood and expanding stage, Bb = Childbearing in second marriage, C = Divorce and single-parent phase, D = Remarriage and stepparenthood, E = School-age children (Stable Stage I), F = Adolescents (Stable Stage II), G = Launching of children (contracting transition), H = Postparental years (stable stages), and F.D. = Family dissolution, surviving widow, widower, divorced.

related to the family developmental process. For example, some people retain high self-esteem despite all sorts of stress, misfortune, or failure; others are extremely satisfied with their marriage whether they are experiencing a developmental crisis or not. It may be the case that self-esteem and/or marital satisfaction vary lawfully over the family life cycle, and such lawfulness would testify to the explanatory power of the life-cycle-stage conceptualization. However, variations in self-esteem and marital satisfaction do not constitute intrinsic elements of family development. In short, there is development itself, and there are potential correlates of development. Research that examines the correlates, hoping to find a developmentally related basis for their fluctuations over the course of the family life cycle does identify the impact of family developmental events on individuals, and it does reveal the explanatory power of the family-life-cycle-stage concept as an independent, contextual variable (the changing family contexts of life satisfaction, for example). However, it is not research that tackles the difficult chore of investigating the actual process of development, and it is not research that is sufficient to establish a theory of family development.

What types of research determine whether the concepts, assumptions, and generalizations of the family development perspective are sufficiently isomorphic to the actual change processes that occur in families? Several examples of important research topics that must be examined in order to test a theory of family development appear below in the form of questions:

1. Do changing plurality patterns within the family (size and density) precipitate the emergence of new roles and their differentiation? Do the changing needs of growing family members (indexed by a changing age composition) bring about changes in reciprocally related positions (structural transformation)?

2. Are there periods of relative equilibrium within families, which are punctuated by periods of disorganization during which families develop new scripts for carrying out their daily activities (role making, negotiation, and consensus seeking)?

3. Is family-developmental-task accomplishment necessary to maintain family cohesion and to satisfy the changing needs of family members? Is success in accomplishing such tasks at one point in time linked to success with tasks later in time?

4. Are there statistically modal or typical family careers? That is, regardless of whether family development occurs in a steady, continuous fashion or as a sequence of sharp ups and downs, can distinct phases of the family career be demonstrated to contain distinct configurations of family roles, different degrees of salience for family tasks, or differing levels of stress and vulnerability? What are the chief "variant" careers that depart from the path of the statistically modal career?

None of the issues raised in the preceding questions invokes the use of the family life cycle solely as an independent variable. Each involves the construction and monitoring of operational indicators of the developmental process in families. It is research that responds to questions such as these that can provide the solid, interrelated, empirical generalizations that are necessary to build a theory of family development.

Analysis of the process of family development is optimally effected by longitudinal methods—methods that require the collection of data on the same families over a long period of time but that have unfortunately been a luxury within social science research. Some retrospective and quasi-longitudinal methods can substitute for actual longitudinal approaches, but these sometimes have serious limitations (see Hill, 1964).

Whatever the method used to investigate family development, it must make the entire family career the target for analysis so that the morphogenic processes of the development of role acquisition, differentiation, consolidation, and integration are adequately portrayed. Unfortunately, the processes of development can become more conspicuous by their absence than by their presence. Among families that adapt to recurrent life stresses with a minimum of turmoil, that can rewrite family role scripts to adjust to the changing demands of family members, and that adequately accomplish their developmental tasks, the analyst may have trouble sifting the processes of development from the complex web of other, situationally specific activities in which the family and its members are involved over time. Development is so intrinsic and expectable that it occurs without much fanfare in effectively functioning families. However, when development is impeded in "dysfunctioning" families, its existence in "functioning" families becomes manifest by comparison. Barnhill and Longo (1978), for example, noted that many of the families that require clinical assistance are those that have become "stuck" in a family-life-cycle stage. Stuck families have managed adequately with one pattern of roles scripted for a given family stage, but at the occurrence of a significant life-cycle event (signaling a mismatch between role scripts and new needs), they are unable to alter their pattern in order to adjust to the new demands of the members. Families whose role scripts have petrified or families whose members cannot attune themselves to one another's needs (parents who cannot do parenting, or spouses who become mismatched in their expectations) are examples of families that can be compared with the baseline of developmentally functioning families in order to yield a better understanding of the ongoing processes of development.

In any case, adequate study of family development requires longitudinal research that focuses on elements of family dynamics that are truly developmental. Some of these elements (the predictable changes in family role complexes at critical life-cycle transitions, the accomplishment of developmental tasks, and the pileups of family stresses at standard points in the family career) have been suggested. They must be kept conceptually distinct from other elements of family and individual behavior, which may vary in synchronization with life cycle events (because they are, in part, caused to vary by those same events), but that are not themselves intrinsic in development (e.g., life satisfaction). The absence of such a conceptual distinction can lead to faulty interpretation of otherwise sound empirical work. The analyst can erroneously conclude that the absence of a hypothesized relationship between an antecedent and its consequences calls into question the existence of the antecedent itself.

Fruitfulness of the Developmental Perspective for Orienting Family Research and Practice

Despite its "unfinished" character, its sometimes major shortcomings, and its theoretical weaknesses (which family scholars have only recently begun to remedy in a systematic way), the family development perspective has been seminal for much family research and theory building as well as for the establishment of clinical and social policy orientations. For the record, let us take an overview of this work.

Family-Development Theory-Building and Research

Hayes's survey (1977) of family scholars in 1975— covering their use of conceptual frameworks (either singly or in combinations) in their teaching, their graduate training programs, and their research—found family development second only to structure function among six theoretical orientations, including symbolic interaction, exchange, and psychoanalysis. Hodgson and Lewis (1979) examined trends in family theory and methodology for the years 1969 and 1976, as evidenced in the major journals publishing articles on family research and theory, and they noted that the developmental framework had increased in use by family researchers to second place, behind structure function (from 14% of all publications in 1969 to 24% in 1976). They speculated, with the disclaimer that such speculation may be premature, that some combination of the family development and systems perspectives may become the major inductive frameworks that will unify social-scientific studies of the family. Less sanguine about the future of the family development perspective is a minority position advanced by Holman and Burr (1980), who observed that the promise of the developmental perspective during the 1960s as a major integrative theoretical approach was subsequently diluted by its attention to the highly specialized "life-span" studies, which deemphasize family process. The relative validity of these two contrasting assessments of the significance of family development as a basis for integrating findings from empirical studies may be revealed by the industry of developmental theorists during the 1980s. In any case, a consensus exists among historians of family theory and research that family development has had a significant impact on family scholarship since 1950. (For additional data on trends in the changing hierarchy of theoretical orientations about family phenomena, see Cerny, Dahl, Kamika, & Aldous, 1974; Hill, 1980; Klein, Calvert, Garland, & Poloma, 1969; Klein, Schvaneveldt, & Miller, 1977; Mogey, 1971).

Research related to or inspired by the developmental perspective has been much too productive quantitatively to be adequately reviewed in the brief space of this section of our chapter. Much of the research falls into the category of "correlates of family life stages" and is research that cuts across many disciplinary and substantive lines. The phenomenon indexed by the stage categories is treated as a "determinant" variable at times and as a "contextual" variable at other times. Examples are seen in the use of the family-life-cycle stages to account for variance in consumership (Hill, Foote, Aldous, Carlson, & McDonald, 1970); levels of living (Blackwell, 1942; Lively, 1932; Rowntree, 1906); housing choices and constraints (Foote, Abu-Lughod, Foley, & Winnick, 1960); use of leisure time (Rapoport & Rapoport, 1975; Szalai, 1972); marital satisfaction (dozens of studies, reviewed by Miller, 1976; Rollins & Feldman, 1970; Spanier, Lewis, & Cole, 1975); equity in marital roles (Shafer & Keith, 1981); parental satisfaction (Veroff & Feld, 1970); general life satisfaction (Campbell, Converse, & Rodgers, 1976); mental disorder and health (Gove, Grimm, Motz, & Thompson, 1972); and participation in voluntary associations (Babchuck & Booth, 1969; Mattessich, 1977). Because the shape of the relationship between stages of the family cycle and virtually all of the phenomena just cited is not only nonlinear but curvilinear, a theoretical puzzle challenges reviewers of this research to explain the life cycle pattern.

In this review, we have sought to focus more consistently on family development as the phenomenon to be described and explained than as the determinant of other phenomena. Research meeting this prescription was almost nonexistent when Hill and Rodgers made their 1964 assessment, and it remains in short supply. The developmental perspective may be credited with stimulating dozens of "period"- or "stage"-bound descriptive researchers that provide teachers and textbook writers with empirical descriptions of the developmental issues encountered by families at each of the seven stages of the family life span. Evelyn Duvall's five editions of her text (1957, 1962, 1967, 1971, 1977) have benefited from these researches, so that the generalizations in the last two editions are much better documented than was possible in the first three editions. Aldous (1978) drew selectively on more than 200 of these period-specific research studies, most of them published since 1964, to ground her own generalizations stage by stage:

Stages treated in chapters of Aldous text	Number of researches cited	Number published since 1964
Establishment stage	26	21
Childbearing stage, infants, and preschool children	50	45
Families with schoolchildren	37	31
Families with adolescents	37	25
Families in postparental and retirement years	61	51

A major shortcoming of the period-specific research studies, of course, is that they tend to be static with respect to the course of development. They present still photographs of everyday family life at specific phases of the family's career. The least static of these studies compare family patterns in two or more periods by retrospective interviewing or, better still, by follow-up interviews in order to obtain panel observations using what Hill (1964) called the segmented longitudinal method (Hill et al., 1970; Paris & Luckey, 1966; Ryder, 1973). Feldman (1971) verified with such a design the negative impacts of both the first and the second child on marital communication and satisfaction by comparing members of his study cohort who remained childless with those who had a first child. The same negative impacts had been inferred from comparisons of childless and childbearing couples in his earlier, cross-sectional sample (1964), but the longitudinal study provided the necessary, conclusive proof that deterioration occurred within the same families over time. Streib and Thompson's segmented longitudinal design (1958) scheduled interviews at preretirement with potential retirees and again after retirement for those who retired and for those who continued to work. This design is a second example of a departure from the period-specific studies, and it opened up to family scholars a glimpse of the processes of adjustment that were retirement-specific in contrast with the processes that were common to all couples in their mid-60s. Retrospective interviewing is another way to give time depth to period-specific studies and has been accomplished for descriptions of the emptying nest and the postparental periods of family development (Deutscher, 1959; Johnson, 1968; Saunders, 1974). These studies have called into question the widely held views that couples without children in the postparental period are bereft and depressed. Indeed, this appears to be a period of recovery, financially and maritally, and of achieving levels of marital satisfaction not recorded since the early years of marriage.

The only longitudinal study covering any major span of "family time" is the research designed by Burgess and Wallin (1953) for assessments at three points in time: in 1939, as engaged couples (1,000 couples); 3–7 years later (1942–1946) as married couples (married 1–6 years) with 666 couples; and 13–18 years later (married 14–24 years) with 400 couples (see Dizard, 1968). The central variable of interest to Burgess and Wallin was marital adjustment, measured at Time 1 as engagement adjustment.

The original sample of engaged couples was far from representative of the general population: urban, predominantly white-collar middle class, white Protestant, and of husband-and-wife homogamous family background. The attrition within this sample from engagement to early marriage was selective, with couples concentrated in the higher levels of adjustment at Time 2, 3 to 6 years into marriage. There was some room for improvement at Time 2 in happiness levels (12% of wives and 14% of husbands were low) and in degree of love (17.5% of wives and 28.5% of husbands were only "somewhat in love"). But

virtually all couples at this point in the marriage were committed to continuing the marriage. (Only 3%–5% affirmatively answered the question, "Have you ever considered seriously separating or divorcing from your spouse?") It was therefore entirely expected that Time 3 would find the survivors of 15 years of marriage lower, rather than higher, on 32 of 36 different measures of marital success (Pineo, 1961). Of the surviving 400 couples, two thirds scored lower on marital adjustment at Time 3 than at Time 2. There is some evidence of a regression effect, as 50% of couples who scored high initially declined at Time 3, and 44% who scored low initially improved their adjustment scores at Time 3. Nonetheless, the large majority of all couples, regardless of initial levels of adjustment, showed declines from the early to the middle years of marriage. Pineo conceptualized this as a process of disenchantment made up of lowered levels of satisfaction, love, and consensus, with evidence of disengagement in activities and commitment.

Dizard (1968), in a further analysis of the longitudinal data, found shifts in the allocation of power from shared power to concentration of decision making in the husband or the wife position, that is, a segregation of power. Similarly, the division of tasks within the home shifted from a joint integration of roles, with many tasks shared, to role segregation along traditional gender lines. Dizard reported that these structural transformations had occurred while the belief system had remained unaltered, providing no consensual or ideological support for the patterns that emerged.

These findings, from longitudinal data, of decline in marital satisfaction and in equalitarian power and task allocation are congruent with findings inferred from a number of cross-sectional studies (from Serbia, France, Belgium, and the United States), which simulated change over the family span by comparing families at different stages of family development (Blood, 1967; Blood & Wolfe, 1960; Buric & Zecevic, 1967; LePlae, 1968; Michel, 1967; Silverman & Hill, 1967).

Cross-sectional studies offer challenging descriptive findings of period-specific episodes, but they often tell us more about cohort-specific experiences than they do about changes in family development over the life span. Generalizations should be checked out longitudinally, as in the examples cited above, regarding the effects of first parenthood (Feldman, 1971; Ryder, 1973), of the impact of retirement (Streib & Thompson, 1958), and of power and role allocation over the life span (Dizard, 1968; Paris & Luckey, 1966; Pineo, 1961).

Maternal employment over the family's career is one developmental phenomenon that looks quite different from simulations of the life span from cross-sectional samples as against longitudinal samples. Cross-sectional data for recent decades show peak participation of women in the labor force in their early 20s and again at ages 40–50, with a dip among women during the child-rearing years and again in their 60s. Rephrased in terms of the careers of families, there is high employment in early marriage, dropping during childbearing and middle par-

enthood, and a sharp rise in the launching and postparental years. A direct interpretation would be that maternal
employment is normatively proscribed during the child-
rearing period, but longitudinal data tell a different story.
Within Hill's three-generation research (Hill *et al.*,
1970), the women in the grandparent generation were
virtually without gainful employment (about 10% employed) throughout their marital career until the postparental period, when 20% entered the work force. In the
parent generation, 20% were already employed at marriage (during the Great Depression); about half dropped
out for the childbearing period; and by the third decade,
50% were in the labor force. Of the wives in the youngest
generation, 60% were employed at marriage, dropping to
25% during the first years of childbearing, but quickly
reaching 40% employed by the tenth year of marriage.
Thus, the inferences about maternal employment careers
from the cross-sectional data were faulty in describing the
careers of any of the three generations in the Hill study.

Research studies that cover the entire family life span
unfortunately continue to be largely from cross-sectional
samples, and family development scholars must make do
with what is available. They tell the same story as the
"correlates-of-family-development" studies: The course
of development is curvilinear in shape and moves from
simple to complex and back to simple again in structural
complexity. Each of the dimensions of structure appear to
follow such a path: the numbers of persons; the numbers
of interpersonal relationships and density (age homogeneity); the cognitive and prosocial competency of the
members; the allocation of power, tasks, and affection;
the ratio of instrumental and expressive resources to
member needs; efficiency in the management of time,
energy, and space; and links to work, to schools, and to
support systems of kinship and friendship networks.
Some research activity has been initiated and reported for
all or portions of the family career for each of these dimensions, but no studies as yet offer an overarching
integration.

A more general family-development theory is required
to explain the invariant cyclic patterning of family performance across types of phenomena. Descriptively, many
achievements appear to rise and fall and rise again con-
jointly. The structural constraints of family size, as well
as the pressure of numbers on family instrumental resources of space, time, and energy, increase and then
decrease together. The "livability quotient" of children
as increasingly competent, resourceful, responsible, and
prosocial improves paradoxically during the very same
period when marital and parental satisfactions are in decline. When children are most egocentric and least
accountable, they would appear to be most "lovable"
and least resented.

Is the confounding factor one of increasing familial
complexity because of the increased numbers of interpersonal relations to be sustained, requiring a more complex
set of rules and roles to manage and coordinate activities
of maturing children whose growing autonomy makes

consensus more difficult to sustain and reaching a peak in
dissension just when the balance of instrumental needs
and resources (the life cycle squeeze) is most precarious?
Family vulnerability to crisis and family dissension about
rules and roles appear to converge to account for the low
level of marital and general life satisfaction at the nadir in
the family's career. Thereafter, with the leave-taking of
young adults, the household quiets down and becomes
more livable for those who remain (Deutscher's highly
satisfied postparental couples).

Running through this account of the curvilinear course
of development are three general variables: (1) the rise
and fall of interactional-structural complexity; (2) qualitative changes in the cognitive and prosocial competencies and coping resources of maturing children; and (3)
the depletion and restoration of the margin of time, energy, and revenue resources available to the adult members.
We hypothesize that the invariance of life cycle patterns
reported by the researches to date reflects the interactions
of these three general variables.

Clinical Applications

With family service as an explicit goal of the family
development framework, it is not surprising that the
framework has received attention from family therapists
and other clinicians. Family development concepts can
help the therapist to think about life cycle events that
establish the context within which family problems and
individual problems occur. Solomon (1973), for example, suggested that both diagnostic understanding and
treatment planning with families can be enhanced by a
developmental perspective on the family. Developmental
thinking has been credited with shedding new light on at
least three principles within the family therapy literature.

A first principle is that the stresses experienced by
family members occur in a relatively predictable fashion
as a consequence of normal, developmental events and
crises, and that these stresses may often account for the
observed physical or mental disorder (see Caplan, 1964;
Gartner, Fulmer, Weinshel, & Goldklank, 1978; Hadley,
Jacob, Milliones, Caplan, & Spitz, 1974; Hill, 1969).
Hadley *et al.* (1974), for example, demonstrated a
positive relationship between family developmental crises and the onset of symptoms for which family members
will seek treatment.

A second principle is that there do, indeed, exist developmental tasks that, if unfulfilled, produce "dysfunctioning" families (i.e., families that cannot adapt and
mobilize their role organization to meet the needs of the
members). Barnhill and Longo (1978) noted that all families face developmental crises and that those who cannot
transform their structures to deal with such crises require
therapy to make developmental progress. In a study of
families in a community mental health center, Gartner *et
al.* (1978) found that the families that came for treatment
tended to do so as a result of difficulty adjusting to expectable events within the family career (e.g., forming a

marital relationship, launching children, and dealing with the death of a family member). Most families, they suggested, manage to resolve maturational crises, but those that do not "are propelled into therapy by their difficulties in resolving specific crises related to their structure or structural change" (p. 57). Eisenberg (1979) discovered that two aspects of parent–child dynamics (labeled "parental coldness" and "mother excitable-rejecting," both of which indicate deficiencies in developmental task accomplishment) are strongly related to aggressive behavior by children. Terkelson (1980) posited that family adequacy must be measured with reference to the extent to which elements of family structure are matched to specific needs. Because needs change over time, it is evident that structure must transform itself to continue need fulfillment. When families cannot transform their structure, then, Terkelson suggested the goal of family therapy is to restore the family's capacity to support need attainment in its members. Steinglass (1980) proposed that the family development perspective may have great use in the analysis of alcoholic families. Alcoholism is intrinsically chronic and longitudinal. Alcoholic families, Steinglass contended, "distort" their family life cycle. In fact, it appears that alcoholic families, rather than progressing stage by stage through the family career, may proceed in a "recycling" fashion, returning to stages (and the associated tasks) already completed.

A third principle that the developmental perspective reiterates for family therapists is that it is frequently necessary to understand, and to work with, an entire family in order to treat individual and family problems. This statement may sound trite to those who take the term *family therapy* literally. However, as recently as 1980, Carter and McGoldrick (1980) and Terkelson (1980), in a major volume on the family life cycle as a framework for family therapy, felt compelled to state that many clinicians persist in thinking about, and in planning treatments for, individuals rather than families. They exhorted their clinical colleagues to recognize the family as an interdependent system that experiences a predictable series of changes over its career. From the description of the family offered earlier in this chapter (interdependence, boundary maintenance, etc.), it becomes evident why effective diagnosis and treatment require attention to an entire family and to its current life-cycle stage.

Social Policy Applications

Beyond the clinical level, where the developmental perspective may enlighten the diagnosis and treatment of individual and family disorders, some scholars have provocatively moved to the community and societal levels where "diagnosis" and "treatment" become social policy. An understanding of individual and family development, it has been proposed, could provide policymakers with a frame of reference for asking questions about community composition by life cycle stage in order to plan for the needs of aggregates of families in a particu-

lar geographic area. It can also provide an estimation of the optimal means and timing of intervention to remedy social problems that have a developmental feature.

Hirschorn (1977) challenged social service professionals to "transcend the present stalemate in social policy theory" and to "rediscover the contents of social life by examining the work-family system in a developmental perspective" (p. 449). He surmised that social policies directed toward a reduction of delinquency and poverty will never succeed unless such policies are made explicitly adaptable to individuals in different developmental contexts. The stage in the life cycle mediates the impact of policy on individuals and families. Hirschorn also proposed that social policies speak to "the inherent problems of transitions." He called for policies that "allow people to make their transitions successfully and in the most positive way," and for policies "based increasingly on the time of life events" (pp. 447–448). Concretely, such policies would provide people with "second chances" and "forgiveness of errors" by means of payment for job moves, financing for retraining in occupational skills, and compensation for unexpected home loss, family legal problems, and health care related to life cycle stressors.

Similar thinking had been evinced in Aldous and Hill's identification (1967) of "strategic points for intervention" to break the poverty cycle: the inheritance of poverty by one generation from its predecessors, partly because of the scheduling problems and resource deficiencies that poverty-stricken parental families bestow on their children and, consequently, their children's families. Aldous and Hill suggested that an understanding of vulnerability to stress over the family life cycle could enable policymakers to establish targets for intervening to bring families out of poverty. Hill (1980) charted these stage-specific vulnerabilities, and the display of his work (Figure 3) suggests a way by which developmental theory can be translated into a practical, policy-relevant model. Recent empirical documentation of cross-generational links with respect to early marriage, early parenthood, and fertility appears in Card's study (1981) of long-term consequences for the children of teenage parents.

Stolte-Heiskanen (1974, 1975) pursued a somewhat different tack in her formulation of the implications of family development for macrolevel policymaking. She proposed that social indicators can be developed that will signal for policymakers the salient ecological, structural, cultural, and social-psychological needs of families. In turn, social policy (defined as the allocation and adminstration of material and nonmaterial resources) can be attuned to these needs.

Mattessich (1976) proposed that both "strategic intervention" and family needs as related to the life cycle could be used by state-level policymakers in the United States. He noted, as did Stolte-Heiskanen, that the demographic data necessary for characterizing communities on the basis of prevalent family characteristics are available in census reports. Abeles and Riley (1978) reported that

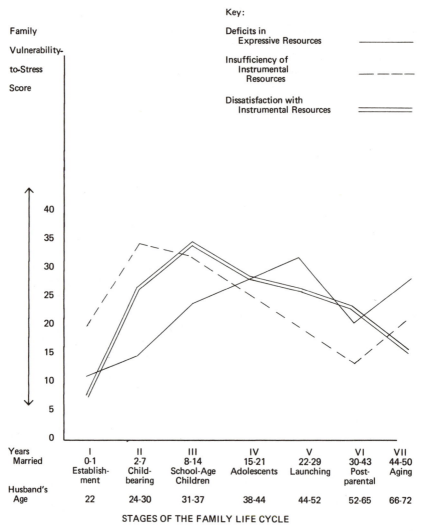

Figure 3. Vulnerability-to-stress scores by stages of the family life cycle. (From Aldous & Hill, 1969.)

the Social Science Research Council was exploring ways of making life course research relevant to policymaking.

Criticisms of the Family Development Perspective

Despite its apparent usefulness for orienting family research and practice, the family development perspective has been strongly criticized for a number of shortcomings and inadequacies. Throughout its history, of course, the developmental perspective, as an emerging and eclectic perspective, has assimilated the relevant features of alternative analytic models—responding, in a sense, to scholarly feedback and profiting from the work of those who

put its deficiencies into relief. Dialogue and controversy that stimulate conceptual innovation and empirical research have been actively encouraged to increase the theoretical stature of the perspective. Hill and Mattessich (1979) formulated what they termed a ''confrontation'' with developmental psychology and life course analysis for the purpose of dissecting and ultimately enhancing the theory of family development. This section contains salient criticisms that the framework has recently come to face.

One of the most thoughtful critiques of the family development perspective is Kerckhoff's *Family Careers: Some Perspectives and Proposals* (1978), which suggests that greater attention be paid to the variety of family careers among families in the United States. This variety is masked when a modal career, such as that presented in Table 1, is taken as representative of the course of family development in American society. Kerckhoff noted three variations that differ from the modal pattern: (1) careers that have an *unusual sequence of stages*, such as in a family founded by childbirth rather than by marriage; (2) careers that are *truncated* and do not pass through the full sequence of stages, such as those of childless marriages or of single-parent families where the marital bond has been broken through death, divorce, or separation; and (3) careers in which the *timing* of life cycle events is "off schedule," such as early or late childbearing, early or late marriage, and unusual gaps between stages. Kerckhoff's observations were taken seriously in the construction of Tables 2–4 and Figure 2. In this section, the criticisms by Kerckhoff and other scholars concerning the family development perspective are discussed in detail.

A Single Modal Life Cycle

A first criticism is that the family-life-cycle stages do not apply to all families (Elder, 1978; Kerckhoff, 1978; Trost, 1977). That is, the pattern of development in many families varies from the seven-stage model in frequent use among family development scholars. Exceptions to the model include single-parent families that have resulted from divorce or death and childless couples. It has been asserted that such exceptions became increasingly frequent in the 1970s and that they have the prospect of even greater frequency during the 1980s.

The issue is not whether development occurs, or whether the concepts of the developmental perspective adequately sensitize analysts to the developmental properties of family systems. Rather, the issue is whether development occurs not just along one pathway (the modal life cycle with some variance around that mode) but along several pathways (each of which constitutes a major type of family development with some variance among the families who fall into that type). The fact that families have specifiable careers or life cycles has been well established historically and cross-culturally. (See, for example, Desai, 1964; Goody, 1962; Haavio-Mannila, 1977; Hareven, 1977; Kamiko 1977; Koyama, Morioka, & Kumagai, 1980). However, do the careers of families in the United States, for instance, have enough in common so that they can be characterized as following a relatively uniform path? The answer, from the statistics presented previously, is that variant paths departing at points from the typical career do exist and must be explicitly recognized, but that the impact of this variability on developmental theory will remain an open question until more data from the 1970s and 1980s become available. "Truncations" of the family life cycle because of divorce occurred in less than one third of all marriages, regardless of the year in which they occurred, through 1977 (Weed, 1980). However, it is predicted that

the number of marriages contracted during the 1960s and 1970s that may eventually end in divorce may approach one in every two, with the large majority then remarrying (Weed, 1980).

Thus, it appears that at least one half, and probably less than two thirds, of existing marriages can be expected to follow (or to have followed) the modal-life-cycle path described earlier. The fact that so many families proceed through a relatively standard life cycle is evidence of the descriptive power of the framework. What, however, of the remaining one third to one half of all families? One significant group of families that differs in its course of development from the two-parent nuclear family is the single-parent family, the vast majority of which are comprised of a divorced woman and her child(ren). However, good reasons exist for pushing the developmental perspective to encompass such families. For example, they are systems with the same system properties as two-parent families, and they must accomplish most of the same developmental tasks as two-parent families (see Table 1). In fact, the principal difference between single-parent and two-parent families is that the former lack the personnel resources to fill the normatively expected positions in the family. This lack of personnel resources places a heavy burden on the remaining family members, who must compensate with increased effort to accomplish family tasks such as physical maintenance and social control.

Permanently childless couples constitute another family type to which the modal family-life-cycle stages do not apply. To date, the percentage of married couples in the permanently childless category has been very small (Glick, 1977; Mattessich, 1979), and scholars working with the developmental perspective have made no substantial attempt to establish a modified set of stages that would describe the career of such families. Remarried couples with children from two or more previous marriages (sometimes called *blended families*) also clearly deviate from the seven-stage model proposed earlier. However, such families, when they have any measure of stability, typically fall into some life-cycle category beyond the first and proceed along a course of development that resembles that of more conventional families (see Table 2).

Thus, this first criticism, which is currently still very active, has led to a stocktaking that has revealed the descriptive efficacy of the family-life-cycle stages for application to the majority of families. It has also led to the identification of some challenges faced by the developmental perspective related to enlarging its scope to become more relevant to single-parent families and possibly other family types.

Timing of Critical Life Events

A second, major criticism of the family development perspective has been that it ignores the timing of critical life events and the duration of stages, especially as these might be affected by historical context (see, for example, Elder, 1978). Great variance, for example, exists in the "typical" ages at which family-life-cycle events occur. For specific families, the effects of encountering certain transitions "early" or "late" relative to other families can be profound.

In fact, these issues are less outside the realm of the family development perspective than they are at its cutting edge. Life course analysts and family historians (e.g., Elder, 1978; Modell, Furstenberg, Hesberg, 1976; Riley, Johnson, & Foner, 1972; Uhlenberg, 1974) have produced data that family development has attempted to incorporate into its theoretical formulations. For several decades, of course, Glick (1947, 1955, 1977) had provided baseline data for the timing of life cycle events (e.g., age at marriage, ages at first and last births, and child spacing). Hill and Mattessich (1979) indicated that the confrontation of family development theory with life-course and age-stratification research showed the need for sifting the developmental features of families that are invariant across social and historical contexts from those family features that are specific to historical periods or particular family cohorts. One difficulty in doing this is that the conceptually equivalent developmental features of families in different social and historical contexts are not necessarily phenomenally equivalent. Analysts need to look carefully at whether a society is, at different periods, merely providing different means for families to proceed along essentially the same career path, or whether it is making fundamental changes in that path itself.

Nevertheless, research has shown—and will continue to show—that families that pass through a similar sequence of stages can have very different life courses. How much these life courses can vary before they constitute disparate paths of development is still an unresolved issue. Life course analysts have demonstrated that the social-historical context makes a difference, but they have not proceeded to indicate the implications of that difference for developmental theory—implications that are of central importance to scholars interested in life span and family development. Rossi (1980) suggested that life course sociologists have been virtually atheoretical in their work, and she proceeded in her research to establish criteria for marking adult development that point out the interactions between critical life transitions and the historical context within which the transitions occur.

The Interaction Effect of Other Careers

A third criticism of the developmental perspective is that it neglects consideration of other careers with which the family career is closely synchronized, and which, in part, may precipitate movement into new stages of the family career. However, the shortcoming of the family development perspective in this regard has been less at the level of acknowledging the synchronization of individual careers inside and outside the family than it has been at the level of constructing an operational model that takes into

account the effects of the confluence of individual careers on the total family career. That is, the seven-stage model used for describing the family career (which, it must be recalled, is only one of several proposals for describing that career) explicitly recognizes the extrafamilial work career of the husband-father and the school career of the oldest child. In addition, Rodgers (1973) argued that careers involving family transactions with other societal institutions are an integral facet of family development; Gove *et al.* (1972) proposed that the family serves as a system of allocation of roles to individuals who pursue their own, separate careers; and Waite (1980) demonstrated that the stage in the family life cycle is a critical determinant of married women's labor-force participation.

Recognition that the careers of all family members are in some way related to family development, coupled with the fact that only the work career of the husband-father and the school career of the oldest child appear as criteria in the most widely used sets of stages for describing the family, has produced dissatisfaction among some family researchers. In response to this dissatisfaction, Voydanoff (1979) proposed one remedy that she tentatively described as the "work-family life cycle," comprised of a set of stages that reflect changes in family composition as well as in the occupational careers of both spouses.

The central issue, however, involves much more than mere recognition of the significant, individual, life-course careers of family members. Rather, it involves our understanding of how development occurs in families. Is it a process with sharp discontinuities demarcating stages containing family role complexes that differ markedly from one another? Or is it a process that occurs continuously, subtly, and almost imperceptibly, so that a family can recognize how its organization at one time differs from its organization earlier but cannot identify any definite disjunctures in its role scripts?

Hill and Joy (1980) suggested that "critical role transitions," a concept borrowed from Rapoport, might be operationalized to generate stages of family development. By definition, movement from stage to stage in the family career is constituted by major changes in the family's complex. Hill and Joy listed a variety of events that exert some amount of pressure on families to alter their patterns of role organization. These events include changes in the number of family members; age composition changes; major status changes (cohabitation, engagement, marriage, parenthood, and empty-nesthood); changes in relationships with external institutions (e.g., school, work, and military service); residential status changes; and changes in social network affiliations. Some of these events may have greater "weight" than others. That is, some may force reorganization independently, whereas others may contribute to reorganization only when they pile up during a relatively brief time interval. Hill and Joy suggested that stages derived from the "critical transition" and "pileup" notions vary according to the demands of a research problem and the availability of data. What is important is that phases of development are seen as a product of the interaction of many different events within a family—events that are often part of the intercontingent career changes of several of the family's members.

The synthesis of the "life-stress" and the "critical-transition" literatures with the literature on family development offers a challenging and promising prospect for building an explicit, comprehensive consideration of the synchrony of individual life-course careers into the operationalization of family development.

Lack of Correlation with Other Measures

A fourth criticism of the family development perspective has been that the family-life-cycle stages correlate very modestly with many other measures of individual and family attributes, in part because the heterogeneity within stages is so great. Nock (1979) and Spanier, Sauer, and Larzelere (1979) have argued that the heuristic conceptual appeal of the life cycle categories has spread among many family researchers in spite of the absence of a critical, empirical examination of the efficacy of those stages as predictors of important marital and family phenomena. Using the example of marital satisfaction, for which the relationship to family-life-cycle stage has been explored empirically, Spanier et al. noted that the stages are very weak predictors.

Nock (1979) assessed the relationships between three family characteristics (the stage in the life cycle, the presence of children, and the length of the marriage) and each of 29 "family life elements," which he grouped into three types: instrumental elements (e.g., income, the number of rooms in the dwelling, and health problems); expressive elements (e.g., the frequency of companionate activities between the spouses, enjoyment of parenthood, and satisfaction with the marriage); and attitudinal elements (e.g., the desire to change residence, the number of voluntary associations, and job satisfaction). He concluded from his analysis that, although the zero-order associations between each of the three family characteristics and each of the 29 family-life elements are similar, the association between the family-life-cycle stage and the family life elements wanes considerably when the length of the marriage is controlled for. His finding is hardly surprising. However, length of marriage is a vacuous concept, and it is still questionable whether life cycle stages (which have theoretical meaning) may be related to family phenomena, which are reasonably expected to vary over the life cycle (as many of Nock's dependent variables are not expected to do).

Spanier et al. (1979) similarly examined the relationships between each of three family characteristics (family-life-cycle stage, age cohort, and marriage cohort) and each of 14 variables measured by the U.S. Census (e.g., the presence of parents or in-laws in the household, family income, and the number of children who have left home). They concluded that the three predictors substan-

tially correspond with one another; that there is "great overlap between stages of the family life cycle on a number of relevant variables"; that none of the three independent predictors is clearly superior to the other two, although age cohort has a slight edge; and that the use of combined information from the three independent variables can at least marginally increase the predictability of the dependent variables that they examined (p. 37). As a result, they recommended that the developmental stage concept be reexamined and refined to take into account a greater number and variety of critical transition points than it currently recognizes, and that the family development framework include a multiplicity of stratification schemes for depicting the process of family development. To date, scholars have not responded to this challenge.

What is the impact of the analytic strategies of these critics on our understanding of the relationship between family-life-cycle stages and other measures of family and individual phenomena? At the empirical level, despite some controversy regarding severe technical shortcomings (see Klein & Aldous, 1979), the results of these analyses provide evidence of the need for better operationalization of the process of family development (a need revealed elsewhere in this chapter along with some proposals for fulfilling it). The results also reveal the need for studies that focus on a set of family variables that are clearly relevant to an examination of family change. The dependent variables in the research of both Nock and Spanier et al. were selected a posteriori because of their availability as secondary data in data sets that permitted only cross-sectional comparisons. The work of both groups of researchers will be enhanced by longitudinal studies that identify a priori those features of family structure and functioning that are expected to vary with developmental regularity over the family career. Nock (1979) exhorted developmentalists to search empirically for "meaningful changes" occurring during the family career (p. 25). He wanted concrete empirical validation of the abstract concepts of family development. Such an exhortation, of course, is not new (see Aldous, 1971; Hill, 1964; Hill & Rodgers, 1964; Klein, Borne, Jache, & Sederberg, 1978).

At the theoretical level, the work of these researchers reintroduced the question of what constitutes development and what is necessary in order to test whether a regular process of development occurs in families. David Klein, in Borne, Jache, Sederberg, and Klein (1979), proposed three models of development that are compatible with the family development perspective. The differences between these models, however, are fundamental, and recognition of the differences suggests possible reasons for the weak empirical associations that research such as that of Nock and of Spanier et al. has revealed between life cycle stages and measures of individual and family phenomena.

Klein pointed out that one model of development as "stage-discrete" predicts that quantitative and qualita-

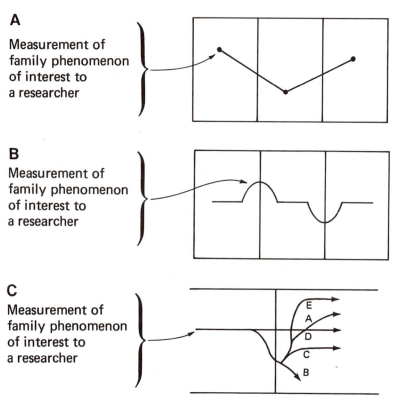

Figure 4. Models of development: (A) as "stage discrete"; (B) as "stage transitional"; (C) as a "stage-transitional branching process." (From Klein, in Borne *et al.*, 1979.)

tive differences exist between adjacent life-cycle stages in such things as marital adjustment. (A graphic representation of these differences appears in Figure 4.) Within a second model of development, a "stage-transitional" model, it is at the periods between stages, the transition points, that disequilibrium occurs within families. Measurement of important individual or family variables during a period of disequilibrium will demonstrate that many of them have different values from those that they have during stable, within-stage periods. That is, attitudes and patterns of behavior may fluctuate wildly during a critical transition, but eventually, the family settles down and "picks up where it left off."

A third model proposed by Klein and his colleagues synthesizes the first two models. They refer to this model as one of a "stage-transitional branching process." This model views "stage transitions as the place to look for variables of interest, but would add the idea that changes result in varying levels of re-equilibrium" (Borne *et al.*, 1979, p. 3). They illustrate this model with a hypothetical illustration of five possible paths that "consensus between spouses" might follow after the birth of their first child. These paths, A through E, appear in Figure 4:

A. The birth of the first child has no effect on spousal consensus.

B. The birth of the first child erodes spousal consensus to such a degree that the relationship ends in divorce or by other means.

C. The birth of the first child erodes consensus, and consensus reestablishes itself at a new, but lower, level.

D. The birth of the first child temporarily erodes spousal consensus, but a full recovery to the pre-birth level eventually occurs.

E. The birth of the first child temporarily erodes spousal consensus, but eventually, a new and higher level of consensus emerges.

What is important about his third model is that it amalgamates a variety of notions that developmental scholars have advanced to describe the process of development: dynamic equilibrium; critical transitions; morphogenesis; family crisis; the "game tree"; and so on. A comparison of the three models illustrates clearly why empirical efforts to "measure" development have produced mixed results. That is, the only model with which statistical procedures of linear and curvilinear association are compatible is the first model in Figure 4. Typical statistical procedures do not detect the processes of development described by the second and third models.

In conclusion, the synopsis of these four criticisms and

of some responses to them is part of the lively dialogue that will undoubtedly continue through the 1980s among family development scholars. In reflecting on these criticisms, it is essential to recall our earlier discussion of "testing the developmental model." Such testing requires the construction and monitoring of operational indicators of the developmental process in families, with the distinction clearly established between the process of development itself and the individual and family phenomena that may be affected by the developmental changes that occur in families. The ultimate goal of this scholarly dialogue is the generation of two types of substantive theory: first, a theory of the phenomenon of family development, for which variety in life-span family-development is the dependent variable to be explained; and second, a family development theory of the economic and social achievements of families, for which "family development" is the antecedent variable in a cause–effect model. It is evident that the four criticisms described here have important implications for both types of theory.

Prospects for the Future

What exists on the horizon for theory and research related to family development? Productive work ought to be undertaken in at least six areas. First, greater refinement is needed of the family career paths for modal and other discernible family types. The statistical overview presented in this chapter suggests differences in family development for families who differ by race, marital status, and marriage order. Some of the data, however, can be only speculative until longitudinal research follows cohorts to determine the precise timing of marriage, divorce, remarriage, first and later births, movement in and out of the labor force, and so on. The concepts of the timing and scheduling of status changes, as they differ across historical contexts and across families of different types within the same historical context, need to be integrated into the family development perspective.

Second, attention needs to be paid to the "faces" within family development. The perspective at present, with its concern about positions and roles and their dynamic counterparts, leaves residual the issue of variability in role performance by the incumbents of family positions, namely, the individual family members. How do the personality type and the competence level of family members interact with the developmental process and affect the family's ability to accomplish its tasks?

Third, the concept of *critical transition* requires improved operationalization. What makes a transition critical, and how are such transitions related to development? Is it the pileup of crises that precipitates change over the family life span? Is development a process wherein family equilibrium, with understanding of role scripts by family members, is punctuated by periods of disequilibrium and the rewriting of scripts, which then provide the basis for a new equilibrium? What produces such pileups? How

are they related to the predictable life-course paths of individual family members?

Fourth, much of the imagery of the family cycle is carried over from the life cycle for individuals. How useful is it as a heuristic for describing the curvilinear path of the family's career: progressive differentiation of role structure from simple to complex into the middle of the cycle, accompanied by increasing demands in excess of resources, followed by a process of dismantling the structure, disengaging from commitments, and lowering the demands on resources? What are the chief variables that, in interaction, explain the rise, the inflection point, and the decline that is life-span family-development?

Fifth, a need exists for better direct study of the phenomenon of family development than has occurred to date. Empirical analysis of correlations between family-life-cycle stage and other individual and family achievements (i.e., where family development is an antecedent) is not necessarily equivalent to an empirical analysis of the phenomenon of development itself (i.e., where family development is the dependent variable). Research topics germane to this issue were mentioned earlier, for example, the effects of changing plurality patterns on the emergence and differentiation of roles; intercontingencies of needs among growing family members in reciprocally related positions; and links of developmental task performance throughout the family career. Research along these lines must incorporate the data organized by family historians and reports on other societies: Do life-cycle invariances persist regardless of historical and societal contexts?

Sixth, family development scholars, informed by their gerontological colleagues, need to attend to the understudied—and perhaps misunderstood—last stage of the family career. The postparental family as an empty nest has been treated as the return to simple structure, but viewed from the perspective of parents (now grandparents), is this an apt characterization? The multilayered set of in-law relationships, grandchildren, and even great-grandchildren may introduce new, important sets of role obligations for the "family of gerontation." Are there important role complex changes at this time that amount to a retirement *to* rather than *from* obligations? Do important transactional relationships develop between the nuclear family (now a couple) and other groups or individuals?

Rodgers (1973) concluded his thoughtful treatise on family development with a chapter entitled "The Challenge of an Incomplete Explanation." To paraphrase his concluding remarks, it appears to us that the inadequacies that family development theory represents in its present form, the ignorance that we still recognize about its empirical support, and the general necessity to probe further and to discover whether it makes good sense are all part of its fascination for us. We hope that some readers will pick up the challenge to deal with the theory's shortcomings. That would be a major accomplishment of this 1986 review!

References

Abeles, R. P., & Riley, M. W. A life course perspective on the later years of life: Some implications for research. *Social Science Research Council Annual Report 1976–1977,* 1978, 11–16.

Aldous, J. *Family Careers: Developmental Change in Families.* New York: Wiley, 1978.

Aldous, J., & Hill, R. Breaking the poverty cycle: Strategic points for intervention. *Social Work,* 1969, *14,* 3–12.

Angell, R. O. *The family encounters the depression.* New York: Scribner's, 1936.

Babchuck, N., & Booth, A. Voluntary association membership: A longitundinal analysis. *American Sociological Review,* 1969, *34,* 31–45.

Baldwin, J. M. *Mental development in the child and the race: Methods and processes.* New York: Macmillan, 1906.

Baltes, P. B., & Brim, O. G. *Life span development and behavior* (Vol. 2). New York: Academic Press, 1979.

Baltes, P. B., & Schaie, K. W. (Eds.). *Life span developmental psychology: Personality and socialization.* New York: Academic Press, 1973.

Baltes, P. B., Reese, H. W., & Nesselroade, J. R. *Life-span developmental psychology: Introduction to research methods.* Monterey, Calif.: Brooks/Cole, 1976.

Barnhill, L. R., & Longo, D. Fixation and regression in the family life cycle. *Family Process,* 1978, *17,* 469–478.

Bengtson, V. *Reconstruction of family development theory: An exercise in the study of micro-social organizations through time.* Prepared discussion of the paper by R. Hill & P. Mattessich, *Reconstruction of family development theories,* 1977, Theory Development and Methods Workshop, National Council on Family Relations, San Diego, California, October 11, 1977.

Berkner, L. K. The stem family and the developmental cycle of the peasant household: An eighteenth-century Austrian example. *American Historical Review,* 1972, *77,* 398–418.

Bigelow, H. F. *Family finance.* Philadelphia: Lippincott, 1936.

Blackwell, G. W. Correlates of the state of family development among farm families on relief. *Rural Sociology,* 1942, *17,* 161–174.

Blood, R. *Love-match and arranged marriage: A Tokyo-Detroit comparison.* New York: Free Press, 1967.

Blood, R. O., & Wolfe, D. M. *Husbands and wives.* New York: Free Press, 1960.

Borne, H., Jache, A., Sederberg, N., & Klein, D. *Family chronogram analysis: Toward the development of new methodological tools for assessing the life cycles of families.* Unpublished manuscript presented at annual meeting of National Council on Family Relations, 1979.

Buckley, W. *Sociology and modern systems theory.* New York: Prentice-Hall, 1967.

Bühler, C. *Der menschliche Lebenslauf als psychologisches Problem.* Leipzig: Hirzel, 1933.

Burgess, E. W. The family as a unity of interacting personalities, *The Family,* 1926, *7,* 3–9.

Burgess, E. W., & Wallin, P. *Engagement and marriage.* Philadelphia: Lippincott, 1953.

Buric, O., & Zecevic, A. Family authority, marital satisfaction and the social network in Yugoslavia. *Journal of Marriage and the Family,* 1967, *29,* 325–336.

Campbell, A., Converse, P. E., & Rodgers, W. L. *The quality of American life.* New York: Russell Sage Foundation, 1976.

Caplan, G. *Principles of preventive psychiatry.* New York: Basic Books, 1964.

Card, J. J. Long-term consequences for children of teenage parents. *Demography,* 1981, *18,* 137–156.

Carter, E. A., & McGoldrick, M. The family life cycle and family therapy: An overview. In E. A. Carter & M. McGoldrick (Eds.), *The family life cycle: A framework for family therapy.* New York: Gardner Press, 1980.

Carus, F. A. *Psychologie: Zweiter Theil: Specialpsychologie.* Leipzig: Barth and Kummer, 1808.

Cerny, V., Dahl, N., Kamiko, T., & Aldous, J. International developments in family theory: A continuance of the initial ''pilgrims' progress.'' *Journal of Marriage and the Family,* 1974 (February), *36,* 169–173.

Christensen, H. T. (Ed.). *Handbook of marriage and the family.* Chicago: Rand McNally, 1964.

Clausen, J. A. (Ed.). *Socialization and society.* Boston: Little, Brown, 1968.

Clausen, J. A. The life course of individuals. In M. W. Riley, M. E. Johnson, & A. Foner (Eds.), *Aging and society, Vol. 3: A sociology of age stratification.* New York: Russell Sage Foundation, 1972.

Cuisenier, J. (Ed.). *The family life cycle in European societies.* The Hague: Mouton, 1977.

Desai, I. P. *Some aspects of the family in Mahuva.* Baroda, India: Sadhana Press, 1964.

Deutscher, I. *Married life in the middle years: A study of the middle class urban post-parental couple.* Kansas City: Community Studies, 1959.

Dizard, J. *Social change and the family.* Chicago: University of Chicago Family and Community Study Center, 1968.

Dowhrenwend, B. S., & Dowhrenwend, B. P. (Eds.). *Stressful life events: Their nature and effects.* New York: Wiley, 1974.

Duvall, E. M. *Family development.* Philadelphia: Lippincott, 1957. (Revised editions, 1962, 1967, 1971, 1977.)

Duvall, E. M., & Hill, R. L. *Report of the Committee on the Dynamics of Family Interaction.* Washington, D.C.: National Conference on Family Life, 1948.

Eisenberg, J. G. The welfare children: An overview of longitudinal findings. *Research in Community and Mental Health,* 1979, *1,* 146–156.

Elder, G. H., Jr. *Children of the Great Depression.* Chicago: University of Chicago Press, 1974.

Elder, G. H., Jr. Age differentiation and the life course. In A. Inkeles, J. Coleman, & N. Smelser (Eds.). *Annual review of sociology,* Vol. 1. Palo Alto, Calif.: Annual Reviews, 1975.

Elder, G. H., Jr. Approaches to social change and the family. *American Journal of Sociology,* Supplement, 1978, *84,* S1–S38.

Eliot, T. D. Family crises and ways of meeting them. In H. Becker & R. Hill (Eds.), *Marriage and the family.* Boston: Heath, 1942.

Erikson, E. H. *Childhood and society.* New York: Norton, 1950.

Feldman, H. *The development of husband-wife relationships.* Ithaca, N.Y.: Cornell University, 1964. (Mimeograph)

Feldman, H. The effects of children on the family. In Andreé Michel (Ed.), *Family issues of employed women in Europe and America.* Leiden: Brill, 1971.

Foote, N. N., Abu-Lughod, J., Foley, M. M., & Winnick, L. *Housing choices and housing constraints.* New York: McGraw-Hill, 1960.

Freud, S. *A general introduction to psychoanalysis.* Garden City, N.Y.: Garden City Publishing Company, 1943. (First German edition, 1916.)

Furstenberg, F. F., Jr. Recycling the family: Perspectives for a neglected family form. *Marriage and Family Review,* 1979, *2*(1), 12–22.

Gartner, R. B., Fulmer, R. H., Weinshel, M., & Goldklank, S. The family life cycle: Developmental crises and their structural impact on families in a community mental health center. *Family Process,* 1978, *17,* 47–58.

Gesell, A. *Infancy and human growth.* New York: Macmillan, 1928.

Glick, P. C. The family cycle. *American Sociological Review,* 1947, *12,* 164–174.

Glick, P. C. The life cycle of the family. *Marriage and Family Living,* 1955, *17,* 3–9.

Glick, P. C. Updating the life cycle of the family. *Journal of Marriage and the Family,* 1977, *39,* 5–13.

Goldberg, S. Social competence in infancy. *Merrill-Palmer Quarterly,* 1977, *23,* 163–178.

Goody, J. (Ed.). *Developmental cycle in domestic groups*. Cambridge, England: Cambridge University Press, 1962.

Goulet, L. R., & Baltes, P. B. (Eds.). *Life-span developmental psychology: Research and theory*. New York: Academic Press, 1970.

Gove, W. R., Grimm, J. W., Motz, S. C., & Thompson, J. D. The family life cycle: Internal dynamics and social consequences. *Sociology and Social Research*, 1972, *57*, 182–195.

Haavio-Mannila, E. Family developmental tasks and happiness. In J. Cuisenier (Ed.), *The family life cycle in European societies*. The Hague: Mouton, 1977.

Hadley, T. R., Jacob, T., Milliones, J., Caplan, J., & Spitz, D. The relationship between family developmental crisis and the appearance of symptoms in a family member. *Family Process*, 1974, *13*, 207–214.

Hall, G. S. *Adolescence: Its psychology and its relation to physiology, anthropology, sociology, sex, crime, religion, and education*. New York: Appleton, 1904.

Hall, G. S. *Senescence: The last half of life*. New York: Appleton, 1922.

Hareven, T. K. The family as process: The historical study of the family cycle. *Journal of Social History*, 1974, *7*, 322–329.

Hareven, T. K. The family cycle in historical perspective: A proposal for a developmental approach. In J. Cuisenier (Ed.), *The family life cycle in European societies*. The Hague: Mouton, 1977.

Havighurst, R. J. *Developmental tasks and education*. Chicago: University of Chicago Press, 1948.

Havighurst, R. J. *Human development and education*. New York: Longmans, Green, 1953.

Havighurst, R. J. Research on the developmental task concept. *The School Review*, 1956, *64*, 215–223.

Havighurst, R. J., Prescott, D. A., & Redl, F. Scientific study of developing boys and girls as set up guideposts. In B. C. Johnson (Ed.), *General education in the American high school*. Chicago: Scott, Foresman, 1942.

Hayes, W. C. Theorists and theoretical frameworks identified by family sociologists. *Journal of Marriage and the Family*, 1977, *39*, 59–67.

Hill, R. *Families under stress*. New York: Harper, 1949.

Hill, R. Generic features of families under stress. *Social Casework*, 1958, *49*, 139–150.

Hill, R. Methodological issues in family development research. *Family Process*, 1964, *3*, 186–206.

Hill, R. Sociological frameworks appropriate for family-oriented psychiatry. *Voices: The Art and Science of Psychotherapy*, 1969, *5*, 65–74.

Hill, R. Modern systems theory and the family: A confrontation. *Social Science Information*, 1971(October), *10*, 7–26.

Hill, R. Status of research on families. In U.S. Department of Health and Human Services, *The status of children, youth, and families 1979*. Washington, D.C.: U.S. Government Printing Office, 1980.

Hill, R., & Hanson, D. A. The identification of conceptual frameworks utilized in family study. *Marriage and Family Living*, 1960, *22*, 299–311.

Hill, R., & Joy, C. *Operationalizing the concept of critical transition to generate phases of family development*. Unpublished paper, prepared for planning meetings with Japanese scholars, Kyoto, Japan, December 15, 1980.

Hill, R., & Mattessich, P. *Reconstruction of family development theories: A progress report*. Paper presented at the Theory Development and Methodology Workshop, National Council on Family Relations, Annual Meeting, 1977.

Hill, R., & Mattessich, P. Family development theory and life span development. In P. Baltes & O. Brim (Eds.), *Life span development and behavior*, Vol. 3. New York: Academic Press, 1979.

Hill, R., & Rodgers, R. The developmental approach. In H. Christensen (Ed.), *Handbook of marriage and the family*. Chicago: Rand McNally, 1964.

Hill, R., Foote, N., Aldous, J., Carlson, R., & McDonald, R. *Family de-velopment in three generations: A longitudinal study of changing family patterns of planning and achievement*. Cambridge, Mass.: Schenkman, 1970.

Hirschhorn, L. Social policy and the life cycle: A developmental perspective. *Social Service Review*, 1977, *51*, 434–450.

Hodgson, J. W., & Lewis, R. A. Pilgrims' progress. III: A trend analysis of family theory and methodology. *Family Process*, June 1979, *18*(2), 163–175.

Holman, T. B., & Burr, W. R. Beyond the beyond: The growth of family theories in the 1970s. *Journal of Marriage and the Family*. 1980, *42*, 729–743.

Holmes, T. H., & Rahe, R. H. The social readjustment rating scale. *Journal of Psychosomatic Research*, 1967, *11*, 213–218.

Hooper, J. O., & Hooper, F. H. *Family and individual developmental theories: Conceptual analysis and speculations*. 1980 revision of a paper presented at the Theory and Methods Construction Workshop of the annual meeting of the National Council on Family Relations, August 1979, Boston.

Johnson, R. E., Jr. *Marital patterns during the middle years*. Unpublished Ph.D. dissertation, Minneapolis, University of Minnesota, 1968.

Kamiko, T. The internal structure of the three-generation household. In J. Cuisenier (Ed.), *The family life cycle in European societies*. The Hague: Mouton, 1977.

Kerckhoff, A. C. *Family careers—Some perspectives and proposals*. Unpublished manuscript, Duke University, 1978.

Kirkpatrick, E. L., Cowles, M., & Tough, R. *The life cycle of the farm family*. Research Bulletin No. 121. Madison: University of Wisconsin Agricultural Experiment Station, 1934.

Klein, D., & Aldous, J. Three blind mice: Misleading criticisms of the "family life cycle" concept. *Journal of Marriage and the Family*, 1979, *41*, 689–691.

Klein, D., Schvaneveldt, J. D., & Miller, B. C. The attitudes and activities of contemporary family theorists. *International Journal of the Sociology of the Family*, 1977, *8*, 5–27.

Klein, D., Borne, H., Jache, A., & Sederberg, N. *Family chronogram analysis: Toward the development of new methodological tools for assessing the life cycles of families*. Unpublished manuscript, University of Notre Dame, 1978.

Klein, J. F., Calvert, G. P., Garland, T. N., & Poloma, M. M. Pilgrims' progress. I: Recent developments in family theory. *Journal of Marriage and the Family*, 1969, *31*, 677–687.

Kohlberg, L. *The development of modes of moral thinking and choice in the years 10–16*. Unpublished doctoral dissertation, University of Chicago, 1958.

Kohlberg, L. Stage and sequence: The cognitive-developmental approach to socialization. In D. A. Goslin (Ed.), *Handbook of socialization theory and research*. Chicago: Rand McNally, 1969.

Koyama, T. *The changing social position of women in Japan*. Paris: UNESCO, 1961.

Koyama, T., Morioka, K., & Kumagai, F. *Family and household in changing Japan*. Tokyo: Japan Society for the Promotion of Sciences, 1980.

Kuhlen, R. G. Social change: A neglected factor in psychological studies of the life span. *School and Society*, 1940, *52*, 14–16.

Lansing, J. B., & Kish, L. Family life cycle as an independent variable. *American Sociological Review*, 1957, *22*, 512–519.

LePlae, C. Structure des tâches domestiques et du pouvoir de décision de la dyade conjugale. In P. de Bie, K. Dobbelaere, C. Le Plae, & J. Piel (Eds.), *La dyade conjugale: Étude sociologique*. Brussels, Belgium: Les Éditions de Vie Ouvrière, 1968.

Lerner, R. M. *Concepts and theories of human development*. Reading, Mass.: Addison-Wesley, 1976.

Lerner, R. M., & Spanier, G. B. (Eds.). *Child influences on marital and family interaction: A life span perspective.* New York: Academic Press, 1978.

Levinson, D. *The seasons of a man's life.* New York: Knopf, 1978.

Lindemann, E. Symptomatology and management of acute grief. *American Journal of Psychiatry,* 1944, *101,* 141–148.

Lively, C. E. *The growth cycle of the farm family* (Bulletin No. 51). Wooster: Ohio Agricultural Experiment Station, 1932.

Looft, W. Socialization and personality throughout the life span: An examination of contemporary psychological approaches. In P. Baltes & K. W. Schaie (Eds.), *Life span developmental psychology: Personality and socialization.* New York: Academic Press, 1973.

Loomis, C. P. *The growth of the farm family in relation to its activities.* Raleigh: North Carolina State College Agricultural Experiment Station, 1934.

Magrabi, F. M., & Marshall, W. H. Family developmental tasks: A research model. *Journal of Marriage and the Family,* 1965, *27,* 454–461.

Mattessich, P. *Family impact analysis.* St. Paul: Minnesota State Planning Agency, 1976.

Mattessich, P. *Kin, friends, voluntary associations: A study of participation in family and non-family networks.* Unpublished Ph.D. dissertation, University of Minnesota, 1977.

Mattessich, P. Childlessness and its correlates in historical perspective. *Journal of Family History,* 1979, *4,* 299–307.

McCubbin, H. Integrating coping behavior in family stress theory. *Journal of Marriage and the Family,* 1979, *41,* 237–244.

McCubbin, H., Joy, C. B., Cauble, A. E., Comeau, J. K., Patterson, J. M., & Needle, R. H. Family stress and coping: A decade review. *Journal of Marriage and the Family,* 1980, *42,* 855–872.

Mead, G. H. The social self. *Journal of Philosophy,* 1913, *10,* 374–380.

Michel, A. Comparative data concerning the interaction in French and American families. *Journal of Marriage and the Family,* 1967, *29,* 337–344.

Miller, B. C. A multivariate developmental model of marital satisfaction. *Journal of Marriage and the Family,* 1976, *38,* 643–657.

Modell, J., Furstenberg, F., & Hesberg, T. Social change and transitions to adulthood in historical perspective. *Journal of Family History,* 1976, *1,* 7–34.

Mogey, J. M. *Sociology of marriage and family behavior 1957–1968: A trend report and bibliography.* The Hague: Mouton, 1971.

Nisbet, R. A. *Social change and history: Aspects of the Western theory of development.* New York: Oxford University Press, 1969.

Nock, S. L. The family life cycle: Empirical or conceptual tool? *Journal of Marriage and the Family,* 1979, *41,* 15–26.

Paris, B. L., & Luckey, E. B. A longitudinal study in marital satisfaction. *Sociological and Social Research,* 1966, *50,* 212–222.

Parsons, T. *Essays in sociological theory: Pure and applied.* Glencoe, Ill.: Free Press, 1949.

Piaget, J. *Le language et la pensée chez l'enfant.* Neuchâtel: Delachaux & Niestlé, 1923.

Pineo, P. C. Disenchantment in the later years of marriage. *Marriage and Family Living,* 1961 (February), *23,* 3–11.

Pressey, S. L., Janney, J. E., & Kuhlen, R. G. *Life: A psychological survey.* New York: Harper, 1939.

Quetelet, A. *Sur l'homme et le développement de ses facultés, ou essai de physique sociale.* Paris: Bachelier, 1835.

Rapoport, R. Normal crises, family structure, and mental health. *Family Process,* 1963, *2,* 68–80.

Rapoport, R., & Rapoport, R. N. *Leisure and the family life cycle.* London: Routledge & Kegan Paul, 1975.

Rawlings, S. W. Families maintained by female householders. *Current Population Reports, Special Studies,* Series P-23, No. 107. Washington, D.C.: U.S. Government Printing Office, 1980.

Riley, M. W., & Foner, A. *Aging and society: Vol. 1. An inventory of research findings.* New York: Russell Sage Foundation, 1968.

Riley, M. W., Johnson, M. E., & Foner, A. (Eds.). *Aging and society: A sociology of age stratification,* Vol. 3. New York: Russell Sage Foundation, 1972.

Rodgers, R. H. *Improvements in the construction and analysis of family life cycle categories.* Kalamazoo: Western Michigan University, 1962.

Rodgers, R. H. Family developmental tasks: A research model. *Journal of Marriage and the Family,* 1965, *27,* 458–461.

Rodgers, R. H. *Family interaction and transaction: The developmental approach.* New York: Prentice-Hall, 1973.

Rodgers, R. H. The family life cycle concept: Past, present, and future. In J. Cuisenier (Ed.), *The family life cycle in European societies.* The Hague: Mouton, 1977.

Rollins, B., & Feldman, H. Marital satisfaction over the family life cycle. *Journal of Marriage and the Family,* 1970, *32,* 20–27.

Rossi, A. S. Aging and parenthood in the middle years. In P. B. Baltes & O. G. Brim, Jr. (Eds.), *Life span development and behavior,* Vol. 3. New York: Academic Press, 1980.

Rowe, G. P. The developmental conceptual framework to the study of the family. In I. Nye & F. Berardo (Eds.), *Emerging conceptual frameworks in family analysis.* New York: Macmillan, 1966.

Rowntree, B. S. *Poverty: A study of town life.* London: Macmillan, 1906.

Ryder, R. Longitudinal data relating marital satisfaction and having a child. *Journal of Marriage and the Family,* 1973, *35,* 604–606.

Saunders, L. Empathy, communication, and the definition of life's satisfaction in the post-parental period. *Family Perspectives,* 1974, *8,* 21–35.

Shafer, R. B., & Keith, P. M. Equity in marital roles across the family life cycle. *Journal of Marriage and the Family,* 1981, *43,* 359–368.

Silverman, W., & Hill, R. Task allocation in marriage in the United States and Belgium. *Journal of Marriage and the Family,* 1967, *29,* 353–359.

Solomon, M. A. A developmental conceptual premise for family therapy. *Family Process,* 1973, *12,* 179–188.

Sorokin, P. A., Zimmerman, C. C., & Galpin, C. J. *A systematic sourcebook in rural sociology,* Vol. 2. Minneapolis: University of Minnesota Press, 1931.

Spanier, G. B., & Glick, P. C. The life cycle of American families: An expanded analysis. *Journal of Family History,* 1980, *5,* 97–111.

Spanier, G. B., Lewis, R. A., & Cole, C. L. Marital adjustment over the family life cycle: The issue of curvilinearity. *Journal of Marriage and the Family,* 1975, *37,* 265–275.

Spanier, G. B., Sauer, W., & Larzelere, R. An empirical evaluation of the family life cycle. *Journal of Marriage and Family,* 1979, *41,* 27–38.

Steinglass, P. A life history model of the alcoholic family. *Family Process,* 1980, *19,* 211–226.

Stolte-Heiskanen, V. Social indicators for analysis of family needs related to the life cycle. *Journal of Marriage and the Family,* 1974, *36,* 592–600.

Stolte-Heiskanen, V. Family needs and societal institutions: Potential empirical linkage mechanisms. *Journal of Marriage and the Family,* 1975, *37,* 903–916.

Streib, G. F., & Thompson, W. E. (Eds.). Adjustment in retirement. *Journal of Social Issues,* 1958, *14,* 1–63.

Sullivan, H. S. *Conceptions of modern psychiatry.* Washington, D.C.: William Alanson White Psychiatric Foundation, 1947.

Szalai, A. (Ed.). *The use of time.* The Hague: Mouton, 1972.

Terkelsen, K. G. Toward a theory of the family life cycle. In E. A. Carter & M. McGoldrick (Eds.), *The family life cycle: A framework for family therapy.* New York: Gardner Press, 1980.

Tetens, J. N. *Philosophische Versuche über die menschliche Natur und ihre Entwicklung.* Leipzig: Weidmanns Erben and Reich, 1777.

Thomas, W. I., & Znaniecki, F. *The Polish peasant in Europe and*

America, Vols. 1 and 2. Chicago: University of Chicago Press, 1918–1920.

Trost, J. The family life cycle: A problematic concept. In J. Cuisenier (Ed.), *The family life cycle in European societies*. The Hague: Mouton, 1977.

Uhlenberg, P. Cohort variations in family life experiences of U.S. females. *Journal of Marriage and the Family*, 1974, *36*, 284–289.

U.S. Bureau of the Census. Marriage, divorce, widowhood and remarriage by family characteristics, Tables 6 and 7. *Current Population Reports*, Series P-20. No. 312. Washington, D.C.: U.S. Government Printing Office, 1977.

Veroff, J., & Feld, S. *Marriage and work in America*. New York: Van Nostrand Reinhold, 1970.

Voydanoff, P. *The implications of work-family relationships for productivity*. Scarsdale, N.Y.: Work in American Institute, 1979.

Waite, L. J. Working wives and the family life cycle. *American Jornal of Sociology*, 1980, *86*, 272–294.

Waller, W. *The family: A dynamic interpretation*. New York: Dryden, 1938.

Weed, J. A. *National estimates of marriage dissolution and survivorship: United States*. Hyattsville, Md.: National Center for Health Statistics, Vital and Health Statistics, Series 3, Analytic studies, No. 19, November 1980.

Werner, H. *Comparative psychology of mental development*. New York: International Universities Press, 1948.

Williams, K. M. *Remarriages: United States*. Rockville, Md.: U.S. National Center for Health Statistics, Series 21, No. 25, December 1973.

CHAPTER 18

Parent–Child Socialization

Gary W. Peterson and Boyd C. Rollins

Introduction

The parent–child relationship initiates a child into the social world and reshapes components of the adult self-concept into identification with parental roles. Much of what occurs between parents and children transforms a biological organism into a human being and confronts adults with a new set of experiences and responsibilities. Through this facet of the socialization process, parents and children acquire the knowledge, attitudes, skills, values, and expectations that allow them to become increasingly integrated into new social relationships.

Since the 1940s, periodic changes have occurred in the research approaches and the theoretical frameworks used in the study of parent–child socialization. Reviewers of the parent–child research in the 1940s and 1950s concluded that little support existed for the psychoanalytic position that maternal styles of caregiving, feeding, weaning, and toilet training shaped the personality development of young children (Orlansky, 1949; Sewell, 1952; Zigler & Child, 1973). In the subsequent two decades, therefore, studies conducted in the parent–child area used approaches derived from the social learning, observational learning, and social power orientations to examine the influence of parental characteristics on children's social and personality outcomes (Bandura, 1976; Bandura & Walters, 1963; Dager, 1964; M. L. Hoffman, 1970, 1980; Maccoby & Martin, 1983; McDonald, 1977, 1979, 1980; Rollins & Thomas, 1975, 1979; Sears, Maccoby, & Levin, 1957; Sears, Whiting, Nowlis, & Sears, 1953; Smith, 1970; Steinmetz, 1979).

Despite such changes, these approaches have been subjected to increasing criticism because all assume that parents "socially mold" their offspring (Bell & Harper, 1977; Hartup, 1978; Hill, 1981). Disillusionment with the assumption that socialization is a unidirectional process indicates that a major effort is under way to reconceptualize the parent–child relationship (Bell, 1968; Walters & Walters, 1980; Wrong, 1961). Increasingly, parent–child socialization has been viewed as a mutual or bidirectional process between the participants, rather than as a unilateral process in which children are molded by adults (Cogswell, 1974). Although over three decades ago, Robert Sears (1951) advocated that investigators begin to address bidirectional models, research reflecting this orientation was virtually nonexistent until the late 1960s and the early 1970s.

Even more recently, another perspective has arisen that proposes that the study of parent–child relations should be expanded beyond dyadic phenomena (Belsky, 1981; Bronfenbrenner, 1979; Klein, Jorgensen, & Miller, 1978; Lewis & Feiring, 1978; Rollins & Galligan, 1978). Those who advocate this approach have concentrated on various social contexts of the parent–child dyad and the interrelated or systemic character of the networks that impinge on and encompass the parent–child relationship. Sources of social influence that originate beyond face-to-face encounters of parents and children have been a focus of this perspective. That is, the parent–child dyad is viewed in terms of such contexts as the parent's marital relationship, sibling relationships, extended kinship ties, the neighborhood, ethnic identification, and interdependence with relevant economic, political, educational, and religious institutions.

Because the study of parent–child relations is in a state of transition, the purpose of this chapter is to review and integrate the social mold, bidirectional, and systemic literatures within the parent–child area. Part of this task involves the application of concepts from the symbolic interaction framework, a sociological perspective used extensively to interpret family structure and interaction (Burr, Leigh, Day, & Constantine, 1979; Holman & Burr, 1980). Concepts from this framework are useful for integrating parent–child research in terms of a "family" perspective and its surrounding social networks.

A related purpose is to reevaluate the existing division of labor between psychologists and sociologists in the study of parent–child relations and the family (Aldous, 1977). That is, psychologists have concentrated on the parent–child dyad, whereas sociologists have focused on the marital dyad. A working arrangement of this kind is

Gary W. Peterson • Department of Child and Family Studies, University of Tennessee, Knoxville, TN 37916. **Boyd C. Rollins** • Department of Sociology, Brigham Young University, Provo, UT 84602. Research support to write this chapter was provided by the Agriculture Experiment Station, University of Tennessee, Knoxville.

unfortunate because conceptual frameworks from sociology are useful for organizing and interpreting much of the bidirectional and systemic research that psychologists have recently conducted. Consequently, the scholarship of these two disciplines in the parent–child area is complementary and should be brought to bear on common issues (Belsky, 1981; Hartup, 1978; Osofsky & Connors, 1979; Parke, 1978).

Following a brief introduction to the symbolic interaction perspective, two major sections on parent–child socialization are presented in this chapter. The first section is concerned with the social mold perspective, and the bidirectional-systemic literature is dealt with in the second section. Concepts from the symbolic interaction perspective are used to interpret the literature reviewed in these sections.

Symbolic Interaction and the Parent–Child Dyad

The symbolic interaction framework was developed out of seminal scholarship by William James, John Dewey, Charles Horton Cooley, W. I. Thomas, and George Herbert Mead (Blumer, 1969; Mains & Meltzer, 1978; Meltzer, Petras, & Reynolds, 1975; Stryker, 1980). Perhaps the basic idea from this perspective is that humans live in a symbolic environment as well as a physical environment. From this perspective, humans are best understood by dealing with the mentalistic symbols and values that influence their interaction within social groups. That is, a dialectical process between individuals and society occurs because the symbols to which humans respond, in turn, emerge from the shared interaction of individuals. Thus, both individual and society are inextricably linked, and each is a product of the other (Berger & Luckman, 1967; Blumer, 1969; Burr *et al.*, 1979; Meltzer *et al.*, 1975; Stryker, 1980).

In family interaction, complex sets of meanings are learned that allow family members to communicate, share experiences, and involve two or more persons in an especially intense social process (Burr *et al.*, 1979; Turner, 1970). Parents, for example, often use words and gestures that express endearment or are intended to control their children. The young, in turn, may respond with meaningful expressions of affection or with counter-control attempts used to assert their independence. The important point here is that parents and children have the ability to share common meanings and to role-take each other. Role taking, then, involves the capacity of individual family members to view both the social world and themselves from the perspective of the other family members. The ability to role-take each other and to share meanings allows them to anticipate the others' responses and to develop a social relationship of special intensity.

Parents and children often define each other as significant others, that is, persons with whom they have an affectionate bond and to whose expectations they assign

special importance. From a young child's perspective, parents attain this status because they control a vast array of resources, including the ability to nurture, to provide for the child's physical welfare, and to offer information in many areas. Parents, on the other hand, define children as significant others because their presence alters many life experiences and adds entirely new dimensions to their self-concepts (LaRossa & LaRossa, 1981; LeMasters, 1974; Turner, 1970).

From a symbolic interaction perspective, parent–child interactions contribute to the emergence of mutually shared norms and expectations. Parents and children perform roles to the extent that sets of expectations begin to guide or constrain their behaviors in the parent–child relationship. Most parents, for example, become responsive to the expectations of their children and other social agents to provide comfort, nurturance, encouragement, and companionship within the parent–child relationship. Such expectations become components of the child socializer role. Likewise, many children occupy a child socializee role by becoming responsive to expectations that they will comform to their parents' wishes, achieve tasks valued by their parents, and be considerate of others.

If parent–child socialization is effective, the taking on and performance of roles in this manner become important components of the self (Cogswell, 1974). That is, adults now ascribe new social definitions to themselves: They are now ''fathers'' and ''mothers,'' with all the responsibilities and rewards of these positions. Children, on the other hand, evolve self-definitions that reflect how well they are ''minding'' and how well they are meeting their parents' achievement expectations.

In addition to considering the ''structured'' aspects of parent–child roles, it is equally important to view children and parents as actors having considerable capacities to restructure their social environments. In other words, there is considerable room for individual differences and innovation because roles provide only general guidelines for interaction, not clear-cut scripts. Much of parent–child interaction, therefore, involves role making, that is, the process of improvising, exploring, and judging what is appropriate on the basis of the situation and the responses of others at the moment (Turner, 1962). Simply stated, expectations are not very clear on such issues as (1) when children should be punished; (2) what form the punishment should take; (3) whether one can ever give a child too much love; and (4) how much achievement pressure is appropriate. Given this lack of clarity, the first phase of interaction between parents and children often involves the establishment of temporary ''definitions of the situation.'' This phase is followed by tentative, probing actions by parents and children, which allow their definitions to be tested against reality and reformulated on the basis of experience.

A wide range of research methodologies are accommodated by the foregoing discussion of symbolic interaction concepts and the recognition that parent–child socialization consists of both "structured" role relations and "dynamic" processes. Contrary to some interpretations of symbolic interaction (Blumer, 1969; Kuhn, 1964), we have taken the position that parent–child research conceptualized in terms of symbolic interaction can benefit from the use of quantitative and qualitative research techniques. That is, parent–child research has benefited and should continue to profit from the use of such quantitative methodologies as experimental designs, scale construction, operational definitions, statistical analyses, survey research, and behavioral observation. This is especially the case when the "structured" aspects of parent–child relations are the subject of study (see Acock & Bengtson, 1980; Gecas, 1976; Steffensmeier, 1982). Qualitative research methodologies, on the other hand, are especially useful for exploring more dynamic processes, for gaining in-depth insights into the experiences of research participants, and for conducting exploratory research. This may include such techniques as participant observation, naturalistic observation, and in-depth interviews (Denzin, 1977; LaRossa & LaRossa, 1981; Lofland, 1976). Because symbolic interaction places emphasis on both the public behavior and the subjective meaning of interaction for the participants, a multiple-methods approach may be necessary to assess these two dimensions (Denzin, 1977; Thomas, Peterson, & Rollins, 1977).

These initial comments about the symbolic interaction perspective only begin to illustrate how this framework can be applied to the parent–child relationship. Subsequent sections of this chapter use concepts from this framework to organize and interpret literature from the social mold, bidirectional, and systemic perspectives.

The Social Mold Tradition

The study of socialization and the parent–child relationship within families was dominated for many years by unidirectional or social mold conceptualizations. Consideration is given in this section to the influence of parental characteristics on the social and personality characteristics of children. Initially this review covers research on parental behavior and parental child-rearing typologies (Baumrind, 1967, 1971; Becker, 1964; M. L. Hoffman, 1970, 1980; Martin, 1975; Rollins & Thomas, 1975; Steinmetz, 1979); parental power (McDonald, 1977, 1979, 1980; Peterson, Rollins, & Thomas, 1985; Smith, 1970); observational learning (Bandura, 1976); and generational transmission (Acock & Bengtson, 1978, 1980; Bengtson & Troll, 1978). Also discussed are the larger social contexts that influence parent–child socialization and that are conceptualized in terms of the social mold perspective: culture (McAdoo, 1978; Mindel & Habenstein, 1975; Peters, 1981b; Staples & Mirandé, 1980); social class (Bernstein, 1964, 1971, 1973; Bronfenbrenner, 1958; Gecas, 1979; Kohn, 1977); history (Elder, 1974, 1981); family structure (Kidwell, 1981;

Schooler, 1972); and gender (Baumrind, 1980; Hoffman, 1977; Maccoby & Jacklin, 1974).

Parental Characteristics and Child Outcomes

The greatest concentration by researchers within the social mold perspective has been given to the parental characteristics and child-rearing behaviors that influence the social and personality development of children. Conceptualized in terms of the symbolic interaction perspective, parents can be viewed as occupying and performing the child socializer role, whereas children are viewed as enacting the child socializee role.

The parents' performance of child socializer roles involves the demonstration of characteristics and behavior that influence children (either consciously or unconsciously) to enact and identify with the child socializee roles. Conceptualized in this manner, children are recipients of socialization who respond to parental expectations for compliance, independence, achievement, and moral behavior.

Child-Rearing Behavior and the Consequences for Children. Much of the research within the social mold perspective has been designed to examine a variety of typologies and dimensions of parental behavior that predict the personality characteristics of and the social outcomes for children. Various psychoanalytic, social learning, and eclectic paradigms have been used to conceptualize the results of this research (Baumrind, 1978; Becker, 1964; M. L. Hoffman, 1970, 1980; Martin, 1975; Rollins & Thomas, 1975, 1979; Schaefer, 1959, 1965; Sears et al., 1957; Sears, Rau, & Alpert, 1965; Shaffer & Brody, 1981; Steinmetz, 1979). The research methodologies have included interviews, self-report questionnaires, and behavior observation. Since the 1940s, numerous studies have consistently identified parental support and control as two generic components of the child socializer role that predict children's performance of the child socializee role (Baumrind, 1966; Becker, 1964; M. L. Hoffman, 1970; Maccoby, 1961; Martin, 1975; Rollins & Thomas, 1975, 1979; Schaefer, 1959; Steinmetz, 1979). Such behaviors are gestures or significant symbols that convey expectations and meaning to children during the socialization process.

The first behavior dimension of the child socializer role is parental support (M. L. Hoffman, 1970, 1980; Rollins & Thomas, 1975, 1979). Other labels for this concept in the parent–child research include *warmth, affection, nurturance,* or *acceptance* (Becker, 1964; Martin, 1975; Schaefer, 1959; Siegelman, 1965). For the most part, parental support has been studied as a unitary dimension. More recent studies, however, have identified several subdimensions of this variable, including companionship, physical affection, rejection, and general support (Ellis, Thomas, & Rollins, 1976; Peterson, Rollins, Thomas, & Ellis, 1980).

Parental support can be viewed as a gesture or a significant symbol communicating that both the child's "self" and the child's actions are valued by the parents. Parents use supportive behavior as a means of encouraging and assigning significance to specific behaviors and internal states of children. Support fosters child behavior that is consistent with parental expectations, that solidifies the parent–child bond, and that enhances the self-image of children.

The second behavioral dimension of the child socializer role, parental control, has been conceptualized in a variety of ways. These interpretations of control include (1) specific behavioral actions or attempts to influence children; (2) the result or outcome of attempts to control children (that is, whether a parent's control attempt actually influences the child); and (3) a general controlling atmosphere (or rule structure) that parents establish in the parent–child relationship (Baumrind, 1966, 1971; Becker, 1964; Maccoby, 1961; Rollins & Thomas, 1979; Schaefer, 1959, 1965; Symonds, 1939).

Despite this conceptual confusion, the most common definitions of control refer to actions used by parents while attempting to modify the behavior and the internal states of children. Much of the parent–child research on parental discipline, induction, dominance, restrictiveness, coercion, and power assertion is concerned with overt influence attempts that parents direct at children. A review of the parent–child research by Rollins and Thomas (1979) referred to this dimension of the child socializer role as "parental control attempts."

A continual problem in the control dimension has been the large number of inconsistent findings for this variable in relation to a variety of child outcomes (Rollins & Thomas, 1979; Thomas, Gecas, Weigert, & Rooney, 1974; Watson, 1957; Yarrow, Campbell, & Burton, 1968). For example, several studies have provided evidence of negative relationships between parental control attempts and children's academic achievement (Jones, 1955; Kagan & Moss, 1962; Kimball, 1953; Morrow & Wilson, 1961; Shaw & Dutton, 1962; Walsh, 1956), whereas other investigators have reported positive relationships (Drews & Teahan, 1957; M. L. Hoffman, 1960; Maccoby, 1961; McCelland, Atkinson, Clark, & Lowell, 1953).

Replication problems have led to several efforts at reconceptualizing the parental control dimension (M. L. Hoffman, 1970, 1980; Maccoby, 1961; Martin, 1975; Rollins & Thomas, 1979; Schaefer, 1959, 1965). One method of addressing this issue has been to examine whether qualitatively different types of control attempts may relate differently to child outcomes. To accomplish this goal, investigators have repeatedly identified three subdimensions of parental control attempts: induction, coercion, and love withdrawal (M. L. Hoffman, 1970, 1980; Rollins & Thomas, 1975, 1979; Staub, 1979).

Parental induction (or love-oriented positive discipline) is an influence attempt by parents that places rational maturity demands on children, offers explanations, and makes children aware that their actions have consequences for others (M. L. Hoffman, 1970; Rollins & Thomas, 1979; Steinmetz, 1979). From a symbolic interactionist perspective, parental induction functions as an information-giving mechanism that communicates parental confidence in the eventual ability of the children to understand and cope successfully with their social and physical contexts. Parental induction encourages role taking in children by providing them with information about the parents' inner experiences, their expectations, and their rationale for their child-rearing actions. It also serves as a primary mechanism through which parents communicate, justify, and encourage the internalization of role expectations (Aronfreed, 1969; M. L. Hoffman, 1980; Staub, 1979).

Another parental control attempt, parental coercion (or power assertion), is the direct and arbitrary application of force (M. L. Hoffman, 1970; Rollins & Thomas, 1979; Steinmetz, 1979). The frequent use of coercion by parents communicates rejection of the child and a low valuation of the child's "self." In contrast to induction, coercion does not communicate the logic underlying a parent's expectations for performance of the child socializee role. Children who are exposed to high levels of coercion often develop values and expectations that differ widely from those of their parents.

A final subdimension, love withdrawal, is a control attempt that threatens to withdraw or temporarily discontinue the affectionate bond with a child (M. L. Hoffman, 1980; Steinmetz, 1979). In other words, this dimension of the child socializer role threatens the bond between parent and child by communicating that the child's "self" and behavior are being rejected (M. L. Hoffman, 1980; Sears *et al.*, 1965; Steinmetz, 1979). Love withdrawal communicates that children must correct a deficiency in their role enactment before a reinstatement of the affectionate bond between parent and child can occur.

Combinations of Parental Behavior. In addition to identifying various subdimensions of parental control, investigators have attempted to resolve inconsistencies in the research by developing models that combine into parental styles certain kinds of parental control attempts and support: A variety of parental styles, therefore, have been conceptualized in which a blend or mix of control and support are used to perform the child socializer role. For example, Baumrind (1967, 1971, 1978) identified "authoritative" as one style that combines high levels of inductive control attempts, maturity demands, and parental support. Authoritative parenting has been found to predict higher levels of children's instrumental competence than either the "permissive" (high support, low control attempts, and low maturity demands) or the "authoritarian" (high coercive control attempts, low support, and low inductive control attempts) parental styles.

Another procedure for examining the combined effects of control and support within the child socializer role has been the development of configurational or circumplex

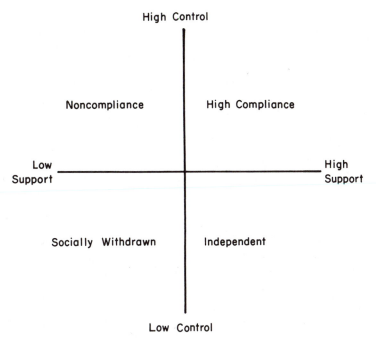

Figure 1. A circumplex model of parental support, control, and child outcomes.

models using multidimensional classification schemes (Becker, 1964; Schaefer, 1959; Straus, 1964; Thomas *et al.*, 1974). Models of this kind have been used to conceptualize the four combinations of levels of parental support and control variables when these variables intersect (and are dichotomized) in two-dimensional space (see Figure 1). These models allow researchers to illustrate how combinations of certain levels of control and support "interact" to produce different outcomes in children. That is, high control and high support might produce high compliance; high control and low support might produce noncompliance; low control and low support might produce social withdrawal; and low control and high support might produce independence in children. The effect of different levels of variables in this combined manner has been referred to as *multiplicative interaction* (Martin, 1975; Rollins & Thomas, 1975, 1979).

Consistent with these ideas, Symonds (1939) set the stage for a complex theory of parental influence on children by suggesting that multiplicative interaction, as well as the additive effects of two or more orthogonal parental behaviors, might predict child outcomes. In this case, the independent variables forming an intersecting circumplex model were parental acceptance–rejection (support) and dominance–submission (control). Becker (1964), on the other hand, extended Symonds's two-dimensional model to a three-dimensional circumplex model of parental behavior that identified warmth–hostility (support), restrictive–permissive (control), and anxious-involvement–calm-detachment as generic parental behaviors

that interact in multiplicative fashion to influence child outcomes. A similar classification scheme is Schaefer's (1965) acceptance–rejection, firm-control–lax-control, and psychological-autonomy–psychological-control dimensions. Closely paralleling the work of Symonds and Schaefer are Siegelman's loving, demanding, and punishing variables (1965).

Besides the development of circumplex models, direct statistical tests have been conducted for multiplicative interaction between parental control and parental support. In a study by Heilbrun and Waters (1968), for example, combinations of high parental support and control were the best predictors of academic achievement in children. By contrast, the relationships between parental support and academic achievement were absent when parents used low levels of control.

A focus on multiplicative interaction and combinations of parental behavior is especially consistent with the symbolic interaction perspective. For example, inductive control attempts combined with high levels of support from parents facilitate role-taking accuracy in the child, maintain a positive affective bond between parent and child, and promote the child's self-esteem. Consequently, tests for multiplicative interaction effects are realistic representations of the complexities involved in performing child socializer roles.

The Child Socializee Role. Investigators using a social mold perspective have concentrated on the effects that dimensions of the child socializer role (performed by parents) have on the social and personality outcomes of children. As a means of conceptualizing child outcomes in terms of symbolic interaction concepts, a specification of the child socializee role is required. To accomplish this, children are viewed in the symbolic interaction framework as being influenced by parents to adjust (1) their self-conceptions; (2) their covert role expectations; and (3) their role behavior within the child socializee role. Many of the dependent variables that are examined in the parent–child research can be reconceptualized in terms of these ideas from the symbolic interaction perspective. Dependent variables have included identification with and dependency on parents (Sears *et al.*, 1957, 1965; Steinmetz, 1979); moral development (M. L. Hoffman, 1970, 1980; Staub, 1979); conformity to parents (Heilbrun & Waters, 1968; Peterson, 1978; Thomas *et al.*, 1974); self-esteem (Coopersmith, 1967; Gecas, 1971; Peterson, Southworth, & Peters, 1982; Thomas *et al.*, 1974); and independence (Martin, 1975; Peterson, 1977).

For example, investigators have examined child-rearing behaviors that predict the identification of children with their parents (Sears *et al.*, 1965). The concept of identification closely parallels the process through which children come to define their parents as significant others, whose expectations they become responsive to. Furthermore, symbolic interaction concepts and the study of children's moral development share a focus on the development of role-taking abilities that allow a person to understand and empathize with the covert experiences of others. These developments, in turn, may be necessary for the development of a moral conscience that is sensitive to the needs and experiences of others.

Children's conformity to their parents is another component of the child socializee role. Investigators of socialization frequently propose that effective socialization involves the development of conformity (Hogan, Johnson, & Ember, 1978; Inkeles, 1968), or responsiveness to the role expectations of social agents (e.g., parents). Later, as development progresses, youthful occupants of the child socializee role increasingly become exposed to expectations requiring less conformity to parents, greater independent decision-making, and greater identification with roles outside the family of origin (e.g., roles in the peer group). Such features of the child socializee role are consistent with the literature on the development of independence in the young.

Another component of the child socializee role is concerned with the common focus of the symbolic interaction and parent–child literatures on children's self-esteem. Symbolic interaction, of course, is especially attentive to the emergence of thoughts and evaluations about the "self" and the interactive processes that contribute to its development. The self or self-esteem of children is partially a product of identifying with and evaluating themselves as occupants of the child socializee role.

The foregoing discussion, therefore, illustrates that several child outcomes from the social mold literature are congruent with the symbolic interaction perspective. Specifically, several dependent variables used in the parent–child research can be viewed as falling within the parameters of the child socializee role.

Parental Antecedents and Child Outcomes. Perhaps the most important issues of the social mold research have been concerned with the relationships between components of the parent's child-rearing performance (of the child socializer role) and the child's social and personality outcomes (child socializee role). Several reviews of research on the correlates of parental support and control have appeared in the literature (Baumrind, 1967, 1972; Becker, 1964; Goldin, 1969; M. L. Hoffman, 1970, 1980; Maccoby, 1961; Martin, 1975; Rollins & Thomas, 1975, 1979; Shaffer & Brody, 1981; Staub, 1979; Steinmetz, 1979; Streissguth & Bee, 1972; Walters & Stinnett, 1971). Despite replication problems, recent reviews of this research have identified several empirical generalizations. Only the major contours of this research are described in this chapter because reviews can be found elsewhere (see especially Maccoby & Martin, 1983; Martin, 1975; Rollins & Thomas, 1979; Shaffer & Brody, 1981; Steinmetz, 1979).

Most of the studies have examined parental behaviors that are hypothesized to predict the self-esteem, achievement, aggression, conformity, morality, dependence, antisocial behavior, and independence of children (Baumrind, 1972, 1978; Thomas *et al.*, 1974). Several of these child-outcome variables define the degree to which children are "socially competent" within the child socializee role. This multidimensional "complex" of child outcomes, referred to as *social competence,* is concerned with the child's relative ability to function effectively within long-term reciprocal role relationships. Thus, young people are socially competent when they demonstrate high levels of self-esteem, conformity to (cooperation with) significant others, moral development, independence, achievement, and internality in locus of control. All of these qualities tend to be consistent with mainstream American values, and parents often desire their children to acquire them (Baumrind, 1972, 1978; Rollins & Thomas, 1979). In contrast, children are less competent within the child socializee role when they are low in these qualities, display substantial antisocial behavior, and/or have identifiable personality disorders. Social competence can be operationalized for research by using its subdimensions as separate dependent variables.

In a review of the parent–child literature, Rollins and Thomas (1979) concluded that empirical evidence on the relationship between parental support and several dimensions of social competence justified the proposition that *the greater the amount of parental support, the greater the amount of children's social competence* (see also Becker, 1964; M. L. Hoffman, 1970, 1980; Maccoby, 1980; Maccoby & Martin, 1983; Martin, 1975; Rollins & Thomas, 1975). Despite substantial agreement on this principle, Baumrind (1980) qualified this generalization by indicating that high levels of maternal nurturance (support) may inhibit the independence and the intellectual achievement of girls. A qualification of this kind suggests that maternal support may be related to dimensions of social competence in a curvilinear manner. In other words, a positive relationship appears as maternal support increases from low to moderate levels, and a negative relationship emerges as higher levels of maternal support become evident. Parental support also may serve as a background variable that enhances the relationship between parental control (see Schaffer & Brody, 1981) and certain aspects of the child socializee role, such as moral development and conformity (see Heilbrun & Waters, 1968; Sears *et al.*, 1957; Yarrow, Scott, & Waxler, 1973). Thus, in addition to the separate or additive effects of parental support, a multiplicative interaction effect between support and control needs to be considered in predicting child outcome variables.

The relationship between different types of parental control attempts and child outcomes has also been a prominent focus within the social mold research. For instance, several reviewers (M. L. Hoffman, 1980; Martin, 1975; Rollins & Thomas, 1979; Steinmetz, 1979) have concluded that parental coercion (or power assertion and physical punishment) exhibits a negative relationship with several dimensions of social competence. This has especially been the case in studies on parental coercion as a predictor of moral internalization, self-esteem, and conformity (Coopersmith, 1967; Hoffman & Saltzstein, 1967; Peterson, Rollins & Thomas, 1981; Staub, 1979). Moreover, several studies reviewed by Rollins and Thomas (1979) indicated that parental coercion is related positively to the development of antisocial aggression—a variable that contributes to low social competence when it reaches higher levels.

Another dimension of the child socializer role, parental induction (or positive love-oriented discipline), exhibits a positive relationship with certain dimensions of social competence. Dependent variables such as conformity to parents, self-esteem, and moral internalization are reported as being related positively to parental induction (M. L. Hoffman, 1970, 1980; Rollins & Thomas, 1979; Shaffer & Brody, 1981; Staub, 1979). A final control attempt, love withdrawal (or negative love-oriented discipline), has been reported as being unrelated to dimensions of social competence (M. L. Hoffman, 1970, 1980; Rollins & Thomas, 1975, 1979; Shaffer & Brody, 1981).

The foregoing discussion illustrates that some of the social mold research has produced enough empirical consensus to construct generalizations. That is, parental support and induction are related positively, whereas parental coercion is related negatively, to several dimensions of social competence in children. Love withdrawal, on the other hand, has demonstrated inconsistent results in relation to dimensions of social competence.

Parental Power. Another research tradition within the social mold perspective has focused on parental power to predict such aspects of the parent–child relationship as child compliance, parent–youth conflict, and parental identification. The conceptualization of parental power used in the parent–child literature is derived from social power theory and consists of several dimensions or social bases of parental power (Cartwright, 1959; French & Raven, 1959). The separate dimensions of parental power refer to the child's perception of the parent's potential ability to reward (reward power), to use force (coercive power), to establish a right to influence (legitimate power), to provide expert information (expert power), and to become an important identification object (referent power) (Edwards & Brauburger, 1973; French & Raven, 1959; McDonald, 1977, 1979, 1980; Peterson, Rollins & Thomas, 1985; Rollins & Thomas, 1975; Smith, 1970).

Insofar as power signifies the potential rather than the actual ability of a parent to influence a child, this concept refers to subjective rather than objective qualities possessed by a parent. Consequently, the power of a parent is a function of the child's perception of the parent–child relationship and does not refer to actual influence attempts (i.e., parental behaviors) used by a parent. Parental power results from "complex conditions" that children perceive as governing the parent–child role relationship. That is, the situational requirements, the socioemotional history, and the instrumental history of the parent–child relationship, as perceived by children, determine their willingness to be influenced. Thus, the "symbolic" environment of the child is the basis for the attribution of parental power by children (Smith, 1983).

The conception of parental power presented here is consistent with a symbolic interaction perspective in that children define the nature of interactive situations and perceive their parents as "significant others." The extent to which parents are viewed as significant others by their children is a reflection of the degree of power or influence that is ascribed to them. That is, children will become responsive to the expectations of parents who are perceived as controlling certain resources, such as rewards, coercion, legitimate authority, and information. Viewed in this manner, the study of parental power concerns the child's perception of the rules for interaction and the status issues that govern the parent–child role relationship.

An important issue that needs further exploration is whether parental power interacts with and determines the impact of parental behavior on the social competence of children. For example, high levels of parental induction (a parental behavior) may have greater impact on children's conformity when the parents are perceived as having high levels of legitimate and/or expert power. Thus, tests for the effects of multiplicative interaction between levels of parental power and parental behavior variables should be a focus of future research.

Thus, the foregoing discussion has illustrated that parental power is an important aspect of the parent–child relationship. It results from the history of the parent–child relationship and refers to the perceived potential (not actual) ability of parents to influence the child. Future research should examine the combined influence of parental power and of behavior dimensions on child outcomes.

Generational Transmission. Investigators within the social mold tradition have also focused on the socialization of attitudes and values across generations (Acock & Bengtson, 1978, 1980; Troll & Bengtson, 1979). Specifically, the contrast and congruence between parents and their offspring on political, moral, sex-role, religious, and achievement attitudes have been examined. A variety of parental qualities that facilitate or hinder generational transmission have been examined in this research (Troll & Bengtson, 1979). To a large extent, generational transmission is the process through which attitudes, values, and expectations associated with the learning and performance of roles are conveyed from one generation to another.

In a survey study of intergenerational differences, Bengtson and Kuypers (1971) found that young people tended to maximize the philosophical and ideological discrepancies between generations, whereas adults concentrated on less fundamental issues, such as lifestyle choices, personal habits, and traits. To explain these results, Bengtson and Kuypers (1971) introduced the concept of *developmental stake,* or the idea that one generation has a particular kind of investment in the other generation. For the parental generation, this investment takes the form of socializing the young as a means of ensuring their own immortality and generational continuity. The developmental stake of youth, on the other hand, is directed toward developing their own lifestyles and attitudes about major social issues, as opposed to validating existing values and strategies. In other words, whereas the young are engaged in role making, the parental generation is committed to passing on the attitudes, values, and expectations associated with existing roles.

A number of contradictions have been identified in the literature on generational transmission. Some of the studies provide evidence of generational similarity (Acock & Bengtson, 1978; Bengtson, 1975; Kandel & Lesser, 1972), whereas other investigations have indicated that value differences exist between parents and children (Connell, 1972; Gallagher, 1974; Payne, Summers, & Stewart, 1973; Tedin, 1974). Part of the confusion results from the practice of comparing across entire cohorts of parents and children (or group comparisons) rather than conducting parent–child comparisons within the same family—a more precise indicator.

Evidence from a study by Acock and Bengtson (1980) clears up more of the confusion. That is, the actual rather than the attributed attitudes (as perceived by the children) of the parental generation considered as a group were more similar to the actual attitudes of the children considered as a group. Results of this kind provide evidence that the so-called generation gap is a product of youth's misattribution of parental orientations and not a poduct of large actual differences. When comparisons between children and parents within the same families were examined,

however, the attributed or perceived attitudes (not the actual attitudes) of individual parents were the best predictors of individual children's self-expressed attitudes. These findings indicate that generational transmission may occur primarily through the attitudes that children perceive their parents to have, rather than through actual parental opinions.

This suggestion that children's attitudes are more strongly predicted by attributed (or perceived) than by actual attitudes corresponds with symbolic interaction concepts. That is, such findings are consistent with the "definition-of-the-situation" concept because children seem to be influenced directly by the meaning that they attribute to their interactions with others and only indirectly by the actual attitudes of others. A child's "definition (or perception) of the situation," therefore, is the immediate reality having the greatest social impact.

Thus, whereas inconsistent findings are apparent in the generational transmission literature, concepts from the symbolic interaction perspective may provide insight into some of the discrepancies. Symbolic interaction concepts are especially useful for interpreting findings related to the cross-generational influences of attributed versus actual attitudes of parents.

Observational Learning. The imitation-modeling tradition proposed by Albert Bandura and his associates (Bandura, 1976; Bandura & Walters, 1963) is another social-mold perspective that is consistent with symbolic interaction (Heiss, 1981). Through a process called *observational learning,* children seem capable of adopting both the behaviors and the internal standards of their parents (or other models). Child outcomes such as aggression, moral behavior, self-esteem, and altruistic behavior have been found to be products of observational learning (Bandura, 1976).

Similar to the symbolic interaction framework, the modeling perspective portrays children as active mediators who acquire information and develop expectancies that guide their actions in the social environment. That is, children can learn the lessons contained in the reinforcements received by others (vicarious reinforcement), provide their own rewards (self-reinforcement), and anticipate their own futures. Capacities of this kind allow children to represent internally and reproduce a complex array of behavior exhibited by a model. Furthermore, Bandura's imitation process may be the same mechanism through which aspects of the parent's role performance are learned and reproduced by children (Biddle, 1979). An important aspect of observational learning is that the parent's role performance socializes children independent of the parent's intention to do so.

Observational learning in children appears to be facilitated by certain attributes of models (e.g., parents), an idea that is similar to the significant-other concept from the symbolic interaction literature. In other words, those models (e.g., parents) who are perceived to be nurturant and powerful are most effective in prompting others to imitate their behavior (Bandura, 1976; Bandura & Huston, 1961). Attributes of this kind determine who will become a significant other for a child, that is, a referent whose opinions and actions are highly valued (Mead, 1934; Webster & Sobieszek, 1974). Likewise, children who identify their parents as significant others are more likely to model parental role behaviors and to internalize parental expectations on subsequent occasions.

The preceding discussion has illustrated that concepts from Bandura's observational-learning perspective are consistent with ideas from the symbolic interaction framework. These concepts provide greater insight into the process through which children learn the roles that adults perform. Socialization for roles occurs on a day-to-day basis, with parents serving as models who consciously or unconsciously teach their children by example.

Critique of Parental Characteristics and Child Outcomes. Criticism of the social mold research on the relationships between parental characteristics and child outcomes has increased. Much of this criticism has been directed at the wide variety of self-report, interview, and behavior-observation methodologies, which may have contributed to inconsistent findings in the parent–child research. These difficulties are compounded by the use of different conceptualizations for the same variables (e.g., see the several interpretations of the parental control dimension described earlier).

The use of different methodologies in this research to operationalize the same or "similar" concepts may be a major contributor to inconsistent results. Blumer (1969), for instance, argued that the typical protocols of scientific measurement bend the empirical world to their premises and evoke different meanings for individual research participants. That is, operational methods, by their very nature, function to create their own reality and meaning. Consistent with this idea, is W. I. Thomas's argument that any situation (including a research situation) involves (1) the objective conditions under which the individual acts; (2) the preexisting attitudes of the individual, which at any given moment influence his or her behavior; and (3) a "definition of the situation" that is both his or her conception of and his or her attitude toward a particular set of circumstances (Thomas & Thomas, 1928).

Other problems with social mold research include the criticism that self-report measures fail to control for response sets and generally have low reliabilities in respondents' answers (Becker & Krug, 1964; Yarrow *et al.*, 1968). Both interview and questionnaire methodologies are also subject to the criticism that the attitudes provided by these measures may not predict behavior.

The most critical comments about measurement, however, have been aimed at the indirect or retrospective nature of the data that are generated. That is, changes across situations and in the self-concepts of respondents inevitably alter how they perceive their relationships. Participants find it difficult or even impossible to recall their specific actions, outlooks, and feelings in an earlier situation. This problem is greatly compounded when respondents are asked to characterize several dimensions of the parent–child relationship in summary across a large number of situations. On the other hand, these problems with retrospective recall in longitudinal designs might be alleviated by providing research participants with memory aids (e.g., diaries, journals, and wall calendars). In other words, memory aids may be used by the respondents to record information on a regular schedule that is intended for later assessment with interviews or questionnaires (Marcus, 1982).

In the case of behavior observation methodologies, critics have pointed to the problem of reactivity, that is, the idea that an observer's presence changes the behavior of parents and children in research settings (Baumrind & Black, 1967; Yarrow & Waxler, 1979). According to this interpretation, observational settings elicit a "definition of the situation" that encourages a different set of role behaviors from those that are typically exhibited by participants in natural or backstage settings. Strategies designed to minimize reactivity include (1) the use of research tasks that are so engrossing that participants forget they are being observed (Straus & Tallman, 1971); (2) the use of familiar settings (e.g., the participants' home) for research purposes (Gottman, 1979); and (3) letting the participants become accustomed to a research setting before recording observations (Haynes, Jensen, Wise, & Sherman, 1979).

Other deficiencies stem from problems in design and analysis. Most of the studies, for example, have small samples and use only bivariate rather than multivariate models. Another problem is the very low (but statistically significant) correlations between child-rearing techniques and child outcomes (Becker, 1964; Hess, 1981; Martin, 1975; Rollins & Thomas, 1979; Sears *et al.*, 1957, 1965; Steinmetz, 1979; Thomas *et al.*, 1974). The failure to conduct analyses for multiplicative interaction and curvilinear relationships also typifies all but a few studies (Rollins & Thomas, 1979; Steinmetz, 1979). Finally, most of the research has failed to examine for effects of the "age variable" (of parents and children) on dimensions of the parent–child relationship.

The most severe criticisms of the social mold approach, however, stem from its portrayal of socialization as a unidirectional process from parent to child (Bell, 1968; Bell & Harper, 1977). Such evaluations have been motivated by more than a decade of research on infancy that underscores the influence of infants on parents. Richard Q. Bell (Bell & Harper, 1977), for example, observed that most of the research in the social mold tradition can be reinterpreted as a child effect rather than a parent effect. Simply stated, this "turnabout" of the social mold position defines the child as an occupant of a parent socializer role and the parent as an occupant of a parent socializee role, with the direction of influence being from child to parent (see the section of this chapter on "Child Effects Research").

Another criticism by advocates of bidirectional models is leveled at the use of static, one-sided summary variables (e.g., parental support or induction) by social mold researchers. According to these critics, a serious problem results because these variables are based on "average scores" calculated across specific indicators, situations, and time periods. Recently, investigators have developed an alternative model of parent–child socialization in which the "sequential exchanges" of specific behaviors between child and parent are examined (Gewirtz, 1969; Lewis & Lee-Painter, 1974). This approach is clearly consistent with the focus of symbolic interaction on dynamic patterns of interaction between parents and children (see the later section of this chapter on "Parent–Child Reciprocity").

Despite the importance of these criticisms, researchers operating within the social mold perspective have countered with some valuable ideas. For example, it is difficult to deny that parents have greater control over environmental contingencies than children and that intentional socialization is primarily an adult-initiated process (Baumrind, 1980). Adults are social agents who have greater insight than children into the expectations, attitudes, and behaviors of their culture. They are more likely than children to have socialization goals that are derived from their culture and to guide their actions.

Even if reciprocal models are sound ideas (and they are!), the meaning and outcome of any given sequence of interaction are not necessarily identical in both directions (Baumrind, 1980; M. L. Hoffman, 1975). This is the case because parents and children are occupants of separate roles having distinctive social expectations and different patterns of role behavior. In short, those who reduce the study of parent–child socialization to the observation of behaviors that move back and forth between parent and child are ignoring a number of fundamental issues. First, these investigators fail to recognize that the relative power of parents and children determines the degree to which "ego" (the child) perceives "alter" (the parent) as a significant other during the socialization process. Such disparities in power are especially relevant during the periods of development that precede late adolescence. Second, these researchers also ignore the idea that parental behavior is motivated by greater intentionality and conveys more complex information than children's behavior.

For the most part, therefore, the research on parental characteristics that predicts child outcomes has been subjected to a variety of methodological and theoretical criticisms. However, the power, intentionality, and sophistication of parents relative to children might still be handled within unidirectional models.

The Larger Social Contexts of the Social Mold Tradition

An important aspect of the parent–child dyad is its interface with the larger social contexts and social structures that encompass this primary relationship. How these larger structures influence parent–child interaction has been a prominent focus of the social mold perspective. Specifically, the most general social environments that encompass the parent–child relationship are cultural (ethnic) variations, historical changes, and the different socioeconomic levels at which socialization occurs. The more immediate contexts reviewed in this section include family structure and parent–child experiences based on gender differences.

These contexts are important for the parent–child dyad because parents and children are influenced simultaneously by both the larger and the more immediate social worlds. Although face-to-face interaction is the most immediate social context, the dimensions of the parent–child relationship are provided additional significance when viewed against a backdrop of larger milieus. This means, of course, that a hierarchy of social contexts provides values, meanings, and goals that become translated into expectations for role behavior within the parent–child relationship. These expectations, in turn, are conveyed to children by significant others (e.g., the parents) who occupy positions in the larger social context and instill a particular conception of social reality in children (Berger & Luckman, 1967).

To a large extent, the roles occupied by parents in larger social contexts influence the child-rearing techniques they use, the meanings they convey to their children, and the outcomes that the children exhibit. Low-income black parents, for example, use child-rearing techniques that reflect both the economic deprivation and the racial discrimination they experience in the larger social context. A frequently cited example is the emphasis within black families on parental practices that encourage self-concept development and coping mechanisms in children (Gutman, 1976; Hill, 1971; Peters, 1976; Richardson, 1980).

Culture and Ethnicity. One of the larger social contexts is the culture or ethnicity of parents and children, that is, their membership in a group of persons who possess a unique social and historical heritage and who seek to convey to their offspring "cultural content" consisting of values, meanings, and goals. These ideal types, in turn, function as sources of expectations that place constraints on behavior in face-to-face interaction. The parent–child relationship, therefore, is an important domain in which cultural meaning becomes translated into role behaviors (Cogswell, 1974). Cultural transmission occurs as parents perform the child socializer role and direct significant symbols at children during the socialization process.

Across different ethnic groups, the performance of child socializer and socializee roles by parents and children demonstrates both unique and common elements (Nisbet & Perrin, 1977; Stryker, 1980). Parents from different ethnic groups often use child-rearing techniques that are derived from their unique set of cultural values and role expectations, which are believed to be adaptive. The various stances of different ethnic groups on important issues are appropriate ways of solving the significant problems within their respective cultures.

A phenomenon that complicates the socialization of ethnic children is the ambiguity or marginality of living simultaneously in two worlds, both the ethnic community and "mainstream" society. Ethnic parents, therefore, are often faced with the challenge of socializing their children for two cultures having substantial conflicts in role expectations (Stonequist, 1937). Peters (1981a), for example, has argued that black families place greater emphasis than white families on the idea that children must respect their elders and authority figures, an orientation that conflicts with expectations of self-assertion and independence within white-dominated institutions (e.g., the school).

While considering "ethnic effects," investigators have frequently sought to identify the similarities and differences between ethnic groups in their performance of parent–child roles (McAdoo, 1978; Mindel & Habenstein, 1975; Staples & Mirandé, 1980). For example, the study of parent–child relations within black families is now being reconceptualized by researchers. Social scientists are moving beyond "pathological" or "deficit" interpretations toward an increased awareness of the adaptive qualities of parent–child socialization within black families. Investigators are now more likely to view the unique socialization practices of black parents as being functional within their own setting (Allen, 1978; Hill, 1971; Peters, 1981b). Current research has also reversed much of the earlier evidence indicating that children's self-esteem was influenced adversely by the experience of socialization in black families (Cross, 1981).

Traditionally, the socialization of black as compared to white children has been portrayed as mother-centered and as characterized by a greater emphasis on parental nurturance, punitiveness, and obedience. Black parents have been reported to use less reasoning, less withdrawal of love, and less rational control than white parents (Bartz & Levine, 1978; Durrett, O'Bryant, & Pennebraker, 1975; Nolle, 1972; Peters, 1981b; Staples, 1976). Certain child-rearing techniques used by black parents prepare black children for the realities of white racism and the early performance of adult roles (Silverstein & Krate, 1975; Staples, 1976). Another proposal is that black parents socialize their children to participate effectively in both the black and the white worlds (Peters, 1981b). Black parents also attempt to buffer the negative images of black people that are conveyed to children by the media, the schools, and other social agents.

A comparative study by Bartz and Levine (1978) adds interesting complexity to the study of socialization within black families. That is, when the effects of social class were controlled, the child-rearing behavior of black parents was similar to Baumrind's concept (1966, 1967, 1971) of authoritative parenting. Such characteristically middle-class behaviors as high support, high control, open communication, and maturity demands were used by black parents.

Socialization processes within Mexican-American, or Chicano, families are another illustration of "ethnic ef-

fects." As in black families, socialization in Mexican-American families has been viewed in negative terms when evaluated from the perspective of Anglo values and culture. Consistent with the "machismo" tradition, the father's performance of the child socializer role within Chicano families has been portrayed as rigid and authoritarian, whereas the mother's performance has been characterized as passive and nurturant (Madsen, 1973; Mindel & Habenstein, 1975). Compared to Anglo children, Mexican-American youth have been described as less independent and as having lower achievement aspirations within the child socializee role. Socialization for traditional gender roles has been reported to be a major emphasis, with male offspring having more freedom than female offspring (Alvirez & Bean, 1975). Children have been described as being taught to display extensive respect for elders and to assume responsibilities for the care of younger siblings (Murillo, 1971).

Researchers have begun to alter some of these conceptions by suggesting that father–child relations within Mexican-American families are warm and compassionate, rather than cold and rigid (Bartz & Levine, 1978; Staples & Mirandé, 1981). In addition, Bartz and Levine (1978) found Chicano parents to be less controlling and more favorably disposed to permissiveness in the child socializer role than black parents. Some of these departures from traditional models of Mexican-American socialization may be a product of historical patterns of change in family structure and dynamics. More specifically, declines in patriarchal roles for men and the participation of Chicano families in urban, middle-class lifestyles may be major trends within Mexican-American families (Alvirez & Bean, 1975). Other authorities have expressed considerable doubt that the type of male dominance represented in the machismo tradition has ever been the behavioral norm within Mexican-American families (Grebler, Moore, & Guzman, 1970).

Future comparative studies should continue to identify similarities and differences in the socialization processes of ethnic families. To the extent possible, investigators must view each ethnic group's construction of "reality" from the inside as a means of understanding the expectations, roles, and behaviors characteristic of each culture.

In summary, ethnic groups create their own versions of social reality within the parent–child relationship. These differences between ethnic groups, in turn, are being viewed increasingly as adaptive responses to their unique circumstances. Some of the research evidence also indicates that socialization practices in Mexican-American and black families are becoming more like those in the mainstream culture.

Social Class and the Parent–Child Relationship. Although societies or cultures have certain widely accepted expectations, no society or culture of any size is governed by a uniform set of norms. In contrast, societies are usually differentiated into a variety of segments that expose the occupants of various social positions to different meaning contexts and organized patterns of behavior.

The concept *social class* or *socioeconomic status* (SES) is descriptive of the principal means through which members of social groups are ordered in relation to each other.

Some authorities have argued that parents from different socioeconomic levels experience disparate conditions of life, develop different conceptions of social reality, acquire different priorities, and develop different expectations for the enactment of the child socializee role. Furthermore, individuals from the same socioeconomic level tend to share definitions of social reality (Berger & Luckman, 1967). Across different SES levels, variability in these definitions has implications for the kinds of gestures and significant symbols that parents use to perform the child socializer role.

To illustrate, investigators have frequently reported that parents of different SES levels exhibit disparate attitudes, values, and expectations for children's performance of the child socializee role (Gecas, 1979; Hess, 1970; Kohn, 1977; Maccoby, 1980). Thus, it has been reported frequently that lower-class parents are more likely than middle-class parents to expect their children to be obedient and respectful and to stay out of trouble. Middle-class parents, on the other hand, tend to emphasize happiness, creativity, ambition, achievement, independence, and self-control (Bayley & Schaefer, 1960; Bronfenbrenner, 1958; Kohn, 1977; Waters & Crandall, 1964). Although white-collar parents tend to consider the "intention" of children's behavior within the child socializee role, blue-collar parents seem especially attentive to the "consequences" of children's behavior (Gecas & Nye, 1974; Kohn, 1977).

By the same token, class variability in the behavior that parents use to perform the child socializer role has been reported by several investigators. For instance, middle-class mothers tend to vocalize with young infants more than lower-class mothers (Messer & Lewis, 1972). During later periods of development, coercive, power-assertive, restrictive, and arbitrary behaviors are more characteristic of lower-class than of middle-class parents (Bayley & Schaefer, 1960; Bronfenbrenner, 1958; Elder & Bowerman, 1963; Erlanger, 1974; Gecas & Nye, 1974; Miller & Swanson, 1960; Sears *et al.*, 1957; Zussman, 1977). In contrast, higher SES parents tend to use more reasoning, support, complex communication, and democratic approaches with their children (Bernstein & Henderson, 1973; Cook-Gumpertz, 1973; Elder & Bowerman, 1963; Hess, 1970; Hess & Shipman, 1965; Kohn, 1977; Miller & Swanson, 1960; Scheck & Emerick, 1976).

Variations in performing the child socializer role by parents of different social classes may have different consequences for children's performance of the child socializee role. Maccoby (1980), for instance, suggested that a particular parental behavior, such as physical punishment, may have different effects on children from distinct socioeconomic backgrounds. That is, physical punishment may have one meaning and consequence for children from lower-class settings, in which such actions

are common, but a considerably different meaning and consequence for middle-class children, whose parents seldom use this tecnique.

Several authorities have also developed formal schemes to explain the impact of social class on the parent–child relationship. Over 25 years ago, for example, Urie Bronfenbrenner (1958) sought to explain why middle-class parents seemed more responsive than lower-class parents to "permissive" child-rearing approaches. He argued that class differences resulted from the disproportionate access of middle-class parents to "expert opinions" on child-rearing practices. Bronfenbrenner seemed to be proposing that middle-class parents used child-rearing experts more frequently than lower-class parents as "significant others" for information on child rearing.

Another social-class framework having only limited empirical support was proposed by Basil Bernstein (1964, 1970, 1971, 1973). Because an important focus of Bernstein's work is the family role system, his work has much in common with the symbolic interaction perspective. Of particular importance are the degrees of role flexibility and different communication styles that are characteristic of families from divergent socioeconomic levels.

Bernstein argued that structured role relationships and communication processes are experienced quite differently within lower- and middle-class families (and parent–child dyads). In other words, the role expectations and conditions of low-income family members become translated into position-oriented family-role systems. Roles tend to be inflexible and rigidly ascribed in low-income families, and status hierarchies are formalized by age and gender. Communication patterns characterized by restricted language codes, and imperative or positional modes of parental control allow only a limited range of child responses (e.g., compliance, rebellion, or withdrawal). Norms within these families tend to be based on social-positional hierarchies (e.g., "Honor thy father").

A substantially different role structure and communication style tends to exist within middle-class families. According to Bernstein, white-collar families are characterized by achieved status, flexible role structures, and a person-oriented milieu. Role compositions and their assignment tend to be flexible, and elaborated language codes encourage information exchange between family members. Personal modes of control that are focused on the individual characteristics of children and the specific circumstances of a situation are used by parents to guide their disciplinary actions.

In addition to Bernstein's work, Melvin Kohn has engaged in another research and theory-building effort to conceptualize the influence of social class on the parent–child dyad (see Gecas, 1979; Kohn, 1959, 1963, 1969, 1977, 1980; Kohn & Schooler, 1973, 1978). This theory has much in common with symbolic interaction because it describes how the parent's role performance in settings outside the family may influence the parent–child relationship.

The basic idea of Kohn's work is that socioeconomic standing exposes parents to certain conditions of life that influence their values and intellectual flexibility. Specifically, Kohn (1977) proposed that work settings (a component of social class) expose parents to particular conditions and values that shape their expectations for their children's performance of the child socializee role.

Kohn suggested that manipulation of symbols, substantive task complexity, and considerable freedom from supervision are conditions and expectations characteristic of middle-class occupational roles. Blue-collar occupations, on the other hand, expose parents to expectations for the manipulation of physical objects, greater standardization of tasks, and closer supervision. These occupational roles, in turn, often become translated into conceptions of social life that parents tend to expect from their children. White-collar parents, for example, tend to value self-direction and internalized standards of behavior from children. Blue-collar parents, on the other hand, prefer conformity, orderliness, neatness, and obedience.

Kohn and others (Gecas, 1981; Kohn, 1977; Scheck & Emerick, 1976; Wright & Wright, 1976) have identified the parents' educational experience as another dimension of social class that influences socialization values and expectations. That is, the ability of parents to attain a particular occupation and to be exposed to its value system is influenced substantially by their level of formal education. Furthermore, greater educational attainment contributes first to higher levels of intellectual flexibility and, in turn, to class disparities in parental values and expectations of children.

Another aspect of Kohn's model is the idea that class differences in parental values and expectations may also produce differences in parental enactment of the child socializer role (Gecas, 1979). For example, the emphasis on self-direction and internalization by white-collar parents may result in higher levels of supportiveness and rational control. By contrast, the conformity–obedience orientations of blue-collar parents are expected to produce higher levels of punitiveness by parents (Gecas, 1979; Gecas & Nye, 1974; Kohn, 1977; Peterson & Peters, 1985). Future researchers need to take Kohn's model one step further and examine the linkages between enactment of the child socializer role by parents and children's outcomes within the child socializee role.

The foregoing discussion illustrates that conditions experienced by parents in their socioeconomic context may have consequences within the parent–child relationship. Specifically, the child outcomes that parents value, their performance of the child socializer role, and the family role system are affected.

Historical Context and the Parent–Child Relationship. Historical processes function as another important context of the parent–child relationship. Parents and children, as members of separate cohorts, have experienced different social-historical events (Troll & Bengston, 1979). Compared to parents, therefore, members of youthful cohorts bring a "fresh view" into interactions with adults (Mannheim, 1952). Exposure to different historical events means that each generation brings unique role expectations and definitions of the situation into the parent–child relationship (Elder, 1974; Volkart, 1951).

A recent historical trend influencing the parent–child dyad, for example, has been the decreased emphasis on economic roles and greater emphasis on affective and companionship roles for children in relation to parents. In other words, children have become objects of economic utility much less, while becoming a focus of nurturant socialization much more (Abramovitz, 1976; Kagan, 1977; Lynn, 1979; Reiss, 1965).

Other important trends have included the movement of mothers into the provider role and fathers into the child socializer role (Hoffman & Nye, 1974; Lamb, 1976; Nye & Rallings, 1979). Given these trends, other changes within the parent–child relationship would seem to follow. For example, compared with mothers of previous eras, today's mothers may experience less guilt about working (and being separated from their children) and may perform the child socializer role more effectively because there are fewer negative sanctions against occupying the provider role (Hoffman & Nye, 1974; Nye & Rallings, 1979). By the same token, recent evidence that infants become attached to fathers may simply reflect the historical trend for fathers to become more involved in child socializer roles (Lamb, 1976; Lerner & Ryff, 1978).

Important insights into the effects of the Great Depression on parent–child relations have been provided in a major study by Glen Elder (1974). He concluded that, during this period, unemployed fathers of economically deprived families suffered declines in power, social prestige, and emotional significance within the family role system. Although the authority of mothers increased relative to that of fathers, this development was insufficient to offset an overall decline in parental influence on children. The offspring from these deprived homes, in turn, became more dependent on significant others outside the family.

Thus, historical trends and events can have a substantial impact on the parent–child relationship. Specifically, the structure, interaction, and meaning of the events that occur between parents and children can be altered by the phenomena that provide each generation with a unique set of experiences.

Family Structure. The structural characteristics of families include several components of the social context that immediately encompass and influence the parent–child relationship. Specifically, family interaction and outcomes may differ as family positions and role relationships become more complex. Three dimensions of family structure receiving empirical and/or theoretical attention are sibling number, child density, and birth order.

In terms of the sibling number, more conflicts in role expectations and greater complexity in family role relationships are expected to result as the number of children increases. Parents often experience role strain, desire greater consensus in role expectations, and have higher levels of frustration when sibling numbers increase. Parents having several children who are faced with these conditions tend to use more control attempts, higher levels of physical punishment, and more authoritarian techniques than parents of fewer children. Furthermore, as the number of children increases, parents often spend less time with and are less supportive of each child. A principle outcome is that roles become inflexible, little negotiation occurs, and expectations become strictly enforced (Bossard & Boll, 1956; Elder & Bowerman, 1963; Peterson & Kunz, 1975; Scheck & Emerick, 1976).

Child density is an additional dimension of family structure that has received limited research attention (Kidwell, 1981). A common belief is that wider spacing of children contributes to the most effective use of a parent's time and performance of the child socializer role (Rossi, 1978; Thompson, 1974). The frustrations, pressures, and conflicting role demands of parents are expected to be alleviated if children are not born close together. Thus, parents are expected to relax their discipline and to exhibit higher levels of supportive behavior as the average spacing between children increases. In contrast, reasoning and support are expected to decrease and punitiveness is expected to increase as children are more closely spaced.

A third feature of family structure receiving empirical attention is birth order. To examine this dimension, most studies have compared only the firstborns and lastborns with general categories referred to as "later"- or "middle"-born children. An important issue in the birth order literature is the influence of this variable on parental behavior. Several researchers, for example, have reported that firstborns, compared to later-borns, receive more parental attention and verbal stimulation during infancy and throughout childhood (Cohen & Beckwith, 1976; Hilton, 1967; Hodapp & Lavoie, 1976; Jacobs & Moss, 1976; Koch, 1954; Lewis & Kreitzberg, 1979; Marjoribanks & Walberg, 1975; Rothbart, 1971; Thoman, Leiderman, & Olson, 1972; Thoman, Turner, & Leiderman, 1970). Some of this "extra attention" to firstborns as compared to later-borns may include intrusive involvements, affectionate behavior, achievement pressure, and stricter training (Hilton, 1967; Kammeyer, 1967; Lasko, 1954; Maccoby, 1980; Rosen, 1961, 1964; Rothbart, 1971; Rubin, Hultsch, & Peters, 1971; Stout, 1960). Elsewhere, certain investigators have suggested that firstborn children are trained within the family to perform "parent surrogate roles" and to assume task-oriented leadership positions (Chemers, 1970; Sutton-Smith & Rosenberg, 1964). In contrast, it appears that lastborn (or youngest) children are exposed to more relaxed forms of discipline and fewer maturity demands.

Although little research evidence exists about children in the "middle" positions, a speculation is that middle-borns may experience parental behavior falling some-where in between the experience of first- and later-borns. In one study of middle-borns, on the other hand, Kidwell (1982) reported that middle-born adolescents demonstrated lower self-esteem than either firstborns or lastborns. Kidwell speculated that middle-borns may experience these deficiencies because they are unable to establish their "uniqueness" within the family. In other words, middle-born children may not experience the same status, recognition, or attention from parents as firstborn or lastborn children.

A possible explanation for "birth order effects" is that parents alter their performance of child socializer roles with subsequent children as they gain increased experience in child rearing. That is, a parent's initial occupation of the child socializer role (for firstborns) is an anxiety-provoking role transition that contributes to high levels of attention, controlling behavior, and achievement pressure (Burr, 1973; Clausen, 1966; Hilton, 1967; Lasko, 1954). Later, with subsequent experiences in the child socializer role, parents may develop a more relaxed or different style of parenting as they adjust to the demands of parenthood.

Despite the foregoing empirical consistencies, a number of contradictions have been identified in the literature on family structure. Schooler (1972), for example, found little evidence that birth order consistently predicted differences in psychiatric disorders, intellectual attainment, occupational achievement, and normal personality dimensions. More recent investigations, therefore, have sought to address the inconsistencies in earlier research by developing multivariate models that incorporate the major family structure variables as well as additional sociodemographic variables. For example, Zajonc and Markus (1975), in their "confluence model," examined the combined influences of family size, child density, and birth order on children's intelligence (Zajonc, 1976). Their model assumes that additional children, the closer spacing of children, and the absence of an older sibling who teaches younger siblings dilute a family's intellectual environment substantially. Other researchers have sought to improve the confluence model by suggesting that "parental attention" to children is another variable that influences children's intellectual development (Marjoribanks & Walberg, 1975). Thus, interaction variables that are influenced by family structure may, in turn, affect children's intellectual development.

In a multivariate study, Kidwell (1981) examined the combined influence of such independent variables as sibling numbers, child spacing, birth order, and gender composition on parental enactment of the child socializer role. Evidence was provided that sibling numbers and sibling spacing had independent influences on parents' use of punitiveness, reasoning, and support. Kidwell also reported that curvilinear relationships existed between sibling spacing and parental behavior. In other words, more positive parent–child relationships were found to exist when children were spaced either close together (12 months or less) or very widely apart (4 years or more), the optimal spacing being about 5 years apart. Intermediate spacing (2–3 years between siblings), on the other hand, was characterized by the highest levels of punitiveness and the lowest levels of support and reasoning. These results provide evidence that role conflicts and role strain are the most severe when children are intermediately spaced (2–3 years apart).

In summary, current research seems to be reversing some of the ambiguities found in earlier studies on family structure and birth order (Kidwell, 1981, 1982; Schooler, 1972). The key to further progress may be the use of multivariate models to examine the influence of several dimensions of family structure simultaneously. Specifically, multivariate models involving such variables as sibling number, child density, birth order, and the gender of siblings should be examined for effects on parent–child interaction and child outcomes.

Gender and the Parent–Child Relationship. A final dimension of family structure that has important effects on parental behavior and the socialization of children is the gender of parents and children. Traditionally, men and women have experienced considerably different social worlds in the family and in the larger social contexts. In their child-rearing roles, parents may function as significant others who mediate these discrepant "male and female realities" to their children. The young, in turn, are expected to internalize and act in accordance with the version of "social reality" pertaining to their own biological gender (Berger & Luckman, 1967). Furthermore, gender has been a means of defining the relative status of family members and of assigning the roles that parents and children are expected to perform (Turner, 1970). Because the gender variable is associated with important cultural and gender-role expectations, it serves as an organizer for child-rearing techniques that parents direct at the young.

Currently, adult gender roles are converging, and therefore, gender differences in the socialization of children may be diminishing as well. For example, Hoffman (1977) argued that the current trends for women to spend less time as mothers, for mothers to be employed, and for fathers to become more involved in child rearing may narrow the existing differences in the socialization experiences of boys and girls. Hoffman (1977) also acknowledged, however, that social trends are not instantly effective, particularly with respect to child-rearing patterns. Consequently, sex differences in the socialization experiences and outcomes of male and female offspring continue to be reported (Peterson, Rollins, Thomas, & Heaps, 1982).

An important facet of the socialization process is the tendency for parents to expect different role behavior from sons and daughters. Parents often expect each gender to respond differently to distinctive types of attention, discipline, and teaching (Birns, 1976; Block, 1980; Serbin, 1980).

For example, female infants receive more attention, stimulation, vocalization, and smiles from mothers, whereas male infants receive a greater variety of responsiveness from fathers (Bell, 1968; Parke & Sawin, 1977; Rebelsky & Hanks, 1971; Thoman, 1976; Thoman *et al.*, 1971, 1972). Male infants who are firstborn receive more vocalizations and stimulation from fathers than female infants (Lamb, 1976; Parke & O'Leary, 1975; Parke & Sawin, 1975, 1977). Compared to infant daughters, infant sons are reported to receive greater frequencies of visual, tactile, and physical stimulation from fathers (Moss, 1967; Parke & Sawin, 1975, 1977), while receiving greater encouragement for gross motor activity by mothers (Smith & Lloyd, 1978).

Beyond infancy, a candid assessment of the research on gender-of-child influences reveals that substantial confusion reigns. Although reports of a moderate number of gender differences are sprinkled throughout the literature, the prevalence of contradictory findings make clear interpretations difficult (Martin, 1975; Rollins & Thomas, 1979; Weitz, 1977). Maccoby and Jacklin (1974), for example, argued that male and female children do not appear to be treated very differently in reference to parental affection, levels of parent–child interaction, type of interaction, autonomy-granting behavior, responses to dependency, and reactions to aggression.

By contrast, researchers have reported somewhat consistently that girls are more cooperative, more conforming to parents, and more identified with mothers than boys (Block, 1973; Devereaux, Bronfenbrenner, & Rodgers, 1969; Martin, 1975), as well as being less independent, assertive, and dominant (Baumrind, 1971, 1972, 1980; Block, 1973; Chodorow, 1978; Devereaux *et al.*, 1969; Dinnerstein, 1977; Martin, 1975; Matterson, 1975). A possible explanation for these findings is that boys are less responsive to parental perspectives because they receive less support, higher levels of punishment, and more coercion from parents than females (Minton, Kagan, & Levine, 1971; Spence & Helmreich, 1978). Furthermore, boys are subjected more extensively to expectations for "agentic behavior" (i.e., taking an active rather than a passive stance in reference to the social environment) by parents and other social agents (Baumrind, 1980). Girls, on the other hand, often develop their sense of self within the context of a strong affective relationship and an extensive personal identification with their mothers. A relationship of this kind may contribute to well-developed social skills but may hinder the process of achieving independence (Baumrind, 1980; Chodorow, 1978; Dinnerstein, 1977). Other research has indicated that maternal support is associated with a feminine orientation in girls, whereas paternal support predicts a masculine orientation in boys (Rollins & Thomas, 1979).

Given these male–female differences, Baumrind (1972, 1980) emphasized that parents should be more demanding with daughters as a means of facilitating intellectual achievement, independence, and agentic behavior, whereas males may require higher levels of nurturance and intimacy as a means of encouraging affiliative qualities. Research consistent with this idea has indicated that female academic achievement demonstrated a negative relationship with parental support and a positive relationship with parental control. In contrast, male academic achievement was best facilitated by higher levels of both parental support and control (Kagan & Moss, 1962; Rollins & Thomas, 1979).

Another suggestion for changing gender-related differences is concerned with the emergence of symmetrical child care, that is, a situation in which both mothers and fathers share child-rearing responsibilities so that girls and boys can be exposed to the agentic and integrative dimensions of child rearing equally (Bakan, 1966; Chodorow, 1978; Dinnerstein, 1977). Hoffman, (1977), for example, argued that trends for mothers to become increasingly employed and for sex-role attitudes to change may eventually contribute to a convergence between the socialization experiences of boys and girls. Specifically, working mothers and parents with nontraditional sex-role attitudes tend to encourage greater independence, autonomy, and achievement orientations in female offspring. Empirical support for part of this argument has been provided by Barnett (1981), who reported that a nontraditional sex-role ideology in parents of girls was associated with early independence granting.

Because the earlier research on the parent–child dyad considered primarily the mother–child relationship, current researchers have sought to examine gender-of-parent differences by focusing on the involvement of fathers in the child socializer role (Biller, 1974; Hetherington & Duer, 1972; Lamb, 1976, 1978a; Lynn, 1974; Nye, 1976; Parke, 1978). Part of this new emphasis has been motivated by changes in family sex-role divisions and trends for fathers to become more involved in child care and socializer roles (Hoffman, 1977). Both Biller (1976) and Weinraub (1978), for example, have concluded that a lack of involvement and warmth by fathers can be detrimental to the development of a healthy sex-role orientation and achievement orientation in children. Biller (1976) added that the sex-role development of boys is facilitated by fathers who are perceived as being powerful and competent.

Authorities also suggest that a father's performance of the child socializer role is a direct influence on children that is ''qualitatively different'' from maternal effects (Biller, 1974, 1976; Lamb, 1978a). Despite this recognition, however, the effects of fathers are often discussed in terms of their influence on children as an indirect effect conveyed through the impact of fathers on mothers (Weinraub, 1978). That is, fathers may have substantial influence on mothers, who, in turn, have impact on children (see the section of this chapter on ''The Systemic Context''). Part of this assignment of fathers to a secondary position in child rearing results from their lower participation in parent–infant interaction relative to mothers (Kotelchuck, 1976). Nonetheless, Parke (1978) concluded that ''fathers, as a member of the network, play an

important, active, and distinctive role in infant social, emotional, and cognitive development'' (p. 583).

One of the most productive areas in the fatherhood literature has been the involvement of fathers in the parent–infant relationship (Lamb, 1976, 1977a; Parke & O'Leary, 1975; Parke & Sawin, 1975). Michael Lamb (1976, 1977b), for example, concluded that father–infant interaction is qualitatively different from mother–infant interaction and directly affects the young child. In comparison to mothers, fathers have been reported to hold infants more while playing with them and to engage in more physically stimulating and innovative forms of play with infants. Furthermore, infants become attached to their fathers, independent of their social attachments to their mothers (Lamb, 1978a). Mothers, on the other hand, hold their infants during instrumental caregiving (e.g., feeding and cleaning) and initiate conventional sensorimotor activites and cognitive games more frequently (e.g., peek-a-boo and pat-a-cake).

The foregoing discussion illustrates that ''gender effects'' within the parent–child relationship are complex. That is, although the influence of fathers within the child socializer role may be increasing, their influence is often described as secondary, and some of their effects may be different from those of mothers. Furthermore, some investigations continue to provide evidence that parents contribute to traditional gender-role differences by having different expectations for sons and daughters and by directing different behaviors at them. Males receive more encouragement toward agentic qualities, and females experience greater pressure toward interdependence. These results remain apparent in spite of other evidence concerning changes in gender-role attitudes in our society.

Critique of the Larger Social Contexts. Like the social mold research on face-to-face relations in the parent–child dyad, the research on the larger social contexts has been subjected to a number of criticisms. Because most investigators within this area use either interviews or self-report methodologies, studies that employ these approaches have the same weaknesses as microlevel research. Moreover, conflicting results have become apparent in studies on the larger social contexts partly because the research designs, the sampling procedures, and the analysis techniques are extremely diverse (Gecas, 1979; Schooler, 1972).

Other difficulties stem from conceptual disputes that are more fundamental. For example, a lack of consensus on several issues about the concept *social class* has contributed to many questions about measurement. Disagreements concern such points as (1) whether social class is a categorical or a continuous variable; (2) whether it is unidimensional or multidimensional (e.g., including income, educational level, and occupational prestige); and (3) whether it is a subjective concept measured by self-report procedures or an objective concept measured by behavioral indicators (Gecas, 1979; Otto, 1975). In the area of cross-ethnic research, on the other hand, a large proportion of the research fails to recognize minority families as autonomous systems governed by their own norms and role relationships. Instead, values and meanings of the white majority are used inappropriately to interpret phenomena within ethnic families having a different cultural experience. Future comparative research must also ensure that adequate controls will be introduced for socioeconomic variability within ethnic groups. Finally, researchers who use the social mold perspective need to develop more comprehensive models to test the links among (1) variables from contexts beyond the family; (2) family structural variables; (3) parental characteristics; and (4) children's social and personality characteristics.

Bidirectional-Systemic Models

The bidirectional-systemic perspective consists of four approaches used to examine the parent–child dyad, all of which reject the idea that socialization is a one-way process from parent to child. One of these approaches, the child effects position, is a reversal of the traditional social-mold perspective and examines how children influence adults (Bell & Harper, 1977; Lerner & Spanier, 1978; Maccoby & Martin, 1983). Thus, investigators of "child effects" examine how children influence the attitudes, behavior, and identities of parents.

A second approach, focusing on reciprocal interaction, examines parent–child interaction as a dynamic process. From this perspective, parent–child relations are a joint enterprise involving tightly woven sequences of interaction (Brazelton, Koslowski, & Main, 1974; Lewis & Lee-Painter, 1974; Osofsky & Connors, 1979; Parke, 1979). In this case, the flow of socialization influence occurs in both directions in the parent–child relationship.

A third approach, dealing with mutual attachment processes, considers the formation of the "initial social bond" between parent and infant from two vantage points. The first vantage point considers the attachment of infants to their parents (Ainsworth, 1973; Bowlby, 1973), and the second examines the attachment of parents to their infants (Klaus & Kennell, 1976). Both of these developments have implicit bidirectional components and may be different stages of the same process.

Finally, the systemic approach has focused on the complex transactions between the parent–child dyad and the surrounding social environment (Belsky, 1981; Bronfenbrenner, 1979; Garbarino, 1982; Klein *et al.*, 1978). This approach tends to view the parent–child dyad in terms of its relationships with the family, the neighborhood, and larger social institutions (e.g., the educational and political systems). Socialization, in this case, is viewed as being multidirectional and occurs through "indirect" as well as face-to-face relationships.

Empirical investigations that deal with newer approaches to the study of parent–child socialization have several deficiencies requiring attention by future investigators. For example, much of the existing work on bidirectionality has been limited to the infancy period, and later periods of development have been neglected. Even more serious has been the failure of researchers to develop theoretical concepts that provide insight into the nature, the antecedents, and the consequences of bidirectional interaction (Osofsky & Connors, 1979). Consequently, bidirectional research has been preoccupied with a descriptive orientation, various methodological issues, and the observation of behavior sequences, without sufficient attention to conceptualizing interaction.

In response to this deficiency, the application of symbolic interaction concepts can assist in organizing and interpreting much of the current research on parent–child socialization. For example, a basic assumption shared by the symbolic interaction framework and the bidirectional-systemic research is that humans are actors as well as reactors within the social environment (Stryker, 1964). That is, infants and children are portrayed as active stimulus seekers as well as recipients of social stimuli (Bell & Harper, 1977; Bruner, 1977; Stern, 1977; White, 1975).

The active quality of infants is provided impetus by certain impressive capacities that facilitate human relatedness (Rollins & Thomas, 1979). As in symbolic interaction theory, the infant is viewed in the bidirectional-systemic research as being socially malleable, as being preadapted for social life, and as having an impact on the social environment. Almost immediately after birth, infants are able to fixate visually on social objects and to attend to configurations similar to the human face (Fantz, 1964; Robson, 1967; Stern, 1977). Certain facial expressions of newborns, such as the smile, elicit social responses from parents and become altered as subsequent social interaction occurs (Charlesworth & Kreutzer, 1973; Parke, 1978; Schaffer, 1977a,b; Sroufe & Waters, 1976; Stern, 1977; Wolff, 1963). Moreover, infants have extensive cognitive and information-processing capacities that facilitate social interaction (Fantz, 1961; Kessen, 1963; Lipsitt, 1963).

Thus, all of the bidirectional-systemic perspectives begin with the premise that infants and children are active agents. Far from being passive organisms, infants begin to structure their world activity and to engage in a dialogue with the social and physical phenomena around them. The following sections of this chapter discuss each of the bidirectional-systemic approaches in greater detail.

Child Effects Research

The first approach to studying bidirectional influences is concerned with the effects of children on adults. Representative of this orientation is Richard Q. Bell's proposal that infants affect parents more than parents affect infants (Bell & Harper, 1977). Support for this argument is derived from observational studies in which infants were found to initiate the majority of interactive sequences and to have certain characteristics that affected their parents.

Because much of this research simply "turned the tables" on the social mold perspective, an appropriate designation for the child effects approach might be the inverted social-mold position.

Child Effects during Infancy. Studies within the child effects tradition frequently indicate that different infant states evoke varied levels of responsiveness from parents (Brazleton *et al.*, 1974; Connors & Osofsky, 1977; Lusk & Lewis, 1972; Moss, 1967; Osofsky & Danzger, 1974; Robson & Moss, 1970; Schaffer, 1977b). For example, infants in alert or awake states evoke parental reactions differing in quality and intensity from responses typically elicited by sleeping infants. Closely related are results indicating that infant responses such as smiling, sighs, helplessness, irritability, and crying are stimuli for parental behavior (Bell & Harper, 1977; Clarke-Stewart, 1978; Korner, 1974; Moss, 1967; Osofsky & Danzger, 1974). Furthermore, maternal responsiveness to an infant is influenced by the degree of discrepancy between her "expectations" regarding an infant's features and the "actual" characteristics of the infant (Klaus & Kennell, 1976).

Other variables that influence parents to respond differently to infants are the age and the gender of the child (Freedman, 1974; Korner, 1974; Lamb, 1977a; Moss, 1974; Parke & O'Leary, 1975; Schaffer, 1977b; Wolff, 1966). In the case of "gender-of-infant effects," mothers tend to stimulate boys by physical means, whereas girls are stimulated more frequently by visual and auditory means (Lewis, 1972). Furthermore, male infants are encouraged by their mothers to engage in greater amounts of gross motor activity than female infants (Smith & Loyd, 1978). "Age effects," on the other hand, are demonstrated by the tendency of mothers and infants to spend increasing amounts of time in the *en face* position during successive phases of development (Moss, 1967; Wolff, 1966; Schaffer, 1977b).

Despite these findings on child effects, very limited rationales have been provided for the influence of infants on parents (Osofsky & Connors, 1979). In response to this atheoretical perspective, concepts from the symbolic interaction framework can be used to organize and interpret much of the child effects research. For example, investigators of child effects suggest that parents impose "definitions" on child-rearing situations and assign social meaning to infant characteristics (Parke, 1978). In addition, the presence of infants socialize a parent's self-conception into identification with the child-care and socializer roles, a result that influences the care and behavior that parents direct at their infants (Parke, 1978; Schaffer, 1977b). Although infants do not socialize their parents intentionally, they do so because the parents impose meaning on their actions and characteristics (Parke, 1978; Schaffer, 1977b). The result of these developments is that infants become occupants of parent socializer roles and influence their parents, who occupy parent socializee roles.

Both symbolic interactionists and bidirectional researchers also share an interest in the contributions of parental expectations, attitudes, and perceptions to parent–infant interactions (Burr *et al.*, 1979; Parke, 1978). Parke (1978), for example, argued that greater emphasis should be placed on these factors as a means of providing investigators with greater insight into the meaning and consequences of interaction for the participants. As an infant's presence, actions, and qualities take on social meaning, these phenomena organize the parent's behavior in accordance with parental roles (e.g., child care and child socializing). "Infant effects" on parents, therefore, result from definitions and meanings that parents impose on the parent–infant relationship.

Attitudes or expectations that guide the behavior of parents in relation to infants have become increasingly apparent to the literature. For example, parents have expectations (or normative standards) regarding certain physical characteristics and behavior of infants. Consequently, when infants exhibit any discrepancies from these norms, the parents often begin to apply such labels to babies as *difficult, unattractive, unresponsive,* or *colicky* (Parke, 1978). Certain children may affect parents by eliciting their own abuse in extreme cases, where severe discrepancies are prevalent (Parke, & Collmer, 1975).

Another infant characteristic having a substantial influence on parental expectations and parent–infant interaction is the infant's gender (Parke, 1978; Schaffer, 1977b). Mothers and fathers often have traditional sex-role expectations of their newborn sons and daughters. Infant daughters are described by parents as being more beautiful, softer, smaller, less attentive, weaker, and cuter than infant sons. Male infants, on the other hand, tend to be viewed as being better coordinated, more alert, stronger, and hardier (Rubin, Provenzano, & Luria, 1974). Parents, in turn, may reflect these traditional sex-role expectations by differentiating their caregiving responses in terms of an infant's gender (Freedman, 1974; Lamb, 1977b; Moss, 1974; Parke & O'Leary, 1975).

Other authorities have examined the impact of infants on the marriage relationship (Hoffman & Manis, 1978; Lamb, 1978b). Of considerable importance has been the finding that a first child's birth has a traditionalizing impact on a couple's marriage. That is, the birth and presence of the infant may result in the withdrawal of the wife from the provider role and the emergence of more traditional sex-role divisions between the marital partners.

In general, therefore, parents are affected by the presence, the actions, and the qualities of infants. A reciprocal role relationship begins to emerge between parent and infant because the adults assign meaning to the infant's characteristics, develop expectations regarding the infant's behavior, and respond to expectations regarding themselves in relation to the infant.

Other Child Effects. Although much of the child effects research concerns the infancy period, later phases of the parent-child relationship are beginning to receive attention as well. Richard Q. Bell, for example, proposed that children's behavior in the parent socializer role may evoke two types of behavior from parents (Bell, 1968; Bell & Harper, 1977). The first type, referred to as *upper-limit control,* is parental behavior designed to reduce or to redirect children's behavior that exceeds parental expectations in intensity and frequency. Upper-limit control is usually evoked when children behave in a noisy, intense, or uncontrollable manner that differs from parental expectations. In contrast, lower-limit control is parental behavior designed to foster certain behaviors that conform to parental expectations. Children who are unusually quiet are likely to evoke such parental control. Support for Bell's proposals was provided in a study by Buss (1981), who reported that parents of highly active children tended to intrude physically, to engage in power struggles, and to become competitive with their children (upper-limit control). Conversely, interactions were generally peaceful and harmonious (lower-limit control) when children exhibited lower activity levels.

An important component of the child effects position is Bell's argument that much of the social mold research can be reinterpreted as a child effect rather than a parent effect (Bell & Harper, 1977). That is, the frequent use of cross-sectional and correlational procedures in the social mold research does not establish the direction of influence in the parent–child dyad. Children who exhibit high levels of socially competent behavior, for example, are probably displaying behavior consistent with parental expectations. Agreement between parental expectations and children's role performance, in turn, is likely to elicit favorable responses (such as support and induction) from the parents who are recipients of this influence. By contrast, socially incompetent role-performance by children (e.g., antisocial aggression) differs usually from parental expectations and is likely to elicit upper-limit controls (e.g., parental coercion).

Elsewhere in the parent–child literature, authorities concerned about cross-generational transmission have suggested that youth movements may affect or "resocialize" the attitudes of parents within a variety of areas (Bengtson & Troll, 1978). To accomplish this, the younger generation often identifies an area of life or a "keynote issue" (e.g., sexual behavior, politics, or religion) and seeks to challenge the existing attitudes, expectations, and role behaviors of their elders in this area. The youth movements of the 1960s were an example of child effects that resulted in such outcomes (e.g., anti-Vietnam-war protests).

The study of power in the parent–child relationship is yet another "parent effect" that could be reconceptualized as a "child effect." In other words, an important speculation for future investigators is that young people are increasingly perceived by parents as having reward, coercive, expert, and legitimate power (Peterson, 1977). Children and youth who increasingly become perceived in this manner will enhance their position as significant others relative to their parents. One result of this process may be that the movement of youth toward independence

and adult status will be facilitated as parents attribute more competence and power to their offspring.

A final "child effect," on the other hand, is the impact of children on family role structures and their parents' marital relationships. Although findings are inconsistent in this area, a number of investigators have reported that the arrival and presence of children may have adverse consequences for marital relationships (Dyer, 1963; Hobbs & Cole, 1976; LaRossa & LaRossa, 1981; LeMasters, 1957; Miller, 1976; Rollins & Cannon, 1974; Rollins & Feldman, 1970; Rollins & Galligan, 1978; Rossi, 1968, 1978; Russell, 1974; Spanier, Lewis, & Cole, 1975). In this tradition, researchers have described the assumption of parenthood as being either a "crisis" or a "transition" for married couples. Furthermore, marital satisfaction has been reported to decline and/or to remain lower during family stages in which children are present in the home (Miller, 1976; Rollins & Galligan, 1978). Apparently, this decline in marital quality occurs because the entrance and continued presence of children contribute to role accumulation, role strain, and less effective performance of marital roles (e.g., the companionship role).

In summary, children who are older than infants have a substantial influence on their parents. That is, the young acquire power in the parent–child dyad, and their role performance elicits behavioral responses from their parents. Youth also identify keynote issues and challenge the attitudes, expectations, and role behavior of adults. Finally, the presence of children may have consequences for the quality of their parents' marital relationship.

Parent–Child Reciprocity

Another approach used by investigators of bidirectional socialization is to examine dynamic processes of reciprocity between parent and child. To conduct this research, investigators have used precise microanalyses of interactive behavior between parents and children (Brazelton *et al.,* 1974; Lewis & Lee-Painter, 1974; Lewis & Roseblum, 1974; Osofsky & Connors, 1979; Parke, 1979). Research on reciprocity shared with behavioral approaches an intent to identify units of behavior emitted by parents and infants. However, unlike traditional stimulus–response (S-R) approaches, investigators of reciprocity have focused on the mutual or symmetrical exchange of S-R units between parent and child, rather than on unidirectional models. There is also an emphasis on examining units of behavior as part of a sequence and not as discrete entities.

One approach to analyzing reciprocity, sometimes referred to as a *flow model,* is concerned with the conditional probability of events (Bakeman & Brown, 1977; Lewis & Lee-Painter, 1974; Martin, Maccoby, Baran, & Jacklin, 1981; Osofsky & Connors, 1979). In this case, researchers calculate the probability of occurrence of a selected behavior by one person (the actor), given the prior occurrence of a selected behavior of the other person (the partner). This probability of occurrence is then compared with the actor's baseline for the behavior of concern, that is, the probability that this action will occur whether or not the partner's behavior has occurred. A key assumption of this approach is that an initial behavior of a pair of behaviors is always responsible for the occurrence of the following behavior.

Further advances in the study of reciprocal interaction include the development of lag sequential analyses (Sackett, 1979). In this case, sequential patterns of behavior are examined without the assumption that a particular behavior is always a function of the behavior that immediately precedes it. That is, probabilities of occurrence can be calculated for behaviors between actor and partner coming later in a sequence than immediately after a criterion behavior.

Investigators of bidirectional interaction have suggested that simultaneous as well as sequentially occurring behavior between parent and child require empirical attention (Osofsky & Connors, 1979; Stern, 1977). Other researchers have recognized the importance of gaining insight into the meaning of behavior sequences for the participants in the interaction (Osofsky & Connors, 1979; Parke, 1978; Schaffer, 1977b; Stern, 1977). Of special concern here are the parents' "definitions of the situation," consisting of the beliefs, attitudes, and values that guide their behavior during sequential exchanges with the infant. Perhaps an unsolvable problem at present is how to gain access to the subjective world of infants and very young children so that they can provide us with glimpses of their psychological experience.

A notable focus of the foregoing approaches to studying interaction, is on the pattern and sequence of behavior, instead of on discrete S-R units. Viewed in this manner, the study of reciprocal interaction is consistent with the intent of symbolic interactionists to examine dynamic patterns of interaction. A focus on the sequences and patterns of interaction correspond with the idea that parents and children bring their lines of action into accord with each other and establish a relationship of fundamental importance. A parent and a child engage in an interaction process, begin to impose meaning on the gestures of the other, and develop mutual expectations. Both participants seem to be engaging in an early version of the role-making process, within the most basic of human relationships (Turner, 1962).

An important quality of parent–infant reciprocity is the mutuality that occurs in this elementary form of role making (Schaffer, 1977a,b). Parent–infant interaction takes the form of mutual gazes, facial displays, and vocalizations, as well as synchronous approach and withdrawal. Changes in head and neck orientation to achieve the *en face* position are additional facets of this process. Reciprocal interactions between infant and parent involving such behaviors have the timing and pattern of a "waltz," an organized quality that has significance as a structured whole. Schaffer (1977b), for example, described these exchanges as an "alternation of roles" or an on-off pattern in which two partners take turns assuming "the actor and spectator role" (p. 66).

Additional research on parent–infant reciprocity has pointed to the cyclical quality of this interaction, which involves constant rhythms of mutual attention (or approach), followed by withdrawal (Brazelton *et al.*, 1974). As part of these cyclical patterns, parents allow their infants to "act" on the social environment and then follow this "indulgence" of infant actions with behavioral programs that modulate and elaborate the actions of the infants (Schaffer, 1977b; Stern, 1977). Competent reciprocity, therefore, requires both moderate levels of stimulation and allowances for periods of withdrawal by the infant. Substantial amounts of redundancy are necessary, tempered with sufficient novelty to encourage further development within the relationship.

An essential idea about the cyclical nature of reciprocity is that parents must "follow in order to lead." For instance, a mother may monitor and fetch an item that has caught the infant's interest. Correspondingly, when an infant discontinues face-to-face interaction, sensitive mothers allow these periodic withdrawals to occur. At other times, parents are responsive to their infant's efforts to initiate bouts of mutual gazing and vocalization.

This tendency for parents to govern their behavior in terms of infant initiatives was supported by Newson (1977), who suggested that mothers tend to act as though infants are communicating actively (or intentionally). In other words, a mother endows the infant's responses with signal value, becomes paced by the infant, and fills in the pauses between the infant's response bursts. In terms of symbolic interaction, these actions seem to be components of the process through which parents supply meaning to the infant's acts by completing them (Stryker, 1964). Gradually, as parents continue this interaction, infants become introduced into a "conversation of gestures" and shared understanding (Mead, 1934). That is, the meaning that parents impose on their reciprocal interaction with their infants originally resides in their own imagination. Nevertheless, the behavior that is guided by these actions starts a process that eventually introduces young children into a world of shared meanings and expectations. A major task of parents, therefore, becomes that of organizing their own activity in synchronous alternation with the behavior of their infants, as a means of facilitating the emergence of a social being.

Investigators of reciprocity use several other concepts that are consistent with the symbolic interaction perspective. For example, literature describing how the parent "reads" the infant's behavior and phases his or her activity with the child's initiatives implies that expectations are beginning to operate in these relationships (Stern, 1977; Thoman, 1976). One of the infant's major achievements during the first six months of life is to develop expectancies about the nature of human interaction (Stern, 1977). Apparently, infants are capable of mastering basic signals and conventions that, in turn, allow the development of patterned behaviors that become interwoven with the parent's actions. The result is a shared program of expectancies leading to an incipient role relationship between parent and child.

Another parallel between the work on reciprocity and symbolic interaction concerns the introduction of children into the symbolic world of human communication (Bruner, 1977; Newson, 1977; Schaffer, 1977b; Stern, 1977). In Mead's conceptualization (1934), symbolic interaction arises out of a selective process in which the random acts of an infant are given significance by his or her interaction partner. Eventually, gestures come to have a common meaning for both the infant and certain significant others with whom interaction occurs. Later, these meaningful actions contribute to the development of role-taking capacities and to the emergence of language (or significant symbols).

As in these ideas from the symbolic interaction perspective, investigators of reciprocal interaction describe the evolution of preverbal dialogues between parent and infant. Exchanges of this kind may function as early antecedents of communication or significant symbol development (Bruner, 1977; Condon & Sander, 1974; Newson, 1977; Schaffer, 1977a; Stern, 1977). Condon and Sander (1974), for example, reported that newborns move in precise rhythm with the speech of their parents. Furthermore, studies of mutual gazing and vocalizing between parent and infant may represent early developments in the process of communication leading to the later acquisition of language content (meaningful symbols) (Bruner, 1977; Condon & Sander, 1974; Newson, 1977; Schaffer, 1977a; Stern, 1977).

An important aspect of this dialogue is that parents take a prominent lead by sustaining interaction and by "imposing" meaning on the process (Bruner, 1977; Schaffer, 1977c). Eventually, infants learn that interactions are reciprocal and that their own behavior communicates during these dialogues (Schaffer, 1977b). That is, infants learn to send out signals deliberately with the expectation that the parents will respond. One speculation is that such behavior on the part of infants represents the inception of intentionality.

Preverbal discourses of this kind between parent and infant seem to have a structure comparable to that of symbolic conversations (Brazelton et al., 1974; Jaffe, Stern, & Perry, 1973). That is, parents and infants either "take turns," interact simultaneously, or permit a continuous back-and-forth flow of gaze behavior and vocalizations. Eventually, these organized patterns of gestures convey meanings and expectations shared by parent and child.

In general, research on reciprocity indicates that, long before children utter their first word, a nonverbal dialogue or "conversation of gestures" develops between parent and infant. A dialogue of this kind conceptualizes the dynamics through which a socially sophisticated adult and a socially unsophisticated infant begin to interpret each other's gestures, acquire shared meanings, and develop predictable expectancies (Blumer, 1969; Stryker,

1964). In short, this research on reciprocity lets us eavesdrop on the emergence of role-making processes between parent and infant.

Attachment

The concept of *attachment* is another aspect of the parent–child relationship that has received substantial research attention (Ainsworth, 1973; Klaus & Kennell, 1976; Maccoby, 1980). In contrast to a unitary trait, attachment has been defined increasingly in terms of particular behaviors that "attached" children and adults exhibit (Rutter, 1979). These behaviors include (1) proximity and/or contact-seeking behavior such as fondling, kissing, cuddling, gazing, soothing, and clinging; (2) showing distress on separation from a particular person; (3) showing joy or relief on reunion; (4) being oriented toward that person even though not in proximity with him or her; and (5) receiving reciprocal attachment behaviors from the other.

The last criterion, referring to the reciprocal nature of attachment behavior, is important in terms of recent conceptualizations. Instead of a unitary trait, attachment has been portrayed increasingly as a developmental process involving mutual behaviors exchanged between parent and infant. Attachment, therefore, is a bidirectional process through which parents and children form the first social bond (Ashton, 1978; Klaus & Kennell, 1978; Maccoby, 1980; Rutter, 1979). Through this process, individual "biological molecules" become tied together in human associations as patterns of interaction emerge and become intertwined (Nisbet & Perrin, 1977). Like investigators of reciprocity, those who study attachment processes examine the emergence of the incipient role relationship between parent and infant. To accomplish this, investigators of attachment have focused on both the attachment of infants to their parents (Ainsworth, 1973; Bowlby, 1969) and the attachment of parents to their infants (Klaus & Kennell, 1976).

Parent-to-Infant Attachment. Taking primarily an ethological perspective, Klaus and Kennel (1976) emphasized the importance of species-specific behaviors that characterize the interaction of mothers with infants. Traditional hospital practices that allow only minimal opportunities for contact between mothers and their newborns are a major focus of this work. Through experimental alterations of prevailing hospital practices, these researchers claim to have identified a number of long-term consequences stemming from early mother–infant contact and separation (Hales, Kennell, & Sosa, 1976; Kennell, Voos, & Klaus, 1979; Klaus, Jerauld, Kreger, McAlpine, Steffa, & Kennell, 1972; Klaus, Kennell, Plumb, & Zuehlke, 1970; Ringler, Kennell, Iavella, Novojosky, & Klaus, 1975). Other investigators, on the other hand, have found the same results to be more transitory in character (Leiderman & Seashore, 1974; Whiten, 1977). Klaus and Kennell (1976) called special attention to the importance of a sensitive period that occurs in the first hours and days immediately after birth. During the first hour after birth, for example, mothers in experimental groups were presented with their nude infants for about one hour of skin-to-skin contact. Extensive contact was also allowed between mothers and infants for several hours during the subsequent days of hospitalization. These experimental groups, in turn, were compared with control groups of mothers who experienced less contact with their infants.

During the period shortly after delivery, the "early-contact" mothers were reported to exhibit species-specific patterns of behavior as they interacted with their infants. The mothers usually began this sequence of behavior with fingertip touching of their infants' extremities and within a few minutes proceeded to palmar massaging of the trunk. The mothers also appeared to be in a state of ecstasy during this process (Klaus et al., 1970). By contrast, these species-specific behaviors developed more slowly in mothers who experienced later contact and mothers of premature infants. Fathers who observed and were involved in the birth process, as well as other individuals who observed the delivery, frequently exhibited signs of attachment.

During later follow-ups, the differences in attachment behaviors between the experimental and the control mothers were quite remarkable. For example, one month after delivery, the early-contact mothers sought greater proximity and engaged in more eye-to-eye contact with their infants than the control-group mothers (Klaus et al., 1972). Similar differences were found to persist in a follow-up study one year after delivery (Kennell, Jerauld, Wolfe, Chester, Kreger, McAlpine, Steffa, & Klaus, 1974).

Differences between experimental and control mothers in terms of their linguistic interaction with their infants were maintained two years after birth, with early-contact mothers using twice as many adjectives and fewer commands than control mothers (Ringler et al., 1975). Studies have also provided evidence of differences in the length and the success of breastfeeding between experimental and control mothers (Sousa, Barros, Gazelle, Bergeres, Pinheiro, Menezea, & Arruda, 1974; Winters, 1973).

A serious criticism of Klaus and Kennell's work is their decision to measure only the mother's side of a reciprocal process. Illustrative of such criticism is Bronfenbrenner's (1979) comment that Klaus and Kennell's "studies provide a glimpse—albeit tantalizingly one-sided—of the process through which the joint activity of mother and newborn leads to the formation of a primary dyad, which, in turn, sets the pace and steers the course of future development" (p. 64). This statement recognizes that parent-to-infant attachment is a reciprocal process and that subsequent reciprocal interaction and social development may be influenced by these early developments. Future research on parent-to-infant attachment would benefit from the same research methodologies used to study reciprocity, including precise micro-analyses of behavior, plus contingent probability and/or lag sequential analyses (Sackett, 1979).

Perhaps in response to such comments, Klaus and Kennell have begun to note that their research may be identifying the onset of mother–infant reciprocity (Kennell et al., 1979). They have proposed that "during the early sensitive period, a series of reciprocal interactions begins between mother and infant which bond them together and insures the further development of attachment" (p. 796). In short, maternal attachment behaviors may initiate the "conversation of gestures" between mother and child as discussed in the previous section on reciprocity. Early contact between mother and child may initiate the process through which shared expectancies and the social construction of a shared understanding develop.

An important parallel of the attachment literature to the symbolic interaction perspective is an emphasis on the emergence of parental expectations. Along these lines, Klaus and Kennell (1978) underscored the need for congruence between parents' expectations and the actual characteristics of their infants. Severe discrepancies between parental expectations and infant qualities, such as infants who are premature or have congenital defects, may interfere with the bonding process and the initiation of reciprocal interaction. In other words, the parent's perception of an infant's ability or inability to occupy and perform a reciprocal role (e.g., the child socializee or parent socializer roles) in relation to the parent may affect how the parent occupies and performs his or her own parental roles. If marked discrepancies are apparent between "expected" and "actual" infants, the parental role enactment may be affected adversely. In some cases, parents who experience these role discrepancies have exhibited high levels of child neglect and abuse (Klaus & Kennell, 1976, 1978).

In summary, the literature on parent-to-infant attachment has examined the onset of a conversation of gestures leading to the first social bond between mother and child. An important task for future investigators is to integrate this issue with the study of reciprocity in the parent–child relationship.

Infant-to-Parent Attachment. A second tradition is concerned with infant-to-caregiver attachment, especially after the first four months of life (Ainsworth & Bell, 1974; Ainsworth, Bell, & Stayton, 1971; Ainsworth & Wittig, 1969; Bowlby, 1969; White, 1975). Although neonates are not attached initially to specific adults, by the age of 4 months, they often begin to exhibit recognition and preference for their mothers. At 7 months, many of them protest separation from their parents and begin to demonstrate a fear of strangers (Ashton, 1978; Maccoby, 1980; Rutter, 1979). Between the ages of 14 and 18 months, protest and distress over separation from the parent reach their peak and subsequently begin to decline. Thereafter, children seem to use their parents as a secure base from which they proceed to expand their exploratory behavior (Ainsworth & Bell, 1974; Carr, Dabbs, & Carr, 1975).

By the age of 3 or 4, children have reduced needs for physical proximity to their parents and have come to realize that the parent–child relationship has continuity, even when the parents are physically absent. As these changes in attachment unfold, children come to view their parents as separate selves having their own patterns of thought and motives. Thus, attachment bonds change from emphasizing physical proximity toward more cognitive representations of relationship continuity.

Early work on attachment tended to portray it as an outcome of social development and as a unitary concept (Coates, Anderson, & Hartup, 1972; Rosenthal, 1973; Stayton & Ainsworth, 1973). More recently, researchers have begun to conceptualize attachment as a developmental process requiring longitudinal investigations. Part of this change has been sparked by results pointing to a lack of consistency in attachment behaviors and to low relationships between the behaviors that are supposed to be indicators of attachment (Masters & Wellman, 1974; Waters, Vaughn, & Egeland, 1980). In response to such results, many researchers and theorists are beginning to argue that attachment is not a unitary trait. Furthermore, as it persists through time, attachment may be represented by different behaviors at successive ages (Cohen, 1974; Lerner & Ryff, 1978; Sroufe & Waters, 1976; Weinraub, Brooks, & Lewis, 1977).

A related idea is that considerable variability exists in the quality of infants' attachment to their parents. For example, in a classic study, Ainsworth, Bell, and Stayton (1971) identified infants who were avoidant, resistant, and securely attached. Children also vary in the number of attachments they form, with multiple attachments of varying intensity being the typical pattern (Ainsworth, 1967; Schaffer & Emerson, 1964). In addition to their mothers, children appear to become attached to their fathers, their siblings, their peers, and a variety of additional significant others (Heineke & Westheimer, 1965; Lamb, 1977b; Rutter, 1979; Schwartz, 1972). Thus, it appears that infants often engage in role-making processes with several significant others at the same time.

Interest in the longitudinal aspects of attachment has stimulated work on the consequences of early bonding for later social development. Despite this emphasis, however, the "causal efficacy" of attachment as a contributor to longitudinal effects has not been established fully. Instead, the existing evidence indicates only that early secure attachment may be "associated" with compliance to maternal demands, appropriate play patterns, and effective problem-solving at later periods of development (Ainsworth & Bell, 1974; Bowlby, 1969; Main, 1973; Matas, Arend, & Sroufe, 1978; Waters et al., 1980). Several investigators, on the other hand, have focused on the early disruption of attachment and its implications for later development. In general, this research has indicated that children often recover from distressed reactions to early separation, and that subsequent recovery is contingent on the quality of the family relations that children experience (Yarrow & Goodwin, 1973; Yarrow, Goodwin, Manheimer, & Milowe, 1973).

Efforts to explain why infant-to-parent attachment occurs have been quite extensive (Ainsworth, 1973; Bowlby, 1969; Erikson, 1963; Freud, 1959; Gewirtz, 1961, 1972; Schaffer & Emerson, 1964). Several investigators have suggested that attachment might be a reciprocal process (Brazelton et al., 1974; Schaffer, 1977b; Stern, 1977). This involves a movement away from describing attachment as an "outcome" at 7 months, to an emphasis on the gradual emergence of a mutually constructed social bond between caretaker and infant. Under special experimental conditions, for example, Carpenter (1975) was able to show that even 2-week-old infants were capable of remarkably refined discriminations between their mothers and strangers. Other investigators have reported that 14- to 20-week-old infants have taken important steps toward attachment (Ambrose, 1961; Bronson, 1973).

Further evidence that attachment is a gradually emerging phenomenon has been provided in studies that specifically examined the mutual or bidirectional aspects of the bonding process, that is, the importance of parents who respond contingently to infants (Ainsworth et al., 1974; Clarke-Stewart, 1978; Lewis & Goldberg, 1969). *Contingent responsiveness,* in this case, refers to the parent's ability to read and react appropriately to the signals of an infant. Data from studies on maternal sensitivity to infant signals indicate that, when parents respond promptly and consistently, infants develop corresponding expectations for these responses (Ashton, 1978). Furthermore, the development of these expectations enhances the parent's position as a primary attachment object and contributes to the emergence of an incipient role relationship.

In studies of reciprocal interaction, certain investigators have begun to identify specific kinds of parent–infant reciprocity that are important in the attachment relationship and consistent with symbolic interaction concepts. Brazelton and associates (1974), for example, underscored the interdependence of rhythms between parent and child, which they believe serve as the root of attachment. These investigators proposed that parents and infants must each learn the behavior patterns of the other and the rules of (or expectations regarding) their developing relationship. In addition, Goldberg (1977) pointed to the importance of parents' ability to *read* an infant in conjunction with the predictability and responsiveness of their own behavior. In this manner, parents and infants seem to develop a sense of efficacy and expectancy in their emerging role relationships.

To a large extent, much of this literature concerns the process by which the infant and the parent gradually come to interpret each other's gestures and to establish mutual expectations. In doing so, these interactants begin to anticipate each other's responses and to adjust their lines of action in accordance with the other. The typical attachment behaviors that appear between 4 and 7 months are simply stages of development in the process of establishing this conversation of gestures. Thus, investigators of infant-to-parent attachment seem to be dealing with emerging role-making processes.

The attachment literature and the symbolic interaction perspective also share a concern with the process by which self–other distinctions emerge out of social interaction. This occurs as the child comes to see himself or herself as an object of the social environment in relation to others. Although more identifiable advances in this process occur in later developmental periods, one outcome of parent–infant transactions is the emergence of a primary relationship with an identifiable person who is separate from the self and is represented internally (Stern, 1977, p. 96). In other words, this is a beginning step, an initial relationship ''in the rough,'' that inaugurates self–other distinctions as parent–infant interactions become intertwined.

Later, with the emergence of further cognitive capacities, the child develops the ability to role-take significant others. One might speculate, therefore, that new role-taking abilities change the attachment relationship by lessening the child's requirements for physical proximity to the parent. That is, the child develops a sense of the parent's intentions to maintain the relationship, despite a temporary absence (Marvin, 1977).

Thus, like the other direction of attachment, research on infant-to-parent attachment is conceptually linked with the study of reciprocity. Simply stated, it is another vantage point from which to view the emergence of the first reciprocal role relationship and may be an important mechanism through which children make their initial self–other distinctions.

The Systemic Context and Parent–Child Socialization

The most recent trend in parent–child research and theory has been to recognize the importance of studying the family and its surrounding networks as holistic entities that socialize children (Belsky, 1981; Bronfenbrenner, 1979; Parke, Power, & Gottman, 1979; Pedersen, 1980). The proponents of systemic models have both incorporated and gone beyond the logic of reciprocal (dyadic) models of socialization. That is, according to this perspective, socialization is not only bidirectional; it is multidirectional.

The major assumption within a systemic perspective is that all members of a given social network (or family) can influence each other simultaneously. In terms of symbolic interaction, this idea is similar to conceptualizing the influence of the entire family-role system on the parent–child role relationship (Klein *et al.*, 1978; Lewis & Feiring, 1978; Rollins & Galligan, 1978). Investigators who take a systemic perspective propose that each role relationship within the family can influence any other role relationship.

Understanding systemic effects requires that families be conceptualized as sets of positions (e.g., husband-father, son-brother) having particular role assignments that form an interdependent system or social network (Aldous, 1978; Rodgers, 1964). Role relationships within these systems are reciprocal, an idea based on the assumption that parental performance of the child socializer and parent socializee role will be reciprocated by children's performance of the child socializee and parent socializer roles. Viewing family role relationships from this perspective implies that the enactment of roles within any family dyad may influence other family relationships, such as the parent–child relationship (Lewis & Feiring, 1978; Nye, 1976; Rollins & Galligan, 1978).

A major component of the systemic orientation is the recognition that direct effects, as a means of conceptualizing parent–child socialization, are much too limited. Instead, systemic approaches are also concerned with indirect influences (or second-order effects) originating with persons or relationships at least ''once removed'' from the children. For example, the influence of Parent A may be conveyed indirectly to a child through the level of support that parent A provides Parent B, who is interacting directly with the child. Some studies have indicated that second-order effects on children occur when one parent (spouse) provides support for the other parent (spouse) in the marital relationship (Belsky, 1979, 1980, 1981; Pedersen, 1980). Yet another way of conceptualizing systemic effects is to consider the possibility that one family relationship can influence another family relationship (in contrast to the effect of one individual on another individual). It is likely, for example, that the quality of the wife–husband relationship has an effect on the kind of parent–child relationship that develops.

Literature on the involvement of fathers with their offspring has been especially attentive to the systemic qualities of families and indirect effects (Belsky, 1979, 1981; Lamb, 1978a; Parke, 1979; Pedersen, 1975, 1980). For example, a father may influence a child indirectly by providing economic support to the mother, who, in turn, is able to spend more time interacting with the child. Conceptualized in role terminology, effective performance of the provider role by a father frees the mother for more time involvement in and effective performance of the child socializer role in relation to the child's performance of the socializee role (see Figure 2, Row A). Another example would be a situation in which a father's use of coercion in the child socializer role contributes to a child's displacement of noncompliant behavior in relation to the mother (see Figure 2, Row B). In this case, the child responds with a lower-quality performance of the child socializee role (e.g., noncompliance) in relation to the mother's performance of the child socializer role. The mother, in turn, may respond to the child with higher levels of coercion in her performance of the child socializer role.

More complex circumstances involve the direct influence of one reciprocal role relationship within the family (e.g., the husband–wife relationship) on another re-

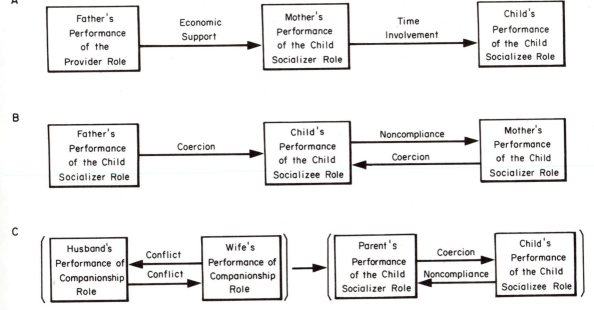

Figure 2. Indirect effects in systemic research.

ciprocal role relationship (e.g., the mother–child relationships). An example would be a situation in which a married couple is experiencing diminished companionship and heightened conflict. The resulting stress, conflict, and frustration may spill over into the parent–child relationship in the form of coercive-noncompliant interactions. From a symbolic interaction perspective, these circumstances may occur when a husband and wife fail to meet each other's expectations within companionship roles (see Figure 2, Row C). Conflict resulting from these discrepancies, in turn, may have a substantial influence on the parent's performance of the child socializer role (e.g., higher levels of coercion) and the child's enactment of the socializee role (e.g., higher levels of noncompliance). Illustrations of this kind only begin to capture the possible complexities in family role relationships.

In the same way that parent–child relations need to be examined in terms of family role systems, additional consideration needs to be given to the social matrix that surrounds the family. Of special interest here is the work of Urie Bronfenbrenner (1979), who called attention to a conceptualization referred to as the *social ecology of childhood.* Bronfenbrenner began at the level of reciprocal interaction between parent and child (or other immediately experienced relationships), which he referred to as the "microsystem." Beyond the parent–child dyad, the surrounding ecological environment is described as a set of nested structures, each being encompassed by a more general level of the social system. In short, a description of concentrically organized social

systems is offered, with special emphasis on the interconnections and the impact that each level of the social system has on the socialization of children. One of Bronfenbrenner's principal goals is to describe both the immediate and the more remote social settings that influence human development and the reciprocity that occurs between levels of the social environment.

More specifically, the level of the social environment that immediately encompasses the microsystem is referred to as the *mesosystem,* a level of social context that conceptualizes the interrelationships among two or more settings in which a particular child directly participates and occupies roles. An example would be a situation in which children simultaneously occupy roles within the parent–child relationship and in the peer group. The *exosystem,* on the other hand, is a more general setting that influences children, but that is not a domain in which children occupy roles directly. An example of an exosystem would be the impact of the parents' work roles on parent–child interactions. In other words, roles within work settings may have a direct impact on parental values, which, in turn, influence parent–child interaction. Finally, the most general level of the social system is the *macrosystem,* a context involving the overarching institutional and structural patterns of the culture or subculture. This generic social system includes the economic, social, historical, educational, legal, and political phenomena at the macrosociological level of analysis.

Notable features of Bronfenbrenner's framework are the concepts that it shares with the symbolic interaction perspective. For example, an important aspect of Bronfenbrenner's analysis of the ecology of childhood and the interrelationships among social settings is the use of such concepts as *role* and *role transition*. For Bronfenbrenner, human development is facilitated through interaction with persons who occupy a variety of roles. It also occurs as individuals make transitions and participate in an ever-broadening role repertoire.

In general, therefore, a systemic orientation places emphasis on conceptualizing parent–child socialization in terms of the family role system and the social networks that surround it. According to this perspective, dyadic conceptions of socialization are too limited because families and social networks are organized systems of inter-contingent role relationships that affect each other directly and indirectly. Besides the family, the parent–child relationship is interconnected with other settings at the same and more general levels of the social environment. That is, the parent–child relationship interfaces with schools, peers, work settings, socioeconomic conditions, and the surrounding ethnic environment. All of these settings, including the parent–child relationship, influence each other.

Critique of Bidirectional-Systemic Models

Although investigators of bidirectional-systemic models have provided important new insights, several complications and problems have become apparent in this research. The child effects research, for instance, suffers from the same limitations as the approach that it was designed to correct. Despite claims to the contrary (Bell & Harper, 1977), the child effects model does not deal with reciprocal causation as much as it does with an inverted one-way model. Thus, it seems as problematic to argue that socialization influence is primarily from child to parent as it does to argue that the influence is from parent to child.

Another problem, referred to as the *tyranny of the data,* is characteristic of investigations on parent–child reciprocity. That is, a prominent obstacle to research on reciprocity is the staggering number of sequential data generated on only a few cases. Furthermore, the complexity of the data and the required analytical procedures encourage researchers to be preoccupied with methodology and to use small, unrepresentative samples. In addressing these complexities, continual improvements in contingent-probability and lag-sequential-analysis techniques will be important (Bakeman & Brown, 1977; Martin *et al.*, 1981; Sackett, 1979). Another data reduction method is the application of multiple-regression techniques to sequential data (Martin *et al.*, 1981; Thomas & Martin, 1976). In this approach, both the actor's prior behavior and the partner's prior behavior are entered as joint predictors of the actor's current behavior. This procedure provides estimates of the independent effects of self-behavior, the partner's behavior, and their interaction.

Another method of addressing the complexity of sequential data is to ascertain the meaning that individuals assign to interactive situations. An approach of this kind may help investigators to conceptualize important components of interaction, to develop hypotheses, and to concentrate their efforts on manageable aspects of the conversation of gestures.

An assessment of both subjective and objective aspects of interaction requires a wider diversity of research methodologies than has previously been used in studies of reciprocity. One approach might be to use interviews and questionnaires in conjunction with observational procedures. This approach would allow the attitudes, perceptions, expectations, and behaviors of the interactants to be assessed (Parke, 1978). In the area of naturalistic research, for example, Denzin (1977) argued for a "triangulated methodology," or an approach in which the observer combines multiple data sources and research methods in studying interaction. According to Denzin, investigators should use "sensitizing concepts" about interaction and multiple methods to link the acts of subjects to their covert self-conversations and, in turn, to tie those acts and thoughts to the subjects' interaction with others.

Although computer technology has provided the capacity to analyze reciprocal interaction at microscopic levels, it remains to be seen if information at this level will be more useful than macroscopic data. As children grow older, parent–child interaction may be less a function of events occurring in immediately preceding time intervals and more a function of events that are remembered and responded to over longer periods of time. The power and the intentional influence within the parent–child relationship must also be considered. Perhaps the greatest utility of microanalytic techniques will be in the examination of parental interactions with infants and younger children.

A final criticism of recent approaches to studying parent–child socialization concerns the complexity of systemic approaches. Thus far, the research and conceptualization within the systemic orientations have been restricted primarily to triadic relationships. For families of more than three persons, the extreme complexities of interdependent role relationships and the countless indirect effects are formidable obstacles to systemic research. However, future investigators must continue to grapple with these sophisticated issues, because systemic models are convincing representations of the socialization process.

In general, therefore, the greatest obstacle to productive research within a bidirectional-systemic orientation concerns the almost overwhelming complexity that confronts investigators. Perhaps the best recommendation is for researchers to develop sound theories, to use sensitizing concepts, and to be realistically selective in the questions that they ask. Although various methodologies and statistics can be used to acquire and to summarize data, scholars ultimately must develop the concepts that give this information meaning. The latter task is the goal, whereas the former is only the means.

Summary and Conclusions

The primary purpose of this chapter has been to review the research on parent–child socialization conducted within the social-mold and the bidirectional-systemic approaches. Part of this involved the application of symbolic interaction concepts to organize and interpret the parent–child research. As a means of concluding this chapter, a conceptual model is presented that summarizes the major ideas of parent–child socialization, followed by suggestions for future research.

The model depicts three interconnecting levels of the social context. At the first level, special recognition is given to the idea that socialization is a bidirectional process at the level of face-to-face or "microlevel" interaction (see Figure 3, Level 1). Insights from both the social-mold and the child-effects approaches are combined to underscore that parents and children "affect" each other. Consequently, each side of the parent–child dyad is portrayed as performing roles, acquiring power, and funda-mentally influencing the other's attitudes, expectations, and role behaviors.

Recognition is also given in this model to the idea that bidirectional socialization has different consequences in each direction of the parent–child dyad. Early in the parent–child relationship, for example, parents have greater power than children and have long-term goals for which they intentionally socialize their offspring. By contrast, very young children affect their parents, to a large extent, through definitions that the parents impose on the presence, the actions, and the characteristics of their offspring. These meanings, plus the immediate requirements of young children, socialize adults for parenting roles. Subsequently, a gradual readjustment in the balance of power and the direction of intentional influence occurs as children acquire knowledge, skills, and resources. By late adolescence or adulthood, these factors have usually become more equalized within the parent–child relationship.

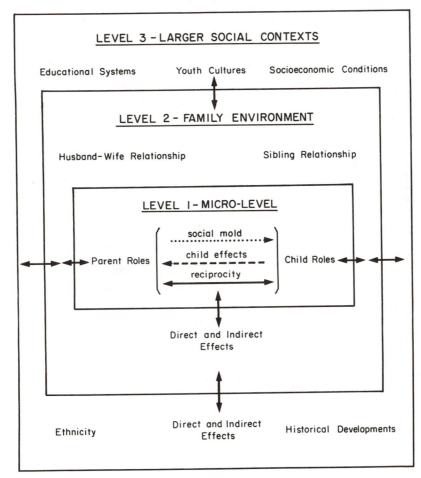

Figure 3. The social context of parent–child socialization.

In addition to "affecting" each other, it is important to remember that parents and children engage in sequential exchanges of behavior referred to as *reciprocity*. That is, an important focus of microlevel studies has been on "conversations of gestures" between infant and parent (see Figure 3, Level 1). Interactions of this kind appear to result in elementary role-making processes, incipient role relationships, and initial social bonds within parent–infant relationships. Presumably, these interactions become altered over time as the imbalance of power and the intentional influence are readjusted within the parent–child relationship.

Interfacing with the parent–child dyad is the larger family environment, in which parents and children occupy intercontingent roles (see Figure 3, Level 2). Because families are interdependent systems of reciprocal relationships, the parent–child, husband–wife, and sibling dyads are continually engaged in complex exchanges of social influence. These avenues of social influence become even more complicated as family structural factors (e.g., sibling number, child density, and birth order) become more numerous and complex (Klein *et al.*, 1978). A further complication is that social influence may be conveyed to parent and child through indirect as well as direct effects. From the perspective of the parent–child dyad, therefore, socialization is a complex and multidirectional process. Consequently, this level of the model both incorporates and goes byond a bidirectional conception of parent–child socialization.

A variety of larger social contexts that interconnect with the family and the parent–child relationship are portrayed in the final level of the model (see Figure 3, Level 3). Included within this dimension are educational systems, youth cultures, socioeconomic conditions, ethnicity, and historical developments. These contexts are direct and indirect sources of attitudes, values, and cultural goals that become translated into a broad framework of expectations in the parent–child role relationship. Thus, if parents and children are shaped by reciprocal interaction, the larger social structures often set broad parameters for these exchanges (Maines, 1977; Stryker, 1980).

In terms of research, a wide variety of designs, analytical procedures, and methodologies are consistent with the foregoing model. Research using the social-mold, child-effects, reciprocal, and systemic designs all have notable strengths and limitations. Investigators need to weigh their research questions carefully and to choose the approach that corresponds most effectively with their resources and the issue at hand. Social scientists need to avoid placing too much credence in any one approach or methodology.

Because parents and children affect each other differently, certain issues may still be examined effectively with unidirectional models. For example, studies on the influence of parental power (McDonald, 1977, 1979, 1980), the socialization of parental attitudes (Acock & Bengtson, 1978, 1980), and family structure (Kidwell, 1981), using survey data and regression techniques, have made important contributions. Tests for curvilinearity in relationships and the use of interaction terms in regression equations have been productive techniques in these studies (Acock & Bengtson, 1978; Kidwell, 1981; Peterson *et al.*, 1985).

Another area in which the social mold perspective can still make significant contributions is the development of comprehensive models that include links among (1) variables from larger social contexts; (2) family structural variables; (3) parental characteristics; (4) and children's social and personality characteristics. To accomplish such contributions, path analysis and structural equation models can be used to examine the relationship between sets of variables that are ordered causally according to theory (Asher, 1976; Jöreskog & Sörbom, 1979). Other investigators who are concerned with the reciprocal rather than the directional influences between different social contexts have emphasized the importance of examining the interconnections between settings that socialize children (Bronfenbrenner, 1979; Garbarino, 1982). Future researchers can benefit by examining how social development is facilitated or hindered by the interrelationships among such settings as the parent–child dyad, the parents' work setting, the school, and the peer group.

In child effects research, on the other hand, attention should be given to the effects of older offspring on adults. Future investigators need to examine the influence of youth power on parents and generational transmission from child to parent (Bengtson & Troll, 1978; Hill, 1975; Peterson, 1977). Child effects of this kind can be examined with the same multivariate designs and regression techniques that have been useful for research on parental effects.

Changes in the expectations and performance of parent–child roles over time should be an additional concern of research. In spite of this need, however, the longitudinal designs needed to examine these issues often require resources that are beyond the reach of many researchers (Hill, 1964; Klein *et al.*, 1978). A means of avoiding this difficulty is to use designs that require more limited resources and time frames. One such design is the segmented longitudinal panel with control groups. In this design, two or more groups of respondents are compared at two or more points in time to monitor the effects of a critical role transition. An experimental group that experiences important changes in role content is identified in advance and is compared to a control group not having the same experience. Another possibility for assessing role change is to combine cross-sectional and longitudinal designs by following several cohorts across limited time periods and then linking the patterns of change in an overall configuration. This procedure has been referred to as *sequential analysis* and permits the researcher to account for developmental and historical effects (Baltes, 1968; Schaie, 1965).

An important component of future parent–child research will be studies of reciprocal interaction involving microanalytic recordings of sequential behavior, contingent probability analysis, and lag sequential analysis (Gottman, 1979; Lamb, Suomi, & Stephenson, 1979; Lytton, 1979; Martin *et al.*, 1981). The application of such procedures is needed especially within parent–child dyads having children who are older than infants. These techniques need to be used in conjunction with interviews and self-report measures to provide insight into the meaning of reciprocal interaction for the participants (Parke, 1978; Pedersen, 1980).

Future investigators also need to concentrate their efforts on studying the parent–child relationship as part of an interdependent system of family roles. This approach will require a focus on the interaction that occurs among three or more family members and a concern with indirect or second-order effects. Special emphasis needs to be placed on devising strategies that are sophisticated enough to handle the many ways in which indirect effects can be mediated. Given the possible complexities of this approach, researchers will need to develop sound theory from which to derive precise hypotheses for empirical scrutiny. The observation of interaction and the quantification of relationships between behaviors are unlikely to be productive unless sufficient theory is developed to guide these efforts and to interpret the results (Lewis, Feiring, & Weinraub, 1981; Parke *et al.*, 1979).

Perhaps the most important undertaking for future investigators is to examine research questions with multiple methods, as few efforts to establish convergent validity and to generalize results across methods have been successful (Miller, Rollins, & Thomas, 1982; Thomas *et al.*, 1977). However, in each case, quantitative, qualitative, experimental, and naturalistic research methodologies can provide complementary information about the generalizability of findings concerning parent–child socialization. For example, experimental and quantitative approaches provide the means through which alternative explanatory factors can be controlled, either by the nature of the design, or through statistical procedures. On the other hand, qualitative and naturalistic approaches provide investigators with a more holistic description of the subjects' lives and perspectives. In addition, such methodologies may reveal whether empirically based principles of socialization operate outside the laboratory in some naturally occurring "reality" (Denzin, 1977; Lofland, 1976).

Even if socialization principles do not generalize from one method to another, the use of multiple methods will help us to understand the role expectations and cues in particular research settings. Apparently, each of these settings encourages participants to construct a unique definition of the situation and to respond in a different manner (Bronfenbrenner, 1979; Thomas & Thomas, 1928; Weisz, 1978).

In conclusion, both conceptually and methodologically, future advances in the area of parent–child socialization will result as investigators increasingly appreciate the complexities involved and devise strategies to accommodate them. Because the parent–child bond is the basic association of the human experience, this complicated task is well worth the effort. Through these relationships, parents add new dimensions to their identities as they act as social agents and are influenced by their offspring. The young, in turn, take their first steps into the social world and become sophisticated participants in the social construction of reality.

ACKNOWLEDGMENTS

Special appreciation is expressed to Jo Lynn Cunningham, David Peters, Marvin Sussman, Roger Swagler, Darwin Thomas, Karl Weddle, and two anonymous reviewers for their helpful comments on earlier versions of this chapter.

References

Abramovitz, R. Parenthood in America. *Journal of Clinical Child Psychology*, 1976, *5*, 43–46.

Acock, A. C., & Bengtson, V. L. On the relative influence of mothers and fathers: A covariance analysis of political and religious socialization. *Journal of Marriage and the Family*, 1978, *40*, 519–530.

Acock, A. C., & Bengtson, V. L. Socialization and attribution processes: Actual versus perceived similarity among parents and youth. *Journal of Marriage and the Family*, 1980, *42*, 501–515.

Ainsworth, M. D. *Infancy in Uganda: Infant care and the growth of attachment*. Baltimore: Johns Hopkins University Press, 1967.

Ainsworth, M. D. The development of infant–mother attachment. In B. M. Caldwell & H. N. Ricciuti (Eds.), *Review of child development research*, Vol. 3. Chicago: University of Chicago Press, 1973.

Ainsworth, M. D., & Bell, S. M. Mother-infant interaction and the development of competence. In K. Connally & J. Bruner (Eds.), *The growth of social competence*. London: Academic Press, 1974.

Ainsworth, M. D., & Wittig, B. Attachment and exploratory behavior of one-year-olds in a strange situation. In B. Foss (Ed.), *Determinants of infant behavior*, Vol. 4. London: Methuen, 1969.

Ainsworth, M. D., Bell, S. M., & Stayton, D. J. Individual differences in strange-situation behavior of one-year-olds. In H. R. Schaffer (Ed.), *The origins of human relations*. London: Academic Press, 1971.

Aldous, J. Family interaction patterns. *Annual Review of Sociology*, 1977, *3*, 105–135.

Aldous, J. *Family careers: Developmental change in families*. New York: Wiley, 1978.

Allen, W. R. The search for applicable theories in black family life. *Journal of Marriage and the Family*, 1978, *40*, 117–129.

Alvirez, D., & Bean, F. D. The Mexican-American family. In C. H. Mindel & R. W. Habenstein (Eds.), *Ethnic families in America: Patterns and variations*. New York: Elsevier, 1975.

Ambrose, J. A. The development of the smiling response in early infancy. In B. M. Foss (Ed.), *Determinants of infant behavior*, Vol. 1. London: Methuen, 1961.

Aronfreed, J. The concept of internalization. In D. A. Goslin (Ed.), *Handbook of socialization theory and research*. Chicago: Rand McNally, 1969.

Asher, H. *Causal modeling*. Beverly Hills, Calif.: Sage Publications, 1976.

Ashton, P. T. The role of the attachment bond in effective parenting. In J. H. Stevens, Jr., & M. Mathews (Eds.), *Mother/child/father/child relationships*. Washington, D.C.: National Association for the Education of Young Children, 1978.

Bakan, D. *The duality of human existence: Isolation and communion in western man*. Boston: Beacon Press, 1966.

Bakeman, R. & Brown, J. Behavioral dialogues: An approach to the assessment of mother-infant interaction. *Child Development*, 1977, *48*, 195–203.

Baltes, B. B. Longitudinal and cross-sectional sequences in the study of age and generation effects. *Human Development*, 1968, *11*, 145–171.

Bandura, A. *Social learning theory*. Englewood Cliffs, N.J.: Prentice-Hall, 1976.

Bandura, A., & Huston, A. Identification as a process of incidental learning. *Journal of Abnormal and Social Psychology*, 1961, *63*, 311–318.

Bandura, A., & Walters, R. H. *Social learning and personality development*. New York: Holt, Rinehart & Winston, 1963.

Barnett, R. C. Parental sex-role attitudes and child-rearing values. *Sex Roles*, 1981, *7*, 837–846.

Bartz, K. W., & Levine, E. S. Childrearing by black parents: A description and comparison to Anglo and Chicano parents. *Journal of Marriage and the Family*, 1978, *40*, 709–718.

Baumrind, D. Effects of authoritative control on child behavior. *Child Development*, 1966, *37*, 887–907.

Baumrind, D. Child care practices anteceding three patterns of preschool behavior. *Genetic Psychology Monographs*, 1967, *75*, 43–83.

Baumrind, D. Current patterns of parental authority. *Developmental Psychology Monograph*, 1971, *4*(1, Pt. 2).

Baumrind, D. Socialization and instrumental competence in young children. In E. Hartup (Ed.), *Research on young children*. Washington, D.C.: National Association for the Education of Young Children, 1972.

Baumrind, D. Parental disciplinary patterns and social competence in children. *Youth and Society*, 1978, *9*, 239–276.

Baumrind, D. New directions in socialization research. *American Psychologist*, 1980, *35*, 639–652.

Baumrind, D., & Black, A. Socialization practices associated with dimensions of social competence in preschool boys and girls. *Child Development*, 1967, *38*, 291–327.

Bayley, N., & Schaefer, E. S. Relationships between socioeconomic variables and the behavior of mothers toward young children. *Journal of Genetic Psychology*, 1960, *96*, 239–276.

Becker, W. C. Consequences of different kinds of parental discipline. In M. L. Hoffman & L. Hoffman (Eds.), *Review of child development research*, Vol. 1. Chicago: University of Chicago Press, 1964.

Becker, W. C., & Krug, R. S. A circumplex model for social behavior in children. *Child Development*, 1964, *35*, 371–396.

Bell, R. Q. A reinterpretation of the direction of effects in studies of socialization. *Psychological Review*, 1968, *75*, 81–95.

Bell, R. Q., & Harper, L. V. *Child effects on adults*. Hillsdale, N.J.: Lawrence Erlbaum, 1977.

Belsky, J. The interrelation of parental and spousal behavior during infancy in traditional nuclear families: An exploratory analysis. *Journal of Marriage and the Family*, 1979, *41*, 62–68.

Belsky, J. A family analysis of parental influence on infant exploratory competence. In F. Pedersen (Ed.), *The father-infant relationship: Observational studies in a family context*. New York: Praeger Special Studies, 1980.

Belsky, J. Early human experiences: A family perspective. *Developmental Psychology*, 1981, *17*, 3–23.

Bengston, V. L. Generation and family effects in values socialization. *American Sociological Review*, 1975, *40*, 358–371.

Bengston, V. L., & Kuypers, J. A. Generational differences and the developmental stake. *Aging and Human Development*, 1971, *2*, 249–260.

Bengtson, V. L., & Troll, L. Youth and their parents: Feedback and intergenerational influence in socialization. In R. M. Lenrer & G. B. Spanier (Eds.), *Child influences on marital and family interaction A life-span perspective*. New York: Academic Press, 1978.

Berger, P. L., & Luckman, T. *The social construction of reality: A treatise in the sociology of knowledge*. New York: Anchor Books, 1967.

Bernstein, B. Elaborated and restricted codes: Their social origins and some consequences. In J. J. Gumpery & D. Hymes (Eds.), *The ethnography of communication*, special publication of the *American Anthropologist*, 1964.

Bernstein, B. A sociolinguistic approach to socialization, with some reference to educability. In F. Williams (Ed.), *Language and poverty*. Chicago: Markham, 1970.

Bernstein, B. *Class, codes and control: Theoretical studies toward a sociology of language*, Vol. 1. London: Routledge & Kegan Paul, 1971.

Bernstein, B. *Class, codes and control: Applied studies toward a sociology of language*, Vol. 2. London: Routledge & Kegan Paul, 1973.

Bernstein, B., & Henderson, D. Social class differences in the relevance of language to socialization. In B. Bernstein (Ed.), *Class, codes and control*, Vol. 2. London: Routledge & Kegan Paul, 1973.

Biddle, B. J. *Role theory: Expectations, identities, and behaviors*. New York: Academic Press, 1979.

Biller, H. B. *Paternal deprivation*. Lexington, Mass.: Heath, 1974.

Biller, H. B. The father and personality development: Paternal deprivation and sex role development. In M. E. Lamb (Ed.), *The role of the father in child development*. New York: Wiley, 1976.

Birns, B. The emergence and socialization of sex differences in the earliest years. *Merrill-Palmer Quarterly*, 1976, *22*, 229–254.

Block, J. H. Conceptions of sex roles: Some cross-cultural and longitudinal perspectives. *American Psychologist*, 1973, *28*, 512–526.

Block, J. H. Another look at sex differentiation in the socialization behaviors of mothers and fathers. In F. Denmark & J. Sherman (Eds.), *Psychology of women: Future directions of research*. New York: Psychological Dimensions, 1980.

Blumer, H. *Symbolic interactionism*. Englewood Cliffs, N.J.: Prentice-Hall, 1969.

Bossard, J. H., & Boll, E. *The large family system*. Philadelphia: University of Pennsylvania Press, 1956.

Bowlby, J. *Attachment*. New York: Basic Books, 1969.

Bowlby, J. *Attachment and loss: Separation anxiety and anger*, Vol. 2. London: Hogarth, 1973.

Brazelton, T. B., Koslowski, B., & Main, M. The origins of reciprocity: The early mother-infant interaction. In M. Lewis & L. A. Roseblum (Eds.), *The effect of the infant on its caregiver*. New York: Wiley, 1974.

Bronfenbrenner, U. Socialization and social class through time and space. In E. E. Maccoby, T. M. Newcomb, & E. L. Hartley (Eds.), *Readings in social psychology*. New York: Holt, Rinehart & Winston, 1958.

Bronfenbrenner, U. *The ecology of human development*. Cambridge: Harvard University Press, 1979.

Bronson, G. W. Infant's reactions to unfamiliar persons and novel objects. *Monograph of the Society for Research in Child Development*, 1973, *37*(3).

Bruner, J. S. Early social interaction and language acquisition. In H. R. Schaffer (Ed.), *Studies in mother-infant interaction*. New York: Academic Press, 1977.

Burr, W. R. *Theory construction and the sociology of the family*. New York: Wiley, 1973.

Burr, W. R., Leigh, G. K., Day, R., & Constantine, J. Symbolic interaction and the family. In W. R. Burr, R. Hill, F. I. Nye, & I. L. Reiss (Eds.), *Contemporary theories about the family*, Vol. 2. New York: Free Press, 1979.

Buss, D. M. Predicting parent-child interaction from children's activity level. *Developmental Psychology*, 1981, *17*, 59–65.

Carpenter, G. Mother's face and the newborn. In R. Lewin (Ed.), *Child alive*. London: Temple Smith, 1975.

Carr, S., Dabbs, J., & Carr, T. Mother-infant attachment: The importance of the mother's visual field. *Child Development,* 1975, *46,* 331–338.

Charlesworth, W. R., & Kreutzer, M. The ontogenesis of smiling and laughter: A perspective on the organization of development in infancy. *Psychological Review,* 1973, *83,* 173–189.

Chemers, M. M. The relationship between birth order and leadership styles. *Journal of Social Psychology,* 1970, *80,* 243–244.

Chodorow, N. *The reproduction of mothering: Psychoanalysis and sociology of gender.* Berkeley: University of California Press, 1978.

Clarke-Stewart, K. A. And daddy makes three: The father's impact on mother and young child. *Child Development,* 1978, *49,* 466–478.

Clausen, J. A. Family structure, socialization, and personality. In M. L. Hoffman & L. W. Hoffman (Eds.), *Socialization and society.* Boston: Little, Brown, 1966.

Coates, B., Anderson, E. P., & Hartup, W. W. Interrelations in the attachment behavior of human infants. *Developmental Psychology,* 1972, *6,* 218–230.

Cogswell, B. E. Socialization into the family. In M. B. Sussman (Ed.), *Sourcebook in marriage and the family* (4th ed.). Boston: Houghton Mifflin, 1974.

Cohen, L. J. The operational definition of human attachment. *Psychological Bulletin,* 1974, *81,* 107–217.

Cohen, S., & Beckwith, L. Maternal language in infancy. *Developmental Psychology,* 1976, *12,* 371–372.

Condon, W. S., & Sander, L. W. Synchrony demonstrated between movements of the neonate and adult speech. *Child Development,* 1974, *45,* 456–462.

Connell, R. W. Political socialization in the American family: The evidence. *Public Opinion Quarterly,* 1972, *36,* 323–333.

Connors, K., & Osofsky, J. D. *Patterning of behaviors during early mother-infant interaction.* Paper presented at the Biennial Meeting of Society for Research in Child Development, New Orleans, 1977.

Cook-Gumperz, J. *Social control and socialization: A study of class differences in the language of maternal control.* London: Routledge & Kegan Paul, 1973.

Coopersmith, S. *The antecedents of self-esteem.* San Francisco: Freeman, 1967.

Cross, W. E. Black families and Black identity development: Rediscovering the distinction between self-esteem and reference group orientation. *Journal of Comparative Family Studies,* 1981, *12,* 19–49.

Dager, E. Z. Socialization and personality development in the child. In H. T. Christensen (Ed.), *Handbook of marriage and the family.* Chicago: Rand McNally, 1964.

Denzin, N. K. *Childhood socialization.* San Francisco: Jossey-Bass, 1977.

Devereaux, E. C., Jr., Bronfenbrenner, U., & Rodgers, R. R. Child-rearing in England and the United States: A cross-national comparison. *Journal of Marriage and the Family,* 1969, *31,* 257–270.

Dinnerstein, D. *The mermaid and the minotaur: Sexual arrangements and human malaise.* New York: Harper & Row, 1977.

Drews, E. M., & Teahan, J. E. Parental attitudes and academic achievement. *Journal of Clinical Psychology,* 1957, *13,* 328–332.

Durrett, M. E., O'Bryant, S., & Pennebraker, J. W. Child-rearing reports of white, black and Mexican-American families. *Developmental Psychology,* 1975, *11,* 871.

Dyer, E. D. Parenthood as crisis: A re-study. *Marriage and Family Living,* 1963, *25,* 196–201.

Edwards, J. N., & Brauburger, M. Exchange and parent-youth conflict. *Journal of Marriage and the Family,* 1973, *35,* 101–107.

Elder, G. H. *Children of the Great Depression.* Chicago: University of Chicago Press, 1974.

Elder, G. H. History and the family: The discovery of complexity. *Journal of Marriage and the Family,* 1981, *43,* 489–519.

Elder, G. H., & Bowerman, C. W. Family structure and childrearing patterns: The effect of family size and sex composition. *American Sociological Review,* 1963, *28,* 891–905.

Ellis, G. H., Thomas, D. L., & Rollins, B. C. Measuring parental support: The interrelationship of three measures. *Journal of Marriage and the Family,* 1976, *38,* 713–722.

Erikson, E. H. *Childhood and society* (rev. ed.). New York: Norton, 1963.

Erlanger, H. S. Social class and corporal punishment in child-rearing: A reassessment. *American Sociological Review,* 1974, *39,* 68–85.

Fantz, R. The origin of perception. *Scientific American,* 1961, *204,* 66–72.

Fantz, R. Visual experience in infants: Decreased attention to familiar patterns relative to novel ones. *Science,* 1964, *146,* 668–670.

Foote, N. N., & Cottrell, L. S. *Identity and interpersonal competence.* Chicago: University of Chicago Press, 1955.

Freedman, D. G. *Human infancy: An evolutionary perspective.* New York: Wiley Interscience, 1974.

French, J. R., & Raven, B. The bases of social power. In D. Cartwright (Ed.), *Studies in social power.* Ann Arbor, Mich.: Institute for Social Research, 1959.

Freud, S. *Outline of psychoanalysis.* New York: Norton, 1959.

Gallagher, B. J. An empirical analysis of attitude differences between three kin-related generations. *Youth and Society,* 1974, *4,* 327–349.

Garbarino, J. *Children and families in the social environment.* New York: Aldine, 1982.

Gecas, V. Parental behavior and dimensions of adolescent self-evaluation. *Sociometry,* 1971, *34,* 466–482.

Gecas, V. The socialization and child care roles. In F. I. Nye (Ed.) *Role structure and the analysis of the family.* Beverly Hills, Calif.: Sage Publications, 1976.

Gecas, V. The influence of social class on socialization. In W. R. Burr, R. Hill, F. I. Nye, & I. L. Reiss (Eds.), *Contemporary theories about the family,* Vol. 1. New York: Free Press, 1979.

Gecas, V. Contexts of socialization. In M. Rosenberg & R. Turner (Eds.), *Sociological perspectives in social psychology.* New York: Basic Books, 1981.

Gecas, V., & Nye, F. I. Sex and class differences in parent-child interaction: A test of Kohn's hypothesis. *Journal of Marriage and the Family,* 1974, *36,* 742–749.

Gewirtz, J. L. A learning analysis of the effects of normal stimulation, privation and deprivation on the acquisition of social motivation and attachment. In B. M. Foss (Ed.), *Determinants of infant behavior.* London: Methuen, 1961.

Gewirtz, J. L. Mechanisms of social learning. In D. A. Goslin (Ed.), *Handbook of socialization theory and research.* Chicago: Rand McNally, 1969.

Gewirtz, J. L. *Attachment and dependency.* Washington, D.C.: Winston, 1972.

Goldberg, S. Social competence in infancy: A model of parent-infant interaction. *Merrill-Palmer Quarterly,* 1977, *23,* 164–177.

Goldin, P. C. A review of children's reports of parent behaviors. *Psychological Bulletin,* 1969, *71,* 222–236.

Gottman, J. M. *Marital interaction: Experimental investigations.* New York: Academic Press, 1979.

Grebler, L., Moore, J. W., & Guzman, R. C. *The Mexican-American people.* New York: Free Press, 1970.

Gutman, H. G. *The black family in slavery and freedom: 1750–1925.* New York: Random House, 1976.

Hales, D., Kennell, J., & Sosa, R. *How early is early contact? Defining the limits of the sensitive period.* Paper presented at the American Pediatric Society and Society for Pediatric Research Annual Meeting, St. Louis, April 1976.

Hartup, W. W. Perspectives on child and family interaction: Past, present, and future. In R. M. Lerner & G. B. Spanier (Eds.), *Child influences on marital and family interaction: A life-span perspective.* New York: Academic Press, 1978.

Haynes, S. N., Jensen, B., Wise, E., & Sherman, D. *Marital interaction and satisfaction: Assessment and impact.* Paper presented at the Annual Meeting of the American Psychological Association, New York, September 1979.

Heilbrun, A. B., & Waters, D. B. Underachievement related to perceived maternal childrearing and academic conditions of reinforcement. *Child Development,* 1968, *39,* 913–921.

Heineke, C. M., & Westheimer, I. J. *Brief separation.* London: Longman, 1965.

Heiss, J. Social roles. In M. Rosenberg & R. H. Turner (Eds.), *Social psychology: Sociological perspectives.* New York: Basic Books, 1981.

Hess, R. D. Social class and ethnic influences upon socialization. In P. D. Mussen (Ed.), *Carmichael's manual of child psychology,* Vol. 2. New York: Wiley, 1970.

Hess, R. D. Approaches to the measurement and interpretation of parent-child interaction. In R. W. Henderson (Ed.), *Parent-child interaction: Theory, research and prospects.* New York: Academic Press, 1981.

Hess, R. D., & Shipman, V. Early experience and the socialization of cognitive modes in children. *Child Development,* 1965, *36,* 867–886.

Hetherington, E. M., & Deur, J. The effects of father absence on child development. In W. W. Hartup (Ed.), *The young child,* Vol. 2. Washington, D.C.: National Association for the Education of Young Children, 1972.

Hill, R. Methodological issues in family development research. *Family Process,* 1964, *3,* 186–205.

Hill, R. Foreward. In R. E. Cromwell & D. H. Olson (Eds.), *Power in families.* New York: Halstead Publications, 1975.

Hill, R. Theories and research designs linking family behavior and child development: A critical overview. *Journal of Comparative Family Studies,* 1981, *12,* 1–18.

Hill, R. B. *The strengths of black families.* New York: National Urban League, 1971.

Hilton, I. Differences in the behavior of mothers toward first- and later-born children. *Journal of Personality and Social Psychology,* 1967, *7,* 282–290.

Hobbs, D. F., & Cole, S. P. Transition to parenthood: A decade replication. *Journal of Marriage and the Family,* 1976, *29,* 383–384.

Hodapp, A., & LaVoie, J. C. Imitation by second borns in adult-sibling dyads. *Genetic Psychology Monographs,* 1976, *93,* 113–128.

Hoffman, L. W. Changes in family roles, socialization, and sex differences. *American Psychologist,* 1977(August), 644–657.

Hoffman, L. W., & Manis, J. D. Influences of children on marital interaction and parental satisfaction and dissatisfaction. In R. Lerner & G. Spanier (Eds.), *Child influences on marriage and family interaction.* New York: Academic Press, 1978.

Hoffman, L. W., & Nye, F. I. (Eds.). *Working mothers.* San Francisco: Jossey-Bass, 1974.

Hoffman, M. L. Power assertion by the parent and its impact on the child. *Child Development,* 1960, *31,* 129–143.

Hoffman, M. L. Moral development. In P. H. Mussen (Eds.), *Carmichael's manual of child psychology* (3rd ed.). New York: Wiley, 1970.

Hoffman, M. L. Moral internalization, parental power and the nature of parent-child interaction. *Developmental Psychology,* 1975, *11*(2), 228–239.

Hoffman, M. L. Moral development in adolescence. In J. Adelson (Ed.), *Handbook of adolescent psychology.* New York: Wiley, 1980.

Hoffman, M. L., & Saltzstein, H. D. Parent discipline and the child's moral development. *Journal of Personality and Social Psychology,* 1967, *5,* 45–57.

Hogan, R., Johnson, J. A., & Ember, N. P. A socioanalytic theory of moral development. *New Directions for Child Development,* 1978, *1,* 1–18.

Holman, T. B., & Burr, W. R. Beyond the beyond: The growth of family theories in the 1970's. *Journal of Marriage and the Family,* 1980, *42,* 729–742.

Inkeles, A. Society, social structure and child socialization. In J. A. Clausen (Ed.), *Socialization and society.* Boston: Little, Brown, 1968.

Jacobs, B. S., & Moss, H. A. Birth order and sex of sibling as determinants of mother-infant interaction. *Child Development,* 1976, *47,* 315–322.

Jaffe, J., Stern, D. N., & Peery, J. C. Conversational complexity of gaze behavior in prelinguistic human development. *Journal of Psycholinguistic Research,* 1973, *2,* 321–330.

Jones, E. The probation student: What he is like and what can be done about it. *Journal of Educational Research,* 1955, *49,* 93–102.

Jöreskog, K. G., & Sörbon, D. *Advances in factor analysis and structural equation models.* Cambridge, Mass.: Abt Associates, 1979.

Kagan, J. The child in the family. *Daedalus,* 1977, *106,* 33–56.

Kagan, J., & Moss, H. A. *Birth to maturity.* New York: Wiley, 1962.

Kammeyer, K. Birth order as a research variable. *Social Forces,* 1967, *46,* 71–80.

Kandel, D., & Lesser, G. S. *Youth in two worlds.* San Francisco: Jossey-Bass, 1972.

Kennell, J. H., Jerauld, R., Wolfe, H., Chester, D., Kreger, N. C., McAlpine, W., Steffa, N., & Klaus, M. H. Maternal behavior one year after early and extended post-partum contact. *Developmental Medicine and Child Neurology,* 1974, *16,* 172–179.

Kennell, J. H., Voos, D. K., & Klaus, M. H. Parent-infant bonding. In J. D. Osofsky (Ed.), *The handbook of infant development.* New York: Wiley, 1979.

Kessen, W. Research in the psychological development of the infant. *Merrill-Palmer Quarterly,* 1963, *9,* 83–94.

Kidwell, J. S. Number of siblings, sibling spacing, sex, and birth order: Their effects on perceived parent-adolescent relationships. *Journal of Marriage and the Family,* 1981, *43,* 315–332.

Kidwell, J. S. The neglected birth order: Middleborns. *Journal of Marriage and the Family,* 1982, *44,* 225–235.

Kimball, B. Case studies in educational failure during adolescence. *American Journal of Orthopsychiatry,* 1953, *23,* 406–415.

Klaus, M. H., & Kennell, J. H. *Mother-infant bonding: The impact of early separation or loss on family development.* St. Louis: Mosby, 1976.

Klaus, M. H., & Kennell, J. H. Parent-to-infant attachment. In J. H. Stevens & M. Mathews (Eds.), *Mother/child father/child relationships.* Washington, D.C.: National Association for the Education of Young Children, 1978.

Klaus, M. H., Kennell, J. H., Plumb, N., & Zuehlke, S. Human maternal behavior at the first contact with her young. *Pediatrics,* 1970, *46,* 187–192.

Klaus, M. H., Jerauld, R., Kreger, N., McAlpine, W., Steffa, M., & Kennell, J. H. Maternal attachment—Importance of the first post-partum days. *New England Journal of Medicine,* 1972, *286,* 460–463.

Klein, D. M., Jorgensen, S. R., & Miller, B. C. Research methods and developmental reciprocity in families. In R. M. Lerner & G. B. Spanier (Eds.), *Child influences on marital and family interaction: A life-span perspective.* New York: Academic Press, 1978.

Koch, H. L. The relation of primary mental abilities in five- and six-year-olds to sex of child and characteristics of his sibling. *Child Development,* 1954, *25,* 209–223.

Kohn, M. L. Social class and parental values. *American Journal of Sociology,* 1959, *64,* 337–351.

Kohn, M. L. Social class and parent-child relationships: An interpretation. *American Journal of Sociology,* 1963, *68,* 471–480.

Kohn, M. L. *Class and conformity: A study in values.* Homewood, Ill.: Dorsey Press, 1969.

Kohn, M. L. *Class and conformity: A study in values* (2nd ed.). Chicago: University of Chicago Press, 1977.

Kohn, M. L. Job complexity and adult personality. In N. Smelser & E. Erickson (Eds.), *Themes of love and work in adulthood*. Cambridge: Harvard University Press, 1980.

Kohn, M. L., & Schooler, C. Occupational experience and psychological functioning: An assessment of reciprocal effects. *American Sociological Review*, 1973, *38*, 97–118.

Kohn, M. L., & Schooler, C. The reciprocal effects of the substantive complexity of work and intellectual flexibility: A longitudinal assessment. *American Journal of Sociology*, 1978, *84*(1), 24–52.

Korner, A. F. The effect of the infants' state, level of arousal, sex and ontogenetic stage on the caregiver. In M. Lewis & L. A. Rosenblum (Eds.), *The effect of the infant on its caregiver*. New York: Wiley, 1974.

Kotelchuck, M. The infant's relationship to the father: Experimental evidence. In M. E. Lamb (Ed.), *The role of the father in child development*. New York: Wiley, 1976.

Kuhn, M. Major trends in symbolic interaction theory in the past twenty-five years. *Sociological Quarterly*, 1964, *5*, 61–82.

Lamb, M. E. *The role of the father in child development*. New York: Wiley, 1976.

Lamb, M. E. Father-infant and mother-infant interaction in the first year of life. *Child Development*, 1977, *48*, 167–181. (a)

Lamb, M. E. A re-examination of the infant social world. *Human Development*, 1977, *20*, 65–85. (b)

Lamb, M. E. The father's role in the infant's social world. In J. H. Stevens & M. Mathews (Eds.), *Mother/child father/child relationships*. Washington, D.C.: National Association for the Education of Young Children, 1978. (a)

Lamb, M. E. Influence of the child on marital quality and family interaction during the prenatal and infancy periods. In R. M. Lerner & G. B. Spanier (Eds.), *Child influences on marital interaction: A life-span perspective*. New York: Academic Press, 1978. (b)

Lamb, M. E., Suomi, S. J., & Stephenson, G. R. (Eds.), *Social interaction analysis: Methodological issues*. Madison: University of Wisconsin Press, 1979.

LaRossa, R., & LaRossa, M. M. *Transition to parenthood: How infants change families*. Beverly Hills, Calif.: Sage Publications, 1981.

Lasko, J. K. Parent behavior toward first and second-born children. *Genetic Psychology Monographs*, 1954, *49*.

Leiderman, P. H., & Seashore, M. J. *Mother-infant neonatal separation: Some delayed consequences*. London, England: CIBA Foundation Conference on Parent-Infant Relationships, 1974.

LeMasters, E. E. Parenthood as crisis. *Marriage and Family Living*, 1957, *19*, 352–355.

LeMasters, E. E. *Parents in modern America*. Homewood, Ill.: Dorsey Press, 1974.

Lerner, R. M., & Ryff, C. D. Implementation of the life-span view of human development: The sample case of attachment. In P. B. Baltes (Ed.), *Life-span development and behavior*, Vol. 1. New York: Academic Press, 1978.

Lerner, R. M., & Spanier, G. B. *Child influences on marital and family interaction: A life-span perspective*. New York: Academic Press, 1978.

Lewis, M. State as an infant-environment interaction: An analysis of mother-infant interactions as a function of sex. *Merrill-Palmer Quarterly*, 1972, *18*, 95–122.

Lewis, M., & Feiring, C. The child's social world. In R. M. Lerner & G. B. Spanier (Eds.), *Child influences on marital and family interaction: A life-span perspective*. New York: Academic Press, 1978.

Lewis, M., & Goldberg, S. Perceptual-cognitive development in infancy: A generalized expectancy model as a function of mother-infant interaction. *Merrill-Palmer Quarterly*, 1969, *15*, 81–101.

Lewis, M., & Kreitzberg, V. S. Effects of birth order and spacing on mother-infant interactions. *Developmental Psychology*, 1979, *15*, 617–625.

Lewis, M., & Lee-Painter, S. The origins of reciprocity: The early mother-infant interaction. In M. Lewis & L. A. Rosenblum (Eds.), *The effect of the infant on its caregiver*. New York: Wiley, 1974.

Lewis, M., & Rosenblum, L. A. (Eds.). *The effect of the infant on its caregiver*. New York: Wiley, 1974.

Lewis, M., Feiring, C., & Weinraub, M. The father as a member of the child's social network. In M. Lamb (Ed.), *The role of the father in child development*. New York: Wiley, 1981.

Lipsitt, L. Learning in the first year of life. In L. P. Lipsitt & C. Spiker (Eds.), *Advances in child development and behavior*, Vol. 1. New York: Academic Press, 1963.

Lofland, J. *Doing social life: The qualitative study of human interaction in natural settings*. New York: Wiley, 1976.

Lusk, D., & Lewis, M. Mother-infant interaction among the Wolof Senegal. *Human Development*, 1972, *15*, 58–69.

Lynn, D. B. *The father: His role in child development*. Monterey, Calif.: Brooks/Cole, 1974.

Lynn, D. B. *Daughters and parents*. Monterey, Calif.: Brooks/Cole, 1979.

Lytton, H. Disciplinary encounters between young boys and their mothers and fathers: Is there a contingency system? *Developmental Psychology*, 1979, *15*, 256–268.

Maccoby, E. E. The choice of variables in the study of socialization. *Sociometry*, 1961, *24*, 257–371.

Maccoby, E. E. *Social development: Psychological growth and the parent-child relationship*. New York: Harcourt Brace Jovanovich, 1980.

Maccoby, E. E., & Jacklin, C. N. *The psychology of sex differences*. Stanford, Calif.: Stanford University Press, 1974.

Macoby, E. E., & Martin, J. A. Socialization in the context of the family: Parent-child interaction. In E. Mavis Hetherington (Eds.), *Handbook of child psychology*, Vol. 4 (4th ed.). New York: Wiley, 1983.

Madsen, W. *The Mexican-American of south Texas* (2nd ed.). New York: Holt, Rinehart & Winston, 1973.

Main, M. *Exploration, play, and cognitive functioning as related to child-mother attachment*. Unpublished doctoral dissertation, John Hopkins University, 1973.

Maines, D. Social organization and social structure in symbolic interactionist thought. *Annual Review of Sociology*, 1977, *3*, 235–259.

Manis, J. G., & Meltzer, B. N. *Symbolic interaction* (3rd ed.). Boston: Allyn & Bacon, 1978.

Mannheim, K. The problem of generations. In K. Mannheim (Ed.), *Essays on the sociology of knowledge*. London: Routledge & Kegan, 1952. (Originally published, 1923.)

Marcus, A. C. Memory aids in longitudinal health surveys: Results from a field experiment. *American Journal of Public Health*, 1982, *72*, 567–573.

Marjoribanks, E., & Walberg, H. Mental abilities: Sibling constellation and social class correlates. *British Journal of Clinical and Social Psychology*, 1975, *14*, 109–116.

Martin, B. Parent-child relations. In R. D. Horowitz (Ed.), *Review of child development research*. Chicago: University of Chicago Press, 1975.

Martin, J. A., Maccoby, E. E., Baran, K. W., & Jacklin, C. N. Sequential analysis of mother-child interaction at 18 months: A comparison of microanalytic methods. *Developmental Psychology*, 1981, *17*, 146–157.

Marvin, R. S. An ethological-cognitive model for the attenuation of mother-child attachment behavior. In T. Alloway, P. Pliner, & L. Kramer (Eds.), *Attachment behavior*. New York: Plenum Press, 1977.

Masters, J., & Wellman, H. Human infant attachment: A procedural critique. *Psychological Bulletin*, 1974, *81*, 218–237.

Matas, L., Arend, R., & Sroufe, L. Continuity in adaptation in the second year: Quality of attachment and later competence. *Child Development*, 1978, *49*, 547–556.

Matteson, D. R. *Adolescence today: Sex roles and the search for identity*. Homewood, Ill.: Dorsey Press, 1975.

McAdoo, H. P. Minority families. In J. H. Stevens & M. Mathews (Eds.), *Mother/child father/child relationships*. Washington, D.C.: National Association for the Education of Young Children, 1978.

McClelland, D. C., Atkinson, R., Clark, R. A., & Lowell, E. L. *The achievement motive*. New York: Appleton-Century-Crofts, 1953.

McDonald, G. W. Parental identification by the adolescent: A social power approach. *Journal of Marriage and the Family*, 1977, *39*, 705–719.

McDonald, G. W. Determinants of adolescent perceptions of maternal and paternal power in the family. *Journal of Marriage and the Family*, 1979, *41*, 757–770.

McDonald, G. W. Parental power and adolescents' parental identification: A reexamination. *Journal of Marriage and the Family*, 1980, *42*, 289–296.

Mead, G. H. *Mind, self and society*. Chicago: University of Chicago Press, 1934.

Meltzer, B. N., Petras, J. W., & Reynolds, L. T. *Symbolic interaction: Genesis, varieties and criticism*. London: Routledge & Kegan Paul, 1975.

Messer, S. B., & Lewis, M. Social class and sex differences in the attachment and play behavior of the year-old infant. *Merrill-Palmer Quarterly*, 1972, *18*, 295–306.

Miller, B. C. A multivariate developmental model of marital satisfaction. *Journal of Marriage and the Family*, 1976, *38*, 643–658.

Miller, B. C., Rollins, B. C., & Thomas, D. L. On methods of studying marriages and families. *Journal of Marriage and the Family*, 1982, *44*, 851–873.

Miller, D. R., & Swanson, G. E. *Inner conflict and defense*. New York: Holt, 1960.

Mindel, C. H., & Habenstein, R. W. *Ethnic families in America: Patterns and variations*. New York: Elsevier Scientific, 1975.

Minton, C., Kagan, J., & Levine, J. A. Maternal obedience and control in the two-year-old. *Child Development*, 1971, *42*, 1873–1894.

Morrow, W. R., & Wilson, R. C. Family relations of bright high-achieving and underachieving high school boys. *Child Development*, 1961, *32*, 501–510.

Moss, H. A. Sex, age and state as determinants of mother-infant interaction. *Merrill-Palmer Quarterly*, 1967, *13*, 19–36.

Moss, H. A. Early sex differences and mother-infant interaction. In R. C. Friedman, R. M. Richart, & R. L. Vande Wiele (Eds.), *Sex differences in behavior*. New York: Wiley, 1974.

Murillo, N. The Mexican-American family. In N. W. Wagner & M. J. Hung (Eds.), *Chicanos: Social and psychological perspectives*. St. Louis: C. V. Mosby, 1971.

Newson, J. An intersubjective approach to the systematic description of mother-infant interaction. In H. R. Schaffer (Ed.), *Studies in mother-infant interaction*. New York: Academic Press, 1977.

Nisbet, R., & Perrin, R. G. *The social bond* (2nd ed.). New York: Knopf, 1977.

Nolle, D. B. Changes in black sons and daughters: A panel analysis of black adolescents' orientations toward their parents. *Journal of Marriage and the Family*, 1972, *34*, 443–447.

Nye, F. I. *Role structure and analysis of the family*. Beverly Hills, Calif.: Sage Publications, 1976.

Nye, F. I., & Rallings, E. M. Wife-mother employment, family, and society. In W. R. Burr, R. Hill, F. I. Nye, & I. L. Reiss (Eds.), *Contemporary theories about the family*, Vol. 1. New York: Free Press, 1979.

Orlansky, H. Infant care and personality. *Psychological Bulletin*, 1949, *46*, 1–48.

Osofsky, J. D., & Connors, K. Mother-infant interaction: An integrative view of a complex system. In J. D. Osofsky (Ed.), *The handbook of infant development*. New York: Wiley, 1979.

Osofsky, J. D., & Danzger, B. Relationships between neonatal charac-

teristics and mother-infant characteristics. *Developmental Psychology*, 1974, *10*, 124–130.

Otto, L. Class and status in family research. *Journal of Marriage and the Family*, 1975, *37*, 315–332.

Parke, R. D. Parent-infant interaction: Progress, paradigms and problems. In G. P. Sackett (Ed.), *Observing behavior: Theory and application in mental retardation*, Vol. 1. Baltimore: University Park, Press, 1978.

Parke, R. D. Perspectives on father-infant interaction. In J. D. Osofsky (Ed.), *The handbook of infant development*. New York: Wiley, 1979.

Parke, R. D., & Collmer, D. A. Child abuse: An interdisciplinary analysis. In E. M. Hetherington (Ed.), *Review of child development research*, Vol. 5. Chicago: University of Chicago Press, 1975.

Parke, R. D., & O'Leary, S. Father-mother-infant interaction in the newborn period: Some feelings, some observations and some unresolved issues. In K. Riegel & J. Meacham (Eds.), *The developing individual in a changing world: Social and enviornmental issues*, Vol. 2. The Hague: Mouton, 1975.

Parke, R. D., & Sawin, D. B. *Infant characteristics and behavior as elicitors of maternal and paternal responsibility in the newborn period.* Paper presented at the Biennial Meeting of the Society for Research in Child Development, Denver, April 1975.

Parke, R. D., & Sawin, D. B. *The family in early infancy: Social interactional and attitudinal analyses.* Paper presented to the Society for Research in Child Development, New Orleans, March 1977.

Parke, R. D., Power, F. G., & Gottman, J. Conceptualizing and quantifying influence patterns in the family triad. In M. E. Lamb, L. J. Suomi, & G. R. Stephenson (Eds.), *Social interactional analysis: Methodological issues*. Madison: University of Wisconsin Press, 1979.

Payne, S., Summers, D. A., & Stewart, T. Value differences across three generations. *Sociometry*, 1973, *36*, 20–30.

Pedersen, F. A. *Mother, father and infant as an interactive system.* Paper presented at the annual convention of the American Psychological Association, Chicago, September 1975.

Pedersen, F. A. *The father-infant relationship: Observational studies in the family setting*. New York: Praeger, 1980.

Peters, M. F. *Nine black families: A study of household management and child-rearing in black families with working mothers*. Unpublished doctoral dissertation, Harvard University, 1976.

Peters, M. F. "Making it" black family style: Building on the strengths of black families. In N. Stinnett (Ed.), *Family strengths: Roots of well-being*. Lincoln: University of Nebraska Press, 1981. (a)

Peters, M. F. Parenting in black families with young children: An overview of the literature. In H. P. McAdoo (Ed.), *Black families*. Beverly Hills, Calif.: Sage Publications, 1981. (b)

Peterson, E. T., & Kunz, P. R. Parental control over adolescents according to family size. *Adolescence*, 1975, *10*, 419–427.

Peterson, G. W. *The familial antecedents of instrumentally competent independence in early adolescence*. Paper presented at the Annual Theory and Methods Workshop of the National Council of Family Relations, October 1977.

Peterson, G. W. *The nature and antecedents of adolescent conformity*. Unpublished doctoral dissertation, Brigham Young University, Provo, Utah, 1978.

Peterson, G. W., & Peters, D. F. The socialization values of low-income Appalachian white and rural black mothers: A comparative study. *Journal of Comparative Family Studies*, 1985, *16*, 75–91.

Peterson, G. W., Rollins, B. C., Thomas, D. L., & Ellis, G. H. *Multiple dimensions of parental control and support*. Paper presented at the Annual Meeting of the National Council on Family Relations, Portland, Oregon, October 1980.

Peterson, G. W., Rollins, B. C., Thomas, D. L., & Heaps, L. K. Social placement of adolescents: Sex-role influences on family decisions regarding the careers of youth. *Journal of Marriage and the Family,* 1982, *44,* 647–658.

Peterson, G. W., Southworth, L. E., & Peters, D. F. Maternal behavior and children's self-esteem in three low-income samples. *Psychological Reports,* 1983, *52,* 79–86.

Peterson, G. W., Rollins, B. C., & Thomas, D. L. Parental influence and adolescent conformity: Compliance and Internalization. *Youth and Society,* 1985, *16*(4), 397–420.

Rebelsky, F., & Hanks, C. Fathers' verbal interaction with infants in the first three months of life. *Child Development,* 1971, *42,* 63–68.

Reiss, I. L. The universality of the family: A conceptual analysis. *Journal of Marriage and the Family,* 1965, *27,* 443–453.

Richardson, B. B. *Racism and child-rearing: A study of black mothers.* Unpublished doctoral dissertation, Claremont Graduate School, 1980.

Ringler, N. M., Kennell, J. H., Jarvella, R., Novojosky, B. J., & Klaus, M. H. Mother to child speech at 2 years—Effect of early post-natal contact. *Behavioral Pediatrics,* 1975, *86,* 141–144.

Robson, K. L. The role of eye to eye contact in mother-infant attachment. *Journal of Child Psychology and Psychiatry,* 1967, *8,* 13–25.

Robson, K. S., & Moss, H. A. Patterns and determinants of maternal attachment. *Journal of Pediatrics,* 1970, *77,* 976–985.

Rodgers, R. Toward a theory of family development. *Journal of Marriage and the Family,* 1964, *26,* 262–270.

Rollins, B. C., & Cannon, K. F. Marital satisfaction over the family life cycle: A re-evaluation. *Journal of Marriage and the Family,* 1974, *32,* 20–27.

Rollins, B. C., & Feldman, H. Marital satisfaction over the family life cycle. *Journal of Marriage and the Family,* 1970, *32,* 20–27.

Rollins, B. C., & Galligan, R. The developing child and marital satisfaction of parents. In R. M. Lerner & G. B. Spanier (Eds.), *Child influences on marital and family interaction: A life-span perspective.* New York: Academic Press, 1978.

Rollins, B. C., & Thomas, D. L. A theory of parental power and child compliance. In R. Cromwell & D. Olson (Eds.), *Power in families.* Beverly Hills, Calif.: Sage Publications, 1975.

Rollins, B. C., & Thomas, D. L. Parental support, power, and control techniques in the socialization of children. In W. R. Burr, R. Hill, F. I. Nye, & I. L. Reiss (Eds.), *Contemporary theories about the family: Research-based theories,* Vol. 1. New York: Free Press, 1979.

Rosen, B. C. Family structure and achievement motivation. *American Sociological Review,* 1961, *26,* 574–585.

Rosen, B. C. Family structure and value transmission. *Merrill-Palmer Quarterly,* 1964, *10,* 59–76.

Rosenthal, M. K. Attachment and mother-infant interaction: Some research impasses and a suggested change in orientation. *Journal of Child Psychology and Psychiatry,* 1973, *14,* 201–207.

Rossi, A. Transition to parenthood: Problems and gratifications. *Journal of Marriage and the Family,* 1968, *30,* 26–39.

Rossi, A. A biosocial perspective on parenting. In A. S. Rossi, J. Kagan, & T. K. Hareven (Eds.), *The family.* New York: W. W. Norton, 1978.

Rothbart, M. K. Birth order and mother-child interaction in an achievement situation. *Journal of Personality and Social Psychology,* 1971, *17,* 113–120.

Rubin, J. Z., Provenzano, R. J., & Luria, Z. The eye of the beholder: Parents' view on sex of newborns. *American Journal of Orthopsychiatry,* 1974, *43,* 518–519.

Rubin, K. H., Hultsch, D. F., & Peters, D. L. Nonsocial speech in four-year-old children as a function of birth order and interpersonal situation. *Merrill-Palmer Quarterly,* 1971, *17,* 41–50.

Russell, C. S. Transition to parenthood: Problems and gratifications. *Journal of Marriage and the Family,* 1974, *36,* 294–305.

Rutter, M. Maternal deprivation, 1972–1978: New findings, new concepts, new approaches. *Child Development,* 1979, *50,* 283–305.

Sackett, G. P. The lag sequential analysis of contingency and cyclicity in behavioral interaction research. In J. D. Osofsky (Ed.), *The handbook of infant development.* New York: Wiley, 1979.

Schaefer, E. S. A circumplex model for maternal behavior. *Journal of Abnormal and Social Psychology,* 1959, *59,* 226–235.

Schaefer, E. S. Children's reports of parental behavior. *Child Development,* 1965, *36,* 552–557.

Schaffer, H. R. Early interactive development. In H. R. Schaffer (Ed.), *Studies in mother-infant interaction.* New York: Academic Press, 1977. (a)

Schaffer, H. R. *Mothering.* Cambridge: Harvard University Press, 1977. (b)

Schaffer, H. R. *Studies in mother-infant interaction.* London: Academic Press, 1977. (c)

Schaffer, H. R., & Emerson, P. E. The development of social attachments in infancy. *Child Development Monograph,* 1964, *29,* 64.

Schaie, K. W. A general model for the study of developmental problems. *Psychological Bulletin,* 1965, *64,* 92–107.

Scheck, D. C., & Emerick, R. The young male adolescent's perception of early childrearing behavior: The differential effects of socioeconomic status and family size. *Sociometry,* 1976, *39,* 39–52.

Schooler, C. Birth order studies: Not here, not now! *Psychological Bulletin,* 1972, *78,* 161–175.

Schwartz, J. Effects of peer familiarity on the behavior of preschoolers in a novel situation. *Journal of Personality and Social Psychology,* 1972, *24,* 276–285.

Sears, R. R. A theoretical framework for personality and social behavior. *American Psychologist,* 1951, *6,* 476–483.

Sears, R. R., Whiting, J. W., Nowlis, V., & Sears, P. S. Some child-rearing antecedents of aggression and dependency in young children. *Genetic Psychology Monographs,* 1953, *47,* 135–234.

Sears, R. R., Maccoby, E. E., & Levin, H. *Patterns of child-rearing.* Evanston, Ill.: Row, Peterson, 1957.

Sears, R. R., Rau, L., & Alpert, R. *Identification and child-rearing.* Stanford, Calif.: Stanford University Press, 1965.

Serbin, L. A. Sex-role socialization: A field in transition. In B. B. Lahey & A. E. Kazdin (Eds.), *Advances in clinical child psychology,* Vol. 3. New York: Plenum Press, 1980.

Sewell, W. H. Infant training and the personality of the child. *American Journal of Sociology,* 1952, *58,* 150–159.

Shaffer, D. R., & Brody, G. H. Parental and peer influences on moral development. In R. W. Henderson (Ed.), *Parent-child interaction: Theory, research, and prospects.* New York: Academic Press, 1981.

Shaw, M. C., & Dutton, B. E. The use of the parent attitude research inventory with the parents of bright academic underachievers. *Journal of Educational Psychology,* 1962, *53,* 203–208.

Siegelman, M. College student personality correlates of early parent-child relationships. *Journal of Consulting Psychology,* 1965, *29,* 558–564.

Silverstein, B., & Krate, R. *Child of the dark ghetto: A developmental psychology.* New York: Praeger, 1975.

Smith, C., & Lloyd, B. Maternal behavior and perceived sex of infant. *Child Development,* 1978, *49,* 1263–1265.

Smith, T. E. Foundations of parental influence upon adolescents: An application of social power theory. *American Sociological Review,* 1970, *35,* 860–872.

Sousa, P. L. R., Barros, F. C., Gazelle, R. V., Bergeres, R. M., Pinheiro, G. N., Menezea, S. F., & Arruda, L. A. *Attachment and lactation.* Fifteenth International Congress of Pediatrics, Buenos Aires, October, 1974.

Spanier, G. B., Lewis, R. A., & Cole, C. Marital adjustment over the family life cycle: The issue of curvilinearity. *Journal of Marriage and the Family,* 1975, *37,* 263–276.

Spence, J. T., & Helmreich, R. L. *Masculinity and feminity: Their psychological dimensions, correlates and antecedents.* Austin: University of Texas Press, 1978.

Sroufe, L. A., & Waters, E. The ontogenesis of smiling and laughter: A perspective on the organization of development in infancy. *Psychological Review,* 1976, *83,* 173–180.

Staples, R. The black American family. In C. H. Mindel & R. W. Habenstein (Eds.), *Ethnic families in America.* New York: Elsevier, 1976.

Staples, R., & Mirandé, A. Racial and cultural variations among American families: A decade review of the literature on minority families. *Journal of Marriage and the Family,* 1980, *42,* 887–903.

Staub, E. *Positive social behavior and morality,* Vol. 2. New York: Academic Press, 1979.

Stayton, D. J., & Ainsworth, M. D. S. Individual differences in infant responses to brief, everyday separations as related to other infant and maternal behaviors. *Developmental Psychology,* 1973, *9,* 226–235.

Steffensmeier, R. H. A role model of the transition to parenthood. *Journal of Marriage and the Family,* 1982, *43,* 319–334.

Steinmetz, S. K. Disciplinary techniques and their relationship to aggressiveness, dependency, and conscience. In W. R. Burr, R. Hill, F. I. Nye, & I. L. Reiss (Eds.), *Contemporary theories about the family,* Vol. 1. New York: Free Press, 1979.

Stern, D. *The first relationship: Infant and mother.* Cambridge: Harvard University Press, 1977.

Stonequist, E. V. *The marginal man: A study in personality and culture conflict.* New York: Scribner's, 1937.

Stout, A. M. *Parent behavior toward children of differing ordinal position and sibling status.* Unpublished doctoral dissertation, University of California, Berkeley, 1960.

Straus, M. A. Power and support structure of the family in relation to socialization. *Journal of Marriage and the Family,* 1964, *26,* 318–326.

Straus, M. A., & Tallman, I. SIMFAM: A technique for observational measurement and experimental study of families. In J. Aldous, T. Condon, R. Hill, M. A. Straus, & I. Tallman (Eds.), *Family problem-solving.* Hinsdale, N.J.: Dryden Press, 1971.

Streissguth, A. P., & Bee, H. L. Mother-child interaction and cognitive development in children. In W. Hartup (Ed.), *Research on young children.* Washington, D.C.: National Association for the Education of Young Children, 1972.

Stryker, S. The interactional and situational approaches. In H. T. Christensen (Ed.), *Handbook of marriage and family.* Chicago: Rand McNally, 1964.

Stryker, S. *Symbolic interactionism.* Menlo Park, Calif.: Benjamin/Cummings, 1980.

Sutton-Smith, B., & Rosenberg, B. G. Sibling association and role involvement. *Merrill-Palmer Quarterly of Development and Behavior,* 1964, *10,* 25–38.

Symonds, P. *The psychology of parent-child relationships.* New York: Appleton-Century-Crofts, 1939.

Tedin, K. L. The influence of parents on the political attitudes of adolescents. *American Political Science Review,* 1974, *68,* 1579–1592.

Thoman, E. B. *Development of synchrony in mother-infant interaction in feeding and other situations.* Proceedings of the 58th Annual Meeting of the Federation of American Societies for Experimental Biology, 1976.

Thoman, E. B., Turner, A. M., & Leiderman, P. H. Neonate-mother interaction: Effects of parity on feeding behavior. *Child Development,* 1970, *41,* 1103–1111.

Thoman, E. B., Barnett, C. R., & Leiderman, P. H. Feeding behaviors of newborn infants as a function of parity of the mother. *Child Development,* 1971, *42,* 1471–1483.

Thoman, E. B., Leiderman, P. H., & Olson, J. P. Neonate-mother interaction during breast-feeding. *Developmental Psychology,* 1972, *6,* 110–118.

Thomas, D. L., Gecas, V., Weigert, A. J., & Rooney, E. *Family socialization and the adolescent.* Lexington, Mass.: D. C. Heath, 1974.

Thomas, D. L., Peterson, G. W., & Rollins, B. C. *Validity in parent-*

child research: A comparison of self-report and behavioral observations. Paper presented at the National Council on Family Relations, San Diego, California, 1977.

Thomas, E. A. C., & Martin, J. A. Analyses of parent-infant interaction. *Psychological Review,* 1976, *83,* 141–156.

Thomas, W. I., & Thomas, D. S. *The child in America.* New York: Knopf, 1928.

Thompson, V. Family size: Implicit policies and assumed psychological outcomes. *Journal of Social Issues,* 1974, *30,* 93–122.

Troll, L., & Bengtson, V. Generations in the family. In W. R. Burr, R. Hill, F. I. Nye, & I. L. Reiss (Eds.), *Contemporary theories about the family,* Vol. 1. New York: Free Press, 1979.

Turner, R. H. Role-taking: Process versus conformity. In A. M. Rose (Ed.), *Human behavior and the social processes.* Boston: Houghton Mifflin, 1962.

Turner, R. H. *Family interaction.* New York: Wiley, 1970.

Volkart, E. H. *Social behavior and personality: Contributions of W. I. Thomas to theory and research.* New York: Social Science Research Council, 1951.

Walsh, A. *Self-concepts of bright boys with hearing difficulties.* New York: Teachers College, Columbia University, 1956.

Walters, J., & Stinnett, N. Parent-child relationships: A decade review of research. *Journal of Marriage and the Family,* 1971, *33,* 70–111.

Walters, J., & Walters, L. H. Parent-child relationships: A review, 1970–1979. *Journal of Marriage and the Family,* 1980, *42,* 807–822.

Waters, E., & Crandall, V. Social class and observed maternal behavior from 1940–1960. *Child Development,* 1964, *35,* 1021–1032.

Waters, E., Vaughn, B. E., & Egeland, B. R. Individual differences in infant-mother attachment relationships at age one: Antecedents in neonatal behavior in an urban, economically disadvantaged sample. *Child Development,* 1980, *51,* 208–216.

Watson, G. Some personality differences in children related to strict or permissive parental discipline. *Journal of Psychology,* 1957, *44,* 227–249.

Webster, M., & Sobieszek, B. *Sources of self-evaluation: A formal theory of significant others and social influence.* New York: Wiley, 1974.

Weinraub, M. Fatherhood: The myth of the second-class parent. In J. H. Stevens & M. Mathews (Eds.), *Mother/child father/child relationships.* Washington, D.C.: National Association for the Education of Young Children, 1978.

Weinraub, M., Brooks, J., & Lewis, M. The social network: A reconsideration of the concept of attachment. *Human Development,* 1977, *20,* 31–47.

Weisz, J. R. Transcontextual validity in development research. *Child Development,* 1978, *19,* 1–12.

Weitz, S. *Sex roles: Biological, psychological, and social foundations.* New York: Oxford University Press, 1977.

White, B. L. *The first three years of life.* Englewood Cliffs, N.J.: Prentice-Hall, 1975.

Whiten, A. Assessing the effects of perinatal events on the success of the mother-infant relationship. In H. R. Schaffer (Ed.), *Studies in mother-infant interaction.* London: Academic Press, 1977.

Winters, M. *The relationship of time of initial feeding to success of breast-feeding.* Unpublished master's thesis, University of Washington, 1973.

Wolff, P. H. Observations on the early development of smiling. In B. M. Foss (Ed.), *Determinants of infant behavior,* Vol. 2. New York: Wiley, 1963.

Wolff, P. H. The causes, controls and organization of behavior in the neonate. *Psychological Issues,* Monograph 17, 1966.

Wright, J. D., & Wright, R. Social class and parental values for children: A partial replication and extension of Kohn's thesis. *American Sociological Review,* 1976, *41,* 527–537.

Wrong, D. H. The oversocialized conception of man in modern sociology. *American Sociological Review,* 1961, *26,* 183–193.

Yarrow, L. J., & Goodwin, M. S. The immediate impact of separation reactions of infants to a change in mother figures. In L. J. Stone, H. T. Smith, & L. B. Murphy (Eds.), *The competent infant.* New York: Basic Books, 1973.

Yarrow, L. J., Goodwin, M. S., Manheimer, H., & Milowe, I. D. Infancy experience and cognitive and personality development at ten years. In L. J. Stone, H. T. Smith, & L. B. Murphy (Eds.), *The competent infant.* New York: Basic Books, 1973.

Yarrow, M. R., & Waxler, C. Z. Observing interaction: A confrontation with methodology. In R. B. Cairns (Ed.), *The analysis of social interaction: Methods, issues, and illustrations.* Hillsdale, N.J.: Lawrence Erlbaum, 1979.

Yarrow, M. R., Campbell, J. D., & Burton, R. V. *Child-rearing.* San Francisco: Jossey-Bass, 1968.

Yarrow, M. R., Scott, P. M., & Waxler, C. Z. Learning concern for others. *Developmental Psychology,* 1973, *8,* 240–260.

Zajonc, R. B. Family configuration and intelligence. *Science,* 1976, *192,* 227–292.

Zajonc, R. B., & Markus, G. B. Birth order and intellectual development. *Psychological Review,* 1975, *82,* 74–88.

Zigler, E. F., & Child, I. L. *Socialization and personality development.* Reading, Mass.: Addison-Wesley, 1973.

Zussman, J. L. *Situational determinants of parental behavior.* Unpublished doctoral dissertation, Stanford University, 1977.

CHAPTER 19

Human Sexuality

Robert T. Francoeur

Orientation

This chapter is an attempt to bring together the main themes and the central insights in our understanding of human sexuality today. As these themes and insights are drawn from researchers working in a variety of different disciplines, I will attempt to emphasize the more significant themes and to structure these in a comprehensive synthesis of sexological research and theory as it appears in 1986. My objective is a clear cognitive and perceptual framework that will provide the reader with a clear understanding of the many factors involved in developing a healthy and positive sexuality.

The origins of sexology, the scientific study of human sexuality and sexual behavior, can be traced back to vague roots in the biological, medical, historical, anthropological, and sociological research of the last century. The idea of *Sexualwissenschaft* gained visibility early in this century with the work of Iwan Block, Magnus Hirschfeld, Wilhelm Reich, Sigmund Freud, Albert Eulenburg, Havelock Ellis, and Albert Moll. The work of these and other researchers eventually led to the statistical studies of American sexual behavior by Alfred Kinsey and his associates in the 1940s and 1950s, and to the physiological and therapeutic research of William Masters and Virginia Johnson in the 1950s and 1960s. Alongside these pioneers were other less public but equally dedicated researchers like Wardell Pomeroy, Paul Gebhard, Alan Bell, John Money, Ira Reiss, Lester Kirkendall, and Helen Singer Kaplan.

The American College of Sexologists includes within the purview of sexology all those aspects, anatomical, physiological, psychological, medical, sociological, anthropological, historical, legal, religious, literary and artistic, that contribute to our understanding of what it means to develop as healthy sexual persons with a positive image of our sexuality in a particular social milieu. These aspects are important elements in the synthesis sketched out in this chapter. In giving some aspects more attention than others, I have tried to highlight central themes and to link these together into a comprehensive, meaningful picture of sexology today.

In setting the perspective for this chapter, I should emphasize that its orientation is more sociological than psychological, biased, if you will, on the side of individuals as they develop in a social milieu rather than on the side of the functioning of individual personalities and their behaviors. Most psychologists view sexual behavior, as they do other behaviors, as being a consequence of personality. The psychologist asks questions like what function a particular behavior plays in the personality, whether this particular sexual (or nonsexual) behavior is functional or dystonic for the individual, and what personality factors motivate a particular behavior. The sociologist asks quite different questions about sexual and nonsexual behavior, questions like what roles particular behavior patterns play in the functioning of the society, and what behaviors are valued or disapproved of and why. The sociologist does not endorse or disapprove of particular behaviors, perferring to report the functioning of a society and its values. This information may then be used by the psychologist or others interested in understanding which behaviors and who in a society are judged to be social adjusted or deviant. But our perspective in this chapter is broader than even the sociological.

Because our sexual development begins on the genetic, anatomical, and hormonal levels nine months before birth, we must begin our synthesis on that very personal and individual level. However, we will quickly expand this individual perspective into its social content.

Sexual Development from Conception to Adolescence

Early Sexual Development and Gender Identity

Sexual and Gender Definitions. The term *sex* is often used without definition and with a variety of implied meanings. Kinsey defined *sex* as behavior that results in orgasm, though many expressions of our sexual behavior do not result in orgasm. Sex can also be used to refer to a person's *sexual anatomy,* or to any behavior involving our sexual anatomy: the penis, testes, and associated structures in the male and the ovaries, vagina, and uterus

Robert T. Francoeur • Department of Biological and Allied Health Sciences, Fairleigh Dickinson University, Madison NJ 07940.

in the female. Some, like Diamond and Karlen (1980), suggest distinguishing between organs that are primarily sexual or erotic in function, organs that are basically "genital" or reproductive, and organs that serve both functions. However, as the sexual hormones that are central to our sexuality flow to every cell of our bodies and create sexually dimorphic (male or female) consequences for such diverse organs as our liver, brain, and muscles, it is probably more accurate to envision human sexuality as permeating every aspect of our personality and anatomy. We can then specify the particular sexual aspect that we wish to discuss or research.

The term *sex* is often used when we are actually talking about gender. *Gender* can be defined as the state of being either male or female, a man or a woman. *Gender identity* is the identification and awareness we have of ourselves as being either male or female. *Gender role,* as defined by John Money (Money & Tucker, 1975), is "everything that a person says or does to indicate to others or to the self the degree that one is male or female or ambivalent" (p. 9). Our gender role includes all the expectations and social messages we get from others about how we should act as sexual persons. These messages, or social scripting, often involve *gender-role stereotyping,* which locks the individual male and female into certain roles and expectations delineated by society.

Finally, the concept of *sex* can include the element of *sexual orientation* or *affectional preference,* traditionally referred to as *heterosexual, homosexual,* or *bisexual.*

Genetic Origins. The beginnings of human sexuality and gender occur at fertilization when the male- or female-determining sperm, carrying a Y or an X sex chromosome plus 22 body chromosomes (autosomes), joins with an ovum containing one X chromosome and 22 autosomes. The result is usually a normal genetic constitution in the zygote, or fertilized egg: 44 autosomes and 2 X chromosomes for a female and 44 autosomes and XY sex chromosomes for a male. Variations occur when abnormal gametes are involved in fertilization. The more common abnormalities are 44 autosomes plus XXY, Klinefelter syndrome, which results in a lanky, often mentally retarded male with degenerated testes; 44 autosomes and a single X, Turner syndrome, resulting in a sexually immature, mentally retarded female; and genetic mosaics with varied anatomies stemming from chromosome number variations in different cells of the body, the multiple fertilization of an ovum, or even the fusion of two fertilized ova.

Gonadal Sex. During the fourth to sixth weeks of pregnancy, primordial undifferentiated gonads (reproductive glands) begin to take shape in the abdominal cavity. The presence or absence of the Y chromosome is the critical factor in this differentiation. In the absence of the Y chromosome, the primordial gonads develop into ovaries. If the Y chromosome is present, the gonads become testes in the sixth to eighth weeks. Very early in this

differentiation, the ovaries and testes begin producing steroid hormones, a predominance of androgenic hormones in males and of estrogens in female fetuses. Small amounts of the opposite sex hormones are produced by the testes, the ovaries, and the cortex of the adrenal glands above the kidneys.

The presence of threshold levels of androgenic hormones, specifically testosterone and dihydrotestosterone (discussed below), are critical in the development of male sexual anatomy and in the imprinting of the brain around the time of birth. Female development proceeds normally whether or not estrogens are present in the fetus. The estrogens, like the male sex hormones, become important in the development of gender-specific secondary sexual characteristics at puberty.

Internal Sexual Development. In the third to sixth weeks of pregnancy, the fetus develops an ambisexual system of internal ducts: a pair of Wolffian ducts and a parallel set of Mullerian ducts. In the sixth through the twelfth weeks, the androgenic hormones in male fetuses cause the Wolffian ducts to differentiate into the vasa deferens, the prostate, the seminal vesicles, and associated structures. At the same time, a newly produced male hormone, the Mullerian inhibiting substance (MIS), causes the Mullerian ducts to degenerate. In the female fetus, the absence of high levels of androgens allows the Wolffian ducts to degenerate and the Mullerian ducts to form the paired fallopian tubes and to fuse into a single vagina and single uterus.

External Sexual Development. At the end of the eighth week, the external sexual anatomy is still ambisexual (undifferentiated), consisting of a genital tubercle, a pair of swellings, and a pair of folds stretching from the tubercle to just in front of the anus. In the third and fourth months of pregnancy, threshold levels of androgenic dihydrotestosterone help the tubercle to become a penis and the swellings and folds to fuse into the scrotal sac and lower shaft of the penis. The testes do not descend from the abdominal cavity into the scrotum until just before birth. In the female fetus, with its low levels of androgens, the tubercle remains small and develops as a clitoris. The swellings and folds remain separated to become the major and minor labia.

Abnormal developments often give us an insight into the normal developmental processes. This is the case with 38 children in the Dominican Republic studied by Imperato-McGinley, Guerrero, Gautier, and Peterson (1979). Seven generations ago, a single woman apparently experienced a mutation in the gene that controls the synthesis of dihydrotestosterone. As a result of intermarriage among the descendants of this woman over the years, children were born with two mutant genes. Over three dozen of these infants have been studied because, though they appeared externally to be female, their chromosomes, gonads, and internal structures were male, a fact not known to anyone until they entered puberty, years later. Without sufficient dihydrotestosterone in the second trimester of pregnancy, the external anatomy of these infants developed in the female track, and they were raised as girls. At puberty, the burst of androgenic hormones induced conversion of the external female anatomy of these children into male anatomy. This shift from female to male is apparently easily handled by both adults and youngsters because of the society's overwhelming patriarchal bias and the premium placed on sons. Various interpretations of this phenomenon have been offered, and several implications have been suggested for our understanding of gender identity and transsexualism as discussed in a later section of this chapter (Imperato-McGinley *et al.*, 1979; Rubin, Reinisch, & Haskett, 1981).

Sexually Dimorphic Imprinting of the Brain. The presence or absence of threshold levels of androgenic hormones in the later months of pregnancy apparently imprints the limbic and hypothalamic regions of the cerebral hemispheres in two ways. First, these regions are imprinted for later production of hormone-releasing factors (FSH-RF and LH-RF or ICSH-RF) in a cyclic pattern for females and in an acyclical or tonic pattern in males. The second type of imprinting is poorly understood at present and involves the imprinting of "masculine" or "feminine" behavior patterns in regions of the brain (Weintraub, 1981).

In *Sexual Signatures* (1975), Money and Tucker summed up the sequence and interactions of sexual development as we understand them today, using the analogy of highways, closed lanes, and barriers (also see Figure 1):

As you approach each gated sex-differentiation point, you could have gone in either direction, but as you passed through, the gate locked, fixing the prior period of development as male or female. Your gonads, for example, could have become either testicles or ovaries, but once they became testicles they lost the option of becoming ovaries, or if they became ovaries they would never again become testicles. In behavior, however, at first you drove all over the highway, but as you proceeded you tended to stick more and more to the lanes marked out and socially prescribed for your sex. The lines and barriers dividing male from female for each kind of sex-linked (gender role) behavior vary according to your culture and experience, and the kind of individual you have become makes a difference in how you feel about crossing them, but you never lose these options entirely. A sufficiently strong stimulus—physical, hormonal, neural, or social—can push you over practically any behavior line or barrier. Your own experience and alterations in the gender stereotypes of your culture can obscure established lines and lower barriers so that crossing becomes easier or harder. (p. 73)

Gender of Assignment and Gender Identity. When parents and family first confront the newborn's sexual anatomy, they react by assigning the infant's gender as either male or female. This assignment immediately sets in motion a whole tapestry of sexual roles and expectations or social scripting to which the infant gradually learns to respond in rewarding ways.

The infant's sexual anatomy also molds its own growing awareness of its body self-image as male or female. Identifying with the same-sex parent and countermodeling with the other-sex parent also aid in the development of a secure gender identity. The use of sexually dimorphic language, with the basic distinctions of *mommy* versus *daddy* and *he* versus *she*, reinforces this gender awareness in the child's second year. This personal conviction about one's maleness or femaleness and one's growing gender identity is gradually integrated into one's personality and gender role as a sexual person. All of this is probably irreversibly set as a definite and distinct gender identity in the first three years of life, despite the anomaly of the "girl-boys" of the Dominican Republic.

The traditional pattern of psychosexual development as it relates to what we call masculine and feminine behavior pictures these two patterns as opposing gradients or currents (Figure 2). If a female is truly feminine, she suppresses or has no masculine traits at all, and a truly masculine male would never exhibit any trait that we see as masculine. This view has been countered by June Reinisch, director of the Kinsey Institute for Research in Sex, Gender and Reproduction, who suggested that every sexual person expresses a basic mixture of what we call masculine and feminine behavioral patterns. Masculinity and femininity are seen as independent but related trends on a general axis rather than as opposing currents. In this view, our sexual potential as male or female is expressed to its fullest when our personalities express a rich and balanced blend of masculine and feminine traits. This androgynous blend expresses a dynamic balance of the yin and yan, poetic and rational, left-handed and right-handed, emotional and intellectual energies that exist as potentials in every woman and man (Singer, 1972).

Sexual Orientation and Affectional Preferences. Current research indicates that our sexual orientation, the "imprinting" that dictates whether we are sexually and affectionally attracted to men, to women, or to both sexes, is probably set by age 5 or 6. In the "imprinting theory" of John Money, our sexual orientation is irreversibly set once and for all early in childhood, though it may take an individual many years to recognize and accept his or her sexual orientation. An alternative and more recent theory suggests that our sexual orientation and affectional preference is panerotic at birth, and that this polymorphic potential is narrowed into socially acceptable expressions by as yet unascertained familial and social factors. (Both of these theories are detailed in the following section.)

In Western societies, sexual orientation, romanticism, and erotic responses are linked together in our consciousness during puberty, when the surge of hormonal changes trigger dramatic changes in secondary sexual characteristics and the maturation of the reproductive capacity. The psychological effects of puberty are equally dramatic. In his *Interpersonal Theory of Psychiatry* (1953), Harry Stack Sullivan highlighted the preadolescent need for intimacy with persons of the same gender.

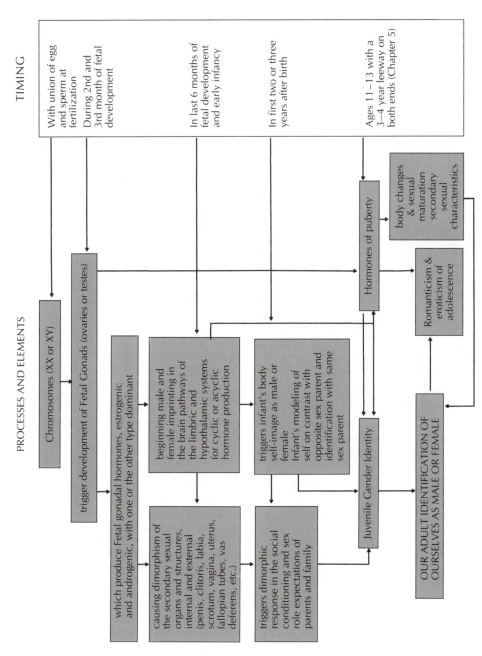

Figure 1. A developmental chart showing the biological, psychological, and social elements that contribute to the formation of our sexuality, our gender identity, and our sexual orientation as these unfold during the life cycle of an individual. (Reprinted with permission from *Becoming a Sexual Person*, by Robert T. Francoeur. New York: Macmillan, 1982.)

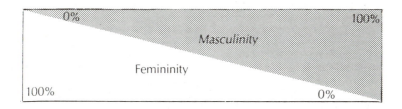

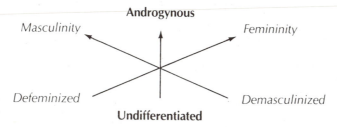

Figure 2. The traditional model (above) and a new paradigm (below) for masculine/feminine development. The diagram at the top presents masculinity and femininity as two opposing poles of development. The second model shows these two as different and relatively independent axes, in which moving along either axis does not of necessity prevent development along the other axis. One can, in fact, combine the two axes in an androgynous balance. (Reprinted with permission from R. T. Francoeur. 1984. *Becoming a Sexual Person: A Brief Edition.* New York: Macmillan, p. 73.)

With puberty, a new need for intimacy, reinforced by a lusty dynamism usually oriented toward persons of the other gender, emerges to conflict with the preadolescent same-sex need for intimacy. Building on this juvenile gender identity and the natural or imprinted sexual orientation, the maturation of puberty and adolescence leads to one's adult identification as a sexual person, a male or a female, with a definite sexual orientation and affectional preference. Throughout this development, familial and social influences are crucial in the scripting and development of a healthy, positive sexual self-identity, as will be evident in subsequent sections of this chapter.

The Sexual Orientation Spectrum

Research Perspectives: Kinsey and Klein. Research on and public discussions of sexual orientations in this country have traditionally focused on the presumed vast majority of ''normal'' heterosexually oriented persons and a very small minority of ''deviant'' homosexually oriented Americans. In keeping with the origins of prejudice, the minority has been described with various derogatory labels, including ''sinner,'' ''criminal,'' ''sexual invert,'' ''psychologically unbalanced,'' ''sick,'' and a wide range of negative colloquial expressions.

The publication of the Kinsey research provided a new research-based concept involving a continuum in sexual orientation that destroyed the assumed dichotomous classification of heterosexually versus homosexually oriented

persons (Kinsey, Pomeroy, & Martin, 1948; Kinsey, Pomeroy, Martin, & Gebhard, 1953). As Kinsey observed in the 1948 study of male sexual behavior:

It would encourage clearer thinking on these matters if persons were not characterized as heterosexual or homosexual, but as individuals who have had certain amounts of heterosexual experience and certain amounts of homosexual experience. Instead of using these terms as substantives which stand for persons, or even as adjectives to describe persons, they may be better used to describe the nature of overt sexual relations, or of the stimuli to which an individual erotically responds. (p. 617)

Among the more important findings on sexual and affectional orientations reported by the Kinsey group were the following: By middle age, half of American men and 20% of American women had experienced some overt erotic interaction with members of their own sex; 37% of the men studied and 13% of the women reported at least one homosexual experience to orgasm; and 4% of the men and 2% of the women identified themselves as exclusively homosexual in their orientation.

In terms of overt behavior and sexual fantasies, the Kinsey data showed that half of American males were 0 on a scale where 0 indicated an exclusively heterosexual orientation and 6 an exclusively homosexual orientation. On the basis of the Kinsey Six Scale, as it is now known, 4% of the men fell in the 6 category. The remaining 46% were distributed in five categories between 1 and 5, to indicate the ratio of their experience and fantasies with both sexes (Figure 3). Of this bisexual group, 15% were

HETEROSEXUAL AND HOMOSEXUAL BEHAVIOR

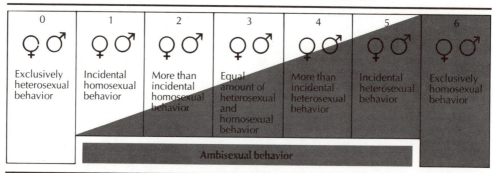

HETEROSEXUAL-HOMOSEXUAL RATING (AGES 20-35)

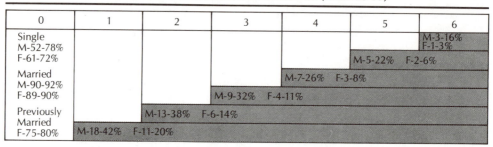

Figure 3. The Kinsey Six Scale for rating the sexual behavior and fantasies of individuals for their heterosexual/homosexual orientation. The seven-category scale, from 0 to 6, and data are from Kinsey's 1948 study of American males and the parallel 1953 study of American females. The range of percentages for males (M) and females (F) in the seven categories represents the ranges found in the subgroups within the survey population. The seven categories, ranging from exclusively homosexual fantasies and behavior to exclusively heterosexual behavior and fantasies, are statistical distinctions. The scale and its categories, however, should be read as a continuum. (Adapted from Kinsey *et al.*, *Sexual Behavior in the Human Female*, 1953; reprinted with permission from *Becoming a Sexual Person*, by Robert T. Francoeur. New York: Macmillan, 1982, p. 514.)

in the Kinsey 1 category, with occasional same-sex but predominantly heterosexually oriented experience and fantasy; 12% rated the Kinsey 2; 9% were equally attracted to and experienced with both sexes; 6% rated the Kinsey 4; and 5% were in the Kinsey 5 category.

An important limitation of these early studies is the lack of information on the developmental or temporal sequence for persons who shifted back and forth across the Kinsey Six Scale during their lifetimes. The Kinsey research assumed that, whatever the unknown causes of sexual orientation might be and the various expressions it might take at different times, one's sexual orientation was set early in life. Because a significant number of American men and women were in the Kinsey 1 to 5 categories, it has become increasingly important for researchers to expand the Kinsey perspective to study the stability or flexibility of sexual orientation.

The belief of post-Kinsey researchers that sexual orientation and erotic, affectional preferences are set by age 5 or 6 has been clearly expressed by Money and Tucker (1975). Questions about the fixed nature of this orienta-

tion arose with the possibility of more in-depth research in the late 1970s, facilitated by the emergence of the self-identified gay community as an increasingly visible and vocal minority seeking civil and political rights.

In expanding the Kinsey research into the developmental life-cycle dimension and adding the temporal dimension, Klein (1978, 1980) has also added five other aspects besides sexual behavior and fantasies. The seven components in the Klein model of sexual orientation and affectional preference are:

1. *Sexual attraction,* answering the question of whom we find attractive as a potential or real sexual partner.
2. *Sexual behavior,* answering the question of who our actual sexual partners have been.
3. *Sexual fantasies.*
4. *Emotional or affectional preferences.*
5. *Social preferences,* answering the question of which sex we are more comfortable with in our leisure and social life.

6. *Lifestyle,* answering the question of the dominant sexual orientation (on the Kinsey Six Scale) of the people with whom we spend most of our time.
7. *Self identification,* the way we view ourselves on the Kinsey Six Scale, from 0 to 6.

In Klein's research, the subject rates himself or herself in these seven areas using the Kinsey Six Scale of 0 to 6. The rating in each aspect is done on the longitudinal basis of five years ago, the current year, and one's ideal state or future goal. Developmental and longitudinal studies using the Klein Sexual Orientation Grid are just beginning. Results and analysis will not provide a more realistic picture of sexual orientation and affectional preference for another decade, that is, until a sufficiently large random sample has been followed for some years. However, preliminary research has already given some idea of what the full research may be likely to confirm, namely, that sexual orientation and affectional preference are for many people a very flexible and dynamic reality rather than something that is irreversibly set in early childhood.

Etiological Theories. Attempts to identify genetic or hormonal factors as critical in determining sexual orientation have not been successful. Kallmann's study (1952a,b) of twins, with a reported 100% concordance for sexual orientation in identical twins and only an 8% concordance in fraternal twins, suggested a possible recessive gene for homosexual orientation. Further research quickly disproved this suggestion. Attempts to find differences in the ratio or amounts of androgenic and estrogenic hormones in gay men, gay women, and heterosexually oriented persons have not yielded significant data (Money & Ehrhardt, 1972; Ehrhardt and Meyer-Bahlburg, 1981). Money and Tucker (1975) suggested that a possible prenatal hormonal influence may be easily overridden by social scripting and environmental factors, though Money believes that sexual orientation is stabilized by age 5 or 6.

Freud's psychosocial theory focused on internal forces and held that homosexual orientation was part of a sexual development arrested at the oral or anal stage. It resulted from an unresolved Oedipal conflict leading to a castration anxiety. He believed that the male homosexual was threatened by the female's lack of a penis and by the castration potential of the vagina. Thus, homosexual men would seek out "phallic women," effeminate men. Subsequent research has shown that most male homosexuals reject the effeminate male partner and that many lesbians prefer "feminine" female partners instead of the "butch" masculine stereotype (Bell & Weinberg, 1978; Bell, Weinberg, & Hammersmith, 1981; Mendola, 1980).

Social learning theorists have also struggled with discerning the causal factors in sexual orientation. The suggestion that the lack of a strong male role image and a domineering, seductive mother reinforcing a son's effeminate behavior may be strong factors in setting a homosexual orientation is often contradicted by studies of gay persons who do not have this background and of heterosexually oriented persons who do have it. McGuire, Carlisle, and Young (1965) linked sexual orientation with the scripting of preadolescent and adolescent sexual behavior. They theorized that a male's earliest erotic experiences with masturbation and accompanying fantasies may be the dominant factor in setting a homosexual orientation. Three independent but sequential components are central to this hypothesis: (1) an early, unpleasant heterosexual experience *or* feelings of inadequacy coupled with a fear of not being able to relate sexually to women; (2) some positive sexual experience that provides substance for homosexual masturbatory fantasies; and (3) "scripting" of the psychological linking of successful and pleasurable homosexual masturbatory fantasies with a successful homosexual experience. Attempts to explain the origins of lesbian orientation have been almost completely avoided by researchers and theoreticians alike.

Cross-cultural studies add a provocative perspective to the theory of social scripting. Ford and Beach (1951) reported that nearly two thirds of the 190 societies they analyzed sanction some form of homosexual activity and relationship. In these cultures, the majority of men and often also women fit into the Kinsey 2 category. In more sexually repressive societies, homosexual behavior is often strongly disapproved of or is severely punished. Yet, despite the social condemnation in these sex-negative cultures, exclusively homosexual and other unconventional behaviors are more common than in more permissive cultures.

Social Scripting and a Panerotic Hypothesis. Kinsey and Klein focused their research on sexual orientation on the interpersonal dimension, ignoring or minimizing other, nonpersonal erotic reactions and relations. Picking up the Freudian concept of the infant's being born with a "polymorphic perversity" that is scripted by society, Stayton (1980) has taken a positive stance that we are born with a "panerotic potential." Figure 4 illustrates Stayton's conception that "Nature's intention seems to be to produce persons who are sexual in the fullest sense of the word" (p. 1). With everything we know containing a potential for sensual and erotic nurturance, Stayton sees the development of a healthy sexual orientation as having two elements: (1) achieving a creative balance between serving one's own needs and being able to delay or substitute (sensual/erotic) gratification, and (2) integrating and resolving the natural tensions between one's own personal erotic preferences and those approved of by society.

In giving some detail to this "panerotic potential," Stayton concentrated on four main dimensions or outlets: (1) autoerotic orientations, (2) animal and inanimate sexual objects, (3) interpersonal relationships, and (4) the erotic potential of mysticism and transcendence. In ad-

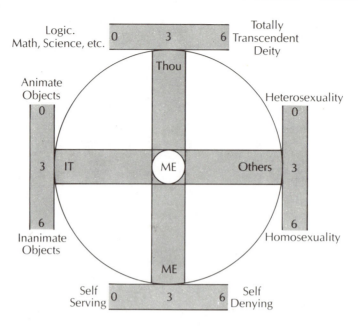

Figure 4. A diagrammatic representation of the human panerotic potential proposed by William Stayton (1978). In this model, the newborn infant has the potential to find nurturance, intimacy, and erotic pleasuring in a variety of directions typified by the four vectors of nature, self, other persons, and the transcendent or mystical. In each direction of erotic potential, Stayton used a modification of the Kinsey Six Scale to indicate the range and the possible balance between two extremes. In effect, in this perspective, each of us is scripted and conditioned to find our nurturance, intimacy, and erotic pleasuring in a unique combination of social, familial, personal, and biological factors, so that the actual paths and outlets we take at particular times in our lives are themselves fluid and unique expressions of our panerotic potential. (Reprinted by permission of William Stayton.)

justing to the sensual-erotic potential of one's own body, it is a question of balancing between a 0 extreme of totally self-serving narcissistic (autoerotic) pleasuring and the other extreme of complete denial of the sensual self. In exploring and developing our erotic potential in the animate and inanimate areas of our world, a healthy sexual orientation balances and integrates the sensual and erotic potentials of the animal world, nature, and the universe. In the interpersonal area of our eroticism, Stayton suggested, the human orientation is, by nature, basically bisexual, predominantly heterosexual, and somewhere in the Kinsey 1 or 2 categories for the majority of persons. In a society with few sexual taboos and a sex-positive value system, Stayton argued, the Ford and Beach (1951) data indicate such a natural bisexual orientation. Only our particular Western cultural values and social scripting dictate that this interpersonal erotic potential be narrowed down to a single heterosexual monogamous pairing for adults.

The fourth dimension of our erotic potential suggested by Stayton is the most controversial and the least documented in human experience. It is supported by many examples in the Eastern religions, which see an intimate connection between sexual relations, human sexuality, and the transcendent goal of mysticism. The Tantric Buddhist tradition and the erotic sculpture of Hindu temples, with the worship of the phallic lingam and the female

yoni, are clear evidence of this erotic potential in religion and mysticism. In Western culture, we are limited to a few scattered examples: the eroticism of Solomon's Song of Songs in the biblical writings of the Jews, the erotic poetry of the Spanish medieval mystics John of the Cross and Theresa of Avila, the Pre-Raphaelite Dante Gabriel Rossetti (1828–1882), and the romantic William Blake (1757–1827), England's great visionary poet.

Figure 5 shows an integration of this pansensual/panerotic potential model with what we know of sexual values in Western Judeo-Christian civilization. Generally speaking, the human erotic potential has been gradually but clearly constricted by social conditioning and scripting from prehistoric times down to its narrowest dimension after A.D. 1200. Linguist-historian John Boswell (1980) has documented the gradual shift in social scripting from a very open, multidimensional eroticism in ancient Greece and Rome through a growing disapproval of anything beyond heterosexual, reproductive, nonerotic sex as Western civilization witnessed the collapse of the Middle Ages. Boswell (1980) also described the burst of homosexual culture in the eleventh and twelfth centuries, followed by the condemnation of all nonmarital, nonheterosexual sex that came with the collapse of Europe's social structure in the fourteenth century.

The overall Western social picture between 1300 and

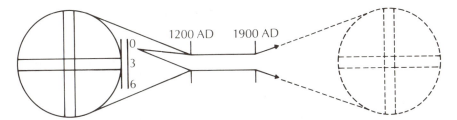

Figure 5. A historical overview of the expression of the panerotic potential in Western civilization. This figure is an attempt to apply the individual panerotic potential shown in Figure 4 to general social trends in Western society. As recently as the days of the Greek and Roman empires, according to Stayton (1980) and Boswell (1980), society endorsed a wide range of sexual outlets in keeping with the broad range of human potential. Between the fall of the Roman Empire and the 1200s, this broad potential was gradually narrowed down to a solitary socially acceptable erotic outlet in exclusive heterosexual monogamy, a repressive standard that remained in effect through to the sexual revolution that swept the United States, Europe, and even the Communist countries starting in the early 1960s. (Reprinted with permission of William Stayton.)

the middle of this century was one of a greatly restricted socially acceptable sexual orientation. Stayton believes that this narrowness began to disintegrate in the early 1960s with the revolution of the civil and women's rights movements, the contraceptive pill, and a freer economy.

Unconventional Expressions of Sexual Orientation and Gender Identity. Since the mid-1960s, restrictive attitudes toward deviant or unconventional sexual behavior have changed considerably in the direction of tolerance, and even acceptance in some areas. The prevalent obsession of Victorians with the debilitating evil of self-pollution has changed to a general acceptance of masturbation as a common and normal sexual outlet for adolescents, for single persons of all ages, and even within marriage. The growing tolerance of homosexuality includes the 1974 decision of the American Psychiatric Association to remove "unconventional sexual orientation" from its list of "mental disorders, diseases and abnormalities," as well as the annual Gay Pride demonstrations across the nation commemorating the 1968 Stonewall Inn riot in Greenwich Village. Nationwide Gallup polls show that the percentage of Americans approving premarital sex rose from 32% in 1969 to 52% in 1973. This trend toward a more comfortable view of our erotic potential and outlets is confirmed in more recent surveys of teenage attitudes on oral and premarital sex. A 1979 survey of 600 teenagers by Hass found that only 12% of the 15- to 16-year-olds thought that a boy should be a virgin when he marries, and that 17% thought a girl should be a virgin at marriage.

Though tolerance for other less conventional sexual objects and roles is less evident in American society, the open discussion of these patterns of behavior in the printed media and on television has contributed to more understanding and the less judgmental view of "It's okay for them if that's what they like, but not for me."

Applying the social-scripting and panerotic-potential models to unconventional behavior gives us a new understanding of these sexual expressions. If we start with a panerotic potential that is somehow scripted in particular and individual directions, then the major factor seems to be the *randomness of the scripting.* The "psychological linking" that connects specific objects, roles, behavior, or stimuli with sexual pleasure and sets up patterns of behavior appears to be random and unpredictable. A male may develop a fetishistic scripting that links a particular item of clothing or body part with sexual stimuli and pleasure because of some adolescent experience(s). Another male, exposed to a seemingly identical experience, may not develop a fetishistic scripting. A boy may link the wearing of feminine apparel with an erotic turn-on as his erotic and sexual behavior develops in adolescence and may become a transvestite as an adult. The roles of dominance and submission, linking pain with sexual arousal and pleasure, can result in sadomasochistic patterns or in the role playing sexual games of bondage and discipline (Gagnon & Simon, 1973; Goleman & Bush, 1977; Simon & Gagnon, 1969a,b; Tollison & Adams, 1979). An unanswered question is why many more males than females develop fetishes and socially deviant sexual orientations.

Unconventional expressions of gender occur in two types: the transgenderist and the transsexual. The transgenderist is usually a heterosexual male with a secure male gender identity. He may be happy expressing himself as a male in heterosexual relations and marriage but feels compelled to play the feminine social role in all other aspects of his life. The transsexual, on the other hand, again usually a male, has a gender identity that is in open conflict with his (her) chromosomes and sexual anatomy. As one's gender identity is irreversibly fixed probably by age 3, psychotherapy alone has proved of little or no help to transsexuals. The most common solution today involves psychological screening and counseling coupled with surgery to allow their anatomy to conform with their gender identity. Because of their deep-seated gender dysphoria and the social conflicts this triggers, many transsexuals suffer severe personality disorders.

The concept of *sexual scripting,* pioneered by Gagnon and Simon and detailed in the next section, emphasizes the importance and the influence of life experiences, especially during adolescence, when our erotic and sexual behavior is just forming. Sexual scripting begins at birth and continues throughout one's life, although some stages are more susceptible to influence and others are fairly resistant to change. In the next section, we examine several aspects of scripting, in the birth process, childhood, and adolescence, with an emphasis on healthy and antisocial consequences.

How Individuals Develop the Self as a Healthy Sexual Person

Affectional Potentials: Causal Relations between Self-Image, Nurturance, Body Pleasure, and Violence

Birthing Nurturance. With the end of World War II, new European concepts in health care and childbirth found a fertile and receptive audience in America. The LaLeche League gained many followers in the more affluent segments of our suburbs and cities with its promotion of breastfeeding. Hospitals and schools promoted workshops in prepared or natural childbirth for prospective parents. In the 1950s, the Lamaze method of childbirth was welcomed by many physicians and women, who had been increasingly disturbed by the common reliance on induced delivery, general anesthesia, and cesarean section (Arms, 1975; Wertz & Wertz, 1977).

In breaking with the traditional American obstetrical practice of delivery, the emphasis and concern shifted from the physician and the mother to making the birth of the new human as natural and comfortable as possible. "Birthing" became an experience to be shared consciously by both father and mother, sometimes even with the whole family present at the birth. In the 1970s, another approach to birthing gained popularity in the United States: The Lebouyer "gentle birthing" emphasizes a delivery environment designed to reduce stress on the newborn and to provide a gentle transition from the warm quiet nurturing womb to the nurturing carresses of the parents. In the Lebouyer delivery, mother and father handle the actual delivery, maintaining physical contact, and touching and stroking the infant from its first emergence from the vagina till it is comfortably nursing at the breast. The physician becomes a resource person in the background.

Specialists in child development began to emphasize the importance of the bonding that can be facilitated in these more natural forms of delivery, bonding between the parents and their child and bonding between the two parents (Money & Tucker, 1975, pp. 161, 204). The key to this earliest of human communications—intimacy and affectional bonding—focuses on a consciously shared experience in birthing communicated continually by nur-turing, loving touches. Touch is commonly acknowledged as the most basic mode of animal communication.

Body Pleasure and the Origins of Violence. This growing emphasis on natural childbirth and the bonding associated with it takes on more significance for the wholesome development of our sexual self-image when linked with the research of developmental neuropsychologist James W. Prescott (1975, 1977, 1978, 1983; Prescott & Wallace, 1976, 1978).

Laboratory experiments initiated by Harry and Margaret Harlow (1965; H. Harlow, 1971) and continued by others have shown that the pleasure and violence centers in the limbic and hypothalamic systems of the mammalian brain have a reciprocal relationship. Stimulation of one center inhibits the activity and development of the other center. When the brain's somatosensory pleasure centers are "turned on," the violence circuits are somehow "turned off": "The reciprocal relationship of pleasure and violence is highly significant, because certain sensory experiences during the formative periods of development will create a neuropsychological predisposition for either violence-seeking or pleasure-seeking behavior later in life" (Prescott, 1975, p. 65).

Using the Textor Cross-Cultural Summary for statistical comparisons, Prescott has found a very high correlation in 39 of 49 contemporary societies, linking high scores on the infant Physical Affection Scale with low adult violence and low physical affection scores with high adult violence levels. This correlation in 39 of 49 societies clearly indicates a strong causal connection between the two variables.

The hypothesis becomes inescapable when the 10 exceptions are examined. In the 6 societies characterized by both low infant physical affection and low adult physical violence, one finds a consistently permissive view of premarital and adolescent sex: "Thus, *the detrimental effects of infant physical affectional deprivation seem to be compensated for later in life by sexual body pleasure experiences during adolescence*" (Prescott, 1975, p. 67; italics in the original). Each of the remaining 4 societies, characterized by both high infant nurturance and high adult violence, have strong taboos against premarital sexual behavior and place a very high value on premarital virginity: "It appears that *the beneficial effects of infant physical affection can be negated by repression of physical pleasure later in life*" (Prescott, 1975, p. 67; italics in the original). When the statistical analysis includes nurturance and body pleasuring during both infancy and adolescence, the reciprocal causal relation of nurturance and violent behavior holds for every one of the 49 cultures for which nurturance values were available.

In subsequent statistical analyses using both contemporary American and other Western cultures, Prescott (1978, 1983) expanded the statistical correlates of adult physical violence to include negative attitudes toward gun control, abortion, nudity, sexual pleasure, premarital and extramarital sex, breastfeeding, and women, along with a glorification of war and through usage of both drugs and alcohol. The correlates of high infant nurturance have been extended to include such social factors as low class stratification, prolonged breastfeeding, a high sense of human dignity and the individual person, acceptance of abortion, premarital and extramarital sex, low sex anxiety and dysfunction, deemphasis of private property and war, few children within an extended family structure, and a peer relationships between men and women.

A Developmental/Descriptive Model of Sexual Violence. Here again, as we found with gender identity and the ''girl-boys'' of the Dominican Republic mentioned earlier, our understanding of the developmental processes that lead to sexually violent personalities can shed considerable light on the conditions and environment that may promote a balanced, healthy sexual maturation and the ability to enter into and maintain mature, rewarding intimate relationships.

In the 1970s, researchers and rehabilitative specialists made considerable progress in gaining answers to two questions: (1) Why do some men and women *need* to control other persons through assault, abuse, or seduction? And (2) why do some persons use sex for this control, whereas others turn to nonsexual but equally antisocial behavior to achieve control? Among the main reasons that have been uncovered are (1) a breakdown or failure in the development of an individual's ability to communicate with others as an equal; (2) a failure to see oneself as *different but equal;* (3) a failure to develop the skills needed to relate in an intimate way to another person; and (4) a socialization process that reduces other people to sexual objects to be used at will (Groth, 1979; McCombie, 1980).

Socially deviant behavior often has its roots in an *inadequate personality.*[1] This is not an inadequate person, but rather a person *who perceives himself or herself as never being equal to his or her peers.* A person with an inadequate personality is never satisfied that he or she has done the best that he or she could have done. If such people get a grade of 98 on an exam, they feel that they should have gotten a 99 or 100. Parental praise is not taken as deserved or earned, but as given by the parent, out of duty. They can only see others as being better than they are; they always see themselves at the bottom of any comparison or ranking.

A child with an inadequate personality has a natural but exaggerated need to please parents and adults. In adolescence, this natural need shifts to a need to please one's

peers and wanting to be accepted as an equal by them. But the feelings of inadequacy hinder attainment of this goal. According to the *developmental-descriptive profile* proposed by William Prendergast (1979), the child with an inadequate personality takes one of three directions in adolescence:

1. Into a middle-of-the road, healthy personal adjustment and socialization.

2. Into the path of denial, where refusal to deal with one's perceived inadequacy drives the individual to compensate with maladaptive but socially tolerated behavior, or with antisocial behavior of various types, the path of the denier.

3. Into a path of acceptance where the individual is resigned to her or his inadequacy and compensates with a variety of maladaptive but socially tolerated (or antisocial) behaviors, the path of the acceptor.

The Path of Healthy Social and Personal Adjustment. A child with an inadequate personality may take a middle-of-the-road path when friends, a teacher, parents, a coach, or others help the youth to work through his or her feelings of inadequacy and to become relatively adjusted and balanced. When the adolescent cannot resolve his or her perceived inadequacy, he or she will compensate for the continued denial or acceptance of perceptions of inadequacy either with maladaptive but socially accepted or tolerated behavior, or with antisocial behavior.

The Path of Denial and Overcompensation. Some people who have not dealt with their feelings of inadequacy react by denial and overcompensation. The denier spends most of his or her time and energy trying to outdo others in sports, academics, or sexual activities. The socially acceptable denier may become the superhero, the corporate executive controlling the lives of thousands of employees and millions of dollars. The male denier may also become the superstud, or Don Juan. However the denier tries to compensate, he or she is seldom content or satisfied. The behavior may be socially tolerated or even highly esteemed by others, though it is personally maladaptive in terms of being expressed in compulsive competitive behavior.

When the denial of inadequacy takes a criminal or antisocial path, the denier may use physical force and terror to gain control: mugging, robbing, spouse or child abuse, or murder. In denying their feelings of inadequacy, some may use sex in an antisocial way, trying to gain control in compulsive, repetitive acts of sexual assault (Figures 6 and 7).

The Path of Acceptance and Seduction. When the adolescent takes the acceptor path, he or she simply ''gives up.'' Gaining the acceptance of one's peers and seeing oneself as equal to them is viewed by the acceptor as an impossible challenge. Socially integrated acceptors tend to find a comfortable niche. They become the clerk or secretary at the fiftieth desk who hardly ever considers the possibility of moving up to the forty-ninth desk, the likable ''Casper Milquetoast'' or Bob Crachitt of Dickens's *A Christmas Carol.* In marriage, the acceptor is on the

---

[1] The terminology used here is based on a developmental and descriptive or pragmatic approach used by psychologists involved in the rehabilitation of sex offenders and convicted criminals. It is *not* concerned with the etiology or description of the personality and behavior types as defined and cataloged in the third edition of the *Diagnostic and Statistical Manual of Mental Disorders* (DSM-III) nor as variously described and defined in clinical terms by abnormal psychology following the gestalt, Rogerian, Adlerian, or other models.

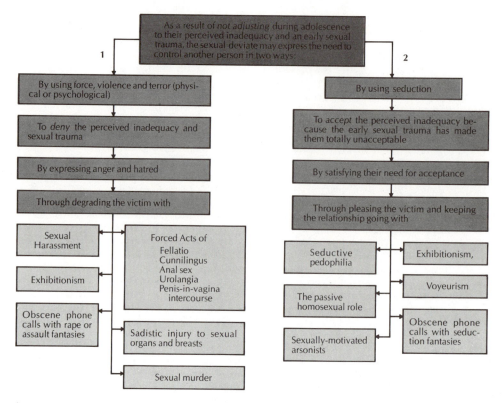

Figure 6. Two behaviors, force (psychological or physical) and seduction, are commonly used by sexual offenders to gain control over their victims. This dichotomy of methods leads the individual into specific antisocial behavioral outlets as shown in this diagram. (Reprinted with permission from *Becoming a Sexual Person,* by Robert T. Francoeur. New York: Macmillan, 1982, p. 413.)

receiving end of verbal or physical spouse abuse and takes the occasional or frequent beatings as evidence that he or she is "really loved and accepted."

Acceptors generally enjoy the dependent role. They need protection and want a certain amount of direction from others. Unless a catastrophe hits, the acceptor will not try to change.

Socially deviant acceptors express their need to compensate for their accepted feelings of inadequacy by controlling others in seductive ways, as embezzlers, forgers, or arsonists. When the acceptor seeks to compensate by gaining control through sexual seduction, she or he will become a pedophile, an exhibitionist, a voyeur, or an obscene phone caller. Male acceptors may also use seduction in seeking acceptance in passive homosexual behavior or with young children who want to please adults.

The obvious questions raised by this developmental-descriptive profile[2] is why some persons with an inade-

---

[2]It is important to remind the reader that the terminology and conceptualization used in this section are pragmatic and descriptive rather than clinical and analytical; they are not intended to follow the third edition of the *Diagnostic and Statistical Manual of Mental Disorders.*

quate personality use nonsexual behavior to gain control through violence or seduction whereas others use sexual assault or seduction to gain the same control. The answer, first proposed by William Prendergast (1979), has been confirmed by psychologists working at the many sex-offender rehabilitation-centers around the United States. In 90% of cases, the crucial factor appears to be an unresolved sexual trauma suffered at an early age, usually between ages 5 and 7. Although this trauma occurs early in development, it usually is not confronted until puberty and adolescence, when the child experiences an erotic/sexual awakening.

Prendergast (1977) described two types of sexual trauma in this profile based on 20 years of work with sex offenders. An active type may include homosexual acts, incest, sodomy, rape, and forced painful sexual relations. When the act does not involve force, the active trauma may be pleasurable at the time because the child with an inadequate personality likes to please older children and adults. The experience may not become traumatic until the child realizes during adolescence that what he or she did and enjoyed is not socially acceptable.

An example from Prendergast's work (1979) illustrates this type of trauma: Larry was a lonely boy whose father

EARLY CHILDHOOD	ADOLESCENCE	ADULT PATH	MEN	BOTH SEXES	WOMEN
AN INADEQUATE PERSONALITY —The person perceives self as being inadequate	Lack of adequate adjustment in relating to peers during adolescence	Denier Path		**Antisocial Non-sexual Deniers** Muggers, Armed robbers, Murderers, Kidnappers, Terrorists Spouse and Child Abusers	
			Playboys, Superstuds, "Citizen Kane" type	**Socially Accepted or Tolerated Deniers** Over achievers in all areas of life	Playgirls, Anti-male lesbians
	Personal adjustment during critical period in relating to peers, made alone or with outside help	Normal Adult Social Adjustment		Socially Adapted	
	Lack of adequate adjustments in relating to peers during adolescence	Acceptor Path	Hen-pecked husband, "Casper Milquetoast" type.	**Socially Accepted or Tolerated Acceptors**	
				Antisocial Non-sexual Acceptors Forgers, Embezzlers, and Profit-motivated arsonists	Helpless women who are attracted to and marry abusive and/or alcoholic men
AN INADEQUATE PERSONALITY plus AN EARLY SEXUAL TRAUMA (Active or passive, conscious or repressed)	Lack of adequate intervention to help the adolescent confront and work through perceived inadequacy and sexual trauma	Denier Path		**Antisocial Sexual Deniers** Rapists, Sexual assaulters, and Anger-motivated Exhibitionists	
	Personal adjustment in relating to peers successfully made during critical adolescent period, alone or with outside help	Normal Adult Social Adjustment		Socially Adapted	
	Lack of adequate intervention to help the adolescent confront and work through perceived inadequacy and sexual trauma	Acceptor Path	Seductive Pedophiles, "Peeping Toms," Obscene Phone Callers Bottomless Male Go-Go Dancers	**Antisocial or Less Tolerated Sexual Acceptors** Exhibitionists motivated by need for acceptance, Some Passive Homosexuals, Sexually motivated Arsonists	Strippers, Topless/Bottomless Go-Go Dancers, Professional "models", Call girls, Some prostitutes

Figure 7. A developmental-descriptive profile of the possible outcomes of compensating behaviors in men and women suffering from an ''inadequate personality'' alone, or from an ''inadequate personality'' combined with an early sexual trauma. (Reprinted with permission from *Becoming a Sexual Person*, by Robert T. Francoeur. New York: Macmillan, 1982. p. 418.)

had died. He was befriended by a neighbor who invited him to his garage workshop. The man showed interest in Larry and also gave him affection. The affection eventually became sexual when the neighbor began to fondle and masturbate Larry. Larry interpreted this activity as affection and came back for more. As an adult, Larry began to do the same thing with young boys in an attempt to find affection and acceptance.

The second type of trauma described by Prendergast is illustrated by another case: As a young boy, Bob was accused by his father of playing with a forbidden gun. Although he pleaded innocence, Bob's father punished him by burning his hand on an electric stove. A second regression session took Bob back to an earlier trauma that Bob linked subconsciously with sex. Continually angry with his mother for not protecting him from his brutal father, and trying to deflect his father's anger to her, Bob picked an occasion when his mother was out with a boy-friend. He called his father at work and asked him to come home. When the father arrived, Bob led his father to a nearby motel, where Bob opened a door to reveal his mother in bed with a sailor. Unfortunately the father's reaction was not what Bob expected. His father calmly closed the door and took Bob back home, where he beat him so badly that he spent three months in the hospital. A 5-year-old expects his mother to protect him. Instead, Bob's mother was out whoring. Bob transferred his anger with his mother to all women and raped six women before he was caught and sent to a diagnostic and treatment center. Once the regression therapy disclosed his trauma and his reaction to it, Bob realized why he raped and began a successful social rehabilitation.

Rehabilitation specialists like Groth (1979), Prendergast (1979), and McCombie (1980) suggest that women who suffer early sexual traumas handle this experience better than men, perhaps because women have more socially acceptable outlets for expressing their emotions and reactions.

Rehabilitative therapies for convicted compulsive-repetitive sex offenders, like the ROARE technique (Reeducation of Attitudes and Repressed Emotions) have a success rate in about 90%. In dealing with the whole developmental process that was diverted from a healthy path, the ROARE reeducation, for instance, includes a thorough sex-education course using explicit films, a rage-induced regression designed to deal with the early sexual trauma when repressed, and reeducation of the self for a positive but reality oriented body image and for a comfortableness with body pleasuring through masturbation and massage.

Sexual Violence and Pornography. In 1970, the Presidential Commission on Pornography and Obscenity concluded that there was no relationship between exposure to erotic presentations and subsequent aggression, particularly sexual crimes. In 1970, only two main types of sexually explicit films and printed material existed: sexually explicit educational or therapeutic material and nonviolent erotica or relational pornography. In the late 1970s, two new forms of pornography appeared: violent or aggressive erotica, which openly degraded and demeaned the role and status of the female participants, and "kiddie porn." The nonaggressive erotica and educational-therapeutic sexually explicit material continue to be produced (Russell, 1980).

The findings of the Presidential Commission are now seriously questioned in view of the new types of pornography (Bart & Jozsa, 1980; Griffin, 1980; McCormack, 1978; Russell, 1980). In laboratory studies, Donnerstein (1979, 1980) used two groups of males; both groups were shown violent-erotic films, but one group had previously mistreated and been angered by women. Both male test groups showed an increase in aggressive reactions after the films, but the angered males showed definite aggression when shown the films with women present. No change in the male reaction was noted when their viewing companions were male.

Neil Malamuth and James Check (1981) extended these findings with nonlaboratory research in which hundreds of college students were sent out to view movies that linked sex and violence. A week later, with no reference to the viewings, the students were given a questionnaire with camouflaged questions related to violence and sex. *Science News* (1980) reported that

the results of the survey indicated that exposure to the films portraying violent sexuality increased male subjects' acceptance of interpersonal violence against women. A similar (though nonsignificant) trend was found for acceptance of rape myths (that women like to be forced to sex). For females the trend was in the opposite direction. Women exposed to violent-sexual films tended to be slightly less accepting of interpersonal violence and of rape myths than were control subjects. "The present findings," say the researchers, "constitute the first demonstration in a nonlaboratory setting . . . of relatively long-term effects of movies that fuse sexuality and violence." (p. 171)

Linking together the work and the theories of Prescott, Prendergast, Donnerstein, and Malamuth and Check provides a provocative, *if still tentative*, picture of normal and antisocial personality development, the development of a wholesome, mature sexual personality capable of relating in an intimate way to other sexual persons.

The Development of Moral Awareness

A key factor in the development of a healthy, wholesome sexuality is the integration of sexual behavior within a personal value system that is at the same time integrated with society's values. Three theories of moral development are relevant here, those of Piaget, of Kohlberg, and of Simon and Gagon.

Jean Piaget's Theory of Moral Development. In Piaget's theory (1965), the newborn infant begins life as a completely *amoral,* totally self-centered being. This stage usually lasts about two years. In the second stage, termed *egocentric* by Piaget, the child has developed only a very general idea of society's moral rules, and these she or he readily changes to suit her or his personal needs between ages 2 and 7. In this period, the child reacts instinctively to her or his environment.

In the third, or *heteronomous,* stage, morality is based on constraint by adults, even though the child begins to assert some degree of logical and moral control over his or her behavior. Between ages 7 and 12, the child begins to distinguish between valid and invalid ideas. Even so, he or she more often accepts an idea without question from a parent, a teacher, or an older child, and issues are clearly set in "black-and-white" terms. There is still little understanding of what is moral because of the total acceptance of a morality imposed by others.

Following a transitional "rest station" in this development, the child enters into the *autonomous* stage of morality, characterized by values based on cooperation rather than on constraint. Peer interactions, discussions, criticism, equality, and respect for others are important factors in this development. The child begins to see other perspectives on moral and ethical issues besides his or her own. The need to question and verify rules and ideas is important, as moral values are internalized and integrated into the child's expanding view of the world and human behavior.

During adolescence in particular, morality is seen in terms of peer consensus and what is mutually beneficial. Social interaction is crucial, along with the necessary ingredient of a parallel cognitive growth. Moral judgments change frequently as the adolescent probes and questions, often rebelling against parental values even though he or she may reaffirm these same values later in life.

Kohlberg's Expanded Theory of Moral Development. Based on his own research, Kohlberg (1967) expanded and modified Piaget's model into six stages clustered on three levels. On the first, or preconventional, level the child responds to cultural rules and "good-bad" labels. In the punishment and obedience-oriented stage of this level, there is total respect for an outside authority that determines behavior, rather than for any internalized morality. In the second, or instrumental relativist-oriented, stage behavior is based on satisfying one's own needs rather than on adjusting to or considering the needs of others or of society.

On the second, or conventional, level of moral discernment, the person conforms to and maintains the moral expectations of her or his family, group, or social system, regardless of the consequences. In Stage 3, the "good-boy–good-girl" stage, a conformity of behavior to moral codes is prompted by the approval that one can expect from others in return for conforming. Stage 4, "law and order," focuses on socially fixed rules, on respect for authority, and on maintaining the social order.

On Kohlberg's third level, the *autonomous, principled, or postconventional* level, the individual makes a clear effort to define his or her morality apart from that of outside authorities. In the fifth, or *social contract,* stage, the moral emphasis is on what is legally binding, and laws are revised to meet social needs. Pluralism is acknowl-

edged, and a shift occurs from an absolutist to a relativistic moral outlook. In Stage 6, the *universal ethical principle* stage, the determination of moral judgment rests in the person's own conscience. Here, abstract qualities such as justice, human rights, and respect for the dignity and equality of all people come into play. Attitudes arise from an internalized set of values without regard to the social system. From even a casual observation of human life, it is obvious that most people do not reach Piaget's autonomous or Kohlberg's postconventional stage of moral sensitivity and development. In fact, most people are guided by outside authority and a conventional morality, the "law-and-order" stage.

Kohlberg's model and conclusions have been criticized by Carol Gilligan, John Gibbs, and Richard Hersh for several important shortcomings. The model is based on research with American boys age 10 and older only while Piaget believes moral development begins for some as early as age four. No females were included in Kohlberg's sample. Gilligan (1982) argued that the apparent sex differential suggested by Kohlberg—namely, that men tend to go to Stage 4 or 5, whereas women tend to base their moral decisions based on Stage 3—may reflect an inadequate articulation of the upper stages. Gibbs pressed this criticism, suggesting that the lack of developmental studies of adults raises the question of whether Stage 6 is ideal or real. There is also so far only a little cross-cultural research to support the claim that this model applies equally to other cultures (Hersh, Paolitto, & Reimer, 1979).

Simon and Gagnon's Social Scripting Theory. Sociologists John Gagnon and William Simon (1965, 1973) based their theory of moral development on two assumptions: (1) that childhood sexual behavior is *not* sexual or erotic in the same sense that this behavior is after puberty, and (2) that sexual behavior may express and serve nonsexual purposes. In focusing on the nature and functions of sexual values, Simon and Gagnon believe that the meanings of behavior change as we mature, so that the values or morality we attach to a particular behavior also changes. Simon and Gagnon believe that the infant's self-exploration and accidental experiences with body pleasure and orgasm, triggered by physical stimuli like exercise, sports, pressure on the sexual organs while sleeping, and the like, are gradually associated with conscious childhood masturbation. As the child matures, this sexual behavior takes on new meanings through interaction with other maturing sexual persons. In adolescence, numerous formal and informal codes of behavior are learned in a type of social scripting. New adolescent experiences with love play, romance, and nurturance add to this picture, gradually transforming and expanding the adolescent's erotic dimensions in new and more intimate interactions and relationships (Gagnon & Simon, 1973; Simon & Gagnon, 1969a,b).

Simon and Gagnon's second assumption contradicts the value system traditional in Western culture whereby men prove their manhood through sexual conquest, whereas women prove their feminity by controlling their sexual desires and limiting sex to a motherhood goal. As sex becomes increasingly only one aspect of a close, mutually shared relationship, these values fade. Sexual conquest and submission are no longer the dominant values in adult intimate relations that they were in Victorian times.

The moral development models of Piaget, Kohlberg, and Simon and Gagnon provide a clearer understanding of the role that society and the family play in molding all of our interpersonal relationships and the values that support them. Both socioeconomic and socioethnic patterns must be taken into account in examining the full picture of sexuality expressed in American society today, with all its subcultures. This picture includes gender roles, sex stereotypes, the purposes of sexual intercourse, the interaction and status of the sexes, acceptable and unconventional sexual behavior, the role and position of the child in the family, the varieties of family structures and their functional roles in society, economic values, and the general structure of each subculture within the larger American culture.

Social Factors in Scripting for Sexual Development, Values, and Roles

Socioeconomic Classes and Sexual Values

Sociologists include the family's income level and the breadwinner(s)' occupation(s) and attained educational level(s) related to a particular type of employment as aspects of general socioeconomic status. Although there is considerable blurring in American class structure today, certain distinctions still seem valid in terms of scripting for sexual behavior and values. Yorburg (1974) proposed as valid distinctions for this purpose (1) upper, middle, and blue-collar working classes; (2) urban and rural classes; and (3) one's ethnic origins. Some economists suggest that the only valid socioeconomic distinction is between the rich and the poor, as the middle class of 15 or 20 years ago has been eroded by inflation. Mass immigrations in the late 1970s, the "boat people" from Southeast Asia, 117,000 Cubans in 1980, and thousands of Mexicans, Arabs, and Muslims have added to the importance of the ethnic dimension in American sexual behavior and values. The resurgence of fundamentalist religious groups in recent years has highlighted the differences in sexual attitudes and values between the followers of the more liberal religious views of the mainstream churches and the literalist, authoritarian "black-and-white" fundamentalist positions.

Valid as the sociological generalizations may be, each distinct cultural, socioeconomic, and religious subgroup contains within it a wide range of behavioral patterns and attitudes, so that stereotyping individuals within any group must be avoided. In general, the higher socioeconomic classes are more likely to adopt such values in human relations as equalitarianism, secularism, tolerance of pluralism, personal achievement, rationalism, the de-

clining influence of sex-role stereotyping, and a reduction in the power politics between women and men. Women in the more educated upper classes tend to be more assertive and the men more sensitive and emotionally expressive. There is a greater acceptance of different sexual behaviors, oral and anal sex, premarital and extramarital sex, and masturbation. Both husbands and wives of the middle class rate their sexual intimacy much more positively than do the upper lower class or the lower blue-collar classes (Rainwater, 1966). There is also considerably more flexibility in lifestyles, with an acceptance of the single life, open or flexible monogamy, and dual-career families with or without children (Rubin, 1977; Yorburg, 1974).

Studies have also shown that, in general, middle-class men and women have more mutuality and sharing than in the blue-collar working class. Working-class males tend to be more ashamed of sharing and reluctant to share household tasks and are more apt to segregate themselves from women at social functions. Working-class women tend to be more passive, nurturing, and emotionally volatile than their middle-class counterparts (Andreas, 1971; Yorburg, 1974).

Ethnic Differences and Sexual Values

In white middle-class American families, adolescent pregnancy is considered a serious, epidemic problem. Yet, in other American subcultures, teenage pregnancy and motherhood are considered a status symbol by all concerned. Often, the more children a young man has fathered, the higher his standing in his peer group. As many ethnic groups have strong extended families, child care is often not a significant problem for the single teenage mother. Social scripting in the ethnic-cultural subgroups often create quite divergent values and attitudes not shared by other subgroups (Guttmacher Institute, 1976, 1981).

Black Americans. Although black matriarchy no longer exists in America, black men, in general, tend to have less authority in blue-collar homes than men of other ethnic groups. Black working-class men are more expressive in their relationships with women. Black women are not as troubled about achieving success as are white women of the same socioeconomic level who come from a much more patriarchal tradition. In many cases, black women have greater opportunities for work than black males and may provide the major support for their families. All of these cultural factors come into play in the formation of sexual values, particularly in giving a positive impetus to early sexual intercourse and a negative image to sexual variations such as masturbation, homosexuality, and oral and anal sex, which are often seen as derogatory to the macho male image (see Peters & McAdoo in McGoldrick, Pearce, & Giordano, 1983; Yorburg, 1974).

There is a serious shortage of young marriageable men in the black community, resulting from a high industrial accident and death rate; inequities in the penal system, with blacks spending more time in prison than whites for the same crimes (Winer, 1981); and high rates of violence and drug use. This situation has favored the evolution of an alternative sexual and family relationship, termed "man sharing" or "extramarital polygamy" by Scott (1980). In what amounts to a functional adaptation to the socioeconomic environment of blue-collar blacks, man sharing spreads the familial contribution and influence of the black male, who maintains a familial and sexual relationship with a single mother and their children alongside his "monogamous" primary relationship. This arrangement gives more stability and social balance to the community than would adherence to the strict monogamous pattern (Allen & Agbasegbe, 1980).

The Jewish-American Tradition. The Jewish ethnic subculture shares some important similarities with the black American tradition, particularly in the area of female power, according to Yorburg (1974). American Jewish women come from a long tradition of importance as economic providers. In their European homelands, Jews were often prohibited by law from owning land. Hence, they often emphasized business ventures in which the wives sharing equally with their husbands, despite the overall patriarchal tradition of Judaism. Such values as achievement, equality of the sexes, and education were part of the cultural heritage that Jewish people brought with them when they immigrated. Many American Jewish women went to college and moved into such male-oriented professions as medicine, law, and business. Studies of college and professional women indicate that Jewish women tend to be more career-oriented than women of other religious backgrounds. Sex-role stereotyping is also less apt to occur in this ethnic group, although it does prevail among the very Orthodox and Hassidic Jewish communities (McGoldrick, Pearce, & Giordano, 1983).

The Japanese-American Tradition. Like many Oriental cultures, the Japanese tend to accept a tradition-oriented authoritarian culture with the male dominant. Studies have shown that Japanese-American wives have less authority in the home than the wives in any other ethnic group. The Japanese tradition insists on strict obedience of the wife and children, and on emotional control in both sexes. There is a strong tendency toward separation of the sexes in Japanese-American families, along with an emphasis on the extended family and the male's need to protect his family's reputation.

These traditional values are often a source of conflict in marriage and family life, especially among young, urban, middle-class Japanese-American women educated in American schools. The conflict is not unusual and appears inevitably when ethnic groups bring with them traditions and sexual values that are not shared by the mainstream of American culture. Interactions and accommodations occur in both directions, with the im-

migrant culture absorbing more from the mainstream in which they are a minority. There is, however, always some cross-fertilization, with immigrant values modifying some local values in the community (McGoldrick *et al.*, 1983; Yorburg, 1974).

The Mexican-American Tradition. The patriarchal tradition is a dominant factor in the Mexican-American culture, especially in the less educated and lower socioeconomic families, where machismo is a prominent attitude and value. These values remain strongest among Mexican-Americans living in rural or border towns and in the segregated barrios of larger urban centers. Even after several generations in the United States, most Mexican-American men are threatened by wives and daughters gainfully employed outside the home. A working wife or daughter is perceived as a threat to the male's machismo image as the sole provider. Mexican-American men also place a high value on many children and thus often refuse to use contraceptives.

Sexual values rooted in the varied Latin American cultures from Mexico, Cuba, Puerto Rico, and the South American countries find quite different expressions when these people emigrate to the United States. Studies are just beginning to reveal some of the many subtle differences among the sexual and family values of the Cuban population in Florida, the Mexican-Americans in the Southwest, and the Puerto Ricans in the large cities of the Northeast. Sex-role stereotyping, male dominance, sexual inequality, and other values are weakening in the culture of younger, educated, urban Latin Americans as their socioeconomic status changes and they become more integrated into the general culture of the United States (McGoldrick *et al.*, 1983).

Islamic-American Traditions. The emergence of a Muslim tradition among black Americans in the 1970s, coupled with the significant increase of immigration from Islamic countries in response to unrest in the Middle East, has produced increasing interactions between Islamic sexual and familial values and the more prevalent values of our Western Judeo-Christian value system. Census figures for the United States provide no clear picture of Islamic and Arabic immigration. The largest concentration of Arab-Americans is in metropolitan Detroit, where over a third of the 150,000–180,000 Arab-Americans are Muslims. The variations in customs and the relative importance given traditional Islamic values among Arab-and/or Islamic-Americans easily match the wide range of ethnic, national, and political realities in the countries from which these people have emigrated to the United States. Muslims from Turkey or Saudi Arabia face problems in adapting to life in the United States that are different from those faced by Muslims from Lebanon, Jordan, Nigeria, or Pakistan.

The patriarchal and other Muslim family traditions may remain in ascendancy, but the harshness of purdah (the custom of "female seclusion") is more often softened in the interaction with Western values. Increasingly, the women attend college and find careers. Their husbands try to adapt to the new lifestyles and values adopted by their wives and and daughters, sharing household chores and parenting in a way that would be unacceptable in their homeland. At the same time, Muslim values, rooted in an open recognition of the sexuality and power of women and the acceptance of bisexual activity, are bound to have some influence on traditional American values as these non-Western attitudes become better known to us. No one knows how these Muslim values may affect an affirmation of equality of the sexes, which nevertheless often contains a radical fear of female sexuality or the open exploration of the human bisexual potential that permeates our mass media (Francoeur, 1981, 1982; Parrinder, 1980).

The Shifting Sex Ratio

In ancient Athens, where males outnumbered females, women held a lower place in society and were more constrained than in Sparta, which had more women than men. In medieval Europe, a shift from a high to a low sex ratio brought a strong feminist movement and greater misogyny among males. The restriction on marital intercourse among Orthodox Jews has resulted in a high sex ratio of 115 males to 100 females. Analyzing these and other data, Guttentag and Secord (1983) argued that a high sex ratio promotes a particular sexual value system that emphasizes marital and sexual commitment, women's place being in the home, centrality of the family, and protection of women. When the ratio is low, adultery is acceptable and normal, marriage is often viewed as temporary, divorce is accepted, sexual liberation is encouraged, women are encouraged to have careers outside the home, women are treated as equal to men, and family life is only part of one's life. This hypothesis suggests some important questions about current sexual values in the United States. The baby boom of the 1950s produced a high surplus of females, who are now in their late 20s and early 30s. Although the sex ratio varies in different age cohorts, the clear surplus of females in American society is likely to have more impact on changing sexual values than any other environmental factor except perhaps our increasing life expectancy and the contraceptive technologies (Guttentag & Secord, 1983).

Variations in Religious Sexual Values

Although religious value systems and attitudes are quite varied, recent efforts to analyze these values have indicated the existence of two distinct moral philosophies. These two philosophies are situated at the two ends of a continuum that encompasses a wide range of approaches to sexual behavior and relationships. Behind every religious system and supporting these two ends of the "moral" continuum are distinct cosmologies, or *Weltanschauungs,* that condition and determine which

sexual behaviors and relationships are to be valued or condemned in what situations. At the *cosmological* end of the continuum is a fixed philosophy of nature, a belief in a universe and in a human nature that was created in finished form by God "in the beginning." Supporting the *cosmogenic* end of the continuum is a belief in a universe and a human nature (including our sexuality) that is always changing and struggling to become what God intends it to become (Francoeur, 1982, Chapter 14).

Out of these two *Weltanschauungs* come distinctly opposing views of human nature, of the origin of evil, and of the nature and purpose of human sex and sexuality. In the cosmological view, evil results from a primeval "fall," and there is a consequent emphasis on redemption through a savior, asceticism and the avoidance of sensual pleasure. In the cosmogenic perspective, physical and moral evil are inevitable, a natural part of the growth pains that humans experience as they explore and develop their potential as sexual persons. The emphasis, then, shifts from a fallen human nature redeemed by adherence to social and moral values established by tradition, to an ongoing creation of human nature in which we participate by our explorations, continued growth, and flexibility (Francoeur, 1983).

Religions rooted in a fixed philosophy of nature tend to stress a patriarchal, exclusively male clergy, fundamentalist or literal interpretations of sacred texts, clear gender roles for men and women, a supernatural life hereafter, and a legalistic morality of conformity to tradition. Sexual activity is more often viewed as a demonic force that must be restrained before it destroys the family and society. Sex is focused on marriage and reproduction, on the "proper use" of the sexual (genital) organs in exclusive heterosexual coitus. Noncoital sex (oral, anal, and masturbatory), nonmarital sex, and homosexual activity are all considered unnatural and immoral, often along with contraceptive (nonreproductive) heterosexual intercourse in marriage.

Religious traditions that accept an evolving or process perspective tend to share authority between male and female clergy and to blur the distinction between clergy and laity. More tolerant of the truths that other religions may express, these churches do not interpret their sacred texts in a literal way, and they accept revelation as an ongoing reality. Gender roles are flexible, and morality emphasizes persons in their environment rather than acts and their conformity to unchanging laws. Human sexuality is viewed as a positive, natural, nurturing, and creative sensual energy. Sexual relations are seen as an important aspect of our growth and maturation as loving, fully human persons. Sex and marriage are linked together, but in a way that allows nonreproductive, nonmarital, and even nonheterosexual expressions as possible vehicles of expressions of love and creativity. This approach is much more tolerant of alternate lifestyles than the fundamentalist religions with their fixed philosophy of nature.

The importance of these two perspectives become evident in the religious views of human sexuality expressed in terms of fundamentalist creationism, biblical covenant, natural law, and situation and humanistic ethics. Genne (1975) compiled a useful synoptic of recent denominational statements on sexuality.

Fundamentalist Creationism. This view of sexual relationships has been clearly expressed in Helen Andelin's *Fascinating Womanhood* (1965) and Marabel Morgan's *Total Woman* (1973), among the top bestsellers in the 1970s, and Audrey Andelin's *Man of Velvet and Steel* (1972). The unchanging, God-given values of the total woman include self-mastery, unselfishness, humility, honesty, chastity, patience, moral courage, benevolent service, self-dignity, gentleness, tenderness, and obedience to her husband. The divinely established masculine virtues are those of the protector and provider and the builder of society, having strong character, confidence, good health, gentleness, understanding of women, attentiveness, youthfulness, humility, and refinement. The true man, in this value system, combines the virtues of Jesus Christ, Sir Lancelot, Abraham Lincoln, and Shakespeare's Petruchio, who tames Kate, the "shrew."

The Covenantal Approach. Most evident in Protestantism, this value system is clearly expressed in the 1970 United Presbyterian Church workstudy document on *Sexuality and the Human Community*. This document lists the following four goals or values for all interpersonal relationships, whether or not they include sexual intimacy:

1. Enhancing rather than limiting one's spiritual freedom.
2. Expressing a compassionate and consistent concern for the well-being of the partner.
3. Strengthening the creative potential of persons called to stewardship in God's world.
4. Expressing joy and opening to persons that flow of grace that enables them to live without despair.

Recognizing that "the Christian community encompasses a wide diversity of racial, ethnic, and cultural groups, and therefore a wide variety of assessments of sexuality and sexual behavior" (p. 7) the covenantal approach emphasizes God's promise of "creating, forgiving and healing love" without attempting to categorize specific sexual acts or relationships as either inherently good or inherently bad. Other formal statements in this perspective are found in *Human Sexuality: New Directions in American Catholic Thought* (Kosnick, Carroll, Cunningham, Modras, & Schulte, 1977), *Towards a Quaker View of Sex* (1963), and *Human Sexuality: A Preliminary Study* (United Church of Christ, 1977).

Natural Law and the Divine Order. The fundamentalist creationist view of sex and marriage has been endorsed in modified, sometimes highly sophisticated for-

mal systems of sexual values by such diverse groups as Orthodox Judaism, the Christian Eastern Orthodox Church, and in statements from the Vatican. This value system was succinctly stated by Pope Paul VI in his 1968 encyclical *Humanae Vitae* in which the Pope claimed that Christian doctrine requires that all sexual (i.e., genital) activity be within the framework of heterosexually monogamous marriage. Homosexuality is viewed as "some kind of innate instinct or a pathological constitution judged to be incurable" (Kosnick *et al.*, 1977, p. 201). All homosexual acts and relationships "are condemned as a serious depravity and even presented in the Bible as the sad consequences of rejecting God" (p. 201). Without condemning homosexuals as persons, the Vatican clearly condemns all homosexual acts as "intrinsically disordered" (p. 201).

Within this divine-order perspective, various positions on contraception, masturbation, and divorce exist, with some Protestant fundamentalists accepting contraception and the Eastern Orthodox accepting divorce and remarriage.

Situation Ethics and Humanistic Values. Joseph Fletcher, an inactive Episcopal priest, ethicist, and humanist, started a major debate and controversy over sexual values with his 1966 book *Situation Ethics: The New Morality:*

According to situation ethics, sexual behavior is morally acceptable in any form—heterosexual, homosexual, bisexual, autosexual (masturbation), or polysexual. What makes any act right or wrong is what it is intended to accomplish—its foreseeable consequences. Sex is a means to an end beyond the sexual act itself. No sexual act is intrinsically right or wrong. No sexual act, in and of itself, should be either blamed or praised apart from whatever human values motivated and guided. (Personal communication)

In 1976, Lester Kirkendall authored "A New Bill of Sexual Rights and Responsibilities," which was endorsed by a wide variety of family-life and sexuality specialists. Published in *The Humanist* magazine, that statement highlights eight major sexual values in the humanist perspective, as follows:

1. *The boundaries of human sexuality need to be expanded to embrace sexual relations as a source of intimacy, pleasure and enrichment for both partners;*
2. *Developing a sense of equity between the sexes is an essential feature of a sensible morality;*
3. *Repressive taboos should be replaced by a more balanced and objective view of sexuality based on sensitive awareness of human behavior and needs, transcending the barriers of age, race, and gender;*
4. *Each person has both an obligation and a right to be fully informed about the various civic, community and personal aspects of human sexuality. This includes those who are handicapped or confined to institutions;*
5. *Sexual morality should come from a sense of caring and respect for others;*
6. *Physical pleasure has worth as a moral value;*
7. *The joy of sexual relations and the need for affection should*

be recognized as a right for every person throughout his or her entire life; and,

8. In all sexual encounters, transitory or long term, there should be a commitment to humane and humanistic values, a respect for the other person and a concern for their happiness. (Kirkendall, 1976, pp. 4–6)

Historical Developments in American Culture

As of 1986, no scholarly history of American sexual customs was available. Two general histories, Bernard Murstein's *Love, Sex, and Marriage through the Ages* (1974) and Reay Tannahill's *Sex in History* (1980), contain a chapter or two on the evolution of American sexual behavior and values. The feminist movement has yielded several histories of women in America. Bradley Smith authored an "informal history" of *The American Way of Sex* (1978), and an interpretive popular study of changing sexual customs between 1940 and 1973 was published under the title *Rape of the A.P.E. (American Puritan Ethic)* (Sherman, 1975). The field desperately requires thorough study by professional historians before we can accurately analyze and interpret the various trends and influences that have affected the evolution of sexual values and behavior in the United States. It is possible, however, in the context of this developmental-descriptive overview of human sexuality to offer a brief characterization of broad periods in our past that have influenced and that continue to influence the changing behavior patterns and values in our pluralistic society. Such a brief sketch is useful as a historical context in which we can locate the earlier summaries of personal development, self-image formation, gender identity and sexual orientation, and socioeconomic, ethnic, and religious influences (Francoeur, 1980–1981).

The Colonial and Revolutionary Eras. In the decades between the discovery of the New World and the American Revolution, early explorers often misunderstood and abused the "sexual permissiveness" of native Americans. The dirth of women suitable for marriage to Christian men led to the custom of "tobacco or trade wives," imported, sight unseen, from Europe. Although the Puritans and the conservative middle-class burghers were very strict about sexual morality, they did accept the naturalness of sex and forgave the numerous violations of formal mores, provided these were publicly confessed. In an adaptation of the Bavarian and Scandinavian customs of "window courting" and "taking your night feet for a walk," the Atlantic Coast colonists commonly accepted "bundling" as a structured form of courtship and premarital sex designed to ascertain the fertility of the soon-to-be-wed female. The more flexible forms of French and English aristocratic marriage and family life were often adopted by upper-class colonists and the leaders of the American Revolution (Murstein, 1974, pp. 299–328; Smith, 1978, pp. 9–86).

The Nineteenth Century. A frontier mentality pervaded American life in the nineteenth century as the new

nation expanded from 16 to 45 states. Three major economic depressions, in 1819, in 1837, and after the Civil War from 1873 to 1878, greatly influenced the development of the dominantly sex-negative values of the last century. The occurrence of two major depressions within 20 years was a major factor in the second Great Awakening of Protestantism in the 1830s, and economic depression and sexual repression went hand in hand.

There was, however, a significant countertrend accompanying the second Great Awakening that explored new patterns of sex and marriage in anticipation of the imminent Second Coming of Jesus. Though few in number, these patterns were considerable in their influence. These groups, led by the Oneida Community (with its 50 years of group marriage) and the polygamous Mormons, included many short-lived communes of social utopians following Rousseau, Fourier, and Marx. Among these were the Harmony Society of George Rapp in Pennsylvania and Indiana, Bronson Alcott's Fruitlands, Brook Farm, and the Amana Community. More religious in their orientation were the Hutterites in the Dakotas, the Moravians in Pennsylvania, and the celibate Shakers of New England. Debates over "free love," the rights of women, and the need for divorce were another aspect of this exploration (Murstein, 1974, pp. 329–366; Smith, 1978, pp. 87–98).

The western frontier offered gold rushes, cattle and sheep raising on scattered farms, battles with Indians, and the massive importation of cheap, often slave, laborers from Latin America, the South Pacific, and the Orient, including thousands of prostitutes. These factors helped to create an attitude toward sex and women that has continued into this century in California and the Southwest (Smith, 1978, pp. 99–132).

On the predominantly sex-negative side was the birth of a "New Chastity Movement" and an obsession with the debilitating consequences of masturbation and excessive sex, which was thought to mean more than once every year or two for married couples! Anthony Comstock's campaign against "obscenity" (any mention of sex in public or private) was another aspect of the triumph of Victorian values (Francoeur & Francoeur, 1977, pp. 10–35).

The Twentieth Century. The end of the Victorian era was signaled by Sigmund Freud's emphasis on the sexuality of women and children, by Havelock Ellis's studies of the importance of touch in sexual relations and his advocacy of sex education for children, and by the family planning work of Margaret Sanger in New York City. Socially, the critical factor in shifting American sexual values was the upheaval that World War I brought to sex roles. The radical shift in sexual values toward a more liberal and exploratory phase came in the "roaring twenties," with the emergence of short skirts coupled with the advent of sanitary menstrual pads, cheek-to-cheek dancing, the "Charleston," and ragtime born in the bordellos of New Orleans. Rudolph Valentino and the vamps of the silent movies reinforced the new attitudes toward sex, though the new independence gained by women who had replaced men in the factories during the war was undoubtedly the crucial social factor in this shift toward more liberal and relaxed behavior patterns (Bullough, 1981; Murstein, 1974, pp. 367–381; Smith, 1978, pp. 133–222).

The Great Depression of the 1930s reversed this liberal trend, returning American culture to a sexually repressive value system that endured well into the 1950s. The pendulum began its return swing to more liberal values with the affluence of the late 1950s; the research of Alfred Kinsey which revealed many hidden secrets of American sexual behavior; the advent of the contraceptive pill; and rock music. The social turmoil of the 1960s—with its emphasis on civil rights, the women's movement, individualism, and self-fulfillment; the emergence of sexually explicit printed media following the birth of *Playboy* magazine; and decisions by the U.S. Supreme Court on what constitutes "obscenity"—brought a gradual, painful shifting of our values.

In the 1970s, some of the key influences were the Vietnam war controversy, which challenged government authority; the permission-giving publicity of alternate lifestyles in the media; the Supreme Court's 1973 decision legalizing abortion; and nudity on the stage and in X-rated movies. The gay rights movement, major advances in reproductive technology (including the birth of the world's first "test-tube baby"), Masters and Johnson's firsthand observations of the human sexual response cycle, and the birth of sex therapy were other important factors in this era (Murstein, 1974, pp. 382–444; Smith, 1978, pp. 223–238).

The Reproductive-Relational Dichotomy.

A major shift in our image and understanding of human sexuality came with the reproductive technologies of the 1970s. Commenting on the psychological and social impact of the contraceptive pill, Ashley Montagu (1969) concluded that

it is a revolutionary development, probably to be ranked with the half-dozen or so major innovations in man's two or more million year history. In its effects I believe that the pill ranks in importance with the discovery of fire, the creation of and employment of tools, the development of hunting, the invention of agriculture, the development of urbanism, scientific medicine, and the release and control of nuclear power. (p. 13)

The psychological and social separation of human reproduction from sexual intercourse was triggered by the advent of the pill. This message has been reinforced by the worldwide publicity given the birth of the world's first test-tube baby on July 25, 1978. In recent years, the media have documented our revolution in reproductive technologies. The media daily carry items about why 20,000–30,000 American women conceive each year by artificial insemination, about the advent of frozen sperm banks, about the development of American clinics specializing in embryo transplants, and about the advent of "prenatal wetnurses" hired to serve as surrogate mothers for women unable to carry their own child. After two or more

million years of experiencing sex and reproduction as inseparable realities, suddenly humans could engage in relational or recreational sex as a form of interpersonal pleasure and communication without the fear of pregnancy. At the same time, humans could now transcend the biological imperatives of sexual reproduction and exercise considerable control over human reproduction as distinct from sexual intercourse.

The Impact of Negative Learning on Sexual Aversion, Desire, Problems, and Dysfunctions

Achieving sexual maturity and health is a lifelong process that each of us experiences in the sociocultural milieu in which we grow up. Lorna and Philip Sarrel (1980) highlighted nine aspects of this development as (1) an evolving positive sense of one's body image and gender identity; (2) learning to deal with, overcome, or moderate the guilt, shame, and childhood inhibitions associated with sexual thoughts and behavior; (3) a gradual loosening of libidinal ties with parents and family; (4) learning what is erotically pleasurable; (5) achieving a comfortableness with and understanding of our sexual orientation; (6) achieving an increasingly satisfying and rich sexual life, free of compulsions and dysfunctions; (7) a growing awareness of being a sexual person and of the place and value of sexual intimacy, communications, and pleasuring in whatever lifestyle we choose; (8) accepting the responsibility for ourselves and our part in the sexual unfolding of our partner; and (9) a gradually increasing ability to experience eroticism as one aspect of intimacy with another person.

Achieving sexual maturity and developing one's self-image as a socially integrated and healthy sexual person is a process filled with risks. These include a variety of internal and external barriers, roadblocks, mistakes made, misadventures, traumas, misinformation, and social scripting by parents, family, and the subculture and society in which we grow up. Each of us reacts to these influences in our own unique way, even as we experience our own unique combination of these factors.

The behavioral research of Masters and Johnson (1966, 1970) gave us some important, if preliminary, insights into the psychological factors involved in sexual dysfunctions. These authors developed the behavioral therapy approach to arousal dysfunctions: painful intercourse (dyspareunia) in both men and women, male erectile problems, and vaginal spasms (vaginismus). They also classified and developed behavioral therapies for orgasmic dysfunctions: premature and retarded ejaculation in men and lack of orgasm in women. In 1974 and 1979, Helen Singer Kaplan expanded our understanding of the "new sex therapy" by integrating the new behavioral therapies with more traditional psychotherapy. She also added a new dimension to the classification of arousal and orgasmic dysfunctions by dealing with antecedent problems of sexual aversion and the lack of sexual desire.

Organic factors such as medications, tranquilizers, poor nutrition, antihypertensive drugs, alcohol, narcotics, physical impairments, diabetes, spinal cord traumas, kidney dialysis, and hormone imbalances may be the primary etiology in an estimated 20% to 30% of the cases of sexual dysfunctions. The psychosocial and relational origins underlying the majority of sexual dysfunctions have taken on new importance with our growing knowledge of the developmental aspects of our sexual unfolding. A healthy sexual development depends on both normal biological development and a positive social scripting from our family, ethnic and cultural background, religious training, and societal roots, as well as on an adequate nurturance. Yet, because every human experiences a mixture of positive and negative inputs into their sexual development (there is no such thing as a perfectly normal and absolutely healthy social and biological environment), every human encounters an occasional or persistent sexual dysfunction.

Sexual aversion is exclusively due to psychological causes: a poor body image and self-image, strong feelings of sexual inadequacy, a traumatic sexual experience in the past, performance anxiety, strong guilt feelings about sex, overwhelming fears of pregnancy or sexually transmitted diseases, strong negative messages from family or society, and fears of becoming involved, vulnerable, or intimate.

The lack of sexual desire is much more often due to psychological factors, although organic causes can certainly be factors. Again, the psychological factors may echo those noted above for the anxiety reactions of sexual aversion, but one can add others, such as hostility toward the other sex or the need for "the lure of forbidden fruit," which can reduce sexual desire in a legitimate relationship.

The same organic and psychological factors that can lead to sexual aversion and the lack of sexual desire can also come into play in dysfunctions that affect sexual arousal and orgasm. To those listed above, we can add others: the failure to develop an ability to relate to another person as a peer; the failure to develop a good sexual self-image, which results in "spectatoring" or constant attempts to "observe" and evaluate one's own performance; misinformation and lack of understanding of what sexual relations may involve; and guilt and anxiety messages about sex in general or about specific sexual behaviors. Questions about what is "normal" or "natural" in sexual relations and behaviors can be based on a variety of criteria, social, religious, legal, statistical, medical, psychological, and personal. Conflicts between what the individual believes is normal and what his or her partner or society views as normal can result in different sexual dysfunctions, depending on the individual's reaction (Haeberle, 1978, pp. 308–400).

Physiological Causes of Sexual Dysfunction

The long-standing American dedication to psychotherapy, the emergence of behavioral therapies for sexual dysfunctions in the 1960s, and their popularity based on simplicity led most sex therapists, until recently, to the belief that 90% or more of all cases of sexual dysfunction are primarily psychological in origin. That belief, however, was never supported with research data. In the early 1980s, new evidence from Wagner and Metz (1980), Wagner and Green (1981), Schumacher and Lloyd (1981), and others seriously challenged this belief. Schumacher, for instance, found that 72% of impotent men had an organic disease, compared with only 12% of men with no erectile problem. Wagner created the first casts of the penile arteries and veins, thus documenting in men with erectile problems a not-uncommon anatomical causes of impotence. These include abnormal arteries incapable of bringing a blood supply sufficient for erection, insufficient cavernous tissue, and faulty vein valves, which reduce erection by allowing blood to leak out instead of being retained.

Four factors must be present for normal sexual arousal; for vasocongestion, which results in penile, clitoral, and labial erection; and for vaginal lubrication in women. These factors are (1) for men, a proper blood supply to the penis; (2) intact pelvic nerves, which tell the arteries and veins when to open and close; (3) normal erectile tissue capable of engorgement; and (4) a reasonable emotional milieu. Until recently, more sex research and therapy focused on the last of these four factors, the psychological. The new awareness stresses the importance of a variety of anatomical and physiological disorders as the main cause in perhaps 30% of all sexual dysfunctions and as a significant contributing factor in another 30% to 50% of dysfunctions.

"Impotence can be caused by virtually every drug listed in the *Physician's Desk Reference*," according to Richard Spark (Brody, 1983, p. C8), an endocrinologist at Harvard Medical School. Antihypertensive medication for high blood pressure, antiasthmatics, narcotics, antidepressants, and tranquilizers are among the more common offending medications. Low testosterone or high prolactin levels, vascular anomalies including those associated with atherosclerosis, and neuropathies (nerve dysfunctions) associated with diabetes, arthritis, and multiple sclerosis are also now part of the etiological picture. However, this research is only starting, and our knowledge of the anatomical and physiological basis of sexual function, especially in the female, is still quite primitive and limited (Leyson, 1985).

Sexual Therapies

Short-term, task-oriented behavioral therapies may be useful in treating many simpler sexual dysfunctions. But many sexual therapists are finding it helpful to use a broader based, multimodal therapy. The new therapies combine behavioral exercises with counseling and psychotherapy to focus on both the current dysfunction and its origins in deficiencies in the individual's sexual unfolding, numerous examples of which have been cited in earier sections of this chapter (Kaplan, 1974, 1979; Leiblum & Pervin, 1980; Tollison & Adams, 1979; Zilbergeld & Evans, 1980).

As with the extensive rehabilitation and reeducation of the compulsive repetitive sexual assaulter mentioned earlier, restoring the person with a sexual dysfunction to a healthy state means dealing with and remedying whatever deficiencies may exist in his or her early psychosexual development. Obviously, this therapy and remedial reeducation have different meanings in different times and settings, depending on what is considered ''normal''— statistically, religiously, socially, or legally—in one's particular subculture and milieu. The precise meaning of sexual health and maturity is dynamic and ever-changing as our culture and subcultures change.

Trends and Projections

There is a possibility that the cyclic pattern of a conservative-repressive phase alternating with an exploratory-permissive phase, both linked closely with the ups and downs of the economic cycle, may continue through the 1980s and beyond. However, several major perturbations in our twentieth-century society may break this cycle and throw the evolution of human sexuality and lifestyles into a quite new orbit. These perturbations include the contraceptive and reproductive technologies separating sex and reproduction, the economic and psychological liberation of women, the political activism of the gay community and other sexual minorities, and the permission-giving and legitimizing impact of the mass media, reinforced by cable and satellite television networks. To these, we can add an increasing life expectancy (doubling between 1900 and 1980, and still rising), population mobility, a certain level of affluence for the majority of Americans despite inflation, the growing number of single adults, earlier sexual maturity coupled with the growing social pressure to delay marriage into the 20s, and the increasing difficulty of the fundamentalist authoritarian churches in maintaining their restricted view of sexuality and acceptable behaviors and relations (Francoeur & Francoeur, 1974, pp. 2–11; Francoeur, 1980, pp. 3–12).

If the cyclic pattern is not continued because of the basic irreversibility of the various social developments just mentioned, particularly the growing economic independence of women and the contraceptive technologies, then six trends may be tentatively projected for the future of American sexuality:

1. ''Decriminalizing'' variant sexual behaviors and relationships as our criminal law relinquishes its efforts to regulate the sexual behavior of consenting adults except where physical harm or public disorder results.

2. ''Demaritalizing,'' with an increasing breakdown of the traditional legal and moral limitations of sexual behavior and intercourse to married couples.

3. ''Degenitalizing'' human reproduction, so that by either coitus or the growing resources of genetic and reproductive technologies, pregnancy becomes a conscious, if less frequent, choice that maximizes the health of the offspring.

4. ''Degenderizing'' sexual behavior and values, with increasing attention to the quality of the intimacy shared by two or more sexual persons, regardless of their sexual anatomies.

5. ''Desexing'' our sexual behavior, with less emphasis on coital and performance pressures; a growing appreciation of the panerotic, nurturing character of all our senses; and a comfortable diffusion of sexuality throughout the whole *bodyspirit* that makes us the sexual persons we are.

6. ''Relationalizing'' our human sexuality, focusing on the ancient biblical concept of human sexual relations as *yahdah,* or ''knowing'' another person in the fullness of her or his being. Sex then becomes a way of transcending the limits of the individual and relating intimately and reverently to other persons and, through them, with the cosmos.

In recognizing our persistent need for nurturance, the ''pluralism'' and ''relationalizing'' of sex will cut across many traditional boundaries of age differences, handicaps, marital status, and gender. The increasing pluralism of human sexuality will create problems and tensions of adaptation. Many people will retreat into their ''shells,'' denying the changes that are occurring all around them. Others, educated for change, decision making, and flexibility, will adapt and grow. But for the majority of Americans, the most common path is likely to be one of stumbling, tension-filled attempts to accept inevitable changes over which they will have little control.

Clinical Implications and Research Suggestions

In this review of human sexual development as we know it in 1986, several implications can be highlighted for clinical practice.

The first implication involves *reconceptualizing* human sexuality to incorporate our new understanding of the nature, meaning, and social functions of human sexuality. This reconceptualization, more sex-positive and much broader than the heterosexual/reproductive/marital concept of Victorian times, will have definite consequences in clinical work with women, children, teenagers, the aged, gay men and women, single persons, the physically handicapped, and the mentally retarded. Our changing concepts of what is ''healthy,'' ''normal,'' ''abnormal,'' ''conventional,'' ''unconventional,'' and ''dysfunctional'' will greatly modify our clinical practice.

A second consequence with clinical significance is the *social restructuring* that will have to occur in the 1980s as we adjust to these new meanings and functions of human sexuality. As the range of conventional and socially acceptable sexual behavior and relations expands, new social and emotional support systems will be needed for sexually active single persons of all ages, for new family forms, and for persons with a gay or bisexual orientation. An important element in this social restructuring will be the legal recognition of these new meanings and functions. Each of these restructurings will impact on clinical practice and education.

A third clinical implication is our obvious need to develop new value systems to guide us in sexual or intimate relations and in reproduction. Although the main focus here will be the articulation of two distinct, general value systems (one for intimacy and the other for reproduction), clinical practice will at the same time require a new sensitivity to the diversity of people's sexual and familial value systems, which stem from their religious, economic, ethnic, and racial diversity. The as-yet-little-studied variations in American ethnic values will very likely become much more important in clincal practice as we expand our knowledge and appreciation of sexuality and erotic pleasure beyond the middle-class, white, educated criteria that have dominated our clinical practice.

The fourth clinical implication is our need to develop a commonly accepted nomenclature and basic models of human sexual response, dysfunctions, and therapy, emphasizing the overriding similarities and the minor differences of male and female patterns (Whipple, Ladas, & Perry, 1982). As we develop new nomenclature and new models, we will need to incorporate and integrate the sexual, erotic, and nurturance dimensions explored by Prendergast (1979), Prescott (1975), Stayton (1980), and others. As this new holistic view emerges and becomes part of clinical practice, human sexuality will again become an integral part of human development, resolving the Kantian dualism of past Western civilization.

Each of the four clinical implications mentioned here contains a variety of obvious issues and problems for productive and promising research in the years ahead. We will need research on each of the four developments mentioned above. Research will also be needed to ascertain how each of these new developments can be used to improve diagnosis and treatment, as well as to provide an improved social climate for personal development.

References

Allen, W. R., & Agbasegbe, B. A. A comment on Scott's "Black Polygamous Family Formation." *Journal of Alternative Lifestyles,* 1980, *3*(4), 375–404.

Andelin, A. *Man of velvet and steel.* Santa Barbara, Calif.: Pacific Press, 1972.

Andelin, H. *Fascinating womanhood.* New York: Bantam Books, 1963.

Andreas, C. *Sex and caste in America.* Englewood Cliffs, N.J.: Prentice-Hall, 1976.

Arms, S. *Immaculate deception: A new look at women and childbirth in America.* Boston: Houghton Mifflin, 1975.

Bart, P., & Jozsa, M. Dirty books, dirty films, and dirty data. In L. Lederer (Ed.), *Take back the night.* New York: Morrow, 1980.

Bell, A., & Weinberg, M. *Homosexualities: A study of diversity among men and women.* New York: Simon & Schuster, 1978.

Bell, A., Weinberg, M. S., & Hammersmith, S. K. *Sexual preference: Its development in men and women.* Bloomington: Indiana University Press, 1981.

Boswell, J. *Christianity, social tolerance and homosexuality.* Chicago: University of Chicago, 1980.

Brody, J. E. How drygs can cause decreased sexuality. *New York Times,* September 28, 1983, pp. C1; C10.

Bullough, V. L. Woman's changing role: Technology's child. *Sexology Today,* 1981, *47*(1), 50–55.

Diamond, M., & Karlen, A. *Sexual decisions.* Boston: Little, Brown, 1980.

Donnerstein, E. *Aggressive erotica and violence against women. Journal of Personality and Social Psychology,* 1980, *39,* 269–277.

Donnerstein, E., & Berkowitz, L. Victim reactions in aggressive erotic films as a factor in violence against women. *Journal of Personality and Social Psychiatry,* 1981, *41,* 710–724.

Ehrhardt, A., & Meyer-Bahlburg, H. Effects of prenatal sex hormones on gender-related behavior. *Science,* 1981, *211,* 1312–1317.

Fletcher, J. *Situation ethics: The new morality.* Philadelphia: Westminster Press, 1966.

Ford, C., & Beach, F. *Patterns of sexual behavior.* New York: Harper & Row, 1951.

Francoeur, A., & Francoeur, R. *Hot and cool sex: Cultures in conflict.* Cranbury, N.J.; A. S. Barnes, 1977.

Francoeur, R. The sexual revolution: Will economic hard times turn back the clock? *The Futurist,* 1980, *14*(2), 3–12.

Francoeur, R. A brief history of American sexual customs. *Sexology Today,* 1980–1981, *47*(2), 14–20; (3), 56–63; (4), 50–55; (5), 14–21; (7), 58–65.

Francoeur, R. Sex behind the Islamic veil. *Sexology Today,* 1981, *47*(6), 12–17.

Francoeur, R. *Becoming a sexual person.* New York: Macmillan, 1982.

Francoeur, R. Religious reactions to alternative lifestyles. In E. D. Macklin & R. H. Rubin (Eds.), *Contemporary families and alternative lifestyles: A handbook on research and theory.* Beverly Hills, Calif.: Sage, 1983.

Francoeur, R., & Francoeur, A. (Eds.). *The future of sexual relations.* Englewood Cliffs, N.J.: Prentice-Hall, 1974.

Gagnon, J., & Simon, W. *Sexual conduct: The social origins of human sexuality.* Chicago: Aldine, 1973.

Genne, W. *A synoptic of recent denominational statements of sexuality.* New York: National Council of Churches, 1975.

Gilligan, C. *In a different voice: Psychological theory and women's development.* Cambridge: Harvard University Press, 1982.

Goleman, D., & Bush, S. The liberation of sexual fantasy. *Psychology Today,* 1977, *11*(5), 48ff.

Griffin, S. Sadism and catharsis: The treatment is the disease. In L. Lederer (Ed.), *Take back the night.* New York: Morrow, 1980.

Groth, A. *Men who rape: The psychology of the offender.* New York: Plenum Press, 1979.

Guttentag, M., & Secord, P. F. *Too many women? The sex ratio question.* Beverly Hills, Calif.: Sage, 1983.

Guttmacher Institute. *11 Million teenagers: What can be done about the epidemic of adolescent pregnacies in the United States?* New York: Alan Guttmacher Institute, 1976.

Guttmacher Institute. *Teenage pregnancy: The problem that hasn't gone away.* New York: Alan Guttmacher Institute, 1981.

Haeberle, E. *The sex atlas.* New York: Seabury Press, 1978.

Harlow, H. *Learning to love.* New York: Ballantine, 1971.

Harlow, H., & Harlow, M. The effect of rearing conditions on behavior. In J. Money (Ed.), *Sex research: New developments* New York: Holt, 1965.

Hass, A. *Teenage sexuality: A survey of teenage sexual behavior.* New York: Macmillan, 1979.

Hersh, R., Paolitto, D., & Reimer, J. *Promoting moral growth: From Piaget to Kohlberg.* New York: Longman, 1979.

Imperato-McGinley, J., Guerrero, L., Gautier, T., & Peterson, R. Steroid 5-alpha-reductase deficiency in man: An inherited form of male pseudohermaphroditism. *Science,* 1974, *186,* 1213–1215.

Imperato-McGinley, J., Peterson, R., Gautier, T., & Sturla, W. Androgens and the evolution of male-gender identity among male pseudohermaphrodites and 5-alpha-reductase deficiency. *New England Journal of Medicine*, 1979, *300*, 1233–1237.

Kallmann, F. Comparative twin study on the genetic aspects of male homosexuality. *Journal of Nervous and Mental Disease*, 1952, *115*, 283–298. (a)

Kallmann, F. Twin and sibship study of overt male homosexuality. *American Journal of Human Genetics*, 1952, *4*, 136–146. (b)

Kaplan, H. S. *The new sex therapy*. New York: Bruner/Mazel, 1974.

Kaplan, H. S. *Disorders of sexual desire*. New York: Bruner/Mazel, 1979.

Kinsey, A., Pomeroy, W., & Martin, C. *Sexual behavior in the human male*. Philadelphia: Saunders, 1948.

Kinsey, A., Pomeroy, W., Martin, C., & Gebhard, P. *Sexual behavior in the human female*. Philadelphia: Saunders, 1953.

Kirkendall, L. A new bill of sexual rights and responsibilities. *The Humanist*, 1976, *36*(1), 4–6.

Klein, F. *The bisexual option: A concept of one hundred percent intimacy*. New York: Arbor House, 1978.

Klein, F. When patients ask: What is bisexuality? *Sexual Medicine Today*, 1979, *3*(4), 10ff.

Klein, F. Are you sure you're heterosexual? Or homosexual? Or bisexual? *Forum* 1980, *10*(3), 41–45.

Kohlberg, L. Stage and sequence: The cognitive-developmental approach to socialization. In D. Goslin (Ed.), *Handbook of socialization theory and research*. Chicago: Rand McNally, 1969.

Kosnick, A., Carroll, W., Cunningham, A., Modras, R., & Schulte, J. *Human sexuality: New dimensions in American Catholic thought*. New York: Paulist Press, 1977.

Leiblum, S., & Pervin, L. *Principles and practice of sex therapy*. New York: Guilford Press, 1980.

Leyson, J. F. (Ed.). *Sexual rehabilitation of the spinal cord injury patient*. Basel: S. Karger, 1985.

Malamuth, N., & Check, J. The effects of mass media exposure on acceptance of violence against women: A field experiment. *Journal of Research in Personality*, 1981, *15*(4), 436–446.

Masters, W., & Johnson, V. *Human sexual response*. Boston: Little, Brown, 1966.

Masters, W., & Johnson, V. *Human sexual inadequacy*. Boston: Little, Brown, 1970.

McCombie, S. (Ed.). *The rape crisis intervention handbook: A guide for victim care*. New York: Plenum Press, 1980.

McCormack, T. Machismo in media research: A critical review of research on violence and pornography. *Social Problems*, 1978, *25*(5), 552–554.

McGoldrick, M., Pearce, J. K., & Giordano, J. (Eds.). *Ethnicity and family therapy*. New York: Guilford Press, 1983.

McGuire, R., Carlisle, J., & Young, B. Sexual deviations as conditioned behavior: A hypothesis. *Behavioral Research and Therapy*, 1965, *2*, 185–190.

Mendola, M. *The Mendola Report: A new look at gay couples*. New York: Crown, 1980.

Money, J., & Ehrhardt, A. *Man and woman, boy and girl*. Baltimore: Johns Hopkins University Press, 1972.

Money, J., & Tucker, P. *Sexual signatures: On being a man or a woman*. Boston: Little, Brown, 1975.

Montagu, A. *Sex, man and society*. New York: Putnam, 1969.

Morgan, M. *The total woman*. New York: Pocket Books, 1973.

Murstein, B. *Love, sex and marriage through the ages*. New York: Springer, 1974.

Parrinder, G. *Sex in the world's religions*. London: Sheldon Press, 1980.

Piaget, J. *The moral judgment of the child*. New York: Free Press, 1965.

Prendergast, W. The sex offender: How to spot him before it's too late. *Sexology*, 1979, *46*(2), 46–51.

Prescott, J. Body pleasure and the origins of violence. *The Futurist*, 1975, *9*(2), 64–74.

Prescott, J. A culture of violence: Philosophical, religious and psychosocial foundations. *Second World Conference of the International Society on Family Law*. McGill University, Montreal, Canada, June 1977.

Prescott, J. *Testimony in the Proceedings of the Senate of Canada, Standing Committee on Health, Welfare and Sciences, Subcommittee on Childhood Experiences as Causes of Criminal Behavior*, April 11, 1978, Issue 15, pp. 5–34.

Prescott, J. *Developmental origins of violence: Psycholobiological, cross-cultural and religious perspectives*. An invited address presented at the annual meeting of the American Psychiatric Association, May 4, 1983.

Prescott, J., & Wallace, D. *Developmental sociobiology and the origins of aggressive behavior*. 21st International Cong'ess of Psychology, Paris, 1976.

Prescott, J., & Wallace, D. The role of pain and pleasure in the development of destructive behaviors: A psychometric study of parenting, sexuality, substance abuse and criminality. *Proceedings Colloquium on the Correlates of Crime and the Determinants of Criminal Behavior*. The National Institute of Law Enforcement and Criminal Justice, 1978.

Rainwater, L. Some aspects of lower class exuality. *Journal of Social Issues*, 1966, *2*, 96–107.

Rubin, L. Sexual liberation and marital strain in the working class. *Sexual Medicine Today*, (September 28, 1977), 19–25.

Rubin, R., Reinisch, J., & Haskett, R. Postnatal gonadal steroid effects on human behavior. *Science*, 1981, *221*, 1318–1325.

Russell, D. The testimony against pornography: Witness from Denmark; and Pornography and violence: What does the new research say? In L. Lederer (Ed.), *Take back the night: Women on pornography*. New York: Morrow, 1980.

Sarrel, L., & Sarrel, P. *Sexual unfolding*. Boston: Little, Brown, 1980.

Schumacher, S., & Lloyd, C. W. Physiological and psychological factors in impotence. *Journal of Sex Research*, 1981, *17*(1), 40–53.

Science News. Sex and violence: Pornography hurts. *118*, 171–172.

Scott, J. Black polygamous family formation. *Journal of Alternative Lifestyles*, 1980, *3*(1), 41–64.

Sherman, A. *The Rape of the A.P.E. (American Puritan Ethic)*. Chicago: Playboy Press, 1975.

Simon, W., & Gagnon, J. On psychosexual development. In D. Goslin (Ed.), *Handbook of socialization theory and research*. Chicago: Rand McNally, 1969. (a)

Simon, W., & Gagnon, J. Psychosexual development. *Trans-Action* (March 6, 1969), 9–17. (b)

Singer, J. *Androgyny: Toward a new theory of sexuality*. New York: Anchor Doubleday, 1972.

Smith, B. *The American way of sex: An illustrated history*. New York: Two Continents/Gemini, 1978.

Stayton, W. A theory of sexual orientation: The universe as a turn on. *Topics in Clinical Nursing*, 1980, *1*(4), 1–7.

Sullivan, H. S. *Interpersonal theory of psychiatry*. New York: Norton, 1953.

Tannahill, R. *Sex in History*. New York: Stein & Day, 1980.

Tollison, C., & Adams, H. *Sexual disorders: Treatment, theory, research*. New York: Gardner Press, 1979.

Towards a Quaker View of Sex. London: Friends Home Service Committee, 1963.

United Church of Chirst, Board of Homeland Ministries. *Human sexuality: A preliminary study*, Eleventh General Synod, 1977.

United Presbyterian Church in the U.S.A. *Sexuality and the human community*. Philadelphia: United Presbyterian Church in the U.S.A., 1970.

Wagner, G., & Green, R. *Impotence: Physiological, psychological, surgical diagnosis and treatment*. New York: Plenum Press, 1981.

Wagner, G., & Metz, P. Impotence (erectile dysfunction) due to vascular disorders: An overview. *Journal of Sex Research,* 1980, *6*(4), 223–233.

Weintraub, P. The brain: His and hers. *Discovery,* 1981, *2*(4), 15–20.

Wertz, R., & Wertz, D. *Lying-in: A history of childbirth in America.* New York: Schocken, 1979.

Whipple, B., Ladas, A., & Perry, J. *The G spot and other recent discoveries about human sexuality.* New York: Holt, Rinehart, and Winston, 1982.

Yorburg, B. *Sexual identity: Sex roles and social change.* New York: Wiley-Interscience, 1974.

Zilbergeld, B., & Evans, M. The inadequacy of Masters and Johnson. *Psychology Today,* 1980, *14*(3), 28–43.

CHAPTER 20

Development of Gender Roles

Susan Losh-Hesselbart

This chapter examines the social roles of women and men. After an assessment of stable and changing social positions related to gender, the chapter summarizes how sex differences in personal traits, as well as the relationships between social gender and societal positions and rewards, are perpetuated. Gender issues are very relevant to family researchers. For example, until recently, many social scientists assumed that women played marginal roles outside the home. Thus, the family became nearly the only social institution studied with respect to women. Our knowledge of how men's family roles relate to other aspects of life has only begun to accumulate. There is also reciprocal feedback across familial and nonfamilial systems. Gender roles within the family influence gender roles outside the family and vice versa.

Terminology

The field of sex roles or gender roles abounds with terminology that reflects the different social-science disciplines. For those who wish to pursue the research literature further, a brief summary of terms will prove helpful. Some psychologists (e.g., Lynn, 1976) differentiate (1) sex-role *orientation;* (2) sex-role *preference;* and (3) sex-role *adoption. Orientation* refers to *self*-definition in terms of culturally defined masculinity and femininity; *preference* refers to desires to adhere to sex-stereotyped norms; and *adoption* refers to *others'* evaluation of the self as masculine or feminine.

Individualized and more structural approaches can also be delineated. Hochschild (1973) differentiated four theoretical areas: (1) *sex differences* in traits and motives, which psychologists examine (Bardwick, 1971); (2) *sex roles,* or the content of the various social roles occupied by each sex, for example, parental or employee roles (Pleck, 1977); (3) the *minority perspective* on prejudice and discrimination, usually against women (Hesselbart, 1976);and (4) the *politics of caste,* or how institutions and social interaction shape the deferent behavior shown by women as a social group to men as a social group (West & Zimmerman, 1977).

Here, I am mainly interested in what have been termed *sex-role orientation, sex-role adoption, sex roles,* and the *minority perspective.* Inevitably, the *sex differences* research must be discussed because many social scientists suggest that male–female differences in orientation, roles, and rewards are caused by sex differences in personality. The *politics-of-caste* perspective can be useful in explaining how gender differences are created and maintained in everyday life.

Currently, debate exists on terms such as *gender, sex,* and *sex role* (Davidson & Gordon, 1979). The term *sex roles* appears to be used in a unique way, as social scientists seldom use such terms as *race roles* or *class roles.* Here, the term *sex* will be used mainly to refer to biologically related research or to personality sex differences. The term *gender* will be used most often to discuss more social issues, such as stereotypes or economic stratification.

"Instrumental" and "Expressive" Roles

The Evolution of "Traditional" Gender Roles

To explore how gender roles are acquired and perpetuated, it is helpful to briefly examine the status of women and men currently and in the past. With every new generation, there is social change and stability. Much social stability exists because children observe patterns of adult behavior and attitudes and adopt parts of these patterns as they develop. The past two decades have produced research that challenges once-established assumptions about the roles of both sexes.

One major school on gender emerged from functional sociology (e.g., Parsons & Bales, 1955). From this perspective, each sex has specialized tasks and privileges. Men are "task" or "instrumental" specialists who represent the family to the world outside, mainly through their occupations, which are increasingly important in achievement-oriented societies. In most countries having electorates, only males—and often only male property-owners—were eligible to vote until the mid-1900s. In many societies, men usually occupied the major roles in institutions outside the family, such as military or religious institutions. Women's roles have been defined as "expressive" or "socioemotional." Women's "jobs"

Susan Losh-Hesselbart • Department of Sociology, Florida State University, Tallahassee, FL 32306.

are to nurture their children and to create a haven for men returning from paid labor. The actual physical labor of housework has not been addressed much by functional sociologists.

It is unlikely that this relatively simple division of roles by gender ever described a majority of households. Certainly, it does not adequately describe gender-role activities before the Industrial Revolution. I doubt that this model describes modern men and women well either.

A Short History of Gender-Role Differentiation

Before the Industrial Revolution, women had important "instrumental" roles in Western societies. The same was—and is still—true in many less developed countries. Using cross-cultural records, Aronoff and Crano (1975) estimated that, on the average, women provided nearly half of world subsistence production. In earlier times and other world areas, women's "traditional" roles have included participation in agriculture, fishing, and animal husbandry. Ironically, as industrialized countries became more involved with less developed countries, industrialized policymakers often assumed that the gender division of labor in both types of countries was similar. Well-meaning advisers often taught skills to the "inappropriate" sex, such as agriculture to men in some African societies. Even the hypothesis that sex differences in physical strength have caused gender occupational segregation is belied by the many women mine workers and construction laborers in India and Japan (Boserup, 1970; United Nations, 1973; Stephens, 1963).

Rather than strength, the physical differences that seem more important in gender segregation relate to procreation. Previously, high mortality rates meant that high fertility rates were needed to replace the population. Survival past the reproductive ages was less common before 1900. High fertility rates implied that much of a woman's adult life was occupied by pregnancy, lactation, and child care. These reproductive constraints have been influential in the gender division of labor. Jobs more frequently held by men, such as hunting, involve geographical mobility. In contrast, women's jobs, such as cooking, are "closer to home" and allow for child care.

As production moved from homes to factories, geographic mobility became more important. Men and single women—and, less often, women with children—left home to join a more cash-oriented economy. Women's productive labor at home, such as textile production, was moved to factories, where it could be done more cheaply and quickly. This practice has continued into the present, with services such as fast-food restaurants as well as with material products.

With greater industrialization, declines occurred in mortality. Thus, women needed to bear fewer children to ensure that some infants would survive into maturity. Children changed from being assets who could work the land or support aged parents to being economic liabilities. For example, in a 1980 press conference, Thomas Es-

panshade of the Brookings Institution estimated that the cost of rearing a child to age 22 (including four years at a public college) was about $80,000. These historical changes have influenced "traditional" gender roles. When productive labor moved from the home, an increased segregation of "home" (women) from "work" (men) occurred. Wage earners in a cash economy have more chances to accumulate power than those without wages; men were and are more likely to earn wages than women. Concurrently, with the lowered "value" of children, women's procreative role became less important. Such factors accentuated social power among men and have influenced many segments of society, including the "traditional family" (Boserup, 1970; Huber, 1976; Oakley, 1974; Stockard & Johnson, 1980).

Relatively few elements labeled *traditional gender roles* by modern social scientists seem recognizable in Western societies before the Industrial Revolution or in many other societies before the nineteenth or twentieth centuries. The elements that have given the most continuity to "traditional" gender roles are women's roles in childbearing and child care and the greater geographical mobility of men.

Women and Men in Industrialized Western Societies

If "traditional" gender roles have a short history, what of those in industrialized societies? Theorists such as Parsons (1942) argued that, with lower productive labor among women at home, wives became "good companions" to their husbands and intensive mothers to their children. In industrialized societies from the nineteenth through the mid-twentieth century, most married women did not enter paid employment.

Even in industrialized societies during the 1900s, the "expressive housewife" has been a luxury few families can afford. Talcott Parsons (1942) felt that the "instrumental–expressive" role differentiation was mainly true of the middle and upper-middle classes; these classes were a minority prior to World War II. Poorer families need a wife's income. Even when a wife does not actively earn income, she contributes needed familial services. As relatively few families had devices such as washing machines until the mid-1900s and few had servants, the wife's cooking, cleaning, and other domestic work have been essential to family life. Before the early 1970s, many social scientists neglected women's housework activities; however, it is difficult to describe a 44-hour housework week among full-time housewives in the mid-1970s as "expressive" (U.S. Department of Commerce, 1977, Table 10/1; Strasser, 1980).

"Traditional" gender roles related to work and family appear to be a recent innovation, probably most accurately applied to those in industrialized societies who were upper-middle class or comfortably middle class before World War II. The realization that women have had important economic roles in the past makes the changes after World War II, which are examined next, part of a continuity of women's productive labor rather than a very recent phenomenon. Later, we shall see that definitions of men's lives with respect to the family have been distorted by definitions of "traditional" gender roles.

Women and Men in the Late Twentieth Century

Productive Labor

Distinct labor-force changes occurred among both sexes in Western societies after the 1940s. Most discussion has centered on the increasing numbers of women in paid employment. The demographic composition of employed women shifted from mainly young, single women before the 1940s to married women in early middle age by the 1960s. Women's labor-force-participation rates remained relatively stable, at around 20%, between 1900 and World War II but had risen to 53% by 1983. These changes were most apparent for married women with children. In 1950, 24% of all married women were in the labor force, compared with 53% by 1984. Whereas 28% of married women with school-aged children were employed or sought work in 1950, 65% were employed by 1984. Rates for married women with preschool children rose from 12% in 1950 to 52% by 1984 (U.S. Department of Commerce, 1970, Table D29/41; 1980, Tables 660, and 662; 1984, Tables 653 and 671).

Less attention has been paid to men's declining labor-force rates. In 1950, 87% of adult men were in the labor force, compared with 77% in 1983. Rates dropped more among black men (85% to 71% between 1954 and 1983) than among white men (86% to 77%). Men of at least 65 were more apt to be in the labor force in 1950 (46%) than in 1983 (17%; U.S. Department of Commerce, 1953, Table 205; 1977, Tables D29/41, D42/48).

These changes are part of the demographic and social changes that occurred after World War II. The postwar "baby boom" increased demands for teachers and nurses. An expanding economy created more secretarial and service jobs. These occupations have been associated with women since the late 1800s and had been staffed by young, single women. With low birth rates from the 1930s through the early 1940s, and high marriage and birthrates from the mid-1940s through the mid-1950s, the demand for "women workers" exceeded the supply of young, single women. Thus, more married women were "pulled" into the labor market (Oppenheimer, 1973).

Other factors seem to be involved in the declining male labor-force rates. One factor is government and private pensions, which allow men to retire at earlier ages than several decades ago. The educational upgrading experienced by Western populations has resulted in persons with more education in the labor force, and currently, younger people have more education than older ones. In 1982, for example, only 73% of adult men with a grammar-school education held or sought jobs, compared with 95% of men holding at least a bachelor's degree (U.S. Department of Labor, 1982). Because employed wives

tend to do less housework and to have more influence in decision making in families, and possibly because retired men may be more likely to spend more time at home, these shifts in employment patterns among both sexes cannot help but affect familial patterns as well.

Economic Rewards

It is unclear how the increase in employment among married women relates to the fears that Parsons (1942) held about familial harmony. Parsons believed that dual "careers" could create problems of familial status attainment if spouses differed on occupational prestige. Two career-oriented persons in the same family could create conflict through competition for time, rewards, or privileges.

Conversely, many American families gain advantages from a wife's employment. In 1983, the median weekly household income was $632 among families with both spouses employed, compared with $413 when only the husband was employed (U.S. Department of Labor, 1984, Report 84-35). For a select number of families in which both spouses have professional or managerial work, a "supercouple" phenomenon has been created. Supercouples can afford the comforts of upper-middle-class life, such as large houses, at a relatively young age. Oppenheimer (1977) reported that a wife's income often sufficed to boost a family at least one notch in social class.

I have already noted that changes in labor force behavior have implications for gender and the family in terms of housework and decision making. Other implications will be explored in later sections of this chapter. Here, it is important to remember that women's and men's attachment to the labor force is converging, and that this trend seems likely to continue. Despite these changes, other aspects of gender and the economy have changed relatively little, and these stabilities have implications for gender roles and family life. In particular, gender segregation among occupations and gender stratification in economic rewards have shown few changes.

In 1939, women employed full time earned about 61% as much as comparably employed men. By 1955, this ratio was about 64%. In 1982, the ratio was about 62%. In 1983, the median income for employed women professionals per week was less than that of the average man employed in any white-collar job (U.S. Department of Commerce, 1984, Table 699; 1979, Tables 9/3, 9/4; 1970, Table G372/415). Part of this earnings difference is due to different labor-force behavior. Men work more years and longer hours in paid jobs, hold more union memberships, and are more likely to have a postsecondary education than women. Even controlling for these factors, men capitalize on education, work experience, occupational prestige or parental social status more than women do (Featherman & Hauser, 1976; Treiman & Terrell, 1975).

On factor related to income is gender labor-force segregation. Although, *on the average*, women and men hold jobs of equal prestige, they hold very different jobs. The typical woman holds a clerical job, whereas the typical man can be found in a skilled trade. In 1968, Gross estimated that about two thirds of men or women would have to change jobs to "integrate" the labor market. According to his calculations, occupational segregation was about the same in 1960 as in 1900. Although there is debate on how much segregation exists, the degree is considerable (Snyder & Hudis, 1976). For example, in 1983, women were 44% of the total labor force but only 6% of engineers, 8% of craft workers, and 39% of public administrators. Men comprised only 16% of librarians, 4% of registered nurses, and 1% of secretaries (U.S. Department of Commerce, 1984, Table 676).

Gender segregation influences women's lower earnings. McLaughlin (1978) divided occupations by the types of required skills, occupational prestige, gender composition, and other variables. When he controlled for occupational prestige, men's jobs had the highest earnings, and those primarily staffed by women had the least.

Educational Training

With current educational trends, more occupational gender integration may result in the long run. Before the 1970s, parents more often sent sons than daughters to college (Marini, 1978). One study of mid-1960s high-school seniors (Lueptow, 1975) found that when parental education and student intelligence test scores were controlled, boys with low achievement values more often planned college attendance (52%) than girls with high achievement values (42%). By 1974, girls were slightly more likely to aspire to college than boys (U.S. Department of Commerce, 1975). In 1960, only about one third of undergraduates were female; by 1982, over half of undergraduates were female (U.S. Department of Commerce, 1980, Table 263; 1984, Table 247). The percentage of baccalaureates awarded to women jumped from recent 24% of the total earned in 1950 to 50% by 1982. Women's share of master's degrees grew from 29% to 51%, and their share of doctorates from 9% to 32% between 1950 and 1982.

Women are also more likely to select college fields that were previously male-stereotyped. The percentage of law degrees awarded to women rose from 4% in 1955 to 33% by 1982. Only 10% of all medical doctorates were awarded to women in 1950; by 1982 that figure was 25%. By 1982, more women majored in business, engineering, or physical science (29% of women college students versus 10% in 1966) (U.S. Department of Commerce, 1984, Tables 249, 267; 1977).

However, considerable gender segregation exists in education. College men were more likely to major in business, engineering, or physical science in 1982 (45%) than in 1966 (38%). In 1977, only 2% of men but 38% of women who were enrolled in vocational programs selected the secretarial or nursing fields. Conversely, among vocational students, 84% of men, but only 25% of

women, were enrolled in mechanics, natural science, engineering, commerce, or police programs in 1977 (U.S. Department of Commerce, 1980, Table 284).

Although, in some instances, women and men are less segregated and more "equal" than they were several decades ago, considerable gender segregation and stratification exist in the economic and academic spheres. These patterns are replicated within the family. The familial division of tasks and decisions tends toward segregation, and each spouse is regarded as having a gender-appropriate area of expertise. The lower wages earned by women are sometimes used to justify lesser male participation in housework, and the time spent by women in housework and childcare frequently limits their efforts to find paid labor or to improve their jobs. To help explain the acquisition and perpetuation of sex-role orientation, adoption, and gender-typed role performances, we must consider what children and adults see when they look at a social system often segregated by gender within and outside the family setting.

Men, Women, and Family Life

The discussion has focused on the roles of women more than on those of men, partly because of the relative dearth of research about male roles until recently.[1] This is true with respect to the family, where, despite Jessie Bernard's warnings (1972), wives' accounts of decision making, household labor, conflict, and companionship have been accepted as veridical reports for husbands, children, and other family members.

The relative lack of research about male roles until about the middle 1970s, coupled with the neglect of earlier data (see Hesselbart, 1978), has created a veritable field day for speculation about male roles. It has been asserted that men are taking a "new interest" in family life. Men are hypothesized as taking more active roles now in household labor and child care than in the recent past. These "changes" have been attributed by some to the "counterculture" of the 1960s and 1970s, which deemphasized men's traditional vocational interests and emphasized greater male expressiveness; to the women's movement, which pointed out an inegalitarian division of domestic labor; and to employed wives, who have less total time for housework and child care than full-time housewives (Bardwick, 1979; Giele, 1978; Pleck, 1979). We will need to examine both assumptions and reported data about gender and familial issues over time and pick our way carefully through these speculations.

A working assumption about gender and family life brings us back to functional sociology and the "tradi-

[1]Certainly, it is the case that "men" have been studied extensively. However, research on male subjects or respondents is often presented as research on "humanity" and is generalized to *both* sexes with few caveats. Research about what is distinctive about *male roles* at home, at work, and in other arenas is far less frequent.

tional'' priorities of women and men. Many social scientists have assumed that a woman's top priority is her family and that a man's top priority is his job (Clark, Nye, & Gecas, 1978; Morgan, 1980). This working assumption may have led social researchers to ignore data about men and the family and to believe that housewives do not really "work."

Existing evidence contradicts some of these assumptions and speculations. We shall see that both sexes rate family life as their highest priority, although this goal has become *less* important in recent years. Men do relatively little housework in general, do no more when the wife is employed, and have not become much more active in domestic labor over the last few decades according to many studies. Perhaps as a result, employed wives, especially those with children, have less leisure and more stress, on the average, than their husbands.

Values about the Family

Surveys available for several years show that both sexes value the family as one of the most important factors in their lives and that the sex differences are relatively small. In a 1964 survey of high-school seniors (Lueptow, 1975), 67% of the boys and 78% of the girls felt that marriage and children were very important personal goals. Identical percentages of both sexes (86%) felt that way about their careers. In one national sample of youth (Institute of Life Insurance, 1974), 40% of boys and 43% of girls ranked a happy family life as *most* important to them; only 11% of boys and 6% of girls rated a fulfilling occupation the same way. Among the national sample of employed persons studied by Pleck and Lang (1978), nearly identical proportions of men rated their family as "one of the most important things" (54%) as rated their job the same way (55%). *Fewer* employed wives than employed husbands rated either their family (46%) or their job (35%) as "one of the most important things." Double the number of men thought about their family "always" or "often" compared with their job (65% versus 32%) as did a similar ratio of women (75% versus 31%).

According to data from some continuing cross-sectional surveys of college students, "the family" has become a less important value for both sexes. In one series surveying entering college students (American Council of Education, 1972; Astin *et al.,* 1977), students rated "raising a family" as *less* important in 1977 than in 1972. Among men, the percentage saying "raising a family" was important dropped from 62% to 59% between 1972 and 1977; the corresponding figures for women students dropped from 69% to 59%. In studies of Dartmouth and University of Michigan male students, Hoge (1976) reported that family relationships were rated as the most important goals by over 60% in 1952 and 1968; this figure dropped to about 50% in 1974. Career or occupational goals were rated as most important by about 25% in both universities in all three surveys. Farley, Brewer, and Fine

(1977) studied Cornell undergraduates in 1952 and 1974. Whereas "family life" was ranked as highest in importance by 60% of men and 87% of women in 1952, in 1974 only 48% of men and 57% of women felt that way. Occupational success was rated most important by 31% of men and 6% of women in 1952; these figures were 29% of men and 23% of women in 1974.

Altogether, these data suggest several things. It is obvious that, at diverse ages, family life is important for both sexes. Among both sexes, family life *and* one's occupation are important priorities. The direction in the 1970s was toward a *lowering* of the value of a "happy family." This phenomenon may be more pronounced among women. Certainly, these data do not indicate that men are now more sensitized to family issues and place a higher value on family life than in the recent past.

Housework

Research on housework contradicts the speculation that large changes are under way in gender roles in the family. Ironically, the domestic labor data suggest that *within* the family *women have instrumental roles and men have expressive roles.* In her study of time budget diaries, Vanek (1974) reported that the amount of domestic labor performed by each sex stayed about the same between the 1920s and the 1960s. Married men spent about the same amount of time in housework whether their wives were employed or not. Vanek suggested that more "labor-saving devices" actually increased the demand for domestic services. For example, with home washing machines, laundry could be done a few times a week rather than just once (also see Strasser, 1980).

In other time-budget research, Robinson (1980; U.S. Department of Commerce, 1977, Table 10/1; Robinson, Yerby, Fieweger, & Somerick, 1977) estimated that, in 1965, full-time housewives spent 56 hours a week in family care, employed wives spent 29 hours, and married employed men spent 8 hours. In 1975, full-time housewives spent 44 hours a week in family care, employed wives 25 hours, and married employed men 10 hours. Robinson found that the 12-hour drop for full-time housewives between 1965 and 1975 was partly an artifact of demographic differences over that time period. With statistical controls instituted for variables such as age, income, and parental social status, the 1975 full-time housewives spent just 22 minutes less per day in housework than those in 1965.

There have also been few changes in the types of tasks done and decisions made by each sex within the home during the past few decades. Certain household jobs continue to be stereotyped as male (yardwork and repairs), and others are stereotyped as female (cooking, laundry, and dusting). Some decisions are "hers" (the food budget and home decoration), and others are "his" (geographical relocations and life insurance; Berk & Shih, 1980; Duncan & Duncan, 1978; Nye, 1976).

One suggestion is that men do less household labor

because of their job responsibilities and that it may take more than flexible job-schedules or more leisure time to increase men's participation in housework (Maklan, 1977). Male blue-collar workers with a four-day work week were compared with those with a five-day work week. Four-day workers spent about 1½ hours more per week on child care than five-day workers and only 24 minutes a week more in housework. The four-day workers *did* spend more time on leisure than the five-day workers: gardening (1 hour more per week); sleep (1½ hours); being outdoors (1½ hours); and "doing nothing" (1 hour). When fathers do participate in child care, their role appears to be more "expressive" than "instrumental." Mothers do most of the routine child care, such as feeding. Fathers watch the child, hold the child, or play with the child (Booth & Edwards, 1980; Lamb & Lamb, 1976; Parke & Sawin, 1976; Rendina & Dickerschild, 1976).

A final example is the differential amounts of free time spent by each sex. In their analysis of 1965 national time-budget diaries, Robinson *et al.* (1977) noted that the husbands of employed women had *less obligatory* time and *more free* time than men married to full-time housewives. For example, fathers of three children (at least one preschooler) had more free minutes per day when their wives were employed (314 minutes) than the comparable husbands of full-time housewives (280 minutes). Full-time housewives with three children averaged more free minutes (296 per day) than comparable employed wives (172 minutes per day). These time differences may be why Robinson *et al.* found that employed wives with children were more likely to feel pressured and harried than full-time housewives.[2] Haynes and Feinleib (1980) suggested that women clerical workers married to blue-collar workers and having children were the most likely of all women to have heart disease, perhaps because the household division of labor is more gender-segregated in blue-collar households with children present. Blue-collar wives may have more pressures than other wives. Taken together, the domestic labor data may be an important reason that the most recent wave of feminism has stressed the egalitarian division of housework.

Marriage, Divorce, and Birth Rates

A constellation of attitude factors (see below), demographics, and social changes have influenced and have been influenced by changes in familial composition. Trends in familial composition are documented in other chapters but can bear a brief summary here. Demographer Charles Westoff (1978) has wondered about the incentives for young women to marry, to remain married, and to bear and rear children:

For centuries, men have exchanged . . . financial rewards, social status and security . . . for the sexual, companionate, and

maternal services of women. . . . But consider a social system in which just as many women as men are engineers, bank presidents, corporation executives, doctors, lawyers, and salespersons. What exactly will be the motivation of women to enter the legal partnership of marriage? (p. 81)

Another demographer, Paul Glick (1975), presented a related but different picture:

[A] significant proportion of men who are . . . in the upper socioeconomic group still hesitate to marry a woman who expects to be a partner in an egalitarian marriage—or who might be a serious competitor for the role of chief breadwinner or "head of the household." (p. 19)

Changes have occurred in forming and dissolving families. First marriage rates dropped from 143 per 1,000 single women in 1946 to 65 in 1981. Those studying familial attitude trends (Duncan & Duncan, 1978) have noted that fewer women chose marriage for the "chance to have children" in the 1970s than in the 1950s. The percentage childless among married women in their early 20s jumped from 24% in 1960 to 40% in 1983. The percentage childless among wives in their late 20s increased from 13% to 27%. More married women expected to bear, at most, two children in 1983 (69%) than in 1967 (39%). Birth rates dropped from 118 per 1,000 women of childbearing age in 1955 to 67 in 1981; the 1977 birthrate was even lower than during the 1930s Depression (79 per 1,000 women).

During the same time, divorce rates rose. Rates per 1,000 married women more than doubled from 9 in 1960 to 23 in 1981. In 1983, 75% of children lived in a two-parent (biological or step) family compared with 92% in 1960. Children living only with their mothers went from 6% to 21% of households between 1960 and 1978; percentages for children in other household arrangements, including fathers only, rose from 2% to 4% of all households with children (U.S. Department of Commerce, 1979, Tables 3/1, 3/2, 4/4; 1984, Tables 65, 82, 90, 120).

Thus, between the 1950s and 1985, Americans married less often, had fewer children, and more often divorced. These demographic data are particularly impressive when it is remembered that the "baby-boom generation" reached young adulthood during the 1960s and 1970s, when demographers expected sharp rises in marriage and birth rates. Changes that occur with respect to major life events such as marriage, divorce, or children relate to core aspects of the self, including sex-role orientation. Remember, however, that other aspects of family life have changed less, most notably the segregation of adult domestic labor and domestic decisions.

Changing Attitudes and Stereotypes about Women and Men

I have waited to discuss gender stereotypes and attitudes, partly because these factors appear important in the acquisition of gender-typed behavior among children.

---

[2]In contrast, some researchers report the largest incidence of anxiety and depression among full-time housewives (Gove & Tudor, 1973).

Also, temporal societal changes suggest that changes in employment and family life cause gender-typed attitude and belief changes rather than the reverse. Women's increase in paid employment began in the late 1940s, and divorce rates began rising in the 1960s. Changes in gender-related attitudes appear to have been greatest in the late 1960s and early 1970s—concomitant with the most visible wave of feminism since the early 1900s. One suggestion (Mason, Czajka, & Arber, 1976) is that demographic changes in marriage, divorce, and labor-force patterns made Americans reassess their attitudes toward women and men.

Attitudes. Systematic attitude surveys date back to at least the 1930s. In 1937, a Gallup Poll question read: "Would you vote for a woman for president if she was qualified in every other respect"? (31% would). No attitude change occurred on this question until the middle 1950s, when over half surveyed would support a woman for president. By 1976—with a reworded item—73% said they would support a "qualified woman" for president (Ferree, 1974).

Other attitude items have shown changes comparable to the "woman president" item. Using several surveys of entering college students, Bayer and Dutton (1976) found that 57% agreed that married women's activities "are best confined to the home and family" in 1967; only 30% agreed in 1974. When white Detroit area wives interviewed in 1962 were reinterviewed in 1977 (Thornton & Freedman, 1979), the percentage agreeing that "husbands should make the major family decisions" dropped from 67% to 33%. On another item, 54% of these wives agreed in 1962 that a wife should *not* expect her husband to "help" around the house; that percentage fell to 38% in 1977.

The survey items receiving the highest endorsement in the 1960s and 1970s related to the nonfamilial roles of women. Most respondents agreed that women and men should have equal job opportunities and that both sexes should receive the same pay for the same work. A majority of adults polled over the last 15 years say that they would endorse a woman for president, senator, mayor, or governor.

The counterpoint to these egalitarian sentiments is that the general public also supports occupational segregation, so that jobs are not equal; supports restrictions on women's combination of paid and family work, which implies that women would have less opportunities than men; and seems to have trouble finding a "qualified" woman candidate to vote for. This ambiguity showed up in the 1976 Gallup "Women in America" poll. Nearly 60% in this survey endorsed the Equal Rights Amendment, and 68% agreed that it was all right for wives to take paid employment. However, a majority of both sexes preferred male physicians and police officers and female nurses. Over 40% preferred male attorneys or dentists and female hairdressers. And 60% of women and 63% of men preferred a male boss.

Perhaps the most accurate word to describe American gender attitudes is *ambivalent*. In one study, Komarovsky (1976) conducted in-depth interviews with Ivy League college men. These men wanted to marry intelligent women—but not women who were smarter than they or who would disagree with them. They seemed enthusiastic about their future wives' having challenging careers—but expected to put their own careers first and did not seem very interested in rearing children.

Sex differences on surveys depend on the type of item; those item differences may provide insight into the factors behind gender attitudes. On abstract issues (e.g., "greater social status for women") or currently unlikely events (e.g., a major female presidential candidate), men often appear more egalitarian than women by a few percentage points. On issues such as housework, employed women, or voting for a woman congressional candidate, women are more egalitarian. There may be a relationship between men's lesser endorsement of everyday egalitarianism and the greater tendency for men to prefer gender-typed behavior in children, especially for boys (Duncan & Duncan, 1978; Gallup, 1976; Huber, Rexroat, & Spitze, 1978; Mason & Bumpass, 1975; Mason *et al.*, 1976; Osmond & Martin, 1975).

Stereotypes. Gender-related attitudes have become more flexible, but it is interesting that stereotypes about the sexes have shown few changes over the past 40 years. Researchers during the 1940s (Fernberger, 1948), the 1950s (McKee & Sherriffs, 1957), the 1960s (Rosenkrantz, Vogel, Bee, Broverman, & Broverman, 1968), and the 1970s (Pedhazur & Tetenbaum, 1979) reported the same stereotypes, despite the changes that had occurred in attitudes, paid employment, marriage, divorce, and childbearing. A "competence cluster," including such traits as logical, self-confident, objective, and active, is stereotypically used to describe men. Associated with women is a "warmth cluster" of traits such as nurturant, emotionally expressive, and sensitive.

In addition, more socially desirable personality traits are associated with the male stereotype than with the female stereotype (Broverman, Vogel, Broverman, Clarkson, & Rosenkrantz, 1972). The mentally healthy adult is often described as comparable to the mentally healthy male and quite differently from the healthy female (Broverman, Broverman, Clarkson, Rosenkrantz, & Vogel, 1970); similar results are found for descriptions of the ideal manager (Schein, 1975) and the desirable adult (Pedhazur & Tetenbaum, 1979).

Different characteristics for males and females are perceived as desirable. A 1974 Roper Poll reported that both sexes ranked intelligence and leadership ability as more valued in males than in females, whereas emotional expressivity and sex appeal were rated higher for females than for males. In a study by Pedhazur and Tetenbaum (1979), traits such as self-reliance, independence, assertiveness, and decisiveness were seen as more socially desirable in men than in women. Indeed, traits such as athletic, assertive, and analytical were seen as desirable for men and *un*desirable for women.

It is useful to juxtapose the relative stability of gender stereotypes held over the last 40 years with the concomitant changes in attitudes toward greater gender equality. Perhaps the small changes in occupational gender segregation and stratification, unequal incomes, or the responsibility for household labor may be related to the pervasiveness and perpetuation of gender stereotyping. Although people may believe that gender equality is fair, the sexes may seem so different that equality seems nearly impossible to attain.

This section has summarized stereotypes and attitudes held by adults about adults. Both children *and* adults are fairly similar in their beliefs about each sex. Perhaps this is not surprising when we consider the degree of gender segregation in employment and familial roles.

Summing Up: The Societal Roles of Women and Men

We will next study the "new generation" and how today's boys and girls become tomorrow's adults. To tell where we are "headed," it has been useful to summarize the roles of women and men now. Just what do today's children see about gender roles and family life?

1. Adults are marrying less, having fewer children, and divorcing more. Today's children see a wider variety of family types than the children of 30 years ago: one-parent families; step parents; step siblings; and cohabitors. As a result, today's children may become more tolerant of departures from the "traditional family."

2. In a home where they live with both parents, children continue to see a gender-stereotyped division of labor in household tasks and decisions. Children see that mothers do most of the routine housework and child care, and that fathers have more of the fun of playing with children.

3. A majority of today's children see both parents working outside the home to share financial responsibility for the family. However, the mothers' jobs are usually more visible to the children than the fathers' jobs. The "typical jobs" held by women—schoolteaching, nursing, and secretarial work—are more visible to children (and the general public) than the jobs held by many men: business executive; electrician, or automobile-assembly-line work. Of course, some male-typed jobs do appear frequently on television, such as physician, lawyer, or police officer, but these are a very small sample of the jobs held by men. Children also find out that jobs at both the top and the bottom of the prestige ladder tend to belong to men rather than to women, that men hold a greater variety of jobs than women, and that men generally earn more than women.

4. Children may hear both parents express egalitarian gender attitudes in several areas: approval of the mother's "outside job" (as long as the housework gets done); approval of some women politicians; or assertions that sons and daughters should be treated nearly the same. However, children may also realize that mothers and fathers (and adult men and women generally) consider the sexes quite different. Sensitive children may be quick to sense the discrepancies in parental attitudes and between parental attitudes and parental behavior.

With this review of gender behavior over time and culture, the stage is set to examine gender socialization, the acquisition of gender identity, and gender-role adoption. In the following sections, we shall see that today's children continue to show gender-typed patterns. This should not be very surprising, given the documentation of gender typing among adults and adult institutions.

A Warning: The "Socialization Copout" Perspective

Most research in the rest of this chapter concerns children and adolescents. This is not because people conveniently stop developing at age 7 or 17. Although changes in self-image and behavior extend into old age, it is often simply easiest to study the relatively captive subjects in grade school, high school, and college. As a result, much social-science knowledge is based on students in restricted social settings.

A focus on student populations can lead to a default assumption that adults change less than children or adolescents. This default assumption I call the *socialization copout*. The socialization copout among researchers or the general public can constrain the study of social gender. For example, a social scientist—or a layperson—might acknowledge that differences exist in the social positions or the social rewards of the sexes. Such an individual might also believe that many of these differences appear to be unfair. That individual may attribute the cause of such differences to personality traits supposed to distinguish the sexes, such as a "fear of success" in women or "inexpressiveness" in men. These personality sex differences, in turn, are explained by the differential socialization of the sexes before adulthood. As a result, our sympathetic individual does not need to examine organizational patterns (e.g., Kanter, 1977) or societal prejudice; instead, he or she can push lower achievement straight onto the "personality" of the person who does not achieve. More political science or sociological approaches, such as the "politics of caste," are not considered.

In the socialization copout, gender-related issues among adults are often ignored. It is often implicitly hypothesized that tremendous changes would be required for adults to live in a less gender-typed manner. For some, "assertiveness workshops," classes in which football is patiently explained to faculty wives, or "household skill" workshops for husbands seem required to produce the greater gender-role flexibility made necessary by changes in life events such as those in the current marriage, divorce, and labor force patterns. Others believe that the effects of these therapies are mild compared with the psychological structures laid down early in life, and only a relative few are exposed to such therapies anyway.

With the socialization copout, the onus for changes related to social gender is placed on the younger generation. Our girls will be raised to be more assertive, our boys more expressive. At some vaguely defined future point, the sexes will be as "equal" as physiology or other restrictions allow them to be. How the gender-typed adults of today will raise the less gender-typed adults of tomorrow is never quite explained.

In summarizing the research and theory on gender socialization, I wish to tread a middle ground. Socialization in childhood lays a foundation for coping and adaptation to all kinds of social rules, including rules relevant to gender orientation and behavior. With social change, social rules change as well, and adults undergo socialization experiences, too. Accordingly, in the later sections of this chapter, socialization in adult life that appears to be related to sex differences and gender roles will receive considerable attention.

Children and Gender Typing: An Overview

Children acquire gender identity very early. By age 2, children appear to know their own sex (Kohlberg, 1966; Lewis & Weinraub, 1979; Maccoby & Jacklin, 1974). Indeed, instances exist in which, because of physical ambiguity, children have had their sex reassigned at some time after birth. If such reassignment is done before about age 3, children appear to easily adopt the congruent gender-typed behavior patterns (Money & Tucker, 1975).

By at least the same time that children gain a gender sense of the self, they also acquire gender-typed stereotypes, interests, and activity patterns. Some research suggests that children under 2 years old prefer to gaze at pictures of same-sex infants, although adults cannot differentiate infant sex in photographs (e.g., Lewis & Weinraub, 1979). Preschool children have greater recall and imitation of same-sex models and figures (Kohlberg, 1966; McArthur & Eisen, 1976). In one study, 3-year-olds were able to tell researchers that fathers were stronger, smarter, and more likely to "be the boss," and that mothers were "nicer" and more likely to give presents (Kagan & Lemkin, 1960). In the mid-1970s, 2-year-olds knew that "girls talk a lot, ask for help and grow up to clean house," whereas boys say "I can hit you" and "grow up to be boss" (Kuhn & Nash, 1976).

By nursery-school age, girls and boys differ markedly in playing behavior: Girls tend to play indoors at crafts or to watch others play, whereas boys more often play outdoors in team games (Lever, 1978; Lott, 1978; Maccoby & Jacklin, 1974). Boys play on teams more than girls do, and boys' games have been described as requiring more participants, having a more complex division of labor, lasting longer, and having more rules than girls' games (Eder & Hallinan, 1978; Lever, 1978). These researchers have suggested that sex differences in "game experience" may lead to greater success for men in the economic marketplace, especially in managerial roles.

It is important to note that, although there are gender-typed activities and stereotypes among youngsters, as well as marked sex differences in play patterns, young boys and girls are more similar than different. Although stereotypes portray females as more sociable or nurturant, and males as more self-confident and achieving, young children do not seem to show actual behavior corresponding to these stereotypes. In their extensive review, Maccoby and Jacklin (1974) reported negligible sex differences in dependence, sociability, amount of physical activity levels, self-esteem, or achievement motivation in *preadolescent* children. Whiting and Edwards (1973) also found relatively few sex differences among children in their review of seven cultures. The one consistent difference over time and culture that has been observed is more "rough-and-tumble play" among boys than among girls. Such play may be linked to the greater interest in dominance and competitiveness that has been observed in boys' games.

Young children seem to take an "ethnocentric" view of gender. Once a young child gains a sense of gender identity, he or she believes that one's own social gender is "better." Young children describe their own sex in more positive terms than the other sex. They see occupations primarily occupied by their own sex as "better" occupations. At the nursery-school and early-primary-school ages, children prefer same-sex friends, book characters, and television figures and imitate same-sex models (Katz, 1979; Kohlberg, 1966; Silvern, 1977; Smith, 1939).

By middle-primary-school age, girls begin to indicate that they believe boys have distinct advantages over girls. Smith (1939) found that between the ages of 8 and 14, boys, initially more positive toward boys than toward girls, became even more positive toward boys. Girls, who originally described girls more favorably than boys, began to describe boys as "better"—a process that Smith attributed to "a general improvement in social comprehension that makes girls more and more free from social prejudice" (p. 22). More recently, Conner and Serbin's study (1978) of reactions to storybook characters found that boys from the fourth through the eighth grades preferred male characters and their activities. Whereas girls would have preferred to be friends more often with female than with male characters, by sixth grade girls would rather *be* the male characters and do the things the male characters did. Studying students from fifth grade through college, O'Bryant, Durrett, and Pennebaker (1980) discovered that, by seventh grade, boys realized that persons in male-typed occupations earned more than those in female-typed occupations—something that girls did not find out until college.

Boys initially believe that boys are better than girls at early ages. Boys also more frequently derogate and reject girls than the reverse. Research indicates that boys are more gender-typed in their choices of toys, playmates, and activities than girls (David & Brannon, 1976; Maccoby & Jacklin, 1974). Some researchers believe that such "compulsive masculinity" reflects a defensive anxiety in boys about admitting to anything typed as "feminine" in their own nature. This perspective may reflect more intense socialization pressures from parents and other important figures for boys to grow up "masculine" than girls receive to grow up "feminine." It is also possible that a shift in identification from other-sex to same-sex models occurs for boys (whose initial attachment is to their mothers), but not for girls. The greater absence of fathers than mothers from the home may give boys less chance to observe concrete models of masculinity (Hartley, 1959; Kohlberg, 1966; Maccoby & Jacklin, 1974; Stockard & Johnson, 1979). The terms I have mentioned related to gender in this section—*modeling, identification,* and *direct pressures*—are major approaches in the general gender-socialization literature and are discussed below.

Perpetuating Sex Differences and Gender Roles

There is an intriguing difference between childhood gender behavior and that of adults. The research on children suggests sex differences in *social* behavior, such as playing games, but relatively few sex differences in personality traits, such as a need for achievement. Among adults, there are far more pronounced sex differences in work roles, domestic roles, and personality attributes. Obviously, something (or a collection of somethings) occurs to rigidify sex differences and gender roles after childhood. In part, knowledge is limited about just what these "somethings" are because of the focus on children and adolescents noted earlier. There are five major approaches to how sex differences and gender roles are acquired:

1. The direct shaping and reinforcement of sex differences in behavior.
2. Imitation and modeling of same-sex figures.
3. The identification with and incorporation of values, personality traits, and behaviors of important same-sex childhood figures.
4. A cognitive-developmental sequence of acquiring gender identity that leads to the acquisition of gender roles.
5. Biological sex differences that influence the responses of socialization agents (the nature–nurture controversy).

Each major approach has supporting evidence, although currently a combination of approaches rather than just one accounts best for gender socialization. These approaches will first be examined. Next, adult socializa-

tion with respect to gender and the implications of adult socialization for future gender roles will be discussed.

Direct Training for Gender Roles and Sex Differences

Probably the most prevalent view among sociologists is that parents, teachers, peers, and other socialization agents directly train children to acquire and reward children for acquiring stereotyped gender behavior (e.g., Weitzman, 1979). These agents purportedly (1) hold stereotypes about the sexes; (2) desire to inculcate gender-typed behavior; (3) interact with children in ways to elicit and directly teach gender-typed behavior; and (4) reward instances of such behavior (and punish gender-inappropriate behavior) when it occurs. Evidence indicates that socialization agents do stereotype infants and children, and that they create an environment that elicits and maintains gender-typed behavior. How much gender-typed behavior is directly rewarded is not clear.

The sex stereotyping of children actually begins before birth with a preference for male babies. Although parents would like at least one boy and one girl, boys are usually preferred as firstborns. Women sometimes continue childbearing until a boy is born. Boys are important in carrying on the family name, whereas girls are seen almost as dolls to "dress up" or to help at home (Hoffman & Manis, 1979; Williamson, 1976). Parents even hold stereotypes about children in the womb. For example, an active, kicking child is often expected to be male (Belotti, 1976).

Parents and other adults view children in stereotyped ways even when children's objective characteristics deviate from gender stereotypes. In their study of the parents of newborns, Rubin, Provenzano, and Luria (1974) found that parents, especially fathers, more often described sons as strong and vigorous and daughters as delicate, although hospital records showed no average sex differences in height, weight, or activity measures. Teachers in another study (Loo & Wenar, 1971) reported that boys were more physically active than girls even though an actometer that the children wore showed no such differences. Kutner and Levinson (1978) reported that toy salespersons selected a wider variety of toys for boys than for girls and that over half of their toy suggestions were gender-stereotyped.

Parents and other socialization agents are concerned about appropriate gender-typed behavior in children, especially in publicly visible behaviors such as dress, toys, household chores, or occupational choices. However, parents also say that they want an "androgynous" child: achieving, neat, self-reliant, and courteous. In national surveys of fathers in 1964 and of both parents in 1975, parents felt that good manners, honesty, good sense, self-control, responsibility, consideration, and obedience to parents were equally desirable in children of either sex (Duncan & Duncan, 1978). In terms of desired personality traits, parents did not report marked distinctions based on the child's sex (see also Maccoby & Jacklin, 1974).

Direct training for adult gender performance parallels the adult attitudes described above. Pressures toward gender-role conformity focus most on areas such as toy choice, chores, clothing, and preparation for adult instrumental roles such as housekeeping or employment. Sidorowicz and Lunney (1980) studied undergraduates who interacted with an infant wrapped in a diaper to disguise its sex. When the infant was "female," 80% of the students handed "her" a doll; when the infant was "male," 65% handed "him" a toy football. In Roper's national survey of adults (1974), both sexes felt that dolls, dollhouses, and tea sets should be given only to girls, and near majorities felt that model kits, war toys, cars, and trains should be given only to boys.

Household chores are also assigned by sex. In their surveys of Detroit mothers in 1953 and 1971, Duncan and Duncan (1978) reported that mothers expected boys more often to shovel snow or wash the car and girls more often to make beds or dust. Adults with a gender-typed division of household chores themselves more often advocated stereotyped chores for children. Girls were more often expected to put away their own clothes at younger ages than boys, and boys were expected to run errands at younger ages than girls, but Duncan and Duncan found no difference in adult expectations for girls and boys to dress themselves or to pick up toys.

The assignment of domestic chores to children on a gender basis is less prevelent now than in past years. Whereas 65% of the Duncans' sample in 1953 felt that only boys should wash the car, only 30% felt this way in 1971. Those saying that only girls should make their own beds dropped from 52% to 29% between 1953 and 1971. Roper also reported less gender stereotyping of household chores for children among adults of both sexes between 1974 and 1980. For example, 39% of women in 1974 felt that children of both sexes should mend their own clothes, whereas 56% felt that way in 1980; the percentages for men increased from 36% in 1974 to 50% in 1980. Increases in feelings that boys and girls should do similar chores also occurred for tasks such as mowing lawns, helping with repairs, helping to cook and clean, and carrying out household trash.

Parents and teachers do pressure children to select gender-stereotyped occupations, such as engineering for boys or secretarial work for girls (Fox, 1975). Parents more often encourage boys to enter college than they do girls. Once in college, parents encourage sons to enter graduate or professional schools more than they do daughters (Marini, 1978).

Direct punishment and rewards for gender-typed behavior are most apparent in matters such as dress or displays of aggression. To instill characteristics such as dependency in girls or achieving behavior in boys, socialization agents behave in more subtle ways. In one study, a nursery school that prided itself on encouraging nonstereotypical gender behavior was observed (Joffe, 1971). Mothers who worked at the center made jokes about the boys' "superior strength" and complimented girls more when the girls wore dresses than when they wore pants. Other studies found that boys receive more punishment than girls from parents and teachers for aggression and more physical punishment for aggression from parents than girls do (Duncan & Duncan, 1978; Maccoby & Jacklin, 1974; Serbin, O'Leary, Kent, & Tonick, 1973). As children who are physically punished often become adults who use physical aggression (see Steinmetz, Chapter 26), perhaps men show more physical aggression than women because they received more physical punishment as children.

On the other hand, children may not be directly reinforced for adopting stereotypical gender behavior in several areas. Some research indicates that parents do not reward girls more nor punish them less than boys for showing dependence (Maccoby & Jacklin, 1974). As noted earlier, boys are punished more for aggression than girls, which may occur because boys show more aggression than girls *or* because parents consider it more important to control aggression in boys. At least among young children, mothers appear to treat both sexes with about equal amounts of warmth, praise, and pressure toward independence (Duncan & Duncan, 1978; Lamb & Lamb, 1976; Maccoby & Jacklin, 1974). One difference in parental behavior that comes through consistently is that both parents, especially fathers, treat little girls as fragile and more often "roughhouse" with sons (Lewis & Weinraub, 1979; Maccoby & Jacklin, 1974). Work by Lewis (see review in Lewis & Weinraub, 1979) suggests that mothers engage sons more than daughters in tactile stimulation before the infants are 6 months old but touch and vocalize more to daughters after the infant reaches 6 months old. Taken altogether, however, the behavior of parents with *preschool children* suggests that, with the exception of encouraging stereotyped gender behavior in areas such as dress or toys, parents treat sons and daughters differently in only a few areas. Of course, these few areas may turn out to be crucial in the development of sex differences and gender roles when the children grow older.

Data from school observations indicate that preschool and elementary-school teachers treat the sexes in different ways. Teacher behavior may contribute to the development of greater self-esteem and independence in boys and greater anxiety and dependence among girls. First, boys receive more total attention from teachers than girls do. Boys receive both more blame, reprimands, and punishment for "bad" behavior and more praise and encouragement for "good" behavior than girls. More often than girls, boys receive explicit instructions on how to solve problems *themselves* from teachers. Serbin's studies (Serbin *et al.*, 1973; Serbin, Conner, & Citron, 1978) suggest that teachers pay attention to girls mainly when the girls are physically proximate to the instructor, whereas boys receive attention regardless of how close to the instructor they are. Whereas girls are praised for neatness and good conduct, boys are praised for creativity and skill (Lott, 1979; Sears & Feldman, 1966; Taylor, 1979). The message coming through to children is that boys and their accomplishments are more deserving of attention than girls and their accomplishments.

Boys receive more attention than girls from teachers and, as we shall shortly see, also generally from fathers. This greater attention may be a mixed blessing. At least until adolescence, pressures on boys to adhere to gender-typed behaviors appear greater than similar pressures for girls. Parents of both sexes are more concerned about ''masculine'' behaviors in boys than about ''feminine'' behaviors in girls. In particular, parents seem to dislike and show anxiety about cross-sex behavior among boys. For example, adults more often allow girls to play with toys such as trucks than they allow boys to play with toys such as cooking sets. Little girls are allowed greater latitude in dress than little boys, and boys receive more discipline than girls (Duncan & Duncan, 1978; Lynn, 1976; Maccoby & Jacklin, 1974; Roper Organization, 1974, 1980; Will et al., 1976).

Socialization pressures for girls to act ''feminine'' increase during late childhood and early adolescence. Parents then become concerned about chaperoning and protecting their daughters (Maccoby & Jacklin, 1974). This time point appears to be more stressful in the development of girls than of boys. It is during late childhood and adolescence that girls begin to fall behind in mathematics, to shift their career choices to stereotypically female fields, to lower their educational aspirations, to lose self-esteem, and to begin to believe that boys and men are superior to girls and women (Aneshensel & Rosen, 1980; Maccoby & Jacklin, 1974; Marini, 1978; Weitzman, 1979). Simmons, Blyth, Van Cleave, and Bush (1979) found that, whereas boys' self-esteem in late childhood increased over time, that of many girls dropped. This loss of self-esteem was particularly marked among girls who started seventh grade at junior high school (rather than continuing at an elementary school), who had begun menstruation, and who had begun dating, that is, among girls who showed earlier physical and social maturity. Meanwhile, boys who matured early *gained* in self-esteem. Also during this time, girls placed increasing importance on physical appearance. The continued shift among females to stereotyped career choices and activities continued during college for those attending (Astin, 1977).

Thus, pressures to adhere to gender-typed role behavior may hit boys and girls at different times. For boys, these pressures begin early, possibly starting before age 1 (Lamb & Lamb, 1976). For girls, these pressures start around puberty, when girls are physically mature and are capable of becoming pregnant.

The instillation of gender typing among children is augmented by the different roles that parents play when they take care of their children. If nothing else, the adult division of labor in child care alerts children to differences in how adult men and women behave. The distinct roles that each parent plays in child care also imply that the parents differ in sheer proximity to the child, in their observations of the child's activities, and in rewarding or punishing the child's behavior.

Fathers frequently are nurturant toward their children: touching, vocalizing, smiling, and playing (Mackey & Day, 1979; Parke & Sawin, 1976; Rendina & Dickerschild, 1976). However, mothers are the primary caretakers for young children: feeding them, cleaning them, and watching out for their safety. Fathers take more interest as children grow older, and their role appears to be the ''fun'' one of playing with their children (Booth & Edwards, 1980; Crano & Aronoff, 1978; Lamb & Lamb, 1976; Parke & Sawin, 1976; Rendina & Dickerschild, 1976). In child rearing, mothers are clearly ''task-oriented'' and fathers are ''socioemotional.'' The above studies suggest that mothers are more exposed to the physical demands, the routine behavior, and the discipline of the child. In contrast, fathers are exposed to the child at play, developing interests and activities. Fathers may have more influence on the child's future aspirations and interests than do mothers because of the different exposure of each parent to different aspects of the child's behavior.

This potential differential impact of parents on children is important because fathers are generally more concerned about appropriate gender behavior in children. Fathers more than mothers believe it is important for children to ''grow up like a girl or boy should'' (Barry, 1980; Duncan & Duncan, 1978; Lynn, 1976); insist more on ''appropriate'' gender-typed toys and chores (Duncan & Duncan, 1978; Roper Organization, 1974, 1980); and differ in their praise and discipline of girls and boys (Lynn, 1976; Maccoby & Jacklin, 1974). Fathers appear to be interested more in the activities of their sons than in those of their daughters—an interest differential that increases as the children grow older (Lamb & Lamb, 1976; Parke & Sawin, 1976; Rendina & Dickerschild, 1976).

Because fathers differentiate more than mothers in their behavior toward their children, fathers may be more important than mothers in the development of gender identity and behavior. For example, girls encouraged by their fathers to do well more often achieve in school and plan less gender-typed occupational careers (Manley, 1977). Fathers may also encourage flirtatious behavior in daughters and stereotypical expressions of femininity, such as wearing dresses as opposed to pants (Maccoby & Jacklin, 1974).

Parents and teachers are important in training children about gender-typed clothing, toys, games, and career aspirations. Beyond these highly visible behaviors, it is unclear just how much direct training influences personality traits or gender-typed patterns of social interaction. Although adult women defer more to men than the reverse, the research literature does not indicate that parents *directly* teach children that men are ''superior.'' The observations about classroom teachers are suggestive in this regard, but it is obviously difficult to do parallel studies of parents in the privacy of their homes. Concerning personal attributes such as dependency, aggression, or school achievement, parents appear to have similar expectations for both sexes and do not seem to reinforce these traits differently. Indeed, Maccoby and Jacklin were surprised when they extensively reviewed the sex differences literature to discover how little difference there was in parental socialization other than highly visible gender-typed behavior.

The relative incompleteness of the direct training approach to explain marked differences among adults in gender-typed personal styles, interaction patterns, and roles has led many to consider other approaches to gender socialization. One of the most popular alternatives emphasizes modeling or imitation in acquiring gender-typed identities and behaviors.

Imitation and Modeling

The approach labeled *social learning* or *modeling* adds more explanatory power about acquiring gender roles and sex-typing than an approach that stresses solely direct training and rewards for behavior. Modeling approaches stress the learning and performance of overt behaviors and imitation of models. Large "chunks" or sequences of behavior are acquired according to these views, rather than the piecemeal, disjointed behaviors implied with a "direct learning" approach. An important distinction made by modeling theories is the separation of learning and actually performing behaviors. A repertoire of potential responses can be acquired by observation. The incentives to perform behaviors can come from direct rewards to the observer *or* from characteristics of the model *or* from rewards presented to the model. A child may imitate a model because the model (but not yet the child) has been rewarded or because the model is nurturant or powerful, that is, because of vicarious reinforcement. Drawing on cognitive consistency research, social learning theorists argue that internalizing gender attitudes and identity occurs because one has already engaged in gender-typed behavior. Thus, changes in attitudes, opinions, or values follow changes in behavior. For example, a boy who plays with trucks, gets dirty in puddles, and wants to be a police officer strengthens his identity as male because he has done these "boylike" things. Depending on the theorist, social learning stresses either the situation specificity of gender-typed responses (e.g., Mischel, 1966) or the generalizability of broad and subtle aspects of gender-typed behavior (Bandura & Walters, 1963; Maccoby & Jacklin, 1974).

Three important types of modeling situations can be distinguished: (1) symbolic presentations, including media models; (2) concrete figures, including parents, teachers, siblings, peers, and even strangers; and (3) the patterning of an individual's behavior in *social* situations after observed *relationships* among others, such as bosses

and employees, students and teachers, or husbands and wives. The first two types of modeling have received far more attention than the third.

Media aimed at both children and adults offer fertile ground for acquiring gender-stereotyped behavior. In newspapers, general magazines, and prime-time television, women seem conspicuous by their absence; most characters are men (Tuchman, Daniels, & Benet, 1978). Saturday morning television and children's storybooks and school texts present a similar picture. In a study of Saturday morning television in the middle 1970s, 68% of the program characters and 80% of the commercial characters were male (McArthur & Eisen, 1976).

Females shown in children's media tend to remain home or indoors more than males. Although males are active and solve problems, females passively watch or are preoccupied with their physical appearance. Men tend to be authorities who tell women what to do or what products to use (McArthur & Eisen, 1976; Tuchman *et al.*, 1978; Weitzman, Eifler, Hokada, & Ross, 1972). Specialized media, such as women's magazines, may currently portray women and men in a larger variety of activities: employed women, or men taking care of children (Tuchman, 1979). However, two studies of children's books, one in Germany (Knopp, 1980) and one in the United States (St. Peter, 1979), suggest that very little reduction of gender stereotyping has occurred in children's stories.

Children apparently respond to media gender stereotypes. Heavy television viewers are more gender-stereotyped than light viewers. McGhee and Frueh (1980) reported that children who were heavy television viewers became more stereotyped between first and fifth grade; among light viewers, children became less stereotyped during the same time (also see Frueh & McGhee, 1975). Children, especially boys, more often imitate same-sex models than other-sex models in the media. Possibly, boys are more likely to imitate filmed male models because more males than females are portrayed in the media and because media males are found in a greater variety of activities (McArthur & Eisen, 1976; Perry & Perry, 1975).

The data on children imitating same-sex parents more than other-sex parents (or other same-sex concrete figures, such as siblings) are ambiguous. Theoretically, modeling approaches are vague in specifying which models will be chosen. Persons high in nurturance and warmth, or those perceived as powerful and as controlling valued resources, are more often chosen as models. However, as mothers are usually perceived by children as more nurturant and fathers as more powerful, there are few clues here about which parent would be chosen as a model more often. The picture becomes more complicated because children are exposed to a variety of models of both sexes, parents are rarely "pure" gender-stereotyped models, the performance of the behavior of the identical model may differ in boys and girls, and the gender-typed behavior of children does not highly resemble gender-typed behavior among adults (Heilbrun, 1976; Mischel, 1966; Maccoby & Jacklin, 1974).

Further, children do not resemble the same-sex parent more than the other-sex parent in attitudes, values, or perceived degree of similarity. College students do not seem more similar to the same-sex parent in terms of self-described attitudes or personality traits (Maccoby & Jacklin, 1974). McDonald (1977, 1980) studied high-school and college students and found that both sexes saw themselves as equally similar to their mothers and fathers. In the preschool years, children are not more likely to imitate the same-sex than other-sex parent—and sometimes imitate a stranger at least as readily as a parent (Lynn, 1976; Maccoby & Jacklin, 1974). Kohlberg (1966) noted that a child may prefer and imitate same-sex peers or strangers at an earlier age than she or he imitates the same-sex parent. Although nursery-school children show clearly gender-typed behavior, the degree of gender typing does not seem to be related to the degree of gender typing among the child's parents (Maccoby & Jacklin, 1974). Intriguingly, boys are more gender-typed overall at earlier ages than girls, even though children are exposed more to concrete female than to concrete male models, for example, mothers, nursery and grade-school teachers, and nurses.

The data on imitating filmed models, where there are tendencies to imitate same-sex models, clash with the parental data, where tendencies to imitate the same-sex parent are, at best, ambiguous. A partial resolution of this apparent contradiction comes from recent retheorizing on social learning and modeling. In these reformulations, two issues are stressed: (1) the original but often neglected distinction between learning and performance and the role of reinforcement and (2) the ability of children to abstract from the performances of several models of both sexes.

Because children are exposed to many models of both sexes, children learn, even if they do not perform, behavior of both "typical" males and "typical" females. Whether the behaviors are actually performed depends on what happens to the model *and* what happens to the imitator. Generally, models who are rewarded are imitated more frequently even if the child who imitates receives no reward. Behavioral rewards to either the model or the imitator in real life probably depend to some extent on the cultural gender-appropriateness of the model or on the child's behavior (Mischel, 1966; Perry & Perry, 1975).

Bandura (Bandura & Walters, 1963) found that, overall, boys were more likely to imitate filmed aggressive responses than girls. When children were directly rewarded for imitation, sex differences in aggressive imitation nearly vanished. Even if boys receive at least as much punishment for aggression from parents as girls, it seems likely that boys learn from television and peers that physical aggression is more appropriate (and perhaps is rewarded *as well as* punished) for males than for females. It

is also probable that children are differentially rewarded for imitative responses in toy choices and chores that are seen as gender-appropriate.

Notice, too, that nothing in the social learning approaches specifies that *only* a parent of the same sex is imitated. Because of the small child's dependence, parents are certainly important models—but other models are also present. Perry and Bussey (1979) believe that children code behavior as gender-appropriate by observing a variety of models of both sexes and noting the differential frequencies of behavior emitted by each sex. If relatively more males than females are associated with a specific behavior (e.g., wearing slacks), that behavior is coded as "male-appropriate." Perry and Bussey found that, when the behavior of *several* models was sharply distinct by sex, children were far more likely to imitate a same-sex model than when equal numbers of both sexes or models performed a behavior. If a majority of one sex performed a specific behavior ("sex-appropriate") and only a minority of the other sex performed that same behavior ("sex-inappropriate"), children were most likely to imitate the behavior of the same-sex "appropriate" model *or* that of the other-sex "inappropriate" model.

Powerful models are more often imitated, but little research has examined the *relative* balance of power between parents and conjugal family power and modeling. Employed wives are generally more powerful in marriage than wives who are not employed outside the home. Daughters of employed wives hold higher aspirations for achievement, have more self-confidence, and choose less feminine-stereotyped occupations than the daughters of full-time housewives (Baruch, 1976; Hoffman & Nye, 1974; Tangri, 1972). These findings suggest some type of modeling of mothers by daughters. Hetherington (1965) reported that girls in "mother-dominant" families and boys in "father-dominant" families were more likely to imitate the same-sex parent. McDonald (1977, 1980) found that adolescents reported themselves as most similar to the parent high in "expert power" or in "referent power" (attractiveness). With one exception, McDonald found that the perceived ability of parents to control rewards and punishments was not related to perceived child similarity. In an apparent contradiction of the results above, McDonald reported that daughters of mothers *high* on "outcome control power" were *less* likely to see themselves as similar to their mothers.

How the different types of power wielded by parents influences modeling and imitation in children deserves further study. Kohlberg (1966) claimed that the power structure between parents does not change with the age of the child. In contrast, many family researchers know that the age of her children influences the wife's employment status: married mothers of preschoolers are (see earlier) slightly less often employed than other women of the same age. In turn, the wife's employment status influences the structure of family power (Hoffman & Nye,

1974). Family power can change as children grow older, and these changes may influence how children imitate their parents.

An avenue that has not been fully explored concerns modeling *relationships* between women and men. Small-group studies indicate that individuals behave differently in same-sex versus mixed-sex groups. In both verbal and nonverbal behavior, women behave vis-à-vis men in ways indicating deference that do not appear in same-sex groupings (Frieze & Ramsey, 1976; Henley, 1977). These interaction patterns are likely to be picked up at early ages by children, who learn that men are the "boss." When small children play games like "house," they perform complementary role patterns (e.g., mother–father) often imitated from parental interaction. How ways of same-sex and cross-sex interactions are learned and performed has important implications for adult roles (e.g., secretary–boss) and deserve further attention.

Refinements of the modeling approaches are promising to explain the acquisition of gender roles. However, many social-learning theorists assume that a child acquires a sense of gender identity *before* imitating same-sex models and gender-appropriate behavior, although these imitations can strengthen gender identity. Other than brief references to a child's learning labels such as *boy* or *girl* from adults, social learning theorists are vague about how a child learns that one is male or female in the first place, as well as the importance of gender identity for larger core self-identity. The acquisition of gender identity has probably been examined most by psychoanalytic approaches to identification and cognitive-developmental theorists.

Gender Identity and Parental Identification

Psychological identification involves the incorporation of the attitudes, values, personality traits, and coping styles of a highly significant other, usually a parental figure. The incorporation usually involves a large segment of the significant figure. For psychoanalytic theorists, gender identity is largely acquired through identification with the same-sex parent: a process woven through a complex schema of love, sexual libido, castration fears, jealousy, and loss. Although imitation is involved, the identification process is more complex than merely modeling the rewarded activities of others (Heilbrun, 1976).

According to psychoanalytic approaches, the earliest identification for both sexes is with the mother. Indeed, it is theorized that the infant is unable to distinguish itself from the mother during the early months of life. The mother is also the first love object (or libido cathexis) for both sexes. The young girl continues to identify with her mother but switches her love object to her father during childhood. Conversely, the mother continues as a love object for the small boy, who later identifies with his father.

Gender identity for both sexes supposedly revolves about the discovery of sex differences in genitalia and, for Freudians, the superiority of male genitals (Freud, 1963, 1965). Boys assume at first that everyone has a penis. When a boy discovers that females do not, he explains this "lack" by either age (little girls will grow a penis when they get older) or castration (women had a penis that was cut off). The boy, viewing his father as a rival for his mother's affection, fears that the larger, stronger father will punish the child with castration. The boy's fears and hostilities toward his father coexist with love. In the context of these conflicts, the boy represses his hostilities toward his father and his libidinous feelings toward his mother and "identifies with the aggressor": his powerful father. The boy finds relief from the castration anxieties and ambivalence by idealizing, imitating, and internalizing his father's values, mannerisms, and attitudes. This process is hypothesized to occur between about the third and the fifth years of the boy's life.

During the same time, girls go through a different Oedipal conflict. Girls originally identify with their mothers, as boys do. When girls discover that they do not have a penis, they blame their mothers, reject them, and turn to their fathers. Then, the girl discovers that her father cannot give her a penis either, and she supposedly envies males because they possess one. The little girl never quite gets over this loss. She realizes that she cannot be a man but sees women, including her mother, as devalued because mothers lack a penis. Eventually, the girl substitutes the wish for a baby instead of a penis: a boy baby bringing the "longed for" penis with him. Only when she becomes a mother will the woman renew a warm identification with her own mother (Freud, 1965). Freud believed that surmounting the Oedipus complex was never as complete for women as for men. He also believed that achieving gender identity was more difficult for the woman, who has to (1) change from an active clitoral to a passive vaginal sexuality and (2) change her primary love object from her mother to her father.

Other psychoanalytic theorists believe that boys have the more difficult task in achieving gender identity for many reasons. Remember that boys show gender-typed behavior earlier than girls, and that males are more concerned that both sexes show appropriate gender behavior than females. These results have been interpreted by some as evidence of greater anxiety and defensiveness about gender identity among males than among females.

First, boys must switch identification from their mothers to their fathers, whereas girls continue to identify with their mothers. The boy's Oedipal crisis is surmised to be more filled with fear, rivalry, and loss (castration) than the girl's. While separating himself from the mother, however, the boy gains a greater sense of self; because of identification continuity with the mother, girls may find it more difficult to achieve individualization later in adulthood, whereas boys face the hard task of establishing a separate self during childhood (Chodorow, 1974,

1975; Maccoby & Jacklin, 1974; Stockard & Johnson, 1979).

Boys and men may also envy women's ability to bear children and the power that mothers have over small children. To compensate, some psychoanalytically oriented theorists suggest that boys develop an exaggerated and defensive sense of maculinity. Stockard and Johnson (1979) suggested that societies institutionalize stereotypes of male superiority as an incentive for boys to develop a masculine identity.

One explanation of potential male problems in identification involves the greater number of concrete female than male models for the growing child. Fathers are more absent from the home and play smaller roles in child caretaking. Children see an aspect of their mother's work in housework but often are not exposed to the work their fathers do. Of course, children may be ignorant of what their mothers do when they are employed; however, as noted earlier, nearly all women do housework, regardless of their labor force status, so even with employed mothers, children still see their mothers' housework activities. Boys may end up acquiring a masculine identity from the media or from other symbolism, and symbolic figures are usually more gender-typed than concrete men. In addition, how boys are supposed to behave is often defined in prohibitions (especially against ''feminine'' behavior) than in prescriptions. Therefore, boys become anxious about exhibiting ''feminine'' behavior, turning to ''compulsive masculinity'' (Chodorow, 1974; David & Brannon, 1976; Hartley, 1959; Stockard & Johnson, 1979).

Finally, boys may have more difficulty establishing gender identity because boys' behavior may be less acceptable to adults than girls' behavior. The greater incidence of ''rough-and-tumble play'' among boys may be seen as disruptive by parents and teachers, and boys do receive more punishment for aggression than girls. Boys may be in a double bind if they see that stereotypical masculine behavior (e.g., aggression or risk-taking) is punished but *also* rewarded in sports and the military and on television programs (Hartley, 1959; Maccoby & Jacklin, 1974).

I have two major objections to the hypothesis that gender identification is more difficult to achieve for males than for females. First, young boys identify with men, and men hold more economic and social power than women. Girls identify with women, and women are seen as less rewarded and less powerful than men. Indeed, socialization theorists who consider power factors important in parental identification often have difficulty explaining why children of both sexes do not identify with men. Kohlberg's elusive answer (1966) to this dilemma was

[A]dult female stereotypes are positive enough to make femininity attractive to young girls. . . . While [these are] inferior to power and competence of the male, [they are] still superior to . . . a child of either sex. . . . ''Niceness'' is a very important value to school-age American girls. . . . Another . . . stereotypical distinction . . . has to do with the supe-

rior attractiveness of females in . . . physical beauty . . . and interpersonal and sexual charm. (p. 121)

Whereas boys are offered the competence and achievement associated with adult males of various ages, the best incentive offered to girls is the sex appeal associated primarily with young women. It is possible that lower self-esteem occurs among girls entering junior high and high school because at those ages girls begin to realize that they are being asked to identify with models holding a less valued societal status.

Second, whereas boys may be taught to avoid many interests and behavior labeled feminine, girls may have difficulty deciphering just *which* feminine behaviors bring approval. At least over the past several decades, there has been tremendous debate about what ''being female'' really is. Girls may perceive demands to be simultaneously sexy and chaste, to have an interesting career but to put their husband's needs first, to be intelligent but not *too* intelligent, and to be healthy but not athletic. Surely, there is at least as much role conflict in being female as there is in being male, and it would be surprising if girls did not sense these conflicts in the course of identifying with their parents and acquiring a stable gender identity.

In addition to the debate over which sex has the greater difficulty in parental identification and gender identity, there are other challenges to the psychoanalytic approach to gender. This approach postulates that children primarily identify with the same-sex parent. Through the incorporation process, the child acquires a stable sense of being male or female and the appropriate gender values and behaviors. Thus, gender identification is hypothesized to cause gender identity and the acquisition of gender-typed behavior.

Some data challenging this causal sequence were reviewed earlier under in the section on modeling. Young children and adolescents often simply do not show marked similarities to the same-sex parent. The relative resources and power of the parent appear to be at least as important as the parent's sex, as family research suggests that children and adolescents are more likely to identify with the parent who has more resources, such as education (Lueptow, 1981), expertise or attractiveness (McDonald, 1977, 1980), or dominance in the family (Hetherington, 1965).

Maccoby and Jacklin (1974) suggested that if both sexes initially identify with the mother, then girls should be more gender-stereotyped and should show stereotypical gender behavior at earlier ages than boys. In fact, the opposite pattern occurs. Greater gender-typed behavior occurs earlier among males and continues among males into adult life.

Perhaps the largest challenge to psychoanalytic frameworks of gender identification and identity comes from cognitive-developmental theory. Both the *sequence* of identity acquisition and the *type of input* hypothetically used by children to establish gender identity have been critiqued. Cognitive-developmental theorists view the focus on bodily zones and parental jealousy and rivalry as less important than the cognitive capacities of growing children.

Cognitive Development and Gender Identity

Cognitive theorists stress the symbol-manipulating abilities of children, which develop with age. Children are viewed as active cognitive processors who question, structure, and interpret information; infer causality; and seek value clarification. The processes of acquiring a stable identity, gender stereotypes, and gender-typed behavior are theorized as being parallel to non-gender-related cognitive tasks such as learning object constancy, generalizing across objects in the same abstract category, and learning social rules of interaction. Gender identity, stereotypes, and behavior change over time as children become able to handle greater cognitive complexity (Constantinople, 1979; Katz, 1979; Kohlberg, 1966; Lewis & Weinraub, 1979).

These theorists agree on other points: It is self-rewarding to express one's values and one's·"core self." Because gender identity is an important component of the core self, expressing this identity in attitudes, dress, activities, and other modes is considered self-rewarding. In acquiring a stable sense of gender identity (or *gender constancy*) for oneself and others, the child usually goes through the phase labeled earlier as *gender ethnocentrism*. Children label behaviors and characteristics more typical of their own sex as "better" because those exhibiting such behaviors and characteristics seem to be similar to the self; this process can also occur for racial, ethnic, religious, and even regional identities. Finally, nearly all cognitive theorists caution that gender identity is not the same as holding cultural stereotypes about the sexes or holding behaviors conforming to gender stereotypes. Although these concepts are conceptually and empirically related, a little girl who plays with trucks can see herself as very female and a little boy who plays with dolls can define himself as very male.

Kohlberg (1966), one of the most influential cognitive-developmental theorists on gender identity, has stressed how children learn object constancies. Until about age 5 or 6, he has speculated that a child does not realize that he or she is *permanently* a boy or girl, that he or she cannot change gender through fantasy, and that others also have a constant biological sex and are similar or not to the child. For Kohlberg, the crucial first step is gender identity, that is, one's initial definition as male or female. Unlike psychoanalytically oriented theorists or learning theorists, Kohlberg believes that gender identity *precedes* the acquisition of gender stereotypes, gender-typed activities, and same-sex friendships; these beliefs and behaviors, in turn, *precede* identification with the same-sex parent.

The child begins to acquire gender identity by hearing labels like *boy* or *girl* applied to the self. At first, the labels are simply linguistic tags, like a proper name. The child next realizes that gender labels are also consistently applied to others. By age 3, the child knows its own gender and begins to apply gender labels to others, using a loose constellation of physical characteristics, such as dress, size, or hairstyle. By age 4, a child applies gender labels to others with few mistakes.

Unlike Freud, Kohlberg does not believe that knowledge of sex differences in the genitals plays the initial crucial role in the acquisition of gender identity and parental identification, although—like Freud—Kohlberg believes that children of both sexes see male anatomy as "superior" to female anatomy. Children given anatomical information by their parents do not have greater awareness of gender constancy than other children. Initially, gross physical characteristics such as size are important. Slightly later, gender typing for children begins to include social and personal characteristics, such as power, prestige, aggression, and nurturance. There are strong similarities between these characteristics and those stressed by modeling theorists, as children tend to imitate models higher in power, prestige, or nurturance. It is not until school begins that children consistently link genital sex differences to gender.

Kohlberg emphasized that the awareness of one's own sex and the beginning of gender-typed activities come before imitation of same-sex models. In his research, boys displayed a preference for same-sex playmates before imitating their fathers over their mothers. Even when the boy seemed to identify with his father, he showed some difficulty in differentiating his father from his general stereotypes about males. For example, a boy might attribute stereotypical interests such as hunting, fishing, and football to his father, even if the father did not do these activities. Thus, parental identification was hypothesized to occur late in the process of gender typing.

Once a child develops a gender identity, he or she is motivated to choose the congruent gender-linked activities and playmates and the same-sex parent. This motivation comes from several sources. Children want competence and mastery over their environment, and adults (especially males) are seen as larger, stronger, and more competent than children. Desires for cognitive consistency make activities and persons associated with one's own sex appear to be more valuable and rewarding. Kohlberg suggested that, once a child begins to model same-sex activities and interests, a stable relationship with a same-sex model is needed for the child to continue developing skills and receiving approval for his or her performances. During this relationship, the child becomes emotionally dependent on the model, and the same-sex parental identification theoretically results.

Like other early writers on cognitive development, Kohlberg was less clear about how gender identity and parental identification operate for girls. He suggested, like the psychoanalytic theorists, that girls do not switch identification from their mothers to their fathers. He also noted that the preference for same-sex activities and models is less pronounced among girls than among boys. Kohlberg suggested that power differences between adult women and men may cause this sex difference in gender-stereotyped preferences among children. Possibly, the father's expectations help girls to develop a female identity, although this process is not fully explained.

Other cognitive-developmental theorists place less emphasis on peers and parents in learning gender identity and a greater emphasis on abstracting general social rules from teachers, siblings, media, and other concrete and symbolic figures. Constantinople (1979) agreed with Kohlberg that children acquire gender identity via parental labels and the use of properties such as size, clothing, toys, or hairstyles to label others. She added to these factors the importance of the child's learning general categories of rules and norms related to gender. These rules specify pronounced and subtle modes of appropriate gender behavior, including interaction with same- and other-sex persons. The rules specify the time and the place of expressing needs (e.g., a father may hug his small crying son at home but not in a store), the appropriate modes of expressing needs, and the proper objects of behavior. Constantinople stressed the importance of reinforcement (which Kohlberg downplayed) and how enforcement of "proper" gender behavior is handled by a wide variety of persons.

One disagreement between cognitive-developmental and psychoanalytic theorists concerns when gender identity and identification are acquired. Those with a Freudian perspective locate these developments around age 5 or 6, following the resolution of Oedipal conflicts. These theorists note that adolescence can bring problems in identity and identification once more into salience. Those more cognitively oriented, such as Kohlberg, suggest that *gender constancy* occurs by age 5 or 6, whereas *gender identity* is fixed by age 3. Constantinople (1979) and Lewis and Weinraub (1979) have suggested that gender identity is acquired by age 2 and possibly as early as early as 18 months. The latter theorists used work by Money (Money & Tucker, 1975) that deals with the gender reassignment of hermaphrodites and infants with prenatal exposure to androgenic hormones. In such cases, Money's work suggests that gender reassignment occurring before age 3 tends to result in a stable gender identity. In any case, the major focus of both psychoanalytic theorists and many cognitive-developmental theorists is on the child's preschool years. Like the other approaches examined thus far, the cognitive-developmental framework can be vague concerning how the child's gender-typed behaviors develop into adult gender roles.

One notable exception is Katz's 1979 theoretical article. Katz stressed the different skills and developmental tasks that occur during childhood, adolescence, adulthood, and late adulthood. Often, these skills are similar in that both sexes must develop the same *type* of skill, although the *form* of the skill may differ for each sex. Both sexes must adjust to bodily changes at adolescence,

develop courting skills, develop marital relationships, and learn parenting skills, although women may develop such skills at slightly younger ages than men. Some experiences are uniquely female: menstruation, pregnancy, childbirth, and nursing. In this country, at least, the young girl's socialization during childhood may not prepare her for these experiences. Other experiences have traditionally been more associated with males: higher education, vocational preparation, employment, and retirement, although more women are now having these experiences.

Katz noted that the sexes are more similar at some time points (childhood and old age) than at others (adolescence and young adulthood). Thus, the skills that each sex must develop differ at different ages. The sources of influence in learning gender roles may also differ by age and sex. Parents may be most important during childhood and early adolescence, one's spouse probably becomes most important during adulthood, and one's own children can influence gender-role performance among parents. Approved gender behavior can differ substantially by age. The coyness and flirtatiousness found among some females may be considered "cute" in nursery school, sexy in adolescence, and affected in adulthood. Highly aggressive behavior among some males may be considered "spunky" in nursery school, heroic in some situations in young adulthood (like wars or sports), and socially disruptive in middle age.

The point that I am making here and that I have stressed earlier is that socialization does not stop at the grade-school or college door. There are so many discontinuities in gender behavior between childhood and adulthood that these cannot be explained solely by reference to reinforcement, modeling, identification, and development during one's early years. At most, childhood experiences expose children to preparation for adulthood and to models of what male and female adults are like and "should be" like. These are important factors indeed, but they leave gender-role development far from complete.

Thus far, the emphasis in this chapter on gender roles and the acquisition of gender roles and gender behavior has been mainly on what others do to the individual and how the individual reacts. *Labeling, reinforcement, shaping,* and *modeling* all refer to experiences that children and adults undergo and to which they react. Brief mention has been made of active, potentially innate human characteristics: language, symbol manipulation, motivations for competence, and motivations arising from the psychological investment in certain bodily zones. A final major approach to the acquisition of gender roles and gender behavior focuses on the potential innate differences between the sexes. Although this more sociobiological orientation includes cultural influences, its greatest emphasis is on how biological sex differences during childhood and adulthood shape the behavior of socialization agents and the structures of societal institutions related to gender.

The Nature–Nurture Controversy

The fifth major approach to the instillation of gender typing and gender roles contains the crucial postulate that innate sex differences in behavior condition the actions of socialization agents. Parents and other socialization agents treat girls and boys differently because they respond to differences in the children's behavior. For example, mothers may verbalize more to girls than to boys because female infants are initially more vocal than male infants (see, for example, hypotheses in Maccoby & Jacklin, 1974, p. 305).

Alternatively, whereas innate sex differences among infants may be small, sex differences could be accentuated when males and females reach puberty and adulthood, marry, and rear children. To anticipate these developments, socialization agents may show different behaviors toward boys and girls to prepare the children for adulthood. Barry, Bacon, and Child (1957) provided an example of this reasoning:

The relevant biological sex differences are conspicuous in adulthood but generally not in childhood. If each generation were left . . . to its own devices . . . sex differences would have to be developed after puberty at the expense of considerable relearning. . . . [A] pattern of child training which foreshadows adult differences can serve the useful function of minimizing what Benedict termed "discontinuities in cultural conditioning." (p. 329)

Barry *et al.* stated that

biological differences . . . make most appropriate the useful division of . . . roles between the sexes. . . . In our training of children, there may now be less differentiation in sex roles than characterizes adult life—so little . . . as to provide inadequate preparation for adulthood. . . . many of the adjustment problems of women in our society today may be partly traced to conflicts growing out of inadequate childhood preparation for their adult role. (pp. 331–332)

Biological approaches obviously deserve attention. If strong innate tendencies shape the behavior of women and men, social changes promoting greater gender-role similarity can have only a limited impact. For some sociobiologists, the amount of social change required to promote both greater gender similarity and equality would be so costly as to damage society (Barash, 1977; Goldberg, 1974; Wilson, 1978).

Nature–nurture arguments use five main types of evidence: (1) cross-cultural comparisons; (2) changes in gender behavior over time; (3) infant behavior; (4) the effects of sex hormones such as estrogens and androgens; and (5) cross-species comparisons. A biological view of human gender behavior is buttressed if other animals, especially primates, show sex differentiation patterns similar to those of humans, if fluctuating hormone levels correlate with gender-typed behavior, if certain aspects of gender behavior are culturally nearly universal, and if small children show sex differences foreshadowing adult gender behavior. Several of these components have already been examined in this chapter, but they will be briefly reviewed here with respect to the interaction of cultural and biogenic gender patterns.

Cross-cultural data and changes in gender behavior across time point toward two major gender behaviors: Males tend more often to display aggression and dominance behavior, and females tend more often to display nurturance. In other respects, humans show a wide variety of gender-typed behaviors in areas such as economic production, religion, and family life. Gender behavior also appears to be responsive to historical events such as war or demographic events such as the "baby boom."

Despite such variety, dominance and nurturance behaviors have important implications for gender behavior. Barry *et al.* (1957) argued that most societies pressure girls toward nurturance, obedience, and responsibility and pressure boys toward achievement and self-reliance: behaviors related to the adult roles of each sex. Nurturance of infants among females and rough-and-tumble play among males also seem to be behaviors associated with primates as well as humans, according to some researchers. "Innate" male dominance is cited frequently among some sociobiologists who argue that men's superior status in many societies is "natural" (Goldberg, 1974).

Thus, it is important to realize that patterns of nurturance and rough-and-tumble play are often modified by culture. Barry *et al.* (1957) reported that these sex differences are greatest in societies characterized by hunting large animals, grain crops, nomadic residence patterns, and large family groupings. Whiting and Edwards (1973) found fewer sex differences in societies in which boys were expected to tend babies and perform domestic chores. In these societies, boys showed more nurturant behavior and girls showed more rough-and-tumble play than in other societies. Whiting and Edwards suggested that children assigned chores close to home receive more adult supervision and demands. Children under these circumstances may also be pressured to show responsibility for others and may be discouraged from aggressive play. Also, remember that substantial evidence shows that fathers play an important expressive role in child rearing and that paternal nurturance varies widely by society (Crano & Aronoff, 1978; Mackey & Day, 1979). Thus, even "universal" behaviors show variation across cultures.

By age 3, it should be recalled, children have acquired gender-typed behaviors and usually a sense of gender identity. Before that age, sex differences among infants appear to be relatively few. There is the suggestion (Lewis & Weinraub, 1979) that infant boys sleep less and may be more irritable than infant girls. Again, small boys do show more rough-and-tumble play than small girls.

Even when sex differences occur among infants and small children, these do not necessarily reflect "nature" factors. Recall that parents stereotype infants before and at birth when few neonatal sex differences exist. Little boys are handled more roughly than little girls, although it is small boys who show higher mortality rates from illness and accidents. Research subjects hand the "wrong toys" to an infant whose sex has been disguised, and the same schoolroom behaviors among girls and boys receive different treatment from teachers. The behavior of infants and small children may tell us more about how parents and other socialization agents treat them than about "natural" sex differences at early ages.

Cross-species comparisons are only modestly helpful in explaining human gender-role behavior. Sex-linked behavior varies widely across different species, and even among groups within a specific species. Some groups of male rhesus monkeys show hostile behavior toward infants, for example, whereas in other groups, male rhesus monkeys are very nurturant toward infants. Other types of monkeys rarely display "paternal" behavior in the wild but will do so under laboratory conditions. Infant female monkeys raised in isolation fail to show normal parenting behavior as adults (Harlow, 1962; Lewis & Weinraub, 1979; Lynn, 1976; Rypma, 1976). Perhaps the most promising research with animals concerns those receiving hormone treatments during pregnancy. The effects of hormone treatments on offspring among mammals have some parallels with those on human infants whose mothers have received similar treatments during pregnancy.

Money (e.g., Money & Tucker, 1975) and Ehrhardt (e.g., Ehrhardt, 1977) have studied gender identity and behavior among children with different kinds of biological sex anomalies. In some cases, mothers who received progestin during pregnancy bore daughters with masculine-appearing external genitalia at birth. In others, girls with "adrenogenital syndrome" produce too much androgen (a "male" hormone); some boys also show this syndrome. Some boys are unable to utilize androgen correctly. Other boys had mothers who took estrogen and progesterone ("female" hormones) during pregnancy. Among still other children, the ambiguous appearance of external genitalia at birth have led to gender assignments inconsistent with their chromosomal sex.

In Money's studies, children exposed to androgens prenatally and girls with adrenogenital syndrome had gender identities congruent with their biological sex and seemed satisfied with their gender identities. However, these groups showed a marked incidence of physical activity, intense energy, and rough outdoor play (see also Reinisch, 1981). Compared with their own sisters, the androgenized girls were more often described as "tomboys," more often played with trucks and blocks, preferred boys as playmates, and showed less interest in dolls, infant care, and makeup. The data on these androgenized girls suggests a parallel with some animal experiments: pregnant rhesus monkeys and rats injected with androgens produce female offspring that show a high incidence of rough-and-tumble play, chasing, and dominance behavior.

Preliminary data on boys whose mothers received estrogen therapy during pregnancy and on boys whose bodies do not sufficiently utilize androgens present a different picture. Boys prenatally exposed to estrogens may be less physically active than other boys (Ehrhardt, 1977), although they have a male gender identity, normal male genitalia, and normal reproductive capacities. Some androgen-insensitive boys have female-appearing genitalia at birth and develop female secondary sex characteristics at puberty. Those androgen-insensitive males raised as boys appear to be quieter and less competitive than boys without this syndrome (Money & Tucker, 1975), results similar to those in the prenatally estrogenized boys. Thus, evidence indicates that hormones differently concentrated in females and males can be linked to behaviors such as physical activity, which, in turn, can be linked to gender-role expectations.

Research by sexology experts such as Ehrhardt or Money, however, also indicates that hormones interact with cultural expectations and rewards. Children raised with a gender identity incomptabile with their genetic composition seem to view themselves in terms of the gender socially assigned to them before age 3. Androgen-insensitive males raised as girls see themselves as female even after medical examinations reveal that they are "really" boys. Money and his colleagues suggested that such children developed to be happier and more "normal" if hormone therapy was given and surgery performed to make their biological sex as compatible as possible with their gender identity. The same appears to be true for androgenized females reared as "boys." Children with hormone abnormalities reared with a chromosomally compatible social gender identity view themselves as the "proper" sex even if the boys are quiet and the girls are tomboys; they marry and can become satisfied parents. In still other instances, girls with only one X chromosome who did not have ovaries and who required supplementary estrogen at puberty were described by Money and Tucker (1975) as "the epitome of conventional femininity" (p. 30). Although hormonal makeup is clearly important, the social identity that one develops as male or female is at least as important in the development of gender-typed behavior.

Finally, there is recent research on "male and female brains" (see brief reviews in Goleman, 1978; Lewis & Weinraub, 1979). It is suggested in these reviews that males develop their speech centers in one brain hemisphere and spatial skills in the other (lateral specialization), whereas females develop spatial and verbal skills bilaterally. This specialization may cause boys' relatively greater tested spatial skills, which have been linked to mathematical ability. Even these hypotheses about sex differences in brain function should be complemented by considering social factors, as the following example suggests.

Suppose that twice as many males as females possess high spatial aptitudes because of brain lateral specialization. These sex differences do not explain why sex differences in mathematics appearing during grade school 20 years ago now do not appear until adolescence (Maccoby & Jacklin, 1974). Nor does such a sex difference prove sufficient to explain gender segregation in fields such as engineering. Suppose that potential sex differences in spatial skills and differential labor-market participation were statistically controlled. Even with controls for sex differences in "brain specialization," spatial skills, and labor market participation, an expected 15%–20% of engineers would be women: a percentage nearly 10 times that now in the labor force. Surely, other factors besides sex differences in aptitude must be involved.

The important issues here are probably *not* whether hormonal sex differences influence individual behavior or whether biological parenthood influences societal institutions. Obviously, there are important factors. It is also obvious that societies take the behavioral potentials associated with biological sex and show considerable variation in shaping institutions such as the family or in setting rules for appropriate gender behavior. Even within American culture, there have been changes in the roles of both sexes over a relatively short time period: the past 30 years. These changes would not be possible unless biology gives potential flexibility to male and female behavior, and unless adults as well as children can modify gender behavior in different ways.

The Case for Adult Learning

One argument used by those emphasizing a biological influence on gender roles is that biology has more impact on adult sex differences and gender roles than on those among children. Children are theorized as receiving socialization pressures toward gender-typed behavior to prepare them for biological developments during adolescence and adulthood. It is unclear how much evidence supports this position: Most hormonal gender research among humans concerns the effects of prenatal and childhood hormonal influences. Research studies that link hormone concentrations or other biological factors to gender-related behavior are just beginning.

Gender socialization pressures during adulthood and developments in gender identity during adulthood are similarly neglected in research. Yet, learning patterns of gender behavior and changes in gender identity at different points in the life cycle must occur during adulthood. There have been too many changes in postsecondary education, marriage, divorce and birth rates, employment rates, and retirement rates among both sexes for adult learning not to take place. This section on the perpetuation of gender-related behavior and roles briefly examines theoretical perspectives and some empirical studies that suggest what types of gender socialization occur after childhood.

Many theorists have been attempting to chart developments in self-identity over the life cycle (e.g., see Erikson, 1978; Katz, 1979; Levinson, Darrow, Levinson, Klein, & McKee, 1978; Rivers, Barnett, & Baruch, 1979). Technical, economic, and demographic factors have contributed to increased longevity. With increased longevity, there is greater recognition of distinct life stages following childhood. Uhlenberg (1969) defined a "typical" life cycle as survival to age 20, marriage, children, and survival with one's spouse to age 55. Only 21% of women born in 1830 epxerienced such a "complete cycle," but Uhlenberg expected 57% of women born in 1920 to do so. Historian Hareven (1978, p. 203) pointed out that Americans "discovered" childhood in the first half of the nineteenth century and then "invented" adolescence at the end of it. These "discoveries" and "inventions" of the life cycle, she suggested, occurred because of the changes brought about by longevity, technical advancement, and the need for increased training to function adequately in an industrialized society.

Precisely what later life stages include differs slightly by theorist. Most theorists include a young, middle, and late adulthood stage. During the "young adult" stage, individuals carve a separate identity and forge new relationships with others. Postsecondary education, military service, starting work, and finding an occupational mentor are parts of this process, especially for men. Marriage, having children, and forming close friendships are also tasks at this stage, traditionally especially for women. Middle adulthood can involve carving out an occupational niche, becoming a mentor oneself, entering community life, and, perhaps for men, discovering one's feelings or the "feminine" side of oneself. For many women after 1950, middle adulthood has meant a new life: entering or reentering school or employment. Divorce in midlife often means a massive reorientation for women who have been full-time career housewives.

Undoubtedly, stages of adulthood touch many aspects of gender identity. Bodily changes such as menstruation, emissions, pregnancy and childbirth, menopause, or prostate troubles contribute to core biological aspects of gender identity, and these bodily events change with age. The social statuses of spouse and parent are also important for gender identity, as is one's occupation for men and, increasingly, for women. It is interesting that relatively few studies closely examine the relationships between such important adult experiences and gender identity. Finding what mechanisms are causing these experiences to become integrated into gender identity remains an important research task for the future. Already, there are some significant studies suggesting how adult socialization into gender roles proceeds.

Direct training and rewards play a role in adult gender-behavior acquisition. Parke and Sawin (1976) cited a Swedish study in which prospective fathers offered the opportunity to practice child-caretaking skills were more involved with their infants than other fathers. In a series of experiments with college students, Hokanson (1970) found that, when *male* students were shocked by a bogus confederate, their stress indicators, such as blood pressure and heart rates, rose and stayed high until these students *returned* the shock. When *female* students received a shock, their stress indicators remained high until they pressed an "appeasement button" giving points to the bogus confederate. Hokanson devised a "reverse rein-forcement" schedule to change the overt behaviors of his subjects: After this schedule, when shocked, more females retaliated directly and more males pressed the appeasement button. More impressively, through this conditioning, Hokanson found changes in autonomic responses. Blood pressure and heart rates now dropped for females who retaliated and for men making appeasement gestures. Hokanson's work suggests that gender-linked behaviors such as aggressive intent among young adults may be more amenable to change than previously supposed. His work is also important to consider when the "costs" and "benefits" of male and female gender roles are compared in the final section of this chapter.

Survey data from college students up through at least the early 1970s suggests that some form of learning occurred to make students more gender-typed at the end of their college years than at the beginning. During college, men raised their aspirations for advanced degrees and higher status occupations, whereas women lowered theirs. Women initially aspiring to fields such as law or medicine switched to elementary or secondary education or to nursing (Astin, 1977; Bielby, 1978; Spaeth, 1977). Further, during college, men increased their skills in areas such as mathematics, whereas women increased their skills in typing (Astin, 1977). Recently, there has been an exception to these trends among women exposed to women's studies courses: Women with this experience appear to raise their aspirations for careers and to become less gender-stereotyped, even when there was a control for initial differences between women electing women's studies courses and those in other courses (Howe, 1977; Rubel, Croke, & Parsons, 1975).

Modeling factors may also influence gender behavior in adulthood. Women attending women's colleges gained more self-esteem and more often planned graduate school than women on other campuses, again with a control for the initial differences among students at coeducational and women's colleges (Astin, 1977). Women in college courses taught by women showed more assertiveness in the classroom than women in courses taught by men (Sternglanz & Lyberger-Ficek, 1977). In one experiment (Jennings, Geis, & Brown, 1980), college women were exposed either to gender-stereotyped "commercials" or to "commercials" that reversed stereotypical gender behavior. Women exposed to the innovative "commercials" conformed less and behaved in a more self-confident way in a later situation than women exposed to the traditional "commercials." Finally, pregnant women and new mothers frequently turn to women who are already mothers for assistance and advice (Rivers et al., 1979).

Virtually all the modeling research I have located that relates to adulthood studies women. Certainly, it would be valuable to know more about modeling effects on men. For example, who do men turn to for advice about fatherhood—or do men go through such a process at all? Are men able to confide in friends and ask for advice

about their love relationships? How does the increased saliency of women in responsible business or professional occupations influence men's judgment of women's ability?

Finally, research indicates that aspects of one's job influence attitudes and psychological functioning. Miller, Schooler, Kohn, and Miller (1979) studied national samples of employed adults. Structural factors of the job such as closeness of supervision, they suggested, can change employees. Those in jobs with a high degree of routinization can become more fatalistic; those experiencing job stress in Miller et al.'s samples became more anxious and showed less intellectual flexibility and less self-confidence. Kanter (1977) carried the logic of these studies directly into gender identity. She suggested that behavior interpreted as "feminine" in employment (e.g., low interest in promotion or an emphasis on social interaction) is a function of jobs with low promotion ceilings and little formal responsibility. Women given the opportunity to "move up" the job ladder began developing ambitions comparable to men in the same types of jobs. It seems likely that a woman working in a "man's field" would change her opinions about what kinds of work and what kinds of behavior might be appropriate for women.

The studies cited and the developing theoretical perspectives on adult identity represent a beginning of a discovery of how gender identity develops during adulthood. This emerging research indicates that the perpetuation of gender roles and gender-typed behavior continues long past childhood. How important these adult experiences are compared with childhood ones cannot be well evaluated without further studies of adults in "noncaptive" situations. Although childhood gender identity and learning influence adult behavior, many adult situations emerge that were not anticipated during childhood, for example, the effect of divorce on middle-aged housewives, the small but increasing numbers of fathers seeking child custody in divorce, and the increasing numbers of nonmarried cohabitors. More knowledge of adult experiences and adult learning related to gender can enable us to predict with more certainty future changes in gender roles, particularly those related to family life.

A Caveat: Traditional Gender Roles Can Be Hazardous to Your Health

In the final section of this chapter, I will speculate about what current trends in gender roles imply for the family of today and tomorrow. We have already seen that some changes have occurred in the roles of men and women that have influenced and have been influenced by family life. In addition, continuities in gender behavior and the perpetuation of gender stereotypes and gender-typed roles exist. The 1960s and 1970s were times of considerable debate about how men and women "should" behave, whether the quality of male–female relationships was "better" in the past, and how changes in gender behavior have affected the family. In this section, I will briefly review some research that suggests that greater flexibility in gender roles may be more beneficial for both sexes—even though a certain amount of stress and confusion is bound to occur with the social changes associated with changes in gender behavior.

Along with many other social scientists now, I suspect that rigid distinctions between the roles of women and men may create a less efficient and less harmonious society. A growing body of research suggests that extreme gender differentiation may harm both sexes, that gender-stereotyped behavior may be stressful, and that gender stratification may be particularly damaging to women. The sources of research that appear to be applicable are those on depression and anxiety, on labor force performance, on epidemiology, on self-esteem, and on "androgyny."

In industrialized societies, gender segregation in general can lead to a underutilization of talent. This can occur in professions and occupations that men or women may hesitate to enter because they are the "wrong" sex. Certainly, societies can use the most talented physicians, repair personnel, grade-school teachers, and other skilled workers, regardless of their gender.

One barrier that hinders the free movement of each sex into fulfilling and productive labor is the separation of home from work that occurred with the Industrial Revolution. Our education–employment schedules are relatively inflexible: In most industrialized countries, there is a relatively rigid sequence of education, followed by employment, followed by retirement. This sequence is particularly pronounced for men and is buttressed by unionization, emphases on seniority, and norms of "commitment" in the professional and managerial occupations. Jobs are structured so that they require continuous time spent away from home. As child care is stereotyped as "women's work," day care is not usually available in the workplace except during the mobilization of nearly the entire population, such as during wars or periods of exceptionally full employment. Women who wish both high-prestige jobs and families often postpone marriage and childbearing into their 30s, or neither marry nor bear children, or face difficulty finding adequate day care for their children (Giele, 1978; Hennig & Jardim, 1977; Kreps & Clark, 1975).

When the demand for labor has been high enough or unions have made strong demands during contract negotiations, employers have responded with more flexible schedules. For example, when there has been a greater demand for than a supply of secretaries or nurses, some employers have experimented with more flexible schedules. If, as in the 1950s, there has been a greater demand for than a supply of elementary-school teachers, school districts have proved willing to hire women with children and to allocate (usually unpaid) maternity leave.

The point is that, if more flexible schedules and timetables in skilled "women's work" can be arranged, other classes of workers can benefit if employers perceive the demand or advantages in these arrangements. More flexible paid employment could allow both sexes an optimal balance of paid work and family activities. Perhaps, if fathers are more visible in a greater range of activities in the family setting, sons may not display the "defensive masculinity" postulated by some socialization theorists. Rather than completing one's total education before full employment, "educational breaks" (similar to academic sabbaticals) might be available to workers, who could use these breaks for additional career training or simply for an enjoyable hobby. Rather than abrupt retirement, workers might ease out of the labor force with part-time employment and flexible schedules (Kreps & Clark, 1975).

The adherence of individuals to gender-stereotyped behavior may also be psychologically, socially, and physically harmful for both sexes. One theoretical innovation during the 1970s was Sandra Bem's concept of "androgyny." An androgynous person is postulated to incorporate the "best of both sexes." He or she is independent, self-confident, and competent (socially desirable traits associated with men) and also warm and sensitive (socially desirable traits associated with women). Such an individual has been considered more flexible and able to perform tasks stereotypically associated with either sex. Although it is not clear whether "androgyny" measures a stable personality trait or simply an orientation toward social situations, individuals who score as androgynous appear to be more able to express affection than male-stereotyped persons and have more confidence in their opinions than female-stereotyped persons (Bem, 1975; Bem & Lenney, 1976; Helmreich, Spence, & Holahan, 1979). For example, Ickes and Barnes (1978) found that persons with stereotyped gender identities in mixed-sex dyads interacted less and liked each other less than those in mixed-sex dyads with at least one "androgynous" participant. It should also be remembered that surveys of parents suggest that both fathers and mothers want an "androgynous" child: one who is both competent and sensitive.

Some research indicates that "traditional sex roles" damage physical and mental health. Women report depressive and anxiety symptomatology more often than men, and these scores in some studies are highest for full-time housewives (Dohrenwend & Dohrenwend, 1976; Gove & Tudor, 1973). One source of epidemiological data is that collected in Framingham, Massachusetts in the late 1970s (e.g., Haynes & Feinleib, 1980). In this research, women employed in clerical occupations had twice the incidence of diagnosed heart disease as professional and managerial women. Married mothers employed in clerical occupations had three times the heart disease rates of full-time housewives or professional and managerial women, and higher rates than men overall. Meanwhile, male professionals and managers had heart disease rates double those of male blue-collar workers and quadruple those of male clerical and sales workers.

Although women may verbally report more anxiety and depressive symptomatology than men, some researchers hypothesize that "playing it cool" causes higher rates of psychosomatic illness, such as ulcers or even heart disease, among men (Harrison, 1978). Attempts to match the adventurous, aggressive, or competitive aspects of stereotypical "masculine" behavior may result in the higher death rates from accidents, suicide, and homocide associated with males in all age groups (U.S. Department of Commerce, 1977, Table 5/8; 1979, Table 2/2; 1980, Table 100).

Psychologically, being placed in an inferior position or receiving fewer rewards for the same work may damage female self-esteem. Earlier, research was reviewed that suggested that young children initially describe their own sex more positively than the other sex. During adolescence, both sexes generally describe males in more positive terms than females. As children grow older, they may become more aware of negative stereotypes associated with females, and it is probably not coincidental that girls' self-esteem drops during adolescence and remains lower than that of boys through the college years.

One consequence of lower self-esteem among women is that females are more likely than males to attribute success to luck or effort and failure to low ability. In contrast, males attribute success to ability and failure to low effort or to biased evaluators (Deaux, 1976). In one recent study, Dweck *et al.* (1980) asked fourth- through sixth-grade children what grades they expected on their first report card of the academic year. Although during the previous year, the average girl attained *higher* grades than the average boy, the girls expected *lower* report-card grades than the boys did. When the children were resurveyed after their first report card was received, once again the girls averaged higher grades than the boys. However, rather than having *higher* expectations for their next report card, the girls held the *same* average expectations for grades that boys did. Perhaps girls lack the self-esteem to believe in their own accomplishments, and this low self-esteem may influence lower career and educational expectations among girls.

To summarize this section, "traditional sex roles" may be too inflexible to permit adaptation to a changing, industrialized society. There is evidence that too rigid adherence to gender-stereotyped behavior may induce social, psychological, and perhaps even physical damage. This damage may be reflected in marriages that no "longer work," in couples who may be afraid to "gamble" on bearing children, or in the increasing documentation of domestic violence.

Gender and the Family: Some Hints for the Future

It is misleading to say that a "revolution" in gender roles has occurred during the past few decades. Nevertheless, there have been some substantial changes that have implications for family life. In this final section, these changes are summarized, the potential influences of

these changes on family life are suggested, and I make some suggestions for further research on the connections between gender roles and family life.

Some of the most important changes in gender roles concern the increased options available to women. An employed woman is less financially dependent on her parents, her husband, or her other relatives, and the rate of labor force participation among women has dramatically increased since the late 1940s. Despite continuing gender segregation and inequity in the labor market, women say that they are less likely now to choose marriage for economic security and are more able to terminate an unhappy marriage through divorce. Through economic modernization and population pressures, there are fewer traditional incentives for women to bear children. With effective and available birth control, women can control their fertility. Two major traditional reasons for women to marry—economic security and children—may be less salient for young women today. Companionship and love are increasingly cited by both sexes as reasons to marry (Duncan & Duncan, 1978; Roper Organization, 1980).

With less emphasis on biological motherhood, women can plan various futures: remaining single and/or childless; increased postsecondary education; entrance into professional careers; entrance into skilled trades; relatively permanent financial contributions to a dual-income marriage; and more flexible schedules of paid work and childbearing. Indicators of these different lifestyles are found in changing employment, education, marriage, divorce, and fertility rates, as well as in changes in attitudes about gender behavior. With increased labor-force participation among women, fewer children, and more options open to women, the balance of power among spouses is probably becoming more ideologically and empirically egalitarian. The increased salience of the norm of conjugal companionship implies that spouses should be friends, and friendship is a relationship that encourages conjugal equality and partnership.

Changes among male roles have been less dramatic. Of course, both men and women are marrying less, having fewer children, and divorcing more often. The retirement age among men has dropped, and this factor may, as some adult socialization theorists suggest, give men more opportunities to explore their "feminine" side of feelings and sensitivities. Nevertheless, the changes in education and employment patterns have not been as great nor as far-reaching among men as among women in the recent past.

Contrary to current folklore, men have not seemed to increasingly turn to more participation in family life. The value of family life to young men, although high, is less than it was a few decades ago, and a similar decline in the "value of the family" has occurred among young women. Men take an active role in rearing children, particularly in expressive play rather than routine care. Because family researchers have "discovered" fatherhood relatively recently, there are not yet any indicators suggesting that men have expanded their role as fathers over past participation. Housework is still highly gender-segregated. Despite a few publicized ''househusbands,'' men do little housework. If the roles of men change relatively little, limits exist on how much relational change can occur within the (two-spouse) family.

Limits on relational changes between the sexes within and outside the family may partly explain the notable and yet limited changes in the gender socialization of children. Although less gender segregation in socialization exists now, children are still raised with gender-stereotyped toys, chores, media, and career expectations. Girls are still treated as though they were physically fragile; boys are still treated as more creative and valuable. The documentation for these phenomena is most thorough in studies of teachers and the media; however, given the interconnectedness of societal institutions and patterns, parents and other socialization agents differentiate as well. Children learn gender stereotypes and status differences between the sexes at early ages, and girls and women continue to deprecate themselves relative to boys and men.

Indeed, perhaps greater changes in gender socialization have occurred among adults than among children in recent years. Marriage, divorce, cohabitation, employment, and children all occupy large blocks of an adult's gender identity. With fewer children, and thus less time spent in child rearing, the components of an adult's socially defined femininity or masculinity are certain to have undergone change. These changes in gender orientation and adoption are very relevant to life within families.

How the socialization of adults into gender roles proceeds is a topic that deserves much additional research. Major approaches to childhood gender socialization (direct training, modeling, identification, and cognitive development) have several limitations in explanatory power for children, let alone adults. Although components of each of these approaches have utility in explaining adult gender socialization, the already-identified drawbacks in these perspectives caution us not to apply them without further thought. To know more about adult socialization, we still need more knowledge about gender roles. In particular, I believe that we need to know far more than we currently do about men's familial roles.

Men in surveys often tell social scientists that the family is the most important thing in their lives. The observational and experimental studies cited here indicate that men enjoy and put time into parenthood. Studies of children and adolescents suggest that fathers play an important part in the acquisition of gender identity and gender-typed behavior. These kernels of information are the tip of the iceberg in our knowledge about men's familial roles. There are many more questions awaiting through empirical research. For example, how do men's feelings about family life compare with women's? What kinds of similarities and differences exist between women and men in their expectations about spouses and children? What kinds of social and psychological characteristics differentiate men who are very involved in parenthood from men who are less involved: What kinds of situations or characteristics make men more or less involved in domestic labor? What kinds of models influence a man's orientation toward the roles of husband and father?

Research about men and the family is just one subset of the unexplored and underexplored subjects pertaining to gender roles and family life. Throughout this chapter, other potential research has been suggested. The study of social gender has grown so much since 1960 that these and other research questions yet unasked are likely to receive at least preliminary answers in the years ahead.

Meanwhile, it is wise to remember that changes in gender roles, like other types of social change, do not proceed in tidy, linear progressions. After two decades of intense debate in the mid-twentieth century about the social meanings of being male or female, many groups are concerned about gender-role changes. The Equal Rights Amendment, sent to the states for ratification in 1972, failed a few states short of ratification in 1982. Laws on legal abortion are being challenged; some religious and civil groups fear that the ''erosion'' of the ''traditional family'' has damaged public order; government programs begun to help some widowed or divorced women have been dismantled; and other programs designed to lessen gender typing in schools no longer receive government funding. Some demographers (e.g., Easterlin, 1973, 1979; Heer & Grossbard-Shectman, 1981) have predicted an increase in fertility and a return to single-earner couples. An improved labor market has been predicted by these demographers when the ''birth-dearth'' babies born during the late 1960s and the 1970s reach maturity. Such an improved labor market, they suggest, would lessen the necessity for both spouses to seek paid employment, and wives would leave the labor market to raise the increased numbers of children such prosperity would make possible. Active feminists may thus seem as quaint in a decade or so as the suffragists of the early twentieth century appeared to many during the ''togetherness era'' of the 1950s.

Will we return to the patterns of gender and the family that have been portrayed as characteristic of the late eighteenth through the mid-twentieth centuries? Personally, I doubt it. Professionally, I intend to keep a close eye on developments in gender roles and family life. I suspect that changes in research related to social gender and the family will more than fill a chapter in the next edition of the *Handbook of Marriage and the Family*.

ACKNOWLEDGMENTS

I appreciate comments by Candace West, Ronald Pavalko and an anonymous reviewer on earlier drafts of this chapter. Mary Mathis provided invaluable assistance on compiling references.

References

American Council of Education. *The American Freshman: National Norms for Fall 1972.* ACE Research Reports, 7, 5. Washington, D.C.: Author, 1972.

Aneshensel, C. S., & Rosen, B. C. Domestic roles and sex differences in occupational expectations. *Journal of Marriage and the Family,* 1980, *42*(1), 121–131.

Aronoff, J., & Crano, W. A Re-examination of the cross-cultural principles of task segregation and sex role differentiation in the family. *American Sociological Review,* 1975, *40,* 12–20.

Astin, A. W. *Four critical years: Effects of college on beliefs, attitudes, and knowledge.* San Francisco: Jossey-Bass, 1977.

Astin, A. W., King, M. R., & Richardson, G. T. *The American freshman: National norms for fall 1977.* Los Angeles: Graduate School of Education, University of California, 1977.

Bandura, A., & Walters, R. H. *Social learning and personality development.* New York: Holt, Rinehart & Winston, 1963.

Barash, D. P. *Sociobiology and behavior.* New York: Elsevier, 1977.

Bardwick, J. M. *Psychology of women: A study of biocultural conflicts.* New York: Harper & Row, 1971.

Bardwick, J. M. *In transitions: How feminism, sexual liberation, and the search for self-fulfillment have altered America.* New York: Holt, Rinehart & Winston, 1979.

Barry, H., Bacon, M. K., & Child, E. L. A cross-cultural survey of some sex differences in socialization. *Journal of Abnormal Social Psychology,* 1957, *55,* 327–332.

Barry, R. J. Stereotyping of sex roles in preschoolers in relation to age, family structure, and parental sexism. *Sex Roles,* 1980, *6*(6), 795–806.

Baruch, G. K. Girls who perceive themselves as competent: Some antecedents and correlates. *Psychology of Women Quarterly,* 1976 (Fall), 38–49.

Bayer, A. E., & Dutton, J. E. Trends in attitudes on political, social, and collegiate issues among college students: Mid-1960s to mid-1970s. *Journal of Higher Education,* 1976, *47*(2), 159–171.

Belotti, E. G. *What are little girls made of? The roots of feminine stereotypes.* New York: Schocken Books, 1976.

Bem, S. L. Sex role adaptability: One consequence of psychological androgyny. *Journal of Personality and Social Psychology,* 1975, *31,* 634–643.

Bem, S., & Lenney, E. Sex typing and the avoidance of cross-sex behavior. *Journal of Personality and Social Psychology,* 1976, *33,* 48–54.

Berk, S. F., & Shih, A. Contributions to household labor: Comparing wives' and husbands' reports. In S. F. Berk (Ed.), *Women and household labor.* Beverly Hills, Calif.: Sage, 1980.

Bernard, J. *The future of marriage.* New York: World, 1972.

Bielby, D. D. V. Career sex-atypicality and career involvement of college educated women: Baseline evidence from the 1960s. *Sociology of Education,* 1978, *51,* 7–28.

Booth, A., & Edwards, J. N. Fathers: The invisible parent. *Sex Roles,* 1980, *6*(3), 445–456.

Boserup, E., *Women's role in economic development.* New York: St. Martin's Press, 1970.

Broverman, I. K., Broverman, D. M., Clarkson, F. E., Rosenkrantz, P. S., & Vogel, S. R. Sex-role stereotypes and clinical judgments of mental health. *Journal of Consulting and Clinical Psychology,* 1970, *34*(1), 1–7.

Broverman, I. K., Vogel, S., Broverman, D. M., Clarkson, F. E., & Rosenkrantz, P. S. Sex-role stereotypes: A current appraisal. *Journal of Social Issues,* 1972, *28,* 59–78.

Chodorow, N. Family structure and feminine personality. In M. Z. Rosaldo & L. Lamphere (Eds.), *Women, culture and society.* Stanford, Calif.: Stanford University Press, 1974.

Chodorow, N. *The reproduction of mothering.* Paper presented at the annual meeting of the American Sociological Association, San Francisco, 1975.

Clark, R. A., Nye, F. I., & Gecas, V. Work involvement and marital role performance. *Journal of Marriage and the Family,* 1978, *40*(February), 9–21.

Conner, J. M., & Serbin, L. A. Children's responses to stories with male and female characters. *Sex Roles,* 1978, *4*(5),637–645.

Constantinople, A. Sex role acquisition: In search of the elephant. *Sex Roles,* 1979, *5*(2), 121–133.

Crano, W. D., & Aronoff, J. A cross-cultural study of expressive and instrumental role complementarity in the family. *American Sociological Review,* 1978, *43*(4), 463–471.

David, D. S., & Brannon R. (Eds.). *The forty-nine percent majority: The male sex role.* Reading, Mass.: Addison-Welsey, 1976.

Davidson, L., & Gordon, L. K. *The sociology of gender.* Chicago: Rand McNally, 1979.

Deaux, K. *The behavior of women and men.* Monterey, Calif.: Brooks/Cole, 1976.

Dohrenwend, B. P., & Dohrenwend, B. S. Sex differences and psychiatric disorders. *American Journal of Sociology,* 1976, *81*(6), 1147–1454.

Duncan, B., & Duncan, O. D. *Sex typing and social roles: A research report.* New York: Academic Press, 1978.

Dweck, C. S., Goetz, T. E., & Strauss, N. L. Sex differences in learned helplessness: IV. *Journal of Personality and Social Psychology,* 1980, *38*(3), 441–452.

Easterlin, R. A. Relative economic status and the American fertility swing. In E. B. Sheldon (Ed.), *Family economic behavior.* Philadelphia: J. B. Lippincott. 1973.

Easterlin, R. A., Wachter, M. L., & Wachter, S. M. The coming upswing in fertility. *American Demographics,* 1979 (February), 12–15.

Eder, D., & Hallinan, M. Sex differences in children's friendships. *American Sociological Review,* 1978, *43,* 237–250.

Ehrhardt, A. A. Prenatal androgenization and human psychosexual behavior. In J. Money & H. Musaph (Eds.), *Handbook of sexology, II: Genetics, hormones and behavior.* New York: Elsevier, 1977.

Erikson, E. H. (Ed.). *Adulthood.* New York: W. W. Norton, 1978.

Farley, J., Brewer, J., & Fine, S. W. Women's values changing faster than men's? *Sociology of Education,* 1977, *50,* 151.

Featherman, D. L., & Hauser, R. M. Sexual inequalities and socioeconomic achievement in the U.S., 1962–1973. *American Sociological Review,* 1976, *41,* 462–483.

Fernberger, S. W. Persistence of stereotypes concerning sex differences. *Journal of Abnormal and Social Psychology,* 1948, *43,* 97–101.

Ferree, M. M. A woman for president? Changing responses: 1958–1972. *The Public Opinion Quarterly,* 1974, *38*(3), 390–399.

Fox, B. *Sex role stereotyping by school teachers: Determinants from teacher's current family roles.* Unpublished doctoral dissertation, University of Michigan, 1975.

Freud, S. *Dora: An analysis of a case of hysteria.* New York: Collier Books, 1963.

Freud, S. Woman as castrated man. *New introductory lectures on psychoanalysis.* New York: W. W. Norton, 1965.

Frieze, I. H., & Ramsey, S. J. Nonverbal maintenance of traditional sex roles. *Journal of Social Issues,* 1976, *32*(3), 133–141.

Frueh, T., & McGhee, P. E. Traditional sex role development and amount of time spent watching television. *Developmental Psychology,* 1975, *11,* 109.

Gallup, G. *Women in America: March 1976 (The Gallup opinion poll,* Report 128). Princeton: Gallup International, 1976.

Giele, J. Z. *Women and the future: Changing sex roles in modern America,* New York: Free Press, 1978.

Glick, P. C. A demographer looks at American families. *Journal of Marriage and the Family,* 1975, *37,* 15–26.

Goldberg, S. *The inevitability of patriarchy*. New York: William Morrow, 1974.

Goleman, D. Special abilities of the sexes: Do they begin in the brain? *Psychology Today*, 1978 (November), 48–59.

Gove, W. R., & Tudor, J. F. Adult sex roles and mental illness. *American Journal of Sociology*, 1973, *78*(4), 812–935.

Gross, E. Plus ça change . . . ? The sexual structure of occupations over time. *Social Problems*, 1968, *16*, 198–208.

Hareven, T. K. The last stage: Historical adulthood and old age. In E. H. Erikson (Ed.), *Adulthood*. New York: W. W. Norton, 1978.

Harlow, H. F. The heterosexual affectional system in monkeys. *American Psychologist*, 1962, *17*, 1–9.

Harrison, J. Warning: The male sex role may be dangerous to your health. *The Journal of Social Issues*, 1978, *34*, 65–86.

Hartley, R. E. Sex-role pressures and socialization of the male child. *Psychological Reports*, 1959, *5*, 457–468.

Haynes, S. G., & Feinleib, M. Women, work, and coronary heart disease: Prospective findings from the Framingham heart study. *American Journal of Public Health*, 1980, *70*(2), 133–141.

Heer, D. M., & Grossbard-Shechtman, A. The impact of the female marriage squeeze and the contraceptive revolution on sex roles and the women's liberation movement in the United States, 1960–1975. *Journal of Marriage and the Family*, 1981, *43*(1), 49–65.

Heilbrun, A. B., Jr. Identification with the father and sex-role development of the daughter. *The Family Coordinator*, 1976, *25*(4), 411–416.

Helmreich, R. L., Spence, J. T., & Holahan, C. K. Psychological androgyny and sex role flexibility: A test of two hypotheses. *Journal of Personality and Social Psychology*, 1979, *37*(10), 1631–1644.

Henley, N. M. *Body politics: Power, sex and nonverbal communication*. Englewood Cliffs, N.J.: Prentice-Hall, 1977.

Hennig, M., & Jardim, A. *The managerial woman*. Garden City, N.Y.: Anchor Press/Doubleday, 1977.

Hesselbart, S. A comparison of attitudes toward women and attitudes toward blacks in a southern city. *Sociological Symposium*, 1976, *17*(Fall), 45–68.

Hesselbart, S. *Some underemphasized issues about men, women and work*. Paper presented at the annual meeting of the American Sociological Assocation, San Francisco, September 1978.

Hetherington, E. M. A developmental study of the effect of sex of the dominant parent on sex-role preference, identification, and imitation in children. *Journal of Personality Social Psychology*, 1965, *2*, 188–194.

Hochschild, A. A review of sex role research. *American Journal of Sociology*, 1973, *78*(4), 1011–1029.

Hoffman, L. W., & Manis, J. D. The value of children in the United States: A new approach to the study of fertility. *Journal of Marriage and the Family*, 1979, *41*(3), 583–596.

Hoffman, L. W., & Nye, F. I. *Working mothers*. San Francisco: Jossey-Bass, 1974.

Hoge, D. R. Changes in college students' value patterns in the 1950s, 1960s, and 1970s. *Sociology of Education*, 1976, *49*(2), 155–163.

Hokanson, J. E. Psychophysiological evaluation of the catharsis hypothesis. In E. I. Hokanson & J. E. Hokanson (Eds.), *The dynamics of aggression: Individual, group, and international analyses*. New York: Harper & Row, 1970.

Howe, F. *Seven years later: Women's studies programs in 1976*. Washington, D.C.: National Advisory Council on Women's Educational Programs, 1977.

Huber, J. Toward a socio-technical theory of the women's movement. *Social Problems*, 1976, *23*, 371–388.

Huber, J., Rexroat, C., & Spitze, G. A crucible of opinion on women's status: ERA in Illinois. *Social Forces*, 1978, *57*(2), 549–565.

Ickes, W., & Barnes, R. D. Boys and girls together—and alienated: On enacting stereotyped sex roles in mixed-sex dyads. *Journal of Personality and Social Psychology*, 1978, *36*, 669–683.

Institute of Life Insurance. *Youth 1974; Finance related attitudes*. New York: Institute of Life Insurance Research Services, 1974.

Jennings, J., Geis, F. L., & Brown, V. Influence of television commercials on women's self-confidence and independent judgment. *Journals of Personality and Social Psychology*, 1980, *38*(2), 203–210.

Joffe, C. Sex role socialization and the nursery school or as the twig is bent. *Journal of Marriage and the Family*, 1971, *33*, 467–476.

Kagan, J., & Lemkin, J. The child's differential perception of parental attributes. *Journal of Abnormal Social Psychology*, 1960, *61*, 440–447.

Kanter, R. *Men and women of the corporation*. New York: Basic Books, 1977.

Katz, P. A. The development of female identity. *Sex Roles*, 1979, *5*(2), 155–178.

Knopp, S. Sexism in the pictures of children's readers: East and West Germany compared. *Sex Roles*, 1980, *6*(2), 189–205.

Kohlberg, L. A cognitive-developmental analysis of children's sex-role concepts and attitudes. In E. E. Maccoby (Ed.), *The development of sex differences*. Stanford, Calif.: Stanford University Press, 1966.

Komarovsky, M. *Dilemmas of masculinity*. New York: W. W. Norton, 1976.

Kreps, J., & Clark, R. *Sex, age, and work: The changing composition of the labor force*. Baltimore: Johns Hopkins University Press, 1975.

Kuhn, D., & Nash, S. *Sex-role concepts of two- and three-year-olds*. Paper presented at the Western Psychological Association Convention, Los Angeles, April 1976.

Kutner, N. G., & Levinson, R. M. The toy salesperson: A voice for change in sex-role stereotypes. *Sex Roles*, 1978, *4*(1), 1–7.

Lamb, M. E., & Lamb, J. E. The nature and importance of the father-infant relationship. *The Family Coordinator*, 1976, *25*(4), 379–385.

Lever, J. Sex differences in the complexity of children's play and games. *American Sociological Review*, 1978, *43*(4), 471–483.

Levinson, D., Darrow, C., Levinson, M., Klein, E., & McKee, B. *The seasons of a man's life*. New York: Ballantine Books, 1978.

Lewis, M., & Weinraub, M. Origins of early sex-role development. *Sex Roles*, 1979, *5*(2), 135–153.

Loo, C., & Wenar, C. Activity level and motor inhibition: Their relationship to intelligence test performance in normal children. *Child Development*, 1971, *42*, 967–971.

Lott, B. Sex-role ideology and children's drawings: Does the jack-o-lantern smile or scare? *Sex Roles*, 1979, *5*(1), 93–98.

Lott, B. Behavioral concordance with sex role ideology related to play areas, creativity, and parental sex typing of children. *Journal of Personality and Social Psychology*, 1978, *36*, 1087–1100.

Lueptow, L. B. Parental status and influence and the achievement orientations of high school seniors. *Sociology of Education*, 1975, *48*(1), 91–110.

Lueptow, L. B. Sex-typing and change in the occupational choices of high school seniors: 1964–1975. *Sociology of Education*, 1981, *54*(1), 16–24.

Lynn, D. B. Father and sex-role development. *The Family Coordinator*, 1976, *25*, 403–428.

Maccoby, E. E., & Jacklin, C. N. *The psychology of sex differences*. Stanford, Calif.: Stanford University Press, 1974.

Mackey, W. C., & Day, R. D. Some indicators of fathering behaviors in the United States: A crosscultural examination of adult male-child interaction. *Journal of Marriage and the Family*, 1979, *41*(2), 287–299.

Maklan, D. M. How blue-collar workers on 4-day work weeks use their time. *Monthly Labor Review*, 1977 (August), 18–26.

Manley, R. O. Parental warmth and hostility as related to sex differences in children's achievement orientation. *Psychology of Women Quarterly*, 1977, *1*(3), 229–246.

Marini, M. M. Sex differences in the determination of adolescent aspirations: A review of research. *Sex Roles*, 1978, *4*(5), 723–753.

Mason, K. O., & Bumpass, L. L. U.S. women's sex-role ideology, 1970. *American Journal of Sociology,* 1975, *80,* 1212–1219.

Mason, K. O., Czajka, J. L., & Arber, S. Change in U.S. women's sex-role attitudes, 1964–1974. *American Sociological Review,* 1976, *41,* 573–596.

McArthur, L. Z., & Eisen, S. V. Television and sex role stereotyping. *Journal of Applied Social Psychology,* 1976, *6*(4), 329–351.

McDonald, G. W. Family power: Reflection and direction. *Pacific Sociological Review,* 1977, *20*(4), 607–621.

McDonald, G. W. Parental power and adolescents; parental identification: A reexamination. *Journal of Marriage and the Family,* 1980, *42*(2), 289–296.

McGhee, P. E., & Frueh, T. Television viewing and the learning of sex-role stereotypes. *Sex Roles,* 1980, *6*(2), 179–188.

McKee, J. P., & Sherriffs, A. C. The differential evaluation of males and females. *Journal of Personality,* 1957, *25,* 356–371.

McLaughlin, S. D. Occupational sex identification and the assessment of males and female earnings inequality. *American Sociological Review,* 1978, *43*(6), 909–921.

Miller, J., Schooler, C., Kohn, M. L., & Miller, K. A. Women and work: The psychological effects of occupational conditions. *American Journal of Sociology,* 1979, *85*(1), 66–94.

Mischel, W. A social-learning view of sex differences in behavior. In E. E. Maccoby (Ed.), *The development of sex differences.* Stanford, Calif.: Stanford University Press, 1966.

Money, J.,& Tucker, P. *Sexual signatures: On being a man or a woman.* Boston: Little, Brown, 1975.

Morgan, C. S. Female and male attitudes toward life: Implications for theories of mental health. *Sex Roles,* 1980, *6*(3), 367–380.

Nye, F. I. *Role structure and analysis of the family.* Beverly Hills, Calif: Sage, 1976.

Oakley, A. *Woman's work: The housewife, past and present.* London: Penguin, 1974.

O'Bryant, S. L. Durrett. M. E., & Pennebaker, J. W. Sex differences in knowledge of occupational dimensions across four age levels. *Sex Roles,* 1980, *6*(3), 331–337.

Oppenheimer, V. K. Demographic influence on female employment and the status of women. *American Journal of Sociology,* 1973, *78,* 946–961.

Oppenheimer, V. K. The sociology of women's economic role in the family. *American Sociological Review,* 1977, *42*(June), 387–406.

Osmond, M., & Martin, P. Y. Sex and sexism: A comparison of male and female sex-role attitudes. *Journal of Marriage and the Family,* 1975, *37,* 744–758.

Parke, R. D., & Sawin, D. B. The father's role in infancy: A re-evaluation. *The Family Coordinator.* 1976, *25*(4), 365–371.

Parsons, T. Age and sex in the social structure of the United States. *American Sociological Review,* 1942, *7,* 604–616.

Parsons, T., & Bales, R. F. *Family, socialization and interaction process.* Glencoe, Ill.: Free Press, 1955.

Pedhazur, E. J., & Tetenbaum, T. J. Bem sex role inventory: A theoretical and methodological critique. *Journal of Personality and Social Psychology,* 1979, *37*(6), 996–1016.

Perry, D. G., & Bussey, K. The social learning theory of sex differences: Imitation is alive and well. *Journal of Personality and Social Psychology,* 1979, *37,* 1699–1712.

Perry, D. G., & Perry, L. C. Observational learning in children: Effects of sex model and subjects' sex role behavior. *Journal of Personality and Social Psychology,* 1975, *31,* 1083–1088.

Pleck, J. H. The work-family role system. *Social Problems,* 1977, *24,* 417–427.

Pleck, J. H. Men's family works: Three perspectives and some new data. *The Family Coordinator,* 1979, *28,* 481–488.

Pleck, J. H., & Lang, L. *Men's family role: Its nature and consequences.*

Wellesley, Mass.: Wellesley College Center for Research on Women, 1978.

Reinisch, J. M. Prenatal exposure to synthetic progestins increase potential for aggression in humans. *Science,* 1981 (13 March), *211*(4487), 1171–1173.

Rendina, I., & Dickerschild, J. D. Father involvement with first-born infants. *The Family Coordinator,* 1976, *25*(4), 373–378.

Rivers, C., Barnett, R., & Baruch, G. *Beyond sugar and spice: How women grow, learn, and thrive.* New York: G. P. Putnam's, 1979.

Robinson, J. P. Housework technology and household work. In S. F. Berk (Ed.), *Women and household labor.* Beverly Hills, Calif.: Sage, 1980.

Robinson, J. P., Yerby, J., Fieweger, & Somerick, N. Sex-role differences in time use. *Sex Roles,* 1977, *3*(5), 443–458.

Roper Organization. *The Virginia Slims American women's opinion poll, Vol. 3: A survey of the attitudes of women on marriage, divorce, the family, and America's changing sexual morality.* New York: Author, 1974.

Roper Organization. *The 1980 Virginia Slims American women's opinion poll: A survey of contemporary attitudes.* New York: Author, 1980.

Rosenkrantz, P., Vogel, S., Bee, H., Broverman, D. M., & Broverman, I. Sex-role stereotypes and self-concepts in college students. *Journal of Counsulting and Clinical Psychology,* 1968, *32*(3), 287–295.

Rubel, D. N., Croke, J. A., & Parsons, J. E. A field study of sex-role attitude change in college women. *Journal of Applied Social Psychology,* 1975, *5*(2), 110–117.

Rubin, J. Z., Provenzano, F. J., & Luria, Z. The eye of the beholder: Parents' views on sex of newborns. *American Journal of Orthopsychiatry,* 1974, *44,* 512–517.

Rypma, C. B. Biological bases of the paternal response. *The Family Coordinator,* 1976, *25*(4), 335–339.

St. Peter, S. Jack went up the hill . . . but where was Jill? *Psychology of Women Quarterly,* 1979, *4*(2), 256–260.

Schein, V. E. Relationships between sex role sterotypes and requisite management characteristics among female managers. *Journal of Applied Psychology,* 1975, *60,* 340–344.

Sears, P. S., & Feldman, D. H. Teacher interactions with boys and girls. *National Elementary Principal,* 1966, *46,* 30–35.

Serbin, L. A., O'Leary, K. D., Kent, R. N., & Tonick, I. J. A comparison of teacher response to the preacademic and problem behavior of boys and girls. *Child Development,* 1973, *44,* 796–804.

Serbin, L. A., Connor, J. M., & Citron, C. C. Environmental control of independent and dependent behaviors in preschool girls and boys: A model for early independence training. *Sex Roles,* 1978, *1*(6), 867–875.

Sidorowicz, L. S., & Lunney, G. S. Baby x revisited. *Sex Roles,* 1980, *6*(1), 67–73.

Silvern, L. E. Children's sex-role preferences: Stronger among girls than boys. *Sex Roles,* 1977, *3*(2), 159–171.

Simmons, R. G., Blyth, D. A., Van Cleave, E. F., & Bush, D. M. Entry into early adolescence: The impact of school structure, puberty, and early dating on self-esteem. *American Sociological Review,* 1979, *44*(6), 948–967.

Smith, S. Age and sex differences in children's opinion concerning sex differences. *Journal of Genetic Psychology,* 1939, *54,* 17–25.

Snyder, D., & P. Hudis. Occupational income and the effects of minority competition and segregation: A reanalysis and some new evidence. *American Sociological Review,* 1976, *41* (April): 209–234.

Spaeth, J. L. Differences in the occupational achievement process between male female college graduates. *Sociology of Education,* 1977, *50,* 206–217.

Stephens, W. N. *The family in cross cultural perspective.* New York: Holt, Rinehart & Winston, 1963.

Sternglanz, S. H., & Lyberger-Ficek, S. Sex differences in student-teacher interactions in the college classroom. *Sex Roles*, 1977, *3*, 345–352.

Stockard, J., & Johnson, M. M. The social origins of male dominances. *Sex Roles*, 1979, *5*, 199–218.

Stockard, J., & Johnson, M. M. *Sex roles: Sex inequality and sex role development*. Englewood Cliffs, N.J.: Prentice-Hall, 1980.

Strasser, S. M. An enlarged human existence? Technology and household work in nineteenth-century America. In S. F. Berk (Ed.), *Women and household labor*. Beverly Hills, Calif.: Sage, 1980.

Tangri, S. S. Determinants of occupational role innovation among college women. *Journal of Social Issues*, 1972, *28*(2): 177–199.

Taylor, M. C. Race, sex, and the expression of sex-fulfilling prophecies in a laboratory teaching situation. *Journal of Personality and Social Psychology*, 1979, *37*, 897–912.

Thornton, A., & Freedman, D. S. Changes in the sex role attitudes of women, 1962–1977: Evidence from a panel study. *American Sociological Review*, 1979, *44*(5), 831–842.

Treiman, D. J., & Terrell, K. Sex and the process of status attainment: A comparison of working women and men. *American Sociological Review*, 1975, *40*, 174–200.

Tuchman, G. Women's depiction by the mass media. *Signs*, 1979, *4*(3), 528–542.

Tuchman, G., Daniels, A. K., & Benet, J. (Eds.). *Hearth and home: Images of women in the mass media*. New York: Oxford University Press, 1978.

Uhlenberg, P. R. A study of cohort life cycles: Cohorts of native-born Massachusetts women, 1830–1920. *Population Studies*, 1969, *23*, 407–420.

United Nations. *Demographic yearbook, 1973*. New York: United Nations, Department of Economic and Social Affairs, 1974.

U.S. Department of Commerce. *Statistical abstract of the United States: 1953*. Washington, D.C.: Bureau of the Census, 1953.

U.S. Department of Commerce. *Historical statistics of the United States: Colonial times to 1970, Part 1*. Washington, D.C.: Bureau of the Census, 1970.

U.S. Department of Commerce. *College plans of high school seniors: October, 1974*, Current Population Reports, Series P-20, No. 284. Washington, D.C.: Bureau of the Census, 1975.

U.S. Department of Commerce. *Social indicators 1976*. Washington, D.C.: Bureau of the Census, 1977.

U.S. Department of Commerce. *A statistical portrait of women in the United States: 1978*, Current Population Reports, Special Studies Series P-23, No: 100. Washington D.C.: Bureau of the Census, 1979.

U.S. Department of Commerce. *Statistical abstract of the United States 1979*. Washington, D.C.: Bureau of the Census, 1980.

U.S. Department of Commerce. *Statistical abstract of the United States, 1985*. Washington, D.C.: Bureau of the Census, 1984.

U.S. Department of Labor. *Educational level of labor force continues to rise*. (*News*: 82-276). Washington D.C.: Bureau of Labor Statistics, 1982.

U.S. Department of Labor. *Earnings of workers and their families*. (*News*: 84-35). Washington, D.C.: Bureau of Labor Statistics, 1984.

Vanek, J. Time spent in housework. *Scientific American*, 1974, *231*(5), 116–120.

Weitzman, L. J. *Sex role socialization: A focus on women*. Palo Alto, Calif.: Mayfield, 1979.

Weitzman, L. J., Eifler, D., Hokada, E., & Ross, C. Sex role socialization in picture books for pre-school children. *American Journal of Sociology*, 1972, *77*, 1125–1150.

West, C., & Zimmerman, D. H. Women's place in everyday talk: Reflections of parent-child interaction. *Social Problems*, 1977, *24*, 521–529.

Westoff, C. F. Some speculations on the future of marriage and fertility. *Family Planning Perspectives*, 1978, *10*, 79–83.

Whiting, B., & Edwards, C. A cross-cultural study of sex differences in the behavior of children aged three through eleven. *Journal of Social Psychology*, 1973, *91*, 171–188.

Will, J. A., Self, P. A., & Datan, N. Maternal behavior and perceived sex of infant. *American Journal of Orthopsychiatry*, 1976, *46*(1), 135–139.

Williamson, N. E. *Sons or daughters: A cross-cultural survey of parental preferences*. Beverly Hills: Sage, Calif.: 1976.

Wilson, E. O. *On human nature*. Cambridge, Mass.: Harvard University Press, 1978.

CHAPTER 21

Marriage, Family, and Fertility

Brent C. Miller

Introduction

The study of human fertility is centrally concerned with conception and childbearing, and with variables related to these events. Biological conditions that affect fecundity (the ability to bear children) are obviously important in understanding fertility, and technology plays a part through the invention and dissemination of devices and procedures that can regulate conception or birth. However, because the vast majority of people are biologically able to reproduce, and technology affects fertility only if it is used, the emphasis of this chapter is on social-cultural variables related to fertility. Social-cultural elements most strongly affect when and with whom sexual intercourse occurs and whether measures are taken to prevent conception or birth. Marriage and the family are major social-cultural elements, and especially in advanced societies, the social-cultural influences on human fertility are of overriding importance (Andorka, 1978).

Generally speaking, children have been conceived only by sexual intercourse between men and women.[1] Rarely or never, however, has random procreative intercourse been socially approved. Sexual relations that might result in pregnancy are regulated in virtually every society by some institutionalized pattern of marriage. In fact, marriage has sometimes been defined as the "socially accepted union of individuals in husband and wife roles *with the key function of legitimizing parenthood*"

(Reiss, 1980; p. 50, emphasis mine). Marriage has different meanings around the world, but in most societies, reproduction is considered a major reason for marrying, and childbearing is expected to follow marriage. In a few cultures, the tie between marriage and reproduction is so direct that separation or divorce are automatic if conception does not occur (Dozier, 1967). In other cultures, marriage was not even allowed (traditionally, at least) until after pregnancy occurred and fertility was proved (Malinowski, 1974; Mead, 1949). In advanced technological societies, the link between marriage and childbearing is less direct, but the normative expectations persist that married couples will have children and that unmarried individuals will not.

Selected Examples of Marriage, Family, and Fertility Patterns

There is an intriguing diversity of marriage, family, and fertility patterns. For example, in some Shipibo Indian villages of the Peruvian Amazon, sexual intercourse begins shortly after the first menstruation, marriage occurs early and is virtually universal (14 is the average age at marriage), and the first birth typically occurs during the fifteenth year (Hern, 1977). Completed fertility of women over age 49 ranges from about 7.5 to 10 children.[2] With 96% of the females 15 and older having experienced at least one live birth, the women are remarkably fecund. Other important elements in their high fertility are the early and nearly universal marriage, lack of any effective contraception, and the consequent early and prolonged childbearing.

Among the !Kung hunter-gatherers of the Kalahari Desert, menarche and marriage also occur almost simultaneously, but not until about age 15 or 16, and the first child is typically born when the mother is between 19 and 20 (May, 1978). Children are breast-fed for three to four years, and apparently because of unusually effective lactational amenorrhea (ovulation prevented by breast feeding), the completed family size is about five children

---

[1] For the first time in history, there are now unquestionable exceptions. At this writing, several infants have been delivered in the conventional way after being conceived *in vitro* (outside the mother's body) and reimplanted in the mother's uterus. It has been medically possible for a somewhat longer time to achieve conception by artificial insemination (manual insertion of semen into the vagina). More dubious accounts of conception without intimate sexual relations have been around for a long time, such as the "Case of the Miraculous Bullet" (1971). In this case, a young woman ostensibly became pregnant after being struck in the abdomen by a bullet that had first passed through the scrotum of a young Civil War soldier who was skirmishing nearby.

[2] The completed fertility figure of 7.5 is probably a low estimate because Hern (1977) reported that problems of remembering stillbirths and early infant deaths were evident.

Brent C. Miller • Department of Family and Human Development, Utah State University, Logan, UT 84322-2905.

(Howell, 1976; May, 1978). This relatively low fertility (compared to that of the Shipibos of the Amazon) is probably due to later ages at menarche, marriage, and first birth, longer birth intervals, and earlier menopause.

Among North American Hutterites, an Anabaptist sect living primarily in the United States and Canada, menarche occurs at about age 13, but marriage and sexual intercourse are culturally postponed until the early 20s. Although not occurring early, marriage is virtually universal and is viewed as being primarily for the purpose of "multiplying and replenishing the earth." Because no form of birth control is used and breast feeding as it is practiced has limited effectiveness in suppressing ovulation, completed fertility averages between 10 and 11 children. Except for the cultural delay of marriage and childbearing, the Hutterites are thought to be near the limits of "natural fertility," or the level of fertility that would be experienced if all women lived in stable marriages throughout their childbearing years and no forms of contraception were used.

Finally, in an advanced society like the United States, marriage occurs later and it is usually less universal and less stable than in primitive cultures or developing countries. Women in advanced societies are biologically similar to the prolific Hutterites—they reach menarche at about age 13 and menopause around age 50—but between these biological markers when menstruation begins and ends, only two or three children are born on the average. Most of the sexually active childbearing years are devoted to contraception, abortion, or sterilization.

The last three of these remarkably different marriage, family, and fertility patterns are portrayed in Figure 1. Along the horizontal lines, the timing and duration of biological, social-cultural, and technological fertility experiences are indicated. The black rectangles represent full-term pregnancies resulting in 5, 11, and 2 children, respectively, in !Kung, Hutterite, and advanced societies.

Basic Fertility Concepts

A number of fundamental concepts are important in understanding fertility and its relation to marriage and family patterns. Basic measures and rates are essential tools for describing what has happened and is happening to fertility. Fertility rates are especially useful because they are, by definition, the number of births per unit of the population; rates make it possible to compare countries with different population bases, and time periods during which the population has changed.

The most basic and widely used fertility measure is the *crude birth rate,* that is, the number of live births per 1,000 population in a given year. It is a rough or crude measure of fertility because the number of births is related to everyone in the population, including children, men, and older women who are not able to bear children. Crude birth-rate data are widely available throughout the world,

but they can be greatly affected by the age and sex distribution in a society.

A more refined measure, which is not affected by the number or age of males and females, is the *general fertility rate.* It is the number of births per 1,000 women of childbearing ages, usually considered 15–44 or 15–49. A related but even more precise measure is the *age-specific fertility rate,* which is the number of births per 1,000 women in a particular childbearing age group. Age-specific fertility rates are usually given in five-year intervals, from 15–19 through 45–49. For example, studies of teenage childbearing often draw on the age-specific fertility rates of young women between the ages of 15 and 19.

Another common measure of fertility is the *total fertility rate.* Unlike the other rates described so far, the total fertility rate is somewhat hypothetical because it is the number of births that a group of 1,000 women *would have* by the end of their childbearing years if they experienced the age-specific rates observed during that particular year. The hypothetical total fertility rate is based on actual age-specific rates, and it expresses the level of childbearing in a particular year by all women of childbearing ages.

The *completed fertility rate* can be calculated only after women have finished having children. It is the number of births that *did occur* per 1,000 women during their reproductive years of life. Completed fertility rates describe past fertility experiences for a cohort of women who are the same age (usually age 49 or older). For this reason, completed fertility rates are sometimes called *cohort fertility rates.*

Any of the fertility rates mentioned above (except the crude birth rate) can be converted to *marital fertility rates.* That is, general, age-specific, or total fertility rates can be computed for married women only, to eliminate the influence of marital status (in other words, to disregard nonmarital births). This would be done if one was interested in either marital or nonmarital fertility and needed to separate them analytically. All of these basic fertility concepts and measures, and some less basic ones, are defined as concisely as possible in Table 1 for ease of reference.

Trends in Fertility

As with most other issues, an understanding of fertility is enhanced by knowing about the past. Fertility trends in the United States, in advanced societies in general, and in developing countries provide an important perspective for studying the relationship among marriage, family, and fertility.

Fertility Trends in the United States

The history of fertility in the United States can be conveniently divided into three time periods (Masnick and McFalls, 1976). The first and longest period was the sustained decline in fertility from the earliest available data

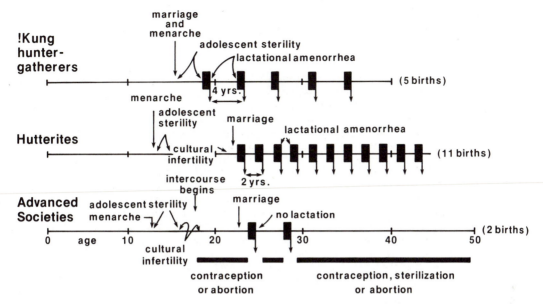

Figure 1. Selected examples of marriage and fertility patterns. The !Kung are thought to approximate primitive hunter-gatherer fertility, Hutterite reproduction is near the maximum level, and the advanced postindustrial pattern is characterized by deliberate control over fertility. (Source: May, 1978, p. 495.)

Table 1. Basic Fertility-Related Concepts

Fertility: Conception and bearing of children; the actual reproductive performance of an individual, couple, group, or population.

Fecundity: The biological potential, or physiological capacity of males and females to reproduce.

Natural fertility: The level of childbearing that would be achieved if all women lived in uninterrupted sexual unions during their childbearing years and no contraception was used (approximately 10 children per woman).

Crude birth rate: The number of births, or live births, per 1,000 population.

General fertility rate: The number of births per 1,000 women of childbearing age (15–44 or 15–49).

Age-specific fertility rate: The number of births by particular age group per 1,000 women in that age group (15–19, 20–24, etc.)

Total fertility rate: The number of children that a cohort of 1,000 women would bear if they went through their reproductive lives with the age-specific rates of fertility observed in the given year; a measure of the fertility of a hypothetical cohort that expresses the level of childbearing observed in a particular calendar year by women of all childbearing ages.

Completed fertility rate: The number of births that occurred per 1,000 women during their reproductive years of life (ages 15–49).

Marital fertility rates: General, age-specific, or total fertility rates computed only for married women, to eliminate the influence of marital status (disregards nonmarital births).

Gross reproduction rate: The average number of daughters that would be born to a woman during her lifetime if she passed through her childbearing years conforming to the age-specific fertility rates of a given year; analogous to the total fertility rate except that only daughters are counted.

Effective fertility ratio: The number of children under 5 years of age per 1,000 women of childbearing ages.

Number of children: The number of children born alive or the number of living children.

Expected number of children: The number of children actually anticipated by the end of the reproductive age.

Desired number of children: The number of children one would like to have.

Planned number of children: The number intended to be borne by those who plan the number of children.

Ideal number of children: The number that is considered ideal in the given culture or society.

through the Great Depression of the 1930s (see Figure 2). Although nationwide data for the early 1800s are not available, fragmentary evidence and demographic estimates suggest that the crude birth rate was about 50 births per 1,000 population (Moore & O'Connell, 1978). In recent years, crude birth rates in the United States have varied between 15 and 17 per 1,000 population annually. Birth rates among blacks have always been higher than among whites in the United States, but these racial fertility differences have greatly diminished over time. U.S. crude birth rates in the 1800s were higher than in Western European nations, according to Moore and O'Connell (1978), primarily because of the young age structure in the United States and the large proportion of women in the childbearing years.

The second major period in the fertility of the United States began in the middle 1930s with slight fertility increases that rapidly accelerated as World War II ended (see Figure 3). For more than a decade beginning in 1946, fertility rates increased each year. This postwar baby boom, as it has come to be known, lasted longer in the United States than in European countries. Fertility indicators in the United States began to fall off again in the late 1950s, and the historical long decline in the nation's fertility was resumed.

The United States is currently in the third period of its

fertility history, characterized initially by declining, and now by relatively stable but low, fertility rates (see Figure 4). Viewing these changes in context, Moore and O'Connell (1978, p. 4) stated:

From a historical perspective, the postwar baby boom appears as an aberration from the long-term decline in fertility in the United States, since the low fertility rates of the early 1970s are of a magnitude comparable to those recorded during the Great Depression. However, fertility rates for women over 35 are significantly lower now than they were during the 1930s.

Fertility Trends in Advanced Societies

Sharply declining fertility has characterized almost all advanced societies (with the exception of Ireland) in recent decades, and some countries now record more deaths than births. The more developed countries had an average crude birth rate of about 23 in 1950 as compared to 16 in 1980 (Mauldin, 1980). The average decline in crude birth rates among these countries has been almost one third (32.3%) over this period.

An overview of fertility in developed countries, and a persuasive argument about the links between future marriage and fertility patterns, has been provided by Westoff (1978a,b). Although being appropriately cautious about predicting future fertility, Westoff has presented a con-

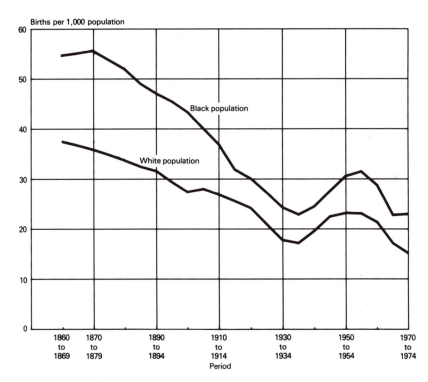

Figure 2. Crude birth rates of the white and black population in the United States: 10-year averages, 1860–1879, and 5-year averages, 1880–1884 to 1970–1974. (Source: Moore and O'Connell, 1978, p. 3.)

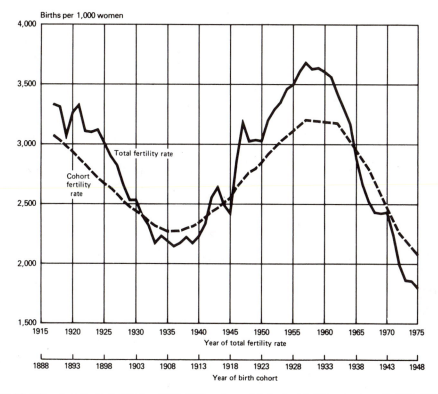

Figure 3. Total fertility rate in the United States, 1917–1975, and completed cohort fertility rate at age 49; 1888–1948. *Note:* rates are estimated from 1890 to 1925 and projected from 1926 to 1948. (Source: Moore and O'Connell, 1978, p. 6.)

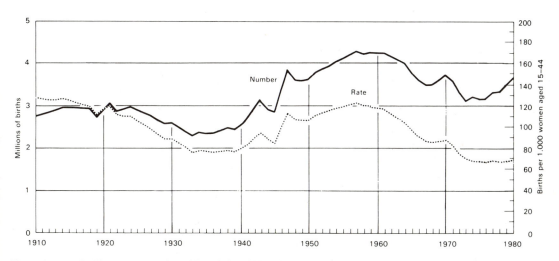

Figure 4. Total fertility rate and number of live births: 1970–1979. *Note:* Beginning 1959, trend lines are based on registered live births: trend lines for 1910 to 1959 are based on live births adjusted for underregistration. (Source: U.S. Bureau of the Census, 1980.)

vincing rationale for why most of the world's developed countries are approaching zero population growth.

Figure 5 shows which countries are experiencing more deaths than births already, and Westoff argued that most other industrialized nations are moving in the same direction. A key element he identified is "a change in the

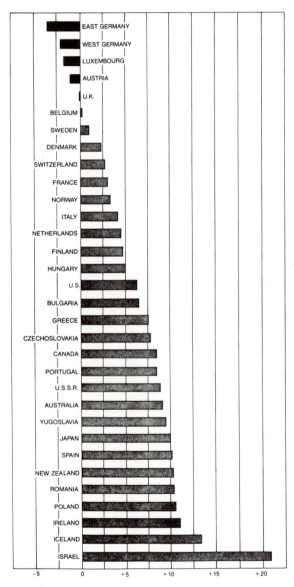

Figure 5. Rate of natural increase (per 1,000 population) for selected developed countries. The rate of natural increase (birth rate minus death rate) is below the zero-population-growth line in a few European countries, and it is approaching that level in most industrialized nations. The data are mostly for 1976; the U.S. figure is for 12 months ending in May 1978. (Source: Westoff, 1978a, p. 52.)

economic value of children, from a source of income in agrarian economies to a considerable drain on income in industrial and post industrial economies'' (Westoff, 1978a, p. 53). Further, he identified a number of pervasive social changes that are essentially irreversible, some of which have yet to run their full course:

The economic transformation of society has been accompanied by a decline in traditional and religious authority, the diffusion of an ethos of rationality and individualism, the universal education of both sexes, the increasing equality of women, the increasing survival of children, and emergence of a consumer-oriented culture that is increasingly aimed at maximizing personal gratification. When these changes are combined with the development and diffusion of sophisticated birth control technology, it is hardly surprising that the institutions of marriage and family show signs of change. (1978a, p. 53)

In addition to these very global outlines of change, Westoff specifically identified marriage and family trends that work against rising birth rates, particularly in the United States. For example, there has been a dramatic decline in the proportion of women in the United States who marry young, there is a clear trend toward unmarried couples living together, the divorce rate has made it apparent that marriage is less stable than was formerly the case, and remarriage has begun to decline (each of these issues will be discussed more thoroughly in later sections). Perhaps even more significant is the changing economic position of women; there is little doubt that women's employment and fertility are negatively related and that an increasing proportion of women will work in the future (Kupinsky, 1977). Other things being equal, the recent trends in marriage and reproductive behavior point toward fertility's remaining low or declining further in advanced societies.

Fertility Trends in Developing Countries

The population of the world has increased by 75% since 1950, from approximately 2.5 billion to 4.5 billion in 1980 (Mauldin, 1980). Changes in fertility in developing countries are especially important because of the large populations in these countries and the fact that they have proportionally higher fertility than more advanced societies. In 1950, approximately two thirds of the world's population lived in developing nations and one third in developed countries. The proportion living in developing nations had increased to approximately three quarters of the world's population (3.3 billion, or 74%) by 1980 (Mauldin, 1980).

Natural population increase occurs when there are more births than deaths. Historically, changes in the birth rates of developing countries have been relatively slight, but death rates plummeted around the world in the years following World War II. According to Mauldin (1978), mortality declined three to five times faster in the decades following World War II than before it. As a consequence, worldwide life expectancy increased from 40 years to more than 53 by 1975. These drastic declines in mortality and increased longevity, combined with nearly stable fertility, brought clearly into focus the spectre of a global population crisis.

Now, however, birth rates have also begun to fall off in the developing countries. The data have been summarized by Mauldin (1978, 1980) and Mauldin and Berelson (1978). These reports compare crude birth rates in 94 developing countries at several intervals between 1950 and 1975. The data show that fertility remained quite high in the majority of developing countries until about 1965, after which crude birth-rate declines were much more pronounced. These findings seem to be related to other data that show that fertility is relatively insensitive to socioeconomic conditions during early stages of societal development (Anker, 1978). The recent falling off of birth rates in developing countries is, perhaps, partially a reflection of the fact that "after middle levels of development fertility becomes fairly sensitive to socioeconomic conditions" (Anker, 1978, p. 68). Table 2 summarizes declines in crude birth rates by region (data for individual countries are presented in Mauldin, 1978, 1980, and Mauldin & Berelson, 1978).

Africa is the only region where crude birth rates remained high and showed little decline up to 1975. The countries in the African region that did show large declines were Egypt (17%), Mauritius (29%), and Tunisia (24%). In the Americas, there was a decline of 14% overall between 1965 and 1975. Countries experiencing more than a 25% decline included Barbados (31%) and Chile (29%). In Asia as a whole, crude birth rates declined by

only 2% between 1950 and 1965, but during the next decade, the crude birth rates declined by 17% and several countries declined by 30% or more (Hong Kong, 36%; South Korea, 32%; Singapore, 40%; Taiwan, 30%).

An important aspect of this decline is that the reductions in fertility have been most substantial in the largest developing countries. Table 3 shows that countries with more than 35 million population experienced approximately double the decline in crude birth rates observed in smaller developing countries.

Summary of Fertility Trends

In the United States and advanced societies generally, there has been an almost continuous decline in birth rates toward approximating death rates and reaching zero population growth. Several countries already experience more deaths than births, and some scholars project that most advanced societies will be having about equal numbers of births and deaths by the year 2000.

From a global perspective, however, population growth is still a critical issue. In developing countries, fertility levels have remained very high until recently; notable declines have occurred only in the last 15 years. With drastically lowered death rates, fertility rates remain high enough to cause rapid population growth in the developing countries and the world. These past and projected worldwide trends in birth, death, and natural increase are summarized in Figure 6.

Table 2. Crude Birth Rates and Crude Birth-Rate Declines in 94 Developing Countries, Selected Regions, 1950–1975[a]

Region	Crude birth rates				Crude birth-rate declines (in percentages)	
	1950–1955	1960	1965	1975	1950–1955 to 1965	1965–1975
Africa[b] (38 countries)	49	48	48	46	1	4
The Americas[c] (21 countries)	42	41	41	36	3	14
Asia and Pacific[d] (35 countries)	41	39	40	33	4	17
Total (94 countries)	42	40	41	35	4	15

[a]All figures are weighted by population of countries within regions. Source: Adapted from Table 1 in Mauldin (1978).

[b]*African countries* studied included Algeria, Angola, Burundi, Cameroon, Central African Republic, Chad, Congo, Dahomey/Benin, Egypt, Ethiopia, Ghana, Guinea, Ivory Coast, Kenya, Lesotho, Liberia, Libyan Arab Republic, Madagascar, Malawi, Mali, Mauritania, Mauritius, Morocco, Mozambique, Niger, Nigeria, Rwanda, Senegal, Sierra Leone, Somalia, Sudan, Tanzania, Togo, Tunisia, Uganda, Upper Volta, Zaire, and Zambia.

[c]*American countries* studied included Barbados, Bolivia, Brazil, Chile, Colombia, Costa Rica, Cuba, Dominican Republic, El Salvador, Guatemala, Haiti, Honduras, Jamaica, Mexico, Nicaragua, Panama, Paraguay, Peru, Trinidad and Tobago, and Venezuela.

[d]*Asian and Pacific countries* included were Afghanistan, Bangladesh, Bhutan, Burma, China, Fiji, Hong Kong, India, Indonesia, Iran, Iraq, Jordan, Khmer/Kampuchea, North Korea, South Korea, Kuwait, Laos, Lebanon, Malaysia, Mongolia, Nepal, Pakistan, Papua New Guinea, Philippines, Saudi Arabia, Singapore, Sri Lanka, Syrian Arab Republic, Taiwan, Thailand, Turkey, North Vietnam, South Vietnam, Yemen, and People's Democratic Republic of Yemen.

Table 3. Crude Birth-Rate (CBR) Declines, by Size of Population, Developing Countries, 1965–1975[a]

35 million or more		15–35 million		5–15 million		.5–5 million	
Country	Crude birth-rate decline (in percentages)	Country	Crude birth-rate decline (in percentages)	Country	Crude birth-rate decline (in percentages)	Country	Crude birth-rate decline (in percentages)
Bangladesh	2	Afghanistan	−2	Angola	4	Bhutan	3
Brazil	10	Algeria	4	Bolivia	1	Burundi	1
China	24	Burma	3	Cameroon	3	Cen. African Rep.	5
Egypt	17	Colombia	25	Chile	29	Chad	2
India	16	Ethiopia	2	Cuba	40	Congo	−2
Indonesia	13	Iran	2	Dominican Rep.	21	Costa Rica	29
Korea, South	32	Korea, North	5	Ecuador	0	Dahomey	3
Mexico	9	Morocco	2	Ghana	2	El Salvador	13
Nigeria	1	Peru	2	Guatemala	4	Fiji	22
Pakistan	1	Sudan	0	Iraq	0	Guinea	2
Philippines	19	Taiwan	30	Ivory Coast	1	Haiti	0
Thailand	23	Tanzania	5	Kenya	0	Honduras	7
Turkey	16	Vietnam, North	23	Khmer/Kampuchea	2	Hong Kong	36
		Vietnam, South	0	Madagascar	0	Jamaica	21
		Zaire	6	Malawi	5	Jordan	1
				Malaysia	26	Kuwait	5
				Mali	−1	Laos	5
				Mozambique	2	Lebanon	2
				Nepal	−1	Lesotho	−4
				Saudi Arabia	0	Liberia	0
				Senegal	0	Libya	−1
				Sri Lanka	18	Mauritania	0
				Syrian Arab Rep.	4	Mauritius	29
				Tunisia	24	Mongolia	9
				Uganda	−4	Nicaragua	7
				Upper Volta	1	Niger	1
				Venezuela	11	Panama	22
				Yemen	1	Papua New Guinea	5
				Zambia	−2	Paraguay	6
						Rwanda	0
						Sierra Leone	0
						Singapore	40
						Somalia	0
						Togo	2
						Trinidad and Tobago	29
						Yemen, P.D.R. of	3
Total weighted by							
Unity[b]	14		7		7		9
Population[c]	13		7		6		6

[a]Source: Mauldin (1978), p. 78.
[b]Each country is given a weight of 1.
[c]Changes in CBRs are weighted by the population of each country.

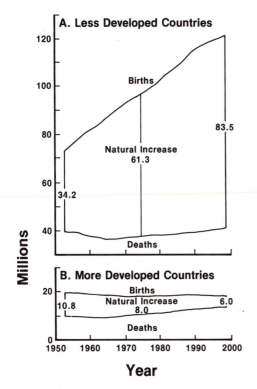

Figure 6. Average number of births, deaths, and population increase, 1950–2000 (United Nations median assumptions). (Source: Mauldin, 1980, p. 155.)

Linkages among Marriage, Family, and Fertility

There are various ways of conceptualizing how marriage, family, and fertility are intertwined (see, for example, the theoretical essays on family and fertility by Burr, 1973, and by Cogswell & Sussman, 1979). One of the earliest and most intensive studies of family and fertility was done in Puerto Rico by Hill, Stycos, and Back (1959). They reported a rank-order correlation of .9 between fertility rates and eight family types, which ranged from being rural consensual unions in which the husband had less than four years of education, to being urban legal unions in which the husband had more than four years of education. Equally high rank-order correlations were reported between fertility rates and the way families were internally structured, ranging from the type in which the wife remained at home under the rule of a strongly dominant husband who placed many prohibitions on her activities, to the type in which the wife worked outside the home, the husband was less dominant, and placed few prohibitions on her activities. These investigators summarized the results of this phase of their research as follows:

The factors which turned out to be most closely related to the dependent (fertility) variables involved family organization and

individual readiness for action. Communication and time of perception of problems of family size are by far the most important factors in predicting competence and success in fertility control. (Hill et al. p. 248)

Lineage or Family-of-Orientation Effects on Fertility

At a second level of conceptualization and study, there are lineage or family-of-orientation effects on fertility. Numerous studies have reported a positive relationship between number of siblings and number of children between number of siblings and number of children (Bumpass, 1975; Bumpass & Westoff, 1970; Duncan, Freedman, Coble, & Slesinger, 1965; George, Ebanks, Nobbe, & Anwar, 1976; Marshall & Cosby, 1977; Stokes & Johnson, 1977). Thornton (1980) critically reviewed and empirically assessed several mechanisms that could produce the relationship between family-of-origin parental characteristics and the fertility of the children. These include (1) family-of-origin socialization toward similar standards of living and economic consumption that appear to be related to childbearing (Easterlin, 1969, 1973; Thornton, 1978b); (2) within-family socialization toward similar aspirations, preferences, and desires about family size (Gustavus, 1973; Gustavus & Nam, 1970; Haskell & Handler, 1977; Marshall & Cosby, 1977; McLaughlin 1974; Paterson, 1972; Stokes & Johnson, 1977; Westoff & Potvin, 1967); (3) the transmission of parental knowledge or ignorance about contraception and its effective use (Westoff & Potvin, 1967); (4) children's attempts to re-create the role relationships that existed in their own families of orientation (Duncan et al., 1965); and (5) the biological transmission of varying fecundity through genetic mechanisms.

It should be apparent that macrosocial, economic, and cultural influences on fertility are often transmitted through the family. Religion, as another example, has been related to both desired family size and completed fertility, and religious affiliation is one of the cultural elements that shows the highest continuity from one generation to the next (Hill, 1971).[3]

Family Events as Intermediate Variables Affecting Fertility

At a third level of analysis, there are specific marital and family events that directly affect childbearing. For example, the age of marriage, the proportion who marry versus the proportion who remain single, the proportion who divorce, and the amount of time before remarriage

[3]Of course, initial ideas about ideal family size and fertility desires are modified by adolescent and adult experiences. The important point is that the family is a key link in shaping the social and psychological parameters that eventually become expressed in actual fertility behavior.

are all related to fertility because they reflect time spent in socially approved relationships for bearing children.

A useful model for examining the specific relationships between family and fertility was developed by Davis and Blake (1956) and adopted by Freedman (1975) in organizing his annotated bibliography on *The Sociology of Human Fertility*. The variables listed in Table 4 are conceptualized as "intermediate variables" that come between macrosocial organizations and norms, on the one hand, and fertility levels, on the other. Many of these variables, especially those in Group A affecting exposure to intercourse, are marriage and family characteristics that have clear and direct ties to fertility.

Age of Entering Sexual Unions. The younger people are when they become involved in sexual unions, the longer they will be exposed to intercourse and, other things being equal, the more children they are likely to have. Because entering a sexual union often means marriage or a marriagelike relationship, another way of expressing this generality is: The younger the age at marriage, the higher the fertility (Bumpass, 1969; Bumpass & Mburugu, 1977).

The age at first marriage reached a low point in the United States during the 1950s. Among those entering their 20s between 1955 and 1959, about 54% of both black and white women were married by age 20.5:

Moreover, by age 21.5, 45 percent of the White women and 61 percent of the Black women had borne at least one child. By way of contrast, women born from 1950 to 1954, who were 20 to 25 years old in 1975, were relatively much slower to enter marriage and motherhood. By age 20.5, only 45 percent of White women and 34 percent of Black women had married. As a result, a far

smaller proportion of these women had become mothers by age 21.5 (29 percent of White women and 34 percent of Black women) than the proportion among women in the 1935–39 cohort. (Moore & O'Connell, 1978, p. 13)

The fertility effects of age at first marriage and first birth carry through to be reflected in the total number of children born. In 1975, among women married long enough to show or project 20 years of marital experience, those who first married before age 19 averaged approximately one child more than those who married after age 21. Women who married between the ages of 19 and 21 had an average number of children intermediate between those who married younger and older (Moore & O'Connell, 1978).

These data supporting the inverse relationship between age of marriage and fertility are all the more salient because of recent evidence of widespread marriage postponement, especially in the United States (see Figure 7). Whereas the median age of first marriage among women has increased only gradually in recent decades, the percentage who have remained single through their early 20s has risen rapidly:

Fully 49 percent of the women 20 to 24 years of age in 1979 had not yet married for the first time—a striking increase of three-fourths since 1960 when only 28 percent of women in their early twenties had never married. The proportion of women remaining never married among those 25–29 approximately doubled between 1970 (10.5 percent) and 1979 (19.6 percent) after showing no change during the 1960's. (U.S. Bureau of the Census, 1980, p. 8)

Similar trends away from early marriage have been observed in developing countries. As shown in Table 5, the largest increase in the percentage of females never

---

Table 4. "Intermediate" Variables Related to Fertility[a]

A. Factors affecting exposure to intercourse (the "intercourse variables").
   1. Those governing the formation and dissolution of unions in the reproductive period.
      a. Age of entry into sexual unions.
      b. Permanent celibacy: Proportion of women never entering sexual unions.
      c. Amount of reproductive period spent after or between unions.
         (1) When unions are broken by divorce, separation, or desertion.
         (2) When unions are broken by death of husband.
   2. Those governing the exposure to intercourse within unions.
      a. Voluntary abstinence.
      b. Involuntary abstinence (from impotence, illness, unavoidable but temporary separations).
      c. Coital frequency (excluding periods of abstinence).
B. Factors affecting exposure to conception (the "conception variables").
   1. Fecundity or infecundity, as affected by involuntary causes.
   2. Use or nonuse of contraception.
      a. By mechanical or chemical means.
      b. By other means.
   3. Fecundity or infecundity, as affected by voluntary causes (sterilization, subincision, medical treatment, etc.).
C. Factors affecting gestation and successful parturition (the "gestation variables").
   1. Fetal mortality from involuntary causes.
   2. Fetal mortality from voluntary causes.

[a]Source: Davis and Blake (1956).

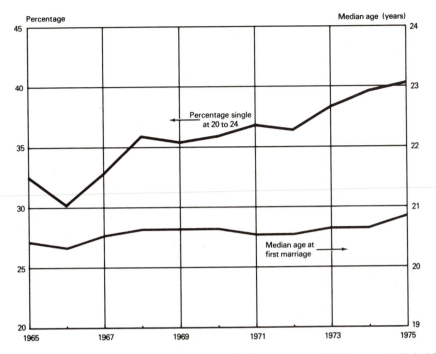

Figure 7. Median age of women at first marriage and percentage single among women 20–24 years old, United States, 1965–1975. (Source: Moore & O'Connell, 1978, p. 14.)

married at various ages is reported from regions where fertility has remained very high (e.g., Africa). Later marriages in these countries will, perhaps, eventually make some contribution to lowering the present high levels of fertility.

Westoff (1978b) tied both later marriage and increasing cohabitation into his argument that fertility will continue to decline in the United States and other developed countries. It is clear that there is an increasing proportion

of unmarried couples in the United States who live together. Between 1970 and 1979, the number of opposite-sex unmarried adults living together more than doubled, and most of this increase occurred among couples without children. Although unmarried-couple households with children present increased by 84 percent during the 1970s, the increase for those with no children rose by 200 percent.

Whether cohabitation is viewed as a postponement and

Table 5. Percentage of Females Aged 15–19 and 20–24 Never Married, Selected Developing Countries, by Region, around 1960 and 1970[a]

Region	Number of countries	Year 1960	Year 1970	Change Absolute	Change Percentages
Females aged 15–19					
Africa	7	55.6	69.2	13.5	24.3
The Americas	13	80.8	81.7	0.9	1.0
Asia and the Pacific	20	64.6	72.7	8.1	12.5
All regions	40	68.3	75.0	6.7	9.8
Females aged 20–24					
Africa	6	15.6	25.3	9.7	62.2
The Americas	13	42.6	47.4	4.8	11.4
Asia and the Pacific	20	24.2	32.9	8.7	35.1
All regions	39	30.1	37.7	7.6	25.2

[a]Source: Mauldin (1978), p. 81.

delaying of marriage or as a more basic change in the institution itself, Westoff (1978a) argued that cohabitation necessarily means lower fertility than marriage because it is a less stable relationship. In any case, it is clear that there is a trend in the United States toward increasing cohabitation and later marriage. These trends are also evident in various countries around the world, and they suggest that there will be lower fertility in the years ahead.

Permanent Celibacy and Polygamy. Those who do not marry or enter into marriagelike sexual unions during their lives are usually a very small percentage of a population. In most societies, marriage is a prerequisite for childbearing in the sense that children born out of marriage are regarded differently from "legitimate" children born to married parents. Consequently, the vast majority of childbearing occurs within marriage. The greater the incidence of celibacy in a population, the lower the fertility because of the social pressures against childbearing among those who are not married or who are at least not in a marriagelike relationship.

Some types of family structure are related to the proportion of the population that remains permanently celibate. Stem families are especially noted for having high rates of celibacy because older sons are likely to receive disproportionate inheritance, often leaving younger sons with fewer resources with which to enter marriage. It is not coincidental that countries with the stem family pattern also have low rates of fertility. There are large differences between the fertility of societies that have traditionally had a stem family (Ireland or Japan) and the fertility of countries with more universal marriage.

Goldstein (1976) pointed out that polyandry can operate to reduce fertility by creating surpluses of celibate women. In Himalayan villages in the Limi Valley (Nepal), the most common form of marriage when a family has more than one son is for two or more brothers to marry the same wife (fraternal polyandry). Polyandry does not seem to have any appreciable effect on the fertility of individual females; the average number of living children was 2.9 for monogamously married women and 2.7 for polyandrously married women. This lack of difference in the fertility of monogamous and polyandrous married women was also reported by Nag (1962) with respect to the Toda and the Jaunsari. However, aggregate fertility of the population is greatly reduced by this marriage practice. In the Limi Valley, approximately one third of the women of childbearing ages have never been married and are restricted from full participation in childbearing.[4] Such a high rate of celibacy created by

fraternal polyandry is apparently a cultural mechanism that evolved to preserve extremely limited family resources (primarily land and animals) and to pass them on intact to a single next-generation family (Goldstein, 1976). In any case, the rates of celibacy in the Limi Valley are even higher than in the much noted European industrial nations during and at the end of World War II. Among the women in Limi, nearly one third remain celibate as compared to 26.3% in Ireland in 1946, 20.9% in Sweden in 1945, and 20.1% in Switzerland in 1941 (Davis & Blake, 1956, p. 218).

The effects of polygyny (multiple wives married to the same man) on fertility are less clear-cut than the case of polyandry just described. Some have argued (Dorjahn, 1958) that polygyny reduces fertility. A possible mechanism for this lowering effect is that polygyny is closely associated with a prolonged postpartum sexual taboo (Lorimer, 1954; Whiting, 1964). However, as Hern (1977) observed:

Polygyny could have two effects; to lower the number of children per married woman by lengthening birth intervals, and to increase the proportion of women married. The former effect would be to decrease individual and overall fertility, and the latter would be to increase overall fertility. (p. 366)

Polygyny might then have the reverse effect of polyandry so far as celibacy is concerned. In societies where polygyny is permitted, virtually every woman of childbearing age is involved in a sexual union. In societies where polyandry is practiced and several men marry the same woman, there may be a surplus of women who never marry or bear children (Goldstein, 1976).

Family Extendedness and Fertility. Some analyses of fertility and family structures have specifically examined family extendedness versus nuclearity (Burch & Gendell, 1971; Davis, 1955; Davis & Blake, 1956; Lorimer, 1954; Nag, 1962, 1967; Ryder, 1976). The basic hypothesis has been that higher fertility occurs in extended families because of (1) the encouragement of early and nearly universal marriage; (2) the reduction of the parents' costs of childbearing and rearing because of the availability of joint economic resources and additional personnel for child care; and (3) the increased motivation of both husband and wife to reproduce through inducements of increased status and potentially increased economic and political positions vis-à-vis other extended families (Ryder, 1976, p. 93).

However, the extended-family–high-fertility link appears to have been developed more conceptually than empirically. According to Burch and Gendell (1971): "There is a striking contrast between the wide acceptance of the proposition that the extended family encourages high fertility and the scarcity of relevant empirical evidence" (p. 227). In fact, Ryder (1976) pointed out that empirical studies have failed to support the supposed relation between family extendedness and fertility. Some studies have found no relation at all, and others have found higher fertility in nuclear families (Freedman,

---

[4]Goldstein (1976) noted that some of the unmarried women in the Limi Valley were obviously part of sexual unions. Approximately half had one or more children. Even though not strongly disapproved, the fertility of unmarried women was limited as compared to that of married women, apparently because of extremely harsh economic conditions. The average fertility of all married women was reported as 3.3 children, whereas the fertility of unmarried women was 0.7 (Goldstein, 1976).

Takeshita, & Sun, 1964; Lui, 1967; Nag, 1967; Pakrasi & Malaker, 1967).

Ryder (1976) suggested that research on this issue had often been flawed by not taking into account the fluid, dynamic, developmental nature of family structure over the life cycle. Often, the cumulative fertility of ever-married women had been related to *current* family structure, but this kind of analysis is not sensitive to the fact that, in many societies, a young couple may start out in an extended-family residence and later move into their own nuclear household. Another common procedure has been to relate cumulative fertility to *initial* family structure. As Ryder (1976) pointed out, neither of these procedures is satisfactory because

The former presupposes that women have lived in only one form of family structure, or that if a woman has lived in other family structures, her previous experience had no effect on her fertility. The latter presupposes that future experiences will not alter fertility, which is related only to initial participation in one type of family structure. (p. 95)

Ryder proposed a more accurate method of calculating the level of fertility as affected by family structure, namely, attributing each birth to the form of family the mother lived in at the time of conception. This refined way of assessing the relationship was used on data collected during Ryder's field studies in Yucatán. Cumulative fertility measures of women aged 15–44 were calculated according to when and how long they had lived in nuclear and extended families. Based on age-specific fertility measures, women who lived in extended families throughout their reproductive years could expect 11.1 live births as compared to 8.9 births to women who lived in nuclear families. Thus, there appeared to be some support for the extended-family–higher-fertility hypothesis. However, when comparing only the women who had lived continuously in either extended or nuclear families (with no change in family structure) throughout their childbearing years, there were no differences in fertility (10.6 and 10.7, respectively). The fertility experience of women who did change family structure during their childbearing years seems to explain part of the difference in these figures. According to Ryder (1976),

These women who have transitional residence in different family structures (the majority of all women) have one or two children in rapid succession in an extended family. They move into a nuclear family where their fertility is higher than that of women wholly resident in an extended family, but lower than that of women wholly resident in a nuclear family. (p. 97)

Relatedly, Bebarta (1974) found that women in joint families in the state of Orissa, India, experienced slightly lower fertility than women in nuclear families (completed fertility of 5.11 compared to 5.45). But women belonging to a changing family type, compared to a stable or pure type, reported the highest completed fertility of all (6.67 children). This finding implies that the changes in traditional extended families associated with industrialization and modernization might temporarily increase fertility, at least in the initial stages of social change.

Marital Disruption and Fertility. When marriage is interrupted by separation, divorce, or death of a spouse during the reproductive years, lower fertility would seem to be a likely result. In fact, the data from U.S. samples generally support this thesis. Cohen and Sweet (1974) found that women who were widowed or divorced had slightly fewer children than women in intact first marriages. This effect seemed to be stronger for nonwhites than for whites. The fertility of nonwhites in discontinuous marriages in 1960 was 70% of that experienced by those in intact marriages, and the fertility of whites in discontinuous marriages was 81% of that of whites continuously married (Lauriat, 1969).

Thornton's analyses (1978) have further specified these relationships with more recent data. His finding that fertility was lower in the years just preceding separation suggests that marital discord reduces fertility while couples are still living together. Some nonmarital fertility follows divorce, of course, but the fertility of women who have experienced marital dissolution is substantially reduced throughout their remaining childbearing years or until they remarry. Remarriage is followed by larger increases in fertility among white women than among nonwhites in the United States (Thornton, 1978a). In effect, the childbearing of remarrying white women catches up to the childbearing of those in stable marriages, but the fertility of nonwhite women who remarry remains substantially lower than the fertility of those in stable marriages. Part of this differential results because white women remarry sooner than nonwhites (Thornton, 1978a).

According to the Davis and Blake (1956) formulation, lower fertility in discontinuous marriages might occur because of reduced exposure to intercourse. However, Levin and O'Hara (1978) suggested an alternative hypothesis for the relationship between disrupted marriage and fertility. According to them, the experience of the previous parenthood has more impact on the lower fertility of remarried women than the reduction in the exposure to intercourse. In other words, remarried partners often have emotional and financial commitments to children of previous marriages that reduce their desire for more children in the subsequent marriage. Remarried partners are also older at the time of remarriage and are likely to make decisions about childbearing with more knowledge and experience than they had in the previous marriage. Thus, they might be more realistic and less romantic about childbearing decisions, and consequently reduce their fertility.

A number of additional factors have been identified that complicate what might at first seem to be a simple relationship between marital disruption and lower fertility. For example, disruption of marriage has a positive effect on fertility in some situations because it allows the possibility of another union. Second or subsequent unions may reinitiate childbearing with the new partner that would not have occurred with the former partner. Ebanks, George, and Nobbe (1974) cited evidence to support this possibility among women in Barbados;

those with only one marital union had an average of 2.6 live births, those with two unions averaged 3.8 live births, and those with four unions averaged 4.7 live births. Although these differences were attenuated when age was controlled, the same pattern remained. A similar pattern was also reported in Ecuador (Chen, Wishik, & Scrimshaw, 1974). Likewise, Marino (1970) contended that, in a society with a shortage of males, marital instability can increase fertility by allowing males to be shared by fecund females who would otherwise be without partners.

Decreasing levels of overall fertility have also been noted as an important factor in the relationship between marital disruption and fertility (Levin & O'Hara, 1978; Onaka, Yaukey, & Chevan, 1977). The average number of two or three pregnancies in advanced societies constitutes a very small proportion of the 25 or 30 years of biological fecundity. Even allowing for marital interruptions of several years, there is still plenty of time, biologically speaking, to achieve the same small family size as in the rest of the population (Thornton, 1978a).

Various investigators have pointed out that several elements bear on the preceding argument (Levin & O'Hara, 1978; Thornton, 1978a). There would be little difference in the fertility of continuously married and remarried women if the overall level of fertility were low and if there were a young age at first marriage, a low age at first divorce, and a low age at remarriage. Under these conditions, there would still be many fecund years left for having as many children in subsequent marriages as in the continuously married population.

Another possible complication in the martial-disruption–lower-fertility idea is the pronatalist tendency for women who remarry after long periods outside marriage to be more fertile than those who remarry quickly (Downing & Yaukey 1979; Thornton, 1978a). Apparently, this makeup or catchup phenomenon lessens reproductive differences that are due to the loss of exposure to intercourse after marital disruption.

Finally, Levin and O'Hara (1978) contended that reports about fertility and remarriage have possibly been misleading because controls for the marital histories of the husbands have usually not been included. Regardless of the woman's marital history, fertility is significantly reduced if she is married to a husband who has been previously married. Apparently, if the husband's marital history is not taken into account, the low fertility of previously married women with remarried husbands combines with the higher fertility of remarried women with once-married husbands to mask the relationship.

A number of investigators have studied the relationship between the stability of various types of sexual unions and fertility (Nag, 1971; Nobbe, Ebanks, & George, 1976; Onaka et al., 1977; Ram & Ebanks, 1973; Stycos & Back, 1964; Williams, Murthy, & Berggren, 1975). Latin American countries, in general, and the Carribean Islands, in particular, are appropriate for analyzing the relationship between fertility and the type and stability of

sexual unions because of the numbers of various unions in existence. The most often analyzed types of unions are legal marriages, which are the most stable, consensual or common-law unions, which are less stable, and visiting unions, which are the least stable and in which the partners do not actually live in the same residence. The most common finding of these studies is that fertility is directly related to the stability of the sexual union, being highest in marriages, intermediate in consensual unions, and lowest in visiting unions (see especially Downing & Yaukey, 1979; Nobbe, et al., 1976). The higher fertility of stable unions appears to be due, at least in part, to the greater reproductive time lost through disruption of the less stable unions. Onaka et al. (1977), for example, showed that the percentage of potential reproductive time lost between 15 and 49 is two or more times as great for consensual unions as for legal ones.

In summary, there has been somewhat conflicting results from studies on the effects of marital disruption on fertility. Some studies in the United States have reported that marital dissolution decreases fertility (Cohen & Sweet, 1974; Lauriat, 1969). Other studies have reported that, especially in Latin America, women married more than once are as fertile as or more fertile than women married only once (Chen et al., 1974; Ebanks, et al., 1974; Marino, 1970). Although the loss of exposure to conception from interrupted marriage is often cited as the cause of decreased fertility, many other factors contribute to or confound this potential effect: the overall fertility rates in the population, the age at time of marital dissolution and remarriage, the effect of previous parenthood on the new union, the pronatalist effect of remarriage, the relative number of males compared to fecund females, the marital history of a remarried woman's husband, the length of time between unions, and so on.

Although fertility is usually positively related to the stability of the union, being highest in stable marriages and lowest in unstable visiting unions, there are cases where fertility is found to be highest among women who have had the most sexual unions. In short, "It seems in retrospect that we and others have been burdened with a simplistic view of the potential causal paths involved in relationships between marital stability and fertility" (Onaka et al., 1977, p. 115). Thornton (1978a) concluded that "marital dissolution probably only substantially decreases the number of children born in populations where remarriage rates are low, fertility in stable first marriages is high, and family planning is limited" (p. 379). This is an area where marriage and fertility patterns are obviously connected, but where much remains to be clarified about the nature of the relationships. As Thornton (1978a) pointed out, timing in the life cycle is critical to future studies, and analyses should be based on completed fertility after the end of the childbearing years.

Frequency of Intercourse. The more often couples have intercourse, the more likely conception is to occur, other things being equal.[5] If intercourse occurs only sporadically, pregnancy is less likely than if sexual relations are frequent. The question then arises: Are there marriage and family patterns related to the frequency of intercourse within unions?

In the preceding section, the argument was presented that disruption or dissolution of sexual unions reduces fertility. In discontinuous relationships, lower fertility occurs, ostensibly, as a consequence of spending less time in sexual unions during the reproductive years. This may, in fact, be the most adequate explanation of differential fertility between continuous and discontinuous relationships. However, when comparing the fertility of the stable marriages, consensual unions, and visiting relationships common in Latin America, an equally plausible explanation seems to be the frequency of intercourse within unions. Lower fertility is related not only to instability and disruption, but also to how frequently intercourse occurs in continuous relationships. This supposition is also consistent with Thornton's finding (1978a) of lower fertility preceding separation, presumably caused by less frequent intercourse.

The conclusion of Nobbe et al. (1976) is especially convincing and lucid:

The basic structural component which makes common-law and married status alike from the standpoint of fertility is the matter of common residence. It is the sharing of the same domicile that affords the couple the opportunity for sexual contact on a regular basis, and this, in turn, increases the exposure to risk of pregnancy. For those in visiting union types, on the other hand, common residence is not involved. As such, the sexual intercourse that occurs is more sporadic and infrequent and the risk of pregnancy is less. (p. 307)

More frequent intercourse does not necessarily result in higher fertility, of course, In the United States, the frequency of intercourse within marriage appears to have increased in recent decades (Westoff, 1974) at the same time that fertility has declined, primarily because of more widespread and effective contraceptive use, and because of abortion.

Fertility Control and Regulation

There are many ways of controlling or regulating fertility. At the societal level, fertility is reduced when family patterns postpone marriage and sexual relations, encourage permanent celibacy, and so on. Individual couples control fertility by using various methods of birth control. *Birth control* is a general term referring to ways of preventing birth from occurring. Births can be prevented by methods that prevent conception (con-

traception) and methods that prevent birth after conception has occurred (abortion).

The study of fertility control in its family contexts was pioneered by Hill et al. (1959). There is little doubt about the importance of marriage and the family in fertility planning, and little doubt that fertility regulation is relevant to the mental and physical health of most of the world's population (Martin, 1978). In spite of some controversy, fertility regulation (especially the use of contraceptives) has become a part of the lives of a large majority of Americans of reproductive age. Family-planning services have been increasingly available, and the use of contraceptives has been steadily rising in the United States, both in and outside marriage (Ford, 1978; Jaffe & Dryfoos, 1980; Westoff & Jones, 1977a; Zelnik & Kantner, 1977, 1980). In 1975, nearly 80% of once-married couples of reproductive age were using contraception (Westoff & Jones, 1977a), an increase of 15% since 1965. Not only were more couples using contraceptives, but more effective methods, including birth control pills, IUDs, and sterilization, had become popular (Westoff & Jones, 1977a). The pill was most often used by wives married fewer than 10 years, and sterilization was cited as the method most often used by couples married 10 years or longer (Westoff & Jones, 1977a).

The Use of Family-Planning Clinics and Services

The increased use of contraceptives by married couples and unmarried sexually active individuals is attributed in large part to the increased use of family-planning agencies and services. The use of organized family-planning services in the United States has steadily increased since the late 1960s (Torres, 1979). The number of teenagers attending family-planning clinics in the United States more than doubled from 1971 to 1976 (Jaffe & Dryfoos, 1980; Zelnik & Kantner, 1977). In 1977, 4.2 million women were served by organized family-planning clinics, and about one third of those served were in their teens (Torres, 1979). In 1977, it is estimated that 9.7 million visits were made to private physicians by women aged 15–44 for family-planning services (Cypress, 1979). This statistic indicates that, for every 1,000 women of reproductive age in 1977, 200 visits were made. In contrast to the one third of visits to clinics made by teens, only 1 out of 10 visits to private physicians was made by a teenager.

The figures thus far presented represent family-planning contacts by women. The number of men who made family-planning visits is considerably lower. Cypress (1979) reported that 12 visits to private physicians were made by women for each visit by a man.

Participation in family-planning services is significantly related to successful fertility regulation (Cutright & Jaffe, 1977). Once a woman is prompted to use a family-planning service, her rate of continuous contraceptive use is increased (Cosgrove, Penn, & Chambers, 1978; Edwards et al., 1980), and the chances of

---

[5]Frequency of intercourse is positively related to fertility only up to a certain point. Extremely frequent intercourse (several times a day over a long period of time, for example) can prevent conception because sperm are not regenerated in sufficient quantities.

contraceptive failure and unplanned pregnancy are decreased (Okada & Gillespi, 1977). It has been estimated that through the use of family-planning programs during the period 1970–1975, 1.1 million unwanted or unplanned births to low-income and marginal-income women were averted in the United States (Cutright & Jaffe, 1977).

Another factor related to birth-planning success has been the method of contraception used (Cutright & Groeneveld, 1978; Okada & Gillespi, 1977). Once a woman attends a medical family-planning facility, she may acquire a prescribed method of birth control such as the pill or an IUD. These methods are technically very effective and have been found to lead to greater success in contraception than several other common methods (Cutright & Groeneveld, 1978).

The outcomes of adolescent participation in family-planning services have been shown to be similar to those of adults. In three high schools in St. Paul, the provision of family-planning services was related to reduced fertility rates and higher rates of contraceptive continuation by clients (Edwards, Steinman, Arnold, & Hakanson, 1980). Over the three-year period of the initial program, the fertility rates of the students declined 56%, and the contraceptive continuation rate was 86% (Edwards *et al.*, 1980).

Across the nation in 1975, 2.4 million of an estimated 4 million sexually active adolescent females were served by organized family-planning clinics and private physicians combined (Dryfoos & Heisler, 1978). It was estimated that 266,000 births to teenagers were averted in the United States by their use of family-planning clinics during the years 1970–1975 (Cutright & Jaffe, 1977). Although there is an increasing trend for sexually active adolescents to use contraception and to use more effective methods, there is still a substantial proportion who report that they never use contraception or use it sporadically (Zelnik & Kantner, 1977, 1980).

In conclusion, it can be said that birth control use in the United States has become normative and increasingly effective among married couples, and that effective contraception has been low but is increasing among adolescents. Participation in family-planning programs and the method of contraception used contribute to birth-planning success. There is evidence that the use of birth control has prevented unplanned births for women of all reproductive age groups in the United States. These facts demonstrate the relevance of contraception to the lives of both married couples and unmarried sexually active individuals.

Factors Related to Contraceptive Use

Many personal and social variables are related to the use of contraceptives. Certainly, access to contraceptives, motivation to use them, and some minimal knowledge about contraceptives precede their use. If we take these prerequisites as givens, the following factors have been shown to be related to contraceptive use.

Ahmed (1977) found that if a couple was situationally stable in their marriage, family planning appeared to be more effective. He stated, ''Fluctuation in income, checkered employment history, fluctuation in marital adjustment and frequency of temporary separations, all tend to suppress the association of ability to plan and fertility planning success'' (p. 105).

Other studies have indicated that, in marriages where communication between spouses was verbal, empathetic, and concurrent, the use of modern methods of birth control and low fertility occurred more often than in marriages where these conditions did not exist (Downs, 1977). Married couples who communicated about contraception had more agreement on contraceptive issues. Similarly, in a study conducted in India, Mukherjee (1975) found that husband–wife communication was positively correlated with the adoption of family planning by the couple. He also found that, the greater the interspouse communication, the greater the wives' knowledge and awareness of various contraceptive methods. One might conclude from these studies that the ability of a couple to communicate, plus specific discussion of contraceptive desires and preferences, leads to more effective fertility planning.

From analyses of the 1973 National Fertility Survey, Ford (1978) reported that age group was not particularly relevant to contraceptive use in marriage. She found that the percentage of contraceptive users was not significantly different for wives aged 15–29 as compared with wives aged 30–44. In addition, Ford reported that contraceptive use did not differ by region of the United States or by employment of the wife, but there were some differences in use by race, income, education, and parity. White wives used contraceptives more than black wives, and those living below the poverty level used contraceptives least when compared to wives at other income levels. Wives who had higher levels of education used contraceptives more frequently than those with less education, and women of higher parity (2–4 live births) used birth control more often than women of lower parity.

Other findings have suggested that religious affiliation is not as strongly related to contraceptive use as it once was. For example, Westoff and Jones (1977b) found when comparing Catholic wives to non-Catholic wives in 1975, that contraceptive use was about the same (a difference of only 3.5% as compared to a difference of 11.5% in 1965). The types of contraceptives used were also similar for the Catholic and the non-Catholic groups. In another study, Ford (1978) found that Protestant use of contraception (72.0%) was greater than Catholic use (66.3%) among whites, but among blacks, Catholic use (70.4%) was greater than Protestant use (59.2%). It appears that religious affiliation, at least when comparing Catholics and Protestants, no longer accounts for major differences in contraceptive use in the United States.

Another factor related to the use of contraception has been attitudes toward population problems. Results from studies conducted in 1965, 1970, and 1975 indicated a correlation between parity and population attitudes (Westoff & McCarthy, 1979). Women who were concerned about population problems in 1970 had fewer children during 1971–1975 than those who did not indicate a concern. In general, though, belief that population increase is a serious problem peaked in the United States in 1970 and has declined since then (Westoff & McCarthy, 1979).

In summary, it is apparent that personal, interpersonal, and situational factors are all important in contraceptive use. Because it has often been reported that contraceptive practice is considered more the woman's responsibility than the man's, there is some value in assessing the similarities and differences between factors affecting male and female use of contraceptives.

Factors Related to Male Use of Contraceptives. Although males do use contraception, they rarely seek out family-planning services (Cypress, 1979; Scales, 1977). Interestingly, research has suggested that any inclusion of males in the contraceptive decision-making process would very likely contribute to use (Fisher, 1979; Maxwell, Sack, Frary, & Keller, 1977; Thompson & Spanier, 1978). For example, in a study of university males, Fisher (1979) found that the use of contraception by men who could plan, discuss, purchase, and use birth control devices was higher than among men who avoided these behaviors.

This notion of planning seems particularly relevant to contraceptive use in teens. Scales (1977) pointed out that, when contraception is used by teens, more than 50% of the methods used are male methods (condoms and withdrawal). Finkel and Finkel (1978) reported that, most often, intercourse for teen males was erratic and that a majority of males felt that using birth control made sex seem planned. In addition, Maxwell *et al.* (1977) found that planning intercourse was relevant to contraceptive use in their sample of both male and female college students. They found that a majority (69%) had not planned first intercourse, and that, of those who had, only 31% had used a reliable method of contraception. In contrast, 46% had not planned their *most recent* intercourse, and the vast majority of planners (87%) had used contraception.

Thompson and Spanier (1978) found that communication with one's sexual partner about birth control increased the use of contraceptives for both males and females. Foreit and Foreit (1978) found that the use of contraceptives varied according to the type of relationship, with men and women in steady relationships using contraceptives more often, and using more effective methods, than those in less steady relationships. One might infer that, in steady relationships, there is a greater opportunity to discuss, expect, and plan intercourse. Maxwell *et al.* (1977) also supported the idea that relationship characteristics were important to contraceptive use. They found, among both males and females, that a higher level of emotional involvement increased the likelihood that reliable contraception would be used.

Hedin-Pourghasemi (1978) found that the men with the least stereotypical gender attitudes were likely to use the most effective methods of contraception. These results might be considered along with Fisher's findings (1979) concerning men who were willing to discuss and be involved in contraceptive use versus men who avoided this behavior. One might suspect some interaction between attitudes toward women and willingness to discuss and participate in contraceptive use. This possibility remains to be empirically examined.

In conclusion, it has been shown that planning intercourse as well as discussing birth control with one's sexual partner has been related to contraceptive use among males. In addition, the type of relationship or emotional involvement a male has with his partner is also important in determining contraceptive use. A male's attitude toward gender roles is also relevant to the use of birth control, but the manner in which this variable interacts with the other variables identified remains unclear.

Factors Related to Female Use of Contraceptives. Some studies have examined women's sex-role orientations and contraceptive use (Brown, 1978; Hedin-Pourghasemi, 1978; Irons, 1978). Among white, never-married university females, Brown (1978) found that successful contraceptors were significantly more sexually assertive than unsuccessful contraceptors. Hedin-Pourghasemi (1978) also reported that women who were less stereotypical in their sex-role orientation with reference to their self-concept, their relationship with their partner, and their attitudes toward males and females were more likely to use effective means of contraception than women who were highly stereotypical. It was also found that women who had less stereotypical self-concepts were more likely to have partners who used effective contraception (Hedin-Pourghasemi, 1978). In addition, Irons (1978) found that there was a significant positive correlation between women who managed their fertility effectively and women who were "profeminist."

The educational experience and the career orientation of the wife have also been found to be relevant to contraceptive use, at least in a sample of well-educated English wives (Woodward, Heath, & Chishold, 1978). The women, for the most part, were successful family planners, with the wife taking the initiative in contraceptive use. It was hypothesized by the authors that the success of these women in family planning was a result of their ability to rationally plan, control, and achieve their goals, which were, in part, a result of their education and professional orientation. Women's employment and gender roles, in relation to fertility, are considered in greater detail in a later section.

Women's orientation toward sexuality and contraception, not surprisingly, is related to contraceptive use. In a female teen sample, Spain (1978) found that sexuality was seen as more positive by effective contraceptive users than by nonusers. Steinlauf (1977) also found that women's attitudes toward contraception correlated positively with use, particularly among those aged 20 and above. Fisher, Byrne, Edmunds, Miller, Kelley, and White (1979) reported similar findings.

Other factors that have been found to be related to contraceptive use by adolescent girls are problem-solving skills (Steinlauf, 1977), a sense of "inner control," and a future planning orientation (Spain, 1978). Contrary to Steinlauf's (1978) findings, Smith (1978) found no significant relationship between locus of control or ego development and contraceptive use.

Relationships with significant others, especially the sexual partner, are associated with family planning among females. Cahn (1978) reported that contraceptors received support for their contraceptive behavior from their peers and their mothers. Thompson and Spanier (1978) reported that peer influence was not significantly related to male use of contraception but was significantly correlated with female use. They also reported that parents, as compared to peers, were less influential in determining contraceptive use.

Apparently, the most influential significant other in determining the use of birth control is the partner. Thompson and Spanier (1978) indicated that communication between sexually active partners about birth control was positively related to the use of birth control by both women and men. Delamater and Maccorquodale (1978) also reported that whether or not contraception was discussed in advance by partners influenced use by women. They also indicated that relative frequency of intercourse with one's partner was positively correlated with contraceptive use by women.

It was pointed out in the section on male use that the type of couple relationship is related to contraceptive use, and the same finding holds true for women. Individuals in steady versus casual relationships were more likely to use contraception and to use more effective methods (Foreit & Foreit, 1978), and those with a higher level of emotional involvement with their partner were more likely to use an effective method of birth control (Fisher et al., 1979).

Another factor that is relevant to contraceptive use is sexual experience itself. In a study of female and male college students, Maxwell et al. (1977) found that a person's sexual experience is a highly significant variable in contraceptive use. Delamater and Maccorquodale (1978) also found that birth control use by women was positively correlated with having had more than one partner and the number of lifetime coital experiences.

Summary of Fertility Control and Regulation

The availability of and some knowledge about contraception are probably necessary, but not sufficient, to ensure their use (Byrne, 1979; Dembo & Lundell, 1979; Fisher, 1979; Irons, 1978; Severy, 1979; Zelnik & Kantner, 1979). The use of family planning has been found to be closely related to individual, social-psychological, and situational variables. Fisher et al. (1979) concluded "that even when sexually active individuals are aware of easily available contraceptive resources, differences in emotions, attitudes, norms and situational factors are corre-

lated with variations in contraceptive behavior" (p. 53). A common thread of influence on contraceptive use throughout all age groups (married or unmarried) has been communication, primarily between partners. Of course, the elimination of unwanted and mistimed pregnancies is not just a matter of communication, but the importance of communication cannot be ignored. It would seem that the more conscious and rational decision-making is about sexual relations and contraception, the less haphazard and more effective family planning would be. But then, sex and children are, perhaps, areas of life about which people are least rational. Although motivations for childbearing and the values of children are sometimes illogical and irrational, they are important. These emotions and values underlie reproductive behavior and are often powerful determinants of actual fertility.

Values of Children and Motivations for Childbearing

Fertility has always been affected by social-cultural expectations and psychological factors. This is probably more true in modern times than formerly because, in a historical sense, having children was not usually the result of a deliberate, rational choice anyway. Less than a century ago in the most advanced societies, pregnancy and parenthood were often unplanned events over which one had very little control. Although contraception has been practiced for thousands of years, only in relatively modern times have couples been able to regulate their fertility with any degree of certainty. Now that the number and timing of children is more a matter of choice than it has been in the past, values and motivations for children are likely to have a more important effect on fertility experiences.

Pronatalism and Antinatalism

Almost all children grow up expecting to become parents. The nearly universal and generally unquestioned anticipation of parenthood reflects strong cultural values that encourage having and rearing children. These values, and the policies that support them, have been referred to as *pronatalism*, meaning in favor of childbearing. Few cultural values are held more universally.

Social rewards, honors, and praise for having children have been referred to by Kammeyer (1981) as a "cultural press for childbearing." Strong values favoring childbearing and rearing are quite understandable when historically high death rates and short life expectancy are considered. Today, infant mortality in the most advanced countries averages about 1 in 100 births, but it has been estimated that 1 infant in 7 died in its first year in relatively advanced England during the eighteenth century, and across time, only about half the infants born ever reached maturity (Kammeyer, 1981).

Throughout the course of human history, childbirth has been no simple task for women either. Only a century ago in the United States nearly one woman in five died of childbirth-related causes. As Kammeyer (1981) stated it:

Throughout history, and up until only a few years ago, having a baby was a dangerous experience for a woman. The possibility of a woman dying in childbirth was very real. Since the threat of dying in childbirth was great, it is not surprising that there had to be some correspondingly high social rewards to get women to take the risk. Those social rewards evolved and they are still strong and pervasive. (p. 171)

Considering short life expectancies, especially the high maternal and infant mortality, it is understandable that pronatalist values and the cultural press for childbearing emerged. Historically speaking, almost every woman had to bear as many children as she could just to *maintain* the population. This is, of course, no longer the case, and recent concerns have been with curbing population growth. Still, in many societies, pronatalist values and social rewards for childbearing are pervasive. Truly, as Margaret Mead (1950) once observed, "every human society is faced not with one population problem but with two: how to beget and rear enough children and how not to beget and rear too many!" (p. 210).

Values and social policies that discourage or are against childbearing are referred to as *antinatalist*. In recent years, antinatalist sentiments have increasingly been expressed in the United States, both by individuals and by groups. Most countries, including the United States, have a history of pronatalist sentiments and government policies, but some countries are now deliberately reducing incentives and support for having children as a way of curbing their population growth. Most of the resistance to the cultural press for childbearing in the past came from individuals and was based largely on personal reasons, but now national and international organizations are using empirical data about the costs and difficulties of having children to communicate some unfavorable aspects of parenthood.[6]

Satisfactions and Costs of Children

In the late 1960s and early 1970s, scientists began studies to gain a clearer understanding of the satisfactions and costs people associate with having children (Arnold, Bulatao, Buripkdi, Chung, Fawcett, Iritani, Lee, & Wu, 1975; Berelson, 1973; Fawcett, 1972, 1973; Hoffman, 1972). As stated by Hoffman, Thornton, and Manis (1978),

While the empirical relationships between fertility behavior and various social, economic, and demographic variables are fairly

[6]Examples of such groups are Zero Population Growth (ZPG) and the National Association for Optional Parenthood (NAOP), formerly called the National Organization for Nonparents (NON). Reasons for not having children have been presented in popular books with such revealing titles as *The Baby Trap* (Peck, 1971), *The Case against Having Children* (Silverman & Silverman, 1978), and *The Myth of Mom and Apple Pie* (Peck & Senderowitz, 1974).

well understood, the causal mechanisms that produce those correlations are still quite obscure. In fact, one of the goals of contemporary fertility research is to identify and estimate the causal mechanisms that produce differences in fertility behavior (Easterlin, 1969; Thornton, 1977). Inasmuch as values concerning children are important elements of models purporting to explain fertility behavior, it seems plausible to expect that these values and their distribution in the population are related to and affect the differentials in actual fertility so often observed. Values concerning children may be one of the important mechanisms producing the largely unexplained differentials in actual fertility behavior. By better understanding the values people perceive in children and the way these perceptions are distributed in the population, it may be possible to gain insights into that behavior. (p. 105)

The effect of values and expectations on fertility depends somewhat on active decisions on the part of potential parents. About half of first births to both married and unmarried women are fully intended (Miller, 1978). Also, 63% of parents and 93% of those who chose not to have children report an active decision-making process (Ory, 1978). However, even passive decisions such as the conscious or unconscious decision "not to decide" may be influenced by underlying values concerning children. An increased understanding of the values of children has implications for fertility forecasts, population policy, and family-planning programs, as well as for the study of family relations.

Values of Children. The value of children is determined by perceptions of the functions they serve and the needs they fulfill. Values change with social and cultural changes, but there seems to be a growing consensus about the important values of children. Hoffman and Manis (1979) identified the following values, which are listed in the order of how frequently they were mentioned as advantages of having children in the United States:

1. Primary group ties, affection (love and companionship, having a complete family, benefiting the marriage, giving love).
2. Stimulation and fun (activity, pleasure from watching them grow).
3. Expansion of self (purpose to life, learning experience, self-fulfillment, life experience).
4. Adult status and identity (maturity, usefulness, societal expectations, sex identity).
5. Achievement and creativity (creating a life, doing a good job, teaching).
6. Economic utility (household labor, old-age security).
7. Morality (being a better person).

In the United States, the most common values reported are primary group ties, affection, stimulation, and fun (Hoffman 1975; Hoffman & Manis, 1979). In more agricultural settings, children may be expected to contribute economically by participating in household labor or by providing financial security in old age (Mueller, 1972; Nag, 1972). In fact, the economic value of children was the most frequent mentioned advantage of having children in Indonesia (Meyer & Singarimbun, 1977) and the Philippines (Bulatao, 1975). These economic values of children have declined in advanced societies because of the curtailment of child labor and the decreased importance of children to parents as sources of old-age financial support (Stern, Smith, & Doolittle, 1975). Although the economic values of children remain important in more rural and ethnic populations (Fawcett, 1972; Hoffman & Manis, 1979), the urban middle class stresses non-economic values such as love, companionship, and fun (Espenshade, 1977). As previously noted, part of Westoff's explanation (1978a,b) for declining fertility around the world is that children will be less and less an economic asset and more and more a financial liability.

In the United States, values concerning children vary by ethnicity, education, and sex (Fawcett, 1972; Hoffman & Manis, 1979; Wyatt, 1967). Women place greater emphasis on love and fun, and men tend to emphasize identity in terms of self-extension and masculinity (Hoffman & Manis, 1979; Humphrey, 1977). Values may also change during the life cycle. For example, whereas the first child may enhance adult status, later children are less likely to do so (Hoffman, 1972).

Of course, it is not just the positive values of children that affect fertility decisions. Hoffman and Hoffman (1973) suggested that five kinds of variables may contribute to fertility ideals and decisions: (1) the positive values of children (already described); (2) the negative values or costs of children; (3) alternative sources of positive values; (4) facilitators; and (5) barriers. These other social-psychological aspects of the motivation for childbearing are explored next.

Costs of Children. The direct cost to raise a child in 1980 was estimated to be about $85,000 (Espenshade, 1980). If the loss of income from a five-year interruption of the mother's employment and the costs of a college education for the child were added, the cost was estimated at between $100,000 and $140,000 (Espenshade, 1980). Many of those who choose to remain childless do so for financial reasons (Hoffman & Manis, 1979). Although costs are generally less with subsequent children, contemporary parents place great importance on financial reasons for limiting family size (Vinokur-Kaplan, 1977).

In addition to the more tangible economic costs of children, there are also psychological costs. Loss of freedom is the most commonly cited disadvantage of children, mentioned by both parents and childless couples (Barnett & MacDonald, 1976; Burnside, 1978; Hoffman, 1972; Hoffman & Manis, 1979; Vinokur-Kaplan, 1977). Another perceived cost of children is the responsibility of parenting, including worry and anxiety (Barnett & MacDonald, 1976; Fawcett, 1972; Francke, Abramson, & Maitlan, 1980; Miller & Myers-Walls, 1983). Hoffman (1972) suggested that this is the other side of the positive value of the challenge or stimulation of child rearing. Parents who expect to be or are successful at child rearing

may perceive it positively, whereas those who expect and experience problems may perceive it more negatively.

The negative effect of children on marriage is another commonly mentioned disadvantage (Barnett & MacDonald, 1976; Fawcett, 1972; Vinokur-Kaplan, 1977). Again, this cost may be thought of as the opposite side of the positive value of marriage enhancement and may depend on other values that determine whether it will be considered negatively or positively. There is much empirical support for the relationship between egalitarian marital values and the desire for a smaller family (Bram, 1975; Burnside, 1978; Scanzoni, 1976; Tobin, 1976; Toomey, 1978). On the other hand, domestic roles related to greater values of children may contribute to a more positive expectation regarding the effect of children on marriage.

Alternatives to Children. Hoffman (1972) reasoned that the value of children would be higher if there were fewer alternatives to meet the needs associated with children, and the evidence agrees (Hoffman et al., 1978). As education, employment, and women's age at marriage increase, childlessness also increases. The greater incidence of childlessness and smaller family size among better educated employed women and among women who marry later may reflect a greater choice of alternatives explored before decisions are made about parenthood (Bram, 1975; Coombs, 1978; Henley & Gustavus, 1976; Norris, 1977; Renne, 1976; Toomey, 1978).

The existence of alternatives appears to influence values directly. Highly educated women mention fewer economic and practical values of children; working women mention less stimulation and fun of children (Hoffman & Manis, 1979). The costs of children because of their interference with the mother's career are of more concern to less traditional women than to the more traditional women, who, Hoffman (1972) suggested, may perceive a value of "success avoidance"; having children to avoid competition with men, especially with their husbands.

Facilitators of and Barriers to Childbearing. The effect of values on fertility behavior is mediated by the individual's definition of the situation (Ory, 1978). Some situational factors make it more difficult or easier to have children. Some examples of barriers are a poor financial situation, poor health, or extreme time demands. Examples of facilitators are prosperity, adequate housing, and assistance with competing work and time demands (Fawcett, 1972; Hoffman, 1972). These structural concerns seem to be more related to decisions regarding family size than to the decision of whether or not to have the first child (Ory, 1978).

A special kind of facilitator is reference group support. Ory (1978) suggested that, in addition to situational factors, the effect of values is also mediated by reference group influences. The reference group may have either a facilitative effect by supporting positive values of children and domestic role definitions, or an alternative effect of supporting childlessness or small family size and egalitarian marital roles. Couples are no doubt influenced by the prevailing norms in their culture and subculture. The family size norms in the United States currently favor two children, one of each sex, a rather narrow ideal (Hoffman & Manis, 1979; Lee & Kahn, 1978). Prescriptions for child rearing are inherent in the cultural values of children, but the social group may also provide proscriptions against either childlessness or large families. Pressures against large families include concerns about the population explosion and world problems (Hoffman, 1972). Pressures against childlessness include ideas that it is selfish, immature, or foolish (Barnett & MacDonald, 1976; Ory, 1978).

Fertility norms vary by religion, race, and career orientation (Henley & Gustavus, 1976; Thornton, 1979), which may help explain group differences in fertility. Group norms seem to be more influential in the decision of whether or not to have children than in the decision of how many to have, which is more influenced by situation (Ory, 1978). Nevertheless, both psychological and sociological factors are related to family size decisions.

Summary of Childbearing Values, Motivations, and Intentions. The values underlying childbearing appear to be quite different in advanced and developing societies. Values of children have been changing historically from largely economic to largely personal, and within marital contexts, values of children and childbearing intentions are also subject to change. Changes in childbearing intentions seem to be more common among those who want more children. Among a group of over 3,000 women asked about their childbearing intentions in 1970 and again in 1975, 23.5% of those intending to have more children changed their minds, compared to only 4% of those who intended to have no more (Westoff & Ryder, 1977, 1979). Intentions are not always accurate predictors of fertility, and many women (34%) who intended to have more children in 1970 had not had another child by 1975; 70% of them had changed their minds primarily for financial reasons. By comparison, only 12% of those who wanted no more children ended up having another child anyway, but only 26% because of a change of mind; the rest "just happened" (Westoff & Ryder, 1977, 1979).

These findings indicate that family size intentions are adjusted downward more frequently than they are adjusted upward. Other researchers have also reported a general downward shift in preferences over time, as well as final parity below initial expectations among those just beginning to have children (Freedman, Freedman, & Thornton, 1980). Westoff and Ryder suggested that fertility forecasts based on the intentions of couples in 1970 may have been as much of an overestimation as those based on the existing fertility rates in 1970. The changing trends in situational facilitators, barriers, values of children, and motivations for childbearing will continue to play major roles in fertility behavior.

Contemporary Issues in Fertility and the Family

In this final section of the chapter, two fertility-related issues of great current interest are addressed. Adolescent pregnancy became an important topic for research and intervention in the 1970s, presumably because of its adverse consequences for those most directly involved. Gender roles and women's status, other major issues, are also closely related to fertility. Accompanying the women's movement and rising women's employment, there has been a growing awareness that fertility behavior is likely to be drastically altered because of changes in traditional definitions of women's roles.

Teenage Pregnancy and Fertility

Adolescent pregnancy in the United States became a national concern during the 1970s. Since that time, there have been over a million pregnancies annually to females 19 or younger (U.S. Bureau of the Census, 1980), and approximately one third of these pregnancies ended in abortion (Jaffe & Dryfoos, 1980; Tietze, 1977). Since the early 1980s, nearly half (45 percent) of adolescent pregnancies in the United States have ended by induced abortion (Jones, Rorrest, Goldman, Henshaw, Lincoln, Rosoff, Westoff, & Wulf, 1985). The personal and social costs of teenage fertility have been widely discussed (Baldwin & Cain, 1980; Freedman & Thornton, 1979; Furstenberg, 1976; McKenry, Walters, & Johnson, 1979; Nye & Lamberts, 1980; Card & Wise, 1978).[7]

Incidence. Although there seems to be a popular impression of a nationwide epidemic of adolescent childbirth, 15- to 19-year-old age-specific fertility rates have actually been declining for more than a decade (National Center for Health Statistics, 1980):

From 1940 through 1960, birth rates to women 15–19 years of age (births per 1,000 women 15–19) increased from 54.1 to 89.1. From 1960 through 1976, however, this rate decreased from 89.1 to 53.6, a 40 percent reduction. (U.S. Bureau of the Census, 1980, p. 1)

Since 1976, teenage fertility rates have shown little change. Rates of teen childbearing have declined in recent decades partly because abortion rates have risen.

[7]Although teenage pregnancy has received concerted research attention only in recent years, some professional journals have devoted special issues to teen pregnancy and parenting (*Family Planning Perspectives*, 1978, *10*, 4; *Journal of Social Issues*, 1980, *36*, 1). There are also a number of excellent reviews available. Some provide general surveys of the issues (Chilman, 1980b; McKenry *et al.*, 1979), and others focus more specifically on adolescent sexuality (Chilman, 1978, 1980a; Gordon, Scales, & Everly, 1979; Zelnik, Kantuer, & Ford 1981).

Overall pregnancy rates (including abortion and live births) appear to have been increasing in the United States (Miller, 1985) and to be considerably higher than in other developed countries (Jones *et al.*, 1985). Another reason for concern has been that birth rates to older mothers have been declining even more, resulting in an increasing *proportion* of all births occurring to teenage mothers. Births to teenage mothers accounted for 14% of all births in 1960, and for 18% in 1976 (U.S. Bureau of the Census, 1980). Concern about teenage childbearing is also based on the fact that births to teens are increasingly nonmarital, placing greater demands on public support systems. Between 1940 and 1977, illegitimacy rates doubled among black and quadrupled among white teens (Campbell, 1980).

Causes and Processes of Teen Fertility. There are analytic advantages in viewing the sequence of events that leads to adolescent childbearing as a series of decisions or issues, even though becoming pregnant is not usually a conscious decision on the part of an adolescent. Figure 8 presents such a series of issues that adolescents face, consciously or not, and the probable outcomes of their choices.

The first decision portrayed in Figure 8 is whether or not to be sexually active. Sexual activity among teenagers, especially among females, is increasing rapidly. From 1971 to 1979, the percentage of 15- to 19-year-old females rose by two thirds, from 27% to 46% (Zelnick & Kantner, 1980). Virtually all studies of sexual attitudes and behavior suggest that there is a considerably higher percentage of young men than of young women who are sexually active (Clayton & Bokemeier, 1980; Reiss & Miller, 1979).

Adolescents who become sexually active face the issues of contraceptive use. Of course, contraceptive use leads to a relatively lower likelihood of becoming pregnant; and the decision not to use contraception (or no decision at all) leads to a higher likelihood of pregnancy. Although earlier studies (Diamond, Steinhoff, Palmore, & Smith, 1973; Furstenberg, 1971; Goldsmith, Gabrielson, Gabrielson, Matthews, & Potts, 1972) reported that one half to two thirds of all sexually active adolescents had never used contraceptives, more recent studies show higher usage. In 1971, less than one in five sexually active adolescents used contraception regularly, and less than 50% had used contraception at last intercourse (Zelnik & Kantner, 1977). By 1976, however, 30% of the adolescents reported that they used contraceptives regularly, and 64% reported use at last intercourse. Not only has there been an increase in the use of contraceptives among teens, they are using more effective methods, such as the pill (Zelnik & Kantner, 1977). Still, the majority of teen contraceptive use is irregular and inconsistent (Finkel & Finkel, 1978). The reasons for contraceptive use are complex (Byrne, 1979; Dembo & Lundell, 1979; Severy, 1979), apparently not depending very much on knowledge (Irons, 1978; Zelnik & Kantner, 1979), but depending more on age, sexual experience, and the nature of the partner relationship (Hornick, Doran, & Crawford, 1979).

Once pregnancy occurs, many young unmarried adolescents face the decision of whether to carry the pregnancy to term and have the child. About 60% of teen pregnancies result in a live birth, 30% end in induced abortion, and the remainder of teen pregnancies terminate spontaneously (Baldwin, 1976; Forrest, Tietze, & Sullivan, 1979; Tietze, 1977). Approximately one third of all abortions involve teenagers (Jaffe & Dryfoos, 1980). If the decision is not to abort (or no "decision" is made), the parenting decision is next to be faced.

During the last two decades in the United States, there has been a strong trend toward adolescent mothers keeping their babies and away from adoption. Only 7% of

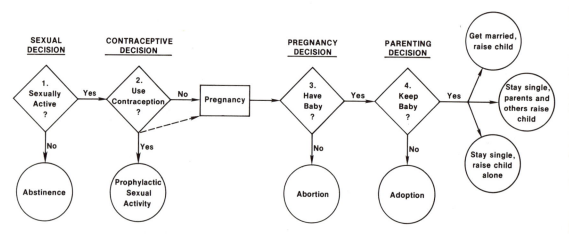

Figure 8. Decisions and outcomes of teenage sexuality, pregnancy, and parenthood.

babies born to white teen mothers were placed for adoption in 1976, whereas corresponding figures were 18% in 1971 and 65% in 1966 (Zelnik & Kantner, 1978). Adoption is rarely even considered as an alternative in the decision-making process (Bracken, Klerman, & Bracken, 1978). There is also a trend away from marrying to legitimize a child; more than half of premaritally pregnant whites in 1971 married before the outcome of their premarital pregnancy, but in 1976, only one third did so (Zelnik & Kantner, 1978). Chilman (1980a) attributed this change to a marked reduction in the stigma of unmarried parenthood. In fact, it appears that there are stronger social pressures and negative stigmas against the teenage girl who chooses to place her child for adoption.

A summary of the causes of teenage sexual intercourse is presented in Chilman's review (1980b) of the variables associated with nonmarital intercourse among adolescents. The chart that she developed from reviewing the literature is presented in Table 6. The factors in the left column are those that have most consistently been found to be related to nonmarital teenage sexual activity.

Consequences of Adolescent Childbearing. Although the consequences of adolescent childbearing have been thought to be extremely detrimental to the child, the parents, the grandparents, and society (Nye & Lamberts, 1980), questions have recently been raised about whether the negative consequences observed are really *caused* by adolescent childbirth. Against a backdrop of prevalent "detrimental consequences" literature, the most recent

Table 6. Summary of Major Factors Apparently Associated with Nonmarital Intercourse among Adolescents[a]

Factors	Males	Females
Social Situation		
Father having less than a college education	unknown	yes, for blacks
Low level of religiousness	yes	yes
Norms favoring equality between the sexes	probably	yes
Permissive sexual norms of the larger society	yes	yes
Racism and poverty	yes	yes
Migration from rural to urban areas	unknown	yes
Peer-group pressure	yes	not clear
Lower social class	yes (probably)	yes (probably)
Sexually permissive friends	unknown	unknown
Single-parent (probably low-income) family	unknown	yes
Psychological		
Use of drugs and alcohol	yes	no
Low self-esteem	no[b]	yes[b]
Desire for affection	no[b]	yes[b]
Low education goals and poor educational achievement	yes	yes
Alienation	no[b]	yes[b]
Deviant attitudes	yes	yes
High social criticism	no[b]	yes[b]
Permissive attitudes of parents	yes[b]	yes[b]
Strained parent-child relationships and little parent-child communication	yes	yes
Going steady; being in love	yes[b]	yes[b]
Risk-taking attitudes	yes[b]	yes[b]
Passivity and dependence	no[b]	yes[b]
Aggression; high levels of activity	yes	no[b]
High degree of interpersonal skills with opposite sex	yes[b]	no[b]
Lack of self-assessment of psychological readiness	no[b]	yes[b]
Biological		
Older than 16	yes	yes
Early puberty	yes	yes (probably for blacks)

[a]Source: Chilman (1980b), p. 796.

[b]Variables supported by only one or two small studies. Other variables are supported by a number of investigations. The major studies on which this table is based are Furstenberg (1976); Jessor and Jessor (1975); Sorenson (1973); Kantner and Zelnik (1972); Udry *et al.* (1975); Simon *et al.* (1972); Zelnik and Kantner (1977); Fox (1980); Cvetkovich and Grote (1975); Presser (1978).

and thorough review based on national data comes to some rather surprising conclusions (Chilman, 1978, 1980b). In her 1980 summary of the consequences of early childbearing, Chilman concluded by saying, "The direct social and psychological effects of early childbearing, *per se,* appeared to be fairly minimal for young people in many aspects of their later lives" (p. 801). Many of the supposed detrimental consequences to young parents thought to have been caused by early childbearing may, in fact, according to Chilman, be due to preexisting personal, social, or economic conditions and not to early parenthood *per se.* Another surprising conclusion made by Chilman is that the consequences of adolescent childbearing may be less severe if the young woman does not marry. According to Chilman's review, early marriage, rather than the timing of the first birth *per se,* is most strongly related to later marital disruption, to dropping out of school, and so on.

Although the long-term negative consequences of early parenthood for adolescents may have been overstated in a causal sense, there is little doubt that teen childbearing is usually associated with heavy psychological, social, and economic costs (Furstenberg, 1980; Lieberman, 1980; Presser, 1980; Trussel, 1980). The detrimental consequences for infants born to young mothers may also be due less to the age and the biological maturity of the mother than to poor diet and inadequate prenatal care (Makinson, 1985), but there are substantial medical risks for infants born to young teen mothers (Menken, 1980).

Women's Roles and Fertility

The relationship between women's roles and fertility is complex and multifaceted (see book-length treatments by Allman, 1978; Kupinsky, 1977; Scanzoni, 1975). The following section briefly highlights selected relationships between how women are regarded and what they do in society, on the one hand, and their fertility, on the other.

Youssef (1978) made a critically important distinction between two components of women's status: the *rights* given to women and the *respect* given to them. This distinction is especially important in the study of fertility because the two factors are sometimes used interchangeably when, in fact, they are often inversely related: "Thus, women receive great respect in certain societies that give them few rights; they receive equality of rights in societies in which they compete with men but have relatively low respect" (Youssef, 1978, p. 77).

Several scholars have analyzed modernization, women's status, and fertility in Muslim societies, which are, of course, among the most traditional in the world (Allman, 1978; Beck & Keddie, 1978). In such societies, women are highly respected in domestic and maternal roles, but there are strong economic, cultural, and structural barriers to their activity in public life. Under these conditions, fertility may remain unchanged or may

change very slowly even with rapid societal development. Youssef (1978) reported that, although economic development varies considerably across Muslim countries, levels of fertility appear not to have reacted to these changes or to differences in global economic-industrial conditions. However, "The critical point is to relate fertility levels of Muslim populations *to women's status and position*" (Youssef, 1978, p. 74; italics mine). When women's status indicators in Muslim countries were combined (female literacy, literacy relative to males, income-earning activity, timing of marriage, and incidence of marriage), two thirds of the variance in gross reproduction rates was explained, with female literacy explaining the largest amount.

As noted earlier, the extent to which women spend their lives bearing and raising children depends, largely, on the alternatives that are open to them (Hoffman *et al.,* 1978). In traditional societies and subcultures, the major role of women is motherhood. But in the process of societal development and technological change, women become more educated and more involved in the nonagrarian labor force. Consequently, in advanced societies, alternatives to motherhood, or at least alternatives to *prolonged* bearing and raising of children, have become extremely important.

Direction of Effects. The inverse relationship between fertility and women's education or employment (indicators of their roles and status) is well documented, but considerable efforts are still being made to understand the causal processes involved (Cramer, 1980; Rindfuss, Bumpass, & St. John, 1980; Weller, 1977). Do women's education and employment reduce fertility? Does earlier or higher fertility curtail education and employment? Are both equally important, or is one direction of effect much stronger than the other? At the societal level, changes in women's roles (higher education and employment) seem likely to reduce aggregate fertility, but at the personal level, the reverse is probably also true: fertility experiences have powerful effects on whatever else women do in life. Stated simply:

> No factor has greater impact on the roles women occupy than maternity. Whether a woman becomes a mother, the age at which she does so, and the timing and number of her subsequent births set the conditions under which other roles are assumed. (Rindfuss et al., 1980, p. 431)

Most scholars would agree that there is some degree of mutual causation in the relationship between employment and fertility, but a majority seem to maintain that the dominant path is from employment to fertility. In a summary and empirical evaluation of the causal direction, Cramer (1980) concluded that in the short run, fertility has a large impact on employment; and that, in the long run, years of employment also have a substantial effect on fertility behavior.

There are, however, some important exceptions to the generally observed inverse relationship between employment and fertility. For example, in developing countries, work and motherhood may not be conflicting roles. Child-care responsibilities may be turned over to extended-family members (grandparents or siblings) as a matter of course, and often, work is located in or near the home. Similarly, in low socioeconomic groups, the obligation for married women to work is included in the traditional role of wife, *along with* maternal and domestic responsibilities. Working is not a choice for these women, it is a necessity. Furthermore, the work they do (with low pay and little intrinsic reward or job satisfaction) does not represent a desirable alternative to motherhood. It follows that this type of work for women is not necessarily accompanied by smaller desired or completed family size (Kupinsky, 1977, pp. 215–216). Kupinsky (1977) highlighted several theoretical perspectives as being particularly helpful in understanding the multifaceted relationship between women's employment and fertility.

Psychological Perspective. Individual personality factors, including the values of children, play an important role in the relationship between female employment and fertility (Hoffman & Hoffman, 1973; Pohlman, 1969). If the psychological rewards and values of childbearing are very high, women are less likely to work, and couples are more likely to have a child or additional children. Conversely, if the psychological rewards of childbearing are low, women are more likely to seek alternative means of gratification, such as occupational roles in preference to motherhood.

Economic Perspective. The decision to bear children is sometimes a rational choice that depends on the perceived economic cost of children vis-à-vis other ways in which money might be spent. At the macrolevel, the relationship can be seen in lower fertility rates during economic depressions and higher rates during times of relative economic prosperity. Of course, the economic cost of rearing a child has increased rapidly (Espenshade, 1980) with accelerating inflation, and the historical economic advantage of having many children to provide labor has all but disappeared. According to the income adequacy hypothesis, the higher the income of the husband, the less likely the well-educated woman is to work or to have low fertility. Conversely, a well-educated woman married to a low earning husband is more likely both to work and to have low fertility (Sweet, 1970). Mason (1974) argued that the higher a woman's potential wage rate, the greater the economic opportunity costs of children, and hence the fewer children chosen. As would be expected, Kupinsky (1977) reported that the negative association between the wife's income and fertility is well documented.

Sociological Perspective. When women enter the labor force, one perspective anticipates role conflicts between parental and work responsibilities. To resolve these conflicts, women usually reduce the obligation to one role or the other. This can be done by lessening parental responsibilities (having fewer children), by dropping out of the labor force when parental roles are especially demanding, or by somehow combining both roles as well as possible by means of surrogate caregivers, part-time work, and so on).

A more social-psychological approach emphasizes the importance of sex-role orientations, especially of women (Mason, 1974; Scanzoni, 1975, 1978, 1979). Some recent findings suggest compelling links between sex-role orientations, women's employment, and fertility. For example, the greater the sex-role egalitarianism and the fewer the children intended or desired, the longer marriage is delayed; the higher the educational attainment, the more work is pursued for intrinsic gratifications and external rewards (Scanzoni, 1975). According to Scanzoni's integration of previous studies and analyses of data in the North Central United States, changes in sex-role orientation have preceded and affected both female employment and fertility. Scanzoni's (1978, 1979) studies have emphasized the explicit marital-negotiation processes of low-fertility egalitarian women.

A final sociological approach emphasizes the importance of the worker role *per se.* Working before having any children, and especially the proportion of years worked since marriage, is consistently related to smaller-family-size desires and expectations (Clifford & Tobin, 1977), to earlier and more effective use of birth control (Kupinsky, 1977), to longer intervals between marriage and the first child (Clifford & Tobin, 1977), and to total fertility (Kupinsky, 1977). The lowest fertility occurs among mothers who have worked during the greatest proportion of their marriage and who worked before their first child was born (Clifford & Tobin, 1977).

Biological Perspective. Although biological explanations of the relationships between women's fertility and their education and employment are not often emphasized, neither can they be ignored. There is evidence that subfecundity influences women both to enter the labor force and, of course, to have lower fertility. Long ago, it was observed that, in every age group, couples with working wives were less likely to be fecund and more likely to be sterile than those with wives not working (Freedman *et al.*, 1959). In other words, the biological hypothesis suggests that this third factor, subfecundity, is a partial explanation for the inverse relationship between women's employment and their fertility (Kupinsky, 1977).

Summary of Women's Roles and Status. Roles of women have historically been closely tied to bearing and raising children. In countries with very high fertility, these traditional female roles continue to be especially prominent. However, women's education and employment are increasing worldwide, both in absolute terms and relative to men.

Fertility desires, expectations, and experiences in the United States have been linked to women's roles (Scanzoni, 1975) and especially to the traditional homemaking role as the appropriate place of women (Thornton & Camburn, 1979). Changes have been documented in the increasingly egalitarian sex-role attitudes of women in the United States (Mason, Czajka, & Arber, 1976). Especially striking are analyses of panel data that found the same women's sex-role attitudes to have become much less traditional over a 15-year period (Thornton & Freedman, 1979). In 1962, 32%–56% of women gave egalitarian responses to sex-role-attitude questions, but by 1977, the percentage had increased to 60%–77%. The changes were not linked to age or maturation, but additional education, paid employment, and divorce were related to shifts toward egalitarian attitudes. These changes in sex-role attitudes, and their correlates, have important implications for understanding fertility, especially when viewed in terms of the links that Scanzoni (1975) identified between sex-role equality, the desire for a small family size, postponement of marriage, increasing education, and employment for intrinsic reasons.

Summary and Conclusions

Fertility levels in the United States and other advanced societies have shown a long-standing decline. In recent decades, similar declines have begun in most developing nations. Biological changes over historical time and biological differences between groups help only minimally to explain these fertility changes and differentials. Technological advances have made control over fertility a practical reality in advanced societies and increasingly possible in developing countries. Clearly, however, fertility patterns do not depend only, or even mostly, on biology or technology for controlling conception or birth. Particularly in advanced societies, fertility patterns depend most fundamentally on the social, psychological, and economic elements of the culture, among which elements marriage and family are especially important.

Historically, marriage has been the social-cultural mechanism for legitimizing childbearing. Lower fertility has resulted when people have not married or when they have spent less time in marriage relations, either because they postponed marriage or because marriages were terminated. Later ages of marriage have recently been observed in the United States and in developing nations. Levels of nonmarital cohabitation increased considerably during the 1970s, and divorce trends in advanced societies, especially in the United States, reflect the fact that marriages are less stable than they have ever been. There have also been signs that remarriage is becoming less frequent and that cohabitation after first marriage is becoming more common. After reviewing these trends, Westoff (1978b) wrote that "such informal arrangements will hardly contribute to increasing fertility and there will probably be less stability in the early (more fertile) years of marriage" (p. 80). These changes in marriage and family patterns appear to be widespread, and they portend low fertility in the foreseeable future.

Other interfaces between fertility and marriage and family patterns are less universal or less well understood than the demographic marital variables just referred to. For example, insights into how polygyny and polyandry affect fertility in specific cultures are of limited value in explaining or predicting general fertility patterns or trends. At a microlevel of analysis, characteristics of marital interaction (especially communication and equality) appear to be important variables in fertility planning and decision making, but these dynamics do not appear to have been as widely studied as the more easily assessed demographic marital characteristics. Recent studies of lineage fertility have, however, illuminated some of the key mechanisms by which differential fertility is transmitted intergenerationally (Thornton, 1980).

At the most general conceptual level, it has been argued that there are pervasive changes toward more heterogeneous life experiences that are inversely related to fertility. Cogswell and Sussman (1979) contended that the effects of heterogeneity operate in both societal and familial contexts, and where there are diverse contacts and experiences, there tend to be lower fertility rates and smaller completed family size. The notion of *heterogeneity* "refers to exposure to and experience with people, ideas, knowledge, organizational systems, cultures, values, and lifestyles which are different from those experienced in the past" (Cogswell & Sussman, 1979, p. 184). It would seem that heterogeneous experiences could influence fertility through their impact on personal modernity which has been defined as an individual's awareness of the range of available options and the degree to which he or she holds values that permit the choosing of options that are best suited to his or her abilities, talents, skills, interests, and preferences (Safilios-Rothschild, 1970).

Heterogeneous experiences and individual modernity are the antithesis of traditional family lifestyles and roles, expecially for women. Perhaps the family-related changes of greatest worldwide significance for fertility are occurring in women's roles and status. Fundamental indicators of these changes are greater access to and involvement in education and employment.

When viewed against the historical marital and family roles of women, the changes described above have important implications for fertility. The extent of change in women's status, and particularly their involvement in the economy, is impossible to predict, but the direction of change is clear: increasing proportions of women will be better educated and will be oriented to employment as well as to the traditional roles of bearing and raising children. Changes in values about children, parenting, and alternatives; sex roles and sex-role orientations; educational and economic activities of women; contraceptive knowledge and practice; and other macrosocial-cultural influences—all will affect fertility through the timing of marriage, marital processes and quality, alternative marital arrangements and structures, and the stability of marriage. Much has been learned about marriage, family, and fertility links, but much remains to be better understood.

ACKNOWLEDGMENTS

Appreciation is expressed to Arland Thornton and two anonymous reviewers for their critical insights and suggestions. I am likewise indebted to Kenneth H. Cannon, Debra Caswell-Madsen, Katrina Day, Wayne Godfrey, Mike Jones, Lori Roggman, and Marilyn Skinner for their assistance in researching and preparing this chapter, and to Vicki Luther for her careful typing of the manuscript.

References

Ahmen, F. Situational stability and fertility planning behavior. Doctoral dissertation, University of Chicago, 1976. *Dissertation Abstracts International*, 1977, *38*, 1049A.

Allman, J. (Ed.). *Women's status and fertility in the Muslim world*. New York: Praeger, 1978.

Andorka, R. *Determinants of fertility in advanced societies*. New York: Free Press, 1978.

Anker, R. An analysis of fertility differentials in developing countries. *Review of Economics and Statistics*, 1978, *60*(1), 58–69.

Arnold, F. A., Bulatao, R. A., Buripakdi, C., Chung, B. J., Fawcett, J. T., Iritani, T., Lee, S. J., & Wu, T. S. *The value of children: A cross national study*, Vol. 1. Honolulu: East-West Population Center, 1975.

Baldwin, W. H. *Adolescent pregnancy and childbearing: Growing concerns for Americans*. Population Bulletin 31 (September), Washington, D.C.: Population Reference Bureau, 1976.

Baldwin, W. H., & Cain, V. The children of teenage parents. *Family Planning Perspectives*, 1980, *12*, 34–43.

Barnett, L. D., & MacDonald, R. H. A study of the membership of the national organization for non-parents. *Social Biology*, 1976, *23*(4), 297–310.

Bebarta, P. C. Family type and fertility in an urbanized village in India. Doctoral dissertation, Utah State University, 1974. *Dissertation Abstracts International*, 1974, *36*, 560-A.

Beck, L., & Keddie, N. (Eds.). *Women in the Muslim world*. Cambridge: Harvard University Press, 1978.

Berelson, B. The value of children: A taxonomical essay. *The Population Council Annual Report*. New York: Population Council, 1973.

Bracken, M. B., Klerman, L. V., & Bracken, B. S. Coping with pregnancy resolution among never married women. *American Journal of Orthopsychiatry*, 1978, *48*(2), 320–334.

Bram, S. To have or have not: A social psychological study of voluntarily childless couples, parents-to-be, and parents. Doctoral dissertation, University of Michigan, 1974. *Dissertation Abstracts International*, 1975, *35*, 4250B–4251B.

Brown, L. S. Do users have more fun: A study of the relationship between contraceptive behavior, sexual assertiveness and patterns of casual attribution. Doctoral dissertation, Southern Illinois University, 1977. *Dissertation Abstracts International*, 1978, *39*, 5002B–5003.

Bulatao, R. A. *The value of children: Across national study, Vol. 2: Philippines*. Honolulu: East-West Population Institute, 1975.

Bumpass, L. L. Age at marriage as a variable in socio-economic differentials in fertility. *Demography*, 1969, *6*, 45–54.

Bumpass, L. L. Data relevant to socialization in the U.S. National Fertility surveys. *Papers of the East-West Population Institute*, 1975, 36.

Bumpass, L. L., & Mburugu, E. K. Age at marriage and completed family size. *Social Biology*, 1977, *24*, 31–37.

Bumpass, L. L., & Westoff, C. F. *The later years of childbearing*. Princeton, NJ.: Princeton University Press, 1970.

Burch, T. K., & Gendell, M. Extended family structure and fertility:

Some conceptual and methodological issues. *Journal of Marriage and the Family*, 1971, *32*, 227–236.

Burnside, B. M. Gender roles and lifestyle: A sociocultural study of voluntary childlessness. Doctoral dissertation, University of Washington, 1977. *Dissertation Abstracts International*, 1978, *38*, 5557A–5558A.

Burr, W. R. *Theory contruction and the sociology of the family*. New York: Wiley, 1973.

Byrne, D. The people glut: Societal problems and the sexual behavior of individuals. *The Journal of Sex Research*, 1979, *15*,(1), 1–5.

Cahn, J. The influence of others on teenagers' use of birth control. Doctoral dissertation, University of New York, 1978. *Dissertation Abstracts International*, 1978, *39*, 1537B.

Campbell, A. A. Trends in teenage childbearing in the United States. In C. Chilman (Ed.), *Adolescent pregnancy and childbearing: Findings from research*. Washington, D.C.: U.S. Government Printing Office, 1980.

Card, J. J., & Wise, L. L. Teenage mothers and teenage fathers: The impact of early childbearing on the parents personal and professional lives. *Family Planning Perspectives*, 1978, *10*(4) 199–205.

Case of the miraculous bullet. *American Heritage*, 1971, *23*(December), 99.

Chen, K. H., Wishik, S. M., & Scrimshaw, S. The effects of unstable sexual unions on fertility in Guayaquil, Ecuador. *Social Biology*, 1974, *21*, 353–359.

Chilman, C. *Adolescent sexuality in a changing american society: Social and psychological perspectives*. NIH Monograph No. 79-1426, U.S. Department of Health, Education, and Welfare. Washington, D.C.: U.S. Government Printing Office, 1978.

Chilman, C. *Adolescent pregnancy and childbearing: Findings from Research*. Washington, D.C.: U.S. Government Printing Office, 1980.(a)

Chilman, C. Social and psychological research concerning adolescent childbearing: 1970–1980. *Journal of Marriage and the Family*, 1980, *42*, 793–806.(b)

Clayton, R. R., & Bokemeier, J. L. Premarital sex in the seventies. *Journal of Marriage and the Family*, 1980, *42*, 759–775.

Clifford, W. B., & Tobin, P. L. Labor force participation of working mothers and family formation: Some further evidence. *Demography*, 1977, *14*(3), 273–284.

Cogswell, B. E., & Sussman, M. B. Family fertility. In W. R. Burr, R. Hill, F. I. Nye, & I. L. Reiss (Eds.), *Contemporary theories about the family*, Vol 1. New York: Free Press, 1979.

Cohen, S. B., & Sweet, J. A. The impact of marital disruption and remarriage on fertility. *Journal of Marriage and the Family*, 1974, *36*, 87–96.

Coombs, L. How many children do couples really want? *Family Planning Perspectives*, 1978, *10*(5), 303–308.

Cosgrove, P. S., Penn, R. L., & Chambers, N. Contraceptive practice after clinic discontinuation. *Family Planning Perspectives*, 1978, *10*, 337–340.

Cramer, J. C. Fertility and female employment: Problems of causal direction. *American Sociological Review*, 1980, *45*, 167–190.

Cutright, P., & Groeneveld, L. Birth planning success: Motivation and contraceptive method. *Family Planning Perspectives*, 1978, *10*, 43–48.

Cutright, P., & Jaffe, F. *Impact of family planning programs on fertility*. New York: Praeger, 1977.

Cvetkovich, G., & Grote, B. *Antecedents of responsible family formation*. Progress report paper presented at a conference sponsored by the Population Division, National Institute of Child Health and Human Development, Bethesda, Maryland, 1975.

Cypress, B. K. Family planning visits to private physicians. *Family Planning Perspectives*, 1979, *11*, 234–236.

Davis, K. Institutional patterns favoring high fertility in underdeveloped areas. *Eugenics Quarterly*, 1955, *2*, 33–39.

Davis, K., & Blake, J. Social structure and fertility: An analytical framework. *Economic Development and Cultural Change*, 1956, *4*, 211–235.

Delamater, J., & Maccorquodale, P. Premarital contraceptive use: A test of two models. *Journal of Marriage and the Family*, 1978, *40*, 235–247.

Dembo, J., & Lundell, B. Factors affecting adolescent contraceptive practices: Implications for sex education. *Adolescence*, 1979, *14*,(56), 657–664.

Diamond, M., Steinhoff, P. G., Palmore, J. A., & Smith, R. G. Sexuality, birth control, and abortion: A decision making sequence. *Journal of Biosocial Science*, 1973, *5*, 347–361.

Dorjahn, V. R. Fertility, polygyny, and their interrelations in Temme society. *American Anthropologist*, 1958, *60*, 838–860.

Downing, D. C., & Yaukey, D. The effects of marital dissolution and remarriage on fertility in urban Latin America. *Population Studies*, 1979, *33*, 537–547.

Downs, P. E. Examining the intrafamily decision making process with respect to contraceptive behavior. Doctoral dissertation, University of North Carolina at Chapel Hill, 1976. *Dissertation Abstracts International*, 1977, *37*, 5377A.

Dozier, E. P. *The Kalinga of Northern Luzon, Phillipines*. New York: Holt, Rinehart, & Winston, 1967.

Dryfoos, T. G., & Heisler, T. Contraceptive services for adolescents: An overview. *Family Planning Perspectives*, 1978, *10*, 223–233.

Duncan, O. D., Freedman, R., Coble, J. M., & Slesinger, D. P. Marital fertility and the size of family of orientation. *Demography*, 1965, *2*, 508–515.

Easterlin, R. A. Towards a socioeconomic theory of fertility: Survey of recent research on economic factors in American fertility. In S. J. Behrman, L. Corsa, Jr., & R. Freedman (Eds.), *Fertility and family planning: A world view*. Ann Arbor: University of Michigan Press, 1969.

Easterlin, R. A. Relative economic status and the American Fertility swing. In E. B. Sheldon (Ed.), *Family and Economic Behavior*. Philadelphia: J. B. Lippincott, 1973.

Ebanks, G. E., George, P. M., & Nobbe, C. E. Fertility and number of partnerships in Barbados. *Population Studies*, 1974, *28*, 449–461.

Edwards, L. E., Steinman, M. E., Arnold, K. A., & Hakanson, E. Y. Adolescent pregnancy prevention services in high school clinics. *Family Planning Perspectives*, 1980, *12*, 6–14.

Espenshade, T. J. The value and cost of children. *Population Bulletin*, 1977, *32*, 2–47.

Espenshade, T. J. Raising a child can now cost $85,000. *Intercom* (Population Reference Bureau), 1980, *8*(September), 10–13.

Fawcett, J. T. (Ed.) *The satisfactions and costs of children: Theories, concepts, methods*. Honolulu: East-West Population Institute, East-West Center, 1972.

Fawcett, J. T. (Ed.). *Psychological perspectives on population*. New York: Basic Books, 1973.

Finkel, M. L., & Finkel, D. J. Male adolescent contraceptive utilization. *Adolescence*, 1978, *13*, 443–451.

Fisher, W. Affective, attitudinal, and normative determinants of contraceptive behavior among university men. Doctoral dissertation, Purdue University, 1978. *Dissertation Abstract International*, 1979, *39*, 4613B–4614B.

Fisher, W. A., Byrne, D., Edmunds, M., Miller, C. T., Kelley, K., & White, L. A. Psychological and situation specific correlates of contraceptive behavior among university women. *Journal of Sex Research*, 1979, *15*(1), 38–55.

Ford, K. *Contraceptive utilization*. DHEW publication No. PHS 79-1978. Office of Health Research, Statistics, and Technology. National Center of Health Statistics, Hyattsville, Maryland, September 1978.

Foreit, K. G., & Foreit, J. R. Correlates of contraceptive behavior among unmarried U.S. college students. *Studies in Family Planning*, 1978, *9*(6), 169–174.

Forrest, J. D., Tietze, C., & Sullivan, E. Abortion in the United States. *Family Planning Perspectives*, 1979, *11*(6), 329–341.

Fox, G. The mother-daughter relationship as a sexual socialization structure: A research review. *Family Relations*, 1980, *29*, 21–28.

Francke, L. B., Abramson, P., & Maitlan, T. Childless by choice. *Newsweek*, January 14, 1980, p. 96.

Freedman, D. S., & Thornton, A. The long term impact of pregnancy at marriage on the family's economic circumstances. *Family Planning Perspectives*, 1979, *11*(1), 13, 18–21.

Freedman, R. *The sociology of human fertility: An annotated bibliography*. New York: Wiley, 1975.

Freedman, R., Takeshita, J. Y., & Sun, T. H. Fertility and family planning in Taiwan: A case study of demographic transition. *American Journal of Sociology*, 1964, *70*, 16–27.

Freedman, R., Freedman, D. S., & Thornton, A. D. Changes in fertility expectations and preferences between 1962 and 1977: Their relations to final parity. *Demography*, 1980, *17*, 365–378.

Furstenberg, F. F. Birth control experience among pregnant adolescents—Process of unplanned parenthood. *Social Problems*, 1971, *19*, 192.

Furstenberg, F. *Unplanned parenthood: The social consequences of teenage childbearing*. New York: Free Press, 1976.

Furstenberg, F. F. The social consequences of teenage parenthood. In C. Chilman (Ed.), *Adolescent pregnancy and childbearing: Findings from research*. Washington, D.C.: U.S. Government Printing Office, 1980.

George, P. M., Ebanks, G. E., Nobbe, C. E., & Anwar, M. Fertility differences between the family of orientation and the family of procreation in Barbados. *International Journal of Sociology of the Family*, 1976, *6*, 57–69.

Goldsmith, S., Gabrielson, M., Gabrielson, I., Matthews, V., & Potts, L. Teenagers, sex and contraception. *Family Planning Perspectives*, 1972, *4*, 32–38.

Goldstein, M. C. Fraternal polyandry and fertility in a high Himalayan valley. *Human Ecology*, 1976, *4*(3), 223–233.

Gordon, S., Scales, P., & Everly, K. *The sexual adolescent: Communicating with teenagers about sex* (2nd ed.). North Scituate, Mass.: Duxbury Press, 1979.

Gustavus, S. O. The family size preferences of young people: A replication and follow-up study. *Studies in Family Planning*, 1973, *4*, 335–342.

Gustavus, S. O., & Nam, C. B. The formation and stability of ideal family size among young people. *Demography*, 1970, *7*, 43–51.

Haskell, S. D., & Handler, L. Personality and background predictors of a young wife's desired family size. *Journal of Clinical Psychology*, 1977, *33*(3), 755–759.

Hedin-Pourghasemi, M. Sex role attitudes and contraceptive practices among never-married university students. Doctoral dissertation, Tufts University, 1977. *Dissertation Abstracts International*, 1978, *38*, 6344A.

Henley, J. R., & Gustavus, S. O. An exploratory technique for measuring fertility norms. *Social Biology*, 1976, *23*(2), 149–157.

Hern, W. M. High fertility in a Peruvian Amazon indian village. *Human Ecology*, 1977, *5*(4), 355–368.

Hill, R. *Family development in three generations*. Cambridge, Mass.: Shenkman, 1971.

Hill, R., Stycos, J. M., & Back, K. W. *The family and population control: A Puerto Rican experiment in social change*. Chapel Hill: University of North Carolina Press, 1959.

Hoffman, L. W. A psychological perspective on the value of children to parents. In J. T. Fawcett (Ed.), *The satisfactions and costs of children: Theories, concepts, methods.* Honolulu: East-West Population Institute, 1972.

Hoffman, L. W. The value of children to parents and the decrease in family size. *Proceedings of the American Philosophical Society,* 1975, *119,* 430–438.

Hoffman, L. W., & Hoffman, M. L. The value of children to parents. In J. T. Fawcett (Ed.), *Psychological perspectives on population.* New York: Basic Books, 1973.

Hoffman, L. W., & Manis, J. D. The value of children in the United States: A new approach to the study of fertility. *Journal of Marriage and the Family,* 1979, *41,* 583–596.

Hoffman, L. W., Thornton, A., & Manis, J. D. The value of children to parents in the United States. *Journal of Population,* 1978, *1*(2), 91–131.

Hornick, J. P., Doran, L., & Crawford, S. H. Premarital contraceptive usage among male and female adolescents. *The Family Coordinator,* 1979, *28,* 181–190.

Howell, N. Toward a uniformitarian theory of human paleodemography. *Journal of Human Evolution,* 1976, *5,* 25–40.

Humphrey, M. Sex differences in attitude to parenthood. *Human Relations,* 1977, *30,* 737–749.

Irons, E. S. The causes of unwanted pregnancy: A psychological study from a feminist perspective. Doctoral dissertation, University of Massachusetts, 1977. *Dissertation Abstracts International,* 1978, *38,* 5354A.

Jaffe, F. S., & Dryfoos, J. G. Fertility control services for adolescents: Access and utilization. In C. Chilman (Ed.), *Adolescent pregnancy and childbearing: Findings from Research.* Washington, D.C.: U.S. Government Printing Office, 1980.

Jessor, S., & Jessor, R. Transition from virginity to nonvirginity among youth: A social-psychological study over time. *Developmental Psychology,* 1975, *11,* 473–484.

Jones, E. F., Forrest, J. D., Goldman, N., Henshaw, S. K., Lincoln, R., Rosoff, J. I., Westoff, C. F., & Wulf, D. Teenage pregnancy in developed countries: Determinants and policy implications. *Family Planning Perspectives,* 1985, *17,* 53–63.

Kammeyer, K. C. W. *Confronting the issues: Sex roles, marriage and the family* (2nd ed). Boston: Allyn & Bacon, 1986.

Kantner, J., & Zelnik, M. Sexual experiences of young unmarried women in the U.S. *Family Planning Perspectives,* 1972, *4,* 9–17.

Kupinsky, S. The fertility of working women in the United States: Historical trends and theoretical perspectives. In S. Kupinsky (Ed.), *The fertility of working women: A synthesis of international research.* New York: Praeger, 1977.

Lauriat, P. The effect of marital disruption on fertility. *Journal of Marriage and the Family,* 1969, *31,* 484–493.

Lee, C. F., & Kahn, M. M. Factors related to the intention to have additional children in the United States: A reanalysis of data from the 1965 and 1970 national fertility studies. *Demography,* 1978, *15*(3), 337–344.

Levin, M. L., & O'Hara, C. J. The impact of marital history of current husband on fertility of remarried white women in the United States. *Journal of Marriage and the Family,* 1978, *40*(1), 95–102.

Lieberman, E. J. The psychological consequences of adolescent pregnancy and abortion. In C. Chilman (Ed.), *Adolescent pregnancy and childbearing: Findings from research.* Washington, D.C.: U.S. Government Printing Office, 1980.

Lorimer, F. *Culture and human fertility.* Paris: UNESCO, 1954.

Lui, P. K. C. Differential fertility in Taiwan. *Contributed papers, Sydney Conference, International Union for the Scientific Study of Population,* 1967, 363–370.

Makinson, C. The health consequences of teenage fertility. *Family Planning Perspectives,* 1985, *17,* 132–139.

Malinowski, B. The principle of legitimacy. In R. Coser (Ed.), *The family, its structure and function* (2nd ed.). New York: St. Martin's Press, 1974.

Marino, A. Family, fertility and sex ratios in the British Carribbean. *Population Studies,* 1970, *24,* 159–172.

Marshall, K. D., & Cosby, A. R. Antecedents of early marital and fertility behavior. *Youth and Society,* 1977, *9,* 191–212.

Martin, J. F. Family planning and family health. *International Nursing Review,* 1978, *25*(6), 172–174.

Masnick, G. S., & McFalls, J. A., Jr. A new perspective on the twentieth-century American fertility swing. *Journal of Family History,* 1976, *1,*(2), 217–244.

Mason, K. O. *Women's labor force participation and fertility.* Research Triangle Park, N.C.: Research Triangle Institute, 1974.

Mason, K., Czajka, J., & Arber, S. Change in U.S. women's sex role attitudes, 1964–1974. *American Sociological Review,* 1976, *41,* 573–596.

Mauldin, W. P. Patterns of fertility decline in developing countries, 1950–75. *Studies in Family Planning,* 1978, *9*(4), 75–84.

Mauldin, W. P. Population trends and prospects. *Science,* 1980, *209,* 148–157.

Mauldin, W. P., & Berelson, B. Conditions of fertility declines in developing countries, 1965–1975. *Studies in Family Planning,* 1978, *9,*(5), 89–147.

Maxwell, J. W., Sack, A. R., Frary, P. B., & Keller, J. F. Factors influencing contraceptive behavior of single college students. *Journal of Sex and Marital Therapy,* 1977, *3,* 265–273.

May, R. M. Human reproduction reconsidered. *Nature,* 1978, *272*(5653), 491–495.

McKenry, P. C., Walters, L. H., & Johnson, C. Adolescent pregnancy: A review of the literature. *The Family Coordinator,* 1979, *28,* 17–28.

McLaughlin, S. Expected family size and perceived status deprivation among high school senior women. *Demography,* 1974, *11,* 57–75.

Mead, M. *Male and female.* New York: Morrow, 1949.

Mead, M. *Male and female: A study of sexes in a changing world.* London: Gollancz, 1950.

Menken, J. The health and demographic consequences of adolescent pregnancy and childbearing. In C. Chilman (Ed.), *Adolescent pregnancy and childbearing: Findings from research.* Washington, D.C.: U.S. Government Printing Office, 1980.

Meyer, P., & Singarimbun, M. *Values and costs of children to Javanese and Sudanese parents: Preliminary results from the Indonesia V.O.C. survey.* Paper presented at a siminar, Population Institute, Gadjah Mada University, Yogyakarta, April 21, 1977.

Miller, B. C. Adolescent pregnancy and childbearing. *Utah Science,* 1985, *46,* 32–35.

Miller, B. C., & Myers-Walls, J. Stresses of parenting. In H. McCubbin & C. Figley, (Eds.), *Stress and the family.* New York: Brunner-Mazel, 1983.

Miller, W. B. The intendedness and wantedness of the first child. In W. B. Miller & L. F. Newman (Eds.), *The first child and family formation.* Chapel Hill: University of North Carolina Press, 1978.

Moore, M. J., & O'Connell, M. Perspectives on American fertility. U.S. Bureau of Census. *Current Population Reports.* Series P-23, No. 70. July 1978.

Mueller, E. Economic motives for family limitation: A study conducted in Taiwan. *Population studies,* 1972, *27,* 383–403.

Mukherjee, B. The role of husband-wife communication in family planning. *The Journal of Marriage and the Family,* 1975, *37,* 655–667.

Nag, M. *Factors affecting human fertility in nonindustrial societies: A cross-cultural study.* New Haven, Conn.: Yale University Publications in Anthropology, No. 66, Yale University Press, 1962.

Nag, M. Family type and fertility. *Proceedings of the World Population Conference at Belgrade.* New York: United Nations, 1967.

Nag, M. Pattern of mating behavior, immigration and contraceptives as factors affecting human fertility in Barbados. *Social and Economic Studies*, 1971, *20*, 111–133.

Nag, M. Economic values of children in an agricultural setting. In J. T. Fawcett (Ed.), *The satisfactions and costs of children: Theories, concepts, methods*. Honolulu: East-West Population Institute, 1972.

National Center for Health Statistics. Selected demographic characteristics of teenage wives and mothers. *Advance Data from Vital and Health Statistics* (HHS Publication No. PHS 80–1250). Hyattsville, Md.: U.S. Government Printing Office, 1980.

Nobbe, C. E., Ebanks, G. E., & George, P. M. A reexploration of the relationship between types of sex unions and fertility: The Barbadian case. *Journal of Comparative Family Studies*, Summer 1976, *7*(2), 295–308.

Norris, P. S. Wife-husband fertility issues in Hawaii: A social psychological analysis. Doctoral dissertation, University of Hawaii, 1977. *Dissertation Abstracts International*, 1977, *38*, 2433-B.

Nye, F. I., & Lamberts, M. B. *School-age parenthood: Consequences for babies, mothers, fathers, grandparents, and others*. Extension Bulletin 0667. Pullman: Washington State Cooperative Extension, 1980.

Okada, L. M., & Gillespi, D. G. The impact of family planning programs on unplanned pregnancies. *Family Planning Perspectives*, 1977, *9*, 173–176.

Onaka, A. T., Yaukey, D., & Chevan, A. Reproductive time lost through marital dissolution in metropolitan Latin America. *Social Biology*, 1977, *24*,(2), 100–115.

Ory, M. G. The decision to parent or not: Normative and structural components. *Journal of Marriage and the Family*, 1978, *40*(3), 531–539.

Pakrasi, K., & Malaker, C. The relationship between family type and fertility. *Milbank Memorial Fund Quarterly*, 1967, *45*(4), 451–460.

Paterson, N. Adolescent family size preferences. *International Journal of Sociology of the Family*, 1972, *2*, 231–245.

Peck, E. *The baby trap*. New York: Bernard Gris, 1971.

Peck, E., & Senderowitz, J. (Eds.). *Pronatalism: The myth of mom and apple pie*. New York: Thomas Crowell, 1974.

Pohlman, E. W. *The psychology of birth planning*. Cambridge, Mass.: Schenkman, 1969.

Presser, H. B. Age at menarche, socio-sexual behavior and fertility. *Social Biology*, 1978, *2*, 94–101.

Presser, H. B. Social consequences of teenage childbearing. In C. Chilman (Ed.), *Adolescent pregnancy and childbearing: Findings from research*. Washington, D.C.: U.S. Government Printing Office, 1980.

Ram, B., & Ebanks, G. E. Stability of unions and fertility in Barbados. *Social Biology*, 1973, *20*, 143–150.

Reiss, I. L. *Family systems in America* (3rd ed.). New York: Holt, Reinhart & Winston, 1980.

Reiss, I. L., & Miller, B. C. A theory of heterosexual permissiveness. In W. Burr, R. Hill, F. I. Nye, & I. L. Reis (Eds.), *Contemporary theories about the family*. New York: Free Press, 1979.

Renne, K. S. Childlessness, health, and marital satisfaction. *Social Biology*, 1976, *23*(3), 183–197.

Rindfuss, R. R., Bumpass, L., & St. John, C. Education and fertility: Implications for the roles women occupy. *American Sociological Review*, 1980, *45*, 431–447.

Ryder, J. W. Interrelations between family structure and fertility in Yucatan. *Human Biology*, 196-76, *48*(1), 93–100.

Safilios-Rothschild, C. Toward a cross cultural conceptualization of family modernity. *Journal of Comparative Family Studies*, 1970, *1*, 19.

Scales, P. Males and morals: Teenage contraceptive behavior and the double standard. *The Family Coordinator*, 1977, *26*, 211–222.

Scanzoni, J. *Sex roles, life styles, and childbearing: Changing patterns in marriage and the family*. New York: Free Press, 1975.

Scanzoni, J. Gender roles and the process of fertility control. *Journal of Marriage and the Family*, 1976, *38*, 678–691.

Scanzoni, J. *Sex roles, women's work, and marital conflict: A study of family change*. Lexington, Mass: D. C. Heath, 1978.

Scanzoni, J. Work and fertility control sequences among younger married women. *Journal of Marriage and the Family*, 1979, *41*(4), 739–748.

Severy, L. Sex, contraception, and fertility attitudes and behavior: An overview. *The Journal of Sex Research*, 1979, *15*(1), 76–83.

Silverman, A., & Silverman, A. *The case against having children*. New York: David McKay, 1971.

Smith, E. M. Psycho-social correlates of regular contraceptive use in young unmarried women. Doctoral dissertation, Washington University, 1978. *Dissertation Abstracts International*, 1978, *39*, 1845A.

Sorenson, R. *Adolescent sexuality in contemporary America*. New York: World, 1973.

Spain, J. S. Psycho-ogical dimensions of effective and ineffective contraceptive use in adolescent girls. Doctoral dissertation, City University of New York, 1977. *Dissertation Abstracts International*, 1978, *38*, 3373B.

Steinlauf, B. Attitudes and cognitive factors associated with the contraceptive behavior of young women. Doctoral dissertation, Wayne State University, 1977. *Dissertation Abstracts International*, 1978, *38*, 2439B.

Stern, D., Smith, S., & Doolittle, F. How children used to work. *Law and Contemporary Problems*, 1975, *39*(3), 93–117.

Stokes, C. S., & Johnson, N. E. Birth order, size of family of orientation, and desired family size. *Journal of Individual Psychology*, 1977, *33*(1), 42–46.

Stycos, J. M., & Back, K. W. *The control of human fertility in Jamaica*. Ithaca, N.Y.: Cornell University Press, 1964.

Sweet, J. A. Family composition and the labor force activity of American wives. *Demography*, 1970, *7*, 195–209.

Thompson, L., & Spanier, G. B. Influence of parents, peers, and partners on the contraceptive use of college men and women. *Journal of Marriage and the Family*, 1978, *40*(3), 481–492.

Thornton, A. D. The first generation family and second generation fertility. In G. J. Duncan & J. N. Morgan (Eds.), *Five Thousand Families* (Vol. 5). Ann Arbor: Institute for Social Research, 1977.

Thornton, A. D. Marital dissolution, remarriage, and childbearing. *Demography*, 1978, *15*, 361–380.(a)

Thornton, A. Religion and fertility: The case of Mormonism. *Journal of Marriage and the Family*, 1979, *41*, 131–142.

Thornton, A. The influence of first generation fertility and economic status on second generation fertility. *Population and environment*, 1980, *3*, 51–52.

Thornton, A., & Camburn, D. Fertility, sex role attitudes, and labor force participation. *Psychology of Women Quarterly*, 1979, *4*, 61–80.

Thornton, A., & Freedman, D. Changes in sex role attitudes of women, 1962–1977: Evidence from a panel study. *American Sociological Review*, 1979, *44*, 831–842.

Tietze, C. Legal abortion in the United States: Rates and ratios by race and age, 1972–1974. *Family Planning Perspectives*, 1977, *9*(1), 12–15.

Tobin, P. L. Conjugal role definitions, values of children, and contraceptive practice. *Sociological Quarterly*, 1976, *17*(3), 314–322.

Toomey, B. G. College women and voluntary childlessness: A comparative study of women indicating they want to have children and those indicating they do not want to have children. Doctoral dissertation, Ohio State University, 1977. *Dissertation Abstracts International*, 1978, *38*, 6944A.

Torres, A. Rural and urban family planning services in the United States. *Family Planning Perspectives*, 1979, *11*, 109–114.

Trussel, T. J. Economic consequences of teenage childbearing. In C. Chilman (Ed.), *Adolescent pregnancy and childbearing: Findings from research*. Washington, D.C.: U.S. Government Printing Office, 1980.

Udry, J. R., Bauman, K., & Morris, N. Changes in premarital coital experience of recent decade-of-birth cohorts of urban America. *Journal of Marriage and the Family*, 1975, *37*, 783–787.

U.S. Bureau of the Census. Population profile of the United States. *Current Population Reports* (Series P-20, No. 350, 1979). Washington, D.C.: U.S. Government Printing Office, 1980.

Vinokur-Kaplan, D. Family planning decision making: A comparison and analysis of parents' considerations. *Journal of Comparative Family Studies,* 1977, *8*(1), 79–98.

Weller, R. H. Wife's employment and cumulative family size in the United States, 1970 and 1960. *Demography,* 1977, *14,* 43–65.

Westoff, C. F. Coital frequency and contraception. *Family Planning Perspectives,* 1974, *6,* 136–141.

Westoff, C. F. Marriage and fertility in the developed countries. *Scientific American,* 1978, *239*(6), 51–57.(a)

Westoff, C. F. Some speculations on the future of marriage and fertility. *Family Planning Perspectives,* 1978, *10*(2), 79–83.(b)

Westoff, C. F., & Jones, E. F. Contraception and sterilization in the United States, 1965–1975. *Family Planning Perspectives,* 1977, *9*(4), 153–157.(a)

Westoff, C. F., & McCarthy, J. Population attitudes and fertility. *Family Planning Perspectives,* 1979, *11,* 93–96.

Westoff, C. F., & Potvin, R. H. *College women and fertility values.* Princeton, N.J.: Princeton University Press, 1967.

Westoff, C. F., & Ryder, N. B. *The contraceptive revolution.* Princeton, NJ.: Princeton University Press, 1977.

Westoff, C. F., & Ryder, N. B. The predictive validity of reproductive intentions. *Demography,* 1979, *14*(4), 431–453.

Whiting, J. W. M. Effects of climate on certain cultural practices. In W. M. Goodenough (Ed.), *Explorations in current anthropology.* New York: McGraw-Hill, 1964.

Williams, S. J., Murthy, N., & Berggren, G. Conjugal unions among rural Hiatian women. *Journal of Marriage and the Family,* 1975, *37,* 1022–1030.

Woodward, D., Heath, A., & Chishold, L. Patterns of family building and contraceptive use of middle-class couples. *Journal of Biosocial Science,* 1978, *10,* 39–58.

Wyatt, F. Clinical notes on the motives of reproduction. *Journal of Social Issues,* 1967, *23*(4), 29–56.

Youssef, N. H. The status and fertility patterns of Muslim women. In L. Beck & N. Keddie (Eds.), *Women in the Muslin world.* Cambridge: Harvard University Press, 1978.

Zelnik, M., & Kantner, J. Sexual and contraceptive experience of young unmarried women in the United States, 1976 and 1971. *Family Planning Perspectives,* 1977, *9,* 55–71.

Zelnik, M., & Kantner, J. F. First pregnancies to women ages 15–19: 1976 and 1971. *Family Planning Perspectives,* 1978, *10*(1), 11–20.

Zelnik, M., & Kantner, J. Reasons for nonuse of contraception by sexually active women aged 15–19. *Family Planning Perspectives,* 1979, *11,* 289–296.

Zelnik, M., & Kantner, J. F. Sexual activity, contraceptive use and pregnancy among metropolitan area teenagers: 1971–1979. *Family Planning Perspectives,* 1980, *12,* 5.

Zelnik, M., Kantner, J. F., & Ford, K. *Sex and pregnancy in adolescence.* Beverly Hills, Calif.: Sage, 1981.

CHAPTER 22

Divorce

Helen J. Raschke

The first goal of this chapter is to examine the many facets of marital separation and divorce[1]—the nineteenth and twentieth century trends and concomitant societal changes, theoretical frameworks, correlates and individual causes, consequences and adjustment, legal aspects, and policy implications. The approach taken here is social-psychological and sociological; the relationships between individuals and between individuals and the larger society are the primary focus. Literature from other disciplines—psychology, psychiatry, social work, law and the judiciary, child and family development, economics, demography, family social science, and others—is included where appropriate.

The second goal is to analyze and synthesize the disparate literature into a coherent whole and to critique each part of the whole. Incorporated is the argument that much of the research was conducted from a deviance perspective, which influenced the original purpose, the questions asked, the variables focused on, and the interpretation of results. The deviance perspective is rooted in Western religious values that interpret the monogamous, lifelong, nuclear family as the only family form that can enable society to survive. Any deviation from that form was considered a basic threat to the survival of society. Currently, the deviance perspective seems to be moving from a threat to society to a threat to the individuals involved in divorce.

With these goals in mind, statistical trends of the incidence of divorce and the accompanying social and economic milieus are examined as the first step.

[1]Because of the scarcity of research on marital separation, it cannot be addressed as fully as divorce. It should be noted that marital separations occur more frequently than divorce (because of reconciliations) and can be as problematic (Weiss, 1975). Therefore, this chapter will be biased toward divorce, which may distort the picture somewhat in certain of the sections; this distortion seems unavoidable in view of the state of the knowledge at this time. Structural consequences, such as single-parent families and remarriage, are topics of separate chapters in this book and will not be included in this chapter.

Helen J. Raschke • West Texas Legal Services, Wichita Falls, TX 76301.

Context

Trends and Societal Changes

Prior to the nineteenth century, the history of marital separation and divorce is sketchy; it is probable, however, that marital separation and divorce are as old as the institution of marriage itself and are two of several mechanisms that evolved over the centuries to relieve the strains of marriage (Goode, 1963).

The incidence of divorce is estimated from census data, including the Current Population Surveys taken between the decennial censuses, or from vital registration statistics on divorce.[2] Two very different demographic approaches—period and cohort—use these divorce statistics to analyze marriage and divorce patterns. The period approach uses marriage, divorce, and mortality vital statistics for a specific period of time, conventionally one year, to depict the patterns of divorce for that time period. This approach includes all divorces for all ages and all lengths of marriages, from less than 1 year to over 50 years. From period divorce statistics, the crude rate and the refined rate are calculated; the crude rate is the ratio of the total number of divorces to the total population and the refined rate is the ratio of the total number of divorces to the number of married couples in the population.

With the cohort demographic approach, generally a group of couples married in the same year is followed over the span of their marriage; their subsequent divorces are recorded and analyzed. The cohort can be an age cohort, as well as a marriage cohort; that is, all those born in a specific year or interval of years (such as 1940–1944) are followed in the same way. An additional refinement is to use the latest vital statistics available and to project the proportion of cohort marriages (age at marriage or year of

[2]Vital registration statistics on divorce are acquired from the 28 states included in the Divorce Registration Area (DRA); divorce statistics for states not participating in the DRA are estimated from information provided by these states by comparing them to DRA states and areas with similar sociodemographic characteristics. The vital registration statistics yield higher levels of divorce than U.S. Census data, most likely because of failure to report a divorce in the U.S. Census (Preston & McDonald, 1979).

marriage) still in existence that would end in divorce if, at each successive interval of marriage duration, the cohort marriages were subject to the divorce and death rates of the current period (Preston & McDonald, 1979; Weed, 1980).

The period demographic approach is illustrated by Figure 1, which represents the refined divorce rate for the 124-year period 1860–1984.

Table 1 represents the cohort demographic approach beginning with the marriage cohort of 1950. It shows the percentage of cohort marriages that actually ended in divorce through 1977 as well as the percentage that was projected to end in divorce before the death of one spouse. This percentage shows a steady increase from 29.5 for the 1950 cohort to 49.2 for the 1973 cohort. Thus, of the couples married in 1973, nearly half of them have ended or will end their marriage by divorce before the death of one spouse, an increase of 66% in 23 years. These projections are based on 1976–1977 divorce and death rates, and as there has been a moderate increase in the divorce rates from 1977 to 1981, and then slight decreases in 1982 and 1983 (National Center for Health Statistics, 1984), these projections may slightly underestimate actual experience. Preston (1975) and Preston and McDonald (1979) developed the procedures used by Weed (1980) in calculating the projections in Table 1. These procedures re-

duced each cohort at each duration of marriage by the estimated number of divorces and by the estimated number of marriages dissolved by the death of one spouse.

As shown in Figure 1, the annual divorce rate has been rising since the mid-nineteenth century, with slight bulges after the Civil War and World War I, a dramatic rise and fall after World War II, and decreases during the Depression years of the 1930s, all reflecting to some degree the social and economic conditions of the time period. The most precipitous increase began in the early 1960s, leveled in 1976–1977, and began climbing again in the late 1970s and early 1980s. A record high was reached in 1979 and 1981 with a crude rate of 5.3 divorces (National Center for Health Statistics, 1982). The crude divorce rate then dropped to 5.1 in 1982, to 5.0 in 1983, and 4.9 in 1984, and again to 4.9 in the first half of 1985 (National Center for Health Statistics, 1983, 1984, 1985a,b). The increase in the divorce rate in the 1960s and 1970s was greater than could have been expected based on the long-term divorce rate up to the beginning of the 1960s (Cherlin, 1981).

In 1860, the earliest year in which data were compiled, the divorce rate was approximately 1 divorce per 1,000 existing marriages and was beginning to alarm some segments of American society (O'Neill, 1967). In the 60-

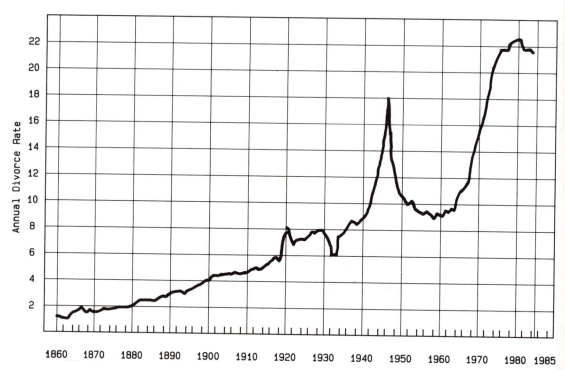

Figure 1. Annual divorce rate for the United States, 1860–1984. (Sources: 1866–1977, Cherlin, 1981; 1978–1980; U.S. Department of Health and Human Services, 1981a,b; 1981–1984, personal communication from Paul Glick, Professor Emeritus, Arizona State University.)

**Table 1. Number of Marriages Ended by Divorce and Percentage of Cohort Marriages
Projected to End in Divorce, United States, 1950–1977**[a]

| Year of marriage | Number of marriages in cohort | Cohort marriages ended by divorce through 1977 | | Percentage of cohort marriages projected to end in divorce |
		Cumulative number	Cumulative percentage	
1977	2,178,367	17,947	0.8	—
1976	2,154,807	92,050	4.3	—
1975	2,152,662	185,584	8.6	—
1974	2,229,667	289,759	13.0	—
1973	2,284,108	381,537	16.7	49.2
1972	2,282,154	448,033	19.6	48.7
1971	2,190,481	482,085	22.0	48.0
1970	2,158,802	535,330	24.8	47.8
1969	2,145,000	565,776	26.4	47.1
1968	2,069,000	560,362	27.1	45.9
1967	1,927,000	545,884	28.3	45.3
1966	1,857,000	539,856	29.1	44.3
1965	1,800,000	538,730	29.9	43.7
1964	1,725,000	512,797	29.7	42.2
1963	1,654,000	489,733	29.6	41.0
1962	1,577,000	468,397	29.7	40.0
1961	1,548,000	457,371	29.5	39.1
1960	1,523,000	461,192	30.3	38.8
1959	1,494,000	445,732	29.8	37.6
1958	1,451,000	428,035	29.5	36.5
1957	1,518,000	445,473	29.3	35.4
1956	1,585,000	457,366	28.9	34.4
1955	1,531,000	450,958	29.5	34.4
1954	1,490,000	438,147	29.4	33.8
1953	1,546,000	440,420	28.5	32.3
1952	1,539,318	445,529	28.9	32.1
1951	1,594,694	446,349	28.0	30.9
1950	1,667,231	448,442	26.9	29.5

[a]From Weed (1980).

year period (1860–1920) between the beginning of the Civil War era and the end of World War I, the divorce rate rose from 1 to 8 divorces per 1,000 existing marriages, with a particularly rapid rise during the Progressive Era (1890–1920)—from 3 to 8.

Major concomitant societal forces during the last half of the nineteenth century were increasing industrialization and urbanization spurred by technological advancements; these events weakened kinship ties and the control of younger people by their elders and the community, especially in the lower strata (Goode, 1963). O'Neill (1967) maintained that the modern form of the conjugal family emerged during the nineteenth century and that divorce became increasingly important as a safety valve for intolerable marriages. Goode (1963) argued that, theoretically, the conjugal family pattern "fit" the needs of the industrial system better than any other, and hence, this

family pattern was encouraged to develop. Both the conjugal family pattern and the industrial system made demands on individuals very different from those made by the older systems; the industrial system was based theoretically on individual achievement and merit, with little concern for the worker's individual satisfaction. As a result of this, plus the loss of many family functions to other emerging modern societal institutions, the family was left with core functions that placed more emphasis on the expressive aspects of marriage and less on the instrumental aspects, a change that made the marital relationship increasingly vulnerable to emotional and psychological stresses (Ogburn, 1953). Although the Industrial Revolution influenced family patterns and can be correlated with change in these family patterns, including divorce, it is difficult to establish positive causality, given the many complex factors involved in the process.

Also embedded in the factors surrounding industrialization and changing family patterns were the ideologies of equalitarianism and the conjugal family. Both emphasized freedom of choice, individualism, merit, and greater equality between the sexes and the classes. Included in these ideologies was the freedom not only to choose one's spouse, but also to end an intolerable marriage (Goode, 1963). Overlapping and interacting with these ideologies was another ideology of equal rights for women, emanating from the feminist movement in the mid-nineteenth century. Rabkin (1980) documented how married women changed, in the eyes of the law, from the property of their husbands into autonomous, legally competent adults in the nineteenth century, a change that laid the foundation for female emancipation and the emergence of the feminist movement.

It can be reasonably concluded that the complex of factors in the industrialization and urbanization processes plus the emerging ideologies and legal changes influenced the divorce rate. This happened gradually over the nineteenth century but was speeded up by the demands of the Civil War for war material, especially by the provision of more opportunities for paid jobs in industry outside the home for women; increased job opportunities, coupled with legal changes, increased the bargaining power of women vis-à-vis their husbands and enabled some women to leave unsatisfactory marriages (Scanzoni, 1979).

In addition, the sharp rise in the divorce rate during the Progressive Era escalated the divorce controversy that had begun in earnest by the mid-nineteenth century. This controversy revolved around the morality, the deviance, and the moral pathology of those involved in divorce (O'Neill, 1967). The stage was set for the study of divorce from a deviance perspective, although with different definitions in different historical periods.

By 1907 more stringent divorce laws had been pushed through by the conservatives (religious and political) in many states; however, Halem (1980) claimed that these laws were more "noteworthy in theory than in effect" and that, "as public sentiment changed, ways of circumventing civil and religious laws were found" (p. 50). By 1920, both opponents (considered the conservatives) and proponents (considered the liberals) realized that the rising divorce rate was beyond the control of civil laws and/or the pulpit.

The societal changes accompanying the fluctuating but steadily rising divorce rate per 1,000 marriages (from 8 to nearly 23) in the 65-year period from 1920 to 1985 are complex and interactive. The feminist movement was often blamed for the rising divorce rate. However, O'Neill (1971) argued that this movement actually became quiescent in the 1920s while at the same time the divorce rate continued to rise. This continuing rise was probably part of the aftermath of both World War I and the feminist movement plus the spirit of the 1920s— flamboyant, free-spending, prosperous, and rebellious. The severe economic depression of the 1930s contributed

to the lower divorce rate of that decade. The social and economic dislocations caused by World War II, in turn, were the major cause of the drastic rise in the divorce rate in the late 1940s. The "familism" of the 1950s, probably more than any other single factor in that decade, influenced the lowering and stabilizing of the divorce rate. Easterlin (1980) and Elder (1974) argued that this familism was greatly influenced by the 1930s economic and psychological deprivations experienced by the children of that decade, who became young adults in the 1950s. These deprivations included severe economic insecurity and family stresses due to unemployment by the father. Childhood deprivations, in turn, caused the Depression children to place high value on family life and family stability, which was made easier by the general economic prosperity of the 1950s.

In the 1960s, feminism and the women's movement(s) were resurrected after 40 quiescent years, and their goal of equal opportunities for education and jobs gave impetus to marketplace opportunities for women and an ideology for women to seek self-realization along with equal rights. In the 1970s, the vicissitudes of the economy— inflation plus recession—actually forced huge numbers of women into the paid labor market, and many women became self-supporting for the first time. The difficult economic situation of the 1970s was very different from that of the 1930s in its combination of serious inflation with recurrent recessions; as a result, the divorce rate was affected quite differently, as shown in Figure 1. In the 1960s, and especially throughout the 1970s and into the 1980s, the economic institutions interacted with family institutions to "pull" women into economic independence and to "push" them out of unsatisfactory marriages.

The ideologies of individualism (Goetting, 1979) and self-realization (Weiss, 1975), although rooted in earlier centuries, became increasingly important in the marital relationship and probably played a role in the drama of the rising divorce rates, especially in the 1960s and 1970s.

Finally, the social stigma attached to divorce began fading during the last 20 years, especially in the 1970s. This change accompanied an increase in divorce among the middle and upper classes, making it more difficult for the pulpit, the media, and the politicians to castigate the divorced. Nevertheless, Halem (1980) claimed that many of the social scientists, family professionals, and those in the medical profession, especially psychiatrists, continued to use the clinical pathology perspective to deal with the divorced: there was something clinically wrong with the individual that would require professional psychiatric or psychological therapy for rehabilitation, or divorce itself was producing clinical symptoms in individuals that would require outside professional help. Thus, the stigma may have faded overtly but, at least theoretically, remained covertly alive in this deviance perspective.

In summary, the concomitant broad societal changes, including economic fluctuations (e.g., prosperity, depressions, recessions, and inflation), political events such as wars, and social movements such as the women's movement, interacted with industrialization, urbanization, and economic conditions to encourage or force more women into the paid labor market, spur the fading of the social stigmas attached to divorce, and strengthen the ideologies attached to feminism, individualism, and self-realization. It would be difficult to disentangle the causal relationships of these complex economic, social, political, and ideological factors, which accompanied and undoubtedly contributed, in various ways, to the rise in the divorce rates during the last 120 years (for a comprehensive analysis of these relationships, see Cherlin, 1981).

Theoretical Context

Related to the statistical trends and broad societal changes are the theoretical perspectives that have accompanied the study of divorce by social scientists and others. These perspectives range from negative to neutral to somewhat positive.

The perspectives with negative connotations far outweigh the neutral and positive connotations and fit into the argument that divorce has been theoretically viewed and empirically studied from a deviance perspective. As Halem (1980) observed, "the assumption lingers that divorce in some way is connected to or results from a defect or weakness in one or both partners" (p. 3).

Sociology and the other social sciences profess to present facts and analyses to enable a more thorough understanding of the phenomena involved in the divorce process, and the helping professions offer various kinds of treatments. The problem arises when divorce is separated from other "problems in living" and is given more deviant treatment than is realistic. This type of perspective and treatment has been a major reason for the ambiguities surrounding divorce, making it more of a problem than it need be.

In the 1970s, both qualitative and quantitative empirical research increased dramatically, much of it atheoretical and of uneven quality. However, by 1980, one sociological theory, social exchange, and two versions of a social psychological theory, crisis (the first more sociologically oriented and the other more psychologically oriented), had been modified and adapted to describe, predict, and/or explain the causes (social exchange) and consequences (crisis) of separation and divorce.

Social exchange theory, based on the work of Homans (1958, 1974), Blau (1964), and Thibaut and Kelley (1959), has been used in various ways to explain the causes of divorce on the individual level. This theory is concerned with the costs and rewards that an individual perceives as being associated with a relationship. These rewards and costs were initially economic but came to include the social and psychological aspects of relationships in the sociological theories. Alternatives to present situations were added: that is, even if present costs outweighed rewards, one would not leave the relationship unless the alternative was perceived as better than the present outcome. Levinger (1965, 1976) changed the terminology to *attractions* and *barriers,* Scanzoni (1972, 1979) used the changing *bargaining power* of the spouses, and Yoder and Nichols (1980) built on Altman and Taylor's theory (1973) of *social penetration,* which posits that both situational determinants and personality factors must be taken into consideration. Yet the underlying assumptions and conceptual ideas of social exchange theory remain central in these versions to explain the causes for divorce and/or marital separation.

Crisis theory, the sociological version as opposed to the psychiatric version (cf. Caplan, 1964), originally developed by Hill and others (e.g., Hansen, 1965; Hill, 1949, 1958) and further elaborated by Burr (1973), has been used by family stress researchers and theorists to describe, predict, and explain when a stressor event will cause a crisis or a disorganization in a family. Hill's ABC-X model (1949) posited that A (the stressor event) was mediated by B (the crisis-meeting resources of the family) and C (the definition of the situation by the family) to produce X (the crisis). Burr (1973) modified the B factor into "invulnerability to stress" and McCubbin and Patterson (1982) suggested further strengthening of the original ABC-X model by the addition of postcrisis variables, such as calling it the "double ABC-X model." The As are the initial stressor event, normal family life changes, and stressors that result from the family's efforts to cope; the Bs are the resources already available and those coping resources strengthened or developed in response to the crisis; the Cs are the family's perception of the stressor event and also their perception of the crisis; and the Xs include family adaptation as well as crisis.

A second theoretical approach to crisis theory was developed in the 1970s by clinically oriented researchers and theorists to deal specifically with the consequences of separation and divorce. This theoretical school of thought is based on overlapping stages that describe some of the psychological-emotional consequences of separation and divorce. These stages are presented in Table 2. Each of these various theorists' stages include the symptoms associated with the stage as well as suggested clinical interventions. As Salts (1979) suggested, these models are basically in agreement, and their variation comes from their different starting and ending points in the separation–divorce process. For example, Wiseman (1975) based her theoretical model on Kübler-Ross's grief model (1953) and Smart (1977) applied Erikson's eight-stage developmental model (1963) in developing her model.

These theoretical developments are quite new, and although their explanatory power appears high, considerably more research is needed for further development and refinement. Other theoretical approaches that have potential for the study of divorce are general systems and family developmental (Price-Bonham & Balswick, 1980). More macro-, middle-range, and microtheorizing need to be done with more cooperation between clinician-practitioners and theorist-researchers.

Table 2. Comparison of Separation and Divorce Adjustment Stages[a]

| | Authors and stages | | | | | | | | | |
Time sequence	Bohannon (1970)	Herrman (1974)	Kessler (1975)	Wiseman (1975)	Weiss (1975)	E. Brown (1976)	Froiland & Hozeman (1977)	Levy & Joffe (1977)	Kraus (1979)	Smart (1979)
Before separation	Station I: Emotional divorce	Stage I: Denial Stage II: Anger	Stage I: Disillusionment Stage II: Erosion Stage III: Detachment	Stage I: Denial Stage II: Loss and depression	Stage I: Erosion of love	Stage I: Decision making	Stage I: Denial Stage II: Anger Stage III: Bargaining		Stage I: Denial	Stage I: Trust vs. mistrust Stage II: Autonomy vs. shame and doubt
Separation		Stage III: Bargaining Stage IV: Depression	Stage IV: Physical separation	Stage III: Anger and ambivalence		Stage II: Physical separation	Stage IV: Depression	Stage I: Separation	Stage II: Anger/guilt/regret	Stage III: Initiative vs. guilt
After separation to legal divorce	Station II: Legal divorce Station III: Economic divorce Station IV: Coparental divorce		Stage V: Mourning	Stage IV: Reorientation of lifestyle and identity	Stage II: Transition	Stage III: Restructuring phase 1. Emotional 2. Legal 3. Parent–child 4. Economic 5. Social			Stage IV: Focus on one's own present functioning	Stage IV: Industry vs. inferiority
Goal: adjustment	Station V: Community divorce Station VI: Psychic divorce	Stage V: Acceptance	Stage VI: Recovering A. Second adolescence B. Hard work	Stage V: Acceptance and new level of functioning	Stage III: Recovery (persistence of attachment)	Stage IV: Restructuring: Fairly stable and autonomous lifestyle	Stage V: Acceptance	Stage II: Individuation Stage III: Reconnection	Stage V: Acceptance of new lifestyle	Stage V: Identity vs. role confusion Stage VI: Intimacy vs. isolation Stage VII: Generativity vs. stagnation Stage VIII: Ego integrity vs. despair

[a]From Price-Bonham and Balswick (1980) and Salts (1979).

Structural and Perceptual Correlates

In this section, correlates of separation and divorce, as revealed by contemporary empirical research, are discussed. Also included are the reasons for the divorce from the individuals' perspectives. Because of the paucity of longitudinal studies plus the extraneous or uncontrolled variables in most studies, these correlates cannot be claimed to present the entire causal chain.

A major limitation in the literature is the inconsistent definition and use of terms such as *marital disruption, instability,* and *dissolution.* A few studies narrowly define them; most studies use them in a somewhat broader sense, often using *marital disruption, instability,* and/or *dissolution* interchangeably with *separation* and *divorce.* In general, the terms as used by the theorists and researchers themselves, and cited in their specific studies, are followed in this chapter.

The correlates examined include socioeconomic status, age at marriage, premarital pregnancy, race, religion, intergenerational transmission, geographic location (rural and urban as well as regional), and children.

Socioeconomic Status

Socioeconomic status (SES), includes occupation (employment status), income, and education. These three components are generally highly related to each other and make analysis of the overall concept of SES difficult.

Overall, socioeconomic status is inversely related to the likelihood of divorce; people in low-status occupations, with less education and less income, are more likely to end their marriages in divorce than are people with high-status occupations, more education, and more income. Before Goode's survey (1956) in 1948, it was assumed that higher-status occupational groups had higher divorce rates. Goode found the opposite, even though he initially discounted his first pretest data because they diverged so much from the assumptions about divorce at that time. Researchers following Goode found the same overall inverse relationship in the 1950s, the 1960s, and the 1970s.

A general trend toward convergence in the divorce rates for men among higher- and lower-SES groups was noted in comparing the 1960 U.S. Census with the 1970 U.S. Census (Norton & Glick, 1979); the rate of increase in the proportion divorced was more rapid among upper-SES men (whose divorce rate had been low) than among lower-SES men. For women, there was a similar trend toward convergence among higher- and lower-SES groups as a result of the divorce rate's increasing more slowly than the average for upper-SES women (whose divorce rate had been high). This trend toward convergence in divorce rates among different SES groups continued throughout the 1970s. From these trends, Norton and Glick (1979) concluded that "the recent increase in divorce has been pervasive with regard to social and economic level, but that socioeconomic differences in divorce are now smaller than they used to be" (p. 14).

Employment Status. The relationship between employment status and marital disruption is not consistent in the literature. Miao (1974) found that the employment rate was positively related to marital instability in the 1950s, but that this relationship ceased to exist for both whites and nonwhites in the early 1960s. However, other researchers, using data collected in the 1960s and the early 1970s, reported findings contradictory to those of Miao for the 1960s.

The first major longitudinal studies that followed a large, representative sample of people over a period of years were conducted from the late 1960s into the 1970s. Ross and Sawhill's study (1975) of a national sample of 5,000 families followed longitudinally for 5 years reported a positive relationship between unemployment and marital instability, a finding also supported by Cherlin (1979). Furstenberg (1976) also found lower-status employment (unskilled work) to be related to higher marital disruption. Coombs and Zumeta (1970) found the likelihood of divorce to be greater when the husband was periodically unemployed. It is possible that unemployment may highlight other problems or cause them to surface, increasing pressure on the marriage.

In addition, given the increasing numbers of married women entering the labor market, the employment status of women must be taken into account. Examining the relationship of the employment of women to subsequent marital disruption, Mott and Moore (1979) found a positive relationship for whites but not for blacks. For women, employment alone does not necessarily predict marital disruption, but when combined with other variables, it may lead to anticipatory behavior, which these researchers termed the "independence" effect—working in anticipation of a subsequent marital separation or divorce. It appears that some women need to establish their economic independence before leaving an unsatisfactory marriage. Booth and White (1980) reported that a wife's employment is an important factor in permitting her thoughts about divorce, a part of anticipatory behavior. Finally, in a comparison study of divorced and currently married people in Great Britain, women in higher-status occupations than their husbands were more likely to be divorced than women in lower-status occupations (Thornes & Collard, 1979). The directions of causality for these relationships are complex and difficult to determine.

In addition, the variable of perception can further complicate these relationships. The subjective meanings attached to being employed and the type and level of employment can differ between a husband and wife. Scanzoni (1968) reported that divorced women are more dissatisfied with their husbands' (or their former husbands') occupational achievement, whatever it is, than married women.

From the above, it can at least be concluded that a zero-order relationship exists between occupational status and marital stability, with lower occupational status leading to lower marital stability or what is less likely but still possible, lower marital stability leading to lower occupational status. In addition, wives' employment status and its relation to husbands' employment status must be taken into consideration. The more likely wives are to be employed, the more likely they are to leave an unsatisfactory marriage, but this relationship is mediated by the husband–wife earnings ratio discussed in the next section.

Income. A second component of socioeconomic status is income. The extant research presents contradictory findings concerning the relationship between income and marital disruption. In several large-scale studies using longitudinal and cross-sectional data, when family income is controlled, neither the occupation nor the education of the husband shows a relationship to marital stability (Cutright, 1971; Hampton, 1975; Johnson, 1975). This finding suggests that, of the three components of socioeconomic status, family income is a more important influence on marital stability than either employment status (occupation) or education. Lower income is significantly associated with higher marital instability. However, instability of income and lower-than-usual income and/or assets, rather than actual amount of income, were found to predict marital disruptions in both the Ross and Sawhill (1975) and the Cherlin (1979) longitudinal studies, as well as the Galligan and Bahr (1978) study using data from the National Longitudinal Surveys. Mott and Moore (1979) did not find direct economic factors to be as important in predicting marital disruptions as other SES and demographic factors. In general, it appears that a lower but dependable income promotes marital stability more than a higher but erratic income, that a higher dependable income promotes marital stability even more, and that additionally, for whites, not being in debt and/or having a certain level of assets increases marital stability.

The relationship between marital disruption and income becomes more complicated when wives' earnings are taken into consideration. Earlier studies ignored the impact of wives' earnings on marital disruption; but by the 1970s, these actual or potential wages had to be taken into consideration because of the huge increase in married women's labor-force participation. Overall, wives' earnings appear to be positively related to marital disruption (Hannan, Tuma, & Groeneveld, 1977; Ross & Sawhill, 1975), but this relationship is mediated by the husband–wife ratio. The numerator of this ratio is the actual or expected hourly wage of the wife, and the denominator is the actual or expected hourly wage of the husband. The larger this ratio, the more likely the wife's earnings are to approach, equal, or exceed the husband's earnings (if the wife's earnings equal the husband's earnings, the ratio would be 1; if they exceed the husband's earnings, the ratio would be 1 plus a fraction; if they are smaller, the ratio would be only a fraction). Using this husband–wife ratio, Cherlin (1979) reported that higher ratios are associated with higher marital disruption. From these findings, it appears that marital stability is promoted when women's actual or potential earnings are relatively small-

er than their husbands', a situation that would make it financially more difficult to leave an unsatisfactory marriage.

There are two opposing ways of viewing the influence of wives' earnings on marital stability. Ross and Sawhill (1975) posited the "income" effect and the "independence" effect. Theoretically, given the generally positive relationship between family income and marital stability, the more wives contribute to the family income, the higher the marital stability should be. This is the "income" effect; but it appears to be weaker than the "independence" effect, in which the higher income of wives is related to a higher likelihood of leaving an unsatisfactory marriage (or to a husband's leaving an unsatisfactory marriage when he knows that his wife can support herself). Whether wives' earnings have an "income" effect or an "independence" effect seems to depend on the husband–wife ratio (Cherlin, 1979).

Thus, it appears that for the income aspect of SES, stability of husbands' income is more important for marital stability than actual level of income, and that the husband–wife ratio mediates the influence of wives' earnings on marital stability—the lower the ratio, the higher the marital stability.

Education. The third and final component of SES is formal education. Higher education has generally been associated with higher marital stability. However, when other variables, such as sex and years of education completed, are taken into consideration, this relationship becomes more complicated. Glick and Norton (1979), using census survey data, reported higher proportions of men and women aged 35–54 who did not finish high school currently divorced in 1975 and even higher proportions among those who started college but did not complete it (13–15 years of education).[3] Based on 1975 data, the lowest proportion of men currently divorced occurred among those who had 16 or more years of education. For women, the lowest point was also 16 years but the proportion rose with 17 or more years of education. Because the rate of divorce among women at this educational level had decreased, whereas it had increased for men, this gap may become smaller in the future. One of the major differences between men and women with 17 or more years of education was that the men remarried faster and the women more slowly than those of each sex with less education. Men in this age range (35–54) had a larger age range of potential partners; that is, societal norms permit men to marry much younger women, whereas the reverse is not true for women. Highly educated men generally have the economic resources to remarry. Highly educated

[3]Glick and Norton (1979) suggested that the "same configuration of personal, social, and economic circumstances that tend to be associated with reaching a terminal educational level tend also to be associated with relatively stable marriages" (pp. 18–19); this explanation has come to be known as the *Glick effect* (Bauman, 1967).

women do not have access to as large a pool of potential marriage partners as men and are financially able to support themselves; hence, they do not need to remarry for economic support.

On the other hand, Mott and Moore (1979) report that education was significantly inversely related to marital disruption for young women when other relevant variables were controlled, that is, the higher the education, the lower the marital disruption. This difference could be caused by the age range in the two studies: 35–54 in Glick and Norton's report (1979), and ages 14–24 in 1968, making the sample 19–29 in 1973 (the time of the last interview) in Mott and Moore's study. Education could have different effects in the two age groups; the subjective meaning given to graduate education could be different between the two age groups with the older age group viewing it as a greater and more difficult accomplishment than the younger group, and hence being less willing to make career sacrifices for their marriages that seem necessary for women but not for men.

In contrast to Mott and Moore's finding of an inverse relationship between education and marital disruption for women under 29, Thornton (1978) reported no significant relationship between education and marital disruption when age at marriage, race, and religion were controlled. Sweet and Bumpass (1974) did find an inverse relationship, but it was considerably weakened when other relevant variables were controlled. Both of these studies used data that encompassed all age ranges.

Age at Marriage

In general, age at marriage is inversely correlated with separation and divorce for those who marry for the first time under age 20 and over age 30—much more for those under age 20, a relationship showing consistency for at least three decades (Bauman, 1967; Glenn and Supancic, 1984; Glick and Norton, 1979; Tarver, 1951).

For those marrying under age 20, the mate selection stage of the family life cycle is disrupted, and according to family developmental theory, if one stage of the life cycle is not completely carried out, the subsequent stages will be adversely affected. Hence, the young are deprived of the emotional, educational, and economic resources to make a success of marriage. In addition, those marrying under age 20 are more likely to be premaritally pregnant; the likelihood of interrupted high-school education for both young spouses—particularly for the teenage wife (U.S. Bureau of the Census, 1973)—and lower income and occupation(s) for one or both, all interact to produce a very high probability of divorce. Perhaps these teenagers have unrealistic expectations of adult roles, caused from insufficient time to mature into these roles; they may have difficulty in breaking their ties with their families before their adolescent developmental tasks are really accomplished. This relationship between marriage under age 20 and a high

subsequent divorce rate remained when length of marriage, level of education, and premarital pregnancy were controlled (Bumpass & Sweet, 1972). However, Frisbie, Bean, and Eberstein (1978) reported that marital instability was related to marrying under age 19 for whites but not for blacks and Mexican-Americans. In this event, the truncating of adolescence as well as of courtship, had different effects depending on race and ethnicity. Frisbie *et al.* suggested familism and Catholicism among the Mexican-Americans and configurations of economic discrimination among the blacks as possible explanations for the marital stability of neither groups' being affected by age at first marriage. This finding needs further replicating, especially for blacks in the Northeast and the South, and also nationally, to clarify contradictory findings by other researchers (e.g., Mott & Moore, 1979).

Those marrying over age 30 may have developed an independent lifestyle, which may hinder the development of interdependence, and for women may mean a greater probability of having established careers with adequate education and income to maintain a desired lifestyle.

Premarital Pregnancy

Premarital pregnancy and teenage marriages have been consistently reported to be associated with high divorce rates (e.g., Bumpass & Sweet, 1972; Christensen & Meissner, 1953; Christensen & Rubenstein, 1956; Hampton, 1979). It also appears that approximately half the marriages in which the wife is premaritally pregnant end in divorce within the first five years (Coombs & Zumeta, 1970; Furstenberg, 1976), more than double the rate for the non-premaritally pregnant in these studies. Furstenberg (1976) concluded that the disruption of the courtship process and the economic problems of the couple, generally caused by an interrupted high school education, create strains too severe for many young couples to cope with. Again, the inability to complete all or most of their adolescent developmental tasks and also to complete satsatisfactorily the courtship emotional and psychological tasks hinder or make impossible appropriate role performance in subsequent stages of the young family's life cycle. Marriages hastened by premarital pregnancies are still not completely accepted by society, even though one third of all first births are premaritally conceived—with 9% of these births occurring before and 24% after marriage (Glick & Norton, 1979).

Race

Most studies find that blacks have higher separation and divorce rates than whites (Bianchi & Farley, 1979; Carter & Glick, 1976; Galligan & Bahr, 1978; McCarthy, 1978; Miller, 1971; Moynihan, 1967; Norton & Glick, 1979; Sweet & Bumpass, 1974; Thornton, 1978; U.S. Bureau of the Census, 1980a). This finding is not surprising, given the strong relationship between socioeconomic status and separation or divorce, and given the relationships of these variables with race. When income is controlled, the results of several major studies show no or almost no black–white differences in rates of divorce (Cutright, 1971; Farley & Hermalin, 1971; Hampton, 1975, 1979; Hoffman & Holmes, 1976). In general, as income increases, the stability of black marriages is very similar to that of white marriages.

However, McCarthy (1978) reported that "overall, the black-white differentials are much smaller for divorce than for separation, since there are significant differences by race in the probability of divorcing after separation" (pp. 350–351). Blacks have much higher separation rates than whites and take much longer to divorce legally than do separated whites. Hence, the findings that report modest differences in black–white divorce rates can be misleading because they hide the large differences in marital separation. Yet, black second marriages are less likely to end in divorce than white second marriages and have a pattern of dissolution similar to white first marriages.

Uncontrolled fertility and racial discrimination are two major explanations put forth by Cutright (1971) for the black–white marital disruption differentials; these two factors existed throughout the 1970s and into the 1980s and, hence, could still be valid explanations for the black–white differentials, if they do exist. Racial discrimination affects socioeconomic status (education, occupation, and income), which, in turn, affects fertility behavior; lower SES is related to higher incidence of unwanted pregnancies and adolescent, illegitimate, or premaritally conceived births.

An early explanation suggested by Moynihan (1967) for black–white differentials is the matrifocal structure of the black family, which emasculates the male and overloads the female, creating a subculture that supports divorce. This explanation has been challenged by the view that social-psychological and economic pressures (possibly caused by racial discrimination) rather than subcultural predispositions influence divorce among blacks. (See Kitson & Raschke [1981] for a review of this literature, and Hampton's institutional decimation argument [1980] as a reason for black marital disruptions.)

Religion

The influence of religion on family variables, including separation and divorce, has been relatively neglected in family research. Religious preference or affiliation is not required on divorce decrees, and the U.S. Census has not asked the question since the 1950s. Therefore, religious data must be obtained by other methods. The few available studies do show relationships between religion and marital disruption (Glenn & Supancic, 1984; for a review see Kitson, Babri, & Roach, 1985). The overall results of these studies indicate that Catholics have lower divorce rates than Protestants, but that more

Catholic marriages end in separation, as would be expected given the Catholic Church's position on divorce. Homogamous Jewish marriages are more stable than Jewish–Gentile marriages, and Protestant–Catholic marriages are less stable than homogamous marriages. Differences within Protestant denominations include those from fundamentalist and conservative denominations having higher divorce rates than those from mainstream Protestant churches. Using data from seven U.S. National Surveys conducted from 1973 to 1980, Glenn and Supancic (1984) reported that the divorce rate varied inversely with frequency of church attendance. Hampton found a similiar relationship for blacks in his analysis of the Panel Study of Income Dynamics (1979). In Thornes and Collard's study (1979) of the divorced and currently married in Great Britain in 1971–1972, both currently married spouses were more likely to belong to and attend church more frequently than the divorced had during their marriages.

Intergenerational Transmission

Intergenerational transmission of divorce is reported in a number of studies. In general, children of divorced parents are themselves slightly more likely to divorce; although this relationship does not appear to be strong, it is consistent in the literature.

Various explanatory models (from Pope & Mueller, 1976) for this relationship include (1) a psychopathological model, in which transmission of the parents' characteristics, problems, and coping styles to their children produces similar problems leading to marital disruption; (2) an economic model of reduced family income and downward social mobility, which often follows divorce, especially for women, reducing the kinds of marital choices available for the children later; (3) a social learning model, in which inappropriate sex-role learning, inappropriate socialization for marriage caused by the conflict in the home before the divorce, and lack of one parent as a gender-role model after the divorce lead to higher marital instability; and (4) a social control model, in which inadequate supervision by the custodial single parent can produce high-risk marriages among the children of divorce: marrying at younger ages, being pregnant at marriage, and marrying husbands with lower-status occupations. For the most part, the relationship between the divorce of parents and subsequent marital disruption for their children is not strong, and in some studies, it almost disappears when relevant background variables are controlled (Kulka & Weingarten, 1979; Mueller & Pope, 1977). Nevertheless, this particular relationship appears to be one that is potentially modifiable by either individual or societal intervention.

Geographic Location

In general, in the United States, urban areas and the West have had the highest divorce rates (Cutright, 1971;

Mott & Moore, 1979). Glenn and Shelton, in their study (1985) using survey data from the 1973–1982 General Social Surveys, found the highest level of maritial dissolution in the West, South Central, Mountain, and Pacific census divisions and also found that this high level can be accounted for by the residential movement in these areas which lead to lower levels of social integration. In addition, Sweet and Bumpass (1974) reported that southern blacks have lower disruption rates than those blacks who moved to the North, and that the highest divorce rates are for those blacks who both grew up and remained in the urban areas of the North. The finding gives added support to the role of social integration being a social glue which helps keep marriages intact. The social and geographic mobility common to people living in the ''divorce belt'' can produce a sense of isolation, anonymity, loss of social supports (kin and community), and anomie. All of these are potential strains on marriage, especially youthful ones.

Children

Children were once thought to be a deterrent to divorce, but now close to 60% of all divorces involve children, with an average of 1 per divorce in 1979. Of all children under age 18, 18.9% were involved in a divorce during 1979 (U.S. Department of Health and Human Services, 1981a). However, women without children do have considerably higher divorce rates than women with children (Bumpass & Sweet, 1972). Part of this realtionship can be attributed to the fact that the highest number of divorces occurs in the very early years of marriage (between the second and third years).

Cherlin (1977) and Hoffman and Holmes (1976) reported that children appear to be a deterrent to divorce only if they are very young—preschool in Cherlin's analysis and under age 2 in Hoffman and Holmes's analysis. It is probable that the extra time, expense, and effort needed to care for young children are the major factors deterring divorce. However, Mott and Moore (1979) found ''no evidence of any pattern of association between childbearing and marital disruption, after controlling for related factors such as education, age, and duration of marriage'' (p. 363). Kanoy and Miller (1980) examined the evidence that children are barriers to or facilitators of divorce and found support for both. They suggested that divorce may be delayed but probably not prevented because of children. Children are more likely to be facilitators of divorce if they are conceived premaritally or soon after marriage and if the child is born with a congenital malformation. Johnson and Johnson (1980) also found significantly higher postmarital instability related to unplanned children.

Given the increasing acceptance of divorce, one could also expect more divorces to include children. This is not to say that children ''cause'' divorce or are even a correlate of it in the same sense as socioeconomic status, yet it could be expected that normal children at least contribute to strains in an already troubled marriage,

given the consistent findings that children, especially in adolescent years, lower marital satisfaction.

Couples' Perceptions of the Reasons for Divorce

Weiss (1975) called the participants' perceptions ''accounts,'' that is, histories of the breakdown that are concerned with only a few dramatic events or factors that thread through the marriage; these accounts are often different for each partner because the events selected to compose the histories are generally very different: what was important to one spouse was not to the other, and vice versa. Hence, when both partners are studied, their accounts are likely to vary drastically, as if two different marriages, instead of one, were involved. An example is Levinger's study (1966) of the reasons given for marital breakup obtained from court-required interviews for child custody in Cleveland, in which he reported that the wives' accounts included significantly more complaints of physical and verbal abuse, financial problems, mental cruelty, drinking, neglect of home or children, and lack of love, whereas the husbands' accounts included in-law troubles or sexual incompatibility.

In an attempt to compare the complaints of women in Goode's study (1956) of Detroit ever-divorced women in 1948 with complaints of divorced women in Cleveland in 1974–1975, Kitson and Sussman (1982) suggested that the 1948 complaints may have been more serious than the 1974–1975 complaints. The 1948 Detroit complaints included nonsupport, issues of authority, the complex of activities involved in being out with the boys, and drinking. The 1974–1975 Cleveland complaints included affective-emotional aspects of marriage, personality, home life, authority, and values. It appears that a shift had taken place during this 27-year period from more instrumental to more expressive reasons for ending a marriage by separation or divorce.

In addition, Kitson and Sussman reported major differences between men and women in their marital complaints. The only agreement between the sexes was ''lack of communication/understanding,'' which was ranked first by both men and women as the most important reason for ending their marriage. Joint conflict over gender roles, ranked second by men, included disagreements over appropriate gender roles for men and women and also complaints of the spouse's being too authoritarian or too paternalistic/maternalistic. Internal gender-role conflict, ranked second by women, was concerned with the individual's own conflicts about independence, a life of one's own, and desires for freedom. When these two responses were combined, their high frequency suggested that ''married couples today are struggling with issues involving the desire for self-growth and the development and allocation of roles within the family'' (Kitson & Sussman, 1982, p. 92).

For men, ''not sure what happened, with attempted explanation'' and ''different backgrounds/incompatible'' tied for third rank in the most frequently mentioned complaints; for women, these two complaints were ranked twenty-ninth and eighth, respectively. "Interests and values changed" was ranked fifth in frequency of complaints by men and seventh by women. Problems with relatives tied with internal gender-role conflict for sixth place for men; for women, these complaints ranked eighteenth and second, respectively.

For women, extramarital sex, immaturity, and drinking tied for third place in frequency of complaints; for men, these complaints ranked twelfth, fourteenth, and nineteenth, respectively. Finally, being out with the boys was the sixth most frequent complaint for women, and being out with the girls ranked sixteenth for men. Aside from the first two complaints, this Cleveland study reveals significant differences in the rankings of complaints of men and women.

The similarity between marital complaints in Albrecht's large study (1979) of ever-divorced men and women in eight western states and those in the Kitson and Sussman Cleveland study is the expressive nature of the top-ranking complaints in both of the studies.

Finally, Hayes, Stinnett, and DeFrain (1980), studying divorce in the middle years, reported little or no conflict over anything; rather, there was a diminishing of communication and pleasurable shared activities over the years, with the marriage not being examined until some crisis occurred. These findings suggest that the reasons given for a divorce may differ with the life cycle stage of a family. The relation of the life cycle stage of a family to marital satisfaction has been well researched (Spanier & Lewis, 1980); its relation to individuals' reasons for their divorce would appear to follow from the marital satisfaction research and would be a valuable addition to the body of divorce knowledge.

Consequences and Adjustment: Adults

What happens after separation or divorce is one process with two interacting components: the consequences and the adjustment to these consequences. Further, these consequences can be positive, neutral, or negative, and adjustment will vary accordingly. Not only do consequences and adjustment interact, but adjustment is often viewed or measured in terms of lack of negative consequences; hence, from this perspective, it could be argued that consequences and adjustment are operationally the same and should not be separated. However, it is necessary, for the analytical purposes of this chapter, to address them separately.

Consequences are the various interacting processes that occur after the separation or divorce and often begin before the physical separation. Several types of consequences have been well researched, especially physical and mental health and economics. Another type, psychological-emotional aspects, was increasingly researched in the 1970s. Other consequences, not so well researched but important, are residential mobility, job-related problems, changes in social and sexual life, role redefinitions, and changes in kin relationships.

Conventionally, consequences of separation or divorce have included those negative events, processes, and states of being and feeling that are possible and sometimes probable. These consequences, then, are what individuals have to adjust to; if there are no negative consequences, then the adjustment process is not difficult. It is asserted here that this adjustment process has been made more difficult than necessary because of the self-fulfilling prophecy of the deviance perspective, a perspective which permeates the consequences-adjustment theory and research and has done much to shape and mold it (Halem, 1980).

For the purposes of this chapter, a conceptual definition of *adjustment* is "developing an identity for oneself that is not related to the status of being married or to the ex-spouse, and performing adequately the role responsibilities of daily life in the arenas of home, family, work, and play" (adapted from Kitson & Raschke, 1981). Hence, adjustment is a process and not an event. McCubbin and Patterson (1982), dealing with family stress and crisis in general, defined adjustment as a "short-term response by a family which changes the situation momentarily, but is not intended to have any long-term consequences" (p. 37). They suggested that the concept *family adaptation* would be more fruitful for describing the long-term outcome of family postcrisis adjustment. However, the term *adjustment* is used in this section because that is the term used in almost all the research in this area.

There are basically two types of operational definitions for divorce adjustment. The first type uses measures originally constructed or designed to measure other concepts that are logically related to divorce adjustment, such as Rosenberg's Self-Esteem Scale (1965), Rotter's External versus Internal Locus of Control (1966), and a variety of others that measure mental health and psychological-social functioning. Most of these adjustment measures focus on the absence of negative feelings or events or states of being, and as a result, they really measure the absence of negative consequences, hence causing the overlap of consequences with adjustment. They rarely measure the presence of positive consequences. Rotter's External versus Internal Locus of Control and Bradburn's Affect Balance Scale (Bradburn & Caplovitz, 1965), with its combination of positive and negative affect, are examples of attempts to measure both the positive and negative dimensions of feelings. The equating of adjustment with the absence of negative consequences has been influenced by the overall deviance mystique surrounding divorce and has permeated the thought and work of social scientists.

In the second type of operational definition, scales or measures have been developed specifically to tap various subdimensions of the divorce adjustment process or experience, such as Goode's trauma scale (1956), Blair's divorcee's adjustment instrument (1969), and Raschke's problems and stress scale (1974). The scales or measures in this category, even those most recently constructed, appear to tap more of the negative than the positive aspects.

Another major problem in these measures, originally wrestled with by Raschke (1974, 1977) and further elaborated on by Holley (1980), is the contamination of the dependent and independent variables, subdimensions of which overlap and hence cause inflated statistical results (see also Price-Bonham & Balswick, 1980; Thoits, 1981). Problems of reliability are introduced when adjustment is assessed by qualitative measures, as is often done by clinicians and practitioners. However, their work is extremely valuable in giving new insight for hypotheses to be tested in empirical, quantitative research. It is essential that theorists, researchers, and practitioners cooperate and collaborate in developing more satisfactory conceptual and more rigorous operational definitions of the divorce adjustment process and experience, with a better balance between the negative, harmful aspects and the positive, constructive aspects.

Physical and Mental Health

The literature relating marital status to physical health consistently shows more problems among the separated and divorced than among the married and almost all other marital-status groups (never-married and widowed). Bloom, Asher, and White's extensive review (1978) reveals a higher incidence of motor vehicle accidents, disease morbidity, alcoholism, suicide, homicide, and disease mortality among the separated and divorced. They reported that illness and disability rates are usually higher for the separated than for the divorced, when these two groups are analyzed separately, a difference also supported by Verbrugge (1979), but only for women. Stack's study (1980) shows a highly significant relationship between divorce and suicide. Lynch (1977) claimed that a person's marital status is one of the best predictors of health, disease, and death.

Verbrugge (1979) attributed the high incidence of physical health problems among the separated and divorced to

especially risky life styles, partly caused by the stress and unhappiness of marital dissolution and to the inclusion of people whose poor health caused marital problems and subsequent divorce or separation, and who have difficulty remarrying. (p. 280)

Verbrugge also concluded that being separated, divorced, or widowed is harder on the physical health of women than on that of men.

Psychological and emotional distress in the newly separated or divorced and other dislocations associated with the transition from the married to the divorced status account for another large part of the difference. Physical illness is often preceded by life events associated with psychological distress, such as that precipitated by marital disruption (Bloom *et al.*, 1978; B. S. Dohrenwend, 1973). However, poor physical health can also be viewed as a stressor on the marriage, and if the marriage is weak, the health problem could highlight other problems in the same way that unemployment does. From the individual's perspective, the deviant mystique surrounding separation and divorce could contribute further strain leading to further health problems. Hence, for some aspects of physical health, the direction of causality is not clear. Longitudinal research is needed to specify the conditions under which marital separation and divorce lead to poorer physical health and vice versa, and also how these variables are related to mental health.

Mental health encompasses psychopathology that is related to psychiatrically diagnosed mental illnesses such as depression, neuroses, and functional psychoses. Psychological and emotional distress is also related to psychopathology because the distress experienced in marital separation or divorce can be a precipitator of these mental illnesses. Mental illness, like physical illness, can also precipitate separation or divorce.

Separated and divorced people are overrepresented in every category of mental illness, whereas married people are underrepresented. In many studies, mental illness is measured by inpatient admission rates and the use of public outpatient clinics. Bloom *et al.* (1978) concluded that admission rates are highest for the separated or divorced, intermediate for the widowed and never-married, and lowest for the married. They also reported that males from disrupted marriages have consistently and substantially higher admission rates than females, and that, regardless of sex or type of facility, the separated have higher rates than the divorced when the two groups are differentiated.

Bachrach (1975) found three theories to explain the relationship between marital status and mental disorder: selectivity theory, role theory, and stress theory. Persons who have physical or mental disabilities are less likely to marry in the first place, are less likely to remain married, and are less likely to remarry if they divorce; hence, the "healthier" people are selected into marriage, providing the basis for selectivity. Role theory asserts that the different social roles, especially the sex roles involved in different marital statuses, entail differential risks to mental and physical disorders. In stress theory, the separation or divorce experience is the stressor event, which, under certain conditions, can lead to crises that may be manifested in physical or mental illness.

Bloom *et al.* (1978), building on Bachrach's study, reduced role theory and stress theory into a single theory, noting:

first, that marital disruption is the product of previously existing disabilities that serve to mediate entrance into and exit from various marital status categories; and second, that various marital statuses or marital status changes may produce enough stress to precipitate psychiatric or other disabilities. (p. 885)

Hence, selectivity theory and role/stress theory end up as two logical explanations for the relationships between mental health and marital status. These relationships are more likely to be interactive than causal; that is, under certain conditions, mental illness leads to divorce, and under other conditions, the roles attached to marriage can produce enough distress to lead to a divorce, which can lead to mental illness. These interactions are very complex, so that their empirical study is very difficult (cf. B. P. Dohrenwend, 1975). Because of the use of cross-sectional data, it is not possible to determine whether mental illness is more likely to lead to separation or divorce, or vice versa.

Psychological and Emotional Consequences

Psychological and emotional consequences of separation and divorce have been confounded with the psychopathological aspects because there can be an overlap, especially if these consequences are severe and have the possibility of leading to mental illness. Even though psychopathology and psychological or emotional consequences are often included in the same category, for the purposes of this chapter they are treated as conceptually different.

The consequences of separation and divorce have been conceptually and operationally defined in a variety of ways—including disorganization, trauma, stress, quality of adjustment, distress, problems and stress, maladjustment, unpleasant or undesirable emotional feelings, and crisis (c.f. Goode, 1956; Kitson & Sussman, 1982; Raschke & Barringer, 1977; Waller, 1967; Weiss, 1975).

In 1975, Weiss's *Marital Separation* appeared, based on three years of his work with Seminars for the Separated at the Harvard Laboratory of Community Psychiatry, which examined separation distress qualitatively; he concluded that separation distress is real but situational, and that it is modified by internal and external factors.

Numerous studies consistently show the separation and divorce process to be associated with psychological pain or unpleasant emotional feelings. The main exceptions are when the marriage has been extremely conflict-ridden and when, for one or both partners, the decision to divorce comes as a relief, even though the relief may be intermingled with separation distress. (See Sell, 1981, for a comprehensive bibliography, and Bloom *et al.*, 1978, for a review of specific studies related to the psychological problems and emotional consequences of divorce.)

In summary, the literature is consistent in documenting negative psychological and emotional consequences. These negative consequences are balanced, for most people, sooner or later, by positive, constructive aspects, which are rarely the focus of study. The psychological and emotional consequences of separation and divorce have been more distorted than any of the other consequences as a result of the deviance perspective.

Economic Consequences

The economic impact of divorce or separation appears to have the greatest effect on women. The largest proportion of female heads of families are divorced or separated mothers with children under age 18, and they are drastically overrepresented among the poor. In 1978, about 3.4 million women (approximately one half of the 7.1 million single-parent mothers at the survey date who had one or more children under age 21) were awarded child support payments; of these mothers, only one half received the full amount awarded, and one quarter received less than they were due. Those women with lower mean incomes were less likely to be awarded or to receive, if they were awarded, child support payments (U.S. Bureau of the Census, 1980b; see also Brandwein, Brown, & Fox, 1974).

The U.S. Bureau of the Census (1980b) also reported that only about 14% of the 14.3 million ever-divorced or separated women had ever been awarded or had any agreement to receive alimony or maintenance payments. In 1978, about 22% of those women who were supposed to receive alimony or maintenance payments actually received them. Data from the Panel Study of Income Dynamics indicate that only 3% of female-headed families received enough alimony and/or child support (with no other source of income) to keep them at or above the poverty level (Jones, Gordon, & Sawhill, 1976). Weitzman and Dixon (1980), in their comprehensive review of the "myth of alimony," argued that our society socializes women to believe that, if they perform the "proper" roles of wives and mothers, giving up all thoughts of careers for themselves, they will always be taken care of—if not directly by their husbands, then indirectly by alimony or by society through Aid for Families with Dependent Children, (AFDC). Weitzman and Dixon dispelled this notion as a cruel hoax on women. Seal (1979) reported that California's no-fault divorce laws are proving to be economically disastrous to women and children, many of whom have been forced to live on AFDC while their ex-husbands continue to live affluent, middle-class lives. Perhaps, this is one of the major reasons that, in 1978, 50% of children in families maintained by women were in poverty versus only 16% of children in families with both parents, and that 32% of families maintained by women were in poverty versus 9% of all persons maintaining families. For both child support and alimony, the lower-income women, who need the support the most, are the least likely to get it. This is one of the more obvious reasons that there were 2 million single-parent mothers below the poverty level in 1979 (U.S. Bureau of the Census, 1980b).

Espenshade (1979) concluded that divorced women and their children fare worse than divorced men; they fall economically in terms of actual income and especially in their income–needs ratio, whereas the men actually rise. The one exception to this consistent finding is when fathers have custody of their children: the children are economically better off with their fathers (Duncan & Morgan, 1976b). When both divorced men and women were compared to intact married couples, the continuously married couples fared economically best of all (rose the most over the five-year survey period, whereas divorced women fared the worst, with divorced men hovering in between).

Given what is known about women and divorce, it is hardly surprising that the economic consequences of divorce for women and their custodial children are, for the most part, devastating. Bane (1976) commented:

There are a number of reasons why women with children but without husbands find themselves in such desperate economic straits. The data suggest the following causes: loss of "economies of scale"; greater prevalence of divorce and death among poor families; low and irregular levels of alimony, child support, and public assistance; fewer opportunities for female heads of families to work; lower wages than men when they do work. (p. 112)

In addition, approximately 90% of children are still being "awarded" to the mother—the parent who generally has less education and less job experience (or none) than the father, and who usually has to look for an entry-level job at an older age, thus putting herself at an extreme economic disadvantage. Hence, the parent least able to provide financially for the child(ren) is still overwhelmingly favored by the courts for custody, even though this pattern is gradually changing in some states. Women themselves also need a different kind of awareness and socialization if the majority of them are to accept the removal of prejudice against fathers' getting custody of the children. As will be discussed under "Legal Aspects," joint custody, relatively new but apparently working out for the children involved, seems to be a reasonable compromise for the parents—and one that would alleviate the mother's financial as well as physical overload.

In addition to the more thoroughly researched consequences discussed above, there are other consequences, perhaps less deleterious or more temporary, that cause specific problems at a specific time and that must be dealt with by all separated and divorced people. These other consequences include residential mobility, job-related problems, changes in social and sexual life, role redefinitions, and, for middle-aged people, changes in relationships with grown children and aging parents.

Other Consequences

Residential Mobility. The more practical consequences include one or both spouses' moving to a new house or apartment, with the ensuing changes in lifestyle caused by high residential relocation for themselves and the children, too, if they move. In addition, low-income single-parent mothers often experience discrimination in housing (Deutscher, 1968), although this has had to take subtler forms, harder to measure, since the advent of antidiscriminatory housing laws. These lifestyle changes are further compounded for women with custody as a result of their downward economic plunge after divorce. Often these women must move to smaller, less expensive, less desirable housing. Men without custody generally move to smaller living quarters. Roles must be reallocated, especially when the care of children is involved, whether custody is single or joint, and no matter how the custody is divided. The family changes from nuclear to binuclear (two families—one mother-headed, the other father-headed) for the children involved (Ahrons, 1979, 1980), and many details must be worked out regarding the children's daily activities. Working out these changes is made more difficult by a residential move (Hetherington, Cox, & Cox, 1979a,b,c; Roman & Haddad, 1978; Weiss, 1979). Many divorced men, especially those from traditional marriages, have initial difficulty and stress in organizing and maintaining a household routine (Hetherington, Cox, & Cox, 1976).

Job-Related Problems. Both men and women have difficulties, caused by the separation or divorce, with routine work on their jobs (Bloom, Hodges, & Caldwell, 1983; Hetherington *et al.*, 1976). Although many women return to school, others must immediately find a paying job to support themselves and, usually, their children. For traditional women who have devoted their lives to being "good" wives and mothers, finding a job can often be traumatic. This job hunt can be especially difficult if they never had job skills or if they have let job skills "rust" over the years. Almost always, the displaced homemaker is on her own, often in middle age, with little or no socialization for the economic tribulations, job problems, and other struggles that usually follow a separation or divorce (e.g., Hetherington *et al.*, 1978, 1979c). These are the kinds of women who generally know little or nothing about the financial aspects of maintaining a home and family.

Social and Sex-Life Changes. Almost all of the research shows loneliness to be a universal human condition in the postseparation or postdivorce period (e.g., Cleveland, 1979; Goode, 1956; Smith, 1980; Waller, 1967; Weiss, 1975). The social life of most people is adversely affected, especially for one to three years after the separation, when it generally returns to normal or to the preseparation level (e.g., Hetherington *et al.*, 1976, 1979c; Raschke, 1977). Old friends are often lost, especially if they are married friends, and developing new friendship networks in the "world of the formerly married" is often difficult at first.

Goetting (1981), among others, commented on the tendency of society to organize social life on the basis of couples and two-parent families, a pattern that often excludes divorced persons from participation in social events. Also, many times, divorced people, especially women, are viewed as "threats" to ongoing marriages, especially those that may be shaky. Given the fact that social participation in activities outside the home is consistently related to better postdivorce adjustment, loneliness and difficulty with social life can hinder such adjustment.

Several studies have reported generally more and/or better sex for the separated or divorced (Gebhard, 1970; Hunt, 1974). When a time dimension is included, the frequency of sexual activity follows the general pattern of overall social activity—low at first, then rising after one year, and by the end of two years (after the divorce), about the same for the divorced as for the married and for both men and women. Cleveland (1979) reported four general patterns of sexual partners or outlets: (1) the estranged spouse; (2) masturbation; (3) short-term partners (either serial or concurrent); and (4) ongoing, monogamous partners. Casual or short-term sexual encounters seem to be the norm and are almost a necessity for some people to "prove" themselves in certain ways during the first year, but after that, both men and women seem to need to move beyond these casual encounters to more intimate relationships (Cleveland, 1979; Hunt, 1966; Hunt & Hunt, 1977).

Role Redefinitions. Role redefinitions are an essential and logical, though painful, part of the aftermath of divorce. Kitson, Lopata, Holmes, and Meyering (1980) compared the divorced with the widowed status and concluded that the role and cultural expectations established for widows are missing for the divorced. This ambiguity of norms for the divorced creates unique problems for them in their attempts to forge the roles necessary to build new lives, separate from their former married life. A lack of norms means that individuals must develop their own, for the most part, to fit their specific situation. This requirement can be frightening to people who fear uncharted waters and especially to those who seek to "escape from freedom."

Related to role redefinitions is role strain; the roles usually performed by the absent spouse are shifted to the remaining parent, creating role overloads that force the custodial parent to reorganize priorities for the new family's life, and often creating problems in parent–child relations as well as stress for the custodial parent. Bloom *et al.* (1983) reported that problems with child rearing were notable in their study of the first eight months of marital separation.

Hetherington *et al.* (1976, 1978, 1979c) also reported child-rearing difficulties for both divorced men (who did not have custody) and divorced women. In the first year, the reorganization of family life was preceded by disorganization in routine household tasks and activities—like eating together and on time, reading to the children at bedtime, and getting them to bed and to school on time. By the end of the second year (after divorce), the disorganization had receded, and mother-headed families as well as divorced fathers seemed to be functioning reasonably well.

Generally, role strain in single-parent families is alleviated by reallocating roles (e.g., giving children more responsibility), eliminating nonessential roles, and setting priorities. For example, the position of the single-parent mother includes the roles of helping her children with schoolwork and keeping them fed and healthy; these roles might have priority over keeping a "spotless house" and also could create role conflict with her personal goals, such as returning to school herself, devoting more time and energy to establishing her career, dating, or engaging

in other self-fulfilling activities. This is one of the reasons that having the ex-husband involved in the children's activities is not only useful for them, but also helpful to the custodial mother in reducing her role strain. (See Pais & White, 1979, for a comprehensive review of family redefinition.)

Intergenerational Relationships. Another consequence is the change, for middle-aged divorced people, in their intergenerational relationships. In an examination of the impact of middle-age divorce on grown children and/or aging parents, Hagestad and Smyer (1980) found that women are more likely to turn to their children, especially their grown children, and their parents for support, whereas men rely more on other resources. Men feel that their children and parents react more negatively to the divorce than do the children and parents of women. These authors commented, "women display impressive strength in an area which seems to be the men's Achilles' heels: interpersonal bonds to family members, across generations" (p. 9). Grown children also experience stress in their feelings of responsibility—financial or emotional or both—especially for the divorced mother. Even though middle-aged men end up better off economically than middle-aged women, their children and parents tend to react to them less supportively. In addition, the divorce may be harder on the grown children than on the aging parents because the children have one set of parents while most aging parents have more than one child (Hagestad & Smyer, 1980).

Adjustment: Research Findings

Two major categories of variables have been isolated by empirical research as being associated with levels of adjustment: unmodifiable factors which are unchangeable and outside the individual's control, and modifiable factors, which are changeable through the individual's efforts and/or through social intervention. Unmodifiable variables include, gender, children, age, length of marriage, divorce decisions and complaints, length of separation, and the legal system. Potentially modifiable variables include: socioeconomic status (education, income, occupation), social supports, and psychological resources. The unmodifiable variables are discussed next.

Gender. The research on the adjustment differences between men and women is inconclusive. Some researchers have found no differences (c.f. Weiss, 1975). Others have found differences in distress in different time periods of the adjustment (Deckert & Langelier, 1978, Bloom and Caldwell, 1981). Brown and Fox (1978), in their review of sex differences in divorce adjustment conclude that, in general, "women experience both more situational stress and more conscious feelings of subjective distress than men during a divorce" (p. 119). They qualify this difference as being influenced by economic resources, custody of children, and early socialization patterns, all of which tend to be gender-linked.

Related to gender and adjustment is mental health. There is an ongoing controversy in the literature over the comparative rates of mental illness in women and men. Gove's review (1972) shows that married women have higher rates of mental illness than married men, but the opposite is true for the other marital statuses; unmarried, divorced, and widowed women have lower rates of mental illness than men in these categories. Gove attributed these differences to the social roles that married men and women experience; marriage is more of a problem for women and more beneficial to men. Hence, women may be better off out of marriage and men worse off, so that divorced women have less mental illness and divorced men more (Gove, 1972, 1978a,b, 1979). Gove and Tudor (1973) also presented evidence supporting this position in studies of both treated and nontreated populations.

Although Dohrenwend and Dohrenwend (1974, 1976, 1977) questioned these conclusions because of the definition and measurement of mental illness and other methodological problems, Gove's recent work (1979), based on large representative samples, continues to support the position that married men experience lower rates of psychiatric treatment than married women, whereas unmarried (especially separated or divorced) men experience higher rates than women in these marital statuses. Glenn (1975), in three national surveys, found that married persons, as an aggregate, reported greater global happiness than any category of unmarried persons, with wives reporting much higher happiness than husbands in one of the surveys. He reported that women, as a whole, exceeded men in both the stress and the satisfaction that they derived from marriage.

On the other hand, Fox (1980) reported that women are more likely to be mentally ill than men, regardless of marital status. Radloff (1975) added "learned helplessness" to their social role as a reason for women's higher depression.

Children. There is no consistency in the research literature on how children affect adjustment for the parent with custody, for the parent without custody, or for parents with joint custody. Day and Raschke (1980) discussed children as being both rewards and costs in helping to determine the intensity of a divorce crisis and the subsequent level of adjustment. This reward–cost ratio of children is probably the reason for the contradictory findings. In Goode's study (1956) of divorced mothers, those women with more children reported greater trauma.

Bloom and Hodges (1981) reported that the presence of children appears to add to the difficulties of the divorcing parents. Hetherington *et al.* (1977, 1978, 1979a,b,c) reported that custodial mothers were still having problems with their male children at the end of two years after the divorce, which probably contributed to mothers' poorer adjustment, given that continuing conflict, especially if it is unresolved, can lead to various kinds of problems for both mothers and sons. Berman and Turk (1981) also found that male children contributed to distress during the postdivorce period. Spanier and Casto (1979) reported that fathers with custody had the same problems as mothers with custody; if so, the fathers' adjustment could also be affected adversely. With the trend of more fathers requesting and obtaining joint or full custody, research on single fathering is badly needed. Any differences and similarities between mothers and fathers in single parenting would be a useful addition to the empirical knowledge.

Children can and do create role strain for the custodial parent, but not enough attention has been given in the research to the kinds of help or support that children may provide for the custodial parent. Weiss (1975) suggested that responsibility for the children may also help keep parents going. Pais's finding (1978) that the greater the satisfaction with mother–child interaction, the greater the mother's adjustment indicates that children can be "adjustment assets" that may partially account for the gender differences in adjustment reported above. Brown, Felton, Whiteman, and Manela's findings (1980) also support this interpretation. (For other research on children of divorce, see Levitin, 1979.)

Age and Length of Marriage. For first marriages, age and length of marriage are generally correlated and hence it is not easy to disentangle their effects on divorce adjustment. Most studies find the longer the marriage, the more difficult the adjustment (c.f., Chiriboga, Roberts, & Stein, 1978; Hetherington, Cox, & Cox, 1978). A few studies show no relationship between length of marriage and adjustment (c.f. Brown, Felton, Whiteman, & Manela, 1980). Again, the findings are inconclusive and the empirical evidence sparse.

Older people, and especially older women, have more difficulty in adjusting to divorce than younger people (e.g., Goode, 1956; Meyers, 1976; Pais, 1978). Kitson and Raschke (1981) point out this relationship could be caused by a "lowered sense of 'marketability' for remarriage or lowered self-esteem and insecurity concerning reentering the 'single scene' after a long absence" (p. 24). It is probable that older people in longer marriages are more affected by the deviance "mystique" surrounding divorce than are younger people.

Divorce Decision and Complaints. Most studies report that initiators and those who make mutual decisions regarding the divorce have less difficulty adjusting (Goode, 1956; Brown *et al.*, 1980; Kitson, 1982). On the other hand, Weiss (1975) found little difference in the adjustment of the "leaver" and the "left", but the "leaver" reported more guilt and the "left" more feelings of hurt and abandonment. It is likely that the "leavers" did most of their adjustment prior to announcing the decision.

The type of divorce complaint, or reason given for the divorce seems to be related to subsequent adjustment (Weiss, 1976; Kitson and Sussman, 1982). When the complaint reflects badly on the divorced individual, such as spouse's alcoholism or marital infidelity, the adjustment appears to be more difficult.

Length of Separation. According to almost all the research, the amount of distress is greatest in the period immediately preceding and immediately following the physical separation. The amount of time since the physical separation is positively correlated with better adjustment: the longer the time lapsed, the better or easier the adjustment (Chester, 1971; Goode, 1956; Kessler, 1975; Spivey & Scherman, 1980). Physical separation is more tumultuous than the actual granting of the divorce, unless it is a bitterly contested divorce or child custody battle. Then, the turmoil and distress can continue until the "dust settles." As a result, in research and theory, the "events" of physical separation and those of divorce in the entire marital separation and divorce process need to be kept conceptually and methodologically separate.

Weiss (1975, 1976, 1979) made a distinction between short-term and long-term adjustment problems. There comes a time when adaptation should be completed, usually between the second and fourth year (Weiss, 1975), depending on other factors that influence it; in fact, Kessler (1975) indicated that, if adjustment is not completed by the end of the third year (after the physical separation), the individual is bogged down in the mourning stage. It is also probable that the deviance "mystique" exacerbates the adjustment process, dragging it out.

The Legal System.[4] Insufficient research exists to determine the effect of the legal system on divorce adjustment, especially no-fault divorce. One of the original ideas behind the no-fault concept was that it would reduce the polarization generally present in fault divorces (Rheinstein, 1972). Dixon and Weitzman (1980) reported that the decline in the number of litigious actions in California suggests that "some of the acrimony and hostility engendered by the former adversary system has been diluted" (p. 306). Whether this reduction of litigious actions also brings about a reduction in distress and hence enhances postdivorce adjustment, as the reformers hoped, is still a largely unanswered question. It has already been pointed out that no-fault divorce in California has had disastrous economic consequences for women and children, given the relationship between inadequate financial resources and adjustment. Adjustment, at least for some women, is more difficult because of the economic implications of no-fault divorce.

Obviously, the legal situation does play a role and has the potential, at least, of alleviating or making worse the

---

[4]The legal system is potentially changeable and modifiable but generally not in a way that would help a specific individual at the specific time when she or he wants a divorce. It usually takes years and a great deal of work by many people to get laws changed.

distress surrounding the divorce, but the evidence is not in on how and under what conditions it affects or is specifically related to divorce adjustment.

Socioeconomic Status. Income is potentially modifiable for most people and is positively related to adjustment (Bould, 1977; Goode, 1956; Spanier & Lachman, 1980). For women, the more economically independent they are, the better their adjustment; and related to this, the higher their sense of personal fate control, the better their adjustment (Bould, 1977). Higher anticipated income (Kitson and Sussman, 1982) is related to better adjustment, and greater anticipated financial strain (Brown, Felton, Whiteman, & Manela, 1980) is indicative of poorer adjustment.

Education and occupation are indirectly related to adjustment because they are both related to income.

Social Supports. Social support has been defined as "formal and informal contacts with individuals and groups that provide emotional or material resources that may aid a person in adjusting to a crisis such as separation and divorce" (Kitson & Raschke, 1981, p. 25). Most studies that have examined the relationship between social participation and adjustment (e.g., lower distress, better coping, and personal growth) have found a positive relationship. Higher social participation is significantly related to better adjustment, no matter how it is measured (Taibbi, 1979; Unger & Powell, 1980; White & Bloom, 1981). Kitson (1982) reported that changes in social activities after the end of the marriage are related to significantly higher distress, but that friends and professional help buffer some of this distress. Some people may find various changes, including social changes very difficult because of the role ambiguity surrounding the divorced status.

Dating is associated with higher adjustment (Goode, 1956; Hetherington *et al.,* 1976, 1978, 1979c; Hunt, 1966; Spanier & Lachman, 1980). Higher sexual permissiveness (Raschke, 1974) and sexual activity (Hunt & Hunt, 1977) have a positive influence on adjustment. In a study of low-income, single-parent mothers, Hynes (1979) reported that higher levels of social support—informally from friends and families, and formally from organizations and public agencies—are related to better adjustment. Satisfaction with social support, as well as degree of support, was related to child-rearing practices in Colletta's study (1979): higher satisfaction and higher support were associated with better child-rearing practices, that is, mothers with more supports were less punitive and less restrictive than those with fewer supports.

Psychological Resources. Separated and divorced people are affected by psychological or internal variables as well as sociological variables. Religion plays a unique role that has not been clearly delineated, but some studies have found that having a religious affiliation and/or considering oneself religious is related to enhanced personal growth and better adjustment (Barringer, 1973; P. Brown, 1976); on the other hand, Raschke (1974) reported no relationship. Given the value placed on religion in our society and the recent emphasis in many churches on special programs for separated and divorced people, religion may prove to be quite strongly related to adjustment.

Gender-role orientations, dogmatism, tolerance of change, anxiety, self-esteem, locus of control, coping styles, and continued attachment are all modifiable factors that research shows to be related to adjustment. Women with equalitarian gender-role orientations show better adjustment and more personal growth (e.g., Felton, Brown, Lehmann, & Liberatos, 1980; Granvold Pedler, & Schellie, 1979;). Higher tolerance of change and lower dogmatism were associated with better adjustment in Raschke's (1974) and Hynes's (1979) studies. Kitson (1982) reported that high anxiety and/or low self-esteem appeared to be related to poorer adjustment. Internal locus of control was related to better adjustment in both Bould's (1977) and Pais's (1978) studies. Dill, Feld, Martin, Beukema, and Belle (1980) found that limited options for addressing a problem and lack of environmental response complicated the coping efforts and, hence, the adjustment of low-income mothers. Finally, continuing attachment (preoccupation with and longing for the ex-spouse but vacillation between love and hate) was conceptualized by Weiss (1975) and operationalized and used in research by Brown *et al.* (1980), and Kitson (1982). Attachment was significantly associated with distress and poorer adjustment. Hynes (1979), using Kitson's measure, found that high attachment was significantly associated with more distress.

Consequences and Adjustment: Children

Consequences

The consequences of marital separation or divorce for children and their effects on children comprise one of the most researched areas in divorce. As Longfellow (1979) stated in her extensive review:

The findings to date are equivocal; they do not permit assertions that divorce has any single broad-reaching impact on children. Nor should they encourage further pursuit of the question: does divorce have negative effects? Instead, our questions should be phrased to discover what it is about divorce that troubles children. (p. 287)

Halem (1980) claimed that post–World War II research reinforces the pathogenic effects of divorce on children:

Generally using cases in which the pathology was already advanced, the researchers proceeded through retrogressive analyses to link the aberration with earlier disruptions in family functioning, most frequently maternal deprivation, father absence, and broken homes. (p. 161).

The widespread notion that divorce is a deviant state has permeated the research and, as a result, perpetuates the deviance perspective.

Levitin (1979) divided research on children of divorce into three categories: (1) the single-parent family-research tradition; (2) the clinical research tradition; and (3) the classic studies of the 1970s.

Most of the studies in the single-parent family tradition were done in the 1950s and 1960s and concentrated on the relationship between living in a single-parent family and some type of deviant behavior; little or no consideration was given to antecedent or intervening variables, and Levitin (1979) claimed that *"post hoc ergo propter hoc* [following this, therefore caused by this] reasoning characterizes many of these studies" (p. 2). In addition, the single-parent family was seen in these studies as an aberrant or deviant form of the normal family—a view that was result and a cause of the larger deviance perspective surrounding divorce. Longfellow (1979) concluded that this kind of research has contributed very little "to an understanding of what it is about divorce that affects the child" (p. 291) and claimed that the absence of the father may have a more indirect impact on the child through the direct impact on the mother. Herzog and Sudia (1971, 1973) concluded that the problems of the child in a single-parent family are not so much affected by the absence of the father as by the functioning of the custodial parent (usually the mother), a conclusion strongly supported by Zill (1978).

The generalizability of the study results are weakened by the conceptual and methodological problems of the clinical research tradition. The selection of the sample, often the most adversely affected children of divorce in the general population, the lack of standardized instruments, and the differences in the clinicians' training or background, which influence their interpretation of behaviors, make the validity and reliability of studies problematic. In addition, the clinical studies generally focus "on problems and failures to cope rather than on strengths and coping capabilities" (Levitin, 1979, p. 4; see Kalter, 1977, for a review of studies in this genre). Generally, these clinical studies portray children as suffering very negative and sometimes long-lasting consequences from divorce.

The classic studies of the 1970s are best represented by the work of Hetherington, Cox, and Cox (1976, 1977, 1978, 1979a,b,c) and Wallerstein and Kelly (1980); they are considered very influential studies. The Hetherington *et al.* study (1977, 1978, 1979a) was multimeasure, multimethod, two-year longitudinal, and quasi-experimental, using 48 nursery-school children from newly divorced single-parent, mother-headed families matched with 48 nursery-school children from two-parent families. In the Wallerstein and Kelly (1980) project, the sample, referred by attorneys, school psychologists, teachers, and other sources, consisted of 60 families with 131 children in affluent Marin County near San Francisco, California. Clinical-type interviews were conducted over a five-year period. Six weeks of child-focused counseling was offered as an incentive to participate in the study. These two studies showed an overall negative impact of the separation and divorce on the children. Most of the Hetherington *et al.* sample had reached a new equilibrium by the end of the second year after the divorce, whereas a significant minority of the Wallerstein and Kelly sample were still disturbed at the end of the five-year survey period. Part of the difference in these two studies stems from different beginning points: the Hetherington *et al.* study began after the divorce, whereas the Wallerstein and Kelly study began shortly after the physical separation. The differences between these studies illustrate how results can be affected by differences in research design, methods of data collection, and analysis and interpretation.

Levitin's first two categories (1979) of research traditions represent Longfellow's criticism (1979) that research on children of divorce asks the wrong questions. The Hetherington *et al.* and Wallerstein and Kelly studies are considered "benchmark" studies by many, but their generalizability to larger populations of children of divorce have been questioned by some family professionals (cf. Cherlin, 1981). The mass media have been most guilty of generalizing their findings to all children of divorce; this erroneous generalizing often produces guilt, anxiety, fear, unnecessary worry, and other negative feelings in separated or divorced parents that could interfere with effective parenting.

Effect of Family Conflict

Goetting (1981), along with Longfellow (1979), reported one important, consistent finding in the literature: the relationship between family structure and marital discord, and the harmful effects that this conflict can have on children from all types of families. Studies reporting such results began in the 1950s and have since continued (e.g., Berg & Kelly, 1979; Hetherington *et al.*, 1979a,b,c; Landis, 1960; Magrab, 1978; McCord, McCord, & Thurber, 1962; Nye, 1957; Raschke & Raschke, 1979; Rutter, 1971; Zill, 1978). Although different in sample type, in time periods, and in research designs, these studies consistently report that marital conflict, as perceived by the children in a two-parent family, is more harmful to the children than their living in a peaceful single-parent family (with little or no postdivorce bickering between the ex-spouses or using the children as pawns in the parents' psychological war). The consequences of marital or postmarital conflict are negative for children's self-concept, personal and social adjustment, family and peer relations, academic achievement, and mental and physical health. Children from happy two-parent families fare best, children from unhappy or conflict ridden two-parent families fare worst, and children from single-parent families are in the middle and are closer to children in two-parent happy families if there is peace in their families. Contrary to these findings, Wallerstein and Kelly (1980)

reported that conflict before the physical separation was not related to the subsequent adjustment of the children, but that their adjustment was adversely affected by postdivorce conflict of the parents. This difference in findings is probably a result of differences in research design, analyses, and interpretation.

Kulka and Weingarten (1979) examined a variety of measures of adult adjustment and psychological functioning from two national surveys, one conducted in 1957 (Gurin, Veroff, & Feld, 1960) and the other in 1976, nearly 20 years apart. Kulka and Weingarten reported very small differences between adults in the 1976 survey who had experienced a childhood divorce and those who had not, and there had been a considerable diminishing of negative effects between 1957 and 1976. Kulka and Weingarten concluded that "these early experiences have at most a modest effect on adult adjustment" (p. 73).

Several important variables in the research seem to aid adjustment: (1) discussion of the impending separation and divorce with the children, including open discussion of the problems involved; (2) involvement with the noncustodial parent, seeing him or her often, and free access to him or her; (3) lack of hostility in the relationship between the parents; (4) good emotional and psychological functioning, that is, good adjustment and adaptation to the divorce; and (5) good parenting ability and maintaining an orderly, stable, organized daily-living routine for the children. In addition, Kurdek, Blisk, and Siesky (1981) also found the psychological variables of high internal locus of control and a high level of interpersonal reasoning to be correlated with higher levels of children's adjustment. This finding is supported by both Hetherington *et al.* (1979a,b) and Longfellow (1979).

Jacobson (1978a,b,c) documented the importance of parents' explaining and discussing the impending separation and continuing the discussion after the separation or divorce (1978c). She reported that the greater the interparental hostility, the greater the maladjustment of the child (1978b). Finally, Jacobson (1978a) emphasized the importance of the noncustodial parents' spending time with his or her children, especially those aged 7–13; for preschoolers, time with the father did not seem to make as much difference. Free access to the noncustodial parent was consistently associated with better child adjustment.

Herzog and Sudia (1971, 1973), on the other hand, concluded that the functioning of the custodial parent was more important for the children's social and personal adjustment than the other parent's being absent. Good emotional and psychological functioning enhanced adjustment to the divorce, or perhaps good adjustment helped to create good emotional and psychological functioning. The direction of causality was not clearly delineated. Related to this functioning is the finding that younger parents, high geographic mobility, and limited financial resources predict maladjustment for children in single-parent families but not for children in two-parent families (Hodges, Wechsler, & Ballantine, 1979).

Parenting ability was found to be a crucial variable in

child adjustment to divorce by both Hetherington *et al.* (1977, 1978, 1979a) and Wallerstein and Kelly (1980). In addition, these studies reported orderly, organized, stable daily routines as contributing to adjustment.

Legal Aspects

A commonly held belief is that liberalization of divorce laws increases divorce. Cherlin (1981) demonstrated, conversely, that divorce behavior changed before the major liberalization laws: the dramatic rise in the divorce rate began in the early 1960s, whereas the change in attitudes toward divorce occurred somewhere in the late 1960s and the early 1970s, after which most states liberalized their divorce laws. Brody (1970) claimed that the laws that affect family life and moral behavior generally change slowly and lag behind what is really happening and accepted. The case of divorce lends support to this argument.

Wright and Stetson (1978) and Sell (1979) found almost no difference in the divorce rates of the states that liberalized their laws and the states that did not. Schoen, Greenblatt, and Mielke (1975) reported similar findings for California.

Given all the other variables that contribute to the rising divorce rate, it is doubtful that, by itself, the liberalization of the divorce laws in the early 1970s could explain much of the variance.

The adversarial system under fault divorce has been heavily criticized as increasing acrimony and escalating conflict (e.g., Herrman, McKenry, & Weber, 1979).

Some of the psychological and interpersonal issues that lawyers are poorly equipped to handle have been moved into various court-attached intervention functions, variously called *mediation arbitration, adversarial intervention,* and sometimes *court-appointed required counseling.*

The two most commonly used alternatives to the adversarial model are mediation and arbitration by a neutral third party. This idea has been adapted from labor–management disputes and other types of conflicts. In recent years, the courts have been given the right to recommend or to require counseling before granting a divorce and also before making custody decisions. In most of these cases, the counseling facilities are attached to the court, especially when children are involved. Another method of intervention is the court-appointed child advocate (guardian *ad litem*), who helps the judge to make decisions regarding custody and visitation when the divorcing parents cannot agree (Kargman, 1979). In Los Angeles County, there is postdivorce counseling as well as counseling before and during the divorce, to help both the ex-spouses and especially the children involved (Elkin, 1977).

These alternative methods appear to be producing the desired results, but they are too recent to have allowed the amassing of sufficient data to assess their effectiveness.

California was the first state, with its 1969 California Family Law Act, to enact no-fault divorce. The concept of fault-linked grounds for divorce, such as adultery, extreme cruelty, willful desertion, willful neglect, and habitual intemperance, was thus replaced with one neutral substitute: "irreconcilable differences leading to the irremediable breakdown of the marriage" (Dixon & Weitzman, 1980). It was hoped that no-fault divorce would make the divorce process less bitter and acrimonious, would eliminate the hypocrisy of the former adversary or fault system, and would enable more rational and equitable property settlements and spousal support (Dixon & Weitzman, 1980). In the 1970s, most states added some form of no-fault divorce, while keeping some forms of fault divorce (see Freed & Foster, 1977, for a review of these changes).

The major study investigating the impact of the new no-fault divorce law was conducted by Dixon, Kay, and Weitzman in the California Divorce Law Project (cf. Dixon & Weitzman, 1980; Kay, 1972; Weitzman & Dixon, 1979, 1980). This study is used here as the basis for the discussion of the impact of the no-fault divorce laws on adults and children. In general, these researchers found that the new California law produced some intended results but also some unintended results.

Impact on Adults

The divorce rate was not reduced in California, but this lack of reduction was attributed to factors other than the new no-fault law. Litigious action dramatically declined, a result strongly suggesting a reduction in hypocrisy and collusion, as well as a dilution of the bitterness and acrimony that can surround a divorce action (Dixon & Weitzman, 1980). It would seem logical that reduction of bitterness would enhance personal and social adjustment to the divorce despite Spanier and Anderson's (1979) not finding any relationship between dissatisfaction with the fault-based legal system and adjustment. Decidedly, relationships between all legal systems (fault and no-fault) and divorce adjustment need considerably more empirical testing before conclusive statements can be made.

More husbands (formerly those most likely to be defendants) are doing the initial filing, as the concept of legal guilt no longer exists. Husbands' filing increased from a constant of 22% from 1966 through 1969 (Schoen *et al.,* 1975) to 29% in 1970, to 33% in 1972, remaining constant through 1977.

Financially, the new law has negatively affected the majority of women (Weitzman & Dixon, 1980); Seal (1979) claimed that its effects have been disastrous for women and children. Yet, before no-fault, most divorced women were not awarded alimony, so a bad situation has become worse. As Weitzman and Dixon (1980) commented: "Under both legal systems, the reality of alimony awards clearly differed from the legal ideal" (p. 158). In their comprehensive study of alimony after no-fault, Weitzman and Dixon reported a significant overall decline in the frequency of both monetary and token awards, suggesting that the courts are applying the minimalist standard of alimony. Their findings include fewer alimony awards after short marriages, unchanged alimony awards after longer marriages, a shift from permanent to transitional awards, fewer awards to employed and high-income wives, and the displaced homemaker's having only a 50/50 chance of getting any kind of alimony if her husband earns $20,000 or less per year. If the husband earns between $20,000 and $30,000, her chances improve (but only if she has been married 18 or more years). If the husbands' earnings are over $30,000, wives of long or short marriages have an excellent chance of getting a good spousal support settlement. It is the 17% of men who earned over $20,000 in 1977 who created the "alimony myth," according to Weitzman and Dixon (1980). This small minority who paid alimony are not representative of divorced men in the general population, and the myth of the wife as an "alimony drone" needs to be dispelled.

Weitzman and Dixon (1980) suggested that, although the law pays lip service to considering all the circumstances of the respective parties, the thrust of the California law is to encourage the wife to become self-supporting; thus, the goal of economic self-sufficiency replaces the goal of supporting a full-time custodial parent. In this case, the children, as under the old adversary system, may end up the losers along with their custodial mothers.

The major unintended and seemingly most disastrous consequence of the no-fault divorce law in California is its effect on the older housewife who has spent 20, 30, or more years helping to build her husband's career and caring for their children. At the time of divorce, this older housewife finds that she has no stake in her husband's career, and even though she helped him build it, the earnings from it are his, not hers; he reaps the benefits of the partnership that she helped to build (Weitzman & Dixon, 1980). This situation also exists under the adversary legal system, but the wife (if she is the "innocent" party) has more economic bargaining leverage.

Finally, the most revealing aspect of the California legal system's treatment of men and women, which should demolish the alimony myth, is the division of the postdivorce income between the households of the former spouses. The husband's postdivorce household retains two thirds to three fourths of the total, and the wife is left with no more than one third. In all income groups, the postdivorce income of men is substantially higher than that of their former wives (Weitzman & Dixon, 1980).

In summary, the no-fault divorce law in California appears to have produced some of its intended goals, such as reduction of the bitterness, hostility, collusion, and hypocrisy surrounding the divorce action. However, the new law also appears to have produced some unintended consequences, such as worsening the financial situation of most women, especially the older displaced homemaker.

Impact on Children

The impact of no-fault divorce on children focuses on three areas: custody, support, and visitation. The California case eliminated the presumption for the mother in 1973 and replaced it with a sex-neutral standard for granting custody.

In the Western world, presumption for the mother has been previously determined socially and historically, that is, according to the social and economic circumstances during a particular historical era. During feudalism, the father was automatically given custody; but after the Industrial Revolution, when fathers moved to factories and offices and off the farms for their work, women's maternal instincts were "discovered" (Foster & Freed, 1978). In the nineteenth century, an 1839 English law "modified the father's absolute right to custody by granting the mother the right to be awarded custody of children who were less than seven years old" (Weitzman & Dixon, 1979). After that, the "tender years" presumption in favor of the mother became prevalent in the United States as well as in England. This maternal preference for child custody became, in the twentieth century, almost a "divine right" and/or "natural law," buttressed by such famous child psychologists as Dr. Bruno Bettelheim (1956), as well as the legal system itself. It was almost as though the granting of custody was socially constructed to align with the needs of the economic system of the historical era. From an objective perspective, the maternal custody preference may have had positive consequences for men in "freeing" them to be more efficient workers in the industrial economic system, but for women, these "advantages" would appear to be outweighed by the negative consequences. Traditional female socialization continues to cause almost all divorcing mothers to want and almost always to gain custody of their children. As of 1975 only three states still had the maternal preference explicitly in their statutes (Mnookin, 1975), but implicitly, the "tender years doctrine" was continued in other states.

In California, the results of the no-fault divorce beginning in 1970 and the elimination of the maternal preference in 1973 show no significant before-and-after changes in custody, support, or visitation, contrary to the general predictions of the researchers in the California Divorce Law Project (Weitzman & Dixon, 1979).

In addressing the impact of no-fault divorce, Weitzman and Dixon reported that, "On the whole, fathers' requests for physical and legal custody were not significantly different, nor was there any significant increase in physical or legal custody awards to fathers" (p. 492). Both years, mothers were awarded physical custody between 85% and 89% of the time; fathers gained sole physical custody 9% of the time in both years in San Francisco but dropped from 9% in 1968 in Los Angeles to 6% in 1972.

Finally, regarding child support, Weitzman and Dixon

(1979) reported no difference between 1968 and 1972. Custodial mothers still ended up having to provide more than half of the child support, even though under the old law and under the new law, over 80% of the noncustodial fathers were ordered to pay child support. The amount awarded the custodial mother was usually less than half the minimal financial cost of rearing a child (Weitzman & Dixon, 1979). The noncustodial father never had to pay more than one half of his net income to his ex-wife and their children—no matter how many there were—so that several people had to try to live on the same amount that one person (the noncustodial father) was left to live on, at least before he remarried.

The California Divorce Law Project later examined the year 1973 (when the maternal preference was legally eliminated) and the year 1977 (when the consequences of the new sex-neutral legal standard for awarding custody should have surfaced). The researchers looked at custody awards and again found no significant changes between 1973 and 1977. Mothers were still being awarded custody in 90% of the cases and fathers in 6%, and split or joint custody was given in the remaining 3–4% of the cases.

In summary, it appears that seven years of no-fault divorce and four years of neutral-sex preference for custody produced relatively few changes for children in California. Given the nine-year time span and the large-scale representative sample used in the California Divorce Law Project, one could argue that these results can be reasonably generalized at least to other large urban areas in the United States.

Conclusions

This chapter has presented a review and an analysis of contemporary theory and research related to marital separation and divorce, along with the argument that the deviance perspective colors the way in which professionals and laypeople have tended to view divorce. As a result, research has generally focused on the problems and the negative aspects of divorce.

In reviewing this field as of the early 1980s, this chapter has examined the contexts, the correlates and causes, the consequences and adjustment, and the legal aspects of marital separation and divorce. In context, statistical trends and concomitant large-scale societal changes show that divorce rates have been affected by social, economic, and political changes accompanying the rise in the refined divorce rate from approximately one divorce per 1,000 existing marriages in 1860 to 23 in 1985. Most empirical research has been atheoretical, but there have been recent attempts to develop modified versions of social exchange theory to describe, predict, and/or explain the causes of divorce, as well as two different crisis theories to deal with the consequences. The sociodemographic correlates include socioeconomic status (income, occupation, and education), age at marriage, premarital pregnancy, race, religion, intergenerational transmission, geographic lo-

cation, and children. The causes or reasons for divorce given by individuals, which are different for men and women, appear to be shifting from the more instrumental to the more expressive aspects of marriage, perhaps following other similar changes in the core functions of the family. It was pointed out that consequences and adjustment overlap, and that, when there are no negative consequences, there is no need for a painful or difficult adjustment. Negative consequences for adults, when they exist, may include poor physical and/or mental health, psychological and emotional problems and distress, economic plunges that are especially devastating to custodial mothers, and problems related to residential relocations, changes in social and sexual lives, role redefinitions, and intergenerational relations.

Children appear to suffer similar negative consequences, but these can be alleviated by continuing open parent–child communication about the separation and divorce; maintaining a peaceful, well-organized home with lack of overt conflict between the parents; and attempting joint custody where possible. The effect of the California no-fault divorce law, although lessening spousal hostility, increases financial stress for women.

Theoretical and Methodological Problems

How we have come to know what we know about this field leaves much to be desired. One problem is that it is difficult to obtain knowledge about the process of divorce from studies designed for other purposes, such as census data, the Michigan Panel Study of Income Dynamics, the National Longitudinal Surveys of Labor Market Experience, fertility studies, mental and physical health surveys, and other tangentially related research. Most studies have been cross-sectional, but in the 1970s, there was a move toward the more expensive, complex longitudinal designs.

In addition to myriad methodological problems, knowing what variables to focus on (as well as to control) and how to define them conceptually and operationally has been a real problem for theorists and researchers alike. The dominance of aberrant behaviors as the crucial variables to focus on has emerged from the deviance perspective that the research has been cast in. As a result, it appears to have been extremely difficult for professionals to conceptualize the divorce experience except as being negative and pathological. The lack of any long-term theoretical development has also hindered the research and the systematic accumulation of knowledge, but recent theoretical developments are encouraging.

These methodological and theoretical limitations, then, impair the conclusions that can be made from the research. These limitations are being recognized, and efforts are currently being made to transcend them. Much more collaboration, cooperation, and informal as well as formal sharing of information are needed among theorists, researchers, and those in the helping professions.

Finally, it should be recognized that divorce is not the fundamental issue; it is merely one of the many consequences of marriage—a formal exit from a perceived intolerable relationship. Other consequences are desertion (historically employed as an informal exit), continuing conflict (*Who's Afraid of Virginia Woolf?*), and empty-shell marriages. Therefore, marriage itself is the fundamental problem and more theoretical and empirical research should be done on the impingement of broad societal forces on the dyadic interaction within marriages. The research reviewed here does raise questions about the influence of societal forces and sociodemographic characteristics on marriages.

Given the popularity of marriage and the fact that some divorce is inevitable, it appears likely that divorce must come to be accepted as a legitimate, normal, viable, nonpathological exit from marriage. Most family demographers believe that the divorce rate will not do much more than level off, as it did in 1976–1977, and again slightly in 1979–1980, or drop slightly as it has from 1982–1985. Therefore, professionals in every interested discipline could more profitably focus on the following questions: (1) What is it about divorce that troubles adults as well as children? (2) What are the strengths that humans need in order to cope with nonnormative life transitions? (3) How are nonnormative life transitions different from and similar to normative life transitions? (4) What can be done to build up coping strengths to prepare for nonnormative life transitions? And (5) How can nonnormative life transitions be used as positive growth experiences?

By reconceptualizing divorce as one of the normal consequences of marriage and hence removing it from the socially created and socially defined deviance milieu of our society, concerned professionals will be taking a step out of the "dark ages of sick deviance" into the "sunlight of healthy normalcy." The millions of men, women, and children whom divorce has already touched and will touch in the future will be the true beneficiaries.

References

Ahrons, C. R. The binuclear family: Two households, one family. *Alternative Lifestyles*, 1979, *2*, 499–515.

Ahrons, C. R. Divorce: A crisis of family transition and change. *Family Relations*, 1980, *4*, 533–540.

Albrecht, S. L. Correlates of marital happiness among the remarried. *Journal of Marriage and the Family*, 1979, *41*, 857–867.

Altman, L., & Taylor, D. A. *Social penetration: The development of interpersonal relationships*. New York: Holt, Rinehard, & Winston, 1973.

Bachrach, L. L. *Marital status and mental disorder: An analytical review*. United States Department of Health, Education, and Welfare (DHHS Publication No. ADM 75–217). Washington, D.C.: U.S. Government Printing Office, 1975.

Bane, M. J. Marital disruption and the lives of children. *Journal of Social Issues*, 1976, *32*, 103–117.

Barringer, K. D. *Self perception of the quality of adjustment of single parents in divorce participating in Parents-Without-Partners organizations*. Unpublished doctoral dissertation, University of Iowa, 1973. (DAI, 34/07A, p. 4446).

Bauman, K. E. The relationship between age at first marriage, school dropout, and marital instability. *Journal of Marriage and the Family*, 1967, *29*, 672–680.

Berg, B., & Kelly, R. The measured self-esteem of children from broken, rejected, and accepted families. *Journal of Divorce*, 1979, *2*, 363–369.

Berman, W. H., & Turk, D. C. Adaptation to divorce: Problems and coping strategies. *Journal of Marriage and the Family*, 1981, *43*, 179–189.

Bettelheim, B. Fathers shouldn't try to be mothers. *Parents Magazine*, October 1956, 124–125.

Bianchi, S. M., & Farley, R. Racial differences in family living arrangements and economic well-being: An analysis of recent trends. *Journal of Marriage and the Family*, 1979, *41*, 537–551.

Blair, M. *Divorcee's adjustment and attitudinal changes about life*. Dissertation Abstracts, 1969, *30*, 5541–5542. (University Microfilms No. 70–11,099.)

Blau, P. M. *Exchange and power in social life*. Chicago: Wiley, 1964.

Bloom, B. L., & Caldwell, R. A. Sex difference in adjustment during the process of marital adjustment. *Journal of Marriage and the Family*, 1981, *43*, 693–701.

Bloom, B. L., & Hodges, W. F. The predicament of the newly separated. *Community Mental Health Journal*, 1981, *17*, 277–293.

Bloom, B. L., Asher, S. J., & White, S. W. Marital disruption as a stressor: A review and analysis. *Psychological Bulletin*, 1978, *85*, 867–894.

Bloom, B. L., Hodges, W. F., & Caldwell, R. A. Marital separation: The first eight months. In E. J. Callahan & K. A. McKluskey (Eds.), *Life-span developmental psychology: Nonnormative life events*. New York: Academic Press, 1983.

Bohannan, P. The six stations of divorce. In P. Bohannan (Ed.), *Divorce and after*. Garden City, N.Y.: Doubleday, 1970.

Booth, A., & White, L. Thinking about divorce. *Journal of Marriage and the Family*, 1980, *3*, 605–616.

Bould, S. Female-headed families: Personal fate control and the provider role. *Journal of Marriage and the Family*, 1977, *39*, 339–349.

Bradburn, N., & Caplovitz, D. *Reports on happiness*. Chicago: Aldine, 1965.

Brandwein, R. A., Brown, C. A., & Fox, E. M. Women and children last: The social situation of divorced mothers and their families. *Journal of Marriage and the Family*, 1974, *36*, 498–514.

Brody, S. A. California's divorce reform: Its sociological implications. *Pacific Law Journal*, 1970, *1*, 223–232.

Brown, C. A. Feldberg, R., Fox, E. M., & Kohen, J. Divorce: Chance of a new lifetime. *Journal of Social Issues*, 1976, *32*, 119–133.

Brown, E. Divorce counseling. In D. Olson (Ed.), *Treating relationships*. Lake Mills, Iowa: Graphic Publishing, 1976.

Brown, P. *Psychological distress and personal growth among women coping with marital dissolution*. Unpublished doctoral dissertation. University of Michigan, Ann Arbor, 1976. (DAI, 37/02B, p. 947.)

Brown, P., & Fox, H. Sex differences in divorce. In E. Gomberg & V. Frank (Eds.), *Gender and psychopathology: Sex differences in disordered behavior*. New York: Brunner/Mazel, 1978.

Brown, P., Felton, B. J., Whiteman, V., & Manela, R. Attachment in adults: The special case of recently separated marital partners. *Journal of Divorce*, 1980, *3*, 303–317.

Bumpass, L. L., & Sweet, J. A. Differentials in marital stability: 1970. *American Sociological Review*, 1972, *37*, 754–766.

Burr, W. C. *Theory construction and the sociology of the family*. New York: Wiley-Interscience, 1973.

Caplan, G. *Principles of prevention psychiatry*. New York: Basic Books, 1964.

Carter, H., & Glick, P. C. *Marriage and divorce: A social and economic study* (rev. ed.). Cambridge: Harvard University Press, 1976.

Cherlin, A. The effect of children on marital dissolution. *Demography*, 1977, *14*, 265–272.

Cherlin, A. Work life and marital dissolution. In G. Levinger & O. C Moles (Eds.), *Divorce and separation: Context, causes, and consequences.* New York: Basic Books, 1979.

Cherlin, A. J. *Marriage, divorce, remarriage.* Cambridge: Harvard University Press, 1981.

Chester, R. Health and marriage breakdown: Experience of a sample of divorced women. *British Journal of Preventive and Social Medicine,* 1971, *25,* 231–235.

Chiriboga, D. A., & Cutler, L. Stress responses among divorcing men and women. *Journal of Divorce,* 1977, *1,* 95–106.

Chiriboga, D. A., Roberts, J., & Stein, J. Psychological well-being during marital separation. *Journal of Divorce,* 1978, *2,* 21–36.

Christensen, H. T., & Meissner, H. H. Studies in child spacing: III-Premarital pregnancy as a factor in divorce. *American Sociological Review,* 1953, *18,* 641–644.

Christensen, H. T., & Rubinstein, B. B. Premarital pregnancy and divorce: A follow-up study by the interview method. *Marriage and Family Living,* 1956, *18,* 114–123.

Cleveland, M. Divorce in the middle years: The sexual dimension. *Journal of Divorce,* 1979, *2,* 255–261.

Colletta, N. D. Support systems after divorce: Incidence and impact. *Journal of Marriage and the Family,* 1979, *41,* 837–846.

Coombs, L. C., & Zumeta, A. Correlates of marital dissolution in a prospective fertility study: A research note. *Social Problems,* 1970, *18,* 92–102.

Cutright, P. Income and family events: Marital stability. *Journal of Marriage and the Family,* 1971, *33,* 291–306.

Day, R., & Raschke, H. J. *A general theory of crisis and its applicability for divorce adjustment.* Paper presented at the annual meetings of the National Council on Family Relations, Portland, Oregon, 1980.

Deckert, P., & Langelier, R. The late-divorce phenomenon: The causes and impact of ending 20-year-old or longer marriages. *Journal of Divorce,* 1978, *1,* 381–390.

Deutscher, I. The gatekeeper in public housing. In I. Deutscher & E. J. Thompson (Eds.), *Among the people: Encounters with the poor.* New York: Basic Books, 1968.

Dill, D., Feld, E., Martin, J., Beukema, S., & Belle, D. The impact of the environment on the coping efforts of low-income mothers. *Family Relations,* 1980, *29,* 503–509.

Dixon, R. B., & Weitzman, L. J. Evaluating the impact of no-fault divorce in California. *Family Relations,* 1980, *29,* 297–307.

Dohrenwend, B. P. Sociocultural and social-psychological factors in the genesis of mental disorders. *Journal of Health and Social Behavior,* 1975, *16,* 365–392.

Dohrenwend, B. P., & Dohrenwend, B. S. Social and cultural influences on psychopathology. *Annual Review of Psychology,* 1974, *25,* 417–452.

Dohrenwend, B. P., & Dohrenwend, B. S. Sex differences and psychiatric disorders. *American Journal of Sociology,* 1976, *81,* 1447–1452.

Dohrenwend, B. P., & Dohrenwend, B. S. Reply to Gove and Tudor's comment on sex differences and psychiatric disorders. *American Journal of Sociology,* 1977, *82,* 1336–1345.

Dohrenwend, B. S. Life events as stressors: A methodological inquiry. *Journal of Health and Social Behavior,* 1973, *14,* 165–177.

Duncan, G. J., & Morgan, J. N. Young children and "other" family members. In G. J. Duncan & J. N. Morgan (Eds.), *Five thousand American families—Patterns of economic progress,* Vol. 4. Ann Arbor: Institute for Social Research, University of Michigan, 1976.(b)

Easterlin, R. A. *Birth and fortune: The impact of numbers on personal welfare.* New York: Basic Books, 1980.

Elder, G. H., Jr. *Children of the Great Depression.* Chicago: University of Chicago Press, 1974.

Elkin, M. Postdivorce counseling in a conciliation court. *Journal of Divorce,* 1977, *1,* 55–65.

Erikson, E. K. *Childhood and society* (2nd ed.). New York: W. W. Norton, 1963.

Espenshade, T. J. The economic consequences of divorce. *Journal of Marriage and the Family,* 1979, *41,* 615–625.

Farley, W., & Hermalin, A. I. Family stability: A comparison of trends between blacks and whites. *American Sociological Review,* 1971, *36,* 1–17.

Felton, B. J., Brown, P., Lehmann, S., & Liberatos, P. The coping function of sex role attitudes during marital disruption. *Journal of Health and Social Behavior,* 1980, *21,* 240–248.

Foster, H. H., & Freed, D. J. Life with father. *Family Law Quarterly,* 1978, *11,* 321–322.

Fox, J. W. Gove's specific sex-role theory of mental illness: A research note. *Health and Social Behavior,* 1980, *21,* 260–267.

Freed, D. J., & Foster, H. H., Jr. Family law in the fifty states: An overview. *Family Law Reporter,* 1977, *3,* 4047–4052. Monograph #28.

Frisbie, W. P., Bean, F. D., & Eberstein, I. W. Pattern of marital instability among Mexican Americans, blacks, and Anglos. In F. D. Bean & W. P. Frisbie (Eds.), *The demography of racial and ethnic groups.* New York: Academic Press, 1978.

Froiland, D. J., & Hozeman, T. L. Counseling for constructive divorce. *Personnel and Guidance Journal,* 1977, *55,* 525–529.

Furstenberg, F. F., Jr. Premarital pregnancy and marital instability. *Journal of Social Issues,* 1976, *1,* 67–86.

Galligan, R. J., & Bahr, S. Economic well-being and marital stability: Implications for income maintenance programs. *Journal of Marriage and the Family,* 1978, *40,* 283-290.

Gebhard, P. Postmarital coitus among widows and divorcees. In P. Bohannan (Ed.), *Divorce and after.* Garden City, N.Y.: Doubleday, 1970.

Glenn, N. D. The contribution of marriage to the psychological well-being of males and females. *Journal of Marriage and the Family,* 1975, *37,* 594–600.

Glenn, Norval D. and Shelton, Beth Ann. Regional differences in divorce in the United States. *Journal of Marriage and the Family,* 1985, *47,* 641–652.

Glenn, Norval D. and Supancic, Michael. The social and demographic correlates of divorce and separation in the United States: An update and reconsideration. *Journal of Marriage and the Family,* 1984, *46,* 563–575.

Glick, P. C., & Norton, A. J. Marrying, divorcing, and living together in the U.S. today. *Population Bulletin,* 1979, *32*(5).

Goetting, A. Some societal-level explanations for the rising divorce rate. *Family Therapy,* 1979, *2,* 71–87.

Goetting, A. Divorce outcome research: Issues and perspectives. *Journal of Family Issues,* 1981, *2,* 350–377.

Goode, W. J. *After divorce.* Glencoe, Ill.: Free Press, 1956.

Goode, W. J. *World revolutions and family patterns.* New York: Free Press, 1963.

Gove, W. R. The relationship between sex roles, marital status, and mental illness. *Social Forces,* 1972, *51,* 34–44.

Gove, W. R. Sex differences in the epidemiology of mental disorder. In E. Gombert & D. Franks (Eds.), *Gender and psychopathology: Sex differences in disordered behavior.* New York: Brunner/Mazel, 1978.(a)

Gove, W. R. Sex, marital status, and psychiatric treatment: A research note. *Social Forces,* 1979, *58,* 89–93.

Gove, W. R., & Tudor, J. Adult sex roles and mental illness. *American Journal of Sociology,* 1973, *77,* 812–835.

Granvold, D. K., Pedler, L. M., & Schellie, S. G. A study of sex role expectancy and female postdivorce adjustment. *Journal of Divorce,* 1979, *2,* 383–393.

Gurin, G., Veroff, J., & Feld, S. *Americans view their mental health.* New York: Basic Books, 1960.

Hagestad, G. O., & Smyer, M. A. *Adult intergenerational relations under stress: The case of divorce in middle age.* Paper presented at the annual meeting of the Gerontological Society, San Diego, California, November 1980.

Halem, L. C. *Divorce reform: Changing legal and social perspectives.* New York: Free Press, 1980.

Hampton, R. L. Marital disruption: Some social and economic consequences. In G. J. Duncan & J. N. Morgan (Eds.), *Five thousand American families—Patterns of economic progress,* Vol. 3. Ann Arbor: Institute for Social Research, University of Michigan, 1975.

Hampton, R. L. Husband's characteristics and marital disruption in black families. *The Sociological Quarterly,* 1979, *20,* 255–266.

Hampton, R. L. Institutional decimation, marital exchange, and disruption in black families. *Western Journal of Black Studies,* 1980, *4,* 132–139.

Hannan, M., Tuma, N., and Groeneveld, L. P. Income and marital events: Evidence from an income maintenance experiment. *American Journal of Sociology,* 1977, *82,* 1186–1211.

Hansen, D. Personal and positional influence in formal groups: Composition and theory for research and family vulnerability to stress. *Social Forces,* 1965, *44,* 202–210.

Hayes, M. P., Stinnett, N., & DeFrain, J. Learning about marriage from the divorced. *Journal of Divorce,* 1980, *4,* 23–29.

Herrman, S. J. Divorce: A grief process. *Perspectives in Psychiatric Care,* 1974, *12,* 108–112.

Herrman, M. S., McKenry, P., & Weber, R. E. Mediation and arbitration applied to family conflict resolution: The divorce settlement. *The Arbitration Journal,* 1979, *34,* 17–21.

Herzog, E., & Sudia, C. E. *Boys in fatherless homes.* U.S. Department of Health, Education, and Welfare, Office of Child Development (DHEW Publication No. OCD 72–33). Washington, D.C.: U.S. Government Printing Office, 1971.

Herzog, E., & Sudia, C. E. Children in fatherless families. In B. M. Caldwell & H. N. Ricciuti (Eds.), *Review of child developmental research,* Vol. 3. Chicago: University of Chicago Press, 1973.

Hetherington, E. M., Cox, M., & Cox, R. Divorced fathers. *Family Coordinator,* 1976, *25,* 417–428.

Hetherington, E. M., Cox, M., & Cox, R. Beyond father absence: Conceptualization of effects of divorce. In E. M. Hetherington & R. D. Parke (Eds.), *Contemporary readings in child psychology.* New York: McGraw-Hill, 1977.

Hetherington, E. M., Cox, M., & Cox, R. The aftermath of divorce. In J. H. Stevens, Jr., & M. Matthews (Eds.), *Mother–child, father–child relations.* Washington, D.C.: National Association for the Education of Young Children, 1978.

Hetherington, E. M., Cox, M., & Cox, R. The development of children in mother headed families. In H. Hoffman & D. Reiss (Eds.), *The American family: Dying or developing.* New York: Plenum Press, 1979.(a)

Hetherington, E. M., Cox, M., & Cox, R. Family interactions and the social emotional and cognitive development of children following divorce. In V. C. Vaugh & T. B. Brazelton (Eds.), *The family: Setting priorities.* New York: Science and Medicine Publishers, 1979.(b)

Hetherington, E. M., Cox, M., & Cox, R. Stress and coping in divorce: A focus on women. In J. Gullahorn (Ed.), *Psychology and women in transition.* Silver Springs, Md.: B. H. Winston, 1979.(c)

Hill, R. *Families under stress.* New York: Harper, 1949.

Hill, R. Social stresses on the family. In M. B. Sussman (Ed.), *Sourcebook in marriage and the family.* Boston: Houghton Mifflin, 1968. (Reprinted from *Social Casework,* 1958, *39,* 139–150.)

Hodges, W. F., Wechsler, R. C., & Ballantine, C. Divorce and the preschool child: Cumulative stress. *Journal of Divorce,* 1979, *3,* 55–68.

Hoffman, S., & Holmes, J. Husbands, wives, and divorce. In G. J. Duncan & J. N. Morgan (Eds.), *Five thousand American families—Patterns of economic progress,* Vol. 4. Ann Arbor: Institute for Social Research, University of Michigan, 1976.

Holley, P. *An analysis of Divorce Adjustment Measures.* Paper prepared for presentation at the Southwestern Sociological Association annual meeting, Houston, Texas, April 1980.

Homans, G. C. Social behavior as exchange. *American Journal of Sociology,* 1958, *63,* 597–606.

Homans, G. C. *Social behavior: Its elementary forms* (rev. ed.). New York: Harcourt Brace Jovanovich, 1974.

Hunt, M. *The world of the formerly married.* New York: McGraw-Hill, 1966.

Hunt, M. *Sexual behavior in the 1970s.* Chicago: Playboy Press, 1974.

Hunt, M. W., & Hunt, B. *The divorce experience.* New York: McGraw-Hill, 1977.

Hynes, W. J. *Single parent mothers and distress: Relationships between selected social and psychological factors and distress in low-income single parent mothers.* Unpublished doctoral dissertation, Catholic University of America, Washington, D.C., 1979. (DAI, 40/3A, p. 1686.)

Jacobson, D. S. The impact of marital separation/divorce on children: I. Parent–child separation and child adjustment. *Journal of Divorce,* 1978, *1,* 341–360.(a)

Jacobson, D. S. The impact of marital separation/divorce on children: II. Interparent hostility and child adjustment. *Journal of Divorce,* 1978, *2,* 3–19.(b)

Jacobson, D. S. The impact of marital separation/divorce on children: III. Parent–child communication and child adjustment, and regression analysis of findings from overall study. *Journal of Divorce,* 1978, *2,* 175–194.(c)

Johnson, F. C., & Johnson, M. R. Family planning: Implications for marital stability. *Journal of Divorce,* 1980, *3,* 273–281.

Johnson, S. B. The impact of women's liberation on marriage, divorce, and family life style. In C. Lloyd (Ed.), *Sex discrimination and the division of labor.* New York: Columbia University Press, 1975.

Jones, C. A., Gordon, N. M., & Sawhill, I. V. *Child support payments in the United States.* Working Paper No. 992–03. Washington, D.C.: Urban Institute, 1976.

Kalter, N. Children of divorce in an outpatient psychiatric population. *American Journal of Orthopsychiatry,* 1977, *47,* 40–51.

Kanoy, K., & Miller, B. C. Children's impact on the parental decision to divorce. *Family Relations,* 1980, *29,* 309–315.

Kargman, M. W. A court appointed child advocate (guardian ad litem) reports on her role in contested child custody cases and looks to the future. *Journal of Divorce,* 1979, *3,* 77–90.

Kay, H. H. Making marriage and divorce safe for women. *California Law Review,* 1972, *60,* 1683–1700.

Kessler, S. *The American way of divorce: Prescriptions for change.* Chicago: Nelson-Hall, 1975.

Kitson, G. C. Attachment to the spouse in divorce: A scale and its applications. *Journal of Marriage and the Family,* 1982, *44,* 379–393.

Kitson, G. C., Babri, K. B., & Roach, M. J. Who divorces and why: A review. *Journal of Family Issues,* 1985, *6,* 255–293.

Kitson, G. C., & Raschke, H. J. Divorce research: What we know; what we need to know. *Journal of Divorce,* 1981, *4*(3), 1–38.

Kitson, G. C., & Sussman, M. B. Marital complaints, demographic characteristics, and symptoms of mental distress in divorce. *Journal of Marriage and the Family,* 1982, *44,* 87–101.

Kitson, G. C., Lopata, H. Z., Holmes, W. M., & Meyering, S. M. Divorces and widows: Similarities and differences. *American Journal of Orthopsychiatry,* 1980, *50,* 291–301.

Kraus, S. The crisis of divorce: Growth promoting or pathogenic. *Journal of Divorce,* 1979, *3,* 107–119.

Kübler-Ross, E. *On death and dying.* New York: Doubleday, 1953.

Kulka, R. A., & Weingarten, H. The long-term effects of parental divorce on adult adjustment. *The Journal of Social Issues,* 1979, *35,* 50–78.

Kurdek, L. A., Blisk, D., & Siesky, A. E., Jr. Correlates of children's long-term adjustment to their parents' divorce. *Developmental Psychology*, 1981, *17*, 565–579.

Landis, J. T. The trauma of children when parents divorce. *Marriage and Family Living*, 1960, *22*, 7–16.

Levinger, G. Marital cohesiveness and dissolution: An integrative review. *Journal of Marriage and the Family*, 1965, *27*, 19–28.

Levinger, G. Sources of marital dissatisfaction among applicants for divorce. *American Journal of Orthopsychiatry*, 1966, *36*, 803–807.

Levinger, G. A social psychological perspective on divorce. *Journal of Social Issues*, 1976, *32*, 21–47.

Levitin, T. E. Children of divorce: An introduction. *Journal of Social Issues*, 1979, *35*, 1–25.

Levy, T. M. & Joffe, W. *Counseling couples through separation: A developmental approach*. Paper presented at the annual meeting of the National Council on Family Relations, San Diego, October, 1977.

Longfellow, C. Divorce in context: Its impact on children. In G. Levinger & O. C. Moles (Eds.), *Divorce and separation: Context, causes and consequences*. New York: Basic Books, 1979.

Lynch, J. J. *The broken heart: The medical consequences of loneliness*. New York: Basic Books, 1977.

Magrab, P. R. For the sake of the children: A review of the psychological effects of divorce. *Journal of Divorce*, 1978, *1*, 233–245.

McCarthy, J. A comparison of the probability of the dissolution of first and second marriages. *Demography*, 1978, *15*, 345–359.

McCord, J., McCord, W., & Thurber, E. Some effects of paternal absence on male children. *Journal of Abnormal and Social Psychology*, 1962, *64*, 361–369.

McCubbin, H. I., & Patterson, J. M. Family adaptation to crises. In H. McCubbin, B. Cauble, & J. Patterson (Eds.), *Family stress, coping and social support*. Springfield, Ill.: Charles C. Thomas, 1982.

Meyers, J. C. *The adjustment of women to marital separation: The effects of sex-role identification and of stage in family life, as determined by age and presence or absence of dependent children*. Unpublished doctoral dissertation, University of Colorado, 1976. (DAI, 37/05B, p. 2516.)

Miao, G. Marital instability and unemployment among whites and nonwhites, the Moynihan Report revisited—again. *Journal of Marriage and the Family*, 1974, *36*, 77–86.

Mika, K., & Bloom, B. L. Adjustment to separation among former cohabitors. *Journal of Divorce*, 1980, *4*(2), 45–66.

Miller, M. H. A comparison of the duration of interracial marriages in Hawaii. *International Journal of Sociology and the Family*, 1971, *1*, 197–201.

Mnookin, R. Child-custody adjudication: Judicial functions in the face of indeterminancy. *Law and Contemporary Problems*, Summer, 1975, 226–234.

Mott, F. L., & Moore, S. F. The causes of marital disruption among young Americans: An interdisciplinary perspective. *Journal of Marriage and the Family*, 1979, *41*, 355–365.

Moynihan, D. P. The Negro family: The case for national action. In L. Rainwater & W. L. Yancey (Eds.), *The Moynihan report and the politics of controversy*. Cambridge: M.I.T. Press, 1967.

Mueller, C. W., & Pope, H. Marital instability: A study of its transmission between generations. *Journal of Marriage and the Family*, 1977, *39*, 83–93.

National Center for Health Statistics. Annual summary of births, deaths, marriages, and divorces: United States, 1981. *Monthly Vital Statistics Report* (DHHS Publication No. PHS 83–1120). Hyattsville, Md: U.S. Government Printing Office, 1982.

National Center for Health Statistics. Annual summary of births, deaths, marriages, and divorces: United States, 1982. *Monthly Vital Statistics Report*. (DHHS Publication No. PHS 83–1120). Hyattsville, Md.: U.S. Government Printing Office, 1983.

National Center for Health Statistics. Annual summary of births, deaths, marriages, and divorces: United States, 1983. *Monthly Vital Statistics Report*. (DHHS Publication No. PHS 84–1120). Hyattsville, Md.: U.S. Government Printing Office, 1984.

National Center for Health Statistics. Births, marriages, divorces, and deaths for June, 1985. *Monthly Vital Statistics Report*. (DHHS Publication No. PHS 85–1120). Hyattsville, Md.: U. S. Government Printing Office, 1985a.

National Center for Health Statistics. Annual summary of births, marriages, divorces, and deaths: United States, 1984. *Monthly Vital Statistics Report*. (DHHS Publication No. PHS 85–1120). Hyattsville, Md.: U.S. Government Printing Office, 1985b.

Norton, A., & Glick, P. Marital instability in America, past, present, and future. In G. Levinger & O. C. Moles (Eds.), *Divorce and separation: Context, causes, and consequences*. New York: Basic Books, 1979.

Nye, F. I. Child adjustment in broken and in unhappy unbroken homes. *Marriage and Family Living*, 1957, *19*, 356–360.

Ogburn, W. F. The changing functions of the family. In R. F. Winch & R. McGinnis (Eds.), *Selected studies in marriage and the family*. New York: Henry Holt, 1953.

O'Neill, W. *Divorce in the progressive era*. New Haven, Conn.: Yale University Press, 1967.

O'Neill, W. L. *Everyone was brave: A history of feminism in America*. Chicago: Quadrangle Books, 1971.

Pais, J. S. *Social-psychological predictors of adjustment for divorced mothers*. Unpublished doctoral dissertation, University of Tennessee, Knoxville, 1978. (DAI, 39/8A, p. 5165.)

Pais, J., & White, P. Family redefinition: A review of the literature toward a model of divorce adjustment. *Journal of Divorce*, 1979, *2*, 271–281.

Pope, H., & Mueller, C. W. The intergenerational transmission of marital instability: Comparison by race and sex. *Journal of Social Issues*, 1976, *32*, 49–66.

Preston, S. H. Estimating the proportion of American marriages that end in divorce. *Sociological Methods and Research*, 1975, *3*, 434–460.

Preston, S. H., & McDonald, J. The incidence of divorce within cohorts of American marriages contracted since the Civil War. *Demography*, 1979, *16*, 1–25.

Price-Bonham, S., & Balswick, J. O. The noninstitutions: Divorce, desertion, and remarriage. *Journal of Marriage and the Family*, 1980, *42*, 959–972.

Rabkin, P. A. *Fathers to daughters: The legal foundations of female emancipation*. Westport, Conn.: Greenwood Press, 1980.

Radloff, L. Sex differences in depression: The effects of occupation and marital status. *Sex Roles*, 1975, *1*, 249–265.

Raschke, H. J. *Social and psychological factors in voluntary postmarital dissolution adjustment*. Unpublished doctoral dissertation, University of Minnesota at Minneapolis, 1974. (DAI, 35/08A, p. 5549.)

Raschke, H. J. The role of social participation in postdivorce adjustment. *Journal of Divorce*, 1977, *1*, 129–140.

Raschke, H. J., & Barringer, K. D. Two studies in postdivorce adjustment among persons participating in Parents Without Partners Organizations. *Family Perspective*, 1977, *11*, 23–34.

Raschke, H. J., & Raschke, V. J. Family conflict and children's self-concepts: A comparison of intact and single-parent families. *Journal of Marriage and the Family*, 1979, *41*, 367–374.

Rheinstein, M. *Marriage stability, divorce, and the law*. Chicago: University of Chicago Press, 1972.

Roman, M., & Haddad, W. *The disposable parent: The case for joint custody*. New York: Holt, Rinehart & Winston, 1978.

Rosenberg, M. *Society and the adolescent self-image*. Princeton, N.J.: Princeton University Press, 1965.

Ross, H. L., & Sawhill, I. V. *Time of transition: The growth of families headed by women*. Washington, D.C.: Urban Institute, 1975.

Rotter, J. Generalized expectancies for internal versus external control of reinforcement. *Psychological Monographs*, 1966, *80*, 1.

Rutter, M. Parent-child separation: Psychological effects on the children. *Journal of Child Psychology and Psychiatry*, 1971, *12*, 233–260.

Salts, C. J. Divorce process: integration of theory. *Journal of Divorce*, 1979, *2*, 233–240.

Scanzoni, J. A social system analysis of dissolved and existing marriages. *Journal of Marriage and the Family*, 1968, *30*, 452–461.

Scanzoni, J. *Sexual bargaining: Power politics in the American marriages*. Englewood Cliffs, N.J.: Prentice-Hall Spectrum, 1972.

Scanzoni, J. A historical perspective on husband–wife bargaining power and marital dissolution. In G. Levinger & O. C. Moles (Eds.), *Divorce and separation: Context, causes, and consequences*. New York: Basic Books, 1979.

Schoen, R. California divorce rates by age at first marriage and duration of first marriage. *Journal of Marriage and the Family*, 1975, *37*, 548–555.

Schoen, R., Greenblatt, H. N., & Mielke, R. B. California's experience with non-adversary divorce. *Demography*, 1975, *12*, 223–243.

Seal, K. A. A decade of no-fault divorce. *Family Advocate*, 1979, *1*, 10–15.

Sell, K. D. Divorce law reform and increasing divorce rates in the United States. In J. G. Wells (Ed.), *Current issues in marriage and the family* (2nd ed., revised). New York: Macmillan, 1979.

Sell, K. D. *Divorce in the seventies: A subject bibliography*. Phoenix, Ariz.: Oryx Press, 1981.

Smart, L. S. An application of Erikson's theory to the recovery-from-divorce process. *Journal of Divorce*, 1979, *1*, 67–79.

Smith, M. J. The social consequences of single parenthood: A longitudinal perspective. *Family Relations*, 1980, *29*, 75–81.

Spanier, G. B., & Anderson, E. A. The impact of the legal system on adjustment to marital separation. *Journal of Marriage and the Family*, 1979, *41*, 605–613.

Spanier, G. B., & Casto, R. F. Adjustment to separation and divorce: An analysis of 50 case studies. *Journal of Divorce*, 1979, *2*, 241–253.

Spanier, G. B., & Lachman, M. E. Factors associated with adjustment to marital separation. *Sociological Focus*, 1980, *13*, 369–381.

Spanier, G. B., & Lewis, R. A. Marital quality: A review of the seventies. *Journal of Marriage and the Family*, 1980, *42*, 825–839.

Spivey, P. B., & Scherman, A. The effects of time lapse on personality characteristics and stress on divorced women. *Journal of Divorce*, 1980, *4*, 49–59.

Stack, S. The effects of marital dissolution on suicide. *Journal of Marriage and the Family*, 1980, *42*, 83–91.

Sweet, J. A., & Bumpass, L. L. Differentials in marital instability of the black population: 1970. 1974, *Phylon*, *35*, 323–331.

Taibbi, R. Transitional relationships after divorce. *Journal of Divorce*, 1979, *2*, 263–270.

Tarver, J. D. Age at marriage and duration of marriage of divorced couples. *Sociology and Social Research*, 1951, *36*, 102–106.

Thibaut, J. W., & Kelley, H. H. *The social psychology of groups*. New York: Wiley, 1959.

Thoits, P. Undesirable life events and psychophysiological distress. *American Sociological Review*, 1981, *46*, 97–109.

Thornes, B., & Collard, J. *Who divorces?* Boston: Routledge & Kegan Paul, 1979.

Thornton, A. Marital instability differentials and interactions: Insights from multivariate contingency table analysis. *Sociology and Social Research*, 1978, *62*, 572–595.

Unger, D. G., & Powell, D. R. Supporting families under stress: The role of social networks. *Family Relations*, 1980, *29*, 566–574.

U.S. Bureau of the Census. *Census of population: Age at first marriage*. Final report. PC(2)-4B. Washington, D.C.: U.S. Government Printing Office, 1973.

U.S. Bureau of the Census. Current Population Reports, Series P-23, No. 104. *American families and living arrangements*. Washington, D.C.: U.S. Government Printing Office, 1980.(a)

U.S. Bureau of the Census. Current Population Reports, Series P-23, No. 106. *Child support and alimony: 1978* (advance report). Washington, D.C.: U.S. Government Printing Office, 1980.(b)

U.S. Department of Health and Human Services. *Advance report of final divorce statistics, 1979*. Monthly Vital Statistics Report, Vol. 30, No. 2, Supplement. Washington, D.C.: U.S. Government Printing Office, May 1981.(a)

U.S. Department of Health and Human Services. *Births, marriages, divorces, and deaths for 1980*. Monthly Vital Statistics Report, Vol. 29, No. 12. Washington, D.C.: U.S. Government Printing Office, 1981.(b)

Verbrugge, L. M. Marital status and health. *Journal of Marriage and the Family*, 1979, *41*, 267–285.

Waller, W. W. *The old and the new: Divorce and adjustment* (3rd ed.). Carbondale, Ill.: Southern University Press, 1967.

Wallerstein, J., & Kelly, J. *Surviving the breakup: How children and parents cope with divorce*. New York: Basic Books, 1980.

Weed, J. A. *National estimates of marriage dissolution and survivorship: United States*. Vital and Health Statistics: Series 3, Analytical Studies, No. 19. (DHHS publication no (PHS) 81–1403. National Center for Health Statistics, Hyattsville, Md., November 1980.)

Weiss, R. S. *Marital separation*. New York: Basic Books, 1975.

Weiss, R. S. The emotional impact of marital separation. *Journal of Social Issues*, 1976, *32*, 135–145.

Weiss, R. S. *Going it alone: The family life and social situation of the single parent*. New York: Basic Books, 1979.

Weitzman, L. J., & Dixon, R. B. Child custody awards: Legal standards and empirical patterns of child custody, support, and visitation after divorce. *University of California Davis Law Review*, 1979, *12*, 473–521.

Weitzman, L. J., & Dixon, R. B. The alimony myth: Does no-fault make a difference? *Family Law Quarterly*, 1980, *14*, 141–187.

White, S. W., & Bloom, B. L. Factors related to the adjustment of divorcing men. *Family Relations*, 1981, *30*, 349–360.

Wiseman, R. S. Crisis theory and the process of divorce. *Social Casework*, 1975, *56*, 205–212.

Wright, G. C., Jr., & Stetson, D. M. The impact of no-fault divorce law reform on divorce in American states. *Journal of Marriage and the Family*, 1978, *40*, 557–580.

Yoder, J. D., & Nichols, R. C. A life perspective comparison of married and divorced persons. *Journal of Marriage and the Family*, 1980, *42*, 413–419.

Zill, N. *Divorce, marital happiness and the mental health of children: Findings from the Foundation for Child Development National Survey of Children*. Report prepared for National Institute of Mental Health Workshop on Divorce and Children, Bethesda, Md., 1978.

CHAPTER 23

The Family in Later Years

Judith Treas and Vern L. Bengtson

Throughout most of human history, the family has been both the primary context of social integration for aged individuals and the principal provider of economic support and physical assistance to the elderly in need. Within the lifetime of those Americans now approaching old age, however, a number of dramatic changes have occurred in social structure and culture—changes that promise to alter traditional assumptions concerning aging, the family, and social supports in meeting the challenges of old age.

In this chapter, we examine both macrosocial and microsocial indicators concerning the family life of today's aging population. We review recent research that documents four macrosocietal trends affecting aging and contemporary families:

1. *Demographic trends:* Although more and more Americans are surviving into their eighth, ninth, and even tenth decades of life, recent cohorts have borne fewer children—a fact suggesting that future families may be increasingly taxed to their limit in providing for elderly members in need.

2. *Marital status:* Although more couples than ever before are surviving to celebrate their golden wedding anniversary, a widening sex gap in mortality has produced a growing population of widows at the same time that the ranks of the divorced aged have increased—a fact suggesting greater needs but fewer familial resources for a substantial segment of older Americans.

3. *Labor-force-participation patterns:* More and more middle-aged women are employed full time outside the home—a fact indicating that the traditional ''kinkeepers'' may find themselves squeezed between the demands of the older and the younger generations within the family.

4. *The growth of public programs and services:* Other social institutions have taken on some traditional family functions in meeting the needs of older members—a fact implying to some observers the decline of families as a primary social institution in American society.

Taken together, these trends suggest that we may be in the midst of a dramatic transition in the family integration of older Americans.

In the face of such changes, we will review evidence indicating the importance of contemporary families in the lives of aged individuals. Families continue to be viewed as the foremost institution for social support of the aged. Even in a fast-changing and ever more complex postindustrial society, current research suggests the following three indicators of continuing familial function:

1. *Direct caregiving:* Families are primary providers of direct assistance in meeting needs associated with the dependencies of aging: transportation, assistance in daily living, and, to a lesser extent, housing and economic support.

2. *Psychological support:* Families provide assistance in negotiating the changes associated with aging by providing meaning, a sense of continuity, and affirmations of value.

3. *Social contact:* Interaction with children and kin provides much of the interpersonal connection for many older people; such interaction is perceived as both frequent and positive.

In short, an evaluation of recent research concerning the family of later life has revealed some surprising continuities of function in the face of a wave of structural change.

The focus on the continued viability of family functions with age has led to some unfortunate discounting of structural changes, however. In reaction against popularly held beliefs in the breakdown of the family and the abandonment of aged kin, family gerontologists have tended to downplay changes in the family life of elders. Transcending the bounds of households, the extended helping network of kin, identified by Sussman (1965), Shanas, Townsend, Wedderburn, Friis, Milhaj, and Stehouwer (1968), and others, led students of aging to discount obvious transformations in the living arrangements of older people. Until the advent of life course analysis (Elder, 1978), family scholars tended either to focus on the early stages of ahistorical conjugal life cycles or to stress the impact of social change on family institutions in general rather than on older families in particular.

In this chapter, we argue for greater consideration by family sociologists of the later stages of the family life

Judith Treas and Vern L. Bengtson • Department of Sociology, University of Southern California, Los Angeles, CA 90089-0032.
Partial support for the preparation of this chapter was provided by grants/AG-04092 and 5-T32-AG00037 from the National Institute on Aging; and grant/MH-38244 from the National Institute of Mental Health.

cycle and greater attention by social gerontologists to changes in the family life of the elderly. In particular, we wish to focus on the interplay between family life as experienced by its members and the larger world of which the family is a part. In addressing the topic of the family life of older people, (1) we shall attend to both the macrosocietal context and the microsocial processes in older families; (2) we shall consider both conjugal and intergenerational dimensions of family life in old age; and (3) we shall recognize that families in later life are affected by social change as well as by individual changes associated with aging. We begin by sketching the broad changes challenging families, before we turn to a consideration of relations within families with older members. As no review can do justice to research on aging and the family, the reader is also referred to other essays on this topic (Aizenberg & Treas, 1985; Bengtson & Robertson, 1985; Bengtson & Treas, 1980; Fogel, Hatfield, Kiesler, & March, 1981; Hagestad, 1981; Streib & Beck, 1980; Sussman, 1976; Treas, 1983; Troll, Miller, & Atchley, 1979).

The Macrosocial Context of Aging Families

On October 2, 1981, the *Los Angeles Times* reported a human interest story:

Joseph Horowitz still doesn't understand why his mother got so upset. He wasn't "missing" from their home in Miami Beach; he had just decided to go north for the winter. Etta Horowitz, however, called authorities. Social worker Mike Weston finally located Joseph in Monticello, N.Y., where he was visiting friends. Etta, 102, and her husband, Solomon, 96, had feared harm had befallen their son, Joseph, 75, a former taxicab driver. "Finding her son was a nice Jewish New Year's present for his mother," Weston said.

This story of a parent's protectiveness and a child's protestations of independence would hardly have been newsworthy had the family members been younger. Given their advanced ages, however, the article serves as testimony to the never-ending negotiation of family roles over the life cycle. The Horowitz family also offers evidence of the social, demographic, and economic changes that have altered the context of family life in later years. Because of declining death rates, Etta and Solomon can look back on a marriage surviving three quarters of a century, and Joseph's adulthood has already overlapped his parents' lives by over 50 years. Residing in a Sunbelt community populated largely by older persons who have lived most of their lives somewhere else, Joseph (and presumably his parents) enjoys the relatively new life-cycle stage of retirement made possible by old age pensions. In times of trouble, they can count on a professional social worker, not merely on friends and relations.

To be sure, no family is exemplary and no two families are ever quite alike, because there are almost infinite combinations of family characteristics: ethnic traditions, private meanings, financial resources, residential milieus, career trajectories, cohort memberships, dyad affections and disaffections, decision-making styles, and so

on. Despite this diversity, two factors account for commonalities across families.

First, families face universal dilemmas in fulfilling such essential functions as the economic maintenance and socialization of their members. A case in point is the tension between offspring, who must ultimately achieve independence, and parents, whose own lives are given meaning by a close link or "developmental stake" in a younger generation (Bengtson & Kuypers, 1971). Such familiar issues are a common thread linking very different families.

Second, families are unified because family "interiors" are marked inevitably by the macrosocietal events outside the household. In the 1930s, for example, many families confronted a common problem: the Great Depression. Their widespread response was to have fewer children. In the 1950s, these children, now grown, confronted unprecedented economic opportunities born of a labor shortage. Their common response to unanticipated affluence—marrying earlier and having more children closer together—gave rise to the baby boom (Easterlin, 1980). What is perhaps most amazing is that very different sorts of married couples—teenagers and mature adults, whites and nonwhites, high-school dropouts and college graduates—opted for larger families as a response to prosperity (Rindfuss & Sweet, 1977). In a review of the research on intergenerational relations, Hagestad (1981) argued the need to emphasize the variation rather than the norm in family life. This stress on the unique microenvironment of the family may serve well to explain the origins of individual heterogeneity (e.g., personality). In the aggregate, however, the common response to common opportunities or problems looms large.

As the experiences of the Horowitz family remind us, the contemporary family of later life is in many ways unprecedented, being a product of demographic change and social innovations altering the content of family functions. Never before have so many persons lived to grow old and to have aging parents, aging spouses, and even aging children. The family has long been the principal context of social integration for the aged and the primary source of financial support and physical care for the elderly. Thus, the family has felt more intimately than any other societal institution the macrosocietal changes affecting the numbers of older persons and their social roles.

The Demographic Revolution: Longer Lives, Falling Fertility

Within the lifetime of today's older Americans, a phenomenal growth in the population of aged individuals has occurred. In 1900, 4,901,000 Americans were 60 years old or older; in 1978, 33,486,000 were in this age group (U.S. Bureau of the Census, 1976, 1979b). Not only has the number of older Americans increased, but their proportion relative to other age groups has grown. In 1900, less than 4% of the population was 65 or older; in 1980, 11%—one out of nine Americans—was over 65.

This dramatic ''graying of America'' may be traced to three demographic developments. First are long-run declines in fertility, which have increased older persons' share of the population by reducing the offsetting numbers of younger Americans. Second are declines in adult mortality, which have permitted more persons to survive into old age. Third is the restriction of immigration, which earlier in the century injected many young adults into the U.S. age structure.

These changes in population age pyramids have registered three important effects on intergenerational relations (Treas, 1977):

1. Because of improvements in mortality, today's middle-aged and older offspring are more likely to have aging parents than were their counterparts in earlier eras.

2. Because of fertility declines, aging parents may have even fewer descendants to call on for help than did their own parents.

3. Younger adults, having grown up in smaller families, may have fewer brothers and sisters to share the support of aging parents.

Though today we take survival into old age for granted, growing old was less certain in previous historical periods when mortality rates were higher. In 1900, only 63% of women who had survived to age 20 could expect to reach a sixtieth birthday (Preston, Keyfitz, & Schoen, 1972). In 1976, by contrast, mortality schedules indicate that 90% of women living to age 20 could expect to reach 60 (National Center for Health Statistics, 1980b). These developments suggest that more middle-aged adults today have elderly parents alive than ever before in our history. This is good news, as it means unprecedented opportunities for the generations to enjoy one another's company in adulthood. It may also imply new challenges to the family support system, however.

Increasingly, an aging parent is very old and is female. In 1930, 29% of Americans over 65 were aged 75 or older. By 1980, 39% of the old were in these advancing years (U.S. Bureau of the Census, 1976, 1981c). Over the same period, the sex gap is death rates widened, contributing to the creation of a population in which two out of three persons 65 and older are women. Over half of these women are widowed. To be sure, today's ''oldold'' may enjoy greater physical well-being and financial security than in the past; however, more older Americans than ever are in the age range associated with declining health, capacities, and resources. It is the frail and widowed elderly who have relied most heavily on the resources of younger relations. Thus, compositional changes in the older population itself may tax the capacities of family members to provide companionship, counsel, services, and financial support to aged kin.

The growing numbers and needs of older Americans have outpaced the growth of the younger population. Historically, this rise in the aged's share of population reflexts long-term declines in fertility more than increases in longevity (Treas, 1981a). Because each successive generation of women has given birth to fewer children than did their mothers, the ratio of young to old has fallen. Figure 1 shows the completed fertility of birth cohorts of women ages 60–64 in selected years. Between 1931 and 1971, the percentage of these older women who had borne four or more children dropped markedly, from 47.1 to 20.7, whereas the percentage childless varied only slightly over the 40-year period. It is true that declines in fertility have been partially offset by the surer survival of those children born. Other evidence, however, points to an overall decline in the numbers of children available to parents in later life. Consider the widening differential between males and females in mortality: today, a mother has a one-in-four chance of surviving her son (Metropolitan Life, 1977).

Looking ahead, we can anticipate other demographic repercussions on family life in old age. The first is a decrease in the numbers of children who might provide care to aging parents. The cohort entering old age in 1981, for example, included the parents of the celebrated baby boom (children born between 1946 and 1958). These women were slightly more likely to have had four or more children than those of the preceding Depression decade (25.5% compared with 20.7%). More important, they were less likely to have been childless (13.9% versus 21.4%). Their greater numbers of offspring may represent a greater potential for support in later life, but this cohort seems likely to offer only a brief reversal of the long-run trend toward smaller families and fewer descendants in old age (Cherlin, 1983). In fact, their children, as members of the baby-boom cohort itself, are evidencing record low fertility. In the face of low levels of fertility, mortality changes loom larger. Extensions of the marked mortality improvements of the 1970s would exacerbate the rapid aging of the population (Crimmins, 1982).

A second implication of fertility trends in the past 20 years involves siblings. If smaller families mean fewer descendants for the aged, they also mean fewer siblings for the middle-aged. Of course, the parents' average family size is not the same as the children's average family size, as youngsters in big families weigh more heavily in the distribution of sibling numbers (Preston, 1976). Nonetheless, changes in the proportion childless and in the distribution of family size suggest that even babyboom children grew up in smaller families, on the average, than did those born before them (Preston, 1977).

The trend toward fewer brothers and sisters suggests that successive generations may have fewer siblings with whom to share the sometimes considerable burden of aging parents. The declining number of descendants is a trend in conflict with the surer survival of aging kin. These facts pose questions about the continuing effectiveness of family support systems for the aged at the same time that they spark controversy over the capacity of an aging society to pick up the slack. In sum, late-life intergenerational relations are now the rule rather than the exception, but the family network potentially available to the older person is less extensive than it once was.

Demographic change in kin networks suggests three

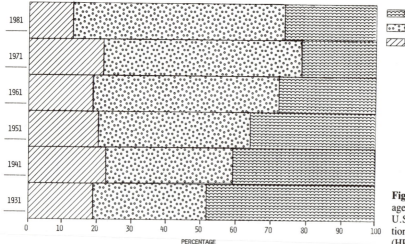

MOTHERS WITH 4+ CHILDREN

MOTHERS WITH 1-3 CHILDREN

WOMEN WITH NO CHILDREN

Figure 1. Cohort fertility of women, ages 60–64, 1931–1981. (Source: U.S. Department of Health, Education, and Welfare Publication No. (HRA)-76-1152, Table 7A).

possibilities. First, intergenerational relations may have become denser and more intense as fewer kin fulfill the functions that once fell to many. As the greater overlap of parents' and children's life spans (because of mortality declines) has afforded more opportunities for mutual socializing and socialization, intense relationships in the small family may well have resulted. Second, the intergenerational family life of the aged may have become impoverished in some way. Some tasks once performed by kin may have atrophied as family functions, perhaps to be taken up by nonrelatives, as is the case in much custodial care of older Americans. Third, a dearth of descendants may have had little effect on the qualitative family life of the aged. Sibling specialization in the division of labor may always have ensured that the support of aging parents would fall only to a few offspring. Smaller families may actually have strengthened the bonds between parents and their children.

To be sure, numbers of grown offspring are an imperfect gauge of familial resources in later life. Siblings and their children, for example, are known to care for elderly persons who do not have children of their own. Similarly, it is widely recognized that not all offspring pitch in to help aged parents. One child often assumes special responsibility for aged parents, because he or she is in the best position to do so, because it simplifies the decision making, or because it provides a tax exemption, whereas financial support contributions split between siblings do not.

There is, nonetheless, some evidence that having fewer children is associated with negative outcomes in old age. Analyzing data from the General Social Surveys, Singh and Williams (1981) reported that the childless aged, especially women, express less satisfaction with family life than do those with children. Beckman and Houser (1982) found that older widows who had either no children or only one child scored slightly lower on measures of social-psychological well-being than widows with more children, even when social background and social interaction factors were controlled for. Soldo and Myers

(1976) found that women who bore fewer than three children had a 15% higher chance of institutionalization than did women with more children. Unfortunately, none of these studies can entirely resolve issues of causation. Are low-parity women at risk of negative outcomes in old age because they have few children or because lifelong disadvantages in mental and physical health lead first to lower fertility and later to lower well-being? As studies have failed to document a positive relation between morale and contact with children (Arling, 1976), the latter interpretation remains plausible.

To sum up, we face an elderly population of unprecedented size relative to other age groups. Although the greater overlap in life spans has meant that intergenerational family life has been enriched, new challenges have also arisen. Despite the improved health and economic well-being of many older Americans, the composition of the older population has tipped toward widowed women and the very old, the very group most dependent on the resources of others. Despite the growing numbers and needs of aging parents, their children (born into smaller families) may have fewer siblings to lend a hand in the care of older relatives. It is likely that demographic developments have already altered traditional generational and age relations within families.

Consider the growing numbers of older persons living apart from kin. Between 1950 and 1980, for example, the percentage of women 65 and older who headed a household containing no kin increased dramatically from 18% to 42% (U.S. Bureau of the Census, 1981a). Although social security allowances may have enabled separate living (undoubtedly the preference of most of these women), Kobrin (1976) pointed out that the burgeoning population of older widows has compromised social customs of multigenerational residence. There are simply too many older mothers and mothers-in-law for offspring to absorb into their homes.

The demographic constraints on family support systems outlined above suggest to some observers that we are in the midst of a radical shift: "Those aspects of housing, recreation, health care, and income maintenance now provided by younger generations to their elderly parents and grandparents will need to be provided by society at large'' (Shanas & Hauser, 1974, p. 91). In light of emerging constraints on the expansion of social services, it may be necessary to develop new partnerships between informal and formal support systems for the elderly.

Work and Welfare in Old Age

If changes in the demographic metabolism of the population have been both a boon and a bane to family life, the introduction of public programs of old-age support marks another innovation with far-ranging implications for older and younger family members. Because the family has been the mainstay of support for the aged, the introduction of alternative mechanisms of support raises the possibility of important shifts in filial norms, in intergenerational dependencies, and in the currency of exchange between aged parents and younger relations.

As sociologists, anthropologists, demographers, and economists have long observed, the desire to ensure one's support in old age has traditionally been a major motive for having children. Before the establishment of adequate societal provisions for the care of the elderly, only the obligations of offspring could be counted on to maintain one's livelihood when one was too old and too sick to work or when one's breadwinning husband died. This necessity led, of course, to customs and strategies to ensure that support would be forthcoming. Parents had many children as a hedge against child mortality, and persons without their own children adopted the children of others. Daughters who forsook marriage to care for aging parents became themselves dependent on kin in old age. Parental control over wealth and the means of production—the family farm—gave the aged the clout to ensure the dutiful attention of their offspring (Greven, 1973). Norms such as the biblical injunction to honor one's father and mother cemented the bonds between aging parents and adult offspring. Traditional Chinese society furnishes perhaps the most impressive example of norms of parental power and prerogative:

In traditional society an individual from childhood to the end of his life was completely immersed in an atmosphere which compelled the observation of filial piety. The lesson of filial piety was carried in nursery stories, in daily exhortations and reprimands, in tales and novels, in textbooks from the first primer to the most profound philosophical discourse, in the numerous ''temples of filial sons and chaste women'' (chieh hsiao tz'u) which studded the land, in dramatized living examples of extremely filial children. (Yang, 1974, p. 432)

Even bolstered by such strong cultural imperatives, familial relations are not an altogether perfect vehicle for the support of the aged. For example, some persons have no children who are willing and able to assist them in their last years. Even though some older persons have no family resources on which they can call and even though old age support may pose a considerable burden to younger families, there have been, until recently, few alternatives.

It has been suggested that industrialization and modernization have acted to lower the status of the aged in families and in the larger society (Cowgill & Holmes, 1972). Technological change, educational expansion, and shifts in the occupational structure make the skills of the aged obsolete. The movement of economic production out of the home and into the factory prompts internal migration that distances kin. A change from ascribed to achieved bases of attainment undermine the importance of lineage. Even the structure of intergenerational relations may change: If work roles are not customarily handed from father to son, the solidarity of the male lineage is weakened, leaving the matrilineal bonds as those that cement families (Sweetzer, 1966).

In contrast to factors setting the stage for a seeming erosion of filial and familial values, economic development has fostered a greater potential for independence from kin in old age. The growth of a market economy presents financial vehicles (e.g., banks) that permit saving for old age. Social insurance programs characteristic of increasing affluence offer another alternative to kin support (Walther, 1980). This is not to argue that the introduction of alternative sources of support necessarily weakens intergenerational support ties. Nor is this to give comfort to the generally unsupportable myth of the abandonment of the elderly by their families. Under some circumstances, savings and investment opportunities may strengthen the position of the elderly by increasing the legacy available to dutiful heirs. In less affluent societies, too, old age pensions may raise the stock of the older person as a valuable, contributing member of the household. Today, in the People's Republic of China, for example, the familial position of the retired industrial worker is bolstered both by pension contributions to the family exchequer and by time spent in household chores and child care (Treas, 1979). Similarly, in nineteenth-century England, even nonrelatives were willing to care for elderly widows receiving pensions from the colliery disaster funds (Anderson, 1977).

In the United States, the introduction of social security, the expansion of private pension schemes, and the proliferation of public social services have been a counterpoint to changes in the economic roles of the aged. Conceived in the Great Depression, the 1935 Social Security Act was intended not only to afford financial support in retirement, but also to reduce unemployment by removing older workers from the labor force. Three other forces contributed to declining employment by aged males: (1) declines in agricultural and self-employment, in which continued work at a reduced pace was possible; (2) the expansion of mandatory retirement in response to seniority systems and private pension plans; and (3) the very institutionalization of retirement, making leisure an acceptable and even desirable part of later life. In combination, these forces caused the labor-force-participation of men 65 and older to drift down from 44.7% in 1950 to 19.1% in 1980 (U.S. Bureau of the Census, 1981c). More and more men have opted for younger and younger ages of retirement. In the 1970s, a trend toward early retirement became evident among working women—a reminder that the rising labor-force participation of women has enabled them to become retirees, too (Treas, 1981c).

The changing balance of work and welfare in the older population has had remarkable implications for family life. First, social security and other public and private programs of income maintenance have afforded older families and older family members a considerably higher living standard than they realized in earlier times. For example, the percentage of persons 65 and older who fell below the government poverty line plummeted from 35.2% in 1959 to a low of 14.0% in 1978 (U.S. Bureau of the Census, 1981b). In conjunction with in-kind goods (such as subsidized housing) and services (such as Medicare and homemaker assistance), higher incomes have permitted older Americans greater economic, residential, and physical independence from offspring. Although individuals continue to prefer family members as confidants and financial counselors, younger cohorts are today quite willing to turn to professional service providers for housekeeping, meal preparation, and personal care (Brody, Davis, & Johnsen, 1979). This is not to suggest that family aid is becoming superfluous to the aged, but rather to observe that the content of filial roles is changing. For example, the very growth of social welfare systems has led to kin becoming mediators between elderly family members and the bureaucracy (Shanas & Sussman, 1977).

Second, the substitution of pensions for earnings has introduced a new stage into the family life cycle. In the past, most individuals worked, perhaps at reduced capacities, until they were too old and ill to do so. Today, most couples experience a period of retirement during which both enjoy reasonably good health and vigor. For those who are healthy, retirement is typically perceived as a positive experience (Foner & Schwab, 1981). Together with greater prosperity, early retirement has probably reordered the preoccupations of later life toward a greater concern with leisure activities—a development most compatible with the historical shift to companionate marriages from marriages of necessity.

If the spread of social insurance programs has affected families, it is also true that family behavior has altered public income-maintenance programs. Before the first social-security check was mailed, for example, the system was altered to recognize the economic responsibilities of workers to support other family members: wives, widows, dependent children, and elderly parents. More recently, rising divorce rates and increases in the labor force participation of married women have prompted criticism of existing eligibility and benefit provisions (Treas, 1981c). Splitting of earning credits between spouses and credits for homemakers have been suggested as ways of protecting women who must take time out of the labor force to raise children.

To sum up, support of the aged has come to rely less and less on the aged's own gainful employment or on the resources of kin. In their place are public programs of old

age support that shift responsibility from the younger generations within the family to those within the broader society. These changes have implications for families of later life. They signal an unprecedented period of vigorous retirement shared by married couples and greater independence for the elderly from younger family members.

Late-Life Living Arrangements

The living arrangements of the elderly represent the dimension of family life most amenable to objective assessments of social change. Through the efforts of social historians (Hareven, 1977), household membership and family structure have been reconstructed from parish records, censuses, and other administrative documents for a range of societies over a broad sweep of time. To be sure, who lives with whom provides us with only limited information on the qualitative aspects of family processes. Who lives with whom, for example, does not tell us who likes whom. Unfortunately, historical information on the delicate affective infrastructure of families is usually available only for a nonrandom selection of the literature minority who leave surviving letters, memoirs, and diaries.

Some limited inferences may be drawn from a knowledge of living arrangements, nonetheless. Persons who live together tend to pool economic resources and to develop a division of labor. The household head and spouse often enjoy some special power and responsibility in decision making. Of necessity, those residing in the same dwelling unit are apt to interact more frequently than persons who live in separate households. On average, they enjoy certain advantages of coresidence, such as economies of scale and efficiencies of household task specialization. When persons live together in the face of free choice and other household options, it may be possible to infer that the benefits (in terms of economic gains, companionship, and conformity with social expectations) exceed the costs (in privacy, independence, and perhaps personal space).

The living arrangements of older persons have undergone substantial changes over time, although the nature of these changes has not been popularly appreciated. Popular opinion holds that the elderly traditionally were incorporated into the multigenerational homes of their offspring and that only in recent years have the aged been abandoned by their families. Historical research, however, suggests that, where such multigenerational living arrangements were adopted, they were not widespread but existed only for a brief period in the family life cycle between the time when a failing father surrendered the control of the farm to his son and the parents' deaths (Berkner, 1972). At least in England and the United States, the evidence indicates that the elderly have long preferred to maintain their own homes rather than to live in the homes of kin. By taking in boarders and lodgers as their children left home, for example, older Americans in the nineteenth century were able to compensate for the loss of their children's, their spouse's or their own earnings in order to remain residentially independent (Modell & Hareven, 1973).

Smith (1979) provided a useful overview of the living arrangements of elderly Americans in 1900 by documenting the persistence of household headship into old age. For example, 94% of married men, aged 70 or older, who were gainfully employed headed their own households at the turn of the century, as did almost half of widows 55 and older. Advancing age, loss of gainful employment, and widowhood decreased the probability of being a head or the spouse of head. Of course, substantial proportions of the aged lived in the same household as a child. Given the tempo of marriage and the emancipation of offspring, the "young-old" were more likely to reside with unmarried offspring and the "old-old" with married children. In 1900, of the households incorporating a member 75 or older, 31% also contained a married child and 38% a grandchild. Residing with a child, however, often meant still being the household head. That status was apparently abandoned only reluctantly when it was no longer possible to maintain independent housing. Only a small proportion of the aged lived alone and apart from kin in 1900. Even for the unmarried without families of their own, 70% of women and 40% of men lived with kin, typically siblings (Smith, 1979).

When the past is compared to the present, it is clear that the elderly exhibit a preference to maintain their own homes, rather than living in the homes of others. What has changed, however, is an increasing probability of heading a household containing no other family members (such as a spouse). As recently as 1950, only 10.3% of men and 18.1% of women 65 and older headed households containing no kin. Thirty years later, the figures were 15.4% and 41.2%, respectively (U.S. Bureau of the Census, 1981a). Nonfamilial living falls more heavily to women because it is they who are more likely to outlive their spouses. Even among the still-married couples where the husband continues to head the household after age 65, a generational separation of living arrangements is seen. Mean family size decreased from 2.63 in 1955 to 2.29 in 1978, mostly because of the exodus of adult members such as grown children (Treas, 1981b).

Admittedly, there are noteworthy variations by racial and ethnic group in the probability of living with kin, suggesting subcultural differences in norms and resources. Table 1 summarizes the living arrangements of the noninstitutionalized aged population in 1980. Among men, older blacks were less likely than Anglos and Spanish-origin elderly to live in families regardless of age, and they were much more likely to be found as nonheads living apart from kin (e.g., as boarders, lodgers, resident employees, and guests). Before age 75, Anglos were most likely to reside with family members, and after 75, the Spanish-origin male was most likely to live with kin. The results for women are especially interesting. For both age groups, women of Spanish origin were most likely to live with their relations and least likely to live as a primary individual. With increasing age, these women were even more likely to be incorporated into families. Among Anglo and black women, however, rates of family living dropped off. This finding implies that women in these two groups tend to maintain separate housing after widowhood, whereas women of Spanish origin are more likely to share housing with kin as they grow older and become widowed. Interestingly, these ethnic differentials in living arrangements parallel results from a Los Angeles survey of elderly in these three groups (Bengtson, Burton, & Mangen, 1981). When asked, "Would you prefer to live with your children, or in a separate residence?" 72% of the Mexican-Americans replied, "Separate resi-

Table 1. Family Status (Percentages) by Age, Sex, Race, and Spanish Origin, 1980[a]

	White		Black		Spanish origin	
	65–74	75+	65–74	75+	65–74	75+
Men						
In families	86.8	77.7	77.3	69.5	78.2	84.2
Not in families	13.2	22.3	22.7	30.5	21.8	15.8
Household head	(11.8)	(21.0)	(18.5)	(28.5)	(17.4)	(15.1)
Other	(1.3)	(1.3)	(4.5)	(2.0)	(4.5)	(0.7)
Total	100.0	100.0	100.0	100.0	100.0	100.0
Women						
In families	62.3	47.2	64.0	55.5	68.8	74.5
Not in families	37.7	52.7	36.0	44.1	31.2	25.5
Household head	(36.6)	(51.6)	(34.6)	(42.8)	(28.3)	(22.4)
Other	(1.1)	(1.1)	(1.4)	(1.3)	(2.9)	(3.0)
Total	100.0	100.0	100.0	100.0	100.0	100.0

[a]Source: U.S. Bureau of the Census. Marital status and living arrangements. *Current Population Reports*, Series P-20, No. 365. Washington, D.C.: U.S. Government Printing Office, 1980.

dence," compared with 83% of the blacks and 98% of the Anglos.

These observations of ethnic differences in living arrangements are reinforced by findings from special tabulations from the 1970 Census of Population. Focusing on the living arrangements of the widowed aged 75 and older, Sweet (1977) reported that men and women of many minority groups (Chinese, Japanese, Mexican, Cuban, Puerto Rican, and southern rural blacks) were more likely to live with children than was the case for their white counterparts. To take an extreme example, 60% of Cuban widows 75 and older lived with offspring, compared to only 25% of non-Hispanic whites (1970 data). Southern urban blacks and American Indians were less likely to reside with children. Sex interactions are apparent for nonsouthern blacks and Filipinos: Men were underrepresented in intergenerational living, and women were overrepresented.

Variations over time and across groups in the household structures of the aged raise inevitable questions about the determinants of living arrangements in late life. The nearly universal coresidence of elderly married couples is to be anticipated, but the disparities in intergenerational living require further consideration. At the microlevel of family functioning, Silverstone and Hyman (1976) identified four common circumstances in which multigenerational households with older members came into being:

1. A parent is widowed (or divorced) and, although physically independent, is emotionally dependent and too fearful or helpless to live alone.

2. A parent, physically incapacitated and incapable of living alone, wants to be cared for by a child rather than strangers or a nursing home.

3. Parents and children decide to pool their finances so that both generations can live more comfortably, or they may live together because they get along well and choose to have a combined household.

4. An older but somewhat active parent escapes a lonely life by living with a child but at the same time fills a useful function, such as babysitter or housekeeper, freeing the child (usually the daughter or daughter-in-law) of many household chores and making it possible for her to pursue a career or a special talent.

Those familiar with the logic of the "new home economics" (Becker, 1976; Sawhill, 1977) will find these scenarios compatible with the economic theory of marriage or, more generally, coresidence. The first case, for example, suggests a "caring" head who reallocates resources among family members to recompense the aging parent for losses, and who derives satisfaction from supporting the parent. The second situation elaborates this theme of caring, and also introduces the element of complementary characteristics: The parent's and the child's enjoyment of caretaking is enhanced because the caretaker is a chip off the old block, sharing the parent's traits and tastes to a greater extent than might be expected of a nursing-home attendant. In the third case, the con-

geniality of kin's complementary characteristics is reinforced by certain economies of scale. The last case introduces the substitution of the parent's "inexpensive" time for a child's "expensive" time, where the value of time is determined by the wage each commands in the marketplace. Despite the intuitive appeal of this formulation, this theory has not been put to empirical test, especially with respect to the living arrangements of aged relatives in households.

Three explanations of secular changes in the households of the elderly have been set forth. Although more complementary than competing, these alternative explanations stress, in turn, demographic, economic, and normative determinants of late-life living arrangements.

Demographic accounts of change have stressed shifts in the populations most "at risk" of various living arrangements as well as more subtle demographic squeezes affecting household decisions.

In the first tradition, Soldo (1977) traced 1960–1970 changes in living arrangements to increases in the numbers of women and very old persons in the aged population. Kobrin (1976) argued a more complex demographic explanation of the rise of the primary individual: Changes in vital rates have created an excess of elderly widows and a shortfall of middle-aged daughters, fostering a generational imbalance that has undermined the rules of intergenerational residence (which were always more supportable in theory than in practice). Demographic explanations are plausible because they acknowledge that coresidence depends on the availability of kin. To take the case of elderly Filipino males, we find comparatively few living in families; poverty, restrictive immigration policies shutting out potential spouses, and prohibitions against interracial marriage consigned a high proportion to lifelong bachelorhood.

A second explanation of changes in the living arrangements of the elderly points to rising affluence, which permitted the aged to purchase more private residential arrangements. More recently, it has been suggested that the contemporary housing crunch will constitute an economic impetus for shared housing in the 1980s, resulting in a greater social integration of the aged. Beresford and Rivlin (1966) were among the first to suggest that the advent of social security might afford greater generational separation of households. Extrapolating time trends from cross-sectional results, Michael, Fuchs, and Scott (1980) argued that 75% of the increase in the percentage of aged widows living alone could be accounted for by changes in average social security benefits. Pampel (1981) distinguished between compositional effects (arising because a larger proportion of the population receives income above some threshold for independent residence) and processual effects (the increase in the propensity to live alone regardless of the level of income). Time series as well as cross-sectional census data for 1960 and 1970 provide evidence of both changing income and changing taste effects.

Of course, the recurrent finding that the growing preference for privacy has outpaced rising income and demographic shifts in population composition raises a good many questions about the determinants and consequences of norms of coresidence. Although issues concerning the aged have not been explicitly addressed, popular commentary has identified profound transformations in societal values falling under the rubric of the "me decade" (Wolfe, 1976) or the "culture of narcissism" (Lasch, 1979). Here, the argument is that familistic orientations championing a collective identity are succumbing to perceptions of the self as an individual not to be bound by the expectations of others. A majority of adults in the United States oppose the idea of older persons' sharing a home with grown children (U.S. Bureau of the Census, 1980a). Similarly, widows have reported a desire for independent quarters, citing the annoying rambunctiousness of grandchildren, the lack of independence, and the folkway against two cooks in the same kitchen (Lopata, 1973). Despite behavioral and attitudinal indicators of a preference for generational separation of living arrangements, however, the antecedents of such cultural values have attracted relatively little attention.

If the causes of changing living arrangements are not entirely understood, neither have the implications of the growing intergenerational separation of residence been adequately explored. Rosenfeld (1979) suggested that inheritance patterns may already be undergoing change in response to changes in the household structure of the elderly. Among the aged living in retirement communities, for example, he detected a tendency to leave bequests to elderly friends and neighbors—a tendency less frequently observed for those older persons residing closer to their children. Similarly, it is questionable whether traditional helping patterns can survive the spatial separation of kin. Caring for an elderly relation is more difficult when two households are involved because travel time and the duplication of many household chores is necessary. In sum, a dramatic transformation in the living arrangements of older Americans has occurred. Fewer and fewer elderly are living with kin. Today, 41% of elderly women and 15% of men live alone. That change merits greater recognition. We remain woefully ignorant of both the causes and the consequences of changes in the residential patterns of the generations.

The Generation in the Middle

The demographic trends outlined above suggest new challenges for kin in the physical and emotional support of aging family members. No account of the constraints on family relations would be complete without a consideration of the changing social roles of mid-life Americans (Bengtson, 1979; Cherlin, 1983; Hagestad, 1981; Treas, 1977). New options for men and women have created aspirations and obligations that, in turn, compete with duties toward aged kin while altering their own course of aging. The transformation in the roles of women has been especially striking. Women have long been the mainstay of family support systems for the aged. Documenting a sexual division of labor in the care of older relatives, Lopata (1973) reported that Chicago area widows described sons as helpful in managing funeral arrangements and financial affairs, whereas daughters were said to foster close emotional ties by visiting and providing services. Considerate though sons may be, the major responsibility for the psychological and physical maintenance of the aged has fallen to female members of the family. It is they who take widowed mothers (and mothers-in-law) into their households, share confidences, run errands, and provide nursing and custodial care.

In a study of homebound elderly in New York City (Cantor, 1980), the major caregivers were, in rank order, children, spouse, relatives, and friends or neighbors. Among the children providing assistance, 75% were women while among other relatives, friends, and neighbors, virtually all persons giving care were women. Only in the case of the spouse were the proportion of male and female caregivers evenly divided: 51% male and 49% female.

At a time when younger women have reduced fertility to accommodate career demands, new roles for women lead us to question the continued willingness and ability of women to meet fully and personally the needs of aging relatives.

First, mothering the baby boom and inspiring "the feminine mystique," middle-aged women today are more likely to have married and to have had children than women of earlier eras. The maiden aunt, devoted to caring for her aging parents, appears to be a vanishing phenomenon (Treas, 1977). Instead, a husband, children, aging in-laws, and her own elderly parents compete for a woman's time.

Second, paid employment represents another claim on the time and energy of women. Over half of all wives aged 45–54 are in the labor force today, compared with only 11% in 1940 (U.S. Bureau of Census, 1973). Time-budget studies suggest that women's greater involvement in paid work has not occasioned a reallocation of housework among family members. Domestic responsibilities still fall largely to women, as indicated by the fact that married women averaged 143 minutes of housework each day, compared with 25 minutes for married men (Waite, 1981). In a New York City study of housebound elderly (Cantor, 1980), 60% of the children who served as the major source of care for an elderly parent were working; the time they spent assisting parents was over and above the time spent on the job. The caregivers (mainly women) reported considerable strain as they attempted to balance the conflicting demands of work, their own families, and care of their aging kin. Only by cutting down on socializing with friends or "free time to attend to one's own needs" could they manage the triple burden imposed by the caring role (Cantor, 1980). Unfortunately, work cuts into the time available to run errands for shut-in kin or to provide nursing care to aging parents. As studies of family helping patterns illustrate, vigorous older people may furnish valuable services to younger generations, but parents needing assistance with daily living can require considerable attention. One study found that two fifths of offspring caring for elderly parents in their homes devoted 40 or more hours a week to custodial tasks (Newman, 1976). When the caregiver and the aging parent maintain separate residences, the duplication of chores and travel time pose additional demands.

Third, cultural changes may well have undermined the influence of traditional norms. As Benton (1981) documented in a meticulous content analysis of popular periodicals, less and less credence has been given over the last decades to notions that one's conduct should be bound by the expectations of others. In the context of the "me decade," we see an unprecedented emphasis on self-expression (Turner, 1976) and midlife renewal activities (Neugarten & Hagestad, 1976). Growing numbers of middle-aged Americans launch second careers, return to college, divorce and remarry, or vacation abroad. If cultural shifts supporting change have transpired, they were made feasible by a postparental era free of the personal and financial responsibilities of childbearing, a consequence of the trend toward early childbearing and small families. To outgrow child-care obligations only to confront parent-care burdens may generate frustration in the face of new norms encouraging personal preoccupations. This dilemma is all the more poignant because the offspring of the frail elderly may themselves be older, retired persons hoping to enjoy the reward of carefree leisure time.

Illustrating this point, one woman, who is the mother of a 45-year-old son and who lives with her 94-year-old mother, expressed the frustrations of the middle generation:

As a "child" I feel guilt often. Why? I think because my mother dominated and still dominates me. I have always felt that I must do as she says. She feels that children are duty bound to care for their parents. Thus now that I have her to care for I feel resentment and bitterness at having to give up all these years while I am growing old, too. I am caught between two generations. (Bengtson & Treas, 1980, p. 421)

To be sure, various historical developments affect not only the capacities of offspring to respond to the needs of elderly parents, but also the personal histories that those offspring bring to their own old age. For example, women's longer work-lives may contribute to their greater independence by assuring them private pensions and experience in negotiating the world beyond home and family (Treas, 1981c). Because couples prefer to share their retirement years, wives' employment and retirement benefits have been found to influence the timing of husbands' retirement, indicating an additional influence of this significant life-cycle transition (Anderson, Clark, & Johnson, 1980). In short, social and cultural changes have both immediate and delayed, positive and negative, effects on older families.

Microsocial Perspectives on Aging Families

We have suggested that macrosocial trends involving fertility, mortality, living arrangements, and labor force participation have had a significant impact on the family life of aging individuals. We turn now to a consideration of the microsociology of the family in old age, that is, the patterns of marital and intergenerational relations in contemporary older families.

Two issues underlie any discussion of microsocial patterns in aging families. The first and most obvious is *change:* inevitable and continuous alteration in the person's immediate social world with the passage of time. As individuals grow up and grow old, their interpersonal world alters in important, if often unnoticed, ways. Marital roles and expectations change; relations with children are altered; and the normal dependencies of aging cause redefinitions of need and responsibility. The second issue is *negotiation.* With the changes that accompany the passage of time, there is the need to redefine familial positions as well as expectations. Functions once undertaken by one family member must be assumed by another, and a negotiation of redefined roles and norms is required. Frequently, this negotiation leads to some form of conflict, actual or perceived, particularly if the negotiation is not explicit.

Intergenerational Relations: Solidarity in the Aging Family

Many Americans believe that family life has significantly changed and that the position of elderly members is being jeopardized—despite recently accumulating historical evidence to the contrary. There are other commonly accepted beliefs that may be questioned in light of contemporary data from family sociology (Bengtson & Treas, 1980; Shanas, 1979a).

One common belief is that most older people do not have frequent contact with offspring because of widespread geographic mobility and the general weakening of family ties. A second concern involves the existence of the "generation gap," the perception that there are serious strains in family ties between generations. A third notion is that older persons are primarily recipients in intergenerational exchanges, receiving more than they give.

Each of these beliefs is a commentary on popular perceptions of contemporary family relations and of the well-being of today's elderly family members. How much truth is there in these perceptions? How can one characterize the intricate bonds of connectedness and the tensions between generations? What are the relevant concepts, variables, and perspectives that inform answers to these questions?

In addressing these specific issues, it is useful to begin by examining the aging family in the light of some basic constructs from general social theory applied to small groups (see Bengtson, Olander, & Haddad, 1976). One important determinant of the process and product of any human group is its structure; a second is the extent of interaction among the members; and a third is the degree of cohesiveness exhibited by those interactions. The family is, of course, a special type of small group, so there is considerable utility in charting the variations between families in structure, in interactions, in feelings of cohesiveness, and in agreement. Each of these dimensions of family structure and process has significant implications for the individuals who comprise it; each of these dimensions changes with the aging of individuals and the passage of time.

A useful construct to describe the parent–child dyad as it develops and changes through time is *solidarity,* a concept drawing from the works of the earliest sociologists down to the present (Bengtson & Schrader, 1981). Intergenerational solidarity can be conceptualized as being comprised of several different but interrelated dimensions:

1. *Family structure:* The number, sex, and age of family members across generations, as well as their geographic proximity.
2. *Association:* The frequency of interaction between individuals and the type or nature of companionate activities shared across generations.
3. *Affect:* The negative or positive sentiment, the feelings and perceptions of closeness or distance between family members of different generations.
4. *Consensus:* The degree of similarity or conflict in general values, specific sociopolitical opinions, and perceptions of agreement.
5. *Exchange or power:* The balance of resources held by each generation, material or nontangible, often evidenced in the degree of exchange of assistance or support between generations.
6. *Norms:* Perceptions of what should be done between generations, reflecting parental and filial responsibility.

These concepts serve as a way to organize the emerging literature concerning intergenerational relations involving older family members, as well as to suggest directions for future research. Table 2 lists the six constructs as well as variables that have been or can be used in survey or ethnographic studies to reflect each.

Contemporary patterns of intergenerational family solidarity can be assessed in a variety of ways. Census tabulations provide evidence concerning family structure and household composition. Large-sample survey data present information concerning interaction, affect, and norms or expectations within families. Legal data draw on testamentary declarations for insight into rewards and punishments between generations. In the following review of the literature, we focus on the three dimensions that are most important in the three common beliefs about the contemporary family life of older people suggested

earlier: questions concerning association, affect, and exchange between generations.

Associational Solidarity between Generations. One dimension of family solidarity involves the activities or encounters that characterize the interaction between the members. The popular stereotype depicts older family members as having infrequent contact with children because of geographic mobility and a gradual weakening of family ties (Shanas, 1979b). Although it is true that few aging parents today share living quarters with their offspring, as reflected in the data reviewed in the first section of this paper, this does not imply infrequent interaction.

Survey data suggest that there is, in fact, a high degree of interaction between generations in contemporary families. For example, in a three-nation survey conducted in 1975, only one in ten older Americans reported that he or she had *not* seen one of his or her children within the past 30 days (Shanas, 1979a,b). (However, the average frequency of contact across all children tends to be much less frequent, as documented by Lopata, 1979.)

Such high frequency of contact may be surprising in view of popular stereotypes, but these findings are typical of other studies. In the 1974 Los Angeles community survey, interaction with children during the previous day was reported by 56% of the Mexican-Americans, 40% of the Anglos, and 33% of the blacks (Bengtson & Manuel, 1976). In New York, a cross-ethnic survey found even higher rates of contact (Cantor, 1975): half saw their children at least once a week, and two thirds at least monthly.

Sussman (1965, 1976, 1977) has argued that such data indicate the persistence of an extended-family kinship structure that has special salience for the elderly. In the face of rapid social and technological change and high geographic mobility, the kinship structure provides many supports to its members. The ongoing contact between adult children and their parents, their sharing of social activities, and the exchange of material and nonmaterial aid are examples of such supports. However, Lopata (1979) found that such interactions involving kin are primarily limited to parent–child relations, suggesting that intergenerational association is much more prevalent than sibling or extended-family contacts.

Thus, aggregate data concerning associational solidarity between aging parents and their middle-aged children indicate relatively high levels of contact and shared activities. However, four factors of social differentiation appear to affect the nature of intergenerational contact. Sex is one such differentiating characteristic. For example, married daughters tend to have closer ties to parents than do married sons (Sussman, 1965, p. 82). This is particularly true for widowed mothers (Lopata, 1979), who see daughters as providers of emotional closeness and comfort and sons as more task-oriented (and less frequent) supporters. Middle-aged daughters have been identified as the more salient "kinkeepers" in terms of both type and frequency of contact by a number of re-

Table 2. Critical Constructs in the Analysis of Relations between Generations and Variables Reflecting Their Measurement

Construct		Variables to be operationalized

A.	Family structure across generations: Parameters of social unions	A-1. Number of living family lineage members of the subject
		    a. Children
		    b. Parents
		    c. Grandchildren or grandparents
		    d. Lineal relatives by marriage (children-in-law, parents-in-law)
		    e. Siblings and siblings' lineal relations

		A-2. Sex-lineage type (male-male; male-female; female-female; female-male)
		A-3. Number and type of lineal "fictive kin"
		A-4. Geographic proximity of each of the above to the subject
		A-5. Household composition of the subject
B.	Associational solidarity or integration	B-1. Frequency of interaction between subjects and lineage members in common activities
		B-2. Type of common activities shared
C.	Affectual solidarity or integration	C-1. Perceived quality of interaction: sentiments of warmth, closeness, trust, understanding, communication, and respect toward the other
		C-2. Perceived reciprocity of interaction: sentiments from the other
D.	Consensual solidarity or integration	D-1. Degree of similarity or conflict in general values
		D-2. Degree of similarity or conflict in specific opinions (sociopolitical or religious orientations)
		D-3. Perception of similarity or contrast and/or conflict
E.	Functional solidarity or integration	E-1. Degree of exchange of services or assistance between lineage members
		E-2. Perception of potential support or assistance between lineage members
F.	Normative solidarity or integration	F-1. Instances of norms enacted concerning associational, affectional, consensual, or functional solidarity
		F-2. Perceptions of norms potentially enacted

searchers (Adams, 1968; Hill, Foote, Aldous, Carlson, & MacDonald, 1970; Shanas, 1962; Rosenthal, 1985). Despite notions that firstborn or lastborn offspring are singled out for special attachments to and responsibilities for aging parents, there is little or no evidence of birth-order effects on either older parents' or grown children's perceptions of the trust, intimacy, fairness, respect, and affection of the filial relation (Treas, Gronvold, & Bengtson, 1980).

Marital status is a second characteristic differentiating the nature of intergenerational contact. Widows, for example, are more dependent on kin than are the married aged (see Lopata, 1973). Unmarried offspring also appear to maintain closer ties to aging parents than do married children, at least in terms of being more likely to share housing with the older generation.

Social class represents a third characteristic affecting contact. Hill *et al.* (1970) found that working-class men engaged in more intergenerational contact than did white-collar males. Adams (1968) noted that the occupational

stratum of the parent affected patterns of contact; upwardly mobile males appearing to be the most likely to give tangible aid to working-class parents. Downward mobility among males had the effect of decreasing contact with kin, whereas upward mobility may increase contact (Schoenholz, 1978). Cantor (1975) found that the lower the social class, the greater the extent of supportive relationships, as measured by frequency of interaction and the amount of help given and received by the elderly. Cantor noted that, as social class rises, nuclear families in a kinship network maintain greater distance between themselves; elderly parents are less intensely involved with their adult children day-to-day. This is not to say that the higher-status elderly are forsaken by their children. Assistance and intervention are given in times of illness and crisis, but socialization with peers, rather than with children, is expected to fill the void of more intensive parent–child interaction (Cantor, 1979).

Ethnicity is a fourth differentiating characteristic in family contact. In a study of three Los Angeles ethnic groups, Bengtson *et al.* (1981) reported that Mexican-Americans had more children and saw them more frequently than either blacks or whites. Similarly, Cantor's cross-ethnic survey (1975) of New York's elderly found that the Hispanic elderly interacted with their children more often, received more help from their children, and reported a significantly greater sense of closeness to their children. Black and white elderly, by contrast, had similar levels of solidarity and interaction except in one area. Blacks, like Hispanics, tended to give more help to their children than did the white elderly, probably because of the greater need on the part of the offspring. This greater sharing of more limited economic and social resources on the part of black and Spanish elderly suggests adaptation to the pressures of poverty and unemployment within a functional family system (Cantor, 1975).

It is important to examine the type, as well as the frequency, of association or interaction between the aged and their children. From one study involving 2,044 members of three-generation family lineages (sample described in Bengtson, 1975; Bengtson, Mangen, Landry, 1984) come several suggestions concerning associational solidarity involving older family members. Reports from both the elderly and the middle-aged concerning the nature and the frequency of intergenerational interaction yielded three dimensions of interaction or "objective solidarity" (Bengtson & Black, 1973): informal activities (recreation, conversation, talking about important matters); ceremonial or family ritual activities (large and small family gatherings, reunions, birthdays); and exchange of assistance (helping and being helped). It should be noted that Lopata (1979) reported the involvement of adult children in 65 separate supports, organized into economic, service, social, and emotional systems.

In Bengtson's study (1984), both generations reported relatively high levels of all types of activities. No significant general differences appeared between the reports of the middle-aged and the elderly in the perception of frequency of contact, although one specific difference concerned the giving and receiving of help. When estimating the amount of help given by the middle-aged child, the child herself or himself reported a higher level than did her or his parent. Moreover, the parents reported giving less help to the children than the children reported receiving. In these data, the old tended to downplay the practical exchanges between generations; they tended to emphasize the affectual or sentimental aspects of family life, as discussed below.

Affectual Solidarity between Generations. A second major dimension of parent–child relations across the life span concerns subjective judgments of the *quality* of interaction. Often this is referred to as *closeness* or *warmth;* affectual solidarity may be defined as "mutual positive sentiment among group members and their expressions of love, respect, appreciation, and recognition of others" (Bengtson & Schrader, 1981, p. 118). We have seen that many studies indicate a high degree of contact or shared activities between middle-aged children and their aged parents. Less research has been carried out on the affectual dimensions of such contact, that is, their subjective quality for the participating generations. Popular stereotypes hold that there is a "generation gap," and that differences between generations lead to feelings of conflict and distance.

But this stereotype appears to be unfounded. In one study, for example, Lopata (1979) queried Chicago area widows about whom they felt closest to, whom they most enjoyed being with, to whom they told problems, who comforted them when they were depressed, who made them feel important, and so forth. The main contribution to emotional supports were adult children, especially daughters. Friends, other kin, and new husbands, in cases of remarriage, were second-order choices.

It should be noted that the problem of the generation gap impinges on contemporary older individuals in two ways (Bengtson, 1971).

First is evidence of differences between the behaviors and standards of the aged individual's own peers and those of younger age groups or cohorts. These contrasts can be attributed to differences in levels of maturation (aging) and to contrasts in historical experience, as was discussed in previous sections. Born during a particular period in history and sharing certain demographic and sociopolitical events, those individuals who are over 65 have orientations that are often perceived as contrasting with those of younger members of the society. To paraphrase the popular jargon, this may be termed a *cohort gap.*

Second are differences between generations within the family. Here, the differences may be even more personally relevant, as they are related to the wishes and fulfillment that parents often seek for in children and grandchildren. Within his or her own family, the aging individual may see the currents of change and the conflict of the broader society as impinging on him or her personally, or as questioning lifelong principles that have governed his or her behavior. Such family differences may be termed a *lineage gap* (Bengtson & Treas, 1980).

At a higher level of abstraction, these sets of life changes, taken together, can be said to give parents and children a different *generational* or *developmental stake* in the other (Bengtson & Kuypers, 1971). Parents and children have an investment ("stake") in their relationship that varies according to how the relationship enables the attainment of personal goals. In the case of the adolescent and her or his middle-aged parent, the parent may be concerned with the creation of social heirs. Aware of his or her own mortality and fearing that his or her contribution or significance may be lost, the parent may wish to perpetuate valued ideals and institutions in his or her offspring. To this end, the older generation may tend to deny or minimize evidence of intergenerational differences. By contrast, the younger generation is concerned with developing distinctiveness, a personal identity of their own. The goal of youth is to create values and institutions for themselves, and their elders' attempts to perpetuate existing values and institutions may be perceived as an imposition rather than as well-intentioned advice. Youths' developmental stake causes them to exaggerate or maximize intergenerational differences.

The available research suggests that high levels of sentiment or liking are expressed between aged parents and their middle-aged children (Brody, 1977; Bengtson & Treas, 1980; Bengtson & deTerre, 1980). At the same time, several studies suggest that there is a slightly higher perception of subjective solidarity on the part of the elderly parent. Family members think of their relations as warm, and this is especially true of the oldest generation.

Exchanges of Assistance and Support between Generations. A third dimension of intergenerational solidarity, the exchange of assistance and support between older persons and their children, has been a topic of much research on intergenerational relations (Adams, 1968; Brody & Brody, 1980; Cantor, 1975, 1980; Hill *et al.,* 1970; Kreps, 1965; Lopata, 1973, 1979; Rosow, 1967; Townsend, 1968; Troll, 1970). In an earlier review, Sussman (1965) summarized empirical data on mutual aid collected since the 1950s, noting a general tendency for families to turn to kin rather than to outside agencies in times of trouble (p. 70). He depicted routine day-to-day exchanges of services (e.g., shopping, child care, and provision of shelter) as well as financial help. The pattern of financial aid described in this article was usually from parents to children, especially during the early years of the child's marriage (p. 69). Lopata (1979) separated financial and service supports and reported that widows considered themselves recipients more frequently than givers of such supports. Siblings rarely appeared in the support network that involved largely sons and daughters.

In their three-generation study, Hill *et al.* (1970) found that, in a crisis situation, all three generations saw kin as their preferred source of assistance (p. 69). Exchange of help within these three generations was greater than all other sources of help, including that from more distant kin and from outside agencies. Over a one-year period, 65% of help received by grandparents was familial; for the parent generation, 53% was familial; and for the married-child generation, 44% was familial (p. 66). Consider the three-nation study of Shanas *et al.* (1968). Although three fifths of older Americans reported that they received help from their children, over half reported that they gave help. A 1974 Harris poll reported similar results, as do data from the Southern California study of generations (Bengtson, 1979).

Cantor's study (1975, 1979) of the elderly in New York City found a similar stress on the importance of the family as a source of social supports. She noted that, in the value system of the present generation of elderly, kin is generally seen as the most appropriate source of social support, regardless of task, followed next by friends and neighbors and lastly by formal organizations. Labeling this "the hierarchical-compensatory model of support," Cantor

found that, when the initially preferred element is absent (i.e., children), other groups may act in a compensatory manner as a replacement. Thus, for the family-less or isolated elderly, friends and neighbors may assume the "familial role" (Cantor, 1979).

Acts of mutual aid were the second most frequent type of interaction mentioned between generations in Adams's study (1968). Sex and occupational status influenced exchanges of help in this as well as in Rosow's study (1967). In the latter, the social class of the *parents* influenced the type of help received. Middle-class parents tended to receive moral support, and working-class parents were the recipients of slightly more material help (p. 150). In Rosow's study, the most powerful predictor affecting whether children aided their parents was the gender of the nearest child. This factor was even more salient than social class. Lopata's studies revealed that the sex, the birth order, and the age of the children were important variables (1973, 1979). Among New York City elderly, Cantor (1975) found that the amount of help parents receive from their children was positively related to age and paucity of income. This finding suggests that as older people become more vulnerable, their children respond with more of the needed assistance.

In sum, another frequently assumed belief about the family life of older people, that the elders are primarily dependent recipients of intergenerational exchanges, is not supported by contemporary data. Those on the threshold of old age are perhaps more correctly categorized as givers than receivers. At least at this stage of life, the old make few financial demands of their offspring, for the percentage receiving contributions *from* their children varies from only 2% of couples to 13% of single women. Although these findings are suggestive, more remains to be known about financial transfers *between households*. Also understudied is the way in which family income is allocated *within* households to elderly kin and others (Moon, 1977).

A 1969 survey of Americans aged 58 to 63 (Murray, 1976) provides data on intergenerational support. For those respondents with parents alive, many reported sharing a household with the elderly or furnishing other support. Whereas 27% of married men and 22% of their wives shared with the aged, fully 54% of men and 43% of women without spouses did so. These figures may be compared with those for respondents with living children: 35% of married persons, 25% of single men, and 10% of single women provided total or partial support to the younger generation.

To summarize the findings concerning dimensions of solidarity, it appears that elderly parents report higher levels of subjective solidarity (affect), whereas middle-aged children report higher levels of both giving and receiving help (objective solidarity). This finding is consistent with the "generational stake" discussed above. Each generation has a different investment in the parent–child dyad that colors her or his perception of the relationship. Whereas the elderly report higher levels of affection, they minimize the amount of assistance or exchange of services. This finding is congruent with their greater "stake" in the relationship, in which the dimension of affect or sentiment is more important than the instrumental dimension of assistance or help. This finding may also reflect the fact that declining health or income may prevent them from helping kin as much as they might wish.

Marital Relations in Old Age: Marriage and Its Alternatives

Marital relations reflect the most obvious horizontal dimension of family life in old age, just as intergenerational relations encompass its most salient vertical dimension. To characterize adequately the microsociology of family life in old age requires data on husband–wife relations as these exhibit change or stability with the passage of time. Also necessary is an awareness of singleness in old age, as less than half of the American population 65 and older are married and living together.

To begin with, consider trends over time in the marital status of individuals above the age of 65. It is often assumed that higher divorce rates mean that the aged of today are more likely to be single than the aged 80 years ago. It is true that there has been an increase in the proportion reporting themselves currently divorced. More surprisingly, those who say that they have never married increased up to 1980. On the other hand, the proportion widowed has actually decreased. Because of these offsetting trends, the proportion married has increased somewhat in recent years.

What is most striking in these data, however, are the sex differences in marital status for older Americans, as seen in Table 3. In 1980, females were about half as likely as males to be currently married (39.7% compared with 77.5%) and more than three times as likely to be widowed (51.0% and 13.6%). These figures reflect the tendency for men to marry women younger than themselves, as well as the greater longevity of females than males. With remarriage rates much lower for older women than for older men (Treas & VanHilst, 1976), the prospect is for greater numbers of older women without spouses in the next several decades. This will be true particularly for those above the age of 75.

Marital Roles and Evaluations. In contrast with the early stages of the family life cycle, marital relations in the second half of life have elicited relatively little scholarly attention. Family researchers with an interest in the aged have more frequently grappled with the sampling complexities of multigenerational studies than with the more straightforward survey of marital dyads. Many of the data available on older couples are a by-product of cross-sectional surveys analyzed by age of head or life cycle stage. Unfortunately, items applicable to younger couples may be inappropriate to older ones. For example, Blood and Wolfe's pioneering study (1960) of marital power contained a query about which spouse decided what job to take—an item that does not apply to retired men and their wives.

Life cycle variations in marital satisfaction have been the subject of numerous studies, although the results are questionable and contradictory. Whereas early re-

Table 3. Marital Status by Sex for Americans 65 and Older (Percentages)[a]

Sex and marital status	1890	1900	1910	1920	1930	1940	1950	1960	1970	1980
Men										
Never married	5.6	5.7	6.2	7.3	8.8	9.8	8.3	7.7	7.5	5.1
Married	70.5	67.1	65.6	64.7	63.2	63.8	(65.5)	(70.7)	(72.4)	(77.5)
Spouse present	—	—	—	—	—	—	61.9	66.8	68.3	75.5
Spouse absent	—	—	—	—	—	—	3.6	3.9	4.1	2.0
Widowed	23.3	25.4	27.1	26.9	26.2	25.1	24.3	19.2	17.1	13.6
Divorced	0.4	0.5	0.7	0.8	1.1	1.3	1.9	2.3	3.0	3.7
Total	100.0	100.0	100.0	100.0	100.0	100.0	100.0	100.0	100.0	100.0
Women										
Never married	5.6	6.0	6.3	7.1	8.4	9.3	8.9	8.5	8.1	5.9
Married	35.4	34.2	35.0	33.9	34.7	34.3	(35.6)	(37.3)	(36.5)	(39.7)
Spouse present	—	—	—	—	—	—	33.2	34.6	33.9	38.0
Spouse absent	—	—	—	—	—	—	2.5	2.7	2.6	1.7
Widowed	58.6	59.3	58.1	58.4	56.0	55.6	54.4	52.1	52.2	51.0
Divorced	0.3	0.3	0.4	0.4	0.6	0.7	1.1	2.0	3.2	3.4
Total	100.0	100.0	100.0	100.0	100.0	100.0	100.0	100.0	100.0	100.0

[a]Source: U.S. Bureau of the Census. *Historical Statistics of the United States,* Part 1. Washington, D.C.: U.S. Government Printing Office, 1975; and U.S. Bureau of the Census. Marital Status and Living Arrangements: March 1980. *Current Population Reports,* Series P-20, No. 365. Washington, D.C.: U.S. Government Printing Office, 1980.

searchers reported a negative association between age and marital satisfaction (Pineo, 1961; Terman, 1938), much recent research has reported a U-shaped relation, with the young and the old expressing greater satisfaction than those in the middle stages of the life cycle. Based on a study of 800 married Mormons, Rollins and Cannon (1974) attributed the greater marital satisfaction of the aged to a lack of career and parenting stresses. Spanier, Lewis, and Cole (1975) identified a U-shaped relation for working-class couples in Ohio, but not for their middle-class counterparts in Ohio or Georgia. Among the explanations they gave for older couples' higher satisfaction was a cognitive consistency theory arguing that the old place a high value on their marriage in order to justify their long investment in the relationship.

Gilford and Bengtson (1979) offered one explanation of the coexistence of linear and curvilinear findings in the relationship between age and marital satisfaction. They argued that there are two orthogonal dimensions to marital satisfaction. A positive dimension focuses on such activities as working cooperatively, having stimulating discussions, and laughing together. A second dimension of negative sentiment singles out sarcasm, disagreements, criticisms, anger, and the like. Considering marital relations in a three-generation sample, the investigators found that negative sentiments declined with age, and that positive interaction had a U-shaped relation with age. Thus, the marriages of the grandparents were reported to be more satisfactory than those of the middle-aged on both dimensions. Among the oldest respondents (aged 71–90), however, both positive interaction and negative sentiment were low.

Schafer and Keith (1981) considered one factor that may underlie general expressions of marital satisfaction. Based on a random sample of Iowa couples, this study explored perceptions of equity in the performance of marital roles. For both husbands and wives, the assessments of fairness tended to be higher for those in later stages of the life cycle. For example, married couples with a wife 60 or older and no children at home saw the accomplishment of cooking and housekeeping tasks as more equitable than did younger couples.

Besides considering the general evaluation of marital relations, some researchers have addressed the issue of how the long-term relationships of the old may differ from the newer relationships of the young. A developmental literature on love suggests that relations are transformed with the passing of time so that the very basis of bonds of affection changes (Levinger, 1974). From this perspective, physical attraction, passion, and self-disclosure facilitate the formation of new relationships, but relations are sustained over the long haul by familiarity, loyalty, and a mutual investment in the relationship.

Reedy, Birren, and Schaie (1981) explored these issues on the basis of Q sorts of love experience statements given by 102 couples identified as happily married. Distinguishing young, middle-aged, and old, the authors found that the age groups were in perfect agreement on the ranking of six components of love. Emotional security (as

reflected in perceptions of trust and caring) was rated as the most important characteristic of love by all groups. This was followed, in order, by respect, communication, help and play behaviors, sexual intimacy, and loyalty to the relationship. Despite the general consensus on what characterizes love, age differences were noted. Older couples placed a greater premium on emotional security and loyalty, giving less weight to sexual intimacy and communication than did younger couples.

Life cycle studies of marital relations have been criticized on a number of counts (Schram, 1979; Spanier et al., 1975). The most serious objection has to do with the inference of aging effects from cross-sectional surveys. In the absence of longitudinal data, any changes in satisfaction over the course of a marriage are confounded with possible cohort differences in perceived satisfaction. Other problems include the failure to control for social desirability bias; the use of data from individual married persons, not dyads; inattention to the bias introduced by the life cycle attrition of unhappy marriages via divorce; and the use of linear statistics to analyze a curvilinear relation.

Despite indications of high marital satisfaction among the old, potential sources of strain and role realignment in old age have been identified. Although most men seem to welcome and to adjust readily to retirement, there is some evidence that sudden togetherness and a reshuffling of domestic chores may impose strains (Foner & Schwab, 1981). Studies of wives' responses to their husbands' retirement have emphasized negative evaluations (Kerckhoff, 1966). For example, the wives of retirees, although acknowledging the gratification of feeling needed, objected to postretirement demands on their time, reductions in personal freedom, and too much togetherness (Bengtson, 1973).

Despite dramatic postwar increases in married women's labor-force participation, the marital implications of the wife's retirement have been the subject of little study. Traditionally, wives have been thought to pattern their own retirement plans on those of their husbands, but women's greater work-force commitment may mean that the wife's job exerts an influence not only on her own retirement decision, but also on that of her husband. Recent research on the labor-force-participation decisions of older husbands and wives demonstrates that labor force withdrawal by one spouse is associated with retirement by the other partner as well (Anderson et al., 1980). Thus, couples show a preference for joint retirement, with its potential for shared leisure. Of course, this may not be financially possible if one partner is much younger or is constrained by the provisions of a private pension plan.

Although women's retirement has traditionally been viewed as a welcome return to favored activities in the home, recent studies have indicated that women may well experience more retirement problems than do men (Atchley, 1976; Fox, 1977; Jaslow, 1976). A qualitative study of 25 couples in which the wife had recently retired from university employment revealed that the wives experienced some difficulty in "settling down" to household tasks even though their retirement did not typically lead to a reallocation of household chores and despite the frequent report of improved marital relations (Szinovac, 1980).

New Family Forms in Later Life? Recent decades have witnessed a growing preoccupation with alternative family lifestyles for the aged. Spectacular changes in national rates of divorce, remarriage, and cohabitation have fueled speculation about the impact of these developments on the family lives of older Americans. Although speculation has outpaced research on this topic, the evidence suggests that marital innovations have been largely a phenomenon of the young, not the old. In other words, the lives of the aged are more likely to be affected by the fallout from their offspring's divorce than by their own marital breakup.

Because more recent cohorts have been more vulnerable to divorce, the divorced have been on the rise among the ranks of the elderly. For those 65 and older, for example, there were 32 divorced men for every 1,000 spouse-present married men in 1970, but this figure had risen to 49 by 1980 (U.S. Bureau of the Census, 1981c). This increase represents largely the accumulation of divorces occurring at earlier stages of the life cycle. Among all 1976 divorces and annulments for which age was reported, only 1.5% involved a husband 65 or older (National Center for Health Statistics, 1980a). To be sure, the divorce rate among the elderly has risen, but this increase has been modest when compared with the meteoric rise for younger Americans (U.S. Bureau of the Census, 1979a). Between 1968 and 1975, for example, the divorce rate rose 70% for those 25–39, but only 35% for those 65 and older. As divorce may disrupt broader kinship ties, and as being divorced has been linked to negative consequences for health and well-being, the growing population of divorced elderly may signal new vulnerabilities in the older population.

If divorce rates are low among the older population, the same may be said for marriage and remarriage rates. In 1976, there were only 2.2 brides for every 1,000 single women 65 and older; among their male counterparts, there were only 15.6 grooms (National Center for Health Statistics, 1980a). As Treas and VanHilst (1976) suggested, these low marriage rates may reflect normative proscriptions against late-life romance; declines in the health, mobility, and income that make courtship possible; or an unwillingness to make major investments in a relationship that can be expected to end relatively soon in death. Women are less likely to wed than are men, because sex differentials in mortality create a shortage of eligible bachelors in the older population and because older women are viewed as less desirable marriage partners than are younger women. Despite the infrequency of late-life nuptials, studies of late marriages have found them to enjoy considerable success (McKain, 1969; Vinick, 1978). Whatever the prognostications for marriages and remarriages among older persons, there is little evidence that new marriages in old age are on the upswing (Treas & VanHilst, 1976).

Before 1979, remarrying widows lost social security benefits, so many persons believe that the aged have opted for nonmarital cohabitation instead of formal unions. Such a marital alternative may be more widely discussed than practiced, however. In 1980, there were only 116,000 unmarried couples in which the householder was 65 or older (U.S. Bureau of the Census, 1981a). Of course, it cannot be inferred that all of these pairings represented romantic attachments. The 1970s witnessed a remarkable 198% increase in the number of couples living together in the general population; for those 65 and older, the increase was only 1%.

In short, in the face of major normative shifts, the aged adhered to more traditional relations. In part, this adherence reflects the fact that the old have fewer opportunities and incentives to alter their marital situation. It also represents less acceptance of cohabitation. A 1977 poll found that 82% of men and 69% of women voiced acceptance of living together. For Americans over 65, however, only 28% of men and 12% of women said that "living together" was either "OK" or "doesn't matter" (Population Reference Bureau, 1978).

As the intimate social network of some older people is quite limited, considerable attention has been focused on noninstitutional communal living as a means of providing older persons with a primary group akin to the residential family unit. Sussman (1976), for example, described a Florida court case in which 11 elderly persons, aged 61–94, were ruled to be a "family" in compliance with local zoning laws. New questions on living arrangements in the 1980 U.S. Census of Population may permit for the first time, estimates of the numbers of aged living in communes and other variant household arrangements It is not known whether older person's house-sharing is rising. McConnell and Usher (1980) noted the advantages that intergenerational house-sharing may offer to older homeowners with extra rooms. In their survey of middle-aged and older homeowners in Los Angeles, these authors found that one third of the respondents expressed positive attitudes toward sharing their homes. Companionship, financial benefits, and help, especially in an emergency, were most frequently cited as advantages of shared residence. Loss of privacy and disruptions in lifestyle were seen as the principal disadvantages. It remains to be seen whether this enthusiasm, coupled with straitened economic circumstances and a housing squeeze, may occasion a return to the boarder and lodger practice that has been on the decline throughout this century.

Widowhood. Although aging inevitably entails a renegotiation of familial roles, no late-life change may be as profound as the transition from married to widowed. Loss of one's spouse involves the loss of an intimate, the disruption of economic support patterns, the everyday assumption of new and unfamiliar tasks, and the reordering of relations with others. As a consequence, widowhood has been associated with negative outcomes, both short- and long-term.

As 7 out of 10 wives survive their husbands, widowhood is largely a woman's issue. In comparison to men, women's greater economic dependency and lower remarriage rates may make widowhood a particular problem for women. On many counts, however, widowhood is more difficult for men. For example, widows demonstrate higher death rates than their married counterparts, but men are more affected by the loss of a spouse than are women (Gove, 1973). Although widowhood seems to contribute to higher rates of mental illness, it is men who are most affected (Gove, 1972). Suicide rates are higher for the widowed population, especially men (Rico-Velasco & Mynko, 1973).

The implications of such findings are that men benefit more from marriage and are more devastated by widowhood. The reasons for this sex difference remain a matter of speculation. Although it has been suggested that widowhood is a "roleless role" (Lopata, 1975) without normative guidelines for behavior, it may be that the prevalence of widowhood among older women affords more behavioral models and anticipatory socialization than are available to men. Alternatively, men's gender roles may ill-equip them for their lives alone. For example, they may not know how to cook for themselves. If they have relied exclusively on their wives as confidantes and have delegated kin-keeping tasks to them, husbands may be socially isolated if their wives die, especially if retirement has severed work friendships.

Bereavement itself is recognized as a complex process. Its normal symptoms might be thought abnormal in another context: confusion, denial, hostility, numbness, intense pining, depression, feverish activity, dependency, and the like (Marshall, 1980; Peterson & Briley, 1977). It appears that this painful and protracted process leads to a reasonably successful adjustment to widowhood for most persons. Indeed, Morgan (1976) suggested that morale differences between widowed and married women are largely eliminated when such factors as age, health, income, and kin contact are taken into account. Disparities in adjustment within the widowed population exist, nonetheless. Balkwell (1981) provided a thoughtful overview of the research on the determinants of successful adaptation to widowhood. As has been noted, widowhood appears to be more difficult for men than for women. Older widowed persons display better adjustment than do their younger counterparts. Whether the death was anticipated may interact with age: forewarning promotes the adjustment of the young and interferes with the adaptation of the old. As Balkwell argued, anticipation of death may provide younger spouses with time to come to terms with the inevitable loss, but a lengthy illness for the old may serve only to exhaust the older spouse and disrupt his or her relations with others.

Ongoing relations with kin may afford some comfort during the transition to widowhood and beyond. It is widely appreciated, however, that much kin support is of a short-term and ceremonial nature. After the funeral, the widow's everyday kinship network may be very circumscribed. For example, relations with in-laws may not survive the death of one's spouse. Focusing on Chicago area widows, Lopata (1978) considered four types of support systems: the economic support system, the service support system, the social support system (of shared activities), and the emotional support system (identifying persons who contribute to feelings about oneself and those who serve particular relational roles such as confidant). Lopata's results demonstrated no support for the notion of an extended helping network of relations on whom widowed women could call. Among those 65 and older, for instance, 87% did not list a brother or sister as providing any service, and 76% reported no social activities shared with a sibling. Rather than relying on "other relatives," the widows in Lopata's study reported links with adjacent generations in the lineage: parents for the younger widows and children for their older counterparts. With the exception of a few gender-typed activities (e.g., car care), it was women who figured in these generational lines of support for widowed women.

To sum up, widowhood represents a profound transition in the lives of the aged. On a number of indices of well-being, it is apparent that this transition involves particular vulnerabilities, although widowhood and the adjustment to widowhood may be more difficult for some groups than for others. The loss of a spouse coupled with the possible decrements of aging itself may suggest a heightened role for kin in the lives of the widowed. Kin involvement, however, seems to be limited largely to the children of the elderly widow. Other relations appear infrequently in their reports of supportive relationships.

Intervention Perspectives: Older Families in Trouble

Despite the strength of intergenerational solidarity in many contemporary families documented in the previous section, it is clear that many families of older individuals are in trouble, are in need of external support, or are not able or willing to provide the aged individual with needed resources. Indeed, much current research suggests that family crises involving the dependency of a previously healthy, active older member are the rule, rather than the exception. As is suggested by the research of Lopata (1979), Cantor (1975, 1980), Brody (1978), and Silverstone (1978), these crises are widespread and increasingly expectable. And as is suggested in the analysis of Bengtson and Kuypers (1985) of the family breakdown cycle in old age, severe stresses await families coping with the normal losses and transitions of aging.

As we attempt to summarize the literature, three additional factors must be given attention with respect to adequate policy responses to the burdens and stresses in the social context of aging individuals.

First, most surveys report the existence of socially isolated aged individuals—widowed and without children because they never had any or because they have outlived them. For example, Lopata (1979) reported that some of the Chicago area widows she interviewed did not even know where one of their children was living, having lost contact years before. The less education a woman had achieved in her youth, and the lower the socioeconomic class, the more restricted was her life space in widowhood. The average contact with all children in Lopata's sample was less than once a week (p. 187), a figure much lower than that for the nonwidowed respondents in other surveys. Over 15% of the inner-city elderly in Cantor's survey (1975) were without any kin they could contact and were thus "family-less."

Second, subcultural and ethnic differentials are increasingly important to recognize in America's pluralistic society. Osaka (1979) documented both the strengths and the strains among Japanese-American families adjusting to old age. Bengtson and Burton (1982) noted factors leading to greater vulnerability of mental health among aged blacks. Cantor (1980) noted the link between family tensions and mental health problems among the Hispanic elderly. Where minority status reflects cultural marginality, the problem of intergenerational conflict—especially with regard to norms concerning taking care of the aged—may be especially severe.

Third, it should be noted that conflict between adult children and aged parents may have a long history in some families, going back to childhood and adolescence (Bengtson & Kuypers, 1985). In such cases, a crisis involving the older member's frailty may be impossible to resolve within the family. More dramatic is the problem of adult abuse, often crassly termed *granny bashing*. Physical and/or emotional harm inflicted on older family members has been increasingly reported in the mass media and by researchers studying violence in the family (Johnson, 1980; Steinmetz & Strauss, 1978).

Burdens of Family Caregiving to the Elderly

Several studies have documented the burdens and stresses that families deal with when providing care to frail elders. The existing research on family caregiving leads to the following sobering conclusion: Although the provision of care by families to impaired members is extensive, such care may produce serious negative consequences for the individuals involved—of whatever generation.

Frequently, the problem of the "generational squeeze" is exacerbated by the advent of illness, such as senile dementia (Smith & Bengtson, 1979). The precursors of institutionalization and its outcome in terms of feelings of well-being doubtless reflect a complex interplay between the needs and the capacities of aging parent and grown child. Consider the following report of a 64-year-old daughter and her 92-year-old mother's institutionalization:

A year ago she fell and broke her pelvis, and after her return from the hospital, we moved her into our home. She needed considerable help and supervision; we hired someone to live in who was to take care of mother's needs.

It didn't work out well. We hired "sitters" for those occasions when I, or we, had to be away, even for short excursions. My preoccupation with my mother's welfare put a strain on my relationship with my husband. Mother's constant presence became a burden to me, too; I dreaded hearing the sound of her slippers shuffling to the kitchen each morning. . . . But mother seemed to become disturbed, coming into our bedroom at night, turning on lights, calling me in the wee hours. The paranoia increased until one morning she became extremely agitated, wanting to leave the house because "someone" . . . was trying to kill us.

Aware that it would be agonizingly difficult for me to make the first move to place mother in a retirement home, I seized the opportunity. With her approval, I arranged for her to move into an excellent place that very day . . . presently behaving quite normally.

We see mother four or five times a week, often taking her for a drive and to lunch, spending an average of three hours each time. Much of my time away from her is concerned with "doing" for her in some way. My own projects are neglected. However, the depression I felt this past year has lessened somewhat so that I hope for an eventual return to equilibrium and some insight as to better ways to handle the traumatic aspects of aging. (Bengtson & Treas, 1980, p. 419)

In a longitudinal study of family burden in caring for a mentally impaired aged relative, Hoenig and Hamilton (1966) found that 66% of the families reported adverse effects on the household as a result of the patient's illness. The most burdensome problems reported by the families were providing physical or nursing care, followed by the patient's excessive demands for companionship. These researchers also found that the families of aged patients more frequently complained of negative effects on the family's feelings and mental outlook because of caregiving than did the relatives of younger patients.

Similar results were reported by Sanford (1975). His research was conducted on families of elderly persons who lived in hospital geriatric units in London. The purpose was to establish which problems encountered by the family prevented them from accepting the older person back into their homes. The most "intolerable" problem reported was the behavior patterns of the increasingly demented elder.

Silverstone (1978) suggested that knowledge of caregiving effects on American aged and their families is limited and tends to be one-sided. That is, the focus has been on young caregivers, who are viewed as experiencing the only problem in the caregiving process. Furthermore, the family caregiving literature appears generally to assume that impaired aged persons expect, willingly accept, and react positively to assistance from their families, although the aged's expectations may be higher than the family's capacity to respond. As yet, research has failed to investigate the possible range of reactions by the aged themselves to their family members' assistance. Arling, Parham, and Teitleman (1978) suggested that family caregiving may have negative effects on the elderly under certain conditions. Despite the benevolent intentions of kin, they may unwittingly take an excessive responsibility for the impaired elder's care, depriving the person of potential opportunities to behave as independently as possible or to have some measure of control over daily functioning. In these situations, the older person is placed in a helpless position vis-à-vis his or her family members. This circumstance may be related to the high prevalence of depression among the physically incapacitated elderly. There is a serious gap in our knowledge of the process by which families deal with the caregiving problem, that is, how the elderly themselves respond to the stresses of the dependent role (Smith & Bengtson, 1979). Furthermore, the responses of the elder can be better understood by examining him or her in relation to the expectations and the caregiving behaviors of other family members, not simply the primary caregiver.

In short, contemporary intergenerational family life among America's aged reflects a diverse picture of strengths and weaknesses, support and problems. Although most of today's elderly are neither isolated nor abandoned by their families in a fast-changing social context, many feel vulnerable to the changes of aging and to the overtaxed resources of multigenerational family units. For these elderly Americans and their families, and for the smaller but more desperate minority experiencing neglect or outright abuse at the hands of overwrought or indifferent children, it is important that more comprehensive and humane social policy be enacted.

Public Policy Pressures: The Changing Context of Family Life

The extension of life to include four and five generations in the family, women entering the labor force in increasing numbers, and the tension between values of filial piety and intergenerational independence are examples of the contemporary demographic and social trends impinging on today's American family. Such trends suggest pressures for a broader range of social policies to meet changing family patterns in the years ahead (Sussman, 1977). An analysis of the evolution of current public policies aimed at enhancing the family's function, however, points to some curious contradictions.

First, many forms of help with young children (e.g., nursery schools, babysitters, and school lunch programs) have been taken-for-granted elements of social institutions. Yet attitudes about providing services to help families with their old are often sanctimonious and judgmental. At what point does the public and professional expectation of "filial responsibility" become social irresponsibility?

Second, most industrialized nations provide services that support family caregiving for older people that are not available in the United States. Gibson's analysis (1980) of policy patterns internationally notes that "these nations have moved beyond the rhetoric of family sup-

port" to implement a wide variety of programs institutionalized in collective public policy. The question is: Why is there such a lag between needs and family-oriented programs in contemporary American society?

A long inventory can be cited of programs that have been suggested—and in some cases implemented—to meet the special needs of families that include a dependent or impaired older person (Brody, 1978; Cantor, 1980; Lopata & Brehm, 1981; Silverstone, 1978; Sussman, 1977). Among these are (1) in-home services such as homemaker and personal care; (2) service-supported living arrangements and quality institutions for older people that need not be regarded with fear and anxiety; (3) financial supports, such as family allowances to help defray parent-care costs; (4) reimbursement for day care (which is now regionally uneven because it is not reimbursable in some states); and (5) respite care.

Gibson's analysis (1980) of policy patterns in other industrialized nations points to actual experiences of implementation. She noted that nearly all industrialized nations except the United States and Canada provide a financial "constant attendance allowance" on behalf of those who need care at home. Home-help and home-health services are widely available (for example, 923 home-help aides per 100,000 population in Sweden, as compared to 29 per 100,000 in the United States). Some nations have implemented innovative housing-assistance provisions (loans or grants to remodel an extra room for an old person in Japan, "granny flats" in the United Kingdom and Australia). Direct payment to family caregivers is available in Sweden; evening and weekend home help aides and nurses are provided in Denmark; and district nurses are available 24 hours a day in the Netherlands.

By contrast, past policies in the United States have, in effect, constrained the family's functioning in caring for older members and have exacerbated problems resulting from demographic and social changes. Among such unintended consequences of previous policy are the following:

1. The social security cutoff of the family maximum for families with more than two children. Refusal to help widows obtain retraining and job opportunities if they have no dependent children in their care and are too young for retirement benefits results in their being left both poor and angry (Lopata & Brehm, 1981).
2. Age-segregated housing, effected by building facilities mandated for seniors alone, makes contact with peers easier but intergenerational contact more difficult (Lawton, 1981).
3. Filial obligation provisions for Medicaid and the insistence that children be responsible for medical care payment (Lopata & Brehm, 1981).

It has been suggested that, as long as social policy in the United States continues to give only lip service to family policy that would help the elderly (as well as their primary caretakers, spouses, and "women in the middle"), all generations are at risk, for their health and well-being are interlocked (Brody, 1980). From the evidence reviewed in this chapter, it is clear that our society is in the midst of demographic and social changes that put the position of the elderly, in some sense, in more jeopardy. We do not know what future impact on parent care will result from the current increase in single-parent families, from the later ages at which women are having children, from the increase in nonmarried couples, and from the rising rates of divorce and remarriage. It is certain that policymakers will feel pressure to develop new policy to deal with increasingly overtaxed family resources in caring for the dependent elderly. Such changes will themselves alter the macroenvironment in which families function.

Conclusion

Our review of the literature on aging and the family suggests a complex picture of change and continuity at both the microsocial and the macrosocial levels of analysis. Aging brings inevitable and predictable changes in individuals. Children grow up and parents grow older. The role of the worker is relinquished for that of the retiree. There is an onset of chronic health conditions that alter capacities for daily activities. Loved ones die. These changes often entail the renegotiation of family roles and the realignment of family networks, social contexts that reflect continuity and stability as well as change.

Change in individuals is paralleled by societal changes. Demographic alterations in fertility and mortality have affected the availability of kin. Changes in economic resources and cultural norms have transformed the living arrangements of the generations. Employment has become less important in the support of the aged, and public pensions have become more important. These changes imply that the context of aging is changing. Many Americans find themselves in very-late-life circumstances different from what they may have imagined when young.

Despite the currents of change in which families are caught up, our review of 163 studies has shown little evidence of family disorganization in reaction to the undeniable burdens of aging. Considerable solidarity is displayed between generations. If a spouse and offspring prove the most important familial resources for the elderly, it is probable that this circumstance represents a continuation of long-standing traditions of American family life into the present. However, decrements associated with aging—loss of spouse, job, health, and the capacity for independent living—place special demands on family relations. These demands may be manifested in guilt, friction, and feelings of inadequacy for young and old alike. If the familial demands of later life are more sorely felt or more openly acknowledged today than in the past, it may be because aging kin have become more commonplace. It may also be because Americans have come to accept that the welfare of older citizens is no longer merely a private concern, but also a public responsibility.

ACKNOWLEDGMENTS

John J. Schneider assisted with the preparation of this chapter.

References

Adams, B. N. *Kinship in an urban setting.* Chicago: Markham, 1968.

Aizenberg, R., & Treas, J. The family in later life: Psycho-social and demographic considerations. In J. Birren & K. W. Schaie (Eds.), *Handbook of the psychology of aging.* New York: Van Nostrand Reinhold, 1975.

Anderson, K., Clark, R., & Johnson, T. Retirement in dual career families. In R. L. Clark (Ed.), *Retirement policy in an aging society.* Durham, N.C.: Duke University Press, 1980.

Anderson, M. The impact on the family relationship of the elderly of changes since Victorian times in governmental income maintenance provision. In E. Shanas & M. Sussman (Eds.), *Family, bureaucracy and the elderly.* Durham, N.C.: Duke University Press, 1977.

Arling, G. The elderly widow and her family, neighbors and friends. *Journal of Marriage and the Family,* 1976, *38,* 757–768.

Arling, G., Parham, I., & Teitleman, J. Learned helplessness and social exchanges: Convergence and application of theories. Paper presented at the 31st annual meeting of the Gerontological Society, Dallas, Texas, 1978.

Atchley, R. Orientations toward the job and retirement adjustment among women. In J. F. Gubrium (Ed.), *Time, roles, and self in old age.* New York: Behavioral Publications, 1976.

Balkwell, C. Transition to widowhood: A review of the literature. *Family Relations,* 1981, *30*(1), 117–127.

Becker, G. S. *An economic approach to human behavior.* Chicago: University of Chicago Press, 1976.

Beckman, L. J., & Houser, B. B. The consequences of childlessness on the social-psychological well-being of older women. *Journal of Gerontology,* 1982, *37*(2), 243–250.

Bengtson, V. L. Inter-age differences in perception and the generation gap. *The Gerontologist,* 1971, Part 2, 85–90.

Bengtson, V. L. *The social psychology of aging.* Indianapolis: Bobbs-Merrill, 1973.

Bengtson, V. L. Generation and family effects in value socialization. *American Sociological Review,* 1975, *40,* 358–371.

Bengtson, V. L. You and your aging parent: Research perspectives on intergenerational interaction. In P. Ragan (Ed.), *Aging parents.* Los Angeles: University of Southern California Press, 1979.

Bengtson, V. L., & Black, K. D. Intergenerational relations and continuities in socialization. In P. Baltes & K. W. Schaie (Eds.), *Life-span developmental psychology: Personality and Socialization.* New York: Academic Press, 1973.

Bengtson, V. L., & Burton, L. Mental health and the black elderly: Competence, susceptibility, and quality of life. *Journal of Minority Aging,* 1982, *7,* 25–31.

Bengtson, V. L., & deTerre, E. Aging and family relations: A decade review. *Marriage and Family Review,* 1980, *3*(2), 51–76.

Bengtson, V. L., & Kuypers, J. A. Generational differences and the developmental stake. *Aging and Human Development,* 1971, *2,* 249–260.

Bengtson, V. L., & Kuypers, J. A. Psycho-social issues in the aging family. In P. Muissen, J. Munnichs, & E. Olbrecht (Eds.), *Life span and change in a gerontological perspective.* New York: Academic Press, 1985.

Bengtson, V. L., & Manuel, R. *Ethnicity and family patterns in mature adults: Effects of race, age, SES and sex.* Paper presented at the annual meetings of the Pacific Sociological Association, San Diego, 1976.

Bengtson, V. L., & Robertson, J. *Grandparenthood.* Beverly Hills: Sage, 1985.

Bengtson, V. L., & Schrader, S. Parent-child relations. In D. Mangen & W. Peterson (Eds.), *Handbook of research instruments in social gerontology,* Vol. 2. Minneapolis: University of Minnesota Press, 1981.

Bengtson, V. L., & Treas, J. Intergenerational relations and mental health. In R. B. Sloane & J. E. Birren (Eds.), *Handbook of mental health and aging.* Englewood Cliffs, N.J.: Prentice-Hall, 1980.

Bengtson, V. L., Olander, E., & Haddad, A. The "generation gap" and aging family members: Toward a conceptual model. In J. F. Gubrium (Ed.), *Time, roles, and self in old age.* New York: Human Sciences Press, 1976.

Bengtson, V. L., Burton, L., & Mangen, D. *Family support systems and attribution of responsibility: Contrasts among elderly blacks, Mexican-Americans, and whites.* Paper presented at the annual meetings of the Gerontological Society of America, Toronto, Ontario, 1981.

Bengtson, V., Mangen, D., & Landry, P. In Garms, Homolova, E. M. Hoerning & Schaeffer (eds). *Intergenerational relationships.* N.Y.: C. J. Hogrefe, 1984.

Benton, J. *The new sensibility.* Unpublished manuscript, University of California at Los Angeles, 1981.

Beresford, J. C., & Rivlin, A. M. Privacy, poverty, and old age. *Demography,* 1966, *3(1): 247–258.*

Berkner, L. K. The stem family and the developmental cycle of the peasant household: An 18th century Austrian example. *American Historical Review,* 1972, *77,* 398–418.

Blood, R., & Wolfe, D. *Husbands and wives: The dynamics of married living.* Glencoe, Ill.: Free Press, 1960.

Brody, E. M. *Long-term care of older people: A practical guide.* New York: Human Sciences Press, 1977.

Brody, E. M. *The formal support network: Congregate treatment setting for residents with senescent brain dysfunction.* Paper presented at the Conference on Clinical Aspects of Alzheimer's Disease and Senile Dementia, sponsored by the National Institutes of Mental Health, Bethesda, Md., December 6–8, 1978.

Brody, E. M. "Women in the middle" and family help to older people. *The Gerontologist,* 1981, *21,* 471–480.

Brody, E. M., & Brody, S. *New directions in health and social supports for the aging.* Paper presented at the Anglo-American Conference, Fordham University, New York, 1980.

Brody, E., Davis, L., & Johnsen, P. *Formal and informal service providers: Preferences of three generations of women.* Paper presented at the annual meetings of the Gerontological Society, Washington, D.C., 1979.

Cantor, M. H. Life space and the social support system of the inner city elderly of New York city. *The Gerontologist,* 1975, *15,* 23–27.

Cantor, M. H. Neighbors and friends: An overlooked resource in the informal support system. *Research on Aging,* 1979, *4(1),* 434–463.

Cantor, M. H. *Caring for the frail elderly: Impact on family, friends, and neighbors.* Paper presented at the annual meetings of the Gerontological Society of America, San Diego, 1980.

Cherlin, A. Changing family and household: Contemporary lessons from historical research. *Annual Review of Sociology,* 1983, *9,* 51–66.

Cowgill, D. O., & Holmes, L. D. (Eds.). *Aging and modernization.* New York: Appleton-Century-Crofts, 1972.

Crimmins, E. M. Implications of recent mortality trends for size and composition of population over 65. *Review of Public Data Use,* 1982, *10*(December).

Easterlin, R. *Birth and fortune: The impact of numbers on personal welfare.* New York: Basic Books, 1980.

Elder, G. Approaches to social change and the family. In J. Demos & S.

S. Boocock (Eds.), *Transitions. American Journal of Sociology* supplement, 1978.

Fogel, R., Hatfield, E., Kiesler, S., & March, J. (Eds.). *Stability and change in the family.* New York: Academic Press, 1981.

Foner, A., & Schwab, K. *Aging and retirement.* Monterey, Calif.: Brooks-Cole, 1981.

Fox, J. H. Effects of retirement and former work life on women's adaptation in old age. *Journal of Gerontology,* 1977, *32*(2), 196–202.

Gibson, M. *Support for families of the elderly in other industrialized nations.* Unpublished paper, International Federation on Aging, 1980.

Gilford, R., & Bengtson, V. L. Measuring marital satisfaction in three generations: Positive and negative dimensions. *Journal of Marriage and the Family,* 1979, *41*(May), 387–398.

Gove, W. R. Sex, marital status and suicide. *Journal of Health and Social Behavior,* 1972, *13,* 204–213.

Gove, W. R. Sex, marital status and mortality. *American Journal of Sociology,* 1973, *79,* 45–67.

Greven, P. J., Jr. Family structure in seventeenth century Andover, Massachusetts. In M. Gordon (Ed.), *The American family in social-historical perspective.* New York: St. Martin's Press, 1973.

Hagestad, G. O. Problems and promises in the social psychology of intergenerational relations. In R. Fogel, E. Hatfield, S. Kiesler, & J. March (Eds.), *Stability and change in the family.* New York: Academic Press, 1981.

Hareven, T. Family time, historical time. *Daedalus,* 1977, *106*(Spring), 57–70.

Hill, R., Foote, N., Aldous, J., Carlson, R., & MacDonald, R. *Family development in three generations.* Cambridge, Mass.: Schenkman, 1970.

Hoenig, J., & Hamilton, M. Elderly psychiatric patients and the burden on the household. *Psychiatria et Neurologia,* 1966, *152,* 281–293.

Jaslow, P. Employment, retirement and morale among older women. *Journal of Gerontology,* 1976, *31*(March), 212–218.

Johnson, M. L. *Criminal victimization and the older American: Fear vs. reality.* Background paper for the White House Conference on Aging, section on Family and Support Systems, 1980.

Kerckhoff, A. C. Family patterns and morale in retirement. In I. H. Simpson & J. C. McKinney (Eds.), *Social aspects of aging.* Durham, N.C.: Duke University Press, 1966.

Kreps, J. The economics of intergenerational relationships. In E. Shanas & G. Streib (Eds.), *Social structure and the family.* Englewood Cliffs, N.J.: Prentice-Hall, 1965.

Kobrin, F. The fall of household size and the rise of the primary individual in the United States. *Demography,* 1976, *13,* 127–138.

Lasch, C. *The culture of narcissism: American life in an age of diminishing expectations.* New York: W. W. Norton, 1979.

Lawton, M. P. *Environment and aging.* Monterey, Calif.: Brooks-Cole, 1981.

Levinger, G. A three-level approach to interaction: Toward an understanding of pair relatedness. In T. Houston (Ed.), *Foundations of interpersonal attraction.* New York: Academic Press, 1974.

Lopata, H. Z. *Widowhood in an American city.* Cambridge, Mass.: Schenkman, 1973.

Lopata, H. Z. On widowhood: Grief, work and identity reconstruction. *Journal of Geriatric Psychiatry,* 1975, *8,* 41–55.

Lopata, H. Z. Contributions of extended families to the support systems of metropolitan area widows: Limitations of the modified kin network. *Journal of Marriage and the Family,* 1978, *40,* 355–364.

Lopata, H. Z. *Women as widows: Support systems.* New York: Elsevier North-Holland, 1979.

Lopata, H. Z., & Brehm, H. *Widowhood: From social problem to federal program.* New York: Praeger, 1981.

Los Angeles Times, October 2, 1981, p. 2.

Marshall, V. W. *Last chapters: A sociology of aging and dying.* Monterey, Calif.: Brooks-Cole, 1980.

McConnell, S. R., & Usher, C. E. *Intergenerational house-sharing: A research report and reference manual.* Los Angeles: Andrus Gerontology Center, University of Southern California, 1980.

McKain, W. C. *Retirement marriages.* Agricultural Experiment Station Monograph No. 3. Storrs: University of Connecticut Press, 1969.

Metropolitan Life Insurance Company. Current patterns of dependency. *Statistical Bulletin,* 1977, *58*(January), 1.

Michael, R. T., Fuchs, V. R., & Scott, S. R. Changes in the propensity to live alone: 1950–1976. *Demography,* 1980, *17,* 39–55.

Modell, J., & Hareven, T. K. Urbanization and the malleable household: An examination of boarding and lodging in American families. *Journal of Marriage and the Family,* 1973, *35,* 467–479.

Moon, M. *The measurement of economic welfare.* New York: Academic Press, 1977.

Morgan, L. A. A re-examination of widowhood and morale. *Journal of Gerontology,* 1976, *31,* 687–695.

Murray, J. Family structure in pre-retirement years. In M. Ireland *et al.* (Eds.), *Almost 65: Baseline data from the retirement history study.* Washington, D.C.: U.S. Government Printing Office, 1976.

National Center for Health Statistics. *Vital Statistics of the United States, 1976, Marriage and Divorce.* Rockville, Md., 1980. (a)

National Center for Health Statistics. *Vital statistics of the United States, 1976, Mortality.* Rockville, Md., 1980. (b)

Neugarten, B. L., & Hagestad, G. O. Age and the life course. In R. H. Binstock & E. Shanas (Eds.), *Handbook of aging and the social sciences.* New York: Van Nostrand Reinhold, 1976.

Newman, S. *Housing adjustments of older people: A report from the second phase.* Ann Arbor: Institute for Social Research, University of Michigan, 1976.

Osaka, M. M. Aging and family among Japanese Americans: The role of ethnic tradition in the adjustment to old age. *The Gerontologist,* 1979, *19*(5), 448–455.

Pampel, F. *Social change and the aged: Recent trends in the U.S.* Lexington, Mass.: Lexington Books, 1981.

Peterson, J. A., & Briley, M. L. *Widows and widowhood: A creative approach to being alone.* New York: Association Press, 1977.

Pineo, P. C. Disenchantment in the later years of marriage. *Marriage and Family Living,* 1961, *23*(February), 3–11.

Population Reference Bureau. Marriage, divorce and living together. *Interchange,* 1978, *7,* 1–3.

Preston, S. Family sizes of children and family sizes of women. *Demography,* 1976, *13,* 105–114.

Preston, S. Reply to comment on "Family sizes of children and family sizes of women." *Demography,* 1977, *14,* 375–377.

Preston, S., Keyfitz, N., & Schoen, R. *Causes of death: Life tables for national populations.* New York: Seminar Press, 1972.

Reedy, M. N., Birren, J. E. & Schaie, K. W. Age and sex differences in satisfying love relationships across the adult life span. *Human Development,* 1981, *24*(1), 52–66.

Rico-Velasco, J., & Mynko, L. Suicide and marital status: A changing relationship? *Journal of Marriage and the Family,* 1973, *35,* 239–244.

Rindfuss, R. R., & Sweet, J. A. *Postwar fertility trends and differentials in the United States.* New York: Academic Press, 1977.

Rollins, B., & Cannon, K. Marital satisfaction over the life cycle: A reevaluation. *Journal of Marriage and the Family,* 1974, *36*(May), 271–283.

Rosenfeld, J. *The legacy of aging.* Norwood, N.J.: Ablex Publishing Corporation, 1979.

Rosenthal, C. Kin-keeping in the familial division of labor. *Journal of Marriage and the Family,* 1985, *45,* 509–521.

Rosow, I. *Social integration of the aged.* New York: Basic Books, 1967.

Sanford, J. R. A. Tolerance of debility in elderly dependents by supporters at home: Its significance for hospital practice. *British Medical Journal,* 1975, *3,* 471–473.

Sawhill, I. Economic perspectives on the family. *Daedalus,* 1977, *106*(Spring), 115–125.

Schafer, R. B., & Keith, P. M. Equity in family roles across the life cycle. *Journal of Marriage and the Family,* 1981, *43,* 359–367.

Schoenholz, K. *Occupational mobility and kin interaction: A reconceptualization.* Paper presented at the annual meetings of the American Sociological Association, San Francisco, 1978.

Schram, R. W. Marital satisfaction over the family life cycle: A critique and proposal. *Journal of Marriage and the Family,* 1979, *41* (February), 7–13.

Shanas, E. *The health of older people: A social survey.* Cambridge: Harvard University Press, 1962.

Shanas, E. The family as a social support system in old age. *The Gerontologist,* 1979, *19*(2), 169–174. (a)

Shanas, E. Social myth as hypothesis: The case of family relations in old age. *The Gerontologist,* 1979, *191,* 3–10. (b)

Shanas, E., & Hauser, P. M. Zero population growth and the family of older people. *Journal of Social Issues,* 1974, *30,* 79–92.

Shanas, E., & Sussman, M. (Eds.). *Family, bureaucracy and the elderly.* Durham, N.C.: Duke University Press, 1977.

Shanas, E., Townsend, P., Wedderburn, D., Friis, H., Milhaj, P., & Stehouwer, J. *Old people in three industrial societies.* London: Routledge & Kegan Paul, 1968.

Silverstone, B. Family relationships of the elderly: Problems and implications for helping professionals. *Aged Care and Services Review,* 1978, *1*(2), 1–9.

Silverstone, B., & Hyman, H. *You and your aging parent.* New York: Pantheon Books, 1976.

Singh, B. K., & Williams, J. S. Childlessness and family satisfaction. *Research on Aging,* 1981, *3,* 218–227.

Smith, D. S. Life course, norms, and the family system of older Americans in 1900. *Journal of Family History,* 1979, *4*(3), 285–298.

Smith, K. F., & Bengtson, V. L. Positive consequences of institutionalization: Solidarity between elderly parents and their middle-aged children. *The Gerontologist,* 1979, *19*(5), 438–447.

Soldo, B. *Determinants of temporal variations in living arrangements among the elderly, 1960–1970.* Unpublished Ph.D. dissertation, Duke University, Durham, N.C., 1977.

Soldo, B., & Myers, G. *The effects of lifetime fertility on the living arrangements of older women.* Paper presented at the annual meetings of the Gerontological Society, New York, 1976.

Spanier, G. B., Lewis, R. A., & Cole, C. L. Marital adjustment over the family life cycle: The issue of curvilinearity. *Journal of Marriage and the Family,* 1975, *37*(May), 263–275.

Steinmetz, S., & Strauss, M. A. *Violence in the family.* New York: Dodd, Mead, 1978.

Streib, G. F., & Beck, R. W. Older families: A decade review. *Journal of Marriage and the Family,* 1980, *42*(4), 937–956.

Sussman, M. B. Relations of adult children with their parents in the United States. In E. Shanas & G. Streib (Eds.), *Social structure and the family: Generational relationships.* Englewood Cliffs, N.J.: Prentice-Hall, 1965.

Sussman, M. B. The family life of old people. In R. H. Binstock & E. Shanas (Eds.), *Handbook of aging and the social sciences.* New York: Van Nostrand Reinhold, 1976.

Sussman, M. B. Family, bureaucracy, and the elderly individual: An organizational/linkage perspective. In E. Shanas & M. Sussman (Eds.), *Family, bureaucracy and the elderly.* Durham, N.C.: Duke University Press, 1977.

Sweet, J. A. *Further indicators of family structure and process for racial and ethnic minorities.* Center for Demography and Ecology Working Paper No. 77-30. Madison: University of Wisconsin Press, 1977.

Sweetzer, D. A. The effect of industrialization on intergenerational solidarity. *Rural Sociology,* 1966, *31*(June), 156–170.

Szinovac, M. E. Female retirement: Effects on spousal roles and marital adjustment. *Journal of Family Issues,* 1980, *1*(September), 423–440.

Terman, L. *Psychological factors in marital happiness.* New York: McGraw-Hill, 1938.

Townsend, P. Isolation, desolation, and loneliness. In E. Shanas *et al.* (Eds.), *Old people in three industrial societies.* London: Routledge & Kegan Paul, 1968.

Treas, J. Family support systems for the aged: Some social and demographic considerations. *The Gerontologist,* 1977, *17*, 486–491.

Treas, J. Socialist organization and economic development in China: Latent consequences for the aged. *The Gerontologist,* 1979, *19*(February), 34–43.

Treas, J. The great American fertility debate: Generational balance and support of the aged. *The Gerontologist,* 1981, *21*(February), 98–103. (a)

Treas, J. Postwar trends in family size. *Demography,* 1981, *18*(August), 321–334. (b)

Treas, J. Women's employment and its implications for the economic status of the elderly of the future. In S. Kiesler, J. Morgan, & V. Oppenheimer (Eds.), *Aging: Social change.* New York: Academic Press, 1981. (c)

Treas, J. Aging and the family. In D. S. Woodruff & J. E. Birren (Eds.), *Aging: Scientific perspectives and social issues* (2nd ed.). New York: D. Van Nostrand, 1983.

Treas, J., & VanHilst, A. Marriage and remarriage rates among older Americans. *The Gerontologist,* 1976, *16*, 132–136.

Treas, J., Gronvold, R., & Bengtson, V. L. *Filial destiny? The effects of birth order on relations with aging parents.* Paper presented at the annual meetings of the Gerontological Society of America, San Diego, 1980.

Troll, L. E. Issues in the study of generations. *Aging and Human Development,* 1970, *1*, 199–218.

Troll, L., Miller, S., & Atchley, R. *Families in later life.* Belmont, Calif.: Wadsworth, 1979.

Turner, R. H. The real self: From institution to impulse. *American Journal of Sociology,* 1976, *81*(March), 989–1016.

U.S. Bureau of the Census. Census of Population: 1970. Subject reports final report PC(2)-6A. *Employment Status and Work Experience.* Washington, D.C.: U.S. Government Printing Office, 1973.

U.S. Bureau of the Census. Demographic aspects of aging and the older population in the United States. *Current Population Reports,* Series P-23, No. 59. Washington, D.C.: U.S. Government Printing Office, 1976.

U.S. Bureau of the Census. The future of the American family. *Current Population Reports,* Series P-20, No. 78. Washington, D.C.: U.S. Government Printing Office, 1979. (a)

U.S. Bureau of the Census. Social and economic characteristics of the older population: 1978. *Current Population Reports,* Series P-23, No. 85. Washington, D.C.: U.S. Government Printing Office, 1979. (b)

U.S. Bureau of the Census. American families and living arrangements. *Current Population Reports* Series P-23, No. 104. Washington, D.C.: U.S. Government Printing Office, 1980. (a)

U.S. Bureau of the Census. Money income in 1978 of families and persons in the United States. *Current Population Reports,* Series P-60, No. 123. Washington, D.C.: U.S. Government Printing Office, 1980. (b)

U.S. Bureau of the Census. Marital status and living arrangements: March 1980. *Current Population Reports,* Series P-20, No. 365. Washington, D.C.: U.S. Government Printing Office, 1981. (a)

U.S. Bureau of the Census. Money income and poverty status of families and persons in the United States: 1980. *Current Population Reports* Series P-60, No. 127. Washington, D.C.: U.S. Government Printing Office, 1981. (b)

U.S. Bureau of the Census. Population profile of the United States, 1980. *Current Population Reports,* Series P-20, No. 363. Washington, D.C.: U.S. Government Printing Office, 1981. (c)

Vinick, B. Remarriage in old age. *The Family Coordinator,* 1978, *27*, 359–363.

Waite, L. U.S. women at work. *Population Bulletin,* 1981, *36*, 1–44.

Walther, R. J. *Intergenerational transfers, family structure and social security.* Paper presented at the annual meetings of the Gerontological Society of America, San Diego, 1980.

Wolfe, T. The "me" decade and the third great awakening. *New Yorker,* 1976, *23*(August), 26–40.

Yang, C. The Chinese family: The young and the old. In R. L. Coser (Eds.), *The family: Its structures and functions* (2nd ed.). New York: St. Martin's Press, 1974.

PART IV

Family Dynamics and Transformation

This concluding part of the handbook is divided into two subparts. The first part has three chapters on family power, stress, and violence—conditions and processes that impinge on marital and family relationships. The second subpart consists of chapters on legal processes, social policy, family life, education, marital and family therapy, and mechanisms for transforming the family.

In the chapter "Family Power," Szinovacz postulates the need for improved multidimensional conceptualizations, operationalizations, and innovative theoretical frameworks of family power. Szinovacz recommends that a historical overview of family power be considered as a research area. The need for imaginative concepts and tools and the handling of bothersome methodological issues are addressed. A theoretical framework is offered that emphasizes the complexity and the dynamic nature of the family "powering" process, with due consideration given to the structural context, the group and member characteristics, the situational contingencies, and the users of power.

Boss, in her "Family Stress" chapter, reviews the research on stress, locating the initiation of interest in the field with the Great Depression of the 1930s. Building on the work of Hill, McCubbin, and other investigators, Boss utilizes the ABC-X model. She examines the stressor "A," coping resource "B," the "X" (consisting of crisis, which she differentiates from stress and elaborates by including family coping), and the meaning and perception of the event—the "C" factor. As a construct for understanding the stress process, boundary ambiguity is discussed and a model is presented. Boss concludes that the *meaning* that an event holds for the family and its individuals is the key to answering why some families cope with stress whereas others fall into crisis.

"Family Violence," by Steinmetz, describes the historical roots of family violence, discusses definitional and methodological problems, and examines the theoretical perspectives and the major variables used in family violence research. Included in this chapter are statistics on the abuse of wives, husbands, children, parents, the elderly, and siblings. A variety of models is presented, and an assessment of future research needs is provided—

specifically, the need for longitudinal research designs and multidisciplinary research efforts.

Liss, in the chapter "Families and the Law," presents a historical overview, legal terminology, and definitions. These are followed by an analysis of the legal and social antecedents and consequences of divorce, child support, child custody, parental rights, parental abuse, interracial adoption, foster care, elderly abuse, and marital rape.

Although legal changes have a direct impact on families, social policies also influence marriage and family life. They determine what resources and options are available to various segments of the population. Moen and Schorr, in "Families and Social Policy," examine a variety of approaches to family policy; the relationship between families, policies, and social change; and the role of social science research in the formulation and evaluation of the social policies that affect families. The authors present three case studies: income support and employment policies; social security for the aged; and workplace policies for parents. They note that the United States is unique among industrialized nations in not providing a wide range of economic supports for families.

In the chapter "Family Life Education," Darling provides approaches, means, and strategies to increase the likelihood of successful family functioning. She describes the scope and focus of family life education, provides a conceptual framework based on an ecosystem approach, and discusses the role of families as educators. She addresses family life education as a public or private issue and the competency of those who are family life educators.

The final chapter, "Marital and Family Therapy," by Kaslow, addresses the options available for couples and families needing intervention. Following a historical scenario, the major schools of marital and family therapy are examined, including psychoanalytic, Bowenian, contextual–relational, experiential, communication–interactional, structural, strategic–systemic, behavioral, and problem solving. Kaslow concludes with a presentation of a multimodal model, essentially a dialectical approach, in an attempt to integrate the similarities of the approaches used by each therapeutic school.

CHAPTER 24

Family Power

Maximiliane E. Szinovacz

First, if so many people at so many different times have felt the need to attach the label power . . . to some Thing they believe they have observed, one is tempted to suppose that the Thing must exist. . . . The second and more cynical suspicion is that a Thing to which people attach many labels with subtly or grossly different meanings in many different cultures and times is probably not a Thing at all but many Things. (Dahl, 1957, p. 201)

It appears we have come full circle: less than two decades ago, power played such an insignificant role in family sociology that the term was not even mentioned in Christensen's handbook (1964). Now, some desperate scholars opt for a deletion of this same concept, claiming its "continued use" to be "conceptually unwarranted" and "misleading" (Turk, 1975, p. 94). Avoiding a concept and on the other hand, confining its use to simple social situations are common attempts to deal with complex social realities, but they do not lead to adequate theoretical solutions. Rather, as Blalock and Wilken (1979) pointed out, "we must . . . come to grips with a very complex reality by constructing models that contain a large number of variables that cannot be measured in any given study" (p. 325). Yet, the above citation from Dahl (1957) very likely conveys two fundamental truths about power: We are all aware that there is, indeed, such a "Thing," and many of us "agree to disagree" on the exact meaning of this "Thing." Thus, it seems vital to identify and address those issues in family power studies that, in the past, constituted major barriers to the improvement of theory and research.

One such barrier is evident in the continuous struggle for valid conceptualization and measurement of family power (cf. Olson & Cromwell, 1975b; Olson & Rabunsky, 1972; Safilios-Rothschild, 1970; Sprey, 1972; Turk, 1975; Turk & Bell, 1972). We learned fairly early that previous attempts to measure power were highly questionable, but we were given very few *concrete* suggestions about how to achieve more sophisticated measurements. Furthermore, failure to integrate such conceptual and methodological considerations led to rather single-handed efforts, particularly in the meth-

odological realm; Berger (1980) speaks rightly of a "measurement morass" (p. 220). It is obviously premature to discuss the validity of measurements without a clear understanding of the concepts that are to be measured. Recent developments show a trend not only to construct new measures rather than "make do with the old ones" (Meyer & Lewis, 1976), but also to address methodological problems with theoretical and conceptual issues in mind (cf. Hill & Scanzoni, 1982; Olson, 1977; Olson & Cromwell, 1975b; Scanzoni, 1979b; Scanzoni & Polonko, 1980; Scanzoni & Szinovacz, 1980; Szinovacz, 1981). Despite these recent efforts, we are still far removed from achieving valid, reliable, and theoretically sound operationalizations of family power.

The other most obvious "dead end" was the rather significant isolation from theory development and research on power relationships in groups other than the family (e.g., general sociological theory and political sociology), as well as in other disciplines (e.g., social psychology). This negligence seems particularly unfortunate because scholars in these fields very often addressed the same issues and dealt with the same problems encountered by family sociologists. Indeed, many of the recent developments in family power studies can be attributed to a reorientation in this respect.

Even though such words of caution are still necessary, some significant progress has been achieved in recent years. There is increasing consensus that family power relations should be studied from a process or *dynamic perspective* through examination of the antecedents and consequences of specific power structures, as well as through investigations of family interactions such as influence strategies, negotiation, or conflict management processes (Berger, 1980; Olson & Cromwell, 1975b; Safilios-Rothschild, 1969b; Scanzoni, 1979a,b; Scanzoni & Szinovacz, 1980). Consideration of the specific power issues pertinent to different stages of such processes or to specific family areas also led to a general demand for a *multidimensional* view of family power relations (Olson & Cromwell, 1975b; Safilios-Rothschild, 1970; Scanzoni, 1979b) and the development of family power typologies (Safilios-Rothschild, 1976a,b). Most important among these efforts are perhaps the various attempts to analyze family power relations within a broader the-

Maximiliane E. Szinovacz • Department of Individual and Family Studies, University of Delaware, Newark, DE 19716.

oretical framework such as exchange, conflict, or negotiation theories (Beckman-Brindley & Tavormina, 1978; LaRossa, 1977; Scanzoni & Szinovacz, 1980).

In order to overcome the current difficulties in family power research, at least two tasks need to be accomplished: the improvement of multidimensional conceptualizations and operationalizations of "family power" and the development of a theoretical framework that accounts for the complexity of "powering" processes (Sprey, 1972) but at the same time achieves that theoretical clarity and simplicity that is necessary to understand and explain complex social phenomena. Hence, the purpose of this chapter is twofold.

The first part deals with conceptual and methodological issues in family power research. Specifically, previous developments in the general sociological power literature are summarized and applied to the recurrent methodological problems encountered by family power researchers. It is hoped that this discussion will further clarify and provide a basis for designing new or improved family-power measures. Even though the purpose of this chapter is not to propose new methodologies, some recommendations concerning power measurement will also be presented.

In the second part of the chapter, a still tentative theoretical framework of family power relations is proposed. This framework emphasizes the complex and dynamic nature of family "powering" processes. Evidence both from family power studies and from small-group research is used to obtain a more complete picture of the many factors that influence ongoing power relationships. This framework should not only lead to a more systematic organization of relevant theoretical and research questions but may also provide some specific directions for future theory construction and research. It should demonstrate that we cannot fully understand power relations by relying on a very limited set of explanatory factors (i.e., tangible resources and gender norms) and on empirical evidence showing some statistical association between these factors and some "outcome power" indicators, while ignoring the conditions under which and the means through which power is exercised. It is not my intention to provide a *comprehensive review* of the many family-power studies conducted within the last two decades. Recent publications of such reviews would reduce this task to mere duplication (cf. Beckman-Brindley & Tavormina, 1978; Berger, 1980; Cromwell & Olson, 1975; McDonald, 1977a, 1980; Rollins & Thomas, 1979; Safilios-Rothschild, 1970; Scanzoni, 1979b; Szinovacz, 1977a).

Conceptual and Methodological Issues in Family Power Studies

Definition and Conceptualization of Power

In defining *power*, family sociologists usually rely on power definitions derived from general sociological or

socialpsychological theories.[1] *Power* is defined as the net ability or capability of actors (A) to produce or cause (intended) outcomes or effects, particularly on the behavior of others (O) or on others' outcomes (McDonald, 1980; Safilios-Rothschild, 1970; Scanzoni, 1979b; Szinovacz, 1977a).[2] However, the conceptual and operational implications of these definitions are not always recognized.

Power as Ability. There seems to be increasing agreement that "power is always potential" (Bierstedt, 1974, p. 236) and is therefore a kind of dispositional concept to be distinguished from behavioral acts indicating the use of power or *control* (cf. Bannester, 1969; Blalock & Wilken, 1979; Blau, 1964; Giddens, 1976; Gulliver, 1979; Lehmann, 1969; Nagel, 1975; Schopler, 1965; Sprey, 1975; Thibaut & Kelley, 1959; Winter, 1973; Wrong, 1979). This ability rests with the actor, even if it is not currently put to the test. But failure to use one's power over an extended time period may be interpreted as lack of power (Nagel, 1975). Dispositional concepts cannot be directly measured (Blalock & Wilken, 1979; Sprey, 1975). Rather, any operationalization of power has to be inferential and may rely either on those factors or "power bases" that are believed to determine this ability or on the observation or perception of the successful use of power. For instance, if we were primarily interested in an individual's physical power, we might assess this power either on the basis of diverse indicators of his or her physical strength (e.g., height or muscular development) or on the basis of his or her success in fighting. But neither indicator is sufficient to fully measure physical power as ability and to predict behavior. Our subject may be confronted by an even stronger person and thus may become the relatively less powerful in this relationship, or she or he may choose not to fight and may thus fail to exercise

---

[1]The most widely used sources are Weber (1947), Cartwright (1959), Homans (1974), Buckley (1967), Thibaut and Kelley (1959), Emerson (1962, 1972a,b, 1976), Winter (1973), and Blalock and Wilken (1979).

[2]In this context, the terms *actor* (A) and *other* (O) refer to individuals, groups, or larger social units. *Behavior* is defined broadly to include attitudes, beliefs, emotions, and so on, as well as overt acts. Power is not always used to achieve behavioral changes; it may also be used to retain the status quo or to reinforce currently existing conditions.

[3]Viewed from this perspective, resource theory is meaningful only if it refers to the *relative importance* of specific resources or power bases. Critics of this theory emphasize that it fails to consider power bases such as relative love or other intangible resources (Safilios-Rothschild, 1970, 1976b). It may very well be that Blood and Wolfe (1960) did not center on the most important power bases, but an extension of the theory to *all possible* power bases would render it very nearly tautological. The theory would then propose that actors who possess power bases do in fact make use of such bases.

her or his ability in a specific situation.[3] The insight that power as ability cannot be directly measured led to the abandonment of a search for *the* valid power measure and to the development of multidimensional power indicators designed to capture the divergent aspects of this ability or potential (Cromwell, Klein, & Wieting, 1975; Olson & Cromwell, 1975b; Olson & Rabunski, 1972; Szinovacz, 1981).[4]

Unit of Analysis. Apparently, family sociologists agree that family power is a 'system property' (McDonald, 1980), but this surmise is questionable. After all, power *is* defined as A's ability, not as a system attribute. *Individual power* refers to A's potency or mastery (A has the power to do *x*). As an actor's attribute it is nevertheless contingent on the object or the situational factors (e.g., the weight of a stone that A wants to lift). *Social power* (A has the power to get B to do *y* or A has power over B) reflects A's *net* ability to affect B's behaviors or outcomes, after the potential resistance forces of Other(s) and/or the costs arising from power exertion have been taken into consideration.[5] Social power, therefore, is "systemic" or "relational" in that it always implies a relationship among the actors (Cartwright, 1959; Champlin, 1970; Dahl, 1957, 1968; Harsanyi, 1962; Lehmann, 1969; Lewin, 1951; Weber, 1947). However, conceiving of power as a relational concept does not render it a "system property." Only the distribution of power, or perhaps more precisely the distribution of power bases, among group members represents a system property (cf. Rogers, 1974). To say that A is able to affect *specific behaviors* of O is obviously different from saying that the balance of power bases in a marriage is in favor of the husband. In addition, power may be viewed as a system property or system disposition if our focus is on the family's power vis-à-vis other social institutions (cf. Parsons, 1958, 1964; Rogers, 1974; Zimmerman, 1947).

Any analysis of power requires specification of the social relationship under consideration. In his review,

McDonald (1980) consequently pled for more stringent conceptualization of *family power* and distinguished marital, parental, offspring, sibling, and kinship power. We may thus describe power relations within the family system as a whole or within specific subsystems (e.g., between spouses, between parents and children, or between siblings). The major difference between power relations in dyads and in larger groups is that the latter allow coalition formation, and the mere possibility of coalitions may affect power relations within dyadic subsystems. Even though power relations within various family subsystems are likely to differ substantially, a general explanation of power relationships should apply to any of these subsystems. The specific characteristics of these subsystems would enter into this general theory as independent or intervening factors.

Intentionality and Effectiveness. Some scholars contend that the concept *power* should be reserved for occasions on which the ability to produce effects on others is "intended" and "foreseen" (Lehmann, 1969; Minton, 1972; Wrong, 1979). Lack of intentionality and/or effectiveness (foreseeable outcomes) indicates social influence, but not social power. This is not to say, however, that power has as its prerequisite the issuing of specific commands on the part of the power holder. Friedrich's notion (1963) of the "rule of anticipated reactions" implies that the other may fulfill the actor's intentions and thus submit to his or her power without receiving explicit commands. For instance, a housewife in charge of the family budget knows that she cannot spend big sums on clothes and that, if she did so, her husband would be likely to apply negative sanctions; that is, her husband has at least some control over her spending behaviors even if the issue is not explicitly discussed. In such cases, the other's behavior must, however, be clearly attributable to the actor, and it should occur without a considerable time-lag (between preferences and outcomes). Unsuccessful control attempts indicate "a breakdown of the (previous) power relation" (Wrong, 1979, p. 6).[6]

If we accept these restrictions, operationalizations of power must refer to the actor's intentions or preferences (cf. Nagel, 1975). To make a decision or to win a conflict (cf. Blood & Wolfe, 1960; Olson & Ryder, 1970) does not indicate power exertion unless it is ascertained that the actor actually *wanted* to make this decision or to win the conflict. Safilios-Rothschild (1976a,b) and Goode (1970) also called attention to this issue by emphasizing that women are often left with the implementation of routine household decisions, and the husband retains his right to veto specific procedures. To carry out such routine deci-

---

[4]Because dispositions are usually viewed as relatively stable, describing power as a disposition may divert the reader from the dynamic and changing nature of power relations. Power is a dispositional concept insofar as it constitutes an ability, but this "disposition" is dynamic and may change from situation to situation as well as over time (Rogers, 1974). The following terminology is used throughout this chapter: *power* constitutes A's net ability to cause intended effects on O; *control* refers to the actual and successful use of this ability and thus reflects exercised power (*control* and *exercised power* are used interchangeably). *Control attempts* are behavioral acts designed to exercise power. They may be successful and may thus result in power exertion by A. If unsuccessful, they indicate control on the part of O.

[5]The distinction between the effects on O's *behavior* and *outcomes* is similar to the differentiation between behavior and fate control (Kelley & Thibaut, 1978; Thibaut & Kelley, 1959).

[6]Dahl (1957) applied the concept of *negative power* to circumstances in which O is led to do the opposite of what A requested. The issue of intentionality is still one of the most widely discussed among power theorists. Some authors reject intentionality as a prerequisite of power (cf. Lukes, 1977, 1978).

sions may be rather costly to the wife (e.g., in terms of time and energy) and is thus not always consistent with her personal wishes (Szinovacz, 1975). If intentionality is not viewed as a necessary condition for control acts, cognitive elements (i.e., preferences) may be disregarded in power measures. Gottman (1979), for instance, defined *power*—or in his terminology, *dominance*—behaviorally as "asymmetry in predictability" (p. 71) (i.e., the degree to which behavior at time 2 can be predicted from A's and O's behaviors at time 1) but rejected the intentionality requirement made by Nagel (1975) and others.

It was precisely the issues of intentionality and effectiveness that led some family theorists to request an abolition of the power concept (cf. Turk, 1974, 1975). However, without such restrictions, the power concept can be applied to such a variety of social phenomena that it becomes virtually meaningless. To eliminate the cognitive element from power conceptualizations entails the same problems that Weber (1947, p. 112ff.) noted when discussing "social" action. On the other hand, eliminating the power concept (and substituting other equally complex concepts) may just enhance confusion and is probably a less effective route than maintaining the concept and increasing our efforts to conceptualize and operationalize specific power dimensions. Obviously, actors are not always fully aware of their preferences or intentions (cf. Roloff, 1980). However. research on power strategies indicates that actors are able to describe "what they do to get their way" (Falbo, 1977a). They also can distinguish between actual and preferred behavior patterns in family relationships (cf. Szinovacz, 1979a). What may be necessary to obtain valid answers to such questions is to concentrate on specific and relatively recent events.

Reputational Power.[7] Power as A's ability to effect intended behavior or outcomes in O should be distinguished from reputational power or power attributions. There can be little doubt that power attributions constitute an important element in power relationships. O's perception that A is powerful may enhance A's ability to affect O's behavior (Wrong, 1979), and A may also gain considerable advantages owing to O's underrating of his or her own potential. Raven and Kruglanski's concept (1970) of informational power implies the conscious use of this possibility on the part of A. Although power attributions are partially based on A's resources and past use of power, they are also contingent on specific perceptions and interpretations by O. For instance, power attributions seem to convey a unidimensional characterization of power relations and contain biases that preserve O's self-image (cf. Kaplowitz, 1978). Attributions not only affect actors' behavior toward each other (cf. Alexander & Lauderdale, 1977; Ryder, 1972) but may also

have important strategic, ideological, moral, and psychological consequences. Specifically, power attributions determine the likelihood of coalition formation, the evaluation of interactions in terms of norms of distributive justice, the assignment of responsibility, and the actors' cooperativeness (Kaplowitz, 1978; Wortman, 1975).

The conceptual and operational differences between power and control and "actual" versus reputational power are summarized in Table 1. Actual power as an ability or potential is never *directly* measurable. Actual control refers to the past use or exercise of power. Behavioral self-report data designed to measure this concept may rely either on comparisons between the actors' preferences and their reports of *specific* behavioral outcomes (cf. Szinovacz, 1979a) or on concrete descriptions of behavioral sequences (cf. Scanzoni & Szinovacz, 1980). Behavioral measures such as the revealed-difference technique (Strodtbeck, 1951), SIMFAM; (Straus & Tallman, 1971), the Inventory of Marital Conflict (IMC; Olson & Ryder, 1970), or Goodrich and Boomer's color-matching game (1963) as well as the major research paradigms used in social-psychological studies (cf. Rubin & Brown, 1975), also represent indicators of actual control. Self-report data such as Blood and Wolfe's decision-making scale (1960) or Heer's question (1962, 1963) "Who is boss?" reflect insiders' attributions of control. In order to obtain attributions of power (as potential), subjects would have to be asked to predict the family members' relative ability to affect specific outcomes. Whenever observers describe power relationships, their reports also constitute power attributions (e.g., interviewers' comments or the reports of participant observers, as in the case of most ethnographic data). According to this perspective, Olson's concept (1977) of insiders' and outsiders' realities requires an additional differentiation, namely, the distinction between observers' power attributions and relatively "pure" behavioral measures derived from the coding of audiovisually recorded interaction sequences.

Presence of Conflict. Another issue in power theory refers to the question of whether conflict functions as a necessary condition for power to be a relevant factor in social relationships (McDonald, 1980, p. 843). Confusion regarding this issue stems partially from the lack of distinction between overt conflict (i.e., conflict behavior or an open struggle) and conflict of interests (cf. Fink, 1968; Kriesberg, 1973). Authors who reject the notion of conflict as an essential element in power situations usually refer to overt conflict. For instance, McDonald (1980) argued that "power differentials may function directly to *suppress potential conflictual situations*" (p. 843; italics mine).

In the following discussion, *conflict* is defined as "incompatibility of goals" (cf. Duke, 1976, p. 237). Obviously, A's ability to effect intended behaviors or outcomes in O cannot be made contingent on whether O resists A's control attempts and thus chooses to engage in

---

[7]This terminology differs from Olson and Cromwell's (1975b) use of *potential* and *actual power*.

Table 1. Definitions and Indicators of Potential versus Exercised and Actual versus Reputational Power[a]

Potential versus exercised power	Actual versus reputational power		
	Actual	Reputational (insiders)	Reputational (outsiders)
Potential	A *can* cause specific effects on O. Not *directly* measurable.	O *perceives* that A *can* cause specific effects on O. Self-reports regarding A's ability to affect O's behavior or outcomes	Observer *perceives* that A *can* cause specific effects on O. Observers' reports regarding A's ability to affect O's behavior or outcomes.
Exercised (control)	A *has* caused specific effects on O. Behavioral self-reports or behavioral measures of control.	O *perceives* that A *has* caused specific effects on O. Self-reports regarding A's relative control over a specific event or outcome.	Observer *perceives* that A *has* caused specific effects on O. Observer's reports regarding A's relative control over a specific event or outcome.

[a]The terminology used here is partially derived from Nagel (1975) and Olson (1977).

an open struggle. O may accept A's suggestion either because he or she agrees with A or because resistance is considered too costly. It is only the former situation that implies power exertion under conditions of nonconflict. In this situation, the significance of A's control attempt depends on whether he or she expected resistance from O. It is proposed that control attempts and control are of relatively little significance to both Actors if both parties initially agree and if resistance on O's part is not expected (cf. Duke, 1976; Rollins & Bahr, 1976). This approach follows research traditions that conceive of resistance as a major factor in power relationships (Weber, 1947) or that insist on the "impositional" nature of power relations (Lehmann, 1969). It is implied not that all of A's goals are opposed by O, but that some divergence of interests between actors exists. For instance, actors may be committed to the same ultimate goals but may disagree on the means of achieving those goals (cf. Blalock & Wilken, 1979).

Of course, some situations occur that exhibit major properties of control events, but that only marginally or indirectly involve conflict over goals. Especially difficult to classify are situations of more-or-less subtle manipulation in which O is not aware of A's control attempts. The processes of redefining and changing subjective realities described by phenomenologists and existentialists (Berger & Kellner, 1964; Laing, 1969) probably constitute power exertion if A's intent is to achieve specific modifications in O's behaviors or outcomes (see also Sprey, 1972).

Also, unless the initiating party can be easily identified, lack of conflicting interests between the parties may cause serious measurement problems. If measurement of control relies on the statistical association between the actors' preferences and specific outcomes, high correlations between the actors' preferences would prevent the assessment of their relative control. Nagel (1975, p. 155)

consequently observed that conflict presence constitutes a necessary condition of power *measurement*. The importance of specific conflict characteristics for power exertion processes will be discussed in a later section of this paper.

Power, Influence, and Dominance. Another shortcoming in the family power literature stems from insufficient differentiation among related but divergent concepts, most notably, power, influence, and dominance. Following the previous discussion and Huston (1983), power differs from influence in regard to the dimensions of ability, intentionality, and effectiveness. In contrast to power, influence consists of causal relations between A's and O's behaviors. These causal relations can be unintentional, and the actors may be unable to achieve their desired goals. Huston (1983) characterized this difference well when he wrote:

Influence is a descriptive term, referring to instances in which events in one partner's chain are causally connected to events in the other's chain. . . . Power . . . refers to the ability to achieve ends through influence. Persons who fail to achieve their own ends (or worse yet, consistently defeat them) may be influential, but they are not generally considered by social scientists to be powerful. (p. 170)

The power definition we have presented above is content- and situation-specific; that is, it refers to A's ability to effect *specific* outcomes or behaviors in O, at a given point in time. Dominance, on the other hand, addresses the *overall* symmetry or asymmetry in relationships (Huston, 1983) and concerns the partners' relative *control* rather than their relative *power*. An individual may thus be said to be dominant if she or he controls a broader range of the other's behaviors and outcomes than vice versa (A's scope of control is greater than O's). We may, of course, extend assessments of power to a wide range of behaviors. But even then, it is still important to distinguish between asymmetries in power and in control. A spouse who is able to exert control may not make use of his or her potential. Or the less powerful partner may be quite dominant if the other fails to counteract his or her control attempts.

Dimensions of Power Relations: Descriptive and Explanatory Power Analysis

Family sociologists generally agree on the multidimensional nature of the power concept (McDonald, 1980; Olson & Cromwell, 1975b; Safilios-Rothschild, 1970; Scanzoni, 1979b; Szinovacz, 1977a). Attempts to specify power "dimensions" led primarily to the development of power typologies (cf. Safilios-Rothschild, 1976a). Here, power dimensions are viewed as the major constituents or elements of power relations (Dahl, 1957, 1968). In order to determine which elements must be considered to achieve a relatively complete picture of power relationships, it is useful to follow Nagel's distinction (1975) between descriptive and explanatory power analyses. At the descriptive level, our main concern rests with the *assessment* of a power relationship at a given point in time. Usually, this description refers to specific control events and may be operationalized as a causal relationship between the actors' preferences and outcomes (Nagel, 1975, p. 29). Nagel's concept of descriptive power analyses thus resembles the concept of outcome power used by family power scholars (cf. Olson & Cromwell, 1975b, p. 6). Because descriptive power analysis focuses on A's (net) effect on O's behaviors or outcomes, it is probably more appropriate to speak of A's *control* (i.e., exercised power) rather than *outcome power*. Such descriptions are necessarily static. Because power relations change continuously, we can assess control only at a given point in time. In order to *describe* control, it is neither necessary to investigate how A obtained the ability to control O nor how she or he went about exercising power. Thus, describing control means answering the following questions: To what degree was A able to achieve a specific goal in a specific relationship and under what costs? Has A been able to achieve similar effects on O in the past? Descriptive power analysis thus assigns a theoretical status to "powering processes" (Sprey, 1972) similar to that assumed by so-called black boxes in cybernetic models. In order to arrive at a relatively complete *description* of control, at least the following constituents or dimensions ought to be specified: the scope, the extension, and the amount of control (Dahl, 1957; Nagel, 1968, 1975, 1976). Harsanyi (1962) suggested the inclusion of two additional dimensions, namely, the opportunity costs to A and to O. These dimensions and their definitions are summarized in Table 3 and are discussed in detail under "outcomes" in the second part of the chapter.

It is only when we attempt to *explain* or predict power

that a dynamic conceptualization and careful investigation of "powering" processes become necessary.[8] Then, we are indeed required to provide answers to questions such as: Under which conditions are the actors most likely to exercise power? How do the actors go about exercising power? Which strategies are the most effective? What are the consequences of power exertion and the use of specific strategies for the relationship as a whole? From this perspective, family power processes are not restricted to acts of assertiveness or control during family interactions (Olson & Cromwell, 1975b); they include dynamics of power acquisition, strategy selection, and interactional consequences. Dimensions that ought to be included in explanatory power analyses are presented in Table 2 and are discussed throughout the second part of the chapter.

Methodological Issues

Recurrent Measurement Problems. Methodological problems continue to plague family power researchers (for critical reviews, see Beckman-Brindley & Tavormina, 1978; Eichler, 1981; Huston, 1983; Jacob, 1975; McDonald, 1977a, 1980; Olson & Cromwell, 1975a; Riskin & Faunce, 1972; Safilios-Rothschild, 1970). The most widely used self-report measure of power is Blood and Wolfe's decision-making scale (1960). Critics have argued that the scale fails to provide a representative sample of family decisions, neglects different stages of decision-making processes, and does not account for differences in the importance and the frequency of the included decision topics (Brinkerhoff & Lupri, 1978; Douglas & Wind, 1978; Gillespie, 1971; Janis & Mann, 1977; Olson, Cromwell, & Klein, 1975; Safilios-Rothschild, 1969a, 1970). Efforts to weigh decisions according to their importance did not produce consistent results (Price-Bonham, 1976). Other reviewers have requested that emphasis be put on contested decisions or on critical points in the decision-making process (Bahr, Bowerman, & Gecas, 1974; Davis, 1970; Davis & Rigaux, 1974; Kelley, 1977; Wilkes, 1975). The latter argument is usually tied to the more general demand for an investigation of decision-making *processes* or phases instead of the static outcome measure used by Blood and Wolfe (cf. Aldous, 1977; McDonald, 1977a). In addition, the relia-

---

[8]Nagel (1975) stated: "Thus, ascending levels of theoretical complexity are implied by different types of power measures. A simple model of the outcomes suffices to estimate exercised power from known preferences and outcomes. To explain exercised power or to attribute potential power, a static theory of power coefficients is needed. . . . To predict exercised power in the near future, one must add hypotheses about preferences. To attribute possible power, one needs a dynamic model of power coefficients; and to make long-term predictions of exercised power (should one wish to be so rash), the dynamic theory of power must be supplemented by extended predictions about preferences" (p. 174ff.).

bility or the unidimensionality of Blood and Wolfe's and similar scales has been questioned. Some studies show that different scaling and coding procedures result in divergent assessments of decision-making outcomes (Bahr, 1973; Cromwell & Wieting, 1975; Hesselbart & Bolling, 1979; Safilios-Rothschild, 1970; Szinovacz, 1977b, 1978; Szybillo, Sosanie, & Tenenbein, 1979).

Researchers using self-report measures also tend to neglect the inputs of family members other than the couple in the decision-making process, even though recent evidence suggests that children or extended-family members may actively participate in such decisions (Filiatrault & Ritchie, 1980; Heer, 1963; Liu, Hutchison, & Hong, 1974; McDonald, 1980). Although it became clear that reliance on one spouse (usually the wife) is methodologically unacceptable, the conceptual and methodological problems involved in studying couples or family groups have not been fully resolved (Huston & Robins, 1982; Thompson & Walker, 1982; Thomson & Williams, 1982). A series of studies were designed to estimate and explain the incongruence between husband and wife responses. The results from these studies generally indicated distinct differences between the spouses' answers, whereas the overall response patterns of husband-and-wife groups proved to be quite similar. Explanations of these differences referred to methodological inadequacies such as question ambiguity or social desirability effects, as well as substantive reasons such as role ambiguity or conflict between the spouses and their divergent interests and perceptions (Booth & Welch, 1978; Davis & Rigaux, 1974; Douglas & Wind, 1978; Granbois & Willett, 1970; Heer, 1962; Munsinger, Weber & Hansen, 1979; Niemi, 1974; Price-Bonham, 1977; Quarm, 1981; VanEs & Shingi, 1972; Wilkening & Morrison, 1963). Szinovacz (1984) argued that self-report data reflect the spouses' personal definition of the situation and may contain a cognitive dissonance bias if the marital reality deviates from their expectations. From this perspective, incongruent responses ought to be treated as "meaningful" evidence rather than as a purely methodological "problem." To obtain a complete picture of marital interaction processes, self-report data should be combined with evidence from observations or behavioral self-report data (McDonald, 1980; Olson, 1977; Olson & Cromwell, 1975a).

Even though self-report data have probably been subject to the heaviest criticism, various behavioral or observational measures of family power (e.g., variations of Bales' Interaction Process Analysis, Strodtbeck's revealed-difference technique, or various simulation games) have fared only slightly better (cf. Dovidio & Ellyson, 1982; Goodrich & Boomer, 1963; Hadley & Jacob, 1973; Mishler & Waxler, 1968; Olson & Ryder, 1970; Osmond, 1978; Raush, Barry, Hertel, & Swain, 1974; Schwartz, Tesser, & Powell, 1982; Straus & Tallman, 1971; Winter & Ferreira, 1967). One of the most widely held objections is that experimental settings and tasks cannot capture everyday marital interactions. Not only do spouses seem to behave differently in the laboratory and in the home (O'Rourke, 1963), but the data may further be biased owing to an "onstage" effect and to the actors' attempts at impression management (Heer, 1963; Liu et al., 1974; Tedeschi, 1981). Concern about the relationship between specific experimental settings and the displayed conflict behaviors, or about the relevancy of experimental tasks for the couple, also reduces the validity of observational or behavioral techniques (Glick & Gross, 1975; Klein, 1978; Klimoski, 1978). However, some researchers have found no task effects on their results (Jacob & Davis, 1973; Zuckermann & Jacob, 1979). Furthermore, coding of marital interactions is rather time-consuming and complex, and different procedures can lead to divergent results (Psathas, 1961; Waxler & Mishler, 1966). As in the case of Blood and Wolfe's scale (1960), many behavioral measures also present a static picture of marital interactions: frequency scores don't suffice to describe the ongoing dynamics of family decision-making, conflict management or negotiations (Aldous, 1977; Kelley, 1977). Some of the more recently developed sequential analyses are a promising step toward truly dynamic or process-oriented measures (Gottman, 1979; Gottman, Markman, & Notarius, 1977; Waxler & Mishler, 1975).

Comparisons of self-report and behavioral data have indicated low convergent and discriminant validity between different methods, but high intercorrelations among self-report and among observational data (Cromwell et al., 1975; Hadley & Jacob, 1973; Meyer & Lewis, 1976; Olson, 1969; Olson & Rabunsky, 1972; Szybillo et al., 1979; Thomas, Peterson, & Rollins, 1977; Turk & Bell, 1972). However, the results presented in these studies may not constitute conclusive evidence regarding the validity of various measurements. Observational and self-report data touch on divergent realities (outsiders' and insiders') and are thus inherently distinct (Olson, 1977, see also Table 1). Basic requirements of the multitrait–multimethod paradigm (Campbell & Fiske, 1959) were also not fulfilled. Specifically, the measures used in these comparisons often addressed different analytical concepts and did not refer to the same tasks or power domains, and the self-report scales were not tested for interitem reliability. If more stringent criteria are applied, somewhat stronger correlations between self-report and observational data can be achieved (Szinovacz, 1981).

Applying Conceptual Issues to Measurement. Failure to apply the conceptual issues discussed above in renewed measurement efforts is probably the single most important reason for the continuing operationalization problems in family power research. Incidentally, the many critical comments brought forward against previous power measures did not result in the development of new measures. With a very few exceptions (e.g., Hill & Scanzoni, 1982; Huston, 1983), power research in the 1970s was based on indicators developed during the 1960s.

Power, Control, and Attributions. One reason for the recurrent measurement problems may be that we were overambitious in our measurement efforts. At least some measures were intended to grasp the full complexity of family power relations. But power can be inferred only from descriptions or observations of past events. Because such descriptions or observations will always be restricted to a selected set of control events, generalizations to overall power structures or power relations in a group are inherently problematic. Such generalizations would require a relatively representative sample of control events, and the achievement of such representative instruments is highly improbable in the near future, if it is at all possible.[9] Rather than striving for representativeness, it may therefore be more realistic to acknowledge that control is always situationally specific and to concentrate our efforts on relatively complete descriptions of specific control events within selected domains (cf. Henshel, 1973; LaRossa, 1977). In order to obtain such descriptions, we may rely either on behavioral self-reports or on extended observations in laboratory or home settings.

Self-report data refer to *control attributions,* which are apparently strongly influenced by role expectations (Olson & Rabunsky, 1972) and by the family members' relative *attention* rather than by *person* control (Mishler & Waxler, 1968; Szinovacz, 1981). The influence of norms on control attributions does not represent a major methodological problem as long as we are aware that attributions are inherently biased by the subjects' perceptions and beliefs. Confounding attention and person control, on the other hand, constitutes a more serious measurement problem. If subjects' reports (or behavioral codes) reflect primarily the family members' *participation* in a discussion or a decision-making process (attention control) rather than their relative *effect* on specific outcomes or on each other's behavior (person control), then the validity of the measures must indeed be questioned. However, careful phrasing of questions and revision of behavioral codes in this regard may suffice to overcome this difficulty. Blood and Wolfe's decision-making scale (1960) and behavioral measures that rely primarily on the quantity of behavior acts (e.g., the number of control attempts and the number of interruptions) are particularly problematic in view of this issue.

Intentionality and Effectiveness

Family power researchers also disregard the issue of intentionality. Even authors who theoretically imply intentionality fail to ask subjects whether they *wanted* to make specific decisions, whether they had the final say on selected issues, or whether they *desired* to control family interactions. The revealed-difference technique implies a

somewhat artificial relationship between "preferences" and outcomes (i.e., the subjects' initial choice or solution and the joint decision outcome). It is not clear, however, whether spouses really strive to impose their initial solution on the partner.[10] Actors may change their preferences because of situational contingencies (shifting from an *individual* to a *joint* decision-making task) and in view of their joint future relationship. And in some cases they may choose not to exert power. This option is often overlooked, but it very likely constitutes an important element in power relations (cf. Molm, 1981a,b; Sprey, 1981).

In addition, the zero-sum character of many revealed-difference methods and the ahistorical character of laboratory tasks (neglect of the couple's conflict-management and power-exertion history) seem to enhance such artificial effects. The social-psychological research literature provides clear evidence that individuals behave differently in zero-sum compared to mixed-motive games (cf. Rubin & Brown, 1975). Behaviors in both settings are important, but restricting experimental settings to one type of situation necessarily results in one-sided findings. Also, experimental tasks can easily be modified to represent either situation. For instance, the IMC could be converted into a mixed-motive task by requesting subjects to come up with their own solution to the problems presented in the vignettes rather than having to choose between two predetermined alternatives. In this case, spouses could come up with new solutions that might not only allow both spouses to "win" to some degree, but that would also enable them to apply a wider variety of conflict-management and power-exertion strategies. It could also be argued that family members are more likely to revert to their habitual interaction patterns if they are presented with relatively unstructured tasks and are allowed to develop their own solutions.

In experimental tasks, family members tend to avoid behaviors that may have adverse consequences for their relationship. This effect can probably be reduced by assuring a high relevancy of the experimental task. One way to achieve high relevancy is to ask the subjects to discuss issues that are known to be conflictual in their relationship (e.g., through previous questions on family conflicts), although such procedures may pose ethical problems.

Without reference to intentionality (e.g., Gottman, 1979), interpretation of the results may become difficult. Is it correct to assume that any causal relationship between past and future behaviors indicates control? What

[9] Some exchange and equity theorists have proposed representative lists of relevant exchanges or inputs/outputs (Longabough, 1963; Traupmann, 1976).

[10] In using the IMC (Olson & Ryder, 1970), I found spouses consciously giving in or taking back their initial solutions so as to achieve relatively balanced win scores. In some cases, such proceedings led to quite illogical solutions; that is, the couple would agree that the husband in the vignette was "responsible" for the conflict but nevertheless decided that things should be done his way. Often, a spouse would comment that she or he wouldn't persist on a solution because the preceding issue had been handled her or his way.

about imitation or coincidental behavior similarities? And what about the delegation of unimportant decisions to the other party, in some cases even against his or her wishes (cf. Safilios-Rothschild, 1976b)?

In order to achieve valid measures that indicate the *amount* of control (see Table 3), some consideration should be given to the relative effectiveness and the consistency of reported or observed control events. Thus, we need to specify to what degree family members modified their own position on an issue owing to control by other family members, and whether specific outcomes are rather exceptional or correspond to previous behavior patterns in the family. Degree of control may be assessed through comparisons of the family members' overall "position modifications" (cf. Scanzoni & Szinovacz, 1980; Spector, 1975) throughout an experimental task or on the basis of detailed behavioral self-reports. Consistency can obviously be disregarded if we are dealing with infrequent control events. In the case of recurrent issues, some information on consistency may be obtained through questions pertaining to the probability of similar outcomes, past experiences in similar situations, or re-tests and longitudinal studies.

Finally, even though some researchers consider weighing the importance, relevance, or frequency of decisions or issues (Olson & Ryder, 1970; Price-Bonham, 1976; Safilios-Rothschild, 1976a,b; Szinovacz, 1977b, 1978), these attempts are only a first step toward measuring the costs of power. The importance of the issue to A or O refers only to *indirect* costs (How essential is it for A to get O to comply with his or her requests? What does O lose if she or he submits to A's wishes?). A complete estimate of costs necessitates the measurement also of *direct* costs (What must A do or risk to get O to comply? What must O do or risk to effectively resist A?). Long-term consequences of power exertion are often overlooked. For instance, A may successfully control O's behavior over some time but, by doing so, exhausts his or her relevant power bases or resources (a husband who gives his wife an additional allowance whenever she threatens to assume gainful employment will eventually end up with very few discretionary funds of his own). Of course, this argument applies only to some resources (e.g., money) and not to others (e.g., self-esteem). Also, the use of specific power means or bases may prove effective in the short run but may decrease A's power in the long run. The continuous use of coercion, for example, may undermine A's other power bases, particularly his or her referent power, and may thus decrease A's ability to affect O's behavior in the long run (French & Raven, 1959; Raven & Kruglanski, 1970). On the other hand, provision of the same reward may lead to satiation (a marginal utility problem). Some information on direct costs could be obtained through evaluation, by the subjects, of the outcomes, as well as of the effectiveness of specific power bases and means. The assessment of long-term consequences probably requires longitudinal data.

Unit of Analysis. Power research may pertain to the family group as a whole or to different family subsystems. Methodologically, it seems important to obtain information from all those family members who usually participate in decisions or negotiations concerning the selected issues. In addition, patterns of coalition formation always need to be considered.

It therefore seems clear that power measurement requires more detailed information than can usually be obtained through a self-report scale or an experimental task. In order to adequately describe even single control events, we need to specify at least the following dimensions: the goals or realistic preferences of each actor[11] and the actual outcome of a decision or negotiation process, the consistency and effectiveness of their control attempts, the identification of those actors usually involved in the control event under consideration, and the costs incurred by each actor. At our current level of knowledge, such information can probably best be obtained through a combination of in-depth interviews and observations. We can hardly hope to achieve valid control measures unless we realize that single scales or brief experimental tasks provide insufficient information to estimate control.

Toward an Explanatory Analysis of Family Power Relations

The focus on resource theory and its modifications in family power research (cf. Blood & Wolfe, 1960; Burr, 1973; Rodman, 1967; Rollins & Bahr, 1976) led to a one-sided perspective of family power dynamics. Specifically, resource theory is restricted to the explanation of determinants of family power and neglects the contingencies and processes of power exertion (control), as well as the consequences of such processes. For a descriptive analysis of power, a static model of control may suffice, but an explanation of power relations must reflect the complexity and dynamics of ongoing "powering" processes.

In the following sections, an explanatory model of family power relations is presented. At the present stage of theory development and research on family power, this model remains tentative. No attempt is made to present a set of interrelated propositions, nor are any claims made about the completeness of the model. The major objective underlying this model is to *integrate existing theory and research* within a *process framework* of family power relations. The model is primarily *orientative* in the sense that it gives structure to current theoretical and empirical contributions. The model draws attention to the *complexity* of ongoing power processes through a relatively detailed discussion of the many factors or variables that have been shown to affect power relations in families and

---

[11]Idealistic desires or wishes (e.g., a housewife dreams of never doing housework again) should not be treated as preferences in this sense.

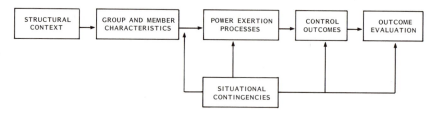

Figure 1. A dynamic model of family power exertion. The causal sequences represent one single power exertion event.

other small groups. In addition, major model dimensions are presented in a causal sequence, but many of these causal linkages require empirical support. It should be emphasized that the model as a whole contains too many factors to be empirically testable. How specific research questions can be derived from the model is discussed in the concluding section of this chapter.

In discussing the model dimensions, some of the problematic issues in family power research will also be addressed. Lack of relevant research, particularly on power exertion processes in families, necessitates reliance on data from other small-group research. Because findings from such studies may not always be applicable to family groups (cf. Reiss & Blehar, 1979; Vincent, Weiss, & Birchler, 1975; Winter, Ferreira, & Bower, 1973; Walters, 1982), such generalizations ought to be taken as hypothetical and as requiring further empirical inquiry.

The theoretical perspective underlying this model is eclectic; it borrows particularly from exchange, conflict, and negotiation theories, but it also uses some basic assumptions from symbolic interaction theory. The basic outline of the model, as demonstrated in Figure 1, was inspired by Strauss's ''general paradigm of negotiation'' (1978) and subsequent modifications of this paradigm by Szinovacz and Scanzoni (1979) and Scanzoni and Szinovacz (1980). It was also informed by other general models of power and bargaining processes (e.g., Blalock & Wilken, 1979; Druckman, Rozelle & Zechmeister, 1977; Gulliver, 1979; Janis & Mann, 1977).

Explanatory power analysis focuses on the dynamics of ''powering'' processes, their determinants, and their consequences (cf. Berger, 1980; Nagel, 1975; Scanzoni, 1979b; Sprey, 1972, 1975). Generally, the model addresses the question: How can we explain ongoing processes of power exertion (or control) in family groups? It is proposed that control processes always occur within a given societal context and are therefore influenced by general sociostructural conditions. In addition, ongoing control processes are shaped by specific group and member characteristics of the family. The structural and the group–member characteristics represent relatively stable dimensions, at least for the time period of ongoing control processes. Although the group and member characteristics are themselves contingent on structural context factors, they feed into the power exertion or control processes. Which group or member characteristics are rele-

vant and in which ways they affect such processes are at least partially determined by situational contingencies. Situational contingencies are also assumed to directly influence the control processes, their outcomes, and their evaluation. Finally, the model postulates direct causal relationships between power exertion processes and outcomes, as well as outcome evaluation and consequences.

The causal sequence outlined by Strauss (1978) and incorporated into this model represents one single control event. Further events build on past experiences and outcomes and are therefore contingent on such prior events. The proposed model deals with *specific control events;* it does not attempt to explain the overall power distribution among family members. The focal points of the general model outlined in Figure 1 are control processes and control outcomes. The concept of control or power exertion processes (see footnote 4) includes all those behaviors and behavioral sequences that occur during a control event and that represent attempts by each actor to affect the other actors' behaviors or outcomes. Control outcomes constitute the result of such processes in terms of A's net effect on O's behaviors or outcomes, at a given point in time.[12] The *specific* dimensions or variables pertaining to the *general* dimensions outlined in Figure 1 are

---

[12]Some authors described similar processes under the general construct of *family decision-making* (cf. Blood & Wolfe, 1960; Scanzoni & Szinovacz, 1980). This terminology may be misleading. Not only has its use led to the unfortunate operationalization of control as *participation* in decisions, but the concept is also widely applied to rational choice behavior in the psychological, home economics, and consumer behavior literature (cf. Janis & Mann, 1977; Paolucci, Hall, & Axinn, 1977). Because these literatures often refer to *family* decision-making, control and rational choice behaviors may be easily confounded. There are, however, important differences between the two concepts. Decision-making as rational choice behavior does not necessarily entail *social* power processes. Individuals can make decisions for themselves that have no immediate consequences for others. What has usually been labeled *family* decision-making (emphasizing rationality and effectiveness) probably comes close to the notion of *family problem-solving* (cf. Klein & Hill, 1979). Power exertion may occur as *part* of the decision-making process, but not all decision-making behaviors involve power exertion. On the other hand, power exertion is not always tied to decision-making processes among family members.

Table 2. Dimensions of a Model of Family Power Exertion[a]

Structural context
Social positions
Opportunity structures
Normative constraints and orientations
Group and member characteristics
Power bases and interdependence (tangible and nontangible resources, authority, compliance, alternatives)
Group composition (coalition, number of children, life cycle stage, household composition)
Personality (authoritarianism, machiavellianism, cognitions, internal-external locus of control, self-concept, power motives)
Other member characteristics (ethnic and cultural background, age, sex, socioeconomic status)
Self–other orientations (interpersonal orientation, bargaining interests, trust, fairness, gender norms, past experiences)
Situational contingencies
Conflict characteristics (content, objectives, target, structure, intensity, duration, available outcomes)
Other situational contingencies (time pressure, presence of third parties)
Power exertion processes
Position modifications
Power exertion strategies (reinforcement control, informational control, ecological control)
Power resistance strategies (psychological reactance, public commitment, anticipatory attitude change, inoculation, blocking outcomes, creating demands, extension of power network, devaluation of contributions)
Control outcomes
Scope, extension, and amount of control
Costs of power exertion

[a]This table contains the component dimensions of the major model dimensions shown in Figure 1.

summarized in Table 2 and are discussed in the following sections.

The most important feature of this model is perhaps that a family member's ability to control other members is viewed as variable; that is, it may change over time, varies according to the power domain or in regard to specific situational contingencies, and so forth. At some times, just one or two of the proposed influence factors may be operant, and at other times, power exertion can be a very involved process and its outcome contingent on a complex interplay of many factors. The model implies a critique of family power theories that rely on only a few explanatory factors (e.g., resource theory).

Structural Context

Exchange theorists explain power relations primarily in terms of the exchange partners' individual contribu-

tions and their relative dependence on each other's need gratifications within the relationship (cf. Blau, 1964; Emerson, 1976). Critics of this approach conceive of this assumption as a legitimization of manifest social discrimination against women rather than as an explanation of their powerlessness (Bell & Newby, 1976; Gillespie, 1971). More general arguments against exchange theory emphasize its neglect of social context variables and its ahistorical perspective (Befu, 1980; McDonald, 1981). It seems clear that power relations in families cannot be separated from the social context in which they occur. Specifically, the family members' positions and roles within and outside the family, their access to opportunity structures, and normative orientations provide the framework within which family power processes occur.

Social Positions. Family members occupy ascribed and achieved social positions and roles that partially define their intrafamilial control potential. Which positions and roles are accessible to or appropriate for each family member depends on sociocultural factors. In our society, the husband still holds the primary responsibility for being the family provider, whereas the wife is expected to take charge of household management even if specific tasks are shared by the spouse (cf. Bahr, 1975; Hesselbart, 1976, 1978; Szinovacz, 1979b,c). Similarly, men are expected to behave in a competitive and sometimes even aggressive manner, whereas women are encouraged to demonstrate emotionality and helplessness (Komarovsky, 1946, 1976; Maccoby & Jacklin, 1974). It is only to some degree that the nature of these positions or roles *per se* has direct implications for the family members' relative power; more important, perhaps, are the societal importance and status value of these positions and roles as well as their consequences for the family members' relative dependence on each other (cf. Berger, Zelditch, Anderson, & Cohen, 1972; Emerson, 1976). As incumbent of the position of provider and household head, the husband-father may be granted *authority* (legitimized control) over a wide range of family decisions. Even though his right to control such decisions can be challenged by his wife, socially reinforced authority— or, more precisely, "formally institutionalized power" (Buckley, 1967, p. 195)—is reinforced by sanctions, ranging from disapproval by relevant others to legally enforced sanctions, that render countercontrol efforts more costly for the wife (Bannester, 1969; Bierstedt, 1974; Nye, 1978).[13]

But legitimized control is certainly not the only structural basis of family members' power relations. *Age and sex norms* can determine which roles selected persons or groups may play and whether or not they may assume specific prestigious societal positions. Some societies at-

[13]Until recently, most countries' laws required that the wife take residence with her husband.

tribute mythical or superhuman power to men (e.g., medicine men); others respect and grant deference to women owing to their presumed association with fate or their intuitive and sometimes prophetic abilities (Janeway, 1975). Also, as Sanday (1981) observed, authority can be "*ascribed* as a natural right due the female sex when a long-standing magicoreligious association between maternity and fertility of the soil associated women with social continuity and social good" (p. 114). Similarly, kinship rules (descent, residence) may be associated with male or female dominance within a broad sphere of activities (Johnson & Hendrix, 1982).

Age norms can qualify the significance of ascribed sex roles. In some relatively patriarchal societies, elderly women or widows are ganted high social prestige that affects their power position vis-à-vis other family members (Queen & Habenstein, 1974, p. 115; Salamon & Keim, 1979; Stephens, 1963, p. 301). And achievement of socially valued positions is only rarely fully determined by normative prescriptions. Ownership of land property, inheritance of property or assets among high-status women, and occupational achievement may all reduce the impact of the husband's authority on marital power relations (cf. Lee, 1977; Pool, 1978; Rogers, 1975; Sussman, Cates, & Smith, 1970).

Occupancy of specific statuses or positions not only affects the family members' power bases (especially authority and tangible and intangible resources) but also regulates *role expectations and behavior patterns,* which may either reinforce or counterbalance the partners' relative resource potential (Burns, 1973, 1977). For instance, women's position as the "weaker sex" allows them to request services and to assume a position of helplessness that evokes feelings of social responsibility in others (Berkowitz & Daniels, 1972; Field, 1974; Schopler & Bateson, 1965; Schwartz, 1975). Also, as long as sex is viewed as something women do *for* men, women can and, indeed, do use sexual favors in bargaining (Komarovsky, 1964; Rubin, 1976). The husband's authority is based on and is therefore contingent on his success in the occupational world. Unemployment or insufficient income consequently reduce his control over family matters (Elder, 1974; Komarovsky, 1964). On the other hand, authority may be used (or better, abused) for manipulative purposes. Specifically, a husband may use his authority to define his power domains and thus extend his impact on family issues beyond the normatively prescribed scope (Claessens, 1970; Joas, 1973; Ryder, 1972).

Family sociologists have tended to overemphasize the husband's authority and his provider role as bases for his power position in the family (cf. Burr, 1973; Rodman, 1967; Rollins & Bahr, 1976). This viewpoint neglects other positions that people can obtain and roles that they may assume that offset the "traditional" and "institutionalized" power (Buckley, 1967) inherent in the husband's position as household head. Because of the diffuse character of family roles (Parsons & Bales, 1955), it is always the *entire range* of positions that family members occupy and the full repertory of roles that they play that enter into family control processes.

Access to Opportunity Structures. Occupancy of specific social positions not only gives the incumbent definite rights and duties but also opens (or bars) access to opportunity structures. Owing to the priority ascribed to the husband's economic roles (cf. Laub-Coser & Rokoff, 1971), women are often denied equal *access to economic and social opportunities* (income, social contacts, and skills). Especially the resulting economic dependence of wives on their husbands was singled out early as the most important barrier to wives' equality in marital relations (Engels, 1884). Changes in the accessibility of these opportunity structures, as evident in the increasing labor-force participation of married women, result in a shift in the spouses' relative material resources and thus possibly in more balanced power relations (cf. Bahr, 1975; Cunningham & Green, 1979; Rank, 1982; Szinovacz, 1979c). Such new opportunities also "allow" women to develop assertive skills, to assume more tough bargaining strategies, or to reject previously tolerated outcomes (Cagle, 1975; Hood, 1983; Scanzoni, 1972, 1975, 1977, 1978).

However, explaining marital power relations entirely in terms of relative economic and social opportunities in the population at large runs the risk of encompassing dual fallacy.

First, *factors other than economic resources* play an important role, particularly in intimate power relations, and these factors have been neglected by both resource and exchange theorists (Boulding, 1962; Chadwick-Jones, 1976; Eichler, 1981; Heath, 1976; Safilios-Rothschild, 1970). The heavy emphasis on tangible resources also obscures the fact that women may have some opportunities that are barred to men. For instance, gender-role differences in socialization that hinder the development of expressive skills in men could constitute an important resource for women in intimate relationships. A husband may very well feel that "he has to make good" for his (learned) inability to express emotions or to demonstrate affection by providing other rewards for his wife. Also, even though men tend to exhibit aggressive behaviors that serve as coercive potential, women may, to some degree, counteract such behaviors through learned response patterns (Maccoby & Jacklin. 1974, p. 242). Hewitt (1976) suggested that "power and authority lessen the need for sensitive or accurate role-taking," and that "accurate role-taking is a useful tool for controlling others" (p. 142). Women may thus learn how to counterbalance socially or even biologically (physical force) predetermined advantages of the partner. On the other hand, sex-role socialization that places heavy emphasis on female submissiveness and dependence may reinforce structural discrepancies in the access to societal positions and may hinder women's performance in positions of authority (Jacobson, Antonelli, Winning, & Opeil, 1977; Santee & Jackson, 1982; Thompson, 1981).

Second, the *aggregate distribution of opportunities* in the population at large may not be characteristic of individual families or selected population groups. Career wives may have equal or more access to economic opportunities than their husbands. Working-class or underemployed husbands whose access to economic resources is limited can also suffer a decrease in their authority (Komarovsky, 1964; Rubin, 1976). This lack of legitimate and resource power may then lead the husband to resort to violence as the "ultimate resource" (Allen & Straus, 1975; Goode, 1971).

Finally, the unequal allocation of opportunities that is reflected in the family members' needs and reward potentials entails not only different rights but also *different obligations* for the family members. In our society, children are highly dependent on their parents for physical and psychological support until they reach late adolescence. Parents, consequently, have the duty to provide for their children for a long time, an obligation strongly reinforced by sanctions, including the removal of the child from the parents' home. In societies that grant children earlier access to opportunity structures (e.g., through alternative social supports—for instance, from extended-family members, and through earlier participation in economic activities), such strong and long-term dependence on the parents may not occur (cf. Aries, 1962). In other words, the exploitive potential inherent in family members' unequal access to opportunity structures is often curtailed by institutionalized norms and regulations that, to some degree, "protect" the weaker parties. The traditional housewife was entitled to economic support from her husband. With the increasing emphasis on equality, some countries are now beginning to adopt laws that make both spouses responsible for economic provisions (cf. Glendon, 1975; Szinovacz, 1979b).

Different access to opportunity structures also evolves from divergent *restrictions of autonomy,* especially according to sex and age. The implicit expectation that women need to be protected from physical or sexual assault (whatever the true motive underlying this assumption) results in a series of strategies that restrict their freedom, such as confinement, close protection, and other normative constraints. These restrictions prevent women from taking part in a series of social activities, at least when alone (Fox, 1977). Changes in gender norms are evident in new family laws curtailing the husband's authority. For instance, several countries are now abandoning previous legislation that restricted women's autonomy both inside and outside the family (cf. Kamerman & Kahn, 1978; Lipman-Blumen & Bernard, 1979). Similarly, close supervision of children and youths may not always be motivated by mere security reasons but may constitute an effort to control their behaviors through restricting otherwise available opportunities.

Normative Constraints and Orientations. Normative contraints and orientations play an important role in power and exchange relations (Cook & Emerson, 1978;

McDonald, 1981; Tallman & Ihinger-Tallman, 1979). Power is directly affected by norms that define the *importance of rewards and costs* that the actors may provide for or impose on each other. Because power is contingent on the partners' relative dependence on each other, perceptions of relative dependence are based on societal and personal evaluations of specific gratifications as well as on the available alternatives (Blalock & Wilken, 1979; Blau, 1964; Burgess & Conger, 1974; Emerson, 1972a, 1976; Tallman & Tallman-Ihinger, 1979). Institutionalized (and internalized) role expectations constitute one element of such evaluations. For instance, a housewife is likely to place great importance on the husband's fulfillment of the provider role and may thus regard herself as highly dependent on his economic contributions, whereas a career woman probably attributes greater importance to the husband's participation in familial tasks and depends on him for the performance of such services. In traditional marriages, the spouses' relative power would then be primarily a function of the spouses' performance of instrumental tasks, whereas modern couples would value the reciprocal fulfillment of emotional gratifications (cf. Ingoldsby, 1980; Scanzoni & Szinovacz, 1980). Such norms could be one reason that working-class wives seem to gain more power owing to employment than middle-class wives (cf. Bahr, 1975). Because working-class spouses rely heavily on same-sex friends for emotional support, power relations between the spouses may be centered on the relative fulfillment of instrumental roles (cf. Komarovsky, 1964; Rubin, 1976).

In addition, the *general market value* of specific contributions constitutes an important element of the spouses' evaluation (cf. Heer, 1963). Housewives may feel dependent on their husbands not because the wives' services are intrinsically unimportant, but because their market value is comparatively low. *Available alternatives* also have to be judged in the light of societal and normative constraints. Because such alternatives are, to some degree, socially predetermined, they result in implicit power asymmetries between the partners (e.g., double standards). Institutionalized (and internalized) norms prescribe the *domains and amount of authority* that may legitimately be used by the incumbents of social positions (Buckley, 1967; Scanzoni, 1979b). If control remains within prescribed or socially accepted limits, it is usually less costly to A and resistance is more costly to O than power exertion beyond such limits. Thus, the acceptance of the husband's authority implies asymmetry in the relationship unless his advantage is counterbalanced by *additional* contributions on the part of the other family members. Nevertheless, even if the husband is granted a high level of authority, there are clear expectations that he should not interfere in certain domains. Most of the studies on family decision-making reveal that some decision areas are defined as the husband's and others as the wife's, and a third group constitutes overlapping decision areas (Blood & Wolfe, 1960; Centers, Raven, & Rodrigues, 1971; Szinovacz, 1978).

Normative orientations also prescribe *when and how power should be used*. For instance, as long as the husband maintains his position as household head, women are expected to demonstrate submissiveness—at least in public. Societal norms thus reinforce a "myth of male dominance" even if the wife predominates within the family (Rogers, 1975). Also, there are often distinct expectations about which power strategies or bargaining tactics are appropriate for specific relationships or within specific social settings. With increasing gender-role modernity, marital negotiations not only may shift from implicit to more explicit tactics but may also involve more competitive or tough negotiating on the part of the wife (Hershey & Werner, 1975; Lantz, Schultz, & O'Hara, 1977; Scanzoni & Szinovacz, 1980). Similarly, social or even legal sanctions can be applied if power exertion exceeds the accepted range of coercive behaviors. For instance, current public concern regarding wife abuse or "marital rape" may indicate decreased societal acceptance of physical coercion on the part of the husband (Gelles, 1974, 1979; Steinmetz, 1977; Straus, 1976, 1978b).

Finally, social norms and role expectations set the *context within which marital exchanges and power relations are evaluated*. What is judged to be fair or acceptable depends not only on the partners' personal values, but also on social norms and contingencies. In a sex-role-traditional marriage, the wife appreciates her husband's help with household tasks as a special favor and thus feels that she ought to reciprocate with special services, whereas a sex-role egalitarian wife may very well take her husband's participation in household tasks for granted. Similarly, normative constraints influence the degree to which exchange partners accept and thus remain in relationships that violate their expectation of distributive justice and fairness (Bagarozzi & Wodarski, 1977; Bredemeier, 1978; Burgess & Conger, 1974). What is acceptable is not always fair, but it may still constitute the best available alternative. Therefore, relatively unsatisfactory marriages are maintained owing to the unfairly treated partner's lack of viable alternatives (cf. Lewis & Spanier, 1979). Partners evaluate their relationship not only in terms of each other's relative contributions, but through comparisons with relevant or similar others (Bahr, 1972; Berger *et al.*, 1972; Homans, 1974). A wife may therefore consider marital exchanges just or at least acceptable if she is "better off" than most other wives, even if she feels that she contributes more to the relationship than does her husband (Willis & Frieze, 1980).

In summary, structural context factors provide a general framework within which family power and exchange relations operate. They influence the availability of selected power bases to individual family members. Social norms prescribe the rights and duties of status incumbents and thus affect the costs of power exertion over specific domains. Such norms may also set standards for appropriate behaviors and may thus set some constraints on the specific power-exertion strategies that family members may use and the costs incurred through the selection of certain strategies. In addition, these norms directly (through social and normative constraints or alternatives) or indirectly (through the internalization of values and norms) predetermine the importance attached to specific contributions, the potential escape routes (Martin, 1977), and the partners' evaluation of power and exchange relations.

Group and Member Characteristics

Power Bases and Interdependence. Whereas the family process literature traditionally focused on the consequences of family power structuring (Beckman-Brindley & Tavormina, 1978; Cromwell & Olson, 1975), family sociologists have concentrated on those factors that determine family power relations. Much of the current research on marital power was initiated by Blood and Wolfe's attempt (1960) to explain power in terms of the family members' relative resources. These authors proposed that socially valued resources such as education, income, or occupational status have become more viable determinants of marital power relations than normative factors, that is, the husband's authority. Studies in the United States and highly industrialized European countries seemed to confirm this notion (Blood & Wolfe, 1960; Centers *et al.*, 1971; Kandel & Lesser, 1972; Lamouse, 1969; Lupri, 1969; Michel, 1967), but research in less developed countries soon revealed that normative factors cannot be discarded as power determinants of marital power relations (Buric & Zecevic, 1967; Cooney, Rogler, Hurrell, & Ortiz, 1982; Cromwell, Corrales, & Torsillo, 1973; Safilios-Rothschild, 1967). Later studies indicated that norms and the spouses' relative resources interact in their impact on marital control or decision-making patterns (Burr, Ahern, & Knowles, 1977; Conklin, 1979; Oppong, 1970; Papanek, 1969; Rank, 1982; Richmond, 1976; Szinovacz, 1978). This insight led to the development of *resource theory in a cultural context* and *normative resource theory*, which integrate both resources and norms into a more comprehensive explanation of marital power relations (Burr, 1973; Lupri, 1970; Rodman, 1967, 1970; Rollins & Bahr, 1976).

Meanwhile, resource theory has been widely criticized. Not only is the empirical evidence on which the theory rests highly questionable (McDonald, 1977a, 1980; Safilios-Rothschild, 1970), it also seems that the theory itself constitutes an oversimplified and rather static approach to marital power relations (cf. Eichler, 1981; Johnson, 1975; Scanzoni, 1979b; Sprey, 1972). The conceptualization by Blood and Wolfe (1960) on *how* resources affect marital power rests on two questionable assumptions:

First, Blood and Wolfe's approach implies that marital power relations are a *direct* function of the number of selected (mainly tangible) objective properties the family members possess. This approach neglects the fact that the relevance of such properties rests on their perception and evaluation by the other family members (Levinger 1959). A similar argument is often brought forward against behavioristic conceptualizations of rewards by some exchange theorists (e.g., Homans, 1974). Critics of this orientation argue that what is rewarding or what is an important contribution depends on the individuals' perceptions and their definition of the situation (Abrahamson, 1972; Singelmann, 1972). More recently, Blalock and Wilken (1979) offered a complex model of power in which a clear distinction is made between objective properties and resources:

A's resources or sources of power will depend upon the goals, utilities, and subjective probabilities of actor B, and perhaps of other actors as well. . . . Thus resources must also be distinguished from any objective properties, positions, or characteristics that A may have. . . . We may look upon the conversion of objective properties into resources as a problem of measurement. . . . This measurement or conversion process. . . will necessarily involve assumptions about the motivational states of other actors. (p. 345)

These authors' work, as well as other statements on bargaining and influence processes, increasingly stress the importance of the actors' subjective perceptions, beliefs, or evaluations (Gulliver, 1979; Tedeschi, 1981). It seems rather paradoxical that such subjective factors have frequently been ignored by students of the highly intimate and particularistic exchange relations typical among family members.

Second, it is probably incorrect to say that relative power is contingent on the family members' relative *contributions*. Rather, if power reflects independence (Emerson, 1962, 1976), it is the relative *neediness* of the family members *and* the degree to which their needs are satisfied in the relationship and can be satisfied *only* in the relationship that determine relative power. Thus, power relations are altered not only by changes in the members' relative resources, but also by decreasing one's dependency on the other (cf. Blau, 1964). Alternative opportunities and/or the spouses' relative commitment to the relationship must be considered if one is to obtain an estimate of their relative dependence on each other and on the maintenance of the relationship (Eichler, 1981; Johnson, 1978; Leik & Leik, 1972; Levinger, 1976; Thibaut & Kelley, 1959).

In addition, there is increasing agreement that resources other than those proposed by Blood and Wolfe (1960) have an important impact on family power relations (Safilios-Rothschild, 1970; Scanzoni, 1979b). A series of attempts have been made to develop comprehensive typologies of power bases and/or resource classes. Despite their differing theoretical foundations, these typologies are remarkably similar.

The earliest and probably the most widely recognized attempt is French and Raven's list (1959) of "power bases." These authors originally proposed five major power bases: legitimate, reward, coercive, expert, and referent power; later, they included informational power as an additional basis. French and Raven's typology

(1959) actually refers to *means* of power exertion rather than to *power bases*. For instance, although both reward and coercive power are based on resources, they differ in regard to *how* these resources are used, that is, whether rewards are promised or punishments are threatened. They can, however, be easily converted into actor characteristics (cf. Tedeschi & Lindskold, 1976). Other authors have added categories to this typology or specified components within selected categories. One of the most commonly mentioned additional categories is trustworthiness (Tedeschi, Bonoma, & Brown, 1971; Tedeschi & Lindskold, 1976). The inclusion of this characteristic rests on the assumption that source credibility affects the effectiveness of diverse resources and other power bases (cf. Hovland, Janis, & Kelley, 1953; Schlenker, Nacci, Helm, & Tedeschi, 1976). Among the specific resources mentioned in other typologies are status and prestige, love or expressiveness, sex, money, services, goods, physical strength, positive self-concept, and metapower (cf. Foa & Foa, 1974; Goode, 1971; Levinger & Huesmann, 1980; Ryder, 1972; Safilios-Rothschild, 1976a; Scanzoni, 1979b; Scanzoni & Szinovacz, 1980). Generally, power bases include tangible and intangible resources that may originate from personal attributes or the individual's position within the family and other social systems (Edwards, 1969; Scanzoni, 1979b).

Whereas resource theory focuses on the relative quantity of tangible resources, other researchers emphasize that the *importance* and the *effectiveness* of specific resources can be assessed only if several other factors are taken into account. Specifically, the volume, the frequency, the magnitude, the intensity, and the stability of the family members' relative contributions, as well as the quality and the value of the exchanged benefits, need to be considered (cf. Beckman-Brindley & Tavormina, 1978; Edwards, 1969; Emerson, 1972a; Gouldner, 1960; Greenberg, 1980; Homans, 1974; Schopler, 1965; Tedeschi, 1974b). Even the disparity between the actors' income, social skills, and so on in itself (Scanzoni & Szinovacz, 1980) does not constitute a viable indicator of relative resources unless this disparity is reflected in the actors' relative contributions to each other and the importance of these contributions.

Because the importance of disparity probably varies with the absolute level of the family members' contributions, both absolute and relative resource levels need to be taken into consideration. Fox (1973) found, for instance, that the relative effect of resource discrepancies varies with the absolute level or amount of the resources owned by the spouses. And outcome scarcity and values of both the actor and the other have been shown to influence power perceptions (Bacharach & Lawler, 1976).

However, utilities in intimate exchange relations may involve recurrent needs and are thus less subject to diminishing returns than would be true in other exchange relations (Blalock & Wilken, 1979). The value of specific benefits thus depends on their utility to A and to O, and the establishment of dependence relations requires that contributions occur with some consistency and in appropriate amounts. Given the complex conversion process of objective properties into resources, a valid assessment of the actors' resources poses a formidable and yet not fully resolved problem (Emerson, Cook, Gillmore, & Yamagishi, 1983; Harsany, 1977; Heckathorn, 1983). Also, dependence may result in increased efforts to conterbalance A's control, particularly if this control violates prevalent societal norms. "Unconventional asymmetries" in couples (e.g., the wife's having a higher social status than her husband) can lead to high defensiveness and thus more restrictive behaviors on the part of the husband (Safilios-Rothschild, & Oijkers, 1978). And the quality of specific contributions is often more important than mere quantity. The motives and resource potential of the donor may enhance or decrease the value of his or her contributions. Benevolent motives and contributions on the part of relatively "poor" donors tend to increase the value of received benefits. Fromkin and Snyder (1980) further suggested that payoff values vary with the degree to which exchange commodities contribute to self-perception of uniqueness.

Another criterion for estimating the value of specific benefits is the similarity of exchanged resources. Several studies indicate that different resource classes cannot be arbitrarily exchanged. Rather, individuals seem to expect reciprocation within the same or at least between similar resource classes and are more satisfied with such exchanges (Donnenwerth & Foa, 1974; Foa & Foa, 1980; Turner, Foa, & Foa, 1971). Tests of resource theory imply that commodities such as income or knowledge (education) generally affect power relations within all familial domains. Thus, the relative income of the spouses is related to control over such diverse issues as the husband's job and disciplining the children. This assumption is questionable not only in the light of the findings by Foa and Foa (1980), but also because the importance of a particular resource is often situation-specific.

Furthermore, specific properties vary in the degree to which they can be mobilized; that is, not all resources are adequate or usable in every exchange situation. Blalock and Wilken (1979) mentioned a series of resource qualities that affect degree of mobilization: divisibility, detachability, interchangeability, generalizability, indispensability, expendability, and replenishment rate (p. 355ff.). Not only is the value of specific properties contingent on their own qualities, but it may also be altered by situational contingencies (Martin & Osmond, 1982; Molm, 1981) and relationship characteristics. Marsden (1983) contended that actors with access to alternative exchange relations may engage in "price making"; that is, they may inflate resources and thus alter exchange terms.

Which resources are used and how they are used to obtain compliance have important consequences both for the probability of achieving compliance and for the quality and future of the relationship. Some authors treat reward and coercive power as one dimension, because both are based on the direct mediation of resources

(McDonald, 1977b, 1979; Smith, 1970, 1977). However, the uses of rewards or punishments and promises or threats are not equally efficient approaches, and they affect the relationship quite differently. Specifically, reward power enhances relationship development and may strengthen referent power, whereas coercion results in dissatisfaction of the partner and reduces the actor's referent power. Expertise as a power basis is restricted to the expert's area of competence and must be recognized by the other.

As in the case of expertise, compliance with authority is based on the assumption that the status occupant will act to further the well-being of the group. Authority is thus restricted to specific positional rights and is contingent on the fulfillment of obligations connected with the status. Reward and coercive power, as well as authority, also seem to be more effective if the other's behaviors are observable (cf. French & Raven, 1959; Raven & Kruglanski, 1970). French and Raven's conception (1959) of referent power implies that the other's identification with the actor serves as a power basis for the actor. Such identification depends on the actor's attractiveness to the other—even positive opinions expressed by an unattractive source increase the target's opposition.

Referent power probably constitutes the most generalizable power basis. Unlike legitimate, expert, or informational power, referent power is not restricted to a predefined range of domains, nor does it require observability of the other's behavior. Referent and expert power lead to acceptance rather than to mere compliance and therefore may have more positive long-term consequences than the use of other power bases (cf. Duck, 1977; French & Raven, 1959; Hallenbeck, 1966; Huston, 1974; Kelvin, 1977; Michener & Burt, 1975; Milgram, 1965; Raven, Centers, & Rodrigues, 1975; Raven & Kruglanski, 1970; Rubin & Brown, 1975; Schlenker et al., 1976; Schopler, 1965; Tedeschi, 1974a; Tedeschi & Lindskold, 1976; Zander & Curtis, 1962).

Compliance as a Resource: A Note on the Power of the Powerless. If tangible resources were the only source of power, children would obviously be quite powerless. However, several studies indicate that children exert power not only vis-à-vis other children (Gellert, 1961), but also vis-à-vis their parents, and that they do participate in family decision-making and problem-solving tasks (Bell, 1968, 1979; Grusec & Kuczynski, 1980; Huston, 1983; Jacob, 1974, 1975; Lerner & Spanier, 1978; McGillicuddy-DeLisi, 1980; Rollins & Thomas, 1975, 1979; Schuham, 1970, 1972; Winter & Ferreira, 1969).

Children, as well as other powerless groups (e.g., the aged), possess an important resource in their compliance (Dowd, 1975; Emerson, 1976). Blau (1964) clearly stressed this point when he described O's "willingness to comply" as a "generic social reward. . . . which can be used (by A) to attain a variety of ends" (p. 22). From this perspective, compliance represents primarily a basis of power differentiation: owing to his or her lack of other resources, O has to comply in order to obtain needed services.

Children's compliance, however, may serve them to achieve more than "needed" services from their parents. Sprey (1977) emphasized, for instance, that children have a part in "public" goods that are available to all users regardless of their relative contributions (e.g., shelter and electricity). Such benefits cannot be denied to children. Therefore, restrictions on the children's use of such benefits and other demands for conformity often have to be acquired through *additional* incentives. Furthermore, children's "good" behavior is a source of pleasure and pride to the parents and thus constitutes a direct reward (Richer, 1968). Consequently, children often use compliance or "good" behavior in order to obtain desired benefits ("If mother doesn't buy me candy in the supermarket, I'll scream and make all the people look at us") or to affect parental responses. Such effects, of course, constitute power exertion on the part of the child. The norm of social responsibility and the application of a distributive-justice norm of need and ability may further increase exploitation of the parents on the part of their children: children's dependency and helplessness arouse feelings of responsibility in the parents and make them vulnerable to the children's control attempts (for a further discussion of this issue see Scanzoni & Szinovacz, 1980, Chapter 8). Or children may apply power exertion strategies that induce their parents to comply with the child's requests. Assuming the role of a martyr constitutes one example of such strategies (cf. Braver & Rohrer, 1975).

As they grow older, children may gain power owing to an increase in tangible resources and alternatives (peers and other adults). Their impact on family matters and/or their power vis-à-vis their parents then depends on the amount of such resources and alternatives, and also on the comparative social status of the parents (Jacob, 1974; Richer, 1968; Scanzoni & Scanzoni, 1976).

Group Composition. Not only did family sociologists often neglect children as participants in family decisions, they also practically "forgot" that control processes in triads and larger groups are prone to *coalition formation* (McDonald, 1975, 1980). The social psychological literature provides ample evidence that power asymmetries among individual group members are often overcome by coalitions whose members are able to resist the more powerful member(s). Among the factors that determine the formation of specific types of coalitions are the coalition utility for the group members, the member's resource differences, liking and conflict among group members, the perceived power distribution in the group, group size, and specific features of the experimental situation (Caplow, 1968; Cassidy & Neave, 1977; Chertkoff, 1971; Komorita, 1978; Komorita & Meek, 1978; Mazur, 1968; McDonald, 1975; Michener, Lawler, & Bacharach, 1973; Oliver, 1980). Because of the possibility of coalition formation, power processes in *families* are

qualitatively distinct from such processes within dyads. For one thing, power exertion processes in three-or-more-person groups are definitely more complex than in the dyad (Midgaard & Underdal, 1977; Rapoport, 1970). In addition, they provide weaker family members with opportunities to pool their resources and to exert additional pressure on another family member. In such cases, comparisons of the family members' *personal* resources are insufficient to predict familial control processes.

Because the group composition of the family varies over time (i.e., according to the *number of children* and the *life cycle stage*), the structural conditions of the group are in constant flux. These variations change the mere content of family decisions and power exertion, and they also affect the relative dependency of the spouses on each other and on the maintenance of the relationship. Some researchers have suggested that the presence of small children increases the mother's dependence (economically and emotionally) and thus undermines her power position in the family (Blood & Wolfe, 1960; Burr, 1970; Lewis, 1972). However, if men do become more involved in child care (cf. Hesselbart, 1978), and if they are interested in maintaining a relationship that ensures daily contact with their children, their dependence on the relationship may also increase.[14] Once the children are older, coalitions between the mother and the children may also weaken the father's control potential.

Finally, the *presence of other persons* (e.g., extended kin) in the household has important consequences for the management of internal family affairs. Extended-family members not only participate in family decisions and may form coalitions with either spouse, their mere presence seems to be related to the decision-making patterns and the power relations within the couple (cf. Liu *et al.,* 1974; Straus, 1975). The availability of alternative sources of gratification for one or both spouses decreases their dependence on each other and thus contributes to more "autonomous" (Wolfe, 1959) decision-making patterns and/or higher segregation of marital control domains (cf. Bott, 1957; Szinovacz, 1977b, 1978). Also, the higher observability of family behaviors, owing to the presence of third parties, reduces the likelihood of specific power-exertion tactics, particularly of violent behaviors (Gelles, 1974, 1979).

Personality. Even though it seems obvious that individual characteristics affect the family members' behaviors and interaction, no *systematic* efforts have been made to assess personality effects on family power processes. The social-psychological literature provides some evidence that personality has an important influence (cf. Gallo & McClintock, 1965; Hermann & Kogan, 1977; Rubin & Brown, 1975; Tedeschi & Lindskold, 1976).

---

[14]The current struggles over custody for the children certainly show that the husband can also become "more interested" in the maintenance of the relationship once a family has been established.

Among the personality factors that have been shown to affect power exertion and dominance behaviors are relatively stable personality dimensions, the individuals' motives, their cognitive structure, and feelings of powerfulness and competence (Minton, 1967; Rubin & Brown, 1975; Terhune, 1970).

Personality dimensions such as authoritarian attitudes or machiavellianism seem to affect individuals' choices regarding whether or not to exert power as well as their choices of power means and the specific bargaining behaviors that they exhibit. *Authoritarian* males seem to be more dominant and seem to abide by traditional roles of male authority (Centers *et al.*, 1971; Craddock, 1977). They are also likely to engage in retaliation (Friedell, 1967) and to bargain competitively rather than cooperatively (cf. Gallo & McClintock, 1965; Rubin & Brown, 1975), but to respect others with high authority (Tedeschi & Lindskold, 1976). Actors who score high on *machiavellianism* (Christie & Geis, 1970) tend to compete and to exploit others while being highly sensitive to interpersonal and situational contingencies (cf. Harrell & Hartnagel, 1976; Rubin & Brown, 1975). They prefer indirect and nonrational influence strategies (Falbo, 1977b), which probably have a higher manipulative potential than direct, rational strategies.

Cognitions such as risk taking, cognitive complexity, and tolerance of ambiguity have also been shown to relate to bargaining and power exertion processes. Risk takers and persons low in cognitive complexity tend toward self-interested, competitive bargaining, whereas tolerance of ambiguity promotes cooperative responses (Rubin & Brown, 1975). Rim (1979, 1980a,b) reported interaction effects of sex of spouse, personality, and cognitive development on means of influence in marriage.

One of the most widely used indicators of powerfulness is locus of control (Rotter, 1966). The evidence on the effect of *internal* versus *external locus of control* on power and control processes is inconclusive. In some cases, internals exploited their partners, whereas other research indicates more authoritarian and punishing behaviors on the part of externals (Assor & O'Quin, 1982; Bobbit, 1967; Goodstadt & Hjelle, 1973; Tedeschi & Gaes, 1977). However, several studies suggest that internals are more likely than externals to resist control attempts (cf. Tedeschi & Lindskold, 1976). In their study on married couples, Doherty and Ryder (1979) found an interaction effect of locus of control and trust. External, high-trusting husbands and internal low-trusting wives proved to exhibit less assertive behaviors than the other groups. Lack of *self-confidence,* low *self-esteem,* and a negative *self-concept* all seem to induce competitive and coercive behaviors, which probably constitute defensive strategies (Hovland *et al.*, 1953; Minton, 1967; Rubin & Brown, 1975), but low-self-esteem subjects may also be more susceptible to persuasion than individuals with high self-esteem (Stimpson, 1970). However, Centers *et al.* (1971) reported no relationship between self-confidence and spouses' decision-making patterns. Price (1973), on the

other hand, indicated that self-actualization is reflected in the decision-making *style* employed by spouses.

Research on the *power motive* shows that individuals differ in the degree to which they strive for power, as well as in their motives for doing so. Specifically, the need for power (*n* power) may rest on an active motive to gain influence, or it may reflect fear of weakness and thus may constitute a defensive motive (McClelland, 1975; Uleman, 1972; Veroff & Veroff, 1971, 1972; Winter, 1973). Winter (1973) linked the development of fear of power to early experiences of dominance, particularly as a function of birth-order effects. McClelland (1975) pointed out that the power motive manifests itself in how people play out ascribed social roles. Thus, men who score high on *n* power exhibit assertive emotional behaviors, whereas women high in *n* power focus "on building up the self which may be the object of that (male) assertiveness" (p. 51). High *n* power seems to induce individuals to stand out in public, for example, through taking high risks (McClelland & Watson, 1973). That power motitivation of the spouses influences marital interactions is evident from a study by Winter, Stewart, and McClelland (1977). These authors found that husbands with high *n* power are less likely than other husbands to have career-oriented wives.

In short, personality factors have been shown to play a role in the degree to which and the manner in which individuals exhibit power-related behaviors, in their susceptibility to control attempts, and in the power exertion strategies that they are likely to use (see also Phillips, 1967). Because the family context restricts an individual's behaviors less than other more formal settings, their personal orientations and motivations probably constitute an important factor in family interactions. Ignoring these factors in family power research means neglecting the more personalized and individualistic facets of family power relations. In addition, the family plays an important role in the development of power-relevant personality characteristics, either through learning and modeling processes or on the basis of structural features of the family group, such as the birth order and the sex of the children (cf. Kraut & Price, 1976).

Other Member Characteristics. Several of the studies on marital decision-making also investigated general background factors in addition to the couple's relative resources. Efforts to assess differences in power relations among various *ethnic groups* generally led to a rejection of the myth of macho dominance among Hispanic groups (Cromwell & Cromwell, 1978; Cromwell & Ruiz, 1979; Hawkes & Taylor, 1975) and of the myth of wife dominance among black families (Centers *et al.*, 1971; Cromwell & Cromwell, 1978; Gray-Little, 1982; Hammond & Enoch, 1976; King, 1969; Willie & Greenblatt, 1978). Evidence from social-psychological research further suggests that blacks tend to be more cooperative bargainers than whites (cf. Rubin & Brown, 1975). Cultural background has also been shown to affect marital power relations (cf. Conklin, 1979; Johnson, 1975; Kumagai, 1979; Kumagai & O'Donoghue, 1978; Liu *et al.*, 1974).

Age effects on power relations remain quite unclear. Existing studies indicate, for instance, that husbands participate less in marital decisions as they grow older (Centers *et al.*, 1971), that both spouses "mellow" with age and thus are more likely to give in to the other's demands (Safilios-Rothschild, 1969b), or that gender differences in bargaining behaviors become more distinct with age (cf. Rubin & Brown, 1975).[15] Because these studies refer to different dimensions of power and divergent features of the power exertion process, the results may not be totally contradictory. Also, age may not affect power relations and control behaviors in a linear fashion. Because psychological studies emphasize age differences among younger groups, whereas the family literature focuses on such differences among older groups, the emergent contradictions could reflect a curvilinear relationship. Some research also suggests that age discrepancies among family members—and not only age *per se*—affect family power relations (cf. Oppong, 1970; Szinovacz, 1975).

Sex differences in power exertion and bargaining indicate that men adopt a profit-oriented approach that leads them to compete or cooperate depending on which strategy maximizes their profits, whereas women respond to interpersonal cues and thus reciprocate the partner's cooperative or competitive behaviors (cf. Rubin & Brown, 1975; Terhune, 1970). Generally, men seem to exhibit tougher bargaining strategies and are more dominance-oriented than women (cf. Bartos, 1970; Bean & Kerckhoff, 1971; McCarrick *et al.*, 1981). They are also more likely to use verbal and direct strategies, whereas women rely on nonverbal and indirect tactics (Falbo, 1977b; Falbo & Peplau, 1980; Hoffman, 1982; Johnson, 1976; Peplau, 1979; Safilios-Rothschild, 1969b). A similar trend did emerge in regard to individuals' sex-role orientations: feminine persons were shown to be less assertive and to use more indirect strategies than their masculine counterparts (Falbo, 1977b).

Findings indicating that the sex composition of the group (opposite vs. same sex) is associated with divergent bargaining behaviors (cf. Rapoport & Chammah, 1965; Smith, Vernon, & Tarte, 1975) would suggest that different family subgroups (e.g., mother–daughter vs. mother–son) may engage in distinct power exertion behaviors. Sex differences also influence power perceptions by others. Several studies indicate sex differences in adolescents' perceptions of parental power (Buehler, Weigert, & Thomas, 1974; Smith, 1977).

A final background characteristic that has consistently been shown to influence family power processes is *socioeconomic status* (SES). Most studies indicate that lower-SES husbands are more dominant and authoritarian than middle-class husbands (cf. Komarovsky, 1964;

Rubin, 1976; Willie & Greenblatt, 1978). However, social-psychological studies suggest that actors high in status and prestige make more influence attempts and are more likely to succeed, but that they are less susceptible to the other's influence than lower-status subjects. One reason for this apparent contradiction may be the different power bases used by low- and high-status subjects and the ways in which power is used. Higher-status individuals obtain control on the basis of their resources and legitimate status and thus through deference to them by others. Their control is voluntarily accepted and may therefore appear to be less pronounced than the defensive use of coercion (often in the form of physical strength) by lower-class husbands. Also, experimental conditions probably prevent lower-status subjects from using coercive tactics such as violence.

Self–Other Orientations. How family members interact with each other, which power strategies they use, and how satisfied they are with the outcomes depend partially on their orientations and expectations. In a conflict or bargaining situation, partners differ in their *responsiveness* to each other as well as in the bargaining *interests* that they pursue. A person low in *interpersonal orientation* follows his or her own approach regardless of the other's reactions, whereas individuals high in interpersonal orientation develop their approach in response to the other's behaviors (cf. Rubin & Brown, 1975). Interpersonal orientation is not to be confounded with bargaining interests, that is, whether individuals act on the basis of *self-interest* (maximization of one's own profits), *group interests* (maximization of joint interests), *competitive interests* (maximization of the other's losses or costs), or *altruistic interests* (maximization of the other's profits) (cf. Blalock & Wilken, 1979; Burns, 1973, 1977; Kelley & Thibaut, 1978; McClintock, 1977; McNeel & Reid, 1975; Rubin & Brown, 1975).[16] The documented bargaining effectiveness of machiavellians provides a good example for the validity of this analytical differentiation. Their success rests on the fact that they combine egotistic or competitive bargaining goals with high interpersonal orientation. Thus, machiavellians behave cooperatively if such behavior will further their own interests, whereas authoritarian personalities tend toward rigidly applied competitive strategies, and such strategies are likely to evoke competitive responses in the opponent (Deutsch, 1973; Kelley & Stahelski, 1970a,b; Raush *et al.*, 1974; Schlenker & Goldman, 1978). Some of the studies on family power relations implicitly portray a powerful person as someone who strives to control all family behaviors and who does so exclusively to promote egotistical goals. Not only may family members refrain

---

[15]It is also unclear whether these effects are due to age or length of marriage.

[16]As Kelley and Thibaut (1978) showed, short-term maximization of altruistic interests may serve long-term goals of the actor, and maximization of the other's interests does not necessarily decrease the actor's outcomes or profits.

from power exertion, but power may also be used to enhance others' welfare. For instance, a husband may refuse his wife's request for money to buy a dress in order to ensure that the whole family will be able to go on an extended trip. Altruistic power use seems to evolve from a different motivational structure from use of "personalized" power for personal gain (McClelland, 1970), and the consequences of competitive and altruistic control are clearly distinct. Epstein and Santa-Barbara (1975) reported that mutually destructive couples ("hawks") perceive each other as competitive and engage in exploitive interactions, whereas "doves" are mutually cooperative and display appeasing behaviors. And lower-status individuals (e.g., women or children) may be more successful in their control attempts if they pursue group goals rather than self-interest motives (Ridgeway, 1982).

How spouses evaluate specific power processes and outcomes also depends on the perceived *fairness* in the relationship. Some exchange theorists have tended to equate distributive justice with equity regardless of relationship type or situational contingencies (Adams, 1969; Homans, 1974; Walster & Walster, 1975; Walster, Walster, & Berscheid, 1978). However, the data on which this interpretation is based are probably inadequate to clearly differentiate between equitable and equality-based exchanges (Cate, Lloyd, Henton, & Larson, 1982). Other scholars have emphasized that equity norms prevail among strangers, that equality principles underlie exchanges among friends, and that the principle of need and ability applies to interactions among relatives (Bar-Tal, Bar-Zohar, Hermon, & Greenberg, 1977; Deutsch, 1975; LaGaipa, 1977; Leventhal, 1976; Peterson, 1975). It is therefore not surprising that a *general quid pro quo* orientation seems to undermine the quality of marital relations (Murstein, Cerreto, & MacDonald, 1977). Thus, it is probably not the application of equity norms *per se,* but the rigid application of one single standard that reduces marital satisfaction. Rather, the fairness of *specific* transactions is evaluated on the basis of divergent distributive-justice principles. For instance, spouses may judge each other's participation in household activities on a principle of equality, contingent on their other work commitments, but they may evaluate each other's emotional gratifications on the basis of need and ability. The evaluation of specific demands or control attempts by family members occurs within the context of previously established expectations and rules. Individuals who develop and apply a relatively rigid conception of justice and who generally believe "in a just world" may be very trusting, but they may also have high expectations and may show little empathy for others' disadvantages (Rubin, 1975). Under such conditions, the justice demands of one partner may be perceived as rather unfair requests or judgments by the other.

Violations of established rules on the "governance" of family matters (Broderick, 1975; Wieting & McLaren, 1975) are also likely to result in feelings of injustice. Thus, fairness evaluations refer not only to the distribu-

tion of contributions among family members, but also to the individuals' expectations as well as procedural norms and rules (cf. Blalock & Wilken, 1979; Kahn, Nelson, Gaeddert, & Hearn, 1982; Morgan & Sawyer, 1979).

Finally, some exchanges may be short-term and restricted, whereas others may involve long-term expectations or univocal benefits (cf. Ellis, 1971). Although spouses may expect some reciprocation of their contributions in the long run, parent–child or generational kin relations are probably governed to an important degree by generalized exchanges based on univocal reciprocity (Ekeh, 1974). Parents do not always expect their children to "repay" them for the services the children once received; rather, they expect their children to render similar services to the next generation. Or assistance among members of the extended-kin group may follow a principle of relative need and ability and expectations of generalized exchange, but it is not expected that each beneficiary will repay the specific person(s) who helped in a crisis situation.

Whenever immediate reciprocation does not occur, *trust* becomes a vital prerequisite for fairness estimates. High trust not only induces cooperative behaviors and, indeed, constitutes a prerequisite for long-term exchanges (Blau, 1964; Deutsch, 1973; Haas & Deserau, 1981; Santa-Barbara & Epstein, 1974; Terhune, 1970), but it may also prevent spouses from one-sided continuous power exertion. Thus, spouses who distrust each other and are inclined toward a critical or even cynical view of each other tend to display dominant and aggressive behaviors (Szinovacz, 1983). Lack of trust and the resulting competitive behaviors are therefore not only a function of egotistical or competitive orientations but could also indicate fear of being unjustly treated or "cheated." The competitive tendencies of persons with a low self-concept would then constitute a defensive strategy (Tedeschi & Gaes, 1977).

Gender norms delineate the degree to which legitimate authority or power (Buckley, 1967) rests with the husband-father and specify the legitimate power domains of the family members. If traditional gender norms are applied, spouses may be able to arrange many family matters on the basis of "spontaneous consensus" (Fox, 1974; see also Scanzoni, 1979b; Scanzoni & Szinovacz, 1980). With the emergence of more egalitarian gender norms (cf. Burchinal & Bauder, 1965; Cherlin & Walters, 1981; Hill, 1970; Hobart, 1981; Thornton, Alwin, & Camburn, 1983), more issues become negotiable as the interest spheres and power domains of the spouses increasingly overlap. Scanzoni (1979b) consequently criticized the assumption "that movement toward egalitarian role structures somehow signals the 'end of power'" (p. 306). Rather, the greater flexibility of role expectations and rules associated with modern gender norms necessitates negotiation of issues that were formerly unchallenged power domains of either spouse. Egalitarian marriages may thus involve more explicit and open control processes than are usual in traditional, gender-norm-segregated relationships. In addition, norms that emphasize democratic procedures in family negotiations enhance control attempts by all family members, including the children, because they render such attempts less costly than under the conditions of the rigid role expectations that the wife and the children ought to submit to the legitimate authority or power of the husband (Scanzoni & Szinovacz, 1980).

Generally, self–other orientations, though linked to personality dispositions, evolve from *past experiences*. Even the most trusting person may become distrusting if she or he feels continuously unfairly treated or distrusted by the partner (Deutsch, 1973; Scanzoni, 1979b). The history of power processes within the family thus constitutes the context within which current power processes take place and the point of view from which they are evaluated (cf. Molm, 1981a; Komorita, 1973; Scanzoni, 1979b; Scanzoni & Polonko, 1980). In addition, it is not only the family members' orientations *per se* that affect power processes but also the *similarity* of their attitudes and their mutual responsiveness or orientation *toward* each other. Attitude similarity not only reduces the conflict potential in the family but, at least under some conditions, also enhances cooperation (Apfelbaum, 1974; Garner & Deutsch, 1974; McNeel & Reid, 1975). In order to reach mutually satisfactory outcomes, spouses must understand each other, demonstrate empathy, and coordinate their responses (Scheff, 1967).

To summarize, specific group and member characteristics constitute major parameters of power situations. Specific characteristics (e.g., resources and authority) determine the family members' relative dependence on each other's contributions and thus the likelihood that they will engage in control attempts, as well as the probability of the success of such attempts. The importance and the efficiency of these power bases depends not only on the quantity and the quality of the members' contributions, but also on other contingencies, including group composition, normative orientations, and so forth (e.g., in three-and-more-person groups, "weaker" members may pool their resources, or the costs of power exertion may be contingent on the perceived legitimacy of control attempts). Furthermore, whether or not and how the family members attempt to exercise power are dependent not only on their mere ability in terms of relative power bases, but also on personal and interactional characteristics. Given equal ability, we may, for instance, expect a relatively high number of control attempts on the part of authoritarians or among partners who distrust each other. Both power bases and other member and group characteristics also influence the quality of control processes. Specific power bases are linked to specific means of control (e.g., lack of material resources may lead husbands to rely on physical force), and certain other group and member characteristics affect the probability of competitive versus cooperative bargaining processes.

Situational Contingencies

Conflict Characteristics. The structure of small, intimate groups renders them prone to frequent and intensive conflicts (Alford, 1982; Blood, 1960; Coser, 1956; Simmel, 1955; Sprey, 1969, 1979). Sprey (1969) thus conceived of the family as "a system in conflict." And it is because of this quality that power struggles and power exertion represent a "normal" feature of family life. Therefore, not conflict *per se*, but the nature and type of specific conflicts influence family stability and members' satisfaction (cf. Bernard, 1964; Sprey, 1979). As mentioned above, conflict does not constitute a necessary condition of power exertion, but it probably increases the importance of control processes. Surely, specific characteristics of conflict situations have important consequences for and are inherently linked to the power exertion processes. At least three dimensions of conflict situations affect the nature of control processes: the conflict content or objectives, the conflict intensity and duration, and the available conflict outcomes.[17]

Family sociologists have tended to assess power relations without giving much attention to the specific issues at hand. Because power exertion, by definition, represents an attempt to accomplish one's goals, explanations of control processes cannot be entirely abstracted from the nature of these goals. Conflict theorists have shown that conflict content and objectives are directly linked to conflict processes. Family conflicts can focus on at least three *content* areas; topic issues (e.g., money and vacations); personal issues (e.g., habits and appearance); and relationship issues (e.g., task allocation and jealousy). In each of these cases, arguments may refer to matters of distribution, values, or goal specification (deKadt, 1965).

Conflicts that imply a *confrontation over core values, general principles, or basic goals* (cf. Coser, 1956; Simmel, 1955; Sprey, 1979) are usually more intense and more difficult to resolve than conflicts over means. Scanzoni and Scanzoni (1976) emphasized that basic conflict involves questioning the "rules of the game" or the relationship, whereas nonbasic conflict occurs *within* such rules and implies consensus over the core issues. Basic conflict, therefore, requires changes in the negotiated order of the relationship; nonbasic conflict does not.

Sprey (1979) suggested an additional differentiation within the category of basic or structural conflicts, namely, whether the conflict concerns a confrontation over *privileges* or over matters of *autonomy*. The first results from perceived violations of distributive justice (Deutsch, 1973). Given the ongoing changes in gender roles, conflict over privileges associated with the husband's status in the family represents a recurring theme of

---

[17]For a full discussion of relevant conflict characteristics see Brehmer and Hammond (1977), Druckman (1977), Kriesberg (1973), Deutsch (1973), Coser (1956), and Mack and Snyder (1957), among others.

confrontation in marriages (Scanzoni, 1972; Schafer & Keith, 1981). In intimate groups, individuals are also constantly engaged in a struggle over the maintenance of individuality versus the maintenance of group integration. Thus, conflicts may originate from discrepancies between the partners' needs for closeness or independence (Napier, 1978).

We can also differentiate between *distributive* and *integrative* conflict situations. Depending on the issue under consideration, the conflict may imply a zero-sum game situation (distributive structure) or a non-zero-sum game situation (integrative structure). In the latter case, both parties may gain in the conflict. Distributive conflict situations, on the other hand, imply that one party must win at the expense of the other if the conflict is to be resolved. Much of the current literature on family power relations either assumes a zero-sum game situation or introduces zero-sum conditions into the experimental setting. Because the two situations are structurally different and have divergent solution possibilities (cf. Kimmel & Havens, 1966; Rapoport, 1970), the generalizability of the results from such research is questionable (see also Sprey, 1972, 1975, for a critique). Indeed, couples who bargain for mutually satisfactory outcomes may consciously attempt to restructure conflicts from zero-sum to mixed-motive conditions. Research on attitudinal conflicts shows, for instance, that cooperative subjects emphasize their similarities, whereas competitive subjects primarily view the divergencies between their positions (Judd, 1978).

Conflict over basic issues and distributive conflicts probably enhance the chances that power will be exerted because the opportunity costs of refraining from power use will be relatively high. Given the competitive potential of such conflict situations, they are also more likely to involve coercive power-exertion strategies. And the emergent power structure in a relationship may be partially contingent on the conflict issue at hand. If resolution of the conflict issue is particularly important to one partner, but not to the other, the more interested party may be at a power disadvantage (cf. Michener *et al.*, 1973).

Of course, different issues may be involved in a single, overt conflict event. Extension of the *number of issues* is likely to intensify the conflict (particularly if intangible issues are involved) and to render agreements more difficult to achieve (Coser, 1956, 1967; Kriesberg, 1973; Sprey, 1979). And the more issues involved, the more complex the power exertion processes are likely to become.

One reason that basic and distributive conflicts are more difficult to resolve is that they usually increase conflict intensity. The implications of *conflict intensity* for power processes have been investigated in a series of experimental studies. This research shows consistently that conflict intensity raises the subjects' preference for and increases the frequency of coercive and competitive strategies (Axelrod, 1967; Goodstadt & Kipnis, 1970; Tedeschi & Lindskold, 1976), as well as the probability of escalation (Deutsch, 1973).

Many of the conditions that relate to conflict intensity and its consequences also apply to *conflict duration*. Coser (1956, 1967) held that conflict will be prolonged if one or several of the following conditions are met: the goals of the opposing parties are not very limited; dissensus over the goals of conflict is relatively high; and the parties have difficulty in correctly interpreting the opponent's symbolic points of victory and defeat (cf. Turner, 1978). Extension of the issues is also likely to intensify and prolong the conflict. In accordance with these assumptions, Kelley, Deutsch, Lanzetta, Nuttin, Shure, Faucheux, Moscovici, and Rabbie (1970) found that an increase in the difficulty of the game situation led to an extension in trial time and hindered agreement. Komorita (1973) reported that competitive acts used against competitive opponents provoked long stalemate situations and prevented cooperative solutions. The nature of power exertion processes is thus contingent on the conflict conditions. Coercive strategies are more likely if conflict characteristics enhance the intensity and the duration of the conflict. And it is under such conflict conditions that power exertion is less likely to result in mutually satisfactory outcomes.

In order to fully understand conflict situations and conflict management processes, we must obtain information not only on the type, duration, or intensity of the conflict, but also on the *available conflict outcomes* (cf. Heilman & Garner, 1975; Kane, Joseph, & Tedeschi, 1977; Kelley, 1965; Patchen, 1970). If conflicts center on the means of achieving mutual goals, conflict outcomes largely depend on the actors' knowledge of the available means as well as on the availability of such means. For instance, the course of a dispute over the wife's work overload and the means of reallocating her responsibilities depends on whether the couple can afford and are willing to engage outside help, on the availability of relatives, or on the spouses' feelings regarding the participation of the children in household tasks. The availability of specific outcome alternatives may also determine the structure of the conflict. If the only alternative available to our couple is a redistribution of household tasks between the spouses, the conflict may acquire a distributive nature, whereas availability of other alternatives allows for the emergence of an integrative conflict situation. In addition, the availability of alternative solutions influences attributions of responsibility, and such attributions have important consequences not only for power exertion processes and outcomes, but also for their evaluation by the participants (Doherty, 1979; Kane *et al.*, 1977; Kelley, 1965).

One of the major limitations of experimental conflict studies seems to be that they often predetermine the potential conflict outcomes (Patchen, 1970). For instance, one of the instruments more widely used to investigate marital conflicts, the Inventory of Marital Conflict, or IMC (Olson & Ryder, 1970), forces spouses to choose between two and only two alternative outcomes, although other solutions might be equally meaningful. Such manipulation of conflict outcomes, though desirable for some research purposes, may seriously distort research findings because the *available* conflict outcomes affect the individuals' behaviors during the control processes.

Other Situational Contingencies. Even though space limitations do not permit a detailed discussion of other situational factors that affect power processes, two conditions deserve brief mention. One of these factors is the *time pressure* during power processes. Whereas bargaining under high time pressure generally seems to enhance the likelihood of agreements (cf. Rubin & Brown, 1975; Yukl, Malone, Hayslip, & Pamin, 1976), prolonging a power struggle may in itself constitute a power exertion strategy. For instance, the indefinite delay of a decision to change existing conditions (e.g., the wife's employment or having children) indicates that the partner interested in maintenance of the status quo has been successful in controlling the other (Scanzoni & Szinovacz, 1980). Similarly, high-stress or crisis situations often require rapid settlement of conflicting ideas and quick decision-making. In such situations, fearlessness and strength may become more important than other resources of the leader, and she or he is likely to be replaced if she or he proves unable to handle the crisis adequately (cf. Bahr & Rollins, 1971; Rosen, Levinger, & Lippitt, 1961).

The second contingency is the *presence of others* while power exertion takes place. If an "audience" is present, the partners are likely to engage in power exertion strategies that are approved and to evoke positive evaluations by the third party (cf. Rubin & Brown, 1975). However, these public behaviors are not necessarily the family members' habitual patterns of interaction and power exertion.

It has also been shown that stress and tension affect individuals' behaviors in power or bargaining situations. In their review of this literature, Hopmann and Walcott (1977) noted that stress tends to decrease the actors' perceptual complexity, tolerance of ambiguity, cognitive flexibility, and performance of problem-solving tasks. It may also lead to enhanced hostility and tough bargaining among the contending parties.

It is noteworthy that both time pressure and the presence of outsiders are usual characteristics of experimental tasks designed to measure power. Unless the influence of such situational contingencies on the results is clearly established, we shall not be able to generalize such results to every day behavior patterns in families.

In short, situational contingencies may be viewed as intervening variables that mediate relationships between the contextual and group member characteristics and the power exertion processes. This brief review of conflict characteristics suggests that conflict features that enhance conflict intensity make it more likely that power will be exerted and will contribute to coercive power-exertion strategies. Under such conditions, conflict outcomes will tend to be regulated or to result in a stalemate. And these outcomes are likely to reduce the members' emphasis on group interest, their mutual trust, or their feelings of fairness and, therefore, can lead to the negative exchange

patterns observed in some clinical couples (cf. Gottman, 1979; Patterson, 1976, 1978). Other situational factors seem to reduce the probability of intense and lengthy conflicts. Time pressure renders the solution of the conflict more important than many other considerations, and the presence of others forces family members to restrict their power-exertion strategies to socially approved forms.

Power Exertion Processes

The family research literature is remarkably devoid of serious attempts to gain information on *how* family members go about exercising power. Even process-oriented studies assessing family members' interactions in a conflict situation have not gone beyond such general measures as the number or frequency of successful control attempts, talking time, leadership behaviors, or, at best, competitive versus cooperative behaviors (cf. Hadley & Jacob, 1973; Olson & Ryder, 1970). This neglect may be due to the fact that experimental settings sharply reduce the available options of power strategies. Specifically, time pressure and the public setting induce family members to use verbal and relatively rational strategies, such as persuasion or reasoning, whereas other strategies are virtually impossible under experimental conditions (e.g., physical coercion and ingratiation through sexual promises). It is thus not surprising that the few self-report studies on marital power processes demonstrate a much wider range of strategies than have been shown in observational studies (cf. Adler, 1977; Hoffman, 1982; Raven *et al.*, 1975; Safilios-Rothschild, 1969b).

Because specific behavioral qualities of power exertion need not be assessed to *describe* the amount of exercised power, it may well be asked why such detailed information is at all necessary to *explain* power processes. How family members go about exercising power affects their success in bringing about desired outcomes, and it influences the outcomes and their evaluation. Thus, a deficit in resources may be offset through the use of highly effective strategies (Gruder, 1970), and specific outcomes may be accepted or rejected depending on how they were achieved.

Power Exertion as Position Modification. In exercising power, family members attempt to alter each other's positions (behaviors or outcomes). Each modification of the original position indicates that power was exercised (cf. Scanzoni, 1979b; Scanzoni & Szinovacz, 1980; Spector, 1975). However, the total amount of exercised power (i.e., outcome power) cannot always be equated with the relative changes in original positions. On the one hand, additional information acquired during bargaining may lead a family member to *voluntarily* abandon his or her initial position. On the other hand, bargaining may be extended to several issues. In this case, position modifications regarding all pertinent domains have to be taken into account to adequately assess outcome power. Consequently, power cannot be easily measured unless the *con-*

tent of the issue(s) and the *sequence* of offers and counteroffers are considered.

Power Exertion Strategies. Classifications of power exertion strategies refer to three major analytical dimensions: (1) the power bases used by the source; (2) the ways in which such power bases are utilized; and (3) changes in others' position through alterations in the power relationship itself.

Compilations of the concrete strategies used to exert power reveal that the actors engage in a variety of behaviors "to get their way." For instance, in a recent unpublished study by this author, spouses named over 50 behaviors in response to the question: "What do you (your spouse) do to get your (his or her) way?" Included in these answers were such divergent strategies as "outtalking" the other, reference to books, pleading, nagging, crying, coalitions, being sexy, being cold or pretending to be busy, or throwing things. Falbo (1977a) also reported that a variety of divergent strategies evolved from responses to a similar question. Choice of the specific strategies varies in regard to personality factors, sex, and age, as well as the group's power structure. For instance, women tend to use emotional, nonverbal, and indirect strategies, whereas men favor rational, direct, and verbal tactics. Women attribute expert power to their husbands, and males believe that their wives use primarily referent power. With increasing age, spouses seem to rely more on referent power and are more likely to give in; younger couples emphasize expert and legitimate power bases in their control attempts. In egalitarian marriages, wives use fewer emotional strategies than in husband-dominant marriages, whereas husbands' strategies change from discursive to argumentative techniques as their own power in the marriage increases (cf. Adler, 1977; Falbo, 1977b; Raven *et al.*, 1975; Rim, 1979; Safilios-Rothschild, 1969b).

Tedeschi, Bonoma, and Schlenker (1972), Tedeschi, Schlenker, and Lindskold (1972), and Tedeschi and Lindskold (1976) proposed a taxonomy of power strategies that is based on the specific power bases mediated by the actors as well as on the ways in which they attempt to exert power.[18] Depending on specific combinations of power bases mediated by the source, three modes of power exertion are distinguished: *reinforcement control* (mediation of resources or attraction); *informational control* (based on informational power); and *ecological control*. The latter may be contingent on diverse power bases of the actor but does not imply direct mediation of such bases as a part of the power exertion attempt. The means of achieving attitudinal or behavioral changes in the target consist of *open* or *direct* and *manipulative* or *indirect* strategies.

Open influence based on the mediation of reinforcement consists of *contingent threats and promises*. Manip-

ulative reinforcement control, on the other hand, involves the noncontingent use of *rewards* and *punishments*. Ecological control is always indirect. In using ecological control, the actor may (1) *construct the environment* in ways that are believed to increase the target's likelihood of behaving in specific ways: (2) *provide cues* that she or he knows evoke particular behaviors in the target; or (3) affect the other's outcomes by *non-decision-making,* that is, by ignoring his or her requests (Tedeschi & Lindskold, 1976, p. 299ff.). Several studies indicate, for instance, that the probability of achieving compliance can be enhanced through variations in the initial demands made by the actor. Both initial requests for very small favors (the foot-in-the-door technique) and for extreme favors (the door-in-the-face technique) seem to enhance compliance under specific conditions (cf. Cialdini *et al.*, 1975; Seligman, Bush, & Kirsch, 1976; Snyder & Cunningham, 1975). Also, tough bargainers who request much while conceding little seem to be able to obtain relatively high concessions from their opponents (cf. Bartos, 1970).

Information control rests on the processing of information in order to obtain the desired changes in the target. Informational control relies on the use of informational power, but it may also include the mediation of other power bases, such as expertise or trustworthiness. For instance, *persuasion* in the form of *recommendations* or *warnings* may—but does not necessarily—imply the use of expertise. Another type of informational control is *activation of commitments,* that is, an appeal to normative values, such as familistic or individualistic motives, fairness, duties, and obligations, and guilt-inducing appeals (Deutsch, 1973; Falbo, 1977a; Raush *et al.*, 1974; Scanzoni, 1978; Tedeschi & Lindskold, 1976). Finally, *ingratiation techniques* are applied in order to increase the subject's attractiveness to the target, that is, to raise the actor's referent power and to enhance the target's influenceability (Jones, 1964; Tedeschi & Lindskold, 1976). Thus, lower-status bargainers were shown to increase the likelihood of a favorable compromise by using face-saving and ingratiation techniques (Tjosvold & Huston, 1978). Whereas persuasion represents an open influence attempt, activation of commitments and ingratiation are manipulative strategies.

In reviewing the results reported above and in comparing French and Raven's list (1959) of power bases with Tedeschi and Lindskold's typology (1976), it becomes evident that means of power exertion cannot be satisfactorily categorized on the basis of only one dimension, that is, the specific power bases used by the spouses. In order to fully explore the effectiveness and consequences of specific power-exertion strategies, it is also necessary to include additional dimensions, such as the degree of directness, rationality, and verbalization. Indeed, ecological strategies cannot be directly assessed through French and Raven's measure (1959). However, unpublished data by this author reveal that ecological control constitutes a power strategy frequently used by couples. Among the specific ecological tactics mentioned by her sample of

---

[18]These authors wrote of "influence strategies," but this concept includes power exertion strategies.

100 couples were such behaviors as pretending to be busy, pacing the room, acting girlish, crying, or assuming a "don't care" attitude. Furthermore, spouses may have less trouble describing specific power-exertion strategies than accurately responding to the relatively abstract instrument developed by French and Raven (1959).

The *effectiveness* of specific strategies is highly relation- and situation-specific. Any assessment of strategy effectiveness requires consideration of both the *short-* and the *long-term consequences* (French & Raven, 1959) of the combination of specific strategies and their appropriateness for specific actors (e.g., males or females) or in given situations (Bell, Chafetz, & Horn, 1982; Hamner & Yukl, 1977; Pruitt & Lewis, 1977; Tedeschi, Bonoma, & Schlenker, 1972; Tedeschi, Schlenker, & Lindskold, 1972). For an excellent summary of the consequences of using unilateral or reciprocal and single or multiple power strategies, see Raven and Kruglanski (1970). There is also some evidence to suggest that the use and the effectiveness of specific strategies depends on the actors' relative power bases. For instance, reported sex differences in strategy use may be more a function of unequal power or resources than of sex differences *per se* (Lamb, 1981; Martin & Osmond, 1975).

Power Resistance Strategies. Much of the power literature focuses on how actors go about altering others' behaviors. It is often overlooked, however, that most power processes consist not only of proposals and counterproposals but also of attempts to resist others' power exertion by techniques other than mere counterattacks. Of course, resistance forces have always been assigned an important role in Lewinian psychology. Heider (1958), for example, defined *power* as a function of difficulty and exertion, a definition that takes resistance directly into account (cf. Tedeschi, Bonona, & Schlenker, 1972; Tedeschi, Schlenker, Lindskold, 1982).

In their literature review, Tedeschi and Lindskold (1976) mentioned four major forms or types of *resisting power exertion attempts.* The first type constitutes what Brehm (1966) called *psychological reactance:* in order to maintain independence, Brehm argued, people may either directly refuse to comply or behave in ways known to be the opposite of other's desired outcomes. Second, *public commitment* to a position has been shown to decrease a target's influenceability. In this case, resistance is heightened because of an increase in the target's stake in the conflict (maintenance of a public image). A third form of resisting control attempts stems from attitudinal changes before the control attempt itself. *Anticipatory attitude change* allows subjects to remain independent by foregoing a conflict situation in the first place. For example, the less powerful partner may change his or her viewpoint if the other partner's divergent opinion becomes known and if attempts to change O's viewpoint appear too costly (cf. Weeks, 1975). Finally, a person may learn to become immune to control, particularly in the form of communicative persuasion. It is doubtful, however, whether

such *inoculation* extends beyond resistance to cultural truisms (cf. Tedeschi & Lindskold, 1976).

Modes of *changing the power relationship* itself consist of the blocking of outcomes, demand creation, extension of the power network, and the devaluation of outcomes (or withdrawal). Each of these modes represents a different way in which the actors alter their relative dependence on each other. *Blocking outcomes* increases A's dependene on O by hindering him or her from obtaining valued outcomes that may or may not be controlled by O. Blocking outcomes that are controlled by third parties seems to be particularly important if O is highly dependent on A. In this case, O's dependence on A's contributions may remain relatively stable, while A's dependence on O increases through the mediating role that she or he plays in allowing or refusing A access to outcomes controlled by others. The involvement of children in marital conflicts often serves this function. Second, O may increase his or her partner's dependence on him or her by *creating demands* in A. Sexual deprivation is a classical example of this strategy. The third mode, *extension of the power network,* decreases O's dependence on A through O's obtaining rewards offered and controlled by A from other sources, at a "better" exchange rate. If a husband refuses to spend a lengthy vacation with his wife, she may choose to go with her mother or her friends instead. Finally, dependence relations can be modified by *devaluing A's contribution* (cf. Blau, 1964; Emerson, 1962, 1964; Tedeschi & Lindskold, 1976). Many conflicts over the custody of children illustrate that the parents are quite willing to do without each other's company but are unwilling to devalue the gratifications derived from living with their children.

The typology of power strategies developed by Tedeschi and Lindskold (1976) and presented in the preceding pages centers primarily on strategy contents. Other typologies pertain to a wider range of dimensions. In their discussion of power means, Blalock and Wilken (1979), for example, also referred to such factors as the concentration of power application, consistency of strategy use, and adherence to the established rules of power confrontations (Chapter 9).

In addition to the specific strategies used by the actors, the effectiveness and consequences of power exertion also depend on specific behavioral qualities and characteristics, such as presentation factors, flexibility, and communication style. Presentation factors are particularly important as determinants of the actor's credibility and trustworthiness (Tedeschi & Lindskold, 1976). Actors who are flexible in their approach are more able to adjust to situational contingencies and to the partner's behaviors and, therefore, are more likely to reach desirable outcomes than more rigid individuals (Raush *et al.,* 1974; Spector, 1975). Accurate communications may facilitate conflict resolution and compromises (cf. Alexander, 1973; Brickman, 1974; Deutsch, 1973), but communication can also be used strategically to gather information about the other's utilities or to manipulate the other's perceptions (cf. Rubin & Brown, 1975; Tedeschi & Lindskold, 1976).

In short, the specific strategies used to exercise power not only depend on group and member characteristics and on situational contingencies but also influence the outcomes and consequences of control processes. Most important, power exertion strategies constitute the specific behaviors through which power exertion takes place. Because the use of particularly effective strategies may offset an uneven distribution of power bases among the group members, the power structure in a relationship and at a given time is never fully determined by the actors' power bases and represents an emergent phenomenon. In addition, how partners behave in a power situation has important consequences for their evaluation of the process and their future behaviors. The same outcome may be more acceptable if it was achieved through ingratiation rather than coercion.

Control Outcomes

Although much of the research on family power has been criticized for its overemphasis on outcome power (cf. Berger, 1980; Olson & Cromwell, 1975b; Sprey, 1972, 1975), it could be argued that only very few of these studies have actually measured outcome power. As previously indicated, outcome control represents the total of the relative position modifications achieved by the actor, but the most common outcome-control measures seem to assess power norms or leadership behaviors (see p. 657). Outcome control regarding a specific issue can be assessed only after negotiations and decision making have come to a relatively stable conclusion. Before some solution has been achieved, power exertion is still in flux, and outcome control, therefore, is uncertain. In conflict situations, outcome control is usually closely linked to the type of conflict management achieved by the partners.

Unilateral power exertion and highly asymmetrical outcome control indicate conflict regulation; that is, one partner submits to the other's demands. Conflict resolution, on the other hand, probably prevails under conditions of relatively balanced power exertion. Even though the final solution may still be closer to one partner's original position than to the position of the other partner, a mutually satisfactory solution would seem to be unlikely unless some compromise between the original positions were reached. A stalemate indicates not that power was not exercised, but that neither partner was able to achieve position modifications that permitted a final solution. Postponement of decision making and negotiation suggests an ongoing power struggle. Of course, long-range postponement of a decision may eventually lead to a one-sided solution of the issue; that is, one partner is able to prevent the other from changing the status quo (cf. Scanzoni & Szinovacz, 1980). The relative frequency of such outcome types not only affects the partners' satisfaction with the relationship but may constitute a structural

feature of the relationship itself. Cuber and Harroff's "conflict-habituated" couples (1965) have obviously "agreed to disagree" over most issues, whereas "total relationships" probably require resolution of most conflicts. And the devitalized and passive-congenial couples may have come to avoid open confrontations as well as *direct* or *overt* power exertion.

Assessment of outcome control requires consideration of at least four dimensions: the scope, the extension, the amount and the temporal reach of control (Dahl, 1957; Huston, 1983; Nagel, 1968, 1975, 1976). These dimensions and their definitions are presented, together with other concepts, in Table 3. These factors reflect variations in O's attributes or responses. Within a given social relationship, A's power may be restricted to specific issues or situational contingencies (*scope*), and it may pertain to some group members, but not to others, as individuals or joined together in coalitions (*extension*). For instance, with increasing participation in child-rearing

Table 3. Power Dimensions and Definitions[a]

A.	Power bases	Tangible and intangible resources that the actor can employ to affect the other's behavior or outcomes.
B.	Power means	Strategies used by the actor to achieve intended effects on the other's behavior or outcomes, including the mediation of resources.
C.	Scope of power	Domains or issues to which the actor's ability to affect the other's behaviors or outcomes pertains.
D.	Extension of power	Number of others (individually or jointly) whose behaviors or outcomes the actor can affect.
E.	Amount of power	Probability and degree of the actor's effect on the other's behaviors or outcomes.
F.	Temporal reach of power	Number of times and length of time the actor is able to affect the other's behaviors or outcomes.
G.	Costs of power	a. Opportunity costs to the actor include forgone alternatives in the case of an unsuccessful control attempt and direct costs incurred during the control attempt.
		b. Opportunity costs to the other include the direct costs of noncompliance and forgone alternatives in the case of compliance.

[a]This table is a synthesis of earlier descriptions of power dimensions by Dahl (1957), Harsanyi (1962), Huston (1983), and Nagel (1968).

activities, husbands may claim and achieve more impact on child-care-related decisions, a previously unchallenged power domain of the mother. This increase in scope may also imply an increase in extension; that is, the father may gain additional power over specific behaviors of the children (cf. Safilios-Rothschild, 1969a). Furthermore, the possibility of coalition formation (e.g., the "weaker" parent coalesces with one or more children) provides one basis for continuous changes in family power structuring. Even if the father alone were more powerful in most domains than any other family member, he may not be able to impose his will on a coalition among all other family members. It should be noted, however, that family negotiations may extend to several issues (e.g., the husband offers to spend less time with his friends if his wife quits her job). In this case, A's concessions regarding another domain constitute part of his opportunity costs.

Amount of power refers to the likelihood or probability of A's effect on O's behavior and the degree of that effect. Let us assume that a couple continuously fights over how to allocate their financial resources. The husband would achieve the maximum amount of outcome control if he *always* ended up having the final say in money matters *and* if the family budget were *entirely* determined by his preferences (cf. Dahl, 1957; Nagel, 1968).

Some authors also consider *temporal reach* an important dimension of outcome control (Cook & Flay, 1978; Huston, 1983). This concept draws our attention to the fact that control may be of short duration and immediate in its consequences or long-lasting and delayed in its effects. Furthermore, the control event may occur only once or may be repeated on a number of occasions.

Harsanyi (1962) argued that a comprehensive description of power situations also requires consideration of both actors' *opportunity costs*. A's costs include the direct costs necessary for the control attempt (e.g., the costs of promised rewards and the costs of information acquisition) and the costs of forgone alternatives if his or her control attempt fails. O's costs, on the other hand, consist of the direct costs of resistance to A's attempt and the forgone alternatives due to compliance with A's demands. The direct costs thus represent the relative effort of the actors to gain compliance or to resist compliance; forgone alternatives constitute losses owing to a failed control attempt or to giving up one's own preferences through submission to A's requests. The powerlessness of martyrs owes itself to the fact that their noncompliance usually costs them their lives, but the unsuccessful control attempt on the persecutor's part (e.g., to obtain a confession) is of little consequence to her or him. The effort invested in a control attempt or in resistance largely depends on the importance of the issue to the actors.

Critics of Blood and Wolfe's study (1960) emphasized that the decisions included in these authors' decision-making scale were of varying significance to the spouses and were thus not comparable; for example, a wife will need more convincing to quit her job than to let her husband purchase his own clothes (cf. Safilios-Rothschild, 1970).

One of the most problematic implicit assumptions in the family power literature is that outcome power (or better, control) is often treated as a dichotomy; that is, the actors are attributed either control or not having had an impact on the issue at hand. At best, the mutual control of the partners is also taken into consideration. The previous discussion of dimensions of outcome control should have made clear that this generalized, dichotomized notion of outcome control is untenable. In many situations, all group members have some input into the negotiations and exert some power. Their relative outcome control depends on the degree to which each partner changed his or her original position *and* on the costs that he or she incurred during the power exertion process.

Another problem in current family-power studies comes from the continuous neglect of power exertion processes in their impact on outcome control. As indicated above, the effectiveness of specific power strategies may offset imbalances in the partners' power bases. Furthermore, actors vary in their efforts and persistence to achieve specific goals. In some cases, the mere persistence and frequency of control attempts (e.g., constant nagging by the wife) induce behavior changes in the partner even if O possesses more relevant power bases (cf. Rollins & Bahr, 1976). And reputational power affects the likelihood of the actors' risking control attempts (Rollins & Bahr, 1976).

Outcome control thus reflects the relative total number of position modifications achieved by each partner, given equal costs. Explanations of outcome control cannot rely only on the actors' relative power bases; they must also include assessments of the effectiveness of their power strategies as well as their efforts invested in the control attempt. Lack of outcome control in specific situations does not necessarily indicate lack of power unless A was clearly unable (rather than unwilling) to exert power. On the other hand, outcome control over specific domains ought not be taken as an indicator of overall power. A may very well fail to obtain control over specific outcomes while still maintaining a position of high power in the relationship.

Consequences of Control Processes

Because of the limitations in existing research findings, the consequences of specific power relations on family interactions and quality are quite unclear. Findings on the relationship between marital power and marital satisfaction indicate that egalitarian or husband-dominant families are more satisfied than wife-dominated families (cf. Bean, Curtis, & Marcum, 1977; Blood & Wolfe, 1960; Corrales, 1975; Kemper & Reichler, 1976; Michel, 1967; Sprenkle & Olson, 1978; Szinovacz, 1978, 1979a). However, the interpretation of these findings is questionable. Most authors stress that wife dominance violates societal norms and therefore results in a negative evaluation of the relationship even by the woman. Although this explanation may apply to the husband's marital satisfaction, it seems unacceptable for the woman. If power exertion constitutes an intentional act to modify others' behaviors or outcomes, the powerful person should not be unhappy about being successful in doing so. Wives may thus be dissatisfied with the fact that they have to carry out decisions that their relatively incompetent husbands are unable to carry out or that a powerful husband has delegated to them (Safilios-Rothschild, 1976a,b; Szinovacz, 1979a). In the former case, the relationship between wife dominance and marital satisfaction is spurious; in the latter case, women are powerful only as far as routine decisions are concerned, whereas their husbands exert "orchestration power" (Safilios-Rothschild, 1976b). Decision making is, therefore, not necessarily a pleasant activity that spouses strive to perform at all times (cf. Janis & Mann, 1977; Safilios-Rothschild, 1976a,b). In those cases in which behavioral power measures were used, the wife's leadership may have constituted a defensive strategy rather than an indicator of high control (Szinovacz, 1981). Also, because wife dominance indeed violates predominant social norms, families with powerful wives may undergo consistent power struggles, and this fact, rather than her dominance, may inflate the wife's marital happiness.

And how should we interpret the fact that some family sociologists and therapists have found that a centralized authority structure in favor of the husband is conducive to marital quality (cf. Craddock, 1980; Ferreira & Winter, 1965; Kolb & Straus, 1974; Shepperson, 1981)? One interpretation of these findings could be that well-adjusted families are more able than disturbed families to present themselves in accordance with socially desirable norms of male dominance, whereas the disturbed families are so involved in their power struggles that they are unable to maintain a public image of male authority. On the other hand, during times of social change, families that adopt new life patterns for which no patent solutions exist may find themselves in a stressful situation, particularly if they themselves undergo normative reorientations (cf. Scanzoni & Szinovacz, 1980). Such families are probably less likely to view their relationship in conventional ways (and, as a result, to have low marital-satisfaction scores) and are more likely to seek expert help (and, as a result, to be labeled *disturbed*) than families that maintain traditional role expectations and a constant pattern of male authority or dominance. And such labeling may function to reinforce images of traditional family structures and, therefore, to distract from the societal bases of family problems (Donzelot, 1979). Maladjustment of the children in wife-dominant families may occur owing to the discrepancy between familial and societal role expectations (Alkire, 1969, 1972).

Generally, the assessment of the consequences of familial power relations cannot be restricted to mere correlations between outcome control or power structure and

marital or familial quality. Different structural arrangements may imply a similar distribution of overall outcome control but are likely to have diverse effects on the members' satisfaction. Thus, the consequences of egalitarian power structures for marital satisfaction vary according to other structural features, namely, whether the pattern is autonomous or syncratic (Bean *et al.*, 1977; Wolfe, 1959). In addition, the *context* within which specific control outcomes occur influences the consequences. Research on problem-solving efficiency indicates, for instance, that a centralized authority structure may enhance problem-solving efficiency among lower-class families, but not among middle-class families (Tallman & Miller, 1974).

Outcome evaluations refer not only to *how much* power was exercised by the actor, but also to the *means* and *strategies* used in exercising power. There can be little doubt that coercive strategies, ranging from threats to physical violence, result in more negative evaluations than, perhaps, equally or even more efficient ingratiation techniques based on referent or reward power (cf. Jones, 1964; Rands, Levinger, & Mellinger, 1981; Raven & Kruglanski, 1970; Raven *et al.*, 1975). Problem-solving efficiency may be enhanced if the leader's power rests on authority and expertise and if she or he uses leadership in a coordinative manner (Klein & Hill, 1979). Similarly, it is not necessarily the amount of overall control that parents exert on their children that affects the children's development and their later personality characteristics, but how such control is exercised. Coercive control tends to prevent the development of such characteristics as creativity, self-esteem. and competence, whereas inductive control furthers the development of the same characteristics (Rollins & Thomas, 1975, 1979). And adolescents' perceptions of parental power, as well as their identification with the parents, are contingent on the parents' perceived possession of *specific* power bases, namely, referent and expert power (McDonald, 1979; Smith, 1970).

The *frequency and consistency* of power exertion and of specific strategies are also likely to affect outcomes and their evaluation. Consistent and frequent use of coercive strategies has been shown to result in patterns of continuous negative exchanges and a vicious circle of coercion with highly destructive consequences (Feldman, 1979; Gottman, 1979; Gottman, Notarius, Markman, Bank, & Yoppi, 1976; Patterson, 1976, 1978; Schlenker & Goldman, 1978). Such patterns can be broken only if the implicit reinforcement contingencies are eliminated. Or some spouses may accept some coercive and aggressive behaviors by their partner as long as the occurrence of such behaviors remains infrequent and within clearly delineated boundaries (cf. Young, 1977).

What family members deem acceptable or fair depends not only on distributive justice, but also on the specific conditions and the motivation underlying their behaviors. Thus, coercive and aggressive acts may be acceptable if they were provoked (cf. Deutsch, 1969). Unilateral and coercive power exertion by one spouse is likely to be particularly destructive for the relationship if it occurs in regard to the other spouse's legitimate power domain or is of great importance to him or her.

A final consequence of family control processes is their modeling and learning effects on the children. As indicated above, children learn power-relevant behavioral dispositions such as machiavellianism from their parents (Kraut & Price, 1976). The very strong modeling effects of coercive and violent behaviors have been demonstrated in a series of studies (cf. Gelles & Straus, 1979; Owens & Straus, 1975; Straus, 1977, 1978a; Straus et al., 1980). And the mother's delegation of power to older siblings has been shown to affect the younger siblings' problem-solving efficiency in the presence or absence of relevant others (cf. Cicirelli, 1975, 1978).

In order to adequately assess the consequences of power relations, it is therefore essential to go beyond mere correlations between ''outcome control'' and familial quality and to consider how power is exercised and which conditions lead to the use of specific power-exertion strategies or certain control outcomes. In addition, the causal direction of relationships between power and other familial behaviors needs to be specified. Egalitarian control patterns may contribute to the partners' marital satisfaction, and they may also be the result of a satisfactory relationship (cf. Szinovacz, 1979a). Or highly coercive children can affect the parents' well-being and relationship (Patterson, 1978), but marital satisfaction has also been shown to affect the parents' relative use of punishments or rewards with their children (Kemper & Reichler, 1976). Steinmetz (1979) presented a similar argument when she emphasized that the effects of specific disciplinary techniques on children (and such techniques are, of course, often power exertion strategies on the part of the parents) are contingent on contextual and relationship factors, such as the general family environment, the day-to-day patterns of interaction, or the timing and consistency of these behaviors.

In order to fully understand the consequences of control processes, it is not enough to assess direct interactional and attitudinal changes brought about through specific control events. Rather, their long-term consequences for future control processes must be considered. In this sense, past control events constitute the interactional and attitudinal context within which future control processes operate. Past control events may lead to a redistribution of power bases among the family members; they may affect the family members' perceptions of fairness, or they may result in different orientations (e.g., the family members may learn to distrust each other). Current behaviors are often fully understandable only in the light of the family's past relationship. The mutually destructive behavior patterns described by Gottman (1979), for instance, have their roots in the perpetuation of negative exchanges and the use of coercive power strategies. Vio-

lence often evolves from continuous psychological abuse (cf. Gelles, 1974; Steinmetz, 1977) and is generationally transmitted through learning and role modeling (cf. Straus et al., 1980).

Conclusion

Some Guidelines for Future Research

During the 1960s and early 1970s, progress in family power research was seriously constrained owing to conceptualization and operationalization problems as well as adherence to an oversimplified theoretical perspective. More recent work in this area suggests that many of these problems may be overcome by the end of the 1980's. The increased sensitivity to measurement problems and the heightened awareness of the complexities of family power relationships and processes constitute a promising basis for methodological and theoretical developments.

The objective of this chapter was to elaborate further on both issues. In the first part of the chapter, conceptual issues were discussed in detail and in view of the current methodological problems in measuring power. Specifically, an attempt was made to show the links between conceptual and measurement issues. The second part of the chapter addressed theoretical issues in family power research. Existing research results from family and small-group research were synthesized within a general theoretical framework of family power processes. The major assumptions underlying the proposed model were that family power relations are subject to sociostructural and specific situational and group conditions, and that they consist of a multidimensional and multiphasic process. In discussing the major model dimensions, an attempt was made to show how contextual factors, group and member characteristics, and situational contingencies are reflected in the family members' power exertion processes and outcomes and how they affect the evaluation and consequences of such processes. The great number of potential influence factors mentioned throughout this discussion surely demonstrates the complexity of powering processes.

Because many of the current approaches to family power tend toward an oversimplified theoretical perspective, this emphasis on complexity seems warranted. However, complexity is certainly not the ultimate goal of theory building, and models that are too complex may discourage researchers. Obviously, empirical investigations of power relations will have to be restricted to partial tests of some relationships implied in such complex models. It may thus seem appropriate to conclude this theoretical discussion with a few examples of research questions that may be generated from this model.

Certainly, the model draws attention to the need for multivariate analyses of family power relations. Even those studies that have investigated the effect of several independent variables have often been restricted to bivariate analyses (cf. Centers *et al.*, 1971). Thus, we know very little about the relative importance of selected influence factors or about potential interaction effects. We may expect, for instance, that the effect of resource disparities between spouses on marital control processes is mediated through specific interaction patterns or is contingent on cultural or subcultural conditions. Low-income husbands may use physical strength only as the "ultimate resource" if cultural prescriptions attribute the responsibility for the provider role primarily to the husband or if his low income remains in constant criticism from his wife.

Another widely neglected field of research is the relationship among power bases, power exertion strategies, and control outcomes. Studies of this relationship could help us to understand to what degree family members are able to offset deficiencies in their power bases through the use of particularly effective strategies and which strategies are chosen for this purpose. In addition, there may be direct links between the specific resources and the power strategies used in a control event. Thus, some resource potentials may be relatively worthless if a family member does not have the necessary skills to also apply the appropriate power strategies. However, each of these questions can be addressed only through multivariate analyses. Such statistical procedures are also necessary in the study of the relative impact of group and member characteristics other than power bases on power exertion processes and outcomes.

Some of the causal sequences implied in the model could be tested on the basis of cross-cultural or subcultural comparisons. We may, for example, investigate how cultural context factors are linked to specific structural features of family groups, including differential patterns of resource distribution among the family members, and how these contextual and structural characteristics interact in their influence on control processes and outcomes. Are the sexual favors that working-class women use to influence their husbands (cf. Rubin, 1976) equally applicable and effective among middle-class couples? And what specific outcomes can wives control by using this strategy?

Similarly, the effect of situational contingencies on family power processes is still quite unclear. We suspect that families behave differently in public settings and in their homes, but most of the research connecting conflict characteristics to power exertion processes and outcomes has been conducted with groups of strangers (Raush *et al.*,'s 1974 study is obviously a major exception). Because family members interact within the context of their history, specific situational contingencies may affect their behaviors quite differently than they would affect the behaviors among strangers. We may be able to enhance competitive behaviors among strangers through increased incentives in experimental games (cf. Deutsch, 1973), but shall we also be able to so induce competitive behaviors in family groups that have established a long history of cooperation? Descriptions of specific power-

exertion events in different situations or in systematic variations of experimental settings (using family groups) may provide useful insights into these relationships.

Finally, the model presented in the second part of this chapter contains a series of specific influence factors that have never or only very seldom been included in studies of family power relations. For example, most of the evidence regarding personality and interpersonal orientation factors is based on social-psychological research with strangers. Surely, family members' personalities and their attitudes toward each other can be expected to affect their behaviors in power situations. To what extent family members deem it important to control others' behaviors or to use power at all and how they go about exerting power may be more contingent on their mutual trust and their positive regard for each other than on their relative power bases. An examination of such relationships will not only contribute to our general understanding of family power processes but may also provide us with some important insights into why some families engage in frequent power struggles and continuously attempt to control each other whereas other families tend to avoid such confrontations. Comparing families that differ in such interpersonal orientations in regard to their other structural features could also enhance our understanding of the family historical antecedents of current power-exertion strategies and outcomes. Obviously, we need longitudinal studies to obtain detailed descriptions of the development of family power relations over time.

Suggestions for Measurement

It is clearly not the purpose of a review to elaborate on the development of new measures. However, a significant part of this chapter dealt with current methodological problems in family power research. Specifically, it was suggested that many measurement problems are based on insufficient conceptual distinctions. Thus, it may seem appropriate to provide some suggestions regarding measurement improvement and to show how some issues raised in the preceding discussion could be applied.

One of the most prominent difficulties with current power measures is that they lack clear theoretical and conceptual foundations. To ask family members about their relative say in specific decisions or to observe who wins in an experimental game provides us with very little information about the family members' control over selected family issues. A family member may be perceived as having the final say if she or he carries out most of the tasks involved in the decision-making process or makes the most suggestions during an experimental task. The meaning of such answers thus remains quite ambiguous. Furthermore, the amount, scope, and extension of outcome control require specification. The currently used measures do not produce sufficiently *detailed* information to adequately assess even outcome control. At this stage of measurement development, in-depth analyses of specific control events may be most needed. Thus, family members could be asked separately or jointly to provide detailed accounts of recent control events or to give detailed explanations of how specific familial arrangements (e.g., task allocation) have been worked out (Beckman, 1982; Frank & Scanzoni, 1982; Hood, 1983; LaRossa & LaRossa, 1981), and the results obtained from such in-depth analyses could then be compared to results obtained through traditional power measures.

Another way to develop new measures is through an extension of the multimethod approach. In addition to obtaining multiple scores on the basis of several self-report and behavioral indicators, family members could be asked to elaborate on their responses. Such procedures may contribute to an explanation of why different power measures lead to divergent results. In all these instances, all family members who usually participate in the relevant control events should be interviewed or observed.

Behavioral measures could be improved by extending the observations to longer and less structured tasks and, particularly if power relations with or among children are concerned, through lengthy observations in natural settings. Obviously, such lengthy (and expensive) procedures are particularly problematic if the study involves a large sample or the analysis of power relations does not constitute the primary goal of the investigation. For such purposes, relatively short and standardized measures are essential. However, as in the case of other scales, the development of such indicators requires in-depth analyses and adequate validity and reliability tests.

Until such newly developed measures are available, even slight modifications of the currently used measures may lead to significant improvements. For instance, social psychological studies of power exertion strategies suggest that respondents can relate relatively easily to the question "What do you do to get your way?" Answers to this question not only indicate that the interviewees are able to describe specific control events and power exertion strategies but also suggest relative high face validity. Instead of asking subjects about their relative final say in decisions, we could instead request estimates of how likely they are able to get their way on specific occasions and to what extent their viewpoint would be accepted by other family members. The validity of current behavioral measures could be enhanced if family members were asked to resolve issues that are known to be relevant to their family (e.g., on the basis of prior questions regarding familial conflicts), if they were allowed to come up with their own rather than predetermined solutions (thus eliminating the zero-sum problem), and if coding procedures were revised to more closely correspond to the theoretical concepts outlined earlier in this chapter.

Alternative Approaches to Family Power

The perspective taken in this chapter is grounded in conventional approaches to family theory in general and to family power relations in particular. The increasing interest in divergent approaches such as those offered by feminists, critical thinkers, and phenomenologists requires some consideration of alternative interpretations. Mainstream sociologists have tended to ignore these more radical approaches in their entirety. It is my contention that several critical points offered in this literature are valid and could, if taken seriously, help advance research on family power relations. Space limitations do not allow an in-depth discussion of each of these viewpoints, but I would nevertheless like to conclude this chapter with a few suggestions for future research that have been informed by such alternative approaches.

The Feminist Critique. One of the most fervent criticisms of family power research, and especially of resource theory, comes from feminist scholars. They have consistently pointed out that (traditional) family-power research depicts increasing symmetry in marital relations (Young & Willmott, 1973) despite persistent sexual stratification at the societal level (Bell & Newby, 1976; Gillespie, 1971), that it ignores sexual inequalities in marriage and other legal contracts (Weitzman, Dixon, Bird, McGinn, & Robertson, 1983), and that it is oblivious to exemplifications of women's dependence and submission in intimate relations as evidenced in the distribution of household work, inequities in sexual gratification, and the extent of physical abuse (Breines & Gordon, 1983; Dobash & Dobash, 1979; Hartmann, 1981; Shulman, 1980; Thorne & Yalom, 1982; Williams, 1980).

There can be little doubt about the substantive claims brought forward by these critics. Every introductory sociology text offers evidence of the inferior position of women in regard to major social-status characteristics, many of which constitute resources in the Blood and Wolfe (1960) framework. Similarly, even employed wives still maintain the primary responsibility for most household and child-rearing tasks and, consequently, have considerably less leisure time than their husbands (Geerken & Gove, 1983; Szalai, 1973; Szinovacz, 1979b). Recent research on the use of physical force against wives and even girlfriends also supports the notion that the dependence of women on the relationship contributes to their abuse (Kalmuss & Straus, 1982) and prevents them from leaving abusive relationships (Cate, Henton, Koval, Christopher, & Lloyd, 1982; Gelles, 1979; Pagelow, 1981).

Family power researchers only rarely pay attention to these arguments. However, the feminist critique points to several important issues that require enhanced consideration. One such issue is the overemphasis on micro-sociological processes and explanations. As conceptualized by Emerson (1976), A's power is a direct function of O's dependence. And dependence is contingent not only on the actors' resources, but also on their alternatives as well as on the costs of pursuing such alternatives. Access to and the acceptability of the alternatives are importantly affected by societal structures and norms. Women as a group are disadvantaged not only in regard to socioeconomic opportunities resulting in economic dependence on men, but also in regard to other demographic factors and gender norms providing differential standards for men's and women's behavior (cf. Eichler, 1981). For instance, it might be worthwhile to investigate the effect on power relations of a skewed sex ratio in the population that favors men's position in the marriage market. Also, despite some decreases in sexual double standards, women's public behavior is still more restricted than men's (Fox, 1977); as a result, the initiation of heterosexual relations is more difficult and probably also more costly for women than for men.

Another issue addressed by the feminist critique concerns the importance of decisions considered in family power studies. Family power researchers generally acknowledge the relevancy of this problem, but little has been done to correct it. However, as long as relatively unimportant decisions or behaviors constitute the basis of our research evidence, our results may very well provide a biased view of current marital relations. We cannot proclaim increased egalitarianism on the basis of joint decision-making in minor areas, while ignoring major inequalities in the division of labor between the sexes or repeated accounts of the use of violence against wives who dare to question their husbands' authority (cf. LaRossa, 1977). Unless our theories can account for these findings, their validity may quite rightfully be questioned.

A Lesson from Critical Theory. One major concern of critical theorists is the inherent conservative bias in empirical research. It is argued that "technique has dictated a view of human behavior which eternalizes the present constraints to which men are subject" (Birnbaum, 1971, p. 226). Empirical research necessarily reflects current societal (or familial) conditions. Such evidence, if interpreted ahistorically and with an implicit claim for general validity, tends to legitimize these current conditions and deflects our thought from the human potential (cf. Gouldner, 1970; Horkheimer, 1970).

Some critics of family power research have applied this argument to resource and exchange theories. For example, Bell and Newby (1976) wrote:

Exchange theory cannot itself . . . provide an explanation of hierarchical relationships. . . . Deference, as any relationship, involves exchange but *we need to know* what is exchanged for what, how the norms of exchange *are established or imposed.* (p. 156)

If accepted uncritically, resource theory (at least in its original formulation by Blood and Wolfe and in their emphasis on tangible resources) may indeed legitimize traditional power hierarchies among family members. Are we not saying implicitly that husbands who control more resources than their wives are *entitled* to have more say in the marriage? What remains unquestioned is that access to these resources is, to a large extent, societally predetermined and that the evaluation of contributions and the fairness of their distribution is based on external

relationship criteria, that is, on status value and referential structures (Berger *et al.,* 1972). There is also relatively little concern about the implications of research findings that show that, even if the traditional resource distribution breaks down, men can and do rely on physical force as the "ultimate resource" (Tellis-Nayak & Donoghue, 1982; Yllo & Straus, 1982).

What are the implications of this critique? The critically informed interpretation of resource theory points to the pervasiveness of norms (ideology) and sociostructural conditions as determinants of marital power relations. To fully understand how ideologies and social structure manifest themselves in family power relations, it will be necessary to abandon our microsociological emphasis, to engage in cross-societal and historical comparisons and to acknowledge physical strength as an important power basis (Collins, 1975).

To avoid interpretations that "eternalize" present societal constraints, we may further profit from in-depth analyses of couples or families who have themselves, at least to some extent, transcended these constrictions. Current power research centers on middle-aged, middle-class individuals. We thus know very little about power relations among families that adhere to alternative marriage and family forms, and we also have very little information on families whose resource distribution is in sharp contrast to the "average" middle-class family (e.g., independently wealthy women in upper-class marriages and elderly spouses who are physically incapacitated).

Finally, the emphasis on human potential and emancipation in critical theory calls for increased consideration of the consequences of asymmetrical power relations for the family members. Family power research has concentrated on the structural dimensions of power relations, but we know very little about family members' feelings and evaluations of power relations. In other words, we may know who participates in certain decisions, but we know hardly anything about feelings of oppression and dependence. And except for a few studies relating power structure and marital satisfaction, we are also quite ignorant about the personal and familial consequences of family power structures and processes. Research in this field certainly could profit from addressing such questions as: How do feelings of dependence relate to family members' relative resources? Under what conditions are family members who are at a resource disadvantage able to develop and maintain self-perceptions of autonomy and independence? What are the relative effects of objective and subjective dependence on interactions (see also Kalmuss & Straus, 1982)?

Power and the Construction of Reality. Much of the present power literature deals with relatively explicit negotiations and decisions that concern specific behaviors or outcomes. However, power can also be used to shape individuals' identities and self-concepts. This view of power and control is perhaps most evident in the works of

Berger and Kellner (1964) and of Laing (1969) (see also McLain & Weigert, 1979).

Berger and Kellner (1964) pointed to the validating function of marital relationships, and they showed that marriage partners engage in a process of reality construction in which both partners' past and present experiences are redefined and modified in order to establish a common reality. Even though the authors viewed this process of "biographical fusion" (McLain & Weigert, 1979, p. 176) as reciprocal and largely unintentional, the actors may engage in active and conscious attempts to shape the other's self-image and to impose their own subjective realities on the partner. Laing (1969) referred to such processes as "attributions." They consist of projections onto the other, and they often serve as a substitute for orders or direct control attempts:

One way to get someone to do what one wants, is to give an order. To get someone to be what one wants him to be . . . is another matter. In a hypnotic (or similar) context, one does not tell him what to be, but tells him what he is. Such attributions, in context, are many times more powerful than orders (or other forms of coercion or persuasion). (p. 78)

Case studies show that such attribution processes are quite common in couples' accounts of decision-making and negotiation processes. Let us examine a brief excerpt from LaRossa and LaRossa's case study materials (1981):

CAROL: I don't think that I realized that I did want to go back to work. And then . . . . when we finally talked about it, I guess it finally came out in the middle of all that, that you know, "Yes, I really would like to go back to work." Sooner than I had thought.

CHESTER: Well, I just don't think you ever really wanted to be a housewife . . . And I think it's great. I didn't marry Carol to be a housewife. (p. 123)

In this dialogue, the husband indicates that he prefers his wife to work, but at the same time, he presents her return to the labor force as her idea. From the wife's account, however, the reader is not fully convinced that it was Carol's idea and that she really wants to resume employment at this time.

It would seem essential that family power researchers pay more attention to such control situations. If A is able to shape and modify O's identity and self-concept, his or her control is likely to extend to a broad range of behaviors, to be long-lasting, and to involve relatively few costs because O is made to believe that he or she acts in his or her own interests.

During the 1960s, we became aware that family power relations constitute an important element of family interactions. The initial efforts to empirically investigate family power relations led to a methodological, conceptual, and theoretical debate that continued well into the 1970s and is still not entirely resolved. Recent theoretical contributions have provided an expanded framework for studying family power relations. Hopefully, the 1980s will bring the research evidence needed to substantiate and expand current theoretical accomplishments in this field.

ACKNOWLEDGMENTS

I would like to thank David Klein, Gerald McDonald, David Olson, John Scanzoni, Jetse Sprey, and an anonymous reviewer for their suggestions and their critical comments on an earlier draft of this paper.

References

Abrahamson, B. Humans on exchange: Hedonism revived. *American Journal of Sociology*, 1972, *76*, 273–285.

Adams, J. S. Inequity in social exchange. In L. Berkowitz (Ed.), *Advances in experimental social psychology*, Vol. 2. New York: Academic Press, 1969.

Adler, E. S. *Perceived marital power, influence techniques and marital violence.* Paper presented at the meeting of the American Sociological Association, 1977.

Aldous, J. Family interaction patterns. In A. Inkeles, J. Coleman, & N. Smelser (Eds.), *Annual review of sociology.* Palo Alto, Calif.: Annual Reviews, 1977.

Alexander, C. N., & Lauderdale, P. Situated identities and social influence. *Sociometry*, 1977, *40*, 225–233.

Alexander, J. F. Defensive and supportive communications in family systems. *Journal of Marriage and the Family*, 1973, *35*, 613–618.

Alford, R. D. Intimacy and disputing styles within kin and nonkin relationships. *Journal of Family Issues*, 1982, *3*, 361–374.

Alkire, A. A. Social power and communication within families of disturbed and nondisturbed pre-adolescents. *Journal of Personality and Social Psychology*, 1969, *13*, 335–349.

Alkire, A. A. Enactment of social power and role behavior in families of disturbed and nondisturbed pre-adolescents. *Developmental Psychology*, 1972, *7*, 270–276.

Allen, C. M., & Straus, M. A. *Resources, power, and husband-wife violence.* Paper presented at the meeting of the National Council on Family Relations, 1975.

Apfelbaum, E. On conflicts and bargaining. In L. Berkowitz (Ed.), *Advances in experimental social psychology*, Vol. 7. New York: Academic Press, 1974.

Aries, P. *Centuries of childhood. A social history of family life.* New York: Vintage, 1962.

Assor, A., & O'Quin, K. The intangibles of bargaining: Power and competence versus deference and approval. *The Journal of Social Psychology*, 1982, *116*, 119–126.

Axelrod. R. Conflict of interest: An axiomatic approach. *Journal of Conflict Resolution*, 1967, *11*, 87–99.

Bacharach, S. B., & Lawler, E. J. The perception of power. *Social Forces*, 1976, *55*, 123–134.

Bagarozzi, D. A., & Wodarski, J. S. A social exchange typology of conjugal relationships and conflict development. *Journal of Marriage and Family Counseling*, 1977, *3*, 53–60.

Bahr, S. J. Comment on "The study of family power structure: A review 1960–1969." *Journal of Marriage and the Family*, 1972, *34*, 239–243.

Bahr, S. J. The internal consistency of Blood and Wolfe's measure of conjugal power: A research note. *Journal of Marriage and the Family*, 1973, *35*, 293–295.

Bahr, S. J. Effects on power and division of labor in the family. In L. W. Hoffman & F. I. Nye (Eds.), *Working mothers.* San Francisco: Jossey/Bass, 1975.

Bahr, S. J., & Rollins, B. C. Crisis and conjugal power. *Journal of Marriage and the Family*, 1971, *33*, 360–361.

Bahr, S. J., Bowerman, C. E., & Gecas, V. Adolescent perceptions of conjugal power. *Social Forces*, 1974, *52*, 357–367.

Bannester, M. E. Sociodynamics: An integrative theorem of power, authority, interfluence, and love. *American Sociological Review*, 1969, *34*, 374–393.

Bar-Tal, D., Bar-Zohar, Y., Hermon, M., & Greenberg, M. S. Reciprocity behavior in the relationship between donor and recipient and between harmdoer and victim. *Sociometry*, 1977, *40*, 293–297.

Bartos, O. J. Determinants and consequences of toughness. In P. Swingle (Ed.), *The structure of conflict*. New York: Academic Press, 1970.

Bean, F. D., & Kerckhoff, A. C. Personality and perception in husband-wife conflicts. *Journal of Marriage and the Family*, 1971, *33*, 351–359.

Bean, F. D., Curtis, R. L., & Marcum, J. P. Familism and marital satisfaction among Mexican Americans: The effects of family size, wife's labor force participation, and conjugal power. *Journal of Marriage and the Family*, 1977, *39*, 759–767.

Beckman, L. J. Measuring the process of fertility decision-making. In G. L. Fox (Ed.), *The childbearing decision*. Beverly Hills, Calif.: Sage, 1982.

Beckman-Brindley, S., & Tavormina, J. B. Power relationships in families: A social-exchange perspective. *Family Process*, 1978, *17*, 423–436.

Befu, H. Structural and motivational approaches to exchange. In K. J. Gergen, M. S. Greenberg, & R. H. Willis (Eds.), *Social exchange: Advances in theory and research*. New York: Plenum Press, 1980.

Bell, C., & Newby, H. Husbands and wives: The dynamics of the deferential dialectic. In D. L. Barker & S. Allen (Eds.), *Dependence and exploitation in work and marriage*. London: Longman, 1976.

Bell, D. C., Chafetz, J. S., & Horn, L. H. Marital conflict resolution: A study of strategies and outcomes. *Journal of Family Issues*, 1982, *3*, 111–132.

Bell, R. A reinterpretation of the direction of effects in studies of socialization. *Psychological Review*, 1968, *75*, 81–95.

Bell, R. Parent, child, and reciprocal influences. *American Psychologist*, 1979, *34*, 821–826.

Berger, C. R. Power and the family. In M. E. Roloff & G. R. Miller (Eds.), *Persuasion: New directions in theory and research*. Beverly Hills, Calif.: Sage, 1980.

Berger, J., Zelditch, M., Anderson, B., & Cohen, B. P. Structural aspects of distributive justice: A status value formulation. In J. Berger, M. Zelditch, & B. Anderson (Eds.), *Sociological theories in progress*, Vol. 2. Boston: Houghton Mifflin, 1972.

Berger, P. L., & Kellner, H. Marriage and the construction of reality. *Diogenes*, 1964, *46*, 1–23.

Berkowitz, L., & Daniels, L. R. Affecting the salience of the social responsibility norm: Effects of past help on the response to dependency relationships. In C. Hendrick & R. A. Jones (Eds.), *The nature of theory and research in social psychology*. New York: Academic Press, 1972.

Bernard, J. The adjustment of married mates. In H. T. Christensen (Ed.), *Handbook of marriage and the family*. Chicago: Rand McNally, 1964.

Bierstedt, R. *Power and progress: Essays in sociological theory*. New York: McGraw-Hill, 1974.

Birnbaum, N. *Toward a critical sociology*. New York: Oxford University Press, 1971.

Blalock, H. M., & Wilken, P. H. *Intergroup processes*. New York: Free Press, 1979.

Blau, P. M. *Exchange and power in social life*. New York: Wiley, 1964.

Blood, R. O. Resolving family conflicts. *Journal of Conflict Resolution*, 1960, *4*, 209–219.

Blood, R. O., & Wolfe, D. M. *Husbands and wives: The dynamics of married living*. New York: Free Press, 1960.

Bobbit, R. A. Internal-external control and bargaining behavior in a prisoner's dilemma game. *Dissertation abstracts*, 1967, *27*, 3266–3267-B.

Booth, A., & Welch, S. Spousal consensus and its correlates. *Journal of Marriage and the Family*, 1978, *40*, 23–34.

Bott, E. *Family and social network*. New York: Free Press, 1957.

Boulding, K. E. An economist's view. *American Journal of Sociology*, 1962, *67*, 458–461.

Braver, S. L., & Rohrer, V. When martyrdom pays. *Journal of Conflict Resolution*, 1975, *19*, 652–663.

Bredemeier, H. C. Exchange theory. In T. Bottomore & R. Nisbet (Eds.), *A history of sociological analysis*. New York: Basic Books, 1978.

Brehm, J. W. *A theory of psychological reactance*. New York: Academic Press, 1966.

Brehmer, B., & Hammond, K. R. Cognitive factors in interpersonal conflict. In D. Druckman (Ed.), *Negotiations*. Beverly Hills, Calif.: Sage, 1977.

Breines, W., & Gordon, L. The new scholarship on family violence. *Signs*, 1983, *8*, 490–531.

Brickman, P. *Social conflict*. Lexington, Mass.: Heath, 1974.

Brinkerhoff, M., & Lupri, E. Theoretical and methodological issues in the use of decision-making as an indicator of conjugal power: Some Canadian observations. *Canadian Journal of Sociology*, 1978, *3*, 1–20.

Broderick, C. B. Power in the governance of families. In R. E. Cromwell & D. H. Olson (Eds.), *Power in families*. New York: Halsted Press, 1975.

Buckley, W. *Sociology and modern systems theory*. Englewood Cliffs, N.J.: Prentice-Hall, 1967.

Buehler, M. H., Weigert, J. A., & Thomas, D. L. Correlates of conjugal power: A five culture analysis of adolescent perceptions. *Journal of Comparative Family Studies*, 1974, *5*, 5–16.

Burchinal, L. G., & Bauder, W. W. Decision-making and role patterns among Iowa farm and non-farm families. *Journal of Marriage and the Family*, 1965, *27*, 525–530.

Burgess, R. L., & Conger, R. D. Distributive justice and the balance of power. *American Sociological Review*, 1974, *39*, 427–443.

Buric, O., & Zecevic, A. Family authority, marital satisfaction, and the social network in Yugoslavia. *Journal of Marriage and the Family*, 1967, *29*, 325–336.

Burns, T. R. A structural theory of social exchange. *Acta Sociologica*, 1973, *16*, 188–208.

Burns, T. R. Unequal exchange and uneven development in social life: Continuities in a structural theory of social exchange. *Acta Sociologica*, 1977, *20*, 217–245.

Burr, W. R. Satisfaction with various aspects of marriage over the life cycle: A random middle-class sample. *Journal of Marriage and the Family*, 1970, *32*, 29–37.

Burr, W. R. *Theory construction and the sociology of the family*. New York: Wiley, 1973.

Burr, W. R., Ahern, L., & Knowles, E. M. An empirical test of Rodman's theory of resources in cultural context. *Journal of Marriage and the Family*, 1977, *39*, 505–514.

Cagle, L. T. *Exchange and romantic love norms*. Paper presented at the meeting of the American Sociological Association, 1975.

Campbell, D. T., & Fiske, D. W. Convergent and discriminate validation by the multitrait-multimethod matrix. *Psychological Bulletin*, 1959, *56*, 81–105.

Caplow, T. *Two against one: Coalitions in triads*. Englewood Cliffs, N.J.: Prentice-Hall, 1968.

Cartwright, D. A field theoretical conception of power. In D. Cartwright

(Ed.), *Studies in social power*. Ann Arbor: University of Michigan Press, 1959.

Cassidy, R. G., & Neave, E. H. Dynamics of coalition formation: Prescriptions vs. reality. *Theory and Decision*, 1977, *8*, 159–171.

Cate, R. M., Henton, J. M., Koval, J., Christopher, F. S., & Lloyd, S. Premarital abuse. A social psychological perspective. *Journal of Family Issues*, 1982, *3*, 79–96.

Cate, R. M., Lloyd, S. A., Henton, J. M., & Larson, J. H. Fairness and reward level as predictors of relationship satisfaction. *Social Psychology Quarterly*, 1982, *45*, 177–181.

Centers, R., Raven, B. H., & Rodrigues, A. Conjugal power structure: A reexamination. *American Sociological Review*, 1971, *36*, 264–278.

Chadwick-Jones, J. K. *Social exchange theory: Its structure and influence in social psychology*. London: Academic Press, 1976.

Champlin, J. R. On the study of power. *Politics and Society*, 1970, *1*, 91–111.

Cherlin, A., & Walters, P. B. Trends in United States' men's and women's sex role attitudes: 1972–1978. *American Sociological Review*, 1981, *46*, 453–460.

Chertkoff, J. M. Coalition formation as a function of differences in resources. *Journal of Conflict Resolution*, 1971, *15*, 371–383.

Christensen, H. T. (Ed.), *Handbook of marriage and the family*. Chicago: Rand McNally, 1964.

Christie, R., & Geis, F. (Eds.). *Studies in Machiavellianism*. New York: Academic Press, 1970.

Cialdini, R. B., Vincent, J. E., Lewis, S. K., Catalan, J., Wheeler, D., & Darby, B. L. Reciprocal concessions procedure for inducing compliance: The door-in-the-face technique. *Journal of Personality and Social Psychology*, 1975, *31*, 206–215.

Cicirelli, V. G. Effects of mother and older sibling on the problem-solving behavior of the younger child. *Developmental Psychology*, 1975, *2*, 749–756.

Cicirelli, V. G. Effect of sibling presence on mother-child interaction. *Developmental Psychology*, 1978, *14*, 315–316.

Claessens, D. *Rolle und Macht*. Munich: Juventa, 1970.

Collins, R. *Conflict Sociology*. New York: Academic Press, 1975.

Conklin, G. H. Cultural determinants of power for women within the family: neglected aspect of family research. *Journal of Comparative Family Studies*, 1979, *10*, 36–53.

Cook, K. S., & Emerson, R. M. Power, equity and commitment in exchange networks. *American Sociological Review*, 1978, *43*, 721–739.

Cook, T. D., & Flay, B. R. The persistence of experimentally induced attitude change. In L. Berkowitz (Ed.), *Advances in experimental social psychology*, Vol. 11. New York: Academic Press, 1978.

Cooney, R. S., Rogler, L. H., Hurrell, R., & Ortiz, V. Decision-making in intergenerational Puerto Rican families. *Journal of Marriage and the Family*, 1982, *44*, 621–631.

Corrales, R. G. Power and satisfaction in early marriage. In R. E. Cromwell & D. H. Olson (Eds.), *Power in families*. New York: Halsted Press, 1975.

Coser, L. A. *The functions of social conflict*. New York: Free Press, 1956.

Coser, L. A. *Continuities in the study of social conflict*. New York: Free Press, 1967.

Craddock, A. E. Relationships between authoritarianism, marital power expectations and marital value systems. *Australian Journal of Psychology*, 1977, *29*, 211–221.

Craddock, A. E. Marital problem-solving as a function of the couples' marital power expectations and marital value systems. *Journal of Marriage and the Family*, 1980, *42*, 185–196.

Cromwell, R. E., & Olson, D. H. Multidisciplinary perspectives of power. In R. E. Cromwell & D. H. Olson (Eds.), *Power in families*. New York: Halsted Press, 1975.

Cromwell, R. E. & Ruiz, R. A. The myth of macho dominance in decision-making within Mexican and Chicano families. *Hispanic Journal of Behavioral Sciences*, 1979, *1*, 355–373.

Cromwell, R. E., & Wieting, S. G. Multidimensionality of conjugal decision-making indices: Comparative analyses of five samples. *Journal of Comparative Family Studies*, 1975, *6*, 139–152.

Cromwell, R. E., Corrales, R., & Torsillo, P. M. Normative patterns of marital decision-making power and influence in Mexico and the United States: A partial test of resource and ideology theory. *Journal of Comparative Family Studies*, 1973, *4*, 177–196.

Cromwell, R. E., Klein, D. M., & Wieting, S. G. Family power: A multitrait-multimethod analysis. In R. E. Cromwell & D. H. Olson (Eds.), *Power in families*. New York: Halsted Press, 1975.

Cromwell, V. L., & Cromwell, R. E. Perceived dominance in decision-making and conflict resolution among Anglo, Black, and Chicano couples. *Journal of Marriage and the Family*, 1978, *40*, 749–760.

Cuber, J., & Harroff, P. *Sex and the significant Americans*. Baltimore: Penguin, 1965.

Cunningham, I. C. M., & Green, R. T. Working wives in the United States and Venezuela: A cross-national study of decision-making. *Journal of Comparative Family Studies*, 1979, *10*, 67–80.

Dahl, R. A. The concept of power. *Behavioral Science*, 1957, *2*, 201–215.

Dahl, R. A. Power. In D. L. Sills (Ed.), *International Encyclopedia of the Social Sciences*, Vol. 12, New York: Macmillan, Free Press, 1968.

Davis, H. L. Dimensions of marital roles in consumer decision-making. *Journal of Marketing Research*, 1970, *7*, 168–177.

Davis, H. L., & Rigaux, B. P. Perception of marital roles in decision processes. *Journal of Consumer Research*, 1974, *1*, 51–62.

de Kadt, E. J. Conflict and power in society. *International Social Science Journal*, 1965, *17*, 454–471.

Deutsch, M. Socially relevant science: Reflection on some studies of interpersonal conflict. *American Psychologist*, 1969, *24*, 1076–1092.

Deutsch, M. *The resolution of conflict*. New Haven, Conn.: Yale University Press, 1973.

Deutsch, M. Equity, equality, and need: What determines which value will be used as the basis of distributive justice? *Journal of Social Issues*. 1975, *31*, 137–149.

Dobash, R. E., & Dobash, R. *Violence against wives*. New York: Free Press, 1979.

Doherty, W. J. *Cognitive processes in intimate conflict: Applications of attribution theory and social learning theory*. Paper presented at the Theory Development and Methods Workshop, National Council on Family Relations, 1979.

Doherty, W. J., & Ryder, R. G. Locus of control, interpersonal trust, and assertive behavior among newlyweds. *Journal of Personality and Social Psychology*, 1979, *37*, 2212–2220.

Donnenwerth, G. V., & Foa, U. G. Effect of resource class on retaliation to injustice in interpersonal exchange. *Journal of Personality and Social Psychology*, 1974, *29*, 785–793.

Donzelot, J. *The policing of families*. New York: Pantheon, 1979.

Douglas, S. P., & Wind, Y. Examining family role and authority patterns: Two methodological issues. *Journal of Marriage and the Family*, 1978, *40*, 35–47.

Dovidio, J. F., & Ellyson, S. L. Decoding visual dominance: Attributions of power based on relative percentages of looking while speaking and looking while listening. *Social Psychology Quarterly*, 1982, *45*, 106–113.

Dowd, J. J. Aging as exchange: A preface to theory. *Journal of Gerontology*, 1975, *30*, 584–594.

Druckman, D. (Ed.). *Negotiations*. Beverly Hills, Calif.: Sage, 1977.

Druckman, D., Rozelle, R., & Zechmeister, K. Conflict of interest and value dissensus: Two perspectives. In D. Druckman (Ed.), *Negotiations*. Beverly Hills, Calif.: Sage, 1977.

Duck, S. W. *Theory and practice in interpersonal attraction*. London: Academic Press, 1977.

Duke, J. T. *Conflict and power in social life*. Provo, Utah: Brigham Young University Press, 1976.

Edwards, J. N. Familial behavior as social exchange. *Journal of Marriage and the Family*, 1969, *31*, 518–527.

Eichler, M. Power, dependence, love and the sexual division of labour. *Women's Studies International Quarterly*, 1981, *4*, 201–219.

Ekeh, P. P. *Social exchange theory: The two traditions*. Cambridge: Harvard University Press, 1974.

Elder, G. H. *Children of the great depression*. Chicago: University of Chicago Press, 1974.

Ellis, D. P. The Hobbesian problem of order. A critical appraisal of the normative solution. *American Sociological Review*, 1971, *36*, 692–703.

Emerson, R. M. Power-dependence relations. *American Sociological Review*, 1962, *17*, 31–41.

Emerson, R. M. Power-dependence relations: Two experiments. *Sociometry*, 1964, *27*, 282–298.

Emerson, R. M. Exchange theory, Part 1: A psychological basis for social exchange. In J. Berger, M. Zelditch and B. Anderson (Eds.), *Sociological theories in progress*. Boston: Houghton Mifflin, 1972. (a)

Emerson, R. M. Exchange theory, Part 2: Exchange relations and network structures. In J. Berger, M. Zelditch, & B. Anderson (Eds.), *Sociological theories in progress*. Boston: Houghton Mifflin, 1972. (b)

Emerson, R. M. Social exchange theory. In A. Inkeles, J. Coleman & N. Smelser (Eds.), *Annual review of sociology*. Palo Alto, Calif.: Annual Reviews, 1976.

Emerson, R. M., Cook, K. S., Gillmore, M. R., & Yamagishi, T. Valid predictions from invalid comparisons: Response to Heckathorn. *Social Forces*, 1983, *61*, 1232–1247.

Engels, F. *Der Ursprung der Familie, des Privateigentums und des Staats*. Zurich: Schweizerische Volksbuchhandlung, 1884.

Epstein, N. B., & Santa-Barbara, J. Conflict behavior in clinical couples: Interpersonal perceptions and stable outcomes. *Family Process*, 1975, *14*, 51–66.

Falbo, T. Multidimensional scaling of power strategies. *Journal of Personality and Social Psychology*, 1977, *8*, 537–547. (a)

Falbo, T. Relationships between sex, sex role, and social influence. *Psychology of Women Quarterly*, 1977, *2*, 62–72. (b)

Falbo, T., & Peplau, L. A. Power strategies in intimate relationships. *Journal of Personality and Social Psychology*, 1980, *38*, 618–628.

Feldman, L. G. Marital conflict and marital intimacy: An integrative psychodynamic-behavioral-systemic model. *Family Process*, 1979, *18*, 69–78.

Ferreira, A. J., & Winter, W. D. Family interaction and decision-making. *Archives of General Psychiatry*, 1965, *13*, 214–223.

Field, M. Power and dependency: Legitimation of dependency conditions. *Journal of Social Psychology*, 1974, *92*, 31–37.

Filiatrault, P., & Ritchie, J. R. B. Joint purchasing decisions: A comparison of influence structure in family and couple decision-making units. *Journal of Consumer Research*, 1980, *7*, 131–140.

Fink, C. F. Some conceptual difficulties in the theory of social conflict. *Journal of Conflict Resolution*, 1968, *12*, 412–460.

Foa, E. B., & Foa, U. G. Resource theory. Interpersonal behavior as exchange. In K. J. Gergen, M. S. Greenberg, & R. H. Willis (Eds.), *Social exchange: Advances in theory and research*. New York: Plenum Press, 1980.

Foa, U. G., & Foa, E. B. *Societal structures of the mind*. Chicago: C. C Thomas, 1974.

Fox. A. *Beyond contract: Work, power, and trust relations*. London: Faber & Faber, 1974.

Fox, G. L. Another look at the comparative resources model: Assessing the balance of power in Turkish marriages. *Journal of Marriage and the Family*, 1973, *35*, 718–729.

Fox, G. L. "Nice girl": Social control of women through a value construct. *Signs*, 1977, *2*, 805–817.

Frank, D. I., & Scanzoni, J. Sexual decision-making: Its development and dynamics. In G. L. Fox (Ed.), *The childbearing decision*. Beverly Hills, Calif.: Sage, 1982.

French, J. R. P., & Raven, B. The bases of social power. In D. Cartwright (Ed.), *Studies in social power*. Ann Arbor: University of Michigan Press, 1959.

Friedell, M. F. A laboratory experiment in retaliation. *Journal of Conflict Resolution*, 1967, *12*, 357–373.

Friedrich, C. J. *Man and government*. New York: McGraw-Hill, 1963.

Fromkin, H. L., & Snyder, C. R. The search for uniqueness and valuation of scarcity. Neglected dimensions of value in exchange theory. In K. J. Gergen, M. S. Greenberg, & R. H. Willis (Eds.), *Social exchange: Advances in theory and research*. New York: Plenum Press, 1980.

Gallo, P. S., & McClintock, C. G. Cooperative and competitive behavior in mixed-motive games. *Journal of Conflict Resolution*, 1965, *9*, 68–78.

Garner, K., & Deutsch, M. Cooperative behavior in dyads: Effects of dissimilar goal orientations and differing expectations about the partner. *Journal of Conflict Resolution*, 1974, *18*, 634–645.

Geerken, M., & Gove, W. R. *At home and at work*. Beverly Hills, Calif.: Sage, 1983.

Gellert, E. Power relations of young children. *Journal of Abnormal Social Psychology*, 1961, *62*, 8–15.

Gelles, R. J. *The violent home*. Beverly Hills, Calif.: Sage, 1974.

Gelles, R. J. *Family violence*. Beverly Hills, Calif.: Sage, 1979.

Gelles, R., & Straus, M. A. Determinants of violence in the family: Toward a theoretical integration. In W. R. Burr, R. Hill, F. I. Nye, & I. L. Reiss (Eds.), *Contemporary theories about the family*. New York: Free Press, 1979.

Giddens, A. *New rules of sociological method: A positive critique of interpretative sociology*. New York: Basic Books, 1976.

Gillespie, D. L. Who has the power? The marital struggle. *Journal of Marriage and the Family*, 1971, *33*, 445–458.

Glendon, M. A. Power and authority in the family: New legal patterns as reflections of changing ideologies. *American Journal of Comparative Law*, 1975, *23*, 1–33.

Glick, B. R., & Gross, S. J. Marital interaction and marital conflict: A critical evaluation of current research strategies. *Journal of Marriage and the Family*, 1975, *37*, 505–514.

Goode, W. J. *World revolution and family patterns*. New York: Free Press, 1970.

Goode, W. J. Force and violence in the family. *Journal of Marriage and the Family*, 1971, *33*, 625–636.

Goodrich, D. W., & Boomer, D. A. Experimental assessment of modes of conflict resolution. *Family Process*, 1963, *2*, 15–24.

Goodstadt, B. E., & Hjelle, L. A. Power to the powerless: Locus of control and the use of power. *Journal of Personality and Social Psychology*, 1973, *27*, 190–196.

Goodstadt, B. E., & Kipnis, D. Situational influences on the use of power. *Journal of Applied Psychology*, 1970, *54*, 201–207.

Gottman, J. M. *Marital interaction. Experimental investigations*. New York: Academic Press, 1979.

Gottman, J. M., Notarius, C., Markman, H., Bank, S., & Yoppi, B. Behavior exchange theory and marital decision making. *Journal of Personality and Social Psychology*, 1976, *34*, 14–23.

Gottman, J., Markman, H., & Notarius, C. The topography of marital conflict: A sequential analysis of verbal and nonverbal behavior. *Journal of Marriage and the Family*, 1977, *39*, 461–478.

Gouldner, A. W. The norm of reciprocity: A preliminary statement. *American Sociological Review*, 1960, *25*, 161–178.

Gouldner, A. W. *The coming crisis of Western sociology*. New York: Basic Books, 1970.

Granbois, D. H., & Willett, R. P. Equivalence of family role measures based on husband and wife data. *Journal of Marriage and the Family*, 1970, *32*, 68–72.

Gray-Little, B. Marital quality and power processes among black couples. *Journal of Marriage and the Family*, 1982, *44*, 633–646.

Greenberg, M. S. A theory of indebtedness. In K. J. Gergen, M. S. Greenberg, & R. H. Willis (Eds.), *Social exchange: Advances in theory and research*. New York: Plenum Press, 1980.

Gruder, C. L. Social power in interpersonal negotiation. In P. Swingle (Ed.), *The structure of conflict*. New York: Academic Press, 1970.

Grusec, J. E., & Kuczynski, L. Direction of effect in socialization: A comparison of the parent's versus the child's behavior as determinants of disciplinary techniques. *Developmental Psychology*, 1980, *16*, 1–9.

Gulliver, P. H. *Disputes and negotiations*. New York: Academic Press, 1979.

Haas, D. F., & Deserau, F. A. Trust and symbolic exchange. *Social Psychology Quarterly*, 1981, *44*, 3–13.

Hadley, T. R., & Jacob, T. Relationship among measures of family power. *Journal of Personality and Social Psychology*, 1973, *27*, 6–12.

Hallenbeck, P. N. An analysis of power dynamics in marriage. *Journal of Marriage and the Family*, 1966, *28*, 200–203.·

Hammond, J., & Enoch, J. R. Conjugal power relations among black working class families. *Journal of Black Studies*, 1976, *7*, 107–128.

Hamner, W. C., & Yukl, G. A. The effectiveness of different offer strategies in bargaining. In D. Druckman (Ed.), *Negotiations*. Beverly Hills, Calif.: Sage, 1977.

Harrell, W. A., & Hartnagel, T. The impact of Machiavellianism and the trustfulness of the victim on laboratory theft. *Sociometry*, 1976, *39*, 157–165.

Harsanyi, J. C. Measurement of social power, opportunity costs, and the theory of two-person bargaining games. *Behavioral Science*, 1962, *7*, 67–80.

Harsanyi, J. C. *Rational behavior and bargaining equilibrium in games and social situations*. Cambridge: Cambridge University Press, 1977.

Hartmann, H. I. The family as the locus of gender, class, and political struggle: The example of housework. *Signs*, 1981, *6*, 366–394.

Hawkes, G. R., & Taylor, M. Power structure in Mexican and Mexican-American farm labor families. *Journal of Marriage and the Family*, 1975, *37*, 807–812.

Heath, A. *Rational choice and social exchange*. New York: Cambridge University Press, 1976.

Heckathorn, D. D. Extensions of power-dependence theory: The concept of resistance. *Social Forces*, 1983, *61*, 1206–1231.

Heer, D. M. Husband and wife perceptions of family power structure. *Marriage and Family Living*, 1962, *24*, 65–67.

Heer, D. M. The measurement and bases of family power: An overview. *Marriage and Family Living*, 1963, *25*, 133–139.

Heider, F. *The psychology of interpersonal relations*. New York: Wiley, 1958.

Heilman, M. E., & Garner, K. A. Counteracting the boomerang: The effects of choice on compliance to threats and promises. *Journal of Personality and Social Psychology*, 1975, *31*, 911–917.

Henshel, A. Swinging: A study of decision making in marriage. *American Journal of Sociology*, 1973, *78*, 885–891.

Hermann, M. G., & Kogan, N. Effects of negotiators' personalities on negotiating behavior. In D. Druckman (Ed.), *Negotiations*. Beverly Hills, Calif.: Sage, 1977.

Hershey, S., & Werner, E. Dominance in marital decision-making in women's liberation and non-women's liberation families. *Family Process*, 1975, *14*, 223–225.

Hesselbart, S. L. *Does charity begin at home? Attitudes toward women, household tasks, and household decision-making*. Paper presented at the meeting of the American Sociological Association, 1976.

Hesselbart, S. L. *Project TAL research report*. Tallahassee: Florida State University, 1978.

Hesselbart, S. L., & Bolling, D. *Item coding: A neglected methodological issue in questionnaire measures of conjugal decision-making*. Paper presented at the meeting of the Southern Sociological Society, 1979.

Hewitt, J. P. *Self and society. A symbolic interactionist social psychology*. Boston: Allyn & Bacon, 1976.

Hill, R. *Family development in three generations*. Cambridge, Mass.: Schenkman, 1970.

Hill, W., & Scanzoni, J. An approach for assessing marital decision-making processes. *Journal of Marriage and the Family*, 1982, *44*, 927–942.

Hobart, C. W. Sources of egalitarianism in young unmarried Canadians. *Canadian Journal of Sociology*, 1981, *6*, 261–282.

Hoffman, S. B. *The interpersonal influence strategies of adult cohorts*. Unpublished PH.D. Dissertation, Pennsylvania State University, 1982.

Homans, G. C. *Social behavior: Its elementary forms*. New York: Harcourt Brace Jovanovich, 1974.

Hood, J. C. *Becoming a two-job family: Role bargaining in dual-worker households*. New York: Praeger, 1983.

Hopmann, P. T., & Walcott, C. The impact of external stresses and tensions on negotiations. In D. Druckman (Ed.), *Negotiations*. Beverly Hills, Calif.: Sage, 1977.

Horkheimer, M. *Traditionelle und kritische Theorie*. Frankfurt/M: Fischer, 1970.

Hovland, C. I., Janis, I. L., & Kelley, H. H. *Communication and persuasion*. New Haven, Conn.: Yale University Press, 1953.

Huston, T. L. A perspective on interpersonal attraction. In T. L. Huston (Ed.), *Foundations of interpersonal attraction*. New York: Academic Press, 1974.

Huston, T. Power. In H. H. Kelley, E. Berscheid, A., Christensen, J. Harvey, T. Huston, G. Levinger, E. McClintock, A. Peplau, & D. Peterson (Eds.), *Close relationships*. San Francisco: Freeman, 1983.

Huston, T., & Robins, E. Conceptual and methodological issues in studying close relationships. *Journal of Marriage and the Family*, 1982, *44*, 901–926.

Ingoldsby, B. B. *Emotional expressiveness and marital adjustment: A cross-cultural analysis*. Paper presented at the meeting of the National Council on Family Relations, 1980.

Jacob, T. Patterns of family conflict and dominance as a function of child age and social class. *Developmental Psychology*, 1974, *10*, 1–12.

Jacob, T. Family interaction in disturbed and normal families: A methodological and substantive review. *Psychological Bulletin*, 1975, *82*, 33–65.

Jacob, T., & Davis, J. Family interaction as a function of experimental task. *Family Process*, 1973, *12*, 415–427.

Jacobson, M. B., Antonelli, J , Winning, P. U., & Opeil, D. Women as authority figures: The use and nonuse of authority. *Sex Roles*, 1977, *3*, 365–375.

Janeway, E. On the power of the weak. *Signs*, 1975, *1*, 103–110.

Janis, I. L., & Mann, L. *Decision-making. A psychological analysis of conflict, choice, and commitment*. New York: Free Press, 1977.

Joas, H. *Die gegenwaertige Lage der soziologischen Rollentheorie*. Frankfurt: Athenaeum, 1973.

Johnson, C. L. Authority and power in Japanese-American marriage. In R. E. Cromwell & D. H. Olson (Eds.), *Power in families*. New York: Halsted Press, 1975.

Johnson, G. D., & Hendrix, L. A cross-cultural test of Collins' theory of sexual stratification. *Journal of Marriage and the Family*, 1982, *44*, 675–684.

Johnson, M. P. *Personal and structural commitment: Sources of consistency in the development of relationships.* Paper presented at the Theory and Methods Workshop, National Council on Family Relations, 1978.

Johnson, P. B. Women and power: Toward a theory of effectiveness. *Journal of Social Issues,* 1976, *32,* 99–110.

Jones, E. E. *Ingratiation. A social psychological analysis.* New York: Irvington, 1964.

Judd, C. M. Cognitive effects of attitude conflict resolution. *Journal of Conflict Resolution,* 1978, *22,* 483–498.

Kahn, A., Nelson, R. E., Gaeddert, W. P., & Hearn, J. L. The justice process: Deciding upon equity or equality. *Social Psychology Quarterly,* 1982, *45,* 3–8.

Kalmuss, D. S., & Straus, M. A., Wife's marital dependency and wife abuse. *Journal of Marriage and the Family,* 1982, *44,* 277–286.

Kamerman, S. B., & Kahn, A. J. (eds.), *Family policy: Government and families in 14 countries.* New York: Columbia University Press, 1978.

Kandel, D. B., & Lesser, G. S. Marital decision-making in American and Danish urban families: A research note. *Journal of Marriage and the Family,* 1972, *34,* 134–138.

Kane, T. R., Joseph, J. M., & Tedeschi, J. T. Perceived freedom, aggression, and responsibility, and the assignment of punishment. *The Journal of Social Psychology,* 1977, *103,* 257–263.

Kaplowitz, S. A. Towards a systematic theory of power attribution. *Social Psychology,* 1978, *41,* 131–148.

Kelley, H. H. Experimental studies of threats in interpersonal negotiations. *Journal of Conflict Resolution,* 1965, *9,* 79–105.

Kelley, H. H. An application of attribution theory to research methodology for close relationships. In G. Levinger & H. L. Raush (Eds.), *Close relationships.* Amherst: University of Massachusetts Press, 1977.

Kelley, H. H., & Stahelsky, A. J. Errors in perception of intentions in a mixed motive game. *Journal of Experimental Social Psychology,* 1970, *16,* 411–438. (a)

Kelley, H. H., & Stahelsky, A. J. Social interaction basis of cooperators' and competitors' beliefs about others. *Journal of Personality and Social Psychology,* 1970, *16,* 66–91. (b)

Kelley, H. H., & Thibaut, J. W. *Interpersonal relations. A theory of interdependence.* New York: Wiley, 1978.

Kelley, H. H., Deutsch, M., Lanzetta, J. T., Nuttin, Jr., J. M., Shure, G. H., Faucheux, C., Moscovici, S., & Rabbie, J. M. A comparative experimental study of negotiation behavior. *Journal of Personality and Social Psychology.* 1970, *16,* 411–438.

Kelvin, P. Predictability, power and vulnerability in interpersonal attraction. In S. Duck (Ed.), *Theory and practice in interpersonal attraction.* New York: Academic Press, 1977.

Kemper, T. D., & Reichler, M. L. Marital satisfaction and conjugal power as determinants of intensity and frequency of rewards and punishments administered by parents. *The Journal of Genetic Psychology,* 1976, *129,* 221–234.

Kimmel, P. R., & Havens, J. W. Game theory versus mutual identification: Two criteria for assessing marital relationships. *Journal of Marriage and the Family,* 1966, *28,* 460–465.

King, K. Adolescent perception of power structure in the Negro family. *Journal of Marriage and the Family,* 1969, *31,* 751–755.

Klein, D. M. *Developmental context, coorientations, and conflict management.* Unpublished doctoral dissertation, University of Minnesota, 1978.

Klein, D. M., & Hill, R. Determinants of problem-solving effectiveness. In W. R. Burr, R. Hill, F. I. Nye, & I. L. Reiss (Eds.), *Contemporary theories about the family,* Vol. 1. New York: Free Press, 1979.

Klimoski, R. J. Simulation methodologies of negotiation. *The Journal of Conflict Resolution,* 1978, *22,* 61–78.

Kolb, T. M., & Straus, M. A. Marital power and marital happiness in relation to problem-solving ability. *Journal of Marriage and the Family,* 1974, *36,* 756–766.

Komarovsky, M. Cultural contradictions and sex roles. *American Journal of Sociology,* 1946, *52,* 182–189.

Komarovsky, M. *Blue-collar marriage.* New York: Random House, 1964.

Komarovsky, M. *Dilemmas of masculinity: A study of college youth.* New York: Norton, 1976.

Komorita, S. S. Concession-making and conflict resolution. *Journal of Conflict Resolution,* 1973, *17,* 745–762.

Komorita, S. S. Evaluating coalition theories. *The Journal of Conflict Resolution,* 1978, *22,* 691–706.

Komorita, S. S., & Meek, D. D. Generality and validity of some theories of coalition formation. *Journal of Personality and Social Psychology,* 1978, *36,* 392–404.

Kraut, R. E., & Price, J. D. Machiavellianism in parents and their children. *Journal of Personality and Social Psychology,* 1976, *33,* 782–786.

Kriesberg, L. *The sociology of social conflicts.* Englewood Cliffs, N.J.: Prentice-Hall, 1973.

Kumagai, F. Social class, power and husband-wife violence in Japan. *Journal of Comparative Family Studies,* 1979, *10,* 1–105.

Kumagai, F., & O'Donoghue, G. Conjugal power and conjugal violence in Japan and the USA. *Journal of Comparative Family Studies.* 1978, *9,* 211–221.

LaGaipa, J. J. Interpersonal attraction and social exchange. In S. Duck (Ed.), *Theory and practice in interpersonal attraction.* New York: Academic Press, 1977.

Laing, R. D. *The politics of the family.* New York: Vintage, 1969.

Lamb, T. A. Nonverbal and paraverbal control in dyads and triads: Sex or power differences? *Social Psychology Quarterly,* 1981, *44,* 49–53.

Lamouse, A. Family roles of women: A German example. *Journal of Marriage and the Family,* 1969, *31,* 145–152.

Lantz, H., Schultz, M., & O'Hara, M. The changing American family from the preindustrial to the industrial period: A final report. *American Sociological Review,* 1977, *42,* 406–421.

LaRossa, R. *Conflict and power in marriage: Expecting the first child.* Beverly Hills, Calif.: Sage, 1977.

LaRossa, R., & LaRossa, M. M. *Transition to parenthood.* Beverly Hills, Calif.: Sage, 1981.

Laub-Coser, R., & Rokoff, R. Women in the occupational world: Social disruption and conflict. *Social Problems,* 1971, *18,* 535–554.

Lee, G. R. *Family structure and interaction: A comparative analysis.* Philadelphia: Lippincott, 1977.

Lehmann, E. W. Toward a macrosociology of power. *American Sociological Review,* 1969, *34,* 453–465.

Leik, R. K., & Leik, A. *Interpersonal commitment as a balancing mechanism in social exchange.* Paper presented at the meeting of the Pacific Sociological Association, 1972.

Lerner, R. M., & Spanier, G. B. *Child influences on marital and family interaction: A life-span perspective.* New York: Academic Press, 1978.

Leventhal, G. S. Fairness in social relationships. In J. W. Thibaut, J. T. Spence, & R. C. Carson (Eds.), *Contemporary topics in social psychology.* Morristown, NJ. General Learning Press, 1976.

Levinger, G. The development of perception and behavior in newly formed social power relationships. In D. Cartwright (Ed.), *Studies in social power.* Ann Arbor: University of Michigan Press, 1959.

Levinger, G. A social psychological perspective on marital dissolution. *Journal of Social Issues,* 1976, *32,* 21–47.

Levinger, G., & Huesmann, L. R. An "incremental exchange" perspective on the pair relationship: Interpersonal reward and level of involvement. In K. J. Gergen, M. S. Greenberg, & R. H. Willis (Eds.), *Social exchange:*

Advances in theory and research. New York: Plenum Press, 1980.

Lewin, K. *Field theory in social science.* New York: Harper & Row, 1951.

Lewis, R. *Satisfaction with conjugal power over the family life cycle.* Paper presented at the meeting of the National Council on Family Relations, 1972.

Lewis, R. A., & Spanier, G. B. Theorizing about the quality and stability of marriage. In W. R. Burr, R. Hill, F. I. Nye, & I. L. Reiss (Eds.), *Contemporary theories about the family,* Vol. 1. New York: Free Press, 1979.

Lipman-Blumen, J., & Bernard, J. *Sex roles and social policy.* Beverly Hills, Calif.: Sage, 1979.

Liu, W. T., Hutchison, I. W., & Hong, L. W. Conjugal power and decision making: A methodological note on cross-cultural study of the family. *American Journal of Sociology,* 1974, *79,* 84–98.

Longabaugh, R. A category system for coding interpersonal behavior as social exchange. *Sociometry,* 1963, *26,* 319–344.

Lukes, S. *Essays in social theory.* New York: Columbia University Press, 1977.

Lukes, S. Power and authority. In T. Bottomore & R. Nisbet (Eds.), *A history of sociological analysis.* New York: Basic Books, 1978.

Lupri, E. Contemporary authority patterns in the West German family: A study in cross-national validation. *Journal of Marriage and the Family,* 1969, *31,* 134–144.

Lupri, E. Gesellschaftliche Differenzierung und familiale Autoritaet. *Koelner Zeitschrift fuer Soziologie und Sozialpsychologie,* 1970, *14,* 323–352.

Maccoby, E. E., & Jacklin, C. N. *The psychology of sex differences,* Vol. 1. Stanford, Calif.: Stanford University Press, 1974.

Mack, R. W., & Snyder, R. C. The analysis of social conflict—toward an overview and synthesis. *Journal of Conflict Resolution,* 1957, *1,* 212–248.

Marsden, P. V. Restricted access in networks and models of power. *American Journal of Sociology,* 1983, *88,* 686–717.

Martin, P. Y., & Osmond, M. W. Structural asymmetry and social exchange. A sex-role simulation. *Simulation and Games,* 1975, *6,* 339–365.

Martin, P. Y., & Osmond, M. W. Gender and exploitation: Resources, structure, and rewards in cross-sex social exchange. *Sociological Focus,* 1982, *15,* 403–416.

Martin, R. *The sociology of power.* London: Routledge & Kegan Paul, 1977.

Mazur, A. A nonrational approach to theories of conflict and coalitions. *Journal of Conflict Resolution,* 1968, *12,* 196–205.

McCarrick, A. K., Manderscheid, R. W., & Silbergeld, S. Gender differences in competition and dominance during married couples group therapy. *Social Psychology Quarterly,* 1981, *44,* 164–177.

McClelland, D. C. The two faces of power. *Journal of International Affairs,* 1970, *24,* 29–47.

McClelland, D. C. *Power: The inner experience.* New York: Irvington, 1975.

McClelland, D. C., & Watson, R. I. Power motivation and risk-taking behavior. *Journal of Personality,* 1973, *41,* 121–139.

McClintock, C. G. Social motivation in settings of outcome interdependence. In D. Druckman (Ed.), *Negotiations.* Beverly Hills, Calif.: Sage, 1977.

McDonald, G. W. Coalition formation in marital therapy triads. *Family Therapy,* 1975, *2,* 141–148.

McDonald, G. W. Family power: Reflection and direction. *Pacific Sociological Review,* 1977, *20,* 607–621. (a)

McDonald, G. W. Parental identification by the adolescent: A social power approach. *Journal of Marriage and the Family,* 1977, *39,* 705–719. (b)

McDonald, G. W. Determinants of adolescent perceptions of maternal and paternal power in the family. *Journal of Marriage and the Family,* 1979, *41,* 757–770.

McDonald, G. W. Family power: The assessment of a decade of theory and research, 1970–1979. *Journal of Marriage and the Family,* 1980, *42,* 841–854.

McDonald, G. W. Structural exchange and marital interaction. *Journal of Marriage and the Family,* 1981, *43,* 825–839.

McGillicuddy-DeLisi, A. V. The role of parental beliefs in the family as a system of mutual influence. *Family Relations,* 1980, *29,* 317–323.

McLain, R., & Weigert, A., Toward a phenomenological sociology of family. In W. R. Burr, R. Hill, F. I. Nye, & I. L. Reiss (Eds.), *Contemporary theories about the family,* Vol. 2. New York: Free Press, 1979.

McNeel, S. P., & Reid, E. C. Attitude similarity, social goals, and cooperation. *Journal of Conflict Resolution,* 1975, *19,* 665–681.

Meyer, R. J., & Lewis, R. A. New wine from old wineskins: Marital power research. *Journal of Comparative Family Studies,* 1976, *7,* 397–408.

Michel, A. Comparative data concerning the interaction in French and American Families. *Journal of Marriage and the Family,* 1967, *29,* 337–344.

Michener, H. A., & Burt, M. R. Components of ''authority'' as determinants of compliance. *Journal of Personality and Social Psychology,* 1975, *31,* 606–614.

Michener, H. A., Lawler, E. J., & Bacharach, S. B. Perception of power in conflict situations. *Journal of Personality and Social Psychology,* 1973, *28,* 155–162.

Midgaard, K., & Underdal, A. Multiparty conferences. In D. Druckman (Ed.), *Negotiations.* Beverly Hills, Calif.: Sage, 1977.

Milgram, S. Some conditions of obedience and disobedience to authority. *Human Relations,* 1965, *18,* 57–78.

Minton, H. L. Power as a personality construct. In B. A. Maher (Ed.), *Progress in experimental personality research,* Vol. 4. New York: Academic Press, 1967.

Minton, H. L. Power and personality. In J. T. Tedeschi (Ed.), *The social influence processes.* Chicago: Aldine, 1972.

Mishler, E. G., & Waxler, N. E. *Interaction in families: An experimental study of family processes and schizophrenia.* New York: Wiley, 1968.

Molm, L. D. The conversion of power imbalance to power use. *Social Psychology Quarterly,* 1981, *44,* 151–163. (a)

Molm, L. D. Power use in the dyad. The effects of structure, knowledge, and interaction history. *Social Psychology Quarterly,* 1981, *44,* 42–48. (b)

Molm, L. D. A contingency change analysis of the disruption and recovery of social exchange and cooperation. *Social Forces,* 1981, *59,* 729–751. (c)

Morgan, W. R. & Sawyer, J. Equality, equity, and procedural justice in social exchange. *Social Psychology Quarterly,* 1979, *42,* 71–75.

Munsinger, G. M., Weber, J. E., & Hansen, R. W. Joint home purchasing decisions by husbands and wives. *Journal of Consumer Research,* 1979, *1,* 60–66.

Murstein, B. L., Cerreto, M., & MacDonald, M. G. A theory and investigation of the effect of exchange-orientation on marriage and friendship. *Journal of Marriage and the Family,* 1977, *39,* 543–548.

Nagel, J. H. Some questions about the concept of power. *Behavioral Science,* 1968, *13,* 129–137.

Nagel, J. H. *The descriptive analysis of power.* New Haven, Conn.: Yale University Press, 1975.

Nagel, J. H. Description and explanation in power analysis. In T. R. Burns, & W. Buckley (Eds.), *Power and control: Social structures and their transformation.* Beverly Hills, Calif.: Sage, 1976.

Napier, A. Y. The rejection-intrusion pattern: A central family dynamic. *Journal of Marriage and Family Counseling*, 1978, *4*, 5–12.

Niemi, R. G. *How family members perceive each other*. New Haven, Conn.: Yale University Press, 1974.

Nye, I. F. Is choice and exchange theory the key? *Journal of Marriage and the Family*, 1978, *40*, 219–234.

Oliver, P. Selective incentives in an apex game. *The Journal of Conflict Resolution*, 1980, *24*, 113–142.

Olson, D. H. The measurement of family power by self-report and behavioral methods. *Journal of Marriage and the Family*, 1969, *31*, 545–550.

Olson, D. H. Insiders' and outsiders' views of relationships: Research studies. In G. Levinger & H. Raush (Eds.), *Close relationships*. Amherst: University of Massachusetts Press, 1977.

Olson, D. H., & Cromwell, R. E. Methodological issues in family power. In R. E. Cromwell & D. H. Olson (Eds.), *Power in families*. New York: Halsted Press, 1975. (a)

Olson, D. H., & Cromwell, R. E. Power in families. In R. E. Cromwell & D. H. Olson (Eds.), *Power in families*. New York: Halsted Press, 1975. (b)

Olson, D. H., & Rabunsky, C. Validity of four measures of family power. *Journal of Marriage and the Family*, 1972, *34*, 224–234.

Olson, D. H.. & Ryder, R. G. Inventory of marital conflicts (IMC): An experimental interaction procedure. *Journal of Marriage and the Family*, 1970, *32*, 443–448.

Olson, D. H., Cromwell, R. E., & Klein, D. M. Beyond family power. In R. E. Cromwell & D. H. Olson (Eds.), *Power in families*. New York: Halsted Press, 1975.

Oppong, C. Conjugal power and resources: An urban African example. *Journal of Marriage and the Family*, 1970, *32*, 676–680.

O'Rourke, J. F. Field and laboratory: The decision-making behavior of family groups in two experimental conditions. *Sociometry*, 1963, *26*, 422–435.

Osmond, M. W. Reciprocity: A dynamic model and a method to study family power. *Journal of Marriage and the Family*, 1978, *40*, 49–62.

Owens, D. J., & Straus, M. A. The social structure of violence in childhood and approval of violence as an adult. *Aggressive Behavior*, 1975, *1*, 193–211.

Pagelow, M. D. *Woman-battering: Victims and their experiences*. Beverly Hills, Calif.: Sage, 1981.

Paolucci, B., Hall, O. A., & Axinn, N. *Family decision-making: An ecosystem approach*. New York: Wiley, 1977.

Papanek, M. L. Authority and sex roles in the family. *Journal of Marriage and the Family*, 1969, *31*, 88–96.

Parsons, T. Authority, legitimation, and political action. In C. J. Friedrich (Ed.), *Authority*. Cambridge: Harvard University Press, 1958.

Parsons, T. Some reflections on the place of force in social process. In H. Eckstein (Ed.), *Internal war: Problems and approaches*. New York: Free Press, 1964.

Parsons, T., & Bales, R. F. *Family, socialization, and interaction process*. New York: Free Press, 1955.

Patchen, M. Models of cooperation and conflict: A critical review. *Journal of Conflict Resolution*, 1970, *14*, 389–407.

Patterson, G. R. The aggressive child: Victim and architect of a coercive system. In L. A. Hamerlynck, E. J. Mash & L. C. Handy (Eds.), *Behavior modification and families*. I. *Theory and research*. II. *Applications and developments*. New York: Brunner/Mazell, 1976.

Patterson, G. R. *Mothers: The unacknowledged victims*. Paper presented at the Pennsylvania State University, 1978.

Peplau, L. A. Power in dating relationships. In J. Freeman (Ed.), *Women: A feminist perspective*. Palo Alto, Calif.: Mayfield, 1979.

Peterson, C. C. Distributive justice within and outside the family. *The Journal of Psychology*, 1975, *90*, 123–127.

Phillips, C. E. Measuring power of spouse. *Sociology and Social Research*, 1967, *52*, 36–49.

Pool, D. I. Changes in Canadian female labour force participation, and some possible implications for conjugal power. *Journal of Comparative Family Studies*, 1978, *9*, 41–51.

Price, D. Z. Relationship of decision styles and self-actualization. *Home Economics Research Journal*, 1973, *2*, 12–20.

Price-Bonham, S. A comparison of weighted and unweighted decision-making scores. *Journal of Marriage and the Family*, 1976, *38*, 629–642.

Price-Bonham, S. Marital decision-making: Congruence of spouses' responses. *Sociological Inquiry*, 1977, *47*, 119–126.

Pruitt, D. G., & Lewis, S. A. The psychology of integrative bargaining. In D. Druckman (Ed.), *Negotiations*, Beverly Hills, Calif.: Sage, 1977.

Psathas, G. Alternative methods for scoring interaction process analysis. *The Journal of Social Psychology*, 1961, *53*, 97–103.

Quarm, D. Random measurement error as a source of discrepancies between the reports of wives and husbands concerning marital power and task allocation. *Journal of Marriage and the Family*, 1981, *43*, 521–535.

Queen, S. A., & Habenstein, R. W. *The family in various cultures*. Philadelphia: Lippincott, 1974.

Rands, M., Levinger, G., & Mellinger, G. D. Patterns of conflict resolution and marital satisfaction. *Journal of Family Issues*, 1981, *2*, 297–321.

Rank, M. Determinants of conjugal influence in wives' employment decision-making. *Journal of Marriage and the Family*, 1982, *44*, 591–604.

Rapoport, A. Conflict in the light of game theory. In P. Swingle (Ed.), *The structure of conflict*. New York: Academic Press, 1970.

Rapoport, A., & Chammah, A. M. Sex differences in factors contributing to the level of cooperation in the Prisoner's Dilemma game. *Journal of Personality and Social Psychology*, 1965, *2*, 831–838.

Raush, H. L., Barry, W. A., Hertel, R. K., & Swain, M. A. *Communication, conflict, and marriage*. San Francisco: Jossey/Bass, 1974.

Raven, B. H., & Kruglanski, A. W. Conflict and power. In P. Swingle (Ed.), *The structure of conflict*. New York: Academic Press, 1970.

Raven, B. H., Centers, R., & Rodrigues, A. The bases of conjugal power. In R. E. Cromwell & D. H. Olson (Eds.), *Power in families*. New York: Halsted Press, 1975.

Reiss, D., & Blehar, M. Family styles of interacting. In *Families today*, Vol. 1. Washington: National Institute of Mental Health, 1979.

Richer, S. The economics of child rearing. *Journal of Marriage and the Family*, 1968, *30*, 462–466.

Richmond, M. L. Beyond resource theory: Another look at factors enabling women to affect family interaction. *Journal of Marriage and the Family*, 1976, *38*, 257–266.

Ridgeway, C. L. Status in groups: The importance of motivation. *American Sociological Review*, 1982, *47*, 76–88.

Rim, Y. Personality and means of influence in marriage. *Human Relations*, 1979, *32*, 871–875.

Rim, Y. Means of influence in marriage. Similarities and discrepancies. *Small Group Behavior*, 1980, *11*, 66–75. (a)

Rim, Y. Personality development and means of influence in marriage. *Personality and Individual Differences*, 1980, *1*, 297–300. (b)

Riskin, J., & Faunce, E. E. An evaluative review of family interaction research. *Family Process*, 1972, *11*, 365–455.

Rodman, H. Marital power in France, Greece, Yugoslavia, and the United States: A cross-national discussion. *Journal of Marriage and the Family*, 1967, *29*, 320–324.

Rodman, H. Eheliche Macht und Austausch von Ressourcen im kulturellen Kontext. *Koelner Zeitschrift fuer Soziologie und Sozialpsychologie*, 1970, *14*, 121–144.

Rogers, M. F. Instrumental and infra-resources: The bases of power. *American Journal of Sociology*, 1974, *79*, 1418–1433.

Rogers, S. C. Female forms of power and the myth of male dominance: A model of female/male interaction in peasant society. *American Ethnologist*, 1975, *2*, 727–756.

Rollins, B. C., & Bahr, S. J. A theory of power relationships in marriage. *Journal of Marriage and the Family*, 1976, *38*, 619–628.

Rollins, B. C., & Thomas, D. L. A theory of parental power and child compliance. In R. E. Cromwell & D. H. Olson (Eds.), *Power in families*. New York: Halsted Press, 1975.

Rollins, B. C., & Thomas, D. L. Parental support, power, and control techniques in the socialization of children. In W. R. Burr, R. Hill, F. I. Nye, & I. L. Reiss (Eds.), *Contemporary theories about the family*, Vol. 1. New York: Free Press, 1979.

Roloff, M. E. Self-awareness and the persuasion process: Do we really know what we're doing? In M. E. Roloff & G. R. Miller (Eds.), *Persuasion: New directions in theory and research*. Beverly Hills, Calif.: Sage, 1980.

Rosen, S., Levinger, G., & Lippitt, R. Perceived sources of social power. *Journal of Abnormal and Social Psychology*, 1961, *62*, 430–441.

Rotter, J. B. Generalized expectancies for internal versus external control of reinforcement. *Psychological Monographs*. 1966, *80*, 1–28.

Rubin, J. Z., & Brown, B. R. *The social psychology of bargaining and negotiation*. New York: Academic Press, 1975.

Rubin, L. B. *Worlds of pain: Life in the working-class family*. New York: Basic Books, 1976.

Rubin, Z. Who believes in a just world? *The Journal of Social Issues*, 1975, *31*, 65–90.

Ryder, R. G. What is power? Definitional consideration and some research implications. In J. H. Masserman (Ed.), *Science and psychoanalysis, Volume 20: The dynamics of power*. New York: Grune & Stratton, 1972.

Safilios-Rothschild, C. A comparison of power structure and marital satisfaction in urban Greek and French families. *Journal of Marriage and the Family*, 1967, *29*, 345–352.

Safilios-Rothschild, C. Family sociology or wives' family sociology? A cross-cultural examination of decision-making. *Journal of Marriage and the Family*, 1969, *31*, 290–301. (a)

Safilios-Rothschild, C. Patterns of familial power and influence. *Sociological Focus*, 1969, *2*, 7–19. (b)

Safilios-Rothschild, C. The study of family power structure: A review 1960–1969. *Journal of Marriage and the Family*, 1970, *32*, 539–552.

Safilios-Rothschild, C. The dimensions of power distribution in the family. In H. Grunebaum & J. Christ (Eds.), *Contemporary marriage: Structure, dynamics, and therapy*. Boston: Little Brown, 1976. (a)

Safilios-Rothschild, C. A macro- and micro-examination of family power and love: An exchange model. *Journal of Marriage and the Family*, 1976, *38*, 355–362. (b)

Safilios-Rothschild, C., & Dijkers, M. Handling unconventional asymmetries. In R. Rapoport & R. N. Rapoport (Eds.), *Working couples*. New York: Harper & Row, 1978.

Salamon, S., & Keim, A, M. Land ownership and women's power in a Midwestern farming community. *Journal of Marriage and the Family*, 1979, *41*, 109–120.

Sanday, P. R. *Female power and male dominance. On the origins of sexual inequality*. Cambridge: Cambridge University Press, 1981.

Santa-Barbara, J., & Epstein, N. B. Conflict behavior in clinical families: Preasymptotic interactions and stable outcomes. *Behavioral Science*, 1974, *19*, 100–110.

Santee, R. T., and Jackson, S. E. Identity implications of conformity: Sex differences in normative and attributional judgments, *Social Psychology Quarterly*, 1982, *45*. 121–125.

Scanzoni, J. *Sexual bargaining: Power politics in the American marriage*. Englewood Cliffs, N.J.: Prentice-Hall, 1972.

Scanzoni, J. *Sex roles, life styles, and childbearing: Changing patterns in marriage and the family*. New York: Free Press, 1975.

Scanzoni, J. Changing sex roles and emerging directions in family decision making. *Journal of Consumer Research*, 1977, *4*, 185–188.

Scanzoni, J. *Sex roles, women's work, and marital conflict*. Toronto: Lexington, 1978.

Scanzoni, J. Social exchange and behavioral interdependence. In R. Burgess & T. Huston (Eds.), *Social exchange in developing relationships*. New York: Academic Press, 1979. (a)

Scanzoni, J. Social processes and power in families. In W. R. Burr, R. Hill, F. I. Nye, & I. L. Reiss (Eds.), *Contemporary theories about the family*. Vol. 1, New York: Free Press, 1979. (b)

Scanzoni, J., & Polonko, K. A conceptual approach to explicit marital negotiation. *Journal of Marriage and the Family*, 1980, *42*, 31–44.

Scanzoni, L., & Scanzoni, J. *Men, women, and change. A sociology of marriage and the family*. New York: McGraw-Hill, 1976.

Scanzoni, J., & Szinovacz, M. E. *Family decision-making: Sex roles and change over the life cycle*. Beverly Hills, Calif.: Sage, 1980.

Schafer, R. B., & Keith, P. M. Equity in marital roles across the family life cycle. *Journal of Marriage and the Family*, 1981, *43*, 359–367.

Scheff, T. J. A theory of social coordination applicable to mixed-motive games. *Sociometry*, 1967, *30*, 215–234.

Schlenker, B. R., & Goldman, H. J. Cooperators and competitors in conflict. *The Journal of Conflict Resolution*, 1978, *22*, 393–410.

Schlenker, B. R., Nacci, P., Helm, B., & Tedeschi, J. T. Reactions to coercive and reward power: The effects of switching influence modes on target compliance. *Sociometry*, 1976, *39*, 316–323.

Schopler, J. Social power. In L. Berkowitz (Ed.), *Advances in experimental social psychology*, Vol. 2. New York: Academic Press, 1965.

Schopler, J., & Bateson, N. The power of dependence. *Journal of Personality and Social Psychology*, 1965, *2*, 247–254.

Schuham, A. I. Power relations in emotionally disturbed and normal family triads. *Journal of Abnormal Psychology*, 1970, *75*, 30–37.

Schuham, A. I. Activity, talking time, and spontaneous agreement in disturbed and normal family interaction. *Journal of Abnormal Psychology*, 1972, *79*, 68–75.

Schwartz, B., Tesser, A., & Powell, E. Dominance cues in nonverbal behavior. *Social Psychology Quarterly*, 1982, *45*, 114–120.

Schwartz, S. The justice of need and the activation of humanitarian norms. *The Journal of Social Issues*. 1975, *31*, 111–136.

Seligman, C., Bush, M., & Kirsch, K. Relationship between compliance in the foot-in-the-door paradigm and size of first request. *Journal of Personality and Social Psychology*, 1976, *33*, 517–520.

Shepperson, V. L. Difference in family coalitions and hierarchies between normals and neurotics. *Family Relations*, 1981, *30*, 361–365.

Shulman, A. K. Sex and power: Sexual bases of radical feminism. *Signs*, 1980, *5*, 590–604.

Simmel, G. *Conflict and the web of group affiliations*. New York: Free Press, 1955.

Singlemann, P. Exchange as symbolic interaction: Convergences between two theoretical perspectives. *American Sociological Review*, 1972, *37*, 414–424.

Smith, N. S., Vernon, C. R., & Tarte, R. D. Random strategies and sex differences in the prisoner's dilemma game. *Journal of Conflict Resolution*, 1975, *19*, 643–650.

Smith, T. E. Foundations of parental influence upon adolescents: An application of social power theory. *American Sociological Review*, 1970, *35*, 860–873.

Smith. T. E. An empirical comparison of potential determinants of parental authority. *Journal of Marriage and the Family*, 1977, *39*, 153–164.

Snyder, M., & Cunningham, M. R. To comply or not comply: Testing the self-perception explanation of the "foot-in-the-door" phenomenon. *Journal of Personality and Social Psychology*, 1975, *31*, 64–67.

Spector, B. I. A social-psychological model of position modification: Aswan. In I. W. Zartman (Ed.), *The 50% solution*. New York: Anchor Books, 1975.

Sprenkle, D. H., & Olson, D. H. Circumplex model of marital systems:

An empirical study of clinic and non-clinic couples. *Journal of Marriage and Family Counseling,* 1978, *4,* 59–74.

Sprey, J. The family as a system in conflict. *Journal of Marriage and the Family,* 1969, *31,* 699–706.

Sprey, J. Family power structure: A critical comment. *Journal of Marriage and the Family,* 1972, *34,* 235–238.

Sprey, J. Family power and process: Toward a conceptual integration. In R. E. Cromwell & D. H. Olson (Eds.), *Power in families.* New York: Halsted Press, 1975.

Sprey, J. *Conflict, power, and consensus in families.* Paper presented at the meeting of the American Sociological Association, 1977.

Sprey, J. Conflict theory and the study of marriage and the family. In W. R. Burr, R. Hill, F. I. Nye, & I. L. Reiss (Eds.), *Contemporary theories about the family,* Vol. 2. New York: Free Press, 1979.

Sprey, J. *Achieving solidarity: Fairness and power use.* Paper presented at the Second Annual Conference on the Alliance of Family Therapy and Family Research, Florida State University, 1981.

Steinmetz, S. K. *The cycle of violence. Assertive, aggressive, and abusive family interaction.* New York: Praeger, 1977.

Steinmetz, S. K. Disciplinary techniques and their relationship to aggressiveness, dependency, and conscience. In W. R. Burr, R. Hill, F. I. Nye, & I. L. Reiss (Eds.), *Contemporary theories about the family,* Vol. 1. New York: Free Press, 1979.

Stephens, W. N. *The family in cross-cultural perspective.* New York: Holt, Rinehart & Winston, 1963.

Stimpson, D. V. The influence of commitment and self-esteem on susceptibility to persuasion. *The Journal of Social Psychology,* 1970, *80,* 189–195.

Straus, M. A. Husband-wife interaction in nuclear and joint households. In D. Narain (Ed.), *Explorations in the family and other essays: Professor K. M. Kapadia memorial volume.* Bombay: Thacker, 1975.

Straus, M. A. Sexual inequality, cultural norms, and wife-beating. *Victimology,* 1976, *1,* 54–76.

Straus, M. A. Societal morphogenesis and intrafamily violence in cross-cultural perspective. *Annals of the New York Academy of Sciences,* 1977, *285,* 718–730.

Straus, M. A. *Family patterns and child abuse in a nationally representative American sample.* Paper presented at the 2nd International Congress on Child Abuse and Neglect, 1978. (a)

Straus, M. A. Wife beating: How common and why? *Victimology,* 1978, *2,* 443–458. (b)

Straus, M. A., & Tallman, I. SIMFAM: A technique for observational measurement and experimental study of families. In J. Aldous, T. Condon, R. Hill, M. Straus, & I. Tallman (Eds.), *Family problem solving.* Hinsdale, Ill.: Dryden Press, 1971.

Straus, M. A., Gelles, R. J., & Steinmetz, S. K. *Behind closed doors: Violence in the American family.* New York: Anchor Press, 1980.

Strauss, A. *Negotiations: Varieties, contexts, processes, and social order.* San Francisco: Jossey/Bass, 1978.

Strodtbeck, F. L. Husband-wife interaction over revealed differences. *American Sociological Review,* 1951, *16,* 468–473.

Sussman, M. B., Cates, J. N., & Smith, D. T. *The family and inheritance.* New York: Russell Sage, 1970.

Szalai, A., Connerse, P., Feldheim, P., Scheuch, E., & Stone, P. *The use of time.* The Hague: Mouton, 1973.

Szinovacz, M. E. *Entscheidungsstruktur und Aufgabenverteilung in jungen Familien.* Unpublished doctoral dissertation, University of Vienna, 1975.

Szinovacz, M. E. Power structure: A component in family dynamics. In S. Goldberg & F. Deutsch (Eds.), *Life-span individual and family development.* Monterey, Calif.: Brooks/Cole, 1977. (a)

Szinovacz, M. E. Role allocation, family structure, and female employment. *Journal of Marriage and the Family,* 1977, *39,* 781–791. (b)

Szinovacz, M. E. Another look at normative resource theory: Contributions from Austrian data—A research note. *Journal of Marriage and the Family,* 1978, *40,* 413–421.

Szinovacz, M. E. Marital adjustment and satisfaction with marital decision-making. *International Journal of the Sociology of the Family,* 1979, *9,* 67–94. (a)

Szinovacz, M. E. *The situation of Austrian women: Economic and family issues.* Vienna: Federal Ministry of Social Affairs, 1979. (b)

Szinovacz, M. E. Women employed: Effects on spouses' division of household work. *Journal of Home Economics,* 1979, *71,* 42–45. (c)

Szinovacz, M. E. Relationship among marital power measures: A critical review and an empirical test. *Journal of Comparative Family Studies,* 1981, *12:* 151–170.

Szinovacz, M. E. Economic resources, wife's skepticism, and marital violence. *International Journal of Family Psychiatry,* 1983, *3,* 419–437.

Szinovacz, M. E. Differierende Antwortmuster in Ehepartnerbefragungen: Ein theoretischer Erklaerungsversuch. In H. Meuleman & K. Reuband (Eds.), *Zur Rekonstruktion sozialer Realitaet bei der Erhebung and Analyse von Interviews.* Frankfurt: Campus, 1984.

Szinovacz, M. E., & Scanzoni, J. *Toward a theory of marital conflict management.* Paper presented at the Theory and Methods Workshop, National Council on Family Relations, 1979.

Szybillo, G. J., Sosanie, A. K., & Tenenbein, A. Family member influence in household decision-making. *Journal of Consumer Research,* 1979, *6,* 312–316.

Tallman, I., & Ihinger-Tallman, M. Values, distributive justice and social change. *American Sociological Review,* 1979, *44,* 216–234.

Tallman, I., & Miller, G. Class differences in family problem solving: The effects of verbal ability, hierarchical structure, and role expectations. *Sociometry,* 1974, *37,* 13–37.

Tedeschi, J. T. Attributions, liking and power. In T. L. Huston (Ed.), *Foundations of interpersonal attraction.* New York: Academic Press, 1974. (a)

Tedeschi, J. T. (Ed.), *Perspectives on social power.* Chicago: Aldine, 1974. (b)

Tedeschi, J. T. *Impression management theory and social psychological research.* New York: Academic Press, 1981.

Tedeschi, J. T., & Gaes, G. G. Aggression and the use of coercive power. *The Journal of Social Issues,* 1977, *33,* 101–125.

Tedeschi, J. T., & Lindskold, S. *Social psychology: Interdependence, interaction, and influence.* New York: Wiley, 1976.

Tedeschi, J. T., Bonoma, T. V., & Brown, R. C. A paradigm for the study of coercive power. *Journal of Conflict Resolution,* 1971, *15,* 199–223.

Tedeschi, J. T., Bonoma, T. V., & Schlenker, B. R. Influence, decision, and compliance. In J. T. Tedeschi (Ed.), *The social influence processes.* Chicago: Aldine, 1972.

Tedeschi, J. T., Schlenker, B. R., & Lindskold, S. The exercise of power and influence: The source of influence. In J. T. Tedeschi (Ed.), *The social influence processes.* Chicago: Aldine, 1972.

Tellis-Nayak, V., & Donoghue, G. O. Conjugal egalitarianism and violence across cultures. *Journal of Comparative Family Studies,* 1982, *13,* 277–290.

Terhune, K. W. The effects of personality in cooperation and conflict. In P. Swingle (Ed.), *The structure of conflict.* New York: Academic Press, 1970.

Thibaut, J. W., & Kelley, H. H. *The social psychology of groups.* New York: Wiley, 1959.

Thomas, D. L., Peterson, G. W., & Rollins, B. C. *Validity in parent-child research: A comparison of self-report and behavioral observations.* Paper presented at the Theory and Methods Workshop, National Council on Family Relations, 1977.

Thompson, L., & Walker, A. J. The dyad as the unit of analysis: Conceptual and methodological issues. *Journal of Marriage and the Family,* 1982, *44,* 889–900.

Thompson, M. E. Sex differences: Differential access to power or sex-role socialization? *Sex Roles,* 1981, *7,* 413–424.

Thomson, E., & Williams, R. Beyond wives' family sociology: A method for analyzing couple data. *Journal of Marriage and the Family,* 1982, *44,* 999–1008.

Thorne, B., & Yalom, M. (Eds.), *Rethinking the family.* New York: Longman, 1982.

Thornton, A., Alwin, D. F., & Camburn, D. Causes and consequences of sex-role attitudes and attitude change. *American Sociological Review,* 1983, *48,* 211–227.

Tjosvold, D., & Huston, T. L. Social face and resistance to compromise in bargaining. *The Journal of Social Psychology,* 1978, *104,* 57–68.

Traupmann, J. *Exchange, equity and marriage: Love's labors cost.* Paper presented at the Theory and Methods Workshop, National Council on Family Relations, 1976.

Turk, J. L. Power as the achievement of ends: A problematic approach in family and small group research. *Family Process,* 1974, *13,* 39–52.

Turk, J. L. Uses and abuses of family power. In R. E. Cromwell & D. H. Olson (Eds.), *Power in families.* New York: Halsted Press, 1975.

Turk, J. L., & Bell, N. W. Measuring power in families. *Journal of Marriage and the Family,* 1972, *34,* 215–222.

Turner, J. H. *The structure of sociological theory.* Homewood, Ill.: Dorsey, 1978.

Turner, J. L., Foa, E. B., & Foa, U. G. Interpersonal reinforcers: Classification, interrelationship, and some differential properties. *Journal of Personality and Social Psychology,* 1971, *19,* 168–180.

Uleman, J. S. The need for influence: Development and validation of a measure, and comparison with the need for power. *Genetic Psychology Monographs,* 1972, *85,* 157–214.

VanEs, J. C., & Shingi, P. M. Response consistency of husband and wife for selected attitudinal items. *Journal of Marriage and the Family,* 1972, *34,* 741–749.

Veroff, J., & Veroff, J. B. Theoretical notes on power motivation. *Merrill Palmer Quarterly,* 1971, *17,* 59–69.

Veroff, J., & Veroff, J. B. Reconsideration of a measure of power motivation. *Psychological Bulletin,* 1972, *78,* 279–291.

Vincent, J. P., Weiss, R. L., & Birchler, G. R. A behavioral analysis of problem solving in distressed and nondistressed married and stranger dyads. *Behavior Therapy.* 1975, *6,* 475–487.

Walster, E., & Walster, G. W. Equity and social justice. *The Journal of Social Issues.* 1975, *31,* 21–44.

Walster, E., Walster, G. W., & Berscheid, E. *Equity: Theory and research.* Boston: Allyn & Bacon, 1978.

Walters, L. H. Are families different from other groups? *Journal of Marriage and the Family,* 1982, *44,* 841–850.

Waxler, N. E., & Mishler, E. G. Scoring and reliability problems in interaction process analysis: A methodological note. *Sociometry,* 1966, *29,* 28–40.

Waxler, N. E., & Mishler, E. G. Sequential patterning in family interaction: A methodological note. *Family Process,* 1975, *14,* 211–219.

Weber, M. *The theory of social and economic organization.* New York: Free Press, 1947.

Weeks, M. O. Toward a theory of the dynamics of marital power in decision-making: An adaptation and test of balance theory. *International Journal of Sociology of the Family,* 1975, *5,* 220–229.

Weitzman, L. J., Dixon, C. M., Bird, J. A., McGinn, N., & Robertson, D. M. The traditional marriage contract. In L. Richardson & V. Taylor (Eds.), *Feminist frontiers.* Reading, Mass.: Addison-Wesley, 1983.

Wieting, S. G., & McLaren, A. T. Power in various family structures. In R. E. Cromwell & D. H. Olson (Eds.), *Power in families.* New York: Halsted Press, 1975.

Wilkening, E. A., & Morrison, D. E. A comparison of husband and wife responses concerning who makes farm and home decisions. *Marriage and Family Living,* 1963, *25,* 349–351.

Wilkes, R. E. Husband-wife influence in purchase decisions—A confirmation and extension. *Journal of Marketing Research,* 1975, *12,* 224–227.

Williams, J. H. Equality and the family. *International Journal of Women's Studies,* 1980, *3,* 131–142.

Willie, C. V., & Greenblatt, S. L. Four "classic" studies of power relationships in black families: A review and look to the future. *Journal of Marriage and the Family,* 1978, *40,* 691–696.

Willis, R. H., & Frieze, I. H. Sex roles, social exchange, and couples. In K. J. Gergen, M. S. Greenberg, & R. H. Willis (Eds.), *Social exchange: Advances in theory and research.* New York: Plenum Press, 1980.

Winter, D. G. *The power motive.* New York: Free Press, 1973.

Winter, D. G., Stewart, A. J., & McClelland, D. C. Husband's motives and wife's career level. *Journal of Personality and Social Psychology,* 1977, *35,* 159–166.

Winter, W. D., & Ferreira, A. J. Interaction process analysis of family decision-making. *Family Process,* 1967, *6,* 155–172.

Winter, W. D., & Ferreira, A. J. Talking time as an index of intrafamilial similarity in normal and abnormal families. *Journal of Abnormal Psychology,* 1969, *74,* 574–575.

Winter, W. D., Ferreira, A. J., & Bowers, N. Decision-making in married and unrelated couples. *Family Process,* 1973, *12,* 83–94.

Wolfe, D. M. Power and authority in the family. In D. Cartwright (Ed.), *Studies in social power,* Ann Arbor: University of Michigan Press, 1959.

Wortman, C. B. Some determinants of perceived control. *Journal of Personality and Social Psychology,* 1975, *31,* 282–294.

Wrong, D. H. *Power: Its forms, bases, and uses.* New York: Harper & Row, 1979.

Yllo, K., & Straus, M. A. *Patriarchy and violence against wives: The impact of structural and normative factors.* Paper presented at the Theory Construction and Methodology Workshop, 1982.

Young, D. M. "Beneficial" aggression. *The Journal of Communication,* 1977, *27,* 100–103.

Young, M., & Willmott, P. *The symmetrical family.* New York: Routledge & Kegan Paul, 1973.

Yukl, G. A., Malone, M. P., Hayslip, B., & Pamin, T. A. The effects of time pressure and issue settlement order on integrative bargaining. *Sociometry,* 1976, *39,* 277–280.

Zander, A., & Curtis, T. Effects of social power on aspiration setting and striving. *Journal of Abnormal and Social Psychology,* 1962, *64,* 63–74.

Zimmerman, C. C. *Family and civilization.* New York: Harper & Brothers, 1947.

Zuckerman, E., & Jacob, T. Task effects in family interaction. *Family Process,* 1979, *18,* 47–53.

CHAPTER 25

Family Stress

Pauline Boss

Introduction: Family Vulnerabilities and Strengths

The family has been characterized as a "puny work group" badly organized to withstand stress and yet engaged in the most stressful of social responsibilities (Hill, 1958, pp. 33–34). Nevertheless, many families succeed and survive because, to varying degrees, their vulnerabilities are counterbalanced by their strengths. Thus, the general challenge to scientists and therapists is to ascertain why some families can cope even in the face of severe stress whereas others crumble under the least amount of pressure; the specific challenge is to identify and understand those elements of a family's internal and external contexts that enhance *or* block this coping process.

Given the inevitability of normative as well as unexpected family stress, we could narrow our view to focus on strengthening the vulnerable family system so that it will better recover from the influence of stress throughout the life cycle. But the more compelling question remains: Why do some families make it even though they are severely stressed? Why are some families relatively invulnerable?

From this more optimistic perspective, researchers and clinicians have studied families to determine their strengths and perceptions so that others may benefit from the identification of preventive and supportive strategies. Indeed, experts in family stress currently focus more on strengths than on vulnerabilities. This chapter follows suit but with an added emphasis on the context and the *meaning* that the family gives to an event of stress. Because of this more subjective focus, it follows that this chapter has a clinical as well as a research orientation.

We define *family stress* as an upset in the steady state of the family. It may be as mild as a bat flying around the house or as severe as a holocaust; it includes anything that may disturb the family, cause uneasiness, or exert pressure on the family system. Not all stressed families are in crisis, however; many avoid crisis by managing to hold the degree of stress to a tolerable level, a process called *coping*. Nor have all families in crisis had long-term stress; they may have been doing well until a disaster struck. Even a strong family will fall into momentary crisis when an accident occurs, when a tornado rips away their house, or when a loved one dies unexpectedly.

It appears, therefore, that some other factors operate in the stress process that influence outcome. Although individual strengths, family strengths, and social supports have recently been identified as predictors of stress outcome, we suggest here that the end result of the stress process is influenced by an even broader *external context*, which, in turn, influences the family's *internal context* and, thereby, the *meaning* they give to a particular stressful event. We therefore build on past and current research but move in a new direction toward more qualitative analysis and phenomenological study of the stress process. Three qualitative variables—the ambiguity in the family's boundary, the family's use of denial, and the family's value orientation—are discussed in this chapter to represent the family's internal context as it affects the stress process and subsequent outcomes of coping or crisis. Viewed from inside the family, boundary ambiguity represents their sociological or structural context; the use of denial represents their psychological context; and the family's value orientation represents their philosophical context. We inductively present these variables as a way of viewing the family stress process from a more contextual approach, internally and externally.

Organizationally, this chapter is divided into three sections. First, we review the classic family stress literature to acquaint ourselves with language and concepts. Thus, basic terms and constructs are clarified to give us a consistent and common base of understanding from which to proceed. If you will, this first section may be regarded as a *basic primer* on family stress.

Second, we move into the present to review current literature on family stress and coping.[1] We focus heavily on everyday family stress and coping across the life cycle and present a selective synthesis of theory and research.

---

[1] For a more comprehensive review of the current research, especially in coping, see McCubbin, Joy, Cauble, Comeau, Patterson, and Needle, 1980.

Pauline Boss • Department of Family Social Science, University of Minnesota, St. Paul, MN 55108.

Third, from the perspective afforded by the literature reviews, we explore future directions for family stress research, theory, and clinical application. The focus is on the search for more inclusive variables in family stress theory. This is a search for what we might call *umbrella variables.*

Within the family's internal context, family boundary ambiguity, family value orientation, and the family's use of denial are submitted as examples of more inclusive variables that are basic to the understanding of the stress process in both therapy and research. By adding these comprehensive variables, the attempt is to codify and simplify rather than to extend family stress theory. The purpose of this chapter, then, is to define terms, to discuss past and current literature, and to examine new and general variables of a more qualitative nature. Ultimately, the purpose is to direct future research more to general theoretical propositions and less to midrange theory.

Historical Overview of Literature on Family Stress

In the Talmud and the Bible, we read that families have been concerned with events of change, trouble, disaster, and ambiguity since the beginning of recorded time. The systematic interest of scholars in these phenomena, however, is relatively recent. The current approach to family stress research began at the University of Michigan and the University of Chicago as a result of a major societal event, the Depression of the 1930s, which provided the situational base for the first studies by Angell (1936) and by Cavan and Ranck (1938). These scientists based their work on the case study approach, in which they used the inductive[2] method, applied social-psychological theory, and examined the group as well as the individuals in the group. The family was viewed as an "organization that is in the constant process of adaptation to changing conditions" (Angell, 1936, p. 14). Not unlike some present-day researchers (e.g., Reiss, 1981), Angell saw families as entering "a new phase of this tentative process" (p. 14) when under stress. In the families studied during the 1930s, the stressor was the sudden loss of income.

Based on this research, Angell (1936) inductively derived the two major determinants of a family's reaction to sudden loss of income: (1) *integration,* which he defined as the family's common interest, affection, sense of economic interdependence, and other bonds of coherence and unity, and (2) *adaptability,* which he defined as the flexibility of the family unit in discussion and decision making. These early findings remain unchallenged today; current research of a more deductive nature presents similar findings regarding family strengths (McCubbin, Boss, Wilson, & Lester, 1980a; Olson, McCubbin, Barnes, Larsen, Muxen, & Wilson, 1983; Olson, Sprenkle, & Russell, 1979).

Predating Boss's work (1980b) on family role flexibility (androgyny) as a coping resource, Angell (1936) noted that "plastic" families (those in which roles are interchangeable rather than rigid) are best equipped to surmount obstacles (p. 17). Of his two factors, Angell concluded that "even a moderate degree of adaptability will pull families with any integration at all through all but the worst crises" (p. 181).

Cavan and Ranck (1938) added to this work with a longitudinal study of families before and during the Depression, spanning the years 1927 to 1935. Supporting the findings of Angell (1936), Cavan and Ranck found that a family's previous methods of meeting difficulty were related to how they met present difficulty; that is, well-organized families, even when Depression losses were great, continued to be organized, whereas disorganized families became further disorganized. Unemployment continued to be the major cause of family stress and was investigated even beyond the Depression (e.g., both Komarovsky, 1940, and Cavan, 1959, studied unemployed males).

A Columbia University scholar named Koos (1946) also emphasized inductive methodology and the social psychological perspective; he, too, focused on economic stress but, for the first time, made explicit the high stress of urban living by studying family abilities to solve troubles and crises in a New York City slum. His major contribution to the literature was his "profile of trouble" (p. 107). It was further developed by Hill (1949) and labeled "the roller-coaster pattern of response to stress." Koos made an early plea for social supports to aid families coping with high stress:

A first need, if the effect of trouble is to be minimized, is the reconstruction of the family as a family. This is not *to be construed as saying that it is up to the family. Quite the opposite. As our industrial culture has provided the elements leading to family disintegration, so must that culture now provide (through social organization) for the reconstitution of the family.* (p. 123)

In his study of stressed[3] families, Hill (1949) made a major contribution to theory with his focus on the family as a culturally conditioned organization that reflects the state of the culture and, at the same time, internal familial behaviors. The stressor event that Hill studied was family separation due to World War II. Based on the earlier findings of Angell (1936), Cavan and Ranck (1938), Komarovsky (1940), and Koos (1946), Hill developed a

---

[2]Induction, according to Burr (1973), is "logical movement from the specific to the general" (p. 20). The process of induction is especially important in theory building because it allows the discovery of general propositions that encompass and explain a range of specific propositions. Deduction, on the other hand, is logical movement from the general to the specific. It is the process of using general propositions and other identifiable conditions as a basis for explaining why specific propositions or conditions exist (Burr, 1973, p. 19). One deduces from general theory to specific hypotheses, whereas one induces from specific observations to a general theoretical level.

[3]In this study, Hill used *stress* negatively; that is, he referred to *distress* in the Selye (1956) sense.

list of 10 items[4] to test family adequacy in relation to the twin concepts of family integration (coherence) and adaptability (flexibility). Hill labeled these items "family resources." They were used to mediate the stress of family separation and reunion brought about by World War II. The methodology of Hill's study was in-home interviews with the case study approach, survey research, and a random sample ($n = 137$). Of the many contributions to the literature stemming from this study, the most lasting has been the ABC-X model (Hill, 1949, 1958). In addition, there was further development of the roller-coaster model of family adjustment (Hill, 1949).

Crisis Model of Family Stress

This roller-coaster model of family adjustment after crisis was originated by Koos (1946), refined and developed by Hill (1949; Hansen & Hill, 1964), and adapted for this chapter (see Figure 1). It illustrates familial adjustment to crisis. According to the model, after the onset of a stressor event the family may go into crisis, that is, a *period of disorganization*, in which previous interactions and coping strategies are inadequate, inoperable, or blocked. Then, the time depending on its vulnerability to stress and its generative power, the family reverses this disorganization and begins to reorganize and recover to go into what Hill (1949) called the *period of recovery*. Finally, the family may reach a new *level of reorganization* above, below, or equal to the one experienced before the onset of the stressor event. What this means is that the family does not have to be destroyed by a crisis. It can recover to a level that is higher than, lower than, or equal to the level of functioning at the time the event occurred. Although this point needs further empirical verification, clinical observations inductively support Koos's and Hill's premises of variation in levels of recovery for families that have been in crisis.

Crisis, according to an often-cited definition from psychology, is the person's reaction to an obstacle that stands in the way of important life goals, this obstacle being, for a time, insurmountable through the usual methods of problem solving (Caplan, 1961). This definition regarding the individual is congruent with the definition of crisis developed by family sociologist Reuben Hill (1949), who

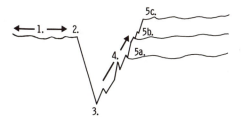

1. Level of family functioning before event occurred
2. Event occurs
3. Low point in period of disorganization "Hitting bottom"
4. Period of recovery
5. Level of reorganization
   a. below previous level of functioning
   b. equal to previous level of functioning
   c. higher than previous level of functioning

Figure 1. Diagram of family crisis model. (Adapted from R. Hill, *Families under Stress.* New York: Harper & Row, 1949; and E. L. Koos, *Families in Trouble.* New York: King's Crown Press, 1946.)

is credited with the original definition of terms in his ABC-X model.

ABC-X Model of Family Stress

With his ABC-X model, Hill (1958) contributed a substantial base for scientific inquiry into family stress. The most succinct explanation of that model was presented by Hill to a group of social workers in 1957. He explicitly joined the work of family sociologists on family crisis-proneness with that of social workers who researched multiproblem families. Hill presented a framework for family stress theory that focused on three variables: A, the provoking event or stressor; B, the resources or strengths the family has at the time of the event; and C, the meaning that the family (individually and collectively) attaches to the event. These three variables remain a foundation of current family-stress theory. This chapter, however, pays most attention to the C factor because, from a clinical perspective, the family's perception of an event is a powerful, if not the most powerful, variable in explaining family stress. From a research perspective, perception is difficult to measure and therefore remains the least investigated variable in the model even though Hansen and Hill (1964) advocated its study.

Hill's ABC-X model is used here heuristically and primarily as a reference point for the reader throughout the chapter. As we move in new directions, it is helpful to know where we have come from. Because of the nature of the variables, however, we do not define and discuss them in their original order. The A factor (stressor event) is defined first, then the X factor (crisis and stress). The B factor (resources) is defined in relation to coping theory

[4]"(1) Previous success in meeting family crisis; (2) Non-materialistic goals predominate; (3) Flexibility and willingness to shift traditional roles of husband and wife or father and mother, if necessary; (4) Acceptance of responsibility by all family members in performing family duties; (5) Willingness to sacrifice personal interest to attain family objectives; (6) Pride in the family tree and ancestral traditions; (7) Presence of strong patterns of emotional interdependence and unity; (8) High participation as a family in joint activities; (9) Presence of egalitarian patterns of family control and decision-making; (10) Strong affectional ties between father–mother, father–children, mother–children, children–children" (Hill, 1949, pp. 17–18).

and research, and the C factor (the meaning of the event) is discussed in relation to the internal context of the family in stress.

Because theoretical definitions directly affect research and clinical strategies, it is essential to review and clarify definitions in this chapter. We focus on family stress theorists who have developed definitions, but we cite individual stress theorists as well. From a general systems perspective, we look at both sets of literature because both individual and group indicators are important to understanding and predicting the outcome of the family stress process.

The Stressor Event: The A Factor

A stressor, according to Hill (1949), consists of those life events or occurrences that are of sufficient magnitude to bring about change in the family system. Although the literature is not always consistent on this point, the stressor event, it should be noted, is not synonymous with change. Burr (1973) and McCubbin, Joy, Cauble, Comeau, Patterson, and Needle (1980) concur, as does Golan (1978); the latter labeled the stressor event as a hazardous event that "is the *starting point* that marks a change in the ecological balance" of a system (p. 64, italics added).

A *stressor event*, therefore, is defined most often in the literature as *an event that is capable of causing change and stress but that does not necessarily do so every time.* Although Selye (1956) originally defined a stressor event as a noxious stimulus, Lazarus (1974) called a stressor event merely a threat, that is, a more neutral stimulus. Clearly, Lazarus went beyond Selye by implying that the end result (degree of stress) depends more on specific reactions to specific stressors than on nonspecific stimuli. Monat and Lazarus (1977) reached this conclusion after investigating such stressor events as the application of heat and the resulting physiological reactions, but their research may also have relevance to family stress situations. For example, family therapists often see a teenager apply "heat" to a family situation that causes the parents' blood pressure to rise at an alarming rate. The high blood pressure depends on quite specific reactions to a specific stressor, in this case, the child's rebellious behavior, but according to Lazarus (1974), specificity can be associated with varied options. The stress disorder (i.e., the parents' high blood pressure) could depend on at least three factors: (1) the formal characteristics of the environmental demands; (2) the quality of the emotional response generated by the individuals facing these demands; and (3) the processes of coping mobilized by the stressful event (Lazarus, 1974, p. 327).

In short, a stressor event is a stimulus that threatens the status quo. It is a stimulus that holds the *potential* for beginning the process of change or stress. It is not change itself. A stressor event does not in itself contain the attribute of stress, only the potential or capacity for producing the process or condition of stress. A stressor event, therefore, is "a stimulus or force" (Brown, 1980) that

has an impact on the individual or family and that may or may not produce stress, depending on the individual's or the family's perceptions, resources, and context. When stressful life events are a *cause,* they are not synonymous with the state of stress, which is a *consequence.* Were they synonymous, we would have a tautology. To circumvent Hansen and Johnson's (1979) point that it is difficult to avoid tautological reasoning in specifying the nature of the stressor on the family because stressors frequently are identified by their effect (that is, change equals change), we emphasize this important point: A stressful life event (a stressor) has only the *potential* to cause stress; it is not synonymous with the state of stress in any degree of intensity.

Based on this definition, the stressor event has no attribution of its own except neutrality;[5] that is, a stressful life event has no positive or negative attribute, so the outcome of a stressful event is not predetermined. The event merely holds the potential for varying levels of stress: optimal, deprived, or excessive (Selye, 1956, 1980). Because it has this capacity as a neutral stimulus, the stressor event depends on the family system's resources and perceptions (the B and C factors) for further attribution (Hill, 1949; Burr, 1973). "Stress is not seen as inherent in the event itself, but rather is conceptualized as a function of the response of the distressed family to the stressor" (McCubbin, Joy, Cauble, Comeau, Patterson, & Needle, 1980b, p. 857). Given that the dimensions of stressor events are variant and multiple, we need to classify and define types.

Normal Developmental Stressor Events. The classification of stressor events is shown in Figure 2. In the left-hand column are listed the types of stressors that usually are predictable because they are part of everyday life and part of the normal human developmental process. Examples are the birth of a child (see Russell, 1974; Ventura & Boss, 1983), adolescents' leaving home, and retirement. Normative stress was addressed by Rapoport (1965) and developed further by Boss (1980a), and Mederer and Hill (1983).

Normative stress, according to Boss (1980a), is defined in terms of family boundary changes of acquisition or loss across the family life cycle, that is, the normal losses and gains of family membership are stressors because they bear the *potential* for stress. As family membership grows or shrinks, changes occur in marital relations (e.g., divorce); work relations (e.g., unemployment or retirement); and personal status (e.g., health). These changes affect family interactions. It is hypothesized that

---

[5]Note that this interpretation is different from Rapoport's statement (1965) that "stress is equated with a stressful event or situation" (p. 23) and Hill's statement (1958) that the hardship of the event is attributable to the event itself. More recently, Hill and others (e.g., McCubbin, Joy, Cauble, Comeau, Patterson, & Needle, 1980) have modified this position to eliminate tautological possibilities.

TYPE :

maturational .... situational

normative .... disaster

developmental .... environmental

predictable .... unexpected

volitional .... nonvolitional

SOURCE :

inside the family .... outside the family

SEVERITY :

chronic.. acute

mild... severe

isolated... cumulative
(multi-problem)

Figure 2. Classification of stressor events.

as family boundaries change as a result of these normal maturational changes, the family experiences an increase in stress, at least until the process of transition and reorganization is accomplished.

Unexpected and Disaster Stressor Events. The right-hand column of Figure 2 lists other types of events, the kind that initially attracted family stress theorists. These events are unexpected and are the result of some unique situation that cannot be predicted and is not likely to be repeated. Examples include wars, floods, nuclear plant disasters, fires, and economic depression. Whereas the accident at the Three Mile Island nuclear power plant in 1979 was attributed to human and mechanical failure (Bartlett, Houts, Byrnes, & Miller, 1983), many disastrous stressor events are caused by nature. Examples are the drought in Bangladesh (Feldman & McCarthy, 1983), an earthquake in Nicaragua, and a flash flood in South Dakota (Bolin & Bolton, 1983). Inasmuch as these events are often called acts of God and are not thought to be the result of an action by someone within the family, they are categorized as nonvolitional.

Volitional Stressor Events. Stressor events can be classified by the degree of choice that they allow, that is, the degree of the family's control of the event's occurrence. An example of a volitional stressor event is a wanted marriage, a wanted job promotion, a wanted divorce, or a test you willingly take as a student (Mechanic, 1978). Examples of nonvolitional stressor events are deaths, unwanted pregnancies, or job promotions that force unwanted household moves.

Source of Stressor Events. Hill (1949) also classified stressor events by source, that is, inside or outside the family. Intrafamily stressors can be unique (e.g., mental disease) or fairly common (e.g., the birth of a premature

infant). Examples of stressful family events from outside the family are primarily environmental, such as the effects of tornadoes, earthquakes, and wars.

Chronic Stressor Situations. Both normative and disaster events can vary on other dimensions, such as chronic versus acute and mild versus severe. The presence of a family member with persistent kidney disease exemplifies a chronic event, whereas a child's breaking a leg represents an acute event. Even within this classification, the stress from both chronic and acute events may be only a minor bother (e.g., poor eyesight [chronic] or a cold [acute]) or a severe stressor (e.g., alcoholism [chronic] or pneumonia [acute]). Because of the current focus of researchers and clinicians on the area of chronic stress, the term is defined in detail here.

A *chronic stressor* is a situation that runs a long course, is difficult to amend, and has a debilitating effect on the family. But there are different types of chronic stressor events. The first characteristic that further specifies the type of chronic stressor event is ambiguity versus predictability; there is uncertainty regarding the facts about the onset, the development, and the conclusion of the event (e.g., missing family members or illness such as renal disease or Alzheimer disease). A second specificity is the context in which the chronic stressor event develops, that is, whether it is a result of the larger context (e.g., inflation, living near an active volcano, or the closing of a factory) or a result of an individual pathology (e.g., persistent illness). A third specificity of type of chronic stressor event is its visibility versus its nonvisibility. Some chronic stressors, such as diabetes, are not physically noticeable, whereas others, such as severe retardation or the loss of a limb, are immediately apparent to the observer and the family members.

Because of the import of both the general characteristics and the specific descriptors of chronic stressors, it is essential that researchers identify and describe categorically the events that they are investigating.

Especially when there is an ambiguous chronic stressor in the family, we must be aware of the possibility of denial or early extrusion of the family member suffering from the chronic illness (Gonzalez & Reiss, 1981). Given the long-term and ambiguous qualities of a stressor event (e.g., end-stage renal disease, sickle-cell anemia, or alcoholism), the family may reorganize itself without the affected member, thereby denying his or her physical presence in the family system.

Denial may also be used by the family in another way. The members may deny that the stressor of chronic illness exists and may view the affected person as normal, as if oblivious of the fact that anything is wrong. In both cases, denial becomes a coping and/or a defense mechanism for dealing with the duration and the ambiguity of the situation. Not being able to come up with the facts surrounding the disease, the family comes up with its own solution: denying that the affected member is present *or* denying that the illness exists. (For additional discussion on denial, see the section, "Meaning and Perception of the Event: The C Factor.")

The subtle characteristics of chronic stressor situations, even more than acute events, call for special consideration in research methodology. That is, research instruments must be able to measure perceptual variables resulting from the duration and the ambiguity of chronic stressor situations. Measuring instruments must be sensitive to the possibility of the family's early psychological extrusion of a chronically ill member or to the family's total denial of the existence of the persisting illness in one of its members.

Another characteristic of chronic stressor situations that influences research as well as therapy is that the family's perception of the situation may change over the family life cycle. According to Wikler (1981), chronic stressors, such as severe retardation, become "recycled" at each juncture across the life span when a developmental step would normally occur in that person. For example, when the retarded child reaches school age and cannot go, the family is reminded acutely of the chronic stressor, and it will be reminded again, at successive developmental junctures, when transitional behaviors should be forthcoming and are not possible.

Another complication of chronic stressor events is that they overlap the normal developmental family life transitions over the life span. From the work of Gonzalez and Reiss (1981), it appears that the family cannot absorb both the stressor of an illness and the stressors of normal family development at the same time. Coping with both becomes too much. Thus, one could predict that families would be critically stressed whenever a chronic illness overlaps a normal developmental transition even though the family was coping with the illness reasonably well before that time.

The chronic stressor, therefore, should be defined as a stressful situation, rather than as a stressful event, that carries with it the inherent qualities of long duration, the high probability of pileup with other events, and the potential of being highly ambiguous in etiology, development, and conclusion.

The Pileup of Stressor Events. More recently, the concept of "stress pileup"[6] (McCubbin, Joy, *et al.*, 1980, p. 861) has added a critical dimension to the classification of stressful life events. Isolated versus cumulative events may affect individuals and families differently. In fact, the accumulation of stressor events may explain family crisis better than any one isolated event. The concept of accumulation is the basis of the Holmes and Rahe Scale (1967), which quantifies stress pileup for individuals, and of the Family Inventory of Life Events and Changes Scale developed by McCubbin, Patterson, and Wilson (1981), which does the same for families. More is said about the concept of pileup later in this chapter.

[6]This concept would be more accurately labeled *stressor pileup* or *event pileup*.

We can conclude from the preceding discussion that stressor events do indeed encompass situations that are complex, and that this complexity points to the need for longitudinal design and multivariate analysis in stress research.

Stress, Crisis, and Strain: The X Factor Redefined

Unlike the stressor event, stress *is* synonymous with change. It is experienced as a process rather than as an event and thus implies change. Caplan (1964) defined *stress* as an upset in the steady state; that is, the system is no longer in equilibrium but is disturbed, uneasy, strained, pressured, and certainly not at rest. To engineers, *stress* means the force exerted when one body presses on, pulls on, pushes against, or has a tendency to compress or twist another body; they measure the intensity of this mutual force in pounds per square inch. On the other hand, medical and social scientists define stress with individual indicators, such as change in anxiety scores or blood pressure, or with family system measures, such as change in role performance or task assignments. More recently, McCubbin, Patterson, and Wilson (1981) developed a series of instruments that quantify the degree of stress on the family as perceived by family members.

Crisis versus Stress. Crisis differs from stress in that it is a change so acute, severe, and overwhelming that the family system is blocked, immobilized, and incapacitated. Stress resulting in crisis is so high that the system's resources are no longer adequate to maintain the structure. For example, in families, boundaries are not maintained, customary roles and tasks are no longer performed within the system, and individuals may no longer function at optimal levels, physiologically or psychologically. If we use the engineering metaphor, crisis would mean that the bridge has collapsed; the structure has broken down so that it no longer functions in transporting people across the water or in preventing them from falling over the sides. The point at which a crisis occurs, then, is determined by the point at which a structure, human or mechanical, can no longer perform its functions.

General indicators of a crisis, therefore, are (1) nonperformance of prescribed roles, (2) nonmaintenance of structural boundaries, and (3) immobilization of the system. The specific indicators of crisis after a sudden death, for example, might be (1) the inability of the adults to take care of themselves, to work, or to take care of their children; (2) the inability of family members to support and take care of each other, so that outsiders are temporarily needed to come in and perform the usual family tasks and roles; and (3) the inability of the family members to make decisions and solve problems.

Crisis, therefore, is a point of *acute* disequilibrium as opposed to stress, which is a state of *disturbed* equilibrium. Crisis is preceded by stress. This stress may build up in a gradual process, or the stress process and the subsequent crisis may both happen within moments, as in disasters and unexpected deaths.

However, stress does not always end in crisis. Many individuals and families live with relatively high amounts of stress throughout their lives; indeed, some seem to thrive on it and never reach the crisis point, just as a creaking bridge may never collapse. Crisis, therefore, is dependent on stress, but stress can occur independently of crisis. Because of these qualitative and quantitative differences, the terms *stress* and *crisis* should never be used interchangeably.

Crisis as a Turning Point for Families. Inherent in the difference between stress and crisis are the variables of *duration* and *severity*. Although family stress can go on for long periods of time, a family crisis is temporally limited and has a turning point. Whereas stress is merely an upset in a steady state, a crisis is an upset of such rigor that the system's support and coping mechanisms are no longer equal to the pressure. Once this ratio shifts again, the crisis is over and recovery is in progress.

We emphasize, therefore, that a crisis does not have to permanently disable a family (as it may a bridge). Human systems, unlike mechanical ones, can learn from their experiences, even painful ones. After a crisis, families can redefine themselves and their resources (Cavan & Ranck, 1938) or reconstruct their reality by changing the rules by which their system operates (Reiss, 1981). Such shifts in the family's perception and organization constitute a turning point, and the recovery process begins. Crisis does not have to break the family structure. It only temporarily immobilizes it and may, in fact, lead to an even higher level of functioning after recovery than before.

Crisis as a Categorical Variable. McCubbin, Joy *et al.* (1980) defined crisis as a continuous variable, that is, as "the amount of incapacitatedness or disorganization in the family where resources are inadequate" (p. 857). Based on our discussion here, we must disagree with this definition insofar as we define family crisis as a categorical variable. The structure either holds or it doesn't. The family is not in crisis until the structure gives way to a stress overload and the concomitant inability to cope. Figure 1 is consistent with our definition of crisis as a categorical variable: The family is either in crisis or it is not. This is an important point for researchers in their search for ways to measure family stress and family crisis. Whereas family stress is a continuous variable ranging from high to low, family crisis is categorical.

Family Stress versus Strain. The difference between the two concepts of family stress and family strain is also most easily understood from the perspective of engineering, where theories of structural failure have been highly developed. In engineering, stress is "the force per unit area," whereas strain is the result of a mismatch or deformity (shear stress) that occurs when one cannot line up the

force (stress) with the supports to absorb it. This mismatch between the point of pressure and the point of strength begins to deform the structure and results in strain. The bridge bends and buckles, but it does not yet collapse. The family still functions, but with great difficulty and at a lowered level.

The danger from strain is that if the shape starts changing, the energy of distortion is applied to the structure and, by definition, limits the degree of the structure's tolerance. When such a structural change occurs, therefore, a collapse or failure is more likely because everything in the structure must move to absorb the mismatch (shear stress). With normal stress, only the appropriate parts of the structure are affected by the pressure.

Applying this analogy to family stress theory, we can predict that strain, defined as a mismatch between the accumulating demands made on the family and the resources to meet those pressures, is detrimental to all families over time. The family is not fortified to meet such demands, so the pressure begins to warp even the basic structure of the family. Despite strong individuals and family strengths, the persistent application of stress in areas where it is unexpected will eventually cause even the staunchest of family systems to buckle. More important than trying to avoid family stressor events, then, is the avoidance of strain. The accumulation of events is relevant to strain in that strain is more likely to occur when stressful events pile up and exert a persistent pressure on the family structure. In order for researchers to delineate the effect of strain on the family structure, longitudinal studies will be necessary. Such research may shed light on the question of why some families collapse under a particular stress whereas others do not.

The next sections of this chapter focus on the B factor of family coping resources, coping as an outcome instead of a crisis (a new additive to the X factor), and, finally, the meaning of the stressor event (the C factor) to the family.

Coping Theory and Research: A Shift in Emphasis from Crisis to Invulnerability in Families

The major emphasis in family stress research during the 1970s and 1980s shifted from crisis to coping.[7] For the first time, researchers are less concerned with why families fail and more concerned with why families succeed (McCubbin, Joy *et al.*, 1980; McCubbin & Boss,

---

[7]The coping studies were begun under the direction of Hamilton McCubbin at the Center for Prisoner of War Studies in San Diego and were continued at the University of Minnesota by McCubbin and at the University of Wisconsin–Madison by Boss. The University of Minnesota Agricultural Experiment Station, the University of Wisconsin Graduate School, and the University of Wisconsin Agricultural Experiment Station have been generous in their support of these research projects.

1980; Ventura & Boss, 1983), a reflection of the assumption that stressor events are inevitable. No family can escape normal developmental stressor events, and few can avoid unexpected events, such as illness, accidents, or disasters. If researchers can identify how strong families cope and survive, we may be able to provide the information that will help to strengthen more vulnerable families before or after an expected or unexpected stress event occurs. Such anticipatory preparation may make families less vulnerable to the effect of stressor events as they move through the life span. Thus, the research and theoretical models of this decade are shifting from a basis of vulnerability to one of *recoverability* or *invulnerability*.

During the 1970s, a new concept called *coping* was introduced into the family stress literature (Boss, McCubbin, & Lester, 1979; McCubbin, 1979; McCubbin, Dahl, Lester, Benson, & Robertson, 1976). At first glance, family coping appears to operationalize Hill's B factor (family resources), but the concept is, in fact, a unique dimension that is not accommodated by Hill's original ABC-X model. An adaptation of Hill's model to accommodate coping is illustrated in Figure 3.

Family Coping Resources: The B Factor. The family's coping resources are its individual and collective *strengths* at the time the stressor event occurs. Examples are economic security, health, intelligence, job skills, proximity, spirit of cooperation, relationship skills, and network and social supports. The family's resources, therefore, are the sociological, economic, psychological, emotional, and physical *assets* on which the members can draw in response to a single stressor event or an accumulation of events. However, having resources does not imply how the family will use them. For example, a family may use a resource such as money to cope with the event of unemployment in a maladaptive way (e.g., to buy more liquor) or more functionally (e.g., to look for another job). Thus, the availability and the amount of family resources remain static (nonprocess) variables that

can be rather easily assessed by researchers and therapists.

Family Coping as an Outcome: A New Addition to the X Factor. Family coping (as opposed to being in crisis), is a *process and outcome variable;* it refers to what the family *does* with its resources. Only if the family brings its coping resources into action is the *process of coping* begun. If the family has few resources, individually and collectively, the coping process may never begin, and crisis may result when a stressful event occurs.

This distinction between coping resources and coping as a process outcome points to a void in earlier stress models (Burr, 1973; Hill, 1958). Because they were primarily models of family crisis or vulnerability (rather than invulnerability or recoverability), they did not include coping as a unique and separate entity. If we change the definition of the X factor in the ABC-X model to reflect results in *varying degrees of stress from coping to noncoping (crisis),* this new concept can be incorporated into the existing model (see Figure 3) as an alternative outcome. Note, however, the broken line in Figure 3 between "Coping" and "Crisis," which indicates a critical level beyond which there is a breaking point and acute disequilibrium.

Coping as a Process: An Interplay among the B, C, and X Factors. Regardless of the theoretical model, researchers from different backgrounds appear to agree that

coping refers to efforts to master conditions of harm, threat or challenge when a routine or automatic response is not readily available . . . environmental demands must be met with new behavioral solutions or old ones must be adapted to meet the current stress. (Monat & Lazarus, 1977, p. 8)

White's definition (1974) is more succinct and refers to a more neutral situation: "Coping refers to adaptations under relatively difficult conditions" (p. 49).

From a cognitive and phenomenological perspective, Lazarus (1966, 1977) defined coping as a cognitive activity incorporating (1) an assessment of impending harm (primary appraisal) and (2) an assessment of the conse-

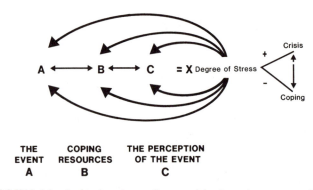

Figure 3. Hill's ABC-X Model revised to show degree of stress and the alternative outcomes of crisis and coping.

$$\begin{array}{ccc}
\textbf{COGNITIVE}^1 & \textbf{EMOTIONAL}^2 & \textbf{COPING}^3 \\
\textbf{APPRAISAL} \longleftrightarrow & \textbf{REACTION} \longleftrightarrow & \textbf{BEHAVIOR}
\end{array}$$

[1]Based on: (a) Degree of perceived threat
                    (b) Stimulus configuration
                    (c) Psychological make-up of the individual

Includes primary appraisal which is the assessment of impending
harm and secondary appraisal which is the assessment of any consequences the coping behaviors might have.

[2]Includes actual reactions to the perceived threat.

[3]Includes (a) direct action behaviors (fight or flight) which
deal with the stressor itself and (b) palliative behaviors (actions or
thoughts which make the person feel more calm).

Figure 4. The coping process. (Source: Lazarus, 1977.)

quences of any coping action (secondary appraisal).[8] Thus, the *coping process*, according to Lazarus (1977), is the cognitive use of primary and secondary appraisals of what is happening, whereas *coping strategies* or activities are the actual responses to a perceived threat. *Coping behaviors* are defined by Lazarus (1976) as (1) *direct action behaviors*, which are an attack on or an escape from threat (fight or flight) and are designed to change a stressed relation with one's physical or social environment; and (2) *intrapsychic forms of coping*, which are defense mechanisms (e.g., detachment or denial) designed to reduce emotional arousal rather than to change the situation. Both *actions* and *thoughts* may make a person feel better even if they cannot change the source of the stress.

Although Lazarus's theoretical work is psychological and is directed to individual stress, it is relevant to family stress theory. The importance of cognition as well as a stressed person's psychological profile (values, beliefs, expectations, and motivations) was emphasized by Lazarus (1966) and is significant in family stress and coping. Implicitly, under Hill's C factor—the meaning of the event—values and beliefs become important in the primary and secondary appraisal of threat. Joining Hill's (1958) and Lazarus's (1966) conceptualizations, re-

searchers may begin to operationalize Hill's C factor by using the indicators of appraisal that Lazarus outlined in his coping process (see Figure 4).

According to Lazarus (1966, 1977), an individual's coping behavior is organized not by emotions but by the *cognitive process* that leads to the *emotional response*. He included the possibility that a coping behavior may be chosen for its multiple purpose, that is, to deal with the problem generated by the stress emotion and to control the emotion. Indeed, socializing with people is a coping behavior that deals with physical isolation, which is caused by separation or divorce, and with the depression and loneliness that arise from the same causes. Deciding to get up and go to a party not only helps to alleviate physical isolation but may ease a depressed emotional state as well. The decision to go to the party may be a result of cognition (recognition of loss) leading to an emotional response (depression or loneliness) that organizes the person's behavior (decision to attend the party).

What Lazarus described, however, is *functional* coping. *Dysfunctional* coping may also take place in some families. Because of learned behavior and implicit family rules or paradigms, coping strategies in abusive families appear to be automatic and not cognitively planned. For example, a parent may cope with job frustration by coming home and abusing the children, or a stressed person may reach for a drink without even thinking. An abusive family member simply moves from an emotional to a behavioral response. Only after the individual's denial is penetrated can he or she move to cognition. If the situation is one of physical or sexual abuse, one purpose of treatment is to help the individuals within each family system to do some cognitive restructuring. This is not an easy task if the dysfunctional pattern of coping has been accepted across generations. The task of the therapist, then, is to stimulate, mediate, or facilitate the family's reconstruction of reality; but first, the denied reality must be recognized by the family. Even one person in the fami-

---

[8]Initially, Rahe (1974) defined coping "rather narrowly as one's ability to reduce his physiological activation" (p. 74). "In sum, a subject's recent life-change experience passes through several steps of perception and defense before body symptoms are perceived and perhaps reported" (p. 76). In this process, there are several chances for coping so that the illness may never be manifested. Meditation, for example, may hold high blood pressure in check. Nevertheless, Rahe reported research that illustrates significant correlations between past experiences, psychological defenses, physiological reactions, coping, the patient's illness behavior, and the doctor's diagnosis. (See diagram in Dohrenwend & Dohrenwend, 1974, p. 75.)

ly can begin the process toward a functional coping process.

Family Coping: Inductive Evidence for a Social-Psychological Definition. The first question is whether the phenomenon of family coping exists or whether some individuals in the family are simply coping collectively. The answer is, we believe, both.

With the assertion that both individual and family coping are important, the theoretical perspective of this chapter is set in the dialectical mode. Although Buckley (1967) presented three variations of systems theory (the mechanistic, the organismic, and the dialectical process), only the dialectical worldview allows the researcher or the therapist to incorporate the complexity and the process dimensions of family stress and coping. Family therapists, such as Carl Whitaker, Marizio Andolfi, and Helm Stierlin, use a dialectical perspective in systems theory, but researchers have only recently begun to consider the perspective valid for the study of families in stress.

The dialectical worldview derives from the work of early Greek philosophers. It holds that the elements of a universe *are held together by opposition*. Thus, dialectics is a philosophy based on process: movement, development, and interaction. The process depends on elements in opposition, such as destruction, emergence, and alteration, which are the basis for change. This same Aristotelian philosophy later became the basis for Hegel's notion of progressive development: From every *thesis* there evolves an opposite (*antithesis*), and these two result in the development of a unified whole (*synthesis*), which, in turn, reacts on the original thesis.

The notion of thesis and antithesis was introduced into the field of psychology by Erik Erikson (1950), who described individuals and society or parents and children as contradictions to each other. Riegel (1976, 1979) carried the case for the dialectical perspective even further by noting the conflicting development of individuals in four areas: the biological, the psychological, the physical, and the cultural. For example, the psychological development of adolescents may not always be in harmony with their physical development.

Recently, Hill and Mattesich (1979) moved family developmental theory into a process model in order to study the movement among normative family transitions over time. Family stress is full of opposing elements: adaptation versus revolution; coping versus crisis; conflict versus solidarity; independence and self-sufficiency versus family cohesion; and that most *elementary* of all opposing elements in family research, the individual versus the family as a group.

From the dialectical perspective, the definition of family coping in this chapter includes both individual and group indicators. The cognitive appraisal of a stressful situation or event, the emotional reaction to it, and the behavioral responses to both the appraisal and the emotion all happen within the individual, although within a systems context. Furthermore, we add from the family

therapy perspective the assumption that individuals are highly influenced by the past and present systems of which they have been or are a part. Thus, family coping is defined as the group's management of a stressful event or situation (McCubbin, 1979). We must add an important note, however: The family as a group is not coping if even *one* member manifests distress symptoms. Even if the family as a whole looks as if it is managing the effect of a particular stressor event, on closer examination we may find that the mother is depressed, an adolescent has psychosomatic problems, or the father's blood pressure is dangerously high. Thus, the exploration of inductively derived group indicators as well as individual indicators is recommended in the assessment of family coping.

In sum, family coping is the management of a stressful event by the family and by each individual in the family. It is the cognitive and affective process by which individuals and their family system adjust to, rather than eradicate, stress.

Following environmental and/or internal stressor events, coping behaviors are elicited when family stress levels fluctuate too much or too little. By activating the coping process, the level of family stress, however extreme, is modified, and a crisis is averted. For example, in some families, everyone retreats behind closed doors when an argument gets too hot; in others, someone may act out mischievously to stir up a family life that is boring and cool. Both the individual and the family system are involved in this process.

Initially, the person or the family may hit on the behaviors that ease the problem accidentally, by trial and error, or by rationally deciding to take a certain course of action that proves effective. In any event, once a coping behavior that works for a particular event is found, it becomes a part of the person's repertoire or the family's paradigm as a *coping* or problem-solving strategy.[9]

The Possibility of "Inherited" Coping Strategies. Although family coping strategies are not inherited, the existence of family patterns of coping that have been passed on from generation to generation is frequently seen by clinicians, especially those who treat abusive family systems. These families pass down coping paradigms that permit physical aggression and submission. Although such behaviors may have had some coping function in a more primitive time, they are now dysfunctional; nevertheless, they continue to be transmitted across the generations. The concept of the *family paradigm* (Reiss, 1981) in relation to family coping patterns may prove a fruitful theoretical base for future research.

Assumptions. At the base of the preceding definition and description of the family coping process are the following assumptions:

[9]See also Klein and Hill's family problem-solving effectiveness (1979) and Reiss's family paradigm, or family construction of reality (1981).

1. Stressor events of different types are an inevitable part of normal, everyday life for both individuals and families and are assumed to be omnipresent.

2. Stressor events, though in themselves benign, may stimulate the production of stress levels that must be coped with if a crisis is to be averted. For this reason, it is valuable to study highly stressed families and individuals to determine how they adapt to and manage stress without detrimental effects to the individual or the family.

3. Coping is a process involving the *cognitive, emotional,* and *behavioral* responses of both *individuals* and the *family* as a collective. Assessment of the coping process must include all those responses from both the individuals and the family as a whole if we are to have valid information on how families manage stress.

4. In this coping process, the contexts of both individual and family systems are salient. The external context is woven out of the family's history, culture, religion, economics, developmental stage, and constitutional state (the health of the family members). The internal context is based on the family's philosophy (its values, beliefs, and paradigms), its psychology (use of defense mechanisms), and its sociology (structure and function). The study of families in stress must be contextual in order to be valid.[10]

5. Inasmuch as context, internal and external, may influence the coping process, the evaluations of specific coping behaviors by both scientist and therapist must be as objective as possible. For example, we must bear in mind that even though different coping mechanisms are used in different cultures, the same end may be achieved: the emotional and physical health of the individual family members, as well as the functional interaction of the system as a whole.

Deductive Evidence for a Social-Psychological Definition of Family Coping. Early coping research, mostly psychological, focused on personality traits as predictors of coping behavior in any given situation. The results were not conclusive. More recently, however, researchers have followed the recommendations of Monat and Lazarus (1977) by observing the coping behaviors of people *after* the onset of a stressor event (Boss, 1977, 1980a, 1983a; McCubbin & Patterson, 1983). The social-

[10]Scientists, primarily from social psychiatry and sociology, who have taken into account either or both external and internal contexts of the family in their study of stress are Arsenian and Aresenian (1948); Bianco (1974); Billings and Moos (1981); Boss (1975a,b, 1977, 1980a,b); Boss and Greenberg (1984); Bruhn, Chandler, Miller, Wolf, and Lynn (1966); Elder (1974); Elder and Rockwell (1979); Guntern (1979); Henry and Stephens (1977); Hill (1949); Insel and Moos (1974); Kellam and Branch (1971); Kellam, Branch, Agrawal, and Grabill (1972); Kellam, Ensminger, and Turner (1977); Kiritz and Moos (1974); Leik, Leik, Ekker, and Gifford (1982); McClosky and Schaar (1965); McCubbin and Patterson (1983); Moos and Billings (1981); Moos, Finney, and Chan (1981); Reiss (1981); and Reiss and Oliveri, (1983).

psychological definition of family coping presented in the preceding section is deductively based on a series of poststressor studies that were carried out during the 1970s, which centered on coping after the stressor event of family separation, father absence in most cases.

Beginning with a sample of military families that manifested prolonged and ambiguous father absence, an instrument was developed to measure the coping behaviors used by the wives called the "Coping with Separation Inventory" (CSI; McCubbin, Dahl, Lester, & Boss, 1975). Subsequently, a refined version of the CSI, now titled the "Family Coping Inventory" (FCI; McCubbin, Boss, Wilson, & Dahl, in McCubbin & Patterson, 1981, pp. 103–105), was used for the testing of other father-absent populations: a nonwartime sample of U.S. Navy aviation pilots and wives, in which the men were absent for about eight months at a time (McCubbin, Boss, Wilson, & Lester, 1980); a nonmilitary sample of corporate executives' wives whose husbands were absent for an average of one week per month (Boss *et al.,* 1979); and a rural and urban sample of women who experienced husband–father absence because of divorce (Davis & Boss, 1980; McCabe, 1981).

The findings from these coping studies are summarized, along with those from McCubbin (1979) and Boss (1983a), in Table 1. It is interesting that, despite the qualitative variations in the type of husband–father absence, certain coping behavior patterns were constant across *all* samples: (1) *establishing independence and self-sufficiency* by the remaining parent and (2) *maintaining family integrity,* in most cases (all except the corporate executive families). It appears from this series of investigations that coping strategies focus on self-development as well as on the integration of the family as a system. This finding is consistent with systems theory (Buckley, 1967) and, most significantly, with the early findings of Angell (1936) and Hill (1949), which suggest that the families that cope the best have strength as a unit as well as in the individual members.

These two major coping strategies (establishing independence and self-sufficiency and maintaining family integrity and stability) indicate the importance of both individual (psychological) and group (sociological) variables in the building of family stress and coping theory. In Burr's model (1973), the individual psychological variables of coping strategies were not made explicit. From recent coping research, however, it appears that a dialectical balance between the individual and the family system may provide the theoretical basis for understanding the coping process.

The coping research also indicates that the coping strategies identified fall into the categories outlined by Lazarus: (1) direct action behavior (e.g., learning new skills and advancing "my" professional career); (2) intrapsychic forms of coping (e.g., never showing fear and believing that "my" life would not be any better if "my" spouse were here); and (3) behavior that controls the emotion generated by the stressor event (e.g., professional

Table 1. Coping Strategies in the Management of the Stress from Husband–Father Absence: Qualitative Variations

Prolonged separation (average 6 years)	Routine separation (8 months)	Repeated separations (average 1 week)	Rural divorce (6 months after)	Urban divorce (6 months after)
McCubbin, Dahl, Lester, Benson, and Robertson, 1976	McCubbin and Lester, 1976	Boss, McCubbin, and Lester, 1979	Davis and Boss, 1980	McCabe, 1981
($N = 17$)	($N = 82$)	($N = 66$)	($N = 28$)	($N = 50$)
Seeking resolutions and expressing feelings				Community involvement
Reducing anxiety				Involvement in divorce-related activities and programs
Establishing autonomy and maintaining family ties				Maintaining family ties and seeking support from relatives
Maintaining family integrity	Maintaining family integration and stability		Doing things with children and maintaining family stability	Doing things with children and maintaining family stability
Maintaining the past and dependence on religion	Believing in God		Religion and relatives	Reliving the past and passivity
Establishing independence through self-development	Establishing independence and self-sufficiency	Establishing independence and self-sufficiency	Establishing independence and self-sufficiency	Self-sufficiency and concentration on hobbies
	Trusting and building relationships	Developing self and interpersonal relationships	Developing relationships with people	Expressing feelings and building close relationships
	Living up to the military's expectations	Fitting into the corporate lifestyle		
	Keeping active in hobbies			

Source: Boss (1983a, p. 70)

counseling, keeping a diary or journal and drinking alcohol). The fact that findings from the present family-coping research are compatible with those of the early research on families of the Great Depression, with Hill's studies of World War II families, and even with Lazarus's individual coping research indicates that we are moving in the right direction in this relatively new area of inquiry. Measurement remains an area for further development since the present coping instrumentation has been found to be wife specific by Ventura and Boss (1983) and may not tap the range of coping behaviors used by husbands in the family.

Coping as a Dependent Variable: Some Complexities. Although coping increases the ability to recover from stress, it is also true that coping can *increase* vulnerability if the adaptations have harmful side effects. Like stress, coping can have both positive and negative consequences for individuals and families. Sometimes a radical change in behavior is preferable to coping and adaptation. For example, a sexually abused child who runs away from home may be coping more positively than the child who learns how to deny and tolerate the abuse. On the other hand, the spouse of an alcoholic who copes by becoming a workaholic may have chosen an adaptive behavior that causes exhaustion, anger, and isolation; thus, the coping strategy increases vulnerability.

According to Monat and Lazarus (1977):

Any evaluation of coping and adaptation must take into account diverse levels of analysis (physiological, psychological, sociological), the short versus long-term consequences, and the specific nature of the situation in question. (p. 11)

McCubbin, Joy *et al.* (1980) and Boss *et al.* (1979) made no judgments about coping strategies when such behaviors as drinking alcohol and taking medications were reported as helping some wives to cope with husband absence. Religious and cultural values influence the choice of coping behaviors. Thus far, coping research indicates only that active versus passive behaviors are most predictive of how adequately individuals and families will function (Boss *et al.*, 1979; Lazarus, 1977; McCubbin, Joy *et al.*, 1980).

Aside from action versus passive individual behavior, another view is possible here: A coping behavior (active or passive) may be more functional if it is used in the context of *socializing with people* and less functional if it occurs in *isolation from people*. Such general variables are encouraged for the next decade of research because they explain more about why some families cope and why some cannot (see also Menaghan, 1983).

Further complexities remain regarding the concept of coping as an outcome variable because a behavior can be simultaneously a coping mechanism and a stressor event. In their review of the literature of the 1970s, McCubbin, Joy *et al.* (1980, p. 859) pointed to radical changes in women's roles as possible causes of family conflict or husbands' hardships. They did not make clear, however, whether the changed roles are events that *increase* or *decrease* family stress. The existing literature never makes clear whether the mother's employment outside the home is a coping mechanism *or* a stressor event. Certainly, outside work may, in fact, *relieve* stress in the family system, economically or psychologically, or *increase* stress because of role overload. Even *both* may be possible simultaneously. A dialectical rather than categorical view of the event of changing women's roles and, particularly, women's employment may be more productive in explaining stress in the families of employed mothers. Cultural and socioeconomic contexts also need to be considered.

The phenomenon of family violence should also be investigated on a more general theoretical level in terms of family stress and coping. Distasteful as it may seem, violence can be a coping mechanism, although a dysfunctional one, based on earlier assumptions. Indeed, violent behavior can stem from an inadequate repertoire of coping resources, which means that the process of functional coping never can begin. Family violence and other forms of family dysfunction (e.g., alcoholism) can be viewed more productively by researchers and clinicians from this more complex and dialectical theoretical base, given that these behaviors and the family patterns that they foster can be simultaneously a way to cope and a stimulus for even more stress.

McCubbin, Joy *et al.* (1980) also pointed out that the complex interrelation of coping mechanisms and stressor events has not yet been investigated to any degree, perhaps because the theoretical base is still not apparent. In the face of the two opposing truths that are so often operating, we suggest that the complexity of family systems interaction is best accommodated by a dialectical view. For example, a man may get drunk and hit his wife in order to cope with a frustrating day on the job, or a woman may adopt a coping mechanism that becomes addictive (e.g., the use of tranquilizers or alcohol or work) in order to cope with marital frustrations. In such cases, the coping mechanism can provide stimuli for the development of even more stress. Vulnerability increases when a particular coping behavior is used so frequently that it becomes a stress producer rather than a stress reducer. Work, alcohol, and medication can all fall into this category.

The complexity of a *chain reaction* concept, first described by Scherz (1966), also needs the attention of investigators. It is important to note that the more qualitative chain-reaction phenomenon is not identical with the quantitative concept of stress pileup as operationalized by Vaughn, Egeland, Sroufe, & Waters (1979) and by McCubbin, Joy *et al.* (1980). For example, the chain reaction phenomenon may manifest itself only when a current loss or separation reactivates an earlier family loss that was never fully grieved or resolved to what Hill (1949) called the "recovery stage." Although clinicians have contributed inductively to this body of knowledge, there is little deductive evidence to explain and predict the resolution of separations over the life span. A related idea is what Klaus Riegel (1979) referred to as the codetermination of events, that is, events occurring in one dimension that can be prior to, the trigger for, or the causes of events occurring in another. He was referring to qualitive as well as quantitative variables. The phenomenon of the chain reaction in family stress and coping is such a qualitative variable and, in all its complexity, is rightly beginning to be incorporated into stress and coping theory (Figley, 1978; McCubbin & Patterson, 1983).

Family and Community Coping with Large-Scale Disasters. Because of current worldwide concern with the nuclear threat and survival, selected research, theory, and issues in the area of survival are reviewed here. Other disasters in Israel and the United States were the bases for major investigations during the 1970s.

In order to examine the effects of family separation and adjustment during the Vietnam conflict, investigators at the center for Prisoner of War Studies in San Diego conducted longitudinal studies on the families of men who were listed as prisoners of war or as missing in action (MIA). These studies are summarized in Boss (1980b);

Hunter (1983); McCubbin, Dahl, and Hunter (1976); and McCubbin, Joy *et al.* (1980). Because of their focus on perception, the Boss studies will be discussed later in this section.

At about the same time, Israeli investigators studied the effects of the Yom Kippur War on families, in particular the event of loss and bereavement (Golan, 1978; Lieberman, 1971; Palgi, 1970, 1973, 1975). While gunfire was still heard in the streets, an international conference on the effects of stress was convened in Jerusalem; it brought together major stress researchers from all over the world and from a variety of disciplines (Caplan, 1979).

Other disasters, not war-related, were also studied during the decade and were discussed at a conference on Family and Disaster[11] in 1980 at the University of Uppsala, Sweden. After presentations on the effects of floods, famine, fires, and nuclear plant disasters, the following observations were made on disasters in relation to family stress and coping:

1. The importance of families when disaster strikes has not yet been fully understood. For instance, in the 1980 earthquake in Algeria, many persons stayed in the disaster area in order to acquire information about missing relatives. Other striking examples of people's refusal to be moved to safety were cited at the Uppsala seminar. In theoretical terms, the problem is one of coordination between a bureaucratic organization (civil defense) and a solidaric organization (the family).

2. There is a tendency for disaster research to be identified with the organizational point of view. Sociologists tend to identify more with the bureaucratic than with the solidaric organization (e.g., in the research on Three Mile Island). The dysfunctions and the harming effects of the rescue operations themselves have not yet been emphasized and studied.

3. More specifically, cross-national research on disaster could yield some understanding of the different effects of relatively comparable events (Dumon, 1980).

In respect to disaster survival, then, the objectives of civil defense and families are at odds. Whereas *community survival* demands rapid evacuation and movement, *family survival* depends on remaining together. Before civil defense plans can be accepted by urban populations, authorities must accommodate to the need for families to be cohesive and continuous in their interactions. Bureaucratic plans have demanded just the opposite and, therefore, the effectiveness of possible evacuations is questioned:

Disasters . . . represent discontinuity, the new and the unknown. They bring a need for adaptation to unknown demands, a

---

need for society, organizations, groups, and individuals to change. Whether functional or dysfunctional, disasters certainly introduce change in society. (Dumon, 1980, pp. 3–4)

In sum, it appears that civil defense and community authorities that work with families in disaster situations are faced with a paradox: To save families, they must first get them to fragment; that is, they must get individuals to flee for safety from wherever they are rather than attempt to go back to the family home. To help people survive, authorities must convince them to evacuate individually and immediately rather than to wait until the family is assembled. Although they were alerted to this fact earlier by Hill and Hansen (1962), researchers and defense authorities are just now beginning to appreciate the strength of families' tendency to cohere, even in the face of disaster. The plans for worldwide coping and survival are just now beginning to take this fact into account.

Meaning and Perception of the Event: The C Factor.
Both meaning and perception are now considered important by individual- and family-stress theorists, but Reuben Hill (1949; Hansen & Hill, 1964) was the first to focus on the "meaning of the event," including it in his model of family crisis under the C factor. More recently, David Reiss (1981) called attention to the "family's construction of reality" as a determinant of how families find solutions to problems.

We recognize that Hill's C factor, the perception of the event, implies the study of qualitative variables. Perhaps this recognition explains why researchers have focused so little on this area. Clinicians, however, know at least intuitively that a family's perception of the situation is critical to how they will react to and cope with stress. Thus, we now turn to a close examination of the family's perception of the event, not because there is definitive research to review, but precisely because of the dearth of research. As examples of a perceptual variable that illustrates the heuristic C factor, we focus on a selected qualitative variable: degree of boundary ambiguity. We also discuss two concepts that are related to the family's perception of who is in and who is out of this family: denial and value orientation. The discussion centers on how these three variables can create barriers to the resolution of stress and the reorganization of the family system after the impact of a stressful event. Because perception of boundaries is related to family context, the chapter closes with the presentation of a contextual model of family stress.

Family Boundary Ambiguity: A New Construct for Understanding the Stress Process—Potential Interplay between A and C Factors

Along with the current shift toward the development of family coping research and theory, a more generalized conceptualization of family stress and coping variables is also sought. That is, we are looking for more inclusive

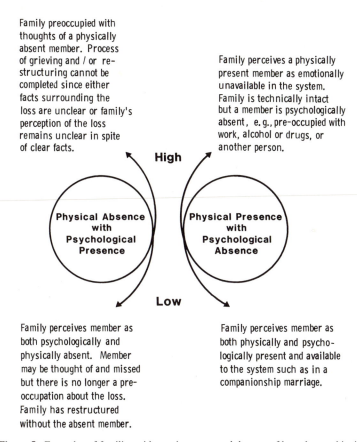

Family preoccupied with thoughts of a physically absent member. Process of grieving and / or re-structuring cannot be completed since either facts surrounding the loss are unclear or family's perception of the loss remains unclear in spite of clear facts.

Family perceives a physically present member as emotionally unavailable in the system. Family is technically intact but a member is psychologically absent, e. g., pre-occupied with work, alcohol or drugs, or another person.

High

Physical Absence with Psychological Presence

Physical Presence with Psychological Absence

Low

Family perceives member as both psychologically and physically absent. Member may be thought of and missed but there is no longer a pre-occupation about the loss. Family has restructured without the absent member.

Family perceives member as both physically and psycho-logically present and available to the system such as in a companionship marriage.

Figure 5. Examples of families with varying types and degrees of boundary ambiguity.

variables (less midrange) that will explain a broader spectrum of stressor events and their effect on families. One of these more encompassing stress variables is family boundary ambiguity. It is discussed here in detail as an example of a variable that explains and predicts the effect of a variety of family stressor events.

The term *family boundary ambiguity* was introduced and operationalized by Boss (1975a) as a state when family members are uncertain in their *perception* of who is in or out of the family or who is performing what *roles* and *tasks* within the family system (see Figure 5).

In relating family boundary ambiguity to the heuristic model, it must be emphasized that the phenomenon can manifest itself under both the A factor (stressor event) and/or the C factor (perception of the event). That is, boundary ambiguity can result from two different situations: (1) one in which the family *cannot* get the facts surrounding the event (e.g., MIA, divorce, joint custody, desertion, and some chronic illness) and/or (2) one in which family members *can* get the facts surrounding the event but, for some reason, ignore or deny or distort them (see for example, Lindemann, 1944). The family's per-

ception of the event, therefore, is different from that of an objective outside observer. For example, such families may perceive a chronically ill family member as normal when he or she has been clearly diagnosed as ill; they may perceive a missing family member as present when he or she is clearly physically absent; or they may perceive an alcoholic family member as absent when he or she is actually physically present.

Indeed, the phenomenon of boundary ambiguity can exist if a family finds itself in either situation, regardless of whether we classify the phenomenon under the A or the C factor. What is of critical importance to researchers' and therapists' understanding of the concept is that its impact on family stress stems primarily from the C factor (perception of the events). That is, whether the ambiguity results from unavailable facts surrounding the event or from the family's skewed perception of reality, *the family's perception of the event and the meaning they give it comprise the critical variable in determining family membership and, therefore, the existence and degree of boundary ambiguity.* Even with the families of men missing in action, we can find some families in which the facts of loss are unclear but the families arbitrarily decide on a reality of who is in and who is out of the family system. Thus, the therapist and researcher must be careful not to be misled by what exists under the A factor (the presence or absence of facts surrounding the event itself) because the family, in the end, gives the event its own meaning and reality. Thus, the family ultimately determines the degree of ambiguity surrounding the event by the congruence between the members' *psychological perception* of who is in and who is out with the *physical reality* of who is in and who is out of the system.

To illustrate the complexity of the phenomenon in relation to the outline provided by the ABC-X model, see Figure 5. Examples show that a *high* degree of boundary ambiguity results from (1) being unable to get clear facts surrounding the event (e.g., in the families of Iranian hostages) and (2) having the facts but, for some reason, denying or ignoring them (e.g., untreated families of alcoholics or of those with chronic illnesses such as end-stage renal disease). Other examples show that a *low* degree of boundary ambiguity results from (3) having clear facts about the event and perceiving the event in congruence with these facts and (4) not having clear facts about the event but arbitrarily deciding on the most realistic perception of the event, given the available information. To be sure, this last case represents a "family gamble," and the boundary ambiguity will remain low only as long as the family's agreed-upon perception is not threatened by new information. When there are reports of seeing men alive in the jungle or when an alcoholic spouse who has stopped drinking tries to reenter the family, the ambiguity may again arise over these family boundaries because the prospect of another boundary change, although positive, is a disorganizing influence on family boundary maintenance. Having been clarified arbitrarily, the family boundary is now again ambiguous.

Given this introduction to the boundary ambiguity variable in relation to the ABC-X outline, a review of the research that established the variable follows. The participants in the early research were families that were facing an event of ambiguous loss: having the husband-father declared missing in action during the Vietnam conflict. The findings, however, clearly indicate that psychological perception was operative and that it was an important variable. Thus, even in this early research, the interrelations of the ambiguity with both the A and the C factors are established.

Review of Boundary Ambiguity Research and Theory Development Project

Initially, we derived the variable of family boundary ambiguity inductively from observations of corporate executive families in a family therapy clinic, and then we empirically described and tested the variable with military families (Boss 1975b, 1977, 1980b). A sample of father-absent families was used in which the father's whereabouts and status as dead or alive were not known.

Boundary ambiguity was operationalized with the indicator of psychological father presence (PFP) in a family in which he was physically absent. That is, he had been officially declared missing in action (MIA) during the conflict in Vietnam and Cambodia. Correlational analysis revealed significant negative covariance between the family's ability to function and the degree of psychological father presence, especially when the father was kept present to perform the expressive role[12] by remaining the person with whom the wife was emotionally involved and with whom she was psychologically preoccupied (Boss, 1977, 1980b).

Overall, the data on the wives gave strong support to the proposition that boundary ambiguity was related to the ability to function, in that the wives' emotional health appeared to be strongly enhanced by their no longer planning to seek evidence for their husbands' return, and by their being closely involved in new relationships with a desire to remarry. For the wives, especially, it appeared to be functional to close out the missing husband's expressive (emotional) role in the family system.

Data from this first study less clearly supported the proposition that PFP would have dysfunctional effects on the children.[13] Nevertheless, the mother's movement toward relieving ambiguity was significantly related to the children's adjustment as well as to her own. The direct effect on the wife versus the indirect effect on the children was examined more closely in a subsequent study. Building on a theoretical reformulation from the first study, the follow-up study of the same population of families with a missing father was based on data collected in 1977 (Boss, 1980b). A more precise way to measure boundary ambiguity (as indicated by PFP) was developed through factor-analytic methods (Table 2) and is presented in Table 3.

Findings from this study added definitive support to the proposition that in a family with a physically absent father, a high degree of PFP was related to wife dysfunction and was a significant predictor of wife as well as family dysfunction. Although PFP remained primarily a wife-focused variable, it was also significant in blocking the regenerative power of the entire family system after the event of the loss. Even though PFP related more to the wife's own psychological state rather than to her ease in performing family roles, it appeared that her psychological well-being as the remaining executive influenced the entire family system. This finding was consistent with findings from Phase 1 of this study (Boss, 1977) as well as with the assumptions of systems theory (Buckley, 1967),

---

[12] In sociology, instrumental roles are task-oriented and tend to be externally oriented, and expressive roles are social or integrative and are more internally oriented (Parsons & Bales, 1955).

[13] According to clinical perspective, the effect on the children may be manifested only at a later time, when they are grown. Longitudinal research is needed to verify this clinical hypothesis.

**Table 2. Items Contained in the Psychological-Father-Presence Subset
Extracted from Wife's Self-Report Inventory and Their Loadings (19 Items)**[a]

Item number	Loading	Items
30	−.8926	I no longer consider myself an "MIA" wife.
57	−.6572	I feel I have prepared myself for a change in status.
61	−.6023	My children are able to talk about their father without becoming emotionally upset.
28	−.5894	My children are aware of all "the facts" and have reconciled their father's loss.
35	−.4998	I feel I am able to plan my future without feeling guilty for not continuing to wait for my husband.
49	−.4680	I hope to remarry.
47	−.4570	The armed services have done everything reasonably possible to account for my husband.
26	.8164	I find myself still wondering if my husband is alive.
23	.8162	I continue to keep alive my deepest hope that my husband will return.
58	.7722	I feel guilty about dating (or wanting to date).
4	.7094	My children still believe that their father is alive.
64	.5791	I will never be satisfied until I have positive proof of my husband's death.
21	.4705	My children and I seem to talk about their father quite often.
20	.4368	I think about my husband a lot.
33	.4255	I feel it will be difficult, if not impossible, to carve out a new life for myself without my husband.
18	.3490	I feel incapable of establishing a meaningful relationship with another man.
11	.2623	Conflicts with my own parents over my husband's change of status have presented a problem for me.
22	.2873	My in-laws do not or would not approve of my plans to develop a life for myself.

[a]Eigen value = 6.25. Total observed variance accounted for is 33%. Total explained variance accounted for is 39%.

which imply a dialectical relation between the system as a whole and the individuals in it.

Based on these cumulative findings, the proposition regarding PFP is now being tested on populations going through less extreme experiences that still manifest the phenomenon of family boundary ambiguity; the logic is that there are theoretical commonalities regarding family boundary ambiguity (or the potential for it) between the disastrous MIA situation and less unusual situations, such as divorce.

According to Hansen and Johnson (1979), ambiguity has been identified "as a fundamental and pervasive quality of stressed conditions that makes the definitional aspect of family interaction especially problematic" (p. 590). The concept of ambiguity is presented as a cognitive and/or evaluative uncertainty of the situation at hand. Supporting Cobb (1974) and Boss (1975b, 1977), Hansen and Johnson wrote, "the uncertainties and unfamiliarities introduced by change are among the most stressful qualities of change" (p. 590). However the events may vary between MIA and divorced families, they have in common the potential for ambiguity because the status of the absent parent within the family boundary is indeed unclear. Although one event grows out of disaster and the other is more normative, theoretical parallels were identified (Boss, 1983a) that may help to explain the impact of these stressor events on the family system:

- Both events represent a loss of membership, either psychological, physical, or both, and, therefore, a change in the family system boundary.

- Both events represent an unclear loss. That is, it was not absolutely clear to family members whether the absent person was in or out of the family system or what roles he or she was in or out of.

- There are no social rituals for clarifying either event of loss (missing in action or divorce), as there are for the event of the death of a spouse. Therefore, the families had to find their own way of coping with the loss without the support and guidance of social rituals to close out the missing member in the family system and to move on to reorganization and recovery at a functioning level. Instead, the family had to arbitrarily decide on a perception of reality.

- Both events involve different types of role assignments—that is, instrumental (task-oriented) and expressive (socioemotional)—and thus, closing out and clarification of the family boundary may have had an instrumental-expressive specificity. The psychological or emotional closeout may have preceded the closeout of instrumental roles, especially that of providing economic support. In divorced families, many instrumental roles, such as providing economic support, continued, just as they did for the MIA families, which continued to accept the missing husband's paycheck as long as the children were young and still at home. This approach may not have been dysfunctional for the family system as long as the individual family members were clear about which roles remained active and which ones were closed out.

- Both events involve the loss of one family executive,

Table 3. Psychological-Father-Presence Scale (18 Items)[a,b]

Item number	Level of PFP	Items
Wife		
1	(−)	I no longer consider myself an "MIA" wife.
2	(−)	I feel I have prepared myself for a change in status (to widow).
3	(−)	I feel I am able to plan my future without feeling guilty for not continuing to wait for my husband.
4	(−)	I hope to remarry.
5	(−)	The armed services have done everything reasonably possible to account for my husband.
6	(+)	I find myself still wondering if my husband is alive.
7	(+)	I continue to keep alive my deepest hope that my husband will return.
8	(+)	I feel guilty about dating (or wanting to date).
9	(+)	I will never be satisfied until I have positive proof of my husband's death.
10	(+)	I think about my husband a lot.
11	(+)	I feel it will be difficult, if not impossible, to carve out a new life for myself without my husband.
12	(+)	I feel incapable of establishing a meaningful relationship with another man.
Children		
13	(−)	My children are able to talk about their father without becoming emotionally upset.
14	(−)	My children are aware of all "the facts" and have reconciled their father's loss.
15	(+)	My children still believe that their father is alive.
16	(+)	My children and I seem to talk about their father quite often.
Parents/In-laws		
17	(+)	Conflicts with my own parents over my husband's change of status have presented a problem for me.
18	(+)	My in-laws do not or would not approve of my plans to develop a life for myself.

[a]Source: Boss (1982).
[b]Key: (+) = high degree of psychological father presence
(−) = low degree of psychological father presence.

if not *the* family executive, when the families were traditional in orientation. Thus, major reorganization was needed for boundary maintenance in these family systems.

Propositions. By means of the composite approach of both induction and deduction, the following theoretical propositions were synthesized from previous research on both disaster and divorce samples and are presented here for the future testing of family separations where ambiguity surrounds the event as well as the family's perception of the event.

Proposition 1. Keeping the physically absent parent psychologically present within the family systems boundaries is more directly dysfunctional for the spouse than it is for the children. That is, the spouse may be able to perform family role responsibilities for the benefit of the children even though he or she is personally preoccupied by and psychologically involved with the missing spouse. Thus, the family-functioning score may not register at the same level as the psychological functioning score of the remaining spouse. Nevertheless, both the family as a whole and the individuals are negatively affected when the family boundaries are ambiguous.

Proposition 2. A high degree of boundary ambiguity is dysfunctional for some roles but *not for all* (e.g., the MIA wife keeping the missing husband present as financial provider, and more recent preliminary findings on instru-

mental role overlap, such as caring for children in joint custody situations, Moskoff, 1980). I propose that keeping the absent family member present for instrumental roles is more functional than keeping him or her psychologically present to fulfill expressive roles.

Normative Boundary Ambiguity in Families across the Life Cycle. Although the boundary ambiguity research began primarily with military dependents and disaster victims, researchers currently are systematically studying people in more normative situations. The events of loss and separation so common to military families also occur in normal everyday family life (Rapoport, 1965). Entries and exits of family members across the family life span are inevitable; thus, births, deaths, leaving home, getting married, and so on, continuously affect the family system's process of boundary maintenance. Learning to clarify family boundaries after loss or acquisition, therefore, is a critical developmental task required of families over the life cycle. The task of being able to let go and take in, being able to adapt to the systemic change that this process of transformation demands, is a major coping strategy for all families and individuals over the life cycle. If we were to theoretically summarize one task as universally essential for family functioning over the life cycle, it would be the task of boundary maintenance (Boss, 1980a; see Aldous, 1978, for other tasks).

The 1970s, therefore, saw renewed interest in normative developmental life events that may be the stimuli for stress. Again, the disciplines of sociology, developmental psychology, and social work participated in research: Pearlin and Radebaugh (1976) identified major role changes during the life cycle as we move through normatively expected entrances into and exits from social roles. They developed "strain scores" to measure the stress of these entrances and exits. Role changes and task realignments during family-life-cycle transition periods were focused on also by Boss (1980a, 1983b), Golan (1975, 1978), Hill (1973), Hill and Joy (1979), and Mederer and Hill (1983). The acquisition of roles was found to be more stressful than the loss of roles (George, 1980; Neugarten & Hegestad, 1977); and "strain scores" related to normative stress were lower than scores for nonnormative events (Pearlin & Lieberman, 1979; Pearlin, Menaghan, Lieberman, & Mullan, 1981).

All these events and situations center on the occurrence and/or the perception of *loss*. Sometimes, it is the clear-cut loss of a family member but, at other times, as in developmental events, it is the loss of how a family member has been perceived or the loss of her or his familiar role. Boundary ambiguity, therefore, can result from developmental changes across the family life cycle as well as from the actual loss of members. When the adolescent leaves home, we lose a dependent child and gain an independent young adult; when an elderly parent grows frail, we lose someone to look up to and lean on and gain a serious and tender responsibility. When our babies grow up and go to school for the first time, we lose someone exclusively dependent on us. Whether these changes result in relief or sadness, they represent a loss of something irretrievable. That is, a role or perception is altered and the boundaries of the family system are changed regarding who is in and who is out and on what basis they are in or out.

Giving up and letting go are, therefore, events that happen to all families across the life span. If families are fortunate enough to have no disastrous losses, they surely will have normative ones. Whether these losses produce crisis or coping may be determined by the degree and the duration of boundary ambiguity in the system after the event occurs. It is for this reason that being able to resolve the boundary ambiguity that arises after an event of loss is important in determining whether the family will reorganize and maintain its boundaries as a viable system or become a system with highly ambiguous boundaries and thereby increase in dysfunction. Indeed, this premise may help to explain why some families can cope with high stress whereas other families crumble with the least amount. The ability to clarify and maintain boundaries after loss may be more relevant in predicting whether a family will cope or go into crisis than continued focus on the specificity of the event itself.

Denial as a Barrier to Clarifying Family Boundaries. No doubt because it is not easily quantified, the concept of denial has received less attention from researchers than from clinicians and counselors who, from the time of Freud, recognized its existence and power. The variable is defined as the refusal to believe what one sees, that is, to acknowledge, cognitively or affectively, a physical reality. Denial, therefore, is the blockage of perception in order not to acknowledge a physical reality. Although it is commonly accepted that denial is a defense mechanism in which external reality is rejected, it is submitted here that one's culture and value orientation influence *what* is acceptable to see and *how* it should be perceived.

The function of denial is debatable. Indeed, it can prevent cognitive preparation for an event of separation and thereby block the coping process and hold the family system in an unresolved state. In essence, it allows the individual or family to defend an old belief system or paradigm. Yet, denial can be functional for the family, especially in the early stages of a stressful event. For example, when a person is diagnosed as having a terminal illness, denial may at first be functional. Indeed, according to Kübler-Ross (1969), denial constitutes the first stage of the grieving process. She considers it, at least for a time, a healthy way of dealing with the uncomfortable and painful situation. She sees denial as "a buffer after unexpected shocking news which allows people to collect themselves and, with time, mobilize other, less radical defenses" (p. 39).

The family, faced with loss, undergoes similar stages of adjustment. At first, the family may deny the fact of terminal illness in the family or "shop around" from doctor to doctor in the vain hope of hearing that this was a wrong diagnosis. According to Kübler-Ross:

They may seek help and reassurance that it is all not true from fortune-tellers and faith healers. They may arrange for expensive trips to famous clinics and physicians and only gradually face up to the reality which may change their life so drastically. (p. 168)

Depending on the patient's perception and attitude and the family's ability to communicate, the family may suddenly shift its perception to an acceptance of reality and a recognition of the impending loss. The family secret, painful as it is, is revealed and recognized, explicitly. Family members talk and cry together and perform the necessary tasks in preparation for the loss (Kübler-Ross, 1969). It would be less functional if the family continued to deny their loss or impending loss.

Does denial prevent cognition or is it in itself a cognitive decision at some level to ignore reality? The determination of its source may be less important in applied settings than the identification of its outcome. If denial of a loss prevents the cognitive preparation that sets in motion the process of grieving and subsequent reorganization, then the outcome of denial will be dysfunctional. If denial is in itself a cognitive decision to "freeze" or "abort" the process of grieving, for example, as in the case of an ambiguous loss with the Iranian hostages, then denial may have a positive influence on the outcome, at least in the short run. Not having grieved out the family members who were taken hostage, these families kept their loved ones psychologically present. They denied a negative outcome and continually hoped for a safe return. Inasmuch as the hostages did, in fact, return, the denial of loss and the maintenance of their place in the family system in this case were functional (see Boss, 1980c).

Denial can also be an effective barrier against stress from a physiological perspective but may have devastating psychological or sociological consequences (Lazarus, 1977). For example, denying the chemical dependence of a husband may keep the wife's blood pressure down, but it may lead to her isolation and the development of depression as well as to poor relationships with her children and others who see her husband more realistically.

Moreover, in any one domain, a response that is optimal in one situation at a particular time may be damaging in some other situation or at a different time. For example, denial may be effective in the physiological domain (i.e., lowering the secretions of stress-related hormones) for the parents of a terminally ill child before the child's death (Wolff, Friedman, Hofer, & Mason, 1964) but may prove ineffective after the child dies (i.e., the stress-related hormones then increase dramatically; see Hofer, Wolff, Friedman, & Mason, 1972). It is clear that what is considered an optimal or beneficial response is highly dependent on one's perspective, judgments, and situational timing (Monat & Lazarus, 1977).

Traditionally, when denial is used as a palliative (cover-up) mode of coping, it is viewed as pathological or maladaptive. This view is supported by studies in which a defensive behavior (e.g., a woman's denying a lump in her breast) prevents active coping behaviors (e.g., going to a doctor or accepting treatment). Nevertheless, denial is a useful defense in many situations, at least initially, in that it prevents a person from being overwhelmed in a situation in which immediate direct action is limited or of little use (Hamburg & Adams, 1967). For example, when nothing can be done to change the event or threat, denying that it is there may be momentarily helpful while one gains some strength and sense of what to do and how to proceed.

Though sparse, the literature relating to the temporal quality of denial appears to be consistent: Denial is more likely to be a useful coping mechanism in the short run (Cohen, 1975; Hamburg & Adams, 1967) and more harmful in the long run. Cohen (1975) further stipulated that short-term denial is useful when (1) a person would be overwhelmed by an unpleasant reality; (2) the likelihood of an actual loss or disaster occurring is small; (3) an individual can do nothing to prepare for the potential threatening event; and (4) a hopeful attitude prevents feelings of giving up.

Continuing in the same direction, Monat and Lazarus (1977) emphasized the importance of *time* and *situation* in determining the positive or negative effects of denial as a coping mechanism:

Palliative modes of coping may be damaging when they prevent essential direct actions but may also be extremely useful in helping a person maintain a sense of well-being. integration or hope

under conditions otherwise likely to encourage psychological disintegration. (p. 10)

There follows a summary of qualitative research on the presence of denial in a family system in which a member was suffering the final stage of long-term chronic renal disease. The illness is so grave and ambiguous in its outcome (patients will die but no one knows when) that families frequently cope by denying either the stress of the ill family member or the normative developmental stress of other family members. In such severe chronic illness, the threat of loss remains "a potent aspect of the family's experience for an indefinite period of time" and "little, if any, of this negative feeling can be expressed openly because the patient is gravely ill and cannot be blamed for the situation" (Gonzalez & Reiss, 1981, p. 6). The family, then, is left little choice but to deny the reality of the situation. By denying the problem, they appear to "buy time." When a family member's status is chronically ambiguous (one does not know if the individual is in or out of the family system), it appears that reorganization of the family system is impossible. Change cannot take place because of the lack of clarity in the status of family membership and boundaries. In order to maintain morale and gain time until more evidence accumulates, the family may need to deny some reality. The early extrusion of a physically present family member from the family system, as reported by Gonzalez and Reiss (1981), demonstrates the qualitative impact of ambiguity in and on family system boundaries. Denying the existence of the disease keeps the chronically ill member inside the family system, whereas acknowledging the inevitable result of the illness may precipitate a closing out (Boss, 1977), a closing of ranks (Hill, 1949), or a premature extrusion (Gonzalez & Reiss, 1981) of that member from the family system.

The studies of ambiguity in stressful situations have focused primarily on populations where the stressor event manifests the ambiguity. That is, the family cannot get clear facts about the event as in missing-in-action and end-stage-renal-disease (ESRD) families; thus, they do not know if the affected family member is in or out of the family. Because boundary ambiguity is externally caused and maintained, denial may be the only coping mechanism available to the family. In the absence of clear facts and, therefore, control of the situation, the family may simply cope by denying reality and making up their own reality based on wishful thinking (e.g., "Mother really isn't sick").

However, in some situations, the quantitative facts regarding family membership are clear to the outside observer, but the family continues to deny or ignore them. In this case, the ambiguity is internally supported because the family's *perception* maintains the boundary ambiguity regardless of the availability of facts. As a coping mechanism, denial is relevant in both externally and internally caused situations of family boundary ambiguity. But as with the variable of boundary ambiguity, the existence or nonexistence of denial flows ultimately from the

C factor, the family's perception of the event. Ultimately then, regardless of the lack of information from the outside, the family's internal perception of the event is what needs to be measured if we are to understand validly what a stressful event of loss means to a family and how they cope with it.

Propositions. With this discussion of denial as it relates to ambiguity in family loss situations, the following propositions are formulated for testing:

1. Denial can be both a functional or a dysfunctional coping mechanism, depending on the duration of the stressor event: The longer the denial of reality, the more dysfunctional it becomes as a coping mechanism, and the more it becomes a barrier to stress reduction and family reorganization.

2. Denial, as a coping mechanism, is used for longer periods of time in situations of high ambiguity (when a family cannot determine clearly if a member is inside or outside the family boundaries) than in clearly bounded situations, such as the death of a family member. Thus, strategies for helping stressed families may be more effective if the therapeutic focus is on clearing up the perception of who is in and who is out of the family, rather than on the denial as resistance.

3. Denial is the prevailing choice of coping mechanism when the stressor event or situation is not only chronic but ambiguous in its course and outcome (e.g., final-stage renal disease, alcoholism, multiple sclerosis, and cancer).

4. Thus, denial correlates highly with ambiguity in family boundary and, ultimately, with family dysfunction.

In sum, denial is a coping mechanism with both structural and psychological dimensions; it has attributes of function or dysfunction, depending on when it is used in ambiguous situations. Although denial can be viewed as preventing cognitive preparation for an event of separation in both expected and unexpected situations, it can be simultaneously viewed as "buying time." Most important to clinicians and researchers, denial is more likely in the context of ambiguity. That is, in order to break the denial, it is more effective to focus on the *perception* of family boundaries than on the denial behavior itself. Not being able to clarify if a family member is in or outside the family boundary may in itself precipitate a cognition, at some level, that, for the moment, there will be no recognition of loss, impending or actual. In the absence of clarity, denial may not be an unreasonable choice of coping behavior.

Just as people may choose whether to let go or to be masterful in a situation, so, too, they may, at some level, choose what events to acknowledge or to deny. It is important for family stress researchers, theoreticians, and clinicians to further examine the variable of denial in all its complexities. It is not *either* functional or dysfunctional but *both,* depending on duration and the availability of clear facts about the event or situation of loss.

The Family's Values and Belief System: An Influence on All Factors

Another variable that affects family members' perceptions of an event and their subsequent ability to cope, especially in the clarification of boundaries after a loss, is the family's value orientation in terms of mastery. This orientation is critical in determining how (or if) a family will begin the coping process. A family with a *mastery* orientation may believe that it can solve anything, that it can control any situation, whatever the event or situation. A family less oriented to mastery may believe in accepting whatever happens rather than trying to remedy or control a situation. Such a family is often described for cultural purposes as *fatalistic.*

In its classic definition, fatalism is a belief that everything that happens is determined by a higher power, that such events are inevitable and cannot be avoided. In short, fatalism signifies a cultural belief that what happens to a person is predetermined and out of his or her control. Thus, a fatalistic value orientation involves the intuitive, the unconscious, and the mystical more than the cognitive and rational aspects of a person and a family.

Although, classically, fatalism is defined as a doctrine holding that volition and effort cannot influence behavior, license is taken here to define a belief system that opposes mastery. In this discussion, the potential use of one's volition to lower stress in a situation is not ruled out. The term *fatalism* is being used to describe a belief system that leans toward acceptance rather than mastery, not because of law or predetermination by a deity, but because of cultural and environmental conditioning that reinforces a sense of powerlessness.

The German word *Schicksal* most accurately represents the opposite of a belief in mastery as defined here. *Schicksal* does not carry with it an implication of inevitability but simply refers to the way life is experienced. It allows room for the concept of cognition. We continue, therefore, to use the English word *fatalism* but to stress the German rather than the English definition.

In my clinical observations of families under stress, it has been apparent that the values and beliefs dictating their problem-solving strategies have a cognitive as well as an unconscious component. Even when they are in a hostile environment and are powerless, people and families make choices both intuitively and rationally either to master a situation or to give in to it. Over time, they may, in fact, do both. Inasmuch as control and mastery may be given up as a result of new facts about the event, there may be a major shift in the family's value orientation and subsequent perception of the event of loss.

When a family is faced with a problem, its beliefs and values determine its action (or lack of it) in the coping process. Indeed, a barrier to the coping process could then be a highly fatalistic value orientation because it implies passivity rather than action; the family would do nothing about the cause of the event on the grounds that the options for change are controlled by forces outside the family. Individuals might discuss options for changing the event or their perception of it, but they would reject any option intuitively. Such a family's conclusion would be, "We just accept what comes"; "We've never been very successful before in coping with problems so why try now"; or "We are losers anyhow, so why fight it." Antonovsky (1979) referred to individuals who saw the world as unmanageable and unpredictable as low in coherence and therefore less able to cope with stress. The same may be true for the family.

The major point that must be kept in mind is that, given the suggestions in the coping literature that *active* coping strategies are more effective than *passive* strategies, it is logical to assume that families with value orientations of mastery cope with stress more functionally than do those with an orientation toward fatalism (in the sense of *Schicksal*). The following review of literature suggests a need for caution about this assumption. The issue of active versus passive coping is more complex than saying one is functional and the other is dysfunctional. Effectiveness, for example, is influenced by larger cultural and contextual variables, as the following indicates.

Value Orientations and Belief Systems as They Affect Families in Stress. In Western thinking especially, "belief in a just world" is held by many people (Lerner, 1971; Lerner & Simmons, 1966). This belief system values—indeed, requires—control and mastery. According to Festinger (1957), for us to hold this belief, we must also believe that there is an objective fit between effort and outcome, and that this logical fit is available to all. If this belief in justness and the assumption of its availability to all people is accepted, then people in crisis and victims can be viewed as somehow deserving what they get. The underlying assumption in this value orientation is that those who are "just" can master and control any event that happens to them and their families. As in the stories of Horatio Alger, the underlying principle is that hard work and mastery will solve problems and keep one out of trouble.

Belief in a "just world" becomes a problem when we see a victim who has been "just" but nevertheless is victimized. Looking at birth-defective children, for example, may bring discomfort because (1) we can see nothing to explain their plight, and (2) we conclude that, if it happened illogically to them, it therefore could also happen to us no matter how "just" we are (Watts, 1984).

Given such beliefs and attitudes, coping behaviors are necessarily influenced. We may deny a person's affliction because it is illogical, or we may fabricate a logical reason to explain the stress that is present. For example, we may conclude that, because a family has always been in trouble, it is no wonder that their baby is defective or that they are poor and on welfare.

People from Eastern cultures that are more fatalistically oriented can more easily tolerate the illogical. They may attribute the misfortune of a defective baby to fate without judgment on justness or unjustness. Therefore, in order to understand the perception of a stressful event and the subsequent coping strategies used by a family, researchers and therapists must first determine the family's beliefs and view of the world. Certainly, the value orientation of mastery is a relevant component in the family's perception of the event and its decision on coping strategies.

Illustrating the idea of mastery and "a just world," it is reported that combat soldiers in Vietnam took seriously the old army adage that "If you do your job right, you'll stay out of trouble" (Bourne, 1969, p. 108). Soldiers held onto this belief, and it appeared to be effective in allowing them to cope with the threat of death in combat. Their fears of death were overshadowed by their feelings of invulnerability and the belief that, if they performed with skill and action as trained, they would be safe (Bourne, 1969). From this research, it is apparent that the fear of death can be mastered even over long periods of time. Denial of the threat of death and a belief in one's invulnerability combine to provide effective coping strategies for soldiers who face even overwhelming odds.

On the other hand, during the Holocaust, many Jews, a notable exception being the Warsaw ghetto uprising, valued a fatalistic passivity over mastery as they coped with the threat of death. According to Hilberg (1961), the two basic coping patterns used by many Jews during that period were (1) an attempt to avert action and, if that failed, (2) automatic compliance with the enemy (p. 666). Their coping patterns were based on what the Jewish culture had learned over the ages, "that in order to survive, they had to refrain from resistance" (Hilberg, 1961, p. 666). Using strategies of cooperation and submission, the Jews, according to Hilberg, dealt with their resistance in the same way that the Nazi captors dealt with guilt: by repression and denial. For example, in the recorded minutes of the 1941 Viennese Jewish Conference of War Invalids, there is an obvious avoidance of direct reference to death. They wrote only of seeing "black" and "tempting fate" (p. 668), with no mention of death or threat of annihilation. It is as if denial was the only coping strategy available to these victims. If they saw discrimination and maltreatment as their heritage and fate, then they perceived that they could do nothing about it. Indeed, if Hilberg was correct, the likelihood of resistance in this context was low.

Prisoners of war during the Vietnam conflict also used submission as a coping mechanism. In order to minimize torture or the threat of death, they reported using a passive model of adaptation. For example, they internalized anger and did not act it out directly (Hall & Malone, 1974; McCubbin, 1979). Some Iranian hostages also reported using passive measures to maintain some vestige of control over their lives in captivity, for example, by refusing food, but other hostages reported using direct expressions of anger at times, for example, yelling and cursing their captors (personal conversations, 1982).

The value orientations of mastery versus fatalism (in the sense of *Schicksal*) were also studied in nonwartime situations by Kluckhohn and Strodtbeck (1961) among various subcultures in the United States. The investigation of one's orientation to nature may have particular relevance to the measurement of a person's beliefs on the continuum (1) subjugation to nature; (2) harmony with nature, or (3) mastery over nature. Indeed, the dominance of each orientation varied according to the subculture tested; for example, the Spanish-American culture in the American Southwest manifested a definite subjugation-to-nature orientation:

The typical Spanish-American sheepherder believed firmly that there was little or nothing a man could do to save or protect either land or flocks when damaging storms descended upon them. He simply accepted the inevitable. In Spanish-American attitudes toward illness and death one finds the same fatalism. "If it is the Lord's will that I die, I shall die" is the way they express it, and many a Spanish-American has been known to refuse the services of a doctor because of the attitude. (Kluckhohn & Strodtbeck, 1961, p. 13)

The value orientation of harmony with nature, according to the investigators, was dominant in many periods of Chinese history. It was strongly evident in Japanese culture historically as well as at the time when Kluckhohn and Strodtbeck did their work; it also existed in earlier Mormon groups.

The mastery-over-nature position is dominant among mainstream Americans. The view, in general, is that it is one's duty to overcome obstacles; hence, there is great emphasis on using technology to master and control problems:

Natural forces of all kinds are to be overcome and put to the use of human beings. Rivers everywhere are spanned with bridges; mountains have roads put through and around them; new lakes are built, sometimes in the heart of deserts; old lakes get partially filled in when additional land is needed for building sites, roads, or airports; the belief in manmade medical care for the control of illness and the lengthening of life is strong to an extreme; and all are told early in life that "the Lord helps those who help themselves." (Kluckhohn & Strodtbeck, 1961, p. 13)

Nuttal's work (1980) in the United States further supports the importance of cultural value orientations in response to family stress and coping. The attribution of stress outcomes to cultural belief systems and values is documented by Kagitcibasi (1983); her research in Turkey explicated how fatalistic belief systems interface with social change in the face of disaster.

Funded by the Disaster Section of the National Institute of Mental Health, Nuttal (1980) took an inductive approach to investigate family coping in American communities that were struck by four different types of natural disaster: (1) the loss of kin from the breaking of a dam; (2) the loss of property from a flood in Johnstown, Pennsylvania; (3) the effects of a nonviolent disaster (blizzard) in Buffalo, New York; and (4) the coastal flooding of three towns in Massachusetts when a seawall caved in. From this diverse research pool, Nuttal inductively identified *Verstehen* (understanding the meaning) as a significant variable. His major finding was that the culture and the

unique meaning that the event had for each community formed a critical variable. When a flood was fatalistically perceived as a message from God, the meaning and the subsequent coping strategies were different from the strategies adopted when the flood was viewed as a failure of technological mastery. With a fatalistic belief system, a family coped passively in the belief that nothing could be done about the imminent destruction. Rather than move away or build a house on stilts, they just accepted the destruction and cleaned up in its wake. On the other hand, more mastery-orientated families coped actively by planning or building a dam, moving away, or building a house on stilts. Such families did not passively accept the destruction but used technology and their own activity to control the event or to prevent it from happening again.

Following Nuttal's (1980) exploratory study, Kagitcibasi (1983) investigated how Turkish families coped with the disaster of earthquakes and floods, and provided support for the importance of the culture, values, and meaning in relation to fatalism. She identified the interference of a fatalistic belief system with social change; that is, believers in fatalism would not relocate even in the face of disaster. The fatalistic tendency among Turkish peasants is well documented (e.g., Frey, 1963; Kagitcibasi, 1983), but Kagitcibasi induced from her and other research the conclusion that fatalistic (high external) locus-of-control tendencies are prevalent among people who are more often victims of natural disasters: the urban poor and rural peasants. They tend to perceive natural disasters as inevitable and as bad fortune that has to be endured because of overpowering mystical and supernatural forces (Kagitcibasi, 1983).

Like Kluckhohn, Strodtbeck, and Nuttal, Kagitcibasi made a strong case for cultural variation in the qualitative meaning of disaster for Turkish peasants. She hypothesized that a fatalistic orientation might at times be functional for the rural peasants and the urban poor in Turkey when they lack access to technology that predicts and controls disastrous events, and when they do not have the economic means to get protection or to move to a safer place. In such situations, their only alternative for coping may be passive acceptance and resignation to "God's will." According to Kagitcibasi (1983), such resignation may "provide psychological relief and social solidarity" through strengthening a sense of community belongingness (pp. 7–8). Nevertheless, passive belief systems negate the likelihood of social change and support the status quo of people in dire stress and hardship. As with the Jews during the Holocaust, passive acceptance may, in the long run, be destructive.

It is therefore apparent that a fatalistic belief system may be functional primarily when nothing can be done to change a situation. Researchers and therapists must be aware that the variables of fatalism versus mastery are, by their very nature, highly related to the variables of supporting the status quo versus change.

The question raised by the research cited is whether the belief system influences the inability to cope actively with the stressor event or whether the lack of resources to cope actively with the event fosters a fatalistic belief system as an adaptation. Because of this question, researchers need to determine not only the context but also the relation of the context to the stressor: Is the context blocking the coping process and thereby reinforcing the status quo, which may harm or even destroy the family? If a family stays on the banks of a flooding river long enough, their coping resources will eventually be depleted. There comes a time when passive acceptance is no longer functional. The family's belief in acceptance may make the stress less psychologically painful, but it will not halt or reverse the process of destruction and crisis. Only active coping will change the direction of that process.

To further complicate the picture, structural as well as perceptual constraints result from the cultural context. For example, it may be impossible for some families to move to higher ground or to resist impending doom even if they want to because of scarce economic resources or membership in the wrong caste. If only monied or upper classes have the higher ground, or if only upper classes are to be spared from going to death camps, then the choice of coping strategy is removed from the remaining individuals or families. Those who remain in the path of disaster may have to choose acceptance as a coping strategy because of economic, structural and institutional constraints that are outside their control. The poor and lower classes, because of their lack of resources and power, are therefore often highly vulnerable to stress and may resort to passive acceptance and/or fatalism as coping strategies simply because that is all they have. The attribution of stress outcomes to cultural belief systems and values was documented by Feldman and McCarthy (1983) in their research into the disaster of famine and its relation to Bangladesh cultural attitudes and macroeconomics.

The Influence of Value Orientation on Stress Outcomes. From the preceding selective review of research, it appears that, in order to cope with a stressor event, passive acceptance is functional at times and dysfunctional at other times. That is, "flowing with the tide" and giving up efforts at control sometimes enhance the movement toward relief of stress. Nevertheless, there are times when one must help oneself, when one must act and take charge of a situation in order to reduce stress levels. Ultimately, lowering the level of stress is what matters, not the value orientation leading to that outcome.

Essentially, we must document when it is functional to use coping strategies that are based on mastery and control, and when it is functional to use coping strategies that are based on passivity and resignation. Because in mainstream America a mastery orientation is primarily valued, the following assumptions relating to families in stress are presented:

1. Family belief systems such as mastery or fatalism (defined as *Schicksal*) influence vulnerability and recoverability levels in stressed families. The introduction of the cultural belief system as a variable in family stress

research represents a more general theoretical variable than those previously delineated in the Burr (1973) and the McCubbin and Patterson (1983) models.

2. With a belief system of fatalism (as opposed to mastery), a family may give a qualitative meaning to any specific stressor event. For example, in their research on family mobility, McFarlane and Sussman determined (1982) that "sources of stress during a move are attributed to *External* and *Uncontrollable* factors" (p. 9), but that family members do not necessarily name the same factors. Wives tended to define moving as stressful if it affected family relationships, whereas husbands classified moving as stressful if they did not want to make the move, that is, if the impetus for the move was out of their control.

3. The effect of a fatalistic belief system is dialectical; that is, it may be both positive and negative: negative when the soldier is in combat, but positive if he is taken prisoner; dysfunctional when control of an event would be possible with some action and effort, but functional when mastery and control are impossible.

4. Although a fatalistic belief system may be functional in the short run when a disastrous event strikes and nothing can be done to reverse it, that same belief system may be dysfunctional in the long run because *it will interfere with social change.* If a person clings to the belief that an event is the result of fate, karma, or God's will, this belief may block the coping process that can change the situation, the use of resources, or the perception of what is occurring. Believing that one has mastery over a situation aids the process of developing active coping behaviors and/or stimulates a revolution that, according to Reiss's description (1981), will change the family's construction of reality and, therefore, their problem-solving strategies.

On the basis of these four assumptions, the following propositions are made:

1. Family belief systems and value orientations influence how families perceive stressor events and how they cope with or solve problems, and thus, the levels of stress stimulated by stressor events are influenced.

2. Families from cultures or subcultures believing in fatalism (e.g., Eastern cultures) cope less well with stressor events that require a high degree of social change than do families from a more mastery-oriented culture (e.g., Western cultures).

3. At the same time, families from cultures or subcultures valuing mastery cope less well with stressor events that require solidarity and maintenance of the status quo.

4. Given that both change and solidarity are critical although opposing elements for the survival of any family system regardless of culture or subculture, it appears that belief systems valuing both fatalism and mastery can be dialectically functional over time for all families facing normative and unexpected stressor events because the families then have the situational flexibility to "flow with the tide" (passively adapt) or to work to change the situation (actively revolt). In fact, the families that have a

history of coping well with stress may be those that select what they will be fatalistic about and what they will master or control, with variations in between, thus making the variable continuous rather than categorical.

5. In situations of potential stress with no chance of change—that is, with no hope—the fatalistic belief system may be more functional for the lowering of stress levels than the belief in mastery. On the other hand, a family with a strong value of mastery may be less likely to give up hope even in what is a hopeless situation, such as the terminal illness of a family member.

6. In chronic, long-term family illness, the value orientation of fatalism may be dysfunctional in that it prevents systemic change. In conditions such as alcoholism, retardation, or anorexia nervosa, or of a comatose patient, a fatalistic orientation encourages denial of reality and the maintenance of the status quo in the family system.

Conclusion

The question asked at the beginning of this chapter was *why* some families cope with stress whereas others fall into crisis. We have posited that the answer lies in the *meaning* that the event holds for the family and the individuals within it. Of all the factors that were originally described as related to crisis, we have here focused on the family's perception of the stressor event or situation as a major determinant of outcome. In the studies on boundary ambiguity, this premise has been supported.

The family's perception, however, is mediated by the context in which the stressful event or situation occurs (see Figure 6). We considered the family's context from a social-psychological and biological perspective on both macro- and microlevels of analysis. The *external* context of the stressor event or situation is comprised of six indicators: historical, economic, developmental, constitutional, religious, and cultural.

The *historical* context refers to the time when the event takes place, for example, during World War II, after the Vietnam conflict, after the women's liberation movement, before the civil rights movement, during the Depression of the 1930s, or after the tunnel was built to bring tourists to a previously isolated mountain village.

The *economic* context is the state of the larger environment's economy. It could also refer to a major change in the family's economic environment resulting from sudden economic gains (or losses) from outside sources, such as lotteries or inheritances.

The *developmental* context is the stage in the life cycle of both individuals and the family itself. A newly formed family of young people, for example, may perceive the event of pregnancy more positively than a mature family in which there are already six children. The different levels of stress caused by the event of pregnancy in these two families can be explained more accurately by their developmental stage, which mediates their perception, than by the event of pregnancy itself.

The *constitutional* context of the family is the biological health and physical strength of the members of that unit. Some people, and therefore families, because of strong genes and a good environment, are simply stronger than others. They have more stamina and resilience, which influence the energy and perseverance they have to activate and maintain the coping process. A good constitution makes it easier to act in defense of oneself and one's family when a stressor event occurs.

The *religious* context also influences how a family perceives an event—especially regarding attempts to control or accept a situation of stress and who is to blame for what is happening and thus the level of guilt that the family

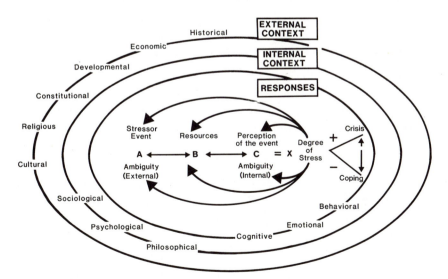

Figure 6. The contexual model of family stress.

carries. People of certain religions in America believe that even the lack of rain or the birth of a defective child is their fault; others believe that there is a larger plan, and so they accept what happens, even disaster, as God's will. Such varying religious beliefs are part of the family's external context, as they are instilled from the outside.

Finally, the *cultural* context, which encompasses some of the former dimensions, makes up a major part of the external context in that it provides the canons and mores by which families define events of stress and their coping resources. The larger culture of which the family is a part provides the rules by which the family operates at the microlevel. Sometimes, however, the family may at the same time belong to a subculture that conflicts with the mainstream culture, for example, military or ethnic groups. The cultural incongruence between internal and external contexts may help answer the question of why these families are highly stressed and often in crisis.

The six dimensions of the family's external context influence the family's internal context. The *internal* context of the family in stress is made up of three dimensions: the sociological, the psychological, and the philosophical.

The *sociological* context is the structure and function of the family regarding its boundaries, role assignments, and perceptions of who is in and who is outside those boundaries. Boundary ambiguity is a major variable in this regard.

The *psychological* context is the family's ability (or inability) to use defense mechanisms when a stressful event occurs. The mechanism of denial was presented to illustrate the point. In the long run, the use of denial adds psychological ambiguity to the sociological ambiguity in a stressed family and thereby blocks resolution and reorganization.

The *philosophical* context of the family is its values and beliefs on a microlevel. The rules of the individual family can, for example, be different from those of the larger culture to which it belongs. Certainly, minority families in American culture have experienced this difference. When the larger culture, for example, provides government support for the institutional care of elderly parents, but not within the family, the external and internal contexts are in conflict, so that even more stress has been created. Also, the military subculture imposes rules on its families that are inconsistent with those of the larger culture, so that its families are additionally stressed.

Even on a microlevel of analysis, rules for coping may be different. Within one community, we can find families that believe that illness is to be accepted, whereas others believe that illness is to be overcome with modern science and technology. Some families believe that fighting back actively is the appropriate behavior, whereas others believe in passive resistance or acceptance. Although these beliefs and values are influenced by the larger cultural and religious context, the family's philosophy most directly influences its perception of a stressful event. Furthermore, the internal context, more than the external con-

text, is in the control of the individual family. Even within the same cultural or religious context, families differ in their individual philosophies. (Note the arrows in Figure 6.) We focus this chapter on the microlevel, therefore, not because the internal context is more important than the external, but because it is more accessible to the individual family.

What we have tried to do in this chapter is to simplify family stress theory. Rather than expanding the number of variables and propositions, we have presented more parsimonious variables, such as boundary ambiguity. This is a necessary step in theory building.

We have also emphasized throughout this chapter that the stressor event or situation does not act directly on the family system. Rather, *it is the perception of the event as mediated by internal and external contexts that determines whether the family will cope or fall into crisis.* Because of the importance of perceptual variables, both phenomenology and logical positivism must be used by family stress researchers and clinicians. The former has been devalued in recent decades, especially in American psychology and sociology. Without knowing how the family perceives the event or situation that is stressing it, neither the researcher nor the clinician has the necessary data for explanation or intervention. Too often, we impose *our own contexts* on the family's circumstance and give their event *our meaning.* The phenomenological approach is helpful in preventing this error precisely because it allows us to focus on *the family's meaning and perception of the stressful event.* Family therapists have done this more routinely than have family researchers.

From the family therapy perspective, and building on Hill's earlier emphasis on meaning, this chapter has incorporated phenomenology with logical positivism, induction with deduction, and qualitative research with quantification to identify unique as well as commonly held qualities in families under stress across the life span. Ultimately, this approach to theory building will bring us closer to the accumulation of knowledge regarding family invulnerability to stress and the answer to our initial question.

ACKNOWLEDGMENTS

I would like to acknowledge my debt to the University of Minnesota Agricultural Experiment Station, to the University of Minnesota Graduate School, and to the University of Wisconsin Graduate School and Experiment Station for supporting the development of this chapter.

Especially, I acknowledge the support of Richard Sauer and Keith McFarland of the University of Minnesota, St. Paul, and Robert Bock, Robert Bray, and Frank Kooistra at the University of Wisconsin–Madison. Appreciation is also expressed to the following graduate students, members of a University of Wisconsin–Madison Family Stress Seminar, who provided rigorous and stimulating discussion during the author's early development of this chapter: Lorraine Beaulieu, Doris Berndt, Pat Friday, Louise Frye, Earlene Harris, Linda Hein, Patricia McDonnell, Roberta Reed, Suzanne Schuler, Anne Speckhard, Jacqueline Ventura, Arden Walz, and Beverly Wolfgram. Appreciation is also due Linda Burkett, Jan Greenberg, Gerald Hadd, Denise Nelson, Anne Speckhard, and Craig Roberts, graduate students at the University of Minnesota, who helped with technicalities in the final manuscript. My thanks to Gloria Lawrence and Nanette McCann for their patience and skill in typing this manuscript, and to Sylvia Rosen, who provided editorial assistance.

References

Aldous, J. *Family careers: Developmental change in family.* New York: Wiley, 1978.

Angell, R. C. *The family encounters the Depression.* New York: Charles Scribner, 1936. (Reprinted in 1965.)

Antonovsky, A. *Health, stress and coping.* San Francisco: Jossey-Bass, 1979.

Arsenian, J., & Arsenian, J. M. Tough and easy cultures: A conceptual analysis. *Psychiatry,* 1948, *11,* 377–385.

Bartlett, G. S., Houts, P. S., Byrnes, L. K., & Miller, R. W. The near disaster at Three Mile Island. In O. Hultaker & J. Trost (Eds.), *The International Journal of Mass Emergencies and Disasters,* 1983, *1*(1), 19–42.

Bianco, C. *The two rosetos.* Bloomington: Indiana University Press, 1974.

Billings, A., & Moos, R. H. The role of coping responses and social resources in attenuating the stress of life events. *Journal of Behavioral Medicine,* 1981, *10,* 57–189.

Blank, A. S. Jr. Stresses of war: The example of Viet Nam. In L. Goldberger & S. Breznitz (Eds.), *Handbook of stress.* New York: Free Press, 1982.

Bolin, R. C., & Bolton, P. A. Recovery in Nicaragua and the U.S.A. In O. Hultaker & J. Trost (Eds.), *The International Journal of Mass Emergencies and Disasters,* 1983, *1*(1), 125–144.

Boss, P. G. *Psychological father absence and presence: A theoretical formulation for an investigation into family systems interaction.* Unpublished doctoral dissertation, University of Wisconsin, 1975. (a)

Boss, P. G. Psychological father presence in the missing-in-action (MIA) family: Its effects on family functioning. *Proceedings: Third Annual Joint Medical Meeting Concerning POW/MIA Matters,* Center for Prisoner Studies, Naval Health Research Center, San Diego, November, 1975, pp. 61–65. (b)

Boss, P. G. A clarification of the concept of psychological father presence in families experiencing ambiguity of boundary, *Journal of Marriage and the Family.* 1977, *39* (February), 141–151.

Boss, P. G. Normative family stress: Family boundary changes across the lifespan. *Family Relations,* 1980, *29,* 445–450. (a)

Boss, P. G. The relationship of psychological father presence, wife's personal qualities, and wife/family dysfunction in families of missing fathers. *Journal of Marriage and the Family,* 1980, *42*(3), 541–549. (b)

Boss, P. G. Précis prepared for the Emergency Meeting of the Task Force on Families of Catastrophe, February 4–5, 1980. In C. R. Figley (Ed.), *Mobilization: Part I: The Iranian crisis. Final report of the Task Force on Families of Catastrophe.* West Lafayette: Purdue University Family Research Institute, 1980. (c)

Boss, P. G. *The measurement of family boundary ambiguity: A general variable in family stress theory.* Paper presented at the National Council on Family Relations, October, 1982.

Boss, P. G. Family separation and boundary ambiguity. In O. Hultaker & J. Trost (Eds.), *Family and disaster.* Special issue of *The International Journal of Mass Emergencies and Disasters,* 1983, *1*(1), 63–72. (a)

Boss, P. G. The marital relationship: Boundaries and ambiguities. In C. Figley & H. I. McCubbin (Eds.), *Stress and the family,* (Vol. 2.). New York: Brunner/Mazel, 1983. (b)

Boss, P. G., & Greenberg, J. Family boundary ambiguity: A new variable in family stress theory. *Family Process,* 1984, *23,* 535–546.

Boss, P. G., McCubbin, H., & Lester, G. The corporate executive wife's coping patterns in response to routine husband-father absence. *Family Process,* 1979, *18* (March), 79–86.

Bourne, P. G. *The psychology and physiology of stress.* New York: Academic Press, 1969.

Brown, B. B. Perspectives on social stress. In H. Selye (Ed.), *Selye's guide to stress research.* New York: Van Nostrand Reinhold, 1980.

Bruhn, J. G., Chandler, B., Miller, M. C., Wolf, S., & Lynn, T. N. Social aspects of coronary heart disease in two adjacent ethnically different communities. *American Journal of Public Health,* 1966, *56,* 1493–1506.

Buckley, W. *Sociology and modern systems theory.* Englewood Cliffs, N.J.: Prentice Hall, 1967.

Burr, W. *Theory construction and the sociology of the family.* New York: Wiley, 1973.

Caplan, G. (Ed.). *Prevention of marital disorders in children.* New York: Basic Books, 1961.

Caplan, G. *Principles of preventive psychiatry.* New York: Basic Books, 1964.

Caplan, G. Mastery and stress: Psychological aspects. *American Journal of Psychiatry,* 1981, *138*(4), 413–420.

Cavan, R. S. Unemployment: Crisis of the common man. *Marriage and Family Living,* 1959, *21,* 139–146.

Cavan, R. S., & Ranck, K. H. *The family and the Depression.* Chicago: University of Chicago Press, 1938.

Cobb, S. A model for life events and their consequences. In B. S. Dohrenwend & B. P. Dohrenwend (Eds.), *Stressful life events: Their nature and effects.* New York: Wiley, 1974.

Cohen, F. *Psychological preparation, coping and recovery from surgery.* Unpublished doctoral dissertation, University of California, Berkeley, 1975.

Davis, E. L., & Boss, P. G. *Rural divorce: How rural wives cope with separation.* Technical report. Madison: University of Wisconsin–Madison, Department of Child and Family Studies, 1980.

Dohrenwend, B. S., & Dohrenwend, B. P. *Stressful life events: Their nature and effects.* New York: Wiley, 1974.

Dumon, W. *Committee on Family Research Gazette,* 1980, *8*(Fall), 3.

Elder, G. H. *Children of the Great Depression.* Chicago: University of Chicago Press, 1974.

Elder, G. H., & Rockwell, R. C. The life-course and human development: An ecological perspective. *International Journal of Behavioral Development,* 1979, *2,* 1–21.

Erickson, E. *Childhood and society.* New York: Norton, 1950.

Feldman, S., & McCarthy, F. E. National trends affecting disaster response and family organization in Bangladesh. In O. Hultaker & J. Trost (Eds.), *The International Journal of Mass Emergencies and Disasters.* Sweden: International University Library Press, 1982.

Feldman, S., & McCarthy, F. E. Disaster response in Bangladesh. In O. Hultaker & J. Trost (Eds.), *The International Journal of Mass Emergencies and Disasters,* 1983, *1*(1), 105–124.

Festinger, L. *A theory of cognitive dissonance.* Stanford, Calif.: Stanford University Press, 1957.

Figley, C. *Stress disorders among Viet Nam veterans.* New York: Brunner/Mazel, 1978.

Frey, F. W. Surveying peasant attitudes in Turkey. *Public Opinion Quarterly,* 1963, *27,* 335–355.

George, L. *Role transitions in later life*. Belmont, Calif.: Brooks/Cole, 1980.

Golan, N. Wife to widow to woman: A process of role transition. *Social Work*, 1975, *20*, 396–374.

Golan, N. *Treatment in crisis situations*. New York: Free Press, 1978.

Gonzalez, S., & Reiss, D. *Families and chronic illness: Technical difficulties in assessing adjustment*. Paper presented in Theory Construction Workshop, National Council on Family Relations Annual Meeting, Milwaukee, 1981.

Guntern, G. *Social change, stress and mental health in the pearl of the Alps*. New York: Springer-Verlag, 1979.

Hall, R. C., & Malone, P. T. Psychiatric residuals of prolonged captivity experience. In H. I. McCubbin *et al.* (Eds.), *Families of prisoners of war and servicemen missing in action*. San Diego: Center for Prisoner of War Studies, Naval Health Research Center, 1974.

Hamburg, D. A., & Adams, J. E. A perspective on coping: Seeking and utilizing information in major transitions. *Archives of General Psychiatry*, 1967, *17*, 277–284.

Hansen, D., & Hill, R. Families under stress. In H. T. Christensen (Ed.), *Handbook of marriage and the family*. Chicago: Rand McNally, 1964.

Hansen, D., & Johnson, V. Rethinking family stress theory: Definitional aspects. In W. Burr, R. Hill, F. Nye, & I. Reiss (Eds.), *Contemporary theories about the family* (Vol. 1). New York: Free Press, 1979.

Henry, J. P., & Stephens, P. M. *Stress, health and the social environment: A sociobiologic approach to medicine*. New York: Springer-Verlag, 1977.

Hilberg, R. *The destruction of the European Jews*. New York: Harper & Row, Colophon Books, 1961.

Hill, R. *Families under stress*. New York: Harper & Row, 1949. (Reprinted Westport, Conn.: Greenwood Press, 1971.)

Hill, R. Generic features of families under stress. *Social Casework*, 1958, *49* (February, March), 139–150.

Hill, R. *Family life cycle: Critical role transitions*. Paper presented at the Thirteenth International Family Research Seminar, Paris, 1973.

Hill, R., & Hansen, D. A. Families in disaster. In G. W. Baker & E. W. Chapman (Eds.), *Man and society in disaster*. New York: Basic Books, 1962.

Hill, R., & Joy, C. *Conceptualizing and operationalizing category systems for phasing of family development*. Unpublished manuscript, Family Study Center, Department of Sociology, University of Minnesota, 1979.

Hill, R. & Mattessich, P. Family development theory and life-span development. In P. Baltes, & O. Brim (Eds.), *Lifespan development and behavior* (Vol. 2). New York: Academic Press, 1979.

Hofer, M. A., Wolff, C. T., Friedman, S. B., & Mason, J. W. A psychoendocrine study of bereavement (Parts I and II). *Psychosomatic Medicine*, 1972, *34*, 481–504.

Holmes, T. H., & Rahe, R. H. The social readjustment rating scale. *Journal of Psychosomatic Research*, 1967, *11*(September), 213–218.

Hunter, E. J. Treating the military captive family. In F. Kaslow & R. Ridenour (Eds.), *The military family: Dynamics and treatment*. New York: Guilford Press, 1983.

Insel, P. M., & Moos, R. H. (Eds.). *Health and the social environment*. Lexington, Mass.: Lexington Books, 1974.

Kagitcibasi, C. How does the traditional family in Turkey cope with disasters? In O. Hultaker & J. Trost (Eds.), *The International Journal of Mass Emergencies and Disasters*, 1983, *1*(1), 145–152.

Kellam, S. G., & Branch, J. D. An approach to community mental health: Analysis of basic problems. *Seminars in Psychiatry*, 1971, *3* (May), 207–225.

Kellam, S. G., Branch, J. D., Agrawal, K. C., & Grabill, M. E. Woodlawn Mental Health Center: An evolving strategy for planning in community mental health. In S. E. Golan & C. Eisdorfer (Eds.), *Handbook of community mental health*. New York: Appleton-Century Croft, 1972.

Kellam, S. G., Ensminger, M. E., & Turner, R. J. Family structure and the mental health of children. *Archives of General Psychiatry*, 1977, *34*(September), 1012–1022.

Kiritz, S., & Moos, R. H. Psychological effects of social environments. *Psychosomatic Medicine*, 1974, *36*, 96–114.

Klein, D., & Hill, R. Determinants of problem-solving effectiveness. In W. Burr, R. Hill, F. I. Nye, & I. Reiss (Eds.), *Contemporary theories about the family* (Vol. 1). New York: Free Press/Macmillan, 1979.

Kluckhohn, F. R., & Strodtbeck, F. L. *Variations in value orientation*. Westport, Conn.: Greenwood Press, 1961.

Komarovsky, M. *The unemployed man and his family*. New York: Dryden Press, 1940.

Koos, E. L. *Families in trouble*. New York: King's Crown Press, 1946.

Kübler-Ross, E. *On death and dying*. New York: Macmillan, 1969.

Lazarus, R. S. *Psychological stress and the coping process*. New York: McGraw-Hill, 1966.

Lazarus, R. S. *Patterns of adjustment* (3rd ed.). New York: McGraw-Hill, 1976.

Lazarus, R. S. Cognitive and coping processes in emotion. In A. Monat & R. S. Lazrus (Eds.), *Stress and coping*. New York: Columbia University Press, 1977.

Leik, R. K., Leik, S. A., Ekker, K., & Gifford, G. A. *Under the threat of Mt. St. Helens: A study of chronic family stress*. Final report for Federal Emergency Management Agency, Washington, D.C. 20472, Office of Prevention, National Institute of Mental Health, February 1982.

Lerner, M. J. Justice, guilt, and veridical perception. *Journal of Personality and Social Psychology*, 1971, *20*, 127–135.

Lerner, M. J., & Simmons, C. Observers' reaction to the innocent victim: Compassion or rejection? *Journal of Personality and Social Psychology*, 1966, *4*, 203–210.

Lieberman, E. American families and the Vietnam War. *Journal of Marriage and the Family*, 1971, *33*, 709–721.

Lindemann, E. Symptomatology and management of acute grief. Paper read at Centenary Meeting of the American Psychiatric Association, Philadelphia, Penn., May 15–18, 1944. Reprinted in A. Monat & R. S. Lazarus (Eds.), *Stress and coping: An anthology*. New York: Columbia University Press, 1977.

McCabe, M. *Coping with divorce in an urban environment*. Unpublished doctoral dissertation, University of Wisconsin, 1981.

McClosky, H., & Schaar, J. H. Psychological dimensions of anomie. *American Sociological Review*, 1965, *30*, 14–40.

McCubbin, H. Integrating coping behavior in family stress theory. *Journal of Marriage and the Family*, 1979, *41*(August), 237–244.

McCubbin, H. I., & Boss, P. G. (Eds.). Family stress, coping and adaptation. *Family Relations*, 1980, *29*(4). (Special issue)

McCubbin, H. I., & Patterson, J. M. *Systematic assessment of family stress, resources and coping: Tools for research, education and clinical intervention*. St. Paul: University of Minnesota, 1981.

McCubbin, H., & Patterson, J. Family stress and adaptation to crisis: A double ABCX model of family behavior. In H. McCubbin, M. Sussman, & J. Patterson (Eds.), *Advances in family stress theory and research*. New York: Haworth Press, 1983.

McCubbin, H., Dahl, B., Lester, G., & Boss, P. *Coping with Separation Inventory (CSI)*. San Diego: Naval Health Research Center, 1975.

McCubbin, H., Hunter, E., & Dahl, B. Residuals of war: Families of prisoners of war and servicemen missing in action. *Journal of Social Issues*, 1975, *31*(Fall), 95–109.

McCubbin, H., Dahl, B., & Hunter, E. Research on the military family: A review. In H. McCubbin, B. Dahl, & E. Hunter (Eds.), *Families in the military system*. Beverly Hills, Calif.: Sage Publications, 1976.

McCubbin, H., Dahl, B., Lester, G., Benson, D., & Robertson, M. Coping repertoires of families adapting to prolonged war-induced separations. *Journal of Marriage and the Family*, 1976, *38*(3), 471–478.

McCubbin, H., Boss, P., Wilson, L., & Lester, G. Developing family invulnerability to stress: Coping patterns and strategies wives employ.

In J. Trost (Ed.), *The family and change*. Sweden: International Library, 1980.

McCubbin, H., Joy, C., Cauble, B., Comeau, J., Patterson, J., & Needle, R. Family stress and coping: A decade review. *Journal of Marriage and the Family*, 1980, *42*(4), 855–871.

McCubbin, H., Patterson, J., & Wilson, L. *Family Inventory of Life Events and Changes (FILE):* Research instrument. St. Paul: Family Social Science, University of Minnesota, 1981.

McFarlane, P. T., & Sussman, M. B. *Residential relocation and family stress*. University of Delaware, Department of Individual and Family Studies, April, 1982. (Mimeo)

Mechanic, D. *Students under stress: A study in the social psychology of adaptation*. Madison: University of Wisconsin Press, 1978.

Mederer, H., & Hill, R. Critical transitions over the family life span: Theory and research. In H. McCubbin, M. Sussman, & J. Patterson (Eds.), *Social stress and the family*. New York: Haworth Press, 1983.

Menaghan, E. G. Individual coping efforts and family studies: Conceptual and methodological issues. In H. I. McCubbin, M. B. Sussman, & J. M. Patterson (Eds.), *Social stress and the family*. New York: Haworth Press, 1983.

Monat, A., & Lazarus, R. (Eds.). *Stress and coping*. New York: Columbia University Press, 1977.

Moos, R. H., & Billings, A. G. Conceptualizing and measuring coping resources and processes. In L. Goldberger & S. Breznitz (Eds.), *Handbook of stress: Theoretical and clinical aspects*. New York: Macmillan, 1981.

Moos, R. H., Finney, J., & Chan, D. The process of recovery from alcoholism: Comparing alcoholic patients and matched community controls. *Journal of Studies on Alcohol*, 1981, *42*, 383–402.

Moskoff, M. *Boundary setting patterns of the divorced co-parenting relationship*. Master's thesis, University of Wisconsin–Madison, June 1980.

Neugarten, B., & Hagestad, G. Age and the life course. In R. H. Binstock & E. Shanas (Eds.), *Handbook on aging and the social science*. New York: Van Nostrand Reinhold, 1977.

Nuttal, R. L. *Coping with catastrophe: Family adjustments to national disaster*. Keynote address at Groves Conference on Marriage and the Family, Gatlinburg, Tennessee, 1980.

Olson, D. H., Sprenkle, D. H., & Russell, C. S. Circumplex model of marital and family systems I: Cohesion and adaptability dimensions, family types, and clinical applications. *Family Process*, 1979, *18*(March) 3–28.

Olson, D. H., McCubbin, H. I., Barnes, H., Larsen, A., Muxen, M., & Wilson, M. *Families: What makes them work*. Beverly Hills, Calif.: Sage Publishing, 1983.

Palgi, P. The adaptability and vulnerability of family types in the changing Israeli society. In A. Jarvus & J. Marcus (Eds.), *Children and families in Israel*. New York: Gordon & Breech, 1970.

Palgi, P. Socio-cultural expressions and implications of death, mourning, and bereavement. In *Israel arising out of the war situation*. Israel: Jerusalem Academic Press, 1973.

Palgi, P. *Culture and mourning: Expressions of bereavement arising out of the war situation in Israel*. Paper presented at the International Conference on Psychological Stress and Adjustment in Time of War and Peace, Tel Aviv, Israel, 1975.

Parsons, T. & Bales, R. F. *The family socialization and interaction process*. Glencoe, Ill.: Free Press, 1955.

Pearlin, L. I., & Leiberman, M. A. Social sources of emotional distress. In R. G. Simmons (Ed.), *Research in community mental health*. Greenwich, Conn.: JAI Press, 1979.

Pearlin, L. I., & Radabaugh, C. W. Economic strains and the coping functions of alcohol. *American Journal of Sociology*, 1976, *82*, 652–663.

Pearlin, L. I., Menaghan, E. G., Lieberman, M. A., & Mullan, J. T. The stress process. *Journal of Health and Social Behavior*, 1981, *22*(4), 337–356.

Rahe, R. The pathway between subjects' recent life changes and their near-future illness reports: Representative results and methodological issues. In B. Dohrenwend & B. Dohrenwend (Eds.), *Stressful life events*. New York: Wiley, 1974.

Rapoport, L. The state of crisis: Some theoretical considerations. In H. Parad (Ed.), *Crisis intervention: Selected readings*. New York: Family Service Association of America, 1965.

Reiss, D. *The family's construction of reality*. Cambridge: Harvard University Press, 1981.

Reiss, D. & Oliveri, M. E. Family stress as community frame. In H. I. McCubbin, M. B. Sussman, & J. M. Patterson (Eds.), *Social stress and the family*. New York: Haworth Press, 1983.

Riegel, K. A manifesto for dialectical psychology. *American Psychologist*, October 1976, pp. 692–693.

Riegel, K. *Foundations of Dialectical Psychology*. New York: Academic Press, 1979.

Russell, C. Transition to parenthood. *Journal of Marriage and the Family*, 1974, *36* (May), 294–302.

Scherz, F. H. Family treatment concepts. *Social Casework*, 1966, *47*(4), 234–240.

Selye, H. *The stress of life*. New York: McGraw-Hill, 1956.

Selye, H. (Ed.). *Selye's guide to stress research* (Vol. 1). New York: Van Nostrand Reinhold, 1980.

Vaughn, B. E., Egeland, B., Sroufe, L. A., & Waters, E. Individual differences in infant mothers attachment at twelve and eighteen months: Stability and change in families under stress. *Child Development*, 1979, *50*, 971–975.

Ventura, J., & Boss, P. G. The family coping inventory applied to parents with new babies. *Journal of Marriage and the Family*, November, 1983.

Watts, W. A. Designing attitude change programs. In R. Jones (Ed.), *Special education in transition: Attitudes toward the handicapped*. Reston, Va.: Council for Exceptional Children, 1984.

White, R. W. Strategies of adaptation: An attempt at systematic description. In G. Coelho, D. Hamburg, & J. Adams (Eds.), *Coping and adaptation*. New York: Basic Books, 1974.

Wikler, L. Chronic stresses of families of mentally retarded children. *Family Relations*, 1981, *30*(2), 281–288.

Wolff, C. T., Friedman, S. B., Hofer, M. A., & Mason, J. W. Relationship between psychological defenses and mean urinary 17-hydroxycortocasteroid excretion rates: I. A predictive study of parents of fatally ill children. *Psychosomatic Medicine*, 1964, *26*, 576–591.

CHAPTER 26

Family Violence

PAST, PRESENT, AND FUTURE

Suzanne K. Steinmetz

Introduction

*Justice between master and slave and between father and child is
not the same as absolute and political justice, but only analogous
to them. For there is no such thing as injustice in the absolute
sense towards what is one's own; and a chattel, or a child till it
reaches a certain age and becomes independent, is, as it were, a
part of oneself, and no one chooses to harm himself; hence there
can be no injustice towards them and therefore nothing just or
unjust in the political sense. For these, as we saw, are embodied
in law, and exist between persons whose relations are naturally
regulated by law, that is, persons who share equally in ruling
and being ruled. Hence Justice exists in a fuller degree between
husband and wife than in father and children, or master and
slaves, in fact, justice between husband and wife is Domestic
Justice in the real sense, though this too is different from Political Justice.* (Aristotle, *The Nicomachean Ethics*, p. 293–295)

Although Aristotle viewed husbands and wives as equals,
the husband's right to dominate and control his wife and
to use physical force to do so is still deeply embedded in
American culture.

This chapter is divided into four major sections. The
first section explores the historical roots of violence between family members; the next section discusses definitional and methodological problems and describes the
levels of violence perpetrated by family members on each
other. In the third section, major theoretical perspectives
are described, and the most frequently used variables and
models elaborating various linkages are presented. The
final section provides a discussion of present and future
research needs.

Although family violence is a relatively new area of
research, the rapid growth of studies makes it necessary
for this chapter to be selective rather than inclusive. Thus,
sexual abuse and marital rape are only briefly examined,
and child molestation, date rape, and rape are not
covered.

George and Wilding (1972) raised the important question, "When does a social fact become a social problem?" When does society recognize a type of behavior or

social phenomenon as a "social problem" rather than as
an isolated occurrence faced by an individual. It appears
that there are several stages in this evolution.

The first stage consists of acceptance of the status quo.
The behavior is seen as normal, although perhaps not
desirable. People are aware of the existence of this behavior but, through selective inattention, disregard the behavior and the consequences. An example of this stage in
the area of family violence is the "discovery" of child
abuse. Early radiological evidence examined by Caffey
(1946) revealed systematic, identifiable childhood battery. However, it was only when this phenomenon was
labeled the "battered child syndrome" by Kempe *et al.*
(1962) that it gained the media's attention. However,
family violence, as an academic topic of research, remained virtually hidden until the early 1970s. In fact,
O'Brien (1971) noted that he was unable to locate a single
title in all the issues of the *Journal of Marriage and the
Family* from 1939 to 1970 that included the word
violence.

Public awareness, the second stage, is best illustrated
by examining the topic of child abuse in the early 1970s.
Newspaper and magazine articles related the plight of
the battered child and, less frequently, the abused wife.
These articles were based on anecdotal case histories of
an abused person, supported with Federal Bureau of Investigation statistics or local homicide or police domes-
tic-disturbance calls when available.

The third stage is characterized by the onset of systematic research, usually limited to body counts and small in-
depth studies (Gelles, 1974; Steinmetz, 1977a), which
attempt to describe interaction and to provide some understanding of the dynamics. These studies, along with
increased local concern and the concomitant generation
of local police and court-related data, are valuable in the
development of the fourth stage, which focuses on public
policy development and the enforcement of services. This
fourth stage characterizes the mid-1980s, when all states
have mandatory child-abuse-reporting acts and most
states have formal or informal mechanisms for aiding
battered wives, including hotlines, shelters, and counseling centers.

Suzanne K. Steinmetz • Department of Individual and Family
Studies, University of Delaware, Newark, DE 19716.

725

A final stage, the elimination of domestic violence, is less likely to be achieved in our autonomous society, which values privacy, independence, and a diverse value system. Thus, we must constantly confront a dichotomy: laws that protect family members from violence and laws that protect family members' privacy and control over their household. However, data from a recently completed national survey (Straus & Gelles, 1985), when compared with the findings of a national study conducted in 1975 (Straus, Gelles, & Steinmetz, 1980), found a 47% decrease in child abuse and a 21% decrease in wife abuse, suggesting that, with adequate public awareness, education, services, and enforced laws, we could considerably reduce the incidence of family violence.

A Historical Perspective

If we were to trace the evolution of this growing field of family research, we would have to start with the special issue of the *Journal of Marriage and the Family* in 1971 that was devoted to the then available data on violence in the family.

Spurred by the concerns of women's groups, interest in this topic grew. Within a few years, edited volumes, several special issues of journals, and a growing number of dissertations that would later become research monographs became available (Steinmetz, 1978c).

This is not to suggest that society has been unaware of family violence. Accounts abound in court records, newspaper articles, and preambles to laws. For example, a Massachusetts law during the colonial period required that cohabitation be peaceful, and yet there were numerous examples of this requirement's not being met.

The First Church of Boston excommunicated Mary Whorten "for reviling of her husband and sticking of him and other vile and wicked courses" (Morgan, 1966, p. 141). One man in Plymouth Colony was punished for abusing his wife by "kiking her off from a stoole into the fier," and another for "drawing his wife in an unciveil manner on the snow." Joan Miller was charged with "beating and reviling her husband and egging her children to healp her, bidding them to knock him in the head and whishing his victual might choke hime" (Demos, 1970, p. 93).

Wife Abuse

Some of our ancient laws decreed that a woman who was verbally abusive to her husband was to have her name engraved on a brick, which would then be used to knock out her teeth (Steinmetz, 1980c). In Greek literature, Euripides argued that "Women should be silent, not argue with men and should not speak first." Roman law even justified the husband's killing his wife for adultery, drinking wine, or other "inappropriate" behavior.

In our country, however, the colonists believed that women represented a very critical resource. Without

women, the very survival of the colonies was in jeopardy. Thus, they insisted that men and women cohabit peacefully, and they provided strong social sanctions to instill this behavior in couples. With industrialization and rapid population growth, our social sanctions of nonviolent marital interactions changed. The husband's right to chastise his wife with a whip or rattan no bigger than his thumb, a remnant of old English law, was upheld by a Mississippi court in 1828. This "rule-of-thumb" law, which prevailed for nearly a half a century, limited the husband's use of corporal punishment to "great cases of emergency," with "salutary restraints" (*Bradley* v. *State*, Walker 158, Miss. 1824).

In 1874, a North Carolina court ruled that the husband had no right "to chastise his wife under any circumstances." This ruling did note, however, that if

no permanent injury has been inflicted, no malice, cruelty, or dangerous violence shown by the husband, it is better to draw the curtains, shut out the public gaze, and leave the parties to forget and forgive. (State v. *Oliver, 70, NC, 60, 61, 1874)*

In 1885, the economic cost to society of providing for the imprisoned wife-beater and his family was a concern of the members of the Pennsylvania legislature. Following the lead set by the state of Maryland, they suggested that public whippings be used as an alternative punishment (Steinmetz & Straus, 1974). It is curious that members of the legislature thought that a public whipping, with the humiliation and pain involved, would stop the violent husband from beating his wife. Apparently, the message was "Do as I say, not as I do."

It is not just the general public that has ignored the issue of family violence. Researchers have often been blind to the actual degree of violence existing in our society and to the damage it causes. In 1974, Maccoby and Jacklin, commenting on newspaper articles describing wife beating, noted that the extent of this kind of violence was rare, suggesting that

although incidents of this kind exist as an ugly aspect of marital relations in an unknown number of cases, an aspect that tends to be unseen or deliberately ignored and denied by outsiders, there can be little doubt that direct force is rare in most marriages. Male behavior such as the described above would be considered pathological in any human (or animal) society, and if widespread would endanger the species. (p. 426)

In discussing women's use of violence to resolve conflicts, Scanzoni (1978) noted: "The frequency of reported active violence is relatively modest among our respondents. Eighty-six percent state that they never hit their husbands" (p. 136).

Recognition of the extent and seriousness of wife abuse is an important first step in increasing public awareness and in providing education, support services, and resources for these women and their families. Thus, the denial of the existence of battered husbands, discussed below, has important ramifications for the violent women, their husbands, and their children.

Husband Abuse

Historically, men have been given the right to control women through abusive means, if necessary, because women and children have often been seen as chattel along with farm animals and property.

There were, however, instances in which society considered the wife justified in using physical force against her husband. The charivari, a post–Renaissance custom, was a noisy demonstration intended to shame and humiliate wayward individuals in public. The target was any behavior considered to be a threat to the patriarchal community's social order. Thus, in France, the husband who "allowed" his wife to beat him was made to wear an outlandish outfit and to ride backward around the village on a donkey while holding onto the tail (Shorter, 1975).

The Britons treated beaten husbands by strapping them into a cart and parading them through the booing crowds. The assaultive wife was also punished by riding backward on a donkey and being forced to drink wine and then wipe her mouth with the animal's tail (Shorter, 1975).

The bumbling husband, or the "Dagwood Bumstead syndrome," is another way in which deprecation of men by women has been permitted in our culture. A systematic examination of domestic relations as pictured by comic strips during the 1950s revealed that males were considerably more likely to be the victims of marital violence (see Table 1).

A favorite theme of the turn-of-the-century comic strips, such as "Katzenjammer Kids" and "Bringing Up Father," was the husband who endured physical and verbal abuse from his wife. The popularity of these domestic relations comics are most likely sustained because they approximated, in a nonserious manner, common family situations, and perhaps they allow men and women to carry out in fantasy those actions that they were unable to carry out in reality (Steinmetz, 1977–1978).

These comics often depict the husband as deviating from the masculine cultural ideal of strength, self-assertion, and intelligence, and as assuming the character traits that have been culturally ascribed to femininity. The wife in the comics, who was "justified" in playing the dominant, chastising, and violent role because her husband didn't fulfill his culturally prescribed role, was simultaneously shown displaying undesirable "feminine" traits.

Gelles provided many examples of husband abuse in

Table 1. Marital Conflict in the Comics[a]

	Perpetrator of aggression	Victims of hostility	Initiates the violence	Recipients of violence
Husband	10	63	10	14
Wife	73	39	7	1

[a]Adapted from Saenger (1963). Based on 156 syndicated comic strips appearing in nine New York City newspapers during October 1950.

his monograph *The Violent Home* (1974). In addition to the tabular data in this study, quotes from his respondents provide ample support of the fact of husband abuse. For example, one respondent noted, "He would just yell and yell—not really yell, just talk loudly, and I couldn't say anything because he kept talking, so I'd swing" (Gelles, 1974, p. 80).

Another respondent, a retired cook, was often verbally and physically attacked by his jealous wife, and still another was quoted as saying: "My wife is very violent. It's a miracle that I didn't go out because she really put a hell of a dent in my head" (p. 83).

Unfortunately, there is a tendency for some feminist writers to deemphasize the importance of women's use of violence, and to attempt to discredit any research that suggests that women may use violence on their spouses (e.g., Field & Kirschner, 1978; Pagelow, 1984; Pleck, Pleck, Grossman, & Bart, 1977–1978; Walker, 1984).

For example, the denial of the consequences of husband abuse in Walker's excellent book on wife battering (1984) is puzzling. She amply demonstrated the cyclical nature of domestic violence in her study of over 400 battered women. She reported that 67% of the women were battered as children (41% by their mothers, 44% by their fathers); that about 20% had brothers and sisters who were also battered; that 44% of their fathers battered their mothers; and that 29% of the mothers battered their fathers. Furthermore, 28% of these battered women reported that they battered their own children, and 5% attributed this behavior to being angry at their husband; 15% used violence against their spouse (either in retaliation or in self-defense) when in a battering relationship; and 5% continued this violent behavior after they left the first relationship and entered into a nonbattering relationship.

Walker's conclusion that these data "refute the 'mutual combat' or 'battered man' problem as being a large one" (1984, p. 150) is difficult to understand. The 29% of her respondents who battered their husbands and the 15% of her sample in which both spouses used violence can not be ignored.

Even if one were willing to assume that the 5% of new relationships characterized by husband battering is relatively inconsequential, the nondirect, "next-generation" effects noted by Walker (the 41% of children battered by their mothers, the 29% of mothers who battered the father, and the 5% of women who batter the child because they are angry at the husband) surely must be considered significant.

In a lengthy attempt to dispute the existence of battered husbands, Pagelow (1984) noted that the number of men battered by their wives is minuscule.[1] Others writers

---

[1]Although Pagelow carefully detailed the criticisms leveled by writers attempting to refute the existence of battered husbands, she ignored rejoinders or other sources of information supporting this phenomenon thus severely limiting the usefulness of her analysis for scholars.

(Field & Kirschner, 1978) take the stance that, by labeling these findings as "flim-flam" (p. 216), one can simply dismiss them.

Unfortunately, this conspiracy of silence fails to recognize that family violence is *never* inconsequential (Steinmetz, 1978d). To deny the existence of women's use of violence also denies them legitimate access to resources that may reduce the stress and conflict that result from the multiple roles faced by women today, and that may help them to develop nonviolent forms of interaction. The impact of public acknowledgment, education, and services on reducing domestic violence can be illustrated by comparing the findings from a 1975 survey (Straus *et al.,* 1980) with those from a 1985 survey (Straus & Gelles, 1985). This resurvey found a 47% reduction in child abuse, a 21% reduction in severe violence toward wives, and a less dramatic reduction (4%) in severe violence toward husbands. Furthermore, although overall husband-to-wife violence was reduced 6.6%, overall wife-to-husband violence actually increased 4.3%.

Child Abuse

The concept of children as property of their parents is illustrated in the Hammurabi code of 2100 B.C. and the Hebrew code of 800 B.C., which considered infanticide an acceptable practice (Bates, 1977).

In Roman times, the Patria Potestae permitted fathers to sell, sacrifice, mutilate, or kill offspring (Radbill, 1968).

The Book of Proverbs provided parents with specific guidelines on education: "He who spares the rod hates his son, but he who loves him disciplines him diligently" (13:24).

The practice of burying children in the foundations of buildings existed throughout history, and as recently as the sixteenth century, German children were buried alive beneath the steps of public buildings (Bates, 1977). During the Industrial Revolution, children endured long hours, extreme physical hardship, and numerous beatings to ensure that they would exhibit no laziness. In fact, the immortalization of the fate of children sentenced to these conditions has persisted in the expression "beating the dickens out of a child," which persists today as evidence of the child abuse that Charles Dickens witnessed and wrote about (Sarles, 1976). (*Webster's Third New International Dictionary* indicates an earlier, euphemistic, use of the word dickens to mean "devil" dating back at least to Shakespeare's time, Gove, 1976.)

Child abuse, although only recently "discovered" by researchers, has its roots in the early history of our country. In 1646, a law that attempted to help parents control their rebellious children noted that, unless the parents

have been very unchristianly negligent in the education of such children or have so provoked them by extreme and cruel correction" any child over 16 years of age and of sufficient understand-

ing who cursed, smited and would not obey his natural mother or father, then "would be put to death." (Bremner, 1970, p. 37)

In 1874, Mary Ellen, a 9-year-old, was finally rescued by social workers who defined her as a member of the animal kingdom so that she might be protected under the law designed to protect animals because none were available to protect children. Public reaction to the need to use the Society for the Prevention of Cruelty to Animals to protect children was instrumental in the founding of the Society for Prevention of Cruelty to Children. However, nearly a century passed before all states had laws mandating the reporting of child abuse, requiring investigation of the reported cases, and providing services to these children and their families.

Elder Abuse

In the late 1970s, elder abuse was hailed as the "new" domestic-violence problem, and social critics mused over this latest indication of the breakdown of the American family (Steinmetz, 1978a). Is elder abuse really new, or is it simply the latest of the areas of domestic violence to be acknowledged as a social problem?

Respected and Despised. Although old age was venerated in colonial America, veneration was construed to mean reverence, respect, and worship, not necessarily affection or love (Fischer, 1977). The Fourth Commandment requires respect of one's parents, but respect or veneration did not automatically come with aging. The special powers assumed to be held by elders might be in the form of God's grace or the Devil's evil powers. Aging brought with it mixed blessings: elders were venerated and respected but also feared, isolated, and despised.

Although the oldest citizens of the church sat in the most prestigious pew as "elders of the church," they also predominated as victims of the Massachusetts witch hunts (Fischer, 1977, p. 34), and they constituted the largest group of paupers. In 1910, 60% of the residents in Ohio state pauper institutions, 62% in Pennsylvania, 87% in Wisconsin, and 92% in Massachusetts were elderly (Fischer, 1977).

Furthermore, children often neglected their aged parents. Cotton Mather, in *Dignity and Duty,* complained that "there were children who were apt to despise an Aged Mother." Landon Carter, in 1771, wrote, "It is a pity that old age which everybody covets and everybody who lives must come to should be so contemptible in the eyes of the world" (Smith, 1980, p. 275).

The elderly poor fared most miserably. Throughout the court records of Connecticut and Massachusetts are instances of attempts to bar these people from entering a given town, as they would increase the population of the almshouses. A 1772 New Jersey law required the justices of the peace to search arriving ships for old persons as well as other undesirables, and to send them away in order to prevent the growth of pauperism (Smith, 1980, p. 61).

Neighbors often ''warned-out'' poor widows and forced them to wander from one town to another.

Control of Property. The transfer of property, through both inheritance and deeds of gift, provides insights into parents' attempts to use economic control as a hedge against maltreatment in their old age. In an attempt to provide for the surviving wife, many husbands' wills included elaborate provisions for her care, which required the children to furnish food, clothing, and shelter or forfeit their inheritance.

Other parents deeded the land to their offspring before their death, but the provision of a lifetime of care was a requirement of keeping the land. For example, Henry Holt, by a deed of gift, gave his original homestead to his 30-year-old unmarried son. The deed required him to ''Take ye sole care of his father Henry Holt and of his natural mother Sarah Holt'' for the rest of their days, and to provide for all their needs, which were very carefully detailed. Failure to supply any of the required articles would result in forfeiture of the property (Greven, 1970, pp. 143–144). Josiah Winslow left all his movable properties to his wife for her to distribute after her death according to their children's performance of their filial duties (Mayflower Descendants XXXIV: 34, as cited by Demos, 1970).

The desire of the father to use economic means to control his adult children produced conflict when these children tried to establish independence. In one family, 32-year-old Robert Carter was forced to spend an additional 10 years under his father's authority because he lacked the financial means to secure complete independence. Bitter arguments, mostly resulting from the middle-aged son's continued dependence on his father, nearly resulted in physical blows. Landon Carter, the father, feared for his life and went around with a pistol. He noted that

surely it is happy our laws prevent parricide or the devil that moves to this treatment would move to put his father out of the way. Good God, that such a monster is descended from my loin. (J. Greene, as cited by Fischer, 1977, p. 75)

Although the Carters faced their problem in the latter part of the eighteenth century, these conflicts have existed throughout America's history. For example, in 1868, the bill for boarding of a poor sick old man was brought to the Board of Commissioners of Brown County, Minnesota. Oliver Mather, the son, had driven off his aged father and did not want to support him (Fischer, 1977).

Historical evidence suggests that family violence is not a new social problem; rather, it has only recently been identified as a social problem by researchers, journalists, social planners, and the judiciary.

The Level of Violence in Families

A Definition of Violence

For the purpose of this chapter, violence is defined as an act carried out with the intention of, or an act perceived as having the intention of, physically hurting another person. This ''physical hurt'' can range from a slap to murder. Although this is the basic definition of violence, it is usually necessary to take into account a number of other characteristics of these violent acts: Was the act *instrumental* to some other purpose, such as disciplining a child for a specific wrongdoing, or was it *expressive,* that is, an end in itself? Is it a culturally permitted or required act, such as spanking a disobedient child, a *legitimate* act, as opposed to one that runs counter to cultural norms such as murder, which is *illegitimate* violence? The basis for the ''intent to hurt'' may range from concern for a child's safety (as when a child is spanked for going into the street) to hostility so intense that the death of the other is desired. The former would be an example of ''legitimate instrumental violence'' and the latter of ''illegitimate expressive violence.''

In an earlier study (Steinmetz, 1977a), it was hypothesized that the conflict resolution methods most likely to be repeated are those deliberate acts that are considered legitimate behavior by society (or at least are perceived as such by the respondents); that are aimed at changing another's behavior (instrumental); and that are perceived to be successful by the individuals participating in the acts (see Table 2).

These relationships are illustrated by the following quote:

I've heard that you shouldn't spank when you're angry, but I can't agree with that, because I think that's the time you should spank; before you have a chance to completely cool off, too. I think that the spanking helps the mother or dad as well as impresses the child that they did something wrong, and when they do something bad, they are going to be physically punished for it. You don't hit them with a stick or a belt, or a hairbrush, but a good back of the hand . . . they remember it. (Steinmetz, 1977a, p. 27)

This quote richly illustrates the dimensions of aggressive interaction noted in Table 2. First, the respondent suggests an expressive dimension (''spanking helps the mother or dad'' to get rid of frustration). Second, the instrumental dimension (''impresses the child that they did something wrong'') is mentioned. A third point is the

Table 2. Variables Influencing the Choice of Methods of Conflict Resolution[a]

Variable	Likelihood of an act's becoming a part of one's conflict-resolution repertoire	
	+	−
Intent	Deliberate	Accidental
Societal view of act	Legitimate	Illegitimate
Perceived goal of act	Instrumental	Expressive
Perceived outcome	Success	Failure

[a]From Steinmetz (1977a).

respondent's differentiation between what she considers legitimate (''a good back of the hand'') and illegitimate (''you don't hit them with a stick or a belt, or a hairbrush''). Furthermore, her action is deliberate (''I think that's the time you should spank; before you have a chance to completely cool off, too'') and is perceived as being successful (''they remember it'').

Methodological Problems

One encounters several methodological problems when studying sensitive topics:

Social Desirability. The first problem to consider is the effect of social desirability on data collection accuracy. Battering one's spouse or child is unacceptable behavior and therefore may be embarrassing for the respondent to discuss. As a result, the respondent may minimize the severity of violent acts (e.g., a brutal beating becomes a few slaps).

This redefintion may also be an attempt to resolve the cognitive dissonance produced when two divergent values or beliefs must coexist. Because love or caring is not considered a normal response to someone who hurts or mistrusts us, the respondent must redefine the violent behavior in order to validate continued love for the batterer and to reduce the dissonance.

Retrospective Data. The second methodological problem is the reliance on data from retrospective studies. As most studies of domestic violence are retrospective in nature, the effect of the accurate recall of details must be considered. Minor incidents may be forgotten or redefined. A battered wife, especially if the violence has ceased, may define an incident that she considered extremely violent when it happened as a ''loss of temper'' or ''a few slaps.'' Likewise, a spanking, because of the age at which it occurred or the emotions surrounding the incident, may be recalled as a battering. Violent parents or partners who have died may be remembered by family members in a more loving light. However, the death of the violent person may allow others to speak freely about the violence.

A Wife's View. A third problem is the tendency for the data to be obtained from one spouse, usually the wife. The congruence of the husband's and the wife's responses, as well as those of the children and third parties, such as a social worker, needs to be considered. For example, Heer's study (1963) of marital power found that marital agreement ranged from a low of 15% to a high of 30%, depending on the type of decision. The range was considerably wider (23%–64% agreement) in Wilkening and Morrison's study (1963) of farm and home-related marital decision-making and was higher (55%–76%) in a study conducted by Safilios-Rothschild (1969). Although a part of these incongruities is probably due to instrument

inadequacies, measurement errors and interview interaction, incongruities also result from the different perceptions held by each partner (Niemi, 1974).

A number of studies have gathered data from several family members in an attempt to examine the different perceptions held. In the first, Straus (1974) compared the responses of 105 students to the responses of 57 fathers and 60 mothers. In this study, each parent was given a separate questionnaire and a return envelope, so that, in some families, each parent returned a questionnaire; in others, neither did. When comparing the student scores with those of the parents, reasoning was correlated .19 with fathers and .12 with mothers; verbal aggression was .51 for the fathers and .43 for the mothers; and violence was .65 for the fathers and .33 for the mothers. Straus suggested that the lower correlations with the mothers' scores may reflect the mothers' (or the students') desire to present the mother in a better light.

A second study (Steinmetz, 1977a) compared the child's responses with a parent's responses for three behaviors (discussion, verbal aggression, and physical aggression) and the husband's response on a questionnaire with the wife's responses in an interview (see Table 3). The parent's and child's reporting of behavior was extremely consistent.

These are group comparisons (e.g., 61% of the parents reported physical aggression), not comparisons of parent and child in each family. Given the consistency between the parents' and the child's reports and the high percentage of individuals engaging in each behavior, one suspects a high degree of consistency in the reporting of the existence of the behavior by different family members. A comparison of family profiles in the uses of verbal and physical violence to resolve family conflicts revealed considerable similarity, a finding that was statistically highly significant. Unfortunately, these percentages re-

Table 3. A Comparison of the Percentage of Parents and Children Using Different Conflict-Resolution Methods[a]

	Reports	
	Parents (%)	Child (%)
Marital		
Discussion	98.0	98.1
Verbal	93.9	92.5
Physical	61.2	60.4
Parent–Child		
Discussion	96.2	98.1
Verbal	96.2	96.2
Physical	84.6	69.2

[a]From Steinmetz (1977a).

flect only the occurrence, not the frequency (how often) or the intensity (how severe). It is quite possible that comparisons focusing on these aspects of family interaction would show considerable differences.

Szinovacz (1983) used a modified version of the Conflict Tactic Scales (CTS) (Straus, 1979b) for gathering data from both the husband and the wife in the *same* family. She found that husbands and wives tended to disagree on both the occurrence and the frequency of violent behavior. In explaining the 50% more violence by husbands and the 20% more violence by wives, Szinovacz noted that they

may very well differ in their definition of violence and accordingly report or fail to report especially minor forms of violence. Thus, husbands may not report or even recall some violent acts by their wives because they did not take these behaviors seriously. (p. 642)

Definitional and Conceptual Problems. Inadequately defined terms and different approaches to operationalizing concepts is the fourth major methodological problem. Sweet and Resnick (1979) noted that it is difficult to interpret and compare child abuse findings because of the inconsistent use of the terms *abuse* and *neglect*. Many studies use Gil's definition (1968, 1970), which includes deliberate acts of omission (emotional and physical neglect) as well as physical and sexual violence. Giovannoni (1976) distinguished between "neglect" (the failure to perform parental duties, i.e., supervision, nurturance, and protection) and "abuse" (exploitation of the rights of parents to control, discipline, and punish). The operationalization of the behavior affects the results. Straus *et al.* (1980) measured positive forms of discipline (e.g., talking it out and mediating), verbal aggression (e.g., yelling and threats), and physical aggression (hitting, biting, shoving, and the use of gun or knife). They did not specifically request information on sexual abuse, although it may have been reported as "other" physical or emotional neglect. It is likely that the amount of sexual abuse reported was much lower in this study than it would have been in one specifically eliciting information on sexual abuse and incest. Therefore, the specific topics covered, the method by which the topic is covered, and the individual from whom the information is requested all influence the responses received.

Inadequate Samples and Research Designs. A fifth methodological concern noted in the child abuse literature is the lack of in-depth, rigorous, empirical studies that use random samples (Polansky *et al.,* 1975). The research has primarily been descriptive, based on case studies from special groups or from "official" records.

A content analysis of 2,700 abstracts in the National Center on Child Abuse and Neglect Services reported that "the literature represented a disproportionate reliance upon 'think pieces' rather than empirical examination" (Bolton, Laner, Gai, & Kaner, 1981, p. 536). These researchers noted that, whereas over 71% were discussion

pieces and nearly 6% were reviews of literature, just under 20% could be described as empirical research. This group of research studies had serious shortcomings: small samples (one fourth of the studies had 20 subjects or fewer, and one half had 60 subjects or fewer); aggregated data from official records (Central Registry Data) and limited use of random samples, with an overreliance on official records; and lack of control groups. Problems arise because "official" records are not representative. Whom one is, whom one knows, and what one has all influence one's likelihood of being cited in an official record. When aggregate data from central registries such as those compiled by the Federal Bureau of Investigation, the police, or the National Center on Child Abuse and Neglect are used, this lack of representativeness is simply enlarged. Lack of control in research design presents another problem. We have all heard the dictum "Abusing mothers were abused children." However, because of the lack of a control group in these studies, the data cannot reveal how many abused children grew up to be warm, loving, and nonviolent parents and spouses.

Although a comparable, in-depth examination of spouse abuse research is lacking, it is reasonable to assume that the same shortcomings noted for the child abuse literature also exist.

Confounding of Correlations and Causation. A sixth concern is the confounding of correlation and causation in the research. The checklist approach to data gathering has provided a wealth of variables that can be interrelated through correlational analysis. Unfortunately, a quantum leap is made when interpreting these data. Thus, we are led to believe that variables such as alcohol or drug abuse, lack of education, unwanted or unplanned pregnancy, and unemployment "cause" domestic violence. Not only are the data collected usually inadequate for making these statements, but *post facto* statistical analysis, such as specification and elaboration that might provide a statistically controlled approximation of the data collected by means of experimental research designs, is rarely performed.

One study (Schumm, Martin, Bollman, & Jurich, 1982) used correlation and discriminant analysis to assess the ability of the variables (total family income, family size, the parents' education, their perceived income adequacy, loneliness, powerlessness, the father's employment, religiosity, and job satisfaction) to discriminate between mothers and fathers who were nonviolent, who were verbally violent (but physically nonviolent), and who were verbally and physically violent. Only the fathers' average weeks employed and the mothers' perceived income adequacy for the rural sample discriminated among the groups. For the urban sample, the variables of the father's religiosity and the mother's education approached significance. Although this study is admirable in its innovative use of statistics, the variables selected were not consistently found to correlate with violence (see the discussion on social class later in this chapter). Furthermore, the standard deviations provided suggest that many of the variables examined in this study had little variance. Thus, one would not expect them to have great discriminant power as a group. A third criticism is that it is not a single crisis or stress that produces violence; rather, a combination of factors together, such as job-related stress, unplanned pregnancy, alcohol abuse, and lack of money, produce violence. Had this study examined the cumulative effects as well as the independent relationships, this approach might have provided stronger discriminant power.

Are We More Violent Today?

The deluge of media coverage of child abuse and marital violence may suggest to the casual observer that these are new problems, the result of an industrialized, highly mobile society. However, researchers such as Radbill (1968) and deMause (1974) have presented evidence that children now are exposed to less neglect, mistreatment, and violence than at any other time in history. Because systematic data on child abuse have not been gathered until recently, and because the available "historical" data have been biased by the tendency to record only the most dramatic incidents (those resulting in permanent injury or death), it is difficult to compare historical accounts and early data collection efforts with the more precise statistics gathered today. A comparison of classical societies during eras when the emphasis was on artistic, cultural, and technological development with societies during eras characterized by power struggles or the acquisition of territory and resources reveals that high levels of interpersonal violence accompany power struggles and acquisition of territory (Steinmetz and Straus, 1974). This theory also finds contemporary support in comparisons of societies on measures of internal and external violence and marital violence (Steinmetz, 1981b) and sibling violence (Steinmetz, 1982; see Table 4).

Another way to indirectly measure attitudes toward certain behaviors is to examine legislation, both proposed and passed. The early colonial laws that gave parents the right to put unruly children to death provide insights into colonial parents' concern about disobedient children and the parents' perceived inability to control these children through parental respect, authority, and social pressures.

Finally, although most individuals over 60 years old are familiar with the strapping behind the woodshed or the belt that hung on the pantry door, parental discipline of this type, once considered quite normal and acceptable, would now be labeled as suspected child abuse if a teacher, a school nurse, a baby-sitter, or a friend saw the welts and reported them to the appropriate agency, as required by law.

To examine violence levels in the recent past, Straus et al. (1980) compared the parent–child violence used by 306 couples with their children aged 13 to 17 and the violence that these parents had experienced when they were teens. Over one third of these parents had used

physical punishment during the year of the survey, and 37.3%, an "almost" identical percentage, had been hit by their parents when they were teenagers. Straus et al. suggested:

The seeming increase in child abuse is probably the result of greater public awareness, less public toleration of cruelty to children, and the uncovering of cases through new laws that require doctors and others to report cases of child abuse. (p. 105)

Data from a second national study of family violence (found in Table 5) show a considerable decline in child abuse rates for all behaviors except "threaten with knife/gun" or "used knife or gun," which doubled from .1% to .2% (Straus & Gelles, 1985).

Marital Violence

Numerous studies have noted that between 50% and 60% of the couples interviewed reported physical violence by a partner at some time during the marriage or relationship (Gelles, 1974; Steinmetz, 1977a; Straus et al., 1980).

However, most of these studies surveyed intact couples and confined their questions to interaction with the current mate. Roughly 20/1,000 married men or women divorce; two thirds (65.5%) of these divorced individuals remarry (Carter & Glick, 1976). Because over one third of the women seeking a divorce in one study cited physical abuse as the reason for dissolving the relationship, studies that ignore marital interaction with a previous spouse have greatly underestimated the actual amount of violence (Levinger, 1966).

For about 1 out of 5 women, the abuse is not an isolated incident but occurs repeatedly, and for 1 out of 15 to 20 women, severe physical battering occurs (Gelles, 1974; Steinmetz, 1977a; Straus et al., 1980; Walker, 1984). There were 1,745 spousal and 690 boyfriend–girlfriend homicides in 1983; women were victims in 59% of these cases (U.S. Department of Justice, 1985).

A nationally representative survey of 2,143 maritally intact families (Straus et al., 1980) revealed that, in almost 7 out of every 100 couples, one spouse had thrown something at the other during the previous year, and in about 1 out of 6 (16%), this had happened at some point in their marriage.[2]

The statistics for slapping a spouse were about the same: 7% in the previous year and 18% at some time. Also, 13% had pushed, shoved, or grabbed during the year, and almost 25% had at some time during the marriage.

At the other extreme, approximately 1 or 2 out of every 100 couples (1.5%) had experienced a "beating-up" in-

---

[2]It is unlikely that this national survey included severely battered women, those labeled "chronic battered women," in the sample. Severely battered women who were still living with the batterer would not risk further violence by being "caught" telling someone about their family life.

Table 4. Comparison of Political Violence Profiles with Marital and Sibling Violence Scores

Collective protest	Score	Hibbs (1973) (1956–1967) Internal war	Score	Feirerabend et al. (1969) (1948–1965)	Score	Gurr (1961–1965)	Rank	Gurr and Bishop (1976) (1950–1960)	Rank	Marital violence[a]	Rank	Sibling violence[b]	Rank
Finland	1.95	Finland	1.61	Finland	0	Finland	98	Canada	68	Finland	1	Canada	1
Puerto Rico	2.92	Puerto Rico	2.64	Israel	8	Puerto Rico	93	Finland	67	Puerto Rico	2	Israel	2
Canada	3.74	Israel	3.09	Canada	10	Canada	80	Puerto Rico	49	Belize	3	Puerto Rico	3
Israel	4.26	Canada	4.68	U.S.	97	U.S.	41	U.S.	24	U.S.	4	Finland	4
c		c		c	109	Israel	21	Israel	17	Canada	5	U.S.	5
U.S.	7.12	U.S.	6.45			c	20			Israel	6		
Scores ranged from low of 0 (9 countries) to a high of 7.12 for the United States.		Scores ranged from a low of 0 (15 countries) to 11.17 for South Vietnam.		Scores ranged from a low of 0 to a high of 190.		Ranking of most violent = 1 to least violent = 114.		Scores ranged from 1 to 83; a low number represents high violence ranking based on structural violence and physical violence measures.		1 = lowest physical violence score; 6 = highest violence score.		1 = lowest level; 5 = highest physical violence score.	

[a]Rankings are based on the average of husbands' and wives' mean frequency scores during the marriage. Data from Steinmetz (1981b).
[b]Data not computed for Belize. Rankings based on average of sibling's mean frequency scores while living at home from ages 3 to 18. Data from Steinmetz (1982).
[c]Data not available for Belize. Data available for Guatemala noted to give some idea where British Honduras might fall (because of numerous similarities between the two countries).

Table 5. Comparison of 1975 and 1985 National Survey of Family Violence[a]

Items	Parent to Child		Husband to Wife		Wife to Husband	
	1975 ($N = 1,146$)	1985 ($N = 1,428$)	1975 ($N = 2,143$)	1985 ($N = 3,520$)	1975 ($N = 2,143$)	1985 ($N = 3,520$)
Threw something	5.4	2.7	2.8	2.8	5.2	4.3
Pushed/grabbed/shoved	31.8	30.7	10.7	9.3	8.3	8.9
Slapped/spanked	52.2	54.9	5.1	2.9	4.6	4.1
Kicked/bit/hit with fist	3.2	1.3	2.4	1.5	3.1	2.4
Hit/tried to hit with object	13.4	9.7	2.2	1.7	3.0	3.0
Beat up	1.3	0.6	1.1	0.8	0.6	0.4
Threatened with gun or knife	0.1	0.2	0.4	0.4	0.6	0.6
Used gun or knife	0.1	0.2	0.3	0.2	0.2	0.2

[a]The 1975 data from Straus *et al.* (1980); the 1985 data from Straus & Gelles (1985).

cident during 1975, and "beating up" had occurred at some time in the marriage of 5% of the couples interviewed.

The rates for actually using a knife or a gun on one's spouse were 1 out of every 200 couples per year, and almost 1 out of 27 couples at some point in the marriage.

The impact on families of these extremely violent forms of family interaction is best understood when they are computed on the total number of couples. In 1975, there were about 47 million couples living together in the United States. Based on the above rates, over 1.7 million Americans had at some time faced a husband or a wife wielding a knife or a gun, and well over 2 million had been beaten up by their spouse.

It seems appropriate to ascertain the point at which the violence exceeds the bounds of "normal" family violence. When does it become "wife beating"? Straus *et al.* (1980) constructed a wife–husband beating index that measured the extent to which the spouse went beyond throwing things, pushing, and grabbing, to hitting with an object, beating up, and threatening to use or using a knife or a gun, acts that carry with them a high risk of serious physical injury. Almost 4 out of every 100 (3.8%) American wives were beaten by their husbands every year. This comes to a total of almost 1.8 million wives each year, and when the question was asked if there ever was a beating, one out of eight couples (12.6%) had experienced a beating sometime during the marriage.

A decade later, in 1985, Straus and Gelles (1985) conducted a similar survey. Minor husband-to-wife violence (threw something; pushed, grabbed or shoved; slapped or spanked) had been reduced by 9.4%; severe violence (kicked, bit, or hit with fist; beat up; threatened or used a gun or a knife) was 21% lower than 10 years earlier (see Table 5). Based on the 54 million couples in the United States in 1985, the 21% decrease represented 375,000 fewer beaten wives. Although this decrease is encouraging, these rates suggest that over 1.3 million wives are still being beaten each year, hardly an indicator of domestic tranquility.

Physical violence is only one form of violence perpetrated against wives. Fourteen percent, 1 out of 7, of the 930 women interviewed in a study of women who were, or who had been married, had been raped by their husband or ex-husband (Russell, 1982).

In a review of the research in this area, Finkelhor and Yllo (1983) reported the following: 36% of 304 battered women in 10 shelters had been raped by their husband or their cohabiting partner (Spektor, 1980); a similar rate was found by Giles-Sims (1979); and 37% of a sample of 119 battered women had experienced marital rape (Pagelow, 1980).

Finkelhor and Yllo surveyed 326 women in a childhood sexual abuse study and reported that the use or the threat of physical force by the partner in order to have sex had been experienced by 10% of the women. However, 3% of the women had had this experience with a stranger. Although forced sex in marriage is possibly the most frequent type of sexual assault, women who have been sexually assaulted by their husband or partner avoid defining themselves as raped (Gelles, 1979).

Although women are both victims and perpetrators of violence, husband abuse, as a topic of investigation, has received little attention (Steinmetz, 1977–1978, 1980c). This is most likely because the extent of injury is considerably less severe than in woman abuse. Furthermore, men's greater resources (money, credit, status, and power) allow them to use private sources of help; thus, their abuse goes unreported.

Studies of infanticide (Radbill, 1968) and homicide (Wolfgang, 1958) have clearly indicated that women have the potential to be violent. Oswald (1980) examined the histories of patients admitted to the Royal Infirmary of Edinburgh because of parasuicide. During 1977 and 1978, 592 admitted women who were married (or living with a man) and who were between 20 and 40 years old answered 30 items that contained questions on the victim and the perpetrator of violence. Oswald found that 51% ($N = 299$) reported domestic violence. Of those women reporting violence, 88% ($N = 263$) were victims, but

Table 6. Cross-Cultural Comparison of Husbands' and Wives' Use of Violence

Study	N	Throw things		Push/ shove		Hit/ slap		Kick		Hit with object		Threaten with knife/ gun		Used knife/ gun		Use of any violence		Mean frequency	
		H	W	H	W	H	W	H	W	H	W	H	W	H	W	H	W	H	W
Gelles (1974)	80	22	11	18	1	32	20	25	9	3	5	5	0	—	—	47	33	—	—
Steinmetz (1977a)	54	39	37	31	32	20	20	—	—	10	10	—	—	2	2	47	43	3.5	4.0
Steinmetz (1977b)	94	31	25	22	18	17	12	—	—	12	14	—	—	—	—	32	28	6.6	7.0
Finland[a]	44	20	23	18	14	16	14	—	—	9	9	—	—	—	—	61	64	2.19	2.18
Puerto Rico	82	28	16	22	11	25	11	—	—	22	11	—	—	—	—	49	25	5.78	6.60
British Honduras	231[b]	24	21	25	23	23	22	—	—	19	18	—	—	—	—	39	38	6.83	6.38
Spanish speaking	103	23	22	27	26	25	20	—	—	20	19	—	—	—	—	40	39	5.85	5.73
Creole	79	24	21	19	17	22	18	—	—	15	15	—	—	—	—	34	29	7.78	7.17
Caribbean	37	31	30	30	27	24	27	—	—	22	19	—	—	—	—	51	54	7.37	6.20
Canada	52	21	21	17	13	13	13	—	—	10	12	—	—	—	—	23	21	6.00	7.80
Israel	127	14	14	13	12	15	14	—	—	13	13	—	—	—	—	22	20	8.42	8.65
Kibbutz	63	16	14	16	14	17	16	—	—	14	14	—	—	—	—	21	16	9.91	12.56
City	64	13	13	11	9	13	13	—	—	13	11	—	—	—	—	22	20	7.59	7.38

Percentage

[a]Cross-cultural data adapted from Steinmetz (1981c).
[b]Contains 12 additional cases which were of mixed families.

41% of the victims ($N = 124$) reported that they were also excessively violent; 36 women (12%) had been perpetrators but not victims of violence.

Although the documentation on husband beating is not as extensive as that on wife beating, we do know that over 3% of 600 husbands in mandatory conciliation interviews listed physical abuse by their wife as a reason for the divorce action (Levinger, 1966). Although this is a far lower percentage than the nearly 37% of wives who mentioned physical abuse, it is consistent with other data suggesting that there is about a 1:13 ratio of husband abuse to wife abuse.

Based on police records and a random sample of New Castle County (Delaware) families in 1975, it was estimated that 7% of the wives and just over a half percent (.6%) of the husbands had been victims of severe physical abuse by their spouse (Steinmetz, 1977c). Statewide data collected between January 1, 1981, and June 30, 1981, revealed that there had been 423 incidents of wife abuse and 33 incidents of husband abuse.

Although the actual number of cases of reported abuse had grown considerably, possibly because of increased services and wide advertisement of their existence, the ratio of 13 abused women to 1 abused man remained constant.

Although these data represent the percentage of husbands and wives who have used physical violence against a spouse, they do not tell us the frequency with which these acts occurred. By comparing the mean scores, it is revealed that, not only does the percentage of wives who have ever used physical violence often exceed that of the husbands who did, but that wives also exceed husbands in the frequency with which these acts occur (see Tables 5 and 6).

There are several limitations in these data. First, for the most part, they report on violence that is considered socially acceptable, "normal" violence, that is, hitting, slapping, pushing, and throwing things (Stark & McEvoy, 1970).

Second, these data do not provide information on the intensity (one or two slaps or 20 minutes of being battered) or the degree of injury. Statistics from women's shelters, crisis lines, and hospital emergency rooms, as well as the police data noted earlier, suggest that because women are usually smaller and lighter than men, they suffer a greater degree of physical injury and are more likely to have been terrorized (e.g., with a knife held to the throat for two hours), threatened, and brutalized by prolonged and repeated attacks.

Parent–Child Violence

Corporal punishment, which fulfills the definition "intent to inflict physical injury," and which differs only in degree of severity from child abuse, is an important aspect of family abuse. First, it is the most prevalent form of family abuse. Numerous studies (Blumberg, 1964–1965; Erlanger, 1974; Stark & McEvoy, 1970) have indicated that between 84% and 97% of all parents have used physical punishment at some point in their child's life. A high percentage of these families continue to use corporal punishment for disciplining their children until the tenth grade (Bachman, 1967) and the twelfth grade (Steinmetz, 1971, 1974; Straus, 1971). The American Humane Association (1978) found that 36% of reported abuse cases involved children between 10 and 18; Gil (1970) found nearly 17% of abused youth were over 12. Knopoka's nationwide study of adolescent girls (1975) revealed that 12% had been beaten and 9% had been raped. Straus *et al.* (1980) found that 66% of youth 10 to 14 years old had been struck; 34% of those 15 to 17 had been hit. Abused levels were highest for two age groups: 3- to 4-year-olds and 15- to 17-year-olds. These two age groups share similarities. Both represent ages at which the children have entered a stage of maximum control over their environment. The 3- to 4-year-old has the ability to open doors, negotiate all household "barriers," and explore the yard and neighborhood. The 15- to 17-year-old is learning to drive, drink, smoke, and explore sex.

Yet, both age groups are viewed by the parents as having the minimum cognitive or commonsense ability to make appropriate and safe decisions regarding these new experiences. The 3- to 4-year-old can explore the house and the neighborhood but lacks the knowledge to do so safely. The 15- to 17-year-old may experiment with adult activities but often lacks adult maturity in these areas. Finally, the activities of both age groups often represent a questioning of parental authority and control. Under these conditions, parents are most likely to resort to physical force in an attempt to regain and maintain this control (Steinmetz, 1977a).

Physical punishment is also used on the very young. Korsch, Christian, Gozzi, and Carlson (1965) interviewed 100 mothers of infants who were outpatients in Los Angeles clinics. Almost half had spanked their infants under 12 months of age, and one fourth had started spanking before the infant had reached 6 months. Wittenberg (1971), using parents with a wide range of socioeconomic status (SES), found no class differences in methods used to discipline children, but 41% had used some form of physical punishment for babies under 6 months of age and 87% had used physical force before their children were 2.

Corporal punishment is also the most accepted form of family violence. Parents are expected to control and mold their children, and they are given considerable freedom in selecting the mechanisms they use to obtain this control. Unlike in Sweden, where a parent can be imprisoned for a month for striking a child (Ziegert, 1983), spanking is considered an acceptable way of disciplining children in the United States. The privilege of spanking a child is rapidly being extended to school administrators, schoolteachers, and school bus drivers.

In fact, the United States and England represent clear dissenters among all major countries and a growing number of Third World countries that ban corporal punishment in schools (Steinmetz, 1986). A final consideration is the existence of a positive relationship between corporal punishment and other forms of family violence. Severe physical punishment has marked the childhood of numerous adults who commit physically violent acts on their family members and on strangers. Several researchers have stated that physical punishment is at one end of a continuum, and that child abuse is at the other end (Gelles, 1973, 1975; Gil, 1970; Steinmetz, 1977a; Straus *et al.*, 1980). With increasing stress, physical punishment can easily develop into child abuse.

The data on reports of suspected child abuse can range from an optimistic 6,000 cases per year (Gil, 1970) to a more realistic 500,000 cases based on Light's reanalysis (1974) of Gil's data. Probably, the most accurate data for estimating child abuse are those provided by Straus *et al.* (1980), which are based on parents' reports of specific "disciplinary" techniques. Unfortunately, limiting the sample to intact families and collecting data only on preselected children between the ages of 3 and 17 eliminate the two populations most likely to experience child abuse: single-parent families, where stress, financial difficulties, and the lack of support and resources contribute to child abuse potential, and infants and toddlers, who are at greater risk for injuries requiring medical attention and, therefore, detection.

As a result, the estimates provided by Straus *et al.* (1980), although accurately reflecting abuse among intact families with posttoddler children, do not provide any insights into the abuse that occurs among single-parent families, nor into violence perpetrated on infants and toddlers, or by the noninterviewed parent, or on another child in the family. We do know that filicide is second to spousal homicide as the predominant form of fatal domestic violence. Although severe violence and filicide are not the predominant forms of parent–child violence, the frequency with which even these extreme forms of violence occur is astounding. Approximately 3 children in 100 are kicked, bitten, or punched by their parents during a single year, and 8 out of 100 experience these acts sometime during their childhood. Slightly more than 1 in 100 children were beaten up by a parent during the interview year; 4 in 100 had been beaten by a parent at some time; 1 child in 1,000 each year faces a parent who threatens to use a gun or knife; and nearly 3 children in 100 have grown up facing a parent who at least once threatened them with guns or knives. The same proportions hold for children who had guns and knives actually used on them.

With the exception of the acts "threatened" or "used a gun or knife," children whose parents were violent to them experienced this violence more than once. For example, children who had something thrown at them had it happen an average of 4.5 times, and children who were pushed or grabbed or shoved experienced that 6.6 times during the 12-month period. As expected, spanking and slapping were the most frequent: an average of 9.6 times a year. The average for kicks, bites and punches was 8.9 times a year, and children were hit with objects 8.6 times a year. For those who were beaten, the beating was repeated almost once every two months, an average of 5.9 times over the year. If a gun or knife was used, it happened "only" once in the survey year.

A resurvey conducted in 1985 found considerably lower rates of parent-to-child violence. A comparison of the rates obtained in 1975 with those obtained in 1985 revealed that the severe violence index (composed of the scores for kicked, bit, or hit with fist; hit or threaten to hit with something; beat up; threatened with gun or knife; and used a gun or knife) was nearly 24% lower in 1985. The very severe index—which was similar to the severe index except that the item "hit or tried to hit with something," which was considered ambiguous, was eliminated—was over 47% lower. Because the very severe violence index represents those acts that are most likely to result in child abuse, a 47% decrease in child abuse is quite dramatic and represents considerable gain in public awareness, education, services, and intervention programs aimed at reducing child abuse (see Table 5).

The violence seems to affect all ages of children: 82% of the 3- and 4-year-olds had had some mode of violence used on them; 82% of the children from 5 years old to 9 had been hit; two thirds (66%) of the preteens and early teenage children (10–14 years old) had been struck; and slightly more than one third (34%) of the children 15 to 17 years old had been hit by their parents (Straus, 1979a; Straus et al., 1980).

Even the most severe forms of parent–child violence are not single events. They occur periodically and even regularly in the families where these types of violence are used. If a beating is considered an indication of "child abuse," then child abuse appears to be a chronic condition for many children, not a rare experience for few.

Parent Abuse

Violence between parents and children is not a one-way interaction. Not only are children the recipients of violence, but children also perpetrate acts of violence of which the parents are the target. Clinical studies of parricide reveal many similarities.

In a study of children who killed a parent, Sargent (1962) reported that not only had the parents used extreme cruelty toward the child, but their cruelty was condoned by other family members. Other studies (Sadoff, 1971; Tanay, 1975) reveal that the victim parent was cruel and frequently beat other members of the family, especially the child's mother.

Compared with an adolescent who committed other types of homicide, an adolescent who murdered a parent was more likely to be chronically abused by his or her father and to have a mother who was abused by the father (Corder, Ball, Haizlip, Rollins, & Beaumont, 1976).

The only national study to examine violence between all family members interviewed 2,143 intact families, 608 of which had adolescent children between 10 and 17 years old (Straus et al., 1980). An in-depth analysis of these 608 families (Cornell-Pedrick & Gelles, 1982) revealed that 9% of the parents (2.5 million families) had experienced at least one attack, and that 3% (900,000 parents) had experienced severe violence: punching, kicking, biting, hitting with an object, being beaten up, or being threatened or attacked with a gun or a knife.

In both single-parent families (Warren, 1978) and intact families (Straus et al., 1980), mothers are more likely to be the victim and sons the perpetrators. Although Harbin and Madden (1979) failed to support the relationship between child abuse or spouse abuse and children who abused their parents, other studies (Cornell-Pedrick & Gelles, 1982; Schumn et al., 1982; Straus et al., 1980) did find this relationship. In fact, Cornell-Pedrick and Gelles reported:

The rate of adolescent to parent violence severity is directly related to the violence severity the child has experienced as well as directly related to the rates of interspousal violence severity. (p. 11)

Violence between Siblings

Sibling violence is probably considered normal childhood behavior by most. However, our complacency needs reexamination. Over 3% of the homicides that occurred in Philadelphia between 1948 and 1952 and 3% of the homicides in New York City in 1965 were sibling homicides (Bard, 1971; Wolfgang, 1958). Although these studies do not constitute nationally representative samples, the 3% rate of sibling homicide appears to be stable over time, and at least, it represents the rates for two large cities. Nationally, approximately 280, or 1.5%, of all reported homicides were between siblings in 1983 (U.S. Department of Justice, 1985).

Although the number of sibling homicides is less than the number of marital or filial homicides that occur during a given year, the national survey (Straus et al., 1980) revealed that, when severe (nonhomicidal) violence is examined with the use of the items "hit or threatened to hit with something," "beating up," and "threat" and "use of a knife or gun," sibling violence exceeds the level of violence that parents use on children or that spouses use on each other.

Sibling violence is not a new phenomenon. An eighteenth-century diary noted the following incident between two adolescent children:

"Before breakfast Nancy and Fanny had a fight about a shoe brush which they both wanted. Fanny pull'd off her shoe and threw it at Nancy, which missed her and broke a pane of glass. . . . They then enter'd upon scratching & c. which methods seem instinctive in women." (Fithian, 1945, pp. 349–350)

A study of college freshmen found that 62% reported that they had used physical violence on a sibling during the last year (Straus, 1971). Other studies, based on broad, nonrandom samples (Steinmetz, 1977b, 1982) and a random sample (Steinmetz, 1977a), found rates ranging from 64% to 78%.

Of the 2,143 families interviewed in the national survey (Straus *et al.*, 1980), 733 had two or more children between 3 and 17 years of age who were living at home. The study revealed that, during the survey year (1975), 75% reported using physical violence that averaged 21 acts per year: 42% of siblings kicked, bit, or punched; 16% beat each other up; .8% threatened to use a gun or a knife; and .3% used a gun or a knife. When we extrapolate these percentages to the 36.3 million children between ages 3 and 17 who have siblings, we find that 6.5 million children have been beaten up by a sibling and that nearly 2 million children, at sometime during their childhood, have faced a gun or a knife.

There were over 36 million attacks that would have been considered assault had they not occurred between siblings: in a single year, 5.8 million beaten up; 14.5 million hit with an object; 15.2 million kicked, bitten, or punched; 290,400 threatened with a gun or a kinfe; and 109,000 attacked with a gun or a knife.

Abuse of the Elderly

Although a great deal of research has been undertaken in the area of domestic violence during the last two decades, elder abuse has been virtually ignored until recently (see Kosberg, 1983, for a review of this topic).

Research has shown that the most frequent abusers of women and children are family members. Thus, it is not surprising that family members predominate as abusers of the elderly. In one study, although only 13% of service providers who responded to a mail survey had reported a case of elder abuse, 88% were aware of the problem (Block & Sinnott, 1979, 1980). Douglas, Hickey, and Noel (1980) found that 17% of their respondents in a similar survey of professionals had reported physical abuse of an elder, and 44% had reported verbal or emotional abuse. In a mail survey of over 1,000 medical personnel, social service professionals, and paraprofessionals, 183 reports of elder abuse were received, and 80% of this abuse was perpetrated by a family member (O'Malley, Segars, & Perez, 1979).

During a 12-month period, Family Service Association of Greater Lawrence, Massachusetts, received 82 referrals of elders suspected of being abused, being neglected, or being in a potentially threatening situation. On investigation, one fourth of those elders who were living with their family had experienced abuse or neglect (Langdon, 1980). In a single year, the Baltimore police reported 149 assaults against individuals 60 years old or older. They noted that nearly two thirds of these assaults (62.7%) had been committed by a relative other than the spouse (Block & Sinnott, 1980).

In the first eight months after passage of the Connecticut Elderly Protective Service Law, 87 cases of physical abuse, 314 cases of neglect, 65 cases of exploitation, and 8 cases of abandonment were reported (Block & Sinnott, 1980).

In a poll conducted by Louis Harris and Associates, 15% of the black and 19% of the white respondents reported that they knew a victim of elder abuse. However, 58% of the blacks (but only 36% of whites) interviewed considered elder abuse a "very serious" problem (Sourcebook of Criminal Justice Statistics, 1982).

The above studies did not limit the abuse to that occurring exclusively within the family. Furthermore, the data in these studies was reported by a third party (a social service agency, medical or legal personnel, police, or a protective service agency) and might reflect a somewhat limited awareness of the complexities involved.

To overcome this limitation in the research, an indepth interview of generationally inversed families (families in which adult children were fulfilling the parenting and caregiving role for their elderly parents) focused on the levels of dependency, stress, conflict, and abuse occurring between the adult child and the elder.

Using a nonrandom sample obtained through a snowball technique (Babbie, 1983), 104 caregivers responsible for 119 elders who met the following criteria were interviewed: the family shared a residence, and the elder was not a house guest or a visitor; the adult child performed some tasks for the elder so that there was some degree of dependency; the elder was over 55 years old; the caregiver was the adult responsible for the household; and if the elder was deceased, death had occurred within the preceding three years (Steinmetz, 1981a, 1984, in press; Steinmetz & Amsden, 1983).

The sample of elders was comprised of predominantly white women, of which 91% were 70 years or older, 85% had experienced diminished physical functioning, and 35% had been hospitalized within the last year. The abusive techniques used by the caregiving children ranged from screaming and yelling (30%), threatening to send the elder to a nursing home (8.5%), threats of physical force (4.5%), confinement to one room or ignoring the elder (5%), withholding or forcing food or medication as a control mechanism (17%), to more physically abusive acts such as restraining the elder (7.5%) and slapping, hitting, or shaking (2.5%). Overall, 12% of the caregivers had used physically abusive acts or the threat of physical violence in an attempt to maintain control. If one considers the abuse to one's dignity as well as the potential for injury resulting from forcing an elder to eat or take medicine (or giving medicine to make them easier to control), then 23%, or nearly 1 in 4 of the caregivers, used physically abusive ways to control their elderly parent or kin. This is in addition to the emotional trauma that a dependent elderly person might suffer from being yelled at or being threatened with being sent to a nursing home (Steinmetz, 1985).

The elderly attempted to maintain control over their environment in a number of ways: 34.5% yelled; 59.5% pouted; 37% cried; 60% manipulated through guilt or sympathy; 24.5% refused food or medication; and 18% hit, slapped, or threw something at the caregiver.

The elder's violence was highly correlated with a high level of dependence; the caregiver's violence was highly correlated with feelings of stress resulting from performing these ''dependency'' tasks and was family-related (Steinmetz, 1987, in press; Steinmetz & Amsden, 1983).

Families characterized by high levels of family-related stress (teenagers, small children, recent death, alcoholism, another family member with physical or emotional or mental problems, both spouses employed, single parenthood, or financial problems) had elder abuse scores that were more than five times higher than those of families with low levels of family stress.

Although the level of dependency (household, personal grooming and health, financial, mobility, social-emotional, and mental health) that an elder had on the caregiver was not highly correlated with abuse, those caregivers who perceived these tasks to be stressful had abuse scores that were 21 times higher than those of families who did not find providing these tasks to be stressful.

Variables and Theories

One of the major difficulties facing the social scientist is the untangling of the effect of one variable from another—a difficulty intensified because a family's day-to-day interaction cannot be studied in a controlled experimental setting. For example, the abused wife is often a member of a family that exhibits numerous characteristics (e.g., alcohol abuse, economic instability, an unplanned or unwanted pregnancy, and lack of resources) that produce a high level of stress and that have been shown to contribute to violence. How does the researcher, without the ability to manipulate family members, discover which of these variables is the major contributor or which variables interact to intensify the violence?

Although multivariate analysis can express the relative contribution of each variable, it does little to explain the overall process by which families increase or decrease their likelihood of experiencing abuse.

Theoretical frameworks and the models developed from these theories can often provide these links. A theoretical perspective predicts, in a logical fashion, the outcome of certain circumstances, attitudes, and behaviors. The choice of a theoretical perspective is important not only in attempting to understand the process by which family violence is initiated and maintained but, more important, in developing mechanisms to help families reduce or eliminate violence and hopefully to prevent it from occurring.

The three groups of theories described below provide a very brief synopsis of major theories being used to explain domestic violence (see Gelles & Straus, 1979, for an extensive review of theories of family violence). These groups are intraindividual, social-psychological, and social-cultural theories. Within each group of theories, the variable most frequently examined will be discussed.

These variables were selected for examination because they represent those most frequently used and most carefully documented. Numerous additional variables—especially those that contribute to stress, such as racial and ethnic discrimination, pregnancy, too many children, crowded living conditions, and marital instability—have also been found to contribute to family violence (see Gelles, 1980; Pagelow, 1984; Straus et al., 1980, for more comprehensive reviews of this research). Finally, a tri-level model of violence is proposed as a mechanism for interfacing the three levels of theories.

Intraindividual Theories and Variables

Intraindividual theories explain violence in terms of some characteristics of the individual actor. Gelles and Straus (1979) discussed psychopathological violence caused by an abnormality, an internal aberration, or a defect, and alcohol and drugs, which act as disinhibitors releasing the violent tendencies that exist in humans. Also, in this group are theories based on instinctual or organic factors, for example, genetic, chromosomal, hormonal, or medically linked violence. Although the psychopathological model was one of the earliest explanations of child abuse (Kempe et al., 1962; Steel & Pollock, 1968; Wasserman, 1967) and wife beating (Snell, Rosenwald, & Robey, 1964), this approach, as the sole cause, has been discredited (see Gelles, 1973; Steinmetz, 1978c; Walker, 1979).

The linking of violence to the XYY chromosome in males has been extensively documented (Lederberg, 1973; Shah, 1970). Although a large Danish study (Jarvik, Klodin, & Matsuyama, 1973; see Mednick, Van Dusen, Gabrielli, & Hutchings, 1982, for a review of these studies) found that low intelligence rather than aggressive personalities appeared to be related to the XYY male, it appears that it is the linking mechanism rather than the actual relationship between XYY and violence that has been articulated. The XYY chromosome tends to produce low intelligence, which, in turn, is correlated with low education, limited occupational opportunities, and increased frustration, which lead to antisocial behavior and violence.

Organic brain syndrome has been linked to episodic, violent outbursts, and clinical observations have found this violence to include domestic violence (Elliot, 1978, 1982; Monroe, 1970). Brain maturation lag is suggested as an explanation for the neurological etiology of violent behavior (Blackburn, 1975, 1980), and temporal lobe and psychomotor epilepsy and EEG abnormalities have been linked to violent and aggressive behavior (Benson & Blumer, 1975; Dossett, Burch, & Keller, 1982; Lewis, Pincus, Shanok, & Glaser, 1982; Williams, 1969).

The hormonal influence on violent behavior (usually the testosterone influence on males' behavior) has most recently been tied to the female hormones in the premenstrual syndrome. The premenstrual syndrome has been used successfully as a defense in France and England (Dalton, 1980), raising the specter of a return to the tactic of prohibiting women from working in certain jobs because of mental and emotional instability linked to their monthly cycle. However, this approach should not be overlooked as contributing to the behavior of a mother who is abusing her child. In fact, in a comprehensive review of the hormonal influence on violence Tardiff (1982), noted that studies found no such influence in "normal" individuals (i.e., no evidence of a relationship between violent behavior and hormonal levels), but relationships were found when the samples were composed of "violent" individuals. He noted that the hormonal levels may act as the straw that breaks the camel's back for individuals with other problems, stresses, and frustrations.

Mental Illness

Because of the incongruence between the view of the family as the unit that provides love, comfort, protection, and support and data that indicate the prevalence of violence between family members, we tend to look for a scapegoat to help us understand the use of extreme violence.

It is easy to comprehend why child abusers or wife batterers are labeled as mentally ill: obviously, normal people would not behave this way. Likewise, a battered wife is described as having psychiatric defects: Why else would she allow herself to become a victim? In this section, mental illness and psychiatric and personality disorders are used to explain victim characteristics as well as offender characteristics (i.e., mentally ill children as victims of abuse and mentally ill parents as abusers).

Child Abusers. Early studies of child abuse tended to attribute numerous psychiatric defects, such as depression, immaturity, impulsiveness, and dependency, to abusing parents (Elmer, 1971; Holter & Friedman, 1968; Steel & Pollock, 1974). For example, 48% of the mothers in one British study were described as being neurotic, and a high percentage of the fathers in this study were diagnosed as psychopaths (Kempe & Helfer, 1972). Although the above finding suggests that the parents' psychiatric disorders resulted in child abuse, the evidence to the contrary is overwhelming. Steel and Pollock (1968) noted that abusive parents did not exhibit excessive aggressive behavior in other areas of their lives and were not much different from a cross section of the general population. Kempe and Helfer (1972) stated that less than 10% of parents who abuse children are seriously mentally ill. Furthermore, electroencephalographic examination of abusive parents found no evidence of a relationship between child abuse and organic dysfunction (Smith, Honigsberger, & Smith, 1973).

From the empirical evidence, it appears that child abusers are no more and no less mentally ill or emotionally disturbed than any randomly selected group of parents. Being identified and labeled as a child abuser appears to be the major distinguishing feature. There are, however, differences in personality between abusive and nonabusive parents.

Comparisons of a matched sample of 65 abusing parents and 65 nonabusing parents found that the abusing parents were significantly more likely to score high on rigidity, unhappiness, and distress factors (i.e., easily upset, often frustrated, angry, mixed up, and rejected) than the nonabusing parents (Milner & Wimberley, 1980). Rosen (1979) compared the interpersonal values of 30 abusing and 30 nonabusing mothers and found that the abusing women valued conformity and benevolence or nurturance less and authority and power needs more than did nonabusing subjects. Six personality characteristics were found to be common to a group of 60 abusers: reliance on the child to satisfy dependency needs, poor impulse control, poor self-concept, disturbances in identity formation, feelings of worthlessness, and misperception of the child (see Sweet & Resnick, 1979, for a comprehensive discussion of this material).

Spouse Abuse. Interviews with 60 patients (38 women and 22 men) in a psychiatric hospital revealed that 48% had been involved in battering-spouse or battering-partner relationships (Post, Willett, Franks, House, Bach, & Weissberg, 1980). Of the females, 50% reported that they had been battered; 14% of the males had been battered; 21% of all these patients reported that they had battered their partners; and 12% had been both victims and perpetrators of spouse abuse.

In their study of 60 battered women, Hilberman and Munson (1977–1978) found that almost the entire sample of 60 women had sought medical help for stress-related complaints and that many evidenced symptoms commonly associated with the rape-trauma syndrome. More than half had evidence of prior psychological dysfunction, including classic depressive illness, schizophrenia, manic-depression, alcoholism, and severe character disorders, and 22% had been hospitalized because of violent psychotic behavior.

The generalizability of small clinical samples that lack control groups, coupled with the lack of description for the sequence of events, is a major problem in many of these studies: Was the "psychological dysfunction" the cause or the result of being abused, or were the abuse and the psychological dysfunction simply two variables in a multiproblem family?

There has been an assertion that, as certain types of women are more apt to be victims, and as these women often appear to avoid taking steps to resolve their problems, they are at fault for being abused. The assumption is made that all women can control their lives if they choose to. Research describing the personality characteristics of a battered wife often leaves an impression that these victims, by their own weaknesses, have enabled the battering to occur. A woman is likely to become a victim of spouse abuse when she displays the characteristics of a weak, vulnerable woman: she is isolated (Gelles, 1979; Prescott & Letko, 1977; Roy, 1977; Straus, 1977–1978); she is overcome by anxiety (Gelles, 1975; Prescott & Letko, 1977; Ridington, 1977–1978); and she is full of guilt and shame (Hilberman & Munson, 1977–1978; Resnick, 1976).

Some researchers suggest that, by changing the woman's social and economic resources, by increasing her education and job skills, by teaching her to be less submissive, by helping her to have a better self-concept, or by teaching her to interpret her husband's moods, the violence can be reduced. Although possessing these skills and resources may be a valid mechanism for helping a victim to escape from the battering environment at its onset or to decrease the likelihood of violence, those who suggest these remedies tend to assume that the battered woman has the ability to control her environment, and that not doing so implies a satisfaction with the status quo. This display of learned helplessness allows these women to be further victimized (Walker, 1977–1978).[3]

It is suggested that, contrary to the notion that the battered woman has personality characteristics or psychiatric conditions that "cause" her to be at risk of being beaten (e.g., she is poor, uneducated, anxious, weak, and lacks self-confidence), it is the dynamics of the beating itself that produce these manifestations (Steinmetz, 1979). This phenomenon is closely related to the processes involved in brainwashing: isolation from family, friends, and social support systems reinforces the victim's dependency on the abuser for confirmation of her worth. Unfortunately, the confirmation supports the woman's negative self-image, filling her with shame and guilt. In this "trapped" learned-helplessness state, even well-educated women with resources are unlikely to leave without intervention because they don't see these resources as valid mechanisms enabling them to leave.

Elder Abuse. In a report on caregivers who battered elderly relatives, it was found that 14% of the abusers were suffering from mental illness and that 2% had made a suicide attempt in the past (Bergman, O'Malley, & Segars, 1980). Stress was also a major contributor to elder abuse: 26% of the abusers had medical problems; 6% had suffered the loss of spouse; 2% had experienced the birth of a child; and 2% had experienced a recent death (Bergman *et al.*, 1980). Furthermore, 63% of the elders

were noted as a source of stress to the abusive caregivers (Bergman *et al.*, 1980): 48% responded that caregiving was stressful; 2% experienced financial stress; and 11% had severe physical and mental disabilities.

Steinmetz and Amsden (1983) investigated the relationship between stress, a sense of burden, the level of dependency, and abuse for 119 elders and their caregivers, usually adult children. The authors found strong and highly significant correlations between mental health dependency and elders' and caregivers' use of verbal and physical violence as a control mechanism. The elders' use of physical violence was also related to grooming, health care, mobility, and social-emotional dependencies. Only help with household tasks and transportation were not significant. Although the level of "task" dependency was related to abuse, the caregivers' report of being burdened was not. However, the caregivers' feelings of stress as a result of performing these tasks were related to abuse. The strongest relationships, however, were between the level of the elders' dependency and the elders' use of control. It appears that being dependent and observing (or being told by the caregiver) how stressful these tasks were was associated with disruptive, abusive behaviors (51 out of 154 possible relationships were significant).

Mental Retardation and Neurological Dysfunction

Although it is difficult to untangle cause and effect in the relationship between mental retardation and child abuse, Sandgrund, Gaines, and Green (1974) and Martin, Beezley, Conway, and Kempe (1974) have provided data to suggest that child abuse is a causal factor in mental retardation. Martin *et al.* determined that only 43% of a sample of children whose abuse did not include head trauma manifested neurological dysfunction, whereas 71% of a sample of abused children with skull fractures (suggesting more severe abuse) did exhibit evidence of neurological dysfunction. Sandgrund *et al.* (1974) noted that, whereas only 3% of children who were not abused or neglected were retarded, 20% of the neglected and 25% of the abused were retarded. These studies seem to indicate that the abuse produced the neurological dysfunctions.

In an investigation of 97 abused children, Johnson and Morse (1968) noted that nearly 70% of the children had exhibited either a mental or a physical handicap before the initial report of abuse. Gil (1970) noted that 27% of abused children had demonstrated a physical or intellectual abnormality in the year preceding the abusive incident. Green (1968) found that 23% of a sample of school-aged schizophrenic children had suffered abuse. Of one sample of abused children, 55% had an IQ below 80 (Elmer, 1977; Elmer & Gregg, 1967), and 43% of another group of abused children were retarded (Morse, Sahler, & Friedman, 1970). Unfortunately, these studies

---

[3]Recently, there has been a controversy over the removal of the diagnosis of "masochistic personality disorder" from the *Diagnostic and Statistical Manual of Mental Disorders* under pressure from feminists, primarily because it is indiscriminately used to inaccurately describe battered women who remain in a violent relationship. Although the objective may be noble, this action should be questioned on two fronts. First, the term replacing masochistic personality disorder, "self-defeating" personality disorder, will no doubt be used in a similarly indiscriminate manner to stigmatize battered women instead of providing them help. Second, should politics rather than science dictate medical and psychiatric definitions? As Simons, a psychoanalyst and a researcher on masochism, noted, "It is not scientifically valid to throw out a category merely because it might be misused" (see *Time,* Dec. 2, 1985, p. 76).

do not assess the sequence of the retardation and the abusive behavior.

Furthermore, caution must be interjected into these findings. The general knowledge of abuse and the reporting of child abuse during the period in which these studies were conducted were questionable; thus, the *initial report* of abuse may not be the same incident as the initial abusive attack. It is possible that abuse was detected because the child was receiving special services for a mental or physical problem.

Other researchers have suggested that retarded children may be more "abuse-prone" or that they become the victims of scapegoating because neurological dysfunctioning results in atypical behavior that is difficult to control, does not meet parental expectations, and does not reinforce positive parent–child interaction. Evidence on congenital defects provides support of the theory that, at least in some cases, the infant's characteristics are a major contributing factor (see Frodi, 1981, for a review of this literature).

An analysis of 14,083 abused children found that 12% of these children had problems that could make fulfillment of the parents' expectations difficult, such as mental retardation, premature birth, chronic illness, a physical handicap, congenital birth defects, and severe emotional problems (Soeffing, 1975). However, this percentage does not appear to differ from the percentage of children with problems found in nonabused populations. Thus, the question of causal link—whether "problem" children are targets for abuse, or whether abused children develop problems—is not sufficiently answered.

These data suggest that, whereas severe abuse contributes to neurological dysfunction, children who exhibit behavior that is perceived as being abnormal by the parents are also likely to be candidates for abuse. In fact, Friedrich and Borisking (1976) suggested that it is not necessary for the child to be abnormal: the parents' perception of the child as abnormal can be sufficient to instigate abuse of the child.

Being abused can result in personality traits that may increase the likelihood of further abuse. Kinard (1980) compared 30 children who had been physically abused at least one year earlier with a control group matched in age, sex, race, birth order, the number of children in the family, parental structure, SES, and the type of residence and neighborhood. Although a battery of psychological tests revealed small differences in self-concept, the abused children were more unhappy, nonconforming, extrapunitive, and aggressive in child–child relationships (but not in parent–child relationships) than the nonabused children.

Premature Infants

In a comprehensive review of the contributions of infants' characteristics to child abuse, Frodi (1981) noted that mental, physical, and behavioral abnormalities increase the child's potential for being abused. The baby's crying, which was perceived by mothers of premature or atypical infants as an aversive stimulus, often triggered abusive behavior.

Parent–child interaction is a reciprocal rather than a unidirectional process. Infants or children who deviate from parental expectations in physical appearance, behavior, or potential are at greater risk of abuse than are children who fulfill parental expectations. As premature babies are more likely to be restless, distractible, and difficult to care for than full-term babies, and as they are usually absent from the mother after birth, at a time when bonding occurs (Mussen, Conger, & Kagen, 1974), prematurity may increase the likelihood of abuse. In an examination of a sample of 20 battered children, Elmer and Gregg (1967) found that one third of them had been premature. In their study of 88 battered children, Klein and Stern (1971) noted that over 12% were premature, and that over 23% of another sample of 51 battered children had had low birth weight, a relationship also reported by other researchers (Fomuford, Sinkford, & Louy, 1975; Martin *et al.*, 1974).

Leiderman (1974) found significant differences in both attitudes and behaviors between mothers of premature infants and mothers of full-term infants. Fanaroff, Kennell, and Klaus (1972) analyzed the visiting patterns of mothers of low-birth-weight infants. Of 146 mothers, 38 visited their babies less than three times in a two-week period. A follow-up investigation identified 11 cases of failure to thrive; in 9 of these cases, the mothers had been in the infrequent visiting group. The concerns with causal links raised earlier also need to be considered in these studies.

Social-Psychological Theories

Social-psychological theories examine the interaction of the individual with the social environment and with other individuals, groups, and organizations. The major theories to be discussed in this section are frustration–aggression, social-learning and role-modeling, symbolic interaction, exchange and resource, and conflict theories.

Frustration–Aggression Theory

The application of frustration–aggression theory to family violence contains two modifications of the original theory: (1) viewing the expression of aggression as a response to the emotion that the individual feels when some goal is blocked and (2) viewing aggression as a response to frustration as the product of learning rather than of an innate drive. Dollard, Miller, Doob, Mowrer, and Sears (1939) hypothesized that the strength of inhibitions against an act of aggression increases with the amount of punishment anticipated by the child as a consequence of that act. Thus, physical punishment would inhibit the child's aggression. However, the frustration–aggression theory would also predict that the physical violence used to control the child's behavior is experienced as a frustration and as a generator of anger, which produces still further aggression in the child.

A reconciliation of these opposing predictions is provided by an examination of the findings from research based on this theory. These data suggest that a curvilinear relationship exists between physical punishment and aggression (Steinmetz, 1978b). It appears that low amounts of physical punishment provide a nonaggressive model for girls to follow, whereas high physical punishment extinguishes aggressiveness. For boys, low physical punishment apparently does not provide enough control, whereas high punishment increases the frustration, both of which conditions result in aggressiveness. Moderate physical punishment for boys provides a balance between control and nonfrustration. The above findings are limited to mother–daughter and father–son interaction.

Social-Learning and Role-Modeling Theories

Social-learning theory, which views violence as a learned phenomenon, has received support in studies using a laboratory setting (Bandura, 1973; Bandura, Ross, & Ross, 1961; Bandura & Walters, 1963; Singer, 1971); in survey research on family interaction (Owens & Straus, 1975; Patterson, Cobb, & Ray, 1973; Steinmetz, 1977a,b); and in clinical studies (Climent & Ervin, 1972; Steel & Pollock, 1968; Wasserman, 1967). The social-learning and role-modeling theories assume that children learn violent behavior when they see their parents, or significant others, resolving problems by means of violence. They then model this role of violent interpersonal interactions when they themselves become parents.

Although social-learning theory, specifically as it explains learned helplessness, has been used to describe the processes of battering (Walker, 1979), Steinmetz (1979) differentiated between "Saturday night brawlers" (typified by reciprocally escalating, violent interaction, with either spouse likely to be the victim in a given fight) and the "chronic battered syndrome" (characterized by powerlessness, intense fear on the part of the victim, and repeated, intense battering by the perpetrator). The Saturday night brawlers' interactions are illustrated by the following quote:

We would get into a big argument and I would just keep needling and pushing until he would slap me to shut me up.
Interviewer: Did you shut up?
No, I would hit back. It just ended up in a bigger argument.
(Steinmetz, 1977a, p. 25)

The dynamics that produce the chronic battered syndrome parallel the techniques used in brainwashing: fear of further beatings to control behavior; isolation from family and friends because of embarrassment and concern over involving them; guilt because the victim sees herself as being at fault and as deserving to be abused; emotional dependency on the abuser; and lack of support from family, friends, and professionals, further reinforcing the victim's total dependency on the abuser. It is unusual for these women to retaliate during the attack because of fear of further escalation. In fact, they will go to great lengths to avoid confrontation or escalation, as described in the quote below:

As soon as my husband and I got into bed, he resumed the intimidation. When he got to his most terrifying threat, one that I had heard repeated so many times, that I knew it by heart, I knew that there was no turning back, so I reached under the bed and pulled the statue [which had been removed from the mantle earlier that evening] up with me so I would be prepared. All the while, I was entreating him to stop talking and go to sleep. I assured him that we could talk more in the morning. I told him how frightened I became when he spoke so. Undeterred, he seized me by my hair, and drew back to hit me. His blow never landed. I hit him first. He fell back into the pillows. Stunned for a minute, I realized that I would have to hit him again. He had told me many times that if I ever hit him, I would have to kill him, because if I did not, he would kill me. (Myers, 1978 pp. 174–175)

Symbolic Interaction Theory

Symbolic interaction theory is concerned with the processes involved in defining the act of violence. Gelles (1974) and Steinmetz (1977a) have suggested that the perspective of the individual is an important component of this process. The individual's perception of the family relationship has been a critical factor in child abuse (Friedrich & Borisking, 1976); family interaction (Niemi, 1974); suicide (Lester, 1968); and family violence (Steinmetz, 1977a). Not just the interaction itself but also the symbolic interpretation placed on the act must be considered. For example, a slap may be labeled as unacceptable violence by one wife who seeks help from a crisis center, whereas a two-minute beating is viewed as a loss of temper not worthy of mentioning by another wife.

Exchange and Resource Theory

Exchange theory asserts that marital interaction is governed by an attempt to maximize rewards and to minimize costs. Therefore, violence would be used to restore distributive justice when the costs are perceived by one individual as exceeding the rewards.

In some ways, this theory is similar to resource theory, in which violence is used as a resource to gain one's wishes in a manner similar to money, status, and the individual's personal attributes. Goode (1971) hypothesized that the greater the nonviolent resources available to an individual, the more force that individual has the ability to use, but the less he or she will actually deploy overtly. Thus, violence is used as a resource when all else fails or is perceived to have failed. Gelles (1976) reported that the fewer the resources a woman has, the more likely she is to remain with a severely abusive husband.

Conflict Theory

A conflict theory of violence assumes that conflict is an inevitable part of all dyads or groups characterized by positions of dominance and submission (which may be reversed with each new interaction) and competing goals. Because the family can be viewed as an arena of confrontation and conflicting interests (Sprey, 1969), violence is a likely outcome and a powerful mode of advancing one's interests when all others fail. Important to an understanding of a conflict theory approach to violence is Weber's clarification (1947) of the terms *authority* ("the probability that a command with a given specific content will be obeyed by a given group of persons") and *power* ("the probability that one actor within a social relationship will be in a position to carry out his own will despite resistance, regardless of the basis on which this probability rests." (cited by Dahrendorf, 1959, p. 166). Confrontations within the family often occur when an individual has the authority but not the power to demand certain behavior. Numerous reports exist of parents severely battering an infant who would not stop crying or a toddler who would not stop wetting the bed. These parents felt that their authority was being questioned by the child, and that they lacked the power to control the child's undesirable behavior.

A widespread example of incongruity between authority and power occurs when parents of teenagers realize that, although they still have the legal authority to "control" the child, they most likely do not have the "power" to carry out their desires if the child rebels (Steinmetz, 1977a). When this happens, parents resort to physical violence (Bachman, 1967; Steinmetz, 1971, 1974; Straus, 1971). This authority without power has also been offered as an explanation of marital conflict and wife beating (Allen & Straus, 1979; Kolb & Straus, 1974; O'Brien, 1971).

Variables Used in Social-Psychological Theories

The major variables used by social-psychological theorists are social class and the components of social class (income, education, employment status, and the occupational environment), alcohol, age, and stage in the life cycle.

Alcohol

Wertham (1972), Gil (1970), and Young (1964) found a relationship between the use of alcohol and child abuse. Alcohol was also found to be closely linked to wife beating (Coleman & Straus, 1979; Gelles, 1974; Prescott & Letko, 1977; Roy, 1977). MacAndrew and Edgerton (1969) suggested that the effects of alcohol on social behavior are influenced by cultural expectation and socialization. Thus, in some societies, the use of alcohol is associated with considerable violence, whereas in others, no relationship exists. In still other societies, violence is associated with alcohol, but only under certain circumstances. An example of this cultural effect is Finland's high level of alcoholism (Wiseman, 1975), yet relatively low level of spouse abuse (see Table 6). Several researchers (Gelles, 1974; Straus *et al.*, 1980) have noted the difficulty of ascertaining the actual sequence: Do men drink, lose control, and then beat their wives? Or do men wish to vent their anger on their wives and drink in order to gain the courage to do so and to provide an excuse for their action? Gelles (1974) suggested that the association between alcohol and violence reflects the process of deviance disavowal: men get drunk in order to have an excuse for their abusive behavior toward their wives.

In a study of 139 persons appearing in family court during three months in 1974 in Hamilton, Ontario, 52% reported physical assaults on their wives, 10% reported assaults on their children, and 46% reported a problem with alcohol (Bayles, 1979). The probability of violence was .74 when alcohol was a major problem and only .31 when alcohol was not viewed as a major problem. Of a sample of abusers of the elderly (Bergman *et al.*, 1980), 28% were reported to be alcohol or drug abusers.

Unfortunately, much of the literature linking alcohol and family violence is subjective, being based on verbal declarations of the abuser or on observations by the victim or a third party, rather than on chemical blood-alcohol levels and an in-depth investigation of all the drinking behavior of the abuser. When this lack of systematic investigation is compounded by the definitional problems of abuse noted earlier (alcohol is almost always associated with physical abuse or neglect rather than with sexual abuse), the relationship becomes spurious. In a comprehensive review of alcohol and child abuse studies, Orme and Rimmer (1981) reported that it was not possible, given the current empirical studies, to establish that the incidence of child abuse among alcoholics is higher than the incidence of child abuse in the general population.

There are difficulties in defining alcoholism. Of the 25 studies examined, 15 had no definition, and the remainder were not specific (e.g., "intoxicated," "excessive drinking," "parents were heavy drinkers") and varied according to the reporter's perception. In summing up their examination, Orme and Rimmer (1981), in an exhaustive review of the literature, stated that they "found no adequate empirical data to support the association between alcoholism and child abuse" (p. 284). In fact, estimates of alcoholism and alcohol problems in the general population appear to be identical to estimates of these problems in the child-abusing population. Furthermore, correlation is not evidence of causation. It appears that authorities have linked one deviant act (excessive drinking) with another (child abuse) and have assumed a causal relationship.

Coleman and Straus (1979) found a curvilinear relationship between the frequency of drunkenness and marital abuse in a nationally representative sample of 2,143 families. Although about 2% of the husbands who "rarely" drank were severely violent and about 18% of those who were "almost always" drunk were likewise violent, those most likely to be violent were those who were "often drunk" (31%). A similar pattern was found for women. Although alcohol may act as a disinhibitor of control, with an increase it becomes a debilitating factor, lessening the ability or the desire to use violence.

Unfortunately, the problems in this study are similar to those noted above: drunkenness and its frequency are based on the respondents' recollections and their perception of the meaning of these terms. Furthermore, although we know the likelihood of both events' occurring in a family, the causal link can not be ascertained.

Age and Stage in the Life Cycle

Spouse Abuse. O'Brien (1971) found that violence was spontaneously mentioned in 64% of longer duration marriages and in 36% of shorter duration marriages. In an examination of 150 cases of battered women, Roy (1977) found that the violence first peaked between 2.5 and 5 years of marriage. Unfortunately, the findings are sparse and inconclusive. Is violence mentioned more frequently in longer duration marriages because of the greater number of opportunities for conflict and stress to have reached the violent stage? Or does violence occur early in a marriage, and for most couples, either the violence is stopped or the marriage dissolved? In marriages of longer duration, is the battered wife (or husband) trapped in a violent home?

Child Abuse. In a national study, Straus *et al.* (1980) found that over 80% of those under 30 years old were more likely than those older to consider the slapping and spanking of 12-year-olds necessary, normal, and good. Less than 66% of the group 50 years and older supported this view. Still, approximately two-thirds of the population over 50 held a view that is contrary to a large body of research, as well as to popular advice on child rearing.

Straus *et al.* (1980) reported that the use of violence on children decreased as both the children and the parents matured. During the survey year, 86% of children 5 to 9 years old, 54% of children 10 to 14 years old, and about 33% of children 15 to 17 years old had been hit by their parents. These data are consistent with earlier reports by Gil (1970), in which over 28% of abuse incidents involved youths over 12 years of age, and by the American Humane Association (1978), which reported approximately 36% of abuse and neglect cases involving 10- to 18-year-olds. Furthermore, 21% of parents under 30 years old, 13% of parents 31 to 50 years old, and 4% of those 51 to 65 years old used abusive violence on a child. No parents 65 or older used abusive violence on a child, perhaps because of the ages of their "children" (30–40 years old), rather than a change in their child-rearing philosophy.

Elder Abuse. The frail or "vulnerable" elderly are those most likely to be abused. Of the abuse reported by professionals, 36% of the victims were 80 years or older, 19% were 75 to 80 years old, 17% were 70 to 74, and 18% were 65 to 69. The elders reporting the smallest percentage of abuse (9%) were those between 60 and 65 years old (Bergman *et al.*, 1980).

By comparing the proportion of abuse citings in each age group with the total population of each group of elders based on national census statistics, Bergman *et al.* (1980) found that a proportionally greater number of elders 75 years or older were abused than were the younger age groups, those between 60 and 75. Apparently, not only is caring for a vulnerable elder (75 years or older) more stressful to the caregiver, but any resulting neglect and abuse is likely to have more detrimental effects than similar acts would have on a younger person.

Social Class

Social class is probably one of the most commonly used variables in family violence research. Based on the definition used and the indices or measures that comprise "social class," different relationships will be found. When a working-class–middle-class or blue-collar–white-collar classification based on type of occupation is used, slightly higher levels of violence are found among blue-collar workers. However, if the components of SES (i.e., type of job, educational level, and income) are examined separately, the data are inconsistent.

Possibly, one of the earliest myths to be examined was the class myth of family violence (Steinmetz & Straus, 1973). Current studies have verified the existence of family violence in all social classes and suggest that the almost exclusive representation of working-class and lower-class child abusers noted by Blumberg (1964–1965), Gil (1970), Holter and Friedman (1968), and Elmer (1971) may have resulted from the practice, in earlier research, of using medical facilities to obtain the study populations. An underrepresentation of reported violence in middle-class families may be a consequence of the privacy surrounding middle-class acts and the services used by middle-class families. Whereas middle- and upper-class families have access to private social support systems (such as family counselors, private doctors, ministers, and lawyers, who maintain the privacy of the professional relationship) lower-class families must rely on social control agencies such as the police, social service or family court workers, and clinics—agencies that keep "public" records. Newberger, Reed, Daniel, Hyde, and Kotelchuck (1977) found that lower-class and minority children with injuries are more likely to be labeled as abused than middle- and upper-class children. Even when the injury level was held constant in mock cases presented to physicians in which the race and the class of the family was varied, the physicians were more likely to label minority or lower-class children as abused (Turbett & O'Toole, 1980).

Although social class differences, when categorized by the middle-class–working-class dichotomy, are small, with working-class individuals tending to use more violence, the individual variables of income, occupation, and education that form the basis of most SES indicators are not consistently in the direction of this relationship. Perhaps because the middle-class–working-class dichotomy is broad, subtle differences are lost.

Blue-Collar–White-Collar. The most common social class categorization is blue-collar–white-collar. Using this broad categorization of working-class–middle-class, we find that, although violence occurs in all social classes, blue-collar status predicts a somewhat greater level of family violence for both males and females (Steinmetz, 1977a; Straus *et al.*, 1980). It may be that this classifications system reflects broad, class-based differences, such as the middle class's use of more efficient communication skills because of the desirability of mediation and compromise rather than overt aggression (Johnson & Morse, 1968). As the inability to communicate is highly related to physical violence between spouses (Prescott & Letko, 1977; Steinmetz, 1977b), it may also contribute to the differences in levels of family violence with respect to social class.

Income. The link between income levels and violence may be primarily an indirect one that provides families with resources useful for mediating many stress-producing and potentially violent situations. Greater financial resources enable parents to procure stress-reducing mechanisms, such as baby-sitters, vacations, nursery schools, and camps, which provide them with "time out" from child-rearing and homemaking responsibilities, thus possibly preventing or reducing violence.

When physical or medical problems arise, possessing a higher income enables one to secure medical and psychological help from a private physician. Prescott and Letko (1977) found that wives of professional men were four times more likely to have contacted a therapist than wives of men in low-status jobs. This finding may reflect a greater awareness of the availability of this resource as well as an income that enabled these expenditures.

Garbarino's study (1976) of 58 counties in New York State analyzed the rates of reported child abuse in relation to socioeconomic and demographic characteristics and found that socioeconomic stress and inadequate resources accounted for a significant amount of the variance (46%) in rates of child abuse.

Finally, mothers in higher-income families have greater access to contraception and abortion, which enables them to have greater control over family size and spacing, a factor related to family conflict and violence (Farrington, 1977; Johnson & Morse, 1968; Straus, 1976; Young, 1964). Among Gil's abused families (1970), 40% had 4 or more children, and in Johnson and Morse's sample (1968) of 101 abused children, 35% were from families with 4 or more children.

In general, there is a consistent decrease in violence as income levels go up. With family incomes under $6,000,

53% of families reported abuse between siblings, 22% reported child abuse, and 11% reported wife and/or husband abuse. In contrast, of those families with incomes of $20,000 and over, 41% reported sibling violence, 11% reported child abuse, and 2% each reported husband and wife abuse (Straus *et al.*, 1980).

Financial pressures resulting from inadequate income were found to contribute to elder abuse. In one study of elder abuse, 23% of caregivers reported that they had financial problems, and 16% were listed as long-term financial problems (Bergman *et al.*, 1980): 27% earned less than $5,200, and 23% earned between $5,200 and $9,000; thus, 50% had extremely low incomes.

An adequate income can ameliorate some conditions of family violence by purchasing services (counseling, medication, child care, household help, and vacations) that reduce the stress and frustration of day-to-day care.

Education. Education is usually considered one of the major components of social class. It defines the range of occupations that one is qualified for and thus is closely linked to income (from the job) and prestige (obtained by working in a given job). Steinmetz (1977a) found that a husband's education showed a strong negative correlation with spousal violence and father–child violence, and that a wife's education showed a similar relationship to spousal violence but virtually no relationship to mother–child violence. Gelles's finding (1974) of an inverse relationship between husbands' educational levels and violence was consistent with that noted by Steinmetz. However, although Gelles noted rather high levels of violence among college graduates, in the national data (Straus *et al.*, 1980) there were fewer college graduates who were offenders or victims of spousal violence, and college graduates were the least violent parents.

Whereas other studies tended to find a negative relationship between education and violence, Straus *et al.* (1980), when they categorized education into four levels (eighth grade or below, some high school, high-school graduate, and college), did not support this finding. For both men and women, there was a positive relationship between the first three levels of education and child abuse (11%, 15%, and 18% for men; 12%, 14%, and 17% for women). It was only among those parents who had been exposed to college that a decrease in child-abuse rates occurred: 11% for both men and women.

A curvilinear relationship also appeared for spouse abuse. Among high-school dropouts, the highest rates of both violence and victimization were found: 6% of both husbands and wives reported being abused, and 7% of both males and females reported being violent toward a spouse. However, those with eighth-grade or less education were less likely to be violent (3% abused their wives, and 4% abused their husbands) or to be victims of violence (4% were abused husbands, and 5% were abused wives). For those with a high-school education, 4% of husbands and wives were abused, and 4% of both had been abusers. However, the impact of a college education on the probability of victimization is noteworthy. Whereas a college education reduced the likelihood of a woman's victimization (only 2% of college-educated women in the sample were abused), it increased the likelihood of victimization for men (5% of college-educated men were abused). One can speculate on the reasons for these differences: Does a college education require a renegotiation of the traditional sex roles, a renegotiation that may, temporarily, result in conflict and violence? Are college-educated males less ''macho'' and/or better at verbal communication and therefore less inclined to use physically violent ways to resolve conflicts? Are college-educated females more aggressive, more strong-willed, and/or less likely to automatically take the submissive role in a marriage? Or are college-educated couples more likely to remember or define as violent, acts of physical aggression, those that may be overlooked among less-educated families as violent?

Employment Status. The employment status of the husband–father and satisfaction with occupational or homemaking roles are also predictors of family violence. Unemployment is often perceived by males as incompetency in fulfilling their provider role, and it has been linked to child abuse and wife beating. Gil (1970) reported that nearly half (48%) of the fathers in his sample of abusers had experienced unemployment during the year preceding the abuse. McKinley (1964) found that the lower the job satisfaction, the higher the percentage of fathers who used severe corporal punishment—a relationship that was not affected by social class.

A study of battered women who replied to a request for information in *Ms.* magazine reported that husbands who were unemployed or who were employed part time were extremely violent, compared with husbands who were employed full time (Prescott & Letko, 1977). Although this sample was a nonrepresentative sample, a national survey (Straus *et al.*, 1980) found similar results: a consistently lower level of child and spouse abuse among families where the husband was employed full time. Furthermore, part-time employment was more likely to predict family violence than was unemployment.

Also related to the use of violence are job satisfaction and perceived inability to fulfill the breadwinner–head-of-household role (Levinger, 1966; O'Brien, 1971; Prescott & Letko, 1977). Because middle- and upper-class parents are usually better educated, they are more likely to have fulfilling jobs and to have the flexibility to change jobs. They are also likely to reside in larger, more comfortable homes and to have adequate resources for carrying out the homemaker and child-rearing roles. As a result, parents in the middle and upper classes are less likely to be locked into unfulfilling jobs in the marketplace and in the home.

Occupational Environment. Occupational environment, a concept that focuses on the tasks and the ideology inherent in specific occupations, was found to predict,

with more accuracy than social class, the parents' use of violence on their children (Steinmetz, 1971, 1974). This same idea is supported in studies of police attitudes, which found that police showed no evidence of abnormal aggressiveness or rebellious tendencies (Neiderhoffer, 1967; Skolnick, 1969) or sadistic or authoritarian attitudes or behavior (MacNamara & Sagarin, 1971). It appears that it is not the individual who selects law enforcement as a career, but the training and the job itself that produce punitive, authoritarian, and violent behavior. Shwed (1979) found similar results for military personnel: the ideology and goals of the unit (not just the tasks that the individuals actually performed) predicted the levels of violence used.

Sexual Inequality and Social Status. Because sexual inequality has been considered a major force behind the abuse of wives, reducing sexual inequality is considered necessary in order to reduce wife abuse (Dobash & Dobash, 1979; Martin, 1976). However, some researchers (Steinmetz & Straus, 1974; Whitehurst, 1974) suggest that violence may actually increase as women strive to obtain greater income, power, and status, while men attempt to maintain their dominant position in these areas. Steinmetz and Straus (1974) suggested:

> It will not be until a generation of men and women reared under egalitarian conditions and subscribing to equalitarian rather than male-superiority norms takes over that we can expect to see a reduction in violent encounters between spouses. In the meantime, the conflict between the emerging equalitarian social structure and the continuing male superiority norms will tend to increase rather than decrease conflict and violence between husbands and wives. (p. 76)

Straus (1976) suggested that the ''long-run'' consequences may be to lessen the frequency of wife abuse, but that the ''short-run'' impact may actually be to increase violence because many men may not easily give up their traditional role of dominance.

Using American states as a unit of analysis, Yllo (1983) obtained measures for the economic status of women, their educational accomplishments, their role in politics, and the laws protecting women's rights. The relationship between the overall status of women and the levels of violence, as measured by the CTS (Straus *et al.,* 1980), was curvilinear; violence is highest in those states where the status of women is lowest, and violence decreases as status improves, but violence increases in states in which the status of women is the highest. This relationship was not affected by measures of urbanization, statewide levels of education, or the state level of violent crime, and it was only slightly affected by state levels of income.

In addition to the husband's and the wife's occupational, educational, and financial achievement and their social status, the compatibility of their statuses is important. Status inconsistency (inconsistent educational and occupational attainment) and status incompatibility (husband and wife with unequal status) were found to predict marital violence (Hornung, McCullough, & Sugimoto, 1981). Although both status inconsistency and status incompatibility in general increase psychological abuse, physical aggression, and life-threatening violence, certain types of status inconsistency (e.g., a husband's occupational underachievement) and status incompatibility (e.g., a woman's high-status occupation relative to her husband's) are particularly likely to result in severe marital violence.

Sociocultural Theories

Sociocultural theories of violence focus on the macro-level of analysis and include systems theory, functional theory, structural theory, culture theory, Marxist theory, and feminist theory (Gelles & Straus, 1979).

Systems Theory

Systems theory views the family as a goal-seeking, purposive, adaptive system and focuses on the processes by which family violence occurs and is maintained (see Straus, 1973, for a carefully developed systems theory of family violence and Giles-Sims, 1983, for application of systems theory to wife abuse). Olson, McCubbin, Barnes, Larsen, Muxen, and Wilson (1983) used two major systems-theory concepts to describe communication in the family that are useful for explaining family violence: *morphogenesis* (the positive feedback that enables the family system to grow, innovate, and change) and *morphostasis* (negative feedback that attempts to maintain the status quo), consisting of *consensual morphostasis,* or genuine stability, and *forced morphostasis,* maintained by force or coercion or power. Olson *et al.* noted:

It is hypothesized that when there is a more free-flowing balance between morphogenesis and morphostasis, there will be a mutually assertive type of communicating, egalitarian leadership, successful negotiation, positive and negative feedback loops, role sharing and role making, and rule making with few implicit rules and more explicit rules. Conversely, dysfunctional family systems will fall at the extremes of these variables. (p. 62)

Whitchurch (in press) noted that in a battering relationship, it appears that violent couples do not engage in a mutually assertive type of communicating, egalitarian leadership, or role sharing or role making, which would be possible only if a free-flowing balance between morphogenesis and morphostasis existed. Systems theorists have focused almost exclusively on morphogenic forces, ignoring morphostatic forces. A communication approach would facilitate an understanding of these negative interpersonal interactions.

Some attempts have been made to categorize couples and families according to their use of verbal and physical violence: Steinmetz has divided battering couples into "Saturday night brawlers" and "chronic battered women" based on the mutual versus one-sided use of verbal

and physical violence, and she has divided families into four categories based on the use of physical and verbal violence[4]; and Cuber and Harroff (1965) described "conflict-habituated" marriages of at least 10 years, characterized by controlled levels of tension and conflict. Whitchurch (in press) suggested that Olson, Sprenkle and Russell's circumplex model (1979), with the 16 categorizations, and the FACES instrument designed to operationalize the model might provide new insights not possible in these rough categorizations. As an example, she suggested that the "rigidly enmeshed" family type may well be those families described as having chronic battered syndrome, and she noted that male-batterer dyads may be quite different in family type than female-batterer or mutually combatant dyads. Finally, communication may be the crucial factor describing the rigidity of violent dyads, as well as the key to unlocking the dynamics of violent interpersonal relationships.

Functional Theory

The functional theory asserts that violence is important in maintaining the adaptability of the family. Coser (1967) noted that violence can serve three positive functions. First, it provides an area of achievement for an individual, such as violence or compulsive masculinity, as illustrated in Brown (1965) and Toby (1966). Second, violence can also act as a danger signal for the community, as in current debates over comparable worth in computing wage levels for males and females. Third, violence can act as a catalyst for change. For example, horrifying, extremely sadistic accounts of child abuse stirred the public consciousness to support state laws for dealing with child abuse, as well as the federal Child Abuse Prevention and Treatment Act. Publicizing the ordeals faced by beaten wives has been instrumental in instituting state legislation to provide protection from abuse, as well as services for victims and their children.

Variants of a functional perspective include Bakan's belief (1971) that child abuse, especially infanticide, serves as a population control mechanism. Although is doubtful that the 2,000 reported deaths per year from child abuse (Besharov, 1975) can be considered a population-control measure in contemporary society, infanticide was a very effective population control mechanism in the past (Radbill, 1968).

Another variant of this theory, identified as the catharsis theory, postulates the necessity of "moderate vi-

[4]Four different types of family problem-solving modes were described: "screaming sluggers," families that were both highly verbally and physically aggressive; "silent attackers," families who are not verbally aggressive but use high amounts of physical aggression; "threateners," families who use verbal aggression, but are low users of physical aggression; and "pacifists," families who use low amounts of both verbal and physical aggression.

olence'' in order to release pent-up frustration and hostility, thus reducing the likelihood of severe violence. Although this position has not been supported by research in child rearing (Bandura & Walters, 1963) or husband–wife interaction (Straus, 1974), it continues to form the basis of treatment offered by some family therapists (Bach & Wyden, 1968), in which freely expressing controlled, lower-level violence is seen as a mechanism for preventing explosive, violent interaction as a result of ''stored-up'' anger.

A third variant of functional theory is sociobiology. Developed from the work of ethnologists, a sociobiological perspective would explain the higher rates of child neglect or abuse among handicapped, foster, or adopted children as a lack of parental bonding between parent and child resulting from the inability of these offspring to continue the genetic line of the parents.

Structural Theory

A structural theory of violence identifies the source of violence as the differential distribution of violence-producing factors such as stress, frustration, and deprivation. Therefore, one would expect a greater prevalence of family violence among certain groups, such as those who live in poverty, with large numbers of children, and in crowded living quarters.

Cultural Theory

The culture-of-violence theory suggests that the differential distribution of violence is a function of cultural norms and values concerning violence (Wolfgang & Ferracuti, 1967). This theory predicts that a greater degree of violence would occur in those families belonging to a culture or a subculture in which socialization practices are deeply embedded in violence, rather than resulting from an excess of deprivation and stress, or from the lack of alternative resources for resolving a conflict.

The image of machismo among Latin males has often been used as an example of cultural attitude toward the appropriateness of violence. Wolfgang and Ferracuti (1967) found that groups with high rates of homicide were also characterized by extremely high rates of rape and aggravated assault, which constitute evidence of a subculture of violence.

Marxist Theory

The Marxist approach sees the source of violence as an economic and political phenomenon. Women are an oppressed economic class deprived of economic control, political power, and status. They are victimized by the patriarchial, capitalistic system, which fosters control of the oppressed (female) class by their oppressors. Violence, as a male's mechanism of controlling females, is a logical extension of this theory.

Feminist Theory

Although feminist theory is closely identified with Marxist theory, Jaggers and Struhl (1978) delineated several feminist perspectives, some of which are not necessarily Marxist in philosophy. An example of the impact of different feminist perspectives on viewing human behavior is provided below in the discussion of battered wives. If one identifies with the perspective that is prevalent among *radical feminists*, wife beating is an example of the victimization of a gender-oppressed class. In a socially produced, male-dominated, and sanctioned pattern of interaction, the abusive husband is simply an expected product of his society. Only by eliminating socially instituted sexism can women reduce their victimization. Furthermore, husband beating would be viewed as an aberration from this perspective.

Socialist feminists believe that wife beating is a political act, the result of the patriarchial capitalistic society's domination over women. Thus, men, as controllers of the capital as well as power holders in society and family, would rarely be victims of domestic abuse. Only by changing the economic, political, and gender-based delegation of powers would it be possible to eliminate domestic violence.

If one adheres to a *liberal feminists'* perspective, liberation is seen in terms of equal opportunities for educational and professional advancement, a resource perspective in which equalization of the resources would produce equal status between males and females.

Although these theories provide insights into wife abuse, they do little to explain child or husband abuse. If women are, by definition, a gender-oppressed class (radical feminism), how can a male be the victim of abuse by his wife? Can the patriarchial capitalistic society, with its domination over women (socialist feminism), ''explain'' the battered husband? As males have greater opportunities for employment and professional advancement (women still earn only 57 cents for each dollar earned by a male), why do men stay in abusive relationships?

Unfortunately, existing feminist theory has been constricted to explaining wife abuse under certain conditions and thus has limited utility as a theory of *family* violence. A feminist perspective general enough to explain all forms of family violence would be a welcome addition to the field.

Variables Used in Sociocultural Theories

Macrolevel analyses such as those discussed in the section on sociocultural theories are by definition comparative or cross-cultural. In this section, we discuss the major variables used in these analyses: measures of political protest violence, ''street'' violence, and belief systems.

Violence has characterized American society from the beginning; it was instrumental in our westward expansion and has been used consistently for controlling even peaceful dissenters (Hofsteader & Wallace, 1970). There has been no period in the history of the United States in which some segment of the population—ethnic or geographic—has not experienced severe conflict and violence (Steinmetz, 1973). The use of physical force to suppress conflict and the general societal sanctioning of these acts can be seen in events such as the Kent State University shooting, the 1968 Chicago Democratic National Convention, the school-desegregation busing programs, the antichoice conservatives' bombing of abortion clinics, and the KKK's far-right violence. It is not surprising that the United States ranks among the highest of all Western countries in violent crime (Gurr & Bishop, 1976; Hibbs, 1973).

One cannot help but wonder if the methods that family members use to resolve family conflict somehow reflect the general attitudes of the society toward the use of physical aggression to resolve other social problems. This becomes a chicken-and-egg problem. Does society influence individual behavior, or is the individual the constructor of society? Although the starting point might be a psychological perspective that sees people's natural aggression as a determinant of their ability to survive (Tiger, 1969), the perspective of this researcher leans toward the sociocultural influence, that is, the influence of the social setting on the learning of aggressive behavior.

Although caution must be expressed in the linking of societal levels of aggression to interpersonal and familial levels of aggression, there is both theoretical and empirical support for this position. Langman (1973) found that the child-rearing methods that parents used and the amount of interpersonal aggression considered tolerable were related to the level of aggression considered appropriate in the culture, an observation that has been supported in the anthropological literature (e.g., Mead, 1935; Whiting, 1965).

In a study of playground behavior, Bellak and Antell (1974) found that the aggressive treatment of a child by his or her parents was correlated with the aggressiveness displayed by the child. The authors found that the levels of both parent and child aggression were considerably higher in Frankfurt, Germany, than in Florence, Italy, or in Copenhagen, Denmark. The rates for suicide and homicide, considered by Bellak and Antell additional indications of personal aggression, were also much higher in Germany. DeMause (1974, p. 42) reported that 80% of German parents admitted to beating their children and that 35% did so with canes. A German poll showed that up to 60% of the parents interviewed believed in beating (not slapping or spanking) their children (Torgerson, 1973, as cited by Bellak & Antell, 1974).

Studies based on the data in the Human Relations Area files are also revealing. The incidence of wife beating in 71 primitive societies was positively correlated with invidious displays of wealth, pursuit of military glory, bellicosity, institutionalized boasting, exhibitionistic dancing, and sensitivity to insults (Slater & Slater, 1965). These descriptions sound curiously similar to the macho male's attempt to dominate, which are often linked to wife abuse in the United States.

Lester (1980), also studying primitive cultures, found that wife beating was more common in societies characterized by high divorce rates and in societies in which women were rated as inferior. Societies that experienced not only high rates of drunkeness but also high rates of alcohol-related aggression also had higher rates of wife beating.

In an examination of wife abuse in 86 primitive societies, Masumura (1979) found that wife abuse was correlated with overall societal violence, for example, homicide, suicide, feuding, warfare, personal crime, and aggression. Whereas matrilocal societies were found to be characterized by intrasocietal "peacefulness" (Divale, 1974; Van Velzen & Van Wetering, 1960) and to exhibit less feuding (Otterbein & Otterbein, 1965), Masumura (1979) reported weak, but positive, correlations between wife abuse and patrilocal residence and patrilineal inheritance, thus providing limited support of the idea that male dominance leads to higher rates of wife beating.

Using specification and elaboration, Masumura (1979) systematically considered alternative explanations for the correlation between wife abuse and other forms of violence. Because these alternative hypotheses were not supported, he concluded, "It becomes more plausible that various types of aggression are separate manifestations of a sociocultural tendency toward violence" (p. 56).

Using the Textor cross-cultural categorization of contemporary societies, Prescott (1975) found that, in 36 of 49 societies, physical violence decreased when physical affection increased, and that physical violence increased when physical affection decreased.

Steinmetz (1981b, 1982) compared the societal violence profiles from a number of studies with marital violence and sibling violence scores from Finland, Puerto Rico, Canada, Israel, Belize (British Honduras), and the United States (see Table 4). In general, similarities were found between political and civil profiles of violence and marital violence scores within each society. Whiting (1965) reported less wife beating in societies that lived in extended-family forms. Therefore, the high levels of violence on the kibbutz, where norms of sexual equality and the availability of numerous kin would have predicted lower levels of spousal violence, as compared to nuclear families in Israel, was surprising. However, Demos (1970) noted that, to survive the cramped living quarters, early American colonists went to great length to avoid family conflict. They apparently vented their hostilities on their neighbors, as the rate of conflict between neighbors was extremely high. Is it possible that preserving the community tranquility is of extreme importance, therefore, the kibbutz family keeps the conflicts within the family in order to preserve the more important communal tranquility? Because deteriorating economic conditions are often linked to increasing domestic violence, the rapid inflation experienced during the 1970s, as well as increased Middle East tension and border conflicts in Israel, may explain the kibbutzim's relatively high level of marital violence, which is not entirely consistent with their profile of societal violence collected during an earlier era.

The United States has the highest levels of societal violence of the societies studied; yet, the marital violence scores place U.S. families in the middle of the group. The numbers of families reported to have used violence, as well as the mean frequency scores, are considerably lower for this sample than for the others (Gelles, 1974; Steinmetz, 1977a; Straus *et al.*, 1980). In these studies, nearly 60% of the families reported using physical violence, and one study (Straus *et al.*, 1980) also reported mean violence scores of 8.8 for husbands and 10.3 for wives. However, these data were collected from husbands and wives, not from their children. Is it possible that U.S. children are less aware of their parents' violent interaction than children in other countries, or could we expect the levels for other societies to be even higher if the parents had reported the information?

The final point to be noted is the very consistently low ranking on all measures of societal violence assigned to Finland, yet the high percentage of both husbands and wives (over 60%) who used marital violence. Of further interest is the extremely low frequency of violence used by each of these couples. Is the use of low levels of violence more acceptable in Finland, or is there less of an attempt to shield negative family interaction from the children?

Sibling violence was also examined cross-culturally. Finland and Puerto Rico, consistently low on all measures, were relatively low on this measure, whereas Canada and the United States, fairly high on all measures, had somewhat higher sibling scores. However, the relationships were not as clearly defined as with the marital violence scores.

Kumagai and O'Donoghue (1978) examined relative power between husband and wife and the effect that it may have on conjugal violence in Japan and the United States. They found that, whereas U.S. couples were egalitarian in power and violence, Japanese wives were more powerful than their husbands but were considerably more likely to be the victims than the offenders in spouse abuse.

Ethnic Comparisons within the United States

In secondary analyses of the national data Cazenave and Straus (1979; Straus *et al.*, 1980) found that blacks were less likely to report sibling or parent abuse than were whites: more than twice as many black husbands as white husbands had slapped their wife during the previous year (5% vs. 11%). Similar rates were found for wife-to-husband slapping (3% vs. 6%) and husband beating (4% vs. 8%) for whites and blacks, respectively. However, when income was controlled for, differences appeared. At the highest income levels ($12,000–19,000 and $20,000 +

per year), blacks were less likely than whites to report sibling abuse or parent abuse. Marital abuse was less for blacks at the two highest income levels and at the $0 to $5,900 level. Only in the group with an income of $6,000 to $11,999 (which constituted the largest group for blacks) was this trend not observed.

When the occupational class of the husband was used as a control, the differences were small among blue-collar families of both races for slapping a child, child abuse, and sibling abuse. However, among white-collar families, a much larger percentage of white families were abusive toward their children; sibling abuse and parent abuse were experienced more by whites in both social-class groups. Only marital abuse scores were higher among black families. This provides considerable support for a cautionary note on the importance of controlling for social class when examining ethnicity as a contributing factor in domestic violence.

In a study of validated cases of child abuse and neglect in Texas during 1975 to 1977, Lauderdale, Valiunas, and Anderson (1980) found that these rates for all types of abuse were highest among blacks, followed by Mexican-Americans, with Anglos having the lowest rates. However, analysis within each group indicated that the Anglos had the highest proportion of abuse, followed by blacks, with Mexican-American families having the lowest proportion of abuse.

A study of child abuse and neglect conducted in Hawaii during 1976 to 1977 revealed that Japanese-Americans had significantly lower rates of abuse as compared to Samoan-Americans (3.5% to 6.5%) (Dubanski & Snyder, 1980). However, Japanese-Americans represented 27% of the population, and Samoan-Americans constituted less than 1% of the population.

Using a series of vignettes, Giovannoni and Becerra (1979) attempted to ascertain ethnic differences in the attribution of seriousness to acts of mistreatment. They found that, 94% of the time, blacks and Hispanics gave a more serious rating to the vignette than did Anglos. Furthermore, education and income were inversely related to the ratings of seriousness.

An examination of the impact of ethnicity on family violence in the United States was undertaken by Blanchard and Blanchard (1983). They administered a modification of the CTS used by Straus *et al.* (1980) to 475 college students in Hawaii. They divided the sample into European, Japanese, Chinese, Filipino, and Hawaiian–part Hawaiian. They asked about violence toward any family member rather than toward a specific family member (i.e., parent, sibling, or spouse). They found that the Hawaiian students had the highest scores, with a mean score of 7.8; the Caucasians the next highest with 4.2; the Filipinos, 3.75; and the Chinese, 3.20. The lowest scores were obtained by the Japanese, who had a mean score of 3.05. These scores, however, did not include slapping, pushing, grabbing, or shoving, as these acts were not violent enough to qualify "as a violent crime charge or . . . inspire a reputation as a bully" (p. 182).

To assess the effect of ethnicity on family violence. Straus *et al.* (1980) categorized respondents as blacks, whites, others (composed of American Indians, Orientals, and others), and Jews. For all categories but wife abuse, the "other" ethnic groups were found to be most violent. In general, the Jews had lower scores for all dyads but husband abuse (they were in the middle range of violence for this category). As was noted in Cazenave and Straus (1979), when income and social class were controlled for, these relationships were altered.

A Cycle of Violence

Perhaps the most consistent finding is the cyclical nature of family violence: violence in the family serves as a training ground for the children, who as adults are more likely to approve of violence as an acceptable way of solving problems and to use violence both within the family and outside the family (Sedgley & Lund, 1979; Steinmetz, 1977a,b; Straus *et al.*, 1980). (See Figure 3.)

In an experimental group of 60 "abused," 30 "neglected," and 30 "normal" children between the ages of 5 and 13, Green (1978) found that the physically abused children demonstrated a significantly higher incidence of self-destructive behavior, including suicide attempts, self-mutilation, and suicidal ideation, than did the neglected or normal children. Green suggested:

The abused child's sense of worthlessness, badness and self-hatred as a consequence of parental assault, rejection and scapegoating formed the nucleus for subsequent self-destructive behavior. (p. 81)

Based on a study of 34 boys and 39 girls in a family treatment program, Galdston (1975) noted that, when children have received significant exposure to violent behavior before the age of 2, they are likely to identify with this pattern of response in a way that is essentially irreversible. Although a great deal can be done, subsequently, to change these patterns, intervention before the age of 18 months greatly enhances the possibility of modifying the child's violent behavior.

Whereas Kinard (1979) found that abused children were more likely than nonabused children to use aggression as a response to frustration with peers (but not adults), studies of parricide found that child abuse was directly related to the murder or the attempted murder of a parent by a child. Corder *et al.* (1976) compared 10 adolescents charged with parricide with a matched sample that had killed another relative or a stranger. Those committing parricide were more likely to have been abused, to have had a father absent or a father who was physically abusive to the mother, to have been overly attached to the mother, and to have been sexually overstimulated by one parent.

A childhood characterized by relentless brutality, personal experience with violent death, and extremely unfavorable home conditions was found to be a common background factor for 33 adolescents who had committed murder (Bender, 1959). In a study of children who killed, Sargent (1962) reported that, not only had the parents used extreme cruelty toward the child, but their cruelty had been condoned by other family members. Studies of adolescents who have committed parricide (Sadoff, 1971; Tanay, 1975) reveal that the victim parent was cruel and frequently beat other members of the family, especially the child's mother. Climent and Ervin (1972) found that approximately three fourths of a sample composed of 30 individuals who were admitted to the emergency room as a result of violent behavior had been assaulted by their mothers. Only one sixth of the control group of 30 emergency-room admissions had been assaulted by their fathers, and only 1 individual had been assaulted by the mother in this study. Palmer (1962) found that murderers were more likely to have suffered severe, physical beatings and traumatic incidents than the control group, which consisted of their brothers.

A brutalizing childhood was found to be characteristic of rapists (Brownmiller, 1975; Hartogs, 1951); individuals with split personalities (Schreiber, 1973); and suicides (Bender & Curran, 1940; Gayford, 1975; MacDonald, 1967). A study of the childhood environment of 14 political assassins revealed disorganized, broken families; parental abuse and rejection; and marginal integration into society (Steinmetz, 1973; 1977a). Connell (1972) and Jacobs (1971) found excessive violence in families of attempted suicide cases.

In a study of 100 battered wives, Gayford (1975) discovered that 5% of the batterers and 23% of the victims had had a violent childhood; 37% of the wives and 54% of the husbands abused their children.

In a secondary analysis of a survey conducted for the Commission on the Causes and Prevention of Violence, Owens and Straus (1975), reported a strong association between exposure to violence, as either an observer or a victim, during childhood as well as violent behavior as an adult, a finding supported by Sedgely and Lund (1979), in a secondary analysis of data compiled by the National Opinion Research Corporation. These patterns were found to have continued over several generations in studies of child abuse, a cycle in which the battering parents had experienced abuse from their own parents (Bryant, 1963; Craft, 1969; Oliver & Taylor, 1971; Silver, Dublin, & Lourie, 1969; Wasserman, 1967; Zalba, 1966). Wilt and Bannon (1976) noted that over one fourth of the individuals who committed assault or murder reported having had frequent arguments with their parents. Furthermore, their analysis of 90 intrafamilial homicides revealed that 62% had been preceded by previous assaults on the same family member. Even in less violent forms, the use of physical force is passed on from generation to generation (Steinmetz, 1977a,b).

In a comprehensive review of the consequences of child abuse, Libbey and Bybee (1979) reported:

Being raised in an abusive environment can result in delays in physical, neurological, intellectual, cognitive, speech, language and general psychosocial development; problems in learning, behavior and personality; and failures in infant–mother bondings. (p. 9)

Furthermore, the violence experienced by these children often "forces" them to run away from the home, contributing to the increasing numbers of homeless youth. In fact, several studies have suggested that, whereas minority and poor women enter prostitution because of a need for money, a rapidly growing number of white middle-class youths are turning to the streets in order to escape a violent home (Baizerman, Thompson, & Stafford-White, 1979; Silbert, 1980).

The relationship between child abuse and spouse abuse also has substantial support. Gayford (1975) reported that 37% of abused wives and 54% of abusive husbands had abused their children. In one sample of battered women, Roy (1977) reported violence in the families of origin of 81% of abusive husbands and 33% of abused wives. In a controlled pilot study, Parker and Schumaker (1977) reported that about 68% of their abused wives had mothers who had been abused, whereas 25% of the nonabused wives had witnessed their mothers being abused.

Rosenbaum and O'Leary (1981) compared 52 self-referred victims of physical marital violence, 20 women who were selected at random and scored satisfactorily on Locke-Wallace Marital Adjustment Test, and 20 women who had not experienced violence, but who had experienced marital discord and were involved in marital therapy. These authors found that the children of the abused wives were more likely to exhibit behavior problems, but the differences were not significant. The abused wives were no more likely to have witnessed parental abuse than were the nonabused wives, but a strong and significant relationship existed between the husband's witnessing of parental spouse abuse and his using physical violence on his wife. Rosenbaum and O'Leary (1981) also found that nearly 82% of the husbands who had witnessed marital violence as children had also been victims of child abuse by their parents. They noted that the male children of couples in which there is wife abuse are clearly at high risk for development into the next generation of abusive husbands.

This finding is consistent with Feshbach's review (1970) of the aggression literature, which showed that boys respond to severe punishment by exhibiting overt agression, girls by exhibiting inhibited, passive behavior and conflict and anxiety about aggression.

These studies clearly support the cyclical nature of domestic violence. Cornell-Pedrick and Gelles (1982), in a test of this theory, found that a family background of violence predicted adolescent violence more than any other variable examined. They noted:

Social, family structural, and situational factors which are associated with adult violence in families are either not or only weakly related to violence by adolescents. Indeed the only important consistency in the analysis of violence towards parents and other forms of family violence is that the presence in a household of one form of violence is related to the occurrence of other types of violence. (p. 13)

Additional evidence for the close link between witnessing and experiencing violence as a child and using or being the victim of violence was provided by a small exploratory study that I conducted in the spring of 1984 with 72 college students, two thirds of whom were juniors and seniors. In this predominantly female class, 36% reported courtship violence. In over half (54%) of these couples, the violence was used by both the student and partner, and 23% (all female) reported student-only violence. For 65% of the students, the violence had occurred more than once, and a similar percentage reported that the violence had occurred with more than one partner; yet, 88% had continued the relationship after the violence had occurred. Of the students who reported that their mothers had used physical means of disciplining them, 41% also reported courtship violence, as compared with only 16% of those whose mothers had been nonviolent. Similar, but not as dramatic, trends were noted for father–student interactions: 26% of students with nonviolent fathers had experience courtship violence, compared with 30% of students with violent fathers.

The finding that most clearly substantiates the intergenerational transmission of violence as a conflict resolution method is the relationship between students' reports of mother–father violence and their own courtship violence experiences. Only 18% of the students who reported that their parents used neither verbal nor physical aggression to resolve marital conflicts had experienced courtship violence. However, 42% of the students who reported mother–father physical violence and 33% of students who parents used verbal aggression to resolve marital conflicts had experienced courtship violence.

Similar findings were reported by Bernard and Bernard (1983) with a sample of 481 college students. Of the 168 males, 15% had abused a partner; 77% of the abusers had also been abused; and 8% had been abused but had not abused their partner. Of the 293 females, 21% had been abusive, and of this group, 82% had also experienced abuse; 16% had been recipients of abuse but had not been abusive. Although there was apparently no difference between experiencing violence or observing violence in the parental home and becoming abusive, both situations were as likely to produce abusive offspring. However, Bernard and Bernard did report that students tended to use the same forms of violence (such as punching or throwing things) as were used in the home. In fact, 74% of the male students from violent homes used the same form of abuse on their partner that they had experienced or observed; 77% of female students from violent homes used similar forms of abuse.

Models

Numerous theories and the major variables subsumed under these theories have been discussed. However, they have been discussed as individual, one-by-one relationships. We know that, in an interpersonal relationship, many variables interact to produce the desired (or undesired) outcome.

Some models are quite simple, such as the balance theory approach (Steinmetz, 1980a). This model posits a balance between stress-, conflict-, and violence-producing variables and stress-, conflict-, and violence-reducing variables that must be maintained if violence is to be prevented. Variables such as unemployment, illness, unwanted pregnancy, and alcoholism, when excessive, "tip" the balance and result in conflict and/or violence, unless resources such as the individual's characteristics, family strength and support, and community services are sufficient to balance the scale (see Figure 1).

Another model, suggested by Walker (1979), describes the phenomenon of wife battering as a cycle of increasing tension, tension release via battering, and positive interaction (see Figure 2). Walker's model, a psychological perspective, depicts the process by which a woman is trapped in a state of "learned helplessness." However, the variables that produce the tension-building section of the cycle can be macrolevel factors (e.g., economic conditions) as well as microlevel variables (such as spousal communication patterns, alcoholism, and individual characteristics). Although developed from the histories of battered women, and explaining how they become trapped, this model can easily be adapted to parent–child interaction.

Another cycle of violence model illustrates the relationship between the violent home and the violent society. In this model, being raised in a violent home often produces violent parents, spouses, and citizens. These individuals are more likely to accept and glorify violence, thus providing an atmosphere in which violence as acceptable behavior influences family interactions (see Figure 3).

In attempting to disentangle the corresponding rates of societal crimes and family violence, Steinmetz (1977a) posited the model shown in Figure 4, in which the relationship between macrolevel conditions (high crime rates) and microlevel conditions in the family violence were explored. In summarizing this model, it was noted that, in order to test the linkages in Figure 4, one would need to identify societies with a similar quality of life but possessing either high crime rates or high levels of family aggression, but not both. Thus, it is suggested that macrolevel conditions cause two separate phenomena: high crime rates and high levels of family aggression. If societies could not be identified filling the above conditions, this fact would argue for the second set of linkages, that is, macrolevel conditions resulting in high crime rates

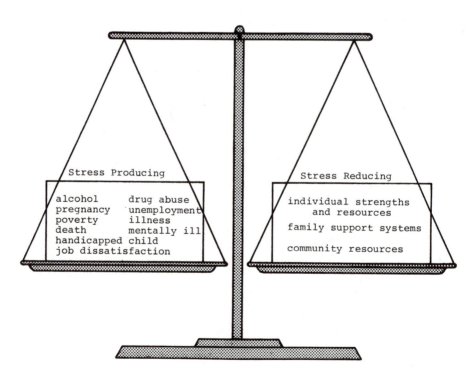

Figure 1. A balance scale model. (Adapted from S. K. Steinmetz, *Journal of Home Economics*, 1980, 72 (2), pp. 32–36.)

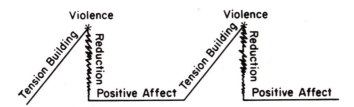

Figure 2. Walker's cyclical theory. (Based on Walker, 1979.)

(and an acceptance or tolerance of aggression and violence), which are translated into higher levels of family violence (Steinmetz, 1977a).

Models have also been developed that consider objective measures of societal, family, and individual variables and behaviors as well as the subjective meanings attributed to these variables and behaviors by the individual, the family, and society (Steinmetz, 1977a). For example, in Figure 5, a relationship is posited between family, societal, and individual characteristics of the acts (Boxes A–C), a precipitating situation (Box E), the response to the precipitating situation (Box K), and the outcome, such as a change in behavior (Box N). This model suggests, however, that the individual's percep-

tion of these attributes (Box D), as well as the actual attributes (e.g., the perception of the social status as well as the actual status), influences behavior. In other words, it matters little that one is viewed by society as a success if one feels like a failure.

Likewise, the definition of the situation, expectations and needs, power and resources, and the sequence of events (Boxes F–I) modify and shape the individual's perception of the precipitating situation (Box J). The actors' perception of the response to the precipitating situation (Box M) is influenced by whether or not the actors accept or reject the response (Box L). The actual success or failure, as well as the perceived success or failure of the outcomes (Boxes O, P), affects the likelihood of these

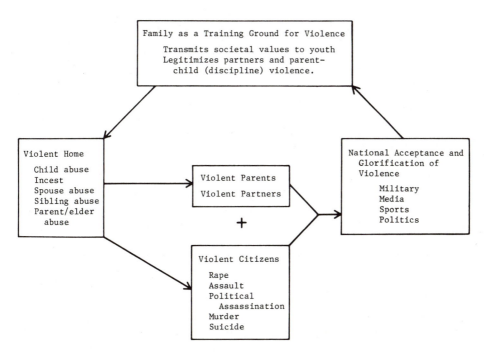

Figure 3. The cyclical nature of violence: Family ↔ Society.

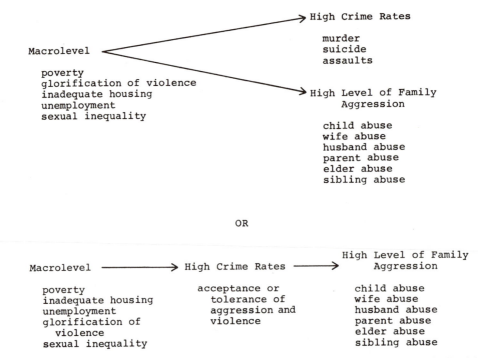

Figure 4. Alternative models for the relationship between macrolevel variables, high crime rates, and family violence.

behaviors' being continued (Box Q) unless modified via intervention, education, or situational changes (Box R).

This model illustrates the importance of considering the subjective meanings attributed to family interaction by the actors as well as objectively measured phenomena in order to adequately understand the dynamic processes of family violence. Systems theory models such as those developed by Giles-Sims (1983) and Straus (1973), incorporate specific decision-making choices that must be completed before the next phase can be considered.

A model that captures not only the cyclical nature of domestic violence but also the interface between the intraindividual, the social-psychological, and the sociocultural levels of violence is needed. The model depicted in Figure 6 attempted to illustrate these relationships. The intraindividual variables listed within the innermost circle identify individual characteristics that explain family violence. Social-psychological theories, based on the interaction between societal and individual characteristics, are found on the second level. The variables associated most frequently with these theories are those found in the triangle. At the third level, represented by a square, are the sociocultural theories, which locate the causes of domestic violence in society. The variables discussed are inside the square.

Although each of these three levels focuses exclusively on a particular level for the explanation, this tri-level model of violence is an intermeshing of all three levels.

Individual characteristics, as evidenced by the intraindividual theories, explain some portion of violence. For example, because of the gap between expectations and reality, as well as the additional stress experienced by the parents, having a premature or handicapped infant explains some portion of child abuse. However, it is the variables used most frequently in social-psychological theories (alcohol or drug abuse, social-class-related variables, and marital status) that increase the likelihood that violence will occur in a family with an "atypical infant." Most important, the tri-level model of violence examines individual and social-psychological variables in a sociocultural context. What is the meaning of the circumstances described above? Does society blame the parents for the birth of this atypical infant, or does it offer the parent support? Does the parents' cultural identification affect their acceptance or rejection of this infant? The tri-level model and attending theory and the model presented attempt to encompass the interaction of all three levels of theory and a wide range of variables used to explain family violence.

Conclusion

Hundreds of studies on some aspect of domestic violence emerge yearly, each one teasing out new variables, usually from small, nonrandom (convenient) samples. Each study often confirms earlier studies with a new twist. Although slowly adding to our knowledge, these studies, because of their tunnel vision, unfortunately fail to answer some larger questions.

This tunnel vision approach can be traced to several causes. Insecure funding, usually for one- or two-year periods, encourages the replication of studies of known outcomes with small, often insignificant variations. Longitudinal studies that allow an in-depth study of families during different stages of the life cycle, such as the Oakland Study, are not possible with today's constantly changing funding priorities.

The supply and demand in the academic and social service section must also be considered: Because of the greater supply of academicians to fill the jobs in a tightening market, should the new researcher put his or her proverbial "research" eggs in one "longitudinal study" basket? Spending five years (or even three years) on a single research project that may or may not produce publishable findings may sound the death knell for young professionals. Even the most established academicians are not free of the constraints of promotions, raises, and other perquisites that are tied to annual productivity rates. This point interrelates with financial concerns since the cost–benefit ratio of grant preparation time in a tight funding market must not be overlooked. Current research often operates to minimize risks and to maximize outcome.

Territoriality is another limiting factor: Can a social scientist find happiness invading the sanctum of medical or psychiatric research? To propose a medical basis of social behavior is the antithesis of the social learning approach currently in vogue. Suggesting a psychiatric approach to understanding either the victim's or the offender's behavior is considered heresy in some circles. To suggest, in the spirit of equality, that men and women have an equal ability (especially when weapons are available) to commit violence is abhorrent to the (Marxist) radical feminists' perspective, as it removes the blame from a patriarchal, capitalistic society (in which women are viewed as an oppressed victimized class) and places it on the shoulders of the individuals perpetrating the violence.

Although theoretically tidy, these approaches limit our ability to explore the full range of variables that contribute to interpersonal violence. Just a few unanswered questions that will require a multidisciplinary approach are briefly noted here. The effect of the extra X chromosome on male violence has been demonstrated. More recently, the premenstrual syndrome (PMS) effect on women's violence has been explored (Dalton, 1980), and has been used as a defense plea for murder in England. The relationship between child-abusing mothers and PMS should be explored. The treatment of PMS is simple and effective, and the diet, exercise, and stress-reduction components are of general benefit to mothers in increasing their health, fitness, and self-concept. The relationship between stress and PMS may explain why

some mothers can withstand a lot of problems and others fall apart quickly. There is some concern among feminist groups that PMS may support the notion that women are unsuitable for certain jobs. However, if a gender-based argument were raised, then men, because of their higher rates of hypertension, heart attacks, and ulcers, should also, as a group, be considered unsuitable for certain jobs, such as high-pressure jobs (e.g., as corporate executives or governmental leaders) or jobs in which the safety of other depends on their performance (e.g., as air traffic controllers, physicians, and pilots).

Neurological data on organic brain syndrome and wife abusers is another rich avenue of exploration. Early research found that certain families over several generations are predisposed to these particular brain-wave patterns (Elliott, 1978, 1982; Monroe, 1970). This finding raises the question of genetic transmission and represents a new dimension in the understanding of the cycle of violence.

Why does alcohol contribute to violence? Without the benefit of scientific research, our own personal observations reveal that some people become the uninhibited life of the party when "drunk," whereas others fall asleep, and still others become nasty and aggressive. We also know that there is a tendency in certain families for the members to become alcoholic. Therefore, the genetic variable of alcoholism and its effect on the cycle of violence between generations must be considered, as well as the social-learning, role-model, and intergenerational influences.

The influence of nutrition on aggressive and violent behavior is perhaps one of the more promising areas of research. The controversial Feingold diet, which examines the effects of artificial flavoring and colors, needs further investigation with larger samples and better controls, which should be conducted over longer periods of time. Sugar and additives have been found to relate to hyperactivity and aggression in numerous studies (Prinz, Roberts, & Hantman, 1980; Stare, Whelan, & Sheridan, 1980) and have formed the basis of one murder defense labeled the *Twinkie defense* (Beck & Reese, 1979). If diets rich in sugars and additives, the diets most likely to be found among teenage mothers and their children, cause hyperactivity and aggressiveness (i.e., difficult-to-control children and mothers who deal with their frustration by using violence on their children), then links between diet and child abuse seem extremely likely.

Atlhough the importance of social-psychological and the sociocultural theories is overriding in explaining family violence, understanding other influences is especially critical for the prevention of domestic violence.

Although assuming that the medical-physiological factors are *the* major cause of family violence is misleading and wrongly removes the responsibility for violent behavior from the violent individual, ignoring these factors when trying to understand family violence—and, more important, when trying to reduce violence or to prevent

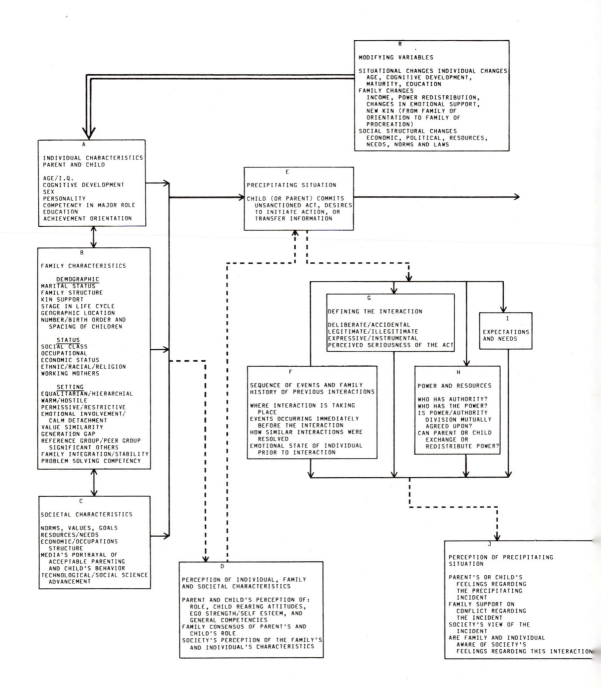

Figure 5. Theoretical model of components and processes involved in goal-oriented parent–child interaction.

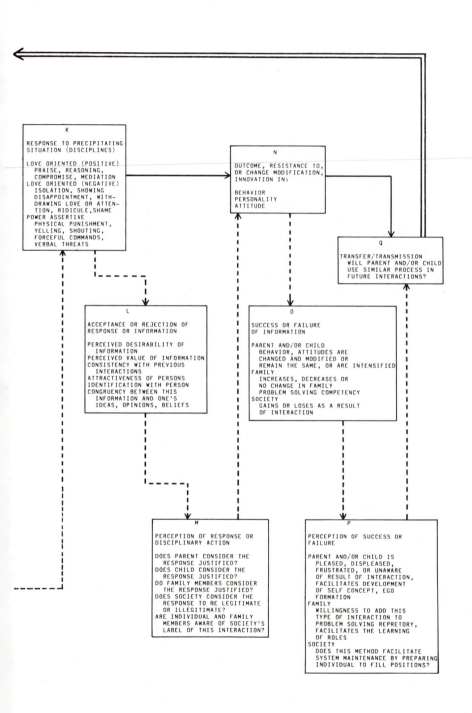

K

RESPONSE TO PRECIPITATING
SITUATION (DISCIPLINES)

LOVE ORIENTED (POSITIVE)
   PRAISE, REASONING,
   COMPROMISE, MEDIATION
LOVE ORIENTED (NEGATIVE)
   ISOLATION, SHOWING
   DISAPPOINTMENT, WITH-
   DRAWING LOVE OR ATTEN-
   TION, RIDICULE, SHAME
POWER ASSERTIVE
   PHYSICAL PUNISHMENT,
   YELLING, SHOUTING,
   FORCEFUL COMMANDS,
   VERBAL THREATS

N

OUTCOME, RESISTANCE TO,
OR CHANGE MODIFICATION,
INNOVATION IN:

BEHAVIOR
PERSONALITY
ATTITUDE

Q

TRANSFER/TRANSMISSION
   WILL PARENT AND/OR CHILD
   USE SIMILAR PROCESS IN
   FUTURE INTERACTIONS?

L

ACCEPTANCE OR REJECTION OF
RESPONSE OR INFORMATION

PERCEIVED DESIRABILITY OF
   INFORMATION
PERCEIVED VALUE OF INFORMATION
CONSISTENCY WITH PREVIOUS
   INTERACTIONS
ATTRACTIVENESS OF PERSONS
IDENTIFICATION WITH PERSON
CONGRUENCY BETWEEN THIS
   INFORMATION AND ONE'S
   IDEAS, OPINIONS, BELIEFS

O

SUCCESS OR FAILURE
OF INFORMATION

PARENT AND/OR CHILD
   BEHAVIOR, ATTITUDES ARE
   CHANGED AND MODIFIED OR
   REMAIN THE SAME, OR ARE INTENSIFIED
FAMILY
   INCREASES, DECREASES OR
   NO CHANGE IN FAMILY
   PROBLEM SOLVING COMPETENCY
SOCIETY
   GAINS OR LOSES AS A RESULT
   OF INTERACTION

M

PERCEPTION OF RESPONSE OR
DISCIPLINARY ACTION

DOES PARENT CONSIDER THE
   RESPONSE JUSTIFIED?
DOES CHILD CONSIDER THE
   RESPONSE JUSTIFIED?
DO FAMILY MEMBERS CONSIDER
   THE RESPONSE JUSTIFIED?
DOES SOCIETY CONSIDER THE
   RESPONSE TO BE LEGITIMATE
   OR ILLEGITIMATE?
ARE INDIVIDUAL AND FAMILY
   MEMBERS AWARE OF SOCIETY'S
   LABEL OF THIS INTERACTION?

P

PERCEPTION OF SUCCESS OR
FAILURE

PARENT AND/OR CHILD IS
   PLEASED, DISPLEASED,
   FRUSTRATED, OR UNAWARE
   OF RESULT OF INTERACTION,
   FACILITATES DEVELOPMENT
   OF SELF CONCEPT, EGO
   FORMATION
FAMILY
   WILLINGNESS TO ADD THIS
   TYPE OF INTERACTION TO
   PROBLEM SOLVING REPRETORY,
   FACILITATES THE LEARNING
   OF ROLES
SOCIETY
   DOES THIS METHOD FACILITATE
   SYSTEM MAINTENANCE BY PREPARING
   INDIVIDUAL TO FILL POSITIONS?

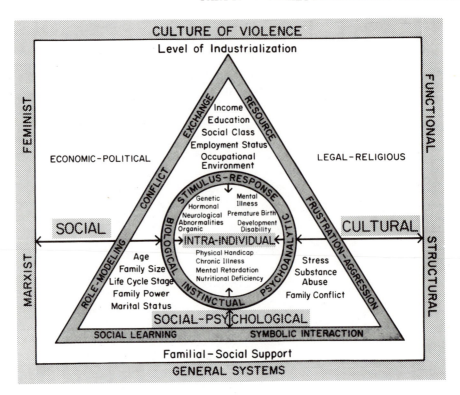

Figure 6. The relationship between intraindividual, social-psychological, and sociocultural levels of theory: A tri-level model of violence.

violence from occurring—will severely hinder our ability to develop a more comprehensive understanding and treatment of the problem.

ACKNOWLEDGMENTS

I greatfully acknowledge the help of the following people: Daniel Saunders, David Finkelhor, and Larry Baron for commenting on earlier drafts; Barbara Settles and Murray Straus for suggestions and insights provided during the development of the manuscript; Dennis Carey for the preparation of the graphics; Cathy Sullivan for typing earlier drafts; and L. Leon Campbell and the University of Delaware for granting me a sabbatical and facilitating the acquisition of a computer, which was invaluable in preparing the final draft.

References

Allen, C. M., & Straus, M. A. Resources, power and husband-wife violence. In M. A. Straus & G. T. Hotaling (Eds.), *The social causes of husband-wife violence.* Minneapolis: University of Minnesota Press, 1979.

American Humane Association. *National analysis of official child neglect and abuse reporting.* Denver: Author, 1978.

Aristotle. *The Nicomachean ethics.* (H. Rackham, Trans.) Cambridge: Harvard University Press, 1968.

Babbie, E. *The practice of social research.* Belmont, Calif.: Wadsworth, 1983.

Bach, G. R., & Wyden, P. *The intimate enemy.* New York: Avon, 1968.

Bachman, J. G. *Youth in transition.* Ann Arbor: University of Michigan Institute for Social Research, 1967.

Baizerman, M., Thompson, J., & Stafford-White, K. An old young friend: Adolescent prostitution. *Children Today,* 1979, (Sept.–Oct.), pp. 20–24.

Bakan, D. *Slaughter of the innocents.* San Francisco: Jossey-Bass, 1971.

Bandura, A. *Aggression—A social learning analysis.* Englewood Cliffs, N.J.: Prentice-Hall, 1973.

Bandura, A., & Walters, R. H. *Social learning and personality development.* New York: Holt, Rinehart & Winston, 1963.

Bandura, A., Ross, D., & Ross, S. A. Transmission of aggression through imitation of aggressive models. *Journal of Abnormal and Social Psychology,* 1961, *63,* 575–582.

Bard, M. The study and modification of intra-familial violence. In J. L. Singer (Ed.), *The control of aggression and violence.* pp. 149–64. New York: Academic Press, 1971.

Bates, R. P. *Child abuse—the problem.* Paper presented at the 2nd World Conference of the International Society on Family Law, Montreal, June 1977.

Bayles, J. A. Violence, alcohol problems and other problems in disintegrating familes. *Journal of Studies on Alcohol,* 1979, *39*(3), 551–563.

Beck, M., & Reese, M. Night of gay rage. *Newsweek* (June 4, 1979), pp. 30–31.

Bellak, L., & Antell, M. An intellectual study of aggressive behavior on children's playgrounds. *American Journal of Orthopsychiatry,* 1974, *44*(4), 503–511.

Bender, L. Children and adolescents who have killed. *American Journal of Psychiatry,* 1959, *116,* 510–513.

Bender, L., & Curran, F. J. Children and adolescents who kill. *Criminal Psychopathology,* 1940, *3*(4), 297–322.

Benson, D. F., & Blumer, D. (Eds.) *Psychiatric Aspects of Neurological Disease.* New York: Grune & Stratten, 1975.

Bergman, J. A., O'Malley, H., & Segars, H. Legal research and services for the elderly and Elder abuse in Massachusetts: A survey of professionals and paraprofessionals. *Elder Abuse: The Hidden Problem* (a briefing). Select Committee on Aging, U.S. House of Representatives, 96th Congress. Boston, Mass., June 23, 1979. Washington, D.C.: U.S. Government Printing Office, 1980.

Bernard, M. L. & Bernard, J. L. Violent intimacy: The family as a model for love relationships. *Family Relations,* 1983, *32* (Apr.), 283–286.

Besharov, D. J. Building a community response to child abuse and maltreatment. *Children Today,* 1975, *4*(5), 2–4.

Blackburn, R. Aggression and the EEG: A quantitative analysis. *Journal of Abnormal Psychology,* 1975, *84,* 358–365.

Blackburn, R. Aggression (physiological). In R. H. Woody (Ed.), *Encyclopedia of clinical assessment* (Vol. 1). San Francisco: Jossey-Bass, 1980.

Blanchard, D. C., & Blanchard, R. H. Hawaii: Violence, a preliminary analysis. In A. P. Goldstein & M. H. Segall (Eds.), *Aggression in global perspective.* New York: Pergamon Press, 1983.

Block, M., & Sinnott, J. (Eds.). *The battered elder syndrome: An exploratory study.* College Park: Center on Aging, University of Maryland, 1979.

Block, M., & Sinnott, J. P. Prepared statement. *Elder Abuse: The Hidden Problem.* Briefing by the Select Committee on Aging. U.S. House of Representatives (96), June 23, 1979. Boston, pp. 10–12. Washington, D.C., U.S. Government Printing Office, 1980.

Blumberg, M. When parents hit out. *Twentieth Century,* 1964–1965, *173,* 39–44.

Bolton, F. E., Laner, R. H., Gai, D. S., & Kane, S. P. The "study" of child maltreatment: When is research . . . research? *Journal of Family Issues,* 1981, *2*(4), 531–539.

Bradley v. *State,* Walker 158 (Miss. 1824).

Bremner, R. H. *Children and youth in America: A documentary history* (Vol. 1.). Boston: Harvard University Press, 1970.

Brown, C. *Manchild in the promised land.* New York: New American Library, 1965.

Brownmiller, S. *Against our will: Men, women and rape.* New York: Simon & Schuster, 1975.

Bryant, H. D. Physical abuse of children: An agency study. *Child Welfare,* 1963, *42,* 125–130.

Caffey, J. Multiple fractures in long bones in infants suffering from subdural hematomas. *American Journal of Roentgenology,* 1946, *56,* 163–173.

Carter, H., & Glick, P. C. *Marriage and divorce: A social and economic study.* Cambridge: Harvard University Press, 1976.

Cazenave, N. A., & Straus, M. A. Race, class, network embeddedness and family violence: A search for potent support systems. *Journal of Comparative Family Studies,* 1979, *10*(3), 281–300.

Climent, C. F., & Ervin, F. R. Historical data in the evaluation of violent subjects. *Archives of General Psychiatry,* 1972, *27,* 621–624.

Coleman, D. H., & Straus, M. A. *Alcohol abuse and family violence.* Paper presented at the American Sociological Assocation Annual Meeting 1979 (Mimeo).

Connell, P. H. Suicidal attempts in childhood and adolescence. In J. G. Howells (Ed.), *Modern perspectives in child psychiatry.* New York: Brunner/Mazel, 1972.

Corder, B. F., Ball, B. C., Haizlip, T. M., Rollins, R., & Beaumont, R.

Adolescent parricide: A comparison with other adolescent murder. *American Journal of Psychiatry,* 1976, *133*(Aug. 8), 957–961.

Cornell-Pedrick, C. P., & Gelles, R. J. Adolescent to parent violence. *Urban and Social Change Review,* 1982, *15,* 8–14.

Coser, L. A. *Continuities in the study of social conflict.* New York: Free Press, 1967.

Craft, M. The natural history of psychopathic disorder. *British Journal of Psychiatry,* 1969, *115,* 39–44.

Cuber, J. F., & Harroff, P. *Sex and the significant Americans.* Baltimore: Penguin, 1965.

Dahrendorf, R. *Class and class conflict in industrial society.* Stanford, Calif.: Stanford University Press, 1959.

Dalton, K. Cyclical criminal acts in premenstrual syndrome. *Lancet,* 1980, *2,* 1070–1071.

deMause, L. *A history of childhood.* New York: Psycho-History Press, 1974.

Demos, J. *A little commonwealth.* New York: Oxford University Press, 1970.

Divale, W. T. Migration extended warfare and matrilocal residence. *Behavior Science Research,* 1974, *9,* 75–133.

Dobash, R. P. and Dobash, R. E. Community response to violence against wives: Charivari, abstract justice and patriarchy. *Social Problems, 28* (5), 563–581.

Dollard, J., Miller, N. E., Doob, L. W., Mowrer, O. H., & Sears, R. S. *Frustration and aggression.* New Haven, Conn.: Yale University Press, 1939.

Dossett, R. G., Burch, N. R., & Keller, W. J. *An electrophysiological profile of violence: The EEG of juvenile offenders.* Presented at the Sothwest Science Forum Symposium on Violence and Aggression, Houston, Texas, October 1982.

Douglas, R., Hickey, T., & Noel, P. *A study of maltreatment of the elderly and other vulnerable adults.* Final report to the U.S. Administration on Aging and the Michigan Department of Social Services, Ann Arbor, Michigan, November 1980.

Dubanski, R. A., & Snyder, K. Patterns of child abuse and neglect in Japanese- and Samoan-Americans. *Child Abuse and Neglect,* 1980, *4*(4), 217–225.

Elliott, F. Neurological aspects of psychopathic behavior. In W. H. Reid (Ed.), *The psychopath: A comprehensive study of antisocial disorders and behavior.* New York: Brunner/Mazel, 1978.

Elliot, F. Neurological findings in adult minimal brain dysfunction and the dyscontrol syndrome. *The Journal of Nervous and Mental Disease,* 1982, *170*(11), 680–687.

Elmer, E. Studies of child abuse and infant accidents. In *The mental health of the child.* U.S. National Institute of Mental Health. Washington, D.C.: U.S. Government Printing Office, 1971.

Elmer, E. A follow-up study on traumatized children. *Pediatrics,* 1977, *59,* 273–279.

Elmer, E., & Gregg, G. S. Developmental characteristics of abused children. *Pediatrics,* 1967, *40,* 596–602.

Erlanger, H. S. Social class and corporal punishment: A reassessment. *American Sociological Review,* 1974, *39* (Feb.), 68–85.

Fanaroff, A., Kennell, J., & Klaus, M. Follow-up of low birth weight infants—The prediction value of maternal visiting patterns. *Pediatrics,* 1972, *49,* 287–290.

Farrington, K. *Family violence and household density: Does the crowded home breed aggression?* Paper presented at the Meeting of the Society for the Study of Social Problems, Chicago, September 5–9, 1977.

Feirerabend, I. K., Feirerabend, R. L., & Nesvold, B. A. Social change and political violence: Cross national pattern. In H. D. Graham & T. R. Gurr (Eds.), *Violence in America: Historical and comparative perspectives.* Washington, D.C.: U.S. Government Printing Office, 1969.

Feshbach, S. *Aggression.* In P. H. Mussen (Ed.), *Carmichael's manual of child psychology* (Vol. 2). New York: Wiley, 1970.

Field, M., & Kirchner, R. M. Services to battered women. *Victimology*, 1978, *3*(1–2), 216–222.

Finkelhor, D., & Yello, K. Rape in marriage: A sociological view. In D. Finkelhor, R. J. Gelles, G. Hotaling, & M. A. Straus, *The Dark Side of Families*. Beverly Hills, Calif.: Sage, 1983.

Fischer, D. H. *Growing old in America*. New York: Oxford University Press, 1977.

Fithian, P. V. *Journal and letters of Philip Vickers Fithian, 1773–1774*. Princeton, N.J.: Princeton University Press, 1945.

Fomuford, A. K., Sinkford, S. M., & Louy, V. E. Mother-child separation at birth: A contributing factor in child abuse. *Lancet*, 1975, *2*, 549–550.

Friedrich, W. N., & Borisking, J. A. The role of the child in abuse: A review of the literature. *American Journal of Orthopsychiatry*, 1976, *46*, 580–590.

Frodi, A. M. Contribution of infant characteristics to child abuse. *American Journal of Mental Deficiency*, 1981, *85*(4), 341–349.

Galdston, R. Preventing the abuse of little children: The parents' center project for the study and prevention of child abuse. *American Journal of Orthopsychiatry*, 1975, *45*(3), 372–381.

Garbarino, J. A. A preliminary study of some ecological correlates of child abuse: The impact of socioeconomic stress on mothers. *Child Development*, 1976, *47*, 178–185.

Gayford, J. Wife battering: A preliminary survey of 100 cases. *British Medical Journal*, 1975, *1*, 195–197.

Gelles, R. J. Child abuse as psychopathology: A sociological critique and reformulation. *American Journal of Orthopsychiatry*, 1973, *43*, 611–621.

Gelles, R. J. *The violent home*. Beverly Hills, Calif.: Sage, 1974.

Gelles, R. J. Violence and pregnancy: A note on the extent of the problem and needed services. *The Family Coordinator*, 1975, *24*(1), 81–86.

Gelles, R. J. Abused wives: Why do they stay? *Journal of Marriage and the Family*, 1976, *38*(1), 127–138.

Gelles, R. J. Etiology of violence: Overcoming fallacious reasoning in understanding family violence and child abuse. In R. J. Gelles (Ed.), *Family violence*. Beverly Hills, Calif.: Sage, 1979.

Gelles, R. J. Violence in the family: A review of research in the seventies. *Journal of Marriage and the Family*, 1980, *42*, 873–885.

Gelles, R. J., & Straus, M. A. Determinants of violence in the family: Toward a theoretical integration. In W. Burr, R. Hill, F. I. Nye, & I. Reiss (Eds.), *Contemporary theories about the family*. New York: Free Press, 1979.

George, V., & Wilding, P. *Motherless families*. London: Routledge & Kegan Paul, 1972.

Gil, D. Violence against children. *Journal of Marriage and the Family*, 1968, *33*(4), 637–648.

Gil, D. *Violence against children: Physical child abuse in the United States*. Cambridge: Harvard University Press, 1970.

Giles-Sims, J. *Wife battering: A systems theory approach*. New York: Guildford Press, 1983.

Giovannoni, J. M. Parental mistratment: Perpetrators and victims. *Journal of Marriage and the Family*, 1976, *33*(4), 649–657.

Giovannoni, J. J., & Becerra, R. M. *Defining child abuse*. New York: Free Press, 1979.

Goode, W. J. Force and violence in the family. *Journal of Marriage and the Family*, 1971, *33*(Nov.), 624–636.

Gove, P. B. (Ed.). *Webster's third new international dictionary of the English language*. Springfield, Mass.: G. & C. Merriam, 1976.

Green, A. H. Self-destructive behavior in physically abusive schizophrenic children: Report of cases. *Archives of General Psychiatry*, 1968, *19*, 171–179.

Green, A. H. Self-destructive behavior in battered children. *American Journal of Psychiatry*, 1978, *135*(May 5), 579–582.

Greven, P. *Four generations: Population, land and family in colonial Andover, Massachusetts*. Ithaca, N.Y.: Cornell University Press, 1970.

Gurr, T. R. A comparative study of civil strife. In H. D. Graham & T. R. Gurr (Eds.), *Violence in America: Historical and comarative perspectives*. Washington, D.C.: U.S. Government Printing Office,

Gurr, T. R., & Bishop, V. F. Violent nations and others. *Journal of Conflict Resolution*, 1976, *20*(Mar.), 79–110.

Harbin, H., & Madden, D. Battered parents: A new syndrome. *American Journal of Psychiatry*, 1979, *136*, 1288–1291.

Hartogs, R. Discipline in the early life of six delinquent and sex criminals. *Nervous Child*, 1951, *9*(Mar.), 167–173.

Heer, D. M. The measurement and bases of family power: An overview. *Family Process*, 1963, *2*, 133–139.

Hibbs, D. A. *Mass political violence*. New York: Wiley, 1973.

Hilberman, E., & Munson, I. Sixty battered women. *Victimology*, 1977–1978, *2*, 460–470.

Hofsteader, R., & Wallace, M. *American violence: A documentary history*. New York: Knopf, 1970.

Holter, J. C., & Friedman, S. B. Principles of management in child abuse cases. *American Journal of Orthopsychiatry*, 1968, *38*(1), 127–138.

Hornung, C. A., McCullough, B. C., & Sugimoto, T. Status relationships in marriage: Risk factors in spouse abuse. *Journal of Marriage and the Family*, 1981 *43* (Aug.), 675–692.

Jacobs, J. *Adolescent suicide*. New York: Wiley-Interscience, 1971.

Jaggar, A. M. and Struhl, P. R. (Eds.). *Feminist frameworks: Alternative theoretical accounts of the relations between men and women*. New York: McGraw-Hill, 1978.

Jarvik, L. F., Klodin, V., & Matsuyama, S. S. Human aggression and the extra chromosome: Fact or fantasy? *American Psycholgist*, 1973, *28*, 674.

Johnson, B., & Morse, H. A. Injured children and their parents. *Children*, 1968, *15*, 147–152.

Kempe, C. H., & Helfer, R. E. (Eds.). *Helping the battered child and his family*. Philadelphia: Lippincott, 1972.

Kempe, C. H. *et al.* The battered child syndrome. *Journal of the American Medical Association*, 1962, *1981*, 17–24.

Kinard, E. M. Emotional development in physically abused children. *American Journal of Orthopsychiatry*, 1980, *50*(4), 686–696.

Kinard, E. M. The psychological consequences of abuse for the child. *Journal of Social Issues*, 1979, *35*(2), 82–100.

Klein, M., & Stern, L. Low birth weight and the battered child syndrome. *American Journal of Diseases of Childhood*, 1971, *122*, 15–18.

Knopoka, G. *Young girls: A portrait of adolescents*. Englewood Cliffs, N.J.: Prentice-Hall, 1975.

Kolb, T. J., & Straus, M. A. Marital power and marital happiness in relation to problem solving ability. *Journal of Marriage and the Family*, 1974, *36*, 756–766.

Korsch, B. M., Christian, J. B., Gozzi, E. K., & Carlson, P. V. Infant care and punishment: A pilot study. *American Journal of Public Health*, 1965, *55*, 1880–1888.

Kosberg, J. I. (Ed.). *Abuse and maltreatment of the elderly: Causes and interventions*. Boston: John Wright, PSG, 1983.

Kumagai, F., & O'Donoghue, G. Conjugal power and conjugal violence in Japan and the U.S.A. *Journal of Comparative Family Studies*, 1978, *9*(2), 211–221.

Langdon, B. Statement presented at the House of Representatives Select Committee on Aging. (96), June 23, 1979. Boston, Mass. Washington, D.C.: U.S. Government Printing Office, 1980.

Langman, L. *Economic practices and socialization in three societies*. Paper presented at annual meeting of American Sociological Association, 1973.

Lauderdale, M., Valiunas, A., & Anderson, M. Race, ethnicity, and child maltreatment: An empirical analysis. *Child Abuse and Neglect*, 1980, *4*(3), 163–169.

Lederberg, J. The genetics of human nature. *Social Research*, 1973, *43*, 387.

Leiderman, P. H. Mothers at risk: A potential consequence of the hospital care of the premature infant. In E. Anthony & C. Koupernik (Eds.),

The child in his family: Children at psychiatric risk (Vol. 3). New York: Wiley, 1974.

Lester, D. Punishment, experiences and suicidal preoccupation. *Journal of Genetic Psychology*, 1968, *113*, 89–94.

Lester, D. A cross-cultural study of wife abuse. *Aggressive Behavior*, 1980, *6*, 361–364.

Levinger, G. Sources of marital dissatisfaction among applicants for divorces. *American Journal of Orthopsychiatry*, 1966, *36*, 5.

Lewis, D. O., Pincus, J., Shanok, S., & Glaser, G. Psychomotor epilepsy and violence in a group of incarcerated adolescent boys. *American Journal of Psychiatry*, 1982, *139*(7), 882–887.

Libbey, P., & Bybee, R. The physical abuse of adolescents. *Journal of Social Issues*, 1979, *35*(2), 101–126.

Light, R. Abused and neglected children in America: A study of alternative policies. *Harvard Educational Review*, 1974, *43*, 556–598.

MacAndrew, C., & Edgerton, R. B. *Drunken comportment: A social explanation*. Chicago: Aldine, 1969.

Maccoby, E. E., & Jacklin, C. N. *The psychology of sex differences*. Stanford, Calif.: Stanford University Press, 1974.

MacDonald, J. M. Homicidal threats. *American Journal of Psychiatry*, 1967, *124*, 475–482.

MacNamara, D. E., & Sagarin, E. *Perspectives on correction*. New York: Thomas Y. Crowell, 1971.

Martin, D. *Battered wives*. San Francisco: Glide Publishers, 1976.

Martin, H. P., Beezley, P., Conway, E. F., & Kempe, C. H. The development of abused children. *Advances in Pediatrics*, 1974, *21*, 25–73.

Masumura, W. T. Wife abuse and other forms of aggression. *Victimology: An International Journal*, 1979, *4*(1), 46–59.

McKinley, D. G. *Social class and family life*. New York: Free Press, 1964.

Mead, M. *Sex and temperament in three primitive societies*. New York: Morrow, 1935.

Mednick, S. A., Van Dusen, K. T., Gabrielli, W. F., & Hutchings, B. *Genetic predispositions for criminal behavior*. Presented at the Southwest Science Forum Symposium on Violence and Aggression, Houston, October 1982.

Milner, J. S., & Wimberly, R. C. Prediction and explanation of child abuse. *Journal of Clinical Psychology*, 1980, *36*(4), 875–884.

Monroe, R. R. *Episodic behavioral disorders—A psychodynamic and neurophysiologic analysis*. Cambridge: Harvard University Press, 1970.

Morgan, Edmund S. *The puritan family*. New York: Harper & Row, 1966.

Morse, C., Sahler, O., & Friedman, S. A three-year follow-up study of abused and neglected children. *American Journal of Disease of Children*, 1970, *120*, 439–446.

Mussen, P. H., Conger, J., & Kagen, J. *Child Development and Personality* (4th ed.). New York: Harper & Row, 1974.

Myers, T. Testimony presented before the subcommittee on domestic and international scientific planning, analysis and cooperation, HR, Committee on Science and Technology (95) Feb. 14–16, 1978, pp. 175–185.

Neiderhoffer, A. *Behind the shield: The police in urban society*. Garden City, N.Y.: Doubleday, 1967.

Newberger, E. H., Reed, R. B., Daniel, J. H., Hyde, J. N., & Kotelchuck, M. Pediatric social illness: Toward an etiologic classificaton. *Pediatrics*, 1977, *60*, 178–185.

Niemi, R. G. *How family members perceive each other*. New Haven, Conn.: Yale University Press, 1974.

O'Brien, J. E. Violence in divorce-prone families. *Journal of Marriage and the Family*, 1971, *33*, 692–698.

Oliver, J. E., & Taylor, A. Five generations of ill-treated children in one family pedigree. *British Journal of Psychiatry*, 1971, *119*(552), 473–480.

Olson, D. H., McCubbin, H. I., Barnes, H. L., Larsen, A. S., Muxen, M. J., & Wilson, M. A. *Families: What makes them work*. Beverly Hills, Calif.: Sage, 1983.

Olsen, D. H., Sprenkle, D., & Russell, C. Circumplex model of marital and family systems I: Cohesion and adaptability dimensions, family type and clinical applications. *Family Process* 1979, *18*, 3–28.

O'Malley, H., Segars, H., & Perez, R. *Elder abuse in Massachusetts: A survey of professionals and paraprofessional*. Boston: Legal Research and Sources for the Elderly, 1979.

Orme, T. C., & Rimmer, J. Alcoholism and child abuse. *Journal of Studies on Alcohol*, 1981, *42*(3), 273–287.

Oswald, I. Domestic violence by women. *The Lancet*, 1980, *D6*, 1253.

Otterbein, K. F., & Otterbein, C. S. An eye for an eye, a tooth for a tooth: A cross-cultural study of feuding. *American Anthropologist*, 1965, *67*, 1470–1482.

Owens, D. J., & Straus, M. A. The social structure of violence in childhood and approval of violence as an adult. *Aggressive Behavior*, 1975, *1*(2), 193–211.

Pagelow, M. D. *Does the law help battered women? Some research notes*. Madison, Wi.: Law and Society Association, 1980.

Pagelow, M. D. *Family violence*. New York: Praeger, 1984.

Palmer, S. *The psychology of murder*. New York: Thomas Y. Crowell, 1962.

Parker, B., & Schumaker, D. The battered wife syndrome and violence in the nuclear family of origin: A controlled pilot study. *American Journal of Public Health*, 1977, *67*, 760–761.

Patterson, G. R., Cobb, J. A., & Ray, R. A. A social engineering technology for retraining families of aggressive boys. In H. E. Adams & I. P. Unikel (Eds.), *Issues and trends in behavior therapy*. Springfield, Ill.: Charles C Thomas, 1973.

Pleck, E. J., Pleck, M., Grossman, M., & Bart, P. The battered data syndrome: A comment on Steinmetz's article. *Victimology*, 1977–1978, *2*(3–4), 680–683.

Polansky, N. A., *et al. Profile of neglect: A survey of the state of knowledge of child neglect*. Washington, D.C.: U.S. Department of Health, Education, and Welfare, 1975.

Post, R. D., Willett, A. B., Franks, R. D., House, R. M., Back, S. M., & Weissberg, M. P. A preliminary report on the prevalence of domestic violence among psychiatric inpatients. *American Journal of Psychiatry*, 1980, *137*(8), 974–975.

Prescott, J. W. Body pleasure and the origins of violence. *The Bulletin of the Atomic Scientist*, 1975, *31*, 10–20.

Prescott, S., & Letko, C. Battered: A social psychological perspective. In M. M. Ray (Ed.), *Battered women: A psychosociological study of domestic violence*. New York: Van Nostrand Reinhold, 1977.

Prinz, R. J., Roberts, W. A., & Hantman, E. Dietary correlates of hyperactive behavior in children. *Journal of Consulting and Clinical Psychology*, 1980, *48*(6), 760–769.

Radbill, S. X. A history of child abuse and infanticide. In R. E. Helper & C. H. Kempe (Eds.), *The Battered Child*. Chicago: University of Chicago Press, 1968.

Resnick, M. Wife beating: Counselor training manual #1. Ann Arbor, Mich.: NOW-Wife Assault Task Force, 1976.

Ridington, J. The transition process: A feminist environment as reconstitutive milieu. *Victimology*, 1977–1978 *2*, 563–575.

Rosen, B. Interpersonal values among child-abusive women. *Psychological Reports*, 1979, *45*, 819–822.

Rosenbaum, A., & O'Leary, D. Children: The unintended victims of marital violence. *American Journal of Orthopsychiatry*, 1981, *51*, 692–699.

Roy, M. A current survey of 150 cases. In M. Roy (Ed.), *Battered women: A psychosociological study of domestic violence*. New York: Van Nostrand Reinhold, 1977

Russell, D. *Rape in marriage*. New York: Macmillan, 1982.

Sadoff, R. L. Clinical observations on parricide. *Psychiatric Quarterly*, 1971, *45*, 65–69.

Saenger, C. Male and female relations in the American comic strip. In D.

M. White & R. H. Abel (Eds.), *The funnies: An American idiom*. Glencoe, Ill.: Free Press, 1963.

Safilios-Rothschild, C. Family sociology of wives' family sociology: A cross cultural examination of decision-making. *Journal of Marriage and the Family*, 1969, *31*, 190–301.

Sandgrund, A., Gaines, R. W., & Green, A. H. Child abuse and mental retardation: A problem of cause and effect. *American Journal of Mental Deficiency*, 1974, *79*, 327–330.

Sargent, D. Children who kill: A family conspiracy. *Social Work*, 1962, *7*, 35–42.

Sarles, R. M. Child abuse. In D. J. Madden & J. R. Lion (Eds.), *Rage, hate, assault and other forms of violence*. New York: Spectrum Publications, 1976.

Scanzoni, J. *Sex roles, women's work and marital conflict*. Lexington, Mass.: Lexington Publishers, 1978.

Schreiber, F. R. *Sybil*. New York: Warner Books, 1973.

Schumn, W. M., Martin, M. J., Bollman, S. R., & Jurich, A. P. Classifying family violence. *Journal of Family Issues*, 1982, *3*(3), 319–340.

Sedgely, J., & Lund, D. Self reported beatings and subsequent tolerance for violence. *Public Data Use*, 1979, *7*(1), 30–38.

Shah, S. A. *Report on the XYY chromosomal abnormality*. Public Health Service publication No. 2103, 1970.

Shorter, E. *The making of the modern family*. New York: Basic Books, 1975.

Shwed, J. A. *The military environment and physical child abuse*. Unpublished master's thesis, University of New Hampshire, Durham, 1979.

Silbert, M. *NIMH study of streetwalkers: Final report*. San Francisco: Delancy Street Foundation, 1980. (Mimeo)

Silver, L. B., Dublin, C. C., & Lourie, R. S. Child abuse syndrome: The "gray areas" in establishing a diagnosis. *Pediatrics*, 1969, *44*, 594–600.

Singer, J. *The control of aggression and violence*. New York: Academic Press, 1971.

Skolnick, J. H. *Justice without trial: Law enforcement in democratic society*. Garden City, N.Y.: Doubleday, 1969.

Slater, P., & Slater, D. Maternal ambivalence and narcissism. *Merrill Palmer Quarterly*, 1965, *11*, 241–259.

Smith, D. B. *Inside the Great House: Planter Family Life in the Eighteenth-Century Chesapeake Society*. Ithaca, N.Y.: Cornell University Press, 1980.

Smith, S. M., Honigsberger, L., & Smith, C. A. EEG and personality factors in baby beaters. *British Medical Journal*, 1973, *3*, 20–22.

Snell, J. R. Rosenwald, R., & Robey, A. The wifebeater's wife: A study of family interaction. *Archive of General Psychiatry*, 1964, *11*, 107–112.

Soeffing, M. Abused children are exceptional children. *Exceptional Children*, 1975, *42*, 126–133.

Sourcebook of Criminal Justice Statistics. Washington, D.C.: U.S. Government Printing Office, 1982.

Spektor, P. Testimony delivered to the Law Enforcement Subcommittee of the Minnesota House of Representatives, February 29, 1980.

Sprey, J. The family as a system in conflict. *Journal of Marriage and the Family*, 1969, *31*(Nov.), 699–706.

Stare, F. J., Whelan, E. M., & Sheridan, M. Diet and hyperactivity: Is there a relationship? *Pediatrics*, 1980, *66*(4), 521–525.

Stark, R., & McEvoy, J. Middle class violence. *Psychology Today*, 1970, *4*(Nov.), 52–65.

State vs. *Oliver*, 70 NC 60, 61 (1874).

Steel, B. F., & Pollock, D. A psychiatric study of parents who abuse infants and small children. In R. E. Helfer & C. H. Kempe (Eds.), *The battered child*. Chicago: University of Chicago Press, 1968.

Steinmetz, S. K. Occupation and physical punishment: A response to Straus. *Journal of Marriage and the Family*, 1971, *33*, 664–666.

Steinmetz, S. K. *Family backgrounds of political assassins*. Paper presented at the American Orthopsychiatric Assocation, 1973. (Reviewed in *Human Behavior*, January 1974.)

Steinmetz, S. K. Occupational environment in relation to physical punishment and dogmatism. In S. K. Steinmetz & M. A. Straus (Eds.), *Violence in the family*. New York: Harper & Row, 1974.

Steinmetz, S. K. *The cycle of violence assertive, aggressive, and abusive family interaction*. New York: Praeger, 1977. (a)

Steinmetz, S. K. The use of force for resolving family conflict: The training ground for abuse. *Family Coordinator*, 1977, *33*(4), 19–26. (b)

Steinmetz, S. K. Wifebeating–husbandbeating—a comparison of the use of physical violence between spouses to resolve marital fights. In M. Roy (Ed.), *Battered women: A psychosociological study of domestic violence*. New York: Van Nostrand Reinhold, 1977. (c)

Steinmetz, S. K. The battered husband syndrome. *Victimology*, 1977–1978, *2*, 499–509.

Steinmetz, S. K. Battered parents. *Society*, 1978, *15*, 54. (a)

Steinmetz, S. K. Disciplinary techniques and their relationship to aggression, dependency, and conscience. In W. R. Burr *et al.* (Eds.), *Contemporary theories about the family*. New York: Free Press, 1978. (b)

Steinmetz, S. K. Violence between family members. *Marriage and Family Review*, 1978, *1*, 1–16. (c)

Steinmetz, S. K. Services to battered women, still our greatest need: A reply to Field and Kirchner. *Victimology*, 1978, *3*,(1–2), 222–226. (d)

Steinmetz, S. K. Wife beating: A critique and reformulation of existing theory. *Bulletin of the American Academy of Psychiatry and the Law*, 1979, *6*(3), 322–334.

Steinmetz, S. K. Investigating family violence. *Journal of Home Economics*, 1980, *72*(2), 32–36. (a)

Steinmetz, S. K. Violence prone families. *Annals of the New York Academy of Sciences*, 1980, *347*, 251–265. (b)

Steinmetz, S. K. Women and violence: Victims and perpetrators. *American Journal of Psychotherapy*, 1980, *34*(3), 334–350. (c)

Steinmetz, S. K. Elder abuse. *Aging*, 1981 (Jan.–Feb.), pp. 6–10. (a)

Steinmetz, S. K. Marital abuse: A cross-cultural comparison. *Sociology and Social Welfare*, 1981, *8*(2), 404–414. (b)

Steinmetz, S. K. A cross-cultural comparison of sibling violence. *International Journal of Family Psychiatry*, 1982, *2*(3–4), 337–351.

Steinmetz, S. K. Family violence towards elders. In S. Saunders, A. Anderson, C. Hart, & G. Rubenstein (Eds.), *Violent individuals and families: A handbook for practitioners*. Springfield, Ill.: Charles C Thomas, 1984.

Steinmetz, S. K. Elder abuse: One-fifth of our population at risk. Testimony presented to the Subcommittee on Health and Long-Term Care. HR. Select Committee on Aging (99), May 10, 1985.

Steinmetz, S. K. Confronting violence in the 1980s: In the street, school, and home. In L. G. Hertzberg, J. F. Ostrom, & J. R. Field, *Violent Behavior: Vol. I. Assessment and intervention*. New York: Spectrum Publications, 1986.

Steinmetz, S. K. *Duty bound: Family care and elder abuse*. Beverly Hills, Calif.: Sage (in press).

Steinmetz, S. K., & Amsden, D. J. Dependent elders, family stress and abuse. In T. H. Brubaker (Ed.), *Family relationships in later life*. Beverly Hills, Calif.: Sage, 1983.

Steinmetz, S. K., & Straus, M. A. The family as cradle of violence. *Society*, 1973, *10*(6), 50–56.

Steinmetz, S. K., & Straus, M. A. (Eds.). *Violence in the family*. New York: Harper & Row, 1974.

Straus, M. A. Some social antecedents of physical punishment: A linkage theory interpretation. *Journal of Marriage and the Family*, 1971 (Nov.), pp. 658–663.

Straus, M. A. A general systems theory approach to a theory of violence between family members. *Social Science Information*, 1973, *12*, 105–125.

Straus, M. A. Leveling, civility, and violence in the family. *Journal of Marriage and the Family*, 1974, *36*(Feb.), 13–29.

Straus, M. A. Sexual unequality, cultural norms and wife-beating. *Victimology*, 1976, *1*, 54–76.

Straus, M. A. Wifebeating: How common and why? *Victimology*, 1977–1978, *2*, 443–457.

Straus, M. A. Family patterns and child abuse in a nationally representative American sample. *Child Abuse and Neglect*, 1979, *3*, 213–215. (a)

Straus, M. A. Measuring intrafamily conflict and violence: The conflict tactics (CT) scales. *Journal of Marriage and the Family*, 1979, *41*(Feb.), 75–88. (b)

Straus, M. A., & Gelles, R. J. *Is family violence increasing: A comparison of 1975 and 1985 national survey rates*. Paper presented at the annual meeting, American Society of Criminology. San Diego, November 1985.

Straus, M. A., Gelles, R. J., & Steinmetz, S. K. *Behind closed doors: Violence in American families*. New York: Doubleday, 1980.

Sweet, J. J., & Resnick, P. The maltreatment of children: A review of theories and research. *Journal of Social Issues*, 1979, *35*(2), 40–59.

Szinovacz, M. E. Using couple data as a methodological tool: The case of marital violence. *Journal of Marriage and the Family*, 1983, *45*(3), 633–644.

Tanay, E. Reactive parricide. *Journal of Forensic Sciences*, 1975, *21*(1), 76–82.

Tardiff, K. *Endocrine effects in aggression and violence*. Presented at the Southwest Forum Symposium on Violence and Aggression, Houston, October 1982.

Tiger, L. *Men in groups*. New York: Random House, 1969.

Toby, J. Violence and the masculine ideal: Some qualitative data. *Annual of the Americal Academy Political and Social Science*, 1966, *364*, 19–27.

Torgerson, D. *Daily Times* (Mamaroneck, N.Y.). February 20, 1973, p. 4.

Turbett, J. P., O'Toole, R. *Physician's recognition of child abuse*. Paper presented at the annual meeting, American Sociological Association, New York, 1980.

U.S. Department of Justice. *FBI uniform crime reports*. Washington, D.C.: U.S. Government Printing Office, 1985.

Van Velzen, H. U. E., Van Wetering, W. Residence, power groups, and intra-societal aggression. *International Archives of Ethnography*, 1960, *49*, 169–200.

Walker, L. E. Battered women and learned helplessness. *Victimology*, 1977–1978, *2*, 525–534.

Walker, L. E. *The battered woman*. New York: Harper & Row, 1979.

Walker, L. E. *The battered woman syndrome*. New York: Springer, 1984.

Warren, C. *Parent batterers: Adolescent violence and the family*. Paper presented at the annual meeting of the Pacific Sociological Association, Anaheim, Calif., April, 1978.

Wasserman, S. The abused parent of the abused child. *Children*, 1967, *14*, 175–179.

Weber, M. *The theory of social and economic organization* (A. M. Henderson & T. Parsons, Trans.). New York: Free Press, 1947. (Reprinted, 1964)

Wertham, F. Battered children and baffled adults. *Bulletin of New York Academy of Medicine*, 1972, *40*, 887–898.

Whitchurch, G. G. Communication and conjugal violence: Linkages in family studies and communication research. In S. K. Steinmetz & G. G. Whitchurch (Eds.), *Family violence: An anthology*. Harper & Row (in press).

Whitehurst, R. Violence in husband–wife interaction. In S. K. Steinmetz, & M. A. Straus (Eds.), *Violence in the Family*. New York: Harper & Row, 1974.

Whiting, B. Sex identity conflict and physical violence: A comparative study. *American Anthropologist*, 1965, *67*, 123–140.

Wilkening, E. A., & Morrison, D. E. A comparison of husband and wife responses concerning who makes farm and home decisions. *Marriage and Family Living*, 1963, *25*, 349–351.

Williams, D. Neural factors related to habitual aggression, considerations of differences between those habitual aggressives and others who have committed crimes of violence. *Brain*, 1969, *92*, 503–520.

Wilt, G. M., & Bannon, J. D. *Violence and the police: Homicides, assaults, and disturbances*. Washington, D.C.: Police Foundation, 1976.

Wiseman, J. P. An alternative role for the wife of an alcoholic in Finland. *Journal of Marriage and the Family*, 1975, *37*, 172–179.

Wittenberg, C. Studies of child abuse and infant accidents. In J. Segal (Ed.), *The mental health of the child: Program reports of the National Institute of Mental Health*. Washington, D.C.: U.S. Government Printing Office, 1971.

Wolfgang, M. E. *Patterns in criminal homicide*. Philadelphia: University of Pennsylvania Press, 1958.

Wolfgang, M. E., & Ferracuti, F. *The subculture of violence: Toward an integrated theory of criminology*. London: Tavistock, 1967.

Yllo, K. Sexual equality and violence against wives in American states. *Journal of Comparative Family Studies*, 1983, *14* (1, Spring), 67–86.

Young, L. R. *Wednesday's children: A study of child neglect and abuse*. New York: McGraw-Hill, 1964.

Zalba, S. A. The abused child: A survey of the problem. *Social Work*, 1966, *11*, 3–16.

Ziegert, K. A. The Swedish prohibition of corporal punishment: A preliminary report. *Journal of Marriage and the Family*, 1983, *45*, 917–926.

CHAPTER 27

Families and the Law

Lora Liss

Introduction

Origins of American Family Law

This chapter traces the origins of the family and the law in the United States, including the movement of marriage from contract (private) to status (state-regulated) relationships and, in the opinion of many social historians, the return to a contractual approach to married and unmarried relationships (Sussman, 1975).

The role of women, central to the institution of the family, is explored from the perspective of their legal subordination in marriage, through the cult of motherhood, the myths and stereotypes as they were incorporated into the law, and the evolution of the new minority—the homemaker.

The chapter marks the silence of the U.S. Constitution on the subject of the family yet notes the development of a body of constitutional law that speaks profusely of rights and responsibilites that impact on the family and that limit state regulation of domestic relations. The interplay between U.S. Supreme Court decisions and state legislation has followed an erratic movement between liberal and conservative approaches to family law (Chastain, 1982). Although the state defines the rights and obligations of marriage, with few exceptions it will not interfere with ongoing relationships between husbands and wives or parents and children. For example, the courts will not inquire into the adequacy of support obligations for wives, but they will intervene to uphold third-party creditors' suits against husbands, and they have begun to hold wives liable for debts incurred for medical necessities during the marriage (*Sillery* v. *Fagan and Fagan,* 1972). Ironically, this case represents the closest that the courts have come to recognizing wives as legal partners in marriage, not in the traditional master–servant relationship of husbands to wives. If the wife can contract and spend the marriage's resources, she can be held liable in a manner that the New Jersey court traced back to a French case of 1559 (Blumrosen, 1982). The decision that the financial burdens of marriage rest equally on husband and wife is

an example of the cumulative effects of constitutional efforts to eliminate discrimination in family law as they have trickled down to the states. Marriage, divorce, privacy, parent–child relationships, custody, child support, alimony, property disposition, parental abuse of children, marital rape, and elder abuse are the major topics that illustrate the current status of the family and the law in the United States today.

From Contract to Status

Historically, marriage existed as a private relationship, often an alliance between families, still practiced by tribes today, with neither the state nor the church involved. In effect, marriage constituted a form of contract, although it lacked enforcement by formal institutions and the terms of the marriage were heavily circumscribed by societal norms. In 1885, Sir Henry Maine noted the extent of state involvement in marriage and predicted a progressive evolution of societies from status, based on one's ascribed position in the community, to contract, based on rational, purposive deliberations (Bernard, 1975). But in 1982, marriage had not yet conferred on individuals the ability to negotiate contracts freely, beyond the decision to enter the institution of marriage. Once entered, rights and duties flow from the collective contract and the relationship cannot be terminated at will.

In one sense, all marriages involve a contract, although one with many hidden provisions unknown to the partners until the marriage breaks down and one or more of the parties seek redress for presumed wrongful behavior. At that point, the parties discover that the state has a third-party interest.

The prestatus contractual marriage has been traced to the later days of the Roman Empire, when marriage was freely terminable by either one of the parties, but the family exercised such strict controls that divorce was rare. When these controls broke down, the absence of any law created a vacuum of restraint, and it became common to change partners frequently, sometimes within a few days (Bodenheimer, 1968).

The Stoic philosophers and the early Christians condemned the sexual chaos of their times and, through their teachings, eventually swung back to the other extreme.

Lora Liss • 7207 Snowden Drive, San Antonio, TX 78240.

The reaction against the Roman way of life caused the complete abolition of divorce in the Middle Ages. Christianity and the law based on its teachings made a unique and unprecedented attempt to create absolutely permanent, indissoluble marriage. By 1880, a papal encyclical of Leo XIII had asserted as doctrine that matrimony was instituted by God, not man, and that no man could rend the bonds of matrimony asunder (Encyclical Letter, 1880, in Wadlington & Paulsen, 1978). Once each of the contracting parties acted out of free will, that marriage became subject to divine law. If there were things in the matrimonial pact that violated the consent that made the marriage, it would not be a true marriage.

Protestants rejected the concept of marriage as a sacrament and insisted that it should be a temporal matter. But Luther, the first to assert this position, did not take the next logical step—to free divorce. The family was the focal point of his social philosophy; consequently, only in the cases of adultery or malicious desertion, threats to family solidarity, was he prepared to concede an absolute divorce, and only the innocent party was free to remarry (Wadlington & Paulsen, 1978, p. 343).

Effect of Religion on U.S. Marriage and Divorce Laws

Religious doctrines still permeate laws in the United States governing marriage and divorce, derived from English common law. For example, annulments are granted only if there is fraud that goes to the essentials of the marriage, including bigamy, incest, impotence, or insanity. Before the reign of Henry VIII, marriage was regarded as a sacrament of the church and therefore indissoluble (Kanowitz, 1969). As a result, the English ecclesiastical courts granted no absolute divorces, although they did permit judicial separations, or divorce *a mensa et thoro* which did not end the marriage or permit remarriage. Between the reign of Charles II (1660–1685) and 1857, when Parliament passed the Matrimonial Causes Act, divorce could be granted only by private acts of Parliament. "Before 1715 there were 60, between 1775 and 1800 there were 74, and between 1800 and 1850 there were 90 private divorce bills" (Areen, 1979, n. 15A).

Although there were no ecclesiastical courts in this country, and ecclesiastical law was not part of the common law adopted here, similar patterns emerged. Only a few states initially established the right to absolute divorce in the courts, although most permitted private legislative bills by the turn of the nineteenth century (Liss, 1982). By the Civil War, all but five states had transferred divorce to the courts. Fears of a licentious society were just as prevalent in colonial America as in the anti-Roman reaction. Divorce was not facilitated: it was treated as a deviance from the norm and legal grounds were stringent, particularly for women initiating divorce (Kanowitz, 1969). Collusion between the parties, merely desiring to live apart, was anathema. The interests of the state in promoting social stability took precedence over the wishes of individual parties. By the mid-nineteenth cen-

tury, state laws prescribed the rights and obligations of the marriage contract and, with local variations, prescribed who might marry, the age at which they might marry, the civil procedures that governed marriage, the effect on property rights and the grounds considered sufficient for dissolution. The forms of limited divorce, *a mensa et thoro* (also known as separation from bed and board), and absolute divorce, *a vinculo matrimonii,* still persist in virtually all states today. Even the advent of no-fault divorce in the 1970s failed to abolish these distinct forms, each with its own jurisdictional requirements and effects.

Separation of Church and State

Just as the state asserted its supremacy over individuals, the supremacy of the state over religious beliefs was enunciated in the United States under the principle of separation of church and state. In a leading early U.S. Supreme Court case, for example, a Mormon attempted to practice polygamy in the territory of Utah in violation of federal law. The Supreme Court established that the U.S. Congress had the power to prohibit bigamy or polygamy even if the individual was practicing his or her religious beliefs. (*Reynolds* v. *United States,* 1878). The Court held that, although marriage was a sacred obligation, it nevertheless was a civil contract regulated by law.

Similarly, in 1976, the issue was raised in Oklahoma, where a Christian wife contended that the court had no authority to grant her husband a divorce in violation of the ecclesiastical obligations of marriage they had assumed (*Williams* v. *Williams,* 1976). The Oklahoma Supreme Court relied on separation of church and state to hold that the state had absolute control over the dissolution of the civil marriage contract, even though it had no right to enforce or dissolve ecclesiastical vows.

From Status to Contract

For most of our history, marriage has been a highly regulated state-controlled institution. Only in recent years have couples begun to negotiate and bargain for the terms of their personal relationships, through either marriage contracts or cohabitation contracts in lieu of marriage. Many states are now willing to enforce express and implied agreements between parties, as in *Marvin* v. *Marvin* (1976), to be more fully discussed later in this chapter. The popularity of marital and nonmarital contracts has been attributed to significant social changes that have disrupted the established order, prominent among which is the diffusion of sex roles (Beck, 1982). Previously, male superiority was legitimized by societal arrangements for support, divorce, and custody. In the last two decades, the growing demand for sex equality has been both reflected in and fostered by changes in family law.

Sex Equality and Its Impact on Family Law

The impact on women of changes in the legal marital relationship has been particularly strong. This section traces the subordination of women in the law, the influence of the idealization of domesticity and the cult of motherhood, and the emergence of the women's movement. It examines the interaction of the law with women's search for equality and economic independence and the concomitant assertion of fathers' rights, as well as children's rights to self-expression.

In the mid-1960s, when the predecessor *Handbook of Marriage and the Family* was published, women's roles and household economics were referred to as "peripheral specialities" that were "either ignored or relegated to subsidiary positions and treated only when they bear upon the family as such" (Christensen, 1964). Today, it is difficult to imagine that reevaluation of women's roles could possibly have been seen as separate from the focus on the family.

Subordination of Women

The subordination of the wife, based in part on biblical notions of the unity of flesh of husband and wife, resulted in the married woman's loss of legal rights under the feudal doctrine of "coverture," described by Blackstone (1854) as follows:

By marriage, the husband and wife are one person in law; that is, the very being or legal existence of the woman is suspended during the marriage, or at least is incorporated and consolidated into that of the husband, under whose wing, protection and cover she performs everything. (p. 442)

In return for suspension of her legal rights in marriage, the husband was obligated to provide financial support to the family.

Incorporation of the concept that the unity of marriage resided in the husband permeated laws affecting women's names, domicile, and rights to contract and to own and manage property. The harshness of the common-law rules was somewhat alleviated by courts of equity, which were granted substantial discretionary powers. Challenges to the basic principle were uncommon, but they were an important part of American history.

As early as 1855, legal disabilities imposed on married women by the common law were rejected by individuals such as Lucy Stone and her husband, Henry Blackwell. In their Marriage Protest, they declared that such laws "confer upon the husband an injurious and unnatural superiority, investing him with legal powers which no honorable man would exercise, and which no man should possess" (Kraditor, 1968, p. 149). The couple deliberately set out to create an emancipated marriage that would allow the wife full freedom for a public career, by signing a contract in which the husband renounced all legal rights to his wife's services and property and in which the wife contracted to keep her maiden name (Lerner, 1977). But such individual contracts were rare indeed and could not sustain a legal challenge.

The Cult of Motherhood

In addition to the civil death imposed on women who married, the subordination of married women was primarily accomplished in many different cultures through ideologies about motherhood (Gordon, 1977, p. 10). The motherhood ideology served two basic functions: property regulation and justification for the sexual division of labor. It ensured that property would remain within the paternal family by enforcement of chastity on mothers, and by defining femininity with the motherly characteristics of softness, self-effacement, passivity, and sensitivity; and it precluded the fatherly ones: power, assertiveness, freedom, and activity. The ideology implied that men cannot do child raising, that women must mother in order to realize themselves, and that the qualities of this feminine motherliness are the essential qualities of all women, defining and limiting their possibilities in the social, economic, and political spheres. This ideology helped to enforce on women a societal need for large families and a moral prohibition on birth control. Although individual women did use birth control despite this powerful prohibition, there was never an organized challenge to the ideology of motherhood until industrialization created a new economic system that did not require a high birth rate (Gordon, 1977, p. 11).

With industrialization, the spheres of men and women became increasingly separated, including the relegation of the sex drive to men exclusively, with women's sexuality reserved only for the respectable purpose of reproduction. The new theory that women had no sex drive supplanted the male view of women that had dominated for most of history—that women had powerful lusts (Gordon, 1977, p. 22). The repression of female sexuality resulted ultimately in a rebellion against the Victorian sexual system. The rebellion was closely connected with the feminist movement that arose in the 1840s against the repression of sex and the subjugation of women, and that was repeated in the 1960s, when the invention of birth control pills had widespread repercussions.

Women's Rights to Property

An example of the rebellion of women against their subordination is found in the area of their legal rights to property (see Cantwell, 1980; Liss, 1980).

The starting point of any inquiry into American women's property rights is usually the various Married Women's Property Acts and, before that, English common law, under which the civil rights of a woman were suspended during marriage. The Married Women's Property Acts are routinely assumed to have been the remedy for the denial of women's property rights, but recent studies show that they merely codified the granting of limited equitable rights to women.

The socialization process transmitted traditional views of women as docile, obedient, and psychologically dependent on men. The legal system effectively reinforced the socialization process by denying economic independence to most women. Male inheritance of real property through primogeniture (inheritance by the eldest son) affected all women, married or single, and seriously limited women's options for economic self-sufficiency. Single women had male guardians until the age of 21, and until the mid-nineteenth century, unmarried women did not live alone. The differences in marital status did not appear to be worth the disapprobation that accompanied the "spinster's" denial of marriage and children as women's raison d'être. Only as industrialization began and the need for new kinds of skilled labor became manifest in offices, factories, and schools were women encouraged to remain single and enter the emerging labor force (Ehrenreich & English, 1979).

The Emergence of the Women's Movement

The subordination of women has been closely linked with the subordination of black Americans. In *An American Dilemma* (1944), Myrdal likened the institution of slavery to that of the family: "When a legal status had to be found for the imported Negro servants in the seventeenth century, the nearest and most natural analogy was the status of women and children" (p. 1073). In the beginning, the fight for the emancipation of slaves became closely associated with the fight for women's emancipation. The Grimké sisters, Angelina and Sarah, for example, first became involved in the 1830s in the abolitionist movement and only gradually came to demand women's rights. They perceived the particular burden that slavery placed on women and stressed the bond of women of all races (Lerner, 1971, p. 161).

The Grimké sisters' political activism heightened their awareness of women's oppression in marriage and society. Their personal experiences as political activists and nontraditional homemakers (Angelina married at 33; Sarah joined the household and carried major child-rearing responsibilities when Angelina's health was undermined by childbearing problems) mirrored the tension between the antislavery and early feminist movements (Lerner, 1971, p. 309).

The next generation of women leaders, separated by only a 20-year time span, but supported by a much larger network, stood on the shoulders of the pioneering Grimké sisters. Reinforced by the first women's convention at Seneca Falls in 1848, Lucretia Mott, Elizabeth Cady Stanton, Susan B. Anthony, and Lucy Stone continued the struggle for women's emancipation from training for inferior, marriage-centered roles and burdensome propagation and domestic chores, as well as for the prohibition of liquor as well as slavery. In later years, only Stanton frontally attacked the institution of marriage, to the dismay of her suffragist allies.

After the emancipation of the slaves was won, Charlotte Perkins Gilman became the leading proponent of equality and economic independence for women in the second half of the nineteenth century. She did not reject marriage or the family but called for changes in the institutions of child rearing and home maintenance to ease the burdens on working women. She argued that by working outside the home, marital relations would be strengthened (Easton, 1978, p. 18). Gilman was considered the "intellectual," above the battles waged by the suffragists and reformers; she designated herself a "sociologist," not a feminist (Rossi, 1973, p. 568).

Each wave of feminism has been marked by the quest for respectability. Attacks on the women's movement have been most effective when they challenged the political activity as disruptive of the home and as threatening the stability of the family as an institution. Like the antislavery movement before it, the suffrage movement also had its detractors of the family as burdensome to women. But the twentieth-century women leaders were skillful in using the sanctity of the family to their advantage, as well as women's special abilities to cope with social problems based on their experience in the home (Chafe, 1972, p. 13). Carrie Chapman Catt's strategy of consensus with prevailing public opinion bore fruit. Deemphasizing criticism of marriage and repressed sexuality, the suffragists concentrated on making the vote for women a prominent item on the agenda of reform (Chafe, 1972, p. 15).

Almost a century later, Simone deBeauvoir (1953) noted the economic and political dependence of woman on man throughout history and termed it the equivalent of two unequal castes, with men holding the better jobs, getting higher wages, and having more opportunities for success than their new competitors. Some recent feminists have concluded that legal marriage is inherently oppressive for women, and have dedicated themselves to its abolition (Kay & Amyx, 1978, p. 62). Not until Kate Millett's *Sexual Politics* (1970) did a feminist theory emerge in the United States that laid the oppression of women at the feet of woman's role in the family (Easton, 1978, p. 23). Millett distinguished between "traditional patriarchy," in which women had no legal standing, and "modern patriarchy," in which women are formally accorded equal rights with men but in which most women do unpaid labor in the home rather than work for wages in the labor force.

Shulamith Firestone (1970) traced the idea of hierarchical power in the family by linking sex roles with power relations in the family. Firestone linked feminism with a protest against social hierarchies in general, which appealed to the largely college-educated, professional white women comprising the radical wing of feminism in 1970. The movement spread to middle-class, working women, whose numbers mushroomed in the 1960s and 1970s (Easton, 1978, p. 24).

As women's ability to support themselves has improved, their underlying dissatisfaction with the structure of the family and women's roles in the family has returned. Women had suppressed this dissatisfaction in favor of the antislavery movement, then women's suffrage, and in the mid-twentieth century World War II. By the 1960s Betty Friedan (1963) had caught the spirit of betrayal represented by the feminine mystique. Without acknowledging Gilman's earlier pronouncements, she blamed the housewife trap for causing the "problem with no name." This time, enough factors converged to enable women to stand their ground. In the past, the attack on the family had left women unacceptable choices: marriage with children or no marriage. Now, with the revolution created by the pill, women could choose marriage and no children or delayed childbearing. Thus, marriage persisted, nonmarital relationships flourished, the birth rate dropped, and egalitarian roles were pursued as the norm.

What is to ensure that this time women will not be persuaded to return to the hearth in the name of family stability? If Maine's progressive evolution of status to contract could be relied on, it would be unnecessary to institutionalize changed family relations by law. In the absence of such proof, legislation protecting women's right to remain in and advance in the labor force is essential. Amending the Constitution to guarantee women equal rights has once again failed, at least temporarily. But other factors distinguish this wave of feminism from all others.

There has been a growing convergence between white and minority women. Although the history of minority women's experiences in the United States differs in many respects because of cultural and societal expectations, today most American women of all races and classes expect to work outside the home for much of their adult lives, including the child-raising years (Chafe, 1972). The pursuit of economic independence through labor force participation has had a profound effect on family structures, affecting the age-old bargain of sexual favors exchanged for promises of economic security.

This section has traced the reemergence of the women's movement in the 1960s. The next part explains how the law has influenced and has been influenced by the changing norms of the family.

Impact of the Law on the American Family

The Law as It Reflects Myths about the Family

In the past, the law largely reflected the prevailing myths about the family, including myths regarding the nuclear family, woman's place in the home, single women as "spinsters," fathers as breadwinners but not child rearers, sexuality for procreation only, and extramarital sex as adulterous and condemned behavior. Over the past decade, changes in the mores that encompass far more variant family forms than have previously been acknowledged have been dramatic in legislation and court decisions. This section describes the myths that are being destroyed by the interaction of legal changes and the way in which the family members actually conduct their lives.

Definition of the Family. The basic myth that has been shattered over the past decade is that of the nuclear family. What is considered the traditional nuclear family? A breadwinner-father, a housewife-mother, and two children under 18, accounted for only 7% of the population in 1975 (U.S. Bureau of Labor Statistics, 1977). Today, people are living together in new combinations for the intimacy and support that was formerly restricted to the nuclear family. Unmarried adults with or without children, single-parent families, multigenerational communes, and various new groupings of the elderly comprise the new definition of the family. The ability of the law to respond to changing family definitions and lifestyles has been varied.

The question of what constitutes a family has proved perplexing to the courts. Zoning ordinances have proved to be an area of controversy in which the test of what constitutes a legal family has emerged. Originally, the purpose for restricting residential zoning was to prevent turning old, large houses into boarding houses with numerous unrelated tenants. In the 1960s and 1970s, when new modes of communal living became popular, the zoning laws aimed at preventing the poor from putting 14 in a room were used to combat people whose views were antithetical to traditional views of the family.

For example, in *Palo Alto Tenants Union* v. *Morgan* (1970), members of communal living groups sought to enjoin various public officials from "harassing" them under the guise of enforcing municipal zoning ordinances limiting certain areas to single-family dwelling. *Family* was defined in the ordinance as "one person living alone, or two or more persons related by blood, marriage, or legal adoption, or a group not exceeding four persons living as a single housekeeping unit" (Wadlington & Paulsen, 1978, p. 44). The California court found no infringement by the ordinance of the family's constitutional right to freedom of association, distinguishing the "traditional family" relationship from the "voluntary family." The former was seen as an institution reinforced by biological and legal ties that are difficult or impossible to sunder. A zoning law that would have divided or totally excluded traditional families would indeed have been suspect. But the communal living groups were held by the court to have fluctuating memberships with no legal obligations of support or cohabitation, not subject to the state's vast body of domestic regulations law, and without the biological links that characterize most families. The court held that the commune's right to form was constitutionally protected, but not the right to insist that these groups live under the same roof in any part of the city they chose.

Similarly, when six unrelated students tried to rent a house, the United States Supreme Court upheld a restrictive zoning ordinance in *Village of Belle Terre* v. *Boraas* (1974). The Long Island ordinance restricted land use to one-family dwellings and defined the family as:

One or more persons related by blood, adoption or marriage, living and cooking together as a single housekeeping unit, exclusive of household servants. A number of persons but not exceeding two (2) living and cooking together as a single housekeeping unit though not related by blood, adoption, or marriage shall be deemed to constitute a family.

The majority found no violation of the right to privacy because even two unmarried people could fit the definition of *family.*

More recently, the United States Supreme Court has expressed its recognition that the "traditional family" includes not just the nuclear group of parents and child but more extended-kin groups as well. The court distinguished *Moore* v. *City of East Cleveland, Ohio* (1977) from *Belle Terre*, which barred unrelated individuals living together, by striking down a city ordinance that made it a crime for a grandmother to live with her grandsons, who were first cousins rather than brothers. Broadening the definition of *family*, as it applied to related individuals, the *Moore* court held that the Constitution protected the sanctity of the family beyond the nuclear family, citing the tradition of uncles, aunts, cousins, and especially grandparents sharing a household along with parents and children as a venerable tradition from which millions of citizens have profited (Wadlington & Paulsen, 1978, p. 46).

The Court stated:

Even if conditions of modern society have brought about a decline in extended family households, they have not erased the accumulated wisdom of civilization, gained over the centuries and honored throughout our history, that supports a larger conception of the family.

The definition of *family* has also been an issue in welfare cases. The Supreme Court invalidated one aspect of federal welfare program on the basis of traditional equal-protection criteria. In *U.S. Department of Agriculture* v. *Moreno* (1973), the justices held unconstitutional a provision of the federal food-stamp program of assistance to "households." A 1971 amendment had redefined *households* as being limited to groups of related persons, excluding any household containing an unrelated person. The classification was held to be wholly without rational basis, clearly irrelevant to the purposes stated in the statute's preamble: to satisfy nutritional needs and help the agricultural economy (Gunther, 1980, p. 693).

The legislative history revealed an intent to prevent "hippies" or hippie communes from participation, which the court found to be an impermissible purpose. A bare congressional desire to harm a politically unpopular group cannot constitute a legitimate governmental interest, according to the Court (Gunther, 1980, p. 694). The majority opinion even rejected the "interest in minimizing fraud" as not rationally related to a legitimate government interest, and one Justice found the restriction against unrelated persons in a household to be a violation of the First Amendment right to associate with whomever one chooses. On the other hand, the two dissenters found it reasonable for Congress to restrict food stamps only to related persons to guarantee that the household exists for some purpose other than to collect food stamps!

Another area in which the definition of the family has played an important role is in the Aid to Families with Dependent Children (AFDC) program. In this case, the law itself has been instrumental in breaking up the family. Based on the myth of the nuclear family, it was assumed that when no breadwinner was present, that the mother should be able to stay home with the children, and that the

state would play the father's role. The system has had a built-in incentive for poor fathers to desert their families because of the man-in-the-house rule, which caused fathers to leave in order for the family to qualify for AFDC. Desertion became economically attractive even for a caring husband and father. One recent report stated that 80% of children on welfare were on the rolls not because their fathers were dead or disabled, but because their fathers were not in the home (Food Research and Action Center, 1979).

Congress tried to patch up the program by permitting states to cover two-parent families in which the father (but not the mother) was unemployed or underemployed. But the Supreme Court declared the sex-discriminatory provisions unconstitutional. Granting benefits only to families where children were dependent because of the father's but not the mother's unemployment was found to be

part of the "baggage of sexual stereotypes" that presumes the father has the "primary responsibility to provide a home and its essentials," while the mother is the center of the home and family life. (Califano v. Westcott, 1979)

Unfortunately, the effect of this decision may well be to increase the pressure on mothers of young children to work even when they have inadequate child care and require skills training to earn more than poverty-level incomes.

The decision to recognize unmarried people on welfare living together as a family is fraught with danger. For example, one of the key issues in welfare reform is the "filing unit," whose income is counted in determining family eligibility. If the filing unit is "all related people living together," a brother with no legal obligation to support his sister and her children would have his income counted in determining the family's needs. This might discourage family members from living together to share expenses and might promote promiscuity because strangers are not included in the filing unit.

In addition to the definition of the family playing an important role in the welfare system, many other income-maintenance programs exist as almost a second whole system of family law. Medicare, medicaid, general assistance, nutrition programs, supplemental security income (SSI), housing assistance, disability programs, and employment-related programs such as unemployment insurance and earned income-tax credits to low-income workers comprise a loose network of programs aimed at poor individuals and families. Although a detailed analysis of the welfare system is beyond the scope of this chapter, it should be recognized as an important element, influencing the configuration of American families.

One little-recognized fact is that most of the poor are women. The next section includes statistical data on the economic status of women.

The Economic Status of Women. In addition to defining the family unit, the law has had to confront a variety of myths about the role and status of women, which should be tested against the facts when court decisions and legislation are evaluated. Some of the key myths and facts include the following:

MYTH: Marriage is a lifetime commitment to one partner.

FACT: In 1977, the divorce rate was 21 per 1,000 married women. Forty percent of marriages begun in the 1980s are expected to end in divorce.

MYTH: In the typical family, children are raised by their natural parents.

FACT: Experts predict that, by 1990, only 50% of the children in the United States will have spent their entire childhood and adolescence with both natural parents.

MYTH: Most women have a man to support them.

FACT: Women without men do tend to be poor, and increasingly, women are becoming heads of households, required to support their families. In 1978, over 8 million women headed families; 63% of them were widowed or divorced; about 33% of female-headed families were living in poverty, compared to only 6% of male-headed households.

MYTH: When divorce occurs, women benefit from receiving alimony and child support.

FACT: Only about 14% of the 14.3 million ever-divorced or separated women were awarded or had an agreement to receive alimony; for those who did actually receive payment in 1977, the average was only $2,850 for the year. Of the women who were supposed to receive child support in 1978, less than half received the full amount due; the mean amount received was only $1,800.

MYTH: At divorce, women receive most of the couple's property.

FACT: As of spring 1979, less than one half of the 12 million women who had been divorced received some form of property settlement. The median settlement value for all women receiving property was only $4,650.

MYTH: Women with children are expected to be homemakers; men are expected to be breadwinners.

FACT: By 1980, 17.5 million women with children were in the paid labor force. Over half of all American children under 18 had mothers who were employed; 7.5 million of them were under 6.

MYTH: When women work they earn dollar for dollar what men earn.

FACT: Employed women today receive, on the average, 59 cents for every dollar paid to men. The gap is worse for minority women.

MYTH: When equally educated, women earn respectively as much as men.

FACT: Women college graduates are paid $400 a year less than men who have only finished elementary school, $11,609 compared to $12,000 in 1979.

MYTH: When families break up, husbands and wives fare equally well.

FACT: A long-term study of 5,000 American families showed wives and children to be 12 times as likely to be on welfare if they experienced separation or divorce. Husbands were able to improve their standard of living by 30% over a seven-year period (1967–1973), whereas the standard of living of divorced women declined 7% (National Organization for Women Legal Defense and Education Fund, 1981).

MYTH: The ''new'' sexual morality is seen as a change for the worse.

FACT: Age and level of education distinguish men and women who fear the effects of the new morality. Single women, women under 30, college-educated women, and women living in the West are the groups most ready to acknowledge positive changes as a result of society's more widespread acceptance of sexual freedom before marriage. Four times as many younger women as those 50 or over see better marriages resulting, and twice as many in the younger group see ''more honest relationships.'' (Virginia Slims American Women's Opinion Poll, 1974)

Clearly, the law is beginning to catch up with the facts in the halls of Congress and the courtrooms of the nation. The tension between the new and the old morality is most evident in the court's handling of contested divorces. With the breakdown of the ''tender years'' doctrine, more men are receiving custody of the children; no-fault divorce has virtually eliminated adultery as grounds for granting divorce, although it still is a factor in awarding alimony and property. The trend has grown toward child support becoming the mutual obligation of both parents; rehabilitative alimony has emerged, although it is limited to short periods of time to help divorced women get training to enhance their ability to support themselves and their children. Other provisions, such as the use of the family home and the use of family possessions, including the family automobile, have tended to ameliorate the status of divorced wives.

In states without community property laws, systems of ''equitable distribution'' or the equivalent have evolved to permit judges to award assets beyond the family home to the dependent spouse. Recognition of the homemaker's contribution to the marriage is increasingly becoming part of the criteria for the distribution of marital property. The contribution may include helping put a spouse through schooling for a profession, such as law, medicine, or architecture, or helping to create goodwill for a business or contributing inherited monies to the investments of the marriage (Liss, 1980).

But these rights have by no means been uniformly established and enforced. The next section explains how the legal system affecting family relations has evolved to protect certain ''fundamental'' rights, to leave others to the individual states, and to relegate other rights to the sphere of private contractual relations.

Constitutional Protection of Family Rights

This section describes the rights and limitations extended to the family as a unit, to individual members of the family, and to parent–child relationships as they have been tested against the Constitution, the embodiment of our fundamental values. Courts at the state and local level are expected to remain within constitutionally valid parameters when formulating their opinions, but it is the United States Supreme Court that is the final arbiter of whether a law or a lower court decision is, in fact, constitutional. It is important, therefore, to recognize that the basic document against which all attempts to regulate individual and family behavior by federal and state governments must be measured is silent on the subject of the family. Various explanations for the constitutional omission have been put forth. Some suggest that the framers recognized that the needs of an emerging industrialized society called for the capacity to avoid inherited status and to bring workers into an expanding economy as fully as possible on the basis of their abilities (Rice, 1977, p. 79). The possibility that the family might occupy central attention within the American Constitution posed the problem of the maintenance of a nobility. The implicit contract of the Constitution was to be between the government and the individual citizen, without reference to the family.

A basic assumption of the American system has been that the rights of the individual outweigh those of the family. A century ago, Sir Henry Maine (1885) characterized the movement toward modernism as the "gradual dissolution of family dependency and the growth of individual obligation in its place" (Rice, 1977, P. 80). A corollary to this individualistic bent is the view that home and family are bastions of privacy, not to be intruded on by the state. But the silence of the Constitution has not prevented the state from asserting a governmental interest in marriage and all of the concomitant rights and obligations that flow therefrom.

The State's Interest in Marriage

The federal government's avoidance of intrusion into matters affecting the family created a vacuum into which the body of law generally referred to as *family law* was introduced. Individual states had to define marriage, divorce, and inheritance rights, ultimately creating a patchwork quilt of government actions and services.

The Uniform Marriage and Divorce Act is the only semblance of a federal standard, and it has not been widely accepted by the states either in its entirety or in sections. State court decisions, based on the common law, prevail unless there are statutes that cover marriage, divorce, child custody, and so on. When state laws come into conflict with federal law or preempt a constitutionally protected individual right, they may reach the Supreme Court, where they are subjected to various standards of judicial review. When the Supreme Court decides such challenges, they become precedents for other states and reflect the Court's assessment of the statute in relation to the Constitution.

In addition to the Bill of Rights, the first ten amendments to the Constitution, the later adoption of the Fourteenth Amendment further limited the federal and state governments from interfering with individual behavior by forbidding any state to "make or enforce any law which shall abridge the privileges or immunities of citizens of the United States," or to "deprive any person of life, liberty, or property, without due process of law nor deny to any person within its jurisdiction the equal protection of the laws." The Supreme Court has, since *Marbury* v.

Madison (1803), been the branch of government to decide what the law is, even to the point of striking down state legislation that unduly interferes with individuals and their property.

Increasingly, the interaction among the courts, Congress, and the public has been influenced by sociological concepts and methods that permeate the legislative history of particular measures, such as Title VII of the Civil Rights Act of 1964, which bars discrimination on the basis of race, color, national origin, religion, or sex. The courts have moved from applying common-law principles in which women's rights were suspended during marriage to striking down sex-stereotyped provisions that denied equal protection to both sexes. Yet, until 1971 (*Reed* v. *Reed*), traditional assumptions about the woman's role in society dominated Supreme Court responses to sex discrimination challenges. Federal legislation protecting women had been upheld because "history discloses the fact that woman has always been dependent upon man" (*Muller* v. *Oregon*, 1908).

In *Reed,* the Court held that men could no longer be given preference over women as administrators of decedents' estates. Applying the rational basis test with unusual bite, such sex-segregated laws were deemed invalid unless an "important" state interest could be established, beyond mere administrative convenience. The heightened scrutiny soon gave way to an intermediate standard of judicial review, which declared sex-discriminatory laws invalid unless they served an "important" state interest, and the classification based on sex was "substantially related" to that interest (*Craig* v. *Boren*, 1976).

The Supreme Court has never established sex discrimination as a "suspect" classification that would require strict scrutiny to determine if a classification based on sex should be permitted. The closest the Court came was in *Frontiero* v. *Richardson* (1973), when four of the nine Justices found unconstitutional the different benefits accorded Air Force personnel, based on sex. In accord with the Fifth Amendment due process clause, the Court rejected the argument of administrative convenience as justification for the sex-based preferential treatment. But without a majority of the Court holding gender-based discrimination invalid *per se,* the standard of judicial review continued to fluctuate through the next decade.

The question of why the Supreme Court has failed to extend the standard of strict scrutiny to sex discrimination cases continues to be widely debated. The Court has admitted withholding suspect classification because of the then pending Equal Rights Amendment (ERA). If one additional justice had agreed with the four-person plurality in *Frontiero*, the ERA would have largely become unnecessary. Sex would have received the same strict scrutiny as race before sex-based classifications would have been held valid.

Even though the ERA failed to receive the requisite states' ratification by June 30, 1982, the Court might still conclude that sex classifications are suspect under the equal protection clause of the Fourteenth Amendment.

But that has become increasingly unlikely with the evolution from the Warren Court to the Burger Court.

As noted in the introduction to this chapter, the persistence of sex discrimination and the subordination of women in society have marked family relations. To the extent that the Supreme Court has invalidated many gender-based statutes, it has contributed to the breakdown of sexual stereotypes within the family as well as within the larger society. For example, when the Court struck alimony laws requiring only men to provide alimony to their spouses at divorce, it was alerting wives to the awareness that they may be held equally responsible for support if their spouse is dependent and they decide to divorce (*Orr v. Orr*, 1979).

The next section examines the Court's interpretations of the rights involved in the institution of marriage itself.

The Right to Marry

The right to marry was established as a "fundamental interest" of the state in the evolution from contract to status, as described in the introduction to this chapter. Initially, the state asserted its interests over religious freedom, restricting polygamous marriages even when they constituted the free exercise of religion, a First Amendment guarantee. Religious beliefs carried into practices contrary to the law of the land were not acceptable. Apart from the supremacy of the state over religion, the earliest Supreme Court decision establishing the state's interest in the institution of marriage and the family was stated in *Maynard v. Hill* (1888):

The [marital] relation once formed, the law steps in and holds the parties to various obligations and liabilities. It is an institution, the maintenance of which in its purity the public is deeply interested, for it is the foundation of the family and of society, without which there would be neither civilization nor progress. (Wadlington & Paulsen, 1978, p. 13)

Thus, parties freely entering a new relationship as individuals suddenly are joined by the state as a third party, with its own separate and often conflicting interests.

Later, state restrictions on marriage based on age, sex, degree of relationship, and race were upheld as long as there was a minimally rational basis for such restrictions.

More recent decisions, however, have established marriage as "one of the basic civil rights of man" (*Loving* v. *Virginia,* 1967) and have subjected alleged state interests in marriage to a standard of strict scrutiny. In *Loving,* for example, the Court held that the racial classifications necessary to meet state antimiscegenation laws in Virginia were unconstitutional on equal protection grounds and also held that the interracial couple had been denied liberty without due process of law.

The *Loving* decision ended the racial restrictions on marriage; it led to legislative reform for some but not all restrictions on marriage, including proscriptions against marriages between paupers, or between very distant relatives. A recent illustration follows, in which the *Loving* rationale invalidated a state provision dealing with financial obligations for marriage.

An indigent father had not met his child-support obligations and was, therefore, denied a marriage license in Wisconsin, in conformance with a statute restricting remarriage for any residents not meeting their court-ordered support obligations for children not in their custody, without court approval (*Zablocki* v. *Redhail,* 1978). Redhail had not applied for court permission because he could not satisfy the requirements: he had not been paying court-ordered support for an illegitimate daughter, and the child had been receiving benefits under the AFDC program since her birth. The woman whom Redhail wished to marry was pregnant; they wanted to legalize their relationship before the birth of the child.

The Court legitimized the new family already begun by striking the statute as unconstitutional.

The Court rejected the Wisconsin statute's rationale of protecting the welfare of the child by encouraging the noncustodial parent to pay support as insufficient justification for the broad infringement on the right to marry. The statute can only prevent the marriage, with no guarantee of any money for the child, and the state has a variety of other methods of ensuring the payment of support obligations, such as wage assignments and civil and criminal penalities. The statute was seen as a direct interference with the right to marry, but the Court made clear that not every state regulation must be subjected tb rigorous scrutiny: "Reasonable regulations that do not significantly interfere with decisions to enter into the marital relationship may legitimately be imposed." Here, the state concern was that the children of the delinquent parent might become public charges. On the one hand, the state interest lay in not permitting remarriage under such circumstances; on the other, the fundamental right to marry was at stake. Somewhat surprisingly, the Court placed the fundamental importance of marriage ahead of state fiscal constraints.

Marital Right to Privacy

Once marriage was established as a fundamental right, the next major extension of constitutional protection was the right of privacy within marriage. That was soon followed by the extension of the right to privacy to the unmarried and then to the home itself, regardless of marital status—at least to the extent of receiving "obscene" information and ideas, protected by the First Amendment.

The leading modern case establishing a constitutional right to privacy in marriage was *Griswold* v. *Connecticut* (1965). The Supreme Court struck down a state prohibition on the use of contraceptives, holding that the very idea of allowing police to search the "sacred precincts of marital bedrooms for telltale signs of the use of contraceptives" prohibited by state law was repulsive to the notions of privacy surrounding the marriage relationship.

Leaving the details of marital intimacy free from state regulation was then extended to the unmarried, based on the interpretation of the equal protection clause of the Fourteenth Amendment that it was invalid to treat unmarried individuals differently from the married. In *Eisenstadt* v. *Baird* (1972), the Supreme Court rejected the state's goal in banning the distribution of contraceptives to unmarried persons except through registered physicians or pharmacists. It upheld the "right of the individual, married or single, to be free from unwarranted governmental intrusion into matters so fundamentally affecting a person as the decision whether to bear or beget a child."

The emphasis on the right to privacy foreshadowed the landmark decision in *Roe* v. *Wade,* in 1973, which protected the right of the woman to decide whether to bear or beget a child.

Reproductive Freedom and the Right to Privacy

The two most significant advances in women's rights within the family over the past two decades were probably the technological invention of the birth control pill and the *Roe* abortion decision, widely known as the woman's right to choose. It has been ironically noted that it was the conservative Burger Court that took the right to privacy in contraception established in *Griswold* to a logical nexus with a woman's right to determine whether or not to terminate her pregnancy. In *Roe,* the Court struck down Texas's criminal abortion laws, which prohibited abortion except to save the mother's life. The Court balanced the right of personal privacy against "important" state interests in regulating abortions. The two state interests recognized as paramount to the individual's freedom of choice were the state's concern after the first trimester of pregnancy with the health of the mother and the potential life of the child. During the first trimester the state was totally prohibited from interfering with the abortion decision. That standard has been gradually eroded to "unduly burdensome interference." Similarly, the original *Roe* distinction between second- and third-trimester state interests has been encroached on by the growing concern about postviability, discussed later, which can begin early in the second trimester.

Although the Court has never held that the fetus is a "person" within the protection of the Fourteenth Amendment, the line of cases since *Roe* v. *Wade* has manifested increasing concern for the fetus. In *Planned Parenthood of Missouri* v. *Danforth* (1976), viability was defined as "that stage of fetal development when the life of the unborn child may be continued indefinitely outside the womb by natural or artificial life-supportive systems." In Pennsylvania, a post-*Roe* statute subjected physicians to criminal liability if they failed to follow a statutorily prescribed standard of care when the fetus "is viable" or "there was sufficient reason to believe that the fetus may be viable." The majority of the Court found the viability determination and standard-of-care provisions unconstitutionally vague, invalidating the law.

In 1977, Supreme Court decisions in several abortion cases were read to limit severely the fundamental right to choose as enunciated in *Roe* v. *Wade.* Three cases concerned public funding and indigents' "unnecessary" nontherapeutic abortions (*Maher* v. *Roe,* 1977; *Beal* v. *Doe,* 1977; and *Poelker* v. *Doe,* 1977). The Court held that it is not unconstitutional for states participating in the Medicaid program to refuse to pay the expenses incidental to nontherapeutic abortions while paying the expenses incidental to childbirth. Three Justices dissented in each of the cases, saying that the majority showed a "distressing insensitivity to the plight of impoverished pregnant women." The dissenting Justices felt that the disparity in state funding between childbirth and abortion clearly coerced indigent pregnant women to bear children that they would not otherwise choose to have. They saw the decisions as an erosion of the fundamental right of pregnant women to be free to decide whether to have an abortion, as well as an impingement on the right to privacy because of the financial pressure that forces poor women to bear children.

In 1980, the majority went even further in removing the protection of the right to choose from poor women. In *Harris* v. *McRae,* the Court held that

Although government may not place obstacles in the path of a woman's exercise of her freedom of choice, it need not remove those not of its own creation. The financial constraints that restrict an indigent woman's ability to enjoy the full range of constitutionally protected freedom of choice are the product not of governmental restrictions on access to abortions but rather her indigency.

Poverty, like sex, has never been declared a suspect classification.

The abortion issue is a noteworthy illustration of the interaction between the legal system and public pressure. Both the Court and the Congress have fluctuated over the past decade, moving with the ebb and flow of public opinion. In the early 1970s, pressure from women's groups to open access to abortions for all women was intense. By the 1980s, a severe backlash had set in from antiabortionists, calling themselves "prolife." At this writing, the latter are in the ascendancy, although a majority of respondents polled in every major poll continue to favor the woman's right to choose, in consultation with her doctor, whether or not to terminate a pregnancy. Meanwhile, Medicaid-funded abortions declined by 98% in 1980, and in 1981, payments were denied to the remaining 2%, victims of rape or incest. Groups of private citizens were organized to help poor women pay for abortions. Mobilization of civil liberties and abortion rights groups was proceeding to meet the threat of a proposed constitutional amendment. A "Human Life Amendment" was introduced in the Ninety-seventh Congress to outlaw abortion entirely and declare the fertilized egg or fetus to be a legal "person" entitled to due process from the moment of fertilization and at every stage of its biological development. Other bills in Congress would circumvent the amendment process and redefine the word *person* in the Fourteenth Amendment to include the unborn, affecting abortion and birth control programs at a minimum. Several bills would limit or nullify previous Supreme Court decisions, including the landmark 1973 decision granting women the right to choose. The irony of the situation is that, if the ''prolife'' efforts succeed, women carrying fetuses would have fewer rights than the fetus. Other ramifications of this win–lose scenario affecting the family have yet to be fully explored.

Spousal and Minors' Rights in Abortion. The Supreme Court has also had to rule on the rights of husbands and parents in the abortion decision. In *Planned Parenthood of Missouri* v. *Danforth* (1976), the Court struck down a provision requiring a husband's consent before a married woman could get an abortion. Since the state had no authority to prevent abortion during the first trimester, it could not delegate that authority, even to the husband, the Court held. It acknowledged the husband's deep and proper concern and interest in his wife's pregnancy but weighed the balance in the wife's favor.

However, since *Danforth,* spousal notice has become a major issue in abortion cases. A Fifth Circuit decision upheld the Florida Medical Practice Act provision requiring a married woman currently living with her spouse to notify her husband of her intent to terminate her pregnancy and to provide him with an opportunity to consult with her concerning the abortion procedure (*Scheinberg* v. *Smith,* 1981). Although the Court recognized that the spousal notice provision left the married woman with something less than the completely untrammeled freedom of choice mandated by *Roe,* it held that the state interests of maintaining and promoting the marital relationship and of protecting a husband's interest in the procreative potential of the marriage overrode the woman's interest. Distinguishing the Florida notice statute from the Missouri requirement of the spouse's consent, which the Supreme Court had struck down in *Danforth,* the Fifth Circuit Court decided that the state's substantial interest in the state-created vehicle for procreation, marriage, should not be abused ''through one spouse perpetually and secretively frustrating the other's desire for offspring'' (*Scheinberg,* at 485).

With regard to parental consent to minors' abortions, the Court upheld a Utah statute that requires a physician to notify, if possible, the parents of a minor seeking abortion. Stating that their previous holding was still valid, that a state may not constitutionally legislate a blanket, unreviewable power of parents to veto their daughter's abortion, the Court distinguished the mere requirement of parental notice in *H.L.* v. *Matheson* (1981). It noted the parent's role in child rearing as basic in the structure of our society. If the minor was not living at home, was mature, needed emergency medical aid, or had hostile parents, the question was left open whether the notification would be required. The dissent found the decision a departure from the protection of families from unwarranted state intrusion, in contrast with the majority's interest in protecting parental authority and family integrity. The dissent felt that state intervention was hardly likely to resurrect parental authority that the parents themselves were unable to preserve.

Abortion is one of the few areas involving conflicting interests between parents and children in the family in which the state has intervened. It has addressed issues between the family and the state, however.

Child Rearing and the State's Interest

To a large extent, the above cases exemplify the family's taking precedence over the state in privacy cases. This is also true in other child-related cases. For example, in *Wisconsin* v. *Yoder* (1972), Amish parents won the right to adhere to their religious values through informal vocational education, rather than being compelled to yield to state interests and have their children attend formal high-school classes.

The Court felt that the Amish had convincingly demonstrated the sincerity of their religious beliefs, the interrelationship of belief with their mode of life, and the endangerment to that way of life represented by the state's violation of the free exercise of their religious beliefs. It was incumbent on the state to show how its strong interest in compulsory education would be adversely affected by granting an exemption to the Amish. The state did not meet that burden.

Parents have not always prevailed in conflicts with the state educational systems' attempts to accommodate the religious clauses of the First Amendment, which prohibit laws respecting an establishment of religion, on the one hand, and which forbid laws prohibiting the free exercise of religion, on the other. For the purposes of this discussion, it is noteworthy that family concerns have surfaced in issues of public transportation of children to parochial schools, school prayers, release time, book purchases, and Bible reading, but the major tension has been between maintaining the wall of separation between church and state and the right of families to choose whether and in what manner to follow their religious values without coercion.

A comprehensive review of the Burger Court's actions noted that the Court has recognized as ''fundamental'' the right of individual autonomy in activities relating to marriage, procreation, contraception, abortion, family relationships, and the rearing and education of children (Gunther, 1980). The most frequently asserted state interests in the regulation of family life cited were ''the state's interest in strengthening the family as a valuable social institution, its police power interest in regulating the public morals, and its responsibility as *parens patriae* to intervene to promote the best interests of the child'' (p. 630).

One additional area of interest to sociologists regarding the states' interests in parent–child relationships concerns illegitimacy. The Court eliminated gender-based barriers, for example, when it overturned presumptions that the natural mother, but not the natural father, of an illegitimate child was fit for custody of the children (*Stanley* v. *Illinois,* 1972). The children of the unwed father became wards of the state on the mother's death because of the statutory presumption that all unmarried fathers could reasonably be presumed to be unqualified to raise their children. The Court ordered the right to a hearing to determine fitness instead. The unwed-father decision had an even more significant impact on adoption. Before *Stanley*, an unacknowledged illegitimate child could be relinquished by the mother alone; post-*Stanley*, the claims of the natural father had to be heard as well (*Caban v. Mohammed, 1979*).

To this point, this section has emphasized the Court's expansive interpretation of the Constitution on family rights. Although its direction has been primarily broadening over the past two decades, it began to falter in the area of family relations over applying the new equal-protection, substantive, and procedural due-process interpretations to nontraditional or variant family forms. The next section describes the limits that the Court has placed on constitutionally protected behaviors.

Limits on Constitutional Rights

This section presents three areas of family-related behaviors that have been challenged in the courts, have reached the level of review by the highest state courts or the Supreme Court, and have been denied constitutional protection. They are support obligations during marriage, the right to marital privacy in the bedroom, and homosexual relations, including marriages. These represent the limits on constitutional rights at the beginning of the 1980s.

Support Obligations in Marriage

The Court has traditionally been reluctant to intervene in intact marriages to ensure the fulfillment of marital support obligations. The classic common-law case illustrating deference to nonintervention in marriage is *McGuire* v. *McGuire* (1953).

Lydia McGuire was the plaintiff in the action against her husband to recover suitable maintenance and support. At the time of the trial, the wife was 66 years of age and he was 80; they had been married 34 years. They lived in a farmhouse without a kitchen sink, an inside toilet, or a bathroom. The wife had no acesss to cash or credit beyond the small amount she raised from selling chickens and eggs and used to buy clothing and groceries. Charles McGuire had land worth $83,000, over $100,000 in government bonds, $13,000 in the bank, and $8,000 income each year. The district court awarded Lydia $50 a month personal allowance, decreed that she was legally entitled to use the husband's credit, and obligated him to pay for home improvements, to purchase a new automobile, and to pay her travel expenses to visit her two daughters at least once a year. But the Supreme Court of Nebraska found no legal basis for the suit and dismissed it.

In 1976, on the eve of elections on equal rights amendments to the state constitutions of Massachusetts and Col-

orado, nationally syndicated columnist Ellen Goodman brought up poor Lydia McGuire, married all those years to "Skinflint" McGuire. Goodman hoped to quiet some of the fanfare being created by anti-ERA organizers who were targeting housewives with propaganda designed to convince them that equal rights would mean the end of their right to be supported by their husbands. Goodman's point was that the right to be taken care of did not exist, at least not in an enforceable way, as the *McGuire* court had long ago said:

The living standards of a family are a matter of concern to the household, and not for the courts to determine, even though the husband's attitude toward his wife, according to his wealth and circumstances, leaves little to be said in his behalf. As long as the home is maintained and the parties are living as husband and wife it may be said that the husband is legally supporting his wife and the purpose of the marriage relation is being carried out. (Wadlington & Paulsen, 1978, p. 282)

Ironically, it is only at divorce that a woman can claim a proportion of her husband's income.

A more recent Pennsylvania court also took a hands-off attitude (*Commonwealth* v. *Glenn, 1966*), when the appeals court overruled a trial court's order requiring a husband to pay his wife the sum of $60 weekly for support of their three children where the parties were living together and the husband was furnishing food, paying rent and utilities, and contributing to the children's needs. The court was reluctant to impose a mandatory budget on a husband as long as the family unit was intact and there was no "startlingly obvious evidence of neglect."

The courts have remained steadfast in refusing to intervene in more traditional family practices, such as support obligations during marriage. It should therefore come as no surprise that they have found some of the more nontraditional aspects of current family behaviors, such as homosexual relationships, "swinging," and communal living to be beyond the protection of the Constitution. The former two are discussed in the succeeding sections; the latter was examined earlier.

Limits on Rights to Marital Sexual Privacy

The section on reproductive freedom described the emergence of the right to privacy over the past two decades. But in examining the limits of the United States Supreme Court's interpretations of the right to privacy, it is necessary to delve deeper into history.

The Supreme Court's first decision striking down a state law on equal protection grounds was in *Skinner* v. *Oklahoma* (1942), when the Court invalidated Oklahoma's Habitual Criminal Sterilization Act. The act required sterilization after a third conviction for a felony involving moral turpitude but excluded such felonies as embezzlement. The Court found that the right of procreation should apply equally to those convicted of grand larceny or embezzlement; immunity for the latter was clear, pointed, and unmistakable discrimination.

Skinner established the right of privacy through judicial interpretation beyond the express language of the Constitution, in which no generalized right of privacy exists. *Skinner* was a key decision that the Court relied on in *Roe* v. *Wade*, where the right of privacy was found to reside in the Fourteenth Amendment's concept of personal liberty and restrictions on state action, where the right was broad enough to encompass a woman's decision whether or not to terminate her pregnancy. But the Court has since shown little inclination to apply the privacy rationale of the abortion cases to some other contexts, for example, to private homosexual relations between consenting adults (*Doe* v. *Commonwealth's Attorney for City of Richmond*, 1976).

The Supreme Court in *Doe* upheld Virginia's law, which treats homosexual acts between two consenting adults in private places as sodomy. The Court distinguished between the right of privacy between homosexuals and the "privacy of the incidents of marriage, the sanctity of the home, or the nurture of family life." Homosexuality, the Court held, is obviously no portion of marriage, home, or family life and may be prohibited, even when committed in the home, when appropriate in the promotion of morality and decency. Thus, even though in earlier cases, contraceptives and pornography were protected for use within the home, private consensual sexual relations between male adults may still be barred.

The next section describes the further limitations on the rights of privacy, that is, on the rights of a married heterosexual couple in sexual activities within the home.

Marital Sexual Activities within the Home. The same Virginia sodomy statute that the Supreme Court affirmed in *Doe* was upheld in a case involving the right of privacy of a married heterosexual couple. In *Lovisi* v. *Slayton* (1976), the right to marital privacy, which was otherwise protected and beyond the power of the state to scrutinize, was dissolved by the presence of an onlooker–stranger in the marital bedroom. The Lovisis had placed advertisements in a magazine, *Swinger's Life*, as a result of which they met Earl Romeo Dunn, who subsequently engaged in sexual activities with them in their marital bedroom. The Lovisis were convicted of sodomy with one another, after Mrs. Lovisi's daughters displayed erotic photographs of the incident at school and police obtained a search warrant and discovered hundreds of erotic pictures in the house. The appellate court sustained the conviction, noting that state law protects married couples from unwelcome intruders, and the federal Constitution protects them from the state in the guise of an unwelcome intruder; but once they accept onlookers, whether close friends, chance acquaintances, observed "peeping Toms," or paying customers, they may not exclude the state as a constitutionally forbidden intruder.

The *Lovisis* case exemplifies the limits that the courts have placed on constitutionally protected marital privacy for heterosexual couples. The next section describes the limits of constitutional protection for homosexual couples wanting to marry.

Lack of Equal Protection for Homosexual Marriages

Homosexuals have not attained the right to marry as a fundamental right guaranteed by the Constitution. In *Singer* v. *Hara* (1974), despite the existence of an Equal Rights Amendment to the Washington State Constitution, the state court of appeals held that the ERA does not require the state to authorize same-sex marriage, because

the refusal of the state to authorize same-sex marriage results from the impossibility of reproduction (a primary societal value) rather than from an invidious discrimination on account of sex. (Wadlington & Paulsen, 1978, p. 38)

The *Singer* court noted a law review article that stated that marriage laws must accommodate same-sex marriages once the state has an equal rights amendment, but the court was unpersuaded. (See "Note, The Legality of Homosexual Marriages," 1973.) The court did take note that the public attitude toward homosexuals is undergoing substantial, albeit gradual, change but felt that the desirability of revising marriage laws to accommodate homosexuals to be included within the definition of marriage was a question for the legislature.

The Supreme Court has never addressed the issue of homosexual marriages, but it is highly unlikely that the Burger Court would be sympathetic.

This section has described the limitations on the rights of individuals within families, according to constitutional protections. Clearly, no general fundamental right of privacy exists. The freedom to live one's life without governmental interference is balanced against assertions of legitimate governmental interest in justifying such restrictions. Some legal scholars have noted that extraordinary protection of individual rights in family contexts has become commonplace, although not all consensual sexual behavior has become protected (Gunther, 1980, p. 607). Those scholars cite John Stuart Mill's autonomy principle as the rationale:

The sole end to which mankind are warranted, individually or collectively, in interfering with the liberty of action of any of their number is self-protection; that government may control the individual only to prevent harm to others. . . . Over himself, over his own body and mind, the individual is sovereign. (On Liberty, 1859/1947, p. 9)

Other scholars see the Burger Court's decisions regarding sex as based not on Mill's principle, but on "stability-centered concerns of moderate conservative family and population policy" (Gunther, 1980, p. 608). The contraception and abortion decisions have been viewed as representing standard conservative views that social stability is threatened by excessive population growth, and that family stability is threatened by unwanted pregnancies, fragile marriages, single-parent families, irresponsible youthful parents, and abandoned or neglected children. The seemingly libertarian choices extended in the abortion and contraception cases were not meant as sexual but procreational choices. Under this view, it has been predicted that, within a few years, fornication and sodomy laws will also be found unconstitutional, in response to the same demands of order and social stability requiring legitimization of the increasing number of unions outside traditional marriage. Similar pressures for legitimacy are seen to be generated by the homosexual community as it becomes an increasingly public sector of our society. Grey (in Gunther, 1980, p. 608) predicted that if legislatures do not change their laws, the Court will step in and "play its traditional role as enlightened conservator of the social interest in ordered stability, and will strike down those laws, in the glorious name of the individual."

The foregoing debate among legal scholars about the significance of Supreme Court decisions in legitimizing family relationships closely parallels the debates among sociologists in the substantive areas covered by the other chapters in this handbook.

The remaining sections of this chapter focus on developments in family law at the state level over the past two decades.

Issues Governed Primarily by State Decisions and Statutes

This section describes the current status and trends in selected areas of family law, governed primarily by state laws and decisions that have not risen to the level of controversy that would bring the issue to the Supreme Court, as addressed in the previous sections. Where the issue has been derived from a constitutional challenge, that fact is noted.

Only in recent years has the law evolved to enable families to negotiate and bargain for the terms of their personal relationships, including marriage, divorce, child support, custody, and property disposition. Historically, such private agreements between husbands and wives were invalid because the state was a third party in interest. Until the nineteenth century, the unity of husband and wife prevented contracts between them. Contracts regarding support obligations, such as antenuptial agreements, were void as a matter of public policy if they could be construed as conducive to divorce. Increasingly, the parties have looked to the courts to enforce those agreements or make the award in lieu of private agreements.

The particular areas selected for presentation in this section are those that have aroused considerable legislative or judicial attention and remain unsettled areas of family law. They include divorce, child support, child custody, parental abuse, parental rights, interracial adoption, foster care, elder abuse, and marital rape.

Divorce

The major reform in divorce law over the past two decades has been the elimination of "fault" as grounds for divorce. As of August 1980, all but two states had some form of "no-fault" divorce. Religious opposition has constituted the major obstacle to freely obtained divorce in the face of marital breakdown. In Illinois and South Dakota, proof of serious marital sin was required (Freed & Foster, 1983). Under current law in most states, living separate and apart pursuant to a separation agreement is proof of irretrievable breakdown or irreconcilable differences.

Although fault has been eliminated as the major ground for granting divorces, it still figures prominently in determining alimony, property disposition, and child custody in most states. The trend is increasingly toward minimizing the importance of marital misconduct in awarding alimony or distributing property, however. In allocating marital assets, an increasing number of states take into consideration the nonmonetary as well as the monetary contribution of each spouse to the marriage.

The gap between common-law and community-property states has been narrowing, with approximately 40 states following the common law derived from England but having the power of "equitable distribution" over marital property (see Liss, 1980). Factors to be considered by the courts generally include the length of the marriage; the age, health, and station in life of the parties; occupation; the amount and sources of income; vocational skills; employability needs; the contribution to or dissipation of marital property; and the need of a custodial parent to occupy the marital home.

Laws requiring alimony only for wives have become sex-neutral, authorizing awards to either spouse, depending on the circumstances. Concomitantly, alimony has often become restricted to limited periods of time to allow the recipient to become self-supporting.

These basic changes have had dramatic effects on many of the accompanying transitional relationships involved—between husbands and wives, between parents and children, and even among more remote relatives who often become embroiled in divorce and custody battles. State intervention in previously private matters has become prevalent, as a highly mobile society complicates the search for equity and justice. The following sections detail some of the efforts toward reciprocity and enforcement of agreements made in one state as the parties move around the country.

Child Support

Since 1970, in about 32 states, statutes specify child support as the obligation of both parents rather than, as formerly, the primary obligation of the father. In a few states, this change has been achieved by court decisions rather than legislation. Some states have adopted the National Conference of Commissioners on Uniform State Laws draft of the Uniform Marriage and Divorce Act Section 309 by statute, to aid the court in determining the extent of duty of support owed by either or both parents (Freed & Foster, 1981, p. 258). The specific statutory criteria considered by the courts include (1) the financial resources and needs of the child; (2) the financial resources and needs of the custodial parent; (3) the standard of living that the child would have enjoyed had the marriage not been dissolved; (4) the physical and emotional condition of the child and his or her educational needs; and (5) the financial resources and needs of the noncustodial parent.

The obligation of parental support usually ends when the child reaches majority, but there are exceptions, for handicapped children, for example (*Elkins* v. *Elkins*, 1977).

Enforcement of Child Support. The first survey report on the receipt of child support and alimony payments revealed that, of the 7.1 million women with children present from an absent father, only about three-fifths had been awarded or had an agreement to receive child support payments in 1978 (U.S. Bureau of the Census, 1978).

The proportion of women who were awarded child support payments was higher for white women (71%) than for black (29%) or Spanish women (44%). Of the women who were supposed to receive child support in 1978, only 49% received the full amount that they were due, and 23% received less than they were due; the rest received none.

Uniform Reciprocal Enforcement of Support Act. A major factor in the noncollection of maintenance and support payments has been the increased mobility of the population. In 1950, the Uniform Reciprocal Enforcement of Support Act (URESA) was promulgated to overcome the limitation of states in restricting enforcement to obligees within the state, and to overcome the indifference of many states that refused or neglected to enforce support in favor of out-of-state dependents on the theory, often only tacitly admitted, that one state had no interest in helping another state rid itself of the burden of supporting destitute families.

By the mid-1970s, all states had adopted some version of the act or similar legislation, but cases were brought because of the conflicts in the varying versions. The United States Constitution requires certain forms of interstate relationships, through the Full Faith and Credit Clause (Art. IV, Sec. 1). Under this requirement, for example, the courts of one state are required to give full effect to a final judgment rendered by a court of competent jurisdiction of a sister state. The limitations on this requirement, however, include decrees awarding custody or child support, in which sister states are not required to enforce judgments rendered in error by courts without proper jurisdiction (*Williams* v. *North Carolina*, 1945), and the decree of one state may be disregarded by a court in another state by a finding of "changed circumstances." The courts attempt to balance the jurisdictional and substantive issues in each case against the best interests of the child. Long-arm statutes specifically applicable to alimony and/or support for wife or children have been enacted in 21 states, attempting to extend the reach of the states granting decrees (Freed & Foster, 1979, p. 126). But limitations on the reach of jurisdiction have been established by a United States Supreme Court decision in *Kulko* v. *Superior Court of California* (1978). The defendant husband was held to have had insufficient minimum contacts with the State of California to warrant jurisdiction over him, when his ex-wife moved to California after remarrying and attempted to increase his child-support obligations. The Supreme Court found it unreasonable to permit California to assert *in personam* jurisdiction because his only connection to the state was his consent to let his daughter live there.

Child Support and Establishment of Paternity Amendments. A new federal role in the collection process, however, has added sharper teeth to the existing state-law framework for support enforcement. The Child Support and Establishment of Paternity amendments of 1974 and 1975 to the Social Security Act permit garnishment of wages of all federal employees, including the military, and permit federal district courts to hear cases certified to them by the Department of Health and Human Services, regardless of the amount in controversy (federal statutes normally require that the amount in controversy exceed $10,000 to be heard in federal courts). A mechanism has been established to refer delinquent court-ordered support payments to the Secretary of the Treasury for collection, and Parent Locator Services have been established at both the federal and state levels using government records cooperatively to recoup promised support payments. Many millions of dollars in arrearages have been collected since this act went into effect.

The goal of paring down otherwise inevitable welfare expenditures has apparently been sufficient to inject the federal government into a traditionally state role. An increasing number of states require payment of maintenance and child support directly to an official of the court, who keeps records of arrears, sends for the delinquent spouse, and often requires security for future payments. A number of states also now provide for wage deduction orders after one or more defaults but forbid employers to discharge employees because of wage deductions for alimony or child support (Freed & Foster, 1979, p. 127).

Child Custody

The factors that have been considered relevant to the "best interests of the child" standard used by the courts in awarding the custody of children at divorce generally include: (1) emotional ties between the child and other family members (separating the children and a child's preference are considered); (2) the interest of the parties in and their attitude toward the child (the psychological parent and which parent places higher priority on child's welfare are considered); (3) the desirability of continuing an existing relationship; (4) preference given to the mother (the "tender years" doctrine); (5) the age, sex, and health of the child; and (6) the conduct, marital status, income, social environment, or lifestyle of a party, only upon showing of present or potential emotional or physical harm to child.

Tender Years Doctrine. The tender years doctrine, in which a mother of young children would generally be given preference for custody if other factors were evenly balanced, held sway for many years as the most appropriate criterion for the best interest of the child. By 1978, the doctrine had been relegated to the status of merely one factor in most states, but it had also been upheld in 1978 in a sex-discriminatory fashion. In Oklahoma's statutory provision, for example, "when the child is of tender years the mother is preferred, but if the child is of an age to require education and preparation for labor or business, the father is preferred" (*Gordon* v. *Gordon,* 1978).

The new trend is toward "joint" custody, in which the child usually switches back and forth. Changing lifestyles and parental roles have made joint custody more appealing, and where workable, is the best available alternative to an intact family. One innovative approach tried by a pair of contemporary architects who separated shortly after painstakingly renovating a New York brownstone was to leave the children in the house and let the parents shift between abodes. One week, the father lived in the renovated townhouse with the children. The next week, the mother came. The children were spared moving, and both parents could continue to enjoy their house. However, such arrangements require a level of compatibility between divorcing spouses that is rarely seen.

Some states require agreement, and others act on the application of either parent for joint custody. In some states, the courts presume that joint custody is in the best interests of the child. The concept is by no means uncontroversial. One problem is the enforced heightened contact between parents who have dissolved the relationship (Roman & Haddad, 1978; "When Fathers Have to Raise Families Alone," 1977).

Uniform Child Custody Jurisdiction Act. A growing number of states have adopted the Uniform Child Custody Jurisdiction Act (UCCJA, 1973), one of the most important developments in family law. Its basic purposes are to discourage continued controversies over child custody in the interest of stability of home environment for the child, to deter child abductions, and to promote interstate assistance in adjudicating custody matters. In 1976, only 9 states had enacted the act into law; by 1985 only Massachusetts had not adopted the UCCJA (Interview, Assistant Director, Family Division, District of Columbia Superior Court, 1985).

Grandparents' Visitation Rights. As a reaction against common-law doctrine that generally held that grandparents had no legal right to visitation with grandchildren if the custodial parent objected, in the 1960s and 1970s some 32 states enacted statutes specifically permitting grandparents to seek visitation rights under certain circumstances. The appropriate circumstances would include death of the child's parent or parents, divorce, or separation (see Foster & Freed, 1978). These laws should decrease the animosity and hostility that denial of grandparents' visitation rights has created in the past.

Child Advocacy In many new statutes, provisions are made for the appointment of guardians *ad litem* (appointed by the court), or an attorney to represent the child's best interests in marital dissolution where custody is contested. Some controversy exists over whether the proper role of the attorney serving as a guardian *ad litem* should be as a vigorous advocate of the position of her or his client, bound by the canons of professional responsibility to represent the child zealously and to the best of her or his ability, or whether the guardian should investigate the facts, interview the persons involved, and make a recommendation to the court based on a view of the best interests of the child.

One critic of the role believes that, because of the uncertainty of the standard, the child advocate is in no better position than the judge to determine the child's best interest (Mlyniec, 1977). Other practitioners have proposed that all separation agreements—even where uncontested—should be scrutinized to ensure adequate protection of the children.

Child Kidnapping Every year an estimated 25,000 to 100,000 child-snatching cases occur, with less attempt at recovery than if they had been stolen cars.

The federal kidnapping statute does not apply to parents, so when a parent kidnaps his or her own child in violation of a custody order, there is no federal charge. Two solutions to this problem have been put forth: (1) a uniform child-custody bill that would make one state's custody decision binding on all other states, and (2) ending the existing exemption under the federal kidnapping statute for parents who abduct minor children from a parent having legal custody.

The first solution has made progress with Massachusetts the only state which has not adopted the UCCJA as of 1985. The UCCJA has proved an excellent tool for returning custody to the custodial parent or preventing conflicting state custody decisions, but it is a civil penalty only. Some parents want more severe penalties, including the arrest of the abducting parent. (Interview, Assistant Director, Family Division, District of Columbia Superior Court, 1985.) Support developed for the second solution, making parental kidnapping a federal crime with severe penalties.

In December 1980, in the last hours of the lame-duck session of the Ninety-sixth Congress, the Parental Kidnapping Prevention Act was passed and signed by President Carter. Its purposes correspond to those of the UCCJA and put full faith and credit in child custody determinations of sister states. The law has three major parts, according to Senator Malcolm Wallop (R-Wyoming), its sponsor: (1) it requires state courts to enforce and refrain from modifying custody and visitation decrees made by sister states; (2) it authorizes the use of the Federal Parent Locator Service to locate parents of children who have been abducted; and (3) it applies the federal Fugitive Felon Act to state felony parental kidnapping cases, making it possible for the FBI to investigate cases that state authorities intend to prosecute (Wallop, 1980). Since enactment, the PKPA has been the subject of controversy among Congressional committees responsible for its oversight, the United States Department of Justice (DOJ), responsible for implementation guidelines, and the FBI, charged with investigation and arrest.

The DOJ guidelines required that independent credible information establish that the child is in physical danger or is being seriously abused or neglected (Wallop, 1981, p. 6). The Congressional committees responsible for PKPA urged greater federal–state cooperation in issuing warrants for arrest under the Unlawful Flight to Avoid Prosecution provisions of the Fugitive Felon Act. Senator Wallop, sponsor of the PKPA, urged that the restrictive criteria of "serious danger" be eliminated, that the requirement for approval by DOJ headquarters staff be dropped, and the FBI be more easily involved in enforcing the parental kidnapping law in the same manner as other state felony cases (Wallop, 1982).

The Department of Justice defended the small number of arrests (26 arrests under Fugitive Felon warrants from 1981–82), as a prudent and reasonable exercise of prosecutorial discretion. A state must be prepared to request FBI assistance, to extradite the fugitive and bring the fugitive to trial (DOJ, 1982, p. 3). Otherwise, the DOJ intends to "avoid any open-ended utilization of FBI investigative resources and the indiscriminate use of Federal criminal process for enforcing what, in many instances, are nothing more than civil obligations." (DOJ, p. 2). Thus, the statutory declaration that child-snatching is a felony has not resulted in an effective enforcement program.

Parental Abuse of Children

Physical Abuse. In the early 1960s, publicity about the extent of the physical abuse of children revealed the "battered-child syndrome," which led to legislation establishing reporting systems and coercive intervention schemes to curb the abuse. The House of Delegates of the American Bar Association (ABA) in 1978 drafted a Juvenile Justice Standards Project, noting that, each year, approximately 150,000 child "neglect" proceedings are heard by juvenile courts throughout the country. As a result, as many as 50% order the child removed from the home, and the remainder order supervision and therapy as a condition of continued custody.

The ABA's perspective was one of limited coercive intervention by state action, recognizing that commentators have pointed out defects in the current system caused by an excess of intervention. Proponents of broad intervention insist that broad, though vague, laws are essential to protect all children needing help. These commentators would leave largely to the discretion of judges and social workers the decisions on when and how to intervene (see Katz, 1971; Mnookin, 1975).

The system proposed by the ABA was designed to allow intervention only where there is reason to believe that the child will, in fact, benefit; to ensure that every effort will be made to keep children with their parents or, if impossible, to provide them with a stable living condition; to ensure that the procedures followed will facilitate decision making; and to ensure the accountability of all decision makers. Family autonomy is a basic tenet of the ABA report.

The dangers inherent in any coercive intervention system by state action, however, weigh heavily against their adoption. Clear protection of parental due-process rights must be maintained in balancing the best interests of the allegedly abused or endangered child.

Termination of Parental Rights

The courts have been extremely reluctant to deprive a natural parent of the right to custody of the child. Such parental rights have not been allowed to be permanently abridged unless demanded "for the most powerful reasons" (*In re Day*, 1937).

However, when the rights of parents and the welfare of their children are in conflict, the welfare of the minor children usually prevails. For example, in *In re Sego* (1973), although the father had been convicted of murdering the children's mother, his wife, the court was reluctant to approve the Department of Public Assistance recommendation, after 1½ years of his 25-year sentence, that Mr. Sego be permanently and totally deprived of all rights to care for his son and daughter and that the children be placed in an adoptive status. He had a remarkable record in rehabilitation at the prison, but the appellate court concluded that there was clear, cogent, and convincing evidence to support the order of permanent deprivation.

In 1982, the Supreme Court held that allegations supporting termination of parental rights must be proved by "clear and convincing" evidence, striking down a statute that relied on a lesser burden of proof (*Santosky* v. *Kramer*, 1982).

Other factors often considered are the age of the child, the closeness of the parent–child relationship, parental therapy, and the child's preference. Permanent deprivation of parental rights is not taken lightly.

Interracial Adoption

Cultural differences based on class, race, and ethnic origin create different problems in family law. For example, in the area of adoption, middle-class white couples have more alternatives in the event of premarital pregnancy than do lower-class nonwhite couples (Ladner, 1972).

Ladner attributed the alternatives to the following race and class differences:

1. In the middle class, it is generally assumed that girls engage in sexual relations at a later age.
2. If pregnancy occurs, abortion or marriage usually follows, reducing the number of out-of-wedlock births.
3. Adoption centers for nonwhite children (especially the poor) are virtually unknown.
4. If white girls become pregnant, they are not forced to keep the child and rear it because of the availability and awareness of adoption facilities.

Ladner noted that whites do most of the adopting, and they do not usually adopt black children, although there has been a recent trend toward interracial adoption. Controversy has accompanied this trend, and it is reflected in court decisions.

In the leading interracial adoption case, *Drummond* v. *Fulton Co. Dept. of Family and Children Services* (1976, *cert. den.* 1978), the issue was whether race was constitutionally permissible as a basis for decisions that a child should not be placed with certain adoptive parents. The plaintiffs were the white foster parents of a child who was considered "racially mixed." Her mother was Caucasian, but the paternity was unknown. The pediatrician testified that he thought she was "racially mixed," although her race was impossible to determine. Georgia law required the placement of children with adoptive applicants who had "the most comparable characteristics of those of the child . . .," language that had been revised from the more offensive "racial suitability" test (Ga. Code Ann., 1977).

The caseworker's supervisor became convinced that the child should be adopted by a black couple. The agency informed the foster parents that race would be a substantial factor in the child's placement for adoption, but that other factors would be considered as well. The child was removed from the foster home, where she had been for 2½ years, and was placed in a black foster home to make a better adjustment to living with a black family. The original foster parents (Drummond) argued that their rights to due process under the Fourteenth Amendment had been violated as there had been no hearing on their right to adopt, and that their rights to equal protection had been violated because they had been denied an adoption application solely on racial grounds. They asserted that they had a constitutionally protected interest in the prospective adoption of their foster child, a due process entitlement based on the right to family privacy.

After the state supreme court rejected the *Drummond* claim, the federal court of appeals ultimately held that the agency's intent was only to serve the child's best interest. Although it was unconstitutional to use race as the *sole* basis for deciding that a child should not be placed with certain adoptive parents, the court said that adoption agencies have both the right and the responsibility to consider race in creating a parent–child relationship, as long as race is not used in an "automatic" fashion.

Interracial adoption remains a sensitive area of family law, particularly in view of the desire of the black community to retain their ethnic identity rather than to accede to white adoptions of black children.

Foster Care

Inherent in the conflict between natural parents and foster parents is the tension between the desire to create a stable environment for the child compared to a temporary one. The leading relevant United States Supreme Court case, *Smith* v. *Organization of Foster Families for Equality and Reform* (OFFER) (1977), highlighted these tensions. Individual foster parents and an organization of foster parents brought a class action suit against New York State and New York City officials, alleging that the procedures governing the removal of foster children from foster homes provided by statute violated the due-process and equal-protection clauses of the Fourteenth Amendment. In the New York system, foster care was defined as a "child welfare service which provides substitute family care for a planned period for a child when his own family cannot care for him for a temporary or extended period and when adoption is neither desirable nor possible" (Child Welfare League of America, 1959).

Foster parents typically are licensed by the state or an authorized foster-care agency to provide care under a contractual arrangement with the agency, and they are compensated for their service. Although the foster parent maintains responsibility for the day-to-day supervision of the child, the natural parent's placement of the child with the agency does not surrender legal guardianship. The failure of a parent with capacity to fulfill his or her obligation to visit the foster child and plan for its future may result in termination of the parent's rights on the grounds of neglect. On the other hand, the agency may move the foster child from the foster home or return the child to the natural parents in accordance with the statute or the placement agreement.

Foster care has been condemned by the natural parents, as a class-based intrusion into the family life of the poor. In New York City, for example, over 50% of all children in foster care are from female-headed families receiving Aid to Families with Dependent Children; 52% of the children are black and 26% are Puerto Rican. The natural parents assert that the "voluntary" placements are coerced by threats of neglect proceedings and reflect social workers' middle-class biases in continuing foster care longer than the natural parents feel is necessary. Furthermore, foster care has serious inadequacies because of excessive caseloads and turnover among social work professionals; lack of adequate supervision and review of placement; and mistreatment, neglect, and abuse of children in foster care.

The Supreme Court in *Smith* noted the unavoidable tension between foster parents and the absolute rights of the natural parent to the return of the child, in the absence of a court order obtainable only on compliance with rigorous substantive and procedural standards. But the Court stopped short of rejecting the concept of a protected liberty interest for foster parents. The Court held that the New York City provision for a full preremoval hearing was constitutionally sufficient to protect whatever liberty interest might exist when the state attempts to transfer the child to another foster home.

The solution proposed by recent welfare-reform programs to help intact families stay together has been to provide federal assistance to the states for better foster-care facilities and procedures, as well as adoption subsidies to aid in the placement of hard-to-place children.

According to one analyst, too many children go into foster care because of a lack of supportive services designed to prevent the need for foster care (Keene, 1978).

The problem of excessive use of foster care has been particularly acute for particular groups, such as the American Indian. The Indian Child Welfare Act was passed in 1980, following more than a decade of efforts and studies that indicated that one fourth of all Indian children in one state had been separated from their families and placed in foster and adoptive homes or institutions. Few of these children had been removed on the grounds of physical abuse. Most had been removed on the vague grounds of "neglect," often resulting from a lack of awareness of and sensitivity to Indian cultural values by many non-Indian social workers, judges, and others in the legal system (President's Advisory Committee for Women, 1980, p. 111).

The Child Welfare Act attempts to reduce the inappropriate placement of children by encouraging the states to use foster care as a temporary measure rather than as a long-term solution. It also attempts to remove barriers to the adoption of hard-to-place children. The act emphasizes working with the family of origin rather than placing children in unfamiliar surroundings (President's Advisory Committee for Women, 1980, p. 83).

Elder Abuse

One of the most recent problems in family law to come to the surface is the physical, mental, and financial abuse of the elderly by their relatives or caretakers. A few major studies have begun to document the mistreatment of the elderly (see, e.g., Block & Sinnott, 1979; Lau & Kosberg, 1979; Steinmetz, 1981).

The types of abuse defined by researchers include psychological abuse, centering on verbal assaults and threats; physical abuse, involving neglect and blows resulting in welts and bruises, rather than bone fractures; medical abuse; violation of rights; and an unsanitary environment. Steinmetz has suggested that many of the problems of indifference and mistreatment derive from the economic, physical, and emotional difficulties of adult children living with the dependent elderly.

Laws are being formulated to protect the elderly, but concerns are being voiced that they not be treated as in-

competents who cannot make decisions about their own welfare merely because of their age.

In many aspects, the emergence of the social problem parallels that of child abuse, and the proposed solutions are being compared to those proffered for neglected and abused children (Katz, 1979).

A six-stage process has been identified by which types of violence such as rape, child abuse, and spouse battering have emerged, including tacit public acceptance, public awareness, coming forth, public policy, enforcement stage, and true control (Haber & Seidenberg, 1978).

Concern about domestic violence against the elderly has been pegged between stage 2, public awareness, and stage 3, coming forth. Just as Congress in 1974 passed the Child Abuse Prevention and Treatment Act, which conditioned states' eligibility for grants to improve their child protective services on their providing for neglect- and abuse-reporting measures, elder abuse is perceived as calling for the same legal measures. The underlying assumptions of such proposals are that state intervention is essential, and that successful treatment is possible. But coercive intervention has often violated family autonomy because of serious flaws in child abuse and neglect statutes (Katz, 1979, p. 706). Sussman has warned of the immense social and constitutional questions raised by creating a system whereby large numbers of people are required to report their suspicions about child neglect; Katz warns of the same concerns in the elder abuse context. Reporting statutes have also revealed defects in overburdening child protective agencies as well as producing biased reports from nonprofessionals encouraged to report suspected or known instances of child neglect and abuse (Besharov, 1977; Katz, 1979, p. 707).

The potential harm is even greater for elder abuse, where a report can trigger an incompetency proceeding if the victim refuses protective services. One of the most ambitious legislative efforts to date has been Connecticut's Protection of the Elderly Act, which includes provisions for lack of consent and the appointment of a conservator for elderly persons lacking the capacity to consent to protective services (Connecticut General Statute, 1977).

Steinmetz (1978) suggested that

battered parents . . . often refuse to report the abuse for fear of retaliation, lack of alternative shelter, fear of the unknown, and the shame and stigma of having to admit they raised such a child. (p. 55)

Katz (1979, p. 711) believes that the elderly have good reason to fear the consequences of state intervention. He cited one study showing that 46% of the abused aged who received protective services became institutionalized which frequently led to premature death. One solution would be voluntary rather than mandatory prevention, treatment, and reporting programs, even though some cases of elder abuse may be hidden from view.

One important distinction between child abuse and elder abuse is the fact that the status of a child in the eyes of the law is incompetency, with the law offering protection against children's own ignorance, helplessness, and vulnerability (see Wald, 1979). However, the ability to make one's own decisions does not disappear with age alone. As Katz (1979) posited:

Because of the potential for misuse of protective measures, we must not lose sight of the fact that, although some of the aged may be dependent and at risk, they are not children who lack decision-making power by virtue of their age. (p. 718)

She cautioned against so-called protective services for the elderly that are given under the guise of protection but that actually deprive the individual of dignity, autonomy, and self-esteem.

In 1981 approximately 26 states had what they considered adult protective-service laws varying widely in scope (Select Committee on Aging, 1981, p. xvi). Only 16 of those states required mandatory reports of suspected elder abuse. Congresswoman Mary Rose Oakar (D-Ohio) has introduced the Prevention, Identification and Treatment of Elder Abuse Act, which would create a National Center for Adult Abuse and provide funds for states that have mandatory reporting laws and that provide for immunity from prosecution for persons reporting incidences of abuse, neglect, and exploitation.

In the final analysis, the right to privacy, to be left to one's own choices, even if they offend another's lifestyle, is a constitutional right that must be respected, and that must be applied to the elderly.

Family Responsibility Laws. Although there was no duty of adult children to support poor parents in common law, the duty now found in current law and court decisions does trace back to the statutory provisions of the Elizabethan Poor Laws in 1601 (*Swoap* v. *Superior Court of Sacramento Co.*, 1973). The California Supreme Court in *Swoap* noted the similarity in language between California's Civil Code codified in 1872 and the Elizabethan Poor Law: "to protect the public from the burden of supporting people who have children able to support them."

In the beginning of the state–county old-age-assistance program, aged persons who had children able to support them were specifically excluded from the system. With modifications, the standard for assistance became "needy persons unable to maintain themselves by work"; however, adult children deemed able to support a recipient owed the county reimbursement.

The court in *Swoap* found the requirement of placing the burden for support on adult children to be constitutional. To the court, the burden on the adult children was "rational" on the ground that the parents, who were now in need, had supported and cared for their children during their minority, and that such children should, in return, support their parents to the extent to which they were capable.

A vigorous dissent by a leading state judge, Justice Tobriner, deplored the court's majority holding, fearing that it would permit the state also to charge the children of

parents in need for the costs of subsidized public-housing projects, medical care, recreational centers, reduced public-transportation fares, and so on. He cited the harsh and self-defeating social effects of the "relative responsibility" provisions and the body of social work opinion that has long maintained that holding relatives liable creates and increases family dissension and controversy and weakens and destroys family ties at the very time that they are most needed.

Two years after the opinion in *Swoap,* the California legislature repealed the Relatives' Responsibility Statute (see California Welfare and Institutions Code, 1976). The constitutionality of the filial support statutes has been analyzed and found in violation of the equal protection clause of the Fourteenth Amendment, as no rational basis existed to hold children liable for the support of indigent parents (Annotation, *American Law Reports,* 1977; Levy & Gross, 1979). Levy and Gross found the filial support laws imposed an economic burden on those least able to sustain it (the employed lower classes), thereby perpetuating a cycle of poverty or near poverty.

The strong sentiment in favor of the repeal of filial responsibility laws is countered by those who demand the use of all possible resources to meet the rising costs of welfare as the proportion and total number of aged persons in our society continues to increase. Cost–benefit analyses aside, it is often the near-elderly (average age 55–65) who are supporting the frail elderly (average age 75). Most are women who themselves have few resources, who are likely to be divorced or widowed, and who are living on the border of poverty. Their limited resources become stretched between the support of their elderly mothers (most often) and the support of their own children and grandchildren. The need for care extends for long periods of time—on the average 10 years, and 15 years is not unusual. The cost of alternative institutional care in private facilities is prohibitive, requiring the expenditure of family income to gain entrance and the loss of personal benefits to the elderly once they are admitted (Steinmetz, 1981).

Conservatorship. Another related area of controversy in the legal rights of the aged is conservatorship proceedings described by Atkinson (1980). Variations exist among definitions in state laws, but once the proposed conservatee is declared incompetent, incapacitated, or impaired, a conservator of his or her estate is appointed.

But all capacity tests are subject to manipulation, as Atkinson noted, citing an example from a New Jersey case (*In re Strittmater's Estate,* 1947). In 1947, Miss Strittmater bequeathed her entire estate to the National Women's Party, a feminist political party. Her relatives introduced testimony based on her marginal annotations in books and on photographs to show that she was psychotic:

My father was a corrupt, vicious, and unintelligent savage, a typical specimen of the majority of his sex. Blast his worm-stinking carcass and the whole damn breed. . . . That moronic she-devil that was my mother. . . . It remains to the [Party] to expose protectors and lovers for what they are.

Despite supportive testimony by her banker and her lawyer as to her mental capacity, her gift to the National Women's Party was ruled invalid. This kind of treatment has been termed the "crazy-old-lady" attitude that tends to deprive the elderly of due process rights. Some states do not even require medical substantiation of an "unsound mind." Once a conservator is appointed by the court, the conservatee loses control over his or her property and civil rights to the same degree under every state statute. The conservatee cannot make gifts or contracts, manage or control property, convey or release contingent property interests, enter into a joint tenancy or tenancy by the entirety, create a trust or exercise power as a trustee, change the beneficiaries of his or her insurance policies, or choose a residence. The ability to marry may also be jeopardized.

It is the state's interest in acting as *parens patriae* in conservatorship proceeding, but it has traditionally been defined as nonadversarial and has provided a lower level of due process protection. The elements of due process at issue are adequate notice, appointment of counsel, and an opportunity to choose a jury trial. Although the differing state approaches offer various protections, none satisfy constitutional requirements for due process. Conservatorship proceedings operate in a netherworld between simple property ownership and civil rights. No property is lost—only the right to control it.

The United States Supreme Court held in *Mullane* v. *Central Hanover Bank* (1950), the pivotal notice case, that notice must be reasonably calculated to apprise interested parties of pending actions and to afford them an opportunity to present their objections under all circumstances. Most proposed conservatees are served while hospitalized or in nursing homes, where freedom to leave is restricted. California relies on a "court visitor," and Illinois requires an attorney to serve as a guardian *ad litem* to explain the petition's contents, and to gauge the conservatee's condition for the court. But clear published standards for incompetency do not exist against which evidentiary standards can be applied.

In a system without a court visitor or guardian *ad litem*'s report, the judge's ability to see the proposed conservatee in person is the crux of the proceeding. In cases where a public guardian has petitioned, the proceedings have been dismissed when an independent and feisty old person has marched into the courtroom demanding to know just who is interfering in her or his life and why. If the courts excluded hearsay evidence, which is now freely admitted, and required the doctor's presence for a medical evaluation, the quality of medical testimony would become more reliable.

When one considers the increasing proportion of society that is over age 62 (the base age of most statutes), it is apparent that protection from abuse under conservatorship statutes warrants balancing administrative costs more closely in favor of due process concerns. The potential loss of rights in these proceedings cannot be measured lightly.

The legal system treats people at both ends of the age spectrum as analogous. The young suffer from a lack of legal recognition until they reach the age of majority; the old experience the disintegration of their legal rights and a resultant loss of autonomy. It is essential that stereotypes be replaced by factual determinations of competence in the case of the elderly, as well as of the young, to make their own decisions.

Marital Rape

In previous times, husbands had the right to use physical punishment on their wives. One of the early cases establishing the precedent of excusing the husband of abusing his wife under certain circumstances was *Joyner* v. *Joyner* (1862). The North Carolina court held that:

The wife must be subject to the husband. Every man must govern his household, and if by reason of an unruly temper, or an unbridled tongue, the wife persistently treats her husband with disrespect, and he submits to it, he not only loses all sense of self-respect, but loses the respect of the other members of his family, without which he cannot expect to govern them [citing Genesis]. *. . . it follows that the law gives the husband power to use such a degree of force as is necessary to make the wife behave herself and know her place.*

In some ways, not much change has occurred since then, as the current state of the law confirms. The following paragraphs, for example, trace the spousal exception for rape, which has protected husbands from prosecution for raping their wives.

By 1985, the number of states that barred a married woman from charging her husband with rape if she is living with him had declined to 21 (National Clearinghouse on Marital Rape, 1985). The spousal exception doctrine stems from the seventeenth-century jurist and misogynist Sir Matthew Hale, who made the exemption for husbands explicit in Pleas of the Crown:

But the husband cannot be guilty of a rape commited by himself upon his lawful wife for by their mutual matrimonial consent and contract the wife hath given up herself in this kind unto her husband which she cannot retract. (Griffin, 1980, p. 23)

Hale is still being cited by the American legal system. For example, in *State* v. *Smith* (1977), the New Jersey appellate court upheld the lower court's finding that a man could not be convicted for the rape of his wife. The court found ample cause to believe that the common-law rule excluding a husband from a statute condemning rape still obtained in New Jersey because it had never been abrogated by legislation or judicial decision. The *Smith* court cited the fatally anachronistic nature of Sir Matthew Hale's view regarding the "external irrevocability of a wife's consent to submit to her husband sexually," but it nevertheless consigned the spousal exception to the status of *implied* statutory law of the state beyond the court's power to abolish.

Although in the following year New Jersey overrode the effects of the *Smith* decision, the holding was detrimental to the 12 other states with similar rape statutes at that time. New Jersey's rape statute had no explicit exclusion or inclusion of husbands, but those states with an explicit statutory spousal exception would require legislative change even more clearly if they were to interpret the common law similarly to the *Smith* court. Drucker (1979), writing about marital rape, disputed the existence of the spousal exemption doctrine and advocated that the courts reinterpret the common law in light of the changed conditions of the times, to avoid legislative action.

New Jersey's amended statute now reads: "No actor shall be presumed to be incapable of committing a crime under this act because of age or impotency or marriage to the victim" (N.J. Sessions Law Service, 1978). It has joined ranks with only five other states in extending the protection of the law to a married woman who has been raped by her husband (Griffin, 1980). California, one of those states, amended its bill to limit spousal rape to cases of force or threat of force, provided the victim was not unconscious or drunk. Laura X (1980), head of the Women's History Research Center, found the California legislators insistent about this limitation: if a couple came home drunk from a party and had sex, they feared that the woman would automatically cry rape in the morning. Ironically noting the very high opinion that the legislators had of their wives, Laura X and other feminists would have preferred the elimination of the marital exemption entirely, subjecting husbands to the same standards of behavior as anyone else.

Although the trend is toward permitting women to bring rape charges against their husbands once they are separated, there is also an expansion in many states to include in the marital exemption live-in lovers and "voluntary social companions" (dates) with whom a woman has had consensual sex over the past year. A chart of current statutory law prepared by the National Center on Women and Family Law noted that two states, Delaware and Hawaii, have deleted the marital exemption, but that the "voluntary social companion" exemption (which applies to first-degree rape) may be extended to spouses (Griffin, 1980, p. 58).

This section has provided an overview of the primary areas of family law at the state level that are controversial and unsettled law today.

The next section treats in depth one final substantive area, unmarried cohabitation, as an illustration of variant family forms. Or is it merely common-law marriage revisited? It is the reader's choice.

Impact of Variant Family Forms

During the 1960s and 1970s, radical shifts in the variety of family forms occurred, causing repercussions in the adjudication of disputes. Roles within the home were given close scrutiny to determine whether allocations of labor were fair and acceptable to each member of the family. After the postwar baby boom, the reduction in the number of children per family required planning for a much longer life span without children in the home. Women began leaving the home in droves to enter or to reenter the labor force. Husbands were expected to help with the household chores, now that wives were not at home all day filling their time with excessive cleaning, laundering and cooking activities. Women were more accepted in the job market, and fathering proved to be a welcome change to many men.

The younger generation, product of the postwar emphasis on suburban child-centered nuclear families, chose in remarkable numbers not to marry, living alone, living with one partner, or living in single-sex or communal groups in experimental families.

This chapter has explored the tangible responses of the legal system to those changes in family behavior. Reading the United States Supreme Court Justices' opinions, one is struck by the amount of sociological emphasis they relied on in reaching their decisions. At first glance, it appears that the courts have made remarkable strides in keeping apace with changed behaviors. But on closer examination, the stopping points beyond which the courts are not likely to go resemble the dominant society. The more nontraditional family groupings, for example, have not been fully accepted. The majority opinions contrasted with the dissents reflect the tensions over new lifestyles. The focus on sex discrimination reflects the impact on family of women rapidly becoming economically independent, yet locked into divorce and support laws predominantly geared to the economically dependent spouse of the past. The courts are struggling to deal with these effects fairly. Decisions by the courts and legislatures on alimony, child support, child custody, and the disposition of property reflect the attempt to keep up with the changing norms and mores affecting the family.

Judges have the discretion to impede or accelerate the changing patterns. If women are no longer confined to mothering roles, why not give custody to the father? If fathers get custody, they also need possession of the family home to maintain stability. If working mothers of children under 6 become the norm, reduced alimony is the result. Yet, recognition of the discrimination that women have suffered and still suffer in the workplace moderates many judicial awards and legislative changes in benefits. "Rehabilitative alimony" has emerged, to help the formerly dependent spouse recoup her skills. Homemakers' contributions to marriage are counted in dividing marital assets. Increasingly, there are more sex-neutral awards of privileges and obligations, such as enforcement of child support orders and custody decrees.

Whether these changes will ultimately equalize family relations is still unclear. Even when court decisions favor equality in domestic relations, they often get modified, diluted, or even reversed.

Once area that illustrates the erratic nature of the courts

is unmarried cohabitation, a new form of common-law marriage, but with a new twist: dependent-partner claims on marital property.

In *Marvin* v. *Marvin* (1976), Lee Marvin, a well-known actor, and Michelle Marvin (she had assumed his surname) had cohabited nonmaritally in California for seven years. She sued him for $1 million when he allegedly kicked her out of the house, in violation of an oral agreement under which she was entitled to half the property acquired during the relationship. This included motion picture rights worth over $1 million. In a trial that captured enormous media attention, Michelle's sacrifice of a lucrative career as a singer–entertainer to devote full time to Lee's career as a companion, homemaker, housekeeper, and cook was highlighted.

The California Supreme Court found several ways in which nonmarital cohabitation could require division of assets: as a result of an express contract between nonmarital partners, except to the extent that the contract is explicitly founded on the consideration of meretricious sexual services; through an implied contract, an agreement of partnership or joint venture, or some other tacit understanding between the parties; as a result of the doctrine of *quantum meruit* ("as much as is deserved"); for example, for reasonable value of household services or equitable remedies such as constructive or resulting trusts, when warranted by the facts of the case. In *Marvin*, the court found that neither an express nor an implied contract to share property existed, but an award was made under the judicial discretion that permitted additional equitable remedies to protect the rights of unmarried people living together. The $104,000 award was intended for rehabilitation purposes so that Michelle Triola Marvin could have the economic means to reeducate herself and to learn new employment skills.

The *Marvin* court recognized the prevalence of nonmarital relationships in modern society and the social acceptance of them, as it distinguished agreements that would be nonenforceable by the courts if they expressly provided for sexual conduct. Such conduct would constitute prostitution under the law. The court was quick to deny the equation of nonmarital relationships with prostitution. Rather, it supported the notion that many young couples today live together without the solemnization of marriage, in order to make sure that they can successfully later undertake marriage. It saw the trial period as preliminary to marriage and as serving as some assurance that the marriage will not subsequently end in dissolution to the harm of both parties. Elaborating on this view, the court stated:

The mores of the society have indeed changed so radically in regard to cohabitation that we cannot impose a standard based on alleged moral considerations that have apparently been so widely abandoned by so many. Lest we be misunderstood, however, we take this occasion to point out that the structure of society itself largely depends upon the institution of marriage, and nothing we have said in this opinion should be taken to derogate from that institution. The joining of the man and woman in marriage is at once the most socially productive and individually fulfilling relationship that one can enjoy in the course of a lifetime. (Wadlington & Paulsen, 1978, p. 57)

The *Marvin* court did not resurrect the doctrine of common-law marriage largely abandoned by most states, and abolished in California in 1895. The court held that Michelle Marvin had the same right to enforce contracts and to assert her equitable interest in marital property acquired through her efforts as does any other unmarried person. The court took particular cognizance of California's community-property system in rejecting the defendant's plea that persons who choose to live together without marriage have deliberately elected to remain outside the bounds of the community-property system. In a burst of sociological insight, reminiscent of Jessie Bernard's predictions about the future of marriage (1975), the court noted that

A deliberate decision to avoid the strictures of the community property system is not the only reason that couples live together without marriage. Some couples may wish to avoid the permanent commitment that marriage implies yet be willing to share equally any property acquired during the relationship; others may fear the loss of pension, welfare or tax benefits resulting from marriage. Others may engage in the relationship as a possible prelude to marriage. In lower socio-economic groups the difficulty and expense of dissolving a former marriage often lead couples to choose a non-marital relationship; many unmarried couples may also incorrectly believe that the doctrine of common law marriage prevails in California and thus that they are in fact married. (Wadlington & Paulsen, 1978, p. 57)

In the aftermath of *Marvin*, many courts generally followed its lead, regardless of whether they were in community-property states or not. For example, Oregon, New York, Connecticut, Michigan, Wisconsin, and Washington have reached decisions similar to that in *Carlson* v. *Olson*, a Minnesota case (1977) in which the Minnesota Supreme Court quoted extensively from *Marvin* in an action for partition of real and personal property accumulated by a man and woman who had lived together for 21 years without being married. The couple had held themselves out to the community as being married, and the court noted that the doctrine of common-law marriage would have covered the parties had it not been abolished by legislation in 1941.

Similarly, in New Jersey, where common-law marriage has been forbidden since 1939, the New Jersey Supreme Court ruled that a businessman's promise to support his former live-in lover was a legal and binding contract, stating in *Kozlowski* v. *Kozlowski* (1979): "An agreement between adults living together is enforceable to the extent it is not based on a relationship proscribed by law or on a mere promise to marry" (Freed & Foster, 1981, p. 229).

Under the illegal consideration doctrine, some courts have denied recovery to women having oral express agreements for sharing assets with a man if sexual relations were part of the bargain. That was considered void as against public policy.

The latest footnote to the *Marvin* case is that, in August 1981, the California Court of Appeals reversed and rejected the $104,000 award. Her lawyer said he would appeal the decision. No decision had been reached by September, 1985.

An unexpected consequence of legalizing experimental family forms, such as cohabitation as in *Marvin,* might be a decrease in living together because it would carry all the hazards of marriage. Sussman (1980) found that the legal system is coopting cohabitation by making legal the mere act of living together under essential agreements that couples make verbally or in writing.

Summary: New Directions in Family Law

Judicial Discretion

Judicial discretion is increasingly important in family law because traditionally the courts have been extremely deferential to the states, with great diversity and little federal uniformity. Despite the conservative tenor of most judicial opinions, variant family forms are gaining greater recognition and legitimacy (Marciano, 1975).

Courts respond to social pressures. When the trend is egalitarian—such as during the 1970s—the courts become more progressive. When the country is interpreted as moving to the far right, the courts tend to retrench. The outcome of increased judicial discretion can have a significant impact on the family. For example, if judges continue to direct awards of custody, support, and property disposition with ever-increasing sex neutrality, women will be expected to work, to be liable for marital debts, to earn sufficient income to support themselves and their children, and to be entitled to an equal share of the assets acquired during marital or nonmarital relationships, including retirement and pension plans. On the other hand, if judges yield to the recent backsliding toward sex-stereotyped role relations, exemplified by the Supreme Court's affirmation of a male-only registration for the draft program (*Rostker* v. *Goldberg,* 1981), the pressure on women to revert to more traditional, dependent roles will increase.

From Status to Contract Revisited

The past decade's trend away from status (state-determined relations) toward contract (negotiated individual relationships) in family law through individual marriage or cohabitation contracts has been termed the first major development in "marriage law" in modern times to come from the people themselves (Sussman, 1975). If the numbers of people asserting their rights through marriage or cohabitation contracts, oral or written, increase, the courts can be expected to continue the trend of honoring them. However, individual contracts require equal bargaining power, still elusive for many women. Otherwise, contracts can merely reinforce the dominant norms of a traditional society, which has in the past relegated women

to a subordinate position. The courts may be more apt to award more generous support and alimony to some women than they can negotiate on their own (Beck, 1982, p. 374).

With the decreased stigma of divorce, women's ability to control reproduction to an unprecedented degree, and technological improvements in housekeeping, it is highly unlikely that women will return to the home or that the high rate of marital dissolution will slacken.

What are the legal implications of this trend toward freer marital and nonmarital relations? To reach the stage of legally enforceable individual contracts, many obstacles would require removal. Two basic concepts essential to consider are discussed next.

Occupation as a Status Determinant

The massive entry of women into the labor force is crucial to the changing family. The decline of marriage as a basic supportive institution and of the family as the primary status-determinant has created shifts toward one's occupation as the status determinant (Glendon, 1980). This shift from family toward occupation is reflected in the tension between benign and disadvantaging sex classifications, for example, as the courts weigh the differences between ending sex stereotyping and approving well-deserved remedies for past discrimination (Blumrosen, 1979). We cannot assume that women generally have been in the labor force, have had pay equal to that of men, and have had the same opportunities for advancement and salary-based fringe benefits. In a sex-fair work world, where one's occupation determines one's share of society's goods, family law can be sex-neutral. Flexibility is still required to determine whether, in the individual case, the wife has, in fact, followed the societal prescriptions for dependence and is therefore entitled to affirmative protective benefits.

With occupation replacing family as the status determinant, equality in the workplace assumes even greater urgency as a prerequisite to the contract model.

Conflict of Values

Perhaps the most critical dilemma for the next decade will be the pressures for individual rights and agreements as opposed to the state interest in family policy. Under a more conservative administration than the country has had for several decades, there may be a return to policies emphasizing "fundamental values" that are no longer adhered to by the majority of our citizens. Integral to the resolution of that dilemma will be the role of the courts in sorting out protected constitutional rights from "compelling" state interests.

Weakened enforcement and changes in federal laws, regulations, and court decisions may slow the rate of closing the gap between desired family behaviors and the societal support necessary to sustain them. For example, cuts in child-care expenditures and elimination of part-time and flexitime positions force women to return to the home. Although it seems unlikely that radically different proposals would garner sufficient constituent support, similar trends did occur after World War II, and after the women's suffrage and antislavery battles were won.

Furthermore, the pattern of past discrimination would portend that economic pressures to reduce the size of the labor force could again operate toward the resumption of traditional family roles. At this time, however, at least the half of the labor force that is comprised of women, as well as the women who work in the home and have derived many benefits from the resurgence of the women's movement, can be expected to rise up and protect their new turf and hard-won gains. The partnership model of marriage has been strengthened by the social reality that the cost of living requires the two-income family.

To move from status to contract relations, the conflict of values currently being waged by organized groups pressing for and against greater equality in the family must be creatively resolved to arrive at a new consensus. Ironically, both those favoring and those opposing greater autonomy in lifestyles require the legal system to legitimize their goals. Conservatives decry big government yet propose massive intervention to arrest the trends that they deplore. Liberals need government to remove the barriers to diverse living patterns.

Forecast

In the short run, economic pressures will keep the dominant trends flowing toward modification of the old common-law system. Applying a cost–benefit analysis to family law as it stands today would probably yield an adverse reaction to risk taking in either liberal or conservative directions. As government assistance programs are cut, those squeezed are protesting. Senior citizens have become a potent political force, and the politicization of women appears to be moving forward in the aftermath of the defeat of the Equal Rights Amendment.

The legal system will be hard-pressed to maintain equality of opportunity, affirmative action, nontraditional training programs, and alternative work structures to combat soaring unemployment. If women are forced back into economically dependent roles, the courts will react accordingly. The influx of women and minority judges, particularly in the federal courts as a result of the Omnibus Judgeship Act implemented by President Carter, may prove to be important to family relations. The appointment of the first woman (although she is a known conservative) to the Supreme Court by President Reagan may also make a difference.

The attempts by reactionary groups, such as the Moral Majority, to bottle up the expanded rights and the changed lifestyles that so many Americans have experienced in the past two decades will produce compromises unforeseeable at present. But in the long run, the changed social behavior of the past two decades, reinforced by the law, will continue the revolution in family law.

References

Annotation. *American Law Reports*, 3d, 1977, *75*, 1159.

Annual editions readings in marriage and the family. Guilford, Conn.: Dushkin Press, 1981.

Areen, J. *Allocating family assets at divorce*. Georgetown University Law Center, 1979.

Atkinson, G. Towards a due process perspective in conservatorship proceedings for the aged. *Journal of Family Law*, 1980, *18*, 1.

Beal v. *Doe*, 432 U.S. 438 (1977).

Beck, P. W. [Review of *Marital and non-marital contracts: Preventive law for the family*]. *Family Law Quarterly*, Winter 1982, *15*, 371.

Bernard, J. *Women, wives, mothers, the future of marriage*. Chicago: Aldine, 1975.

Besharov, D. J. The legal aspects of reporting known and suspected child abuse and neglect. *Villanova Law Review*, 1977–1978, *23*, 458.

Blackstone, H. *Commentaries on the laws of England*. New York: Harper Brothers, 1854.

Block, M., & Sinott, J. *The battered elder syndrome: An exploratory study*. College Park, Md.: Center on Aging, University of Maryland, 1979.

Blumrosen, R. Wage discrimination, job segregation, and Title VII of the Civil Rights Act of 1964. *University of Michigan Journal of Law Reform*, 1979, *12*, 3.

Bodenheimer, B., Reflections on the future of grounds for divorce. *Journal of Family Law*, 1968, *8*, 185–193.

Caban v. *Mohammed*, 441 U.S. 380 (1979).

Califano v. *Westcott*, 443 U.S. 76 (1979).

California Welfare and Institutions Code, Section 12350, Supp. (1976). Relatives Responsibility Statute (repealed).

Cantwell, W. P. *Man plus woman plus property equals?—Pondering the marital equation*. Unpublished paper, Denver, Colorado, 1980.

Carlson v. *Olson*, 256 N.W. 2d 249 (1977).

Chafe, W. *The American woman*. London: Oxford University Press, 1972.

Chastain, R. M. Introduction, 45 landmark decisions. *Family Advocate*, Summer 1982, *5*, 32.

Child Support and Establishment of Paternity Amendments to Title IV, Social Security Act, 42 U.S.C. AY 651 (1975, 1974).

Child Welfare League of America, Standards for Foster Family Care, 1959.

Christensen, H. T. (Ed.). *Handbook of marriage and the family*. New York: Rand McNally, 1964.

Civil Rights Act of 1964, 42 U.S.C. 2000(e) *et. seq.*

Commonwealth v. *Glenn*, 208 Pa. Super. 206 (1966).

Connecticut General Statute, Chapter 814, S. 46a-19, 46a-20 (1977). Protection of the Elderly Act.

Craig v. *Boren*, 429 U.S. 190 (1976).

DeBeauvoir, S. *The second sex*. New York: Knopf, 1953.

Doe v. *Commonwealth's Attorney for City of Richmond*, 425 U.S. 901 (1976).

Domestic Violence Prevention and Services Act, HR 2977 (1980) (not passed).

Drucker, D., The common law does not support a marital exception for forcible rape. *Women's Rights Law Reporter*, 1979, *5*, 181.

Drummond v. *Fulton Co. Dept. of Family and Children Services*, 408 F. Supp. 382 (N.D. Ga. 1976); rev'd. 547 F.2d 835 (5th cir. 1977); revised on rehrg. en banc, 563 F.2d 1200 (5th cir. 1977); *cert. denied*, 98 S.Ct. 3103 (1978).

Easton, B. Feminism and the contemporary family. *Socialist Review*, 1978, *8*(3), 11–36.

Ehrenreich, B., & English, D. *For her own good*. Garden City, N.Y.: Anchor Books, 1979.

Eisenstadt v. *Baird*, 405 U.S. 438 (1972).

Elkins v. *Elkins*, Ark. 553 S.W.2d 34 (1977).

Firestone, S. *The Dialectic of Sex.* New York: William Morrow, 1970.

Food Research and Action Center. *Guide to welfare reform.* Washington, D.C.: Author, 1979.

Foster, H. H., Jr., Freed, D. J. Grandparents visitation: Vagaries and vicissitudes. *New York Law Journal,* 1978, *6*(24).

Freed, D. J., & Foster, H. H., Jr. Divorce in the fifty states: An overview as of 1978. *Family Law Quarterly,* Spring 1979 *13,* 116.

Freed, D. J., & Foster, H. H. Jr. Divorce in the fifty states: An overview as of 1980. *Family Law Quarterly,* Winter 1981, *14,* 229.

Freed, D. J., & Foster, H. H. Jr. Divorce in the fifty states: An overview as of 1982. *Family Law Quarterly,* Winter 1983, *16,* 315.

Friedan, B. *The feminine mystique.* New York: Norton, 1963.

Frontiero v. *Richardson,* 411 U.S. 677 (1973).

Georgia Code Ann. S74-409, 410, 411 (Supp. 1977).

Glendon, M. A. Modern marriage law and its underlying assumptions: The new marriage and the new property. *Family Law Quarterly,* 1980, *13,* 4.

Goodman, E. The right you can't lose. *Boston Globe,* October 29, 1976, p. 33.

Gordon, L. *Woman's body, woman's right.* New York: Penguin Books, 1977.

Gordon v. *Gordon,* 577 P.2d1271 (1978), *cert. denied* 99 S.Ct. 185.

Griffin, M. K. In 44 states, it's legal to rape your wife. *Student Lawyer,* 1980, *9,* 21.

Griswold v. *Connecticut,* 381 U.S. 479 (1965).

Gunther, G. *Constitutional law* (10th ed.). Mineola, N.Y.: Foundation Press, 1980.

H. L. v. *Matheson,* 67 L. Ed. 2d 388 (1981).

Haber, S. & Seidenberg, B. Society's recognition and control of violence. Kutash, Kutash, & Schlesinger (Eds.), *Violence.* San Francisco: JosseyBass, 1978.

Harris v. *McRae,* 448 U.S. 297 (1980).

In re Day, 189 Wash. 368, 65 P. 2d 1049 (1937).

In re Sego, 82 Wash. 2d 736, 513 P. 2d 831 (1973).

In re Strittmater's Estate, 140 N.J. Eq. 94 (1947).

Interview, Assistant Director, Family Division, District of Columbia Superior Court, November, 1985.

Joyner v. *Joyner,* 59 N.C. 322 (1862).

Kanowitz, L. *Women and the law.* Albuquerque: University of New Mexico Press, 1969.

Katz, S. *When parents fail.* Boston: Beacon Press, 1971.

Katz, S. Elder abuse. *Journal of Family Law,* 1979–1980, *18,* 4.

Kay, H., & Amyx, C. *Marvin* v. *Marvin:* Preserving the options. In W. Wadlington & M. G. Paulsen (Eds.), *Domestic relations.* Mineola, N.Y.: Foundation Press, 1978.

Keene, N. Foster care and adoption reform: An Overview. *Journal of Family Law,* 1977–1978, *16,* 752.

Kozlowski v. *Kozlowski,* 80 N.J. 378 (1979).

Kraditor, A. *Up from the pedestal: Selected writings in the history of feminism.* Chicago: Quadrangle Press, 1968.

Kulko v. *Superior Court of California,* 436 U.S. 84, 1978.

Ladner, J. *Tomorrow's tomorrow.* Garden City, N.Y.: Doubleday, 1972.

Lau, E. & Kosberg, J. R. Abuse of the elderly by informal care providers. *Aging,* September–October 1979, p. 299.

Laura X. *Greta Rideout indicts marital rape project. Berkeley, Calif.: Women's History Research Center, 1980.*

Lerner, G. *The Grimké sisters.* New York: Schocken, 1971.

Lerner, G. *The female experience.* Indianapolis: Bobbs Merrill, 1977.

Levy, M. and Gross, S. Constitutional implications of parental support laws. *University of Richmond Law Review,* 1979, *13,* 517.

Liss, L. *Women's right to property and divorce.* Unpublished paper, Washington, D.C., 1980.

Liss, L. *Women's right to property and divorce in early Maryland.* Unpublished paper, Washington, D.C., 1982.

Loving v. *Virginia,* 388 U.S. 1 (1967).

Lovisi v. *Slayton,* 539 F.2d 349 (4th Cir., 1976).

Maher v. *Roe,* 432 U.S. 464 (1977).

Maine, H. S. *Ancient law.* New York: Henry Holt, 1885.

Marbury v. *Madison,* 1 Cranch 137, 2 L.Ed. 60 (1803).

Marciano, T. D. Variant family forms in a world perspective. *The Family Coordinator,* October 1975, *24,* 408.

Marvin v. *Marvin,* 176 Cal. Rptr. 555 (2d Dist. 1981), 557 P.2d 106, Supreme Court of California, en banc (1976).

Maynard v. *Hill,* 125 U.S. 190 (1888).

McGuire v. *McGuire,* 157 Neb. 226 (1953).

Mill, J. S. *On liberty.* New York: Appleton-Century-Croft, 1947. (Originally published, 1859.)

Millett, K. *Sexual Politics.* Garden City, N.Y.: Doubleday, 1970.

Mlyniec, W. The child advocate in private custody disputes: A role in search of a standard. *Journal of Family Law,* 1977–1978, *16,* 1.

Mnookin, R. Child custody adjudication: Judicial functions in the face of indeterminancy. *Law and Contemporary Problems,* 1975, *39,* 226.

Moore v. *City of East Cleveland, Ohio,* 431 U.S. 494 (1977).

Mullane v. *Central Hanover Bank,* 339 U.S. 306 (1950).

Muller v. *Oregon,* 208 U.S. 412 (1908).

Myrdal, G. *An American dilemma.* New York: Harper & Row, 1944.

National Clearinghouse on Marital Rape. *State Law Chart.* Berkeley, Ca., 1985.

National Organization for Women Legal Defense and Education Fund. *Myths of equality.* New York (1981).

New Jersey Sessions Law Service, Ch. 95 No. 20:14–5(b) (1978).

Note. The legality of homosexual marriages. *Yale Law Journal,* 1973, *82,* 573.

Orr v. *Orr,* 440 U.S. 268 (1979).

Palo Alto Tenants Union v. *Morgan,* 321 F.Supp. 908, 1970, N.D. Cal. aff'd. 487 F.2d 883 (9th Cir. 1973).

Parental Kidnapping Prevention Act, HR. 8406 amends Section 1073, Social Security Act, signed January 1981.

Planned Parenthood of Missouri v. *Danforth,* 428 U.S. 52 (1976).

Poelker v. *Doe,* 432 U.S. 519 (1977).

President's Advisory Committee for Women. *Voices for women,* December 1980.

Prevention, Identification, and Treatment of Elder Abuse Act of 1981, H.R. 769, 97th Congress (1981).

Reed v. *Reed,* 404 U.S. 71 (1971).

Reynolds v. *United States,* 98 U.S. 145 (1878).

Rice, R. M. *American family policy.* N.Y.: Family Service Association of America, 1977.

Roe v. *Wade,* 410 U.S. 113 (1973).

Roman, M. & Haddad, W. The case for joint custody. *Psychology Today,* September 1978, pp. 96–105.

Rossi, A. S. *The feminist papers.* New York: Columbia University Press, 1973.

Rostker v. *Godlberg,* 69 L.Ed.2d 478 (1981).

Santosky v. *Kramer,* 102 U.S. 1388 (1982).

Scheinberg v. *Smith,* 659 F.2d 476 (1981).

Select Committee on Aging, U.S. House of Representatives, 97th Congress, Hearings on Elder Abuse (1981).

Sillery v *Fagan and Fagan,* 120 N.J. Super. 416 (1972).

Singer v. *Hara,* 11 Wash. App. 247, 522 P.2d 1187 (1974).

Skinner v. *Oklahoma,* 316 U.S. 535 (1942).

Smith v. *Organization of Foster Families* (OFFER), 431 U.S. 816 (1977).

Stanley v. *Illinois,* 405 U.S. 645 (1972).

State v. *Smith,* 148 N.J. Super.219, 372 A.2d 386 (Essex County Court, 1977).

Steinmetz, S. Battered parents. *Society,* July–August, 1978, pp. 54–55.

Steinmetz, S. Elder Abuse. *Aging,* January–February 1981, pp. 6–10.

Sussman, M. B. *Marriage contracts: Social and legal consequences.* Presented at the 1975 International Workshop on Changing Sex Roles in Family and Society, Dubrovnik, Yugoslavia, June 17, 1975.

Sussman, M. B. *Marriage and the family: Current critical issues.* New York: Haworth Press, Critical Essay Series, 1980.

Swoap v. *Superior Court of Sacramento County,* 10 Cal. 3d 490, 111 Cal. Rptr. 136 (1973).

Uniform Child Custody Jurisdiction Act, Section 14-13-101 *et seq.* C.R.S. 1973.

Uniform Marriage and Divorce Act. National Conference of Commissioners on Uniform State Laws. Chicago: 1974.

Uniform Reciprocal Enforcement of Support Act, 1950, 9 Uniform Laws Annotated 888.

U.S. Bureau of the Census. *Child support and alimony: 1978,* Advance Report, Special Studies P-23, No. 106.

U.S. Bureau of Labor Statistics. News release, USDL 77-191, March 8, 1977.

U.S. Department of Agriculture v. Moreno, 413 U.S. 528 (1973).

U.S. Department of Justice. *Letter to Senator M. Wallop,* March 30, 1982.

Village of Belle Terre v. *Boraas,* 416 U.S. 1 (1974).

Virginia Slims American Women's Opinion Poll, Roper Organization Inc., 1974.

Wadlington, W., & Paulsen, M. G. (Eds.). *Domestic relations.* Mineola, N.Y.: Foundation Press, 1978.

Wald, P. Children's rights: A framework for analysis. *University of California-Davis Law Review,* 1979, *12,* 255.

Wallop, M., Senator. *Letter to friends,* December 17, 1980.

Wallop, M., Senator. *Letter to U.S. Attorney General,* January 20, 1982.

Wallop, M., Senator. *Statement before the House Judiciary Committee on Crime,* September 24, 1981.

Weitzman, L. J. *The marriage contract: Spouses, lovers and the law.* N.Y.: Free Press, Macmillan, 1981.

When fathers have to raise families alone. *U.S. News and World Report, 1977.*

Williams v. *North Carolina,* 325 U.S. 226 (1945).

Williams v. *Williams,* 543 P.2d 1401 (1976).

Wisconsin v. *Yoder,* 406 U.S. 205 (1972).

Zablocki v. *Redhail,* 434 U.S. 374 (1978).

CHAPTER 28

Families and Social Policy

Phyllis Moen and Alvin L. Schorr

The 1970s and the early 1980s have witnessed the politicization of the American family. Conservatives and liberals alike have couched political agendas in a family rhetoric. Concurrently with this war with words, with advocates on both sides of the political spectrum invoking such goals as family welfare, stability, and sanctity, it is fair to say that the well-being of families, especially their economic well-being, has steadily declined. This chapter seeks to move beyond rhetoric to an examination of the interplay between public policies and families in the United States.

To look at families in relation to social policy is to bridge the private and public aspects of human existence. Typically, the family is seen, even reverenced, as a private institution, closed off from the rest of the world and exempt from public scrutiny. Social policy, on the other hand, functions in the open, often in the marketplace; linking policies to families rejects an arbitrary division between public and private interests. Families are very much affected—enhanced, troubled, and changed—by public action (and inaction). Similarly, political choices are shaped by the actions of individual families. It is this recursive relationship—the feedback between political decisions and family decisions—that is the subject at hand.

The chapter is organized into six principal sections. First, we consider various approaches to family policy, examining alternative definitions of family policy as well as factors influencing the development of policies affecting families in the United States. Second, we review the relationship between families, policies, and social change, suggesting reasons for the burgeoning interest in family issues and placing this interest in both historical and political contexts. From this, we examine how the family interest can be defined, delineating possible directions for family policy. The fourth section describes three case studies: income support and employment policies, social security for the aged, and workplace policies for

parents. The fifth section explores the role of social science research in the formulation and evaluation of policies affecting families. The sixth and concluding section forecasts the future of policies affecting families in the United States.

Approaches to Family Policy
Alternative Definitions

The expression *family policy* is very much in vogue, but its referent can be broad or narrow, depending on how one chooses to define the term. As Gilbert Steiner (1980) pointed out, family policy can incorporate everything that touches the lives of family members or it can include next to nothing because specific policies can be subsumed under headings such as ''health policy'' and ''employment policy.'' If one looks only at how government intends to affect families, ''family policy'' almost disappears, for individuals, rather than families, are the basic targets of government action.

The first task, therefore, is to assign meaning to this imprecise concept. Bane (1980) opted for an expansive definition, including ''all those aspects of government policy which affect family life'' (p. 156). Similarly, Steiner (1980) called it ''whatever policy makers do that affects family relationships'' (p. 238). Others, by contrast, narrow the focus to particular types of families, such as those raising children, suggesting that ''family policy comprises publicly supported programs and practices that enable parents to provide at least a minimum level of nurture and support for their children'' (Lynn, 1980, p. 205) or that it refers to ''governmental goals concerned with family well-being and resultant activities directed toward families with children'' (Aldous & Dumon, 1980, p. 255).

In a measure, one can choose the definition one likes. In this chapter, we reserve the term *family policy* to mean *a widely agreed-on set of objectives for families, toward the realization of which the state (and other major social institutions) deliberately shapes programs and policies.* Such a definition incorporates the sense that family policy is coherent and more-or-less deliberate. Much public and professional discussion seems to aim at such policy. Ex-

Phyllis Moen • Department of Human Development and Family Studies, and Sociology, Cornell University, Ithaca, NY 14853. **Alvin L. Schorr** • School of Applied Social Sciences, Case Western Reserve University, Cleveland, OH 44106.

cluded, then, is what Martin Rein (1977) called "tacit" family policy, which may be uncovered by analyzing a broad range of government policies and inferring the priorities and norms that appear to have been assigned to family matters. Admittedly, those, too, are policies that affect families. They deserve attention, though their development may have been inadvertent.

Such a definition limits the discussion to policies with intended, as opposed to unintended, repercussions for families. However, such policies can be further subdivided according to whether they are direct or indirect, long- or short-term, affecting the structure of families or their functioning. In short, *family policy* is a most heterogeneous concept, incorporating a spectrum of issues. Family policies are distinguishable from general policies whenever one can perceive the *group* (i.e., the family group) impact of a policy or the second-order effects of a policy aimed at one individual, yet affecting other family members as well.

Defining *family policy* brings up another conceptual issue: the problems in establishing a definition of the family. Allen (1979) has summarized a number of possible definitions, ranging from "Any group of two or more persons with a legal or biological relationship" (p. 24) to legalistic, moral, functional, and social-psychological definitions. Her proposed definition for the family of the 1980s turns on the family's function as an economic unit: "A group of people who are bound by their common work efforts, from which their common consumption derives" (p. 35). The operationalization of the concept of the family has obvious policy implications, as one definition may be more inclusive than another, and policies aimed at families would, hence, incorporate some living arrangements and relationships while neglecting others. Rather than settling for a particular definition, it seems more appropriate to define families according to the particular issues involved. For example, policies concerned with the socialization of children should use a definition including households with children. In sum, definitions of the family should be relative to the issue at hand rather than sacrosanct.

Family Policy in the United States

For various institutional reasons, the United States has never achieved consensus on a core of family goals. Schorr (1962) pointed to three major traditions that have resulted in policies for American families that are tacit rather than explicit, and that are contradictory rather than consistent in their effects. The first is the supremacy of the individual. Since colonial times, a New World ideology nurtured the democratic disposition to deal with individuals instead of families (Calhoun, 1945). The interests of the individual—his or her achievement, development, or happiness—are the habitual American emphasis. The family is apt to be regarded as a vehicle for individual satisfaction.

The second tradition that has prevented a systematic focus on families has been a deep commitment to free enterprise. The laissez-faire orientation of our society has underscored the preeminence of economic interests. Therefore, families moved in search of better land or more work; family members worked at home and then in factories as economic needs dictated, and they learned the social skills and forms that were necessary for economic betterment. Only government could have influenced or redirected this institutional molding of family life, and Americans were deeply distrustful of government intrusion into their lives. Even in the last 40 years, when government has come to have unprecedented power and public support, there has continued to be widespread ambivalence about its actions.

The third tradition that has inhibited the development of family policy is the pluralistic nature of our political system, and of families themselves. Families are diverse and heterogeneous. Regional and ethnic as well as religious variations in values have precluded a consensus on what is meant by *family well-being* or on the development of policies promoting family interests. Until recently, the national government has studiously avoided the conflicts inherent in any attempt to legislate family values. The divisiveness and bitterness that have arisen in disputes about family planning and abortion, particularly where these issues were joined in Congress, are an indication of how divided we are on family values (see discussion about these controversies in Steiner, 1981).

Since the 1930s, there has been an incremental shift in dominance from the local level to the federal level for policies in general, including those relating to families. Moreover, the federal government has played a major role in supporting research, demonstration projects, and evaluations linked to family concerns (Grotberg, 1981). However, beginning in the Nixon years and culminating in the Reagan adminstration, there has been a swing in the pendulum back to state and local control. The point remains that there are layers of government, all of which affect family life, more often than not as a consequence of a composite patchwork of unrelated programs.

No analysis of family policy in the United States would be complete without mention of the increasingly active role of the courts in such family-related issues as civil matters, disability, women's rights, and abortion. Although there has been a historical debate about government intrusion into family affairs versus the sanctity of the family, the courts have been less reluctant than the other branches of government to intervene in family matters, though in an arbitrary and sometimes contradictory fashion (Wallach, 1981).

Families, Policies, and Social Change

Why the Focus on Families?

Steiner (1980) called family policy the social policy "fad" of the late 1970s, the "subject of the year" (p. 235). It continues to retain its prominence in the 1980s.

There are several reasons—all involving pervasive social changes—that scholars, policymakers, and citizens' groups have chosen to focus their attention on families as a target group. (Other, possibly more potent, reasons, pragmatic and political, will be attended to in a later section.) Demographic changes in the structure and composition of families, ideological changes concerning the nature of men's and women's roles, and a perceived increase in the incidence of social pathology have thrust the family into the political arena.

Americans tend to appraise the nation's families on the basis of comparisons, real or idealized, with families of the past. Whether the family as an institution is thriving or dying depends on preferences and expectations concerning its "proper" functioning. There is little doubt that the family has changed. However, seeing the family as a public problem is typically a perception based on negative comparisons with the classic family of Western nostalgia (Goode, 1968).

Demographic Changes. Families are experiencing unprecedented changes in structure and form. Demographic shifts in the population of the United States manifest themselves in the altered composition of individual families. It is important, however, to place these changes in a larger historical context. Some, like the markedly increased employment of married women, are revolutionary in nature. Others, such as the declining birth rate, are continuations of long-term trends (in which the 1950s was a perturbation; see Masnick & Bane, 1980). Still others represent compositional changes, such as the transformation of the single-parenthood group from predominantly widows to primarily divorced and single persons. But whatever the impetus for these transformations, the statistical trends listed below have intruded into the policy realm, as changing family shapes have resulted in corresponding changes in needs and demands for programs and services:

1. *Aging population.* By 1990, it is expected that the median age of the population will be 33 years, compared to 30 in 1979 (Joint Economic Committee, 1980a). The 65-plus population of the United States is currently growing at a rate twice that of the general population. Although in 1969 those 65 and over constituted 9.8% of the population, by 1979 they had grown to 11.1% and are projected to reach 12% by 1990 (Joint Economic Committee, 1980a).

2. *Declining birth rate.* American women gave birth to only half as many babies in the late 1970s as they did during the peak of the baby boom in the late 1950s. The fertility rate during the 1970s was 1.8, the lowest in American history. The average family in the early 1900s included four children, but two children is the norm in today's families (Glick, 1979).

3. *More women in the labor force.* About three out of five people entering the labor force in the 1970s were women. Nearly 52% of women were in the labor force at the beginning of 1980, compared to only 43% a decade

earlier. Participation is expected to increase to about 60% by 1990 (U.S. Department of Labor, 1980). The greatest increase has been in the labor force participation of married women, especially those with young children. Indeed, 62% of women who work outside the home have children under 18. In 1979, more than 30 million youngsters under 18 had working mothers (U.S. Department of Labor, 1980).

4. *Increasing divorce rate.* Forty percent of people marrying today will ultimately divorce. During the 1970s, the divorce rate increased 51% (U.S. Department of Commerce, 1980). (Still, half of 45- to 49-year-old women will in 1990 be living with their first husbands; see Bane, 1976.) This rising divorce rate has resulted in a steady rise in the number of one-parent households. In fact, in 1978, 19% of the 63 million children under 18 were living in one-parent households (Glick, 1979). The implications for children are startling. About one half of the children now being born are likely to live in female-headed households sometime before they reach age 18 (U.S. Department of Commerce, 1980). That proportion represents 40% of white children and 75% of minority children.

5. *Postponement of marriage.* A decline in the pool of eligible males, the increase in employment of women, and increasing numbers of couples who choose not to marry have resulted in apparent postponement of marriage. In 1978, for example, 48% of the women 20 to 24 years of age were in the "never-married" category, compared to only 36% in 1968. And the longer marriage is postponed, the more likely it is that individuals will remain unmarried. It is estimated that 8% to 9% of adults now in their 20s will never marry, compared to the current rate of 4 to 5% for older cohorts (Glick & Spanier, 1980).

Whereas some observers point to these changes as evidence of family disintegration, others read these trends as contributing to an improvement of family life (Glick, 1979). For example, lower birth rates may mean devoting greater attention to the children who are born. More working mothers may mean higher self-esteem and greater satisfaction for mothers, benefiting their children as well. Postponement of marriage may produce a better economic base for new families.

These shifts in family structure and composition have repercussions in the political environment. Demographic changes affecting family functioning create new "needs," arguing for a policy response. But these changes in families may also foster changes in public attitudes about the family and the role of government intervention in family affairs. As examples a declining death rate has placed heavier burdens on the social security system. In the latter case, the relative good health of 65-year-olds has challenged assumptions on which a policy such as mandatory retirement is based.

Changing Ideologies. The women's movement and concomitant changes in the definitions of women's and men's family roles have forced a reexamination of family lifestyle and political actions affecting that lifestyle. Embedded within this changing gender orientation is a shift in conceptions of family life. As Rainwater (1974) pointed out, there has emerged in the United States a general belief that "each person should live only with the people he finds it satisfying to live with" (p. 30). This attitude is reflected in the increased incidence of cohabitation and in the escalation of divorce rates. But from a long view, this is simply a deepening and broadening of individualist and liberationist values that reach far back in American history.

Increasing Social Pathology. The perception that child abuse, delinquency, and teenage pregnancy are increasing and that the welfare rolls are expanding exponentially has led to a search for preventive measures. In fact, welfare rolls have declined as a proportion of the population in the last decade. Teenage pregnancy increases as a proportion only because the overall birth rate has declined so sharply; that is, it is not really increasing. Still the public perception is otherwise. (And the impacts, on mothers and children, of out-of-wedlock births are profound.) Whereas families had previously been viewed as primarily closed systems (Aldous, 1975, 1978), there has been increasing recognition of the vulnerability to forces outside the boundaries of the family itself. The Advisory Council on Child Development of the National Academy of Science (1976) recognizes the importance of supports for families as critical for the development of children, placing families in their larger social and economic contexts:

Many of the difficulties faced by families are intricately linked with larger societal concerns: inequality, poverty, the decline of cities, poor housing, unemployment, inadequate health care, lack of transportation, the deterioration of the environment, inadequate education. (p. 12)

Similarly, the Carnegie Commission, headed by Kenneth Keniston (1977), underscored the plight of parents:

Parenthood is deeply rewarding but it is not easy and it is not cheap. We believe that those who choose to bear children must be expected to support and care for them, barring unexpected catastrophes—poor housing, unemployment, inadequate health care, lack of transportation. . . . Today far too many parents are unable to accept the full responsibilities of parenthood because there are no jobs or supports for them, or jobs they can find do not pay a living wage. (p. 77)

More generally, the world today is not the world we have known; the family is somehow held accountable for that fact.

Historical and Political Perspectives

Emerging Interest in the Family. The family as an institution has been a subject of interest since the nineteenth century, when Calhoun and DeToqueville provided background information on families in the United States. More recent interest in the links between policy and families can be seen as an outgrowth of the larger appreciation of knowledge as an "essential element in effective political action" (Henriot, 1972). It is said that policymakers are becoming more interested in having a foundation of facts on which to base their decisions. Alterations in the ideological, demographic, and social-problem landscapes in the 1970s resulted in an increased sensitivity of family scholars and government officials to the family in transaction with other institutions and a growing recognition of the implications, for families, of governmental actions (Hill, 1980).

A landmark event in this developing concern about family policy was the 1973 hearings held by the Senate Subcommittee on Children and Youth. The hearings (chaired by then Senator Walter Mondale) examined emerging trends and pressures on families; some of those testifying urged the preparation of family impact statements, similar to environmental impact statements, in order to evaluate the consequences, for families, of governmental actions. One result of this discussion was the establishment of a Family Impact Seminar at George Washington University in 1976 (Hubbel, 1981).

Interest in family policy has also been manifested in a variety of academic programs and training programs across the country. Two such programs were funded by the National Institute of Mental Health (NIMH) at the University of Minnesota's Family Study Center and at Duke University's Institute of Policy Sciences and Public Affairs. NIMH has also provided support to the Wellesley Center for Research on Women. Other groups established, in part, to examine family policy include Vanderbilt University's Center for the Study of Families and Children, the Cross-National Studies program at Columbia University's School of Social Work, and the American Enterprise Institute for Public Policy Research.

Still further evidence of the growing academic interest in family policy was the creation in 1979 of a new journal, the *Journal of Family Issues;* the development of the Family Impact Seminar; and the allocation of an entire issue of the *Journal of Marriage and the Family* to policy concerns (Hill, 1980). Important reviews of family policy issues have been provided by McDonald and Nye (1979); Rice (1977, 1979); Levitan and Belous (1981); Zigler, Kagen, and Klugman (1983); Aldous and Dumon (1980); and Cherlin (1983). Also noteworthy are the national dialogues on the salience of family issues widely disseminated in the National Academy of Science's *Toward a National Policy for Children and Families* (1976) and the Carnegie Council's *All Our Children* (Keniston, 1977).

Family policy won its recent currency during Jimmy Carter's first campaign for the presidency, when he sought to placate the Catholic bishops who thought him insufficiently opposed to abortion. In a speech in the summer of 1976, Carter promised to chart a "profamily policy" and to hold a White House Conference on the Family. One of the effects of the fracas that ensued between prolife and freedom-of-choice people, aggrieved minorities, various professional factions, and others who declared themselves parties to the argument was to rename it the White House Conference on *Families*. The Coalition for the White House Conference on Families, composed of a diverse body of organizations concerned with families, was active in disseminating information about the White House Conference in particular, and also about policies relevant to families. The fruits of the regional meetings that constituted the White House Conference on Families have yet to be ascertained (though the removal in 1981 of the Marriage Tax Penalty—taxing married couples at a higher rate than two nonmarried individuals—can be seen as one possible consequence). The White House Conference on Families has been aptly described as more of an arena than a forum (Wallach, 1981).

Political Context. Over the long run, the national government has tended to avoid deliberate influence of any sort on family patterns. Only in 1980 was an Office for Families established in the Department of Health and Human Services. Before that time, no agency of government was given prominence as being directly concerned with the well-being of all families. From time to time, responding to pressure from church and other profamily groups, the government has had employees and occasional offices directed toward family concerns. Their duties were usually quite special (concerning welfare families, for example) and their responsibilities and authority scant. Political support for family policy has, in the main, been nonexistent.

There has been no scarcity of political rhetoric and expressions of good intentions, of course, for example, the references to "a decent home and suitable living environment for every American family" in the Housing Act of 1949 and "preserving, rehabilitating, reuniting or strengthening the family" (the Social Security Act). But from our very beginnings, it has been this country's democratic disposition to concern itself with individuals, not families. The forces discussed earlier, of free enterprise, individualism, and pluralism, have prevented consensual family goals from developing in the political arena. Policies aimed at families did emerge, but only by an incidental and circuitous route. Historically, the United States government has influenced families either by accident or in order to use them as mechanisms for attaining other national objectives. Alvin Schorr (1962, 1968) has offered three insights concerning the formulation and implementation of policies directed toward families.

1. *Principle of coherence.* The government's image of its client is the individual, not the family. Until recently, family concerns have been an afterthought on the policy agenda. To the extent that family goals are seen as pertinent to meeting the needs of individuals, they are more likely to be supported by government policy. The Social Security Act of 1935 is one example of policy seen as beneficial both to individuals and to families. This legislation was intended to serve two goals: to provide economic security for the elderly and to encourage retirement in order to provide jobs for the unemployed. Each program—for retirement, for disability, and for single-parent children—was enacted first with respect to the needs of the individuals; provision for dependent wives, mothers, and children always came afterward.

2. *Pickaback principle.* To the degree that family goals coincide with other national interests, social or economic, they are more likely to be embraced. For example, the Housing Act of 1949 was passed primarily out of Congressional concern about the possibility of postwar deflation. That new housing starts would be beneficial to families as well was a convenient and acceptable result.

3. *Principle of direct response.* Issues that can be narrowly defined in terms of a specific target population or a specific family function are likely to be supported. Because of the highly diverse views of the family, it is only on narrow issues that a politically actionable consensus can be reached. One illustration of such a narrowly defined issue is the Congressional extension of Aid to Families with Dependent Children to two-parent families with an unemployed breadwinner (AFDC-UP). This amendment was a response to anxiety concerning the effects of the public assistance program on marital stability.

Family concerns have not occupied a prominent position on the policy agenda, in part, because they are dissimilar to other issues. In terms of clientele, there exists no powerful and articulate interest group to speak for families in the same way as for industry and labor. Unlike in environmental issues, for example, there are seldom clearly defined and widely agreed-on objectives that are pursued in the name of family well-being. As Steiner (1980, 1981) has observed, family issues are more ethical and moral than merely political. Consensus is rarely achieved on what constitutes the dimensions of family well-being.

Neither are there clearly defined mechanisms by which to achieve these goals even if they were satisfactorily articulated. Formulating workable solutions to family problems requires a theory about the causes of family problems. A case in point: Various theories of the factors underlying "the welfare mess," held at different times or simultaneously held by different decision-makers, implied solutions that are widely at variance with one another (Goodwin & Moen, 1980).

Europeans know what they want from family policy; for example, in Sweden a better quality of child care and equality for women and men, and in France a higher birth rate. (Europeans also have greater cultural homogeneity than is found in the United States, making such agreement far easier to come by.) In the United States, on the other hand, *family policy* is a term of art—the art of advertising. Laying claim to the term is an instrument to use in gaining public support for one's own distinctive objectives, whatever their source or rationale. Family policy in the United States has yet to find a constituency; though much is invoked in the name of family policy, little effort is aimed at its coherent development.

In the Family Interest

Almost everyone, including politicians, is "for" families, but that can mean vastly different things to different individuals. Some proponents of the family interest speak in favor of increased social supports for families, whereas others are for removing governmental fetters and letting families alone. Although there is rampant controversy about what would be most helpful for families, there is a general consensus that promoting family well-being is a good thing, both for society at large and for individuals in particular.

Social policies, observed Alva Myrdal (1941), tend to be ameliorative or symptomatic—dealing with consequences rather than causes. Truly preventive or prophylactic policy must concern itself more deeply with families and with children. Cooley (1909) aptly described the family, like other primary groups, as an essential bridge between the individual and the larger society, transmitting, mediating, interpreting, and sustaining society's norms. There is growing acceptance that the family's larger interest is also in the interest of the nation. For men and women, young and old, families have been and are the major source of emotional support. For many, especially the young, they are also providers of economic support. Strong, economically independent families are nothing less than an essential national resource.

Family well-being has historically been promoted for religious and moral considerations. Concern for individuals, especially children, has also been reflected in an emphasis on families. The Advisory Committee on Child Development of the National Academy of Science (1976) emphasized that the family's interest is inseparable from the best interests of the child. The central policy question raised by this committee, therefore, is "what can be done to help families remove or lessen the constraints they face in raising their children?" (p. 9) Opportunities and access to resources for all family members are very much bound to one's social status, which is typically defined in terms of the occupation and income of the major breadwinner. Lifestyle as well as life chances—for children and for adults—are deeply connected to the family's position in this status hierarchy.

Interest in families has recently turned to financial inducements. This has reflected concern not so much about the economic well-being of families as about the burden they impose on the welfare system and on government in general. Moroney (1980) emphasized this concern when he reminded us that most of the handicapped are cared for by families, asking what would happen if those 5% to 10% of families caring for handicapped members suddenly required the public sector to take over this responsibility. When policies fail to support family functioning, the public sector must often take over the services normally provided by families. Public recognition of this role of families as important service providers and as basic economic units has begun to grow concomitantly with the call for policies directed toward furthering the family interest.

Observers from all points on the political spectrum are recognizing the significance of the family's position between the individual and other institutions of society. As Gerald Caplan (1976) succinctly put it, the family serves as a "collector and disseminator of information about the world" (p. 22). One direction of this information flow, quite logically, is "downward" from parents to children. But it also flows from grandparents to their adult children and "upward," from members of younger generations to their elders.

Underlying the drive beginning in the 1980s to scale down or dismantle large social-welfare programs is the oft-stated goal of encouraging families and individuals to be autonomous, to thrive or survive on their own skills and resources. This position was well articulated by Berger and Neuhaus (1979) of the American Enterprise Institute. Naming the family a "mediating structure," they suggested the need for public support for it in order to nurture the values and well-being of the next generation (p. 19). Public policy, they wrote, should "cease and desist" from interfering with mediating structures. Rather, families, neighborhoods, churches, and voluntary associations, instead of government agencies, should be the primary institutions relied on for the realization of social purposes. This approach, they contended, would "expand government services without producing government oppressiveness" (p. 7). One may wonder how many of the most needy would fail to be served in such a fashion, and whether neighborhoods, churches, and voluntary associations, free of government "oppression," would serve their own distinct purposes rather than those of government or families. More important, it is doubtful that the private philanthropic and voluntary sectors have the resources to fill the gaps left by government retrenchment.

Families have a disadvantageous, unequal, uneven relationship to other institutions, being forced to respond to economic and political winds of change without much ability to influence or control change themselves. Inflation, interest rates, and the federal budget have powerful repercussions for families. The effects of economic decisions and conditions are often not in the family's interest. The words of Hill in 1949 have an uncomfortably familiar ring today:

For too long the family has been called upon to take up the slack in a poorly integrated social order. If fiscal policies are bungled producing inflation, the family purse strings are tightened; if depressions bring sudden impoverishment, family savings and family's capacity to restrict consumption to subsistence levels are drawn upon; if real estate and building interests fail to provide housing, families must adapt themselves to filtered down, obsolete dwellings or double up into shoehorned quarters with other families. For too long the family has been ignored in social planning, and the strains are telling. (p. ix)

Family Policy: Possible Directions

The fact that there has been no explicit family policy in the United States has not prevented scholars from proposing the alternative directions that such policy might take. One notion that some favor is limiting the scope of family policy to particular family types or target groups. Bane (1980), for example, argued that families with children are especially deserving of attention. Giele (1979) and Kamerman and Kahn (1978) have singled out certain population groups as most relevant to family policy: the aged, children, and women, among others. Still others have suggested that the domain be narrowed not only to particular families or population groups, but to particular issues as well. For Kamerman and Kahn (1978), these would include various types of policy that are relevant to family functioning, such as health, housing, personal social services, income, and taxes. Giele (1979) similarly proposed actions to support four areas of family functioning: nurturance, economic, residential, and cultural. Some have focused on only one issue—*income*—as the prime domain of family policy. A seminar of American and European scholars concluded that "the most important family programs in terms of political appeal, financial commitment, and general effect are economic measures directed toward families with children (Aldous & Dumon, 1980, p. 255). Economic factors were also a major concern for Featherstone (1979): "The strength of this new outlook (new liberalism) is its realization that inequality is the central issue, and that the major long-term item on the national agenda for families has to be income distribution" (p. 46).

A second and intimately related domain of family life that has been perceived as relevant to policy development is the *socialization of children*. The United States has a history of both direct and indirect subsidies for child care. The 1967 amendments to the Social Security Act provided day-care services for handicapped children as well as day care for children of welfare recipients. Title XX of the 1975 Social Services amendments allocated money for states to provide for protective services for children, foster-care services, and child-care services for poor families. There has been, in addition, indirect subsidization; for example, the Tax Reform Act of 1976 and the Economic Recovery Act of 1981 have enabled employed parents to deduct a portion of their child-care expenses from their income tax.

Though no all-inclusive child-care legislation has been enacted into law, several major bills, such as the Comprehensive Child Development Act of 1971 (S. 2007; vetoed by President Nixon), the Child and Family Services Act of 1975 (S. 626), and the Child Care Act of 1979 (S.4), have underscored the significance some have attached to the child-care issue. The failure of each of these proposals has turned on a basic question: "Should parents or should others care for children?" (McCathren, 1981, p. 131) This question, of course, ignores the fact that many children have working parents—mothers and fathers—who are employed outside the home, and that these children are therefore in someone else's care for a portion of each week. Regardless of their stand on government-supported child care, both scholars and politicians have recognized that the nation has a vested interest in facilitating the healthy development of the next generation (cf. Bronfenbrenner & Weiss, 1983).

A third, important area on the policy agenda might well be labeled *families under stress*. This area includes families faced with major traumas such as natural disasters, plant closings, and critical illness, as well as chronic stresses such as those faced by families with a handicapped child. The government has had a mixed role in supporting families in crisis situations, generally providing aid in public situations (such as an earthquake) rather than helping families with personal hardships (such as a critical illness). Government has also been reluctant to intervene in the day-to-day problems of living. Families with a handicapped child have generally been expected to manage on their own. Similarly, families with two earners or single parents encountering problems juggling domestic and child-care responsibilities with the demands of work have had little help from the public or private sectors in the form of paid parental leaves, flexible job scheduling, day care, or the possibility of working a reduced number of hours.

A "neutral" family policy, one that neither encourages nor discourages particular family forms, is another possible goal. Examining welfare policies, MacDonald and Sawhill (1978) defined a neutral family policy as one that "does not alter the costs and benefits of making decisions about marriage, births, and household composition" (p. 92). The principle may seem attractive but is difficult to apply in concrete situations.

Discrepancies between what was and what is have focused public attention on the nation's families. But the more useful questions should be phrased in terms of the discrepancies between what exists and what we as a people feel *should* exist. The shape of this prescriptive argument depends not only on the individual's location in the social structure but on his or her location in the family structure as well. Racial, ethnic, and class differences abound in the variant definitions of the family situation. But definitions also vary according to one's position with the family. Husbands, for example, may define family issues differently from wives, and the aged may have a quite different perspective from the parents of young children. However, the absence or impracticality of broad family *policy* does not preclude the development of *policies* for families. These can be achieved in relatively narrow arenas when consensus, or at least the absence of opposition, has been achieved. We will return to this matter.

Family Policies: Three Case Studies

Families are critical to the nation, as economic systems, as child-rearing systems, and as adaptive systems that respond to changing conditions and circumstances while simultaneously satisfying the unique needs of their members. Focusing on families rather than on individuals differentiates those policies that have family repercussions from those that affect individuals alone. Although there are a number of policies that affect families directly (such as income support), even more affect families indirectly, by touching the lives of individuals and, through them, the lives of other family members. Aid to the handicapped, the mentally ill, and the retarded is an example of a policy with indirect family effects, as are employment and workplace policies affecting the work lives of parents. We will examine here two areas of existing family policies: income-support and employment policies and social security for the aged. Then, we will turn to an issue of emerging concern, that of workplace policies affecting parents.

Income-Support and Employment Policies

Income support and employment are basic to any analysis of family policy, as economic security affects virtually every aspect of daily life. Income defines and limits the choices of families, determining life chances and lifestyle (Moen, Kain, & Elder, 1983). Yet, neither employment nor income adequacy are guaranteed in the United States.

Rein (1977) suggested that analysis of the "claim packages" (the different ways in which kin, the market, and government enter the income packages of families) provides a strategic way of locating "tacit" government family policy because it reveals the *de facto* priorities which are assigned to different claims structures. Similarly, an examination of the deliberate mechanisms that government uses to provide for the economic welfare can be a way of learning about explicit policies directed towards families.

Most families are supported by one or more jobs. The largest welfare system is, in one sense, the family, with income shared between wage-earner and nonwage-earner members. Because a secure job at a living wage is critical for family economic independence, it would seem that available employment at sufficient wage levels would be the most fundamental of family policies. But employment is labeled, in the United States, as an individual rather than a family concern. Moreover, it is too often defined as a private trouble rather than a public issue. In brief, we have, in the United States, no coherent employment policy, much less a family-oriented one.

The focus on individual aspects of employment has meant that family repercussions tend to go unnoticed. Clearly, a wage sufficient for an individual is often inadequate to support a family (see Bell, 1975; Furstenberg, 1974). Job loss should also be viewed from a family perspective because it is a family as well as an individual crisis. A study by Moen (1979, 1983) of the 1975 recession found that nearly 17% of all families with children present in the home had a breadwinner who was unem-

ployed at some time during 1975. The families most likely to face job loss were those with preschool children. This is reasonable, as the employed parents of young children are workers with little seniority or job experience. Moreover, the "cushion" of unemployment insurance is not equally available to all families. Moen found that, in 1975, less than half (46%) of the families of the unemployed received unemployment benefits. Women heading families were the least likely to be protected by insurance. The economic impacts of unemployment are colored by the availability of unemployment insurance and the duration of job loss. But they are also determined by family factors, such as the number of earners in the household and the number of dependents to be supported.

Whereas employment and unemployment policies have continued to focus on individuals, welfare policies have shifted from the individual to the family as the appropriate unit of concern. From 1935 to, perhaps, 1960, income-support policies were largely shaped by a social insurance ideology. This ideology reflected the philosophy that Alva Myrdal (1941) noted had been gaining ground in Western societies, that it is a social obligation to provide for the maintenance of human beings, even during those times when they are not productive. The nation identified major risks to income—old age, disability, widowhood, being orphaned, and unemployment—and added a program that would guard against each new risk. The programs were designed to protect those who were likely to be poor, and the payment formula was developed to favor those who had the least income. These programs make up the social security and unemployment insurance systems. In principle, they were designed to *prevent* poverty. To these were added welfare programs, provided out of need rather than entitlement; need was determined primarily by income level. Originally relatively small, the program grew in the 1950s and 1960s and came to preoccupy public attention. With such programs as food stamps and medicaid, so-called means-tested programs became, by the 1970s, of almost overwhelming importance. A fundamental question in the income-support policies of the United States had come to be the question of entitlement versus need, with family rather than individual income determining need.

The largest of the welfare or means-tested programs is Aid to Families with Dependent Children (AFDC), a program providing federal dollars to the states for payments to single-parent (fatherless) families and, in some (25) states, to two-parent families where the parent is unemployed or unable to hold down a full-time job. Benefit payments at the end of 1980 averaged $304 per family per month and $105 per recipient per month, though there are wide differences in payments among the states (U.S. Department of Health and Human Services, 1981).

Historically, a distinction has been drawn between the "deserving" and the "undeserving" poor. This was a major component of the Elizabethan Poor Law in 1601 (Stein, 1971), a legacy that is still with us today. The deserving are seen as being economically dependent through no fault of their own. This attribution of blame for one's financial state is reflected in public support of aid for different groups of the population. A study of the attitudes of Chicago-area residents revealed that the disabled are seen as more deserving of government help than are the poor. Moreover, the poor elderly and poor children are regarded as more deserving of help than are poor adults under 65 (Cook, 1979). These distinctions are also reflected in the social meanings commonly attached to various types of income support; unemployment compensation and social security payments are largely devoid of stigma, whereas AFDC carries with it a connotation of disrepute.

The distinction between deserving and undeserving implies that the undeserving poor are categorically different from the rest of the population. Research suggests, however, that the proportion of families permanently dependent is relatively small, whereas the size of the population at risk of economic need is quite large. Longitudinal analysis of a nationwide sample of over 5,000 families has documented the movement in and out of the poverty level of a sizable proportion of families over time (Duncan, Coe, & Hill, 1981). Similarly, a study of women-headed families across the nation by Rein and Rainwater (1977) verifies the transitory character of economic dependency, with nearly 40% of these families on welfare for one year or less.

Major paradigms in the area of public welfare policy have offered explanations of poverty based on the characteristics of individuals and their families, including the human capital resources (such as job skills and education) of the breadwinner. Other theories designate institutional and economic structures as the principal course of economic inequality and, hence, the deprivation of some families. Welfare reform measures have tended to follow the dictates of the prevailing paradigm at particular times in history (see Goodwin & Moen, 1980). From the perspective of the indirect repercussions of family policy, it is important that only a minority of those who receive income transfers are defined as recipients of welfare, with the stigma that the term implies. Regardless of cause, economic deprivation results in occupying the role of welfare recipient. As Street, Martin, and Gordon (1979) pointed out, poverty status is socially constructed, emerging from "the actions of agencies, communities and groups which take part in the institution of welfare" (p. 20).

Families facing poverty confront a related difficulty— dealing with the public assistance bureaucracy:

The poor need not only the ability to deal with the bureaucracy, but also great amounts of patience (as when welfare officials refuse to make appointments and keep recipients waiting interminably), high tolerance for rudeness and insult (as when indigent users of hospital emergency rooms find that no one even notices they are trying to ask questions), and a rare readiness to make their private lives public (as when one is questioned about

one's sex life by a stranger in an open cubicle of a welfare office). (Street et al., 1979, p. 69)

Welfare provides economic support for poor families, but in a capricious manner:

Public assistance policies and practices are in almost perpetual flux, reflecting the complex permutations of the phasings of federal, state, county, local administrative and fiscal processes, the vagaries of political decisions, pressures, cycles of virtue and terror, and local grassroots demands, and the organizational disarray induced by shifts in caseload size, turnover of employees, and so on. (Street et al., 1979, p. 40)

The reduction in social programs in the early 1980s underscored the vulnerability of low-income families to political and economic change.

Welfare payments serve to assuage the *economic* plight of poor families, but they also foster feelings of inadequacy and stigma, reflecting a discrepancy between what is publicly valued and what is practically administered. Prevailing ideology underscores the right of needy children to government support; still, the mechanism for providing that support is aid to the *families* of dependent children. Income goes to the adults who are the caretakers of children, bringing down on all members of the families the social attitudes accorded to those adults.

There have been periodic attempts to shift people from welfare. The Work Incentive Program (WIN), which was funded in 1968, was designed to train AFDC mothers for work and to help them find jobs, private if possible and in public service if necessary. Subsequent improvements of the WIN program provided additional supports for the WIN participants, including allowances for child care and medical expenses. The program had mixed results at best, making no appreciable dent in the welfare caseload. Parents employed in marginal, low-wage jobs simply do not earn enough to achieve financial independence. Moreover, our economy does not provide a sufficient number of jobs for all those wanting work. Training programs and short-term public-service employment do little to alter this situation.

The dilemma of how to provide for children and at the same time not to reward parents who do not work has been a major impediment to welfare reform. It is said that, by its very nature, public welfare encourages dependency. But public concern with dependency must confront the fact that most of the welfare poor want to work. A major study of welfare recipients found that the poor had the same work ethic, goals, and values as the middle class but had far lower *expectations* of achieving success in employment (Goodwin, 1972).

Perhaps the most widely discussed question about the family effects of welfare has been whether it encourages separation and divorce. An income maintenance experiment (to be discussed further along) has seemed to lend support to the view that guaranteed assistance does disrupt marriages. However, a wide variety of other evidence points to the opposite conclusion. AFDC was extended to unemployed *parents* (rather than mothers alone) in order to prevent marital dissolution. Yet, divorce statistics in the states that adopted the program reflect no change in this respect from earlier years, or from other states. If spouses were separating in response to welfare, the application for welfare should have come quickly after separation. On the average, it took a year or more. The question is still hotly contested among scholars (Bahr, 1979, 1981; Draper, 1981). Public opinion notwithstanding, the evidence for so-called fiscal desertion has been almost entirely anecdotal. Indeed, fiscal desertion must happen on occasion, but we do not design public policies to deal with exceptions.

Rainwater (1977) postulated that it is impossible to understand social issues or policies in the United States without coming to grips with the fact that our economic system "does not need and will not make use of all those who, according to our cultural standards, are expected to work. Some of the society's members are not needed or wanted at all" (p. 4). Perhaps that is the question central to welfare dependency and reform. In looking at income support and employment policies one must face, therefore, a profoundly important social issue. In *Beyond the Welfare State* (1960), Gunnar Myrdal warned that we are developing a "permanent underclass": people with chronically inferior incomes and a characteristic employment pattern. The dual-labor-market theorists (cf. Doeringer & Piore, 1975) argue that we have two distinct pools of labor, one of them essentially low paid, nonunion, and dead end. As the balance of public policy shifts heavily toward means-tested provision of food, housing, medical care, day care, and higher education—not hypothetical examples—we move toward a duplex society. One portion of the population copes successfully in a free market while an economic underclass barely survives in a world of welfare, public clinics, and housing administrators.

Family policy, as its bottom line, should be concerned with increasing the quantity and quality of work and with a more equitable distribution of income (Schorr, 1977). The National Academy of Science, in *Toward a National Policy for Children and Families* (1976), recommended as a reasonable and feasible goal that "no child should be deprived of access to a family living standard lower than half of the median family income level" (p. 5). And yet, of course, children—and their families—continue to live in deprivation.

Social Security for the Aged

The enactment of the Social Security Act in 1935 represents a landmark in family policy in the United States:

If we were to single out the one event in the depression which is likely to have the most far-reaching permanent effects on the American family as an institution, we might point to the passage of the Social Security Act. The passage of the Act symbolizes the recognition of greater state responsibility for the protection of the unemployed, the youth, the disabled, and the aged. (Stouffer & Lazarsfeld, 1937, p. 37)

Originally titled the Economic Security Act, this legislation, as described in the report of the Committee on Economic Security, sought to achieve six goals: to provide for the basic needs of the aged; to prevent dependence; to slow the growth of public assistance; to encourage thrift (by excluding a means test for benefits); to prevent a decline in wages by removing old workers and providing opportunities for younger workers; and to promote a stable economy by maintaining the purchasing power of older persons (Stein, 1980). When amended in 1939, the act also provided payments for wives and dependent children as well as retired workers, underscoring the worker's role as family breadwinner. Clearly the Social Security Act embodies both the pickaback principle and the principle of coherence, aiding the economy while furthering the well-being of individuals and families.

The provision of a national system of retirement benefits has had widespread repercussions for families (for a fuller discussion, see Schorr, 1980). It was estimated that, in 1928, one third of the aged population were economically dependent on either relatives or organized charity. But by 1970, less than 1 person in 10 of age 60 or over was in such a dependency position (Grad, 1977). Largely as a result of the Social Security Act, the incidence of poverty among the elderly has been steadily falling; it was 35.2% in 1959, 24.5% in 1970, 14.6% in 1974, and 14.0% in 1978 (Joint Economic Committee, 1980b).

The social security system provides a basic income floor for the aged, although it is one that is exceedingly modest. In early 1981, the average monthly benefit was $343 for an individual and $390 for a married couple (both over 65). Estimated poverty income levels in 1981 were $357 per month for an individual and $451 for a couple. Private pensions, earned income, and support from other government programs (such as S.S.I.) in many cases supplement social security payments. However, it is estimated that over half of the income of 56% of aged couples and 73% of single elderly individuals is derived from social security. Most (90%) of all Americans over 65 are eligible for social security benefits (VanGorkum, 1979).

The financial security afforded by the retirement insurance program offers the elderly greater options in their living arrangements. In 1952, for example, one aged person in three lived with his or her adult children; by 1976, only one person in six did so. Such income also permits greater geographical mobility for the elderly (Schorr, 1980).

From a larger view, the provision of social security benefits has reduced the claims of the elderly for support from their adult children, freeing up income for these families to use in raising their own children. It quite possibly smoothes the interpersonal relationships between generations even as it reduces the financial dependency of the aged on their children. Along these lines, it is important to note the countertrend of deinstitutionalization, which, in effect, dumps handicapped and other dependent individuals back on families and on communities. Social security has provided a measure of relief for families, but countervailing pressures have emerged in other directions.

To see the wide-ranging impact of social security insurance on families one has only to imagine life without it: uncertainty about retirement would be a major source of anxiety for middle-aged adults, many elderly would be impoverished, and still others would be forced to reside with their children, regardless of their respective preferences. It is no wonder that discussion about limiting social security payments or pushing back the age of eligibility has brought out such an impassioned response from both present and future beneficiaries.

Workplace Policies for Parents: An Emerging Policy

Changes in working patterns in the United States as well as in European countries are an example of emerging policies that have a direct impact on family life. Alternatives to traditional practices regarding the amount and scheduling of work hours are now widely accepted in European countries and are beginning to gain acceptance in the United States as well (see discussion in Kamerman, 1980; Kamerman & Kahn, 1981).

The impetus toward alternative work patterns has diverse origins, ranging from concern with energy conservation and transportation problems, to an awareness of the changes wrought by the industrial technology, to a general goal of enhancing the quality of working life. Another important factor has been the growing awareness of changes in the traditional family roles of men and women and the wish to accommodate to them by giving workers greater flexibility and options in integrating working life with their family life (Miller, 1978).

The adoption of alternative work patterns is an example of the "pickaback" model of family policy. Working parents may benefit from increasing flexibility in the time and timing of work, but so do students, older workers, and handicapped persons. Even more germane to the issue are the potential benefits available to employers, especially those providing part-time jobs, in the form of minimal or substandard wages and employment conditions, including few benefits and little security in part-time employment. Considering the substantial number of people who work part time involuntarily, this alternative creates an *apparent* reduction in unemployment rates, as well.

Innovative work patterns particularly beneficial to working parents include flexible working hours (flexitime), compressed work weeks, part-time work, job sharing, and parental leaves.

Flexitime. Flexible working hours are the most popular work schedule innovation and include a variety of practices giving employees some choice in determining their working hours. Flexitime, which had its origin in Germany in 1967, has spread quite rapidly throughout the industrialized world, particularly as a device for attracting workers to places where labor shortages are acute. It is an especially common practice in Germany and Switzerland, where 29% and 40%, respectively, of the workers are on flexible schedules.

In the United States, in 1980, 7.6 million workers, or 12% of the full-time workers, were on flexible schedules, and another 2.7 million part-time employees were also able to choose, within limits, their working hours. Over one fourth (26.5%) of full-time sales workers and more often a fifth (20.2%) of those in management and administrative positions had control over their working hours. Other occupations with a high proportion of flexitime workers were professional and technical workers (15.8%) and transport equipment operatives (14.3%). About 13% of the parents who were employed in May 1980 could choose their beginning and ending hours; this flexibility was somewhat more common among employed fathers (14%) than among mothers (10%) (*U.S. Department of Labor News,* 1981).

In 1978, Congress adopted the Federal Employees Flexible and Compressed Work Schedules Act (Public Law 95-390) to encourage experimentation with flexible schedules throughout the federal government. At the end of a three-year experimental period, the Office of Personnel Management evaluated the program and reported back to Congress the generally favorable effects of alternative work schedules on, among other things, employee morale, welfare, and family life.

Compressed Schedules. The United States, rather than Europe, has taken the lead in adopting the compressed work week, an arrangement whereby employees work more daily hours in exchange for fewer days per week. Begun during the 1960s, this practice has involved about 2% of the labor force (Maklan, 1977). However, the number of full-time workers employed 4½ days or less per week has been increasing, and in May 1980, 2.7% of the work force were on such reduced-week schedules. The majority of those on compressed time worked a 4-day week, with an extended weekend (Monday or Friday off). Service workers were the occupational group most likely to work full time in less than 5 days (6.7% of this category had schedules of 4½ days or less in 1980), and managers and administrators were least likely to work a compressed week (1.1%). The industry having the greatest proportion of workers on compressed schedules was local government, where over 1 in 10 (10.8%) had less than a 5-day schedule. Many of these represented police and fire personnel. Men and women were equally likely to work a shortened work week (*U.S. Department of Labor News,* 1981). Married workers were not enthusiastic about the compressed work week, possibly valuing free midweek evening hours more than an extra day off (Maklan, 1977).

Part-Time Employment. Part-time employment provides the largest alternative to the standard work pattern in the United States today. In the United States, about one worker in seven works less than 35 hours a week, the accepted dividing line between full- and part-time (Leon & Bednorzik, 1978). About 17% of the work force in the United Kingdom works part time; over 20% of the Swedish workers have part-time jobs (Miller, 1978).

Part-time workers put in, on the average, an 18-hour week. It must be recognized, however, that many of those working part-time in the United States would prefer full-time employment; approximately one fifth of the part-timers are *involuntarily* working part-time, being unable to locate or arrange full-time employment.

Some groups of workers are particularly inclined to seek out part-time jobs: women, students, and older workers. Women hold most part-time jobs, being twice as likely as men to work less than full time. In fact, a recent study found that over half of the women employed at some time during a five-year period spent at least a portion of that time working part time (Moen, 1985). This pattern is largely due to the domestic and child-care responsibilities that have traditionally been the province of women, making part-time jobs a strong preference, if not a necessity, at various stages of the life course.

Students use part-time employment as a way of combining work and education roles. In May 1977, teenagers constituted almost half of the male and one fifth of the female part-time workers who were voluntarily working part time (Leon & Bednorzik, 1978).

Older workers may use part-time employment as a semiretirement option. In May 1977, over half of the employed women 65 and older were working part-time; two fifths of the employed men in this age group were employed less than 35 hours a week.

Part-time employment is also used to supplement the earnings of a main full-time job (moonlighting). Part-time jobs may be held in addition to a regular full-time job, and some piece together two part-time jobs to constitute full-time employment.

The Federal Employees Part-Time Career Employment Act of 1978 (Public Law 95-437) provides for the option of part-time employment in the federal service.

Job Sharing. One variant of part-time employment is job sharing, where the duties of a single otherwise full-time job are divided between two people. There are a number of alternative arrangements: each person working half of the year, one working mornings and the other afternoons, and working on alternating days. Because these jobs are actually full time, the wages and employment conditions are apt to be better than those usually found in part-time jobs.

In a demonstration project sponsored by the U.S. Department of Labor in Wisconsin among state government employees, 45 full-time jobs have been divided into 87 shared part-time positions. As reported, the program appears to be popular with employees and to have a positive effect on productivity (U.S. Department of Labor, 1979).

Parental Leaves. Since 1974, Sweden has had a nine-month paid leave of absence to be provided to one of the employed parents of newborn infants. The leave can be taken by either the mother or the father, or the total may be shared by them. Moreover, parents can take this leave on a part-time basis, extending the period of time that they can remain at home with the child at least part of the day. Pay during the period of parental leave is provided by the government and represents 90% of the parent's salary.

Other European countries also have various forms of parental leave. In Norway, either parent may take an unpaid leave of absence of up to one year without loss of job or seniority. In France, such unpaid leaves can be taken for up to two years following the birth of a child. And in Israel and Austria, mothers (only) can take a one-year leave of absence. In Hungary, mothers on such leave are paid half their salary. Poland provides mothers a three-year leave, but without pay.

Conclusions. Alternative work patterns illustrate both the principle of coherence and the "pickaback" model of family policy. Working parents may benefit from increasing options in the amount and timing of work, but so, too, can students, older workers, and handicapped persons. Although the focus is on the individual worker, alternative work patterns can be beneficial to both workers and families. But not to be undervalued are the gains made by employers (e.g., reduced absenteeism and the provision of services at odd hours, as well as a cheaper work force) and the benefits perceived by government (e.g. the reduction of traffic congestion and the conservation of energy) as well. It is interesting, in this regard, that, in the United States, there is a considerable trend toward scheduling changes and much less interest in the provision of day care for the children of employed parents.

Because alternatives to the traditional workday and work week are useful on a number of levels, they have a high likelihood of success as policy innovations. They are responsive to the family needs generated by women's increasing labor force participation and to the changing ideologies concerning the roles of men and women. Options in the time and the timing of work aid parents—mothers *and* fathers—to better integrate occupational and family roles. But these policies should not obscure the fact that many workers, especially women, will continue to be faced with low pay and economic insecurity even as their options in scheduling expand.

Evaluating Policies: The Role of Social Science Research

Family Impact Analysis

Family impact analysis refers simply to the process of assessing the consequences for families of the intended and unintended effects of policies. Most social and economic policies affect families to some degree; what is required is an estimate of these effects overall, and of the various types of families most likely to be touched. Much that affects families is *unanticipated*. Much that affects families is also *indirect,* a by-product of policies concerned with such basic economic issues as the gross national product or balancing the budget. But however unanticipated, however circuitous these repercussions may be, they should not be ignored. Hence, the need for a broad-ranging family impact analysis.

The process of estimating the effects on families of public and private policies should take account of the following considerations:

1. *Intensity.* How large are the projected consequences? Are they potentially profound or superficial?
2. *Extent.* Are the effects long- or short-term? Are they dynamic or static, coextensive or sequential? Is there a primary outcome of overriding importance or a number of first-order and second-order effects?
3. *Range.* Does the impact portend consequences for all families or merely for particular subgroups of the population? Do effects vary with life cycle stage?
4. *Importance.* How significant are the expected consequences likely to be for the families involved? Are the changes apt to be irrevocable?
5. *Value.* Would the families affected see the anticipated consequences as beneficial or harmful to their interests? Would policymakers define them as desirable or undesirable?

In spite of abundant discussion about the need for family impact analysis (cf. Johnson & Ooms, 1979; McDonald & Nye, 1979; Ory & Leik, 1983; Sussman, 1971), little good analysis has been accomplished thus far. An excellent piece of work from the Family Impact Seminar is Bohen and Viveros-Long's *Balancing Jobs and Family Life: Do Flexible Work Schedules Help?* (1981). Robert Moroney's *Families, Social Services, and Social Policy: The Issue of Shared Responsibility* (1980), examining policies related to the elderly and the severely retarded, serves as a model for policy analysis in any field. There has also been research sponsored by the Office of Policy Development and Research of the U.S. Department of Housing and Urban Development on the effects of restrictive rental practices on families with children (Greene & Blake, 1980; Marans, Colten, Groves, & Thomas, 1980). These studies leave little doubt that families with children are indeed excluded from much of the rental housing market, with particular difficulty encountered by single-parent families, poor and large families, and black and Hispanic families.

Still, by and large, policy analyses with a focus on families are conspicuously absent, notwithstanding the convocation of a White House Conference on Families, the creation of an Office for Families, and a growing emphasis on families as a unit of political concern. One explanation for this neglect is the very complexity of the process required to analyze family effects. No small part of the difficulty in accomplishing such analyses concerns the matter of outcome measures. What kinds of conse-

quences for families should be the focus of family impact analysis? This is a question that, for the present, has no accepted answer.

The Development of Family Indicators of Well-Being

As Campbell (1981) pointed out, governments rarely do anything about a problem until they have learned to count it. Until conditions affecting families can be identified and their salutary and deleterious effects can be measured, it is unlikely that policy will attend to these conditions. The difficult task is the construction of indicators of family well-being and the linking of these indicators to policy or programmatic decisions. What is required are (1) multiple indicators (rather than an aggregate index); (2) causal modeling (rather than merely descriptive statistics); and (3) adequate conceptualization and the linking of measurement to concepts (for a fuller discussion, see Moen, 1980a,b).

Because families are diverse, and because even the same family changes in structure, function, and needs over time, no single measure of family well-being will suffice. For example, in looking at the economic situation of families, measures would be required to assess the distribution of financial resources across families as well as the changes in the economic circumstances of particular family types. Moreover, evaluating financial impacts should include, beyond objective data, the family's own subjective appraisal of its financial resources and prospects (cf. Katona, 1972). A simple indicator of overall economic well-being would only obscure more than it revealed.

In order for family policy analysis to be useful, the links between particular policies and outcomes must be made explicit. This linking requires a dynamic rather than static approach in looking at the *changes* that families experience as a consequence of *changes* in public policy. It also argues for an anticipatory, "armchair" procedure of prospective analysis, of teasing out the intended and the unintended potential family outcomes of emergent policies.

Indicators, unfortunately, are often mistaken for what they are taken to represent. Hence, we are presented with divorce statistics cited as evidence of the proposition that the American family is "in trouble" and the increasing employment rates of mothers as evidence of the inadequacy of care for children. Just as the number of hospital beds do not reflect the health of a community, neither do many of the current yardsticks used for family problems accurately gauge the well-being of American families.

What, then, might be some more accurate indices of family outcomes? We suggest that family indicators be developed with both objective and subjective components. The attitudes and perceptions of family members, including their expectations of the future, cannot be ignored if one is to gauge the impact of government policies on families. But even more critical are the objective conditions under which families live their lives. Income levels, health care, housing, and employment—all contribute to the welfare of families and must be taken into account.

Social Science Research and Policy Development

Whether social science research can make a contribution to the formulation of family policy depends on the type of research that is done and on the manner in which it is integrated into the policy process. Because the goals of family policy are often ill defined, analyses of family impacts may be similarly unclear. Moreover, it is difficult to separate specific policy impacts from the effects of other external influences or from ongoing changes within the family itself. Another, even more serious problem is that social science research is all too often not policy-oriented. Research is typically more concerned with the illumination of an issue than with the delineation of policy-manipulable variables. Compounding the problem is the fact that social scientists usually operate within the relatively narrow confines of their own discipline, examining only a partial slice of a much broader reality.

The obstacles preventing the use of social science information by policymakers include problems of access, timing, and perceived relevance. Researchers seldom have ready access to policy officials. But even with access, social science research often requires too much time to provide information useful to deliberations about pending legislation. To often, the final report is submitted only after the critical vote has been taken. Moreover, policymakers and administrators are often unimpressed by empirical research; relevant findings, therefore, may well be ignored. In discussing this issue, Nathan Caplan (1976) suggested that social scientists and policymakers inhabit different worlds, characterized by conflicting values, rewards, and language.

A report of the National Academy of Sciences and the Social Science Research Council (1969) underscored this point:

Many academic scientists value the prestige that their contributions to basic research and theory give them in the eyes of their peers more than whatever rewards might be obtained from clients who find their work useful. It . . . leads not only to scientific knowledge but also to respect and status tendered by those whose judgments they value most. (p. 193)

The cleavage between scholarly research and policymaking is reflected by the characteristic underutilization of social science information in the formulation of policy. Where research is used, it may serve as no more than a political tool in the promotion of a particular position among contending interests. The links between research on families and family policies are therefore quite tenuous. However, two cases where social science information *has* been instrumental in the policy process are the evaluations of the Head Start program and of the income maintenance experiments.

Head Start Evaluation. Social science research, like social policy, is a product of the historical milieu in which it is embedded. Concern about the effects of preschool programs on children from low-income families was part of the larger concern about poverty that characterized the social legislation of the 1960s. Though Project Head Start, which was begun in 1965, focused primarily on individuals (preschool children), it also had a family component, with a goal of encouraging the fuller participation of parents in the emotional, social, and intellectual development of their children. Objectives of the Head Start program, in addition to improving the child's physical, social, and cognitive development, included strengthening the family's ability to relate to the child, developing (within the child and the family) a responsible attitude toward society, and increasing the dignity and self-worth of all family members (Cooke, 1965). Project Head Start was, from a larger view, very much a *family* policy because it was conceived of as a long-term remedy for the intergenerational transfer of poverty. However, early analysis of the Head Start program concentrated primarily on one outcome, the child's intellectual development, and found no beneficial impact (Westinghouse Learning Corporation, 1969). More recent evaluations have examined a number of outcomes of programs similar to Head Start, still, however, focusing on the child as the unit of analysis (*Consortium for Longitudinal Studies*, 1983; Darlington, Royce, Snipper, Murray, & Lazar, 1980; Lazar, 1980; Lazar & Darlington, 1982). These studies assessed three outcome measures: placement in special-education classes, maintenance of proper grade level, and completion of high school by the age of 18. These reports by the Consortium for Longitudinal Studies, unlike the Westinghouse study, document beneficial effects for preschool programs. These findings, widely disseminated among policymakers, appear to have positively influenced Congressional appropriations for the Head Start budget (Lazar, 1980).

The impact on families of these programs, however, has yet to be ascertained, partly because of their focus on preschool education as a mechanism for breaking the culture of poverty, and for enabling poor children to improve their situation through education. But it also reflects the absence of appropriate family outcome measures: What kinds of family changes can the involvement of parents (read, "mothers") in the preschool programs of their children be expected to achieve? Whereas data on IQ and school performance are readily accessible to the scholar, family outcome measures are neither accessible nor even adequately conceptualized.

Income Maintenance Experiments. In the late 1960s, the Office of Economic Opportunity undertook a series of experiments to test the effects on families of guaranteeing a minimum level of income. Four experiments, involving thousands of families, were conducted in New Jersey, Pennsylvania, and rural parts of North Carolina and Iowa; Gary, Indiana; and Seattle and Denver. Although the specifics of the experiments varied, all low-income families involved received a specified amount of money in order to bring their total income up to at least the poverty level. The experiments generally ran for a period of three years, though the Seattle–Denver experiment lasted five years.

Studies of these income-maintenance experiments documented little change in the work effort of husbands in the face of a guaranteed income. However, wives and single-parent women in the experimental group showed a tendency to reduce their work hours somewhat (Moffitt, 1981). This outcome may reflect the time pressures that women experience in combining both family and work responsibilities.

The results that have received the greatest publicity are the findings concerning the higher rates of marital dissolution among participants in the Seattle–Denver program (Hannon, Tuma, & Groenveld, 1977). In this experiment, the women receiving the lowest income guarantees were the most likely to dissolve their marriage. A variety of theories have been offered to interpret this finding, although the quality of the experiment has been debated (cf. Goodwin, 1979, 1983). One theory is that, whereas families with generally higher levels of income are less likely to dissolve, where the wife gains an income of her own she might choose to dissolve a marriage that she would otherwise be compelled to continue.

From the point of view of social policy analysis, the almost exclusive emphasis on marital dissolution in the income maintenance experiments is quite significant. Vast quantities of data were collected, but we don't know, for example, the impact of a guaranteed income on family nutrition, on the use of health services, or on the quality of the time the parents spent with their children. A single family outcome, marital dissolution, dominates the discussion about guaranteed income. Because one experiment arrived at a negative finding, for some, that finding effectively ended the debate.

The Role of the Social Scientist: Conclusions. Analysis of existing or prospective family policies poses a number of ethical, conceptual, and methodological as well as political perplexities. Ethical dilemmas turn on the question of values. It is values that determine how problems are defined. For example, is welfare dependency a consequence of personal deficiencies, such as laziness, or is it endemic to the free enterprise system (Goodwin, 1983)? Ethical issues also enter into the establishment of goals and priorities. Policies beneficial to particular individuals within the family might also jeopardize the family as a unit, or vice versa. Similarly, policies supportive of families might also be seen as detrimental to the economy. The functionalist dilemma is ever present; one cannot ask which alternative is "best" without adding, "Best for whom?"

In fact, Butler (1981) made an important distinction between matters of *fact* and matters of *value,* noting that the most important contributions that social scientists make to policy formulation are often nonscientific value

statements rather than data on families *per se.* Similarly, Lichtman (1981) pointed out that the issues addressed by the National Academy of Science (1976) and by Keniston and the Carnegie Council (1977) are fundamentally a question of values. It is important, in this regard, to view policy analysis in terms of the interests and ideologies being served (cf. Doris, 1982). To quote Lichtman (1981):

The social science of policy questions is grounded simultaneously in the researcher's participation in the commonwealth and his participation in the community of scientists. It is not the researcher's disinterest, but his dual set of interests that gives his work value and integrity. (p. 67)

Where social scientists do attempt to engage in policy-oriented research, they are beset with a number of difficulties. The conceptual and methodological problems include the absence of outcome measures and theory. There is always the danger that the available information will itself define the problem, even though it may be irrelevant or inadequate. Research design and analysis are also constrained by political pressures that limit the focus and establish the variables of interest, as was true in the income maintenance experiments. A great deal of social research is dominated by the government's needs and interests. To ignore that fact is to be naive.

There remains the problem of access to relevant decision-makers. As Wallach (1981) pointed out, social scientists need to spend more time and effort getting their messages across: "The extent to which social scientists can use their contributions to influence social policy may depend upon the degree to which they can sharpen what they have to say and how they say it" (p. 168).

In spite of these drawbacks, we feel that the process of family impact analysis is a useful one, presenting, in the words of Rivlin (1970), two major messages: "It is better to have some idea where you are going than to fly blind," and "It is better to be orderly than haphazard about decision-making" (p. 2).

Forecasts for the Future

Moroney (1980) reminded us that the largest social-service agency in the nation is the family. The family is responsible for the care of children, the sick and disabled, and the aged, as well as for the economic welfare of all its members. The critical question is how government and, given today's political climate, other institutions can help families to accomplish these tasks. This question raises a parallel issue in the research realm: How can social scientists facilitate the development of policies supportive of families?

Family Impact Analysis as a Sensitizing Device

There are, we feel, four orientations that, if adopted by scholars and decision makers, would greatly improve the likelihood of policies in the family interest. The first is an *orientation toward families as active rather than passive entities.* Families do not merely respond to external circumstance; they may resist, negotiate, or collaborate in order to achieve their own private agendas. Seeing families as acting rather than as simply reacting provides a fresh perspective on family problems. Families can be defined as part of the solution rather than as merely the repository of the problem. As Featherstone (1979) pointed out, "a sense of the elusive, complex poetry of family matters is a reminder of how resistant families can be to public policy, meddling, good works, and other efforts of reformers to straighten out the human race" (p. 51). This viewpoint would be conducive to policies supporting families in achieving their own goals rather than to policies replacing families by substituting public services for private ones.

A second contribution to enlightened policymaking would be a greater *awareness of the changing nature of families.* This awareness would involve the obvious alterations in family structure and composition (especially the increase in single-parent families), but it would include as well a sensitivity to the transitions of families as their members move from one role to another (e.g., mothers entering the labor force, fathers and/or mothers becoming unemployed, separation, and divorce) and as they move from one stage of the life cycle to another (e.g., becoming parents and "launching" the last child). Acknowledgment of variations across families as well as changes within the same family over time could produce policies and programs better tuned to the different needs of differing family types. This emphasis on the pluralistic and changing nature of families removes, we feel, the necessity or even the desirability of framing a definition of the family as a basis for formulating policy. Families can be described in terms of the issue at hand; for example, if the concern is with the socialization of children, then those households involved in the care and raising of a child would constitute the target group.

A third orientation would be to *consider families rather than individuals as units of analysis.* Teenage pregnancies, for instance, have repercussions beyond the teenager. Furstenberg (1976) demonstrated that the parents of a young girl can do much to lessen the detrimental effects of pregnancy. Policies directed toward aiding young women should not ignore their family context. Similarly, records on child abuse or spouse abuse are often kept by the victim's name, with no effort made to trace the history of the abuse of various siblings or to link marital problems with parental ones. Families are the appropriate unit for policy analysis when one is considering either family-level variables (such as marital stability or economic adequacy) or individual effects that are mediated by family effects (as when child nutrition is affected by programs such as food stamps).

Finally, a "family impact" orientation could *sensitize researchers and decision makers to look for the possible inadvertent impact of policies on families, especially on families beyond the targeted group.* What, for example, is the impact of mortgage interest deductions on those who can't afford to purchase homes? What are the effects of a program like Head Start on the *mothers* as well as the children? What are the implications for parents and their other children of moving the handicapped back into the community? When is the process of getting services— medical, welfare, and legal—more stressful than doing without? What is the effect on the father–child relationship of trying to collect support payments from divorced or separated fathers? Although there will rarely be "data" sufficient to answer these questions, the act of framing them will in itself illuminate possible unintended and even deleterious consequences.

The best time to contemplate the family effects of policies and programs is at their beginning, when they are first being discussed. That there will be effects on families is a given. What must be determined is what these effects are likely to be and whether or not, on balance, they are desirable.

Opportunities for Family Policies

There are, we feel, several opportunities for the development of policies with a deliberate focus on families and their well-being.[1] The strategy for developing such family policies is simple: draw on existing ideological and economic strengths. The first step in developing this strategy requires an emphasis on *issues that unite rather than issues that divide.* By this, we mean exploiting fully the principles of coherence and pickaback in the family interest. Many policies that would be useful to families (such as alternative patterns in the scheduling of work) can also be seen as beneficial both to individuals and to other institutions (business or government, in particular). A concern with the family can be incorporated within the larger issues of decentralization and public (i.e., government) interference in the lives of individuals. Policies with multiple goals, including goals for the family, can be developed that would fit within the current policy agenda; what is required are imagination and sensitivity to the prevailing political currents, looking for consensus issues, not just controversial ones.

A second opportunity is to *examine existing programs for their benefits to families, and to build on these.* What are some of the positive aspects, for families, of established policy, such as the Social Security Act? This approach requires building on existing limited resources, rather than lobbying for unrealistic reform.

The third opportunity for enhancing family policies is to *move to new sources of policy initiatives,* both at the local level and in the private sector. It may be that the national government will not (or cannot) respond to the needs of families, at least not in the short run. Com-

[1]This section draws on private communication with Urie Bronfenbrenner.

ing to terms with that possibility necessitates a focus on other governments, at other levels, and on the more contained interests of business and labor. What is required is the development of new social inventions that preserve the autonomy of families and that at the same time promote their economic security.

Outlook for Families

It appears that the 1980s will be a time of continued economic and employment insecurity for a significant proportion of American families (Moen, 1983). Moreover, unlike in the period of the New Deal in the 1930s, one can expect little in the way of social services and programs either to reduce the threat of hard times or to mitigate their effects. Given the dominant governmental concerns with fiscal restraint and major cutbacks in social programs, it is highly likely that increasing numbers of families will experience financial setbacks, either from job loss or from failure to keep pace with the spiraling cost of living.

The United States is unique among the industrialized nations in failing to provide wide-ranging economic supports for families, particularly families raising children (Kamerman & Kahn, 1981). Most American families rely exclusively on earned income in order to make ends meet. When that income is jeopardized by unemployment or inflation, the family faces financial trouble. Thus, family resources and options are constrained by a political climate that limits public supports for families experiencing hard times.

We have, therefore, the contradiction of an increased concern with the strengthening of family life at the same time that programs designed to that end are dismantled or cut back and macroeconomic conditions only exacerbate the difficulties that families face. This chapter has underscored the importance of family economic viability for both family well-being and the well-being of the nation. Policymakers with liberal and conservative ideologies alike appear to have a vested interest in promoting family values. Those committed to strengthening family life would do well to attend to policies promoting job and income security. Establishing economic security for families is a fundamental issue of family policy. Identifying other concerns must necessarily take a backseat to this most basic requirement.

Berger and Neuhaus (1979) exhorted decision makers to replace the cynical axiom "Politics is the art of the possible" with the more positive "Politics is the art of discovering *what* is possible" (p. 43). No government can avoid decisions and programs affecting families. Given that families have more influence on the objective welfare and the subjective well-being of individuals than any other institution, we are of the persuasion that policies for families are not only possible but essential. The task is to recognize shared interests and to develop and achieve common goals and common values.

ACKNOWLEDGMENTS

The authors appreciate the comments of Richard P. Shore and the (considerable) bibliographic work of Maxine Schoggen.

References

Aldous, J. The intermingling of governmental policy, social structure, and public values: The case of changing family. In N. J. Demerath, O. Larsen, & K. F. Schuessler (Eds.), *Social policy and sociology*. New York: Academic Press, 1975.

Aldous, J. *Family careers: Developmental changes in families*. New York: Wiley, 1978.

Aldous, J., & Dumon, W. (Eds.). *The politics and programs of family policy: United States and European perspective*. Notre Dame, Ind.: Center for the Study of Man, University of Notre Dame and Leuvan Press, 1980.

Allen, C. M. Defining the family for post-industrial public policy. In D. P. Snyder (Ed.), *The family in post-industrial America: Some fundamentals for public policy development*. Boulder, Colo.: Westview Press, 1979.

Bahr, S. J. The effect of welfare on marital stability and remarriage. In G. McDonald & F. I. Nye (Eds.), *Family policy*. Minneapolis, Minn.: National Council on Family Relations, 1979.

Bahr, S. J. Welfare and marital dissolution: A reply. *Journal of Marriage and the Family*, 1981, *43*, 302.

Bane, M. J. *Here to stay*. New York: Basic Books, 1976.

Bane, M. J. Toward a description and evaluation of United States family policy. In J. Aldous & W. Dumon (Eds.), *The politics and programs of family policy*. Notre Dame, Ind.: Center for the Study of Man, University of Notre Dame and Leuvan Press, 1980.

Bell, C. S. Should every job support a family? *Public Interest*, 1975, *40*, 109–118.

Berger, P. L., & Neuhaus, R. J. *To empower people: The role of mediating structures in public policy*. Washington, D.C.: American Enterprise Institute for Public Policy Research, 1979.

Bohen, H. H., & Viveros-Long, A. *Balancing jobs and family life: Do flexible work schedules help?* Philadelphia: Temple University Press, 1981.

Bronfenbrenner, U., & Weiss, H. Beyond policies without people: An ecological perspective on child and family policy. In E. Zigler, S. L. Kager, & E. Klugman (Eds.), *Children, families and government: Perspectives on American social policy*. Cambridge: Cambridge University Press, 1983.

Butler, J. A. Social science and the formulation of policy toward children. In H. C. Wallach (Ed.), *Approaches to child and family policy*. Boulder, Colo.: Westview Press (AAAS), 1981.

Calhoun, A. W. *A social history of the American family: From colonial times to the present* (3 vols.). New York: Barnes & Noble, 1945.

Campbell, A. *The sense of well-being in America: Recent patterns and trends*. New York: McGraw-Hill, 1981.

Caplan, G. The family as support system. In G. Caplan & M. Killilea (Eds.), *Support systems and mutal help*. New York: Grune & Stratton, 1976.

Caplan, N. Social research and national policy: What gets used, by whom, for what purposes and with what effects?" *International Social Science Journal*, 1976, *28*, 187–194.

Cherlin, A. Family policy: The conservative challenge and the progressive response. *Journal of Family Issues*, 1983, *4*(3), 427–438.

Consortium for Longitudinal Studies. *As the twig is bent—Lasting effects of preschool programs*. Hillsdale, N.J.: Lawrence Erlbaum, 1983.

Cook, F. L. *Who shall be helped? Public support for social services.* Beverly Hills, Calif.: Sage, 1979.

Cooke, R. *Recommendations for a Head Start program by a panel of experts.* Washington, D.C.: Office of Economic Opportunity, 1965.

Cooley, C. H. *Social organization.* New York: Scribner, 1909.

Darlington, B., Royce, J. M., Snipper, A. S., Murray, H. W., & Lazar, I. Preschool programs and later school competence of children from low-income families. *Science,* 1980, *208,* 202–204.

Doeringer, P. B., & Piore, M. J. Unemployment and the "dual labor market." *The Public Interest,* 1975, *2*(38), 72.

Doris, J. Social science and advocacy: A case study. *American Behavioral Scientist,* 1982, *26,* 199–234.

Draper, T. W. On the relationship between welfare and marital stability: A research note. *Journal of Marriage and the Family,* 1981, *43,* 293–299.

Duncan, G. J., Coe, R. D., & Hill, M. S. *Poverty.* Ann Arbor: Institute for Social Research, Survey Research Center, 1981. (Mimeograph)

Featherstone, J. Family matters. *Harvard Educational Review,* 1979, *49,* 20–52.

Furstenberg, F. F., Jr. Work experience and family life. In J. O'Toole (Ed.), *Work and the quality of life: Resource papers for work in America.* Cambridge: Massachusetts Institute of Technology, 1974.

Furstenberg, F. F., Jr. *Unplanned parenthood: The social consequences of teenage childbearing.* New York: Free Press, 1976.

Giele, J. Z. Social policy and the family. *Annual Review of Sociology,* 1979, *5,* 275–302.

Glick, P. Children of divorced parents in demographic perspective. *Journal of Social Issues,* 1979, *35,* 170–182.

Glick, P. C., & Spanier, G. B. Married and unmarried cohabitation in the United States. *Journal of Marriage and the Family,* 1980, *42,* 19–30.

Goode, W. J. The theory of measurement of family change. In E. B. Sheldon & W. E. Moore (Eds.), *Indicators of social change: Concepts and measurements.* New York: Russell Sage, 1968.

Goodwin, L. *Do the poor want to work?* Washington, D.C.: Brookings Institute, 1972.

Goodwin, L. Limitations of the Seattle and Denver income maintenance analysis. *American Journal of Sociology,* 1979, *85,* 653–657.

Goodwin, L. *Causes and cures of welfare: New evidence on the social psychology of the poor.* Lexington, Mass.: Lexington Books, 1983.

Goodwin, L., & Moen, P. The evolution and implementation of family welfare policy. *Policy Studies Journal,* 1980, *80,* 633–650.

Grad, S. *Income of the population aged 60 and older, 1971* (Staff Papers No. 26). Washington, D.C.: Office of Research and Statistics, Social Security Administration, 1971.

Greene, J. G., & Blake, G. P. *How restrictive rental practices affect families.* Washington, D.C.: U.S. Government Printing Office, 1980.

Grotberg, E. The federal role in family policies. In H. C. Wallach (Ed.), *Approaches to child and family policy.* Boulder, Colo.: Westview Press (AAAS), 1981.

Hannan, M. T., Tuma, N. B., & Groenveld, L. P. Income and independence effects on marital dissolution. *American Journal of Sociology,* 1977, *84,* 611–633.

Henriot, P. J. Political aspects of social indicators: Implications for research. *Social Science Frontiers* (No. 4). New York: Russell Sage Foundation, 1972.

Hill, R. *Families under stress.* New York: Harper & Row, 1949.

Hill, R. *Status of research on families* (Chap. 8). Rockville, Md.: NIMH, 1980.

Hubbell, R. The family impact seminar: A new approach to policy analysis. In W. C. Wallach (Ed.), *Approaches to child and family policy.* Boulder, Colo.: Westview Press (AAAS), 1981.

Johnson, S., & Oorns, T. Is government helping or hurting families. *Pennys Forum,* 1979 (Spring, Summer), pp. 4–5.

Joint Economic Committee of the Congress of the United States. *Special study on economic change: Vol. 1. Human resources and demographics: Characteristics of people and policy.* Washington, D.C.: U.S. Government Printing Office, 1980. (a)

Joint Economic Committee of the Congress of the United States. *Special study on economic change, social security and pensions: Programs of equity and security. A staff study.* Washington, D.C.: U.S. Government Printing Office, 1980. (b)

Kamerman, S. *Parenting in an unresponsive society: Managing work and family life.* New York: Free Press, 1980.

Kamerman, S., & Kahn, A. J. *Family policy: Government and families in fourteen countries.* New York: Columbia University Press, 1978.

Kamerman, S., & Kahn, A. J. *Child care, family benefits and working parents: A study in comparative policy.* New York: Columbia University, 1981.

Katona, G. The human factor in economic affairs. In A. Campbell, & P. E. Converse (Eds.), *The human meaning of social change.* New York: Russell Sage Foundation, 1972.

Keniston, K. Carnegie Council on Children. *All our children: The American family under pressure.* New York: Harcourt Brace Jovanovich, 1977.

Lazar, I. Social research and social policy—Reflections on relationships. In R. Hoskins & J. J. Gallagher (Eds.), *Care and education of young children in America: Policy, politics, and social science.* Norwood, N.J.: Ablex, 1980.

Lazar, I., & Darlington, R. Lasting effects of early education: A report from the Consortium for Longitudinal Studies. *Monographs of the Society for Research in Child Development,* 1982, *47,* 2–31 (Serial No. 195).

Leon, C., & Bednorzik, R. A profile of women on part-time schedules. *Monthly Labor Review,* 1978, *101*(10), 3–12.

Levitan, S. A., & Belous, R. S. Working wives and mothers: What happens to family life. *Monthly Labor Review,* 1981, *104,* 26–30.

Lichtman, A. J. Language games, social science, and public policy: The case of the family. In H. C. Wallach (Ed.) *Approaches to Child and Family Policy.* Boulder, Colo.: Westview Press (AAAS), 1981.

Lynn, L. E. Fiscal and organizational constraints on United States family policy. In J. Aldous & W. Dumon (Eds.), *The Politics and Programs of Family Policy.* Notre Dame, Ind.: Center for the Study of Man, University of Notre Dame and Leuvan Press, 1980.

MacDonald, M., & Sawhill, I. V. Welfare policy and the family. *Public Policy,* 1978, *28,* 89–119.

Maklan, D. M. *The four-day workweek: Blue collar adjustment to a nonconventional arrangement of work and leisure time.* New York: Praeger, 1977.

Marans, R. W., Colten, M. E., Groves, R. M., & Thomas, B. *Measuring restrictive rental practices affecting families with children: A national survey.* Ann Arbor, Mich.: Institute for Social Research, 1980.

Masnick, G., & Bane, M. J. *The nation's families 1960–1990.* Boston: Auburn, 1980.

McCathren, R. R. The demise of federal categorical child care legislation: Lessons for the '80s from the failures of the '70s. In H. C. Wallach (Ed.), *Approaches to child and family policy.* Boulder, Colo.: Westview Press (AAAS), 1981.

McDonald, G., & Nye, F. I. (Eds.). *Family policy.* Minneapolis: National Council on Family Relations, 1979.

Miller, A. R. Changing work life patterns: A twenty-five year review. *The Annals of the American Academy of Political and Social Science,* 1978, *435,* 83–101.

Moen, P. Family impacts of the 1975 recession: Duration of unemployment. *Journal of Marriage and the Family,* 1979, *41,* 561–572.

Moen, P. Developing family indicators: Financial hardship, A case in point. *Journal of Family Issues,* 1980, *1,* 5–30. (a)

Moen, P. Measuring unemployment: Family considerations. *Human Relations,* 1980, *33*(3), 183–192. (b)

Moen, P. Unemployment, public policy, and families: Forecasts for the 1980s. *Journal of Marriage and the Family*, 1983, *45*, 751–760.

Moen, P. Continuities and discontinuities in women's labor force activity. In G. H. Elder, Jr. (Ed.), *Life course dynamics: 1960s to 1980s*. Ithaca: Cornell University Press, 1985.

Moen, P., Kain, E. L., & Elder, G. H., Jr., Economic conditions and family life: Contemporary and historical perspectives. In R. Nelson & F. Skidmore (Eds.), *American families and the economy: The high costs of living*. Washington, D.C.: National Academy Press, 1983.

Moffitt, R. A. The negative income tax: Would it discourage work? *Monthly Labor Review*, April 1981, pp. 23–27.

Moroney, R. M. *Families, social services and social policy: The issue of shared responsibility*. Washington, D.C.: U.S. Government Printing Office, 1980.

Myrdal, A. *Nation and family: The Swedish experiment in democratic family and population policy*. Cambridge: M.I.T. Press, 1941.

Myrdal, G. *Beyond the welfare state*. London: Methuen, 1960.

National Academy of Sciences and the Social Science Research Council. *The behavioral and social sciences, outlook and needs*. Washington, D.C.: National Academy of Sciences, 1969.

National Academy of Sciences and the Social Science Research Council. *Toward a national policy for children and families*. Washington, D.C.: National Academy of Sciences, 1976.

Ory, M. G., & Leik, R. L. A general framework for family analysis. In D. Olson & B. C. Miller (Eds.), *Family studies review yearbook* (Vol. 1). Beverly Hills, Calif.: Sage, 1983.

Rainwater, L. Work, well-being and family life. In J. O'Toole (Ed.), *Work and the quality of life*. Cambridge: M.I.T. Press, 1974.

Rainwater, L. *Welfare and working mothers. Family policy note 6*. Joint Center for Urban Studies of M.I.T. and Harvard University, 1977.

Rein, M. *Notes for the study of tacit family policy. Family policy note 1*. Cambridge: Joint Center for Urban Studies, 1977.

Rein, M., & Rainwater, L. *The welfare class and welfare reform. Family policy note 4*. Cambridge: Joint Center for Urban Studies of the M.I.T. and Harvard University, 1977.

Rice, R. M. *American family policy: Content and context*. New York: Family Service Association of America, 1977.

Rice, R. M. Exploring American family policy. *Marriage and Family Review*, 1979, *2*, 3.

Rivlin, A. M. *Systematic thinking for social action*. Washington, D.C.: Brookings Institution, 1970.

Schorr, A. A. Family policy in the United States. *International Social Science Journal*, 1962, *14*, 452–467.

Schorr, A. A. *Explorations in social policy*. New York: Basic Books, 1968.

Schorr, A. A. *Testimony before welfare reform subcommittee*, House of Representatives on H.R. 9030, 1977. (Mimeograph)

Schorr, A. A. *Thy Father and Thy Mother. A Second Look at Filial Responsibility and Family Policy*. U.S. Department of Health and Human Services, Social Security Administration, 1980.

Stein, B. *On relief: The economics of poverty and public welfare*. New York: Basic Books, 1971.

Stein, B. *Social security and pensions in transition*. New York: Free Press, 1980.

Steiner, G. Y. Looking for family policy—Big tickets on moral judgments. In J. Aldous & W. Dumon (Eds.), *The politics and programs of family policy*. Notre Dame, Ind.: Center for the Study of Man, University of Notre Dame and Leuvan Press, 1980.

Steiner, G. Y. *The futility of family policy*. Washington, D.C.: Brookings Institute, 1981.

Stouffer, A., & Lazarsfeld, P. F. *Research memorandum on the family in the depression* (Bulletin 29). New York: Social Research Council, 1937.

Street, D., Martin, G. T., & Gordon, L. K. *The welfare industry: Functionaries and recipients in public aid*. Beverly Hills, Calif.: Sage, 1979.

Sussman, M. B. Family systems in the 1970's: Analysis, policies and programs. *The Annals of the American Academy*, 1971, *396*, 40–56.

U.S. Department of Commerce, Bureau of the Census. *Social Indicators III*. Washington, D.C.: U.S. Government Printing Office, 1980.

U.S. Department of Health and Human Services. *Characteristics of state plans for aid to families with dependent children*. Washington, D.C.: Social Security Administration, Office of Family Assistance, 1981.

U.S. Department of Labor, Bureau of Labor Statistics. *Perspective on working women: A databank*. (Bulletin 2080). Washington, D.C.: U.S. Government Printing Office, 1980.

U.S. Department of Labor News, February 1981.

VanGorkum, J. W. *Social security revisited, Studies in social security and retirement policy*. Washington, D.C.: American Enterprise Institute for Policy Research, 1979.

Wallach, H. C. Conclusion. In H. C. Wallach (Ed.), *Approaches to child and family policy*. Boulder, Colo. Westview Press (AAAS), 1981.

Westinghouse Learning Corporation. The impact of Head Start on children's cognitive and affective development, executive summary. *Ohio Report to the Office of Economic Opportunity* (EDO S6321). Washington, D.C.: Clearinghouse for Federal Scientific and Technical Information, 1969.

Zigler, E., Kagen, S. L., & Klugman, E. *Children, families and government: Perspectives on American social policy*. Cambridge: Cambridge University Press, 1983.

CHAPTER 29

Family Life Education

Carol A. Darling

Introduction

Interest in the family and in family life education has become widespread and multifaceted during the past few decades. This interest, however, is not a new phenomenon; it evolved during the latter part of the nineteenth and early part of the twentieth centuries. Its beginning had many characteristics of a reform movement arising during the social-cultural upheavals of that period. During this time, there were a number of related social, economic, and scientific forces that inevitably impacted on the functions of the home and the family and led toward an increased interest in the problems of modern family life in the 1920s. Industrialization, urbanization, and smaller families were altering the established patterns of marital and parent–child relations; the result was a recognition of certain felt inadequacies and frustrations in American family life. Increasing numbers of women were entering the labor force; however, their expanding interests and roles were inextricably tied to a concurrent commitment to their homes and families. As a consequence, traditional family patterns began to change, as did expressed needs for assistance with family problems (Kerckhoff, 1964; Rockwood, 1948).

Although the intended focus of this chapter is to examine some of the current trends and issues facing family life education, a brief overview of its origins will contribute to a clearer understanding of its current status.

The onset of the twentieth century gave rise to a period of change and ferment providing impetus for the development of the disciplines and professions that are now an integral part of family life teaching. Psychiatry, psychoanalysis, and the mental health movement, as well as home economics, psychology, and the progressive education movement, originated during these years. As many groups were still in the process of conceptualizing their own approaches to a new field of education, they had not yet reached a stage in their own development where they could confer with persons of dissimilar orientations and backgrounds to consider problems of common interest. Hence, some of the current breadth and diversity in family

life education had its beginnings in the earliest years of its inception (Kerckhoff, 1964).

The highlighting of some specific dates will help to establish a chronology of events during this period:

1888—The Child Study Association was formed to discuss problems of childhood and child nature.

1900—A body of knowledge was evolving in psychology, sociology, biology, and economics.

1908—The American Home Economics Association was established to provide opportunities for home economists and other professionals to cooperate in the attainment of individual and family well-being, the improvement of homes, and the preservation of values significant to home life.

1914—The American Social Hygiene Association was formed because of the interest of professionals in the topics of sex education, the prevention of venereal disease, and the prevention of prostitution.

1919–1920—A sex education boom occurred during World War I.

1922—The first college course in marriage preparation was taught by Ernest Groves at Boston University.

1929—The National Council of Parent Education was organized to provide cooperation and coordination among family professionals, organizations, and agencies.

1934—The Groves Conference on Marriage and the Family was organized to discuss ways of preserving family values in our society by encouraging a multidisciplinary approach to enhance research, counseling, and family-life education techniques.

1938—The National Conference on Family Relations, which later changed its name to the National Council on Family Relations, was organized to bring together within one association leaders in research, teaching, and professional service in the field of marriage and the family (Hendrickson, 1963; *Home Economics New Directions*, 1959; Kerckhoff, 1964; Rouner, 1969).

This overview of family life education indicates that several disciplines and organizations were interested in studying the family, but their foci of attention and degrees of involvement varied. In the past, some disciplines avoided teaching courses in marriage and family living

Carol A. Darling • Department of Home and Family Life, Florida State University, Tallahassee, FL 32306.

because a functional orientation, as taught in home economics, did not have an equivalent status with the theoretical or research perspectives. Some disciplines were not willing to risk their professional reputation by offering functional courses and thus took a traditional approach to the subject matter. But as student interest and demand increased, several subject-matter areas, in addition to home economics, became involved in the study of families, such as health, sociology, psychology, biology, medicine, and, more recently, even history, economics, and mass communications (Somerville, 1971).

Historians who had not previously been concerned with the private and routine affairs of the average person have begun to recognize the historical and social importance of links between the family and religion, revolutions, and migration. For example, most of what is distinctive in American culture can be traced to our colonial roots and the willingness of individuals and families to move to increase their chances of success and their opportunities. Hence, many American values and qualities, both positive and negative, have evolved from this historical tendency toward mobility. Such qualities as optimism, individualism, achievement orientation, and love of novelty, in contrast to superficiality, alienation, loneliness, and materialism, have had an important impact on family life (Slater, 1980). Both the detachment from and the establishment of friendships, as well as strains on intimate bonds, have had a pervasive effect on families in our culture. With social-emotional ties becoming transitory, permanent reference points such as those found in family or marriage relationships have become essential for bearing this burden of isolation from close personal relationships.

The field of economics has also turned its attention to the study of families by carefully examining household consumption and production. This "new home economics" is an attempt to apply economic analyses to understanding household problems. Although home economists, such as Reid (1934), were active pioneers in the study of household production and consumption, there has been an increasing recognition by economists that much of the investment in the economy is made in human beings rather than in physical capital. Fertility is also shaped in important ways by economic considerations and has led to renewed interest in the economics of household decisions. In addition, decisions related to consumption, savings, mobility, labor force participation, investments in human capital, and, in a sense, marriage itself are all important elements of family life that are now being studied by economists.

Mass communications via several forms of popular media have also turned their focus toward the family. Coverage of family issues through television, movies, and major journals has illustrated that the current sense of crisis over the family is both newsworthy and interesting to consumers. However, the mass media are not only examining family changes, but also playing an important role in the process of shaping new cultural mores by publicizing and legitimizing a variety of role models for interpersonal relationships.

Whereas the early years of family life education evolved from an era of social ferment and the diverse involvement of disciplines and organizations, recently there has been a multidimensional surge of attention to the family. Because this increased interest has brought forth several problems and issues within the field, the broad objectives of this chapter are to identify and discuss the trends and issues in family life education, to present a proposed model for organizing family programs, and to suggest program recommendations. To further these objectives, this chapter explores such concerns as the dilemma regarding the definition of family life education, the lack of a broad conceptual framework to guide family educators, and the limited role given to families as participants in the educative process. In addition, the dissemination of family life education, as well as the changing concerns and transitions within the field, will be examined. It is hoped that this overview of issues and concerns in family life education will not only help to clarify the past and present situations, but will also give some direction for the future.

The Scope and Focus of Family Life Education

Scope of Family Life Education

In addition to an increasing interest in families, there has been a concurrent expansion of family-life education programs. As these education endeavors have wide variations in purpose, sponsoring agent, target group, topic, and instructional design, some definitional problems and confusion exist about what actually constitutes family life education. In addition, an examination of the literature reveals several purposes being espoused by program leaders, such as prevention, education, intervention, remediation, and therapy. Although all of these goals have some similarities in preserving and improving the quality of family life, there is also a major difference. There appears to be an implied time element, in that prevention, education, and enrichment would happen "before" some occurrence in order to provide a protective or readiness orientation. In contrast, intervention, remediation, and therapy suggest that some incident or problem has already occurred and that some corrective measures are needed. Although these differences in purpose exist, family life education is perceived, in general, as the foremost preventive measure for the avoidance of family problems.

Another problem in defining family life education results from the wide assortment of family-life education programs that now exist for a variety of audiences. These programs can be both general (covering multiple content areas) or specific (involving several specialty topics such as divorce adjustment, expectant parenting, single lifestyles, or stress management). However, according to Fisher and Kerckhoff (1981), this diversification has brought about an active subspecialization that could splinter the field and cause a destructive impact. Over-specialization can result in a duplication or overlap of services, as well as difficulties in preparing professionals for the potentially overwhelming task of having to be an expert in too many areas. Thus, Fisher and Kerckhoff called for a restatement and reintegration of the field and a return to training professionals as generalists.

During the course of its existence, family life education has been offered in both formal and nonformal settings and has employed a wide variety of instructional methods. All too often, people view educational programs as being restricted to formal institutional settings that provide instruction from kindergarten through high school and beyond, at the university level. Whereas several family-life programs have been established within this context, other nonformal settings also provide for family life education experiences. For example, the Cooperative Extension Service (CES) is recognized as the world's largest publicly supported nonformal education organization and is dedicated to the development of people and the improvement of the quality of their lives. Family life education is an important component of CES and is implemented by professional staff who utilize various delivery methods, including informal discussions, support groups, self-help groups, workshops, and mass media techniques. Program priorities are influenced by input from several sources and, in the 1980s, are focused on some of the following concerns: (1) the impact of public policy, communities, institutions, and services on the well-being of families and what families can do to mediate this impact; (2) family empowerment, which emphasizes the strengths of families; (3) stress management; and (4) parent education. With a network of 4,000 strategically placed professionals, CES has the potential of making a significant contribution to family life education during this decade (Daly, 1981).

Other nonformal programs can be found in various religious settings, as the church is one institution whose members span the life cycle from birth to death. The church is also an institution in society that serves and relates to the total family. One of the important areas in which churches are greatly involved is marriage, including premarriage education, education of the newly married, marital enrichment, and postmarriage education. Other topics of interest are family enrichment, family-life-cycle concerns, and sexuality (Swain, 1981). Although the church has provided numerous family living programs that have served both individuals and families, religious sponsorship of programs may not be available to or compatible with the needs of some segments of the population.

A third location of nonformal family life education can be found in community settings. As early as 1948, a committee of the Family Service Association of America supported the call for family life education. Most community agencies have both a mandate to provide multiple services and a mandate to service a large geographical location. Counseling is often a major component of community agencies, along with opportunities for referrals. One of the most distinctive characteristics of community family-life education programs is their broad appeal. Often, providers such as churches, businesses, and schools are responsive primarily to their own members. On the other hand, community agencies have the potential for a broad and continuous appeal. In this age of financial and program accountability, however, agencies are facing some important questions and pressures from consumers and funding bodies. Hence, evaluation and research appear to be necessary, along with improved training, standards, and supervision (Bowman, 1981).

Whereas the family-life education programs that take place within schools often use more conventional methods of instruction, nonformal programs enjoy an endless methodological latitude. This inherent flexibility can be best examined by employing a categorical format containing three basic modes of instruction: the mass mode, the group mode, and the individual mode.

The mass mode encompasses all those family living activities that address an anonymous mass audience in which there is no direct contact between the learners and the educators. Examples of such methods include printed materials (books, pamphlets, magazines, and newspapers); audiovisual materials (films, filmstrips, and videotapes); the mass media (television and radio); lectures; and technological instruction through simulators or computers. The group mode is directed toward clientele organized into learning groups specially constituted for the purpose of participating in family life education by means of group discussion, therapy, or question-and-answer periods. Although groups may vary in structure, format, or process, their function remains the same: to utilize group interaction and instruction models in order to influence the attitudes and practices of the participants. The individual mode is primarily oriented to counseling and guidance.

Family counselors and therapists are most concerned with effecting a systemic change in the family in an effort to improve the functioning of its members. As there is clearly no single best mode, the choice should be based on the specifics of the situation and the needs and characteristics of the participants (Harman & Brim, 1980).

The absence of any systematic effort to gather data on the myriad of family-life education activities makes it difficult to accurately assess the numbers and characteristics of the participants. The task is further complicated by multiple sponsors and modes, as well as the wide diversity of people involved. Printed material is the method by which family life education is most often dispersed. Harman and Brim (1980) cited Clarke-Stewart, who reported that the average annual sale of child-care books is 44,000, and that, between 1970 and 1975, approximately 23 million books on child rearing were sold. Even the circulation of journals and magazines regularly featuring articles on child care is over 26 million. Although not all Americans have attained functional reading levels, the outreach of books, pamphlets, journals, and magazines is still extensive. If the participants in adult education programs, public-school programs, and mass media were added to these figures, the resulting number would not only be vast, but inaccurate; that is, many persons would be counted either more than once or not at all. As family life education occurs at several different levels, from preschool through lifelong education, it is very difficult to obtain an accurate determination of the numbers and characteristics of its participants or nonparticipants.

Definition of Family Life Education

As a result of this multidimensionality, family life education has become increasingly difficult to define; often, definitions appear to be too limited. For example, Avery and Lee (1964) proposed the following definition:

Family life education involves any and all school experiences deliberately and consciously used by teachers in helping to develop the personalities of students to their fullest capacities as present and future family members—those capacities which equip the individual to solve most constructively the problems unique to his family role. (p. 28)

Their emphasis on "school experiences deliberately and consciously used by teachers" suggests that schools are the exclusive agent in disseminating family life education, that schoolteachers are the only legitimate educators, and that teachers are totally purposive in their education activities. Educators attempt to be aware of the substance and the effect of their instruction, but teachers, as well as parents and other professionals, are not always cognizant of the unintentional results of their actions.

Another view of family life education mentioned by Kerckhoff (1964) states:

Family life education includes facts, attitudes, and skills relating to dating, marriage, and parenthood. Obviously, then, it includes—but is more than—homemaking education, or parent education, or family sociology, or sex education. Throughout the content is woven the idea of relationships—parent-child, husband-wife, boy-girl, and so on. (p. 883)

Although family life education does include facts, attitudes, and skills, it also includes values and their relationship to a much broader scope of concepts than dating, marriage, and parenthood. The idea of relationships is very important; the notion of individual development is another concept central to the current focus of family life education.

A more comprehensive statement has come from the National Commission on Family Life Education, a task force of the National Council on Family Relations:

Family life education is a fairly new educational specialty, but one for which there is a steadily increasing demand. It is a multi-professional area of study which is developing its philosophy, content, and methodology from direct experiences with families and the collaboration of such disciplines as home economics, social work, law, psychology, sociology, economics, biology, physiology, religion, anthropology, philosophy, and medicine. It includes a number of specialized areas, among which are interpersonal relationships, self understanding, human growth

and development, preparation for marriage and parenthood, child rearing, socialization of youth for adult roles, decision making, sexuality, management of human and material family resources; personal, family and community health; family-community interaction, and the effects of change on cultural patterns. ("Family Life Education Programs: Principles, Plans, Procedures, A Framework for Family Life Education," 1968, p. 211)

Although this discussion is broad-based and inclusive, it is also somewhat cumbersome. Rather than conceptualizing what is meant by family life education, it merely lists professions, disciplines, and specialized areas of study. As a result, this list of professions and content is subject to continual change to include other disciplines and new topics of familial interest.

A few years later, the National Commission of Family Life Education prepared a Position Paper on Family Life Education (1970, p. 186). This document stated that the purpose of family-life education programs is to guide individuals and families in improving their interpersonal relationships and realizing their potential to improve their quality of life. It was suggested that there was an urgent need for the development of family-life programs in schools, churches, and other social institutions, as well as the development of family life materials based on scholarly research. The National Council on Family Relations (NCFR) further recommended that comprehensive and sequential family living programs incorporate sex education and be a planned portion of the regular curriculum from preschool through college. This position statement contained components critical to family life education and also emphasized a lifelong perspective.

Cromwell and Thomas (1976) proposed a more succinct definition: "Family life education promotes the delivery, coordination, and integration of family development resources to individual family units in order to improve family life" (p. 15). Although generally the educational potential of the family system for its members has been ignored and there is a definite need to focus on the family as a basic unit, family-life education programs have also been designed for singles in an effort to attend to the needs of this group as well.

After examining the expanded interest in the family and its diverse educational contexts, family life education is conceptualized herein as an interdisciplinary field of study concerned with preserving and improving the quality of human life by the study of individuals and families as they interact with the resources in their multifaceted environments. This view of family life education implies the breadth of the field; there are no boundaries on professional or disciplinary involvement and there are no exclusions of individuals because they may not currently comprise a family unit. Thus, any individual, regardless of her or his stage in the life cycle, can participate in and benefit from family-life education programs. The program content can also range from a broad coverage of topics to in-depth studies of specialized areas. Central to this concept is the notion of interaction with environmental resources. These resources may be human or non-human and may include other individuals, organizations, systems, values, time, energy, or any element that may influence or be influenced by individuals or families.

Although one definitional problem has resulted from using a definition of family life education that has been too narrow, another has evolved as a result of public controversy. Part of the early turbulence over family life education was that it clearly included sex education. Although family life education involved a great number of topics, one that was consistently highlighted was sexuality. Consequently, the words *family life education* became obtrusive to certain elements of the population. Because parent education had not received similar controversial publicity, it did not immediately connote sexuality. Hence, it has become safer politically for some organizations and school systems to offer courses in parent education. Although it is recognized that these courses also includes components of human sexuality, there appears to be less opposition to the programs.

How does family life education differ from parent education? Though both have the problem of self-definition, family life education is generally concerned with the broad spectrum of individuals, families, and their multifaceted environments, whereas parent education is concerned with enhancing parental competence and self-esteem in the parental role. Parent education is, in fact, only one part of family life education. Although parenting programs are not new, recently there has been a surge of interest in them. Problems such as adolescent pregnancy, substance abuse, and parent–child communication have motivated parents to seek assistance in coping with the loss of equilibrium in their families. While the scope of parent education differs from that of family life education, the choice of implementing either program depends on the individual interpretations of teachers and sponsoring agencies.

An examination of the issues involved in family life education begins with several questions: What is family life education? How broad is its scope? And, what does it include? Although individual programs may tailor their definitions to suit their specific purposes, this investigation of trends and issues in family life education uses a broad conceptualization that is more inclusive than limiting.

A Conceptual Framework for Family Life Education: An Ecosystem Approach

One of the criticisms of many family-life education programs is that they do not use a conceptual framework in organizing the study of family behavior. Many programs are quick to use popular teaching methods and to discuss timely topics. However, without a framework for the reciprocal relationships among families and their environments, many meaningful insights and long-range goals of family-life education programs may not be achieved.

In the past, a number of conceptual frameworks have been integrated in differing degrees into family living courses. Some of the early and current texts were examined for their conceptual frameworks. The developmental approach has been prevalent for several years (Duvall, 1971; Schulz & Rogers, 1980; Stroup, 1966); however, the interactional, the structural-functional, the exchange, and the systems approaches have also been implemented. Although a majority of texts contain no mention of conceptual frameworks (Bowman & Spanier, 1978; Cox, 1981; Knox, 1979; McCary, 1980; Orthner, 1981; Saxton, 1980), some contain either a few paragraphs or a single chapter describing them (Bell, 1979; Dyer, 1979; Eshleman, 1981; Scanzoni & Scanzoni, 1981; Schulz, 1982; Smart & Smart, 1980). As a result, many family-life students and future educators have not been well informed about existing frameworks and have not been integrating them into the organization of their programs. Although several approaches are in existence, the focus of this chapter is on an emerging framework, an ecosystem approach, which captures the essence of the other frameworks while adding a new ecological dimension.

The ecosystem approach to studying the issues that face individuals and families has received considerable attention from a number of content areas, including home economics, education, social work, sociology, psychology, anthropology, and biology. Whereas this approach may have a somewhat different meaning to different people, wholeness and integration are the unifying concepts.

Numerous perspectives can be incorporated into an ecosystem approach. A sociological view emphasizes the family as a constellation of roles and norms; the developmental view stresses the changing nature of the family throughout the life span; and the social-exchange view describes the family as a group that seeks to maximize rewards and minimize costs. By perceiving events and relationships from a holistic perspective, an ecosystem approach can provide integration by incorporating the idea of the family as a set of interrelated roles that change through time while the family is trying to maximize quality of life (Andrews, 1977; Melson, 1980). This approach can provide a framework in which multidisciplinary study can be accomplished and in which various theories and approaches can also be combined. It has been closely associated with the study of ecology and has evolved from general systems theory and a social systems approach (Bertalanffy, 1969; Broderick & Smith, 1979; Kantor & Lehr, 1975; Tansley, 1935). However, an ecosystem approach attaches critical attention to the biological and physical dimensions of the organism–environment relationship, its psychosocial characteristics and interactions, and the families' transactions with other environments (Andrews, Bubolz, & Paolucci, 1980).

Components of the Family Ecosystem Model

The model of the family ecosystem depicted in Figure 1 has evolved through the individual and collective efforts

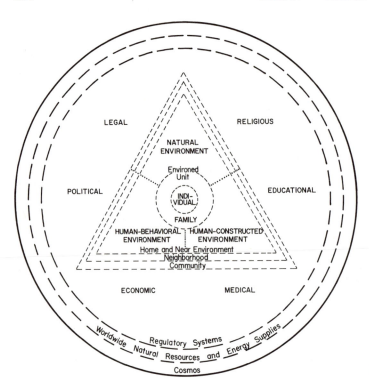

Figure 1. Family ecosystem approach.

of faculty and students at Michigan State University's College of Human Ecology and is adapted from Morrison (1974) and Bubolz, Eicher, and Sontag (1979). Basically, an ecosystem model consists of three main elements: the organism or environed unit, its environment, and the network of interactions and transactions between them.

The Organism or Environed Unit. The family, as the environed unit, can be defined as a bonded group of interacting and interdependent persons who have some common goals and resources and, for part of their life cycle, share living space (Andrews *et al.*, 1980; Hook & Paolucci, 1970). This broad definition of the family embraces differing family forms of varying sizes, ages, and role patterns and is therefore nonexclusionary. Because many people in the family field choose the family or the household kin group as a central focus, the family has likewise been considered the center of interest in the family ecosystem approach. Because the term *environed unit* may be conceptualized as a broad kin network or a subsystem within the nuclear family, the notion of the family as it is discussed in this chapter can encompass several forms of families. By utilizing this approach, an analysis of relationships within the family can also be achieved. The family is therefore conceived of as a collection of interdependent, yet independent, individuals whose corporate entity differs from the characteristics of its individual members. When the family is viewed as an in-

teracting group of individuals who are emotionally, physically, and socially interdependent, the focus is on the relationships among the family members rather than on the attributes of the group or the individual.

Environment. The environmental component incorporates a complex integration of the natural, human-behavioral, and human-constructed components of the family's internal and external environments. In addition, consideration is also given to a combination of the regulatory systems, the natural resources, and the energy supplies that surround the environed unit. The organism of major interest is the family and all peripheral elements are considered its environments. However, the referent environment may change as the system of interest changes. At times, the center of interest may be the individual and his or her interactions within the family; the individual then becomes the organism of central focus, and the family unit constitutes the environment. At other times, the family unit is examined as it interacts with other components of its external environment, such as work, school, or the neighborhood. Hence, the family is both a system itself and an interdependent subsystem of the larger social system.

The environment of the family can be understood to contain three central components that permeate several levels of the environment. These three components are the natural environment, the human-behavioral environment, and the human-constructed environment. The natural environment provides the fundamental resources for survival, such as food, air, and water, within a context of space and time. Whereas the natural environment furnishes the resources for sustaining life, the human-constructed environment plays a critical role in mediating between families and nature. It contains human modifications of the physical and biological environments, such as roads, buildings, and machines, as well as human alterations of the sociocultural environment (i.e., values, laws, and language). The human-constructed environment is both vulnerable to the limitations of the natural environment and protective against the natural elements. Equally important are the emotions, sentiments, and social patterns that constitute the human-behavioral environment because it is within this environment that family members are socialized and human beings are nurtured (Bubolz *et al.*, 1979).

The natural, human-behavioral, and human-constructed components of the environment not only exist within the internal environment of the home, but are also integrated within other levels of the external environment. The various external environments of family can be identified by their relative distance from the family unit. The immediate living space, or home environment, is of special interest in the ecosystem approach because many of the resources necessary for human existence are contained in it. As one goes beyond the home and becomes progressively more global, other levels of the environment take on importance, such as the neighborhood, the community, and various regulatory systems.

The regulatory systems, including medicine, education, religion, economics, politics, and the legal system, have been developed to facilitate energy exchanges between families and their social and physical environments. In addition, these regulatory systems interact with each other, as well as with the broader natural environment. Although the natural elements in one's near or microenvironment are important to everyday living, the entire ecosystem—individuals, families, and their multiple environments—is critically dependent on the world's supplies of natural resources and energy. Thus, regulation of the macroenergy environment and its sources is essential. Ultimately, all energy is derived from the sun; therefore, an ecosystem approach can not omit the environment that exists beyond the boundaries of the earth. Although much of this cosmic environment is still unknown, its present and future impact should not be taken for granted.

Interaction. The third organizing component of the family ecosystem consists of the interactions between the organism and its environment. These reciprocal transactions between families and their environments are essential for the transformation of the energy needed to facilitate family survival and goal achievement. These interactions can occur in many ways, that is, within the organism, among components in an environment, among the

environments, and between the organism and one or more of its environments. In addition, these interactions often take place simultaneously and interdependently, as illustrated by the following example:

Two single parents decide that they will combine their independent families through marriage (interaction among individual organisms creates a new family organism). They realize, however, that their lives are going to become more complicated and possibly more stressful. Because they will all be living within one household, a residential relocation will involve new relationships among stepsiblings and stepparents, alterations of space allocations, and shifts in roles and responsibilities (interactions are occurring simultaneously and interdependently within the organism, among components of the near environment, and between the organism and its environment). Furthermore, the visitation patterns of the children with their noncustodial parents may have to be adjusted, financial resources will have to be redistributed, and new interactions will be formed between the family members and other environments, such as friends, neighbors, schools, and other systems (interactions are occurring simultaneously and interdependently within the organism and between the organism and its external environments). The employment of both parents necessitates the blending of schedules and responsibilities with the procedures and time patterns of other systems (interaction between the organism and its environments and interactions among the environments external to the family).

This example depicts only a few of the potential interactions that could occur within and between families and their environments; nevertheless, it provides some insight into the complex network of interdependent transactions. Traditionally, the socialization process has been viewed as a one-way transaction of adults socializing children. Because of an increased emphasis on ecological inquiry, all elements—the children, the family system, and the environment—can be seen as having reciprocal interactional effects.

Implied in the concept of transactions between families and their environments is the existence of a boundary that serves either to separate the individuals within the family or to separate the family from the components of its environment. Family internal boundaries define familial subsystems and regulate interaction among the members such as husband–wife, parent–child, or siblings. The family unit can also set itself off from the external environment by establishing permeable boundaries ranging on a continuum from open to closed (Kantor & Lehr, 1975). Families that have a high level of exchange with the outside environment are considered more open than those families that have little interaction with the environment. Over time, it is the development of this transactional patterning that characterizes a family's boundary permeability and interdependence with its environment.

Application of the Family Ecosystem Approach to Family Life Education

Although only some of the basic elements of the family ecosystem have been outlined, there are several emerging implications for programs in family life education. Many disciplines use a systems approach emphasizing the interactions of humans with their environments, but the ecosystem approach creates an increased awareness of the interdependency of all life. Hence, further attention can be given to the family as a unit in relationship to a total environmental context. Because an ecosystem approach attends to the family's internal and external environments, several areas of study within the family field can use this perspective of linkage to arrive at a level of integration.

An examination of the number and the interrelationship of problems facing families (e.g., family violence, adolescent pregnancy, and economic pressures) reveals that none of these problems can be solved within the framework of any single discipline. Although several disciplines espouse an interdisciplinary approach, progress is rarely made because each contributor maintains the vantage point of his or her own discipline. The frameworks of each can be expanded to include concepts borrowed from other disciplines, but only those concepts that pose no serious threats or difficulties would be allowed (Auserwald, 1968). The major focus of a profession, in contrast to a discipline, is the integration of knowledge from science, philosophy, and art for the purpose of solving problems. However, a profession may also have conceptual myopia, resulting in the omission of critical interfaces between other disciplines and professions. When this omission occurs, the interactions between different arenas of life are also ignored, for example, the family's interaction with the biological, psychological, social, and economic aspects of the environment.

Rather than using an interdisciplinary approach in developing family life programs, an ecological approach can be used to establish a more effective means of dealing holistically with persistent problems of family life. From an ecological perspective, knowledge can be realigned to incorporate the behavioral sciences, as well as the physical and biological sciences. This added dimension contributes to the wholeness of family study by allowing disciplines and professions to work cooperatively rather than in competition with each other.

The application of an ecological approach can also be an advantage from a theoretical perspective. Because this framework clarifies the interfaces between disciplinary approaches and environmental systems, several theoretical models concerned with interactional processes and information exchanges can be incorporated. Various conceptual approaches (i.e., developmental, exchange, structural-functional, symbolic interaction, crisis, and role theory) can be integrated in explaining family behavior. These approaches also represent bodies of research and knowledge that can be readily assimilated into the field of family study. Through the use of the ecological approach, diversity in family study can lead to greater synthesis and understanding.

Instead of using cause–effect relationships to analyze family issues, the ecosystem approach examines internal family processes, as well as families and their dynamic interaction with multiple environmental factors. Thus, this approach provides a view of reality as an interconnected whole. For example, when family life educators focus their attention on dual-career families, several conceptual frameworks can be integrated, such as the exchanges that occur between family members, the interaction processes involved in cooperation and negotiation, and the links between developmental tasks during the life span and the world of work. Internal and external environments also affect dual-career families. Within the home, the values and attitudes of family members regarding work, age, health, and time all influence family decisions about dual careers. Families may look to neighborhoods and communities for assistance in child care, mass transportation, and convenience services. Regulatory systems also become involved. The economics of inflation and recession, the politics of affirmative action and equal pay acts, and the educational needs of children and adults all interact and impinge on the family unit. Finally, it is critically important to consider both the natural resources of the environment, which are necessary for the production of goods and services, and the dwindling energy supplies, which are being used to maintain our industrial complex, homes, and interfaces between these two environments. Without energy, how could the entire system continue to operate?

Although this example portrays only a few of the interdependent links between families and their environments, examining the total environment helps family life educators, related disciplines, and students to gain keener insights into family issues. Using the family ecosystem approach can therefore alleviate one of the problems in family life education, namely, the lack of a broad conceptual framework to guide family life educators. However, other problems continue to exist, in particular, the limited view given to the role of families in the educative process.

The Family as Educator

Although the family does not perform all the child-rearing functions that it once did, it is still regarded as the primary educator of children. Children acquire their most fundamental lessons in basic life tasks and human relationships within the family. The pervasive impact of the family environment profoundly affects the capacity for intimacy; for communicating love and anger; for sharing and withholding; for giving and taking; for accepting or rejecting one's own sexuality and that of others; and for participating in the entire range of human experiences from birth to death (Chilman, 1978). The importance of families and their needs has been recognized by family life educators; nevertheless, the powerful role of families as critical agents of education has often been overlooked.

Because the family encompasses emotionally significant relationships, it is both a major factor in a child's socialization and an important element in a child's development and education. The use of these terms involves not only some similarities, but also some differences: (1)

socialization concerns the process of acquiring the ability to participate in society and includes enculturation, whereby individuals learn the ways of a particular culture; (2) the *development* of humans considers the time dimension of change and growth; and (3) *education* entails those processes used to assist and/or to enhance the learning of skills, knowledge, and other life tasks of one person from another. Thus, family members educate one another consciously and unconsciously and can be considered both teachers and learners (Paolucci, 1979).

The experiences of children have often been divided into socialization and education. As a result, the family is considered the agent of socialization, but not of education, and the school is considered the agent of education, but not of socialization. Because of the discontinuity between these concepts, a narrow perspective of families has evolved (Leichter, 1974). Society has taken over some of the socializing and educating tasks of the family and has deemphasized the family's importance as a partner in the educative process, therefore, family-life educators need to become more acutely aware of the educative potential of the home, so that this resource can become more effective. It is proposed that the approach used by family life educators employ a broad view of the family as an environment in which both socialization and education occur to effect the development of human resources, either explicitly or implicitly.

The family is the arena of the earliest and usually the most intensive socializing interactions. Although most socialization is unplanned, inadvertant, and a by-product of activities that serve other purposes, the family is also a place of deliberate socialization designed to bring about desired outcomes. Adults—and sometimes older siblings—consciously attempt to socialize children. Generally, children understand that acceptance of and cooperation with socializing efforts is expected. Even though socialization attempts may appear to be ineffective, children's private acceptance of social messages can occur in conjunction with overt noncompliance (Turner, 1970).

For years, the family environment has been the primary setting in which family members develop their human resources and learn basic life tasks. A family organizes and uses resources such as materials, time, labor, talents, skills, and space to achieve its particular set of goals. Some of these resources are invested in the development of the human resources of its members, so that they can become productive and self-fulfilled persons (Paolucci, 1979). Human resources are the physical, psychological, social, cultural, and economic attributes that an individual possesses to fulfill his or her changing roles (Liston, 1974). The sum of these attributes is not nearly as significant as the unique interactive process that occurs in the achievement of some goal that the person wishes to attain. The family environment constitutes the primary input system for developing an individual's human resources by facilitating direct transfers and exchanges of goods and services while integrating the content of societal norms and values (Paolucci, 1979).

By using a family ecosystem approach and recognizing the importance of families as educators, the concept of families can be returned to the central focus of family life education (Paolucci, Bubolz, & Rainey, 1976). The study of families has too often tended to focus on family problems and pathologies, leaving families in a weak and helpless position. In contrast, a positivist view of families emphasizes strengths. This view, in turn, leads to a belief that families constitute a powerful force in enhancing their own quality of life.

Some programs are recognizing the vital importance of families as educators. The establishment of parent drop-in centers in elementary schools, where parents can learn about child development and early childhood education, borrow toys, and communicate with teachers, is a step in this direction (Sullivan, 1980). In Falls Church, Virginia, an integrated sex-education program was instituted through the coalescence of five groups: students, parents, faculty, administrators, and the school board. This program is a combination of student courses, parent education classes, and a parent–community support group for the educators (Tatum, 1981). Merrill (1980) examined the family–school relationship in the context of parent education and counseling in the elementary school and found that the best avenue for helping youngsters with problems is through their parents. Community agencies are also increasingly incorporating family life education into their programs serving families and children. For this reason, Prochaska and Fallon (1979) conducted a workshop for community agency professionals to explore some of the issues contained in initiating programs that would focus on the enrichment and strengthening of families. It is through programs like these that family-life educators can become family-life facilitators, helping families to see their potentials and restoring or increasing the family's feelings of self-confidence and inherent worth.

Family Life Education: Public or Private Issue?

With the increased attention being given to the role of families as educators, an important question that evolves in sponsoring family life education is whether family affairs are a private or a public issue. Although the family can be looked to as the primary socializer, educator, and developer of human resources in children, its inability to meet all the needs of its members within a complex technological society has resulted in the development of many social and educational support systems (Leichter, 1974). Although the family plays a critical role in child rearing, society has also been investing a significant part of its resources in providing assistance to families that are unable, on their own, to assure their children of a reasonable start in life or that need supplementary assistance from educational institutions. This educational training system not only contributes to the development of children and the enhancement of family life, it also does much more. It replaces, for better or worse, a large part of the family's socializing tasks by emphasizing societal norms, strengthening certain behaviors, and reinforcing particular values (Ginsberg, 1976).

Human affairs remain private when the consequences of an act by a person or a group of people are confined mainly to the person or the group directly involved. When the consequences are recognized as having an effect on society as a whole, and there is an effort to influence these consequences, they become a public affair. Child abuse, family financial management, divorce, juvenile crime, and the sexual behavior of adolescents and adults go beyond the interaction of the immediate dyad or family and can affect other elements of the family system, peers, educational systems, health delivery systems, and societal support systems.

In addition to various family problems becoming public affairs, family life education itself has become a public issue. At the White House Conference on Families regional hearings, family life education was ranked eighth as an issue of concern and was mentioned in all but 1 of the 33 state reports. However, a compilation of recommendations from the National Conference indicated that increasing family life education was not rated as highly, as it ranked 25th out of 34 recommendations. Although 74.8% of the delegates approved of this recommendation, its diminished priority represents the opposition of individuals who oppose teaching values in school and/or those who disapprove of government involvement in family matters. Conservative groups disseminated materials that objected to family life education as an intrusion of the public domain into the private realm of the family. As a result, although family life education had strong support from some quarters, it was also opposed by an unwavering and vocal minority (Alexander, 1981; *Listening to America's Families*, 1980).

Because of the opposition and difficulties that family life education has faced, many individuals favor the government's granting higher priority to this issue. Although the U.S. Department of Education does not have the authority to require the teaching of any subject, it could encourage other levels of government to give family life education more consideration by emphasizing its importance. It is unlikely, however, that the federal government will take this role in the 1980s, because the Secretary of Health and Human Services went on record against federal involvement in either contraceptive or sex education, believing this topic to be the business of the parents (Goodman, 1981).

At the state level, only 30 states and the District of Columbia have specific policies regarding family life and sex education in the public schools and directions on the implementation of this instruction. Although no states prohibit sex education, only 2 states and the District of Columbia actually require schools to provide family life and sex education; 6 additional states encourage its offering at the local level, and 22 states leave the decision entirely to the local authorities. In the remaining 20 states, 13 include family life and sex education as an optional element of health and/or other curricula; 1 state requires family life and sex education to be a part of the health curriculum; and 6 states have no written policy (Kenney & Alexander, 1980).

Although governmental support may not be available in the near future, the state and national recommendations from the White House Conference on Families suggest that many people would like the government to give more priority to this issue. Therefore, family advocates will be needed to help governmental officials realize that families desire family life education for themselves and their children. Government could help by:

1. Acknowledging the important role that this subject can play in strengthening families
2. Developing and providing a curriculum
3. Providing technical assistance in developing, implementing, and evaluating family life education programs
4. Funding programs
5. Training personnel (Alexander, 1981)

Although budget cuts in social programs tend to be the current trend, in actuality education as a preventive model would be far less costly than the expense of remedial social services to families. As governmental officials are politically wary of becoming involved in family life education, a strong base of community support will have to be built to demonstrate families' interests and needs.

Issues in the Dissemination of Family Life Education

As the controversy surrounding government intrusion into family matters and family life education has intensified, other issues regarding the dissemination of family life education have also come to the forefront: Are family life education programs effective? Are the teachers qualified? Should teachers be certified?

Program Evaluation

One of the most neglected aspects of early family life education has been program evaluation in terms of both quantity and quality. However, because of current budgetary decreases in educational funding and the increased importance of financial accountability, stronger attention needs to be given to the effectiveness of family-life education programs. Several articles have been published about specific course offerings, but most of these articles simply describe the programs and give little attention to their results or implications. Evidence about the effectiveness of family life education is minimal in light of the abundance of programs in operation.

Interest in program evaluation accelerated in the late 1970s, but evaluation methodology still needs further scrutiny. Several programs have been evaluated by the use of pre- and postmeasurements to determine the change accounted for by the programs. However, the reported effectiveness can be greatly influenced by the number of participants, the attrition rate, and/or the quality and focus of the instrument. Moreover, only a few studies utilize control groups, and in many, the educator is also the researcher. When the evaluation is done by the person who teaches the course, the results are suspect.

Courses offered in an institutional setting have frequently been evaluated, but the increasing assortment of teaching settings and methods in family life education are necessitating more creative evaluation designs. The interest in and quality of program evaluation have improved during the past few years; however, evaluation of and research on family life education have generally been minimal, especially when one looks at the longitudinal impact of the programs. Some exceptions are studies by Davis, Hovestadt, Piercy, and Cochran (1982) and Avery, Haynes-Clements, and Lamke (1981), who, respectively, completed 12-week and one-year follow-up studies to assess the effectiveness of their programs over time. Furthermore, Story (1979) and Gunderson and McCary (1980) reported that positive affective and cognitive effects from sex education classes were retained over at least two years. Longitudinal evaluations, however, must be able to attribute results to program participation and not to other intervening events.

The instruments used in program evaluation have often been problematic as determinations of reliability and validity have frequently been overlooked. Thus, it is important to note some of the investigations that have included this vital component. In a study by Hinkle, Arnold, Croake, and Keller (1980), one of the main purposes was to determine the reliability of three measurement scales appropriate for assessing the effects of family education programs. Pinsker and Geoffroy (1981) paid heed to reliability concerns by using scales with established reliability, as well as by obtaining interobserver reliability. Although such assessments are valuable, generalizations cannot be made to others who have participated in similar programs. Family life education appears to have an impact on some participants, but uncertainty still exists regarding the replicability of effects with other clientele in other contexts.

An examination of program results as demonstrated by course evaluations indicates both encouragement and a need for further research and program development. Using sex education as an example, numerous studies have reported some favorable effects on adolescents and young adults, for example, a reduction of sexual guilt, inhibitions, and the double standard; the maintenance of traditional values of love and fidelity; and the development of more comfortable and responsible attitudes toward sex (Gunderson & McCary, 1980). In addition, students have displayed an increase in knowledge and a tolerance of the sexual practices of others (Kleininna & McClure, 1981; Parcel & Luttman, 1981). On the other hand, it appears that the magnitude and the momentum of the trends indicated by large, nationally representative samples will keep the adolescent pregnancy rate at or

near its current level for another decade or two (Jorgenson, 1981; Zelnik, Kantner, & Ford, 1981). The potential effectiveness of sex education programs continues to be reduced by formidable barriers: Barriers include intentional pregnancies, lack of support from others in the adolescent's social network, the inconsistencies and uncertainties that characterize efforts to formulate educational policy, and emotional obstacles, which interfere with decisions on whether sex education should be available and, if so, under what conditions. This indecision is due to a lack of adequate information from educational and social scientists, who have not yet been able to determine empirically which combination of conditions (the age to begin, the duration and comprehensiveness of programs, parental or community involvement, curriculum guidelines, or teacher preparation), if any, is the best for reducing pregnancy risk (Jorgenson, 1981).

The example of sex education and its relationship to research and evaluation points up several critical issues. Concentrated empirical investigations using sound research designs are needed to determine the optimal circumstances for teaching family life education. This research, however, cannot be based solely on course evaluations. Therefore, an important component of such research is the investigator's determination of what are the most meaningful criteria for success. If the success of sex education programs was based on the adolescent pregnancy rate, these programs would be deemed failures. Other programs claim success because the attendance was high or participation was sustained. However, program assessments using attendance as a criterion do not provide information about the program's aims. Instead, educators must develop some pragmatic and meaningful objectives and goals for what family life and sex education programs can realistically deliver. Program evaluation should consider two questions: Were the individual expectations and needs of the participants met? Were the intended program goals achieved?

Underlying much of family-life education programming is the notion that education results in knowledge leading to attitude change and later behavior modifications. However, pre- and postmeasurement instruments do not measure behavioral change, though they may indicate knowledge gains. Consequently, investigations such as that of Pinsker and Geoffroy (1981), which used six different measures including a series of five home observations of parent–child interaction, are valuable contributions to the evaluation literature. Whereas the aim of some programs is to change knowledge, attitudes, and behaviors to meet the diverse needs of the participants, other programs have a goal of impacting on children. Conceptually and methodologically, the effects of family life education on children are the most complicated to determine. A researcher not only has to carefully define the effect being investigated, but also has to control for several potential intervening variables. Examples of such attempts are Pinsker and Geoffry's pre- and postintervention observations of parent–child interaction (1981) and Hinkle *et al.*'s examinations (1980) of the relationship of changed parental attitudes and behaviors to the self-esteem of children. Although studies of this type are few, the feature that is becoming increasingly apparent is that family life education can have effects on both the participants and their families.

There are important ties among family research, education, and educational evaluation. Research on families provides an important information base that teachers can use in the classroom to correct myths and misconceptions. Educators must be able to understand how research is conducted, to interpret published research, and to apply research findings in their particular learning environments. Moreover, teaching family life education generates important questions that need to be addressed by systematic research. Therefore, teachers also need to assess what and how learning takes place and what factors are associated with the utility and effectiveness of their programs. It is evident that a vast number of courses are inadequately evaluated, and that many questions remain unanswered (Miller, Schvaneveldt, & Jensen, 1981).

Teacher Preparation

The quality of family-life teachers is an important part of the delivery system for family life education; therefore, teacher preparation is of critical concern. The rapid increase in family-life education programs during the 1970s created a demand for teachers, but as teacher preparation takes time, several "band-aid" approaches were instituted, such as preservice training, in-service training, sensitivity training, human relations laboratories, and sexuality workshops. These approaches can enhance teacher preparation, but they are inadequate as the sole training method. These measures may have reduced the original need for the quantity of teachers, but the emphasis is now on teachers possessing a breadth and depth of preparation. Although there is still controversy at both the high-school and the college levels over who should teach family life education, the larger issues are (1) the need to develop well-defined and effective teacher preparation programs to prepare competent family educators and (2) the need to develop a uniform set of teacher-training standards that will allow for a nationally recognized certification process to ensure teacher and program quality.

It is obvious that the professional and political demands on today's family-life education teachers are numerous and complex. As a result, the preparation of teachers has become a topic of importance to parents and school systems. Parents have always wanted competent teachers for their children in traditional subject areas, but when the course topic is family life and sex education, parents are even more vocal over course content and teacher qualifications. Whether or not school systems include human sexuality in family life education, they may not always hire teachers who are sufficiently

competent to teach in either area. Although some schools have family living as a separate course, others include it within several courses and therefore may enlist teachers from a variety of disciplines to become family life educators. At times, individuals who have had no courses in family living and whose educational training is in such fields as history, English, or science teach such courses. Thus, the success of family life education is often based on the comfort or discomfort, the competence or incompetence, and the knowledge or ignorance of these teachers about both the subject matter and the interpersonal skills needed to teach it.

The preparation of qualified family-life education teachers is no simple task, as it involves the unification of many elements. Whereas some recommended subject areas are content-oriented (i.e., human development through the life span, family relationships, parent education, and human sexuality), others deal with processes (i.e., family–environment exchanges, interpersonal skills, and evaluation). The family, as examined from an ecosystem perspective, interacts with many elements of its environment, so that teachers must be aware of community resources and the effect of various legal, political, economic, and medical systems on the family. Decision-making skills are important, too, as families deal with both internal situations and the management of external environments.

The learning of family content and environmental exchanges is not enough. Family educators need to develop communication skills so that they can deal with students and society at large. Family educators also need to become adept in communicating their program to community groups and in handling controversy and dissension. Several family-life educators have recognized the importance of an interface with the community and have conducted workshops for local agencies, have organized programs for youth through youth agencies, and have built coalitions between community leaders and school educators (Cassell, 1981; Chethik, 1981; Prochaska & Fallon, 1979; Quinn, 1981; Wagman & Bignell, 1981). Good public relations are also required to gain community support and to encourage policymakers to overcome their reluctance to establish policies supporting the teaching of this subject. Finally, family educators should become more able evaluators. To increase their awareness of the long-term effects of family life education and the consequences of family life programs for individuals, families, and communities, educators have to become more skillful in collecting, analyzing, and using data to implement program changes (Jorgenson & Alexander, 1981). It is evident that family life education is a particularly diverse and complex topic for individuals, families, and teachers and, thus, requires special training and skills.

Because of the lack of uniformity in teacher preparation, inadequacies and inconsistencies have evolved in family-life education programs. As a result, a majority of the delegates to all three conferences of the White House

Conference on Families noted the critical nature of the training and certification procedures for course leaders. They additionally supported the development of bilingual, multidimensional, and technically relevant courses to better meet the needs of today's students (Alexander, 1981). It is widely believed that the certification of family educators will improve the quality of family life teaching in this complex and sensitive area, will introduce family life courses into more schools, and will facilitate increased enrollments of both male and female students (Jorgenson & Alexander, 1981; Kerckhoff & O'Connor, 1978).

Teacher Certification

Although teacher certification is a worthwhile goal, the implementation of this policy under the jurisdiction of state governments may not be feasible in the near future. A survey of high school family life teachers found few states specifically certifying people as family life educators. Although enthusiasm for such certification was identified in a few more states, the dominant impression was that professional standards for family educators can best be obtained by means other than specific certification, that is, through inservice training and improvement of college programs (Kerckhoff & O'Connor, 1978).

Why has there been a lack of interest in teacher certification? Because the prevalent philosophy in state educational institutions favors more general teacher certification, there is little interest in the specific certification of family educators. Moreover, there is a fear that such a move would make family life education a target of controversy, endangering the status quo (Kerckhoff & O'Connor, 1978). Conflict might also evolve from the disciplines and professions that would compete for the collegiate program designated to certify family life educators. The vested interests of academic departments in times of reduced funding and enrollments could be a major hindrance to states' progress toward certification.

In general, most of the support for certification comes from professional groups associated with the educational movement. For example, the National Council on Family Relations reactivated the Committee on Standards and Criteria for Certification of Family Life Educators, which has prepared a position paper providing the NCFR with a basis for credentialing family life educators. This committee has addressed the procedure of identifying those persons qualified to be family life educators by exploring two forms of recognition: accreditation and certification. Accreditation is a process by which an agency or organization evaluates and recognizes an institution or program of study as meeting certain predetermined standards. Certification is a process by which a professional agency or association grants recognition to an individual who has met certain predetermined qualifications. Although accreditation offers some exciting future possibilities, it does not appear to be feasible at the present time because of its complexity, time constraints, and financial costs. Consequently, the NCFR Committee on Standards and Criteria for Certification of Family Life Educators has concluded that the certification of individuals is the appropriate precursor for the accreditation of educational institutions and has recently formulated guidelines for this procedure. This committee still strongly encourages a continued effort toward the establishment of specific standards at the state level, but in the meantime, individual certification has been established by the NCFR that would enable teachers in all states and educational settings to have a credentialing mechanism verifying their expertise in the field of family life education (*Standards and Criteria for the Certification of Family Life Educators, College/University Curriculum Guidelines, and Content Guidlines for Family Life Education: A Framework for Planning Programs over the Life-Span,* 1984). With the existing diversity of family life professionals and programs, the training and certification of family life educators, as well as the setting of standards to evaluate educators and curricula, are essential for strengthening programs.

Changing Concerns and Transitions within Family Life Education

Political controversy has developed over both the topic of family life education and the subissues of sexuality, government assistance, program effectiveness, and teacher preparation and certification. Although none of these issues has been resolved, their degree of importance has changed over time and is apparent in the professional writings of family educators. Although family life education has existed for decades, there have been several recent shifts in interest. Partly because of the effects of changing environmental conditions on the needs of families and the diversity of goals, philosophies, backgrounds, and funding sources of sponsoring agencies, a variety of family-life education programs have emerged. The issues of concern to family professionals have also fluctuated. For example, in the late 1960s, a furor existed over including family life and sex education in the public schools, and major controversies raged in several communities. Although this problem appeared to be somewhat resolved during the latter part of the 1970s, it has now resurfaced and has become a volatile issue at local, state, and federal levels.

To gain some perspective regarding current developments and recent shifts of interest for family life educators, an examination was made of the last two decades of articles contained in *The Family Coordinator* (now entitled *The Journal of Family Relations*). *The Journal of Family Relations,* a journal published by the National Council on Family Relations, has long been regarded as a journal for practitioners serving family interests through education, counseling, and community service.

To determine what family professionals considered as issues of concern in their field, a compilation of articles relating to family life education was made and is presented in Table 1. Although several articles contained content about families that would be of interest and use to educators, only articles relating more specifically to family-life education materials, methods, programs, or issues were included in this analysis. One hundred and seventy-two articles met these criteria and were categorized according to the topics listed in Table 1. Some articles were entered in more than one category as their content is applicable to more than one area (e.g., public policy as it relates to sexuality).

On the whole, the data reveal an increasing interest in family life education from the 1960s to the 1970s: 51 articles (29.7%) on family life education were published from 1960 to 1969, and 121 (70.3%) articles were published from 1970 to 1979, an increase of 137%. In addition to the total number of articles per decade, the results also indicate some interesting trends regarding specific issues and content areas.

Because of professional and public concerns about quality teaching, teaching materials and methods received considerable attention in the late 1960s and the early 1970s, but this interest, especially in materials, diminished in the later years. Expanding programs in the early 1970s were incorporating, as teachers, individuals from differing backgrounds who were in need of supportive materials to facilitate their educative goals. Because entire programs were not necessarily functioning as part of the total required curriculum, many educators and school systems believed that the use of certain techniques, films, or materials constituted family-life and sex education. For instance, menstruation films, venereal-disease cassette presentations, and class visits by the school nurse and open-minded parents were used by many school systems to pacify outcries for family-life and sex education (Luckey, 1978). The current situation is somewhat different. There may be a need for quality printed materials for certain topics and age groups, but a plethora of books, movies, filmstrips, and pamphlets has been produced in response to the earlier void. As a result, the educator's task is now to evaluate and select the best materials for his or her use.

As family life educators rely heavily on printed and audiovisual materials, educators need to be particularly alert to biased or inaccurate materials. According to criteria established by Griggs (1981, p. 549) for evaluating resources, content should:

1. Reflect family members of all ages
2. Portray nonsexist roles for family members
3. Include information about families of different racial, ethnic, and cultural backgrounds

Table 1. Family Life Education: Two Decades of Varying Interests[a]

	1960–1964	1965–1969	1970–1974	1975–1979	Total (%)
Teaching materials	2	4	7	1	14 (8.1)[a,b,c]
Teaching methods	3	5	16	11	35 (20.3)
Use of conceptual framework	0	1	3	3	7 (4.1)
Program evaluation	0	9	3	10	22 (12.8)
Teacher preparation	1	3	8	3	15 (8.7)
Teacher certification	0	0	0	4	4 (3.1)
Definition of family life education	2	4	0	0	6 (3.5)
Public policy	0	2	8	0	10 (5.8)
General information	1	3	4	5	13 (7.6)
Course topics	7	29	40	34	110 (64.0)
Sexuality	5	15	22	6	48 (27.9)
Parent education	0	4	3	13	20 (11.6)
Marriage	1	4	4	4	13 (7.6)
Enrichment	0	0	1	5	6 (3.5)
Premarriage	0	1	1	3	5 (2.9)
Communication	0	1	3	1	5 (2.9)
Values	0	2	3	0	5 (2.9)
Adolescent pregnancy	0	0	1	1	2 (1.2)
Crisis	1	0	1	0	2 (1.2)
Family planning	0	2	0	0	2 (1.2)
Interpersonal relationships	0	0	1	0	1 (.6)
Expectant parents	0	0	0	1	1 (.6)

[a]Source: *Family Coordinator Journal of Family Relations*, 1960–1979.
[b]N = 172 articles (1960–1969, N = 51; 1970–1979, N = 121).
[c]Total percentage exceeds 100 as content of articles can apply to more than one category.

4. Recognize the uniqueness of individuals and families regardless of age, race, ethnicity, and cultural and socioeconomic backgrounds
5. Recognize that the composition of families varies
6. Be based on contemporary research

In addition to these criteria, a number of others can also be used to evaluate family life materials; thus, the teacher must judge which criteria are the most critical and which should be applied in a particular situation.

Other previously discussed trends and issues listed in Table 1 show that, at the beginning of the 1970s, teacher preparation was receiving the attention of family educators, followed by a focus on teacher certification in the late 1970s. This shift of concern occurred during the early 1970s as a response to the rapid influx of teachers from varying backgrounds and because of a concomitant concern about quality teachers and programs. Whereas defining family life education was a prominent issue during the 1960s, an examination of the 1970s discloses an increasing emphasis on the use of program evaluation and conceptual frameworks.

One curious trend is the interest in public policy during the late 1960s and the early 1970s. Recently, family life professionals and other concerned citizens have become increasingly involved with public policies and issues that affect families, but according to Table 1, public policy was more an issue between 1970 and 1974 than from 1975 to 1979. An examination of these articles has revealed that the focus was not on public policy *per se*, but on public policy as it related to teaching family life education, especially sex education. The growing concern over increased sexual activity among adolescents and young adults in the late 1960s and the early 1970s provided the impetus for confrontations regarding the inclusion of sex education in the school curriculum. Would sex education prevent or encourage sexual involvement and pregnancy? The answer was unknown at that time, but the importance of sex education definitely made the transition from a private to public issue.

In the 1960s and 1970s, sexuality was not only a major interest of public policy, but also a topic receiving considerable attention in course offerings. Of all content areas, sex education had the largest percentage (27.9%) of articles published in *The Family Coordinator/Journal of Family Relations*. Interest in this topic declined in the last half of the 1970s; nevertheless, sexuality was one of the major interests of this two-decade period. Why is the topic of sex so important to family life educators? Primarily because of the political controversies regarding sexuality, the reported increases in sexual activity among younger adolescents, the degree of impact that an unwanted pregnancy can have on the life of a teenager, and the needs of family life educators to increase their feelings of competence and comfort in dealing with the topic of sexual and contraceptive behavior.

Another prevalent course topic in the 1970s that gained considerable momentum during the latter part of the decade was parent education. Parenting programs were not new, but there was a surge of interest in parent education. Problems such as adolescent pregnancy, substance abuse, and parent–child communication motivated parents to seek assistance in coping with the loss of equilibrium in their families. Parent education, however, has not been limited merely to parents. Earhart (1980) suggested that an individual involved in parent education may not yet be a parent but can store knowledge for future use. Thus, parent education programs can have considerable variation in format and clientele.

Along with courses in sexuality and parent education, another topic of changing interest in the late 1970s was marriage and family enrichment. The enrichment model encompasses an assortment of family programs, courses, and experiences that are more structured, short-term, and definable than family therapy, but more experiential and affective than family life education (L'Abate & O'Callaghan, 1977; Otto, 1976). Family enrichment programs are designed for persons who believe that they have a fairly well-functioning family and who wish to make their family life even better. Family enrichment programs are concerned with enhancing family communication and emotional life in order to reinforce family strengths and to develop individual and family potential. Similarly, marriage enrichment programs seek to develop individual and marital potential while maintaining a primary focus on the relationship of the couple. As a rule, enrichment programs are viewed from a positive perspective because they do not operate from a pathology-centered model (Otto, 1975).

Course topic trends in sexuality, parent education, and enrichment displayed the greatest degree of change during the 1970s, but several other course topics were also of interest to family life educators, such as marriage and premarriage, communication, values, adolescent pregnancy, crisis, family planning, interpersonal relationships, and expectant parenting. Within this constellation of courses, an inter- and intragenerational focus is apparent. Programs that provide for intergenerational interaction help to establish meaningful ties, in order to moderate significant life changes and to reduce negative age stereotypes and attitudes (Powell & Arquitt, 1978). On the other hand, intragenerational interaction has been of interest because siblings can have an important effect on each other's development, and an understanding of these relationships can be used as socialization for parenthood (Essman, 1977).

Although political issues, program organization, and topics of content have changed over the years, family life education itself has retained its critical importance. The proliferation of programs, workshops, and band-aid measures were expected to cause the self-destruction of family life education (Luckey, 1978), but that does not seem to have been the case. Rather, it appears that families are turning to family-life education programs to meet current needs, to solve problems, and to satisfy aspirations for enriching and improving their quality of life.

Challenges for the Future

The intent of this chapter has been to examine the current status of family life education by giving a broad perspective of the multiple and complex issues in this field. Although some problems are more controversial than others, a general overview of these difficulties includes the following:

1. The current breadth and diversity of family life education, originating during the early years of its inception, have become more pronounced and have resulted in a lack of cohesion among disciplinary endeavors.

2. Definitional dilemmas exist because of the current multidimensionality in family-life education programming and a prior limited scope and focus.

3. The absence of a broad conceptual framework has resulted in a lack of focus and organization in educational programming.

4. A limited view of the critical role of family members as educators in the learning process has lessened the potential strength of family programs.

5. The private versus public nature of family affairs has been an intensely debated issue affecting public support for family problems, as well as public funding for family life education.

6. The quality of family life education, the effectiveness of programs and program evaluation, the competence of teachers and their preparation, and the pros and cons of teacher certification have all been questioned.

Although individual family educators may be concerned only with a few specific issues, the complexity and interdependence of all these issues provide dilemmas when examining current family-life education programs. There is no all-encompassing solution to these problems; thus, an awareness of their existence and the resultant agitation to families, educators, disciplines, and governments is important and necessary.

The advent of family life education can be compared to a firecracker exploding with a burst of energy in multitudinous directions. Whereas parts of the explosion result in rays of enlightenment, other parts create either pain and difficulties or merely fizzle. Family life education also exploded with considerable energy from its founding individuals and organizations and has since gone in numerous directions. As indicated by the current interest in family life education, the public believes in the inherent value of these programs and has expressed a need for them. Several controversies have also exploded, but family life education is still surging forth in an attempt to meet the changing needs of families. Topics such as the "how-to's" of weddings, budgets, and child care have been superseded by analyses of the interpersonal relationships involved in sexuality, parenting, and family crises. Although neither an exploding firecracker nor family life education can be contained, the recognition of its amorphous, energized nature can lay a foundation for increased understanding of the field.

What does the future hold for family life education?

Definitional, organizational, and political problems will probably be on the scene for some time, but neither the family nor family life education is going to die. Consequently, what challenges lie ahead for family life educators?

A major challenge is the further development and use of a conceptual framework that will integrate disciplines, conceptual approaches, and content relating to families and their environments. Within the family ecosystem approach, family life educators will be able to work interdependently. The resulting synergistic effect should add strength to the field. The application of the ecosystem approach will not only enhance professional cohesion but also assist educators and families in recognizing the interrelatedness of family problems. This holistic approach would enable families to better understand transactions with their environments and the internal processes of their family. Families would then be able to receive a broad, integrated perspective of the stresses and strengths in their lives, rather than an isolated view.

Although the family ecosystem approach has no time restrictions as far as datedness is concerned, the importance of certain topics to educators and families will vary, as indicated by the examination of *Family Coordinator/Journal of Family Relations'* articles over a two-decade span. Behaviors that had occurred infrequently in the past (e.g., cohabitation, childfree marriages, and dual-career marriages) became increasingly frequent and more visible, and traditional values regarding virginity and uninvolved fatherhood were increasingly replaced by sexual permissiveness and father power. The microelectronic revolution will also have impacts on families and family life education. Home computers and the implementation of telebuying will add new dimensions to family lifestyles and informal education. Families may spend more time at home viewing and discussing products than strolling through the malls. Even the structure of family decision making may undergo a transformation as greater amounts of information become available to those who have the ability and the willingness to use it (Goldsmith & Goldsmith, 1982). Consequently, a challenge for family educators will be to keep up with the most current information and research regarding the family's changing behavior and environment. It is a truism that one who dares to teach must never cease to learn.

Many issues of concern to family life educators are incorporated within the political arena challenging them to become more adept in their interactions with community organizations, public service groups, and different levels of government. Groups under many family labels are quite vocal regarding their own concerns, but family educators have maintained virtual silence. However, it is critically important that advocates for family life education make their views known to the appropriate officials and institutions and to solicit their support and action. Without such involvement, family life education will receive only infrequent and random attention from politicians.

As family educators become family advocates, they will also be challenged to examine the value implications of various policies, and to consider the following questions:

1. To what degree might certain policies disenfranchise familial investment in the human resource development of family members?
2. How can parents have more control over educative and social services to their families?
3. To what extent are family professionals influencing policies that affect their own vested interests?
4. How can the efforts of families and professionals be made more cooperative than competitive? (Darling & Bubolz, 1980)

If our goal is truly to enhance the well-being of families, then the dynamics, the value implications, and the outcomes of our role as policy advocates will need some careful thought before action is taken.

As can be seen, the future holds several challenges to family educators in a changing society. Not only will it be necessary to use a broad conceptual approach for family study, to keep up-to-date on new trends, and to become involved as family advocates, but we must also remember to keep the lifelong development of families as a central focus. The term *family life education* is composed of three words: *family, life,* and *education.* Education is regarded as primary intervention, but what about the two words *life* and *family?*

All too often, family-life education programs are designed for a narrow age group: school-aged children to young adults. What about the rest of the population? Family interaction is a lifelong process and occurs in a variety of settings with a variety of needs and problems. Children and young adults are not the only ones with questions, a desire for information, or problems in forming and maintaining close relationships. Preschool children, parents, single adults, and senior citizens also have questions and needs that require attention. Might broad-based community programs facilitate such an approach to family life education and support interpersonal communication from a developmental life-span basis? This type of program would promote the integration of males and females of all ages and would be more beneficial than segregating children and young adults into educational settings for cognitive learning that lack a vital link to real-life family experiences and family affectional support systems.

An integrative family-life education program does have some inherent problems. Sometimes, parents do not perceive themselves as being effective family educators because they feel they must (1) know everything about families; (2) be comfortable discussing everything related to family life; or (3) be avant-garde in their attitudes or their children will not respect them or listen to them. Consequently, receiving community acceptance, stimulating parent involvement, and making parents, students, and teachers more comfortable in their coeducator

roles will provide some additional challenges for family educators. Some programs are already working on this cooperative task (Merrill, 1980; Prochaska & Fallon, 1979; Sullivan, 1980; Tatum, 1981), but many community groups are influenced by local resistance to family life education or by confusion about what the term *family life education* really means. Thus, it is vitally important that those individuals and groups interested in family life education coalesce to provide strength and support for community efforts toward lifelong programs in family living.

It is indeed both an exciting and a stimulating time for family professionals. The increasing volume and variety of program options, public concerns, professional issues, and familial needs are all converging to establish new challenges for family educators. Although the issues presented in this chapter require some creative problem-solving, the task is not solely ours. Family members, too, are willing to take part in the educative process, providing that we include them in the way they want to be involved rather than in the way we perceive they should be involved. It is important to keep in mind that the home is the most dynamic learning center available. Hence, a major goal of professional family-life educators should be cooperation with the nonformal educators in the family setting in order to help facilitate the family's understanding of the processes involved in maintaining and enhancing its quality of life.

References

Alexander, S. J. Implications of the White House Conference on Families for family life education. *Family Relations,* 1981, *30,* 643–650.

Andrews, M. P. *Exploring ecosystems: Research considerations.* Paper presented to the faculty of the Division of Home Economics, Oklahoma State University, Stillwater, Oklahoma, August 22, 1977.

Andrews, M., Bubolz, M., & Paolucci, B. An ecological approach to the study of the family. *Marriage and Family Review,* 1980, *3½,* 29–49.

Auserwald, E. M. Interdisciplinary versus ecological approach. *Family Process,* 1968, *7,* 202–215.

Avery, A., Haynes-Clements, L., & Lamke, L. Teaching shy students: The role of the family life educator. *Family Relations,* 1981, *30,* 39–43.

Avery, C. E., & Lee, M. R. Family life education: Its philosophy and purpose. *The Family Life Coordinator,* 1964, *13,* 27–37.

Bell, R. *Marriage and family interaction* (5th ed.). Homewood, Ill.: Dorsey Press, 1979.

Bertalanffy, L. von. *General systems theory: Essays in its foundation and development.* New York: Braziller, 1969.

Bowman, H., & Spanier, G. *Modern marriage* (8th ed.). New York: McGraw-Hill, 1978.

Bowman, T. A dream taking form: Family life education in community settings. *Family Relations,* 1981, *30,* 543–548.

Broderick, C., & Smith, J. The general systems approach to the family. In W. R. Burr, R. Hill, F. I. Nye, & I. L. Reiss (Eds.), *Contemporary theories about the family* (Vol. 2). New York: Free Press, 1979.

Bubolz, M. M., Eicher, J. B., & Sontag, M. S. The Human ecosystem: A model. *Journal of Home Economics,* 1979, *71,* 28–30.

Cassell, C. Putting sex education in its place. *The Journal of School Health,* 1981, *51,* 211–213.

Chethik, B. Developing community support: A first step toward a school sex education program. *The Journal of School Health,* 1981, *51,* 266–270.

Chilman, C. S. *Adolescent sexuality in a changing American society: Social and psychological perspectives.* Washington, D.C.: U.S. Department of Health, Education and Welfare, Public Health Service, National Institutes of Health, 1978.

Cox, F. *Human intimacy: Marriage, the family, and its meaning.* St. Paul: West Publishing Company, 1981.

Cromwell, R. E., & Thomas, V. L. Developing resources for family potential: A family action model. *The Family Coordinator,* 1976, *25,* 13–20.

Daly, R. A forward look: Family life education in the Cooperative Extension Service. *Family Relations,* 1981, *30,* 537–542.

Darling, C. A., & Bubolz, M. M. Public policy and the family: An integrative course. *Journal of Home Economics,* 1980, *72,* 20–23.

Davis, E., Hovestadt, A., Piercy, F., & Cochran, S. Effects of weekend and weekly marriage enrichment formats. *Family Relations,* 1982, *31,* 85–90.

Duvall, E. *Family development* (4th ed.). Philadelphia: Lippincott, 1971.

Dyer, E. *The American family: Variety and change.* New York: McGraw-Hill, 1979.

Earhart, E. M. Parent education: A lifelong process. *Journal of Home Economics,* 1980, *72,* 20–23.

Eshleman, J. R. *The family: An introduction* (3rd ed.). Boston: Allyn & Bacon, 1981.

Essman, C. S. Sibling relations as socialization for parenthood. *The Family Coordinator,* 1977, *26,* 259–261.

Family life education programs: Principles, plans, procedures, A framework for family life education. *The Family Coordinator,* 1968, *17,* 211–215.

Fisher, B., & Kerckhoff, R. Family life education: Generating cohesion out of chaos. *Family Relations,* 1981, *30,* 505–509.

Ginzberg, E. *The human economy.* New York: McGraw-Hill, 1976.

Goldsmith, E., & Goldsmith, R. Telebuying. *Forum,* January 1982, pp. 24–25.

Goodman, E. So who's going to tell them the facts of life? *Washington Post,* February 10, 1981.

Griggs, M. Criteria for the evaluation of family life education materials. *Family Relations,* 1981, *30,* 549–555.

Gunderson, M., & McCary, J. Effects of sex education on sex information, and sexual guilt, attitudes, and behaviors. *Family Relations,* 1980, *29,* 375–379.

Harman, D., & Brim, O. *Learning to be parents: Principles, programs, and methods.* Beverly Hills, Calif.: Sage Publications, 1980.

Hendrickson, N. J. *A brief history of parent education in the United States.* Columbus: The Ohio State University Center for Adult Education, 1963.

Hinkle, D., Arnold, C., Croake, J., & Keller, J. Adlerian parent education: Changes in parents' attitudes and children's self esteem. *American Journal of Family Therapy,* 1980, *8,* 32–43.

Home Economics New Directions. Prepared by the Committee on Philosophy and Objectives of Home Economics, American Home Economics Association, Washington, D.C., 1959.

Hook, N., & Paolucci, B. Family as an ecosystem. *Journal of Home Economics,* 1970, *62,* 315–318.

Jorgenson, S. *The promise of sex education: Implications of research on adolescent pregnancy risk.* Paper presented at the Annual Meeting of the National Council on Family Relations, Milwaukee, Wisconsin, October 1981.

Jorgenson, S. R., & Alexander, S. J. Reducing the risk of adolescent pregnancy: Toward certification of family life educators. *The High School Journal,* 1981, *64,* 257–268.

Kantor, D., & Lehr, R. *Inside the family.* San Francisco: Jossey-Bass, 1975.

Kenney, A. M., & Alexander, S. J. Sex/family life education in the schools: An analysis of state policies. *Family Planning/Population Reporter,* 1980, *9,* 44–52.

Kerckhoff, R. K. Family life education in America. In H. Christensen (Ed.), *Handbook of marriage and the family.* Chicago: Rand McNally, 1964.

Kerckhoff, R., & O'Connor, T. Certification of high school family life teachers. *The Family Coordinator,* 1978, *27,* 61–64.

Kleinginna, A., & McClure, G. Introduction of an undergraduate course in the psychology of human sexuality. *Teaching of Psychology,* 1981, *8,* 34–35.

Knox, D. *Exploring marriage and the family.* Glenview, Ill.: Scott, Foresman, 1979.

L'Abate, L., & O'Callaghan, J. B. Implications of enrichment model for research and training. *The Family Coordinator,* 1977, *26,* 61–64.

Leichter, H. J. Some perspectives on the family as educator. In H. J. Leichter (Ed.), *The family as educator.* New York: Teachers College Press, 1974.

Listening to America's families. Report from the White House Conference on Families, Washington, D.C.: U.S. Government Printing Office, 1980.

Liston, M. *Human resource development research.* Paper presented at the NCRS-3 Meeting, St. Louis, September 1974.

Luckey, E. B. In my opinion: Family life education revisited. *The Family Coordinator,* 1978, *27,* 69–73.

McCary, J. L. *Freedom and growth in marriage* (2nd ed.). New York: Wiley, 1980.

Melson, G. F. *Family and environment an ecosystem perspective.* Minneapolis: Burgess, 1980.

Merrill, J. Parent education and counseling. *Texas Personnel and Guidance Journal,* 1980, *8,* 79–86.

Miller, B., Schvaneveldt, J., & Jensen, G. Reciprocity between family life research and education. *Family Relations,* 1981, *30,* 625–630.

Morrison, B. M. The importance of a balanced perspective: The environments of man. *Man-Environment Systems,* 1974, *4,* 171–178.

Orthner, D. *Intimate relationships: An introduction to marriage and the family.* Reading, Mass.: Addison-Wesley, 1981.

Otto, H. A. Marriage and family enrichment in North America—Report and analysis. *The Family Coordinator,* 1975, *24,* 137–142.

Otto, H. A. *Marriage and family enrichment: New perspectives and programs.* Nashville, Tenn.: Abington, 1976.

Paolucci, B. *Invisible family production: The development of human resources.* Paper prepared for the National Science Foundation, National Center of Scientific Research Roundtable on the Productive Function of Non-Market Goods and Services of American and French Families, Oise, France. In A. Michel (Ed.), *Les femmes dans la société marchande.* Paris: Presses Universitaires de France, 1979.

Paolucci, B., Bubolz, M., & Rainey, M. *Women, families, and non-formal learning programs.* East Lansing: Institute for International Studies in Education, Michigan State University, 1976.

Parcel, G., & Luttman, D. Evaluation of a sex education course for young adolescents. *Family Relations,* 1981, *30,* 55–60.

Pinsker, M., & Geoffroy, K. A comparison of parent effectiveness training and behavior modification training. *Family Relations,* 1981, *30,* 61–68.

Position paper on family life education. *The Family Coordinator,* 1970, *19,* 186.

Powell, J. A., & Arquitt, G. E. Getting the generations back together: A rationale for development of community based intergenerational interaction program. *The Family Coordinator,* 1978, *27,* 421–426.

Prochaska, J., & Fallon, B. Preparing a community for family life education. *Child Welfare,* 1979, *58,* 665–672.

Quinn, J. Sex ed at the "Y": New approaches to a not-so-new problem. *Children Today,* 1981, *10,* 18–21.

Reid, M. *Economics of household production.* New York: Wiley, 1934.

Rockwood, L. *Highlights of a study of the sources and history of family life education*. Unpublished manuscript. Cornell University, Ithaca, New York, 1948.

Rouner, E. *The role of colleges and universities in family life education*. Mount Pleasant: Central Michigan University Press, 1969.

Saxton, L. *The individual, marriage, and the family* (4th ed.). Belmont, Calif.: Wadsworth, 1980.

Scanzoni, L., & Scanzoni, J. *Men, women, and change: A sociology of marriage and family* (2nd ed.). New York: McGraw-Hill, 1981.

Schulz, D. *The changing family: Its function and future* (3rd ed.). Englewood Cliffs, N.J.: Prentice-Hall, 1982.

Schulz, D., & Rogers, S. *Marriage, the family, and personal fulfillment* (2nd ed.). Englewood Cliffs, N.J.: Prentice-Hall, 1980.

Slater, P. Some effects of transcience. In E. Douvan, H. Weingarten, & J. Scheiber (Eds.), *American families*. Dubuque: Kendall/Hunt, 1980.

Smart, L., & Smart, M. *Families: Developing relationships* (2nd ed.). New York: Macmillan, 1980.

Somerville, R. M. Family life and sex education in the turbulent sixties. In C. B. Broderick (Ed.), *A decade of family research and action*. Minneapolis: National Council on Family Relations, 1971.

Standards and Criteria for the Certification of Family Life Educators: College/University Curriculum Guidelines, and Content Guidelines for Family Life Education: A Framework for Planning Programs Over the Life Span. Minneapolis, Minn.: National Council on Family Relations, 1984.

Story, D. A longitudinal study of the effects of a university human sexuality course on sexual attitudes. *Journal of Sex Research*, 1979, *15*, 184–204.

Stroup, A. *Marriage and family: A developmental approach*. New York: Appleton-Century-Crofts, 1966.

Sullivan, E. Parent drop in center. *Teacher*, 1980, *98*, 46.

Swain, M. Family life education in religious institutions: Catholic, Jewish, and Protestant. *Family Relations*, 1981, *30*, 527–535.

Tansley, A. G. The use and abuse of vegetational concepts and terms. *Ecology*, 1935, *16*, 284–307.

Tatum, M. L. The Falls Church experience. *Journal of School Health*, 1981, *51*, 223–225.

Turner, R. H. *Family interaction*. New York: Wiley, 1970.

Wagman, E., & Bignell, S. Starting family life and sex education programs: A health agency's perspective. *Journal of School Health*, 1981, *51*, 247–252.

Zelnik, M., Kantner, J., & Ford, L. *Sex and pregnancy in adolescence*. Beverly Hills, Calif.: Sage Publications, 1981.

CHAPTER 30

Marital and Family Therapy

Florence W. Kaslow

Setting the Stage: A Historical Scenario

Although the major objective of this chapter is to delineate, compare, contrast, and, to some extent, integrate, the extant *major* theoretical schools of marital and family therapy in the mid 1980s, it seems important to provide a brief historical backdrop against which one can view them and bring each into the spotlight for serious analysis. (Despite a conscious effort to be extremely objective and accurate, this retrospective portrait necessarily reflects the author-as-scholar's own biases accrued through her experience and her vast reading about and contact with many of the leading personalities in fhe field. Given the space restrictions, the intent is to be comprehensive; yet there is full realization that this discussion is far from all-inclusive.)

From Marriage Counseling to Marital Therapy

Initially, marriage counseling and family therapy evolved separately, the former preceding the latter by about 20 years. They did not begin to coalesce into a unified field until the early 1970s, as will become apparent later in this chronology.

During the turbulent two decades following World War I, there was a period of social instability, reflected in heightened mobility and weakening of parental authority in the family constellation, paralleled by a loosening of family ties and an upswing in divorce rates. This phenomenon alarmed leaders in law, religion, and medicine as well as in the mental health professions in the United States and in Europe. They observed that the consequent family dysfunctioning contributed to severe intrapsychic and interpersonal stress and that the family, a basic institution and cornerstone of society, was in serious jeopardy.

In the late 1920s and early 1930s, although avant-garde psychotherapists were already attuned to the strong influence that patients' changing attitudes and behaviors had on their significant others, most notably their spouse, the

Florence W. Kaslow • Florida Couples and Family Institute, Northwood Medical Center, Suite 202, 2617 North Flagler Drive, West Palm Beach, FL 33407.

prevailing mode of treatment was still individual, psychoanalytically oriented psychotherapy. However, one by one, the least doctrinaire and most sensitive clinicians realized that it might be more efficacious to see the marital partners together in order to ascertain a fuller picture of the situational problems and the sexual and relational difficulties as each viewed them and as they were actually played out in the therapist's presence. These clinicians hypothesized that they then would be better able to assess the couples' vulnerabilities and strengths, as individuals and as a pair and, on the basis of this assessment, to mazimize therapeutic leverage in terms both of interpretations of feelings and actions and of strategies to modify noxious behaviors that inflamed the conflict areas and to enhance growth (Kaslow, 1975, 1977).

Gradually, these enterprising pioneers learned of each other's efforts and met together to share ideas. This mutual reenforcement of the idea that the pathway each had separately embarked on made good clinical sense, and that the spiralling divorce rates indeed signified a clarion call to rapid action, led to the founding in 1932 of three marriage-counseling centers in the country, in New York, Los Angeles, and Philadelphia (Mudd, 1974). Because working with the couple as a dyadic unit necessitated (1) generating new theoretical constructs based on interactions and transactions as well as intrapsychic dynamics' and (2) experimenting with new therapeutic modes suited to this special patient population, these practitioners increasingly departed from their orthodox psychoanalytic heritage. They were, in a sense, punished for their heresy by being criticized and discredited by their more traditional peers and former teachers. The censoring mounted when, in addition, they began to claim that marriage counseling constituted a distinct specialization and that training in psychiatry, psychology, or social work for the treatment of individual patients did not prepare a clinician for the conjoint treatment of couples; instead, they posited that additional and different training was essential. This provocative stance and the negative reaction to the feisty leaders that it engendered in establishment quarters led the practitioners of marriage counseling to the formation of their own separate professional organization. The American Association of Marriage Counselors had its inception in 1942; its objectives were to provide a forum for the interchange of ideas among the leaders in this young field and to offer training for those interested in becoming marriage counselors.

The original small group had high standards for membership and became somewhat provincial in outlook in the 1950s and 1960s. The proportion of physician and lawyer members declined, and more pastoral counselors and social workers joined and became active. Around 1970, the name was changed to American Association of Marriage and Family Counselors (AAMFC) to reflect the increasing number of members who were engaging in family counseling. At that time, the organization numbered 1,000 (Olson, Russell, & Sprenkle, 1980). In 1978, the name was again changed, this time to American Association for Marital and Family Therapy (AAMFT), signaling the fuller shift to doing therapy, rather than counseling, as the major orientation of the membership. Martin (1976) stated succinctly in *A Marital Therapy Manual* that he would avoid using the term "marriage counselor since marriage 'counseling' frequently has an unfortunate and misleading connotation of being neither an important nor a depth approach psychotherapy" (p. 1). The same realization about the superficial implications of the term *counseling* contributed to the organization's most recent name change.

As of 1986, the AAMFT's membership has skyrocketed to approximately 13,000 people. During the huge expansion phase from 1970 to 1975, the membership requirements were less stringent. But by 1976, the organization's leadership, which by then had helped spearhead licensing or certification laws through six states (it had become ten by 1985), began accrediting agency- and university-based training and degree-granting programs and was vitally interested in upgrading the education and training requirements as these pertained to raising the standards for practitioners. Consequently, they tightened up the qualifications for clinical membership, specifying such requirements as (1) completion of a master's or doctoral degree in marital and family therapy from a regionally accredited educational institution, or an equivalent course of study as defined by the board; (2) 1,000 hours of direct clinical contact with couples and families; (3) 200 hours of approved supervision of that work; (4) two years of work experience under approved supervision; and (5) endorsement by two clinical members of the association attesting to suitable qualities for the conduct of marital and family therapy (AAMFT, 1983).

The proportion of psychologists and psychiatrists who have joined has been on the upswing since the late 1970s, and the percentage of clergy members had taken a decided downturn. The membership, composed of individuals originally trained in a variety of disciplines, has great vitality at present. No one theoretical or philosophical orientation is espoused; each of the theories to be discussed has adherents within the membership. The binding force has been more a commitment to the global ideals and purposes of marriage and family therapy (now expanded to include sex and divorce therapy) than a shared, slavish devotion to one or several theoretical ideologies.

Family Therapy: A Grand Entrance

The roots of family therapy were more farflung and multifaceted. Yet, some similarities are apparent. Just as classic marriage counseling partly emerged as a response to concerns about deterioration of the strength and viability of marriage and the family following World War I, family therapy had its inception during a comparable period of social upheaval and family disorganization following World War II. Once again, various therapists and communications theorists practicing in different locales and diverse settings from the East to the West Coast—including Philadelphia, New York, Atlanta, Topeka, and Palo Alto—had become increasingly disenchanted with the slowness and often the lack of definitive improvement in their patients, whom they were treating through customary insight-oriented psychoanalytic psychotherapy. These theorists and clinicians seem to have come from a different heritage from that of the early marriage counselors and were either unaware of the early treatment advances and contributions to the therapeutic literature or simply disregarded these and forged ahead on their own. They reinvented some concepts, like the importance of conjoint treatment (Satir, 1964), and fashioned new ones like pseudomutuality (Wynne, Ryckoff, Day, & Hirsch, 1958) and undifferentiated family ego mass (Bowen, 1974).

Several detailed histories of family therapy have appeared (see, for example, Guerin, 1976; Kaslow, 1980b; Olson, 1970; Olson *et al.*, 1980). Only a brief synopsis of those historical facts that are most pertinent to the main focus of this chapter are provided here. (The reader interested in a fuller account should find the aforementioned sources helpful.)

As psychiatry in the early twentieth century moved slowly away from being a specialty with a medical and biological base and began to incorporate concepts drawn from anthropology, sociology, and psychology, an interactional model for understanding, interpreting, and treating patients seemed to be needed. The family as a system moved into the foreground as the obvious unit for treatment, for it is the matrix in which the child lives and learns, and it is one's most significant others who help shape—and, in turn, are influenced by—one's attitudes and actions.

The child guidance movement—which originated in 1909, when juvenile courts decided that they should endeavor to treat delinquent children—was also a major contributor. Staffs of child guidance clinics rapidly recognized that treatment of their young patients would be of little avail unless it was supported by the parents and reenforced by their learning better child-rearing techniques and ways in which to relate more consistently and affectionately while accepting and exercising rational parental firmness. At some of these clinics, practitioners also saw developmentally disabled and emotionally disturbed children and adolescents. They became aware that parents who became more distressed about the improvement in the child than they had been about the original problems for which they had sought help would sabotage or terminate the treatment. What other logical conclusion could an empathic, intelligent, nonrigid staff reach than that it was advisable to enlist the parents' cooperation by involving them? If the parents also benefited, this was an additional bonus. In the early child-guidance clinics, a concurrent model was customary, with a psychiatrist seeing the child and a social worker, the parent(s). Frequently, only the mother attended the sessions, either because of her own internal stress or because of the external agency's insistence to do so, accompanied by school or other community pressure. If the father was declared by the mother to be too busy, too uninterested, or generally unavailable, her comments were accepted as valid, and little initiative was taken to reach him. This modus operandi remained a dominant one until the ascendance of the family-as-a-system perspective in the middle 1960s. Nonetheless, the "peripheral" father remains a concern (Kaslow, 1980c), and some therapists refuse to see a family unless he is present (Keith & Whitaker, 1981).

Therapists' disillusionment with the standard interventions used with "schizophrenics" in either inpatient or outpatient settings led them to experiment with more novel strategies. In some cases, they observed on visiting day that the patient's behavior looked less bizarre and more symbolic and reactive in the company of his or her family; in others, they arranged to see the patient along with his or her family to maximize the use of time in overcrowded facilities. In either case, the astute therapist recognized the causal links in the transactions, saw the scapegoating and rejecting mechanisms in operation, observed the schizophrenogenic family dynamics, and decided that the nuclear family contributed to the creation and maintainence of the "psychotic" process. Therefore, if the psychosis was to be disrupted or "cured," these relatives also had to be involved and had to change in significant ways.

On the West Coast, a group of theorists were exploring the dynamics of interpersonal communication, the nature of feedback, and the impact of different styles of communication on recipients of messages, "metamessages," and what they came to label *double-bind messages* (Bateson, Jackson, Haley, & Weakland, 1956). And in academia, social scientists like Talcott Parsons (1951) were publishing their latest formulations on social systems, thus providing a solid theoretical foundation for the work of clinicians, who were already viewing the family unit as a complex system.

A little-mentioned part of what became the ground swell was the family service agency, where families were increasingly being seen as units—partly to pare down the huge waiting lists in a cost-efficient way, and partly because those who had the courage to question existing dogma and to generate their own techniques realized that the family they saw often appeared to be quite different from the one that any individual member of the family described. At the least, distortion could be minimized, better reality-testing encouraged, and faulty communication patterns commented on and intercepted when all family members came together.

As each small group of practitioners became intrigued with the potency of their new technques, they began to talk about the strides they were making. Others sensed their enthusiasm and came to hear them at conferences and to talk with them where they worked. Given the zeal and pioneering spirit and the tremendous interest being generated by what appeared to some to be a panacea for all psychopathology, the leaders were willing to have others view their interviews through one-way mirrors, or sit in and observe a live session, or even pitch in and serve as a cotherapist. With the advent of audio- and videotapes, the leaders, great and not so great, recorded their work for distribution to eager, curious clinicians throughout the world.

By the late 1950s, the various forces alluded to earlier had converged into what seemed to be a family therapy movement. It gained many adherents and great momentum during the late 1960s and the 1970s. Some of the leaders became "gurus," traveling around to lecture about and demonstrate their brand of family therapy. Various major and minor schools of thought gained prominence. In 1977, the American Family Therapy Association (AFTA) was born because some of the luminaries wanted an organization of just family therapists.

By 1986, AFTA had 850 members. It has purposely kept its growth slow and admits senior, often well-known, clinicians, teachers, and researchers from the U.S. and abroad. It has become an influential scientific forum in the family therapy field. La Perriere (1985), then president of AFTA, stated that higher participation characterized the organization and that members consider it a "burn-out center for the prevention and cure of professional fatigue."

Although family therapy is viewed by some as no more than seeing a family together as an adjunct to individual treatment, others have hailed (or maligned) it as a radical new therapy. For many, family systems theory represents a new, holistic way of viewing experience and behavior and undergirds the practice of conjoint therapy (Framo, 1979). The family, traditionally viewed by some analysts as an interfering factor in individual treatment, is perceived instead as a resource and support system and is used creatively as a force to bring about positive and lasting change in both the individual and the family unit. The pioneer theoreticians and therapists stimulated a true paradigmatic shift in the manner in which human problems were seen, reorienting their thinking regarding the nature of and the ways of modifying relationships and pathology (Kuhn, 1962).

Such a shift precipitated the development of further new concepts to enhance and/or replace traditional thinking regarding etiology, symptom formation, diagnosis, and treatment. As a result of this ongoing process of proliferation and redefining concepts of psychopathology and treatment, various schools of thought have branched out from the family therapy tree since the mid 1950s. Differentiations have been made, and models and typologies have emerged. As the field has expanded, confusion has increased concerning whether the theories are distinct entities, similar conceptualizations conveyed in different terminology, or theories that partially overlap in some ways and diverge in others.

In this chapter, an attempt is made to clarify the relationships between the schools of thought called collectively *family therapy*. Most do not exist as *totally* distinct from one another. Nonetheless, they need to be differentiated through an understanding of both the similarities that bind them together and the unique perspectives that give each theory its own coloration and identity.

The "Major" Schools of Marital and Family Therapy

Initially, when people study the field of marital and family therapy, they may become confused by the various theories that are presented. (Because similar schools exist in marital and family therapy, from here on, we will speak just of "family therapy.") Family therapy is not monolithic; this rubric subsumes approaches ranging from those derived from traditional psychoanalytic theory to techniques emerging from structural and strategic theory, and from learning theory.

Overview of Conceptual Models

The presentation of the various schools of family therapy to fledgling clinicians and to converts from other mental health disciplines needs to be articulated as clearly and precisely as possible. At present, there are several ways of approaching the complex task of training family therapists. One seems to be to present all of the theories as distinct entities and to assign the task of assimilating them to the trainee. When this is the strategy, the theories may be elaborated with or without a sense of relatedness. The novice is hard put to distinguish which theory is which, not because differences do not exist, but because the notion that the theories are *totally* distinct is inaccurate and deceiving. What results is a sense of blurred boundaries between the schools rather than a notion of related but distinguishable theories. The commonalities need exploration; the teacher can translate the terminology from one theoretical framework into that of other conceptual schools, indicating when different terms or concepts are used to mean the same thing, as for example, Minuchin's "enmeshed family" (Minuchen & Fishman, 1981) and Bowen's "undifferentiated family ego mass" (1974). Whether this pedagogical approach is adopted or whether the trainee is asked to make these links, the unifying factors that do exist between the schools become evident. In all schools, the family is viewed as a system, and the

members as interdependent parts; it is comprised of several subsystems with generational links and boundaries, communication networks, splits and alliances, rules, secrets, and myths. Olson *et al.* (1980) attempted to integrate principles from various schools of thought into a "circumplex model of marital and family systems." They found that "three dimensions emerged from the conceptual clustering of concepts from six social science fields, including family therapy" (p. 59–74). These dimensions are *cohesion, adaptability,* and *communication*. These authors derived their evidence for the importance of these particular dimensions from the fact that numerous theorists and therapists have independently evolved concepts related to them as critical to their work. The majority hold that a paramount goal of therapy is to change the family system of interaction, with individual change occurring as a product of systems change (Sander, 1979). The main divergence occurs on issues like the importance of history versus the centrality of the here-and-now, and the emphasis to be placed on intrapsychic versus interpersonal dynamics.

Another approach to training is to present only one theory, suggesting to the trainee, overtly or covertly, that there is only one true way to conceptualize and work with families, and that this is it. Such a doctrinaire approach creates the danger of raising narrow-minded clinicians or technicians, who may emerge armed with techniques and strategies, but who lack a comprehensive understanding of family functioning and pathology. They do not acquire a sense of relatedness among the theories nor of the value of professional cross-fertilization. The false presentation of any theory as unique and as distinct from and superior to all other theories fosters a professional narcissism and competitive loyalty to one's guru that ultimately does a disservice to the patients, who are forced to fit into the theory, and to the trainee, who is encouraged to emulate the trainer rather than to distill the essence from various teachers and utilize this in a unique and creative way.

Neither a dogmatic approach presenting one theory nor an eclectic potpourri is adequate. The various perspectives should be presented in an accurate, fair, and understandable manner so that eventually the family therapy trainee will acquire exposure to the myriad schools and select one or two for intensive study and training.

For this author, the best way of conceptualizing the theories is in the form of a continuum, suggesting that the schools of thought are indeed distinguishable but not totally discrete, and expressing a sense of relatedness and overlap.

Marital and family therapy theories and techniques have been classified in various ways in the past. Beels and Ferber (1972) attempted to classify the leading therapists by personality and style. They divided the therapists into two main categories. They described the *conductors* as the

vigorous personalities who can hold their audiences spellbound by their talks and demonstrations. They have a keen, explicit sense of their own values and goals, which they . . . hope to get the family to adopt. Some of them are regarded by their critics as sadistic, manipulative, exhibitionistic, and insensitive.

The reactors *are those who have less compelling public personalities . . . [and] present themselves to the families not only as themselves but in various roles dictated by the tactics or the . . . dynamics of the family. They refer in their writings to the danger of being swamped, confused, inveigled, or extruded. They have goals and values, but they are more likely to [have] . . . a secret agenda in therapy.* (Beels & Ferber, 1972, pp. 175–176)

The conductors are overtly more dominant and try to enter the family by quickly asserting control. The reactors seem to respond more to what the family presents, are less aggressive, and take more of an observer role. They may consult more with a cotherapist or family members regarding impressions and interpretations. Beels and Ferber grouped Minuchin, Ackerman, Bowen, and Satir as conductors and Nagy, Wynne, Whitaker, Haley, and Zuk as reactors. Others would disagree with who is listed in these groups; these therapists have certainly changed with time.

In the early 1980s, the personality of the leaders is still so inextricably intertwined with the theories and the development of the field that, like Beels and Ferber, I find it difficult to disentangle them. However, I will focus mostly on substantive matters, for if the field is to continue to mature, we must extract and highlight the theoretical underpinnings of therapeutic technique; these constitute the knowledge base that makes therapy a science that is teachable and transmissible in writing. Yet, the personality of the therapist is also an intrinsic part of the process; it is the special ingredient that can add art to the science in establishing a therapeutic alliance and enabling healing or growth to occur.

In the literature, four or five major schools of thought are usually differentiated. For example, Gurman (1979) did a fine comparison of approaches in marital therapy from three perspectives (psychoanalytic, systems, and behavioral) by exploring various *dimensions,* including: the role of the therapist, the importance of the past and the unconscious in treatment, the nature and meaning of the presenting problem, the role of assessment, the importance of mediating goals, and the identified ultimate goals of therapy. Stanton (1980) reviewed systems approaches to family therapy, identifying strategic systems, structural systems, and Zuk's triadic go-between model (1971) as the three distinct approaches. Goldenberg and Goldenberg (1980) identified four theoretical models of family interaction: family psychodynamic theory, communications theory, structural theory, and behavioral theory.

The typologies cited above do not seem to me to be sufficiently adequate, in that they tend to merge some theoretical positions that are significantly different from one another; also, each has some important omissions. I have identified 10 distinct theoretical perspectives on the family and its treatment, and these comprise the nosology to be presented here. This schema includes treatment modalities and also classifies them with an eye to theories of normal and pathological behavior. The theory and the therapy are not differentiated, as each perspective has produced a corresponding therapeutic approach, so that such a distinction is artificial and misleading. A number of intervention strategies exist within the context of each of the various theories, but these are not considered schools of thought in and of themselves because the approach to treatment is consistent with a broader theory.

The 9 approaches (Kaslow, 1981a) that represent the major theories of family therapy are the (1) psychoanalytic; (2) Bowenian; (3) contextual-relational; (4) experiential; (5) problem-solving; (6) communicational-interactional; (7) structural; (8) strategic-systemic; (9) behavioral and (10) integrative, diaclectic, or multimodal. Before discussing these theories in depth, several continua are presented to emphasize the relationships that exist between the various epistemologies. The continua avoid the notion of a digital view, an either-or comparison, and at the same time do not fuse closely related theories to one another. Each theory offers a different view of the "reality" of the family. Some techniques and terminology may be similar, yet, they are not identical because they exist within the context of a different epistemology or reality. For example, even though both the contextual and the behavioral approaches speak of reciprocity in relationships, the term bears a meaning that is unique to its theoretical context. Both structural and communications theorists have what each describes as an ahistorical approach, but their interpretations of what this implies are quite divergent.

A temporal dimension is used in Figure 1 to compare the theories noted above.

The role of the past, in both theory and technique, is emphasized in the psychoanalytic and Bowenian models, which stress the importance of the history of relationships, past conflicts, and past experiences. The contextual model stresses the loyalties to one's family of origin and the ledger of balances accrued from the past and how these influence and should be rebalanced in the present (Boszormenyi-Nagy & Spark, 1973). At the other extreme lies the behavioral model, which considers history and past conflicts of little import in treatment (Gurman, 1979).

The substance or focal point of a therapy is used as the parameter for the continuum in Figure 2. At one end is the centrality of the intrapsychic world (psychoanalytic), and at the other is centrality of external behavior (behavioral).

Commonalities among the Theories

The continua suggest differences of varying degrees between the schools in both the focus of the theory and the theory's concept of the important time dimensions, but some basic similarities do exist and these are briefly discussed before the theories are examined more closely.

Gurman (1979) noted that all the theories stress assessment as a very important first phase of therapy, although the approaches to assessment vary. Systems therapy,

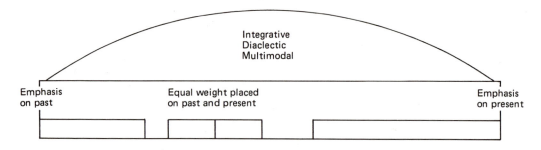

Figure 1. Theoretical perspective of time. I believe that much more consideration has to be given to the future, that is, the long-range goals and consequences of changes that the therapy mobilizes. There is too little future orientation in the field.

which he subdivided into Bowenian and communications, assesses a family system by actively intervening and observing the affects of these moves on the system; how the family respond becomes part of the diagnosis. Behavioral therapists stress a thorough, systematic assessment, in contrast to the more informal or less structured diagnostic procedures of the psychoanalytic therapists.

The schools also share a belief in the importance of certain mediating goals in therapy, including the specification of the problem, the redefinition of the problem to "fit" the particular theoretical perspective, the recognition of mutual contributions to the problem by all family members, and a moving in therapy toward increased give-and-take and responsibility and decreased blaming and coercion. Finally, all therapists consider the recognition and modification of the communication patterns. However, the weight put on these various mediating goals differs from school to school. For example, the strategic therapist accepts the presenting problem as stated and intervenes accordingly. The contextual belief is that it is essential to get beyond what is presented as the problem.

The role of the therapist is defined differently in each theory, but some similarities do exist. All attempt to clarify communications, and all but the psychoanalytic approach may sometimes assign tasks or homework, but even here there are variations. The assignment of home-

work varies in the manner in which the tasks are given and in the supporting rationale behind the assignment (Gurman, 1979). The suggestions of the contextual therapist tend to be of an evocative type, in contrast to the task-oriented prescriptions of the structural and strategic therapists.

Despite the seemingly divergent pathways taken by practioners of the 9 schools, they do have some similar outcome goals. Those that are recognized as important by all the schools include the development of role flexibility and adaptability; a balancing of power, particularly in marital therapy; the establishment of individuality within the family collectivity; and greater clarity and specificity of communications.

Understanding Family Therapy: Toward an Integration of Concepts

The notion of the theories of family therapy relating along a continuum undergirds the thrust of this chapter; it seems to facilitate a clear and accurate presentation and should contribute to stimulating the reader toward a personal integration of his or her own theories of choice. We are not attempting to pick the "winner," that is, which theory is best in working with all kinds of families. That would be a formidable and perhaps impossible task. A theory that has explanatory power with one family may

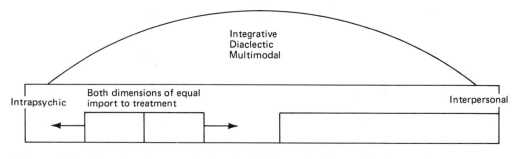

Figure 2. Theoretical focal points.

prove inadequate for conceptualizing the dynamics of another, and an intervention strategy that works well with one type of symptomatology or syndrome may result in an impasse with another. Which is most efficacious and under what conditions can be determined only by the psychotherapy process and by outcome research. Part of the complexity of conducting this research is that empirical research is governed by the model it proposes to test.

The notions of *problem* and *solution* have unique meanings within each particular school. Also, there is no universal agreement on who constitutes the family—that is, whether it should be nuclear, extended and how far, by blood, or by who lives together—nor on who must be present at the therapy session.

Although each school has one or several principle therapists or spokespersons, here we are concerned more with the theories than with the therapists themselves. Yet as Whitaker (1976) accurately posited, the person of the therapist is at least as important as the techniques that he or she uses. Suffice it to say that I concur that each individual unavoidably adds his or her own style and personality to the interpretation and application of a theory (Kaslow, Cooper, & Linsenberg, 1979). But the cornerstones of practice must be the choice of a theory or concepts from several theories and the learning of the skills necessary for the interventions selected. One's beliefs determine what one sees and how one perceives it and, in turn, determine what one then does. The concepts that one accepts are therefore vital to what one does in therapeutic practice. A true "eclectic" understands several or many theories and chooses to pick concepts and to integrate these in the manner that is best suited to himself or herself. It is hoped that the continuum concept will facilitate such personal understanding and synthesis, leading to a professional belief system that will then allow the therapist to carry out effective and consistent therapy. This has already been done by the Duhls in their integrative model (1979), by Lazarus in his multimodal approach (1976) and in his more recent work, which he calls "selective eclecticism";[1] and in my "diaclectic" model. Here, the words *dialectic* and *eclectic* are blended to convey a comprehensive approach (Kaslow, 1980a,c).

A more in-depth look at the theories on the continua follows. Then, the final section in this chapter attempts a synthesis into a "diaclectic" model.

Psychoanalytic Family Therapy

History and Theoretical Development. Of the various schools of thought and practice, psychoanalytic family therapy is the nearest descendant of individual psychoanalytically oriented psychotherapy. One early leading proponent was Nathan Ackerman, a psychoanalyst and child psychiatrist who crystallized his interest in the family as a unit in an article called "The Unity of the Family"

in 1938. At that time, he was on the staff of the children's unit at the Menninger Clinic in Topeka, Kansas. Later, he moved to New York, where he taught at Columbia University and worked at the Jewish Family Service. His interest in the family unit flourished, and his reputation as a compassionate, intuitive, and sagacious therapist spread. As younger therapists and colleagues who were trained in other modalities expressed mounting interest in his work, the need for some systematic training became apparent. In response to this need, Ackerman founded the Family Institute of New York in 1965, which was intended both to treat troubled families and to train clinicians in family therapy (Guerin, 1976; Kaslow, 1980b). Since its inception, the staff of the institute have encouraged innovativeness and challenging of dogma (LaPerriere, 1979).

Donald Bloch replaced Ackerman as director of the institute, and in 1971, following the death of its founder, this facility was renamed the Ackerman Institute. (Although the prevailing orientation remains psychodynamic, some of the key training staff have become deeply imbued with systemic-strategic principles and techniques[2] and are using this approach in their research, treatment, and training endeavors.)

Because many of the pioneers in the first generation of family therapists were psychiatrists and psychologists with analytic training, these roots, though often somewhat hidden under the guise of new terminology, break through in the use of concepts drawn from object relations theory (Fairbairn, 1952), the debates about what happens to the transference in family therapy, and disagreements over whether any lasting change can occur if one only treats the symptom or changes the family structure without attending to etiology and arrested development. Certainly in Bowenian, contextual, experiential, and integrative or diaclectic family therapy, the psychoanalytic heritage is evident (Kaslow, 1981a).

Those practicing psychoanalytic family therapy adhere to the belief that unconscious factors and one's past history play an important role in present behavior and symptomatology. By adapting this concept from the individual to the family, the analytic group first developed the art of family-history taking. The concern with the past, coupled with recognition of the systems properties of the family, undergirds what happens in treatment.

The Family and the Therapist in Treatment. Given the importance of the past as it contributes to and shapes the present, *assessment* plays a central role. Variations in how assessment is accomplished are manifold, reflecting the particular therapists' ideas of what it is important to ascertain and in what kind of sequence. Some use a rather specific history-taking format; others use what the patients are discussing to ask related, if seemingly tangential, questions about the past. Major presenting problems are considered, particularly their underlying meaning and

---

[1]Speech made by Arnold Lazarus at Hahnemann Medical College, June 1980.

[2]Keynote presentation by Lynn Hoffman, AAMFT Regional Conference, Denver, Colorado, May 1980.

significance, but the primary focus is on interactional themes (Gurman, 1979). All members of the family unit, as well as the relationships between and among them, are considered the patient.

Because the marital pair create the family unit, it is important to explore the unconsious as well as the conscious reasons for their choice of mate, the evolution of their relationship, the conflicts and experiences that predated their marriage, and the influence of these on the current marital and family interactions and affective quality.

The clinician quickly strives to establish a strong therapeutic alliance. The salient objectives (what Gurman, 1979, called "mediating goals") in this kind of therapy include the delineation of problem(s) and their redefinition so that they are more accessible to resolution; the recognition by all family members of their mutual contributions to the perpetuation of the conflicts; the clarification of boundary issues; the explication of individual needs and desires and how these can be fulfilled within the marital-family system; the modification of extreme narcissistic or inappropriate demands; an increase in expressive and listening skills; the diminishing of coercive and blaming statements; the facilitation of problem-solving and conflict-resolution skills; an increase in interaction; insight into current family dynamics and transactions; the modification of dysfunctional rules and communication patterns; the individuation of each family member; and the resolution of spousal and therapist–patient transferences.

When these goals are achieved during the course of therapy, they make possible its continuation until more "ultimate goals" (Gurman, 1979) are accomplished. These include, but are not limited to, greater trust and closeness, more role flexibility, heightened appreciation of uniqueness, greater comfort with and enjoyment of one's sexuality, a more balanced power relationship between the couple as parents and spouses, improved balance between the cognitive and affective realms of living, an improved self-image for each and family esteem for all, clearer communication, and the resolution of neurotic conflicts. Many of these are concordant with the dimensions that appear in the various discussions of the healthy family (Kaslow, 1980a, 1982; Lewis, Beavers, Gossett, & Phillips, 1976).

In order to realize these goals, the therapist encourages and supports affective communications and greater demonstrations of affectionate feelings; clarifies the nature of the family's communications; interprets the reasons for and the meaning of actions and feelings; challenges assumptions and beliefs and tries to dislodge constricting and rigidly adhered to, outdated patterns; fosters and interprets the transference; and facilitates the development of insight into the self and deeper awareness of other family members. The therapist may share something about his or her own values and beliefs and may discuss the countertransference. This is primarily a verbal psychotherapy, used by both conductors and reactors, predi-

cated on understanding intrapsychic and interpersonal dynamics, and geared to improving overall individual and family functioning and self-esteem, while reducing conflicts and the need for symptomatology.

Bowenian Family Therapy

Brief Commentary on Bowen. Murray Bowen is a psychiatrist who did some of his early work with schizophrenics at the Menninger Clinic and then moved on to conduct research and to treat schizophrenics and, later, their families, too, under the auspices of the National Institute of Mental Health (NIMH). Following that, he became the acknowledged leader of the Family Center at Georgetown University Medical School in Washington, D.C., which is primarily a training center. Now past seventy, Bowen is one of the founders of the American Family Therapy Association (1977) and became its first president. In 1976, Bowen wrote:

I have spent almost three decades on clinical research in psychotherapy. A major part of my effort has gone toward clarifying theory and also toward developing therapeutic approaches consistent with the theory. (p. 42)

One of the gains he anticipated was the improvement in making predictions and in shaping the outcome of therapy as intervention strategies became more closely linked to theoretical underpinnings.

Theory and Treatment. Bowen (1976) posited that "the successful introduction of a significant other person [i.e., the therapist] into an anxious or disturbed relational system has the capacity to modify relationships within the system" (p. 47). Clearly, this kind of pronouncement makes the Bowenian approach one of the systems approaches to family therapy.

Bowen proposed that another characteristic of a system in which the emotional forces are in opposition is that, the greater the level of anxiety or tension, the more the members tend to withdraw from outside relationships and to compartmentalize themselves with each other. Thus, the most disturbed and upset families, who are most in need of assistance, are least likely to reach out for it, or if they do, they have so insulated themselves as to be least accessible to interventions by an outsider. How they get to the therapist and how he or she gains their attention and trust is part of the challenge to the therapist. Bowen came to believe that the significant other is a variable in the outcome of therapy. Thus, voodoo experts, tribal healers, or charismatic spirtual leaders who assume or are assigned magical and supernatural powers can sometimes, because of the high level of emotionality and the low level of reality that they conjure up, produce rapid change or instantaneous conversion. Although psychotherapists do not usually claim to have magic, Bowen (1978) asserted that the degree of assigning and assuming overimportance in the therapeutic relationship is sometimes excessive and that the clinician makes few convincing efforts to correct the distorted perception. This inflation is analogous to overvaluing and idealizing someone with whom we fall in love, as she or he, too, generates a high level of emotionality.

Based on the above observations, coupled with his early research in treating schizophrenics, Bowen expended much effort in "eliminating the assumed and assigned importance from the therapeutic relationship." He achieved much better results in treating schizophrenics by virtue of "successfully managing the transference" than did his colleagues and found that this experience later led to his "staying out of the transference" found in those being treated in family therapy. In so doing, he attempted to ensure that the intensity of the relationship would be centered on the original family members and not siphoned off into an intense transference relationship. This marked a major departure from psychoanalytic theory and practice and became a cornerstone of his systems approach. As Bowen perceives family therapy as quite different from conventional psychotherapy, he used another vocabulary to avoid confusion. He has written of "supervising" the effort that a family makes on its own behalf, and of "coaching" a family member in working with his or her family of origin (Bowen, 1976, pp. 50–51).

The crux of Bowenian theory lies in the degree to which individuals are able to distinguish between the feeling process and the intellectual process. In his earlier research, he had found that parents of schizophrenics, who superficially seemed to function well, had trouble differentiating between the subjective feeling process and the more objective thinking process. Such fusion and confusion of affective and cognitive processes was found to be most marked in close personal relationships. As those with "the greatest fusion between feeling and thinking function the poorest and those who function best demarcate these processes, Bowen and colleagues began to stress the concept of differentiation of self" (1974). Bowen (1974) spoke of the schizophrenic family as being characterized by an "undifferentiated family ego mass"; it followed that an objective of treatment was to foster the individuation of all members.

Bowen's ideas on family systems evolved rapidly and became consolidated into a theory between 1957 and 1963. In addition to the aforementioned notions about the nuclear family's emotional system, he talked about the necessity of grasping and working with the family projection process, the "process through which parental undifferentiation impairs one or more children." Operating through the father–mother–child triangle, this process revolves around the mother as the principal caretaker of the infant and results in primary emotional impairment of the child. Some of the amount of undifferentiation in the parents is projected onto the child, as is some of the mother's anxiety. When the anxiety level is high and the projection occurs, the father plays a supportive role in the projection process. The child responds with anxiety and is then labeled as "the problem." If the child is physically or mentally impaired, the anxiety is likely to escalate, so

more gets projected in overpermissiveness and oversolicitousness, or in overdemandingness, rigidity, and rejection. When families are asked to do their genogram (a family tree of the extended family), who the most triangulated child in each nuclear unit was or is becomes apparent, and one can zero in to work toward detriangulation or extrication from the triad.

A triangle exists when there is a relatively close dyad and a third person, who is more of an outsider, would like to be closer to one of the original dyad. One member of the original pair may be attracted to the idea of a new coupling; the other may fear the intrusion and the potential pair. The dynamics are constantly in flux; sometimes, each plans a strategy until a new, more comfortable equilibrium is established by the one who has become most disconcerted by the triangle. The third party, who may stabilize as well as disrupt the original dyad, may be a child, a friend, a lover, a parent, or a therapist. Those who cannot tolerate intimacy often create triangles to diffuse the intensity of a dyadic relationship; others use it to stir up feelings of jealousy or to find someone to fulfill needs unmet by the original partner. It is critical that the therapist not get triangulated by his or her patients, for in doing so, he or she gets so caught up in their emotional systems that the objectivity and neutrality essential for changing the dysfunctional dynamics is lost. Sometimes, in learning how the parents attempt to triangulate the therapist, he or she becomes aware of how they have triangulated the child as they repeat the patterned maneuvers. Bowen often works with parents toward detriangulation; when this occurs, they will act differently at home, and the fusion of family members will begin to resolve.

Other key concepts include the multigenerational transmission process (of mental illness slowly building in each successive generation) and sibling position. In the middle 1970s, Bowen added his more recently evolved ideas on the "emotional cutoff" (handling unresolved emotional attachments by running away, withdrawing, or negating the importance of the original family) and "societal regression"; that is, when a family is subjected to chronic sustained anxiety, it begins to lose contact with its intellectually determined principles and resorts increasingly to emotionally determined decisions to allay anxiety. This process leads to regression and symptom formation. A similar process occurs at the societal level during periods of disorganization and impacts on the family, placing added stress on it.

The Family and the Therapist in Treatment. Because the natural tendency of a family system is to maintain its homeostatic balance, any movement by a member toward differentiation is perceived as a threat to the status quo and is resisted by the others. The therapist supports the individuation efforts and prevents the person from being drawn back into the too-tight togetherness. Differentiation can be successfully accomplished only if the patient is sufficiently motivated; otherwise, he or she is doing it for the therapist and becomes too tightly linked to the therapist—a new version of the symbiosis from which he or she has so recently been extricated. Satisfactory progress in this process is also contingent on the stage in the patient's own developmental cycle when he symbolically and emotionally separates from the family. This progress can best be assessed when one sees how the patient later copes with long-term severe stress; the process is probably never fully completed.

In sum, a Bowenian therapist sees as vital the assessment of the multigenerational history and the relationships within the family of origin. The presenting problems are likely to be interpreted in light of the concepts of fusion and differentiation. The individual members of the family as well as the relational system are the patient unit. Problems are reframed; voyages home to work through unresolved emotional attachments are encouraged and coached by the therapist; patients' needs and desires are clarified; increased reciprocity and cooperation fostered; and the transference is avoided. The therapist attempts to modify nonfunctional system rules. Above all, the goal is to foster positive differentiation, as contrasted to emotionally cutting oneself off from one's family of origin. Philip Guerin and Thomas Fogarty (1972), two psychiatrists who trained under and worked with Bowen, have done some useful elaborations and extensions on the use of the genogram, on the dimensions of self (Fogarty, 1976), and on the multigenerational model of family therapy (Guerin & Guerin, 1976). A recent book by McGoldrick (1986) further illuminates the language and technique of genograming.

Contextual-Relational Theory and Therapy

Theoretical Development. The originator and leading proponent of contextual family therapy is Ivan Boszormenyi-Nagy. Born in Hungary, and trained as a psychiatrist, Nagy began to establish his reputation through his work with families at Eastern Pennsylvania Psychiatric Institute (EPPI) in Philadelphia. His colleagues there included James Framo, with whom he coedited *Intensive Family Therapy* (1965), a book that reflects a somewhat traditional psychoanalytic approach to family therapy. By 1973, when he and his then colleague Geraldine Spark coauthored *Invisible Loyalties,* the emphasis on one's indebtedness to his or her family of origin, the continuing profound influence of one's biological relatedness (even if it is unknown or disowned), and conceptualization in an ethical-existential framework had become paramount. In this theory, as in Bowenian theory, the family of origin is central. Nagy and Spark stressed concepts of entitlement and a ledger of balances and obligations, predicated on one's biological heritage. Whereas Bowen emphasizes the voyage home to rework unfinished business from the past, contextual therapists are now apt to engage in multigenerational family therapy, gathering various members of the clan together to resolve problems, to unearth the hidden loyalties, and to repair the ruptured or strained relationships. Nagy is currently a professor at

Hahnemann Medical University, and Spark is in private practice in Philadelphia.

The loyalties concepts are particularly thought-provoking for those working in the arenas of adoption, custody, child abuse, and foster placement. The emphasis on the importance of the biological ties and the claims of the natural parents to their offspring is at great variance with the stance that Goldstein, Freud, and Solnit (1973) took concerning the primacy of psychological parenting and object constancy.

Therapist and Family in Treatment. The contextual model perceives the family coming into a treatment situation as a result of a sense of hurt and unfairness on the part of a member or members of the family. There exists an imbalance in the family relational ledgers and a corresponding breakdown of trust between family members, resulting in stagnant relationships and a lack of resources for trust building. This imbalance may be manifested systemically by the presence of a scapegoat within the family or by an inability of the members to ask for or receive anything from other family members. The relational imbalances result in a sense of unfairness between family members, seen in a sense of overentitlement or overindebtedness in these members.

The assessment process involves developing a three-generational picture of the family through the use of a genogram. The therapist assesses the fairness and violations of fairness between family members and between generations, particularly in parent–child relationships. Often, unresolved issues between the parents and their parents (the grandparents) affect the second-generation parent–child relationship negatively. For example, a child may be "parentified" by the parent(s) when the parent tries to satisfy unmet emotional needs through the child, needs that have not been met in that parent's relationship with his or her mother and father and are not being fulfilled by current adult relationships. The parent takes without giving back, creating a nonreciprocal, imbalanced relationship. This may be perpetuated through future generations if not recognized and corrected. This type of exploitative pattern can best be detected through the use of a three-generational genogram, which shows what legacy issues are involved and identifies the patterns of interaction in past generations. The inclusion of history taking in the assessment process is therefore a vital part of the therapy. Content as well as process is important. The history-taking session also serves as a vehicle for the beginning of trust building between the therapist and the family.

The contextual therapist initially addresses the presenting problem and allows all the family members present to express their opinion concerning the difficulty. A shift away from the problem takes place quickly thereafter, and a move is made toward the more basic dynamic issues, the symptom generally being viewed as an expression of an underlying factor concerning loyalty to one's family of origin and the concomitant imbalance in the family relationships. This emphasis on loyalty and connective ties is in direct contrast to the approach of the structuralists, which zeros in on the presenting problem and pursues the goal of symptom relief.

The therapist's role revolves around recognition of the multilateral nature of the issues. Because of the existential nature of relationships, there always exist as many sides to an issue as there are people involved. It is essential to the contextual approach that the therapist recognize all the sides to an issue and convey this notion of multilaterality to the family. Acknowledging each person is the first step toward developing trustworthiness between the family and the therapist.

The therapist's acknowledgment of each person's side is referred to as *multidirected partiality,* which, in effect, provides everyone with an opportunity to be heard, so that her or his position on the issue is acknowledged. This multidirected partiality is the cornerstone for the rebuilding of trust in relationships. Once people know that they will be given the opportunity to speak and will be listened to sensitively, they are more likely to begin to hear and acknowledge the other side(s) of an issue. Then, the process of give-and-take begins to function within the family, forming the basis for trustworthiness in the relationships. Within this multipartiality, the therapist may take sides in an effort to involve a particularly distant or exploited member, but always with the realization that a rebalancing must take place at some point.

Boszormenyi-Nagy (1979) defined the goal of contextual therapy as the "rejunction," which includes the acknowledgment of equitable multilaterality, a commitment to a fair balance of give-and-take, and a process of reengagement in living mutuality. In other words, the therapist encourages exploration by the family members of their own capacities for correcting imbalances through both increased availability to others and the redefined use of others as resources.

Through such rebalancing, the therapist helps the family to develop trustworthiness, which is viewed as the fundamental resource of family relationships. The therapist cannot set trustworthiness in motion by manipulation or by forming tactical power alliances. Rather, he or she must be able to see the people before him or her as human beings, realizing the pain of the struggle. A combination of deep, active, empathic concern, a recognition of multilaterality, and a stance of multidirected partiality by the therapist will enable the family to begin to mobilize their own healing resources. Boszormenyi-Nagy (1979) stated that, "as soon as therapeutic efforts are directed at balances of merit rather than at the nature of feelings or transactions, the self reinvestment process of mutual trustbuilding has begun" (p. 5).

This approach has been criticized as being too intellectual and as being inappropriate for treating families from the lower economic classes and those who are not highly articulate. Yet, Nagy feels that the theory is built on basic human principles that are applicable regardless of race, creed, or economic standing. The concepts of trust, fairness, and reciprocity are not limited to any one class of people; rather, they are basic relational concepts. The contextual approach is not only applicable to present problems but also stresses the preventive aspect anchored in the rebalancing of present relationships for the benefit of future offspring.

Experiential Therapy

And How It Came to Be: Creative Artistry. Carl Whitaker, another of the great pioneers in family therapy, came also from a professional heritage of being a psychiatrist in a mental hospital assigned to treating the severely disturbed, including many schizophrenics. Elsewhere, he did play therapy with children. From each of these experiences, he gleaned a good deal about the nature and utility of "craziness"; about entering a patient's world intuitively by allowing his own unconscious the freedom to spontaneously comprehend the metacommunication of the patient's unconscious, no matter how covert or tangled; and about the importance of the therapist's fashioning a style harmonious with his or her own nature.

He began practicing and writing about family therapy in Atlanta in the early 1950s. He and his colleagues, Warkentin and Malone, experimented with cotherapy as early as 1956; they saw their inpatients in conjunction with family members and found that this pairing, plus bringing in the patient's significant others, both increased their (the therapists') insight into the family dynamics and symptomatology of the identified patient and also heightened the impact that they made in untangling the web and enabling positive growth to occur (Whitaker & Malone, 1981).

In the 1960s, Whitaker moved to the University of Wisconsin Medical School to become a professor in the Department of Psychiatry and to teach family therapy. His warmth, playfulness, sense of humor, genuine compassion, intuitive giftedness, keen knowledge of people, and sound grounding in the conventional theories of therapy, which he publicly eschews as inadequate and restrictive, have drawn many interns, residents, and well-established professionals to his courses and training workshops. He attempts to set those who would be disciples (of any leader) free by encouraging them not to be "carbon copies of the master" and stresses that "technical approaches do not seem to succeed for second generation therapists" (Whitaker, 1976, p. 155).

He cautions against engaging in symptom relief only because of what may happen if the symptom has developed as an adaptation (perhaps the best possible one?) to an extremely pathological family or societal situation. The implication is that the consequence could be the precipitation of a worse dilemma in another member of the family, or even the disintegration of the unit. Thus, he often views the symptom as "an exquisite experience of regression in the service of the ego." It cannot be abandoned until the patient perceives it as too weighty and no longer necessary. For this reason, he may resort to framing a paradox, thereby exacerbating the symptom by prescribing it until it becomes so exaggerated that it topples under its own weight. Whitaker was doing "psychotherapy of the absurd" for many years, well before others began describing their use of paradox in family therapy. Because of his keen empathy with the patients' pain and adaptation, he seems to be able to generate a paradox that is extremely appropriate and to convey to the patient that, in some uncanny way, she or he is beautifully understood. At times, Whitaker and his colleagues, in expressing their own craziness, seem to be able to provoke their patients back into sanity. However, a therapist who lacks the skill to speak metaphorically or to frame paradoxes that are attuned to the particular patient's "pathology" and the family's way of maintaining it may indeed make the situation worse. It is a technique to be used with wisdom, warmth, and humor, and not as a gimmick.

Whitaker writes as he does therapy, and quoting him is the best way—short of being treated by him or watching him work—to illustrate how he experiences life, of which therapy, for him, is a part:

One of the effects of a therapeutic orientation based on theory is that the therapist becomes an observer. In doing so, he not only avoids his chance of being a person, but he also tends to help the family avoid their courage to be. (Whitaker, 1976, p. 156)

Certainly, implicit here is a clarion call for the experience of therapy to be an authentic encounter for all involved, and one becomes aware of Whitaker's kinship to the humanists and existentialists.

For the experientialists, the nontechnical process of family therapy involves a deliberate attempt to heighten anxiety. Whitaker generally recommends (and often uses) a cotherapy team to increase the therapist's potency and give each therapist support and a partner to bail her or him out if she or he gets ensnared by the family. This approach makes it possible to play more roles, to alternate functions consistent with his idea that "members of the family should be able to play all positions on the family team," and to go beyond stereotypical roles. The team exhibits a pattern of caring, so the family can risk becoming more anxious instead of "escaping into protective, defensive patterns." The therapist establishes an I–thou relationship, characterized by flexibility and caring, in order to pressure the family into tolerating additional anxiety. In the therapist's modeling through sharing her or his own "secret language," including metaphorical allegories, free associations, and fantasies, he or she releases the patients to trust the therapist enough to share their own zany and idiosyncratic inner world (Whitaker, 1976, pp. 160–163).

In his set of rules to help keep the therapist alive, Whitaker (1976) included the following (partial list below), which convey some of his essence and spirit:

1. *Learn how to love. Flirt with any infant available.*
2. *Develop a reverence for your own impulses, and be suspicious of your behavior sequences.*
3. *Enjoy your mate more than your kids and be childish with your mate.*
4. *Learn to retreat and advance from every position you take.*
5. *Build long term relations so you can be free to hate safely.*
6. *Face the fact that you must grow until you die. Develop a sense of the benign absurdity of life and learn to transcend the world of experience.*
7. *Develop your primary process living. Evolve a joint craziness with someone you are safe with.* (pp. 160–163)

In *The Family Crucible* (1978), Gus Napier and Carl Whitaker discussed their thoughts about therapy and illustrated the rhythmic process as they choreograph it by chronicling what transpires with vignettes of a prototypical family in therapy with them. It is a moving saga of the family's presenting problem, tensions, anxieties, turmoil, spurts of growth, and the great moments when an "aha" flashes into one member's consciousness. Because of the vivid descriptions of the therapeutic interventions and their teamwork as cotherapists, the reader has an opportunity to view the treatment process from behind an invisible mirror. It is a superb therapeutic dance, according to such rules of movement as "retreating and advancing from every possible position." There is a gripping scene in which Whitaker sits on the obstreperous teenage son on the floor, in order to immediately convey the power and authority that the senior generation has over the junior generation, and to model how this can be done, when necessary, for the father. This dramatic and drastic strategy mobilizes the father to become more actively and physically in touch with his son and changes the family's ways of interacting. Because of the fine timing and extreme appropriateness of this behavior, it goes beyond the kind of techniquism and power maneuvering that it would be if used by a less skilled and caring clinician. One begins to comprehend the heart of experiential family therapy in experiencing its cadences while reading this gripping book.

David Keith, another experiential therapist who did part of his residency training and some co-therapy with Whitaker at Wisconsin, co-authored several challenging and delightful articles characteristic of their style (Keith & Whitaker, 1978, 1981). They draw an analogy between play therapy and family therapy, depicting the importance of playing with the entire family, actually, symbolically, or metaphorically. In so doing, the therapists convey permission to play, freeing the patients to engage in having fun together, thereby making family life less serious and constrained. Keith and Whitaker also articulate some of the basic tenets in their heretofore allegedly atheoretical model. Besides the art of playing, chief among these is that the therapist allow his or her own primary-process thinking to connnect with the primary-process thinking of the patients, so that they feel sufficiently appreciated, cared about, and understood to be able to want to get better. Clearly, in this system, a strong therapeutic alliance is essential, and the personality of the therapist encompasses warmth, flexibility, tenderness, firmness, and a sense of absurdity and humor.

Another proponent of experiential family therapy is Walter Kempler (1981). In his variation, *the goals of therapy are negotiated by vigorous attention to, and manipulation of, our current encountering. The current encounter is the focal point. The therapist keeps the encounter vital by insisting that the members stick to the present moment, by insisting on the fullest measure of participation appropriate to the context of that moment, and by actively challenging any encounter-diminishing behavior.* (p. 29)

Kempler posits that the approach is a phenomenological one that is characterized by experimentation, exploration, and spontaneity. Thus, an environment conducive to expressing the free flow of feelings between family members is created. Behavior is deemed the more critical index of where one is than feelings are; what one does or does not do is considered more persuasive than one's excuses, tears, or promises. In Kempler's writings, there seems to be a blending of the existential perspective of Nagy and the effervescent, in-the-moment encounter of Whitaker.

Communicational-Interactional Therapy

History and Theoretical Development. Palo Alto, California, was the site of the inception of the communications school of family therapy in the early 1950s. There, Gregory Bateson, Don Jackson, John Weakland, and Jay Haley, who all shared an interest in the nature of the communication process, joined forces to do research. With their diverse backgrounds, they were able to apply anthropological methods of participant observation and objective scrutiny as well as social systems theory to their work with the families of schizophrenics. Jackson, a psychiatrist, established the Mental Research Institute (MRI) in 1959; it has had a continuous history since, as a major center for training, research, and therapy. Haley, who had worked with Jackson on the Bateson research project some years earlier, joined Jackson at the MRI in 1962, when the Bateson project ended. Virginia Satir, a social worker who moved from Chicago to Palo Alto, joined the group and rapidly moved into the foreground of the dynamic band of family therapy pioneers. In her family therapy primer, *Conjoint Family Therapy* (1964), Satir presented in outline form the core ideas of the communications wing of family systems, theory and therapy (Kaslow, 1980b). Both her clearly articulated publications and her vibrant, magnetic presentations prompted many clinicians to decide to explore and ultimately to take some training in family therapy. Today, her followers are loosely banded together in Satir's Avanta Network.

The Palo Alto group, out of their careful research into the patterns of communications in schizophrenic families, formulated the concept of the double bind. In *Toward a Theory of Schizophrenia* (1956), Bateson, Jackson, Haley and Weakland spelled out this conceptualization. The essential elements they identified in the development of the cognitive distortions and other difficulties associated with schizophrenia include:

1. Two or more persons.
2. Contradictory messages, such as "(I insist you) be

spontaneous," as a repetitive occurrence in the experience of the victim.

3. A primary negative injunction, for example, "if you do not do what I say, I will spank you," or "do not do that, or I will punish you."
4. A secondary injunction which contradicts the first and is sent at a more abstract logical level; like the first, it will be enforced by sanctions or punishments that seem to be life threatening. The secondary injunction is generally communicated nonverbally through facial expression, posture or gesture and its intent is masked by the verbal message.
5. A tertiary negative injunction which forbids the receiver of the communique (the victim) any channel of escape. By way of illustration, consider the father who forbids his son's aggressive actions and then beats him for being too passive and getting picked on by the neighborhood bullies.

Once the hapless child victim has learned to perceive the world in terms of these contradictory "damned if you do" and "damned if you don't" messages, any portion of the sequence is enough to activate the feeling of being trapped. The entire series of elements is no longer needed to trigger the confused, panicky reaction.

Several other concepts that have been contributed to family systems theory by members of this group merit inclusion here. Jackson (1959) developed the notion of family homeostasis; that is, the family unit desperately attempts to maintain the status quo and is highly resistant to any internal or external threat to that equilibrium. Given this situation and the therapist's potential as a change agent, he or she is likely to be perceived with mistrust. Thus, it is difficult to gain entrée into the family system, so deft strategies and shrewd and accurate understanding of the family's dynamics as revealed in their verbal and nonverbal messages are imperative. Satir (1964) showed that, if one member of the family is troubled, and all are interdependent in their functioning, then all the members are, in some way and at some level, in pain. Leverage for gaining entrance can be found in recognizing this shared, reciprocal pain and in indicating that all can potentially contribute to improved family functioning and can find ways of having their own needs met and the pain reduced through conjoint family therapy.

Because of her sensitivity to the nuances of nonverbal communication, and her realization of its cogency, Satir developed such techniques as family sculpting, as a means of having people depict how they view their family without the use of words filtered through secondary-process thinking. Sculpting has been further developed and elaborated in the literature by others, like Duhl, Kantor, and Duhl (1973), Constantine (1978), and Papp (1976).

Haley (1971), like Whitaker, became intrigued with the potency inherent in the use of paradox to disrupt rigidified relational and communication patterns. He personified the communication theorists' interest in strategic interventions, based on evaluation of the current structure and functioning of the family system.

Haley became the first editor of *Family Process* in 1962; this was the first journal to be devoted entirely to family theory and therapy. Shortly thereafter, he left California to join Minuchin at the Child Guidance Clinic in Philadelphia, bringing with him his strong theoretical beliefs in the importance of changing family structure.

Weakland and the others now at the MRI, including Jules Riskin, Paul Watzlawick, and Art Bodin, have developed brief family intervention and crisis techniques. The major orientation there now seems to be a combination of communications, strategic, and structural theory and techniques. Rapid problem resolution conducive to positive change is what is pursued (Watzlawick, Weakland, & Fisch, 1974; Weakland, 1977).

The Therapist and the Family in Treatment. The communications therapist is likely to be an active interventionist who directs and structures the sessions and places a high value on clarifying communication. Teaching skills, imparting knowledge, and giving practical advice are not his or her priorities. The methods that these practitioners are apt to use include, in addition to the aforementioned, manipulating the environment, assigning ''homework'' or tasks, and challenging the family's beliefs (Gurman, 1979). There is overt, candid recognition of the rules, secrets, and communication patterns of the group, and straightforward strategies are employed to modify the dysfunctional modes.

Therefore, these therapists see a rapid and complete assessment as constituting the imperative first stage of treatment. As with the Bowenites, the treatment is not standardized. Rather, the course it follows emanates from the therapist's clinical acumen and focuses on key themes presented by the particular patient system. The evaluation is concerned with specific problem behaviors, and these are deemed to be metaphors for the basic thematic interaction patterns. The original problem presented is viewed as a statement about the power distribution and the conflicts. The *relationships* between members—and not the members *per se*—constitute what are to be treated.

A developmental history of the couple and the family is believed to be useful, as is an understanding of the reasons for the spouses' choice of each other. Little interest is evinced in the intrapsychic life, past or present, of the family members. It is the contemporaneous interactions that are of paramount import. Therefore, the communications therapist does not seek to heighten and analyze any transference phenomenon, or to foster the development of insight.

It follows that the end goals include replacing stereotypical role concepts and behavior with greater breadth and flexibility, seeking resolution of the presenting difficulties, redistributing power for a more equitable balance, and enabling the participants to communicate more clearly and accurately what they think, feel, and desire. When these goals are achieved, the family can function at a more satisfying and productive level. By working *in vivo* with the communication network in the therapy sessions, and by highlighting what is occurring at that moment, potent zeroing-in to disrupt pathological functioning is attempted, and an effort is made to keep therapy brief and efficient.

Structural Family Therapy

Theoretical Development. The structural model of family therapy has been developed primarily by Minuchin and his colleagues (1967, 1974, 1978). Born in Argentina, Minuchin obtained his M.D. and pursued a practice in pediatrics. He later journeyed to the United States and received further training in child psychiatry. He then spent time in Israel working with displaced children and Jewish families who had immigrated from Arab lands. These experiences sparked his interest in the concept of working with families in treatment. After his return to the United States, he became involved in a research project at the Wiltwyck School in New York, studying the structure and process of the interactions of families of low socioeconomic status who produced delinquent children (Minuchin *et al.*, 1967). The basic tenets of structural theory took shape through the course of this work, including the notions of family structure and boundaries, the concept of subsystems, and the importance of observing the process of family communication and intervening to disrupt faulty messages. Concrete, action-oriented techniques emerged and proved successful in treating families that were not functioning on a sophisticated verbal level and that wanted tangible signs of fairly rapid improvement.

The theory continued to evolve to its present form at the Child Guidance Clinic of Philadelphia, where Minuchin served as director from 1965 to 1981. Braulio Montalvo and Bernice Rossman accompanied Minuchin from the Wiltwyck School, and Jay Haley joined this group in 1967 and became one of its leading lights. The Child Guidance Clinic staff turned an existing, small, intercity clinic into the largest facility of its kind in the country, serving low-income families as its major clientele. The clinic also became the headquarters of the structural-family-therapy school, becoming an internationally recognized center for training professionals and paraprofessionals alike.

Structural family therapy is based on the concept of perceiving people as a part of their environment, interacting with rather than acting on it. People cannot be understood without taking into account their context or the circumstantial aspects of their reality. The family, of course, is a vital part of this reality, largely determining how one experiences the world. The theory stresses that this interactional concept must be central to the *practice* of therapy; the dichotomy between the individual and her or his context is artificial and must be dismissed.

While at Wiltwyck, the Minuchin group focused not on the intrapersonal dynamics of the delinquent act, but on the family environment that had produced and supported the child's style of coping. This coping style, when it came into conflict with the extrafamilial milieu, was labeled as being "delinquent." In studying these families carefully, the therapist researchers were able to perceive a sense of order in these seemingly disorganized families. There was a structure to the family, which included invisible walls that separated certain individuals and groups of individuals and prevented closeness. They also lacked intergenerational boundaries. The family contained subsystems and a definable pattern of communication and behavior that was maintained by the structure and the rules. Minuchin found this structure to be very powerful, and through manipulating the subsystems and boundaries, he was able to bring about change, giving rise to new patterns of interaction. Further work at Wiltwyck led to an appreciation of the importance of the family's communicational system (who related to whom—the splits, schisms, and alliances), particularly nonverbal, as well as the notion of a continuum describing the family structure, with the axis being disengagement–enmeshment. These therapists found that dysfunctional families tend toward one or the other extreme (Minuchin *et al.*, 1967).

From this research project and their clinical experiences, the structuralists concluded that it was essential to focus on the here-and-now, because what was important about the past is reenacted in present transactions and is visible in the therapy session and the current behavior. The family is viewed as more than just a collection of individuals; it is the sum of all plus the dynamics of how the members relate within the structure that they have created. It is this arrangement that determines their style of interaction (Minuchin, 1974). It then follows that the structure is of central importance to the therapist attempting to facilitate change in the system. Minuchin pointed out that, when this structure is modified, each person's experience of the family changes; the result is a new position in the family and altered behavior. It is the experiences within the family context that determine each member's behavior both intrafamilially and extrafamilially.

A central tenet of this approach is the notion of a hierarchical organization within the family. A family should not be a group of equals. The parents should be in charge as the executives. The subsystems include the spouse subsystem, composed of the marital dyad; the parental subsystem, which may include a grandparent or other adult in a central role and/or a parentified child; the parent–child dyads; and the sibling subsystem, which acts as the child's first peer group (Minuchin, 1978). Knowledge of these subsystems and the boundaries separating them is necessary to an understanding of the health or pathology of the family. The growth of all family members is partially contingent on constructing or reinforcing the appropriate boundaries.

The family is always experiencing transitions as its members grow and develop as individuals. The structure must adapt to these changes in order to allow continued growth. The family goes through a developmental life cycle (Haley, 1973), necessitating an adaptive capacity to meet new circumstances and at the same time continuing to provide a stable environment for its members.

When a family cannot adapt, rigid patterns of interaction develop and, even when perceived as dysfunctional, cannot be altered. Such inflexible patterns of interaction and boundaries prevent the family from exploring new alternatives. As indicated above, Minuchin *et al.* (1978) noted that dysfunctional families are often overly enmeshed or disengaged, terms that refer not to specific behavior but to the characteristic way in which family members establish contact with each other. In disengaged families, the members do not seem to care about or react to one another. One can sense a disconnected quality and a lack of contact between family members. Enmeshed families lie at the opposite end of the spectrum. They exhibit a tight interlocking of family members, so that any change attempted by one member is met with immediate resistance by the other members. The characteristics of such families include power conflicts, difficulty in verbalizing affect or concern, and immediate reactivity to each member's shifting activity.

The structural approach has been applied to a wide range of families, problems, and symptoms. All economic levels have been treated. Stanton (1981) noted that the criticism directed at this approach's inability to treat intellectualizing upper-middle-class families is not well founded. The disorders treated include psychosomatic problems (Minuchin, 1978); drug addiction (Stanton, 1978); delinquency (Minuchin *et al.*, 1967); elective mutism (Rosenberg, 1978); and encopresis (Andolfi, 1978). This approach is usually utilized when the *identified* patient is a child or adolescent and the treatment of choice appears to be family therapy.

This is a *brief therapy* approach, usually lasting no longer than five or six months. The family members who interact day-to-day are involved in the therapy sessions; distant family members are not usually called in. When the situation is critical, as when an anorectic child is in serious danger, the patient may be hospitalized, and the family may be brought in either to live in at the hospital temporarily or to undergo intensive outpatient family-therapy sessions (Minuchin, 1978).

The Family and the Therapist in Treatment. Minuchin feels that a family enters treatment when stress has overloaded the system. The family has adapted to changed circumstances in a dysfunctional manner and, when it is stressed, continues to maintain its homeostatic balance by repeating the pathological behavior without variation. The task of therapy is to *restructure* the family, introducing to the members alternate ways of interacting. The therapist monitors the proximity and the distance of members, as the dysfunction is often a result of enmeshment or disengagement. The therapist plays a strong and directive role, as the family has sought his or her help because of his or her expertise. These therapists believe that the family has the capacity to adopt new patterns of behavior and/or interaction and to change in the direction of more adaptive functioning.

The therapist joins the family as rapidly as possible in order to collect data and to diagnose the problem. By entering the family system, the therapist learns how they experience reality, getting a sense of their rules, myths, and themes, as well as how it feels and what it actually means to be a member of that family.

The presenting problem is accepted by the therapist as the real problem, and interventions are designed to relieve the symptom and, in so doing, to improve the system's functioning. Once this occurs, the family has greater confidence in the therapist and may decide to work on other problems, being more optimistic about the outcome. This is a more symptom-oriented approach than psychoanalytic therapies; yet, it is not as symptom-focused as the strategic therapies.

In order for the structural therapist to be consistent with the theory, he or she must be willing to plunge in actively and directly. Interventions are usually concerned with the family structure. The stance is taken that, within the hierarchy, the parents should have the power, and when necessry, they are supported by the therapist in asserting it. Process (or how the family interacts) rather than content (or what is said) is the key to therapy. Nonverbal aspects of the communication process are noted as important data.

Spatial interventions are made in an effort to restructure the family. These may entail rearranging seating in a session, removing members temporarily, or having certain members observe the session from behind a one-way mirror, taking them out of the action for a while and forcing others to relate. This is a way of changing interpersonal boundaries in an effort to alter the perspectives of the family members. Again, the therapist concerns herself or himself with the distance or proximity between family members.

Another means of changing the imbedded pattern involves the therapist's use of self in unbalancing the homeostasis of the system. The clinician can join or support one individual or a subsystem at the expense of other family members, thus modifying the usual hierarchical organization and introducing the possibility of new combinations or alternatives.

To change how the family members perceive life, the therapist attempts to transform the linear view of the family (that one member is the problem or the identified patient) to one of complementarity (we are all involved). The notion that "You, the family, must come to therapy and change so that your symptomatic member will improve" is basic to all schools of family therapy.

The therapist can add information in an effort to restructure the family. He or she can educate the family by conveying a model of normal family functioning based on sharing his or her own experience and knowledge. The introduction of paradox can be used to confuse family members, to disrupt their stuck thinking, and to jolt them into a search for alternatives. By adding new information,

the therapist can help the family construct a new, workable reality as an alternative to their dysfunctional and stereotyped reality.

The structural therapist searches for competence within the family rather than exploring the roots of dysfunctional behavior. This approach is linked with the theoretical notion that the family has its own resources and is capable of coping in a more functional manner when it becomes aware of what that may be.

Finally, the therapist may work to reenact a dysfunctional transaction and then intervene in the process by increasing the intensity, by prolonging its occurrence, by introducing new variables (new family members), or by indicating alternate transactions. Then, by having the family enact a changed pattern of transaction, the session serves as a viable model for interaction outside the therapy room. A prime example is the family lunch with the anorectic patient and his or her family, in which the symptom and the interaction are confronted as it is in the session and then is reenacted differently (Minuchin *et al.,* 1978).

Minuchin (1974) sees therapy as inducing a more adequate family organization, one that will enable family members to realize their own growth potential. Why do they change? He noted three reasons: (1) the perception of reality has been challenged; (2) the family has been presented with alternate ways of interacting; and (3) because it is in the nature of the family that, once new transactional patterns have been tried out and new, more fruitful relationships develop, they become self-reinforcing.

This model has achieved great popularity. Its theory and the techniques are explicit and lend themselves to being taught systematically and to being imitated. At the Child Guidance Clinic, visitors from all over the world can view sessions through one-way mirrors. They can see videotapes made by the teaching staff there or purchase them for use in their home communities. And leading proponents travel worldwide to do workshops, demonstrating and discussing what they do. It is our impression that, to utilize this approach effectively, the therapist must be comfortable being a *conductor* (Beels & Ferber, 1972), an active and powerful therapist who conveys his or her expertise and belief in his or her abilities to assist the family to mobilize their capacity to change.

Strategic-Systemic Therapy

Historical Roots. The theorists of this persuasion share many commonalities with those of the communications and structural schools. All concur that, as the actors in a system are to some extent interdependent, the behavior of any one member affects all other members, and that the important time and relational dimension is the here-and-now. Given that the family is more than the sum of the individual personalities and includes their interactions, it is *nonsummative* (Olson, 1970). Whether an action makes a temporary impact or leads to lasting change depends on the power that has accrued to the one engaging in the behavior from any or all of the sources from which power is derived: (1) society, or the external system; (2) the particular family's history and tradition of power allocation and dominance; and (3) the specific family unit's equilibrium and need for survival and system maintenance at the given time (Stanton, 1981).

In the Palo Alto group, Haley helped interweave ideas from communications and cybernetic systems theory. He was also intrigued by Milton Erickson's innovative use of hypnotic and unorthodox, metacognitive therapeutic techniques. Out of these streams, he fashioned his *Strategies of Psychotherapy* (1963), and his pioneering work has been labeled *strategic family therapy*. In the section on structural family therapy, his collaboration with Minuchin in Philadelphia is discussed. This phase partially ended when Haley and Madanes left the Child Guidance Clinic in Philadelphia in the late 1970s to found the Family Therapy Institute of Washington, D.C., where strategic family therapy is taught and practiced.

Another bastion of strategic family therapy is in Texas. There, Robert MacGregor, Harry Goolishian, Alberto Serrano, and their colleagues charted the path in devising multiple-impact family therapy (Beels & Ferber, 1972, pp. 179–180, 184), bringing families who lived a distance from their therapy center into the area for several days of marathon treatment by a high-powered team. They recognized that potent strategic maneuvers were necessary to dislodge existing rigid patterns and structures. Later Goolishian and Dell, like Haley, were attracted to the use of paradoxes and metaphors. In the late 1970s, the Galveston Family Institute emerged as a training and treatment site for this particular theory and methodology. In the early 1980s, the Galveston group became very involved in the new epistemology, cybernetics, recursiveness, and the work of Humberto Maturano (Dell, 1981; Maturano, 1975).

The Milan group, headed by Mara Selvini-Palazzoli, has become internationally acclaimed by strategic-systemic theoreticians and clinicians. Palazzoli, a psychiatrist who traveled from Italy to study in the United States, came into contact with researchers and therapists at the MRI and the Philadelphia Child Guidance Clinic. Influenced by their ideas, she returned to Milan and tried out her notions on family systems, the treatment of disturbed children through brief therapy of their parents (Selvini-Palazzoli, Boscolo, Cecchin & Prata, 1974), the therapy of families with an anorectic child (1974), the role of the referring person in the therapy (1980), and the use of paradox (Selvini-Palazzoli, Cecchin, Prata, & Boscolo, 1978). The Milan group has devised new methods for treating families who live long distances from the clinic and can come for therapy only monthly (Selvini--Palazzoli, Boscolo, Cecchin, & Prata, 1978).

Subsequently, Selvini-Palazzoli returned to the United States, and her work made a major impact on some of the staff at the Ackerman Institute, among them, Lynn Hoffman, whose early work with Haley (Haley & Hoffman, 1967) ran in a similar vein. Other Americans have also been incorporating ideas and techniques derived from the Milan group into their practice, particularly the use of the therapeutic team observing behind the one-way screen and serving as colleagues of and consultants to the therapist in formulating the systemic hypothesis and shaping the prescription to be given or sent in telegram form to the patient's family. The influence of the Milan contingent is also substantial throughout Europe (see the July 1981 special international issue of *Journal of Marital and Family Therapy,* which many of the European contributors liberally credit the work of the Milan group as being seminal to their current thinking and practice) and apparently is deemed applicable to many families on the Continent. More recently, Selvini-Palazzoli has been working with *ritualized prescriptions* for schizophrenic families.

Also in Italy, there is a Family Institute in Rome under the leadership of Maurizio Andolfi. He calls his interventive mode "provocative therapy," and its major divergence from the other systemic-strategic approaches is that he confronts the patients early in the session, literally provoking a strong reaction to unfreeze the existing dynamics and structure, while the others are more apt to wait until later in the session or even until after the session to provoke the upheaval (Andolfi, 1979).

In strategic therapy, the clinician initiates what occurs in treatment and tailors a particular approach to each problem. The therapist overtly assumes the responsibility for influencing the patients; further, he or she attempts to maximize his or her power in order to effect change.

The causal sequence within the family system is believed to be nonlinear and complex. Family system change is perceived to be essential as a forerunner to individual change. A vicious cycle occurs when misdirected efforts to improve a problem situation lead instead to a worsening of the difficulty. Haley (1973) stated that a symptom, which serves as a communicative act and brings about contact between two or more people in the family unit, generally appears when an individual is "in an impossible situation and is trying to break out of it" (p. 44). Symptom formation usually occurs at transitional points in the family's life cycle when the task is not mastered well and a crisis ensues. Someone's development becomes fixated or "stuck," and the symptom evolves as an expression of the unresolved crisis. Strategic therapists believe that all mental and psychosomatic illnesses can be treated by their methodologies.

The Therapist and the Family in Treatment. The adherents of strategic therapy seek to perfect techniques that work, even if they do not appear logical to the family or to observers. They are pragmatic and symptom-focused; their approach is primarily a behaviorally oriented one in which insight and awareness are not deemed to be essential for change to occur. Perceptions and subjective feelings are seen more as dependent than as independent variables because these change when alterations in interpersonal relationships take place. Because the repetitive, dysfunctional behavioral sequences and transactions occur in the present and are being perpetuated by continuing, current behavior, modification of them dictates intervention in the present system and not consideration of past events and emotions (Stanton, 1981). The therapist must therefore take deliberate, forceful steps to change enough facets of the repetitive pattern so that the symptom will no longer be needed and will wither away.

Diagnosis is based on the observations gleaned when an intervention is made and the family members' reactions are noted. How they relate to each other becomes clear in the session, and the therapist not only constructs specific questions to draw out patterned responses but also comments on what the family members do. In terms of process and efficiency, the conceptualization is that every therapeutic move has diagnostic value, and every diagnostic interpretation has therapeutic potential. Traditional diagnostic labeling is avoided so as not to reinforce the individual's pathology or the family's identification of one member as the patient.

In strategic therapy à la Haley, the focus is usually kept on the index patient and his or her problem until it is worked through, going with rather than against the family's definition of the perplexing situation. Once this is successfully accomplished, additional dilemmas that have surfaced may be tackled. By having enabled the family to achieve their original problem resolution, the therapist gains their confidence and augments his or her power and leverage for further interventions. All problems are articulated in a form that makes them solvable, and agreement on an acceptable objective and measurable aim is sought early.

Here, as in behavior therapy, the major therapeutic tools are tasks and directives. These are predicated on the data derived earlier so that they are on target and lead to structural change. Although part of the session may be devoted to discussing how the assignment is to be carried out, the actual doing is programmed to occur between sessions, so that the beneficial effects of treatment spill over into the external real-life world. If the problem behavior is deeply entrenched and chronically pervasive, as in a psychosomatic disorder, emphasis may be placed more on the management of the symptom than on the problem itself. The aim is to bring the parental disagreement out into the open where it can be dealt with, so that the parents can cooperate to make the child behave better, despite his or her affliction.

A core premise here is that therapeutic change comes about when new interactional modes are triggered by the therapist's direct and active interventions in the family system (Haley, 1971, p. 7). The therapist endeavors to replace the repetitious, dysfunctional behavior and communication patterns with new, healthier ways of communicating and acting. In terms of logical levels, strategic therapists differentiate between *first-order change*, which is allowable because it entails only superficial modifications that do not change the system or its members in a significant way, and *second-order change*,

which results from major modifications in the interaction and transaction patterns. It is this second-order change that the strategic theorists deem essential to a successful therapeutic outcome (Watzlawick *et al.*, 1974).

Second-order change may be brought about through different approaches, often employed in conjunction with one another, as appropriate. Used singly, these approaches may not be potent enough to penetrate and dislodge the rigidly maintained homeostasis. Several are briefly described here by way of illustration.

The therapist may engage in *symptom prescription*, suggesting that the symptomatic behavior should be increased rather than attempting to alleviate it. In so doing, the therapist is apparently sanctioning the behavior that others have considered undesirable. Thus, the therapist does not arouse resistance from the identified patient, who does not need to defend his or her right to maintain the problem behavior. By recommending exacerbation of the symptom, the therapist intends to intensify it to a pitch where it will crumble. Also, if the person can deliberately make the symptom more severe, the therapist acquires leverage to point out that, as he or she can control the behavior by increasing it, then he or she can also exercise control to decrease it.

There is frequent use of *paradoxical instructions*, the framing of therapeutic double binds. Whichever half of the contradictory message the patient chooses to follow will engage her or him in some aspect of improvement. A directive that seems to go counter to the desired goals is, in fact, used to propel the patient toward it. In effect, once the problem is clearly defined, definite goals have been set, and the paradoxical instructions have been given, the responses are observed and the therapist continues to encourage the customary behavior (symptom prescription), thus ruling out "rebellious improvement." The therapist then expresses bewilderment at the changes that occur, refusing to take credit for them. Haley posited (1963) that the basic rule seemed to be to encourage the symptom in such a way that it is no longer of any use to the patient. The Milan group formulates a paradoxical prescription that involves the entire family in its execution.

Reframing is another favorite technique. By taking behaviors that have been criticized as crazy or disturbed and relabeling them positively, the therapist introduces a new view of reality. For instance, an acting-out, belligerent adolescent may be relabeled the family savior; his or her behavior is interpreted as a marvelous sacrifice in the service of holding the parents' marriage together, as the only time they agree and act in consort is when the adolescent gets into trouble. The symptom/problem is developed to avert a more devastating problem from erupting. The family is maneuvered into being grateful rather than critical or is forced to begin to resolve the underlying marital conflict.

Palazzoli and her colleagues (Selvini-Palazzoli, Boscolo, Cecchin, & Prata, 1978) generally do not work in cotherapy pairs. Instead, they often use the "Greek chourus," a group of observers in an adjoining room, who may call the therapist out and make suggestions or "take sides" or may participate in a postsession deliberation about what the written prescription should contain when it is sent. To address the conflicting pulls to change and yet remain the same—the team may frame and deliver a "split message"—each side advocating a different course of action.

It remains for research to document the effectiveness of these dramatic, sometimes startling, and generally "catchy" techniques.

Behavioral and Problem-Solving Therapies

Theoretical Development. The behavioral approach is predicated on a great amount of research done on human as well as animal behavior, carried out in both the laboratory and natural settings. Currently, this approach, specifying concrete, observable behaviors, is being applied in the treatment of both couples (Jacobson & Margolin, 1979) and families, having been expanded from the traditional individual approach to behavioral treatment (Bandura, 1969). A behaviorist attempts to look at behavior in relation to the environment, which, in turn, leads to the definition of a cause or causes associated with the presenting problem. The behavior therapist is concerned with (1) environmental events that precipitate certain behaviors, acting as a stimulant, and (2) the events that follow behavior and serve to reinforce it, thereby increasing the likelihood of its recurrence. Both operant conditioning à la Skinner (1953) and respondent or classical conditioning à la Pavlov (1941) are used in the assessment and treatment of marital and family problems.

This model in its present form is no longer based just on experimental psychology; it has expanded to the application of experimentally based principles of social and cognitive theory as well. It is both a cross-sectional model, describing the interactions of a couple or a family in reinforcement terms, and a longitudinal, developmental model that attempts to describe the antecedents to behavior and interactional patterns (Jacobson & Margolin, 1979). For this reason, we have subsumed the social-learning, cognitive-behavioral (Beck, 1976), and rational-emotive (Ellis & Grieger, 1977) theories and therapies under the larger rubric of behavioral theory and therapy.

Most behavioral therapists involved in treating couples or families acknowledge the systems concept, emphasizing the interdependent nature of the behavior patterns between a couple or among family members. Liberman (1970) carried this systems approach to the point of making home visits and involving other components of the family system in treatment, including community members and school personnel. He believes it is misleading to regard one person's behavior as the cause of another's behavior, without considering the reciprocal contribution made by the other person. People maintain each others' behavior through reinforcement. Control is therefore a circular or reciprocal process.

Behavior therapists stress the learning or relearning of ways to relate. Lieberman's "contingency contracting" (1970) seeks to influence behavior by changing the basis for a family's concern and acknowledgment from the patient's maladaptive behavior to that which is desired and adaptive. In addition to contigency contracting, therapists focus on training in communicational skills and the application of reinforcement principles to increase positive relational behavior (Jacobson & Margolin, 1979). Stuart's operant-interpersonal therapy (1969) operates on a similar premise, a quid pro quo, the notion that you must give something in order to get something.

It would be inaccurate, however, to view this school as just a discipline involved in applying techniques. It is grounded in the premise that individuals have diverse, *unique* learning histories; therefore, a rigid "cookbook" application of techniques is not advocated or sanctioned. Rather, principles derived from experimentation are applied in clinical situations, so that behavioral therapy is both a method of inquiry into clinical problems and a body of intervention strategies. The process of assessment, as well as the execution of the strategy, is vital to successful treatment.

In addition to the analysis of problems and the application of behavioral principles to treatment, some behaviorists stress the establishment of a positive working alliance with the couple or family (Liberman, 1970). Without such an alliance, they believe, little or no success can be realized. This recognition of the import of the therapist–client relationship is a departure from the traditional behavioral approach, promulgated by Skinner (1953), Wolpe (1958), and other narrow-band behaviorists who minimized the need for a therapeutic alliance and seemed to suggest that gains were accrued from the interventions *per se* and that therapists who followed similar procedures were interchangeable.

It is difficult to decide just where to classify the approach developed by Epstein, Bishop, and Levin (1978) and their colleagues. This approach, originally called the *McMaster model*, is now frequently labeled the *problem-solving model*, apparently because the core group of proponents have left McMaster Hospital in Canada:

The model utilizes a general systems theory approach to describe the structure, organization and transactional patterns of the family unit. It allows examination of families along the total spectrum ranging from healthy to severely pathological in their functioning. (Epstein *et al.*, 1978, p. 19)

The conceptual framework was first published under the title "The Family Categories Schema" (Epstein, Segal, & Rakoff, 1962). It was predicated on a study of 110 nonclinical families. It continues to undergo revisions based on research and clinical experience.

The McMaster model addresses itself to the following family dimensions: problem solving, communication, roles, affective responsiveness, affective involvement, and behavioral control. It outlines a procedure to use in dealing with each dimension. As the main thrust is toward problem solving geared to better behavioral control and functioning, this aspect will be described. The model includes a sequential listing of the stages in the process:

(1) Identification of the problem, (2) Communication of the problem to appropriate resources within or outside of the family, (3) Development of alternative action plans, (4) Decision regarding a suitable action, (5) Action, (6) Monitoring that action which is taken, (7) Evaluation of the success of the action. (Epstein *et al.,* 1978, p. 22)

Problems are subdivided into affective and instrumental ones, a useful distinction for the task at hand.

It may be in the seventh stage that this model differs most from other approaches and contributes an aspect worthy of incorporation where it is not incompatible, as it might be with systemic-strategic therapy. In this problem-solving paradigm, the patients are guided to evaluate the success of their efforts, reviewing what has transpired in order to learn when appropriate problem-solving behaviors have occurred and which approaches have proved most successful. They discover that chaotic behavioral control is least effective and flexible behavioral control is most effective.

Given the emphasis on clarity of procedures, specific sequential stages to be followed, here-and-now activity and resolution, and behavioral change as the goal, rather than the development of insight and change in feelings, this approach seems to best fall under the behavioral rubric.

The Family and the Therapist in Treatment. A family or couple enter treatment locked into a pattern of interaction that does not seem to be meeting their respective needs and that is usually marked by the use of self-defeating control or power maneuvers by various family members. For example, a husband may withhold money from his wife until she performs the desired behavior, or parents may deal with undesirable behavior, such as a child's acting out, by covertly conveying that it is acceptable, although overtly they criticize it or think they are being punitive. The respondent may interpret the punishment as rewarding, in that he or she is deriving much-desired parental attention because of the behavior. The attention serves as a reinforcer rather than a deterrent.

Central to this theory is the tenet that these patterns and all other recurring behaviors are rewarded in some manner or else they would not be repeated. The couple or the family need to be presented with more desirable alternatives and taught the contingencies through which they can obtain more satisfying behavior in their relationships.

The therapist does not assign a "sick" role to any member. In a relational context, all members contribute to the system of relating and, therefore, to each other's behavior. In the treatment context, the behavior therapist does not blame the patient for lack of change. He or she has the responsibility of designing effective interventions. The patient is always right (Liberman, 1970). The therapist has two vital preliminary tasks: making an accurate, functional assessment of the presenting problem and establishing a therapeutic alliance, that is, communicating genuineness, empathy, and warmth to the family or the couple.

The behavior therapist follows several themes when working with a family or a couple. These cut across different strategies and are presented here to give a sense of unity to the behavioral approaches, which may sometimes seem to be dissimilar because of the specific techniques that are emphasized.

Positive teaching refers to the therpist's efforts to emphasize the positive aspects of the particular relational system. Throughout the course of treatment, strengths are identified, and strategies are designed to complement and build on these. This goal can often be achieved by differentiating between the act and the intention of the act. Family members and spouses seem always to assume the worst intentions for offending behaviors. A positive interpretation of the act by the therapist is often helpful in that it provides the other members with a new, less critical perspective. An adolescent's delinquent behavior may be *reframed* as a sacrificial cry for help for the parents' poor marital relationship, rather than being interpreted as meant to hurt or embarrass the family members.

The therapist is also attempting to replace aversive control contingencies with *positive control strategies,* emphasizing an increase in positive, desirable behavior rather than focusing on decreasing undesirable behaviors. This is a subtle but important point to emphasize. In most dysfunctional relationships, people try to get what they want through the use of aversive stimuli, including threats, punishment, and the withholding of rewards. Such contingencies may work for a short while, but eventually such behavior is reciprocated, and as these aversive strategies begin to dominate, the satisfactions derived from the relationship plummet (Jacobson & Margolin, 1979). Thus, it is important for the therapist to emphasize change through the use of positive reinforcement rather than punishment or negative reinforcement. *Shaping* plays a key role in this task, that is, rapidly reinforcing successive approximations of the desired behavior. Expectations of quick, sweeping changes are unrealistic. Modification of the patients' expectations tends to lead toward a more lasting change.

The concept of *reciprocity* is integral to the behavioral approach. Communication training, *contingency contracting,* and problem-solving strategies depend on the clients' ability to understand the reciprocal nature of relationships. Often, people view themselves as victims of situations or other people's behavior. Therefore, they accept virtually no responsibility for what transpires or for attempting to improve matters. As they acquire an understanding of reciprocity, they begin to realize that they do possess power and influence that can be used to bring about change in a relationship. Hopelessness can be transformed into realistic optimism if the therapist is able to demonstrate to each person her or his role (and power) in the maintainance of undesirable behavior and, conversely, her or his ability to unlearn these behaviors and to replace them with more satisfying ones.

Finally, the therapist acts as a teacher, aiding the family or the couple in learning new modes of relating and generalizing what they learn to the extratherapeutic context. Relational skills and concepts are taught not only to solve the presenting problem but to prevent future crises, endowing the family with new skills and enhancing their problem-solving capabilities. The therapist may educate through *modeling, didactic training sessions, reading assignments,* and other specific *homework tasks.* Behavioral therapy is clearly distinguished from other schools by this educational and skills-training emphasis. Strategic therapists, for example, put the burden of change on the family and do not assume a position of teaching. The contextual model sees the therapist as playing the role of catalyst; that is, he or she functions as a resource for mobilizing the trust-building capacity within the family (Boszormenyi-Nagy & Spark, 1973).

Behavioral therapy has been widely applied to marital problems, as well as in family therapy. Paterson (1971), for example, emphasized teaching parents behavioral management skills and encouraging them to take control. Liberman's contingency contracting approach (1970) has been applied primarily to marital problems. Jacobson and Margolin (1979) focused on using social learning therapy and behavior exchange principles in marital therapy. This mode of therapy continues to grow in popularity, largely because of the clearly delineated, widely applicable techniques that have evolved from and continue to be generated from research on human relational behavior. It is a model that lends itself well to psychotherapy outcome research because the presenting symptom is what is treated and specific changes are desired. These tend to be observable, and indices for measurement can be decided on. Because of the specificity of the techniques, replication studies are more feasible than they are likely to be when one uses a psychoanalytic or a Bowenian model.

Toward an Integration of Concepts: A Current and Future Perspective

A brief history of marital and family therapy has been presented. It was (selectively) culled from (1) a review of the literature; (2) my conversations with leaders in the field; and (3) my personal immersion in the field for several decades as a teacher, a therapist, an author, an editor of one of the major journals, a guest lecturer, and a workshop leader throughout the United States and many countries of the world, including Canada, Mexico, Japan, Israel, Norway, and South Africa. As one works with families in many lands, interviewing them to demonstrate theory in action through technique and process, and trains professionals working in various countries with seemingly extremely diverse populations, a multicultural perspective evolves. It is essential to recognize and respect the

uniqueness and idiosyncratic rules, myths, symptoms, and structural forms that characterize different ethnic, racial, religious, class, cultural, and subcultural groups. It is equally necessary not to overgeneralize; not all families within a group are represented by the prototypical profile. Each society generates families that are dysfunctional, midrange, and healthy; in each, flexibility, differentiation of the self, a sense of belonging, and coping skills are vital for effective and reasonably content functioning.

Along with the uniquenesses, one also is struck by the profound similarities: the universals of humankind such as the desire for security and continuity, love and affection; respect for oneself and of one's significant others; a sense of relatedness to one's family and the larger society; freedom from poverty, war, and extreme personal and familial anxiety and tension; a position as a contributing member of one's world; and optimism about the future. The ability to perceive, understand, and appreciate both the uniquenesses and the similarities among very different families, using a multicultural perspective, is an absolute must for the teacher/therapist who attempts to treat couples and families and to train other clinicians to do so.

However, although such a perspective is necessary, it is not sufficient. One must also be soundly grounded in theory—both theory of marital and family functioning and theory of therapy and the techniques and processes through which the therapeutic interventions occur, for this is the scientific aspect of the field.

For a body of knowledge to be worthy of the appellation *theory,* it must contain all of the following elements:

1. Explanatory power regarding the *etiology* of the symptom, disorder, or dysfunction.
2. Methodology and vocabulary for *diagnostic* assessment of the malady or problem, be it of the identified patient, or of the couple or family system, or both.
3. A system for intervening to bring about the desired changes, some format or mapping of the *therapeutic process* during the beginning, middle, and ending phases of therapy, and for any needed follow-up. This system includes a firm grasp of the vital ingredients for bringing about positive change, growth, and healing.
4. *Prognostic power,* that is, tools and concepts for predicting outcomes.
5. *Evaluative potential;* that is, it must lend itself to being evaluated through psychotherapy process and outcome research.
6. *Preventive capability;* that is, because of the changes wrought in the therapy, a more wholesome environment should be produced, and the children should grow up to be emotionally healthier and capable of creating less symptomatic, disturbed families. Also, principles derived from studying healthy families (Kaslow, 1980d; Lewis *et al.,* 1976), as

well as from treating distressed families, can be taught in family-life education courses and marriage encounter groups and therefore fall under the *prevention* rubric.

Given that the field of marital therapy is just 56 years old, that the younger field of family therapy has been in existence only slightly over 36 years, and that the amalgamation of these two as a separate discipline is still incomplete, it is not surprising that few, if any, of the schools of thought presented contain all of the elements integral to a conceptual schema that merits consideration as a complete or grand theory. Yet, all of the schools have made a sufficient contribution to the development of the field to warrant inclusion, and it is anticipated that, during the 1980s, as Olsen and his colleagues (Olsen *et al.*, 1980) have said so well, the field will exhibit more intellectual and scientific rigor in the pursuit of theory development and conceptual clarity.

An Integrative, Diaclectic, or Multimodal Model

I have tried in the foregoing discussion to highlight the commonalities and to contrast the differences in the various schools of thought. It is apparent that, during the infancy and adolescence of the field, the separateness of the schools contributed to its richness and have made it a multihued tapestry. Continued sharpening of the differences is certainly being advocated and encouraged.

However, a parallel development also began to emerge in the late 1970s as a few theoretician/therapists realized that the pioneers who had had the audacity and courage to depart from the analytic tradition had now created their own orthodoxies, and that many of their former students had become doctrinaire purists, slavishly adhering to their master's teachings rather than continuing to refine these and to use them creatively. Also, unflinching devotion to their way as the only right way by "disciples" of each school has led to the kind of divisiveness, fragmentation, and argumentative conflict in the field typical of unhealthy families, rather than to the clear boundaries accompanied by open and continuous interchanges and the room for disagreement characteristic of healthy families (Beavers, 1977).

Therefore, some of today's leaders have begun to search for the basic premises common to all schools. These were elucidated earlier in this chapter. The pursuit of a synthesis of the various notions, nomenclature, partial theories, techniques, and strategies has been attempted in an effort to distill the essence of each school. In so doing, these critics of atrophy hope to add renewed vigor to the field by setting creative individuals free to choose the theory of family dynamics and functioning that has the best explanatory power for a given family and to draw from a broad-based knowledge of process and technique those strategies that are likely to bring about the desired change most rapidly and effectively.

This line of reasoning is reflected in the experiential school described earlier. It is also the crux of the *integrative family therapy* being practiced and taught by Fred and Bunny Duhl, currently codirectors of the Boston Family Institute. They lucidly described "structured spontaneity" as the crux of the "thoughful art of integrative family therapy" (Duhl & Duhl, 1979). They use metaphors, sculpting, home visits, and play therapy. They speak of doing metatherapy and drawing from "anthropology, linguistics, education, developmental psychology, as well as general systems and family therapy" (p. 61). They seek to train therapists who "will be free to integrate all their own skills, experiences and personal history with metatheory, and an ethical approach to strategies, techniques and tactics of therapy." They want their trainees to become "proactive in the discovery of theory and techniques, and to be free to risk trying the new as well as to risk repeating the old" (pp. 59–76).

Arnold Lazarus's *multimodal therapy* (1976) flows from a similar penchant for using theoretical interpretations and interventions drawn from various approaches; in the past decade he has begun to refer to his *modus operandi* as "systematic eclecticism," a designation selected to differentiate his brand of treatment from a hit-or-miss eclecticism based only on playing hunches, doing whatever strikes one's fancy, and not having a sufficient base in theory to be soundly grounded.

My own activities and thinking have followed a route similar to that taken by the Duhls. I have called it a *diaclectic approach* (Kaslow, 1980b,c). *Diaclectic* is a word blended to designate the seeking of the *dialectic* synthesis between two seemingly opposite approaches (the thesis and the antithesis) and of the *eclectic* in what seems appropriate, pragmatic, dramatic, soothing, or unsettling, in accordance with the needs of the specific family and what appears to contain the best potential for resolution of the current trouble and the deep-seated unhappiness and inner turbulence. One can use a psychodynamic understanding of the individual and of the family's developmental cycle and incomplete transitions, and one can see these within the context of the family's multigenerational history and legacy. One might decide to intervene by sculpting, by using paradox or symptom prescription, by a task assignment, or through family art therapy. What is selected comes from a simultaneous intuitive and cognitive response to both the family's primary-process thought and their secondary-process rational behavior and communications. The therapist's pace is attuned to the family's rhythm.

Judicious selection from what is known, predicated on what is likely to prove most effective is a hallmark of adult behavior and of the maturation of a professional field. Because strict adherence to any one model or the attempt to duplicate someone else's style can imprison the therapist and limit the possibility of a successful outcome, it is reasoned that an integrative, diaclectic approach that permits the clinician the greatest authenticity and freedom born of discipline should also stimulate these qualities in the patients. This approach springs from a flexible, open systems paradigm that enables all parties in the therapeutic encounter to remain dynamic, growing, and nondogmatic. It veers away from narrow, absolutist formulations and is pragmatically concerned with what works, that is, what brings about progress in therapy and living.

In 1974, Lunde considered criticisms of therapeutic eclecticism. These include that such an approach is opportunistic, fragmentary, and piecemeal; that it glosses over irreconcilable differences and mutually exclusive viewpoints; and that it includes contradictory positions within a model. Others charge that eclecticism is vague, indecisive, and geared to expediency, and that it does not lend itself to replication and evaluation. Certainly, these criticisms may be true, but they are not necessarily so, as these qualities are not inherent in eclecticism *per se.* Lunde (1974, p. 382) concluded that the greatest benefits lie in seeking to maintain an open mind, in finding the element(s) of truth in each theory, and in remaining skeptical about unproven facts.

In Figures 1 and 2, the integrative, diaclectic model has been drawn as overarching because it seeks an orderly combination of the compatible elements of various systems. At its best, diaclecticism is not a conglomeration of incongruent theories and conflicting concepts of health, dysfunction, and change, but a challenging approach that promotes judicious and appropriate selectivity and continued creativity. With the great advances in the various wings of the field that marked the 1970s, I believe that the major parallel trends of the 1980s are—and should be—expansion and clarification within each school of theory and therapy *and* ongoing efforts to integrate their compatible aspects in a systematic and rational manner.

ACKNOWLEDGMENTS

Appreciation is expressed to Gregory Soehner for his assistance in the preliminary work on this chapter.

References

Ackerman, N. The unity of the family. *Archives of Pediatrics,* 1938, *55*(1), 51–62.

American Association for Marital and Family Therapy (AAMFT). *Membership Brochure,* Washington, D.C., 1983.

American Association of Marriage and Family Counselors (AAMFC). *Membership Brochure,* Clarmont, Calif. 1976.

Andolfi, M. A structural approach to a family with an encopretic child. *Journal of Marriage and Family Counseling,* January 1978, *4*(1), 25–30.

Andolfi, M. *Family therapy: An interactional approach.* New York: Plenum Press, 1979.

Bandura, A. *Principles of behavior modification.* New York: Holt, Rinehart & Winston, 1969.

Bateson, G., Jackson, D. D., Haley, J., & Weakland, J. Towards a theory of schizophrenia. *Behavioral Science,* 1956, *1,* 251–264.

Beavers, W. R. *Psychotherapy and growth: A family systems perspective.* New York: Brunner/Mazel, 1977.

Beck, A. T. *Cognitive therapy and the emotional disorders.* New York: International Universities Press, 1976.

Beels, C., & Ferber, A. What family therapists do. In A. Ferber, M.

Mendelsohn, & A. Napier (Eds.), *The book of family therapy.* New York: Science House, 1972.

Berger, M. M. *Beyond the double bind.* New York: Brunner/Mazel, 1978.

Boszormenyi-Nagy, I. Contextual therapy: Theraputic leverages in mobilizing trust. In I. Zwerling (Ed.), *The American family* (Report No. 2). Philadelphia: Smith, Kline, & French, 1979.

Boszormenyi-Nagy, I., & Framo, J. L. *Intensive family therapy.* New York: Harper & Row, 1965.

Boszormenyi-Nagy, I., & Spark, G. M. *Invisible loyalties: Reciprocity in intergenerational family therapy.* New York: Harper & Row, 1973.

Bowen, M. Toward the differentiation of a self in one's family of origin. In F. Andres & J. Lorio (Eds.), *Georgetown Family Symposium Papers, I.* Washington, D.C.: Georgetown University Press, 1974.

Bowen, M. Theory in the practice of psychotherapy. In P. J. Guerin (Ed.), *Family therapy: Theory and practice.* New York: Gardner Press, 1976.

Bowen, M. *Family therapy in clinical practice.* New York: Jason Aronson, 1978.

Colapinto, J. The relative value of empirical evidence. *Family Process,* 1979, *18,* 427–441.

Constantine, L. L. Family sculpture and relationship mapping techniques. *Journal of Marriage and Family Counseling,* April 1978, *4*(2), 13–24.

Dell, P. Paradox redux. *Journal of Marital and Family Therapy,* April 1981, *7*(2), 127–134.

Duhl, F. J., & Duhl, B. S. Structured spontaneity: The thoughtful art of integrative family therapy at BFI. *Journal of Marital and Family Therapy,* July 1979, *5*(3), 59–76.

Duhl, F., Kantor, D., & Duhl, B. Learning, space and action in family therapy. In D. Bloch (Ed.), *Techniques of psychotherapy: A primer.* New York: Grune & Stratton, 1973.

Ellis, A., & Grieger, R. (Eds.). *Handbook of rational emotive therapy.* New York: Springer, 1977.

Epstein, N. B., Segal, J. J., & Rakoff, V. *Family categories schema.* Unpublished manuscript. Presented by authors in Family Research Group, Department of Psychiatry, Jewish General Hospital, Canada, 1962.

Epstein, N. B., Bishop, D. S., & Levin, S. The McMaster model of family functioning. *Journal of Marital and Family Counseling,* 1978, *4*(4), 19–31.

Fairbairn, R. *Object relations theory of personality.* New York: Basic Books, 1952.

Fogarty, T. Systems concepts and the dimensions of self. In P. J. Guerin (Ed.), *Family therapy: Theory and practice.* New York: Gardner Press, 1976.

Framo, J. Family theory and therapy. *American Psychologist,* 1979, *34,* 988–992.

Goldenberg, I., & Goldenberg, H. *Family therapy: An overview.* Belmont, Calif.: Wadsworth, 1980.

Goldstein, J., Freud, A., & Solnit, A. J. *Beyond the best interests of the child.* New York: Free Press, 1973.

Guerin, P. J. Family therapy: The first twenty five years. In P. J. Guerin (Ed.), *Family therapy: Theory and practice.* New York: Gardner Press, 1976.

Guerin, P. J., & Fogarty, T. Study your own family. In A. Ferber, M. Mendelsohn, & A. Y. Napier (Eds.), *The book of family therapy.* New York: Science House, 1972.

Guerin, P. J., & Guerin, K. B. Theoretical aspects and clinical relevance of the multi-generational model of family therapy. In P. J. Guerin (Ed.), *Family therapy: Theory and practice.* New York: Gardner Press, 1976.

Gurman, A. S. Dimensions of marital therapy: A comparative analysis. *Journal of Marital and Family Therapy,* January 1979, *5*(1), 5–18.

Gurman, A. S., & Kniskern, D. P. Research on marital and family therapy: Progress, perspective and prospect. In S. L. Garfield & A. E.

Bergin (Eds.), *Handbook of psychotherapy and behavior change: An empirical analysis* (2nd ed.). New York: Wiley, 1979.

Haley, J. *Strategies of psychotherapy.* New York: Grune & Stratton, 1963.

Haley, J. *Changing families.* New York: Grune & Stratton, 1971.

Haley, J. *Uncommon therapy: The psychiatric techniques of Milton H. Erickson.* New York: Norton, 1973.

Haley, J., & Hoffman, L. *Techniques of family therapy.* New York: Basic Books, 1967.

Jackson, D. D. Family interaction, family homeostasis and some implications for conjoint family psychotherapy. In J. H. Masserman (Ed.), *Science and psychoanalysis: Individual and familial dynamics.* New York: Grune & Stratton, 1959.

Jackson, D. D., & Satir, V. A review of psychiatric developments in family diagnosis and therapy. In N. W. Ackerman, F. L. Beatmen, & S. N. Sherman (Eds.), *Exploring the base of family therapy.* New York: Family Service Association of America, 1961.

Jackson, D. D., & Weakland, J. H. Conjoint family therapy: Some considerations on theory, technique and results. *Psychiatry,* 1961, *24,* 30–45.

Jacobson, N., & Margolin, G. *Marital therapy: Strategies based on social learning and behavior exchange principles.* New York: Brunner/Mazel, 1979.

Kaslow, F. W. Training of marital and family therapists. In F. W. Kaslow (Ed.), *Supervision, consultation and staff training in the helping professions.* San Francisco: Jossey-Bass, 1977.

Kaslow, F. W. Divorce and divorce therapy. In A. Gurman & D. Kniskern (Eds.), *Handbook of family therapy.* New York: Brunner/Mazel, 1980. (a)

Kaslow, F. W. History of family therapy in the United States: A kaleidoscopic overview. *Marriage and Family Review,* 1980, *3*(1/2), 77–111. (b)

Kaslow, F. W. Profile of the healthy family. *Focus pa Familien* (Norwegian Journal of Family Therapy), 1980. (c); *The relationship,* 1982, *8*(1), 9–24.

Kaslow, F. W. Stages in the divorce process: A psycholegal perspective. *Villanova Law Review,* 1980, *25*(4/5), 718–751. (d)

Kaslow, F. W. A dialetic approach to family therapy and practice: Selectivity and synthesis. *Journal of Marital and Family Therapy,* July 1981(a), *7*(3), 345–351.

Kaslow, F. W. Involving the peripheral father. In A. Gurman (Ed.), *Questions and answers in the practice of family therapy* (Vol. 1). New York: Brunner/Mazel, 1981. (b)

Kaslow, F. W., Cooper, B., & Linsenberg, M. Therapist authenticity: A key factor in family therapy effectiveness. *International Journal of Family Therapy,* Summer 1979, *1*(2), 184–199.

Keith, D. V., & Whitaker, C. A. Struggling with the impotence impasse: Absurdity and acting-in. *Journal of Marriage and Family Counseling,* January 1978, *4*(1), 69–78.

Keith, D., & Whitaker, C. Play therapy: A paradigm for work with families. *Journal of Marital and Family Therapy,* July 1981, *6*(3), 243–254.

Kempler, W. Experiential psychotherapy with families. *Family Process,* 1968, *7,* 88–99.

Kempler, W. *Experiential psychotherapy within families.* New York: Brunner/Mazel, 1981.

Kuhn, T. *The structure of scientific revolutions.* Chicago: University of Chicago Press, 1962.

LaPerriere, K. Family therapy training at the Ackerman Institute: Thoughts of form and substance. *Journal of Marital and Family Therapy,* July 1979, *5*(3), 53–58.

La Perriere, K. AFTA—An evolving professional organization. *AFTA Newsletter,* Winter 1985, *22,* p.l.

Lazarus, A. *Multi-modal behavior therapy.* New York: Springer, 1976.

Lewis, J. M., Beavers, W. R., Gossett, J. T., & Phillips, V. A. *No single thread: Psychological health in family systems.* New York: Brunner/Mazel, 1976.

Liberman, R. Behavioral approaches to family and couple therapy. *American Journal of Orthopsychiatry,* 1970, *40,* 106–118.

Lunde, D. T. Eclectic and integrated theory: Gordon Allport and others. In A. Burton (Ed.), *Operational theories of personality,* New York: Brunner/Mazel, 1974.

Martin, P. A. *A marital therapy manual.* New York: Brunner/Mazel, 1976.

Maturana, H. R. The organization of living: A theory of living organizations. *International Journal of Man–Machine Studies,* 1975, *7,* 313–332.

McGoldrick, M., & Gerson, R. *Genograms in family assessment.* N.Y.: Norton, 1985.

Minuchin, S. *Families and family therapy.* Cambridge: Harvard University Press, 1974.

Minuchin, S. Structural family therapy: Activating alternatives within a therapeutic system. In I. Zwerling (Ed.), *The American family.* Philadelphia: Smith, Kline & French, 1978.

Minuchin, S., & Fishman, H. C. *Family therapy techniques.* Cambridge: Harvard University Press, 1981.

Minuchin, S., Montalvo, B., Guerney, B. G., Rosman, B., & Schumer, F. *Families of the slums: An exploration of their structure and treatment.* New York: Basic Books, 1967.

Minuchin, S., Rosman, B. L., & Baker, L. *Psychosomatic families: Anorexia nervosa in context.* Cambridge: Harvard University Press, 1978.

Mudd, E. H. *Marriage counseling and the related professions.* Paper presented at a meeting of the College of Physicians, Philadelphia, November 1974.

Napier, A. Y., with Whitaker, C. A. *The family crucible.* New York: Harper & Row, 1978.

Olson, D. H. Marital and family therapy: Integrative review and critique. *Journal of Marriage and the Family,* November 1970, *32*(4), 501–538.

Papp, P. Family choreography. In P. J. Guerin (Ed.), *Family therapy: Theory and practice.* New York: Gardner Press, 1976.

Parsons, T. *The social system.* Glencoe, Ill.: Free Press, 1951.

Patterson, G. *Families: Application of social learning to family life.* Champaign, Ill.: Research Press, 1971.

Pavlov, I. P., *Conditioned reflexes and psychiatry* (trans. by W. H. Gantt). New York: International Publications, 1941.

Rosenberg, J. B. Two is better than one: Use of behavioral techniques within a structured family therapy model. *Journal of Marriage and Family Counseling,* 1978, *4*(1), 31–40.

Ruesch, J., & Bateson, G. *Communication, the social matrix of psychiatry.* New York: W. W. Norton, 1951.

Sander, F. *Individual and family therapy: Toward an integration.* New York: Jason Aronson, 1979.

Satir, V. *Conjoint family therapy.* Palo Alto, Calif.: Science and Behavior Books, 1964. (Revised, 1967.)

Satir, V., Stachowiak, J., & Taskman, H. *Helping families to change.* New York: Jason Aronson, 1975.

Selvini-Palazzoli, M. *Self starvation: From the intrapsychic to the transpersonal approach to anorexia nervosa.* London: Chaucer, 1974.

Selvini-Palazzoli, M., Boscolo, L., Cecchin, G., & Prata, G. The treatment of children through brief therapy of their parents. *Family Process,* 1974, *13*(4),

Selvini-Palazzoli, M., Boscolo, L., Cecchin, G., & Prata, G. A ritualized prescription in family therapy. *Journal of Marital and Family Therapy,* July 1978, *4*(3), 3–9.

Selvini-Palazzoli, M., Cecchin, G., Prata, G., & Boscolo, L. *Paradox and counterparadox.* New York: Aronson, 1978.

Selvini-Palazzoli, M., Boscolo, L., Cecchin, G., & Prata, G. The problem of the referring person. *Journal of Marital and Family Therapy*, January 1980, *6*(1), 3–9.

Skinner, B. F. *Science and human behavior,* New York: Macmillan, 1953.

Skynner, A. C. R. *Systems of family and marital therapy.* New York: Brunner/Mazel, 1976.

Sprenkle, D. H., & Olson, D. H. L. Circumplex model of marital systems: An empirical study of clinic and nonclinic families. *Journal of Marriage and Family Counseling,* 1978, *4*(2), 59–74.

Stanton, M. D. An integrated structural/strategic approach to family and marital therapy. *Journal of Marital and Family Therapy,* 1981, *7*(4), 427–440.

Stierlin, H. *Psychoanalysis and family therapy.* New York: Jason Aronson, 1977.

Stuart, R. B. Behavioral contracting within the families of delinquents. *Journal of Behavior Therapy and Experimental Psychiatry,* 1971, *2,* 1–11.

Watzlawick, P., Weakland, J., & Fisch, R. *Change: Principles of problem formation and problem resolution.* New York: Norton, 1974.

Weakland, J. H. Family somatics: A neglected edge. *Family Process,* 1977, *16,* 263–272.

Whitaker, C. Psychotherapy of the absurd: With a special emphasis on the psychotherapy of aggression. *Family Process,* March 1975, *14*(1), 1–16.

Whitaker, C. The hindrance of theory in clinical work. In P. J. Guerin (Ed.), *Family therapy: Theory and practice.* New York: Gardner Press, 1976.

Whitaker, C. A., & Malone, T. P. *The roots of psychotherapy.* New York: Brunner/Mazel, 1981.

Wolpe, J. *Psychotherapy by reciprocal inhibition.* Stanford, Calif.: Stanford University Press, 1958.

Wynne, L., Ryckoff, I., Day, J., & Hirsch, S. H. Pseudo-mutuality in schizophrenia. *Psychiatry,* 1958, *21,* 205–220.

Zuk, G. H. *Family therapy: A triadic-based approach.* New York: Behavioral Publications, 1971.

Notes on Contributors

Vern L. Bengston is Director of the Andrus Center's Gerontology Research Institute and Professor of Sociology at the University of Southern California. His publications include *The Social Psychology of Aging; Youth, Generations, and Social Change* (edited with Robert Laufer); and *Grandparenthood* (edited with Joan Robertson). Dr. Bengston directs a longitudinal study of three-generational families at USC.

Pauline Boss is an Associate Professor in the Department of Family Social Science at the University of Minnesota. Her research and theoretical work focus on the effects of psychological absence of family members in intact corporate and military families and psychological presence in families in which members are dead or missing. Dr. Boss is completing a book on family stress.

Carol A. Darling, Associate Professor in the Department of Home and Family Life at Florida State University, has served as a member of the National Council of Family Relations' Committee on the Standards and Criteria for Certification of Family Life Educators. Dr. Darling has written a curriculum guide for family life education programs in public schools.

Robert T. Francoeur is Professor of Human Sexuality and Embryology in the Department of Biological and Allied Health Sciences at Fairleigh Dickinson University. Dr. Francoeur's research focuses on the impact of changing values and new technologies. Among his books are *Utopian Motherhood: New Trends in Human Reproduction; Eva's New Rib: 20 Faces of Sex, Marriage and Family; Hot and Cool Sex: Cultures in Conflict;* and *Becoming a Sexual Person.*

Frank F. Furstenberg, Jr., is Professor of Sociology at the University of Pennsylvania. His books include *Recycling the Family* (with Graham B. Spanier); *The New American Grandparent* (with Andrew Cherlin); and *Adolescent Mothers in Later Life* (with Jeanne Brooks-Gunn). Dr. Furstenberg is currently examining data from a national survey on the impact of marital disruption on child development.

Patricia A. Gongla is employed at the IBM Scientific Center in Los Angeles and also holds an appointment in the Department of Psychiatry and Biobehavioral Sciences at the University of California in Los Angeles. Dr. Gongla has conducted research related to the evaluation of organizational programs and the diagnosis of post-traumatic stress disorder.

Tamara K. Hareven is Professor of History and Director of the History of Family Program at Clark University and a Research Associate at the Center for Population Studies at Harvard University. Dr. Hareven's books include *Transitions: The Family and the Life Course in Historical Perspective; Amoskeag: Life and Work in an American Factory City* (with R. Langerbach); *Family Time and Industrial Time;* and *Aging and the Life Course: An Interdisciplinary and Cross-Cultural Perspective* (with K. Adams).

Susan Losh-Hesselbart is an Associate Professor of Sociology at Florida State University. Dr. Losh-Hesselbart is the author of articles on gender stereotypes, work and family roles, and gender and social change. She has served as the sociology editor for *Sex Roles: A Journal of Research* and is presently conducting an examination of the changes in gender ideology during the 1970s and 1980s.

Reuben Hill (deceased, 1985) was Regents' Professor at the Family Study Center of the University of Minnesota. Dr. Hill's research dealt with family problem solving and adjustment to crises in a series of studies on war separation and reunion, of family adjustments to rapid urbanization, of the planning and control of family size, and a three-generation longitudinal panel study of family decision making and timing in preplanning family consumption. His most recent research examined the critical transitions families experience over the family life cycle.

Sharon K. Houseknecht, Associate Professor of Sociology at Ohio State University, has published articles on voluntary childlessness and has edited a special issue of *Journal of Family Issues* on "Childlessness and the One-Child Family." Dr. Houseknecht is now doing research on career and family patterns of professional women.

Florence W. Kaslow is Director of the Florida Couples and Family Institute and an Adjunct Professor in the

Department of Psychiatry at Duke University Medical Center. Dr. Kaslow is a Diplomate in Clinical, Forensic, and Family Psychology. She is the author of *The International Book of Family Therapy; The Military Family: Diagnosis and Treatment;* and *Psychotherapy with Psychotherapists.*

David M. Klein is an Associate Professor of Sociology at the University of Notre Dame. Dr. Klein is the author of *Theories of Family Life.* His research interests include conflict management in marriage, family problem solving, the development of families over the life cycle, and the history of family sociology.

Lauren Langman is an Associate Professor of Sociology at Loyola University in Chicago. Much of Dr. Langman's research focuses on the effects of social class and cultural variations on socialization practices. Currently he is interested in the Frankfurt School of Critical Theory and the General Systems Theory.

Robert E. Larzelere is an Associate Professor in the Rosemead School of Psychology at Biola University. Dr. Larzelere's research interests include statistical procedures, trust in intimate relationships, parental discipline of toddlers, and conflicts between religion and the social sciences.

Gary R. Lee is Professor of Sociology and Rural Sociology at Washington State University. Dr. Lee is the author of *Family Structures and Interaction: A Comparative Analysis* and has also published numerous articles dealing with family structure from a cross-cultural perspective. He also conducts research in the area of social gerontology.

Lora Liss is a trial attorney at the San Antonio District Office of the U.S. Equal Employment Opportunity Commission. Dr. Liss holds a doctorate in sociology and has taught at Fairleigh Dickinson University. Her research interests encompass women's rights to property at divorce, women's legal history, and employment discrimination.

Eleanor D. Macklin is an Associate Professor and the Director of the Marriage and Family Therapy Program in the Department of Child, Family and Community Studies at Syracuse University. Dr. Macklin has published articles on nonmarital cohabitation and nontraditional family forms. She is the coeditor of *Contemporary Families and Alternative Lifestyles: Handbook of Research and Theory.*

Teresa Donati Marciano is Professor and Chair of Sociology in the Department of Sociology and Anthropology at Fairleigh Dickinson University. Dr. Marciano's recent publications include articles on "Families and Cults," in *Marriage and Family Review* and "Family Coalitions and Religious Observance after Divorce," in *Jewish Social Studies.* She is the coauthor of *Family and the Prospect of Nuclear Holocaust* (with Marvin B. Sussman).

Paul Mattessich is the Director of the Wilder Foundation's Office of Research and Statistics, an organization that specializes in studies related to human services for individuals and families. This organization received the 1983 Distinguished Contribution to Families Award from the Minnesota Council on Family Relations.

Brent C. Miller is a Professor in the Department of Family and Human Development at Utah State University. Dr. Miller has coedited three volumes of the *Family Studies Review Yearbook* (with David Olson); *Marriage and Family Development* (with Evelyn Duvall); and *Family Research Methods.* His current research interests are on the relationships between family variables and adolescent sexual behavior, pregnancy, and fertility.

Phyllis Moen is an Associate Professor of Human Development and Family Studies and Sociology at Cornell University. Dr. Moen's research has investigated policy-related issues involving the relationships between work and the family. Currently she is preparing a book on working parents in Sweden.

Marie Withers Osmond is an Associate Professor of Sociology at Florida State University. Dr. Osmond's major research interests and publications are in the areas of cross-societal family comparisons and the sociology of sex/gender. Her monograph, *Gender and Family Analysis,* is nearing completion.

Gary W. Peterson is an Associate Professor in the Department of Child and Family Studies of the University of Tennessee. His research interests and publications include parent–child relations, adolescent socialization, and family theory. Dr. Peterson is coeditor of *Adolescents in Families.*

Chaya S. Piotrkowski is an Associate Professor in the Department of Psychology at St. John's University in New York. Her research has dealt with work and the family and women's roles. She is the author of *Work and Families.* Dr. Piotrkowski is currently examining the relationships between parents' occupational stress, family dynamics, and children's well-being.

Karen A. Polonko is an Assistant Professor in the Department of Sociology at Old Dominion University. She is now doing research on family, fertility, and sexuality. Dr. Polonko was the winner of the Reuben Hill Award (1982) for outstanding research and theory for an article on childlessness (written with Jay D. Teachman and John Scanzoni).

Rhona Rapoport is the Cofounder and Codirector of the Institute of Family and Environmental Research in London. Dr. Rapoport has written *Sex, Career and Family* (with Michael Fogarty and Robert Rapoport); *Dual Career Families; Dual Career Families Re-examined; Leisure and the Family Life Cycle; Fathers,*

Mothers and Society; and *Families in Britain* (all with Robert Rapoport).

Robert N. Rapoport is the Cofounder and Codirector of the Institute of Family and Environmental Research in London. Among Dr. Rapoport's books are *Community as Doctor; Sex, Career and Family* (with Michael Fogarty and Rhona Rapoport); *Dual Career Families; Dual Career Families Re-examined; Leisure and the Family Life Cycle; Fathers, Mothers and Society;* and *Families in Britain* (all with Rhona Rapoport).

Helen J. Raschke is the Private Attorney Coordinator for the West Texas Legal Sevices in Wichita Falls, Texas. Dr. Raschke is currently conducting research on the differences between low-income battered women who file for divorce and those who subsequently drop the case.

Boyd C. Rollins is Professor of Sociology, Coordinator of the Interdepartmental Family Studies Ph.D. Program, and Associate of the Family and Demographic Research Institute at Brigham Young University. Dr. Rollins's major theory and research publications are in the areas of parental influence in the socialization of children and marital satisfaction and conjugal power relationships in the marital dyad.

John Scanzoni, Professor of Family Relations at the University of North Carolina—Greensboro, has published in the areas of family theory, gender roles, decision making, and family demography. Dr. Scanzoni's recent books include *Family Decision-Making: A Developmental Sex Role Model* (with Maximiliane E. Szinovacz) and *Shaping Tomorrow's Family: Theory and Policy for the 21st Century.* At this time he is preparing a book entitled *Family and Close Relationships: A Paradigm Shift.*

Alvin L. Schorr is Leonard W. Mayo Professor of Family and Child Welfare in the School of Applied Social Sciences at Case Western Reserve University. Formerly he was Director of Research and Planning for the Office of Economic Opportunity and Deputy Assistant Secretary in the Department of Health, Education, and Welfare. Professor Schorr has published widely on public policy and is now completing his book *The New Welfare State.*

Barbara H. Settles is Professor of Individual and Family Studies at the University of Delaware. Dr. Settles's research interests and publications deal with the cost and quality of foster care, parenting inputs for the care of exceptional children, and the development of educational materials for adults to help them prepare for their later years. She is currently editing a book *Families on the Move: Immigration, Migration and Mobility* (with Suzanne Steinmetz).

Arthur B. Shostak is Professor of Sociology at Drexel University. He is the author, editor, and coeditor of twelve books and over 100 articles. Dr. Shostak's recent books include *Putting Sociology to Work; Men and Abortion; Blue-Collar Stress,* and *Modern Social Reforms.*

Graham B. Spanier, Vice President for Academic Affairs at Oregon State University, is also Professor of Human Development and Family Studies, and Sociology. Dr. Spanier's research has focused on the quality and stability of marriage, family demography, divorce and remarriage. His books include *Parting: The Aftermath of Separation and Divorce* (with Linda Thompson), and *Recycling the Family: Remarriage after Divorce* (with Frank F. Furstenberg, Jr.).

Suzanne K. Steinmetz, Professor of Individual and Family Studies at the University of Delaware, has over 75 publications treating such topics as family violence, aging, socialization, sex roles, and family theory. Dr. Steinmetz's books include *Violence in the Family* (with M. Straus); *Cycle of Violence: Assertive, Aggressive and Abusive Interaction; Behind Closed Doors: Violence in the American Family* (with M. Straus and R. Gelles); *Marriage and Family Life* (with S. Clavan and K. Stein); and *Duty Bound: Family Care and Elder Abuse.* Currently she is completing *Violence in the Family: An Anthology* (with G. Whitchurch).

Marvin B. Sussman is Unidel Professor in the Department of Individual and Family Studies at the University of Delaware. He was the recipient in 1980 of the Ernest W. Burgess Award of the National Council on Family Relations for his continuous contributions to family theory and research. In 1985, he received the Distinguished Family Scholar Award given by the Society for the Study of Social Problems. Founder and editor of *Marriage and Family Review,* Dr. Sussman has authored, coauthored, edited, or coedited 31 monographs and books and approximately 100 journal articles dealing with the family, community rehabilitation, organizations, the sociology of aging, and the sociology of medicine.

Maximiliane E. Szinovacz is a Research Associate in the Department of Individual and Family Studies at the University of Delaware. Dr. Szinovacz's research interests and publications focus on marital power and decision making, sex roles, female employment, and women's retirement. She has published *Family Decision-Making: A Developmental Sex Role Model* (with John Scanzoni) and *Women's Retirement: Policy Implications of Recent Research.* She is currently working on a monograph on family power.

Jay D. Teachman is an Associate Professor of Sociology at Old Dominion University. He is the author of over 25 articles. Dr. Teachman's research utilizes a life-course perspective in examining the number, timing, and sequencing of events such as marriage, divorce, and birth.

Darwin L. Thomas is a Professor of Sociology at Brigham Young University and the editor of *Family Perspectives*. He has published four books and numerous journal articles. In his research, Dr. Thomas concentrates on the socialization processes and products in the family and religion interface.

Edward H. Thompson, Jr., is an Associate Professor and Chair of the Department of Sociology at Holy Cross College, Worcester, Massachusetts. Dr. Thompson's research interests and publications are in the areas of family burdens, management of stress, single-parent families, men's roles, and patient compliance with structural expectations.

Judith Treas is an Associate Professor and Chair of the Department of Sociology at the University of Southern California and a Research Associate at the Andrus Gerontology Center. Dr. Treas has published numerous articles on demographic and historical aspects of aging. Her research at this time focuses on trends in family income inequity and on income-pooling patterns between spouses.

Jean Edmondson Wilcox is an Assistant Professor and Extension Specialist in the Department of Family and Human Development at Utah State University. Dr. Wilcox's research interests include mate selection and family dysfunction. Currently she is performing content analysis of the professional literature on child sexual abuse.

Doris Wilkinson is a Professor of Sociology at the University of Kentucky. She has published widely on topics dealing with black and minority families, included among them ''Afro-American Women and Their Families'' in *Marriage and Family Review* and ''The Black Family Past and Present: A Review Essay'' in *Journal of Marriage and the Family*. Dr. Wilkinson also edited the book *Black Male/White Female*.

Index

865

Politics (*Cont.*)
events in, 601
factors in, 77
groups in, 159, 161, 162, 167, 173
issues in, 809
orientations to, 228
planning in, 157
pressures in, 809
problems in, 165
processes in, 162, 212
of sexuality, 104, 115, 116–119
supervision in, 75
of youth, 489
Polyandry, 576
Polygamy, 220, 525, 528, 576, 768, 775
extramarital, 525
Polygyny, 61, 67, 336, 340, 420, 576
Polymorphic perversity, 515
Polymorphic potential, 511
Polysexual, 527
Population, 531, 597, 649
change, 566, 570–571, 573, 583, 797
control mechanisms for, 748
ethnic, 183–190, 192
growth, 377–378, 726, 779
natural increase, 570–571, 573
policy on, 582–583, 770
problems of, 580–581, 583, 585
study of, 376
world, 579
zero growth, 570, 571, 583
Pornography, 118, 779
kiddie, 522
laboratory studies of, 522
new types of, 522
Portugal, 422
Position, 106, 160, 164, 194, 378, 465, 483–485, 494, 542
intrafamilial, 445, 446–447, 483–485, 665
modification of, 673, 677
social, 160, 542, 661, 665
Positional appeal, 239
Position-oriented roles, 242
Positivism, 82, 91, 94–99, 105, 106, 108, 110–111
alternatives to, 94–98
in American sociology, 83, 91
and antipositivism, 109
decline of certainty and, 106, 109
definition of, 82, 83
logical, 720
in philosophy of science, 94–95
and the postpositivist future, 98–100
Postconventional morality, 241, 523
Postindustrial economy, 570
Postindustrial society, 164, 181, 412, 570
Postmarriage, 172, 334, 607, 817
Postparental stage, 450–451, 453, 454, 458, 465
Postseparation period, 426
Poverty, 3, 24, 45, 51, 161, 172, 190, 197, 198, 200, 203, 231, 232, 233, 254, 270, 328, 336, 405, 410, 414, 419, 446, 459, 580, 587, 610, 772, 773,

Poverty (*Cont.*)
776, 784, 786, 798, 802, 803, 804, 808, 809
adaptation to, 637
characteristics of, 231
culture of, 197, 200, 232, 808
cycle of, 459, 786, 808
family violence and, 749, 755
feminization of, 190
Filipino males and, 632
gender differences in, 773
levels of, 328
and paupers, 728
Power, 105–106, 108, 111, 112, 116, 117–119, 121, 125–127, 129, 136, 144, 147, 149, 165, 166, 170, 181, 223, 228, 229, 235, 239, 242, 251, 257, 263, 267, 305, 337–338, 477–478, 480, 483, 496, 497, 498, 524, 536, 547, 548–550, 551, 552, 558, 651–693, 718, 740, 755, 769, 780, 796.
See also Control; Family power; Influence; Marital power; Parental power
ability as, 652–653, 655, 667, 670, 671
access to, 164, 184
assertion of, 239, 240, 242, 474, 477, 482
asymmetries in, 656, 663, 666, 667, 682
behavior and, 850–851
communication and, 748
costs of, 659, 661, 663, 676
definitions of, 652–656, 675, 676, 677, 744
descriptive analyses of, 656
determinants of, 684
dimensions of, 654, 656–679
distribution of, 667, 848
dynamics of, 659
economic, 184
effectiveness and, 653–654
explanatory analyses of, 656, 659, 679
feelings of, 668
hierarchical, 770
higher, 715
institutionalized, 662
measurement of, 655, 656
men and, 164, 184, 263, 305
models of, 660, 665
perceived versus actual, 333
political, 184, 185, 202, 212–213, 245, 524, 749
and position, 662, 667
processes of, 656, 659–679, 682
resistance to, 675
sexual, 116, 118–119
social, 234
sources of, 665
situations of, 677
strategies of, 654, 664, 669, 673, 675, 677, 678, 680, 854
structures of, 651, 678, 682
struggles for, 680
systems of, 105, 164
theory and, 649, 679
types of, 477, 489, 653
typologies of, 656

Power (*Cont.*)
use of, 663, 842, 852
women and, 218–219, 525–526, 681–682, 747
world, 173
Power bases, 652, 661, 662, 664, 669, 671, 676, 680
coercive, 477, 489, 665, 666
expert, 477, 489, 548, 550, 665, 674, 677, 678
informational, 654, 665, 666, 674
legitimate, 384, 477, 489, 665, 674, 679
physical strength, 652, 669, 671, 680, 682
position, 239
referent, 477, 548, 659, 665, 666, 674, 678
reputational, 654, 655
reward, 477, 489, 665, 666, 678
typologies of, 665, 666, 674
Power exertion, 653, 656, 658–661, 663, 664, 667–679
processes of, 659–661, 667–669, 673, 677
strategies of, 661, 664, 667, 668, 674–676, 678–681
means of, 665
dimensions of, 661
Powerlessness, 197, 202, 233, 245, 271, 362, 661, 715, 731, 743
unemployment and, 271
Power relations, 116, 117, 118, 271, 653, 656–679, 681, 770, 854–855
dimensions of, 656–679
ethnicity and, 668–669
in the family, 59, 68–73, 654, 669, 849
marital, 662, 668, 669, 682
Practioners, 601, 609
Pragmatic theory, 69
Praxis, 104, 105, 120
Prayer, 181
Preadolescents, 513, 515, 543
Preconventional morality, 523
Predestination, 290
Prediction, 479
models of, 173–178, 343
Predivorce phase, 412
Pregnancy, 220, 336, 340, 374, 510–511, 524, 529–531, 536, 552, 554, 555, 565, 566–567, 579, 580, 603, 605, 606, 719, 776, 779, 783, 810
adolescent, 203, 524, 585–588, 822, 828–829
family violence and, 739
fear of, 529–530
premarital, 603, 605, 783
rates of, 578, 585–586
unplanned, 398, 580, 582, 731, 732
unwanted, 336, 606, 699, 754, 779
and wanted versus unwanted child, 15
women and, 556, 776
Prehistoric times, 516
Preindustrial era, 39, 40, 41, 52, 53, 65, 67, 115, 162, 341
communities in, 40, 52
economy of, 222
in England, 419

ACKNOWLEDGMENTS

We gratefully thank the following students for their help: Mary Cannon for indexing, editing, and preparing the final index and Beth Cohen, Joy Pellicciaro, Lynn Worden, and Nancy Wilson for their help with indexing.